S0-BBS-618

Oxford Dictionary of National Biography

Volume 49

Oxford Dictionary of National Biography

IN ASSOCIATION WITH
The British Academy

From the earliest times to the year 2000

Edited by
H. C. G. Matthew
and
Brian Harrison

Volume 49
Sartorius–Sharman

Great Clarendon Street, Oxford OX2 6DP

Oxford University Press is a department of the University of Oxford.
It furthers the University's objective of excellence in research, scholarship,
and education by publishing worldwide in

Oxford New York

Auckland Bangkok Buenos Aires Cape Town
Chennai Dar es Salaam Delhi Hong Kong Istanbul Karachi
Kolkata Kuala Lumpur Madrid Melbourne Mexico City Mumbai Nairobi
São Paulo Shanghai Taipei Tokyo Toronto

Oxford is a registered trade mark of Oxford University Press
in the UK and in certain other countries

Published in the United States
by Oxford University Press Inc., New York

First published 2004

British Library Cataloguing in Publication Data
Data available

Library of Congress Cataloging in Publication Data
Data available: for details see volume 1, p. iv

ISBN 0-19-861399-7 (this volume)
ISBN 0-19-861411-X (set of sixty volumes)

Text captured by Alliance Phototypesetters, Pondicherry
Illustrations reproduced and archived by
Alliance Graphics Ltd, UK
Typeset in OUP Swift by Interactive Sciences Limited, Gloucester
Printed in Great Britain on acid-free paper by
Butler and Tanner Ltd,
Frome, Somerset

LIST OF ABBREVIATIONS

1 *General abbreviations*

AB	bachelor of arts
ABC	Australian Broadcasting Corporation
ABC TV	ABC Television
act.	active
A$	Australian dollar
AD	*anno domini*
AFC	Air Force Cross
AIDS	acquired immune deficiency syndrome
AK	Alaska
AL	Alabama
A level	advanced level [examination]
ALS	associate of the Linnean Society
AM	master of arts
AMICE	associate member of the Institution of Civil Engineers
ANZAC	Australian and New Zealand Army Corps
appx *pl.* appxs	appendix(es)
AR	Arkansas
ARA	associate of the Royal Academy
ARCA	associate of the Royal College of Art
ARCM	associate of the Royal College of Music
ARCO	associate of the Royal College of Organists
ARIBA	associate of the Royal Institute of British Architects
ARP	air-raid precautions
ARRC	associate of the Royal Red Cross
ARSA	associate of the Royal Scottish Academy
art.	article / item
ASC	Army Service Corps
Asch	Austrian Schilling
ASDIC	Antisubmarine Detection Investigation Committee
ATS	Auxiliary Territorial Service
ATV	Associated Television
Aug	August
AZ	Arizona
b.	born
BA	bachelor of arts
BA (Admin.)	bachelor of arts (administration)
BAFTA	British Academy of Film and Television Arts
BAO	bachelor of arts in obstetrics
bap.	baptized
BBC	British Broadcasting Corporation / Company
BC	before Christ
BCE	before the common (*or* Christian) era
BCE	bachelor of civil engineering
BCG	bacillus of Calmette and Guérin [inoculation against tuberculosis]
BCh	bachelor of surgery
BChir	bachelor of surgery
BCL	bachelor of civil law
BCnL	bachelor of canon law
BCom	bachelor of commerce
BD	bachelor of divinity
BEd	bachelor of education
BEng	bachelor of engineering
bk *pl.* bks	book(s)
BL	bachelor of law / letters / literature
BLitt	bachelor of letters
BM	bachelor of medicine
BMus	bachelor of music
BP	before present
BP	British Petroleum
Bros.	Brothers
BS	(1) bachelor of science; (2) bachelor of surgery; (3) British standard
BSc	bachelor of science
BSc (Econ.)	bachelor of science (economics)
BSc (Eng.)	bachelor of science (engineering)
bt	baronet
BTh	bachelor of theology
bur.	buried
C.	command [identifier for published parliamentary papers]
c.	*circa*
c.	*capitulum pl. capitula*: chapter(s)
CA	California
Cantab.	Cantabrigiensis
cap.	*capitulum pl. capitula*: chapter(s)
CB	companion of the Bath
CBE	commander of the Order of the British Empire
CBS	Columbia Broadcasting System
cc	cubic centimetres
C$	Canadian dollar
CD	compact disc
Cd	command [identifier for published parliamentary papers]
CE	Common (*or* Christian) Era
cent.	century
cf.	compare
CH	Companion of Honour
chap.	chapter
ChB	bachelor of surgery
CI	Imperial Order of the Crown of India
CIA	Central Intelligence Agency
CID	Criminal Investigation Department
CIE	companion of the Order of the Indian Empire
Cie	Compagnie
CLit	companion of literature
CM	master of surgery
cm	centimetre(s)

Cmd	command [identifier for published parliamentary papers]
CMG	companion of the Order of St Michael and St George
Cmnd	command [identifier for published parliamentary papers]
CO	Colorado
Co.	company
co.	county
col. *pl.* cols.	column(s)
Corp.	corporation
CSE	certificate of secondary education
CSI	companion of the Order of the Star of India
CT	Connecticut
CVO	commander of the Royal Victorian Order
cwt	hundredweight
$	(American) dollar
d.	(1) penny (pence); (2) died
DBE	dame commander of the Order of the British Empire
DCH	diploma in child health
DCh	doctor of surgery
DCL	doctor of civil law
DCnL	doctor of canon law
DCVO	dame commander of the Royal Victorian Order
DD	doctor of divinity
DE	Delaware
Dec	December
dem.	demolished
DEng	doctor of engineering
des.	destroyed
DFC	Distinguished Flying Cross
DipEd	diploma in education
DipPsych	diploma in psychiatry
diss.	dissertation
DL	deputy lieutenant
DLitt	doctor of letters
DLittCelt	doctor of Celtic letters
DM	(1) Deutschmark; (2) doctor of medicine; (3) doctor of musical arts
DMus	doctor of music
DNA	dioxyribonucleic acid
doc.	document
DOL	doctor of oriental learning
DPH	diploma in public health
DPhil	doctor of philosophy
DPM	diploma in psychological medicine
DSC	Distinguished Service Cross
DSc	doctor of science
DSc (Econ.)	doctor of science (economics)
DSc (Eng.)	doctor of science (engineering)
DSM	Distinguished Service Medal
DSO	companion of the Distinguished Service Order
DSocSc	doctor of social science
DTech	doctor of technology
DTh	doctor of theology
DTM	diploma in tropical medicine
DTMH	diploma in tropical medicine and hygiene
DU	doctor of the university
DUniv	doctor of the university
dwt	pennyweight
EC	European Community
ed. *pl.* eds.	edited / edited by / editor(s)
Edin.	Edinburgh
edn	edition
EEC	European Economic Community
EFTA	European Free Trade Association
EICS	East India Company Service
EMI	Electrical and Musical Industries (Ltd)
Eng.	English
enl.	enlarged
ENSA	Entertainments National Service Association
ep. *pl.* epp.	*epistola(e)*
ESP	extra-sensory perception
esp.	especially
esq.	esquire
est.	estimate / estimated
EU	European Union
ex	sold by (*lit.* out of)
excl.	excludes / excluding
exh.	exhibited
exh. cat.	exhibition catalogue
f. *pl.* ff.	following [pages]
FA	Football Association
FACP	fellow of the American College of Physicians
facs.	facsimile
FANY	First Aid Nursing Yeomanry
FBA	fellow of the British Academy
FBI	Federation of British Industries
FCS	fellow of the Chemical Society
Feb	February
FEng	fellow of the Fellowship of Engineering
FFCM	fellow of the Faculty of Community Medicine
FGS	fellow of the Geological Society
fig.	figure
FIMechE	fellow of the Institution of Mechanical Engineers
FL	Florida
fl.	*floruit*
FLS	fellow of the Linnean Society
FM	frequency modulation
fol. *pl.* fols.	folio(s)
Fr	French francs
Fr.	French
FRAeS	fellow of the Royal Aeronautical Society
FRAI	fellow of the Royal Anthropological Institute
FRAM	fellow of the Royal Academy of Music
FRAS	(1) fellow of the Royal Asiatic Society; (2) fellow of the Royal Astronomical Society
FRCM	fellow of the Royal College of Music
FRCO	fellow of the Royal College of Organists
FRCOG	fellow of the Royal College of Obstetricians and Gynaecologists
FRCP(C)	fellow of the Royal College of Physicians of Canada
FRCP (Edin.)	fellow of the Royal College of Physicians of Edinburgh
FRCP (Lond.)	fellow of the Royal College of Physicians of London
FRCPath	fellow of the Royal College of Pathologists
FRCPsych	fellow of the Royal College of Psychiatrists
FRCS	fellow of the Royal College of Surgeons
FRGS	fellow of the Royal Geographical Society
FRIBA	fellow of the Royal Institute of British Architects
FRICS	fellow of the Royal Institute of Chartered Surveyors
FRS	fellow of the Royal Society
FRSA	fellow of the Royal Society of Arts

FRSCM	fellow of the Royal School of Church Music
FRSE	fellow of the Royal Society of Edinburgh
FRSL	fellow of the Royal Society of Literature
FSA	fellow of the Society of Antiquaries
ft	foot *pl.* feet
FTCL	fellow of Trinity College of Music, London
ft-lb per min.	foot-pounds per minute [unit of horsepower]
FZS	fellow of the Zoological Society
GA	Georgia
GBE	knight or dame grand cross of the Order of the British Empire
GCB	knight grand cross of the Order of the Bath
GCE	general certificate of education
GCH	knight grand cross of the Royal Guelphic Order
GCHQ	government communications headquarters
GCIE	knight grand commander of the Order of the Indian Empire
GCMG	knight or dame grand cross of the Order of St Michael and St George
GCSE	general certificate of secondary education
GCSI	knight grand commander of the Order of the Star of India
GCStJ	bailiff or dame grand cross of the order of St John of Jerusalem
GCVO	knight or dame grand cross of the Royal Victorian Order
GEC	General Electric Company
Ger.	German
GI	government (*or* general) issue
GMT	Greenwich mean time
GP	general practitioner
GPU	[Soviet special police unit]
GSO	general staff officer
Heb.	Hebrew
HEICS	Honourable East India Company Service
HI	Hawaii
HIV	human immunodeficiency virus
HK$	Hong Kong dollar
HM	his / her majesty('s)
HMAS	his / her majesty's Australian ship
HMNZS	his / her majesty's New Zealand ship
HMS	his / her majesty's ship
HMSO	His / Her Majesty's Stationery Office
HMV	His Master's Voice
Hon.	Honourable
hp	horsepower
hr	hour(s)
HRH	his / her royal highness
HTV	Harlech Television
IA	Iowa
ibid.	*ibidem*: in the same place
ICI	Imperial Chemical Industries (Ltd)
ID	Idaho
IL	Illinois
illus.	illustration
illustr.	illustrated
IN	Indiana
in.	inch(es)
Inc.	Incorporated
incl.	includes / including
IOU	I owe you
IQ	intelligence quotient
Ir£	Irish pound
IRA	Irish Republican Army
ISO	companion of the Imperial Service Order
It.	Italian
ITA	Independent Television Authority
ITV	Independent Television
Jan	January
JP	justice of the peace
jun.	junior
KB	knight of the Order of the Bath
KBE	knight commander of the Order of the British Empire
KC	king's counsel
kcal	kilocalorie
KCB	knight commander of the Order of the Bath
KCH	knight commander of the Royal Guelphic Order
KCIE	knight commander of the Order of the Indian Empire
KCMG	knight commander of the Order of St Michael and St George
KCSI	knight commander of the Order of the Star of India
KCVO	knight commander of the Royal Victorian Order
keV	kilo-electron-volt
KG	knight of the Order of the Garter
KGB	[Soviet committee of state security]
KH	knight of the Royal Guelphic Order
KLM	Koninklijke Luchtvaart Maatschappij (Royal Dutch Air Lines)
km	kilometre(s)
KP	knight of the Order of St Patrick
KS	Kansas
KT	knight of the Order of the Thistle
kt	knight
KY	Kentucky
£	pound(s) sterling
£E	Egyptian pound
L	lira *pl.* lire
l. *pl.* ll.	line(s)
LA	Lousiana
LAA	light anti-aircraft
LAH	licentiate of the Apothecaries' Hall, Dublin
Lat.	Latin
lb	pound(s), unit of weight
LDS	licence in dental surgery
lit.	literally
LittB	bachelor of letters
LittD	doctor of letters
LKQCPI	licentiate of the King and Queen's College of Physicians, Ireland
LLA	lady literate in arts
LLB	bachelor of laws
LLD	doctor of laws
LLM	master of laws
LM	licentiate in midwifery
LP	long-playing record
LRAM	licentiate of the Royal Academy of Music
LRCP	licentiate of the Royal College of Physicians
LRCPS (Glasgow)	licentiate of the Royal College of Physicians and Surgeons of Glasgow
LRCS	licentiate of the Royal College of Surgeons
LSA	licentiate of the Society of Apothecaries
LSD	lysergic acid diethylamide
LVO	lieutenant of the Royal Victorian Order
M. *pl.* MM.	Monsieur *pl.* Messieurs
m	metre(s)

m. *pl.* mm.	membrane(s)
MA	(1) Massachusetts; (2) master of arts
MAI	master of engineering
MB	bachelor of medicine
MBA	master of business administration
MBE	member of the Order of the British Empire
MC	Military Cross
MCC	Marylebone Cricket Club
MCh	master of surgery
MChir	master of surgery
MCom	master of commerce
MD	(1) doctor of medicine; (2) Maryland
MDMA	methylenedioxymethamphetamine
ME	Maine
MEd	master of education
MEng	master of engineering
MEP	member of the European parliament
MG	Morris Garages
MGM	Metro-Goldwyn-Mayer
Mgr	Monsignor
MI	(1) Michigan; (2) military intelligence
MI1c	[secret intelligence department]
MI5	[military intelligence department]
MI6	[secret intelligence department]
MI9	[secret escape service]
MICE	member of the Institution of Civil Engineers
MIEE	member of the Institution of Electrical Engineers
min.	minute(s)
Mk	mark
ML	(1) licentiate of medicine; (2) master of laws
MLitt	master of letters
Mlle	Mademoiselle
mm	millimetre(s)
Mme	Madame
MN	Minnesota
MO	Missouri
MOH	medical officer of health
MP	member of parliament
m.p.h.	miles per hour
MPhil	master of philosophy
MRCP	member of the Royal College of Physicians
MRCS	member of the Royal College of Surgeons
MRCVS	member of the Royal College of Veterinary Surgeons
MRIA	member of the Royal Irish Academy
MS	(1) master of science; (2) Mississippi
MS *pl.* MSS	manuscript(s)
MSc	master of science
MSc (Econ.)	master of science (economics)
MT	Montana
MusB	bachelor of music
MusBac	bachelor of music
MusD	doctor of music
MV	motor vessel
MVO	member of the Royal Victorian Order
n. *pl.* nn.	note(s)
NAAFI	Navy, Army, and Air Force Institutes
NASA	National Aeronautics and Space Administration
NATO	North Atlantic Treaty Organization
NBC	National Broadcasting Corporation
NC	North Carolina
NCO	non-commissioned officer
ND	North Dakota
n.d.	no date
NE	Nebraska
nem. con.	*nemine contradicente*: unanimously
new ser.	new series
NH	New Hampshire
NHS	National Health Service
NJ	New Jersey
NKVD	[Soviet people's commissariat for internal affairs]
NM	New Mexico
nm	nanometre(s)
no. *pl.* nos.	number(s)
Nov	November
n.p.	no place [of publication]
NS	new style
NV	Nevada
NY	New York
NZBS	New Zealand Broadcasting Service
OBE	officer of the Order of the British Empire
obit.	obituary
Oct	October
OCTU	officer cadets training unit
OECD	Organization for Economic Co-operation and Development
OEEC	Organization for European Economic Co-operation
OFM	order of Friars Minor [Franciscans]
OFMCap	Ordine Frati Minori Cappucini: member of the Capuchin order
OH	Ohio
OK	Oklahoma
O level	ordinary level [examination]
OM	Order of Merit
OP	order of Preachers [Dominicans]
op. *pl.* opp.	opus *pl.* opera
OPEC	Organization of Petroleum Exporting Countries
OR	Oregon
orig.	original
OS	old style
OSB	Order of St Benedict
OTC	Officers' Training Corps
OWS	Old Watercolour Society
Oxon.	Oxoniensis
p. *pl.* pp.	page(s)
PA	Pennsylvania
p.a.	per annum
para.	paragraph
PAYE	pay as you earn
pbk *pl.* pbks	paperback(s)
per.	[during the] period
PhD	doctor of philosophy
pl.	(1) plate(s); (2) plural
priv. coll.	private collection
pt *pl.* pts	part(s)
pubd	published
PVC	polyvinyl chloride
q. *pl.* qq.	(1) question(s); (2) quire(s)
QC	queen's counsel
R	rand
R.	Rex / Regina
r	recto
r.	reigned / ruled
RA	Royal Academy / Royal Academician

RAC	Royal Automobile Club
RAF	Royal Air Force
RAFVR	Royal Air Force Volunteer Reserve
RAM	[member of the] Royal Academy of Music
RAMC	Royal Army Medical Corps
RCA	Royal College of Art
RCNC	Royal Corps of Naval Constructors
RCOG	Royal College of Obstetricians and Gynaecologists
RDI	royal designer for industry
RE	Royal Engineers
repr. *pl.* reprs.	reprint(s) / reprinted
repro.	reproduced
rev.	revised / revised by / reviser / revision
Revd	Reverend
RHA	Royal Hibernian Academy
RI	(1) Rhode Island; (2) Royal Institute of Painters in Water-Colours
RIBA	Royal Institute of British Architects
RIN	Royal Indian Navy
RM	Reichsmark
RMS	Royal Mail steamer
RN	Royal Navy
RNA	ribonucleic acid
RNAS	Royal Naval Air Service
RNR	Royal Naval Reserve
RNVR	Royal Naval Volunteer Reserve
RO	Record Office
r.p.m.	revolutions per minute
RRS	royal research ship
Rs	rupees
RSA	(1) Royal Scottish Academician; (2) Royal Society of Arts
RSPCA	Royal Society for the Prevention of Cruelty to Animals
Rt Hon.	Right Honourable
Rt Revd	Right Reverend
RUC	Royal Ulster Constabulary
Russ.	Russian
RWS	Royal Watercolour Society
S4C	Sianel Pedwar Cymru
s.	shilling(s)
s.a.	*sub anno*: under the year
SABC	South African Broadcasting Corporation
SAS	Special Air Service
SC	South Carolina
ScD	doctor of science
S$	Singapore dollar
SD	South Dakota
sec.	second(s)
sel.	selected
sen.	senior
Sept	September
ser.	series
SHAPE	supreme headquarters allied powers, Europe
SIDRO	Société Internationale d'Énergie Hydro-Électrique
sig. *pl.* sigs.	signature(s)
sing.	singular
SIS	Secret Intelligence Service
SJ	Society of Jesus
Skr	Swedish krona
Span.	Spanish
SPCK	Society for Promoting Christian Knowledge
SS	(1) Santissimi; (2) Schutzstaffel; (3) steam ship
STB	bachelor of theology
STD	doctor of theology
STM	master of theology
STP	doctor of theology
supp.	supposedly
suppl. *pl.* suppls.	supplement(s)
s.v.	*sub verbo* / *sub voce*: under the word / heading
SY	steam yacht
TA	Territorial Army
TASS	[Soviet news agency]
TB	tuberculosis (*lit.* tubercle bacillus)
TD	(1) *teachtaí dála* (member of the Dáil); (2) territorial decoration
TN	Tennessee
TNT	trinitrotoluene
trans.	translated / translated by / translation / translator
TT	tourist trophy
TUC	Trades Union Congress
TX	Texas
U-boat	*Unterseeboot*: submarine
Ufa	Universum-Film AG
UMIST	University of Manchester Institute of Science and Technology
UN	United Nations
UNESCO	United Nations Educational, Scientific, and Cultural Organization
UNICEF	United Nations International Children's Emergency Fund
unpubd	unpublished
USS	United States ship
UT	Utah
v	verso
v.	versus
VA	Virginia
VAD	Voluntary Aid Detachment
VC	Victoria Cross
VE-day	victory in Europe day
Ven.	Venerable
VJ-day	victory over Japan day
vol. *pl.* vols.	volume(s)
VT	Vermont
WA	Washington [state]
WAAC	Women's Auxiliary Army Corps
WAAF	Women's Auxiliary Air Force
WEA	Workers' Educational Association
WHO	World Health Organization
WI	Wisconsin
WRAF	Women's Royal Air Force
WRNS	Women's Royal Naval Service
WV	West Virginia
WVS	Women's Voluntary Service
WY	Wyoming
¥	yen
YMCA	Young Men's Christian Association
YWCA	Young Women's Christian Association

2 Institution abbreviations

All Souls Oxf.	All Souls College, Oxford
AM Oxf.	Ashmolean Museum, Oxford
Balliol Oxf.	Balliol College, Oxford
BBC WAC	BBC Written Archives Centre, Reading
Beds. & Luton ARS	Bedfordshire and Luton Archives and Record Service, Bedford
Berks. RO	Berkshire Record Office, Reading
BFI	British Film Institute, London
BFI NFTVA	British Film Institute, London, National Film and Television Archive
BGS	British Geological Survey, Keyworth, Nottingham
Birm. CA	Birmingham Central Library, Birmingham City Archives
Birm. CL	Birmingham Central Library
BL	British Library, London
BL NSA	British Library, London, National Sound Archive
BL OIOC	British Library, London, Oriental and India Office Collections
BLPES	London School of Economics and Political Science, British Library of Political and Economic Science
BM	British Museum, London
Bodl. Oxf.	Bodleian Library, Oxford
Bodl. RH	Bodleian Library of Commonwealth and African Studies at Rhodes House, Oxford
Borth. Inst.	Borthwick Institute of Historical Research, University of York
Boston PL	Boston Public Library, Massachusetts
Bristol RO	Bristol Record Office
Bucks. RLSS	Buckinghamshire Records and Local Studies Service, Aylesbury
CAC Cam.	Churchill College, Cambridge, Churchill Archives Centre
Cambs. AS	Cambridgeshire Archive Service
CCC Cam.	Corpus Christi College, Cambridge
CCC Oxf.	Corpus Christi College, Oxford
Ches. & Chester ALSS	Cheshire and Chester Archives and Local Studies Service
Christ Church Oxf.	Christ Church, Oxford
Christies	Christies, London
City Westm. AC	City of Westminster Archives Centre, London
CKS	Centre for Kentish Studies, Maidstone
CLRO	Corporation of London Records Office
Coll. Arms	College of Arms, London
Col. U.	Columbia University, New York
Cornwall RO	Cornwall Record Office, Truro
Courtauld Inst.	Courtauld Institute of Art, London
CUL	Cambridge University Library
Cumbria AS	Cumbria Archive Service
Derbys. RO	Derbyshire Record Office, Matlock
Devon RO	Devon Record Office, Exeter
Dorset RO	Dorset Record Office, Dorchester
Duke U.	Duke University, Durham, North Carolina
Duke U., Perkins L.	Duke University, Durham, North Carolina, William R. Perkins Library
Durham Cath. CL	Durham Cathedral, chapter library
Durham RO	Durham Record Office
DWL	Dr Williams's Library, London
Essex RO	Essex Record Office
E. Sussex RO	East Sussex Record Office, Lewes
Eton	Eton College, Berkshire
FM Cam.	Fitzwilliam Museum, Cambridge
Folger	Folger Shakespeare Library, Washington, DC
Garr. Club	Garrick Club, London
Girton Cam.	Girton College, Cambridge
GL	Guildhall Library, London
Glos. RO	Gloucestershire Record Office, Gloucester
Gon. & Caius Cam.	Gonville and Caius College, Cambridge
Gov. Art Coll.	Government Art Collection
GS Lond.	Geological Society of London
Hants. RO	Hampshire Record Office, Winchester
Harris Man. Oxf.	Harris Manchester College, Oxford
Harvard TC	Harvard Theatre Collection, Harvard University, Cambridge, Massachusetts, Nathan Marsh Pusey Library
Harvard U.	Harvard University, Cambridge, Massachusetts
Harvard U., Houghton L.	Harvard University, Cambridge, Massachusetts, Houghton Library
Herefs. RO	Herefordshire Record Office, Hereford
Herts. ALS	Hertfordshire Archives and Local Studies, Hertford
Hist. Soc. Penn.	Historical Society of Pennsylvania, Philadelphia
HLRO	House of Lords Record Office, London
Hult. Arch.	Hulton Archive, London and New York
Hunt. L.	Huntington Library, San Marino, California
ICL	Imperial College, London
Inst. CE	Institution of Civil Engineers, London
Inst. EE	Institution of Electrical Engineers, London
IWM	Imperial War Museum, London
IWM FVA	Imperial War Museum, London, Film and Video Archive
IWM SA	Imperial War Museum, London, Sound Archive
JRL	John Rylands University Library of Manchester
King's AC Cam.	King's College Archives Centre, Cambridge
King's Cam.	King's College, Cambridge
King's Lond.	King's College, London
King's Lond., Liddell Hart C.	King's College, London, Liddell Hart Centre for Military Archives
Lancs. RO	Lancashire Record Office, Preston
L. Cong.	Library of Congress, Washington, DC
Leics. RO	Leicestershire, Leicester, and Rutland Record Office, Leicester
Lincs. Arch.	Lincolnshire Archives, Lincoln
Linn. Soc.	Linnean Society of London
LMA	London Metropolitan Archives
LPL	Lambeth Palace, London
Lpool RO	Liverpool Record Office and Local Studies Service
LUL	London University Library
Magd. Cam.	Magdalene College, Cambridge
Magd. Oxf.	Magdalen College, Oxford
Man. City Gall.	Manchester City Galleries
Man. CL	Manchester Central Library
Mass. Hist. Soc.	Massachusetts Historical Society, Boston
Merton Oxf.	Merton College, Oxford
MHS Oxf.	Museum of the History of Science, Oxford
Mitchell L., Glas.	Mitchell Library, Glasgow
Mitchell L., NSW	State Library of New South Wales, Sydney, Mitchell Library
Morgan L.	Pierpont Morgan Library, New York
NA Canada	National Archives of Canada, Ottawa
NA Ire.	National Archives of Ireland, Dublin
NAM	National Army Museum, London
NA Scot.	National Archives of Scotland, Edinburgh
News Int. RO	News International Record Office, London
NG Ire.	National Gallery of Ireland, Dublin

NG Scot.	National Gallery of Scotland, Edinburgh
NHM	Natural History Museum, London
NL Aus.	National Library of Australia, Canberra
NL Ire.	National Library of Ireland, Dublin
NL NZ	National Library of New Zealand, Wellington
NL NZ, Turnbull L.	National Library of New Zealand, Wellington, Alexander Turnbull Library
NL Scot.	National Library of Scotland, Edinburgh
NL Wales	National Library of Wales, Aberystwyth
NMG Wales	National Museum and Gallery of Wales, Cardiff
NMM	National Maritime Museum, London
Norfolk RO	Norfolk Record Office, Norwich
Northants. RO	Northamptonshire Record Office, Northampton
Northumbd RO	Northumberland Record Office
Notts. Arch.	Nottinghamshire Archives, Nottingham
NPG	National Portrait Gallery, London
NRA	National Archives, London, Historical Manuscripts Commission, National Register of Archives
Nuffield Oxf.	Nuffield College, Oxford
N. Yorks. CRO	North Yorkshire County Record Office, Northallerton
NYPL	New York Public Library
Oxf. UA	Oxford University Archives
Oxf. U. Mus. NH	Oxford University Museum of Natural History
Oxon. RO	Oxfordshire Record Office, Oxford
Pembroke Cam.	Pembroke College, Cambridge
PRO	National Archives, London, Public Record Office
PRO NIre.	Public Record Office for Northern Ireland, Belfast
Pusey Oxf.	Pusey House, Oxford
RA	Royal Academy of Arts, London
Ransom HRC	Harry Ransom Humanities Research Center, University of Texas, Austin
RAS	Royal Astronomical Society, London
RBG Kew	Royal Botanic Gardens, Kew, London
RCP Lond.	Royal College of Physicians of London
RCS Eng.	Royal College of Surgeons of England, London
RGS	Royal Geographical Society, London
RIBA	Royal Institute of British Architects, London
RIBA BAL	Royal Institute of British Architects, London, British Architectural Library
Royal Arch.	Royal Archives, Windsor Castle, Berkshire [by gracious permission of her majesty the queen]
Royal Irish Acad.	Royal Irish Academy, Dublin
Royal Scot. Acad.	Royal Scottish Academy, Edinburgh
RS	Royal Society, London
RSA	Royal Society of Arts, London
RS Friends, Lond.	Religious Society of Friends, London
St Ant. Oxf.	St Antony's College, Oxford
St John Cam.	St John's College, Cambridge
S. Antiquaries, Lond.	Society of Antiquaries of London
Sci. Mus.	Science Museum, London
Scot. NPG	Scottish National Portrait Gallery, Edinburgh
Scott Polar RI	University of Cambridge, Scott Polar Research Institute
Sheff. Arch.	Sheffield Archives
Shrops. RRC	Shropshire Records and Research Centre, Shrewsbury
SOAS	School of Oriental and African Studies, London
Som. ARS	Somerset Archive and Record Service, Taunton
Staffs. RO	Staffordshire Record Office, Stafford
Suffolk RO	Suffolk Record Office
Surrey HC	Surrey History Centre, Woking
TCD	Trinity College, Dublin
Trinity Cam.	Trinity College, Cambridge
U. Aberdeen	University of Aberdeen
U. Birm.	University of Birmingham
U. Birm. L.	University of Birmingham Library
U. Cal.	University of California
U. Cam.	University of Cambridge
UCL	University College, London
U. Durham	University of Durham
U. Durham L.	University of Durham Library
U. Edin.	University of Edinburgh
U. Edin., New Coll.	University of Edinburgh, New College
U. Edin., New Coll. L.	University of Edinburgh, New College Library
U. Edin. L.	University of Edinburgh Library
U. Glas.	University of Glasgow
U. Glas. L.	University of Glasgow Library
U. Hull	University of Hull
U. Hull, Brynmor Jones L.	University of Hull, Brynmor Jones Library
U. Leeds	University of Leeds
U. Leeds, Brotherton L.	University of Leeds, Brotherton Library
U. Lond.	University of London
U. Lpool	University of Liverpool
U. Lpool L.	University of Liverpool Library
U. Mich.	University of Michigan, Ann Arbor
U. Mich., Clements L.	University of Michigan, Ann Arbor, William L. Clements Library
U. Newcastle	University of Newcastle upon Tyne
U. Newcastle, Robinson L.	University of Newcastle upon Tyne, Robinson Library
U. Nott.	University of Nottingham
U. Nott. L.	University of Nottingham Library
U. Oxf.	University of Oxford
U. Reading	University of Reading
U. Reading L.	University of Reading Library
U. St Andr.	University of St Andrews
U. St Andr. L.	University of St Andrews Library
U. Southampton	University of Southampton
U. Southampton L.	University of Southampton Library
U. Sussex	University of Sussex, Brighton
U. Texas	University of Texas, Austin
U. Wales	University of Wales
U. Warwick Mod. RC	University of Warwick, Coventry, Modern Records Centre
V&A	Victoria and Albert Museum, London
V&A NAL	Victoria and Albert Museum, London, National Art Library
Warks. CRO	Warwickshire County Record Office, Warwick
Wellcome L.	Wellcome Library for the History and Understanding of Medicine, London
Westm. DA	Westminster Diocesan Archives, London
Wilts. & Swindon RO	Wiltshire and Swindon Record Office, Trowbridge
Worcs. RO	Worcestershire Record Office, Worcester
W. Sussex RO	West Sussex Record Office, Chichester
W. Yorks. AS	West Yorkshire Archive Service
Yale U.	Yale University, New Haven, Connecticut
Yale U., Beinecke L.	Yale University, New Haven, Connecticut, Beinecke Rare Book and Manuscript Library
Yale U. CBA	Yale University, New Haven, Connecticut, Yale Center for British Art

3 *Bibliographic abbreviations*

Adams, *Drama*	W. D. Adams, *A dictionary of the drama*, 1: *A–G* (1904); 2: *H–Z* (1956) [vol. 2 microfilm only]
AFM	J O'Donovan, ed. and trans., *Annala rioghachta Eireann / Annals of the kingdom of Ireland by the four masters*, 7 vols. (1848–51); 2nd edn (1856); 3rd edn (1990)
Allibone, *Dict.*	S. A. Allibone, *A critical dictionary of English literature and British and American authors*, 3 vols. (1859–71); suppl. by J. F. Kirk, 2 vols. (1891)
ANB	J. A. Garraty and M. C. Carnes, eds., *American national biography*, 24 vols. (1999)
Anderson, *Scot. nat.*	W. Anderson, *The Scottish nation, or, The surnames, families, literature, honours, and biographical history of the people of Scotland*, 3 vols. (1859–63)
Ann. mon.	H. R. Luard, ed., *Annales monastici*, 5 vols., Rolls Series, 36 (1864–9)
Ann. Ulster	S. Mac Airt and G. Mac Niocaill, eds., *Annals of Ulster (to AD 1131)* (1983)
APC	*Acts of the privy council of England*, new ser., 46 vols. (1890–1964)
APS	*The acts of the parliaments of Scotland*, 12 vols. in 13 (1814–75)
Arber, *Regs. Stationers*	F. Arber, ed., *A transcript of the registers of the Company of Stationers of London, 1554–1640 AD*, 5 vols. (1875–94)
ArchR	*Architectural Review*
ASC	D. Whitelock, D. C. Douglas, and S. I. Tucker, ed. and trans., *The Anglo-Saxon Chronicle: a revised translation* (1961)
AS chart.	P. H. Sawyer, *Anglo-Saxon charters: an annotated list and bibliography*, Royal Historical Society Guides and Handbooks (1968)
AusDB	D. Pike and others, eds., *Australian dictionary of biography*, 16 vols. (1966–2002)
Baker, *Serjeants*	J. H. Baker, *The order of serjeants at law*, SeldS, suppl. ser., 5 (1984)
Bale, *Cat.*	J. Bale, *Scriptorum illustrium Maioris Brytannie, quam nunc Angliam et Scotiam vocant: catalogus*, 2 vols. in 1 (Basel, 1557–9); facs. edn (1971)
Bale, *Index*	J. Bale, *Index Britanniae scriptorum*, ed. R. L. Poole and M. Bateson (1902); facs. edn (1990)
BBCS	*Bulletin of the Board of Celtic Studies*
BDMBR	J. O. Baylen and N. J. Gossman, eds., *Biographical dictionary of modern British radicals*, 3 vols. in 4 (1979–88)
Bede, *Hist. eccl.*	*Bede's Ecclesiastical history of the English people*, ed. and trans. B. Colgrave and R. A. B. Mynors, OMT (1969); repr. (1991)
Bénézit, *Dict.*	E. Bénézit, *Dictionnaire critique et documentaire des peintres, sculpteurs, dessinateurs et graveurs*, 3 vols. (Paris, 1911–23); new edn, 8 vols. (1948–66), repr. (1966); 3rd edn, rev. and enl., 10 vols. (1976); 4th edn, 14 vols. (1999)
BIHR	*Bulletin of the Institute of Historical Research*
Birch, *Seals*	W. de Birch, *Catalogue of seals in the department of manuscripts in the British Museum*, 6 vols. (1887–1900)
Bishop Burnet's History	*Bishop Burnet's History of his own time*, ed. M. J. Routh, 2nd edn, 6 vols. (1833)
Blackwood	*Blackwood's [Edinburgh] Magazine*, 328 vols. (1817–1980)
Blain, Clements & Grundy, *Feminist comp.*	V. Blain, P. Clements, and I. Grundy, eds., *The feminist companion to literature in English* (1990)
BL cat.	*The British Library general catalogue of printed books* [in 360 vols. with suppls., also CD-ROM and online]
BMJ	*British Medical Journal*
Boase & Courtney, *Bibl. Corn.*	G. C. Boase and W. P. Courtney, *Bibliotheca Cornubiensis: a catalogue of the writings … of Cornishmen*, 3 vols. (1874–82)
Boase, *Mod. Eng. biog.*	F. Boase, *Modern English biography: containing many thousand concise memoirs of persons who have died since the year 1850*, 6 vols. (privately printed, Truro, 1892–1921); repr. (1965)
Boswell, *Life*	*Boswell's Life of Johnson: together with Journal of a tour to the Hebrides and Johnson's Diary of a journey into north Wales*, ed. G. B. Hill, enl. edn, rev. L. F. Powell, 6 vols. (1934–50); 2nd edn (1964); repr. (1971)
Brown & Stratton, *Brit. mus.*	J. D. Brown and S. S. Stratton, *British musical biography* (1897)
Bryan, *Painters*	M. Bryan, *A biographical and critical dictionary of painters and engravers*, 2 vols. (1816); new edn, ed. G. Stanley (1849); new edn, ed. R. E. Graves and W. Armstrong, 2 vols. (1886–9); [4th edn], ed. G. C. Williamson, 5 vols. (1903–5) [various reprs.]
Burke, *Gen. GB*	J. Burke, *A genealogical and heraldic history of the commoners of Great Britain and Ireland*, 4 vols. (1833–8); new edn as *A genealogical and heraldic dictionary of the landed gentry of Great Britain and Ireland*, 3 vols. [1843–9] [many later edns]
Burke, *Gen. Ire.*	J. B. Burke, *A genealogical and heraldic history of the landed gentry of Ireland* (1899); 2nd edn (1904); 3rd edn (1912); 4th edn (1958); 5th edn as *Burke's Irish family records* (1976)
Burke, *Peerage*	J. Burke, *A general* [later edns *A genealogical*] *and heraldic dictionary of the peerage and baronetage of the United Kingdom* [later edns *the British empire*] (1829–)
Burney, *Hist. mus.*	C. Burney, *A general history of music, from the earliest ages to the present period*, 4 vols. (1776–89)
Burtchaell & Sadleir, *Alum. Dubl.*	G. D. Burtchaell and T. U. Sadleir, *Alumni Dublinenses: a register of the students, graduates, and provosts of Trinity College* (1924); [2nd edn], with suppl., in 2 pts (1935)
Calamy rev.	A. G. Matthews, *Calamy revised* (1934); repr. (1988)
CCI	*Calendar of confirmations and inventories granted and given up in the several commissariots of Scotland* (1876–)
CClR	*Calendar of the close rolls preserved in the Public Record Office*, 47 vols. (1892–1963)
CDS	J. Bain, ed., *Calendar of documents relating to Scotland*, 4 vols., PRO (1881–8); suppl. vol. 5, ed. G. G. Simpson and J. D. Galbraith [1986]
CEPR letters	W. H. Bliss, C. Johnson, and J. Twemlow, eds., *Calendar of entries in the papal registers relating to Great Britain and Ireland: papal letters* (1893–)
CGPLA	*Calendars of the grants of probate and letters of administration* [in 4 ser.: *England & Wales, Northern Ireland, Ireland, and Éire*]
Chambers, *Scots.*	R. Chambers, ed., *A biographical dictionary of eminent Scotsmen*, 4 vols. (1832–5)
Chancery records	chancery records pubd by the PRO
Chancery records (RC)	chancery records pubd by the Record Commissions

CIPM	*Calendar of inquisitions post mortem*, [20 vols.], PRO (1904–); also *Henry VII*, 3 vols. (1898–1955)
Clarendon, *Hist. rebellion*	E. Hyde, earl of Clarendon, *The history of the rebellion and civil wars in England*, 6 vols. (1888); repr. (1958) and (1992)
Cobbett, *Parl. hist.*	W. Cobbett and J. Wright, eds., *Cobbett's Parliamentary history of England*, 36 vols. (1806–1820)
Colvin, *Archs.*	H. Colvin, *A biographical dictionary of British architects, 1600–1840*, 3rd edn (1995)
Cooper, *Ath. Cantab.*	C. H. Cooper and T. Cooper, *Athenae Cantabrigienses*, 3 vols. (1858–1913); repr. (1967)
CPR	*Calendar of the patent rolls preserved in the Public Record Office* (1891–)
Crockford	*Crockford's Clerical Directory*
CS	Camden Society
CSP	*Calendar of state papers* [in 11 ser.: *domestic, Scotland, Scottish series, Ireland, colonial, Commonwealth, foreign, Spain* [at Simancas], *Rome, Milan*, and *Venice*]
CYS	Canterbury and York Society
DAB	*Dictionary of American biography*, 21 vols. (1928–36), repr. in 11 vols. (1964); 10 suppls. (1944–96)
DBB	D. J. Jeremy, ed., *Dictionary of business biography*, 5 vols. (1984–6)
DCB	G. W. Brown and others, *Dictionary of Canadian biography*, [14 vols.] (1966–)
Debrett's Peerage	*Debrett's Peerage* (1803–) [sometimes *Debrett's Illustrated peerage*]
Desmond, *Botanists*	R. Desmond, *Dictionary of British and Irish botanists and horticulturists* (1977); rev. edn (1994)
Dir. Brit. archs.	A. Felstead, J. Franklin, and L. Pinfield, eds., *Directory of British architects, 1834–1900* (1993); 2nd edn, ed. A. Brodie and others, 2 vols. (2001)
DLB	J. M. Bellamy and J. Saville, eds., *Dictionary of labour biography*, [10 vols.] (1972–)
DLitB	Dictionary of Literary Biography
DNB	*Dictionary of national biography*, 63 vols. (1885–1900), suppl., 3 vols. (1901); repr. in 22 vols. (1908–9); 10 further suppls. (1912–96); *Missing persons* (1993)
DNZB	W. H. Oliver and C. Orange, eds., *The dictionary of New Zealand biography*, 5 vols. (1990–2000)
DSAB	W. J. de Kock and others, eds., *Dictionary of South African biography*, 5 vols. (1968–87)
DSB	C. C. Gillispie and F. L. Holmes, eds., *Dictionary of scientific biography*, 16 vols. (1970–80); repr. in 8 vols. (1981); 2 vol. suppl. (1990)
DSBB	A. Slaven and S. Checkland, eds., *Dictionary of Scottish business biography, 1860–1960*, 2 vols. (1986–90)
DSCHT	N. M. de S. Cameron and others, eds., *Dictionary of Scottish church history and theology* (1993)
Dugdale, *Monasticon*	W. Dugdale, *Monasticon Anglicanum*, 3 vols. (1655–72); 2nd edn, 3 vols. (1661–82); new edn, ed. J. Caley, J. Ellis, and B. Bandinel, 6 vols. in 8 pts (1817–30); repr. (1846) and (1970)
DWB	J. E. Lloyd and others, eds., *Dictionary of Welsh biography down to 1940* (1959) [Eng. trans. of *Y bywgraffiadur Cymreig hyd 1940*, 2nd edn (1954)]
EdinR	*Edinburgh Review, or, Critical Journal*
EETS	Early English Text Society
Emden, *Cam.*	A. B. Emden, *A biographical register of the University of Cambridge to 1500* (1963)
Emden, *Oxf.*	A. B. Emden, *A biographical register of the University of Oxford to AD 1500*, 3 vols. (1957–9); also *A biographical register of the University of Oxford, AD 1501 to 1540* (1974)
EngHR	*English Historical Review*
Engraved Brit. ports.	F. M. O'Donoghue and H. M. Hake, *Catalogue of engraved British portraits preserved in the department of prints and drawings in the British Museum*, 6 vols. (1908–25)
ER	The English Reports, 178 vols. (1900–32)
ESTC	*English short title catalogue, 1475–1800* [CD-ROM and online]
Evelyn, *Diary*	*The diary of John Evelyn*, ed. E. S. De Beer, 6 vols. (1955); repr. (2000)
Farington, *Diary*	*The diary of Joseph Farington*, ed. K. Garlick and others, 17 vols. (1978–98)
Fasti Angl. (Hardy)	J. Le Neve, *Fasti ecclesiae Anglicanae*, ed. T. D. Hardy, 3 vols. (1854)
Fasti Angl., 1066–1300	[J. Le Neve], *Fasti ecclesiae Anglicanae, 1066–1300*, ed. D. E. Greenway and J. S. Barrow, [8 vols.] (1968–)
Fasti Angl., 1300–1541	[J. Le Neve], *Fasti ecclesiae Anglicanae, 1300–1541*, 12 vols. (1962–7)
Fasti Angl., 1541–1857	[J. Le Neve], *Fasti ecclesiae Anglicanae, 1541–1857*, ed. J. M. Horn, D. M. Smith, and D. S. Bailey, [9 vols.] (1969–)
Fasti Scot.	H. Scott, *Fasti ecclesiae Scoticanae*, 3 vols. in 6 (1871); new edn, [11 vols.] (1915–)
FO List	*Foreign Office List*
Fortescue, *Brit. army*	J. W. Fortescue, *A history of the British army*, 13 vols. (1899–1930)
Foss, *Judges*	E. Foss, *The judges of England*, 9 vols. (1848–64); repr. (1966)
Foster, *Alum. Oxon.*	J. Foster, ed., *Alumni Oxonienses: the members of the University of Oxford, 1715–1886*, 4 vols. (1887–8); later edn (1891); also *Alumni Oxonienses … 1500–1714*, 4 vols. (1891–2); 8 vol. repr. (1968) and (2000)
Fuller, *Worthies*	T. Fuller, *The history of the worthies of England*, 4 pts (1662); new edn, 2 vols., ed. J. Nichols (1811); new edn, 3 vols., ed. P. A. Nuttall (1840); repr. (1965)
GEC, *Baronetage*	G. E. Cokayne, *Complete baronetage*, 6 vols. (1900–09); repr. (1983) [microprint]
GEC, *Peerage*	G. E. C. [G. E. Cokayne], *The complete peerage of England, Scotland, Ireland, Great Britain, and the United Kingdom*, 8 vols. (1887–98); new edn, ed. V. Gibbs and others, 14 vols. in 15 (1910–98); microprint repr. (1982) and (1987)
Genest, *Eng. stage*	J. Genest, *Some account of the English stage from the Restoration in 1660 to 1830*, 10 vols. (1832); repr. [New York, 1965]
Gillow, *Lit. biog. hist.*	J. Gillow, *A literary and biographical history or bibliographical dictionary of the English Catholics, from the breach with Rome, in 1534, to the present time*, 5 vols. [1885–1902]; repr. (1961); repr. with preface by C. Gillow (1999)
Gir. Camb. opera	*Giraldi Cambrensis opera*, ed. J. S. Brewer, J. F. Dimock, and G. F. Warner, 8 vols., Rolls Series, 21 (1861–91)
GJ	*Geographical Journal*

Gladstone, *Diaries* — *The Gladstone diaries: with cabinet minutes and prime-ministerial correspondence*, ed. M. R. D. Foot and H. C. G. Matthew, 14 vols. (1968–94)

GM — *Gentleman's Magazine*

Graves, *Artists* — A. Graves, ed., *A dictionary of artists who have exhibited works in the principal London exhibitions of oil paintings from 1760 to 1880* (1884); new edn (1895); 3rd edn (1901); facs. edn (1969); repr. [1970], (1973), and (1984)

Graves, *Brit. Inst.* — A. Graves, *The British Institution, 1806–1867: a complete dictionary of contributors and their work from the foundation of the institution* (1875); facs. edn (1908); repr. (1969)

Graves, *RA exhibitors* — A. Graves, *The Royal Academy of Arts: a complete dictionary of contributors and their work from its foundation in 1769 to 1904*, 8 vols. (1905–6); repr. in 4 vols. (1970) and (1972)

Graves, *Soc. Artists* — A. Graves, *The Society of Artists of Great Britain, 1760–1791, the Free Society of Artists, 1761–1783: a complete dictionary* (1907); facs. edn (1969)

Greaves & Zaller, *BDBR* — R. L. Greaves and R. Zaller, eds., *Biographical dictionary of British radicals in the seventeenth century*, 3 vols. (1982–4)

Grove, *Dict. mus.* — G. Grove, ed., *A dictionary of music and musicians*, 5 vols. (1878–90); 2nd edn, ed. J. A. Fuller Maitland (1904–10); 3rd edn, ed. H. C. Colles (1927); 4th edn with suppl. (1940); 5th edn, ed. E. Blom, 9 vols. (1954); suppl. (1961) [see also *New Grove*]

Hall, *Dramatic ports.* — L. A. Hall, *Catalogue of dramatic portraits in the theatre collection of the Harvard College library*, 4 vols. (1930–34)

Hansard — *Hansard's parliamentary debates*, ser. 1–5 (1803–)

Highfill, Burnim & Langhans, *BDA* — P. H. Highfill, K. A. Burnim, and E. A. Langhans, *A biographical dictionary of actors, actresses, musicians, dancers, managers, and other stage personnel in London, 1660–1800*, 16 vols. (1973–93)

Hist. U. Oxf. — T. H. Aston, ed., *The history of the University of Oxford*, 8 vols. (1984–2000) [1: *The early Oxford schools*, ed. J. I. Catto (1984); 2: *Late medieval Oxford*, ed. J. I. Catto and R. Evans (1992); 3: *The collegiate university*, ed. J. McConica (1986); 4: *Seventeenth-century Oxford*, ed. N. Tyacke (1997); 5: *The eighteenth century*, ed. L. S. Sutherland and L. G. Mitchell (1986); 6–7: *Nineteenth-century Oxford*, ed. M. G. Brock and M. C. Curthoys (1997–2000); 8: *The twentieth century*, ed. B. Harrison (2000)]

HJ — *Historical Journal*

HMC — Historical Manuscripts Commission

Holdsworth, *Eng. law* — W. S. Holdsworth, *A history of English law*, ed. A. L. Goodhart and H. L. Hanbury, 17 vols. (1903–72)

HoP, *Commons* — *The history of parliament: the House of Commons* [*1386–1421*, ed. J. S. Roskell, L. Clark, and C. Rawcliffe, 4 vols. (1992); *1509–1558*, ed. S. T. Bindoff, 3 vols. (1982); *1558–1603*, ed. P. W. Hasler, 3 vols. (1981); *1660–1690*, ed. B. D. Henning, 3 vols. (1983); *1690–1715*, ed. D. W. Hayton, E. Cruickshanks, and S. Handley, 5 vols. (2002); *1715–1754*, ed. R. Sedgwick, 2 vols. (1970); *1754–1790*, ed. L. Namier and J. Brooke, 3 vols. (1964), repr. (1985); *1790–1820*, ed. R. G. Thorne, 5 vols. (1986); in draft (used with permission): *1422–1504*, *1604–1629*, *1640–1660*, and *1820–1832*]

IGI — *International Genealogical Index*, Church of Jesus Christ of the Latterday Saints

ILN — *Illustrated London News*

IMC — Irish Manuscripts Commission

Irving, *Scots.* — J. Irving, ed., *The book of Scotsmen eminent for achievements in arms and arts, church and state, law, legislation and literature, commerce, science, travel and philanthropy* (1881)

JCS — *Journal of the Chemical Society*

JHC — *Journals of the House of Commons*

JHL — *Journals of the House of Lords*

John of Worcester, *Chron.* — *The chronicle of John of Worcester*, ed. R. R. Darlington and P. McGurk, trans. J. Bray and P. McGurk, 3 vols., OMT (1995–) [vol. 1 forthcoming]

Keeler, *Long Parliament* — M. F. Keeler, *The Long Parliament, 1640–1641: a biographical study of its members* (1954)

Kelly, *Handbk* — *The upper ten thousand: an alphabetical list of all members of noble families*, 3 vols. (1875–7); continued as *Kelly's handbook of the upper ten thousand for 1878* [1879], 2 vols. (1878–9); continued as *Kelly's handbook to the titled, landed and official classes*, 94 vols. (1880–1973)

LondG — *London Gazette*

LP Henry VIII — J. S. Brewer, J. Gairdner, and R. H. Brodie, eds., *Letters and papers, foreign and domestic, of the reign of Henry VIII*, 23 vols. in 38 (1862–1932); repr. (1965)

Mallalieu, *Watercolour artists* — H. L. Mallalieu, *The dictionary of British watercolour artists up to 1820*, 3 vols. (1976–90); vol. 1, 2nd edn (1986)

Memoirs FRS — *Biographical Memoirs of Fellows of the Royal Society*

MGH — Monumenta Germaniae Historica

MT — *Musical Times*

Munk, *Roll* — W. Munk, *The roll of the Royal College of Physicians of London*, 2 vols. (1861); 2nd edn, 3 vols. (1878)

N&Q — *Notes and Queries*

New Grove — S. Sadie, ed., *The new Grove dictionary of music and musicians*, 20 vols. (1980); 2nd edn, 29 vols. (2001) [also online edn; see also Grove, *Dict. mus.*]

Nichols, *Illustrations* — J. Nichols and J. B. Nichols, *Illustrations of the literary history of the eighteenth century*, 8 vols. (1817–58)

Nichols, *Lit. anecdotes* — J. Nichols, *Literary anecdotes of the eighteenth century*, 9 vols. (1812–16); facs. edn (1966)

Obits. FRS — *Obituary Notices of Fellows of the Royal Society*

O'Byrne, *Naval biog. dict.* — W. R. O'Byrne, *A naval biographical dictionary* (1849); repr. (1990); [2nd edn], 2 vols. (1861)

OHS — Oxford Historical Society

Old Westminsters — *The record of Old Westminsters*, 1–2, ed. G. F. R. Barker and A. H. Stenning (1928); suppl. 1, ed. J. B. Whitmore and G. R. Y. Radcliffe [1938]; 3, ed. J. B. Whitmore, G. R. Y. Radcliffe, and D. C. Simpson (1963); suppl. 2, ed. F. E. Pagan (1978); 4, ed. F. E. Pagan and H. E. Pagan (1992)

OMT — Oxford Medieval Texts

Ordericus Vitalis, *Eccl. hist.* — *The ecclesiastical history of Orderic Vitalis*, ed. and trans. M. Chibnall, 6 vols., OMT (1969–80); repr. (1990)

Paris, *Chron.* — *Matthaei Parisiensis, monachi sancti Albani, chronica majora*, ed. H. R. Luard, Rolls Series, 7 vols. (1872–83)

Parl. papers — *Parliamentary papers* (1801–)

PBA — *Proceedings of the British Academy*

Pepys, *Diary*	*The diary of Samuel Pepys*, ed. R. Latham and W. Matthews, 11 vols. (1970–83); repr. (1995) and (2000)
Pevsner	N. Pevsner and others, Buildings of England series
PICE	*Proceedings of the Institution of Civil Engineers*
Pipe rolls	*The great roll of the pipe for* ..., PRSoc. (1884–)
PRO	Public Record Office
PRS	*Proceedings of the Royal Society of London*
PRSoc.	Pipe Roll Society
PTRS	*Philosophical Transactions of the Royal Society*
QR	*Quarterly Review*
RC	Record Commissions
Redgrave, *Artists*	S. Redgrave, *A dictionary of artists of the English school* (1874); rev. edn (1878); repr. (1970)
Reg. Oxf.	C. W. Boase and A. Clark, eds., *Register of the University of Oxford*, 5 vols., OHS, 1, 10–12, 14 (1885–9)
Reg. PCS	J. H. Burton and others, eds., *The register of the privy council of Scotland*, 1st ser., 14 vols. (1877–98); 2nd ser., 8 vols. (1899–1908); 3rd ser., [16 vols.] (1908–70)
Reg. RAN	H. W. C. Davis and others, eds., *Regesta regum Anglo-Normannorum, 1066–1154*, 4 vols. (1913–69)
RIBA Journal	*Journal of the Royal Institute of British Architects* [later *RIBA Journal*]
RotP	J. Strachey, ed., *Rotuli parliamentorum ut et petitiones, et placita in parliamento*, 6 vols. (1767–77)
RotS	D. Macpherson, J. Caley, and W. Illingworth, eds., *Rotuli Scotiae in Turri Londinensi et in domo capitulari Westmonasteriensi asservati*, 2 vols., RC, 14 (1814–19)
RS	Record(s) Society
Rymer, *Foedera*	T. Rymer and R. Sanderson, eds., *Foedera, conventiones, literae et cuiuscunque generis acta publica inter reges Angliae et alios quosvis imperatores, reges, pontifices, principes, vel communitates*, 20 vols. (1704–35); 2nd edn, 20 vols. (1726–35); 3rd edn, 10 vols. (1739–45), facs. edn (1967); new edn, ed. A. Clarke, J. Caley, and F. Holbrooke, 4 vols., RC, 50 (1816–30)
Sainty, *Judges*	J. Sainty, ed., *The judges of England, 1272–1990*, SeldS, suppl. ser., 10 (1993)
Sainty, *King's counsel*	J. Sainty, ed., *A list of English law officers and king's counsel*, SeldS, suppl. ser., 7 (1987)
SCH	Studies in Church History
Scots peerage	J. B. Paul, ed. *The Scots peerage, founded on Wood's edition of Sir Robert Douglas's Peerage of Scotland, containing an historical and genealogical account of the nobility of that kingdom*, 9 vols. (1904–14)
SeldS	Selden Society
SHR	*Scottish Historical Review*
State trials	T. B. Howell and T. J. Howell, eds., *Cobbett's Complete collection of state trials*, 34 vols. (1809–28)
STC, 1475–1640	A. W. Pollard, G. R. Redgrave, and others, eds., *A short-title catalogue of* ... *English books* ... *1475–1640* (1926); 2nd edn, ed. W. A. Jackson, F. S. Ferguson, and K. F. Pantzer, 3 vols. (1976–91) [see also Wing, *STC*]
STS	Scottish Text Society
SurtS	Surtees Society
Symeon of Durham, *Opera*	*Symeonis monachi opera omnia*, ed. T. Arnold, 2 vols., Rolls Series, 75 (1882–5); repr. (1965)
Tanner, *Bibl. Brit.-Hib.*	T. Tanner, *Bibliotheca Britannico-Hibernica*, ed. D. Wilkins (1748); repr. (1963)
Thieme & Becker, *Allgemeines Lexikon*	U. Thieme, F. Becker, and H. Vollmer, eds., *Allgemeines Lexikon der bildenden Künstler von der Antike bis zur Gegenwart*, 37 vols. (Leipzig, 1907–50); repr. (1961–5), (1983), and (1992)
Thurloe, *State papers*	*A collection of the state papers of John Thurloe*, ed. T. Birch, 7 vols. (1742)
TLS	*Times Literary Supplement*
Tout, *Admin. hist.*	T. F. Tout, *Chapters in the administrative history of mediaeval England: the wardrobe, the chamber, and the small seals*, 6 vols. (1920–33); repr. (1967)
TRHS	*Transactions of the Royal Historical Society*
VCH	H. A. Doubleday and others, eds., *The Victoria history of the counties of England*, [88 vols.] (1900–)
Venn, *Alum. Cant.*	J. Venn and J. A. Venn, *Alumni Cantabrigienses: a biographical list of all known students, graduates, and holders of office at the University of Cambridge, from the earliest times to 1900*, 10 vols. (1922–54); repr. in 2 vols. (1974–8)
Vertue, *Note books*	[G. Vertue], *Note books*, ed. K. Esdaile, earl of Ilchester, and H. M. Hake, 6 vols., Walpole Society, 18, 20, 22, 24, 26, 30 (1930–55)
VF	*Vanity Fair*
Walford, *County families*	E. Walford, *The county families of the United Kingdom, or, Royal manual of the titled and untitled aristocracy of Great Britain and Ireland* (1860)
Walker rev.	A. G. Matthews, *Walker revised: being a revision of John Walker's Sufferings of the clergy during the grand rebellion, 1642–60* (1948); repr. (1988)
Walpole, *Corr.*	*The Yale edition of Horace Walpole's correspondence*, ed. W. S. Lewis, 48 vols. (1937–83)
Ward, *Men of the reign*	T. H. Ward, ed., *Men of the reign: a biographical dictionary of eminent persons of British and colonial birth who have died during the reign of Queen Victoria* (1885); repr. (Graz, 1968)
Waterhouse, *18c painters*	E. Waterhouse, *The dictionary of 18th century painters in oils and crayons* (1981); repr. as *British 18th century painters in oils and crayons* (1991), vol. 2 of *Dictionary of British art*
Watt, *Bibl. Brit.*	R. Watt, *Bibliotheca Britannica, or, A general index to British and foreign literature*, 4 vols. (1824) [many reprs.]
Wellesley index	W. E. Houghton, ed., *The Wellesley index to Victorian periodicals, 1824–1900*, 5 vols. (1966–89); new edn (1999) [CD-ROM]
Wing, *STC*	D. Wing, ed., *Short-title catalogue of* ... *English books* ... *1641–1700*, 3 vols. (1945–51); 2nd edn (1972–88); rev. and enl. edn, ed. J. J. Morrison, C. W. Nelson, and M. Seccombe, 4 vols. (1994–8) [see also *STC, 1475–1640*]
Wisden	*John Wisden's Cricketer's Almanack*
Wood, *Ath. Oxon.*	A. Wood, *Athenae Oxonienses* ... *to which are added the Fasti*, 2 vols. (1691–2); 2nd edn (1721); new edn, 4 vols., ed. P. Bliss (1813–20); repr. (1967) and (1969)
Wood, *Vic. painters*	C. Wood, *Dictionary of Victorian painters* (1971); 2nd edn (1978); 3rd edn as *Victorian painters*, 2 vols. (1995), vol. 4 of *Dictionary of British art*
WW	*Who's who* (1849–)
WWBMP	M. Stenton and S. Lees, eds., *Who's who of British members of parliament*, 4 vols. (1976–81)
WWW	*Who was who* (1929–)

Sartorius family (*per.* *c.*1730–1831), painters, became prominent in the eighteenth century. **John Sartorius** (*supp. fl.* 18th cent.), reputed animal painter, is frequently cited as the German-born founder of a dynasty of British sporting artists, descended from Jacob Christoph Sartorius of Nuremberg (*fl.* 1694–1737), engraver. No reliable evidence of his career survives, nor any signed or securely documented painting. The list of exhibits of his paintings at the Free Society of Artists as published by Algernon Graves (1907) seems to have been conflated with those of (his son?) Francis [i] Sartorius [*see below*]. Where, rarely, the paintings given by Graves to 'Sartorius Senior' can be identified from the list of titles, they are invariably by other members of the family. Thus, for instance, the oil painting of the thoroughbred racehorse Whirligig exhibited at the Society of Artists in 1770 (catalogue no. 218) as by 'John Sartorius' is in fact signed by Francis Sartorius. Considerable doubt, therefore, must attach to his being a working artist.

By contrast **Francis** [i] **Sartorius** (1733/4–1804), sporting painter, was exceptionally prolific and left a large corpus of signed, documented, and engraved work. Although based in London, where he maintained studios at various addresses in Soho, he was certainly itinerant, visiting race meetings (notably Newmarket) and gentlemen's seats and studs. He may have received some instruction from Thomas Butler, a print dealer and publisher in Pall Mall. His equestrian and canine portraiture has a charming if wooden air which attracted considerable patronage among the sporting gentry and nobility, including such notable figures as the duke of Cumberland and Lord Rockingham. He exhibited frequently at the main London venues, the Society of Artists, the Free Society of Artists and the Royal Academy. On 24 October 1757 he married Frances Lynn, who died before 1793 when he married, second, Grizel Dickson on 17 February.

Francis [i] Sartorius was among the first sporting artists to visit and paint in Ireland, where he worked for the second earl of Aldborough at Baltinglass, co. Wicklow (1787). He was also working on Irish commissions towards the end of his life. His sole published autograph letter is from Belmont, Cheshire, and is addressed to John Smith-Barry in Merrion Square, Dublin, and dated 11 August 1800. It confirms a commission for a painting of mares and foals on 'a piece of canvas six foot long by two foot' for which the price is to be 'three guineas a horse': the 'foles' Sartorius 'give[s] in, which I don't think but will please' (*Repository of Arts*). The accompanying sketch shows five mares, implying a price of 15 guineas for the painting—at a time when such painters as Sir William Beechey in London were charging 100 guineas for a human portrait of comparable size.

Sartorius's productivity did not compensate for the low prices he charged: he died intestate, administration of his goods valued at just £100 being granted in June 1804 to his only surviving son from the first of his two marriages, John Nost Sartorius.

John Nost Sartorius (1759–1829), animal painter, was born on 20 May 1759 and baptized on 10 June at St James's, Westminster, the son of Francis [i] Sartorius and his wife, Frances. His unusual forename, frequently, and erroneously, given as John Nott, may derive from the sculptor John Van Nost, who was perhaps a godfather and whose family were neighbours in Piccadilly.

The striking similarity of early works by the son to those of his father suggests ineluctably that he was his pupil and collaborator. Father and son lived from at least 1775 in Soho and its environs, John Nost settling in a house at 2 Spur Street, Leicester Square, in the parish of St Martin-in-the-Fields in 1785, where he was joined by his father. Towards the end of his life John Nost Sartorius moved to a house in suburban Kennington, Surrey, where he died intestate. Curiously, the letters of administration granted in April 1829 to his son John Francis Sartorius [*see below*] describe him as 'Gentleman', despite his leaving an estate valued at only £20.

John Nost Sartorius was an extremely prolific painter, though his subject matter is restricted solely to that of a sporting and animal nature. The wide geographic spread of his work throughout the United Kingdom implies that he was regularly itinerant, and views of patrons' houses and estates regularly feature in the background of his paintings. Among his many patrons' commissions are numbered those for Lord Foley at Epsom and in Herefordshire; Lord Derby both at Newmarket and at Knowsley in Lancashire; Sir Charles Bunbury at Newmarket and in Cheshire; Christopher Wilson in Yorkshire; and the duke of Cleveland at Raby Castle, co. Durham.

John Nost Sartorius exhibited widely at the major London venues: the Society of Artists (1778), the Free Society of Artists (1776–83), and the Royal Academy (1781–1824). Numerous popular prints were produced after his paintings, both copperplate-engravings and mezzotints. His huge popularity with the sporting gentry has left us with a library of images of the famous racehorses of his day that they owned, and a record of the country sports that they enjoyed. While the style of his paintings is somewhat wooden and naïve, they are none the less an endearing, enduring, and valuable record of a way of life which had changed beyond recognition by the middle of the nineteenth century: they have remained very popular with collectors in modern times.

With his wife, Margaret (*née* Watkins), whom he married on 24 June 1777 at St Anne's, Soho, John Nost Sartorius had three sons and two daughters. The eldest, **John Francis Sartorius** (*bap.* 1779, *d.* 1831), who was baptized on 21 March 1779, at Macclesfield Street, continued the family tradition of painting sporting pictures in what was rapidly becoming an archaic style. Shortly after the death of his grandfather in 1804 he moved from the old artistic milieu of Soho to the new one of Chelsea, where he had a studio in Queen's Elms Gardens, off the King's Road. By the time of his death, his retardataire style of hunting and racing pictures had left him with few patrons, and he was producing small and undistinguished still lifes of dead birds, which he continued to send to the Royal Academy until 1829. None of his three children with his wife, Zara Adamson, whom he married on 17 April 1805 at St Marylebone Church, was a painter.

Francis [ii] **Sartorius** (*bap.* 1781, *d.* after 1808), marine painter, was baptized on 9 September 1781, the second son of John Nost Sartorius. He first exhibited at the Royal Academy at the age of eighteen in 1799, and lastly in 1808. He seems never to have lived anywhere other than central London. His productions are of modest quality; there are seven in the National Maritime Museum, Greenwich.

Charles James Sartorius (*bap.* 1794, *d.* after 1821) was baptized on 23 April 1794 at St Pancras parish church, the fourth child and third son of John Nost Sartorius. Like his brother Francis [ii] Sartorius, he was a marine painter, exhibiting five pictures at the Royal Academy between 1811 and 1821. The younger daughter of John Nost Sartorius, Louisa Margaret, baptized on 17 June 1795 at St Martin-in-the-Fields, Westminster, exhibited one painting (a still life) at the British Institution in 1813 but is not otherwise known.

G. (George?) William Sartorius (*fl.* 1773–1779) was a painter of 'fruit pieces' and occasional portraits. His middle name is known only from occasional signed pictures, his initials from the records of the Free Society of Artists from 1773 to 1779. His relationship with the other members of the Sartorius family is unknown; the style of his paintings suggests he was a contemporary of Francis Sartorius the elder. CHRISTOPHER FOLEY

Sources Graves, *Soc. Artists* • Graves, *RA exhibitors*, vol. 7 • F. Siltzer, *The story of British sporting prints* [1929] • *Repository of Arts Magazine* (autumn 1987) [letter of Francis [i] Sartorius] • parish register, Westminster, St James's, 10 June 1759 [baptism, John Nost Sartorius] • *IGI* • parish register, Soho, St Anne's, 21 March 1779 [baptism, John Francis Sartorius] • house plaque, 3 Queen's Elms Gardens, Chelsea [John Francis Sartorius] • parish register, Soho, St Anne's, 9 Sept 1781 [baptism, Francis [ii] Sartorius] • admon, PRO, PROB 6/205, fol. 94*v* [John Nost Sartorius] • admon, PRO, PROB 6/180, fol. 505*r* [Francis [i] Sartorius]

Wealth at death £100—Francis [i] Sartorius: administration, PRO, PROB 6/180, fol. 505*r* • £20—John Nost Sartorius: administration, PRO, PROB 6/205, fol. 94*v*

Sartorius brothers (*act. c.*1857–1925), army officers, were the three sons of Admiral Sir George Rose *Sartorius (1790–1885), naval officer, and his wife, Sophia, daughter of John Lamb. They chose not to follow their father into the navy but entered the army, and were as successful in their profession as he had been in his. Their careers followed similar interests and patterns of service: dedication in the training of men, experience in military administration, service in India, war in Afghanistan, awards for bravery in battle. In retirement the brothers, with homes in Surrey, maintained a family closeness.

The eldest son, **George Conrad Sartorius** (1840–1912), was born on 2 April 1840. He joined his brothers at Victoria College, Jersey, in 1856, went on to the Royal Military Academy, Woolwich, and entered the Royal Artillery as a lieutenant in 1857. In India he was attached to the Bombay staff corps and served with the native infantry regiments, was captain in 1869, and deputy assistant quartermaster-general of the Bombay district in 1876. He married in 1863 Anna Lucas (*d.* 1869), daughter of General Charles Lucas, and they had a son and two daughters. His second wife, whom he married in 1870, was Ernestine Isabella Ross, author, daughter of George Ross. During the Russo-Turkish War in 1877 Sartorius took leave to travel to Bulgaria, becoming one of the group of correspondents and observers attached to the camp of General Valentine Baker (who was serving with the Turkish army), and took responsibility for its day-to-day organization. He served in the Second Anglo-Afghan War as a major, being attached to the 29th Bombay native infantry, with the southern Afghanistan field force, and was mentioned in dispatches.

In 1882 Sartorius was in Egypt on Wolseley's campaign which culminated in the battle of Tell al-Kebir and the British occupation. He stayed in Egypt as deputy to Valentine Baker, then inspector-general of a new semi-military gendarmerie. In December 1883 the Egyptian government decided to send an expedition to the Sudan to defend Egyptian garrisons against the Mahdists; for political reasons, instead of the army the inadequate, ill-prepared, and ill-equipped gendarmerie was dispatched to Suakin on the Red Sea. Sartorius, sent on ahead of Baker, took charge of military training for the force. With him were his wife and daughter: Ernestine Sartorius acted as her husband's secretary and kept a detailed journal (published as *Three Months in the Soudan*, 1885). The expedition ended in disaster in February 1884 at the first battle of al-Teb when the gendarmerie fled from the Mahdists, and Baker, Sartorius, and the other officers struggled to control the rout: of nearly 4000, fewer than 1500 returned. Sartorius was awarded the second-class Mejidiye. On his return to Cairo he found that his gendarmerie position had been abolished in an attempt at administrative reform, and he returned to the Bombay staff corps.

Further distinguished service followed during the Upper Burma expedition of 1886–8: Sartorius was made brevet colonel, was twice mentioned in dispatches, and was made CB. With him in Burma was his son, George Charles Francis, who had joined his father in the Bombay staff corps. Sartorius continued with the Indian (formerly Bombay) Staff Corps as colonel and commandant. On his retirement in 1897 he received the reward for distinguished services. During his years in India he enjoyed big game hunting (claiming the record for the largest buffalo ever shot), with expeditions to Africa to shoot lion and buffalo. In retirement he lived at Thorwald, near Godalming, Surrey. He died on 2 November 1912.

The second son, **Reginald William Sartorius** (1841–1907), was born on 8 May 1841. He entered Victoria College, Jersey, with his younger brother in 1855, and joined the army in January 1858 in the Bengal infantry, becoming a lieutenant in May. During the Indian mutiny he carried dispatches through the encircling enemy at the relief of

Azamgarh and was in operations in the Gorakhpur district. Further active service followed, including the Bhutan campaign. In 1868 he became captain, Bengal infantry, at the same time extending his activities and responsibilities as squadron subaltern of one of the cavalry regiments. In 1873, as captain, 6th Bengal cavalry, he joined the Asante expedition of Captain John Hawley Glover.

The Asante army invaded the Gold Coast (a British protectorate) in 1873 and, overcoming local people, occupied British coastal fortified posts. The British government accepted the offer of Captain Glover, an experienced administrator in west Africa and held in high esteem among the Africans, to raise a local army against the Asante. An imperial expedition under Sir Garnet Wolseley was also sent. Glover's force was to travel by steamer up the River Volta, advance west towards Kumasi, the Asante capital, and thus provide a diversion for Wolseley's force advancing from the coast.

In spite of Glover's experience and standing there were delays, poor communications, little success in persuading the inhabitants, and conflict with the Asante. At one encounter at Abogoo on 17 January 1874 Sartorius, under heavy fire, rescued a Haussa non-commissioned officer and placed him under cover. Wolseley's force, advancing towards Kumasi, repulsed attacks from the Asante and, having entered the town, waited for the Asante king to accept peace terms. When there was no response the town was destroyed: Wolseley, uncertain of the Asante army and fearing treachery, withdrew. Glover, ignorant of Wolseley's actions, sent Sartorius ahead to Kumasi. With a small group of Haussas, on 11 February he rode into and through the ruins of the deserted town, unhindered by the enemy, and on to Wolseley's camp. It was evidence that the Asante were defeated.

The incident brought Sartorius to the attention of the British press and public, and he was featured in the *Illustrated London News* (21 March 1874) and appeared in various photographs, including some with his dog which accompanied him on the campaign. On their return Glover and Sartorius, 'the renowned Ashantee officers', were guests of honour at a banquet in Liverpool town hall (9 April 1874). Sartorius was twice mentioned in dispatches, made brevet major, created a CMG, and in October was awarded the Victoria Cross for the incident at Abogoo.

As a consequence of the publicity Sartorius was appointed to the staff of the prince of Wales on his visit to India in 1875–6. Sartorius married in 1877 Agnes Maria, daughter of Dr J. Kemp; they had a son, Gerald (*d.* 1967), who also served in the Indian army, and was awarded the Military Cross for his actions at Ypres in November 1914, and a daughter, Esme, who served in the VAD during the First World War. His preference was for action, and through his insistence (the 6th Bengal cavalry was not involved) Sartorius joined the Afghan campaign. He continued as major and lieutenant-colonel to carry out dual responsibilities, with the infantry and as squadron subaltern and then commander of a cavalry regiment. In 1886 he became colonel of the Bengal infantry, and his active career came to an end in 1893, when he left India and went to live in Italy.

In 1895 he was listed as major-general, Bengal infantry, and in 1897 was placed on the retired list. In England he resided at Haslemere, Surrey. He was a member of the Royal Yacht Squadron, and died suddenly on 8 August 1907 when sailing at Cowes, Isle of Wight. In his obituaries his moment of fame was recalled, emphasizing that his ride into Kumasi summed up his character: 'he was then as he was throughout his life' (*Daily Telegraph*, 9 Aug 1907).

The third son, **Euston Henry Sartorius**, count of Penhafirme in the Portuguese nobility (1844–1925), was born on 6 June 1844 in Cintra, Portugal. With his brother Reginald he entered Victoria College, Jersey, in 1855; he went on first to the Royal Naval School, New Cross, then, deciding on an army career, he attended the Royal Military Academy, Woolwich, followed by the Royal Military College, Sandhurst, where he passed out first in his year. He joined the 59th (2nd Nottinghamshire) regiment as an ensign in 1862. In June 1869 at Broadstairs he rescued three girls from drowning, for which he received the Humane Society's bronze medal. He passed the Staff College in December 1870. He was for four years instructor in military surveying at Sandhurst, and then travelled for a year overland, through Persia, to India to rejoin his regiment. Sartorius married in 1874 Emily (*d.* January 1915), daughter of Sir Francis Cook, and had two daughters and a son, Euston Francis Frederick, who served in the Grenadier Guards and died of wounds in 1915.

In the Second Anglo-Afghan War three British army columns invaded Afghanistan in November 1878. The 59th foot was part of the southern Afghanistan field force, moving from Quetta to Kandahar. In this march Sartorius's company escorted the Royal Artillery guns. Kandahar was reached on 8 January 1879, and despite continuing transport and supply problems in an inhospitable country, British victory resulted in a treaty in May 1879. A British resident was established in Kabul, and the forces began their return to India. In September, when the resident, Sir Pierre Louis Napoleon Cavagnari, was murdered, war erupted again. The southern field force was recalled and was once more engaged in fighting in and around Kandahar. The 59th foot and the 29th Bombay infantry were involved in the capture of Kalat-i-Ghilzai and in the move towards Ab-i-Tazi on 10 October, with Sartorius present as assistant field engineer. Later that month he was with the small force of 350 men which advanced upon the large Ghilzais force assembling at Shahjui. Under fire from the British heavy guns the Ghilzais retreated, taking refuge in an old fort on a precipitous hill. On 24 October Sartorius with a small party led the attack on the hill against the full force of the enemy and captured the hilltop post; the rest of the British force followed, there was fierce hand-to-hand fighting, and the Ghilzais fled. Sartorius was badly wounded by sword cuts in both hands. For this action he was made brevet major, and in May 1881 awarded the Victoria Cross. He was twice mentioned in dispatches, and received special commendation for 'excellent work and gallant conduct' in connection with his surveying (Survey Department, Report of proceedings of the Government of India, 17 May 1880, Creagh and Humphris).

Sartorius partially lost the use of his left hand and, unable to continue as an active field officer, was appointed to headquarters duties as deputy assistant adjutant-general and quartermaster-general at Aldershot. In the 1882 Egyptian campaign he was deputy assistant adjutant-general and quartermaster-general, responsible for base and communications: he was made brevet lieutenant-colonel, was mentioned in dispatches, and received the fourth-class medal of Osmanieh. He became colonel in 1886, and was assistant adjutant-general in Portsmouth from 1891 to 1894. In 1896 he was made CB, and went to Japan as military attaché. Major-general in 1899, he retired in August 1901 but continued colonel of a volunteer battalion of the South Lancashire regiment. He undertook further diplomatic duties and attended the Siamese princes at Queen Victoria's jubilee and at the coronations of Edward VII and George V.

Through his father's connections with Portugal, Sartorius was entitled to bear the title count of Penhafirme when residing there. In retirement he lived at Holmbury St Mary, Surrey, and in London. Following a short illness he died at his residence, 17 Chelsea Embankment, London, on 19 February 1925.

The careers, the interests, and the achievements of the three brothers were similar, but there were marked differences in personalities. The best known was Reginald William, with his public image as the daring captain of the Second Anglo-Asante War, riding on a pony through the ruins of Kumasi, with his dog at his side. He was the unconventional soldier, intent on action and successful in persuading authorities to allow him his way, as in the Anglo-Asante and Anglo-Afghan wars. Euston Henry was the clever brother, successful at military studies and, as a staff officer, an effective organizer and administrator who, in retirement, was able to adjust to the different skills of diplomatic life. Their Victoria crosses were awarded for incidents on the battlefield in Africa and Afghanistan which show similar qualities of quick courage, coolness, and determination. The career of George Conrad, the eldest, was less spectacular, marred by the disaster at al-Teb, for which neither he nor the other gendarmerie officers were responsible. His career was steady, and as uneventful years in the Bombay staff corps passed he found his outlet for action and excitement in big game hunting.

In the history of the Victoria Cross only one other pair of brothers has been honoured (the Gough brothers, during the Indian mutiny). For the Sartorius brothers there were administrative problems relating to their awards. In public opinion Reginald Sartorius deserved the VC for his ride through Kumasi. But the circumstances of that ride did not fall within the terms of the VC warrant: that is, no superior officer had been present to provide testimony to his conduct. His action at Abogoo, however, had been witnessed: hence the decision was taken to specify that incident in the VC award. Sartorius himself believed that his VC was for the ride (*Daily Telegraph*, 2 Nov 1967). The action of Euston Sartorius at Shahjui did not come within the existing definition for the VC award, because his conduct had been part of 'his duty in leading his men'. A redefinition of the VC warrant was suggested, and various drafts were circulated which included the addition of phrasing such as 'marked gallantry in the performance of their duty'. Such wording was not, however, incorporated in the VC warrant of April 1881, but Sartorius's action was re-examined and his award was approved.

DOROTHY ANDERSON

Sources 'Sartorius, Sir George Rose', *DNB* • *Hart's Army List* (1857–1912) • *WW* • *WWW, 1897–1915* • *WWW, 1916–28* • *Army List* (1910) • M. Harding, ed., *The Victorian soldier: studies in the history of the British army, 1816–1914* (1993) • T. A. Heathcote, *The Afghan wars, 1839–1919* (1980) • B. Robson, *The road to Kabul: the Second Afghan War, 1878–1881* (1986) • E. Sartorius, *Three months in the Soudan* (1885) • *LondG* (26 Oct 1874) • *LondG* (17 May 1881) • M. J. Crook, *The evolution of the Victoria cross: a study in administrative history* (1975) • E. Hebden, 'The VC and his dog', *Daily Telegraph* (2 Nov 1967) • H. M. Stanley, *Coomassie and Magdala: the story of two British campaigns in Africa*, 2nd edn (1874), 205–6 [full text of Sartorius's report to Glover on his ride through Kumasi, dated 3 Feb 1874] • H. J. Stannus, *Curiosities of the Victoria Cross* (1992) • V. Baker, *War in Bulgaria: a narrative of personal experiences*, 2 vols. (1879) • *The Times* (6 Nov 1912) • *The Times* (1 Jan 1913) • O'M. Creagh and E. M. Humphris, *The V.C. and D.S.O.: a complete record*, 3 vols. [1920–24] • *The Times* (9 Aug 1907) • *Daily Telegraph* (9 Aug 1907) • *ILN* (21 March 1874) • *Gore's Directory of Liverpool* (1885); facs. edn as *An everyday history of Liverpool* (1965) • H. Brackenbury, *The Ashanti war*, 2 vols. (1874); facs. edn (1968) • S. H. Shadbolt, ed., *The Afghan campaigns of 1878–1880*, 2 (1882) • *The Times* (21 Feb 1925) • *The Times* (9 May 1925) • L. Maxwell, *The Ashanti ring: Sir Garnet Wolseley's campaigns, 1870–1882* (1985) • D. Anderson, *Baker Pasha: misconduct and mischance* (1999) • letter of administration, 14 Oct 1909 [Reginald William Sartorius] • W. J. Elliott, *The Victoria Cross in Afghanistan and on the frontiers of India during the years 1877, 1878, 1879 and 1880: and how it was won* (1882) • 'Storming a hill in Afghanistan', *The Graphic* (27 Dec 1879) • *The Times* (25 Aug 1967) • A. Lloyd, *The drums of Kumasi: the story of the Ashanti wars* (1964) • archives, Victoria College, Jersey, Channel Islands • NAM, Sartorius files • D. Anderson, 'The interpretation of "Valour": the Sartorius brothers and their V.C.s', *Orders and Medals: the Journal of the Orders and Medals Research Society*, 40/4 (Dec 2001), 249–56

Likenesses Maull & Co., photograph, 1874? (Reginald William Sartorius), priv. coll. • group portrait, photograph (George Conrad Sartorius), repro. in Sartorius, *Three months in the Soudan*, p. 169 • group portrait, photograph (George Conrad Sartorius, Reginald William Sartorius, Euston Henry Sartorius), Victoria College, Jersey • photograph (Reginald William Sartorius), repro. in Creagh and Humphris, *The V.C. and D.S.O.* • photograph (Euston Henry Sartorius), repro. in Creagh and Humphris, eds., *The V.C. and D.S.O.* • portraits, repro. in Anderson, 'The interpretation of "Valour"'

Wealth at death £20—Reginald William Sartorius: administration, 14 Oct 1909, *CGPLA Eng. & Wales* • £2266 2*s*.—George Conrad Sartorius: resworn probate, 24 Dec 1912, *CGPLA Eng. & Wales* • £22,560 9*s*. 11*d*.—Euston Henry Sartorius: probate, 5 May 1925, *CGPLA Eng. & Wales* • £18,199 7*s*. 4*d*.—Euston Henry Sartorius: further grant, 14 Aug 1925, *CGPLA Eng. & Wales*

Sartorius, Euston Henry, count of Penhafirme in the Portuguese nobility (1844–1925). *See under* Sartorius brothers (*act.* *c*.1857–1925).

Sartorius, Francis (1733/4–1804). *See under* Sartorius family (*per. c.*1730–1831).

Sartorius, Francis (*bap.* 1781, *d.* after 1808). *See under* Sartorius family (*per. c.*1730–1831).

Sartorius, George Conrad (1840–1912). *See under* Sartorius brothers (*act. c.*1857–1925).

Sartorius, Sir George Rose (1790–1885), naval officer, born on 9 August 1790, was the eldest son of Colonel John Conrad Sartorius (*d.* 1801) of Württemberg, an officer of the East India Company's engineers, and his wife, Annabella, daughter of George Rose and granddaughter of Admiral Harvey. He entered the navy on the books of the yacht *Mary* in June 1801. In October 1804 he joined the *Tonnant* (Captain Charles Tyler) and was present at Trafalgar. He was then sent to the *Bahama*, one of the Spanish prizes, and in June 1806 to the frigate *Daphne*, in which he was present at the operations in the Rio de la Plata. On 5 March 1808 he was promoted lieutenant of the *Success*, which, after a season in protection of the Greenland fishery, went to the Mediterranean, where she took part in the capture of Ischia and Procida and the defence of Sicily against Joachim Murat's threat of invasion. Sartorius, on different occasions, commanded the boats in bringing out merchant vessels from under heavy fire on shore. The *Success* was afterwards employed in the defence of Cadiz, and on 1 February 1812 Sartorius was promoted commander. In August he was appointed to the gun-brig *Snap* (12 guns) on the home station. He was moved to the brig-sloop *Avon* (18 guns) in July 1813 and was posted from her on 6 June 1814. On 14 December he was appointed to the *Slaney* (20 guns) in the Bay of Biscay, which was in company with the *Bellerophon* when Napoleon surrendered himself on her. She was paid off in August 1815.

In 1831 Sartorius was engaged by Dom Pedro to command, with the rank of admiral, the Portuguese regency fleet against Dom Miguel, and he gained some marked successes over the usurper's forces. His difficulties were, however, very great: there was factious opposition from the Portuguese leaders; and promised supplies were not forthcoming, and his men were consequently mutinous or deserted at the earliest opportunity. He spent much of his own money keeping them together, and he threatened to carry off the fleet as a pledge for repayment. Dom Pedro sent two British officers on board the flagship with authority, one to arrest Sartorius and bring him on shore, the other to take command of the squadron. Sartorius captured both of them as soon as they appeared on board and temporarily conciliated his men. Such a situation, however, could not last; and without regret, in June 1833, Sartorius handed over his disagreeable command to Captain Charles Napier, who, warned by his predecessor's experience, refused to stir until the money payment was secured. Sartorius gained only the grand cross of the Tower and Sword, together with the grand cross of St Bento d'Avis and the empty title of viscount of Piedade for life. His name had, meantime, been struck off the list of the British navy, but was restored in 1836. He married, in 1839, Sophia, a daughter of John Lamb. They had three sons, all of whom served in the army.

On 21 August 1841 Sartorius was knighted and at the same time appointed to the *Malabar* (72 guns), which he commanded in the Mediterranean for the next three years. In 1842 he was thanked by the president and congress of the United States for his efforts to save the American frigate *Missouri*, burnt in Gibraltar Bay. In July 1843 off Cadiz he received on his ship the regent of Spain, Baldomero Espartero, driven out of the country by the revolutionary party. The *Malabar* was paid off towards the end of 1844, and Sartorius had no further service afloat, though he offered to serve in the Crimean War. He received further Portuguese titles of nobility: viscount of Mindello on 8 July 1845, and count of Penhafirme on 19 August 1853, both for life, but never used them.

Sartorius continued for the rest of his long life to take great interest in naval matters. As early as 1855, he claimed, he had proposed to the Admiralty to revive the ancient practice of ramming an enemy ship; and though the idea probably occurred to others about the same time, he was one of the earliest to bring it forward, and was generally acknowledged as the pioneer. In the 1850s and 1860s he repeatedly advocated, in letters to the Admiralty and to *The Times* and elsewhere, the construction of steam rams (warships designed primarily to ram). He published pamphlets on defence and naval topics. His 1839 pamphlet on naval manning warned of possible invasion. His controversial lengthy pamphlet *Coast Defences and Naval Warfare* (1862), partly responding to the 1859 royal commission on the defences of the United Kingdom proposals for fortification, advocated anti-invasion defence by mobile land artillery, riflemen, steam rams, and armed merchantmen; asserted that steam rams were the most effective warships; and criticized the *Warrior* as inferior to the *Gloire* and 'a beautiful ship … an admirable work of art, but for the purposes of war … an utter failure'.

Sartorius became a rear-admiral on 9 May 1849, vice-admiral on 31 January 1856, and admiral on 11 February 1861. He was made a KCB on 28 March 1865, became vice-admiral of the United Kingdom in 1869, was promoted admiral of the fleet on 3 July 1869, and was made a GCB on 23 April 1880. He died at his house, East Grove, Lymington, Hampshire, on 13 April 1885, preserving to the last his faculties, and to a remarkable extent his physical energy and a relatively young appearance. Two of his sons, Major-General Reginald William *Sartorius and Major-General Euston Henry *Sartorius, won the Victoria Cross. A third son, George Conrad *Sartorius, also entered the army, serving in Egypt and Upper Burma [*see under* Sartorius brothers (*act. c.*1857–1925)].

J. K. Laughton, *rev.* Andrew Lambert

Sources Devon RO, Somerset MSS [incl. biographical memoranda] · N. Macaulay, *Dom Pedro, 1798–1834* (1986) · O'Byrne, *Naval biog. dict.* · *The Times* (14 April 1885) · *Army and Navy Gazette* (18–25 April 1885) · P. Mackesy, *The war in the Mediterranean, 1803–1810* (1957) · J. J. Colledge, *Ships of the Royal Navy: an historical index*, 1 (1969) · Kelly, *Handbk* · Burke, *Peerage* · R. Gardiner and A. Lambert, eds., *Steam, steel and shellfire: the steam warship, 1815–1905* (1992) · *Annual Register* (1885)

Archives Bedford estate office, London, Russell MSS • Devon RO, Somerset MSS • Woburn Abbey, Bedfordshire, letters to Lord George William Russell
Likenesses portrait, repro. in *ILN*, 86 (1885), 431 • portrait, repro. in *The Graphic*, 19 (1879), 216
Wealth at death £3866 15*s*. 3*d*.: probate, 5 June 1885, *CGPLA Eng. & Wales*

Sartorius, John (*supp. fl.* **18th cent.**). *See under* Sartorius family (*per. c*.1730–1831).

Sartorius, John Francis (*bap.* **1779**, *d.* **1831**). *See under* Sartorius family (*per. c*.1730–1831).

Sartorius, John Nost (**1759–1829**). *See under* Sartorius family (*per. c*.1730–1831).

Sartorius, Reginald William (**1841–1907**). *See under* Sartorius brothers (*act. c*.1857–1925).

Sass, (John) Henry (**1787–1844**), artist and art teacher, was born in Bloomsbury, London, on 29 April 1787 and baptized at St George's, Bloomsbury, on 22 May, the second child of John Henry Sass (*d. c*.1824/5), formerly of Kurland, Russia (now Courland, Latvia), and his wife, Elizabeth North. In 1786 Sass senior advertised that he drew and made embroidery patterns for ladies, and his wife gave instruction in embroidery, filigree work, and the making of artificial flowers. By the 1790s, in addition to supplying material for filigree work and artificial flowers, Sass senior and his kinsman **Richard Sass** (1774–1849), landscape painter, were in practice together. Richard Sass was born in London on 29 April 1774, the son of Henry Sass and his wife, Elizabeth. With Sass senior he sold drawings of figures 'after the best masters' and landscapes, fruit, and flowers, undertaking, among other things, 'copies of figures from masters'; Richard also took on teaching 'within ten miles of London' (*Morning Herald*, 16 Jan 1793). Richard Sass exhibited at the Royal Academy from 1791 to 1813, and counted among his pupils Princess Charlotte Augusta of Wales. He worked in Ireland and published a series of etchings of Irish and Scottish landscapes. In connection with his watercolour and teaching practice, his book *Patterns from Nature* was published in 1810, a copy of which is held in the V&A. In 1825 he moved to Paris, where he died in 1849. Sass senior seems to have worked at Upper King Street and then in High Holborn until about 1818. Two, or possibly three, of his daughters were artists. He probably died about 1824–5.

His father's background clearly influenced Sass in his choice of career and he was admitted as a student to the Royal Academy Schools on 9 March 1805, as a painter. His early career was fairly typical of many art students of his day. He started exhibiting at the Royal Academy for the first time in 1807 with *A Study*, possibly a self-portrait. Apart from his studies at the academy he worked at the British School at the British Institution in 1808. In 1809, on the recommendation of John Soane, he was given permission to make sketches from the sculptures and antiquities in the British Museum. In 1808 his Royal Academy exhibit *Ulysses's Descent into Hell* announced his ambitions to paint in the grand style, while in 1812 his *Themistocles Taking Refuge at the Court of Admetus*, the subject for the gold medal in painting in 1811, shows that he had been in contention for the highest honours, unsuccessfully as it transpired.

Conceivably such a lack of success caused Sass to change direction, though with some hindsight, and perhaps not without having identified a real gap in the London art world at the time, he implied that this change rested on his awareness, while still a pupil, that there was little opportunity for young men to learn drawing to a level that would qualify them for admission to the Royal Academy Schools: that, indeed, 'such teaching has not been worthy of the attention of men of talent' (Sass, liii–liv). Thus it must have been Sass, advertising from his father's address, who in 1813 announced the establishment of a 'School for Drawing and Studying the Human Figure' to remedy these deficiencies (*The Times*, 16 Aug 1813). The school held drawings and models from the antique and books of prints from which students could work.

In 1815 Sass married Mary Robinson of Lincolnshire. In the same year he set off for Italy, returning home in 1817, a tour which resulted in a book, *A Journey to Rome and Naples in 1817*. This was published in May 1818 just after Sass had re-advertised his School of Design at the beginning of the exhibition season in April. Described as a 'probationary school' for the Royal Academy, the British Institution, and study of the Elgin marbles at the British Museum, it taught drawing (including figure drawing), with an emphasis on line and the handling of light and shade, as well as painting in oil and watercolour (*The Times*, 20 April, 29 April, 22 May, 24 June 1818). By the end of 1818 Sass's School for Drawing and Painting, with room for a live-in pupil, was established at 50 Great Russell Street, opposite the British Museum. By the beginning of 1820, capitalizing on the proximity and popularity of the Elgin marbles at the British Museum, he had moved to larger premises nearby at 6 Charlotte Street, where there was board and lodging for pupils. Here Sass remained until the school was taken over by his former pupil F. S. Cary in 1842, Sass, according to Richard Redgrave, having become insane. The first signs of this insanity were noticed during the late 1830s by his student W. P. Frith (Frith, 1.52). Sass died on 21 June 1844.

For more than two decades Sass and his academy, housed in an elegant building with a bust of Minerva over the porch, stood uniquely at the centre of art education in England, a position that was fully recognized by the art establishment. Sass enjoyed the friendship of leading artists and Royal Academicians including Sir Thomas Lawrence, John Constable, and William Etty. Outside this milieu Sass, who was a radical and admired Napoleon, counted Daniel O'Connell as a friend. Of his many students who went on to be admitted to the Royal Academy Schools, some in their turn became distinguished, for example Charles West Cope, Augustus Egg, W. P. Frith, W. E. Frost, J. C. Horsley, J. E. Millais, D. G. Rossetti, and Abraham Solomon; Mrs E. M. Ward also studied with Sass. The best account of Sass, his school, and his thorough teaching methods, is given by W. P. Frith. He believed that Sass had 'great qualities as a teacher' (Frith, 1.55) and singled out for mention one of the mottoes which Sass put on the walls of the school and which sums up his teaching philosophy and, it can be added, suggests one reason for the growth of Pre-Raphaelitism in the late 1840s: 'those models which have passed through the approbation of ages are intended for your imitation, and not your criticism' (ibid., 1.43). Outside his teaching Sass's long acquaintance with the arts of design led to him giving evidence to the House of Commons select committee on the arts and their connection with manufactures in 1836.

It is difficult to pass judgement on Sass's qualities as an artist since so little of his output seems to have survived. Yet he exhibited eighty-four works at the Royal Academy between 1807 and 1839, most of them portraits, and eight works at the British Institution between 1809 and 1821. His Royal Academy exhibit of 1808, mentioned above, also shown at the British Institution in 1809, was etched by Sass (impression, BM). It shows the strong influence of Henry Fuseli. Sass's portrait of Francis Willis was mezzotinted by William Ward and published by the artist in May 1813 (impression, V&A). It shows Sass dealing rather awkwardly with the standard half-length seated figure. Sass, somewhat vain, seems to have compensated for an obvious failure to cut a figure in exhibitions by becoming 'extraordinarily pompous' and given to wearing 'the most extravagant waistcoats of cut velvet', as J. C. Horsley put it (Horsley, 24). In the case of his *Journey to Rome*, severely reviewed in the *Annals of the Fine Arts* (3/9, 1819, 311–18), Sass was no doubt flattered by a letter praising it which he received from Stendhal. Significantly, in 1826 the *Literary Gazette* (27 May 1826, 351) announced that Sass was preparing a grandly titled 'History of the arts and painting and sculpture in England, as far as is connected with his own time' but this does not seem to have been published.

The history of portraits of Henry Sass is slightly confused because he had the same name as his father. Those most certainly of him, as self-portraits, were exhibited at the Royal Academy in 1811 and 1813, and other portraits 'of an artist' by him shown at the academy in 1821 and 1827 might fall into the same category. The portrait of 1821 might perhaps be that engraved and published by E. Stalker in 1822 (impression, BM). It shows Sass, porte-crayon in hand, standing next to a bust of Raphael: Sass's prototype seems to have been Sir Joshua Reynolds's *Self-Portrait as a Doctor of Civil Law* (exh. British Institution, 1813; RA) and it thus shows something of the artist's misguided wish to put his own abilities and ambitions on a par with those of the great president of the Royal Academy. A miniature by W. J. Newton (exh. RA, 1808) could be of either Sass or his father. A bust by W. G. Nicholl (exh. RA, 1822) could also be of the father or son since Nicholl showed a bust entitled *The Late H. Sass Esq* (which must be the father), at the Society of British Artists in 1825. A self-portrait was in the possession of Edwin Etty Sass in 1897, perhaps that after which the engraving was taken. Two views by Sass, *The Interior of Mr Sass's Gallery*, were exhibited at the Royal Academy in 1830 and 1831. ROBIN HAMLYN

Sources parish register, Bloomsbury, St George, LMA, R.297, 22 May 1787 [baptism] • *Daily Universal Register* (25 Nov 1786), advertisement • S. C. Hutchison, 'The Royal Academy Schools, 1768–1830', *Walpole Society*, 38 (1960–62), 123–91, esp. 162 • *The Examiner* (6 Nov 1808), 718 • committee meeting minutes, 8 July 1809, BM, vol. CE 3/9, 2424 • *Art-Union* (Nov 1844), 332 • H. Sass, *A journey to Rome and Naples in 1817* (1818) • *The Times* (16 Aug 1813); (20 April 1818); (29 April 1818); (22 May 1818); (24 June 1818); (5 Dec 1819); (10 Dec 1819); (19 Dec 1819); (24 March 1820); (10 April 1820); (17 May 1820) [advertisements] • Redgrave, *Artists*, 44 • W. P. Frith, *My autobiography and reminiscences*, 2nd edn, 2 vols. (1887), vol. 1 • *Recollections of a Royal Academician by John Callcott Horsley RA*, ed. E. Helps (1903) • W. T. Whitley, *Artists and their friends in England, 1700–1799*, 2 vols. (1928), 282–3 • will, PRO, PROB 11/2008, sig. 857

Likenesses W. J. Newton, miniature, exh. RA 1808 (of Sass?) • H. Sass, self-portrait, exh. RA 1811 • H. Sass, self-portrait, exh. RA 1813 • H. Sass, self-portrait?, exh. RA 1821 • W. G. Nicholl, bust, exh. RA 1822 (of Sass?) • E. Stalker, line engraving, pubd 1822, BM • H. Sass, self-portrait?, exh. RA 1827 • C. H. Lear, pencil drawing, *c.*1845, NPG • H. Sass, self-portrait; in possession of Edwin Etty Sass, in 1897

Sass, Richard (1774–1849). *See under* Sass, (John) Henry (1787–1844).

Sassamon, John (*c.*1620–1675), translator and minister in America, was born in coastal Massachusetts before it became an English colony. Little is known of his early life. His parents, both Algonquian Indians, may have converted to Christianity in 1633 during a smallpox epidemic occasioned by the recent arrival of English colonists in Massachusetts Bay. Sassamon appears to have been orphaned during the epidemic and was subsequently raised among puritans in Dorchester, Massachusetts, possibly in the home of Richard Callicott, where he learned English and converted to Christianity. In 1637 he served alongside colonial forces during the Pequot War. On his return to Dorchester (along with a Pequot captive who may have become his wife) he began assisting John Eliot, minister of the adjacent town of Roxbury, in his efforts to learn Algonquian and in his missions to the Indians. Throughout the 1640s he worked closely with Eliot in translating the Bible and other religious tracts into Algonquian, and in 1650 aided him in establishing the first 'praying town' of converted Indians in Natick, Massachusetts. At Natick, Sassamon served as a schoolmaster. In 1653 Eliot arranged for him to attend Harvard College briefly.

Literate, bilingual, and better educated than nearly all of his Indian peers (and most colonists), Sassamon lived the greater part of his life among the English. Increase Mather, minister of Boston, called Sassamon a man 'of very excellent parts' (Mather, 49), and William Hubbard, minister of Ipswich, wrote that he 'was observed to conform more to the English Manners than any other Indian' (Hubbard, 1.61). Yet in 1662 Sassamon abandoned colonial society to live among non-Christian Wampanoags ruled by King Philip (also known as Metacom), whose territory ranged over parts of Rhode Island and Plymouth colonies. For much of the 1660s he laboured as scribe and interpreter to Philip, who was himself illiterate. During this time he may actually have continued to serve Eliot, working essentially as a missionary among the Wampanoags. In the early 1670s he left Philip's employ to become minister of the praying town of Namasket. There, in the winter of 1674–5, he learned of Philip's plans to wage war against the colonists. Demonstrating his ultimate loyalty to the

English, he betrayed Philip's plans to Josiah Winslow, governor of Plymouth.

Soon after his meeting with Winslow, Sassamon disappeared and, when his body was found under the ice of nearby Assawompset pond in February 1675, suspicion immediately fell on Philip. In a trial conducted on 1 June the Plymouth court (that comprised an extremely unusual jury of twelve Englishmen and six Indians) determined the murder to have taken place on 29 January and convicted three of Philip's chief men, Mattashunannamo, Tobias, and Wampapaquan, of murdering Sassamon as punishment for his betrayal of their sachem, claiming that they had strangled him and then shoved his body through a hole in the ice to make it appear as though he had drowned. Their execution, held on 8 June 1675, immediately propelled Philip to action: his warriors were reported arming just three days later, and on 24 June 1675 they began attacking English towns, starting a war that would ultimately devastate the Indian population and claim nearly half of all English settlements in New England. JILL LEPORE

Sources W. Hubbard, *A narrative of the troubles with the Indians in New-England* (1677); repr. in *The history of the Indian wars in New England*, ed. S. G. Drake, 2 vols. (1865) • I. Mather, *A brief history of the war with the Indians in New-England* (1676); repr. as *The history of King Philip's war*, ed. S. G. Drake (1862) • J. Lepore, 'Dead men tell no tales: John Sassamon and the fatal consequences of literacy', *American Quarterly*, 46 (1994), 479–512 • J. Lepore, *The name of war: King Philip's War and the origins of American identity* (1998) • J. P. Ronda and J. Ronda, 'The death of John Sassamon: an exploration in writing New England history', *American Indian Quarterly*, 1 (1974), 91–102 • J. Winslow and T. Hinckley, 'Narrative shewing the manor of the begining of the present warr with the Indians of Mount Hope and Pocassett', *Acts of the commissioners of the united colonies of New England*, ed. D. Pulsifer (1859), vol. 9 of *Records of the colony of New Plymouth in New England*, ed. N. B. Shurtleff and D. Pulsifer, 362–5

Sassie, (Charles) Victor Vincent (1915–1999), restaurateur, was born at 73 West Bank, Cwmtillery, Abertillery, Monmouthshire, on 28 August 1915, the youngest son of Louis Sassi, a colliery carpenter, and his wife, Linda Mambriani. His family later moved to Barrow in Furness, where his Italian-born father worked in the shipyards. After basic schooling, Sassie travelled in Europe working in a range of jobs before settling into the restaurant business; he learned about Hungarian food in Budapest and Vienna before the Second World War, most notably at the Three Hussars. After his return to Britain he worked first as a grocer's assistant. On 5 May 1948 he married Elizabeth Varadi (*b*. 1929/30), with whom he had a daughter. Sassie opened a Hungarian restaurant in Soho that operated under a number of names and in a number of locations before becoming the Gay Hussar in Greek Street in 1953. The Labour MP Tom Driberg adopted the restaurant and its owner and made it synonymous with the group of left-wing politicians allied to Aneurin Bevan and known as the Bevanites—though Bevan himself did not become a regular.

It was this association that transformed the Gay Hussar from an eating place into an institution. The food was a once-fashionable representation of mittel European cooking, centred on a version of Hungarian food still served in tourist restaurants in Budapest but in few other locations. The menu remained virtually unchanged from the beginning of the operation and was oblivious to culinary fashion. But the food was not really the point of the atmosphere that Sassie created in the Gay Hussar. The Bevanites' presence as regular eaters brought in trade unionists and journalists. The *Daily Mirror* began to use the Gay Hussar for leaving parties, encouraged by the fact that Robert Maxwell, the paper's owner for much of the restaurant's heyday, was banned by Sassie for failing to pay his bills.

The upstairs room became the scene of regular conspiratorial dinners. By the 1960s the Gay Hussar was the most famous political restaurant in London. In addition to old Bevanites such as Michael Foot, a new generation of Labour politicians, not necessarily of the left, adopted the place, including Roy Hattersley. Sassie created an atmosphere in which political gossip, intrigue, and discussion could flourish. Personally, he was in part showman and in part father confessor and friend to his many regulars. Roy Hattersley recalled:

> My first book, a biography of Horatio Nelson, was savagely reviewed in the Daily Telegraph and my publisher suggested a consoling lunch at the Gay Hussar. Victor Sassie was out when we telephoned to book a table, and when I later complained that he was absent from his post, he said: 'I was out buying your book.' I told him that I could only assume that he had not read the *Daily Telegraph*. 'That's all I have read,' he replied. 'It seemed a good day for your friends to buy a copy.' I believed then—and I believe now—that he was telling the exact truth. (*The Guardian*)

Sassie played the front-of-house role with such skill and personality that he became as much a part of the experience of eating at the Gay Hussar as the food or the wine. One foundation of the restaurant's success was the idea that it was in some sense a safe neutral ground where different elements in the political process could mix. The restaurant suffered a temporary decline when the confidentiality of what happened at these dinners was once breached. The shop workers' union hosted a Soviet distributive workers' delegation to a substantial dinner. The *Daily Mail* acquired the bill and put it on the front page. The political clientele deserted Sassie and he was forced to hire a Gypsy fiddler. But gradually, and at the urging of some of his most loyal customers, the politicians returned.

By the 1980s the golden age of the Gay Hussar, like the golden age of the left, had passed. A good measure of a restaurant's evolution from being genuinely a significant cultural entity to being a tourist attraction is the appearance of framed photographs of famous clientele. Though the Gay Hussar retained a close association with the left, the London that it served, with Fleet Street and Transport House near by, disappeared during the 1980s. Sassie retired in 1988, sold the business, and never returned. He died on 7 June 1999 at University College Hospital, Camden.

Sassie's lasting significance is as one of the great restaurateurs of the twentieth century: he created an eating place in the Gay Hussar that transcended its confines as a business to sell food and became a national institution.

BRIAN BRIVATI

Sources *The Times* (9 June 1999) · *Daily Telegraph* (9 June 1999) · *The Guardian* (9 June 1999) · *The Independent* (10 June 1999) · b. cert. · m. cert. · d. cert.

Likenesses photograph, repro. in *The Times* · photograph, repro. in *Daily Telegraph* · photograph, repro. in *The Guardian* · photograph, repro. in *The Independent*

Sassoon family (*per. c.*1830–1961), merchants, came to commercial prominence with **David Sassoon** (1792–1864), a Jewish merchant. Born in Baghdad in October 1792, the son of Sason ben Saleh (1750–1830) and Amam Gabbai, David belonged to a Sephardic family that, though originating in Spain, had prospered in Mesopotamia, and was active in both financial and religious affairs. David's father held the position of state treasurer to the governor of Baghdad for nearly forty years. The office carried with it automatic leadership of the Jewish community as well as tremendous commercial power.

David joined his father's business in Baghdad at an early age, after receiving a traditional Hebrew education and a counting-house apprenticeship. In 1818 he married Hannah (*d.* 1826), daughter of Abdullah Joseph of Baghdad, and they had two sons and two daughters. The eldest son, **Sir Abdullah David Sassoon**, first baronet (1818–1896), was born in Baghdad; he was known later, particularly after his father's death, as Albert. His younger brother, **Elias David Sassoon** (1820–1880), was born in Baghdad in 1820. Hannah died in 1826 and two years later David Sassoon married Farha Hyeem (1812–1886), aged sixteen, the daughter of a Baghdad merchant; they had six sons and three daughters. At some point in the late 1820s, persecution of the Jewish community in Baghdad forced the family to flee. David was the first to leave, moving initially to Bushehr on the Persian Gulf before settling in Bombay. By 1832 he had been joined by his family and had begun trading from a small office at 9 Tamarind Street. He transferred later, as the firm grew, to larger premises in Forbes Street. He traded mainly with the Gulf ports, exchanging British cotton goods for commodities such as hides, silks, spices, and pearls.

As trade grew David embarked on an expansionist policy. At home the firm bought up wharfages in Bombay, aware that the new steamship service between Britain and India would drive up the value of such property. Overseas the opening up of five Chinese ports to foreign traders after the treaty of Nanking (Nanjing) in 1842 had a profound effect on the firm's fortunes. Located midway between Europe and China it was ideally placed to take immediate benefit, trading Lancashire textiles and Indian yarn and opium for Chinese goods. Cotton and opium were the two commodities on which the firm rose to prominence.

Although the firm's interests were spread across the world, it was David Sassoon's policy to keep the control of the business in his own hands and in those of his sons. In

Sassoon family (*per. c.*1830–1961), by unknown photographer [David Sassoon (seated), with his sons (left to right), Elias David, Sir Abdullah David, and Sassoon David Sassoon]

1844 Elias, his second son, was sent to the Far East to supervise the firm's operations there. Branches were established in Shanghai (which after Bombay became the second centre of Sassoon activities), Canton (Guangzhou), Hong Kong, and Yokohama and Nagasaki in Japan.

In 1858 David sent his eldest son from his second marriage, Sassoon David Sassoon (1832–1867), to establish the London office of David Sassoon & Co. in Leadenhall Street in the City of London. This office played a central role in the boost to the Sassoon fortunes resulting from the outbreak of the American Civil War in 1861. The war disrupted the supply of American cotton to Lancashire's mills, which turned to India as a replacement source. London became a main centre of the firm's operations and, as a consequence, branches were established in Liverpool and Manchester. From this time both the business and the family began to gravitate to England.

David Sassoon poured vast amounts of the fortune he acquired as a merchant into public benefactions; on his death he was one of Bombay's most energetic, wealthy, public-spirited, and benevolent citizens. He funded some of the most important cultural and civic institutions in Bombay: hospitals, libraries, museums, orphanages, and schools. He became a British subject in 1853, signing his naturalization certificate in Hebrew as he neither spoke nor wrote English. When he died in Poona on 7 November 1864 he was buried in the mausoleum in the courtyard of the synagogue which he had funded.

On joining David Sassoon & Sons, Albert Sassoon was sent to Baghdad to re-establish the firm's trading links and to recruit staff for the various offices in China. In 1838, aged twenty, he married Hannah (*d.* 1895), daughter of

Meyer Moses, a Baghdad merchant. They had three daughters and two sons. From Baghdad, Albert moved to China and then back to Bombay to assist his father in his last years. He became a partner in David Sassoon & Sons in 1852 and took over the leadership on his father's death.

Under Albert's direction David Sassoon & Sons rose to the peak of its prosperity, as one of India's most important businesses. Albert significantly extended the business from trade to industry by opening one of the first great textile mills in Bombay. Through his activities India became a manufacturing centre for cotton and woollen goods rather than an exporter of raw cotton to England for manufacture. Wool was imported from Australia to stimulate the woollen industry and the firm also established the Sassoon Spinning and Weaving Company and the Sassoon and Alliance Silk Manufactory Company.

Further diversification of the firm's interests took place when between 1872 and 1875 it constructed a wet dock at Bombay, the first on the west coast of India. Enormously successful in stimulating the commercial development of the port, it was bought four years later by the Bombay government. Trade also diversified overseas as the firm involved itself in the cultivation and export of Indian tea and the importation of sugar from Java, and the network of branches was extended into Singapore. Although Albert was later to become involved in the founding of the Hongkong and Shanghai Bank (in 1865) and was a member of the board of the Imperial Bank of Persia (in 1889), the focus of the firm's activities remained overwhelmingly mercantile.

Albert's interests began to develop away from business. He became a leading member of the Bombay chamber of commerce, and served on the Bombay legislative council from 1867 to 1871. He became one of the governor's inner circle of advisers on educational and building projects. His commitment to civic affairs was recognized in 1867, when he was awarded the Order of the Star of India, and in 1872 on his retirement from the legislative council when he was awarded a knighthood. In 1873 Sir Albert visited England and was the first Indian and first Jew to receive the freedom of the City of London in recognition of his philanthropic work in both India and Britain. He became a member of the Worshipful Company of Fishmongers.

In 1876 Sir Albert decided to move to London, which immediately became the focus of the firm's activities, with all major policy decisions and directives emanating from Leadenhall Street. Albert was a great success socially, becoming part of the aristocratic social circle that revolved around the prince of Wales, later Edward VII, whom he had entertained during the latter's state visit to India beginning in 1875. The triumph of his social career was his reception in London in 1889 for the shah of Persia, from whom he had already received the order of the Lion and the Sun. He settled at 25 Kensington Gore and bought a second mansion at 1 Eastern Terrace, Kemp Town, near Brighton. Links with the eminent banking family of Rothschild followed when in 1887 Edward Albert Sassoon (1856–1912), Albert's only surviving son and heir, married Aline, the second daughter of Baron Gustave de Rothschild. On 22 March 1890 Albert was created baronet in recognition of his role in the industrialization of India. On 24 October 1896 Albert died at his home, 1 Eastern Terrace, Kemp Town, of a heart attack; he was buried in a private mausoleum next to his property. His son, Edward, succeeded to the chairmanship of the firm and to the baronetcy.

Sir Albert's younger brother, Elias David Sassoon, married Leah Gubbay (*d.* 1878) in 1840 and they had five sons and two daughters, one of whom, Hannah, married the financier Sir Sassoon Jacob David, first baronet. Their son, Sir Percival Victor David Ezekiel *David, achieved prominence as a collector of Chinese art. In 1844 Elias was sent to China to develop the firm's interests and within five years his firm enjoyed a secure footing along the entire China coast. Its trade was primarily in textiles and opium, but it also diversified into small-scale broking and banking activities. Elias joined Albert as a partner in the firm shortly after 1852.

On the death of their father in 1864 Elias saw himself as his brother's permanent deputy, but three years later he resigned from David Sassoon & Sons. Taking his eldest son, Jacob (1844–1916), into partnership, he established a rival firm, E. D. Sassoon & Co., based in Bombay with offices in Shanghai, which carried on identical activities trading with the same centres as David Sassoon & Sons. It was soon competing significantly in opium and Indian yarn and opened offices in Europe, Africa, and America, outstripping the original firm. The two houses remained separate and rivals. Elias died in 1880, aged fifty-nine, in Colombo, Ceylon, while visiting tea plantations, and the business passed into the hands of his sons Jacob, Edward (1853–1924), Meyer (1855–1924), and David (1866–1938).

At the end of the nineteenth century the Sassoon family, pre-eminent in trading and aristocratic social circles, moved into politics when in 1899 Sir Edward, Albert's son, was elected Conservative MP for the Hythe constituency in Kent. Sir Philip *Sassoon, Sir Edward's son, succeeded to the baronetcy, the chairmanship of David Sassoon & Co., and the Hythe seat on his father's death in 1912. (Sir Philip's sister, Sybil, married in 1913 the earl of Rocksavage, heir of the marquess of Cholmondeley.) Sir Philip died in 1939 without an heir and his second cousin, Sir Victor Sassoon (1881–1961), grandson of Elias David Sassoon, took over as head of the Sassoon family. Sir Victor was the nephew of Jacob and had become chairman of E. D. Sassoon & Co. in 1924. He also became the third holder of the baronetcy to which Jacob had been elevated in 1909 for his civic and philanthropic activities. Sir Victor's death in 1961 ended both the second baronetcy and the last family connection with his companies in the direct male line. A later prominent member of the family was the poet and writer Siegfried *Sassoon (1886–1967), a grandson of Sassoon David Sassoon. SERENA KELLY

Sources S. Jackson, *The Sassoons* (1968) • C. Roth, *The Sassoon dynasty* (1941) • *The Times* (26 Oct 1896) • C. Roth, ed., *Encyclopaedia Judaica*, 16 vols. (Jerusalem, 1971–2) • *Presentation to the freedom of the City of London to Sir A. D. Sassoon C.S.I. at the council chamber, Guildhall*

on Thursday 6 Nov 1873, [n.d.], London *Jewish Chronicle* office · P. Fletcher Jones, *Jews of Britain* (1990) · R. P. T. Davenport-Hines and G. Jones, eds., *British business in Asia since 1860* (1989) · D. Englander, *Documentary history of the Jewish immigrants in Britain* (1994)

Likenesses T. Woolner, statue, 1870 (David Sassoon), Mechanics' Institute, Bombay · Pet, caricature, chromolithograph (Albert Sassoon), NPG; repro. in *Monetary Gazette and Mining News* (4 April 1877) [supplement] · Spy [L. Ward], caricature, chromolithograph (Albert Sassoon), NPG; repro. in *VF* (16 Aug 1879) · group portrait, photograph, unknown collection; copyprint, NPG [*see illus.*] · photograph (Albert Sassoon), repro. in Jackson, *Sassoons*, facing p. 32 · photograph (David Sassoon), repro. in Jackson, *Sassoons*, facing p. 32 · photograph (Elias David Sassoon), repro. in Jackson, *Sassoons*, facing p. 32 · wood-engraving (Albert Sassoon; after photograph by Dickinson and Foster), NPG; repro. in *ILN* (31 Oct 1896)

Wealth at death £385,249 12*s*. 3*d*.—Albert Sassoon: probate, 1 Dec 1896, *CGPLA Eng. & Wales*

Sassoon, Sir Abdullah David, first baronet (1818–1896). *See under* Sassoon family (*per. c.*1830–1961).

Sassoon, David (1792–1864). *See under* Sassoon family (*per. c.*1830–1961).

Sassoon, Elias David (1820–1880). *See under* Sassoon family (*per. c.*1830–1961).

Sassoon, Sir Philip Albert Gustave David, third baronet (1888–1939), politician and art collector, was born in Paris on 4 December 1888, the only son of Sir Edward Albert Sassoon, second baronet (1856–1912), and his wife, Aline Caroline (*d.* 1909), daughter of Baron Gustave de Rothschild, of the French branch. He was grandson of Sir Abdullah David Sassoon (known as Albert), first baronet, who had been born at Baghdad in 1818 and had accompanied his father, David Sassoon, when he moved to Bombay and there founded the great merchant house of David Sassoon & Co. The Sassoons had been settled in Mesopotamia for many centuries, and local tradition claimed that they had been driven out of Spain in the fifteenth century.

Philip Sassoon was educated at Eton College and at Christ Church, Oxford, where he took a second in modern history in 1911. At nineteen years of age he chose British nationality, having, on account of his birth in France, the right to elect for one country or the other. In 1912 his father, who had been Unionist member for Hythe since 1899, died, and he was returned to parliament in the same interest for the same constituency. He represented it without a break for twenty-seven years, until his death. In 1933 he received the freedom of the borough. When war broke out in 1914 he held a commission in the Royal East Kent yeomanry, and in December 1915 he was appointed private secretary to Sir Douglas Haig, commander-in-chief of the British armies. In this important position, which he held until after the armistice, his cosmopolitan social gifts were fully called into play, and he obtained a unique view of the war and of the statesmen and generals who were conducting it. It was to Sassoon that Haig handed the piece of paper on which he had written the famous 'backs to the wall' order of the day, and the field marshal subsequently gave it to him. He retained it until his death, when he bequeathed it to the British Museum.

In the years immediately following 1918 Sassoon busied himself with politics, with travelling, and with entertaining. He completed Port Lympne, near Hythe, the country residence which he had begun before the war, and on which he spent freely his great fortune. This house soon became famous for its meetings between the various statesmen and soldiers who were conducting the lengthy peace conference in Paris, and their host showed his own particular qualities of tact and considerateness.

In 1924 Sassoon was appointed under-secretary of state for air, a post which he held until 1929 and again from 1931 until 1937. During the second period the secretary of state for air sat in the House of Lords, and in consequence Sassoon represented his ministry in the House of Commons. His annual speech on the introduction of the air estimates, invariably delivered without a single written note, was followed with attention by members of all parties, because of its careful reasoning and mass of skilfully presented detail. Sassoon's quick comprehension of the meaning of air power did much to rouse the public, while the personal interest which he took in the Royal Air Force and the enthusiasm with which he always sought to promote its welfare were of great service to the country.

In 1929 Sassoon's only book, *The Third Route*, appeared; an account of his flying tour of British overseas air stations in India and the Middle East, it is notable for its descriptive skill and for its power of humorous exaggeration, both of which distinguished equally his conversation. In 1937 he was appointed first commissioner of works, a post which synthesized many of his energies, and wherein he was most happy. Although death cut short his tenure of this office, several memorials remain to his taste, notably his restoration of Sir James Thornhill's Painted Hall at the Royal Naval Hospital, Greenwich.

Honours, like great wealth, came to Sassoon early. He was sworn of the privy council in 1929; held numerous orders and decorations, British and foreign (including appointment as GBE, 1922); and was for many years a trustee of the National Gallery (chairman of the board from December 1932 to 1936), the Tate Gallery, the Wallace Collection, and the British School at Rome. But, despite his successful career, his gifts were perhaps more those of an artist than of a politician. His kindnesses were, like his wit, creative, and in Port Lympne and Trent Park, New Barnet, he made works of art. The first preserved the qualities of his fire and brilliance as a young man, while the second reflected his more mature judgement. Besides being a judge of pictures, he was a connoisseur of furniture, china, and old silver—in fact of all beautiful or decorative objects. The exhibitions, such as 'Conversation Pieces' and 'The Age of Walnut', which were held, in aid of charity, each spring for many years in his London house were famous among art-lovers. These exhibitions were organized by Sassoon and by his cousin Mrs David Gubbay, who acted as hostess for him at Trent and Port Lympne. No picture of life between the wars is complete without some account of one of these houses, filled always with politicians, painters, writers, professional golfers, and airmen. His great entertainments were imbued with his personality and with imagination, as if with a kind of magic, and he seemed to be surrounded by a constant activity in house and garden.

Sassoon died, after a month's illness, at his London house, 45 Park Lane, on 3 June 1939. He was unmarried, and the baronetcy became extinct. His only sister married the fifth marquess of Cholmondeley.

Osbert Sitwell, *rev.*

Sources P. Sassoon, *The third route* (1929) • personal knowledge (1949) • private information (1949) • *CGPLA Eng. & Wales* (1939)
Archives BL, corresp. with Lord Northcliffe, Add. MS 62160 • Herts. ALS, letters, mainly to Lady Desborough • HLRO, letters to David Lloyd George • Houghton Hall, King's Lynn, corresp. mostly with Lord Esher • Lpool RO, corresp. with seventeenth earl of Derby | FILM BFI NFTVA, news footage • IWM FVA, home footage | SOUND IWM SA, oral history interview
Likenesses M. Beerbohm, caricature, 1913, Yale U. • W. Stoneman, photograph, 1921, NPG • J. S. Sargent, oils, 1923, Tate collection • H. Coster, photographs, 1929, NPG • W. Stoneman, photograph, 1931, NPG • G. Philpot, portrait, priv. coll. • J. S. Sargent, charcoal drawing, priv. coll.
Wealth at death £1,946,892 17*s*. 8*d*.: probate, save and except settled land, 12 Aug 1939, *CGPLA Eng. & Wales*

Sassoon, Siegfried Loraine (1886–1967), poet and writer, was born on 8 September 1886 at Weirleigh, Brenchley, near Paddock Wood in Kent, the second of the three sons of Alfred Ezra Sassoon (*d.* 1895), financier and sculptor, and his wife, Georgina Theresa, daughter of Thomas *Thornycroft and Mary *Thornycroft, sculptors, and sister of Sir J. I. and Sir W. H. *Thornycroft. He was educated at Marlborough College (1902–4) and Clare College, Cambridge (1905–6), of which he was later an honorary fellow. His father left home when Siegfried was seven and died in 1895, so that the boys were entirely brought up by their mother and her talented family.

In his *Memoirs of a Fox-Hunting Man* Sassoon would depict himself as a lonely child, adding: 'as a consequence of my loneliness, I created in my childish day-dreams an ideal companion who became much more of a reality than such unfriendly boys as I encountered at Christmas parties'. His life can be seen as a quest for that ideal companion. Discovering at Cambridge that he was homosexual, he lived briefly with one such companion, David Thomas, whose death on the western front in March 1916 would prompt such poems as 'The Last Meeting' and 'A Letter Home'.

Sassoon left Cambridge without taking a degree and lived as a country gentleman, hunting, playing cricket, collecting books, and writing poems, of which he privately printed nine pamphlets between 1906 and 1912. These early verses, on the strength of which he was encouraged by Edmund Gosse, Edward Marsh, and Robert Ross, are graceful, often imitative, full of poetical intent, but without body. He was always 'waiting for the spark from heaven to fall', and when it fell it was shrapnel, for the First World War turned him from a versifier into a poet.

Sassoon enlisted as a trooper in the Sussex yeomanry, and in 1915 was commissioned in the Royal Welch Fusiliers and posted to France. He soon became well known for his bravery and was nicknamed Mad Jack. He was awarded the MC for bringing back a wounded lance-corporal under

Siegfried Loraine Sassoon (1886–1967), by Sir Cecil Beaton, 1920s

heavy fire, and later unsuccessfully recommended for the VC for capturing a German trench single-handedly.

Sassoon was wounded in April 1917 and while convalescing in England he felt impelled to write a violent attack on the conduct of the war ('I am making this statement as an act of wilful defiance of military authority, because I believe that the war is being deliberately prolonged by those who have the power to end it'). This he contrived to have read out in the House of Commons, but instead of the expected court martial, the under-secretary for war declared him to be suffering from shell-shock, and he was sent to Craiglockhart War Hospital, near Edinburgh. During his three months there he made two important friendships: with the young poet Wilfred Owen, whom he encouraged and helped, and with the psychologist and anthropologist W. H. R. Rivers, who became a loved and revered father figure to him. Eventually he decided to fight again and early in 1918 was posted to Palestine. In May he rejoined his old battalion in France, and in July was wounded again, this time in the head. So finished his military service.

Meanwhile in *The Old Huntsman* (1917) and *Counter Attack* (1918) Sassoon's savagely realistic and compassionate war poems had established his stature as a fully-fledged poet, and despite all his later prose and verse, and his growing aversion to the label, it was mainly as a war poet that he was regarded for the rest of his life.

In 1919 Sassoon was briefly involved in Labour politics and was the first literary editor of the reborn *Daily Herald*. This uncongenial task brought him into contact with the younger poet Edmund Blunden, who became a lifelong friend. In 1920 he read his poems on a lecture tour in the United States. Thereafter he lived in London, hunted for a few seasons in Gloucestershire, and brought out volumes of poetry—*Selected Poems* (1925), *Satirical Poems* (1926), and *The Heart's Journey* (1927)—which greatly increased his reputation and represent his full flowering as a poet.

All his life Sassoon kept copious diaries. Those for the years 1920–25 show him torn politically, the possessor of a private income with an uncomfortable socialist conscience; torn artistically, preferring eighteenth-century poetry to that of his modernist contemporaries, and longing—but unable—to write a Proustian masterpiece; and torn emotionally by a succession of disappointing homosexual relationships. The most enduring and important of these was with the artist Stephen Tennant (1906–1987).

In the late 1920s Sassoon turned to prose, drawing on his pre-war diaries and those for the first quarter of 1916 for his *Memoirs of a Fox-Hunting Man*. This was published in 1928, anonymously, though his name appeared in the second impression. This lightly fictionalized autobiography of his early years in Kent, in which he figures as the narrator George Sherston, was an immediate success, was awarded the Hawthornden and James Tait Black memorial prizes, and was quickly accepted as a classic of its kind—an elegy for a way of life which had gone for ever. He continued the story in *Memoirs of an Infantry Officer* (1930) and *Sherston's Progress* (1937).

On 18 December 1933 Sassoon married Hester, daughter of Sir Stephen Herbert Gatty, and they settled at Heytesbury House, near Warminster in Wiltshire, where Sassoon spent the rest of his life. Their son was born in 1936, and, although the marriage ended in 1944 in sadness and separation, at Heytesbury, Sassoon continued to find the beauty and the solitude that his writing needed, and he became steadily less inclined to leave home for any reason.

Once established there Sassoon began to write his factual autobiography, beginning with *The Old Century and Seven More Years* (1938), his favourite among his books, dedicated to his loved and admired friend Max Beerbohm, and continuing with *The Weald of Youth* (1942) and *Siegfried's Journey* (1945), which carried his story up to 1920. In 1948 he published a critical biography of George Meredith, and all the time he was writing poetry, published in private or public editions, which culminated in the *Collected Poems* of 1947 (enlarged edn, 1961).

In 1957 Sassoon's quest for an ideal companion ended with his 'unconditional surrender' to God. He was received into the Roman Catholic church, and the comfort and joy with which his religion filled his last years was celebrated in a spiritual anthology of his poetry, *The Path to Peace* (1960), printed and published by his dear friends the nuns of Stanbrook Abbey. If those devotional poems lack the vitality and power of his war poems, it may be because he was, by nature, a poet of polarity and protest rather than of union and acceptance.

Sassoon was strikingly distinguished in appearance, his large bold features expressing the courage and sensitivity of his nature, and he retained his slimness and agility into old age, playing cricket well into his seventies. A dedicated artist, he hated publicity but craved the right sort of recognition. He was appointed CBE in 1951, and was pleased by the award of the queen's medal for poetry in 1957 and by his honorary degree of DLitt at Oxford in 1965, but he pretended that such honours were merely a nuisance. A natural recluse, he yet much enjoyed the company of chosen friends, many of them greatly his juniors, and was a witty and lively talker. He loved books, pictures, and music, and was a brilliant letter writer. Sassoon died at his Heytesbury home on 1 September 1967, and was buried in Mells churchyard, Somerset, near his friend Monsignor Ronald Knox. RUPERT HART-DAVIS, *rev.*

Sources *Siegfried Sassoon diaries* [1915–25], ed. R. Hart-Davis, 3 vols. (1983–5) · [S. Sassoon], *Memoirs of a fox-hunting man* (1928) · personal knowledge (2004) · private information (2004) · b. cert. · m. cert. · d. cert.

Archives BL, letters and poetical MSS, Add. MSS 62941–62942 · BL, papers, Add. MSS 75285–75294 · Col. U., Rare Book and Manuscript Library, corresp., literary MSS, and papers · CUL, corresp. · CUL, letters and poetical MSS · IWM, corresp. · NAM, notebooks and papers · Rutgers University, New Jersey, corresp., poems, and papers | BL, corresp. with Sir Sydney Cockerell, Add. MS 52752 · BL, letters to Sir William Thornycroft, Add. MS 56099 · Bodl. Oxf., letters to Robert Nichols with drafts and poems · Bodl. Oxf., letters to E. J. Thompson · Col. U., Rare Book and Manuscript Library, corresp. with Wilfred Owen and family · CUL, corresp. with Edward Dent and MS poems · CUL, corresp., incl. with Faber & Faber · CUL, letters to Hans Hodson · CUL, letters to Geoffrey Keynes · King's Cam., letters to E. M. Forster · Ransom HRC, letters to Edmund Blunden · Sheff. Arch., letters to Edward Carpenter · Southern Illinois University Library, Carbondale, letters to Robert Graves · U. Leeds, Brotherton L., letters to Edmund Gosse · U. Leeds, Brotherton L., letters to Philip Gosse · V&A NAL, letters mainly to Dame Hildelith Cumming

Likenesses M. Beerbohm, caricature, drawing, 1913, Yale U. · G. Philpot, oils, 1917, FM Cam. · C. Beaton, vintage bromide print, 1920–29, NPG [*see illus.*] · H. Coster, photographs, 1929, NPG · W. Stoneman, photographs, 1929–31, NPG · M. Beerbohm, cartoon, 1931, *The Spectator* offices, London

Wealth at death £97,128: probate, 17 Jan 1968, *CGPLA Eng. & Wales*

Sastri, Valangiman Sankaranarayana Srinivasa (1869–1946), social worker and politician in India, was born at Valangiman, Tanjore district, Madras, on 22 September 1869, the son of a Brahman priest, Sankaranarayana Sastri. He was educated at the Native High School and the Government College, Kumbakonam, and the teachers' training college, Saidapet, Madras. As a young man he became a schoolmaster. He married Parvati in 1883, and they had a son. His wife died in 1896, and in the following year he married Lakshmi (*d.* 1934), with whom he had two daughters.

In 1899 Sastri was appointed headmaster of the Hindu High School, Triplicane, Madras, and while there came under the influence of Gopal Krishna Gokhale, who in 1905 founded the Servants of India Society with the object of forming 'a select, compact and trustworthy corps of young men' prepared by study, observation, travel, and work of a probationary character to take a real part in public life. Sastri was admitted as a member of that society in January 1907, and on the death of Gokhale in 1915 became its president. Before that he had been elected a fellow of

Madras University and nominated by the government to the Madras legislative council, by which he was elected in 1916 to the central legislative council. From an early age Sastri had shown unusual proficiency in the English language, and he was soon recognized as one of the most eloquent Indian speakers of his time. Turning from social questions, such as marriage reform, to which he had first given his attention in the Servants of India Society, he became interested in two main problems: self-government for India and the rights of Indians within the empire. During his active years he never turned away for long from these subjects.

Sastri was one of the nineteen members of the central legislative council who in 1916 signed a memorandum proposing wider plans of constitutional reform than the British government and the recently appointed viceroy, Lord Chelmsford, seemed prepared to sanction; and under the auspices of the Indian National Congress he took part in an active campaign for Indian home rule. British policy became more liberal towards Indian aspirations in 1917–18, and Sastri eventually withdrew from the Congress when the report on constitutional reform signed by E. S. Montagu and Lord Chelmsford was published (1918) and, with other moderate reformers who disapproved of agitation against the government and especially of the civil disobedience preached by M. K. Gandhi, helped to form the National Liberal Federation, of which he became president in 1922. Though not a wholehearted admirer of the scheme of diarchy introduced by the Government of India Act of 1919, he supported it and had been one of the three Indian members of the committee under Lord Southborough which devised the electoral scheme embodied in that act. In 1921 he was elected a member of the council of state and in that year represented India at the Imperial Conference in London. That was his first great opportunity of pleading the cause he had most at heart. He contended that where Indians were lawfully settled they should be admitted into the general body of citizenship with no deductions made from the rights that other British subjects enjoyed; and the conference—South Africa dissenting—agreed to a resolution admitting in principle the claim of Indians to equality of citizenship. While in England for that conference Sastri received the freedom of the City of London which, he said, he accepted not as a personal distinction, 'but in all sincerity and hopefulness as a symbol of, and prelude to, the conferment on India of the freedom of the British Empire'. Later in the year he represented India at the League of Nations assembly at Geneva and at the conference in Washington on the limitation of armaments.

To help in arriving at a practical interpretation of the resolution passed at the Imperial Conference, Sastri was sent by the government of India in 1922 to Australia, New Zealand, and Canada, and in his report on that mission he urged the promotion of personal intercourse as the best solvent of prejudice. Nowhere was prejudice more firmly rooted than in South Africa. An Indian suggestion that a committee of inquiry should visit the union was made in 1923 but both J. C. Smuts and J. B. M. Hertzog were opposed to it, and it was not until 1926 that a proposal for a round-table conference in South Africa on the status of the Indian population was accepted. Sastri was an obvious choice for that task. An agreement was reached in 1927 whereby the union government would seek to aid Indians domiciled in the union to attain a European standard of life and to secure the help of the government of India in repatriating Indians who could not be assimilated in the population. The agreement was much criticized in South Africa; but the appointment of Sastri in 1927 as the first agent-general of the government of India in South Africa, in order to secure more effective co-operation between the two governments, did much to allay resentment and was greeted with such satisfaction by the union government that it at once extended an amnesty to all Indians illegally present in its territory. Sastri was then at the height of his popularity and prestige, and the charm of his personality and his remarkable gifts as a speaker served him well in fighting his countrymen's battles in England and the British colonies. He had too the distinction of going to South Africa as a privy councillor, the first Indian, apart from members of the judicial committee, to receive that honour (1921). In 1930 he was the first Indian to be appointed a Companion of Honour.

He visited Malaya in 1936 to advise the government of India on the conditions of labour there. Earlier he had gone to east Africa to help the Indian community in stating their views on proposals made for the closer union of Kenya, Tanganyika, and Uganda, and on his return he suggested in his report the lines on which Indian representation in the Kenya legislative council should be based. He was a member of the royal commission on labour in India appointed in 1928, and was a delegate to the first two of the three round-table conferences held in London (1930–31) to consider a new constitution for India. His last work of importance—he had resigned the presidency of the Servants of India Society in 1927—was as vice-chancellor (1935–40) of the recently formed Annamalai University at Annamalainagar in the Madras presidency. In 1937 he was invited to form a ministry in Madras, when the Congress Party refused to take office. He declined the offer. He exercised little influence in nationalist politics, after the advent of mass politics under the leadership of Gandhi, even though he had excellent personal relations with him. He was widely respected for his intellect, eloquence, and integrity, but events had moved too fast for him and his associates in the moderate party who stood for the gradual evolution of their country into a self-governing and undivided India as a dominion of the British empire. Sastri died at Madras on 17 April 1946.

S. T. Sheppard, *rev.* B. R. Nanda

Sources P. K. Rao, *V. S. Srinivasa Sastri: a political biography* (1963) · T. N. Jagadisan, *V. S. Srinivasa Sastri* (1969) · *Letters of the Right Honourable Srinivasa Sastri*, ed. T. N. Jagadisan, 2nd edn (1963) · B. R. Nanda, *Gokhale: the Indian moderates and the British raj* (1977) · *Sastri speaks: being a collection of the speeches and writings of V. S. Srinivasa Sastri*, ed. S. R. Naidoo and D. Bramdaw (1931) · V. S. S. Sastri, *Life of Gopal*

Krishna Gokhale (1937) • *Indian Year Book* • *Times of India* (18 April 1946) • *The Times* (20 April 1946) • *Hindu* (18 April 1946)
Archives National Archives of India, New Delhi • Nehru Memorial Museum and Library, New Delhi
Likenesses C. Nageswara Rao, oils, Annamalai University, Tamil Nadu, India, Sastri Hall • photograph, repro. in Jagadisan, ed., *Letters of … Srinivasa Sastri*, frontispiece

Satchwell, Benjamin (1732–1810), philanthropist, was born on 3 January 1732 at The Mill, Leamington Priors, Warwickshire, and baptized there at All Saints' Church on 16 January 1732, the fourth of the six children of William Satchwell (*d.* 1749), a miller and parish clerk, and his wife, Frances (*d.* 1789). In 1746 he was apprenticed in the neighbouring village of Offchurch to a shoemaker, Edward Whitehead, who seems to have encouraged him to read widely. In 1753 Satchwell completed his apprenticeship and returned to Leamington, which then had a population of some 300, to work as a shoemaker. By the time of his marriage in 1764 to Mary Whitmore he had amassed £200 and also bought a cottage in New Street, Leamington, which was his home for the rest of his life. He and his wife had four sons and four daughters.

Satchwell became a friend of William Abbotts, the landlord of the Black Dog tavern, with whom from 1784 he developed a mineral spring, the second in the village, and they made a substantial commercial success of their spa in Bath Street. Satchwell was also known locally for his involvement in various charitable and community ventures. On Whit Monday 1777 he founded the village's first friendly society, named the Fountain of Hospitality, and in 1806 he helped to set up the Leamington charity, which provided free baths and accommodation for those who were too poor to pay for hydrotherapy. Satchwell established a postal service for the parish in 1788 and served himself as the first postmaster. In 1808 he was one of the three local worthies who laid foundation stones for the 'new town' north of the River Leam. He was a modest poet, although only two examples of his verse are known to have survived, and he wrote regularly in praise of Leamington's cures in both the local and the London press. Involved in parish government from an early age, he seems to have been regarded as a wise voice in local disputes. He was active in the development of Leamington, and erected Satchwell's Buildings for visitors in 1807; a street in the town was named after him.

Satchwell's cartoon portrait shows how contemporaries viewed him, for in it he clutches a churchwarden's clay pipe, while a copy of William Dugdale's *Antiquities of Warwickshire* lies open on his knee. He died at his home in New Street, Leamington, aged seventy-eight, from a chest condition on 1 December 1810, a month after making his will, attended by an eminent consultant from Northampton Hospital, William Kerr, who had formerly practised in Leamington. His wife had probably predeceased him. He was buried on 4 December 1810 in All Saints' churchyard, Leamington, near the south porch of the parish church, where a substantial chest tomb was placed by one of his daughters two years later. Satchwell's obituary notice in the *Warwick Advertiser* commended his 'honest zeal' and 'rustical roundelays', and he featured as a character in local guidebooks for most of the nineteenth century.

Joan Lane

Sources T. B. Dudley, *A complete history of Royal Leamington Spa* (1896) • 'Life of Benjamin Satchwell', Warks. CRO, CR1563/261 • S. Pratt, *A brief account of the progress and patronage of the Leamington Spa charity* (1812) • J. C. Manning, *Glimpses of our local past* (1894) • W. T. Moncrieff, *New guide to the spa of Leamington* (1818) • W. Smith, *County of Warwick* (1829) • *Warwick Advertiser* (8 Dec 1810) • parish register and banns of marriage, Leamington Spa, All Saints', Warks. CRO, DR 514/1, DR 514/8 [baptism] • inquisition post mortem, Warks. CRO, CR 1563/262 • *GM*, 1st ser., 82/2 (1812), 358
Archives Warks. CRO, *Life* MS, CR 1563/261
Likenesses cartoon, engraving, repro. in Dudley, *Complete history*, 55
Wealth at death house, garden, and land in Leamington Priors: will, Warks. CRO, CR 1563/261

Satchwell, Leonard (1888–1963), electrical engineer, was born on 30 August 1888 in the village of Attleborough, just outside Nuneaton, Warwickshire, the third and youngest child of Walter Satchwell, a Baptist minister, and his wife, Rachel Hore, previously Herbert, *née* Baker, of Dover, Kent. Information is scant on his education and apprenticeship, but it seems that he gained much of his engineering experience in Scotland, and it was apparently there that he met and married his first wife, Christian (*d.* 1940).

In 1921 Satchwell, in partnership with a Mr Johns, founded the Rheostatic Company in Slough, which, with its staff of six, operated from a cowshed on the Slough trading estate. The company's function was to manufacture unbreakable power resistors, used for varying the speed of trams and trolleybuses. In 1927 the company introduced the world's first commercially available thermostat, the 'C' type, for the control of electric heaters, and soon after the more modern 'Q' type room thermostat, which became one of the best-known thermostats of its kind in public and private premises over the next twenty years. At the end of the 1920s, when the company was steadily expanding, a move was made to larger premises on the Farnham Road, Slough.

Satchwell became chairman and managing director of the Rheostatic Company, posts which he held until 1947. The company continued to expand, so that from 1938 to 1939 he was also a director of the Harland Engineering Company and from 1939 to 1947 of a French subsidiary, La Thermostatique. In 1938 he was a director of the British Electric Plant Company. From 1946 to 1949 Satchwell was a director of Janitor Boilers, and from 1947 chairman. That same year he was also chairman of Weatherfoil Heating Systems.

The Rheostatic Company was introduced as a public company on the London stock exchange in 1937. The premises were destroyed by fire under somewhat suspicious circumstances on 2 February 1939, but were completely rebuilt in six weeks. As a result of the need for fuel economy in the Second World War a compensator was developed that enabled heating systems in public buildings to be controlled automatically, depending on the temperature of the weather. The firm's resistors were also in demand for use by the Royal Navy and the Royal Air Force, especially to shield shipboard equipment from the harmful influence of nearby magnetized instruments.

Following the death of Christian in London in early 1940, Satchwell married Winifred Ada Doris (*b.* 1902/3), the daughter of Edwin Henry Stevens, a retired oil company salesman, and fourteen years his junior, whom he had known for some years through business contacts when the directors went to South Africa to form a subsidiary company, Contractors in Paarl, Cape Province. The marriage took place in Westminster, London, on 3 June 1940. The new Mrs Satchwell was a director of Rheostatic from 1945 to 1947. A divorce then took place, however, and Mrs Satchwell married M. J. Gartside, who took over as chairman of Rheostatic in 1948 following Leonard Satchwell's retirement. Satchwell's long-standing association with Winifred had been the cause of considerable bitterness in the Gartside family.

In 1953 the company sold its resistor business and concentrated on temperature control systems. In 1967 it was acquired by Elliott Automation, which was itself absorbed by the English Electric Company and so became part of the General Electric Company (GEC), the largest electrical manufacturer in Britain.

Meanwhile, in the mid-1950s, and probably in Guernsey, where he had made his home following his retirement, Satchwell had married Marion, his third wife. There were no children of any of the three marriages.

Satchwell died of heart failure at the Princess Elizabeth Hospital, St Martin's, Guernsey, on 9 June 1963, and that same year the Rheostatic Company was renamed Satchwell Controls (Satchwell Control Systems from 1964) in commemoration of its founder. Satchwell's widow survived him into the 1990s, when the company was still based in Slough. ADRIAN ROOM

Sources *Satchwell Control Systems Limited: a potted history* (1986) • private information (2004) • b. cert. • m. cert. [Winifred Ada Doris Stevens] • d. cert.

Satow, Sir Ernest Mason (1843–1929), diplomat and scholar, was born on 30 June 1843 at 10 Buccleuch Terrace, Upper Clapton, Hackney. He was the third son and eighth child of (Hans) David Christophe Satow (1801–1874), merchant, of Wismar (in Mecklenburg) and Riga, who had settled in London in 1825, and his wife, Margaret (1812–1899), elder daughter of Edward Mason, a law stationer. Satow was educated at Newcombe's schools in Lower Clapton (1852–6) and at Mill Hill (1856–9), and at University College, London, where he took his BA in 1861. In that year he came first in the examination for student interpreterships to the Far East. Of precocious talent, especially linguistically, Satow's career in Japan and China was to last more than forty years.

It was never Satow's desire originally to serve in China, but—more romantically—in Japan, only recently reopened to the West by the gunboat diplomacy of the 1850s. That 'diplomacy' itself prompted violent political upheaval, and the young Satow lived life to the full, accompanying further punitive naval expeditions and encouraging what he himself subsequently described as the 'revolutionary' tendencies then abroad in Japan. At the same time, as a student interpreter in the consular service, he developed an almost unprecedented proficiency in the language (for a foreigner), which the successive British ministers in Japan, Rutherford Alcock and Harry Parkes, were not slow to exploit. However, after the overthrow of the humiliated Tokugawa dynasty of shoguns in 1868, and its replacement mainly by the leaders of the Satcho group, the role of the British legation diminished. Satow was appointed Japanese secretary in that year. He turned his attention to scholarship, becoming the first of a triumvirate of great British Japan scholars, the others being W. G. Aston and B. H. Chamberlain. He also started a family with Takeda Kane (1853–1932), his *musumé* (mistress, or common-law wife), who made a home for him in Tokyo from the 1870s until he left Japan for Bangkok in 1884. They had two sons.

Unlike Aston and Chamberlain, who became full-time scholars, Satow moved on in public life. In 1884 he secured his first independent posting, as consul-general at Bangkok, where he began to work to undermine the system of extra-territorial jurisdiction which represented the most insidious encroachment on the sovereignty of the Asian polities still free of Western colonialism, and to sustain Siam's independence in the face of both French and British ambitions. He was promoted to the rank of minister in 1885, but his health broke down. He spent four years in recuperation as minister at Montevideo in Uruguay from 1889; at the nadir of his career he experienced a religious revelation that nearly turned him into a Roman Catholic. He returned to the firing line in 1893, going as envoy-extraordinary and minister-plenipotentiary to Morocco, where he was active in defending its independence, mainly against France.

In 1895 Satow was made KCMG and appointed minister-plenipotentiary to Japan, the job he had hitherto always coveted. During his further five years in Tokyo he sought to build on his old personal contacts with the Satcho leadership, on Britain's abandonment of its extra-territorial rights in Japan, and on Britain's refusal to join the triple intervention powers (Russia, Germany, and France) in their attempts to cancel out Japan's victory in its first modern war with China over Korea. In this context, and foreseeing an eventual confrontation between Russia and Japan, Satow favoured Japan's influence in Korea and even in China, and also supported a full-scale alliance between Japan and Britain, which was not to materialize until after he had transferred to Peking (Beijing). Back in Tokyo, he resumed regular contact with his Japanese family.

The final phase of Satow's official career saw him transferred reluctantly to China to help sustain China's independence and territorial integrity in the aftermath of the Boxer uprising. As the leading figure at the year-long Boxer Conference, he found himself for the first time a major player in international affairs, and earned the GCMG that was his reward for the agreement signed between China and the Western powers in Peking in September 1901. Ironically, however, Sir Claude Macdonald, who had been the previous minister at Peking, and who had been moved to Tokyo to make way for Satow, was promoted ambassador in 1905 as a consequence of the 1902 Anglo-Japanese alliance and Japan's success in its war with Russia of 1904–5, while Satow was refused translation to a Western embassy and retired early, in 1906, still a mere minister.

Satow had gone far in the diplomatic service, thanks to almost unswerving loyalty and discretion, the word he virtually lived by: few of his inner thoughts appear outside his voluminous diaries and private correspondence. But he had not progressed as far as he had hoped, and he returned to England in the summer of 1906 a disappointed man. In particular, he evidently concluded that his association with the East had ultimately counted against him back in London. Moreover, his final reception in Tokyo, *en route* for England, at the hands of the two Japanese he had considered his special friends, Ito Hirobumi and Inoue Kaoru, had seemed almost devoid of gratitude on their part. The Campbell-Bannerman government's surprise invitation to Satow to be Britain's second delegate at the second peace conference at The Hague in 1907 helped to give him a new direction. The Foreign Office expected little enough of Sir Edward Fry and Lord Reay, the other principal delegates to the 44-country jamboree, and therefore looked to Satow to take the lead in pursuing its strictly mundane and nationalistic aims. Initially, he sought instead to express his own more idealistic principles. In particular, his sympathies were with the small countries, outside and also within Europe, but amid the confusion of the conference it became impracticable to sustain such a stance. Thus it was his own proposal to defer much of the conference's business to the twelve-country major power conference in London in 1908–9 that effectively disposed of this important effort to realize a permanent international organization before 1914.

Now fully retired, Satow settled at Ottery St Mary in east Devon, and threw himself into local politics, his magistracy, and charitable work. He made no further journeys abroad after a final visit to Germany in 1914, but he supported Christian missionary endeavour around the world, especially in China. His disillusion with his Eastern career led him to dispose of much of his Japan library, and for the rest of his life he had as little to do with the East as he could, while maintaining his friendships with many 'old Japan hands'. He had his younger son over to England for six years (1910–16) to study botany, an old interest of his own, before the boy returned to his mother in Japan. At an earlier stage he had already organized the emigration of his tubercular older son to the healthier climate of Colorado in the United States, where he died in 1926. But Satow revealed their existence only to those close to him; he did retain to the end of his days his Japanese manservant, Honma Saburo. Almost as an afterthought he issued his memoirs of sixty years before, *A Diplomat in Japan*, in 1921, which nevertheless became a minor classic. Another book, *A Diplomat in Siam*, was not published until 1996.

Satow turned scholar, and anti-German soon after. On the latter score, for much of the rest of his life he strove to refute all suggestions that he and his family were part-German, with the consequence that he found himself variously described as Polish, Swedish, Russian, and even Dutch-Russian. Of course, his family connections with Germany had been strong, and he had paid the country many visits in his youth. As for scholarship, after early contributions on the Far East to the *Cambridge Modern History* (vol. 19, 1909) and a couple of articles for the *Quarterly Review*, his first major work was *The Silesian Loan and Frederick the Great* (1915), which helped him justify his changed attitude to Germany and to compensate for his failure to secure a university chair in international law. The climax to this new phase of his life came shortly before the outbreak of the First World War, when he was signed up to compile a *Guide to Diplomatic Practice*, otherwise known simply as 'Satow', which was still in print in 2002. It originally appeared in two volumes in 1917; Satow was much occupied thereafter in expanding it for a second edition in 1922. Strangely, the work led to a close association with the inter-war internationalist historian Harold Temperley, a critic of the pre-war diplomacy of which Satow had been an exponent. Thus Satow pre-read much of Temperley's *Foreign Policy of Canning* (1925); Temperley later wrote Satow's biography for the *Dictionary of National Biography*. It was also thanks to Temperley that Satow was able to place some of his work on international law with the *Cambridge Historical Journal*. Prior to this he had already published on the post-war reorganization of Europe, and like others with Eastern experience, and unlike Temperley, he always remained sceptical of the League of Nations, which he considered no more constructive than the 1907 conference at The Hague, and perhaps more likely to contribute to a new age of dictatorship and war than of peace. But seen widely by this time as just an old fogey, he exerted little influence, and did not live to see his fears realized. He died on 26 August 1929 at his home, Beaumont, in Ottery St Mary, at the age of eighty-six and was buried in Ottery parish churchyard.

Despite his own somewhat attenuated education, Satow was a highly cultivated man. He had a love of music, art, and literature, and, if he had disappointed his father by preferring Japan to Cambridge, he maintained links there (he delivered the Rede lecture there in 1908) and at Oxford, both of which universities awarded him honorary doctorates. During home leaves he had also studied law, at Marburg in 1875 and Lincoln's Inn in 1883, and was called to the bar in 1887 after passing the examinations with distinction. His wide circle of acquaintances among scholars, extended by family connections with Oxford and Cambridge colleges, included such distinguished figures as Herbert Spencer, C. H. Firth, and Gilbert Murray. But with the greater part of his life apparently wasted in the effort to promote a broad world-view, Satow always kept the intellectual world essentially at bay. In the end, his privately printed *Family Chronicle of the English Satows* (1925) was a testament to what probably mattered to him most.

N. J. Brailey

Sources Satow MSS, PRO, Foreign Office Archives • Siam and Japan series, PRO, FO 69 and FO 46 • E. M. Satow, *A diplomat in Japan* (1921) • E. M. Satow, *A diplomat in Siam*, ed. N. Brailey (1996) • E. M.

Satow, *Family chronicle of the English Satows* (1925) • B. M. Allen, *The Rt. Hon. Sir Ernest Satow* (1933) • H. Cortazzi and G. Daniels, eds., *Britain and Japan, 1859–1991* (1991) • I. H. Nish, *Biographical portraits: Britain and Japan*, 2 vols. (1994–7) • G. A. Lensen, *Korea and Manchuria between Russia and Japan* (1966) • N. J. Brailey, 'Sir Ernest Satow, Japan and Asia', *HJ*, 35 (1992), 115–50 • N. J. Brailey, *The Satow Siam papers*, 1 (1997) • C. O. Davis, *The United States and the second Hague Peace Conference* (1975) • C. O. Jan, 'The East Asian diplomatic service and observations of Sir Ernest Satow', PhD diss., Florida University, 1976 • b. cert. • d. cert. • N. Hagiwara, *Toui gake* (1980), 49–76 ['A cliff far away']

Archives PRO, corresp., diaries, and papers, PRO 30/33 | Bodl. Oxf., corresp. with Lord Kimberley • Bodl. Oxf., letters to Sir Matthew Nathan • Mitchell L., NSW, letters to G. E. Morrison • NL Scot., letters to Sir James Lockhart • PRO, letters to Sir James Macleod, PRO 30/26/85

Likenesses Spy [L. Ward], chromolithograph caricature, NPG; repro. in *VF* (23 April 1903) • cartoon, repro. in Lensen, *Korea and Manchuria* • photographs, Yokohama Archives of History, Japan • photographs, repro. in Allen, *The Rt. Hon. Sir Ernest Satow* • portrait, repro. in *ILN* (29 Sept 1900)

Wealth at death £19,872 19s. 11d.: resworn probate, 1929, *CGPLA Eng. & Wales*

Saul, Arthur (*d.* **1586**), Church of England clergyman, was a native of Gloucestershire. Admitted demy at Magdalen College, Oxford, in early 1545, he graduated BA and became a fellow in 1546, proceeding MA early in 1549. One of the college's many committed protestants, whose acknowledged leaders were Thomas Bentham, John Foxe, and Laurence Humphrey, Saul was accordingly expelled by Bishop Stephen Gardiner's visitors in October 1553 and departed for the continent for the rest of Mary's reign. In 1554 he was at Strasbourg and was one of those who declined to migrate to Frankfurt. In December that year he was a beneficiary, to the tune of ten florins, of the bounty of the duke of Württemberg.

Saul removed to Heidelberg, where, on 23 June 1556, he was registered as a student from the diocese of Bristol. Probably, therefore, he was by now attached to the household of Katherine Bertie, duchess of Suffolk, settled at nearby Weinheim. On the arrival in Heidelberg in July 1556 of the English government agent John Brett, Saul and 'one Tremayne' (probably Richard) at first attempted to bribe him and then apparently threatened to use him 'with force' and do him 'displeasure', whereupon Brett hastily departed (Leadam, 128–9).

Upon Saul's return to England at the beginning of Elizabeth's reign he was one of twenty-eight protestants (including Foxe, Humphrey, and Richard Tremayne) whose preferment was urged on Lord Robert Dudley, later earl of Leicester, on the grounds that they had rejected 'Antichriste and al his Romishe rags' (Magd. Cam., Pepys Library, 'Papers of state', 2.701). On 2 November 1559 and 25 January 1560 Saul received letters patent for the prebend of Bedminster and Redclyffe in Salisbury Cathedral and the first prebend in Bristol Cathedral respectively. By the beginning of 1562 he had become chaplain to Sir Nicholas Bacon, lord keeper of the great seal. In that capacity Saul made a number of recommendations for crown livings in Bacon's gift between 1562 and 1575, and successfully petitioned on his own behalf on no fewer than four occasions. On 25 April 1562 he received letters patent for the prebend at Gloucester vacated by Richard Cheyney on his elevation to the bishopric and subsequently acquired from Bacon the benefices of Porlock, Somerset (12 September 1562), Ubley, Somerset (12 June 1564), and Doynton, Gloucestershire (11 October 1566).

As proctor for the dean and chapter of Gloucester during the convocation of 1562–3 Saul voted in favour of radical liturgical reform. In 1565 he was appointed by Thomas Bentham, now bishop of Coventry and Lichfield, to visit his diocese and in 1576 was one of a commission of four empowered by Archbishop Edmund Grindal to visit that of Gloucester. On 26 October 1579 he was appointed a chaplain to John Aylmer, bishop of London.

Higher preferment eluded Saul. He resigned his Gloucester canonry in 1580 in favour of his son-in-law, Laurence Bridger, rector of Slimbridge, and made his will on 6 August that year. He requested burial in Bristol Cathedral next to his wife (her identity is unrecorded), leaving his property to his five children, Arnold, William, Anne Bridger, Elizabeth, and Justine. Laurence Bridger was appointed sole executor (his sons were still minors) and George Savage, archdeacon of Gloucester, was one of his overseers. A short codicil was added on 12 June 1586 and Bridger was granted probate on 16 July. Saul died in possession of his canonries at Salisbury and Bristol.

BRETT USHER

Sources J. R. Bloxam, *A register of the presidents, fellows … of Saint Mary Magdalen College*, 8 vols. (1853–85) • W. D. Macray, *A register of the members of St Mary Magdalen College, Oxford*, 8 vols. (1894–1915) • C. H. Garrett, *The Marian exiles: a study in the origins of Elizabethan puritanism* (1938) • J. Brett, 'A narration of the pursuit of English refugees in Germany under Queen Mary', ed. I. S. Leadam, *TRHS*, new ser., 11 (1897), 113–31 • *Fasti Angl., 1541–1857*, [Salisbury; Bristol] • BL, Lansdowne MS 443, fols. 114*v*–229*v*, *passim* • Inner Temple Library, London, Petyt MS 538, vol. 47, fols. 575*r*–576*r* • LMA, DL/C/333, fol. 108*r* • C. Litzenberger, *The English Reformation and the laity: Gloucestershire, 1540–1580* (1997) • will, PRO, PROB 11/69/38, fols. 294*v*–295*r*

Wealth at death see will, PRO, PROB 11/69/38, fols. 294*v*–295*r*

Saul, Arthur (*d.* **1614x18**), writer on chess and supposed spy, is a figure about whom much remains obscure. He was possibly a kinsman of Arthur *Saul (*d.* 1586), canon of Bristol and of Gloucester, and may be the Arthur Sale who graduated BD from Magdalen College, Oxford (the college which the canon had attended), on 8 July 1572.

Saul's little book, *The Famous Game of Chesse-Play*, was first published in 1614, with a splendid woodcut frontispiece showing two gentlemen about to start playing. While not of great depth as an aid to technique, it was the first European book to include the curious rule (contrary to modern practice) that a player whose king is stalemated wins the game, which was justified by the argument that his opponent 'hath unadvisedly stopped the course of the game, which is to end onely by the grand Check-mate' (Saul, 1614, unpaginated). The book was dedicated to Lucy, countess of Bedford, whose deceased father, Lord Harington of Exton, had been one of Saul's friends. In it Saul stated that he had played the game for many years. In 1618 John Barbier printed an amended edition which mentioned that the author was now dead, and this edition was reprinted in 1640, 1652, 1672, 1673, and 1676.

The only certain information about Saul lies within the cover of his book. However, his name appears in manuscript sources in a number of contexts, and one or more of these references to Arthur Saul may well apply to the chess writer. In 1600 or 1601 Arthur Saull of London, gentleman, complained to the court of Star Chamber that on 18 August 1600, after he and his wife had been staying for about six months at the house of Walter Shipman in Gloucestershire, it was violently attacked by Richard Jones, shipwright of Chepstow, and about sixty armed men, who claimed that they were acting in the queen's name and threatened to burn down the house and strip Saull's wife of all her clothes.

Most intriguing are the references to Arthur Saul, spy for the English government, who appears in the record about 1600 and then between 1615 and 1617. Suitably for a secret agent, it is not entirely certain that the spies in the two periods are the same man, let alone the chess writer; their signatures appear significantly different! However, the plausibility that the writer on chess was also a spy is strengthened by the compatibility of the death date of Arthur Saul, author (between 1614 and 1618), with that of Arthur Saul, spy (spring of 1617). In a letter of about 1600, probably to Sir Robert Cecil, Saul reported on an unsuccessful search for someone in London, despite seeing the man he was pursuing a week earlier on Ludgate Hill and looking for him since in crowded places such as St Paul's and many eating houses, 'and here in the court' (*Salisbury MSS*, 10.449).

About 10 September 1615 Saul was (according to his own account) asked by Sir Ralph Winwood, secretary of state, to go to the continent to discover which English Catholics were sent to Douai and elsewhere. Upon his return a few months later he accordingly reported to Winwood and to George Abbot, archbishop of Canterbury. He then proceeded to make it his business to find out about priests who had returned to England from St Omer and Douai, and who had resorted to the Spanish ambassador's house and to a brick house in Petticoat Lane where Saul went to mass with them. On 19 February 1617 Saul, described as a yeoman of London, was arrested and charged with the rape of one Hester Hopkins in the church porch of St Mary Abchurch. He was imprisoned in Newgate gaol, where a number of Catholic priests were also held, and on 5 April he made a statement before Sir Thomas Bennett and Thomas Wilson about his secret service for the state and supplied dramatic information about the recent escape of two women recusants and two priests. Shortly afterwards, Saul fell victim to the unhealthiness of a seventeenth-century prison. He died in Newgate on 29 April 1617, having been sick for nine days of 'a pineing sicknes' which carried off five other prisoners (Bowler, 98).

C. G. Lewin

Sources A. Saul, *The famous game of chesse-play* (1614); rev. J. Barbier (1618) • bill of complaint of Arthur Saull of London to star chamber, PRO, STAC 5/575/1 • information of Arthur Saule, prisoner in Newgate, April 1617, PRO, SP 14/91/20 • H. Bowler, ed., *London sessions records, 1605–1685*, Catholic RS, 34 (1934), 97–8 • letter from Arthur Saull, Hatfield House, archives of the marquess of Salisbury, CP 83/38 [also microfilm copy in BL, manuscripts room] • *Calendar of the manuscripts of the most hon. the marquis of Salisbury*, 10, HMC, 9 (1904), 449 • Foster, *Alum. Oxon.* • city of London sessions file, April 1617, CLRO, SF 76 • H. J. R. Murray, *A history of chess* (1913)

Wealth at death died in Newgate prison

Saull [Saul], **William Devonshire** (1783–1855), radical philanthropist and geological collector, was born on 21 April 1783 at Byfield, Northamptonshire, the son of William Saul and Elizabeth Devonshire. Nothing is known of Saull's early years, except that he married nineteen-year-old Elizabeth Weedon (1789–1860) at Chesham on 8 December 1808. Shortly after, his company, Saull and Saddington, wine and brandy merchants, was established at 19 Aldersgate Street in the City of London. Wm Devonshire Saull & Co. remained at this address until about 1830, when the firm moved to 15 Aldersgate Street. Saull was a wealthy Owenite and freethinker who not only talked of materialist science as a force to smash 'tyranny and priestcraft', as he said at the Rotunda in 1832 (*Isis*, 1, 1832, 60), but acted on it. Poorly educated himself, he used his wine importation profits to help build the Owenites' City Road Hall of Science and John Street Institution, as well as run the Rotunda and fund the infidel missionaries Robert Taylor and Richard Carlile.

Radicals equated knowledge with liberation, and Saull, an avid collector, built a large geological museum adjoining his house at 15 Aldersgate Street (geology being a dangerous science that in radical eyes demolished ideas of supernatural creation). He became a fellow of the Geological Society in 1831 and in 1833 opened his museum to working people. An appreciation of the natural rise of life pointed out by palaeontology, he believed, would blow away religious 'phantasies'. His mooting of the 'simian hypothesis'—the evolution of a 'naked savage' from 'the ape or monkey tribe'—even flummoxed some socialists ('Lecture of Mr Saull in Bristol', *Crisis*, 3, 1833, 37). Saull's fossils, which (from 1831) incorporated James Sowerby's collection, were therefore stratigraphically arranged (although this was not the practice of the British Museum). The public was admitted every Thursday, with Saull on hand to illustrate the ascent of fossil life. Many radicals saw social progress—accelerated by phrenological practice—as a continuation of this natural development. Saull himself became a member of the London Phrenological Society, and his own cranial collection eventually contained the head of the atheist patron of the radical Rotundists, Julian Hibbert.

In 1835 Saull rebuilt his museum. Ironically it was here that the tory anti-transmutationist Richard Owen saw the fused sacral vertebrae of an Isle of Wight *Iguanodon*, which he made one of the defining characteristics of his new order, the Dinosauria, in 1841–2. Another hollowed vertebra from early Cretaceous rocks Owen identified as belonging to a huge saurian, *Cetiosaurus*, later recognized as a sauropod dinosaur.

By 1841 Saull was supporting the Chartists at their Political and Scientific Institute, Old Bailey. That year he became a fellow of the Society of Antiquaries and from

1841, when he lectured the members on the Celtic and Roman remains of Dunstable, until 1854 he delivered a string of papers. From the mid-1840s he spoke at the congresses of the British Archaeological Association on ancient fortifications and early villages. His *Notitia Britanniae* (1845) used the evidence from barrows to argue for the progressive ascent of the 'aborigines' of Great Britain and to castigate those who would impede the continuing progress of so much of mankind. He was an active council member (1850–55) of the Ethnological Society, where he talked on the Celts, Norse, and Saxons, and his pamphlet *Observations on the Aboriginal Tribes of Britain* (1848) originated as an Ethnological Society paper. While everyone acknowledged his kind-heartedness, Saull's radical science and politics were badly received by the gentlemen at the Geological and Astronomical societies. His new edition in 1832 of Sir Richard Phillips's *Essay on the Physico-Astronomical Causes of the Geological Changes of the Earth's Surface* (which deplored Newton's occult explanation of gravitation) was attacked in print, while his paper on the subject to the Geological Society in 1848 had to be reprinted privately as *An Essay on the Connexion between Astronomical and Geological Phenomena* (1853).

In old age, Saull's radical science kept pace with his politics. In 1850 and 1851 he presided at the John Street Institution over the celebrations of Robert Owen's seventy-ninth and eightieth birthdays, in Owen's presence. By then Saull was owner of Owen's town house and mortgagee of Rosehill, the estate at the centre of Owen's co-operative experiment at Harmony Hall in Hampshire.

To the end Saull was financing the cause. In 1848 he purchased unconsecrated ground in Kensal Green cemetery for his family and fellow freethinkers, which his friend Henry Hetherington was the first to occupy, in 1849. Saull joined him here on 11 May 1855, having died, at his home, 15 Aldersgate Street, on 26 April 1855 of a haemorrhage. By then his museum comprised Roman antiquities from the City, coins, and 20,000 geological specimens valued at over £2000. It was unclear from his will whether it should be bequeathed to the John Street Institution or the Metropolitan Institution Company. In court the vice-chancellor settled in favour of the latter, which received the museum, library, and £500. The museum was sold in 1863; 200 fossils, including the *Iguanodon* sacrum, went to Richard Owen's department at the British Museum, as did many of Sowerby's invertebrates.

ADRIAN DESMOND

Sources 'Saull, William Devonshire', *Geological Curator*, 3 (1981–3), 247–8, 296 • *Journal of the British Archaeological Association*, 12 (1856), 186–7 • *GM*, 2nd ser., 44 (1855), 102 • *The Reasoner*, 3 (1847), 83; 5 (1848), 429; 7 (1849), 164; 9 (1850), 84; 10 (1851), 252; 11 (1851), 20; 15 (1853), 208; 16 (1854), 97; 18 (1855), 38–9; 19 (1855), 31, 47, 55, 296; 20 (1856), 74; 21 (1856), 96, 115; 24 (1859), 191; 26 (1861), 14 • minutes of the Ethnological Society, Archives of the Royal Anthropological Institute, London • *IGI* • W. Holden, *Holden's triennial directory* (1809–11) • 'Pigot's directory', 1828–9, GL • R. Cooter, *The cultural meaning of popular science: phrenology and the organization of consent in nineteenth-century Britain* (1984) • I. McCalman, *Radical underworld: prophets, revolutionaries, and pornographers in London, 1795–1840* (1988) • J. O. Farlow and M. K. Brett-Suiman, *The complete dinosaur* (1997)

Archives NHM, fossil collection | NHM, letters to Owen and Sowerby

Wealth at death at least £2500

Saulles, George William de (1862–1903), medallist, was born on 4 February 1862 at Villa Street, Aston Manor, Birmingham, and baptized there on 13 April 1863 at St Philip's Church, the son of William Henry de Saulles, glass merchant, and his wife, Elizabeth Anne. His grandfather was French, or possibly Swiss, but his father had settled in Birmingham. He began his art training at the Birmingham School of Art under E. R. Taylor and gained several prizes there. He was then apprenticed to John Wilcox, die-sinker, in Birmingham, from whom he gained varied experience, including the execution of dies for large labels for Manchester manufactured goods, which sometimes included figures in their design. He moved to London in 1884, and worked for John H. Pinches, the die-engraver, then in Oxenden Street, Haymarket. In 1888 he returned to Birmingham and worked for Joseph Moore, the medallist.

During 1892 de Saulles was commissioned to work on new coinage for the Royal Mint, following the death of Leonard Charles Wyon, the chief engraver. In January 1893 he was appointed 'engraver to the mint' (*Annual Report of Deputy Master of the Mint*, 1893, 30), and from that time until his death was actively engaged in the production of dies for English and colonial coins and for official medals. He was a highly skilled craftsman who worked with great rapidity, and who designed, modelled, and engraved most of his dies. He was in some degree influenced by the French school of L. O. Roty and J. C. Chaplain, but in his official work there was little scope for innovation or the exercise of imagination.

De Saulles's medallic work between 1894 and 1903 included large numbers of official and private medals and several plaques, many of which were exhibited at the Royal Academy from 1898. Notable among these were the diamond jubilee medal of Queen Victoria (1897), the coronation medal of Edward VII (1902), and the Stokes jubilee medal with a portrait of Professor Nathaniel Stokes (1899).

De Saulles's first commission from the mint was to execute the dies for the new issue of coins of Queen Victoria in 1893, designed by Thomas Brock. He designed the Britannia reverse of the English bronze coins of 1895, and the issue of English coins made in 1902 after the accession of Edward VII. His signature on the coins is De S. He also designed and engraved the dies for various colonial coins, such as the British East Africa copper coins (1897), the British Honduras coins (1894), and the British dollar for India (1895). He made the last great seal of Queen Victoria (1899), and many designs for official seals for the colonies. At the time of his death he was preparing the models for the great seals of the United Kingdom and those of Ireland and Scotland, subsequently executed by F. Bowcher. (His work is listed in more detail by Pinches, 312–13; Hocking, 2.301; and Brown, vols. 2–3.)

De Saulles was regarded as a kind-natured man and was entirely devoted to his profession. He died on 22 July 1903 at his home, 31 Fairfax Road, Bedford Park, Chiswick, and was buried on 25 July in the churchyard of St Nicholas's, Chiswick. He left a widow, Myra Elizabeth. Works and designs on paper by de Saulles are among records of the mint at the Public Record Office, London.

CHRISTOPHER MARSDEN

Sources J. H. Pinches, 'George William de Saulles', *Numismatic Chronicle*, 4th ser., 3 (1903), 311–13 • C. P. Barclay, 'G. W. de Saulles: engraver to the mint', *The Medal*, 20 (1992), 56–68 • L. Forrer, ed., *Biographical dictionary of medallists*, 1 (1902), 385; 7 (1923), 217 • C. E. Challis, ed., *A new history of the royal mint* (1992) • W. J. Hocking, *Catalogue of the coins, tokens, medals, dies, and seals in the museum of the royal mint*, 2 vols. (1906–10) • L. Brown, *A catalogue of British historical medals, 1760–1960*, 3 vols. (1980–95) • private information (1912) [J. H. Pinches] • *The Times* (24 July 1903) • *CGPLA Eng. & Wales* (1903) • Thieme & Becker, *Allgemeines Lexikon* • *IGI*

Archives PRO, records of the Royal Mint, designs on paper

Likenesses photograph, repro. in C. P. Barclay, 'G. W. de Saulles', 57

Wealth at death £867: administration, 6 Aug 1903, *CGPLA Eng. & Wales*

Sault, Richard (*d.* 1702), mathematician and writer, whose origins are obscure, is first heard of in connection with John Dunton's *Athenian Gazette*, a single half-folio which advertised itself as 'resolving weekly all the most nice and curious Questions propos'd by the Ingenious'. Sault, a mathematics teacher, was married to Sarah, Dunton's stepsister. The first two numbers of the gazette, issued on 17 and 24 March 1691, carried numerous and diverse questions ostensibly sent in by the general public, but which were in fact written entirely by Sault and Dunton as a lead-in. Before the third number, Sault recruited the moral philosopher John Norris (1657–1712) and Dunton brought in his brother-in-law Samuel Wesley, rector of South Ormsby, Lincolnshire, and father of John and Charles Wesley. Norris declined payment but Sault, Wesley, and Dunton signed articles of agreement, and were, it seems, the 'Athenian Academy' under whose aegis the *Athenian Mercury*, as it was now called, appeared regularly until 1697. Its success inspired several imitators, and on one occasion Sault was roused to put hand to sword against Tom Brown, editor of the rival *Lacedemonian Mercury*, before being calmed by an apology.

By 1693 Sault was keeping a mathematical boarding-school in Adam's Court, Broad Street, near the Royal Exchange, London, and teaching by correspondence. He contributed 'A treatise on algebra', which included Joseph Raphson's 'Converging series for all manner of adfected equations', to William Leybourne's *Pleasure with Profit* (1694), and afterwards reprinted this section for his own pupils. Also in 1694 he published a translation of Nicolas Malebranche's *Recherche de la vérité*, with a defence and life of the author. On 22 February 1695 John Houghton's *Collections for Husbandry and Trade* advertised the prospectus for a new 'royal academy' where mathematics would be taught in Latin, French, or English by Sault and Abraham De Moivre. An algebraic note extracted from Sault's work and published in the Royal Society's *Philosophical Transactions* (vol. 20, 1698, p. 425) demonstrated his acquaintance with Newton's geometrical theory of vanishing quantities and with the notation of fluxions; he was not, however, a member of the society. His translation into English of the *Breviarum chronologicum* of Gyles Strauch, professor of divinity at Danzig, was published in 1699, and again in 1702 and 1722.

Controversy was aroused by a curious work published by Dunton as *The second Spira, being a fearful example of an atheist who had apostasised from the Christian religion, and died in despair at Westminster, Dec. 8 1692*, 'by J.S.'. Sault claimed he knew the author, who nevertheless remained unidentified. The original Spira was an Italian lawyer and reputed atheist whose tragic death had been the subject of a popular biography, published in 1548 and repeatedly reprinted in Italian and French. Dunton later concluded that Sault was both author and subject of *The Second Spira*, and that he was depicting his own remorse and religious alienation brought about by his immoral life. To make his point, Dunton included in his memoirs a letter from Sault's wife in which she accused her husband of loose living, and in reply to which Sault allowed that she was one of the best of wives, and admitted his guilt.

Sault moved to Cambridge about 1700, where his mastery of algebra earned him a considerable reputation. He shortly fell into a terminal illness and, being in great poverty, was supported by the friendly contributions of the scholars, collected without his knowledge. He died in Cambridge in May 1702 and was buried in the church of St Andrew the Great there on 17 May.

H. F. BAKER, *rev.* ANITA MCCONNELL

Sources C. H. Cooper, 'Account of Richard Sault, mathematician, and one of the editors of the *Athenian Mercury*', *Cambridge Antiquarian Society: Communications*, 3 (1864), 37 • S. Parks, 'The Athenian Society', *John Dunton and the English book trade* (1976), 74–108 • *The life and errors of John Dunton*, [rev. edn], 1, ed. J. B. Nichols (1818), 154–8, 189–91 • E. G. R. Taylor, *The mathematical practitioners of Tudor and Stuart England* (1954), 289

Saumarez, James, first Baron de Saumarez (1757–1836), naval officer, was born at St Peter Port, Guernsey, on 11 March 1757, the third son of Matthew Saumarez (1718–1778), physician of Guernsey, and his second wife, Carteret, daughter of James le Marchant. Richard *Saumarez was his younger brother. His father, a younger brother of Captain Philip *Saumarez (1710–1747), who had sailed round the world with George Anson, was the son of Matthew, colonel in the Guernsey militia, whose ancestry dated to the reign of Henry II. In 1767, while James was at Elizabeth College, Guernsey, his father, who had six sons and a limited income, persuaded Captain Lucius O'Brien to enter the boy's name on the books of the *Solebay* (28 guns) where it remained for two years and nine months while he finished his schooling.

Early naval career In August 1770 Saumarez joined the *Montreal* (36 guns, Captain James Alms) and he went with Alms to the Mediterranean, where he moved that November into the *Winchelsea* (32 guns, Captain Samuel Goodall) before shifting in February 1772 to the *Levant* (28 guns, Captain Samuel Thompson); he returned with Thompson after three years in 1775. Having passed for lieutenant that September he went with Commodore Sir Peter Parker in

James Saumarez, first Baron de Saumarez (1757–1836), by Thomas Phillips, 1809

the *Bristol* (50 guns) to North America, carrying Lord Cornwallis to assume the military command; the latter's flattering offer of a commission in his old regiment was declined. The young officer first saw action in the unfortunate attack on Fort Sullivan (28 June 1776) where he was literally blooded and became the sole survivor of his gun's crew. His very steady behaviour earned him an acting order (11 July) which was extended when he went with Parker to the *Chatham* (50 guns) where he came to the notice of his Uncle Philip's contemporary circumnavigator, now Admiral Augustus Keppel; Lord Howe confirmed his promotion (25 January 1778) and gave him his first command, the galley *Spitfire*, in which he was active on the coast of New England until she was burnt to prevent her capture that August.

Saumarez returned to England in the *Leviathan*, went home on leave, and, hearing that he had been appointed to the *Edgar* (74 guns) fitting out at Woolwich, he took passage for England early in 1779 in the *Ambuscade* (32 guns) with his friend Captain Phipps. Off Portsmouth, Phipps, hearing that the Channel Fleet had sailed, determined to follow and captured a Frenchman going down the channel. The first lieutenant of the *Victory* (100 guns), Sir John Borlase Warren, was appointed to command her and Saumarez went to the flagship as a supernumerary. By 1781 he had become her first lieutenant, and successive captains testified to those qualities which had so impressed Cornwallis; when Hyde Parker shifted his flag to the *Fortitude* (74 guns) he took Saumarez with him and after the miniature but classic action on the Dogger Bank (5 August 1781) made him acting captain of the *Preston* (50 guns), whose captain had been killed. He was thus presented with the other commanding officers to George III who, on learning that he was related to Anson's captain, told Saumarez that he was a worthy descendant. It is no surprise that though only second lieutenant of the *Fortitude*, Saumarez was promoted master and commander (23 August) into the fireship *Tisiphone* (20 guns), then serving as a sloop. Under Saumarez she joined Admiral Richard Kempenfelt's detachment to North America and it was the *Tisiphone* which, on 12 December 1781, warned the admiral of a large French trooping convoy escorted by twenty sail of the line who were on the far side of the ships. This intelligence allowed Kempenfelt to take the majority of the French troop ships whose escort had foolishly fallen to the leeward of their charges. Saumarez was subsequently sent to warn Hood at Barbados of the advent of their survivors, which he could only do with reasonable dispatch by some particularly hazardous navigation among rocks hitherto thought impassable. The admiral was impressed, and Hood ordered Saumarez's move to the *Russell* (74 guns).

Battle of the Saints to battle of Cape St Vincent, 1782–1797 Made post on 7 February 1782, aged almost twenty-five, Saumarez fought brilliantly at the battle of the Saints eight weeks later, surprising and astonishing George Bridges Rodney who broke the enemy line to find his junior had already done so. Although the French flagship struck to Hood's, she did so only when the *Russell* bore down on her. Rodney's reaction was to declare with an oath that Saumarez's action had distinguished him above all others in the fleet, while Hood referred to him as 'that excellent young man' whom he sent back with the trade to England—and to half pay. By now he had fought in three general actions: Nelson, three years his senior, had commanded only frigates and had seen no fleet action.

During the ten years of peace Saumarez divided his time between Guernsey and Exeter, taking the opportunity to make his only visit to France, visible from the family home, to inspect the new breakwater at Cherbourg. Otherwise his peace was disturbed only by brief commissioning of the *Ambuscade* (32 guns) in 1787 and the *Raisonnable* (64 guns) in 1790. Meanwhile he married (8 October 1788) Martha (*d.* 1849), daughter of Thomas le Marchant and his wife, Mary Dobree. They had three sons and four daughters; the eldest boy, James, spent some time in the Baltic with his father before taking holy orders.

When war broke out in 1793 Saumarez was given the *Crescent* (36 guns) which he manned without difficulty; it was with equal ease that on 20 October 1793 he took the French *Réunion*, of equal rate. Although she carried 320 men to Saumarez's 260, they were inexperienced seamen and indifferent gunners, and after two hours and 120 casualties she struck to the *Crescent*, which despite damaged rigging had not lost a man. Saumarez was called to London to be presented and knighted, and to receive a large piece of plate, the start of a splendid collection. In June 1794 his seamanship and the discipline of his men were notable in the channel when the *Crescent*, in company with the *Druid* (32 guns) and *Eurydice* (24 guns), met two 36-gun French frigates and two 54-gun ships (cut-down 74s). A change in the wind required a controlled retreat to Guernsey which Saumarez carried out with great skill, allowing the slower *Eurydice* to escape supported by the *Druid*. Seeing them enter harbour, the disappointed enemy were confident of taking Saumarez when his ship disappeared through a channel into St Peter Port never before attempted: even he felt obliged to query the master's confidence. The latter, Jean le Breton, replied simply 'I am quite sure—there is your house—there is mine'.

In the following March Saumarez was appointed to command the *Orion* (74 guns). His heart, as A. T. Mahan pointed out in 1893, was on a ship of the line, 'whose high organization and steady discipline … appealed to a temperament naturally calm, methodical and enduring' (*Atlantic Monthly*, 71/427, 1893, 608). Chance and choice combined to further his career. He was active in Lord Bridport's running action off the Île de Groix which was 'though a victory, not a very great one'; in blockading Brest and Rochefort for eighteen months; and, under Sir William Parker, in reinforcing Sir John Jervis shortly before the latter's action off St Vincent on 14 February 1797. Jervis put Parker's squadron in the van; fresh from home waters, the ships were cleaner and faster. Saumarez took his opportunities. He claimed that though the *Salvador del Mundi* (112 guns) struck to the *Victory*, she had already been engaged by the *Orion*, which had put a boat's crew on board. More visible was his disappointment over the *Santissima Trinidad* (136 guns) which had already surrendered to him, first with a white flag and then with the British colours over the Spanish. But as the *Orion* ceased fire, *Victory* signalled the fleet to wear and Saumarez had no realistic chance to secure that prestigious prize, but only the mortification of seeing her rehoist her own colours and then of having no reference made to the incident in the admiral's dispatch. Instead he spoke petulantly of the affair to Nelson, who had assured him that Spanish officers confirmed the facts, 'Whoever doubted it Sir?' replied Saumarez. 'I hope there is no need for such evidence to establish the truth of a report by a British officer', an early example of the unfortunate intemperance which occasionally tarnished an otherwise urbane, courteous, and essentially Christian character.

But Saumarez and Nelson were never comfortable with one another. The next year's pursuit of Brueys found Saumarez, the senior captain in Nelson's squadron, *ex officio* his second in command in the Nile campaign. It is A. T. Mahan's opinion that neither Nelson nor St Vincent saw in him the necessary qualifications for a surrogate but could not easily replace him with Thomas Troubridge, their preferred incumbent, while Nelson could not afford to send home so notable a ship. They might not have been surprised had they known that as the ships chased eastwards, Saumarez recorded his relief to a journal intended as an eventual letter home that 'fortunately I only act here *en second*; but did the chief responsibility rest with me, I fear it would be more than my too irritable nerves would bear' (Ross, 1.207). With Troubridge missing the battle when his ship grounded while entering Abu Qir Bay, it would have been on Saumarez that praise or blame fell had Nelson's head wound proved fatal. As it was, Saumarez received his only wound at the same time, when a large piece of splintered wood, which had already killed two men, struck him hard enough to cause a severe contusion on the thigh. Whether to spare Troubridge embarrassment, or to avoid identifying Saumarez as his second, the admiral did not mention in his dispatch either officer as in any way senior to the other. But when Saumarez began to talk about dividing the line Nelson ended the discussion by walking away, saying what a 'good thing it was that there was no order given'. Saumarez then took six prizes and seven of the squadron slowly home. Frequently becalmed off Malta, he was humiliated by the French reply to his demand that they surrender; furthermore the few small arms he landed for the Maltese insurgents were of questionable value to their resistance. None the less on reaching England there were two large gold medals, a colonelcy in the marines, and more plate to console him.

Algeçiras In 1799 Saumarez went to the *Caesar* (84 guns), the navy's first two-decked ship of that rate, and was in the Channel Fleet when Jervis (now Lord St Vincent) returned from the Mediterranean determined to introduce a similar degree of discipline to that achieved in his recent command. He found in Saumarez one of the very few men to whom he could entrust the blockade of Brest, though it reduced his physique until he resembled 'a shotten herring'. Increased now to six or eight of the line close in within 2 miles of the harbour's mouth, this was a command requiring calm, steadfast, and professional seamanship. The change of pace from two gold medal actions to the prolonged strain of close blockade is hard to imagine; both forms of warfare were equally important in their consequence if different in public impact. Saumarez was honoured by St Vincent's assurance that 'with you there I sleep as soundly as if I had the keys of Brest in my pocket' (from the *Ville de Paris* off Ushant, 15 Sept 1800) and consoled by promotion to the flag list as a rear-admiral of the blue on 1 January 1801 and the creation of a baronetcy on 13 June. Next day he sailed to blockade Cadiz.

In fact Saumarez was soon to lift it on hearing that Linois's squadron, leaving Toulon to reinforce the Spaniards, had been forced into Gibraltar Bay to shelter off Algeçiras, a safe haven. Leaving only Captain Richard Keats, who may have been too far north to see the recall, Saumarez emulated Nelson and sought a close and instant engagement on 6 July, a boldness which was thwarted by wind and tide. During the inevitable retreat, the *Hannibal* (74 guns) grounded and was forced to surrender, though her captain was honourably acquitted: the other ships were also damaged, two seriously. Saumarez showed greater and more successful leadership in his conversion of defeat into victory. While his ships were repairing at Gibraltar, Keats appeared in the *Superb*, closely followed by a Spanish detachment of nine ships, including the *Hannibal*, from Cadiz. Repair work went on faster than was imaginable and on the afternoon of 12 July 1801 Saumarez led out his five ships in pursuit. Keats was sent ahead, and in a night action caused two Spaniards to sink one another in a single conflagration while capturing a French ship with no British losses.

Saumarez was made KB, the insignia sent out for his immediate investiture by the governor of Gibraltar. In addition he received fulsome tributes in the Lords from St Vincent and Nelson, a valuable sword from the City, yet more plate, and, after some correspondence, an annuity of £1200. But again Saumarez contrived to take offence where none was intended. Despite a singularly tactful letter (13 August 1801) from St Vincent pointing out their Lordships' inability to avoid passing him over for the command of a detachment from Admiral Lord Keith's extended Channel Fleet, Saumarez formally objected to their decision. This earned him a tremendous put down from St Vincent (*Letters*, 1.211), though another officer would probably have been ordered to strike his flag. However, he must have been consoled six months later by the offer of the Mediterranean Fleet, which he declined in May 1802, when, having superintended the restoration of Minorca to Spain, he returned to Guernsey.

In 1803 Saumarez hoisted his flag at the Nore (11 March) before taking up the command in the Channel Islands, pivotal while invasion seemed imminent but something of a domestic sinecure thereafter, disturbed occasionally, for example, by the bombardment of Granville (15 September). After a hint from St Vincent, Thomas Grenville declared his intention to bring him back into the Channel Fleet. In 1806 a special promotion of flag officers was made, to include him among the vice-admirals. In January 1807 he became second in command of the Channel Fleet, again under St Vincent, though now it was the latter who generally lived ashore, the junior again bottling Brest. When Alan Gardner succeeded St Vincent, Saumarez was superseded by John Thomas Duckworth and returned to the Guernsey command, declining Lord Mulgrave's offer of the East India station. There seemed little to do after Trafalgar. But he was soon selected for the Baltic command which had been formed in the wake of the Franco-Russian alliance signed at Tilsit in July 1807, and the subsequent continental blockade to exclude British military, political, and commercial interests from mainland Europe. Saumarez was to hold this command from March 1808 until October 1812, his flag in the *Victory* (100 guns) in which he had served as a lieutenant, and his load lightened by the appointment of Sir Samuel Hood and Richard Keats as his rear-admirals.

Baltic command The appointment was a major career change and marks something of a high point in Saumarez's career, not just as a naval officer but also as a tactician and diplomat engaged in a patient and ultimately successful loosening of the Franco-Russian hold on Baltic trade. That Saumarez's achievement is now so highly regarded only serves to throw into sharper relief the bathetic tone previously adopted in memoirs such as those by Mahan and J. K. Laughton.

Early in 1808 there was every indication that the blockade was firmly in place, with all but Sweden pledged to close their ports to British trade. However, Saumarez's deployment of line-of-battle ships in defence of its merchant interest gradually served to expose 'the Baltic ports to the pressures of a British commercial offensive' (Ryan, xx). By imposing its own blockade on these ports the British forced traders to co-operate and to seek to circumvent the blockade using covert means. By 1809–10 Saumarez was able to report a tangible increase in the volume of trade despite the formal continuation of a united Franco-Russian policy, which itself began to deteriorate after French offensives in northern Europe in late 1810. In these months Saumarez also saw the first signs that the continental system was weakening following the Swedes' rejection of French demands to declare war on Britain. For the remainder of 1810 and 1811 he worked to convince the Swedes that it would be better for them to adopt an independent (and hence not anti-British) line. By 1812 Russia, facing the prospect of war with the French, offered to assist Sweden in its attack on Denmark, thus fully vindicating Saumarez's careful, pragmatic, and diplomatic approach to the crisis. As A. N. Ryan has argued, Saumarez's 'greatest asset … was his ability to estimate realistically the workings of national interest and to use the power at his disposal accordingly' and, while heavily armed, he kept his guns silent and 'the gates of Northern Europe open after Napoleon had decreed that they be closed' (Ryan, xxiii, xxv). The Swedish leadership also showed its appreciation:

> You have been the guardian angel of the country. By your wise, temperate and loyal conduct you have been the first cause of the plans which have been formed against the demon of the continent … you were the first cause that Russia dared to make war with France. Had you fired one shot when we declared war against England, all had been ended and Europe would have been enslaved. (Ross, 2.293–4)

He also received the grand cross of the order of the Sword and a 2000 guinea sword.

In 1814 Saumarez was promoted admiral and in 1815 advanced to GCB on the expansion of the Bath; in 1819 he was appointed rear-admiral of the United Kingdom and in 1821 advanced to vice-admiral. From 1824 to 1827 he was port admiral at Plymouth, and in 1830 he received his last naval promotion, to admiral of the red on 22 July. In 1831 he was belatedly raised to the peerage as Baron de Saumarez of Saumarez, in 1832 promoted to general in the Royal Marines (after which the rank was abolished), and in 1834 elected an elder brother of Trinity House where his installation may have accounted for his absence from the funeral of his old friend Richard Keats at Greenwich. He died calmly, aged seventy-nine, on 9 October 1836 in St Peter Port, Guernsey, and he was buried in his native parish of Câtel; a 99 foot obelisk was built in his memory (1887–9) but demolished by German forces in 1943.

Saumarez was a tall and graceful man, lofty in height and demeanour. Hotham found him

> rather formal and ceremonious in his manner but without the least tincture of affectation or pride—more than ordinarily attentive to his duty to God but with the meekness of a Christian having the boldness of a lion when necessary.

Certainly no Gambier, he was liked by both his officers and men, had no difficulty in manning his ships, and, though punctiliously correct and civil in public, relaxed in ward room and cabin. This rather unbending public attitude—which many, including Nelson, mistook for aloofness or even arrogance—was a natural defensive reserve, not always successful in masking an almost pathological sensibility. Byam Martin, who knew him well, observed a tendency towards depression which at times made him hardly fit for duty, a situation compounded by his tendency of brooding alone and of taking offence when none had been intended. He was nevertheless seen by St Vincent as 'an officer whose merit cannot be surpassed'.

Saumarez was survived by his wife, who died on 17 April 1849, and by his younger brother **Sir Thomas Saumarez** (1760–1845), army officer, who was born on 1 July 1760 at St Peter Port, Guernsey, the fourth son of Matthew Saumarez and Carteret le Marchant. He joined the army in January 1776, and survived the middle years of the American War of Independence, but was captured at the surrender of Yorktown on 19 October 1781. He was later appointed brigade-major of the Guernsey militia and was knighted on 15 July 1795 after presenting the island's congratulations to the prince of Wales on his marriage. He was assistant quartermaster-general (1786), inspector of the Guernsey militia (1799), major-general (1811), commander-in-chief at New Brunswick (1813), and garrison commander at Halifax, Nova Scotia (1812–14). Following his return to England he became groom of the bedchamber to the duke of Kent and was promoted general on the coronation of Queen Victoria in June 1838. In 1787 he had married Harriet (*d.* 1858), daughter of William Brock. He died at his Guernsey home, Petit Marche, on 4 March 1845 and was survived by his wife, who died on 18 February 1858. A. B. SAINSBURY

Sources *DNB* • *Memoirs and correspondence of Admiral Lord de Saumarez*, ed. J. Ross, 2 vols. (1838) • A. T. Mahan, 'Admiral Saumarez', *Atlantic Monthly*, 71/427 (May 1893) • *The Saumarez papers: selections from the Baltic correspondence of Vice-Admiral Sir James Saumarez, 1808–1812*, ed. A. N. Ryan, Navy RS, 110 (1968) • 'An ambassador afloat – Vice Admiral Sir James Saumarez of the Swedish court 1803–12', ed. A. N. Ryan, *British navy and the use of seapower*, ed. J. Black and P. Woodfire (1988) • *The private correspondence of Admiral Lord Collingwood*, ed. E. Hughes, Navy RS, 98 (1957) • *Letters and papers of Admiral of the Fleet Sir Thos. Byam Martin, GCB*, ed. R. V. Hamilton, 3 vols., Navy RS, 12, 19, 24 (1898–1903) • G. L. Newnham Collingwood, *Life and correspondence of Lord Collingwood* (1829) • *Letters of admiral of the fleet, the earl of St Vincent: whilst the first lord of the admiralty, 1801–1804*, ed. D. Bonner-Smith, 2 vols., Navy RS, 55, 61 (1921–7) • E. P. Brenton, *Life and correspondence of John, earl of St Vincent*, 2 vols. (1838) • J. Ralfe, *The naval biography of Great Britain*, 4 vols. (1828) • J. Marshall, *Royal naval biography*, 4 vols. (1823–35) [with 4 suppls.]

Archives NRA, priv. coll., corresp. and MSS • Shrubland Hall, Coddenham, corresp. and papers • Suffolk RO, Ipswich, dispatches, corresp., and letter-books; letter-books of his command of the Baltic squadron | BL, corresp. with T. Martin, Add. MSS 43165–43166 • BL, letters to Lord Nelson, Add. MSS 34906–34931, *passim* • NA Scot., letters to Lord Melville • NMM, letters to S. Hood; letters to R. Keats; letters to C. Yorke • Northumbd RO, Newcastle upon Tyne, letters to C. Fenwick • PRO, statement of the services of Sir James Saumarez, ADM 1/16 • Som. ARS, letters to Sir Richard Keats

Likenesses P. Jean, miniature, 1801, NPG • T. Phillips, portrait, 1809, priv. coll. [*see illus.*] • J. Steell, statue, 1840, NMM • attrib. S. Lane, oils, NMM • C. Turner, mezzotint (after Carbonier), BM, NPG; repro. in E. P. Brenton, *The naval history of Great Britain*, 5 vols. (1823–5) • E. Williams, oils (after T. Phillips), NMM

Saumarez, Philip (1710–1747), naval officer, was born in St Peter Port, Guernsey, on 17 November 1710, the second of the five sons of Matthew de Sausmarez of Guernsey and Anne Durell of Jersey. The eldest son, John, became *procureur du roi* (attorney-general) of Guernsey in 1744; Philip and the other three sons served in the navy, and on joining the service Anglicized their surname to Saumarez. In 1719 Philip was sent to Jersey, first to receive tuition from his godmother, Lady de Carteret, and later to attend a grammar school there; he went on to attend Isaac Watts's school in Southampton in 1721, and a school in Greenwich in 1723. He joined the navy as a volunteer in February 1726, and served in the Mediterranean, channel, and Caribbean as midshipman and then master's mate, until, in 1737, he received his commission as a lieutenant.

On 28 December 1739 Saumarez was appointed third lieutenant on the *Centurion*, then preparing for her voyage to the South Sea as the flagship of Commodore George Anson. After long delays the squadron sailed from Spithead on 18 September 1740 on a voyage remarkable for its casualties and disappointments, and for a belated triumph in the capture of the Acapulco galleon off the Philippines. Saumarez, who became first lieutenant on the *Centurion* on 18 February 1741, was an important figure on the voyage. Not only did he become Anson's right-hand man, but he kept a fuller set of journals than any other member of the expedition. In many instances they give a different interpretation of events from that of the authorized account of the voyage published in 1748 under the name of Richard Walter.

One of Saumarez's most notable achievements was his success as temporary commander of the *Tryal* sloop (from 27 February to 14 April 1741) in bringing his tiny vessel round Cape Horn at a time when the atrocious weather conditions forced back two of Anson's larger ships. To judge by a letter he wrote to Anson, but perhaps never sent, Saumarez felt that this feat had gone unrecognized, and that he had a 'very indifferent prospect' (Heaps, 96, 97).

There is, however, no evidence that Saumarez's contributions were undervalued or unappreciated during the rest of the voyage, as Anson came to rely heavily on the Guernsey man. He commanded prize vessels, and was in charge of the *Centurion* when Anson was not on board. During one such period, in September 1742, one of the most dramatic episodes of the voyage occurred when the *Centurion*—the last remaining ship of the squadron—was driven out to sea from its anchorage at the island of Tinian in the north Pacific, leaving Anson and most of the crew marooned.

With only a quarter of the ship's normal complement on board, it took Saumarez nineteen days to beat through heavy seas back to the anchorage. As he wrote in a wry aside, he did not know 'whether I should be a captain in spite of my teeth at last' (abstract of journal, 7 Dec 1742, priv. coll.). After refitting at Macao, the *Centurion* captured the *Covadonga* treasure galleon on 20 June 1743. The most detailed and dispassionate account of the action comes from Saumarez, who, in contradiction to the heroic version later given in the authorized narrative, admitted that 'we engaged the enemy with great advantages on our side' (Williams, 200). He commanded the captured galleon on its run into Canton (Guangzhou), but returned to the *Centurion* for the voyage home. The ships arrived back at Spithead in 1744, having circumnavigated the globe.

The homecoming was marred by a prolonged legal dispute over prize money between the officers of the *Centurion* and those who had served as supernumeraries. Saumarez appeared as the senior officer among the flagship's officers, who eventually won their case, but at a cost. He referred to 'this fatal law suit' which had separated him from his friends, and longed to be at sea again (Heaps, 255). In this he had his wish, for in June 1745 he was appointed captain of the *Sandwich*, and in September 1746 he moved to the *Nottingham* (60 guns). On 11 October Saumarez captured the French ship *Mars* (64 guns) with the loss of only three men killed. As captain of the *Nottingham* he fought under Anson at the first battle of Cape Finisterre (3 May 1747), but on 14 October 1747, while serving under Vice-Admiral Edward Hawke, he was killed at the second battle of Cape Finisterre while trying to intercept the *Intrépide* and *Tonnant*.

Captain Keppel, Saumarez's old shipmate from the voyage round the world, wrote to Anson with the news: 'Poor Saumarez died like he was, alongside the *Tonnant*, much regretted by the whole squadron' (Sausmarez, 6). His body was brought to Plymouth for burial in St Peter's Church by his cousin, Philip Durell, captain of the *Gloucester*. Durell reported to John de Sausmarez the surgeon's opinion that Philip had had no more than a year to live, his lungs being 'much wasted' (Heaps, 258–9). Philip Saumarez died a wealthy man, leaving more than £15,000, most of this prize money from the capture of the *Covadonga* and the *Mars*.

Philip Saumarez's influence lived on beyond his death, for the uniform adopted by captains in the navy in 1748 was a modified version of the dark blue uniform he had designed the year before. Saumarez had acted in response to Anson's wish that captains in the Royal Navy, like those in other navies, should wear a regular uniform. At least twice on the voyage round the world, at Macao in 1742 and at Canton in 1743, Anson had improvised a uniform for his officers and men in an attempt to impress the Chinese authorities. Two of the extant portraits of Philip Saumarez show him wearing the new uniform, one painted before and the other after his death.

Saumarez was survived by his brother **Thomas Saumarez** (1720–1766), naval officer, who was born in April 1720 at St Peter Port and served as midshipman on the *Centurion* during Anson's voyage round the world. He is not mentioned by name in the published accounts, but must have performed to Anson's satisfaction, for on his return in 1744 he was given a commission and on 27 November 1748 promoted post captain. In 1752 he served in the Caribbean as captain of the *Wager* in command of a small squadron, but his most noteworthy feat came in home waters during the Seven Years' War.

On 2 November 1758, while in command of the *Antelope* (50 guns), Saumarez captured the *Belliqueux* (64 guns). The French ship, homeward bound from Canada, was in some distress off Ilfracombe, and surrendered as soon as the *Antelope* opened fire. The *Belliqueux* was taken into the Royal Navy, and Saumarez was appointed to command her. In November 1759 he was under Hawke's command, but missed the battle of Quiberon Bay by three days.

In 1761 he sailed in her to the Caribbean, but poor health forced him to relinquish his command and to return home. On leaving the navy Thomas Saumarez married Katharine Mountstevens, and settled at Rickmansworth, Hertfordshire, where he died on 21 September 1766, he and his wife having had no children.

GLYNDWR WILLIAMS

Sources H. de Sausmarez, *Captain Philip Saumarez, 1710–1747, and his contemporaries* (1936) • L. Heaps, *Log of the Centurion, based on the original papers of Captain Philip Saumarez* (1973) • G. Williams, ed., *Documents relating to Anson's voyage round the world, 1740–1744*, Navy RS, 109 (1967) • P. Saumarez, abstract of journal, priv. coll.

Archives NMM, log of *Centurion Prize*, ADM L/C/301 • priv. coll., abstract of voyage to South Seas • Royal Court House, St Peter Port, Guernsey • The Greffe, Guernsey, corresp. and papers

Likenesses two portraits, in or before 1747 • H. Cheere, monument, Westminster Abbey

Wealth at death approx. £15,000

Saumarez, Richard (1764–1835), surgeon, fifth son of Matthew Saumarez (1718–1778) and his wife, Carteret, daughter of James le Marchant, was born in St Peter Port, Guernsey, on 13 November 1764. Both Richard's parents died when he was a boy, causing him to be placed under the care of his eldest brother, John, a childless army surgeon, who lived in the family house in the Plaiderie, St Peter Port. Richard was born into a well-known Guernsey family, and two elder brothers added to this reputation. James *Saumarez became an admiral fighting under Nelson, and Thomas *Saumarez [*see under* Saumarez, James] was knighted after achieving the rank of general. Saumarez did not wish to be a burden on his brother John, and so he entered himself as a medical student at the London Hospital about 1781. There he was apprenticed to William Blizard, who was a recent appointment himself as surgeon. Saumarez was admitted a member of the Company of Surgeons on 7 April 1785 when he received a modified licence which forbade him to practise in London or within 7 miles of the City. This restriction was abolished the following year. From 1786 he was living at Newington Butts in Southwark, just south of the Thames.

On 6 January 1786 Saumarez married Marthe, daughter

of Jean le Mesurier, lawyer, and governor of Alderney, at St Peter Port, Guernsey. They had two daughters, Carteret and Martha, and three sons, who went into the navy, medicine, and the church. Two sons, the Revd Paul Saumarez and Frederick Walshman Saumarez, surgeon, became mentally ill before their father's death and were placed under the care of the court of chancery. The third son, Richard (1791–1866), became an admiral, and spent twenty years campaigning on behalf of the mentally ill and against the vast expense of chancery proceedings. He also acted as a member of the committee protecting his brothers' interests. Between 1824 and 1861 the brothers were moved on fourteen occasions to different lodgings and asylums depending on their state of health.

In 1788 Saumarez was appointed surgeon to the Magdalen Hospital, Streatham, an office which he resigned on 1 March 1805. He then became an honorary governor in recognition of the services he had rendered the hospital. He gradually developed a large and lucrative practice in London until 1818, when he retired to Bath. On 13 November 1801 Marthe had died of consumption, and Saumarez subsequently married Elizabeth Enderby, a rich widow and a great-aunt of General Gordon of Khartoum. It was at her desire that they retired to Bath.

Saumarez produced a number of works and was a polemical writer, adopting a controversial stance on several issues. He felt a great debt of gratitude to his teacher Blizard, to whom he dedicated two books, and believed that the excellent clinical training he had provided was an isolated example, and that in general the medical corporations were failing students. When the Surgeons' Company lost its charter in 1796 Saumarez was one of those who actively opposed its reconstruction until there were assurances that it would be better managed. When these were unforthcoming the bill for reconstruction of the company was thrown out of the Lords, and the College of Surgeons was re-established later in 1800.

In 1798 Saumarez published his *A New System of Physiology*, in which he commented on the state of Oxford and Cambridge universities and on the Company of Surgeons. In it Saumarez opposed the Brunonian philosophy which was fashionable at the time, challenging the model in which all diseases were divided into the sthenic and asthenic, depending on the level of excitement in the body. Saumarez suggested that doctors should concentrate on identifying the interdependency of various organs, viewing the body as a whole system. He also accused John Brown (the founder of the system) of plagiarism from John Hunter. In *The Principles of Physiological and Physical Science* (1812) Saumarez attacked less skilful practitioners for cruelty to animals in their needless attempts to replicate Hunter's experiments. In 1813, in his oration to the Medical Society of London, Saumarez attacked Richeraud for inconsistency in regard to his ideas on the impenetrability of matter, as Richeraud had also suggested that particles of matter acted on each other. In this volume Saumarez again returned to the state of English universities and the College of Surgeons, while praising the examinations introduced at Oxford University. In general, though, the content of his monographs was a mishmash of ideas drawn from other sources. He was elected FRSE in 1822 and FRS in 1834.

Saumarez died at his residence at 21 The Circus, Bath, on 27 January 1835. His will specified that he was to be buried in the family vault next to his first wife. He left his house and goods to his second wife, and properties and money to his son Richard and two daughters. Specific provision was made for his two mentally ill sons, while his son Richard's wife was specifically excluded from the management of any moneys. NICK HERVEY

Sources dockets, PRO, Chancery RO, J 103/2 • PRO, PROB 11/1846, sig. 259 • *DNB* • *GM*, 2nd ser., 3 (1835), 333
Wealth at death large estate; house and goods in The Circus, Bath, to wife; two children received houses; investments to yield annual income left to children; daughter-in-law received £75 p.a., but excluded from control over any money: will, PRO, PROB 11/1846, sig. 259; PRO, PROB 12/237

Saumarez, Thomas (1720–1766). *See under* Saumarez, Philip (1710–1747).

Saumarez, Sir Thomas (1760–1845). *See under* Saumarez, James, first Baron de Saumarez (1757–1836).

Saumarez, Thomas (1827–1903), naval officer, born at Sutton, Surrey, on 31 March 1827, was the great-nephew of James, first Baron de Saumarez (1757–1836), and the son of Captain (afterwards Admiral) Richard Saumarez (*d.* 1864). After attending Western Grammar School, Brompton, London, for a few years, he entered the navy in 1841 and served on the east coast of South America, at Buenos Aires, at Montevideo, and in the Rio Parana. He was made lieutenant in March 1848 and served principally on the west coast of Africa, where on 31 March 1851 he saved a man from drowning and received the Royal Humane Society's silver medal. Later that year he commanded a division of gunboats at Lagos, Nigeria, and was severely wounded. In September 1854 he was promoted commander, and in that year also married a daughter (*d.* 1866) of S. R. Block of Greenhill, Barnet, in Hertfordshire. They had no children.

In May 1858 Saumarez commanded the screw gunvessel *Cormorant*, and he served with distinction at the capture of the Taku (Dagu) forts, where the *Cormorant* led the attack, broke through a formidable boom, and with her first broadside, fired at the same moment, dismounted the largest of the enemy's guns. He afterwards took part in the operations in the Peiho (Beihe) and in the occupation of Tientsin (Tianjin), and on the coast of China. His promotion to captain was dated 27 July 1858, and he had no further active service. In 1868 he married his second wife, Eleanor, daughter of B. Scott Riley of Liverpool; they had no children. On 12 April 1870 he was retired, and was made a CB in 1873. He became by seniority a rear-admiral in 1876, vice-admiral in 1881, and admiral in 1886. He died at Elmina, Albion Road, Ramsgate, Kent, on 22 January 1903. His second wife survived him. J. K. LAUGHTON, *rev.* ANDREW LAMBERT

Sources D. Bonner-Smith and E. W. R. Lumby, eds., *The Second China War, 1856–1860*, Navy RS, 95 (1954) • *The Times* (23 Jan 1903) •

W. L. Clowes, *The Royal Navy: a history from the earliest times to the present*, 7 vols. (1897–1903), vol. 7 • personal knowledge (1912) • O'Byrne, *Naval biog. dict.* • W. E. F. Ward, *The Royal Navy and the slavers* (1969) • J. J. Colledge, *Ships of the Royal Navy: an historical index*, 1 (1969) • G. S. Graham, *The China station: war and diplomacy, 1830–1860* (1978) • Kelly, *Handbk* • *CGPLA Eng. & Wales* (1903)

Wealth at death £1717 8s. 11d.: resworn probate, Oct 1903, *CGPLA Eng. & Wales*

Saundby, Sir Robert Henry Magnus Spencer (**1896–1971**), air force officer, was born at 83A Edmund Street, All Saints, Birmingham, on 26 April 1896, the second son in the family of three sons and one daughter of Robert Saundby FRCP (1849–1918), a consulting physician at Birmingham General Hospital and professor of medicine at Birmingham University, and his wife, Edith Mary Spencer (1856–1943).

Saundby was educated at King Edward's School, Birmingham, from 1909 to 1913 and, having gained his London matriculation, joined the London and North-Western Railway Company in 1914 as a probationer in the traffic department. He had served in the Officers' Training Corps at school, and on 15 June 1914 was commissioned in the 1st/5th territorial battalion, the Royal Warwickshire regiment. In mid-February 1915 he had a severe attack of cerebro-spinal meningitis, which immobilized him for eight months. He was cleared by a medical board on 11 October and on the 23rd applied to join the Royal Flying Corps (RFC)—an application which proved successful. He was then nineteen and strongly built (6 feet 1 inch tall and weighing over 12 stone), and in his letter applying for a transfer said that he had flown previously, and had a practical knowledge of petrol engines and training as a machine-gun officer.

Saundby began flying with 12 reserve squadron at Thetford, Norfolk, on 28 February 1916 and went solo on 31 March. He gained further air experience with the same squadron at Dover, with the Central Flying School at Upavon, and with 40 squadron at Gosport. He was then posted to 24 squadron, British expeditionary force. This squadron operated DH2 single-seater, pusher-engined fighters—the pilot sitting out ahead of the biplane wings, with a machine-gun and an unrestricted view.

Through the autumn and winter months of 1916–17 Saundby flew offensive patrols, then in late February 1917 he was transferred as a flight commander to 41 squadron, which also had 'pusher'-type fighters (FE8s). After a month's operations and two forced landings, in one of which his machine turned over, he was posted home at the end of March. He had destroyed nine enemy aircraft in combat over the western front. On 13 April he joined the experimental station at Orfordness, where he evaluated different types of aircraft and was again in action: on the night of 16–17 June when he participated in the destruction of Zeppelin L48, flying a DH2 in darkness for the first time. For this brave feat he was awarded the Military Cross.

Saundby vividly recorded his impressions of western front air fighting, and the destruction of Zeppelin L48, in words and watercolour paintings, in a book called *Flying Colours* (1919). The preface, by Major-General E. B. Ashmore, described him as 'one of a very gallant band of pilots who fought under the late Major Lanoe Hawker VC DSO during the Somme offensive of 1916'.

With a greatly expanded RFC training programme in 1917, to provide pilots for home defence and the British expeditionary force, Saundby was posted for instructor duties, first to Catterick Bridge and then, from October, to 11 training squadron. He also evaluated many different types of fighter aircraft, including the Sopwith Camel and SE5A. From November 1918 he was at no. 38 training depot station, Tadcaster, and by the end of that year had done 650 hours 45 minutes' flying. He was awarded the Air Force Cross in the 1919 new year honours.

At that time the newly formed RAF had still to find its peacetime role. Flight Lieutenant Saundby might have been destined for a maritime squadron, for during 1919 he took seaplane and navigation courses at Lee-on-Solent and Calshot. But by February 1920 he was again on instructional duties—at 1 flying training school, Netheravon—and expressed his relief at being 'back on Avros'. He was also able to indulge his lifelong enthusiasm for fly-fishing, in the nearby River Avon. He flew an Avro 504 in a relay race at the RAF aerial pageant at Hendon on 3 July 1920, and by the end of 1921 had done over 940 hours' flying on some forty-five different types. His experience was soon to be put to the test in a new role—bomber operations, which were to influence the rest of his career.

At the March 1921 Cairo conference, presided over by Winston Churchill (then secretary of state for the colonies), the RAF was given the role of peace-keeping in Iraq and Transjordan by the use of aircraft and armoured cars; and in February 1922 Sandy Saundby was posted to join one of the squadrons involved—no. 45, based at Almaza, Cairo. It was equipped with Vickers Vernon twin-engined biplane bomber/transports, a type bigger than any he had previously flown, and he was required to operate in hot, dusty desert conditions. On 45 he first met the then squadron leader A. T. Harris, later to be his air officer commanding-in-chief at Bomber Command headquarters.

Saundby first flew to Baghdad in April 1922, and in February–March 1923 took part in bombing operations, as he did in November–December of that year. The squadron also held bomb-dropping competitions, in which great emphasis was placed on accuracy, and in September–October 1924 it provided VIP transport for the secretary of state for air, Lord Thomson, who was flown by Harris and Saundby on a round of visits to RAF stations in Egypt and Transjordan.

In 1925, however, Saundby's association with 45 squadron ended: in January he was posted to 4 flying training school at Abu Sueir, near Isma'iliyyah in Egypt, as an instructor. But after only two months there he was ordered to take over command of the Aden flight because of the commanding officer's sudden illness. He resented this posting, which he considered unfair after his two years in Iraq, but was subsequently glad to have had the experience.

The flight's two-seater Bristol Fighters were used to implement a policy of air control, similar to that in Iraq but on a smaller scale; in an article reminiscing about its operations Saundby asserted that these 'opened a new chapter of peace, order and prosperity for the Protectorate' (J. R. W. Taylor, ed., *Aircraft Sixty-Eight*, 1968). In recognition of his command he was awarded the Distinguished Flying Cross in the 1926 new year honours.

By then Saundby was again at Abu Sueir, for in December 1925 he had been posted back to 4 flying training school, this time as chief instructor. But he filled this role for only six months: by October 1926, after a posting home and four months' leave, he was a flight commander on 58 (bombing) squadron at Worthy Down. This squadron was equipped with Vickers Victoria and Virginia twin-engined biplanes, and his commanding officer was again A. T. Harris. This association, like his involvement in the RAF bomber world, was to last for the next two decades of his service career.

By July 1927, when he took part in the RAF display at Hendon, Saundby had done over 2000 hours' flying; in September his log book was marked with four 'exceptional' endorsements by his commanding officer—a resounding citation for his service career as a pilot, but also an epilogue to it. For, although he continued to fly many different types of aircraft until 1938, he was now set on a senior officer's upward progress to air staff appointments.

Thus Saundby attended the 1927–8 RAF Staff College course, following which he was posted successively to the headquarters of the Wessex bombing area for air staff duties and, in May 1931, to the Air Ministry directorate of operations and intelligence. Earlier in 1931, on 10 January, he married Joyce Mary Rees-Webbe (1904–1986), whom he had met when she accompanied her father, Major Marmaduke Oswald Norman Rees-Webbe, on one of his fly-fishing expeditions. The marriage, which produced a son and two daughters, was a notably happy one.

Saundby's first Air Ministry tour was followed by three years (1933–6) as an instructor at the RAF Staff College, a period characterized by writing and lecturing on defence themes against the background of the rise of Nazism and Fascism. In 1932, when on an Imperial Defence College course, he won the Gordon Shephard memorial prize, awarded annually for 'the best essays on reconnaissance and kindred subjects', and in 1933 and 1935 he came third and second respectively.

By now a wing commander, Saundby went from the Staff College back to the Air Ministry, where he was first deputy director of operations, then deputy director of operational requirements, as a group captain. From December 1938 he served as director of operational requirements (DOR), and a year later was promoted acting air commodore. In his DOR posts he advocated the development of four-engined bombers, which eventuated as the wartime Stirling, Lancaster, and Halifax types.

In April 1940 Saundby was appointed assistant chief of the air staff (operational requirements and tactics), and in November he was moved to headquarters, Bomber Command, as senior air staff officer. His experience of bombing operations in Iraq and Aden, his service in the Wessex bombing area at squadron and staff levels, and his views on the application of air power made him naturally suited to such an appointment. In February 1943 his long friendship with Sir Arthur Harris was consolidated when he was appointed deputy air officer commanding-in-chief, at Harris's insistence. Then an air vice-marshal, he was promoted air marshal in the autumn and appointed KBE in the 1944 new year honours.

At Bomber Command headquarters in High Wycombe, Saundby played an important supporting role to Harris, his air officer commanding-in-chief, deflecting the criticisms of bombing policy which emanated from the Air Ministry through the deputy chief of the air staff, N. H. Bottomley, and the director of bomber operations, Sidney Bufton. He also helped to maintain good relations between Harris and the chief of the air staff, Sir Charles Portal. Saundby's relaxed and approachable manner, which, coupled with his enthusiasm for butterfly collecting, sometimes caused him to be likened to an absent-minded professor, was appreciated by the headquarters staff, who found Harris aloof and introspective. His own relationship with Harris was exactly as it had been during their squadron days—one of unswerving loyalty. He himself had held only one minor command, that of the Aden flight. Harris had always been his commanding officer, and this status was maintained at Bomber Command headquarters. He also had a particular friendship there with the United States Army Air Force 8th Air Force commander Ira C. Eaker, which was reinforced by a shared enthusiasm for model railways.

In a lecture to the Royal United Services Institute in October 1945 Saundby expressed the view that the experience of the war had confirmed that there were two chief ways in which a powerful bomber force could contribute to victory. One was the destruction of vital industrial centres and the other the systematic paralysing of all forms of communication.

Ill health (osteoarthritic lumbar spine and an osteoarthritic hip, resulting initially from injuries received in his forced landings in the British expeditionary force) beset him in the autumn of 1945, and in April 1946 he was placed on the retired list, with a disability pension; he retained the rank of air marshal.

Saundby was extremely active in retirement, being particularly concerned with the welfare of ex-members of the RAF and their dependants. From 1945 to 1958 he chaired the council of the Royal Air Forces Association (RAFA), and from 1952 to 1959 was a council member of the RAF Benevolent Fund and also a trustee, representing the RAFA. In the 1956 new year honours he was appointed KCB (civil), and in 1960 he became deputy lieutenant of Berkshire. He wrote and lectured frequently on the RAF and defence subjects, and he also edited the papers which formed *The Book of the Piscatorial Society, 1836–1936* (1936), reflecting his interest in fly-fishing. He died on 26 September 1971, in Edgecombe Nursing Home, Hampstead Marshall, Berkshire, and after cremation his ashes were scattered on the bank of his beloved River Avon, near Netheravon, where he had served in 1920–21.

HUMPHREY WYNN

Sources Ministry of Defence, Air Historical Branch (RAF) • Ministry of Defence, Army Historical Branch • b. cert. • d. cert. • private information (2004) [R. P. Saundby] • RAF Innsworth, Gloucestershire, PMA (Sec) 1b 1 (RAF) • PRO, WO, 374/6041 • C. Messenger, *'Bomber' Harris and the strategic bombing offensive 1939–1945* (1984) • D. Saward, *'Bomber' Harris: the authorised biography* (1984) • royal regiment of fusiliers, St John's House, Warwick • Oxford crematorium

Archives NHM, entomological diaries • Royal Air Force Museum, Hendon, corresp. and papers, incl. flying logbooks, lectures, articles, and photos | IWM, corresp. with Sir Henry Tizard • Wolfson College, Oxford, corresp. with H. B. D. Kettlewell

Likenesses W. Stoneman, photograph, 1940–49, NPG • photograph, 1942, IWM • T. C. Dugdale, oils, *c.*1946, IWM • H. Coster, photographs, NPG

Wealth at death £11,018: probate, 14 Dec 1971, *CGPLA Eng. & Wales*

Saunders, Sir Alexander Morris Carr- (1886–1966), sociologist and academic administrator, was born at Reigate, Surrey, on 14 January 1886, by some fifteen years the youngest child of James Carr-Saunders, a wealthy underwriter, and his wife, Flora Anne Tower. He was proud of his descent from the architect Robert Morris and conscious of his affinity with two other relatives, W. W. and Edward Saunders, both entomologists and fellows of the Royal Society. In childhood he was lonely and at Eton College intensely unhappy. He left, aged sixteen, to spend two years in Paris and the French Alps. In this period he came to believe that it was in biology that the greatest advancement of learning would be made in the years ahead, and it was to read this subject that he went up to Magdalen College, Oxford. He took a first in zoology in 1908, was elected to the biological scholarship at Naples for a year, then returned to Oxford as a demonstrator in comparative anatomy.

It became clear to Carr-Saunders, however, that his interests extended beyond the laboratory. His imagination had been fired by the prospects for human betterment, opened by Mendel's rediscovered paper of 1865, and by the work of William Bateson on heredity. In 1910 he moved to London, where he studied biometrics under Karl Pearson, became secretary of the research committee of the Eugenics Education Society, and served as subwarden of Toynbee Hall. He was elected to Stepney borough council, and in 1914 was called to the bar by the Inner Temple.

At the outbreak of the First World War Carr-Saunders enlisted in the ranks of the infantry but he was commissioned in the Army Service Corps and, after a year in France, was posted to a depot at Suez, where he remained, against his will, for the rest of the war. His duties left him leisure to plan a work on population that would 'view the whole problem … from an historical and evolutionary standpoint'. He came back in a state of depression and indecision, and accepted an offer to return to Oxford as a demonstrator in zoology. Here, however, he accomplished his grand design rapidly; his book *The Population Problem* (1922) did much to establish his reputation among his contemporaries, although it did not attract wide attention at the time. Forty years later it was claimed as having anticipated later developments in ethology by its stress on behaviour that contributes to the survival of the group, and on the practices by which groups are secured of their territory. His concern for the problems of population was to lead him to serve as chairman of the population investigation committee from 1936, and of the statistics committee of the royal commission on population from 1944 to 1949; he was instrumental in establishing the study of demography, and unflagging in his leadership of the Eugenics Society, which awarded him its first Galton medal in 1946.

In 1923 he was called to Liverpool as the first holder of the Charles Booth chair of social science. The task of directing a department proved highly congenial to him; the air of detachment that his colleagues felt in him did not prevent him from entering fully into the life of a civic university. His own publications meanwhile added to his reputation, especially the pioneering account of the history and structure of the professions (in a book of that title, with P. A. Wilson, 1933). He married in 1929 a former Oxford pupil, Teresa, daughter of Major Edmund Harington Molyneux-Seel, a professional soldier and Lancashire landowner; they had two sons and a daughter.

The appointment to Liverpool had been quite unforeseen. Equally unforeseen but readily accepted was the call to Carr-Saunders in 1937 to succeed Sir William Beveridge as director of the London School of Economics (LSE). In the next nineteen years he held the school together through its exile during the war and presided over its ensuing expansion of numbers and activities. When he joined it he found an academic community agitated and divided by his predecessor's style of administration; he himself established his authority and restored harmony in the community by a style that was an absence of style. His simple and quiet approach to business flowed from his self-image; he saw himself as no more than a scholar among scholars animated by a common devotion. He was vigorous, even combative when necessary, and was able to transact business in the office rapidly. But in council his touch was as light as it was deft. Where sectional interests were latent his own selflessness diffused disinterest; discussions in which he never forcibly intervened served their therapeutic purpose and moved to generally accepted conclusions that seldom ran contrary to his own judgement.

When in 1943 Carr-Saunders joined the commission under Sir Cyril Asquith on higher education in the colonies he took up a task to which he was drawn alike by his scholarly and his humanitarian concern for its object. He created and became chairman both of the University of London senate committee, which guided the development of university colleges in east Africa, Sudan, central Africa, Nigeria, the Gold Coast, and the West Indies, and of the Inter-University Council, through which the help of all the British universities was given to the colleges and universities of the dependent territories. He was chairman in 1947 of the commission which promoted the University of Malaya, and in 1952–3 of the commission which led to the foundation of the multiracial University College of Rhodesia and Nyasaland. On his retirement from the LSE, in December 1965, he devoted himself to this work more than ever, travelling continually to maintain personal contacts with the new colleges. He carried out the survey of the manpower requirements of the African universities presented to the Tananarive conference of 1962; his book *New Universities Overseas* (1961) gives an account of these developments.

Two interests formed in early years remained with Carr-Saunders throughout life. In the French Alps he had learned the craft of the mountaineer; he had a special knowledge of the Aiguilles Rouges and, while he was at Liverpool, he climbed Tryfan more than a hundred times. His first sight of Raphael's frescoes in the Vatican had opened a new world to him and he continued to find a lively pleasure in paintings and to collect them. He also had a lifelong interest in farming and country pursuits, finding happiness in their practical and creative aspects. He once remarked that the farmer is 'the man who does the only job that really matters'. Seemingly withdrawn and remote he was keenly observant and warm in his attachments. In his private judgement of men he made sharp distinctions but in his dealings with them he was uniformly tolerant. His lean frame and ascetic, somewhat melancholy mien concealed great energy; the strength of his hands marked the tenacity which enabled him to carry through on his retirement a task that would have extended most men fully in the prime of life. His exertions responded to the breadth of his intellectual interests and his deep sense of social responsibility. As a young man he had been a sceptic in the tradition of the Victorian rationalists but his philosophic bent and concern for right action drew him insistently towards theology, and he found a faith within the Anglican fold.

Carr-Saunders was knighted in 1946, in which year he also became a fellow of the British Academy, and was appointed KBE in 1957. He received honorary doctorates from the universities of Glasgow, Columbia, Natal, Dublin, Liverpool, Cambridge, Grenoble, Malaya, and London; he was also honorary fellow of Peterhouse, Cambridge, of the University College of East Africa, and of the LSE. He died near Dale Head, Thirl Moor, St John's in the Vale, Cumberland, on 6 October 1966.

HENRY PHELPS BROWN, *rev.*

Sources E. H. Phelps Brown, 'Sir Alexander Morris Carr-Saunders, 1886-1966', *PBA*, 53 (1967), 379–89 · *The Times* (8 Oct 1966)

Archives BLPES, research papers · PRO, corresp. and papers relating to inter-university council, BW90 | BLPES, corresp. with Lord W. Beveridge · BLPES, corresp. with the editors of the *Economic Journal* · BLPES, corresp. with R. H. Tawney · Bodl. Oxf., corresp. relating to Society for Protection of Science and Learning · Bodl. RH, corresp. with Margery Perham · NL Wales, letters to John Glyn Davies · Rice University, Houston, Texas, Woodson Research Center, corresp. with Sir Julian Huxley | SOUND BL NSA, recorded talk

Likenesses W. Coldstream, oils, 1955, London School of Economics

Wealth at death £64,640: probate, 3 Jan 1967, *CGPLA Eng. & Wales*

Saunders, Sir Charles (*c.*1713–1775), naval officer, was possibly the son of James Saunders of Bridgwater, Somerset. He entered the navy in the *Seahorse* (20 guns) on 17 October 1727, under a relative, Captain Ambrose Saunders, who died in March 1730; after this the boy was sent to the *Hector* (44 guns) under the command of Captain Peter Solgard, with whom he served in the Mediterranean until 1734. Saunders passed his lieutenant's examination on 7 June of that year and on 8 November he was promoted third lieutenant of the *Exeter* (60 guns), which served in Sir John Norris's fleet and was later a guardship at Sheerness. On 28 July 1738 Saunders was appointed to the *Norfolk* (80 guns), and in June 1739 to the *Oxford* (50 guns); from this ship he was moved a fortnight later to the *Sunderland* (60 guns) and on 14 August to the *Centurion* (60 guns), again as third lieutenant, then fitting out for her celebrated voyage under Captain George Anson.

On 19 February 1741 in an anchorage in Patagonia, Saunders was promoted by Anson commander of the brig *Trial* in which he reached the Juan Fernandez Islands in a deplorable state: only Saunders, the lieutenant, and three men were able to do duty. After leaving the islands the *Trial* was condemned and scuttled as not seaworthy, and Saunders and the crew moved into a Spanish prize which Anson commissioned as a frigate, giving her commander post rank on 26 September 1741. In the following April, when Anson was preparing to leave the coast of America, this frigate also was destroyed, her officers and men being divided between the remaining ships, the *Centurion* and the *Gloucester*; the latter was abandoned and burnt as unseaworthy during the Pacific crossing. Following the *Centurion*'s arrival at Macao in November Saunders, charged with Anson's dispatches, returned to England in a Swedish merchant ship; he arrived in late May 1743. On 1 June his commissions as commander and captain were confirmed to their original date, and on 29 November he was appointed to the *Plymouth* (60 guns), from which, on 20 December, he was moved to the *Sapphire* (44 guns), which was employed during the following spring in watching Dunkirk under the orders of Sir John Norris.

In March 1745 Saunders took command of the *Gloucester* (50 guns), a new ship, on the home station, and in company with the *Lark* (44 guns), on 26 December 1746, he captured a Spanish homeward-bound register-ship, valued at £300,000; Saunders's share amounted to between £30,000 and £40,000. In August 1747 he was appointed to the *Yarmouth* (64 guns), in which he played a distinguished role in helping to secure the result of the second battle of Finisterre under Rear-Admiral Edward Hawke on 14 October. In December he was moved into the *Tiger* (50 guns), which was paid off on the peace.

On 6 April 1750 Saunders entered parliament as MP for Plymouth, though his political career did not fully develop until after the Seven Years War. On 26 September 1751 he married the only daughter of a London banker, James Buck; the following years were ones in which Saunders gained rapid promotion. In February 1752 he was appointed to the *Penzance* (44 guns) as commodore and commander-in-chief on the Newfoundland station. In April 1754 he was appointed treasurer of Greenwich Hospital, an office which he held for the next twelve years; and in May he was returned through Lord Anson's influence as MP for Hedon in Yorkshire, a constituency he continued to represent until his death. In January 1755 Saunders was appointed to the new ship *Prince* (90 guns), which remained at Spithead through the year, and in December he resigned the command on being appointed comptroller of the navy, a post he held from 25 November 1755 to 24 June 1756. On 4 June 1756 he returned to active service; he was promoted rear-admiral, and sent out to the Mediterranean as second in command under Hawke. On Hawke's return to England in January 1757 Saunders was left commander-in-chief until May, a period described shrewdly and entertainingly by Augustus Hervey in his *Journal*, from which a good impression of Saunders's character can be gained.

On 14 February 1759 Saunders was promoted vice-admiral of the blue, and appointed commander-in-chief of the fleet for the St Lawrence, which sailed from Spithead three days later. By late June he reached Quebec, with twenty-two ships of the line, thirteen frigates, numerous small craft, and transports carrying some 8,000 troops, under the command of Major-General James Wolfe. In the face of strong French resistance, Saunders succeeded in occupying such positions off Quebec and in the lower river as to block the possibility of any supplies or reinforcements reaching the garrison. Relations were good between the navy and army, and Saunders's contribution was the successful organization of a large fleet up a difficult river. He also consolidated the position of the army after the battle for Quebec with energy and skill. On 18 October, Saunders withdrew from the St Lawrence with the greater part of the fleet, and sailed for England. In the entrance of the channel he had intelligence of the Brest fleet's having put to sea, and immediately turned aside to join Hawke. He had scarcely done so, however, when he had news of the victory at Quiberon Bay, whereupon he resumed his route, landed at Cork, and proceeded by land to Dublin; he arrived there on 15 December, having been made lieutenant-general, Royal Marines (10 November 1759) en route.

Saunders had a flattering reception from the king when he arrived in London, and, on taking his seat in the House of Commons on 23 January 1760, he received the thanks of the house from the speaker. In April he was appointed commander-in-chief in the Mediterranean, where he successfully blockaded Cadiz, while his frigates harried enemy shipping and watched Toulon. He also added substantially to his fortune through prize money. On 26 May 1761 he was installed, by proxy, as a knight of the Bath.

On 31 July 1765 Saunders was appointed one of the lords of the Admiralty in Lord Rockingham's administration, close as he was to the Rockinghamite Keppel family. When the administration collapsed, Chatham appointed Saunders first lord on 15 September, but he resigned on 11 December 1766 when the Rockinghamites were provoked by Chatham. Although a close, trusted, and valued follower of Rockingham, Saunders received a less favourable verdict from Lord Harcourt, who claimed he was unequal to the job of first lord, and from Horace Walpole, who described him as 'a most gallant, but weak man' (Walpole, *Memoirs*, 2.282).

Saunders, who was promoted admiral on 18 October 1770, did not serve again, though on 23 April 1773 he was once more nominated to the command in the Mediterranean during the Swedish crisis on the threat of French re-armament. He died of gout in the stomach at his house in Spring Gardens, London, on 7 December 1775, and was privately buried in Westminster Abbey on 12 December. He left no children, and bequeathed the greater part of his considerable property in Norfolk and Suffolk to his niece, Jane. He also left an annuity of £1200 to Augustus, Lord Keppel. J. K. LAUGHTON, *rev.* ROGER KNIGHT

Sources J. Charnock, ed., *Biographia navalis*, 6 vols. (1794–8) • W. H. Whiteley, 'Saunders, Sir Charles', *DCB*, vol. 4 • PRO, Admiralty MSS, ADM 6 • HoP, *Commons, 1754–90* • J. Brooke, *The Chatham administration, 1766–1768* (1956); repr. (Westport, CT, 1976) • N. Tracy, *Navies, deterrence and American independence: Britain and seapower in the 1760s and 1770s* (1988) • H. W. Richmond, *The navy in the war of 1739–48*, 3 vols. (1920) • [earl of Bristol], *Augustus Hervey's journal*, ed. D. Erskine (1953) • R. Middleton, *The bells of victory: the Pitt–Newcastle ministry and the conduct of the Seven Years' War, 1757–1762* (1985) • R. Walker and B. Robins, *A voyage round the world … by George Anson*, ed. G. Williams (1974) • N. A. M. Rodger, *The wooden world: an anatomy of the Georgian navy* (1986) • J. C. Sainty, ed., *Admiralty officials, 1660–1870* (1975) • J. M. Collinge, *Navy Board officials, 1660–1832* (1978)

Archives Harvard U., Houghton L., letter-book while in command at Quebec • New Jersey Historical Society Library, papers relating to HMS *Neptune* and HMS *Terror* | PRO, Admiralty MSS, ADM 6

Likenesses J. Reynolds, oils, *c.*1765, NMM • R. Brompton, oils, 1772–3, NMM • J. Chapman, stipple, pubd 1800, BM, NPG • J. Macardell, mezzotint (after J. Reynolds), BM • stipple and line engraving (after bust), NPG; repro. in F. Hervey, *The naval history of Great Britain*, 5 vols. (1779)

Wealth at death estates in South Walsham, Stokesby, Thrigby, and Kinsham, Suffolk and Norfolk; also at Hedon, Yorkshire: will, PRO, PROB 11/1014

Saunders, Christopher Thomas (1907–2000), economist, was born on 5 November 1907 at a private hospital at 70 Newhall Street, Birmingham, the son of Thomas Bekenn Avening Saunders (1870–1950), a Church of England clergyman and later canon residentiary of Carlisle Cathedral, whose mother was the daughter of a German protestant clergyman named Bekenn from Bremen, and his wife, Mary Theodora Slater (1869–1928). He was educated at the Craig School, Windermere, and St Edward's School, Oxford (1921–5). He then read philosophy, politics, and economics at Christ Church, Oxford, graduating in the second class in 1929. He was a long-standing member of the Labour Party and close to the Fabian Society. With M. P. Ashley he published his first book, *Red Oxford*, in 1929.

Saunders's professional life embraced a wide range of activities. He worked for the University of Liverpool on the social survey of Merseyside (1930–33), and held an appointment in the economics research department of the University of Manchester (1933–5) and an appointment with the joint committee of cotton trade organizations in Manchester, later converted into the official Cotton Control (1935–44). He was then seconded to the combined production and resources board in Washington for the rest of the Second World War. In 1945 he joined the civil service, first with the Ministry of Labour (1945–7), and subsequently with the central statistical office (1947–57), ending as deputy director. In 1953 he was appointed CMG. On 16 June 1947 Saunders married Cornelia Jacomijntje Gielstra (*b.* 1911), a graduate of the Nederlandsche Economische Hoogeschool; they had one son. The family lived in Eton Avenue, Hampstead, London, until their move to Geneva in 1965. After their return to England in 1972, they took up residence in Hove, Sussex, and subsequently moved to Edinburgh to join their son, taking up residence at Flat 17, 4 Gillsland Road, Edinburgh.

The work of Saunders on wider economic issues began in 1957 when he was seconded from the central statistical office to take over the directorship of the prestigious National Institute of Economic and Social Research (NIESR), a position he held until 1965. During this period he greatly enhanced the NIESR's work in forecasting and other fields. When he joined the institute its governing bodies had just decided to embark on the regular publication of analyses of national economic trends and prospects, that is, the activity of a 'Konjunktur Institut'. This scheme had been formulated earlier by Christopher Dow, with the support of Brian Hopkin, the then director of the NIESR. Christopher Saunders oversaw the vital initial stage in which, with Robert Nield as editor, the first issue of the *National Institute Economic Review* was planned and produced, appearing in January 1959. In 1965, when Saunders was fifty-eight, the NIESR was anxious to extend his term of office for a further period, and other tempting offers, including the directorship of the central statistical office, also presented themselves. However, his interests in world and particularly European and East–West economic affairs took Saunders to Geneva, where he subsequently became director of the economic analysis division of the United Nations (UN) Economic Commission for Europe. In this work he managed a multinational research team and maintained the tradition of independent, even-handed research established by Gunnar Myrdal and the division's first director, Nicky Kaldor. This position he held until his retirement at the age of sixty-five in 1972. But far from settling into a true retirement, he continued work as a consultant to the UN in both Geneva and New York. From 1973 he was also a professorial fellow in the Centre for Contemporary European Studies at the University of Sussex. His deep knowledge of both eastern and western European economies greatly benefited the University of Sussex's research activities in this field. From 1974 Saunders became actively associated with the Vienna Institute for Comparative Economic Studies as a member of the steering committee of the Workshops on East–West European economic interaction. Next to the UN Economic Commission for Europe, this institute was one of the important bridges during the cold war for East–West European economic relations. Saunders edited a great number of volumes in the institute's Workshop series.

The deep-rooted interest and concern of Saunders in a wide range of economic issues is evident from the list of his publications. His work at the central statistical office was closely related to the development and use of national income statistics, and it was thanks to him that the monumental volume *National Income Statistics: Sources and Methods* could finally be published by the central statistical office in 1956. In later years he concentrated more on problems of incomes policies, earnings, and pay patterns, and on problems arising from the concentration and specialization of industries in Western economies. He subsequently turned his attention to structural world economic problems and to the precarious subject at the time of East–West economic co-operation, which involved him in extensive travels throughout eastern Europe and the former Soviet Union.

Saunders's books and a wide range of papers were outstanding in providing valuable guidance to policy makers. Most of his work as a civil servant and with the UN was published under the auspices of the authorities concerned, as at his time civil servants were not normally allowed to publish under their own names. However, important publications appeared under Saunders's own name during the 1930s, and there was again a flood of signed publications from the time he joined the NIESR in 1957.

Christopher Saunders was a very special person to his friends and colleagues. His courtesy and kindness, his generous appreciation of others, and the painstaking care he took in giving help and advice to younger economists and graduate students was remembered with deep gratitude. Christopher Saunders died, on 13 January 2000, aged ninety-two, at the Royal Infirmary, Edinburgh, and was cremated at the Warriston crematorium, Warriston Road, Edinburgh, on 19 January 2000. His wife and son survived him. STEPHEN F. FROWEN

Sources personal knowledge (2004) · private information (2004) [Cora Saunders, widow] · *WWW* · S. F. Frowen, ed., *Controlling industrial economies: essays in honour of Christopher Thomas Saunders* (1983) [includes bibliography]

Archives BLPES, corresp. relating to Royal Economic Society

Likenesses R. Pepys, oils, *c.*1960, priv. coll. · L. Silbert, photograph, 1975, priv. coll.

Saunders, David Hogg (*d.* **1904**). *See under* Saunders, George (1859–1922).

Saunders, Edith Rebecca (**1865–1945**), botanist, was born in Brighton on 14 October 1865, the daughter of John Saunders, hotel keeper, and his wife, Jane Rebecca Whitwell of Islington. She was educated at Handsworth Ladies' College and at Newnham College, Cambridge, where she took both parts of the natural sciences tripos (1887, 1888), obtaining first-class honours. She held a Bathurst studentship from 1888 to 1889. She was an alpine climber as a

Edith Rebecca Saunders (1865–1945), by Maull & Fox

young woman, and throughout her life an excellent skater. In 1889 she was appointed demonstrator in botany at Newnham College, and along with her colleague Marion Greenwood she organized the Balfour Laboratory, of which she became director in 1899. For more than twenty years she taught most of the practicals in the natural sciences for the women students of Newnham and Girton colleges. She was recognized as a stimulating teacher who demanded high-quality work.

Saunders's research was in two areas, plant genetics and floral morphology. Early in her career she undertook collaborative research with William Bateson on plant breeding experiments on *Biscutella laevigata*. The work involved a study of what came to be known as dominant and recessive characters; the results were published in 1898 and 1902. The rediscovery in 1900 of Gregor Mendel's work gave a special impetus to these investigations; by 1902 Saunders and Bateson had established the existence of Mendelian inheritance in *Lychnis*, *Atropa*, and *Datura*, and it is likely that they had rediscovered some of Mendel's laws before his work was known to them.

From about 1902 Edith Saunders and Bateson were the leading members of the team which started the modern study of plant genetics in Britain; indeed, she has been called the mother of British plant genetics. Her later research in this area involved a study of the complex genetic interactions in *Matthiola incana*, on which she published twenty-two papers. Her selection as president of section K (botany) of the British Association in 1920 reflected her prominent position in the field.

By the 1920s, stimulated largely by observations on plant structure made during her genetics work, Edith Saunders was turning increasingly to problems in floral morphology: in a long series of papers in the *Annals of Botany* and the *New Phytologist* she recorded her observations on vascular and carpellary structure in a wide range of flowers. Her results and theories were summarized in her two-volume work *Floral Morphology* (1937–9). The overall impact of her morphological work was to some extent diminished by the fact that she held to her theory of carpel polymorphism, despite the overwhelming criticism levelled against it. Nevertheless, her contribution to floral anatomy is regarded as important and her papers were frequently cited many years after her death.

Edith Saunders enjoyed travelling, and went with the British Association to Australia, New Zealand, South Africa, China, Japan, and North America. She was one of the first women to be elected to the fellowship of the Linnean Society (1905). She later served on its council (1910–15), and was vice-president from 1912 to 1913. She was president of the Genetical Society in 1936. The Royal Horticultural Society awarded her the Banksian medal in 1906.

Edith Saunders was a well-known and highly respected figure in Cambridge for many decades. With the outbreak of the Second World War she gave up her research and worked in the Cambridge offices of the YMCA and WVS, and also in Addenbrooke's Hospital Library (1940–43). In addition she was honorary treasurer of the WVS Services Club from 1941 to 1945. She was in the process of resuming her scientific work when she died, unmarried, on 6 June 1945 in Cambridge, following a bicycle accident. Her passing, at the time of the end of the war in Europe, received comparatively little notice for a person of her scientific stature. MARY R. S. CREESE, *rev.*

Sources G. I. Elles, E. Shakespear, J. McL. Thompson, and J. B. S. Haldane, *Nature*, 156 (1945), 198–9, 385 • H. H. Thomas, *Proceedings of the Linnean Society of London*, 158th session (1947), 75–6 • H. Godwin, A. R. Clapham, and M. R. Gilson, *New Phytologist*, 45/1 (1946), 1–3 • R. Schmid, 'Edith Saunders and floral anatomy: bibliography and index to families she studied', *Botanical Journal of the Linnean Society*, 74 (1977), 179–87 • *CGPLA Eng. & Wales* (1946) • M. R. S. Creese, *Ladies in the laboratory? American and British women in science, 1800–1900* (1998)

Likenesses Maull & Fox, photograph, Linn. Soc. [*see illus.*] • photograph, Newnham College, Cambridge, archives; repro. in *Newnham College Roll Letter* (Jan 1946)

Wealth at death £19,623 8*s*. 4*d*.: probate, 4 Feb 1946, *CGPLA Eng. & Wales*

Saunders, Sir Edmund (*d*. 1683), judge and law reporter, came from obscure parentage. According to his will Saunders 'drew my first breath' (PRO, PROB 11/374, fols. 355*v*–356*r*) in the parish of Barnwood, near Gloucester. His will also refers to his father and mother Gregory, suggesting that they were his adoptive parents, and to the widow of a Mr Russell, schoolmaster at Gloucester, perhaps an early teacher. According to Roger North, Saunders was 'no better than a beggar boy', who acquired a living in Clement's Inn by 'courting the attorney's clerks for scraps'. His diligence led him to be employed as a copyist by the clerks, and from there he progressed to be 'an exquisite entering clerk' (North, 1.293–4). Thus 'having been four years of

New Inn' (MacGeagh and Sturgess, 163), he entered the Middle Temple on 4 July 1660, giving his address as the city of Gloucester. He was called to the bar on 25 November 1664.

In 1666 Saunders commenced his reports of cases in king's bench which he continued until 1672. These were first published in 1686 (first English edn, 1722), with the records in Latin and the arguments in French, as *The Reports of Divers Pleadings and Cases in the Court of King's Bench*. These were glossed by John Williams and became *Williams' Saunders* (1799), 'a classic on Pleading' (Simpson, 460). More notes were added by E. V. Williams and J. Patteson (1824). The reports demonstrate that Saunders quickly acquired a large legal practice in king's bench: in 1680 he was the leading pleader on the pleas side, and fifth on the crown side. His cases included defending Anne Price in 1680 from the charge of attempting to suborn one of the witnesses to the Popish Plot, and he was the only barrister to be assigned to the defence of all five Catholic lords indicted for the plot. In 1681 Saunders appeared for the crown against Edward Fitzharris and against the earl of Shaftesbury, both of whom faced charges of high treason. In May 1682 he moved unsuccessfully in the king's bench for the discharge of the earl of Danby from the Tower, and in June he defended William Pain against the charge of writing and publishing letters which suggested that the magistrate Sir Edmund Godfrey had committed suicide. In July Saunders advised the lord mayor of London in the legal dispute over the disputed election for sheriffs, which led to the tories taking control of the city.

No doubt as a reward for his efforts on behalf of Charles II, on 13 November 1682 Saunders was made a king's counsel, and on 24 November he became a bencher of the Middle Temple. He was knighted on 21 January 1683, and on the 23rd he was sworn a serjeant-at-law at the common pleas bar, his two sponsors being the lord chamberlain, the earl of Arlington, and the secretary of state Sir Leoline Jenkins, and then sworn in as lord chief justice of the king's bench at the bar of that court. Saunders was appointed a judge to ensure that the king obtained a verdict against the City of London in the *quo warranto* proceedings, which Saunders himself had helped to draw up having found the irregularities which formed the legal basis for the forfeiture. To Burnet, his advice on how to 'overthrow the charter' made Saunders 'a learned but a very immoral man' (*Bishop Burnet's History*, 2.342). However, Saunders was not a well man, and although he presided over the trial at the Guildhall in February 1683 of some whigs for riot during the poll for sheriffs the previous year, he was reported as indisposed later in the month. In May he continued to preside at the trial arising from the shrieval riots, and also presided at the trial of Sir Patience Ward for perjury in the duke of York's action against Thomas Pilkington. On 22 May, while he was presiding at the Guildhall, he was 'taken very ill, and was forced to go off the bench' (Luttrell, 1.259). He was absent from king's bench when the judgment against the City of London was delivered on 12 June. Saunders, who was unmarried, 'lived humbly in Butcher Row with the Earles, Jane Earle being suspected, probably wrongly, of being his mistress' (Simpson, 460). He died in London on 19 June 1683 'of the palsy, stone, and a complication of other distempers' (Luttrell, 1.262), and was buried on the 28th in the Temple Church.

Saunders was a very able lawyer, who according to North 'never in all his life betrayed a client to court a judge', nor did he have a regard for fees, 'but did all the service he could, whether feed double or single' (North, 3.91). In his will he described his body as 'so vile and loathsome as not to be endured above ground', a point of view shared by North who saw him as 'very corpulent and beastly; a mere lump of morbid flesh' (North, 1.294), and who referred to 'the very great stench of his carcass at the bar' (North, 3.92). Some of his physical condition was put down to his fondness for alcohol: on one occasion a case involving the question of whether brandy was subject to excise duty saw samples handed to the jury, and ended with the admission that Saunders had drunk the remainder of the evidence. However, Saunders had other good points: 'wit and repartee in an affected rusticity were natural to him' (North, 1.294), and an easy accessibility to law students who were often in his company. He spent most of his time as a barrister under the care of Nathaniel Earle and his wife, his landlords, to whom he left most of his estate 'as some recompense for their care of me and attendance upon me for many years'. Nor did Saunders forget his origins, leaving money to the poor whom he defined as not only 'such as receive alms of the people, but likewise such as have a great charge upon them and nothing but their daily labour to sustain themselves' (will). His final year was spent in a house on the corner of Parson's Green. STUART HANDLEY

Sources will, PRO, PROB 11/374, sig. 147 • Baker, *Serjeants* • Sainty, *Judges* • Sainty, *King's counsel* • R. North, *The lives of … Francis North … Dudley North … and … John North*, ed. A. Jessopp, 3 vols. (1890), vol. 1, pp. 293–6; vol. 3, pp. 90–93 • N. Luttrell, *A brief historical relation of state affairs from September 1678 to April 1714*, 6 vols. (1857) • H. A. C. Sturgess, ed., *Register of admissions to the Honourable Society of the Middle Temple, from the fifteenth century to the year 1944*, 1 (1949), 163 • D. Lemmings, *Gentlemen and barristers: the inns of court and the English bar, 1680–1730* (1990), 268, 271 • *Bishop Burnet's History*, 2.342, 345, 442 • *State trials*, 7.906–7, 1242; 8.270–71, 779, 1039–58, 1264–5, 1378; 9.187–352; 11.831 • *Register of burials at the Temple Church, 1628–1853* (1905), 25 [with introduction by H. G. Woods] • Foss, *Judges*, 8.160–64 • A. F. Hauighurst, 'The judiciary and politics in the reign of Charles II', *Law Quarterly Review*, 66 (1950), 244–5 • A. W. B. Simpson, ed., *Biographical dictionary of the common law* (1984)

Wealth at death see will, PRO, PROB 11/374, sig. 147

Saunders, Sir Edward (1506–1576), judge, was born on 4 April 1506, the eldest surviving son of Thomas Saunders (*d*. 1528) of Sibbertoft, Northamptonshire, and Margaret, daughter of Richard Cave of Stanford in that county. His younger brother was the Marian martyr Lawrence *Saunders. Cooper says he studied at Cambridge, though there is no convincing evidence to support the claim. In 1524 he was admitted to the Middle Temple, and, after spending some time in Cromwell's service, rose very rapidly in his profession. He became reader of the Middle Temple in the summer of 1539, perhaps already knowing that he was destined to receive a serjeant's writ, and was created serjeant-at-law (at a remarkably early age) in June 1540. In 1541 he was chosen recorder of Coventry, and in 1547 was the first new king's serjeant appointed by Edward VI (at the instance of Thomas Wriothesley). As recorder, he was elected to represent Coventry in the parliament of 1542; he was member for Saltash in 1553.

In 1553 Saunders persuaded the mayor of Coventry to refuse Northumberland's command to proclaim Lady Jane Grey as queen and to proclaim Mary instead. Mary duly appointed him a justice of the common pleas on 4 October 1553 and conferred a knighthood upon him in 1555. On 8 May 1557 he was translated to the king's bench as chief justice. Elizabeth renewed his office on her accession, but two months later, on 22 January 1559, demoted him to be chief baron of the exchequer. The reason was probably religion, as in the case of his colleague Sir Anthony Browne of the common pleas, though Saunders had recently been involved in a jurisdictional dispute with the admiralty and had also opposed Bedford and Dudley over their interference with offices in the common pleas. During his time as a judge he kept law reports, which survive in manuscript copies; some extracts were printed in 1994.

Saunders died on 12 November 1576 and was buried in accordance with his testamentary directions at Weston under Wetherley, Warwickshire, where there is a crude kneeling effigy wearing a mantle over armour. A poetic 'Epitaph upon the Death of Syr Edward Saunders', of indifferent merit, was published by Lodowick Lloyd the same year. Besides his estates in Warwickshire (including a house at Sherbourne) and Northamptonshire, Saunders left a London house in the Whitefriars, adjoining Serjeants' Inn, which he bought when a serjeant in 1546 and which in 1614 was conveyed to trustees for the Society of Serjeants' Inn. He left one daughter (Mary) by his first wife, Margaret (*d.* 1563), who was the daughter of Sir Thomas Englefield, justice of the common pleas, and widow of George Carew (*d.* 1538) of Suffolk. His second wife, Agnes Hussey, survived him. To his kinsman Francis Saunders (*d.* 1585), bencher of the Middle Temple, he left a silver-gilt ewer with the arms of Saunders, 'my circuite gowne of London russett faced with martyn, my greatest byble beinge at Sherborne, my abridgmentes of Fitzherbert being also there', and £160. J. H. BAKER

Sources HoP, *Commons, 1509–58*, 3.271–2 • Foss, *Judges* • Cooper, *Ath. Cantab.*, 1.359–60, 565 • *Reports from the lost notebooks of Sir James Dyer*, ed. J. H. Baker, 1, SeldS, 109 (1994) • C. H. Hopwood, ed., *Middle Temple records*, 1: *1501–1603* (1904) • Sainty, *Judges* • introduction, *The reports of Sir John Spelman*, ed. J. H. Baker, 2, SeldS, 94 (1978) • Baker, *Serjeants*, 168, 535 • PRO, PROB 11/58, sig. 41 • H. C. King, *Records and documents concerning Serjeants' Inn, Fleet Street* (1922), 108–11 • inquisition post mortem, PRO, C142/182/32(2)

Likenesses sandstone and marble effigy on monument, 1576, St Michael's Church, Weston under Wetherley, Warwickshire

Saunders, Edward (1848–1910), entomologist, was born on 22 March 1848 at East Hill, Wandsworth, the youngest of seven children (four sons and three daughters) of the entomologist William Wilson *Saunders (1809–1879) and his second wife, Mary Ann (*née* Mello). His elder brother George Sharp Saunders (1842–1910) was also an entomologist, and editor of the *Journal of the Royal Horticultural Society* (1906–8). Their youngest sister, Mary Anne Saunders (*d.* 1927), married the zoologist Thomas Roscoe Rede Stebbing (1835–1926). She was not only an accomplished field naturalist, but also one of the first woman fellows of the Linnean Society.

Saunders was educated entirely at home, and no doubt acquired his interest in natural history (and in particular entomology) from his father. He began work on his father's collections at an early age, writing a paper on Coleoptera for the first volume of the *Entomologist's Monthly Magazine* at the age of sixteen. In 1865 he entered his father's office as an underwriter at Lloyd's, an appointment which marked the beginning of a long business career. Thereafter Saunders's daytimes were spent largely in the Royal Exchange; his natural history studies and collecting were primarily carried out during his spare time. In 1865 he became a fellow of the Entomological Society, later serving as treasurer (1880–90), and a vice-president (1874, 1899, 1901, 1906, and 1907). He joined the Linnean Society in 1869, and contributed several papers to the society's journal. He was also a member of the Stockholm Entomological Society, and an editor of the *Entomologist's Monthly Magazine*, to which he made about 140 contributions.

Saunders became particularly interested in the Buprestidae (jewel beetles), which formed the basis of several contributions to the *Transactions of the Entomological Society* from 1866 to 1869. He published *Catalogue of the Species Contained in the Genus Buprestis, Linn* in 1870, and in the following year his *Catalogus Buprestidarum synonymicus et systematicus* appeared. For this latter work he undertook his only foreign field trip, visiting museums across Europe to examine their specimens. Between 1872 and 1874 he described several new genera and numerous new species. About this time he also began work on the British Hemiptera which were issued in a series of notes, and subsequently he produced *Hemiptera Heteroptera of the British Isles* (1892).

Similarly, Saunders began work on a third group, the Hymenoptera Aculeata. His interest in these was probably aroused when his father purchased William E. Shuckard's collection of British Hymenoptera. In turn his attention became especially drawn to the Aculeates, and his chief work was at the time was considered to be the *Hymenoptera Aculeata of the British Isles* (1896). In time, he formed an impressive collection, which included specimens given to him by his father's cousin, Sir Sydney Smith Saunders, a former consul-general in Albania and writer on Hymenoptera.

In 1872 Saunders married Mary Agnes, daughter of Edward Brown (*d.* 1866), an East India merchant, of East Hill, Wandsworth. The couple had five sons and four daughters. Between 1872 and 1887 Saunders lived successively in Reigate, Surrey, Wandsworth, London, and Bromley, Kent (all were close to his business), before settling at Woking, Surrey, in 1887. On 5 June 1902 he was elected FRS. He was also author of *Wild Bees, Wasps, and Ants, and other Stinging Insects* (1907), which included illustrations by his daughter. Saunders died on 6 February 1910 at 4 Lansdowne Place, his seaside lodgings, in Bognor Regis, Sussex. He was survived by his wife and all but one of his children, and buried in the cemetery at Brookwood, near Woking. YOLANDA FOOTE

Sources T. R. R. Stebbing, *Proceedings of the Linnean Society of London*, 122nd session (1909–10), 94–8 • *Entomologist's Monthly Magazine*, 46 (1910), 49–53 • presidential address, *Proceedings of the Entomological Society* (1910) • *Entomologist's Record*, 22 (1910) • *Catalogue of scientific papers*, Royal Society, 19 vols. (1867–1925) • *Nature*, 83 (1910), 17 • Desmond, *Botanists*, rev. edn • A. T. Gage and W. T. Stearn, *A bicentenary history of the Linnean Society of London* (1988) • *CGPLA Eng. & Wales* (1910) • b. cert.

Archives NHM, entomological notes • Oxf. U. Mus. NH, Hope Library • Oxf. U. Mus. NH, diary, incl. details of captures | Oxf. U. Mus. NH, letters to Sir E. B. Poulton • Oxf. U. Mus. NH, letters to G. A. J. Rothney; corresp. with J. O. Westwood • Royal Entomological Society, London, letters to C. J. Wainwright

Likenesses Maull & Polyblank, photograph, 1855, NPG • Elliott & Fry, photograph, repro. in *Entomologist's Monthly Magazine*, 46 (1910), 49–53 • Maull & Co., photograph, RS

Wealth at death £2878 7*s*. 6*d*.: resworn probate, 26 April 1910, *CGPLA Eng. & Wales*

Saunders, Sir Edwin (1814–1901), dentist, was born in London on 12 March 1814, the son of Simon Saunders, senior partner in the firm of Saunders and Ottley, publishers, in Brook Street, London. From an early age Saunders showed an aptitude for mechanical objects and ideas, and from the age of twelve to fourteen he experimented with methods of replacing steam with hydraulic power for the propulsion of ships; he also invented a sweeping machine for city streets. Despite this aptitude Saunders was not encouraged to pursue a career in civil engineering. However, the practical aspects of dentistry attracted him, and about 1830 he was apprenticed in London to Mr Lemaile, a dentist in Southwark.

At the end of three years Saunders was thoroughly grounded in dental mechanics, and he started to practise in Surrey. He also gave a course of lectures on elementary mechanics and anatomy at a mechanics' institute. Frederick Tyrrell, surgeon to St Thomas's Hospital, London, happened to be present at one lecture and was so impressed that he invited Saunders to lecture at St Thomas's. Saunders lectured there unofficially from 1837, until, having obtained the diploma of the Royal College of Surgeons, in 1839, he was appointed dental surgeon and lecturer on dental surgery to St Thomas's Hospital, a post he occupied until 1854. In 1855 he was elected FRCS. Saunders was also dentist from 1834 to the Blenheim Street Infirmary and Free Dispensary. In 1837 he moved his practice to the West End of London and in 1840 he started, in conjunction with Mr Harrison and Mr Snell, a small institution for the treatment of the teeth of the poor. It was the first charity of its kind, and lasted about twelve years.

While working on prosthetic devices for cleft palate, Saunders came to know Alexander Nasmyth, who was researching the same problem and who had a large dental practice in London. After 1846, when Nasmyth was incapacitated by an attack of paralysis, Saunders took charge of and later bought Nasmyth's practice, which he carried on at Nasmyth's house, 13A George Street, Hanover Square, until he retired to Wimbledon about 1890. He succeeded Nasmyth in 1846 as dentist to Queen Victoria, the prince consort, and the other members of the royal family. In 1848 he married Marian, eldest daughter of Edmund William Burgess.

Saunders held that dentistry was a part of medicine. A good organizer and a man of considerable scientific attainments, he was deeply involved in the attempts to turn dentistry into a profession. As part of the Dental Reform Association, in 1856 he was among those who petitioned the Royal College of Surgeons to grant a diploma in dental surgery, which eventually led to the college obtaining powers, in 1859, to examine candidates and grant a diploma in dentistry. The Odontological Society was founded at Saunders's house in 1857 in an initiative to unite those who practised dental surgery. Saunders was the first treasurer, and was president in 1864 and 1879. After the Dentists Act was passed in 1878 he took a leading role in the establishment of the British Dental Association. He was also a trustee of the first dental hospital and school established in London, in Soho Square in 1859. The institution prospered, largely through his energy and generosity, and in 1874 the Dental Hospital in Leicester Square was opened—and handed over to the managing committee free of debt. Saunders's involvement was commemorated by the school's Saunders scholarship. Saunders himself remained on the management committee until he resigned over the decision to rebuild.

Saunders was president of the dental section at the meeting of the International Medical Congress in London in 1881, and in the same year he was president of the metropolitan counties branch of the British Medical Association. In 1883 he was knighted, being the first dentist to receive that honour. In 1886 he was president of the British Dental Association. He died at Fairlawn, Wimbledon Common, Surrey, on 15 March 1901, and was buried at Putney cemetery. He was survived by his wife.

D'A. POWER, *rev.* PATRICK WALLIS

Sources *BMJ* (23 March 1901), 746–7 • *The Lancet* (23 March 1901) • *Medico-Chirurgical Transactions*, 85 (1902), cii–civ • *Journal of the British Dental Association*, 22 (1901), 200–03 • *The advance of the dental profession: a centenary history, 1880–1980*, British Dental Association (privately printed, London, 1979) • V. G. Plarr, *Plarr's Lives of the fellows of the Royal College of Surgeons of England*, rev. D'A. Power, 2 vols. (1930) • Z. Cope, *The Royal College of Surgeons of England: a history* (1959) • *CGPLA Eng. & Wales* (1901)

Wealth at death £109,081 0*s*. 3*d*.: resworn probate, July 1901, *CGPLA Eng. & Wales*

Saunders, Emma (1841–1927), philanthropist, was born on 2 March 1841 in Middleton Stoney, near Bicester, Oxfordshire, the third daughter and the youngest of the five children of Joshua Saunders (1811–1900), a subagent of the Bank of England, and his wife, Mary Magdalene, *née* Morris. In April 1845 Joshua Saunders was elected as subagent to the Manchester branch of the Bank of England, and Emma moved with the family to that area. In June 1847 she moved again as her father was made subagent to the Bristol branch. Emma, who never married, remained in the Bristol area for the rest of her life.

Little is known of Emma Saunders's education or Anglican background, but her life was changed through a Christian mission held at Christ Church, Clifton, Bristol. She taught in an industrial home for girls in the area, a boys' class in St James's Sunday school, and at a nearby ragged school. Her Christian mission work among railwaymen began in 1878 with a Sunday Bible class, which she ran in an upper room at Bristol Temple Meads railway station. She also organized a mothers' meeting on Monday afternoons in the same room, which seated about a hundred people. Soon afterwards she began visiting on site those involved in the construction of the Severn Tunnel (1873–86) and other railway projects in the area. Such activities predated (but later became part of) the Railway Mission, which was founded in 1881.

Work among railwaymen succeeded to such an extent in the 1880s that, in conjunction with the Great Western Railway (GWR) Temperance Society, a hall was built in Pyle Hill goods yard, Mead Street, which sat 300 people. The benches were given by the railway company and the rostrum was obtained from the chapel in the old gaol, which was then being demolished. Here the mission under Emma Saunders held its various meetings and annual teas for all grades of railwaymen.

But it was Emma Saunders's visits to the places they worked which established her as the Railwaymen's Friend. She would visit railway workers only if invited to do so, but the popularity of her calls was such that this work took up most of her time, and assistants were recruited. She covered every station, depot, signal box, and grade and class of worker on the railway in the Bristol area, and she gave every one of the 2000 workers whom she visited monthly a Christian text or message and personal token, such as flowers, a seaweed or shell card, a lavender bag, or something else which she herself had made. Hence she was also known as the Lady with the Basket. She also visited railway workers or their families when they were ill. In 1910 she established the Bristol and West of England Railwaymen's Institute, which had a canteen and games rooms and held engineering classes. Her love of animals led her to give a copy of Anna Sewell's *Black Beauty* to every railway carter to encourage them to treat their horses kindly.

Emma Saunders's work among railwaymen continued until just after the First World War. If cautioned about going out in the wet when in her seventies she would reply, 'I'm not sugar, I won't melt'. To mark her eightieth birthday, on 2 March 1921, more than 5000 railway employees subscribed to an illustrated address, settee, and armchair.

Emma Saunders, who was described on her death certificate as 'of independent means', died at her home, 6 Sion Hill, Clifton, Bristol, on 27 February 1927 and was buried on 2 March at Redland Green cemetery. On 1 July 1928 a memorial tablet (showing her in profile holding a basket) was unveiled at Bristol Temple Meads to the Railwaymen's Friend, in remembrance of her 'fifty years devoted Christian service'.

PETER STREET

Sources *The life-story of the Railwaymen's Friend … compiled by her niece* (1927) • *Railway Signal* (April 1927); (Aug 1928) • b. cert. • d. cert.

Likenesses white marble portrait, 1928 (after photograph), Bristol Temple Meads railway station

Wealth at death £9997 13*s*. 1*d*.: probate, 23 April 1927, *CGPLA Eng. & Wales*

Saunders, Erasmus (1670–1724), Church of England clergyman, was born in the parish of Clydau, north Pembrokeshire, the son of Tobias Saunders (*d*. 1719/20), weaver and landowner, of Cilrhedyn, Pembrokeshire, and Lettice Phillipps of Pen-boyr, Carmarthenshire. He matriculated at Jesus College, Oxford, on 20 March 1690, being described as 'pauper puer', though he belonged to the ancient family of Saunders (later Saunders-Davies) of Pentre, near Clydau. Saunders graduated BA in 1693, MA in 1696, BD in 1705, and DD in 1712. He made the acquaintance of the naturalist and Celtic scholar Edward Lhuyd, and assisted him in his fieldwork in Pembrokeshire and Carmarthenshire.

Saunders received the patronage of Bishop William Lloyd and followed Lloyd's son as vicar of Blockley, Gloucestershire, on 13 August 1705. He also held the rectory of Helmdon, Northamptonshire, in 1706–21, and was prebendary of Brecon, in the diocese of St David, from 1709 until his death. He married Dorothy, daughter of Humphrey Lloyd of Aberbechan, near Newtown, Montgomeryshire, at Blockley in 1714. They had at least one son, also Erasmus, who matriculated in 1734 and graduated DD from Merton College, Oxford, in 1753; he was canon of Windsor (1751), vicar of St Martin-in-the-Fields, and prebendary of Rochester (1756). He died at Bristol in 1775.

Saunders, a keen supporter of the SPCK, was a man of distinguished piety and an active church reformer. He is best known as the author of a work, written at the suggestion of Bishop Bull, entitled *A view of the state of religion in the diocese of St. David's about the beginning of the eighteenth century, with some account of the causes of its decay* (1721). This work paints a gloomy portrait of poverty and ecclesiastical malpractices in the diocese of St David and, although his evidence has been widely quoted by historians, it should be borne in mind that Saunders, resentful and embittered at being refused promotion to a bishopric, exaggerated evidence of ruined churches, pluralism, absenteeism, and non-residence. Saunders is also credited with having written *Short Illustrations of the Bible*, but this should probably be identified with another work of his entitled *A Domestick Charge, or, The Duty of Household-Governours* (1701); a translation into Welsh was executed by Samuel Williams, but it does not appear to have been published. Saunders died from apoplexy on 3 June 1724, at Aberbechan, and was buried two days later at St Mary's, Shrewsbury, where an inscription to his memory was placed in the chancel. He was survived by his wife. Another memorial was erected at Blockley in 1771 by his son, Erasmus.

D. L. THOMAS, *rev.* DYLAN FOSTER EVANS

Sources F. Green, 'Saunders of Pentre, Tymawr, and Glanrhydi', *West Wales Historical Records*, 2 (1911–12), 161–88 • M. Clement, ed., *Correspondence and minutes of the SPCK relating to Wales, 1699–1740*

(1952) • I. James, 'Correspondence', *Archaeologia Cambrensis*, 4th ser., 10 (1879), 72–3 • Llallawg [T. James], 'Correspondence', *Archaeologia Cambrensis*, 4th ser., 4 (1873), 384 • Foster, *Alum. Oxon.* • *GM*, 1st ser., 46 (1776), 47
Archives Bodl. Oxf., letters to Edward Lhuyd
Likenesses oils (of Saunders?), NL Wales

Saunders, Sir George (**1670/71–1734**), naval officer, whose place of birth and parentage are unknown, after nine years at sea in the merchant service entered the navy in 1689 as a volunteer on the *Portsmouth*, with Captain George St Lo; in 1690 he became for a short time a prisoner of war when the ship was captured. In December of that year he joined the *Ossory*, in which he was present in the battle of La Hogue. On 28 December 1692 he passed his examination, being then twenty-one, and having served in the navy for not quite three years. On 5 December 1694 he was promoted lieutenant, and in January he was appointed to the *Yarmouth*. From 1696 to 1699 he was in the *Pendennis* with Captain Thomas Hardy; in 1700 he was in the *Suffolk*; in 1701 he was in the *Coventry*, again with Hardy; and in 1702 he was first lieutenant of the *St George*, the flagship of Sir Stafford Fairborne with Sir George Rooke at Cadiz and at Vigo. On 1 May 1698 he had married Ann (*d.* 1740), daughter of Charles Dartiquenare.

Saunders was next promoted to the command of the bomb-vessel *Terror*, which he brought home in November after a stormy and dangerous passage. A few weeks later he was posted to the small frigate *Seaford*, on the Irish station, in which, and afterwards from January 1705 in the *Shoreham*, he continued until 1710, cruising in the Irish Sea, chasing and sometimes capturing the enemy's privateers, and convoying the local trade between Whitehaven, Hoylake, Milford, and Bristol on the one side, and on the other from Belfast to Kinsale. From 1710 to 1716 he commanded the *Antelope* (50 guns) in the channel.

During the 1715 Jacobite rising Saunders's ship was part of a squadron attempting to inspect suspected Jacobite vessels at Havre-de-Grace, and when the French resisted he was sent to Paris to pursue the matter. In 1716 he was appointed to the *Superbe*, which in the following year was one of the fleet in the Baltic with Sir George Byng. Byng, when appointed in 1718 to the command of a fleet in the Mediterranean, selected Saunders as first captain of his flagship, the *Barfleur*. In that capacity Saunders had an important share in the defeat of the Spanish fleet off Cape Passaro, and in the subsequent operations on the coast of Sicily and Naples.

While on his way to England overland with Byng and his sons, Saunders stopped at Hanover where he was knighted by George I on 21 August 1720. He served as a commissioner of the victualling from 1721 until he became extra commissioner of the navy in January 1728; a year later, on 15 January 1729, he moved again, to become comptroller of the treasurer's accounts. He held that office for the remainder of his life, additionally gaining promotion to rear-admiral on 9 June 1732. Saunders was also member of parliament for Queenborough from 20 February 1728 until his death on 5 December 1734; he was buried at St Olave, Hart Street, London.

By his will, dated 20 September 1732 and proved on 14 December 1734, Saunders left the bulk of his estate to his wife, Ann. The will also made bequests to his daughter Anna Maria Egerton, his three granddaughters, and his executors, Thomas Revell and Seth Jermy of the victualling office. J. K. Laughton, *rev.* J. D. Davies

Sources summaries of officer's services, PRO, Admiralty MSS, ADM 6/424, 7/549 • lieutenant's passing certificate, PRO, Admiralty MSS, ADM 107/1, p. 22 • *Portsmouth* paybook 1689, PRO, Admiralty MSS, ADM 33/117, ticket 211 • *The Byng papers: selected from the letters and papers of Admiral Sir George Byng, first Viscount Torrington, and of his son, Admiral the Hon. John Byng*, ed. B. Tunstall, 3 vols., Navy RS, 67–8, 70 (1930–32) • *Pattee Byng's journal, 1718–1720*, ed. J. L. Cranmer-Byng, Navy RS, 88 (1950) • will, PRO, PROB 11/668, fols. 340–41 • R. S. Lea, 'Saunders, Sir George', HoP, *Commons, 1715–54* • J. M. Collinge, *Navy Board officials, 1660–1832* (1978) • *Report on the manuscripts of Lord Polwarth*, 5 vols., HMC, 67 (1911–61) • *Calendar of the manuscripts of the marquess of Ormonde*, new ser., 8 vols., HMC, 36 (1902–20), vol. 8 • NMM, Sergison MSS, SER/136 • marriage register, St Martin-in-the-Fields, London
Archives PRO, Admiralty MSS • TCD, corresp. with William King
Wealth at death £5000 left to wife; £3000 left to eldest granddaughter on reaching twenty-one or on marriage; £1000 left to each of younger granddaughters on reaching twenty-one or on marriage; plus a house in Great Burlington Street, Westminster: will, PRO, PROB 11/668, fols. 340–41

Saunders, George (*bap.* **1762**, *d.* **1839**), architect, was baptized on 26 September 1762, the son of Joseph Saunders, a London carpenter who resided at 252 Oxford Street, and his wife, Grace. His first (and only) exhibit at the Royal Academy was a design for a public bath, shown in 1781.

Little is known of Saunders's architectural output but it is clear that he was a more interesting figure than has generally been recognized. In 1790 he published *A Treatise on Theatres*, a learned European-wide survey (dedicated to Charles Greville, his patron) that considered their optical and acoustic properties, and included designs for a theatre and an opera house. Saunders had visited Italy and France in 1787–90, and made a special study of continental methods of construction such as the fireproof floors made of hollow earthenware pots used in the Palais Royal in Paris. One of his earliest known works was the Theatre Royal and assembly rooms in New Street, Birmingham, commenced in 1793 behind the façade of 1780 by Samuel Wyatt. Other work in this field included the lecture theatre of the Royal Institution in Albemarle Street (*c.*1800) and the reconstruction of the roof of Wren's Sheldonian Theatre in Oxford (1801–2).

Saunders was architect to the trustees of the British Museum, and in 1802 was asked to prepare designs for new galleries to receive the Townley collection of classical statuary and for artefacts newly arrived from Egypt. Parliament granted £4000 for their construction in 1804 and they were opened by Queen Charlotte in June 1808. Saunders's designs, demolished in 1849, were important for being among the earliest top-lit public galleries in the country, and their conventional Palladian exteriors masked an interior of sophistication which owed much to the work of Henry Holland. The same influence can be discerned at his extensive additions (1793–6) to Kenwood

House, Hampstead, for the second earl of Mansfield, where he added two wings and a vast service range. Saunders's other known gallery designs were an 'antiquaries' closet' (*c*.1805) at the Bodleian Library, which housed several manuscript collections, and a sculpture gallery (*c*.1790) for the earl of Cawdor, a noted collector of antiquities, at his London house.

Much of Saunders's later career was spent administering rather than designing. He was employed by the Treasury to investigate the finances of the office of works under James Wyatt in the period 1809–12, and for twenty-eight years until his death was chairman of the Westminster commission of sewers. He was also a magistrate for the county of Middlesex, and in 1826 was one of three JPs appointed to consider the question of the county's bridges, and was joint author of their printed report.

Saunders was a learned man of diverse achievement, who was in contact with Sir Joseph Banks and the French archaeologist Quatremère de Quincy. He reviewed books on architecture for the *Monthly Review* from 1795 to 1815, and was elected fellow of the Society of Antiquaries in 1808 and fellow of the Royal Society in 1812, an indication of the intellectual esteem in which he was held. His printed works, in addition to *A Treatise on Theatres*, consisted of a number of scholarly papers: 'The origin of Gothic architecture' (*Archaeologia*, 17, 1814), 'The situation and extent of London at various periods' (*Archaeologia*, 26, 1836), and 'Observations on brick bond as practised at various periods' (*Civil Engineer and Architect's Journal*, 1, 1838). He died, unmarried, at his Oxford Street residence (an illustration of which appears in Tallis, 180) on 26 July 1839.

F. M. O'Donoghue, *rev.* Roger Bowdler

Sources Colvin, *Archs.* • *DNB* • I. Jenkins, *Archaeologists and aesthetes in the sculpture galleries of the British Museum, 1800–1939* (1992) • J. Ingamells, ed., *A dictionary of British and Irish travellers in Italy, 1701–1800* (1997) • private information (2004) • *IGI* • J. Tallis, *Tallis's London street views*, 72 (1838–40), 180 • Westminster Commissioners of Sewers, minutes for 2 Aug 1839

Likenesses F. Chantrey, two pencil sketches, *c*.1830, NPG • B. Cheverton, bust (after F. Chantrey), RIBA

Wealth at death £12,000: PRO, death duty registers, IR 26/1531, entry 571

Saunders, George (1859–1922), journalist, was born at Rattray, Perthshire, the elder son of **David Hogg Saunders** (*d.* 1904), writer, editor, and merchant, of Dundee and Craigmill, Blairgowrie. David Saunders, a staunch believer in God and the Liberal Party, published poems and articles under the pseudonym 'The Christian Democrat' in his paper, the Dundee *People's Journal*. His reputation as an insightful political moderate spread beyond his native Dundee, winning the grateful recognition of Gladstone.

George Saunders was marked by his father's values; a strict Presbyterian, he knew his Bible nearly by heart. He was educated at Rattray parish school and Dundee high school, then went to the University of Glasgow where he won prizes in moral philosophy, English literature, and foreign languages. He matriculated, a Snell exhibitioner, at Balliol in 1881. Drawn by his deep interest in German philosophy, Saunders studied textual criticism and did research on the New Testament at the universities of Bonn and Göttingen. He spoke French and German fluently, but with a pronounced Scottish burr, and read Greek and Latin for pleasure throughout his life. Another literary passion was poetry; he knew his Burns as well as his Bible.

Saunders inherited his father's interest in politics, as well as his devout Presbyterianism. Although his political sentiments were modelled on his father's, he was not liberal in his moral judgements; if a person, or a nation, offended his sense of propriety or his self-conscious dignity, his strictures were harsh and unyielding. In 1884 Saunders was admitted to the Inner Temple. A chance introduction to the peripatetic editor of the *Pall Mall Gazette*, W. T. Stead, intervened and Saunders found himself in France interviewing General Boulanger. Pleased with Saunders's work, Stead hired him as his personal assistant for a trip to Russia to interview Tsar Alexander III. Being a foreign correspondent appealed to Saunders's love of facts and accuracy, his skill with foreign languages, and his political interests. He felt, as a journalist, 'like a trout lying with its nose upstream' (Wilson, 4). Travelling home from Russia, Saunders stopped in Berlin, where he accepted a job as a correspondent for the London *Morning Post*. It was a momentous year for Germany; two emperors were buried in quick succession and the young Wilhelm II came into his fateful inheritance. For the next twenty years Saunders, once described as 'Scottish to the bone' ('Note on George Saunders', Saunders MSS), lived and worked in Berlin, first for the *Post* and from 1897 as 'Our Own Correspondent' for *The Times*.

George Saunders was moderately tall and large-boned, with bright blue eyes and a luxuriant moustache. A vital man, he walked fast, loved to play golf, and astonished Berliners by playing at curling on their city's frozen rivers. His words, like his actions, were forceful and direct and he had the courage born of strong convictions. Shrewd and observant, Saunders's outward reserve masked—but did not diminish—his passionate patriotism and his moral fervour. Saunders was no stranger to Germany, although by the 1890s the country he had known as a student was vanishing. Along with the desires of a grandiose young emperor, burgeoning prosperity fostered demands for expansion and international prestige. Saunders was intensely aware of the effect these changes had on both people and politics, turning Germany, in his view, into a 'parvenu' country with all of the attendant moral failings. His marriage in 1893 to Gertrude Hainauer, the daughter of Oscar Hainauer, a Berlin banker and art collector, was a personal and a professional asset. It was a happy marriage, producing three sons and two daughters; one son, Malcolm, rose to the rank of commander in the Royal Navy. Through his German relatives, Saunders had social contact with many prominent people in Berlin. This advantage, along with a thorough knowledge of the language, literature, and history of Germany, often provided Saunders with privileged information.

Diligent and productive during his years with the *Morning Post*, Saunders made his name writing for *The Times*. For

Germans wielding political power—thanks to his heated and repeated warnings as to the true aim of Germany's foreign policy and the unhealthy nature of her government—that name became anathema; the Kaiser himself called him 'a first class swine' (*History of The Times*, 3.462). In England it was the reverse; to the editor of *The Times*, Saunders was 'a Prince of Correspondents' (ibid., 3.649). Sir Edward Grey, the foreign secretary, admitted later: 'We now know that the line [he] took sprang from knowledge, [and] a good many of his countrymen owe some apology to the memory of Mr George Saunders for having underrated his sincerity and knowledge' (ibid., 3.371, n. 3). *The Times* moved Saunders to Paris in 1908. Germany was not spared his deeply critical attention while he worked to solidify the occasionally shaky entente between Paris and London. When his dire warnings came true in 1914, Saunders wanted to 'do his bit'; he joined the political intelligence department of the Foreign Office where his experience and expertise were welcomed, earning him an OBE at the war's end. Glasgow also honoured him with an LLD. Saunders lost one son in the war and survived it himself by only four years. His final crusade was against the imposition of an impossible peace on a Germany verging on economic, political, and moral collapse, but he was not heard. Saunders died of cancer at his home, Potswarn, Woking, on 10 September 1922.

LINDA BRANDT FRITZINGER

Sources O. J. Hale, *Publicity and diplomacy, with special reference to England and Germany, 1890–1914* (1940) • P. Kennedy, *The rise of the Anglo-German antagonism, 1860–1914* (1980) • A. J. A. Morris, *The scaremongers: the advocacy of war and rearmament, 1896–1914* (1984) • [S. Morison and others], *The history of The Times*, 3 (1947) • 'George Saunders on Germany, 1910–1920: correspondence and memoranda', ed. K. M. Wilson, *Proceedings of the Leeds Philosophical and Literary Society*, 21/1 (1987) [whole issue] • A. J. Ll. Morris, 'George Saunders, *The Times*' Berlin correspondent: a case study in diplomacy and publicity, 1896–1914', *Moirae*, 6 (1981), 16–41 • Saunders MSS, News Int. RO

Archives CAC Cam., corresp., diaries, and notes • News Int. RO, papers | PRO, Foreign Office index

Saunders, Helen Beatrice (1885–1963). *See under* Vorticists (*act.* 1914–1919).

Saunders, Henry. *See* Sanders, Henry (1727–1785).

Saunders, Henry Victor Parker. *See* Parker, Henry Victor (1910–1978).

Saunders, Howard (1835–1907), ornithologist, was born in London on 16 September 1835, the son of Alexander Saunders and his wife, Elizabeth (*née* Laundy). He was educated at a private school in Leatherhead and at Dr Gavin Smith's school at Rottingdean. On leaving school he entered Anthony Gibbs & Sons, a firm of bankers and South America merchants. In 1855 he left England to take up a post at Callo in Peru. During the journey across the Atlantic he made the observations on albatrosses which formed the subject of his first paper (published in *Ibis* in 1866). Indeed, his love of natural history led to his resigning his business position some time in or before 1860. In that year he crossed the Andes to reach the headwaters of the Amazon; he followed the river downstream, ultimately reaching Pará in Brazil. Until his return to England in 1862, his time was spent in zoological and antiquarian researches. Thereafter he devoted himself to ornithological studies, and between 1863 and 1872 he made a number of expeditions to Spain and other parts of Europe in the course of his research. In 1868 he married Emily (*d.* 1906), youngest daughter of William Minshull Bigg. The couple had two daughters.

In 1882 Saunders succeeded the dilatory Alfred Newton as editor of the two final volumes of Yarrell's *British Birds*. His own *Illustrated Manual of British Birds* was published in 1889 (2nd edn, 1899). It was described as 'perhaps the best and most widely appreciated of his works, [which] will always remain a model of accuracy and learning compressed into the smallest possible bulk' (*The Zoologist*, 436). He also published a revision of Mitchell's *Birds of Lancashire* and memoirs on the eggs collected on the transit of Venus expedition (1874–5). He was joint editor (with P. L. Sclater) of *Ibis* (1883–8 and 1894–1900). He was recorder of Aves for the *Zoological Record*, and wrote articles and reviews in *The Field* and *The Athenaeum*.

Saunders was regarded as a great authority on gulls; he wrote the monograph on the terns, gulls, and skuas for the catalogue of the birds in the British Museum (vol. 25, 1896), and had a large collection of gull skins (acquired by the British Museum in 1894). Other important works included his report on the gulls and terns (*Laridae*) collected during the voyage of HMS *Challenger*, and the article 'Birds' in the Royal Geographical Society's *Antarctic Manual* (1901). (Saunders had a great interest in the geography of the Arctic and Antarctic regions.)

Saunders was a fellow of the Linnean, Zoological, and Royal Geographical societies, and served on the councils of all three bodies. From 1880 to 1885 he served as honorary secretary to section D (zoology) of the British Association for the Advancement of Science. In 1901 he became secretary of the British Ornithologists' Union. He was also the first secretary and treasurer of the British Ornithologists' Club on its foundation in 1892.

Saunders's work was considered to be exceptionally careful and accurate. Along with Alfred Newton, he was regarded as one of the greatest contemporary authorities on British birds. His readiness to assist those engaged in similar activities earned him universal respect. He died at his residence, 7 Radnor Place, London, on 20 October 1907 after a long illness, and was interred at Kensal Green cemetery.

J. C. EDWARDS

Sources *The Auk*, 25 (1908), 103 • *The Zoologist*, 4th ser., 11 (1907), 436–8 • *The Ibis*, 9th ser., 2 (1908), 169–72 • W. H. Mullens and H. K. Swann, *A bibliography of British ornithology from the earliest times to the end of 1912* (1917)

Likenesses photograph, repro. in *The Zoologist*, 437

Wealth at death £3080 13*s*. 2*d*.: probate, 11 Nov 1907, *CGPLA Eng. & Wales*

Saunders, Sir Hugh William Lumsden (1894–1987), air force officer, born in Johannesburg, Transvaal republic, on 24 August 1894, was the son of Frederick William Saunders and his wife, Annie Eliza Lumsden. He was educated at the Marist Brothers' College, Johannesburg, from 1904 to 1910, and employed as a metallurgy student in the gold-mining industry until August 1914, when he joined the 10th infantry, Witwatersrand rifles, as a private. He served in South-West Africa and then from July 1915 with the 8th South African horse in east Africa. He was promoted to sergeant and earned a Military Medal before being discharged when his unit disbanded in February 1917. He had also earned the lifelong nickname Dingbat (often shortened to Ding): the word means a piece of money or a tramp or a 'thingummy'.

Saunders sailed to England in April 1917, joined the Royal Flying Corps in May as an air mechanic, learned to fly with 4 training squadron at Northolt, Middlesex, in July, and was commissioned in October. He served as a fighter pilot on the western front in 84 squadron (equipped with the SE 5a, an excellent single-seater biplane, armed with two machine-guns) from December 1917 until August 1918. By then he was that squadron's senior flight commander and acted as commanding officer whenever Major Sholto Douglas was absent. Douglas regarded him as 'very solid and imperturbable' (Douglas, 259): part of the squadron's backbone. 'A large, burly man and as steady as a rock when things were going badly, he has changed over the years [some forty-five of them, when Douglas was writing] less than almost anyone I know'. He certainly destroyed two kite balloons and five enemy aircraft, drove six others down, apparently out of control, and was awarded both a Military Cross and a Distinguished Flying Cross.

Saunders was granted a permanent commission in the RAF as a flying officer in August 1919 and was sent to the Middle East in March 1920. He rejoined 84 squadron (now equipped with the DH 9a, a large two-seater bomber-reconnaissance biplane) in Iraq and was promoted to flight lieutenant in January 1921. He earned a bar to his DFC in October for flying low over a besieged British garrison at Samawah (on the Euphrates, 150 miles south of Baghdad) and dropping supplies despite accurate rifle fire from the ground, which hit his machine several times. While in Iraq he married Phyllis Margaret Gertrude (*d.* 1980), daughter of Major P. W. Mabbett, on 28 November 1923 in St Peter's Church, Basrah. They had two sons: one became a soldier in the Royal Artillery; the other, a flight cadet at Cranwell, died in 1951.

Saunders returned to England in December 1923 and after six months' leave was employed on training duties in the Air Ministry from July 1924 until December 1928. He attended the RAF Staff College at Andover, Hampshire, during 1929 and was promoted to squadron leader in May. After staff duties at the Uxbridge headquarters of the air defence of Great Britain in 1930 and 1931, Saunders went to Egypt as commanding officer of 45 (bomber) squadron from January 1932 until September 1935, flying Fairey IIIF biplanes. He was promoted to wing commander in January 1936 and returned to training duties in the Air Ministry until his selection for a course at the Imperial Defence College in 1938. 'The aim was to give selected officers of the three Services, the Commonwealth Services and UK civil servants the opportunity to study problems of national and international strategy and security, and international relations,' recalled Saunders in 1977 (Gray, 34). 'We carried out studies and wrote appreciations covering a major war in Europe, a Mediterranean war, invasion of India by Russia and a Far Eastern war involving Japan.'

In the first of these four scenarios Saunders would play a prominent part, but before then he was promoted to group captain and seconded for duty as head of the Royal New Zealand Air Force from February 1939 to January 1942. He actively encouraged a rapid expansion of military aviation there and travelled to Canada to help finalize the empire air training scheme, which would make a vital contribution to British aircrew strength throughout the war. He had been promoted to air commodore in January 1941 and, on returning to England in February 1942, was promoted again—to air vice-marshal—and sent to Bentley Priory, north London; he was Fighter Command's chief administration officer there until November, when he became head of that command's famous 11 group.

During the next two years Saunders was responsible for the defence of London and south-east England, for offensive fighter sweeps and bomber escort duties across the English Channel, and for covering the landing beaches on and after D-day, 6 June 1944. In April 1948 the president of the United States made him a member of the Legion of Merit in the degree of commander because, according to the citation, 'the loss of American medium bombers to enemy fighters while escorted by fighters of his command were the lowest of any American bomber units in any theater of operations throughout the entire war.'

Saunders returned to the Air Ministry in November 1944 and was director-general of personnel there until July 1945. He again escaped from Whitehall, on promotion to air marshal, as air commander in Burma (August 1945 to November 1946) and then as head of Bomber Command (January to October 1947). In October 1947, however, Lord Tedder, chief of the air staff, had him appointed air member for personnel (AMP) and gave him the vital task of building the third RAF, to replace the air forces that had been virtually extinguished at the end of each world war.

For two years, until October 1949, Saunders was responsible for attempting, after the distortions caused by rapid demobilization in 1945–6, to create a balanced service, capable of operating swiftly and effectively in many parts of the world. He also had to incorporate, for the first time, national servicemen into a regular force, and cope with rates of pay and working conditions that were poor. Worse still was an ever-widening gap between the quality of both aircraft and ground equipment left over from 1945 and that needed to face alarming challenges from the Soviet Union, culminating in the Berlin airlift (1948–9). All this was against a background of severe austerity, as Britain tried to recover from the immense costs of a long war. Tedder and Saunders organized a major conference in May 1949 which was intended to harmonize service and civilian needs for men and women of intelligence and technical skill. Its object was 'so to dovetail civil and military employments as to make them continuous parts of the recipient's general education and development and not, as they have been in the past, phases which interrupt each other' (Narracott, 6).

Saunders was promoted to air chief marshal in May 1950 and served as the RAF's inspector general until he was appointed to command air forces western Europe (January–April 1951) and then to be air deputy to General Dwight D. Eisenhower, supreme allied commander, Europe, until September 1953. He became special air adviser to the Danish ministry of defence and head of the Royal Danish Air Force from June 1954 to July 1956. In retirement he found many occupations: chief co-ordinator of Anglo-American hospitality activities in the United Kingdom (1956–9), vice-chairman of the National Savings Committee (1956–70), and ten years on the council of the RAF Benevolent Fund.

Saunders was appointed CBE in July 1941, CB in June 1943, KBE in June 1945, KCB in January 1950, and GCB in June 1953. The president of the Polish republic conferred on him the order of Polonia Restituta in 1945. He was also made an officer of the Légion d'honneur in June 1947, and received from the king of Denmark in November 1956 the grand cross of the order of the Dannebrog. He died at his home, Rhodes House, 1 South Lane, Downton, near Salisbury, Wiltshire, on 8 May 1987. VINCENT ORANGE

Sources C. Shores and others, *Above the trenches: a complete record of the fighter aces and units of the British empire air forces, 1915–1920* (1990), 331–2 • A. H. Narracott, 'Biography: Air Marshal Sir Hugh W. L. Saunders', *RAF Quarterly*, new ser., 2 (Jan 1950), 4–7 • P. H. Liddle, *The airman's war, 1914–18* (1987) • T. I. G. Gray, ed., *The Imperial Defence College and the Royal College of Defence Studies, 1927–1977* (1977) • D. Neate, *Scorpion's sting: the story of no. 84 squadron, RAF, 1917–92* (1994) • C. G. Jefford, *The fighting camels: the history of no. 45 squadron, RAF* (privately printed, 1995) • S. Douglas, *Years of combat* (1963) • *The Times* (11 May 1987) • *Daily Telegraph* (12 May 1987) • Burke, *Peerage* (1967) • private information (2004)

Likenesses photograph, repro. in Shores and others, *Above the trenches* • photograph, repro. in Liddle, *Airman's war*

Saunders, John (1811–1895), writer and editor, born at Barnstaple, Devon, on 2 August 1811, was probably the son of John Saunders and his wife, Sarah Northcote, both of Exeter, of whom little is known. Saunders was self-educated and seems to have been left to fend for himself from as early as nine years old. The early 1830s found him living in Lincoln with his sister Mary [*see below*] and working as a publisher. There in 1834 they jointly produced *Songs for the Many, by Two of the People*. The poems won the commendation of Bulwer Lytton and Leigh Hunt, and were reissued in 1838 in a volume entitled *Songs, Sonnets, and Miscellaneous Poems*. About this time Saunders moved to London and married Katherine Nettleship (*d.* 1887), daughter of John Henry Nettleship, merchant of Ostend and Brussels. They had twelve children, nine of whom survived childhood. Their eldest son seems to have become a painter and their eldest daughter, Katherine [*see below*], made a name as a novelist.

In struggling to establish his career in London, Saunders was assisted greatly by Charles Knight, publisher to the Society for the Diffusion of Useful Knowledge, who praised his 'imaginative turn of mind' (Knight, 2.193). Saunders wrote a series of articles on Chaucer for the society's *Penny Magazine*, which formed the basis of an introduction to a modernized version of the *Canterbury Tales*, published in 1845 and reissued in 1889 with illustrations from the Ellesmere manuscript. He was made responsible for the topic of national antiquities in the New Orbis Pictus series, and with Knight wrote the volumes entitled *Old England*. Another important relationship, though one which was to end in conflict, was that with the author William Howitt. In 1840 Saunders collaborated with Howitt in producing *Portraits and Memoirs of Eminent Living Political Reformers*, illustrated by George Hayter and others. In 1846 Saunders founded the *People's Journal*, an illustrated weekly paper; Howitt, along with his wife, Mary, was from the first a regular contributor and soon a joint proprietor. W. J. Linton contributed engravings to the paper, and several series of articles by Harriet Martineau appeared there, including one entitled 'Household education', the plan of which was suggested by Saunders. However, following a disagreement, Howitt broke away to found the rival *Howitt's Journal* in 1847. By the time the two journals were amalgamated in 1849, Saunders had lost his position as editor and was reduced to acting as clerk in a Fulham brewery for several years.

During this period Saunders wrote *Love's Martyrdom*, a quasi-Elizabethan five-act play in blank verse, which describes the conflicts arising from the jealous mistrust by a deformed Lincoln merchant of his faithful fiancée and philandering brother. Tennyson characterized the author as 'a man of *true* dramatical genius'; Landor found in the play 'passages worthy of Shakespeare'; and Dickens also admired it, while suggesting alterations to fit it better for the stage (Saunders, *Love's Martyrdom*, preface). It was produced by John Buckstone at the Haymarket in June 1855, with Barry Sullivan, William Farren, and Helen Faucit playing the leading roles, though it was acted for only seven nights.

From November 1856, together with the dramatist John Westland Marston, Saunders conducted his own *National Magazine*, a finely illustrated monthly to which Walter Thornbury was a major contributor. Though he had resigned his financial interest in the journal as early as 1857, Saunders's first novel, *The Shadow in the House*, appeared as a serial there in 1860–61. He went on to write a further nineteen novels, occasionally in collaboration with his eldest daughter. *Abel Drake's Wife, or, The Story of an Inventor*, in which a strike and other features of life in industrial Lancashire are interwoven with a love story, was the most popular. It was first issued in 1862 and frequently reprinted. *Hirell, or, Love Born of Strife* (3 vols., 1869), detailing the tragic consequences of an encounter between a philandering English aristocrat and the daughter of a stern Welsh Calvinist, was dedicated to Gladstone. *Israel Mort, Overman*, serialized in the *Cardiff Weekly Times* in 1874 and published in three volumes in 1876, was a powerful story of life in the south Wales coalfields; it was dedicated to Lord Aberdare, Gladstone's home secretary, who had sponsored legislation protecting miners. Saunders also returned to the drama successfully during the 1870s.

Arkwright's Wife, a story of the inventor of the spinning jenny written in collaboration with Tom Taylor, was performed in Leeds before opening at the Globe, London, in October 1873 and running through the season. This was followed by a dramatization of his most popular novel under the title *Abel Drake*, again in collaboration with Taylor, which ran at the Royal Princess's Theatre in London following provincial performances in 1874. Saunders's last novel to appear in volume was *Miss Vandeleur* (3 vols., 1884), following syndication by Tillotsons Fiction Bureau. However, a number of later serial works never appeared in book form, including 'Atonement' and 'Ezekiel Rodda' which ran respectively in *Lloyd's Weekly* (1891) and *The People* (1892).

Saunders's financial circumstances were precarious almost throughout his life. Publishing ventures had led him into bankruptcy in both 1838 and 1848, and he was forced to apply to the Royal Literary Fund on a dozen occasions between 1839 and 1894. His name was twice put forward for a civil-list pension, the first time in 1883 with the support of George Eliot and Charles Reade and the second in 1894 sponsored by Walter Besant and R. D. Blackmore. However, both proposals failed. Saunders died at his home at 3 Orchard Cottages, Lower Richmond Road, Surrey, on 29 March 1895, and was buried at Richmond cemetery.

Saunders's sister Mary made her name as a novelist rather earlier. She was known as **Mary Bennett** (1813–1899), following her marriage on 12 February 1838 to John Bennett (1815–1894), publisher, journalist, and novelist. At the same time she had begun to write a series of popular historical melodramas in the style of Harrison Ainsworth, including *The Jew's Daughter* (1837), *The Cottage Girl* (1838), and *The Gipsey Bride* (1840), all of which appeared in weekly numbers and were still being reprinted in the 1880s. With her husband she collaborated on a number of literary projects, including editing the *Boys' and Girls' Companion* from 1857, and writing for John Maxwell's periodicals. Among her last publications was a series of articles in the early 1870s in the *Dublin University Magazine*, where her husband held an editorial position. She made a series of applications to the Royal Literary Fund from 1879, and lived in penury following the deaths of her husband and brother. She died on 1 December 1899 at 39 Churchfield Mansions, Fulham.

Saunders's daughter **Katherine Saunders** (1839/40–1894), later Katherine Cooper on her marriage in 1876 to the Revd Richard Cooper, rector of Swayfield, Lincolnshire, from 1878, published more than a dozen works of fiction, many with nautical or Welsh settings. Her first effort was the tale 'Matthew's Puzzle', written at the age of sixteen, which was later included in the novel *Martin Pole* (2 vols., 1863), published under her father's name. She also collaborated with him on *The Lion in the Path* (3 vols., 1875), a romance set during the reign of James II. Her better-known works included: the tales collected under the title *Gideon's Rock* (1874); the triple-decker *The High Mills* (1875); the novella *Sebastian* (1878), a coy tale of an Anglican clergyman's brush with martyrdom, initially serialized in *Macmillan's Magazine*; and *Nearly in Port, or, Phoebe Mostyn's Love Story* (1886), the first of a series of devotional novels for the Religious Tract Society. She died shortly before her father, on 7 August 1894 in Swayfield. GRAHAM LAW

Sources BL, Royal Literary Fund Archives, file 974 (1839–96) • *The Echo* (3 April 1895) • *The Times* (4 April 1895) • *Richmond and Twickenham Times* (6 April 1895) • *The Athenaeum* (6 April 1895) • W. Besant, *Queen* (20 April 1895) • C. Knight, *Passages of a working life*, 3 vols. (1864–5), 2.193, 322; 3.11, 20 • private information (1897) • Boase, *Mod. Eng. biog.* • Crockford (1870–95) • J. Saunders, *Love's martyrdom: a play and a poem*, 2nd edn (1882), preface, v–xiv • *The Times* (12 June 1855) [review of performance of *Love's martyrdom*] • *Era* (17 June 1855) [review of performance of *Love's martyrdom*] • *The Times* (8 Oct 1873) [review of performance of *Arkwright's wife*] • *Era* (12 Oct 1873) [review of performance of *Arkwright's wife*] • *Era* (18 Oct 1874) [review of performance of *Abel Drake*] • *BL cat.* • *Wellesley index* • *DNB* • d. cert. [Katherine Saunders] • m. cert. [Mary Bennett] • d. cert. [Mary Bennett]

Archives BL, letters to Royal Literary Fund, loan 96

Saunders, John Cunningham (1773–1810), ophthalmic surgeon, the youngest son of John Cunningham Saunders and his wife, Jane, formerly Tasker, was baptized on 10 October 1773 at St James's Church, Huish by Hatherleigh, Devon. He was sent to school at Tavistock when he was eight years old, and afterwards to South Molton, where he remained until 1790. He was then apprenticed to John Hill, surgeon, of Barnstaple, for five years and went subsequently to London, where in 1795 he entered the combined hospitals, St Thomas's and Guy's, in Southwark. An enthusiastic student of anatomy under Astley Paston Cooper, whose house pupil he was and to whom he acted as dresser, in 1797 he was appointed demonstrator in that subject at St Thomas's Hospital. He resigned his demonstratorship in 1801 and went into the country for a short time, but on his return to London in 1803 he was reappointed demonstrator, and held this post until his death. On 7 April 1803 he married Jane Louisa, daughter of Daniel Colkett. Their only daughter died in infancy.

With John Richard Farre (1775–1862) Saunders was a co-founder of a charitable institution established to care for diseases of the eye and ear. As the London Infirmary for Curing Diseases of the Eye, it opened for patients in Bloomfield Street, Moorfields, on 25 March 1805. Within a few years treatment was limited to diseases of the eye. In 1899 it moved to City Road and became Moorfields Eye Hospital.

Saunders was an able surgeon and a skilful operator. He was the first surgeon to devote himself exclusively to ophthalmology and he made significant contributions to this speciality, notably in the management of congenital cataracts. His first book, written under the influence of Astley Cooper, was *Anatomy of the human ear, with a treatise of its diseases, the causes of deafness and their treatment* (1806), which went through three editions. His second, *A Treatise on some Practical Points Relating to Diseases of the Eye* (1811), was published posthumously by J. R. Farre. A new edition was issued in 1816 at the expense of the institution and for the benefit of his widow.

Saunders became ill in 1809 with severe pain in the head

and then partial paralysis. He died, of a cerebral haemorrhage, on 9 February 1810 at his residence in Ely Place, Holborn. He was buried in St Andrew's, Holborn, on 21 February 1810. His wife survived him.

D'A. POWER, *rev.* NOEL RICE

Sources J. R. Farre, *A treatise on some practical points relating to diseases of the eye by the late John Cunningham Saunders* (1816), 5–35 • E. T. Collins, *The history and traditions of the Moorfields Eye Hospital: one hundred years of ophthalmic discovery and development* (1929) • N. Weir, *Otolaryngology: an illustrated history* (1990) • N. S. Rice, 'John Cunningham Saunders (1773–1810): his contribution to the surgery of congenital cataracts', *Documenta Ophthalmologica*, 81 (1992), 43–51 • parish register, 10 Oct 1773, Huish by Hatherleigh, Devon, St James [baptism]

Likenesses A. Condon, stipple (after A. W. Devis), repro. in J. C. Saunders, *A treatise on some practical points relating to diseases of the eye* (1811) • A. W. Devis, portrait, Moorfields Eye Hospital, London

Saunders, Katherine (1839/40–1894). *See under* Saunders, John (1811–1895).

Saunders, Lawrence (*d.* 1555), protestant martyr, was the son of Thomas Saunders (*d.* 1528) of Sibbertoft, Northamptonshire, and his wife, Margaret Cave. The judge Sir Edward *Saunders was his elder brother. In 1538 he was elected from Eton to King's College, Cambridge, where he graduated BA in 1541. He then left university and was bound apprentice to Sir William Chester in London, but returned to Cambridge on the voluntary cancelling of his indenture. He proceeded MA in 1544 and had received the degree of DTh by the time he was granted a licence to preach in the early months of Edward VI's reign.

Around the same time Saunders was appointed divinity reader at Fotheringhay College, Northamptonshire. In this position, according to John Foxe, Saunders 'by doctrine and life … edified the godly, drew many ignorant to Gods true knowledge, and stopped the mouth of the adversary' (Foxe, *Actes and Monuments*, 1583, 1494). After the dissolution of the college he was made reader at Lichfield Cathedral by Protector Somerset in July 1548. It was while he was at Lichfield that he married a woman named Joanna, with whom he had a son, Samuel. He subsequently became rector of Church Langton in Leicestershire, and on 27 August 1552 prebendary of Botevant in York Minster. On 28 March 1553 he was collated by Archbishop Cranmer to the rectory of All Hallows, Bread Street, in London, a plum living which had been earlier intended by the privy council for John Knox.

After Mary's succession Saunders continued to preach in both London and Leicestershire. According to Foxe, Saunders's arrest in 1554 was proceeded by an apparently chance meeting with Sir John Mordaunt, a councillor to Queen Mary, who advised him against preaching. When Saunders rejected this advice Mordaunt immediately went to Bishop Bonner to inform him of Saunders's intentions. In the meantime Saunders returned to his lodgings, where:

> because hee seemed to bee somewhat troubled, one whiche was with him there, asked him how he did: In very dede (sayeth he) I am in prison til I be in prison: meaning that his mind was unquiet, until he hadde preached, and that then he shoulde haue quietnesse of mind, though he were put in prison. (Foxe, *Actes and Monuments*, 1583, 1494)

Saunders was arrested in October 1554, having just given a sermon at All Hallows, Bread Street, and spent the next three months in a London prison. On 29 January 1555 he was arraigned by Bishop Stephen Gardiner at Southwark Cathedral, convicted of heresy, and executed by burning at Coventry on 8 February 1555. The decision to execute him in Coventry may have been taken in reference to the known protestantism of this midlands town, or to Saunders's evangelical work in nearby Lichfield, or to his family background in Northamptonshire. After his martyrdom Joanna Saunders went into exile with Robert and Lucy Harrington. The latter died shortly afterwards and by 18 June 1556 Robert Harrington had married Saunders's widow and had probably adopted his son.

Many of Saunders's letters were published in 1564 in the collection edited by Miles Coverdale entitled *Certain Most Godly, Fruitful, and Comfortable Letters of True Saintes and Holy Martyrs of God*. These are addressed from prison, probably the Marshalsea, to people who included Ridley and Latimer in Oxford, Saunders's wife (although it is worth noting that her first name, Joanna, is not used by her husband in these letters), the godly in Lichfield, and Lucy and Robert Harrington. A number of the letters addressed specifically to Lucy Harrington contain passionate spiritual guidance, while in one of his letters to his wife Saunders gives precise directions about the shirt he wishes to wear on the day of his execution, writing, 'Wyfe I would you sent me my shirte which you know wherunto it is consecrated. Let it be sowed downe of both the sydes and not open' (Coverdale, 205). Saunders has also been credited with the authorship of the tract *A trewe mirrour of glase, wherin we maye beholde the wofull state of thys our realme of Englande, set forth in a dialogue or communication betwene Eusebius and Theophilus* (1556; *STC* 21777), but there are doubts about the accuracy of this ascription.

Two letters apparently written by Edward Saunders to Lawrence while the latter was in prison were published by Foxe in the 1583 edition of *Actes and Monuments*. In them Edward tries to persuade his younger brother to give up his heretical opinions. It seems at least possible that the source of these letters was Saunders's widow, Joanna. Their tone and the Catholic beliefs they express are such that Edward himself would almost certainly not have wanted to see them published after 1558.

TOM BETTERIDGE

Sources J. Foxe, *Actes and monuments* (1563) • J. Foxe, *Actes and monuments*, 4th edn, 2 vols. (1583) • M. Coverdale, ed., *Certain most godly, fruitful, and comfortable letters* (1564) • D. MacCulloch, *Thomas Cranmer: a life* (1996) • Venn, *Alum. Cant.*, 1/4.14

Archives BL, Harley MS 416 • BL, Lansdowne MS 389 • Emmanuel College, Cambridge, MS 260, fols. 42, 123, 254 • Emmanuel College, Cambridge, MS 262, fols. 166, 167, 169

Likenesses woodcut (being burned at the stake), NPG; repro. in H. Holland, *Herōologia* (1620)

Saunders, Margaret (1686–1745), actress, was born in Weymouth, Dorset, the daughter of Jonathan Saunders, a wine cooper, and the granddaughter on her mother's side of Captain Wallis, a 'sea officer'. According to *The History of* *the English Stage* she was educated at a boarding-school in Steeple Ashton, Wiltshire, and apprenticed to Mrs Fane, a milliner, of Catherine Street, Strand, London. Margaret apparently provided information herself for this source, which reports that she made her début at Drury Lane 'at the earnest Request of her hearty friend Mrs Oldfield, tho' but 16 Years of Age' (Betterton, 161).

Mrs Saunders's earliest recorded performance was as Flareit in Colley Cibber's *Love's Last Shift* on 18 October 1707 at the Queen's Theatre. The numerous roles she played that year, including Mrs Littlewit in Ben Jonson's *Bartholomew Fair*, Fainlove in Richard Steele's *The Tender Husband*, Lucy in William Congreve's *The Old Bachelor*, and Lady Haughty in Jonson's *The Silent Woman*, suggest this was not her first season with the company. She moved between the Haymarket and Drury Lane, taking an annual shared benefit, and was considered 'a very good actress in parts of decayed widows, nurses and old maids' (Davies, 3.259). For her 1709 performance as Dorothy in Susannah Centlivre's *The Man's Bewitched*, she came to the attention of the *Female Tatler*, which commented: 'nor is Mrs Saunders, though ranked below Belinda [Oldfield], to be less applauded for her natural trembling and faltering in her speech when she apprehended Sir Jeffrey to be a ghost' (Morgan, 140). In 1710 she returned to Drury Lane for a salary of £50, and remained with the company until her retirement. Her parts included Emilia in *Othello*, Dol in Jonson's *The Alchemist*, and Busie in John Gay's *The Wife of Bath*, as well as such roles as Lady Laycock in Thomas Betterton's *The Amorous Widow*, Lady Wishfort in Congreve's *The Way of the World*, and Widow Lackit in Thomas Southerne's *Oroonoko*. The final performance recorded for her was as Tattleaid in Steele's *The Funeral* on 13 April 1721.

After her asthmatic condition forced her to retire—'my ill State of Health obliged me to quit it [the stage] in 1720' (Betterton, 73)—Mrs Saunders seems to have remained a dependant in Ann Oldfield's household, and much detail about her comes as a result of her lifelong friendship with Oldfield. In 1709 Saunders witnessed Oldfield's contract with Owen Swiny at the Haymarket. In 1712 she wrote to the Churchills, patrons of Oldfield and her husband, Maynwaring, with an account of Maynwaring's illness. Saunders nursed Ann through her final illness and organized her funeral with a care satirized by Alexander Pope. Ann left her an annuity of £10 as the only non-family beneficiary in her will. E. Curll dedicated his *Faithful Memoirs of Ann Oldfield* to Saunders in 1731.

After Oldfield's death there is little information about Margaret Saunders, who returned to the stage one final time as Lady Wishfort for Mrs Younger's benefit performance on 11 March 1743. The following January, Covent Garden gave her her own benefit in which she did not perform: *Julius Caesar*, as commanded by the prince of Wales. The playbill for this production makes much of Margaret's reduced circumstances and illness. She died, unmarried, some time before 6 March 1745, when her will was proved by her sister Anne Morrison of Martlett Court, Bow Street. In her will she left a picture of Oldfield and one of herself to Mrs French of Bushey, Hertfordshire, and £20 and a ring to Newborough Swingland for 'the care and pains taken by him in my affairs' (*BDA*). J. Milling

Sources Highfill, Burnim & Langhans, *BDA* · T. Betterton, [W. Oldys and others], *The history of the English stage* (1741) · T. Davies, *Dramatic miscellanies*, 3 vols. (1784) · J. Lafler, *The celebrated Mrs Oldfield* (1989) · E. L. Avery, ed., *The London stage, 1660–1800*, pt 2: *1700–1729* (1960) · A. H. Scouten, ed., *The London stage, 1660–1800*, pt 3: *1729–1747* (1961) · F. Morgan, ed., *The female tatler* (1992) · W. Egerton [E. Curll], *Faithful memoirs of the life, amours and performance of … Anne Oldfield* (1731) · BL, Add. MS 61461, fol. 165
Archives BL, Add. MS 61461, fol. 165

Saunders, Sir Owen Alfred (**1904–1993**), engineer and university administrator, was born on 24 September 1904 at 53 Rudloe Road, Streatham, London, the only son of Alfred George Saunders (1877–1954), engineer, and his wife, Margaret Ellen (1877–1935), daughter of David Jones, believed to have been descended from Owain Glyn Dŵr. He had one sister, Nancy Gwynneth Myfanwy, who became a concert pianist. His parents were both gifted, his father being the inventor and designer of the Beckmeter petrol pump, which at one time almost monopolized the forecourts of petrol filling stations in Britain. He eventually rose to become managing director of the engineering firm Beck & Co. Saunders's mother was a teacher who had a great influence on his formative years. His formal education began at Emanuel School, Wandsworth Common, where he remained from 1913 to 1919. He then left school and studied at home. During his last year at school, where he reached the classical upper sixth form, he won the school prizes in both chemistry and logic, though he had not attended the lessons in either, much to the embarrassment of the headmaster and his colleagues. He enrolled at Birkbeck College in January 1921, joining the chemistry department, and achieved a first-class pass in the London University external general science degree in June 1923. After attending evening classes in honours physics he won a scholarship to Trinity College, Cambridge, in December 1922, entering the college in October 1923. He obtained first-class honours in part one of the mathematical tripos in June 1924, having been awarded an additional open scholarship in mathematics and physics at Trinity in March of that year.

Saunders was offered several possible lines of research in Cambridge but decided to undertake applied research as it was better paid. He joined the fuel research station at Greenwich early in 1927. There he was involved in the design and performance of industrial furnaces from 1928 until 1931, working with Dr Margaret *Fishenden. They jointly produced a book, *The Calculation of Heat Transmission*, which was published in 1932 and rapidly established itself as a reference book and a classic text. While at Greenwich, Saunders continued his connection with the external department of London University and obtained the BSc in special mathematics with first-class honours in part one in 1927 and part two in 1928. Finally, in 1929, he was awarded an MSc in physics.

In 1932 Saunders was appointed a lecturer in applied

mathematical physics at Imperial College; Margaret Fishenden also joined the staff. Saunders gave a ten-lecture course on the new subject of heat transfer, which was a great success. Unlike that of many specialists, his style was clear, relaxed, and authoritative. On 27 July 1935 he married Marion Isabel McKechney (1908–1981); they had two daughters and a son. Saunders became the first Clothworkers' reader in thermodynamics at Imperial College in 1937, an appointment which he held until 1946. By 1939 his work had extended to designing and testing ejector exhaust systems for piston aero-engines. In 1942 he was seconded to the Ministry of Aircraft Production as deputy director of turbine engine research. This led to contacts with Frank Whittle and his jet engine team under the overall leadership of Dr Roxbee Cox, later Lord King's Norton. He made valuable contributions to the design of combustion chambers and other items connected with this new form of aircraft propulsion.

By 1946 Saunders had returned to Imperial College and was appointed to the chair of mechanical engineering and headship of the department, in which post he continued until September 1964, retaining his connections with engineering work relating to defence. He was chairman of the naval engineering committee and strongly supported the use of aero-derivative gas turbines in place of the steam turbines hitherto used for the propulsion of naval ships. In addition to overseeing skilfully a substantial building programme at Imperial College, Saunders recruited several gifted members of staff who distinguished themselves in fields derived from his work. Saunders's achievements were recognized by his election to fellowship of the Royal Aeronautical Society, of the Institute of Fuel in 1957, and of the Royal Society in 1958. He became president of the Institution of Mechanical Engineers in 1960 and an honorary fellow in 1965, the year in which he was created knight bachelor. He served on the Council for Scientific and Industrial Research until its dissolution in 1965, and in 1962–3 was a member of the committee which produced *Engineering Design* (the Feilden report), which became a bestseller. He retired from headship of the Imperial College mechanical engineering department in 1964 and was elected pro-rector, in which post he served for the nominal term of two years. With the sudden death of Sir Patrick Linstead, Saunders found himself acting as rector from 1966 to 1967, in which year he became vice-chancellor of the University of London, a post he filled until 1969. When the university wished to merge Bedford College and the Royal Holloway College, Saunders played a major part, becoming the first chairman of the council of the combined college.

On retirement from the vice-chancellorship Saunders sought to spend more time in his country house at Middleton-on-Sea, Sussex, and to see more of his family. His first wife, Marion, died in January 1981, and on 18 July the same year he married Mrs Daphne Holmes (*b*. 1909), who had been a close friend of Marion and Saunders for many years. In his later years he suffered from failing eyesight and his knee joints troubled him, so that his visits to London became less frequent. Nevertheless he had a warm reunion with Sir Frank Whittle after the latter was appointed to the Order of Merit in 1986.

Saunders was remembered as a very clever academic and engineer who made no enemies but had great achievements to his credit, including the unexpected one of being a member of the Magic Circle—a skill on which he drew at many family and office Christmas parties. He died in Reigate, Surrey (where he and his second wife had moved in 1989), on 10 October 1993, and was buried at Randells Park crematorium, Leatherhead, on 15 October. He was survived by his second wife and by two of his three children, the elder of his two daughters having predeceased him. G. B. R. FEILDEN

Sources H. Ford, *Memoirs FRS*, 41 (1995), 379–94 · *The Independent* (15 Oct 1993) · *The Times* (18 Oct 1993) · *The Guardian* (9 Nov 1993) · *WWW, 1991–5* · personal knowledge (2004) · private information (2004) · b. cert.

Archives RS, autobiographical notes

Likenesses photograph, *c*.1960, repro. in Ford, *Memoirs FRS*, 378 · M. Noakes, oils, 1967, ICL; repro. in *The Independent* · photograph, repro. in *The Times*

Wealth at death under £125,000: probate, 5 Nov 1993, *CGPLA Eng. & Wales*

Saunders, Richard (1613–1675), medical practitioner and astrologer, was born on 2 May 1613, probably in a house known as Saunders' Manor in Bedworth, Knightlow, Warwickshire, the youngest child of William Saunders and his wife, Elizabeth, daughter of R. Purifoy of Drayton in Leicestershire. The Saunders family, originally from Northamptonshire, had settled in Warwickshire by the sixteenth century. The family arms appear in engravings of 1653 and 1671. According to one authority, the manor was held 'of the King as of the earldom of Warwick' (*VCH Warwickshire*, 6.28). Richard had four brothers, Michael, the male heir, Humphrey, Roger, and Nicholas, and one sister, Maria.

Saunders and his wife, Elizabeth, had four sons and one daughter; as an astrologer, he took an interest in the hours of their birth. His son Charles was born on 22 November 1652 at 10.20 p.m. and baptized on 3 December at 3.30 p.m. Another son, Richard, was born in 1654, attended St John's College, Oxford, and later, in 1673, became a student of Lincoln's Inn. Nothing is known of Saunders's own education. He was widely read in his field, and appears to have been literate in Latin, Greek, and Hebrew. With regard to his career, he may have been at one time a 'baker in London's Grub Street' (Capp, 329). From at least 1650 until his death in 1675 he resided at the Three Cranes, Chancery Lane, and earned his living as a medical practitioner and astrologer. Although obscured by the huge reputation of William Lilly, Saunders was not an insignificant astrologer or physician, and was quite renowned in his day.

Saunders was probably most widely known as the author of the almanac *Apollo Anglicanus*, which he published every year from 1654 until his death. Indeed, it continued to be published in his name, then in the name of one Richard Saunder, until at least 1781. However, his first publication was an expensive and profusely illustrated folio entitled *Physiognomie and Chiromancie, Metoposcopie* (1653). This was his major work and brought him to the notice of the wealthy buyers of such books. In 1671 he put out a second, slightly enlarged, edition, again in folio, at a price of 10 shillings. Between 1663 and 1676 there were four editions of another work, entitled *Palmistry*, which was basically a cheaper pocket version of the 1653 folio, aimed at a wider market.

Saunders's work was not original, being essentially compilations from and translations of earlier and contemporary continental works such as those of Michael Scot, Paracelsus, Della Porta, Cardano, Goclenius, Robert Fludd, and Jean Belot. Apart from a small piece entitled *Two Groatsworth of Wit for a Penny, or, The English Fortune-Teller*, (*c*.1675), which he co-authored with Dr Coelson, his only other work, *The Astrological Judgment and Practice of Physick*, was published posthumously in 1677. Once again it appears to be a composite work reflecting his practice as an astrological physician.

Saunders was a member of William Lilly's circle, and acted as physician to Lilly and Elias Ashmole. He was referred to explicitly in condemnations and praises of astrologers alongside the more familiar names of Wharton, Gadbury, Booker, and Culpeper. Lilly once referred to him as 'Philotheoros'. However, he seems to have been closest to Ashmole who, apart from being godfather to Richard's son Charles, also bought some of Saunders's books after he died. He stands out from the rest of Lilly's circle in that he seems to have been the only one to have published on physiognomy.

In religion Saunders was probably Anglican. Politically, he blew with the wind. In 1654 he followed Lilly in supporting Cromwell, yet he was a monarchist at heart and welcomed the Restoration. In 1653, the year of Barebone's Parliament, he advocated the abolition of lawyers, an important theme during this period. Yet in the same year he could write 'most of those that have the forehead [great and spatious], are people of good consciences, not given to do any hurt, they are very fit to become lawyers' (R. Saunders, *Physiognomie*, 161). As with Lilly, Saunders was critical of both established medical and scientific authorities as well as quacks and Gypsies. The signs of degeneration he saw around him in the tempestuous 1650s and 1660s led him to dream of improving the human race by scientific breeding, an idea he probably derived from Campanella's *Civitas solis* (1643). Among other things this involved observing the stars in the process of reproduction. This astrological medical view had a political nuance to it in that Saunders combined it with apocalyptic speculation on a 'sabbatical revolution' (Capp, 173) and a 'messianic emperor' (Capp, 171). He died at his home, the Three Cranes, on 23 December 1675, between the hours of 10 a.m. and 11 a.m.

M. H. PORTER

Sources B. S. Capp, *Astrology and the popular press: English almanacs, 1500–1800* (1979) • W. Camden, *The visitation of the county of Warwick in the year 1619*, ed. J. Fetherston, Harleian Society, 12 (1877), 371 • *Elias Ashmole (1617–1692): his autobiographical and historical notes*, ed. C. H. Josten, 5 vols. (1966 [i.e. 1967]) • *VCH Warwickshire*, 6.28 • A. C. Fox-Davies, ed., *Armorial families: a directory of gentlemen of coat-armour*, 7th edn, 2 (1929), 1718–19 • L. G. H. Horton-Smith, *The Saunders and Lumley families of the county of Northampton in the 16th century* (1941) • T. H. Saunders, *The Saunders, Sanders, Sandars family and its blood connections* (privately printed, Liverpool, [1932])

Archives N. Yorks. CRO, book of palmistry with horoscopes | Bodl. Oxf., MSS Ashmole

Likenesses T. Cross, line engraving, BM, NPG; repro. in R. Saunders, *Physiognomie and chiromancie* (1653) • line engraving, BM, NPG; repro. in R. Saunders, *The astrological judgment and practice of physick* (1677) • line engraving, BM, NPG

Saunders, Richard Huck- (1720–1785), physician, whose parents were named Huck (his mother's maiden name was Harrison), was born Richard Huck, in Westmorland. He was educated, under the direction of his uncle, at the grammar school of Croughland in Cumberland, where he received extensive training in Latin. Huck intended to continue his classical studies at Oxford, under the direction of another uncle, but a fall from a hay cart, which resulted in a fractured leg, prevented him from doing so. As a result of this injury and his subsequent convalescence, however, he decided that he wanted to pursue a career in surgery.

After a five-year apprenticeship with a surgeon at Penrith named Neal, Huck became a student at St Thomas's Hospital, London, where he was a pupil of John Girle. In 1745 he entered the army, and was appointed surgeon to Lord Sempill's regiment, the 25th foot, which fought at Culloden the next year. Huck served with the regiment until the peace of 1748. He then settled at Penrith, and on 13 October 1749 received the degree of MD from Marischal College, Aberdeen, after being 'examined with a solution of a case of medicine and aphorism of Hippocrates'. He practised at Penrith for two years, and in 1750 he was appointed surgeon to the 33rd regiment, which was then at Minorca. Saunders remained there for three years. From 1753 to 1755, while quartered with his regiment at Edinburgh, he took the opportunity to attend the medical classes at Edinburgh University. He returned briefly to England and then went to America under the earl of Loudoun, by whom he was promoted to the rank of physician to the army. As physician he served during the Seven Years' War. After the successful expedition against Havana, in 1762, he returned to England in poor health. Nevertheless, he immediately began a continental tour. Throughout this period he corresponded at length with Sir John Pringle.

Saunders finally settled in Spring Gardens, London, as a physician, and was admitted a licentiate of the Royal College of Physicians on 1 April 1765. He was elected a fellow of the college, *speciali gratia*, on 18 September 1784, and was elected a fellow of the Royal Society in 1768. Huck became physician to the Middlesex Hospital in September 1766, and physician to St Thomas's Hospital on 14 December 1768, when he resigned his office at the former institution. He held his post at St Thomas's until 1777, when he was succeeded by Henry Revell Reynolds. That same year he married Jane Saunders (*d*. 1780), niece and heir of Admiral Sir Charles *Saunders; he thus acquired a large fortune, both in land and money. In addition, he assumed the name and armorial bearings of the Saunders family. The couple had two daughters: Anne, who married Robert Dundas, second Viscount Melville, in August 1796; and

Jane, who became the wife of John Fane, tenth earl of Westmorland, in 1800.

Saunders died in the West Indies on 24 July 1785, leaving 'a reputation for humanity, candor, disinterestedness, and medical knowledge' (*Medical Commentaries*, 12).

W. W. Webb, *rev.* Jeffrey S. Reznick

Sources 'A short account of the late Dr John Parsons, Dr Richard Huck Saunders, Dr Charles Colingnol, and Sir Alexander Dick', *Medical Commentaries* [Edinburgh], 10 (1786), 12, 322 ff. • Munk, *Roll* • Burke, *Gen. GB* (1940) • private information (1897)

Wealth at death probably very wealthy through marriage to heiress Jane Saunders

Saunders, Thomas (1712/13–1775), administrator in India, was appointed as an eighteen-year-old writer in the company's service in 1731, possibly through connections on his mother's side, the family of Thomas Hall, an influential ship's husband. Nothing else is known about his antecedents or early life. He was sent first to Sumatra, an outpost of the company; his private commercial prospects were not promising because his father could only provide him with a small starting capital. However, he was soon transferred to the hub of the company's business on the Coromandel coast in India, rising steadily over the next twenty years in the service, with postings at Vizagapatam, Ingeram, and Fort St David. He obviously recommended himself to the directors for his probity and ability, because in 1750 he was put in charge of all the company's operations on the coast, replacing Governor Charles Floyer, who was dismissed with other councillors for gaming and allowing 'Extravagant Expenses' and for 'the general neglect and want of order in every branch of our Affairs' (Love, 2.418).

Saunders had not only to clean up the company's service at Madras, but also to cope with an emerging unstable political situation among the Mughal authorities governing the Carnatic, where the company traded. At the end of the War of the Austrian Succession (1740–48), during which the French and British had attacked each other's main settlements on the Coromandel coast, the peace of Aix-la-Chapelle had supposedly restored the political *status quo ante* between the warring Europeans in India. But soon after, the French, under their ambitious and dynamic governor Joseph Dupleix, chose to intervene in the contest in progress between rivals to become nawab of the Carnatic, by giving military support to the claims of Chanda Sahib. Fearing that if Chanda were successful, Dupleix would use his influence to hobble severely the company's commerce, if not exclude it altogether from the Carnatic, Saunders and his council, without reference to London but also without any initial imperial intent, decided to back the rival Indian prince Muhammad Ali Khan. Saunders's general conduct was later strongly approved by the directors. The war which ensued lasted for eleven years, long after the murder of Chanda Sahib in 1752 and the end of Saunders's term of office in 1755, being transformed by the outbreak of the Seven Years' War in 1756 into essentially an Anglo-French struggle to become masters of the Carnatic and other areas in India.

In the first phase of the war (1750–55), until substantial national military and naval forces were introduced in 1756, neither side could field armies big enough to deal a decisive blow to the other. Operations resolved themselves into a few skirmish battles and a prolonged blockade of Trichinopoly, the most important fortified town in the interior, held by Muhammad Ali and his British allies, who usually had fewer forces than the French and their allies. In consequence, the British were generally on the defensive, sometimes desperately, during Saunders's governorship, despite Clive's celebrated capture and defence of Arcot. The company's military commander-in-chief, Major Stringer Lawrence, sometimes seen as the father of the British Indian army, was a highly professional and redoubtable soldier who played a crucial role in upholding the company's cause. But he was a reluctant associate with Saunders in formulating a grand strategy for the war, and his choleric disposition and support for his favourites among the military led to bruising encounters with the cool and rational civilian governor. Part of the problem lay with the ill-defined division of power and responsibility between the civilians and the military. Lawrence was very prickly over his assumed prerogatives, whereas the governor was designated overall commander-in-chief. Robert Orme, a contemporary Madras civil servant and later first historian of British India, and no friend of Saunders, rated him as having 'a much Superior Sagacity to the Soldier' (Orme to John Payne, director, 26 Oct 1755, BL OIOC, Orme MSS, OV 28, fols. 1–29). Considering that Saunders was confronting complex political and strategic problems of which he had no previous experience, he performed very creditably in defending the company's interests and supporting its armies in the field, especially since, aside from having to placate the cantankerous Lawrence, he was facing the opposition of a self-serving cabal on his own council. He seems to have been equal to the challenge. As Orme later remarked, he was 'the Man on Earth I should dread [most] as an Enemy' (Love, 2.469). And a royal officer serving in the Carnatic at the time, critical of Saunders for the way he was treating his regiment, wrote sourly in his journal that he was 'a man of reported great knowledge in the Company's interest and affairs in India, who did most of the business himself not being of a disposition fond of gayety … he was withal of a cunning turn … seldom speaking but with some design' ('Major Corneille's journal of an expedition to India, in 1754', BL OIOC, MS Eur. B/215, fol. 71).

In 1754, aware of the growing distress among the directors at the seemingly interminable war which had halted trade on the coast and was thrusting the company into horrendous military expense and consequent debt, Saunders negotiated a truce with Dupleix's more cautious and amenable successor, Charles Godeheu. Before events in Europe precipitated a resumption of hostilities in 1756, Saunders resigned for the sake of his health and left for Europe on 14 January 1755, carrying with him what Orme approvingly considered only a 'Moderate fortune' when a corrupt man in his position might have made much more (Orme to John Payne, 26 Oct 1755, BL OIOC, Orme MSS, OV 28, fols. 1–29).

Back in England, Saunders does not appear on the public record again until 1758, when the East India Company director John Payne got him elected to its board as a useful man because of his recent Indian experience. However, Saunders disappointed his patron through scant attendance at the board and discourtesy. Payne wrote to Orme: Saunders 'lives in a most strange way, I think I may almost say despised by all the world' (Parker, 236). Saunders lost his seat the following year and did not return until 1763, as a member of the Clive faction in the great political turmoil which split the company during these years. Although he was made deputy chairman in 1767, Saunders did not progress to the chair, perhaps because, as another director wrote, he had a 'want of knowledge to conduct a party and … a want of skill to debate in General Courts' (ibid., 236). Having fallen out with Clive later that year, Saunders did not contest the company election of 1768, but still remained active in company affairs, representing the interests of its servants in India who were creditors of Muhammad Ali, the nawab of the Carnatic (among whom he probably numbered himself).

Saunders's private life is shadowy. He was married, probably to the sister of Thomas Pitt of Cornwall, and may have lost a son in his early years on the Coromandel coast since there is a record in 1740 of the death of a child called Thomas Saunders at Madras. A second son, also called Thomas Saunders, is mentioned in his will, and there was at least one daughter, Elizabeth, who later married William Pye, of the Pyes of Faringdon, who was wounded at Plassey (1757) as aide-de-camp to Clive. They had a daughter, Elizabeth, who married a Dr Walker. Saunders left a substantial estate, Pittcroft, long associated with the family, at Brill near Aylesbury in Buckinghamshire, to his son; other bequests, to Saunders's brother and sister, are also mentioned. Thomas Saunders died on 16 October 1775 in Upper Brook Street, London, and was interred in the family vault at Brill. Although not perhaps a likeable man, Saunders's solid political achievements in the service of the East India Company have been perhaps unjustly eclipsed by the lustre of Clive and Hastings.

G. J. Bryant

Sources J. G. Parker, 'The directors of the East India Company, 1754–1790', PhD diss., U. Edin., 1977 • H. D. Love, *Vestiges of old Madras, 1640–1800*, 4 vols. (1913) • C. E. Buckland, *Dictionary of Indian biography* (1906) • BL OIOC • Burke, *Gen. GB* (1833) • M. Wilks, *Historical sketches of the south of India, in an attempt to trace the history of Mysoor*, 3 vols. (1810–17) • will, PRO, PROB 11/1014

Archives BL OIOC, India Office and Orme MSS

Wealth at death estate at Brill, value apparently substantial: will, PRO, PROB 11/1014

Saunders, Thomas Harry (1813–1870), paper manufacturer, was born in Limehouse, London, on 19 September 1813, the youngest in the family of two sons and three daughters of John Saunders, hoop bender, and his wife, Mary. Very little is known about his early life. He seems to have entered the paper-making trade in the late 1830s at a boom time and eventually owned six paper mills in Kent and Buckinghamshire, branching out from the family businesses of coal and timber merchants and, especially, seed crushing. His first partnership in a paper mill was in 1840 in Hawley, south of Dartford on the Darent. On 11 July 1844 he married Mary, daughter of Thomas Bold Marchant of Brenchley in Kent. There were no children.

Saunders's mills had a reputation for supplying everything from newsprint (for *The Times* in the 1850s and 1860s) to security paper, in which he built up a huge export business to Europe, the British empire, and South America for stamps and banknotes (his customers included almost all the best-known banks). His name is first found in the watermark of a postage stamp for Barbados as early as 1840. The quality of his paper is confirmed by the fact that he exhibited, and won some twelve prize medals, at international exhibitions from 1851 onwards, though not at the more parochial trade shows. In the run-up to the Great Exhibition of 1851 he produced sample sheets with a watermarked light and shade portrait of Queen Victoria: later these exquisite watermarks became part of his stock-in-trade and were described as a 'degree of perfection … the quintessence of the papermaking craft'. More prosaically it was predicted that they could 'form a valuable addition to bank note paper for the prevention of forgery'.

Saunders's business expanded entirely by acquisition. One of his mills was probably the largest in the country by the 1880s, though it seems not to have been a paper mill when he acquired it. He rebuilt the Phoenix mill in Dartford as one of the major industrial buildings in the south-east of England. During his career he created an 'immense, flourishing and progressive business' of six mills with some eighteen hand-making vats and three paper machines.

On the national scene, during the 1860s Saunders was twice in small deputations to the prime minister, the third Viscount Palmerston, concerning controversy about the abolition of paper duties and the continuing import duties on rags. His evidence to the parliamentary select committee revealed that he was not one of those who believed that straw could ever be an adequate substitute for rags. In 1862, with his mill manager, he took out a patent on an improved way of drying machine-made paper and of regulating the supply of pulp to the paper machine. He was an active nonconformist of Baptist tendencies and employed a metropolitan missionary to preach indoors and out. His substantial charitable activities included strong support of the Shaftesbury Society (though this did not stop his widow owning a public house next to one of the mills). He was also a member of the Royal Society of Arts.

Saunders died on 5 February 1870 at Spring Wood, Dartford, following a debilitating stroke two years earlier which had put an end to his trade activities. His estate was valued at under £120,000.

Colin Cohen, *rev.*

Sources T. H. Saunders, *Illustrations of the British paper manufacture* (1855) • *Dartford Chronicle* (12 Feb 1870) • *The Paper Mills Directory* (1859) [1859 onwards] • management letter-books of *The Times*, News Int. RO • d. cert. • m. cert.

Wealth at death under £120,000: probate, 28 Feb 1870, *CGPLA Eng. & Wales*

Saunders, Thomas William (1814–1890), police magistrate, second son of Samuel E. Saunders of Bath, and his wife, Sarah, was born on 21 February 1814. He was entered as a student at the Middle Temple on 16 April 1832, and called to the bar on 9 June 1837. On 16 August 1854 he married Frances Gregory, daughter of William Galpine of Newport, Isle of Wight; they had a son, William Edgar Saunders (*b.* 1856), a barrister and author. From 1855 to October 1860 Saunders was recorder of Dartmouth, and from that date to 1878 recorder of Bath. For some years he was a revising barrister, and in December 1872 he became a commissioner for hearing municipal election petitions. Richard Assheton Cross appointed him a Metropolitan Police magistrate on 2 September 1878, and he sat at the Thames police court until his resignation a few days before his death. His decisions were seldom reversed, and tended to err on the side of leniency. He was a member of the Reform Club and of the Burlington Fine Arts Club. He died at St Michael's Road, Bournemouth, on 28 February 1890.

Thomas William Saunders (1814–1890), by unknown engraver, pubd 1890

Saunders was author of a great number of works on legal subjects, especially on common law and criminal matters. G. C. Boase, *rev.* Eric Metcalfe

Sources J. Foster, *Men-at-the-bar: a biographical hand-list of the members of the various inns of court*, 2nd edn (1885), 413 • *The Times* (3 March 1890), 7 • *The Times* (4 March 1890), 3 • *The Graphic* (8 March 1890), 275 • *Debrett's Illustrated House of Commons and the Judicial Bench* (1886), 338
Likenesses engraving, NPG; repro. in *The Graphic*, 275 [*see illus.*]
Wealth at death £2843 5*s*. 5*d*.: probate, 14 April 1890, *CGPLA Eng. & Wales*

Saunders, William (1743–1817), physician, was born in 1743 in Banff, Scotland, the son of James Saunders, physician. He was educated at the University of Edinburgh, where he was a pupil and friend of William Cullen. He graduated MD in 1765, with a thesis on antimony.

Saunders began practice in London about 1766, and gave lectures on chemistry with W. Keir at Red Lion Court, and materia medica at Guy's Hospital, which were well attended. He also lectured on medicine and in 1770 became the first in London to advertise clinical lectures. He is said to have made £1000 a year from his lectures, which he published.

Saunders did experiments on lead for Sir George Baker, and it was largely through Baker's influence that he was elected physician to Guy's Hospital in 1770, becoming a governor both there and at St Thomas's Hospital. Saunders helped his friends in their careers, and at the same time the circle of governors at Guy's, as well as former students settled in the army, navy, and East India Company, were a great help to him in establishing his own large practice. Sir William Farquhar was a friend. He was appointed extra-physician to the prince regent in 1807. Saunders was elected licentiate of the Royal College of Physicians in 1769, and a fellow in 1790; he served as censor four times. He was a fellow of the Royal Society of Edinburgh (1792), the Society of Antiquaries, and the Royal Society (1793). His publication on red Peruvian bark (1782), translated into French, German, and Latin, quickly led to the displacement of quilled bark in the treatment of fevers.

In his Goulstonian lectures, which he afterwards published as *A Treatise on the Structure, Economy, and Diseases of the Liver* (1793), Saunders was probably the first English physician to observe that in some forms of cirrhosis the liver became enlarged and afterwards contracted. In his Harveian oration in 1796 he praised the recent discovery of the cause of Devonshire colic by Sir George Baker. He also published between 1768 and 1809 works on mercury, antimony, stones in the bladder, and mineral waters. Saunders never professed to be a profound classical scholar, but was quick and amiable. Astley Cooper said of him that he was a 'most entertaining lecturer, but superficial person, with a considerable share of genius' (Wilks and Bettany, 113).

On 22 May 1805 Saunders was chairman of the meeting which led to the formation of the Medical and Chirurgical Society and he was its first president. He resigned from Guy's Hospital in 1802, and retired from practice in 1814, moving from Russell Square to Enfield, Middlesex, where he died on 29 May 1817. An obituary said he had an 'arterial irregularity about the brain' (*London Medical and Physical Journal*, 392). He was buried in Enfield parish church; his children put up a monument to him in the church and his son J. J. Saunders gave his portrait to the Royal College of Physicians. Norman Moore, *rev.* Jean Loudon

Sources S. Wilks and G. T. Bettany, *A biographical history of Guy's Hospital* (1892), 109–16 • *London Medical and Physical Journal*, 38 (1817), 388–92 • J. M. H. Moll, 'William Saunders, 1743–1817', *Journal of Medical Biography*, 1 (1993), 235 • *GM*, 1st ser., 87/1 (1817), 571 • Munk, *Roll* • location of Dr William Saunders's house, *c*.1790, Wellcome L., RQ529 • *Nomina eorum, qui gradum medicinae doctoris in academia Jacobi sexti Scotorum regis, quae Edinburgi est, adepti sunt, ab anno 1705 ad annum 1845*, University of Edinburgh (1846) • G. Clark and A. M. Cooke, *A history of the Royal College of Physicians of London*, 2 (1966), 571–2 • S. C. Lawrence, *Charitable knowledge: hospital pupils and practitioners in eighteenth-century London* (1996)
Archives Wellcome L., lecture notes
Likenesses C. Townley, mezzotint, pubd 1792 (after L. F. Abbott), BM; repro. in R. Burgess, *Portraits of doctors and scientists in the Wellcome Institute, London* (1973) • J. R. Smith, mezzotint, pubd 1803 (after his earlier work), BM • H. Ashby, oils, 1809, RCP Lond. • H. Meyer, stipple (after drawing by R. W. Satchwell), BM; repro. in

European Magazine (1817) • coloured lithograph, Wellcome L. • photogravure • portrait, repro. in Moll, 'William Saunders, 1743–1817', 235

Saunders, William (1823–1895), newspaper proprietor and politician, was born on 20 November 1823, at Russell Mill, Market Lavington, Wiltshire, the youngest son of Amram Edward Saunders, mill owner, and Mary Box. He was educated at Devizes grammar school. After leaving school he worked for his father at Lavington and Bath, and then opened his own quarries, supplying stone for the construction of the Great Western Railway. On 27 April 1852 he married Caroline Elizabeth, the eldest daughter of L. C. Spender, a physician. In 1860, with the journalist William Hunt, and his brother-in-law, Edward Spender, Saunders started the *Western Morning News* of Plymouth. The paper began as politically independent, but Spender's whig sympathies gradually dominated, giving an anti-radical, and later, anti-home rule bias. Saunders disapproved and eventually severed all connection with the newspaper. In 1864 he founded another penny daily, based on Hull, the *Eastern Morning News*. The following year he acquired the Newcastle upon Tyne *Northern Daily Express*. Taking advantage of the new telegraph service, in 1863 Saunders and Spender set up the Central Press Agency, the first of its kind. An agreement made with Reuters in 1868 allowed the Central Press a monopoly outside London. Although the agency's active promoters were Liberal, they sought to achieve political balance in the stories they supplied. The tory whips were not persuaded that this arrangement was to their party's advantage, and so, in 1871, purchased the agency. Saunders, in breach of the agreement of sale, blithely continued as before until, in 1873, an injunction obliged him to change his agency's name to Central News.

Saunders was a pioneer in syndicating news to his several newspapers, provoking very different responses from his editors. James Macdonell, editor of the *Northern Daily Express*, deprecated the arrangement. 'Under him [Saunders] the *Express* will have no creed, no principles, no anything, but a sneaking determination to pay' (W. R. Nicoll, *James Macdonell, Journalist*, 1890, 107). This was an unfair estimate. For Saunders, his political principles meant much more than profit: he obliged the mainly tory readers of his Hull newspaper to suffer homilies on the sins of landlordism, or the virtues of land nationalization, and would sometimes write to express disagreement with an article or editorial, but he was no tyrant to his editors. His sympathy and advocacy of a variety of radical causes gave Saunders his prominence in local and national affairs. A fanatical supporter of Henry George, he involved himself in various land nationalization campaigns. He was treasurer and a substantial contributor to the unsuccessful English Land Restoration League, which sought to convert agricultural labourers to Georgite ideas. He was also closely associated with Joseph Chamberlain's 'radical' or 'unauthorized programme', on which he fought and won the East Hull parliamentary constituency in 1885. Nominally a Gladstonian Liberal, his support of a Labour candidate against a whig in the neighbouring Central Hull constituency succeeded in splitting the Liberal vote and losing the seat. Neither this, nor his spirited advocacy of 'advanced' ideas, endeared Saunders to the local Liberal Association. In 1886 he lost his parliamentary seat. Undismayed, he was soon involved in a campaign to keep Trafalgar Square open for public meetings, an episode that ended with the futile if notorious 'battle of bloody Sunday' on 13 November 1887. In 1889 he was elected for the Walworth constituency to serve on the newly created London county council. As well as speaking about the taxation of ground values he wrote several substantial pamphlets on the subject, and also a *History of the First London County Council* (1892).

In July 1892 Saunders was again returned to parliament, this time for Walworth, a constituency he retained until his death. At Westminster he once more demonstrated his passionate radicalism, advocating federal home rule, the eight-hour working day, and prohibition. Temperance he saw as a means of radicalizing the Liberal Party. The executive of the United Kingdom Alliance, the leading temperance body, exercised highly centralized, oligarchic rule. Saunders sought the democratization of the alliance, and blamed the leadership for the failure of its campaigns. His disillusion was reflected in his substantially reducing the large contributions he had previously made to the movement.

Saunders died at his home, The Hollies, Market Lavington, on 1 May 1895. He was a man of formidable conviction. He did not always win acclaim or success for his ideas, but he earned and enjoyed the respect of friend and foe alike. A. J. A. MORRIS

Sources J. A. Spender, *Life, journalism and politics*, 1 (1927) • *Weekly Dispatch* (5 May 1895) • *ILN* (13 Feb 1886) • L. Brown, *Victorian news and newspapers* (1985), 33, 92, 116–17, 123 • S. E. Koss, *The rise and fall of the political press in Britain*, 1 (1981), 332 • A. J. Lee, *The origins of the popular press in England, 1855–1914* (1976), 63, 91, 124, 135, 138–9, 144, 152, 254 • T. H. S. Escott, *Masters of English journalism* (1911), 298, 300, 316 • *CGPLA Eng. & Wales* (1895)

Likenesses portrait, repro. in *ILN*, 106 (1895), 570

Wealth at death £9522 0s. 9*d*.: probate, 19 June 1895, *CGPLA Eng. & Wales*

Saunders, William Wilson (1809–1879), entomologist and botanist, was born on 4 June 1809 at Little London, near Wendover, Buckinghamshire, the second son of the Revd James Saunders (1770–1838), rector of Kirtlington, Oxfordshire. His name at birth was William Saunders, but owing to a proliferation of people with the same name, he later opted to include Wilson. This name change was carried out with the blessing of his friend William Wilson, father of George Fergusson Wilson, the chemist.

Saunders was educated privately until 1827, when he was sent to the East India Company's military academy at Addiscombe, Surrey. He passed as an officer, second in examination, and obtained his commission in the Royal Engineers in August 1829. He joined his corps at Chatham immediately, and proceeded to India in August 1830, but resigned the following year. During that year in India, however, he managed to amass a substantial collection of plants and insects which he brought home with him. On

William Wilson Saunders (1809–1879), by Maull & Polyblank, 1855

returning to England, he joined his uncle and future father-in-law, Joshua Saunders, in business as an underwriter at Lloyd's where, for many years, he was a member of the committee, and also of the shipping committee. He settled at East Hill, Wandsworth, Surrey, and in 1832 married his cousin, Catharine Saunders.

Saunders was an enthusiastic naturalist throughout his life, and considered an 'accurate artist in Natural History subjects' (*Entomologist's Monthly Magazine*, 120). It was also believed at the time that few contributed more to the advancement of entomology and botany than Saunders. He was one of the original 101 members of the Entomological Society of London, and was twice its president (1841–2 and 1856–7). He read his first entomological paper, 'On the habits of some Indian insects', to the society on 7 April 1834, and it was published in the *Transactions* (1, 60–66). He also wrote a number of other papers on Indian insects, but his entomological papers numbered no more than thirty in total. He edited *Insecta Saundersiana* (1850–69), which contained descriptions of many of the insects in his collection by Francis Walker, Henri Jekel, and Edward *Saunders, his son. Furthermore, some of the illustrations featured in Hewitson's *Exotic Butterflies* were drawn from specimens in Saunders's collection.

After the death of his first wife Saunders married, on 24 June 1841, Mary Anne (*b.* 1819/20), daughter of Abraham Mello, of Middleton Stoney, Oxfordshire. In 1857 Saunders moved to Hillfield, Reigate, Surrey, where he started the Holmesdale Natural History Club in the same year. At Wandsworth he had made a large herbarium, and at Reigate he established a private museum and a notable well-stocked garden. He accumulated not only a vast collection of insects, but also of plants (including many exotic specimens) from abroad. He edited a number of botanical works including *Refugium botanicum* (1867–73), with descriptions of plants in his possession by Heinrich Gustav Reichenbach, John Gilbert Baker, and others, and illustrated by William Hood Fitch; and two parts of *Mycological Illustrations* (1871 and 1872), edited with Worthington George Smith, and including some of his own illustrations. He contributed materials for Brewer's *Flora of Surrey*, and was also author of more than thirty-five papers between 1831 and 1877.

In 1833 Saunders was elected a fellow of the Linnean Society, of which he acted as treasurer from 1861 until 1873. He was elected FRS on 2 June 1853, and fellow of the Zoological Society in 1861. He was also a treasurer, secretary, and vice-president of the Royal Horticultural Society. In 1873, following the loss of over-insured unseaworthy vessels at sea, and the collapse of the marine insurance business, Saunders was left almost ruined financially; he was forced to dispose of his large collections of insects (mostly to the British Museum and the Hope Museum, at Oxford), plants (both living and dried), and watercolour drawings. In 1874 Saunders retired to Worthing, Sussex, where he devoted himself to horticulture. After the death of his second wife he married, on 10 July 1877, Sarah, daughter of Robert Cholmeley, of Findon, Northamptonshire. He died on 13 September 1879, at his residence, Raystead, Worthing, and was survived by his wife, three sons, and two daughters. Saunders's seven children (four sons and three daughters) included William Frederick Saunders FLS (1834–1901); George Sharp Saunders FLS (1842–1910), entomologist; Edward Saunders (1848–1910), also an entomologist; and Mary Anne Saunders (*d.* 1927), a naturalist who married the zoologist Thomas Roscoe Rede Stebbing FRS (1835–1926). YOLANDA FOOTE

Sources *Entomologist's Monthly Magazine*, 16 (1879–80), 119–20 · *Nature*, 20 (1879), 536–7 · *Gardeners' Chronicle* (4 Feb 1871), 136 · private information (1897) [G. S. Saunders] · *Catalogue of scientific papers*, Royal Society, 19 vols. (1867–1925) · *BL cat.* · A. T. Gage and W. T. Stearn, *A bicentenary history of the Linnean Society of London* (1988) · Desmond, *Botanists*, rev. edn · H. R. Fletcher, *The story of the Royal Horticultural Society, 1804–1968* (1969) · M. Hadfield, R. Harling, and L. Highton, *British gardeners: a biographical dictionary* (1980) · *CGPLA Eng. & Wales* (1879) · m. certs. [W. W. Saunders and Mary Anne Mello; W. W. Saunders and Sarah Cholmeley]

Archives Bucks. RLSS, diaries and family corresp. · NHM, natural history notes and papers · Oxf. U. Mus. NH, Hope Library, corresp. and entomological notebooks, incl. details of captures | Oxf. U. Mus. NH, letters to J. O. Westwood · RBG Kew, letters to Sir William Hooker

Likenesses Maull & Polyblank, albumen print, 1855, NPG [*see illus.*] · Maull & Co., sepia photograph, RS · portrait, repro. in *Gardeners' Chronicle*, 136 · portrait, repro. in Hadfield, Harling, and Highton, *British gardeners*

Wealth at death under £450: probate, 13 Nov 1879, *CGPLA Eng. & Wales*

Saunderson, Edward James (1837–1906), politician, was born on 1 October 1837 at Castle Saunderson, co. Cavan, the third son of Alexander Saunderson (*d.* 1857), landed gentleman and MP, and his wife, Sarah Juliana (*d.* 1870), eldest daughter of the Revd Henry Maxwell, sixth Baron

Edward James Saunderson (1837–1906), by Elliott & Fry, 1890s

Farnham. Saunderson had three brothers and two sisters, but he alone inherited the family seat, Castle Saunderson, and the bulk of the family land in Cavan. This amounted to some 12,000 acres, which had been built up in the seventeenth century: the estate survived virtually intact through to the late nineteenth century. Because of this background and inheritance Saunderson identified strongly with the Irish gentry class and with the protestant planter tradition: indeed, he devoted the last ten years of his political career to a defence of Irish landlordism.

Between 1845 and 1857 Saunderson and his parents spent much time on the continent. He was educated in France at a time of constitutional upheaval, and the legacy of these years was borne throughout his career. He acquired not only a good knowledge of the French language, but also a European political vision, and a profound loathing of political disruption. These years of exile imbued him with a sentimental Irish patriotism, which—despite his ferocious commitment to the union—he retained throughout his life.

Saunderson returned to Ireland after his father's death in 1857, and inherited the Castle Saunderson estate in 1862, on reaching the age of twenty-five. On 22 June 1865 he married the Hon. Helena Emily de Moleyns (*d.* 1926), youngest daughter of Thomas, third Baron Ventry. They had four sons and a daughter. He maintained the family tradition of parliamentary involvement when, in 1865, he was returned as MP for county Cavan; he also maintained the whig traditions of his family through his stand as a Palmerstonian Liberal. He was unopposed at the general election of 1868, but was beaten by a home-ruler in 1874. During his first parliamentary tenure, Saunderson was a painfully inhibited, largely silent MP, intimidated by those of superior political talents. Indeed, at this time he was more conspicuous as a spiritual than as a political campaigner: his evangelical protestantism provided him with a renewed spiritual confidence, with an informal training in public oratory, and—ultimately—with a new sense of political purpose.

The land war (1879–82) brought Saunderson back into national politics. Intensified rural violence, combined with the looming electoral challenge of the home-rule movement, nudged him towards a more militant loyalist position than that which he had hitherto occupied. In 1882 he joined the Orange order, and on 12 July 1882 he marked his political comeback through a fiery Orange speech delivered at Ballykilbeg, co. Down. His alarm was intensified by the prospect of parliamentary reform, which looked set to strengthen further the electoral position of the home-rule movement. Saunderson was active in resisting the reform and redistribution scheme of 1884–5; and, when this endeavour failed, he vigorously promoted a separate Irish loyalist grouping within the House of Commons. The apparent betrayal of Irish loyalist interests by British parties, and the continued development of the home-rule cause stimulated the growth of independent loyalist institutions in Ireland throughout 1885. Saunderson was highly active in this movement, and demonstrated his commitment to an independent loyalism by seeing off John Monroe, the officially nominated Conservative candidate in the ferociously Orange North Armagh constituency. Monroe withdrew in October 1885, leaving the way clear for Saunderson's election victory in the following month.

Saunderson sat for North Armagh from 1885 until his death in October 1906. He was one of the key architects of the semi-autonomous Irish Unionist parliamentary party which emerged in January 1886. He was also one of the most active critics of Gladstone's first Home Rule Bill in that year. After the defeat of this measure, and the return of the Conservatives to power, Saunderson came to occupy a position of first-rate significance in national politics. In command of a small but influential group of Irish Unionist MPs, he was courted by Conservative leaders as diverse as Lord Salisbury and Lord Randolph Churchill. He was a popular and effective speaker inside the Commons, although perhaps not a great debater; he was much in demand as a stump orator in the later 1880s, when the British Conservatives did not possess popular and accessible public speakers. After the Salisbury government was defeated in 1892, Saunderson was widely regarded as the single most influential Irish Unionist, and he was therefore one of the most prominent critics of Gladstone's second Home Rule Bill (1893).

The defeat of this measure, coming after the split in the Parnellite party, temporarily robbed Irish Unionism of its central purpose. After 1893 Saunderson modified his leadership stand by concentrating more directly upon the economic interests of the Irish gentry than upon the broader political interests of Irish Unionism. He was a bitter opponent of both the Liberal Land Bill of 1895 and the Conservative Land Act of 1896, and deemed both measures to be prejudicial to the interests of Irish landlords. Saunderson's defiance simultaneously angered the Conservative leadership and the tenant lobby within Ulster Unionism. He was increasingly seen, not as a consensual leader for Irish Unionism, but as a narrow spokesman for the landlord interest. At the general election of 1900 he was opposed in North Armagh by James Orr, a local businessman, with substantial tenant farmer support. Saunderson triumphed—but many of his followers defected to the opposition camp.

Saunderson's political style and enthusiasms at this time recalled an age of landed ascendancy. His leadership was no longer automatically accepted within Unionism, where the working men of Belfast, the farmers, and the Presbyterians were pressing their claims with increasing force. The land agitation in Ulster of T. W. Russell, combined with the devolution controversy of 1905, provoked younger Unionists to undertake a complete reorganization of Ulster Unionism. But Saunderson played little part in this. After 1904 he was increasingly ill, racked at first by pneumonia and later by a weakened heart. He returned to active membership of the Commons in June 1905, and was re-elected for North Armagh in January 1906. In a House of Commons denuded of Unionist representation, he had a position of potentially first-rate significance. But this was never realized. For Saunderson remained weak, and on Sunday 21 October 1906, after a short period of renewed ill health, he died at Castle Saunderson.

As a speaker, Saunderson could be blunt or acidic; but he won admiration for his directness, even from political opponents. In public life he cared for the interests of his church, his caste, and the union: other issues, and especially matters of detail, bored him. He was a whig, paternalist and mild; his approach to public life was that of the *grand seigneur*. ALVIN JACKSON

Sources R. Lucas, *Colonel Saunderson MP* (1908) • A. Jackson, *Colonel Edward Saunderson* (1995) • H. Saunderson, *The Saundersons of Castle Saunderson* (1936) • A. Jackson, *The Ulster party: Irish unionists in the House of Commons, 1884–1911* (1989) • Burke, *Gen. Ire.*

Archives PRO NIre., corresp. and papers | Hatfield House, Hertfordshire, Salisbury MSS

Likenesses E. Long, oils, 1890; in possession of Mr Burdett-Coutts, 1912 • Elliott & Fry, photograph, 1890–99, NPG [*see illus.*] • R. P. Staples, crayon drawing, 1899; in possession of Mr Burdett-Coutts, 1912 • H. Harris Brown, oils, 1905, Castle Saunderson • W. G. John, bronze statue, 1910, Portadown, Northen Ireland • Ape [C. Pellegrini], chromolithograph caricature, NPG; repro. in *VF* (26 Feb 1887) • W. Burton, etching (after photograph by Elliott & Fry), NPG • S. P. Hall, pencil on paper, NG Ire.

Wealth at death £25,178 6*s*. 9*d*.: resworn probate, 7 Dec 1906, *CGPLA Ire.* • £1270 1*s*. 4*d*.—effects in England: Irish probate sealed in London, 19 Dec 1906, *CGPLA Ire.*

Saunderson, Frances Lumley- [*née* Lady Frances Hamilton], **countess of Scarbrough** (*c.*1700–1772), courtier, was the second daughter of George *Hamilton, first earl of Orkney (*bap.* 1666, *d.* 1737), and his wife, Elizabeth *Villiers (*c.*1657–1733), presumed mistress of William III. She was probably educated at home; her parents were important figures at the courts of William III, Anne, and George I, which allowed their daughters to grow up close to the heart of British politics and diplomacy. On 27 June 1724 Frances married Thomas Lumley-Saunderson (1690/91?–1752), the fourth son of Richard *Lumley, first earl of Scarbrough, and his wife, Frances Jones. Lumley had taken the additional name Saunderson in 1723 upon inheriting the estates of James Saunderson, earl of Castleton. He became third earl of Scarbrough in 1740, when he succeeded his brother Richard, the second earl. After a period as envoy-extraordinary to Portugal from 1722 to 1725, Scarbrough allied himself formally with Frederick, prince of Wales, serving as treasurer of the household from 1738 until Frederick's death in 1751. Lady Scarbrough was a lady of the bedchamber to Frederick's wife, Augusta. These appointments owed more to Lady Scarbrough's connections than her husband's. Her father had been a close friend of George I, which was itself a recommendation to Frederick. Her elder sister, Anne, *suo jure* countess of Orkney (*d.* 1756), leased her house at Cliveden in Buckinghamshire to Frederick. Lady Orkney's husband, William O'Brien, fourth earl of Inchiquin, became a member of Frederick's household in 1744.

If Frederick had become king, the Scarbroughs would undoubtedly have benefited through lucrative patronage appointments, something that they needed badly to support a growing family of two sons and three daughters. While Scarbrough was a poor money manager, his financial prospects had also been twice blighted: first by the South Sea Bubble, and second by the will of his brother the second earl, which bequeathed the Lumley estates in co. Durham and Sussex to their youngest brother, James, along with an annual income of £6000, and only a lump sum of £20,000 to the third earl. When her husband died in 1752, Lady Scarbrough was left in a difficult situation. Richard, the only son to survive his father, became fourth earl of Scarbrough and married Barbara Savile (through whom the Scarbroughs later inherited estates in Yorkshire and Nottinghamshire), as well as becoming heir to the co. Durham portion of his uncle James's estate.

Lady Scarbrough had two unmarried daughters, Frances and Anne, to provide for (her third, Harriot, had died in 1747), and the king's enmity to overcome if she wished to obtain any kind of future family advancement. Perhaps this is why she focused the majority of her determination and energy on securing patronage for her son-in-law, Peter Ludlow, whose support for the king's ministers was unquestionable, and thus indirectly for her daughter Frances, whom he married in 1753. Although she did seek patronage for herself and her other children, she devoted most of her energy between 1754 and 1760 to securing an Irish earldom for the untitled Ludlow. She bombarded Thomas Pelham-Holles, duke of Newcastle, first lord of the Treasury for most of the period, with written requests, and repeatedly brought up her requests in person when they met socially. In true eighteenth-century fashion she conveniently ignored her husband's unpalatable allegiance to the prince of Wales and based her claims instead on his diplomatic service and her own family's loyalty and service to the crown. She also never allowed Newcastle to forget that Ludlow had used his own fortune when standing as the government candidate in a recent hotly contested election. By granting patronage to Ludlow, she argued that the king would be recognizing the loyalty and service of the wider Scarbrough family:

> Your Grace may believe it is No small Mortification to me, After All the service of My poor Lord, without his ever having had, or Asked one favour, to see My Children disappointed of every thing they, or I ask, it has been the happiness of My Lord and family; to serve his Majesty; but it has Allways been, And Now is At the Expence of Our fortunes; whilst other familys Not More Attach'd; or better known to yr. Grace, & pardon me if I say Not More deserving; have made their fortunes by the Crown, & have every thing they wish. (BL, Add. MS 32735, fol. 376v, Lady Scarbrough to the duke of Newcastle, 19 March 1755)

Underlying all of these arguments was Lady Scarbrough's pressing need to retrieve her daughter's rank and reinforce her family's prestige. She was convinced that both had suffered as a result of the Ludlow marriage. When Ludlow accepted an Irish barony in 1755 as the first step towards the earldom, however, she was mortified. She would have preferred that he remain untitled rather than have her daughter descend to the rank of an Irish baroness. Even three years later, when Princess Amelia with her usual tactlessness had accosted her at a drawing-room for allowing her daughter to lose her rank, she still felt the incident strongly enough to relate it to Newcastle and blame him for her embarrassment. Finally, after many letters and much badgering, her persistence paid off and she attained her goal: in 1760 Ludlow was created Earl Ludlow in the Irish peerage.

Lady Scarbrough's use of the patronage system was not in itself unusual for an aristocratic woman who knew the workings of the eighteenth-century political world from the inside out. Nor was it unusual for aristocratic widows to request patronage based on their own past political loyalty and service or those of their birth or marital family. As the recognized heads of their families and, consequently, often as territorial political figures in their own right, these women often operated in the same way and as forcefully as their male counterparts and were treated accordingly by male politicians. What makes her campaign for Ludlow particularly interesting is the way in which an ostensibly straightforward patronage request for a man could serve multiple purposes—in this case, not only retrieving a woman's status but, by extension, preserving the reputation of a family as a whole. Having succeeded in getting what she wanted from the patronage system, Lady Scarbrough appears to have withdrawn from it. Little is known about her later years. She died at Bath on 27 December 1772 and was 'carried away' (GEC, *Peerage*) on 6 January 1773; in her will she requested that she be buried next to her husband in Saxby church, Lincolnshire.

E. H. Chalus

Sources T. W. Beastall, *A north country family* (1975) • E. Milner, *Records of the Lumleys of Lumley Castle* (1904) • BL, Newcastle papers, Add. MSS 32735, 32861, 32877, 32882, 32889, 32907–32908, 32987 • will, PRO, PROB 11/985, sig. 79 • A. Collins, *The peerage of England: containing a genealogical and historical account of all the peers of England*, 4th edn (1768) • GEC, *Peerage* • Burke, *Peerage* (1967) • R. R. Sedgwick, 'Lumley (afterwards Saunderson), Hon. Thomas', HoP, *Commons, 1715–54* • R. R. Sedgwick, 'Lumley, Hon. James', HoP, *Commons, 1715–54* • L. B. Namier, 'Ludlow, Peter, 1st Earl Ludlow', HoP, *Commons, 1754–90*

Archives BL, corresp. with duke of Newcastle, Add. MSS 32735, 32861, 32877, 32882, 32889, 32907–32908, 32987

Wealth at death £8000–£9000—bequeathed in will: 3 Feb 1773, PRO, PROB 11/985 (proven)

Saunderson, Nicholas (*bap.* **1683**, *d.* **1739**), mathematician, baptized on 20 January 1683, was the eldest son of John Sanderson (or Saunderson), an exciseman, and his wife, Ann, of Thurlstone, near Penistone, Yorkshire. At the age of twelve months he lost by smallpox not only his sight, but his eyes. As a youth he reportedly taught himself to read by tracing out letters on gravestones with his fingers. He was taught arithmetic by his father whom he assisted in his excise work, devising an ingenious counting board at which he was extremely adept. He first learned classics at the free school of Penistone, and became competent in Latin and Greek and fluent in French. When he was eighteen he was tutored in algebra and geometry (he is said to have drawn mathematical diagrams by pricking holes in a soft sheet of paper), and in 1702 he was sent to Attercliffe Academy, near Sheffield, to be tutored in logic and metaphysics. Then, at the age of twenty-four, he went to Cambridge with Joshua Dunn (*d.* 1709), a fellow-commoner of Christ's College, also from Attercliffe. He resided at Christ's with his friend, and was given library privileges, but was not admitted a member of the university. He wanted to teach mathematics, and with the consent of the Lucasian professor, William Whiston, he formed a class, to which he lectured on the Newtonian philosophy and on all the usual topics of mixed mathematics, as well as on astronomy and optics. He was highly respected as a teacher, and considered skilled in imparting to students a capacity to distinguish between truth and falsehood.

On 30 October 1710 Whiston was expelled from his professorship; on 19 November the following year Saunderson was made MA by special patent upon a recommendation from Queen Anne, in order that he might be eligible to succeed Whiston, and the next day 'he was chosen [fourth Lucasian] mathematick professor' in spite of some opposition (Luard) and without Newton's support. Indeed, Edmond Halley commented that 'Whiston was dismissed for having too much religion and Saunderson preferred for having none' (Dyer, 142–3). On 21 January 1712 Saunderson delivered his inauguration speech, in a very elegant and rhetorical Latin style and concluding with a long encomium on how knowledge of mathematics leads students to reason correctly. From this time he applied himself closely to the reading of lectures and tutoring, continuing in residence at Christ's College until 1723, when he took a house in Cambridge, and married Abigail Dickons, daughter of William Dickons, rector of Boxworth, Cambridgeshire. They had a son, John, and a daughter, Anne. In 1728, when George II visited Cambridge, Saunderson attended him in the Senate House, and was created doctor of laws.

Nicholas Saunderson (*bap.* **1683**, *d.* **1739**), by John Vanderbank, 1718–19

Saunderson's main significance is as an excellent and popular teacher in the years that mathematics began to emerge as the centre of a Cambridge education. He differed from his predecessors in the Lucasian chair both in his almost exclusive emphasis on the communication of mathematical ideas, and in his apparent lack of interest in theology. Philip Dormer Stanhope, later the fourth earl of Chesterfield, who was at Trinity Hall (1712–14) and attended Saunderson's lectures, described him as a professor who had not the use of his own eyes, but taught others to use theirs. Saunderson spent seven or eight hours a day in teaching. Notes taken by students from his lectures are extant in several university libraries, and in his time they also circulated outside Cambridge; John Harrison (1693–1776), the clockmaker whose chronometers eventually helped solve the problem of longitude, was apparently assisted in his mathematical self-education by a set of manuscript notes of Saunderson's lectures that he encountered as a young man.

Saunderson had a good ear for music, and could readily distinguish to the fifth part of a note; he was a good flautist. He could judge the size of a room and his distance from the wall, and recognized places by their sounds. He had a keen sense of touch; he 'distinguished in a set of Roman medals the genuine from the false, though they had … deceived a connoisseur who had judged by the eye' ('Life' in Saunderson). He was a man of outspoken opinions in general; his reverence for Newton was extreme. As Lucasian professor he was the recipient of one of four copies of the 'Commercium epistolicum', justifying Newton's position in his dispute with Leibniz, that the Royal Society sent to Cambridge in 1713. He was elected a fellow of the Royal Society on 6 November 1718. He corresponded with William Jones (1675–1749) and was acquainted with De Moivre, Machin, and Keill. In his capacity as Lucasian professor he sat with Newton, Halley, Cotes, Flamsteed, and Keill on the board of longitude formed by parliament to award prizes for research which would help to solve the problem of determining longitude at sea. He was also a member of the Spitalfields Mathematical Society.

Saunderson died of scurvy on 19 April 1739 and was buried in the chancel of the parish church at Boxworth (a village about 8 miles north-west from Cambridge), where there was placed a monument to his memory. He had published no books during his lifetime. His *Algebra*, prepared by him during the last six years of his life, was published by subscription in 1740 by his widow and children with the help of John Colson, his successor as Lucasian professor. The treatise is a model of careful exposition and it was used as a text at the Royal Military Academy at Woolwich. Some of Saunderson's manuscripts were printed in 1751, under the title *The method of fluxions applied to a select number of useful problems, together with … an explanation of the principal propositions of Sir Isaac Newton's philosophy.*

H. F. BAKER, *rev.* JAMES J. TATTERSALL

Sources 'Life', N. Saunderson, *The elements of algebra in ten books* (1740) • *Biographia Britannica* (1776) • C. Hutton, 'Dr Nicholas Saunderson', *A mathematical and philosophical dictionary*, 2 vols. (1795–6) • G. Dyer, *The privileges of the University of Cambridge* (1824); repr. (New York, 1978) • E. G. R. Taylor, *The mathematical practitioners of Tudor and Stuart England* (1954); repr. (1967) • H. R. Luard, *The diary of Edward Rudd, 1709–1720* (1860) • S. P. Rigaud and S. J. Rigaud, eds., *Correspondence of scientific men of the seventeenth century*, 2 vols. (1841); repr. (1965) • *Correspondence of Sir Isaac Newton and Professor Cotes*, ed. J. Edleston (1850) • A. De Morgan, *A budget of paradoxes* (1872) • E. Burke, *A philosophical essay into the origins of our ideas of the sublime and beautiful* (1766) • Venn, *Alum. Cant.*

Archives BL, lecture notes, Add. MS 59488 • Bodl. Oxf., lecture notes • CUL, lecture notes and papers • Gon. & Caius Cam. • Norfolk RO, lecture notes • Sidney Sussex College, Cambridge • Stanford University, California, lecture notes and papers • U. Leeds, Brotherton L. • UCL, lecture notes • Wellcome L., lecture notes | Babson College, Babson Park, Wellesley, Massachusetts, commentary on Newton's *Principia*

Likenesses J. Vanderbank, oils, 1718–19, Old Schools, Cambridge [*see illus.*] • G. Vandergucht, line engraving (after J. Vanderbank, 1718–19), BM, RS; repro. in Saunderson, *Elements of algebra* • oils, Christ's College, Cambridge

Saurin, Susan [*name in religion* Scholastica] (**1829–1915**), Roman Catholic nun, was born on 21 September 1829 at Garballagh House, Duleek, co. Meath, Ireland, the youngest of six children of Michael Saurin, landowner, and his wife, Brigid, *née* Mathews. Two sisters were Carmelite nuns, one brother, Matthew, was a Jesuit priest, and another, Patrick, was a lawyer. Her brother Michael died in 1863.

Susan entered Baggot Street Convent of Mercy, Dublin, in November 1850. Under the name Sister Scholastica, she became a fully professed nun on 3 October 1853, taking vows of poverty, chastity, and obedience. She was selected to join the founding nuns of a new Mercy convent first at

Clifford, in the West Riding of Yorkshire (1856), and subsequently in Hull. Her superior in Clifford and Hull was Mother Mary Starr (Sister Joseph), whose mother assistant (deputy) was Mother Julia Kennedy (Sister Magdalen). All three nuns had trained together in Baggot Street.

Under Starr's direction Saurin undertook a variety of menial duties in the convent, but in every task she seemed to incur the displeasure of her inexperienced superior, who excelled at highlighting Saurin's faults. Starr's displeasure reached its zenith when Saurin refused to disclose to her the substance of her conversation with a priest in confession and when Saurin wrote to her uncle, a priest in Drogheda, asking him to arrange a transfer for her to another convent in Ireland. These were deemed to be sins of disobedience and of the writing of clandestine letters. Bishop Robert Cornthwaite of Beverley (the local ordinary) received two requests to intervene. Starr insisted that he help her to get rid of Saurin by dispensing her from her vows. The Saurin family, on the other hand, insisted that he investigate the convent because of the ill treatment being meted out to Susan.

A commission of inquiry was appointed, with a panel of five priest commissioners. Saurin was the only nun to be interviewed and cross-examined on twelve charges of faults against obedience, poverty, charity, and truth. The panel reported unanimously to the bishop against Saurin, although in their individual reports on the inquiry four of the panel had highlighted mitigating circumstances in Saurin's favour, including 'unrefuted testimony to several instances of extraordinary and unexemplary severity' (Leeds Diocesan Archives, *Saurin* v. *Starr* MSS). Saurin was required to leave the convent. Her family was furious and vowed to seek justice in the courts. Saurin refused to leave the convent and to acknowledge the bishop's power to dispense with her vows without her consent. Starr and Kennedy ignored her views. Deeming her to be no longer a member of the community, they confined her to an attic room with many privations. She remained there for more than thirteen months until she almost starved to death. In May 1867, on the advice of her brother Patrick and a Hull physician, she left the convent quietly, unknown to Starr and Kennedy.

The next time they met was on 3 February 1869 at Westminster Hall, London, to answer the case of *Saurin* v. *Starr and another* before the lord chief justice and the court of the queen's bench. The case lasted a record twenty-one days and made significant history as 'The Great Convent Case'. Nuns, priests, parents, schoolchildren, the physician, and Bishop Cornthwaite were all called to give evidence. Starr and Kennedy were found guilty of wrongfully and maliciously compelling Saurin to leave the convent and of subjecting her to various indignities, assaults, persecutions, and annoyances, including trying to libel her before the bishop. The trial was given extensive media coverage and caricatures of the key figures occupied pages in *Vanity Fair* and *Punch*. The solicitor-general described the case as a scandalous affair in which no scandal had been discovered. The legal costs to the Hull nuns came to £6000.

Details of Saurin's subsequent life as recorded in the Mercy annals are scant and misleading. Five years after the case, under the assumed name of Mary Brown, she entered the Visitation Convent at Westbury-on-Trym, near Bristol. As Sister Michael she remained incognito for many years, and died in the Visitation Convent at Harrow on the Hill on 10 February 1915, aged eighty-five years. She was buried first at the Visitation Convent and then reinterred at Kensal Green cemetery, London.

MARIA G. MCCLELLAND

Sources M. G. McClelland, 'Early educational endeavour: a study in the work of the Hull Mercy Nuns, 1855–1930', MPhil. diss., 1993 • W. L. Arnstein, *Protestant v. Catholic in mid-Victorian England: Mr Newdegate and the nuns* (1982) • A. Carroll, *Leaves from the annals of the Sisters of Mercy*, 4 vols. (1881–8) • *The inner life of the Hull nunnery exposed* (1869) [a transcript of the trial] • J. McCullen, *The call of St Mary's* (1984) • G. Porter, *The Rev. Porter on the Hull convent case* (1869) • Baggot Street Archives, Dublin, Mercy Convent records • Waldron, East Sussex, Visitation Sisters archives

Archives Leeds Diocesan Archives | Baggot Street Archives, Dublin • Leeds Diocesan Archives, Cornthwaite and Clifford MSS • Sacra Congregazioni di Propaganda Fide, Rome, Propaganda Fide archives • Waldron, East Sussex, Visitation Sisters archives

Likenesses double portraits, drawings (with Starr), repro. in McCullen, *The call of St Mary's*, 39, 40 • drawing, repro. in *The Times* (1869), frontispiece • drawing, repro. in *Illustrated Weekly News* (20 Feb 1869)

Saurin, William (1757–1839), lawyer and politician, was born in Belfast and baptized at St Anne's Church, Belfast, on 13 July 1757, the second son of James Saurin (1719–1772) vicar of St Anne's, and his wife, Jane (*d.* 1760), daughter of William Johnston, of New Forge, co. Antrim, and widow of James Duff. He was descended from a notable Languedoc family who were firmly attached to the Reformed church. Following the revocation of the edict of Nantes in 1685, his grandfather Louis Saurin (*d.* 1749) was compelled to leave France, and settled in Ireland. Louis was presented to the deanery of Ardagh on 22 March 1727, and on 3 June 1736 installed archdeacon of Derry. He and his wife, Henriette Cornel de la Bretonnière, had four daughters and one son, James, who succeeded Richard Stewart as vicar of St Anne's, Belfast, in 1747. Aside from William, James and his wife had three other sons: Louis, James (later bishop of Dromore), and Mark Anthony.

William Saurin received his early education at the Revd Saumarez Dubourdieu's school in Lisburn, co. Antrim, before entering Trinity College, Dublin, as a fellow-commoner in 1775. He graduated BA in 1777. He proceeded to London where he entered Lincoln's Inn, and was called to the Irish bar in 1780. On 21 January 1786 he married Mary (*d.* 1840), widow of Sir Richard Eyre Cox, fourth baronet, and the eldest daughter of Edward O'Brien, younger brother of the first marquess of Thomond, and Mary Carrick. Her two brothers, William and James, later succeeded as the second and third marquesses of Thomond respectively. Saurin and his wife had a large family. The eldest son, Admiral Edward Saurin (*d.* 1878), married on 15 July 1828 Lady Mary Ryder (1801–1900), second daughter of the first earl of Harrowby.

Saurin first attracted wider attention as a result of the capable manner in which he acted in the 1790 election for

County Down as agent to the Hon. Edward Ward against Robert Stewart, afterwards Viscount Castlereagh. In 1796 he was elected by the members of the Irish bar to the position of captain of their first company of yeoman infantry. He was granted a patent of precedence immediately after the prime serjeant, attorney-general, and solicitor-general on 6 July 1798. He served the government during 1798 in some of the trials arising out of the Irish rising. He was offered the post of solicitor-general, vacant through the elevation of John Toler, afterwards first earl of Norbury, to the attorney-generalship, but declined on the grounds that he could not support the government's plans to implement a union between Ireland and Great Britain. It was at first his intention to convene a meeting of the lawyers' yeomanry corps on 2 December 1798 to consider 'a question of the greatest national importance' (Blackstock, 181). However, this was postponed at the last moment to avoid the impropriety of discussing political subjects in the character of a military unit. Instead, a general bar meeting was summoned for Sunday 9 December 1798. At the meeting Saurin proposed the motion 'that the measure of a legislative union of this kingdom and Great Britain is an innovation, which it would be highly dangerous and improper to propose, at the present juncture, to this country' (Bolton, 78). In a closely argued and temperate speech he stressed the inappropriateness of the measure and the potential neglect of Irish interests at Westminster. It was a shock to the Dublin government when a motion to adjourn the debate was heavily defeated, and immediately afterwards Saurin's original motion was carried with approval.

Saurin was not content with this. He hoped to persuade the Dublin corps to lay down their arms and thereby encourage the rest of the Irish yeomanry to follow suit. As a consequence the government determined to strip him of his legal and yeomanry positions. However, Lord Castlereagh, then Irish chief secretary, received a commitment from Saurin that he would make no further efforts to involve the yeomanry and so the orders to relieve him of his positions were subsequently rescinded. In July 1799 the lower house of Dublin corporation approved a motion that proposed presenting Saurin with the freedom of the city, 'for his manly resistance to the legislative union' (Bolton, 130–31). However, the board of aldermen deleted all references to his anti-unionist activities, and confined themselves to a simple grant of the city freedom.

Saurin was returned for the borough of Blessington by the influence of the anti-unionist magnate Lord Downshire in 1799. He made three lengthy speeches against the union in February, March, and June 1800, the first of which was later published. During the union debates in March 1800 Saurin attempted to establish the doctrine of the will of the people, to justify resistance to a law passed contrary to the nation's will. Lord Castlereagh led the attack on this dangerous principle, which he described as Jacobin, and as Edward Cooke, under-secretary, reported: 'he said these doctrines went to excite and justify rebellion' (Geoghegan, 111). Although Saurin's opposition to the union may appear contradictory in light of his subsequent career, it derived from a combination of professional interest and narrow protestant nationalist beliefs. He defended this political world in terms of the protestant 'nation', as he was committed to upholding protestant 'ascendancy'. Thus his later conduct, far from being illogical, was consistent with the beliefs that had inspired his anti-union opposition.

On 21 May 1807 Saurin, at the age of fifty, was appointed attorney-general for Ireland under the administration of the duke of Richmond. He became exceptional among Irish law officers for retaining the office for an unsurpassed span of fifteen years. During this period he was at the centre of opposition to further Catholic concessions. In 1811 he conducted the prosecution of Dr Edward Sheridan under the provisions of the Convention Act of 1793, and though he failed on that occasion to secure a conviction, he was successful in a similar charge against Thomas Kirwan in the following year.

In 1812 Saurin recognized that Robert Peel, the new Irish chief secretary, shared his views with regards to the maintenance and protection of the protestant establishment. They worked closely together and Saurin was an influential adviser during Peel's tenure. He conducted the prosecution of John Magee, editor and proprietor of the *Dublin Evening Post*, who was charged with seditious libel for printing an attack on the duke of Richmond. Aside from the explicit cause of the case, the underlying motivation stemmed from the newspaper's close identification with the Catholic Board and in particular Daniel O'Connell. The case opened on 26 July 1813 with the defence led by O'Connell, who concluded his case by delivering a scathing attack on the governance of Ireland and a personal attack on Saurin. When Magee came up for sentencing, Saurin denounced O'Connell for his conduct at the trial and O'Connell reciprocated by stating that it was only out of respect for the court that he would refrain from horsewhipping the attorney-general. However, by the summer of 1814, Peel and Saurin had effectively emasculated the pro-Catholic press and suppressed the Catholic Board.

The appointment of Lord Wellesley as lord lieutenant in 1822 prompted Saurin's removal from the post of attorney-general. The decision was unexpected and, indignant at his treatment, he refused a judgeship coupled with a peerage, and returned to his practice at the chancery bar. Lord Wellesley commented:

> I have been told that I have ill-treated Mr Saurin. I offered him the chief-justiceship of the king's bench: that was not ill-treating him. I offered him an English peerage: that was not ill-treating him. I did not, it is true, continue him in the viceroyalty of Ireland, for I am viceroy of Ireland. (Grattan, 5.123n.)

Though deprived of office Saurin was still an influential figure within the country. He was an active promoter of the Brunswick clubs, which were formed with the purpose of defending the protestant constitution and resisting Catholic emancipation. In February 1829 he spoke at the second general meeting of the Brunswick Constitutional Club of Ireland held in the Rotunda, Dublin.

Saurin finally retired from the law in 1831 as father of the bar. He died at his residence in St Stephen's Green, Dublin, on 11 January 1839. Undoubtedly he had a vested interest in the existing constitution, which would have been jeopardized by the admission of Catholics to full political rights. However, his motivation was not solely sectarian and thus it would be unfair not to attribute at least some of his passion and intensity to genuine convictions about the rectitude of the constitution.

DAVID HUDDLESTON

Sources *Clergy of Connor from patrician times to the present day* (1993) • J. Wills, *Lives of illustrious and distinguished Irishmen*, 6 (1847), 328–47 • A. J. Webb, *A compendium of Irish biography* (1878) • *DNB* • Burke, *Peerage* • *GM*, 2nd ser., 12 (1839), 88 • H. Cotton, *Fasti ecclesiae Hibernicae*, 6 vols. (1845–78) • G. C. Bolton, *The passing of the Irish Act of Union* (1966) • B. Jenkins, *Era of emancipation: British government of Ireland, 1812–1830* (1988) • A. Blackstock, *An ascendancy army: the Irish yeomanry, 1796–1834* (1998) • P. M. Geoghegan, *The Irish Act of Union* (1999) • H. Grattan, *Memoirs of the life and times of the Rt Hon. Henry Grattan*, 5 vols. (1839–46), vol. 5, pp.15, 120–23 • J. Hill, 'The legal profession and the defence of the *ancien régime* in Ireland, 1790–1840', *Brehons, serjeants and attorneys: studies in the history of the Irish legal profession*, ed. D. Hogan and W. N. Osborough (1990), 181–209 • M. O'Connell, *Daniel O'Connell: the man and his politics* (1990) • GEC, *Baronetage*

Archives BL, corresp. with R. Peel, Add. MSS 40211–40389, *passim*

Sausmarez, Lionel Maurice de (1915–1969), painter and writer on art, was born on 20 October 1915 in Sydney, Australia, the second son of Clarence Montgomery de Sausmarez (1880–1918), a marine engineer of an old and distinguished naval family from Guernsey, and Jessie Rose Macdonald, *née* Bamford (1878–1963). She was the widow of an explorer, and had become a professional pianist and teacher. The family moved to Grenada in the West Indies when Maurice was one year old, and he was first educated there before attending St Michael's, Highgate, when the family moved to England, and then going to Harvest Road primary school, Willesden. He was awarded a scholarship to Christ's Hospital in 1926. At school he excelled in playing the piano and organ as well as in art.

From 1932 to 1936 de Sausmarez attended Willesden Art School and from there had to choose whether to go to the Royal College of Music or to study art; in the event he became a royal exhibitioner at the Royal College of Art (1936–9). He won a continuation scholarship in 1939 but relinquished it because of the outbreak of war. That year he married Kate Elizabeth Lyons (*d.* 2000), with whom he had a daughter. During the war he was exempt from military service as he had suffered rheumatic fever as a child, and became a volunteer firefighter in Sheffield when teaching at the Edward VII School.

De Sausmarez's first one-man show of paintings was at the Paul Alexander Gallery in Kensington in 1949. He was commissioned by the Pilgrim Trust to contribute work to *Recording Britain*, the four illustrated volumes of which were eventually published between 1946 and 1949. He also began showing in mixed exhibitions, which included those of the Royal Academy (from 1945), the New English Art Club (member, 1950), the Royal Society of British Artists (member, 1953), the Leicester Galleries, and the London Group.

From 1942 de Sausmarez taught part-time at Harrow School, Goldsmiths' College, and the Willesden, City and Guilds, and Camberwell schools of art. He became chairman of the Artists' International Association (1946–8), and helped to establish its permanent home in Lisle Street. In 1947 he became head of the school of drawing and painting at Leeds College of Art, and in 1950 was invited to set up the department of fine art at the University of Leeds, as its first head, a post he held until 1959. Leeds City Art Gallery possesses three of his paintings of this period, including *Winter* (oil on canvas, *c.*1955). His work is also in the collections of the Victoria and Albert Museum, London, the Ferens Art Gallery, Hull, Bedford Art Gallery, the Whitworth Art Gallery, the City of Wakefield Art Gallery, and the National Gallery of New Zealand, Wellington. He had pictures in Contemporary Art Society exhibitions at the Tate Gallery in 1951 and 1956.

In the late 1950s de Sausmarez had a close relationship with Bridget Riley, who became one of the most distinguished abstract painters of her generation, and about whom he later wrote a book (*Bridget Riley*, 1970). He was appointed head of fine art at Hornsey School of Art in 1958, and in 1962 became principal of the Byam Shaw School of Drawing and Painting, a post in which he remained until his death.

As a painter, de Sausmarez's work was characterized by a classical approach to composition, and he was preoccupied with the use of colour to explore light and space. A fine draughtsman, his earlier work included landscapes, still lifes, interiors, and a number of commissioned portraits, including those of Vice-Chancellor Nicholson of the University of Hull and the poet James Kirkup. He later mostly painted landscapes directly from the motif, and he also worked in the studio from colour studies and drawings, on compositions which became essays in fragmented and faceted shapes, analogous to those of Jacques Villon, whose works, after those of Cézanne and Poussin, he particularly admired. In 1964 he was elected associate of the Royal Academy and in that year also published his widely acclaimed and frequently reprinted book *Basic Design: the Dynamics of Visual Form* (1964). He subsequently wrote books on Poussin (*Poussin's Orpheus and Eurydice*, 1969) and on his friend Ben Nicholson (1969), as well as giving broadcast talks and writing many articles on the visual arts and on art education. A deep commitment to art teaching led him to become president of the Society for Education through Art, and he was a member of the Council for Diplomas in Art and Design from 1968, among many other official appointments.

De Sausmarez travelled before the war in Belgium, the Netherlands, France, and Germany, and later in Italy and east Africa. He had a house in the Vaucluse from 1962 and subsequently worked there every year. In 1963 he was divorced from his first wife and in May that year he married, second, Jane Elisabeth Boswell (*b.* 1938), artist and printmaker, with whom he had two sons. Having bought a house in north London in 1943, he lived there, in Leaside Avenue, for the rest of his life after his years in Yorkshire. He was a handsome, saturnine man, tall and slim, who wore a beard at earlier periods in his life. He died in London of heart trouble on 27 October 1969, and was cremated at Golders Green. A thanksgiving service was held at St Paul's, Covent Garden, on 15 December of that year. His second wife survived him. A memorial group of his pictures was exhibited at the Royal Academy in 1970.

ALAN WINDSOR

Sources *WWW*, *1961–70* • *The Times* (30 Oct 1969) • *The blue book: leaders of the English-speaking world* (1969) • private information (2004) [Jane de Sausmarez, wife]

Archives Tate collection, corresp. and notebooks | SOUND Tate collection (for broadcasts)

Likenesses L. M. de Sausmarez, self-portrait, oils, 1960, priv. coll. • L. M. de Sausmarez, self-portrait, pencil drawing, priv. coll.

Saussure, César-François [César] **de** (1705–1783), travel writer, was baptized in Lausanne, Pays de Vaud, Switzerland, on 24 June 1705, the eldest of the three sons and two daughters of François-Louis de Saussure (*bap.* 1676, *d.* 1724), minister of the Reformed church, and his wife, Jeanne-Emilie (Elisabeth; *bap.* 1680, *d.* 1762), daughter of César Gaudard, controller-general of Lausanne, and Elisabeth d'Aubonne. Although descended on both sides from leading noble families in the city, he did not apparently attend the Académie de Lausanne.

After the death of his father Saussure embarked on fifteen years of travel, which included two extended visits to England during which he recorded his impressions. He left Lausanne on 8 April 1725 and arrived in London on 24 May. Here he lodged first in the City itself, then in East Sheen and in Islington. In 1728 his family firmly opposed his plans to marry a merchant's daughter. In October 1729—presumably through the influence of the friends in England he mentions but does not name—Saussure left for Constantinople as secretary to George Hay, Lord Kinoull (*d.* 1758), the English ambassador there, but by 1732 he was at Rodosto, on the Marmara Sea, in the service of Prince Francis II Rakoczy, an exiled Hungarian rebel. After the prince's death in 1735 Saussure returned in January 1736 to Lausanne, but late in 1738 was again in London, ready to leave for America with Charles, Lord Cathcart. Yielding to the pleas of his mother, Saussure abandoned his plans; in the event it was his younger brother Henri de Saussure (1709–1761) who established himself at Charlestown, South Carolina, and whose four sons were all later active in the American War of Independence, though it is not clear on which side.

Saussure, meanwhile, remained for a while in London where, before June 1739, he overcame initial suspicions and joined the freemasons, an organization that he described in detail and defended vigorously in his manuscript notebook. A lodge was formed in Lausanne in 1738 and constituted by the London grand lodge in 1740, but it was suppressed in 1745 by the Bernese rulers, along with all other manifestations of freemasonry in their territories. Saussure was concerned to demonstrate to a Swiss audience that the movement had flourished for a long time in England without trouble; it drew support from the highest echelons of society, including the prince of Wales.

César-François de Saussure (1705–1783), by Joseph Lander, 1758

In 1740 Saussure returned to Lausanne, where he lived from the revenues of his estates and joined the oligarchic ruling council. In 1742 he finished the first draft of an account of his travels, based on his notes, and for more than twenty years this passed through the hands of many people—including Voltaire—in Bern, Geneva, and Lausanne. Saussure married, at Lausanne Cathedral, on 22 June 1743, Elisabeth-Françoise (1717–1783), daughter of Jost Gaudard of Bern and Lausanne, and his wife, Françoise Bergier: they had two daughters who survived to adulthood, Henriette-Marie, or Henriette (1751–1815), and Elisabeth-Henriette-Louise-Marguerite, or Isabelle (1752–1831). Saussure revised his manuscripts and collected them into three large volumes for his children (Bibliothèque cantonaire et universitaire de Lausanne, MS 363), recasting his experiences of England in the fashionable form of letters to an anonymous friend. He signed a covering preface to his daughters on 15 November 1765, but publication was left to his descendants Anne van Muyden-Baird and Berthold van Muyden, who edited respectively *A Foreign View of England in the Reigns of George I and George II* (1902; repr. 1995) and *Lettres et voyages de Monsr César de Saussure en Allemagne, en Hollande et en Angleterre* (Lausanne, Paris, and Amsterdam, 1903). These writings apparently draw on only a part of Saussure's manuscripts; ostensibly set in the years 1725 to 1729 they are silently updated by impressions culled from Saussure's second visit, which introduces some anachronisms. None the less, they provide a lively, detailed, and valuable account of the impact on a foreign visitor of a wide variety of London sights and customs in the early eighteenth century, complementary in its concern with everyday aspects of civic, mercantile, and low life to Voltaire's contemporary, much more literary and aristocratic, analysis. Saussure was conscious of being one of many commentators, English and Swiss, and to avoid duplication on specific points he referred his readers, for instance, to John Chamberlayne's *The Present State of England* or his fellow Lausannois Sébastien-Isaac Loys's evidently well-known account of Waltham Abbey in 1727. An enthusiast for English countryside and architecture, Saussure considered St Paul's Cathedral—with St Sophia's in Constantinople and St Peter's in Rome—as one of the most beautiful churches in the world. Impressed by England's civic and parliamentary ceremony as well as its markets, entertainments, newspapers, scientific achievement, and abundant water supply, he was more equivocal on English justice, which he thought was largely humane but unfair to women who had murdered their husbands. Moral corruption, crime and varieties of criminals, and the insolence of the common people earned his censure. Saussure saw English tolerance as generally a virtue, but was not overly enamoured of any of the religious or political parties: Anglicans, with honourable exceptions, were lazy pluralists and the Book of Common Prayer was almost a mass book; Presbyterians were mostly ignorant, rigid, and hypocritical; Quakers (described at length) were simply ridiculous. Without such dangerous divisions, Saussure concluded, the English would be the happiest and most fortunate nation in the world.

In the remaining years of his life Saussure compiled histories of France and of Switzerland, as well as memoirs of notable events in the Pays de Vaud and accounts of his visits to the celebrated healer Michel Schüppach in search of a cure for long-standing health problems. His will of June 1774 acknowledged his painful and mysterious infirmities, but reaffirmed his ardent protestant faith. He died in Lausanne on 8 March 1783 and was buried in the cathedral there. His *Lettres de Turquie* was published in a parallel French and Hungarian version in 1909.

VIVIENNE LARMINIE

Sources *Recueil des généalogies vaudoises*, Société Vaudoise de Généalogie, 3 (Lausanne, 1950), 161–3 • *Lettres et voyages de Monsr César de Saussure en Allemagne, en Hollande et en Angleterre, 1725–1729*, ed. B. van Muyden (Lausanne, 1903) • W. de Charnière de Sévery, 'César de Saussure et la Société des francs-maçons de Londres, en 1739', *Revue Historique Vaudoise* (1917), 353–66 • J.-C. Biaudet, 'César de Saussure et Michel Schüppach', *Revue Historique Vaudoise* (1956), 107–48 • will, Archives cantonales vaudoises, Bg 13 bis/12, fols. 86*v*–90*v*

Likenesses J. Lander, portrait, 1758, Musée Historique de Lausanne [*see illus.*] • oils, Musée Historique de Lausanne, Place de la Cathédrale, Lausanne; repro. in Biaudet, 'César de Saussure', following p. 112

Wealth at death considerable wealth in land and vines: will, Archives cantonales vaudoises, Bg 13 bis/12, fols. 86*v*–90*v*

Savage family (*per. c.*1280–*c.*1420), gentry, of Bobbing, near Sittingbourne, Kent, first appears in the twelfth century. But the true founder of the family's fortunes was **Sir John** [i] **Savage** (*d.* 1298), both by his marriages and by his service to Edward I. His first wife, Mary Abelyn, was the heir of both her father and brother and of Iseult, widow of Henry of Appulderfield. His second wife, and cousin to Mary, Margaret (*d.* 1298/9), daughter of Roland of Oxted, brought the manor of Oxted, Surrey, to the Savages. With his first wife Sir John had at least two sons, Ralph [i], a canon of Chichester, and **Sir John** [ii] **Savage** (*b.* 1277, *d.* after 1324); Roger [i] (*b.* after 1278, *d.* 1299), his son from his second marriage, died while still a royal ward. Before his nineteenth year John [ii] Savage was married to Lucy, one of his stepbrother's young aunts, a move doubtless designed to strengthen the family's claim to both the Oxted estate and to a share of Roger's inheritance. Between his father's death and his coming of age in September 1298 John was briefly the ward of Edmund, earl of Cornwall, the king's brother, and he was among those knighted with Prince Edward in 1306. Three years later he was serving against the Scots.

The life of John [ii] Savage was not without blemish: in 1311 he was imprisoned in Canterbury for forestalling; the next year he and a Ralph Savage were among a mob that allegedly attacked Justice William Inge's Kentish manors; and in the same year he was recorded as owing nearly £10 in the county. Sir John may well have regarded service against Scotland from 1313 to 1315 as a temporary escape from his problems at home, since it brought with it a suspension of pleas against him. He served under Aymer de Valence, earl of Pembroke, in 1315, but in 1318 he was pardoned as an adherent of Thomas, earl of Lancaster. In 1320 he again owed money, this time £700, and from 1315 to 1321 he was involved in land deals which may represent attempts to restore his finances. While he sat in the parliaments of 1318, 1319, 1321, and 1322, it was not until 1322–3 that he is found again in royal service, raising and leading Kentish contingents against the Scots. His return to active service under the Despensers may suggest a political reorientation after Lancaster's fall, but he was also bailiff of Queen Isabella's liberty of Milton, Kent, and in 1324, following her fall from favour, a commission of oyer and terminer was appointed to investigate his alleged oppressions as bailiff.

Sir John [ii] Savage's descendants made little impression. A more substantial figure was **Sir Roger** [ii] **Savage** (*d.* in or before 1320), possibly Sir John's brother. By 1295, when he accompanied Edward I on campaign in Gascony, he had already been involved in maritime defence. In 1297–8 he served in Flanders and Scotland, and in 1311 in Scotland again, but his real contribution to Edwardian foreign policy lay in his diplomatic skills. In 1300 and 1302 he accompanied embassies to Rome, and in 1306 he was Edward I's ambassador to the curia in the matter, among others, of Edward's claim on the monastery of Scone. Two years previously he had represented the Cinque Ports' grievances against Calais to the king of France. In November 1306, as Prince Edward's attorney, he received seisin of the duchy of Aquitaine. In 1311 he was once again preparing for an embassy to France, and in 1314 he was part of Sir Gilbert Peche's mission to the marchese di Ancona. In what appears to be his final diplomatic assignment, in 1317 he received two visiting cardinals at Dover and accompanied them to London. In February 1308 he was summoned to Edward II's coronation, and three months later he was among the justices summoned to parliament. Under the new king he was keeper of the castles of Windsor and Leeds, Kent. From 1311 until his death he was a frequent Kentish commissioner, justice, and conservator of the peace.

Sir Ralph [ii] **Savage** (*d.* 1344x6) was probably Sir Roger [ii]'s son with his wife, Claricia. He was with the latter at Edward II's coronation, and he also accompanied Sir Gilbert Peche in Gascony. He maintained the family presence in Kentish administration into the reign of Edward III. In 1316 he represented Kent in parliament, and in 1324 he was summoned to a great council. In 1321–2 he was sheriff of Kent and constable of Canterbury Castle, and thereafter he was often seen on Kentish commissions. In 1324 he was an enthusiastic commissioner of array for the Gascony campaign, and again in 1326, when he was also an admiral. With his wife, Lara, daughter of Stephen Chelsfield and heir of Reginald Preston, he had a son, Sir Arnold *Savage (*d.* 1375) [*see under* Savage, Sir Arnold (1358–1410)]. Largely through Sir Arnold's service to Edward, the Black Prince, the family entered upon a new stage of wealth and influence.

Another Sir Arnold *Savage (1358–1410), his son, brought the Savages to their zenith, becoming a notable speaker of the Commons. But under his son, a third **Sir Arnold Savage** (*c.*1382–1420), the Savages of Bobbing quietly faded from history. In 1399 Arnold was married to Katherine, daughter of Roger, fourth Baron Scales, and his wife, Joan, daughter of John Northwood, and through this marriage he added several leading Norfolk gentry to the existing family connection. In 1414 he was knighted and sat as a Kentish MP, and he served in the Agincourt campaign, but after 1415 he withdrew from public life. He died in 1420, survived by his widow (who lived for another sixteen years), and his sister and heir, Elizabeth, widow of Sir Reynold Cobham (*d.* 1405) of Rundale and Allington, and wife of William Clifford. PETER FLEMING

Sources *Chancery records* • *CIPM*, 3, nos. 487, 529 • C. Moor, ed., *Knights of Edward I*, 4, Harleian Society, 83 (1931), 214–19 • J. S. Roskell, 'Sir Arnald Savage of Bobbing', *Archaeologia Cantiana*, 70 (1956), 68–83 • HoP, *Commons*, *1386–1421*, 4.306–11 • G. O. Bellewes, 'The last Savages of Bobbing', *Archaeologia Cantiana*, 29 (1911), 164–8 • E. F. Jacob, ed., *The register of Henry Chichele, archbishop of Canterbury, 1414–1443*, 2, CYS, 42 (1937), 205–6, 547–9 • *CDS*, 2.1903; 5.566(d) • J. B. Sheppard, ed., *Literae Cantuarienses: the letter books of the monastery of Christ Church, Canterbury*, 1, Rolls Series, 85 (1887), 70–72

Archives BL • CKS | PRO

Savage family (*per.* 1333–1519), landowners and administrators, styled in the late middle ages lords of Lecale, in co. Down, came from an old Anglo-Norman family of Ulster. The William Savage who witnessed a charter of John de Courcy, first lord of Ulster, was probably related to the twelfth-century Cheshire landholders of that name. Courcy's charter establishing Black Abbey on the Ards peninsula (*c.*1183) mentions the nearby castle of Ardkeen, later recorded as *caput* of the Savage family's estates. After the assassination of William de Burgh, third earl of Ulster, in 1333 the influential post of seneschal of the liberty of Ulster passed from the guilty Mandevilles to **Sir Robert Savage** (*d.* 1360), who earned a legendary reputation among the Anglo-Irish for his defence of the neglected colony against Irish attacks. Later the office of seneschal was held by **Edmund Savage** (*fl.* *c.*1385–*c.*1398), named with dislike and fear in letters of Irish chiefs to Richard II. From *c.*1452 **Janico** [Seinicín] **Savage** (*d.* 1468), styled 'captain of his nation', was seneschal. He instigated a dramatic appeal for support to Edward IV about 1467, comparing the Ulster colonists to the children of Israel in bondage to the pharaoh. The annals of Ulster (1469–70) equate the title of seneschal with that of lord of Lecale, the last remnant of English Ulster, by stating that the great Ó Néill, Éinrí son of Eoghan, assisted Patrick White to capture **Patrick Savage** (*d.* in or after 1481), expel his family, and seize the lordship of Lecale, but that the Savages took back Lecale and the seneschalcy from Patrick White the following year. Patrick Savage was still seneschal in 1481, but in that year he was blinded and exiled. On 2 August 1482 **Roland Savage** (*d.* 1519) was appointed seneschal by the Dublin government. However, an anonymous tract of about 1515 lists Roland as 'one of the English great rebels' living outside Dublin's control. The ninth earl of Kildare expelled him from the lordship of Lecale, substituting the Prior Mág Aonghusa. Roland died soon after, of grief, the annals suggest, leaving an attenuated patrimony to his son Edmund, who was inaugurated chief in his place.

KATHARINE SIMMS

Sources S. Duffy, 'The first Ulster plantation: John de Courcy and the men of Cumbria', *Colony and frontier in medieval Ireland*, ed. T. B. Barry, R. F. Frame, and K. Simms [forthcoming] • T. E. McNeill, *Anglo-Norman Ulster* (1980), 79–84, 118–20 • J. T. Gilbert, ed., *Chartularies of St Mary's Abbey Dublin … and annals of Ireland*, 2 vols. (1884–6) • E. Tresham, ed., *Rotulorum patentium et clausorum cancellarie Hibernie calendarium* (1828) • *State papers published under … Henry VIII*, 11 vols. (1830–52), vol. 3, pt. 1 • A. M. Freeman, ed. and trans., *Annála Connacht / The annals of Connacht* (1944); repr. (1970) • W. M. Hennessy, ed. and trans., *The annals of Loch Cé: a chronicle of Irish affairs from* AD *1014 to* AD *1590*, 2 vols., Rolls Series, 54 (1871), vol. 2 • E. Curtis, *Richard II in Ireland and the submissions of the Irish chiefs* (1927) • W. Reeves, 'Notice of a record preserved in the chapter house, Westminster', *Proceedings of the Royal Irish Academy*, 5 (1850–53), 132–6 • D. B. Quinn, 'Guide to English financial records for Irish history, 1461–1558', *Analecta Hibernica*, 10 (1941), 1–69 • K. Simms, '"The King's Friend": O'Neill, the crown and the earldom of Ulster', *England and Ireland in the later middle ages*, ed. J. Lydon (1981), 214–36 • W. M. Hennessy and B. MacCarthy, eds., *Annals of Ulster, otherwise, annals of Senat*, 4 vols. (1887–1901)

Savage family (*per.* *c.*1369–1528), gentry, originated in Derbyshire. The Savages established an important interest in Cheshire in the late 1370s after **John (I) Savage** (*d.* 1386) married as his second wife the heiress Margaret Danyers. The lands she brought to him, which included Clifton, Cheshire, had been granted to Geoffrey of Dutton by John, constable of Chester, during the reign of Henry II. John Savage had risen to prominence in the service of Edward, the Black Prince, in France: one of the remaining garrison commanders after 1369 when the days of large-scale musters had passed, he held Salveterre in 1373. John died in 1386, leaving an heir, John (II), and three daughters, Elizabeth, Blanche, and Lucy. Margaret survived him and went on to marry Piers Legh, younger son of Robert Legh of Adlington; but it was her Savage descendants to whom she gave the liberty of bearing her arms, argent, four (or five) fusils in pale, sable.

Sir John (II) Savage (*d.* 1450) achieved success in royal service. Like his father, he served in France: Froissart records his complaint in 1390 at the tournament of St Inglevert that he had not crossed the sea merely to run one lance. Under Richard II he was appointed keeper of the park of Macclesfield, along with Piers Legh of Macclesfield. Yet he made the transition to the Lancastrian allegiance: soon after Bolingbroke's accession, Savage was granted a fee and in the first year of the reign he led troops in Henry IV's Scottish campaign. John (II) consolidated his interest around Macclesfield, receiving a lease of its mills in 1408, and he was often a justice on eyre in Cheshire. Knighted at Agincourt, in 1418 John (II) led 250 Cheshire men to Calais; he also received significant rewards from a ransom. Early in Henry IV's reign he married Maud, daughter of Robert Swinnarton, heir to a valuable inheritance which included all the lands once held by Hugh Despenser, earl of Winchester, in Staffordshire and Cheshire; these included the manor of Great Barrow, Cheshire. With Maud, John had five sons, John (III), William, Arnold, George, and Roger,-and three daughters: Margaret, who married John, eventual heir to Sir Piers Dutton of Dutton; Maud, who married Sir Thomas Booth of Barton; and Isabel, who married Robert Legh of Adlington. In 1428, after Maud's death, John married again, his second wife being Ellen, daughter of Sir Ralph Vernon; they were jointly granted the manors of Picton, Shipbrook, and the church of Davenham, which had formed part of the dower of Margaret, wife of Ralph Vernon. Sir John (II) died on 1 August 1450; his son and heir, John (III), born in 1409 or 1410, was already aged forty and more, and the foundations for a transition of power from father to son were laid in 1439 when they were jointly appointed to office in Macclesfield for life.

Sir John (III) Savage (1409/10–1463) extended Savage interests by obtaining a stake in the Middlewich salt industry. He married Elizabeth, daughter of Sir William Brereton, with whom he had John (IV), his son and heir (born in 1421 or 1422, when John (III) was still very young), and three daughters: Margery, who married first Edmund Legh of Baguley, and second Thomas Leycester of Nether Tabley, as his second wife; Margaret, who also married twice, first to John Maxfield, and second to Randle Mainwaring of Carincham, third son of Randle Mainwaring of Peover; and third, Ellen, who married Piers Warburton. John (III) died on 29 July 1463, aged fifty-three, leaving John, his heir, aged forty and more.

John (II) Savage was retained in 1441–2 by Humphrey Stafford, first duke of Buckingham, but Buckingham's intervention in the politics of Cheshire was short-lived. More productive and long-lasting connections were formed with the houses of York and Stanley. Although there is a possibility that John (III) entered the service of the house of York, it seems more likely that it was his son **Sir John (IV) Savage** (*c.*1423–1495) who did so. He was therefore well placed to benefit from Henry VI's deposition. John (III) served as deputy to Sir Thomas *Stanley, afterwards Baron Stanley, as steward of the duchy lordship of Halton, Cheshire. John (IV) married Stanley's daughter Katherine; the couple's children were many and prominent. Aside from John (V), Savage's son and heir, there was Thomas *Savage (*d.* 1507), who rose to be bishop of Rochester in 1492, and of London in 1497, and archbishop of York in 1501, Sir Humphrey, Lawrence, James, Sir Edmund, Christopher, William, George, and Richard. His daughters made good matches, with Ellen being married to Peter Legh of Lyme, Katherine to Thomas Legh of Adlington, Margaret to Edmund Trafford of Trafford, Lancashire, Alice to Roger Pilkington (*d.* 1527) [*see under* Pilkington family], and Elizabeth to John Leek of Langford, Derbyshire. John (IV) was knighted at Elizabeth Woodville's coronation in May 1465, became a knight of the body to Edward IV, and a banneret after the Scottish campaign of 1482; he was also very prominent in local affairs in Cheshire and the north midlands. In 1484, as mayor of Chester, he presided when his sons were made freemen of the city.

Sir John (V) Savage (*d.* 1492), who fought for Edward IV at Tewkesbury, became a royal carver and knight of the body, and was second in order of precedence when Edward was buried. He received many important grants, including that of the constableship of Hanley Castle, Worcestershire. As such close supporters of Edward IV, and associates of the Stanleys, it is not surprising that John (V) and his father seem to have been mistrusted by Richard III. Thomas Savage may have been abroad during the latter's reign and possibly acted as the Savages' direct contact with Henry Tudor. According to Polydore Vergil, John (V) was one of those who 'invited' Tudor to invade. He certainly played an important role at Bosworth, where he commanded the left wing. The author of *Bosworth Feilde* described him and his men, clad in their distinctive white livery hood:

> Sir John Savage, that hardy Knight,
> deathes dentes he delt that day
> with many a white hood in fight,
> that sad men were at assay.
> (Hales and Furnivall, 3.255)

As a result of this support, in 1486 he received an extensive grant in the north midlands of the forfeited estates of John, Lord Zouche, and Francis, Viscount Lovell, valued at £158 p.a. or more. He also received extensive grants of office, especially in Worcestershire and Gloucestershire. The support of the Savages for Henry Tudor guaranteed them a growing prominence at court, and at eight out of eleven council meetings for which evidence survives during the period June–July 1486 either John (V), or Thomas, or both, were present. Sir John (V) Savage led the force that seized Humphrey Stafford from sanctuary at Culham in 1486. He married Dorothy, daughter of Sir Ralph Vernon of Haddon, and the marriages of his daughters suggest the extending interest of the family: Alice married Sir William Brereton; Felicia married Robert Milward of Eaton, Derbyshire; Ellen married John Hawarden; and Maud married Sir Robert Needham of Shenton, Shropshire. Sir John (V) Savage was also notable for his illegitimate offspring: George Savage, parson of Davenham, who himself fathered several illegitimate sons, including George Savage, chancellor of Chester, John Wilmslow, archdeacon of Middlesex, and perhaps Edmund *Bonner, bishop of London. John (V)'s brothers also enjoyed successful careers: Sir Humphrey established a position in Staffordshire and served in the parliament of 1491–2 as knight of the shire for the county; Sir Edmund was knighted at Leith in May 1544 and married Mary, widow of Roger Legh of Ridge, and daughter and heir of William Sparke of Surrey.

Yet the Savages suffered the same difficulties as the Stanleys, in spite of their support for the king. When Richard Savage, brother of John (V), failed to appear on a murder charge, his father was imprisoned. Sir John (V) was killed at the siege of Boulogne in 1492, and Sir Humphrey was already suspected of involvement in the activities of Perkin Warbeck in September 1493, when his house was attacked by two royal servants. The Savage family's remarkable success in winning office and land in the north midlands had already made them enemies, most notably (and in spite of John (V)'s marriage) the Vernons of Haddon. For a few years immediately after 1485 the Savages could rely on the support of others with influence in the region, including the Stanleys, to whom they were related. But by March 1494 this alliance had dissolved, as the Stanleys moved to support the Vernons; Stanley violence, most clearly seen in the murder of William Chetwynd in June 1494, may have helped to forge an alliance between the Savages and Henry Willoughby. Yet Savage and Stanley interests had already clashed, most obviously in the Pilkington–Ainsworth dispute over the manor of Mellor on the Derbyshire–Cheshire border. The Savages, and particularly Bishop Savage, pressed the claims of John Ainsworth, although his adversary Robert Pilkington, who relied on the good lordship of the earl of Derby and his heir, claimed to be able to show his ancestors in possession for eight generations. Conflict flared in 1493, when Sir John (IV) Savage distrained the tenants for rents and evicted those who would not pay, and trouble continued intermittently into the next century. The attack on Sir Humphrey in that same year may also reflect his family's residual loyalty to the Yorkist succession, and fears aroused in Cheshire by the intrusion of the council in the marches of Wales into the palatine administration.

Sir John (IV) Savage died on 22 November 1495 at the age of seventy-three. His grandson **Sir John (VI) Savage** (*d.* 1527) succeeded to his father's offices after the latter's death at Boulogne and became a knight for the body by 1501. John (VI) married Anne, daughter and heir of Ralph Bostock, and thereby acquired a claim to the Venables of Kinderton inheritance. Although the Venables interest had the case dismissed from Star Chamber to common law, John (VI) Savage used the influence of the earl of Shrewsbury, Sir Thomas Lovell, and Edmund Dudley to secure victory. With Anne he had seven sons, John (VII), Edward, George, Richard, Lawrence, Roger, and Thomas, and a daughter, Anne, who married Thomas, sixth Baron Berkeley, in 1533. The fall of Sir Humphrey Savage did not affect John (VI)'s career. The most obvious sign of his success at court was the marriage of his heir John (VII) to Elizabeth, the daughter of Charles Somerset, later earl of Worcester. Yet, especially after the death of Archbishop Thomas, the Savages' position was still open to challenge. In 1498 John (VI) lost the stewardship of the High Peak, Derbyshire, and a combination of personal extravagance and royal policy left him in debt to the crown. By 1515 some Savage estates were taken into royal hands to secure payment.

Although John (VI) provided a contingent for the campaign against France in 1512, and his son **Sir John (VII) Savage** (*d.* 1528) led a company in 1513 and was knighted at Tournai, the Savages' continued contempt for royal authority in their regional power bases in the west and north-west soon made them a target for Cardinal Wolsey's determination to administer 'indifferent' justice. The immediate occasion for action against them was the murder on 31 March 1516 by John (VII) and his associates of John Pauncefote, a JP in Worcestershire and potential rival to the Savages in that region. Both Johns were taken into custody in the Tower in June 1516. By the time the two men were brought into king's bench in February 1517 the number of indictments had grown to at least sixty-seven. After a long series of hearings, which also provided the occasion for a radical reinterpretation of the laws of sanctuary, the alleged violation of which had formed the central plank of John (VII)'s response to an appeal of murder, both Johns abandoned their defences, and in November 1520 were granted royal pardons. Clearly, a deal had been concocted behind the scenes, involving the king's sister Mary and John (VII)'s brother-in-law, the earl of Worcester. The settlement was not to the Savages' advantage, however, for John (VI) lost his offices and had substantial fines imposed. For the payment of these nearly all the Savage estates outside Cheshire were entrusted to royal feoffees and leased back to the family at an annual rent of £160, while for additional security those in Cheshire were also taken over by the crown. Despite their consequent heavy indebtedness the Savages seem to have failed to learn their lesson, continuing in subsequent years a long-standing quarrel with Sir Piers Dutton of Halton, and feuding with Ralph Leche over the manor of Ilkeston. John (VI) died in 1527, and his son John (VII) in 1528, only a few months after the crown had foreclosed on his father's debt. John (VI) was probably buried in Macclesfield church, where his son was interred. What was left of the Savage inheritance passed to John (VII)'s infant son, John Savage (*d.* 1597), who grew up 'to be a worshipful Elizabethan gentleman' (Ives, 319). TIM THORNTON

Sources G. Ormerod, *The history of the county palatine and city of Chester*, 2nd edn, ed. T. Helsby, 3 vols. (1882) • *26th report of the deputy keeper of the public records* • *Report of the Deputy Keeper of the Public Records*, 31 (1870) • R. Somerville, *History of the duchy of Lancaster*,

1265–1603 (1953) · J. Varley, ed., *Middlewich cartulary*, 1, Chetham Society, new ser., 105 (1941) · J. Varley and J. Tait, eds., *Middlewich cartulary*, 2, Chetham Society, new ser., 108 (1944) · *Report on manuscripts in various collections*, 8 vols., HMC, 55 (1901–14), vol. 2, pp. 28–56 [summarizes N. Yorks. CRO, ZDV XI] · W. A. Shaw, *The knights of England*, 2 vols. (1906), vol. 1, p. 17 · *Report of the Deputy Keeper of the Public Records*, 37 (1876), 646 · J. H. E. Bennett, ed., *The rolls of the freemen of the city of Chester*, 1, Lancashire and Cheshire RS, 51 (1906), 8–9 · *CPR, 1476–1509* · *Three books of Polydore Vergil's 'English history'*, ed. H. Ellis, CS, 29 (1844) · J. Gairdner, ed., *Letters and papers illustrative of the reigns of Richard III and Henry VII*, 1, Rolls Series, 24 (1861), 1 · S. B. Chrimes, *Henry VII* (1972) · E. W. Ives, 'Crime, sanctuary and royal authority under Henry VIII: the exemplary sufferings of the Savage family', *On the laws and customs of England: essays in honour of Samuel E. Thorne*, ed. M. S. Arnold, T. A. Green, and others (Chapel Hill, NC, 1981), 296–320 · C. G. Bayne and W. H. Dunham, eds., *Select cases in the council of Henry VII*, SeldS, 75 (1958) · J. W. Hales and F. J. Furnivall, eds., *Bishop Percy's folio manuscript*, 3 vols. (1868), vol. 3 · effigy, Macclesfield church, Cheshire [probably Sir John (IV) Savage] · effigy, Macclesfield church, Cheshire [probably Sir John (V) Savage] · effigy, Macclesfield church, Cheshire [probably Sir John (VI) Savage] · effigy, Macclesfield church, Cheshire [Sir John (VII) Savage]

Archives Cheshire County RO, Cholmondeley of Cholmondeley collection (DCH)

Likenesses effigy (Sir John (V) Savage?), Macclesfield church · effigy (Sir John (IV) Savage?), Macclesfield church · effigy (Sir John (VI) Savage?), Macclesfield church · effigy (Sir John (VII) Savage), Macclesfield church

Savage, Sir Arnold (*d.* 1375). *See under* Savage, Sir Arnold (1358–1410).

Savage, Sir Arnold [Arnald] **(1358–1410)**, administrator and speaker of the House of Commons, was born on 8 September 1358 and baptized in St Bartholomew's Church at Bobbing, near Sittingbourne in Kent, where his family had been settled since the thirteenth century. His father, also **Sir Arnold Savage** (*d.* 1375), was a member of the household of Edward, the Black Prince, and served at Crécy in 1346 in the retinue of Michael, Lord Poynings (*d.* 1369), whose daughter Margery became Savage's first wife. The first Sir Arnold was several times a commissioner of array in Kent, sheriff and escheator of the county in 1348–9, knight of the shire in 1352, and warden of the Kentish coasts in 1355. From 1359 to 1363 he was mayor of Bordeaux, being employed in the latter year in negotiations with Castile, and in 1371 and 1373 with France. He died on 27 July 1375, at the Black Prince's manor of Wallingford, shortly after going to Bruges as a member of an embassy led by John of Gaunt, duke of Lancaster. Eleanor, his second wife and mother of the second Sir Arnold, died in October of the same year.

The second Sir Arnold Savage was not yet seventeen when his father died. He proved his age in 1380, but it was not until May 1382 that he was granted seisin of his father's lands, comprising the manors of Bobbing and Tracies in Newington, Kent, and other small properties nearby. Before that he had undertaken to pay £40 for the right to marry whom he pleased, a payment that was remitted in consideration of the good services of his mother, Eleanor, to the king—she had nursed the future Richard II in his infancy. When Savage did marry, it was to Joan, daughter of Sir William Eckingham, with whom he had one son, another Sir Arnold, and one daughter. The third Sir Arnold married Katherine, daughter of Roger, Lord Scales, while his sister Eleanor married successively Sir Reynold Cobham (*d.* 1405) and William Clifford.

After the revolt of 1381 Savage served on a commission to restore peace in Kent, becoming sheriff of the county in 1381–2; and in 1385 he took part in the king's expedition to Scotland, with only one archer in his company. Knighted during this campaign he was to serve Richard II as a king's knight or chamber knight for the remainder of the reign. In 1387 he joined the earl of Arundel's raid on La Rochelle. This time his greatly enlarged retinue comprised one other knight, twenty-eight esquires, and thirty-six archers. He was returned as one of the knights of the shire for Kent to both parliaments of 1390, meeting in January and November. After the end of the second parliament Savage was appointed, with Sir William Hoos and others, to inquire into the shortcomings of Thomas Kempe, late escheator for Kent and Middlesex, and on 31 December 1390 he was granted 40 marks yearly from the issues of Kent, in consideration of his father's good services to the Black Prince and of his own to the present king. In 1396 this grant was replaced by one of £50 yearly from the petty custom of London. His meagre landed inheritance doubtless made him dependent on such grants to maintain his knightly status. In November 1391 he was once more returned to parliament for Kent, and continued in the following years to be appointed to various commissions for the county, including the commissions of the peace from 1396 to 1399. In 1393 he was granted the custody of Queenborough Castle in Sheppey for life.

Savage is not known to have taken any active part in the politics of the last years of Richard II, and was not even a member of parliament in September 1399, but had evidently no difficulty in changing his allegiance. On the accession of Henry IV he was immediately confirmed on the commission of the peace for Kent, and remained on it for the rest of his life, while the new king also renewed his annuity of £50. By January 1401, when he was again returned to parliament for Kent, he was a member of the prince of Wales's council; and this time the Commons chose him as their speaker. Then it immediately became clear that he enjoyed lecturing the king, the Lords, and the Commons, whom he later described as a 'Trinity'; according to Thomas Walsingham, Savage's eloquence earned universal praise. He requested that the Commons should not be hurried, and three days later asked the king not to listen to talebearers. Then he said that the needs for good government were 'sense, humanity and richness' (*RotP*, 3.456), and that the Commons should avoid conduct by which they might be seen as flatterers. But when he presented himself a third time, the king, evidently tired of listening to his copious advice, asked that further petitions should be put in writing. At the end of the session, in a demand anticipating much in the later history of parliament, Savage asked that Commons' petitions should be answered before a grant was made. To this proposal, that redress should precede supply, Henry gave no direct answer. Finally Sir Arnold likened the meeting of parliament to the mass. Three days later his own grant of £50 yearly from the petty custom was confirmed.

Whether Savage sat in the next parliament in January 1402 is unknown because the returns are lost, but about Michaelmas of that year he became a member of the king's council with a yearly salary of £100, by far the largest grant that he ever received; and in January 1404 he was again returned to parliament for Kent, and for the second and last time elected speaker. The Commons sat for sixty-seven days and Savage voiced their criticisms; the king's manors and castles were in a ruinous state, a large number of grants were neither rightly nor discreetly made, and the cost of the royal household was excessive. Restrictions were then imposed on the royal household, a rather grudging new tax on knights' fees and income was granted, and the revenue from it entrusted to four treasurers of war—hardly a satisfactory session for the king. The position of a speaker like Savage, simultaneously a royal councillor and spokesman of the Commons, was inevitably ambivalent. But it does not seem to have been held against him that he had given voice to so much in the way of criticism and complaint. Although he was not returned to the Commons again, he remained an active member of the council, his attendance being regularly recorded until 1409. As a councillor he was sent on three embassies in 1408 and 1409 to treat for peace with France. He died on 29 November 1410, and was buried in St Bartholomew's Church, Bobbing, where his brass still survives. J. L. KIRBY

Sources *CIPM*, 14, 15, 19 • *RotP*, 3.455–6, 466, 523, 530 • *Return of MPs*, 1.53–284 • *Chancery records* • N. H. Nicolas, ed., *Proceedings and ordinances of the privy council of England*, 7 vols., RC, 26 (1834–7), vols. 1–2 • Rymer, *Foedera*, 3rd edn, 4/1 • T. Otterbourne, *Chronica*, ed. T. Hearne (1732), 232 • F. C. Hingeston, ed., *Royal and historical letters during the reign of Henry the Fourth*, 1, Rolls Series, 18 (1860), 69 • E. Hasted, *The history and topographical survey of the county of Kent*, 2nd edn, 3 (1797), 446; 6 (1798) • W. Warwick, 'On Gower, the Kentish poet, his character and works', *Archaeologia Cantiana*, 6 (1866), 83–107, esp. 87 • J. G. Waller, 'The lords of Cobham, their monuments, and the church [pt 1]', *Archaeologia Cantiana*, 11 (1877), 49–112, esp. 91 • G. O. Bellewes, 'The last Savages of Bobbing', *Archaeologia Cantiana*, 29 (1911), 164–8 • J. S. Roskell, 'Sir Arnald Savage of Bobbing', *Archaeologia Cantiana*, 70 (1956), 68–83 • J. S. Roskell, *The Commons and their speakers in English parliaments, 1376–1523* (1965) • W. Stubbs, *The constitutional history of England in its origin and development*, new edn, 2 (1896), 2.29–31 • J. H. Ramsay, *Lancaster and York* (1892), 1.29, 69, 73, 98 • J. L. Kirby, 'Councils and councillors of Henry IV', *TRHS*, 5th ser., 14 (1964), 35–65 • J. L. Kirby, *Henry IV of England* (1970) • H. M. Colvin and others, eds., *The history of the king's works*, 6 vols. (1963–82) • A. L. Brown, 'The Commons and the council in the reign of Henry IV', *EngHR*, 79 (1964), 1–30 • E. F. Jacob, ed., *The register of Henry Chichele, archbishop of Canterbury, 1414–1443*, 2, CYS, 42 (1937), 205–6

Likenesses brass sculpture, St Bartholomew's Church, Bobbing, Kent

Savage, Sir Arnold (*c.*1382–1420). *See under* Savage family (*per. c.*1280–*c.*1420).

Savage, Edmund (*fl. c.*1385–*c.*1398). *See under* Savage family (*per.* 1333–1519).

Savage [*née* Darcy], **Elizabeth**, *suo jure* **Countess Rivers** (**1581–1651**), courtier and victim of popular violence, was the daughter of Thomas Darcy, third Baron Darcy of Chiche (*d.* 1640), later created Viscount Colchester (1621) and Earl Rivers (1626), and his wife, Mary Kitson (*d.* 1644), daughter of Sir Thomas Kitson of Hengrave, Suffolk. On 14 May 1602 she married Thomas Savage (*c.*1586–1635), with whom she had a large family of eleven sons and eight daughters. Savage was the eldest surviving son of Sir John Savage of Cheshire and his wife, Mary Allington, daughter and coheir to Sir Richard Allington, from which family he inherited the manor of Melford Hall, Suffolk. Savage inherited his father's baronetcy in 1615; in November 1626 he was created Viscount Savage. At his death, on 20 November 1635, Elizabeth inherited Melford Hall, which together with St Osyth Priory in Essex formed her principal residences. Her father died in February 1640 and was succeeded by her eldest son, John Savage, as Earl Rivers; fourteen months later, on 21 April 1641, she herself was created Countess Rivers *suo jure*, for life.

Elizabeth Savage inherited from her father and husband the political and religious allegiances that were to bring her ruin in the civil war. Both men were closely associated with the court of Charles I, both had links with the duke of Buckingham, and both played a role in their respective counties (Essex in the case of the former and Lancashire and Cheshire in the case of the latter) in the enforcement of Caroline policy. Elizabeth and her husband both served at the court of Charles I, Thomas as chancellor to Queen Henrietta Maria; Elizabeth, as a lady of the bedchamber, was a close companion of the queen, after whom she named one of her daughters. These appointments reflected the family's strong Catholic links. Elizabeth's father was suspected of being a church papist, but he enjoyed royal protection against recusancy legislation. The houses at both St Osyth and Long Melford formed little islands of Catholicism surrounded by neighbouring communities with a strong commitment to puritanism. Knowledge of the family's Catholicism and of the presence of Jesuit priests had made them an object of popular rumour as well as of official action, her father being excluded from the county magistracy.

The political instability brought about by the collapse of Charles I's personal rule and parliament's emphasis on a Catholic conspiracy as the explanation for their inability to secure a settlement with the king heightened rumour and suspicion. In January 1642 Countess Rivers's sister spoke of being daily threatened by the common sort of people. Parliament's call for action against Catholics worsened the family's position. Elizabeth was presented to the Essex courts as a recusant and her house was searched for arms on the order of parliament. In August 1642 the crowds at Colchester who had attacked Sir John Lucas there went on to attack Catholics in the belief that this was what parliament really wanted. Although many Catholic families were affected, Countess Rivers became the most famous victim. Edward Hyde, earl of Clarendon, included an account of her fate in his *History of the Rebellion* and the royalist newsbook writer Bruno Ryves gave a detailed (and colourful) account in his newsbook, *Mercurius Rusticus*. At St Osyth the crowds ransacked and plundered the house. Forewarned, the countess had fled to her other house at Long Melford but the crowds followed her there and all but destroyed that house as well, the countess claiming only just to have escaped as the crowds broke in. The family of the present incumbent at Melford Hall, Sir Richard Hyde Parker, have preserved a colourful story of the countess's fleeing the house and throwing into a nearby pond a box with the strings of pearls that are to be seen in her portrait at the hall. Seven years later the Essex minister Ralph Josselin, on a trip to Melford, noted, 'I saw the ruines of that great [house], plundered out and desoloate without inhabitants', while St Osyth was later said to have remained uninhabited for the next seventy years (*Diary of Ralph Josselin*, 174). The countess put her losses at some £100,000 and claimed not to have been left even a change of apparel.

Although the popular attacks on her may have attracted wider support from those opposed to the family's association with Charles I's regime and offended by their estate policies as major landowners and their use of their extensive religious patronage to appoint ministers of crypto-papist or Arminian leanings (several of whom were also attacked), Countess Rivers was able to secure support from those who shared neither her religion nor her politics. The earl of Holland in asking Sir Thomas Barrington to support her acknowledged the difference in religion, but noted that in the countess her Catholicism 'is governed with more modesty and Temper than I ever sawe it in any person' (BL, Egerton MS 2646, fol. 197*r*). Parliament ordered the restitution of her goods, but this seems to have had only limited effect, her problems being compounded by a rent strike by her tenants. After a second episode in which parliamentarian soldiers invaded her house and took away her goods, she sought permission to go to France in May 1643. In 1648 she petitioned successfully to be allowed to compound for her estates sequestrated by parliament. However, the attacks, combined with the fines imposed on her and her son Earl Rivers, declared a notorious papist by parliament in July 1642, took a heavy toll. At her death, on 9 March 1651, she was said to be bankrupt. She was buried at St Osyth with her Darcy ancestors. JOHN WALTER

Sources J. Walter, *Understanding popular violence in the English Revolution: the Colchester plunderers* (1999) • L. Dow, 'The Savage hatchment at Long Melford', *Proceedings of the Suffolk Institute of Archaeology*, 26 (1952–4), 214–19 • BL, Harley MS 33, fols. 19–21 • HLRO, Main papers collection, HL, 29/8/1642, 9/9/1642 • PRO, SP 16/446/28; SP 16/352/50; SP 16/023, 57 • *JHL*, 5 (1642–3), 201–2, 331 • *JHL*, 6 (1643–4), 19, 57, 89–90 • B. Ryves, *Mercurius Rusticus, or, The countries complaint of the morthers, robberies, plundrings* … (1643) • M. A. E. Green, ed., *Calendar of the proceedings of the committee for compounding* … *1643–1660*, 3, PRO (1891), 1857 • BL, Egerton MS 2646, fol. 197*r* • C. M. Hibbard, 'The role of a queen consort: the household and court of Henrietta Maria, 1625–42', *Princes, patronage and the nobility: the court and the beginning of the modern age, c.1450–1650*, ed. R. G. Asch and A. M. Birke (1991), 393–414 • Essex RO, Q/S Ba 5/1/3; Q/SR 317/34 • CUL, Hengrave MSS • J. A. Rush, *Seats in Essex, comprising picturesque views of the seats of the nobility and gentry* [n.d., 1897?], 143 • Clarendon, *Hist. rebellion* • *The diary of Ralph Josselin, 1616–1683*, ed. A. MacFarlane, British Academy, Records of Social and Economic History, new ser., 3 (1976), 174 • GEC, *Peerage* • BL, Harley MS 6071, fol. 79*v*

Archives CUL, Hengrave MSS

Likenesses attrib. P. Lely, oils, *c*.1640, Melford Hall, Suffolk

Wealth at death died in debt: GEC, *Peerage*

Savage, Ethel Mary. *See* Dell, Ethel Mary (1881–1939).

Savage, Sir George Henry (1842–1921), psychiatrist, was born at 65 Edward Street, Brighton, Sussex, on 12 November 1842, the son of William Dawson Savage, a chemist and druggist at Balham and then Brighton, and his wife, Elizabeth Wallace. Educated at private schools in Brighton and then at Brighton College, Savage attended chemistry classes and was apprenticed locally to a firm of doctors; he subsequently matriculated from London University with honours in botany. For the next two years he was a pupil at Sussex County Hospital, and studied medicine from 1861 at Guy's Hospital, London, where he won the treasurer's gold medal. He qualified MRCS in 1864, LRCP and MB (London) in 1865, and MD in 1867. After being appointed resident house surgeon at Guy's in 1865 he moved to general practice, working for four years as medical officer for a lead mining company at Nenthead, Alston, in Cumberland, often being required to ride 20 miles a day visiting his patients. It was here that he met his first wife, Margaret, daughter of Jacob Walton, of Alston Moor, who died of a pulmonary embolism little more than a year after their marriage on 9 September 1868; they had one child. Savage was appointed assistant medical officer to Bethlem Royal Hospital in 1872 under Rhys Williams. Succeeding to the post of physician superintendent in 1879, Savage served in that capacity until 1888, when he retired to take up private practice and was made a governor of the hospital. He took the MRCP in 1878, and was elected FRCP in 1885.

Savage's shift towards private practice was discernible by the 1880s, as he sought to reach a more popular market with his writings and began to be a frequent absentee from Bethlem, something that aroused criticism from his colleague J. C. Bucknill. As a private practitioner, Savage was not only one of the most fashionable but one of the first, among a number of leading Victorian specialists in mental diseases, to seek success outside the asylum and to develop a practice based on the consulting room. Savage also became consulting physician to several private asylums, including The Priory, Roehampton, and Chiswick House. As a private consultant he was also frequently consulted by the Home Office in difficult mental cases. Savage was additionally a lecturer on mental diseases at Guy's Hospital for thirty years. His straightforward, authoritative teaching at Bethlem and Guy's attracted students from all over the world. He was in demand too as a postgraduate teacher, especially for the London University MD degree, serving as an examiner in mental pathology. Throughout his career Savage was a supporter of medical education for women, providing both financial and moral backing. However, in his writings he supported the commonly held belief in the danger of over educating females of frailer nerves.

Savage also served for over twenty years as consulting physician to the Royal Institution for the Mentally Deficient, Earlswood, and was on its board of management. He was elected president of the Medico-Psychological Association (MPA) in 1886, giving a presidential address on insanity's relationship to bodily and functional disorders. He was an original member of the Neurological Society and was elected president in 1897, when he spoke on heredity and neurosis.

Savage jointly (with Daniel Hack Tuke and Thomas Clouston) edited the *Journal of Mental Science* from 1878 to 1894. He was a prolific writer, publishing over a hundred articles in this and other medical journals, capitalizing on the clinical material provided by his extensive hospital experience. While at Bethlem he had joined Klein's physiology classes and made the most of the hospital's rather limited pathological opportunities, making a number of contributions to the Neurological Society and to its journal, *Brain*. Despite devoting much attention to the central nervous system, Savage was essentially a clinician, and his contributions to psychiatry were supplemental rather than seminal. His publications covered a wide range of subjects, from catalepsy, epilepsy, puerperal insanity, the neuroses, and general paralysis of the insane, to the pathology of insanity and restraint. Early articles (1879 and 1881) on the administration of chloral and hyoscyamine are of note for their criticisms of excessive chemical restraint. Savage used sedation sparingly and mostly for violent and dangerous cases, although for deterrent as well as quietening purposes. Savage's relatively large scale use of mechanical restraint at Bethlem, on the other hand, aroused considerable controversy in the press and within the profession, drawing particular criticism from J. C. Bucknill. Savage's association with the pro-restraint lobby seems to have been one of the reasons that his relations became strained with Henry Maudsley too—not a single article by Maudsley appeared in the *Journal of Mental Science* during Savage and Tuke's joint editorship. Savage also appears to have been quite positively disposed to the benefits of sexual surgery for insanity, giving early support to such surgery on a few cases at Bethlem, and later being one of a number of psychiatrists sympathetic towards sterilization for the mentally 'unfit'.

In 1907 Savage gave the Lumleian lectures before the Royal College of Physicians, entitled 'The increase of insanity', on which Savage offered a traditional perspective, convinced that the increase was real and directly related to the progress of civilization. While he accepted that the transmission of insanity might lead to the extinction of the race, his preventive and eugenic concerns with controls over reproduction and immigration did not prevent him from being critical of alarmist contemporary theories. In 1909 he lectured at the college on experimental psychology and hypnotism as the Harveian orator for that year. His lecture offered a slightly more hopeful assessment of the likely benefits and medical uses of psychological observations and hypnotism than those given by many of his professional contemporaries.

Savage also published on forensic psychiatry, becoming known as an expert witness in insanity pleas, and extending his public profile by expounding on the Jack the Ripper case. His status as an authority on a variety of medico-psychological matters is underlined by the fact that he wrote twenty of the articles in Daniel Hack Tuke's *Dictionary of Psychological Medicine* (1892) and six in T. C. Allbutt's *System of Medicine* (1896–9). His publications also included a number of influential papers on the association of insanity with marriage, which showed that he was not prepared to go as far as some of his more eugenically minded colleagues in advocating state regulation of espousal and fertility. Savage's major single authored work was a textbook entitled *Insanity and Allied Neuroses* (1884), which was praised as being an accessible, standard reference book for students and junior practitioners, but was also criticized for its neglect of pathology; it went into a fourth revised edition in 1893 and was further enlarged in 1907. Savage moved further than most of his colleagues towards recognizing that general paralysis was the result of structural changes in the nervous system associated with syphilis. He also emphasized the influence of individuals' environment in determining their mental state, often seeing insanity as being as much to do with maladjustment to changing social and environmental factors as with organic disease and constitutional predisposition.

Savage was knighted in 1912, and in the same year was elected first president of the newly formed psychiatric section of the Royal Society of Medicine. He also took an active role in the management of the After-Care Association, acting as its treasurer until his death. He remained relatively active well into the twilight of his life, continuing to publish and deliver papers. During the First World War he served as a consultant to Knutsford's hospitals for officers and spoke before the MPA on wartime mental disabilities.

Savage's most famous private patient was the novelist Virginia Woolf, about whose mental problems he was intermittently consulted between 1904 and 1913, having long been both friend and physician to her family. Historical and literary scholarship on his treatment of Woolf has tended to pronounce negatively, censuring his espousal of a strict rest-cure regime as inappropriate and profoundly out of sympathy with Woolf's needs as a woman and a writer. Woolf was hostile from the outset to Savage's prescription and her family also gradually lost faith in his advice, the final straw being her attempted suicide at the very moment the family was explaining to Savage why they had called in a second opinion. Woolf exacted her revenge through her portrayal of him in her novel *Mrs Dalloway*, Savage serving as one of the models for the sinister and domineering society nerve specialist, Sir William Bradshaw. Yet despite Woolf's (and others') characterization of Savage as tyrannical and shortsighted, his prescriptions of rest, a ban on reading and writing, isolation from friends, simple regimen, confinement in a nursing home or in natural surroundings away from the city, and holidaying in the country and at the coast, were relatively mild and conventional fare for mentally and physically ill patients in late Victorian times.

Savage enjoyed a breadth of non-medical interests. He was an enthusiastic alpine climber, making a record ascent of the Matterhorn and being a member and one-time vice-president of the Alpine Club. He was also a keen cyclist, golfer, fisherman, gardener, and fencer, as well as an avid mineralogist and botanist, devoting much of his spare time to gathering and cataloguing a considerable collection of rock and flora samples. Well-connected socially, Savage took pains to become a prominent member of numerous gentlemen's social and recreational clubs and associations, from the 'Sunday Tramps', to the Organon Club and the Casual Club. Savage had also joined and (for a time) presided over the Old Union Masonic Lodge, but abandoned masonry on his second marriage, on 3 May 1882, to Adelaide Mary Sutton (*b.* 1856/7), daughter of Henry Gawen Sutton, physician. Savage was seen by contemporaries as a candid, humorous, sociable, clubbable, vigorous bodied man; he was a great supporter of the physical and psychical virtues of exercise and sport. Suffering from progressive deafness and bodily debility later in life, he died after 'an attack of hemiplegia' on 5 July 1921, at his home, 26 Devonshire Place, London. He was cremated and his ashes were interred at Sevenoaks. His second wife had died in the early 1900s. He left a son, Harold Savage, who was a medical practitioner in the Malay States, and a daughter, Mrs Droeser.

JONATHAN ANDREWS

Sources *The Lancet* (16 July 1921), 155 · *BMJ* (9 July 1921), 63 · *BMJ* (16 July 1921), 98–9 · *BMJ* (30 July 1921), 174 · R. P. Smith, *Journal of Mental Science*, 67 (1921), 393–404 · Munk, *Roll* · E. Showalter, *The female malady: women, madness and English culture, 1830–1980* (1985); repr. (1988) · S. Trombley, *All that summer she was mad: Virginia Woolf: female victim of male medicine* (1982) · A. Scull, C. MacKenzie, and N. Hervey, *Masters of Bedlam: the transformation of the mad-doctoring trade* (1996) · P. Fennell, *Treatment without consent: law, psychiatry and the treatment of the mentally disordered people since 1845* (1996) · *The diary of Virginia Woolf*, ed. A. O. Bell and A. McNeillie, 5 vols. (1977–84) · Q. Bell, *Virginia Woolf: a biography*, 2 vols. (1972) · *The letters of Virginia Woolf*, ed. N. Nicolson, 6 vols. (1975–80) · b. cert. · m. cert. [Adelaide Mary Sutton] · *CGPLA Eng. & Wales* (1921)

Archives Bethlem Royal Hospital, Beckenham, Kent

Likenesses photograph, 1886, RCP Lond., book of presidents of the Medico-Psychological Association · Vincent Brooks for Day & Son Ltd, cartoon, lithograph, 1912, repro. in *VF Supplement* (7 Feb 1912); copy, RCP Lond. · Adlard & Son & West Newman Ltd, photograph, repro. in Smith, *Journal of Mental Science*, 393 · colour reproduction (after lithograph), Yale U., Clements C. Fry print collection · photograph, RCP Lond., College Club · photograph, RCP Lond. · photograph (after lithograph), Yale U.

Wealth at death £27,038 8s. 5d.: probate, 1 Sept 1921, *CGPLA Eng. & Wales*

Savage, Sir (Edward) Graham (1886–1981), schoolteacher and educational administrator, was born on 31 August 1886 at Upper Sheringham, Norfolk, the eldest in the family of three sons and two daughters, the surviving children of Edward Graham Savage and his wife, Mary Matilda Dewey, whose family were small farmers at Donhead, near Shaftesbury in Dorset. His parents were the teachers at Upper Sheringham elementary school which he attended before King Edward VI School, Norwich, and Downing College, Cambridge. At Cambridge he obtained firsts in part one of the natural sciences tripos (1905) and part two of the historical tripos (1906).

Before the First World War Savage held various teaching appointments at Bede College, Durham; St Andrew's College, Toronto; and Tawfiqieh School and the Khedival Training College, Cairo. He also joined the Territorial Army.

In 1911 he married May, daughter of Percy Thwaites, an artist, of Southchurch, Essex. They had two sons and a daughter. On the outbreak of war he was commissioned in the Royal West Kent regiment, as a captain and later major, fighting at Gallipoli and in France, being severely wounded at Ypres.

In 1919 Savage became an inspector of schools for the Board of Education and began a career of rapid advancement in the public service. After a stint as a district inspector (1919–27) he became successively staff inspector for science (1927), divisional inspector for the north-west (1931–2), chief inspector of technical schools and colleges (1932), and senior chief inspector from 1933 to 1940.

When E. M. Rich, the education officer to the London county council, retired in 1940, Savage jumped at the opportunity to exchange the role of a school inspector for that of senior local authority educational administrator. The London job was a challenge which appealed to him; it was also better paid. Savage's early years in London were spent improvising schooling for children who drifted back to the capital in the lulls between the bombing. It was a period of extreme difficulty when a depleted education service was at full stretch and educational standards inevitably suffered.

By 1943 Savage was looking ahead to post-war reconstruction. Labour had controlled the London county council since 1934. Soon after taking over, Labour members had been frustrated in attempts to eliminate the sharp distinctions between grammar and senior elementary schools. Savage thought along similar lines. The London school plan (1947) provided for comprehensive schools, not separate county grammar, technical, and modern schools. He claimed later that his ideas arose from a visit he had paid, as a school inspector, to Canada and the United States in the winter of 1925–6. He admired the comprehensive character of the American high schools though much of his subsequent report dwelt on their failure to provide for the differentiated needs of the whole school community.

The London plan bore Savage's authentic stamp, but he was also a realist and recognized that this was the answer his political masters wanted. He remained ambivalent about many aspects of comprehensive education. He wanted all kinds of pupil together under the same roof, but he expected them to pursue markedly different courses, with a strong practical, technical, and vocational input. The current assumption was that these schools would have to be very large—360 to 390 children in each year group—to yield a big enough academic sixth form.

Moreover, as the law stood, London's fifty-five aided grammar schools remained largely unscathed, to continue alongside the so-called comprehensives.

To the end of his life Savage remained a grammar-school man at heart, with a special regard for the direct-grant schools, which he described in a *Times* interview in 1965 as 'the scaffolding on which a good state system of secondary education is slowly being built'.

A large man with a large personality, a bald dome of a head, and a face scarred by war wounds with a bristling moustache, Savage was not an easy man to know, even for those who worked closely with him for many years. There was a warmer side to his personality which his family knew, which came out in visits to children and teachers injured in the bombing.

After his retirement in 1951, Savage acted between 1956 and 1964 as chief assessor to the Industrial Fund for the Advancement of Science Teaching in Schools, channelling money to independent schools for laboratories and equipment. His many other distinctions included being chairman of the League of the Empire (1947–62), the Simplified Spelling Society (1949–68), and the Board of Building Education (1956–66). He was president of the Science Masters' Association (1952–3) and from 1967 to 1971 vice-president of the City and Guilds of London Institute. He was made an honorary fellow of the Institute of Builders in 1966. He was appointed CB in 1935 and knighted in 1947. Savage died on 18 May 1981 in Highgate, London.

STUART MACLURE, *rev.*

Sources *The Times* (20 May 1981) • S. Maclure, *One hundred years of London education, 1870–1970* (1970) • private information (1990) • *WWW* • b. cert. • m. cert. • d. cert.

Wealth at death £36,824: probate, 6 Oct 1981, *CGPLA Eng. & Wales*

Savage, Henry (*c.*1604–1672), college head, was one of the sons, probably the second, of Francis Savage (*d.* 1617) of Dobshill in the Worcestershire parish of Eldersfield, a wealthy gentleman who named eleven living children by at least two wives in his will of 1614. Savage was a commoner of Balliol College, Oxford, by 1622, and by 1624 an exhibitioner on the foundation of John Bell, bishop of Worcester, but he delayed matriculation until some months before graduating BA in 1625. Elected a fellow of Balliol in 1628, he proceeded MA in 1630 and BD in 1637, and resided in college until early in the civil war, when he withdrew to travel in France with his pupil William Sandys (1626/7–1668).

In 1648 Savage was presented to the vicarage of Sherborne St John in Hampshire, a Sandys family advowson. That year he failed to appear as required before the Oxford parliamentary visitors, and nearly lost his fellowship, but in 1651, the year in which he gained the degree of DD, they appointed him master. In 1653 and 1655 he published minor works on infant baptism. About 1655 Savage married Mary Sandys (*d.* 1683), sister of his former pupil William, and daughter of Henry Sandys (*d.* 1644), of Sherborne St John, who had been a royalist colonel. Over the next seventeen years the couple had at least seven children, five of whom survived their father.

Despite owing the mastership to parliamentary authority, Savage retained it at the Restoration and enjoyed royal patronage in the ensuing decade. In 1660, the year which saw the publication of his anti-presbyterian work on church government and the successful claim of his brother-in-law to the Sandys barony, he became a chaplain-in-ordinary. He was made rector of Sherborne St John in 1662 and a prebendary of Gloucester in 1666, and was also given dispensation in 1662 and 1670 respectively to hold the Oxfordshire rectories of Bladon and Crowmarsh Gifford, in plurality with the Lincolnshire rectory of Fillingham, a Balliol benefice he had taken in 1661. Savage also claimed another Balliol rectory in Lincolnshire, that of Riseholme. Meanwhile he published a work on toleration, *The dew of Hermon which fell upon the hill of Sion, or, An answer to a book entitl'd 'Sion's groans'* (1663).

Balliol fell into financial difficulties during the civil war, and its position deteriorated under Savage. This was partly because London property was lost in the 1666 conflagration, but mainly because of mismanagement and abuse. In 1670 the college's visitor, Bishop William Fuller of Lincoln, intervened. Fuller was shocked by what he found and formally admonished Savage, ordering him to hand over £20, the corrupt proceeds of selling a college cook's place. This was perhaps by way of a specimen charge; several other complaints against Savage were never resolved. Balliol continued under visitation for the remainder of his mastership, and after his death there was suspicion that he had embezzled benefactions. Reflecting in 1676, his successor, Thomas Good, who had instigated the visitation although an old friend, wrote 'had D[r]. Savage livd but a year longer the colledge gates had been shutt up', but judged him 'a good schollar, and in himself an honest man but unaequally yoaked' (Lincs. Arch., VV2/4/22).

Savage's main published work was *Balliofergus, or, A commentary upon the foundation, founders and affaires of Balliol Colledge, gathered out of the records thereof, and other antiquities: with a brief description of eminent persons who have been formerly of the same house* (1668). It contains much harping on financial misfortune, in the forlorn hope of raising funds. Anthony Wood was very critical of it, although he had provided some of the material. It is not entirely reliable, but gives a valuable outline of early Balliol history, and is of general interest to antiquarians as the first history of any college based on original documentation. Savage died in Balliol on 2 June 1672. He was buried at night near the altar steps in the college chapel two days later.

JOHN JONES

Sources Wood, *Ath. Oxon.*, 2nd edn, 2.499–500 • J. Jones, *Balliol College: a history*, 2nd edn (1997) • *The life and times of Anthony Wood*, ed. A. Clark, 5 vols., OHS, 19, 21, 26, 30, 40 (1891–1900), esp. vol. 2, pp. 246–7 • papers of the bishops of Lincoln, 1670–76, Lincs. Arch., VV2 [as visitors of Balliol] • H. Savage, *Balliofergus* (1668) • first Latin register, Balliol Oxf. • plate records, Balliol Oxf., archives, 2, fols. 2–3 • M. Burrows, ed., *The register of the visitors of the University of Oxford, from AD 1647 to AD 1658*, CS, new ser., 29 (1881), 164 • N. Crouch, diary, 1634–72, Balliol Oxf., MS 355 • H. Savage, MS of Balliofergus, etc., Balliol Oxf., MS 429 [with notes by A. Wood] • *CSP dom.*, *1662*; *1669–70* • A. T. Butler, ed., *The visitation of Worcestershire, 1634*, Harleian

Society, 90 (1938), 88 • H. Savage, autograph will, made 1671, proved 1672, Oxf. UA, Hyp B32/84 • will, made 1614, proved 1617, PRO, PROB 11/129, sig. 37 [Francis Savage] • burial register, St Mary Magdalen parish, Oxford

Archives Balliol Oxf., MS copy of his history of Balliol, notes, and drafts, MSS 255, 429 • Balliol Oxf., papers and drafts for *Balliofergus* (incl. notes provided by Anthony Wood) and *The dew of Hermon*, MS 429 | Balliol Oxf., autograph submission to the Act of Uniformity, between pp. 263 and 264 in First Latin register • Balliol Oxf., inventory of the contents of his rooms in Balliol, plate records 2, fols. 2v–3 • Lincs. Arch., MSS of the bishops of Lincoln as visitors of Balliol, letters, VV2 • Oxf. UA, court case 1652, CC papers 1652/7

Likenesses attrib. J. Taylor, oils, *c.*1665, Balliol Oxf.

Wealth at death estate worth a few hundred pounds and some long leases: will, Oxf. UA, Hyp B32/84

Savage, James (1767–1845), antiquary and editor of newspapers and journals, was born in Howden, Yorkshire, on 30 August 1767, a son of James Savage, clockmaker, and elder brother of William *Savage (1770–1843), printer and engraver; their mother's name was unrecorded. The family claimed descent from a younger branch of the long-established Savages of Rock Savage, near Runcorn, Cheshire, whose family took the title of Earl Rivers. He married Diana (*bap.* 1769, *d.* 1806), eldest daughter of Thomas Swainston of Hatfield, near Doncaster, at the latter place on 21 March 1796. Their only son, Thomas James Savage, was born in 1798.

Savage published articles in local journals and in 1790 went into business with his brother as booksellers and printers in Howden. In 1799 Savage published anonymously *History of Howden Church* and *Historical Account of the Parish of Wressle*, the second of which reappeared as *History of the Castle and Parish of Wressle* (1805). In 1797 William Savage migrated to London, where he became a noted fine printer and worked for the Royal Institution. James Savage followed in 1803, working successively for the publishers Richard Phillips, Joseph Mawman, and William Sherwood. He contributed to the *Monthly Magazine* and *Universal Magazine* and edited Charles Reinhard's *Concise History of the Present State of Commerce of Great Britain* (1805). *Observations on the Varieties of Architecture in … Parish Churches* (1812), attributed to Savage by the *Dictionary of National Biography*, is almost certainly the work of his namesake James Savage (1779–1852), the architect (Colvin, *Archs.*, 851).

Following the establishment of the London Institution in 1806 in Old Jewry, Savage was appointed clerk to its librarian, Richard Porson, and cared for him during his final illness, which is described in Savage's *Account of the Last Illness of Richard Porson*, reprinted in J. S. Watson's *Life of Porson* (1808). William Upcott was sub-librarian. Newly widowed, Savage married, second, Margaret Luckfield (*d.* 1818), a widow, at St Olave Jewry on 31 May 1807. A daughter, Margaret, was born on 17 January 1808.

In 1808–9 Savage edited a well-received journal called *The Librarian* (printed by his brother), which carried accounts of libraries and archives, reviews of books of bibliographical interest, and his account of Porson (1.274–81). In 1810 the managers decided that a clerk was superfluous. Savage disappeared, and it emerged that he had been pocketing commissions on sales of shares in the institution. He apparently fled to Birmingham, but the managers declined to take action on the ground that transactions between individual proprietors were a private matter.

A change of employment was necessary, and in 1811 Savage reappeared as the author of *An Account of the London Daily Newspapers*, in which he examined their circulations and political opinions and provided a plan for a provincial newspaper. He revealed that he had edited a newspaper in the midlands (its title is not given) and that he wished to continue in that line. Savage was living in London, but in that year was invited to Taunton to manage a new conservative weekly newspaper, the *Taunton and Bridgwater Journal*. The newspaper, of which only four issues survive (Som. ARS), lasted until November 1816, when it suddenly ceased. The reason is unknown, but he later referred to 'peculiar circumstances in which he was unfortunately involved' (*Taunton Courier*, 13 Nov 1817); the printing press was put up for sale. He had already established a bookshop, circulating library, and reading room, run by his wife, in the Parade, Fore Street, which moved to High Street in 1819.

Savage continued with interests in London. In 1817 he registered a printing press at his brother's home, 77 Lower Thames Street, and in 1818 and 1821 at other addresses. In September 1818 his wife died, aged thirty-eight, followed by his son on 15 May 1819. Savage published *Memorabilia* (1820), a collection of historical anecdotes, and, most importantly, a rewritten edition of Joshua Toulmin's *History of Taunton* (1822).

In November 1822 Savage relinquished business to become librarian of the newly established Somerset and Taunton Institution (later the Taunton and Somerset Institution) in the Market (*Taunton Courier*, 4, 25 Dec 1822, 1 Jan 1823). In 1827 he issued prospectuses for a proposed topographical dictionary of Somerset and a history of its western parts. Only *A History of the Hundred of Carhampton* (1830) materialized, but his extensive manuscript collections were acquired by Sir Thomas Phillipps and eventually found their way to local repositories.

Although Savage had found a congenial position and was respected for his fund of literary and historical knowledge, he had not abandoned his old ways. He accepted money from members to purchase non-existent books and diverted subscriptions to his own pocket. He was dismissed in 1829 and whisked to a debtors' prison in London. He still possessed friends, for on his release he was appointed editor of the *Dorset County Chronicle*, another conservative newspaper. He worked in Dorchester for fourteen years and published *Dorchester and its Environs* (1832), reissued as *The History of Dorchester* (1833). He retired to Taunton shortly before his death at his home in St James Street there on 19 March 1845; he was buried at St Mary Magdalen on the 25th. A staunch tory and churchman, he was praised by his obituary writers for his amiable qualities and integrity, but his failings precluded any successful career.

K. A. Manley

Sources *GM*, 2nd ser., 23 (1845), 557–8 • J. Savage, *GM*, 2nd ser., 21 (1844), 98–100 [obit. of William Savage] • J. Savage, *GM*, 1st ser., 89/1

(1819), 493–4 • London Institution, managers' minute books, GL • minute books, Taunton and Somerset Institution, Som. ARS • L. Brooke, *Somerset newspapers* (1960), 69 • *Taunton Courier* (17 Oct 1816); (21 Nov 1816); (20 Feb 1817); (13 Nov 1817); (10 Sept 1818); (29 March 1820); (4 Dec 1822); (25 Dec 1822); (1 Jan 1823) • W. B. Todd, *A directory of printers and others in allied trades, London and vicinity, 1800–1840* (1972), 169 • I. Maxted, *The London book trades, 1775–1800: a preliminary checklist of members* (1977), 198 • *Dorset County Chronicle* (27 March 1845) • J. Hunter, memorandum, BL, Add. MS 36527, fol. 177 • parish register of St Peter, Howden, East Riding of Yorkshire Archives Service, Beverley [baptism] • parish register of St Lawrence, Hatfield, Doncaster Archives, South Yorkshire [marriage] • parish register, Taunton, St Mary Magdalen, Som. ARS [burial]

Archives AM Oxf., antiquities of Somerset • Bath Central Library, collections for history and genealogies of Somerset • Exeter Central Library, West Country Studies Library, collections relating to history of Somerset • Exeter Central Library, collections • Som. ARS, collections for the history of Bridgwater • Som. ARS, collections for a history of Somerset • Som. ARS, collections relating to monastic lands in Somerset, 1535 • Som. ARS, MS of his history of Somerset | GL, London Institution minute books • Som. ARS, Taunton and Somerset Institution minute books

Savage, James (1779–1852), architect, was born on 10 April 1779 at Hoxton, London. Of his parents nothing is known. He was educated at Mr Adams's school, Stockwell, before being articled in 1793 to D. A. Alexander, whom he served for some years as clerk of works, assisting with Maidstone gaol. He was admitted to the Royal Academy Schools in December 1798, and exhibited at the academy between 1799 and 1832. About 1815 he married Ann (*c*.1790–1841x51), herself a Londoner; they had two sons and two daughters. From about 1815 they lived at 34 Walbrook, in the City of London, before moving to 31 Essex Street about 1829, where he was still living, a widower, at the time of the 1851 census.

In 1800 Savage won second prize (£150) for designs for improving Aberdeen. He was particularly interested in construction, and was successful in a number of competitions for building bridges, including rebuilding Ormond Bridge over the Liffey, Dublin (1805; not executed), Richmond Bridge, Dublin (1808), and Temsford Bridge over the Ouse, Bedfordshire (1815). He read a paper on bridge-building to fellow members of the London Architectural Society in 1806 (printed in their second volume of *Essays*, 1810). In 1823 his design for rebuilding London Bridge was defeated by the casting vote of the chairman of the House of Commons committee in favour of Sir John Rennie's design, which Savage then criticized in *Observations on the Proposed New London Bridge* (1823). He published a plan in 1825 for embanking the south side of the Thames from London Bridge to Lambeth. He carried out repairs to bell-frames at Lincoln Cathedral and St Mary-le-Bow Church. His constructional interests also found expression in his daring design for St Luke's Church, Chelsea (1820–24), probably the earliest successful revival of a medieval solid stone groined vault supported by flying buttresses also of stone; this was a landmark in the Gothic revival, though criticized as lacking true Gothic spirit. It proved too expensive, however, to use in his other Gothic churches, nearly all in the environs of London: All Saints', Upper Norwood (1827–9); Holy Trinity, Sloane Street (1828–30; dem.); Holy Trinity, Tottenham Green (1828–9); St Mary's, Ilford (1829–31); St Mary's, Speenhamland, Berkshire (1829–31; rebuilt); St Michael's, Burleigh Street, Strand (1832–3; dem.); St Thomas's, Brentwood, Essex (1835; rebuilt); and St Paul's, Addlestone, Surrey (1836–8).

In 1825 Savage was called in to report on L. N. Cottingham's proposals for raising the tower of Rochester Cathedral, and in 1829 he advised on the competition designs for restoring Magdalen College chapel, Oxford. Savage's one classical church, St James's, Bermondsey (1827–9; assisted by George Allen), offered a solution to the problem of combining a Grecian portico with a tower. He also built church schools at Chelsea, Ilford, and Brentwood, and three union workhouses in Kent. In 1831 he joined Cottingham in successfully protesting against a threat to demolish the lady chapel of St Saviour's, Southwark; they published a significant pamphlet, *Reasons Against Pulling Down the Lady Chapel* (1832), advocating conservative restoration. Savage was one of the seventeen architects consulted by the House of Commons committee on rebuilding the House in 1833: he recommended a circular chamber for its acoustic advantages. For the subsequent competition for new houses of parliament in 1835 he submitted an unfinished design in the castle style; his failure provoked his widely circulated pamphlet *Observations on style in architecture, with suggestions on the best mode of procuring designs for public buildings* (1836), in which he analysed both the faults of the competition and the role of the architect, who should not merely imitate past styles.

An adviser on architectural and engineering questions under litigation, Savage frequently also served as an arbitrator. He was a key defence witness in 1827–30 in the government's action against the contractor for the new custom house, Henry Peto, who attributed his success to Savage's evidence. In 1830 he succeeded Henry Hakewill as surveyor to the Middle Temple, completing his works there, and adding a clock tower. This appointment led to his undertaking the restoration of the Temple Church for the Middle and Inner Temples. Costs soaring above Savage's estimates provoked an inquiry by Sir Robert Smirke; he was consequently superseded in 1842 by Sydney Smirke and Decimus Burton, who completed the restoration, mainly to Savage's designs, at a high cost. His reputation and his business suffered as a result.

Savage was elected president of the Surveyors' Club for 1825, and was chairman of the fine arts committee of the Royal Society of Arts. He was a member of the Institution of Civil Engineers, but resigned his fellowship of the Institute of British Architects because he wanted a qualifying examination for membership. A freeman of the City of London, he belonged to the Skinners' Company. For several years a martyr to gout and rheumatism, Savage died on 7 May 1852 at his home at North Place, Hampstead Road, St Pancras, and was buried at St Luke's, Chelsea, on 12 May. His personal estate was assessed for legacy duty at some £350. M. H. Port

Sources *Civil Engineers and Architect's Journal*, 131 (July 1852), 226–7 • *GM*, 2nd ser., 38 (1852), 206–7 • H. Savage, memoir of James Savage, RIBA BAL, MS SP 11(iv) • census returns, 1841, PRO, HO 107/731, fol. 12; 1851, HO 107/1512, fol. 3 • will, PRO, PROB 11/2162 • death duty register, PRO, IR 26/1948 • J. M. Crook, 'The restoration of the Temple Church', *Architectural History*, 8 (1965), 39–46 • M. H. Port, *Six hundred new churches: a study of the church building commission, 1818–1856, and its church building activities* (1961) • *London Directory* (1820–41) • Graves, *RA exhibitors* • J. Myles, *L. N. Cottingham, 1787–1847, architect of the Gothic revival* (1996) • M. H. Port, ed., *The Houses of Parliament* (1976) • S. C. Hutchison, 'The Royal Academy Schools, 1768–1830', *Walpole Society*, 38 (1960–62), 123–91, esp. 158

Archives GL, St Mary-at-Hill: papers about general repairs

Wealth at death approx. £350—personal estate: will, PRO, PROB 11/2162; PRO, death duty registers, IR 26/1948

Savage, Jane (1752/3–1824). *See under* Savage, William (1720–1789).

Savage, Janico (*d.* 1468). *See under* Savage family (*per.* 1333–1519).

Savage, Sir John (*d.* 1298). *See under* Savage family (*per.* *c.*1280–*c.*1420).

Savage, Sir John (*b.* 1277, *d.* after 1324). *See under* Savage family (*per.* *c.*1280–*c.*1420).

Savage, John (I) (*d.* 1386). *See under* Savage family (*per.* *c.*1369–1528).

Savage, Sir John (II) (*d.* 1450). *See under* Savage family (*per.* *c.*1369–1528).

Savage, Sir John (III) (1409/10–1463). *See under* Savage family (*per.* *c.*1369–1528).

Savage, Sir John (IV) (*c.*1423–1495). *See under* Savage family (*per.* *c.*1369–1528).

Savage, Sir John (V) (*d.* 1492). *See under* Savage family (*per.* *c.*1369–1528).

Savage, Sir John (VI) (*d.* 1527). *See under* Savage family (*per.* *c.*1369–1528).

Savage, Sir John (VII) (*d.* 1528). *See under* Savage family (*per.* *c.*1369–1528).

Savage, John (*d.* 1586). *See under* Babington, Anthony (1561–1586).

Savage, John (*fl.* 1683–1701), engraver and printseller, was a minor figure whose career has yet to be properly studied. George Vertue, the eighteenth-century historian of English art, mentions him only once: 'I think Jo. Nutting who learnt of him said he was a Frenchman' (BL, Add. MS 23078, fol. 52). If so, like many other members of the London print world, he was probably a Huguenot refugee. The earliest sign of his activity yet noted is as engraver of plates for the *Philosophical Transactions* of the Royal Society from 1683 onwards. Savage entered the printselling business when he bought the shop of Isaac Beckett at the Golden Head in the Old Bailey from his widow, who had initially continued the trade after her husband's death in May 1688. This happened soon after 4 October 1688, when she remarried. According to a card in the Bagford collection:

> John Savage engraver who bought Mr Isaac Beckett's mezzotinto plates & prints and lived at his house at the Golden Head in the Old Bayly is removed to the Golden Head in St Paul's Church Yard. Where you may be furnished with all sorts of mezzo-tinto prints, frames, glasses &c. (BL, Harley 5947, fol. 34, no. 110)

This move took place before 17 September 1698, when an advertisement in the *Post Boy* refers to his shop at the south side of St Paul's Churchyard.

Savage's publishing business cannot have flourished, and few of the plates in his stock were made by any others besides himself. The last sign of his activity yet found is an advertisement in the *Post Man* for 27 February 1701 for a portrait of Philip V of Spain, which gives his address as 'near Doctor's Commons'. This suggests that he had by now ceased operating a shop and was selling from his home.

Savage's own plates cover a wide range of subjects, from portraits, book illustrations, and title-pages to trade and playing cards, and are in etching and engraving; he never made a mezzotint. His finest works are for Tempest's *Cries of London* in 1688; although only two plates are signed, he clearly made all seventy-two. ANTONY GRIFFITHS

Sources A. Griffiths and R. A. Gerard, *The print in Stuart Britain, 1603–1689* (1998), 260 [exhibition catalogue, BM, 8 May – 20 Sept 1998] • *Post Boy* (17 Sept 1698) • *Post Man* (27 Feb 1701) • private information (2004) [J. A. Ganz]

Savage, John (1673–1747), scholar and Church of England clergyman, was born probably in Westminster, but possibly in Hertfordshire, the son of Ann Savage and her husband, probably called William. He was educated at Westminster School, where he was a king's scholar (1687). In February 1691 he entered Emmanuel College, Cambridge, where he graduated BA in 1695 and proceeded MA in 1698. After Cambridge he travelled for eight years in Europe as tutor to James Cecil, fifth earl of Salisbury, a minor who had succeeded his father in 1694 at the age of three. Salisbury appointed Savage chaplain and eventually presented him, successively, to the Hertfordshire livings of Bygrave (1701–8) and the wealthier Clothall (1708–47).

On their return from abroad Savage, a Cambridge graduate, was incorporated into Oxford University in May 1705 and admitted to Christ Church. Salisbury matriculated there a month later, and the following January commemorated Savage on a foundation stone laid in the new Peckwater Quad. Savage then proceeded BD and DD (1707) and continued to travel in Italy at least until 1716. In March 1732 he was made lecturer at St George's, Hanover Square, London, and from there he showed great fondness for his old school, reportedly attending plays, elections, and exercises and furnishing the pupils with extempore epigrams. He 'grew young again and among the boys was a great boy himself' (Nichols, *Lit. anecdotes*, 142n.). William Cole described him as 'A stately man, rather corpulent' (Cole, 86); he was elsewhere described variously as a 'very jolly convivial priest' (*Old Westminsters*, 821) and 'a lively, pleasant facetious old man' (*Works of … Newton*, 44). He was also president of the Royston Club, which clerics rarely joined.

A colourful character and a hedonist, known by some as

the 'Aristippus of the age' (Nichols, *Lit. anecdotes*, 141n.), he was also a prolific writer and translator. He published a translation from Italian of sixty satirical letters in Moscheni's *Brutes Turned Critics* (1695), and an abridgement of Knolles's and Rycaut's *Turkish History* (1701). He wrote the first volume, and superintended the second, of *A Compleat History of Germany* (1702), based on German and Latin sources, claiming that 'the like [was] never extant in any language'. Among later works were *Letters of the Antients* (1703) and *A Full View of Popery* (1704), translated from Spanish. His sermons include one preached at Hertford assizes on 7 August 1704, entitled *The Security of the Established Religion, the Wisdom of the Nation*.

Savage died at the rectory, Clothall, on 24 March 1747, after falling from the scaffolding erected in Westminster Hall for Lord Lovat's trial. It is unlikely that he married; though a deletion on his will could have referred to a deceased wife a sister seems more likely. He clearly wished to be remembered. His will requested Westminster scholars to commemorate him with a marble stone in the east cloister; though allegedly they subscribed for it, Savage's estate doubtless met the cost, as his will directed. Another epitaph at Clothall, in words again composed in his will, records his enlargement of the rectory. He was buried at Clothall.

William Savage (*c*.1670–1736), college head, was born at Ickleford, Hertfordshire, and was possibly related to John Savage. He entered Emmanuel as a sizar in April 1686, graduated BA in 1689, and proceeded MA (1693), BD (1700), and DD (1717); he was fellow of the college from 1692 to 1703. Meanwhile in December 1692 he was ordained deacon at St Botolph, Aldersgate, London, and in June 1696 James Gardiner, bishop of Lincoln, ordained him priest at Buckden, Huntingdonshire. Clearly tory in political orientation, he was appointed chaplain to the lord keeper, Sir Nathan Wright; it was presumably through Wright's influence that Savage was presented to the crown living of St Ann Blackfriars (1702–36), united since 1670 with St Andrew by the Wardrobe. He also held the Kentish living of Gravesend (1704–20), which in 1720, after a spell as Bishop Francis Atterbury's chaplain, he exchanged for another Kent parish, Stone (1720–36).

In September 1719 Savage was elected master of Emmanuel. In 1720 he resigned, on his preferment to Stone, but only briefly, to fulfil the requirements of college statutes. Little is known of his tenure as master but, not apparently a distinguished scholar, he displayed considerable administrative and financial acumen, which he used to Emmanuel's advantage. New buildings—Founder's Range—already planned before his election, were now completed under his skilled financial management. Acting also as college bursar he oversaw Emmanuel's finances with meticulous care, and after surveying the library, buttery, and kitchens, he reformed their operation. In 1724 he was vice-chancellor of the university. He died at Cambridge on 1 August 1736, after falling from a horse, and was buried at Sampford, Essex. Two of his sermons were published in 1707. WILLIAM MARSHALL

Sources Foster, *Alum. Oxon.* • Venn, *Alum. Cant.* • *Old Westminsters* • Nichols, *Lit. anecdotes*, vol. 2 • *The works of … Thomas Newton*, 3 vols. (1782) • R. Clutterbuck, *Hertfordshire* (1827) • W. Cole, 'Athenae Cantabrigienses', BL, Add. MS 6880, fol. 86 • *GM*, 1st ser., 83/2 (1813) • H. L. Thompson, *Christ Church* (1900) • F. H. Forshall, *Westminster past and present* (1884) • A. Kingston, *A history of Royston* (1906) • J. Ingamells, ed., *A dictionary of British and Irish travellers in Italy, 1701–1800* (1997) • *Emmanuel College Magazine*, 8 (1897–8) • S. Bendall, C. Brooke, and P. Collinson, *A history of Emmanuel College, Cambridge* (1999) • G. Hennessy, *Novum repertorium ecclesiasticum parochiale Londinense, or, London diocesan clergy succession from the earliest time to the year 1898* (1898) • London register of ordinations, GL, MS 9535/3, fol. 69 • C. H. Fielding, *The records of Rochester* (1910) • Rochester diocesan muniment books, CKS, DRb/Am1, fol. 83v; DRb/Am2, fol. 80v, 92r • Lincs. Arch., MS REG 35, fol. 31 • *A sermon … at … St Lawrence Jewry, September 29 1707* (1707) • Emmanuel College, Cambridge, MS BUR. 6.2, fol. 7 [26 Sept 1719, 4 Nov 1720]; COL. 9.1, vol. 1, p. 83

Archives Herts. ALS, letters to second Earl Cowper

Likenesses M. Vandergucht, line engraving, 1702 (after T. Foster), BM, NPG; repro. in J. Savage, *A compleat history of Germany* (1702)

Savage, John (1828–1888), poet and journalist, was born in Dublin on 13 December 1828, the son of a United Irishman from Ulster. After attending a school at Harold's Cross in Dublin, he entered the modelling and ornament schools of the Royal Dublin Society in 1844. In 1845 and 1847 he won premiums for work on landscape and ornament. He became a member of Young Ireland and of the Irish Confederation, and contributed to John Mitchel's *United Irishman*, and, when that paper was suppressed, to its successor, the *Irish Tribune*. He was a founder of *Irish Felon*, and also founded *The Patriot*, which was suppressed.

Savage joined in the abortive rising at Ballingarry, co. Tipperary, and took part in attacks on police barracks at Portlaw with John O'Mahony. He escaped to New York late in 1848, where he became a proofreader for the *Tribune*, and afterwards one of its contributors. When Mitchel started *The Citizen* in New York in 1854 Savage was appointed literary editor. In the same year, he married, in New York, Louise Gouverneur, daughter of Captain Samuel Reid. In 1857 he moved to Washington, where he became editor, and ultimately proprietor, of the *Washington States Journal*. He is said to have fought with the Irish brigade in the American Civil War under Thomas Francis Meagher. With John O'Mahony he was active in the Fenian movement in America, and in 1868 was appointed Fenian agent in Paris. After the movement split in 1867 Savage continued to follow the O'Mahony wing, favouring armed intervention in Ireland. He was offered the post of United States consul in Leeds but declined it. In 1875 he was given the degree of LLD of St John's College, Fordham, New York. He died in New York on 10 October 1888. Savage is best known for his books on the rebellions of 1798 and 1848, and for his memoirs of Fenians. He also wrote plays and poetry; his most popular poem was *Shane's Head*.

D. J. O'DONOGHUE, *rev.* MARIE-LOUISE LEGG

Sources D. J. O'Donoghue, *The poets of Ireland: a biographical and bibliographical dictionary* (1912); repr. (1970) • D. J. Hickey and J. E. Doherty, *A dictionary of Irish history* (1980); pbk edn (1987) • *Freeman's Journal* [Dublin] (11 Oct 1888) • *The Nation* (13 Oct 1888) • T. W. Moody, ed., *The Fenian movement* (1968)

Likenesses Montbard, portrait, repro. in *The Irishman* (1869–70)

Savage, Sir John Boscawen (1760–1843), marine officer, of a family long settled at Ardkeen, co. Down, son of Marmaduke Coghill Savage, and grandson of Philip Savage of Rock Savage, Ballygalget, was born at Hereford on 23 February 1760. On 5 December 1762 he was gazetted to an ensigncy in the 91st foot, by virtue of a commission obtained for an elder brother who had since died. In September 1771 he was exchanged into the 48th, and in 1772–3 served with it in Dublin and in Tobago. In 1775 he is said to have fought a duel with his colonel, which was possibly the cause of his selling out in 1776. He married, in 1786, Sophia, eldest daughter of Lieutenant William Cock RN and his wife, Elizabeth Ward, a cousin of Robert Plumer Ward, the novelist. In January 1777 he obtained a commission as lieutenant of marines. In 1778 he embarked on the *Princess Amelia*; in 1779–80 he was in the *Bedford* in the channel, in the action off Cape St Vincent, and at the relief of Gibraltar; in 1782–3 he was in the *Dolphin* in the West Indies. In 1793 he was in the *Niger*, on the coast of the Netherlands; on 24 April he was promoted captain, and embarked in command of the detachment on board the *Orion*, with Sir James Saumarez. In her he was at the actions off Lorient, off Cape St Vincent, and at the Nile, when he was bruised by a cannon ball that passed between his arm and side. It is said that before the battle, Saumarez, having addressed the officers and ship's company, turned to Savage with, 'Will you say a few words to your men?' On which Savage spoke: 'My lads, do you see that land there? Well, that's the land of Egypt, and if you don't fight like devils, you'll damned soon be in the house of bondage.' The speech has been erroneously attributed to many other officers. In 1801 Savage was in the *Ganges* at Copenhagen. On 15 August 1805 he was made a major; on 1 January 1812 a brevet lieutenant-colonel; on 24 March 1815 lieutenant-colonel of marines; and on 20 June 1825 colonel-commandant of the Chatham division. He was made a CB on 26 September 1831, a KCH on 22 February 1833, and a KCB on 25 October 1839. On 10 January 1837 he was promoted major-general unattached. By the death of his cousin in 1808 he succeeded to Rock Savage, and the family estate of Ballygalget. During his later years he lived at Woolwich, was friendly with the duke of Clarence, and was a favourite of Princess Sophia, whom he used to delight with stories of the war. He died at Woolwich Common, Kent, on 8 March 1843, and was buried there in the parish churchyard. His wife survived him only three months, dying on 12 June; she was buried in the same vault as her husband. A monument to them was erected in the church. Their eldest surviving son, Henry John Savage (1792–1866), became colonel of the Royal Engineers, and lieutenant-general, and, having sold Rock Savage, died at St Helier. The next son, John Morris, a colonel in the Royal Artillery, settled in Canada, where he died in 1876.

J. K. Laughton, *rev.* Roger T. Stearn

Sources *United Service Magazine*, 1 (1843) • G. F. Armstrong, *The ancient and noble family of the Savages of the Ards* (1888) • R. Muir, *Britain and the defeat of Napoleon, 1807–1815* (1996) • J. L. Moulton, *The royal marines* (1973) • *Belfast News-Letter* (13 Nov 1876) • *GM*, 2nd ser., 19 (1843), 534

Savage, John Percival (1895–1970), industrialist, was born at 8 Watt Street, Nottingham, on 18 November 1895, the son of Robert Louther Savage, a railway guard, and his wife, Mary, *née* Pakes, who was a Primitive Methodist. In 1911, when he was fifteen, he left Mundella secondary school, Nottingham, without qualifications and joined Boots, the retail chain and pharmaceutical manufacturers, as an office boy. At the time the founder, Jesse Boot, was trying to improve the standard of recruits by taking them from the local secondary schools; though his eyes were thought to be weak, young Savage was sent into the accounts department.

Savage's rise through the business was undoubtedly due to his shrewdness and dedication to the company, but can be adequately understood only by reference to the internal organization of Boots during that period. In 1921, after Jesse Boot sold his controlling interest in the company to the American firm Rexall, John Greenwood was appointed expense controller and Savage became one of his assistants. It was recognized that with the rapid growth of payroll, retail branches, and manufacturing, the need for co-ordination of policy on expenditure was vital. Although the company as a whole had profit objectives, it was virtually impossible to allocate individual targets to sections within it because, with the exception of the shops, individual profit-earning units could not be defined. Central direction of expenditure was therefore inevitable, and in the course of a few years the expense control department acquired considerable executive authority. Savage allowed it to become a kind of clearing-house for numerous problems which did not easily belong elsewhere; his major assets were his earthy common sense, his easy rapport with the men he had grown up with, and his growing reputation as a mediator. On 20 April 1922 he married Beatrice Maude, daughter of Henry Hodgson, a painter.

During the twenty years or so that Savage was his assistant, Greenwood allowed him a very free hand and he represented the finance director on various Boots committees on which Greenwood really ought to have been sitting. This delegation not only gave Greenwood more time for hunting and fishing but, in particular, saved him from having to disagree too often with Lord Trent (Jesse Boot's son and successor), who took the chair at some of these meetings. The arrangement was no doubt also congenial to Trent, who hated difficult personal encounters and found Savage an easier person to deal with. In 1936 Trent appointed Savage as his personal assistant and in 1941, when the chairman effectively moved to government service as a civil commissioner, Savage became general manager. Having been Trent's right-hand man for eighteen years, he was the only executive who knew enough of the business to succeed him.

This career background serves to explain the main achievements of Savage's seven years as Boots' chairman and managing director (1954–61). It can fairly be regarded as a period of transition from the Trent autocracy to managerial government by committee. During the years in which Savage was administrative general manager but lacked the authority of appointment as chief executive, he had to form policy from a feeling for the consensus—given the jealousy of his rivals there was no practical alternative. When he was finally appointed chairman, he continued to be reasonable and considerate to those whom he regarded as of similar rank and social background; in office Savage allowed the executive to argue with him and worked for agreement. He had few original ideas of his own and seldom visited the branches, so was also prepared to listen to younger men. He was a good organizer of managers in the sense that he provided the right conditions to enable them to work together as a team. One of the Boots buyers at the period recalled that he suddenly acquired so much more freedom that he hardly knew how to use it. However, the benefits were still limited; a small circle of 'buddies' gained most.

In later years Savage was sensitive about his lack of formal education; 'superior' accents grated with him and the Boots' managers recruited at Cambridge made him feel insecure. Greenwood tried to give him some polish by taking him to his London club and to a Savile Row tailor, but he never enjoyed such surroundings or formal occasions. He was immensely proud of his achievement in climbing from the lowest rung of the ladder to the top but he was not entirely at ease there, particularly on formal occasions. He was popular in his own circle but nervous at shareholders' meetings. He had never worked for any other firm, did not join employers' organizations, would not take directorships in other firms, and knew little of the world of business outside Boots. In any situation he took his inspiration from what Lord Trent would have done. Trent had trusted him to maintain his policies and Savage was loyal to the end; his chairmanship was really an extension of Trent's. Shy and truculent, Savage too often bristled at strangers and subordinates, and his habitual swearing intimidated or alienated some of the rising generation of managers. By the time he was Boots chairman one of his family could describe him as a 'fallen Methodist', and he had a great liking for pink gins. Savage died at his home, 612 Derby Road, Nottingham, on 22 February 1970. S. D. CHAPMAN

Sources S. D. Chapman, *Jesse Boot of Boots the Chemists* (1974) • J. E. Greenwood, *A cap for Boots: an autobiography* (1977) • private information (2004) • *Nottingham Evening Post* (29 Dec 1953)

Wealth at death £83,063: probate, 27 April 1970, *CGPLA Eng. & Wales*

Savage, Marmion Wilme (1804–1872), novelist and journalist, was born in Dublin on 22 February 1804, the only son of the Revd Henry Savage (*d.* 1820), vicar at Ardkeen, and his wife, Sarah Bewley Savage. Savage spent his early youth in northern Ireland before returning to Dublin where he matriculated as a pensioner on 6 October 1817 at Trinity College. An excellent student, Savage received a scholarship, then given only for the classics, in 1822, and graduated BA on 2 March 1824. He went on to study law, graduating from the Inner Temple in London in 1828, but he retained his ties to Trinity, acting as auditor of the Externe College Historical Society from 1829 to 1830. In 1829 he married Olivia Clarke (*d.* 1843), a niece of Sydney, Lady Morgan. He became a barrister at King's Inns in Dublin in 1832.

1832 was also the year of Savage's first publication, an article entitled 'The gnostics' which appeared in *The Amulet* and formed something of a nervous display of his classical learning. His interest in religious matters is also clearly demonstrated in his review of Thomas Brown's *The Fudges in England* (*Westminster Review*, 24 Jan 1836, 79–92), in which he details his dislike of protestant extremism and supports the position of tolerance taken in Brown's work. During this time Savage had become a valued writer for *The Examiner*, as well as co-authoring with Edward Berwick an important article suggesting a number of improvements to the commission on Irish railways (*Edinburgh Review*, 69, 1839, 156–88). He had also, in 1837, been appointed usher and keeper of the council chamber at Dublin Castle, although he was to leave the post in 1852 when, at his own request, the office was abolished in order to save funds.

Savage's only son, Henry Arthur, was born in the early 1840s; little is known of his life, although he was to live long enough to serve briefly in the London Irish corps under the guidance of the poet Samuel Lover. Savage's wife, Olivia, died in 1843, and before his second marriage in 1855 to Rosa Narissa Rosevo (or Rosava) of Dublin he had published four novels. His fiction is characterized by a lightly satiric or slowly progressive ridicule, but each novel ends in full condemnation of the central objects, while consistently replacing extreme attitudes with moderation and common sense. Refreshing in its lack of bigotry and easy sensationalism, Savage's work is also marked by his possession of an immense fund of native Irish lore combined with a remarkably wide-ranging classical scholarship. In *The Falcon Family* (1847), the Falcons serve as Savage's metaphor for the Anglo-Irish. The novel presents a stark political warning to sponging governors and accidental supporters, but the 'young Irelanders' (Savage coining the term) and tractarians are disparaged. *The Bachelor of the Albany* (1847), felt by many to be his best novel, comments on the flood of events which cause one 'angular' Peter Barker's development into a husband responsible for the welfare of many, while, once again, the tractarians and the Irish church do not fail to escape criticism. *My Uncle the Curate* (1849), an adventure story set in the 1830s, features exotic scenes in the wilds, a tithe collection robbery, and an abduction of the vicar's daughter. It none the less articulated many of the inequities of life in Ireland, and is considered to have 'well reflect[ed] the politics of the age' (Nield, 424). His fourth novel, *Reuben Medlicott* (1852), demonstrates that the hero's public school experiences lead to a life of mistaken choices and comic futility, effectively mocking parenting and pedagogy, which Savage saw as compromised by avarice and complacency.

During this time Savage had continued with his journalistic efforts, writing an article entitled 'Lord Clarendon's administration' (*Edinburgh Review*, 93, Jan 1851, 208–303), and going on to produce several pieces for the *Dublin University Magazine* in 1853 and 1854. In 1855 he edited and wrote an introduction to the collected writings of an Irish Catholic barrister, *Sketches Legal and Political, by the Rt Hon. Richard Lalor Shiel*. The following year saw the publication of his novella, *Clover Cottage* (1856), which was later adapted as a one-act comedietta by Tom Taylor and renamed *Nine Points of the Law*. Also in 1856 Savage moved to London to become editor of *The Examiner*, in which capacity he served for three years, until he was forced to retire for health reasons. The Savages consequently moved from their home in Kensington Gate, London, to Torquay in Devon. Savage published only occasionally thereafter: his 'Religion and philosophy reconciled in prayer' (*Fortnightly Review*, 3, 1 Jan 1866, 474–6) is discursive, while 'The Irish judicial establishment' (*Fortnightly Review*, 4, 1 March 1866, 129–41) criticizes the wasteful number of judges appointed in Irish districts. A final novel, *The Woman of Business* (1869–70), takes to task the absurd trappings of sensationalist mystery novels, as well as the foibles of the spoiled and wealthy. At the end of the twentieth century, the most recent edition of a Savage novel was the 1927 Rescue series edition of *The Bachelor of the Albany*, introduced by Bonamy Dobrée, who describes the effect of all of Savage's novels on the reader: 'We feel that we are in the presence of a man of culture and kindliness, not wanting in power or deftness, but skeptical of reforming human nature, though hopeful of cultivating the mind' (Dobrée, 14). Savage died of heart failure complicated by bronchitis at Belgrave Crescent, Torquay, on 1 May 1872. He was buried on 3 May at the Church of England municipal cemetery in Torquay. PARALEE NORMAN

Sources admission papers and barrister papers: council of the Honourable Society of King's Inns, Dublin: memorial papers, Marmion Wilme Savage, Trinity Term, 1832 • J. B. Leslie, 'Biographical index of the clergy of the Church of Ireland', RCB Library, Dublin, RCB Library MS 61.4.4. • 'Reports of the committees of inquiry into public offices', *Parl. papers* (1854), 27.33, no. 1715 • J. Nield, 'Semi-historical novels and tales', *A guide to the best historical novels and tales*, rev. edn (1929), 424 • P. Norman, *Marmion Wilme Savage, 1804–1872: Dublin's Victorian satirist* (2000) • B. Dobrée, introduction, in M. W. Savage, *The bachelor of the Albany* (1927), 14 • P. Norman, 'The island of Higgledy-Piggledy: Marmion Savage's *My uncle the curate*, 1849', *Éire–Ireland*, 25/4 (1990), 93–110 • *Annual report*, College Historical Society, Trinity College, Dublin (Dublin, 1956–7); (1960–61) • *The College Historical Society* (1932), 11, appxs 6–7 • *The life and labours of Albany Fonblanque*, ed. E. B. de Fonblanque (1874), 37 [his nephew] • Calendar abstract of the will of Marmion Wilme Savage, PRO Ire., Dublin [some particulars about the Savage family records were destroyed at the burning of the Four Courts, Dublin, 1922] • *Torquay Directory and South Devon Journal* (7 May 1872) • P. Norman, 'A neglected Irish novelist: Marmion W. Savage', *Books at Iowa*, 35 (Nov 1981), 3–13 • P. Norman, 'Light satire and Hogarth's pictorial composition: Marmion Savage's novel, *The Falcon family, or, Young Ireland*, 1845', *Éire–Ireland*, 23/1 (1988), 129–43 • d. cert. • Burtchaell & Sadleir, *Alum. Dubl.*

Archives University of Iowa, Iowa City, Leigh Hunt MSS

Wealth at death under £1500—in England: Irish probate resealed in England, 11 July 1872, *CGPLA Eng. & Wales* • under £3000: probate, 26 June 1872, *CGPLA Ire.*

Savage, Patrick (*d.* in or after **1481**). *See under* Savage family (*per.* 1333–1519).

Savage, Sir Ralph (*d.* **1344x6**). *See under* Savage family (*per.* *c.*1280–*c.*1420).

Savage, Richard, fourth Earl Rivers (*c.***1654–1712**), army officer and politician, was born about 1654, the second son of Thomas Savage, third Earl Rivers (*c.*1628–1694), and his first wife, Elizabeth Scrope (*b.* *c.*1627), the second of the three illegitimate daughters and coheirs of Emmanuel Scrope, earl of Sunderland (1584–1630), and Martha Jeanes or James. The Savage family had been established in Cheshire since the fourteenth century. Savage was the great-grandson of Elizabeth *Savage, *née* Darcy, Countess Rivers, and her husband, Thomas Savage, first Viscount Savage, and although he inherited their court connections he does not seem to have shared his great-grandmother's Roman Catholicism.

Early career In autumn 1672 Savage was commissioned a captain in the Royal English regiment, a marine regiment that was just forming in Ireland. In April 1673 he received a commission as captain in the duke of Buckingham's regiment, which he retained until February 1674. On 23 February 1674 Savage was implicated, along with his elder brother, Thomas, then known as Viscount Colchester, and three others, in the death of William Cole, who was killed during a drunken brawl. On 26 December 1674 Charles II granted Savage's petition for a pardon for felony and the murder of Cole, extending and renewing the pardon to all other felonies whatsoever, on the grounds that it could not be shown that Savage was more guilty than the others. Allowed to return to Buckingham's regiment, he remained with it until it was disbanded in February 1679, when he was given a commission as captain in Lord Gerard's regiment of horse. On 21 August 1679 he married Penelope, the daughter of Roger Downes of Wardley, Lancashire. Savage's only legitimate child, Elizabeth Savage (*d.* 1714), was born from this marriage.

Following the death of his elder brother about 1680, Savage became known as Viscount Colchester. Through the patronage of a kinsman, William Stanley, ninth earl of Derby, he became colonel of foot militia in Cheshire, and in 1681 he was returned as member of parliament for Wigan. There is no record of his participation in parliament, but he did accompany James Scott, duke of Monmouth, on his journey through the north-west, and he and his father entertained him at Rocksavage and at Wardley, both in Cheshire, in June 1683. Later that summer Colchester volunteered for service against Monmouth's rising, and following his father's second marriage in 1684, to Arabella, the eldest daughter of Robert Bertie, third earl of Lindsey, the court looked more favourably upon him. Colchester retained Wigan until 1685, when, on account of his earlier support for Monmouth, he became unacceptable to the gentry. He relinquished the seat to Lord Charles Murray, Derby's nephew. At the 1685 election Colchester stood for Lancaster with Derby's support, but was defeated.

On 23 May 1686 Colchester was commissioned as lieutenant and lieutenant-colonel of the 4th troop of Horse Guards under Henry Jermyn, Baron Dover, and in 1687 he became justice of the peace in Lancashire. It was during this period that his evening escapades with friends, such as John, third Baron Lovelace, William, Lord Cavendish, and Charles, fourth Baron Mohun, created the initial basis for his long-lived reputation as 'one of the greatest Rakes in England in his younger days, but always a lover of the Constitution of his country' (*Memoirs of the Secret Services*, 144). At the end of James II's reign Colchester was the principal leader of the Treason Club, an informal gathering of like-minded whig army officers, aspiring politicians, and former army officers with ties to Monmouth who met at the Rose tavern in Russell Street, Covent Garden, London. Under Colchester's informal leadership the group laid a plan for army officers to defect from James II to William III. On 28 January 1688, his first wife having died, Colchester married Margaret (*d. c.*1692), the daughter of Sir Richard Stydolf, bt, of Norbury, Surrey, and the widow of Thomas Tryon of Bullwick, Northamptonshire.

In the service of William III On the first news that William had landed, Colchester set out to greet him with Henry Wharton, William Jephson, and Charles Godfrey. They joined William at Exeter on 13 November. Four members of Colchester's troop of life guards joined them, along with some sixty other men on horseback. In doing this, Colchester became the first English nobleman to defect to William after his landing in England, and he later accompanied William to London.

When the 4th troop of guards had been disbanded, Colchester received a commission on 31 December 1688 in Colonel Fenwick's troop, the 3rd dragoon guards. Meanwhile Derby continued to search for an appropriate parliamentary seat for Colchester, but was unsuccessful. Although Colchester opposed the withdrawal of James II's writs, he found a seat at Liverpool and was elected to the Convention Parliament. He was a member of eight committees and moved on 28 January 1689, in the committee for elections and privileges, that the grand committee immediately report that the throne was vacant. He was among those requested to report on the essentials for securing law, liberty, and religion. On 12 February he carried the amended proclamation of the new reign to the House of Lords.

During summer 1689 Colchester served with his regiment at the siege of Edinburgh Castle. On returning to London he was sent to the House of Lords on 19 July to ask for a conference on the declaration of rights. After the recess he served on the committee for the Mutiny Bill and also served on the committee to consider restoring corporations. Twice he acted as a teller in his support for the disabling clause. He was reappointed justice of the peace in Lancashire in 1689, served as a commissioner for assessment in Cheshire and Lancashire in 1689–90, and was deputy lieutenant of Cheshire from 1689 to 1695. In 1690 he was elected to parliament for Liverpool, voting thereafter with the whigs.

Colchester took part in William's expedition to Ireland, and in September 1690 distinguished himself in taking Cork, leading the grenadiers in the van of the attacking force. On 24 November 1691 William reviewed Colchester's regiment on Hounslow Heath before they went to serve in Flanders. About that time Colchester reportedly asked William for a vacant regiment. Not disposed to grant the request, the king said only that he would think about it, to which Colchester replied, 'Then, Sir, I won't' (*Egmont Diary*, 1.509). Amused by his reply, William acquiesced and in January 1692 made Colchester colonel in command of the 3rd troop of Horse Guards, a post he retained for eleven years. Meanwhile Colchester's defection to William was not forgiven among Jacobites. In giving a general pardon in 1692, James II explicitly excluded Colchester by name.

On 1 April 1693 Colchester was promoted major-general, and, on his father's death in London on 14 September 1694, he left his seat in the Commons and succeeded to the peerage as fourth Earl Rivers. In January 1695 the king granted him and his heirs £500 a year for a hundred years. On 3 April 1695 he became *custos rotulorum* and lord lieutenant of Cheshire, serving until 1704. Meanwhile, by the middle of 1694 he had begun a sexual relationship with Anne Gerard, *née* Mason, countess of Macclesfield (*c.*1668–1753) [*see* Brett, Anne]. Lady Macclesfield was separated from her husband, Charles Gerard, second earl of Macclesfield (who as Lord Gerard had been Rivers's commanding officer from 1679 to 1686); she and Rivers had two children: Anne (*b.* 1695), who died in infancy, and Richard (*b.* 1697), about whom nothing is known after 1698. His identity was claimed by the poet Richard *Savage. The affair and the pregnancies led to the Macclesfields' notorious divorce in 1698, but the relationship between the two had probably ended before Lady Macclesfield married Henry Brett in 1700.

On 27 April 1697 Rivers was promoted lieutenant-general. His place among the intimate friends of William III was shown when, on 14 January 1698, he joined the king in his private visit to Peter I of Russia in London, alongside Henry Sidney, earl of Romney, and Arnold van Keppel, earl of Albemarle. Three years later, in November 1701, Rivers received additional appointments as constable of Liverpool Castle and lord lieutenant of Lancashire. In 1702 he became vice-admiral of Lancashire.

The War of the Spanish Succession On 9 March 1702 Rivers's commission as lieutenant-general was renewed and he served under Marlborough in Flanders. In the House of Lords in January 1703 he exemplified the tension between Commons and Lords when he accused the Commons of attempting to tack the occasional conformity issue to the money bill. He was also one of the peers who signed the protest against grants to Prince George of Denmark. In March 1703 he sold his commission as colonel of the 3rd Horse Guards to Charles Butler, earl of Arran, for £3000 and his regiment of horse to Colonel William Cadogan for another £3000. Rivers was given a commission as general of horse on 16 September 1703, and in 1705 he was appointed lord lieutenant of Essex and vice-admiral of Lancashire. About this time John Macky described him as:

> a gentleman of very good sense and very cunning; brave in his person, a lover of play, and understands it perfectly well; hath a very good estate and improves it every day; something covetous; is a tall handsome man of very fair complexion. (*Memoirs of the Secret Services*, 144)

Aspiring for appointment as a commander-in-chief,

Rivers was, on 25 March 1706, made commander-in-chief of the land forces in an expedition of 10,000 infantry and 1200 cavalry that was to land at the mouth of the Charente River in the hope of inciting the protestant Cevennois into an open revolt against France. Although they embarked in a squadron commanded by Sir Cloudesley Shovell in July, continuing light and contrary winds prevented the force from leaving the channel during the entire summer. By October the government in London had abandoned this plan and ordered Shovell and Rivers to proceed to the coast of Spain, where they were first to seize Seville and then move on the long-desired objective of Cadiz. As the expedition entered the Bay of Biscay it encountered heavy storms that scattered the transports and severely damaged the fleet. The ship in which Rivers had embarked, *Barfleur*, sprang a serious leak and was ordered to return to England. Rivers and his staff officers transferred at sea to Shovell's flagship, *Association*, in which they eventually reached Lisbon. After a month at sea the ships needed a further month there to repair and refit. Upon arrival in Portugal, Rivers found himself facing a series of conflicting demands and misunderstandings, with changing and inconsistent orders from London. London had ordered him to attack Seville and Cadiz, but Archduke Charles of Austria, regarded by the allies as Charles III of Spain, wanted English forces to go to Catalonia. At the same time the Portuguese wanted the forces to remain in Portugal to support their purposes. Adding to the confusion, Henri Massue de Ruvigny, earl of Galway, was named overall commander-in-chief in the Peninsula, while Rivers was given an unclear choice either of succeeding Galway, should he choose not to accept the command as he had threatened, or—as the government in London now preferred—to serve as Galway's second in command and have command only in Galway's absence. Meanwhile, Charles Mordaunt, third earl of Peterborough, was making separate plans of his own and asking for Rivers's participation. The lord treasurer, Sidney Godolphin, first earl of Godolphin, had already sent orders from London that Rivers was not to heed Peterborough's demands. While the long period in transports and in port at Lisbon reduced the number of soldiers capable of fighting, Rivers was unsure of what course to follow. Finally, in late January 1707, over the strenuous protests of the Portuguese, Rivers took his troops to Alicante on the Spanish Mediterranean coast. Faced with confusion about his objectives, changing expectations as to whether or not he would succeed Galway, and rising tensions created through the differing political connections of the two generals at Charles III's court, Rivers chose to return to England in April 1708. While he had been away, and without his knowledge, his only daughter, Elizabeth, had become the second wife of Colonel, later Lieutenant-General, James *Barry, fourth earl of Barrymore (1667–1748).

At Marlborough's recommendation, Rivers was sworn of the privy council on 25 November 1708, but by 1709 he was already distancing himself from the whig interest. When the post of constable of the Tower became vacant, Rivers consulted Robert Harley, who suggested that he speak to Marlborough about it. When Marlborough hesitated about giving him the office, Rivers asked Marlborough's permission to approach the queen. Marlborough consented, assuming that the queen would turn to Marlborough for the final decision, as she had normally done. To Marlborough's consternation, the queen immediately granted Rivers's request. Marlborough responded by asking the queen to cancel Rivers's appointment, but the queen refused—the first event of an unfolding political crisis that eventually led to the end of Marlborough's power.

Having become a close political ally of Robert Harley, Rivers was a member of the 'juntilla', along with Charles Seymour, sixth duke of Somerset, Charles Talbot, duke of Shrewsbury, Peterborough, Henry St John, and Harley, which actively worked to undermine the Marlborough–Godolphin ministry. In 1710, during the formation of Harley's ministry, Rivers was mentioned as a candidate for the Admiralty board, but was not appointed.

In high favour with the new government, Rivers was appointed to undertake a special diplomatic mission in August–October 1710 to Hanover to reassure the Electress Sophia and her son, George, elector of Hanover, and eventually George I of Great Britain, that the new government in Great Britain remained faithful, both to her sceptical allies and to the protestant succession. Delayed briefly by illness, Rivers sailed from Harwich on 22 August, had a meeting with the grand pensionary of Holland, Anthonie Heinsius, in The Hague on 1 September, and arrived in Hanover on 19 September. Marlborough suspected that Rivers's mission was also part of a plot to remove him from command of the army and to persuade George to take his place, although Rivers was instructed to say that Marlborough would not be replaced unless he wished to resign. Public discussion and the political climate alone were enough to motivate George to protest to the queen that Marlborough was a keystone in the military affairs that bridged the alliance. Rivers left Hanover in late October and returned to England, 'neither satisfied with them nor they with him' (Halifax to Newcastle, 26 Oct 1710, *Portland MSS*, 2.223).

In 1711 Rivers regularly attended the House of Lords and drew closer to Harley, now earl of Oxford; he also became noted for his hostility to the Marlboroughs. His repeated requests to return to active military service were ignored, but in October and November 1711 he returned to Hanover on a special diplomatic mission to discuss proposed terms for a peace. Following Marlborough's dismissal at the end of 1711 and his replacement in January 1712 by James Butler, second duke of Ormond, Rivers became colonel of the Royal Regiment of Horse Guards on 4 January 1712 and Marlborough's successor as master-general of the ordnance. On 18 January he was additionally appointed general and commander-in-chief of the army in Great Britain to serve whenever Ormond was absent from the country.

Death Shortly after receiving these appointments, Rivers became seriously ill and went to Bath, from where rumours soon circulated of his death. He returned to his home at Ealing Grove, Middlesex, and died there on 18 August 1712. He was buried at Savage Chapel, Macclesfield, Cheshire, on 4 October. Swift wrote: 'I loved the man and detest his memory' (J. Swift, 2.563). In addition, Swift famously, but inaccurately, related that Rivers:

> has left legacy to about 20 paultry old whores by name, and not a farthing to any Friend, Dependant, or Relation; he has left from his only child, lady Barrimore, her mother's estate, and given the whole to his heir-male, a Popish priest, a second cousin, who is now earl Rivers, and whom he used in his life like a footman. After him, it goes to his chief wench and bastard. (ibid., 562–3)

In fact Rivers granted to the two executors of his will, Shrewsbury and Oxford, £500 apiece. To his mistress, Mrs Elizabeth Johnson, the daughter of Sir Peter Colleton, bt, he left £1000 and the remaining ninety-six years' annual payments of the Treasury grant of £500, together with all his plate, household goods, and property associated with his two mansion houses, Rivers House, Great Queen Street, London, and Ealing Grove. He also left £10,000 to Bessy Savage (*c.*1699–1746), the illegitimate daughter of Rivers and Elizabeth Johnson, to be given at age twenty-one or at marriage with her mother's permission. Aged fifteen Bessy married Frederick van *Nassau van Zuylestein, third earl of Rochford (1682/3–1738) [*see under* Nassau van Zuylestein, William van, second earl of Rochford]. An additional legacy of land valued at £1500 was purchased for the sole benefit of Mrs Arabella Field and her children at Great Charleton, Essex, along with additional small legacies to Mrs Honor Hawke and her son and Mrs Katherine Dutar and her daughter, as well as to his servants, his surgeon, and his godson, Thomas Valley. The principal family seat, Rocksavage in Cheshire, and its furnishing devolved on the heir to his title, John Savage, fifth and last Earl Rivers (1665–1737), a Roman Catholic priest and later canon of Liège, but Rivers's son-in-law Barrymore moved into Rocksavage and took control of the estate.

Although he had the reputation of being the most notorious womanizer of his time, Rivers played an important role as the *de facto* leader among army officers who defected from James II and joined William III in 1688. A courageous man, he never was given the opportunity to become the great combat commander that he wished. The high military and diplomatic appointments that he acquired in 1710–12 represented very public symbols of Marlborough's political downfall, over and above their expression of Rivers's own merits.

JOHN B. HATTENDORF

Sources *CSP dom., 1672–5; 1686–7; 1697–8; 1700–02* • *Manuscripts of the earl of Egmont: diary of Viscount Percival, afterwards first earl of Egmont*, 3 vols., HMC, 63 (1920–23), vol. 2 • *The manuscripts of his grace the duke of Portland*, 10 vols., HMC, 29 (1891–1931), vols. 2, 4, 9–10 • *Report on the manuscripts of the marquis of Downshire*, 6 vols. in 7, HMC, 75 (1924–95), vol. 1 • G. Hampson, 'Savage, Richard', HoP, *Commons, 1660–90* • GEC, *Peerage* • C. Dalton, ed., *English army lists and commission registers, 1661–1714*, 6 vols. (1892–1904) • *The Marlborough–Godolphin correspondence*, ed. H. L. Snyder, 3 vols. (1975) • A. D. Francis, *The First Peninsular War, 1702–1713* (1975) • A. D. Francis, *The Methuens and Portugal* (1966) • G. S. Holmes, *British politics in the age of Anne*, rev. edn (1987) • J. Childs, *The army, James II and the Glorious Revolution* (1980) • *Memoirs of the secret services of John Macky*, ed. A. R. (1733) • J. Swift, *Journal to Stella*, ed. H. Williams, 2 vols. (1948) • *IGI*

Archives Longleat House, Wiltshire, Bath MSS, corresp. and related material • PRO, corresp. relating to visit to Hanover, SP 104/48 | BL, letters to Sir Willoughby Aston, Add. MSS 4903, 36913 • BL, letters, Stowe MSS 214, 223–224 • CAC Cam., corresp. with Thomas Earle • CKS, corresp. with James Stanhope, U1590/0136–41

Wealth at death approx. £15,000 in legacies and two mansion houses: will, 1712, PRO, PROB 11/529, fols. 319–21

Savage, Richard (1697/8–1743), poet and playwright, claimed to be the illegitimate offspring of Richard *Savage, fourth Earl Rivers (*c.*1654–1712), and Anne Gerard, countess of Macclesfield (1667/8–1753) [*see* Brett, Anne]. He said that he was born on 10 January 1698 and baptized Richard Savage at St Andrew's, Holborn, with Earl Rivers as his godfather.

Lady Macclesfield (separated from her husband Charles *Gerard, second earl of Macclesfield, since 1685) bore two children by Rivers: a girl in 1695, and a boy on or shortly before 16 January 1697, when the birth was registered. This child was delivered in private rooms at Fox Court, Gray's Inn Lane, Holborn. Baptized Richard Smith on 18 January 1697 by Isaac Burbidge, minister of St Andrew's, Holborn, the boy was styled son of John and Mary Smith. Rivers attended as godfather, signing himself Captain John Smith; the other godparents were Rivers's agents, Newdigate and Dorothy Ousley.

The subsequent history of this child (of whom Lady Macclesfield, in order to conceal her identity from the midwife, was delivered in a mask) is impossible to determine. His name and residence appear to have been periodically changed, to deprive Lord Macclesfield of evidence of adultery (Tracy, 11). Macclesfield, after a protracted and bitter contest beginning in 1697 in the House of Lords (during the course of which Earl Rivers's name was never mentioned), nevertheless obtained on 15 March 1698 a divorce which declared the countess's two children illegitimate. Her personal fortune was returned to her as part of the settlement. She married Colonel Henry Brett in 1700 and subsequently gave birth to their daughter.

In the meantime her illegitimate son was put out to nurse to Mary Peglear in Hampstead, who was at first told his surname was Lee and, later, Smith. He was then transferred to the care of Ann Portlock in Maiden Lane, Covent Garden, who called him Richard Portlock. It is unclear what became of this boy. There is evidence to support Lady Macclesfield's assertion that both illegitimate children died young. The girl was given a formal funeral, which is fully documented, at Chelsea church in 1698. A Richard Portlock was buried in St Paul's, Covent Garden, in November 1698, but as Ann Portlock had a son of her own, and as her husband's name was Richard, this body cannot be conclusively identified as that of Lady Macclesfield's son. Narcissus Luttrell believed in 1698 that he was still alive, under the name of Savage (Luttrell, 350).

Early life There are several discrepancies between the known facts about Lady Macclesfield's son and various accounts (which in their turn differ from one another) published by Savage and his supporters. According to these latter narratives, Savage was born in January 1698, not 1697 as the parish registration shows. His mother determined from his birth to abandon him. He was committed to the care either of a poor anonymous nurse in London, or of his godmother Mrs Lloyd, or to both women in succession.

Thanks to the intervention of Mrs Lloyd and his supposed maternal grandmother, Lady Mason, the story continues, Savage was sent to a small grammar school at or near St Albans, Hertfordshire. His mother thwarted Rivers's deathbed wish to bequeath Savage £6000 by informing him that his son had died. She endeavoured by indirect means to have Savage secretly kidnapped and removed to the West Indies, but, when that scheme failed, apprenticed him to a shoemaker in Holborn, where he could be raised in poverty and obscurity. After Mrs Lloyd or his anonymous nurse died, Savage alighted on some correspondence among her papers narrating the secret circumstances of his birth. Breaking his indentures, he began to use his real name and sought repeatedly to force his claims on his mother.

Each contemporary account of Savage's life supports a version of this story, and each is based to some extent on information derived from Savage himself. The first is a brief narrative in Giles Jacob's *Poetical Register* (1719) stating that Rivers gave his own name and stood godfather to his son at St Andrew's. It claimed that Mrs Lloyd's executors had embezzled a legacy of £300 intended for her charge (Jacob, 1.297–8). The second account consists of a series of three essays, intended to prompt public sympathy and financial support, in Aaron Hill's *Plain Dealer* (1724). Issue number 15, which published one of Savage's poems, was dedicated to his cause. Hill returned to Savage in number 28, printing a brief sketch of his life that included an account of him walking by night beneath his mother's window (*Plain Dealer*, 28.1–2). The third instalment contained a response to number 28 from Savage, referring to a file of 'convincing *Original Letters*' which Hill (although studiously ambiguous about its contents) considered 'Proofs' of his identity 'too *strong*, to be easily mistaken' (*Plain Dealer*, 73.2).

Eliza Haywood's lurid and factually unreliable *roman-à-clef*, *Memoirs of a Certain Island* (1724), relayed the thinly disguised story of Lady Macclesfield's adultery and Savage's childhood, introducing the attempt to have him removed to the plantations. The fullest early account is an anonymous *Life of Mr. Richard Savage* (1727), the work of Charles Beckingham and (probably) Thomas Cooke (Tracy, 90). This asserts that Savage was committed not to Mrs Lloyd, but to 'a poor Woman, with Orders to breed him up as her own, and […] never to let him come to the Knowledge of his real Parents' (Beckingham and Cooke, 5–6). Yet Savage later told Elizabeth Carter that 'the mean nurse' was 'quite a fictitious character', that he had been raised solely by Mrs Lloyd (whom he claimed as guardian, not godmother) and passed under another name until the age of seventeen (Pennington, 59).

In his preface to *Miscellaneous Poems and Translations* (1726), Savage reiterated his claims with little further substantiation. Samuel Johnson compiled his celebrated *Account of the Life of Mr. Richard Savage, Son of the Earl Rivers* (published anonymously in 1744) from most of the above materials, with supplementary information provided by conversations with Savage and the publisher Edward Cave.

No documents to confirm Savage's assertions have been found. Research has not established the existence of Mrs Lloyd in the capacity of godmother or guardian. In the register of St Andrew's, Savage is allotted only one godmother, Dorothy Ousley, whom he never mentioned. No record exists of any communication or relationship between Savage and Lady Mason, his alleged grandmother, although she did not die until 1717. Newdigate Ousley, who lived until 1714, was apparently unknown to him. Mrs Brett (the former Lady Macclesfield) always maintained that he was an impostor.

In Savage's favour, perhaps, are the facts that Lord Tyrconnel, Mrs Brett's nephew, received him into his household, and that Rivers's daughter Bessy Savage, countess of Rochford, recognized his claim. John Savage, Rivers's cousin and heir, subscribed to *Miscellaneous Poems*.

Early writings, 1715–1727 Savage's putative nobility and early works were first brought to light by the Jacobite rising. Before the rising broke out in September 1715 he had composed at least two pieces of doggerel, *An Ironical Panegyrick on his Pretended Majesty G—* and *The Pretender*. He was arrested in November on the charge of possessing a treasonable pamphlet and brought before Mr Justice Woolaston. The *Weekly Packet* of 5–12 November reports that he gave his name as 'Mr. Savage, natural son to the late Earl Rivers' and 'impeach'd one of Mr. Berington the Printer's Men' to escape further prosecution (p. 2).

Robert Girling, a government agent, tracked Savage after his release and in 1717 submitted a report with copies of five seditious poems (including *An Ironical Panegyrick* and *The Pretender*) that he declared were Savage's work. Parliament intervened with an act of amnesty, made law on 6 July 1717, which covered the transgression of composing treasonable libels during the late revolt and thus forestalled any legal action against Savage.

In the meantime, Savage was moving in theatrical circles. Mrs Lucy Rodd Price of Gray's Inn apparently translated Calderón's play *La dama duende* and gave a copy of it to Savage in 1716 with the intention that he should adapt it to the London stage. Savage seems to have delayed the work so long that Mrs Price passed it on to Christopher Bullock. He extensively revised the text and produced the play, *Woman is a Riddle*, on 4 December 1716 at Lincoln's Inn Fields. It ran for twelve performances.

In 1717 Savage published *The Convocation, or, A Battle of the Pamphlets*. The lower house of convocation, which was predominantly high-church, had condemned Benjamin Hoadly (the whig bishop of Bangor) for two of his sermons. As a result, the government prorogued convocation and forbade it to transact synodical business. This arbitrary action prompted a pamphlet war of which Savage was self-appointed historian. The poem, which he later attempted to suppress, gives an account of the dispute from a high-church viewpoint.

In 1718 Savage wrote *Love in a Veil*, another play taken from an original by Calderón, *Peor está que estaba*. Mrs Price may once again have provided the translation, since it is unlikely that Savage was familiar with Spanish. It was produced at Drury Lane on 17 June 1718, running for four performances, and published later that year. The author received two benefits, and came into contact with Richard Steele and the actor Robert Wilks. Savage's dedication of the play to Lord Lansdowne, which contained the first public allusion to his purported identity, gained him powerful supporters.

Wilks is reported to have secured for Savage the sum of £50 from Mrs Brett, with the promise of a further £150. However, Mrs Brett had invested most of her fortune in South Sea stock, and 'when that *Grand Bubble broke*, the other Hundred and Fifty Pounds *evaporated* with it' (Beckingham and Cooke, 11–12). Steele proposed that Savage should marry his illegitimate daughter, Miss Ousley, but the match was broken off when Steele failed to raise the promised dowry of £1000. Savage later asserted that he could never be induced to see Miss Ousley (Pennington, 60). He quarrelled with Steele when the essayist claimed that Savage had ridiculed him.

The actress Anne Oldfield offered Savage financial support, although Robert Shiels and a recent biographer of Oldfield dispute the claim that she settled on him a regularly paid annuity of £50 (Cibber and Shiels, 33; Lafler, 151). In 1720 he met Aaron Hill, who introduced him to the poets James Thomson and John Dyer, as well as to Eliza Haywood and Martha Fowke Sansom. Savage addressed light verse to the Hillarian coterie throughout the 1720s. He may have fathered Haywood's first child (*Selected Fiction and Drama*, ed. Backscheider, xv).

In 1723, while he was 'without Lodging, and often without Meat' (Johnson, 21), Savage wrote and produced the tragedy *Sir Thomas Overbury*. Hill corrected the play, contributing a prologue and epilogue. The *Life* states that the author's performance in the title role at Drury Lane was rewarded 'with much Applause', but Johnson (relying on Savage's private opinion or on witnesses) considered it a failure (Johnson, 12, 24). The play opened on 12 June, ran for three nights, and was revived once more in October for the author's benefit. Savage earned £100 from its production and publication, 'which he thought at that Time a very large Sum, having never been Master of so much before' (ibid., 24). He appeared for the last time on stage as the Duke of York in Theophilus Cibber's adaptation of Shakespeare's *King Henry VI*.

On 11 May 1724 Hill began to publicize Savage's misfortunes in the *Plain Dealer*. A subscription set in train by the periodical enabled Savage finally to publish *Miscellaneous Poems* in 1726, with a preface inveighing against Mrs Brett 'in a very uncommon Strain of Humour' (Johnson, 27). The collection boasted contributions by Hill, John Dyer, and a number of female poets, as well as the greater part of Savage's poetry to date. The most considerable omission was his *Authors of the Town*, a discursive satire published anonymously in 1725, no doubt excluded because it abused some friends and collaborators. As a result of its outspoken attack on Mrs Brett, 'some very considerable Persons' (Beckingham and Cooke, 19), possibly Mrs Brett and Tyrconnel, insisted that *Miscellaneous Poems* be withdrawn. In compensation, they gave Savage an annuity of £50. A revised edition appeared in September with the objectionable preface removed, although the title-page and headings to Savage's own poems continued to describe him as Rivers's son.

Savage now entered a period of relative security. He left his lodgings at Westminster and, 'for the Benefit of the Air, and the Convenience of his Studies' (Beckingham and Cooke, 20), moved to Richmond. He published little in the next year except *A Poem, Sacred to the Glorious Memory of … King George* (1727), a brief and fruitless appeal for patronage.

Trial, conviction, and liberation Savage's prospects were gradually improving, 'when both his Fame and his Life were endangered by an Event, of which it is not yet determined, whether it ought to be mentioned as a Crime or a Calamity' (Johnson, 30). On 20 November 1727 during a visit to town, he embarked on a drinking spree with two companions, William Merchant and James Gregory. At 2 a.m. the trio entered Robinson's Coffee House in Charing Cross and demanded accommodation for the night. A brawl ensued when they forced themselves into a room being vacated by another party, kicked over a table, and placed themselves in front of the fire. Swords were drawn; Savage turned on James Sinclair, and ran him through the belly. Someone then put out the candles and in the ensuing confusion a maid was cut on the head while trying to restrain Savage and Merchant. They were soon arrested nearby. Sinclair died the next morning, having identified Savage as his assailant. The three men were committed to Newgate prison and charged with murder on 22 November.

Their trial took place on 7 December 1727 at the Old Bailey. Johnson's account, derived partly from Savage, provides the fullest extant report. Savage conducted the defence himself—his main speech to the jury, which has not survived, lasted for over an hour—to no avail. He and Gregory were found guilty of murder; Merchant, who had been unarmed, was convicted of manslaughter. Brought into court for sentencing on 11 December, Savage submitted a plea for mercy. He and Gregory were, however, condemned to death by the infamous hanging judge Sir Francis Page.

It is asserted that after Savage's conviction Mrs Brett employed all her influence to obtain his execution (Johnson, 36); Savage wrote her a letter from prison that is now lost. A movement began at once among his friends to appeal to the throne for a pardon. Hill commissioned the anonymous *Life* as part of the campaign for clemency; it ended with his open letter to Tyrconnel, who was apparently critical of his aunt's behaviour. Tyrconnel, thanks to Hill, had seen Savage's 'convincing *Original Letters*', and took charge of bringing a petition before the king and queen. He was granted an audience on 19 December, and a free pardon was obtained for Savage and Gregory on 6 January. Released on bail on 20 January 1728, they were formally freed by 28 February. Savage owed his life to the intercession of many people, chiefly Tyrconnel, although Johnson gives major credit to Frances Seymour, countess of Hertford (ibid., 38).

Later works, 1728–1738 Savage's first undertaking on his release was to complete his energetic confessional poem *The Bastard*, published on 18 April 1728 and unblushingly '*inscrib'd with all due reverence to Mrs BRET, once Countess of MACCLESFIELD*' (Savage, *Works*, 87). It was an immediate success, running to five editions in London during the year, as well as one in Dublin. *The Bastard* opened with 'a pompous Enumeration of the imaginary Advantages of base Birth' (Johnson, 70–71) in which Savage exulted in his illegitimacy:

Blest be the *Bastard*'s birth! through wondr'ous ways,
He shines eccentric like a Comet's blaze.
No sickly fruit of faint compliance he;
He! stampt in nature's mint of exstasy!
He lives to build, not boast, a gen'rous race:
No tenth transmitter of a foolish face.
(Savage, *Works*, 89)

The poem went on to attack Mrs Brett with renewed animosity. She was at the time of its publication in Bath and, as Savage subsequently related 'with great Satisfaction', could not enter any public place 'without being saluted with some Lines from *The Bastard*' (Johnson, 71). He followed up this piece of reckless vilification by advertising a new edition of *Miscellaneous Poems*, with the previously excluded preface reinstated, in June. It is probable, however, that this was not a new edition but the remaining stock of the suppressed first issue (Tracy, 94–5).

Oscillating between plenty and wretchedness, fêted liberally by his friends yet lacking any regular income, Savage remained without a settled residence until Tyrconnel offered about this time to shelter him in his house in Arlington Street and to grant him a fixed annuity of £200. Thus began 'the Golden Part of Mr. *Savage*'s Life […] his Appearance was splendid, his Expences large, and his Acquaintance extensive' (Johnson, 44). Johnson was wrong to believe that the motive of Tyrconnel's generosity was to shield Mrs Brett from further harassment; he thought that *The Bastard* was not printed until 1735, and that Savage held it in reserve to publish the moment his terms ceased to be met (ibid., 70). He did not know that Tyrconnel had intervened to rescue Savage from the gallows. Under Tyrconnel's roof Savage completed what he considered to be his masterpiece, *The Wanderer: a Vision* (1729), a lengthy discursive poem containing horrified fragmentary reflections on murder and a depiction of the figure of Suicide which Johnson thought 'terrific' (ibid., 54). He dedicated *The Triumph of Health and Mirth* (1730) to Lady Tyrconnel's recovery from prolonged illness.

The victims of Pope's *Dunciad* (1728) held Savage to be the chief source for the literary gossip that informs *The Dunciad Variorum* (1729). Savage's prose work *An Author to be Lett* (1729), published under the pseudonym Iscariot Hackney and a by-product of Pope's war with the dunces, earned him many enemies. Although it casts aspersions on the lowly origins of various authors (Savage's friends included), *An Author* is primarily concerned to draw the composite portrait of a typical Grub Street hack. It was republished, with some alterations, in *A collection of pieces in verse and prose, which have been publish'd on occasion of the DUNCIAD* (1731).

When Laurence Eusden, poet laureate, died on 27 September 1730, Savage endeavoured to be nominated his successor. Through Tyrconnel's influence with Mrs Clayton, woman of the bedchamber to Queen Caroline, he gained support for his appointment. At the last moment, however, the laureateship was conferred on Colley Cibber. Undeterred, Savage published on 1 March 1732 an ode on the queen's birthday and assumed the title of volunteer laureate. The queen granted him a pension of £50, on condition that he celebrate her birthday annually. Notwithstanding Cibber's sarcastic remonstrances, Savage continued his yearly tribute until her death.

In August 1732 Savage published *Religion and Liberty: an Epistle to … Sir Robert Walpole*, a panegyric addressed to a figure whom he otherwise mentioned 'sometimes with Acrimony, and generally with Contempt' (Johnson, 51). He later claimed, implausibly, that Tyrconnel had bullied him into writing the poem (ibid.); his efforts to secure a government pension did not, in fact, cease until 1737.

By the early 1730s Savage was moving in opposition whig and dissenting circles. His political sympathies were complicated, paying little heed to party divisions. Never wholly abandoning the emotionally fraught Jacobite strain of his early verse, he identified passionately throughout his life with attempts to legitimize outcasts: specifically, with the tory iconography of a martyred Charles I, lamenting, exiled, and disinherited from the riches and status that were his birthright.

Minor verses aside, Savage's next project was a vivid and effective anti-clerical satire, *The Progress of a Divine* (1735). Savage gave in vitriolic outline the composite character of a fornicating, embezzling, and paedophiliac churchman, swiping at Edmund Gibson, bishop of London—recently accused of obtaining the acquittal of a clergyman charged with depravity—and his associates Henry Stebbing and William Venn. The poem was also prompted by a vicious dispute (1733–4) between Gibson and the lord chancellor, Charles Talbot, over the Arian divine Thomas Rundle's preferment to the see of Gloucester. Savage characteristically became 'a warm Advocate' for the exiled Rundle's cause (Johnson, 83); thanks to a smear campaign conducted by Stebbing and Venn, he had eventually lost the Gloucester vacancy to Gibson's theologically orthodox candidate, Martin Benson, and accepted the bishopric of Derry.

As a result of this publication Savage may have been prosecuted for obscenity (Johnson, 85–6; there is no other evidence for this claim). The episode, combined with Savage's habitual drunkenness, insolence, and extravagance, brought his increasingly uneasy relations with Tyrconnel to a head. He assumed 'the Government of the House', raided his host's wine cellar, and pawned a collection of valuable books stamped with Tyrconnel's crest (ibid., 59–60). By 1735 he was demanding the payment of his annuity as a 'debt' and serenading his patron as 'Right Honourable Brute and Booby'. They parted, it seems, by mutual consent.

Savage had already aligned himself with a hybrid political opposition by joining the freemasons. He made his allegiance public with a poem *On the Birth-Day of the Prince of Wales* (1736), later enlarged and republished as *Of Public Spirit in Regard to Public Works* (1737). Walpole duly reneged on his promise of a place at £200 a year, and Savage was left to bewail the plight of the government hireling in *A Poet's Dependance on a Statesman* (1736). In February 1737 he issued a proposal in the *Gentleman's Magazine* to print his collected works by subscription. Although repeatedly advertised, this design was never executed. Following the death of the queen (20 November 1737), he was struck off the pension list in September 1738 and thus deprived of his last resource.

Reduced to utmost indigence, Savage retained the fitful assistance of many friends and former literary associates; he seems to have assumed that such aid was no more than a disenfranchised aristocrat's right. His lofty ingratitude and readiness to take offence at the slightest perceived reference to his dependent station repeatedly tested their affections to the limit: 'he scarcely ever found a Stranger, whom he did not leave a Friend; but it must likewise be added, that he had not often a Friend long, without obliging him to be a Stranger' (Johnson, 60).

By 1738 Johnson had arrived in London and become Savage's bosom companion in wretchedness and indignation. Johnson later recalled that his friend lodged, when he could afford to, 'in mean Houses' or 'in Cellars'. At other times, he 'walked about the Streets till he was weary, and lay down in the Summer upon a Bulk, or in the Winter with his Associates in Poverty, among the Ashes of a Glass-house' (Johnson, 97). At night, 'in high spirits and brimful of patriotism', they roamed the streets of London together, denouncing ministerial corruption and vowing to stand by their country. Savage's licentiousness may have led his protégé 'into some indulgencies which occasioned much distress to his virtuous mind' (Boswell, *Life*, 1.164).

Retirement and last illness In 1739 Pope raised a fund by subscription to enable Savage to retire to Swansea. He departed in July but, fourteen days later and still on the road, requested further funds from London. He then lingered at Bristol, finally reaching Swansea in December. Little is known about his sojourn in Wales, but he moved in high social circles and made unsuccessful overtures to a local beauty, Mrs Bridget Jones of Llanelli. He composed in 1741 or 1742 a passionate Valentine's day valediction to her. Contrary to the wishes of his subscribers, he had decided to return via Bristol to London, in order to stage a revised version of *Sir Thomas Overbury*.

Savage arrived in Bristol by September 1742. Here 'he was not only caressed and treated, but had a Collection made for him of about thirty Pounds' (Johnson, 118). Yet on or about 10 January 1743 he was arrested for a debt of £8 owed to a Mrs Read—'Madam Wolf Bitch', as Savage called her (*GM*, 1st ser., 57, 1787, 1040)—and committed to Bristol Newgate prison. Here he remained with little financial assistance for the last six months of his life, endeavouring to conceal his imprisonment and poor health. He was tenderly cared for by Abel Dagge, keeper of Newgate, who attempted in vain to secure his release.

In a mysterious letter of 19 June Savage referred to a sister whom he urged a London acquaintance 'for God's sake' to contact 'and let her know the state of my affairs' (*GM*, 1st ser., 57, 1787, 1040). The identity of this 'sister' is unknown; she may be the legitimate daughter of Colonel and Mrs Brett. The *Gentleman's Magazine* records the marriage in October 1737 of a Miss Brett, 'half Sister to Mr *Savage* Son to the late E. *Rivers*', to Sir William Leman of Northall. Another Miss Brett (possessed of a £12,000 fortune) married George Bincks of New Bond Street in July 1735 (*GM*, 1st ser., 7, 1737, 637; *GM*, 1st ser., 5, 1735, 387).

Provoked by Savage's intolerable demands, Pope severed all relations with him. Savage's last poem, composed in Newgate and published posthumously in 1744, was *London and Bristol Delineated*, an acidulous satire addressing Bristol as 'Thou Blank of Sciences! Thou Dearth of Arts!' (Savage, *Works*, 260) and berating its inhabitants for their hypocrisy and barbarity.

On 25 July Savage was confined to his room with pains in his back and side, and rapidly lapsed into a coma. He may have suffered liver failure brought on by drinking (Holmes, 226). On 31 July, the last occasion that Dagge saw him, Savage said, 'with an uncommon Earnestness, *I have something to say to you, Sir*'. Unable to recall what he was about to communicate, he 'moved his Hand in a melancholy Manner' and said, '*'Tis gone*' (Johnson, 135). He died in Newgate on the morning of 1 August 1743, and was buried the next day at Abel Dagge's expense in the churchyard of St Peter's, Bristol. The location of his grave is unknown, but a tablet was erected to his memory in the south wall of the church. Benjamin Victor mentioned a portrait of Savage, which has never been identified, in a letter of the 1750s (Victor, 264).

Savage's most highly regarded works are *The Bastard*, with its peculiarly spirited mock encomium on illegitimacy, and *The Wanderer*, which, although uneven, contains arresting descriptions of mental torment and remorse. *The Progress of a Divine* is one of the most accomplished and furiously animated political satires of its time.

There is an alternative to accepting or rejecting the story of Savage's origins, first suggested by Tyrconnel's relative Francis Cockayne Cust. He conjectured that Savage was the son of Richard Smith's nurse, who substituted him for Lady Macclesfield's child when the latter died and raised him to believe that he was a natural lord (Tracy, 26–

7). This suggestion, however far-fetched, is not impossible. As Boswell concluded, 'The world' must continue to 'vibrate in a state of uncertainty' about his real identity (Boswell, *Life*, 1.174). Whatever the truth may have been, Savage seems to have believed what he said.

FREYA JOHNSTON

Sources C. Tracy, *The artificial bastard: a biography of Richard Savage* (1953) • W. Moy Thomas, 'Richard Savage', *N&Q*, 2nd ser., 6 (1858), 361–5, 385–9, 425–8, 445–9 • R. Holmes, *Dr Johnson and Mr Savage* (1993) • S. Johnson, *An account of the life of Mr Richard Savage*, ed. C. Tracy (1971) • [G. Jacob], *The poetical register, or, The lives and characters of all the English poets*, 2 vols. (1723); repr. (1969) • [C. Beckingham and T. Cooke (?)], *The life of Mr. Richard Savage* (1727); repr. (1988) • *Plain Dealer*, 15 (1724), 1–2 • *Plain Dealer*, 28 (1724), 1–2 • *Plain Dealer*, 73 (1724), 2 • R. Savage and others, *Miscellaneous poems and translations* (1726) • *European Magazine and London Review*, 6 (1784), 189–94, 277–82 • Thomas Birch, unpublished papers, BL, Add. MS 4318 • secretaries of state, state papers domestic, George I, PRO, SP 35/7/78 • *The manuscripts of the House of Lords*, new ser., 12 vols. (1900–77), vol. 3 • E. Timberland, *History and proceedings of the House of Lords*, 2 (1742) • M. Pennington, ed., *Memoirs of the life of Mrs. Elizabeth Carter*, 2nd edn, 1 (1808) • L. Howard, ed., *A collection of letters and state papers*, 2 (1756) • R. Shiels, *The lives of the poets of Great Britain and Ireland*, ed. T. Cibber, 5 vols. (1753) • N. Luttrell, *A brief historical relation of state affairs from September 1678 to April 1714*, 4 (1857) • *The correspondence of Alexander Pope*, ed. G. Sherburn, 3–4 (1956) • Boswell, *Life*, vols. 1–5 • [E. Haywood], *Memoirs of a certain island adjacent to the kingdom of Utopia*, 1 (1724) • R. Savage, *Poetical works*, ed. C. Tracy (1962) • B. Victor, *Original letters, dramatic pieces, and poems*, 1 (1776) • R. Carruthers, *The life of Alexander Pope*, 2nd edn (1857) • J. Hawkins, *The life of Samuel Johnson, LL.D.*, 2nd edn (1787) • *GM*, 3rd ser., 1 (1856), 267–77 • *Weekly Packet* (5–12 Nov 1715), 2 • G. F. Whicher, *The life and romances of Mrs. Eliza Haywood* (1915) • *Selected fiction and drama of Eliza Haywood*, ed. P. R. Backscheider (1999) • J. Lafler, *The celebrated Mrs Oldfield* (1989)

Archives BL, letters to Thomas Birch, unpublished papers, Add. MS 4318 • BL, William Cole, unpublished notebooks, Add. MS 5832, fol. 169 • PRO, secretaries of state, state papers domestic, George I, SP 35/7/78

Wealth at death died in debtors' prison

Savage, Sir Robert (*d.* 1360). *See under* Savage family (*per.* 1333–1519).

Savage, Sir Roger (*d.* in or before 1320). *See under* Savage family (*per.* c.1280–c.1420).

Savage, Roland (*d.* 1519). *See under* Savage family (*per.* 1333–1519).

Savage, Samuel Morton (1721–1791), Independent minister and tutor, was born in London on 19 July 1721. He believed himself to be the lineal descendant and heir of John Savage, second Earl Rivers (*d.* 1654), but did not pursue the claim. His grandfather, John Savage, was pastor of the Seventh Day Baptist Church, Mill Yard, Goodman's Fields. Another relation on his father's side was Hugh Boulter, archbishop of Armagh; hence his friends expected him to seek a career in the established church. However, he first thought of medicine, and spent two years with his uncle Toulmin, an apothecary in Old Gravel Lane, Wapping. Then, after a religious experience, and encouraged by Isaac Watts, he entered the academy in Moorfields supported by the Congregational Fund Board and headed by John Eames. In 1744, while still a senior student, he was chosen as assistant tutor to Eames's successor, David Jennings, to teach mathematics and science. At this point the academy, which was now supported by the trustees of William Coward, moved to a house in Wellclose Square, London, where Savage resided.

In 1747 Savage became assistant minister at Isaac Watts's former church in Bury Street, St Mary Axe. He was ordained there as co-pastor to Samuel Price in 1753, and became sole pastor in 1757 after Price's death. In addition he was afternoon preacher (1759–66) and Thursday lecturer (1760–67) to the presbyterian congregation in Hanover Street under Jabez Earle DD. He was Friday lecturer (1761–90) at Little St Helen's—an appointment in the gift of the Coward trustees—and afternoon preacher (1769–75) for Philip Furneaux at Clapham.

On the death of Jennings in 1762, the Coward trustees appointed Savage his successor as divinity tutor and moved the academy to larger premises in Hoxton Square, formerly the residence of Daniel Williams. As head of the academy, Savage 'encouraged free enquiry', in the Coward tradition, and 'threw no difficulties in the way of those who embraced views of Christianity different from his own' (Toulmin, 17). Among these were his two assistants, Andrew Kippis, a Socinian, and Abraham Rees, an Arian. Although they worked harmoniously with Savage, who was a moderate Calvinist, making the academy an embodiment of the shifting tides of belief within eighteenth-century dissent, it was not viewed with much favour, and was dissolved in 1784.

By this time Savage's early brilliance of mind had faded, and he longed to bury himself in his ample library. He resigned his pastorate at Christmas 1787. Like his tutoring, it had lasted forty years, but latterly had not been well supported. The church closed under his successor. His publications were eight single sermons, of which those on the accession of George III and the death of Jennings are the most noteworthy. Savage was made BD by King's College, Aberdeen, in 1764 and DD by Marischal College, Aberdeen, in 1767.

Savage was one of the originators of the appeal to parliament to relieve dissenting ministers from subscription to the doctrinal articles of the Church of England, which succeeded in 1779. Though never a Coward trustee, he was among the original trustees of two other dissenting charities, the Bury Street Trust (1767) and Mrs Jackson's Trust (1768), which later merged with Coward.

Savage was married twice, first, on 14 May 1752 at Allhallows, to Mary Houlme, the only daughter of George Houlme, a stockbroker of Wellclose Square. She died in 1763, leaving two daughters. He married, secondly, on 14 August 1770 at Tonbridge, Hannah Wilkin, who survived him. Savage died on 21 February 1791 of a contraction of the oesophagus which reduced him virtually to a skeleton. He was buried in Bunhill Fields. A sense of underachievement in ministry and teaching is well caught by a contemporary obituarist in the *Gentleman's Magazine*: 'his skill in the languages of antiquity, joined to a sound judgment, matured by reading and study, qualified him to have shone in a more enlarged sphere than he acted in, as well as to have written more.'

JOHN HANDBY THOMPSON

Sources J. Toulmin, *The life of Dr Samuel Morton Savage* (1796) • W. D. Jeremy, *The Presbyterian Fund and Dr Daniel Williams's Trust* (1885) [NB. first forename wrongly given as George on p. 56] • *GM*, 1st ser., 61 (1791), 190–91 • W. Wilson, *The history and antiquities of the dissenting churches and meeting houses in London, Westminster and Southwark*, 4 vols. (1808–14), vol. 1, pp. 324–6 • S. Newth, 'Memorials of the academical institutions sustained by the Coward Trust … to 1850', c.1890, DWL, fols. 195–9 • W. Bennet, *A sermon occasioned by the death of Revd Samuel Morton Savage DD* (1791) • T. Towle, *Address at the grave* (1791) • H. McLachlan, *English education under the Test Acts: being the history of the nonconformist academies, 1662–1820* (1931), 123–4 • *DNB* • *IGI*

Archives DWL, minutes and corresp. of the Coward Trust

Likenesses line engraving, pubd 1796, BM

Savage [*née* Henry], **Sarah** (1664–1752), diarist, was born on 7 August 1664 at Broad Oak, Flintshire, the eldest daughter and third child of a prominent nonconformist minister and diarist, Philip *Henry (1631–1696), and his wife, Katherine Matthews (1629–1707). Precocious, she was taught while very young to read English by the Revd William Turner and Hebrew by her father; at six or seven she could already read and construe a Hebrew psalm. In childhood she also began a practice continued into old age of summarizing the sermons she had heard preached, because she found reading such reminders comforting and instructive. At sixteen she began participating in holy communion, wherein 'through [the Lord's] goodness, I found great sweetness' (Williams, 30). Thereafter, following the teachings of her father, she aimed to show her faith by zeal for good works. On 25 March 1687, with some reluctance, she married a pious widower with one child, her relative John Savage (*d.* 1729), a farmer and land agent living at Wrenbury Wood, near Nantwich in Cheshire. The marriage was ultimately a happy one, and their home became a meeting place for fellow dissenters. Throughout her life she would be fond of reading religious works. She also became known in her community as a generous giver of alms.

Diary-keeping was an important part of the Henry family's religious observance. Sarah's father began his in 1657 and continued it until his death, and her brother Matthew *Henry and her sister Ann Hulton also kept diaries. Sarah's began in August 1686 and, like those of the rest of her family, her diary was concerned with the close scrutiny of the use of her time, and scrupulously analysed her sinful nature. She became the conscientious recorder of her own lapses, albeit concerned also that her husband should not become over-involved in worldly concerns. Sarah had resolved to follow the four rules for a godly woman set down by her father: 'obedience to her husband, chastity in conversation, sobriety in adornment, and a "meek and quiet spirit"' (Crawford, 'Katharine and Philip Henry', 50). Men and women were to respect the division of labour between the sexes, and a woman's highest achievement was to be 'a fruitful vine and a nursing mother' (ibid.). Although Sarah's diary is primarily a spiritual self-examination, in the first years of her marriage it reveals also her desires for a child, sometimes very directly. Thus, supported by her faith but conflicted by desire and fearing barrenness, in October 1687 she writes:

> If God should see good to delay or totally deny the mercy of children to me still by his grace I will wait on him, and love him not one jot the less, tho' I sometimes can scarce quiet my spirit as I would. (Crawford, 'Attitudes to pregnancy', 44)

In 1688, the year when she came safely through smallpox, she also finally bore a premature but surviving son in December (there had already been one miscarriage earlier), but he died on the 18th. After these early disappointments, however, she proved fruitful; on 13 May 1701 she bore her eighth child, Hannah. She produced in all nine children, four of whom, all girls, would survive her and marry. Other disappointments than the death of her firstborn (and of her fourth child, a son, on 29 December 1705) were that Philip, her only son to survive birth, died of smallpox at twenty-two in 1721, and that on 27 September 1729 her husband died after forty-two years of marriage. But she never repines in her diary at God's will, ever grateful instead for divine goodness while assured of her own unworthiness. The diary is not entirely limited to self-examination or even personal matters, though her religious concerns dominate it. She is patriot enough to note, for example, King William's part in the battle of the Boyne in 1690 and his death in 1702. Her dedication to her family is a continual theme; her resolution that children are 'arrows in the hand and need to be rightly guided' (Crawford, 'Katharine and Philip Henry', 45) reflects her wish to bring up her children in godliness. However, her diary reveals a tension between Christian love for her children and 'creature love': in 1702 she writes that her greatest sin is 'too much love, and too many cares for, my children' (ibid., 51). Domestic work is seen as necessary and part of a woman's duty but unavoidably worldly, and in her correspondence Sarah frequently apologizes for her attention to family life for its own sake rather than for its spiritual significance.

Following her husband's death, and after living for a while with her children and with friends, in 1736 Sarah Savage moved to West Bromwich, Staffordshire, her home until her sudden death on 27 February 1752. She was buried in the churchyard of West Bromwich; her funeral sermon was preached on 15 March 1752 by the Revd Mr Howell, dissenting minister. She left behind her diary, continued until her final year, of which only the first original volume survives, at Chester Record Office, although transcripts exist elsewhere. With the aid of these, the nineteenth-century nonconformist writer John Bickerton Williams, a relative of the Henry family, compiled a memoir of her life and thoughts for publication in 1818 as an example of 'female virtue … for the imitation and guidance of succeeding generations' (Williams, v). Williams selected examples from the diary that would emphasize his subject's piety and showed little interest in, for example, the family's financial matters, but this attempt to present Sarah Savage as an example of the religious life to nineteenth-century women would not have surprised her. She had, indeed, continued her record hoping that posthumously 'it may be useful to some of mine … for their quickening … in the narrow way' (Williams, 236).

HARRIET BLODGETT

Sources J. B. Williams, *Memoirs of the life and character of Mrs Sarah Savage* (1845) • P. Crawford, 'Katharine and Philip Henry and their children: a case study in family ideology', *Transactions of the Historic Society of Lancashire and Cheshire*, 134 (1984), 39–73 • P. Crawford, 'Attitudes to pregnancy from a woman's spiritual diary, 1687–8', *Local Population Studies*, 21 (autumn 1978), 43–5 • *DNB*

Archives Bodl. Oxf., MS, MS Eng. misc. E. 331 • Ches. & Chester ALSS, MS, DB8 • DWL, MS

Savage, Thomas (*d*. 1507), administrator and archbishop of York, was the second son of Sir John *Savage of Clifton, Cheshire (1423–1495) [*see under* Savage family], and Katherine, his wife, daughter of Sir Thomas *Stanley, later first Baron Stanley (*d*. 1459). Sir John *Savage (*d*. 1492) [*see under* Savage family] was his elder brother. Savage studied at Oxford, graduating BA some time before 1474, then at Bologna before 1477, and then at Padua, where he was admitted DCL and was rector of the jurists in 1481–2. His father set him on the path to comfortable pluralism with his first living, the rectory of Davenham, Cheshire, to which he was instituted on 3 December 1470, but it was the service of Henry VII, for which he was well equipped by education and family connections, that made him great. As he later claimed, it was 'as thawe his highnes had made hym out of claye and brought hym to the honor that he is cumed to' (PRO, STAC 10/4, pt 7, fol. 80*v*). On 21 September 1485, already a royal chaplain, he was appointed chancellor of the earldom of March, and in 1489 he became dean of the Chapel Royal. In 1495 the king recommended him to the University of Oxford as a possible chancellor, but he was not chosen.

Savage served Henry as a diplomat, travelling to Spain in 1488–9 to negotiate the treaty of Medina del Campo, which provided for the marriage of Prince Arthur and Katherine of Aragon. In later years he sometimes negotiated with foreign ambassadors in and around London, and in 1503 he accompanied Princess Margaret to Edinburgh for her wedding, which took place on 8 August. Meanwhile he was named to commissions to let the royal lands and to levy the benevolence of 1491, and to numerous commissions of the peace. He sat regularly in the king's council from at least 1486, and by 1495 became its president, a position he probably retained until 1501. In 1492 he left the deanship of the chapel for the bishopric of Rochester (provided on 3 December), and in 1496 he was translated to London by a bull of 3 August. In lawsuits before the council involving his family and friends he is alleged to have shown blatant partiality.

In 1501 Savage was translated to York (bull of 18 January) and with this promotion came a new role in the government of the north, as 'the king's lieutenant and high commissioner' chairing the 'council of the king at York'. He sat regularly as a JP and oversaw prosecutions for retaining, riots, and other offences, but his activity seems to have declined after an affray at Fulford on 23 May 1504 between his entourage and that of Henry Percy, fifth earl of Northumberland (*d*. 1527). This incident, sparked by competition for local influence between the two men, brought down the wrath of the king on both parties. Though his record of residence at York looks impressive—he spent 90 per cent of his time within his diocese—Savage was content to delegate much of his pastoral work to others. He never ordained at York and seems to have done so only once at London. Yet he delegated well. He brought with him to York many of his Rochester and London administrators, and it is a mark of his sound judgement that these would survive him and run the diocese in succeeding decades. In the same way he introduced to northern government such clerics as the treasurer of his household Thomas Dalby, and his secretary Thomas Magnus (*d*. 1550), who would prove mainstays of the council of the north.

Savage was a flamboyant figure, an avid hunter, who kept peacocks and allegedly swore oaths by his priesthood and his father's soul. He evidently inspired great loyalty, as in Thomas Magnus, who requested burial next to the archbishop forty-three years after the latter's death. He accumulated considerable wealth: his probate inventory valued his goods at £4037 15*s*. 10¾*d*., including £1127 18*s*. 3¼*d*. in plate and £232 1*s*. 8*d*. in tapestries. He built at Cawood Castle (south of York, his main residence as archbishop) and at Scrooby in the West Riding. He died at Cawood on 2 or 3 September 1507, leaving what were by the standards of his episcopal contemporaries unusually large sums for provision for his soul. His body was buried in York Minster, where his tomb and large wooden chantry chapel, completed by 1518, remain, but his heart was buried at Macclesfield, in his ancestral county of Cheshire, where he had intended to found a college.

S. J. GUNN

Sources Emden, *Oxf*. • C. G. Bayne and W. H. Dunham, eds., *Select cases in the council of Henry VII*, SeldS, 75 (1958) • R. W. Hoyle, 'The earl, the archbishop and the council: the affray at Fulford, May 1504', *Rulers and ruled in late medieval England: essays presented to Gerald Harriss*, ed. R. E. Archer and S. Walker (1995), 239–56 • *Report on manuscripts in various collections*, 8 vols., HMC, 55 (1901–14), vol. 2, pp. 28–56 • [J. Raine], ed., *Testamenta Eboracensia*, 4, SurtS, 53 (1869), 308–33 • S. Thompson, 'The pastoral work of the English and Welsh bishops, 1500–58', DPhil diss., U. Oxf., 1984 • *Joannis Lelandi antiquarii de rebus Britannicis collectanea*, ed. T. Hearne, [3rd edn], 6 vols. (1774), vol. 4 • *Chancery records* • G. E. Aylmer and R. Cant, eds., *A history of York Minster* (1977) • will, 1550, Borth. Inst., register 29, fol. 95*v* [Thomas Magnus] • Lichfield Joint RO, register of John Hales, B/A/1/13, fol. 105*r* • PRO, STAC 10/4

Archives Borth. Inst., York register, register 25 • CKS, Rochester register, DRb/Ar 1/12 • GL, London register, MS 9531/8 • PRO, STAC 10/4, pt 7, fol. 80*v*

Likenesses tomb effigy, York Minster

Wealth at death goods valued at £4037 15*s*. 10¾*d*.: Raine, ed., *Testamenta Eboracensia*

Savage, Thomas (1594/5–*c*.1633), interpreter in America, may have come from a family in Cheshire, the Savages of Rock Savage, but nothing certain is known of him until January 1608, when he arrived in Virginia, aged thirteen, as one of many labourers on the first supply ship. A month later Captain Christopher Newport gave Savage (as his own 'son') to Powhatan, paramount chief of the Powhatan confederacy of Algonquians. In return Powhatan presented Newport with a large basket of beans and his servant Namontack, to be 'sent to King James his land, to see him and his country' (Hamor, 38). About a month later Powhatan dismissed Savage, apparently because he knew too much about the chief's intentions towards the colonists, but Powhatan soon relented, requested the boy's return, and retained him for nearly three years.

During his time among the Powhatans, Savage learned their language and customs. The chief seems to have been fond of the lad, fed him 'at his oune Table messe' (Spelman, ciii), and used him often as a messenger and interpreter. Probably in late 1610 Savage escaped to Jamestown under the guise of visiting his English friends, fearing for his safety amid Powhatan's intermittent wars with the colony and with other tribes. For the next several years the Powhatans perceived Savage as an enemy and included him by name ('Thom. Newport') in a 'scornefull song' about their battles with the English (Strachey, 85–6). But Savage survived to be one of Virginia's essential bilingual intermediaries. He may have been present in 1613 when Captain Samuel Argall lured Pocahontas into captivity and perhaps helped the Revd Alexander Whitaker convert her to Christianity. A year later he served as interpreter for Ralph Hamor, the colony's secretary, in an unsuccessful attempt to arrange the marriage of Powhatan's youngest daughter (and sister or half-sister of Pocahontas) to Sir Thomas Dale. At that meeting Powhatan chided Savage for deserting him four years earlier but expressed renewed friendship for him and the colony.

In 1621 Savage was the colonial secretary John Pory's interpreter on two expeditions to the Eastern Shore of Chesapeake Bay, which inaugurated trade with local tribes. Those ties proved critically important the next year when a Powhatan uprising under Opechancanough cost hundreds of colonists' lives—a catastrophe that might have been avoided had colonial authorities taken seriously the warnings Savage relayed from Indians on the Eastern Shore. In the aftermath of the massacre Virginians relied heavily on supplies from the Eastern Shore. In 1624 Pory attested that 'with much honestie and good successe' Savage had 'served the publike without any public recompence, yet had an arrow shot through his body in their service' (*Complete Works of Captain John Smith*, 2.290). Governor George Yeardley was less considerate of Savage, trumping up a judicial case that forced Savage to serve private interests rather than the colony's for several years. At some time in the 1620s Savage married Hannah (*d.* 1641), whose surname is unknown, and settled on the Eastern Shore, where he became a substantial planter and landowner. He continued to be an influential interpreter until his death about 1633. He was survived by his wife, who in 1638 married Daniel Cugley. ALDEN T. VAUGHAN

Sources *The complete works of Captain John Smith (1580–1631)*, ed. P. L. Barbour, 3 vols. (1986) • T. Spelman, 'Relation of Virginea', *Travels and works of Captain John Smith*, ed. E. Arber and A. B. Bradley, 2 vols. (1910), vol. 1, pp. ci–cxiv • R. Hamor, *A true discourse on the present estate of Virginia* (1615) • W. Strachey, *The historie of travell into Virginia Britania* (1612), ed. L. B. Wright and V. Freud (1953) • J. F. Fausz, 'Middlemen in peace and war: Virginia's earliest Indian interpreters, 1608–1632', *Virginia Magazine of History and Biography*, 95 (1987), 41–64 • S. M. Kingsbury, ed., *Records of the Virginia Company of London*, 4 vols. (1906–35) • M. B. Stiles, 'Hostage to the Indians', *Virginia Cavalcade*, 12 (summer 1962), 5–11 • V. M. Meyer and J. F. Dorman, eds., *Adventurers of purse and person: Virginia, 1607–1624/25* (1987) • S. M. Ames, ed., *County court records of Accomack-Northampton, Virginia, 1632–40* (1954) • S. M. Ames, ed., *County court records of Accomack-Northampton, Virginia, 1640–1645* (1973) • N. M. Nugent, ed., *Cavaliers and pioneers: abstracts of Virginia land patents and grants, 1623–1800*, 5 vols. (1934)

Likenesses group portraits, repro. in T. de Bry, *Historiae Americanae*, ed. M. Merian, pt 13 (1634)

Savage, Thomas (*c.*1607–1682), merchant and army officer, was born in England. Although nothing definite can be established about his parentage, he was described by Edward Randolph as 'a gentleman of very good family in England' (*CSP col.*, 9.408). By 1635 he was resident in the parish of St Albans, Hertfordshire, and that year departed for Massachusetts Bay on board the *Planter*. Having settled in Boston, he joined the church (January 1636), became a freeman of the colony (May 1636), and in 1637 helped found the artillery company, later the ancient and honorable artillery company of Massachusetts. By 1637 he had married Faith Hutchinson (1617–1652), daughter of William Hutchinson and Anne *Hutchinson (*née* Marbury). He offered his mother-in-law modest support in her conflict with the colonial government and the Boston church. In March 1637 he signed a petition defending another protagonist in the controversy, John Wheelwright, accused of incendiary preaching, and for this he was temporarily disarmed. He acknowledged his error in November and the sentence was rescinded. When the Boston church placed Anne Hutchinson on trial for spiritual errors the following March, he spoke in her favour and refused to vote to admonish her, he and another relative being themselves admonished as a result. Following Anne Hutchinson's banishment, he considered relocating in Rhode Island with his wife's family, took up land in Portsmouth, and resided there intermittently for a year or two. Ultimately, though, the Savages chose to remain in Boston, where Thomas used his connections to Faith's relations to build up his economic enterprises. On 20 February 1652 his first wife died, and on 15 September he married Mary Symmes (1628–1710) of Charlestown, the daughter of a minister.

Savage pursued a career as a Boston merchant, participating in the town's development and in the burgeoning Atlantic trade networks. Despite his past involvement with the Hutchinsonians, he was to be fully integrated into the orthodox community. He rose to the rank of captain in 1651 and was identified as a military officer suitable to oversee a proposed attack on Dutch New Netherland in 1653. He served as a Boston selectman, and held the position of deputy on the general court thirteen times, on five of which occasions he acted as speaker. In 1658 he signed a petition against the Quakers and attended major church synods in 1662 and 1679.

In religion and politics Savage came to be associated

with a group that advocated a relaxation of certain policies and was a founding member (in 1669), and one of the most influential supporters, of the Third Church of Boston, which favoured liberalizing admission and baptism procedures. Like many other merchants he advocated co-operation with the Restoration government. The Massachusetts government summoned him and a few others to answer for a petition expressing this view in 1666 but they were 'dismist with a kinde of reproofe' (Thomas Brendon to the earl of Clarendon, 22 Oct 1666, 'Clarendon papers', *Collections of the New York Historical Society*, 1870, 129). He finally led troops into battle as a major of the Massachusetts forces in King Philip's War (1675–6), and was described as 'of loyal principles' and 'chief in the soldiers' affections, being the only field officer that faced the Indians' (*CSP col.*, 9.408). His portrait, painted in 1679, shows him in military garb with Boston harbour in the background to symbolize his mercantile calling, while the Savage arms are displayed. For two years prior to his death he served as assistant to the governor. He died 'suddenly' on 15 February 1682 at the age of seventy-five, and was buried at the King's Chapel burial-ground, Boston. A funeral elegy (printed as a broadside) and a funeral sermon emphasized his military career as well as his godly care of the Lord's people. The sermon, by Samuel Willard, is a classic of the 'declension' genre so popular in that period in New England. CARLA GARDINA PESTANA

Sources L. Park, 'Old Boston families, III: the Savage family', *New England Historical and Genealogical Register*, 67 (1913), 198–200 • N. B. Shurtleff, ed., *Records of the governor and company of the Massachusetts Bay in New England*, 5 vols. in 6 (1853–4) • O. A. Roberts, *History of the military company of the Massachusetts*, 1 (1895), 24–6 • *Report of the record commissioners of the city of Boston*, 1–28 (1876–98) • *Records relating to the early history of Boston*, 29–39 (1900–09) • *Note-book kept by Thomas Lechford, esq., lawyer, in Boston, Massachusetts Bay, from June 27, 1638, to July 29, 1641*, ed. [E. E. Hale jun.] (1885) • R. D. Pierce, ed., *The records of the First Church in Boston, 1630–1868*, 3 vols. (1961) • H. A. Hill, *History of the old south church (third church), Boston, 1669–1884*, 2 vols. (1890) • E. Battis, *Saints and sectaries: Anne Hutchinson and the antinomian controversy in the Massachusetts Bay colony* (1962) • D. Lawson, *A funeral elegy upon the … expiration of … Thomas Savage* (Boston, 1682); repr. in 'Nine Massachusetts broadsides, 1677–1699', *Proceedings of the American Antiquarian Society*, 93 (1983), 197–221, esp. 204–8 • S. Willard, *The righteous man's death* (1684) [printed with separate title-page in *The child's portion* (1684)] • D. E. Leach, *Flintlock and tomahawk: New England in King Philip's War* (1958) • D. Pulsifer, ed., *Acts of the commissioners of the united colonies of New England* (1859), vol. 10 of *Records of the colony of New Plymouth in New England*, ed. N. B. Shurtleff and D. Pulsifer (1855–61)

Likenesses attrib. T. Smith, 1679, repro. in L. B. Miller, 'The Puritan portrait: its function in Old and New England', *Seventeenth-century New England*, ed. D. D. Hall and D. G. Allen (1984), fig. 10

Wealth at death £3447 8*s*. 9*d*.: inventory, 23 June 1682, probate records, Suffolk county, Massachusetts; on deposit at the office of the register of probate of Suffolk county; summarized in Thwing project, Mass. Hist. Soc.

Savage, Thomas (1651/2–1668), apprentice and murderer, was said to have been born in the parish of St Giles-in-the-Fields, London. All that is known about his early life is that his father, John, a brewer or alehouse keeper, died when he was young, his mother remarried, and his parents 'endeavoured to have their son well-educated' (*God's Justice*, 2). In December 1666 he was apprenticed to Francis Collins, a vintner who lived at the Ship tavern at Ratcliff Cross in Stepney. He apparently led a dissolute life, and frequented a nearby brothel, where he consorted with Hannah Blay. When he ran out of money on Sunday 28 June 1668, Blay is reported to have encouraged him to steal from his master. When he said this was not possible because a maidservant was always present in the house Blay told him to 'knock her on the head' (*God's Justice*, 3–4). That afternoon Savage found himself alone with the servant, Judith Jones, alias Benson, and attacked her repeatedly with a hammer. She died from the wounds three days later. He broke open his master's cupboard, stole £62, and fled, but was apprehended on 29 June and was committed to Newgate prison. He then implicated Blay, who was committed that same day. He was tried at the Old Bailey on 24 October and was sentenced to death. On 28 October, aged sixteen, he was hanged outside the scene of the crime in Ratcliff. The body was taken down and carried to a tavern, where signs of life were detected. He recovered, but was hanged a second time four hours later. He is said to have been buried in Islington, where his mother then lived, but perhaps because he was an executed felon the burial did not take place in the church grounds. Blay, who was sentenced to death at the same sessions, pleaded pregnancy and was reprieved. She was hanged in the same place on 26 February 1669.

This was an atypical murder for the time in that the offenders were so young, it took place in a private house, and the assault was unprovoked (most murders occurred in taverns or outdoors, in the context of arguments and fights). It must have shocked contemporaries; it attracted the attention of five nonconformist clergymen (Hugh Baker, Thomas Doolittle, Robert Franklin, James Janeway, and Thomas Vincent) as well as one other contemporary and several subsequent publishers of criminal biographies, who saw in this case a morality tale indicating the causes of sin and the possibilities of repentance. All accounts ascribe Savage's downfall to his initial sins of sabbath breaking and frequenting alehouses, and document his redemption through spiritual conversion while awaiting trial. This was the typical narrative of murderers' lives found in criminal biographies of the time; the clergymen's pamphlet, *A Murderer Punished, and Pardoned*, which forms the basis of all subsequent published accounts, appropriated this genre to demonstrate the power of puritan godliness. These pamphlets, which are the primary source of information concerning Savage's life, are thus of limited reliability for that purpose. Although the basic facts of the case are confirmed in the judicial records, there is at least one significant difference: while the published accounts indicate that he confessed the crime when he appeared at the Old Bailey (a sign he acknowledged his sins), his indictment indicates that he pleaded innocent. There are other hints that his conversion was incomplete: he was said to be drunk at his trial, and to have struggled with the executioner when he was hanged the second time.

Accounts of the Savage case were frequently reprinted. *A Murderer Punished, and Pardoned* went through thirteen editions to 1708. In 1710, at a time when the societies for the reformation of manners were engaged in a vigorous campaign against profanation of the sabbath, another account of the case was published which went through twenty-two editions in twenty-five years. In 1734 the story was guaranteed lasting fame when it was included in Charles Johnson's *A general history of the lives and adventures of the most famous highwaymen, murderers, street-robbers, etc.*

ROBERT B. SHOEMAKER

Sources *God's justice against murther, or, The bloudy apprentice executed* [1668] · R. F. [R. Franklin], T. Vincent, T. Doolitel [Doolittle], J. Janeway, and H. Baker, *A murderer punished and pardoned, or, A true relation of the wicked life and shameful-happy death of Thomas Savage*, 12th edn (1669) · sessions roll, LMA, MJ/SR/1360, indictments 50–51 · gaol delivery calendar, LMA, P83/MRY1/1167 · P. Lake, 'Popular form, puritan content? Two puritan appropriations of the murder pamphlet from mid-seventeenth-century London', *Religion, culture and society in early modern Britain*, ed. A. Fletcher and P. Roberts (1994), 313–34 · L. B. Faller, *Turned to account: the forms and functions of criminal biography in late seventeenth- and early eighteenth-century England* (1987), 28–31 · *A warning to youth: the life and death of Thomas Savage* [n.d., 1710?] · register of apprentice bindings, Vintners' Company, GL, MS 15220/1

Savage, William (*c*.1670–1736). *See under* Savage, John (1673–1747).

Savage, William (1720–1789), singer and organist, was born probably in London and was a pupil of J. C. Pepusch and Francesco Geminiani. As a boy he sang solo roles for Handel in the opera *Alcina*, in the masque *Acis and Galatea*, and in the oratorios *Athalia*—in which his performance as the young king, Joas, 'met with universal Applause' (Dean, 259)—*Esther*, and *Israel in Egypt*. He remained a prominent and evidently successful Handel singer and, after a short period as an alto, in the early 1740s was bass soloist in the operas *Imeneo* and *Deidamia* and the oratorios *L'allegro ed il penseroso*, *Saul*, *Samson*, and *Messiah*. He also sang in many of William Boyce's court odes, and was said to have 'a pleasant bass voice of the compass of two octaves: he had a clear articulation, perfect intonation, great volubility of voice, and chaste and good expression. In sacred music particularly, his pathos and feeling were excellent and very impressive' (Farmer, 194). In 1743 he was organist of Finchley parish church, and in 1744 he became a gentleman-in-ordinary at the Chapel Royal.

Savage was appointed vicar-choral, almoner, and master of the choristers at St Paul's Cathedral in 1748. There his responsibilities included supervising the musical studies of the boys of the choir, who all lived with him at his house in Paul's Bakehouse Court. One of them, R. J. S. Stevens, later defended Savage against Charles Burney's accusations of pomposity and self-importance, and remembered him as a thorough, if demanding, teacher. He could be 'violent and impatient in his temper to the greatest degree: and his impetuosity, sometimes drove him into chastising the boys almost to cruelty' (*Recollections*, 13), yet 'by constant attention to their elementary rules every morning before breakfast, he made them correct and ready performers' (Farmer, 195). Stevens was bound apprentice to Savage, as was Jonathan Battishill, who was also a cathedral chorister, and his other pupils included C. F. Reinhold, James and William Evance, and his successors at St Paul's, Robert Hudson and Richard Bellamy. Savage resigned the posts of almoner and master of the choristers in 1773 owing to ill health—according to Stevens he was asthmatic—and having on 5 April 1777 resigned also as vicar-choral he went to live in Tenterden, Kent. He returned to London three or four years later and advertised his readiness to take pupils.

In addition to church music Savage wrote secular songs, rounds, and catches—he was a member of the Catch Club—and some violin music. He was a member of both the Academy of Ancient Music and the Beef Steak Club. He was married to Mary Bolt (*d.* 1788), and they had three children: George (*d.* 1816), who became vicar of Kingston and Richmond, Jane, and William. **Jane Savage** (1752/3–1824), who was a notable keyboard player, published a number of *galant* keyboard compositions and vocal works. In 1793 she married Robert Rolleston, a merchant. William Savage died in London on 27 July 1789 and was buried at the end of Gray's Inn Lane in ground belonging to the parish of St George the Martyr, Bloomsbury. His library was later bought by Stevens.

PETER LYNAN

Sources *Recollections of R. J. S. Stevens: an organist in Georgian London*, ed. M. Argent (1992) · H. G. Farmer, 'A forgotten composer of anthems', *Music and Letters*, 17 (1936), 188–99 · *New Grove*, 2nd edn · D. Dawe, *Organists of the City of London, 1666–1850* (1983) · W. Dean, *Handel's dramatic oratorios and masques* (1959)

Wealth at death wife had £19,000 at marriage; predeceased him: Farmer, 'A forgotten composer of anthems'

Savage, William (1770–1843), printer and engraver, was born at Howden, in the East Riding of Yorkshire, the youngest son of James Savage, a clockmaker. Descended from the Savage family of Rock Savage, Cheshire, William was educated at the local church school at Howden, excelling at both geometry and mathematics. In 1790 he began a business as a printer and bookseller in his home town in partnership with his elder brother, James *Savage (1767–1845). In 1797 he moved to London. About two years later—on the recommendation of Dr Barrington, bishop of Durham, and Count Rumford—he was appointed printer to the Royal Institution in Albemarle Street, where he remained until 1804. Savage held various positions at the Royal Institution: for ten years he was assistant secretary to the board of managers, as well as secretary to the library committee, secretary to the committee of chemistry, and superintendent of the printing office.

Presses were registered to Savage in 1801 and 1804 and about 1803, while retaining his appointments at the Royal Institution, he commenced business as a printer at St James Street, Westminster, London. With the financial support of a partner he traded as Savage and Easingwood. He became independent enough to trade as Savage in 1806 and moved premises to 28 Bedfordbury, Covent Garden.

Savage's fame was secured in 1807—the year in which he was commissioned to print Foster's *British Gallery of Engravings*. Printing ink in England at that time was of a very poor quality and Savage, by various experiments, made a printing ink without any oil in its composition. This made it more serviceable for artistic work and easier to manufacture. In *Preparations in Printing Ink in Various Colours* (1832) Savage summarized and assessed the work of earlier ink makers, commenting on the defects and qualities of their inks. In one section he explained how he achieved his results and stated:

> I can truly assert, that every statement I have made is the result of my own practice, and that there is not a direction for preparing an ink but what I have prepared and used myself to a great extent, and found them answer in the most satisfactory manner. ('On the preparation of printing inks', 244)

In recognition of his services the Society for the Encouragement of Arts awarded him their large medal and a sum of money 'for his imitations of drawings, printed from engravings on wood, with inks of his own preparing' (*GM*, 2nd ser., 21, 1844, 99).

From 1822 to 1832 Savage was occupied in arranging the materials which he had been collecting for nearly forty years. His resultant *Dictionary of the Art of Printing* (1840–41) became recognized as one of the authorities on printing. Savage originally intended to produce fourteen separate parts in 1840, but with the advances in printing he held back publication in 1840 and instead completed seventeen parts, issued together in one volume, of 815 pages, in 1841. Although relying heavily on Joseph Moxon's work from the previous century, *The Dictionary* brought articles and practical examples that were now available together in one comprehensive volume. He also produced *Observations on Emigration to the United States* (1819), and *Practical Thoughts on Decorative Printing* (1812). Engravings from Callcott, Varley, Thurston, Willement, and Brooke illustrated this work. The edition was limited and caused some controversy as Savage promised to destroy the blocks of his engravings for the benefit of his subscribers (*GM*, 1st ser., 85/2, 1815, 303).

Savage died at his home in Doddington Grove, Kensington, London, on 25 July 1843. He left three daughters.

E. I. Carlyle, *rev.* J.-M. Alter

Sources *GM*, 2nd ser., 21 (1844) • Redgrave, *Artists* • P. A. H. Brown, *London publishers and printers, c.1800–1870* (1982) • I. Maxted, *The London book trades, 1775–1800: a preliminary checklist of members* (1977) • R. Myers, *The British book trade* (1970)

Savage-Armstrong, George Francis. *See* Armstrong, George Francis Savage- (1845–1906).

Savaric (*d.* 1205), bishop of Bath and Glastonbury, was the son of Geldwin whose father, Savaric Fitzcana, was lord of Midhurst, Sussex. Savaric Fitzcana's wife, Muriel, was the daughter of Richard de Meri and the granddaughter of Humphrey (I) de Bohun, and the bishop was thus a cousin of Reginald de Bohun, or Reginald Fitzjocelin (*d.* 1191), who preceded him as bishop of Bath. The origins of Bishop Savaric's mother, Estrangia or Extranea, are unknown but it seems likely that she came from Burgundy and so provided the link with the emperor Henry VI (*d.* 1197) who described the bishop as a kinsman and whose mother, Beatrix, was the daughter of the count of Burgundy. The relationships with the emperor and Reginald de Bohun were both to prove important in Savaric's appointment to the bishopric of Bath.

At the time of his election to the episcopate, Savaric was described as archdeacon of Northampton (to which position he was appointed in 1175) and treasurer of Salisbury. He had also served as archdeacon of Canterbury and perhaps of Salisbury. Little is known of his activities in any of these posts, though he was on a number of occasions heavily in debt to Henry II, who wrote to Urban III (*r.* 1185–7) to complain of the injuries that Savaric had done to him. Savaric's forfeiture of his archdeaconry in the years 1182–4 may well be connected to this matter.

Savaric's undoubted ambition for promotion to the episcopate came to fruition in the particular circumstances of the Canterbury vacancy following the death of Archbishop Baldwin in November 1190. Having taken the cross, in April 1191 Savaric obtained from Richard I in Sicily letters patent addressed to the justiciars (and, according to Richard of Devizes, involving a bribe) that granted the royal assent should he be canonically elected to any vacant bishopric. The letters, which the king later claimed were forced out of him, were sent to Reginald de Bohun, while at the same time the emperor Henry VI and the French king Philip Augustus both wrote to the monks of Canterbury supporting Reginald's candidature for the archiepiscopate and praising Savaric. On 27 November 1191 Reginald was elected archbishop by the monks of Canterbury (his support for them in their dispute with Archbishop Baldwin over the foundation of a secular college at Hackington assured their favour). He then made a visit to Bath, during which he successfully put Savaric's case to the cathedral priory. On his return journey he fell ill, and at Dogmersfield in Hampshire he passed to Prior Walter of Bath the king's letters giving assent to Savaric's election, and then on 26 December died. Acting on the authority of the letters, the chief justiciar, Walter de Coutances, confirmed the election despite the protests of the canons of Wells, who claimed that their exclusion from the process rendered it invalid. Accordingly, Savaric was ordained priest and then consecrated bishop in Rome on 19 September 1192.

In 1193 the bishop spent many months in Germany negotiating with the emperor for Richard's release, and did not return to England until the end of the year. It may have been about this time, when Henry VI was considering enfeoffing Richard with the kingdom of Arles, that Savaric was appointed imperial chancellor of Burgundy, though he does not appear in the position for certain until 1197. He was one of the hostages given for the payment of the king's ransom early in 1194, and throughout his career continued to spend much time in royal and imperial service, while pursuing his own interests in the dispute for which his episcopate is perhaps best known, that with the monks of Glastonbury over his annexation of the abbey to the see of Bath. This was achieved by bringing pressure to bear through the emperor on the captive King Richard, to whom Savaric granted the city of Bath in exchange for the abbey. At the same time the bishop wrote to Celestine III (*r.* 1191–8) suggesting the union of the churches of Bath and Glastonbury. On 5 December 1193, having arranged the promotion of Henry de Soilli, abbot of Glastonbury, to the see of Worcester, Savaric summoned the prior and two monks to Bath and announced that he was their abbot. On the same day his agents went to Glastonbury and took possession of the abbey in his name and with royal authority.

The monks appealed to the king, and in 1194 Richard deprived Savaric of the abbey; but in Lent 1195 the bishop received a privilege from Celestine III uniting the two churches. It is presumably from this time that he adopted the style 'bishop of Bath and Glastonbury' which he used for the rest of his episcopate. Following the monks' appeal against the papal privilege, Savaric travelled to Rome and in the summer of 1196 obtained further deeds from Celestine confirming the union and forbidding the monks to elect an abbot. The monks' appeal to the archbishop of Canterbury was unsuccessful, and from November 1197 the bishop's proctors administered the abbey for him, producing an inventory of the estates in 1198. With the death of Celestine III in January of that year, however, events began to turn in the monks' favour. On 29 August Richard again deprived Savaric of the abbey and took the administration into his own hands, and in October he gave them permission to elect an abbot and wrote to the cardinals of the curia stating that he had granted Savaric the abbey under duress while in captivity. On 25 November 1198 the monks elected as their abbot William Pica, whom Savaric immediately excommunicated.

On Richard's death in April 1199 Savaric, according to Adam of Domerham, bought from King John agreement to his possession of the abbey. On 6 June he went to Glastonbury and having broken into the church and treasury by force was enthroned there. All except eight of the monks opposed the enthronement and were kept imprisoned until the following day, when Savaric held a chapter meeting at which some monks were beaten and most made their submission to him. Those who did not were later taken to Wells and then dispersed to other monasteries. Both parties continued to pursue their claims in Rome and although Innocent III (*r.* 1198–1216) revoked William Pica's excommunication, Savaric managed to secure the quashing of his election. When Pica died in Rome shortly afterwards in September 1200, the monks of Glastonbury believed that he had been poisoned by Savaric. In the end, however, Innocent seems to have been persuaded (perhaps by the erroneous claim, which Savaric is known to have advanced, that there had been long-standing strife between the monks and the bishop of the diocese) of the need to ratify the union sanctioned by his predecessor, and in August 1202 he appointed judges-delegate in England to arrange the necessary details. They granted the bishop a quarter of the abbey's manors and a share in patronage and other rights, and, despite appeals from many quarters on Savaric's death, their settlement endured until Glastonbury regained its independence in 1219.

In matters of pastoral provision and diocesan administration Savaric's episcopate saw developments consistent with those in other sees at this time. There is a greater diplomatic and stylistic uniformity apparent in his *acta* than in those of earlier bishops of Bath, and he was responsible for appointing the first bishop's official in the diocese, probably a response both to his own lengthy absences from Bath and to the changing role of the archdeacons. Savaric's surviving charters also reveal an increase in episcopal business concerning parish churches, aimed at securing adequate emoluments for the clergy serving them and upholding the bishop's own interests at a local level. He showed favour to the church of Wells, where some members of his household held prebends and whose canons had, according to Adam of Domerham, supported his attacks on Glastonbury. Most notably he founded prebends for several abbots whose houses lay within or had connections with the diocese, while probably continuing the building of the new church begun by Reginald Fitzjocelin and making a number of grants to the common fund of the canons. He also made provision for masses to be said in veneration of the Virgin and for benefactors of the church.

Savaric died on 8 August 1205 at 'Scienes la Vielle', while on a mission to Rome with Peter des Roches, and was later buried at Bath. FRANCES RAMSEY

Sources F. M. R. Ramsey, ed., *Bath and Wells, 1061–1205*, English Episcopal Acta, 10 (1995) • Adam of Domerham, *Adami de Domerham historia de rebus gestis Glastoniensibus*, ed. T. Hearne, 2 vols. (1727) • A. L. Poole, 'England and Burgundy in the last decade of the twelfth century', *Essays in history presented to Reginald Lane Poole*, ed. H. W. C. Davis (1927), 261–73 • *Chronicon Richardi Divisensis / The Chronicle of Richard of Devizes*, ed. J. T. Appleby (1963) • C. R. Cheney, *Innocent III and England* (1976) • D. Knowles, *The episcopal colleagues of Archbishop Thomas Becket* (1951) • W. Stubbs, ed., *Chronicles and memorials of the reign of Richard I, 2: Epistolae Cantuarienses*, Rolls Series, 38 (1865) • *Fasti Angl., 1066–1300*, [Lincoln] • *Fasti Angl., 1066–1300*, [Salisbury] • *Chronica magistri Rogeri de Hovedene*, ed. W. Stubbs, 4 vols., Rolls Series, 51 (1868–71) • W. Stubbs, ed., *Gesta regis Henrici secundi Benedicti abbatis: the chronicle of the reigns of Henry II and Richard I, AD 1169–1192*, 2 vols., Rolls Series, 49 (1867) • [H. Wharton], ed., *Anglia sacra*, 2 vols. (1691) • F. Godwin, *De praesulibus Angliae commentarius* (1616) • BL, Southwark annals, Cotton MS Faust. A VIII, fol. 137*v*

Savarkar, Vinayak Damodar (1883–1966), Hindu nationalist, was born on 28 May 1883 in Bhagur village (near Nasik, then part of the Bombay presidency), the second of four children of Damodarpant and Radhabai. He had two brothers, Ganesh and Narayan, and a sister, Mainabai, and belonged to a Chitpavan Brahman family with some ancestral property and a reputation for Sanskrit learning. Savarkar was educated at Shivaji high school, Nasik, and Ferguson College, Poona, before going to London to study law in 1906, and married in 1901 Mai, daughter of a minister of the petty princely state of Jawhar near Nasik.

Savarkar grew to maturity in a high-caste Hindu milieu where traditions of Maratha Hindu valour under Shivaji and his Peshwa successors against Mughal rulers in the seventeenth and eighteenth centuries were being constructed to provide sustenance for an emergent nationalism, within which anti-British and anti-Muslim strands commingled in varying proportions. Aged ten, after hearing about a Hindu–Muslim riot in a distant part of India, Savarkar led schoolfriends in an attack upon a neighbouring mosque. He became well known, however, as a fervent anti-British patriot from about 1900 onwards, organizing the Mitra Mela revolutionary secret society in the Bombay presidency (it was renamed Abhinava Bharat—Young India—in 1905), and translating the works of the Italian nationalist Mazzini into Marathi. In England from 1906 to 1910, Savarkar tried to send bomb manuals to Indian revolutionaries from London, and celebrated the fiftieth anniversary of the 1857 rebellion as a prime example of united struggle against British rule: it was the subject of his first book, *The First Indian War of Independence*, which was immediately banned. Extradited to India in 1910 for his alleged role in organizing the killing of a British official in Nasik (a case which also involved his elder brother, Ganesh Damodar), Savarkar attempted to escape at Marseilles, and the British intrusion onto French soil to recapture him became a celebrated case in international law.

The British transported Savarkar to the Andaman Islands (1911–21), imprisoned him in Ratnagiri, Bombay presidency (1921–4), and kept him interned in that district until 1937: these experiences confirmed his stature as Veer (heroic) Savarkar, the epithet by which he came to be generally known. Savarkar's *The Story of my Transportation for Life* (1927), however, indicates that prison life was decisive in his transition to a consistently anti-Muslim nationalism. He urged Hindu prisoners to give up caste prejudices in order to unite against alleged efforts at conversion by Muslim warders, made an abortive offer of co-operation with the British in 1914 in the context of Ottoman Turkey's alliance with Germany, and during the non-co-operation–Khilafat united anti-colonial upsurge under Gandhi (1919–22) quarrelled with prisoners imbued with 'vitiated and eccentric … notions of … Hindu-Muslim unity' (Savarkar, *Transportation*, 544).

In Ratnagiri prison Savarkar wrote his immensely influential *Hindutva / Who is a Hindu?* (1923), in which a Hindu was defined as anyone, irrespective of specific religious beliefs or rituals, who acknowledged India as both fatherland and 'holyland that is the cradle-land of his religion' (pp. 74–5). Nationalism was thus implicitly merged with a Hindutva (Hindu-ness) that soared over differences of caste or sect, but insisted on a common history and culture, grounded in an 'Aryan' conquest of the subcontinent that had assimilated non-Aryan elements in a hierarchized unity. Simultaneously, Indian Muslims and Christians were declared incapable of full patriot status: with holy lands in Arabia and Palestine, 'their names and their outlook smack of foreign origin' (Savarkar, *Historic Statements*, 1).

Savarkar, who prided himself on his rationalist and 'modern' views, won a reputation while interned as a social reformer who encouraged inter-dining among castes and the opening of schools and temples to untouchables—but he condemned Ambedkar's call to the latter to convert to Buddhism. He also became a well-known writer of Marathi plays, novels, and anti-Muslim histories, who campaigned for Sanskritized Marathi and Hindi (as the 'national' language) purged of 'Muslim', Urdu influences. After 1937 Savarkar tried to build up the Hindu Mahasabha (of which he was president, 1937–42) as a political alternative to the Indian National Congress and the Muslim League, around the central slogan: 'Hinduise all politics and militarise Hindudom.' He urged Hindus to join the army, opposed the anti-British Quit India movement (1942), and denounced Gandhi for 'appeasing' Muslims during the Hindu–Muslim riots associated with the emergence of independent India and Pakistan in 1947. Anti-Brahman crowds attacked his house when Gandhi was murdered in January 1948 by Nathuram Godse, a disciple who in his trial (where Savarkar was a fellow accused) assumed sole responsibility for the crime but hailed Savarkar as the ideological alternative to Gandhian non-violence which 'would result in the emasculation of the Hindu Community'. Savarkar was acquitted, and went on advocating virulently militaristic, anti-Muslim and anti-Christian policies (there was a 'menace of Christianistan', he declared in 1953, in missionary schools and hospitals). Savarkar's last statement before his death in Bombay on 26 February 1966 called on the Indian government to 'immediately … equip India with … nuclear weapons and missiles' (Savarkar, *Historic Statements*, 244). Organizationally marginalized in his last years (the Mahasabha was routed in every election after 1946), Savarkar, and particularly his *Hindutva* text, remained a principal ideological influence on the eventually more successful alternative Hindu-nationalist formation built up around the Rashtriya Swayamsevak Sangh of K. B. Hedgewar, which became embodied politically in the last decades of the twentieth century in the Bharatiya Janata Party.

SUMIT SARKAR

Sources D. Keer, *Veer Savarkar* (1950–66) • V. D. Savarkar, *The story of my transportation for life* (1927) • V. D. Savarkar, *Historic statements* (1967) • *Samagra Savarkar Wangmaya*, 6 vols. (1963–4) [collected works, vols. 1–4 in Marathi, 5–6 in Eng.]

Archives Nehru Memorial Library, New Delhi

Savery, Servington (*c.*1670–*c.*1744), natural philosopher, was almost certainly born on the family estates at Shilston, near Modbury, Devon, the only child of Christopher Servington Savery, sheriff of Devon, and his wife, Elizabeth, daughter of Colonel Cloberry, whom he married in 1669. Related through his grandfather to Thomas Savery, he belonged to a distinguished Devon family that traced its origins back to immigrants from Brittany in the early sixteenth century; his father, a fervent anti-papist, played an active role in William III's accession to the throne. In 1691 Savery married Elizabeth, the daughter of John Hale of Bowringsley and a close relative of Lord Chief Justice Hale; they had three sons and three daughters. He appears not to have been educated at university, unlike close relatives. Although he corresponded with London instrument makers and fellows of the Royal Society, he seems to have spent his entire life in Shilston, studying, experimenting, and inventing scientific instruments. Best known for his work on magnetism, Savery exemplifies the significant numbers of wealthy, reclusive, provincial natural philosophers of the seventeenth and eighteenth centuries.

Savery started to experiment with magnets while still at school, and after several years of private research was encouraged by John Huxham to communicate his results to the Royal Society. His long paper in the *Philosophical Transactions* (1730) summarized previous knowledge about magnetism, discussed practical techniques for magnetic experiments, and described an elaborate machine based on a rotating terrella (small spherical lodestone) to test theories about the magnetic structure of the earth. The most influential section of the paper concerned the production of artificial magnets from steel bars, introducing new techniques and giving detailed instructions. Savery's artificial steel magnets were important because they provided the first reliable, cheap substitutes for natural lodestone, essential for remagnetizing compass needles on long voyages and for carrying out experiments. Although lacking influence because he was operating from a distance, Savery was respected in metropolitan circles for his work. However, unlike his successor Gowin Knight, he gained little personal advantage from his magnets, which were marketed in Exeter and London by the Lovelace family.

In addition, Savery devised a telescope that had two adjustable object glasses and incorporated a micrometer, and engaged in lengthy correspondence with George Graham about it. Graham used Savery's instrument to measure the diameter of the sun, and recommended it to Lord Macclesfield and James Bradley, the astronomer royal. But it was not until 1753 that James Short arranged for Savery's paper to be published in the *Philosophical Transactions*, and not until about 1755 that John Dollond built a Savery heliometer. Savery's other inventions included a barometer with a sensitive measuring device based on alcohol floating above the mercury.

A descendant of Savery recorded that this 'man of a very studious turn of mind, and of very retir'd habits: amusing himself in philosophical pursuits' died when he was about seventy-four, presumably at Shilston (J. Savery, fols. 83, 92). PATRICIA FARA

Sources J. Savery, 'Account of the Savery family', 1809, BL, Add. MS 44058, fols. 2–13, 65–93 • P. Fara, '"A treasure of hidden vertues": marketing natural philosophy', in P. Fara, *Sympathetic attractions: magnetic practices, beliefs, and symbolism in eighteenth-century England* (1996), 31–65 • S. Savery, 'Magnetical observations and experiments', *PTRS*, 36 (1729–30), 295–340 • R. T. Gunther, *Early science in Oxford*, 2: *Astronomy*, OHS, 78 (1923), 328–30 • H. Horne, letter to John Canton, 15 Feb 1751, RS, Canton MSS, vol. 2, fol. 16
Archives BL, Add. MSS, 4433, 4051, 4053, 44058

Savery [Savory], **Thomas** (**1650?–1715**), engineer, was born at Shilstone, a manor house near Modbury, Devon, one of two sons of Richard Savery and grandson of Christopher Savery of Totnes. He became a military engineer, and by 1696 had attained the rank of trench-master. He spent his spare time on mechanical experiments, and in 1696 he patented (no. 347) a machine to grind and polish plate glass, and a contrivance for rowing ships in a calm using two paddle-wheels worked by a capstan. William III thought highly of the second invention, but although Savery demonstrated its practicability by fitting it to a small yacht, official jealousy prevented its adoption in the navy. Undeterred, he published an account of his invention in a work entitled *Navigation Improved* (1698), and this contained a denunciation of his treatment in official circles.

Savery, who lived at Exeter for a time and whose youth was spent near a mining district, had often turned his attention to the difficulty of keeping the mines free from water. To remedy this he invented a machine for raising water, and on 25 July 1698 he obtained a patent (no. 356) for fourteen years, which was extended by an act of parliament passed on 25 April 1699 for a further twenty-one years. The patent contained no description of the machine, but this deficiency was supplied in a book which he published in 1702, entitled *The Miner's Friend*. A model of the machine, which raised water by utilizing steam pressure and the vacuum produced by the condensation of steam, was demonstrated to William III at Hampton Court, and in June 1699 shown to members of the Royal Society.

In 1702 Savery established a workshop at Salisbury Court, London, very close to St Bride's Church, where he had married Martha Davis (1654/5–1759) on 5 October 1697. At this workshop, mine and colliery owners could see the engine demonstrated before purchase. However, it is doubtful that any machines were actually sold for use in mines, although at least two were later installed for water-supply purposes in London, namely at Campden House, Kensington, and at the York Buildings waterworks in Villiers Street. The engine was satisfactory for raising water short distances, but the intense heat required to lift water from greater depths, as in mines, tended to melt the soldered joints of the machine, which lacked proper safety features and used energy inefficiently. The workshop closed about 1705 and Savery, therefore, was not as successful as he had anticipated, but later he became associated with Thomas *Newcomen, who designed a greatly improved machine; and Savery's patent apparently covered all Newcomen's improvements. Savery has been accused of obtaining ideas from others, but even if he did know about another inventor's theory, he was the first to apply it to produce a practical working pump for sale. The principle was also later used in the pulsometer.

By 1702 Savery had become a captain in the engineers, and his translation of Coehoorn's *The New Method of Fortification* was published in 1705. The same year, through the patronage of Prince George of Denmark, he was appointed treasurer of the commission for sick and wounded seamen. In the following year he was elected a fellow of the Royal Society, and also patented (no. 379) a double hand-bellows, which could melt any metal in an ordinary wood or coal fire. On 5 March 1707 an application was made by Savery for a patent for 'a new sort of mill to perform all sorts of mill-work on vessells floating on the water', but no patent seems to have been granted. In June 1713 his employment at the commission ended, and the following year, again through Prince George, he obtained the post of surveyor to the waterworks at Hampton Court. Within a few days of signing his will on 15 May 1715, Savery died at his home in Marsham Street, Westminster, and was buried at the church of St Giles, Camberwell, on 22 May 1715.

Savery was considered a passionate, self-willed, and parsimonious man, and it appears he had debts when he died. Although he bequeathed all his property and patent rights to his wife (from whom his engine patent, which expired in 1733, was acquired and managed by a committee), she seems never to have administered the will. As late as 1796 letters of administration, with the will annexed, were granted to Thomas Ladds, the executor of Charles Caesar, one of Savery's creditors.

E. I. Carlyle, *rev.* Christopher F. Lindsey

Sources R. Jenkins, 'Savery, Newcomen and the early history of the steam engine, pt I', *Transactions* [Newcomen Society], 3 (1922–3), 96–130, esp. 96–118 • R. L. Hills, 'A steam chimera: a review of the history of the Savery engine', *Transactions* [Newcomen Society], 58 (1986–7), 27–44 • L. T. C. Rolt and J. S. Allen, 'Thomas Savery and his pump', *The steam engine of Thomas Newcomen*, [rev. edn] (1977), 24–30 • J. S. P. Buckland, 'Thomas Savery: his steam engine workshop of 1702', *Transactions* [Newcomen Society], 56 (1984–5), 1–20 • A. Smith, 'Steam and the city: the committee of proprietors of the invention for raising water by fire, 1715–1735', *Transactions* [Newcomen Society], 49 (1977–8), 5–20 • 'Savery's will', *The Engineer* (30 May 1890), 442 • will, with letters of administration, 10 June 1796, PROB 11/546, fol. 170

Archives BL, extracts from family papers, Add. MS 44058 • RS, MSS | BL, letters patent

Likenesses W. Fry (after unknown artist), repro. in T. Savery, *The miner's friend*, repr. (1827)

Wealth at death see will and administration, 10 June 1796, PRO, PROB 11/546, fol. 170

Savile family (*per. c.*1480–1644), gentry, formed a branch of an ancient family which accumulated substantial landed estates largely through the well-tried expedient of marriage with heiresses. Thus John Savile (*d.* 1337) secured part of the Rishworth estate near Halifax and Sir John Savile (*d.* 1399), his grandson, acquired a group of estates centring on Elland, while to his successor, Henry (*d.* 1412), fell the greater prize of Thornhill near Wakefield, where his son Sir Thomas (*d.* 1449) established the senior branch of the family on the death of his mother, Elizabeth, Henry's widow; he founded a chantry on the north side of the chancel of Thornhill church that became the family's place of burial. His successor, Sir John Savile of Thornhill (1415–1482), an active and influential Yorkist, was appointed to the coveted stewardship of Wakefield in 1461, and played an important part in local government under Edward IV as sheriff, MP, JP, and commissioner. His son John, who had married Jane Harrington, predeceased Sir John, who was succeeded by his grandson John.

Knighted and made banneret by Richard, duke of Gloucester, in 1481, **Sir John Savile** (*d.* 1505), of Thornhill, succeeded his grandfather as steward of Wakefield, but was required to resign the post on his appointment as captain of the Isle of Wight—a condition he appears to have resented. Although a trusted retainer of Richard III, he benefited immediately on the victory at Bosworth of Henry Tudor, under whom he was restored to the stewardship and appointed the new king's first sheriff for the county. Nevertheless he soon found himself called before the court of Star Chamber, where he failed to make good his claim to certain townships appurtenant to the manor of Elland, and was ordered to desist from infringing the common rights of the tenants. Savile died on 16 March 1505. There was no issue of his first marriage, to Alice Vernon, and it was his second wife, Elizabeth Paston (*d.* 1547), who was the mother of his children. She is apparently represented on the splendid oak monument in Thornhill church generally considered to be his tomb. The inscription, dating from 1529, may have been added by his son Sir Henry.

The wardship and marriage of Sir John's son **Sir Henry Savile** (1499–1558), of Thornhill, who was aged six at his father's death, was committed by his father to trustees who included the boy's mother, Elizabeth, and Thomas Howard, earl of Surrey, who were to offer the king £1000 for the privilege, which they later disposed of to George Talbot, fourth earl of Shrewsbury. A position was obtained for Henry in the household of Cardinal Wolsey, with whom he remained on good terms. On 29 August 1518, his marriage having been sold by Shrewsbury to Thomas Sotehill of Dewsbury, Henry was married to Thomas's daughter and coheir, Elizabeth; three years later his coming of age in the spring of 1522 marked the re-emergence of the family to an active position of power in the West Riding. Its recent absence had made possible the rise of Sir Richard Tempest, some twenty years Savile's senior and a man of less wealth, to a pre-eminence in local gentry society that was soon challenged when Savile's reassertion of his father's unsuccessful claim to the mesne lordship of the townships appurtenant to Elland was contested by Tempest as steward of Wakefield on behalf of the king. The ensuing bitter legal battle developed into a personal vendetta and continued unabated and with mounting venom until Tempest's death in 1537. With his enemy now out of the way the matter was eventually resolved in Savile's favour.

His friends found Savile affectionate and hospitable; for example, to William Plumpton he writes that 'I perceve … ye say ye will com over and hunt with me And it please you to do so, ye shall be as hertyly welcome as any man that can heare of a good space' (Kirby, no. 241). But in 1526 his wife made an unsuccessful request to Wolsey for a divorce on the grounds of his cruelty, and as one of the most powerful men in the West Riding he must be held responsible for the lamentable state of law and order that was described in a letter of about 1534 to Cromwell from an unknown correspondent who averred that the greater gentry were far more culpable in this matter than the local magnates. Unlike Sir Richard Tempest, who supported the rebels in 1536 and died in the Fleet, Sir Henry (created KB in 1533) remained loyal to the king. In the aftermath he and the earl of Cumberland were temporarily unchallenged at the helm of West Riding affairs and rewards followed: the stewardship of Pontefract, membership of the council in the north, appointment to the bench for all three ridings, and two terms, 1537–8 and 1542–3, as sheriff. Sir Henry died on 23 April 1558 in possession of an estate in Yorkshire worth £450 a year, according to an inquisition *post mortem* taken at Pontefract. In addition his lease of the mills and bailiwick of Wakefield provided a substantial addition to his income. His wife survived him.

His heir must have been a deep disappointment to Sir Henry, for Edward Savile (*d.* 1604) was adjudged to be imbecile, although it appears that he may not have been as incapable as he was represented. Sir Henry's hopes therefore were centred on his beloved illegitimate son, Robert, born of his liaison with a waiting woman named Margaret Barkston (or Barlaston), for whose provision he was intent on releasing as much property as possible out of entail. As he confided to William Plumpton: 'if his brother dy without isew, in all by gift he shall have v hundreth mark land' (Kirby, no. 242). In spite of two marriages Edward did indeed die childless but, probably through the influence of his guardian, George Talbot, sixth earl of Shrewsbury, he entered into settlements in favour of the descendants of Thomas Savile of Lupset (*d.* 1506), by now represented by Henry Savile of Lupset and his son, George, to the latter of whom the earl married his daughter Mary.

Possibly with the intention of making further provision for Robert, Sir Henry formed a syndicate to acquire part of the Kirkstall Abbey estate, including extensive non-demesne lands around Leeds. By 1584 **Sir Robert Savile** (*d.* 1585), of Howley, was in possession of the entire estate in fee, including the abbey site and ironworks. Marriage to a Lincolnshire heiress, Anne Hussey, widow of Sir Richard Thimbleby, brought him an estate in Doddington, and he served as sheriff of the county in 1572. His return to Yorkshire was signalled by his purchase of the Howley estate near Batley in 1578, where he began building the splendid house that was afterwards completed by his son. Knighted on 8 December 1583, he purchased the former chantry of St Anne in Batley church and was buried there on 2 June 1585. His son John *Savile, first Baron Savile of Pontefract, and grandson Thomas *Savile, later first earl of Sussex, would both play significant, though deeply controversial, roles in national politics. The Howley line ended in 1671 with the death without issue of Sir Thomas's son James, second earl of Sussex.

With **Sir Henry Savile** (1517/18–1569), of Lupset, who was living at Thornhill by about 1564, the estates of the senior branch were about to pass to a junior. Following family precedent Henry contracted two fortunate marriages, the first in 1545, with the Nottinghamshire heiress Margaret Fowler or Fuller, the second with Joan Vernon, through which he acquired estates in the midlands, notably Barrowby in Lincolnshire. Known in 1564 as a 'favourer of sound religion' (HoP, *Commons, 1558–1603*, 3.349), his career suggests a man of energy and ability: MP for Grantham 1558, for Yorkshire 1559, JP from 1562 for all three ridings, surveyor for the crown of the northern counties by 1552, common law member of the council in the north from December 1558 until his death (which suggests a legal training but there is no mention of him in the registers), sheriff of Yorkshire in 1567–8, commissioner for Yorkshire chantries 1548, and commissioner to enforce the Acts of Uniformity and Supremacy in the province of York 1561. Some time in or after 1558 he made a third marriage, to Dorothy Wilbraham (*née* Grosvenor), who long outlived him, and died about the end of 1615. Henry Savile died between 1 January and 16 May 1569.

Savile's eldest son, **Sir George Savile**, first baronet (1549/50–1622), was probably still a student at Lincoln's Inn when his father died, having proceeded there from St John's College, Oxford. Knighted on 18 June 1587, his few public offices—MP for Boroughbridge 1586–7 and for Yorkshire 1592–3—were undertaken before he succeeded to Thornhill in 1604. His first wife, Lady Mary Talbot, through whom the family acquired the Rufford estates in five midland counties, died in or before 1599, and in 1611 George was one of the first to purchase a baronetcy from the ever impecunious King James I. Trouble arose after his second marriage, to Elizabeth Ayscough (*d.* 1625/6), and consequent desire to benefit the children of this union to the detriment of his heir, George, with whom he was on bad terms.

Sir George Savile (*c.*1583–1614) had a short life that followed a familiar pattern: University College, Oxford, and the Inner Temple; knighthood in 1603; election to parliament for Morpeth in 1601, a seat he may have owed to Edward Talbot (whose patronage may also have helped secure George's knighthood), and for Appleby in 1614. His first wife, Sarah Rede, had died childless in January or February 1605. He committed his two young sons George and William [*see below*], from his second marriage, to Anne (*d.* 1633), sister of Sir Thomas Wentworth (later earl of Strafford), to the care of his brother-in-law and of his Oxford tutor, George Abbot, then archbishop of Canterbury. The boys and their mother were indeed to have need of a champion, for on the younger Sir George's death in August 1614 his father's resumption of the estate that had been provided for his maintenance left Lady Anne with two sons and no means. Wentworth, who had a sincere affection for his brother-in-law, took up their cause with vigour. The ensuing legal battle continued in the courts until the baronet's death. In 1617 Sir George and Lady Elizabeth were committed to prison for contempt of court and were reported by Sir George Radcliffe to be in good heart and the good company of prisoners of equal rank to their own. At last, on 2 June 1617 Wentworth's unflagging efforts produced a verdict in favour of his nephews. He was also deeply concerned with negotiations to protect their title to the Rufford estates settled on them through their Talbot grandmother. Sir George the younger is commemorated by a splendid tomb in Thornhill church, 'probably erected by Wentworth as a token of affection' (Whitaker, *Loidis and Elmete*, 323). Meanwhile the old baronet settled Lupset on his issue from his second marriage but owing to bad estate management he was forced to sell substantial property in Yorkshire. He died on 12 November 1622 aged seventy-two. He is represented by an alabaster effigy on his tomb at Thornhill.

Of the brief life of Sir George the younger's son Sir George Savile, second baronet (1611–26), there is little to say save that he was born at Thornhill, matriculated at

University College, Oxford, on 5 May 1626, and died in college on 19 December following of smallpox. His inheritance thus passed to his brother **Sir William Savile**, third baronet (1612–1644), of Thornhill, who was himself at University College at the time, and proceeded thence two years later to Gray's Inn. On 29 December 1629, probably as a result of Wentworth's influence, he married Anne (*d.* 1662), daughter of Lord Coventry of Aylesborough, a woman who was to be celebrated as one of the heroines of the civil war. Sir William was undoubtedly a young man of impetuous self-assurance whom his solicitous uncle showered with advice not to be 'too positive, or take too much upon you, till you fully understand the course of proceeding' (Whitaker, *Loidis and Elmete*, 315). That he applied himself to the improvement of his estates is demonstrated by the fact that at his death he left an estate of over 50,000 acres producing an income in normal conditions of £7000 a year. Included were three main residences: Thornhill Hall (destroyed by parliamentary forces), Rufford Abbey, and a house in York.

Selected by Wentworth to be deputy lieutenant of the West Riding before 21 September 1633, Sir William Savile was appointed to the council in the north in July 1636, but took no pains to conceal his contempt for the vice-president, Sir Edward Osborne, a man of inferior wealth, and Wentworth eventually intervened to reinforce Osborne's authority against Savile's attempts to undermine it. As the civil war approached Sir William devoted his energies to raising the regiment of '900 very able fellows' from the West Riding who marched through Newcastle on 9 May 1639, the king coming to the court gate to see them (Hodgson, 9). The following April, sitting for Yorkshire in the Short Parliament, he signed the petition against forced billeting and spoke against ship money, afterwards lamenting that the moderation of his speech had precluded him from sharing the fate of those bolder spirits who had been sent to the Fleet. Nevertheless he remained loyal to the king. Defeated in the election of 1640, he was returned for Old Sarum in a by-election early the following year and was thus present throughout the trial of Strafford, in whose favour he gave evidence and whom he supported to the end. For some unspecified offence he was himself committed to the Tower on 12 June and released on the 29th after a reprimand on his knees at the bar of the house from the speaker.

On 22 August 1642 Sir William Savile was with the king at Nottingham when the royal standard was raised; the following month, branded as a 'suspicious man', he was expelled from the Commons by parliament. Towards the end of 1642 Newcastle marched into the West Riding and Sir William was placed in command at Leeds, but on 23 January 1643 Fairfax captured the town after a furious attack and Savile escaped by swimming across the river. Appointed governor of the town and castle of Sheffield, his letters at this time 'breathe much of the high tone and heroic spirit which animated supporters of the royal cause' (Hunter, 107). His last is dated 19 January 1644 from York, whither he had been transferred and where he died in arms for the king five days later. His widow, described as a woman 'of incomparable affection to his Majesty, of singular Prudence … and of great interest and power' (Foxcroft, 29), was permitted to leave Sheffield Castle with her children and baggage. Their son, Sir George *Savile, baronet, who was then aged ten, was subsequently created marquess of Halifax. Henry *Savile (1642–1687) was their younger surviving son. With the death without male issue of the second marquess in 1700, the Thornhill and Rufford estates passed ultimately to Sir George Savile, the seventh baronet, a descendant of the first Sir George through his second marriage. Thus the first baronet's hopes came to fulfilment. JOAN KIRBY

Sources J. W. Clay, 'The Savile family', *Yorkshire Archaeological Journal*, 25 (1918–20), 1–47 · J. T. Cliffe, *The Yorkshire gentry from the Reformation to the civil war* (1969) · R. B. Smith, *Land and politics in the England of Henry VIII: the West Riding of Yorkshire, 1530–46* (1970) · J. P. Cooper, ed., *Wentworth papers, 1597–1628*, CS, 4th ser., 12 (1973) · T. D. Whitaker, *Loidis and Elmete* (1816) · T. D. Whitaker, ed., *The life and original correspondence of Sir George Radcliffe* (1810) · A. Gooder, ed., *The parliamentary representation of the county of York, 1258–1832*, 1, Yorkshire Archaeological Society, 91 (1935); 2, Yorkshire Archaeological Society, 96 (1938) · J. C. Hodgson, ed., *Six north country diaries*, 1, SurtS, 118 (1910) · G. Radcliffe, *The earl of Strafforde's letters and dispatches, with an essay towards his life*, ed. W. Knowler, 2 vols. (1739) · *The life and letters of Sir George Savile … first marquis of Halifax*, ed. H. C. Foxcroft, 1 (1898) · H. B. McCall, ed., *Yorkshire Star Chamber proceedings*, 2, Yorkshire Archaeological Society, 45 (1911) · W. Brown, ed., *Yorkshire Star Chamber proceedings*, 3, Yorkshire Archaeological Society, 51 (1914) · *LP Henry VIII*, vols. 3/2–4, 7 · *The Plumpton letters and papers*, ed. J. Kirby, CS, 5th ser., 8 (1996) · J. Hunter, *Hallamshire: the history and topography of the parish of Sheffield* (1869) · HoP, *Commons*, 1558–1603, vol. 3 · HoP, *Commons*, 1509–58, 3.280–81, 614–15 · M. Sheard, *Records of the parish of Batley in the county of York* (1894) · monuments, Thornhill church

Archives Notts. Arch., estate papers and title deeds · West Yorks. AS, Kirklees, maps and plans; papers and title deeds | West Yorks. AS, Kirklees, Denby Dale sale plan and particulars

Likenesses oak effigy, 1529 (John Savile), Thornhill church, Yorkshire · engraving, 1635 (William Savile; after oil painting), priv. coll.; repro. in E. Hailstone, ed., *Portraits of Yorkshire worthies*, 1 (1869) · M. Colt, alabaster effigy on monument (George Savile), Thornhill church, Yorkshire · two recumbent effigies on a tomb chest (George Savile), Thornhill church, Yorkshire

Wealth at death £427 p.a. value of estate in Yorkshire, Henry Savile: Clay, 'The Savile family', 14 · £7000 p.a., value of estate, William Savile: Cliffe, *The Yorkshire gentry*, 30–31

Savile, Bourchier Wrey (1817–1888), Church of England clergyman and theological writer, was born in Westminster, London, on 11 March 1817, the second son of Albany Savile MP, of Okehampton (*d.* 1831), and Eleanora Elizabeth, daughter of Sir Bourchier Wrey, seventh baronet. He was admitted to Westminster School in 1828, and was elected a king's scholar there in 1831. He became a pensioner of Emmanuel College, Cambridge, in 1835, and graduated BA in 1839 and MA in 1842. He married on 28 April 1842 Mary Elizabeth, daughter of James Whyte of Pilton House, Devon. They had four sons and five daughters.

Savile was successively curate of Christ Church, Halesowen, Shropshire, in 1840, of Okehampton, Devon, in 1841, and of Newport, Devon, in 1848; chaplain to Earl Fortescue from 1844; rector of West Buckland, Devon, in

1852; and curate of Tawstock, Devon, in 1855, of Tattingstone, Suffolk, in 1860, of Dawlish, Devon, in 1867, of Combeinteignhead, Devon, in 1870, and of Launcells, Cornwall, in 1871. In 1872 Sir Lawrence Palk (later Baron Haldon) presented him to the rectory of Dunchideock with Shillingford St George, Devon. He died at Shillingford rectory on 14 April 1888, and was buried on 19 April.

Savile was a contributor to the *Transactions of the Victoria Institute* and to the *Journal of Sacred Literature*, and the author of more than forty volumes. His works, chiefly theological and in tone evangelical, display much learning. His volume *Anglo-Israelism and the Great Pyramid* (1880) exposed the fallacies of the belief in the Jewish origin of the English people. Savile expressed his premillennial views in a commentary on 2 Thessalonians chapter 2 (1853), in which he equated the Roman Catholic church with the anti-Christ. He also wrote on the historicity of the Pentateuch (1863) and on the reality of the spirit world (1874). G. C. Boase, *rev.* Ronald Dent Kuykendall

Sources Venn, *Alum. Cant.* • Boase, *Mod. Eng. biog.*
Wealth at death £896 18*s.* 4*d.*: probate, 20 Sept 1888, *CGPLA Eng. & Wales*

Savile, Sir George, first baronet (1549/50–1622). *See under* Savile family (*per.* *c.*1480–1644).

Savile, Sir George (*c.*1583–1614). *See under* Savile family (*per.* *c.*1480–1644).

Savile, George, first marquess of Halifax (1633–1695), politician and political writer, was born on 11 November 1633 at Thornhill Hall, near Dewsbury, Yorkshire, the second of seven children and eldest son of Sir William *Savile, third baronet (1612–1644), landowner [*see under* Savile family (*per.* *c.*1480–1644)]. His mother was the Hon. Anne (*d.* 1662), eldest daughter of Thomas *Coventry, first Baron Coventry, and his second wife, Elizabeth. Henry *Savile (1642–1687) was his brother.

Minority, 1633–1654 Savile's great-grandfather, the first baronet, was of the minor gentry but married a daughter of the sixth earl of Shrewsbury and in 1604 succeeded a cousin as head of the Saviles of Thornhill. In 1622 he left somewhat under 40,000 acres in Yorkshire and Lincolnshire to the second baronet, who in 1625 also inherited, from the Shrewsbury side of the family, 16,800 acres in Nottinghamshire, including Rufford Abbey in Sherwood Forest, and over 7000 acres in Yorkshire, Derbyshire, Staffordshire, Oxfordshire, and Shropshire. In 1651 the Savile estate rental was £6550.

After entering the Long Parliament following a by-election in January 1641 the third baronet, Sir William, placed his heir in the private school of Charles Croke DD in Amersham, Buckinghamshire. While George was there his great-uncle Thomas *Wentworth, earl of Strafford, was beheaded and his father was briefly committed to the Tower. Sir William withdrew his son from school by April 1642, when he left London for the last time, and in June joined the king's army at York. Seeking refuge, in September Lady Savile moved from Rufford to Thornhill, later to Durham, and in February 1643 to a sister in Shropshire.

George Savile, first marquess of Halifax (1633–1695), attrib. Mary Beale, *c.*1674–6

George and his brother William attended Shrewsbury School from then until May, when their mother moved to Sheffield Castle. Their father was appointed governor there in May, and in November also at York, where he died in January 1644. In August, after enduring the two-week siege of the castle, the family returned to Rufford.

Although the court of wards was petitioned by various parliamentarians, including the first baronet's eldest son by his second wife, a pre-emptive ordinance of parliament in July 1645 granted the wardship of the body, but not the marriage, of Sir George and £4000 from his estate to Lord Wharton. Wharton was paid by November 1647. Because of Sir William's delinquency and loans to Charles I, however, the estate suffered further exactions.

To evade Wharton's clutches his ward was sent abroad 'ere he was full 13 years of Age', as Sir Edward Sherburne, employed in the Savile household from 1651 to 1655, later recalled (*Poems and Translations*, xxviii). The earliest evidence shows him in France by July 1647. Under the general supervision of Eleazar Duncon DD he travelled with a Scottish presbyterian tutor, George Anderson MA. He spent a year at a Huguenot academy in Paris and some months in Angers and Orléans, a year in Italy, and at least two months in the Netherlands. His library later included books in French, Latin, Italian, and Spanish.

In 1648 Thornhill Hall, garrisoned and besieged during the family's absence, was accidentally destroyed by explosion and fire on the day of surrender. Lady Savile, moreover, risked helping Sir Marmaduke Langdale to plan the capture of Pontefract and later escape. In 1660 Wharton claimed to have used influence 'to preserve S[r] George still under her Education' when 'a Person then in greate power would have gott him into his hands', apparently after 1649 (Wharton, fol. 252*v*).

After returning to England in June 1652 Savile proceeded to Worcestershire, where his mother was staying with Dorothy *Pakington, Lady Pakington (*d.* 1679), her sister. There he impressed Henry Hammond with his intelligence and gravity, but two years later Hammond urged fellow clergyman Gilbert Sheldon to counteract, by 'friendly converse', unspecified dangers of his 'delight in company' (*Life and Letters*, 2.340). He also had a temper. His father's surviving trustee, having denied liability for £6000 of Sir William's debts, threatened Sir George in 1653 that he could lawfully take possession of the estate. As the trustee later recounted when sued, 'the plt: gave the Defendt: such an Answere beinge in passion as he refirreth the Relacon and consideracon of it to the Plt' (Brown, 'George Savile', 31).

Royalist conspiracy and politics, 1654–1669 By April 1654 Savile's family was involved in a royalist plot. In January 1655 his uncle, Sir John Pakington, second baronet, was arrested for receiving shipments of weapons. On 7 March his uncle William *Coventry rode post-haste from London to meet Langdale's associate Charles Davison and Sherburne at Rufford. That night about two hundred armed men assembled at the nearby inn but dispersed when warned that they had been betrayed and that the rising in Yorkshire had failed. Cromwell wrote to the local commander that Savile and Sir Roger Cooper were undoubtedly involved and should be seized. Savile, however, had remained in London. (From 1653 to 1672 he leased Carlisle House in Lincoln's Inn Fields, except from 1659 to 1662, when he lived in St John's Street, Clerkenwell.) Apparently no action was taken against him.

By this time four of Savile's siblings had died: Mary in 1635, Margaret and Talbot in 1650, and William in 1652. In May 1656 Anne (*d.* 1667) married Lord Windsor, who complained about underpayment of her £7000 portion. On 29 December 1656 Savile married Lady Dorothy (1639x42–1670), daughter of Henry *Spencer, first earl of Sunderland, who brought him £10,000. By 1660 he had paid debts of £20,000 and still owed £10,000.

From Charles II's restoration Savile expected a role in public life, recognition of his loyalty, and compensation for his losses. Despite disqualification because of his father he was elected MP for Pontefract in 1660. In July he petitioned the Lords, unsuccessfully, to exclude Wharton's £4000 from the Bill of Indemnity and Oblivion. In 1661 he made preliminary enquiries about re-election. Sir John Dawnay, who had supported his candidacy in 1660, wished to stand at Pontefract if he did not, while Sir John Goodricke offered to step aside for him in the county election. He deferred to both and retired from the Commons.

Appointed deputy lieutenant and colonel of foot in the Yorkshire militia under Langdale in 1660, Savile continued under the duke of Buckingham. At Rufford in 1665 he lavishly entertained James, duke of York, who subsequently recommended him for a peerage, seconded by his uncle Sir William Coventry (now York's secretary) and Buckingham. The earl of Clarendon thwarted this attempt, objecting in part that Savile's remarks about religion made him suspect of atheism.

Besides Buckingham only Savile was favoured in 1666 with a special commission for raising a troop of horse in Yorkshire, where he acted as Buckingham's second in a duel. He followed his patron out of office in February 1667 and in again seven months later, after Clarendon's downfall. On 13 January 1668 he was created Baron Savile of Eland and Viscount Halifax. His recent appointment to the independent commission of accounts made the timing somewhat compromising.

Halifax's politics in the House of Lords were royalist but factional, and he drifted away from Buckingham. In a debate against Buckingham of November 1669 he asserted that royal authority was too restricted for the glory of the kingdom and the interest of the peers themselves, whom he compared to rays that shine only when majesty is at its brightest. In Charles's presence York told Henry Savile that his brother Halifax had done his duty well.

Privy council and opposition, 1672–1679 On 17 April 1672, one month after the declaration of indulgence and the declaration of war against the Dutch, Halifax was admitted to the privy council. Sent in June to congratulate Louis XIV upon the birth of a son he was joined with Buckingham and the earl of Arlington in negotiating an Anglo-French peace with the states general of the United Provinces. Yet he disapproved of the war as upsetting the balance of power. In helping to draft the terms he tried to minimize demands upon the Dutch, and after returning to England he did not endorse his colleagues' proposal to invade Zeeland.

His wife had given birth to five children: George (1660; died 10 months later), Henry (1661), Anne (1663), William [*see below*] (1664/5), and George (1667). She died on 16 December 1670. About 19 November 1672 Halifax married Gertrude (1640/41–1727), whose presbyterian father, William Pierrepont of Thoresby (younger son of the earl of Kingston), had been a politician before the Restoration. A daughter, Elizabeth, was born in 1675.

Before parliament met in February 1673 and passed the Test Act, Halifax learned privately of York's conversion to Roman Catholicism. During a debate on the declaration of indulgence he remarked that 'if we could make good the eastern compliment, O king, live for ever! he could trust the king with every thing; but since that was so much a compliment, that it could never become real, he could not be implicit in his confidence' (*Bishop Burnet's History*, 2.103).

Prior to the October session Sir William Temple thought that Halifax and Coventry hoped to gain office by attacking the government and the war. If so, they were frustrated by the separate peace with the Dutch and the earl of Danby's rise to power. Opposition lords tried to exploit fears of popery—in 1674 Halifax moved to confiscate firearms from Catholics—but were outflanked by Danby's appeal to narrow Anglican and cavalier interests. In 1675, seemingly apprehensive of absolutism, even without Catholic or French influence, Halifax opposed the passage of Danby's non-resisting test. On 6 January 1676 his uncle Henry *Coventry, secretary of state, notified him that the king, without explanation, had dismissed him from the privy council.

A few days before parliament met in October 1678 Halifax and Buckingham confided to the French ambassador, Barrillon, that the opposition would pursue the Popish Plot far enough to alienate York from Danby and prevent the voting of additional supplies for the troops raised to fight the French but kept in England. Halifax, his uncle by marriage the earl of Shaftesbury, Buckingham, and the earl of Essex led the investigation in the Lords. Halifax concurred with Lord Holles that men's lives should not be taken on the testimony of the disreputable informers, yet he did not scruple to exploit the plot politically. He jointly moved an address to bar the king's brother from the royal presence and councils and voted to remove the queen from Whitehall. When the previous year's negotiation for a French subsidy was betrayed to the opposition leaders he secretly communicated with Barrillon (through Algernon Sidney, his first wife's uncle) about overthrowing Danby, who subsequently was impeached.

Parliament was dissolved and Danby resigned, receiving not only a pardon but also a pension and a warrant (never executed) for a marquessate. Halifax told the Lords in March 1679 that it was 'impossible to imagine that the King cou'd ever be prevailed upon to doe an act soe ungratefull to his people' (Thompson, 1.185). Charles, sitting in the gallery, was furious.

Influence, real and illusory, 1679–1682 One month later, when the king adopted Temple's scheme for a privy council of thirty to include members of the opposition, he resisted Halifax's inclusion more than anyone else's, acquiescing only when his principal advisers offered to beg on their knees. Once admitted, Halifax resented not being within the inner circle consisting of Temple, Essex, and the second earl of Sunderland, his brother-in-law. He was co-opted despite Sunderland's warning that he 'could draw with no Body, and still climbing up to the Top himself' (Temple, 31). He, Sunderland, and Essex became known as the triumvirate. Royal favour towards him, noticeable by 3 May, continued to grow. Years later Gilbert Burnet attributed this to Halifax's calculated 'lively and libertine conversation' (*Bishop Burnet's History*, 2.206).

More to the point Halifax sought to defuse the growing constitutional crisis by accommodating both the public's fears of the Popish Plot and the king's refusal to consider excluding his brother from the royal succession. He argued with Temple that several priests convicted under a long dormant Elizabethan statute should be executed on the grounds that the plot 'must be handled as if it were true, whether it were so or not, in those Points that were so generally believ'd' (Temple, 49). When the Commons rejected the royal proposal for statutory limitations upon the powers of a Catholic successor, he and Essex advised Charles to dissolve parliament and summon another for October. On 16 July 1679, four days after the dissolution, he was promoted to an earldom.

That autumn, as the king adopted a more confrontational policy towards the opposition and shifted his confidence to Sunderland, Lawrence Hyde, and Sidney Godolphin, Halifax fell ill with symptoms of depression. He wavered between staying in the government and leaving; he and Essex complained to friends that they were merely dupes. In December he, Temple, and Essex opposed the decision to postpone parliament until the following November. In January 1680 he withdrew to Rufford.

At Sunderland's urging Halifax met the ministers in June and conditionally agreed to return upon assurances that the triumvirate's strategy, reinforced by Spanish and Dutch alliances, would be followed. Afterwards he wrote to a cousin, the future Viscount Weymouth:

> A little time will shew the reality of this, or expose the deceipt if there is any; in the mean time I am the same free man … and … ready to serve the King when ever hee closeth with the interest of the Nation, and if … hee goeth against it, I will be none of the instruments, to carry on that scheme. (*Works*, 1.11)

Halifax returned to London in mid-September. At the opening of parliament in October the king promised security for the protestant religion consistent with the succession: two days later Halifax duly introduced a bill penalizing Catholics. The Commons passed the second Exclusion Bill, which when brought up to the Lords on 15 November was rejected on the first reading, following a 10 hour debate in which Halifax and Shaftesbury led the opposing sides. Charles had refused to be intimidated and the outcome had been predicted, but as principal royal spokesman Halifax was credited with defeating the bill.

Halifax was now regarded as the chief minister, Sunderland having defected to the exclusionists. On 7 January 1681 the Commons resolved that Halifax, the marquess of Worcester, and the second earl of Clarendon were enemies to the king and kingdom because they advised the king to reject exclusion in his latest message.

Charles dissolved parliament on the 18th and summoned another to meet at Oxford. Halifax, the only minister who opposed the dissolution, left for Rufford on the 24th. There he told Sir John Reresby that 'he intended to goe to Parlament whenever it assembled, but that afterward he would leave the Court and business, except his Majesty would be advised to doe such things as were for the publique good' (*Memoirs of Sir John Reresby*, 215). In March, when the Commons rejected a regency scheme and brought in another exclusion bill, parliament was dissolved and he went back to Rufford, intending to remain until autumn.

On 19 May, however, the king commanded Halifax to return at once; he arrived a week later. There was reason to believe that his advice would be followed. The continued exile of York, the early meeting of parliament, and the renewed offer of expedients were consistent with his recommendations. The latest dissolution, moreover, could be justified by whig intransigence, and the king's declaration on 8 April had promised frequent parliaments. Accordingly, between about 19 May and 9 June Halifax apparently refuted the opposition's counterblast to the royal declaration. *Observations upon a Late Libel*, first noticed on 16 June and ascribed to him four days later, sarcastically exposed the hypocrisy and selfish ambitions of the whig leadership.

Although supposedly in the king's confidence Halifax was ignorant of the secret French treaty of 1681. (He learned of it by 1684.) Thus he lent needed credibility to the royal pretence of independence from French influence. Believing the opposition's extremism responsible for Charles's reluctance to call another parliament, Halifax could justify repressive measures against whigs, like those against Catholics, on the grounds of expediency.

After returning to the government, therefore, Halifax took an active role in purging the commission of the peace, arranging for Stephen College to be indicted at Oxford, and seeking evidence against Shaftesbury. In a privy council committee he argued that if the king engaged himself against France and secured Shaftesbury a parliament could safely be held, the duke of Monmouth would be unable to prevent its success, and if the duke of York 'prove but complyable in this, then wee tramble all those little pretenders in peeces' (*Works*, 1.31).

Halifax's usefulness lessened in 1682 when the power of the whigs began to ebb, the French lifted the siege of Luxembourg, and a powerful faction hostile to him emerged at court. The duchess of Portsmouth arranged for York's return from Scotland in March and Sunderland's readmission to the ministry in July. Halifax had threatened to leave if Sunderland returned: as consolation he was promoted to a marquessate on 22 August. On 25 October he was also appointed lord privy seal, a post worth about £3000 annually. It had been intended for Sir Edward Seymour, but Halifax insisted that Charles keep a previous promise of the next vacant office.

In August, Halifax's daughter Anne married, with a portion of £10,000, Lord Vaughan (afterwards third earl of Carbery), twenty-four years her senior, whose previous vote against Halifax as an enemy to the king and kingdom prompted Sir Charles Sedley to comment: 'never was any age so comicale as this' (*Chesterfield, his Correspondence*, letter 90).

Loss of influence and office, 1683–1688 By 1683, because of Spanish refusal to accept English arbitration, whig weakness after the Rye House Plot, and increased revenues, another parliament was not needed. In January 1684 Halifax warned Charles that not summoning one would soon violate the Triennial Act, which might discontent 'thos which were for the service of the Crown, but for his Majesty observeing the lawes at the same time'. Nevertheless he added that if the king 'thought not fit to doe it, he would not relinquish his service, but if he could find out any reasons as an excuse for his not doing it, would study to doe it' (*Memoirs of Sir John Reresby*, 327). When discontented previously Halifax had withdrawn from court. He was no longer indispensable, however, and statecraft had its charms.

Although Halifax's influence was eclipsed by that of his rivals the king tolerated his scheming against them, if only to avoid being completely dominated by a single faction. Thus in November 1683 Halifax secretly arranged an abortive reconciliation between Charles and his son, the duke of Monmouth. Earlier he had clashed with Lawrence Hyde, now earl of Rochester, over Treasury accounts: with tacit royal approval he renewed his attacks in 1684. In July he secured the nominations for two vacancies on the Treasury commission, from which (in a phrase he coined) Rochester was 'kicked up stairs' to the presidency of the privy council (*Bishop Burnet's History*, 2.445). He also supported Danby's release from the Tower, hoping to bring him into play against Sunderland.

In May 1683 the queen, Catherine of Braganza, had appointed Halifax to her privy council; in April 1684 she made him chancellor and keeper of her great seal and granted a fee-farm rent of £550 from her jointure lands. He soon settled this income upon his troublesome son Henry (Lord Eland), whose £1500 allowance had to be increased to gain the hand in marriage, and £20,000, of the Huguenot marquise de Gouvernet's daughter. His brother Henry, the English envoy in Paris, had arranged the match.

At the cabinet council Halifax opposed freeing all Catholics who had been imprisoned during the Popish Plot under the recusancy laws; opposed issuing Irish army commissions to Catholics in contravention of the Test Act; and opposed omitting a representative assembly from the intended new charter for Massachusetts as being inconsistent with the rights of Englishmen.

Citing various reasons including this last issue, towards the end of 1684 York, Portsmouth, Sunderland, and Barrillon began a concerted effort to have him dismissed. Charles remained evasive, initially saying that he would wait for a pretext, subsequently that he preferred Halifax to leave voluntarily. He let him keep attacking Rochester and apparently had him prepare another attempt to reconcile with Monmouth. He also continued to enjoy Halifax's company. In February 1685, on the eve of his fatal illness, Charles was laughing as they walked side by side from the council chamber to Portsmouth's lodgings.

In January, Halifax had anonymously distributed three manuscript copies of *The Character of a Trimmer*, one to the archbishop of Canterbury with a letter asking him to deliver it to the king. It circulated in manuscript until pirated for publication in 1688. In it he alluded to policies that he had opposed in council; the genre of a character and arguments balanced on the notion of the golden mean enabled him to do so without betraying his authorship, which he disclosed after 1688.

Tory journalists had been denouncing trimmers, a supposed third party of neutrals and traitors, in order to intimidate moderate tories and Anglicans who did not support thorough repression of whigs and dissenters. Halifax's pamphlet, ostensibly a defence of the centre against both extremes, was designed to undermine tory support for repression at home and inaction abroad. It argued that ruling in accordance with the laws was in the interest of both prince and people; that the Church of England was best served by comprehension of protestant dissenters or some leniency towards them (less towards Catholic laymen, and only to promote conversions); and that the balance of power was in the national interest. For tactical reasons Halifax both understated his sympathy for protestant dissenters and refrained from stating outright his conviction that Charles was secretly a Catholic and still in the pay of Louis XIV.

In 1685 James II, despite having urged Halifax's dismissal, thought it prudent for him to be in office when parliament met. James's brothers-in-law, however, were rewarded at Halifax's expense. Rochester became lord treasurer, Halifax was kicked upstairs to the presidency on 18 February 1685, and Clarendon was given the privy seal.

In two audiences Halifax spoke his mind 'with that planess in relation to his service in point of government that he wondered the King (considering his temper) took it with that calmness' (*Memoirs of Sir John Reresby*, 361). At the privy council he opposed granting commissions to Catholics contrary to the Test Act; in several further audiences he opposed repealing the Test Act and Habeas Corpus Act. James dismissed him on 21 October, telling Barrillon that he made an example of Halifax to show that only unreserved attachment to his own interests could gain credit at court. The queen dowager, obliged to accept Halifax's resignation, later gave his wife a diamond ring worth more than £1300.

Evidently Halifax spent much of his enforced leisure in reading and writing. Current concerns were reflected in his notes on the prerogative, the sacramental test, and monasticism. (Whether former monastic lands, like Rufford Abbey, were secure under a Catholic monarch had been questioned.) Before as well as after the revolution, moreover, he may have worked on his sympathetically nuanced character of Charles II, published posthumously.

Halifax began but abandoned a character of his aunt Dorothy, Lady Pakington. Passages from it are echoed in 'Advice to Betty', written at the end of 1687 for his younger daughter (aged twelve) and privately distributed in a few manuscript copies. It was pirated as *The Ladies New-Year's Gift, or, Advice to a Daughter* (1688); his name appeared in the sixth edition (1699). Although urging the conventional virtues expected of a young woman of quality he did so as a counsel of prudence, explaining how, despite the natural and legal inequality of the sexes, she should manage herself and others to her best advantage. This work remained popular for decades, reaching its fifteenth numbered edition by 1765, and was translated into French and Italian.

Halifax's letters to William of Orange, 1686–8, were optimistic that James, whether from his own mistakes or unforeseen accidents, would be unable to obtain repeal of the Test Act. In June 1687 Halifax and other governors of the Charterhouse—he had been elected in February 1683, succeeding Shaftesbury—defied the king by refusing to admit a Catholic. Twelve months later he drafted a petition for the imprisoned seven bishops, which they declined to use. He also risked prosecution for seditious libel by sending to the press two pamphlets against royal policy, apparently in the belief that protestant public opinion, if properly informed, would obstruct James's designs. Although anonymous they were soon suspected to be his.

A Letter to a Dissenter (1687) appeared at the beginning of September, went through six editions (more than 20,000 copies in print), and provoked twenty-four replies. It purported to be 'upon Occasion of' the declaration of indulgence in April but was prompted by the dissolution of parliament in July. Taking the illegality of the declaration for granted Halifax wrote to dissuade protestant dissenters from supporting parliamentary repeal of those laws which penalized Catholics as well as themselves and to assure them of more understanding from Anglicans in the future. According to the nonconformist preacher Richard Baxter most of his brethren did not address the king to thank him for the indulgence: they 'waited in expectation of seeing the Effects of the Marquesses Declaration on behalf of the Church Party' about an Anglican change of heart towards them (*Works*, 1.88).

The Anatomy of an Equivalent (1688) was written after the birth of the prince of Wales in June heralded a Catholic dynasty. The second declaration of indulgence, in April 1688, had vaguely promised to provide a secure liberty of conscience without oaths or tests—the concept of an 'equivalent' that originated in March 1687 but gained currency following publication of Halifax's *Letter*, eight replies to which mention it. The word 'equivalent' itself was much less current. Dissecting it, however, enabled Halifax to anticipate any specific royal proposal to a parliament by instilling distrust of the very notion of anything preferable to the sacramental test. The pamphlet was described as 'sharp and biting, though the application be veiled over' (*Works*, 1.111).

In office and opposition, 1688–1695 When questioned on 1 November 1688 Halifax assured the king that he had not invited William to intervene. On the 27th, when a group of peers assembled by royal command, he joined in urging James to summon parliament, dismiss Catholics from office, and send commissioners to negotiate with William. The following week he, Sidney, Lord Godolphin, and the earl of Nottingham were sent to William's camp. Returning to news of the king's disappearance he promptly committed himself to William's cause. He chaired the peers who met at Whitehall on 13 December and, following James's unexpected reappearance, did so again at Windsor on the 17th. William sent Halifax, the earl of Shrewsbury, and Lord Delamere to tell the king to leave London. On the 22nd, following James's flight to France, Halifax chaired the peers at Westminster who asked William to assume provisional administration of the government.

When the convention met in January 1689 the Lords elected Halifax speaker. In 1681 he had supported the expedient of a regency, but William told him privately that he would leave rather than accept one. So Halifax voted that the throne was vacant. He had not been privy to William's coming, he told his tory friend Reresby, but 'now that he was here, and upon soe good an occasion, we were obliged to defend him' (*Memoirs of Sir John Reresby*, 547). He even proposed making William sole monarch and opposed deleting 'rightful and lawful' from the oath of allegiance. As speaker he formally offered the crowns to William and Mary at their coronation; as confidential adviser he had drafted the speech of acceptance.

The queen dowager reappointed Halifax as her chancellor and lord keeper on 2 February 1689. On the 28th William III signed a warrant for his appointment, on 8 March, as lord privy seal. These manifestations of royal favour greatly offended the whigs. In June and July the Commons considered addresses to remove both Halifax and Danby, now marquess of Carmarthen, because they had been censured by former parliaments; in August a motion for an address against Halifax alone was defeated. In the Lords a motion to depose him from the speakership failed in July.

On 18 October, the last day of the prorogation, Halifax declined to continue as speaker. In November a Lords' committee investigated the complicity of former ministers, especially Halifax, in repressing whigs and favouring Catholics during previous reigns. In December an address was proposed in the Commons against the three commissioners whom James had sent to William.

In August, Halifax had noted hints of William's subsequent reliance upon the tories led by Carmarthen, who by December anticipated nominating a new lord privy seal. Halifax was now less willing than in 1682 to retain office while losing influence to a hated rival. On 8 February 1690 (two days after the dissolution of parliament was proclaimed) he returned the seal to the king, saying 'it was for his service I did it'. William contradicted him, shut the door, and refused the seal until Halifax promised to resume office, if health permitted, 'when it was for his service' (Foxcroft, 2.248). A successor was not appointed until 1692.

From office Halifax drifted into opposition. He continued to serve the queen dowager but ceased to attend the privy council and was dismissed on 23 June 1692. Burnet believed that he went 'in to the Intrests of the Jacobites' and 'studied to … shelter that party upon all occasions' (Foxcroft, 2.194). Despite occasional contacts with Jacobite agents, however, Halifax remained committed to the revolution settlement. He supported neither Carmarthen's tory nor, after 1693, Sunderland's whig government: rather, he associated with the country opposition, led in the Commons by Robert Harley. His views found expression not only in the House of Lords but also in three anonymous works, initially circulated in manuscript copies and later published by others.

The Following Maxims were Found amongst the Papers of the Great Almanzor (1693) purported to be written by a medieval Muslim conqueror. Its twenty-three political maxims (comparable to the ten inserted in *Observations*) indirectly criticized William's policies and choice of ministers.

A Rough Draught of a New Modell at Sea (1694) was written and circulated in 1693. In 1692 and 1693 the questionable official conduct of an aristocratic whig admiral had been followed by that of a commission of three tory admirals, thereby reviving a much earlier controversy over the relative merits of gentlemen and seamen commanders. In parliament Halifax supported the commission. His pamphlet maintained that, because England was a mixed monarchy, both gentlemen (if brought up at sea) and seamen should command ships. One-third of the text discusses forms of government, defending the English constitution as better suited to the nation than either absolute monarchy or a commonwealth.

Some cautions offered to the consideration of those who are to chuse members to serve in the next parliament (1695), written after March 1693 and circulated about April 1694, was posthumously revised and published during an election, perhaps at Harley's instigation. Implicit in its characterization of twenty unsuitable types is Halifax's ideal candidate: someone capable of protecting the nation's interest against the court.

Other writings from this period remained unpublished. The sheets headed 'Fundamentalls', 'Kings and queens', and 'Ministers' (possibly chapter titles) contain rough notes and maxims written from an insider's perspective, as if for the benefit of monarchs and ministers. 'Raillery' is a draft essay on the species of wit in which Halifax excelled. He also jotted down a great number of maxims on sheets headed 'Misc.'. Similar manuscripts in the possession of his granddaughter were the source for *A character of King Charles the Second: and political, moral and miscellaneous thoughts and reflections* (1750), edited by Alexander Pope. Halifax had praised Montaigne's *Essais* for its 'true Picture of himself and of Mankind' (*Works*, 3.23). His own writings, reticent about himself, are more suggestive of Machiavelli and La Rochefoucauld.

Private concerns 'His heart', Burnet observed, 'was much set on raising his family'. Contemptuous of titles Halifax claimed to have acquired his own because they 'might be of use to his family'. He also 'made a vast estate for them' (*Bishop Burnet's History*, 1.493). Indeed, by 1695 property acquired or improved after 1651 had increased his rental income (excluding fines) from £6550 to £14,704; parks and residences, if let, would have added £700 to that. At twenty-one years' purchase for freehold and eleven for leasehold his real estate was worth £313,469.

Halifax was knowledgeable about financial matters. Sir William Petty's *Quantulumcunque Concerning Money* (1682; printed 1695) was addressed to him. In 1683 he led a syndicate that offered to farm the excise with a £600,000 advance to the exchequer. For decades, moreover, he systematically sold life annuities. Like marriage portions, they presumably provided much of the capital for enlarging his estate. Sixteen years after his death, when approximately fifty annuities (including several sold by his son) were still outstanding, they represented principal of over £40,500.

Among other conspicuous expenditures befitting Halifax's dignity, after 1669 he built Halifax House, designed by William Taylor, a mansion of about fifty rooms on a double lot in St James's Square. (Additional work in 1678 included piping river water to his bathtub.) In 1724, when dilapidated, it sold for £6500. After 1677 he demolished some monastic remains and doubled the size of Rufford Abbey, valued at £20,000 in 1720. Fire damage to the 123-room structure in 1692 cost more than £2000 to repair. In 1686, for £760, he purchased a smaller (9 acre) more accessible retreat: Berrymead Priory in Acton, Middlesex.

Any satisfaction Halifax had in elevating his family would have been tempered with anxiety about ensuring the continuation of its male line. When this was threatened he made settlements of his estates in 1688, 1693, and 1695, which by-passed female heirs in favour of more distantly related males. In October 1687 Halifax's brother died unmarried and his eldest son died childless. The second son, William, married one month later and had a son who died in infancy before his wife's death in 1694. In February 1689 the third son, George, died unmarried. Of Halifax's daughters, Anne died in July 1689, leaving a daughter, while Elizabeth, with £20,000, married Lord Stanhope in March 1692; their son, the future fourth earl of Chesterfield, was born two years later.

On 31 March 1695, probably at his house in St James's Square, Halifax ate an undercooked chicken. A violent fit of vomiting pushed his constipated intestine through an old rupture, and gangrene set in. Although his condition quickly worsened he refused to let his son Lord Eland be notified lest Eland's wedding, on 2 April, should be delayed. He took the Anglican sacrament and asked forgiveness for the scandal caused by his loose way of talking about religion. Speechless by the time Eland arrived on 5 April, he died an hour later. On the 11th he was buried in Westminster Abbey. His widow survived him, and died on 1 October 1727.

The writer Henry *Carey later claimed to be his illegitimate son.

Reputation With a double chin, a nose he considered ugly, and a dark complexion (he was known as the Black Marquis, Carmarthen as the White), Halifax was not noted for good looks. What impressed contemporaries was his intellectual brilliance. In 1682 even a satire acknowledged his 'prodigious Wit' (*Poems on Affairs of State*, 127). Burnet thought him 'a man of a great and ready wit … much turned to satire'. 'The liveliness of his imagination', however, 'was always too hard for his judgment' (*Bishop Burnet's History*, 1.491, 492). When his vivacity and judgement declined, 'while he studyed to support all w[th] Witt and Mirth w[th]out considering w[t] became his Age and Post, he lost a great deal of that esteem w[ch] he had formerly both as to his parts and his Integrity' (Foxcroft, 2.194).

As a frequent target of Halifax's raillery after 1688 Burnet was undoubtedly biased. Nevertheless, he was not alone in suspecting Halifax of atheism and republicanism. 'He let his wit run much on matters of religion: so that he passed for a bold and determined atheist; though he often protested to me he was not one.' (He claimed to be 'a Christian in submission: he believed as much as he could' and hoped God would not blame him 'if he could not digest iron'.) As for politics, he 'seemed full of comonwealth notions: yet he went into the worst part of King Charles's reign' (*Bishop Burnet's History*, 1.491–2).

Halifax's private maxims convey a more subtle impression. They depict men as guided by passion rather than reason, more governable by manipulation than appeal to external authority. They regard both organized religion and hereditary monarchy as exploitation and most of what passes for virtue as selfishly motivated. But they also show that their author preferred the people to believe wrongly rather than not at all, and to be frightened or flattered into good behaviour if incapable of it otherwise. In an age when radical ideas in religion and politics threatened the traditional structure of society in which Halifax was exalted, he could be cynical about the ideology of both the established church and the monarchy while remaining sincerely devoted to preservation of the status quo.

Halifax could afford political outspokenness and independence. As his son reminded the Commons in 1689, Halifax had no need to be at court to maintain himself according to his rank, since God had given him more than enough. Burnet, however, saw another need. 'His Spirit was restlesse, and in spite of all his pretences to Philosophy, he could not bear to be out of business' (Foxcroft, 2.195). From Burnet's whig perspective Halifax's independence was self-defeating: 'he went backwards and forwards, and changed sides so often, that in conclusion no side trusted him' (*Bishop Burnet's History*, 1.492).

During his lifetime Halifax was better known as a politician than an author. His eight publications, five of which were first circulated in manuscript, were all anonymous. His literary reputation, for both content and style, was established by the publishers' collected edition entitled *Miscellanies* (1700; reprinted 1704, 1717, and 1751) and Pope's edition of unpublished pieces (1750).

Those seeking to understand Halifax through his writings were apt to presume strict candour even in his political pamphlets, the underlying motives and disingenuous aspects of which both literary artifice and the passage of time obscured. Changing sides was not neutrality: in 1685 contemporaries neither called him a trimmer nor recognized his authorship of the trimmer pamphlet. Yet in 1757 Hume supposed that he 'was esteemed the head' of those called trimmers, who 'affected' neutrality between the parties (*Works*, 1.xx–xxi). After 1848 Macaulay's opinion prevailed: that in changing sides he 'assumed … and vindicated' the nickname Trimmer, being one by principle and temperament rather than self-interest (Macaulay, 234).

H. C. Foxcroft's 1898 biography and edition determined the Halifax canon, to which in 1940 Hugh Macdonald added *Observations*. Sir Walter Raleigh, reprinting the 1700 and 1750 editions in 1912, emphasized Halifax's modernity and Englishness. In an edition of 1969 (based upon Foxcroft's) J. P. Kenyon, modifying Macaulay's characterization, depicted a politically moderate intellectual who both loved and hated politics. Although ambivalent about Halifax's contemporary reputation Kenyon considered the trimmer pamphlet his political testament. An edition by M. N. Brown of 1989–90, which included previously unedited material, contrasted Halifax's public arguments and private observations.

William Savile, second marquess of Halifax (1664/5–1700), landowner and politician, was probably born at Rufford Abbey, Nottinghamshire.

He was educated at Geneva, 1679–81, and Oxford, where he matriculated at Christ Church on 5 December 1681 aged sixteen. He does not appear to have taken a degree. He travelled in France, Italy, and Spain, 1684–6, and in the Netherlands, 1686–7. On 6 October 1687 he succeeded his brother as Lord Eland and subsequently took up residence at Norfolk House (St James's Square) and Barrowby, Lincolnshire. On 28 November 1687 Eland married Elizabeth (*bap*. 19 Jan 1671, *d*. 1694), eldest daughter of Sir Samuel Grimston, baronet, a presbyterian. (Of her £20,000 portion half was not due until the death of her father, whom she, the first marquess of Halifax, and Eland all predeceased.) They had both a son and a daughter who predeceased Eland and another daughter, the future Lady Bruce. Elizabeth died in August 1694. By December the first marquess of Halifax had arranged a match with Lady Mary (*bap*. 18 May 1677, *d*. 1718), eldest daughter of Daniel Finch, earl of Nottingham. The marriage settlement (for £20,000) was sealed in February 1695, but because of Nottingham's official duties in Westminster the wedding, in Rutland, was postponed until 2 April. They had two sons, both of whom predeceased their father, and three daughters who survived him—one who died unmarried and the future countesses of Burlington and Thanet.

In 1689 Eland represented Newark, his late uncle's constituency, and was appointed a deputy lieutenant of Nottinghamshire. A tory, and less pragmatic than his father, he voted that the throne was not vacant; after succeeding his father on 5 April 1695, he allied with Nottingham in the Lords. Burnet thought him 'an honest man, but far inferior to' his father, 'which appeared the more sensibly, because he affected to imitate him; but the distance was too wide' (*Bishop Burnet's History*, 1.493).

On 31 August 1700, at Acton, he succumbed to 'an inward feavour' (Luttrell, 4.680) and on 6 September was buried in St Michael's, St Albans, beside his first wife. His widow survived him, and died on 19 September 1718. His peerage became extinct but the baronetcy continued until 1784.

The second marquess's executors and trustees, led by Nottingham, faced obligations amounting to £55,000 for portions and £1899 for debts, legacies, and arrears of annuities. In 1706 the first marriage portion, not paid until 1713, became due and the Lords rejected the trustees' petition for a private bill to raise money by selling land. Litigation, 1706–22, resulted in the seventh baronet, who had inherited much of the family estate, contributing £23,800 (plus £3222 interest) towards the two remaining portions. Orders in chancery and private acts of parliament in 1713, 1719, and 1721 permitted the trustees to sell various properties to raise portions and in 1743, after the last annuity expired, to distribute the residue to the coheirs. MARK N. BROWN

Sources *The life and letters of Sir George Savile ... first marquis of Halifax*, ed. H. C. Foxcroft, 2 (1898) • *The works of George Savile, marquis of Halifax*, ed. M. N. Brown, 3 vols. (1989) • *Bishop Burnet's History* • T. B. Macaulay, *The history of England from the accession of James II*, new edn, ed. C. H. Firth, 6 vols. (1913–15) • J. W. Clay, 'The Savile family', *Yorkshire Archaeological Journal*, 25 (1918–20), 1–47 • W. Temple, *Memoirs: from the peace concluded 1679*, ed. J. Swift (1709) • *Memoirs of Sir John Reresby*, ed. A. Browning, 2nd edn, ed. M. K. Geiter and W. A. Speck (1991) • M. N. Brown, 'George Savile marquis of Halifax', PhD diss., Harvard U., 1964 • Notts. Arch., Savile of Rufford papers • indentures of Savile family settlements, 1687–95, priv. coll. • 'Acco[ts] of the trust estate for four years viz[t] 1712 1713 1714 1715', Northants. RO, Finch-Hatton MSS, F.H.286 • inquisitions post mortem of George Savile, knight, 1626, and George Savile, second baronet, 1634, PRO, Ward 7/74/98; 7/86/145 • D. Finch, earl of Nottingham and Winchelsea, letters and papers, 1694–1730, Leics. RO, Finch MSS, DG.7/4950–4951 • Chatsworth House, Derbyshire, Savile–Finch MSS, boxes 1, 4–5 • W. Turner, accounts, 1670–90, Sheff. Arch., M.D. 150–51 (A–O) • Catherine of Braganza's privy council, minute books, 1681–95, PRO, LR 2/131–2, 168 • minutes of meetings, 1683–95, Charterhouse, London, assembly orders vol. C, committee orders vol. D • Phillip, Lord Wharton, 'The case betwixt the Ld Wharton and Sr George Savill', [1660], Bodl. Oxf., MS Carte 203, fols. 252–3 • E. M. Thompson, ed., *Correspondence of the family of Hatton*, 2 vols., CS, new ser., 22–3 (1878) • W. Trumbull, autobiography (to 23 May 1687) and verses, [n.d.], All Souls Oxf., MS 317 • N. Luttrell, *A brief historical relation of state affairs from September 1678 to April 1714*, 6 vols. (1857) • *The poems and translations of Sir Edward Sherburne*, ed. F. J. van Beeck (1961) • *Poems on affairs of state ... by the greatest wits of the age*, 3 (1704) • *Philip Stanhope, second earl of Chesterfield: his correspondence with various ladies ... and letters exchanged with Sir Charles Sedley, John Dryden, Charles Cotton, Mr. Bates* [1930] • B. H. Nuttall, *The Saviles of Thornhill: life at Thornhill Hall in the reign of Charles I* [1986] • PRO, C 38/344; C 54/4655/22 • GEC, *Baronetage* • M. N. Brown, 'Trimmers and moderates in the reign of Charles II', *Huntington Library Quarterly*, 37 (1974), 311–36 • J. Charlesworth, ed., *The register of the parish of Thornhill, part I*, Yorkshire Parish Register Society, 28 (1907) • monument, Westminster Abbey • *GM*, 2nd ser., 34 (1850), 367 • J. L. Chester, ed., *The marriage, baptismal, and burial registers of the collegiate church or abbey of St Peter, Westminster*, Harleian Society, 10 (1876) • *The parish of St James, Westminster*, 2 pts in 4 vols., Survey of London, 29–32 (1960–63) • A. I. Dasent, *The history of St. James's Square* (1895) • BL, Add. MS 17677 HH, fol. 253 • parish register, St Michael's, St Albans, 6 Sept 1700 [burial, William Savile]

Archives BL, notes, Add. MS 51511 • BL, Spencer MSS, corresp. and papers • BL, Trumbull MSS, diplomatic letter-book, ref. 66 • Chatsworth House, Derbyshire, Devonshire MSS, corresp. and papers • CUL, library catalogues, Dd.II.14, IX.3, 51; Oo.VI.108c • Leics. RO, Finch MSS, literary papers • Leics. RO, original of rough draft of a New Model at Sea • Notts. Arch., corresp. and papers • W. Yorks. AS, estate records | BL, letters to Finch, Add. MS 28569 • Bodl. Oxf., letters to Gilbert Burnet • CKS, corresp. with Alexander Stanhope • CUL, Alexander Sion papers • Longleat House, Wiltshire, Coventry MSS • Longleat House, Wiltshire, Thynne MSS • Northants. RO, Finch-Hatton MSS • Notts. Arch., manuscript accessions, M7428–M7443 • Notts. Arch., Foljambe of Osberton papers • Notts. Arch., Portland papers • Sheff. Arch., Wentworth Woodhouse Muniments • U. Nott. L., letters to Sir Philip Monckton • W. Yorks. AS, Leeds, letters to Sir John Reresby • W. Yorks. AS, Savile (Mexbrough) MSS

Likenesses oils, *c*.1661–1666, Chatsworth House, Derbyshire • attrib. M. Beale, oils, *c*.1674–1676, NPG [*see illus.*] • J. Houbraken, engraving, 1740 (after M. Beale), repro. in T. Birch, *The heads and characters of illustrious persons of Great Britain* (1743) • M. Beale, oils (original or copy of her earlier work), priv. coll. • J. Cole, engraving (after monument), repro. in J. Dart, *Westmonasterium*, 2 vols. (1723) • effigy on marble monument (after M. Beale), Westminster Abbey

Wealth at death approx. £350,000: PRO, C 38/344; PRO, C 54/4655/22; Notts. Arch., DDSR. 225/3/1; F. H. W. Sheppard, ed., *The parish of St. James 1: south of Piccadilly*, 1, Survey of London, 29 (1960), 157

Savile, Sir George, eighth baronet (1726–1784), politician, was born on 18 July 1726 at Savile House, Leicester Square, London, the only son of Sir George Savile, seventh baronet (1679–1743), MP for Yorkshire, and Mary, only daughter of John Pratt of Dublin, deputy vice-treasurer of Ireland. A descendant of the marquess of Halifax, 'the Trimmer', Savile's main estate was at Rufford, Nottinghamshire, adjoining the properties of Portland and Newcastle at Welbeck and Clumber, but like his father he pursued his parliamentary career in Yorkshire, where his seat was at Thornhill, near Dewsbury (where there is still a district called Savile Town). He inherited the baronetcy in 1743 at the age of seventeen. Two years later, during the Jacobite rising, he became a lieutenant-colonel in the young Rockingham's regiment, and contributed £200 to the defence fund. Admitted to Queens' College, Cambridge, in January 1745 as a fellow-commoner, he graduated MA and LLD in 1749.

In 1753 Savile made one of the few false moves of his political career. Anticipating the general election, he presumed, with the strong backing of Rockingham, that the sitting member for Yorkshire, Sir Conyers Darcy, nearly seventy, would retire, and offered himself as a candidate. But Darcy refused to stand down and Savile wrote to Rockingham that he would not be 'bambouzled' (Hoffman, 15). Over-eager, Rockingham attended a meeting at York on 16 July and called upon Darcy to make way for a younger man. This went down badly and Savile withdrew. Rockingham, chastened and angry, could have brought him in for Higham Ferrers or York, but Savile preferred to wait for the county vacancy. When it came, he was elected in place of Darcy in January 1759 without opposition. None of his four subsequent elections was contested.

Savile made his mark in the Commons quickly. In his first week in the house he was put on eleven committees, no doubt as a courtesy as well as encouragement, and at the beginning of the new parliament in 1761 he was considered for the speakership in succession to Arthur Onslow. He was also offered the comptrollership of the household, but declined. Further offers came his way, but he was already suffering from asthma, did not relish constant attendance, and doubted whether his constituents would admire a placeman. In a list for a Rockingham ministry in May 1765 he was pencilled in for a seat at the Admiralty board, and when Pitt was negotiating the following month he was mentioned as a possible secretary at war.

Meanwhile he followed Rockingham's political line. His house in Leicester Square was used for party meetings and in 1767 Rockingham referred to him as 'my mentor' (Hoffman, 152). In April 1765 Horace Walpole noted that Savile had 'shone' in a debate on French encroachments in Newfoundland (Walpole, *Corr.*, 38.528). On 7 February 1766 he spoke in opposition to Grenville's motion to enforce the laws in America, and he spoke and voted in favour of the

Sir George Savile, eighth baronet (1726–1784), by Benjamin Wilson, in or before 1770

repeal of the Stamp Act, a basic Rockingham measure. On 22 April 1766 he successfully seconded Sir William Meredith's motion that the use of general warrants in Wilkes's case had been illegal. When, towards the end of that parliament, a dispute between Sir James Lowther and the duke of Portland in Cumberland caused considerable concern about property rights, Savile was the ideal man to bring forward a bill to limit the rights of the crown (the Nullum Tempus Bill), though Rockingham had to push him hard to undertake it. His speech of 17 February 1768 failed to carry the day, though Burke praised it as one of the most elegant he had ever heard, but Savile succeeded in the new parliament on 24 February 1769.

Behind the scenes Savile was much consulted. His advice was usually moderate. He did not much like the tone of Burke's *Thoughts*, which he saw in draft. He warned Rockingham against those who were always calling for 'pulling down, coming in, etc.', and in a comment aimed probably at Burke begged Rockingham to remember 'my cold hesitations. Don't keep your room too hot' (Brooke, 'Savile, Sir George', 406; Hoffman, 148). On America he was particularly cautious. He warned correspondents in the colonies not to drive things to extremes, but to welcome the repeal of the Stamp Act as a generous measure.

But in a private letter to Rockingham he confessed that he believed that Grenville's tough attitude had done little more than bring on the inevitable crisis 'twenty or possibly fifty years sooner than was necessary' (Keppel, 2.76).

Two issues in the parliament of 1768–74 brought Savile to the forefront of politics—Wilkes and America. The decision in April 1769 to seat Luttrell for Middlesex angered him greatly since he saw it as the House of Commons flagrantly ignoring the wishes of the voters. In October 1769, when a Yorkshire meeting resolved to petition on the issue, Burke wrote that Savile had 'never spoken with more ability', bringing tears to the eyes of his listeners (*Correspondence*, 2.96–7). On 9 January 1770 he caused a sensation in the house by declaring that parliament had betrayed its trust and, when called upon to withdraw his remarks, threatened to repeat them. Horace Walpole, with some exaggeration, commented that Savile's remarks implied rebellion, and a number of Rockinghamites, including the duke of Richmond, were appalled at Savile's 'violence' (Walpole, *Corr.*, 39.121). On 7 February 1771 he moved for a bill to secure the rights of electors, insisting that the house, by itself, could not make law: he was defeated by 167 to 103. He repeated the motion in 1772, 1773, and 1774, each time without success. Ill health was already taking its toll and on 16 February 1771 Burke thought Savile 'ill and out of spirits. I never saw any man out of his sick-bed look worse' (*Correspondence*, 2.199). Later in the year he had a bad fall while hunting and his parliamentary activity was curtailed. He refused to take part in debates on the East India Company since he totally disapproved of colonial acquisition. But he exerted himself in February 1772 to make a long speech supporting the application of certain Church of England clergymen to be excused from subscribing to the Thirty-Nine Articles, arguing that several of the articles were inconsistent with reason, that the petitioners were respectable men, and that the church should keep its doors open as wide as possible. John Lee, a future attorney-general, wrote that he had never been so affected by 'the power of pious eloquence' (Trevelyan, 415), but the petition was rejected by a large majority. On 17 March 1773 Savile supported a bill to relieve protestant dissenters, telling the house that Christians should embrace as brothers, and on 5 May 1774 seconded Meredith's motion to allow relief from the Thirty-Nine Articles.

At the end of the parliament Savile's wish was to retire, but the entreaties of his friends persuaded him to stand once more. The parliament of 1774 was dominated by the American crisis and the issues arising from it. Savile had already protested against the punitive measures directed at Massachusetts Bay, complaining that they were 'an extraordinary exertion of legislative power', threatening chartered rights (Cobbett, *Parl. hist.*, 16.1277). He watched with horror as relations deteriorated into war. He was, he told the house on 10 February 1775, a mere novice at ruining commerce and on 1 December 1775 he predicted that France and Spain would intervene. The lack of success of the opposition made him despondent. To Rockingham he wrote in January 1777 deploring the unpromising prospect of affairs: 'we are not only patriots *out of place*, but patriots out *of the opinion of the public*' (Keppel, 2.304), and concluded that there was no point in struggling to achieve a minority of seventy-one rather than sixty-nine. Much of his time he devoted to his duties as colonel of the West Riding militia. But in the following session, on 14 May 1778, he attended and moved with success a small bill to relieve Roman Catholic subjects from a few of their disabilities. This had clearly been concerted with the leaders of the Catholic community who had submitted a loyal petition on 1 May, and Savile contented himself with arguing that protestants ought never to persecute. The consequences were delayed, but momentous.

The parliamentary opposition was rescued from its hopeless position by the misfortunes and cost of war. On 30 December 1779 a meeting was called at York to petition for economical reform to give some relief from wartime taxation. Savile attended and told his constituents that he had long hoped for such a move. His speech of 8 February 1780 introducing the petition was a major effort. He apologized for a sore throat: 'the venerable patriot', wrote the *Parliamentary History* respectfully, was heard 'in deep silence' (Cobbett, *Parl. hist.*, 20, 1778–80, 1374). The property of the petitioners, he told the house, was greater than that of its members, and should their wishes be ignored, he would not contemplate the consequences. North noted the menace, but the debate continued incongruously with an intervention by Lord George Gordon, increasingly eccentric, declaring that true reform must begin with religion. As the association movement showed signs of becoming an anti-parliament and adopted a plan of parliamentary reform, Rockingham's enthusiasm cooled, leaving Savile in an awkward position. Meanwhile in the summer of 1780 Gordon's Protestant Association erupted into violence, in the course of which Savile, though anti-Catholic, was denounced as the champion of the papists and proponent of the 1778 Catholic Relief Bill, his coach was smashed, his London house attacked, and much of his furniture destroyed. On 23 June 1780, in a gesture of conciliation to the outraged protestants, Savile moved for a bill to prevent papists from keeping schools attended by protestant children.

After considerable hesitation Savile endorsed the association programme in the autumn of 1780. At the general election in September 1780 he was once more returned for Yorkshire but he advised his constituents that they were not to expect regular attendance. In the new house he pursued what was almost a personal vendetta against North, pressing him closely on the pensions issue and criticizing the terms of his loans. His relations with Rockingham were under strain and on 7 May 1782 he supported Pitt's motion for parliamentary reform, asserting that the constitution was rotten within. He was too ill to attend the York meeting on 19 December 1782. He disliked the coalition which Fox and his allies made with North in the spring of 1783, writing to his friend David Hartley that they were uniting with men they ought to impeach. He made a last speech on 6 May 1783 in support of Pitt's second motion for reform of parliament, but was obliged to sit down, 'to the great mortification of the House, who were distressed to see so good a man in so weak a state of health' (Cobbett, *Parl. hist.*, 23, 1782–3, 846). In November 1783 he announced that he must retire. Fitzwilliam, who had taken over Rockingham's interest, begged him to continue even if he never set foot at Westminster. But Savile was a dying man and knew it. There was little point, he told his constituents, in 'breaking my neck at the next hedge' (Wyvill, 3.281) and he wanted to take his tired horse home. He died, 'universally lamented' (*GM*), a few weeks later, on 10 January 1784 at Thornhill, where he was buried on 24 January. He was unmarried.

Savile had some of the attributes of the typical country gentleman. He was proud to represent his county of Yorkshire, and deferred constantly to his constituents; he was suspicious of encroachments by the executive upon the liberties of the subject; he was reluctant to hold office, and often weary of the burden of public business which so important a constituency imposed upon him. But his extensive estates in Yorkshire, Nottinghamshire, and co. Fermanagh gave him far more wealth than most gentlemen; his property in the West Riding provided contacts with trade and industry, which he fostered; his relations with his close neighbours Rockingham and Portland gave him party connections, though he maintained a certain independence; and he won a respected position in the House of Commons as a more than useful debater.

Wyvill, writing years later, saw Savile as a bridge between the aristocracy and the people—'the keystone, to use language nearly his own, by which the nobles and the people, as parts of the same political arch, were united and kept together' (Wyvill, 4.165 n.). But the bridge was breaking and though Savile's nephew Francis Ferrand Foljambe took his seat for the county, he lost it three months later at the general election to an associator. More than twenty years later 'Independent Savile' was fondly remembered in ballads at the Yorkshire election of 1807 (Gooder, 108).

John Cannon

Sources Cobbett, *Parl. hist.* • G. Thomas, earl of Albemarle [G. T. Keppel], *Memoirs of the marquis of Rockingham and his contemporaries*, 2 vols. (1852) • R. J. S. Hoffman, *The marquis: a study of Lord Rockingham, 1730–1782* (1973) • C. Wyvill, ed., *Political papers*, 4 vols. [1794–1804] • *The correspondence of Edmund Burke*, ed. T. W. Copeland and others, 10 vols. (1958–78) • Walpole, *Corr.* • H. Walpole, *Memoirs of the reign of King George the Third*, ed. D. Le Marchant, 4 vols. (1845) • *JHC* • *The manuscripts of the Right Honourable F. J. Savile Foljambe, of Osberton*, HMC, 41 (1897) • GEC, *Baronetage* • *The correspondence of King George the Third from 1760 to December 1783*, ed. J. Fortescue, 6 vols. (1927–8) • J. Brooke, 'Savile, Sir George', HoP, *Commons* • *GM*, 1st ser., 54 (1784), 73 • E. A. Smith, *Whig principles and party politics: Earl Fitzwilliam and the whig party, 1748–1833* (1975) • I. R. Christie, *The end of North's ministry, 1780–82* (1958) • I. R. Christie, *Wilkes, Wyvill and reform: the parliamentary reform movement in British politics, 1760–1785* (1962) • P. Langford, *The first Rockingham administration, 1765–1766* (1973) • A. Gooder, ed., *The parliamentary representation of the county of York, 1258–1832*, 2, Yorkshire Archaeological Society, 96 (1938) • E. C. Black, *The Association* (1963) • *The historical and the posthumous memoirs of Sir Nathaniel William Wraxall, 1772–1784*, ed. H. B. Wheatley, 5 vols. (1884) • P. C. Yorke, *The life and correspondence of Philip Yorke, earl of Hardwicke*, 3 vols. (1913) • G. O. Trevelyan, *The early history of Charles James Fox*, new edn (1908) • *Correspondence of William Pitt, earl of Chatham*, ed. W. S. Taylor and J. H. Pringle, 4 vols. (1838–40) • R. I. Wilberforce and S. Wilberforce, *Life of William Wilberforce*, 5 vols. (1838) • N. C. Philipps, *Yorkshire and English national politics, 1783–4* (1961) • J. Cannon, *The Fox–North coalition: crisis of the constitution, 1782–4* (1969) • *Memorials and correspondence of Charles James Fox*, ed. J. Russell, 4 vols. (1853–7) • J. Brooke, *The Chatham administration, 1766–1768* (1956) • F. G. Stephens and M. D. George, eds., *Catalogue of political and personal satires preserved … in the British Museum*, 5–11 (1935–54) • *Report on manuscripts in various collections*, 8 vols., HMC, 55 (1901–14), vol. 8 • Venn, *Alum. Cant.*

Archives Berks. RO, corresp. and MSS • Notts. Arch., personal corresp., personal, family, and political corresp. and papers | BL, corresp. with duke of Newcastle, Add. MSS 32723–32991, *passim* • East Riding of Yorkshire Archives Service, Beverley, letters to John Grimston • N. Yorks. CRO, corresp. with Christopher Wyvill • PRO, corresp. and MSS relating to fourth earl of Scarbrough's affairs, C 104/30, C 112/19 • Sheff. Arch., corresp. with Lord Rockingham • U. Nott. L., letters to the third duke of Portland

Likenesses B. Wilson, portrait, in or before 1770; Sotheby's, 8 March 1989, lot 43 [*see illus.*] • B. Wilson and J. Basire, etching and line engraving, pubd 1770 (after B. Wilson), BM • J. Fisher, statue, 1784, York Minster • J. Nollekens, bust, 1784, FM Cam.; replica, V&A • B. Bartolozzi, engraving (after Fisher) • B. Wilson, portrait, Trinity House, Hull • B. Wilson, portraits, Osberton, Nottinghamshire • B. Wilson, portraits, Rufford, Nottinghamshire

Wealth at death substantial: will, in *Yorkshire Archaeological Journal*, 25 (1920), 36; *DNB*

Savile, Sir Henry (1499–1558). *See under* Savile family (*per. c.*1480–1644).

Savile, Sir Henry (1517/18–1569). *See under* Savile family (*per. c.*1480–1644).

Savile, Sir Henry (1549–1622), mathematician and classical scholar, was born on 30 November 1549 in Over Bradley, West Riding of Yorkshire, one of eight children and the middle of three sons of Henry Savile (*d.* 1566) of Over Bradley and his wife, Elizabeth, daughter of Robert Ramsden of Yorkshire and his wife, Elizabeth. John *Savile (1546–1607) was his elder brother and Thomas *Savile (*d.* 1593) was his younger brother. His father studied civil and canon law at Oxford University and was a moderately prosperous landowner. The family valued learning highly and Henry Savile the elder made provision in his will for the division of his library between his sons, leaving money specifically for the purchase of books.

Early years and education, 1549–1570 John Savile left an account of the many tutors he had as a boy—relations and local churchmen, in the main—from whom he received a solid classical education: the four years before he went up to Oxford in 1561 were spent reading Terence, Ovid, Virgil, Horace, and Cicero. This style of education may have been a consequence of turmoil in the grammar school system in the wake of disruptive legislation during Edward VI's reign. It is most likely that Henry Savile, only three years younger than his brother, received similar early education and probably under the same tutors.

The Savile clan was large, and other branches of the family—notably the Saviles of Thornhill, Derbyshire—were among the wealthiest landowners in the region. Some were also known for their puritanism and founded schools which were supervised by puritan clergy. The Saviles of Over Bradley have left no such explicit evidence of

Sir Henry Savile (1549–1622), by Marcus Gheeraerts the younger, 1621

their confessional inclination. They were, however, very clearly protestant: John Savile records that one of his first reading books, set to him at the age of eight, was the *Dialogi sacri* by the freethinker Sebastian Châteillon. Thomas Savile, moreover, mentioned in a letter to William Camden that one of his childhood tutors had been rejected from a university post by a 'fanatical gang of Catholics' on the grounds that he was a puritan (W. Camden, *Gulielmi Camdeni, et illustrium virorum ad G. Camdenum epistolae*, 1691, 14–15). While later in Europe, Henry Savile befriended both Roman Catholic and protestant humanists, but his closest association was with the former Catholic Andreas Dudith, bishop of Cinq-Églises, in Wroclaw, Poland, whose drift away from his original confession carried him through Calvinism to Arianism and unitarianism.

The Savile brothers attended Oxford University. Henry Savile, like his father, matriculated at Brasenose College in 1561, aged twelve. He excelled in mathematics and astronomy, but his interests also embraced classical scholarship, English history, patristic theology, and much else besides. His protégé Richard Montague famously described him—not without bias, perhaps, but certainly with justice—as the 'Magasin of learning' (R. Montague, *Diatribae upon the First Part of the Late History of Tithes*, 1621, 126). In 1565 (a year before he graduated BA on 14 January 1566), he was elected to a fellowship at Merton College. He subsequently held a series of college offices: second dean in 1574–5, principal postmaster in 1575–6, and third bursar from 1576 to 1578. In 1575 he was also elected proctor with John Underhill, a protégé of Robert Dudley, earl of Leicester. At Leicester's insistence, both men had their offices extended to a second year.

Savile's intellectual interests during his student years are very well documented by his own manuscript writings and annotations in printed books. Although he is best known today as the translator of Tacitus and editor of John Chrysostom, the last work he published before he died was a set of lectures on Euclid, delivered at the inauguration of the Savilian professorships. His interest in mathematics was not a late development: the sciences were, in fact, his first interest as a youth, and took second place to theology only in his middle age. While studying for his MA, and perhaps even earlier, Savile immersed himself in astronomy and geometry, both ancient and modern. After proceeding MA on 30 May 1570, he was chosen as one of the regent masters in astronomy for the year 1570–71. This office entailed delivering the 'ordinary lectures' in that subject—the only form of teaching that the university provided for undergraduates.

Early work, 1570–1578 The text of the lectures survives in three manuscript volumes in the Bodleian Library (Savile MSS 29, 31, 32). In these lectures Savile describes something of the programme of study he pursued at the beginning of his scientific career. His earliest interest, he tells us, was in philosophy; a friend recognized, however, that his talents lay elsewhere, and advised him to turn his attention to mathematics. He began his studies with Euclid's *Elements*, perhaps as part of the university's compulsory geometry curriculum. He worked systematically through it, book by book, and recalls that he found the subject so enthralling—especially the fifth and sixth books on the theory of proportion, a subject that remained a lifelong interest—that he would forget to eat or sleep. By the middle of the notoriously difficult tenth book (on irrational quantities), however, he found himself mentally exhausted, and decided to abandon geometry for astronomy. Typically, he began not with one of the simplified handbooks on the subject, but with Ptolemy's *Almagest* itself, which he read in the original Greek assisted by an assortment of translations. The difficulty of the mathematics, however, defeated him, and eventually he returned to geometry, completing his reading of the *Elements*. On the advice, he says, of his elders, he then broadened his mathematical education by studying the works of Archimedes and perhaps learning some algebra, before finally turning back to Ptolemy.

With this thorough grounding in geometry, Savile found the *Almagest* much more accessible on the second reading. He now realized, in fact, that the existing translations, both medieval and Renaissance, were entirely unsatisfactory, and often mathematically flawed. In 1568 he therefore embarked on his first scientific project: a new translation of the *Almagest*; this survives in manuscript in the Bodleian Library (Savile MSS 26–28). His translation covers approximately half of the Greek original, the text taken from the *editio princeps* by Simon Grynaeus of 1538—Savile's annotated copy of this edition is also extant (Bodl. Oxf., MS Savile W. 14). He also translated the commentaries of Theon, Pappus, and Cabasilas which Grynaeus printed alongside the ancient text. Savile's translation is technically very accurate and is written in an elegant and clear Latin style. The mathematical competence derives largely from his study of the works of the great fifteenth-century reformer of astronomy, Johannes Regiomontanus, whose interpretations and additions Savile wrote carefully into the margin of his printed *Almagest*.

While he was translating the *Almagest*, Savile began to lay the ground for his next project. At the back of one of the notebooks, he made a list of all astronomers and mathematicians, ancient and modern, whom he had encountered in his reading, together with brief biographies and bibliographical details: what works they wrote, whether they had been published, and where manuscripts of their unprinted works could be found. The list, which Savile entitled 'Auctores mathematici', contained some 700 entries. This was the raw material for a history of the sciences; while in the midst of translating Ptolemy, Savile even settled on a title for the projected work: 'Compendium historiae mathematicae'. The work was never published, but formed a large section of his ordinary lectures, occupying much of the first volume of the manuscript. It is a remarkably comprehensive and historically detailed survey of ancient science, organized biographically, beginning with the legendary foundations of the sciences by the Hebrew patriarchs and ending with Ptolemy. In the *Praelectiones* he delivered fifty years later, Savile drew attention especially to his demonstration in the life of Euclid that the author of the *Elements* was not the same person as Euclid of Megara, the philosopher and contemporary of Plato, as was almost universally believed at the time (by, for instance, Henry Billingsley, whose translation of the *Elements* was published in 1570, the same year as Savile's lectures).

The lectures following Savile's history of the sciences contain the most advanced treatment of astronomy in sixteenth-century England, with the possible exception of the papers of Thomas Harriot. The range of sources known to Savile, and the depth of his understanding of them, is astonishing, particularly given the young age at which he delivered these lectures. He showed a mastery of astronomers from Ptolemy, through the Arabs, to Regiomontanus and Copernicus. His analysis of the astronomical hypotheses of various astronomers through history is comparable in its technical skill to that of contemporary continental astronomers, such as Erasmus Reinhold. Savile's teaching far surpassed the usual instruction in astronomy at Oxford, which rarely went beyond the basics of the sphere and sometimes concerned itself only with judicial astrology (which he expressly rejected in his lectures and continued to condemn throughout his life).

Savile appears to have been the first to teach the new astronomy of Copernicus at an English university. He did not, however, subscribe to the heliocentric world-view. In his lectures he presented the Ptolemaic and Copernican systems side by side, and made no comment on the fact that the two systems contradicted each other, although elsewhere in the same lectures he made it clear that he believed the earth to be fixed in place in the centre of the universe. His attitude is typical for most astronomers of the period: they revered Copernicus, whom they considered to have matched or surpassed Ptolemy in skill, but were little interested in heliocentrism *per se*. Savile's pragmatic approach to the problem of the two world-systems is well illustrated by an anecdote (from later in his life) related by his contemporary, Nathanael Carpenter. When he was once having dinner with Savile, Carpenter relates in his *Geography*, the conversation turned to astronomy, and he asked whether, in Savile's view, the earth really travelled around the sun (as Copernicus had it) or was in fact stationary at the centre of the universe, as Ptolemy maintained. Savile answered that he was entirely indifferent as to the truth of either hypothesis so long as (in the ancient formula) the appearances were saved—and on this criterion either hypothesis 'would indifferently serve an Astronomer'. He illustrated this with a homely simile: 'is it not all one … sitting at Dinner, whether my Table be brought to me, or I go to my Table, so I eat my meat?' (N. Carpenter, *Geography Delineated Forth in Two Bookes*, 2 pts, 1625, pt 1, p. 143).

Most unusually for a scientific writer in England of this period, Savile's lectures on mathematics and astronomy concentrated entirely on theoretical issues. He emphasized to his students that both sciences had been part of—in fact, central to—the ancient liberal-arts curriculum; he also maintained that the true scholar should waste no time mastering practical applications in either field. His prejudice was partly personal: his own intellectual interests lay wholly within the theoretical sphere and he repeatedly identified himself as a Platonist, stating at one point that his avoidance of practical arts was the consequence of his 'disgust for external things'. He also hoped to improve the institutional standing of the sciences at Oxford: most well-bred Oxford students neglected mathematics and astronomy, some because they seemed difficult and obscure arts to master, a great many more because of the widespread assumption that they were the province of vulgar merchants and sailors. To combat these prejudices, Savile made humanism central to the model of the sciences he presented in his lectures, not only in order to win the interest of students who had come to Oxford to study the humanities, but also because he believed that the humanist could make a real contribution to mathematics—as he himself had done in his historical researches into the lives of ancient mathematicians.

Savile's understanding of the sciences was largely

formed by his study of contemporary continental publications. He frequently compared the poor state of the sciences at Oxford with the great esteem they enjoyed at European universities. There, he declared, scholars were as familiar with Ptolemy's *Almagest* as students at Oxford were with Greek grammar. If Oxford were to make up the gap in the sciences, it would not be through studying handbooks or popular, practical expositions but by absorbing the original sources of ancient science. Savile also contrasted the poor state of the sciences in late sixteenth-century Oxford with the achievements of medieval Oxford mathematicians and natural philosophers, especially those of his own college (now known as the Merton school). This was a theme to which he frequently returned, most notably during Elizabeth I's visit to Oxford of 1592, when he gave a speech in his role as adjudicator of a debate held for her entertainment. He chided the scholars of Oxford for their squeamishness, unable to bring themselves to read the works of these scientists because of the barbarous Latin they employed. In the same speech (which was published posthumously and subsequently reprinted by Charles Plummer) he decided in favour of the proposition 'Should astrologers be banished from the state?'.

Savile's lectures of 1570 were disrupted by outbreaks of the plague in Oxford and were rescheduled several times. Despite these obstacles, the remarkable nature of these lectures firmly established his scholarly reputation—as Anthony Wood said, he became 'famous for his learning, especially for the Greek tongue and mathematics'. In part, his success can be attributed not only to the content of the lectures, but to their lively style and careful pacing and explanation of the difficult material—Savile was a gifted teacher as well as a fine scholar. The *Praelectiones* of 1620 (unfortunately, the only other lectures of his to survive) exhibit the same qualities, and an anecdote from a few years previously shows that Savile remained an inspiring teacher. Henry Gellibrand, who went up to Trinity College, Oxford, in 1615, was an indifferent student until he stumbled into one of Savile's lectures by accident—or rather, to avoid the fine that would have been levied if he did not attend. He soon became so absorbed by it that he 'immediately fell to the study of that noble science'—and eventually became Gresham professor of astronomy (J. Ward, *The Lives of the Professors of Gresham College*, 1740, 81). As well as confirming Savile's expertise as a lecturer, this story suggests that he at times delivered the compulsory or ordinary lectures in mathematics, a task he perhaps assumed in the absence of any recent graduates capable of teaching the sciences to his standard. No doubt it was this circumstance which led him to found the Savilian professorships, thereby providing a permanent replacement for the teaching of mathematics through the regency system.

Savile continued to value the theoretical branches of the sciences more highly than the practical. The scientific books which he annotated later in his life are, with very few exceptions, theoretical; in books where both types of science appear, such as astronomical books, the annotations concentrated in areas such as planetary theory and neglected subjects like the construction of instruments. In his Savilian professorships, however, he did attempt to strike a balance.

European tour, 1578–1585 Savile's most notable contemporary at Merton was Thomas Bodley. Their relationship at first seems to have been uneasy. In 1566–7, soon after his arrival at Merton, Savile became embroiled in factionalism at the college. Bodley, then dean, headed the conservative grouping; Savile—for perhaps the only time in his life—was one of the 'rebel hotblades' (Martin and Highfield, 159), putting his name to a letter questioning Bodley's authority. A close friendship between the two men developed despite this incident. In 1576 Bodley embarked on a European tour, and left his rooms at Merton to be occupied by Savile. In 1578, supported by a small allowance from Merton, Savile himself left for the continent, travelling first to Paris, where Bodley was then residing.

Savile remained abroad for four years, travelling as far east as Wroclaw in Poland, and as far south as Rome. His travelling companions included George Carew, Henry Neville, and Philip Sidney's younger brother Robert. The latter, like so many travelling Englishmen of the time, was on tour primarily to meet important political figures and to acquire a cosmopolitan 'polish' and smattering of foreign languages, all of which were considered useful for a gentleman, especially a courtier. No doubt Savile shared these goals, but his notes and the letters that document his tour reveal in addition an altogether more serious purpose. He was on tour primarily to further his mathematical and humanistic education, and much of his time was spent in the great libraries of Europe; the manuscripts he copied out were later to form the core of the Savilian professors' collection, and are now in the Bodleian Library. He also established friendships with many important scholars. In Altdorf (near Nuremberg) he was the guest of the professor of mathematics Johannes Praetorius, who remained in correspondence with Savile for many years afterwards. Praetorius sent him on to his friend Tadeaš Hájek (Thaddaeus Hagecius), the imperial physician in Prague, who was also a fine astronomer. Hájek in turn sent him to Dudith in Wroclaw, where he stayed for six months. While there he worked extensively with Paul Wittich, an astronomer who had, until a couple of months before, been a colleague and confidant of Tycho Brahe; he and Savile were preoccupied in particular with the problem of reconciling Ptolemy and Copernicus, one of the central problems of European astronomy in this period. In Padua he passed his time in the library of Gian Vicenzo Pinelli—one of the greatest in Europe—and then spent several weeks in the Biblioteca Marciana in Venice, where he hunted out mathematical manuscripts for himself and theological and rhetorical works for Pinelli. Savile returned to England late in 1582 and, according to Wood, was appointed tutor in Greek to Elizabeth shortly thereafter—the start of his career as a courtier which was to lead rapidly on to higher academic office.

Warden of Merton and provost of Eton, 1585–1595 In 1585, Savile became warden of Merton by rather unorthodox means. The warden was, according to the college's own statutes, elected by the fellows. Despite—or perhaps because of—his long association with the college and familiarity with the fellows, Savile invested no faith in this democratic process and obtained the post instead through his influence with the queen. In a letter to the college of 1586, William Cecil, first Lord Burghley, lord treasurer, and Sir Francis Walsingham, principal secretary, recognized that the fellows had, by tradition, the freedom to choose their own warden, but trusted that they would 'concur with Her Majesty's wishes' (Martin and Highfield, 169–70). They of course did, but clearly this imposition from above rankled with some of the fellows. William Aubrey recorded that one fellow complained until his dying day that Savile's closeness to the queen made it impossible to deal with him in a normal manner. The same fellow asserted that Savile was 'too much inflated with his learning and riches', and 'did oppresse the fellows grievously'. After his appointment, it seems, Savile made little effort to restore normal relations with his colleagues. The college register (as might be expected) contains no complaint against him, but a set of letters now in the Merton archives reveals that the fellows' displeasure was expressed very forcefully more than a decade after his appointment (ibid., 173–7).

Savile was said to be tall and extremely handsome. He married Margaret (*d.* in or after 1622), daughter of George Dacres of Cheshunt, Hertfordshire, and his wife, Elizabeth, and widow of George Gerrard of Dorney, Buckinghamshire, in either 1591 or 1592. She had two daughters from her first marriage, including Anne (1585/6–1627), who married Sir Dudley Carleton. Savile and his wife had two children, Henry (*d.* 1604) and Elizabeth (*b. c.*1595, *d.* after 1651), known as Bess, who married Sir John Sedley, second baronet. After he secured the provostship of Eton College in 1595 Savile was rarely in residence at Oxford—and even before then, his constant attendance at court (in part to lobby for the provostship, in part because of his office of Greek tutor) meant he was in college only infrequently. As early as 1587 he nominated a sub-warden, Thomas Master, to run the affairs of the college during his absence. Savile's appointment to Eton made it obvious that this arrangement was to be permanent, and two years later, when Master took a living which disqualified him from holding his position in the college, the fellows seized the opportunity and lobbied the visitor, John Whitgift, archbishop of Canterbury, to have the sub-warden removed. The fellows also complained to Thomas Ravis, vice-chancellor, about Savile's irregular behaviour, accusing him of holding more offices than he was permitted to and ruling Merton as an absentee warden, as well as favouritism and corruption in his administration of college properties. The matter was settled by Elizabeth's intervention and the summary dismissal of several fellows. The chancellor of the university, Sir Thomas Sackville, however, felt obliged to write to Savile condemning in general terms the absence of heads of colleges and, when they were present, their habitation with their wives in college—another rule that Savile had flouted since his marriage. The chancellor implicitly demanded Savile's resignation; Savile wrote a letter to Whitgift defending himself. He admitted that he stayed in Merton only six or seven times a year, but previous wardens, he argued, had not always resided in college—and his absences saved the college money in food and heating bills. He went on in his letter to describe some of the substantial improvements he had made at Merton (including, ironically, greatly increasing the number of fellows); and although some of his colleagues may not have agreed at the time, there is no doubt the college benefited from Savile's wardenship. He enlarged the library (more than tripling its holdings of printed books) and introduced continental-style bookstacks, in which the books were stored standing up, rather than lying flat as was the usual practice in England. These stacks can still be seen in the college library. He also had built, between 1608 and 1610, the fellows' quad and the handsome façade looking out onto Christ Church meadow, employing Yorkshire builders who had worked on his family's properties. As well as appointing many new fellows to enhance the college's intellectual reputation, he made the first two Savilian professors, Henry Briggs and John Bainbridge, fellows of Merton—perhaps hoping that his college would regain the leading role in the sciences it had enjoyed in the fourteenth century.

Savile was one of the first donors to the Bodleian Library. In 1599 Merton, at his instigation, delivered £40–£50 worth of books to the new library. Bodley was to call on his assistance many times in the early days of the library—a reflection not only of their long friendship, but of Savile's experience in improving the libraries of Merton and Eton. In 1598 Bodley and Savile together made sketches for the design of the arts end, and the actual building was done by the same Yorkshire masons who had worked on the Savile family estates and whom Savile had contracted for the construction of the fellows' quad. The design of the 'tower of the five orders' in the schools quadrangle is almost certainly due to Savile, since these masons had only recently built one of the few other examples in England of superimposed classical orders, at a property in Yorkshire belonging to Savile's older brother John Savile. Moreover, the idea for the tower probably comes from an illustration in Daniele Barbaro's edition of Vitruvius's *De architectura* (Venice, 1567), a book that Savile owned and had studied. He was also involved in the selection of worthies for the frieze in what is now the upper reading room. After Bodley's death in 1613, Savile was largely responsible for the completion of the library.

Savile campaigned long for the provostship of Eton and, in 1595, finally obtained his wish. His appointment was, once again, rather irregular, not least because the provost was supposed to be in orders. In a letter of April 1595 to Sir Robert Cecil, Savile urged him to ask his father to use his influence with Elizabeth to secure the provostship: 'one commendation [from him] in cold blood, and seeming to proceed of judgement, shall more prevail with the Queen then all the affectionate speech that my lord of Essex can use'. He promised Cecil a sum of 300 angels in return for his help (*Salisbury MSS*, 5.188–9). The queen informed the fellows on 14 January 1596, through Cecil, that they were to delay their election until she made her pleasure known to them. On 18 May the fellows received a letter from her informing them that 'we have made choise of our trustie and wellbeloved servant Henry Savill as of one, whom for his knowledge and judgement and integritie … we do thinke to be most meet and worthie thereof'. Recognizing that the provost was customarily chosen by an election of the fellows, she instructed them to elect Savile. As for the fact that 'he is no Preste', she ordered him to be appointed 'notwithstanding anie such defecte of qualitie by Statute required' (Bodl. Oxf., MS Rawl. B. 268, fol. 38*r*). Again, as with the Merton appointment, he was indebted to Burghley.

Aubrey relates that at Eton, Savile was:

> a very severe Governour, the scholars hated him for his austerity. He could not abide Witts: when a young scholar was recommended to him for a good Witt, 'Out upon him, I'le have nothing to doe with him; give me the ploding student. If I would look for witts, I would go to Newgate: there be the Witts.' (*Brief Lives*, 267)

He may not have been loved but, as at Merton, he did much to improve the college, expanding the holdings of the library and surrounding himself with fellows who, if not 'Witts', were certainly to be numbered among the best classical scholars in the country. The number of pupils and faculty members increased during his tenure and extensions were made to the college: the building Savile erected to house his printing press later became the headmaster's residence.

Essex and Tacitus, 1595–1601 Although, in his letter to Cecil petitioning for the provostship, Savile professed little faith in Robert Devereux, second earl of Essex, two months later, on 27 July (no doubt at Savile's request), the earl himself wrote to Cecil urging him to ensure Savile's 'advancement' (*Salisbury MSS*, 5.291). Savile's friendship with Essex dated back to at least 1591. In that year he published his translation of Tacitus's *Histories* and *Agricola* under, it seems, Essex's patronage. Immediately after his prefatory dedication of the book to the queen, there is an address to the reader by a writer who identifies himself only as 'A. B.'. According to Ben Jonson and to Edmund Bolton, the author of this preface was Essex himself. John Florio seems to refer obliquely to the earl's authorship in his *Worlde of Wordes* (1598). In the *Apollogie* which Essex wrote to Anthony Bacon, he cited his friendship with 'that most learned and trulie honest Mr Savile' as evidence for his love of scholarship (Bodl. Oxf., MS e Museo 55, fol. 73*r*). Savile was a friend of Henry Cuffe, whom he made a tutor at Merton in 1586, and it was perhaps through Cuffe—later to be the earl's secretary and according to some (including Essex himself) the cause of his downfall—that Savile was drawn into his circle of intellectuals.

English interest in Tacitus originated in the 1580s within a small group of correspondents which included Cuffe and Savile's younger brother Thomas Savile, as well as Camden and Jean Hotman. It was probably Cuffe who encouraged the application of the Tacitean critique of power to contemporary politics. The most notorious instance of such an interpretation was Sir John Hayward's play *Henry IV* (1599). Hayward was another member of Essex's circle. This study of the seizure of regal power—and the legitimacy of such power obtained through force of arms—could not but suggest uncomfortable contemporary parallels. Asked by Elizabeth whether the play was treasonable or not, Francis Bacon quipped that the author's crime was not treason but theft, having stolen so much from Tacitus. Whatever Hayward's intention, the play was used in evidence against Essex and his co-conspirators to demonstrate that their attempted coup had been long premeditated. Savile, in his work on Tacitus, appears to imply similar comparisons between imperial Rome and Elizabethan England, although he avoids Hayward's extremes.

In his translations, Savile attempted—with mixed success—to convey Tacitus's style as well as his meaning in English prose, in particular his use of aphorism and irony. His commentaries are exhaustive and learned, particularly his lengthy excursus on Roman warfare, which was later translated into Latin (without his permission) for the benefit of continental scholars. More remarkable than the translations and scholarly commentary, however, was the original composition placed first in the volume, entitled *The Ende of Nero and Beginning of Galba*, a work covering events at Rome in the years 68 to 69 AD—between, that is, the end of the period covered in the *Annals* and the beginning of that covered by the *Histories*. This is written in the spirit, as well as the style, of the ancient historian. As Savile remarked in his notes, Tacitus set 'us downe a theoreme of history … that an historiographer is to give knowledge of counsailes and causes', and *The Ende of Nero*, with its focus on power and factions, has been identified as the first example of English 'politic history' (A. T. Bradford, 'Stuart absolutism and the utility of Tacitus', *Huntington Library Quarterly*, 46, 1983, 133). In common with many continental Taciteans, Savile was also profoundly influenced by Niccolo Machiavelli, particularly in his explanation of Nero's fall from power. In Savile's account Nero is not a moral monster whose pitiful end was a fitting punishment for his wicked life (as some contemporary English writers portrayed him), but a weak ruler who was neither loved by his subjects nor able to instill sufficient fear in them to maintain his virtue (that is, the *virtù* of *The Prince*). In his praise of Julius Vindex, a conspirator against Nero, he implicitly supports the view that it is permissible for a military commander, at least, to rebel against a bad monarch—quite against the political orthodoxy of his time, and certainly significant in the light of his association with Essex. The translation of Tacitus and the *Ende of Nero* were much admired at the time. Henry Peacham recommended Tacitus as the 'prince of historians', difficult in Latin but now speaking 'the most pure and excellent English' (H. Peacham, *Complete Gentleman*, 1622, 47). Bolton and Jonson exalted Savile as a reincarnation of Tacitus, and wished that he would now produce a Tacitean history of England. His Tacitean writings were his most successful publication and went through six editions by 1640, and a further edition in 1698. From the second edition of 1598, Savile's work was accompanied by Richard Greneway's much inferior translation of the *Annals* and *Germania*. In 1649 Savile's notes on Tacitus and his *Ende of Nero* were translated into Latin and published in Amsterdam by Isaac Gruter.

Meagre evidence survives for Savile's relationship with Essex after 1591. In 1594 he stayed with the earl, and may have travelled with him to Oxford; and in 1597 he leased Merton College lands to him for a rent well below the market rate, a favour that the latter perhaps repaid with a gift of cash to Savile. The fellows of Merton included this corrupt deal in their catalogue of complaints against the warden. After the failure of Essex's rebellion in 1601, Savile was arrested and briefly imprisoned and all papers relating to the earl and his circle were seized from his study at Eton. The authorities were particularly interested in his relationship with Cuffe, questioning a member of Savile's household about the two men's recent meetings. He was released unpunished, and it is unlikely that he had taken any part in the conspiracy. He was certainly even less involved than Neville, his travelling companion in Europe and lifelong friend, who was imprisoned in the Tower of London and fined heavily, it seems, for having been aware of the plot. Immediately after the arrest of Essex the earl's son and heir, Robert Devereux (later third earl of Essex, then a pupil at Eton), was placed in Savile's care. He was subsequently an undergraduate at Merton, and lived in the warden's lodgings. When James VI and I came to the throne two years later, Savile, like many of Essex's former associates, found the new king to be very well disposed towards him; Savile was knighted by the king on his visit to Eton on 21 September 1604 after a banquet there.

Savile, Scaliger, and Casaubon, 1595–1600 In 1579, on his arrival in Paris, Savile made the acquaintance of the great humanist scholar Joseph Scaliger. In the spring of 1595 Savile, in common with many other mathematicians throughout Europe, received a letter from Scaliger seeking public endorsement for his most recent publication, *Cyclometrica* (Leiden, 1594). This beautifully and expensively printed book purported to square the circle and trisect the angle. Modern mathematics has demonstrated that these ancient problems cannot be solved using the Euclidean tools of compasses and straight-edge (as Scaliger claimed to have done). In 1595, however, it was not known that any attempt at solution was bound to fail—and most mathematicians believed the problems could be solved even if no solution had ever in fact been discovered. Scaliger cannot be faulted, then, for attempting a solution; unfortunately, it was painfully evident that the great philologist had not mastered elementary geometry, and the book was crammed with woeful misunderstandings of basic concepts and errors in simple mathematical reasoning. He never wavered in his belief that his solutions were correct, and in his letter to Savile he asked him, for the sake of their long-standing friendship, to defend the *Cyclometrica* against the spiteful and groundless attacks that were being prepared against it. Unknown to him, however, Savile himself had read the *Cyclometrica* with a sharply critical eye and had filled the margins of his copy (extant in the Bodleian Library) with a comprehensive and frequently sarcastic refutation. Apart from the mathematical errors, Savile found particularly galling Scaliger's intemperate attacks on Archimedes, whom he had castigated for using *reductiones ad absurdum*—a form of argument which, Scaliger insisted, had no validity in mathematics. In his *Praelectiones tresdecim in principium elementorum Euclidis* (1621) Savile quoted at length the reply he sent to Scaliger, 'a better philologist than logician', in which he argued that any logically valid argument (such as a *reductio*) was also mathematically valid (pp. 231–2). Scaliger's reaction to Savile's rebuttal is not recorded.

Savile had a long interest in the quadrature of the circle. In his lectures of 1570, he told his students that a solution was possible and would surely be discovered one day. Scattered through his papers, however, are refutations of several purported quadratures, some of much greater sophistication than Scaliger's; his examination of these failures seems to have led him to a less sanguine view of the problem, and by the time Scaliger wrote to him, he put more faith in the approximate methods first used by Archimedes (that is, in finding a more accurate, but not exact, value for π). His interest in the problem also extended to its history. In the margins of his printed copy of Simplicius's commentary on Aristotle's *Physics*, for instance, he reconstructed from the very corrupt text the several 'quadratures of lunes' discovered by the pre-Euclidean geometer Hippocrates of Chios; he was apparently the first modern scholar to do so. He was thus also well qualified to comment on Scaliger's own history of quadrature which appeared in the *Cyclometrica*. His friend Johannes Praetorius recognized Savile's aptitude for the task and urged him by letter to refute Scaliger on every front. Extant in Savile's papers are fragmentary drafts for a book which, if he had completed it, would have provided a complete history of the problem and refuted several quadratures, including Scaliger's. Several European mathematicians, however, soon published works against Scaliger, and Savile seems to have abandoned the entire project, despite the historical perspective he had to contribute. This was, unfortunately, a recurrent pattern in his mathematical work: his papers contain several unfinished projects to which he had clearly devoted much effort (such as his insightful work on the theory of proportion in the *Elements*) and others which did not get beyond a promising outline (such as his plans to write a history of the homocentric hypothesis in astronomy).

Long after the *Cyclometrica* episode Savile came to know Scaliger's closest friend, Isaac Casaubon, who emigrated from France to England in 1610. Savile's brother Thomas Savile first wrote to him in 1590 while in Germany, submitting some notes on the ancient geographer Strabo for the elder scholar's appraisal. In 1596 Casaubon contacted Henry Savile and Camden to ask their assistance with his work on Polybius—he had been informed by Richard Thomson that the two men were the most learned students of Greek in England. Subsequently, Casaubon helped Savile extensively in obtaining manuscripts from French libraries for the Chrysostom project. Savile's letters to Casaubon concerning their scholarly projects are businesslike—even, at times, rather imperious—and evince no great warmth towards his correspondent. In a letter of December 1611 Savile upbraided him for having dared to question his attacks on Scaliger's mathematical abilities—which Casaubon had only done, no doubt, out of loyalty to his friend, who had died two years before. The criticisms of Scaliger's mathematics which Savile rehearsed to Casaubon are correct enough, but the letter is written in an unpleasant, triumphalist tone, quite inappropriate in the circumstances: 'I cannot marvel enough that so insignificant a man is valued so highly by so fine a man as yourself', he concludes one paragraph (BL, Burney MS 366, fol. 68*r*). In the same letter Savile also mocks Casaubon for having referred to François Viète as 'great'. Most modern historians would rank him as the finest late sixteenth-century mathematician; Savile, however, had met him in Paris and was underwhelmed by his abilities.

Savile's self-confidence, not to say arrogance, could not be more in contrast to Casaubon's gentle and affable character, and on at least one occasion the latter remarked on Savile's conviction of his superiority to all other scholars. However, the antipathy between the two men has been exaggerated. Casaubon visited Savile at Eton in April 1611 and his son Meric went to stay with him there on at least one occasion (November 1611). Casaubon mentions once in his diary that he stayed with Savile when attending the court at Windsor, which may have been his regular practice. In May 1613 he travelled to Eton and then, with Savile, journeyed on to Oxford. Savile spent three days with him at Merton before returning to Eton; Casaubon stayed on another fortnight, but seems to have regretted that he was no longer Savile's guest, but was now in the care of William Goodwin, dean of Christ Church. By Casaubon's account, Savile seems to have been an exemplary host; nor, despite the evident differences between the two men, does he ever give any hint of dislike for him.

Chrysostom, 1600–1613 In the preface to his eight-volume edition of the works of Chrysostom, Savile explained that he had been 'consumed with love' for the church father since his earliest youth, and that he decided about 1600 to publish a complete *concursus* of his works, appalled that his writings should be scattered piecemeal in mouldering manuscripts and partial editions (Savile, preface, 1, sig. ¶4*r*). The work was published by the London bookseller, John Norton, using a press set up at Eton by the London printer Melchisidec Bradwood between 1610 and 1612. Though no evidence remains for his early interest in this author, Savile may have been introduced to patristic literature while on his European tour, where some of his new acquaintances (most notably Luca Pinelli and his humanistic circle) were students of Eastern theology. Savile's correspondence on Chrysostom with Casaubon, Jacques du Thou, and others begins about the turn of the century.

Savile was assisted in his enterprise by classical scholars such as John Bois, Thomas Allen, and Andrew Downes, all of whom contributed critical notes to the edition, as well as John Hales, a fellow of Merton, and Richard Montague. In the preface of the edition he thanked many librarians and scholars in France, Germany, Austria, and Italy who contributed manuscripts and information to the project—correspondence with some of these men is still extant. Samuel Slade, a fellow of Merton, journeyed extensively through the East in search of manuscripts of Chrysostom. The printer's copy of the work is in the Bodleian Library, and it sheds valuable light on editorial practice in the early modern period. As well as manuscript copies of ancient tracts, the large bound volumes contain earlier printed versions of Chrysostom's works; both manuscript and printed texts are marked up with emendations by Savile and his collaborators, and with Savile's instructions for layout to the printer.

The edition was not a financial success. The sales may have been affected by the appearance in 1614 of a six-volume collection of Chrysostom's works accompanied by Latin translations, and other similar bilingual editions in the following few years—Savile's edition contained only the Greek text. Wood states that Savile's text was stolen by Fronto Ducaeus (Fronton du Duc) for the 1614 edition. Du Duc's edition was certainly close to Savile's, but at least some of the labour in establishing the text may have been borne by du Duc himself, whom Savile in his edition named as one of his foreign collaborators. In any case, by printing a text that is still admired to this day Savile made it possible for these more accessible editions to be published. The cost of the edition of 1000 copies was, according to Wood, £8000, an enormous sum largely met from Savile's own resources. The price was initially fixed at £9 for the set, but soon was dropped to £8 (after Savile's death, Eton was selling copies for £3 per set). In his will Savile left fifty copies of the work to Merton and the same number to Eton; he accounts for yet another fifty in the hands of the printer, as well as several others in his possession and that of his son-in-law, Carleton. Carleton assisted him for a year in the preparation of the edition and, after the publication, attempted—with little success—to sell copies of the work in Venice, where he was resident ambassador.

Other scholarly works, 1598–1613 In 1598 Savile published a collection of chronicles and histories of England under the title *Rerum Anglicarum scriptores*. Even at the time the work was considered to be poorly executed. It does, however, uniquely preserve the text of Æthelweard's *Chronicle*, of which the only manuscript was almost entirely destroyed in the Cotton Library fire of 1731. In 1604 Savile wrote a tract on the question of union between England and Scotland entitled 'Historical collections'; it exists in several manuscripts (one of which is dedicated to James VI and I). He largely restricted himself to considering the relationship through history between the two kingdoms without committing himself to an answer on the question of union. He might have been expected to ingratiate himself with the new king but showed considerable independence of thought by opposing in this tract several of James's expressed intentions.

Also in 1604 Savile was enlisted into the 'fifth company' of translators for the Authorized Version of the Bible. He seems to have headed this group, which was responsible for the gospels, Acts of the Apostles, and Revelation and met in the warden's lodgings at Merton. Among the distinguished Oxford scholars who convened in Savile's rooms was the Calvinist divine and master of University College, George Abbot. In 1618 he commissioned from Savile an edition of Thomas Bradwardine's *De causa Dei*. Savile himself found the 'geometrical' style of this anti-Pelagian treatise of the greatest interest, and indeed in the preface to the volume he identified his fellow Mertonian Bradwardine—whose scientific works were well represented in his library—as the finest mathematician of his age.

The Eton press not only published the work on Chrysostom. Savile himself edited for the press Xenophon's *Cyropaedia* (1613)—clearly meant for use as a textbook in the college. Montague edited Gregory Nazianzen's *In Julianum invectivae duae* and other works from a manuscript in Savile's library (1610); and in the same year Matthew Bust edited the *Versus iambici* of Johannes Euchaitensis—both men praised Savile extravagantly in their prefaces. The press also published Theophilus Cangiserus's paraphrases of the Psalms (1613) and, *In usum scholae Etonensis* ('as used at Eton'), the *Oikumene* of Dionysius Periegetes (1613?). Savile was also the prime mover behind the edition of Barlaam's *Logistica* (Paris, 1600) by his old friend John Chamber; the manuscript of the work was obtained by him on his European tour and he urged Chamber to publish it.

Professorships and *Praelectiones*, 1620–1621 Perhaps Savile's most important contribution to the sciences was his foundation in 1620 of two professorships at Oxford in geometry and astronomy, which—as he recommended in the statutes for the chairs—replaced the old regency system of ordinary lectures. He laid down very precise instructions both for the selection of the professors and for their duties. The two men were to be of good character, drawn from any Christian nation, and should 'have imbibed the purer philosophy from the springs of Aristotle and Plato' before thoroughly learning the sciences—just, in fact, as Savile himself had done as a young man (S. Gibson, ed., *Statuta Antiqua universitatis Oxoniensis*, 1931, 528–40). The curriculum was to be centred on the study of the ancients: geometry would be based on Euclid's *Elements*, Apollonius's *Conics*, and all the works of Archimedes, and astronomy on Ptolemy's *Almagest*. The astronomy professor was also required to supplement his teaching with the discoveries of Copernicus and the Arab astronomers. The two professors were to share the teaching of trigonometry, which should be based on the ancient treatises on spherical trigonometry by Theodosius and Menelaus.

This curriculum—with its concentration on the study of ancient science at its most advanced—is remarkably similar to Savile's ideas on proper mathematical education first expressed in his lectures of 1570. Half a century on, however, there are some new elements which reflect, perhaps, a more sophisticated view of the sciences than the naïve Platonism of his youth with its lofty dismissal of the practical. It certainly embodies a more realistic pedagogy, no doubt formed by half a century's experience of teaching undergraduates who had little or no prior mathematical training. Although the goal was still to teach students the best science of antiquity, Savile allowed his professors to start slowly with simple ancient handbooks and, for those students who needed them, to provide classes in the vernacular on basic arithmetic. All of the practical mathematical arts—optics, music, mechanics, geography, navigation, and so on—also fell within the professors' provinces, although any kind of astrological divination or the constructing of horoscopes was completely forbidden. The geometry professor was even enjoined to demonstrate occasionally the art of surveying 'in the fields or other places near the University'. Finally, the professors were to be researchers as well as teachers. The professor of astronomy 'in imitation of Ptolemy and Copernicus' was to make nightly observations of the skies; the records of his discoveries were to be added to the Savilian library (which already included, of course, Savile's own notes on the sciences). This accretion of knowledge, he maintained, was 'the only way to confirm or correct the astronomy of the ancients'. Both were also to deposit in the library their 'notes and observations' on the set books (ibid.). Although the later Savilian professors (who included John Wallis, Edmond Halley, and Sir Christopher Wren) may not have strictly adhered to Savile's prescriptions for textbooks and pedagogical practice, his library remained an essential part of the professorship and manuscripts in his collection formed the basis for many editions of ancient texts by Savilian professors for the next century. Savile inaugurated his professorships on 12 July 1620 by delivering a series of lectures on the first book of Euclid's *Elements*. These were published the following year as his *Praelectiones*. He discussed the definitions, axioms, postulates, and the theorems as far as the eighth proposition of book 1, whereupon he handed over the task of expounding Euclid to Briggs, the first professor of geometry. Savile's lectures are very accomplished and are still of scholarly worth.

Aubrey records that Savile's first choice for the geometry professorship was Edmund Gunter, an Oxford graduate and from 1619 the professor of astronomy at Gresham College in London. The interview did not go well:

> [Gunter] came and brought with him his Sector and Quadrant, and fell to resolving of Triangles and doeing a great many fine things. Said the grave knight, 'Doe you call this reading of Geometrie? This is shewing of tricks, man!' and so dismisst him with scorne, and sent for Henry Briggs, from Cambridge. (*Brief Lives*, 268)

Clearly, Savile's interest in practical mathematics still did not run very deep. Briggs (a Yorkshireman) was at that time also a professor of geometry at Gresham and celebrated in particular for his *Logarithmorum chilias prima* of 1617. The professorship of astronomy went to John Bainbridge, whose description of the comet of 1618 had impressed Savile.

Savile died at Eton on 19 February 1622 and, probably in late March, was buried in Eton College chapel next to his son Henry. He was 'buried by torchlight to save expense, though he left £200 for his funeral' (*CSP dom.*, *1619–23*, 371). His grave is marked by a simple tombstone in the chapel. A magnificent monument was placed by his widow in Merton chapel (now in the ante-chapel), on which Savile's bust is flanked by life-size statues of Ptolemy, Euclid, Tacitus, and Chrysostom. R. D. GOULDING

Sources H. Savile, preface, in St John Chrysostom, *Ta heuriskomena*, ed. H. Savile, 8 vols. (1610–12) • M. Aubineau, *Codices Chrysostomici Graeci, I: Britannia et Hibernia*, Documents, Études et Répertoires publiés par l'Institut de Recherche et d'Histoire des Textes, 13 (Paris, 1968) • M. Aubineau, 'Textes hagiographiques dans les dossiers de Sir Henry Savile', *Analecta Bollandiana*, 86 (1968), 83–5 • M. R. A. Bullard, 'Talking heads: the Bodleian Library frieze, its inspiration, sources, designer and significance', *Bodleian Library Record*, 14 (1994), 461–500 • J. W. Clay and J. Lister, 'Autobiography of Sir John Savile of Methley, knight, baron of the exchequer, 1547–1607', *Yorkshire Archaeological Journal*, 15 (1900), 420–27 • P. Costil, *André Dudith, humaniste hongrois, 1533–1589: sa vie, son œuvre et ses manuscrits grecs* (Paris, 1935) • M. Feingold, *The mathematicians' apprenticeship: science, universities and society in England, 1560–1640* (Cambridge and New York, NY, 1984), 47–8, 124–30 • R. D. Goulding, 'Henry Savile and the Tychonic world system', *Journal of the Warburg and Courtauld Institutes*, 58 (1995), 152–79 • R. D. Goulding, 'Testimonia humanitatis: the early lectures of Sir Henry Savile', *Sir Thomas Gresham and Gresham College: studies in the intellectual history of London in the sixteenth and seventeenth centuries*, ed. F. Ames-Lewis (1999), 125–45 • R. D. Goulding, 'Studies on the mathematical and astronomical papers of Sir Henry Savile', PhD diss., U. Lond., Warburg Institute, 1999 • S. L. Greenslade, 'The printer's copy for the Eton Chrysostom, 1610–13', *Studia Patristica*, 7 (1966), 60–64 • J. R. L. Highfield, 'An autograph commonplace book of Sir Henry Savile', *Bodleian Library Record*, 7 (1963), 73–83 • M. F. Iovine, 'Henry Savile lettore di Bernardino Telesio: l'esemplare di 537.C.6 del *De rerum natura*, 1570', *Nouvelles de la République de Lettres*, 18 (1998), 51–84 • J. Lister, 'Bradley Hall: the home of a distinguished family', *Papers, Reports etc. read before the Halifax Antiquarian Society*, 16 (1919), 1–28 • C. Maccagni and G. Derenzini, 'Libri Apollonii qui … desiderantur', *Scienza e filosofia: saggi in onore di Ludovico Geymonat*, ed. C. Mangione (Milan, 1985), 678–96 • G. H. Martin and J. R. L. Highfield, *A history of Merton College, Oxford* (1997) • D. B. Quinn and N. M. Cheshire, *The new found land of Stephen Parmenius* (Toronto, 1972) • R. B. Todd, 'Henry and Thomas Savile in Italy', *Bibliothèque d'Humanisme et Renaissance*, 58 (1996), 439–44 • *Aubrey's Brief lives*, ed. O. L. Dick (1949); pbk edn (1992) • D. Womersley, 'Sir Henry Savile's translation of Tacitus and the political interpretation of Elizabethan texts', *Review of English Studies*, new ser., 42 (1991), 313–42 • Wood, *Ath. Oxon.*, new edn, 2.310–17 • will, PRO, PROB 11/139, fols. 345*v*–347*r* • *CSP dom.*, *1619–23* • *The manuscripts of the Right Honourable F. J. Savile Foljambe, of Osberton*, HMC, 41 (1897) • *Calendar of the manuscripts of the most hon. the marquis of Salisbury*, 5, HMC (1894)

Archives Bodl. Oxf., corresp. and papers • LPL, corresp.

Likenesses M. Gheeraerts the younger, oils, 1621, Bodl. Oxf. [*see illus.*] • M. Gheeraerts the younger, oils, second version, Eton • portrait (after M. Gheeraerts), MHS Oxf. • portrait (after M. Gheeraerts), Merton Oxf.

Wealth at death moderately wealthy: will, 27 Sept 1621, PRO, PROB 11/139, fols. 345*v*–347*r*

Savile, Henry, of Banke (1568–1617), collector of manuscripts, was born on 20 October 1568 at Blaithroyd (sometimes known as the Banke, or Southowram Bank), Halifax, Yorkshire, the second (but oldest surviving) son of Henry Savile (*d.* 1607) and Frances Moyser. There are hints that some of his family were Catholics, but Savile himself seems to have conformed to the established church. He matriculated from Merton College, Oxford, in 1588, during the wardenship of his distant cousin and namesake, Sir Henry Savile, the translator of Tacitus and editor of Chrysostom. Savile graduated BA from St Alban Hall on 30 May 1592, proceeded MA on 30 June 1595, and was licensed to practise medicine on 28 November 1601. Thereafter, he travelled to France, Germany, and Italy, returning as an accomplished scholar in painting, heraldry, and antiquities. With the exception of one letter to William Camden, such activity has left little trace.

Savile is best remembered for his collection of manuscripts, which were in part inherited from his father and perhaps from his grandfather; possibly these had been acquired after the dissolution of the Yorkshire monasteries. Another thirty-one manuscripts came from the collection of a fellow Yorkshireman, John Nettleton, who may himself have been holding them in hope of a restoration of Catholicism. In any event, Byland, Fountains, and Rievaulx abbeys were well represented on Savile's shelves. Details of the collection are in two lists (BL, MSS Harley 1879 and Add. 35213) and a letter of William Crashaw to Isaac Casaubon, though Savile's will suggests that the two lists represent no more than a fraction of it. The library was particularly strong in texts of the chroniclers and in works of theology. While Savile's manuscripts were used for antiquarian purposes by Archbishop James Ussher, Lord William Howard, and others, the most famous instance of such use occurred when William Camden published a passage purportedly from Asser's *Life of Alfred* proving the antiquity of Oxford University, and then claimed that it came from a manuscript in Savile's possession. It is unclear whether Camden was referring to our Henry Savile of Banke or to his father, and the manuscript has disappeared. Though Savile tried to sell his collection during his lifetime, in the end the collection was broken up, with volumes coming to Sir Simonds D'Ewes, Ussher, the earl of Arundel, and Sir Robert Cotton.

Savile died in the parish of St Martin-in-the-Fields, London, on 29 April 1617, and was buried in the old church. There is no record of him having married or had children. F. J. LEVY

Sources A. G. Watson, *The manuscripts of Henry Savile of Banke* (1969) • M. A. Hicks, 'John Nettleton, Henry Savile of Banke, and the post-medieval vicissitudes of the Byland Abbey library', *Northern History*, 26 (1990), 212–17 • J. P. Gilson, 'The library of Henry Savile, of Banke', *Transactions of the Bibliographical Society*, 9 (1906–8), 127–210 • *DNB* • Wood, *Ath. Oxon.*, new edn, 2.201–2 • *Asser's Life of King Alfred: together with the 'Annals of Saint Neots' erroneously ascribed to Asser*, ed. W. H. Stevenson (1904), xxiii–xxviii • J. Parker, *The early history of Oxford*, OHS, 3 (1885), 39–45

Archives BL, Add. MS 35213 • BL, Harley MS 1879

Wealth at death exact sum unknown: Watson, *Manuscripts of Henry Saville*, 10–11

Savile, Sir Henry, first baronet (1579/80–1632). *See under* Savile, Sir John (1546–1607).

Savile, Henry (1642–1687), courtier and diplomat, was born at Rufford Abbey in Nottinghamshire, the younger surviving son of Sir William *Savile, baronet (*d.* 1644) [*see under* Savile family (*per. c.*1480–1644)], of Thornhill near Leeds, and Anne (*d.* 1662), daughter of Thomas *Coventry, first Baron Coventry (1578–1640). George *Savile, later marquess of Halifax (1633–1695), was his elder brother; their only surviving sister, Anne (1634–1667), later married Thomas *Windsor, first earl of Plymouth.

Family and upbringing Although little information has survived on the upbringing of the Savile children, some time was probably spent in France; while the education of the brothers seems to have been piecemeal, they had an excellent command of the French language. In 1661 Henry went to France on a tour which also took him to Spain in the company of Henry Sidney and Robert Spencer, earl of Sunderland (whose sister had married his brother George); he was away for two years. The royalist credentials of the family stood the Saviles in good stead after the Restoration. In 1665 Henry secured the position of groom of the bedchamber to James, duke of York. In 1666 Savile accompanied the duke, who was lord high admiral of the fleet, aboard his flagship the *Royal Charles*, and in the following year was with him when James went to Chatham to inspect the docks after the audacious capture of the *Royal Charles* by Dutch raiders. Savile's final naval service with the duke took place in May 1672 in a battle between the English and Dutch fleets. Later in the year Savile moved into the royal household as groom of the bedchamber to Charles II.

The courtier Savile's attachment to the York household introduced him to the royal court, where he gave full rein to the wilder side of his character. He formed a close friendship with John Wilmot, earl of Rochester, and their circle of associates came to include such egregious courtiers as Harry Killigrew, Francis Rogers, and Arundel Bull. Savile and the others consumed drink and were entertained by prostitutes on a scale that caused comment even at the Caroline court; there were also rumours of nefarious activities involving young boys. In addition to his general debauchery, Savile was at the centre of various scandalous escapades, some of which led to his suspension from court. He became emotionally entangled with the duke of York's wife, Anne Hyde. In 1669 he was imprisoned for having carried a challenge to a duel from his uncle, Sir William Coventry, to the duke of Buckingham; after being released Savile was barred from court and took himself off to Paris. In 1671, while a guest at Althorp, the residence of his former travelling companion the earl of Sunderland, he attempted to seduce Elizabeth, widow of Joceline Percy, earl of Northumberland. He entered her bedroom during the night, but she resisted and created a commotion. Savile fled the house, and according to one report the infuriated Sunderland and his wife 'breath[ed] nothing but battell murther and suddain death' against the miscreant (*Letters of John Wilmot*, 70). In 1674 Savile engaged in fisticuffs with John Sheffield, earl of Mulgrave. They then fought a duel in which Rochester served as Savile's second. Savile was suspended again from court in 1675 for having insulted the duke of York; as on other occasions, he retired to Paris. The years of heavy drinking and dissolute behaviour took their inevitable toll. Although physically robust and bulky (Rochester occasionally made fun of his corpulence), he fell victim to venereal disease. In 1678 he complained that 'the return of my venereall paines have throwne mee back to dry mutton & dyett drinke' (ibid., 182), and he was forced to resort to the standard treatment of the day: 'I confesse I wonder att myself and that masse of mercury that has gone downe my throate in seven monthes' (ibid., 197–8).

This is one theme in Savile's life: that of the irresponsible younger son of a noble family, who lacked paternal control, mixed with court rakes, had no landed property (although he had an annual income of £1000 from one of his father's estates and received an allowance from his brother, George), frequented the royal court, but had a deplorable reputation which ruled him out as a serious contender in the marriage stakes: he never succeeded in securing the wealthy wife that he fervently desired. There was, however, more to him than the jovial, drunken buffoon. He acquired public responsibilities in which he displayed considerable intelligence and acumen. Indeed, had his personal conduct been more circumspect, these qualities might have been put to more systematic use by the crown.

The diplomat In September 1672 Savile was sent to Paris as envoy-extraordinary in support, first, of the ambassador Sidney Godolphin, and then of his replacement, Sunderland. Earlier in the year France and England had declared war on the United Provinces, where William III of Orange was swept to power on a wave of popular support. William sought better relations with Charles II of England. Savile went to France to co-ordinate action by the French and English fleets, but also to reassure Louis XIV that Charles II's resolution was not wavering. Savile remained in Paris for about three weeks; he had an audience with the king and met senior political figures such as Pomponne and Seignelay. He also took the opportunity to heal the breach with Sunderland. This experience of diplomacy pleased Savile. He wrote to Lord Arlington, asking to be used further:

> if I am capable of serving the King at all, I think my small talents will be of most use abroad, where I have spent soe much of my life, that I shall hardly bee an absolute stranger to any place his majestye or yr lp may be pleased to send me. (Durrant Cooper, 28)

His request was not immediately granted, but he was rewarded with the aforementioned post in the royal household.

In 1673 Savile added another dimension to his career by securing an uncontested seat in parliament for the new constituency of Newark. However, questions arose over the legality of the writ that authorized the election and in 1677 a new one was issued. On this occasion Savile defeated a rival, but only after 'more news and tumult then ever poor mortal was troubled with', and 'four days swallowing more good ale and ill sack than one would have thought a country town could have held' (Durrant Cooper, xvii).

In 1678 Savile was sent again to France as envoy-extraordinary. He arrived in Paris in August and remained until October, when he returned to England. Over the winter Sunderland, the ambassador, was recalled and to his delight Savile was appointed in his place. Savile's joy was tempered when he learned that he would not have the title of ambassador, only of envoy-extraordinary. He went in February 1679, and apart from a brief visit to England in July 1680 remained there until his recall in March 1682. Three major topics occupied him. One was the Dutch War (1672–8) and its aftermath. Peace terms, mediated by the English, were reached at an international congress in Nijmegen. Savile observed how far France fulfilled the terms which it signed in the treaty, but was soon reporting a new crisis: Louis XIV's policy of *réunions* (the occupation of territory whose status had not been clarified at Nijmegen). In conjunction with Dutch representatives, Savile submitted joint objections to the French actions, especially the seizure of Luxembourg. The second main subject to interest Savile was the marriage between Charles II of Spain and Marie-Louise d'Orléans in 1679. In one sense this could be seen simply as the latest in a sequence of Franco-Spanish marriages celebrated since early in the century. On the other hand it heralded a possible *rapprochement* between France and Spain, which would have implications for international relations in Europe. The third topic was the persecution of the Huguenots by Louis XIV, and to this Savile devoted an increasing proportion of his time.

To his superiors in London, Savile described the prohibition placed on Huguenots from visiting their sick, the destruction of Huguenot churches, the offer of tax incentives by the French government to gain converts, and the use of *dragonnades*: the billeting of soldiers on Huguenot families. 'In Poictou', wrote Savile, 'the quartering souldiers upon them has made soe many proselytes that the same trick is to bee tried in Languedoc' (Durrant Cooper, 198). Savile risked diplomatic impropriety by attending the Huguenot church at Charenton near Paris; members approached him for help in leaving France, or in finding spouses in England for their children. Such importuning placed him in a delicate situation, for the French government had forbidden Huguenot emigration, and Savile could not be seen to be aiding Huguenots to break the law. In private he favoured England accepting as many Huguenots as possible, not least because a high proportion practised economically beneficial trades and crafts.

A more immediate concern was the status of English protestants in France. Savile had an audience with Louis XIV on 14 January 1681, during which he argued that English subjects should be exempted from anti-Huguenot legislation. 'Hee [Louis XIV] seemed to hearken favourably enough to what I said … and told mee hee would have the matter examined' (Durrant Cooper, 171). Three days later Savile was informed that the king agreed, subject to the English government's extending similar immunity to French Catholics in England. Savile regarded this as a major achievement, but incidents occurred that required his intervention. In February 1681 a Mistress Bikerton lay on her deathbed in Paris, and was visited by a Catholic priest who urged her to convert. Savile made a formal protest. In July 1681 Sir William Hamilton fell dangerously ill; a priest from St Sulpice gained access to him at midnight and put pressure on him to convert. Once again Savile protested, and on this occasion secured an apology from the priest. When he met French ministers and appealed for lenient treatment of the Huguenots, Savile was rebuffed. He was challenged over the persecution and execution of Catholics in England, and when Oliver Plunket, Catholic archbishop of Armagh, was executed in July 1681, this was held up to Savile as an example of English intolerance and barbarity.

Return to England When Savile returned to England in March 1682, two positions awaited him. During his visit in July 1680 he had been appointed vice-chamberlain to the king, and in January 1682 he was made commissioner of the Admiralty. Most of his time thereafter was occupied by the responsibilities attaching to these posts. By the mid-1680s several of his former friends, including Rochester, had died, and his own health was giving cause for concern. In September 1687, 'his viscera gangrened and his liver parched' (Kenyon, 241n.), he went to Paris for an operation. He failed to recover and died on 6 October 1687.

Savile's life illustrates many of the vicissitudes of the civil war and post-Restoration periods, although he himself was not given to lengthy introspection on the subject. He approached life with an attitude of amused and detached acceptance, and formed friendships on the basis of affection rather than political calculation (one of his closest friends of later years was the republican Algernon Sidney, hardly a name to flaunt before the Stuarts). His correspondence is largely silent on his cultural tastes; it is hard to assess what literature, theatre (apart from the bawdy variety), or music meant to him. His religious observances were minimally conventional, although his encounters with Huguenots gave him a respect for people willing to make material sacrifices in defence of their principles. The most constant threads running through his life were his devotion towards his brother and nephews, and his love of Paris. Many of his happiest years were spent there, and there is a certain congruity in the fact that it was in that city that he died.

DAVID J. STURDY

Sources W. D. Cooper, ed., *Savile correspondence: letters to and from H. Savile*, CS, 71 (1858) • *The letters of John Wilmot, earl of Rochester*, ed. J. Treglown (1980) • Pepys, *Diary*, vols. 6, 9 • *CSP dom.*, *1666–7*; *1671–2*; *1683–4* • J. P. Kenyon, *Robert Spencer, earl of Sunderland, 1641–1702* (1958) • A. Sydney, *Letters … to the honourable Henry Savile, ambassador in France in the year 1679* (1742) • J. Scott, *Algernon Sidney and the English republic, 1623–1677* (1988) • J. Scott, *Algernon Sidney and the Restoration crisis, 1677–1683* (1991) • [H. Savile], *A true relation of the engagement of his majesties fleet under the command of his royal highness, with the Dutch fleet, May 28. 1672, in a letter from H.S. … to the earl of Arlington* (1672) • PRO, SP78 (Foreign) France, 126–136, 143–145, 151 • *DNB*

Archives BL, letter-books, ref. (70–71) • Chatsworth House, Derbyshire, corresp. • Notts. Arch., papers | BL, letters to Sir R. Bulstrode, Egerton MS 3678 • BL, letters to Lord Essex, Stowe MSS 200, 210, 212 • BL, letters to Lord Halifax and earl of Clarendon, Add. MS 17017 • BL, letters to Sir L. Jenkins, copies, Add. MS 4205 • BL, corresp. with H. Coventry and Sir L. Jenkins, Add. MS 72582 • BL, key to his cypher with Lord Sunderland, Add. MS 40677 • BL, letters to H. Sydney, Add. MS 32680

Savile, Jeremy [Jeremiah] (*d.* in or before **1667**?), composer, was named by John Playford among the principal London teachers 'For the Voyce or Viole' during the Commonwealth (*Musicall Banquet*, 1651). He is known as a composer of songs and glees and is reasonably well represented in the anthologies of such pieces that were published in the second half of the seventeenth century. Among his earliest published pieces are 'I will not trust thy tempting graces', 'No more blind boy', and ''Tis but a frown', all of which appeared in Playford's *Select Musicall Ayres and Dialogues* of 1653. His songs were included also in Playford's *The Musical Companion* (1667), compiled for and containing much of the repertory of the Old Jewry music society, a catch club of which Playford and Savile were members. Savile's 'Here's a health unto his majesty', which is contained in the collection, may have been the club anthem and was possibly in use before the Restoration. Savile is not listed as a member of the society in *The Musical Companion*, suggesting that he had died by the time it was published, perhaps during the plague in 1666.

PETER LYNAN

Sources I. Spink, *English song: Dowland to Purcell* (1974) • C. L. Day and E. B. Murrie, *English song-books, 1651–1702* (1940) • *New Grove*, 2nd edn

Savile, Sir John (*d.* **1505**). *See under* Savile family (*per. c.*1480–1644).

Savile, Sir John (**1546–1607**), judge, was born on 26 March 1546 at Elland in Yorkshire, the first of three sons of Henry Savile (*d.* 1566), landowner, of Over Bradley, Yorkshire, and his wife, Elizabeth, daughter of Robert Ramsden of Yorkshire and his wife, Elizabeth. His brothers were Sir Henry *Savile (1549–1622), the mathematician and classical scholar, and Thomas *Savile (*d.* 1593), the scholar and translator. He received a basic grounding in the classics, reading, among others, works by Horace and Cicero in the four years before matriculating at Brasenose College, Oxford, in 1561. He left without taking a degree, and set to the study of law under the auspices of his father. He entered Clement's Inn in October 1564, but moved to the Middle Temple in February 1565.

Savile succeeded his father on 11 October 1566. He was called to the bar in February 1573, after which he began to practise on the northern circuit. On 11 April 1575 he married Jane (1554–1587), daughter of Richard Garth of Morden in Surrey. The couple had one son, Sir Henry Savile, baronet [*see below*], and two daughters. John Savile was made a bencher of the inn in autumn 1586, when he read—tediously, it is said—fifteen lectures on the statute expropriating chantries (1 Edward VI c. 14). Jane Savile died on 11 January 1587, and Savile married Elizabeth (*d.* 1593), daughter of Thomas Wentworth of North Elmsall, Yorkshire, and widow of Richard Tempest of Bowling, Yorkshire, on 23 December. They had one son, John Savile (*d.* 1651), and two daughters. Elizabeth Savile died on 7 January 1593. John Savile was created sergeant-at-law in 1594. On 16 June 1597 he married Dorothy (*d.* 1602), daughter of Thomas Wentworth, second Baron Wentworth of Nettlestead, and his second wife, Anne or Agnes, and widow of Sir Martin Frobisher. They had no children. Savile was appointed baron of the court of exchequer on 1 July 1598 and reappointed on 14 April 1603; he held the office until his death. His wife died on 3 January 1602, and he married Margery Weston (*d.* in or after 1607), daughter of Ambrose Peake of London and widow of one Thwaites of London and of Sir Jerome Weston of Essex, on 24 December 1603. Like his previous marriage, this one produced no children.

Like many lawyers of his time, Savile played his part in public life. He represented Newton, Lancashire, in the parliament of 1572 (probably gaining the seat because of his connection with William Fleetwood, then recorder of the borough). Among other offices, he served as JP for co. Durham from about 1576 and for the West Riding of Yorkshire from about 1580 (he was added to the quorum for both in 1583), and as commissioner for ecclesiastical causes in the diocese of Durham from 1576 to 1577. As justice of assize on the northern circuit from 1598 to 1607, he could not avoid getting embroiled in the politics surrounding the council in the north, to which he was appointed in 1599, following the orthodox common lawyers' line of restraining its jurisdiction and subordinating it to the courts of common law. However, Savile did not descend to the overt rudeness of his circuit companion, Christopher Yelverton, who blatantly snubbed the lord president, Thomas Cecil, second Baron Burghley, when he attempted to sit on the bench in 1601. Savile was named of the quorum of the peace for Cumberland, Northumberland, and Westmorland in 1601.

Throughout his life Savile maintained strong Yorkshire connections. He lived at Bradley Hall, near Halifax, from 1580, and in 1590 purchased the manor of Methley, near Leeds, where he substantially rebuilt the house, which served as his principal residence from 1593. He was a member of the Society of Antiquaries from about 1591, and a law report (BL, Lansdowne MS 1101), edited and printed by John Richardson as *Les reports de Sir John Savile* (1675), has been attributed to him. He died at Serjeants' Inn, London, on 2 February 1607 and was buried at St Dunstan-in-the-West, London, the next day. His heart was interred at Methley church, where a monument was erected to his memory.

Savile's son **Sir Henry Savile**, first baronet (1579/80–1632), landowner, entered the Middle Temple in 1593 and matriculated at Merton College, Oxford, on 4 February 1594, aged fourteen, but did not take a degree. James VI and I knighted him on 23 July 1603. He was returned as MP for Aldborough, Yorkshire, in 1604 and 1614. Savile was created a baronet on 29 June 1611. He was appointed vice-president of the king's council in the north before 1627, was sheriff of Yorkshire from 1628 to 1629, and was knight of the shire in 1629. Savile married Mary (*d.* in or after 1632), daughter of John Dent of London and his wife, Alice. The couple had three sons, all of whom predeceased Savile. He died on 23 June 1632, and was succeeded by his half-brother, John Savile. DAVID IBBETSON

Sources 'Autobiography of Sir John Savile', ed. J. W. Clay and J. Lister, *Yorkshire Archaeological Journal*, 15 (1898–9), 420–42 • HoP, *Commons, 1558–1603*, 3.350–51 • J. Savile, *Les reports de Sir John Savile*, ed. J. Richardson (1675) • R. R. Reid, *The king's council in the north* (1921) • H. S. Darbyshire, *History of Methley*, Thoresby Society, 35 (1937) [for 1934] • Baker, *Serjeants*, 535 • J. H. Baker, *Readers and readings in the inns of court and chancery*, SeldS, suppl. ser., 13 (2000), 167 • H. A. C. Sturgess, ed., *Register of admissions to the Honourable Society of the Middle Temple, from the fifteenth century to the year 1944*, 3 vols. (1949) • C. T. Martin, ed., *Minutes of parliament of the Middle Temple*, 4 vols. (1904–5), vols. 1–2 • Sainty, *Judges* • T. W. Hanson, 'Halifax builders in Oxford', *Transactions of the Halifax Antiquarian Society* (1928), 253

Likenesses effigy on monument, *c.*1607, Methley church, Yorkshire • oils (in robes), Harvard U., law school • painting (in robes; different), repro. in E. Hailstone, *Yorkshire worthies* (1868), no. 22; belonged to family in 1868

Savile, John, first Baron Savile of Pontefract (1556–1630), politician, was the eldest son of Sir Robert *Savile (*d.* 1585) [*see under* Savile family (*per. c.*1480–1644)] of Barkston, Lincolnshire, and Anne, daughter and coheir of Sir Robert Hussey of Linwood in Blankney, Lincolnshire, and widow of Mathew Thimbleby of Poolam in Edington, Lincolnshire. Educated at Trinity College, Cambridge, and Lincoln's Inn, he began his parliamentary career in 1588 as MP for Hull, but afterwards settled in Yorkshire at Howley Hall, a grandiose house near Batley. By 1597 he had obtained the influential office of *custos rotulorum* for the West Riding, and was shortly afterwards knighted. Savile married twice: first, Katherine, daughter of Charles Willoughby, second Baron Willoughby of Parham, who died without issue; and second, on 20 November 1586, Elizabeth (*b. c.*1568), daughter of Sir Edward Carey or Cary of Aldenham, Hertfordshire. They had five sons, including Thomas *Savile, and three daughters.

Described as 'extremely ambitious, arrogant, hot tempered and unscrupulous' (Cliffe, 262), Savile was also intelligent, articulate, and opinionated. Possibly his reputation has suffered as a result of his behaviour during the notorious parliamentary election of 3 October 1597 for the Yorkshire county seats, when he prevented a poll by forcing his way out through the gates of York Castle. A formal complaint dated 13 February 1614 from Sir Edmund Sheffield, lord president of the council in the north, criticizing Savile's disorderly conduct as *custos rotulorum*, resulted in a citation before Star Chamber. Sheffield may have had his own reasons for impugning Savile, but the latter (having resigned the office to forestall imminent dismissal), assigned it to Sir Thomas Wentworth in the belief that in the fullness of time he would step down. When invited to do so by Buckingham three years later, however, Wentworth declined, quoting the deceased Lord Ellesmere's opinion that Sir John's behaviour had 'ill beseemed a man of his place and calling' (Cooper, 83, 99). Savile never forgave him and their resulting enmity became a dominant factor in Yorkshire politics for more than a decade.

Nowhere was their hostility more brazenly paraded than during the elections for the county seats between 1620 and 1628. Both sides made prodigious efforts to muster support, and after his electoral defeats in 1620 and 1625 Savile's allegations of Wentworth's malpractice became the subject of Commons inquiries. It is, however, as a House of Commons man that Savile may be seen at his best. Not given to withholding his opinions, his frequent contributions to debates seem to have been shrewd, apposite, sometimes witty, and, on at least one occasion, innovative. Commons privileges, supply, and redress, and fierce promotion of local interests were recurring themes. In King James's first parliament Savile scorned the Bill of Purveyors as a recipe for 'Hanging the innocent, damning the ignorant, raysing rebellion and starving the king' (*Diary of Robert Bowyer*, 121–2, 123n.). Suspicious of James's intentions in 1624, he declared that 'It was fit to enable the people before they charged them' (Russell, 181), but offered generous supply in return for the abolition of pretermitted customs, for which he had long been campaigning.

In the crucial debate on the six subsidies, Savile's proposal that a grant be made conditional upon establishing the 'proper procedure', namely the right of parliament to decide questions of military objectives and campaigns, was at first eagerly espoused, but eventually defeated by those who argued that it constituted an unwarranted trespass upon the rights of the executive. In the Commons, Savile was ready with statistical evidence to defend the interests of the northern clothiers, as in his oft-quoted summary of the state of the industry during a debate on 20 May 1604 on a proposed new patent for dyeing and dressing cloth. Though by 1626 he was Buckingham's 'man' in Yorkshire, Savile could still insist that the king 'should not presume of more from [his subjects] than can be paid', for 'No man will be willing to give his money to a bottomless gulf' (Bidwell and Jansson, 249).

In 1626 Savile's relentless pursuit of primacy in the West Riding was furthered by the rewards of Buckingham's favour: in June came his appointment to the coveted post of comptroller of the household, and the following month to the vice-presidency of the council and to a commission for augmenting the king's revenues. Then Wentworth's removal from the commission of the peace in July during his shrievalty allowed Savile at last to regain his former place as *custos rotulorum*. On 13 July 1626 the royal charter he had been negotiating on behalf of the leading townsmen of Leeds was granted and he took office as the alderman (with John Harrison as his deputy). On 8 November he was sworn of the privy council. In the following year he was appointed receiver of the compositions of northern recusants, and on 21 July 1628 was created Baron Savile of Pontefract.

Through his alliance with Buckingham, his enthusiastic espousal of the privy seal loan of 1627, and leniency towards the papists, however, Savile laid up for himself a fund of resentment in Yorkshire which contributed to his rapid downfall after the duke's death on 23 August 1628, which, unfortunately for Savile, coincided with Wentworth's return to favour. Within two months his enemy had urged upon the privy council a complaint against him for defrauding the king's revenue by taking substantial bribes from northern recusants. By the end of the year Savile had been removed not only from the receivership but also from his places as vice-president of the council and *custos rotulorum*, although he remained on the bench. He also retained the comptrollership—until June 1629, when he was replaced by Sir Henry Vane—but was debarred from exercising the office in person. Wentworth's triumph was complete by December 1629, when he succeeded Scrope as president of the council.

Sir John Savile died at his home, Howley Hall, on 31 August 1630. His burial on 14 September in St Anne's Chapel, Batley parish church, is recorded in a fulsome inscription by his daughter, Anne Leigh, on a monumental brass. Ownership of the great Kirkstall ironworks on the Aire made Savile one of the leading ironmasters of the period. He had inherited the property together with extensive former abbey lands in the West Riding from his father, an illegitimate son of Sir Henry Savile of Thornhill, who had provided handsomely for him. The valuation of £2200 per annum placed upon his estate in 1631 was said by his son to be a conservative estimate. JOAN KIRBY

Sources J. J. Cartwright, *Chapters in the history of Yorkshire* (1872) • R. R. Reid, *The king's council in the north* (1921) • J. P. Cooper, ed., *Wentworth papers, 1597–1628*, CS, 4th ser., 12 (1973) • GEC, *Peerage* • *Calendar of the manuscripts of the most hon. the marquis of Salisbury*, 7, HMC, 9 (1899), 411–13 • HoP, *Commons, 1558–1603* • S. P. Salt, 'Sir Thomas Wentworth and the parliamentary representation of Yorkshire, 1614–1628', *Northern History*, 16 (1980), 130–68 • J. T. Cliffe, *The Yorkshire gentry from the Reformation to the civil war* (1969) • W. Notestein, *The House of Commons, 1604–1610* (1971) • W. Notestein, F. H. Relf, and H. Simpson, eds., *Commons debates, 1621*, 7 vols. (1935) • R. E. Ruigh, *The parliament of 1624: politics and foreign policy* (1971) • W. B. Bidwell and M. Jansson, eds., *Proceedings in parliament, 1626*, 2: *House of Commons* (1992) • *The parliamentary diary of Robert Bowyer, 1606–1607*, ed. D. H. Willson (1931) • T. L. Moir, *The Addled Parliament of 1614* (1958) • C. Russell, *Parliaments and English politics, 1621–1629* (1979) • F. Pogson, 'Wentworth, the Savites and the office of *Custos rotulorum* of the West Riding', *Northern History*, 34 (1998), 205–10 • M. Sheard, *Records of the parish of Batley* (1894), 137–8, 275 • *The Plumpton letters and papers*, ed. J. Kirby, CS, 5th ser., 8 (1996), 220

Wealth at death £2200 p.a.: PRO, court of wards Feodaries' Surveys, wards 5/49; Borth. Inst., wills 1630–31, vol. 41/A, fols. 314–16

Savile [*formerly* Savile Lumley], **John, first Baron Savile of Rufford (1818–1896)**, diplomatist, born on 6 January 1818, was the second, but first surviving, illegitimate son of John Lumley-Savile, eighth earl of Scarbrough (1788–1856), his mother, Agnes, being of French origin. His grandfather, John Lumley (1761–1835), elder brother of Sir William Lumley, was the fourth of the seven sons of Richard Lumley Saunderson, fourth earl of Scarbrough, and Barbara, sister and heir of Sir George Savile (1726–1784) of Rufford Abbey, and a descendant of the Saviles of Thornhill and Lupset [*see* Savile, George, marquess of Halifax]. Soon after graduating from King's College, Cambridge, in 1782, John Lumley, the grandfather, assumed the name of Savile by royal licence, according to the will of his uncle, Sir George. Having taken orders, he became a prebendary of York, and he succeeded as seventh earl of Scarbrough on the death of his brother, Richard, in 1832, but never took his seat in the House of Lords. On his death three years later from the results of a fall in the hunting-field, he was succeeded by his son, John Lumley-Savile, eighth earl of Scarbrough, who graduated MA from Trinity Hall, Cambridge, and represented Nottinghamshire in parliament (1826–35). He was maimed as a boy, owing, it is said, to his father's violence. He never married, but left five illegitimate children. His large property at Rufford, Nottinghamshire, and in the West Riding he bequeathed to his second surviving son, Henry, a captain in the 2nd Life Guards, owner of the famous racehorse, Cremorne, winner of the Derby in 1872 and the Ascot Cup in 1873. On his death in 1881 the estate passed to the fourth surviving son, Augustus William (1829–1887), who held the post of assistant master of the ceremonies in the royal household for many years previous to his death at Cannes in April 1887.

John Savile Lumley, as he was called at that time, obtained a nomination in August 1841 as supernumerary clerk in the librarian's department at the Foreign Office, and in the following November he accompanied John Fane, eleventh earl of Westmorland, to Berlin as private secretary and attaché. On 5 July 1842 he was appointed attaché at Berlin, and obtained a grasp of diplomatic practice during the next seven years, while his chief was endeavouring to mediate in the Schleswig-Holstein difficulty between Denmark and Prussia. In 1849 he was transferred to St Petersburg, and in October 1854 he became secretary of legation at Washington, being employed on special service at New York some months before his removal to Madrid in February 1858. On 14 April 1860 he was appointed secretary to the embassy at Constantinople, but at the end of that year he was transferred in the same capacity to St Petersburg, where he acted from time to time as chargé d'affaires, and where he was in January 1866 elected member of the Russian Imperial Academy of Fine Arts. The next summer he was promoted envoy to the king of Saxony; and when, a few months later, that mission was withdrawn, he went as envoy to the Swiss confederation. In October 1868 Savile Lumley was transferred to Brussels, and in August 1883, after forty-two years' service, he was promoted to be British minister at Rome; he was sworn of the privy council in the same year. While at Rome he represented Great Britain at the International Sanitary Conference (1885), and started some valuable excavations at Civita Lavinia (Lanuvium). Of the numerous objects there found in marble, terracotta, bronze, and glass, some were presented to the British Museum, while others went to form the Savile Gallery in the Nottingham Castle Museum (1891).

In September 1888 Savile Lumley was succeeded at Rome by the marquess of Dufferin, and retired from the service; the following month he was raised to the peerage as Baron Savile of Rufford in Nottinghamshire; he sat as a tory. In the previous year he had dropped the name of Lumley, and had succeeded to the estate and mansion of Rufford Abbey on the death of his brother Augustus.

Baron Savile greatly improved the abbey and its demesnes. In the former he placed his fine collection of pictures. He showed great judgment as a collector, had a fine perception and a wide knowledge of art, and himself painted some vigorous landscapes and sea pieces. He was elected an honorary member of the Royal Academy at Antwerp, and from 1890 was a trustee of the National Gallery, to which he presented *Christ at the Column*, by Velázquez, and other oil paintings. He was created a CB in 1873, KCB in 1878, and GCB in 1885. He died unmarried at Rufford Abbey on 28 November 1896 and was buried at Bilsthorpe, Nottinghamshire. The title passed to his nephew, John Savile Lumley (1853–1931), son of his brother, Frederick Savile Lumley, rector of Bilsthorpe, who entered the diplomatic service in 1873.

THOMAS SECCOMBE, *rev.* H. C. G. MATTHEW

Sources *The Times* (30 Nov 1896) • *Nottingham Daily Guardian* (30 Nov 1896) • *FO List* (1896) • GEC, *Peerage* • *GM*, 3rd ser., 1 (1856), 771
Archives Notts. Arch., corresp. and papers | BL, letters to Sir Austen Layard, Add. MSS 39038–39119, *passim* • Bodl. Oxf., corresp. with Sir John Crampton • Lpool RO, corresp. with Lord Derby
Likenesses S. van den Kerkhove, bronze bust, Gov. Art Coll.
Wealth at death £43,766 5*s.* 6*d.*: resworn probate, Feb 1898, *CGPLA Eng. & Wales*

Savile, Sir Robert (*d.* 1585). *See under* Savile family (*per.* *c.*1480–1644).

Savile, Thomas (*d.* 1593), scholar and translator, was born at Over Bradley, near Halifax, the second son of Henry Savile (*d.* 1566) of Over Bradley and his wife, Elizabeth Ramsden. Sir Henry *Savile (1549–1622), one of the most famous scholars of his generation, was Thomas's elder brother. Sir John *Savile (1546–1607) was another brother. The precise date of Thomas's birth is unknown, but since he obtained his bachelor's degree at Merton College, Oxford, in 1580 it may have been about 1560. He became a fellow of Merton College in 1581 and master of arts in 1584. He taught the Greek language, and had special interests in Aristotelian philosophy, which at the time was undergoing a revival at Oxford due to the influence of John Case, and also in ancient mathematics and astronomy. In religion he was a supporter of puritanism, as is evident from his friendship with John Rainolds. Like his brother, Thomas travelled extensively in Europe, and made contact with leading scholars. Between 1588 and 1591 he visited several continental centres of learning, notably Breslau, where he stayed with the polymath Andreas Dudith, and Padua, where he had prolonged contact with Gian Vincenzo Pinelli. Letters from Italy reveal a passionate appreciation of Italian scenery and architecture. After his return to England he served as senior proctor at Oxford University in 1592, and in September that year presided over a visit by Elizabeth I. He died suddenly from causes unknown, while on a visit to London, on 12 January 1593. He was buried that month in Merton College chapel.

Savile's range of scholarly contacts is evident from his correspondence with eminent contemporaries such as Isaac Casaubon, Jean Hotman, and William Camden. He was also a friend of the celebrated Hungarian explorer Stephen Parmenius. He published nothing, but there are three surviving manuscripts of his Latin translation of 'Introduction to the phenomena' by the ancient astronomer Geminus (two at Milan and one at Munich), along with extensive notes, and also of two mathematical treatises, 'De rationum additione et subtractione' and 'De rationibus' (also at Milan). His *adversaria* on the ancient geographer Strabo and on some works of Ptolemy, as well as transcriptions and notes in manuscripts are in the Savile collection in the Bodleian Library, Oxford. So accomplished a Greek philologist, mathematician, and astronomer might, given a longer life, have accomplished scholarly work on ancient mathematical and astronomical texts that would have complemented, if not surpassed, the achievements of his better-known brother.

ROBERT B. TODD

Sources R. B. Todd, 'Geminus and the Pseudo-Proclan *Sphaera*', *Catalogus translationum et commentariorum*, 8 [forthcoming] • R. B. Todd, 'Henry and Thomas Savile in Italy', *Bibliothèque d'Humanisme et Renaissance*, 58 (1996), 439–44 • M. Feingold, *The mathematicians' apprenticeship: science, universities and society in England, 1560–1640* (1984), 130–33 • Wood, *Ath. Oxon.*, new edn, 1.591; 2.257–8 • Wood, *Ath. Oxon.*: *Fasti* (1815), 227 • *Reg. Oxf.*, 2/1.93, 246; 2/2.190, 194; 2/3.88–9 • C. Plummer, ed., *Elizabethan Oxford: reprints of rare tracts*, OHS, 8 (1887), 250, 252, 256 • J. M. Fletcher, ed., *Registrum annalium collegii Mertonensis, 1567–1603*, OHS, new ser., 24 (1976) • P. Costil, *André Dudith: humaniste hongrois, 1533–1589. Sa vie, son oeuvre, et ses manuscrits grecs* (1935), 306–7 and index • *The new found land of Stephen Parmenius: the life and writings of a Hungarian poet, drowned on a voyage from Newfoundland, 1583*, ed. and trans. D. B. Quinn and N. M. Cheshire [1972], 13–16, 26–37, 216 • 'Savile, Sir Henry (1549–1622)', *DNB*
Archives Biblioteca Ambrosiana, Milan, Pinelli MSS • Bodl. Oxf., Savile MSS

Savile, Thomas, first earl of Sussex (*bap.* 1590, *d.* 1657x9), politician, was baptized on 14 September 1590 at Doddington-Pigot, Lincolnshire, the third son and heir of John *Savile, first Baron Savile of Pontefract (1556–1630), and his second wife, Elizabeth (*b.* *c.*1568), daughter of Sir Edward Carey or Cary of Aldenham and Berkhamsted, Hertfordshire, and his second wife, Katherine. Thomas's grandfather Sir Robert *Savile (*d.* 1585) [*see under* Savile family (*per.* *c.*1480–1644)] purchased the Howley estate near Batley and began work on a fine family house completed by the first Baron Savile. Thomas's father was probably the wealthiest man in Yorkshire and served as vice-president of the council of the north from 1626 to 1628. Championing the interests of the West Riding freeholders and clothiers, he was notorious for his ongoing quarrel with Sir Thomas Wentworth, later earl of Strafford. His spectacular mansion house at Howley was completed about 1590. Situated on the hill south of Morley township, in the parish of Batley in the West Riding, its construction took many years and allegedly cost £100,000.

Thomas Savile lived at Howley from about 1593 and was admitted to Peterhouse, Cambridge, on 2 October 1608, and the Inner Temple in November 1610. He was knighted at Whitehall on 6 March 1617 and soon after was appointed steward of Wakefield. He was also a trustee of Batley grammar school from about 1620. His first wife was Frances (*d.* 1634x40), widow of Sir John Leveson and daughter of Sir Thomas Sondes of Throwley, Kent, and his second wife, Margaret, daughter of William Brooke, Baron Cobham; they had no children, and his wife was still alive in 1634. In conjunction with his father Savile defeated Wentworth in the county election on 10 January 1624. After the contest his argument with Sir Francis Wortley at Castle Hall, York, led to a lengthy feud and an inconclusive duel between them. In the first county election of 1625 popular support for the Saviles thronged the castle yard at York and Sir Richard Beaumont described the occasion as more like 'a rebellion than an election' (Cust, 148).

Early political career From 1626 the reputations of Sir Thomas and his father as 'country' politicians declined as the duke of Buckingham drew them into his patronage. Sir Thomas was appointed a gentleman of the privy chamber on 29 December 1626 and elected MP for York city on 3 March 1628. Created Viscount Savile and baron of Castlebar in the Irish peerage on 11 June 1628, he also succeeded his father as second Baron Savile of Pontefract in the English peerage at his death on 31 August 1630. On the same day he seized his sister Mrs Anne Leigh's interest in his father's valuable ironworks at Kirkstall, allegedly compelling her trustee Mr James Field to sign a refutation of her claim at knife-point. His actions provoked the tenants to riot and he was accused of tampering with witnesses' depositions in the ensuing Star Chamber case. In 1634 he directed his lawyers to settle his estate in a manner less prone to heavy fines. He invited further unpopularity in 1638 when he enclosed land on the highway from West Ardsley to the clothing towns of Bradford, Halifax, Huddersfield, and Birstall. He subsequently suffered plebeian poaching and robbery on his estates at Lindle Hill and New Park, Wakefield. In 1638 Sir Edward Osborne, vice-president of the council of the north, complained of Savile's frequent attempts to mislead or obstruct the council, reflecting that he 'hath always carried a disaffected heart, not only to me but my Lord Deputy' (K. Sharpe, *The Personal Rule of Charles I*, 1992, 450). Savile was later imprisoned in the Fleet in 1639, having to petition the House of Lords for his liberty.

During the bishops' wars Savile secretly undermined the king's war effort, and Clarendon's later claims of his correspondence with the covenanters were well founded. Savile wrote to the Scots in early July 1640 encouraging them to invade, promising aid from the high sheriff and gentry of Yorkshire. Clarendon explained Savile's activism as rooted in 'particular malice to the earl of Strafford, which he had sucked in with his milk' (Clarendon, *Hist. rebellion*, 6.393). When the Scots rejected his unqualified offers as insufficient, Savile allegedly sent them an engagement promising military support in which he skilfully forged the signatures of disaffected peers. On 28 August he signed the twelve peers' petition calling for a parliament, and he was among the nobles named to treat with the Scots commissioners at Ripon that September.

Courtier Soon after the summoning of the Long Parliament, Savile married Lady Anne Villiers (*b. c.*1623), daughter of Christopher *Villiers, first earl of Anglesey (*d.* 1630), and his wife, Elizabeth, daughter of Thomas Sheldon of Howby, Leicestershire. Savile was appointed a privy councillor on 19 February 1641, and was also given custody of New Park in the Forest of Galtres, and Sheriff Hutton Park, formerly held by Strafford. That April he briefly succeeded Strafford as lord lieutenant of Yorkshire and lord president of the council of the north.

Savile was among the witnesses against Strafford at his trial, but after attempted delays 'wherein to recollect his notes' (Russell, 296–7), actually voted in favour of Strafford at his attainder, objecting to it as an infringement of the House of Lords' privileges. When the earl of Stamford answered him impolitely, another duel nearly ensued. By the spring of 1641 his limited sympathy for the Scots 'was rapidly detaching him from his former allies' (ibid., 269), and he condemned the London tumults in his speech of 14 June as a 'rabble of the base multitude' (Fletcher, 108). There was also much talk in London of his heated exchange with the earl of Essex over the Star Chamber bill that month. Parliament's abolition of his lord presidency and removal of his lord lieutenancy further inclined him to the court. Confessing his dealings with the Scots, begging forgiveness, and promising future loyalty, he was appointed treasurer of the household on 26 November 1641. Thomas Wiseman commented on 2 December that Savile 'has very ill luck to be neither loved nor pitied by any man' (*CSP dom.*, *1641–3*, 189).

In March 1642 Savile was among the sixteen royalist peers who protested against parliament's militia ordinance and on 29 March the House of Lords drafted reasons excusing him from attending the king. By May he joined the king at York, having 'thought better of his earlier refusal' (Russell, 512). He found that many of Yorkshire's gentry remembered his dealings with the Scots and declined his company. The king charged him not to leave York and Savile complained to the earl of Holland 'I saw great Joy in many herein, to see me so used in the Face of my Country' (*JHL*, 5, 1642–3, 73). On 19 May he was debarred from sitting in the Lords' current session and on 3 June he suppressed an anti-royalist petition at Heworth Moor, outside York. Sir John Bourchier alleged that Savile violently interrupted his private reading of the petition and that Savile sent a Captain Playne to goad him. Rumours in London of this incident extended to Savile's having torn up a peace petition. For these reported actions and for abandoning his seat in the House of Lords, on 6 June he was disabled from sitting in parliament, and declared 'a publick Enemy to the State and an Incendiary between the King and his People' (*JHC*, 2, 1640–42, 607).

Civil war Alarmed by this, Savile failed to fully commit himself to the royalists; he advised against the siege of Hull in July 1642, returning to Howley in August rather than accompany the king to Nottingham. He protested against the earl of Cumberland's royalist commission, arguing that Cumberland's taxation measures were contrary to the people's liberties. Savile lamented his situation to Lady Temple that November:

> you write that you are sorie to heare that I have absolutelie declared my self against the pliament, which I wonder at

> this time to heare, when all the gentlemen of this countie complaine of me to the King for being affectionate to the pliament. (Cartwright, 1)

He added later that he would be glad to come to London and that 'I would not have the King trample on the pliament nor the pliament lessen him so much as to make a way for the people to rule us all' (Cartwright, 6). He claimed he had only attended the king as his treasurer and had always urged moderation to him.

In September 1642 Savile arranged through Lady Bland's assistance to pay Captain John Hotham £1000 in money and goods in order to procure a parliamentary protection sparing Howley from plunder. Consequently the royalist earl of Newcastle suspected Savile of conspiring with the rebels to seize the queen upon her expected landing in Yorkshire. He sent Sir Thomas Glemham with 200 cavalry to arrest Savile at Howley one night in November. Glemham escorted him to Newark Castle where he was imprisoned for twenty-six weeks.

In his absence, on 17 January 1643, Savile's tenants invited 250 local parliamentarian insurgents to Howley, whose officer, Nicholas Greathead, voiced rumours that Lord Savile had turned parliamentarian. Savile's tenants now profited from his absence, wasting his estates. Howley's subsequent parliamentarian garrison, commanded by his distant cousin, Sir John Savile of Lupset, was not overpowered by Newcastle's royalists until 22 June 1643. Destroying Savile's estate papers, the royalists plundered Howley, allegedly to the value of £10,000.

During his confinement Savile managed to correspond with the parliamentarian Lady Temple in a disguised hand, while also writing to Viscount Falkland, pleading for a trial. Summoned to Oxford on 13 May 1643, his skilful defence during his examination by the king forced an exoneration. Receiving a sealed pardon, and a public apology from Newcastle, he resumed his duties as privy councillor and lord treasurer.

Savile was created earl of Sussex on 25 May 1644 and sat in the king's Oxford parliament, but his espousal of peace upon terms which the king regarded as disgraceful led to his arrest upon grounds of negotiating with rebels and speaking disrespectfully of the king and the Oxford parliament. He was imprisoned again on 11 January 1645 and the king established his guilt by producing his letter to John Hotham during the trial. Lord Digby impeached Sussex for high treason and the Oxford parliament proposed that he should be tried by martial law, but the Lords refused to agree. In mid-March he was released on condition that he depart overseas, but instead he surrendered himself to parliament and was received in London with a pass from the earl of Essex. He was committed to black rod from 18 to 22 March, and on 5 April released on parole for health reasons to reside at Ashley House, Surrey. He entered into secret peace negotiations with the Scots, claiming he enjoyed the king's full trust and high regard, while publicly maintaining he had always been in parliament's favour. Rightly distrustful, the Scots refused to negotiate, so he turned to the Independents, promising them defections from the royalist command and that William Legge would open Oxford's gates. Meanwhile the Scots accused him of corresponding with royalists in Oxford. Sussex responded by accusing Bulstrode Whitelocke and Denzil Holles of conspiracy with royalists during their visit as parliamentary envoys to Oxford the previous winter. Refusing to name his informant, the duchess of Buckingham, he was imprisoned in the Tower on 20 June for contempt of parliament. Granted permission to prosecute Sussex for damages, Whitelocke recalled how Sussex 'had no proof but his own honour (which was not in much esteem)' (B. Whitelocke, *Memorials of the English Affairs*, 1853, 1.470).

Granted the liberty of the Tower from 31 July 1645 to 22 January 1646, Sussex's wife was permitted to join him from 21 November. He compounded for delinquency on 26 March 1646, taking the national covenant and negative oath at St Margaret's, Westminster, on 28 April. After many failed petitions for bail in which he complained of suffering from the stone, on 5 May he wrote to Henry Marten, requesting his case be brought before parliament and consenting to reveal his informant. On 23 May he was released on bail for £3000. On 8 October his composition fine was reduced to £4000, of which £1000 was considered discharged by his payment to Hotham in 1642.

Last years and reputation During the interregnum Sussex retreated from public life. In 1650 he leased St Mary's chapel at Morley, in Batley parish, to presbyterian trustees for 20s. per year for 500 years. On 3 December 1651 Sussex was shown to have undervalued his estate by £500 in his composition, and £2000 of his fine remained unpaid. In 1655 Colonel George Gill of Beeston was still petitioning for £2000 of his army pay arrears out of Sussex's estate. During the interregnum Sussex purchased for £2500 twenty pictures previously owned by the king, which his widow was later ordered to return. His alleged intention was to hold them in trust for when the king's son returned. Upon his petition to the lord protector, he was exempted from the decimation tax on 18 July 1656. Sussex died in retirement some time between 3 November 1657 when he drew up his will, and 8 October 1659, when it was proved, although not at Howley, as he is not buried in the family vault at Batley. His wife survived him and he was succeeded as second earl by his son James (1647–1671), on whose death the title became extinct.

Clarendon commented that Sussex was 'a man of an ambitious and restless nature; of parts and wit enough; but in his disposition and inclination so false that he could never be believed or depended upon' (Clarendon, *Hist. rebellion* 6.393). Gardiner summarized him likewise as 'a man born to bring disgrace upon every party which he joined' (Gardiner, 9.339). Sussex understood how to appeal to both royalists and parliamentarians, stressing the fear of 'popularity' and using the language of anti-Catholicism as ways to appeal to each. His duplicitous conduct was a natural consequence of his desire for an active political role without committing himself to either side.

He was sincere only in his desire for peace and in his priority of protecting his fortune from plunder or confiscation by whichever side was to triumph.

ANDREW J. HOPPER

Sources GEC, *Peerage*, new edn, vols. 11–12/1 • J. J. Cartwright, ed., 'Papers relating to the delinquency of Lord Savill, 1642–6', *Camden miscellany, VIII*, CS, new ser., 31 (1883) • PRO, SP 23/179/173–239 • *CSP dom.*, 1620–60 • M. R. Pickering, 'Yorkshire', HoP, *Commons, 1558–1603*, 1.280–84 • I. Cassidy, 'Savile, John II', HoP, *Commons, 1558–1603* • *JHL*, 5 (1642–3) • *JHL*, 7 (1644–5) • *JHL*, 8 (1645–6) • *DNB* • C. Russell, *The fall of the British monarchies, 1637–1642* (1991) • J. T. Cliffe, *The Yorkshire gentry from the Reformation to the civil war* (1969) • A. Fletcher, *The outbreak of the English civil war* (1981) • M. A. E. Green, ed., *Calendar of the proceedings of the committee for compounding … 1643–1660*, 5 vols., PRO (1889–92) • R. Cust, 'Politics and the electorate in the 1620s', *Conflict in early Stuart England: studies in religion and politics, 1603–1642*, ed. R. Cust and A. Hughes (1989), 134–67 • Clarendon, *Hist. rebellion* • S. R. Gardiner, *History of England from the accession of James I to the outbreak of the English civil war, 1603–1642*, 10 vols. (1904), vol. 9 • H. Cary, ed., *Memorials of the great civil war in England from 1646 to 1652*, 1 (1842) • F. Barber, ed., 'West Riding sessions rolls', *Yorkshire Archaeological and Topographical Journal*, 5 (1877–8), 362–405 • J. Lister, ed., *West Riding sessions records*, 2, Yorkshire Archaeological Society, 54 (1915) • D. Scott, '"Hannibal at our gates": loyalists and fifth-columnists during the bishops' wars—the case of Yorkshire', *Historical Research*, 70 (1997), 269–93 • *Fourth report*, HMC, 3 (1874) • *Fifth report*, HMC, 4 (1876) • *Sixth report*, HMC, 5 (1877–8) • *Seventh report*, HMC, 6 (1879) • *JHC*, 2 (1640–42) • *JHC*, 4 (1644–6) • J. W. Clay, ed., *Abstracts of Yorkshire wills in the time of the Commonwealth*, Yorkshire Archaeological Society, 9 (1890) • will, PRO, PROB 11/296, fols. 33*r*–34*v* • will, PRO, PROB 11/296, sig. 515 • M. Sheard, ed., *Records of the parish of Batley in the county of York* (1894) • G. Wood, *The story of Morley* (1916) • R. Lockyer, *Buckingham: the life and political career of George Villiers, first duke of Buckingham, 1592–1628* (1981)

Archives BL, Add. MS 32093, fol. 211 • Northants. RO, deeds and papers, family and estate collections • W. Yorks. AS, Leeds, memorial records and estate papers, family and estate collections | PRO, SP 23/179/173–239

Likenesses G. P. Harding, watercolour, *c*.1800–1840 (after unknown artist), NPG

Wealth at death see will, PRO, PROB 11/296, fols. 33*r*–34*v*; PRO, PROB 11/296, sig. 515

Savile, Sir William, third baronet (1612–1644). *See under* Savile family (*per. c*.1480–1644).

Savile, William, second marquess of Halifax (1664/5–1700). *See under* Savile, George, first marquess of Halifax (1633–1695).

Savill, Sir Eric Humphrey (1895–1980), estate administrator and horticulturist, was born at 18 Royal Avenue, Chelsea, London, on 20 October 1895, the second son in a family of three sons and a daughter of Edwin Savill, partner in the firm of Alfred Savill & Sons, chartered surveyors, of Lincoln's Inn Fields, and Helen Webster, *née* Kemp. His mother, a woman of strong character and conviction, was an avid supporter of the campaign for women's rights who on occasions had been an orator for that cause at speaker's corner, Hyde Park. She also practised as a horticulturist. To Savill's distress his parents separated. He never married and cared devotedly for his mother until her death on 10 April 1956.

Savill was educated at Malvern College, where he was a pupil from 1909 to 1913, and at Magdalene College, Cambridge. At the outbreak of the First World War he voluntarily terminated his studies at Cambridge and enlisted in the ranks of the Officers' Training Corps. In December 1914 he was commissioned in the 8th Devonshire regiment. The following year he went with his regiment to France and during the battle of the Somme in July 1916 he was awarded the MC. Later he was severely wounded in the chest and left leg.

After the war Savill returned to Cambridge, and graduated BA in 1920 (MA, 1930). Also in 1920 he joined his father's firm and was elected a professional associate of the Royal Institution of Chartered Surveyors (he advanced to the fellowship in 1930). In 1926 he became a partner in the family firm where he remained until 1930, when he was offered the post of deputy surveyor at Windsor, which he readily accepted. This involved the management of an extensive estate extending from Virginia Water to Bagshot, which incorporated farmland, forests, and mature woodland. During the thirty years he held this position he knew four monarchs and their consorts. This made possible the creation of the Savill Gardens and Valley Gardens at Windsor as an enduring living memorial. Indeed it was by command of George VI in 1951 that the woodland and bog gardens at Windsor were to be designated the Savill Gardens. In 1937 Savill was promoted to deputy ranger, a post he held for twenty-two years. In 1958 Savill became director of forestry to the crown estate, and in 1959 he was made director of the gardens, Windsor Great Park. He retired in 1970.

Savill was an inspired yet highly controversial gardening genius. The individual gardens which he created at Windsor are a testimony to his instinctive flair. Clever use was made of the natural features of Windsor Park, its woodlands, heaths, hillsides, streams, and lakes, and he created what was claimed by contemporaries as the most outstanding garden of the twentieth century in England. In 1954 Savill became a founder member of the Ministry of Transport's landscape advisory committee and from 1962 to 1969 he was its chairman.

Savill held office on two hospital boards—those of King Edward VII Hospital, Windsor, and the Hospital for Sick Children in Great Ormond Street, London. He was generous and unassuming, softly spoken, and with a natural dignity. Yet he could be sharply critical and forthright in expressing his views. He was of medium build and physically tough, though his activities were plainly restricted by his war injuries which he bore uncomplainingly and which, with frequent bronchial attacks, remained painful. Nevertheless, he actively engaged in tennis, athletics, and golf, and in later life fishing became his principal joy.

Savill was appointed MVO (1938), CVO (1950), KCVO (1955), and CBE (1946). He was prominent in the affairs of the Royal Horticultural Society, on whose council he served (1952–68) and whose vice-president he became. In 1955 he received the society's highest accolade, the Victoria medal of honour, and in 1963 a gold Veitch memorial medal. He died on 15 April 1980 at King Edward VII Hospital, Windsor.

GEORGE TAYLOR, *rev.* JOHN MARTIN

Sources J. Watson, *Savills: a family and a firm* (1977) • *WWW, 1971–80*, 705 • personal knowledge (1986) • private information (1986) • *The Times* (17 April 1980), 16h • *The Times* (23 May 1980), 16d • b. cert. • d. cert. • *CGPLA Eng. & Wales* (1980)
Archives NL Scot., corresp. with Sir George Taylor
Likenesses photograph, repro. in J. Watson, *Savills*, 136 • photograph, Harry Smith horticultural photographic collection
Wealth at death £159,927: probate, 20 June 1980, *CGPLA Eng. & Wales*

Savill, Harriet Elizabeth (1789–1857). *See under* Saville, John Faucit (1783?–1853).

Savill, Thomas Dixon (1855–1910), physician, the only son of Thomas C. Savill and his wife, Eliza Clarissa Dixon, was born at Kensington, London, on 7 September 1855. His family owned a firm of printers and publishers who for a time produced *The Lancet*. He was educated at Stockwell grammar school and subsequently entered St Thomas's Hospital with a scholarship in natural science. As an undergraduate Savill had a distinguished career, gaining the William Tite scholarship and many prizes. He continued medical studies at St Mary's Hospital in London, at the Salpétrière in Paris, in Hamburg, and in Vienna. In 1881 he graduated MB with honours of the University of London, becoming MD in the following year and being admitted as a member of the Royal College of Physicians of London in the same year. Successively he became registrar, pathologist, and assistant physician to the West London Hospital and showed early evidence of a lifelong interest in neurology by translating, in 1889, volume 3 of J. M. Charcot's lectures 'Diseases of the nervous system'. In 1885 Savill was appointed medical superintendent of Paddington Infirmary, newly opened, an appointment which gave him an intimate knowledge of the working of the poor-law hospitals. He subsequently became president of the Infirmary Medical Superintendents' Society and was a recognized authority on many of the questions raised in both the majority and minority reports of the poor-law commission in 1909.

Savill's experience as a medical superintendent was reflected in his chief work, *A System of Clinical Medicine*, published in two volumes between 1903 and 1905. His approach was essentially symptomatological in that each system of the body was discussed in turn, and under each he described and grouped prominent symptoms pointing to diseases in specific systems. In the section on arterial diseases he described thickening of the medial coat of the arteries, a condition which he called arterial hypermyotrophy; his descriptions were based upon extensive personal investigations, both macroscopic and microscopic. His book was warmly welcomed by the medical profession, being based, as it was, upon the approach of an excellent clinical teacher.

Savill also developed a reputation as a dermatologist and became, in 1897, physician to St John's Hospital for Diseases of the Skin. However, he decided to retire in 1892 from the Paddington Infirmary in order to become a consulting physician, and particularly in order to pursue his growing interest in neurology. Soon afterwards he was appointed physician to the West End Hospital for Diseases of the Nervous System, and in 1899 he published a book based on a course of clinical lectures on neurasthenia which he had delivered both in Paddington and at the West End Hospital. This work showed him to be an original thinker and clear expositor. He discussed exhaustively the essential nature and clinical features of neurasthenia as then understood, suggesting an aetiological classification which was regarded by contemporary observers as being more satisfactory than any previously advanced. He published in 1909 further observations in lectures on hysteria and allied vasomotor conditions, postulating a possible vascular cause for hysterical phenomena, while admitting that his hypothesis would not explain 'all the various symptoms of this protean and strange disorder' of hysteria. Savill also contributed, mainly to *The Lancet*, between 1888 and 1909 many papers on neurological and dermatological topics and a valuable report on the Warrington smallpox outbreak (1892–3).

Savill married, in 1901, Dr Agnes Forbes Blackadder, then assistant and later full physician to St John's Hospital for Diseases of the Skin. She helped her husband to write his book on clinical medicine and enjoyed a distinguished career in her own right.

Savill was highly regarded as a physician by his colleagues and patients alike. Before his thirtieth year he suffered three attacks of rheumatic fever which left him somewhat disabled and at first nearly penniless. He was a man of firm will and determination and had a manner which at times bred a certain abruptness and an outward reserve which belied his underlying sympathy and understanding towards the ill and the distressed. It was a great surprise to many that he was never elected to the fellowship of the Royal College of Physicians, although the complaint that he lodged with the censors' board of that body against a fellow of the college in 1891, alleging defamation, a complaint which led to protracted deliberations by the board (which ultimately dismissed the complaint), may well have been a factor. The regard in which he was held resulted in the endowment in 1910 by his colleagues at the West End Hospital of a lectureship in his honour, which the author of this note was privileged to deliver in October 1963. Savill's premature death on 10 January 1910 at the early age of fifty-four resulted from a fracture of the base of the skull caused by a fall from his horse in Algiers. He was survived by his wife. WALTON OF DETCHANT

Sources *DNB* • *The Lancet* (15 Jan 1910) • letter from trustees of West End Hospital, *The Lancet* (23 April 1910) • *WWW, 1897–1915* • minutes, censors' board, 24 March 1891, RCP Lond. • *CGPLA Eng. & Wales* (1910)
Wealth at death £6348 13*s*. 5*d*.: resworn probate, 9 Feb 1910, *CGPLA Eng. & Wales*

Saville, Edmund Henry Faucit (1811–1857). *See under* Saville, John Faucit (1783?–1853).

Saville [Savill], **John Faucit** (1783?–1853), actor, theatre manager, and playwright, was reportedly seventy years old when he died, but neither his date of birth nor his parents' names are known. Perhaps his real name was, as is usually supposed, John Savill[e] Faucit: some early signatures and his initial stage name, Mr Faucit, support this.

Yet most official documents, from his marriage record on, give Savill or Saville as surname, often with Faucit as middle name. His career began at Stepney fair, probably in his late teens: here he joined 'Muster [John] Richardson's' company, which toured the fairs with a large, portable booth, acting in pantomimes and abbreviated, highly stereotyped dramas. In 1804, at about twenty-one, the small but personable actor was engaged at the Theatre Royal, Richmond, Surrey, where he played dashing, if secondary, roles such as Frank Rochdale in *John Bull* and Courtall in *The Belle's Stratagem*. He and the fifteen-year-old actress Harriet Diddear [*see below*] became mutually attracted; in 1805, when he was again at Richmond and she was in her father's company at Margate, they eloped to London and were married—under the name Savill—on 2 September. Shortly afterwards, having been reconciled with the Diddears, they acted at Margate, then Dover, as Mr and Mrs Faucit.

In 1806 the couple joined the prosperous Norwich circuit, whose company travelled to seven towns and acted throughout the year; except for a brief hiatus (with Macready at Newcastle), they remained with it for seven years. Faucit acted 'second juvenile' roles and 'Country Boys' in conventional drama and principal parts in 'both serious & comic Pantomimes'; Mrs Faucit eventually played all the leading female characters. In 1813 they were engaged at a major London theatre, Covent Garden. Four children had been born during the Norwich years—John, Harriet, Edmund Henry [*see below*], and Alfred; after the move to London, there were two more—Helena [*see* Faucit, Helen] and Charles. All had careers as actors with the possible exception of Charles. At Covent Garden, although his wife was regularly employed, Faucit appeared only sporadically, mostly in minor comic parts such as Old Gobbo in *The Merchant of Venice*; in 1817, however, he acted Gratiano in that play, winning critical approval for his innovative seriousness in the trial scene. His chief activity was in managing provincial theatres. In Greenwich, where he had his first theatre, he faced opposition from the religious dissenters, but, with the support of prominent citizens, he prevailed. By 1817 he was also operating the Theatre Royal, Margate, becoming its fully-fledged proprietor in 1820.

Faucit's wife left him in 1821 but continued to bill herself as Mrs Faucit, in consequence of which he reversed his names to Faucit Savill(e). According to an obituary in an unidentified journal (New York Public Library) he obtained a legal divorce from his first wife and remarried twice: his second wife was Mrs Ann Amthos (*née* Collier), the widow of an actor, and his third, whom he married after Ann's death, was the daughter of a Yorkshire clergyman. The divorce was undoubtedly a polite fiction (the expense alone would have been prohibitive); but a Mrs Faucit Savill was listed in the Margate playbills beginning in 1822, and an Emily Moody was married (whether legally or not) to a John Faucit Saville on 11 April 1829. He had at least two more children, both apparently with Ann Amthos: Ann, who acted for a while, and Phoebe.

While continuing to manage the theatres at Greenwich and Margate, Saville from time to time undertook the running of others as well—at Woolwich, Gravesend, Ramsgate, Deal, Dover, Sandwich, and Sheerness. After many fluctuations in success, he was brought near ruin by disastrous fires at Ramsgate (December 1829) and Greenwich (January 1831). But this 'unlucky devil', as he was known, remained resilient: recalling Richardson's booth, he replaced his lost theatres with one ingeniously constructed of cast-iron pieces, put together with screws, which could be disassembled and transported from town to town. After he gave up management (his last season at Margate was in 1840), he held an office for a while in the 'treasorial department' of the City of London Theatre.

Saville's career as a dramatist, not counting an early Norwich effort, began with a melodrama, *Justice*, first performed at Drury Lane on 28 November 1820. Of some dozen other plays, several achieved considerable popularity. Notable successes were the melodrama *The Miller's Maid* (English Opera House, 1821), the nautical drama *Wapping Old Stairs* (Surrey, 1837), and the comedy *The Aldgate Pump* (Strand, 1841); the first of these had occasional revivals, in London and the provinces, for years afterwards. (A number of his plays and one by his first wife are preserved in the Larpert Collection, Huntington Library, San Marino, and among the Lord Chamberlain's MSS, PRO.) Later in life he wrote a 'penny-dreadful' novel, *The Heads of the Headless*. On 28 September 1853 the veteran returned to his old Margate theatre to act Benjamin Bowbell in *The Illustrious Stranger* for the benefit of his son Edmund. Shortly afterwards, on 31 October 1853, he died during his sleep at the home of his widowed daughter (probably Ann Wilkins), 31 Primrose Street, Bishopsgate, London.

Harriet Elizabeth Savill [*née* Diddear; *other married name* Farren; *known as* Mrs Faucit] (1789–1857), actress, was the daughter of provincial theatre manager John Diddear and his wife, Elizabeth. When not quite seven she made a successful début at the Theatre Royal, Brighton, under her father's management, as Edward in *Everyone has his Fault*. She continued to act during childhood and adolescence, at Brighton, Dover, Richmond, and Margate. Mrs Faucit's London début, as Desdemona in *Othello*, was at Covent Garden on 8 October 1813; critics approved her appearance and voice but deplored her tendency to play to the audience and to turn Desdemona into an arch, vivacious Congreve heroine. Her most important part that season was Cleopatra in a lavishly mounted *Antony and Cleopatra*, with a text combining Shakespeare and Dryden. Although overshadowed by Eliza O'Neill, who arrived in 1814, she had a substantial metropolitan career for more than two decades, always at Covent Garden, Drury Lane, or the Haymarket. In 1821, after an unsuccessful attempt to have her marriage to John Faucit Saville annulled, she became the common-law wife of the eminent comedian William *Farren, with whom she lived from then on. Their two sons, William *Farren and Henry *Farren, also became actors. On 16 November 1853, shortly after Saville's death, she and Farren were legally married. Mrs Faucit was very successful in certain comic parts (such as Celia in *The*

Humourous Lieutenant) and as the heroine of melodramas and musical plays. Her serious acting, which seemed meretricious in characters such as Lady Macbeth, was genuinely affecting in Meg Merrilies and similar roles; her handsome face and Junoesque figure were assets in regal parts such as Elizabeth in *Richard III*, Gertrude in *Hamlet*, and the empress in *The Exile*. She died in London on 16 June 1857.

Edmund Henry Faucit Saville (1811–1857), actor, was, next to Helen Faucit, the most prominent of John Faucit Saville's children. Although he was trained in medicine, he chose the family profession. After several years of mainly provincial acting, he made his first important London appearance at the Surrey Theatre on 8 May 1837, as Abelard in Buckstone's new drama *Heloise and Abelard*. For sixteen years, until incapacitated by alcohol-related liver disease, he was a leading actor at the London 'minors', especially the Surrey, the Victoria, and the City of London, primarily in melodramatic roles such as the bold sailors in his father's nautical dramas and the villainous Bill Sikes in *Oliver Twist*. Occasionally he acted legitimate parts, including Hamlet and Othello, but his concentration on melodrama had coarsened what was evidently a genuine tragic talent. Saville was married twice, each time to an actress: with his first wife, Anne, he had a son, Edmund, and with his second, Clementina Sobieska Grant, he had a daughter, Harriet, who acted when young, and a son, Henry, who became a dramatist. CAROL J. CARLISLE

Sources P. Egan, *The pilgrims of the Thames in search of the National* (1839) · playbills, BL · playbills, Theatre Museum, London · playbills, Folger · playbills, Brighton Public Library · playbills, Margate Public Library · playbills, Norwich Public Library · playbills, Richmond (Surrey) Public Library · letters, Harvard TC · 'Diddear falsely called Faucit, otherwise Savill against Faucit', County Hall RO, London, Consistorial and Episcopal Court of London, Assignation Book, 1820, DL/C/129 · 'Memoir of William Farren', *Oxberry's Dramatic Biography*, 3/35 (1825), 37–47 · 'Memoir of Mrs Faucit', *Oxberry's Dramatic Biography*, 3/10 (1825), 127–35 · *Theatrical Journal* (11 March 1843), 79 · *Theatrical Times* (29 Aug 1843), 89–90 · *Sunday Times* (6 Nov 1853) · *Kentish Mercury* (12 Nov 1853) · 'The late John Saville Faucit', NYPL for the Performing Arts · review, *Theatrical Inquisitor, and Monthly Mirror*, 3 (1813), 253–4 · review, *Theatrical Inquisitor, and Monthly Mirror*, 11 (1817), 70–71 · *Morning Post* (1 Nov 1817) · *The Scourge* (Nov 1813), 431 · M. Morley, *Margate and its theatres, 1730–1965* (1966)

Saville [*formerly* Salberg], **Victor Myer** (1897–1979), film producer and director, was born on 5 September 1897 at his parents' home, 8 Speedwell Road, Edgbaston, Birmingham, the second of the three children of Gabriel Salberg, a fine art and china dealer, and his second wife, Rebecca, daughter of David Lavenstein. His father, an Orthodox Jew born in Poland, had escaped from the Polish pogroms during the 1880s, and had brought with him to Britain two children from his first marriage; Saville's mother, one of fifteen children, was of English origin. Saville adopted his chosen surname in 1920, on the advice of his wife, who suggested a change to something less Germanic. In his unpublished autobiography Saville described the Salbergs as 'a comfortable middle-class family that was never in want for anything' (Saville, 2). He was brought up in the Jewish faith and educated at King Edward VI Grammar School, Birmingham. His father intended him to read law, but when war broke out in 1914 he enlisted in the 18th regiment of the Territorial Army, the London Irish Rifles, and was invalided out in 1916 following a head wound at the battle of Loos.

Victor Myer Saville (1897–1979), by unknown photographer

As a civilian, Saville began to find modest work in the business to which he devoted his life. He worked for Solomon Levy, a leading film distributor and proprietor, based in Birmingham. Then in 1919 Saville formed his own outfit, Victory Motion Pictures, in which he joined forces with a boyhood friend, Michael Balcon, later a leading film producer himself. Aside from renting and importing, Victory produced advertising films. In 1921 Saville cut his teeth as a director on two short items singing the praises of petroleum. On 26 May 1920 he married Phoebe Vera Teller (1899–1984), daughter of a house furnisher, Lewis Teller, and niece of C. M. Woolf, the film distributor (who helped back his first feature). There were two children: David (*b*. 1926), and Ann (*b*. 1931), who subsequently married Woolf's son John Woolf, himself a leading film producer.

In 1923 Saville and Balcon ventured into feature production with *Woman to Woman*, directed by Graham Cutts, a wartime romance based on a West End play. Other films from the same team failed to match its popular success; Saville found better luck in the late 1920s, when he worked in association with the Gaumont Company, and served as producer for *Hindle Wakes* and two other war stories, *Mademoiselle from Armentières* and *Roses of Picardy*. His own first feature as a director was *The Arcadians* in 1927, based on the musical comedy.

Saville eagerly embraced the new world of talking pictures, and hit his stride as a director in the 1930s, working again with Balcon, now head of production at Gaumont-British Picture Corporation. His films followed conventional patterns of the time—many were based on popular novels or plays—but they were highly polished in treatment. Saville was versatile, and lavished the same panache on a wartime story such as *I Was a Spy*, the omnibus film *Friday the Thirteenth* (1933), and the northern drama of *Hindle Wakes* (one of his numerous remakes). But he showed a special flair for musicals, and guided the singer and dancer Jessie Matthews to great popularity in *Evergreen* (1934), *First a Girl* (1935), and *It's Love Again* (1936).

Saville's success continued once he left Gaumont-British in 1936 to form Victor Saville Productions, working under Alexander Korda's umbrella at Denham Studios. *Dark Journey* (1937) was a vivid spy melodrama, while *South Riding* (1937), based on Winifred Holtby's novel of Yorkshire life, summoned up the social scene with unusual precision. Saville considered it his best work. Since his films had almost a Hollywood sheen, it was not surprising that Hollywood itself took notice; and in 1937 Saville replaced Balcon as head of production for the short-lived British venture of Metro-Goldwyn-Mayer (MGM), MGM-British, where he produced *The Citadel* and *Goodbye Mr Chips*. He announced himself pleased with the change—'I have never considered myself highly as a director', he told the magazine *Film Weekly* (National Film Archive)—and continued with MGM in Hollywood during the Second World War. But he grew to chafe at uncongenial assignments, and returned to directing with the musical *Tonight and Every Night* (1945), made for Columbia. Numerous films made from popular novels followed: their charms have mostly faded. In 1950 he became an American citizen.

In 1952 Saville's son David, was killed in a car crash. Seeking projects that would not need emotional involvement, Saville acquired rights to the hard-boiled thrillers of Mickey Spillane, as far removed from Saville's English work as may be imagined. By 1960 he had moved back to London, and emerged from semi-retirement to produce the attractive *The Greengage Summer*, based on Rumer Godden's novel. An urbane man, he continued in old age to enjoy reading and playing golf, and maintained a lively interest in industry matters, particularly film censorship. Saville's long years in Hollywood brought comparatively few creative rewards, certainly compared with Alfred Hitchcock, who had worked on his very first productions in the 1920s. But his early career in Britain was outstanding: not even Hitchcock managed such a run of popular hits, and the sheer polish of his films and sensitivity to performers (particularly female) easily compensated for their lack of a personal viewpoint. Saville died on 8 May 1979, in Westminster Hospital, London, following a haemorrhage from a ruptured aortic aneurysm.

GEOFF BROWN

Sources National Film Archive, *Victor Saville* (1972) • V. Saville, 'Shadows on a screen', unpubd autobiography, 1974, BFI • R. Moseley, ed., *Evergreen: Victor Saville in his own words* (2000) • b. cert. • m. cert. • d. cert. • *CGPLA Eng. & Wales* (1981)

Archives BFI, Special Collections | FILM BFI NFTVA | SOUND BL NSA, performance footage

Likenesses photographs, 1931–49, Hult. Arch. • photograph, BFI [*see illus.*]

Wealth at death £9110—in England and Wales: probate, 11 Nov 1981, *CGPLA Eng. & Wales*

Saviolo, Vincentio (*fl.* 1595), swordsman and writer on fencing, was born in Padua. Nothing is known of his early life, but he recalls witnessing a quarrel in Slavonia (in the sixteenth century a vague term, denoting the Balkans) and may have travelled widely in Europe before arriving in England. Of his introduction to fencing he reveals only that 'I myself have had many teachers, and found them all to differ one from the other' (Saviolo, 6), but of these one of the earliest may have been a M. Angelo, whom he recalls as an inhabitant of the town of his birth. Most of the little known about Saviolo comes from a hostile account in *Paradoxes of Defence* (1599), by an English writer, George Silver. It seems that Rocco Bonetti, an Italian fencing master, had taken over from William Joyner, its founder, a fencing school located in rooms under what became the second Blackfriars playhouse, and had employed an apprentice named Ieronimo to be his assistant. On the death of Bonetti, perhaps about 1588 or 1589, Saviolo and Ieronimo took control of the school. They 'taught rapier fight at the court, at London, and in the country, by the space of seven or eight years or thereabouts' (Silver, 66). By 1596 the school had passed to one Thomas Brunskill. According to Silver, Saviolo had claimed 'that Englishmen were strong men, but had no cunning, and they would go back too much in their fight which was great disgrace unto them' (ibid.). Provoked by these remarks, Silver and his brother Toby issued a challenge. Saviolo and Ieronimo are said to have accepted, but to have failed to appear out of cowardice; Silver told of a second quarrel, equally discreditable to Saviolo, which occurred at Wells, and condemned his teachings as having 'cost the lives of many of our brave gentlemen and gallants' (ibid., 77). All this should be treated with caution, not least because it may reflect resentment that Italian teachers were becoming fashionable among gentlemen in the capital.

It seems that Saviolo enjoyed the patronage of the earl of Essex. In 1595 he issued *Vincentio Saviolo, his practise, in two bookes, the first intreating of the use of the rapier and dagger, the second, of honour and honourable quarrels* (licensed on 19 November 1594), the first manual of fencing to be published in England. Its preface was addressed to the earl, as the one 'whose bounty most bindeth me' and characterizes the book as 'a new year's gift proceeding from a minde most dutifully affected towards you' (sig. A3). The second of the two works given in the title was substantially a translation of an earlier Italian book on the duel, Girolamo Muzio's *Il duello* (Venice, 1551), but it also contained original material by Saviolo, including a chapter setting out his own thoughts on the duel and a section on the nobility of women, which praises Queen Elizabeth. The five kinds of lies described by Saviolo in the section 'On the manner and diversitie of lies' have been taken as a possible source for the seven kinds of lies described by Touchstone in act v, scene iv of *As You Like It* (although the types of lie described in William Segar's *The Booke of Honor and Armes* [1590] have also been taken as a source for Shakespeare's satirizing of the books of honour and good manners popular in England at the time).

Saviolo's death is recorded by Silver in his *Paradoxes of Defence*, and must therefore have occurred before it was registered by the Stationers' Company on 30 January 1599. STEPHEN WRIGHT

Sources G. Silver, *Paradoxes of defence* (1599) • V. Saviolo, *Vincentio Saviolo, his practise, in two bookes, the first intreating of the use of the rapier and dagger, the second, of honour and honourable quarrels* (1595) • J. L. Jackson, ed., *Three Elizabethan fencing manuals* (1972) • H. Berry, *The noble science: a study and transcription of Sloane MS 2530, papers of the masters of defence of London, temp Henry VIII to 1590* (1991) • L. Barbasetti, *The art of the foil: with a short history of fencing* [1933] • E. K. Chambers, *The Elizabethan stage*, 4 vols. (1923), vol. 2, pp. 500–03

Savona, Laurence William of. *See* Traversagni, Lorenzo Guglielmo (*c*.1425–1503).

Savory, Sir William Scovell, first baronet (1826–1895), surgeon, son of William Henry Savory and his second wife, Mary Webb, was born on 30 November 1826 in the parish of St Mary-at-Hill in the City of London. His father, a merchant, was churchwarden of the parish. He became a student at St Bartholomew's Hospital in 1844, and remained associated with the hospital for the rest of his life. He qualified in 1847, when he became a member of the Royal College of Surgeons. In 1848 he graduated MB (London), having obtained gold medals in physiology, surgery, and midwifery as well as honours in medicine. This outstanding academic achievement indicated his promise as a distinguished surgeon. In 1852 he became a fellow of the Royal College of Surgeons.

On 30 November 1854 Savory married Louisa Frances, daughter of William Borradaile of Croydon; she died in 1868 from blood poisoning, contracted after she had dressed her husband's septic finger. They had one son.

In 1849 Savory was appointed to his first post at St Bartholomew's Hospital medical school, as demonstrator of anatomy and of operative surgery. In 1850 he also took on responsibility for supervising the studies of students reading for degrees in the University of London. In 1859 he gave up both these appointments when he was elected lecturer on general anatomy and physiology at St Bartholomew's, succeeding James Paget. Savory's lectures were very different from those of his predecessor, but were no less admired.

Savory carried out a number of researches in pathology and morbid anatomy and acted as curator of St Bartholomew's pathology museum. In a paper, 'On the valves of the heart', which he read before the Royal Society on 18 December 1851, he described the structure, connections, and arrangements of the valves. He also published another paper, 'On the development of striated muscular fibres in mammalia', in the Royal Society's *Proceedings*. In

Sir William Scovell Savory, first baronet (1826–1895), by Walter William Ouless, 1893

1857 a further study, 'On the relative temperature of arterial and venous blood', appeared in the *Proceedings*. The following year he was elected a fellow of the Royal Society. Throughout his career he published widely, contributing several articles to the *St Bartholomew's Hospital Reports*, *The Lancet*, and the *Transactions of the Royal Medical and Chirurgical Society*. He also wrote and published memoirs of the surgeons Sir William Lawrence and Frederick Carpenter Skey.

In 1861 Savory became assistant surgeon to St Bartholomew's Hospital, and in April 1867 surgeon, an office which he held until 1891, when, on his retirement from active practice, he was appointed consulting surgeon and a governor of the hospital. He was elected lecturer on surgery in 1869, and held the office for twenty years. The lectureship was usually divided, but from 1879, on the death of his friend and colleague George Callender, to 1889, at the particular request of the staff Savory was sole lecturer. In 1881–2 he received in excess of £2000 for his lectures and clinical duties, probably the largest income yet received for surgical teaching in London. He spoke on all aspects of surgery with great authority and erudition.

Savory became a member of the council of the Royal College of Surgeons in 1877, and in 1885 was elected president, an office he held for four years. At that time this represented the longest tenure in the history of the college. He was opposed to any change in the college's constitution and successfully resisted much agitation for radical reforms. He was involved in securing a supplementary royal charter in 1888 and in extending the curriculum for medical education to five years. He was also involved in the project to build an examination hall for the college. He was Hunterian professor of comparative anatomy and physiology from 1859 to 1861, and in 1884 gave the Bradshaw lecture, on 'The pathology of cancer', which provided a critical overview of contemporary theories. He delivered the oration in praise of John Hunter (1728–1793) in 1887, which outlined Hunter's work and background, and indicated Savory's admiration for the individual credited with raising surgery from the barber's craft to a scientific art.

In 1879 Savory delivered a controversial address at the British Medical Association meeting at Cork against Lister and his antiseptic methods. Savory was suspicious of Lister's techniques, preferring to keep to the older traditions of British surgery as practised by Hunter and Lawrence. However, like his colleagues Howard Marsh and George Callender, fellow surgeons at St Bartholomew's, he was an advocate of cleanliness, good diet, and careful nursing. His success as an operator lay in his adherence to these basic conservative principles.

Savory received many honours. He became surgeon-extraordinary to the queen in 1887, and in 1890 was created a baronet. He served on the royal commission on vaccination, and in 1892 on the Gresham University commission. Savory died after a short illness on 4 March 1895, at his house, 66 Brook Street, Grosvenor Square, London. His son, Borradaile Savory, rector of St Bartholomew's the Great, succeeded him as second baronet.

Savory's was an imposing figure with expressive features. His voice was distinct and pleasing, though he never spared his opponents, and usually won his arguments. His surgical practice was considerable but did not prevent him from devoting time to the affairs of the Royal College of Surgeons, where for many years he exerted more influence than any of his contemporaries.

NORMAN MOORE, *rev.* STELLA BUTLER

Sources H. Marsh, *St Bartholomew's Hospital Reports*, 31 (1895), 1–18 • V. C. Medvei and J. L. Thornton, eds., *The royal hospital of Saint Bartholomew, 1123–1973* (1974), 218–19 • *BMJ* (9 March 1895), 564–5 • Burke, *Peerage* • personal knowledge (1897) • m. cert. • *CGPLA Eng. & Wales* (1895)

Likenesses G. Jerrard, portrait, 1881, Wellcome L. • H. R. Hope Pinker, marble bust, after 1890, St Bartholomew's Hospital, London; replica, 1896, RCS Eng. • W. W. Ouless, portrait, 1893, St Bartholomew's Hospital, London [*see illus.*] • H. J. Brooks, group portrait, oils (*Council of the Royal College of Surgeons of England, 1884–5*), RCS Eng. • wood-engraving, Wellcome L.

Wealth at death £93,190 19*s.* 4*d.*: probate, 1 April 1895, *CGPLA Eng. & Wales*

Savoy, Boniface of (1206/7–1270), archbishop of Canterbury, was probably the seventh son of Thomas (I), count of Savoy (1178–1233), and Marguerite (*d.* 1258), daughter of either Guillaume, count of Geneva (1137–1195), or the lord of Faucigny.

Early career Described by Matthew Paris as a man 'of noble stature and elegant bearing' (Paris, *Chron.*, 4.104), Boniface was intended, like four of his brothers, for an ecclesiastical career, but was the only one who appears to have had a religious vocation. By 1224 he was probably a novice in the Carthusian order at Portes, a daughter house of the Grande Chartreuse south of Chambéry, but he never took his monastic vows because, as part of his father's policy of consolidating his hold on strategic sees and providing for his sons, Boniface was elected bishop of Belley and prior of Nantua in 1232. In the following year these appointments were confirmed after he had taken subdeacon's orders, and he inherited, on the death of his father, a share of his family inheritance, including the castle of Ugine.

Boniface might have remained in Savoy had it not been for the marriage in 1236 of his niece, *Eleanor of Provence, to Henry III, who strongly promoted his career, and that of his brother, Peter of *Savoy, in England. After narrowly failing to secure for him the bishopric of Winchester (he had earlier tried to procure it for Boniface's elder brother William of Savoy), the king induced the cathedral chapter of Canterbury, which was labouring under a ban of excommunication imposed by the former archbishop Edmund of Abingdon (*d.* 1240), to elect him archbishop and primate of England on 1 February 1241. Anxious to win support in his dispute with Frederick II, and under Savoyard influence, Innocent IV (*r.* 1243–54) confirmed the appointment on 16 September 1243. The temporalities were restored some time after 27 February 1244. Despite having promised to come as soon as he could, another seven months passed before Boniface travelled to England, probably because of a dispute with Étienne (II) de Thoire-Villars about jurisdiction over the priory of Nantua. The delay was significant for the future: although Boniface had renounced his claim to the succession in 1238, his links with Savoy remained close, and he often returned to his homeland.

Retrenchment and reform When Boniface eventually arrived in England on 25 April 1244, he was warmly welcomed by the king, who had commissioned for him a mitre decorated with precious stones worth 300 marks, and thoughtfully restocked the archiepiscopal wine cellars. He was ordained into the priesthood by Walter de Cantilupe, bishop of Worcester (*d.* 1266), and lost no time in grappling with Canterbury's vast debts, in part the result of his predecessors' extravagance. After his suffragans refused to help, Boniface left England on 26 November 1244 for Lyons, where the exiled Innocent IV consecrated him on 15 January 1245, and later agreed that the first fruits of vacant benefices in the province of Canterbury for up to seven years, or to the value of 10,000 marks (later doubled), should be applied to paying off the debts, a decision the suffragans accepted only after Boniface suspended them. By also reorganizing the Canterbury administration, exacting all dues and services from his tenants, felling timber, and reclaiming part of Romney Marsh, Boniface had paid debts amounting to 22,000 marks by 1261, including those incurred by his predecessors in the construction of the great hall of the archbishop's palace. 'Thus it seems to me', he jested, 'that I have built it, for I have paid their debts' (*Works of Gervase of Canterbury*, 2.251). Boniface then embarked on his own building schemes, including a hospital at Maidstone, Kent.

Except for two brief visits to Savoy, Boniface stayed at the papal court in exile at Lyons from 1244 to 1249. While there he worked to secure the canonization of his predecessor, Edmund of Abingdon, and at the general council summoned by Innocent IV (June–July 1245) was one of the four archbishops chosen to codify the privileges of the church previously acknowledged by emperors and kings. To the annoyance of Henry III he also helped to arrange the marriage of his niece Béatrice, sister of Queen Eleanor, to Charles of Anjou, the younger brother of Louis IX of France. Most important of all, his long stay at Lyons engendered in him a determination to defend the liberties of the church, resist secular control, and pursue ecclesiastical reform, not least by centralizing provincial administration in his own hands.

In September 1249 Boniface returned to England from Lyons bearing the first news of the fall of Damietta to Louis IX, and at Canterbury on 1 November he was enthroned as archbishop in the presence of the king and queen, and most of the prelates. Although Matthew Paris condemned him as 'a man … insufficient for such a dignity … in learning, manners and years' (Paris, *Chron.*, 4.104), Robert Grosseteste, the eminent bishop of Lincoln (at whose funeral Boniface was to officiate in 1253), and the Franciscan scholar Adam Marsh (*d.* 1259) hoped to find in him a like-minded ecclesiastical reformer with the ear of the king. What his suffragans were determined to resist was any attempt to supervise their activities. Despite this, in the spring of 1250, while resentment at his financial demands was at its height, Boniface asserted his metropolitan rights by undertaking a visitation of the clergy of his province. Soon after, at the priory of St Bartholomew's, London, a brawl seems to have occurred about which Adam Marsh, who accompanied the archbishop, claimed 'extremely false accounts have been spread throughout the province both by the clergy and by the populace' (Brewer, 1.163). Matthew Paris's contribution was a damning account of the archbishop, who, he said, wore armour under his vestments and manhandled the sub-prior. After the disputants had appealed to Rome, Boniface left for the continent on 13 June 1250, where he stayed, except for a brief visit to his archiepiscopal see in the following summer, until the end of 1252. During his absence the bishops ignored Marsh's pleas not to disrupt the work of the archbishop, and assembled on several occasions to assert their liberties. The pope, for his part, eventually vindicated Boniface's right of visitation, but exempted parish churches from the payment of procurations in May 1252. That same year his elder brother, Count Amadeus (IV), assigned to him the castle of Tournon and the manor house of Ste Hélène-des-Millières in the Tarentaise.

After Boniface's return to England on 18 November 1252 he was more conciliatory, and even Matthew Paris raised no objection to his conduct during later visitations, which continued intermittently until 1262. Yet there was no weakening in his resolve to protect his rights and supervise his province with strictness. In 1258–9 he successfully defended his jurisdictional liberties by arranging agreements with three of his most powerful vassals by knight service: the priory of Christ Church, Canterbury, the see of Rochester, and the earl of Gloucester. On 22 May 1261 he strengthened his *sede vacante* jurisdiction, and settled a long-running dispute with the diocese of Lincoln, by securing recognition of his authority to appoint members of his own household, rather than officials of the diocese, to take charge during an episcopal vacancy. This agreement became the model for others with the dioceses of London (21 August 1262) and Salisbury (18 January 1263). He also asserted his authority over his suffragans by sanctioning the development of a new 'court of Canterbury' at London to hear appeals from their courts, and other business, and by insisting on receiving personally the profession of obedience of all but three of the thirty-seven bishops consecrated during his archiepiscopate. Consecrations usually took place at Canterbury, and whenever practicable his bishops were required to attend these ceremonial occasions.

Relations with Henry III Much to Henry III's anger and disappointment Boniface was equally vigorous in his defence of ecclesiastical privileges and resistance to the king's interference in episcopal elections, taking up a position he was to defend resolutely for the rest of his life. Even before his first visit to England, he had opposed the king's vindictive efforts to prevent William of Raleigh (*d.* 1250) from becoming bishop of Winchester, and later in 1244 he quashed Henry's attempt to make his clerk, Robert Passelewe (*d.* 1252), bishop of Chichester, after an examination by Grosseteste had found him unfit for office. Boniface was also offended by the arrogance and brutality of the Lusignan half-brothers of the king, who came to England in 1247 and competed for royal patronage with the Savoyard relatives of the queen. In 1252, after he had clashed with one of their number, Aymer de Lusignan (*d.* 1260), bishop-elect of Winchester, over the patronage of the hospital of St Thomas at Southwark, the archbishop's manor of Lambeth was ransacked and one of his officials was abducted. Those responsible were excommunicated, and Boniface and Aymer were not reconciled until 13 January 1253.

Henry took the cross at the hands of Boniface, who may himself have pledged to go, at Westminster on 6 March 1250. After he had persuaded the clergy to grant Henry III a crusading subsidy in return for the king's agreement to reissue Magna Carta, Boniface and thirteen bishops pronounced a sentence of excommunication on 13 May 1253 against those violating the charters and the liberties of the church, a decision confirmed by the pope on 28 September 1253. In Gascony in the following summer, and later in Savoy, he furthered papal policy and the interests of his family in Italy by taking part in the negotiations that resulted, to the dismay of his suffragans, in the diversion of the crusading tenth to the conquest of Sicily.

While again away, mainly in Savoy, between October 1254 and November 1256 Boniface joined his brothers Peter and Philip in an unsuccessful attempt in the summer of 1255 to rescue their brother Count Thomas from captivity at Turin. Meanwhile Henry III's financial exactions had continued. In May 1257 the clergy consented to extend the financial assistance granted to him provided he removed grievances, and did not use this agreement as a precedent for new taxes. The pope urged a compromise, but the king was incensed, and forbade the prelates and other clergy to attend a meeting that Boniface summoned to London in August 1257. Most prelates defied his prohibition and discussed a list of their grievances, as well as authorizing the use of spiritual sanctions against those infringing ecclesiastical liberties. In June 1258 Boniface summoned another meeting for Merton, Surrey, later moved to Westminster, at which the clergy approved a long list of provisions defining the rights of the church.

Boniface and the baronial reform movement Although the clergy may have kept away from the reforming parliament held at Oxford later in the same month, Boniface participated in its work, and must have welcomed some features of the baronial takeover. Along with his brother Peter he was appointed to the new ruling council of fifteen, while Aymer de Lusignan and the king's other Lusignan half-brothers were forced into exile. The barons undertook to seek funds for the Sicilian war, and a promise to reform the church was included in the provisions of Oxford. The archbishop also conducted the impressive ceremony which proclaimed a sentence of excommunication against those who opposed the provisions.

Boniface became increasingly disenchanted with the baronial government when, despite his protests at the infringement of his jurisdiction, the castles of Canterbury and Rochester were given to baronial castellans, the barons failed to finance the papal wars in Sicily, his brother Peter was forced off the council, and no action was taken about the reform of the church. In March 1260 he opposed Simon de Montfort's attempt to hold a parliament in defiance of Henry's wishes, and later he helped Richard, earl of Cornwall (*d.* 1272), the king's brother, who was married to Sanchia, another of the archbishop's nieces, to reconcile the king and his son, the Lord Edward, after a dispute. In the spring of 1261 Alexander IV (*r.* 1254–61) issued a bull absolving Henry from his oath to support the provisions, though he was careful to insist that the king was bound by any changes that were to the advantage of the church. Boniface headed the list of those authorized to absolve the prelates and magnates from their oaths. In August, Boniface published the papal absolution and threatened Hugh Bigod (*d.* 1266), the justiciar, with excommunication if he refused to surrender the castles granted to him under the terms of the provisions.

Responding to a papal request for financial assistance against the Tartar invasion of Hungary, Boniface summoned an ecclesiastical council to meet at Lambeth on 8 May 1261, at which he complained that neither the king nor the barons were prepared to improve the condition of the church. Although an angry Henry III sent a delegation headed by Peter of Savoy and the Lord Edward to press his objections, Boniface and the clergy issued the constitutions of Lambeth on 13 May 1261, a formal restatement of the decisions taken in June 1258, and sought papal confirmation of them. Henry responded by sending proctors to the court of Rome to urge the rejection of the constitutions, which he described as 'to the prejudice of the king's right and dignity and the liberties, law and customs of the realm' (*CPR, 1258–66*, 155). New proctors were appointed in the following January:

> to show the grievances done to the king and the realm by the archbishop of Canterbury and his suffragans, and to obtain the revocation of certain statutes issued by them to the great prejudice of the king and the crown. (*CPR, 1258–66*, 197)

On 25 February 1262 Urban IV (*r.* 1261–4) confirmed the decree of his predecessor, and instructed Boniface and others to absolve the king from any oaths he had taken. All promises made by the prelates and magnates contrary to the dignity of the crown and prejudicial to its rights were declared null and void.

Boniface and the civil war After Boniface left England on 8 October 1262, presumably to secure papal confirmation of the constitutions of Lambeth and to attend to family affairs in Savoy, he found himself increasingly isolated and powerless. His tendency, at times, to exceed his canonical authority had long been a source of anxiety at Rome. Innocent IV had been obliged to use his plenitude of power to confirm Boniface's appointment of Richard of Wyche (*d.* 1253) as bishop of Chichester in 1244, while Alexander IV had overruled the archbishop when he tried to have Adam Marsh made bishop of Ely in preference to Hugh of Balsham (*d.* 1286) in 1256. The archbishop's encroachments on the jurisdiction of diocesan courts had also caused concern. Now the papacy could not allow Boniface's insistence on ecclesiastical reform to compromise its support for Henry III. In January 1263, out of deference to the king, Urban IV refused to approve the constitutions, even though he admitted that he could see nothing wrong in them, and by appointing Guy Foulquois, cardinal-bishop of Sabina, as legate to England in November he deprived Boniface of much of his authority. The increasing disorder in England, especially the ravaging of his lands in Kent, which made it impossible for him to return safely, further undermined Boniface's influence. With their archbishop in exile many of the reforming clergy rallied behind Walter de Cantilupe and other bishops sympathetic to Simon de Montfort, and the disruption in communications enabled a Canterbury monk, Adam of Chillenden, to trick Boniface into appointing him prior of Christ Church. After Henry III's defeat at Lewes on 14 May 1264 Boniface rejected the demands of the Montfortian government that he return to England, or delegate his authority, 'otherwise his emoluments will not be allowed to go out of the realm' (*CPR, 1258–66*, 328). Instead, using the power granted to him by the pope in the spring of 1264 to exercise jurisdiction while resident abroad, he refused in January 1265 to consecrate Walter Giffard (*d.* 1279) as bishop of Bath and Wells until he had appeared before him in France. Meantime, with his future uncertain, and perhaps already often bedridden with the stone, Boniface had made his will at Tournon on 11 October 1264. The experiences of twenty years of incessant travel no doubt explain why one of his many bequests was money to build a bridge over the Rhône on the road between Savoy and France.

It was not until 29 May 1266, almost ten months after Montfort's defeat at Evesham, that Boniface returned to England and recovered possession of his plate and treasure, worth over 6000 marks, which had been safeguarded by his officials throughout the civil war. By then Ottobuono Fieschi, cardinal-deacon of St Adrian (*d.* 1276), who had been appointed legate on 4 May 1265, had already taken charge of ecclesiastical affairs and instituted proceedings against the Montfortian bishops. Although the two men were on friendly terms (the cardinal's sister Béatrice had been married to the archbishop's late brother Thomas), Boniface's authority was effectively in eclipse until Ottobuono's departure in July 1268, the same month in which the archbishop settled a *sede vacante* dispute with the cathedral chapter of Worcester. Despite being disheartened by the ravaging of his estates, he showed continued determination to defend his rights and privileges from whatever quarter they appeared to come under threat, as he demonstrated in April 1266, when he astonished the king by objecting to an appointment to a prebend in Herefordshire. Yet it says much for his weakened standing that Giffard, the official collector of a new crusading subsidy, was able to command him to submit on pain of excommunication.

Although Boniface probably attended the council summoned by Ottobuono to discuss church reform at St Paul's, London, in April 1268, there is no evidence that he played any part in drawing up the important canons it produced, which were in any case published under the name of the legate. When Boniface was too ill to attend the celebration of the feast of St Edward the Confessor at Westminster on 13 October 1268, Giffard, who had been appointed archbishop of York in the previous year, reopened an ancient dispute by having his cross carried before him in the southern province. If the angry Canterbury suffragans showed their feelings by sitting stony-faced in their stalls, Boniface demonstrated his by imposing an interdict on London. He left England for the last time on 14 November 1268, and after his death on 14 July 1270 at Ste Hélène, he was buried with other members of his family in the Cistercian abbey of Hautecombe.

Significance and reputation On the continent, where he spent the greater part of his career of twenty-nine years as archbishop of Canterbury, Boniface was held in high esteem. By the late fourteenth century, his grave, over which an impressive bronze effigy had been erected soon after his death, was the centre of a cult, and it was claimed that Boniface had performed miracles in England during his lifetime. When his tomb was opened in 1580, his body was found to be perfectly preserved. Although the effigy was melted down during the French Revolution, Boniface's remains were reburied under the high altar, and he was beatified by Gregory XVI (*r.* 1831–46) in 1839, when a new stone tomb modelled on the original effigy was erected. In England, by contrast, despite the eulogies of the chroniclers after his death, and the provision in his will of 1000 marks for the poor of his estates, and 20 marks for impecunious scholars at Oxford, most later historians accepted uncritically Matthew Paris's initial vilification of him as a violent, greedy, and neglectful foreigner. Boniface was undoubtedly aggressive and high-handed, he failed to resolve the conflict between family loyalties, the needs of the crown, the interests of his suffragans, and his obligations to the papacy, and he was often absent from England on church and family business at critical times. The civil war, moreover, broke the unity of the ecclesiastical reformers, devastated the archiepiscopal lands, and severely curbed the archbishop's authority. Yet earlier, Boniface's stubborn defence of the prerogatives of the church and of his office had made him the unlikely champion of ecclesiastical liberties, won over many of his former critics, and helped persuade Matthew Paris to modify his first censorious verdict. With papal support Boniface established the rights of provincial visitation in the see of Canterbury, and by clarifying and settling the relationship between the archbishop and his cathedral chapter, largely removed a long-standing conflict between them. His constitutions of Lambeth of May 1261 'became the focus of the continued conflict over the reform of the church up to the seventeenth century' (Wilshire, 65). Although none of his registers has survived, he was clearly also an able administrator who built up an unusually large household and administration, composed almost entirely of university men. So the continuator of Gervase of Canterbury's *Gesta regum* had justification for claiming that 'with great labour and at great expense he procured much good for his church and liberties for himself and his successors' (*Works of Gervase of Canterbury*, 2.250).

CLIVE H. KNOWLES

Sources *Chancery records* · D. A. Williams, 'Aspects of the career of Boniface of Savoy, archbishop of Canterbury, 1241–70', PhD diss., U. Wales, 1970 · L. E. Wilshire, *Boniface of Savoy, Carthusian and archbishop of Canterbury, 1207–1270*, Miscellanea Cartusiensia, 1 (1977) · E. L. Cox, *The eagles of Savoy: the house of Savoy in thirteenth-century Europe* (1974) · F. Mugnier, *Les Savoyards en Angleterre au XIIIe siècle* (1890) · G. Strickland, 'Ricerche storiche sopra il B. Bonifacio di Savoia', *Miscellanea di storia Italiana*, 3rd ser., 32 (1895) · F. M. Powicke and C. R. Cheney, eds., *Councils and synods with other documents relating to the English church, 1205–1313*, 2 vols. (1964) · *The historical works of Gervase of Canterbury*, ed. W. Stubbs, 2 vols., Rolls Series, 73 (1879–80) · R. Foreville, 'L'élection de Boniface de Savoie au siège primatial de Canterbury (1241–1243)', *Bulletin Philologique et Historique* (1960), 435–50 · F. R. H. Du Boulay, *The lordship of Canterbury: an essay on medieval society* (1966) · *CEPR letters*, vol. 1 · F. M. Powicke, *King Henry III and the Lord Edward: the community of the realm in the thirteenth century*, 2 vols. (1947) · J. S. Brewer, ed., *Monumenta Franciscana*, 1, Rolls Series, 4 (1858) · Paris, *Chron.*, vols. 4, 5 · S. Guichenon, *Histoire généalogique de la royale maison de Savoie*, 1 (1660) · A. Gransden, *Historical writing in England*, 1 (1974)

Likenesses engraving (after bronze effigy [destroyed in French revolution]), repro. in Wilshire, *Boniface of Savoy*, 3

Wealth at death numerous bequests: will, Williams, 'Aspects of the career', 487–9

Savoy, Peter of, count of Savoy and *de facto* earl of Richmond (1203?–1268), magnate, was the sixth or seventh son of Thomas (I), count of Savoy (*d.* 1233), and Marguerite, daughter of Guillaume (I), count of Geneva. He was later said to have been born at his family's castle of Susa in 1203.

Early career in Savoy and England As a younger son Peter was intended for a career in the church, and it is as a clerk that he is first recorded, in 1224. By 1226 he was a canon of Lausanne, where in 1229 he was appointed to administer the vacant see, probably in the unfulfilled expectation of his being elected bishop. By 1233 he was probably contemplating the abandonment of his clerical career, for through the agency of his brother William, bishop of Valence, he was then betrothed to Agnès (*d.* 1268), the second daughter of Aymon (II), lord of Faucigny, with the promise of all the Faucigny lands except those already assigned to an elder sister. The marriage took place in 1238. This represented a major expansion of Savoyard influence to the south of Lake Geneva. Peter's attempts to establish a new power base in the western Alps, combined with an aggressive policy towards the neighbouring lords of Geneva, led to a bitter war, and in the winter of 1236–7 Peter was ambushed and briefly taken prisoner. But with family assistance the count of Geneva was worsted, and forced to promise the surrender of various castles and an indemnity of 20,000 marks. In 1237, following the death of his brother Amon, Peter succeeded to an apanage in the Chablais and the Valais, which in turn led to a fierce struggle against the pope and the local ecclesiastical authorities. This dispute may have contributed to the decision of Peter and his brothers to welcome the emperor, Frederick II, to Turin in 1238, and from there to assist in the imperial campaign of reconquest in Lombardy.

By this time the Savoyard ruling family had already obtained an unprecedented position in international affairs, not least through the marriage of Peter's niece Marguerite to Louis IX of France in 1234, followed in 1236 by the marriage of another niece, *Eleanor, to Henry III of England. Various of Peter's kinsmen, including his brothers William and Thomas, count of Flanders from 1237, had already established contacts with the English court, and it was in an attempt to emulate their success that Peter himself sought a meeting with Henry III. In 1240, following a brutal armed assault upon the city of Lausanne which failed to secure the election of his brother Philippe as bishop, Peter made his way to England, where he arrived about Christmas. Thereafter, for the remainder of his life, he was to divide his time and his energies equally between his estates in Savoy and a newfound position at the English court. In England he was afforded an extravagant welcome, and was knighted by the king at Westminster on 5 January 1241. Shortly afterwards his brother, Boniface of *Savoy, was elected archbishop of Canterbury.

In May 1241 Peter was granted the lordship of Richmond in Yorkshire. He appears as a member of the king's council, hearing legal disputes from May 1241, and in September 1241 was granted custody of the heir and lands of William (V) de Warenne, earl of Surrey, and of the castles of Lewes, Pevensey, and Canterbury. This was rapidly followed by custody of Rochester Castle and the Cinque Ports. Native resentment against his promotion was smoothed by Peter's undertaking to surrender Dover, Rochester, and Canterbury castles, and in January 1242 it was Peter who delivered the king's offer of concessions to the barons assembled in parliament. In the same month he received the Sussex honour of Aigle, together with Pevensey Castle, in custody for the next ten years, subsequently transformed into a hereditary fief. Throughout his time in England he appears deliberately to have refrained from claiming the title of earl, describing himself merely as lord of Richmond, perhaps as a sop to baronial opinion.

Consolidation in two countries Peter returned to the continent from June until September 1241, on a mission from Henry III to the barons of Burgundy, and was in Savoy again by December 1241, perhaps to recruit supporters for Henry III's forthcoming campaign in Poitou. In the meantime his previously tense relations with the king's brother, Richard, earl of Cornwall, were eased by Richard's decision to marry yet another of Peter's nieces, Sanchia of Provence, sister of Queen Marguerite and Queen Eleanor. In February 1242, to prepare for the arrival of the English expeditionary force, Peter was sent to Poitou, where he narrowly escaped ambush. He travelled on to Provence, finalizing the arrangements for the marriage of Richard of Cornwall. From Provence he made his way to Savoy, where he resumed the military struggle against Geneva that was to preoccupy him for the next ten years; he secured the strategic lordships of Arlod and Gruyère, and in December 1242 obtained more favourable terms from a marriage negotiated earlier between his daughter Béatrice and Guiges (VII), *dauphin* of the neighbouring province of the Viennois. By the summer of 1244, through a combination of military threats, diplomacy, and purchase, he had effectively imposed his lordship over the entire Pays de Vaud.

Peter then returned to England, where in July 1244 he served as royal spokesman to the clergy in parliament, and in the following year led a major contingent against the Welsh. In February 1246 he was granted a house in the Strand outside London, the origins of the Savoy Palace and, later, the hotel. Having returned briefly to his homeland, in February 1247 he was back in England, bringing with him two Savoyard heiresses, married to Edmund de Lacy, earl of Lincoln, and to Richard, son of the late Hubert de Burgh, one-time earl of Kent, marriages that are said to have bred discontent among the native English baronage. Throughout this period Peter's income from his English estates, together with loans from Richard of Cornwall, served to fund yet further additions to his lordship in Savoy, where in 1248 he was able to purchase the fortified town of Vevey. In October 1249, while still abroad, he was appointed to treat with Louis IX for an extension of the Anglo-French truce, and in the same month was granted custody of Rye Castle and the honour and castle of Hastings, formerly held by the counts of Eu. In 1250 he once again set out for Savoy, *en route* negotiating a further prolongation of the truce with France. While overseas he successfully put down an outbreak of resistance from the lord of La Tour-du-Pin and from his principal rivals, the house of Geneva, obtaining custody of half a dozen of the count of Geneva's most strategically important castles, in theory pending the payment of an indemnity of 10,000 marks, in practice for life.

Peter then returned to England briefly in March 1251, and then became intimately involved in the negotiations for Simon de Montfort's withdrawal from Gascony and in the decision to award the duchy to the Lord Edward, Peter's nephew, rather than to Richard of Cornwall. Throughout this process he served as a staunch supporter of Simon de Montfort, helping to smooth the anger of the king. In August 1251, with his father-in-law on the point of death, he was officially invested with the lordship of Faucigny, used thereafter to tighten his grip over the entire Pays de Vaud as far north as Fribourg and Bern. This process culminated in 1255 in a request from the citizens of Bern and Morat that Peter act as their protector, followed by Peter's award of charters to the two cities, saving whatever loyalty they might owe to the emperor as overlord. In this way, in little more than a decade, backed by the financial resources made available to him from England, Peter had effectively annexed the whole of western Switzerland as a Savoyard fief.

Royal counsellor and diplomat Meanwhile, during one of his occasional visits to England, in November 1252 Peter was appointed keeper of the honour and castle of Tickhill during the Lord Edward's minority, and in the same month became embroiled in the dispute between his brother, Archbishop Boniface of Savoy, and Aymer de Lusignan, bishop-elect of Winchester, that was to escalate into a full-scale factional struggle between the king's Savoyard and Poitevin–Lusignan kinsmen. In the following year he took the cross, being promised the enormous sum of 10,000 marks towards the expenses of his proposed crusade, and receiving a substantial advance payment of 5500 marks in cash so that he might settle his affairs in Savoy. This was accompanied by the award of various lands and wardships, including custody of William de Vescy, who was to be married to a Savoyard heiress at the discretion of Peter and Queen Eleanor.

In July 1253 Peter took charge of various charters relating to the Lord Edward's lands and to the appointment of Eleanor as regent in the event of the king's death, and in the following month accompanied Henry III's expedition to Gascony. There, over the next year, he served as a leading diplomatic adviser, closely involved in the negotiations for the marriage of the Lord Edward to Eleanor of Castile, and in the king's bid for Sicily, intended as a portion for Henry III's younger son, Edmund. Having spent much of 1255 in the Alps, completing his conquest of Bern, by November 1255 he was back in England, passing *en route* through Gascony to give counsel to the Lord Edward. In the following year he was once again appointed to negotiate with Louis IX of France, and thereafter, no doubt because of his experience in papal and imperial politics, was asked to join in discussions over 'the Sicilian business'.

In the summer of 1256 Peter was once again in Savoy, besieging the cities of Turin and Asti whose citizens had in the previous year captured and attempted to ransom his brother Thomas, since 1253 recognized as count of Savoy. He did not return to England until November 1256, at which time the king issued a notorious order, forbidding any writ prejudicial to Peter to be issued by the chancery. In January 1257 he was sent overseas, probably to negotiate the release of his brother Thomas. He was back in England by April 1257, and in the following month, acting together with Queen Eleanor, purchased the wardship of the heir to the Ferrers earldom of Derby, for 6000 marks paid to the Lord Edward. Thereafter he continued to play a part in negotiations over Sicily, and in June 1257, together with Simon de Montfort, travelled to Paris for discussions with the French.

Involvement in the barons' wars With the outbreak of baronial rebellion in the spring of 1258, far from being proscribed by the English barons, Peter joined his other Savoyard kinsmen in a sworn conspiracy against Henry III's Lusignan half-brothers, and in May 1258, at Paris, sealed a provisional draft of the peace treaty with France. In August he advised the barons on their negotiations with the papacy over Sicily, and was sent north, to Scotland, in an effort to prevent disturbances on the northern march. He was subsequently appointed to the council of fifteen that was set to oversee reform. In January 1259 he was sent by the baronial council to greet Richard of Cornwall on his return from Germany, in an attempt to reconcile Richard to the programme of baronial reform. That summer he was in France for the final settlement of Anglo-French disputes under the treaty of Paris. Over the next few months he appears to have crossed and recrossed from France to England on at least two occasions.

By this time Peter had become disenchanted with Simon de Montfort, over Montfort's attempts to exploit the negotiation of the Anglo-French treaty for private interest. As a result he faced attempts by Montfort to secure his removal from the council. In February 1260 he once again set out for Savoy, where, in his absence, his local representatives had continued to make territorial gains at the expense of the neighbouring lords of Geneva and Sion. In 1260 Peter led a successful campaign against the castle of Charousse, obtained various new lordships through pressure placed upon the bishop of Sion, and began the fortification of various outposts in the region of Bern. These had been conceded to him by Richard of Cornwall as king of the Romans in the previous year, and included the lordship of Yverdon on Lake Neuchâtel, where Peter set about the building of a castle. He did not return to England until November 1260, when he rejoined the royalist campaign to suppress baronial reforms, perhaps at least in part because baronial inquiries had threatened various of Peter's own interests in Sussex.

In March 1262 Peter received royal licence to demise Richmond freely after his death, and in June he agreed an exchange with the Lord Edward, surrendering his estates in East Anglia in return for Edward's lordship of Hastings. In July 1262 he accompanied the king to France. He seems to have travelled on to Savoy, where he is to be found in June 1263 at the time of his recognition as count of Savoy in succession to his nephew Boniface, the son of his eldest brother, Amadeus. In the process he effectively usurped the rights of his other nephews, the sons of his brother Thomas, who had been promised the succession to Savoy, but whose military power was no match for Peter's. Thereafter, although he returned briefly to England in November 1263, Peter was increasingly preoccupied with his alpine lordship. During his absence in 1263–4 his English lands were attacked in the opening stages of the baronial revolt led by Simon de Montfort. Peter remained an exile from England throughout the ensuing civil war, although for at least part of this time he is to be found in attendance upon Queen Eleanor in northern France, engaged in attempts to raise money and military support for the king. Since 1259 he had faced the threat that the honour of Richmond would be permanently wrested from him and conferred upon its rightful heir, John of Brittany, who had been reconciled to Henry III under the terms of the Anglo-French peace of 1259.

Last years: achievement With the baronial defeat at Evesham in 1265 Peter's lands were restored, but in May 1266 Richmond was once again seized and conferred upon John of Brittany. Peter himself seems never to have abandoned his claim and he continued to grant charters conferring parts of the Richmond estate, although he made no certain return to England after 1263. From 1265 he was engaged in warfare against Rudolf von Habsburg in the Alps, ended by a treaty negotiated at Löwenburg on 8 September 1267. In May 1268 he drew up a final version of his will, and he died at Pierre-Châtel on 16 or 17 May after a long illness. He was buried in the family abbey of Hautecombe on 18 May 1268. He willed his estates at Faucigny, together with detached portions of the ancestral Savoyard lands, to his only daughter, Béatrice, *dauphine* of Viennois, and his English estates to the sons of Thomas of Savoy, with the exception of the Savoy Palace which he conferred upon the monks of the Grand-St Bernard, and Richmond, which Peter intended for Queen Eleanor. In practice, Eleanor and the Lord Edward proved the principal beneficiaries of his entire English estate. He was succeeded as count of Savoy by his younger brother Philip (*d.* 1285). Peter's widow, Agnès, died shortly after him on 11 August 1268.

From 1240 onwards Peter had shuttled ceaselessly between England and Savoy. However, it was Savoy that appears to have remained closest to his heart. In England he made only a handful of awards to the religious, for the most part simple confirmations of land, although he did attempt to relocate and rebuild the chapel of Pevensey Castle. By contrast, in Savoy he was a generous monastic patron, and it was Savoyards who headed his household, even for his English estates. His principal achievement lay in the conquest of western Switzerland, ensuring that ever afterwards French rather than German would be the language of the western Swiss cantons. The administrative reforms that he instituted there, modelled in part upon the highly centralized government that he and his officials had observed in England, did much to lay the foundations of the later Swiss state. It was Peter who established a fixed financial office at Chambéry, and who, by means of a series of statutes enacted after 1263, transformed the administration of law and justice. Here, ironically, he may well have learned from the reforms attempted by Simon de Montfort and the other baronial rebels against Henry III. In England he is best remembered for his part in the early promotion of the Lord Edward, for his status as a property owner, and in particular for his acquisition and the consequent renaming of the future Savoy Hotel. Although an alien, and therefore suspect to the native English baronage, his activities in 1258–9 serve as a reminder that the baronial rebellion of those years was directed more against the narrow clique of the Lusignans, than against the aliens *en masse*.

NICHOLAS VINCENT

Sources *Chancery records* • Paris, *Chron.* • J. L. Wurstemberger, *Peter der Zweite, Graf von Savoyen, sein Haus und seine Lande*, 4 vols. (1856–8) • E. L. Cox, *The eagles of Savoy: the house of Savoy in thirteenth-century Europe* (1974) • F. Mugnier, 'Les Savoyards en Angleterre au XIIIe siècle', *Mémoires et documents publiés par la Société Savoisienne*, 29 (1890) • J.-P. Chapuisat, 'A propos des relations entre la Savoie et l'Angleterre au XIIIe siècle', *Bulletin Philologique et Historique* (1960) • Cartulary roll of Peter of Savoy, PRO, C47/9/1 • Campbell Charter IX.9 (Rumburgh cartulary), BL, Additional Charters, 11294–7 • H. W. Ridgeway, 'The politics of the English royal court, 1247–65, with special reference to the role of aliens', DPhil diss., U. Oxf., 1983 • H. W. Ridgeway, 'King Henry III and the "aliens", 1236–1272', *Thirteenth century England: proceedings of the Newcastle upon Tyne conference* [Newcastle upon Tyne 1987], ed. P. R. Coss and S. D. Lloyd, 2 (1988), 81–92 • H. W. Ridgeway, 'Foreign favourites and Henry III's problems of patronage, 1247–58', *EngHR*, 104 (1989), 590–610 • J. R. Maddicott, *Simon de Montfort* (1994)

Likenesses tomb effigy, Hautecombe

Savundra, Emil [*formerly* Marion Emil Anacletus Pierre Savundranayagam] (**1923–1976**), swindler, was born on 6 July 1923 in Ceylon. His father was stated to have been a Ceylonese judge. He attended school in Ceylon, and although he never attended university, he gained a doctorate of civil law from the Greek Apostolic Church of St Peter, and in Britain from the 1960s called himself Dr Emil Savundra. With his wife, Pushpan, who came from a rich Ceylonese family and whom he married *c.*1950, he had four sons and a daughter.

During the 1940s, as a Ceylonese army officer, Savundranayagam was involved in dubious military contracts and corrupt sales of surplus equipment. He engaged in shipping frauds and a deal to supply oil to China in which $1 million disappeared (1950). In Ceylon he formed Modern Industries Ltd, which served as a front to obtain $750,000 from Kredietbank of Antwerp on a non-existent cargo of rice to the government of Portuguese Goa (1954); this swindle caused one suicide and another premature death. Extradited from London, Savundranayagam served fifteen months of a five-year prison sentence in Belgium. After his release, he formed four companies with nominal value of £350 million and posed as an economic saviour of Ghana, but was deported after the Camp Bird scandal (1958). In 1959 he perpetrated a coffee bean swindle on the Costa Rican government. He often claimed to be the secret agent of foreign powers. Mandy Rice-Davies, after the death of her protector, the slum landlord Peter Rachman

Emil Savundra (1923–1976), by unknown photographer

in 1962, became the mistress of Savundra, and their relationship figured in the vice trial of Stephen Ward, in which Savundra was referred to as 'the Indian doctor' (1963).

After returning to London, Savundra formed (February 1963) the Fire, Auto, and Marine Insurance Company (FAM), offering motorists cover at about half the price quoted by major companies (which operated a cartel). In an astute ploy he promised insurance brokers (who had hitherto been discouraged as intermediaries in motor business) 20 per cent commission on premiums brought to FAM. He introduced a pioneering computer system and regarded himself as a genius. Although Savundra introduced welcome competition to motoring insurance, his conduct was consistently dishonest. English libel laws gave him indispensable protection. He lied to the auditors when they queried FAM's finances, forged a certificate of government securities worth £540,000 (1965), and invented 'blue-chip' shareholdings worth £870,000 for FAM's balance-sheets (1966). Meanwhile FAM's income was transferred to the Merchant Finance Trust (MFT), a bank formed by Savundra in Liechtenstein. He borrowed £500,000 from MFT at fixed interest of 3 per cent non-repayable for twenty years; Stuart de Quincy Walker, a marine engineer who was managing director of FAM and London manager of MFT, borrowed £224,848 on the same terms. Other sums were lost or misappropriated. Savundra sold his shares in FAM and resigned his directorship in June 1966: within days FAM collapsed. Some 400,000 motorists who had paid premiums found themselves uninsured; unsettled claims exceeded £1.25 million. New insurance legislation was enacted in 1967 and 1973 to prevent further swindles of Savundra's type.

In a disastrous act of braggadocio, Savundra appeared on a BBC television programme (3 February 1967) in which he was confronted with his crimes by David Frost. Savundra disavowed any legal or moral responsibility, strutted like a peacock, and repelled viewers with his wheedling self-righteous hypocrisy. Confronted by a widow who had been deprived of a pay-out after her husband was killed while insured with FAM, he replied, 'I am not going to cross swords with peasants; I am going to cross swords with England's finest swordsmen' (*The Times*, 4 Feb 1967, 1e). Although the directorate of public prosecutions had hitherto been doubtful of success in prosecuting Savundra, inaction was impossible after the Frost programme, and on 10 February he was arrested.

Savundra's trial lasted forty-two days from 10 January to 7 March 1968. His conceit remained irrepressible, and he hampered his counsel by interrupting the proceedings and questioning witnesses. He was such a pompous martinet that Judge King-Hamilton warned him, 'Nobody is going to say "Hail, Caesar" or stand to attention when you come into or out of the witness box' (*The Times*, 15 Feb 1968, 3d). He was sentenced to eight years' imprisonment and fined £50,000.

Released in 1974, Savundra (who was a diabetic with long-standing heart disease) died on 21 December 1976, at his home, 12 Ouseley Road, Old Windsor, Berkshire. His death certificate described him as a retired banker.

RICHARD DAVENPORT-HINES

Sources *The Times* (22 Dec 1976) • *Sunday Times* (11 July 1966) • *Sunday Times* (5 Feb 1967) • T. R. Fehrenbach, *The gnomes of Zurich* (1966), 150–56 • D. Frost, *An autobiography* (1993), 244–53 • *The Times* (Jan–March 1968) • P. Knightley and C. Kennedy, *An affair of state: the Profumo case and the framing of Stephen Ward* (1987) • d. cert.

Archives FILM BBC TV, The Frost Programme (3/3/1967)

Likenesses photograph, News International Syndication, London [*see illus.*]

Sawbridge, Catharine. *See* Macaulay, Catharine (1731–1791).

Sawbridge, George, the elder (*b.* in or before **1621**, *d.* **1681**), printer and bookseller, was born at Hilmorton near Rugby, the son of George Sawbridge, a Warwickshire husbandman. On 19 February 1638 he was apprenticed to the London bookseller Edward Brewster, and after seven years won his freedom on 14 April 1645; about 1646 he also won the hand of Brewster's daughter, Hannah (*c.*1625–1686). When Brewster died in 1647, Sawbridge succeeded him within the Stationers' Company as treasurer of the company's joint-stock venture, the English Stock, a post he held for thirty-two years; he also served as master of the Stationers' Company for 1675–6. From 1647 he operated a shop at the sign of the Bible on Ludgate Hill and sometimes sold books from his house on Clerkenwell Green. He was a leading publisher of medical literature, particularly the posthumous works and translations of Nicholas Culpeper, including a 1679 edition of the London

Pharmacopoeia. He also held shares in the chief publications of his day. He partnered with other printers throughout his career, including Edward Brewster the younger in 1653, and after the Restoration, Sawbridge was a partner in the king's printing house with Samuel Mearne, Richard Roycroft, and others. Ten apprentices were bound to Sawbridge over the years, including two Thomas Sawbridges (the first, probably George's brother, freed in 1666; the second, probably his son, freed by patrimony in 1685).

In 1668, as an executor of the estate of the Cambridge University printer John Field, Sawbridge camouflaged his purchase of Field's printing materials and the leasehold of the university printing house, which still had thirty-four years to run. He paid John Hayes, whose appointment as new university printer Sawbridge had secured, to pose as the owner of Field's business, though Hayes was really only Sawbridge's agent. By company ordinance Sawbridge could not have simultaneously held his post as treasurer of the English Stock and university printer, and should have reported the profits on his Cambridge business to the English Stock account. In January 1679 Sawbridge's secret connection to Hayes was exposed, and he did not stand for another term as treasurer two months later. The company, astounded by Sawbridge's deception, duly revised its rules so that subsequent treasurers had to give up their bookselling businesses entirely and furnish £1000 in securities through guarantors from outside the company. Inventories of Sawbridge's property, mostly investments in the book trade, show him to have been a very wealthy man when he died in London in July 1681; his estate was valued at £11,000, plus a further £15,000 owed to him. In 1683 Sawbridge's widow paid the company £158, a sum that a committee investigating his Cambridge swindle had decided was due to the company.

Hannah Sawbridge maintained the shop at the Bible for five years after her husband's death; her imprint can be found on fifty-two works. She and her son Thomas both died in 1686. The fellow bookman John Dunton remarked on four Sawbridge daughters provided for by their parents, but there was concern about the absence of lands for inheritance. Some confusion persists over the relationship of the Sawbridges to the bookseller George Sawbridge the younger, probably a grandson or grandnephew, who succeeded Thomas Sawbridge at the Three Golden Fleur de Luces in Little Britain, London, in 1692. Despite his misappropriation of English Stock moneys, the elder George Sawbridge left a reputation in the trade that prompted Dunton to describe him as 'the greatest bookseller that has been in England for many years' (*Life and Errors*, 291). ELIZABETH LANE FURDELL

Sources will, PRO, PROB 11/382, sig. 7 [Hannah Sawbridge] • H. R. Plomer and others, *A dictionary of the booksellers and printers who were at work in England, Scotland, and Ireland from 1641 to 1667* (1907) • C. Blagden, *The Stationers' Company: a history, 1403–1959* (1960) • D. F. McKenzie, ed., *Stationers' Company apprentices*, 3 vols. (1961–78), vols. 1–2 • E. Arber, ed., *The term catalogues, 1668–1709*, 3 vols. (privately printed, London, 1903–6) • G. Mandelbrote, 'From the warehouse to the counting house', *A genius for letters*, ed. R. Myers and M. Harris (New Castle, DE, 1995), 49–84 • J. Dunton, *The life and errors of John Dunton … written by himself* (1705) • administration, PRO, PROB 6/56, fol. 89*r* [George Sawbridge]

Wealth at death £11,000: administration, 1681, PRO, PROB 6/56, fol. 89*r*; inventory • £15,000 owed to him • will, PRO, PROB 11/382, sig. 7, fols. 53*r*–54*v* [Hannah Sawbridge]

Sawbridge, John (1732–1795), politician, was the third child of John Sawbridge (1699–1762), a landowner, of Olantigh, Kent, and Elizabeth (1710/11–1733), the daughter of a London banker, George Wanley. He was educated at King's School, Canterbury. According to Horace Walpole he served in the army until 1762, when he inherited from his father extensive estates in Kent and Middlesex. He soon added to his fortune by two marriages, first on 15 November 1763 to Mary Diana (*d*. 1764), the daughter of Sir Orlando Bridgeman, fourth baronet (1695–1764), and Anne Newport, with a dowry of £100,000. She died two months later, and on 16 June 1766 Sawbridge married Anne, the daughter of a London distiller, Sir William Stephenson. He became a partner in the business and fathered three sons and a daughter.

Wealth stimulated political ambition. At the general election of 1768 Sawbridge was returned for Hythe, a borough 10 miles from his home. But he owed his success in that Cinque Port to government support, and since he always acted with the opposition in parliament his subsequent candidatures there, in 1774 and 1784, were unsuccessful. Sawbridge promptly became a champion of John Wilkes in the famous Middlesex elections controversy, proposing the latter's nomination at the third by-election of 13 April 1769, and being a founder member of the Society of Supporters of the Bill of Rights. His role as a prominent Wilkite secured him election that summer as a City of London alderman, for life, and as one of the City's two annual sheriffs. But in 1771 he was among the radicals who believed the society should widen its objectives beyond what seemed to be the sole purpose of paying Wilkes's debts, and who seceded to form a new club, the Constitutional Society. Wilkes, deeming Sawbridge 'an absolute dupe' of his enemies, commented to Junius: 'I allow him honest, but think he has more mulishness than understanding, more understanding than candour' (*Letters of Junius*, 415). Sawbridge, widely respected for his probity and independence of mind, soon became aware of the advantage government gained in London politics from the radical split. Before the general election of 1774 he made a private arrangement with Wilkes that gave him a parliamentary seat for London on the Wilkite ticket in return for his support of Wilkes's candidature for lord mayor. Sawbridge headed the London poll and succeeded Wilkes as lord mayor in 1775. As part of this arrangement Sawbridge endorsed the political programme of the Society of Supporters of the Bill of Rights, including parliamentary reform. His personal hobby horse was annual parliamentary elections, and for a decade from 1771 an annual feature of the parliamentary calendar was his motion for a shorter parliaments bill.

On America, Sawbridge challenged ministerial policy when few did so after the Boston Tea Party. At the introduction of the Boston Port Bill on 14 March 1774 he met a hostile reception when he denied parliament's right to tax America, arguing that 'there can be no such thing as liberty when you can be taxed without your consent' (Simmons and Thomas, 4.65). The Massachusetts Justice Act, providing for the transfer to Britain of trials of soldiers and officials, incurred his repeated condemnation as unfair and unworkable. Sawbridge often made the point that his support of the colonies did not derive 'from a desire of gaining popularity. For certainly the cause of America is not a popular cause in this country. It doth proceed from a love of liberty' (ibid., 4.400). But the Quebec Act, giving the Catholic church official status in that former French colony, enabled Sawbridge and other radicals to whip up popular feeling in London against a measure that seemed to threaten protestantism as well as liberty. That anti-Catholic reaction in 1774 presaged the Gordon riots of 1780, which gave Sawbridge ground to demand repeal of the Catholic Relief Act that had precipitated that disorder.

Denunciation of the North ministry on 12 November 1775 as 'the most unprincipled prostitute tools that ever disgraced this country' (Almon, 3.156) was typical of the repeated attacks Sawbridge made on that administration with what the diarist Nathaniel Wraxall recalled as 'his republican bitterness' (Wraxall, 3.64–5): many suspected Sawbridge of the republican views of his elder sister, the historian Catharine *Macaulay. He was indeed falsely denounced for involvement in a plot to assassinate George III, and he in turn accused the government of framing him. At the 1780 election the ministry contrived to bring about his defeat in London, but he was soon returned at a by-election there. In the political reshuffle of 1782 he became a Foxite and remained one for the rest of his life, narrowly retaining his London seat in 1784 and 1790 contests. He never lost his zeal for 'civil and religious liberty'; in practice this meant parliamentary reform, which he himself proposed in 1784, shorter parliaments, and repeal of the Test Act. Contemporaries assumed that he would have opposed war with the French in 1793 had he not been paralysed for his last three years—his death at his town house in Gloucester Place, Portman Square, on 21 February 1795 being seen as a merciful release. He was buried at Olantigh.

Sawbridge was evidently a rough diamond. Wilkes commented to Junius in 1771 that he was 'not the best-bred man in the island' (*Letters of Junius*, 415). Wraxall was more forthright: 'He was … almost hideous in his aspect … of a coarse figure, and still coarser manners; but possessing an ample fortune, and a strong understanding'. But he ended the pen-portrait with this tribute: 'No individual in our time, that had filled the post of lord mayor, if we except Wilkes, attained to greater popularity than Sawbridge' (Wraxall, 5.105). And the reminiscence of Horace Walpole was a tribute to his character:

> His soul was all integrity, and his private virtues all great and amiable. His capacity, though not deficient, was not bright … He was more respected in his party, than followed, his honesty restraining the dictates of his zeal, and his bigotry being founded on principle, not on doctrines and creeds. (Walpole, 3.192)

PETER D. G. THOMAS

Sources P. D. G. Thomas, *John Wilkes: a friend to liberty* (1996) • I. R. Christie, 'Sawbridge, John', HoP, *Commons, 1754–90* • *The letters of Junius*, ed. J. Cannon (1978) • R. C. Simmons and P. D. G. Thomas, eds., *Proceedings and debates of the British parliaments respecting North America, 1754–1783*, 4 (1985) • H. Walpole, *Memoirs of the reign of King George the Third*, ed. G. F. R. Barker, 4 vols. (1894) • N. W. Wraxall, *Historical memoirs of his own time*, new edn, 4 vols. (1836) • N. W. Wraxall, *Posthumous memoirs of his own time*, 2nd edn, 3 vols. (1836) • J. Almon, ed., *The parliamentary register, or, History of the proceedings and debates of the House of Commons*, 17 vols. (1775–80) • *DNB* • *GM*, 1st ser., 65 (1795), 216–18 • B. Hill, *The republican virago: the life and times of Catharine Macaulay* (1992)

Likenesses R. Houston, group portrait, mezzotint, pubd 1769, BM, NPG • T. Watson, mezzotint, pubd 1772 (after B. West), BM, NPG • J. Sayers, caricature, etching, pubd 1785, NPG • J. Sayers, caricature, soft-ground etching, pubd 1788 (after unknown artist), NPG • J. Sayers, caricature, etching, pubd 1789, NPG • Ridley, stipple, pubd 1798 (after unknown artist), NPG • B. Smith, group portrait, stipple, pubd 1801 (after portrait, *Lord Mayor Newnham taking the oaths*, 1782 by W. Miller), BM • J. Hopwood, stipple, pubd 1805, BM

Sawer, George (*d.* 1627), parish officer, was possibly a son of Edmund Sawer (*d.* 1556) of Scottow, Norfolk, and his wife, Elizabeth (*d.* in or after 1556). Edmund Sawer's will, dated 23 March 1556, refers only to a son named Edmund, suggesting that George was a posthumous child if the identification of his parentage is correct. Little is known about George's early life, beyond notes about the estate of his possible father, whose widow married John Reve of Cawston in Norfolk; George Sawer occupied lands of John Reve in 1601. At some point he studied surveying, signing maps of estates in Felbrigg (1598) and Mannington in Norfolk; maps of Thurning and Sall (or Salle) in the same county and Alvington Field in Cawston in a similar style are attributed to him. He married in or before 1579; his wife, whose name is unknown, was buried at Cawston on 29 April 1619. They had one son, Edmund (1579–1670), MP and auditor of the exchequer, and one daughter who married Francis Phelips of Toddington, Bedfordshire, later also an exchequer official.

Sawer is unremarkable save for the extraordinary collection of his papers that has survived: his career and family illuminate several important dimensions of late sixteenth- and early seventeenth-century England. While the parish register which recorded his death described him as a gentleman, in earlier years he was referred to as a yeoman, and manorial rentals in Cawston never accord him gentry status. Like many men of new wealth in the early Stuart period Sawer sat on the uncertain boundary of gentry status, though his family was on the way up.

Sawer was active in parish affairs from the mid-1590s until about 1620, serving as churchwarden at least twice, and overseer of the poor at least six times. He also helped to co-ordinate a lawsuit brought by the tenants of Cawston against the farmer of the fold-course in 1602. Sawer, described by the rector of Cawston as a 'precise' in 1592 (Norfolk RO, DEP/30, Book 32, Funston con Sawer,

1598), reflects much of what we might expect from a puritan gentleman of the period: his papers indicate almost equal obsessions with order and adequate provision for the poor. The earliest of his parish papers is a draft complaint about a disorderly villager; the following documents how resources for feeding the poor in the town were organized in the famine years of 1596–7. These include a weekly schedule of who was to bring how much grain to market for sale at subsidized rates in 1596 and 1597; lists of those eligible to buy subsidized grain, distinguished by the level of subsidy in 1596–7; lists of the poor, by age and with numbers in each household; lists of the poor which sorted them by level of need; and detailed rating lists. These papers show how both need and ability were defined in response to the crises of the 1590s in a town suffering both from poor harvests and the collapse of the cloth trade. Sawer used his training as a surveyor in his parish work, and ensured that determinations of need and of ability to pay were made rationally. As churchwarden in 1604 he oversaw an extensive rebuilding of the church; before levying the rate he estimated the values of all estates in the parish.

Sawer's family also illustrates the rising gentry. Through his son and son-in-law Sawer received regular news of events in London and at court. They helped him with business in London, while he helped them with Norfolk property. Although he apparently rarely left Cawston, the letters he received kept him well informed of both family and political events in the capital. Kinship was not only instrumental: he kept a charming thank-you note from his grandson, Francis Phelips, when he had just become a grammarian. At various times he provided a home for his niece and a grandson. Sawer, with his care for his neighbours and contacts with the larger world through his family, not only provides connections among puritan parish notables, the rising gentry, and responses to poverty, but also gives them a human face. He died in 1627 and was buried at Cawston on 30 October.

SUSAN D. AMUSSEN

Sources Norfolk RO, NRS 2604, 12B2; MC 148/5–39; MC 254 • parish register, Cawston, 29 April 1619, Norfolk RO, PD 193/1 • parish register, Cawston, 30 Oct 1627, Norfolk RO, PD 193/1 • T. Wales, 'Poverty, poor relief and the life-cycle: some evidence from seventeenth century Norfolk', *Land, kinship and life-cycle*, ed. R. M. Smith (1984), 351–404 • S. D. Amussen, *An ordered society: gender and class in early modern England* (1988) • S. D. Amussen, 'A Norfolk village: Cawston, 1595–1605', *History Today*, 36/4 (1986), 15–20 • PRO, E. 134 43/44, Eliz. I Mich. 7 • will, 1556, Norfolk RO, NCC 319 Beeles [Edmund Sawer] • Norfolk RO, Map 4521E

Archives Norfolk RO, letters, accounts, and MSS, NRS 2604 12B2; MC 148/5–39; MC 254 • Norfolk RO, maps, NRS 5863/1; ACCN 19.11.70 P150B4

Sawrey, Solomon (1765–1825), surgeon, received his professional education from Andrew Marshal, who taught anatomy privately in Bartlett's Court, Thavies' Inn, from 1791 to 1799. Sawrey attended Marshal's lectures in 1794, and attracted his attention by a dissection of the nerves of the eye. Sawrey was admitted a member of the Company of Surgeons in July 1796, and for some years he was demonstrator and assistant lecturer to Marshal. He lived first in Bucklersbury and afterwards in Chancery Lane, London. He practised in both places, and in later life he turned his attention more especially to ophthalmic surgery.

Sawrey published two slight works in 1794 and 1802, and a work on the eye in 1807, but he is remembered for editing Marshal's *Morbid Anatomy of the Brain in Mania and Hydrophobia* (1815) with a useful 34-page memoir of Marshal. Sawrey died in 1825.

D'A. POWER, *rev.* JEAN LOUDON

Sources A. Marshal, *Morbid anatomy of the human brain in mania and hydrophobia*, ed. S. Sawrey (1815) [with a memoir] • private information (1897, 2004) • S. C. Lawrence, *Charitable knowledge: hospital pupils and practitioners in eighteenth-century London* (1996)

Sawston [Sansetun], **Benedict of** (*d.* 1226), bishop of Rochester, was probably a native of Sawston, Cambridgeshire. Nothing is certainly known of his education, though he seems to have had legal training and it has been conjectured that he studied in Paris under Stephen Langton. His opinions are quoted in the Cambridge manuscript of Langton's *Questiones*. He appears in the 1190s as Master Benedict, witnessing charters concerning St Paul's Cathedral. He had been appointed precentor of St Paul's by 26 March 1204, when King John, at the request of the bishop of London, endowed the precentorship with the church of Shoreditch; he also held the prebend of Neasden. Sawston sought to improve the uniquely low standing of the precentor of St Paul's by appropriating the stall of the archdeacon of London, Peter of Blois, but without success. While precentor, he acted as a papal judge-delegate on four occasions.

At the time of his election as bishop of Rochester, on 13 December 1214, on the recommendation of Archbishop Stephen Langton, Sawston was teaching in the schools of Paris. A fourteenth-century Rochester source refers to him as *thesaurarius regis*, but this probably indicates confusion with another Master Benedict [*see* Benedict of Ramsay] who had been active in the king's service. He was consecrated by the archbishop at Osney, near Oxford, on 22 February 1215, and on 15 June of that year he was among the king's advisers at the sealing of Magna Carta. He attended the Fourth Lateran Council in November 1215. A month earlier, while besieging Rochester Castle, King John had occupied the city, quartered soldiers in the cathedral, destroyed manuscripts, and carried off plate and money. In 1218–19, Benedict headed the justices on eyre for the counties of Sussex, Surrey, Kent, and Middlesex. He is found witnessing royal charters at Westminster in January and March 1224. His own episcopal chancery is notable for introducing the dating of documents by time and place at Rochester. In October 1225 he was a member of the last of three embassies sent in that year to treat for peace with Louis VIII of France—none of them was successful. Sawston died on 18 December 1226, and was buried in Rochester Cathedral on 21 December.

M. N. BLOUNT

Sources *Fasti Angl., 1066–1300*, [St Paul's, London] • *Fasti Angl., 1066–1300*, [Monastic cathedrals] • M. Gibbs, ed., *Early charters of the cathedral church of St Paul, London*, CS, 3rd ser., 58 (1939) • T. D. Hardy, ed., *Rotuli litterarum clausarum*, 2 vols., RC (1833–4) • *CPR, 1216–25* •

M. Gibbs and J. Lang, *Bishops and reform, 1215–1272* (1934) · K. Major, 'The "familia" of Archbishop Stephen Langton', *EngHR*, 48 (1933), 529–57 · 'Libellus a monachis Roffensibus anno MCCCLX oblatus de jure eligendi', *Anglia sacra*, ed. [H. Wharton], 1 (1691), 384–6 · C. R. Cheney, *Pope Innocent III and England* (1976) · S. Kuttner and E. Rathbone, 'Anglo-Norman canonists of the twelfth century', *Traditio*, 7 (1949–51), 279–358 · J. E. Sayers, *Papal judges delegate in the province of Canterbury, 1198–1254* (1971) · J. A. Robinson, 'Peter of Blois', *Somerset historical essays* (1921), 100–40 · M. N. Blount and M. Brett, eds., *Rochester*, English Episcopal Acta [forthcoming] [Sawston's Episcopal Acta]

Archives BL, Rochester monastic registers, chronicles, and charters · CKS, Rochester episcopal and other registers · GL, St Paul's Cathedral archives · Medway Archives and Local Studies Centre, Rochester, Kent, Rochester dean and chapter archives

Sawtre [Sawtrey], **William** (*d.* **1401**), Lollard martyr, was serving as a parish chaplain at St Margaret's, Bishop's Lynn, and Tilney, also in Norfolk, when he was initially tried on 30 April and 1 May 1399 before Bishop Henry Despenser of Norwich, accused of preaching ten heretical opinions. He had declared that he would rather venerate a living monarch, or the bodies of the saints, or a confessed and contrite man, than any crucifix; that priests should preach or teach rather than say canonical services; and that money used for pilgrimages would be better spent on the poor. Most significantly, he also held that real bread remained on the altar after the words of consecration, which according to orthodox doctrine transubstantiated it into the body of Christ. At first defiant, a few weeks later he was persuaded or pressured into abandoning these beliefs, abjuring them publicly at Lynn, and swearing never again to preach or hold them.

By early 1400 Sawtre had moved to London, as parish chaplain of St Benet Sherehog. There, however, he apparently maintained links with other Lollard suspects (including the Oxfordshire gentleman Thomas Compworth), and certainly continued to preach heresy. On 12 February 1401 he was therefore arraigned as a relapsed heretic before a full convocation at St Paul's, presided over by Archbishop Arundel. Having been allowed six days to consider his defence, he is said to have returned ingeniously temporizing answers to most of the charges, but was interrogated closely by the archbishop himself concerning the vital question of transubstantiation. For several hours Arundel unremittingly rephrased his questions as Sawtre 'vacillatingly' rephrased his answers, sometimes replying 'as if mockingly' and sometimes protesting ignorance. But at last he asserted that he could only accept the church's ruling if it did not conflict with the will of God, and declared that following the words of consecration the altar bread 'remained true bread, and the same bread as before' (Wilkins, 3.255–7).

Sawtre was thus condemned as an avowed heretic, his relapse being formally established by documentary proof of his earlier abjuration (which he had hitherto denied). He made no plea for mercy. Indeed, according to the chronicler Adam Usk, he prophesied imminent ruin for clergy, king, and kingdom. On 26 February, therefore, he was ceremonially stripped of his priestly orders before a large congregation at St Paul's, to whom the archbishop expounded the condemned man's offences in English. He was then handed over as a layman to the secular powers, and soon afterwards (perhaps on 2 March) burnt at Smithfield, 'bound, standing upright, to a post set in a barrel with blazing wood all around, and thus reduced to ashes' (*Chronicle of Adam of Usk*, 123).

Sawtre's execution was authorized by direct royal command, since the statute *De haeretico comburendo* (which decreed death for relapsed heretics) was not formally promulgated until some weeks later. According to Thomas Netter's *Fasciculi zizaniorum*, Sawtre had appealed for trial before parliament, but without success. The statute may thus have been intended to strengthen the common law against future offenders. Reinforced by the example of Sawtre's death, it proved beyond doubt that the state would henceforth back the church to the utmost.

The first of the small company of Lollard martyrs, Sawtre was reviled by orthodox chroniclers but honoured by his underground co-religionists: one such, William Emayn of Bristol, in 1429 called Sawtre 'a holy man … worshipped in heaven' (Holmes, 1.79), and he later figured prominently in Foxe's protestant book of martyrs.

CHARLES KIGHTLY

Sources D. Wilkins, ed., *Concilia Magnae Britanniae et Hiberniae*, 3 (1737) · *RotP*, vol. 3 · P. McNiven, *Heresy and politics in the reign of Henry IV* (1987) · C. Kightly, 'The early Lollards', DPhil diss., University of York, 1975 · K. B. McFarlane, *John Wycliffe* (1966) · *The chronicle of Adam Usk, 1377–1421*, ed. and trans. C. Given-Wilson, OMT (1997) · [T. Netter], *Fasciculi zizaniorum magistri Johannis Wyclif cum tritico*, ed. W. W. Shirley, Rolls Series, 5 (1858) · J. Foxe, *Acts and monuments*, 7th edn, 3 vols. (1632) · *Thomae Walsingham, quondam monachi S. Albani, historia Anglicana*, ed. H. T. Riley, 2 vols., pt 1 of *Chronica monasterii S. Albani*, Rolls Series, 28 (1863–4), vol. 2 · *Chancery records* · A. Hudson, *The premature reformation: Wycliffite texts and Lollard history* (1988) · J. A. F. Thomson, *The later Lollards* (1965) · A. K. McHardy, 'De haeretico comburendo, 1401', *Lollardy and the gentry in the later middle ages*, ed. M. Aston and C. Richmond (1997), 112–26 · T. S. Holmes, ed., *The register of John Stafford, bishop of Bath and Wells, 1425–1443*, 1, Somerset RS, 31 (1915)

Sawyer, Edmund (*b.* after **1687**, *d.* **1759**), lawyer, born shortly after 1687, was probably the younger son of Edmund Sawyer of White Waltham, Berkshire, and his wife, Mary, second daughter of John Finch of Fiennes, Berkshire. He was of the Inner Temple, but on 28 April 1719 was admitted member of Lincoln's Inn. By 1725 Sawyer had clearly acquired some prominence in the household of John, second duke of Montagu, and was acting as his principal 'man of business', being engaged by Montagu on various law matters, including the holding of manorial courts on the duke's extensive Northamptonshire estates. For these services Montagu had Sawyer created gentleman-usher to the order of the Bath when the order was set up under the duke's close supervision in May 1725, and the following year, under a revision of the order's statutes, he was given the office of Brunswick herald (albeit this was an office peculiar to the order, and did not as such attach him to the College of Arms). He did, however, participate in the ceremonies of the order in June 1725 and June 1732, and officiated with the other heralds at the coronation of George II in October 1727. He relinquished his Bath offices in July or August 1738 (probably at the same time he became a master in chancery), in which latter month a warrant for his successor was issued. In 1750 he and Richard Edwards were nominated commissioners to examine the claims of the creditors of the Royal African Company. He died in possession of the dignity of master in chancery on 9 October 1759. Sawyer compiled the valuable *Memorials of Affairs of State in the Reigns of Queen Elizabeth and King James* (1725), a work which was chiefly derived from the papers of Sir Ralph Winwood and Sir Henry Neville. W. A. SHAW, *rev.* ROBERT BROWN

Sources W. Berry, *County genealogies: pedigrees of Berkshire families* (1837) · Watt, *Bibl. Brit.* · W. P. Baildon, ed., *The records of the Honorable Society of Lincoln's Inn: admissions*, 2 vols. (1896) · *GM*, 1st ser., 20 (1750), 237 · *GM*, 1st ser., 29 (1759), 497 · *GM*, 1st ser., 8 (1738), 277

Sawyer, Elizabeth (*d.* 1621), convicted witch, was a poor woman of obscure origins living in Edmonton, Middlesex, convicted under the Witchcraft Act in April 1621 and hanged for murdering her neighbour by diabolical means. What is known of her life comes from *The Wonderfull Discoverie of Elizabeth Sawyer, a Witch*, the account of her trial and prison confession written by Henry Goodcole, ordinary (chaplain) of Newgate prison. No formal trial records survive.

Elizabeth Sawyer was a married woman with children, pale faced with a stoop which left her body 'bending together' (Goodcole, sig. A4*v*). She had only one eye, a condition which Goodcole says that she shared with at least one of her unnamed parents. Sawyer herself said that she had been injured in an accident: when bending down beside the bed of her dying mother she had stabbed her eye on a stick held by one of her children.

Sawyer had long been suspected of witchcraft by her neighbours. Suspicion had hardened 'to great presumptions, seeing the death of Nurse-children and Cattell, strangely and suddenly to happen' (Goodcole, sig. A4*r*) and crystallized into a resolution to prosecute after a traditional method of identifying a witch—burning thatch from her house to see whether she would be summoned by the act—confirmed local fears. The investigating magistrate, Arthur Robinson, who had long shared local suspicions and had already examined Sawyer several times, committed her to Newgate to await trial at the Old Bailey. She was tried on 14 April 1621, accused of murdering Agnes Ratcleife and two children whose names are not known. Goodcole sited the motivation for these killings in a generalized malice towards neighbours who would not buy the brooms which Sawyer sold, adding that in Ratcleife's case there had been a more specific quarrel. Ratcleife had hit a sow of Sawyer's which had eaten some soap of hers, and Sawyer had vowed revenge. Ratcleife had fallen ill, foaming at the mouth in her sickness, and died four days later naming Sawyer as her killer. Sawyer pleaded not guilty to all three charges.

Agnes Ratcleife's husband witnessed to his wife's dying words (which according to Goodcole made a great impression on the jury), while children testified that they had often seen Sawyer feed two white ferrets with bread and milk. Sawyer's husband also spoke against her: he had seen what was thought to be a spirit or devil in the form of a white ferret run through the thatch of their house. The jury were uncertain of their verdict, and asked the presiding judge, Heneage Finch, recorder of London, to advise them. He referred them to God's guidance, but Arthur Robinson suggested that Sawyer be searched for a witch's mark. Three disinterested women were fetched, who searched Sawyer's body. Although she resisted, 'sluttishly and loathsomely' (Goodcole, sig. B3*r*), a teat-like growth was found near her anus which Sawyer continued to deny existed. She was then convicted of Ratcleife's murder, though acquitted of killing the children.

Sawyer was visited in Newgate by Goodcole on 17 April and, answering leading and prurient questions, said that she had met the devil eight years earlier when he appeared to her when she was cursing, swearing, and blaspheming. Subsequently he visited her secretly three times a week as a black or white dog called Tom. Sawyer had fearfully given her body and soul to the devil-dog and he had told her to pray to Satan, using part of the Latin paternoster. He had sucked her blood through the teat under her clothes. She said that the sucking took a quarter of an hour, but was not painful. Tom did whatever she wished, and although he threatened her for disobeying and mocking his instructions she spoke of stroking and petting him. She denied the murder of Agnes Ratcleife, but confessed that of the children, reversing the finding of the court. She confirmed every aspect of her confession to Goodcole and replied piously to his questions when she was hanged at Tyburn on 19 April.

Goodcole's pamphlet was written in three or four days and registered with the Stationers' Company on 27 April. He would have preferred to have remained silent, he explained, 'knowing the diversitie of opinions concerning things of this nature, and that not among the ignorant, but among some of the learned' (Goodcole, sig. A3*r*). He was publishing it because he was being continually pestered for copies of Sawyer's confession. Evasive, indeed panicky, as he was in locating his account in relation to current debates about witchcraft, he claimed merely to relate the truth of the case. Furthermore, he wished to correct the stories spread by 'most base and false Ballets [ballads], which were sung at the time of our returning from the Witches execution', which by their exaggerations and absurdities undermined belief in the truth of the case. These told of 'a Ferret and an Owle dayly sporting before her, of the bewitched woman brayning her selfe, of the Spirits attending in the Prison': all stories 'fitter for an Ale-bench then for a relation of proceeding in Court of Justice' (Goodcole, sig. A3*v*). Goodcole presented Sawyer's fate as the working out of God's providential justice, an awful warning of the consequences of sin to those who, like her, were given to cursing and blasphemy. Her evil tongue had brought the devil to her and had finally betrayed her at her trial. Unable to 'speake a sensible or ready word for her defense', she had given out 'many most fearefull imprecations for destruction against herselfe then to happen, as heretofore she had wished and indeavoured to happen on divers of her neighbours' (Goodcole, sig. B*r*).

Goodcole's narrative of sin, final penitence, and potential redemption was drawn on within the year by John Ford, Thomas Dekker, and William Rowley in *The Witch of Edmonton*, which was probably first performed at the Cockpit Theatre and was certainly acted at court on 29 December 1621. Elizabeth Sawyer's relationship with the devil-dog became central to the play: the speaking dog is played by an actor, and his combination of friendliness with evil leaves the audience pitying her for her lonely dependence on her Satanic pet. Sawyer is shown as a poor and ugly victim of vicious abuse by the rich and corrupt, a unique portrayal of a witch which owes much to Reginald Scot's *Discoverie of Witchcraft* (1584). MARION GIBSON

Sources H. Goodcole, *The wonderfull discoverie of Elizabeth Sawyer, a witch* (1621) • M. Gibson, *Early modern witches: witchcraft cases in contemporary writing* (2000) • M. Gibson, *Reading witchcraft: stories of early English witches* (1999) • K. J. Leuschner, 'Creating the "known true story": sixteenth and seventeenth century murder and witchcraft pamphlets and plays', PhD diss., U. Cal., 1992 • W. Rowley, T. Dekker, and J. Ford, *The witch of Edmonton*, ed. P. Corbin and D. Sedge (1986)

Sawyer, Herbert (*b.* in or before **1730**, *d.* **1798**), naval officer, details of whose parents and upbringing are unknown, entered the navy in 1747. He served for six years, more than half the time in the *Gloucester* with Commodore George Townshend on the Jamaica station. On 30 August 1753 he passed his lieutenant's examination when it was stated that he was 'more than 22'. On 4 March 1756 he was promoted lieutenant, and in 1757 he was serving in the *Grafton*, one of the fleet off Louisbourg, under Vice-Admiral Francis Holburne. On 19 May 1758 he was promoted to the command of the sloop *Happy*, from which, in October, he was moved to the *Swallow*, one of the squadron on the coast of France, under the orders of Lord Howe. On 26 December he was posted to the *Chesterfield*, and in February 1759 he was appointed to the *Active* (28 guns), in which he continued during the war, and in which off Cadiz on 21 May 1762, in company with the sloop *Favourite*, commanded by Philemon Pownoll, he captured the Spanish treasure ship *Hermione*, with a total cargo of over £500,000 in cash and bullion; of this Sawyer's share amounted to £65,053 13*s.* 9*d.*, one of the largest amounts realized at one haul in the period. Now an extremely wealthy man, Sawyer married the daughter of a Lisbon merchant.

Sawyer was appointed to the *Boyne* in 1777, joined Rear-Admiral Samuel Barrington in the West Indies in 1778, and took part in the defeat of d'Estaing at St Lucia on 15 December; he was in the action off Grenada, under Vice-Admiral John Byron on 6 July 1779, and in the autumn returned to England. In 1780–81 he commanded the *Namur* in the channel, and at the relief of Gibraltar in April 1781, but quitted her when she was ordered to the West Indies in December. From 1783 to 1785 he commanded the guardship *Bombay Castle* at Plymouth.

Sawyer was next appointed commodore of the small peacetime North American base at Halifax, and his principal task was to guard the coasts against American intruders and, with the military, ensure the safety of the new settlements of disbanded soldiers and loyalist refugees. Upon his arrival in June 1785 he authorized the frigate *Mercury* to escort a merchant vessel to Boston to fetch a shipment of live cattle, in an attempt to break the monopoly of the Nova Scotia suppliers. It was the first time since March 1776 that a British warship had freely entered the harbour. When her captain refused to salute the state flag flying from Castle William, a mob assaulted the landing party, led by her captain, and besieged them in a magistrate's home. After days of negotiations to effect their release, they made their departure. In 1787, while visiting Quebec with his ships, Sawyer was embarrassed by a French squadron of three ships of the line and four frigates, which sailed unchallenged along the Nova Scotia coast bound for Boston. He returned to England without orders in August 1788, and never again went to sea.

On 24 September 1788 Sawyer was promoted rear-admiral. He became vice-admiral on 1 February 1793, and admiral on 1 June 1795, but his failing health did not permit him to accept any command. He died at Bath on 4 June 1798. His eldest son, Sir Herbert Sawyer, who was also later in command of the North American squadron, at the outset of the Anglo-American War of 1812–14, died an admiral in 1833. J. K. LAUGHTON, *rev.* JULIAN GWYN

Sources J. Gwyn, 'The culture of work: in the Halifax naval yard before 1820', *Nova Scotia Historical Society*, Journal 2 (1999) • P. Webb, 'British squadrons in North American waters, 1783–1793', *Northern Mariner*, 5 (April 1995), 19–34 • R. A. Evans, 'The army and navy at Halifax in peacetime, 1783–1793', MA diss., Dalhousie University, 1970 • J. Charnock, ed., *Biographia navalis*, 6 vols. (1794–8) • *GM*, 1st ser., 60 (1790), 540 • R. Beatson, *Naval and military memoirs of Great Britain*, 2nd edn, 6 vols. (1804)

Sawyer, Sir Robert (*bap.* **1633**, *d.* **1692**), lawyer and politician, was baptized on 20 September 1633 at White Waltham, Berkshire, the sixth but only surviving son of Sir Edmund Sawyer (*d.* 1676) of Heywood, Berkshire, and his wife, Anne, daughter of Sir William Whitmore of Shropshire. In 1648 Sawyer matriculated as a pensioner from Magdalene College, Cambridge, where he shared rooms with Samuel Pepys. Sawyer took his BA in 1652 and MA in 1655. By this time he had entered the Inner Temple, where he became a barrister in 1661. On 1 July 1665 he married Margaret Suckley (*b.* *c.*1647), daughter of Ralph Suckley, in Islington.

Having begun chiefly in the court of exchequer, Sawyer's legal practice flourished, enabling him to purchase Highclere in Hampshire in 1671. On 1 November 1673 High Wycombe chose him at a by-election as a member of parliament. A petition against his election by some townsmen came to nothing and the new member immediately took a leading role in the house. In 1674 and again in 1675 Sawyer was given particular responsibility in efforts to produce a bill to provide relief to prisoners by making writs of habeas corpus more effective. He was also asked to help produce a bill for suppressing popery and he sat on a committee for a bill to prevent Catholics from sitting in parliament.

Sawyer played a leading role in 1675 in the contest of *Shirley* v. *Fagg*, which pitted the two houses against each other. Dr Thomas Shirley, having failed in a chancery suit against Sir John Fagg, had taken his appeal to the House of Lords. Trouble arose because Fagg was a member of the House of Commons. When Fagg went to the Lords to answer the appeal, the Commons committed him to the Tower of London for a breach of Commoners' privilege against prosecution; likewise the house committed those of Fagg's lawyers who were MPs for pleading at the Lords' bar. Sawyer was the principal actor in the conference between the two houses in May 1675, where he argued the even more aggressive view that the Lords' powers to hear appeals in equity were restricted. A week later Sawyer, joined by Serjeant Sir John Maynard and other leading lawyers, was ordered to inspect ancient records concerning habeas corpus, since those imprisoned on the Commons' orders now tried to use the writ to gain their freedom. Having played a prominent part during the last two years in parliamentary efforts to expand the writ's utility, Sawyer now did what he could to undermine its effect against the Commons' own orders of commitment. Despite these efforts, the Lords' claims to be the ultimate tribunal in all matters and for all subjects—including MPs—prevailed.

Sawyer remained prominent in the Commons. Later in 1675 he was one of those appointed to a committee preparing a bill 'to prevent the illegal exaction of money from the subject' (*JHC*, 361). During the same period he promoted efforts for a bill to force Englishmen serving in French military posts to leave them. And it was Sawyer who reported the finding of another Commons committee that the growing tendency of courts of equity to hear matters pleadable at common law was a grievance to the subject. In short, Sawyer seems to have assumed a leading role in attacking many of those things dearest to royal authority, from wide powers of imprisonment, to close relations with the French king, to the lengthening of equity's reach. None the less his name appeared increasingly between 1675 and 1677 on lists of MPs friendly to the crown.

On 17 October 1677 Sawyer was knighted. Then, in April 1678, he became speaker of the House of Commons, though speculation immediately arose that he would not hold the chair for long. Less than a month later he resigned, pleading illness. An observer suggested that Sawyer was not supported by the court, which asked him to feign sickness, 'and for his cure he was promised 3000 guineas … and, that which made it more comical, he desired the prayers of the House, and was thereupon prayed for' (Thompson, 1.160). Throughout 1678, when not in the speaker's chair, Sawyer increasingly clashed with opposition members in debate, in particular with the witty Welsh lawyer William Williams. When Sawyer spoke in favour of the establishment of a public register of lands to prevent frauds in the sale of property, Williams opposed him. Likewise, Sawyer promoted the king's power to raise troops against Williams's opposition; later that year, he questioned the impeachment of the earl of Danby, which Williams supported.

Sawyer joined eagerly with his Commons colleagues to pursue the Popish Plot. He served on a committee charged with drawing up an address asking the king to remove his queen and other Catholics from court and on another concerned with disbanding royal forces. Likewise he opposed making any exceptions for the duke of York in bills against Catholics. But Sawyer did not sit in the highly charged parliaments of 1679 to 1681, and instead returned his full attention to the courtroom. In July 1679 he prosecuted Sir George Wakeman and others for their alleged part in Catholic conspiracies. Despite having the testimony of Titus Oates to assist his case, Wakeman and the others were acquitted. This failure notwithstanding, Sawyer was one of the leading lawyers of London, with one of the largest client lists and case loads of any practitioner before the court of exchequer and the House of Lords.

On 14 February 1681 Sawyer became attorney-general—as many believed, to reward his support of the court. As the so-called 'tory reaction' of the following years gathered steam, the crown's response to political opposition increasingly took legal form; as attorney-general Sawyer took the lead in these prosecutions. Joined by solicitor-general Heneage Finch and Sir George Jeffreys, Sawyer prosecuted Edward Fitzharris in June. Later that summer he failed to gain a true bill from a London grand jury to an indictment for treason against Stephen College, the 'protestant joiner'. Quite controversially, Sawyer prosecuted College instead at Oxford, where he was convicted. But in November, Sawyer could not convince another grand jury to return a true bill for treason against the earl of Shaftesbury; Sawyer reacted angrily to the crowd's cheers for the earl.

Not long thereafter Sawyer brought an information in the nature of *quo warranto* against London in a move designed to force the City to surrender its charter in order to permit the issuance of a new one on terms more friendly to royal control. When the court at last heard arguments in April 1683, Sawyer took six hours to open the crown's case. After prevailing against the City, Sawyer asked that the justices delay entering the judgment in hopes that the City might be convinced to surrender its charter. But the City baulked, judgment was entered, and the City's charter was forfeit to the crown. This confirmed the long-standing precedent that by *quo warranto* urban corporations—'subordinate governments', as Sawyer called them (*State trials*, 8.1178)—could lose their charters for the slightest misconduct. As attorney-general he now oversaw the process by which more than 130 corporations received new charters during the next four years, threatened as they were with the complete loss of their charters by *quo warranto* if they refused.

Throughout 1683 and 1684 Sawyer led the prosecutions against Lord Russell, Algernon Sidney, Sir Thomas Armstrong, and others; he drew the charges against a whiggish group of rioters at Nottingham's mayoral election; and in 1684 he prosecuted Titus Oates for *scandalum magnatum* against the duke of York, and in 1685 for his perjured testimony in the Popish Plot trials. Russell, Sidney, and Armstrong suffered traitors' deaths and the Nottingham rioters paid huge fines; Oates was fined £100,000 in the first instance and whipped and pilloried in the second. Sawyer also successfully argued the case of the East India Company against Thomas Sandys for his illegal trading there. Sawyer demonstrated that a royal charter granting a trading monopoly to a company was good in law, founded as it was on 'the king's just prerogative' (*State trials*, 10.458).

In 1683 some believed that Sawyer might be named chief justice, and in September 1685 rumours pointed to him as a possible successor to the great seal after Lord Guilford's death; neither promotion came to pass. With James II now on the throne, Sawyer proved increasingly reluctant to implement the king's friendly policies towards Catholics. New rumours arose that dismissal, not promotion, would soon be Sawyer's lot. In April 1686 he refused to draw up the warrants that would permit Catholics to assume church and university posts without taking the oaths normally required, arguing that doing so would be contrary to law. Despite his express disavowal of the king's claimed power to dispense with statute, Sawyer continued as attorney-general until December 1687, when he was finally removed from office.

Sawyer returned to his lucrative legal practice, retaining enough favour at court to enable him to number the queen dowager among his clients. But his service as one of the counsel to the seven bishops in June 1688 put him even more firmly against the interest of the king. Sir William Williams, who prosecuted the bishops, tried to undermine Sawyer's representation of them by pointing to Sawyer's recent service to the crown, to no avail. Sawyer and his co-counsel became the darlings of protestant crowds when the bishops were acquitted of seditious libel. In September 1688, as the nation prepared for what was thought to be an imminent parliamentary election, Sawyer planned to stand for a seat for the University of Cambridge, suggesting to the archbishop of Canterbury that he did so to dishearten the 'enemies of our religion' (Bodl. Oxf., MS Tanner 28, fol. 178).

But revolution intervened. After James II's departure Sawyer was one of a group of leading lawyers consulted in December 1688 about how the nation should proceed in the king's absence. The following month he was indeed elected for Cambridge to serve in the Convention Parliament of 1689. There Sawyer argued vigorously that James's actions were 'an abdication importing a renunciation' (Bodl. Oxf., MS Rawl. D.1232, fol. 7). Thus the crown necessarily descended to the person next in the succession, James's daughter Mary; in the Commons vote, Sawyer opposed declaring that the crown should go as well to her husband. But he soon convinced himself that he could swear allegiance to them jointly since William 'is joined to the Queen and the Queen will be in of her legal title by descent' (ibid.).

In the next parliament Sawyer defended a strict adherence to the Anglican monopoly on power. He also found himself under attack for his actions while attorney-general. Sir William Williams, James II's former solicitor-general, challenged Sawyer to explain why he, when attorney-general, prosecuted Williams for obeying a Commons order to print a pamphlet that allegedly defamed the then duke of York. But it was Sawyer's denial of a writ of error to Sir Thomas Armstrong after his conviction for treason in 1684 that produced a vote of censure by the Commons and his removal from the house in January 1690. Cambridge immediately re-elected Sawyer, who continued his work as an opponent of a comprehension of protestant dissenters and of a standing army. Despite his shifting political fortunes, rumours continued throughout 1691 and early 1692 to name Sawyer as a possible justice or baron of the exchequer.

Sawyer died at Highclere on 28 July 1692, 'in the communion of the holy Catholic Church and of the Protestant Church established by the laws of England' (will, PRO, PROB 11/411, fol. 227). He left Highclere and his other property to his wife, entailing it thereafter on the children of his only daughter, who had married the earl of Pembroke. He was buried on 6 August in the church at Highclere, the building of which he had funded a year earlier. He also left £50 to Magdalene College to help build what would become the Pepys Library. Though sometimes accused of having traded his support of the opposition in parliament in the 1670s for support of the crown—allegedly motivated by cash as well as by offers of the speakership and the attorney-general's office—Sawyer's actions reflected his adherence to two principles: the sanctity of the Church of England and the sanctity of the law as he understood it. Like other lawyers, Sawyer simultaneously believed that it was well within the law for the king to rewrite urban charters and that there was no legal ground for James II's desire to dispense with statute. Both positions derived from his clear sense of the prerogative as an integral, if carefully delimited, part of English law. For his commitment to the church, Sawyer joined vigorously in the hunt for 'popish' plotters in the late 1670s and just as vigorously in the attack on whiggery and protestant dissent in the 1680s; and for the same commitment, he ultimately lost his highest office in 1687 and defended the seven bishops the next year.

PAUL D. HALLIDAY

Sources HoP, *Commons, 1660–90*, 3.399–403 • Foster, *Alum. Oxon.* • Venn, *Alum. Cant.* • Wood, *Ath. Oxon.*, new edn • *The life and times of Anthony Wood*, ed. A. Clark, 2, OHS, 21 (1892), 250, 308; 3, OHS, 26 (1894) • *CSP dom.*, *1678; addenda, 1660–85; 1680–81; 1683–5; 1689–90* • *Fifth report*, HMC, 4 (1876) • *Seventh report*, HMC, 6 (1879) • *Ninth report*, 2, HMC, 8 (1884) • *The manuscripts of S. H. Le Fleming*, HMC, 25 (1890) • *Calendar of the manuscripts of the marquess of Ormonde*, new ser., 8 vols., HMC, 36 (1902–20), vols. 4–6 • *Report on the manuscripts of the marquis of Downshire*, 6 vols. in 7, HMC, 75 (1924–95), vol. 1 • *State trials*, vols. 6–9 • R. North, *The lives of … Francis North … Dudley North … and … John North*, new edn, 3 vols. (1826) • A. Grey, *Debates from the year 1667 to the year 1694* (1763), vols. 5–9 • N. Luttrell, *A brief historical relation of state affairs from September 1678 to April 1714*, 6 vols. (1857) • *The correspondence of Henry Hyde, earl of Clarendon, and of his brother Laurence Hyde, earl of Rochester*, ed. S. W. Singer, 2 vols. (1828) • E. M. Thompson, ed., *Correspondence of the family of Hatton*, 2 vols., CS, new ser., 22–3 (1878) • Pepys, *Diary*, vols. 8–9 • *JHC*, 9 (1667–87) • Sainty, *King's counsel* • *Memoirs and travels of Sir John Reresby*, ed. A. Ivatt (1904) • *The autobiography of Sir John Bramston*, ed. [Lord Braybrooke], CS, 32 (1845) • *The diaries and papers of Sir Edward Dering, second baronet, 1644 to 1684*, ed. M. F. Bond (1976) • 'Debate in the

Convention Parliament on the status of the crown (1689)', *A parliamentary history of the Glorious Revolution*, ed. D. L. Jones (1988) • *Burnet's History of my own time*, ed. O. Airy, new edn, 2 vols. (1897–1900) • J. L. Chester and G. J. Armytage, eds., *Allegations for marriage licences issued by the dean and chapter of Westminster, 1558 to 1699; also, for those issued by the vicar-general of the archbishop of Canterbury, 1660 to 1679*, Harleian Society, 23 (1886) • *Le Neve's Pedigrees of the knights*, ed. G. W. Marshall, Harleian Society, 8 (1873) • *VCH Berkshire*, vol. 3 • *VCH Hampshire and the Isle of Wight*, vol. 4 • will, PRO, PROB 11/411, fols. 227–229v

Likenesses R. White, line engraving, 1688 (*Counsel for the seven bishops*), BM, NPG • G. Kneller, oils, Harvard U.

Wealth at death extensive lands at Highclere and Burghclere, Hampshire; a house in Lincoln's Inn Fields; and other properties: will, 8 Sept 1692, PRO, PROB 11/411, fols. 227–229v

Saxby, Henry Linckmyer (1836–1873), physician and ornithologist, was born in London on 19 April 1836, the second son of Stephen Martin Saxby, of the Royal Navy, and his wife, Mary Ann (*née* Lindeman). His boyhood and early youth were passed in the Undercliff, Ventnor, Isle of Wight, and in north Wales. After being educated at home he went to Edinburgh University in 1857, and received a diploma in medicine in 1860. He married on 16 December 1859 Jessie Margaret (*b*. 1842), a daughter of Dr Edmondston of Unst, Shetland Islands. During part of 1860 and 1861 he was assistant to Dr Edmondston in his practice in Shetland. In 1862 Saxby graduated MD from St Andrews.

After returning to Unst, Saxby entered into practice with his father-in-law, in 1863, and became the parochial medical officer. He remained in Shetland after Dr Edmondston's retirement until 1871, when ill health forced his return to Edinburgh. In 1872 he moved to Inveraray, where he died on 4 September 1873. His wife and five children survived him.

Saxby, who was a good draughtsman, was a born naturalist. He contributed seven papers on ornithological subjects to the *Zoologist* between 1861 and 1871, and was author of *The Birds of Shetland* (1874), which was edited and published after his death by his brother S. H. Saxby.

B. B. WOODWARD, *rev.* PATRICK WALLIS

Sources private information (1897) • *BMJ* (11 Oct 1873), 451 • *London and Provincial Medical Directory* (1867)

Saxby, Jessie Margaret Edmondston (1842–1940), author and folklorist, was born on 30 June 1842 at Halligarth in Unst, Shetland, the ninth of the eleven children of Laurence Edmondston (1795–1879), medical practitioner, and his first wife, Eliza Macbrair (1801–1869), daughter of a Glasgow merchant. Saxby said that she 'had no education more than that acquired by much reading and a close study of nature, and the society of literary and scientific parents'. She grew up in a household of authors: her father wrote ornithological and other natural history papers for scientific journals, and some brilliant 'General observations on the county of Shetland' (1841); his wife published *Sketches and Tales of the Shetland Islands* in 1856; and Jessie's elder brother Thomas Edmondston (1825–1846) produced a precocious *Flora of Shetland* in 1845, before his untimely death. Later Saxby and another brother, the Revd Biot Edmondston, wrote a moving account of their family as seen in childhood, *The Home of a Naturalist* (1888). On or about 16 December 1859, aged seventeen, she married Henry Linckmyer Saxby (1836–1873), her father's assistant and a native of London. They had five sons, and a daughter who died as a child, and meanwhile moved to Inveraray in Argyll. Henry Saxby died there in 1873, still a young man. For the next quarter of a century Jessie Saxby lived in Edinburgh with her children. She had been publishing stories and poetry since 1860—a book of verse, *Lichens from the Old Rock*, had appeared in 1868—and for many years after her husband's death relied on her pen to sustain her family.

Jessie Margaret Edmondston Saxby (1842–1940), by unknown photographer, *c*.1891

Saxby's literary output was vast. A draft bibliography in the Shetland Archives (D. 11/135/2) comprises nearly 150 items, forty-seven of them books. One of her specialities was books for boys, sometimes with a Shetland setting or flavour: *The Lads of Lunda* (1887) is a good example, reprinted several times. She also produced romantic novels for women, on one occasion (*Vita vinctis*, 1887) in collaboration with Annie S. Swan and Robina Hardy. At the same time she was writing a flood of articles and serials for journals and newspapers: 'A bit of bush life' in the *Boy's Own Paper* of July 1884, for instance, or 'A daughter of the sea kings' in *Life and Work*, October 1889. Saxby's house in Edinburgh was much frequented by literary people, and she took a special interest in writers from her native Shetland. As a labour of love she edited the poetry of Basil R. Anderson, a young native of Unst who had died in Edinburgh. The resultant volume, *Broken Lights* (1888), is a classic volume of Shetland dialect verse.

Saxby took a lively interest in current political and cultural matters, and spoke and wrote about them with vigour. 'You know my principles are widely Liberal', she said in 1885, intervening in a newspaper controversy about land reform (Saxby). 'I hold that God's soil—like his Sea—belongs to "the people", not to individuals. I believe a "war-policy" to be a remnant of barbarism' (ibid.). She was a keen supporter of home rule for Ireland, and participated in the temperance movement. During the second half of her life, she took a deep interest in the folklore and antiquities of Shetland, especially after she returned to her native Unst in the late 1890s. It was a relief for her to escape from the necessity of writing potboilers, and she took to scholarly work with alacrity. In 1892 she was the guest speaker at the first meeting of the Viking Club, an antiquarian society for expatriate Shetlanders and Orcadians in London. She was subsequently a member of the 'foundation committee' of the club's journal, *Orkney and Shetland Miscellany* (later *Old-Lore Miscellany*), and contributed vivid articles to it about folklore. In 1932, at the age of ninety, she produced a collection of these papers as *Shetland Traditional Lore*, perhaps her best work; and two years later she collected her verse in *Threads from a Tangled Skein* (1934).

In old age Saxby was an institution in Shetland. A remarkable photograph of her, a spirited figure of eighty-five years, accompanies her obituary in the *Shetland Times* of 11 January 1941. On her ninetieth birthday friends and admirers at home and abroad presented her with an illuminated address:

> That which has endeared you more than anything else to your fellow countrymen and countrywomen is that Shetland is so very dear to your heart, and your vivid fancy and powers of literary expression have been so often and so ably employed in painting and describing Shetland scenes and people, their folklore and traditions … that you embody for thousands in every quarter of the world the very spirit of Shetland.

Jessie Saxby died at her home, Wulver's Hool, Unst, on 27 December 1940, and was buried in the Edmondston family's burial-ground at Halligarth. BRIAN SMITH

Sources *Shetland Times* (11 Jan 1941) • *Shetland News* (2 Jan 1941) • B. Edmondston and J. M. E. Saxby, *The home of a naturalist* (1888) • J. M. E. Saxby, *Shetland Times* (19 Dec 1885) • draft bibliography, Shetland Archives, D. 11/135/2 • m. cert.

Likenesses photograph, *c.*1891, Scot. NPG [*see illus.*] • photograph, 1927, repro. in *Shetland Times* (11 Jan 1941)

Wealth at death £2501 5*s.* 8*d.*: confirmation, 10 April 1941, *CCI*

Saxby [*née* Howell], **Mary** (1738–1801), vagrant and memoirist, was born in London, the daughter of John Howell, a silk weaver, and his wife, Susanna, who died soon afterwards during childbirth. Mary's father remarried and had two further sons, one of whom—together with Mary's daughter Kezia—was responsible for publicizing Mary's posthumous *Memoirs of a Female Vagrant, Written by Herself* (1806), the sole source of information on her life and the reason for her place in the historical record. With her father abroad, Mary was brought up by an uncle and educated at the Revd Whitefield's school in Moorgate until John's return. A turbulent childhood was attributed largely to what she described as her 'wicked and impetuous temper' and 'proud, perverse temper' (*Memoirs*, 2, 5), which she now dedicated to the vexation of her stepmother. After several failed attempts Mary succeeded in absconding and, without provisions or money, left London for the 'country'—principally the borders of Bedfordshire, Northamptonshire, and Buckinghamshire—whereupon she began a period of destitution, scrounging food while resisting the temptation to steal and the advances of 'wicked men' (ibid., 7).

Numerous acquaintances with itinerant labourers and gypsies followed until ill health forced Mary to return to her father in search of medical attention. Once recovered, she journeyed to Kent and then to Epping in Essex, where an innocent association with a 'common woman' (*Memoirs*, 15) led to her being detained in the local bridewell. On gaining her freedom, she fell in once more with a Gypsy with whom she had previously cohabited and who now kept her in a 'state of slavery' (ibid., 17). Mary's release was secured when John Saxby (*d.* 1782), a former acquaintance from Kent, fought and defeated the Gypsy 'and took me away in triumph' (ibid.). Soon pregnant, she was separated from Saxby by his family and was forced to give birth alone to their first child at Woburn, Bedfordshire: attempts to trace John revealed that he had enlisted, an event which shocked his family and prompted their abandonment of Mary, whom they blamed for John's actions. However, with his regiment disbanded, Saxby returned to Mary and pressed her to marry him, though the practicalities of their situation, impoverished and itinerant, meant that they were on several occasions refused by the clergy. Two more children were born to the couple before Mary and John were married at Olney, Buckinghamshire, on 3 January 1771; a further seven children followed, with six of the ten predeceasing their mother.

The period following her marriage saw Mary Saxby first consider religious worship in the wake of several disasters in the family, though such sentiments quickly subsided and she 'returned to my former evil practices', given that she was 'to jests, filthy ribaldry, and profane swearing … grossly addicted' (*Memoirs*, 27). A stern rebuke from her sister-in-law finally proved a turning point in Mary's life, if not in her family's wretched circumstances, and prompted her to look to religion for personal salvation, though it was a year before she began attending regularly at a local meeting-house in Stratford, Essex. Mary's increasingly intense religiosity, evident in the highly emotional language of the second half of her memoir, owed much to the influence of Wesleyan preachers who visited her meeting-house as well as to the hymns of Charles Wesley, which she first encountered in book form.

Saxby's conversion to Methodism was not shared by her husband, John, who remained a fixture at ale houses and a source of domestic discord. But serious ill health in turn prompted a religious experience in John, producing a deathbed confession in autumn 1782. During the following decade Mary continued to sell drapery and haberdashers' goods on the road, often lodging her remaining children with the minister's wife. However, these years also saw the Methodists leave Stratford and Mary's own debate about whether to join the Church of England. Pressed by the parish to quit her lodgings, she returned in April 1791 to Olney, joined the local Independent congregation, and briefly kept a shop before debts and injury following a fall forced her to abandon this venture. In June 1794 Mary's son Thomas, then eighteen, drowned while bathing; at that point, after a description of his burial, Saxby's narrative ends abruptly. According to one of her surviving daughters, Kezia, she continued her memoir after this event, though the material was presumed lost by Samuel Greatheed when he prepared the manuscript for publication soon after Mary's death.

Discussions with Kezia none the less provided Greatheed with sufficient information to sketch a conclusion to Saxby's narrative. During the final seven years of her life she continued her itinerant work, including latterly selling cheap religious tracts, as well as mediating in the domestic crises of her four remaining daughters, the youngest of whom died from smallpox in 1801. Herself increasingly weakened by asthmatic attacks, Saxby died at Olney on 20 December of the same year, having been observed 'to continue in prayer, till about forty minutes before her death' (*Memoirs*, 79). She was buried there two days later.

Saxby's manuscript, the details of whose composition are unknown, was edited by Greatheed at the request of Joseph Wilson of Islington, London, and was published in 1806 by J. Burditt of Paternoster Row with profits to the recently widowed Kezia. Publication of the memoir, then and now a remarkable study of life in an early modern subsistence economy, was justified by Greatheed as a way of highlighting the 'vices and miseries of a vagrant life', which might in turn 'prompt the active beneficence of the present age', and in particular the Society for Bettering the Condition and Improving the Comforts of the Poor, 'to extend their humane and patriotic care to these numerous bands of semi-savages dispersed amidst our highly civilised countrymen' (*Memoirs*, iv). That the study merited this response owed everything to Mary's piety, which, conveyed in a dramatic conversion narrative, was in Greatheed's view relevant to readers of all circumstances.

To modern historians Mary Saxby's memoir represents one of the few apparently genuine accounts of the experience of itinerancy and poverty in the eighteenth century to survive, and is particularly valuable because its author and main subject was a woman. It compares well with works such as *An Apology for the Life of Bampfylde-Moore Carew* (1749), which has generally been assumed a work of fiction, and the autobiography of Charlotte Charke, the daughter of Colley Cibber, whose theatrical background undermines the typicality of her experiences. And, while the work of memoirists such as Francis Place later gave greater literary polish to working-class autobiography, Saxby's efforts are significant for the creation of the genre and an all-important source for understanding the experience of non-élite people.

Published at a time when saccharine tales of religious conversion were frequently juxtaposed to accounts of childhood profligacy, Saxby's narrative stands out for the variety and apparent veracity of her story and provides a unique perspective on the experience of the eighteenth-century poor. Most eighteenth-century paupers were women and Saxby's memoir gives voice to this most unrepresented of historical actors. PHILIP CARTER

Sources [M. Saxby], *Memoirs of a female vagrant, written by herself* (1806) • E. J. Hobsbawm, 'The tramping artisan', *Labouring men* (1968), 34–63 • L. B. Faller, *Turned to account: the forms and functions of criminal biography in late seventeenth- and early eighteenth-century England* (1987) • D. Vincent, ed., *Testaments of radicalism* (1977) • I. Rivers, 'Strangers and pilgrims: sources and patterns of Methodist narrative', *Augustan worlds*, ed. J. C. Hilson and others (1978) • S. King, *Poverty and welfare in England, 1700–1850: a regional perspective* (2000) • T. Hitchcock, 'The publicity of poverty in early eighteenth-century London', *Imagining early modern London: perceptions and portrayals of the city from Stow to Strype, 1598–1720*, ed. J. F. Merritt (2001)

Saxl, Friedrich [Fritz] (**1890–1948**), art historian and a founder of the Warburg Institute, London, was born in Vienna, on 8 January 1890, the son of Ignaz Saxl, a distinguished lawyer who collaborated in the formation of the new Austrian civil code, and his wife, Wilhelmine Falk. Educated at the Maximilian Gymnasium in Vienna and at the universities of Vienna (under Max Dvořák), and Berlin (under Heinrich Wölfflin), Fritz Saxl, as he was known, began his scholarly career with research into the authenticity and dating of Rembrandt's drawings; this work was published in 1912. In 1911 he had been awarded a scholarship at the Oesterreichisches Historisches Institut in Rome, and while there he began to compile his *Catalogue of Astrological and Mythological Illuminated Manuscripts of the Latin Middle Ages*, a work originally sponsored by the Heidelberg Academy. The first volume of this work was published in 1915, the second in 1927, and the third (posthumously) in 1953. The commission was the outcome of Saxl's acquaintance with Aby Warburg, whom he had met through their mutual interest in the imagery of pagan cults and myths and its survival through the middle ages into the Renaissance period. By that time Warburg had already made his most important contributions to the study of fifteenth-century Florentine culture, and had begun to assemble a private library which became the basis of the Warburg Institute. In 1913 Saxl became Warburg's assistant and settled in Hamburg. In the same year he married Elise Bienenfeld, daughter of a Vienna cloth merchant. They had one son, a promising painter and architect who died young, and one daughter.

From 1914 to 1918 Saxl served as a first lieutenant in the Austrian army on the Italian front; after the war he became an army education officer under the first Austrian Labour government. In 1919 he was called back to Hamburg where Warburg had fallen dangerously ill. There he took charge of Warburg's library which he began to turn into a centre for research on the significance of the classical heritage in the history of European civilization. With the financial support of Warburg's brothers in Hamburg and New York, he made the library more widely accessible, invited scholars of international standing for lectures and research, and began to publish the series *Studien der Bibliothek Warburg*, which was later continued as *Studies of the Warburg Institute* and in 1939 became the *Journal of the Warburg and Courtauld Institutes*. The newly founded University of Hamburg provided the academic background for the project, and in 1927 it conferred the title of professor on Saxl. However, the institute remained a private undertaking which Saxl directed after Warburg's death in 1929. Saxl's writings, combined with the publications of the institute issued under his editorship, focused attention on the classical tradition, and the institute became a centre for research in this field. In 1933, when the rise of national socialism seemed likely to endanger the institute, Saxl moved it to London, assisted by a group of sponsors including Samuel Courtauld and Lord Lee of Fareham. It remained a private centre, continuing its lectures and publications, until it was incorporated in the University of London in 1944. Saxl's own account of the history of the institute can be found in E. H. Gombrich's 1970 biography of Aby Warburg. Saxl became a naturalized British subject in 1940 and was elected FBA in 1944.

Moving to England gave to Saxl's work a fresh impetus and a new direction. To his earlier studies of English manuscript painting he now added the study of English medieval sculpture, stressing the features linking it to classical and continental art. He helped to establish as an academic subject the history of art, which had only recently been introduced into British universities by the foundation of the Courtauld Institute. However, he considered that his work ranged beyond the boundaries of the new discipline, describing himself as 'a labourer tilling the soil of the border strip between art history, literature, science and religion' (Gombrich, 'Introduction', *A Heritage of Images*, 7). To the *Journal of the Warburg and Courtauld Institutes* Saxl contributed articles on such varied subjects as pagan sacrifice in the Italian Renaissance, Aniello Falcone and his patrons, the classical inscription in Renaissance art and politics, and a spiritual encyclopaedia of the later middle ages. Among his other publications in English are *Classical Mythology in Mediaeval Art* (with E. Panofsky), *Classical Antiquity in Renaissance Painting* (1938), *British Art and the Mediterranean* (with R. Wittkower, 1948), *English Sculptures of the Twelfth Century* (ed. H. Swarzenski, 1954), and *Saturn and Melancholy* (with E. Panofsky and R. Klibansky, 1958). A selection of his lectures was published posthumously by the institute in 1957, and a complete bibliography of his publications may be found in a later selection of his essays and lectures, *A Heritage of Images* (1970), edited by Hugh Honour and John Fleming.

Saxl was a small, slightly built man who attracted and bewildered by the mercurial quality of his action. His great gift was an ability to communicate the excitement of scholarship. This was never more apparent than in the library of his institute, where he would not accept defeat in finding the precise information needed. If it fell outside the scope of his own field he usually knew to whom to turn, for he was alert to the work of others and in a seemingly casual way was often able to further the cause of scholarship by bringing together people of like interests. His self-effacing manner and his dislike of anything resembling compulsion concealed a strong will and high expectations of others which he never thought it worth while to make explicit. Often misinterpreted, for those who understood him he set a sure standard of scholarly and personal behaviour and the example of an unusual charity. Saxl died on 22 March 1948, at his home, 162 East Dulwich Grove, Dulwich. His wife and daughter survived him. GERTRUD BING, *rev.* CHRISTOPHER LLOYD

Sources G. Webb, *Burlington Magazine*, 90 (1948), 209–10 • preface, *Journal of the Warburg and Courtauld Institutes*, 10 (1947) • G. Bing, 'Fritz Saxl, 1890–1948: a memoir', *Fritz Saxl, 1890–1948: a volume of memorial essays from his friends in England*, ed. D. J. Gordon (1957), 1–46 • E. H. Gombrich, *Aby Warburg: an intellectual biography* (1970) • E. H. Gombrich, 'Introduction', *A heritage of images: a selection of lectures by Fritz Saxl*, ed. H. Honour and J. Fleming (1970) • personal knowledge (1959) • *CGPLA Eng. & Wales* (1948) • d. cert.

Archives Warburg Institute, London, corresp. • Warburg Institute, London, notebooks

Likenesses three negatives, *c.*1912–1930, Warburg Institute, London • O. Fein, photograph, *c.*1946, Warburg Institute, London • W. Höffert, negative (as baby), Warburg Institute, London

Wealth at death £1145 14*s*. 9*d*.: administration, 21 Aug 1948, *CGPLA Eng. & Wales*

Saxon, James (*b.* 1772, *d.* in or after 1819), portrait painter, was born in Manchester in 1772, the son of John Saxon, and baptized at the city's collegiate church on 1 March that year. He entered Manchester grammar school in January 1783. During the mid-1790s he practised as a portrait painter in Manchester and London. In 1795 he made his début at the Royal Academy, exhibiting *Portrait of an Artist*. He followed this in 1796 with *John Palmer in the Character of Cohenberg*, a depiction of the famous actor who had been injured while playing Colonel Cohenberg in a London production of James Cobb's comic opera *The Siege of Belgrade* in January 1791.

Thereafter Saxon moved to St Petersburg, which he seems to have visited at least twice, since his departure from the Russian capital was noted in 1805 and 1819. During his first stay he is known to have painted a portrait of Jonathon Rogers (1739–1811) (*c.*1803; State Hermitage Museum, St Petersburg), a British doctor whose long service with the Russian fleet was rewarded in 1803 with his being named chief physician to the imperial navy and two years later the first physician general to Tsar Alexander's new naval ministry. The work is realistic and informal with the half-figure placed against a monochrome background and treated with a softened finish to the highlighted face, hair and shirt in the style of Henry Raeburn and Archibald Skirving. About the same time he also painted James Leighton (*c.*1804), a Scottish doctor with the imperial navy and physician-in-ordinary to the court of Tsar Alexander I. This work was engraved by the Russian artist Grigory Yanov. A portrait of the former director of the Carron ironworks, then in Russian service, Charles Gascoigne, has also been attributed to him (*c.*1804–5; State Hermitage Museum, St Petersburg).

Upon his return to Britain in 1805 he lived for brief periods in London, Edinburgh, and Glasgow. He continued to paint images of those connected with naval and theatre life, including the Drury Lane company actor James Raymond as Macbeth (exh. RA, 1806), Miss R. Boughton as Lavinia (exh. RA, 1807), and John Clerk of Eldin (*c*.1805; Scot. NPG). The latter was probably painted when Saxon was in Edinburgh, and it recognized Clerk as the author of *An Essay on Naval Tactics* and the inventor of the 'breaking the line' manoeuvre, which had been successfully employed against the French fleet in the battle of the Saints in 1782. It did so by depicting Clerk seated with his plans at a table before a view of distant ships on manoeuvre, the latter painted by the marine artist William Anderson. The same year Saxon painted Walter Scott's portrait (Scot. NPG), again choosing to show the author seated, in this case with his dog Camp and before rows of books. This work was engraved in stipple by James Heath, as an illustration for *Lady of the Lake* (1810). Saxon is said to have become the favourite painter of Scott's wife, Charlotte Charpentier, and he completed a companion portrait of her in 1810 (priv. coll.). During his stay in Glasgow he painted the portrait of a leading architect, David Hamilton. His Scottish period was also marked by some humorous portraits of urban characters. These included 'Crihee the taylor, dealer in old shoes, broker, and picture pimp, the son of an Aberdeen appleman, ironically represented in the character of a connoisseur criticising a picture' and 'the honest old Edinburgh Eggman, its companion' (Ramsay, 443–4), which by 1808 were in the collection of Robert Brown, New Hall House, Midlothian. Saxon's English portraits included that of the sheriff of London, C. Smith (exh. RA, 1808), and the radical Sir Richard Phillips (1806, exh. RA, 1808; NPG), the latter very much adhering to the formula of the Rogers portrait. He is also known to have painted the portrait of the Irish advocate and wit John Philpot Curran aged sixty (*c*.1810). This was engraved in stipple by T. Wageman and published in 1818. His final exhibition appearance was at the Royal Academy in 1817, where he showed the portraits *Mr Stratton* and *Young Gentleman and a Cottager*. It is assumed that he left for his second short sojourn in Russia about this time. There are no records known of his activities after 1819 and it is therefore presumed that he died shortly after leaving St Petersburg that year. JEREMY HOWARD

Sources Graves, *RA exhibitors* • B. Allen and L. Dukelskaya, eds., *British art treasures from the Russian imperial collections in the Hermitage* (1996), 112–13 [exhibition catalogue, Yale U. CBA, 5 Oct 1996 – 5 Jan 1997] • P. J. M. McEwan, *Dictionary of Scottish art and architecture* (1994) • K. K. Yung, *National Portrait Gallery: complete illustrated catalogue, 1856–1979*, ed. M. Pettman (1981), 447 • James Saxon file, Courtauld Inst., Witt Library • A. Ramsay, *The gentle shepherd: a pastoral comedy; with illustrations of the scenery* (1808), vol. 2 • *DNB*

Saxton, Sir Charles, baronet (1732–1808), commissioner of the navy, was the youngest son of Edward Saxton, a London merchant. In January 1745 he became a 'captain's servant' in the *Gloucester* (Captain Charles Saunders); he remained in her for three years, and was then in the *Eagle* with Captain Collins, and in the *St Albans* on the coast of Guinea with Captain John Byron. He was promoted lieutenant on 2 January 1757, and served in the East Indies under Vice-Admiral Charles Watson, and Vice-Admiral George Pocock.

Saxton returned to England in 1760 and on 11 October of that year was promoted commander. On 28 January 1762 he became captain of the *Magnanime* with Commodore Lord Howe, and subsequently in the fleet under Sir Edward Hawke. After the conclusion of the Seven Years' War he commanded the *Pearl* on the Newfoundland station, where he was employed in the Gulf of St Lawrence in part to deter the claims of the French. The *Pearl* was paid off in 1766. In 1770 he commanded the *Phoenix* during the Spanish armament. He married in July 1771 Mary Bush, daughter of Jonathan Bush of Burcott, Oxfordshire.

In 1779 he commissioned the *Invincible*, which during 1780 formed part of the Channel Fleet, and at the end of the year he went out with Sir Samuel Hood to the West Indies. There Saxton was obliged to leave the *Invincible* for some months, owing to ill-health; but he commanded her again in 1781, with Hood, on the coast of North America, and in the action off the Chesapeake on 5 September, in which Hood's division of the fleet was only slightly engaged. He was still with Hood at St Kitt's in January and February 1782, and was then sent to Jamaica, where he remained until the conclusion of the American War of Independence; he returned to England in the summer of 1783. In 1787 he was a member of a commission set up to examine the working of the impress system, and in 1789 was appointed commissioner of the navy at Portsmouth, then the principal dockyard; here he presided over operations central to the expansion of the sailing navy almost to its greatest size. He was created a baronet on 19 July 1794. A low-profile commissioner who disliked administrative innovations, he held the post until 1806 when he was retired on a pension of £750 a year, with a remainder of £300 p.a. to his wife if she survived him. He died in November 1808. J. K. LAUGHTON, *rev.* ROGER MORRISS

Sources J. Charnock, ed., *Biographia navalis*, 6 vols. (1794–8) • R. Morriss, *The royal dockyards during the revolutionary and Napoleonic wars* (1983) • D. Syrett and R. L. DiNardo, *The commissioned sea officers of the Royal Navy, 1660–1815*, rev. edn, Occasional Publications of the Navy RS, 1 (1994)

Archives NMM, notebooks and papers

Likenesses S. W. Reynolds, mezzotint, pubd 1795 (after J. Northcote), BM

Saxton, Christopher (1542x4–1610/11), map maker, was born at Sowood in the West Riding of Yorkshire, between 1542 and 1544. His father was probably Thomas Saxton (*d.* 1600), a man of sufficient means to be assessed for tax in 1567, and his mother's name was most likely Margery. Saxton was brought up in Dunningley, near Wakefield in Yorkshire. Details of his early schooling are obscure, and although he went to Cambridge University it is not known to which college. About 1570 he was apprenticed as a map maker to John Rudd, vicar of Dewsbury, and probably used some of Rudd's survey, collected in the 1550s. Saxton's principal achievement was to make the first national atlas, for which he received considerable patronage and assistance, and also significant reward, including Queen Elizabeth I's favour. Thomas Seckford, the master of the queen's requests, was Saxton's most significant patron, financing his grand cartographic project.

In 1575 the queen required that Saxton be given assistance wherever he went on his county survey. The following year an open letter was written to justices of the peace and mayors in Wales, asking that he be assisted in the principality, and he was also given a 'pass' by the privy council. This and other passes ensured that people with local knowledge would assist him in his operations. In 1577 the queen issued letters patent giving Saxton sole right to publish his own maps for the next ten years—an important safeguard against the common practice of plagiarism.

Saxton's atlas, although the term was not used at the time, first appeared in 1579. The frontispiece and the county maps were never produced as a standard edition; rather, many states and variants are found. Most original copies have an engraved frontispiece with Queen Elizabeth enthroned under a canopy. A map of Anglia (including Wales) is followed by thirty-four county maps, nine of which combine more than one county. Some show internal divisions of counties into hundreds and similar units. It is thought that Saxton himself may have engraved the maps of the Welsh counties and Herefordshire.

Although Saxton has been described as 'the father of English cartography' (Tyacke and Huddy, 5), it has also been alleged that he did not receive adequate recognition during his lifetime. However, the many passes and privileges he was given, and the rewards he received for his accomplishment, suggest that this conclusion needs to be revised. In 1573, for instance, the queen granted him Grigston manor in Suffolk, by 1579 he had been granted armorial bearings, and in 1580 he was given a sixty-year lease on waste ground in the city of London with permission to build houses, in spite of a royal proclamation against such construction.

The sixteenth century has been described as witnessing 'a cartographic revolution in England' (Harvey, 7). Successive maps of Britain as a whole showed gradual but sustained improvements upon one another. The anonymous 'Angliae figura', dated about 1534, was the first to show latitude, longitude, and a scale of miles. A little later, in 1546, 'Britanniae insulae', probably the work of George Lily, showed the coasts of eastern England more accurately. In 1564 Gerardus Mercator produced 'Angliae, Scotiae & Hiberniae nova descriptio', which made Wales clearly recognizable, showing Cardigan Bay for the first time, although the length of the south coast of England was still exaggerated by 15 per cent. Of this process of development, Saxton's maps represent the culmination.

In producing a complete set of county maps of England and Wales, Saxton brought to fruition an idea that had been long germinating. Map-consciousness had been growing in the minds of statesmen, developing simultaneously with surveying techniques. Robert Beale, in his 'List of duties of a secretary of state' of 1592, suggested that ministers should have a map of the kingdom divided into counties and hundreds, and setting out where nobles and gentlemen lived. Saxton's county maps gained instant recognition at the highest political levels—even while they were still in course of production, between 1574 and 1578, Lord Burghley pulled and annotated early proofs. Saxton's maps were planimetrically superior to those of his predecessors. A simple examination reveals that the relative proportions of the land masses are much more faithfully shown. This is fundamentally because Saxton's maps, unlike most of the earlier ones, were not derivative—his map of England and Wales was itself based on his more detailed county maps. It has been suggested that Saxton may have constructed a framework for each map using triangulation.

Saxton is less well known as a local estate surveyor, perhaps because many of his detailed local maps have only recently been discovered. However, it was this profession which dominated his later years. At least twenty-five of his detailed local maps are now known, as well as fourteen written surveys, and there is evidence that a number of other maps or surveys were prepared. His employers included the governors of St Thomas's Hospital in Southwark as well as private landowners. His estate maps were innovative: his 1598 map of Old Byland in Yorkshire, for instance, provides an early example of a cartographic summary of evidence relating to a boundary dispute.

Details of Saxton's death are as unclear as many of those about his life. It appears that he died in 1610 or 1611, and he is believed to have been buried at Woodkirk, near Wakefield in Yorkshire, not far from his birthplace. However, there can be no doubt about his importance. His maps helped to put English cartography in the forefront of European cartography, an area in which it had previously been a laggard. John Speed, Jan Blaeu, and Jan Jansson successively adopted what was essentially his outline of Britain. Soon after his county maps had been published John Norden was revising them, and they exerted a considerable influence upon the maps of John Speed. As late as about 1760 Philip Lea produced a 'Traveller's guide' which he described as 'the best Mapp of the Kingdom of England and Principality of Wales', and which he acknowledged was based on Saxton and 'carefully corrected' by Lea (BL Maps 187 n. 3.). That Saxton's maps were not displaced as the master geographical representation of England and Wales until the Ordnance Survey began publication of 'one-inch' (1:63,360) maps in 1801 shows literally that they stood the test of time. DAVID FLETCHER

Sources I. Evans and H. Lawrence, *Christopher Saxton, Elizabethan map maker* (1979) · S. Tyacke and J. Huddy, *Christopher Saxton and Tudor map-making* (1980) · F. W. Steer and others, *Dictionary of land surveyors and local map-makers of Great Britain and Ireland, 1530–1850*, ed. P. Eden, 2nd edn, ed. S. Bendall, 2 vols. (1997) · W. Ravenhill, 'Christopher Saxton's surveying: an enigma', *English map-making, 1500–1650: historical essays*, ed. S. Tyacke (1983) · W. Ravenhill, 'Introduction', in *Christopher Saxton's 16th century maps: the counties of England and Wales* (1992) · H. G. Fordham, *Christopher Saxton of Dunningley: his life and work*, Thoresby Society, 28 (1928) · *APC*, 1575–7 ·

P. D. A. Harvey, *Maps in Tudor England* (1993) • R. W. Shirley, *Early printed maps of the British Isles*, rev. edn (1991) • BL, Maps 187 n. 3
Archives BL, examples of his atlas

Saxulf. *See* Seaxwulf (*d. c.*692).

Say, Frederick Richard (*bap.* **1805**, *d.* in or after **1858**). *See under* Say, William (1768–1834).

Say, Geoffrey de, second Lord de Say (**1304/5–1359**), soldier, of Codham and Birling, Kent, was the eldest son of Geoffrey de Say, first Lord de Say (*d.* 1322), lord of the manors of Birling, Codham, Burham, and West Greenwich in Kent, as well as of manors and lands in Middlesex, Hertfordshire, and Sussex, and of Idonea, daughter of William, Lord Leyburn (*d.* 1309). He was seventeen at his father's death in 1322. On 11 January 1323 John Triple, citizen of London, bought his wardship and marriage from the king for £200. In June 1326, having proved his age, he received seisin of his father's lands, and in 1333 he obtained view of frankpledge and other liberties in his mother's former dower lands.

Say was summoned for the Scottish expedition in 1327, and in 1333 he received his first summons to parliament and attended the Dunstable tournament; by this time he was also active in the king's service overseas. Over the following two years he served at Berwick and Newcastle. From July 1336 until December 1358 he was often on commissions of the peace, of inquiry, and of oyer and terminer in Kent, Sussex, and Surrey. He was appointed admiral of the western fleet on 10 April 1336, and was frequently at sea from July to October. He was replaced as admiral in January 1337, but from 30 May until August he held this office again with Sir Otho Grandison as joint admiral. During this time he served with four knights, twenty men-at-arms and thirty archers, and was himself described as a banneret. In 1338 he served in Flanders, and the following year he was given two ships to attend the king overseas. During the 1340s he was in Brittany under the earl of Northampton: in 1342 he was constable of the castle of Goy la Forêt, and in March 1346 his good service was rewarded with the prize of a captured Spanish ship. He fought at Crécy, but after his return in June 1347 his activities were largely confined to south-east England.

Campaigning may not have brought great financial rewards: by the time of his death Say had added only two manors to the estates inherited from his father, and he had numerous creditors, most notably William Clinton, earl of Huntingdon, to whom he owed £666 from 1344 until at least 1352, when Say mortgaged his manor of West Greenwich to Huntingdon until the sum was paid off. From 1345 until at least 1351 he was one of the attorneys of Joan de Bar, countess of Surrey, from whom he held his Sussex manors of Hammes and Street. In 1348 and 1349 he had the keeping of the archbishop of Canterbury's parks and chases during the latter's infirmity and the subsequent vacancy of the see. In June 1349 the king retained him for life with £133 per annum in return for his service with twenty men-at-arms and twenty archers. In January 1354 he replaced the earl of Huntingdon as keeper of Rochester city and constable of the castle. An inquiry in 1369 alleged that during his constableship he and his brother Roger as under-constable quarried the castle for building materials, removing lead, tiles, and timber. He was at Roxburgh in January 1356, where he witnessed the Anglo-Scottish treaty.

Say died on 26 June 1359. By his death the total rental value of his property was probably a little over £130 per annum. His widow, Maud (*d.* 1369), daughter of Guy de *Beauchamp, earl of Warwick, and Alice, daughter of Ralph de Toni, whom he had married by 1340, received his Sussex property as jointure and his Kentish manors of Birling and Burham as dower. The wardship and marriage of his nineteen-year-old son and heir, William, was given to Queen Philippa. PETER FLEMING

Sources GEC, *Peerage* • *Chancery records* • Rymer, *Foedera* • *Inquisitions and assessments relating to feudal aids*, 3, PRO (1904) • *CIPM*, 6, no. 327; 10, no. 517 • *Calendar of the fine rolls*, PRO, 7 (1923), 113 • *CPR*, *1361–4*, 48
Wealth at death approx. £130 p.a. in rental value: *CIPM*, 10, no. 517

Say [Fynys], **Sir John** (*d.* **1478**), administrator and speaker of the House of Commons, was of unknown parentage, though certainly related to James Fiennes, Lord Say and Sele (*d.* 1450), in whose company he is often recorded—in 1449 he was even referred to as 'John Fynys that is now speaker of the parliament' (Davis, 1.236). His brother, William, was dean of St Paul's (1457–68). John Say is first recorded in the king's service in 1444, as a yeoman of the chamber, with a daily allowance of 6*d.* Then, and for several years to come, he was closely associated with the regime of William de la Pole, earl of Suffolk, whom he accompanied to France in 1444 on the embassy that negotiated the marriage of Henry VI to Margaret of Anjou, and for whom he became an active partisan in East Anglia. In 1445 not only was he granted the keepership of the privy palace of Westminster, but he also became escheator of Cambridgeshire and Huntingdonshire. In 1446–7 Say was escheator of Norfolk and Suffolk, MP for Cambridge borough in 1447, and a justice of the peace for Cambridgeshire in 1448. At Christmas 1448, as a squire of the body, he was granted an annuity of 50 marks from the counties of Hampshire and Devon.

In February 1449 Say was returned to the Commons for Cambridgeshire and elected speaker. The only man to serve as speaker in both a Lancastrian and a Yorkist parliament, he appears to have won favour with both Henry VI ('in whose service' as he said in his will 'I was brought up and preferred') and Edward IV, and he remembered both kings in his will (PRO, PROB 11/6 35/Wattys). In June 1449 he was rewarded with the office of chancellor of the duchy of Lancaster, and in 1449–50 was sheriff of Norfolk and Suffolk. In 1450, however, when Suffolk fell from power, Say was attacked by the rebels and in 1451 the Commons demanded his banishment from the court; however, he was pardoned in 1452.

From 1454, when he was serving as an MP for Hertfordshire, although this time not speaker, he was summoned to attend the king's council. In May 1455 as deputy of Henry, Viscount Bourchier, afterwards earl of Essex, he was appointed clerk of the treasurer, or under-treasurer of the exchequer, one of the first laymen to hold the office, and one of the first who had not previously served in any minor office in the exchequer. On this occasion both he and Bourchier only held office for little over a year, until September 1456. However, both returned to office from the autumn of 1460 until March 1462, and Bourchier, by then earl of Essex, became treasurer for a third time in April 1471, Say again becoming his deputy from 1475 to 1478. Like his Bourchier patrons, Say had no difficulty in accepting the change of dynasty, and he retained his offices in the duchy of Lancaster, and his membership of the council, into the new reign.

Whether Say was a member of the last parliament of Henry VI or the first of Edward IV is unknown, but in the much adjourned parliament of 1463–5 he again sat for Hertfordshire, was again elected speaker, and earned the new king's gratitude, even if the parliament's grant of taxation was not overgenerous. Among other rewards he was given £40 yearly in 1464 so long as he remained a councillor. On 26 May 1465, at the ending of the parliament and the coronation of Queen Elizabeth (Woodville), he was knighted. To the next parliament, of 1467–8, he was again returned for Hertfordshire, and for the last time elected speaker. Again there were a number of short sessions, and by promising to go to war with France the king secured a grant of two tenths and fifteenths; for his own part Say secured a grant of the wardship and marriage of the heiress of Walter Raleigh, a Devon lawyer. In 1471 Say was pardoned by the governments of both Henry VI and Edward IV on their respective restorations. From 1476 he was keeper of the great wardrobe, and from 1475 until his death in 1478 once more under-treasurer of the exchequer.

John Say first married Elizabeth, daughter of Lawrence Cheyne of Fen Ditton, Cambridgeshire, and widow of Sir Frederick Tilney of Ashwellthorpe, Norfolk. She died in 1473, and in 1477 he married, as her third husband, Agnes, daughter of Sir John Danvers of Cokethorpe, Oxfordshire, widow of Sir John Fray (one of his predecessors as under-treasurer) and of John, Lord Wenlock. Say died on 12 April 1478, and Agnes shortly afterwards. He had held twenty-two manors, the majority in Hertfordshire, while Agnes had three in Kent and two in Essex, along with the advowson of Rowney Priory, Hertfordshire. He left plate and silver cups to three sons and five daughters, and wished to be buried at Broxbourne church beside Elizabeth, his first wife, where their brasses, his now headless, survive.

J. L. Kirby

Sources R. A. Griffiths, *The reign of King Henry VI: the exercise of royal authority, 1422–1461* (1981) • J. S. Roskell, *The Commons and their speakers in English parliaments, 1376–1523* (1965) • J. S. Roskell, 'Sir John Say of Broxbourne', *East Hertfordshire Archaeological Society Transactions*, 14/1 (1959), 20–41 • *Members of parliament: return to two orders of the honorable the House of Commons*, House of Commons, 1 (1878) • *RotP*, 5.141–2, 497, 572 • J. L. Kirby, 'The rise of the under-treasurer of the exchequer', *EngHR*, 72 (1957), 666–77 • R. Clutterbuck, ed., *The history and antiquities of the county of Hertford*, 3 (1827), 193–5 • J. E. Cussans, *History of Hertfordshire*, 11–12, 43, 141 • inquisition post mortem, PRO, C140, 18 Edw.IV, no. 143 • PRO, prerogative court of Canterbury, wills, PROB 11/6 35/Wattys • J. Gairdner, ed., *Three fifteenth-century chronicles*, CS, new ser., 28 (1880), 101 • J. C. Sainty, ed., *Officers of the exchequer: a list* (1983), 198–9 • *Collectanea Topographica et Genealogica*, 4 (1837), 44, 310 • W. Worcester, *Annals*, ed. T. Hearne (1728), 465, 471, 475, 502, 508 • N. Davis, ed., *Paston letters and papers of the fifteenth century*, 1 (1971), no. 135, p. 236

Likenesses double portrait, brass effigy (with his wife), Broxbourne church, Hertfordshire

Say [*née* Bemister; *other married name* Vint]**, Mary** (1739/40–1832), printer and newspaper publisher, bore the maiden name of Bemister. She may have originated from Somerset but on her marriage to the London printer and newspaper publisher Charles Green Say (1721?–1775) at St George's, Botolph Lane, on 9 November 1769 she was described as a spinster of St Botolph Lane in the City of London. On her husband's death in July 1775 she took over the printing of his three newspaper titles at his printing office in 10 and 11 Ave Maria Lane and continued to conduct them with success, at times playing a considerable editorial role in the production of *The Gazetteer*. Ten years later, in 1785, John Pendred listed her as still printing the daily morning newspaper *The Gazetteer*, the *General Evening Post*, published on Tuesdays and Saturdays, and *The Craftsman, or, Say's Weekly Journal*, published on Saturdays. Say was in trouble with the authorities on a number of occasions, being indicted for a libel on the constitution in July 1778 and fined £50 on 25 April the following year. On 4 July 1781 she was sentenced to six months' imprisonment and fined £50 for a libel on the Russian ambassador, and on 8 February 1788 the House of Commons voted to prosecute her for libel following disparaging remarks about Pitt the younger with reference to the impeachment of Sir Elijah Impey.

On 11 November 1787 Say married Edward Vint, calico printer, of Crayford, at St Martin Ludgate but retained the name Mary Say as printer of *The Gazetteer* until March 1790. In 1794 she was joined at Ave Maria Lane by John Vint, a relative originally from Newcastle upon Tyne, who published *The Courier* from that address before moving to Manchester and, later, the Isle of Man, where he died in 1814. Mary Vint established a new title in 1796, *The Selector, or, Say's Sunday Reporter*, which continued publication until at least 1808. She played an active role in the printing industry, being the only woman among the master printers who signed the compositors' scale of wages in 1785, registering her press with the authorities under the Seditious Societies Act on 25 August 1799, and binding six apprentices through the Stationers' Company; three further apprentices were turned over to her between 1776 and 1793. Among her apprentices was another relative, William Bemister, son of John Bemister, shearman, of Frome, Somerset, bound in 1785, who received his freedom only in 1813. She was a tough businesswoman, successfully conducting a conflict with the proprietors of *The Gazetteer* in the 1790s and engaging in a lengthy lawsuit with the former proprietors after *The Gazetteer* was taken over by the *Morning Post* in 1797. She appears to have retired about 1810; she died in Dartford on 9 February 1832 in her ninety-third year, having been widowed for a second time.

IAN MAXTED

Sources R. L. Haig, *The Gazetteer, 1735–1797* (1960) • H. R. Fox Bourne, *English newspapers: chapters in the history of journalism*, 1 (1887), 237–8 • I. Maxted, *The London book trades, 1775–1800: a preliminary checklist of members* (1977), 198–9, 233 • *GM*, 1st ser., 102/1 (1832), 187 • D. F. McKenzie, ed., *Stationers' Company apprentices*, [3]: *1701–1800* (1978), 309, 358 • J. Pendred, *The London and country printers, booksellers and stationers vade mecum* (1785); repr. with introduction and appx by G. Pollard as *The earliest directory of the book trade* (1955), 40–42 • A. Aspinall, 'Statistical accounts of the London newspapers in the eighteenth century', *EngHR*, 63 (1948), 201–32 • A. Aspinall, 'Statistical accounts of the London newspapers, 1800–36', *EngHR*, 65 (1950), 222–34, 372–83 • H. Barker, *Newspapers, politics and public opinion* (1998) • H. Barker, 'Women, work and the industrial revolution', *Gender in 18th century England*, ed. H. Barker and E. Chalus (1997) • C. H. Timperley, *A dictionary of printers and printing* (1839), 735, 853 • E. Howe, *The London compositor* (1947), 49, 74 • W. B. Todd, *A directory of printers and others in allied trades, London and vicinity, 1800–1840* (1972), 200 • L. Werkmeister, *The London daily press, 1772–1792* (1963) • parish register, London, St George's, Botolph Lane, 1769, GL, MS 4796 [marriage] • parish register, London, St Martin Ludgate, Ludgate Hill, 1787, GL, MS 10216/1 [marriage] • parish register, London, St Martin Ludgate, Ludgate Hill, GL, MS 10,214 [burial]

Archives PRO, Chancery masters exhibits (*Unit* v. *Sotheby et al.*), C104/67–8

Say, Samuel (1676–1743), dissenting minister, was born on 23 March 1676 at Castle Green in the parish of All Saints', Southampton, the second son of Gyles Say (1632–1692), nonconformist preacher, and his second wife. He was baptized by Francis Mence. His father, who was of Huguenot descent on his mother's side, was vicar of All Saints', Catherington, Hampshire, from 1656 to 1657 and of St Michael's, Southampton, from 1657. Ordained by presbyters at Bishopstoke on 8 May 1660, he was ejected in 1662 and preached as a nonconformist at Southampton, where he was licensed as a 'Congregational Teacher' on 2 May 1672. He moved to London about 1685 and was minister of the Congregational church at Guestwick, Norfolk, from 1687 until his death, on 8 April 1692.

Samuel Say was educated at schools in Southwick, Hampshire (until 1689), and Norwich (1691–2) before entering the dissenting academy of Thomas Rowe at Newington Green, London, to train for the ministry. Isaac Watts was his fellow student and intimate friend. After leaving the academy Say acted as chaplain for three years to Thomas Scott of Lyminge, Kent. He ministered for a short time at Andover and, from 6 July 1704, at Great Yarmouth, before settling at Lowestoft, Suffolk, in 1707. There he remained for eighteen years but was unable 'to bring the people into a regular church order' (Hughes, 41) and was not ordained pastor. Despite his troubles he declined a call to the Independent congregation in Norwich in 1712. He married, probably on 27 February 1718, Sarah Hamby (1674/5–1745) at Runham, Norfolk. Her uncle was Nathaniel Carter (1635–1722), who married a granddaughter of Oliver Cromwell and founded an important dissenting trust. They had only one child, Sarah, who married Isaac Toms (1709–1801), minister at Hadleigh, Suffolk.

In 1734, after much hesitation, Say accepted the charge of the congregation at Long Ditch (later Princes Street), Westminster, which had been without a minister since the death of Edmund Calamy in June 1732. There his ministry proved successful. Say was indifferent to the doctrinal differences that divided the church and wished to see an end to all party distinctions. He was opposed to attempts to impose human formulas of doctrine and instead 'followed wheresoever his reason, his conscience, and the scriptures led him' (Hughes, 42). A diffident character, he published only a few sermons. Some juvenile verses, which owed much to his favourite author, Milton, and two essays of poetical criticism were edited by William Duncombe and published after his death, in 1745. From 1695 until three days before his death he kept a journal in which he recorded observations about nature and the weather in an idiosyncratic shorthand. Say died on 12 April 1743, of 'a mortification in the bowels', and was buried in Bunhill Fields, London. He was survived by his wife, who died on 9 February 1745, aged seventy.

ALEXANDER GORDON, *rev.* S. J. SKEDD

Sources O. Hughes, *The righteous man's hope in death consider'd … in a sermon … preached on occasion of the death of the late Revd Mr. S. Say* (1743) • 'A sketch of the life and character of the Rev. Samuel Say', *Protestant Dissenter's Magazine*, 1 (1794), 297–302, 345–9, 403–6 • R. Aspland, 'Brief memoir and Say papers', *Monthly Repository* (1809–10) • W. Wilson, *The history and antiquities of the dissenting churches and meeting houses in London, Westminster and Southwark*, 4 vols. (1808–14), vol. 4, pp. 91–5 • *Calamy rev.* • A. Gordon, ed., *Freedom after ejection: a review (1690–1692) of presbyterian and congregational nonconformity in England and Wales* (1917) • J. Browne, *A history of Congregationalism and memorials of the churches in Norfolk and Suffolk* (1877), 241, 391, 521, 529, 598 • J. A. Jones, ed., *Bunhill memorials* (1849), 242 • *IGI*

Archives Bodl. Oxf., journal • DWL, corresp. and MSS • Yale U., Beinecke L., corresp.

Likenesses C. Hall, line engraving (after drawing by J. Richardson), BM, NPG • J. Hopwood, stipple, BM, NPG; repro. in Wilson, *Dissenting churches*, vol. 4, facing p. 91 • oils, DWL

Say, William (1604–1666?), politician and regicide, was the second son of William Say (*d.* 1613) of Slinfold, Sussex, and his wife, Anne, daughter of Sir Edward Fenner a judge of king's bench. Admitted to University College, Oxford, in 1619, he graduated in 1623; he entered the Middle Temple in 1622, was called to the bar in 1631, and became a bencher in 1654. While a young student during the personal rule of Charles I he was fined as the ringleader of a group who drank a toast to a meeting of parliament. By the early 1640s he was a friend of Bulstrode Whitelocke and in 1642 married Ellen, a daughter of Sir Anthony Weldon. Like these two men he became a zealous parliamentarian during the civil war. On 12 April 1647 he was returned to parliament as member for Camelford, Cornwall, and became an active Independent in the Commons. He served as steward to parliament's commissioners treating with Charles I on the Isle of Wight in 1648, and appears to have been an enthusiastic supporter of the king's trial. He attended the proceedings regularly and signed the death warrant [*see also* Regicides]. During the Rump he was one of the most important lawyer members, heavily involved in legislative activity as well as in show trials such as that of John Lilburne in 1649. He was also chairman of the standing grand committee to determine the future of parliament, and was twice nominated to the council of state, in February 1651 and in November 1652. Inactive during the protectorate, he returned to prominence during 1659, as a supporter of parliament rather than the army, although he and Edmund Ludlow sought to reconcile the two groups. Appointed to the council of state in December 1659, he briefly deputized for William Lenthall as speaker of the Commons in January 1660. He was hostile to any return to monarchical government and sought to ensure that royalists would not be able to influence forthcoming parliamentary elections. After Charles II was restored to the throne, Say was exempted from the Act of Indemnity by a vote of the House of Commons on 30 May 1660. He escaped to the continent, however, and in October 1662 joined Ludlow at Lausanne, and subsequently lived with other exiles at Vevey. In 1664 he left to seek a place of greater safety in Germany. In 1665 he was at Amsterdam, and in the following year was concerting in the Netherlands a movement against England. He probably died in 1666, or shortly afterwards. J. T. PEACEY

Sources HoP, *Commons, 1640–60* [draft] • *JHC*, 2–7 (1640–59) • *JHL*, 4–10 (1628–48) • *CSP dom., 1649–64* • C. H. Firth and R. S. Rait, eds., *Acts and ordinances of the interregnum, 1642–1660*, 3 vols. (1911) • *The diary of Bulstrode Whitelocke, 1605–1675*, ed. R. Spalding, British Academy, Records of Social and Economic History, new ser., 13 (1990) • *The memoirs of Edmund Ludlow*, ed. C. H. Firth, 2 vols. (1894) • E. Ludlow, *A voyce from the watch tower*, ed. A. B. Worden, CS, 4th ser., 21 (1978) • G. J. Armytage, ed., *Middlesex pedigrees*, Harleian Society, 65 (1914), 160–61 • PRO, PROB 11/122, fol. 48 • J. G. Muddiman, *The trial of King Charles the First* (1928) • C. H. Hopwood, ed., *Middle Temple records*, 2–3 (1904–5)

Say, William (1768–1834), engraver, was born at Lakenham on the outskirts of Norwich, the only son of William Say (*d.* 1773), land steward to several neighbouring estates, and his wife (*d.* 1771), the daughter of a clergyman. Left an orphan at the age of five, he was brought up by his mother's sister, and after trying unsuccessfully several pursuits he went to London in 1788, armed mainly with his drawing ability. He married Eleanor Francis on 30 December 1790 at St Marylebone, Marylebone Road, and immediately afterwards went to study under James Ward, who was already practising as a mezzotint engraver, in which art Say was to become eminent. His first independent plate came about 1795, and in 1807 he engraved William Beechey's portraits of the duke and duchess of Gloucester, to whom he was appointed engraver. By this time Say had a family of six children, only four of whom survived him: Edward (*bap.* 3 March 1793), Mary Anne (*bap.* 28 Sept 1794), who married John Buonarotti Papworth, Leonora (*bap.* 22 July 1798), who married W. A. Nicholson, Emma (*bap.* 31 Aug 1800), Frederick William (*bap.* 5 Oct 1803), and Frederick Richard [*see below*].

Between 1811 and 1819 Say engraved eleven mainly landscape plates for J. M. W. Turner's *Liber Studiorum*, together with the unpublished nos. 72 and 73. By 23 May 1812 he had been appointed engraver to the prince regent. In January 1820 he executed in mezzotint a portrait of Queen Caroline after A. W. Devis, the first to be so done on a block of soft steel supplied by Jacob Perkins, which, when hardened, produced 1200 copies, nearly ten times the number obtained from a copper plate. Say engraved many portraits, five of which were shown in 1821 at W. B. Cooke's exhibition of engravings, and his plates of two groups of the Dilettante Society after Sir Joshua Reynolds were highly regarded. His address at this time was 92 Norton Street, Fitzroy Square, London. Turner's series *The Rivers of England* contained two of his plates, dated 1825 and 1827, and Sir John Ross's *Narrative of a Second Voyage* (1835) included three mezzotint plates, printed in colour, which were among his last works. His total of 335 plates, signed 'W. Say', contained works after old masters as well as contemporary artists. He kept copies of all his works, which nearly complete collection his son presented to the British Museum in 1852. Reticent but kindly to the outside world, Say was outgoing with young people. Shortly before his contemplated retirement, he died at his home in Weymouth Street, Portland Place, London, from overwork after a short illness, on 24 August 1834, aged sixty-six. His plates and prints, consisting mainly of portraits, although a number of unfinished and unpublished plates were included, were sold by Christies on 23 July 1835.

Frederick Richard Say (*bap.* 1805, *d.* in or after 1858), engraver, the youngest and only surviving son of William Say, was baptized on 1 February 1805 at St Marylebone, Marylebone Road, Middlesex, and enjoyed a highly successful practice as a portrait painter. Among his sitters were George IV (of whom he made a drawing, *c.*1827, which was engraved in mezzotint by his father and published in May 1827), Prince Albert, the archbishop of York, Earl Grey, and Edward Bulwer-Lytton, which last portrait was considered to be his best. His works were engraved by Samuel Cousins, James Thomson, G. R. Ward, and William Walker. He exhibited at the Royal Academy, the British Institution, and Suffolk Street from 1826 to 1854, and his address from 1837 to 1858 was 18 Harley Street. In 1851 his domestic arrangements included two nurses and five servants. The National Portrait Gallery, London, the Scottish National Portrait Gallery, the National Trust, and the India Office, London, hold examples of his work.

B. HUNNISETT

Sources *GM*, 2nd ser., 4 (1835), 660–61 • Bryan, *Painters* (1903–5) • Wood, *Vic. painters*, 3rd edn • A. M. Hind, *A history of engraving and etching*, 3rd edn (1923), 284 • A. J. Finberg, *The history of Turner's Liber Studiorum, with a new catalogue raisonné* (1924) • *IGI* • St Catherine's Index • R. Walker, *National Portrait Gallery: Regency portraits*, 2 vols. (1985) • B. Stewart and M. Cutten, *The dictionary of portrait painters in Britain up to 1920* (1997)

Archives BM, department of prints and drawings

Likenesses J. Green, oils, NPG

Sayaji Rao III. *See* Gaikwar, Sayaji Rao, maharaja of Baroda (1863–1939).

Sayce, Archibald Henry (1845–1933), orientalist and philologist, was born at Shirehampton, near Bristol, on 25 September 1845, the eldest son of Henry Samuel Sayce (*d.*

*c.*1890), perpetual curate of Shirehampton, and his wife, Mary Anne, *née* Cartwright. The father came from a Glamorgan family. Sayce was a sickly child who suffered from pulmonary tuberculosis until the age of seven; consequently he learnt the alphabet late. By the age of ten, however, he was reading Virgil and Xenophon and being tutored in Homeric Greek and English literature. In 1858, when his parents moved to Batheaston with his father's new job, he was sent to day school at Grosvenor College, Bath, where he became especially interested in Hebrew and comparative philology. At fourteen he learned the hieroglyphic 'alphabet' and the names of the Egyptian pharaohs, and he drew oriental inscriptions and works of art. While recovering from typhoid fever he studied cuneiform, thus laying the foundations of his later career as an Assyriologist. At sixteen he developed an interest in theology; and while still at school he began to learn Assyrian, Persian, Arabic, and Sanskrit, hoping to join the Indian Civil Service.

In 1865 Sayce went to university in Oxford. Although he originally intended to go to Brasenose College he won a scholarship at Queen's College at the time of his matriculation and so went there instead. He read Vedic hymns with Friedrich Max Müller in his first year; Müller and John Rhys were to remain lifelong friends. Just after he had gained a first class in classical moderations, in 1866, his eyesight failed him (and was not cured until 1874) and his earlier lung complaint returned, for which he was sent to recuperate at Pau and Biarritz, where he learned Basque. In 1868, while still ill with pneumonia, he obtained a first class in *literae humaniores*; but a second attack in the following year led him to withdraw from the honours school of law and modern history. In 1869, shortly after taking his BA degree, he was elected a fellow and classical lecturer at Queen's College, Oxford. In 1870 he became a college tutor, and was also ordained.

In the early 1870s Sayce was a regular weekly contributor to *The Times* and the New York *Independent*. In 1874 he gave a talk on the first translations of astronomical and astrological tablets from Nineveh to the Society of Biblical Archaeology, of which he was president from 1898 until it ceased to be an independent body in 1919. He acted as one of the University of Oxford's representatives in the Old Testament Revision Company from 1874 to 1884; in 1876, after taking up Indo-Germanic Philology, he became deputy professor of comparative philology.

From 1872 onwards Sayce spent most of his summers travelling in Europe. In 1877–8 he was in Greece as special correspondent of *The Times*, and in 1878 he was nominated by the Italian government as delegate from Oxford to the Fourth Oriental Congress at Florence. He resigned his tutorship in the following year and was then free to devote all his time to his special interests, including exploration of the East. Thereafter, almost until his death, he spent much of each year abroad, partly for his health; he visited almost every European and Asian country, the Far East, and also north Africa and America. In 1879 he helped to found the Society for the Promotion of Hellenic Studies. Two years later he copied and published as *The Ancient Hebrew Inscription Discovered at the Pool of Siloam in Jerusalem* an inscription thought to have been cut during the reign of Hezekiah in a tunnel which brought water into Jerusalem. One of his most notable achievements was to decipher (without any bilingual text) the Urartian ('Vannic') inscriptions, which he published in two articles in the *Journal of the Royal Asiatic Society* (vol. 14, 1882) as 'The cuneiform inscriptions of Van, deciphered and translated'.

In 1890, after his father's death, Sayce resigned his professorship and other university offices, retaining only his college fellowship. He moved to Egypt, where he helped to found the Alexandria Museum in Cairo and was also instrumental in securing for the British Museum two important Greek works previously thought to be lost: Aristotle's *Constitution of Athens* and the *Mimes* of Herondas. In 1891, however, Sayce was tempted back to Oxford by the university's offer of a personal professorship in Assyriology. In addition to his base in Oxford, he spent a good deal of his time in a large Nile-boat which he fitted up with his considerable library. In 1891 he gave up his London flat and bought a house in Edinburgh, which he occupied at intervals until his death.

From 1908 to 1910 Sayce also spent a good deal of time in the Sudan and helped Professor John Garstang of the University of Liverpool in excavating the ancient capital city of Ethiopia, Meroe. In 1911–12 he travelled in the Far East, and in 1915 he resigned his professorship. His last years were spent in Edinburgh, Oxford, and Egypt, where he wrote many articles and reviews.

Sayce's many publications reveal an active imagination. As early as 1870 his paper 'An Accadian seal', published in the *Journal of Philology*, laid the foundations of Sumerian grammar. With his *Assyrian Grammar* (1872), *Elementary Grammar with Reading-Book of the Assyrian Language* (1875), and *Lectures upon the Assyrian Language and Syllabary* (1877), he pioneered Assyrian studies in England, managing to persuade Semitic scholars to take the 'new' language seriously. From 1874 he also contributed several Assyrian translations to *Records of the Past*, the second series of which (1888–93) he also edited. His contribution to linguistic theory of the day was represented by *Principles of Comparative Philology* (1874–5), which relied on the principle of analogy, and *Introduction to the Science of Language* (2 vols., 1880; 2nd edn, 1883; 3rd edn, 1890). He devoted several books to the history of Israel and to the Hebrew language, such as *The Early History of the Hebrews* (1897), *Early Israel and the Surrounding Nations* (1898), and he wrote introductions to, and commentaries on, certain books of the Old Testament. In *The 'Higher Criticism' and the Verdict of the Monuments* (1894) he contested current theories, especially German ones, concerning the authorship of the Pentateuch, citing the evidence of archaeological remains and discoveries to defend the supposed veracity of traditional interpretations of the books of Moses. With A. E. Cowley he edited another work which defended Christian orthodoxy, *Aramaic Papyri Discovered at Assuan* (1906).

In 1882 Sayce published a long article, 'The bilingual Hittite and cuneiform inscriptions of Tarkondêmos' (*Transactions of the Society of Biblical Archaeology*, vol. 7), and between then and the end of his life he produced many studies on Hittite history and language, works which were ridiculed as his approach had been superseded by the 'higher criticism' increasingly favoured by British, as well as continental scholars. His attempt to decipher Hittite hieroglyphs was equally unsuccessful.

Sayce was chiefly known as an Assyriologist, and published many books and articles on the countries, peoples, history, religion, and literature of the Babylonians and Assyrians. His work was drawn upon in the ninth edition (1896) of Murray's *Handbook for Travellers in Egypt*, and he published many useful copies of Egyptian inscriptions as well as writing several books on the general archaeology of the Near East. His translation of Herodotus, books I–III (1883), contained a number of philological errors and was severely criticized. His last book was a stout volume, *Reminiscences* (1923), in which the events of his seventy-eight years are chronicled, interspersed with an abundance of anecdotes showing a lively sense of humour.

Sayce was an energetic lecturer, who gave talks in many parts of the world, and enjoyed publicizing his discoveries through lectures. His Hibbert lectures on Babylonian religion were published in 1887, his Gifford lectures on Egyptian and Babylonian religion in 1902, and his Rhind lectures entitled 'The archaeology of the cuneiform inscriptions' in 1907. He received honorary degrees from the universities of Oxford, Edinburgh, Aberdeen, Dublin, and Oslo, and the triennial gold medal of the Royal Asiatic Society (1925). In 1919 he was elected a corresponding member of the Institut de France, a lifelong ambition.

Sayce was a great popularizer of the importance of oriental archaeology in understanding the Bible. He read and wrote voraciously, and his energy was considered remarkable. He could write in at least twenty ancient and modern languages, and corresponded assiduously with three generations of oriental scholars. As an Assyriologist his strength lay in his ability to decipher, but he was also among the first to appreciate the significance of Heinrich Schliemann's discoveries, and he argued for the existence of pre-Hellenic civilization in Greek lands long before the Mycenaean age was accepted by scholars. By the end of his life, however, he was considered a dilettante rather than a specialist, was criticized for his lack of intellectual penetration, and was made something of a laughing-stock through his vehement and outdated opposition to the work of continental orientalists. He nevertheless made a number of important contributions to oriental philology and archaeology, was much loved by many colleagues and pupils, and evidently felt at home in Egypt and Mesopotamia. Given his long history of recurrent illnesses such as pneumonia and typhoid, and physical set-backs such as blood poisoning, weak eyesight, a car accident, and a snake-bite, the amounts of work he accomplished and travel he undertook are all the more impressive. Sayce died, unmarried, at Bath on 4 February 1933, having bequeathed his oriental books to Queen's College, his notes and transcriptions to the Bodleian Library, and his collections of Middle and Far Eastern antiquities and ceramics to the Ashmolean Museum in Oxford.

BATTISCOMBE GUNN, *rev.* O. R. GURNEY

Sources A. H. Sayce, *Reminiscences* (1923) • F. L. Cross, ed., *The Oxford dictionary of the Christian church*, 2nd edn, ed. A. E. Livingstone (1974); repr. (1983), 1240 • *The Times* (6 Feb 1933) • F. Ll. Griffith, 'Professor A. H. Sayce', *Journal of the Royal Asiatic Society of Great Britain and Ireland* (1933), 497–9 • *Oxford Magazine* (16 Feb 1933) • J. Pelikan, *Jesus through the centuries* (1985) • A. E. McGrath, *The making of modern German Christology, 1750–1990* (1994)

Likenesses Mrs Attwood Mathews, oils, *c.*1902, Queen's College, Oxford • G. F. Watt, oils, 1919, Queen's College, Oxford

Wealth at death £29,063 1*s.* 1*d.*: confirmation, 18 March 1933, *CCI*

Saye and Sele. For this title name *see* Fiennes, James, first Baron Saye and Sele (*c.*1390–1450); Fiennes, William, first Viscount Saye and Sele (1582–1662).

Sayer, Augustin (1790–1861), physician and sanitarian, was born on 10 October 1790 at Bexley, Kent, one of several children of William Augustin Sayer and his wife, Anne; his grandfather Valentine Sayer (*d.* 1766), had been mayor of Sandwich in 1752, 1753, and 1760. When he was twelve years old Sayer travelled to France with his parents and brothers William Henry (*b.* 1791) and Charles Frederick (*b.* 1794) during the short peace of 1802, but with the onset of war again in 1803 he was taken prisoner. However, he was soon permitted to go on parole within a certain radius and supported himself by becoming a tutor in a French school, which made him an excellent French scholar, a good classicist, and an able mathematician. Sayer was detained for several years and when he returned to England began his medical studies. He graduated BA in 1811 and MA in 1813 (the university is not known); he was also registered as a *licencié ès sciences* at the Imperial University of France in 1813. On 31 January 1815 he enrolled as a student at Leiden University and four days later graduated MD. It is said that he was afterwards an army surgeon but his name does not appear on any British army medical list.

Sayer was admitted a licentiate of the Royal College of Physicians on 22 December 1820 and was elected a fellow on 11 July 1843. He was a fellow of the Epidemiological Society, instituted in 1850 for the investigation of epidemic diseases, and was their foreign and colonial secretary from 1855 to 1857. He was a fellow of the Royal Medical and Chirurgical Society (president 1840), and a member of the Medical Society of London. For some years he took an active part in the proceedings of the Westminster Medical Society, serving as vice-president in 1843.

From 1846 to 1847 Sayer was resident English physician in Brussels to the duke of Kent, and honorary physician to Prince Frederick of the Netherlands. His main appointment from 1848 was that of physician to the Lock Hospital and Asylum, Harrow Road, Paddington. Throughout his long professional life he was an earnest advocate of sanitary reform, working alongside Sir Joseph Bazalgette, the chief architect of underground London, and Thomas Cubitt the master builder. Furthering his interest in mains drains and sewage disposal he was a member of the sewers committee of the Marylebone vestry committee (1859). He published three major works on the disposal of town sewage: *Inquiry to Ascertain the Maximum Limit of the Annual Taxation Required from the Sewers Ratepayers* (1855), *Metropolitan and Town Sewage: their Nature, Value and Disposal* (1857), and *London Main Drainage: the Nature and Disposal of Sewage* (2nd edn, 1858).

In the 1851 and 1861 censuses Sayer was entered as a widower but nothing is known of his wife's identity. On 15 November 1861 he died at his home, 28 Upper Seymour Street, Portman Square, London, where he had lived for thirty years with his unmarried sisters. He bequeathed to the library of the Royal Medical and Chirurgical Society a copy of the *Dictionnaire de science medicale* in sixty volumes which was later deposited in the Marcus Beck Library of the Royal Society of Medicine, London.

W. W. WEBB, *rev.* SUE WEIR

Sources *Proceedings of the Royal Medical and Chirurgical Society*, 4 (1861–4), 81 • *The Lancet* (23 Nov 1861), 512 • *Medical Times and Gazette* (23 Nov 1861), 544 • Munk, *Roll*, 3.229–30 • *London and Provincial Medical Directory* (1848) • *London and Provincial Medical Directory* (1855) • *London and Provincial Medical Directory* (1861) • Marylebone sewers committee minutes, City Westm. AC, II/104, 181 • *Transactions of the Epidemiological Society, Quarterly Report of Proceedings*, 72 (1856), 20 • parish register, Bexley, St Mary, CKS, Ac 15337, 16 Feb 1791 [baptism] • census returns for London, 1851, 1861

Wealth at death under £5000: probate, 20 Dec 1861, *CGPLA Eng. & Wales*

Sayer, Isabelle (*d.* 1473). *See under* Women traders and artisans in London (*act. c.*1200–*c.*1500).

Sayer, Robert [*name in religion* Gregory] (1560–1602), Benedictine monk and moral theologian, was born at Redgrave, Suffolk, the son of John and Alice Sayer or Seare 'mediocris fortunae' ('of modest means'). He went to school at Botesdale, Suffolk, for seven years, and was admitted to Gonville and Caius College, Cambridge, as a minor pensioner 'secundis ordinis, literarum gratia' ('of the second rank, by reason of his education') on 5 July 1576. The college refused to allow him to take the degree of BA for the following causes:

> First, for that he by seacret conference had laboured to pervert divers schoolers, and some had perverted; secondly, for that he had used divers allegations against divers poyntes of Mr Jewells booke; thirdly, for that he had bene of greate and familiar acquayntaunce with Fingeley, a pernicious papist; fourthly, for that he had used to gather together papisticall bookes, and to convey them seacretly into the country. (Heywood and Wright, 1.319–20)

Migrating to Peterhouse, he graduated BA as a member of that college in 1581.

Soon afterwards Sayer proceeded to the English College of Douai, then temporarily removed to Rheims. He and William Flack, another Cambridge man, arrived there on 22 February 1582 and after three days were admitted to the common table. On 6 November 1582 Sayer was admitted into the English College at Rome, where, on 21 July 1585, he received all the holy orders. In this troubled period of the college's history he was one of the minority of students who supported their Jesuit superiors, though not their pro-Spanish politics. In 1586 he fulfilled his oath to go on the English mission, was betrayed at the house of Lord Vaux in Hackney, but evaded arrest. On 28 December 1589 he was professed at Monte Cassino, taking the name Gregory, the first Englishman to become a monk since the dissolution of the monasteries. He was professor of moral theology at Monte Cassino for several years. In 1595 he transferred to the monastery of San Giorgio in Venice, possibly to be nearer the printers of the many learned books which he now embarked on publishing, all of which went into many editions. His prodigious editorial activity during these last seven years of his life have caused many to wonder how much he would have achieved had he not died so young. Nevertheless he counted as one of the major moral theologians until the coming of St Alphonsus Liguori. The most widely known of his works was the *Clavis regia sacerdotum casuum conscientiae*, published at Venice in 1605, but more momentous for the development of moral theology was his *Thesaurus casuum conscientiae* (Venice, 1601) which shows his affinities with the later school of probabilism. He died at San Giorgio, Venice, on 30 October 1602, being buried the same day. A collected edition of his principal works, edited by Father Leander à Sancto Martino (John Jones), was published at Douai in 1620.

THOMPSON COOPER, *rev.* DAVID DANIEL REES

Sources E. J. Mahoney, *The theological position of Gregory Sayrus, O.S.B.* (1922) • G. Anstruther, *The seminary priests*, 1 (1969), 302 • J. Pitts, *De illustribus Angliae scriptoribus* (1619), 800–01 • H. Foley, ed., *Records of the English province of the Society of Jesus*, 6 (1880), 155 • B. Weldon, *Chronological notes … of the English congregation of the order of St Benedict* (1881), 39 • Venn, *Alum. Cant.*, 1/4.36 • W. Kelly, ed., *Liber ruber venerabilis collegii Anglorum de urbe*, 1, Catholic RS, 37 (1940) • T. F. Knox and others, eds., *The first and second diaries of the English College, Douay* (1878), 185 • M. Ziegelbauer, *Historia rei literariae ordinis S. Benedicti*, 4 vols. (1754), vol. 1, chap. 2 • J. Heywood and T. Wright, eds., *Cambridge University transactions during the puritan controversies of the 16th and 17th centuries*, 2 vols. (1854) • 'Libri ordinationum', Archivio di Vicariato di Roma • Cooper, *Ath. Cantab.*, 2.384

Archives Monte Cassino Abbey, Italy, MSS of uncompleted works

Sayer, Robert (1724/5–1794), print, map, and chart publisher, was born in Sunderland, the youngest of three sons of James Sayer (1695–1736) of Stockton, a lawyer and descendant of the Sayer family of Worsall, Yorkshire, and his wife, Thomasine Middleton.

Sayer's first known link with the map and print trade was the marriage, in January 1747, of his elder brother James to Mary *Overton [*see under* Overton family (*per. c.*1665–*c.*1765)], proprietor of the map and print business of her late husband, Philip Overton, at the sign of the Golden Buck in Fleet Street, London. Mary continued trading for a year or more after her marriage, after which Robert Sayer, then aged about twenty-four, acquired her stock and shop. Sayer became a freeman of the Stationers' Company by redemption on 6 September 1748, and the first advertisement placed by him trading on his own appeared in December that year. There is no evidence of any apprenticeship or whether he had already received early training in the trade with the Overton family, but whatever his experience it seems that he enjoyed the support of his brother and sister-in-law for several years, as until 1751 the land tax on the Fleet Street premises was charged to James Sayer.

Overton had built up a large collection of plates, mainly by the purchase of successful plates from their original publishers and by the use of a network of contacts for the sale of prints in the provinces and abroad. The cartographic side of the business had recently been strengthened by the purchase of plates of the publisher John Senex, who had died in 1740. Overton had also shared a number of publishing ventures with the Bowles family of St Paul's Churchyard. Sayer recognized the strengths of this pattern of business and adopted similar strategies.

In the 1750s London was fast becoming the centre of the European print trade, and Sayer catered for the explosion of interest in topographical views of English scenery, houses, and gardens and played a central role in the distribution and publication of design books disseminating architectural and decorative ideas to a large public. Sporting prints and books on penmanship were among other popular lines which reached provincial and colonial markets through his network of local contacts. He also sold large numbers of humorous mezzotints or 'drolls', though these did not reach the height of their popularity until the 1770s and 1780s.

In 1753 Sayer entered the county atlas market, joining John Rocque in publishing an edition of Thomas Read's *Small British Atlas*, and he then went on to join other partnerships publishing county atlases. The most important English atlas in which he had a share was the *Large English Atlas* (1760), published with Thomas Bowles, John Bowles & Son, and John Tinney.

In 1760 Sayer and his first wife, Dorothy Carlos (*d.* 1774), whom he had married in 1754, and their young family moved to slightly larger premises a little further east at 53 Fleet Street. He was by now operating on a very large scale with his own printing presses and engravers and printers. He began to move into fine print publishing, taking a lead in publishing engravings of contemporary English paintings, including works by Edward Penny, Angelica Kaufmann, and particularly Johan Zoffany. He published Zoffany's royal portraits, had a share in his theatrical mezzotints, and owned several of the artist's works himself.

Sayer's financial strength enabled him to acquire important stock, plates, and drawings from Thomas Jefferys's business after the latter's bankruptcy in 1766, and he became the dominant partner with Jefferys in several cartographic publications, including *A General Topography of North America and the West Indies* (1768). He also acquired stock from John Rocque's estate after his death.

In 1774 Sayer took John Bennett, previously his apprentice, into partnership, and a period of increased productivity followed. An important series of American atlases was based on plates Sayer had acquired from Jefferys: *The West India Atlas* (1775), *The American Atlas* (1775), *The North American Pilot* (1775), and *The Western Neptune* (1778). These took the firm into chart publishing and were quickly followed by *The Channel Pilot* and *The East India Pilot*, and during the 1780s by charts of the northern and western coasts of Britain, the Baltic, the Mediterranean, and west Africa. Many of the charts were based on the work of other cartographers, but in contrast to much of Sayer's publishing the partners were the sole owners of all the plates from the outset. Within a decade Sayer and Bennett had become the leading British chart publisher, while maintaining its prominent position in maps and prints. The firm's new atlases included Samuel Dunn's *New Atlas of the Mundane System* (1774), Bernard Scale's *Hibernian Atlas* (1776), and *The American Military Pocket Atlas* (1776), the last of these catering for topical interest in the American colonies.

In the early 1780s John Bennett began to show signs of insanity, and the partnership came to an end in 1784 or 1785. Sayer was now sixty and made no innovations after Bennett left. By 1791 he was in ill health, relying increasingly on his assistants and eventual successors, Robert Laurie and James Whittle, and spending much time in Bath and at his house in Richmond.

Sayer was by now a rich man, but he declined the City of London honours of sheriff and mastership of the Stationers' Company and turned his mind to improving the large house on Richmond Hill which he had bought in 1776. Zoffany painted a family group here, showing Sayer in the grounds of the enlarged mansion, which he barely lived to see, with his second wife, Alice Longfield, *née* Tilson, the widow he married on 8 February 1780, and James Sayer, the surviving son of his first marriage. It shows a solid, plainly dressed man, untouched by extravagances of dress or manner that his wealth might have brought, but well content to be portrayed as a country gentleman.

Sayer's success was based on commercial rather than creative skills. He achieved a leading position in the print, map, and chart trades by benefiting from common production facilities and distribution channels and exploiting the expanding markets in all three fields. As a publisher he was shrewd and cautious, at first venturing into the risky atlas market only in partnership with others, and spotting trends in popular taste but building his vast collection of plates by buying plates which had already proved successful. As a seller he developed his provincial, colonial, and foreign contacts to reach a wide market. It was only in the second half of his career, operating from this strong base, that he became more adventurous, moving into fine prints of contemporary pictures and later into chart publishing.

Sayer died at Bath aged sixty-nine on 29 January 1794 'after a lingering illness' (*The Times*, 3 Feb 1794, 4c) and was buried at St Mary's, Richmond, on 7 February. He was survived by his second wife and by one but probably no more of his six children. SUSANNA FISHER

Sources S. Fisher, *The makers of the blueback charts: a history of Imray, Laurie, Norie and Wilson Ltd.* (2001) • T. Clayton, *The English print, 1688–1802* (1997) • D. Hodson, *County atlases of the British Isles published after 1703: a bibliography*, 2 (1989) • private information (2004) • S. C. Cox, *Reports of cases determined in the courts of equity* (1816) • J. B.

Harley, 'The bankruptcy of Thomas Jeffreys: an episode in the economic history of eighteenth-century map-making', *Imago Mundi*, 20 (1966), 27–48 · parish register, Christ Church, Spitalfields, London · parish register, St Dunstan-in-the-West, Fleet Street, London · parish register, St Mary's, Richmond, Surrey · V. Manners and G. C. Williamson, *John Zoffany RA: his life and works, 1735–1810* (1920) · J. Cloake, 'Cardigan House and its architects', *Richmond History*, 15 (1994), 18–26 · R. Sayer, *New and enlarged catalogue for the year M.DCC.LXVI of new useful, and correct maps … prints … books of architecture, drawing and copy-books* (1766) · *Sayer and Bennett's enlarged catalogue of new and valuable prints* (1775); repr. (1970) · *Robert Sayer's catalogue* (1786–8) · *The Times* (3 Feb 1794), 4c · City of London land tax assessments, GL, MS 11316 · D. F. McKenzie, ed., *Stationers' Company apprentices*, [3]: *1701–1800* (1978)

Likenesses J. Zoffany, group portrait, oils, *c.*1793, repro. in Manners and Williamson, *John Zoffany RA*

Wealth at death owner of a thriving business (with large stock of copper plates, own printing presses, freehold Fleet Street premises, and leasehold Fleet Street area warehouse), profits from which were £4600 in 1781 and unlikely to have declined; also owned mansion on Richmond Hill, other unspecified freehold and copyhold property in Richmond, and property (messuages and tenements) in Birmingham area: will, PRO, PROB 11/1242, fols. 105–6

Sayers [*married name* Fleming], **Dorothy Leigh** (**1893–1957**), writer and scholar, was born on 13 June 1893 in the old Choir House at 1 Brewer Street, Oxford, the only child of the Revd Henry Sayers (1854–1928) and his wife, Helen Mary, *née* Leigh (1856–1929). The Sayers family came originally from co. Tipperary, Ireland. Henry Sayers, whose father was also a clergyman, was born in Tittleshall, Norfolk, while Helen Sayers, born in Shirley, near Southampton, was the daughter of a solicitor who was also a fine Latin scholar. Sayers's mother descended from an old landed family with holdings on the Isle of Wight, and as a writer, Sayers always insisted that the middle initial 'L' be used in her name. With a history of churchmen on one side of the family and a scholarly solicitor for her maternal grandfather, Sayers's interest in both theology and crime might be said to come out of family history.

Early life and education Dorothy Sayers began life amid the bustle of Oxford, where her father was choirmaster at Christ Church, but when she was four years old Henry Sayers accepted the more remunerative living of Bluntisham-cum-Earith in the remote fen country of East Anglia, which would later provide the backdrop for one of Sayers's finest novels, *The Nine Tailors* (1934). Each year of her childhood from that time on, she saw the bleak fenland washes flooded to protect the pastures enclosed by the Fens' extensive system of dykes, a memory no doubt summoned thirty years later, as she was composing some of the novel's most eloquent scenes. (During Sayers's adolescence, her parents moved even deeper into the fens, when her father became rector at Christchurch in Cambridgeshire.) Life in the spacious Georgian rectory at Bluntisham was both spartan and elegant. There was no running water, but the family and any guests dressed for dinner in the evening. Later in life, Sayers remembered wistfully the cool linen of her mother's well-appointed table and the sheltering old trees of the rectory's gracious

Dorothy Leigh Sayers (1893–1957), by Sir William O. Hutchison, *c.*1949–50

gardens. By virtue of her class and location, as well as her lack of siblings, the youthful Dorothy Sayers was essentially isolated from others her own age. Like many future authors, she lived largely a life of books and stories, and from early childhood she showed a special talent for languages and story-telling. Able to read by the age of four, she began devouring books from the rectory's library. The young Dorothy Sayers also wrote sketches and plays which she performed to the delight of an indulgent household. Her closest friend, a cousin eight years her senior named Ivy Shrimpton, who had been brought up on a farm in California, often made extended visits to the rectory. Through a youthful sharing of books, imagination, and confidences, the two girls forged a remarkable friendship that would support Sayers during severely trying times in adulthood.

Dorothy Sayers was educated chiefly at home. Yet perhaps because he had no son, Henry Sayers seems to have always assumed that his precocious daughter would eventually study at Oxford, even though women were not admitted as fully-fledged members of the university until 1920, five years after Dorothy Sayers finished her studies there. Nevertheless, her father began her Latin studies at home, before she was seven, and a succession of governesses instructed her in other areas, including French and German. When she was nearing sixteen, her parents decided it was time for her to go away to school, sending her to the Godolphin School in Salisbury, an unhappy experience which Sayers later recalled in 'Cat O' Mary'. Although she was a lifelong believer and communicant, Dorothy Sayers was always repelled by the sanctimonious, an apparently apt description for some teachers at Godolphin. No doubt it was her experience there which led her to remark in her first novel that 'the atmosphere of the Close pervades every nook and corner of Salisbury, and no food in that city but seems faintly flavoured with prayer-books' (*Whose Body?*, 1923, 76). In March 1911 measles spread through Godolphin and Dorothy Sayers became acutely ill; she was near death when her mother came to nurse her. This illness seems to have predisposed her thereafter to lose most of her hair during times of stress. She was relieved to go home, where she could recuperate and prepare for her examinations for Oxford. In the autumn of 1912 she went up on the Gilchrist scholarship to Somerville College, Oxford.

Somerville, with its tradition of nurturing strong women who go on to leadership roles in the public arena as well as the arts, suited Dorothy L. Sayers perfectly. Her college days were among her happiest; while at Somerville, she would later write to her son, she acquired a scholarly method and habit of mind which served her throughout life (*Letters*, 15 Jan 1940). She also forged lifelong friendships there, including one with Muriel St Clare Byrne, who was responsible, in the 1930s, for turning Sayers towards a career in the theatre by convincing her to write the Wimsey play *Busman's Honeymoon* (1937), upon which the novel of the same name was based. While at Somerville, Sayers experienced the first of her 'grand passions' for unattainable men, an intense infatuation with the director of the Oxford Bach Choir, Dr H. P. Allen. Another man who caught her eye was a student named Maurice Roy Ridley, a future chaplain of Balliol, who would influence her characterization of Lord Peter Wimsey years later.

Sayers was a distinguished student, and the liberal education she acquired at Oxford is reflected in her particularly literate novels and essays. In 1915 she took a first in modern (medieval) French. Her early work in languages prepared her well for the translations she was to publish, beginning at the end of the 1920s with *Tristan in Brittany* and stretching to the end of her life, with a translation of *Roland* coming out in 1957 even as she was attempting to finish her most significant work in both literary criticism and translation, the first Penguin edition of Dante's *Divine Comedy*.

Early writing and career Sayers had begun writing verse in childhood and, after her graduation from Oxford, she brought out two slim volumes of poetry, *Op. I* (1916) and *Catholic Tales and Christian Songs* (1918). Her novels reflect a thorough knowledge of English poetry, with special emphasis on Donne, Tennyson, Shakespeare, and Milton, and one of her curious legacies is that many readers must have met the work of some of these writers first, or perhaps only, in the popular novels of Dorothy L. Sayers. Sayers herself was not a great poet, but her early work in traditional poetic devices taught her an attention to form and the careful employment of language which would later distinguish her novels from the average detective story of her day.

After graduation Sayers tried teaching, beginning in Hull and later in London. She never really cared for the classroom, however, and between these two positions took employment, first as a publisher's apprentice to Basil Blackwell and then as a secretary at a school in France, where she assisted a dashing young Oxford friend with whom she fell in love, Eric Whelpton. Whelpton did not return the feeling, but he provided yet more elements of that great male figure she would later envision and conquer legions of readers with, Lord Peter Death Bredon Wimsey. In the years after college, when Sayers was casting about for her life's work, another future novelist, Doreen Wallace, knew her at Oxford and later recalled her:

> I have never known anyone so brimful of the energy of a well-stocked mind: even at 24 … she knew an enormous amount about all sorts of subjects … and nothing would content her but fact. There was, however, a lighter side to this impressive character. Long and slim in those days, small head held alert on slender neck, she loped around Oxford looking for fun. (Reynolds, *Dorothy L. Sayers*, 76)

This seems very much in line with Basil Blackwell's assessment of Sayers as an editor, that she seemed 'a racehorse harnessed to a cart' (Brabazon, 75). Finally, in 1922, she landed a job as copywriter at S. H. Bensons, then Britain's largest advertising agency, where she was to earn her living over the next decade, while turning out increasingly serious novels at the rate of roughly one per year. At Bensons she again enjoyed some of the fun and camaraderie she had experienced as a student at Oxford. Although she had ethical concerns about advertising, she was good at it. A creator of what became known as the Campaign of the Century, the wildly popular and financially successful Mustard Club scheme for Colman's mustard, she also penned the slogan associated to this day with Guinness stout, 'My goodness, my Guinness!' Her work in advertising also supplied one of the most memorable settings in her fiction, the believable office life at Pym's Publicity in *Murder must Advertise* (1933).

The detective fiction Some time about 1920, when thrillers were all the rage, Sayers had conceived the idea of writing detective stories for money. Then one day, while she was plotting a story, the immortal Lord Peter Wimsey walked blithely into her mind, as she would later describe the experience, setting up a residence there more permanent than she might have wished or even believed ('How I came to invent the character of Lord Peter', *Harcourt Brace News*, 15 July 1936, 1–2). He became, indeed, a permanent occupant of her mind, and perhaps because he was so believable to her and had so conquered her imagination, he became, like Sherlock Holmes before him, eminently believable to untold others. In fact, to many around the globe, Lord Peter, as scholar, aesthete, and wit, represents the very epitome of the English gentleman, and the Englishness of Sayers's novels, and their delineation of English life between the wars account for much of her enduring appeal to those of other cultures and eras. As Sayers's essays and plays deal directly with the issues and concerns of her society, so do her novels reflect the very texture of English life in her day.

Sayers was not so successful with men in real life, falling

in love in the early 1920s in London with an unsatisfactory sort, a minor writer named John Cournos, who spurned her, and finally becoming pregnant by a man she did not love, Bill White. In 1924 she gave birth in secrecy to their son, whom she named John Anthony, and whom she took care of from a distance through the ministrations of Ivy, the companion of her youth. On 13 April 1926 she married a Fleet Street journalist and photographer, (Oswald) Atherton Fleming (1881–1950), known as Mac, who shortly thereafter began suffering, like Wimsey, from the effects of his experience in the First World War. They never managed to take her son into their home, as she had hoped upon marriage, but John Anthony took the Fleming name and was represented publicly as their adopted son. Despite a troubled marriage, Sayers stayed with Mac Fleming until his death in 1950. This was the sad domestic drama being played out while she composed her ebullient fiction and self-assured essays.

Sayers was an important scholar and critic of mystery and detective fiction, and in her twelve novels—all but one of which features Wimsey—she set out to bring the modern detective story up to the standards of serious literature, while at the same time making it appeal, as she said, not only to those with a 'caviar' taste in art, but also to 'those in the back-kitchens' ('The present status of the mystery story', *London Mercury*, Nov 1930, 47). This comment, in characteristically earthy language, shows how little real snobbery she had, although she never suffered fools gladly. In her fiction, she wanted to reach an audience as wide and diverse as possible, and by general agreement she succeeded at this goal more than anyone else working in her genre, arguably surpassing even her own ideal mystery writer, Wilkie Collins, especially in novels like *The Nine Tailors* (1934), which is as much a meditation on time and change as it is a murder mystery, and in *Gaudy Night* (1935), where she combines a sensational detective story with a genuine English novel. In this, Sayers's best work of fiction, the heroine wrestles with a crucial moral choice, while the hero undergoes significant change, so that they may come together in parity by the novel's end, in the manner of Jane Austen. In the course of the novels, Lord Peter also develops from caricature into a fully realized human personality.

Sayers worked in the so-called golden age of mystery in the 1920s and 1930s, but she transcended her own time, and her novels will continue to appeal to readers who appreciate a high level of verbal wit, keen intelligence, fascinating characters, and a realistically rendered, vibrant fictional world. Among the best are those which can stand on their own against more manifestly serious fiction of their day, especially *Gaudy Night* and *Busman's Honeymoon*, as well as *The Nine Tailors*, with the flawed but brilliant *Murder must Advertise* falling somewhere below them. The transitional epistolary novel, *The Documents in the Case* (1930), is one of the finest examples of that form in the modern period. It shows Sayers tackling significant social issues while brilliantly evoking early twentieth-century British life. Employing one of the oldest of novelistic formats, this book renders contemporary life with both comedy and profundity. It is also a kind of rehearsal for the four novels featuring Harriet Vane: *Strong Poison* (1930); *Have his Carcase* (1932); *Gaudy Night* (1935), and *Busman's Honeymoon* (1937). Like *Documents*, these books develop an extended treatment of the marriage question and the issue of relationships between men and women, with Harriet and Peter coming to terms gloriously at the end of *Gaudy Night*.

Sayers's novels consider the themes of individual responsibility, order versus anarchy, the spectre of consumption and waste in the modern world (*Murder must Advertise*), the situation of women (*Unnatural Death*, and all the Harriet Vane books), the devastating effects of war (*The Unpleasantness at the Bellona Club* and Wimsey's character generally), the meaning of work (in the characters of Wimsey, Vane, Miss Climpson, and Jack Munting), and the modern argument between science and religion (see especially *The Documents in the Case*). In all her fiction, she examines the implications of the class system. She also wrote a number of workmanlike short stories which were gathered into several collections, but by comparison with her novels they are thin, both thematically and stylistically.

Much of Sayers's thinking on the mystery novel and literature generally can be gleaned from her influential reviews for the *Sunday Times*, published in the early 1930s. In them she responded to virtually every mystery writer of her day, including Agatha Christie and Margery Allingham, and in the process revealed much about her attitude to art. Her other important critical work includes the landmark introductions to the three-volume *Omnibus of Crime* series (1929, 1932, and 1935), as well as a comical and insightful romp entitled 'Aristotle on Detective Fiction' (1935), which was based on an Oxford lecture in which she playfully demonstrated the essential classicism of her genre. Later in life she would produce many essays of Dante criticism.

Other writings and later life No one knows why Sayers stopped writing mystery fiction in the mid-1930s, but the success at that time of her first Wimsey play, *Busman's Honeymoon*, led quickly to a Canterbury Festival commission, for which she wrote *The Zeal of thy House* (1937). With this turn she began writing for the theatre, her culminating accomplishment being the cycle of twelve radio plays composed for the BBC on the life of Christ, *The Man Born to be King* (1941), which was broadcast to a huge audience of Britons during the darkest days of the Second World War. Indeed, in these plays and in works like *Begin Here* (1941) and the Wimsey Papers (1939–40), she offered her countrymen a stirring argument for fighting. The choice, as she saw it, was proposed in the bold title of one of her essays, 'Creed or chaos?' (1947). Her greatest essay, *The Mind of the Maker* (1941), which is both artistic autobiography and examination of the Christian doctrine of the Trinity, was also inspired by these difficult days. It remains one of the best inquiries into the creative process ever written.

Some time in the early 1940s, Sayers began work on the last great passion of her life, the poetry of Dante Alighieri, and she would spend most of the rest of her days working on a verse translation of his *Divine Comedy*. When death overtook her suddenly on 18 December 1957, she had just viewed a new portrait of herself by Sir William Hutchison, a picture now in the National Portrait Gallery, London. She was cremated and her ashes were deposited at St Anne's House, Dean Street, London, on 23 December. She did not live to finish the third volume of the Dante translation, but her Penguin editions had succeeded in introducing *Inferno* and *Purgatorio* to a new generation. Sayers ended life as she began it, as a scholar and wordsmith. At the end of the twentieth century, she was held in higher esteem in Britain for her theological writings than for her fiction, with the opposite being true in the United States. This may change somewhat as a result of the 1998 publication of her last Wimsey novel, *Thrones, Dominations*, which she abandoned in the early 1940s and which was finished by another novelist, Jill Paton Walsh. The book was an immediate best-seller on the *Sunday Times* list in the winter of 1998.

A woman of deep enthusiasms, wide-ranging intellect, and a great zest for living, Dorothy L. Sayers was large of body and of heart. Her work has inspired many writers, most notably P. D. James, and a literary society is named for her. In 1997 a statue of her was unveiled in Witham, Essex, opposite 24 Newland Street, the house she had shared with Fleming and in which she died.

CATHERINE KENNEY

Sources *The letters of Dorothy L. Sayers*, ed. B. Reynolds (1996–) • B. Reynolds, *Dorothy L. Sayers: her life and soul* (1993) • J. Brabazon, *Dorothy L. Sayers: the life of a courageous woman* (1981) • R. E. Hone, *Dorothy L. Sayers: a literary biography* (1979) • C. Kenney, *The remarkable case of Dorothy L. Sayers* (1990) • papers, Wheaton College, Illinois, Marion E. Wade Center • Witham Library, Witham, Essex, Sayers papers • A. S. Dale, ed., *Dorothy L. Sayers: the centenary celebration* (1993) • B. Reynolds, *The passionate intellect: Dorothy L. Sayers' encounter with Dante* (1989) • b. cert. • m. cert. • d. cert.

Archives Ransom HRC, corresp. and literary papers • Wheaton College, Illinois, Marion E. Wade Center • Witham Library, Witham, Essex | BL, corresp. with Society of Authors, Add. MS 56798 • Bodl. Oxf., letters to R. W. Chapman • Col. U., Rare Book and Manuscript Library, letters to Ifan Kyrle Fletcher • Harvard U., Houghton L., letters to John Cournos • ICL, corresp. with Herbert Dingle • Society of the Sacred Mission, Milton Keynes, letters to H. H. Kelly • U. Sussex, letters to Maurice Reckitt • UCL, letters to Arnold Bennett | SOUND BBC WAC

Likenesses H. Coster, photographs, 1938, NPG • W. O. Hutchison, oils, *c.*1949–1950, NPG [*see illus.*] • J. Doubleday, statue, 1997, Newland Street, Witham, Essex • Mac Fleming, sketches, repro. in Brabazon, *Dorothy L. Sayers* • photographs, repro. in Brabazon, *Dorothy L. Sayers* • photographs, repro. in Reynolds, *Dorothy L. Sayers*

Wealth at death £36,276 13*s.* 7*d.*: probate, 3 Aug 1958, *CGPLA Eng. & Wales*

Sayers, Frank (1763–1817), poet and scholar, was born on 3 March 1763 in East Ham, Essex, the only child of Francis Sayers (1724–1763/4), a merchant, and his wife, Ann (1732–1790), daughter of John Morris, a merchant of Great Yarmouth. After her husband's death Ann Sayers returned to her parental home, where Sayers spent the first decade of his life. In 1773 he was sent to boarding-school at North Walsham, then transferred the following year to the newly opened school at Palgrave run by Rochemont and Anna Laetitia Barbauld (1743–1825). There Sayers excelled his fellow pupils, began writing poetry under the influence of Mrs Barbauld, and made an important, lifelong friend in William Taylor (1765–1836). Withdrawn from the school in 1777, he was given mercantile employment in Great Yarmouth. Sayers disliked this, eventually giving it up with a view to studying medicine. His mother had moved to the village of Thorpe, outside Norwich, where he joined her in 1783. Here Sayers's friendship with Taylor was resumed in a 'truly intense' manner (*Works*, xix); it is possible both men were homosexual.

Between 1783 and 1788 Sayers studied medicine at Edinburgh University and in London, but eventually decided he was unfit for the profession. In retrospect these years were more important for an intense study of Greek and philosophy that culminated in plans for a 'history of metaphysical literature' (*Works*, xxix), a project possibly shelved when Sayers discovered that William Enfield (1741–1797), dean of the Norwich literati, was preparing an abridgement of Jacob Brucker's *Historia critica philosophiae*. Sayers's thinking became extremely heterodox under the influence of Hume. In 1788, after a mental breakdown, he decided to take a degree at the University of Harderwijk before settling in Norwich to pursue a literary career. His thesis, *De animi affectionibus complectens*, submitted on 7 August 1789, evidenced the range of his reading in philosophy, and hinted at his own radical sentiments. Before returning to England, Sayers toured the Netherlands and France, staying in Paris to view something of the revolution, which he enthusiastically supported. During his absence his mother moved into Norwich, where he joined her on his return, probably in October 1789.

Sayers immediately began writing a series of dramas on Nordic themes that combined blank verse with odic passages. The following year 'Moina', 'Starno', and 'The Descent of Freya', all muted protests at the deadly effects of superstition, were published by Joseph Johnson (1738–1809), the radical bookseller, as *Dramatic Sketches of the Ancient Northern Mythology*. This publication established Sayers's name as a poet in both Britain and Germany, where two translations were made. In 1792 a revised second edition was published with several additions, including, notably, two 'monodramas', a form Sayers pioneered in English, and which enjoyed a certain vogue in the 1790s. He had been inspired to attempt it by Taylor's admiration for continental versions, particularly Goethe's *Proserpina*. The death of his mother in 1790 had a profound impact on Sayers, who thereafter 'endeavoured to discipline his mind to religion' (*Works*, lvii). His essay 'On the evidence of the truth of Christianity', published in the Unitarian periodical the *Christian Miscellany* between February and March 1792, was a turning point, a clear attempt to shake off Hume's influence. Financially independent after his mother's death, some time in the early 1790s Sayers moved into the cathedral close and 'progressively became a frequenter of the cathedral-worship' (*Works*, lxvi); his movement from atheism to a dogmatic Anglicanism was rapidly completed. Alongside this sea change in his religious opinions, Sayers's political opinions veered round to an extreme toryism that shocked many of his former friends. His friendship with the radical and heretical Taylor was maintained, although it gradually cooled.

Sayers's *Disquisitions Metaphysical and Literary* (1793) represented a significant movement away from poetry. The volume included the essay from the *Christian Miscellany* with others on aesthetics and psychology; the dominant influence on Sayers's thinking was then David Hartley (1705–1757). *Disquisitions* was respectfully reviewed, but did little to enhance Sayers's established reputation. Thereafter he largely lost interest in writing. As early as May 1793 William Enfield was obliged to admit that Sayers was 'too indolent' even to write reviews on a regular basis (Bodl. Oxf., MS Add. C.89, fol. 73*v*). A very slim volume of new poetry, *Nugae poeticae* (1803), showed a tendency towards humour and parody, while a second volume of essays, *Miscellanies, Antiquarian and Historical* (1805), a collection of very slight pieces, demonstrated Sayers's later interest in English, and specifically Anglo-Saxon, history. He revised his earlier poems 'with a sensitive fastidiousness, directed … particularly to the suppression of every word which a perverse ingenuity might imagine to be an emanation of his discarded early opinions' (Robberds, 2.476). There was a third edition in 1803, a fourth in 1807, and two posthumous editions. Sayers adopted a life of cultured leisure, socializing extensively with members of the cathedral clergy. He never married. A large inheritance in 1799 made him rich, and he became a generous contributor to local charities. He rarely left Norwich and 'disliked sleeping from home' (*Works*, lxxx). A sufferer from hypochondria, he died at his home, Lower Close, Norwich, on 16 August 1817 and was buried on 23 August in Norwich Cathedral, where a mural monument was erected in his memory.

Sayers's was a major literary talent squandered. Almost everything he wrote of value was written between 1789 and 1792. *Dramatic Sketches* was one of the most original and influential poetic works of the early 1790s, and exerted a particularly potent spell on the young Robert Southey. Its success in Germany briefly opened the possibility of an Anglo-German school of 'Romanticism'.

DAVID CHANDLER

Sources *Collective works of the late Dr. Sayers; to which have been prefixed some biographic [sic] particulars by W. Taylor of Norwich*, ed. W. Taylor, 2 vols. (1823) • D. J. Chandler, 'Norwich literature, 1788–97: a critical survey', DPhil diss., U. Oxf., 1997 • J. W. Robberds, *A memoir of the life and writings of the late William Taylor of Norwich*, 2 vols. (1843) • D. Chandler, 'Cowper in the *Christian Miscellany*', *N&Q*, 242 (1997), 222–5 • transcript of Great Yarmouth parish registers, Genealogical Society • Bodl. Oxf., MS Add. C .89

Likenesses W. C. Edwards, line engraving (after J. Opie, *c*.1800), BM, NPG; repro. in Taylor, ed., *Collective works of the late Dr. Sayers*, frontispiece

Wealth at death approx. £500 left to various charities: Taylor, ed., *Collective works*, cxxiv–cxxv

Sayers [Sayer], **James** (1748–1823), caricaturist and political propagandist, was born at Yarmouth, Norfolk, in August 1748, the son of the master of a trading vessel. He was articled as a clerk in an attorney's office at Yarmouth, and became a member of the borough council. At this time he composed poetical satires in verse and drew caricatures. After inheriting a small fortune from his father, Sayers went to London in 1780 or 1781 to try his hand at caricature, hoping to exploit the growing popularity of this vehicle for political and social satire. Unlike the majority of political caricaturists who took the side of the opposition against the governments of the day, Sayers consistently devoted his energies to supporting Pitt. His most effective blows were struck against the Fox–North coalition: in November 1783, five days after the publication of Fox's India Bill, he produced *A Transfer of India Stock*, showing Fox making off with India House and all the patronage of India. His most famous print followed two weeks later on 5 December: *Carlo Khan's Triumphal Entry into Leadenhall Street* showed Fox as an Indian potentate mounted on an elephant with the face of Lord North, being led by Burke to India House. M. D. George noted that it was 'one of the most influential political caricatures ever published' (George, *English Political Caricature*, 169) and Lord Eldon later noted Fox's admission that 'Sayers's caricatures had done him more mischief than the debates in Parliament or the works of the press' (Twiss, 1.162). The theme of Carlo Khan became common currency for some time as a satire on the supposed rapacity of the whig party. Pitt rewarded the artist with the sinecure of marshal of the court of exchequer. Further prints attacked the coalition in 1784, but in the general election of that year Sayers returned to East Anglia to write pro-tory squibs for the Norfolk election.

Sayers resumed political caricature in 1785 with a series on Burke's campaign against Warren Hastings. He again attacked Fox in the regency crisis of 1788–9 and in the following two years over his support of the French Revolution. Sayers was the first caricaturist to point up the parallel between Foxites and Jacobins. The *St James's Chronicle* of 20 February 1790 described these prints as 'the most forcible strokes of satire, that, since the time of *Hudibras*, have been aimed at the cause of fanaticism' (George, *Catalogue*, 6.663). Sayers's attitude reflected his connection with the loyalist movement in Norwich, where he was now settled, and his part in the local contest with the dissenters and reformers there. His cousin, the poet and essayist Dr Frank Sayers, a prominent citizen, was a member of the radical club at the start of the French Revolution but turned to loyalism in 1791, it was said through the influence of Burke, but perhaps also owing to the example of his cousin. He died in 1817 and James, his heir, placed a memorial wall tablet to him in the cathedral (Goodwin, 153).

In the 1780s Sayers produced a number of prints on social topics, especially on the theatre and literature, featuring well-known actresses, singers, and literary associates of Dr Johnson. After 1794 he reverted to pamphleteering in the main and he wrote *Outlines of the opposition in 1795, collected from the works of the most capital Jacobin artists* (Norwich City Library, Colman collection). On the death of

Pitt in 1806 he wrote 'Elijah's Mantle', a poem once attributed to Canning. Sayers died in Curzon Street, Mayfair, on 20 April 1823, and was buried in St Andrew's, Holborn. He was a feeble artist whose ideas elevated him into an influential caricaturist and useful asset to Pitt. His most celebrated work, drawn early in his career, was also his worst artistically and was parodied by Gillray who, at times, adopted his signature as a tease. His later caricatures were improved by the addition of soft ground etching and aquatint. His name is sometimes spelt Sayer, but he used the name Sayers on some of his caricatures. A large collection of these is in the print room at the British Museum.

L. H. CUST, *rev.* E. A. SMITH

Sources F. G. Stephens and M. D. George, eds., *Catalogue of political and personal satires preserved … in the British Museum*, 5–7 (1935–42) • M. D. George, *English political caricature: a study of opinion and propaganda*, 2 vols. (1959) • H. T. Dickenson, *Caricature and the constitution, 1760–1832* (1986) • *EdinR*, 150 (1879), 41–76 • 'Sayers, Frank', *DNB* • A. Goodwin, *The friends of liberty: the English democratic movement in the age of the French Revolution* (1979) • *Collective works of the late Dr. Sayers; to which have been prefixed some biographic [sic] particulars by W. Taylor of Norwich*, ed. W. Taylor, 2 vols. (1823) • *The public and private life of Lord Chancellor Eldon, with selections from his correspondence*, ed. H. Twiss, 1 (1844) • J. Cannon, *The Fox–North coalition: crisis of the constitution, 1782–4* (1969) • J. Sayers, *Outlines of opposition in 1795* (1795) • M. Bryant and S. Heneage, eds., *Dictionary of British cartoonists and caricaturists, 1730–1980* (1994)

Likenesses M. Gauci, lithograph (aged sixty-five; after J. Sayers), BM

Sayers, John Edward [Jack] (**1911–1969**), newspaper editor and social commentator, was born on 13 July 1911 in King Street, Birkenhead, the eldest of three children of John Sayers (1880–1939), journalist, of 16 Cyprus Avenue, Belfast, and his wife, Elizabeth Lemon (1886–1957).

Educated at Miss Corry's and Miss Brown's school, Cyprus Road, and then Methodist College, Belfast (1920–30), Sayers became an apprentice reporter at the *Belfast Telegraph* in 1930, there joining his father and his uncle. All three would in time become editor, so ensuring a continuous familial succession from 1937 until 1969. Jack, as he was known, had risen to parliamentary reporter when the Second World War broke out and barely a month later he was serving on HMS *Courageous* when she was torpedoed in mid-Atlantic with the loss of 700 on 17 September 1939. As with many of his generation, the experience of war cast in stone the ideals that were to dominate his later career: patriotism and the values of empire, duty in the service of the community, and the moral responsibility of those in authority to pursue the cause of justice. At the same time his secondment (on 24 October 1939) to Churchill's private map room exposed him to the exotic world of the 'high ups'. Here he observed his mercurial leader and met the great and good, from Churchillian cronies such as Lord Beaverbrook and Brendan Bracken to world leaders such as Roosevelt, Eisenhower (whom he once tried to lock out of the map room on grounds of security), de Gaulle, and even Chiang Kai-shek.

With the war over Sayers married, on 4 October 1945, a war widow, Daphne Mary Godby (1916–1998), daughter of Roger Hardy Parnell, chartered accountant, and his wife Amy Sarah, at Holy Trinity, Brompton, rejoining the *Belfast Telegraph* a month later as political correspondent (with John Cole as his deputy). At the same time (January 1946) he began a radio career for the BBC on such programmes as *Ulster's Half Hour*, *Your Questions*, and the influential, often controversial *Ulster Commentary*. This, together with his freelance articles for the *Daily Telegraph*, the *Observer*, and the *Round Table* (1948–69), ensured that by the time he became editor-in-chief in 1961 Sayers had emerged as the foremost political commentator of his day.

Slightly swarthy and owlish as he peered through his glasses, he looked distinctly archaic for the 1960s in his neat, dark suits with a tight knot to his tie in a stiff white collar. Yet Jack Sayers was to prove one of the most remarkable editors Ulster had ever produced. Under him the *Belfast Telegraph* commanded a daily readership that approached two out of three households in the province, straddling the sectarian divide and offering for many, both protestant and Catholic, a common ground for debate amid the political turmoil of the 1960s. Convinced of the need for change in Ulster he determined through his paper to transform Ulster unionism into an inclusive, supra-class political movement. These ideas, emanating as they did from a traditional Unionist organ, won considerable support in the late 1950s and 1960s. And, with traditional unionism floundering in the wake of this articulate assault, Sayers quickly found himself the confidant of prime ministers, especially Terence O'Neill. Indeed, with O'Neill's conversion to liberalism always a little ambiguous, it was Jack Sayers who proved the most coherent exponent of 'O'Neillism'. With his 'Viewpoint' leaders in the *Telegraph* and most famously the 'I back O'Neill' coupons in December 1968, he led the fight against the sectarian and unbending in the Unionist movement in what he saw as a 'classic struggle between forces of progress and reaction' (Gailey, 110).

None of this made Sayers any the less Unionist. Indeed he held that it was the failure after 1945 to incorporate the identities and aspirations of the minority that imperilled the union and led to the humiliation of direct rule. Such attitudes bred many enemies and the onset of the troubles and O'Neill's fall in 1969 saw Sayers overwhelmed by events and by his failure to recognize that Paisleyism also represented a genuine constituency and not just an antediluvian creed. Journalistically too, as one of the last of the great writing editors, he was finding himself outflanked in the end by the media of television and soundbites. With his health failing, he retired on 31 March 1969, and died in Belfast on 30 August at the Royal Victoria Hospital, after suffering a major heart attack; he was survived by his wife and two daughters, Diana and Sarah. As befitted an Ulster romantic, he was buried, four days later, at Carnlough in co. Antrim, where his planter ancestors had first settled in the seventeenth century.

Under his editorship he gathered together an unusually talented group of young journalists, including John Cole, W. D. Flackes, Martin Wallace, Eric Waugh, and Dennis Kennedy—many of whom later made their names on television. And through them the *Belfast Telegraph* sustained and moulded a popular moderate consensus which, however fragile, remains a unique achievement in twentieth-century Ulster. With his constant emphasis on British standards and with the wide coverage given to all parties he contributed to the civil rights strategy of seeking justice within the system, which was so to unnerve unionism. It was therefore ironic, given his firm belief in the union, that the lasting consequence of his crusade was the permanent division of unionism in Ulster and the subsequent abolition of Stormont with all that that implied for unionism as a philosophy of government. On the other hand, it said much for his integrity that he did not shrink from embracing such conclusions in public. For he recognized that questions over the purpose of unionism and its relationship to the Catholic minority lay at the very heart of the Unionist dilemma. ANDREW GAILEY

Sources A. Gailey, *Crying in the wilderness: Jack Sayers, a liberal editor in Ulster* (1995) • *Belfast Telegraph* (30 Aug 1969) • private information (2004) • *CGPLA NIre.* (1970) • m. cert.
Archives priv. coll., diaries | PRO NIre., Conolly Gage MSS | SOUND BL NSA, current affairs recording • Northern Ireland Home Service, 'Proud his name', BBC Radio 4, 30 Aug 1970
Likenesses R. Friers, cartoons, repro. in Gailey, *Crying in the wilderness*, cover • photographs, *Belfast Telegraph* offices, photographic archive
Wealth at death £23,246 8*s.* 0*d.*: probate, 3 March 1970, *CGPLA NIre.*

Sayers [*married name* Ó Gaoithín or Ó Guithín], **Peig** (**1873–1958**), storyteller, was born in Vicarstown, co. Kerry, in 1873 (she was baptized on 29 March 1873), one of thirteen children born to Tomás Sayers, small farmer and labourer, and his wife, Peig Ní Bhrosnacháin, only four of whom survived to adulthood. From the age of six she was educated in the national school at Dunquin, co. Kerry, but left school early to go into domestic service with a shopkeeper's family in Dingle, where she remained for four years until health problems forced her to return home. She then thought to emigrate to America and in order to secure the funds for such a journey she went into service for a second time. She was very unhappy with her position in this second household and again returned home. Her brother made a match for her with a man from the Blasket Islands, Pádraig 'Flint' Ó Gaoithín (*c.*1862–*c.*1920), a farmer and fisherman. The couple married on 13 February 1892 and went to live on Great Blasket Island, initially with Ó Gaoithín's parents. By 1911 Peig had given birth to ten children, of whom seven survived into adulthood. Of the adult children one died tragically in a fall from a cliff, and five emigrated to America.

Peig Sayers was the most renowned storyteller from west Kerry. Robin Flower, the noted scholar, wrote that Peig:

> is one of the finest speakers on the Island … she is wont to illustrate her talks with tales, long and short, which come in naturally along the flow of conversation, and lighten up all our discourse of the present with the wit and wisdom and folly and vivid incident of the past. (*The Western Island, or, The Great Blasket*, 1944)

Peig told her stories in her home, to neighbours and visitors; with the ability to remember and reinterpret folktales, legends, and local history, her stories included references to proverbs, folk practices and beliefs, and traditional prayers and blessings. A collection of her stories and anecdotes about life on the Great Blasket was published as *Machtnamh seana-mhná* (1939) and translated into English by Sean Ennis as *An Old Woman's Reflections* (1962). In the introduction to the translation, W. R. Rogers noted some features of Peig's storytelling prowess:

> Great artist and wise woman that she was, Peig would at once switch from gravity to gaiety, for she was a light-hearted woman, and her changes of mood and face were like the changes of running water. As she talked her hands would be moving too; a little clap of the palms to cap a phrase, a flash of the thumb over the shoulder to mark a mystery, a hand hushed to mouth for mischief or whispered secrecy.

While Peig could neither read nor write Irish she dictated her autobiography in Irish to her son, with the encouragement of the scholar Máire Ní Chinnéide. Published as *Peig* in 1936, it was awarded the Chraoibhin prize in 1937. A mine of information about life on the Great Blasket, *Peig* was a set school text for Irish school children from 1936 until it was removed from the secondary school syllabus in 1995. The writer Bryan MacMahon translated the book into English in 1973.

In 1942 Peig Sayers moved back to the mainland to live with her son in Vicarstown. She died in Dingle Hospital on 8 December 1958 and was buried in the cemetery at Dunquin. MARIA LUDDY

Sources P. Sayers and M. Ní Chinnéide, *Peig*, ed. M. Ó Guitín (1936) • P. Sayers, *Peig: the autobiography of Peig Sayers*, trans. B. MacMahon (1973) • D. Breathnach and M. Ní Mhurchú, *Beathaisnéis a Cúig: 1882–1982*, 5 ([Dublin], 1997) • R. Welch, ed., *The Oxford companion to Irish literature* (1996)
Archives University College, Dublin, Irish folklore department
Likenesses H. A. Kernoff, charcoal on paper, 1932, NG Ire. • photograph, repro. in Sayers, *Peig*

Sayers, Richard Sidney (**1908–1989**), economist, was born on 11 July 1908 in Bury St Edmunds, Suffolk, the fifth in the family of five sons (the eldest of whom died in infancy) and two daughters of Sidney James Sayers, county accountant for West Suffolk county council, and his wife, Caroline Mary Watson. He attended a succession of schools in Bury St Edmunds from 1912 to 1926, becoming head prefect in his last two years at West Suffolk county school. He entered St Catharine's College, Cambridge, in 1926, taking first classes (division two) in both parts of the economics tripos (1928 and 1929). Although he was made a member of J. M. Keynes's Political Economy Club, it was to Dennis Robertson that he habitually sent drafts of his work before publication.

After postgraduate study in Cambridge Sayers was appointed assistant lecturer at the London School of Economics (LSE) in 1931 and remained there for four years before moving in 1935 to lecture in Oxford, where he became a fellow of Pembroke College in 1939. In 1936 he published *Bank of England Operations, 1890–1914*, which established Sayers's reputation as a monetary historian. Two years later, in need of additional income with the approaching birth of his second child, Sayers produced the first of seven editions of his internationally known textbook, *Modern Banking* (1938). Although a textbook, it gave expression to many original thoughts that are prominent in his later writings: his emphasis on liquidity; his judgement that the bank rate is 'a halting, clumsy, indeed a brutal instrument'; and his scepticism of unsupported monetary policy ('I know of no case in monetary history of a dear money policy alone producing a general deflation of money incomes').

During the Second World War, Sayers worked in the Ministry of Supply, where his duties carried him into the secret area of the atomic bomb and negotiations for the development of uranium supplies. At the end of the war he was persuaded by James Meade to serve as deputy director of the economic section of the Cabinet Office, but after two years opted to resume his academic career, accepting the Sir Ernest Cassel chair of economics at the LSE in 1947 and remaining there until he took early retirement in 1968.

In the 1950s Sayers produced or edited half a dozen books, including one of his major works—some would say his best—*Financial Policy, 1939–45*, which was part of the official war history. This took over five years to complete, appearing finally in 1956. It recreated the atmosphere of the wartime Treasury and dealt with both economic and political issues with great skill. Another work—his favourite though not his best—was his history of Lloyds Bank (1957).

In the spring of 1957 Sayers was appointed a member of the committee on the working of the monetary system, chaired by Lord Radcliffe, the most important assignment of his life. He played a dominant part in the committee's affairs, undertaking much of the examination of witnesses and drafting the key sections of its report (1959). The reception accorded to the report was a bitter disappointment to Sayers. 'Two years of my life—two years wasted!' he once exclaimed.

Sayers's disappointment did not prevent a considerable volume of new work, most of it essays and articles but also a centenary history of Gillett's discount house (1968). He was much in demand as a historian of banking institutions. He was considered as a possible historian of the federal reserve system and invited to produce a sequel to J. H. Clapham's history of the Bank of England to 1914. This was completed in 1976, in three volumes covering the years from 1891 to 1944, in celebration of the 250th anniversary of the founding of the bank. The history was highly praised but left Sayers dissatisfied.

Apart from his academic duties, Sayers was editorial adviser and 'chief architect' of the *Three Banks Review* for twenty years from its foundation in 1948, was closely associated for a time with the editorial side of *Economica*, and from 1969 to 1974 was publications secretary of the British Academy, of which he was made a fellow in 1957 and became vice-president in 1966–7.

Sayers was a superb lecturer, taking immense pains over his lectures and expressing himself, both in lectures and in conversation, slowly and with deliberation. He took great trouble over his graduate students—most of them from abroad. His former pupils are said to have included nineteen ministers of finance.

Sayers was temperamentally a loner who preferred to get on with his work without much social activity. This tendency was accentuated after the war by a bad back, which obliged him to rest for long spells. None the less he was basically a healthy and vigorous man and would walk for hours over rough country even with arthritic hips. Latterly, however, his health deteriorated and in his last few years he was more or less bedridden. Music, art, and walking were his main non-academic interests. In appearance he was tall and lean, clean-shaven, and good-looking.

In 1967 the universities of Warwick and Kent conferred honorary degrees on Sayers and the University of Cambridge sought to do so unsuccessfully. He was an honorary fellow of his old Cambridge college, St Catharine's, and of the LSE and the Institute of Bankers. After the publication of *The Bank of England* he was offered, but refused, a knighthood.

In 1930 Sayers married an old classmate, Millicent, daughter of William Henry John Hodson, bookkeeper in a brewery. They had a son and a daughter, but the marriage eventually broke down. In 1985 he finally left his wife and went to live with Audrey Taylor, an old associate, at 1 Laleham Close, Eastbourne; he died at Eastbourne after a long illness, separated from his family, on 25 February 1989.

Alec Cairncross, *rev.*

Sources A. Cairncross, 'Richard Sidney Sayers, 1908–1989', *PBA*, 76 (1990), 545–61 · *The Times* (6 March 1989) · personal knowledge (1996) · private information (1996) [Theodore Barker, Leslie Pressnell, J. S. G. Wilson, family] · *CGPLA Eng. & Wales* (1989)

Likenesses photograph, repro. in Cairncross, 'Richard Sidney Sayers', *PBA*, 547

Wealth at death under £70,000: probate, 29 March 1989, *CGPLA Eng. & Wales*

Sayers, Tom (1826–1865), pugilist, was born in Pimlico (later Tichborne Street), Brighton, on 25 May 1826, the son of William Sayers (*b.* 1793) and his wife, Mary (or Maria) Hopkins. He was baptized at St Nicholas, Brighton, on 31 December 1826; on 11 August 1846 he married there Mary Lucas Cross, daughter of John Cross. His father was a shoemaker by trade, but Sayers became a bricklayer. He was first employed on the Brighton and Lewes Railway, and afterwards (1848) on the London and North-Western Railway at Camden Town. He was only 5 feet 8½ inches in height, with a fighting weight that varied from 10 stone 2lb to 10 stone 12lb, and was under rather than over the average of middleweight champions; but so great were his strength and courage that he became the most distinguished fighter of his day, and the unconquered champion of England. He acquired the sobriquets of the Brighton Boy and the Little Wonder. His extraordinarily muscular neck and shoulders, combined with the extraordinary quality of his hands, which never gave way, accounted for the power of his hitting; his arms were of medium length, and not particularly muscular. His good-humoured but determined face was so hard that after the severest punishment little trace was visible.

Sayers's pugilistic career commenced on 19 March 1849,

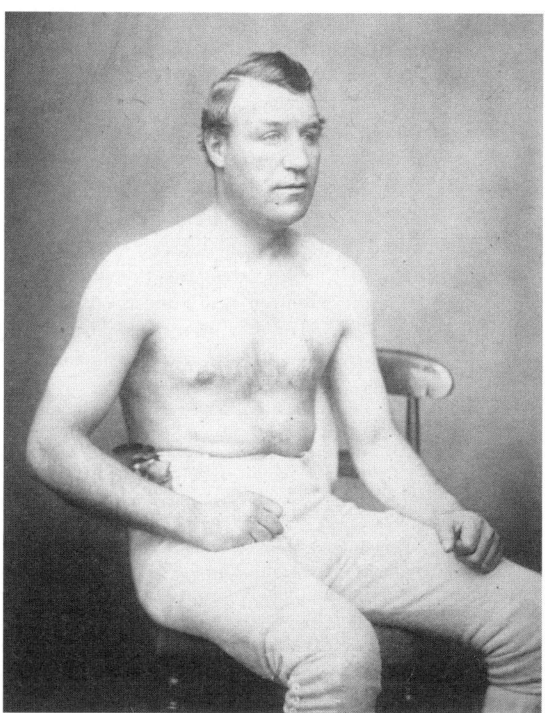

Tom Sayers (1826–1865), by unknown photographer, pubd 1860

when he beat Crouch at Greenhithe. Subsequently he beat Collins at Chapman's Marshes, Long Reach, on 29 April 1851, Jack Grant at Mildenhall on 29 June 1852, and Jack Martin at Long Reach on 26 January 1853. He met, for £100 a side, on 18 October 1853, near Lakenheath, Suffolk, the most accomplished boxer of the period, Nat Langham, who was somewhat past his prime and had to combat youth and strength with science. He did this so successfully that at the end of sixty-one rounds, which took two hours and two minutes, Sayers, blinded though otherwise strong, was decisively beaten. This was Sayers's only defeat, and he learned from it, for he appreciated Langham's tactics and utilized them when he met men heavier than himself. His next victories were over Sims at Long Reach on 28 February 1854; over Harry Poulson at Appledore on 26 January 1856; over Aaron Jones, on the banks of the Medway on 19 February 1857; and over Bill Perry (the Tipton Slasher), a much bigger man and a heavyweight, at the Isle of Grain, on 16 June 1857. The last fight won for Sayers the champion's belt. He subsequently beat Bill Benjamin at the Isle of Grain on 5 January 1858, Tom Paddock at Canary Island on 16 June 1858, Bill Benjamin near Ashford on 5 April 1858, and Bob Brettle in Sussex on 20 September 1859. It has been said that 'your pugilist is the publican in chrysalis' (Miles, *Tom Sayers*, 37), and by 1853 Sayers was established at the Bricklayer's Arms, Camden Town.

Sayers's last and most famous fight was with the American John C. Heenan (the Benicia Boy), for £200 a side and the championship. They met at Farnborough on Tuesday 17 April 1860, and fought thirty-seven rounds in two hours and six minutes. The event attracted the keenest interest in both hemispheres, and a large crowd, including Lord Palmerston. It was chronicled in *Punch* (28 April 1860), in 'The Fight of Sayerius and Heenanus, a Lay of Ancient London'. Heenan stood 6 feet 1½ inches in his stockings, and was a powerful heavyweight with an extraordinarily long reach. Time after time Sayers was knocked down by blows, each of which seemed sufficient to finish the fight; but he always returned good-humoured, though serious, and delivered blow after blow on the American's eyes, and on one occasion he actually knocked his opponent down. Heenan then closed with Sayers whenever possible, and on one occasion got him in such a position on the ropes that strangulation appeared imminent. The ropes were cut, the crowd surged into the ring, and the referee was forced from his place. The fight continued amid increasing disorder, but was finally declared a draw. Each man received a belt, and Sayers retired from the championship on 20 May 1860. The sum of £3000 was raised by public subscription, the interest of which was paid to him on condition that he did not fight any more. The money was afterwards divided among his children when they came of age.

Sayers died on 8 November 1865 at 257 High Street, Camden Town, reportedly of consumption and diabetes, though he was also said towards the close of his life to have shown symptoms of 'childishness' (presumably brain damage). He was buried on 15 November at Highgate cemetery; over his grave there is a monument with a medallion portrait by Morton Edwards, below which is a recumbent mastiff. The inscription is almost effaced. Sayers's 'name was associated with all that was bold, generous, manly, and honest in the practice of pugilism' (*Bell's Life*, 11 Nov 1865). In November 2002 the later champion, Sir Henry Cooper, inaugurated a blue plaque at 257 Camden High Street—only the third commemorating a sporting figure.

William Broadfoot, *rev.* Julian Lock

Sources *Bell's Life* (11 Nov 1865) • H. D. Miles, *Tom Sayers: his life and pugilistic career* (1866) • Boase, *Mod. Eng. biog.* • A. Lloyd, *The great prize fight* (1977) • [F. Dowling], *Fistiana* (1868) • H. D. Miles, *Pugilistica: being one hundred and forty-four years of the history of British boxing*, 3 vols. (1880–81), vol. 3, pp. 359–443 • personal knowledge (1897) • H. Cleveland, *Fisticuffs and personalities of the prize ring* (c.1923) • D. Brailsford, *Bareknuckles: a social history of prize fighting* (1988) • N. S. Fleischer, *The heavyweight championship, 1719–1949* (1949) • R. Dillon, *Great expectations: the story of Benicia, California* (c.1976) • D. Johnson, *Bare fist fighters of the 18th and 19th century: 1704–1861* (1987) • parish register, Brighton, St Nicholas, 31 Dec 1826 [baptism] • *IGI* • www.english-heritage.org.uk, Jan 2003

Likenesses R. Childs, coloured lithograph, pubd 1860, BM • photograph, pubd 1860, V&A [*see illus.*] • M. Edwards, medallion on tomb, 1866, repro. in Cleveland, *Fisticuffs and personalities*, 164–5 • A. Bezzi, bronze cast, NPG • A. Bezzi, plaster cast of statuette, NPG • double portrait, print (with Heenan), repro. in Dillon, *Great expectations* • engraving, repro. in Brailsford, *Bareknuckles*, 128 • portrait, repro. in Miles, *Pugilistica* • portraits, repro. in *Illustrated Sporting News*, 1–5 (1862–6) • prints, repro. in Fleischer, *The heavyweight championship*, 50, 67

Wealth at death under £4000: probate, 24 Nov 1865, *CGPLA Eng. & Wales*

Sayle, William (*d.* 1671), colonial governor, was a member of the Somers Islands Company which founded the colony of Bermuda in 1612. Nothing is known about his early life; he arrived in Bermuda some time before 1630, when his name first appears in that colony's records as a member of the governor's council. From 1638 to 1640 he was its sheriff, and in 1641 he was appointed governor by the Somers Islands Company. He served for one year, during which time he was allied with the puritan dissidents in Bermuda. Due to religious factions in the colony's politics during the English civil wars, he was replaced by Josias Forster in 1642, and then reappointed to the governorship in 1643. He served until 1646. Though Sayle and his wife, Frances (*d.* 1684), were associated with the puritans who founded an Independent church in 1644, as governor he maintained a 'moderate and temperate carriage' towards those who supported the Church of England (Lefroy, 1.608) in Bermuda.

In 1646, after he left the governorship, Sayle took a more active part in the growing struggle between the crown and its opponents. He went to England, and in 1647 procured a grant from parliament giving him proprietary rights over Segatoo, an island in the Bahamas, which was renamed Eleutheria. Sayle, his son Thomas, and twenty-three other shareholders formed a 'Company of Eleutherian Adventurers' (Craton and Saunders, 1.74) with Sayle to be governor for three years. At this time he was also rumoured to be plotting to take over Bermuda by force, sailing to the island colony with 'at least 400 musketts' (Lefroy, 1.622–3). These rumours proved false, but parliamentarian–royalist tensions in Bermuda mounted.

In 1649, when the news of Charles I's execution reached the colony and 'the country in general rose up in arms' (Lefroy, 2.8–9), Sayle and a group of other dissidents including the clergyman Patrick Copeland were banished by the outraged Bermuda royalists. About seventy persons in all, they sailed to Eleutheria to establish a settlement where 'every man might enjoye his owne opinion or Religion, without controll or question' (*Journal of John Winthrop*, 720). The ship and its company arrived safely but a storm later wrecked the vessel and destroyed all its provisions. Sayle and a few of the men took a shallop and sailed to Virginia, where sympathetic supporters of the dissidents' cause gave them a larger vessel and provisions to return to Eleutheria. New England puritans, hearing of the castaways' plight, raised £800 to aid them.

The Eleutheria settlement endured but it did not prosper, and many of the colonists—including Sayle, his wife, and their three sons, Thomas, Nathaniel, and James—returned to Bermuda in 1656. Sayle was appointed governor again in 1658, over protests by Bermudians who were suspicious of his previous involvement with dissidents. But he managed to placate his opponents, and all celebrated the restoration of Charles II in 1660. His final term as governor established a new survey of the entire island colony, legislation for the conservation of Bermuda's cedar trees, and the administration of the free school for the colony's children.

After leaving the governorship in 1662 Sayle served as a member of the Bermuda assembly and as a captain in the militia. In 1669 he was a member of the governor's council. In 1670 he was appointed governor of the new colony of South Carolina. He sailed from Bermuda on 26 February 1670. Barely a year later, on 4 March 1671, aged 'at least 80 years of age' (*CSP col.*, 7.187), he died at Albemarle Point, South Carolina. At the time of his death he owned a mansion, slaves, and land in Bermuda, and another mansion and lands in South Carolina. He was survived by his wife and sons, two grandchildren, and a niece. His will of 15 February 1670, a codicil of 30 September 1670, and estate inventories are in books of wills and inventories in the Bermuda Archives. Frances Sayle died in 1684.

VIRGINIA BERNHARD

Sources J. H. Lefroy, *Memorials of the discovery and early settlement of the Bermudas or Somers Islands*, 2 vols. (1878–9), vol. 1, pp. 622–3, 629–30, 700–01, 719, 724; vol. 2, pp. 112–13, 119–20, 124, 133, 134, 138, 139, 195–6, 235–6, 241–2, 262, 303 • *The journal of John Winthrop, 1630–1649*, ed. R. S. Dunn, J. Savage, and L. Yeandle (1996), 720–21 • books of wills and inventories, 15 vols., 1629–1835, Bermuda Archives, Hamilton, Bermuda, vol. 1, pp. 145, 149–51, 323 • M. Craton and G. Saunders, *Islanders in the stream: a history of the Bahamian people*, 1: *From aboriginal times to the end of slavery* (1992), 74–80 • H. C. Wilkinson, *The adventurers of Bermuda: a history of the island from its discovery until the dissolution of the Somers Island Company in 1684* (1933), 102n., 108n., 280, 284–5, 330–31 • A. C. Hollis Hallett, *Chronicle of a colonial church: Bermuda, 1612–1826* (Pembroke, Bermuda, 1993), 46, 53–4, 55, 98 • W. H. Miller, 'The colonization of the Bahamas, 1647–1670', *William and Mary Quarterly*, 2 (1945), 33–46 • *CSP col.*, vol. 7, pp. 169, 187 • L. B. Wright, *South Carolina: a bicentennial history* (New York, 1976), 45, 47

Archives PRO, Shaftesbury papers

Wealth at death 'mansions' in Bermuda and South Carolina; slaves; land: books of wills and inventories, 15 vols., 1629–1835, Bermuda Archives, Hamilton, vol. 1, pp. 145, 149–51

Sayles, George Osborne (1901–1994), medieval historian, was born on 20 April 1901 at Buckingham Terrace, Unstone, Derbyshire, the sixth of seven children of Larret Pearson Sayles (1867–1942), a dissenting minister working as a commercial traveller at the time of George's birth but subsequently ordained to Anglican orders, and his wife, Margaret (1862–1932), the daughter of Robert Brown of Lanark. He attended Scargill Boys' School at West Hallam in Derbyshire between 1912 and 1914 and the newly opened Ilkeston county secondary school from 1914 to 1919. In 1920 he entered the University of Glasgow as an arts student, intending to major in French, but subsequently decided to major in history and was awarded first-class honours in 1923. His interest in the English medieval parliament was initially awakened by the teaching of Professor Dudley Julius Medley (1861–1953).

Sayles successfully applied for a Carnegie research fellowship to do research with A. F. Pollard, the director of the newly established Institute of Historical Research in London and known to Sayles from his book, *The Evolution of Parliament*, published in 1920. His intended topic was the role of the king's council in the administration of justice in the parliaments of the reign of Edward I. He spent only a year in full-time research in London as in the autumn of

1924 he was offered a junior appointment back in the Glasgow history department. He was to remain there for the next two decades. Sayles continued research on his thesis during the vacations and over the next eight years concentrated his efforts on a thorough reading of the plea rolls of king's bench for the reign of Edward I. These had much less material of relevance to parliament than he had expected and so he decided to utilize the material he had found for a thesis centred on the court of king's bench itself. He was awarded a DLitt for this by Glasgow in 1932. Sayles then turned his thesis into the three volumes of *Select Cases in the Court of King's Bench in the Reign of Edward I* published by the Selden Society in 1936, 1938, and 1939. His primary interest, however, remained the history of the medieval parliament.

In 1927 Sayles met for the first time in the Round Room of the Public Record Office (then in Chancery Lane) a more senior scholar who shared his enthusiasm, Henry Gerald Richardson (1884–1974). That meeting led to a long and close collaboration between the two men which first bore fruit in a joint article published in 1928. Just how infuriating a collaborator Richardson had been emerges clearly from Sayles's posthumous memoir of Richardson in the *Proceedings of the British Academy* but the partnership would not have continued for so long had Sayles not valued the contribution his collaborator made or might make to their joint work. Initially, they quickly produced a series of articles on various aspects of the later thirteenth- and fourteenth-century English parliament, concentrating on its procedures, its surviving records, and what the records of parliament revealed about the business with which parliament dealt. Almost from the beginning there were plans to turn these articles into a book but in the end only a slim volume on the English parliament appeared and then only in 1975, after Richardson's death. The collaborators were also drawn into investigating the medieval history of the Scottish and Irish parliaments and their work on the latter eventually led to the publication in 1952 of what is certain to remain the classic work on that institution, *The Irish Parliament in the Middle Ages*, and to subsidiary volumes of related documents and lists of office-holders in the Irish medieval administration. Other offshoots from their joint work included a projected (but ultimately abortive) new edition of the *Modus tenendi parliamentum* and of various associated treatises; an important pair of articles on the early statutes published in 1934; and (as a by-product of their work on the origins of bill procedure) a joint volume for the Selden Society of *Select Cases of Procedure without Writ under Henry III*, which appeared in 1941.

With the departure from the Glasgow history department of D. C. Douglas in 1934 Sayles for the first time had the opportunity to give lectures on English medieval history and it was probably in this year that he gave the first version of the lectures which were subsequently to become a successful undergraduate textbook, *The Medieval Foundations of England*, when published in 1948. The mid-1930s were also a time of major changes in his personal life. In 1935, while on a cruise round the Western Isles, he met his future wife, Agnes Jessie (1908–1996), the daughter of George Sutherland, a partner in a Glasgow firm of yarn merchants. They married on 2 September 1936 and had a son, Michael, born in 1937, and a daughter, Hilary, born in 1940. George Sayles was too old for service in the Second World War and went on lecturing and examining at Glasgow. He played his part in local civil defence and in the management of his wife's family firm when his brother-in-law was called up. He also started work on a new joint edition (with Richardson) of the late thirteenth-century legal treatise *Fleta*.

At the end of the war Sayles moved (in late 1945) to a chair at the Queen's University, Belfast, and his existing interest in Irish medieval history led him to initiate a project for publishing the eight surviving fifteenth-century registers of the archbishops of Armagh. Much of the work on the register of Archbishop John Mey (edited by his doctoral students W. G. H. Quigley and E. F. D. Roberts) which appeared in 1972 was completed before Sayles left Belfast for Aberdeen in 1955; after his departure and his forced resignation from its general editorship the project languished. While at Aberdeen, Sayles resumed work on the court of king's bench, publishing two further Selden Society volumes in 1957 and 1958 covering the period down to 1340. It was also during this period that he and Richardson wrote their best-known work, *The Governance of Medieval England* (1963), a masterpiece of invective and polemic, whose chief target was the long-dead, if still revered, Bishop Stubbs, though this was only published after Sayles had taken early retirement from Aberdeen in 1962. Generous financial support from the Rockefeller fund made it possible for Sayles to write free of administrative and teaching responsibilities: this allowed the production of two further volumes of *Select Cases in the Court of King's Bench* in 1965 and 1971 and enabled him to continue work on a number of joint projects with Richardson, but of these only a slim volume, *Law and Legislation from Aethelberht to Magna Carta* (published in 1966), ever achieved completion.

On retirement Sayles went to live at Crowborough in Sussex, not far from Richardson's house at Goudhurst, but Richardson's second wife discouraged all visits from his collaborator and Richardson died in 1974 without completing work on any more of their joint projects. After his death Sayles at least felt free to republish (with corrections) in 1981 their joint papers as *The English Parliament in the Middle Ages*, and to publish a second volume of texts illustrating *The Functions of the Medieval Parliament of England* (in 1988). George Sayles died on 28 February 1994 in Crowborough Hospital after a fall in his home. His widow Agnes survived him for less than two years, dying on 27 November 1996. Their ashes now lie buried in a lair in the Glasgow necropolis. PAUL BRAND

Sources P. Brand, 'George Osborne Sayles, 1901–1994', *PBA*, 90 (1996), 441–63 • G. O. Sayles, 'Henry Gerald Richardson, 1884–1974', *PBA*, 61 (1975), 497–521 • priv. coll., Sayles MSS • private information (2004) [family]

Archives priv. coll.

Likenesses M. Sayles, oils, probably priv. coll.; repro. in Brand, 'George Osborne Sayles', 440

Wealth at death £125,000: administration with will, 27 April 1995, *CGPLA Eng. & Wales*

Saywell, William (1642/3–1701), religious controversialist and college head, was born at Pentridge, Dorset, where his father, Gabriel Saywell (*d.* 1658), was rector. He had at least three brothers, Samuel (*b.* 1651/2), James (*b.* 1656/7), and John (all of whom were, like him, educated at St John's College, Cambridge) and a sister. After a few months at Cranbourne School, Hampshire, William was admitted sizar at St John's in 1659, aged sixteen. He graduated BA in 1663, was elected a fellow of his college in April 1666, and proceeded MA in 1667. He was incorporated MA at Oxford in 1669 and proceeded DD in 1679.

Saywell's career was advanced by Peter Gunning, master of St John's, bishop of Chichester (1669–75) and of Ely (1675–84). He served as Gunning's chaplain. In 1672 he was collated to the prebendary of Sutton in Chichester Cathedral and was rector of Birdham and vicar of Pevensey, both in Sussex; on 28 November of that year he was appointed chancellor of the diocese of Chichester. He retained the last post until his death, but resigned the prebendary to go with Gunning to Ely. When Saywell published his first book Richard Baxter regarded it very much as the work of the bishop's mouthpiece, describing him as Gunning's 'Amanuensis, or Chaplain', who 'speaketh his Lord and Masters sence' (Keeble and Nuttall, 2.210). In March 1679 Saywell was installed as a prebendary of Ely Cathedral and in December was elected as Humphrey Gower's successor as master of Jesus College, Cambridge. On 22 January 1681 he was collated to the archdeaconry of Ely upon the resignation of Barnabas Oley.

A skilled writer of Latin verse, Saywell contributed to *Hymenaeus Cantabrigiensis* in 1683 and to *Academiae Cantabrigiensis affectus* in 1685. However, he was best known as a staunch Anglican apologist, equally opposed to popery and to presbyterianism, and as the author of several controversial treatises. The Church of England, he maintained, was 'truly Catholick and apostolick' (Saywell, *Original*, title-page). He proclaimed that

> She only here teaches … the true old way, and the plain doctrines of the Catholick Church, and She is the only particular church to whom by the laws of God and Man you are bound to yield submission; and this has been fully made out not only against Papists, but all other schismatics and dissenters. (Saywell, *Necessity*, sig. A2*v*)

This remained the constant theme of Saywell's polemics, the emphasis of individual works shaped by his perception of where circumstances at the time of writing suggested the main threat to the Church of England to be coming from and with whom he was engaged in polemical controversy. In the tense years of the exclusion crisis and the ensuing tory reaction he produced three main works concerned with the threat from 'the Furious Papist, and Cruel Fanatick' alike (Saywell, *Original*, sig. A3*v*): *The original of all plots in Christendom: with the danger and remedy of schism* (1680), *A serious enquiry into the means of a happy union, or, What reformation is necessary to prevent popery?* (1681), and *Evangelicall and Catholick unity maintained in the Church of England, or, An apology for her government, liturgy, subscriptions* (1682). Saywell's *A Serious Enquiry* countered pleas for protestant unity through comprehension or toleration with the argument that true union lay only in strict conformity to the Church of England; schism and dissent only helped the papists and by creating religious uncertainty allowed ignorance and profanity to flourish: 'the first step to publick reformation and a happy union is, effectually to take away all their conventicles, and at least make them all rest satisfied with a private worship in their own families' (Saywell, *Serious Enquiry*, 40). *Evangelicall and Catholick Unity* was written in reply to Baxter's *Apology for the Nonconformist Ministry* (1681) and John Owen's *An Enquiry into the Original Nature … of Evangelical Churches* (1681).

In 1688 Saywell responded to the Catholic threat under James II in general and to the republication of what he claimed was a distorted account of a debate in the 1650s held between two Catholic priests and Peter Gunning and John Pearson in particular, by publishing anonymously *The Reformation of the Church of England justified, according to the canons of the council of Nice and other general councils* (1688). His final major work, published in the wake of the Toleration Act, was *The necessity of adhering to the Church of England as by law established, or, The duty of a good Christian, and particularly of parents and masters of families under the present toleration* (1692), in which he linked the causes of religious conformity and a reformation of manners. The toleration of protestant dissenters was merely a matter of taking off temporal punishments. The state

> does so far disapprove of the Wayes, that all the obligations in conscience to conform to the church still remain, both by the laws of the Church and State also. Neither is any man thought fit to be admitted to any office or place of trust that does not joyn in communion with the Church of England. (Saywell, *Necessity*, sig. A2*v*)

Saywell's will, made on 2 October 1700, left all his estate, which included property in Cambridgeshire and Kent, to his brother Samuel. However, a codicil made on 14 November acknowledged his wife—whom he does not name—to whom he left an annuity of £150, and left legacies to his sister, nephews and nieces, and cousins. Other money was to go after his wife's death to Ely Cathedral, Jesus College, and St John's College. The schoolmaster of Willingham, Cambridgeshire, and his successors were to receive £10 per annum 'for an encouragement to the said schoolmasters to teach the children of the same parish their catechism and prayers' (PRO, PROB 11/461, fol. 130*r*), while he left doles to the poor of three parishes, including his birthplace. Saywell died in London on 9 June 1701 and was buried in the chapel of St John's College five days later.

SARAH CARR

Sources Venn, *Alum. Cant.* • Foster, *Alum. Oxon.* • T. Baker, *History of the college of St John the Evangelist, Cambridge*, ed. J. E. B. Mayor, 2 vols. (1869) • will, PRO, PROB 11/461, sig. 105 (fols. 129*r*–130*r*) • Wood, *Ath. Oxon.*, new edn • *Calendar of the correspondence of Richard Baxter*, ed. N. H. Keeble and G. F. Nuttall, 2 (1991), 210–12, 225 • *Fasti Angl., 1541–1857*, [Chichester] • *Fasti Angl., 1541–1857*, [Ely] • W. Saywell, *A serious enquiry into the means of a happy union* (1681) • W. Saywell, *The necessity of adhering to the Church of England* (1692)

Scafe, John (1776–1843), poet and writer on geology, was born on 19 June 1776 in London, the only son of William

Scafe (1744–1808), barrister, of The Leazes, Tanfield, Durham, and his wife, Frances, *née* Hodgson, of Fieldhouse, Darlington. Scafe matriculated at University College, Oxford, on 21 January 1794 but never graduated. In 1799 he obtained a commission as ensign in the army, and in 1805 attained the rank of captain in the 43rd regiment of foot. He resigned from the army in 1808 on the death of his father.

At Oxford, Scafe penned an 'Elegy to the River Isis'. While on army service on Minorca in 1800, he composed other verses on 'Beautiful scenery' and these, together with poems written while serving in Dublin in 1806, were subsequently published. Scafe first ventured into print in 1815 with a hesitant edition (six copies) of *Poems in Four Parts* published by J. Graham at Alnwick, where Scafe was then living. Four further volumes in similarly small editions were issued in 1817 and 1818. In 1818 Emerson Charnley of Newcastle published Scafe's collected *Poems* (150 copies). Scafe's publishers' lists of subscribers show that the majority were gentry living in Alnwick and its neighbourhood. One poem, *The Velocipede* of 1819, suggests an interest in technology, this early form of bicycle having been invented in Germany only two years previously.

Scafe, of whose poems it was later noted 'few are very bad' ('Alnwick poets', 334–5, 351), might have remained forgotten had not one of his volumes, a *jeu d'esprit* called *King Coal's Levee* (issued at Alnwick in 1818 in an edition of twenty-five copies), come to the attention of members of the Oxford school of geology late in 1818. The work treated the order of stratification of English rocks, and the utility of such knowledge, as a poetic court scene, and it was inspired by William Phillips's *Outlines of the Geology of England and Wales*. Geology was being popularized by the Geological Society in London (to which the last three editions of Scafe's *Levee* were dedicated). William Daniel Conybeare helped to expand the second edition (1819), with explanatory notes by William Buckland 'comprehending all the leading features of geology' (Buckland to Greenough, 26 March 1819, Greenough archives, UCL). Third (500 copies) and fourth editions (750) appeared in London in 1819 and 1820.

The book caused a sensation. Some accused Scafe of 'intending Personalities in it as Meaning to ridicule the Duke of Northumberland's Publick Days at Alnwick Castle' (Buckland to Mary Cole, 13 July 1819, NMG Wales). Others saw wider, national significance in such seditious times, with 'King Coal' the symbolic monarch and 'The Pebbles' the rabble—Robert *Bakewell (1767–1843) published a mocking commentary on this interpretation in his *Geological Primer in Verse* (1820), a work long thought to be by Scafe himself. In Germany, Goethe was differently impressed, since the book 'contains all the knowledge of geology a man wants' (Morley, 369) and showed how the English 'disseminate through both serious and light poetry what everyone ought to know' (Goethe, 332). Goethe planned a translation (1824) which was never completed.

The success of *King Coal's Levee* led to a sequel issued anonymously in 1820, *Court News … and the Errants*, the latter inspired by Buckland's 'Table of the order of … strata' of 1818, in an edition of 250. This was printed and published by those involved with the earlier volume, so Scafe's authorship seems certain.

Scafe may have become interested in geology through the Newcastle Literary and Philosophical Society, of which he appears to have been a member from 1814. In 1852 Scafe's posthumous 'Minutes of the geology of Holy Island', with an originally coloured geological plan, appeared in Raine's *History and Antiquities of North Durham*. Scafe never married and lived at Alnwick from 1815. By 1838 he had moved to Bamburgh, where he was one of those who first brought the heroic exploits of Grace Darling (1815–1842) in 1838 to public attention. Here he died on 24 December 1843 intestate, leaving an estate of under £450.

H. S. Torrens

Sources J. C. Hodgson, 'John Scafe: a Northumbrian minor poet', *Proceedings of the Society of Antiquaries of Newcastle upon Tyne*, 3rd ser., 10 (1921–2), 14–18 • J. Henning, 'Goethe's interest in British mineralogy', *Mineralogical Magazine*, 28 (1947–9), 534–46 • *Henry Crabb Robinson on books and their writers*, ed. E. J. Morley, 1 (1938), 369–73 • R. Surtees, *The history and antiquities of the county palatine of Durham*, 2 (1820), 233–5 • J. Oxenford, *Conversations of Goethe with Eckermann and Soret*, 1 (1850), 169–71 • J. W. von Goethe, *Schriften zur Geologie und Mineralogie, 1812–1832*, ed. G. Schmid (Weimar, 1949), pt 1, vol. 2 of *Die Schriften zur Naturwissenschaft*, 331–5 • *Laws of the Literary and Philosophical Society of Newcastle upon Tyne* (1794), 18 • 'The Alnwick poets, XX: John Scafe', *Alnwick Journal*, 3 (March–April 1867), 334–5, 351 • *Army List* (1799–1808) • H. S. Stooks, *An alphabetical list of the officers of the forty-third or Monmouthshire light infantry from 1800 to 1850* (1851) • papers concerning the administration of Scafe's estate, 1844, Northumbd RO, 530/20/244 • administration of John Scafe, consistory court of Durham records, 1844, U. Durham • d. cert. • *IGI*

Archives Newcastle Central Library

Wealth at death under £450: administration, consistory court of Durham records, 1844, U. Durham

Scalby, John de. *See* Schalby, John (*d.* 1333).

Scales, Thomas, seventh Baron Scales (1399?–1460), soldier and administrator, was the younger son of Robert, fifth Baron Scales (1374?–1402), and of either his first wife, Joan, daughter of William, fourth Lord Bardolf, or of his second wife, Elizabeth. Thomas was born and baptized at Middleton, Norfolk. He inherited his title on the death without issue of his elder brother Robert on 1 July 1419, and was granted seisin of his estates in February 1421, probably at the end of the month.

Scales spent the next thirty years almost continuously engaged in the war in France. Together with Sir John Fastolf, he was placed in charge of the campaign in Maine by the duke of Bedford after the English victory at Verneuil on 17 August 1424. He was elected a knight of the Garter in the following year. In December 1428 he joined the siege of Orléans, and in June 1429 he was captured in the course of the English defeat at Patay. It is not clear how long it took to secure his release, but he was certainly free by April 1430, when he was among the lords who attended Henry VI on his arrival in France. In 1435 he was appointed lieutenant-general of western Normandy, a command which he was to retain until the truce of Tours in 1444; it was also in 1435 that he was named steward of Normandy by Bedford. Among the captaincies he held were those of Domfront, St Lô, Vire, and Cherbourg. In 1440 he was granted a life annuity of £100 from the exchequer in recognition of his military service. His commitment to the war is evident not only in the fact that he was prepared to continue on campaign, despite the worsening conditions and diminishing prospects of success as the 1440s wore on, but also in his willingness to lend a substantial amount of money to the government; the patent rolls record the repayment in 1444, for example, of a loan of 2000 marks which he had made to the king.

In the course of this military service Scales developed close connections with Richard, duke of York, who took command in France temporarily in 1436–7, and again from 1440 after the death of the earl of Warwick. He stood godfather for York's eldest son, Edward, in 1442. However, in a domestic context his closest political association in his native East Anglia was with William de la Pole, successively earl, marquess, and duke of Suffolk, with whom he had also served in France and for whom he acted as a feoffee. It may be an indication of this association that one of the very few local appointments he received before his return to domestic politics at the end of the 1440s was a commission in the summer of 1440 to arrest Sir Robert Wingfield, a servant of the duke of Norfolk, who was involved, with Norfolk's backing, in a dispute in which he faced opposition from members of Suffolk's affinity.

Scales had been appointed to the commission of the peace in both Norfolk and Suffolk since 1445, but it was only from 1449, after his return from France, that he became a prominent figure in domestic politics. He seems to have become active at court in 1449, and in 1450 was appointed a commissioner to deal with Cade's uprising; before the end of June of that year he was appointed to hold the Tower of London against the rebels. From this point onwards he also took a much greater role in East Anglian affairs, which had been thrown into confusion by the fall of the duke of Suffolk. Despite his links with Suffolk, Scales's active involvement in the region during the previous decade had been extremely limited, and Sir John Fastolf and John Paston, who had opposed Suffolk's affinity in the later 1440s, hoped that Scales might offer them support in their attempt to undermine the local power of Suffolk's servants during the months after the duke's death. However, by the end of 1450 it was clear that Scales was instead offering his lordship to the de la Pole connection. In June 1451 custody of Suffolk's estates during the minority of his heir was granted to Scales and Sir Miles Stapleton, another of the duke's associates—a grant which effectively marked the re-emergence of the de la Pole affinity under the new leadership of Scales, together with the dowager duchess. Despite the renewed efforts of the duke of Norfolk to establish his authority in the region, this connection, with Scales at its head, continued to dominate East Anglian politics throughout the 1450s.

Scales and his wife became closely associated with Queen Margaret of Anjou during the years after 1450, a link which both reflected and reinforced the alignment of the de la Pole connection in East Anglia with the queen and court against the duke of York. As political division grew, it became clear that a workable government could only be sustained by an attempt to maintain some degree of noble consensus, and Scales, among others associated with the court, was therefore a member of the council during York's protectorate in 1454. However, his allegiance was never in doubt when division gave way to outright confrontation at the end of the decade. In 1459 Scales was reported to be attending on the prince of Wales. In the following year, with Robert, Lord Hungerford, he led the unsuccessful attempt to hold the city of London against the Yorkists, eventually having to take refuge in the Tower. There Scales and Hungerford held out against a Yorkist siege until the capture of the king at the battle of Northampton on 10 July made it clear that their position was hopeless. On 25 July Scales attempted to escape by river to sanctuary at Westminster, but was recognized and killed by boatmen near Southwark. According to William Worcester, his naked body lay exposed for several hours before being given honourable burial by his godson the earl of March and the earl of Warwick.

Scales was married to Emma, according to Francis Blomefield the daughter of Sir Simon Whalesburgh of Whalesburgh in Cornwall. They had a son, Thomas, who died a minor. Scales's heir was their daughter Elizabeth, who first married Henry Bourchier, second son of Henry *Bourchier, first earl of Essex. Bourchier died probably in 1458, and Elizabeth then married Anthony *Woodville, son of Lord Rivers, who took the title of Lord Scales in right of his wife. HELEN CASTOR

Sources *Chancery records* • *The Paston letters, AD 1422–1509*, ed. J. Gairdner, new edn, 6 vols. (1904) • A. J. Pollard, *John Talbot and the war in France, 1427–1453*, Royal Historical Society Studies in History, 35 (1983) • J. Stevenson, ed., *Letters and papers illustrative of the wars of the English in France during the reign of Henry VI, king of England*, 2 vols. in 3 pts, Rolls Series, 22 (1861–4) • GEC, *Peerage*, new edn, 11.504–7 [incl. reference to William Worcestre] • F. Blomefield and C. Parkin, *An essay towards a topographical history of the county of Norfolk*, [2nd edn], 11 vols. (1805–10) • *A collection of the chronicles and ancient histories of Great Britain … by John of Wavrin*, trans. E. L. C. P. Hardy, 3, Rolls Series, 40 (1891) • J. Anstis, ed., *The register of the most noble order of the Garter*, 2 vols. (1724) • J. L. Watts, *Henry VI and the politics of kingship* (1996) • R. A. Griffiths, *The reign of King Henry VI: the exercise of royal authority, 1422–1461* (1981) • P. A. Johnson, *Duke Richard of York, 1411–1460* (1988) • H. Castor, *The king, the crown, and the duchy of Lancaster: public authority and private power, 1399–1461* (2000) • H. L. Gray, 'Incomes from land in England in 1436', *EngHR*, 49 (1934), 607–39 • J. Gairdner, ed., *Three fifteenth-century chronicles*, CS, new ser., 28 (1880) • *CIPM*, vol. 20

Wealth at death £376 p.a., assessed in 1436: Gray, 'Incomes', 607–39, esp. 617

Scambler, Edmund (*c.*1520–1594), bishop of Peterborough and of Norwich, was born at Gressingham, Lancashire; the identity of his parents is unknown. He was educated at Cambridge University, graduating BA in 1542, and probably took orders soon after, as he was a probationary fellow at Peterhouse in 1547 but did not complete his year. Whether this was due to his religious views and the

Edmund Scambler (*c.*1520–1594), by unknown artist

change of regime is not known, but by the reign of Mary, Scambler had become a convinced protestant and ministered to a secret community in London during those years. At this time he established relations with Matthew Parker, who also remained in England. At the accession of Elizabeth, Scambler was instituted vicar of Rye in Sussex, a town with a protestant pedigree, and was appointed chaplain to Parker, the new archbishop of Canterbury. With the resignation of many leading Marian clergy Scambler soon received promotion, in the form of prebends at York and Westminster in 1560. Through the influence of William Cecil, who had estates in the area, Scambler was elected bishop of Peterborough on 22 February 1561, preaching before the queen the following week. In 1564 he was created DTh at Cambridge, as of Queens' College.

Scambler proved an active bishop in the recently established see. His experience under Mary made him sympathetic to the first generation of puritan clergy, some of whom had been in exile in Europe and many of whom were, like himself, graduates of Cambridge. Supported by such magnates as the earl of Leicester and major landowners like Sir Richard Knightley, experiments were conducted to improve the quality of the preaching ministry by means of preaching exercises in which the less able listened to their more able colleagues preach, and then discussed the text. These were organized on an area basis and had the support of the bishop who also, more radically, was persuaded in 1570 to lend his support to the 'order of Northampton', a non-episcopal presbyterian form of church government for the county town which had been devised by the preacher and former exile Percival Wiburn. This was too much for the authorities and Scambler withdrew his support. By the end of 1571 he had suppressed the order, while Wiburn was removed to Whiston, a village 8 miles away where he continued to attract support from the town. The exercise or prophesying attended by the clergy of the neighbourhood survived the suppression of the order and was to lead to future confrontation. More immediately Wiburn's removal resulted in Scambler's losing the support of the earl of Leicester. Scambler's relations with Cecil remained close, however, and in 1574 the latter benefited from the endowments of the see when the bishop granted him leases of three lives on the manors of Thirlby and Lowthorpe as well as other rights, amounting in all to a third of the temporalities. By this time the exercises in the diocese had also attracted the attention of central government for the radical measures they proposed, and after the suspension in 1576 of Archbishop Edmund Grindal for refusing to suppress them, relations between the bishop and the puritan clergy of the diocese became more strained. There was lack of leadership in the diocese, reflecting the condition of the church generally, and the bishop was unable or unwilling to act vigorously against local puritan clergy who were backed by powerful lay patrons.

This stalemate was resolved on 15 December 1584 when, somewhat surprisingly for a man in his sixties, Scambler was translated to the wealthier see of Norwich. No doubt the influence of Cecil can be detected in this move but there were also other considerations, financial and religious. As part of his promotion Scambler appears to have agreed to the alienation of sixty-one manors and rectories belonging to the bishopric, and these ultimately passed through the crown to Sir Thomas Heneage. This act, in addition to the grant that he made to Cecil when at Peterborough, has ensured Scambler's reputation as a despoiler of church lands, but although members of his family also benefited from leases, he was also a doughty fighter for rights of the church in matters concerning concealed lands, protecting the rectory of Measham for the Norwich dean and chapter against predatory laymen. His translation also made sound ecclesiastical sense, for whereas Peterborough was dominated by the issue of puritanism his new diocese was riven by rows between Catholic and puritan gentry which had bedevilled the administration of his predecessor, Edmund Freake. His sympathy for puritan clergy made him acceptable to the protestant gentry of both counties in the diocese and he actively sought the removal of the more aggressive papist gentry from local government, though with limited success. He supported the puritan gentry of Bury St Edmunds in their attempts to restore godly government in the town through the combination lectures organized by John Knewstub. Furthermore, and somewhat against the grain of government policy, he drew up a plan in 1589 for exercises in the diocese in which the preaching clergy, many of them nonconformist, would supervise their less learned brethren.

Nothing came of this, for under Whitgift's leadership the time had passed for such experiments, but the attempt shows the bishop committed to a form of churchmanship associated with the first generation of godly reformers. In any case there were limits to his support for radicals. During his episcopate two heretics were put to death for denying the divinity of Christ, the most famous being Francis Kett, a native of Norfolk and a former fellow of Corpus Christi, Cambridge, who was burnt to death at Norwich on 14 January 1589. By now Scambler was an old man somewhat out of touch and, it would appear from his will, with parsimonious or modest instincts which did not fit the ideals of episcopal hospitality; his reputation suffered with his contemporaries and has continued to do so. He was, however, formed in the evangelical priorities of the early phase of the English Reformation, and was a reasonably learned scholar who contributed the translations of the gospels of Luke and John to the Bishops' Bible. He married Julyan Frauncys at St Dionis Backchurch in London on 21 January 1561 and they had at least four sons and two daughters alive at his death, in Norwich, on 7 May 1594, by when he had become the longest-serving bishop of Elizabeth's reign, with an episcopate of thirty-three years. Scambler was buried in Norwich Cathedral where a splendid alabaster tomb was erected to his memory. The tomb was destroyed during the civil wars, allegedly because of some verses inscribed on it, though this seems unlikely. In 1691 a wall monument, probably with the same verses as the original monument, was erected by his great-grandson James Scambler, and is now placed above the monks' door into the cloister.

William Joseph Sheils

Sources H. I. Longden, *Northamptonshire and Rutland clergy from 1500*, ed. P. I. King and others, 16 vols. in 6, Northamptonshire RS (1938–52) • Cooper, *Ath. Cantab.*, 2.167–8 • W. J. Sheils, *The puritans in the diocese of Peterborough, 1558–1610*, Northamptonshire RS, 30 (1979) • P. Collinson, *The Elizabethan puritan movement* (1967) • D. MacCulloch, *Suffolk and the Tudors: politics and religion in an English county, 1500–1600* (1986) • A. Hassell Smith, *County and court: government and politics in Norfolk, 1558–1603* (1974) • F. Heal, *Of prelates and princes: a study of the economic and social position of the Tudor episcopate* (1980) • J. Finch, 'The monuments', *Norwich Cathedral: church, city and diocese, 1096–1996*, ed. I. Atherton and others (1996), 467–93 • M. McClendon, *The quiet Reformation: magistrates and the emergence of protestantism in Tudor Norwich* (1999)

Likenesses W. C. Edwards, line engraving, 1822 (after unknown artist), BM, NPG • oils on panel, unknown collection; copyprint, NPG [*see illus.*]

Scamp, Sir (Athelstan) Jack (1913–1977), industrial conciliator, was born on 22 May 1913 in Handsworth, Birmingham, the second son of a house decorator, Edward Henry Scamp, and his wife, Jane Lamb. There was also one daughter. The Scamp family were very active locally in the Church of England, where Jack became a choirboy. He remained in good voice throughout his life, although his latter-day choral efforts were largely private. From childhood he was also a very keen all-round sportsman and was especially good at association football. His height—he was about 6 feet 3 inches—and powerful build gave him a considerable advantage, and he played in goal, as an amateur, for West Bromwich Albion. He was also a useful cricketer.

After he left a local elementary school at the age of fourteen Scamp's first job was on the clerical staff of the Great Western Railway in Birmingham. There he gained his first experience of life on the shop floor and began to develop the skills that would later establish his reputation as Britain's principal industrial conciliator. The big change in his life came with his marriage in 1939 to Jane, daughter of John Kendall, a midlands builder; they had one daughter and one son. After war service with the Royal Artillery he had a number of temporary jobs, including periods of insurance work, before joining his father-in-law's building business. But he decided not to remain in the family firm and in the 1950s moved into personnel work in the engineering industry. He started in a post with the Rover car company, then moved on to Butlers in Birmingham, and after that to the personnel department of Rugby Portland Cement.

It was at Rugby Portland that Scamp experienced an incident which was to have a profound influence on his later career. He agreed a pay deal for Rugby Portland lorry drivers while the company's general manager was on holiday. On his return Scamp's boss instructed him to repudiate the deal; Scamp refused and resigned. It was an act of great courage, since Rugby Portland was a large company with considerable influence at the highest levels of industry. It could have ended his career. In fact it enhanced his reputation for fairness as well as courage, and established his credentials with the trade unions. He went on to join the Plessey Company and then to Massey-Ferguson (UK), before eventually joining Arnold Weinstock's General Electric Company (GEC) in 1962 as personnel director. It was a crucial time for the newly formed group, drawn together by Weinstock from three major electrical engineering companies. Thousands of jobs were at risk because of the merger and Weinstock put Scamp in charge of the transformation. Few men in recent industrial history have had a more daunting challenge. It amounted to a complete reorganization of Britain's electrical engineering industry, which laid the basis for an even broader industrial regeneration.

Weinstock and Scamp formed a formidable partnership in the course of that change and the two men became very close personal friends as well as colleagues. The chairman of GEC regarded Scamp's role as crucial to the company's development and he became known, in the industrial establishment of the day, as 'the smiling face behind Arnold Weinstock'. His handling of the GEC redundancy problems—which involved several thousand workers—was so caring, sensitive, and skilful in the face of enormous human difficulties that there was a huge demand for his services in a range of government-appointed industrial inquiries. During the 1960s he was a member of a dozen such inquiries and chairman of several, covering disputes in railways, docks, shipbuilding, steel, and inevitably the troublesome car industry. His reputation was such that after the 1964 general election and the formation by George Brown of the Department of Economic Affairs he was appointed by Brown as one of his team of industrial advisers. The prime minister, Harold Wilson, then appointed him as chairman of the newly created

Motor Industries Joint Labour Council (MIJLC), for which he was knighted in 1968.

In many ways Scamp's conciliation role with the MIJLC was one of the most difficult of his career. The car industry's labour relations were in turmoil and registering a record number of disputes, many of them unofficial. Yet he had the ability to settle even the most intractable problem. His calm, friendly, informal approach, his sense of humour, his personal empathy with the shop floor, and his relationships with trade union leaders both nationally and regionally enabled him to achieve what others may have regarded as impossible. All this went to underline a unique reputation for being trusted by both sides of industry as well as government. It was similar with journalists. His handling of the press was quite brilliant and he quickly earned the sobriquet of 'Britain's chief industrial peacemaker'. The title was justified. It also enabled the Wilson government to appoint him to some especially difficult tasks—such as non-executive director to the Fairfields (Glasgow) shipyard when it was taken into public ownership in 1967–8.

Inevitably the scene began to change after the 1970 general election, which brought the Conservatives back to office under Edward Heath. Scamp had already been appointed chairman of a court of inquiry into a major pay dispute affecting all local authorities. His report came out shortly before the June election of 1970 and recommended pay increases for local authority manual workers, including dustmen. The report was attacked by the Heath government, and the issue was seen—wrongly—as a challenge to the government's pay policy. The result was that the Scamp report became a main focus of government criticism against this form of resolving industrial conflict. It was a quite unfair attack on Scamp and he resented it. But the effect was that the great conciliator was rarely used by government after that event.

Even so Scamp was still consulted—often privately—by management and unions and, informally and under cover, by ministers of the Heath government, especially during the wage policy crisis of 1972–3. In his later years he suffered badly from heart trouble and tended to remain in the background, enjoying a very private life with his family which he so much treasured.

In 1970 Scamp became associate professor of industrial relations at Warwick University. He resigned his executive responsibility at GEC in 1972 due to ill health, though he remained a director of the company and a confidant of Lord Weinstock to the end. He also became chairman of Urwick, Orr & Partners, the management consultancy firm. He was companion of the Institution of Electrical Engineers, served on the board of the Engineering Employers' Federation, and was a fellow of both the Institute of Personnel Management and the British Institute of Management. He remained an active supporter of the Church of England, serving on numerous charitable bodies, and held the chairmanship of Coventry City Football Club—which did not prevent him retaining a sentimental attachment to West Bromwich Albion. He sat regularly as a magistrate in the midlands and was deputy lieutenant of Warwickshire. He died at Moretonhampstead, Devon, on 31 October 1977. GEOFFREY GOODMAN

Sources *The Times* (1 Nov 1977) • *The Times* (5 Nov 1977) • private information (2004) [friends; colleagues; Engineering Employers' Federation] • J. Jones, *Union man* (1986) • *DNB* • personal knowledge (2004) • *CGPLA Eng. & Wales* (1978)
Archives U. Warwick Mod. RC, papers
Wealth at death £27,540: probate, 8 March 1978, *CGPLA Eng. & Wales*

Scandrett, Stephen (1631?–1706), clergyman and ejected minister, was the son of Stephen Scandrett (*d.* 1643), yeoman of the wardrobe to Charles I. It was intended that he would be a king's scholar at Westminster School but this was prevented by his father's death, after which, 'waiting on my Lord Lovelaces Son', he was instructed in grammar learning by his tutor until 'he was fit for the university' (Calamy, *Abridgement*, 2.656). He matriculated at Wadham College, Oxford, on 12 December 1654, and graduated BA on 19 March 1657 and MA on 28 June 1659. According to Edmund Calamy 'he spent several years in hard study, to fit him for the ministry, to which he was from the first inclined, never entertaining thoughts of any other employment' (ibid.). He was incorporated MA at Cambridge in 1659, and became 'conduct' (a chaplain) of Trinity College, Cambridge, between 1659 and 1660. At the Restoration he refused to obey the order of the vice-master, James Duport, to read the prayer book service in the college chapel. After an unseemly altercation he was expelled from his office by the master, Henry Ferne.

Scandrett became assistant to a Mr Eyres at Haverhill, Suffolk and, having received presbyterian ordination, was prosecuted in the church courts for preaching after having been silenced in 1662. In 1667 he married Abigail Walker (*d.* 1717); the licence by which they were married, dated 30 November, gave his age as thirty-five and described her as the daughter of one Walker of Little Waldingfield, Suffolk. They had at least six children, three sons and three daughters. In 1669 Scandrett was reported as preaching at Thaxted and Great Sampford in Essex, as well as at Haverhill and other parishes in Suffolk. At Great Thurlow he was joint pastor to a congregation of '60 sometimes 100'; at Long Melford 'John Sconderell' (one of a variety of manglings of his name) preached to a congregation of fifty or sixty 'inferior people & most women' (Turner, 1.102, 104).

At Haverhill, Scandrett was alleged to have preached to a congregation of 'Presbyterians and Quakers' (Turner, 1.103)—an unlikely combination which can be explained by the authorities' misreading of two public disputations which Scandrett held with the Quaker George Whitehead in Essex in 1668–9. Following these, in 1669 Robert Ludgater and others published a tract, *The Glory of Christ's Light within Expelling Darkness*, the latter part of which was written by Whitehead. In this Scandrett was attacked for setting up scripture as the only rule and described as 'a shallow bragging and vapouring man … who showed himself in his Ribbonds like a Fiddler' (Whitehead and others, 9). In reply Scandrett wrote *An Antidote Against Quakerisme*

(1671), in which he called the Quakers 'a misguided flock' (epistle, sig. A2) and criticized them for emphasizing the inner light at the apparent expense of scripture. In turn Ludgater responded to this in *The Presbyter's Antidote Choking himself.*

In 1670 Scandrett was excommunicated for preaching at Walsham-le-Willows, Suffolk, and afterwards sent to the gaols at Bury St Edmunds and Ipswich. In May 1672 he was licensed under the declaration of indulgence to teach at the house of Joseph Alders, which adjoined his own house at Haverhill. At a later date, after the withdrawal of the declaration, he was prosecuted again for preaching at Waterbeach, Cambridgeshire, and at Mr Thurlow's in Cambridge. After the revolution and the Toleration Act Scandrett preached in the places around Haverhill and once a month at Cambridge. From 1690 to 1692 he received a grant from the Common Fund for his services at Haverhill. Edmund Calamy recorded that he was:

> a man of primitive piety and good works. It was his honour in a declining age, when others disputed away truth and duties, to stand up in a vigorous defence of both. He never declined his work at home or abroad, but with an unwearied diligence continued in it as long as he lived. (Calamy, *Continuation*, 2.805)

Scandrett died at Haverhill on 8 December 1706, aged seventy-five, and was buried four days later in the chancel of Haverhill church. His will left small bequests to his children and to the poor of Haverhill. His widow was buried in Haverhill church on 15 May 1717.

W. A. SHAW, *rev.* CAROLINE L. LEACHMAN

Sources E. Calamy, ed., *An abridgement of Mr. Baxter's history of his life and times, with an account of the ministers, &c., who were ejected after the Restauration of King Charles II*, 2nd edn, 2 vols. (1713), vol. 2, pp. 655–8 • E. Calamy, *A continuation of the account of the ministers … who were ejected and silenced after the Restoration in 1660*, 2 vols. (1727), vol. 2, p. 805 • *Calamy rev.*, 428–9 • Foster, *Alum. Oxon.*, 1500–1714, vol. 4 • J. Browne, *A history of Congregationalism and memorials of the churches in Norfolk and Suffolk* (1877), 503–5 • T. W. Davids, *Annals of evangelical nonconformity in Essex* (1863), 623–6 • R. Ludgater, G. Whitehead, and others, *The glory of Christ's light within expelling darkness* (1669) • A. Gordon, ed., *Freedom after ejection: a review (1690–1692) of presbyterian and congregational nonconformity in England and Wales* (1917) • J. L. Chester and J. Foster, eds., *London marriage licences, 1521–1869* (1887) • G. L. Turner, ed., *Original records of early nonconformity under persecution and indulgence*, 1 (1911) • will, Bury St Edmunds RO, J545/48–549

Scanlan, James Donald (1899–1976), Roman Catholic archbishop of Glasgow, was born on 24 January 1899 at 511 Duke Street, Glasgow, the fifth of the seven children of Joseph Scanlan (1861–1950), medical practitioner, and his wife, Sarah Veronica Walls (1861–1922). Scanlan was born into a Roman Catholic family and, after schooling in the city at St Mungo's Academy and St Aloysius' College, he matriculated in 1915 in the faculty of medicine of Glasgow University. It was, however, wartime, so in November 1916 he entered Sandhurst and the following September was commissioned second lieutenant in the Highland light infantry. After service in Egypt from May 1918 to January 1919 he resigned his commission in July. In 1920 he matriculated at Glasgow once again, this time in law, and graduated BL in 1923. Having studied at St Edmund's College, the seminary at Ware, Hertfordshire, from 1924, he was ordained priest for Westminster diocese on 29 June 1929. That autumn he entered the canon law faculty of the Institut Catholique, Paris, graduating licentiate in 1930, then went on to the Apollinare in Rome and graduated doctor in 1932.

After returning to London, Scanlan became assistant priest at St James's, Spanish Place. However, his work in the diocesan marriage tribunal took up increasingly more of his time, until at last in 1938 he became chaplain to a convent in Hammersmith (where during the war he and the nuns were twice bombed out). In 1937 he was appointed diocesan vice-chancellor and was created a domestic prelate (colloquially a monsignor). He succeeded as chancellor in 1944. In 1945 he was made vicar delegate for the United States forces in Britain, with merely nominal duties.

The year 1946 saw Scanlan's return to Scotland. Appointed coadjutor bishop of Dunkeld (with the titular see of Cyme), he received episcopal ordination at Dundee on 20 June 1946. He succeeded as bishop of Dunkeld on 31 May 1949, was translated to Motherwell diocese on 23 May 1955 and finally, on 29 January 1964, was appointed archbishop of Glasgow, a position he held until he resigned on 23 April 1974. His health thereafter declined rapidly. He returned to London but died only three weeks after his arrival there, on 25 March 1976. His body was brought to Glasgow and lay in the cathedral until its interment in Dalbeth cemetery; in December 1979 it was re-interred in the cathedral crypt.

Although as bishop in Motherwell he oversaw much progress and expansion, it is for his ten years in Glasgow that Scanlan is most remembered. J. D., as he was often referred to, retained great affection for his native city and used to reminisce about the Great Exhibition of 1912, during his boyhood. His recreation as archbishop was to walk round the city and he greatly appreciated the honorary DD he received in 1967 from Glasgow University. His was a striking personality, with apparently opposing traits. His military and legal training showed itself in various ways: a meticulous use of language in all his pronouncements, a punctilious insistence on rules in business dealings with his clergy, a refusal to talk shop outside office hours. In his private life and spiritual duties he was most orderly. Yet he combined this with a liking for ceremonial and full formal dress. A raconteur, with archaic turns of speech, he yet gained the respect and liking of his priests, whose backgrounds and careers were so different from his own.

In Motherwell and Glasgow he established good relations with civic and other leaders. All doors were opened to him. At Westminster his work had made him widely known; at the Second Vatican Council in the 1960s he took the opportunity to meet eminent churchmen from all over the world. It was this trait that brought about the achievement he is most remembered for. In January 1971 sixty Glasgow Rangers supporters were crushed to death at a football match against their local rivals, Celtic. The archbishop at once arranged a requiem mass in his cathedral, to which he invited the city leaders and both clubs, despite the religious bigotry which poisoned their relations, and both accepted. It was a truly historic occasion.

Physically, though not tall he was broad and strong. Indeed, shortly after his promotion to Glasgow, he vaulted on to the stage at a public meeting, letting everyone see that at sixty-five he was not too old for the job! Academically gifted though he was, he published little. He translated two books from French: one was *Pastors and People* by Étienne Magnin (1930), on canon law, and the other was *Judaism* by Auguste Vincent (1934). In the Stair Society's *An Introduction to Scottish Legal History* (1958) he provided an article on medieval marriage law. MARK DILWORTH

Sources J. Darragh, *The Catholic hierarchy of Scotland: a biographical list, 1653–1985* (1986) • *Catholic Directory for Scotland* (1947–77) • *Catholic Directory for Scotland* (1981) • Glasgow Roman Catholic Archdiocesan Archives, Glasgow • *Catholic Directory* (1946) • private information (2004)
Archives Glasgow Roman Catholic Archdiocesan Archives, Glasgow, corresp. and papers • Scottish Catholic Archives, Edinburgh, corresp. and papers
Likenesses A. Goudie, oils on plaque, *c.*1971, Glasgow curial offices

Scanlen, Sir Thomas Charles (1834–1912), politician and lawyer in Cape Colony, was born on 9 July 1834 at a mission station near Grahamstown in the eastern Cape, Cape Colony, the elder child of Charles Packenham Scanlen (1809–1871), politician and businessman, and his first wife, Anne (1813–1843), daughter of George and Hannah Dennison. The Scanlen family (originally from Longford, Ireland) and the Dennison family (from Nottinghamshire) had emigrated under the 1820 settler scheme, an enterprise backed by the British government for settling farmers along the eastern frontier of the Cape Colony to provide security against tribal incursions. It was a hard life for the newcomers, and Scanlen was brought up in modest circumstances, attending local schools, while his father pursued business opportunities in different regions of the eastern Cape, settling finally in Cradock. At the age of sixteen Scanlen, who had already seen military service and had twice taken care of his father's affairs during the latter's absence fighting in two of the numerous frontier wars between Africans and Europeans, left school to work in the family business. He soon became interested in the law, which he studied on his own, and in 1855 he was admitted to practise as a notary public. That same year he married Emma Thackwray, who died in February 1862. In July 1863 Scanlen married his cousin, Sarah Ann Dennison (*d.* 1903). There were twelve children of the two marriages, but only four of them survived to adulthood, three of the children tragically dying during the same scarlet fever epidemic. Scanlen was a good lawyer and his practice thrived.

Following in the footsteps of the father he much admired, Scanlen held several elective government positions until ultimately, in 1870, he took over the seat in the Cape parliament that the senior Scanlen had held for twelve years. His father had steadfastly opposed responsible government for the Cape Colony and had favoured a separate eastern colony under representative government, but Thomas Scanlen supported responsible government for a single Cape Colony and soon became a trusted ally of the first prime minister under the new constitution, John Molteno. He was a hard-working member of parliament and established a reputation as an expert in constitutional and fiscal affairs and in parliamentary procedures. His knowledge of these subjects, eschewed by most of his colleagues, gave him more influence than a new member would normally enjoy, especially one as precise and taciturn as he was. Scanlen also became an expert on defence, a subject of intense interest to his constituents, living, as they did, in a region of intermittent border warfare. He was an outspoken opponent of the 'policy of vigour' for handling, or waging war against, black people, which was advocated by Gordon Sprigg, Scanlen's fellow easterner and perdurable parliamentary rival. Scanlen's views on defence and black affairs were not typical of those held by his constituents, but his reputation for integrity, for finding objective solutions to problems, and for paying attention to local concerns earned him sustained support at the polls, both from English- and Afrikaans-speaking voters. Scanlen, acceptable to all elements of a fractious opposition, became prime minister in 1881 when Sprigg's government fell as a result of waging the disastrous 'gun war' against the Sotho. A healthy economy and the support of Afrikaans house members gave an encouraging start to the Scanlen ministry, the first headed by a southern Africa-born politician, but its popularity was short-lived. Within a year the economy had soured and J. H. Hofmeyr, Scanlen's Afrikaner minister, had resigned. Territorial issues affecting the Cape became paramount. The boundaries of the colony were being determined, and passions ran high on all sides over land issues. Under Scanlen's leadership Basutoland became a British protectorate and the Transkei nearly did; the stage was set for Germany to take over South-West Africa, and Transvaal's president, Paul Kruger, was prevented from getting control of Bechuanaland, thereby keeping open the road to the north for British interests. The Scanlen ministry had an excellent legislative record, enacting a host of laws to provide the Cape with efficient administration, but it was to no avail. In 1884, following the defeat of several supporters at general elections, Scanlen resigned and the Sprigg faction took over once again. Scanlen had an undistinguished five years as leader of the opposition. He did not have the street-fighter qualities required to contend with confrontational politics and influence peddling. And his personal life began to unravel. He became estranged from his wife, his drinking became a problem, and he lost everything he had in a wild speculation in the Transvaal's new gold mining industry.

In 1894, at the invitation of his erstwhile protégé, Cecil Rhodes, Scanlen left the Cape, resigning the parliamentary seat he had held for twenty-six years to become a leading official of Rhodesia's administrator on behalf of the crown, the British South Africa Company. His legal services over a fourteen-year period provided the new Rhodesia with the essential laws for good government of that colony. During his life Scanlen set up three legal practices in Cradock, Cape Town, and Salisbury, all successful and all well regarded. He died at his Salisbury home, Greenwood, in North Avenue, on 15 May 1912, having redeemed his reputation; he was buried in Salisbury.

BASIL T. HONE

Sources B. T. Hone, *The first son of South Africa to be premier* (1993) • J. H. Hofmeyr and F. W. Reitz, *The life of Jan Hendrik Hofmeyr (Onze Jan)* (1913) • P. Lewsen, *John X. Merriman: paradoxical South African statesman* (1982) • R. I. Rotberg, *Cecil Rhodes and the pursuit of power* (1988) • T. R. H. Davenport, *South Africa: a modern history*, 3rd edn (1987) • T. R. H. Davenport, *The Afrikaner Bond* (1966) • T. C. Scanlen and A. D. Scanlen, memoranda, Cape Archives, Kilpin MSS • d. cert. [Sarah Ann Dennison]

Archives National Archives of Zimbabwe, Harare, diary of journey in Rhodesia | Bodl. RH, corresp. with Rhodes relating to annexation of Bechuanaland • Cape Archives, Kilpin MSS • Derbys. RO, Gell MSS • National Library of South Africa, Cape Town, Merriman MSS

Likenesses photographs, 1873–7, National Library of South Africa, Cape Town, PHA 1023 • photograph, *c.*1900, National Archives of South Africa, Cape Town, AG3104 • cartoons and sketches, repro. in Hone, *First son of South Africa*

Wealth at death £3500: inventory, Masters Office, Salisbury, Zimbabwe

Scarbrough. For this title name *see* Lumley, Richard, first earl of Scarbrough (1650–1721); Saunderson, Frances Lumley-, countess of Scarbrough (*c.*1700–1772); Lumley, Lawrence Roger, eleventh earl of Scarbrough (1896–1969).

Scarburgh, Sir Charles (1615–1694), physician and natural philosopher, son of Edmund Scarburgh, gentleman, of the parish of St Martin-in-the-Fields, and Hannah Butler, was born in London on 29 December 1615 and was sent to St Paul's School. He entered Gonville and Caius College, Cambridge, as a sizar on 4 March 1633 and graduated BA in 1637 and MA in 1640, at which time he was elected a fellow and concentrated on medicine and mathematics. He studied the latter with Seth Ward, then at Emmanuel College. They chose William Oughtred's *Clavis mathematica* as their text, and Oughtred was pleased by their visiting him at Albury in Surrey to ask an explanation of difficulties they had encountered with his text. Scarburgh, a royalist, was ejected from his Cambridge fellowship about 1644 during the civil war and entered Merton College, Oxford, where he probably intended to serve in a royalist regiment. At Merton he befriended another Caius alumnus, William Harvey, who was then Merton's warden. According to John Aubrey, Harvey told Scarburgh: 'Prithee leave off thy gunning and stay here … I will bring thee into [medical] practice' (J. Aubrey, *Brief Lives*, 1.299). By June 1645 Scarburgh was assisting Harvey in writing his *De generatione animalium*. Supported by letters from Harvey, Scarburgh was created MD by the chancellor of Oxford University on 23 June 1646, one day before Sir Thomas Glenham surrendered Oxford to General Fairfax and parliament. (In 1660 Scarburgh's MD was incorporated at Cambridge.) About 1647 he moved to London, joined a group of natural philosophers organized by John Wallis known as the '1645 Group', and was admitted as a candidate by the College of Physicians on 25 January 1648. He maintained ties with his

Sir Charles Scarburgh (1615–1694), by unknown artist, *c.*1660

Oxford colleagues, arranging in 1649 with the ejected Savilian professor of astronomy, John Greaves, for Seth Ward, his mathematical friend from Cambridge, to be appointed Greaves's successor despite Ward's high-church and royalist convictions. On 8 October 1649 Scarburgh was elected anatomical reader at Surgeons' Hall, where he engaged Christopher Wren, then between Westminster School and matriculating at Oxford, as his assistant in demonstrating and making anatomical experiments. Scarburgh's association with William Oughtred and John Wallis, a founder of the Royal Society, included a shared interest in placing astrology on a solid mathematical footing, a desire that reflects the lack of a definite boundary between astrology and mainline natural philosophy and medicine in seventeenth-century England.

Scarburgh was elected a fellow of the College of Physicians on 26 September 1650 and served as censor in 1655, 1664, and 1665; elect in 1677 (in place of Francis Glisson); and consiliarius in 1684, 1685, 1686, 1688, and 1689. In 1656 Harvey chose him as his successor as Lumleian lecturer in the college. Harvey bequeathed 'my velvet gowne to my lovinge frined, Mr. Dr. Scarburgh', as well as 'all my little silver instruments of surgerie' (Munk, *Roll*). When Harvey's friend and patient Henry Pierrepont, first marquess of Dorchester and a virtuoso of natural philosophy, was admitted as a fellow of the college in 1658 Scarburgh introduced him with a well-received Latin speech. Scarburgh delivered the Harveian oration in 1662. On 28 February 1663 Samuel Pepys recorded that he went with Scarburgh to the dissection of a seaman hanged for robbery. Scarburgh also read the anatomy lectures 'with great applause' (Munk, *Roll*) at the Barber-Surgeons' Hall for many years. Early in the Restoration Charles II appointed him first physician, and knighted him on 15 August 1669. He attended the king in his final illness and left an account in manuscript (S. Antiquaries, Lond., MS 206), which was transcribed and translated in Raymond Crawfurd's *Last Days of Charles II* (1909). He also served as physician to James II, before and after his accession, to the Tower of London, to Prince George of Denmark, and to William and Mary. He was MP for Camelford, Cornwall, from 1685 to 1687.

Scarburgh published a short guide to human dissection, *Syllabus musculorum* (1676), which was a textbook for many years. He was also a member of the earl of Roscommon's 'literary academy' and wrote an elegy on the poet Abraham Cowley, who had been a member of Harvey's circle at Oxford; he stood bail of £1000 for Cowley in 1656. Scarburgh left materials for an English edition of Euclid, which his son Charles published in folio in 1705. Scarburgh also accumulated a valuable library concentrated on mathematical texts. According to John Evelyn's *Diary* for 10 March 1695, the earl of Sunderland

> showed me his library, now again improved by many books bought at the sale of Sir Charles Scarburgh, an eminent physician, which was the very best collection, especially of mathematical books, that was, I believe, in Europe; once designed for the King's library at St James's; but the Queen dying, who was a great patroness of that design, it was let fall, and the books were miserably dissipated.

A catalogue of Scarburgh's library was issued in 1695.

Scarburgh died in London on 26 February 1694 and was buried at Cranford, Middlesex, where his monument, erected by his widow, was set on the north side of the chancel. ROBERT L. MARTENSEN

Sources *DNB* • Munk, *Roll* • Pepys, *Diary* • *The diary of Samuel Pepys*, ed. R. N. G. Braybrooke (1825) • *The diary of John Evelyn*, ed. E. S. De Beer (1959) • R. French, *William Harvey's natural philosophy* (1994) • S. Young, *The annals of the Barber-Surgeons of London: compiled from their records and other sources* (1890) • R. G. Frank, *Harvey and the Oxford physiologists* (1980) • B. S. Capp, *Astrology and the popular press: English almanacs, 1500–1800* (1979) • J. Browne, *Mygraphia nova* (1698) • C. Webster, *The great instauration: science, medicine and reform, 1626–1660* (1975) • *IGI* • Wood, *Ath. Oxon.*

Archives S. Antiquaries, Lond.

Likenesses R. Greenbury?, oils, 1651, Barber-Surgeons' Hall, London • oils, *c.*1660, RCP Lond. [*see illus.*] • M. Vandergucht, line engraving, 1710 (after J. Demetrius), Wellcome L. • J. Brown, stipple (after R. Greenbury; after G. P. Harding), Wellcome L.

Scardeburgh [Scardeburg], **Sir Robert** (*d.* in or after **1348**), justice, originated at Scarborough in the East Riding of Yorkshire, where he acquired property and in 1332 obtained for the town a grant of customs to maintain its quay. He trained as a lawyer and at Michaelmas 1318 became a serjeant, acting in that capacity in the bench and also at the Northamptonshire and Bedfordshire eyres held between 1329 and 1331. In the latter year he was appointed successively chief justice for an eyre in the Channel Islands (10 June) and chief justice of the Dublin bench (2 December); in 1332 he was made a knight-banneret. In Ireland he also acted as 'chief keeper' of the lands of Elizabeth de Clare. Back in England early in 1333, Scardeburgh returned to Ireland in April with instructions for the government there relating to the resumption of Anglo-Scottish hostilities, and then accompanied the justiciar John Darcy on his expedition to Scotland. Replaced as chief justice on 19 January 1334, on 1 February he was made a justice of the justiciar's bench, a position he held until 1 August following. On 16 July he was made chief baron of the Dublin exchequer, but the appointment did not take effect. Instead he began to be employed in England, where on 24 September 1334 he was made a justice of king's bench, and immediately afterwards started to receive commissions, on 4 October being appointed to negotiate the payment of a subsidy in Lincolnshire. On 28 July 1337 he was once more named chief justice of the Dublin bench but never acted, while his transfer to the Westminster bench, ordered on 6 September 1339, was countermanded six weeks later.

A trier of petitions in parliaments of 1340 and 1341, Scardeburgh was employed early in the latter year hearing complaints against ministers and justices disgraced in 1340. But on 5 August he was summarily dismissed in circumstances that make it clear that he had himself come under suspicion of misusing his position. His reputation may already have been shaky—in July 1340 a litigant insulted him in court, describing him as 'false and faithless' (Sayles, *Select cases*, 5.121–3)—and subsequent investigations did nothing to restore it. Essex jurors presented in 1341 that he and Sir Richard Willoughby had taken bribes from suspects, and that he had had an innocent man imprisoned so that he could extract money from him for his release. In January 1342 he was also in trouble for ignoring instructions to return his judicial records into chancery. After his dismissal Scardeburgh received no further commissions until 30 July 1344, when he was sent back to Ireland as chief justice of the justiciar's bench. But he proved no more satisfactory in that capacity, and was replaced on 12 July 1345. He returned to England, and received a few more commissions, all in Yorkshire, where he was a collector of an aid in 1347 and a commissioner of the peace in the East Riding on 10 July 1348. There is no certain reference to him after the latter date, and it is not known when he died. He had a son named John, recorded in 1357; the name of his wife is unrecorded.

HENRY SUMMERSON

Sources *Chancery records* • assize rolls, PRO, JUST/1/258 • H. G. Richardson and G. O. Sayles, *The administration of Ireland, 1172–1377* (1963) • *RotP*, vol. 2 • W. P. Baildon, ed., *Feet of fines for the county of York, from 1327 to 1347, 1–20 Edward III*, 1, Yorkshire Archaeological Society, 42 (1910) • G. O. Sayles, ed., *Select cases in the court of king's bench*, 7 vols., SeldS, 55, 57–8, 74, 76, 82, 88 (1936–71), vols. 4–6 • D. W. Sutherland, ed., *The eyre of Northamptonshire: 3–4 Edward III, AD 1329–1330*, 2 vols., SeldS, 97–8 (1983) • R. Frame, *English lordship in Ireland, 1318–1361* (1982) • D. Crook, *Records of the general eyre*, Public Record Office Handbooks, 20 (1982) • Baker, *Serjeants*, 154, 535 • *CClR, 1354–60*, 396 • *CPR, 1348–50*, 160

Scarfe, Francis Harold [Frank] (**1911–1986**), French scholar and academic administrator, was born on 18 September 1911 at 539 Stanhope Road, South Shields, Tyneside, co. Durham, the son of John James Scarfe, a marine engineer in the merchant service, and Margaret Ingham

(Maggie), *née* Dobson. His parents died when he was young, and he grew up in a naval orphanage. He was later educated at King's College, Durham, Fitzwilliam House, Cambridge, and the Sorbonne in Paris. In 1938 he married Margarete M. Geisler, with whom he had a son, (Francis) Bruno. Before the Second World War he was a university lecturer in French. His views in the early 1930s were pacifist, but the Spanish Civil War made him see the need for active resistance to fascism. When the Second World War began he was conscripted into the Royal Army Ordnance Corps as a private, but he transferred to the education corps and by 1945 was a lieutenant-colonel. He was offered promotion to brigadier if he would stay in the army.

After demobilization Scarfe was supervisor of studies and secretary to the extension lectures committee of the University of Oxford from 1946 to 1947. From 1947 to 1959 he was senior lecturer in French at the University of Glasgow, though during this time his home (to which he returned in vacations) was at 433 Banbury Road, Oxford. From 1959 he was director of the British Institute in Paris until his retirement in 1978. He was also professor of French at the University of London from 1965 to 1978, continuing as professor emeritus. These activities reflected one of his main achievements, which was to bring the British Institute in Paris into the British university system. In 1965 he was made an OBE, in 1967 made Chevalier des Arts et Lettres and awarded the prix de l'Île St Louis, in 1972 made CBE, and in 1978 made chevalier of the Légion d'honneur.

As a young man Scarfe was active as a poet. As a student of French he was drawn to surrealism and contributed to the leading British magazine of surrealism of the 1930s, Roger Roughton's *Contemporary Poetry and Prose*. During the latter years of the decade he was one of the group published in Julian Symons's *Twentieth Century Verse*. Over the next ten years he published three volumes of poetry: *Inscapes* (1940), *Forty Poems and Ballads* (1941), and *Underworlds* (1950). Undoubtedly his most widely read work was *Auden and After: the Liberation of Poetry* (1941): as an introduction to the new poetry of the period, this book's freshness has endured. His later studies include *Auden* (1949), *Paul Valéry* (1954), and *La vie et l'œuvre de T. S. Eliot* (1964). Scarfe also published three novels: *Promises* (1950), *Single Blessedness* (1951), and *Unfinished Woman* (1954). In his retirement he returned to poetry with *Grounds for Conceit* (1984), all the poems in which were composed in 1982–3. He produced editions of Baudelaire (1951) and Andre Chénier (1961) and translated work by Baudelaire and La Fontaine.

The vocation to which Scarfe was drawn as a young man was undoubtedly poetry; but, while he knew all the writers of new poetry in the late 1930s and early 1940s, and indeed was instrumental in introducing them to the poetry-reading public in *Auden and After*, his own published poetry was rather conventional, and his best poems are notable for their simple and direct handling of personal themes. During his later years in Paris he appears to have written very little.

The achievements for which Scarfe attained public distinction were in the fields of educational and cultural organization, marked by his unusual rise from private to lieutenant-colonel in the education corps in the Second World War and by his appointment to the senior British Council post abroad as head of the British Institute in Paris. On retirement he returned to his home, 433 Banbury Road, Oxford. He died in the John Radcliffe Hospital, Oxford, on 13 March 1986. A. T. TOLLEY

Sources A. T. Tolley, *The poetry of the thirties* (1975) • A. T. Tolley, *The poetry of the forties* (1985) • *WW* • I. Hamilton, ed., *The Oxford companion to twentieth-century poetry in English* (1994) • personal knowledge (2004) • d. cert.

Archives Boston University, Boston, Massachusetts, corresp. and literary MSS

Wealth at death £24,803: probate, 1986, *CGPLA Eng. & Wales*

Scargill, Daniel (1647–1721), Church of England clergyman, was born on 31 August 1647 in the village of Knapwell, Cambridgeshire, the son of John Scargill (*d.* 1683). He entered Corpus Christi College, Cambridge, as a sizar in January 1662, matriculating later in the same year. In 1666 he won the Manners scholarship and graduated BA. On 30 August 1667 he was elected to the Norwich fellowship left vacant by the election of John Spencer as master. On 7 December 1668 Scargill was suspended from his degree for upholding atheistical tenets in a public disputation. The university consistory court forced him to make a public recantation. On 12 March 1669 Scargill was expelled from his college and the university. After his expulsion he managed to secure royal intervention in his case and was permitted to recant again in the university church of Great St Mary's on 25 July 1669. In his recantation Scargill confessed to being a follower of the controversial philosopher Thomas Hobbes and he declared that he had 'gloried to be a Hobbist and an Atheist' (*Recantation*, 1). He admitted to upholding propositions that included the ideas that 'all right of Dominion is founded onely in power' (ibid.); that 'all moral Righteousness is founded onely in the Law of the Civil Magistrate' (ibid.); that 'the Holy Scriptures are made law onely by the Civil Authority' (ibid.); and that 'Whatsoever the Civil Magistrate commands is to be obeyed notwithstanding contrary to Divine moral Laws' (ibid.). He also confessed to maintaining that 'there is a desireable glory in being and being reputed an Atheist' (ibid., 4). The recantation was published as a pamphlet immediately afterwards, and Scargill became notorious as a disciple of Hobbes. It is far from clear that Scargill was sincere in the heavily edited confession; his *Recantation* may have registered more accurately the anxieties of the university authorities about the contemporary popularity of Hobbes's ideas. Hobbes himself wrote a (now lost) response to the affair (*Brief Lives*, 1.360–62).

Although Scargill was absolved from his suspension and restored to the university, he was not readmitted to his college, which had fought against his reinstatement. In spite of his misdemeanours he was ordained on 28 June 1672. On 8 July Scargill became rector of Mulbarton, Norfolk, upon presentation by Sir Edwyn Rich. On 2 February 1673 he married Sarah Le Neve (1650–1680) of Aslacton, Norfolk, and, after her death on 22 August 1680, he married Sarah Garman (*d.* 1718), of All Hallows, London, on 20

March 1682. In 1690 Scargill's brother Dudley Scargill presented him to the adjoining parish of Swardeston, which he held in plurality until his death in 1721, aged seventy-four. He was buried at Mulbarton parish church on 31 May. After his recantation Scargill was reputed to have lived a 'pious and exemplary life'. It was reported that he 'was often in conversation reproach'd wth his former Errors, to wch He often used to answer that He hoped He met with with his punishmt for them in this world [*sic*]' (CUL, MS Collect.admin.35, fol. 204). JON PARKIN

Sources C. L. S. Linnel, 'Daniel Scargill, a penitent Hobbist', *Church Quarterly Review*, 156 (1955), 256–65 • J. L. Axtell, 'The mechanics of opposition: Restoration Cambridge *v.* Daniel Scargill', *BIHR*, 38 (1965), 102–11 • J. Parkin, 'Hobbism in the later 1660s: Daniel Scargill and Samuel Parker', *HJ*, 42 (1999), 85–108 • D. Krook, 'The recantation of Daniel Scargill', *N&Q*, 198 (1953), 159–60 • *The recantation of Daniel Scargill* (1669) • records for Great St Mary's Church, 1587–1669, CUL, department of manuscripts and university archives, CUR 18 6 (also numbered as 13) b–e • LPL, MS 941, fols. 107–9 • parish register, Mulbarton, Norfolk RO, PD 494/10, fols. 1–7 • Venn, *Alum. Cant.*, 1/4.28 • annotated MS copy of Daniel Scargill's recantation, U. Cam., archives, MS Collect.admin.35, fol. 204 • C. A. Thurley and D. Thurley, eds., *Index of the probate records of the court of the archdeaconry of Ely, 1513–1857* (1976) • *Brief lives, chiefly of contemporaries, set down by John Aubrey, between the years 1669 and 1696*, ed. A. Clark, 2 vols. (1898)

Archives BL, letters concerning him, Harley MS 7377, fols. 1, 4 • BL, letters to Thomas Tenison, Add. MS 38693, fols. 30, 126–8 • CUL, Baker MSS, account of his trial proceedings, MS mm 1.38, fols. 143–4 • CUL, consistory court records for his trial, CUR 18 6 (also numbered as 13) b–e • LPL, letters concerning him, MS 674, fol. 9

Scargill, William Pitt (1787–1836), Unitarian minister and writer, was born in London. Originally intended for a business life, he attracted the notice of Hugh Worthington, minister at Salters' Hall, under whose advice he studied for the ministry at Wymondley Academy. For six months (March to August 1811) he was assistant to James Tayler at High Pavement Chapel, Nottingham. In 1812 he succeeded Thomas Madge as minister of Churchgate Street Chapel, Bury St Edmunds, and held this charge for twenty years. His ministry was not successful, and he turned to literature as a means of augmenting a narrow income, contributing to periodicals, and producing original tales and sketches, some of which were published in *Essays on Various Subjects* (1815), and other titles such as *Blue-Stocking Hall* (1827) and *Tales of a Briefless Barrister* (1829). He had been a Liberal in politics, but displeased his congregation by becoming a writer for the tory press. He resigned his charge in 1832 and became an adherent of the established church, publishing a series of moral novels including *The Usurer's Daughter* (1832) and *The Puritan's Grave* (1833). At the end of 1834 he published anonymously *The Autobiography of a Dissenting Minister*, in which he plays the part of a candid friend to his former co-religionists. The book is often classed with the anonymous *Particulars of the Life of a Dissenting Minister* (1813) by Charles Lloyd; but Lloyd's is a genuine autobiography, Scargill's a romance, though possibly based on his early life and education. It attracted some attention and was reprinted twice in the same year. Scargill made a precarious living by his pen, yet his sketches are brisk and readable, with a curious vein of paradox. An essay entitled 'The blessings of biography' opens with the advice, 'If you think a man to be a devil, and want to make him an angel, sit down to write a biography of him.' He was famed as a punster. He died of brain fever at Bury St Edmunds on 24 January 1836. He was survived by his wife, Mary Anne, daughter of Robert Cutting of Chevington, Suffolk, and two children. His widow edited some of his contributions to periodicals, many from *The Atlas* newspaper, with the title *The Widow's Offering: a Selection of Tales and Essays* (1837). Of this a pirated edition appeared as *The English Sketchbook* (1856). His widow republished the collection with the title *Essays and Sketches* the following year.

ALEXANDER GORDON, *rev.* CLARE L. TAYLOR

Sources *GM*, 2nd ser., 5 (1836) • M. S. Scargill, *The widow's offering: a selection of tales and essays*, ed. M. A. Scargill (1837)

Scarisbrick [*alias* Neville], **Edward** (1639–1709), Jesuit, was born in Lancashire, the second of the five sons (there were four daughters) of Edward Scarisbrick (*d.* 1652) and his wife, Frances, *née* Bradshaigh (*d.* 1667), of Scarisbrick Hall, Lancashire. Four of the five brothers became Jesuits. Edward Scarisbrick was educated at the English College at St Omer (1653–9) and joined the Jesuits in September 1659 assuming then the name Neville. After completing the studies for the priesthood at Liège he was ordained there on 6 April 1672. He had already taught humanities at St Omer from 1664 until 1670 and he returned there in charge of the studies in 1675. In 1679 he was named by Titus Oates as one of his intended victims. He returned to Lancashire in 1680 as a missionary but in 1686 he was in London and in 1687 was living at the newly opened Jesuit college in the Savoy and was appointed a royal preacher. Two of his sermons, *A Sermon Preached before Her Majesty the Queen Dowager* (1686), on spiritual leprosy, and *Catholick Loyalty: upon the Subject of Government and Obedience* (1688) were published in London, and reprinted, with the sermons of other royal preachers, in 1741 in *A Select Collection of Catholick Sermons*. In 1688 at the outbreak of the revolution he succeeded in escaping to France and soon after his arrival, if not before, he began writing *The life of the Lady Warner of Parham in Suffolk, in religion called Sister Clare of Jesus—written by a Catholick gentleman*. Printed on the press at the English College at St Omer, it was published in 1691. A second edition was published in 1692 to which was added 'An abridgement of the life of her sister-in-law, Mrs Elizabeth Warner, in religion Sister Mary Clare'. A third edition appeared in 1696. He is thought by some to have been the author of *Rules and Instructions* for the sodality of the Immaculate Conception published anonymously in 1703 (Blom and others, 267). After a year at the English Jesuit house at Ghent he returned to Lancashire in 1693 and either then or later became chaplain to the Culcheth family at Culcheth Hall; he remained there until his death on 19 (or 15) February 1709. He was buried at Winwick, Lancashire. GEOFFREY HOLT

Sources H. Foley, ed., *Records of the English province of the Society of Jesus*, 7 (1882–3), 686, 969 • G. Holt, 'Edward Scarisbrick, 1639–1709: a royal preacher', *Recusant History*, 23 (1996–7), 159–65 • G. Holt, *The English Jesuits, 1650–1829: a biographical dictionary*, Catholic RS, 70

(1984), 220 • J. S. Hansom and J. Gillow, eds., 'A list of convicted recusants in the reign of Charles II', *Miscellanea, V*, Catholic RS, 6 (1909), 75–326, esp. 246 • J. Gillow, 'The Catholic registers of Culcheth, 1791–1825', *Miscellanea, VIII*, Catholic RS, 13 (1913), 370–96, esp. 371 • G. Holt, *St Omers and Bruges colleges, 1593–1773: a biographical dictionary*, Catholic RS, 69 (1979), 231 • A. de Backer and others, *Bibliothèque de la Compagnie de Jésus*, new edn, 7, ed. C. Sommervogel (Brussels, 1896), 695 • G. Oliver, *Collections towards illustrating the biography of the Scotch, English and Irish members, SJ* (1838), 134 • T. H. Clancy, *English Catholic books, 1641–1700: a bibliography*, rev. edn (1996), 144 • F. Blom and others, *English Catholic books, 1701–1800: a bibliography* (1996), 267, 270 • C. Dodd [H. Tootell], *The church history of England, from the year 1500, to the year 1688*, 3 (1742), 493 • T. Jones, ed., *A catalogue of the collection of tracts for and against popery*, 2, Chetham Society, 64 (1865), 64, 454, 456 • Archives of the British Province of the Society of Jesus, London

Scarle, John (*d.* **1403**), administrator, was a Lincolnshire man whose family was linked with North Scarle (his parents were buried in the adjacent parish church of Eagle) and who followed his uncle and namesake, with whom he is sometimes confused, into crown service. Granted his first benefice by royal patronage (Holme next the Sea, Norfolk) in 1369, and from 1370 a pensioner of Westminster Abbey, Scarle probably entered crown employment in the late 1360s; his uncle had been a chancery clerk, and from June 1375 the younger John Scarle was a chancery clerk receiving attorneys. Scarle had a parallel career as chancellor of the county palatine of Lancaster, an office to which he was appointed in November 1382, and one he had relinquished by August 1395. He was clerk of parliament from 1384 to 1394, and in July 1394 was appointed keeper of the rolls of chancery, but resigned in September 1397. He was a receiver of petitions in parliament from October 1382 to February 1397, and was keeper of the great seal during Richard II's absences in Ireland (30 September 1394 – 15 May 1395) and in France (10–22 August and 27 September – 23 November 1396). Scarle was appointed chancellor on 5 September 1399 on the instructions of Henry Bolingbroke, but was removed from office on 9 March 1401, as the result of a political coup against Lancastrian servants mounted in the parliament of early 1401. However, he continued to attend council meetings, and to act as a crown servant under a variety of commissions, until January 1403.

Scarle's official duties made him a popular choice to act as a parliamentary proctor; twenty-seven appointments by ten abbots, two bishops, and a cathedral chapter are recorded for the years 1380–1401. He had notably strong links with Bury St Edmunds, whose abbot employed him on eight occasions, and with Westminster. Scarle's ecclesiastical career was comparatively undistinguished. He was ordained, rising from acolyte to priest, in the diocese of London between June 1370 and March 1371, and held a succession of benefices in the eastern counties, including the parish of St Mary, South Kelsey, Lincolnshire (1379–82), Desborough, Northamptonshire (1382–5), and Woolpit, Suffolk, to which he left a generous legacy. Rector of St Bride's, Fleet Street, London, from 1396, Scarle made bequests to the scribe Roger Donk, and of a book that Donk had copied, suggesting that he was a patron of the London book trade. Promotions to cathedral prebends at York (1388), Salisbury (1395), and Lichfield (1395) came comparatively late in his career, and he became archdeacon of Lincoln, on 27 September 1401, only after his dismissal as chancellor. Scarle's dual career, his wide clientele, and his extensive moneylending activities made him wealthy. He lent substantial sums to Richard II (£200 in 1394 and 1397) and Henry IV (£100 in 1402). Scarle's Lancastrian affiliations are clear: he described Archbishop Thomas Arundel (*d.* 1414) in his will as 'my dearest master'; his first cathedral promotion was made during the Merciless Parliament (13 February 1388); he resigned the keepership of the rolls of chancery on 11 September 1397, on the eve of the parliament that proceeded against the former appellants; and he was the choice of the usurper Bolingbroke as chancellor once Richard II was in custody. Scarle had long and close links with Westminster Abbey, and his position as clerk of parliament (1384–94) enabled him to provide the Monk of Westminster with records of the Merciless Parliament. It is John Scarle, therefore, whom historians should thank for the very detailed accounts of that episode which the Westminster chronicle contains. Scarle's will is dated 22 April 1403 and he was dead by 25 April. He was buried at St Bride's Church, Fleet Street, London. A. K. McHardy

Sources *Chancery records* • [J. Raine], ed., *Testamenta Eboracensia*, 3, SurtS, 45 (1865) • PRO, special collection 10 (parliamentary proxies), files 34–40 • Tout, *Admin. hist.*, vols. 3–4, 6 • *Fasti Angl., 1300–1541*, [Lincoln; Salisbury; Coventry; York] • *Fasti Angl., 1300–1541*, [Coventry] • *Fasti Angl., 1300–1541*, [York] • *Fasti Angl., 1300–1541*, [Salisbury] • L. C. Hector and B. F. Harvey, eds. and trans., *The Westminster chronicle, 1381–1394*, OMT (1982) • C. W. Smith, 'A conflict of interest? chancery clerks in private service', *People, politics and community in the later middle ages*, ed. J. Rosenthal and C. Richmond (1987), 176–91 • A. Rogers, 'The political crisis of 1401', *Nottingham Mediaeval Studies*, 12 (1968), 85–96 • *Registrum Simonis de Sudbiria, diocesis Londoniensis, AD 1362–1375*, ed. R. C. Fowler, 2, CYS, 38 (1938) • R. Somerville, *History of the duchy of Lancaster, 1265–1603* (1953)

Archives PRO, special collection 10 (parliamentary proxies)

Wealth at death over £500 in bequests, excl. bequests in kind: will

Scarlett, James, first Baron Abinger (**1769–1844**), judge, was born on 13 December 1769 in Duckett's Spring, St James's parish, Jamaica, the second son of Robert Scarlett of Duckett's Spring and his wife, Elizabeth Wright, a widow, and daughter of Colonel Philip Anglin of Paradise estate, Jamaica. His younger brother, Sir Philip Anglin Scarlett (*d.* 1831), was for some years chief justice of Jamaica. In the summer of 1785 James was sent to England in order to complete his education and he was admitted a member of the Inner Temple on 9 September 1785. After a short period at a public school, he was admitted as a fellow commoner at Trinity College, Cambridge, where he took up residence in November 1785. While at the university he refused to join the 'True Blue Club', and was known as being extremely studious; he formed a friendship with John Baynes, a fellow of Trinity, from whom he received much assistance with his studies. Anxious to establish a career, Scarlett did not wait to take honours, and graduated BA in June 1789. On the advice of his mentor, Samuel Romilly, after taking up his quarters in the Temple Scarlett studied law for a year by himself, and subsequently became the pupil of George Wood, the special pleader, who afterwards became a baron of the exchequer. He was called to the bar on 28 July 1791, and graduated MA in 1794. After some doubts, for he was entirely without professional connections, he joined the northern circuit and the Lancashire sessions. His success was gradual and the result of steady application.

On 22 August 1792, a year after he had been called to the bar, Scarlett married Louisa Henrietta (*d.* 1829), the third daughter of Peter Campbell of Kilmory, Argyll. They had three sons, Robert Scarlett, second Baron Abinger (1794–1861), James Yorke *Scarlett, and Peter Campbell *Scarlett, and two daughters, Mary Elizabeth (*d.* 1860) and Louise Lawrence (*d.* 1871). Scarlett's marriage was a bold venture, as his professional income did not exceed his expenditure until 1798, when his father died. He left the Lancashire sessions, where he had obtained a great deal of work, in 1807. Although soon afterwards he found his services in wide demand, he ultimately confined himself to the court of king's bench and the northern circuit. Although he applied to Lord Eldon for silk in 1807, he did not become a king's counsel until March 1816.

But from this time until 1834 Scarlett 'had a longer series of success than has ever fallen to the lot of any other man in the law' (Scarlett, 71). As the most successful advocate of his day, the largest income which he made in one year at the bar appears to have been £18,500, but his income as a judge was considerably higher. Even after being elected to parliament, Scarlett frequently took long absences in order to make money at the bar—a practice widely condemned by political pamphleteers, including William Hone in *The Political A-Apple Pie* (8th edn, 1820). He purchased the seat and estate at Abinger in Surrey in 1813, and was called to the bench of the Inner Temple three years later.

As Scarlett was neither a great legal thinker nor a particularly eloquent speaker, his reputation as a lawyer rests on his advocacy, shown at its best in his defences of Lord Cochrane and John Hatchard. His quick perception, lucid presentation of evidence, and single-minded focus on the achievement of a favourable verdict, enhanced by his handsome appearance and finely modulated voice, made him a compelling presence in court. He was an effective cross-examiner, but excelled particularly in re-examinations. His persuasiveness as an advocate won him influence over judges as well as juries; indeed, his influence over Lord Tenterden was so marked as to become a subject of complaint at the bar. A joke circulated among lawyers that Scarlett had developed a machine which made judges nod their assent at his arguments. His determination as a prosecutor was apparent at the trial of Henry Hunt, where he was counsel for the crown; his skill was in fact crucial to the success of the government's case against the Peterloo protesters. As a judge, he proved less memorable. Occasionally, he could seem both biased and vain while presiding in court, and he rarely presented more than one side of the case to the jury, who sometimes refused to submit to his dictation.

From 1812, Scarlett coupled political interests with his legal career. He unsuccessfully contested the borough of Lewes as a whig candidate in October that year and again in March 1816. Several offers of a seat were made to him if he would consent to support the tory government, but, though their acceptance would have led to immediate advancement to office, Scarlett refused them all. At last, through the influence of Earl Fitzwilliam, he won a seat at Peterborough at a by-election early in February 1819. He spoke for the first time in the House of Commons during the debate on the Windsor establishment on 22 February. His speech on that occasion was pronounced by Lord Brougham to have been 'one of the most able speeches that any professional man ever made' (H. Brougham, *Life and Times of Henry, Lord Brougham*, 1871, 3.471), but his subsequent parliamentary orations were rarely as memorable as his maiden speech, and Scarlett failed to sustain in the House of Commons the high reputation which he had gained in the law courts. On 3 March 1819 he supported Sir James Mackintosh's motion for the appointment of a select committee on criminal law and was named for it himself. In June he opposed Vansittart's demand for additional taxation, and spoke strongly against the Foreign Enlistment Bill.

Although Scarlett had prosecuted riot and sedition cases arising from the Peterloo massacre in 1819, on 13 December he protested against the Seditious Meetings Prevention Bill, viewing its provisions as 'inimical to the liberties of the country'. He also spoke against the Blasphemous Libel Bill in the same month, and eventually sponsored a liberal reform act which abolished banishment as a penalty in seditious and blasphemous libel cases, a modification of the terms of the Six Acts.

Scarlett was re-elected for Peterborough at the general election in March 1820. On 26 June he denounced the appointment of a secret committee of inquiry into the queen's conduct, and he continued his support for Caroline in January 1821, when he attacked the government for having prejudged the queen's case by omitting her name from the liturgy. Other matters soon claimed his attention. On 8 May 1821 he introduced a bill to amend the English poor law which was read a second time on the 24th of the same month, but was subsequently withdrawn. On 31 May 1822 he moved the second reading of his Poor Removal Bill. Although the measure was defeated, some of its provisions were regarded by Beatrice and Sidney Webb, in their seminal work *English Poor Law History* (1927–9), as the groundwork for the more celebrated reforms of the 1830s.

Scarlett resigned his seat at Peterborough in order to contest Cambridge University at a by-election in November 1822. Although there were two tory candidates in the field, he was easily beaten, and in February 1823 he was re-elected for his old constituency, which he continued to represent until July 1830. In a memorable speech in March 1824 he expressed his resentment at Lord Eldon's attack on the whig James Abercromby. In the following year he unsuccessfully opposed the third reading of the bill for altering the law of principal and factor.

When the liberal tory Canning became prime minister

in 1827, Scarlett, with the consent of the whig leaders, accepted the post of attorney-general, and was knighted (30 April). When Canning's successor, Lord Goderich, was in power, Scarlett proposed the repeal of the Foreign Enlistment Act and the two libel acts of 1819. Although invited by the king and the duke of Wellington to continue in office, Scarlett resigned on the duke's accession to power in January 1828. While supporting the bill making provision for Canning's family on 22 May, Scarlett declared him to be the politician with whose views he most sympathized.

Scarlett succeeded Sir Charles Wetherell as attorney-general in the duke of Wellington's administration on 29 June 1829, declaring that he reserved the right of acting independently of the government on the question of reform. As chief law officer he exhibited much hostility to the press, and at his instance several informations were filed against the *Morning Journal*, *Atlas*, and other papers, for libels on the duke of Wellington and the lord chancellor. On 9 March 1830 he introduced a bill for improving the administration of justice, which received the royal assent on 23 July 1830. By this act separate jurisdiction for the county palatine of Chester and the principality of Wales was abolished, and provision was made for the appointment of three additional judges. At the same time the court of exchequer was opened to general practice, and fixed days were appointed for the commencement and close of terms. At Lord Fitzwilliam's request Scarlett retired from the representation of Peterborough at the dissolution of parliament in July 1830, and became a candidate for the borough of Malton, for which he was returned at the general election in the following month. On the duke of Wellington's downfall in November 1830 Scarlett resigned his office.

Scarlett appears to have thought himself badly treated by the new whig ministry, and was offended by the appointment of Lord Lyndhurst, instead of himself, to the exchequer in January 1831. He had never had much interest in parliamentary reform, and after some hesitation he decided to oppose the Reform Bill. On 22 March 1831 he spoke against the second reading, arguing that if the bill passed it would destroy first the House of Commons, and then the entire British constitution. A few days later he accepted the Chiltern Hundreds. Casting in his lot with the tory party, he was returned for Lord Lonsdale's borough of Cockermouth in the general election of April 1831. On 19 September 1831 he protested strongly against the third reading of the second Reform Bill with dire predictions of the repeal of the corn laws and the confiscation of church property.

At the general election in December 1832 Scarlett and Lord Stormont stood as the tory candidates for Norwich and were returned at the head of the poll. The return was petitioned against, but an investigating committee declared the election valid; Scarlett continued to sit for Norwich until the dissolution of parliament.

Scarlett was appointed lord chief baron of the exchequer on 24 December 1834 in the place of Lord Lyndhurst, who had been made chancellor for the second time. Before his appointment to the exchequer, Scarlett was sworn of the privy council and made a serjeant-at-law. He was created Baron Abinger of Abinger in the county of Surrey and of the city of Norwich on 12 January 1835, and took his seat in the House of Lords for the first time on 20 February 1836. He was the first chief baron to gain a peerage while in office. In the same year he was created an LLD of Cambridge.

Abinger took little part in the debates of the upper house. Several of his judicial opinions, however, were of lasting consequence, particularly in cases of tort (*Winterbottom* v. *Wright*, 1842) and contract law (*Carrington* v. *Roots*, 1837). In the 1837 decision of *Priestley* v. *Fowler*, Abinger promulgated the rule that an employer was not responsible for the negligence of his agents or employees, provided that the person injured was also an employee (and thus a 'fellow-servant' of the negligent party). The fellow-servant ruling was used by subsequent judges in England and the United States as a method of keeping the costs of workplace accidents from falling on employers.

On 21 February 1843 the radical politician T. S. Duncombe called the attention of the House of Commons to the 'partial, unconstitutional, and oppressive' conduct of Abinger while presiding over the special commission issued for Lancashire and Cheshire. The language used by Abinger in his charges to the grand juries on this occasion was undoubtedly indiscreet and seemed motivated by his fear of Chartism. Although the motion for an inquiry was defeated by 228 votes to 73, Abinger was obliged to defend his conduct.

On 28 September 1843 Abinger married his second wife, Elizabeth (*d.* 1886), widow of the Revd Henry John Ridley, rector of Abinger, and daughter of Lee Steere Steere of Jayes, in Wotton, Surrey. He did not long survive this marriage, of which there were no children. Having presided in the exchequer court for more than nine years, Abinger attended the Norfolk circuit in the spring of 1844, apparently in good health. But after a day's work in court at Bury St Edmunds on 2 April, he suffered a stroke and died at his lodgings in the town on 7 April. He was buried in the family vault in Abinger churchyard on 14 April.

G. F. R. Barker, *rev.* Elisabeth A. Cawthon

Sources P. C. Scarlett, *A memoir of the right honourable James, first Lord Abinger* (1877) • *Law Times* (13 April 1844), 27–9 • *The Times* (9 April 1844) • [A. Hayward], 'The first Lord Abinger and the bar', *QR*, 144 (1877), 1–45 [review] • Holdsworth, *Eng. law*, 15.466–75 • Foss, *Judges* • L. W. Levy, *The law of the Commonwealth and Chief Justice Shaw* (1957) • HoP, *Commons* • GEC, *Peerage* • Burke, *Peerage* • *Hansard 2* • E. A. Cawthon, 'Origins of the fellow-servant rule', MA diss., University of Virginia (1981) • C. Tomlins, 'A mysterious power: industrial relations and the legal construction of employer relations in Massachusetts, 1800–1850', *Law and History Review* (1988), 375–438

Archives BL, corresp. with Lord Holland, Add. MS 51813 • BL, corresp. with Sir Robert Peel, Add. MSS 40379–40530 • N. Yorks. CRO, corresp. with Christopher Wyvill • Sheff. Arch., letters to Earl Fitzwilliam and Lord Milton

Likenesses B. Holl, stipple, pubd 1824 (after C. Penny), BM, NPG • J. Doyle, pencil caricature, 1829, BM • H. Cousins, mezzotint, pubd 1837 (after M. A. Shee), BM, NPG • W. Derby, portrait, exh. South Kensington 1868 • Bentivoglio, caricature, etching, BM, NPG

Scarlett, Sir James Yorke (1799–1871), army officer, born in London on 1 February 1799, was the second son of James *Scarlett, first Baron Abinger (1769–1844), and his first wife, Louisa Henrietta (*d.* 1829), daughter of Peter Campbell of Kilmory, Argyll. Peter Campbell *Scarlett was his younger brother. Educated at Eton College and Trinity College, Cambridge (matriculated 1816), he was gazetted cornet 18th light dragoons in 1818, and, being placed on half pay, studied for a year at the senior department of the Royal Military College, Sandhurst. In December 1822 he transferred to the 6th dragoon guards as lieutenant, and in June 1825 got his captaincy. In 1830 he was gazetted major 5th dragoon guards. On 19 December 1835 he married Charlotte Anne, daughter and coheir of Colonel Hargreaves of Burnley, Lancashire; they had no children, and Charlotte survived him.

From 1836 to 1841 Scarlett was Conservative MP for Guildford, taking no very active part in political life, but voting unwaveringly with his party. In July 1840 Major Scarlett was promoted to the command of his regiment, and henceforward the 5th dragoon guards became known as especially efficient. He commanded for nearly fourteen years. In 1853 he was considering retiring into private life, but in 1854 he was appointed to the command of the heavy brigade in the eastern campaign. He sailed for Turkey; at Varna, where a large proportion of his former regiment, the 18th, had been suddenly struck down by cholera, he at once made his way to the hospitals, and by his cheerful manner reduced the panic that had seized the men. Towards the end of September 1854 he went with the heavy brigade, following after the bulk of the army which had fought the battle of the Alma, to the Crimea, and as brigadier before Sevastopol saw his first shot fired.

Early in the morning of 25 October a large Russian force, including a strong force of cavalry under Liprandi, attacked and captured some of the earthworks which protected the allied rear; advancing rapidly, the Russians began to threaten the British base and harbour near Balaklava. At the first sign of attack Scarlett had his brigade under arms, and, after making some show of threatening the enemy, received orders from Lord Raglan to move from the picket lines in rear of the right of the British army to Kadikoi, an important tactical point. While they were marching there the terrain concealed the further Russian advance, so that Scarlett suddenly discovered, nearby on his left flank, about 2000 enemy cavalry. Both the forces were astounded at the encounter. The Russians halted first, but, perceiving their opportunity, began to advance at a rapid trot, with the apparent intention of charging Scarlett's exposed flank. The threat was met with audacity: Scarlett ordered 'left wheel into line' to the three squadrons nearest to him—Inniskilling and Scots Greys—and, placing himself at the head of this small force of barely 300, drove straight uphill at the enemy, who gradually slackened to a slow trot, a walk, and finally halted. Shortly after, the charge was supported by the remaining squadrons, about 400 men, and then the unwieldy column of Russian cavalry heaved, swayed to and fro, and finally broke up.

Sir James Yorke Scarlett (1799–1871), by E. Goodwyn Lewis, 1861

The famous charge of the light brigade occurred later that day. When its remnants came straggling back, and the previous flanking fire from the Russian guns had been almost silenced, Scarlett attempted to secure some substantial advantages from the tragic exploit. Putting himself at the head of his dragoons, which had been drawn up in reserve, he led the way to a second charge down 'the valley of death'. While advancing at a sharp pace, his aide-de-camp, Colonel Beatson, shot up alongside of him and shouted out that he was charging the Russians alone; his brigade had gone 'threes about'. Angry, Scarlett galloped back, and was told by Lord Lucan, the cavalry commander, that he had ordered the retreat. Scarlett maintained thereafter that if he had been allowed to persevere he might have captured and carried off the twelve Russian guns at the head of the valley, and would certainly have cut off a large number of fugitive cavalry near the Traktir Bridge. For his services at Balaklava he was promoted a major-general, and in 1855 he was made a KCB.

In April 1855 Scarlett returned to England, but was soon appointed to succeed Lord Lucan in the command of the British cavalry in the Crimea, with the local rank of lieutenant-general. Although family reasons made him at first reluctant to accept the post, he returned to the Crimea. The original splendid force of cavalry which had landed there in 1854 had, by the time he assumed chief command in 1855, been almost annihilated by active service, climate, and disease. Large drafts of recruits had been sent out to fill up the gaps, and by unremitting labour and drill Scarlett, by the spring of 1856, had brought them to a condition of efficiency, though he said he would not have fought another Balaklava with them.

At the end of the war Scarlett was appointed to command the cavalry at Aldershot; from there he was transferred to Portsmouth, and in 1860 was gazetted adjutant-general to the forces and lieutenant-general in 1862. In 1865 he was selected for the prize of home appointments, command of the Aldershot camp. During the latter part of his tenure of office Prussian victories caused a revolution in tactics. New conditions of warfare necessitated a change in instruction. Scarlett said that he was too old for this and had better leave the task to younger men.

In his closing years Scarlett was one of the last survivors of the blue and buff school of tories. In 1869 he was created a GCB, and on 1 November 1870, on resigning the Aldershot command, he retired from active duty with the rank of general. He died suddenly on 6 December 1871 at his residence, Bank Hall, near Burnley, Lancashire.

HENRY KNOLLYS, *rev.* JAMES FALKNER

Sources *Army List* • Marquess of Anglesey [G. C. H. V. Paget], *A history of the British cavalry, 1816 to 1919*, 2 (1975) • A. W. Kinglake, *The invasion of the Crimea*, 8 vols. (1863–87) • *Hart's Army List* • *Journal of the Society for Army Historical Research*, 19 (1940), 98 • S. J. G. Calthorpe, *Letters from head-quarters … by a staff officer*, 2 vols. (1856) [with illustrations by G. Cadogan]; abridged edn as *Cadogan's Crimea* (1979) • GEC, *Peerage* • Burke, *Peerage* • Walford, *County families* • *Parliamentary Pocket Companion* (1858) • Boase, *Mod. Eng. biog.* • Venn, *Alum. Cant.* • *CGPLA Eng. & Wales* (1872)

Likenesses group portrait, photograph, 1860 (with staff), NAM • E. Goodwyn Lewis, pastel drawing, 1861, Towneley Hall Art Gallery, Burnley, Lancashire [*see illus.*] • E. Havell, drawing, 1868, Towneley Hall Art Gallery, Burnley, Lancashire • M. Noble, marble bust, 1873, Towneley Hall Art Gallery, Burnley, Lancashire; related plaster cast, NPG • P. Grant, oils, priv. coll. • engraving, repro. in *ILN* (16 Dec 1871), 567 • two photographs, Towneley Hall Art Gallery, Burnley, Lancashire • woodcut, NPG; repro. in *Illustrated Times* (16 Dec 1871), 377

Wealth at death under £200,000: administration with will, 14 Nov 1872, *CGPLA Eng. & Wales*

Scarlett, Nathaniel (1753–1802), bookseller and translator, was born on 28 September 1753, the son of Bartholomew Scarlett and his wife, Elizabeth. He was educated at Kingswood School, Wiltshire, and from 1767 at Merchant Taylors' School, London. Originally apprenticed as a shipwright, he was afterwards an accountant and projected the *Commercial Almanac*. Eventually he became a bookseller at 349 Strand, London.

Originally a Methodist, Scarlett became a Universalist and therefore came to believe in universal redemption. He joined the Parliament Court Universalist congregation in Artillery Lane, Bishopsgate, London, where the American Elhanan Winchester was pastor, and was closely associated with Winchester's successor, William Vidler. Vidler was briefly a partner in Scarlett's book shop but withdrew when Scarlett published *The British Theatre*. Their closest association was in a Universalist New Testament translation project based on a manuscript translation by an Anglican clergyman, James Creighton. Once a week Vidler, Creighton, John Cue (a Sandemanian), and Scarlett met at Scarlett's house for breakfast and 'compared Creighton's translation with all Mr. Scarlett's collations and with the Greek, and disputed on them till they could agree' (*Monthly Repository*, 13, 1818, 6). Passages on which they disagreed were taken home after tea for private consideration, and resolved by majority voting. The final arrangement, *A Translation of the New Testament from the Original Greek: Humbly Attempted by Nathaniel Scarlett Assisted by Men of Piety and Literature* (1798), was arranged in dramatic form, and Scarlett calculated that it would take fourteen hours to read. The translation distinguishes between 'the saved' who needed no future punishment and 'the restored' who did. Hence God, who is love, is the saviour of the elect, but the restorer of all. Scarlett also contributed prose and verse to Vidler's *Universal Theological Magazine*.

Scarlett was married, although the identity of his wife is unknown; the couple had at least one child. He died on 18 November 1802.

ALEXANDER GORDON, *rev.* ANDREW M. HILL

Sources *Monthly Repository*, 12 (1817), 193 • *Monthly Repository*, 13 (1818), 6 • *Universal Theological Magazine* (Nov 1802), 279–80 • T. Whittemore, *The modern history of Universalism from the era of the Reformation to the present time* (1830), 293–7 • *Historical catalogue of the printed editions of Holy Scripture in the library of the British and Foreign Bible Society*, 1 (1903), 314–15 • V. Berch, 'The London book trades of the later 18th century', ed. I. Maxted, www.devon.gov.uk/library/locstudy/bookhist/berch.html, 8 May 2002

Scarlett, Peter Campbell (1804–1881), diplomatist, born in Spring Gardens, London, on 27 November 1804, was the youngest son of James *Scarlett, first Baron Abinger (1769–1844), and his wife, Louisa Henrietta (*d.* 1829), daughter of Peter Campbell of Kilmory, Argyll. General Sir James Yorke *Scarlett was his brother. After education at a private school at East Sheen and at Eton College, he went in 1824 to Trinity College, Cambridge. He had been intended for the bar, but George Canning seems to have persuaded his father to send him into the diplomatic service. Accordingly on 10 October 1825 he became an attaché at Constantinople in the suite of Sir Stratford Canning. Having moved to Paris on 1 June 1828, he was a witness of the revolution in 1830 and was for a time made prisoner by the mob. He was appointed paid attaché to Brazil in February 1834, and left England for Rio de Janeiro on 2 August 1834. In the course of 1835–6 he made an excursion across the Pampas and Andes, a full account of which he published under the title of *South America and the Pacific* (2 vols., 1838). The book has an interesting appendix on Pacific steam communication. Ill health interrupted his diplomatic career, and he acted as marshal to his father, then chief baron of the exchequer. On 3 April 1844 he resumed work abroad as secretary of legation at Florence, and was made a CB on 19 September 1854. On 31 December 1855 he was promoted to be envoy-extraordinary and minister-plenipotentiary at Rio, but on 13 December 1858 went back to Florence as minister. After the union of Italy in 1860 the mission was abolished, and Scarlett retired on a pension. On 12 June 1862 he was again employed as envoy-extraordinary at Athens, and in

November 1864, after a prolonged stay in England, was transferred to the court of the emperor Maximilian in Mexico. There, as at Athens, he witnessed the deposition of the reigning sovereign. On 11 October 1867 he retired finally on pension.

Scarlett during his retirement gathered materials for the life of his father, published as *A Memoir of the Right Honourable James, First Lord Abinger* (1877). He married twice: first, Frances Sophia Mostyn, who was the second daughter of Edmund Lomax of Parkhurst, and who died in 1849; second, on 27 December 1873, Louisa Anne Jeannin, daughter of J. Wolfe Murray, and widow of Edmond Jeannin. Scarlett died at his house, Parkhurst, Dorking, on 15 July 1881, leaving one son, Leopold James Yorke Campbell, a colonel in the Scots Guards, and one daughter, Florence, who married Sir John *Walsham.

C. A. Harris, *rev.* H. C. G. Matthew

Sources *FO List* (1880) • *The Times* (16 July 1881)
Archives Hants. RO, corresp. with third earl of Malmesbury and others • PRO, corresp. with Lord John Russell, PRO 30/22
Wealth at death £13,123 17*s*. 11*d*.: probate, 15 Aug 1881, *CGPLA Eng. & Wales*

Scarlett, Robert [*called* Old Scarlett] (**1495x9–1594**), sexton, has long been a celebrated figure in the communal memory of Peterborough, notable alike for his functions and his longevity. According to a verse inscription accompanying a portrait which now hangs above the south side of the west door of Peterborough Cathedral, he buried two queens there—Katherine of Aragon and Mary, queen of Scots—and also oversaw the burial of two generations of townsfolk in the town cemetery to the north of the cathedral precinct. No independent evidence confirms his role in the royal funerals, but his ecclesiastical employment, primarily by the churchwardens and parishioners of the church of St John the Baptist in the market place, is well attested. He is first recorded in 1532/3, when he paid 4*d*. for having the church's great bell rung, presumably to mark the death of a relative. In 1541 he received 2*d*. for putting out a hearse, and further payments to him are recorded at least into the 1570s. As well as gravedigging, his tasks included ringing bells, keeping the churchyard and church roofs clean, and supplying the communion bread and wine. Only once was he employed directly by the cathedral authorities, when in 1548/9 he received 4*d*. for taking lead to the chapter house.

In 1572/3, in recognition of his services and his poverty and old age, Scarlett received 8*s*. in addition to his wages, 'beyng a poore olde man and rysing oft in the nightes to tolle the bell for sicke persons, the wether beyng grevous, and in consideracion of his good service towardes a gowne to keep him warm' (Mellows, *Churchwardens' Accounts*, 176). A householder in the market place by 1538, he was still living there in 1585, and in all likelihood until his death. He died in 1594, still sexton, his burial being recorded in the parish register on 2 July. The date is repeated on a stone at the west end of the cathedral, which adds that he was aged ninety-eight; however, a manuscript note claims that he was no more than ninety-five. His wife, Margaret, had died ten years earlier, but on 5 December 1585 he married Maud Gosling, presumably the Maud Scarlett of Peterborough, widow, who made her will on 20 July 1608 and had died by 19 March following.

Robert Scarlett's fame was such that his image was preserved within the cathedral. The earliest portrait, in a mural over the north side of the west door, shows a spare and upright figure in doublet and hose, with keys in one hand and a long spade in the other, and one foot in an arcaded structure probably representing a sepulchre. It differs considerably from the oil painting which subsequently concealed it. The latter, a copy made in 1747 (itself restored in 1961) of a picture painted in 1665, shows a shorter, stouter man wearing a skullcap, with a whip in his belt, and likewise holding spade and keys; a skull lying on the ground illustrates his employment. Subsequent commemorations have included a column in a local newspaper, the name of a public house, and a cantata performed at the Peterborough Cathedral organ festival in 1982.

Henry Summerson

Sources G. Dixon, *Old Scarlett*, 2nd edn (1997) • W. T. Mellows, ed., *Peterborough local administration … 1107–1488*, Northamptonshire RS, 9 (1939) • W. T. Mellows, ed., *Peterborough local administration: the foundation of Peterborough Cathedral, AD 1541*, Northamptonshire RS, 13 (1941) [1941 for 1939] • W. T. Mellows, ed., *Peterborough local administration: the last days of Peterborough monastery*, Northamptonshire RS, 12 (1947) • W. T. Mellows and D. H. Giffard, eds., *Peterborough local administration: Elizabethan Peterborough*, Northamptonshire RS, 18 (1956) • S. Gunton, *The history of the church of Peterburgh* (1686); repr. (1990) • W. D. Sweeting, 'Monumental inscriptions in Peterborough Cathedral, IV: Old Scarlett', *Northamptonshire Notes and Queries*, 1 (1886), 249–51 • *DNB* • Northants. RO, MW 88 250 1608 P. Will
Likenesses W. Williams, etching (after oils, Peterborough Cathedral), BM, NPG • mural, Peterborough Cathedral; repro. in Dixon, *Old Scarlett* • oils, Peterborough Cathedral; repro. in Dixon, *Old Scarlett*

Scarning, Roger of (*d*. **1278**), bishop of Norwich, probably came from Scarning in north Norfolk. He became a monk at Norwich Cathedral priory, where he was elected prior in 1257, probably between 23 June and 9 December. Nothing is known of his life as prior, but he must have found favour with the monks, for on 23 January 1266 they elected him as bishop of the diocese. His election was confirmed by the papal legate, Ottobuono, temporalities were restored on 17 March, and he was consecrated on 4 April, again by the legate. Throughout his life he retained a close interest in the affairs of the priory. His *acta* show him granting the church of Great Cressingham to the cellarer because that office was overburdened, the church of St Etheldreda was transferred to the refectioner when that official took over the supply of linen for the refectory, and the church of St Gregory was given to the hosteler so that he might better supply those visiting the priory.

Scarning's episcopate was anything but peaceful. First he was forced to flee Norwich and take refuge in Bury St Edmunds when the city was attacked by the 'disinherited', those remnants from the barons' war holding out in the Isle of Ely. More disturbing was the riot of 11 August 1272, when the cathedral priory was attacked and despoiled by townspeople. The outraged monks appealed to both the secular and the ecclesiastical authorities. It was inevitable that the bishop would side with the priory. Scarning called a meeting of the clergy at Eye, and on 29 August excommunicated the leaders of the riot and put the city under an interdict. A more balanced approach was taken by Henry III who went to Norwich on 14 September. The priory was taken into the king's hands, and the prior was persuaded to resign on 27 September. The interdict, which had been relaxed on the king's coming to Norwich, was reimposed on 18 October, and although it was relaxed again for Christmas, was later renewed. The case was sent to Rome and long negotiations ensued. Matters were not finally settled until 1275, when the interdict, which with sundry relaxations had lasted throughout the proceedings, was finally removed. Scarning may well have played a part in these negotiations. The priory had also to organize an expensive repair and cleaning operation, to which the bishop contributed at least £15. Scarning died on 22 January 1278 at the episcopal manor of South Elmham and was buried in the lady chapel of the cathedral on 28 January. BARBARA DODWELL

Sources *Bartholomaei de Cotton … Historia Anglicana*, ed. H. R. Luard, Rolls Series, 16 (1859), 137, 141, 148–50, 153, 156, 395 · T. Arnold, ed., *Memorials of St Edmund's Abbey*, 2, Rolls Series, 96 (1892), 36 · T. Arnold, ed., *Memorials of St Edmund's Abbey*, 3, Rolls Series, 96 (1896), 31 · A. Gransden, ed. and trans., *The chronicle of Bury St Edmunds, 1212–1301* [1964], 51–2, 65 · *Fasti Angl., 1066–1300*, [Monastic cathedrals], 57–8, 61 · H. W. Saunders, ed., *The first register of Norwich Cathedral priory*, Norfolk RS, 11 (1939), 142–6 · B. Dodwell, ed., *The charters of Norwich Cathedral priory*, 1, PRSoc., 40, new ser., 78 (1974), 128–37 · F. Blomefield and C. Parkin, *An essay towards a topographical history of the county of Norfolk*, [2nd edn], 11 vols. (1805–10), vol. 3, pp. 53–6, 493–4 · E. M. Goulburn, H. Symonds, and E. Hailstone, *The ancient sculptures of the roof of Norwich Cathedral* (1876), 369–86 · Norfolk RO, DCN 1/4/3

Scarsdale. For this title name *see* Curzon, Nathaniel, first Baron Scarsdale (1726–1804).

Scarth, Alice Mary Elizabeth (1848–1889). *See under* Scarth, Harry Mengden (1814–1890).

Scarth, Harry Mengden (1814–1890), antiquary, born at Durham on 11 May 1814, was the son of Thomas Freshfield Scarth of Keverstone, Staindrop, co. Durham, chief agent to successive dukes of Cleveland, and his wife, Mary, *née* Milbank, of Gainford, near Darlington. After having received his early education at the Edinburgh Academy he entered Christ's College, Cambridge, as a pensioner in 1833, graduated BA in 1837, proceeded MA in 1841, and was admitted *ad eundem* at Oxford on 1 December 1842. He was ordained deacon at Lichfield in 1837 and priest in 1840, and from 1837 to 1841 held the curacy of Eaton Constantine, Shropshire. He left in 1841, having been presented by William Henry, first duke of Cleveland, to the rectory of Kenley in the same county. By the same patron he was presented in 1841 to the rectory of Bathwick, Bath, with Woolley, Somerset. In 1871 Harry George, fourth duke of Cleveland, presented him to the rectory of Wrington, Somerset, which he held until his death. He was prebendary of Wells from 1848 to 1890 and was rural dean of Portishead from about 1880.

On 15 November 1842 Scarth married Elizabeth Sally (*d.* 1876), the daughter of John Leveson Hamilton (*d.* 1825), rector of Ellesborough, Buckinghamshire. They had seven children, of whom a son, Leveson Edward Scarth, and two unmarried daughters survived him. Scarth was a moderate high-churchman and a good parish priest. He was much esteemed in Bath, and a window was erected to his memory by public subscription in St Mary's Church, Bathwick.

Scarth ranked among the best English authorities on Roman antiquities, especially the relics of the Roman occupation of Britain, but he overstated the influence of the occupation. His principal publications are *Aquae Solis, or, Notices of Roman Bath* (1864) and *Roman Britain* (n.d. [1883]) in a series entitled Early Britain (Society for Promoting Christian Knowledge). From 1885 he was a constant contributor to the *Proceedings of the Society of Antiquaries*, and his paper 'The camps on the River Avon at Clifton' was published in *Archaeologia* (no. 44, p. 428). He also contributed to the journals of the Archaeological Institute, the Archaeological Association, and the Somersetshire Archaeological and Natural History Society.

Scarth died at Tangier, Morocco, on 5 April 1890, and was buried at Wrington.

His eldest daughter, **Alice Mary Elizabeth Scarth** (1848–1889), writer, born in Bath on 24 December 1848, published *The story of the old Catholic and other kindred movements leading up to a union of national independent churches* (1883). WILLIAM HUNT, *rev.* ELIZABETH BAIGENT

Sources *Proceedings of the Society of Antiquaries of London*, 2nd ser., 13 (1889–91), 141 · Crockford (1837–90) · Venn, *Alum. Cant.* · *The Guardian* (16 April 1890) · *CGPLA Eng. & Wales* (1890) · *Proceedings of the Somersetshire Archaeological and Natural History Society*, 36/2 (1890), 198–9 · private information (1897) · *Saturday Review*, 56 (1883), 769–70

Wealth at death £4400 4*s*. 4*d*.: probate, 16 Aug 1890, *CGPLA Eng. & Wales*

Scatcherd, Felicia Rudolphina (1862–1927), journalist and spiritualist, was born on 10 August 1862 at 7 Chepstow Place, Kensington, London. Her father, Watson Scatcherd (*fl.* 1825–1901), had retired from the Indian Civil Service on marrying her mother, Emily Frances Crofton (*d.* 1901), two years previously. Her family, the Croftons of Mohill in co. Galway, had a long tradition of service to the British state.

Felicia Scatcherd lived with her parents until her mother's death in 1901. Emily introduced her to W. T. Stead, crusading editor of the *Pall Mall Gazette* who set her, as with so many other young women, on the path towards fulfilment. Like Stead she was active in two principal fields: spiritualism and international politics. Her talent for journalism led to her becoming editor of the *Psychic Review*. Fluent in French, she wrote and lectured on the continent in support of mediums, and as an expert in spirit photography. She was a means whereby Sir Arthur Conan Doyle gained access to the—later notorious—photos of the Cottingley fairies. Stead enlisted her as a member of Julia's Bureau, his clearing-house of information from the other side (named after the American Julia Ames, who died in 1891).

Scatcherd was proud of her ancestor Richard 'Humanity' Martin (1754–1834), one of the founders of the Society for the Prevention of Cruelty to Animals (1824), and author of the first modern act of parliament preventing cruelty to cattle (3 Geo. IV c. 71). Her concern for animal welfare, especially on the continent, brought her into contact with the Humanitarian League and its supporter the Greek politician, writer, and founder of the socialist labour movement in Greece, Platon Soterios Drakoulès. Scatcherd lived with Drakoulès and his wife for many years, involving herself in his interests, including socialism and town planning, and sharing their travels, whose principal object was to negotiate a means of preventing a European war. At Constantinople they urged members of the Committee of Union and Progress—the Young Turks—to form an alliance with Britain, an initiative that came to nothing in 1913 when Enver Pasha opted to support Germany. In January 1912 Scatcherd was received at Cairo by ʿAbd al-Bahaʾ, leader of the Bahaʾi faith, whom the Young Turks had released from the prison city of Acre in 1908. Her book, *A Wise Man from the East*, told how she urged influential Turks to encourage such a movement in order 'to bring out the spiritual truths of Islam' (*International Psychic Gazette*, 1914), an intervention that was not well received.

As editor from 1916 to 1919 of the *Imperial and Asiatic Quarterly Review*, Scatcherd's object was to advance the allied cause. Success came when Greece declared war on Germany. Her friends also credited her with a decisive voice in the decision to call off the socialist-inspired conference for peace at Stockholm in 1917, to the great relief of the British government. An obituarist noted that she 'regarded the British empire as the greatest living force for world peace' (*Imperial and Asiatic Quarterly Review*, 191). In 1920, as a member of the council of the East India Association, she launched a fierce attack upon Annie Besant and Henry Hyndman for their support of home rule for India. Her own work to improve conditions for women in India (as also in Turkey) was done strictly in the context of the raj.

Felicia Scatcherd died of breast cancer at her London home, 14 Park Square East, St Pancras, on 12 March 1927, and was cremated at Golders Green five days later. Tributes were paid to her overflowing energy, and enthusiasm so unbridled it caused problems: 'Concentration on one subject with her was seldom for long' (*'Jordan Past': a Series of Communications from Felicia Rudolphina Scatcherd*, 1939, v). Conan Doyle portrayed her as Delicia Freeman, a small, determined lady always fishing in her bag extracting 'sometimes a leaflet on Armenia, sometimes a pamphlet on Greece, sometimes a note on Zenana missions, and sometimes a psychic manifesto' (*Land of Mist*, 1926, 205–6). A note of caution can be detected: 'her great heart coupled with her acute mind [elsewhere described as entirely masculine] would not allow her to become a crank', he reassured himself (*Imperial and Asiatic Quarterly Review*, 192). Crankiness is an effective disguise should one be needed. Whether Scatcherd's activities were entirely self-imposed or otherwise directed cannot now be known; notwithstanding, in serving the greater good of the British empire they were in the best tradition of the Crofton family.

ANNE TAYLOR

Sources *Imperial and Asiatic Quarterly Review*, new ser., 23 (Jan–Oct 1927), 191–2 • *Light* [Journal of the College of Psychic Studies], 47 (26 March 1927); (2 April 1927) • Burke, *Peerage* (1999) [Crofton of Mohill] • b. cert. • d. cert. • A. Conan Doyle, *The land of mist* (1926), 205–6 [portrays her as Delicia Freeman] • P.-E. Blanrue, 'Les "fées de Cottingley"', www.zetetique.ldh.org/cottingley.html, April 2001 • *Hastings and St Leonard's Observer* (19 March 1927) • P. Drakoulès, 'Greece, the Balkans, and the federal principle', *Imperial and Asiatic Quarterly Review* (27 Feb 1915) • [A. Drakoulès?], *Jordan past: a series of communications from Felicia Rudolphina Scatcherd* (1939) • J. Joll, *Europe since 1870* (1976), 226–7 • *CGPLA Eng. & Wales* (1927)

Likenesses photograph, repro. in *Light*

Wealth at death £2505 3s. 1d.: probate, 20 July 1927, *CGPLA Eng. & Wales*

Scatcherd, Norrisson Cavendish (1780–1853), antiquary, born at Morley, Yorkshire, on 29 February 1780, was the eldest son of Watson Scatcherd, a successful barrister on the northern circuit. His family had been resident at Morley for two centuries. After attending Hipperholme School he was called to the bar from Gray's Inn on 28 November 1806. His considerable private wealth, however, allowed him soon to leave the law to follow literary and antiquarian pursuits. On 16 January 1851 he was elected a fellow of the Society of Antiquaries. He died at Morley on 16 February 1853, leaving a widow and six children.

Scatcherd was author of *The History of Morley … Yorkshire* (1830), compiled from original sources, and two studies of a noted criminal and philologist: *Memoirs of the Celebrated Eugene Aram* (1832) and *Gleanings after Eugene Aram* (1840). He also wrote on Edward III's chapel (1843) and contributed to the *Gentleman's Magazine* and William Hone's *Year* and *Table* books.

GORDON GOODWIN, *rev.* H. C. G. MATTHEW

Sources W. Smith, *History of Morley* (1876) • W. Smith, *Morley, ancient and modern* (1886) • *GM*, 2nd ser., 39 (1853), 205 • *N&Q*, 6th ser., 2 (1880), 514 • *N&Q*, 6th ser., 3 (1881), 15, 158

Scattergood, Anthony (*bap.* 1611, *d.* 1687), Church of England clergyman, was baptized on 18 September 1611 at Ellastone, Staffordshire, the eldest of the twelve children of John Scattergood (*d.* 1662), attorney, of Chaddesden, Derbyshire, and his wife, Elizabeth (*bap.* 1591, *d.* 1663), daughter of Francis Baker, yeoman, of Ellastone and his wife, Ann. John Scattergood, unsuccessful in his king's bench practice and often in debt, had an uncle, William Fletcher, recorder of Nottingham, who paid for Anthony's schooling and may have helped send him to Cambridge. There he matriculated from Trinity College as a sizar on 17 December 1628, graduated BA in 1633, and proceeded MA in 1636. He was one of Trinity's four chaplains from 1637 to 1640, and a tutor in 1640.

Scattergood's commonplace book (BL, Add. MS 44963), dating from the 1630s, includes various Cambridge items—academic exercises, topical verses, a Latin play by Samuel Brooke—and most interesting selections from the contemporary poets Thomas Carew, Richard Corbet, Henry King, Thomas Randolph, William Strode, and others. W. C. Hazlitt printed some of the unpublished poems in *Inedited Poetical Miscellanies* (1870); H. J. Davis printed others (Davis, 684–90). Scattergood contributed his own poetry to the university's collections celebrating the births of royal children: *Ducis Eboracensis fasciae* (1633), *Carmen natalitium* (1635), and *Synōdia musarum Cantabrigiensium* (1637). He also composed Greek verses prefixed to James Duport's *Thrēnothriambos, sive, Liber Job* (1637).

Through the patronage of John Williams, bishop of Lincoln, Scattergood was installed as rector of Winwick, Northamptonshire, on 2 April 1641 and collated prebendary of Norton Episcopi in Lincoln Cathedral two weeks later. On 27 June 1644, while living in London, he married Martha Wharton (*bap.* 1617, *d.* 1654), daughter of Thomas Wharton, a Bishopsgate grocer. Their two sons and daughter were baptized at Winwick, and Martha was buried there on 13 December 1654. Scattergood remained rector of Winwick through the interregnum and is so described on the title page of his published sermon *The High Court of Justice*, preached at Leicester assizes on 30 July 1652. John Williams, when bishop of Lincoln, had entrusted him with the organization and care of his library, where he found an interesting bible commentary, compiled at some time since the 1570s. Having lost touch with Williams, who had soon become archbishop of York, Scattergood could never discover the author of the manuscript; he published it in 1653, as *Annotationes in Vetus Testamentum et in epistolam ad Ephesios*, and it was reprinted in 1704 and 1722.

On 8 March 1662 convocation appointed Scattergood, with Samuel Dillingham, to read the proofs of the revised Book of Common Prayer. Later that year he was created DD at Cambridge by a royal mandamus, dated 10 June, which singled out 'the Pains he hath taken to digest and fit that great Work the *Critici sacri* for the Press' (Kennet, 708). *Critici sacri* (1660), planned by the publisher Cornelius Bee as a companion to Brian Walton's polyglot Bible (1655–7), had been six years in production. Its nine folio volumes—nearly 10,000 pages—brought together at a price of £13 10*s.* some ninety bible commentaries and tracts by sixty-four sixteenth- and seventeenth-century scholars. Scattergood edited almost all of volumes 1–7 and a great part of volume 8. The other editors were John Pearson, Francis Gouldman, and Richard Pearson. In 1666 Bee complained of a rival project and of losing 1300 copies in the great fire; his proposed reprinting came to nothing, but new editions were later published at Frankfurt (1695–6) and Amsterdam (1698).

In three later scholarly enterprises it is hard to determine exactly what Scattergood did. On 9 January 1662 John Worthington wrote that Scattergood, 'an expert linguist', was revising Cornelius Schrevel's Greek lexicon (*Diary and Correspondence*, 2.95–6), but subsequent English editions of Schrevel make no mention of his contribution. He was also credited with increasing by some thousands of words the parallel texts cited in Cambridge bibles printed by John Hayes, but the sole copy of the first edition (dated or misdated '1678'), said to contain the additional citations, is no longer in Lambeth Palace Library. If that edition never actually existed Scattergood would have to have contributed either the additions of 1677 (beginning 'Psal. 102.25' beside Genesis 1: 1) or those of 1683 (beginning 'Joh. 1.1'), or perhaps both. Francis Gouldman's *Copious Dictionary* of English and Latin presents a different problem: the fourth edition's title page (1678) refers to 'many Thousand Words more added, by the Skill and Pains of Dr *Scattergood*', but it is hard to see where so many extra words could be.

In 1664 Scattergood published his Northampton assize sermon *Jethro's Character of Worthy Judges*. He continued to write poetry: a Greek ode of his is prefaced to James Duport's *Dabidēs emmetros, sive, Metaphrasis libri psalmorum* (1666). Duport wrote him a Latin poem in *Musae subsecivae* (1676), which plays on his name, 'Spargibonum', and praises his knowledge of Greek. On 16 August 1666 Scattergood was collated prebendary of Pipa Minor in Lichfield Cathedral, and on 18 February 1670 he was installed as rector of Yelvertoft, Northamptonshire. On 13 July 1669 he was incorporated DD at Oxford in the newly opened Sheldonian Theatre. He was chaplain to the bishop of Lichfield, John Hacket, a protégé and subsequently the biographer of Archbishop Williams. One of Hacket's sons had been apprenticed to a brother of Scattergood's in London. On 16 November 1670 Scattergood preached Hacket's funeral sermon. In 1672 he edited the second volume (*Forty-Seven Sermons*) of Anthony Farindon's *Eighty Sermons* and may have revised the first.

Scattergood resigned his Lichfield and Lincoln prebends in 1682 and 1683. He died on 30 July 1687 and was buried in the chancel of Yelvertoft church two days later. On 27 August letters of administration (archdeaconry of Northampton) were granted to his son Samuel. His library, sold after Samuel's death, is described below.

Samuel Scattergood (*bap.* 1646, *d.* 1696), Church of England clergyman, was baptized at Winwick on 16 April 1646, the elder son of Anthony Scattergood and his wife, Martha Wharton. He was admitted pensioner at Trinity College, Cambridge, on 20 May 1662 with James Duport as his tutor, and was elected scholar in 1664 and fellow in 1668. He graduated BA in 1666; in 1669 he proceeded MA and was incorporated at Oxford, like his father, at the Sheldonian's opening. He contributed a Greek poem to *Threni Cantabrigienses* (1669) on the death of Queen Henrietta Maria. Having been ordained priest by the bishop of Ely on 19 September 1674, he was successively vicar of St Mary's, Lichfield (1678–81), of Ware (for four months of 1681), and of Blockley, Gloucestershire (1681–96). His *Sermon Preached before the King at Newmarket* (1676) was published by royal command. On 12 September 1681 he married, at Tettenhall, Staffordshire, Elizabeth Gilbert (*d.* 1729). Like himself she was a Lichfield resident; they had two daughters. He was collated to the prebends his father resigned, at Lichfield on 2 June 1682 and at Lincoln on 26 April 1683 respectively. He published his thanksgiving day *Sermon Preached at Blockley* (1683). He died in 1696 and was buried at Blockley on 10 December. His wife survived him; she was buried at Winwick on 31 January 1729.

Samuel Scattergood is remembered as a preacher: his

two published sermons were never reprinted, but from the rest his brother John collected *Twelve Sermons* (1700), later enlarged to *Fifty-Two Sermons* (1723). After Samuel's death his father's library was advertised for auction in London: almost two thousand items in a learned, mostly Latin, collection, to which Samuel had continued to add. Predictably it included Gouldman's *Dictionary* (1678), Hayes's Bible (1683), and an annotated copy of *Annotations upon All the Books of the Old and New Testament* (1651) by John Downame and others; but it also included, without listing them, 'betwixt Fourscore and an Hundred Italian plays'.

HUGH DE QUEHEN

Sources H. I. Longden, *Northamptonshire and Rutland clergy from 1500*, ed. P. I. King and others, 16 vols. in 6, Northamptonshire RS (1938–52), vol. 10 • H. J. Davis, 'Dr Anthony Scattergood's commonplace book', *Cornhill Magazine*, [3rd] ser., 54 (1923), 679–91 • J. Bridges, *The history and antiquities of Northamptonshire*, ed. P. Whalley, 2 vols. (1791) • *Fasti Angl., 1541–1857*, [Lincoln] • W. W. Rouse Ball and J. A. Venn, eds., *Admissions to Trinity College, Cambridge*, 2 (1913) • *Catalogue of the library of the reverend and learned Dr. Scattergood* (1697) • C. Bee, *The case of Cornelius Bee and his partners* (1666?) • W. Kennett, *A register and chronicle ecclesiastical and civil* (1728) • *The diary and correspondence of Dr John Worthington*, ed. J. Crossley, 2/1, Chetham Society, 36 (1855) • T. Plume, *An account of the life and death of … John Hacket*, ed. M. E. C. Walcott (1865) • H. Cotton, *Editions of the Bible*, 2nd edn (1852) • *DNB* • G. W. G. Leveson Gower, ed., *A register of … the parish of Saint Peeters upon Cornhill*, 1, Harleian Society, register section, 1 (1877) • F. J. Wrottesley, ed., *Ellastone parish register*, 2 vols., Staffordshire Parish Registers Society (1907–12) • H. R. Thomas and G. R. Mander, eds., *Tettenhall parish register*, 1 (1930)

Archives BL, commonplace book and papers relating to him, Add. MSS 42121, 44963–44964

Scattergood, Samuel (*bap.* **1646**, *d.* **1696**). *See under* Scattergood, Anthony (*bap.* 1611, *d.* 1687).

Scawen, William (**1600–1689**), Cornish-language revivalist, was born at St Germans in Cornwall, where his family had resided at Molenick since the time of Edward I. He was the eldest of the six sons and four daughters of Robert Scawen (*c.*1568–1627), a landowner, and Isabella Nicoll or Nicholles (*d.* in or after 1627). Before 1634 he married Alice Sawle (*bap.* 1604, *d.* 1664), daughter of Nicholas Sawle of Penrice and Alice Rashley, and they had four sons and two daughters. William was MP for St Germans in the Short Parliament of 1640, failed to get elected there again later in 1640, and it is possible that he was returned again for St Germans in November 1646 but did not take up his seat. He was one of Charles I's commissioners in Cornwall. After an active military role in the civil war he was briefly incarcerated by the parliamentary side in Pendennis Castle. With the Restoration he was appointed by Charles II as vice-warden of the stannaries, and held that position for many years.

At a time when the Cornish language was rapidly dying out, Scawen 'had long had a proposal and a desire for the recovery of our primitive tongue' (Pryce, 3). This seems to have involved generally unsuccessful attempts to secure Cornish-language manuscripts from his contemporaries. He was stung into a more active interest at the 1678 assizes in Launceston, when chided by the lord chief justice, Sir Francis North, about the decay of the language. Scawen was in possession of the original of a fifteenth-century Cornish-language poem, 'Pascon agan Arluth', generally known as 'Mount Calvary' or the 'Passion Poem' (BL, Harley MS 1782). In response to North's interest he sought to have it translated into English. Two translations were made: an execrable effort by William Hals, produced in 1679–80 (BL, Add. MS 28554), and a second by Scawen's nephew John Keigwin, dated 1682 (LPL, MS 806, art. 17).

Keigwin's translation is included in one of three manuscript versions of Scawen's own work 'Antiquities Cornu-Britannick' or 'Observations on an ancient manuscript, entitled "Passio Christi"', produced between 1678 and his death in 1689. A version of this work was published in 1777 and reprinted several times, notably by Davies Gilbert in 1838, but it differs somewhat from all three extant manuscript versions. In this work Scawen gives sixteen often-quoted reasons for the decay of the language, including factors such as cessation of contact with Brittany, the ending of performances of the miracle plays, destruction of records during the civil war, the lack of a Cornish translation of the Bible, the antipathy of the gentry to the language, and the closeness of English-speaking Devon and its influences. In the manuscript Scawen acknowledges the assistance of John Keigwin and of his father, Martin (1606–1667)—thus suggesting an earlier start to the translation of 'Pascon agan Arluth' than 1678—as well as that of Nicholas Boson and John Read. He also mentions encouraging these other scholars to correspond in Cornish, beginning a tradition which they and their successors in the language revival movement carried on into the eighteenth century.

Scawen was buried at St Germans on 18 November 1689. The family had all left St Germans before 1730.

MATTHEW SPRIGGS

Sources parish register, St Germans, Cornwall [burial] • J. L. Vivian, ed., *The visitations of Cornwall, comprising the herald's visitations of 1530, 1573, and 1620* (1887), 344, 421–3 • W. Pryce, *Archaeologia Cornu-Britannica* (1790), 3–4 [unpaginated] • Boase & Courtney, *Bibl. Corn.*, 1.88; 2.629 • B. O. Murdoch, *The medieval Cornish poem of the passion* (1979) • A. Hawke, 'A missing manuscript of the Cornish Ordinalia?', *Cornish Studies*, 7 (1979), 45–60 • A. Hawke, 'The manuscripts of the Cornish Passion Poem', *Cornish Studies*, 9 (1981), 23–8 • O. Padel, *Exhibition of manuscripts and printed books on the Cornish language* (1975), 5–6 [unpaginated] • W. Scawen, *Antiquities Cornu-Britannick, or, Observations on an ancient manuscript written in the Cornish language* (1777); repr. in F. Grose, *The antiquarian repertory*, 2 (1779), 61–88; 3 (1808), 208–34 • W. Scawen, 'Observations on an ancient manuscript, entitled "Passio Christi"', in D. Gilbert, *The parochial history of Cornwall*, 4 (1838), 190–221 • C. S. Gilbert, *An historical survey of the county of Cornwall*, 2 (1820), 710 • J. Polsue, *A complete parochial history of the county of Cornwall*, 2 (1868), 39, 44, 45, 55 • W. Borlase, *Natural history of Cornwall* (1758), 296–7, 306 • J. Vicar, *The burning bush* (1646), 383–4 • *Calendar of the Clarendon state papers preserved in the Bodleian Library*, 2: *1649–1654*, ed. W. D. Macray (1869), 274, 293 • D. Brunton and D. H. Pennington, *Members of the Long Parliament* (1954), 22, 219 • M. Coate, *Cornwall in the great civil war and interregnum, 1642–1660* (1933), 118, 185, 207, 226, 373, 375, 377 • M. Stoyle, *West Britons: Cornish identities and the early modern British state* (2002), 134–56 • W. P. Baildon, ed., *The records of the Honorable Society of Lincoln's Inn: admissions*, 1 (1896), 183 • Foster, *Alum. Oxon.*

Archives Cornwall RO, 'Antiquities Cornu-Britannick', MS D.d.Enys 1999 • Cornwall RO, 'Antiquities Cornu-Britannick', MS (Fortescue collection) F2/39 • Royal Institution of Cornwall, Truro, 'Antiquities Cornu-Britannick', MS

Wealth at death £800 p.a. in 1660: *Western Antiquary*, 7/2 (1887), 38–9 · son and heir inherited Molenick and later left property as a vicarage for St Germans church: Vivian, *Visitations of Cornwall*, 422–3; Polsue, *Complete parochial history of Cornwall*, 44, 55

Schafer, Sir Edward Albert Sharpey- (1850–1935), physiologist, was born Edward Albert Schafer at Tottenham Lane, Hornsey, London, on 2 June 1850, the third son and fifth child of Jacob William Henry Schafer, a City merchant, and his wife, Jessie, daughter of W. H. Brown of London. The father had come from Hamburg as a young man and taken British nationality. Schafer, after attending small schools in early childhood, was educated at Clewer House School, Windsor, and later at University College School, Gower Street, and University College, London. His elder brothers, like the other members of his family, had gone into business, but Schafer astonished his parents by saying that he wished to continue his education and study medicine. His parents agreed to this break with tradition, and when he showed his capacity and won prizes and medals they were proud of him. In due time he qualified as a medical practitioner. He was elected the first Sharpey scholar at University College in 1871. This award carried with it teaching duties, William Sharpey, who was professor of general anatomy and physiology, being the first to institute classes in the practical side of these subjects. Schafer owed much to Sharpey, who has been described as the founder of English physiology; the name Sharpey had been given as a second name to Schafer's eldest son, who was killed in 1918, and as Sharpey had no descendants Schafer adopted it as a tribute of gratitude and affection.

Schafer became assistant professor of physiology in 1874 on J. S. Burdon-Sanderson's succeeding Sharpey, and was appointed Jodrell professor in 1883 when Burdon-Sanderson went to Oxford. Schafer was also Fullerian professor at the Royal Institution from 1878 to 1881. He resigned his professorship at University College in 1899 on being elected to the chair of physiology in the University of Edinburgh. He held this post until 1933 when he became emeritus professor, having completed more than sixty years as a teacher.

Schafer's early research work was in histology, and he maintained his interest in this subject throughout his life, holding that it was essentially a part of physiology, being necessary for a proper understanding of functional activity. His investigations on the wing structure of insects and on the absorption of fat by the villi of the small intestine of mammals attracted considerable notice. He was fond of recalling the fact that his first paper, which was on the nerves of the jellyfish and their mode of working, was rejected by the Royal Society's referee, Ray Lankester, but when Oscar and Richard Hertwig made identical discoveries which were printed in a foreign journal, Schafer's paper was hurriedly published, and (as if to make amends) he was elected FRS in 1878 a few days after his twenty-eighth birthday.

In 1883 Schafer published the results of his first researches on cerebral localization and in the following

Sir Edward Albert Sharpey-Schafer (1850–1935), by Charles D'Orville Pilkington Jackson

year he showed how the beat of the frog's heart could be recorded with the aid of photography. In 1886 in conjunction with Victor Horsley he studied muscular contraction produced by stimulation of different parts of the motor tract, and he recorded the muscular rhythm that resulted from volitional impulses in man. Furthermore, with Sanger Brown, he investigated the effect of ablation of portions of the cortex of the brain and the effect of stimulating the visual area in monkeys and the working of the ciliary muscle. These investigations occupied him until about 1893.

The remarkable effect of an extract of the suprarenal gland when injected into the circulation in causing a constriction of the arterioles and a marked rise of the blood pressure was discovered by George Oliver and Schafer in 1894. It led to the opening up of a field of research which proved of the greatest importance to practical medicine. Schafer subsequently published further papers on the internal secretions (with Oliver, Benjamin Moore, Swale Vincent, and P. T. Herring). The study of these secretions, subsequently called hormones, by E. H. Starling was later termed endocrinology, and Schafer did much to develop it. Before leaving University College he also did work (with Moore) on the innervation and contraction of the spleen and on the alleged sensory function of the motor cortex.

After going to Edinburgh Schafer continued his researches and published papers on the effects of partial transection of the spinal cord and circumsection of the motor cortex. In 1902 he demonstrated a direct communication of canaliculi with blood capillaries in the liver. Later he did work (with H. J. Scharlieb) on the action of chloroform on the heart and vessels, (with A. N. Bruce) on the cerebellar tracts of the spinal cord, and (with Walker May) on the effects of section of the vagus and cervical sympathetic nerves. He also investigated the pulmonary circulation, and the influence of the vagus nerve on respiration and the action of the intercostal muscles. Among his latest researches on nerve function was one which involved the cutting of a nerve in his own arm.

Schafer communicated his prone pressure method of employing artificial respiration on persons apparently drowned to the Royal Society of Edinburgh in 1903. By this method the respiratory exchange was much greater than that occurring under existing methods, and it was subsequently adopted by the Royal Life Saving Society, which awarded him its Distinguished Service Medal in 1909.

Schafer was the author of several textbooks on physiology. He was one of the founders of the Physiological Society in 1876, and published its history in 1927. At its jubilee he was the sole survivor of its original members. He also founded in 1908 the *Quarterly Journal of Experimental Physiology*. He was editor until his retirement in 1933, when a bound volume was presented to him, containing articles by twenty-nine of his past and present assistants. It constitutes volume 23 of the *Journal*.

Schafer received many distinctions and held many posts. He was general secretary to the British Association from 1895 to 1900 and was president in 1912. He was president of the International Congress of Physiologists in 1923, and of the Royal Society of Edinburgh in 1933. He received honorary degrees from several British and various other universities, including Bern, Groningen, and Louvain. He obtained the highest award of the Royal Society of London, the Copley medal, in 1924, and numerous other medals. In 1913 he was knighted.

Schafer had a strictly evangelical upbringing and although he relinquished his religion he maintained throughout his life the high ethical standards of conduct and outlook which his parents had taught him, and he never forgot his Bible, which he could quote in such a way as to astonish even students of religion. He had a sincere regard for the truth and a hatred of intellectual dishonesty. At the same time he was liberal and tolerant as is shown, for example, by his championship of the rights of women, especially in the matter of their admission to the medical profession. He earned the appreciation of all members of his staff, many of whom themselves became distinguished workers. Moreover, he was a fine lecturer and won the admiration of his students. With a somewhat stern exterior he was one of the kindliest of men, and with those who came to know him well initial respect grew to permanent affection. He took a delight in hospitality and he invited every member of his class to large student parties which gave him unfeigned pleasure. At North Berwick, where he lived during his Edinburgh days, he was a regular player on the golf links.

Schafer married twice. On 2 April 1878 he married Maud (1859/60–1896), daughter of Adolphus William Dixey, head of the firm of opticians of that name in Bond Street, and sister of Frederick Augustus Dixey FRS, the entomologist; on 10 October 1900 he married Ethel Maude, youngest daughter of John Henry Roberts FRCS. There were four children of his first marriage: two sons, both of whom were killed in the First World War, and two daughters, the elder of whom died young. He died at his home, Park End, 12 Westgate, North Berwick, East Lothian, on 29 March 1935. F. H. A. MARSHALL, *rev.* ANITA MCCONNELL

Sources L. Hill, *Obits. FRS*, 1 (1932–5), 401–7 • *The Times* (30 March 1935) • private information (1949) • personal knowledge (1949) • *BMJ* (6 April 1935), 741–2; (13 April 1935), 801; (29 June 1935), 1331 • b. cert. • m. certs. • d. cert.

Archives U. Edin. L., corresp. • Wellcome L., corresp. and papers

Likenesses C. D'O. P. Jackson, two bronze medals, 1922, Scot. NPG • C. D'O. P. Jackson, bronze medal, NPG [*see illus.*] • photograph, repro. in *Obits. FRS*, 1 (1935)

Wealth at death £6866 12*s*. 6*d*.: confirmation, 12 June 1935, *CCI*

Schalby [Scalby], **John** (*d.* 1333), ecclesiastical writer, was of unknown origins, but his surname may well derive from either Scawby, Lincolnshire, or Scalby, in the North and East Ridings of Yorkshire. He had become a priest by 1298, indeed probably by 1290 when he became rector of Sutton-le-Marsh. From 1294 to 1333 he was rector of Mumby, and between 1299 and 1333 he held three prebends in succession in Lincoln Cathedral. Registrar to Bishop Oliver Sutton of Lincoln from 1281 to 1299, and probably also to Sutton's successor, John Dalderby (*d.* 1320), until 1308, he has been identified with 'Q', the redactor of the *Registrum antiquissimum* of the church of Lincoln. He must have entered the bishop's registry before June 1280, when he was given the important task of compiling the roll of entries for the archdeaconry of Lincoln (his hand appears in the manuscript from 1280). In the spring of 1284 he appears to have been responsible for a thorough reorganization of the episcopal archives (recorded in the court book of Stow), sorting the royal charters and instruments into separate baskets for each reign and storing them in a cupboard, while other important documents were filed and put in 'a certain long chest' (*Register of Sutton*, 3.xxviii). He could not finish this work because the bishop, whom he constantly attended and in whose household he lived, had to move away from Lincoln in the course of his visitations. Nevertheless, the records of Sutton's episcopate were meticulously kept, and in 1290, probably on the initiative of Schalby himself, the method of recording was changed from the rather inconvenient rolls to folios, which led to their better preservation. After 1290 Schalby (who could draw cleverly in pen and ink, and showed a talent for caricature) frequently served as examining chaplain for acolytes and subdeacons for ordination.

In 1308 Schalby settled in the cathedral close in a house called Pollard's, on a repairing lease of 33*s*. 4*d*. paid annually to the chapter. A sum of 3*s*. 4*d*. was to be returned to him as a mark of the chapter's regard. His unrivalled knowledge of the muniments caused him to take a leading part in cathedral affairs, especially in the dispute in 1312 between the dean, Roger Martival (*d.* 1330), and the chapter concerning rights of internal jurisdiction. This case was settled by an award of Bishop Dalderby in 1314. About 1330 Schalby finished a valuable work called 'The book of John de Schalby concerning the bishops of Lincoln and their acts'. This contained short biographies of the bishops from Remigius (*d.* 1092) to Henry Burghersh, bishop from 1320 to 1340. The lives of bishops Sutton and Dalderby, with whom Schalby had been closely associated, are rather fuller than the others. The book also contains notes apparently copied from the *Martilogium*, a document now lost, concerning the official business of the bishops, dean, and chapter. In his dedication of the work to 'all the faithful of the cathedral', Schalby says that he has included material found in the archives as well as information from his elders and some drawn from his own observation.

Schalby died at his home, Pollard's House, Lincoln, in the autumn of 1333. Before his death he seems to have become blind, since Walter Grenewyk, the chapter clerk, was appointed coadjutor to look after him and his prebend. This appointment was made at Schalby's own request, so he must have remained clear-headed until at least a few weeks before his death. He would have been glad of this. ROSALIND HILL

Sources R. M. T. Hill, ed., *The rolls and register of Bishop Oliver Sutton*, 8 vols., Lincoln RS, 39, 43, 48, 52, 60, 64, 69, 76 (1948–86) [esp. vol. 3] • register of Bishop Dalderby, Lincs. Arch. • *The book of John de Schalby, canon of Lincoln, 1299–1333, concerning the bishops of Lincoln and their acts*, trans. J. H. Srawley (1949) • C. W. Foster and K. Major, eds., *The registrum antiquissimum of the cathedral church of Lincoln*, 1, Lincoln RS, 27 (1931) • C. W. Foster and K. Major, eds., *The registrum antiquissimum of the cathedral church of Lincoln*, 3, Lincoln RS, 29 (1935) • K. Major, *Lincoln Cathedral: some materials for its history in the middle ages* (1992) • H. Bradshaw and C. Wordsworth, eds., *Statutes of Lincoln Cathedral*, 3 vols. (1892–7)
Archives Lincs. Arch., register of Bishop Dalderby

Schalch, Andrew (1692–1776), gun-founder, was born in Schaffhausen in Switzerland and was trained in Douai arsenal, but little else is known about his early life. He married and had at least two sons and two daughters. At that time Britain was one of the leading producers of iron cannon in the world, and Moorfields foundry was the only one capable of casting brass guns. In May 1716 Moorfields blew up, killing Matthew Bagley, the last brass-founder, and fifteen others. In consequence, when the Board of Ordnance decided to build a new foundry at Woolwich they had to look abroad for a trained founder; in August 1716 they engaged Andrew Schalch at 5*s*. a day to build the furnaces, subject to a good character's being obtained. By April 1717 Schalch was making moulds and the board's minutes record that his coehorn mortars had proved 'beyond expection' (PRO, WO 47/29–81). In May 1718 he was appointed master founder of his majesty's brass ordnance at 12*s*. a day.

At first Schalch was very diligent, casting cannon, mortars, howitzers, and machine parts. However, by the 1740s officials were irritated by delays and the deterioration in the guns' quality. From 1742 to 1744 they ordered guns from William Bowen, a Southwark brass-founder. In addition, Schalch's contract was changed: although he was still paid for attending the foundry, he had to compete with other founders for orders and pay for workmen and repairs to the furnace. He claimed he had been promised £50 per ton for guns, instead of £30, and an allowance for life. In 1755 the board suspended Schalch while the attorney-general investigated the claims, which were found in the board's favour on most points.

The outbreak of the Seven Years' War prevented the board from dismissing Schalch, however, since they urgently needed guns. The board's minutes record the deterioration in relations between Schalch and his employers, who insisted on weekly progress reports, but to no avail; in July 1758 they ordered Schalch to prepare 24-pounders or 'Answer the Contrary at his Peril'. By December they accused him of being 'dilatory and Negligent' and in February 1759 they were still 'much Surprized at the slowness of Mr Schalch's proceedings' (PRO, WO 47/29–81). Again Schalch was suspended, which apparently had some effect since guns began to appear for proof. However, between July and December 1760 one gun was cast at the foundry and production remained low throughout the decade. Government demands were instead being met by two Southwark founders, Richard Gilpin and William Bowen. Schalch continued to ignore the board's repeated requests to hasten work, while drawing his quarterly allowance.

The reason for the deterioration in Schalch's castings is not documented, but after the board obtained the services of Pieter and Jan *Verbruggen, Schalch was finally retired, in January 1770, on half pay. The parting was acrimonious and took several years to settle. He died on 5 February 1776 at Greenwich and was buried at Woolwich. Schalch took as apprentice in 1719 his brother Jacob, who became foreman at Woolwich and later a founder in Hanoverian service in 1755. He also trained his nephew Lewis Gaschlin, who set up a brass foundry at Greenwich after his uncle's dismissal, and eventually became modeller at the Royal Military Depository, and John and Henry King, who ran the royal brass foundry after Pieter Verbruggen's death. RUTH RHYNAS BROWN

Sources minute books, Board of Ordnance, 1716–72, PRO, WO 47/29–81 • bill books and quarter books, Board of Ordnance, 1716–76, PRO, WO 51/97–269 • M. H. Jackson and C. de Beer, *Eighteenth century gunfounding* (1973) • O. F. G. Hogg, *The Royal Arsenal: its background, origin, and subsequent history*, 2 vols. (1963) • *GM*
Archives Fort Nelson, Hampshire, royal armouries, guns • Museo Millitar, Lisbon, guns • Museum of Artillery, Woolwich, guns • Quex Park, Kent, guns • Southsea Castle, Hampshire, guns • Tower of London, royal armouries, guns

Schank [Schanck], **John** (1740–1823), naval architect and naval officer, was born near Castlerig, Fife, the son of Alexander Schank. He first went to sea in the merchant service, then served for six years as able seaman, midshipman, and master's mate in the warships *Duke*, *Shrewsbury*, *Tweed*, and *Guernsey*. He gained his lieutenant's certificate on 10 January 1766, but continued to serve as a rating—in the *Emerald*, *Princess Amelia* (George Bridges Rodney's flagship), and *Asia* in North America until 2 June 1776, when he became lieutenant in command of the armed vessel *Canceaux* (*Canso*), employed on the St Lawrence. While in the *Emerald* with Captain Charles Douglas, he went to North Cape with the astronomer William Bayley to observe the 1769 transit of Venus.

Schank's mechanical aptitude got him an appointment

superintending the construction of small craft at St John's in Canada, and on the Great Lakes, and building floating bridges for the army. The *Inflexible* (18 guns) was transported in pieces to St John's and reassembled there; commanded by Schank, she played the major role in the defeat of an American flotilla on Lake Champlain on 11 and 13 October 1776. In this or the next year he married a Miss Grant, sister of William *Grant, judge and master of the rolls; he became a commander on 8 April 1780, and a post captain on 15 August 1783.

After the war Schank pursued his practical interests, joining the Society for the Improvement of Naval Architecture in 1791. His early inventions had included a cot which, by means of pulleys, could be raised and lowered by the occupant, but his greatest innovation was the 'sliding keel', a form of centreboard, permitting the design of very-shallow-draught vessels which sailed faster and, it was claimed, steered more easily and tacked and wore more quickly than conventional craft.

Having obtained the patronage of the duke of Northumberland, Schank had the first such vessel built at Boston, Massachusetts, in 1774, and sliding keels were fitted to some small craft on the Great Lakes during the American War of Independence. In 1790 the Navy Board ordered two similar 13 ton vessels to be built, one conventional in design, the other to Schank's specification, namely flat-bottomed and with three sliding keels raised by winch into central wells, one forward, one aft, and one amidships. Comparative trials conducted on the Thames at Deptford bore out Schank's claims, and the board ordered a 120 ton cutter with sliding keels to be built at Plymouth. This vessel, appropriately named the *Trial*, performed well in tests off Teignmouth in February and March 1791, commanded by Schank's protégé, Lieutenant Micajah Malbon. Several more vessels were built with sliding keels, notably the sloop *Cynthia* in 1795, all forty-three of the Acute class of gunboat in 1797–9, and the *Lady Nelson*, which, between 1800 and 1802, sailed with Matthew Flinders to the coast of New South Wales. His expertise in the design of shallow-draught vessels led to Schank's being commissioned by the duke of Bridgewater to design, for use on his canal, a steam tug, *Buonaparte*, which was built at Worsley between 1796 and 1799. In 1800 Schank designed the first of the two paddle steamers named *Charlotte Dundas* for Thomas, Lord Dundas, and the Forth and Clyde Navigation Company.

Another of Schank's ideas was much less successful: during 1798 the brig-sloop *Wolverine* was converted to enable her to carry fewer but heavier guns which, by means of guides in the deck, could be moved from one side of the ship to the other, permitting all the guns to bear on either side. However, it took too long to haul the guns across the deck, and the weight of them all on one side gave the vessel a dangerous list. In an engagement in January 1799 she suffered many casualties as she was unable to bring her main armament into action; and when engaged by a French privateer in the Atlantic in 1804, she was swamped through her open gunports and sank.

Schank served as transport agent with the 1791 expedition to Martinique and Guadeloupe, and with the army in Flanders in 1794 and the Netherlands in 1799. On its formation in September 1795 he was appointed a commissioner of the transport board. Also that year he was employed planning a naval stores depot at Cork. As superintendent of coastal defences about 1802 he designed gunboats and 'gun-rafts'—simple floating batteries. He retired to Dawlish in Devon where he died, probably in June 1823, an admiral of the blue. RANDOLPH COCK

Sources *DNB* • J. Sewell, ed., *A collection of papers on naval architecture* (1791); 3rd edn, 2 vols. (1800) • E. Doran, 'The origin of leeboards', *Mariner's Mirror*, 53 (1967), 39–53 • J. Charnock, *An history of marine architecture*, 3 vols. (1800–02), vol. 3, pp. 337–65 • R. J. G. Griffiths, 'The short and active life of a brig-sloop at war: HMS *Wolverine*, 1798–1804', *Mariner's Mirror*, 84 (1998), 218–23 • *Public characters*, 10 vols. (1799–1809) • [J. Watkins and F. Shoberl], *A biographical dictionary of the living authors of Great Britain and Ireland* (1816) • B. Lavery, *Nelson's navy: the ships, men, and organisation, 1793–1815*, rev. edn (1990) • lieutenant's passing cert., PRO, ADM 107/6 • commission and warrant books, PRO, ADM 6/21 • W. A. Baker, notes, *Mariner's Mirror*, 56 (1970), 410–13 • W. A. Baker, 'Notes', *Mariner's Mirror*, 65 (1979), 350 • L. G. Michaud, ed., *Biographie universelle ancienne et moderne*, new edn, 45 vols. (1843–1865?), vol. 38, p. 249 • W. S. Harvey and G. Downs-Rose, *William Symington: inventor and engine builder* (1980)

Archives PRO, ADM

Likenesses oils, *c.*1795–1805, NMM • C. Turner, mezzotint, pubd 1799 (after J. J. Masquerier), BM • engraving, 1805, NL Aus. • J. J. Masquerier, oils, NPG

Schapiro, Leonard Bertram (1908–1983), historian and barrister, was born in Glasgow on 22 April 1908, the elder son and second of three children of Max Schapiro and his wife, Leah Levine. His father, educated at the universities of Riga and Glasgow, was the son of a wealthy sawmill owner at Bolderaa near Riga, in Latvia, his mother the daughter of a rabbi and cantor of the Garnethill synagogue in Glasgow. His great-uncle, Jacob Shapiro, was a constitutional democratic deputy in the second Duma. From 1912 the family resided in Riga, moving in 1915 to Petrograd in wartime conditions and remaining there until 1921, when the father's newly acquired citizenship of Latvia, which became independent of Russia in 1918, enabled them to leave and settle in London.

Already fluent in English, German, and Russian, Schapiro was educated at St Paul's School and at University College, London, where he read law. In 1931, still a student, he married Ynys Mair, an art student and daughter of David Evans, a Newport pharmaceutical chemist. The marriage was dissolved in 1937. Called to the bar (Gray's Inn) in 1932, he practised in London and on the western circuit, supplementing his income, and gaining his first experience as a teacher, by coaching public school and university entrants.

In 1940 Schapiro became a supervisor at the BBC monitoring service at Evesham, where close study, first of German and from 1941 of Soviet news and information, established an intellectual interest and the foundation of a future academic career. There, among a remarkable group of central European intellectuals, he made friends with G. Katkov and V. Frank, who were to share his growing

Leonard Bertram Schapiro (1908–1983), by Michael Werner, exh. RA 1972

interest in Russian culture and history. Also at Evesham he met and in 1943 married Isabel Margaret, daughter of Salvador de *Madariaga (1886–1978), King Alfonso XIII professor of Spanish studies in Oxford University, 1929–31, and his wife, Constance Helen, *née* Archibald. Isabel later became professor of Russian studies in the University of London. Recruited in 1942 into the intelligence corps, Schapiro was commissioned in early 1943, moved to the general staff at the War Office, and in 1945–6 served in the intelligence division of the Allied Control Commission for Germany, attaining the rank of acting lieutenant-colonel.

Schapiro returned to the bar in 1946 and published a number of articles on subjects of international law, but his experience of Soviet military administration in post-war Germany had reinforced a desire to discover the well-spring of Soviet attitudes to law and government practice, and in 1955 he quit law and devoted himself to Soviet studies.

The Origin of the Communist Autocracy (1955; 2nd edn, 1977), a study of the socialist opposition in the early years of Soviet government, in which Schapiro analysed the Bolsheviks' abuse of their political monopoly, established him as a penetrating critic of the Soviet regime and he was offered a lectureship at the London School of Economics, where he inspired and created a generation of Russian historians and political scientists. From 1963 to 1975 he was professor of political science with special reference to Russian studies at LSE. One of his chief contributions to the field, *The Communist Party of the Soviet Union*, was published in 1960 (2nd edn, 1970). For Schapiro, as an undogmatic constitutionalist, the acid test of political credibility was respect for the law, a test the Soviet regime consistently failed, based as it was on the same principle of arbitrary rule as tsarism. This was the theme of his Yale lectures, published as *Rationalism and Nationalism in Russian Nineteenth-Century Political Thought* (1967). His view that the Stalinist state was the continuation of Lenin's heritage aroused controversy, and he later modified it to allow that Stalin had committed excesses that Lenin might not have countenanced, and still later, in his posthumously published *1917: the Russian Revolutions and the Origins of Present-Day Communism* (1984), he conceded that Stalinism was a possible but not a necessary consequence of Leninism. Had he lived to see the opening of the Soviet archives only a few years later he would have found his earlier stand vindicated.

Born into an Anglophile Riga family, Schapiro based his political ideals on his experience as a lawyer; he particularly admired the English common law and he believed that the rule of law was essential for the creation of a civilized polity. In Russian culture his ideal was the liberal, cosmopolitan novelist Ivan Turgenev, of whom he wrote a sensitive intellectual biography, *Turgenev: his Life and Times* (1978). Never a Zionist or practising Jew, in his youth he had occasionally frequented East End synagogues for their ethnic colour, but he rejected a perceived nationalism in Judaism; moved by Christianity, as by strong religious feeling in general, but unable to accept the divinity of Christ, he was inclined towards a non-specific spirituality. The Jewish aspect of Schapiro's background was not publicly expressed until relatively late in his life and was as much an outcome of his professional concerns as it was of any 'racial' emanation. As chairman of the editorial board of *Soviet Jewish Affairs* (which later became *East European Jewish Affairs*) and a member of the Institute of Jewish Affairs, he took an active part in exposing Soviet antisemitism.

Schapiro was a member of the council of the School of Slavonic and East European Studies from 1956 to 1981. He was elected a fellow of the British Academy in 1971, and in 1980 appointed CBE. He was chairman of the Institute for the Study of Conflict from 1970; a member of the research board of the Institute of Jewish Affairs; a council member of the Institute for Religion and Communism; chairman of the editorial board of *Government and Opposition* from 1965; long-time legal adviser and vice-president from 1976 of the National Council for One-Parent Families; and foreign honorary member of the American Academy of Arts and Sciences (1967).

In 1976, after his second marriage was dissolved, he married (Dorothy) Roma Thewes (*née* Sherris), a journalist and friend from Evesham days, and daughter of Cyril Sherris, a medical practitioner. Spiritual father to innumerable students, he had no children, but derived great joy from his last wife's grandchildren. He died in London on 2 November 1983 and was cremated at Golders Green.

HAROLD SHUKMAN, *rev.*

Sources P. Reddaway, 'Leonard Bertram Schapiro, 1908–1983', *PBA*, 70 (1984), 515–42 · S. E. Finer, *Government and Opposition*, 19/1 (1984) · H. Seton-Watson, 'Leonard Schapiro's legacy', *Encounter*, 62/4 (1984), 40–42 · personal knowledge (1990) · private information (1990) · *CGPLA Eng. & Wales* (1984)

Likenesses M. Werner, bronze bust, exh. RA 1972, RA [*see illus.*]

Wealth at death £59,700: probate, 24 Jan 1984, *CGPLA Eng. & Wales*

Scharf, Sir George (1820–1895), artist and gallery director, was born on 16 December 1820 at 3 St Martin's Lane, London. He was the elder son of the artist George Johann

Sir George Scharf (1820–1895), by William Edward Kilburn, 1847

*Scharf (1788–1860) and Elizabeth Hicks (1785–1869), who married at St Martin-in-the-Fields on 20 August 1820. When the family moved to 14 Francis Street in 1830, George and his younger brother, Henry (1822–1887), were among the first scholars to attend the newly opened University College School. George Scharf senior taught both his sons to draw but whereas Henry showed little interest and later went on the stage, George was eager to learn and often accompanied his father on drawing expeditions, one of which was to the ruins of the burnt-out Palace of Westminster in 1834. The Royal Society of Arts awarded him the silver palette in 1835 and the silver medal for drawing in 1836. In 1838 he entered the Royal Academy Schools.

Like his brother, George Scharf was also attracted by the stage. He found a sponsor in the tragedian William Macready, who gave him the freedom of Covent Garden Theatre 'to encourage him as an artist' (*Macready's Reminiscences*, 2.129), and in 1839 he published *Recollections of Scenic Effects*, a series of etchings illustrating Macready's Shakespearian productions and plays by contemporary authors. They constitute the only substantial visual record of theatrical productions of the 1830s. Later, when Scharf had gained a reputation as a classical scholar, Edmund Kean also employed him to ensure the accuracy of the costumes and scenery in his classical productions at the Princess's Theatre.

Scharf's interest in ancient civilizations began in 1840 when he accompanied Sir Charles Fellows on his second exploration of Asia Minor. Three years later he returned as official artist to the government expedition which went out to obtain and ship home the valuable collection of Lycian antiquities which is now in the British Museum. A selection of the drawings Scharf made at the time was published in 1847 and six of his paintings were exhibited at the Royal Academy. Between his two visits to Asia Minor he found time to contribute a large cartoon, *Caractacus*, to the competition to design frescoes for the Palace of Westminster, exhibited in Westminster Hall in 1843.

Several books on classical antiquities were published with Scharf's illustrations, notably the works on Nineveh by Austen Henry Layard and the various classical dictionaries of Dr William Smith. Macaulay's *Lays of Ancient Rome*, which Longmans published in 1847 with his illustrations, was an immediate success. In 1850 Scharf discovered an unrecorded fragment of the Parthenon frieze at Marbury Hall in Cheshire which was subsequently sent to the British Museum; a drawing of it by Scharf was published in the *Illustrated London News* on 30 November 1850. When the Crystal Palace was rebuilt in south London at Sydenham, Scharf's specialized knowledge was called upon for the creation of the Greek, Roman, and Pompeian courts, and he wrote the catalogue notes describing them when the exhibition opened in 1854.

Scharf was elected a fellow of the Society of Antiquaries in 1852 and became a very active member. He compiled a catalogue of the pictures in the society's possession and supervised their hanging in Somerset House. In 1861 he examined the portraits in the Royal Collection at Windsor and by identifying them against the inventories he was able to correct several attributions. When he delivered a paper at the Society of Antiquaries on this subject Queen Victoria permitted him to borrow three portraits with which to illustrate his talk. Altogether he contributed seventeen papers to *Archaeologia* and numerous communications to the *Proceedings*.

Scharf superintended the art classes at Queen's College, Harley Street, London, and became a successful lecturer, even giving lectures on fine art to ladies at his home for a fee of 2½ guineas for twenty lectures. In 1857 he was appointed secretary to the great royal jubilee Art Treasures Exhibition at Manchester, and when the trustees of the newly formed National Portrait Gallery were looking for their first secretary, the choice fell naturally on George Scharf. He was appointed on 4 March 1857. During the forty-odd years that he held this post he became the recognized authority on historical portraiture, travelling all over the country visiting great houses to identify paintings and authenticate attributions. He made careful sketches of every portrait he saw and his 243 small sketchbooks, filled with meticulous pencil drawings, can be seen in the library of the National Portrait Gallery. They are a testimony to his tireless industry.

At this time Scharf was living at 1 Eastcott Place, Camden Town, London, but upon his appointment as secretary he was given rooms for his office at 29 Great George Street, Westminster, a mid-eighteenth-century building which the National Portrait Gallery had purchased to house its collection. He took up his duties in May 1857 and for over a year he supervised the hanging and cataloguing of the collection, which had now grown to fifty-six paintings; on 15 January 1859 the new National Portrait Gallery was opened to the public. By 1860 Scharf was not only working but living at 29 Great George Street and he was given permission for his mother and aunt to occupy the rooms on the third floor. They moved in, with Sarah, their maid, on 3 April. His ailing father, although not included in the move, was now too ill to be left alone and he joined the family only to die six months later.

By 1869 the collection had outgrown the cramped rooms at Great George Street and in December it was moved to a new home in South Kensington, which was opened on 28 March 1870. With the move Scharf lost his comfortable accommodation over the gallery but, now alone (his mother having died a few months before the move and his aunt in 1864), he went to live at 8 Ashley Place, Westminster. In 1882 he was made a director of the National Portrait Gallery and the same year saw his appointment as life governor of his old school, University College School. On 9 January 1885 he received the companionship of the Bath.

A fire broke out at South Kensington in 1885 and the trustees, fearing for the safety of the collection, had it moved to Bethnal Green Museum in east London. Scharf did not accompany it and when he petitioned the office of works for premises for his office he found himself back at Great George Street, no. 20 having been allocated to him 'for business purposes' (PRO, WORK 17/15/1–3). The move to Bethnal Green was not popular and prompted letters of protest in the press. In May 1889 a sum of £100,000 was offered by William Henry Alexander for the building of a brand-new gallery providing the government would find a suitable site. The offer was accepted and a plot of land in St Martin's Place was decided upon. Ewan Christian was appointed architect and work began in 1890.

In 1892 Scharf had passed the age for compulsory retirement but a special dispensation was made on his behalf so that he could supervise the final move of the collection to its new home. But he never lived to see it finished. Early in 1895 illnesses from which he had suffered for many years forced him to abandon all work. On 12 February he was made knight commander of the Bath and appointed a trustee of the gallery but he was able to enjoy these belated honours for only a few weeks. On 19 April 1895 at his home, 8 Ashley Place, he died, unmarried, of dropsy; he was buried in Brompton cemetery on 23 April.

PETER JACKSON

Sources *DNB* • A. W. Franks, *Proceedings of the Society of Antiquaries of London*, 2nd ser., 15 (1893–5), 377–9 • *The Times* (20 April 1895), 7 • *The Athenaeum* (27 April 1895) • P. Jackson, *Drawings of Westminster by Sir George Scharf*, London Topographical Society, 147 (1994) • P. Jackson, *George Scharf's London* (1987) • PRO, WORK 17/15/1–3 • Boase, *Mod. Eng. biog.*, 3.434–5 • parish register, St Martin-in-the-Fields, London • *Macready's reminiscences, and selections from his diaries and letters*, ed. F. Pollock, 2 vols. (1875) • J. F. Boyes, 'The National Portrait Gallery', *Art Journal*, new ser., 11 (1891), 296–9 • G. Scharf, *Recollections of the scenic effects of Covent Garden Theatre* (1839)

Archives BL, travel diaries, Add. MS 36488 • McGill University, Montreal, McLennan Library, MS history of Greek art • NPG, corresp., diaries, journals, and notebooks | BL, letters to Sir Austen Layard, Add. MSS 38978–39100, *passim* • BL, letters to W. B. Squire, Add. MS 39680 • Bodl. Oxf., corresp. with Lord Lovelace • Castle Howard, North Yorkshire, letters to Lord Carlisle • DWL, letters to Henry Crabb Robinson • U. Edin., letters to David Laing • Yale U., Beinecke L., letters to Frederick Locker-Lampson

Likenesses W. E. Kilburn, photograph, 1847, NPG [*see illus.*] • G. Scharf, self-portrait, pen-and-ink drawing, 1869, NPG • G. Scharf, self-portrait, watercolour drawing, 1872, NPG • photograph, 1876, NPG • Bassano, photograph, 1885, NPG • W. W. Ouless, oils, 1885, NPG • H. J. Brooks, group portrait, oils, 1888 (*Private view of old masters exhibition, Royal Academy, 1888*), NPG • J. Fisher, photograph, 1889, NPG • E. Edwards, cartes-de-visite, NPG • A. Langdon, chalk drawing, NPG • Maull & Polyblank, cartes-de-visite, NPG • Nadar, cartes-de-visites, NPG • G. Scharf, self-portrait, ink and watercolour drawing, BM • G. Scharf, two self-portraits, watercolour drawings, NPG • Southwell Bros., cartes-de-visite, NPG • J. C. Stodart, photograph, NPG • wood-engraving (after photograph by J. Fisher), repro. in *ILN* (27 April 1895)

Wealth at death £1349 4*s*. 1*d*.: probate, 30 May 1895, *CGPLA Eng. & Wales*

Scharf, George Johann (1788–1860), draughtsman and lithographer, was born in Mainburg, Bavaria, on 19 April 1788, the son of Andreas Scharf, a tradesman, and his wife, Franziska, *née* von Pfeffenhausen. His father's business was apparently ruined during the wars which followed the French Revolution, and at the age of thirteen Scharf left home to live in the nearby village of Geisenfeld. In 1802 he began taking drawing lessons from Herr Kiermayer, a painter of religious subjects, and in 1804 he secured a place in the Royal Academy of Arts and Sciences in Munich. Here Scharf learned the art of lithography from his tutor, Professor Joseph Hauber, one of the earliest exponents of the newly invented medium, and by the time he left the academy in 1810 he was not only an expert lithographer but an accomplished miniaturist. He began wandering around France and the Low Countries seeking commissions and became involved in the military ferment resulting from Napoleon's activities. After escaping from the siege of Antwerp in 1814, he enlisted in the British army as a lieutenant of baggage in the engineers. He saw action at the battle of Waterloo, and accompanied the allies to Paris, where he made drawings of the soldiers encamped in the Bois de Boulogne.

On new year's day 1816 Scharf left Paris and travelled to London, where he was to spend the rest of his life. His first address was 3 St Martin's Lane, a grocer's shop owned by Mary Hicks and her younger sister Elizabeth (1785–1869), whom he married at St Martin-in-the-Fields on 20 August 1820. Four months later, on 16 December 1820, their son Sir George *Scharf was born. Their second son, Henry, was born on 8 December 1822 and, after failing as an artist, went on the stage with some success, particularly in America, where he died in 1887.

Scharf soon abandoned the idea of becoming a miniaturist and turned to lithography in order to earn a living. As one of the only artists in London with any knowledge of lithography he was befriended by the lithographic printer Charles Hullmandel, who gave him one of his first commissions, a view of the coronation procession of George IV in 1821. However, his main source of income was as an illustrator for scientific journals, for example, the *Transactions of the Zoological Society of London* and the

George Johann Scharf (1788–1860), self-portrait

Transactions of the Geological Society, and he was employed by Sir Richard Owen and Charles Darwin, who appreciated his meticulous attention to detail and his painstaking accuracy. But he found the drawing of bones and fossils tedious work, and for recreation he wandered around London recording in innumerable sketches the workaday people of the city's streets. These, in bundles and packets each containing several hundreds, were sold by his widow to the British Museum in 1862. The family moved to 14 Francis Street in 1830 when the southern end of St Martin's Lane was demolished with the construction of Trafalgar Square.

Having been commissioned by the City corporation to record the building of New London Bridge, Scharf produced several watercolours, including two, each 5 feet long, which were destroyed during the Second World War but survive as lithographs. When, in 1834, the houses of parliament were burnt down, he made dozens of drawings on the site, among them a panoramic painting now in the Palace of Westminster collection. His most successful work was a portfolio of lithographs of the London Zoo which he published in 1835, and although he exhibited frequently at the Royal Academy and the New Watercolour Society, of which he was an original member, he never, during forty years, sold anything at an exhibition. His work as a scientific illustrator during the 1830s and 1840s brought him an income of around £200 per annum.

In 1845 Scharf went to Germany to visit his ailing brother, Joseph, only to find that he had already died and left Scharf a legacy of 4000 florins. This enabled him to stay on for two years, during which he produced a fine panorama of Regensburg. On his return in 1848 the family moved to 1 Torrington Square, and on the expiry of the lease in 1856 Scharf rented a room for himself at 37 Preston Street, Camden Town, where his health declined rapidly. Financial difficulties around this time were compounded by the dishonesty of a housemaid who stole money intended for local tradesmen. Too ill to be left alone Scharf went to live with his son George who, as secretary of the new National Portrait Gallery, had private rooms over the gallery at 29 Great George Street, Westminster. Here he died, probably from bronchitis, on 11 November 1860. He was buried on 15 November in Brompton cemetery. A self-effacing man who often undervalued his work (for which he was admonished by Hullmandel), Scharf was scrupulously honest. He charged clients by the hour at 2*s.* an hour. Rising at five or six in the morning, he worked for ten to fifteen hours a day. PETER JACKSON

Sources G. Scharf, journals and notebooks, 14 vols., 1833–59, NPG, Heinz Archive and Library • *The Athenaeum* (17 Nov 1860), 673 • *DNB* • H. Detter, *Mainburghs Geschichte von 825 bis 1967* [n.d.] • F. S. Schwarzbach, 'George Scharf and early Victorian London', *Victorian artists and the city*, ed. I. B. Nadel and F. S. Schwarzbach (1980) • P. Jackson, *George Scharf's London* (1987) • Graves, *RA exhibitors* • L. Binyon, *Catalogue of drawings by British artists and artists of foreign origin working in Great Britain*, 4 vols. (1898–1907)

Archives NPG, journals and notebooks

Likenesses G. J. Scharf, photograph (after his self-portrait, miniature), NPG • G. J. Scharf, self-portrait, priv. coll. [*see illus.*]

Scharlieb [*née* Bird], **Dame Mary Ann Dacomb** (**1845–1930**), gynaecologist, was born at 6 Essex Place, Grange Road, Dalston, Middlesex, on 18 June 1845, the only daughter of William Candler Bird, a merchant's clerk, and his wife, Mary Ann, *née* Dacomb. Her mother died of puerperal fever ten days after her birth and Mary was left in the care of her grandmother until, aged two, she rejoined her father—by then working in Manchester. Five years after the death of his wife William Bird remarried, and three more daughters were eventually added to the household. Mary paid tribute in later life to her stepmother for securing her a good education, first in schools in the Manchester area, next at New Brighton, and then in London, at Mrs Tyndall's school in St John's Wood.

In 1865 Mary Bird met William Mason Scharlieb (1827/8–1891), who was in England reading for the bar before returning to India to take up a law practice. His father, Charles, was a member of the Indian Civil Service. Initially opposed to the marriage on the grounds of Mary's age and the distance between England and India, her parents eventually relented and the couple married on 19 December 1865. Mary left England in 1866 and set up home in Madras, where her sons were born in 1866 and 1868 and a daughter in 1870. In 1875, after William Bird's bankruptcy, the Scharliebs were joined in India by her father and stepmother.

Mary Scharlieb was active in helping her husband in his legal practice and it is said that in editing the *Madras Jurist* with him she came across descriptions of the suffering in childbirth of Hindu and Muslim woman prevented by their religion and social position from seeking medical

Dame Mary Ann Dacomb Scharlieb (1845–1930), by Hugh Goldwin Riviere, 1908

attention from male European doctors. This was the origin of her decision to seek medical training. In Britain the argument that female modesty necessitated the provision of women doctors helped to prise open the doors of the medical establishment to women, while the particular needs of Indian women for female medical attendance mobilized support even among those generally opposed to the idea.

Scharlieb took steps to train as a midwife at the Madras Lying-in Hospital, which treated both low-caste Indian and European women. Because it was thought improper for a married woman to sleep overnight at the hospital, Scharlieb found she could not meet the residence qualifications—one of a number of institutional and cultural obstacles that she encountered. Instead she sought a route into the Madras Medical College, to which she was admitted in 1874 with three other European women. She was awarded the diploma of the college in 1877 and then moved to England, where she entered the London School of Medicine for Women, affiliated to the Royal Free Hospital. She qualified MB in 1882 and obtained the gold medal for obstetrics and a scholarship which allowed her to study operative midwifery under Politzer at the Frauenklinik in Vienna. She received support from philanthropic and missionary organizations, and, in 1883, the imprimateur of royalty, when she was granted an audience with Queen Victoria arranged for her by Sir Henry Acland.

Scharlieb returned to India in 1883 to found a hospital for Indian women. The relationship between Western medicine and the Christian missions was, however, uneasy. Scharlieb believed she had a Christian vocation to help the suffering but she warned against proselytizing, arguing that the example of a good life was more efficacious as an instrument of conversion in the long run. She was lecturer and examiner at the Madras Medical College from 1883, and in the period 1884–6 she helped to found the Royal Victoria Hospital for Caste and Gosha Women. She also had a substantial private practice in India which included Indian and European patients; at her own estimate it earned her around £2000 a year. Although primarily called upon in gynaecological and obstetric cases she also treated children and a few Indian men who entrusted themselves to her care.

In 1887 Scharlieb left Madras for London. She disliked the Indian climate and she wanted to pursue her medical career. The parting from her husband was amicable and they were, according to her own account, regularly reunited during his leaves of absence until his death in England in 1891. Scharlieb obtained her MD degree from London University in 1888, the first woman to do so, and in 1889 the London School of Medicine for Women appointed her a lecturer on the diseases of women. Scharlieb set up a private practice at 149 Harley Street, helped by her Indian connections and by the patronage of Sir James Paget, thus also providing a home for her father and children.

Mary Scharlieb was senior surgeon and consultant at the New Hospital for Women from 1892 to 1903. She became MS (London) in 1897. In 1902 she became gynaecologist at the Royal Free Hospital, a considerable triumph since she was in open competition with male applicants, one of whom became her assistant. In 1905 she retired officially from her hospital appointments, though not from private practice. A period of active engagement in public affairs followed, leading to her appointment as CBE in 1917 and DBE in 1926.

Scharlieb had begun writing for the press in 1888. Her articles and books were aimed at a general readership and gave her an enhanced public profile and an opportunity to mould opinion on women's health topics. Her publications included *The Mother's Guide to the Health and Care of her Children* (1905), *A Woman's Words to Women on the Care of the Health in England and in India* (1895), *Womanhood and Race-Regeneration* (1912), and *How to Enlighten our Children* (1926).

As one of the most illustrious representatives of the first generation of medical women, Scharlieb was called on to carry out various public duties. She was appointed a commissioner for lunacy and in 1920 became one of the first women magistrates. From 1913 to 1916 she served on the royal commission on venereal diseases. She supported the recommendations of the commission to set up free clinics and for a public campaign of information and education about the dangers of venereal disease. However, in 1917 she backed efforts to block the issue of prophylactics to serving soldiers. She regarded this as tantamount to state support for prostitution, condoning the double standard and contrary to Christian principles.

After the commission reported, Scharlieb was in great

demand as a speaker on this and other health topics. She believed that, as well as the promotion of Christian principles, she had a duty to advance the cause of women. She threw her weight behind the right of married women to pursue a professional career, believing she had a mission 'to convince the world that constant attention to professional duties is by no means incompatible with the natural and paramount duties of a wife to her husband and a mother to her children' (Scharlieb, 164). She argued the importance to the nation of motherhood, the adoption of measures to encourage healthy mothers and babies, more humane treatment of unmarried mothers and prostitutes, and sex education for the young.

Dame Mary Scharlieb died at her home, 19 York Terrace, London, on 21 November 1930. By this time her reputation among a new generation of medical women was beginning to suffer. Her social attitudes looked increasingly old-fashioned. She was suspicious that birth control would promote sexual hedonism, and the more relaxed social mores of the 1920s disturbed her. None the less she retained her status as a scientific expert on gynaecological and obstetric problems, her work being quoted by the medical establishment and by the proponents of free love alike. Her importance as a pioneer in expanding women's opportunities and reaching the top of her profession remained undiminished. GRETA JONES

Sources M. Scharlieb, *Reminiscences* (1924) · *The Lancet* (29 Nov 1930), 1211–13 · Scharlieb letters and testimonials, Wellcome L., GC/190 · Wellcome L., Sir Edward Sharpey-Schafer MSS, PP/ESS/P67–70 · M. Lal, 'The politics of gender and medicine in colonial India: the Countess of Dufferin's Fund', *Bulletin of the History of Medicine*, 68 (1994), 29–66 · b. cert. · m. cert. · d. cert. · *WWW*
Archives Bodl. Oxf., letters · Wellcome L., letters and testimonials | Wellcome L., letters to Sir Edward Sharpey-Schafer and Maud Sharpey-Schafer
Likenesses H. G. Riviere, oils, 1908, Royal Free Hospital, London [*see illus.*]
Wealth at death £33,050 7*s*. 3*d*.: probate, 24 Dec 1930, *CGPLA Eng. & Wales*

Scharpe, George (*c*.1583–1638), physician, was born in Scotland, and studied medicine at Montpellier University, France. He graduated there in 1607, published his thesis, *Quaestiones medicae*, in 1617, and in 1619 was the successful candidate out of eleven applicants for the chair of medicine left vacant by the death of Varandé. In 1632, in the absence of Ranchin, he became vice-chancellor of the faculty. He was apparently unpopular with his colleagues; in 1631, as proctor, he had been admonished for arrogance at public examinations and for his quarrelsome tendencies. He was threatened with a fine and deposition if he again transgressed; yet in 1634 he had a confrontation with André, who had charge of the botanical garden, and walked out of a meeting of the faculty. For this he was formally censured. However, he was desirable intellectual property, and in 1634 Padua, Venice, and Bologna were competing for him. The latter was successful, and in October 1634 Scharpe moved to Bologna with his family to take up a lucrative chair at the medical school.

Meanwhile in Montpellier, though the faculty declared the professorship vacant, the bishop of Montpellier, Fenouillet, maintained that Scharpe intended to return to his post. The dispute was referred to the Toulouse parliament, but before it pronounced judgment against Scharpe, he died at Bologna in 1638.

Scharpe left six sons, and his widow was pregnant with another child. One of his sons, Claude, had also studied at Montpellier, and became professor of logic and philosophy there. After his father's death, he published the latter's lectures under the title of *Institutiones medicae* (1638). J. G. ALGER, *rev.* SARAH BAKEWELL

Sources V. Busacchi, 'L'Écossais Georges Scharpes, lecteur à Montpellier et à Bologna', *Bulletin et Mémoires de la Société Internationale d'Histoire de la Médecine* (1959), 116–20 [*Comptes Rendus du XVIe Congrès International d'Histoire de la Médecine*, vol. 1] · V. Busacchi, 'La chiamata di Cartesio alla cattedra eminente di teorica della medicina nello studio di Bologna nel 1633', *Pagine di Storia della Medicina*, 11/2 (1967), 9–13 · G. Zaccagnini, *Storia dello studio di Bologna durante il Rinascimento* (1930), 308–9 · J. Astruc, *Mémoires pour servir à l'histoire de la faculté de médecine de Montpellier* (1767), 255–6 · N. F. J. Eloy, *Dictionnaire historique de la médecine ancienne et moderne*, 4 vols. (Mons, 1778), vol. 4, pp. 201–2
Archives Archivio di Stato, Bologna, Archivio dell'Università, Assunteria di Studio, Busta 25, nos. 40, 41
Likenesses I. B. Coriolanus, line engraving, 1637–1638? (aged fifty-seven), Wellcome L.

Schaub, Sir Luke (1690–1758), diplomatist, was born at Basel in Switzerland. In October 1714 he became secretary to Richard Temple, Baron Cobham, ambassador plenipotentiary at Vienna. When Cobham returned to England on 16 May 1715, Schaub acted in his place until Abraham Stanyan arrived as envoy-extraordinary and plenipotentiary in December 1716, a service for which he received an allowance of £2 a day and for which in January 1717 the secretary of state, James, Earl Stanhope, procured him a pension of £200 a year. Having then served as Stanyan's secretary, Schaub left Vienna in October 1717 and went to England as confidential secretary to Stanhope. In February and June 1718 he was actively though unofficially engaged in Paris in the signing of the Quadruple Alliance, and about 9 August he arrived in Madrid with Stanhope on a special mission to prevent a hostile Spanish expedition to Italy. They left on 27 August, when diplomatic relations were broken off. In 1719 Schaub was in Hanover, but he returned to Madrid on 8 February 1720, in charge of affairs in order to prepare a resumption of those relations. He left once more on 21 July. On 8 October 1720 Schaub was knighted in Hanover by George I. Among those congratulating him was the beleaguered South Sea Company director John Craggs, whose death soon negated his promise to share in all Schaub's concerns.

In March 1721 Schaub was sent to Paris as envoy, at first jointly with Robert Sutton and from November 1721 as sole ambassador, a post he owed to his good relations with Cardinal Dubois, foreign minister until his death in 1723, and his favour with Lord Carteret, 'his fast friend and Patron' (BL, Add. MS 32686, fol. 380). Schaub could be an able judge of affairs: an undated proposal for settling the affairs of northern Europe is clear and organized. His diplomatic skills were tested, though, by the intransigence of Philip V over the need for Britain to restore Gibraltar to

Spain, when George I was declaring that he would continue the war for ten years longer sooner than comply. Townshend, secretary of state for the northern department, and Sir Robert Walpole were planning to oust John Carteret from the southern secretaryship, and Schaub, his nominee, was to be either won away from Carteret or recalled. Horace Walpole was accredited to Paris in October 1723, relying on the power of his political supporters to gain co-operation from other foreign ministers and to overcome the attempt by Schaub and Carteret to confine his own role to the accession of Portugal to the Quadruple Alliance.

The duke of Newcastle, who was to take over from Carteret in April 1724, was already directing Walpole's conduct in his mission to displace Schaub, of whom both men professed a poor opinion. Schaub was of unusually small stature, and this may have caused his bustling air to be seen as inappropriate and therefore arrogant. His enemies constantly refer to his height and his insolence together. Walpole complained of his:

> insolent behaviour during the Cardinal's time, wch has drawn upon him the contempt of almost all the foreign ministers, as well as of the persons of Quality here … but the little Gentleman still keeps up the Air of being as considerable as ever. (BL, Add. MS 32686, fol. 379)

Schaub was 'a foreigner, of no family, and of no consequence but as a clerk' (ibid., fol. 380). Newcastle commented:

> I have known my friend Schaub now many years, He certainly has parts, knows a good deal of foreign affairs, but has such an arrogancy, pertness, & is so meddling & intriguing wth every thing & every body, that I don't wonder he has made himself thoroughly obnoxious to the French Court. (ibid., fol. 404)

Even Lord Stanhope, Newcastle believed, saw Schaub as only a clerk and would never have employed him as a foreign minister. The regent, the duke of Orléans, finding among Dubois's papers politically partisan letters from Schaub and Carteret, was willing to see Schaub removed.

The 'Jackanapes' was recalled in May 1724. Schaub, though, did not lose the favour of George II, who employed him from late September 1730 to November 1731 to conclude a treaty with the king of Poland in their joint capacities as electors. This brought Schaub a pension of £600 per annum, payable in Ireland without deduction of the usual 4 per cent tax. In August 1744 he projected a Quadruple Alliance of Britain, the Empire, the United Provinces, and Poland. As late as 1754 he advised Newcastle on delicate negotiations, in which George II had a particular interest, to settle differences with Prussia. His main association, though, was with the 'patriot' opposition, and when Schaub travelled to France on personal business in June 1736 Sir Robert Walpole pressed the English ambassador in Paris, Lord Waldegrave, to 'watch his motions' in case 'the little Swiss goes an emissary from the patriots here' (Coxe, 3.322). Schaub remained on close terms with Carteret and other opposition figures, and became an intimate of Frederick, prince of Wales, whose chaplain and adviser Caspar Wetstein was a warm friend of both Schaub and his wife. Schaub married a French protestant widow. Thomas Gray's poem of 1750 'A Long Story' celebrates her beauty and flirtatiousness in a mock epic narration of a visit by her and Lady Cobham's niece, Henrietta Speed, when Gray was out. Schaub died at his home in Bond Street, London, on 27 February 1758. His wife, who long survived him, died on 25 August 1793.

PHILIP WOODFINE

Sources BL, Schaub MSS; Add. MSS 4204, 4299 · L. Schaub, 'Proposals for mediation and peace, 1718–19', BL, Add. MS 4193 · BL, Wetstein MSS, 1718–1755; Add. MSS 32414–32420 · letters to Carteret, 1719–22, BL, Add. MSS 22521–22522 · correspondence with lords Carteret and Polwarth, 1722–3, BL, Add. MSS 37389–37393 · Walpole, *Corr.* · W. Coxe, *Memoirs of the life and administration of Sir Robert Walpole, earl of Orford*, 3 vols. (1798) · W. A. Shaw, ed., *Calendar of treasury books and papers*, 2, PRO (1898) · correspondence between H. Walpole and Newcastle, BL, Add. MS 32686, fols. 379, 380, 404 · *DNB*

Archives BL, corresp., Add. MSS 4204, 4299 · BL, 'Proposals for mediation and peace, 1718–19', Add. MS 4193 · NYPL, corresp. and papers | BL, letters to Lord Carteret, Add. MSS 22521–22522 · BL, corresp. with lords Carteret and Polwarth, Add. MSS 37389–37393 · BL, letters to Sir Thomas Robinson, Add. MSS 23780–23783 · BL, letters to C. Wetstein, duke of Newcastle, and others, Add. MSS 32414–32420 · BL, corresp. with Charles Whitworth, etc., Add. MSS 37362–37394, *passim* · NYPL, Hardwicke MSS

Wealth at death pictures sold: Walpole, *Corr.*, vol. 21, pp. 199–200

Schaw, William (1549/50–1602), architect and a founder of freemasonry, was a younger son of John Schaw of Broich, now Arngomery in Stirlingshire. He was probably employed at the Scottish court from his youth, but nothing certain is known until 21 December 1583, when he was appointed master of works to James VI; subsequent references to him as an 'architect' are the earliest usages of the word in Scotland. His epitaph reveals that he travelled widely in Europe, studying the liberal arts and especially architecture. In January 1584 he accompanied George, fifth Lord Seton, on a diplomatic mission to France; in October 1589 he travelled to Norway with James VI, when the king sailed to meet his new wife, Anne of Denmark. In November, Schaw was sent home to make preparations for Anne's arrival.

Schaw is known to have worked on the palace of Holyroodhouse and Holyrood Abbey, on Dunfermline Palace and Abbey, and on Stirling Castle, where he was responsible for the new Chapel Royal built for the baptism of Prince Henry in 1594. In addition to his work for the king, Schaw won the patronage of Robert, sixth Lord Seton (later first earl of Winton), and his brother Alexander Seton (later first earl of Dunfermline). He probably worked on Pinkie House and Fyvie Castle, as well as on Seton Palace. At court Schaw performed a wide range of duties: he was, for example, in charge of entertaining three Danish ambassadors in 1585, and was evidently also employed as master of ceremonies. His work at Dunfermline Palace, Queen Anne's main residence, brought him her friendship, and he became her chamberlain.

Schaw was repeatedly accused of being a Roman Catholic, evidently being one of the small circle of Catholics who survived at court with the connivance of James VI. He played a key role in the creation of freemasonry, on the basis of the documents known as the first and second Schaw statutes (now in the possession of the grand lodge of Scotland), issued on 28 December 1598 and 28 December 1599. In these statutes Schaw legislated as master of works and general warden of the craft of stonemasons in Scotland: thus it seems that, as the king's master of works, he claimed authority over all Scottish stonemasons. In laying down the organization and practices of the craft, the statutes drew much on medieval tradition, but there were major innovations. While 'lodges' had sometimes been mentioned previously as working places for masons engaged on individual building projects, the statutes were concerned with lodges as regulatory organizations for the mason craft, based mainly in major towns but coming under the jurisdiction of the 'general warden' rather than of the burgh authorities. Schaw seems to have been inspired by the Renaissance exaltation of architecture as the greatest of the arts, and built on old traditions of the primacy of masons (as the agents of architects) to claim a special status for them. While much of his proposed reorganization concerned the working practices of masons, there are also hints at secrets and rituals, mixing medieval and Renaissance elements. The issue of the two sets of statutes evidently followed meetings of masons held on the day of their patron saint, St John the Evangelist (27 December), and representatives of a number of the new lodges signed the statutes. The development of these lodges and their rituals was to be central to the emergence of freemasonry.

Schaw died, apparently unmarried, on 18 April 1602 at the age of fifty-two, and was buried in Dunfermline Abbey, where a monument (which still survives) was erected to him by Alexander Seton on the orders of Queen Anne. DAVID STEVENSON

Sources D. Howard, *Scottish architecture: Reformation to Restoration, 1560–1660* (1995), vol. 2 of *The architectural history of Scotland* • J. W. Saunders, 'William Schaw, master of works to King James VI and his connection with the Schaws of Sauchie', *Ars Quatuor Coronatorum*, 50 (1937), 220–26 • D. Stevenson, *The origins of freemasonry: Scotland's century, 1590–1710* (1988) • *DNB*

Schaw, William (*c.*1714–1757), physician, was born in Scotland and educated at the University of Edinburgh. He graduated MD there on 27 June 1735, having presented a thesis on diseases due to mental emotion. He was a friend of Swift's physician, William Cockburn, to whom he dedicated *A Dissertation on the Stone in the Bladder* (1738), which was published during the discussions in the House of Commons on granting money for the purchase of a solvent for stones in the bladder. The dissertation describes the method of formation of such stones and the qualities necessary in a solvent, and shows that the proposed solvents probably did not possess these qualities. Schaw became a licentiate of the College of Physicians of London in 1752, and was created MD at Cambridge by royal mandate in 1753. He was elected a fellow of the College of Physicians on 8 April 1754. His only other work was *A Scheme of Lectures on the Animal Oeconomy* (1739). Schaw died in 1757.

NORMAN MOORE, *rev.* CLAIRE L. NUTT

Sources Munk, *Roll*

Schechter, Solomon (1847x50–1915), Hebraist, was born in the small Romanian town of Focsani, the son of Isaac and Hayya (Chaia) Schechter, Jews of Russian origin. He was given the Hebrew name Shneur Zalman, after the founder of the Hasidic sect of Lubavitch or Habad, to which Isaac, the ritual slaughterer (German *Schächter*), belonged and which stressed study and intellect as well as mystical communion with God.

In continental Europe One of a family of five boys and one girl, young Shneur Zalman (or Solomon, as he styled himself when he moved westwards) was a physically powerful and intellectually brilliant red-head with blue eyes, who later claimed that he had inherited passion and energy from his mother while attributing his religious and scholarly tendencies to the influence of his father, who had been his first teacher. The other pervading influences were those of the eastern European *shtetl* (small-town Jewry), the Hasidic *shtiebel* (small and informal place of worship), and the *yeshivah* (academy for rabbinic studies). In addition, he obtained access, apparently through a local *maskil* (modernist intellectual), to books and articles that broadened his mind, at least within the sphere of Jewish scholarship, and led him to seek further education elsewhere. As a teenager he moved on to Lemberg (Lwów), the capital of the Austro-Hungarian province of eastern Galicia, and studied with the outstanding Talmudist and interpreter of Jewish religious law Rabbi Joseph Saul Nathanson. The master was critical of Hasidism, opposed 'progressive' Judaism but without encouraging communal separatism, and made lenient rulings when circumstances demanded them. Schechter, still religiously and educationally unsure of himself, returned to his native town for a while, continued his studies, and even contracted an unhappy marriage.

The combination of a commitment to Judaism, a passion for broader learning, and an undoubtedly radical streak led Schechter to the institutions of Jewish learning in central Europe that were committed to a more historical and scientific approach. Having earlier divorced his wife (whose name is unknown) after only a year of marriage, he abandoned the *shtetl* for ever (physically if never altogether spiritually) and entered the Vienna rabbinical seminary in 1875. The mission of its founder, Adolf (Aaron) Jellinek, was to spread scientific Jewish learning, a moderately liberal interpretation of Judaism, and a love of Jewish community and culture. As well as coming under Jellinek's influence, Schechter acquired a historical approach to the study of rabbinic literature from Isaac Hirsch Weiss, and the ability to subject *midrash* to text criticism and modern exegesis from Meir Friedmann (Ish-Shalom), both teachers more sympathetic to Jewish tradition and the continuity of the Hebrew language than Jellinek himself. It was indeed perhaps because of their similar background, restlessness, and religious outlook that Friedmann was so dear to Schechter in his Vienna years. While in that city, Schechter improved his general education with some university courses, made a living as a Hebrew teacher, and obtained rabbinical ordination.

Solomon Schechter (1847x50–1915), by unknown photographer

By 1879 Schechter was ready to travel further along the road of Westernization, this time via the Hochschule für die Wissenschaft des Judentums, founded in Berlin in 1872. Though not officially aligned, the *Hochschule* was certainly associated more with progressive than with orthodox trends. Indeed, at this stage of his development Schechter was less enchanted with his background than he would later lead us to believe, and the only publications to have come from him by that time had been two vitriolic and pseudonymous satires on Hasidism, for which he later in life atoned with an essay that offered a more favourable assessment of that movement. Now available to him in Berlin, in addition to his own students, were personally orthodox teachers, such as the critical Talmudist Israel Lewy, at the *Hochschule*, and more clinical and sceptical scholars such as the renowned bibliographer Moritz Steinschneider. Lewy inspired Schechter with his text-critical and philological analysis of rabbinic literature and encouraged him to compare manuscript variants and alternative recensions. At the personal level, Schechter was closest to Pinkus Fritz Frankl. This centrist rabbi and scholar whom he had known in Vienna was now Abraham Geiger's successor in Berlin and a teacher at the *Hochschule*, and Schechter found lodgings in his home. Perhaps under Frankl's influence, he deepened his love of scientific Jewish studies, retained an attachment to traditional observance if not to orthodoxy, and nurtured a growing animosity to the kind of German intellectual antisemitism that he encountered when attending university lectures. He had still to find his ideal milieu, and his students in Berlin, Claude Montefiore from England and Richard Gottheil from the USA, both of them religiously liberal, beckoned to him to exchange the Germany that he was finding politically and socially uncomfortable for a potentially more attractive Anglo-Saxon environment.

In England Schechter arrived in England in 1882 as Montefiore's private tutor, destined to spend twenty years there, but always subsidized by the generosity of his English pupil. Though he did not find in the Anglo-Jewish community the appreciation of Jewish culture that he was anxiously seeking, Schechter taught and inspired a group of leading Jewish intellectuals in London called the Wanderers, read widely in English, and began to master that language. Though unthreatened by the relaxed and inclusive orthodoxy championed by Chief Rabbi Nathan Marcus Adler and his son and successor Hermann Adler, Schechter never took to the centralized bureaucracy of the chief rabbinate and the United Synagogue, nor to the Anglo-Jewish cleric, whom he regarded as a mere flunkey or religious functionary with little scholarly achievement. But he did enjoy England's liberal environment, and the Anglo-Jewish establishment accepted him as one of its own despite his biting criticisms. The close company in which he best expressed himself, the Wanderers, was dominated by the writer Israel Zangwill, the critic Joseph Jacobs, and Schechter himself. Other participants were the journalist Asher Myers, the scholar Israel Abrahams, and the historian Lucien Wolf. He developed a close relationship with Herbert and Susie Bentwich, whose daughter, Margery, later recalled his learning, intensity, and warmth:

> Schechter was the ideal of an inspired scholar. The fastidious cavilled at his wildness. He would tramp the room like a caged lion, and roar at his own sallies. His wide mouth would almost eat you; on the other hand, his blue eyes had such a childlike expression, his hand and voice such a warmth, that every child loved him, and their acme of happiness was to run errands for him. (M. Bentwich, *Lilian Ruth Friedlander: a Biography*, 1957, 10)

While in England, Schechter established his scholarly credentials by the critical study of Hebrew manuscripts in the rich collections of that country, as well as in other parts of Europe; by his trail-blazing publication of first scientific editions of such works as *Avot de Rabbi Nathan* and of more general articles in the newly founded *Jewish Quarterly Review*; by teaching at Jews' College; and by contributing learned items to the *Jewish Chronicle*. Given his character and opinions, he inevitably became involved in controversies with other scholars, and the press reverberated with the accusations that he and Solomon Marcus Schiller-Szinnesy, who taught Talmudic and rabbinic literature at Cambridge, unashamedly hurled at each other. His marriage in June 1887 to Mathilde Roth of Breslau (born in Guttentag, Silesia, in 1857; died in New York in 1924) brought him the kind of personal and domestic security, affection, and support that certainly smoothed some of the rougher edges of his personality and toned down at least the religious side of his radicalism. It also brought him a daughter, Ruth, and a son, Frank, both born in London, and a second daughter, Amy, born later in Cambridge. Mathilde was a cultured, literate woman who undoubtedly assisted her husband with his English, encouraged his ambitions, and built a hospitable home in which they could entertain colleagues, visitors, and students. But Schechter had still not found his professional ideal and his next venture, lasting from 1890 to 1902, was to be in the rarefied academic atmosphere of Cambridge.

At Cambridge If an intensely scholastic environment in which to continue his textual studies was all that he was seeking, Schechter might well have remained in Cambridge for the rest of his life, since it was there that he made his most important contributions to Jewish learning. He prepared for the *Jewish Quarterly Review* descriptions of those manuscripts that his predecessor, Schiller-Szinessy, had not included in his catalogue of the Hebraica at Cambridge University Library. Editions of *Aggadat shir ha-shirim* (1896) and *Midrash ha-Gadol* (1902) were published in Cambridge, and he also undertook the kind of Jewish theological summaries that Montefiore desperately wanted and that were ultimately included in his collections of essays. He also admired and sought to emulate the text-critical work done by Oxford and Cambridge classicists and to promote its adoption in the field of rabbinic scholarship. With the Anglo-Jewish cleric Simeon Singer he had in 1896 published some twelfth-century Talmud fragments that he recognized as important for both their content and the new source of such early material to which they had pointed. His greatest and most original coup was his expedition to Cairo in 1896–7 in search of the origin of precisely such medieval Hebrew fragments and his return to Cambridge with what turned out to be 140,000 items of inestimable significance for rewriting the Jewish social, literary, and religious history of the medieval Mediterranean.

Schechter himself has little to say about what precisely inspired him to travel to Cairo in the winter of 1896–7 in search of manuscripts, and to arrange for the costs to be privately met by Charles Taylor, master of St John's College, Cambridge. The undertaking was clearly important enough for him to cancel his projected participation in Herbert Bentwich's Zionist pilgrimage to the land of Israel with the Maccabeans. Undoubtedly, the kind of medieval Hebrew, Aramaic, and Arabic fragments that S. A. Wertheimer and G. Chester had sent to Oxford and Cambridge, and that had appeared in other centres of learning in the previous few years, and the fact that some of them had been written in Cairo had made him consider the possibility of further discoveries. It is equally likely that the success of the Anglo-Jewish lawyer Elkan Nathan Adler in bringing home a sack of palaeographical treasures from the Egyptian capital a year before, during his second visit there, had not gone unnoticed. Surely, however, Schechter's excitement about a Ben Sira (Ecclesiasticus) fragment brought to him by his Scottish Presbyterian friends Agnes Lewis and Margaret Gibson, and his determination to find more such early medieval manuscripts of the Hebrew text preserved by the Jews, were major factors in his decision to travel east. He had resolved to steal a march on Oxford in this connection and to refute D. S. Margoliouth's theory that the authentic voice of Ben Sira was to be found in the Greek and Syriac texts and not among the Jews.

As a result of Schechter's imagination and enthusiasm, as well as of his erudition, the recovery of the 'hoard of Hebrew manuscripts' from the genizah (repository) of the Ben-Ezra Synagogue in medieval Cairo became a reality. His energy and single-mindedness ensured that the major areas represented in that collection began to be carefully investigated before he left Cambridge in 1902. Not only did a number of original studies result from his genizah discoveries; the example he set inspired the composition of hundreds of books and thousands of articles in the century following his Cairo expedition. He ushered in a new age of learning about Jews and Judaism as they existed in the medieval Orient, his discoveries making an impact no less than the Dead Sea scrolls fifty years later. What has become famous as the Cairo genizah shed light not only on what Jewish scholars wrote in the biblical and rabbinic fields but also on the daily lives and relations of Jews, Christians, and Muslims in the early centuries of the second millennium. He was promoted from lecturer to reader in 1892 and made a DLitt in 1898.

But to imagine that Schechter ever felt fully at home in the Cambridge courts, cloisters, and combination rooms is to underestimate the gap that still existed between such an exotic personality and his conventional surroundings. It is true that the Bible scholar William Robertson Smith had supported his appointment as university lecturer and his acceptance as a member of Christ's College. In addition, many leading members of the university, such as Charles Taylor, master of St John's College, and Francis Jenkinson, Robertson Smith's successor as university librarian, enjoyed his wit, valued his remarkable mind, and admired his prodigious learning. Nevertheless, his main friendships were with those outside the established academic society, such as Margaret Gibson and Agnes Lewis, and the literary raconteur and librarian Erik Magnusson. His warmest friendship was undoubtedly the one he enjoyed with the pioneering anthropologist James Frazer, a fellow of Trinity for most of his professional life who never obtained a tenured teaching appointment at Cambridge. On their many afternoon walks, Frazer and Schechter apparently exchanged complaints about the Cambridge establishment and its conventionality, but it would not be accurate to lay the entire blame on the university for the further failure of Schechter to settle down fully. Having gradually abandoned intensely religious institutions for enthusiastically academic ones, he had somewhere lost the close Jewish connection and needed to return to a milieu in which he could combine the best of both traditions, train a future generation of intellectual rabbis, and bring religious advantage to his three children. They were having to be brought up in a tiny Jewish community where synagogue services were held only during term time, where sabbath could be a lonely affair except when visitors came from London, where observing the Jewish dietary laws was not easy, and where apostate Jews were more common than observant ones.

In America So it was that Schechter's final move was to America, to the Jewish community that had for a number of years signalled to him that it required his ideas, industry, and fire. There he re-established the Jewish Theological Seminary as a scholarly and educational institution with a commitment to traditional Judaism, provided an intellectual powerhouse that propelled the conservative movement and its United Synagogue of America for about three-quarters of a century, and disseminated popular presentations of Jewish learning that were, by the time of his death in 1915, having a broad impact. He located a galaxy of scholarly stars for his new faculty and passed on to them some of his genizah finds for research and publication. After much thought about their interpretation, he published some remarkable religious tracts from the genizah in his *Documents of Jewish Sectaries* (1910), including the first text of what was later identified among the Dead Sea scrolls as the Damascus document. He also published collections of lively, thoughtful, and sound essays on Jewish topics and supported the expanding Zionist movement and the growing use of Hebrew, while remaining uncomfortable about their secular aspects. It was not, however, easy for such a maverick personality to become a figure of authority and to weigh himself down with administrative burdens. He resented the failure of the Jewish Theological Seminary's supporters to create an adequate financial endowment and regretted that scientific Jewish scholarship was under-valued. His relations with colleagues, inside and outside that institution, were sometimes strained, and he eventually had to acknowledge the need to create not an umbrella Judaism to cover left and right—one that truly represented the achievements and ideals of what he admiringly called 'Catholic Israel'—but another denomination that was neither Orthodox nor Reform but conservative. It was not uncommon for Schechter in his American years to express frustration and a sense of failure; as Mel Scult has recently put it, 'the Seminary succeeded, but unfortunately Schechter did not know it' (Scult, 'Schechter's seminary', 89).

His personality For Schechter, learning meant application, depth, and accuracy, and he could not easily tolerate superficiality, ignorance, or philistinism. His family links were close and demanded love and loyalty, and he was generous and considerate to those in need. He made adjustments to his inherited religious commitment, perhaps in the light of his personal brilliance and independence of mind, without betraying its most central values. He had a respect for piety, an admiration for integrity, and a suspicion of the bureaucratic and clerical aspects of organized religion. He found it difficult to be anything but the magnetic personality he was, and it was perhaps for this reason that children warmed to him so easily. It has even been suggested that the many friendships he made with women, particularly unattached women, may be attributed to their intuitive feminine capacity for distinguishing the genuine from the pretentious.

But Schechter was never the Cambridge gentleman. He made a noisy impact on company, was sloppy and unkempt in appearance, and was cruelly dismissive of the professional rabbinate. He quickly made and unmade friendships, and fellow scholars often attracted his outspoken derision. He regarded certain scholarly topics as his own and sometimes resented, or even prevented, encroachment on them by academic competitors, preferring to share them with a chosen few almost as an act of patronage. Absent-minded and volatile, radical and unpredictable (characteristics that undoubtedly left their impact on his children), Schechter was nevertheless desperately ambitious, and anxiously searched during most of his life for a milieu in which he could win total acceptance and on which he could exercise an authoritative influence. The paradox is that when he located it, he felt disappointed that it did not measure up to his standards of learning on the one hand and of radicalism on the other.

Schechter died on 20 November 1915 in New York, where he was buried. STEFAN C. REIF

Sources N. Bentwich, *Solomon Schechter: a biography* (1938) · A. S. Oko, *Solomon Schechter M.A. Litt.D.: a bibliography* (1938) · A. Marx, 'Solomon Schechter', *Essays in Jewish biography* (1947) · C. Adler, 'Solomon Schechter: a biographical sketch', *American Jewish Year Book* (1916), 24–67 · S. C. Reif, 'Jenkinson and Schechter at Cambridge: an expanded and updated assessment', *Jewish Historical Studies*, 32 (1990–92), 279–316 · S. C. Reif, 'The Cambridge genizah story: some unfamiliar aspects', ed. M. A. Friedman, *Te'uda*, 15 (1999), 413–28 [Hebrew] · S. C. Reif, 'The Damascus document from the Cairo genizah', *The Damascus document: a centennial of discovery*, ed. J. M. Baumgarten, E. Chazon, and A. Pinnick (2000), 109–31 · S. C. Reif, *A Jewish archive from Old Cairo: the history of Cambridge University's genizah collection* (2000) · J. Sussmann, 'Schechter the scholar', *Jewish Studies*, 38 (1998), 213–30 [Hebrew] · M. Scult, 'The Baale Boste reconsidered: the life of Mathilde Roth Schechter (M.R.S.)', *Modern Judaism*, 7 (1987), 1–27 · M. Scult, 'Schechter's seminary', *The making of an institution of Jewish higher learning* (1997), vol. 1 of *Tradition renewed: a history of the Jewish Theological Seminary*, ed. J. Wertheimer, 43–102 · J. D. Sarna, 'Two traditions of seminary scholarship', *Beyond the academy* (1997), vol. 2 of *Tradition renewed: a history of the Jewish Theological Seminary*, ed. J. Wertheimer, 55–80 · D. J. Fine, 'Solomon Schechter and the ambivalence of Jewish *Wissenschaft*', *Judaism*, 46/1 (1997), 3–24 · B. Hirson, *The Cape Town intellectuals: Ruth Schechter and her circle, 1907–1934* (2001)

Archives Library of the Jewish Theological Seminary of America, 3080 Broadway, New York 10027, archive

Likenesses photographs, Library of the Jewish Theological Seminary of America, New York [*see illus.*]

Scheemakers, Peter Gaspar (*bap.* **1691**, *d.* **1781**), sculptor, was baptized in Sint Jacobskerk, Antwerp, on 10 January 1691, the fifth child and first son of Peeter Scheemakers (*bap.* 1652, *d.* 1714), sculptor, and Catharina van der Hulst. He was apprenticed without indenture to his father and spent three years about 1718 in Copenhagen with the court sculptor, J. C. Sturmberg (*d.* 1722). He came to London about 1720 where he joined the workshop of Pierre-Denis Plumier (1688–1721). Plumier died leaving designs and models for a monument to John Sheffield, duke of Buckingham, in Westminster Abbey which Scheemakers and another assistant, Laurent Delvaux, completed in 1722; George Vertue recorded that Scheemakers was responsible for 'the lady. & other parts' (Vertue, *Note books*,

Peter Gaspar Scheemakers (*bap.* 1691, *d.* 1781), by Andreas Bernardus de Quertenmont, 1776

1.101). In 1722 he also carved a life-sized *Omphale* for Lord Castlemaine's gardens at Wanstead (now lost), paired with a *Hercules* by Delvaux; also for Wanstead, he carved vases with reliefs of a *Sacrifice to Apollo* and a *Sacrifice to Hercules* (Anglesey Abbey). After working briefly for Francis Bird he joined forces about 1723 with Delvaux, working from premises in Millbank, Westminster. They provided the monument to Sir Thomas Grantham at Bicester church, Oxfordshire (*c.*1723), and large standing monuments for the first earl and countess of Rockingham at Rockingham church, Northamptonshire (1724–5), and Sir Samuel Ongley at Old Warden church, Bedfordshire (1727–8). After 1725 he carved a group of *Apollo and Venus* for Cannons, Middlesex (St Paul's, Waldenbury).

In 1728 the partners auctioned their stock, announcing that they were going to Rome 'to improve their studies' (Vertue, *Note books*, 3.36). Travelling with them was William Hoare, who later drew Scheemakers's profile portrait in formal dress; an etching exists in the British Museum, London. Scheemakers was 'assiduous in his studies … after the best antique Statues … makeing of most exact & correct. Moddels in Clay' (ibid., 44–5): one of his several Rome sketchbooks survives in the Huntington Library, San Marino. Returning alone to Millbank in 1730, he completed two imposing monuments to Dr Hugh Chamberlen (1728–31) in Westminster Abbey, London, and Sir Michael Warton (1728–32) in Beverley Minster, Yorkshire. A monument to Mountague Garrard Drake in Amersham church, Buckinghamshire, was in hand in 1730–31 and in 1731 he received another Westminster Abbey commission, for Dr John Woodward's monument. Scheemakers competed unsuccessfully in 1733 against Michael Rysbrack for a commission to cast an equestrian statue of William III for Bristol, but the citizens of Hull accepted his model; the statue was completed in 1734.

Dr Richard Mead, the sculptor's most important patron, gave the first of nearly ten commissions to Scheemakers in 1732—the monument to Topham Foot for St John the Baptist Church, Windsor. Other Mead commissions included monuments for Samuel Mead (1733–4; Temple Church, London) and Sir Thomas Reeve (1739; St John the Baptist Church, Windsor). Mead's involvement in the great London hospitals secured commissions for Scheemakers for two life-sized bronze statues of Thomas Guy (1733–4; Guy's Hospital) and Edward VI (1737–9; St Thomas's Hospital). Mead presented Scheemakers's evocative bust of William Harvey to the Royal College of Physicians in 1739 and in 1740 used his influence to secure the contract that made Scheemakers's name, the memorial to Shakespeare for poets' corner in Westminster Abbey. Raised in time of war, this testament to a national hero won 'disproportionate' acclaim and 'tossd this Sculptor above on the summit of the wheel' (Vertue, *Note books*, 3.116). Success apparently went to his head: Vertue commented: 'this little fellow … since he has done Shakespeare Mon[t] thinks himself above all others' (ibid., 3.108). He noted with distaste the sculptor's acute business sense, 'in the management of his affairs, boldness and also allwayes underworking the others [Rysbrack's] price' (ibid., 3.116).

At Christmas 1741 Scheemakers moved to new premises with an adjacent dwelling in Vine Street, Piccadilly. Although the prospect of commercial expansion was no doubt the main reason, he also needed an improved dwelling, having contracted a 'clandestine' marriage to Barbara la Fosse (*d.* in or before 1781), who had in 1740 given birth to his only son, Thomas [*see below*]. During the decade from 1741 he directed work on nearly forty monuments, notably to Marwood William Turner (1741–2; Kirkleatham church, Yorkshire), General Kirke (1741–3; Westminster Abbey), Sir Christopher Powell (after 1743; Boughton Monchelsea church, Kent), Dr Marmaduke Coghill (1743; Drumcondra church, Ireland), Lord Aubrey Beauclerk (1743–5; Westminster Abbey), General Monck (1743–6; Westminster Abbey), Admiral Balchen (1744–6; Westminster Abbey), and Admiral Wager (1743–7; Westminster Abbey). Although these vary in quality, most have well-executed figural elements, suggesting the sculptor's personal involvement. In 1747 he produced his only work for the City of London, the statue of Sir John Barnard for the Royal Exchange.

The workshop was also involved in garden and library commissions. In 1736–7 Scheemakers had worked for Richard Temple, first Viscount Cobham, at Stowe, Buckinghamshire, on busts of British worthies, four statues of ancient worthies and then an ambitious relief for the Palladian bridge, *Britannia Receiving Gifts from the Four Quarters of the World* (1738–42); between 1739 and 1742 he carved four or more finely characterized patrician heads of Cobham's boy patriots for the Temple of Friendship. Between 1739 and 1743 he worked at the Dormer family estate of Rousham in Oxfordshire; another landscape garden directed by William Kent, sending down several busts and terms and two works for focal positions, *A Lion Attacking a Horse* and a *Dying Gladiator*. In 1743 he received a major order for fourteen marble library busts for Trinity College, Dublin, which was completed in 1749; L.-F. Roubiliac appears to have carved six of them, working in subcontract. Scheemakers embarked on a speculative exercise in 1747, advertising sets of five plaster casts from his models made in Rome, at 5 guineas each; their success led to other ventures in the same medium.

In 1751 Scheemakers won his most lucrative contract, for the massive Shelburne monument (High Wycombe church, Buckinghamshire), in which his most able apprentice, Joseph Nollekens, probably took a part. Sickness led to auctions of workshop contents in 1755 and 1756, but in 1759 he rallied and went into partnership with the architect James (Athenian) Stuart, whose knowledge of the antique now superseded his own. In that year he carved a delicate relief for the *Shepherd's Monument* at Shugborough, Staffordshire, at Stuart's instigation, and several major monuments designed by Stuart followed, for Admiral Howe (1759; Westminster Abbey), Admiral Watson (1763–6; Westminster Abbey), and Lord Chancellor Philip Yorke, earl of Hardwicke, at Wimpole church (1764–6), a work which prefigures the sculpture of the Greek revival. Although Scheemakers was by now well into his seventies all work went out in his name until 1771, when he retired and returned to Antwerp with his savings, estimated at '3 or £4,000' (Farington, *Diary*, 5.1792). Investments from property in Antwerp enabled him to live in the affluent quarter by Sint Jacobskerk and to have his portrait painted in 1776 by a rising artist, A. B. de Quertenmont. He died there in 1781 and was buried on 12 September in Sint Jacobskerk.

Scheemakers, 'a little man in person, but handsome' (Farington, *Diary*, 8.2494), played a major role in popularizing a severe classical style, the prelude to the Greek revival. His moderate prices encouraged new clients from the professional and mercantile communities to order commemorative sculpture.

Thomas Scheemakers (1740–1808), sculptor, the son of Peter Scheemakers and Barbara la Fosse, began entering models of ideal subjects at exhibiting society competitions from Vine Street in 1763 and won premiums from the Society of Arts. He and Stuart worked on several monuments in the 1770s, notably those for Dr Ralph Freman (*c*.1773; Braughing church, Hertfordshire), Joseph Cockes (1775) and Mrs Mary Cockes (1779; both Eastnor church, Herefordshire), all relations of the Yorkes; Stuart also designed the monument carved by the young Scheemakers for Thomas Bentley (1780; Chiswick church). Scheemakers worked alone on two other monuments for his father's patrons, Sir Jemmet Raymond (after 1771; Kintbury church, Berkshire) and Anthony, Lord Feversham (1784; Downton church, Wiltshire). His talent is evident from a sheaf of designs now in the Victoria and Albert Museum, London, and particularly the monument to Mrs Mary Russell (1786; Powick church, Worcestershire), but he lacked his father's drive and appears to have stopped working in 1792. His effects were sold in 1805 and he died on 15 July 1808 leaving a widow, Barbara (1747–1810). He was buried in St Pancras churchyard.

INGRID ROSCOE

Sources I. M. Roscoe, 'Peter Scheemakers', *Walpole Society*, 61 (1999), 163–404 • I. Roscoe, 'Peter Scheemakers and classical sculpture in early Georgian England', PhD diss., U. Leeds, 1990 • M. Whinney, *Sculpture in Britain, 1530 to 1830*, rev. J. Physick, 2nd edn (1988), 157–9, 183–90 • I. Roscoe, 'Peter Scheemakers at Rome', *Gazette des Beaux-Arts*, 6th ser., 110 (1987), 1–10 • M. Baker, 'The making of portrait busts in the mid eighteenth century: Roubiliac, Scheemakers and Trinity College, Dublin', *Burlington Magazine*, 137 (1995), 821–31 • M. Baker, 'Lord Shelburne's "costly fabric": Scheemakers, Roubiliac and Taylor as rivals', *Burlington Magazine*, 132 (1990), 841–8 • D. Solkin, 'Samaritan or Scrooge? The contested image of Thomas Guy in eighteenth century England', *Art Bulletin*, 78 (1996), 467–84 • T. F. Friedman, 'Scheemakers's monument to the best of sons', *Burlington Magazine*, 122 (1980), 61 • I. Roscoe, 'James "Athenian" Stuart and the Scheemakers family: a lucrative partnership between architect and sculptors', *Apollo*, 126 (1987), 178–84 • Vertue, *Note books*, vols. 1, 3 • A. Buesching, *Nachrichten von dem Zustande der Wissenschaften und Kunste in den koniglichen danischen Reichen*, 3 (Leipzig, 1754–7), 194 • P. Baert, 'Mémoires sur les sculpteurs et architectes des Pays-Bas, recueillis en 1778–9', *c*.1870, V&A, MS 86.EE.64, 74–5 • R. Gunnis, *Dictionary of British sculptors, 1660–1851* (1953); new edn (1968) • Antwerp City Archives, PR 55 [baptism] • Antwerp City Archives, PR 300 [burial] • *kerk* registers, OL Vrouwerk-Zuid, Antwerp City Archives, 17 Oct 1769 [parents' marriage]

Likenesses W. Hoare, etching, *c*.1738, BM • A. B. de Quertenmont, oils, 1776, NPG [*see illus.*]

Wealth at death 'had saved 3 or £4,000' in England: Farington, *Diary*, 5.1792 • regular income in Antwerp from compound interest on house in the Eiermarkt, De Zeven Sterren, and on butcher's stall in the Vleeshuis: Acts of Schepenbriefen, Antwerp City Archives, SR.1227, fols. 229v, 300v; SR 1234, fols. 70r–71v

Scheemakers, Thomas (1740–1808). *See under* Scheemakers, Peter Gaspar (*bap.* 1691, *d.* 1781).

Scheener, Edward Schencker (1789–1853), civil servant and half-brother of Queen Victoria, was born in Geneva, Switzerland, on 24 November 1789, the natural son of *Edward, duke of Kent, and Anne Gabrielle Alexandrine Moré. Scheener passed his youth in Geneva in the family of his ostensible father, Thimothée Schencker. Kent undertook to find a place for Scheener in the civil service, and in 1809 he was appointed a supernumerary clerk in the Foreign Office, having previously occupied a position in the council office as an assistant examiner of public accounts. He was appointed to the regular establishment in 1814 and was promoted to the second class in 1823. After being ordered to absent himself permanently from the Foreign Office in September 1826 he was retired on a pension of £272 10*s*. 0*d*. on 5 July 1830.

Royal patronage was at this time fairly common in the Foreign Office; Richard Mellish and Adolfus Kent Oom both had court connections, so Scheener was hardly exceptional. However, it has always been supposed that the duke of Kent, unlike his brothers who had many acknowledged natural children, had just one child, Queen Victoria. Whatever may be the real story of Kent's long liaison with Mme Julie St Laurent and their 'invisible' children, there can be no doubt that Kent fathered two children in Geneva shortly before his sudden and unexplained departure in January 1790; one was Edward Scheener, and the other Adelaide Victoire Auguste Dubus, whose mother died in childbirth.

As soon as Scheener appeared in the Foreign Office in 1809, one of the clerks reported that before George Canning left office he had put Scheener on the establishment as an extra clerk and that 'he had the interest of the Duke of Kent to whom he bears a strong resemblance and whom report says to have a nearer relation to him than their being both sons of Adam' (FO, 95/8/14, fol. 900). The duke of Clarence, always the most solicitous of Kent's elder brothers, took Scheener on his staff as private secretary in 1814, in which capacity he accompanied Europe's royalties to and fro across the channel.

Scheener went abroad again in 1818 but was never able to recover to his satisfaction his expenses from Castlereagh's Foreign Office. After Canning returned to office in 1822, Scheener took up the cause again, but so completely lost his head that Canning declared that he 'would rather copy all the Foreign Office despatches himself than rely upon an individual so wrong-headed, of a nature so suspicious and of a temper so ungovernable' (Bourne, 447). The duke of Clarence was called upon to remind Canning that Scheener was the natural son of the duke of Kent, and that Clarence wished to save Scheener from utter ruin. Scheener was in consequence only suspended (1826), but in 1830, with his patron now king, Scheener succeeded, by dint of publicizing his case in two pamphlets, *Memoirs of an Employée* and *Statement of Facts to his Majesty's Ministers*, in getting his case reviewed by Lord Palmerston. Palmerston refused to take Scheener back and he was placed on the pension list.

It may not be entirely coincidental that Scheener returned to Geneva with his wife, Harriet (*b.* 1781), daughter of David Boyn of London, in 1837, the same year that Victoria ascended the throne. Harriet died on 20 January 1852; they had no children. Scheener died at his home, 280 rue Verdaine, Geneva, on 31 January 1853, a pall of official silence then falling over his very existence.

R. A. JONES

Sources C. R. Middleton, *The administration of British foreign policy, 1782–1846* (1977) • R. Jones, *The nineteenth-century foreign office: an administrative history* (1971) • H. Temperley, *The foreign policy of Canning, 1822–1827*, 2nd edn (1966) • K. Bourne, *Palmerston: the early years, 1784–1841* (1982) • P. A. Tunbridge, 'Field-Marshal the duke of Kent as a freemason', *Transactions of the Quatuor Coronati Lodge* (1965) • private information (2004) • J. M. Collinge, ed., *Office-holders in modern Britain*, 8: *Foreign office officials, 1782–1870* (1979) • Geneva, Archives d'État • BL, Ellis MSS, BL Add. MS 41315

Archives University of Geneva | BL, Ellis MSS, Add. MS 41315 • PRO, FO 95/591 • PRO, FO 95/8/14

Wealth at death see will, dated 29 Aug 1852, Archives d'État, Geneva, Jur. Civ. AAQ. 10, 189

Scheerre [Scheere, Skereueyn], **Herman** [Herman of Cologne] (*fl.* *c.*1388–*c.*1422), manuscript artist, was an illuminator of German or Flemish origin who worked in London *c.*1405–*c.*1422. He is probably to be identified with the illuminator Herman of Cologne whose name occurs in the household accounts of Duke William of Gueldres about 1388–9, and who was working for Philip the Bold, duke of Burgundy, in Dijon in 1401–3. His name, in the various forms of Hermannus Scheere, Herman Skereueyn, or Herman, occurs in connection with the rent of a shop in Paternoster Row, London, some time before 1410, and as witness to two wills of Cologne men in London in 1407; it also appears in three illuminated manuscripts of London provenance from the period *c.*1405–1422 (offices and prayers, BL, Add. MS 16998; the Bedford hours and psalter, BL, Add. MS 42131; the Chichele breviary, London, Lambeth Palace Library, MS 69). The illuminator has also been identified with the Herman of Cologne who was working in Paris for the French queen, Isabel of Bavaria, in 1419. Various manuscripts not signed with his name have been attributed to the artist both on grounds of style and from the occurrence of a motto in the decoration *Si quis amat non laborat* ('He who loves does not labour'). There is controversy over both the dating and the amount of illumination of these books which can be attributed to Scheerre and it has recently been suggested by Kathleen Scott that the motto was also used by his workshop and does not always imply his personal involvement.

If Herman Scheerre is indeed identical with Herman of Cologne, there is very little in his art which derives from Cologne painting, except perhaps some iconographic features. Closer parallels with his style of painting and iconographic types can be found in the work of illuminators of Bruges and Ypres. If Scheerre did originate from Cologne it seems his art was formulated mainly within a Flemish context, perhaps at Dijon when he was working for the duke of Burgundy in 1401–2. He came to England *c.*1405 and remained there until at least 1419, perhaps as late as 1422. While in England he collaborated with other illuminators in London, particularly the leading figure Magister Johannes who, like Scheerre, seems to have been a foreigner, perhaps of Flemish origin. Scott has attempted to analyse more precisely the relative contributions of these two artists, and of the other artists employed in their workshops, in the approximately twenty books illuminated in their styles. The main books whose decoration is mostly by Scheerre himself are: the *c.*1405 book of hours (CUL, MS Ee.1.14); the book of offices and prayers of about 1405 to 1410 (BL, Add. MS 16998); the Nevill hours of about 1405–10 (Berkeley Castle, trustees of the late earl of Berkeley); the *c.*1410 book of hours (Bodl. Oxf., MS Gough liturg. 6); the breviary done for Henry Chichele, perhaps when bishop of St David's (1408–14), before he became archbishop of Canterbury in 1414 (London, Lambeth Palace Library, MS 69); the prayer book of Charles, duke of Orléans (who was imprisoned in London), perhaps of about 1415–17 (Paris, Bibliothèque Nationale, MS Lat. 1196); and, finally, the book of hours and psalter of John, duke of Bedford (BL, Add. MS 42131). His authorship of the annunciation with two donors of an unknown family, in the *c.*1410 Beaufort–Beauchamp hours (BL, Royal MS 2 A.xviii, fol. 23*v*), is not accepted by all.

Herman Scheerre and Johannes were the leading illuminators of early fifteenth-century England and Scheerre's iconographic compositions and ornamental decoration continued to influence English artists up to the 1440s. NIGEL J. MORGAN

Sources K. L. Scott, *Later Gothic manuscripts, 1390–1490*, 2 vols. (1996), nos. 16, 21–3, 29–30, 49, 51, 54, 57, 59 • M. Rickert, 'Herman the Illuminator', *Burlington Magazine*, 66 (1935), 39–40 • C. L. Kuhn, 'Herman Scheerre and English illumination of the early fifteenth century', *Art Bulletin*, 22 (1940), 138–56 • M. Rickert, *The reconstructed Carmelite missal* (1952), 138, 141 • N. J. Morgan, 'Scheerre, Herman', *The dictionary of art*, ed. J. Turner (1996) • G. Spriggs, 'The Nevill hours', *Journal of the Warburg and Courtauld Institutes*, 37 (1974), 104–30 • C. P. Christianson, *A directory of London stationers and book artisans, 1300–1500* (1990), 157–8

Archives Berkeley Castle, Gloucestershire, Nevill book of hours • Bibliothèque Nationale, Paris, MS Lat. 1196 • BL, Add. MSS 16998, 42131 • BL, Royal MS 2 A.xviii, fol. 23*v* • Bodl. Oxf., MS Gough liturg. 6 • CUL, MS Ee.1.14 • LPL, MS 69

Schetky, John Alexander (1785–1824), watercolour painter, was born in March 1785 in Foulis's Close, Edinburgh, and was baptized in the Old Episcopal Church of St Michael in Edinburgh, one of the eleven children of Johann Georg Christoff Schetky (1728/9–1824), composer and violoncellist (who had arrived from Hungary in 1772), and his wife, Maria Anna Theresa (*d.* 1795). His mother, an artist, was the eldest daughter of Joseph Reinagle, also a Hungarian composer, and his wife, Anne Laurie; John Christian *Schetky (1778–1874) was his brother.

After attending the high school, Edinburgh, John Alexander Schetky studied medicine at Edinburgh University and art at the Trustees Academy under John Graham. After graduating, he was appointed assistant surgeon in the 3rd dragoon guards (October 1804) and in April 1809 accompanied his regiment to Portugal where he served with distinction, and conspicuous altruism, in the Peninsular War. In August 1812, Schetky was promoted to the rank of surgeon to the Portuguese forces under Marshall Beresford and remained attached to the 7th division until the end of the war in 1814. He then returned to Edinburgh where he continued to study and practise medicine (he became a fellow of the Royal College of Surgeons of Edinburgh in July 1818) and resumed his art studies at the Trustees Academy.

Schetky's first exhibited work was *A Composition*, which appeared at the Royal Academy in 1808. He sketched constantly during his years abroad and sent work home (usually to his brother John Christian to whom he was very close) for exhibition with the Associated Artists in Water-Colours; in 1810 he was listed as an exhibitor, in 1811 and 1812 as a member. *Celerico*, shown in 1811, received high praise from the president of the society. After his return, Schetky exhibited four works at the Society of Painters in Water Colours in 1816 and 1817, two of these depicting scenery in the Pyrenees and one showing military action in Portugal: *Scene in the Serra da Estrella, in Portugal, with the Flight of the Peasantry on Massena's Invasion*. He also exhibited a *Recollection of the Serra da Estrella, Portugal* at the Royal Academy in 1821. A considerable number of Schetky's landscapes portrayed Scottish scenery (five of these, including three of Loch Lomond, were lent for exhibition at the Royal Scottish Academy in 1863 and 1880); in 1822 and 1823 Rodwell and Martin of New Bond Street published engravings from two drawings by him, *Hawthornden* and *Dunbar Castle*, which were later included in Sir Walter Scott's *Provincial Antiquities and Picturesque Scenery of Scotland* (1826), of which Turner was also an illustrator. An anonymous writer praised Schetky's ability to give 'exquisite detail' in 'romantic scenes of grandeur' (Maclagan, 6–7).

Schetky was recalled to active service in 1819. Following an appointment at the General Hospital at Fort Pitt, Chatham, his artistic skills were also employed in the medical field and he contributed many drawings to the Museum of Morbid Anatomy established by Sir James McGrigor. He also finished the lithographic engravings that comprise *The Fasciculus of Morbid Anatomy* (*c.*1825) published by the medical board—a collection that has been termed 'a valuable addition to the illustration of pathology' (Maclagan, 3). In August 1823, Schetky was promoted to the post of deputy inspector of hospitals on the west coast of Africa where he hoped to visit and sketch the region explored by Mungo Park. Soon after his arrival in Sierra Leone (in February 1824), he was appointed a member of the colonial council. Schetky contracted a fever while travelling from Sierra Leone to Cape Coast Castle and died shortly after his arrival there, on 5 September 1824. His brother John Christian had collaborated with him on two paintings, depicting naval actions, exhibited at the Royal Academy in 1825. CHARLOTTE YELDHAM

Sources D. Maclagan, *Biographical sketch of the late John Alexander Schetky* (1825) • P. J. M. McEwan, *Dictionary of Scottish art and architecture* (1994) • [S. F. L. Schetky], *Ninety years of work and play: sketches from the public and private career of John Christian Schetky … by his daughter* (1877) • Redgrave, *Artists*, 2nd edn • Bryan, *Painters* (1886–9) • Graves, *RA exhibitors* • *The Royal Watercolour Society: the first fifty years, 1805–1855* (1992) • J. L. Roget, *A history of the 'Old Water-Colour' Society*, 2 vols. (1891) • exhibition catalogue (1863) [Royal Scot. Acad.] • exhibition catalogue (1880) [Royal Scot. Acad.] • *DNB*

Archives Royal College of Surgeons, Edinburgh, MSS

Schetky, John Christian (1778–1874), marine painter, fourth son of Johann Georg Christoff Schetky, was born in Ainslie Close, Edinburgh, on 11 August 1778. His father, descended from the ancient Transylvanian family of von Teschky of Hermannstadt, was a well-known composer and cellist, who settled in Edinburgh and died there in 1824 at the age of ninety-five. His mother was Maria Anna Theresa Reinagle (*d.* 1795), eldest daughter of the composer Joseph Reinagle (1762–1825) and sister to Philip Reinagle RA (1748–1833). She was an accomplished musician and artist with a particular skill in miniature painting. Schetky was educated at Edinburgh high school, where he formed a lifelong friendship with his contemporary Walter Scott. An early love of the sea developed into an intense desire to join the navy. He signed up on the *Hind* for two years, but was subsequently persuaded to leave by his parents, to his lifelong regret. He consoled himself, however, by drawing the sea and the great naval vessels. Like Willem van de Velde, whose work influenced his own, he painted with his left hand. In his mid-teens he helped his mother teach drawing, and also began to teach on his own, while studying under Alexander Nasmyth. In autumn 1801 he travelled with a friend to Paris, walking from there to Rome, where he stayed for two months. Early in 1802 he returned to settle in Oxford, where he lived for six years and made many friends. He first exhibited a seapiece at the Royal Academy in 1805 and continued to exhibit there at intervals until 1872. He also showed with the Associated Artists in Water-Colours from 1808 to 1812. In 1808 he accepted the junior professorship of civil drawing in the Royal Military College at Great Marlow, Buckinghamshire. He retired from this post in spring 1811 after spending the Christmas vacation visiting his brother, John Alexander *Schetky (1785–1824), a watercolour painter who was then serving as assistant surgeon with his regiment in Portugal. In the same year he became professor of drawing at the Royal Naval College, Portsmouth, where he remained until the college was dissolved in 1836. During this time he married Charlotte Trevenen (*d.* 1867) on 13 April 1828 at the church of St George, Bloomsbury, London, and returned to live at Buckland House, Kingston, near Portsmouth. Schetky was remembered by his pupils in Portsmouth for his interest in their well-being and his enthusiasm as a teacher. He was described by one of them as a 'fine tall fellow … with all the manners and appearance of a sailor' (Schetky). After leaving Portsmouth he obtained a similar appointment at the East India College in Addiscombe, Kent, which he held until he retired in 1855. While there his practice of making sepia and ink drawings earned him the affectionate nickname All Sepia. The Schetkys had three daughters. In 1837 the family was living at Waddon Lodge near Croydon, Surrey. In 1819 Schetky was appointed painter in watercolours to the duke of Clarence and during his career he received royal commissions as marine painter in ordinary to George IV and William IV and was reappointed to the post under Queen Victoria in 1844. In this capacity he painted two pictures commemorating the visit of King Louis Philippe to Queen Victoria at Portsmouth in October 1844 (one exh. RA, 1845). As well as royal events he painted historic sea battles and actions, ship portraits, and general shipping scenes. Other paintings of note include the *Battle of Trafalgar, 1805* (exh. British Institution, 1825); the *Sinking of the Royal George at Spithead, 1782* (1840; Tate collection), and the *Battle of La Hogue, 1692* (1847), painted for a competition for the decoration of the new houses of parliament. It was exhibited at Westminster Hall in 1847 and purchased by the duke and duchess of Bedford for Woburn Abbey. He was a prolific painter and his work is well crafted. The ships and vessels in his oil paintings are notable for their attention to detail and his depictions of the sea are the result of patient observation. Rocky landscape is often a feature of his work, as shown for example in a pair of paintings entitled *Salvage of Stores and Treasures from HMS Thetis at Cape Frio, Argentina, 1830* (1833, exh. RA, 1834; NMM). Schetky was also an accomplished watercolour painter of naval subjects. His work includes twelve watercolour views engraved by James Heath to illustrate Walter Scott's *Lay of the Last Minstrel* (1808). He also illustrated John Manners's *Sketches and Notes of a Cruise in Scotch Waters on board His Grace the Duke of Rutland's Yacht, Resolution* (1850) with twenty-nine lithographic plates. In 1867, the year of his wife's death, Schetky published *Reminiscences of Veterans of the Sea*, a series of photographs of twenty of his paintings and drawings selected to illustrate the great wooden fighting vessels of the British navy. Of his character his daughter observed that 'to obtain a favour for another was all his life one of his greatest pleasures … at the same time he was the most unbusiness-like of men and rarely took any trouble about his own affairs' (Schetky). He played the cello, flute, and guitar, and sang Scottish ballads and Dibdin's songs with great feeling. Schetky died on 29 January 1874 at his home, 11 Kent Terrace, Regent's Park, London, from an acute attack of bronchitis. He was buried at Paddington cemetery, London, on 5 February 1874. Further examples of his work may be found in the National Gallery of Scotland, Edinburgh; the Castle Museum, Norwich; the Royal Collection; and the Peabody Essex Museum, Salem, Massachusetts.

LINDSEY MACFARLANE

Sources *DNB* • [S. F. L. Schetky], *Ninety years of work and play: sketches from the public and private career of John Christian Schetky … by his daughter* (1877) • *Concise catalogue of oil paintings in the National Maritime Museum* (1988) • E. H. H. Archibald, *Dictionary of sea painters*, 2nd edn (1989) • Graves, *RA exhibitors* • W. Greenaway, 'Artistic passion for sea and ships: John Christian Schetky and his work', *Country Life* (10 April 1980) • N. Surry, *The Portsmouth papers: art in a dockyard town: Portsmouth, 1770–1845* (1992) • J. Turner, ed., *The dictionary of art*, 34 vols. (1996) • *CGPLA Eng. & Wales* (1874) • will, probate department of the principal registry of the family division, London

Archives NRA, priv. coll., report of loss of *Royal George* in 1782

Likenesses J. Napier, oils, 1861, priv. coll. • F. Grant, portrait, priv. coll. • D. Hill and R. Adamson, photograph, Scot. NPG • W. Howard, oils • wood-engraving, BM; repro. in *ILN* (1874)

Wealth at death under £12,000: resworn probate, Aug 1874, *CGPLA Eng. & Wales*

Scheuchzer [Scheutzer], **John Gaspar** (1702–1729), physician and naturalist, was born in Zürich, Switzerland, the son of John James Scheuchzer (1672–1733), professor of mathematics at Zürich and well-known natural historian. He graduated in philosophy at Zürich in 1722, with a dissertation 'De diluvio'. He was a noted naturalist and antiquary, and on coming to England he became librarian to Sir Hans Sloane. Elected a fellow of the Royal Society on 7 May 1724, he was for some time the society's foreign secretary. He received the licence of the Royal College of Physicians on 22 March 1725. In 1728 he was created doctor of medicine at Cambridge, when George I visited the university.

Scheuchzer's most significant publication was *An Account of the Success of Inoculating the Small Pox, for the Years 1727–1728* (1729). This work continued the series of annual pamphlets with the same title written by the physician James Jurin since 1723. In 1728, after Jurin indicated that he would no longer draw up these accounts, Scheuchzer announced that he planned to continue the series. Following Jurin, he compared the mortality rates for natural and inoculated smallpox for the years 1727 and 1728, and provided a comprehensive summary of all the accounts concerning inoculation in England from 1721 to 1729. According to Scheuchzer's figures, an individual had a one in six chance of dying from natural smallpox, and a one in fifty chance of dying from inoculated smallpox. Both Jurin's and Scheuchzer's works were instrumental in establishing smallpox inoculation in Britain.

Scheuchzer also published a paper in the *Philosophical Transactions* on the method of measuring the heights of mountains. He translated an account of the history of Japan from a manuscript by Engelbertus Kaempfer, which Sir Hans Sloane had purchased: *The History of Japan*, beautifully illustrated, was published in London in 1727. At the time of his death Scheuchzer was working on an English translation of Kaempfer's travels to Muscovy, Persia, and the West Indies. Scheuchzer died on 10 April 1729 at Sloane's house in Chelsea and was buried in the Chelsea churchyard. ANDREA RUSNOCK

Sources Munk, *Roll* • N. F. J. Eloy, *Dictionnaire historique de la médecine ancienne et moderne*, 4 vols. (Mons, 1778) • *DNB* • Venn, *Alum. Cant.* • *The record of the Royal Society of London*, 4th edn (1940)
Archives BL, Sloane MSS
Likenesses J. H. Heidegger, portrait, repro. in Munk, *Roll*

Scheves, William (*b.* in or before **1440**, *d.* **1497**), courtier and archbishop of St Andrews, may have been the son of John Scheves, clerk register and official of St Andrews during the reign of James II. Probably born shortly before 1440, he was a determinant in the faculty of arts at the University of St Andrews, together with his predecessor in the archbishopric, Patrick Graham, in 1454. Two years later he was presented for a licence in arts; and by 1460 he was already teaching in the university, a role which he seems to have performed throughout the next decade. This was the unremarkable beginning to the career of one of the most powerful men in James III's Scotland.

Scheves's first recorded appearance at court occurs in 1471, when he is to be found receiving a modest annual pension of £20 Scots for his services as a physician. It may well be asked where he acquired his medical knowledge. A century later George Buchanan gave a possible answer, claiming that Scheves had studied for several years at Louvain under 'John Spernic (Spierinck), a celebrated physician and astrologer' (Buchanan, 2.137). John Spierinck can be identified as a doctor of medicine, rector of the University of Louvain in 1457, 1462, and 1479; yet no record of Scheves's presence at Louvain can be found in the 1460s, a period when he appears in any case to have been teaching at St Andrews. Scheves undoubtedly had a Louvain connection, but it may have dated from much later in his life. In 1491 Jasper Laet de Borchloen dedicated a book on astronomy—specifically on the eclipse of the sun in May 1491—to Scheves; and Laet would subsequently describe himself as a doctor of medicine and astrologer at the University of Louvain.

In the early 1470s Scheves's court duties were more practical than esoteric. His general tasks as physician included obtaining drugs from Bruges for King James and prescribing green ginger for two sick royal servants, but also extended to buying velvet for the king, looking after the silver for the harness of three royal horses, and even making payments for the sewing of the king's shirts. These modest beginnings in royal service brought Scheves into close contact with James III, and his opportunity for spectacular advancement arrived in 1473–4, when the king and the Scottish episcopal hierarchy united to condemn Scheves's former fellow student at St Andrews, Archbishop Patrick Graham. A general council of February 1474 ordered the seizure of the temporalities of Graham's see, and continuing royal attacks on the archbishop paralleled Scheves's insinuation, with James III's support, into St Andrews. By 15 April 1474 Scheves had obtained the archdeaconry of St Andrews; on 13 July 1476 a papal bull appointed him coadjutor of the see on account of Patrick Graham's excommunication and insanity; in February 1478 Scheves was provided to the archbishopric, and in the spring of 1479 he was duly consecrated at Holyrood Abbey.

Scheves's spectacular rise was deeply resented by some other members of the Scottish episcopate; but of even wider concern was his role as court 'fixer', the only individual throughout the reign who countersigned—and perhaps prepared—royal letters on subjects as varied as relations with England, royal gifts and admonitions, local affairs, and finance. In acting thus he was often performing functions which would normally have been the responsibility of Archibald Whitelaw, the king's official secretary. Scheves's closeness to the king at a time when James III and his policies had become deeply unpopular, coupled with the fact that the archbishop held no major office of state, made him an obvious target during the Lauder crisis of 1482. When James was seized, Scheves saved himself by flight and in the autumn of 1482 ran the serious risk of losing his archbishopric, coveted by Andrew Stewart, bishop-elect of Moray, James III's half-uncle, who had already acquired the keepership of the privy seal. While King James's recovery of power in 1483 rescued Scheves's position as archbishop, he had proved himself a broken reed, and never again enjoyed the same intimacy with the king. In the 1480s James looked to new familiars for support, among them Master John Ireland, another hated rival of Scheves from St Andrews student days.

The remainder of Scheves's life was spent in a rearguard action to attempt to preserve and consolidate his career gains. In March 1487 Pope Innocent VIII made the archbishop primate of Scotland; but this status would be of value only if he could secure the obedience of the Scottish episcopate. He was not given the time. In the spring and early summer of 1488 a huge rebellion overwhelmed James III and brought his fifteen-year-old son to the throne as James IV. More alarming for Scheves was that a key role in the successful rebellion had been played by Robert Blackadder, bishop of Glasgow. He was duly rewarded with James IV's support and an archbishopric in 1492, and it was he, not Scheves, who crowned James king, shortly before 26 June 1488. Scheves struggled to assert his primatial status, with no real success, until his death on 28 January 1497.

Scheves acquired a reputation as a scheming and aspiring cleric in the late sixteenth-century history of George Buchanan. This perhaps does him less than justice. His more enduring legacy includes his books, theological texts, medical treatises, and two editions of the *Scotichronicon*, as well as his medallion, struck in the Low Countries in 1491, which not only preserves his portrait, but also boldly asserts his primacy.

NORMAN MACDOUGALL

Sources G. Burnett and others, eds., *The exchequer rolls of Scotland*, 8–10 (1885–7) • *APS*, 1424–1567 • J. M. Thomson and others, eds., *Registrum magni sigilli regum Scotorum / The register of the great seal of Scotland*, 11 vols. (1882–1914), vol. 2 • T. Dickson, ed., *Compota thesaurariorum regum Scotorum / Accounts of the lord high treasurer of Scotland*, 1 (1877) • [G. Buchanan], *The history of Scotland translated from the Latin of George Buchanan*, ed. and trans. J. Aikman, 6 vols. (1827–9), vol. 2 • J. Herkless and R. K. Hannay, *The archbishops of St Andrews*, 5 vols. (1907–15), vol. 1, pp. 80–164 • L. J. Macfarlane, 'The primacy of the Scottish church, 1472–1521', *Innes Review*, 20 (1969), 111–29 • N. Macdougall, *James III: a political study* (1982) • N. Macdougall, *James IV* (1989) • *CDS*, vol. 4 • W. Fraser, ed., *The Annandale family book of the Johnstones*, 2 vols. (1894) • J. Stuart, ed., *The miscellany of the Spalding Club*, 4, Spalding Club, 20 (1849)

Archives BL, books from his library • U. Edin. L., books from his library • U. St Andr. L.

Likenesses attrib. Q. Metsys, bronze medallion, 1491, BM, Musée des Antiquités, Rouen, France • bust, BM • plaster cast, NG Scot.

Schiavonetti, Luigi [Lewis, Louis] (**1765–1810**), printmaker, was born on 1 April 1765 in Bassano del Grappo, Italy, the eldest of eight children of Sante Schiavonetti, a paper manufacturer, and his wife, Gaetana, *née* Viaro. He was taught to draw by the painter Julius (Giulio) Golini, with whom he was sent to study at the age of thirteen. Following the death of his master three years later he subsequently received instruction from the engraver Ambrosio Orio. He then worked for Remordini, whose large enterprise produced illustrated books. About 1790 he went to London to work under Bartolozzi, with whom he lived for a while at North End, Fulham, and gained a thorough grounding and versatility in the graphic arts. After leaving Bartolozzi's employ he and his brother Niccolò [*see below*] lived at 12 Michael's Place (now 231 Brompton Road), Brompton. Here they pursued their engraving careers and entered into print publishing, which seemed to be successful; extant letters indicate they had a continental trade.

Luigi's versatility in stipple, line, and etching ensured a varied output. His talents were required for book illustrations, decorative prints, calling cards, and works after old masters, portraitists, and historical artists. The most important works in which he was involved include Francis Wheatley's *Cries of London* (1793–7): he engraved three plates in stipple and directed the engraving of two others—his task being made more exacting as this series was an early, major one in which the stipple engravings were printed in colour from a single plate.

For the nine-volume *The Dramatic Works of Shakspeare* (1802–3) revised by George Steevens and published by John Boydell he engraved *As You Like It* (1791) after W. Hamilton (3, p. 101); *King Lear* (1792) after R. Smirke (9, p. 71); *All's Well that Ends Well* (1797) after F. Wheatley (3, p.37); and *A Midsummer Night's Dream* (1799) after Sir Joshua Reynolds (2, p. 27). For the folio-size *A Collection of Prints, from Pictures Painted for the Purpose of Illustrating the Dramatic Works of Shakspeare by the Artists of Great Britain* (2 vols., 1803, with a dedication of 1805), Schiavonetti engraved *Two Gentlemen of Verona* (1792; vol. 1, no. 7) and *Troilus and Cressida* (1795; vol.2, no. 35) both after Angelica Kauffman. For each of these he received £315. A new edition of Robert Blair's *The Grave*, published in 1808 by R. H. Cromek, was illustrated by twelve of Schiavonetti's etchings after original designs by William Blake, together with a copperplate line engraving after a portrait of Blake by Thomas Phillips (1807), which was also used as a frontispiece to the second edition of Alexander Gilchrist's *Life of William Blake* (1880), volume 2, and A. C. Swinburne's *William Blake: a Critical Essay* (1906).

While the series of four stipple prints (1793–5) after Charles Benazech and William Miller depicting incidents directly related to Louis XVI are among his finest works, Schiavonetti's *St John* after Van Dyck was considered by William Paulet Carey to be 'among the most perfect line engravings' (*New Monthly Magazine*, December 1815, 112), and in 1807 he received a silver medal set in gold (this particular award was a rare achievement) from the Society of Arts for his engraving (published 1804) of Philippe de Loutherbourg's *Landing of the British Troops in Aboukir*. By 1808 he was a member of the Venetian Academy.

According to Cromek (*GM*, 1st ser., 80, 1810, 662–5), Schiavonetti was tall, gentle, responsible, and unassuming. This character description accords with the engraver's comments after his failure to be elected associate engraver in 1806: he expected the result, for, apart from being a foreigner, he believed it wrong to canvass for votes. Further, his concern for fellow artists extended to membership of a committee, intended to relieve those in financial distress, which preceded the establishment of the Artists' Benevolent Fund.

Having suffered ill health from 1806, Schiavonetti died at his home in Brompton on 7 June 1810 and was buried in a vault on 14 June in St Mary's churchyard, Paddington. His funeral was attended by many painters and engravers; Benjamin West, then president of the Royal Academy, was one of the pallbearers. His portrait was painted by Henry Edridge. Major unfinished works included one after a drawing (*Pandora*) by James Barry, but the most significant was that after Thomas Stothard's *Canterbury Pilgrims*.

Niccolò [Nicholas] **Schiavonetti** (*c*.1771–1813), printmaker, was born in Bassano del Grappo and moved to England after his brother Luigi. Described by a contemporary as 'an engraver of great eminence', he produced a number of outstanding works, including *The Last Effort and Fall of Tippoo Sultan* (after Henry Singleton, published 1802) for the Seringapatam series; *New Mackrel* (stipple, 1795), for *Cries of London*, and several military prints, one, of the

Westminster volunteer cavalry (stipple, 1801), after Sydenham Edwards, being nearly all portraits. A facility in portraiture ensured that he engraved (and published) Phillips's portrait of Joseph Banks (1812) on the recommendation of the artist, in spite of Banks preferring William Sharp. An 'amiable … upright and benevolent individual' (*GM*, 1st ser., 83/1, 1813, 494), Schiavonetti died on 23 April 1813 at the house of his brother-in-law in Hammersmith, aged forty-two. VIVIENNE W. PAINTING

Sources *DNB* • *Transactions of the Society of Arts*, 25 (1807), 20 • J. Boydell, list of payments to artists and engravers, Folger, Y. d. 369 • A. Calabi, *La gravure italienne au XVIII siècle* (1931) • J. Landseer, *Lectures on the art of engraving delivered at the Royal Institution* (1807), 304–5 • *GM*, 1st ser., 80 (1810), 662–5 • *GM*, 1st ser., 83/1 (1813), 494 • *Annual Register* (1813), 598 • P. Cannon-Brookes, *The painted word: British history painting, 1750–1830* (1991), 99–100 [exhibition catalogue] • letters, Free Library of Philadelphia, rare book department • D. Alexander, 'Schiavonetti [Luigi and Niccolò]', *The dictionary of art*, ed. J. Turner (1996) • W. Roberts, *Francis Wheatley: his life and works* (1910) • *The dramatic works of Shakspeare*, ed. J. Boydell, rev. G. Steevens, 9 vols. (1802) • *A collection of prints from pictures painted for the purpose of illustrating the dramatic works of Shakspeare by the artists in Great Britain*, 2 vols. (1803–5) • H. B. Carter, *Sir Joseph Banks (1743–1820): a guide to biographical and bibliographical sources*, St Paul's Bibliographies (1987) • Farington, *Diary*, vol. 7 • W. L. Pressly, *The life and art of James Barry* (1981) • J. Pye, *Patronage of British art* (1970) • C. Clair, *A history of European printing* (1976) • *The poetical works of John Milton*, 3 vols. (1794–7) • *Regency portraits*, R. Walker, National Portrait Gallery, 2 vols. (1985) • G. E. Bentley, *Blake records* (1969) • *An alphabetical catalogue of plates, engraved … after the finest pictures and drawings of the Italian, Flemish, German, French, English and other schools, which compose the stock of John and Josiah Boydell, etc.* (1803)

Archives Free Library of Philadelphia, rare book department, letters | Folger, MS list of payments made by Boydell to artists and engravers, Y. d. 369

Likenesses A. Cardon, stipple, pubd 1811 (after H. Edridge), BM, NPG • H. Edridge, oils

Schiavonetti, Niccolò (*c.*1771–1813). *See under* Schiavonetti, Luigi (1765–1810).

Schiff, Sydney Alfred [*pseud.* Stephen Hudson] (**1868–1944**), novelist, translator, and patron of the arts, was born in London, the illegitimate child of Alfred George Schiff (*c.*1840–1908), a stockbroker, and Caroline Mary Ann Eliza Cavell, *née* Scates (1842–*c.*1896). Caroline had married John Scott Cavell in 1861: he filed for divorce in 1867 on the grounds that Caroline had committed adultery with an unknown person in 1865 and had borne a daughter (Carrie Louise) from this relationship, and that she had cohabited with Alfred Schiff since November 1865. Sydney Schiff's birth was registered under another, untraceable name; the date which the family used as his birthday, 12 December 1868, cannot be confirmed. Caroline married Alfred Schiff in 1869, and they had four further children, one son and three daughters.

Schiff was educated at G. T. Worsley's Preparatory School at Hillingdon, Middlesex, and at Wellington College, Crowthorne, Berkshire. In 1886 he was unsuccessful in his efforts to enter Oxford to read law, and in 1887 he travelled first to Canada, to work for a friend of his father, and subsequently to the United States, to work for his uncle Charles. Travelling in the States, Schiff met Marion Fulton Canine (*b.* 1867/8, *d.* after 1932), whom he married on 29 August 1889 in Ontario. The couple returned to Europe, but the marriage was not a success. In spite of the family wealth, Marion's expectations of luxury were not fulfilled; moreover, she antagonized her mother-in-law, and mocked Sydney's literary aspirations. The couple separated in 1908; Marion filed for divorce in June 1910, and the decree absolute was declared on 8 May 1911.

Schiff married Violet Zillah Beddington (1874–1962) on 10 May 1911. Violet and her family were more encouraging of artistic endeavour than Schiff's parents or his first wife, and he turned his attentions to writing fiction and to patronage of the arts. His first novel, *Concessions* (1913), was published under his own name, but *War-Time Silhouettes* (1916) and subsequent works appeared under the name Stephen Hudson. The pseudonym was adopted in anticipation of the appearance of *Richard Kurt* (1919), the first of a sequence of autobiographical novels. Schiff had begun work on these in 1911, but during the First World War he and Violet had enthusiastically read Proust's *Du côté de chez Swann*. *À la recherche du temps perdu* provided a precedent for the scale, if not the manner, of Schiff's autobiographical sequence. Schiff later extensively revised and combined several of his novels as *A True Story* (1930). His championing of Proust in British literary circles also led to his translating *Time Regained* (1923) after the death of C. K. Scott Moncrieff.

During the war Schiff developed his role as a patron of the arts, supporting Isaac Rosenberg with small gifts of money and painting materials. He subsidized the short-lived but influential periodical *Arts and Letters* (1918–20), as well as contributing to it and editing one issue. In the post-war period he encouraged and supported other modernist artists and writers through purchases and gifts of money, and through correspondence, hospitality, and conversation. His manner was recalled by Jacob Isaacs as being 'fastidious, punctilious' and 'exquisitely courteous', while his appearance, on account of his moustache and conservatively tailored jackets, was that of a military man (Beddington-Behrens, 59–60). His circle included Wyndham Lewis, T. S. Eliot, Katherine Mansfield, John Middleton Murry, and Frederick Delius. Though the Schiffs retained a base in London, they frequently travelled and lived elsewhere in the south of England and on the continent, and in consequence a substantial body of correspondence has survived. They became more settled with the move to Abinger Manor, near Dorking, in 1934. Their house was damaged by a stray German bomb in August 1944, and the shock may have been a contributing factor in Schiff's death at the Sackville Court Hotel, Kingsway, Hove, Sussex, from heart failure on 29 October 1944.

MICHAEL H. WHITWORTH

Sources T. E. M. Boll, 'Biographical note', *Richard, Myrtle and I*, ed. V. Schiff (1962), 15–40 • T. S. Eliot, 'Mrs Violet Schiff', *The Times* (9 July 1962) • E. Beddington-Behrens, *Look back, look forward* (1962) • *Cavell* v. *Cavell*, PRO, J77/76/485 • *Schiff* v. *Schiff*, PRO, J77/1003/459, J77/1011/678 • M. Proust, *Correspondance*, ed. P. Kolb, 21 vols. (1970–93) • m. certs. • *The Times* (13 Nov 1944) • *CGPLA Eng. & Wales* (1945)

Archives BL, papers • BL, corresp., Add. MSS 52916–52923 | Cornell University, Ithaca, New York, Wyndham Lewis papers •

Harvard U., William Rothenstein papers • Merton Oxf., letters to Max Beerbohm • Tate collection, corresp. with Richard Eurich
Likenesses W. Lewis, portrait, 1922–3, repro. in W. Michel, *Wyndham Lewis: paintings and drawings* (1971) • M. Beerbohm, caricature, 1925, repro. in M. Beerbohm, *Observations* (1925) • photograph, *c*.1930, repro. in Beddington-Behrens, *Look back, look forward*, facing p. 60 • photographs, *c*.1930–1933, repro. in Schiff, ed., *Richard, Myrtle and I*
Wealth at death £2221 9*s*. 10*d*.: probate, 30 Jan 1945, *CGPLA Eng. & Wales*

Schiller, Ferdinand Canning Scott (1864–1937), philosopher, was born at Ottensen, near Altona, Schleswig-Holstein, on 16 August 1864, the second son of (John Christian) Ferdinand Schiller, a German merchant, of London and Calcutta, and his wife, Rosa De Castro. He was educated at Rugby School (scholar) and Balliol College, Oxford (exhibitioner), where he obtained a first class in classical moderations (1883) and in *literae humaniores* (1886) and was Taylorian scholar in German (1887). After graduating he worked for a year as a German master at Eton College, to finance a further year at Oxford, during which he wrote *Riddles of the Sphinx*. He became instructor in philosophy at Cornell University in 1893, and formed a friendship with William James that greatly influenced his intellectual development. In 1897 he was appointed to a tutorial fellowship at Corpus Christi College, Oxford, a post which he held until 1926, when he resigned after a severe illness, though remaining a fellow until his death. From 1926 he spent part of each year at the University of Southern California. He became professor of philosophy there in 1929, and emeritus professor in 1936. He was elected a fellow of the British Academy in 1926. In 1935 he married Mrs Louise Luqueer Griswold, eldest daughter of S. Bartow Strang, of Denver, Colorado, USA, and settled in California. There were no children of the marriage. He died at Los Angeles on 6 August 1937.

Schiller's chief publications were *Riddles of the Sphinx* (1891; rev. edn, 1910), *Studies in Humanism* (1907; 2nd edn, 1912), *Formal Logic* (1912; 2nd edn, 1931), and *Logic for Use* (1929). His first book, *Riddles of the Sphinx*, was a brilliant effort to combine the ideas of Darwinian evolution with those of philosophical idealism. Herbert Spencer had already treated philosophical problems from an evolutionary standpoint, but he was far from being an idealist.

Soon after Schiller settled at Oxford in 1897 he became conspicuous as the advocate of what was called by himself and William James 'pragmatism'; this meant an insistence upon the importance of action in human affairs and upon the formation of human opinions. The main feature in Schiller's pragmatism was the doctrine that truth was a kind of valuation; this meant that truth can be equated with usefulness and that an opinion can be regarded as true so far as it is practically useful. The majority of Schiller's contemporaries refused to accept this definition of truth; it seemed to neglect the fact that real things have a nature and qualities of their own. If an opinion is to be regarded as true, it must correspond to objective reality, whether it is useful or not. Whatever may be thought of Schiller's definition of truth, his general position that action is one of the main features of human experience cannot reasonably be disputed. No one can refute his arguments that people are creatures of action; that they take an interest in things and learn about things mainly for the sake of action; and that action is the supreme test of truth, because if people fail in action, they can feel assured that the scheme of thought that guided them was false.

If Schiller's work is looked at broadly, it can be said that his main service was to promote the humanization of philosophy. He saw clearly that the business of philosophy is to explain human experience as exemplified in ordinary persons, and that no important element of human experience should be omitted in the philosopher's survey. In defending this standpoint he attacked vigorously thinkers who, like Plato and Hegel, regarded imaginary beings such as Ideas or the Absolute as more real and more important than ordinary human experience, and who therefore produced systems that are useless and inhuman. Another object of Schiller's attack was formal logic, which he regarded as useless and false, and as having no value as a guide to action or as an explanation of human thinking.

Schiller had many of the gifts of a first-rate thinker: intellectual enthusiasm, vivid imagination, keen critical acumen, great originality, and fertility of ideas; but his powers of analysis and synthesis were less remarkable. Although he did not produce a satisfactory comprehensive synthesis in any department of philosophy, and pragmatism in Britain did not attract a strong following, his lively attacks on F. H. Bradley helped to undermine the dominance of philosophical idealism and impelled British thought towards reviving the empiricist tradition.

Schiller had many interests outside philosophy. He was an ardent mountaineer, a persevering though unskilful golfer, and an inveterate punster. He was an excellent linguist and knew a great deal about physical science. He wrote several tracts on eugenics, and his views in this area are illustrated by his advice to C. P. Blacker of the Eugenics Society 'to conduct campaigns … to legalize voluntary sterilisation, to extend the benefits of the Birth Control Clinics to the classes which need and desire them most' (Jones, 108). His political views 'tended to be pro-aristocracy' (Jones, 111, n. 66). He took a deep and lifelong interest in the work of the Society for Psychical Research, of which he was president in 1914. He was for thirty-five years the able treasurer of the Mind Association.

HENRY STURT, *rev.* C. A. CREFFIELD

Sources *The Times* (9 Aug 1937) • R. R. Marett, 'Ferdinand Canning Schiller, 1864–1937', *PBA*, 23 (1937), 538–50 • J. I. McKie, *Mind*, new ser., 47 (1938), 135–9 • R. Abel, 'Schiller, Ferdinand Canning Scott', *Routledge encyclopaedia of philosophy*, ed. E. Craig (1998), vol. 8, pp. 523–4 • S. Brown, 'Schiller, Ferdinand Canning Scott', *Biographical dictionary of twentieth-century philosophers*, ed. S. Brown, D. Collinson, and R. Wilkinson (1996), 703 • J. Passmore, *A hundred years of philosophy* (1957) • G. Jones, *Social hygiene in twentieth century Britain* (1986), 108 • personal knowledge (1949) • J. Foster, *Oxford men, 1880–1892: with a record of their schools, honours, and degrees* (1893) • *CGPLA Eng. & Wales* (1937)
Archives U. Cal., Los Angeles, corresp., literary MSS, and papers • University of Southern California, Los Angeles, *Ethics of pessimism*

and lecture notes | BL, corresp. with Macmillans, Add. MSS 55163–55164 • JRL, letters to Samuel Alexander • McMaster University, Hamilton, Ontario, letters to Bertrand Russell
Likenesses W. Stoneman, photograph, 1930, NPG
Wealth at death £9874 14s. 5d.—in England: probate, 29 Oct 1937, *CGPLA Eng. & Wales*

Schilling, Richard Selwyn Francis (1911–1997), biochemist and occupational physician, was born on 9 January 1911 at Kessingland, Suffolk, the youngest of the four children of George Schilling (1866–1935), a general practitioner, and his wife, Florence Louise Loweth (1874–1950), daughter of a Lincolnshire farmer. George Schilling had studied medicine at St Thomas's Hospital, London, after which he held various hospital appointments and served as a ship's doctor. He then combined a one-man general practice with other local appointments including assistant medical officer to the Great Western Railway works hospital. An alcoholic, he died suddenly in May 1935.

Richard Schilling boarded from the age of fourteen at Epsom College, where he excelled in rugby football, cricket, and boxing, and from which he passed the first MB. A scholarship enabled him to study medicine at St Thomas's Hospital, which he also represented at sport. He became a member of the Royal College of Surgeons and licentiate of the Royal College of Physicians in 1934, and this allowed him to start immediately in practice; thus, when his father died Richard was able to maintain the general practice until it could be sold as a going concern. He completed the MB BS London in 1937, and on 28 August that year he married Heather, daughter of Clem Norman, a Dorset general practitioner. In a supremely happy marriage they raised a son and two daughters.

Schilling began his career in occupational medicine late in 1935, when he joined ICI Metals as an assistant industrial medical officer. In 1939 he became a medical officer of factories in Manchester. He had joined the Royal Army Medical Corps in 1938 as a lieutenant. At the outbreak of war he was in France with a field ambulance and was evacuated from Dunkirk. Recalled to the factory inspectorate in 1940, he was seconded as secretary of the industrial health research board in 1942, when he participated in field studies with Donald Hunter in his department for research in industrial medicine at the London Hospital. In 1947 Schilling joined Professor R. E. Lane at the Manchester University department of occupational health, combining this work with part-time practice in an engineering works. In 1956 he was appointed director of the Rockefeller occupational health unit within the department of public health at the London School of Hygiene and Tropical Medicine, and a reader in the University of London. The unit became an independent department in 1959, with Schilling as its professor from 1960. In 1968 the department became an institute endowed by the Trades Union Congress (TUC) and it was formally opened by HM the queen mother in 1971.

Schilling was a key figure in the expansion of occupational medicine from a minor interest to a recognized field of medicine, with its own faculty of occupational medicine formed in 1978 within the Royal College of Physicians, London. Although he was involved in early discussions and became a fellow of the faculty, Schilling remained largely detached from its development and it is not mentioned in his autobiography. He published on his investigations into byssinosis of cotton workers, the role of carbon disulphide in heart disease, and the health of seafarers, and he contributed to the committee of inquiry into trawler safety, whose report was published in 1969.

A big man physically, Schilling was easy to deal with, but had firm principles and strong but well controlled feelings and a warm, infectious sense of humour. He was outstanding not only for his leadership, his scientific contributions and pre-eminent position in what was a relatively new and developing field, and as a teacher, but also for his humanity. He regarded himself as being the odd man out in his family in holding liberal or left-wing views and in being concerned for the underprivileged; his idealism and humanity shines through his autobiography, *A Challenging Life: Sixty Years in Occupational Health* (1998). Associated with the *British Journal of Industrial Medicine* (now *Occupational and Environmental Health*) since 1942 and as editor from 1951 to 1955, he established the journal as one of international scientific merit, and himself contributed numerous articles.

Various presidencies, honorary fellowships, and other academic qualifications were conferred on Schilling; these culminated in his appointment as CBE in 1975. When he retired in 1976 his institute had an outstanding international reputation for teaching and research, but it was disbanded in September 1990, allegedly because the university was disenchanted by its links with the TUC and by the difficulty of recruiting a professor of suitable stature. In his autobiography Schilling himself referred to the closure of the institute as 'an act of economic vandalism [which] was the greatest blow to my professional career' (*A Challenging Life*, 158). Latterly, as a consultant to Possum Controls, he was involved in improvements in the quality of life for the disabled. Schilling died of cancer at his home, 11C Prior Bolton Street, Canonbury, London, on 30 September 1997. After a plain funeral at the church he had attended at Hackney he was cremated at Finchley on 7 October 1997. R. IAN MCCALLUM

Sources R. S. F. Schilling, *A challenging life: sixty years in occupational health* (1998) • S. J. Gillam and W. I. McDonald, eds., *Lives of the fellows of the Royal College of Physicians of London continued to 1997* (2000) • H. A. Waldron, 'Academic occupational health under threat', *BMJ* (8 July 1989) • 'The British Journal of Industrial Medicine: 50 years on', *British Journal of Industrial Medicine*, 50 (1993), 1–3 • *The Times* (28 Oct 1997) • V. Bloom, *The Guardian* (3 Oct 1997) • R. Doll, *The Independent* (7 Oct 1997) • *WWW*
Likenesses photograph, repro. in Schilling, *A challenging life*, jacket

Schimmelpenninck [*née* Galton], **Mary Anne** (1778–1856), author, was born in her grandfather's house in Steel House Lane, Birmingham, on 25 November 1778, the eldest child of Samuel Galton and his wife, Lucy Barclay (*d.* 1817). Both parents were members of the Society of Friends, and brought up their children strictly. In 1785 the family moved to Barr in Staffordshire, where among their

Mary Anne Schimmelpenninck (1778–1856), by Henry Adlard, pubd 1858 (after Fisher)

frequent visitors were James Watt, Richard Lovell Edgeworth, Thomas Day, Joseph Priestley, and Erasmus Darwin, whose daughter Violetta married Mary Anne's eldest brother, Samuel Tertius Galton. At an early age Miss Galton showed intellectual tastes, which her parents and their friends helped to develop. When about eighteen she visited her cousins the Gurneys of Earlham, and Catherine Gurney, the eldest daughter, remained her friend throughout the rest of her life. Mary Martha Butt (afterwards the novelist Mrs Sherwood) met Miss Galton at Bath about 1801, and described her as 'a simple, agreeable person, without the smallest display' (Kelly, 228–9).

On 29 September 1806 Mary Anne Galton married Lambert Schimmelpenninck (*c.*1766–1840), a Dutchman involved in the shipping trade at Bristol. They settled at his home in Bristol, and she took an active part in local charities and education, holding classes for young people at their house in Berkeley Square. About 1811 her husband fell into financial difficulties. At the same time a dispute regarding her marriage settlements led to a breach between her and the members of her family which was never healed. She turned her attention to literature for a livelihood. Hannah More had, about this period, sent her some of the writings of the Port-Royalists, and in 1813 Mrs Schimmelpenninck published a compilation based on one of those volumes, *Narrative of a Tour to La Grande Chartreuse and Alet, by Dom. Claude Lancelot*. It ran to several editions. In 1815, during a tour on the continent, she visited Port-Royal, and in 1816 issued a *Narrative of the Demolition of the Monastery of Port Royal des Champs* (3 vols.). The two works were republished, with additions, in 1829 as *Select Memoirs of Port Royal*. The style and mode of thought show the influence of Pascal.

Mary Anne Schimmelpenninck's interests were wide, including history, religion, and aesthetics, and among her books on those subjects was *The Theory and Classification of Beauty and Deformity* (1815), a work of learning rather than insight. She also studied Hebrew, and embodied the result in *Biblical Fragments* (2 vols., 1821–2).

Mrs Schimmelpenninck passed through various phases of religious belief. Even as a child, when attending the Friends' meetings with her parents, she was troubled with doubts. She told Caroline Fox that she had 'suffered from an indiscriminate theological education', and found it difficult to associate herself with any particular body (Fox, 215). In 1808 she was baptized by a Methodist minister, and ten years later she joined the Moravians. Although towards the end of her life she was nearly drawn into the Roman Catholic church, she remained a Moravian until her death.

In 1837 Mrs Schimmelpenninck was suddenly attacked with paralysis, and moved to Harley Place, Clifton, where her health improved slowly. After her husband's death, on 6 June 1840, she led a retired life. She died at Harley Place on 29 August 1856, and was buried in the grounds of the Moravian chapel at Bristol.

Mary Anne Schimmelpenninck was good-looking, high-spirited, and genial in society, though she was said to be inconsiderate towards her family. Elizabeth Gurney said of her: 'She was one of the most interesting and bewitching people I ever saw' (Hare, 86–7).

ELIZABETH LEE, *rev.* K. D. REYNOLDS

Sources C. C. Hankin, ed., *Life of Mary Anne Schimmelpenninck*, 2nd edn (1858) · private information (1897) · Boase, *Mod. Eng. biog.* · A. J. C. Hare, *The Gurneys of Earlham*, 2 vols. (1895) · C. Fox, *Memoires of old friends* (1882) · S. Kelly, *Life of Mrs Sherwood* (1884) · Allibone, *Dict.*

Likenesses H. Adlard, stipple (after Fisher), NPG; repro. in Hankin, *Life of Mary Anne Schimmelpenninck*, frontispiece [*see illus.*]

Schindler, Sir Albert Ashershund Houtum- (**1846–1916**), Persian scholar and employee of the Persian government, was born in Germany on 24 September 1846. No details are known of his family background, early life, or education. Some sources suggest that he was in fact Dutch, though educated at Leipzig University, but during his own lifetime he divulged no information to biographical dictionaries, and in a brief obituary note his son was unable, or reluctant, to add any details. His extraordinary career in Persia began in 1868 as an employee in the Indo-European telegraph company, which recruited several of its engineers and superintendents from Germany. In 1876 he joined the Persian telegraph service as inspector-general of Persian telegraphs and was given the rank of general in the Persian army, though he was never in any sense a soldier. He established a close relationship with the minister of telegraphs, ʿAli Quli Khan, Mukhbir al-Dauleh. He was responsible for extending the telegraph system to some of the regional centres. He was also employed by the shah in mining for gold in Azarbaijan, and by Mukhbir al-Dauleh in managing the turquoise mines in Khorasan. In 1870 he married Louise, who was the eldest daughter of a Swedish physician, Conrad Fagergen (1818–1879), resident for many years in Tehran and Shiraz, and the granddaughter of an Italian general in the Persian army, Barthelemy Semino. She died about 1879, and a few years later, in 1884, he married an English woman, Florence.

From the late 1880s Houtum-Schindler played an important part in the more systematic attempts of Persian and European capitalists and entrepreneurs to explore and develop the country's natural resources. His advice was important in establishing the Imperial Bank of Persia in 1889, and he was subsequently appointed as its inspector of branches, as well as inspector-general of the Persian Bank mining rights corporation. He was also nominally in charge of the road concessions held by the bank. Neither of these subsidiaries flourished, and he was dismissed in May 1894. Thereafter he was nominally director of Persia's foreign office control department but, as he put it himself, 'used as advisor to the Government in nearly all matters' (RGS, correspondence, block 1881–1910. Houtum-Schindler to John Scott Keltie, secretary of the RGS, 4 Sept 1896), or, in Curzon's description, 'a sort of *deus ex machina* required to assist in the solution of most Persian problems' (Curzon, 1.477). He stayed on in Tehran through the years of the 'constitutional revolution', living in his house situated between the Austrian legation and Mukhbir al-Mulk's property just north of Lalehzar. For a time he was in charge of the passport office in the ministry of foreign affairs, and was the honorary Swedish consul-general. He eventually left Persia in the spring of 1911, disappointed at what he felt was the lack of appreciation of his years of long service to the Persian government. The government of India made him a CIE in 1900, and a KCIE in 1911.

In the course of the forty-two years that he had spent in Persia, Houtum-Schindler acquired more precise information about the state of the country than any other European had ever done, either before or most probably since. While supervising the telegraph and mining operations he travelled extensively throughout the Persian empire, across the central plateau, into the tribal areas and the most remote border regions, often leaving Tehran for months at a time. Everywhere he went he collected precise details of distances, routes, archaeological and historical sites, dialects, ethnography, flora and fauna, and population and revenue statistics. He frequently surveyed the territory, and his accurate readings helped to produce maps of the regions through which he travelled. As a result of his friendship with leading Persian notables and ministers he had access to official government records and used them in the many published descriptions of his itineraries. His unique access to these sources of information made him invaluable to the European commercial organizations for whom he worked, foreign legations, and the governments of India and Persia. Unusually self-effacing himself, he allowed others to make use of his remarkable knowledge, notably Lord Curzon who obtained from Houtum-Schindler most of the detailed statistical information on the army, population, distances, revenue, and much else in his great work, *Persia and the Persian Question* (1892), and generously acknowledged that 'few men so excellently qualified to write a first-rate book themselves would have lent such unselfish exertion to improve the quality of another man's work' (Curzon, 1.xiii).

To his study of Persia, Houtum-Schindler brought the exactitude and industry of a genuine scholar *manqué*. His understanding of literary and colloquial Persian was impressive; he built up a valuable library, and published over fifty articles in the leading English, German, and Austrian orientalist and geographical journals of the day, as well as encyclopaedias and reference works. His most important study was the one book which he compiled himself, *Eastern Persian Irak* (1896), a meticulous account of the region between Tehran and Esfahan. His work on the Zoroastrian community in Yazd and Kerman, 'Die Parsen in Persien, ihre Sprache und einige ihrer Gebräuche' (*Zeitschrift der Deutschen Morgenländischen Gesellschaft*, 36, 1882), and his pioneering studies on dialect, are still of value, as is the accurate information provided in the many succinct, exact accounts of his travels. Some of the rare manuscripts he collected came from the libraries of great nineteenth-century Persian bibliophiles and scholars such as Bahman Mirza, Farhad Mirza, and Iʿtimad al-Saltaneh. The best of those manuscripts and lithographs, with some of his translations and annotations, were bought after his death by E. G. Browne, and subsequently went to the Cambridge University Library.

After his return from Persia in 1911, Houtum-Schindler, who had become a naturalized British subject (probably in 1884, but certainly by 1888), settled at first in Wimbledon and then at Fenstanton, a few miles outside Cambridge. Although crippled by gout and increasingly house-bound, he re-established his acquaintance with the two Cambridge orientalists, E. G. Browne and Guy Le Strange, both of whom he had met many years earlier in Persia. He died at his home, Petersfield, Fenstanton, Huntingdonshire, on 15 June 1916, leaving his wife, Florence, and two sons, Alexander, who had joined the Imperial Bank of Persia, and Leonard. JOHN GURNEY

Sources E. G. Browne, 'The Persian manuscripts of the late Sir Albert Houtum-Schindler, KCIE', *Journal of the Royal Asiatic Society of Great Britain and Ireland* (1917), 657–94 • A. Houtum-Schindler, *Eastern Persian Irak* (1896) • G. N. Curzon, *Persia and the Persian question* (1892) • A. Houtum-Schindler, 'Safarnamah-i Khurasan', *Seh safarnamah: Harat, Marv, Mashhad*, ed. Q. A. Rawshani Za'faranlu (Tehran, 1968), 145–211 • BL OIOC, Curzon MSS • d. cert.
Archives RGS | BL OIOC, Curzon MSS
Wealth at death £3312 14s. 3d.: probate, 25 July 1916, *CGPLA Eng. & Wales*

Schinkel, Karl Friedrich (1781–1841), architect, was born in Neuruppin, Mark Brandenburg, on 13 March 1781, the son of a pastor, Johann Cuno Christian Schinkel (*d.* 1787), and his wife, Dorothea, *née* Rose (*d.* 1800). He studied with the architect David Gilly, between 1798 and 1800, and at the Bauakademie, Berlin, in 1799–1800. In 1809 he married Susanne Berger (1782–1861); they had four children. He had travelled to Italy in 1803–4 and was to go again in 1824, but made only one visit to Britain, between 24 May and 5 August 1826. As Prussian privy counsellor for public works he went to Paris and London to study the construction of museums, especially the British Museum, then at an early stage of construction, in preparation for his own work on the Berlin Museum (now the Altes Museum). The study of the British Museum was only one episode in a wide-ranging and eventful visit that took him from London through England, Scotland, and Wales. It is recorded in the manuscript travel diary of seventy-five sides and accompanying letters and additional drawings, known as 'The English journey' ('Die englische Reise', Nationalgalerie, Berlin).

Schinkel's many visits to workshops and factories were set up by his travelling companion Peter Beuth, director of trade and industry in the Prussian finance ministry, whose agenda was to buy samples of and to observe innovative British technology. Consequently their route through Britain was strongly biased towards workshops, factories, and commercial buildings, though Schinkel was able to view the buildings of London and cities on the route. He was generally disdainful of British architecture and speculative building, but was deeply impressed by the innovative use of iron-frame construction he saw almost everywhere. He responded admiringly to engineers he met, such as Henry Maudslay, but had little contact with architects.

Schinkel arrived in London, after three weeks in Paris, on 24 May, and stayed in the capital until 14 June. He visited numerous buildings, workshops, and factories, with trips to the Brighton Pavilion, Greenwich, and Windsor. On 15 June he, Beuth, and Count Danckelmann, went north, passing through Oxford, Birmingham, visiting the Thomason workshop, Dudley—the chimneys here he described as 'smoking obelisks' (Bindman and Riemann, 128)—the Gospel Oaks ironworks, and the Badnal cotton mill at Leek. Admiringly they passed by the Belper mills, and then through Sheffield to Leeds, where they met the industrialist Benjamin Gott at Armley House. Their next extended stop was Edinburgh, where Schinkel expressed a grudging surprise at the quality of the city's new architecture. He made two splendid panoramic drawings of the city (ibid., plates 140 and 142), and after two days there the party went on to Glasgow, via Robert Owen's New Lanark. In their one full day in Glasgow they visited Charles Tennant's chemical works, Charles Todd's textile mills, and the Hunterian Museum, before heading north-west for a short holiday towards the Hebrides, or 'Ossianic Islands' as Schinkel called them. Their objective was the romantic site of Fingal's Cave, where the Prussians sang in harmony to the sound of the waves (ibid., 170).

Following this break of one week the party returned to London via the west of England and Wales. They reached Manchester on 16 July and Schinkel was appalled by the prospects the industrial city offered of overproduction, financial slump, and dreadful living conditions. He describes the 'dreadful and dismal impression' (Bindman and Rieman, 175) made by the huge cotton mills of Ancoats, but the brilliant drawings he made in the journal of them and the Manchester canal system reveal their fascination for him (ibid., plates 164 and 165). He conversed in Liverpool with the city architect John Foster the younger, before the party left for Wales. They went through Conwy as far as the Menai Bridge, before returning to England via the great Pont Cysyllte viaduct. Here Schinkel expressed unequivocal enthusiasm for the designer of these two works and the Conwy suspension bridge, noting that they are 'All the work of Mr Telford, whose road construction is so arranged that from the Menai Bridge all his great works can be observed' (ibid., 188). The party went towards Bristol, and Schinkel remarked appreciatively on the ironwork in the Stanley Mill at King's Stanley, near Stroud. They spent a busy day in Bristol and two hours in Bath, which Schinkel found 'rather boring and wholly in the mean English style' (ibid., 197), before arriving back in London on 30 July. They remained in London until 5 August, then returned to Berlin by way of Calais and Belgium.

The effects of Schinkel's experience of British industrial buildings are clearly to be seen in his later architecture, in the Bauakademie (1831–6) and the Neue Packhof warehouses (1829–32), and the influence of his experience of ancient buildings is visible in many neo-Gothic works, but the most profound effect of 'the English journey' was perhaps in his later emphasis on function as a determinant of architectural design. He continued to live in Berlin, a high official of the Prussian government, until his early death, brought about, it was widely believed, by overwork, on 9 October 1841. He was buried three days later in the Dorotheenstadt cemetery, Berlin. DAVID BINDMAN

Sources D. Bindman and G. Riemann, eds., *Karl Friedrich Schinkel 'The English journey': journal of a visit to France and Britain in 1826* (1993) · G. Riemann, ed., *Karl Friedrich Schinkel: Reise nach England, Schottland und Paris im Jahre 1826* (Berlin, 1986) · M. Snodin, ed., *Karl Friedrich Schinkel: a universal man* (New Haven and London, 1991) · P. Betthausen, *Karl Friedrich Schinkel* (Berlin, 1983)

Archives Staatliche Museen zu Berlin, Sammlung der Zeichnungen, Nationalgalerie, 'Tagebuch der Reise nach England, Schottland und Paris'

Schipton, John of (*d.* 1256), administrator and prior of Newburgh, may have taken his name from Skipton-on-Swale in the North Riding of Yorkshire. Having become a canon of the Augustinian house of Newburgh, also in the North Riding of Yorkshire, he entered royal service as chaplain to John Mansel (*d.* 1265). In 1248 he was employed as a messenger, first to Scotland and later overseas. By May 1249 he had become a royal chaplain. Between November 1250 and January 1251 he was elected prior of Newburgh, although he remained more often at court or on diplomatic missions abroad than at Newburgh. Between June 1252 and July 1253 he was particularly active in authorizing royal writs and witnessing royal charters. In the summer of 1253 he accompanied the king to Gascony, but returned briefly to London in the autumn to arrange supplies for the king's forces. In May 1254 the king sought unsuccessfully to arrange Schipton's election to the bishopric of Carlisle. In July, with John Clarel, he was sent on a mission to Flanders. Schipton's written account of the disturbances there was later used by Matthew Paris in his *Chronica majora*. By May 1255 Schipton was back at court, and was present with the king in September and October 1255 when news arrived of the alleged ritual crucifixion of Hugh of Lincoln. In late October he departed on his last diplomatic expedition, to Germany. On his return he remained at court until July 1256, using his connections to promote the construction of a deer park and fish ponds at Newburgh. He died in the autumn of 1256, perhaps in October. ROBERT C. STACEY

Sources *Chancery records* · Paris, *Chron.* · private information (2004)

Schleger [*formerly* Schlesinger], **Hans** [*pseud.* Zero] (**1898–1976**), graphic designer, was born on 29 December 1898 in Kempen, Posen, Prussia, the second of two sons of Eduard Schlesinger (1859–1932), doctor of medicine, and his wife, Bianca Mendelsohn (1871–1941/2). Both his parents were Jewish. About 1904 the family moved from Kempen to Berlin where Hans attended day school, bored by academic studies but showing precocious talent at drawing. He served unwillingly with the German pioneer corps in the First World War, throwing away the Iron Cross which he was awarded when war ended. He shortened his name to Schleger by the time he was twenty and was studying painting and drawing at the Kunstgewerbeschule in Berlin.

Schleger's modernist vivacity as a designer and the range of his activity in a career that was to embrace the design of posters, packaging, exhibitions, trade marks, and corporate images can be traced back to the influence of the Bauhaus, strong in Berlin culture in the early 1920s. He consistently followed Bauhaus principles of reduction to essentials and he believed in demolishing barriers between fine and applied arts. Poster art as a populist, modernist medium attracted him: he was an early admirer of the work of A. M. Cassandre and Lucian Bernhard.

After leaving the Kunstgewerbeschule, Schleger's first job was for John Hagenbeck's idiosyncratic film company, where he was responsible for everything from publicity design to film sets. At a time when consumer advertising was emerging as a fully-fledged profession Schleger was intrigued by new techniques of visual persuasion, with their roots in behavioural sciences and the interpretation of desire.

In 1924 Schleger set off adventurously to New York, travelling on an oil tanker from Bremen. He spoke only limited English, had very little money and no contacts. It was now he adopted the signature Zero, a wry comment on his status as a designer starting out from scratch as well as an assertion of his emancipation from graphic traditions of the past. His creative originality was obvious in the advertising work that soon came the way of 'the *Wunderkind*, Hans Schleger, the young Berlin graphic artist, who is of all the post-war émigré artists the most successful', as he was already being described in the German professional journal *Gebrauchsgraphik* for February 1926.

Schleger's techniques were sophisticated. His famous series of advertisements for men's outfitters Weber and Heilbroner use photography in a then enterprising way, integrate text and image with reductionist aplomb, and introduce one of the earliest of Schleger's masterly trade marks, the three linked Homburg-hatted men about town. The illustrations made by Schleger for Park and Tilford Candies and Gunther Furriers, gently satiric of the luxuries they advertise, have a wonderful elegance of line. His dramatic magazine advertisements for the Empire State Engraving Company show Schleger's own ambivalent response to New York city, at once a place of nightmare and of fascination.

The Wall Street crash encouraged Schleger to give up his Madison Avenue office. Another influence was his first cousin, Annemarie Mendelsohn (*b.* 1906), whom he married soon after his return to Germany, on 1 December 1929. Schleger was now employed as an art director by W. S. Crawford, a branch of the progressive London advertising agency recently set up in Berlin. In the dislocated atmosphere of Berlin at that period he arrived at images of beautiful decadence, notably in a series of airbrush illustrations used as advertisements for Hudnut, the perfumiers.

Unnerved by the growing political intolerance Schleger left Germany in 1932, and arrived in England, a country he had never even visited in spite of his American reputation as a connoisseur of English upper-class style. His contacts among Crawford's modernist designers, Ashley Havinden and E. McKnight Kauffer in particular, were helpful in establishing him quickly at the centre of London avant-garde design. Schleger and his wife moved into a penthouse flat in Swan Court, Chelsea, adjacent to that occupied by McKnight Kauffer and the American textile designer Marion Dorn.

Schleger's work in the 1930s had a wit and sureness that did much to spread the visual language of modernism in the Britain of that time. His posters for Shell, London Transport, and various government departments were widely circulated. In 1935 Frank Pick commissioned the famous London Transport bus-stop sign which survived for many decades. Schleger's series of advertisements for the corset maker Charnaux harnessed surrealism to commercial art. Success encouraged him to remain in England and he became a British citizen in 1939.

The early years of the Second World War were traumatic for Hans Schleger. Work dried up. He left London and rented a cheap isolated cottage in Cobham, Surrey. His mother, whom he had failed to persuade to join him in London, was taken in November 1941 on the first transport train from Berlin to Teresienstadt and then to the ghetto in Minsk. The exact date of her death remains unknown. Schleger's wife left him and they were divorced in 1943. The strain of these events was extreme, and he began psychoanalysis which continued until his second marriage, to his design assistant, Patricia Marigold (Pat) Maycock (*b.* 1928) on 11 February 1956.

But professionally Schleger was soon in demand again. He designed cheerfully demotic war propaganda posters: for example 'Grow your Own' for the Dig for Victory campaign. After the war he expanded his practice, becoming a consultant to the advertising agency Mather and Crowther and setting up his own office, Hans Schleger and Associates at 14 Avenue Studios in Chelsea, a purpose-built studio occupied by John Singer Sargent at the turn of the century.

Schleger became the most important pioneer of British corporate identity, comparable only with F. H. K. Henrion, another European émigré. He was responsible for brilliant new visual interpretations of MacFisheries and Finmar, Fisons, and ICI. For twelve years he designed the graphics for the Edinburgh Festival, a formative influence in establishing its cultural significance. Schleger's rare combination of subtlety and boldness made him especially adept at the trade mark, evolving memorable symbols for Penguin Books, John Lewis, the Design Centre, and Hutchinsons. Examples of his designs are in the Victoria and Albert Museum, the London Transport Museum, and the Imperial War Museum, London, and the National Gallery of Australia, Canberra.

Schleger became a royal designer for industry in 1959. But in spite of many subsequent accolades and international honours Schleger never lost his edginess, easy to mistake for arrogance, and he was most at ease with his young office staff, his wife, and his two daughters. On the genial continental pattern, Schleger's domestic and office lives were merged. He died at his home, 15 The Boltons, London, of heart failure on 18 September 1976. His funeral service was held at St Mary the Boltons, and Schleger was cremated on 24 September at Putney Vale crematorium; he was an outstandingly resourceful and idealistic artist-designer who affected profoundly the visual life of his adopted land. FIONA MACCARTHY

Sources P. Schleger, *Zero: Hans Schleger—a life of design* (2001) • P. Reilly, 'Zero: Hans Schleger, London', *Gebrauchsgraphik*, 1 (1956) • M. Gowing, 'Hans Schleger', *Graphis*, 93 (1961) • P. Rand and G. Him, 'Hans Schleger', *Graphis*, 188 (1976) • 'Hans Schleger, New York', *Gebrauchsgraphik* (1928) • personal knowledge (2004) • private information (2004) [widow]
Archives priv. coll., archive • RSA, collection
Likenesses S. Buzas, photograph, 1966, priv. coll.
Wealth at death £49,758: probate, 13 April 1977, *CGPLA Eng. & Wales*

Schlich, Sir William Philipp Daniel (1840–1925), forester, was born on 28 February 1840 at Flonheim in Rheinhessen (Germany), the sixth of ten children of Daniel Schlich (1792–1875), a Lutheran pastor who from 1865 was appointed *Kirchenrat* (church / parish councillor), and his wife, Charlotte Frank (1801–1867). Both parents came from Hessian families. The boy was baptized Wilhelm Philipp Daniel. After he had had one year of schooling in Flonheim, in 1848 Schlich's family moved to Langgöns in Hesse, where he was educated at home by his strict father. From 1851 he was taught at preparatory schools at Gross-Gerau near Darmstadt, Essenheim in Rheinhessen, and

Sir William Philipp Daniel Schlich (1840–1925), by Walter Stoneman, 1921

Schotten in Hesse, during which periods he often lived with relatives. In autumn 1855 he entered Darmstadt technical high school where he studied mainly sciences. In the summer of 1858 he took a course in mathematics at the University of Giessen, and then in October of that year proceeded to a one-year course in mechanical engineering at the polytechnic institute at Karlsruhe. In October 1859 Schlich matriculated as a forestry student at the University of Giessen where he was taught by the renowned Professor Gustav Heyer. After graduating in 1862, Schlich began working for the Hesse state forestry service, and following success in the Hessian civil service examination of 1865 was appointed the following year assistant to the *Oberforster* in Homberg. In 1867 he gained his doctorate from the University of Giessen for a dissertation on the financial aspects of forestry.

Territorial changes resulting from the Austro-Prussian War of 1866 resulted in Schlich's being made unemployed, but on Heyer's recommendation he was appointed to the Indian forest service; he arrived in India on 16 February 1867. He was posted first to Burma, where he was promoted from assistant conservator to deputy conservator, and in 1870 he was transferred to Sind. In 1872 he was again transferred, on promotion, to the conservatorship of forests of the province of Bengal. Schlich's first marriage, in 1874, was to Mary Margaret, daughter of William Smith, a Bengal civil engineer. They had one son, who died in childhood, and one daughter. It was also in 1874 that Schlich substituted the use of 'William' for 'Wilhelm'. In 1878 his wife died, and he travelled to Europe on leave.

On his return to India in 1880 Schlich was posted to the Punjab as conservator of forests, but late in the following year he was appointed to act as inspector-general of forests to the government of India in place of Sir Dietrich Brandis. He was confirmed in this appointment in April 1883, when Brandis retired from the service, and held it until February 1885, when he finally left India in order to organize the forestry department at the Royal Indian Engineering College at Coopers Hill, Englefield Green. Perhaps the most important measure passed during Schlich's term as inspector-general was the formation of the imperial working plans branch, which ensured the preparation of forest working plans on approved lines and their scrutiny by a central authority. Schlich also played an important part in the reorganization of the Dehra Dun forest school. Although he left India in 1885, he did not actually retire from the service until 1 January 1889. He became a naturalized British subject in 1886, and in the same year married his second wife, Adèle Emilie Mathilde, daughter of Hermann Marsily, of Antwerp. They had one son and three daughters.

Schlich's appointment to the professorship of forestry at Coopers Hill gave him the opportunity to demonstrate his considerable abilities as a teacher, his contemporaries commenting on the facility with which he won the confidence and affection of his pupils. His duties were concerned primarily with the training of recruits for the Indian forest service, although a few of his pupils obtained appointments in other parts of the British empire.

On the closure of the college in 1905 its forestry branch was transferred to Oxford University, and although he was by then sixty-five and his health was showing signs of decline, Schlich succeeded in building up a fine school of forestry there. In its earlier years the Oxford school continued the tradition of Coopers Hill in being primarily a training centre for the Indian forest service, and Schlich maintained an official connection with the India Office until 1911, when under civil service rules he was obliged to retire. The university then appointed him reader with the status of professor of forestry. Schlich's services to India, which were rewarded by appointment in 1891 as CIE and in 1909 as KCIE, are demonstrated by the fact that he was responsible, while at Coopers Hill and at Oxford, for the training of no fewer than 272 out of a total of 283 officers who joined the Indian forest service during that period. At Oxford he worked strenuously to obtain full recognition for forestry as a branch of scientific learning in the university, first by having it included among the subjects of the BA degree, and second by securing the endowment of a permanent professorship, R. S. Troup being awarded the first chair in 1919. Schlich retired from his university post on 1 January 1920, but continued to live in Oxford, occupying himself with writing until his death.

Schlich's activities were not confined to academic work, and his advice on matters concerning forestry was widely sought throughout the British empire. Among other things, he constantly urged on the British government the importance of increasing supplies of home-grown timber by afforestation and by improving the condition of British woodlands. He was a member of the forestry subcommittee of the reconstruction committee which was appointed in 1916 to consider this question, and whose final report, issued in 1918, led to an extensive scheme of state afforestation under the Forestry Commission. He was elected a fellow of the Royal Society in 1901, an honorary fellow of St John's College, Oxford, in 1909, and was a fellow of the Linnean Society. He was president of the Royal English Arboricultural Society in 1913–14, and was on the governing council of the Empire Forestry Association at the time of his death.

Schlich died on 28 September 1925 at his home, Ferlys Lodge, 29 Banbury Road, Oxford, following a short bronchitic illness. He was buried at Wolvercote, Oxford, on 1 October. Among his published writings, his *Manual of Forestry*, in five volumes (1889–96)—three by himself and two by his colleague W. R. Fisher—ranks as a classic work. Each volume went through two or more editions, the last (vol. 3, 5th edn) being published in 1925, when Schlich was eighty-five. His other publications include *Forestry in the United Kingdom* (1904), and numerous papers and reports. He was the first honorary editor of the *Indian Forester*, a professional journal started in 1875, and was a contributor to it until the year of his death.

R. S. Troup, *rev.* Andrew Grout

Sources D. P. [D. Prain], *PRS*, 101B (1927), vi–xi • E. Mammen, M. S. Tomar, and N. Parameswaran, 'A salute to Dr William Schlich', *Indian Forester*, 91 (1965), 77–82 • *Nature*, 116 (1925), 617–18 • 'Dr William Schlich', *Indian Forester*, 15 (1889), 45–51 • *Indian Forester*, 51 (1925), 625–32 • F. A. Stafleu and R. S. Cowan, *Taxonomic literature: a selective guide*, 2nd edn, 5, Regnum Vegetabile, 112 (1985) • *India Office List* (1925), 665 • *The Times* (1 Oct 1925), 16 • private information (1937) • *CGPLA Eng. & Wales* (1925)

Archives U. Oxf., Forestry Institute, corresp.

Likenesses photograph, *c.*1913, repro. in *Quarterly Journal of Forestry*, 8 (1914), facing p. 1 • W. Stoneman, photograph, 1921, NPG [*see illus.*] • photograph, *c.*1921, repro. in Prain, *PRS*, facing p. vi • photograph, *c.*1924, repro. in *Indian Forester*, 51 (1925), facing p. 625 • effigy on a memorial plaque, U. Oxf., Sir William Schlich Lecture Room, Department of Forestry; repro. in *Indian Forester*, 91 (1965), facing p. 78

Wealth at death £2626 18*s.* 6*d.*: probate, 24 Dec 1925, *CGPLA Eng. & Wales*

Schloss, David Frederick (1850–1912), economist and civil servant, was born in West Derby, Lancashire, on 5 April 1850, the first son of Sigismund Schloss, merchant, of West Derby, and his wife, Rebecca Mocatta. He was educated at Manchester grammar school before matriculating at Corpus Christi College, Oxford, in 1869. He was one of the first Jews to be elected to a college scholarship, which he held from 1869 until 1874, when he graduated BA. His college career was illustrious: he was placed in the first class of classical moderations in 1871 and in the first class of *literae humaniores* in 1873. He was called to the bar of Lincoln's Inn in 1875. On 14 April 1886 Schloss, aged thirty-six, then resident at 17 Davies Street, Berkeley Square, London, and already established as a barrister, married Rachel Sophia Waley, aged twenty-one, at the West London Synagogue, Marylebone. She was the daughter of Professor Jacob *Waley. Schloss was well connected in Anglo-Jewish circles: the philanthropist F. D. Mocatta was his uncle and the banker Leonard Lionel Cohen became his brother-in-law.

Schloss demonstrated in intellectual and practical ways his concern for the lives of the poor of London and particularly for those of Jewish immigrants. In 1885 he printed 'The homes of the poor' in *Time*, addressing the implications of the recent royal commission's report. In 1887 Schloss served as treasurer of the East London Tailoresses' Union and was active in the movement promoting the foundation of women's trade unions. He also supported a short-lived co-operative tailors' workshop, managed by a Mr Risenbury of Backchurch Lane. Schloss's interest in tailoring stemmed from his activities as a member of the Jewish Board of Guardians. He had regular contact with the Charity Organization Society and published several articles on 'sweating' in the *Charity Organisation Review*.

In October 1887 Beatrice Potter, hoping for information about 'sweating practices', obtained an interview with Schloss in his role of sanitary inspector (1884–1912) for the Jewish Board of Guardians. She was disappointed, although he did introduce her to the chief rabbi and his wife. Potter described Schloss as 'Gentleman Jew … Ugly little swarthy fellow, with loud and familiar manners and very full of his own importance but a good natured little soul' (Beatrice Potter's holograph diary, BLPES). Schloss's reluctance to help her stemmed perhaps from his own essay on 'The sweating system' in the *Fortnightly Review* and his understandable unwillingness that she should steal his thunder. Charles Booth was sufficiently impressed to employ him to study the East End boot and shoe trades for *Life and Labour of the People in London*. Assisted by Jesse Argyle, Schloss's investigation comprised over 220 interviews, and he spent much time himself in precise observation of the workers of Mr Fox's workshop in Ogle Street. He collected a good deal of material about women's work in the trade.

Schloss is best described as a 'social radical', a member of the Fabian Society who criticized Gladstonian Liberalism and proposed in 1892 the formation of a fourth party, focusing on MPs such as R. B. Haldane and A. H. D. Acland, which was not socialist but progressive. By the early 1890s he had also established for himself a reputation as an economist whose work was based upon minute observation of carefully collected statistics. In 1893 Hubert Llewellyn Smith, a former associate of Charles Booth and commissioner for labour in the Board of Trade since 1892, appointed Schloss to a position of investigator in the labour department of the Board of Trade. In 1893 Schloss presented to the Royal Statistical Society, of which he was a fellow, a paper entitled 'The reorganisation of our labour department', which caused something of a stir in government circles. He produced several official reports for the department, including *Foreign Immigration to the USA* (1893), *Profit Sharing* (1894), *Gain-Sharing*, *Strikes and Lockouts of 1898*, and the *Report on Trade Unions in 1898* (1900). He was promoted to senior investigator in 1903 before becoming director of the census production office in 1907. A founder member of the London Economic Club, his highly regarded *Insurance Against Unemployment* (1909) and *Methods of Industrial Remuneration* (in its several editions from 1892) were both in use at Cambridge until the 1930s. He was also a regular and respected reviewer for the *Economic Journal*. Schloss died on 15 October 1912 at his home, 18 Hornton Court, Kensington, London, and was survived by his wife and two sons, (Sigismund) David *Waley, and Arthur David *Waley, both of whom assumed the family name of their mother in 1914. ROSEMARY O'DAY

Sources Foster, *Alum. Oxon.* • b. cert. • m. cert. • d. cert. • D. Lewis, *The Jews of Oxford* (1992) • BLPES, Passfield MSS, 7/1/8.2, 8.27 • BLPES, Schloss MSS, Coll. misc. 0762 • C. Collett, letter to Charles Booth, 23 Oct 1903, U. Lond., Booth correspondence • *Economic Journal*, 22 (1912), 636–8 • will, proved, 7 Dec 1912 • R. O'Day and D. Englander, *Mr Charles Booth's inquiry: 'Life and labour of the people in London' reconsidered* (1993) • R. Davidson, *Whitehall and the labour problem in late Victorian and Edwardian Britain* (1985)

Archives BLPES, Coll. Misc. 0002552/A/0004 • BLPES, corresp., notebooks, and papers

Wealth at death £55,033 15*s.* 7*d.*: probate, 7 Dec 1912, *CGPLA Eng. & Wales*

Schlüter, Auguste (1849–1917), domestic servant, was born on 27 June 1849, probably in Hanover, of which state she was a native. At the age of seventeen and speaking very little English she arrived in England, where she joined the household of William and Catherine Gladstone as lady's maid to the unmarried daughters of the family, Mary and Helen. Schlüter kept a diary for many of the years she spent in service to the Gladstones; it was published in 1922. Apparently written in an old exercise book discovered after she left England, it reads in part like a conventional diary, in part as excerpts from letters: 'Here I am, dearest', she wrote on 10 October 1878. 'You will be surprised to find me at the seaside' (Schlüter, 31). The diary provides a fascinating account of the life of a lady's maid in an upper-class household in the last quarter of the nineteenth century.

Gladstone's first three ministries, and politics in general, made almost no impact in Schlüter's diary—its editor observed unkindly that, 'supremely unconscious of the historic background, she watched the great events of her time like a cow gazing at a passing train' (Schlüter, 7). For her, it was enough that 'our Gentleman' (as she invariably called Gladstone) was in charge. She was not, however, entirely divorced from the political functions of the household, as in June 1882 she noted that she sometimes did a little writing for 'the gentlemen secretaries when they have to deal with German letters' (ibid., 82).

In an age when young women were closely chaperoned, lady's maids had considerable opportunities to witness, and mimic, the social round of the upper classes. Schlüter accompanied Mary Gladstone to concerts and plays, on country house visits, and on trips abroad (notably to Darmstadt in 1878, when she took the chance to visit her mother in Hanover). Like her employers, the lady's maid had social circles both in London and at Hawarden, to whom she paid regular calls and with whom she corresponded. It is reported that when Mary Gladstone Drew read her erstwhile maid's diary, she commented with amused condescension on 'the way she gives us all back seats while she occupies the front seat!' (Gladstone, 102).

Schlüter's world, although troubled by homesickness, concern for her mother in Germany and sister in New York, and occasional poor health and melancholy, seems from her diary to have been a comfortable one, illuminated by her devotion to her employers. It therefore came as a considerable and unpleasant shock to her when her 'beloved Lady', Mary Gladstone, her last remaining charge, announced her marriage to Harry Drew in December 1885. 'When I saw Mr Drew', she wrote, 'I felt like a tigress wishing to throw herself on the enemy' (Schlüter, 135). But she was soon reconciled, especially as Catherine

Gladstone took her on as her personal maid. By March 1890 Schlüter recognized that her usefulness to the Gladstones was receding, while her own mother was in financial difficulties and needed her at home. In November 1890 she left England with some cash supplied by Mary Drew and a letter of recommendation from Mr Gladstone, which she carefully copied into her journal, 'for perhaps I might sell it some day when I am in need' (ibid., 177). She remained in touch with the Gladstones for the rest of her life and visited them occasionally. The First World War did not end their correspondence, but she died in Hanover in the autumn of 1917; her last letter to Mary Drew, dated 20 March 1917, did not reach England until after the armistice. K. D. Reynolds

Sources A. Schlüter, *A lady's maid in Downing Street*, ed. M. Duncan (1922) • P. Gladstone, *Portrait of a family: the Gladstones, 1839–1889* (1989) • *Mary Gladstone (Mrs Drew): her diaries and letters*, ed. L. Masterman (1930)

Likenesses photograph, 1884, repro. in Schlüter, *Lady's maid in Downing Street*, ed. Duncan, frontispiece

Schmidt, Johann Christoph (1683–1762/3). *See under* Smith, John Christopher (1712–1795).

Schmitt, Charles Bernard (1933–1986), historian of philosophy and science, was born on 4 August 1933 in Louisville, Kentucky, USA. After graduating from the University of Louisville in 1956 with a bachelor's degree in chemical engineering, he spent a year working for the American Cyanamide Company in Stamford, Connecticut. In 1957 he entered the Columbia University school of engineering in New York, transferring in 1960, the year in which he married, to the philosophy department, where he was supervised by Paul Oskar Kristeller, a leading authority on Renaissance thought.

Although the rest of Schmitt's life was devoted to the history of philosophy, his training as an engineer left a permanent mark on his approach to scholarship, discernible in his informed interest in the history of science and his belief that generalizations should be treated as hypotheses in need of rigorous testing. His doctoral dissertation, completed in 1963 and published in 1967, concerned Gianfrancesco Pico della Mirandola, a Renaissance philosopher who drew on arguments from the ancient Greek sceptic Sextus Empiricus to construct a searching critique of Aristotelian philosophy. This research, much of it conducted in Italy, sparked his enthusiasm for the two subjects which dominated his scholarly career: the rediscovery of ancient scepticism in the Renaissance, and the pervasive influence of Aristotle on European philosophy and culture from 1150 to 1650.

Apart from the academic year 1965–6, when he was a visiting assistant professor at the University of California, Los Angeles, Schmitt taught at Fordham University, New York, from 1963 to 1967, reaching the rank of associate professor. In 1967 he moved to the United Kingdom, which became his adopted country, taking up a research fellowship in the philosophy department at the University of Leeds. He remained there until 1972, spending 1970 to 1971 in Florence as a fellow of the Harvard University Center for Italian Renaissance Studies at Villa I Tatti.

From 1963 onwards, Schmitt published articles and book reviews on various aspects of Renaissance science and philosophy at a prodigious rate; a selection of this material appeared in three collections (1981, 1984, and 1989). In *A Critical Survey and Bibliography of Studies on Renaissance Aristotelianism, 1958–1969* (1971), he underlined the importance of bibliographical research for the history of philosophy, remarking that it 'may be despised only after it has been done' (p. 13). His investigations into the recovery of ancient scepticism continued with *Cicero Scepticus: a Study of the Influence of the 'Academica' in the Renaissance* (1972), in which, with a characteristic blend of modesty and pugnacity, he both encouraged and challenged readers who found flaws in the volume 'to publish a rectification, so we can all gain thereby' (p. x).

From 1973 until his death Schmitt was lecturer in the history of science and philosophy at the Warburg Institute of the University of London. The institute's remit to advance the study of the classical tradition readily accommodated his interest in Aristotelianism, which assumed a more central position within its library, teaching, colloquia, and publications. Dislike of academic hierarchies led him to refuse the promotion merited by his impressive body of work and growing international reputation.

Universities, the main vehicles for the transmission of Aristotelian philosophy from the late middle ages to the seventeenth century, increasingly occupied Schmitt's attention. In 1981 he became the founding editor of *History of Universities*, a journal which sought to place institutions of higher learning within a broad intellectual and cultural context. In *Aristotle and the Renaissance* (1983; Italian translation, 1985; French translation, 1992), based on the Martin classical lectures delivered at Oberlin College in 1980, he argued for the breadth, depth, and continuity of Aristotle's influence in the Renaissance and described the different 'Aristotelianisms' which flourished at the time. Although he insisted that his views constituted no more than a 'first approximation' (p. 110), they were quickly accepted as authoritative. His monograph on John Case (1983) singled out this little-known English Aristotelian as representative of an unjustly neglected aspect of Elizabethan intellectual history; while his extensive addenda and revisions to F. E. Cranz's *Bibliography of Aristotle Editions, 1501–1600* (1984), provided indisputable evidence of the vast diffusion of Aristotelianism in the sixteenth century.

In an effort to secure for the Renaissance its rightful place within the history of Western philosophy, Schmitt was working on two general accounts at the time of his sudden death, on 15 April 1986, while in Padua to deliver a series of lectures. Both books, which greatly enhanced the profile of philosophical developments in this period, were published posthumously: *The Cambridge History of Renaissance Philosophy* (1988), of which he was the general editor; and *Renaissance Philosophy* (1992), completed by Brian Copenhaver.

During the final years of his life Schmitt left his wife, Catherine, and established a permanent relationship with Constance T. Blackwell; both survived him. He was buried on 18 April 1986 in the municipal cemetery, Padua; on 15 June 1998 he was reinterred at the University of Padua chapel.

At the centre of a wide international circle of friends, Schmitt organized and attended innumerable scholarly conferences in Europe and North America, where the new material he invariably presented compensated for his somewhat lacklustre delivery. Distrustful of clever oratory and rhetorical flourishes, whether wielded by Renaissance humanists or modern historians, he cultivated a plain, at times plodding, writing style, impatient to move quickly on to the next project rather than waste time on polishing his prose. JILL KRAYE

Sources personal knowledge (2004) • Warburg Institute, London, archives • B. P. Copenhaver, 'Science and philosophy in early modern Europe: the historiographical significance of the work of Charles B. Schmitt', *Annals of Science*, 44 (1987) • J. B. Trapp, 'The legacy of Charles Schmitt' and 'List of publications by C. B. Schmitt', *Aristotelismus und Renaissance: in memoriam Charles B. Schmitt*, ed. E. Kessler and others (Wiesbaden, 1988), 17–22, 217–32 • L. Giard, 'Charles Schmitt (1933–1986): reconstructor of a history of Renaissance learning', *New perspectives on Renaissance thought: essays in the history of science, education and philosophy in memory of Charles B. Schmitt*, ed. J. Henry and S. Hutton (1990), 264–90 • C. T. Blackwell, 'Towards a history of Renaissance philosophy: a bibliography of the writings of C. B. Schmitt', *New perspectives on Renaissance thought: essays in the history of science, education and philosophy in memory of Charles B. Schmitt*, ed. J. Henry and S. Hutton (1990), 291–308 • J. B. Trapp, *The Times* (5 May 1986) • C. Webster, *Isis*, 78 (1987), 80–81 • N. Siraisi, *History of Universities*, 6 (1986–7), xi–xv • W. F. Ryan, *Archives Internationales d'Histoire des Sciences*, 37 (1987), 148–50 • J. Henry, *British Journal for the History of Science*, 19 (1986), 337 • P. O. Kristeller and R. Popkin, *Journal of the History of Philosophy*, 26 (1988), 347–8 • T. Gregory, *Nouvelles de la République des Lettres* (1987), 7–11 • L. Panizza, *Renaissance Studies*, 1 (1987), 317–19

Archives Warburg Institute, London, archives

Likenesses photograph, repro. in C. B. Schmitt, *Studies in Renaissance philosophy and science* (1981), frontispiece • photograph, repro. in Copenhaver, 'Science and philosophy in early modern Europe', 509

Schmitthoff, Clive Macmillan [*formerly* Maximilian] (**1903–1990**), jurist, was born Maximilian Schmitthoff in Berlin on 24 March 1903, the eldest in the family of one son and two daughters of Hermann Schmitthoff, a prominent Berlin lawyer, and his wife, Anna. After a classical education at the Friedrichsgymnasium in Berlin he read law at the University of Freiburg im Breisgau and later at the University of Berlin, studying under the well-known jurist Professor Martin Wolff, with whom he quickly established a warm rapport and later collaborated in publications. Awarded his doctorate in law at Berlin in 1927, he joined his father's flourishing law practice and quickly became a successful advocate in the Berlin *Kammergericht* (court of appeal). But in 1933 he was forced to leave Germany for England, where he lived for the rest of his life, assuming the name Clive, and altering Maximilian to Macmillan. Having obtained an LLM degree at the London School of Economics in 1936 he was called to the bar in Gray's Inn, becoming a tenant in the chambers of Valentine Holmes, where he had served his pupillage. Lacking the contacts to make a full-time living at the bar, he became a part-time lecturer in German at the City of London College (later the City of London Polytechnic) and wrote books on commercial German and German poetry and prose. In 1940 he married Ilse (Twinkie), daughter of a leading Frankfurt lawyer, Ernst Moritz Auerbach, and herself a lawyer; they had no children. A cultured man, he maintained a keen interest in literature, art, and music throughout his life. He was naturalized in July 1946.

After wartime service in the Pioneer Corps and Canadian Engineers as a warrant officer, during which he took part in the Normandy landings and received several medals, Schmitthoff returned to England, to the War Office. He then went back to the City of London College, initially in the language department but later becoming a lecturer in law in the department of professional studies (lecturer 1948–58, senior lecturer 1958–63, principal lecturer 1963–71). Right up to the time of his retirement he had an abiding loyalty to his first academic home, resisting all blandishments to accept university chairs.

Schmitthoff was in love with the law in all its manifestations. A superb teacher and devoted to his students, he also maintained a successful consultancy practice at the bar. Of medium build and thoughtful demeanour, he had an infectious enthusiasm and humour which captivated students and clients alike. He combined prodigious energy with enterprise and vision. In 1948 he founded the Mansfield Law Club, also establishing a highly successful summer school in English law for foreign students. He developed the MA in business law, the first postgraduate law degree to be offered in the polytechnic sector. He co-founded the Association of Law Teachers in 1966 and was its honorary vice-president until the time of his death. He was a prolific and scholarly writer, with countless articles to his credit in legal periodicals around the world. His first major English law textbook, *A Textbook of the English Conflict of Laws*, was published in 1945. He also wrote a book on the sale of goods, and for many years from 1960 co-edited *Charlesworth's Mercantile Law*. He was general editor of *Palmer's Company Law* for nearly thirty years, from 1959. He was also the founder and editor of the *Journal of Business Law* (1957–89). In 1953 he received the degree of LLD from the University of London in recognition of his scholarship.

Schmitthoff's most striking achievements lay in the field of international trade law, which he created as a subject of academic study and made peculiarly his own. His classic textbook, *The Export Trade*, first published in 1948 and translated into several languages, was the first work to give an overall picture of the law, practice, and institutional structure of international trade law and practice, and in 1979 he became vice-president of the Institute of Export. It was his report *The Progressive Development of the Law of International Trade* (1966), commissioned by the United Nations, that led to the establishment of the United Nations Commission on International Trade Law, devoted to the harmonization of international trade law; and it is he who is credited with first propounding the new *lex mercatoria*, the transnational law of international trade, a subject on which he wrote extensively.

Schmitthoff's retirement in 1971 was purely notional. His scholarly publications continued unabated. His seventieth birthday was celebrated with a Festschrift in his honour, *Law and International Trade* (ed. Fritz Fabricius). He continued to lecture extensively in England and abroad. He held the Gresham chair in law at City University, London, from 1976 to 1986, and honorary and visiting professorships at a number of universities, including the University of Kent at Canterbury, City University, the Ruhr University Bochum, and Notre Dame University, and received honorary doctorates from several universities in Britain and abroad, and from the Council for National Academic Awards. In 1974 he received the grand cross of the German order of merit. In 1983 his colleagues at Kent published a collection of essays by way of tribute, *Essays for Clive Schmitthoff* (ed. John Adams).

The passing of the years seemed to have little impact on Schmitthoff. In 1985, his ninth decade, he became joint vice-chairman of the Centre for Commercial Law Studies at Queen Mary College, University of London, where he introduced and co-taught an LLM course on international trade law, at the same time establishing and organizing a series of annual conferences on international commercial law. A new edition of *Palmer* appeared in 1987 and of *The Export Trade* in 1990. A week before his death he was busy editing a set of conference papers and arranging a meeting with his publishers to discuss new projects. Despite his huge following he was essentially a private man, at his happiest working alone in his study. He died on 30 September 1990 at the Charing Cross Hospital, London, survived by his wife. ROY GOODE, *rev.*

Sources F. Fabricius, ed., *Law and international trade* (1973) · C. M. Schmitthoff, *Clive M. Schmitthoff's select essays on international trade law*, ed. C.-J. Cheng (1988) · *The Independent* (6 Oct 1990) · *The Times* (15 Oct 1990) · personal knowledge (1996) · private information (1996)
Likenesses photograph, repro. in *The Independent*
Wealth at death £28,926: probate, 7 May 1991, *CGPLA Eng. & Wales*

Schmitz, Leonhard (1807–1890), classical scholar and author, was born at Eupen, near Aix-la-Chapelle, France, on 6 March 1807. Schmitz, who lost his right arm in a childhood accident, was educated at the *Gymnasium* at Aix-la-Chapelle, then took a scholarship to the University of Bonn, where he was taught by the distinguished historian of Rome, Barthold Georg Niebuhr. After graduating in 1833 Schmitz taught in the *Gymnasium* and took private pupils, among them Prince Albert of Saxe-Coburg, later the prince consort, who studied at Bonn University from 1836 to 1838. After his marriage in 1836 to an Englishwoman, Eliza Mary Machell, Schmitz found a post as a private tutor in Yorkshire. He became a naturalized British subject, and soon formed a lifelong friendship with Connop Thirlwall, historian and priest. In 1841 Schmitz was awarded his PhD from Bonn, and the following year he published, with the classical scholar William Smith, a translation of the third volume of Niebuhr's *History of Rome*; the first and second volumes had been translated by Thirlwall and Julius Hare in 1828–32.

Leonhard Schmitz (1807–1890), by unknown engraver, pubd 1890

With the support of such influential scholars as Thirlwall, George Cornewall Lewis, George Grote, George Long, Baron Christian von Bunsen, William Smith, and others, Schmitz founded and edited the quarterly *Classical Museum: a Journal of Philology and of Ancient History and Literature*, of which seven volumes were published between 1844 and 1850. In 1844 he published a translation of Niebuhr's *Lectures on the History of Rome*, based on the notes he had taken at Niebuhr's lectures in Bonn. This work made Schmitz's reputation. It was also published in German, and the king of Prussia awarded Schmitz the gold medal for literature and science.

In December 1845 Schmitz became rector of the Royal High School, Edinburgh, a post he held with distinction for twenty years, thus continuing the close connection between Scotland and Germany which had been established in the 1790s, when Schmitz's mentor Niebuhr had studied in Edinburgh and the young Walter Scott had learned German in order to translate Goethe's historical drama *Götz von Berlichingen*. In his induction speech at the school, Schmitz expressed his desire to 'strengthen and increase the intellectual sympathy' between Britain and Germany, and over the next few years he extended the school curriculum to include modern languages, science, and music. In 1859 Prince Albert sent the prince of Wales to Edinburgh to receive instruction in various subjects before matriculating at Oxford. Schmitz was chosen to tutor the prince in Roman history, as he had previously tutored Prince Albert in Bonn.

While living in Edinburgh, Schmitz contributed on classical subjects to the *Penny Cyclopaedia*, edited by George Long; to the eighth edition of the *Encyclopaedia Britannica*; and to several other classical reference works. He also contributed to a series of classical school books published by the Edinburgh firm of W. and R. Chambers, and later wrote histories of England, Greece, and Rome for Collins's School Series of books for junior classes.

Schmitz's contribution to classical scholarship was recognized by his election to the Royal Society of Edinburgh in 1846, and by the award of the degree of LLD by the University of Aberdeen in 1849. He was, however, unsuccessful in his candidature for the chair of Greek at Edinburgh University in 1852. He stayed on at the Royal High School until 1866, when he moved to London. Until 1874 he was principal of the London International College at Isleworth, after which he acted as classical examiner in the University of London, at the same time actively carrying on with his writings on languages and history. In January 1881 he received a civil-list pension. His scholarly work was further recognized by the conferral in 1886 of the degree of LLD by the University of Edinburgh. In 1889 Schmitz had a serious accident at Portsmouth from which he never fully recovered. On hearing of it, a group of friends and former pupils, including the prince of Wales, presented him with a testimonial of over £1400.

Schmitz died of influenza on 28 May 1890 at his home at 53 Gloucester Road, Regent's Park, and was buried in Hampstead parish churchyard. He was survived by his wife and five sons and six daughters. His daughter Dora had already followed in her father's footsteps as a contributor to Anglo-German literary relations by means of her translations in the 1870s and 1880s of several German critical works on Shakespeare, and of the correspondence between Goethe and Schiller. His eldest son, Carl Theodor Schmitz (*d.* 1862), MD of Edinburgh University, went to India on the medical staff in 1861, and, after a heroic career during the cholera epidemic in the Punjab, died on his way home.

Leonhard Schmitz was remembered affectionately by former pupils (who included the inventor of the telephone, Alexander Graham Bell) as 'Lay-on-hard, with his one arm and snuff-box'. His obituarist in *The Athenaeum* (7 June 1890) described him as 'intensely industrious, personally unambitious, and almost devoid of the art of "getting on"; content to labour for scant reward, and never apparently expecting more'. The same writer described Schmitz as a devoted family man of simple habits, concluding that he was 'a model of that type of scholar to whom knowledge is its own exceeding great reward'.

ROSEMARY ASHTON

Sources *The Athenaeum* (7 June 1890), 739 • J. Murray, *Schola regia Edinensis* [forthcoming] • *The Times* (30 May 1890) • Albert, the prince consort, *Letters of the prince consort, 1831–1861*, ed. K. Jagow, trans. E. T. S. Dugdale (1938) • Allibone, *Dict.* • Ward, *Men of the reign* • W. Steven, *The history of the high school of Edinburgh* (1849)
Archives NRA Scotland, priv. coll. | Edinburgh City Archives, school and miscellaneous corresp. • NL Scot., corresp. with George Combe • NL Scot., letters to William Mure • UCL, letters to Society for the Diffusion of Useful Knowledge
Likenesses wood-engraving, NPG; repro. in *ILN* (7 June 1890) [*see illus.*]
Wealth at death £1834 2*s.* 6*d.*: probate, 9 July 1890, *CGPLA Eng. & Wales*

Schmoller, Hans Peter (1916–1985), typographer, was born on 9 April 1916 at Klopstockstrasse 6, Berlin, the son of Hans Schmoller (*b.* 1879), a doctor of medicine and viola player, and Marie Elisabeth Behrend (1887–1944?), an artist who set up an atelier in Berlin for making elaborate pleated paper lampshades. His father died of natural causes in a concentration camp (if this is a natural death) in Germany; his mother was last heard of on a transport to Auschwitz in May 1944.

After leaving the Kaiser Friedrich Schule, Berlin, at the age of seventeen Schmoller hoped to study art history, but the Nazis had made it impossible for Jews to enter a university. He applied to become a pupil of the great lettering artist and type designer Rudolf Koch at Offenbach—foreseeing, remarkably early, his future career—but Koch insisted on his prior training in a craft. Schmoller began a four-year compositor's apprenticeship in the Jewish book-printing firm of Siegfried Scholem: by a day release agreement he was able to study typography at the great Staatliche Kunstbibliothek in Berlin, and in the evenings he studied calligraphy under Johannes Boehland. In 1933 he made the first of several visits to London. After four years at Scholem, he passed his apprenticeship with high praise. He then enrolled in a monotype keyboard and caster course in Fetter Lane, London. The Monotype Corporation was asked by the manager of a missionary printing works in Basutoland if they could recommend someone to help out at their printing press for a year during the manager's absence. Hans Schmoller was offered the job and accepted with pleasure, since he knew that as an alien he might have difficulty in obtaining employment in Britain, and could not return to Germany.

Schmoller now started on his true career in the Morija printing works, staying there from 1938 to 1946 (with an interruption during the Second World War while he was interned as an enemy alien) and in 1942 became production manager. His fine work as a designer for Morija began to be mentioned in the South African newspapers: his work, often in the Curwen Press style, was being sent round the world, and the Limited Editions Club of New York commissioned him to design and print (at Morija) Olive Schreiner's *The Story of an African Farm* (1883), but the work was cancelled by the war, and Schmoller's design was eventually printed twenty-three years later by the Westerham Press in Kent.

When the war ended, Schmoller became a British subject, returned to England for a holiday, and in 1947 was offered a job at the Curwen Press as manager of the bindery and typographic assistant to the director, Oliver Simon—a most valuable appointment. After converting to Methodism on 29 April 1947, in May Schmoller married Dorothée Wachsmuth, midwife and assistant matron in a girls' school, the daughter of his aunt's friend Elisabeth Carson-Carlebach. She bore a daughter, Monica, but sadly died of cancer in 1948. On the advice of Oliver Simon to Allen Lane a job was then offered to Schmoller at Penguin Books. This was due to the departure of Jan Tschichold, who left Penguin in September 1949 after three years spent (in Tschichold's own words) making sure 'that its books, produced as cheaply as possible in millions for the millions, are every bit as well set and designed as the most expensive in the country—indeed, better than most!' (McLean, 147). Under their creator Allen Lane (1902–1970) Penguin Books had become the most important publishing firm in Britain—and for a time, perhaps, in the world.

Allen Lane himself has been called one of the makers of the twentieth century. By the time Schmoller arrived in 1949 the Penguin firm was producing not only millions of paperbacks every year but also distinguished and important works in hardback, all subsequently to be designed by Schmoller, who soon earned Lane's respect and warm support.

Schmoller was not experimental in typography: he worked in the severely traditional (but often decorative) English style pioneered by Oliver Simon. His eye for every kind of printing detail was so infallible that his initials of H. P. caused him to be known, in printing circles, as Half-Point Schmoller. Examples of his work are well illustrated in the special number of the *Monotype Recorder* (6, April 1987) published to commemorate his life and work after his death in 1985. Among his most admired books were the *Penguin Book of Spanish Verse*, edited by J. M. Cohen (1956, for which he designed the decorated paper cover); James Joyce's *Ulysses* (1969 edn, with his calligraphic cover); and the *Four Gospels*, edited by E. V. Rieu (1952).

Schmoller retired as director of Penguin Books at the age of sixty in 1976. On 7 September 1950 he had married second Tatyana Mary Kent (*b.* 1918), secretary to Allen Lane, who had joined Penguin Books before Schmoller in order to assist with a South American publishing scheme which fell through. They had one son, Sebastian (*b.* 1952). Tanya Schmoller was a collector of decorated papers, and when Hans retired they travelled the world in pursuit of collecting. They also built up a remarkable collection of every published Penguin book which was eventually given to the British Library of Political and Economic Science, who later sold it (with Mrs Schmoller's permission) to Japan.

Schmoller was also an able writer and contributed articles on typography and decorated paper to newspapers and leading journals. He edited and translated several books, including Giovanni Mardersteig's *The Officina Bodoni: an Account of the Work of a Hand Press, 1923–1977* (Verona: Edizioni Valdonega, 1980). His last publication, in collaboration with Henry Morris and his Bird and Bull Press in Pennsylvania, was a charming small work about Japanese paper, *Mr Gladstone's Washi* (1984).

Among the honours Schmoller received were the Francis Minns memorial award, 1974, and the prestigious gold medal of the International Book Design Exhibition at Leipzig, 1971. In 1977 he was appointed royal designer for industry. Schmoller died in Wexham Park Hospital, Slough, on 25 September 1985 and was cremated on 3 October 1985 at Slough crematorium.

RUARI MCLEAN

Sources *The Monotype Recorder*, 6 (April 1987) [special issue dedicated to Hans Schmoller] · private information (2004) [Mrs Tanya Schmoller] · d. cert. · R. McLean, *Jan Tschichold: typographer* (1975)
Archives RSA, Archive of Royal Designers for Industry · St Bride Institute, London, St Bride Printing Library · U. Reading L., department of typography and graphic communication, examples of typographical work

Schnadhorst, Francis (1840–1900), political organizer, was born on 24 August 1840 in Birmingham, the younger son and second of the three children of a draper of German extraction. His father died while he was still young and he was brought up by his mother and paternal grandfather, who owned a tailor's shop in Moor Street, Birmingham. He was educated at King Edward VI's Grammar School, Birmingham, and at the age of sixteen, following the death of his grandfather, he took charge of the family business.

Francis Schnadhorst (1840–1900), by Stuff (Henry Charles Seppings Wright?), pubd 1892

Schnadhorst was brought up as a nonconformist and as a young man he acted as secretary to the Revd R. W. Dale, the pastor of Carr's Lane Congregational Church. The alliance between nonconformity and radicalism was particularly close in Birmingham, so Schnadhorst joined the Birmingham Liberal Association soon after its formation in 1865 as a matter of course. He first became involved in the active work of the association in 1867, when he was elected vice-chairman and joint secretary of the St George's ward committee. In 1870, as secretary of the Central Nonconformist Committee he was engaged in educational reforms, especially with respect to endowed schools. In 1872 he served briefly on Birmingham town council, being elected to fill a casual vacancy in October only to be defeated at the municipal elections a month later, but by this time it was apparent that he was a talented organizer and in 1873 he was appointed full-time secretary of the Birmingham Liberal Association in succession to William Harris.

The Birmingham Liberal Association was already regarded as a model of efficiency, following the success of its 'vote as you are told' campaign at the 1868 general election, which had secured the return of Liberal members for all of Birmingham's three seats, but Schnadhorst fine-tuned its organization to an even higher pitch. He quickly engineered the overthrow of the Conservative and Anglican majorities on the town council and the school board and put in place a political machine which carried all before it for well over a decade. This was the heyday of the 'Birmingham caucus' and to its detractors Schnadhorst, with his Teutonic name and 'spectacled, sallow, sombre' features, was the perfect embodiment of its sinister power.

In 1877 Schnadhorst was appointed part-time secretary of the newly formed National Liberal Federation (NLF), while retaining his post with the Birmingham Liberal Association. The work involved in the dual appointment eventually proved too onerous even for someone of his energy and dedication and in 1884 he resigned the Birmingham post to become full-time secretary of the NLF at a salary of £800 per annum. Two years later the Liberal Party organized a national testimonial for him and over £10,000 was raised.

In 1885 Schnadhorst was given a seat on the standing committee of the Liberal Central Association, the party headquarters, and in July 1886 he was appointed secretary of this body. He remained secretary of the NLF, thus becoming the link between the leadership and the constituency associations and hence the key figure in rebuilding the party following the split over Irish home rule and the defection of the Liberal Unionists. Schnadhorst's achievement in keeping the NLF Gladstonian rather than Chamberlainite in 1886 was of considerable importance to the Liberal Party. He reorganized the NLF to make it more responsive to the needs of local associations, so encouraging affiliations, and revolutionized the Central Association's conduct of elections, the improvements being reflected in a series of favourable by-election results at the end of the 1880s. The work of co-ordinating the activities of the NLF and the Central Association proceeded more slowly but some progress was made, most notably in candidate selection. In 1889 Schnadhorst's own candidature in Newcastle under Lyme was approved but he stood down in the following year because of ill health.

Schnadhorst's health continued to decline and within two years of masterminding the Liberal victory at the 1892 general election, so enabling Gladstone to form his fourth ministry, he resigned all his offices with the party. He had always been very highly-strung and eventually suffered a complete mental and physical breakdown before dying at The Priory, a private lunatic asylum in Roehampton, on 2 January 1900. He was survived by his wife, Mary, the daughter of a Birmingham provision merchant, two sons, and a daughter. ERIC TAYLOR, *rev.*

Sources B. McGill, 'Francis Schnadhorst and liberal party organization', *Journal of Modern History*, 34 (1962), 19–39 • *Birmingham Mail* (4 Jan 1900) • *The Times* (5 Jan 1900) • A. T. C. Pratt, ed., *People of the period: being a collection of the biographies of upwards of six thousand living celebrities*, 2 vols. (1897)

Archives BL, Gladstone MSS • Duke U., miscellaneous papers • King's Cam., Browning MSS • U. Birm., Chamberlain MSS

Likenesses W. & D. Downey, woodburytype, NPG; repro. in W. Downey and D. Downey, *The cabinet portrait gallery*, 3 (1892) • Stuff [H. C. S. Wright?], watercolour caricature, NPG; repro. in *VF* (2 July 1892), pl. 542 [*see illus.*] • portrait?, repro. in *ILN*, 116 (1900), 43

Wealth at death £33,556 2s.: administration with will, 30 April 1900, *CGPLA Eng. & Wales*

Schnebbelie, Jacob (1760–1792), topographical draughtsman, was born in Duke's Court, St Martin's Lane, London, on 30 August 1760. His father was a native of Zürich and had served in the Dutch army at Bergen-op-Zoom, before settling in England to become a confectioner in Rochester. Jacob, after carrying on the same business for a short time—first at Canterbury and then at Hammersmith, Middlesex—abandoned it, and became a drawing-master at Westminster and other schools. It is likely that he was self-taught, although it is sometimes claimed that he was a pupil of Paul Sandby. Through the influence of Lord Leicester, the president of the Society of Antiquaries, Schnebbelie was appointed draughtsman to the society. Several views of ancient buildings published in the second and third volumes of *Vetusta monumenta* were drawn by him. He also made many of the drawings for Richard Gough's *Sepulchral Monuments of Great Britain* and John Nichols's *History of Leicestershire*. In 1788 he published a set of four views of St Albans, drawn and etched by himself and aquatinted by Francis Jukes. In 1791 Schnebbelie commenced the publication of the *Antiquaries' Museum*, illustrating the ancient architecture, painting, and sculpture of Britain, a series of plates etched and aquatinted by himself; but he lived to complete only three parts. The work was continued by his friends Gough and Nichols, and issued as a volume, with a memoir of him, in 1800. He was also associated with James Moore and J. G. Parkyns in the production of their *Monastic Remains* (1791), his name appearing as the publisher on some of the plates. A view of the Serpentine River, Hyde Park, London, etched by Schnebbelie in 1787, was aquatinted by Jukes and published in 1796. Schnebbelie died of rheumatic fever at his residence, 7 Poland Street, London, on 21 February 1792, leaving a widow, Margaretha Pollard of Canterbury, and three sons, for whom provision was made by the Society of Antiquaries. Another son was born on the day of Schnebbelie's burial, in the parish of St James's, London, on 26 February 1792, and two sons and a daughter had died in the year before his death.

Robert Bremmel Schnebbelie (*d.* 1847), his son, also practised as a topographical artist, occasionally exhibiting views of old buildings at the Royal Academy between 1803 and 1821. He made the drawings for many of the plates in Wilkinson's *Londina illustrata* (1808–25), Hughson's *Description of London*, and similar publications, but died in poverty in 1847. He was found dead, in Camden

Town, on 15 March; the coroner noted that there was no blame to the parochial authorities. The Victoria and Albert Museum, London, has two watercolours by him.

F. M. O'Donoghue, *rev.* Rosie Dias

Sources *GM*, 1st ser., 62 (1792), 189–90 • C. F. Bell, 'Fresh light on some watercolour painters of the old British school', *Walpole Society*, 5 (1915–17), 47–83 • Redgrave, *Artists* • Graves, *RA exhibitors* • Bryan, *Painters* • *Vetusta monumenta* (1747–1896), vols. 2–3 • J. Moore, *Monastic remains and ancient castles in England and Wales* (1792) • will, PRO, PROB 11/1339 • d. cert. [R. B. Schnebbelie]

Archives Bodl. Oxf., description of seats in Chatham church | S. Antiquaries, Lond., sketchbook and corresp. with Richard Gough and John Nichols

Wealth at death Robert Schnebbelie: died in poverty: *GM*, 1st ser., 62/1 (1792), 189–90

Schnebbelie, Robert Bremmel (*d.* 1847). *See under* Schnebbelie, Jacob (1760–1792).

Schneider, Henry William (1817–1887), industrialist and politician, was born on 12 May 1817 at Beaver Hall, Southgate, Middlesex, son of John Henry Powell Schneider (*bap.* 1768, *d.* 1861) and his second wife, Elizabeth Moule. The family had moved from Switzerland in the eighteenth century. Schneider's father was second-generation head of John Schneider & Co., merchants, London.

After 1824 the Schneider firm was primarily associated with mineral exploration in several countries. Aged eighteen, Schneider was made secretary of an associated organization, the Mexican and South American Company. In 1839 he travelled to the English Lake District and the Furness area, suspecting unexploited deposits of hematite iron ore. While remaining prominent in his family firm, this expedition anticipated his ensuing career.

In 1840 Schneider leased from the earl of Burlington the royalty of Park Farm, Dalton in Furness, Lancashire. He purchased nearby Whitriggs mine in 1842, subsequently leasing Mouzell mine in 1845 to form Schneider, Davis & Co. These operations achieved modest success. A major breakthrough followed in 1850, when renewed speculation at the previously unprofitable Park estate uncovered huge reserves of ore. The subsequent Burlington pit supplied substantial markets in south Wales and the Staffordshire ironworks.

Schneider's original partner, James Davis, withdrew before the discovery was fully recognized. Schneider had also succeeded his father as chairman of the Anglo-Mexican Mining Company, with further mineralogical interests in Exmoor, south Wales, Australian copper, and Cornish tin. In 1853, needing extra capital for Burlington pit, he joined Kirkcudbrightshire landowner Robert Hannay, establishing Schneider, Hannay & Co.

Schneider was still resident in London, travelling on business whenever required. Eloquent in advocating free trade and commerce, he also developed political aspirations, being elected in March 1857 as a Liberal MP for Norwich. Although he played no prominent part in the Commons, he was re-elected in 1859. But charges of electoral malpractice led to his being unseated the following year.

Following improvements to local railways, success at the Park mine, and increasing dominance within the Furness iron industry, Schneider eventually moved north. During 1859 Schneider, Hannay & Co. began building blast furnaces at Hindpool, within the expanding town of Barrow in Furness. Competition from a new steel works (established in 1863 by a partnership involving the duke of Devonshire, the duke of Buccleuch, and Furness Railway manager, James Ramsden) led to the amalgamation of the two companies in 1866. The Barrow Iron and Steel Company mainly manufactured railway lines. Schneider continued as a director until his death.

Schneider married first on 14 September 1842, Augusta Smith (*bap.* 1821), daughter of Richard Smith of Urswick. They had three sons, and she died in 1862. His second marriage, on 1 October 1864, to Elizabeth Turner (1830/31–1881), daughter of Canon Joseph Turner of Lancaster, doubtless aided his renewed attempts to enter parliament. At a by-election in February 1865 he was returned unopposed for Lancaster, and was re-elected the following July at the general election. Once again, the opposition raised allegations of bribery. A royal commission of inquiry, appointed in 1866, delivered a critical report—and for the second time Schneider was ejected from the house, with Matthew Fenwick, his fellow candidate, being likewise removed. The borough of Lancaster was disenfranchised the following year.

Schneider returned to Barrow, immersing himself in local affairs. The town achieved borough status in 1867, with James Ramsden the first mayor. Schneider became an alderman, serving the remainder of his life. He supported the development of the dock system, the Barrow Shipbuilding Company, the Flax and Jute Company, and other smaller industries. He participated on local school boards, contributing lavishly towards the development of local schools, churches, hospitals, and clubs. He was mayor of Barrow from 1875 to 1878, besides being chairman of the borough finance committee, a leading freemason, and a supporter of the local volunteer force. He owned several residences, purchasing Belsfield, an Italianate mansion at Bowness-on-Windermere, in 1869. He was a justice of the peace in both Lancashire and Westmorland.

Barrow became a parliamentary constituency in 1885, James Ramsden declining nomination. Schneider stood for the Conservatives but lost the election to David Duncan. In a curious reversal of previous events, Schneider himself alleged corruption and unseated Duncan on petition—but then waived his claim on the seat. Shortly afterwards, his health broke down. He died at Belsfield on 11 November 1887, being buried in Bowness cemetery four days later. His wife Elizabeth, with whom he had four daughters, had died in 1881 while holidaying at Dresden.

Schneider's greatest success was as the driving force behind the Furness iron industry. But his political career, bedevilled by accusations of electoral corruption, never got off the ground, in spite of his ability as a speaker. His other talents were recognized in 1866 with election as an associate of the Institution of Civil Engineers. At the institution's subsequent meeting he skilfully defended the advantages of steel for railway lines, while in 1880 the *Proceedings* of the Institute of Mechanical Engineers recorded in detail his comments on Furness iron.

Schneider was a constant churchman. Following his death, newspapers mentioned his munificent support for local causes—which he had seldom attempted to conceal. Contemporaries often thought him autocratic—but the author Robert Casson also mentions praise for 'the most generous and liberal despot in Lancashire'. He never openly expressed remorse about his political troubles—although these significantly increased pressure for electoral reform. Furthermore, despite intermittent difficulties, Schneider also considered himself a good employer. He recounted how the Park mine discovery occurred while certain workmen—opposed to the imminent abandonment of exploration—were offering one final week's labour without payment.

Schneider lived ostentatiously, regularly traversing Windermere on his yacht *Esperence* to catch his private train to Barrow. But his eventual fortune proved less than expected, and his memorial in Bowness cemetery is relatively simple. Nevertheless his services to Furness and his business acumen were well recognized—particularly in 1891, when a life-sized statue, provided by public subscription, was unveiled in Barrow. AIDAN C. J. JONES

Sources A. G. Banks, *H. W. Schneider of Barrow and Bowness* (1984) • R. Casson, *A few Furness worthies* (1889), 68–73 • J. D. Marshall, 'Corrupt practices at the Lancaster election of 1865', *Transactions of the Lancashire and Cheshire Antiquarian Society*, 63 (1952–3), 117–30 • *Barrow Herald* (12 Nov 1887) • *Barrow News* (12 Nov 1887) • *ILN* (5 June 1858) • J. Fisher, 'Popular history of Barrow-in-Furness', *North Lonsdale Magazine & Furness Miscellany*, 2/12 (April 1898), 254–7 • *Hansard 3* (1859), 746; (1866), 1871 • 'Royal commission to inquire into … corrupt practices at the last election', *Parl. papers* (1867), vol. 27, no. 3777 [borough of Lancaster] • J. L. Shaw, 'On the hematite iron mines of the Furness district', *Institution of Mechanical Engineers: Proceedings* (1880), 363–79 • J. D. Marshall, 'The founding of modern Barrow', *North West Evening Mail* (14 May 1952) • J. D. Marshall, 'The founding of modern Barrow', *North West Evening Mail* (21 May 1952) • J. D. Marshall, 'The founding of modern Barrow', *North West Evening Mail* (28 May 1952) • J. D. Marshall, 'The founding of modern Barrow', *North West Evening Mail* (4 June 1952) • J. Melville, 'Schneider—iron master of Furness', *North West Evening Mail* (29 Nov 1974) • J. Melville, 'Schneider—iron master of Furness', *North West Evening Mail* (13 Dec 1974) • R. P. Williams, 'On the maintenance and renewal of permanent way', *PICE*, 25 (1865–6), 353–66 [see also p. 203] • A. G. Banks, 'A Barrow industrialist's gift to Burra Burra', *North West Evening Mail* (20 April 1999) • d. cert. • *Lancaster Gazette* (16 Nov 1887)

Likenesses P. Wood, statue, 1891, Schneider Square, Barrow-in-Furness, Cumbria • W. Roffe, engraving (after photograph by J. Hughes), repro. in J. Richardson, *Furness past and present*, 2 (1880), 185 • photographs, repro. in Banks, *H. W. Schneider of Barrow and Bowness*, frontispiece and 70 • photographs, repro. in Fisher, 'Popular history of Barrow-in-Furness', 254 • portrait (damaged)

Wealth at death £204,939 10s. 7d.: probate, 15 Dec 1887, *CGPLA Eng. & Wales*

Schoberl, Frederic. *See* Shoberl, Frederic (1775–1853).

Schofield, Herbert (1882–1963), educationist, was born at Halifax, Yorkshire, on 8 December 1882, the elder son of James and Alice Schofield. On leaving the Trinity higher grade school, Halifax, at fourteen, he joined his father's small mechanical engineering firm to serve a seven-year apprenticeship. He also attended classes in engineering at Halifax Municipal Technical College winning a Carnegie engineering scholarship to the Royal College of Science in South Kensington, where he obtained a BSc honours degree in physics from the University of London. He subsequently took up a post as physics master at Dover county school and director of further education in charge of a small technical institute. It was from this post that, in September 1915, Schofield came to Loughborough as principal of the Technical Institute which had been established only six years earlier.

Schofield's long-term aim was to transform Loughborough College, as the institute soon became known, into a high-level engineering college. His own experience in industry was very probably a motivating factor and he also had a lifelong admiration for American industrial methods which he sought to emulate to a degree in the practical slant he gave his training methods in his college. The first major stage in the college's growth began in January 1916 when Schofield introduced short training courses for women munitions workers, a development that was to expand enormously during the next few years and for which he was made MBE in August 1917. He based his courses on the principle for which he was to become famous, 'training on production', whereby workers were trained under conditions as similar as possible to those in industry. He was later to apply this philosophy to the courses for his students in the post-war college. In September 1918 he introduced a five-year full-time diploma course in mechanical engineering for former officers; the diploma of Loughborough College grew rapidly in the next few years and extended into other branches of engineering and commerce.

Meanwhile, in 1918, Schofield married Clara Johns (*b.* 1890); they had a daughter and adopted a son. His wife died in 1928 and he never remarried. He was awarded a London doctorate of philosophy in 1923 for research into the thermal combustion and mechanical efficiency of high-speed multi-cylinder internal combustion engines. In the college, major developments in the inter-war period included the setting-up of a department for training handicraft teachers in 1930; the establishment of the annual summer school in August 1931, offering courses mainly in physical education and arts and crafts; the creation of an aeronautical engineering department in 1935; and the gradual extension of the college's work in physical education. During these years, Schofield was busily acquiring property for use as student hostels, while at the same time there was a gradual shift in the centre of gravity of the college from its original buildings in the centre of the town to another more spacious site on the western edge of Loughborough, later the campus of Loughborough University. Throughout this period, the work of the original Technical Institute in offering part-time lower-level courses continued. Thus, by the outbreak of the Second World War in 1939, Schofield, with the aid of his able lieutenants, had built up a remarkable institution of international repute, considerable diversity, and with a wide range of residential and sporting facilities.

During the war, Schofield endeavoured to keep the normal diploma and teacher-training courses going, albeit in shortened forms and with fewer students. In addition, the college made a direct contribution to the war effort by providing a wide range of technical courses for personnel of all three services, and by housing the RAF medical rehabilitation unit. The immediate post-war period brought a substantial increase in student numbers as former servicemen flocked into the college. Schofield, always eager to start something new, added another string to his bow, with the introduction of a full-time course in librarianship in January 1947. Nationally and regionally, he continued to be very active. He was chairman of the Council of the Institution of Production Engineers in 1946 and its president from 1948 to 1950; he was appointed vice-chairman of the National Advisory Council on Education for Industry and Commerce; and he was a lay canon of Leicester Cathedral, an honour of which he was very proud. For his contribution to technological education, Schoey, or the Doctor, as he had become known by this time, was made CBE in 1947. However, he was now well into his sixties and finally retired in December 1950 at the age of sixty-eight, after thirty-five years as principal of Loughborough College. After his retirement, Schofield remained in Loughborough and, in addition to becoming a local town councillor, continued to be active in the Rotary movement in which he had been a leading figure for many years, having been president of Rotary International of Great Britain and Northern Ireland in 1931–2.

The empire which Schofield created during his lifetime did not survive very long after his retirement and broke up into four separate institutions: the College of Technology which in 1966 was to become Loughborough University; Loughborough College of Education, which in 1977 amalgamated with the university; Loughborough College of Art and Design, which merged with the university in 1998; and Loughborough Technical College, now renamed simply Loughborough College.

Schofield was an educational entrepreneur, ever ready to grasp an opportunity, and his courage and foresight were exemplified by the extraordinary growth of his college, especially during the harsh economic climate of the inter-war years. His major contribution to technological education was his policy of 'training on production', considered by some to be the precursor of the modern sandwich course. Though not physically large, Schofield had a masterful presence and, the possessor of enormous energy, he drove himself and his staff very hard. A determined and in many ways an autocratic man, he put his life's work into Loughborough College, a unique institution in its time, one which was essentially his creation and which he dominated for so long. He died in a nursing home at Radmoor Road, Loughborough, on 18 September 1963. LEONARD CANTOR

Sources L. M. Cantor and G. F. Matthews, *Loughborough: from college to university* (1977) • L. M. Cantor and G. F. Matthews, *Herbert Schofield at Loughborough: a pictorial history* (1982) • J. M. Harvey, *Herbert Schofield and Loughborough College* • F. E. Foden, 'Herbert Schofield and Loughborough College', *Vocational Aspect of Education*, 32 (1963), 231–46 • L. Cantor, *Loughborough University of Technology: past and present* (1990)

Likenesses O. Birley, oils, 1950, Loughborough University

Wealth at death £35,288 6s. od.: probate, 12 Dec 1963, *CGPLA Eng. & Wales*

Scholderer, (Julius) Victor (1880–1971), bibliographer, was born in Clarendon Road, Putney, London, on 9 October 1880, the only child of German émigrés Otto Scholderer (1834–1902) and his wife, Luise Steurwaldt. His father, a distinguished painter of the Frankfurt school, first left Germany for Paris, and then as a result of the Franco-Prussian War of 1870 moved to London. Both parents became naturalized British citizens, but never really settled down happily to life in Britain; they returned to Germany in 1899.

Educated at St Paul's School and Trinity College, Oxford, Victor Scholderer entered the service of the British Museum Library in June 1904, filling the gap caused by the premature death the previous autumn of R. G. C. Proctor (1868–1903). Thereafter he gave his undivided attention to the library for the next sixty-six years, and some of his best work was completed after his official retirement in 1945. Armed with a formidable knowledge of Latin and Greek literature, bilingual in English and German, and with an excellent command of French already perfected during a year's residence in Paris in his student days, he was ideally equipped to face his life's work. This was the bibliographical study of early printed books, particularly those of the fifteenth century, of which the British Museum had already the best collection in the world and the British Library now has about 10,500 editions. Scholderer quickly developed an acute eye for early typefaces, and worked for many years on the specialized catalogue of the British Museum's incunabula (known as BMC), which is still incomplete. From parts 2 and 3 (Germany), through parts 4–7 (Italy), to the massive part 8 (France), Scholderer was responsible for more of this immensely exacting work than any other individual member of staff. He could inspire awe, even fear, in his colleagues, but was never unjust or unfair, and, as far as anyone else was aware, was hardly (if ever) guilty of an error in his work. He never wrote a full-scale book, but one of the best results of his career was a steady stream of articles, mostly short, all exquisitely written, and not without the occasional touch of wry humour. Each solved some problem, outlining in as few words as possible the career of some early printer or humanist scholar, and paving the way for further research. After his official retirement he gave more of his attention to the museum's collections of Italian and German books of the sixteenth century, and was largely responsible for the publication of the invaluable short-title catalogues of these books, Italian in 1958 and German in 1962, each of which for the first time presented the scholarly world with comprehensive indexes of the printers and booksellers.

In 1927 Scholderer designed a Greek type (New Hellenic), of which he was very proud. The first book printed with it was the *Prometheus Bound* of Aeschylus, prepared by Scholderer himself in 1930, and the type was used by *The*

Times. In the same year, 1930, Scholderer gave the Sandars lectures in bibliography at Cambridge. Entitled 'The invention of printing: facts and theories', they remained unpublished, but he returned to the same theme in later lectures, such as that read before the Bibliographical Society in London in March 1940 and published in *The Library* in 1941. Then he wrote a short booklet, necessarily technical but very readable, on Johann Gutenberg, which the British Museum published in 1963 and later reprinted. In 1948 he gave the annual Italian lecture of the British Academy, under the title 'Printers and readers in Italy in the fifteenth century', published in 1949. During the Second World War he supervised the evacuation of the museum's incunabula from London to Wales, and lived with them, and worked on them, in Aberystwyth for the duration of the war.

In the 1950s Scholderer felt obliged to enter the controversy raging over the so-called Constance missal, a book not to be found in any British library. A copy had recently been acquired by the Pierpont Morgan Library of New York, and Scholderer was never in agreement with the keeper of printed books of that library, Curt F. Bühler, as to a very early date for the missal. He believed it to have been printed between about 1465 and 1473, probably at Basel, and his conclusions were apparently justified by the later researches of another American scholar, Allan H. Stevenson, an expert on paper studies of the fifteenth century. Nevertheless, it was characteristic of Scholderer that he always held Bühler in the highest regard as a fellow incunabulist and also as a personal friend. He was on friendly terms with all the leading bibliographical scholars of continental Europe. Perhaps not enough honours came his way, but he was an honorary doctor of the universities of Durham and Wales, president and gold medallist of the Bibliographical Society of London, fellow of the British Academy, and honorary fellow of the Pierpont Morgan Library (although he never visited America), and in 1961 he was appointed CBE.

Victor Scholderer married Frida Marie, daughter of Otto Semler of Berlin, on 8 May 1913; there were no children. After her death in 1950 he was a lonely widower in a dingy London flat; but he loved cats, poetry, the music of Beethoven, and above all writing another poem or yet another short article or book review in his incomparable style, still tinged with a slight Teutonic formality at times, but never less than stimulating, briefly even amusing, and eminently instructive. The bibliography of his vast output of published writings appeared three times: in *The Library* in 1955, in the selection of his *Fifty Essays* (1966), and in the imposing Festschrift presented to him for his ninetieth birthday in 1970. Even at the third attempt, the bibliography was still not quite complete. The poems which he published at his own expense in two slim volumes (*The Avenue, and other Verses*, 1959, and *Women of Troy*, 1965) are sensitive, tender, introspective, and difficult to understand. One of his greatest loves in literature was Goethe, on whose exhibition in the King's Library at the British Museum in 1949 he wrote a poem in German. Scholderer died on 11 September 1971 at Aberystwyth, which he had come to love during his wartime sojourn there. His body was cremated, possibly at Shrewsbury.

Dennis E. Rhodes

Sources V. Scholderer, *Reminiscences* (1970) • F. Francis, 'Victor Scholderer, 1880–1971', *PBA*, 58 (1972), 429–46 • G. D. Painter, 'Victor Scholderer: in memoriam', *Gutenberg Jahrbuch* (1972), 192–6 • D. E. Rhodes, ed., *Essays in honour of Victor Scholderer* (1970) • *WWW*, 1971–80

Likenesses photograph, *c*.1971, repro. in Francis, 'Victor Scholderer'

Wealth at death £67,185: probate, 9 Nov 1971, *CGPLA Eng. & Wales*

Scholefield, James (1789–1853), classical scholar, was born on 15 November 1789 at Henley-on-Thames, where his father, Nathaniel, was an Independent minister. He was educated at Christ's Hospital, where he won many distinctions. In October 1809 he went up to Trinity College, Cambridge, and in 1812 was elected scholar of the college. He was Craven scholar in 1812, graduated as a senior optime in 1813, and won the first chancellor's medal in 1813 and the members' prize in 1814 and 1815. Scholefield was ordained before taking his degree, and in October 1813 became curate to Charles Simeon, the prominent evangelical, at Trinity Church, Cambridge. He won a fellowship at Trinity in October 1815, and from 1815 to 1821 took resident pupils at Emmanuel House. He proceeded MA in 1816. In July 1823 he accepted the perpetual curacy of St Michael's, Cambridge, and under his ministry the church became very popular with undergraduates preparing for orders. He examined in the first classical tripos held at Cambridge (1824); and on the death of Peter Paul Dobree in 1825, he was appointed regius professor of Greek.

Scholefield was not a scholar of great distinction, but he was the first professor of Greek to lecture regularly: he gave lectures on Greek authors three times a week each Lent term and missed only four courses in twenty-seven years. Although his lectures were not profound, he was a successful teacher who presented the views of other scholars with admirable clarity at a time when few of his contemporaries lectured at all.

Scholefield's published classical works showed little originality: he produced a new edition of Porson's *Four Plays of Euripides* (1826), the first book to be printed using the elegant type based on Porson's own Greek script. His edition of Aeschylus (1828) was highly conservative and closely based on the work of earlier scholars, and his chief undertaking—the collection and publication of the notes and marginalia of his predecessor Peter Paul Dobree—was flawed by inaccuracy. His other works included numerous sermons and papers on the text and translation of the New Testament and a popular *Psalm and Hymn Book* (1828).

Scholefield resigned his fellowship in 1827, and on 27 August, at Trinity Church, married Harriet, daughter of Dr Samuel Chase of Luton, Bedfordshire. In 1837 he accepted the living of Sapcote, Staffordshire, but, having scruples about how he could retain St Michael's and his university connection with a distant benefice, resigned Sapcote without taking up office. In 1849 he succeeded Dr French, master of Jesus, as canon of Ely, a preferment that had recently been attached to the Greek chair. Without it the regius professorship was worth only £40 a year. Scholefield at once abolished fees for admission to the professor's lectures.

On 11 November 1849 St Michael's was seriously damaged by fire, and from this time to his death Scholefield was continuously harassed by disputes over the restoration of the church. Himself a low-churchman, he was also constantly assailed on points of doctrine: the result was a disastrous division among the parishioners. Scholefield preached for the last time at St Michael's on 26 September 1852. He died suddenly at Hastings on 4 April 1853, and was buried at Fairlight, Hastings. He was survived by his wife and one son.

Scholefield examined for several years at Christ's Hospital, and he did a vast quantity of unremunerated work for Cambridge charities and for candidates for orders. He spoke constantly at missionary meetings, and was sole trustee of the Cambridge Servants' Training Institution from its foundation. Other duties included acting as a syndic of the Pitt Press, general editor of the publications of the Parker Society and treasurer of the Clerical Education Society. He combined these and other offices with an unusually busy parochial ministry: he performed single-handed three full services each Sunday for thirty years. The Scholefield theological prizes, founded at Cambridge in 1856 by public subscription, appropriately commemorated him. E. C. Marchant, *rev.* Richard Smail

Sources [H. C. Scholefield], *Memoir of the late Rev. James Scholefield … by his widow* (1855) • *GM*, 2nd ser., 39 (1853), 664–7 • Venn, *Alum. Cant.*

Likenesses J. B. Hunt, mezzotint, pubd 1855 (after G. F. Joseph), NPG • J. B. Hunt, stipple, pubd 1855 (after unknown artist), NPG • portrait (presented by G. F. Joseph); in the possession of his son, 1897

Scholefield, Joshua (1774/5–1844), politician and businessman, though a Yorkshireman by birth, was by 1800 well established in Birmingham. He prospered as an iron manufacturer, merchant, and banker, and became the director of two large banks—the National Provincial Bank of England and the London Joint Stock Bank—and of the Metropolitan Assurance Company. He married three times. His first wife, whom he married at St Phillip's, Birmingham, on 7 July 1804, was Mary Cotterill, the second daughter of Clement Cotterill, of Birmingham. Their younger son, William *Scholefield (1809–1867), was to become the city's first mayor. The family lived in a house in Old Square, but Scholefield later moved to Edgbaston. Following the death of his first wife he married her sister, the youngest daughter of Clement Cotterill, in 1824. In 1835 he married his third wife, Mary Anne Swaine, daughter of Thomas Rose Swaine of Highgate.

An ally of Thomas Attwood, Scholefield became deputy chairman of the Birmingham Political Union, which was formed in 1830 to promote parliamentary reform. Historians have not given him much credit for the union's success, and, if he is judged as a radical organizer, their opinion may be considered a fair one. However, his wealth and standing, as well as his whig connections, gave him advantages over his mostly ultra-tory colleagues in the union leadership. In the tense days of May 1832, when even the union became nervous about its radical posturing and wished to reassure those in authority, it was Scholefield who was received by Lord Grey. After the Reform Bill was passed he joined Attwood as one of the preordained MPs for the new borough of Birmingham. He was returned at every election until his death.

If anyone expected Scholefield to become a spokesman for commercial interests they would have been disappointed. Only once in the Commons did he speak directly on such issues, when he made a minor intervention in a railway debate. Nor, unlike Attwood, was he obsessed with currency reform. In his maiden speech on 21 March 1833 he said: 'He did not believe … distress could be remedied by a change in currency, unless it was accompanied by a reduction of taxation' (*Hansard* 3, 16, 1833, 945).

Scholefield's defence of the common people was both strong and blunt. In 1835 he charged that when the mostly socially superior yeomanry met the lower classes they were apt to be 'more anxious to ride over them than to meet their demands in a fair and proper way' (*Hansard* 3, 27, 1835, 1156). On 12 July 1839 he told the house that 'the Chartists wished for nothing but justice' (ibid., 49, 1839, 274). Their idea of justice and his were similar. He was one of the small minority that had steadfastly opposed the passage of the new poor law in 1834, and just a week before his defence of the Chartists he had restated his own solution: 'The way to relieve the poor was, for the rich to take the burden on their own shoulders' (ibid., 48, 1839, 1413).

Scholefield also displayed some of the more widely held hallmarks of radicalism. He supported the ballot, triennial parliaments, and repeal of the corn laws, and he was a champion of municipal reform. Yet despite the mauling that the successful bill of 1835 received in the Lords, he felt compelled to disown an 1836 Birmingham petition for reform of the upper house. Nor was he ready to concede the Chartists' sole formal objective, a democratic political structure. He may, however, have helped to keep alive their faith in politics. Scholefield died in Edgbaston on 4 July 1844, aged sixty-nine, and was buried in Edgbaston churchyard. R. W. Davis

Sources *Hansard* 3 (1833–42) • *GM*, 2nd ser., 21 (1844), 431 • C. Gill, *Manor and borough to 1865* (1952), vol. 1 of *History of Birmingham* (1952–74) • C. Flick, *The Birmingham Political Union and the movements for reform in Britain, 1830–1839* (1978) • *IGI*

Archives NA Scot., corresp. with Andrew Leith-Hay • U. Durham L., letters to Charles, second Earl Grey

Scholefield, William (1809–1867), politician, born in August 1809 in the Old Square, Birmingham, was the second son of Joshua *Scholefield (1774/5–1844), MP for Birmingham, and his wife, Mary, the second daughter of Clement Cotterill. In 1837 William, after travelling through the United States and Canada, settled down at Birmingham, where he took part in his father's business and engaged in public affairs under his father's guidance. He had married Jane Matilda (*d.* 1843), daughter of John Miller of New York. In 1837 Scholefield became high bailiff of the court leet of Birmingham, and on 26 December 1838 he was chosen as the first mayor of the newly incorporated town. In 1839 he was elected to the town council and his presence paved the way for a closer partnership in the future between local commerce and government in Birmingham.

On his father's death in July 1844 Scholefield stood for the vacant seat in parliament, and expressed views even more radical than those of his father. He was defeated by Richard Spooner, a conservative. But at the general election of 1847 he was returned with George Frederick Muntz in what was to become a landmark in the history of radical Birmingham politics. In 1852 and 1857 Muntz and Scholefield were again elected, though Muntz's highly independent tory radicalism jarred violently with Scholefield's Liberalism. In 1857, on Muntz's death, his place was taken by John Bright without opposition, and Scholefield and Bright continued to hold the seat together until Scholefield's death.

Scholefield pursued an orthodox radical Liberalism, in parliament supporting the expansion of popular political rights, commercial freedoms, and religious liberty. He was one of the twelve members of parliament who voted for the People's Charter, and actively supported bills for repealing the paper duties and 'taxes on knowledge', for lowering income tax, and for preventing the adulteration of food. He supported the movements for working-class land and building societies and mechanics' institutions and assisted the introduction of limited liability clauses into the laws governing industrial partnerships and co-operative societies. Party ties did not destroy his independence of judgement, and, unlike the majority of his political friends, he opposed Lord John Russell's Ecclesiastical Titles Bill, and he supported the northern states during the American Civil War. Scholefield died on 9 July 1867 at his home in Glasshouse Street, Regent Street, London. He had at least seven sons and one daughter; his seventh son, Clement Cotterill Scholefield (1839–1904), became vicar of Holy Trinity, Knightsbridge.

SAMUEL TIMMINS, *rev.* MATTHEW LEE

Sources *Birmingham Daily Post* (10 July 1867) • *GM*, 4th ser., 4 (1867), 262 • personal knowledge (1867) • *Debrett's Illustrated House of Commons and the Judicial Bench* (1867), 204 • Boase, *Mod. Eng. biog.* • D. Fraser, *Urban politics in Victorian England* (1976) • Venn, *Alum. Cant.* • *CGPLA Eng. & Wales* (1867)

Likenesses P. Hollins, bust, 1860, Birmingham Museums and Art Gallery • D. J. Pound, stipple and line engraving (after photograph by Whitlock of Birmingham), NPG; repro. in D. J. Pound, *Drawing room portrait gallery of eminent personages* (1859–60) • portrait, repro. in *ILN*, 15 (1849), 13 • portrait, repro. in *ILN*, 22 (1853), 312 • portrait, repro. in *Edgbastonia*, 1 (1881), 18

Wealth at death under £35,000: administration, 5 Dec 1867, *CGPLA Eng. & Wales*

Scholes, James Christopher (1854–1890), antiquary, son of James Scholes, printer and bookbinder, and his wife, Hannah Elizabeth Thompson, was born at Bolton, Lancashire, on 27 March 1854 and educated at Holy Trinity School in that town. He was trained as a printer and became a reporter on the *Bolton Evening News*, but subsequently he went into business as a draper with premises in Newport Street, Bolton. Scholes served as a member of the Bolton board of guardians from 1887 to 1890 and of the school board from 1888. He married Ann Frost on 9 May 1877; their only child died in infancy. Scholes's wife ran the drapery store while he devoted his attention to antiquarian and genealogical studies. His principal publications were the *Bolton Bibliography and Jottings of Book Lore, with Notes on Local Authors and Printers* (1886) and *A History of Bolton*, which was completed by W. Pimblett and published in 1892. He also wrote several articles for local journals and for the Bolton newspapers. He died on 18 June 1890 at his home, 46 Newport Street, Bolton, and was buried in the town's Tonge cemetery.

C. W. SUTTON, *rev.* ALAN G. CROSBY

Sources *Bolton Evening News* (19 June 1890) • *Transactions of the Lancashire and Cheshire Antiquarian Society*, 8 (1890), 211–12 • A. Sparke, *Bibliographia Boltoniensis* (1913) • *CGPLA Eng. & Wales* (1890)

Wealth at death £1758 12*s.* 7*d.*: probate, 25 July 1890, *CGPLA Eng. & Wales*

Scholes, Percy Alfred (1877–1958), musical writer and encyclopaedist, was born at Headingley, Leeds, on 24 July 1877, the third child of Thomas Scholes, commercial agent, and his wife, Katharine Elizabeth Pugh. Ill health limited his attendance at school (he was a lifelong sufferer from severe bronchitis), but he gave much time to miscellaneous reading and the assiduous study of the elements of music. After a couple of years earning 10*s.* a week as assistant librarian of the Yorkshire College (later the University of Leeds), he taught music at Kent College, Canterbury (1901), and Kingswood College, Grahamstown, Cape Province (1904). On his return to England at the age of twenty-eight his career began to take a more definite direction. He became an extension lecturer to the University of Manchester on what was coming to be known as 'musical appreciation', and continued in this way very successfully for the next six years. Meanwhile he took his ARCM diploma and (after a false start at Durham) entered St Edmund Hall, Oxford, gaining his BMus in 1908.

In 1907, following a series of lectures for the Co-operative Holidays Association, Scholes formed the Home Music Study Union, whose organ, the *Music Student* (in later years the *Music Teacher*), he edited from its foundation in 1908 until 1921. He married Dora Wingate, daughter of Richard Lean, civil engineer, in 1908 and in 1912 made the decisive step of moving to London, his only guaranteed income being £40 a year as assistant to J. S. Shedlock, music critic of *The Queen*. With the support of such men as H. C. Colles and Percy Buck, he was soon making his mark as a journalist and as an extension lecturer for the universities of Oxford, Cambridge, and London. From 1913 to 1920 he was music critic of the *Evening Standard*.

When war broke out in 1914 he was on a lecture tour of

Percy Alfred Scholes (1877–1958), by Elliott & Fry, 1948

colleges in the United States and Canada. On his return he headed, until 1919, the 'music for the troops' section of the YMCA in France, further developing his twin gifts of detailed organization and the ability to hold the attention of the unpractised listener. From this work came his very successful *Listener's Guide to Music* (1919).

Early in 1920 Scholes became music critic of *The Observer*, following the abrupt departure of Ernest Newman who had accepted a substantial offer from the rival *Sunday Times*. For the next five years Scholes filled the position with notable success. His style, always fluent and readable, gained distinction. He continued to regard his role as primarily that of an educator, and was undoubtedly among the first to see the educational potentialities of broadcasting, the gramophone, and the player-piano. He gave a weekly radio talk commenting on the previous week's broadcasts: from 1926 to 1928 he was musical editor of the *Radio Times*. He was usually at work on several books at once. His home was a busy office with as many as six or more typists and co-workers, including his devoted wife.

A contract to provide pianola-roll annotations for the Aeolian Company provided him with the means to detach himself from journalism. In 1928 he moved to Switzerland, and thenceforward lived in the neighbourhood of Montreux. The following year he organized an Anglo-American Music Educators' Conference at Lausanne, which was repeated in 1931. He made four further lecture tours of the United States. He was now able to give time to more solid scholarship and his thesis 'The puritans and music' gained him in 1934 his DLitt from Lausanne University.

For some time Scholes had planned a more comprehensive work, tentatively called 'Everyone's musical encyclopedia', for the great new body of listeners brought into being by radio and the gramophone. The book finally appeared as the *Oxford Companion to Music* in the autumn of 1938. Scholes's varied experience as teacher, lecturer, journalist, critic, and scholar was at last drawn together in one accomplishment—'the most extraordinary range of musical knowledge, ingeniously "self-indexed", ever written and assembled between two covers by one man' (*New Grove*, 5). It remained for many years a most attractive and much used work of reference.

In 1940 Scholes made his way to England just before the fall of France; his wartime homes were first at Aberystwyth, then at Oxford, where he was elected to the board of the faculty of music. He completed a monumental biography of Dr Charles Burney (2 vols., 1948; James Tait Black memorial prize), a model of humane scholarship, and continued his lexicographical labours with his *Concise Oxford Dictionary of Music* (1952) and *Oxford Junior Companion to Music* (1954). After the war he returned to Switzerland, and built a house at Clarens. In 1950 the devaluation of the pound drove him back to Oxford, where he spent much of the following years losing inch by inch his battle against the complications in his lifelong bronchitis brought on by advancing age and an inimical climate. Every winter he returned to Switzerland; and there, at Vevey, he died on 31 July 1958. He was survived by his wife; they had no children. Scholes valued his well-earned academic distinctions which in addition to those already mentioned included: from Oxford the honorary degree of DMus (1943), MA (by decree, 1944), and DLitt (1950), and from Leeds an honorary LittD (1953). He was an honorary fellow and trustee of St Edmund Hall, Oxford; an officer of the Star of Romania (1930), FSA (1938), and OBE (1957). His remarkable library, one of the largest of its kind in private hands, was acquired by the National Library of Canada, Ottawa.

Scholes was of middle height, and although not robust, was an active walker. He worked long hours with great concentration, with methodical interruptions for exercise. His conscience was strongly protestant, totally divorced from any conventional religious expression. He was warmly humanitarian; a long-standing and articulate vegetarian and opponent of blood sports. There were those for whom his clarity of thought, total absence of humbug and affectation, and ironic humour made him seem something of a philistine. He was charitable in good causes, warm and generous in personal dealings, at the same time disinclined to give ground in business matters. Traces of his native Yorkshire speech remained with him to the end. In a letter to his publisher he once wrote, 'the epitaph I should desire for myself, were it not already applied to another and a greater man, would be "The common people heard him gladly".' J. O. Ward, *rev.*

Sources private information (1971, 2004) · personal knowledge (1971) · *The Times* (2 Aug 1958) · *WWW* · 'Scholes, Percy', *New Grove* · *CGPLA Eng. & Wales* (1958)

Archives National Library of Canada, Ottawa, papers relating to *Oxford Companion to Music* | BL, corresp. with Society of Authors, Add. MSS 56799–56800 • U. Edin., corresp. with Charles Sarolea | SOUND BL NSA, documentary performance
Likenesses Elliott & Fry, photograph, 1948, NPG [*see illus.*] • photograph, Oxford University Press, London
Wealth at death £39,406 12*s*. 2*d*.: probate, 19 Dec 1958, *CGPLA Eng. & Wales*

Scholes, Theophilus Edward Samuel [*pseud.* Bartholomew Smith] (*c*.1858–*c*.1940), medical practitioner and political commentator, was born in Jamaica and brought up in Stewart Town. Good schooling and access to steady funds enabled him to study medicine at St Mungo's College, Glasgow, where he qualified LRCS (Edinburgh) in 1884. He became a licentiate of the Royal College of Physicians of Edinburgh on 25 October 1884. He then toured Scotland and Ireland with other black people, speaking of the Christian salvation of Africa 'by the people of that country' and gathering financial support. In February 1886 he, with Jamaican carpenter John Ricketts, left Liverpool for the Congo. He ran a sanatorium at Mukimvika, possibly for two years; the *Medical Directory* for 1887 has Wiverton Road, south-east London, as his address.

Scholes took his MD at Brussels in 1893, the year he visited the African Institute at Colwyn Bay, north Wales. Established by Baptist missionary William Hughes as a practical and Christian training school for Africans, it soon attracted blacks from the Caribbean and the Bahamas, one individual from South Carolina, and Virginia-born former slave Thomas Lewis Johnson, who had travelled in Ireland with Scholes. Scholes, with John Ricketts and his wife, went to Calabar, Nigeria, for the institute. As a witness of the colonizing process he wrote *The British Empire and Alliances: Britain's Duty to her Colonies and Subject Races* (1899), in which he rebutted the standard dismissal of Africans. He asked whether any group or race had ever made permanent advances without external influences, and observed that ancient Greece and Rome and modern European nations had themselves needed outside influences. He also emphasized the similarities between Africa's traditional societies and modern societies in the recent past. Colour prejudice was, he claimed, based on an illusion.

Now based in London, Scholes joined the African Society in 1903, the Incorporated Society of Authors, and the Ethnological Society. He attended parliamentary debates on colonial matters, and wrote (as Bartholomew Smith) *Chamberlain and Chamberlainism: his Fiscal Policies and Colonial Policy* (1903), an attack on the colonial secretary, Joseph Chamberlain. He returned to a study of racist beliefs and the ill-founded justifications for British imperialism with his *Glimpses of the ages, or, The 'superior' and 'inferior' races, so-called, discussed in the light of science and history* (1905); a second volume appeared in 1908, when four more volumes were promised. Scholes exposed double standards, bigotry, coercion, broken pledges, lies, misreporting, and the unsuitability of colonial whites to rule (taking Natal as his detailed example); the advancement of black people was, he claimed, being held back.

Scholes's prose style is indicated by the lengthy titles of his books, but he had read widely, kept newspaper clippings, and his contacts included people with imperial experience. The Guyana-born, London-trained Dr William W. Campbell was thanked for his assistance in *Glimpses*. Pixley Seme, New York graduate, Oxford law student, and later a founder of South Africa's African National Congress, arranged for Pennsylvania Rhodes scholar Alain Locke (who published the influential *New Negro* in 1925) to meet Scholes in London in 1908, and for the Sierra Leonean doctor William Renner to make contact. The organizers of the Universal Races Conference in London (1911) knew of Scholes and his books. South African journalist Sol Plaatje persuaded Scholes to read the manuscript of his *Native Life in South Africa* (1916). American former-slave journalist John E. Bruce also knew about Scholes. Also New York-based, the bibliophile Alphonso Schomburg knew of Scholes in the 1920s and may have met him in London in 1926. And in the 1930s the future first president of Kenya, Jomo Kenyatta, and his friend the Caribbean-born nationalist Ras Makonnen visited Scholes to thank him for his writings.

Scholes was described by contemporaries as tall, with an imposing appearance. How he funded his scholarly activities is unknown; perhaps there was income from property in Jamaica, or occasional work in medicine. In 1908 the *Medical Directory* noted that he was retired. The London decades seem to have been spent at the British Museum. No trace of his death has been uncovered in British records; he may have returned to Stewart Town in the 1930s.

Scholes's writings moved black commentary forward from comments on white failure to conform to Christian standards into arguments based on economics and historical evidence. His books clearly expounded the need to co-operate across artificial barriers and the injustice of racial barriers. His influence on other black people from his base in London places him firmly within the history of pan-Africanism. JEFFREY GREEN

Sources *Medical Directory* (1887–1908) • F. E. Guinness, *The new world of central Africa* (1890) • T. L. Johnson, *Twenty-eight years a slave* (1908) • J. Green, 'Thomas Lewis Johnson (1836–1921): the Bournemouth evangelist', *Under the imperial carpet*, ed. R. Lotz and I. Pegg (1986), 54–68 • U. Wales, Bangor, African Institute MSS • I. Geiss, *The pan-African movement* (1974) • H. T. Thomas, *The story of a West Indian policeman* (1927), 367–73 • J. P. Green, *Black Edwardians: black people in Britain, 1901–1914* (1998) • Royal College of Physicians of Edinburgh
Likenesses portrait, *c*.1893 (after photograph), U. Wales, Bangor, African Institute files

Schomberg, Sir Alexander (1720–1804), naval officer, was born in London, the fifth son of Meyer Löw *Schomberg (1690–1761), a physician of German descent who established a successful London practice in Fenchurch Street. His elder brothers, Isaac *Schomberg and Ralph (Raphael) *Schomberg, followed their father into the medical profession; two more, Moses *Schomberg [*see under* Schomberg, Meyer Löw] and Solomon *Schomberg [*see under* Schomberg, Meyer Löw] entered the law.

Although born into a Jewish family, and brought up as a

Sir Alexander Schomberg (1720–1804), by William Hogarth, 1763

Jew, Alexander Schomberg attended St Paul's School, London, and subsequently renounced, in common with his brothers, the Jewish faith, publicly receiving the sacrament according to the rites of the Church of England. This, under the Test Act, paved his way into the Royal Navy, which he entered as a midshipman in 1743, serving under Captain Edward Pratten on the *Suffolk* (70 guns). He passed his lieutenancy examination on 3 December 1747 and was promoted to the sloop *Hornet* eight days later. In spring 1750, being in the West Indies, he exchanged into the sloop *Speedwell*, which returned to England, and was paid off in the following July. He was then placed on half pay, and so remained until February 1755, when he was appointed to the *Medway* with Captain Peter Denis, one of the fleet on the home station and in the Bay of Biscay. In June 1756 he was again placed on half pay, but in October he was appointed to the *Intrepid* (formerly the French *Serieux*, 64 guns), again with Pratten.

On 5 April 1757 Schomberg was promoted captain of the frigate *Richmond*, from which towards the end of the year he was moved into another frigate, the *Diana*, attached in the following year to the fleet under Admiral Edward Boscawen at the reduction of Louisbourg. Before the troops were landed Boscawen, with the other admirals and generals, went in the *Diana* to examine the coast. The *Diana* was afterwards one of the frigates employed in covering the landing, and when a party of seamen was landed for the batteries, Schomberg was placed in command, subsequently receiving a commemorative gold medal to celebrate the capture. In 1759 the *Diana* was attached to the fleet under Sir Charles Saunders at the reduction of Quebec, where Schomberg was closely associated with General James Wolfe. In the following year the *Diana* was one of the squadron which, under Lord Colvill, repulsed an attempt of the French to regain Quebec, and was afterwards sent home with the news. Schomberg was then appointed to the *Essex* (64 guns), and in 1764 he took part in the reduction of Belle Île, under the command of Commodore Keppel. He retained command of the *Essex* in the fleet off Brest and in the Bay of Biscay until the peace in 1763. In August of that year he married Arabella Susannah, only child of the Revd James Chalmers and Arabella, sister and heiress of Sir Edmond Alleyne, baronet, of Hatfield Peveril; the couple's five children, including Charles Marsh *Schomberg, were baptized in the Christian faith.

At the end of 1770 Schomberg was appointed to the *Prudent*, one of the ships commissioned on account of the dispute with Spain about the Falkland Islands; she was paid off when the dispute was settled. Towards the close of 1771 he was appointed to command the *Dorset*, the yacht attached to the lord lieutenant of Ireland, in spite of the protest of Lord Sandwich, first lord of the Admiralty, who made it clear that he considered Schomberg's acceptance of the post as tantamount to retirement from the line of active service. Schomberg soon regretted his move but was prevented by Sandwich from returning to active service. He therefore remained in command of the *Dorset*, and was knighted by the lord lieutenant in 1777. He was author of *A sea manual recommended to the young officers of the Royal Navy as a companion to the signal book* (1789). Sir Alexander died in Dublin on 19 March 1804 having for many years headed the list of captains. He was buried in the churchyard at St Peter's, Dublin.

Schomberg's second son, **Alexander Wilmot Schomberg** (1774–1850), naval officer, was born on 24 February 1774. He served for some time in his father's yacht, the *Dorset*, and afterwards in the *Porcupine*, *Lowestoft*, *Impregnable*, and *Trusty*. He was promoted lieutenant on 26 July 1793. In that rank he served at the reduction of Martinique and the defence of Guadeloupe, and in the *Boyne* with Sir John Jervis, and the *Glatton* with Sir Henry Trollope. He was promoted commander on 2 April 1798 and advanced to post rank on 1 January 1801; and he served actively during the war, holding several important commands, including the frigate *Loire* (1807–12). He became a rear-admiral on 22 July 1830, vice-admiral on 23 November 1841, and admiral on 9 October 1849. He was twice married and had three sons.

Schomberg's *Naval Suggestions* was privately printed in 1818, and he published at Chichester in 1832 *Practical Remarks on the Building, Rigging and Equipping of Warships*. He died in January 1850. Schomberg's three sons were: Herbert (*d.* 1867); Charles Frederick (*d.* 1874); and George Augustus who entered the armed forces. Herbert and Charles became naval officers and achieved the rank of rear- and vice-admiral respectively.

J. K. LAUGHTON, *rev.* PHILIP MACDOUGALL

Sources G. L. Green, *The Royal Navy and Anglo-Jewry* (1989) • J. Charnock, ed., *Biographia navalis*, 6 (1798), 273 • G. W. Place, 'Parkgate and the royal yachts: passenger traffic between the north-west and Dublin in the eighteenth century', *Transactions of the Historic Society of Lancashire and Cheshire*, 138 (1988), 67–83

Archives PRO, official letters to admiralty • PRO, journals of Admiral Boscawen • PRO, logs of HMS *Richmond, Diana, Essex, Prudent, Dorset*

Likenesses W. Hogarth, oils, 1763, NMM [*see illus.*]

Schomberg, Alexander Crowcher (1756–1792), poet and writer on jurisprudence, was born in Great Yarmouth, Norfolk, on 6 July 1756, the son of Ralph (or Raphael) *Schomberg (1714–1792), physician and writer, and his wife, Elizabeth Crowcher (1719–1807). He was admitted a scholar of Winchester College in 1770 from Southampton School, and in his fourteenth year he wrote a tragedy in collaboration with Herbert Croft (1751–1816). He matriculated at Queen's College, Oxford, on 9 May 1775, was elected a demy of Magdalen College, Oxford, in 1776, graduated BA on 20 January 1779, and commenced MA on 9 November 1781. He was a probationer fellow of Magdalen College from 1782 to 1792 and became senior dean of arts in 1791. Schomberg took religious orders but did not receive any preferment in the church. The myrtle wreath of Lady Anna Miller's literary salon was often awarded to his poetical productions, some of which were reprinted in her volumes. He was likewise a contributor to the periodical *Olla Podrida* edited by Thomas Monro (1788). Subsequently he studied political economy.

Schomberg's works include *Ode on the Present State of English Poetry … by Cornelius Scriblerus Nothus*, with 'a translation of a fragment of Simonides' (Greek and English, Oxford, 1779); *An Historical and Chronological View of Roman Law. With Notes and Illustrations* (1785; 2nd edn, 1857; translated into French by A. M. H. Boulard, 2nd edn, Paris, 1808); *A Treatise on the Maritime Laws of Rhodes* (1786); and *Historical and Political Remarks on the Tariff of the Commercial Treaty with France* (1787). While he was at Bath, Schomberg was attacked by a painful disease. He died there on 6 April 1792 and was buried in the abbey. He was the earliest patron of William Crotch, the composer.

THOMPSON COOPER, *rev.* REBECCA MILLS

Sources Foster, *Alum. Oxon.* • S. Halkett and J. Laing, *A dictionary of the anonymous and pseudonymous literature of Great Britain*, 1 (1882), 210 • D. Turner, *Sepulchral reminiscences of a market town* (1848), 75 • *Letters from the late Lord Chedworth to the Rev Thomas Crompton* (1828), 72 • T. F. Kirby, *Winchester scholars: a list of the wardens, fellows, and scholars of … Winchester College* (1888), 265 • J. R. Bloxam, *A register of the presidents, fellows … of Saint Mary Magdalen College*, 8 vols. (1853–85), vol. 7, p. 51 • *N&Q*, 5th ser., 5 (1876), 288 • *N&Q*, 5th ser., 7 (1877), 54 • *GM*, 1st ser., 62 (1792), 389 • *GM*, 2nd ser., 41 (1854), 114 • Nichols, *Illustrations*, 5.278 • Watt, *Bibl. Brit.*, 2.838

Schomberg, Alexander Wilmot (1774–1850). *See under* Schomberg, Sir Alexander (1720–1804).

Schomberg, Charles de, second duke of Schomberg (1645–1693). *See under* Schomberg, Frederick Herman de, first duke of Schomberg (1615–1690).

Schomberg, Sir Charles Marsh (1779–1835), naval officer and colonial governor, was born in Dublin, the youngest son of Sir Alexander *Schomberg (1720–1804) and his wife, Arabella Susannah, daughter of the Revd James Chalmers. In 1788 he was entered on the yacht *Dorset*, commanded by his father, as captain's servant, and in 1793 on the *Cumberland* with Captain Thomas Louis, whom he followed to the *Minotaur* (74 guns). On 30 April 1795 he was promoted lieutenant of the *Rattler*. He returned to the *Minotaur* in August 1796 and was in her, as lieutenant, in the battle of Abu Qir Bay in 1798, and afterwards in the operations on the coast of Italy. On 3 September 1800 he commanded the boats of the *Minotaur*, under Captain James Hillyar of the *Niger*, in cutting out two Spanish corvettes at Barcelona, for which he was moved into the *Foudroyant* (80 guns) and served through the Egyptian campaign as flag lieutenant to Lord Keith. In August 1801 he was put in command of the *Charon*, employed, with a reduced armament, in carrying the French troops from Egypt; for his services he received the Turkish order of the Crescent. On 29 April 1802 he was promoted commander, and captain on 6 April 1803, when he was appointed to the *Madras* (54 guns), stationed at Malta until spring 1807. The *Madras* was then put out of commission, and he returned to England after an absence of ten years.

In November 1808 Schomberg was appointed to the *Hibernia* (120 guns) as flag captain to Sir William Sidney Smith, with whom he went to Lisbon and from there, having moved into the *Foudroyant*, to Rio de Janeiro. In January 1809 he was appointed by Smith to the *President* (50 guns) but, as another captain for the *President* was sent out by the Admiralty, he returned to England, arriving in April 1810. In June he was appointed to the frigate *Astraea* (36 guns), fitting for the Cape of Good Hope, whence he was detached as senior officer at Mauritius. On 20 May 1811, with two other frigates and a sloop, he fell in with three large French frigates carrying troops sent out from France as a reinforcement for their garrison at Mauritius, of whose capture they had been ignorant. After a brisk action one of the French frigates, the *Renommée* (40 guns), surrendered to the *Astraea*; the other two escaped for the time, but one, the *Néréide*, surrendered at Tamatave in Madagascar a few days later. In April 1813 Schomberg was moved into the *Nisus* (38 guns), in which he went to Brazil, and convoyed a large fleet of merchant ships to England, arriving at Spithead in March 1814. On 4 June 1815 he was made a CB. From 1820 to 1824 he commanded the *Rochefort* (80 guns) in the Mediterranean, as flag captain to Sir Graham Moore; and from 1828 to 1832 he was commodore and commander-in-chief at the Cape of Good Hope, with his broad pennant in the *Maidstone*. On 21 September 1832 he was made a KCH. He also received the order of the Tower and Sword from the prince of Brazil. In February 1833 he was appointed lieutenant-governor of Dominica. He died (unmarried) on 2 January 1835 on the *President*, flagship of Sir George Cockburn, in Carlisle Bay, Dominica, and was interred in St Paul's Chapel on the same day.

J. K. LAUGHTON, *rev.* ANDREW LAMBERT

Sources D. Syrett and R. L. DiNardo, *The commissioned sea officers of the Royal Navy, 1660–1815*, rev. edn, Occasional Publications of the Navy RS, 1 (1994) • J. Marshall, *Royal naval biography*, 2/2 (1825), 817 • W. James, *The naval history of Great Britain, from the declaration of war by France, in February 1793, to the accession of George IV, in January 1820*,

[2nd edn], 6 vols. (1826) • O'Byrne, *Naval biog. dict.* • private information (1897) • 'Capt. Sir C. M. Schomberg', *GM*, 2nd ser., 4 (1835), 90–91 • P. Mackesy, *The war in the Mediterranean, 1803–1810* (1957)

Archives BL, corresp. with Lord Nelson, Add. MSS 34920–34929, *passim*

Likenesses W. Beechey, three portraits; in family possession, 1897

Schomberg, Frederick Herman de [*formerly* Frederick Herman von Schönberg], **first duke of Schomberg (1615–1690)**, army officer, was born on 6 December 1615 at Heidelberg, the only son of Hans Meinhard von Schönberg (1582–1616), army officer and diplomat, and his wife, Anne (*d.* 1615), second daughter of Edward Sutton or Dudley, fifth Baron Dudley, and his wife, Theodocia. His father, marshal of the Palatinate, governor of Jülich-Cleve, and sometime ambassador to England, was instrumental in arranging the marriage of the Elector Frederick V to Princess Elizabeth, daughter of James I, and his mother was her childhood companion and lady-in-waiting. Frederick was his godfather.

Early life and the Thirty Years' War Schomberg's mother having died in childbirth and his father before he was one year old, he was placed under the guardianship of his paternal uncles and brought up by his grandmother, Dorothea Riedesel von Bellersheim. The ill-judged attempt by the young elector to seize the Bohemian throne led to the invasion and destruction of the Palatinate, and ended Schomberg's prospects of a career there. He attended an academy at Sedan from 1625 to 1630 and, after a short interval in Paris and a brief visit to his grandfather Lord Dudley in England, spent two years at the University of Leiden in the United Provinces.

The Thirty Years' War gave Schomberg his first taste of military life. Aged about seventeen, he served as a volunteer in the army of Frederick Henry, prince of Orange, and was present at the siege of Rheinberg in May 1633. Subsequently he joined the semi-mercenary protestant army of Bernard of Saxe-Weimar, then in Swedish service in Germany. He fought with the infantry regiment of Pfhul at the battle of Nördlingen in 1634, and retreated to Alsace with the remnants of Bernard's forces, participating in the many skirmishes along the way at the side of Bernard's second-in-command, Reinhold von Rosen. Following Bernard's transfer to the French service in 1635 Schomberg purchased a company in the German infantry regiment of Josias de Rantzau. He was stationed in the neighbourhood of Calais and Gravelines in support of Marshal Châtillon's successful attempt to link with the Dutch. His fluency in both French and German helped to quell dissension between the two nationalities in the army. In 1636 he served in the French campaign in Franche-Comté where he took part in the siege of Dôle and the relief of St Jean-de-Losne on the Burgundian frontier. In 1637 he entered Westphalia to recruit for a new cavalry regiment that was being raised by Rantzau. Joining him in Holstein, Schomberg advanced into east Friesland and surprised Nordhausen. However, he left Rantzau's service following a duel with another officer in which both men were wounded.

Frederick Herman de Schomberg, first duke of Schomberg (1615–1690), by John Smith, 1689 (after Sir Godfrey Kneller, 1689?)

For a brief period Schomberg took over the management of his property in the Palatinate, fixing his residence at Geisenheim on the Rhine. On 30 April 1638 he married his first cousin, Johanna Elizabeth (*d.* 1664), daughter of his paternal uncle, Heinrich Dietrich, graf von Schönberg auf Wesel. They had six sons: Otto (1639–1656), Frederick (1640–1700), Meinhard *Schomberg, later third duke of Schomberg (1641–1719), Heinrich (1643–1667), Charles [*see below*], and Wilhelm (*b.* 1647, died in childhood). In 1639 Schomberg re-entered the service of Frederick Henry, prince of Orange. He held a series of junior military appointments and was present at the capture of Gennep in 1641, Sas-van-Gent in 1644, and Hulst in 1645. He was a favourite of the prince who appointed him first gentleman of his chamber. He was heavily implicated in Frederick Henry's attempt to seize Amsterdam in the summer of 1650, which may explain his prompt departure from The Hague after the prince's death the following November.

French army, 1651–1660 In 1651 a new phase in Schomberg's career began when he joined the French army as a volunteer. He won rapid promotion under Marshal Turenne in the war in Flanders against the prince de Condé and Spain, becoming *maréchal-de-camp* and captain-lieutenant of the *gensdarmes écossais* in October 1652, and lieutenant-general in 1655, when he raised an infantry regiment in Germany for the French service. From about this time he styled himself *comte de Schomberg*, adopting the same spelling of his surname as that followed by the two marshals of France of the Meissen family of Schönberg, to whom he was unrelated. His title of count of the holy Roman empire he apparently inherited. He participated in the capture of Rethel and Sainte-Ménéhould in Champagne in 1653; in the relief of Arras and the capture of Le Quesnoy in 1654; and in the capture of Landrecies and Condé in 1655. He was wounded at the capture of St Ghislain in 1655, and was then made governor of the town on 25 August. Soon afterwards he prevented its betrayal by a group of Irish officers. In 1656 he was present at Turenne's defeat before Valenciennes where his eldest son, Otto, was killed before his eyes. In 1657, for seventeen days, he defended St Ghislain against 12,000 Spaniards before surrendering on 22 March to Condé and Don Juan of Austria. The following September he captured and became governor of the strategic town of Bourbourg, thereby denying it to the enemy. At the beginning of 1658 he raised another regiment of German infantry, and in June of that year he commanded the second line on the French left wing in Turenne's decisive victory at the battle of the Dunes. Subsequently he led the attack on Winoxbergen, of which, with Gravelines, Furnes (Veurne), and Diksmuide, he was appointed governor.

Portuguese War, 1660–1668 On the conclusion of peace between France and Spain, Schomberg, in search of employment, accepted a command with the Portuguese in their struggle against Spain. Under the terms of his appointment, agreed in August 1660, he was to be general of the forces in the province of Alentejo, with the rank of *maréchal-de-camp*, receiving a yearly salary of 12,000 crusadoes and a further daily sum towards his maintenance. His sons, Frederick and Meinhard, also received appointments. A small, 750-strong French force in Portugal was to come under his command. He undertook the project on Turenne's recommendation and with the secret support of Louis XIV. To disguise the French involvement, however, the final arrangements were completed in England where he travelled after a short visit to Gesenheim. A 3000-strong brigade of English troops, led by the earl of Inchiquin, which was also to come under his command, was to be sent to support the Portuguese. Although ill-supplied and -paid, and on poor terms with their allies, the English provided the professional backbone of the Portuguese army. Schomberg was on familiar terms with Charles II whom he had known in The Hague, and for whom in February 1652, as 'a right worthy person who will spare nothing to serve the king' (W. D. Macray, ed., *Calendar of Clarendon State Papers, 2.1649–1654*, 1869, 119), he had undertaken a diplomatic mission to Mainz. He advised the king to send to Portugal 'the military men that had served under Cromwell, whom he thought the best officers he had ever seen' (*Bishop Burnet's History*, ed. Burnet and Burnet, 1.97). His advice was heeded: the 2000 infantry dispatched in 1662 were drawn entirely from three regiments of the New Model Army whose disbandment had been deferred while they served in Scotland. The 500 cavalry—half the promised number—was a more composite force, made up from the Dunkirk garrison and volunteers. Schomberg became colonel of the cavalry regiment in 1665. A further 2500 reinforcements were sent from Britain and Ireland over the years, but when the final evacuation took place in 1668 only 1000 remained, a wastage of 80 per cent. Charles II ignored Schomberg's more general political advice that he should take over the leadership of protestant Europe and retain possession of Dunkirk.

Sailing from the Downs, Schomberg disembarked at Lisbon on 13 November 1661, and was received there with every mark of distinction. He quickly familiarized himself with the general situation and the complexities and divisions of the Portuguese court. He inspected the fortifications in Alentejo and recommended their improvement. However, before this work could be completed, the Spaniards under Don Juan of Austria crossed the Guadiana and captured Arronches. Although Schomberg's plan to cut them off from their base was frustrated by the shortcomings of the Portuguese he succeeded in checking Don Juan who retired after some skirmishing. He spent the winter superintending the fortification of Evora, Xerumenha, and Estremoz, and in training and reorganizing the Portuguese army. Throughout his service in Portugal he was severely handicapped by the tardiness and indecision of the Portuguese government, the arrogance and incompetence of their generals, and shortages of money, supplies, and equipment. He took the field in April 1662, but when Marialva, the Portuguese commander, ignored his advice not to risk battle, he withdrew to Elvas. He was recalled when Alentejo was overrun by the Spaniards, and against his better judgement was persuaded to attempt to relieve Xerumenha. Having failed in this enterprise, and deeply frustrated by the divisions and inadequacies of the Portuguese, he contemplated resignation. However, he was encouraged to remain when the patriotic party in Lisbon persuaded King Afonso to give him more support, and Louis XIV and Charles II promised reinforcements. In 1663 his position was strengthened by the arrival in Lisbon of Frémont d'Ablancourt, the unofficial French envoy.

News of the unexpected fall of Evora to Don Juan on 20 May was a serious setback to the Portuguese. Schomberg, who had been seriously ill for some months, recommended a counter-attack, and on 8 June he won an overwhelming victory over Don Juan at Ameixial, where the British brigade fought with great distinction. The Spanish forces retreated back across the border. Schomberg was rewarded with command, under certain restrictions, of all the Portuguese forces and he was given the Portuguese title count of Mertola in the same year. Badajoz and Valencia de Alcántara were captured in a Portuguese offensive into Spain in 1664, before commissariat failures forced a frustrated Schomberg to return to Lisbon. In 1665 the Spanish army, now commanded by the marquess of Caracena, again invaded Portugal. Vila Viçosa was stormed, but its citadel held out until the Spaniards were forced by Schomberg and Marialva to give battle at Montès Claros near Estremoz on 17 June. The battle was won for the Portuguese by the British infantry which routed the Swiss and German cavalry of the Spaniards by using their empty matchlocks as heavy clubs. Schomberg was in the thick of the action. His horse was killed beneath him at one point, and on another occasion he narrowly escaped death in personal combat with the prince of Parma whose sword shattered on his cuirass. The crushing victory, which cost the Spaniards two-thirds of their army, sealed the independence of Portugal and contributed to Schomberg's growing international reputation. He took part in the invasion of Galicia the following October, but returned to Alentejo after the capture of La Guardia, frustrated by Portuguese obstruction of his plan to attack Bayona. This was the last major campaign of the war and Schomberg's subsequent military activity was confined to minor border actions in which he twice crossed the Guadiana into Andalusia in 1666, and looted Alburquerque in 1667. His final role was to use his influence with the army to support the establishment of Don Pedro de Braganza's regency government in place of that controlled by the count of Castelo Melhor in the name of Pedro's feeble-minded brother, King Afonso. Peace followed in 1668, in which Spain formally recognized the independence of Portugal. The title of duke, by which Schomberg was afterwards known, was probably awarded to him at about this time by the Portuguese, rather than the French as is commonly supposed. His role in the Peninsula ended, Schomberg sailed from Lisbon on 1 June, arriving in La Rochelle a fortnight later.

Service in England and France, 1668–1686 Schomberg's first wife had died at Gesenheim in 1664 and his fourth son, Heinrich, at Brussels in 1667, of wounds received in a skirmish in Flanders. Together with his sons, Meinhard and Charles, he became a naturalized French subject on his return to France, and purchased the lordship of Courbet near Paris. On 14 April 1669 he married Susanne d'Aumale (*d.* 1688), youngest daughter of the Huguenot Daniel d'Aumale, sieur d'Harcourt, chamberlain to the prince de Condé. She was constantly in ill health and the marriage was childless. In the summer of 1671 he paid a visit to Germany. On the outbreak of the third Anglo-Dutch War he was offered no command in the French army. On 3 July 1673, after attending the siege of Maastricht, he crossed to England, then an ally of France, and took command, under Prince Rupert and with the rank of captain-general, of an army of more than 6000 infantry and some cavalry that was preparing at Blackheath for an attack on Zeeland. On 20 July this force left Gravesend by sea for Yarmouth where it camped, pending the establishment of Anglo-French naval superiority in the North Sea. This was frustrated by the Dutch at the battle of Texel in August. Although his military reputation, knowledge of the United Provinces, and experience of commanding the English in Portugal appeared to qualify him for his command, Schomberg was confronted by serious problems of disorganization and indiscipline with his forces at Yarmouth. The widespread perception that he was the agent of the king of France made him unpopular. His appointment over the heads of Englishmen was resented and gave rise to much bickering, including at one point an unpleasant dispute with Prince Rupert. Constrained by English politics from employing martial law, he found he could only maintain some sort of order in the army by the use of threats. There were complaints by the officers that the severity of the French standards of discipline he sought to impose were unacceptable in England. Summoned to court, he drew up memorials on the maintenance of a standing army and the improvement of its discipline. Charles II apparently gave him a patent for the title of Baron Tetford (which was never enrolled) before he returned to France in November.

Schomberg's first command in the winter of 1673–4 was of the French army between the Sambre and the Meuse. In April 1674 he was given command of the small army in Roussillon which opposed the Spaniards along the Pyrenees. His 10,000 infantry, including a regiment of which he was colonel, were drawn almost entirely from the inexperienced Languedoc militia. After suffering early setbacks in the loss of Bellegarde and a defeat in the field at Maureillas he managed to stabilize the situation when much of the Spanish strength was withdrawn to suppress the revolt in Sicily. From Elne, which he fortified, he raided the Cerdanya, the mountainous region of Catalonia on the Spanish slope of the Pyrenees. In July 1675 he took Ampurias-la-Pila, recovered Bellegarde, and re-entered the Cerdanya, which he intended to use as a logistical base for an attack on the key mountain fortress of Puigcerda. However, not being commanded to undertake the siege, he put the army into winter quarters.

Turenne's death at Salzbach offered Schomberg the opportunity to advance his career. He was created a marshal of France on 30 July 1675. For the campaign of 1676 he was recalled to Flanders to serve with the army deployed under Louis XIV's personal command. In May he dissuaded a bellicose Louis from fighting a field battle against the Dutch and Spaniards at Denain, arguing that he should not be deflected from the main objective of besieging Bouchain which fell to the French immediately afterwards. On the king's return to court in early July, Schomberg was left in command of his army. In August he relieved Maastricht which had withstood a seven-week siege by William of Orange, and skilfully outmanoeuvred an attempt by William to cut him off from his base at Charleroi before both armies went into winter quarters. In 1677 he was reappointed to the army in Flanders and served under Louis at the capture of Valenciennes in March and Cambrai in April. However, after the king's departure in May, command of the main army went to the able Marshal de Luxembourg, with Schomberg, perhaps because of his steadfast adherence to protestantism, being relegated to commanding the army of observation on the Meuse. In 1678 he again served with the king at the capture of Ghent and Ypres in March, but he subsequently returned to the army on the Meuse until the peace of Nijmegen ended the war with the Dutch. The peace treaty included a special article in Schomberg's favour, safeguarding his personal interests in the Palatinate. In 1679 he briefly occupied Cleves with 20,000 French troops to compel the elector of Brandenburg to surrender some of his territorial gains in Pomerania to the Swedes. In June

1684, on the renewal of the war with Spain, he commanded a corps at the successful blockade of Luxembourg, and in August he was deployed with 30,000 men ready to invade Germany to persuade the emperor to agree to the treaty of Ratisbon.

Exiled Huguenot, 1686–1688 The revocation of the edict of Nantes in 1685 brought Schomberg's career in France to an end. In religious belief he remained a devout Calvinist throughout his life and a personal attempt by Louis to persuade him to abjure his faith was met with a refusal. He left the army and was allowed to retire with his family to Portugal, where he arrived in May 1686. Nominally he was on a semi-diplomatic mission, but in fact he was being exiled until such time as he conformed to Catholicism. For the time being, as a mark of Louis's favour, he was allowed to retain his French pensions and property. In Lisbon both the French ambassador and Pedro II made every effort to gain his conversion, but without success. He drew up a memorial for the better discipline of the Portuguese army, which he translated into Portuguese. Eventually, tired of inactivity, he requested Louis's permission to enter the service of Brandenburg. He received no response, and after the Inquisition denied him permission to practise his religion privately he embarked in January 1687 on a Dutch vessel bound for the Netherlands. There he had an interview with William of Orange, which may have included some discussion on Schomberg's possible role in William's long-term plans. In April he proceeded to Berlin where Frederick William, the great elector, welcomed him into his service. He was immediately appointed privy councillor, governor of Prussia, commander-in-chief of the army, and colonel of a dragoon regiment. He purchased as his family residence the Dohna Palace on the boulevard Unter Den Linden, Berlin, where his wife died in 1688.

While still in France, Schomberg had petitioned Louis to restore the edict of Nantes. Both then and after he went into exile he strove to find employment abroad for Huguenots dismissed from the French army. The image of Louis as a persecutor of protestants was a useful propaganda tool for his enemies and to some extent explains the honour and position William of Orange and the great elector accorded Schomberg, who was regarded as the unofficial general of the military exiles. In Berlin his house became the focus for scores of Huguenot refugees, both soldiers and civilians, who looked to him for money and patronage. Subsequently Huguenots were closely associated with Schomberg in the invasion of England and the war in Ireland.

The revolution of 1688–1689 In July 1688 Schomberg was contemplating Austrian offers of a command in the Turkish War, when he received a message from William of Orange to prepare for a campaign in the west. The new elector of Brandenburg, Frederick III, more anti-French than his predecessor, agreed to support William's projected invasion of England. In September, to forestall the French, a strong force of troops from Brandenburg under Schomberg occupied Cologne, where the succession to the archbishopric was in dispute. Schomberg was then allowed to transfer to the Dutch service where William appointed him his second-in-command for the English invasion.

Taking advantage of the French army's deployment in the Rhineland, William sailed with an army of 15,000, landing at Torbay on 5 November 1688. Schomberg was by his side when they rode into Exeter two days later. They encountered scarcely any resistance as they advanced on London. The English army disintegrated, most of its leading personalities changed sides, and James and his family fled to France. Schomberg advised William against arming the peasantry that flocked to his support and expressed his contempt for officers, such as John Churchill, who had so readily deserted their colours. He was appointed commander-in-chief of all the British and foreign forces in England, but the position was little more than notional with real authority in the hands of Churchill and Hans Willem Bentinck. He became colonel of the Queen's foot on 31 December 1688. In April 1689 the Order of the Garter was conferred on him by William. He became a naturalized English citizen, a privy councillor, and master-general of the ordnance. On 8 May he was raised to the English peerage as Baron Teyes, earl of Brentford, marquess of Harwich and duke of Schomberg. His adherence to William having cost him his French estate and a Portuguese pension, parliament compensated him with a grant of £100,000.

Service in Ireland In June 1689 Schomberg was appointed commander of the expedition to Ireland, his mission being to bring a speedy end to Irish resistance to William. The army mustered at Chester, where Schomberg joined it in the third week of July. He was beset with problems: shipping and provisions were slow to arrive, and he complained strongly of the inadequacies of John Shales, who was in charge of supplies. Schomberg landed with the first contingent at Belfast Lough on 13 August, and by late September 13,500 men, with baggage, horses, and a small artillery train, had been transported from Hoylake. The army was very uneven in quality. The bulk of the troops, newly raised in England, were raw and inexperienced. Schomberg formed a poor opinion of the officers, many of whom were Irish protestants. The most professional units were two battalions of Dutch infantry and four regiments of Huguenots. Schomberg was colonel of the Huguenot cavalry regiment and noted for his partiality to the French, claiming they were worth twice the same number of any other troops. He was embarrassed subsequently when it transpired that many of the ordinary soldiers in the Huguenot regiments were Catholics, some of whom were discovered to be in communication with the enemy. The addition of 6000 Ulster protestants, the defenders of Londonderry and Enniskillen, brought his total strength to almost 20,000. His initial impression of the Ulstermen was unfavourable: he described the officers as peasants and compared their men to Croats on account of their fondness for plunder. In time, however, their fighting qualities won his respect.

Schomberg's first action on landing was to reduce the

Jacobite garrison at Carrickfergus which capitulated on terms after a week. As the garrison marched out, Schomberg was obliged to intervene, pistol in hand, to protect them from being murdered by the Ulster Scots. The 105-day siege of Londonderry had been lifted in July, following the city's relief by the dilatory major-general Kirke who had broken the blockading boom and entered the city only on receipt of a peremptory order from Schomberg to take immediate action. A few days later the Jacobite defeat at Newtownbutler also relieved Enniskillen. By the time of Schomberg's arrival the Jacobite army had largely withdrawn from Ulster and was in considerable disarray. The circumstances seemed favourable for a quick march on Dublin, which, it was thought, would prove decisive. Schomberg, still short of transport and supplies, had misgivings, but nevertheless commenced his offensive south on 2 September. A Jacobite force under the duke of Berwick burned Newry before retreating, and Schomberg entered Dundalk, which had not been burned, without opposition. For the next two months, despite William's urgings, he insisted on remaining there on the defensive. He combined pessimism about his own army with an exaggerated respect for the military capacity of his opponents. Bad weather and shortage of supplies had dogged his progress south, and the plan to supply the army by sea through Carlingford was only partially successful. The Jacobites sensed he was in difficulty. James II advanced almost as far as Dundalk with 20,000 men, but Schomberg declined to give battle, and the Jacobites eventually withdrew to Ardee. Meanwhile, at Dundalk, a serious outbreak of disease had occurred in the insanitary Williamite camp. Schomberg himself was ill for a month, suffering from 'une fluxeon sur la poitrine' ('a swelling on the chest'; *CSP dom.*, *1689–90*, 320). In November the army withdrew to Ulster, where sickness continued to ravage the troops in winter quarters. The Army Medical Services were ill-equipped for such an epidemic, and 7000 men died in a disastrous culmination of the disappointing campaign. Schomberg was refused permission to return to England for his health and a change of air. He spent the winter at Lisburn, and in May 1690 took the field to capture Charlemont, a significant Jacobite stronghold in Armagh.

In England there was much criticism of the mismanagement of the Irish campaign. Commissary-General Shales was made the scapegoat and arrested, but Schomberg's reputation also suffered severely. At the advanced age of seventy-four he had proved incapable of showing the spontaneity, flexibility, or drive needed for the quick victory desired by William over what was still a weak and demoralized opponent. William was greatly disappointed in his performance and reluctantly concluded that only by coming to Ireland himself would the campaign there be brought to a rapid conclusion and the forces it tied up be released for service on the continent. He took care to avoid the mistakes of Schomberg's expedition. His army was built up to 37,000, including strong contingents of Dutch and Danish professionals, and with adequate transport, a well-organized commissariat, and improved medical services. To help finance the campaign Schomberg gave William his grant from parliament in return for a £4000 annuity. Although he was retained as the principal general, the king, after he crossed to Ireland in mid-June, tended to ignore his advice and to treat him with noticeable coldness. Schomberg's proposal to march south via the western roads was overruled by William in favour of the Moyry pass. Likewise, at the council-of-war that preceded the battle of the Boyne, Schomberg's suggestion of a flanking movement rather than a direct assault across the river was not adopted, though the substantial diversionary force sent upstream with his son, Meinhard, was some concession to his point of view.

The Williamite infantry forded the Boyne at Oldbridge on 1 July, encountering substantial opposition from the Jacobite cavalry. The Huguenot battalions were soon in considerable difficulty on the south bank, and Schomberg, much concerned, crossed the river to rally them. Wearing his blue Garter ribbon, he was a prominent target and at about noon, having received two sabre cuts to the head from the Irish troopers, he was killed instantly by a shot in the neck, possibly a stray Williamite round. Captain Foubert, one of his Huguenot aides, brought off his body. William was reported to have wept on learning of his death and to have declared he had lost a father. However, it was suggested at the time that Schomberg's hurt at William's discourtesy may have impelled him deliberately to place his life at risk on the battlefield. He was buried on 10 July in St Patrick's Cathedral, Dublin. Only in 1731 was a memorial erected over his grave at the expense of the cathedral chapter, his descendants having incurred the wrath of Dean Swift by failing to contribute towards the cost.

Personality and significance In appearance Schomberg was of middle stature, well proportioned, and fair complexioned. He was a good rider, active and physically fit up to the end of his life. He was well-educated, a good linguist, neat in his appearance, pleasant in his conversation, calm in his manner, and courteous to all. Burnet considered that Schomberg thought much better than he spoke, but regarded him as a man of true judgement and great probity. Louis XIV trenchantly remarked 'Ne trouvez-vous pas bien extraordinaire que M. de Schomberg, qui est né Allemand, se soit fait naturaliser Hollandois, Anglois, François et Portugois?' ('Do you not find it rather extraordinary that M. de Schomberg, who was born German, has been naturalized as Dutch, English, French, and Portuguese?'; *Journal … Dangeau*, 2.190). Most contemporaries, however, took the view that Schomberg's changes of allegiance had not compromised his honour. He belonged to the international military profession of the seventeenth century. Those with the ability and experience to organize and command the larger armies of the time were few and far between, and the rulers who drew on their expertise were little concerned with their nationality or even their religion, but the etiquette, which Schomberg scrupulously observed, was never to transfer allegiance during a campaign. Probably he would never have left the service of

France if his position as a lifelong and committed Calvinist had not been made impossible. The circumstances in which he did, and the price he ultimately paid, only served to enhance his reputation, at least outside France. He avoided politics after his early involvement in the Netherlands, and expressed the view that military matters were best left to military men.

As a soldier Schomberg was personally courageous and his lengthy and varied career ensured that he became very experienced. Contemporaries considered him a great general, and he won the respect and praise of Turenne. Schomberg, who was not given to vainglorious remarks, believed the French rated him their best general after Turenne and Condé. As a strategist, however, he certainly did not equal these commanders, nor his later contemporary, Luxembourg. He was reliable and competent and fought with distinction in both Flanders and the Pyrenees, but mainly in lesser commands. His successful conduct of the war in Portugal brought him an international reputation, which failed, perhaps, to take fully into account the weakness of the Spanish opposition. He was of a professional caste of mind, working hard in the belief that military victory owed more to careful preparation than to good fortune. In the makeshift campaigning conditions that prevailed in Ireland, where he commanded a very inexperienced army, Schomberg's caution, fondness for elaborate planning, and distrust of improvisation were serious defects. It would have been better for his reputation if he had retired earlier: though the blame was not all his, on his final campaign in Ireland his failure to achieve victory ensured that his place in history is not among military commanders of the first rank.

Charles de Schomberg [von Schönberg], second duke of Schomberg (1645–1693), army officer, was born at 's-Hertogenbosch, the Netherlands, on 5 August 1645, fifth son of the first duke. He served with his father in Portugal and Roussillon, where he was captured. On his release he served under Marshal de Créqui in Flanders. In 1686 he accompanied his father to Portugal, but then entered the service of the emperor before transferring to Brandenburg after his father became commander-in-chief of the elector's army. He was appointed governor of Magdeburg and major-general of infantry. He accompanied his father to England in 1688, taking the oath of naturalization with his father in 1689 before returning to the Netherlands where he was wounded in June at the siege of Kaiserwerth. On the death of his father he succeeded to his title by a special limitation and to his £4000 annuity. He took his seat in the House of Lords in November 1690, and the following month was appointed colonel of the 1st foot guards. In April 1691 he was appointed lieutenant-general to command the auxiliary forces, mainly Huguenot *émigrés*, in Savoy. He arrived at Turin in June and took part in the relief of Conti. In 1692 he led an expedition into the Dauphiné, which failed in its principal purpose of raising the Huguenots in revolt. On 4 October 1693, commanding the left wing of the centre at the battle of Marsaglia, he was mortally wounded, and he died twelve days later at Turin. He was buried in the cathedral at Lausanne, Switzerland, but his heart was brought to London and interred in the French church in the Savoy where a memorial slab was erected. He was unmarried, and his successor and heir was his brother, Meinhard.

ROBERT DUNLOP, *rev.* HARMAN MURTAGH

Sources J. Kazner, *Leben Friedrich von Schomberg, oder Schoenburg* (Mannheim, 1789) • *Allgemeine Deutsche biographie*, 56 vols. (1875–1912), vol. 32, pp. 260–62 • C. de Courcelles, *Dictionnaire historique et biographique des généraux français: depuis le onzième siècle jusqu'en 1823*, 9 (Paris, 1823), 135–7 • GEC, *Peerage* • D. C. A. Agnew, *Protestant exiles from France in the reign of Louis XIV, or, The Huguenot refugees and their descendants in Great Britain and Ireland*, 2nd edn, 3 vols. (1871–4) • J. Childs, 'The English brigade in Portugal, 1662–1668', *Journal of the Society for Army Historical Research*, 215 (autumn 1975), 135–47 • C. F. Dumouriez, *Campagnes du maréchal de Schomberg en Portugal, 1662–1668* (1807) • [G. Story], *A true and impartial history of the most material occurrences in the kingdom of Ireland during the last two years* (1691) • J. Childs, 'A patriot for whom? "For God and for honour": Marshal Schomberg', *History Today*, 38 (July 1988), 46–51 • J. Childs, *The army of Charles II* (1976) • J. Lynn, *The wars of Louis XIV, 1667–1714* (1999) • *Bishop Burnet's History of his own time*, ed. G. Burnet and T. Burnet, 2 vols. (1724–34) • J. G. Simms, *Jacobite Ireland, 1685–91* (1969) • J. G. Simms, 'Schomberg at Dundalk, 1689', *The Irish Sword*, 10 (1971–2), 14–25 • H. Murtagh, 'Huguenot involvement in the Irish Jacobite war, 1689–91', *The Huguenots and Ireland: anatomy of an emigration*, ed. C. E. J. Caldicott, H. Gough, and J.-P. Pittion (1987), 225–34 • *CSP dom., 1689–93* • *Journal du marquis de Dangeau*, ed. E. Soulié and others, 19 vols. (Paris, 1854–60), vol. 2 • K. P. Ferguson, 'The army in Ireland from the Restoration to the Act of Union', PhD diss., TCD, 1980 • *Memoirs of the transactions in the Savoy during the war … made English from the original* (1697) • C. Dalton, ed., *English army lists and commission registers, 1661–1714*, 3 (1896), 3, 136, 214

Archives priv. coll., diary and archives | BL, letters to Lord Nottingham and William Blathwayt, Add. MS 38014 [Charles Schomberg] • Bodl. Oxf., letters to officers of the ordnance and Sir Henry Goodriche [Charles Schomberg] • U. Nott. L., letters to first earl of Portland • Yale U., Beinecke L., letters to William Blathwayt [Charles Schomberg]

Likenesses attrib. G. Kneller, oils, *c*.1675, repro. in A. Guy and J. Spencer-Smith, eds., *1688 Glorious Revolution? The fall and rise of the British army, 1660–1704* (1988) [exhibition catalogue, National Army Museum]; trustees of tenth duke of Leeds will trust • J. Smith, mezzotint, 1689 (after G. Kneller, 1689?), NPG [*see illus.*] • P. Vanderbank, engraving (after portrait by G. Kneller), repro. in *The Irish Sword*, 10 (1971–2), facing p. 14 • W. Wissing, oils; reported in collection of Earl Spencer, 1900 • portrait, repro. in *History Today*, 38 (July 1988), 47

Schomberg, Isaac (1714–1780), physician, eldest son of Meyer Löw *Schomberg (1690–1761), and twin brother of Ralph or Raphael *Schomberg, was born at Schweinsberg, Germany, on 14 August 1714. He was a pupil at Merchant Taylors' School, London, from 1726 to 1731, and subsequently received a doctorate in medicine from the University of Giessen. He began to practise medicine in London, under the auspices of his father. Schomberg's father was determined to avenge himself on the Royal College of Physicians, who had fined him £4 in 1738 for grossly unethical conduct. He used his son in an attempt to punish and humiliate the college. In February 1747 Isaac was summoned before the president and censors of the College of Physicians to present himself for examination as a licentiate, but, at his father's instance, he declined the invitation in a discourteous letter. In the early part of 1747 he entered Trinity College, Cambridge, as a student at

Isaac Schomberg (1714–1780), by Thomas Hudson

physic. On 3 April 1747 he notified the censors of this, with a request that he might be examined after he had procured his Cambridge medical degree. This request was refused, and, as he still declined to be examined, his practice was interdicted by the *comitia minora* of the College of Physicians on 25 June 1747. On 7 August of that year he was baptized at St Mary Woolnoth, London.

On 21 July 1749 Schomberg obtained the degree of MD at Cambridge by royal mandate, and then, in order to become a candidate for admission to the College of Physicians, he asked to be examined; but the censors were ordered by the college not to examine him until his prohibition from practice had been removed on proper submission. On the following 1 December he again came before the censors, and on this occasion with an apology, but it was deemed insufficient. Schomberg then demanded (2 February 1750) to be admitted as a fellow as a right, on the ground that he was a doctor of medicine of Cambridge University. The examination was allowed, and his fitness for the profession was established; but at the next *comitia majora*, his admission to the college was rejected by fifteen votes to two, and the interdict on his practice remained in force. He was naturalized in 1750, and made repeated applications for admission to the college, but they were all refused.

William Battie was one of Schomberg's principal opponents at the college, and was consequently satirized in the *Battiad*, which is said to have been the joint composition of Moses Mendez, Paul Whitehead, and Raphael Schomberg. Two cantos were published (1750), and reprinted in Isaac Reed's *Repository* (1. 233–46).

Schomberg's next step was to appeal for justice to the visitors of the college, and the case came before the lord chancellor and others on 29 November 1751. After several hearings it was determined on 25 July 1753, when the court decided that it had no jurisdiction in the matter. He then applied for examination by the college as a favour; but, on account of the heavy expense of the protracted litigation, the application was refused. On 23 December 1765 he was admitted a licentiate, on the initiative of William Battie and Sir William Browne, who had formerly opposed his admission. He was admitted a fellow on 30 September 1771; in 1773 and 1778 he was a censor at the college.

Schomberg gained an influential position among the physicians of London. His acumen and his generosity of character won him many friends, and a short poem by Samuel Bishop on his death lauds his 'warm benignity of soul'. Schomberg was called in, after several other doctors had been in attendance, at the last illness of David Garrick, when the patient, rousing himself from his lethargy, shook the doctor by the hand and exclaimed, 'Though last not least in love'. Hogarth gave Schomberg first impressions of all his engravings, and he was a legatee in Hogarth's will. Schomberg died, unmarried, at his home, Conduit Street, London, on 4 March 1780, and was buried at St George's, Hanover Square, London.

W. P. Courtney, *rev.* Edgar Samuel

Sources G. Clark and A. M. Cooke, *A history of the Royal College of Physicians of London*, 2 (1966), 552–62 • *Minutes of the proceedings of the College of Physicians, relating to Dr Isaac Schomberg from February the 6th, 1746, to December, 1753* (1753) • Munk, *Roll* • E. R. Samuel, 'Dr Meyer Schomberg's attack on the Jews of London, 1746', *Transactions of the Jewish Historical Society of England*, 20 (1959–61), 83–111 • S. Bishop, *Poems on various subjects*, 2nd edn, 2 (1800), 149 • J. M. S. Brooke and A. W. C. Hallen, eds., *The transcript of the registers of … St Mary Woolnoth and St Mary Woolnoth Haw … 1538 to 1760* (1886) • *GM*, 1st ser., 21 (1751), 569 • *GM*, 1st ser., 23 (1753), 342 • *GM*, 1st ser., 50 (1780), 154 • Mrs E. P. Hart, ed., *Merchant Taylors' School register, 1561–1934*, 2 vols. (1936) • J. Knight, *Life of David Garrick* (1894), 289 • Nichols, *Lit. anecdotes*, 3.26–7 • A. Sakula, 'The doctors Schomberg and the Royal College of Physicians: an eighteenth-century shemozzle', *Journal of Medical Biography*, 2 (1994), 113–19 • J. M. Shaftesley, 'Jews in regular English freemasonry, 1717–1860', *Transactions of the Jewish Historical Society of England*, 25 (1973–5), 150–209, esp. 188 • Venn, *Alum. Cant.*

Likenesses T. Hudson, oils, *c*.1749, priv. coll. • W. Gainsborough?, oils, *c*.1770, priv. coll. • W. P. Sherlock, stipple, 1799 (after T. Hudson), Wellcome L. • T. Hudson, oils, Hunt. L. [*see illus.*] • W. P. Sherlock, engraving (after T. Hudson, *c*.1749), repro. in *European Magazine* (1 Aug 1799)

Schomberg, Isaac (1753–1813), naval officer and historian, was born on 27 March 1753 in Great Yarmouth. His grandfather, Meyer Löw *Schomberg, a German physician of Jewish descent, had brought the family to England in 1721. Isaac was the eldest surviving son of the ten children of Ralph *Schomberg (1714–1792), physician and author, and his wife, Elizabeth (1719–1807), daughter of Joseph Crowcher, a London merchant. His younger brother Alexander Crowcher *Schomberg achieved recognition as a poet.

In October 1770 Schomberg entered the Royal Navy and joined the yacht *Royal Charlotte* (Captain Sir Peter Denis) but six weeks later he transferred to the *Prudent* (64 guns), commanded by his uncle Alexander *Schomberg at Spithead. In June 1771 he joined the *Trident* (64 guns), Denis's flagship, and for over three years thereafter he was in the Mediterranean, spending short periods in the frigate *Montreal* and the sloop *Scorpion* (Commander George Elphinstone, later Lord Keith). In March 1775 he joined the *Romney* (50 guns), flagship at Newfoundland of Rear-Admiral Robert Duff and then Vice-Admiral John Montagu, and commanded initially by Elphinstone. Having been promoted lieutenant on 21 August 1777, he commanded for short periods the schooner *Labrador* and the brig *Hinchinbrook*, and sailed home in November 1778 as second lieutenant of the *Europe* (64 guns).

In April 1779 Schomberg transferred to the *Canada* (74 guns, captains Dalrymple and Collier) as second lieutenant, and in October he became first lieutenant on Collier's recommendation, for showing 'great science and ability in his profession' (NMM, SAN/F/27/97). He was present at Admiral Darby's relief of Gibraltar in April 1781 and the *Canada's* capture of the Spanish frigate *Santa Leocadia* off Cape Finisterre on 2 May. In July 1781 the *Canada*, now commanded by William Cornwallis, sailed to the West Indies; she played a distinguished part at St Kitts in January and Rodney's victory at the battle of the Saints on 12 April 1782. A week later Schomberg transferred to the *Barfleur* (98 guns), Sir Samuel Hood's flagship, and returned home in June 1783.

After the war Schomberg was unemployed until April 1786 when Hood, mindful of his distinguished service in the *Canada*, selected him as first lieutenant of the frigate *Pegasus* and mentor to Prince William, the future William IV, in his first command. It was a difficult situation: William, promoted captain after only one year as lieutenant, was aged twenty, Schomberg thirty-three. Moreover they had served together in the *Barfleur* as midshipman and lieutenant. The self-willed, opinionated, and petulant young prince soon showed his dislike of receiving advice from his vastly more experienced lieutenant and matters came to a head in the West Indies. In January 1787, after a number of minor disagreements, William provoked Schomberg into applying to Captain Horatio Nelson (the senior officer on the station) for a court martial on himself to clear his name—on the petty matter of not sending a boat inshore to collect sheets from the hospital. On Nelson's orders Schomberg was put under arrest in his cabin until a court martial could be convened. When, after some months, this proved impracticable for shortage of captains, Schomberg was sent to England. He arrived on 22 July 1787 and was put on half pay.

With hindsight it was an unfortunate appointment. Apart from the age difference and William's determination to be his own man, the prince's pleasures were alcoholic parties lasting long into the next morning, whereas Schomberg's interests were more sober and scholarly. For example, he had an 'excellent little library' on board (*Letters and Papers of ... Martin*, 1.69) and was later to write a history of the navy. But tact was not Schomberg's strong point and the clash when it came was almost inevitable. Nevertheless within three months Schomberg was appointed second (and soon afterwards first) lieutenant of *Barfleur* (again Hood's flagship, as commander-in-chief, Portsmouth), an appointment which prompted William to write a series of extraordinarily offensive letters to Hood.

In October 1788 Schomberg was appointed first lieutenant of the *Crown* (64 guns), flagship of his old captain, Cornwallis (now Commodore Cornwallis, commander-in-chief, East Indies). 'Poor Schomberg is happy beyond expression', wrote Hood to Cornwallis (Cornwallis-West, 148). From 3 March 1790, when the *Crown*'s captain was invalided home, Schomberg was in temporary command with the rank of commander—a position he held until 10 July when he took command of the sloop *Atalanta*. On 13 September, when *Atalanta* was entering Madras Roads, the East India Company's fort failed to hoist its colours, the customary form of salute. Despite the presence of a senior officer (Captain Strachan) Schomberg wrote 'a violent letter' to the Madras government in response to a supposed insult, following it up with a second letter to the same effect.

The governor of Madras referred the letters to Strachan, commenting on their impropriety in the light of Schomberg's junior officer status. Cornwallis, when he arrived at Madras, thought Schomberg's conduct 'so exceedingly improper' that he relieved him of his command. As it was not practicable to hold a court martial on the station Cornwallis sent him back to England, recommending to the Admiralty that the matter be allowed to drop. To his former captain in the *Canada* Schomberg had been a disappointment, though Cornwallis believed the dispute with Prince William had changed his character. Schomberg arrived home in poor health in the summer of 1791. Meanwhile on 22 November 1790, before Cornwallis's report reached London, he had been promoted captain, and on his return home he was put on half pay.

On 13 August 1793, at Pangbourne, Berkshire, Schomberg married Amelia (1764–1840), daughter of the Revd Lawrence Brodrick (*d.* 1786) of Stradbally, Queen's county, Ireland. They had several children of whom four sons survived infancy. For a month at the end of 1793 Schomberg commanded the *Vanguard* (74 guns) and in April 1794 he took command of the *Culloden* (74 guns). At the battle of 1 June 1794 the French *Vengeur*, having been pounded into a wreck by *Ramillies* and *Brunswick*, surrendered to a party from the *Culloden*. Her captain was taken to the *Culloden* shortly before his ship sank, and 127 men were saved by *Culloden*'s boats. Schomberg's last command was the *Magnanime* (44 guns), escorting convoys from Cork, between November 1794 and November 1795.

Thereafter Schomberg retired to Seend, Wiltshire, to write his *Naval chronology, or, An historical summary of naval and maritime events from the time of the Romans to the treaty of peace, 1802*, 5 vols. (1802), dedicated to Lord Hood. The comprehensive lists of ships, captains, and actions in volumes 4 and 5 are of particular value. Throughout 1801 Schomberg commanded the sea fencibles from Southend to Harwich, and from the renewal of war in 1803 until their disbandment in 1808 he commanded the sea fencibles of the Hastings district. In December of that year he was appointed a commissioner of the navy, a reward for suggesting that the sea fencibles had become an unnecessary burden to the country. He died, still a commissioner, at Cadogan Place, Chelsea, on 21 January 1813, and was buried in the family vault in St George-in-the-East, Stepney, London, on 28 January. C. H. H. Owen

Sources captain's letters, PRO, admiralty documents, ADM 1 • C-in-C East Indies (Cornwallis), PRO, admiralty documents, ADM 1/167 • sea fencibles, PRO, admiralty documents, ADM 28/145 • ships' muster books, PRO, admiralty documents, ADM 36 • passing certificate, PRO, admiralty documents, ADM 107/6 • B. McL. Ranft, ed., 'Prince William and Lieutenant Schomberg, 1787–1788', *The naval miscellany*, 4, Navy RS, 92 (1952), 267–93 • *Naval Chronicle*, 29 (1813), 175–6 • G. Cornwallis-West, *The life and letters of Admiral Cornwallis* (1927) • *Letters and papers of Admiral of the Fleet Sir Thos. Byam Martin, GCB*, ed. R. V. Hamilton, 1, Navy RS, 24 (1903) • parish register, Great Yarmouth, 8 April 1753 [baptism] • parish register, London, St George-in-the-East, 28 Jan 1813 [burial] • parish register, London, St George-in-the-East, 10 April 1807 [burial: Elizabeth Crowcher, mother] • parish register, Pangbourne, Berkshire, 13 Aug 1793 [marriage] • *GM*, 1st ser., 62 (1792), 674 • *GM*, 2nd ser., 13 (1840), 667

Likenesses E. M. Booth, oils, *c*.1790–1799, priv. coll. • Bartolozzi, Landseer, Ryder, and Stow, group portrait, line engraving, pubd 1803 (*Commemoration of the victory of June 1st, 1794*; after R. Smirke), BM • J. Downman, chalk and watercolour drawing (of Schomberg?), Royal Collection

Wealth at death under £17,500: PRO, death duty registers, IR 26/591/151

Schomberg, Meinhard, duke of Leinster and third duke of Schomberg (1641–1719), army officer, was born at Cologne on 30 June 1641, the third son of Frederick Herman de *Schomberg, first duke of Schomberg (1615–1690), and his wife, Johanna Elizabeth (*d.* 1664), daughter of Heinrich Dietrich von Schönberg auf Wesel. He joined his father in the service of Portugal, as lieutenant-colonel of his father's cavalry regiment (1663–5) and then colonel (1665–8). He then settled in La Rochelle with his father and was naturalized a French subject. He attained the rank of brigadier and, afterwards, *maréchal-de-camp*, during the Franco-Dutch War (1672–8). Under Marshal de Créqui he distinguished himself at Kochersburg (7 October 1677), before Freiburg-im-Breisgau (14 November), and at Rheinfelden (6 July 1678) and Kinzing (23 July). After the revocation of the edict of Nantes (1685) he emigrated and fought against the Turks in Hungary during the 1686 campaign. Afterwards he joined his father in Berlin, where he entered the service of Elector Frederick William as general of cavalry and colonel of dragoons.

Having travelled to England in the spring of 1689, Meinhard was sent by William III during August with dispatches for his father in Ireland. Shortly afterwards he visited Berlin, probably to secure permission to leave the Brandenburg service, returning to England early in 1690. He was gazetted colonel of a cavalry regiment on 10 April 1690, and commissioned general of the horse on 19 April. At the Boyne he commanded the right wing of William's army, fording the river at Rosnaree, and fought with particular fury to avenge his father's death at that battle. He was present at the abortive siege of Limerick in 1690, returning to England with William at the end of August. He received letters of naturalization on 25 April 1691 and, in order to ensure equality with his younger brother, Charles de *Schomberg (1645–1693) [*see under* Schomberg, Frederick Herman de], who had succeeded their father (by limitation) as duke of Schomberg, Meinhard was created Baron Tara (baron of Tarragh), earl of Bangor, and duke of Leinster in the Irish peerage on 3 March 1691. From May 1691 until the end of the Nine Years' War in 1697, he was commander-in-chief in England during William's absences abroad in Flanders. During the spring and early summer of 1692 he was placed in command of the abortive descent on St Malo before proceeding with his corps to undertake the remainder of the campaign in Flanders. He took considerable interest in mechanical devices, inventing a diving bell 'for working of wrecks', premièred successfully on the Thames on 8 September 1692 (Luttrell, 2.559): he was subsequently granted all wrecks on the coast of America between latitude 12° S and 40° N recoverable within twenty years.

On the death of his brother Charles at the battle of La Marsaglia, Meinhard succeeded to the English dukedom of Schomberg on 16 October 1693, taking his seat in the House of Lords on 19 November. He was made a privy counsellor on 9 May 1695. On 22 December 1696 the annuity of £4000 payable to his late brother—actually the interest at 4 per cent on the grant of £100,000 made by parliament to his father but lent to the crown—was transferred to him and later increased to 5 per cent by Queen Anne. His father's French estates were restored to the family after the peace of Rijswijk (1697), but were again confiscated on the outbreak of the War of the Spanish Succession in 1702. He was one of the six ducal pallbearers at William's funeral on 12 April 1702, and was created knight of the Garter in 1703.

Because of both his own and his father's earlier contributions towards securing Portuguese independence from Spain, on 16 August 1703, at the particular request of King Pedro II, Schomberg was appointed commander-in-chief of the forces sent to Portugal. Marlborough agreed: 'his name would be of great use there' (*Marlborough–Godolphin Correspondence*, 1.201–2). Having arrived in Lisbon in March 1704, this impatient, impetuous man with a hot, fiery temperament went to pieces under the pressures of independent command. Dithering and indecisive, he concentrated on inessentials rather than the welfare of his troops, who were in poor condition after the voyage from England. Isolated south of the Tagus from the main Portuguese forces under Minas in April 1704, Schomberg became thoroughly depressed, lapsing into inertia and allowing the enemy under Count Tserclaes de Tilly to march past his camp at Estremoz without interference. Wrangles over rank and seniority among the English, Dutch, and Portuguese generals further weakened his resolve and authority. Unable to agree on much else, the generals were united on the fact that Schomberg's performance had been disastrous. Although 'it is impossible to give a more mortal stroke to a general than to recall him in the middle of a campaign' (*Marlborough–Godolphin Correspondence*, 1.342), in July 1704 he was sacked, replaced by the earl of Galway, and sent home in September. He was never employed on active service again. William III had recognized these weaknesses and, apart from short spells in Ireland in 1690 and Flanders in 1692, had employed him exclusively in command positions within England.

In the House of Lords, Schomberg showed some interest in ecclesiastical affairs, voting against occasional conformity in 1703, in favour of the impeachment of Dr Sacheverell in 1710, and against the Schism Bill in 1714. In 1711 he resigned the colonelcy of his cavalry regiment in favour of his son, Charles, and was pallbearer at the funeral of the earl of Rochester. He performed the same office for the earl of Godolphin in the following year. The death of his son on 5 October 1713 greatly depressed him. On the accession of George I he resigned the additional £1000 on his annuity and retired from public life to his country house at Hillingdon, on the London road near Uxbridge, completed in 1717. His town residence, known as Schomberg House, Pall Mall, was built during the period of the Commonwealth.

In La Rochelle, on 3 August 1667, Schomberg had married Barbara Luisa, daughter of Giovanni Girolamo Rizzi and his wife, Maria Margarita Callovi of Montferrat. On 4 January 1683 he remarried; his new wife was Raugräfin Caroline Elizabeth (1659–1696), daughter of Karl Ludwig, elector palatine, and his wife, Maria Susanne Louis von Degenfeld. She was born on 19 November 1659, died at Kensington on 28 June 1696, and was buried in Westminster Abbey on 11 July 1696. Schomberg died, suddenly, at Hillingdon on Sunday 5 July 1719, and was buried on 4 August in the duke of Ormond's vault in Henry VII's chapel in Westminster Abbey. He had three children by his second marriage. Charles, styled marquess of Harwich (1691–1713), died unmarried. Two daughters survived him. The elder, Lady Frederica, was the mother of Robert d'Arcy, fourth earl of Holdernesse, while the younger and coheiress, Lady Mary, born on 16 March 1692, married a cousin, Christoph Martin von Degenfeld, from whom the family of Degenfeld-Schomberg descended.

JOHN CHILDS

Sources A. D. Francis, *The First Peninsular War, 1702–1713* (1975) • *The Marlborough–Godolphin correspondence*, ed. H. L. Snyder, 3 vols. (1975) • F. J. A. Kazner, *Campagnes de maréchal de Schomberg en Portugal, 1662–1668* (1807) • F. J. A. Kazner, *Leben Friedrich von Schomberg oder Schönburg* (1789) • N. Luttrell, *A brief historical relation of state affairs from September 1678 to April 1714*, 6 vols. (1857) • C. Dalton, ed., *English army lists and commission registers, 1661–1714*, 6 vols. (1892–1904) • D. C. A. Agnew, *Protestant exiles from France in the reign of Louis XIV, or, The Huguenot refugees and their descendants in Great Britain and Ireland*, 2nd edn, 3 vols. (1871–4) • H. Borkowski, ed., *Les mémoires du burgrave et comte Frédéric de Dohna, 1621–1688* (1898) • *The diplomatic correspondence of the Right Hon. Richard Hill*, ed. W. Blackley, 2 vols. (1845) • *Journal du marquis de Dangeau*, ed. E. Soulié and others, 19 vols. (Paris, 1854–60) • BL, Add. MS 28948 • GEC, *Peerage* • *DNB*

Archives BL, letters to William Blathwayt, Add. MS 21487 • BL, letters to William Blathwayt and William III, Add. MS 38014

Likenesses G. Kneller, *c.*1693, Althorp House, Northamptonshire • J. Smith, mezzotint (after G. Kneller), BM, NPG

Schomberg [Schamberg, Chambers], **Meyer Löw** (1690–1761), physician, born in Vetzburg (or Fetzburg), Württemberg, Germany, was probably the eldest son of Löw Schomberg, a physician of that town. Schomberg entered the University of Giessen, studied classics, then medicine, and completed his MD degree in 1710. His brothers, Salomon, Hertz, and Gerson Löw also took medical degrees at Giessen. Schomberg practised at Schweinsberg, Blankenstein, and then Metz, before settling in London in 1721, where to begin with he was employed by the wardens of the Great Synagogue to attend to their poor at a salary of £30 a year. He was admitted as a licentiate of the Royal College of Physicians on 19 March 1722 and obtained leave to defer payment of the £20 fee on giving his bond. On 12 January 1726 he was admitted as fellow of the Royal Society. In 1730 he joined the freemasons' lodge at the Swan and Rummer, Finch Lane, and in 1734 he served as grand steward. According to Sir William Browne, Schomberg built up a successful practice by befriending and offering hospitality to young surgeons, so that by 1740 he was reputed to have a professional income of 4000 guineas a year.

Schomberg was intensely jealous of his contemporary, Jacob de Castro Sarmento. In 1729 he tried unsuccessfully to block Sarmento's election to the Royal Society, by denigrating his character. In 1738 Sarmento treated Benjamin Mendes da Costa, a former patient of Schomberg, for acute abdominal pain, and prescribed an opiate. Schomberg, who was convinced that the patient was short of breath and that opium would kill him, told the apothecary that Sarmento's prescription was dangerous and induced him to visit the family, to warn them and to urge them to seek other advice. Schomberg exhibited the prescription to the surgeons in Janneway's Coffee House, and denounced Sarmento as an ass and a fool. Sarmento complained to the censors of the Royal College of Physicians, who fined Schomberg £4 for a breach of its moral statutes. From then on, he ran a vendetta against the college, using his son Isaac *Schomberg as a weapon, and became embroiled in a series of expensive lawsuits. Schomberg's essay of 1746, *Emunat omen* ('The faith of a physician'), written in excellent classical Hebrew, explained his alienation from the Jewish community and castigated the Jews of London, especially, it seems, Sarmento and his allies, but he never published it. He had by then become a deist.

Schomberg had a numerous family of at least seven sons and one daughter. He educated his sons for the liberal professions and, from about 1742, encouraged them to join the established church, if this would help their careers. His twin sons, Isaac and Ralph or Raphael *Schomberg became physicians; so did his son Joel, who practised medicine in Metz and Thann. His sons Moses and Solomon qualified as notaries public, as did Ralph. **Moses Schomberg** (1720–1779) was born in Lemburg, Germany, and studied law at the University of Leiden; in 1749 the archbishop of Canterbury granted him a faculty as a notary public, and he entered into partnership in London with Solomon da Costa Athias (1690–1769) and Isaac Netto (1687–1773) in Castle Alley, on one side of the Royal Exchange. **Solomon Schomberg** (1724–1774) was born in London; he received his notary's faculty in 1740 and entered into partnership with Solomon da Costa Athias and Isaac Netto in Castle Alley until 1755, when he acquired his own shop in the Royal Exchange. In 1761 he moved to Threadneedle Street. He can be presumed to have been baptized, because in 1758 he was admitted as a member of the Inner Temple, and while George, Viscount Townshend, was lord lieutenant in Ireland from 1768 to 1772, he served on his staff and was sworn in as an Irish privy councillor in 1770. Henry Schomberg was commissioned in the regular army and reached the rank of lieutenant-colonel. Alexander *Schomberg (1720–1804) was sent to St Paul's School, entered the Royal Navy, reached the rank of captain and was knighted. Meyer Schomberg also had a daughter, Rebecca (1719–1742), who died young.

Meyer Schomberg died at his house in Fenchurch Street, London, on 4 March 1761, and was buried in Hackney churchyard. He left 1s. each to Ralph, Solomon, and Henry, and the residue of his estate in equal shares to Isaac and Alexander. EDGAR SAMUEL

Sources M. Schomberg, 'Emunat omen', trans. H. Levy, *Transactions of the Jewish Historical Society of England*, 20 (1959–61), 101–11 [Heb. text with Eng. trans.] • E. R. Samuel, 'Dr Meyer Schomberg's attack on the Jews of London, 1746', *Transactions of the Jewish Historical Society of England*, 20 (1959–61), 83–111 • E. R. Samuel, 'Anglo-Jewish notaries and scriveners', *Transactions of the Jewish Historical Society of England*, 17 (1951–2), 113–59 • Munk, *Roll* • *Quatuor Coronatorum Antigrapha*, 10 (1913), 166 • P. Blachais, 'L'incroyable histoire des Schombourgs, famille juive d'Alsace', *Bulletin du Cercle Généalogique d'Alsace* (1988), 540–45 • R. D. Barnett, 'Dr Jacob de Castro Sarmento and Sephardim in medical practice in 18th-century London', *Transactions of the Jewish Historical Society of England*, 27 (1978–80), 84–114 • E. Carmoly, *Histoires des médecins juifs anciens et modernes* (1844) • *DNB* • G. L. Green, *Anglo-Jewry and the Royal Navy, 1740–1820: traders and those who served* (1989) • C. Roth, *The Great Synagogue, London, 1690–1940* (1950) • A. Sakula, 'The doctors Schomberg and the Royal College of Physicians: an eighteenth-century shemozzle', *Journal of Medical Biography*, 2 (1994), 113–19 • University of Giessen registers • Society of Genealogists, Colyer Fergusson Genealogical Collection • annals, RCP Lond.

Archives Jewish Theological Seminary, New York

Likenesses T. Hudson, portrait, priv. coll.; repro. in Sakula, 'The doctors Schomberg and the Royal College of Physicians'

Schomberg, Moses (1720–1779). *See under* Schomberg, Meyer Löw (1690–1761).

Schomberg, Ralph [*formerly* Raphael] **(1714–1792)**, physician and writer, son of Meyer Löw *Schomberg (1690–1761) and twin brother of Isaac *Schomberg (1714–1780), was born at Schweinsberg, Germany, on 14 August 1714 and moved to England with his father in 1721. He attended Merchant Taylors' School, London, from 1726 to 1731, and entered the University of Giessen in 1733 but he overspent his £100 p.a. allowance, got into debt, and was ordered to return home before he had completed the medical course. At his request, his father procured him a faculty as a notary public from the archbishop of Canterbury on 24 June 1737, placed him in partnership with Samuel Willett on 12 July 1737, and set them up in a shop in the Royal Exchange, London. Willett complained of Schomberg's neglect of the business and the partnership was ended. In 1738 Schomberg went out to Barbados, at the expense of a Mr Lascelles, as tutor to two young gentlemen there, at a salary of £20 p.a., but he overspent once more and drew bills of exchange on his father in London without authority. When these were refused, he had to leave Barbados. Schomberg then wrote a contrite letter to his father from Amsterdam and returned to England, now with the intention of becoming a surgeon. In April 1742 Schomberg made a lucrative marriage to Elizabeth (1719–1807), only daughter and heir of Joseph Crowcher, a rope maker of Wapping.

In April 1744 Schomberg received an MD degree, by correspondence, from Marischal College, Aberdeen, on the recommendation of his father and two other physicians. In the same year he was master of the Old Dundee masonic lodge when he is described as 'surgeon'. It appears that Schomberg's advantageous marriage did little to temper his avaricious nature, as in 1747 he unsuccessfully sued his long-suffering father in the chancery court for a fictitious debt. He then established himself in medical practice at Great Yarmouth, Norfolk, and was resident there on 16 July 1752, when he was elected as FSA. About 1761 he moved to Bath, where in 1772 Thomas Gainsborough painted his full-length portrait (this painting, on which his continued reputation largely rests, was sold to the National Gallery, London, by J. T. Schomberg in 1862). In 1778 Schomberg was accused by Philip Thicknesse of 'being detected last Sunday in stealing money out of his own plate at the church door', although having £40,000 or £50,000 (Gosse, 154). A caricature of this incident was published in London by J. Macarius. Schomberg left Bath and settled in Pangbourne and then in Reading, where he died at his home in Castle Street on 29 June 1792; he was buried at St George-in-the-East, Stepney, London. His wife, who survived him, died in the same house in 1807 and was buried next to him. Their ten children were baptized in infancy. Most of them died young: two surviving sons were Isaac *Schomberg (1753–1813) and Alexander Crowcher *Schomberg (1756–1792).

Schomberg was a prolific professional writer (and plagiarist), who was described as 'long a scribbler without genius or veracity'. He published articles on both medical and literary topics and wrote plays. Several of his letters to Emanuel Mendes da Costa have been published (J. Nichols, *Literary Ancedotes of the Eighteenth Century*, 1812–16, vol. 4). W. P. COURTNEY, *rev.* EDGAR SAMUEL

Sources E. R. Samuel, 'Anglo-Jewish notaries and scriveners', *Transactions of the Jewish Historical Society of England*, 17 (1951–2), 113–59 • E. R. Samuel, 'Dr Meyer Schomberg's attack on the Jews of London, 1746', *Transactions of the Jewish Historical Society of England*, 20 (1959–61), 83–111 • *Schomberg* v. *Schomberg*, 1747–8, PRO, C 12/2230/13 • P. J. Anderson and J. F. K. Johnstone, eds., *Fasti academiae Mariscallanae Aberdonensis: selections from the records of the Marischal College and University, MDXCIII–MDCCCLX*, 3 vols., New Spalding Club, 4, 18–19 (1889–98) • P. Gosse, *Dr Viper: the querulous life of Philip Thicknesse* (1952), 154 • A. Rubens, 'Anglo-Jewry in caricature, 1780–1850', *Transactions of the Jewish Historical Society of England*, 23 (1969–70), 96–101, esp. 98, pl. XI • A. Sakula, 'The doctors Schomberg and the Royal College of Physicians: an eighteenth-century shemozzle', *Journal of Medical Biography*, 2 (1994), 113–19 • J. M.

Shaftesley, 'Jews in regular English freemasonry, 1717–1860', *Transactions of the Jewish Historical Society of England*, 25 (1973–5), 150–209 • B. Waterhouse, *Gainsborough* (1958), no. 268

Likenesses T. Gainsborough, oils, 1772, National Gallery, London • J. Macarius, caricature, 1788, repro. in Rubens, 'Anglo-Jewry in caricature' • W. T. Fry, stipple (after T. Gainsborough), Wellcome L.

Wealth at death £40,000–50,000, *c*.1778: Gosse, *Dr Viper*

Schomberg, Reginald Charles Francis (1880–1958), army officer and explorer, was born on 19 September 1880 at 4 Russell Terrace, Lower Walmer, Kent, the elder of two children, and only son, of Reginald Brodrick Schomberg (1849–1932), barrister, and his wife, Frances Sophia (1839–1922), daughter of Thomas Charles Morris, gentleman, of Llansteffan and his wife, Mary. He was descended from the physician Meyer Low Schomberg (1690–1761). His parents were Roman Catholic: his father had converted while a student at New College, Oxford. Schomberg spent a happy childhood at the family home in Upper Richmond Road in south-west London. Educated at the Oratory School, Edgbaston, Birmingham (1892–8), he then went up to New College, Oxford, where he graduated in 1901. In 1901 he was commissioned in the 1st battalion Seaforth Highlanders and from 1902 to 1911 he served in India. He saw action as part of the Indian frontier expedition in 1908, and used every leave to visit remote parts of the Himalayan foothills and central Baluchistan. In 1911 he went home to Chasewood Lodge, Ross-on-Wye, the house to which the family had moved in 1910, before taking up a post with the Malay states' guides. In Malaya he spent his leave trekking across remote parts of the Malay peninsula.

In 1915 Schomberg returned to the Seaforths in Mesopotamia and in 1916 he was severely wounded during an attack on Turkish positions at Sunnaiyat, an action for which he was awarded the DSO. After a period of recuperation in Britain he returned to Mesopotamia. On the way, his ship was torpedoed 150 miles east of Malta. He was again wounded, less severely this time, during the attack on Tikrit in 1917, an action for which he received a bar to his DSO. From 1917 to 1919 he commanded the 1st battalion in Mesopotamia and Palestine. While in Palestine he took the opportunity to wander round Jerusalem and other sites central to his faith. After the war he returned to Malaya. From 1919 he was commandant, Singapore volunteer corps, and from 1920 inspector of prisons, Straits Settlements. He resigned in 1921, partly for health reasons. The return of the Seaforths to Scotland and a dislike of life in Britain after the war saw him transfer to the 2nd battalion, with the rank of major, and return to India in 1922. After a visit to Changchenmo, Ladakh, in 1923, he revived plans which he had made before the war to visit Central Asia and Tibet. He retired in December 1927.

The first journey was made in 1926 and was followed by longer journeys in 1927–9 and 1930–31, for which Schomberg received the Royal Geographical Society's Gill memorial medal. He inspired great loyalty in the small group of men whom he often referred to as his 'slaves'. These were led by Daulat Shah, who managed his camp and transport. He enjoyed big game hunting, but there was a more serious side to his explorations. Like many other people at the time, he saw a danger to India if communism were to infiltrate Sinkiang (Xinjiang). He therefore combined intelligence-gathering with his recording of geographical, ethnographical, and botanical information as he wandered over areas rarely, if ever, visited by Europeans. He wrote a popular account of these journeys entitled *Peaks and Plains of Central Asia* (1933). Travels between 1933 and 1936 in remote areas across the north-west frontier of India, from Afghanistan to Ladakh, were related in three further books: *Between the Oxus and the Indus* (1935), *Unknown Karakorum* (1936), and *Kafirs and Glaciers* (1938). He wrote many articles and reviews for the *Alpine Journal*, the *Geographical Journal*, the *Himalayan Journal*, the *Journal of the Royal Central Asian Society*, and the *Scottish Geographical Journal*. Schomberg's reports of conditions in Sinkiang in the 1920s and 1930s are at the Public Record Office and in the British Library oriental and India Office collections. Photographs and accounts of later travels are at the Royal Society for Asian Affairs. From 1936 to 1944 Schomberg served in a number of diplomatic posts. During 1936–7 and 1938–41 he was British consul-general in the French establishments in India; from November 1939 he was in addition consul-general for Portuguese possessions in India. He was consular liaison officer, Persia (1942–3), and then customs, Perso-Indian frontier (1943–4). In 1937 he was made a CIE. From 1944 to 1945 he was colonel, force 136 (part of the Special Operations Executive), China. Throughout these years he continued to explore new territory whenever he could: Baltistan in 1937 and Ladakh in 1944, 1945, and 1946.

Schomberg was 5 feet 8 inches tall and weighed about 10 stone. He was fit and was once described as having walked from Kashmir to Kashgar six times. An honours degree in history and competence in Latin, French, Urdu, Pushtu, Persian, and Turkish were combined with an acutely observant eye and a dry wit which made him an entertaining companion. He was impatient with hypocrisy, pomposity, and what he saw as unnecessary bureaucracy: an India Office memo in 1929 described him as a candid but by no means factious critic. Friends described him not only as tough but also as courteous, considerate, and possessing a natural charm. His army life and what a friend called the spirit of a born traveller, going where the spirit moved him, made Schomberg unsuitable for a settled life. He never married but remained devoted to his parents, his unmarried sister Mary, and his aunts.

Schomberg was a deeply religious man and in 1947 he decided finally to devote the remainder of his life to his church. From 1947 to 1951 he studied for the priesthood at the Collegio Beda, Rome, and was ordained at the basilica of St John Lateran. Between 1952 and 1953 he assisted with parish work at Ringwood, Hampshire; from 1953 to 1954 he was chaplain to the Assisi Home, Grayshot, and from 1954 to 1957 chaplain to the convent of the Sisters of St Joseph, Boars Hill, Oxford. Shortly after he retired in December 1957, Schomberg had a fall at home and fractured his skull. He died at Hereford General Hospital on 1 March 1958 and was buried at Belmont Abbey, Hereford.

M. J. Pollock

Sources *WWW*, 1951–60 · *LondG* (22 Dec 1916) [suppl.] · *LondG* (11 Jan 1919) [suppl.] · *LondG* (1 March 1937) [suppl.] · *Cabar Feidh* (May 1958), 78 · *Journal of the Royal Central Asian Society*, 45 (1958), 112–13 · *The Times* (4 March 1958) · *The Times* (6 March 1958) · *The Times* (7 March 1958) · *CGPLA Eng. & Wales* (1958) · b. cert. · d. cert. · b. certs. [parents] · d. certs. [parents] · private information (2004)

Archives BL OIOC, reports, L/P&S/12/2336; L/P&S/12/2346 · PRO, travel notes, FO 371/12472; FO 371/14720 · Royal Society for Asian Affairs, London, drafts for unpublished works: 'Cold desert'; 'Baltistan journey'; 'Karakorum finale'; 'Tibetan journey'; photographs · U. Oxf., Pitt Rivers Museum, photographs, collection of glass plates | BL OIOC, corresp. with F. M. Bailey, MS Eur. F 157 · BL OIOC, corresp. with Sir George Taylor, MS Eur. C 371 · Bodl. Oxf., corresp. with E. J. Thompson · PRO, CO 273/417, 514, 516 · RGS, MSS, incl. corresp. with Royal Geographical Society

Wealth at death £12,828 9*s*. 8*d*.: probate, 2 Dec 1958, *CGPLA Eng. & Wales*

Schomberg, Solomon (1724–1774). *See under* Schomberg, Meyer Löw (1690–1761).

Schomburgk, (Moritz) Richard (1811–1891). *See under* Schomburgk, Sir Robert Hermann (1804–1865).

Schomburgk, Sir Robert Hermann (1804–1865), surveyor and traveller, was the son of the Revd Johann Friedrich Ludwig Schomburgk, a protestant minister in Thuringia, and Christine Julian, the daughter of J. Krippendorf, counsellor of the princes of Reuss-Gera. Schomburgk was born at Freiburg in Saxony on 5 June 1804, the eldest of four brothers and one sister, and was educated in Germany. He entered business with his uncle and in 1826 went to the USA. His taste for natural history led him in 1830 to the West Indies, and in 1831 he surveyed, at his own cost, the littoral of Anegada, one of the Virgin Islands. His results were printed in the *Journal of the Royal Geographical Society* (1831, 2.152–70), and attracted some notice. During 1835–9, under the direction of the Royal Geographical Society, he explored the rivers Essequibo (the sources of which he was the first European to reach), Corentyn, and Berbice, and investigated in detail the capabilities of the colony of British Guiana. In 1837 he discovered and sent to England the giant water lily *Victoria regia* now renamed *Victoria amazonica*. By his journey across the interior from the Essequibo to Esmeralda on the Orinoco he was enabled to connect his observations with those of his countryman, Humboldt, and to determine astronomically a series of fixed points extending across the watershed of the great rivers of equatorial America (*Journal of the Royal Geographical Society*, 35, 1865, cxxi–cxxii). For these services the Royal Geographical Society conferred on him in 1840 one of its gold medals.

On his return to Europe, Schomburgk represented to the British government the necessity of settling the actual boundary of British Guiana, for commercial and humanitarian reasons. He had witnessed the forcible abduction by Brazilians of Amerindians from what he later declared to be British territory and wished to ensure the native peoples' safety from such practice. In April 1840 he was appointed a commissioner for surveying and marking out the boundaries of the colony, and before returning to South America he wrote *A Description of British Guiana, Geographical and Statistical* (1840), which was in its original

Sir Robert Hermann Schomburgk (1804–1865), by William Brockedon, 1840

form a report to the Colonial Office and is the first detailed account of the colony. For more popular consumption he published by subscription *Twelve Views in the Interior of Guiana* (1841), and two volumes in The Naturalist's Library (ed. W. Jardine) entitled *The Fishes of Guiana* (1841–3).

Schomburgk returned to British Guiana in 1841 and began by marking the line on the north-west with Venezuela. During 1841–3 he extended his survey southward, making Pirara his headquarters, and finishing by a journey thence overland to the headwaters of the Corentyn, down which river he descended to Demerara (*Journal of the Royal Geographical Society*, 15, 1845, 1–104). Some of his journeys were made under extremely arduous conditions and would be as difficult to complete today as when Schomburgk undertook them. His delimitation proposals, known as 'the Schomburgk line', subsequently became famous during the prolonged boundary disputes between British Guiana and the neighbouring countries of Brazil and Venezuela. This 'line' formed the basis of negotiations until the frontier with Venezuela was settled by arbitration in 1899 and that with Brazil in 1904, and then proved decisive in the final delineation of the boundaries.

On Schomburgk's return to England he was knighted by patent on 26 December 1844. While waiting to obtain the further government appointment he sought, he visited Barbados as a director of the Barbados General Railway Company and wrote as a result of his stay a worthy if dull tome, *The History of Barbados Comprising a Geographical and*

Statistical Description of the Island (1848). He also occupied his time in editing for the Hakluyt Society *The Discovery of the Empire of Guiana by Sir W. Raleigh* (1848), an edition of great merit, and in translating from the German *Travels of his Royal Highness Prince Adalbert of Prussia, in the South of Europe and in Brazil* (1849).

Schomburgk was gazetted British consul in Santo Domingo on 25 May 1848, and was made a plenipotentiary to conclude a treaty of amity and commerce between Great Britain and the Dominican Republic on 23 February 1849. However, while his overt remit was to encourage British trade, his more important role was to implement the British policy of maintaining the status quo in the area by blocking the geopolitical aspirations of any European power or the United States. He was appointed British consul at Bangkok, Siam, on 1 May 1857 and arrived there in December of that year. While there he undertook in 1859–60 an important journey from Bangkok to Chiengmai, the capital of the tributary kingdom of Laos, and then across the mountains to Moulmein on the Gulf of Martaban. He also prepared an invaluable report on whether it would be practicable to cut a ship-canal across the isthmus of Kra, whereby the detour by the Strait of Malacca might be spared ships trading between Siam and British India. His health declined (having suffered during his South American journeys) and he retired from the public service with a pension in December 1864. From the University of Königsberg he received the degree of doctor of philosophy, and from the University of Jena that of doctor of medicine. He accepted decorations from the governments of Prussia, Saxony, and France. He died at Schöneburg, near Berlin, on 11 March 1865. After 1826 Schomburgk had spent very little time in Europe and he never married. Nor did he write an account of his travels for the public as many other Victorian explorers did and his name and achievements were later little known.

Schomburgk's brother, **(Moritz) Richard Schomburgk** (1811–1891), botanist, was born at Freiburg in Saxony on 5 October 1811, the second youngest of the five siblings. He was educated at Freiburg, Berlin, and Potsdam, paying special attention to botany, and receiving an appointment in the royal Prussian gardens at Sans-Souci, near Potsdam. In 1840 he accompanied Robert Schomburgk as botanist on the British Guiana boundary survey; he returned to Germany in 1844. In 1847 he published, in German, his account of the boundary expedition, dwelling chiefly on the botanic aspect, entitled *Reisen in Britisch-Guiana*, published in English as *Travels in British Guiana* in 1922. Because of political unrest and a lack of opportunities in Germany, he emigrated to South Australia in 1849 with another brother, Otto, and embarked on the cultivation of the vine, meeting with considerable success. Just before leaving Germany he married Pauline Kneib. In 1865 he became director of the botanic gardens at Adelaide. He died at Adelaide on 24 March 1891. He was a member of many scientific societies, and received several foreign decorations. G. C. Boase, *rev.* Peter Rivière

Sources R. Schomburgk, *The fishes of Guiana*, part I (1841) [incl. partly autobiographical memoir] • PRO, CO 111/218 • P. Rivière, *The Guiana travels of Sir Robert Schomburgk, 1835–43*, Hakluyt Society [forthcoming] • *FO List* (1865) • P. Ojer, *Robert H. Schomburgk* (1969) • P. Rivière, *Absent-minded imperialism* (1995) • R. Schomburgk, *Travels in British Guiana*, 2 vols. (1922) • RGS, Schomburgk MSS • *Journal of the Royal Geographical Society*, 35 (1865), cxxi–cxxii • P. Payne, 'Dr Richard Schomburgk and Adelaide Botanic Garden, 1865–1891', diss., University of Adelaide, 1992 • *AusDB*, vol. 6 [M. R. Schomburgk] • D. Graham Burnett, *Masters of all they surveyed: exploration, geography, and a British El Dorado* (2000)

Archives BL, journal of expedition to British Guiana, Add. MS 34205 • Linn. Soc., papers • NHM, drawings and papers • PRO, Foreign and Colonial Office papers • RBG Kew, papers • RGS, diary and papers | NL Scot., Melville MSS • RGS, letters to Royal Geographical Society • Royal Museum, Edinburgh, letters to Sir William Jardine

Likenesses W. Brockedon, chalk drawing, 1840, NPG [*see illus.*] • M. Gauci, lithograph, pubd 1840 (after drawing by E. U. Eddis), BM • photograph (Moritz Richard Schomburgk), RBG Kew

Wealth at death under £800: probate, 28 Aug 1865, *CGPLA Eng. & Wales*

Schonell, Sir Fred Joyce (1900–1969), educationist and university administrator, was born on 3 August 1900 in Perth, Western Australia, the son of Edward William Schonell, a headmaster, and his wife, Agnes Mary, *née* Mawer. His early education was at Perth modern school. Having taught between 1921 and 1922, he graduated BA in English from the University of Western Australia in 1925. In the following year he moved to London, where he returned to teaching. With a Hackett scholarship awarded by the University of Western Australia he was a research student under Cyril Burt and Percy Nunn at the Institute of Education and King's College, London, between 1929 and 1931, gaining a PhD in education in 1932. On 22 December 1926 he married Florence Eleanor Waterman, with whom he collaborated closely on a number of educational projects until her death in 1962; she was the daughter of William de Bracey Waterman of Perth, Western Australia. They had a son and a daughter.

Partly in step with his postgraduate research, Schonell had taken additional courses in educational theory and teacher training at Cambridge and the Institute of Education in London, obtaining a teaching diploma from the latter in 1929, while still continuing to teach and to research into aspects of educational psychology. He evolved his diagnostic and remedial techniques in schools in London and Kent while a lecturer in education at Goldsmiths' College, University of London. He held that post from 1931 until 1942, when he was appointed professor of education at University College, Swansea, where he built up a major department. In 1946 he succeeded Charles Wilfrid Valentine as professor of education at the University of Birmingham, where he was closely concerned with setting up a new institute of education, a research department, and a remedial education centre. He was awarded a DLit from London in 1943 and an MA from Birmingham in 1947.

Schonell returned to Australia in 1950 to become professor of education at the University of Queensland where he built up the education faculty and established a remedial centre on similar lines to that in Birmingham. In 1960 he became the first vice-chancellor of the university to be appointed from the academic community (a position previously held by prominent lay figures in an honorary capacity), playing a prominent role in promoting and developing the university during his nine-year tenure from 1960 until his death.

Schonell was a considerable researcher and a prolific author with a particular interest in children who would be diagnosed today as having learning difficulties. Between 1932 and 1962, for instance, he published over fifteen books, including *Backwardness in the Basic Subjects* (1942), *Diagnostic and Attainment Tests* (1949), and *Diagnosis and Remedial Teaching in Arithmetic* (1957). His major long-term interest was in the problems that such children encountered with reading, spelling, and simple arithmetic. This concern took in both the detection and the improvement of deficiencies in such key skills. His widely utilized diagnostic tests for arithmetic and intelligence can be seen as directly expressing this interest, as can his series of elementary books designed to improve performance in English and arithmetic. His Happy Venture series of reading books sold in millions to primary schools in Britain and the Commonwealth. The regime that his books for use in schools promoted was that the material should be arranged in strictly increasing order of difficulty, and that progression from the easier to the more demanding material should be based on a rigorous grading scheme.

Schonell served on numerous committees and professional bodies. He was at various times honorary secretary of the education section, president of the midland branch, and council member of the British Psychological Society (BPS). He was made an honorary fellow of the BPS in 1966. After 1950 he was equally active in the Australian branch of the BPS, later becoming a fellow of the newly autonomous Australian Psychological Society. In 1959 he was elected a fellow of the Australian College of Education. He was president of the Australian and New Zealand Association for the Advancement of Science from 1965 to 1966 and national chairman of the Winston Churchill Fellowship selection committee from 1966, as well as serving on the council of the Association of Commonwealth Universities. Outside his academic life, his main interests were in art, music, and, especially, Elizabethan theatre.

Schonell was made a knight bachelor in 1962 and received honorary doctorates from the universities of Western Australia (1963) and Sydney (1965). He died of lymphatic cancer on 22 February 1969 at his home in Rutledge Street, Indooroopilly, Brisbane, a few months before his intended retirement date. After a funeral service at St John's Anglican Cathedral in Brisbane he was cremated at the Mount Thompson crematorium, Brisbane, on 26 February. A. D. LOVIE and P. LOVIE

Sources *The Times* (25 Feb 1969) · *Courier-Mail* [Brisbane] (24 Feb 1969) · *Courier-Mail* [Brisbane] (26 Feb 1969) · *The Telegraph* (24 Feb 1969) · *WWW, 1961–70* · R. Aldrich and P. Gordon, *Dictionary of British educationists* (1989), 219 · University of Queensland · private information (2004) · Burke, *Peerage* (1967)

Archives University of Queensland, Brisbane, MS Collection 197

Likenesses photograph, British Psychological Society, Grace Rawlings Visual Archive

Schonfeld, Solomon (1912–1984), rabbi and rescuer of persecuted Jews, was born on 21 February 1912 at 125 Green Lanes, Stoke Newington, London, the second of seven children (six boys and one girl) of Victor (Avigdor) Schonfeld (1880–1930), rabbi and teacher, and his wife, Ella (Rachel-Leah) Sternberg (1890–1971). Schonfeld was educated at the Highbury county school (1923–7), and studied at the *yeshiva* in Tyrnau (Trnava), Czechoslovakia (1927–9), with Rabbi Michael-Ber Weissmandl (his distant relative, mentor, and inspiration for rescue efforts). Schonfeld returned to London in December 1929 intending to study law but, as a consequence of his father's sudden death in January 1930 and his being chosen to assume his father's role, he went back to rabbinical school, subsequently transferring to the *yeshiva* of Slobodka, Lithuania, simultaneously studying for a doctorate at the University of Königsberg.

In 1933, at the age of twenty-one, Schonfeld returned to London with a beard, ordination, and a PhD to assume his father's positions as rabbi of the Adath Yisroel Synagogue and presiding rabbi of the Union of Orthodox Hebrew Congregations. He greatly expanded both the union and his father's Jewish secondary school (renamed the Avigdor School after his father), the first Jewish Orthodox day school in England. Later he founded the Hasmonean Grammar Schools. He eventually established four Jewish primary schools, whose goal was to instil in the students a pride as Orthodox Jews, comfortable in both Jewish and general society. This reflected the deep-seated commitment by father and son to the Hirschian ideology (so called after Rabbi Samson Raphael Hirsch) of combining strict, independent Orthodoxy with secular education.

Beginning in 1933 the massive refugee problem caused by Hitler's antisemitism resulted in large-scale immigration of German and later Austrian Jewish refugees, for whom the Anglo-Jewish establishment provided a guarantee to the British government to prevent their becoming a public charge. Since the ultimate destination for these refugees was re-emigration elsewhere, including Palestine, the organizations gave priority to the young and the Zionist orientated. This resulted in discrimination against the Orthodox, especially against rabbis, teachers, and other religious functionaries, who were deemed most unassimilable by the secular Jewish organizations, with whom they feared to be identified. Prompted by pleas from Weissmandl to aid those forsaken, Schonfeld changed his focus to rescue. To gain access to governmental agencies and important non-Jewish personalities Schonfeld associated with the chief rabbi, Joseph H. Hertz, in early 1938, creating the Chief Rabbi's Religious Emergency Council (known as the Chief Rabbi's Council or the CRREC). The chief rabbi publicly supported Schonfeld despite the vehement opposition of the Anglo-Jewish establishment, Hertz's natural constituency, which considered Schonfeld a loose cannon. Their refusal to support his rescue efforts necessitated Schonfeld's personal guarantee for every refugee. Since he eventually had full personal responsibility for the physical and spiritual well-being of more than 2000 people, including children and rabbis, he had to raise funds and intercede with the government and non-Jewish leadership. Although the council had a formal secretary, close associates, and a volunteer staff, it was essentially a one-man operation. The chief rabbi gave Schonfeld complete freedom in matters of rescue, and lent Schonfeld the full prestige of his office. One result of Schonfeld's frequent contact with Hertz was meeting his eldest daughter, Judith (1913–1987), whom he married on 16 January 1940; they spent their honeymoon in Palestine. They had three sons, Victor (*b.* 1940), Jonathan Benedict (*b.* 1944), and Jeremy (*b.* 1951).

In addition to his creative approach Rabbi Schonfeld was blessed with a dynamic personality and an awesome physical presence. He was described by Rabbi Hertz, his newly acquired father-in-law, as 'an exceptionally handsome man, six-foot high, blue eyes, a renowned *shnorrer* [fund-raiser]', persuasive and affable, willing to do everything in his power, including bending rules, and displaying 'fearlessness toward the assimilated [Jewish] aristocracy' (private information), to save Jewish lives. Raising half a million pounds for relief and rescue while living solely on the meagre salary paid by his congregation he earned the respect and admiration of both government officials and lay leaders. He mobilized all his incredible strengths to meet his greatest challenge: saving Jewish lives.

During the year and a half before war broke out Schonfeld obtained permission from the Home Office, which was most co-operative, to bring more than 1300 rabbis, teachers, and their families from Germany. He also organized a transport of 300 children from Vienna, whom he placed in Jewish homes or kosher hostels. In order to bring out about 200 rabbinic students aged sixteen to eighteen he created and staffed a *yeshiva* (Ohr Yisroel). At the same time he helped Weissmandl and the Revisionist Zionists organize an illegal transport from Vienna to Palestine. He also obtained 340 Mauritius visas that served as protective papers for many Jews in Nazi-occupied territories.

During the war his efforts shifted back to Britain. When in 1940, due to fear of a German invasion, 25,000 aliens, mostly Jewish refugees, were interned Schonfeld was the first, and for a long time the only person to tour the camps and obtain physical and spiritual improvements for all, including the release of 1000 hardship cases. When he learned that two million Jews had been murdered he devised a rescue plan in January 1943, with the help of Eleanor Rathbone MP, to convince 277 MPs to offer a rescue resolution that would provide sanctuary for Jews throughout the dominions. However, due to Zionist objections to the omission of Palestine, this resolution never materialized. He also conveyed, unsuccessfully, Weissmandl's plea for the allies to bomb the rail lines to Auschwitz. Schonfeld obtained permission for thirty rabbis and families to leave Siberia for Palestine via Tehran. He likewise provided 25,000 Jewish servicemen in Britain and abroad with free kosher food packages and religious articles. He supervised the evacuation of 550 students from the Avigdor School during the London blitz to the village of Shefford, where, throughout the war, he provided them with a complete Jewish educational programme and kosher facilities.

The conclusion of the war presented Schonfeld with a new array of challenges. First, he fitted out twelve large mobile synagogue–ambulances with kosher food, religious articles, medicine, and clothing. They were sent to newly liberated territories including the Netherlands, Germany, France, and Czechoslovakia, and displaced persons camps. Their objective was to set up Orthodox communities and help the broken survivors regain their physical, psychological, and spiritual health, and especially a renewed pride in being Jewish. Schonfeld brought hundreds of youngsters from Prague (the last in 1948), and made five trips to post-war Poland to help returning survivors reconstruct Orthodox communities and above all, rescue 500 orphans (Orthodox and non-Orthodox) from a dangerous situation. In the process he narrowly escaped assassination. When another situation required immediate exodus, Schonfeld simply purchased a boat to take 150 children to England. In 1946 he went on a mission to Cyprus to improve the physical as well as spiritual lives of thousands of Jewish internees. By 1948 Schonfeld concluded the council's work. In all more than 3700 refugees were virtually single-handedly rescued by Rabbi Schonfeld. In addition countless thousands of others directly benefited from his efforts. He now focused on his rabbinic, education, and writing projects. During the 1960s he set up a community centre in Ashdod, Israel, complete with a synagogue and *yeshiva*. His writings included *Jewish Religious Education* (1943), *The Universal Bible* (1955), *Message to Jewry* (1959), *Why Judaism* (1963), *Standard Siddur-Prayer Book* (1973), and *A New–Old Rendering of Psalms* (1980). His health deteriorated following an operation in 1965 for a benign tumour. By 1982 he was an invalid, cared for by some of those he saved. He died at the Whittington Hospital, Archway, Islington, on 6 February 1984. He was buried next day in the cemetery of the Adath Yisroel Synagogue in Cheshunt, Hertfordshire.

DAVID H. KRANZLER

Sources S. Schonfeld, *Message to Jewry* (1958) [incl. 'Report on the Chief Rabbi's Religious Emergency Council, 1938–1948' and articles on Jewish education] · P. Shatzkes, 'Anglo-Jewish rescue and relief efforts, 1938–1944', PhD diss., U. Lond., 1999 · G. Alderman, *Modern British Jewry* (1992) · A. Gottlieb, *Men of vision: Anglo-Jewry's aid to victims of the Nazi regime, 1933–1945* (1998) · N. Bentwich, *They found refuge* (1956) · M. D. Weissmandel, *Torat hemed* (1958); rev. edn (1994) [Heb.; incl. correspondence with Schonfeld] · D. Kranzler, *Solomon Schonfeld: his page in history* (1982) · private information (2004) [J. Schonfeld, M. Retter] · R. Bolchover, *British Jewry and the Holocaust* (1993) · N. Lipschutz, *In memoriam: [of] Rabbi Dr V[ictor] Schonfeld* (1930) · E. D., 'Schonfeld, Victor', *Encyclopaedia Judaica*, ed. C. Roth (Jerusalem, 1971–2) · d. cert.

Archives U. Southampton L., personal and family corresp. and papers | Central Zionist Archives, Jerusalem, Selig Brodedsky MSS

Schonland, Sir Basil Ferdinand Jamieson (1896–1972), physicist and meteorologist, was born at 1 Francis Street, Grahamstown, Cape Colony, southern Africa, on 2 February 1896, the eldest of three sons (there were no daughters) of Selmar Schönland (*b.* 1860), botanist and curator of the Albany Museum of Grahamstown, and his wife, Flora, daughter of Professor MacOwan, rector of Gill College, Somerset East, Cape Colony. Schonland attended St Andrew's College School and then in 1914 took a BA degree in physics at Rhodes University College, Grahamstown. He entered Gonville and Caius College, Cambridge, in 1914, gained a first class in part one of the mathematical tripos (1915), and was elected to an exhibition. Immediately after the examination he enlisted in the Royal Engineers, and as a second lieutenant was placed in charge of a team learning to lay communication cables. Early in 1916 he went to France with his team as officer in charge of the Royal Engineers' 43rd airline section, and for two years without a break he endured the gunfire and mud of Flanders, receiving severe concussion at Arras. He was mentioned in dispatches for bravery, appointed OBE (military), and finished the war as an acting major with the rank of captain and chief instructor, wireless communications. He was demobilized in March 1919 and completed part two of the natural sciences tripos (physics, first class, 1920), winning the Francis Schuldham plate of the college and a George Green studentship for research. He then worked for two years in the Cavendish Laboratory, on the scattering of beta particles. He also discussed atmospheric electricity and thunderstorms with C. T. R. Wilson, a world authority on the subject.

In 1922 Schonland returned to the Cape as senior lecturer in physics at Cape Town and after completing experiments he had started in Cambridge he switched over to atmospheric electricity, measuring electric fields under thunderclouds. He returned to Cambridge with an 1851 Exhibition scholarship in 1928 and met C. V. Boys, who had made a special camera with which to photograph lightning. Alas, Boys never encountered lightning in England during the night hours. It was a simple camera: a photographic lens mounted near to the outer rim of a metal disc which could rotate about its axis at known speed. The image formed by the lens fell on a large photographic plate set parallel to the disc. If the camera, pointing to a thundercloud, happened to secure a picture of the lightning the image would have been sharp if the flash were instantaneous, but if the flash consisted of several separate discharges, lasting, say, for a tenth of a second from start to finish, several images would have been recorded and the time interval between them would be known. Schonland borrowed this camera and chased storms as they developed over the Rand. From many photographs taken with his small team of collaborators the complex sequence of events in the flash were unravelled and were correlated with the measurements of electric field changes at ground level as the storm approached and receded. All this pioneering work has stood the test of time and is of great benefit to the electrical engineer concerned with overhead transmission lines.

Schonland used to spend summer months at his wife's parents' home, 2500 feet above sea level, a site well placed to observe storm clouds approaching from the west. In addition to measuring thunderstorm fields he planted a medium-sized tree in a pot isolated from the ground and measured the electric current flowing up from its branches as the thundercloud passed overhead. This was the first of many attempts to estimate the total current flowing in the lower atmosphere. In 1932 he equipped a small mobile laboratory to follow storm clouds. He showed for the first time that a flash consists of several strokes and measured the time intervals between them. The most important information was related to the way the air broke down from cloud to earth; he found that the first discharge, having relatively weak illumination, travelled from the cloud in a jerky fashion, step by step, branching as it travelled. He called this the leader stroke. When it reached the earth the main stroke of high luminosity travelled back to the cloud. The current flowing in the leader stroke is of the order of amperes but in the main stroke it can reach 100,000 amperes and it is this which can cause great damage to trees and buildings and, travelling on power station lines, can reach the station and put it out of action; alternatively as the lightning enters soil or sand it can fuse particles into a glassy condition and produce fulgurites. Schonland explained the occurrence of the separate strokes in the flash as follows: after the first main stroke has discharged some part of the electrified cloud a leader stroke can extend from that volume to a neighbouring part of the cloud still highly charged and so provide an ionized path to ground over exactly the same route, and this process can continue until the whole of the cloud has delivered its charge to earth. He also explained why spires and towers are so vulnerable to be struck by lightning: as the leader stroke from a cloud descends the stress at the tip of a tower increases until a small leader stroke rises out of the high point and this may then join the descending leader and thus bring the whole stroke to the high rod or steeple.

As a result of this excellent beginning, financial support for a permanent laboratory was forthcoming from Bernard Price, chairman of the Victoria Falls and Transvaal Power Company, and from the Carnegie Institute. By 1937 the Bernard Price Institute for Geophysical Research had been built at Witwatersrand University, with Schonland as its director; his work won him election as FRS in 1938.

With the coming of the Second World War, Schonland was invited by General J. C. Smuts to establish a unit in the South African corps of signals to develop radio direction finding (RDF) and his group moved with the forces up Africa, joining Sir A. P. Wavell before the great desert offensive of December 1940. His army experience was invaluable in persuading army and air force chiefs to accept new ideas; his personality was right, for he was a good listener, a kindly persuasive speaker, and an obvious authority. He went to England to gather information from Sir John Cockcroft at the Air Defence Research and Development Establishment and was asked to remain as his deputy, but after a short time he joined anti-aircraft command where he trained the Royal Engineers to dismantle the German Wurtzburg radar during the successful Bruneval raid. In 1941 he moved on to the army operational research group, as lieutenant-colonel; he was promoted colonel in January 1942 and brigadier in May 1944 just prior to joining Twenty-First Army group as scientific adviser to General B. L. Montgomery. When his chief of staff, General de Guingand, told Montgomery that Schonland was to be his scientific adviser and go with Twenty-First Army group to observe the progress of the war Monty replied 'I observe my own battles', but when Monty presented the CBE (military division) to Schonland he said 'If you have any more like you I will take them' (Allibone, 642).

In 1945 Smuts called Schonland home to establish the South African Council for Scientific and Industrial Research while still remaining in charge of the Bernard Price Institute. In 1951 he became the first chancellor of Rhodes University, and in 1952, president of the South African Association for the Advancement of Science; he received the gold medal of the Franklin Institute (1950). At this time Schonland was worried over some of the winds blowing in South Africa and he urged his young graduates to remember the university motto, the last word of which is truth, to defend the truth, to examine with an open mind whether ideas they may hold are based on truth or on prejudice: 'Remember', he said to them, 'Cromwell's angry outburst, "I beseach you by the Bowels of Christ, consider well lest ye be mistaken"' (Allibone, 649). Schonland was a kind and moral man, and was an enthusiastic supporter of an organization which campaigned vigorously for the rights of the black population.

In 1954 Schonland moved to the Atomic Energy Research Establishment at Harwell as deputy to Cockcroft. He became director in 1958, and was knighted in 1960. He retired in 1961, but remained chancellor of Rhodes and addressed the university with many fine speeches, although he was greatly worried by some of the changes he saw coming in South Africa. He was appointed CBE in 1945, and had honorary degrees from the universities of Cambridge, Cape Town, Rhodes, Witwatersrand, Southampton, and Natal. In 1959 he became an honorary fellow of Gonville and Caius College.

Schonland's great achievement was his immense contribution to our knowledge of lightning. He remained truly modest, a scientist in the pursuit of truth. In 1923 he married Isabel Marian (Ismay), daughter of James Craib of Somerset East, teacher of mathematics and later inspector of schools in Cape Province. They had one son and two daughters; their family life was extremely happy. Schonland's last years were clouded by illness, and he died in Bracken Lea Nursing Home, Shawford, Compton, Hampshire, on 24 November 1972 after a long period of suffering in silence. T. E. ALLIBONE

Sources T. E. Allibone, *Memoirs FRS*, 19 (1973), 629–53 • *The Times* (26 Nov 1972), 16f • *The Times* (5 Dec 1972), 18g • M. Gowing and L. Arnold, *Independence and deterrence: Britain and atomic energy, 1945–1952*, 1 (1974) • d. cert.

Archives Atomic Energy Research Establishment, Harwell, MSS • CAC Cam., papers realating to Atomic Energy Research Establishment • CUL, papers | CAC Cam., corresp. with Sir Edward Bullard

Likenesses W. Stoneman, photograph, 1957, NPG • photograph, repro. in Allibone, *Memoirs FRS*, facing p. 629

Wealth at death £8097: probate, 26 Feb 1973, *CGPLA Eng. & Wales*

Schorlemmer, Carl (1834–1892), chemist, was born on 30 September 1834 at Darmstadt, the eldest child of Johannes Schorlemmer, a master carpenter, and his wife, whose maiden name was Roth. He went first to the elementary school, and then to the *Realschule*. At the urging of his mother (but much against his father's inclination), he attended, between the ages of sixteen and nineteen, the *Höhere Gewerbeschule* in Darmstadt, where he learned elementary science. His father then forced him to abandon his idea of following a learned profession requiring a university education; at Easter 1854, probably at the suggestion of his friend Wilhelm Dittmar (1833–1892), he became the pupil of an apothecary named Lindenborn at Gross-Umstadt. After two and a half years, during which he employed his leisure in acquiring an extensive practical knowledge of botany, he obtained his diploma as pharmaceutical assistant, and went in that capacity to an apothecary named Odenwald at Heidelberg. There he attended the lectures of the chemist Robert Wilhelm Bunsen, which led him to adopt chemistry as a profession. He gave up his business in May 1859 and entered the University of Giessen, where he studied in the laboratory of Heinrich Will and under Hermann Kopp, from whom he derived his interest in the history of chemistry. In the autumn of 1859 he replaced Dittmar as the private assistant of Henry Enfield Roscoe, professor of chemistry at Owens College, Manchester. Schorlemmer remained connected with the college until his death. In March 1861 he was appointed (again to replace Dittmar) as assistant in the college laboratory. In 1873 he was made lecturer, and in 1874 he became the first professor of organic chemistry in England. He was naturalized on 20 May 1879.

In 1861 Schorlemmer began his first original researches, analysing a sample of the light oils from cannel coal tar (*Journal of the Chemical Society*, 15, 1862, 419). This interest in organic chemistry determined the greater part of his life's work. Professor Edward Frankland's observations arising from his commitment to the chemical theory of radicals had led to the general belief that certain important hydrocarbons, now known as the normal paraffins, were capable of existing in two isomeric forms, as 'alcohol radicles', and as 'hydrides of the alcohol radicles'. By a long and patient examination of normal paraffins occurring in coal tar, in natural petroleums, and produced synthetically, Schorlemmer showed that these substances form a single and not a double series. Although Friedrich August Kekulé (1829–1896) and Archibald Scott Couper had (in 1858) independently suggested that in organic compounds each carbon atom is 'tetravalent', it was Schorlemmer's observations in 1862 which proved unequivocally that the four 'valencies' are equivalent. This hypothesis subsequently became one of the fundamental concepts of modern organic structural theory. During the early 1860s Schorlemmer investigated aniline dyes for the Manchester firm of Roberts, Dale & Co. In the course of his work on the paraffins, Schorlemmer prepared a considerable number of new substances. He also

Carl Schorlemmer (1834–1892), by Warwick Brookes

investigated the action of chlorine on the paraffins, described a valuable general method for the conversion of secondary alcohols into the corresponding primary compounds, and made several interesting speculations on the vexed question of the constitution of bleaching powder. With his student and later collaborator Richard Samuel Dale (a son of one of the founders of Roberts, Dale & Co.), he published a valuable series of observations on the phenol-derived aurin and on suberone. Their work on aurin contributed to the structural elucidation of aniline dyes, finally resolved by Emil and Otto Fischer in 1878.

As the years passed Schorlemmer's literary work gradually took him from the laboratory, and, by 1883, absorbed all his time. In 1867 he translated Roscoe's *Elementary Lessons on Chemistry* into German, and in 1870 Roscoe's *Spectrum Analysis*. In 1871, the year in which he became a fellow of the Royal Society, Schorlemmer published independently his *Lehrbuch der Kohlenstoffverbindungen*, of which a translation appeared in 1874 as *Manual of the Chemistry of the Carbon Compounds, or, Organic Chemistry*. In 1874 he also published a short work, *The Rise and Development of Organic Chemistry*, in which the chief historical events are attractively sketched. A French translation of *Rise and Development* … was published in 1885 and a second edition appeared in Germany in 1889; the English second edition was revised and published by Schorlemmer's pupil Professor Arthur Smithells in 1894. The last chapters of the work emphasized the significance of synthetic alizarin, the dye previously obtained from the root of the madder plant, and predicted the industrial synthesis of indigo (achieved in 1897). This book was also notable as it considered the development of science from the point of view of scientists themselves and in a wider social context. In 1877 appeared the first volume of a great *Systematic Treatise on Chemistry*, written jointly by Roscoe and Schorlemmer. This work, of which the successive volumes were published in English and German, was never completed. Schorlemmer gave courses on chemical philosophy in the 1880s. In 1884 he was elected to the committee of the Society of Chemistry and Industry; he was made honorary LLD of Glasgow in 1888. After a lingering illness, he died, unmarried, on 27 June 1892 at his home, Hyde Grove, Chorlton upon Medlock, Manchester.

Schorlemmer was a man of keen insight and he possessed remarkable erudition, patience, and enthusiasm for science. These qualities made him, in spite of imperfect English and a dislike of administrative detail, a respected teacher, and his influence, united to that of Roscoe, of whom he was a close friend, raised the Owens College school of chemistry to the first rank. Though genial and humorous, Schorlemmer was retiring by nature. However, he mixed freely with academic and industrial chemists in Manchester, many from Germany, who met at Owens College and on Saturdays at the Thatched House tavern in Market Street (where he first met Friedrich Engels). Schorlemmer's convivial personality earned him the nicknames Chlormayer and Jollymeyer. Through Engels he became acquainted with Karl Marx, whose views he shared (F. Engels, *Vorwärts Tageblatt*, 3 July 1892), and Samuel Moore, translator of *Das Kapital*. Schorlemmer made use of his scientific ideas in his political philosophy. In 1884 Schorlemmer and Engels visited the United States together.

At the time of his death Schorlemmer had carried the German manuscript of a new history of chemistry down to the end of the seventeenth century. This manuscript was never published. In all, he published forty-six papers independently, two with Harry Grimshaw, eleven with R. S. Dale, and one with Thomas Edward Thorpe. The memorial Schorlemmer Laboratory for research in organic chemistry at Owens College, which in 1881 became a segment of Victoria University, was founded by public subscription and was opened in May 1895. Schorlemmer's influence on communist ideologies (though he was never a practising communist) was acknowledged in the Soviet Union and much of eastern Europe until the end of the 1980s. In the former German Democratic Republic the *Technische Hochschule* of chemistry at Leuna-Merseberg was named after him.

P. J. Hartog, *rev.* Anthony S. Travis

Sources P. Scriba and A. Spiegel, *Berichte der Deutschen Chemischen Gesellschaft*, 25 (1892), 1107–10 · H. E. R. [H. E. Roscoe], *PRS*, 52 (1892–3), vii–ix · H.-J. Bittrich, C. Duschek, and G. Fuchs, *Carl Schorlemmer* (1984) · K. Heinig, *Carl Schorlemmer, Chemiker und Kommunist ersten Ranges* (1981) · O. T. Benfey and A. S. Travis, 'Carl Schorlemmer: the red chemist', *Chemistry and Industry* (15 June 1992), 441–4 · F. Engels, *Vorwärts Tageblatt* (3 July 1892)

Archives JRL · Technische Hochschule, Leuna-Merseberg | Deutsches Museum, Munich, Caro Nachlass, corresp. with Heinrich Caro

Likenesses group portrait, 1887, Technische Hochschule, Leuna-Merseberg • B. Frank, oils, 1983 • W. Brookes, photogravure, NPG [*see illus.*] • Walker & Boutall, photogravure (after photograph by W. Brookes), NPG • group portrait, Technische Hochschule, Leuna-Merseberg • portrait, Deutsche Akademie der Naturforscher Leopoldina; repro. in Scriba and Spiegel, *Berichte der Deutschen Chemischen Gesellschaft*, 1106 • portrait (after photograph), Hebrew University, Edelstein Center

Wealth at death £1954 12*s.* 11*d.*: probate, 18 Aug 1892, *CGPLA Eng. & Wales*

Schorne, John (*d.* in or before **1315**), reputed saint, should not be assumed to have come from the village in Kent of that name. Unlike other English 'saints' of his time, Schorne was neither political in his appeal nor of reported charisma in his life, of which next to nothing is known. There was a minor, uninfluential theme in his posthumous reputation that he had come by abnormally horny knees from long hours in prayer. Schorne's real fame in picture and text lay invariably in his exploit of trapping the devil in his boot, but what, if any, incident or allegory underlay this celebration remains completely obscure. He was evidently a magister by 1273 (of Oxford University, according to the fifteenth-century antiquarian William Worcester), when he was presented to the rectory of Steppingley, Bedfordshire, by Dunstable Priory. This he vacated by May 1282. Perhaps it was then, rather than in 1290 as often supposed, that the priory presented him to the rectory of North Marston, Buckinghamshire, where his cult was to develop, and which he held until his death. One of his name and style was acting as deputy for the absentee archdeacon of Buckingham (the brother of the future Pope Adrian V) in Chesham on 11 May 1280.

Since Schorne was described in an episcopal record in 1273 as a subdeacon and became an incumbent with cure of souls at that time, it is probably wrong to identify him with the namesake collated by Archbishop John Pecham to the rectory of Monks Risborough, Buckinghamshire, on 24 September 1289, a man who had been ordained subdeacon on the title of that benefice just twelve days earlier in Kent. (This man became a deacon on 17 December 1289 and a priest on 27 May 1290 and still held that rectory in 1294.) In what purports to be his will (BL, Lansdowne MS 762, fol. 2; dated 9 May 1313), which is singular in style, Schorne speaks of old age and renders to God what was God's (his soul), to the earth what was the earth's (his body, in a tomb he had designated before the high altar of North Marston), and his goods to be divided between intercessors and the poor, for the welfare of his soul. While some very local cult developed quickly, it spread only in the mid-fifteenth century, from which time come all the extant depictions of him (complete with diabolical captive), in groups from Norfolk (Cawston, Suffield, Gateley), Suffolk (St Gregory's, Sudbury, and possibly Bury St Edmunds Abbey), and Devon (Hennock, Alphington, and Wolborough); two texts of a lengthy invocation to him; and the prosecution (in 1448) of the then vicar of North Marston for counterfeiting his head from an exhumed skull. (Three bloody wounds were a regrettable excess of artistic licence.)

The perpetual spring Schorne had divined for his parish in time of drought came replete with gypsum, Epsom salts, and carbonic acid, and thereby lent considerable support to his posthumous reputation, principally as a healer of rheumatic and eye afflictions, but with an occasional talent in respect of dead oxen and the drowned. So substantial was his fame and profitability that on 7 April 1478 Richard Beauchamp, bishop of Salisbury and dean of Windsor, secured a licence from Pope Sixtus IV to relocate his bones. In fact, in 1480 the chapter of Windsor secured the appropriated rectory of North Marston itself, presumably to control and maximize the market. Schorne's lavish new shrine was the first part of St George's Chapel, Windsor, to be built, in the prime south-east corner. Even without his well, he proved the reliable crowd-puller and money-spinner he had been thought to be, although neither records nor general report substantiate the enormous revenues and popularity sometimes claimed for him. He continued also to thrive at North Marston, where the chapter took pains to market their investment with a modish development of the church. Although deplored by Lollards and reformers such as Erasmus (and later John Bale and John Foxe), pilgrimages to both shrines were used by the church as a reputable penance and remained popular, in southern England, down to the Reformation.

Despite the fame of the boot, Schorne's cult seems to have been a sensitive one, neither coarse nor exhibitionist. It may be compared with the gentle popularity in Exeter of Bishop Edmund Lacy. Significantly, both escaped the long pre-Reformation decline of saints generally. Schorne's image at North Marston was sent to London for destruction by the commissioner to Thomas Cromwell, Dr John Stokesley, in September 1537. In 1585 his chapel at Windsor was redeployed as a tomb for Edward Clinton, earl of Lincoln. Schorne had died by February 1315.

MARIOS COSTAMBEYS

Sources W. Simpson, 'On Master John Schorn', *Journal of the British Archaeological Association*, 23 (1867) • W. Simpson, 'Master John Schorn, his church and well', *Journal of the British Archaeological Association*, 23 (1867) • E. C. Rouse, 'John Schorne's well at North Marston', *Records of Buckinghamshire*, 15 (1951–2) • E. C. Rouse, 'John Schorne's well at North Marston', *Records of Buckinghamshire*, 18 (1970) • Emden, *Oxf.* • W. H. St J. Hope, *Windsor Castle* (1913)

Schotz, Benno (**1891–1984**), sculptor, was born on 28 August 1891 at Arensberg (Kuressaare), on the island of Oesel (Saare), Estonia, the youngest of the four sons and two daughters of Jacob Schotz (*d.* 1920), watchmaker, and his wife, Cherna Tischa Abramovitch (*d.* 1917). His parents were Jewish. At the age of two he moved to Pärnu on the mainland and attended the *Gymnasium* there until 1911. He then studied at the Grossherzogliche Technische Hochschule in Darmstadt, Germany (1911–12), and from 1912 to 1914 at the Royal Technical College, Glasgow, where he gained a diploma in engineering. He settled in Glasgow and in 1930 became a naturalized British citizen. From 1914 to 1923 he worked in the drawing-office of Messrs John Brown, shipbuilders, Clydebank, while attending evening classes in sculpture at the Glasgow School of Art from 1914 to 1917. Although without a formal art qualification, he took a studio in the city centre and began his long association with the Royal Glasgow Institute of the Fine Arts in 1917, exhibiting more than 100 works altogether and being elected honorary president in 1973. At the same time he formed an association with the Royal Scottish Academy, showing more than 200 works and becoming an associate in 1933 and an academician in 1937. He also contributed to shows at the Leicester Galleries, London, from 1921 and the Royal Academy from 1925, exhibiting at the latter twenty-nine works. In 1919 he was a founder member of, and in 1921 president of, the short-lived Society of Painters and Sculptors in Glasgow.

Encouraged by the architect John Keppie, Schotz became a full-time sculptor. His first solo Glasgow exhibition was at Reid's Gallery in 1926 and his first in London at Alex Reid and Lefevre Ltd (Lefevre Gallery) in 1930. He married Milly Stelmach (1902–1971), a dressmaker, on 4 January 1927; they had two children, Cherna Schotz (*b.* 1930) and Amiel Moshe Schotz (*b.* 1936). On the death of Archibald Dawson in 1938, Schotz took up the post of head of sculpture at the Glasgow School of Art, which he held until his retirement in 1961. An enthusiastic teacher, it surprised him years later to learn that students would tremble when he entered a class (*Bronze in my Blood*, 219). A lively host to many artists, writers, actors, and politicians in his homes at 207 West Campbell Street (from 1932) and 2 Kirklee Road (from 1950), he also assisted refugees from eastern Europe, including the painters Jankel Adler and Josef Herman. An ardent Zionist, he began to see the new state of Israel as his true home. His connections led to a solo exhibition in 1955 at the Bezalel National Art Museum, Jerusalem, and the Municipal Museum of Modern Art, Haifa.

Schotz's immense output runs to several hundred portraits and compositions. His bronzes were produced in editions of up to ten. The largest public collections of his work are in the Scottish National Portrait Gallery, Edinburgh, which has fourteen works, including *Lord Boyd Orr* (bronze, 1950), *James Bridie* (terracotta, 1953), and *Stanley Baxter* (plaster, 1983); and the Glasgow Art Gallery and Museum, which has twelve works, including *John Keppie* (bronze, 1922), *The Exile—Ura Collins* (mahogany, 1926), *Alexander Reid* (bronze, 1927), *Milly* (terracotta, 1953), and *Self-Portrait* (terracotta, 1953). A typically appealing portrait of a child is that of his daughter Cherna (bronze, 1932, formerly Dundee Art Galleries and Museums, now McManus Galleries, Dundee). He considered *Hugh McDiarmid* (1958, bronzes in Scottish National Portrait Gallery, Edinburgh, Aberdeen Art Gallery, and BBC Scotland) to be 'the high water mark of my portraiture' (*Bronze in my Blood*, 173). His group of Israeli leaders includes *David Ben-Gurion* (bronze, 1963, Israel Museum, Jerusalem) and *Golda Meir* (bronze, 1970, Israeli embassy, London). Notable large compositions are *Painting and Sculpture* (sandstone relief, 1928–9, Mercat building, Glasgow Cross, Glasgow; for John Keppie), *Moses the Sculptor* (sandstone, 1949, priv. coll.), and the altar cross (iron, welded bronze, and plastic metal, 1958) in St Paul's Roman Catholic Church, Glenrothes, Fife.

Schotz was one of the most important Scottish twentieth-century sculptors, spanning the period between Pittendrigh Macgillivray and Sir Eduardo Paolozzi. Principally a modeller renowned for his portraiture, he took his inspiration from Donatello and Rodin and was a spiritual brother of Jacob Epstein, though he resisted the title of 'the Scottish Epstein'. His vigorous, sometimes craggy heads betray the directness and speed with which they were modelled, a slight exaggeration of features and variation in expression adding movement and life. His carvings in wood and stone have a more stylized, even geometric character. He was generally a traditionalist but about 1960 moved towards abstraction, introducing modern techniques and materials such as welding, plastic metal, and cement. Tree trunks, stone, and shells became the inspiration for expressionistic figures or pure abstracts, developed through countless pen-and-ink drawings.

With prominent cheekbones, alert eyes, a receding brow, and a thick mop of swept-back hair, Schotz would emphasize his bohemian air by sporting a bow-tie. He expressed his opinions in a forthright manner in an accent which recalled his eastern European roots. On 16 April 1963 he was created her majesty the queen's sculptor-in-ordinary for Scotland, as successor to Sir William Reid Dick. A corresponding member of the National Sculpture Society of New York in 1956, he received the honorary degree of LLD from Strathclyde University, Glasgow, in 1969 and the freedom of the city of Glasgow in 1981. He died of old age at his home, 2 Kirklee Road, Glasgow, on 11 October 1984 and was buried on 19 October in Jerusalem. HUGH T. STEVENSON

Sources *Bronze in my blood: the memoirs of Benno Schotz* (1981) · *Benno Schotz: retrospective exhibition* [1970] [exhibition catalogue, Royal Scot. Acad., 13 Feb – 6 March 1971, and elsewhere] · H. Stevenson, ed., *Benno Schotz: portrait sculpture* (1978) [exhibition catalogue, Glasgow Art Gallery and Museum, Glasgow, 23 Aug – 25 Sept 1978] · *Studio sale of Benno Schotz* (1997) [sale catalogue, Christies, Glasgow, 24 Sept 1997] · private information (2004) · *Glasgow Herald* (12 Oct 1984)

Likenesses B. Schotz, self-portrait, terracotta sculpture, 1953, Glasgow Art Gallery and Museum

Wealth at death £59,937.46: confirmation, 4 Dec 1984, *CCI*

Schreiber [*née* Bertie; *other married name* Guest], **Lady Charlotte Elizabeth** (1812–1895), translator, businesswoman, and collector, eldest child of Albemarle Bertie, ninth earl of Lindsey (1744–1818), former army general and tory MP for Stamford, and his second wife, Charlotte Susanna Elizabeth, *née* Layard (1780–1858), was born at Uffington House, Lincolnshire, on 19 May 1812. Her father died when she was six, and in 1821 her mother married the Revd Peter Pegus, to whom Lady Charlotte took an instant—and lasting—dislike. She had two younger brothers and two half-sisters. Educated at home, she soon demonstrated an aptitude for study. Introspective and uninterested in the usual accomplishments thought fit for a young lady, she taught herself Arabic, Hebrew, and Persian, describing 'improvement in my studies' as 'that great object of my existence' (Lady Charlotte, journal, 25 Aug 1829). From the age of nine until she was seventy-nine she wrote in a journal for up to an hour daily.

Lady Charlotte Elizabeth Schreiber [Guest] (**1812–1895**), by William Walker, pubd 1852 (after Richard Buckner)

In the early 1830s this clever young aristocrat with an oval-shaped face and large, expressive eyes became acquainted with the young Benjamin Disraeli, but Lady Charlotte married, on 29 July 1833, aged twenty-one, the wealthy 48-year-old Welsh widower (Josiah) John *Guest (1785–1852). Merthyr's first MP (a whig), he ran the Dowlais Iron Company. Having disliked her stepfather and life at home, Lady Charlotte gladly moved to Dowlais House in the midst of the works. The firm, started by John Guest's grandfather, flourished, becoming the largest ironworks in the world, employing over 7000 workers. Lady Charlotte interested herself in the business, translating into English and publishing a French pamphlet on the use of hot blast. She accompanied her husband on business trips, discussed technical matters with leading scientists such as Charles Babbage, helped write company letters and keep the company's books, and had her own room in the company's London office. In a telling comment in 1836 she exclaimed:

> I am *iron* now—and my life is altered into one of action, not of sentiment—Ambition is not my idol—but my plaything … I have a restless active mind and can I wonder that (when I have health withal) I am tempted to apply its powers to the acquisition of any object I may have in view. (Lady Charlotte, journal, 12 April 1836)

Yet her journal is also a useful reminder that even such a highly privileged and intelligent woman as Lady Charlotte, married to a man who was, in comparison to his fellow ironmasters, both understanding and cultured, nevertheless was constrained by, and felt the constraints of, her gender. She might canvass and pen anonymous political squibs but she could not vote in elections. Fellow businessmen did not always want to take her seriously, and for much of her marriage, especially in the early years, she was pregnant. In the journal she constantly debated with herself about what a woman might do that would both challenge her intellect and talents and yet not rock the boat too much, since she was also determined to be a dutiful wife and mother.

The Guests had ten children in thirteen years, five boys and five girls. At the same time Lady Charlotte furthered her interest in languages by studying Middle Welsh, another unusual step for an ironmaster's wife. Working with Welsh clerics, and drawing upon the research prompted by the Romantic revival and translations started by Welshmen such as William Owen Pughe, she undertook the mammoth task of transcribing and translating twelve Welsh tales into English. Initially published in parts—the first, an Arthurian romance, 'The Lady of the Fountain', appearing in 1838—the enterprise culminated in the magnificent three-volume production *The Mabinogion* (1849). Eleven of the tales were from the medieval *Llyfr coch o Hergest* (Red Book of Hergest), and consisted of the four branches of the Mabinogi, three Arthurian romances (Lady Charlotte has been credited as the first to recognize their European analogues), and four independent tales. She also included the sixteenth-century tale 'Taliesin', illustrations, and her own learned notes. In 1877 an abbreviated one-volume edition appeared. Lady Charlotte made available to the English-speaking world what has since become recognized as a Welsh and Celtic classic, translated into many languages; it was 1929 before an attempt was made to supersede her translation. Tennyson praised her English as the finest he knew, and based his *Idylls of the King* on one of the tales.

Lady Charlotte also involved herself in social welfare. Her husband had instigated a progressive educational system for Dowlais workers, which she now developed with fully trained teachers and a ladder of education for both sexes reaching from infancy into adulthood. In the mid-1850s Sir Charles Barry designed the Dowlais Central Schools—the buildings costing £20,000. Recreational schemes for the workforce were enlivened by the occasional appearance of Henry Layard, discoverer of Nineveh, and Lady Charlotte's cousin. He helped sharpen her social conscience. He married Enid, one of her daughters, and became ambassador at Constantinople where Lady Charlotte visited him. She helped to promote in London the sale of embroidery by Turkish refugees. Barry had already remodelled Canford Manor, the Dorset estate purchased by the Guests in 1846. Lady Charlotte was only too aware of the taint of marrying into trade and of the social damage posed by her mother's unfortunate second marriage. She sought therefore to secure for the future the Guest children's acceptance in 'Society'. In 1838 her husband was made a baronet, but this she considered but a 'paltry distinction' (Lady Charlotte, journal, 3 July 1838). She disparaged the London social round yet carefully and relentlessly pursued it like a business contract: 'Even pleasure is but a business—for balls and parties are only pleasure to me as contributing to one of my objects—Society' (ibid., 12 April 1836).

In 1839 Lady Charlotte wrote:

> whatever I undertake I must reach an eminence in. I cannot endure anything in a second grade. I am happy to see we are at the head of the iron trade. Otherwise I could not take pride in my house in the City and my Works at Dowlais, and glory (playfully) in being (in some sort) a tradeswoman. (Lady Charlotte, journal, 27 April 1839)

Her choice of personal pronouns, even tempered by the qualifications in parentheses, was significant. Her influence at the works increased as her husband's health declined, and late in 1852 Sir John Guest died. As sole active trustee Lady Charlotte now ran the gigantic works for a few years. She felt equal to the task: 'It is a curious position! a woman here quite by myself among all these wild fiery spirits. But thank God I am well—and quite up to all my work and all the exertion that the situation requires' (ibid., 24 July 1853). Yet during this period the iron trade experienced hard times, and in the summer of 1853 there was a strike. In the negotiations leading up to this strike the tensions between her class and gender were really put to the test. The newly widowed Lady Charlotte now had to enter into business discussions with the oligarchy of ironmasters used to seeing women as dinner-party guests but not as colleagues and equals. She was shocked by their attempts to coerce the workers into submission and spoke out against this. Yet as 'a woman and in argument *alone* against the opposition of *five* experienced men of business' (ibid., 1 July 1853) she reluctantly felt she had to concede to their demands. Fearing lest they interpret her objections as 'a woman's weakness' (ibid., 1 July 1853) she proceeded to speak out more resolutely. In the process she denied the masters the opportunity to portray her as a feeble, indecisive woman. Yet she also abandoned her conciliatory attitude towards her workforce. This was sacrificed to a new obduracy. She resolved to resist the Dowlais men should they even threaten to strike (which they did) and then tellingly declared 'I will be their master' (ibid., 11 July 1853).

In less than two years Lady Charlotte's life underwent a further dramatic change. On 10 April 1855 she remarried, thus terminating her position at the ironworks. Charles Schreiber (1826–1884) of Melton, Suffolk, was fourteen years her junior, and employed as a tutor to prepare the Guests' eldest son for Cambridge University. A classics scholar who had won fifteen prizes at Cambridge, he became tory MP for Cheltenham in the mid-1860s and was elected for Poole in 1880. Lady Charlotte, however, retained her whig sympathies.

The Schreibers had no children and spent much of their married life on the continent as passionate, apparently indefatigable, collectors and connoisseurs of china, scouring Europe for bargains—which they usually found. Their collection of eighteenth-century English china, reckoned to be among the finest in the world, is housed at the Victoria and Albert Museum, London, some of it displayed in the Schreiber Room. Lady Charlotte wrote a comprehensive catalogue to accompany the 1800 or so pieces she bequeathed in memory of her second husband, who died in Lisbon in 1884. Her European china was either sold at auction or given to her large family. Her son Montague Guest published her ceramics journal in 1911.

The British Museum acquired Lady Charlotte's eighteenth-century fans, playing cards, and board games. The catalogue for her playing cards alone itemizes 1066 packs, about a third of them German. Her fans, fan leaves, and cards were reproduced and described in five folio volumes, which she worked on from the late 1880s. The final volume of *Playing Cards of Various Ages and Countries* was published posthumously, edited by Sir Augustus Wollaston Franks of the British Museum, who had worked closely with her. In December 1891 Lady Charlotte became the first woman to receive the freedom of the Worshipful Company of Fanmakers. The philanthropist Baroness Coutts was then the only other freewoman of a City of London guild.

Lady Charlotte had a cab shelter built at Langham Place, close to her London home. She bombarded cabmen with long red woollen comforters which she knitted daily, one of the few jobs possible with fast diminishing eyesight. She had always loathed idleness and worked hard at whatever currently occupied her. She lived her last years with her eldest son, Ivor, and his wife, Lady Cornelia Spencer Churchill, daughter of the seventh duke of Marlborough. He had become Baron Wimborne in 1880, thus recouping the social status surrendered when Lady Charlotte married into trade. The family's status was sealed by the marriages of her children to some of the country's most eminent families: her second son married a daughter of the marquess of Westminster, while four of her daughters married into the families of peers. A woman of remarkable talent and determination, whose long life demonstrated her versatility, vitality, and powers of perseverance, Lady Charlotte, after suffering from congestion of the lungs, died, aged eighty-three, on 15 January 1895, at Canford Manor. She was buried on 24 January at Canford church.

ANGELA V. JOHN

Sources journals of Lady Charlotte, NL Wales [and priv. coll.] • *Lady Charlotte Guest: extracts from her journal, 1833–1852*, ed. earl of Bessborough (1950) • *Lady Charlotte Schreiber: extracts from her journal, 1853–1891*, ed. earl of Bessborough [V. B. Ponsonby] (1952) • R. Guest and A. V. John, *Lady Charlotte: a biography of the nineteenth century* (1989) • R. Bromwich, 'The *Mabinogion* and Lady Charlotte Guest', *Transactions of the Honourable Society of Cymmrodorion* (1986), 127–41 • D. J. Jones, 'Lady Charlotte Guest: Victorian businesswoman', *History Today*, 23 (1973), 38–45 • L. W. Evans, 'Sir John and Lady Charlotte Guest's educational scheme at Dowlais in the mid-nineteenth century', *National Library of Wales Journal*, 9 (1955–6), 265–86 • O. Van Oss, 'Lady Charlotte Schreiber', *Transactions of the English Ceramic Circle*, 4/1 (1957), 15–28 • E. Jones, *A history of GKN*, 1: *Innovation and enterprise, 1759–1918* (1987) • A. V. John, 'Beyond paternalism: the ironmaster's wife in the industrial community', *Our mother's land: chapters in Welsh women's history, 1830–1939*, ed. A. V. John (1991), 43–68 • A. Eatwell, 'Private pleasure, public beneficence: Lady Charlotte Schreiber and ceramic collecting', *Women in the Victorian art world*, ed. C. C. Orr (1995), 124–45 • A. J. Miller, *Stories from Dorset history* (1987) • *Cardiff Times* (19 Jan 1895) • *Poole and Bournemouth Herald Times* (17 Jan 1895), 5 • *The Times* (16 Jan 1895), 6 •

Merthyr Express (19 Jan 1895) · private information (2004) · *CGPLA Eng. & Wales* (1895)

Archives BM · NL Wales, journals · V&A | BL, Layard MSS · Bodl. Oxf., corresp. with Sir Thomas Phillipps · Glamorgan RO, Cardiff, Dowlais estate and ironworks corresp. · Northants. RO, Wickham MSS

Likenesses J. Edwards, wood and plaster bust, 1841, Cyfarthfa Castle Museum, Merthyr Tudful, Wales · Hensel, drawing, 1842, priv. coll. · A. E. Chalon, oils, exh. RA 1845, priv. coll. · P. Williams, oils, exh. RA 1845, possibly priv. coll. · R. Buckner, oils, exh. RA 1848, priv. coll. · W. Walker, mezzotint, pubd 1852 (after R. Buckner), BM, Glamorgan RO, Cardiff [*see illus.*] · G. F. Watts, portrait, 1854, priv. coll. · V. Palmeroli, oils, 1871, priv. coll. · sketch, 1891, repro. in *Daily Graphic* (18 Dec 1891) · mosaic (after G. F. Watts, 1854), V&A · photograph, Glamorgan RO, Cardiff · photograph (as elderly widow), repro. in Earl of Bessborough, ed., *Lady Charlotte Schreiber: extracts from her journal, 1853–1891*, 2 (1952) · photographs, NL Wales

Wealth at death £24,680 16*s.* 2*d.*: probate, 8 March 1895, *CGPLA Eng. & Wales*

Schreiner, Olive Emilie Albertina (1855–1920), author and social theorist, was born on 24 March 1855 at Wittebergen Wesleyan mission station, on the border of Basutoland, Cape Colony, the ninth of the twelve children of Rebecca Lyndall (1818–1903) of London and her husband, Gottlob Schreiner (1814–1876), a German-born missionary sent to South Africa in 1837 by the London Missionary Society. Only six of Olive Schreiner's brothers and sisters survived childhood. The loss of her one younger sister, Ellie, when Schreiner was nine, shaped her rebellious temperament and unconventional outlook. Schreiner's own survival did not come easily: at the age of nine months she almost died of lung inflammation. For much of her adult life bouts of asthma and angina spasms afflicted her. When she was eleven her parents' poverty, worsened by her father's expulsion from his missionary post for private trading to supplement his meagre salary, impelled her departure from home with her younger brother, William (Will) *Schreiner (1857–1919), to live with two older siblings in Cradock. Thereafter, until she found work as governess for Boer families, she resided with relatives and family friends.

Schreiner received no formal education. Her mother's excellent tutoring, coupled with the child's quick probing mind, sparked her wide and voracious reading. As an adolescent she wrote fiction and dreamed of becoming a physician. Medical ambition prompted her to visit England in 1881, but her unsystematic education and unstable health blocked her pursuit of this career. Schreiner turned to professional prose, hoping to bring her scientific and healing interests into her fiction.

The Story of an African Farm (2 vols., 1883), Schreiner's second novel (published by Chapman and Hall initially under the pseudonym Ralph Iron), secured her reputation as an evocative storyteller, a daring and perceptive freethinker, and feminist. It is easily the best-known South African work of fiction of the nineteenth and early twentieth century. Like her intellectually and aesthetically less sophisticated first novel, *Undine* (published posthumously in 1928), *The Story of an African Farm* wrestles with her most painful childhood and adolescent experiences. Focused on two primary figures, the novel mingles linear sequences, flashbacks, extended allegories, authorial moralizing, comic and introspective passages, and haunting descriptions of the South African Karoo—a mix critics of Schreiner's time and after deplored (though the novel was always popular with general readers). Judgements were reversed, however, with changes in late twentieth-century literary criticism. Through the poetic spirit of Waldo the novel depicts the terrifying stages of a young person's loss of Christian faith and his search for spiritual and moral direction within a world of natural and human cruelty inseparable from goodness and beauty. Schreiner's second protagonist, the orphan Lyndall, permits the reader to follow the psychological development of a young woman's struggle for self-determination. In the face of societal ridicule and expulsion, male privilege and domination, sexual double standard, sparse work options, and a persistent undertow of Victorian gender norms in her psyche, Lyndall pursues a utopian love that fuses erotic, emotional, and intellectual comradeship. Lyndall's tragic death and Waldo's more ambiguous fate proclaim the futility of a rebel's quest for self-realization within an arbitrary cosmos and within a colonial society riddled with race, class, and gender inequality.

While in England (1881–9) this short, energetic celebrity, with keenly observant and sensitive, large, dark eyes, formed close ties with pioneering authors and reformers, notably Havelock *Ellis, Edward Carpenter, Karl Pearson, and Eleanor Marx. From 1885–6 Schreiner became an outspoken member of the Men and Women's Club, an association committed to frank discussion of sexuality and gender relations. Throughout the 1880s she met numerous of her prominent admirers, including William Gladstone. After her private midday lunch with the former and future prime minister, she recounted to friends their animated and probing exchange of views. She deemed Gladstone a child of genius, though in later years, according to her husband, she would describe his sly, wary, flashing eyes as evocative of a Bengal tiger.

Engaged during her England years in a variety of literary and non-fiction projects, Schreiner took particular pride in her transcendental, feminist, and socialist allegories she collected as *Dreams* (1890). One of these allegories, 'Three dreams in a desert', offered so haunting a drama of present sacrifice in the gain of future ideal that it inspired British suffragettes imprisoned for acts of civil disobedience two decades later. She also published, as Ralph Iron, *Dream Life and Real Life* (1893). Painfully shy except in intimate relationships (and then remarkably open, expressive, and witty), Schreiner entered into various problematic romances and demanding friendships that vied with her time to write and exacerbated her allergies, leading ultimately to a nervous breakdown. In 1889, longing for her South African Karoo landscape and missing her family there, she returned to her homeland.

Focused in the 1890s on her country's social and political problems, Schreiner wrote a series of articles for diverse journals—articles posthumously gathered as *Thoughts on South Africa* (1923). Her parable, *Trooper Peter*

Halket of Mashonaland (1897), was written in 1895–6 as a powerful indictment of Cecil Rhodes. Halket, an English soldier in Cecil Rhodes's Chartered Company, is engaged in efforts to suppress the Mashonaland rebellion. Through a dream dialogue between Halket and a disguised Jesus, the novella charts Halket's gradual conversion from a supporter of British imperialist, racist, and misogynist policies in South Africa to a resolute opponent. Halket's life climaxes when, upon helping one of his company's African prisoners to escape, he is shot to death.

Schreiner's literary fame and her brother Will's rising political prominence (in 1898 he became prime minister of the Cape Colony) facilitated bonds with South Africa's distinguished British and Boer political figures and their families. By the late 1890s Schreiner's political treatises, polemical fiction, public addresses, and personal advocacy made her South Africa's foremost critic of British imperialism, ethnocentrism, and racism. She prophesied the disastrous military and political outcome of the Second South African War (1899–1902) and the South African Union's racist legislation and constitution.

With her politics opposed by most of her family and friends, and as a member of a small, reviled, inter-racial band of South African anti-imperialists, Schreiner drew the support of Samuel Cron Cronwright, whom she married on 24 February 1894. A successful cattle breeder, he shared many of his wife's convictions and, as she asked, took Cronwright-Schreiner as his surname, while she continued to use her maiden name. Although Schreiner's marriage initially fulfilled her ideal of marital love as fusing intellectual and political comradeship with emotional and erotic intimacy, difficulties arose. Her asthma necessitated that her husband sell his thriving farm at Krantz Plaats to enable them to move to Kimberley, the first move of a series and wrenching for him. Cronwright-Schreiner's pursuit of a legal career complicated their residence issues, as did his 1902 election to parliament. The inexplicable death in 1895 of their apparently healthy daughter shortly after her birth, and subsequent miscarriages, further strained their marriage. Before the Second South African War, Schreiner sought asthma relief in Hanover, a Boer village 5000 feet above sea level. Cronwright-Schreiner planned to join her, but martial law required he first secure medical exception. British soldiers looted their abandoned Johannesburg home, destroying most of Schreiner's papers.

After the peace of Vereeniging (1902) concluded the war Schreiner pressed on with her bold campaign for a democratic and socially just nation. (In 1903, to honour her efforts, the esteemed black leader of South African nationalism, Sol Plaatje, named his newborn daughter Olive.) The most mature statement of her political beliefs appeared in *Closer Union* (1909), her eloquent case for a federal constitution based upon sexual and racial equality. Two years later she published her brilliant feminist classic *Woman and Labour*. Although much of this treatise, by emphasizing the social construction of gender identity and roles, rows against the current of prevalent feminist thinking of her time, her chapter 'Woman and war' offers both biological and cultural reasons for most women's predisposition toward non-violence. Schreiner ends *Woman and Labour* with an apocalyptic vision of loving and equal comradeship between the liberated 'new man' and 'new woman' in all spheres of their lives.

Schreiner's most ambitious novel, *From Man to Man* (begun in the 1880s, left unfinished, and published posthumously in 1926), presented in narrative and expository form the social, political, and literary philosophy of a writer at the forefront of her generation's progressive thinkers. *From Man to Man* depicts the South African childhood and adult experience of two sisters. The elder, Rebekah, finds her scientific and intellectual passions stymied in her marriage to a dishonest, philandering husband whose views on white and male superiority echo those of most white male South Africans. After struggling in vain to preserve her marriage, she leaves him and their Cape Town home to bring up their three sons and adopted mixed-race daughter (offspring of her husband's liaison with an African servant) in a home on a country vineyard she had bought years earlier. Late in the uncompleted novel, without even searching for a male comrade who would embody her ideal of the 'new man', Rebekah meets an approximation of her ideal in the person of the married Mr Drummond. The optimism expressed in Rebekah's evolution contrasts with the life of her beloved younger sister, Baby Bertie. Seduced by her tutor, Bertie is the victim of the Victorian sexual double standard. Discarded by her fiancé and tormented by her community's gossip and ostracism, she seeks protection from a stereotyped wealthy Jewish merchant and moneylender. Rabidly in love with Bertie, he whisks her off to London where he suffocates her with food, jewellery, clothing, and jealousy. Yet when he mistakenly concludes she has seduced his young cousin, he, too, casts her out. The contrasting tales of these two sisters afford Schreiner more than an opportunity to expose the toll of sexual injustice on women's lives. At every moment that her daily busyness permits reflection, Rebekah launches into pioneering enquiry into the dynamics of historical change and the nature of gender, class, and race, including a witty and withering critique of social Darwinism. Her fertile mind expresses itself through dreams, letters, and scattered introspective musings on the nature of art and literature, violence and non-violence, intimacy and honesty. She even invents science fiction stories for her children that mock the smug convictions of her contemporaries. The unfinished *From Man to Man* never enjoyed the large readership of *The Story of an African Farm*.

Schreiner's health problems spurred her journey in 1913 to Europe for treatment, an exile prolonged by the First World War. Re-establishing London residence, she spent the war years promoting women's suffrage and pacifism. In June 1920 Cronwright-Schreiner sailed to England to join her. Their reunion was brief. Sensing that death was imminent and wishing to die in her homeland she returned to South Africa on 13 August 1920. Heart failure claimed her life in the night of 10–11 December 1920 at her home, Oak Hill, Wynberg. Early in her marriage, Schreiner and her husband had chosen as their family burial site Buffelskop, Cradock, a stony summit overlooking a boundless expanse and diverse Karoo vegetation. There on 13 August 1921 she was reinterred. Schreiner's will embodied her lifelong egalitarian values: it set up at the South African College, Cape Town (the University of Cape Town's precursor), a medical scholarship for women irrespective of their race, colour, or religion, with preference given to the poor. JOYCE AVRECH BERKMAN

Sources J. A. Berkman, *The healing imagination of Olive Schreiner: beyond South African colonialism* (1989) • R. First and A. Scott, *Olive Schreiner* (1980) [with bibliography] • S. C. Cronwright-Schreiner, *The life of Olive Schreiner* (1924) • *Olive Schreiner letters, 1871–1899*, ed. R. Rive (1988), vol. 1 of *Olive Schreiner letters* • Y. C. Draznin, ed., *'My other self': the letters of Olive Schreiner and Havelock Ellis, 1884–1920* (1992) • M. V. W. Smith and D. Maclennan, eds., *Olive Schreiner and after* (1983) • C. Clayton, ed., *Olive Schreiner* (1983) • I. Vivar, ed., *The flawed diamond* (1989) • G. Monsman, *Olive Schreiner's fiction: landscape and power* (1991)

Archives Albany Museum, Grahamstown, South Africa • BL, papers, Add. MSS 70571–70572 • LUL, corresp. • National English Literary Museum, Grahamstown, South Africa • National Library of South Africa, Cape Town • Ransom HRC, papers • Rhodes University, Grahamstown, Cory Library for Historical Research • Rhodes University, Grahamstown, Thomas Pringle Collection for English in Africa • University of Cape Town, Cape Town, corresp. and papers • University of the Witwatersrand, Johannesburg, Cullen Library | BL, Add. MSS 70524–70589 • Bodl. RH, Rhodes MSS • Borth. Inst., file of papers on South Africa • Knebworth House, Hertfordshire, Constance Lytton MSS • National Library of South Africa, Cape Town, Innes MSS; Merriman MSS • Sheff. Arch., letters to Edward Carpenter • UCL, corresp. mainly with Karl Pearson; papers • University of the Witwatersrand, Johannesburg, Cullen Library, Findlay MSS • Women's Library, London, letters to Alys Russell

Likenesses photographs, National English Literary Museum, Grahamstown, South Africa • photographs, South African Library, Cape Town, South Africa • photographs, University of the Witwatersrand Library, Johannesburg, South Africa • photographs, Sheffield City Libraries • photographs, Albany Museum, Grahamstown, South Africa

Schreiner, William Philip (1857–1919), politician in Cape Colony, was born in the Wittebergen reserve, northern Cape Colony, on 30 August 1857. He was the sixth son in the family of twelve of Gottlob Schreiner (1814–1876), a German artisan missionary of Fellbach in Württemberg, and his English wife, Rebecca Lyndall (1818–1903), daughter of the Revd Samuel Lyndall of Moorfields, London. The author Olive Emilie Albertina *Schreiner (1855–1920) was an older sister. After a promising early education in the eastern Cape and at the South African College, Schreiner consistently took the top place in degrees in literature and science in the University of the Cape of Good Hope (for which he received the overseas Porter scholarship), in the London LLB at the Inner Temple, and, while at Downing College, Cambridge, in the Cambridge law tripos. In 1882 he was admitted to the English and the Cape bars. His characteristically unremitting toil made his law practice in Cape Town a solid success. On 3 January 1884 he married Frances Hester Reitz, whose brother F. W. Reitz successively became president of the Orange Free State and state secretary of the Transvaal republic. The Schreiners had two sons and two daughters. Schreiner's wife outlived him.

William Philip Schreiner (1857–1919), by James Russell & Sons

His profession brought Schreiner into public life. He became Cape parliamentary draftsman in 1885, took silk in 1892, and between 1889 and 1893 assisted the imperial high commissioner and the Cape in negotiations with Transvaal on the future of Swaziland, for which work he was created CMG (1891). These negotiations and retainer work for De Beers also brought Schreiner to the notice of Cecil Rhodes, the Cape premier, who made him the colonial attorney-general in 1893. His growing rapport with Rhodes was confirmed by his election, alongside his mentor, for Barkly West in 1894. During the closure of the Vaal River drifts in 1895 he helped to commit the Cape to possible war by drafting the ultimatum to the Transvaal republic; but he was appalled by the Jameson raid later that year and soon afterwards broke finally with Rhodes. Although he opposed ending the British South Africa Company's charter, he chaired the Cape select committee which condemned Rhodes's conduct. In 1897 he gave evidence at the raid inquiry in London.

With Cape politics polarizing after the raid, Schreiner and other moderates like J. X. Merriman, who were concerned to obstruct Rhodes, moved into cautious association with Afrikaner Bond MPs. The latter were prepared to support a Schreiner ministry from 14 October 1898, after the close general election earlier that year. However, this awkwardly aligned colonial cabinet had difficulty in mitigating the growing hostility between the British imperial government and Transvaal.

Schreiner's attempts with other concerned South Africans to bring President Kruger and Sir Alfred Milner to compromise—for example, at the conference in Bloemfontein in May 1899—were largely vitiated by Milner's carefully concealed campaign to 'work up to a crisis' (Headlam, 1.222). With his eye mainly on Rhodes, Schreiner was perhaps insufficiently assertive towards Milner, who kept his Cape premier out of the Bloemfontein conference and out of much of the diplomacy leading up to the Second South African War in October 1899.

As a loyal subject of the queen, Schreiner did all he could to limit the rising in the northern Cape districts in late 1899, but he had difficulty persuading Milner that the Cape's own forces should as far as possible remain within the colony to protect it. Meanwhile Chamberlain insisted, and Schreiner reluctantly accepted, that Cape rebels should be punished with a minimum penalty of five-year disfranchisement. Yet this encountered Afrikaner Bond resistance which brought about the downfall of his so-called 'South African party' ministry on 17 June 1900.

In defence of his independent position Schreiner subsequently resigned his Malmesbury seat and, returning to law, remained out of parliament until 1908. Offered a Cape place in the national convention by Merriman, Schreiner unselfishly honoured his prior undertaking to defend the putative Zulu king, Dinuzulu, against what he viewed as racially motivated Natal colonial charges arising out of the Bambatha uprising. He fought the long, unremunerative case to vindicate his conversion over the years to a strongly held liberalism and succeeded in clearing Dinuzulu of most charges.

Standing forth by 1909 as the determined champion of Cape non-racialism, Schreiner led a deputation including the African and 'coloured' politicians W. Rubusana, J. T. Jabavu, and A. Abdurahman to Westminster to protest at the limitation and vulnerability of the Cape's non-racial franchise in the draft South Africa Constitution Act of Union. But they failed to secure modifications which would have enabled non-whites to stand for parliament or even to make the two-thirds altering majority apply to MPs from the Cape especially. The protectorates were, however, safeguarded from an offhand transfer to the Union.

After union, Schreiner accepted the invitation of the new prime minister, General Botha, to enter the senate to speak for black African interests. He joined M. K. Gandhi in criticizing the Immigration Act of 1911 and, later, was highly censorious of the discriminatory Natives' Land Act of 1913.

Overtaken by the First World War while overseas in mid-1914, Schreiner would enjoy a swan-song as union high commissioner in London. Here he exhausted himself physically caring for South African interests and troops until his death in harness at Trefaldwyn, Llandrindod Wells, Radnorshire, Wales, on the day peace was signed, on 28 June 1919. He was cremated at Golders Green crematorium and afterwards buried near his parents at Woltemade cemetery, Cape Town. As scholar, sportsman, humanitarian, lawyer and, above all, colonial statesman, Schreiner stood for all that was finest in the old Cape, especially its liberal tradition. JOHN BENYON

Sources E. A. Walker, *W. P. Schreiner: a South African* (1937) • S. C. Cronwright-Schreiner, *The life of Olive Schreiner* (1924) • *Selections from the correspondence of J. X. Merriman*, ed. P. Lewsen, vols. 2–4 (1963–9) • J. Rose-Innes, *James Rose Innes, chief justice of South Africa, 1914–27: autobiography*, ed. B. A. Tindall (Cape Town, 1949) • E. A. Walker, *Lord de Villiers and his times: South Africa, 1842–1914* (1925) • R. First and A. Scott, *Olive Schreiner* (1980) • T. R. H. Davenport, *The Afrikaner Bond* (1966) • J. H. Hofmeyr and F. W. Reitz, *The life of Jan Hendrik Hofmeyr (Onze Jan)* (1913) • *The Milner papers*, ed. C. Headlam, 2 vols. (1931–3) [esp. vol. 1] • G. H. L. Le May, *British supremacy in South Africa, 1899–1907* (1965) • *The reminiscences of Sir Walter Stanford*, ed. J. W. MacQuarrie, 2 vols. (1958–62) • W. Butler, *Sir William Butler: an autobiography*, ed. [E. Butler] (1911) • B. Williams, *Cecil Rhodes* (1921) • J. G. Lockhart and C. M. Woodhouse, *Cecil Rhodes: the colossus of southern Africa* (New York, 1963) • R. I. Rotberg, *The founder: Cecil Rhodes and the pursuit of power* (1988) • V. Buchanan-Gould, *Not without honour: the life and writings of Olive Schreiner* (1948)

Archives National Library of South Africa, Cape Town | BL, letters to Sir Charles Dilke, Add. MS 43921 • BL, corresp. with Lord Gladstone, Add. MSS 46077–46083 • National Library of South Africa, Cape Town, J. X. Merriman MSS • National Library of South Africa, Cape Town, Olive Schreiner MSS

Likenesses two photographs, *c.*1898–after 1901, repro. in Walker, *W. P. Schreiner* • J. Russell & Sons, photograph, NPG [*see illus.*] • bust, Houses of Parliament, Cape Town • group photographs, repro. in Walker, *W. P. Schreiner* • group photographs (with family), repro. in Buchanan-Gould, *Not without honour* • photographs, repro. in *The prominent men of the Cape Colony, South Africa* (Portland, ME, 1902) • photographs, repro. in *Men of the times: old colonists of the Cape Colony and Orange Free State* (Johannesburg, 1906) • portrait, repro. in F. H. Gale, *Who's who in the Union parliament* (1911) • sketch, repro. in R. S. S. Baden-Powell, *ILN* (15 Feb 1890)

Wealth at death £3588 15*s.* 2*d.*: probate, 15 Aug 1919, *CGPLA Eng. & Wales*

Schröder, (Rudolph) Bruno, Baron Schröder in the Prussian nobility [*known as* Baron Bruno] **(1867–1940)**, merchant banker, was born on 14 March 1867 in Hamburg, Germany, the eighth of the nine children of Johann Rudolph Schröder (1821–1887), merchant and merchant banker, and his wife, Clara Louise, a daughter of John Henry Schröder (1784–1883), who in 1818 founded the London merchant bank J. Henry Schroder & Co. Bruno was educated in Hamburg and performed his military service in the second Mecklenburg dragoons, achieving the rank of captain.

Apprenticeship In 1888, aged twenty-one, Schröder began his training with the family firm, Schröder Gebrüder. Established in 1846 by his father and uncle, it was a Hamburg merchant and merchant-banking firm, specializing in trade in sugar, coffee, and saltpetre. For three years he worked as an unpaid 'volunteer' at J. Henry Schroder & Co., London, by then one of the City's leading merchant banks and the most important of the international nexus of Schröder family firms. In 1891–2 he toured the USA and Central America, familiarizing himself with clients and conditions. After his return to Hamburg in July 1892 he joined Schröder Gebrüder, but a few months later 'the

(Rudolph) Bruno Schröder, Baron Schröder in the Prussian nobility (1867–1940), by Philip A. de Laszlo

exceptional chance of a lifetime', as a nephew put it, came his way (*DBB*, 71). His childless uncle, Baron Sir John Henry William *Schröder (1825–1910), the senior partner of J. Henry Schroder & Co., invited him to join the London firm with a view to succeeding him as senior partner.

Schröder's move revitalized the bonds between the Schroder firms and families in Hamburg and London. For half a century thereafter, years when the ties to Germany of other Anglo-German houses loosened and the younger generation was distracted from business by politics and society, Schroders continued to be strongly committed to German clients. When the senior partner was not at his desk, inspired by his uncle's example he devoted himself to family and private pastimes, orchid cultivation, and art collection, notably German Renaissance silver. He regarded himself as a trustee charged on behalf of his ancestors and family with a duty to continue the firm and its traditions and to enhance its standing. He was a devout Lutheran and a staunch supporter of London's Lutheran churches and their charitable works, especially the German Hospital at Dalston. For these works and for his charitable activities in his native Hamburg, he was made a Prussian baron (*Freiherr*) in July 1904, and henceforth was known as Baron Bruno.

Bruno Schröder started at J. Henry Schroder & Co. on 1 January 1893. Two years later, aged twenty-seven, he joined his uncle and Henry Tiarks in the partnership. Both these partners were in their sixties and executive management of the firm was soon assumed by Bruno Schröder. He was joined in the partnership in 1902 by Frank Tiarks (1874–1952), the son of Henry Tiarks, thereby continuing the business association of their families for a second generation. Bruno Schröder and Frank Tiarks, though in many ways temperamentally opposites, made a formidable team. So thoroughly had the younger generation taken control of the firm that the retirement of Henry Tiarks in 1905 and Baron Sir John Henry William Schröder in 1909 made almost no difference to the day-to-day conduct of business.

Merchant banker *par excellence* The 1890s and 1900s were prosperous times for City firms, especially Schroders. The volume of the firm's core international trade finance business more than doubled in these decades, and balance sheet acceptances outstanding at year end rose from £5 million in 1893 to £11 million in 1913, the second largest level of activity in the City. Underlying the expansion was the rapid growth of German international trade, though Schroders' success in winning business owed much to Bruno Schröder's outstanding capabilities as a commercial banker. His strengths were his ability to make sound judgements regarding people and propositions, and his mastery of the technicalities of the bill of exchange. Above all he had an expert knowledge of the trades that Schroders financed, and he kept a careful eye on the business of clients. The tale is told of his meeting with Caesar Czarnikow, the sugar magnate, when he insisted that Czarnikow should accept a larger credit line than he had asked for and was proved justified by developments in the sugar market. Such was his standing as a money market expert that in the 1920s he was consulted by the Federal Reserve Bank of New York and the Banque de France for advice on the development of discount markets in New York and Paris.

Schröder's personality inspired faith in his judgement and dependability. He was quiet and sober in manner, but possessed of such dignity and authority that his very presence commanded respect. His integrity was beyond question and he was tempted neither by an apparently easy profit nor to compromise on a strict standard of straightforwardness. He was outraged, for instance, when in the 1920s it was suggested that the firm might very profitably join an issuing syndicate for a new bond issue for the Romanian government before compensation had been arranged for the holders of pre-war bonds, and he flatly refused to add a first-class name to the prospectus of a second-class borrower. His practice in business was to listen carefully and courteously to the requests of clients and to make an immediate decision upon which a client could rely with absolute confidence. 'I do not think it can have occurred to anyone', wrote Henry Andrews, a manager at Schroders between the wars:

> that Baron Schröder could let him down … he was a great gentleman and without doubt one of the very small

company on whom depended the good name of London in the world of finance and the leadership of London in that world. (*DBB*, 73)

Boom years, 1905–1914 Schroders was already well-established as an issuing house specializing in finance for overseas railway construction and for Latin American governments. Under Baron Bruno's leadership, the firm participated energetically and profitably in London's issuing boom of the years 1905–14. Schröder became closely involved in some of the enterprises, notably in devising the San Paulo coffee valorization scheme of 1908, and he became chairman of the committee responsible for the sale of the collateral coffee. The sovereign bond issues that the firm made for Bulgaria and Romania just before the First World War marked the extension of Schroders' issuing business into central Europe, a development resulting from Baron Bruno's contacts with continental cousins and friends which was to be taken much further after 1919.

Baron Bruno's ties to Germany remained strong despite his move to England. On 5 April 1894 he had married Emma, *née* Deichmann, the daughter of a Cologne banker; they had two sons and two daughters. His principal interest apart from business was the extensive and largely German Schröder family. Both at his Hamburg home, which he visited each July, and at Dell Park, Englefield Green (near Windsor), the estate he purchased in 1900, the visitors were predominantly relatives. In the inter-war period, especially during the inflation of 1923 and the depression of the 1930s, he gave financial assistance to family members, and in October 1931 he created the Rudolph–Clara Schröder Stiftung, a charitable foundation designed to help impoverished descendants of his parents. He continued to support the charities established by his uncle to care for indigent Germans in London. His charitable work was publicly acknowledged not only when he was made a baron in 1904, but again in 1937 when on his seventieth birthday he was awarded an honorary DMed by the University of Hamburg.

As the antagonism between Britain and Germany intensified during the decade prior to 1914, Baron Bruno remained resolutely Anglo-German and actively fostered understanding between the two nations; in 1905 he joined with other Anglo-German financiers including Sir Ernest Cassel, Alfred Beit, and Edgar Speyer to found the Anglo-German Union Club; in 1907 he entertained a group of visiting British journalists at his mother's home in Hamburg; in 1910 he endowed a chair in German at Cambridge University.

Naturalization The outbreak of war between Britain and Germany in August 1914 posed not only commercial problems for Schroders but an immediate threat to the firm's continued existence. Schröder himself was a German citizen, raising the danger that the firm would be seized as enemy property. He was promptly naturalized by the home secretary, Reginald McKenna, who had received urgent representations to do so from the governor of the Bank of England. McKenna explained to the House of Commons that prompt action was essential because:

It is a very large, I believe the largest, accepting house in the City of London, and the very highest commercial authority in the City represented to me that it would be a disaster—no less a word was used—if the doors of Baron Schröder did not open on the following morning, and, unless he had been naturalised at once, they would not have opened. (*DBB*, 74)

Anti-German sentiment ran high in England during the war and Schröder and his family suffered much abuse and even threats. The court of aldermen of the City of London protested against his naturalization as did a number of MPs, some of whom called for his internment. Schröder's position as a trustee for various German charities, particularly the Kaiser Jubilee Fund, established in 1913, and his contributions to the funds of the emergency committee formed to relieve the plight of German nationals interned in England were cited as evidence of his disloyalty. Another purported justification for suspicion was that his eldest son, who was on holiday in Germany when war broke out, was called up into the German army. The news of his disappearance on the Russian front in 1915 was a cruel blow. When challenged to reveal his loyalties in the conflict he replied, 'I feel as if my father and my mother have had a quarrel' (*DBB*, 74).

If the German connections of firm and family led to difficulty and tragedy during the hostilities, in the post-war period they once again created opportunities. The seizure of the City subsidiaries of German banks by the British authorities during the war created problems for the clearance of their transactions in London after 1919, particularly during the period of the German hyperinflation. Much of this business came to Schroders, briefly swelling the firm's staff from some 200 to more than 600 in 1924.

Recovery and depression Baron Bruno's close connections with central European banks led Schroders to participate in the placement of their shares during the 1920s, and to his appointment to the board of the Österreichische Boden Creditanstalt. His links with the Deutsche Bank led to the controversial episode in 1923 when a British syndicate led by Schroders took control of the Baghdad Railway through the acquisition of the Deutsche Bank's interest. The following year, Baron Bruno played a crucial part in the re-establishment of the creditworthiness of the Deutsche Bank after the devastation of its balance sheet during the period of inflation.

Schroders worked closely with other leading City firms both before and after the war. The celebrated Barings–Rothschild–Schroders syndicate started in 1921, though issues continued with other merchant banks. Baron Bruno, like his uncle, preferred to keep distractions from Schroder business to a minimum. Outside directorships were taken only in firms with which Schroders had close commercial connections, such as the North British Mercantile Insurance Company or the New Zealand Loan and Mercantile Agency. Unlike his partner, Frank Tiarks, Schröder did not play a prominent part in the institutions of the City or in public life.

The early 1920s saw the emergence of New York as an important centre for international trade finance and the international capital market. In October 1923 Schröder and Tiarks established a New York bank with a capital of $3 million, the J. Henry Schroder Banking Corporation, the only London merchant bank to take such an initiative. Baron Bruno became chairman of the board, and he visited the concern annually in the 1920s. The Schroder banks specialized in fund-raising for clients in Germany and in the other countries of central Europe. Schröder's name became particularly closely associated with the rationalization of the German potash industry and Schroders made several large issues for the German potash syndicate in the years between the wars.

As German trade revived after 1924 German merchants turned once again to London for trade finance. The volume of Schroders' German acceptances grew rapidly and by the end of the 1920s it had the biggest international trade finance business in the City. Working capital for German industry was also in short supply as a result of the depredations of the hyper-inflation of 1923. In 1924 Baron Bruno organized the formation of the Continental and Industrial Trust to meet the demand for equity and loan capital to medium-sized industrial firms in Germany.

While the international economy remained buoyant Schroders prospered. However, the virtual collapse of the central European banking system in the summer of 1931 and the ensuing suspension of the settlement of international obligations posed a grave threat, since the amount owing was several times the firm's capital. The 'standstill agreements' of the 1930s, in which the leading negotiator on the part of the creditors was Frank Tiarks, averted the immediate danger of failure, but it was not until the early 1950s that the funds were recovered, severely curtailing the business of the firm in the 1930s and 1940s.

Final years Although remaining senior partner until his death, Baron Bruno played a less active part in the firm in the 1930s. While consulted on major matters, he left the day-to-day running of the business to his partners, who since 1926 had included his son, Helmut (1901–1969), and Frank Tiarks's son, Henry (1900–1995). Baron Bruno died on 10 December 1940 at his home, Dell Park, Englefield Green, Surrey, being laid to rest at St Jude's, Englefield Green. He was succeeded in the firm as senior partner by his son Helmut. RICHARD ROBERTS

Sources R. Roberts, *Schroders: merchants and bankers* (1992) · R. Roberts, 'Schröder, Baron Rudolph Bruno', *DBB* · d. cert. · *CGPLA Eng. & Wales* (1941) · *Windsor, Slough and Eton Express* (13 Dec 1940)
Archives Schroders plc, London | SOUND BL NSA, oral history interview
Likenesses P. A. de Laszlo, portrait, priv. coll. [*see illus.*] · portrait (as senior partner), Schroders PLC, London
Wealth at death £502,502 13*s.* 8*d.*: probate, 8 Aug 1941, *CGPLA Eng. & Wales*

Schröder, Sir John Henry William [*formerly* Johann Heinrich Wilhelm], **first baronet, and Baron Schröder in the Prussian nobility** [*known as* Baron Sir John Henry Schröder] (**1825–1910**), merchant banker, was born on 13 February 1825 in Hamburg, Germany, and baptized Johann Heinrich Wilhelm, though he was known in adulthood by the English names John Henry. He was the fourth of the twelve children of Johann Heinrich, Baron Schröder (1784–1883), merchant banker, and his wife, Henriette (1798–1889), daughter of Heinrich von Schwartz (1763–1832). Both parents were offspring of prosperous and prominent Hamburg merchants; his maternal grandfather was the Prussian consul-general in the city state, and his paternal grandfather was burgomaster from 1816 to 1821.

Early life The elder Johann Heinrich Schröder was one of the foremost merchants of his generation in Hamburg. During the Napoleonic wars he lived in London, where he built up a mercantile business with his brother. In 1818 he established his own merchant banking firm, J. Henry Schroder & Co. The following year he returned to Hamburg, married, and set up home. He also established a second firm, henceforth having concerns in London and Hamburg, and later in Liverpool, and travelling regularly between these cities.

John Henry Schröder joined his father's London firm in 1841, aged sixteen, learning the business under the supervision of a resident partner. The London partnership was restructured in 1849, the new resident partners being John Henry and Alexander Schlüsser. The latter was a specialist in trade with Russia, being related to a firm of St Petersburg merchants with which Schroders did business. In 1850 the bond between the partners reflected kinship as well as commerce, when Schröder married Alexander's niece Dorothea Eveline Schlüsser (1828–1900). The newlyweds took up residence in London's fashionable Bayswater.

Schroders prospered in the 1850s and 1860s under the direction of John Henry and Alexander Schlüsser, and revenues from trade finance, the firm's principal activity, quadrupled over these decades. Adroitly, the partners avoided serious losses in the commercial crises of 1857 and 1866. Much of the firm's business was conducted in Hamburg and other commercial centres with John Henry's brothers and cousins, who formed an extensive network of family firms. Schroders' prominent position in trade with Russia was reflected by John Henry's involvement in the affairs of the Baltic exchange. From 1854 to the 1870s, he served as a member of the governing body, playing an active part in bringing about improvements.

International bond issuing Schroders made its début as an issuer of international bonds in 1853, bringing out a loan for a Cuban sugar freight-carrier, the Matanzas and Sabanilla Railroad Company; a director of this firm was a German merchant who had been John Henry's landlord during his bachelor days. In 1863, in the middle of the American Civil War, Schroders audaciously handled the London end of a controversial issue for the Confederate states; it was the only foreign loan raised by either side during the conflict. It was a highly profitable transaction for the Schroder partners. The proceeds financed John Henry's purchase of The Dell, a large house with 160 acres of land abutting Windsor Great Park, in 1864. In the same year he became British by naturalization. In 1865 he was elected as a member of the Society of Merchants Trading to the Continent, the exclusive London merchant bankers' dining club. John Henry paid an annual visit to Hamburg to report on the business and to see his relatives, until 1883, when his father died aged ninety-eight. However, his home was England. He and his wife became close friends of their Windsor neighbours Princess Christian of Schleswig-Holstein, a daughter of Queen Victoria, and her German husband. The Schröders received invitations to court and to attend important royal celebrations, such as the 1887 jubilee service in Westminster Abbey. From 1868, when his father was made a Prussian baron (*Freiherr*), John Henry was known as Baron Schröder, and he inherited the title formally on his father's death in 1883. In 1892 the queen conferred a baronetcy upon him for services to the royal household. He was also given a special dispensation to permit him to continue to use his Prussian title, henceforth being known as Baron Sir John Henry Schröder, bt.

The Confederate loan issue had been made in conjunction with Emile Erlanger, an important business associate and a friend of John Henry. In 1870 their firms jointly made an issue for Japan, the first Japanese external loan. The Erlanger connection also led to Schroders' participation in loans for undertakings in Russia, Chile, and possibly South Africa. In the 1880s and 1890s Erlanger was frequently a guest in John Henry's shooting parties in Scotland.

Alexander Schlüsser's retirement in 1871 led to a recasting of the Schroder partnership. Henry Tiarks (1832–1911), the son of a pastor to London's Anglo-German community who had worked at the firm as a clerk since 1847, was made a partner. He was also a relative, by adoption, of John Henry and Schlüsser, having married the latter's adopted daughter in 1862.

International trade finance The 1870s and 1880s were John Henry's heyday as a businessman. At the start of the 1870s, he secured Schroders' very profitable appointment as principal agent for the worldwide distribution of Peruvian guano, an important fertilizer. The assignment even led to an entrepreneurial involvement in fertilizer manufacture in London's East End. Much of Schroders' business being the finance of international trade, the firm maintained close links with the shipping and marine insurance industries. Since 1863 John Henry had been a director of the North British and Marine Insurance Company. In 1892 he became deputy chairman, and he served as chairman between 1889 and 1900. In 1888 he became a director of the West India Dock Company, and two years later a member of Lloyd's of London.

More and more, John Henry left the day-to-day business of the firm to his partners and devoted himself to other pursuits. He rented Bicester Hall for the hunting season, riding with the Bicester hounds between forty and fifty times each winter. In summer he went on a shoot in Scotland, where he spent July and August. Being childless, John Henry had no offspring to succeed him in the business. In 1895 he brought in a nephew from Hamburg, Bruno *Schröder (1867–1940), to represent the family in the partnership.

Assisted by Henry Tiarks and his son Frank, who was made a partner in 1902, Bruno Schröder soon assumed control of the firm's affairs. But John Henry remained senior partner and still had his say; for some years he refused to allow a telephone in the office to avoid the distraction of incoming calls, and when he was asked to consent to Frank Tiarks's appointment to the court of the Bank of England he declined, replying that he didn't want one of his partners wasting time on outside business.

Pastimes and philanthropy Orchid cultivation had been a pastime since the 1860s, but more assiduous application from the 1880s resulted in John Henry's plants winning three Royal Horticultural Society gold medals and ten silver medals between 1891 and 1904. He played an active part in the affairs of the society, contributing handsomely to the Royal Gardeners' Benevolent Institution. He took great pride in the upkeep of the 10 acres of grounds surrounding The Dell, employing a staff of fifty to tend the garden and run the adjacent 150 acre farm.

Schröder was also an avid collector of works of art, and he amassed a considerable collection. The pictures were for the most part works by fashionable contemporaries, both English and continental. At the turn of the century, full-length portraits of John Henry and his wife were painted by the leading portrait artist Hubert von Herkomer. The paintings and statuary were left to the Hamburg Kunsthalle. His exquisite collection of *objets d'art*—porcelain, Renaissance cameos, jewellery, and snuffboxes—raised £138,000 when sold at auction; *The Times* called it one of the greatest collections to be sold for a generation (10 June 1910).

Throughout his life, Schröder was a generous benefactor of charitable causes, particularly London's German institutions and charities. From the outset he was treasurer of the German Hospital, Hackney, founded in 1843 to serve impoverished Germans living in the East End. In 1862 he became a trustee of the Hamburg Lutheran Church, London's oldest German institution. Among the appeals that enjoyed his financial support were those of the German Orphanage, 1879; the German Work Colony, 1900; the Christus-Kirche, 1904; the German Hospital's convalescent home, 1908; and the German Sailors' Home, opened posthumously in 1912. 'Baron Schröder', observed an obituarist, 'gave more in charity than all the rest of the Germans in this country put together' (*Surrey and Middlesex Journal*, 30 April 1910).

Numerous local causes in the Windsor area also received assistance; notably Schröder made a gift of 5 acres of land to the local council to build an isolation hospital. In recognition of these services he was presented with an illuminated address by the corporation of Windsor on the occasion of his golden wedding in 1900.

Retirement and death John Henry retired from the Schroder partnership early in 1910, aged eighty-five. As usual with partnerships his capital was withdrawn, but a ten-year loan of £1 million to Bruno Schröder, who succeeded him as senior partner, ensured that the firm's business was not disrupted. John Henry did not enjoy a lengthy retirement; he died a few months later on 20 April 1910 in Sidmouth, Devon. He left £2,079,000, one of only thirty fortunes in excess of £2 million in the years 1895 to 1914.

RICHARD ROBERTS

Sources R. Roberts, *Schroders: merchants and bankers* (1992) • *Surrey and Middlesex Journal* (30 April 1910) • Schroder archives, London
Archives Schroders plc, London, archives
Likenesses H. von Herkomer, portrait, 1900, Kunsthalle, Hamburg, Germany • statuary, Kunsthalle, Hamburg, Germany
Wealth at death £2,079,000: Schroders plc, London, archive

Schroeder, Henry [*pseud.* William Butterworth] (**1774–1853**), topographer and engraver, was born at Bawtry, Yorkshire. He ran away from home at an early age and spent three years at sea in slave ships. On his return he settled at Leeds, where he successfully practised engraving for nearly twenty years under the name of William Butterworth. He engraved a series of 111 plates as illustrations for Darcy Lever's *The young sea officer's sheet anchor, or, A key to the leading of rigging and practical seamanship* (1808 and 1819). In 1822 he published *Three Years' Adventures of a Minor*, an account of his time at sea. In 1851 Schroeder published *The Annals of Yorkshire*, a miscellaneous chronicle beginning at the flood and ending with a list of Yorkshire exhibitors at the Great Exhibition. He was also one of the chief compilers of *Pigott's General Directory*, and composed several poems and provincial songs. Usually poor and struggling, he was for a time landlord of the Shakspere Head public house, Kirkgate, and died at Leeds on 18 February 1853.

THOMPSON COOPER, *rev.* WILLIAM JOSEPH SHEILS

Sources W. Butterworth [H. Schroeder], *Three years' adventures of a minor in England, Africa, the West Indies, South-Carolina and Georgia* (1822) • *Leeds Intelligencer* (26 Feb 1853), 8 • Boase, *Mod. Eng. biog.* • *N&Q*, 3rd ser., 9 (1866), 405, 479 • *N&Q*, 3rd ser., 10 (1866), 363–4
Likenesses H. Schroeder, self-portrait, *c.*1821, repro. in Butterworth, *Three years' adventures of a minor*, frontispiece

Schulenburg, (Ehrengard) Melusine von der, *suo jure* duchess of Kendal and *suo jure* duchess of Munster (**1667–1743**), mistress of George I, was born at Emden, Brandenburg, Germany, on 25 December 1667, the second daughter and fourth child (of eight) of Gustav Adolf, Baron von der Schulenburg (1632–1691), and his first wife, Petronilla Ottilia, *née* Schwenke (1637–1674). The Schulenburgs had been nobles in the mark of Brandenburg since the thirteenth century. Melusine's father was a member of the privy council of the elector of Brandenburg. Members of German noble families usually sought employment outside their home territories: Melusine's eldest brother, Matthias Johann von der Schulenburg, rose to eminence as a military commander in the service of Brunswick-Wolfenbüttel, Saxony, and Venice, and in 1690 Melusine joined the court of Sophia, duchess of Hanover (electress from 1692), as a maid of honour. During the next year she became pregnant by Sophia's son, the hereditary prince George Lewis (Georg Ludwig), later King *George I of Great Britain (1660–1727), and gave birth to a daughter, (Anna) Louise Sophia (*d.* 1773), in January 1692. Another daughter, (Petronilla) Melusina *Stanhope (1693–1778) [*see under* Stanhope, Philip Dormer, fourth earl of Chesterfield], followed the next year. Neither were acknowledged as the children of George and Melusine, but instead were described as the daughters of Melusine's sister (Margarethe) Gertrud (1659–1697), who had married a kinsman, Friedrich Achaz von der Schulenburg (1647–1701).

Melusine was referred to during 1692 as George Lewis's mistress in correspondence between George Lewis's wife, Sophia Dorothea, and her lover, Philip Christopher, Count Königsmark, and this may suggest that her status was by then established at the Hanoverian court. The divorce between George Lewis and Sophia Dorothea allowed Melusine's status to become openly acknowledged. Following the accession of George Lewis as elector of Hanover in 1698, Melusine was given precedence over all other ladies at court with the exception of the dowager electress Sophia and visiting queens or princesses, and all but officiated as George's consort. Melusine gave birth to a third daughter, Margarethe Gertrud (*d.* 1726), in 1701, who was registered as the daughter of her sister Sophia Juliane von Oeynhausen (1668–1755), and like her earlier children was never acknowledged as the child of the elector and Melusine. Margarethe Gertrud married Count Albrecht Wolfgang of Schaumburg-Lippe in 1722, a princely marriage that implicitly acknowledged her royal paternity.

Melusine and her daughters accompanied George I to London in September 1714. The gossip that 'She even refus'd comeing hither at first, fearing that the people of England (who she thought were accustom'd to use their Kings barbarously) might chop off his Head in the first Fortnight' (*Lady Mary Wortley Montagu: Essays*, 87) seems unfounded. They moved into apartments at St James's Palace, and later lived in a new court built for them at Kensington Palace. Melusine, with whom George took supper every evening, was described by Lady Mary Wortley Montagu as 'so much of [the king's] own temper that I do not wonder at the Engagement between them' (ibid., 86–7). Although Lady Mary's assessment as a whole was unflattering, it acknowledged the compatibility between Melusine and George. She was recognized by British courtiers as having great influence with the king, and it was sometimes rumoured that she was to be formally acknowledged as the king's wife and as queen. This never happened, and there is no evidence that Melusine and George ever married; George probably wished to avoid drawing attention to his troubled marital history and thereby weaken the Hanoverian dynasty's prospects. Her position in the life of George I received formal recognition in Germany when she was created a countess of the Holy Roman empire in 1715, a rank achieved at the same time by her siblings; the promotion also rewarded her brother the field marshal. Following her naturalization as a British subject in 1716, she was created duchess of Munster in the Irish peerage.

George I preferred to concentrate on business rather than on display, but Melusine usually accompanied him on his visits to the theatre. In November 1717, as the breach between the king and the prince and princess of Wales became public knowledge, she took a prominent part in the assemblies held every night at St James's Palace, a sign that in London she assumed a social role similar to that which she had enjoyed in Hanover. Until then Melusine had enjoyed friendly relations with Caroline, princess of Wales, and had tried to use her influence to keep the prince aligned with the king and his ministers. Melusine was able to turn her ambivalent position, an independent noblewoman who was at the same time practically the king's consort, to the king's advantage during the royal estrangement. In 1718 she negotiated with Robert Walpole, then leading the opposition whigs aligned with the prince, attempting to bring him into the ministerial fold. She also helped George I's existing British ministers, Charles Spencer, third earl of Sunderland, and James, first Earl Stanhope, against the prevailing influence of Baron Andreas Gottlieb von Bernstorff over the king's foreign policy. In persuading George I to allow Sunderland to join the king and Stanhope in Hanover in summer 1719, she gave the British ministers crucial support in their successful bid to exclude Bernstorff from British policy making. In April 1720, two months before Walpole returned to the ministry, he told William, Earl Cowper, that 'he would not wait upon Duchess of Kendal'—the title in the British peerage Melusine had been given on 19 March 1719—'till Things were far advanced; that now he intended it, and that her Interest did Everything; that she was, in effect, as much Queen of England as ever any was; that he did Everything by her' (*Diary of Mary, Countess Cowper*, 132). Some correspondence from British diplomats abroad shows that they would also approach Melusine to smooth the way before asking for a new posting or introducing the king to a new proposition; as the Holy Roman emperor's representative recognized, she 'often "broke the first ice" with the king' (Beattie, 242).

Melusine and her fellow Germans were often accused of avarice by contemporaries and by subsequent commentators on the court of George I. It is true that she accepted large sums of money from those seeking patronage if it was offered: James Brydges, first duke of Chandos, recorded that he gave her £9500 between August 1715 and February 1720, of £25,104 in total given to German courtiers. The opportunities through which German courtiers could make money in the king's service were in fact few, and the cost of living in London has been estimated at four times more expensive than it was in Hanover. Accepting presents in return for influence was an efficient way of maintaining the standard of living demanded of royal courtiers, and the proximity of Melusine and other Germans to George I, particularly in the early years of the reign, inflamed the jealousy of British courtiers, who felt that foreigners were helping themselves to patronage that should have remained in British hands. It was estimated that George I paid her a pension of £7500 a year, and she also invested in Bank of England stock and in property in Holstein and in London. In February 1720, as part of the South Sea Bubble, Melusine received £15,000 worth of stock, for which £120 would be paid for every point the price of stock rose above £154. Her two younger daughters received £5000 of stock each with a similar arrangement. Other public figures also received gifts of stock, and when Melusine appeared on the king's birthday 'in a dress covered with jewels valued at £5000' (Carswell, 127) she was celebrating a prosperity that many believed court and country would share, and not just her own new-found wealth. After the collapse of the bubble she retained her stock and claimed to have made a reasonable profit, although not as much as she would once have expected. In 1722 she was compensated by George I with a patent to produce coinage in Ireland, which she sold to the ironmaster William Wood for £10,000. This act of concern by the king associated Melusine with an act that for many in Ireland epitomized their economic exploitation by the British government, but the crisis counted for little at court.

After 1721 Melusine was a close ally of Charles, second Viscount Townshend. She helped him and Walpole keep in the king's good offices, and Townshend, in turn, kept her potential rivals at court at bay. Chief of these were Sophia Charlotte, Baroness von Kielmansegg, and (residing at Hanover) Sophia Caroline, Countess von Platen, who were George's half-sister and possible half-sister-in-law respectively, although many at the British court chose to believe they were mistresses or potential mistresses of the king. Townshend declared the ministry's 'eternal and inviolable attachment' (Beattie, 244) to Melusine. Her support for the restoration of Henry St John, Viscount Bolingbroke, to his estates was interpreted subsequently as a threat to the administration, as was the friendship Melusine was said to have developed with Bolingbroke's wife, Marie-Claire, marquise de Villette. The idea that Walpole might have been replaced by Bolingbroke at Melusine's suggestion, had George I returned from his visit to Germany in 1727, although unlikely, became part of whig political mythology in the next generation.

Melusine had always accompanied George I on his visits to Germany, and reached Osnabrück a few hours after his death on 11 June 1727. Despite her German origins and princely status there—she had been created princess of Eberstein by Emperor Charles VI on 17 April 1722—she chose to sell her German estates and return to Britain with her two surviving daughters, Louise (who after a failed marriage had been made countess of Delitz by Charles VI in 1722) and Melusina (who married the earl of Chesterfield in 1733). George I left her £22,986 2*s.* 2*d.* in his will, about two-thirds of which was held in trust by Sir Robert Walpole. She received £6993 1*s.* 1*d.* of this sum from Walpole in 1730, perhaps to complete the purchase (or pay the construction fees) of Kendal House in Isleworth, Middlesex, where she moved in 1728. She lived in retirement until her death, at Kendal House on 10 May 1743, and was buried in the vault established for herself and her two elder daughters in South Audley Street Chapel, London.

Unlike George I, Melusine became proficient in English, but like her king her British contemporaries found her difficult to know, and her position in the king's life was often misunderstood. Despite the prominence George I gave her at court, the private life which the king and those close to him led encouraged several otherwise well-informed people to assume that Melusine was just the most senior of many mistresses. Arthur Onslow, speaker of the House of Commons, told his son that she was 'always considered and treated as the King's *private* wife' (*Buckinghamshire MSS*, 515), but John, Lord Hervey, and later Horace Walpole, believed that Sophia Charlotte, Baroness von Kielmansegg, had also been the king's mistress, and their misunderstanding prevailed in English-language works until the late twentieth century. Melusine became the rapacious 'Maypole' (a nickname reputedly given to her by the London mob in her lifetime), the painfully tall and thin favourite of George I whose relationship with Britain was epitomized in this anecdote:

> Melusine and Sophie Charlotte [von Kielmansegg] shared a carriage which was stopped by an unfriendly mob. The following exchange then took place. *La Schulenburg*: 'Good people, why do you plague us so? We have come for your own goods.' Mob: 'Yes, and for our *chattels* too.' (Hatton, 131)

Late twentieth-century research, particularly that of Ragnhild Hatton and of John Beattie, went a great way towards restoring Melusine's reputation in British historiography. She does not loom as large in the historical imagination as she would had she been a queen consort, but her discretion and good sense had a stabilizing effect on the politics of the reign of George I.

MATTHEW KILBURN

Sources R. Hatton, *George I, elector and king* (1978) • J. M. Beattie, *The English court in the reign of George I* (1967) • J. Carswell, *The South Sea Bubble*, rev. edn (1993) • *Diary of Mary, Countess Cowper*, ed. [S. Cowper] (1865) • *The manuscripts of the earl of Buckinghamshire, the earl of Lindsey … and James Round*, HMC, 38 (1895), 515 • *The manuscripts of his grace the duke of Portland*, 10 vols., HMC, 29 (1891–1931), vol. 5, pp. 536, 538, 549, 554, 568, 615, 616; vol. 7, pp. 226, 447, 453 • *Report on the manuscripts of Lord Polwarth*, 5 vols., HMC, 67 (1911–61), vol. 2, p. 432; vol. 4, pp. 139, 145, 328 • GEC, *Peerage*, new edn, 7.111–112; 14.406 • M. W. Montagu, [Account of the court of George I], in *Lady Mary Wortley Montagu: essays and poems and 'Simplicity, a comedy'*, ed. R. Halsband and I. Grundy (1977), 82–94 • *Reminiscences of Mr. Horace Walpole written in 1788*, ed. P. Toynbee (1924) • *Calendar of the Stuart papers belonging to his majesty the king, preserved at Windsor Castle*, 7 vols., HMC, 56 (1902–23), vol. 5, p. 287; vol. 6, p. 328; vol. 7, p. 375 • D. Schwennicke, ed., *Europäische Stammtafeln*, new ser., 19 (Frankfurt am Main, 2000), 69 • will, PRO, PROB 11/726/167, fols. 187r–189r

Archives BL, corresp. with Lord Whitworth, Add. MS 37384, fols. 80, 237, 299; Add. MS 37385, fols. 21, 88; Add. MS 37386, fols. 29, 115, 141, 194, 198; Add. MS 37389, fol. 181 • BL, letter to Charles, third earl of Sunderland, Add. MS 61496, fol. 139

Likenesses portrait, Landesgalerie, Hanover • print, BM

Wealth at death exact value unknown, but legacies (to be paid from total value of estate) of at least £60,000: will, PRO, PROB 11/726/167 (15 April 1743)

Schulz, Fritz Heinrich (1879–1957), legal historian, was born in Bunzlau in German Silesia (now Boleslawiec in Poland) on 16 June 1879, the son of a factory manager. He studied principally in Berlin, where the main influences on him were A. Pernice and E. Seckel, members of the generation of German Roman lawyers who had embarked on the attempt to distinguish within the texts in the *Digest* the classical law from the alterations wrought in it by Justinian's interpolations. This search for interpolations occupied much of Schulz's scholarly life. To the end, if one took him a puzzling text, he would offer a reconstruction of the classical original which might explain the puzzle. In 1914 he married Martha Plant; the couple had two sons and a daughter.

Until the advent of the Nazis, Schulz's career followed the usual pattern, culminating in his appointment to a chair at Berlin University in 1931. The Nazis took away his chair, but he quietly continued his academic work until, shortly before the outbreak of war and on the urging of his wife, he fled first to the Netherlands and finally to Oxford, where he spent the rest of his life. In Oxford he found no official position, though he did some tutorial teaching (in which his enthusiasm could make him prolong the tutorial much beyond the customary hour), but the university press gave him some financial assistance and he embarked on a remarkably fruitful period, in which, as he put it, he gathered in his harvest. Always an unassuming man, he wrote in a letter in 1946 that, though he had no position or money, he had no resentment against Germany and was in one sense grateful to the Nazis because he would never have achieved so much in Germany as he had in 'free England and above all in beautiful Oxford, which has no equal in the world' (private information). Indeed the harvest was remarkable: he turned his attention to English legal history in four important articles on Bracton, but above all he wrote two fundamental works on Roman law.

Until Schulz's expulsion from his chair in Berlin his writing had focused on the search for interpolations and in 1916 he had published his first book, *Einführung in das Studium der Digesten* as a sort of guidebook. In 1934, however, he produced a book of a quite different kind, *Principles of Roman Law*, of which the second edition was published in English in 1936. In it he stood back from the minutiae of textual analysis and isolated certain broad identifying characteristics of Roman law, such as abstraction, tradition, and authority. In its broad sweep the book echoes some aspects of R. Ihering's much vaster work from the previous century, *Geist des römischen Rechts*.

This breadth of view is combined with detailed scholarship in Schulz's greatest book, the principal product of his Oxford years, *History of Roman Legal Science* (1946). It is concerned, not with Roman law itself, but with a history of the ways in which the law was made, applied, expounded, and transmitted. For this purpose he divided his history into four periods, which he termed archaic, hellenistic, classical, and bureaucratic. For each period he studied in turn the jurists and the legal profession, the character and tendencies of the jurisprudence (or legal thinking), and the forms and transmission of the literature. The book was unrivalled for its breadth, learning, and insight, and also for the sometimes vigorous idiosyncrasy of its opinions. These characteristics were also found in his last book, *Classical Roman Law* (1951), which, unlike other textbooks, was concerned only with the classical law, as opposed both to the law of Justinian and the early law. Its simplicity suggests a book intended for students, but it embodied Schulz's own views on the extent and nature of Justinian's interpolations, which are now generally rejected. It can almost be said that the more vigorously certain were his statements, the more controversial they were likely to be.

Schulz died at his home, 5 Tackley Place, Oxford, on 12 November 1957, but had suffered a severe stroke some years before. He was survived by his wife.

J. K. BARRY M. NICHOLAS

Sources W. Flume, *Zeitschrift der Savigny Stiflung für Rechtsgeschichte Romanistische Abteilung*, 75 (1958), 496–507 [obituary] • *The Times* (21 Nov 1957) • private information (2004) • personal knowledge (2004) • H. Niedermeyer and W. Flume, eds., *Festschrift Fritz Schulz*, 2 vols. (1951) [incl. list of writings] • d. cert.

Likenesses photograph, repro. in Niedermeyer and Flume, eds., *Festschrift Fritz Schulz*

Schumacher, Ernst Friedrich [Fritz] (**1911–1977**), economist and writer, was born in Bonn, Germany, on 16 August 1911, the third of the five children of Hermann Albert Schumacher (1868–1952), professor of economics at Bonn and Berlin universities, and his wife, Edith Zitelmann (1884–1975). Having been educated at the Arndt Gymnasium, Berlin, he went on to study politics and economics as a Rhodes scholar (1930–33) at New College, Oxford, and at Columbia University, New York. Having returned to Germany in 1934, he opposed his father's advice to conform to the pressure already evident on professionals to accommodate the Nazi regime, and, after marrying Anna Maria (Muschi) Petersen (1911–1960) on 10 October 1936, he took a post in a financial firm in London.

The outbreak of war in 1939 coincided with the loss of his job and home, and Schumacher was grateful to obtain accommodation and work as a farm labourer through his Oxford friend David Astor. As such work was essential to the war effort it ensured his rapid release when he was interned as an 'enemy alien' in a camp on Press Heath, near Whitchurch, Shropshire, in the summer of 1940. While at the internment camp he came across some German economists who had been working at the Oxford University Institute of Statistics. That institute had set aside its peacetime programme of research in favour of war economics, to be researched mainly by refugee scholars from European countries; they included Czechs, Poles, and Hungarians as well as Germans and Austrians. Early in 1942 a vacancy occurred at the institute, to which Schumacher was appointed.

As the war progressed the balance of the Oxford institute's programme was tilted away from war economics towards post-war recovery and reconstruction. A team of six of its members addressed the question of the economics of full employment, which was published in book form in 1944. The keynote chapter was written by the Polish economist Michal Kalecki, and Schumacher's contribution was on public finance in relation to full employment. Meanwhile William Beveridge had embarked on his own report on full employment. To assist him he recruited a number of younger economists in the forefront of the new economics. Schumacher acted as liaison with the team working at the Institute of Statistics.

Ernst Friedrich [Fritz] **Schumacher** (**1911–1977**), by Sophie Baker

By the end of the war Schumacher had become an applied economist of distinction. Extensive reading of Marx influenced his ideas about the organization of production and the distribution of income. On questions of employment and unemployment he had absorbed the message of Keynes. In addition, he had spent three years in Oxford working side by side with Kalecki. In his writing he appeared as a materialist and a scientist, not standing apart from other economists writing about policy: in the post-war years his position was to change. His return to Germany came as the war was ending, and he was recruited by J. K. Galbraith, the head of the American strategic bombing survey, established to find out why the bombing of German industrial targets had been so apparently ineffective. He was able to return home with his family; he also saw at first hand what a huge task lay ahead in the economic reconstruction and political rehabilitation of Germany.

In 1946 the British government appointed him economic adviser to the Allied Control Commission in the British zone of western Germany. To take up the post he would first have to become a British citizen, which he did in the spring of 1946. His own assessment of what was needed was set out in a paper, the 'Socialisation of German industry', but this paper had less influence than he had hoped. He was also highly critical of the currency reform which he feared would make the rich richer and the poor poorer. But, while the role of the currency reform in triggering the 'economic miracle' of the 1950s may have been exaggerated, there is no doubt that Schumacher appeared to have backed the wrong horse. And he experienced a less dramatic set-back when the Organization for European Economic Co-operation established a European Payments Union, which fell short of his own ideas on multilateral clearing.

Schumacher felt his own influence in Germany to be declining, and in 1950 he welcomed the invitation of the British government to return to England as economic adviser to the National Coal Board (NCB), a post he held for twenty years. It enabled him to stabilize his family life. Since their marriage he and his wife, and their growing family, had lived for short spells in England and in Germany, sometimes apart, but now they could acquire a house in Caterham, Surrey, the family home until his death.

Coal, whether used directly or as an input into gas and electricity, was almost as dominant in Britain in 1950 as it had been a hundred years before. As for the future, one could expect a continuation of the substitution of oil, and there was a growing idea that, in the longer term, nuclear power might be the source of cheap and plentiful energy. While it might seem natural enough for an adviser to the coal industry to be critical of the new industry, it was perceptive of Schumacher to stress not so much any competition with coal but to point out the huge problem which would build up of the disposal of nuclear waste, which would last for hundreds, even thousands, of years. By the end of the 1950s the climate of coal shortage which had prevailed since the end of the war was at an end, and from then on the main aim of policy seemed to be to secure such stability of output as would enable any required reduction in manpower to happen by natural wastage.

At this time Schumacher's eyes were increasingly turning towards the East. In the first place he became interested in questions of economic development, especially in how poverty in countries such as India might be alleviated; secondly he became a Buddhist. In 1955 he received an invitation from U Nu, the prime minister of Burma, to take the post of economic adviser. He declined the offer, but arranged three months' leave from the coal board to visit the country. He found the Burmese people colourful and delightful. While in Rangoon he arranged to spend weekends in a monastery, to be trained in the early steps of meditation, which he believed improved the quality of his thinking. Early in 1960 he received two invitations to work in India, one from the leading socialist and Gandhian J. P. Narayan, which he was tempted to accept. However, his wife developed symptoms of what was to prove a terminal cancer, and she returned to her family home in Germany, where she died. Schumacher's position at the NCB was meanwhile altered on the appointment, in 1961, of Alfred Robens as chairman. Robens encouraged him to remain at the NCB—where he also became director of statistics from 1963 to 1970—and was sympathetic to the ideas on economic development which Schumacher went on to expound.

On 29 January 1962 Schumacher married Verena (Vreni) Rosenberger (*b.* 1941), a Swiss, who had originally joined the family *au pair*, and with whom he had four more children. By the end of that year he felt able to take up an invitation to spend six weeks in India. In a report which he prepared for the Indian planning commission in 1963 he set out the ideas which he continued to develop until his death. He thought Western economics was misleading in its approach to the reduction of poverty in countries such as India. It worked with economic models representing aggregates such as consumption, investment, and gross national product. Income could be raised by following the paths already trodden by the Western economies, building industrial plants in towns and installing in them equipment embodying the most up-to-date technology. But little of the ensuing growth of output would benefit the inhabitants of the millions of villages where the deepest poverty was to be found. What was needed was to provide help directly to the villages in the form of training and know-how. The aid-givers should promote the study and application of simple improvements in the methods of cultivation and related production already in use in the rural areas. By this means the poverty in each village could be relieved in ways not achievable through the conventional economic approach.

When Schumacher presented his idea of what came to be called 'intermediate technology' at a conference of distinguished economists held in Cambridge in September 1964, he made little headway. But he found support elsewhere. In August 1965 an article in *The Observer* newspaper brought a remarkable response, leading to the foundation of an Intermediate Technology Development Group (1966), which brought together people from all over the world who were trying to improve farming methods, and designing simple improved methods of brick making, pottery, and so on.

In 1971 Schumacher resigned from the coal board to devote himself full-time to intermediate technology, and also in that year (September 1971) he became a Roman Catholic. The intermediate technology movement acquired additional impetus when he published in 1973 a collection of his lectures and articles with the inspired title of *Small is Beautiful*. It became a best-seller and was translated into at least fifteen languages. Schumacher began to receive invitations from all over the world to give lectures and to meet prominent politicians, including the president of the United States, where his ideas were disseminated widely, especially among the young, to whom he became something of a guru. After the success of *Small is Beautiful* he brought together his more philosophical pieces in *A Guide to the Perplexed*, which was published just after his death. In the six years after he left the coal board Schumacher pursued an arduous programme of lectures and conferences. He was also a keen promoter of organic cultivation, and was from 1970 president of the Soil Association. In 1974 he was appointed CBE and in 1975 he was made an honorary fellow of the University of Manchester Institute of Science and Technology. He died suddenly on a train, while travelling in Switzerland on a lecture tour, on 4 September 1977, and was buried at Caterham, Surrey, a few days later. Several thousand people attended his memorial service in Westminster Cathedral. After his death an E. F. Schumacher Society was founded in England (1979), and another in South Berkshire, western Massachusetts (1980), to implement his ideas and sponsor annual lectures. G. D. N. WORSWICK

Sources B. Wood, *Alias Papa: a life of Fritz Schumacher* (1984) · *DNB* · *The Times* (6 Sept 1977) · *The Times* (9 Sept 1977) · N. J. Todd, 'introduction', *People, land and community: collected E. F. Schumacher Society lectures*, ed. H. Hannum (1987) · private information (2004) [Barbara Wood, daughter]
Archives E. F. Schumacher Society, 140 Tag End Road, Great Barrington, Massachusetts, papers · Intermediate Technology Development Group, Bourton-on-Dunsmore, Warwickshire, corresp. and papers | Scott Bader Company, Wallingborough, Northamptonshire, corresp. with Ernest Bader
Likenesses S. Baker, photograph, priv. coll. [*see illus.*] · photographs, repro. in Wood, *Alias Papa*
Wealth at death £76,796: probate, 15 May 1978, *CGPLA Eng. & Wales*

Schunck, (Henry) Edward (1820–1903), chemist, was born in Manchester on 16 August 1820, the youngest son of Martin Schunck (1788–1872), an export shipping merchant, and his wife, Susanna, a daughter of Johann Jacob Mylius, senator of Frankfurt am Main. His father had spent some time in Malta before settling in Manchester in 1808 and founding the firm of Schunck and Mylius (later Schunck, Souchay & Co.).

After attending a private school in Manchester, and acquiring analytical skills in the laboratory of William and Charles Henry's chemical works, Schunck went to Germany. He first studied chemistry at Berlin University, where Heinrich E. Rose and Heinrich Gustav Magnus were among his teachers; from 1839 to 1841 he attended Giessen University, where he worked under Liebig, and graduated DPhil. On returning to Manchester, Schunck entered his father's calico-printing works in Rochdale, but within a few years he began full-time chemical researches, particularly in regard to the colouring matters of vegetable substances. In 1841 he published in Liebig's *Annalen* his first paper on research conducted in the Giessen laboratory. This dealt with the action of nitric acid on aloes. (He published under the name Edward Schunck, by which he was generally known.) The following year he presented to the Chemical Society of London (*Memoirs and Proceedings of the Chemical Society*, 1, 1841–3) an investigation made at Liebig's suggestion 'On some of the substances contained in the lichens employed for the preparation of archil and cudbear'. This inquiry he pursued in a paper on the substances contained in the *Roccella tinctoria* (*Memoirs and Proceedings of the Chemical Society*, 1, 1845–8). He isolated and determined the formula of the crystalline substance lecanorin.

From 1846 to 1855 Schunck undertook exhaustive researches on the colouring matters of the madder plant (*Rubia tinctorum*), communicating the results to the British Association in 1846, 1847, and 1848. In the *Philosophical Transactions* for 1851, 1853, and 1855 he gave further account of his investigation in his memoir 'On rubian and its products of decomposition', and described the peculiar bitter substance which he had isolated and named 'rubian'. From rubian Schunck isolated alizarin (the colouring matter obtained from madder root by Colin and Robiquet in Paris during the 1820s). His analyses first showed the chemical nature of alizarin and other constituents of the root. He demonstrated that they were glucosides, and separated alizarin from attached glucose by hydrolysis. This was adapted to an industrial process used, from 1851, for producing a more useful form of the natural colourant. With R. Angus Smith and Henry Roscoe he prepared and communicated for the British Association (Manchester meeting, 1861) a comprehensive report, 'The recent progress and present condition of manufacturing chemistry in the south Lancashire district'. Schunck and others prepared the way for the synthesis of alizarin by Graebe and Liebermann in 1868; further investigations in 1869 by William Henry Perkin in London and Heinrich Caro at BASF in Germany made alizarin a commercial product. Schunck collaborated with Hermann Roemer in the analysis of by-products obtained in Perkin's alizarin process. They published a series of eighteen papers in the *Berichte der Deutschen Chemischen Gesellschaft* and elsewhere on the chemistry of colouring matters (1875–80).

In October 1851 Schunck had married Judith Howard (*b.* 1826/7), daughter of John Brooke MRCS, of Stockport. About the same time he also began researches on indigo which had much practical importance. In 1853 he extracted from the plant *Isatis tinctoria* an unstable syrupy glucoside which he named indican—researches published in the *Memoirs* of the Manchester Literary and Philosophical Society in 1855, 1856, 1857, and 1865. He also published in 1901 a monograph, illustrated with coloured plates, *The Action of Reagents on the Leaves of Polygonum tinctorium*. Study of the constitution and derivatives of chlorophyll, the green colouring matter of plants, occupied Schunck's later years. His initial results appeared in the *Proceedings of the Royal Society* for 1884; later research was carried out in collaboration with the Polish chemist, Leon Marchlewski (1869–1946). They prepared phylloporphyrin, a crystalline substance chemically and spectroscopically resembling haematoporphyrin (a compound obtained from haemoglobin). Schunck suggested that the chlorophyll in the plant performed a function similar to that of haemoglobin in the animal, carrying carbon dioxide rather than oxygen. He wrote 'Chlorophyll' (1890) in Watts's *Dictionary of Chemistry*.

Schunck was a founder member of the Chemical Society of London in 1841. He was elected a fellow of the Royal Society on 6 June 1850 and he was Davy gold medallist for 1899. Elected into the Manchester Literary and Philosophical Society on 25 January 1842, he was secretary (1855–60), and president (1866–7, 1874–5, 1890–91, 1896–7), receiving in 1898 the society's Dalton bronze medal (struck in 1864 but not previously awarded). He was also an original member of the Society of Chemical Industry (1881), chairman of its Manchester section in 1888–9, president in 1896–7, and gold medallist in 1900 for his conspicuous services in applied chemistry. In 1887 he was president of the chemical section of the British Association at the Manchester meeting. Victoria University, Manchester, conferred on him the honorary degree of DSc in 1899.

Schunck carried on his investigations in a private laboratory which he had built near his home at Oaklands, Kersal, Manchester, and housed there a fine library and large collections. He was one of the first chemists to use absorption spectrometry in identification of coloured compounds. He was deeply interested in travel, literature, and art, and in works of philanthropy connected with his native city. He died at his home on 13 January 1903, and was buried in St Paul's churchyard, Kersal. His wife, three of his five sons, and one of two daughters survived him. His estate was valued at almost £150,000. On his death he left to the Victoria University of Manchester his private laboratory, which according to his obituary in *Nature* was 'probably the finest in the kingdom'; this formed the university's Schunck Research Laboratory.

T. E. JAMES, *rev.* ANTHONY S. TRAVIS

Sources H. B. D., *PRS*, 75 (1905), 261–5 • *Nature*, 67 (1902–3), 275 • 'Dr. Edward Schunck', *Manchester Faces and Places*, 9 (1897–8), 1–6 • W. V. Farrar, 'Edward Schunck, FRS: a pioneer of natural-product chemistry', *Notes and Records of the Royal Society*, 31 (1976–7), 273–96 • *Journal of the Society of Chemical Industry*, 22 (1903), 84 • *Manchester Courier* (19 Jan 1903) • H. E. Roscoe, 'Indigo and its artificial production', *Notices of the Proceedings at the Meetings of the Members of the Royal Institution*, 9 (1879–81), 580–94 • m. cert.

Archives Bayerische Staatsbibliothek, Munich, letters to Justus Liebig • CUL, letters to George G. Stokes

Likenesses portrait, repro. in 'Dr Edward Schunck' • portrait, repro. in Farrar, 'Edward Schunck, FRS'

Wealth at death £147,239 11*s*. 6*d*.: resworn probate, Sept 1903, *CGPLA Eng. & Wales*

Schuster, Sir Arthur [*formerly* Franz Arthur Friedrich] (**1851–1934**), physicist, was born on 12 September 1851 in Frankfurt am Main, Germany, the middle son of the three sons and one daughter of Francis Joseph Schuster (1823–1906), textile merchant and later banker, and his wife, Marie S. Pfeiffer (*b*. 1830), daughter of Hofrath Max Pfeiffer, banker, of Stuttgart. Following their marriage in 1849 his parents converted from Judaism to Christianity. Their children were baptized in 1856 and brought up in that faith, although Arthur Schuster apparently had little subsequent interest in religion.

Schuster started elementary school in 1856. His interest in science began during his years at the Frankfurt Gymnasium (1863–8), encouraged by his private tutor, Harald Schütz (later professor of mathematics at the *Gymnasium*). Following Frankfurt's annexation by Prussia in 1866, Schuster's father made 'financial arrangements' (Schuster, *Biographical Fragments*, 40), to ensure that Arthur and his brothers became Swiss citizens, thereby avoiding the threat of service in the Prussian army, and in 1868–70 he attended the academy in Geneva. In 1869 his father moved with his family to take up a position in the family textile business which had transferred to Manchester, then centre of the cotton trade, in 1811. Schuster rejoined his parents in 1870, and he and his siblings became British citizens in 1875. His elder brother, Ernest Joseph (1850–1924), would become a barrister and authority on international

Sir Arthur Schuster (1851–1934), by Sir William Orpen, 1912

law; his younger brother, Sir Felix Otto *Schuster a leading banker; and his sister Paula (*b*. 1863) later married Sir Lawrence Jones.

Schuster determined on a scientific career after a frustrated year as a wages clerk in Schuster Brothers, partly alleviated by attendance at Henry Roscoe's evening classes in chemistry at Owens College. His mother and Roscoe persuaded his father to let him begin full-time studies in October 1871. He took mathematics under Thomas Barker and physics under Balfour Stewart, and began research with Roscoe on the spectra of hydrogen and nitrogen. After a rather disappointing year with G.-R. Kirchhoff (1824–1887) at the University of Heidelberg, Schuster gained his PhD and returned to Owens as an unpaid demonstrator in physics. He spent the summer and autumn of 1874 working with W. E. Weber (1804–1891) in Göttingen and H. L. F. von Helmholtz (1821–1894) in Berlin. On return to England he was invited, because of his knowledge of spectrum analysis, to lead an expedition to Bangkok, Siam, to photograph the coronal spectrum during the total solar eclipse of 6 April 1875. This aim was not entirely successful, but he later participated in similar expeditions to Colorado in 1878, to Egypt (where he took the first successful photograph of the coronal spectrum) in 1882, and to the West Indies in 1886.

Schuster returned to Owens in November 1875 and lectured on James Clerk Maxwell's *Treatise on Electricity and Magnetism*. In May 1876 he visited Maxwell at the Cavendish Laboratory, Cambridge, to discuss undertaking research on the diamagnetism of rocks but, on entry that October, he began a study of oxygen emission spectra. Following Maxwell's death in November 1879, Schuster worked with J. W. Strutt (Baron Rayleigh) to obtain a more accurate value of the standard ohm as a unit of electrical resistance.

In 1881 Schuster was appointed professor of applied mathematics at Owens, which had become one of the colleges of the newly constituted Victoria University; he would succeed Stewart as professor of physics in 1888. On 18 September 1887 he married Emma Caroline Elizabeth (known as Cary; 1867–1962), eldest of the four daughters of George Loveday, gentleman, of Wardington, Oxfordshire. They had one son and four daughters. Both Schuster and his wife were strong supporters of emancipation for women; she played a leading role in the Owens Athletic Union and the staff bicycling club, and acted as hostess at her husband's weekly physical colloquia.

In 1883 Schuster moved on from 'spectroscopy' (a term he introduced in 1882), to continue research which he had begun at Cambridge on low-pressure electrical discharge in gases. He suggested in 1884 that the mechanism involved must be analogous to that of electrolysis in liquids, involving 'dissociation' of the gas into two chemically alike, but oppositely charged, 'particles' (ions). He was the first to use magnetic deflection to determine the ratio of the average charge to mass of the particles present in the luminous discharge of nitrogen. However, because of uncertainty in his experimental result ($10^3 < e/m < 10^6$ e.m.u.), Schuster concluded that 'to an order of magnitude' the ratio was sufficiently similar to that for 'an atom of hydrogen in water' (10^4 e.m.u.), that it confirmed his hypothesis ('The discharge of electricity through gases', *PRS*, 47, 1889, 526–61). In 1897 J. J. Thomson improved on Schuster's experimental method (finding $e/m = 10^7$ e.m.u.) and deduced that the fundamental particles involved, named 'electrons' by George Stoney (1826–1911) in 1894, must be subatomic in size. Feffer in 1989 has argued that, contrary to earlier claims that Schuster's work anticipated Thomson's discovery, Schuster had no interest in the nature of cathode rays—named by Eugen Goldstein (1850–1930) in 1876—nor the carrier particles *per se*.

By 1896 Schuster's experimental work had broadened into electrochemistry, optics, and X-radiography. Encouraged by Stewart he now turned to earth-physics and used the mathematical technique of harmonic analysis to disprove C. G. Knott's claim of periodicity in earthquake occurrences (1897). Schuster's lasting legacy is, however, his development of the periodogram (1897–8), the first practical tool for identifying statistically important frequencies present in a time series of observations. He used it to support Stewart's conjecture that variation of the terrestrial magnetic field was related both to electrical currents in a conducting layer of the upper atmosphere—the Heaviside layer discovered in 1902 by the physicist Oliver Heaviside (1850–1925)—and induced electrical earth-currents, showing both had recurrence periods of about twenty-six days.

Having presided over the building of the new physical laboratory of Owens College in 1900, when the University of Manchester was created in 1903 Schuster became dean of the faculty of science (1903–5); in 1907, partly as a result of strain and partly from a wish to further the cause of international science, he resigned his chair, having first ensured that Ernest Rutherford would become his successor. Although regarded by his contemporaries as a mathematical physicist of exceptional ability, Schuster was also a capable administrator and teacher, and a passionate advocate for the role of science in education and industry. Elected a fellow of the Royal Society in 1879, he began service as its secretary in 1912, moving home in 1913 from Kent House, Victoria Park, Manchester, to Twyford, near Reading, Berkshire, in order to facilitate this work. A strong supporter of scientific links between Britain and Germany, in 1899–1904 he helped the International Association of Academies to become fully established.

Refusing to credit rumours of Germany's growing militarism, Schuster was travelling to the Crimea to observe an eclipse when the First World War began, and had hurriedly to return via Egypt. In the previous year he had attended the Berlin conference of the British–German Foundation to discuss exchange studentships, and his elder brother (president of the German Colony in London), had organized a banquet to celebrate the jubilee of the Kaiser's reign. The Schuster family now found itself subjected to anti-German prejudice both in the press and, in Schuster's case, from some in the Royal Society such as H. E. Armstrong (1848–1937), A. B. Bassett (1854–1930) and E. R. Lankester (1847–1929). Felix Schuster had eventually to issue a press statement pointing out the family's loyalty to Britain and that they all had sons serving in the British army (on the day of Arthur Schuster's presidential address to the 1915 British Association meeting in Manchester, he learned that his own son, serving in the Dardanelles, had been wounded). Admirably supported by the council of the Royal Society, Schuster served as secretary throughout the war, and was then elected vice-president (1919–20) and foreign secretary (1920–24). He also served as secretary of the International Research Council (1919–28) and on the management committees for the Meteorological Office (1905–32) and National Physical Laboratory (1899–1902, 1920–25). During his career he published six books, including *Introduction to the Theory of Optics* (1904), and some 150 scientific papers.

Schuster's honours included appointment to the order of the White Elephant of Siam (1880) and a knighthood in 1920; doctorates from the universities of Geneva (1909), St Andrews (1911), and Oxford (1917); and the award of the royal, Rumford and Copley medals of the Royal Society (1893, 1926 and 1931).

Schuster's rather refined features were always graced by a beard and moustache and his use of spectacles in later life gave him a serious look. Although described as having a generally serious demeanour and retiring nature, he was regarded as kindly, a good conversationalist, and something of a wit, although he could occasionally upset others by espousal of unconventional views (such as his disapproval of the granting of external degrees by London University, and the need for a radical reorganization of the Meteorological Office). Rutherford wrote that Schuster 'unlike most professors is a wealthy man' (Eve, 167), but he was generous with it, purchasing radium for the Physical Laboratory and two seismographs for the Eskdalemuir observatory, endowing readerships in mathematical physics at Manchester and meteorology at Cambridge, and contributing generously to the funds of the Royal Society and the International Union for Co-operation in Solar Research. In his youth Schuster enjoyed walking and climbing, and later cycling and motoring. Since boyhood he had enjoyed sketching and landscape-painting and 'usually carried his complete outfit with him' (Hale, 105) when travelling, even to scientific meetings. Unfortunately, this ended in 1923 when he lost an eye in a golfing accident and his health, apparently never very robust, gradually declined. He died of cerebral thrombosis at his home, Yeldall, Twyford, on 14 October 1934 and was buried at Brookwood cemetery, Woking, on 17 October. RICHARD J. HOWARTH

Sources 'Professor Sir Arthur Schuster', *The Outlook* (13 July 1907) • *Professor Sir Arthur Schuster, F.R.S., 1881–1906, jubilee celebration* (1906) • *The physical laboratories of the University of Manchester: a record of 25 years' work* (1906) • S. Chapman, 'Arthur Schuster, 1851–1934', *Terrestrial Magnetism and Atmospheric Electricity*, 39 (1934), 341–5 • P. J. Davies, 'Sir Arthur Schuster, FRS, 1851–1934', PhD diss., University of Manchester Institute of Science and Technology, 1983 • A. S. Eve, *Rutherford* (1939) • S. M. Feffer, 'Arthur Schuster, J. J. Thomson and the discovery of the electron', *Historical Studies in the Physical and Biological Sciences*, 20 (1989–90), 33–62 • F. W. D. [F. W. Dyson], *Monthly Notices of the Royal Astronomical Society*, 95 (1934–5), 326–30 • G. E. Hale, 'Sir Arthur Schuster', *Astrophysical Journal*, 81 (1935), 97–106 • R. H. Kargon, 'Schuster, Arthur', *DSB* • C. H. Lees, 'Sir Arthur Schuster, FRS', *Proceedings of the Physical Society*, 47 (1935), 1130–34 • B. Schonland, *The atomists (1805–1933)* (1968) • A. Schuster, autobiography, 1905, JRL, SCH/A23 • A. Schuster, *Biographical fragments* (1932) • N. Schuster, 'Early days of Roentgen photography in Britain', *BMJ* (1960), 1164–6 • G. C. Simpson, *Obits. FRS*, 1 (1932–5), 409–23 • m. cert. • d. cert. • *WW* (1934)

Archives JRL, MSS • JRL, corresp. and papers • NRA, priv. coll., lectures and diary • RAS, diary, accounts, and photographs of expedition to Siam to observe solar eclipse • RAS, diary, corresp., and papers • RAS, letters to officers of the Royal Astronomical Society, and its joint permanent eclipse committee • RS, corresp. • Scott Polar RI, letters • St John Cam., letters | Air Force Research Laboratories, Cambridge, Massachusetts, letters to Lord Rayleigh • CUL, corresp. with Lord Kelvin, Add. MSS 7342, 7656 • CUL, letters to Lord Rutherford, Add. MS 7653 • CUL, letters to Sir G. G. Stokes, Add. MSS 7342, 7656, 7675 • CUL, corresp. with Sir J. J. Thomson, Add. MS 7654 • JRL, letters to R. S. Hutton • St John Cam., letters to Sir Joseph Larmor • Trinity Cam., corresp. with Joseph John Thomson • UCL, letters to Sir Oliver Lodge, Add. MS 89 • University of Manchester Institute of Science and Technology, corresp. with G. E. Hale [microfilm]; corresp. with Royal Society [copies] • Wellcome L., photographs and documents of the early use of X-rays

Likenesses photographs, *c.*1888–1920, Wellcome L. • photographs, 1902–*c.*1906, repro. in Schuster, *Biographical fragments* • group photograph, 19 June 1906, repro. in *Professor Sir Arthur Schuster*, frontispiece • J. Collier, oils, 1907, Manchester University • W. Orpen, portrait, 1912, RS [*see illus.*] • photograph, repro. in Chapman, 'Arthur Schuster, 1851–1934', frontispiece • photograph, repro. in *Obits. FRS*, frontispiece • photograph, repro. in Hale, 'Sir Arthur Schuster'

Wealth at death £283,307 4*s.* 11*d.*: resworn probate, 17 Dec 1934, *CGPLA Eng. & Wales*

Schuster, Claud, Baron Schuster (1869–1956), civil servant, was born in Manchester on 22 August 1869, the only son of Frederick Leo Schuster, merchant, and his wife, Sophia Ellen, daughter of Lieutenant-Colonel Herbert William Wood, Madras Army. Schuster belonged to the famous Jewish family which had its origins in Frankfurt am Main. He was a second cousin of Sir Arthur Schuster and Sir Felix Schuster. Schuster's father and uncles were born in England, their father, Samuel Schuster, having come from Frankfurt in 1824. One of the uncles, the Revd William Percy Schuster, became curate at Corfe Castle and later vicar of Lulworth. As a boy Schuster used to stay with him and became so fond of Dorset that in later life he made his country home there. Schuster was educated at Winchester College and New College, Oxford, where he obtained a second class in history in 1892. He was called to the bar by the Inner Temple in 1895 and joined the northern circuit. In 1896 Schuster married Mabel Elizabeth (*d.* 1936), daughter of W. W. *Merry, rector of Lincoln College, Oxford. They had one son, who was killed on active service in France in 1918, and one daughter.

His father having lost his money, Schuster had to earn his own living. He doubted whether he would succeed quickly at the bar and in 1899 was appointed secretary to the London Government Act commission, where he remained until 1902. There he caught the eye of Robert Morant in the Board of Education and he moved to that department, becoming Morant's legal assistant (1903), legal adviser (1907), and principal assistant secretary (1911). His experience under Morant was invaluable and confirmed his grasp of the importance and the working of local government. He was closely involved, with Sir Arthur Thring, on the drafting of education bills under two governments with widely differing policies on church schools; and he was actively concerned in the consequent litigation.

When Morant transferred to national insurance in 1911 he insisted on taking Schuster with him. The change taught Schuster new lessons. The education office had been highly specialized, while the National Health Insurance Commission faced the multifarious task of implementing Lloyd George's complicated scheme of insurance. Schuster became one of the able team of commissioners who used the whole civil service as a single instrument of policy to bring the act into operation within six months and thereafter to administer it. He served in various capacities with the commission, but most usefully as legal adviser.

In 1915 the offices of clerk of the crown in chancery and permanent secretary in the Lord Chancellor's Office were due to fall vacant upon the retirement of Lord Muir Mackenzie. Lord Haldane with good reason chose Schuster, a lawyer with twelve years' experience of constructive administration and with the machinery of government at his fingertips. The appointment, though, caused some surprise at the time, 'having regard to the name and ancestry of the nominee' (*The Times*, 29 June 1956), and it showed some courage on Haldane's part. Haldane regarded the office of chancellor as an intolerable burden for one minister to carry. His mind was moving towards a division of the duties between the chancellor and a minister of justice, to be appointed after the war. Schuster, he thought, would be the man to create the new ministry when the time came.

By the time that Schuster took up his post on 1 July 1915, however, Haldane had ceased to be lord chancellor and his proposals were later rejected by Lord Birkenhead, the first chancellor to be appointed after the war. The lord chancellor continued therefore to bear an exceedingly heavy burden and his staff had to make it possible for him to sustain it. Schuster, until his retirement in 1944, played a key role in enabling ten successive chancellors to perform their varied and arduous duties.

For this task Schuster had natural advantages. He was a quick reader and thinker, fluent on paper, and lucid in stating a case. He was, on principle, as anxious as Haldane himself to see that the right men were put in the right places with the best possible conditions of service, in both the public interest and their own. He had to adapt his technique of a higher civil servant to a new environment in which judges receive with circumspection any advice from an emissary of the executive. A chancellor, although head of the judiciary, does not command judges, but seeks their advice. Schuster's role was often to suggest who should be asked to advise, what should be referred to a committee, who should be invited to serve, and what should be done with the report. He saw to it that action swiftly followed; and the judges, the bar, the Law Society, and members of both houses were the more ready to give the chancellor their help when they found that it yielded practical results.

The chancellors' reforms during Schuster's tenure of office were many and technical. They included the Law of Property Act, 1922, and the acts of 1925 which replaced and superseded it. The most fruitful committees which he suggested and on which he sat were the Swift committee of 1919, which led to much greater efficiency in the county court system; the Law Revision Committee of 1934, from which sprang the first series of acts reforming defects in the common law; and the Rushcliffe committee of 1944, which gave birth to legal aid. But executive action is not all initiative. It is also the response to what happens; and the chancellor's being a kind of universal joint between cabinet, judiciary, and parliament, there was hardly a public event which did not call for action of some sort on his behalf. Schuster was always alert, his course of action soundly planned and quickly put in train, and he was active behind the scenes during events such as the Easter rising, the general strike, and the abdication crisis. Schuster's efficient discharge of his duties furnished the chancellor with the time and the information necessary to formulate the appropriate response to any given problem.

Schuster's 'decisive and directive' style (Stevens, 24) was not always popular with the judges, who resented the contemporary decline in their real power relative to the civil service. As author in 1932 of the report of the committee on ministers' powers, he helped to narrow the judiciary's scope in administrative matters, allowing civil servants to retain wide decision-making powers. He was the subject of a particularly outspoken personal attack by Lord Hewart, the lord chief justice, who had a deep-rooted antipathy to administrators, in the House of Lords on 11 December 1934. Nevertheless, Schuster stilled the movement for a ministry of justice (proposed in 1919 by Haldane's report for the committee on the machinery of government), and thus enabled chancellors to retain for a generation the duty of choosing judges.

From 1944 to 1946 Schuster was head of the legal branch of the Allied Control Commission (British zone) in Austria. Although he was now over seventy-five, he tackled the task with the zest of a young man. After his return he initiated a debate in the House of Lords on Austria, 28 January 1947, in which he sought a clearer definition of Britain's policy towards that country. Schuster advocated a positive and constructive approach that, by restoring the economy and rebuilding the society, would keep Austria free from communist influence. In the same year he did good work as treasurer of the Inner Temple in its reconstruction after the bombing of the war. His mind never lost its vigour, and he died at Charing Cross Hospital, London, on 28 June 1956 after being taken ill while attending an old Wykehamist dinner.

As a young man Schuster had black hair, piercing blue eyes, and the neat, spare figure which he kept all his life. He climbed in the Alps from the age of seventeen and took to skiing in 1921. He was the first man to be president both of the Ski Club of Great Britain (1932–4) and of the Alpine Club (1938–40). Like Leo Amery, who later followed him in holding both these offices, Schuster was an effective liaison officer between the two sports, and he helped to reconcile the old guard of mountaineers to the new breed of ski-racers. As president of the Alpine Club he was responsible for changing the method of membership election, substituting an open vote at a general meeting for the secret ballot. At the age of sixty-four he took to hunting again, which he had not done since he was a boy in Cheshire.

Schuster's love of natural beauty and his sensitive appreciation of literature, and especially classical literature, are reflected in the style and matter of his various writings on mountains and mountaineers. He contributed articles to *The Times* and the *Cornhill Magazine*, as well as to the specialist climbing journals. These, and his various addresses to bodies such as the Alpine Club, were collected in his books *Peaks and Pleasant Pastures* (1911) and *Postscript to Adventure* (1950). He chose mountaineering as the subject of his 1948 Romanes lecture at Oxford.

Schuster was a sociable man and a good conversationalist, regarded by many as an exemplar of 'the wide culture of an earlier generation' (*Alpine Journal*, 373). He was unshakeable in his friendship, but had many of the prejudices widespread among Englishmen of his class, and he often gave pungent expression to his aversions. He detested, for example, modern poetry. 'His dislikes, in fact, were as confident and as catholic as his enthusiasms, and almost by choice he made enemies as well as friends' (ibid., 374).

Schuster was knighted in 1913, appointed CVO in 1918, KC in 1919, KCB in 1920, and GCB in 1927. He served as high sheriff of Dorset in 1941 and was raised to the peerage in 1944. He was an honorary fellow of St Catharine's College, Cambridge. ALBERT NAPIER, *rev.* MARK POTTLE

Sources *The Times* (29 June 1956) • *The Times* (4 July 1956) • *The Times* (11 July 1956) • *Alpine Journal*, 61 (1956), 371–4 • *British Ski Year Book*, 17/38 (1957), 283–9 • C. Schuster, *Men, women and mountains: days in the Alps and Pyrenees* (1931) • C. Schuster, *Postscript to adventure* (1950) • C. Schuster, *Peaks and pleasant pastures* (1911) • personal knowledge (1971) • private information (1971) • R. F. V. Heuston, *Lives of the lord chancellors, 1940–1970* (1987) • R. Stevens, *The independence of the judiciary: the view from the lord chancellor's office* (1993)

Archives Alpine Club, London, diaries • NRA, papers | Bodl. Oxf., corresp. with Sankey • Bodl. Oxf., corresp. with Gilbert Murray

Likenesses W. Stoneman, photographs, 1920–45, NPG • H. Collinson, oils; in possession of family in 1971 • W. Rothenstein, lithograph (as young man), NPG

Wealth at death £24,896 15*s.* 2*d.*: probate, 3 Sept 1956, *CGPLA Eng. & Wales*

Schuster, Sir Felix Otto, first baronet (1854–1936), banker, was born on 21 April 1854, at Frankfurt am Main, in the Land of Hesse, the third son of Francis Joseph Schuster (1823–1906), and his wife, Marie (1829/30–1890), daughter of Hofrath Max Pfeiffer, of Stuttgart in the kingdom of Württemberg. His father was a merchant banker with special interests in cotton who converted from Judaism to Christianity in the 1850s, and emigrated to the 'cottonopolis' of Manchester in 1869, following the Prussian annexation of Hesse in 1866. Around 1858 his mother succumbed to Graves' disease, which was initially treated as a nervous ailment; in addition to her lifetime of pain one eye was excised in the 1860s in an unsuccessful attempt to save the sight of the other from glaucoma. Felix Schuster was educated at Frankfurt Gymnasium, Owens College, Manchester, and Geneva Academy. He had a boyish ambition to be a great musician, and trained as a pianist with Ernest Pauer. His musical technique was proficient and austere; he became a liveryman of the Musicians' Company, and the friend and benefactor of musicians. While a student at Geneva, he took up mountaineering, and belonged to the generation of mountaineers which succeeded the pioneer climbers. He became a prominent official of the Alpine Club, visited the Alps regularly, and took formidable mountain walks when he became too old to climb.

In 1873 Felix Schuster entered the family firm at Frankfurt am Main and after a few months settled in London. As a result of his cosmopolitan education he was an accomplished linguist. He was naturalized in 1875 at the same time as his brother Arthur *Schuster. He became a partner in Schuster, Son & Co. of Cannon Street about the time of his marriage in 1879 to (Alwine) Meta (1860–1918), daughter of Hermann Weber (1823–1918), a physician from the Rhineland who settled in England because he wished to live in the country of Shakespeare's tongue and who was knighted in 1899 for his work on tuberculosis. Her sister Hilda had in 1876 married Schuster's brother Ernest (1850–1924), afterwards a king's counsel and grandfather of the poet Stephen Spender. Felix and Meta Schuster had one son and four daughters (of whom the third in 1906 married Rayner Goddard, later lord chief justice).

Sir Felix Otto Schuster, first baronet (1854–1936), by Lafayette, 1927

The Schuster firm was in 1888 taken over by the Union Bank of London, which was one of the leading London firms engaged in transatlantic finance, and the only such business that had begun as a joint-stock company. Its unique position was partly attributable to its early connection with the Schuster family. Felix Schuster became a director of the Union Bank after this merger, deputy governor in 1893 and governor in 1895 following the appointment of Charles Ritchie, afterwards Lord Ritchie of Dundee, as president of the Board of Trade. Unusually for the head of an English joint-stock bank, Schuster exercised strict control over his bank's daily business rather than trusting routine tasks to general managers. He monitored every account and scrutinized the activities of each branch. This involved him in a constant regime of overwork; this, combined with his shyness and his mastery of the technical minutiae of banking, made him an intimidating employer and colleague.

Schuster's interventionist management, which was more customary in continental than English banking practice, resembled that of his great contemporary, Sir Edward Holden of the Midland Bank. These two men were indeed the leading clearing-bankers in the two decades before 1914. Union's growth in this period was second only to the Midland Bank, with deposits rising from £16,099,945 in 1895 to £45,832,803 in 1914. Schuster was more concerned to strengthen the bank as an institution, and to maintain strong relations with its clients, than to pursue high dividends, and eschewed speculative business. He believed that clearing-bankers should never supply traders with working capital, and was chary of providing long-term finance to industry.

In 1902 Schuster initiated a process of growth by amalgamation by taking over Smith, Payne, and Smith, a firm associated with the family of whom the merchant banker Vivian Hugh Smith was a cadet. The Union of London and Smiths took over other private banking concerns in 1903. In the ensuing decade this new combine showed that the functions and resources of joint-stock and merchant banks could be successfully united. Ultimately in 1918 Schuster and James Mackay, Baron Inchcape, organized Union's merger with the National Provincial Bank. The new National Provincial and Union Bank became one of the 'big five' of the clearing-banks, but was known after 1924 as the National Provincial. Schuster retired as governor in 1918, but remained a director of the amalgamated board, and continued in almost daily attendance at the office, although his influence diminished with age.

In his heyday Schuster was a leading theorist of the banking community whose speeches at his shareholders' half-yearly general meetings and at the Institute of Bankers were highly influential. In December 1903, addressing the institute, he enunciated the bankers' case against tariff protectionism in a speech stressing the City of London's position as the world's dominant financial centre and its role in helping the balance of payments with invisible earnings. His prominence in the controversy over Chamberlain's tariff proposals reached its climax when he unsuccessfully contested the City of London as Liberal free trade candidate in the general election of 1906. His anti-protectionist views earned him the enmity of many right-wing figures, and following the outbreak of war in 1914 he and his family were vilified as German Jews by publicists associated with Leo Maxse, Hilaire Belloc, and G. K. Chesterton. He had an unusually pale face, framed by a square black beard, and semitic features which further incited the racial prejudice against him. Violet Bonham Carter in 1905 thought he looked 'as if he came straight out of an illustrated Old Testament' (Bonham Carter, 95).

Schuster had a high sense of responsibility, and cherished the ambition to help direct British financial policy with the disinterestedness of a civil servant. After Ritchie became chancellor of the exchequer in 1902, Schuster was regularly consulted by the Treasury: 'a very intelligent and shrewd man', judged Sir E. W. Hamilton (diary, 11 March 1902, BL, Add. MS 48679). Schuster served on the royal commission on London traffic (1903–4), the Board of Trade commission on amending company law (1905), the India Office committee on railway finance and administration (1907–8), and the Treasury committee on Irish land purchase finance (1907–8). He was created a baronet in 1906, in which year he was appointed by Lord Morley at an annual salary of £1200 as finance member of the Council of India in London. His position briefly became invidious in 1912 through a secret arrangement for the merchant bank of Samuel Montagu to obtain silver bullion for the Indian government, bypassing the Bank of England and breaking a 'ring' that had rigged the market against that government. The Union of London and Smiths Bank was banker to Montagu & Co., and in the wake of the Marconi revelations, Schuster was the object of much criticism from tories and antisemites. In 1916 he retired from the Council of India.

Schuster was prominent as president of the Institute of Bankers (1907–9) in protesting at David Lloyd George's budget of 1909, and specifically at its increased death duties, and gave notably lucid testimony to the United States National Monetary Commission in 1910. As chairman of the Central Association of Bankers (1913–15), he and Holden were crucial figures in settling complex new financial arrangements when war erupted in 1914. Maynard Keynes believed that Schuster and Holden 'behaved badly' and that Schuster was 'cowardly'. By no means all the clearing bankers 'trusted Schuster or Holden or agreed with their immediate proposals; but they were timid, voiceless and leaderless and in the hurry of the times they did not make themselves heard' (*Collected Writings of John Maynard Keynes*, 30–31). Schuster afterwards worked with Walter Cunliffe on the wartime foreign exchange committee and was president of the British Bankers' Association (1925). Both personally and on behalf of the Association of Chambers of Commerce he urged a return to the gold standard in 1924; by 1930 his Victorian Liberal's faith in the panacea of free trade was shaken.

Schuster usually declined non-executive directorships: he was, however, a director of the German Bank of London, which merged in 1913 with the London and Liverpool Bank of Commerce, and later of the Grand Trunk Railway of Canada; he chaired the British Italian Banking Corporation until 1931. He died of cerebral anaemia and high blood pressure on 13 May 1936, at Ruthin Castle, Denbighshire, and was buried, close to his home, at Fernhurst church, near Haslemere. He was succeeded in the baronetcy by his son, (Felix) Victor.

RICHARD DAVENPORT-HINES

Sources D. Kynaston, *The City of London*, 2 (1995); 3 (1999) • Y. Cassis, *City bankers, 1890–1914*, trans. M. Rocque (1994) [Fr. orig., *Banquiers de la City à l'époque édouardienne, 1890–1914* (1984)] • C. Goodhart, *The business of banking, 1891–1914* (1972) • H. Withers, *National Provincial Bank, 1833 to 1933* (1933) • A. Schuster, *Biographical fragments* (1932) • S. Spender, *World within world: the autobiography of Stephen Spender* (1951) • *The Times* (15 May 1936) • *The collected writings of John Maynard Keynes*, ed. D. Moggridge and E. Johnson, 16 (1971) • *Lantern slides: the diaries and letters of Violet Bonham Carter, 1904–1914*, ed. M. Bonham Carter and M. Pottle (1996) • diary, Sir E. W. Hamilton, BL Add. MS 48679 [entry for 11 March 1902] • *CGPLA Eng. & Wales* (1936) • Y. Cassis, 'Schuster, Sir Felix Otto', *DBB* • *DNB* • d. cert.

Archives BL, diary of Sir E. W. Hamilton, Add. MS 48679 • HSBC Group Archives, London, Midland Bank archives, diary of Sir Edward Holden • PRO, Treasury papers

Likenesses H. von Herkomer, oils, presented in 1903, priv. coll. • photograph, *c.*1914, repro. in Cassis, 'Schuster, Sir Felix Otto' • portrait, oils, presented in 1915, priv. coll. • Lafayette, photograph, 1927, NPG [*see illus.*] • Spy [L. Ward], mechanical repro., NPG; repro. in *VF* (28 June 1906)

Wealth at death £605,499 4*s.* 11*d.*: resworn probate, 18 June 1936, *CGPLA Eng. & Wales*

Schuster, Sir George Ernest (1881–1982), government adviser, was born on 25 April 1881 in Hampstead, London, the elder son (there were no daughters) of Ernest Joseph Schuster (1850–1924), barrister, and his wife, Hilda, daughter of Sir Hermann Weber MD. His father came from a Jewish family of bankers who had left Frankfurt am Main in 1866. One uncle, Felix *Schuster, was given a baronetcy by H. H. Asquith, and another, Sir Arthur *Schuster, became a fellow and secretary of the Royal Society. George Schuster was a scholar of Charterhouse and an exhibitioner of New College, Oxford, where he obtained a second class in classical honour moderations in 1901 and a first in *literae humaniores* in 1903. After reading for the bar (Lincoln's Inn, 1905) he accepted a business post with H. R. Merton & Co. In 1908 he married Gwendolen (*d.* 1981), daughter of Robert John Parker, Baron Parker of Waddington, a judge. They had two sons, one of whom was killed in action in 1941. His marriage was the central happiness of his life.

Schuster's idealistic and active turn of mind was attracted by politics and in 1911 he was adopted as Liberal candidate for North Cumberland. He was considered a promising recruit but, owing to his German name, had to relinquish any political ambitions in August 1914. He joined the Oxford yeomanry. The war suited his mentality and his ideals. In May 1916 he was appointed a chief administrative staff officer at First Army headquarters. After the armistice he went to Murmansk, with the rank of lieutenant-colonel, to deal with the financial and currency problems which beset the White Russians.

When the Murmansk operation was wound up Schuster embarked on training as a teacher on the first course at Birmingham University and felt very frustrated when the whole project was abandoned for lack of funds. At just this time he was selected by a City syndicate to report on practical measures for reviving the economy of what remained of the Austro-Hungarian empire. Though his report to the syndicate contained no effective proposals, it led to a post with Frederick Hull & Co. and another with the finance committee of the League of Nations. He also became a member of the economic research organization of the Labour Party. His growing reputation in economic expertise led to what he styled 'a new adventure'—a request from the Foreign Office that he should go for five years as financial secretary to the Sudan (1922–7). Later he always looked on these years as the most rewarding experience of his life and a 'chance to take part in one of the finest chapters in the history of the British Empire'. This was a disturbed period during which Sir Lee Stack, the governor-general, was assassinated, but Schuster won praise not only for his performance of his financial and administrative tasks, but also for his contribution to the handling of political problems.

In October 1927 a request came from the India Office for Schuster to accept the post of finance member of the viceroy's council. The Colonial Office agreed to release him from the Sudan on condition that the appointment be deferred for a year and that he first travel round east and central Africa as a member of the Hilton Young commission, to report on proposals for the closer union of certain African colonies and then act as financial adviser to the Colonial Office on several economic development projects in the area. Schuster's years in India as finance minister (1928–34) covered an important stage in the transition from British rule to independence. From the first he felt it his prime duty to work for Indian interests. He had to effect large economies in government and military expenditure. It was ironical that he should be the only person wounded, though not seriously, when a bomb was thrown in the assembly, during the introduction of legislation which he himself had suggested should be deferred. He returned to Britain in September 1930 to advise the British delegation at the first round-table conference held in London to plan the political future of the subcontinent. The final effort of his period in India was to be the establishing of a reserve bank as the currency authority for India, independent of the government.

Schuster was fifty-three when he returned from India and still considered himself a young man, with a personal career to make. He was soon invited on to the boards of important companies. Unilever asked him to undertake the chairmanship of Allied Suppliers—the largest retailing group in Britain. His work here brought him to his special interest in relations between management and labour. In 1938 he was elected as Liberal National candidate in the by-election at Walsall. Soon he was working for Sir Stafford Cripps, an old Oxfordshire friend, in the Ministry of Aircraft Production. He spoke often in the Commons, especially on measures of social policy such as the Beveridge plan, which he regarded as totally inadequate as a conception of welfare 'defined in exclusively material terms'. He was a good constituency member and it came as a great shock when he was defeated in 1945.

On his return from India, Schuster had joined the governing body of Charterhouse and by 1939 had become deputy to the statutory chairman, the archbishop of Canterbury. He was constantly in demand as a committee member of proven experience in drafting and lobbying. His own interest focused more and more on industrial relations, and he worked closely on this and economic planning with the post-war Labour government. At the request of the government he went in 1950 as financial and economic adviser to Malta. He was convinced the Maltese were justified in asking for financial help from Britain and finally persuaded them to raise more by local taxation. As a result Cripps immediately recommended a grant of £1.5 million to be met from the colonial development fund. Early in 1953 Schuster was invited by the federation of the Indian chamber of commerce to return to their country and advise them on future policy. He advised that the foundation of India's prosperity must be in the development of agricultural production rather than in large-scale industry, and in village communities rather than in vast urban concentrations.

Schuster was never unoccupied. From 1951 to 1963 he was chairman of the Oxford Regional Hospital Board and from 1953 he was for twenty-two years a most active member of the Oxfordshire county council. He found the work congenial as most of his colleagues were local, voluntary, and non-party. In 1961 came a new 'adventure', the development of Voluntary Service Overseas. These three words summed up his enthusiasms. He became honorary treasurer and eagerly set about creating an orderly administration to support A. G. Dickson's imaginative vision, and within two years he had received generous support from many private sources plus an annual grant of £500,000 from government funds.

When already over eighty he threw himself into his last great activity, the creation of Atlantic College, which he came to prize more highly than anything else he had done. He was chairman of its board of governors from 1963 to 1973. He was much inspired by discussions with Kurt Hahn and Sir Robert Birley. The fact that funds were missing merely spurred him on. He drew on every possible source, reasoning rather than wheedling, involving trade union personalities as well as leaders of finance. He threw himself into every aspect of the project, making it his business to know the pupils and to ensure that staff had frequent opportunities for meeting the governors. His ninetieth birthday was celebrated at St Donats with great display and he remained deeply proud that he had been involved in the college, and also that so constructive a project should have been started in Britain, 'as I do not believe it could have got off the ground in any other country'.

Schuster's long life thus ended on a note of triumph. On his ninety-eighth birthday he went up to London to be measured for two new suits. In his 102nd year he was still writing to headmasters on educational matters. He had published innumerable pamphlets and three books: *India and Democracy* (with G. Wint, 1941), *Christianity and Human Relations in Industry* (1951), and *Private Work and Public Causes* (1979), his autobiography. He listed his recreations in *Who's Who* as 'all country sports'. He was a tall man with an upright and soldierly bearing, with finely marked features and with excellent health. He had a great capacity for work and delighted in it—he nearly always fitted in an hour before breakfast. His financial acumen and his clarity of exposition were widely appreciated, as was his gift for warm friendship and for creating a team spirit in any undertaking. He was a rare mixture of intellectual, man of action, and idealist, who never failed the ideal he had set himself as an undergraduate, believing intensely in hard work, personal service, and the values of the British empire. Reading his slim autobiography, one gets a vivid picture of the life of a public servant in the closing years of that empire.

Schuster was appointed CBE in 1918, KCMG in 1926, and KCSI in 1931. Oxford University awarded him an honorary DCL in 1964. He died on 5 June 1982 at Nether Worton House, the seventeenth-century manor he had owned at Middle Barton, near Banbury, since 1919.

OLIVER VAN OSS, *rev.*

Sources G. Schuster, *Private work and public causes* (1979) • *The Times* (8 June 1982) • private information (2004)

Archives Bodl. Oxf., corresp. and papers | Bodl. RH, corresp. with J. H. Oldham • JRL, letters to *Manchester Guardian* • PRO NIre., corresp. with Lord Dufferin • U. Durham L., letters to Sir Harold MacMichael | SOUND BL NSA, performance recordings

Wealth at death £497,417: probate, 6 April 1983, *CGPLA Eng. & Wales*

Schütz, Christopher [*known as* Jonah, Jonas] (**1521–1592**), metallurgist and furnace engineer, was born in Annaberg, Saxony, the son of Christoph Schütz (*b.* 1505) of Chemnitz and an unknown mother. Having learned his craft in the Lutheran mining communities of the Erzgebirge, he was approached by William Humfrey, assay master at the Tower of London, who needed Schütz's expertise in the zinc-rich ores known as calamine which were required to make 'latten' or brass. In 1563 Humfrey personally paid for his passage to England, where in 1564, with the help of twenty German-speaking assistants, Schütz built the country's first blast furnace, exploiting the Angiddy at Tintern to pump the bellows, much as illustrated in Georg Agricola's *De re metallica* (1556). His dramatic appearances from his large and noisy furnace, resembling a man emerging from a whale, seemingly gave rise to his widely circulated nickname of Jonah or Jonas. A royal licence granted to Humfrey and Schütz on 17 September 1565 to prospect for, mine, and process calamine in England and the pale of Ireland led to their discovering calamine ore in the Mendips early in 1566. To use it in the Tintern furnace Schütz introduced a stamping and sieving process suggested by Daniel Hoechstetter.

On 9 April 1568 Schütz was made an English denizen in recognition of his work at Tintern. His employment may have owed something to a desire to foster the production of weapons and armaments in England, but if that was the case the hopes of his patrons were soon disappointed, for by 1568, facing costs of £333 for calamine extracted from Worle Hill, Humfrey had decided that the ore was too expensive to make the brass needed for wool-combs, ordnance, and scientific instruments, and from 28 May a newly chartered Society of Mineral and Battery Works (with shares held by Humfrey and Schütz) took over the Tintern furnace, converting it to make iron wire. Then late in that year rulings in the exchequer case brought by the crown against the seventh earl of Northumberland, securing the queen's right to mine copper on the earl's lands, led to a boom in metalliferous mining and smelting, promising Schütz and Humfrey supplementary incomes from licensing and advising on applications of their patented furnace design. Thus Schütz was paid to advise on commissioning a new steel furnace at Robertsbridge, Sussex. He also co-operated with the queen's physician Burcot Kranich in using calamine lotion to treat furnace burns, a development confirmed by the archaeological discovery of lotion pots at other Sussex furnaces. In 1570 he commissioned a new smelter at Beauchief Abbey, near Sheffield, and then non-ferrous smelters in Bristol, Nottingham, and London, all for the Company of Mineral and Battery Works, which according to Pettus was soon employing 8000 people. The accounts of the Mines Royal Company for 1575 show that Daniel Hoechstetter three times sought Humfrey's agreement for Schütz's leaving the Sheffield smelters to commission a new furnace at Keswick, and in 1576 Schütz did stay in Keswick for seventeen weeks.

In January 1577 Schütz's London assays played a key role in causing Michael Lok and Sir William Winter, the master of the ordnance, to recommend that Martin Frobisher return to Meta Incognita (south-east Baffin Island) and there collect gold-bearing ores to be selected by Schütz. The latter himself conducted assays on Kodlunarn Island in August 1577, and then in November and December supervised two exploratory assays of Meta Incognita ore in Winter's London garden, using a small new 'footblast' furnace. He beguiled official commissioners for Meta Incognita ores, including John Dee, into considering a bigger blast furnace, possibly at Bristol, to extract more gold, but on 16 December 1577 chose instead a site at Dartford that would better accommodate big water-powered bellows, finishing it to carefully drawn plans in November 1578. The resulting smelting complex disappointed many, although he fired it with coal from Newcastle and metalliferous additives from north-west England and the west country. A report of 1581 criticized the furnace's design, but Schütz's failure was essentially due to the fact—confirmed by modern research—that Meta Incognita's hornblende ores contained no gold. With a speculative investment of over £20,000 obviously lost, including £583 on the Dartford complex, litigation followed, entangling Lok for decades and leading to Schütz's making unavailing offers in 1579 and 1580 to fire the Dartford furnace with other metalliferous ores. After a statute of 1581 forbade the use of the furnace to smelt iron it was sold, and by 1586 was serving John Spilman as England's first paper mill. Schütz escaped prosecution for the Meta Incognita débâcle, but a chancery decree of 20 December 1582 criticized him by name for devastating the woods near Tintern for his smelter there, and limited the amount he could take.

Thereafter Schütz, now the sole surviving patentee of his furnace design and successful in litigating to protect his rights in it, helped many landowners to identify their mineral resources, for instance on the Derbyshire estates of the Hodgkinson family. He also introduced other innovative Germanic practices, as when he identified a market for the graphite deposits of Seatoller and Borrowdale, both in Cumberland, in making cupels and other furnace ware; from 1578 this boosted the entry fines that Roger Robinson paid for leases of Seatoller's mineral-rich land. From at least 1574 Schütz had a house in London's Cripplegate. His will, drawn up on 8 February 1574 but not proved until 8 June 1592, records his wish for burial in St Giles Cripplegate. He left £100 to his brother Balthazar and £5 to Mr Wheeler—the goldsmith who concurred in his erroneous assays of Frobisher's ores in 1576–7. Most of his estate was left to Francis Barty, his executor and probably his legal counsel. Bequests totalling £10 went to the parish and its minister. Nothing was left to his wife (probably named Orothea) though letters patent of 11 January 1578 had once promised Schütz a pension of £100, of which £20 were intended for her. R. C. D. BALDWIN

Sources chancery, patent rolls, PRO, C66/1016, 1047, 1173 • will, PRO, PROB 11/35 • state papers domestic, Elizabeth I, PRO, SP 12/50/36, nos. 17–18 • maps and plans, PRO, MPF 304 • NL Wales, Badminton estate records, 8924–5 • [E. Keswick], *Elizabethan Keswick: extracts from the original account books, 1564–1577, of the German miners, in the archives of Augsburg*, ed. W. G. Collingwood, Cumberland and Westmorland Antiquarian and Archaeological Society, tract ser., 8 (1912); repr. (1987) • J. Pettus, *Fodine regales* (1670); repr. (1981) • R. C. D. Baldwin, 'Speculative ambitions and the reputations of Frobisher's metallurgists', *Meta Incognita: a discourse of discovery: Martin Frobisher's Arctic voyages, 1576–8*, ed. S. Alsford, T. H. B. Symons, and C. Kitzan, 2 vols. (1999), vol. 2, pp. 401–76 • J. McDermott, 'The construction of the Dartford furnaces', *Meta Incognita: a discourse of discovery: Martin Frobisher's Arctic voyages, 1576–8*, ed. S. Alsford, T. H. B. Symons, and C. Kitzan, 2 vols. (1999), vol. 2, pp. 503–21 • S. D. Coates, *The water powered industries of the lower Wye valley: the River Wye from Tintern to Redbrook* (1992)

Wealth at death over £100: will, PRO, PROB 11/35, 8 Feb 1574

Schütze [*née* Raphael; *other married name* Mendl], **(Gladys) Henrietta** [*pseud.* Henrietta Leslie] **(1884–1946)**, writer and pacifist, was born at 42 Portland Place, London, on 6 July 1884, the only child of Arthur Lewis Raphael and his wife, Marianna Floretta (*née* Moses). In her memoirs she recalled her early childhood in a wealthy, cosmopolitan, and assimilated Jewish family. Her mother surrounded herself with artists and became a painter in her own right. Henrietta was a delicate child and a hip injured in infancy plagued her throughout her life.

About 1890 Arthur Raphael's persistent gambling caused him to be excluded from the family firm and he died shortly afterwards. Henrietta and her mother were supported by the family and spent their summers at 2 Hanover Terrace, Regent's Park, London, while wintering by the sea. Marianna Raphael, though loving, was strict and often unavailable to her daughter as she established her own career as a painter. Henrietta grew into a shy and timid child, isolated by her illness, educated by a series of much-loved governesses and tutors. In this period she formed two of her strongest ideals: she fell out of sympathy with Judaism when it required an Orthodox aunt to shave her head and wear a wig, and her precocious reading of William Hickling Prescott's *The Conquest of Mexico* left her with a profound hatred of war.

In April 1902 Henrietta married Louis Mendl (youngest brother of her uncle by marriage Sigismund Mendl), a corn merchant. The marriage was troubled from the beginning and she later recalled with some horror the betrayal of her appalling innocence, both sexual and domestic. The couple spent their first winter in Galatz, Romania, while Louis learned the business. She loved living abroad but was baffled by the practicalities of running her London house. While the ill-matched couple drifted further apart, she gravitated to the company of writers who encouraged her to try writing herself. She worked for the Liberals in the general election of 1906 and a friend's mother introduced her to the Women's Social and Political Union (WSPU). Work for the suffrage brought her most deeply held ideals into conflict—while she supported women's civil rights she hated and feared the violence of the WSPU's campaign, admitting that she had to force herself to take part in demonstrations. She left

Mendl about 1910, and published her first novel, *The Roundabout*, in 1911, as Gladys Mendl, following it with *The Straight Road*.

In 1913 Henrietta married Harrie Leslie Hugo Schütze (1882–1946), who was born and educated in Australia; after studying at Würzburg he became a bacteriologist at the Lister Institute in London. They settled in Glebe House, Chelsea. This marriage was happy; Schütze supported the women's suffrage campaign and respected the growing independence and self-confidence participation in the movement gave his wife. Although she took part in many rallies, she avoided arrest, thanks on one occasion to her husband's timely intervention. She liked Mrs Pankhurst and once hosted her together with her twenty-woman 'bodyguard'; Mrs Pankhurst spoke from her balcony and the police prowled outside. She acted as a courier for the movement, carrying documents rolled inside her hair and clothing, and took part in an unsuccessful deputation to the king, during which she was kicked by a police horse, causing the old weakness in her hip to return with disabling force.

During the First World War the Schützes suffered ostracism because of their German name and pacifist convictions; Henrietta was forced to leave the Society of Women Journalists and the Literary Club. They became friendly with Olive Schreiner, who also suffered the twin social disadvantages of pacifism and a German name. Henrietta used this episode in their lives as the basis for her most popular novel, *Mrs. Fischer's War* (1930, later dramatized in collaboration with Joan Temple). In 1916 she adopted the pseudonym by which she was best-known, Henrietta Leslie.

Between 1919 and 1923 Schütze worked as a reporter on the socialist *Daily Herald*. She loved reporting and felt it consolidated her status as a professional writer and made up for her years as a lady amateur. Her newspaper writing was outspoken and controversial; her editor nearly dismissed her over an article on Turkish baths which he considered indecent. Her friendship with a fellow pacifist, Dick Sheppard, led her to join the Church of England about 1923. Renewed hip trouble forced her to quit the *Herald*, and she travelled to warmer climates whenever she could. She became an honorary organizer of the Save the Children Fund, a post she held from 1924 to 1933. She supported its controversial fund to help German children, organized charity events, and travelled to Bulgaria in 1928 to report on conditions following a severe earthquake. As Henrietta Leslie she was the author of over twenty novels, three plays, and an account of life in Bulgaria, *Where East is West* (1933). She was a member of the PEN Club, an international group of writers whose president was John Galsworthy.

In the 1930s Schütze was torn between her pacifism and her dawning knowledge that only war would stop Hitler's aggression. She had uneasily accepted the policy of appeasement before reluctantly laying her pacifism aside with the outbreak of war. She began to feel a need to reaffirm a Jewish identity that she had scarcely believed she possessed, helping refugees and sheltering many both at Glebe House and in the Schützes' country house. They were in America when war was declared and returned to England, resisting offers to remain in America for the duration. She died on 19 July 1946 at the Salem Hospital, Bern, Switzerland. Her husband died three weeks later.

In her memoirs Schütze wrote of the writer's trade: 'One must be willing to live hard, and welcome, unafraid, any experience that comes one's way' (Leslie, 178). If she was afraid, she conquered it in pursuit of justice, or of a story. She was indefatigable when researching a novel, once travelling with a theatrical company and earning acceptance as a member of the troupe when gathering background for her novel *Mother of Five* (1934), about a stage family. She incorporated aspects of her own life in her writing, often depicting women at odds with conventional society and the conflicts they experienced between marriage and career. She was an outspoken critic of the limitations society placed on women and a tireless worker for women's rights, for children's welfare, and for peace. Above all, she asserted her right to be accepted as a professional, both as a journalist and as a writer of fiction. H. G. Wells once called the young Henrietta Leslie an amateur; she spent a lifetime proving him wrong.

ELIZABETH J. MORSE

Sources H. Leslie, *More ha'pence than kicks* (1943) • *WWW, 1941–50* [Henrietta Leslie and Harry Schütze] • Blain, Clements & Grundy, *Feminist comp.* • S. J. Kunitz and H. Haycraft, eds., *Twentieth century authors: a biographical dictionary of modern literature* (1942) • *CGPLA Eng. & Wales* (1946) • b. cert. • m. cert.

Likenesses S. Solomon, oils, c.1889, repro. in Leslie, *More ha'pence than kicks* • group portraits, photographs, repro. in Leslie, *More ha'pence than kicks*

Wealth at death £4128 2s. 9d.: probate, 17 Dec 1946, *CGPLA Eng. & Wales*

Schuyler, Philip John (1733–1804), revolutionary army officer and politician in the United States of America, was born on 10 November 1733 at the south-east corner of Pearl and State streets, Albany, New York, the third of the five children that survived childhood of John Schuyler (1697–1741), merchant and politician, and his wife, Cornelia Van Cortlandt (*d.* 1762), daughter of Stephen Van Cortlandt, first lord of Cortlandt Manor. Raised in the aristocratic traditions of the Hudson valley Dutch squirearchy, he was tutored at home and in the Albany schools. In 1748 he was enrolled in an academy in New Rochelle, run by the Revd Peter Stouppe, eccentric pastor of the French protestant church. There, while learning French and mathematics, he suffered attacks of rheumatic gout, a hereditary disease that plagued him for the remainder of his life. Mingling with the New York aristocracy, including the Livingstons and DeLanceys, he masked youthful ambitions under the guise of a frivolous social life. He joined trading expeditions into American Indian country, learning practical aspects of commerce and the Mohawk language, and befriending leaders of the Six Nations. His marriage to Catherine Van Rensselaer (1734–1803) on 7 September 1755 linked him even more closely to the Dutch aristocracy. They had fifteen children, eight of whom survived childhood.

In 1755, at the commencement of the Seven Years' War,

Schuyler was commissioned by his cousin, Lieutenant-Governor James DeLancey, to raise and command a company in Colonel William Johnson's expedition against Crown Point. After the fighting he escorted French prisoners to Albany, then returned to Fort Edward and organized a military depot. For the remainder of the war he worked with Colonel John Bradstreet, British deputy quartermaster-general, as a commissary officer, making substantial profits and learning the intricacies of army supply. In 1756 he assisted Bradstreet in delivering supplies to Oswego. Two years later he served under James Abercromby as a deputy commissary with the rank of major in an expedition against Fort Ticonderoga and was with Bradstreet at the fall of Fort Frontenac. During the campaigns of 1759–60 he was at Albany, collecting and forwarding provisions to General Sir Jeffrey Amherst's army. In February 1761 he went to England to settle Bradstreet's accounts with the war office. Travelling extensively in the British Isles, he studied English business practices and canal building, with a view to improving his own and America's commercial prospects.

Schuyler returned to New York in 1762 and settled into the life of a country gentleman on his vast estate at Saratoga. Having inherited huge amounts of property from his father and uncle, Philip Schuyler, he increased these holdings by acquiring with Bradstreet thousands of acres in the Mohawk valley. He developed water power to run sawmills, gristmills, and flaxmills, and acquired a small fleet of merchant ships for commerce with the West Indies. Having already served on the Albany city council (1756–8), he was elected to the provincial assembly of New York in 1768. In that body he became involved in the partisan wrangling between the DeLancey and Livingston factions over how America should respond to British attempts to establish firmer controls over the colonies. Opposing British coercion, he also disliked the violently radical rhetoric of the Sons of Liberty. In 1775 he rejected the DeLancey position, which he considered too pro-British, and was branded a troublemaker by Lieutenant-Governor Cadwallader Colden. He hoped for a reconciliation between the crown and America, but when that was no longer possible he reluctantly led the assembly's opposition to British policies. In April 1775 he attended a revolutionary New York convention that elected him a delegate to the second continental congress. On 15 June congress appointed him a major-general of the continental army with command of the northern department (New York).

Immediately Schuyler began preparations for an invasion of Canada, acquiring provisions, manufacturing weapons, mobilizing troops, and negotiating with the Iroquois to secure their neutrality for the forthcoming campaign. His intention was to lead his forces against Montreal, advance down the St Lawrence River, and capture Quebec. In September, however, he was debilitated by illness and compelled to turn over command of the army to General Richard Montgomery. He returned to Ticonderoga and directed the provisioning of Montgomery's army, thereby helping that officer to capture Montreal and march to the gates of Quebec. When the Americans were compelled to retreat from Canada in the spring of 1776, Schuyler was blamed for the débâcle by the New Englanders, who already disliked him because he supported New York's claims to the New Hampshire grants and because he was too aristocratic for their tastes. In the summer of 1776 he quarrelled with generals David Wooster and Horatio Gates over jurisdictional problems in the northern department but nevertheless managed to organize a successful resistance against Sir Guy Carleton on Lake Champlain. In March 1777, at the instigation of New England legislators, congress castigated him for patriot defeat in Canada and gave Gates an independent command at Ticonderoga. Two months later Schuyler persuaded congress that Gates's appointment undermined his authority, and the latter was recalled. But Gates immediately began to manoeuvre for reinstatement.

In the summer of 1777 Schuyler worked at Albany to prepare for an invasion from Canada by General John Burgoyne. Commanding a weak and dispirited army, he was compelled in July to order General Arthur St Clair to evacuate Ticonderoga when Burgoyne reached that post. Thereafter he handled his army masterfully in retreat, delaying Burgoyne's advance while building up his own forces and ordering Benedict Arnold to relieve Fort Stanwix in the Mohawk valley. Congress was dismayed by Schuyler's loss of Ticonderoga and refusal to stand and fight the enemy. Heeding ugly rumours that the general was either incompetent or disloyal, the legislators replaced him with Gates on 4 August. While Gates went on to inspirit the army, encourage New England militia to enter the fray, and win a triumph over Burgoyne on 17 October at Saratoga, Schuyler deserved credit for laying the groundwork for the victory. Nevertheless, all he could show for his efforts was the destruction of his country home at Saratoga by the British and continued disgrace for his supposed failures and treason.

In 1778, at his own insistence and after months of acrimonious wrangling in congress, Schuyler finally was charged with incompetence and put on trial. Although he was completely exonerated in the autumn, his reputation was irreparably damaged. He continued to bicker with politicians and soldiers, and he was disliked by the troops. Hence on 19 April 1779 he resigned his commission and was elected to congress. He served in that body until April 1780, working on the reorganization of army departments and urging currency reforms. He also was a member of the board of commissioners for Indian affairs until 1785, using his influence to warn of the danger posed by the Native Americans along the New York frontier and advising officials concerning the campaign of General John Sullivan against the Iroquois in 1779. From 1780 to 1797 he held in New York the offices of state senator and state surveyor-general, and was a member of the New York council of appointment. In all these positions he worked to enlarge the powers of the state and central government, and he favoured the constitution of 1787. In 1789–91 and 1797–8 he was a United States senator, working closely with his son-in-law Alexander Hamilton to implement Hamilton's financial programme. He was a regent of the University of the State of New York from 1784 to 1804. Dispirited by the death of his wife in 1803, he died in Albany on 18 November 1804, a very rich man. He was buried in Albany rural cemetery. PAUL DAVID NELSON

Sources D. R. Gerlach, *Philip Schuyler and the American revolution in New York, 1733–1777* (1964) · D. R. Gerlach, *Proud patriot: Philip Schuyler and the war of independence, 1775–1783* (1987) · M. H. Bush, *Revolutionary enigma: a re-appraisal of General Philip Schuyler of New York* (1969) · B. J. Lossing, *The life and times of Philip Schuyler*, 2 vols. (1860–73) · B. Tuckerman, *The life of General Philip Schuyler* (1903) · J. H. G. Pell, 'Philip Schuyler: the general as aristocrat', *George Washington's generals*, ed. G. A. Billias (1964) · D. R. Gerlach, 'Schuyler, Philip John', *ANB* · J. G. Rossie, *The politics of command in the American revolution* (1975) · P. D. Nelson, *General Horatio Gates: a biography* (1976) · *DAB*

Archives New York State Library, Albany, MSS · NYPL, MSS | L. Cong., Washington MSS

Likenesses J. Trumbull, miniature, oils, 1792, Yale U.

Wealth at death very rich: Gerlach, *Philip Schuyler and the American Revolution*, 43–62

Schwabe, Gustav Christian (1813–1897), shipowner and financier, the only son of Philipp Benjamin Schwabe and his second wife, Rosalie Levi, was born in Hamburg on 10 May 1813. Philipp Schwabe, a very wealthy Jewish merchant, had an older son, Ludwig Philipp, from his first marriage, to a woman called Jette. In June 1819 Gustav, together with the rest of his family, was forcibly baptized into the Lutheran church. In the 1820s many members of the Jewish business community in Hamburg established businesses in Britain, where trading conditions were more liberal. The Schwabe family participated in this trend, establishing a calico-printing business in Manchester. Salis, Gustav's uncle, was head of the firm, which quickly opened a Glasgow branch. It is not known when Gustav Schwabe went to Liverpool but by 1838 he was in partnership with Edward Little in a firm of commission agents, and when Little died the following year Schwabe seems to have acquired his house and his business interests. Later he became involved with another Jewish concern, the East Indies shipping firm of J. S. de Wolf & Co., investing in their ships and learning the business of ship management in the Far Eastern and Australian trade.

In May 1842 Schwabe married Helen Dugdale, the daughter of John Dugdale, of Dovecote, in the Wirral, a leading member of the Liverpool and Manchester business communities and a rich man. Shortly afterwards, in partnership with his father-in-law, Adam Sykes, and Benjamin Rutter, Schwabe established the merchant house of Sykes, Schwabe & Co. By 1844 the firm was reported to be doing a very respectable business with Manila and Singapore and by 1849 its capital had reached £50,000. It seems to have been involved in the merchanting of printed calicos and in importing raw cotton and silk, partly for the other family business interests.

The import–export business had naturally led Schwabe to maintain and extend his shipping investments. During the 1840s he had become a junior partner in John Bibby & Sons, the Liverpool shipping firm established in 1805. His marriage had also brought him in touch with an ambitious young shipbuilder, Edward Harland, a distant cousin of his wife. Schwabe sought Harland's advice when Bibbys switched to screw steamers in 1850 and encouraged him to move to Belfast in 1854 in the expectation that its proximity to Liverpool would make it a successful shipbuilding centre. Three years later Schwabe's nephew Gustav Wilhelm Wolff joined Harland there, becoming his partner in Harland and Wolff in 1861. Most of the working capital for this new venture came from Gustav Schwabe and his sister Fanny, Wolff's mother. Schwabe also secured contracts from Bibbys and other shipowners, including the young Thomas Henry Ismay, whom he helped to acquire the bankrupt White Star Line in 1867. Within two years he had persuaded Ismay to adopt the high-risk strategy of entering the north Atlantic passenger market in competition with Cunard; he would provide the funds while Harland and Wolff built the ships. At once the partners commissioned new tonnage of novel design from the Belfast yard. In 1873 the Bibby fleet was sold to Frederick Leyland and Schwabe, one of his backers, withdrew from active participation in that enterprise. He still retained a diversity of interest in textiles and shipping in Liverpool and Manchester, but he spent an increasing amount of his time at his magnificent London home, 19 Kensington Palace Gardens. By this time both Harland and Wolff had luxurious homes nearby.

Although his business career was entirely in the United Kingdom, Schwabe, like Gustav Wolff, remained in close contact with the Jewish community in Hamburg and, unlike the Rothschilds, was an admirer of united Germany. He was a confidant and a backer of Albert Ballin, the managing director of the Hamburg-Amerika Line and the so-called 'Kaiser' of Hamburg. In October 1886 he presented a magnificent collection of 128 pictures to the newly established Hamburg Kunsthalle and in return was made an honorary freeman of the city. He began to withdraw from business in 1893, passing some of his enormous fortune on to his nieces and nephews in the United Kingdom and Germany. He died at 19 Kensington Gardens, London, on 10 January 1897, leaving no children.

The settlement of Schwabe's estate seems to have precipitated the formation of the ill-fated International Mercantile Marine in 1901 in which the White Star, Hamburg-Amerika, and Norddeutscher Lloyd all participated. During the negotiations George Plate, the Norddeutscher Lloyd representative, commented: 'Ballin is the only one who has seen from the first how the land lay—our dear friend Schwabe has left us nicely in the lurch!' (A. J. Balfour to W. J. Pirrie, 1902, PRO 30/60/48). Schwabe's career was not unusual at the time. There were many men who made a livelihood as merchants and financiers, and there were many who had extensive interests in continental Europe, particularly in the rapidly expanding German economy. Schwabe is also a reminder that acceptance of Christianity and marriage outside the Jewish faith, in the nineteenth century at least, did not result in automatic ostracization. MICHAEL S. MOSS

Sources M. Moss and J. R. Hume, *Shipbuilders to the world: 125 years of Harland and Wolff, 1861–1986* (1986) · E. W. Paget-Tomlinson, *Bibby line: 175 years of achievement*, privately printed (1982) · information supplied by the Staatsarchiv, Hamburg, Germany • Bank of England agents' letter-books, Bank of England archives, London • d. cert.

Archives PRO NIre., Harland and Wolff archive

Wealth at death £125,135 7*s*. 10*d*.: probate, 1 April 1897, *CGPLA Eng. & Wales*

Schwabe [*married name* Salis-Schwabe], **Julia** [Julie; *formerly* Ricke Rosetta] (**1818–1896**), philanthropist and educationist, was born at Bremen on 31 January 1818, daughter of the Jewish merchant Gottschalk Herz Schwabe, and was educated at Hamburg and Leipzig. In London on 14 October 1837 she married her older kinsman Salis *Schwabe (1800–1853), a wealthy calico printer who had adopted Unitarianism and been naturalized British by act of parliament on 11 March 1835. She was often known thereafter by the hyphenated form Salis-Schwabe. Mistress of two grand homes—Crumpsall House near Manchester and Glyn Garth near Beaumaris—she entertained lavishly, hosting contemporary 'lions' like Chopin, Jenny Lind, Baron Christian Bunsen, and Ary Scheffer, whose 1850 portrait of her shows a bright, buxom woman with dark hair, full lips, and a challenging gaze. She had an insatiable urge to befriend people, at the risk of mixing them up. Among her assorted acquaintances were the Cobdens, the Brownings, Dickens, Ferdinand Gregorovius, Alexander Herzen, George Eliot, Jane Welsh Carlyle, and Elizabeth Gaskell who, while noting the gay flow of her existence, was one of many to salute her exceptional kindness, her help to anyone in sorrow. Her sensitivity to pain was seen when she walked out disgusted from a bullfight in Madrid. Like her husband, who not only built a colossus of a chimney for his factory at Rhodes, near Middleton, but did all that a benevolent capitalist could for both workers and society, she was enthusiastic for every good cause, from imprisoned Chartists to the German Hospital in Dalston. She found time also to give birth to three daughters and four sons, raising them with the help of governesses including Malwida von Meysenbug.

Salis's unexpected death on 23 July 1853 deprived his wife (as she humbly avowed) of 'quiet, clear reasoning power' (BL, Add. MS 45789, fols. 199–204). Julia Schwabe's was an effervescent personality, passionate, impulsive, even indiscriminate, as she bounced from cause to cause. When she spoke, she intermingled half of Europe's languages. But in debate she was shrewder than critics contended. To one who thought foreign recipients of her charity might feel demeaned she wisely observed: 'I do not understand what scruples of delicacy should limit the freedom of all men to unite on the common ground of humanity in an act of benevolence' (Schwabe to A. Panizzi, 13 May [1862], BL, Add. MS 36720, fols. 434–5). Moreover, in devoting her energies to the happiness of others, she was seldom wasteful. If she lent money to Wagner (whose music sent her to sleep), she later defied his indignation by reclaiming it for a better cause. Ambitious, persuasive, and determined to succeed, she was never shy of knocking at famous doors in the hope of sponsorship. Few dared disobey her, be it to give money, run errands, or draft correspondence. Unlike Salis Schwabe, who had held that socialism was a subtle poison that needed replacing with Christianity, she cared little for the creed as long as it fed the belly and did not close the mind.

Russian and Italian exiles found in Mrs Schwabe an ally for their political struggle. In 1860 she shipped tents, mattresses, and ambulance supplies to Garibaldi's troops, and raised money for the wounded; the first she induced to contribute was Florence Nightingale. In 1861 she became British representative of the Italian Ladies' Philanthropic Association, which Garibaldi, at her suggestion, had exhorted to provide food, work, and education for the masses. She quickly raised £2000 in subscriptions, and a further £1000 through a Jenny Lind concert. Long shocked by squalor and ignorance in Naples, she hastened to establish a girls' elementary school there under the direction of Emilie Reeve; on the latter's untimely death from cholera in 1865, it had to be disbanded. Meanwhile she continued charitable works at home, frequently visiting the family schools at Rhodes, donating cloth for the children's uniforms, and arranging parties and outings. She increased her ability to help by personal economies, such as travelling third class on the railways. When the injured Garibaldi was confined at Varignano in 1862 she rushed to his side, made his first clean shirt, and procured a waterbed for him from Paris.

Truly international in spirit, Julie Schwabe funded medical relief for victims of conflict everywhere—Poles in 1863, Germans in 1866, French in 1870, Russian Jews in 1891. But her heart was set on Naples. After extensive negotiations she was granted in 1873 the lease of a large public building, the disused Collegio Medico. Earlier inspired by the ideas of William Ellis (1800–1881), she was convinced by friends to work also with Froebel methods. She opened first a kindergarten and a mixed elementary school, and with the proceeds of art sales in London and Berlin added in 1877 a training college and in 1879 secondary classes for girls, whose parents helped cover the costs of poorer pupils. At the Brussels pedagogical congress in 1880 she expounded her belief in the moral basis of education and the removal of prejudice. Despite malicious opposition from the church she persevered until, in 1887, her establishment was publicly incorporated as the Istituto Froebeliano Internazionale; in 1890 a handicrafts centre was added. Meanwhile she had conceived for England something more influential still: the Froebel Educational Institute in West Kensington, for which she liberally supplied both money and encouragement; its training college was officially opened by her friend the Empress Frederick in 1895. That same year she republished in its support her intriguing book about Richard Cobden, whose devotion to free trade she shared more for cosmopolitan than for commercial reasons. (It had come out first in French, in 1879, in aid of the Naples schools.)

Julie Schwabe died suddenly of pneumonia at the former Collegio Medico on 20 May 1896, and was buried three days later at the British cemetery in Naples in the presence of Italian and foreign dignitaries. In a subsequent tribute

Claude Montefiore praised 'her tremendous faith in the supreme importance of the cause, her unshaken conviction that persistent pegging away will at last overcome every obstacle' (*Middleton Guardian*, 17 July 1897, 5).

PATRICK WADDINGTON

Sources S. Brookshaw, *Concerning Chopin in Manchester*, [2nd edn] (privately printed, Manchester, 1951) • *The letters of Mrs Gaskell*, ed. J. A. V. Chapple and A. Pollard (1966) • A. von Portugall, 'Mrs Salis Schwabe's Froebel Institution in Naples', *Time* (May 1888), 513–20 • C. C. Aronsfeld, 'A prophetess of liberal education: the life of Julia Salis Schwabe and the founding of the Froebel Institute', *New Era*, 58/3 (1977), 49–53 • A. I. Gertsen, *Sobraniye sochineniy*, 30 vols. (1954–65) • M. von Meysenbug, *Memoiren einer Idealistin und ihr Nachtrag: der Lebensabend einer Idealistin*, 2 vols. (Stuttgart, 1927) • E. M. Lawrence, ed., *Friedrich Froebel and English education* (1952); facs. edn (1969) • F. Bunsen, ed., *A memoir of Baron Bunsen*, 2 vols. (1868) • H. S. Holland and W. S. Rockstro, *Memoir of Madame Jenny Lind-Goldschmidt*, 2 vols. (1891) • W. S. Sichel, *The sands of time: recollections and reflections* (1923) • H. F. Lord, 'An account of the international model educational institution at the ex-Collegio Medico, Naples', *Transactions of the National Association for the Promotion of Social Science* (1875), 453–9 • R. Ashton, *Little Germany: exile and asylum in Victorian England* (1986) • *Froebel's letters on the kindergarten*, ed. E. Michaelis and H. K. Moore (1891) • *The Roman journals of Ferdinand Gregorovius, 1852–1874*, ed. F. T. Althaus, trans. G. W. Hamilton (1907) • *The George Eliot letters*, ed. G. S. Haight, 9 vols. (1954–78) • m. cert. • d. cert. • private information (2004) [James Albisetti]

Archives BL, Nightingale MSS

Likenesses A. Scheffer, portrait, 1850, Froebel Institute College; repro. in Aronsfeld, 'Prophetess of liberal education', 53 • photograph (in old age), repro. in Brookshaw, *Concerning Chopin in Manchester*, facing p. 34

Wealth at death £7774 14*s*. 4*d*.: probate, 22 June 1896, *CGPLA Eng. & Wales*

Schwabe, Randolph (1885–1948), draughtsman and printmaker, was born at Alsbach House, Barton, Lancashire, on 9 May 1885, the son of Lawrence Schwabe, a cotton manufacturer whose father emigrated from Germany in 1820, and his wife, Octavie Henriette, formerly Ermen. Schwabe was educated at a private school in Hemel Hempstead, Hertfordshire, where he demonstrated an early talent for drawing. At fourteen he enrolled at the Royal College of Art, and in 1900 transferred to the Slade School of Fine Art, where he stayed for four and a half years. He studied at the Académie Julian in Paris for eight months in 1906, under Jean Paul Laurens, then travelled and worked in Italy, acquiring a knowledge of Italian architecture. He gradually became known as a draughtsman, etcher, and lithographer.

On 19 April 1913 Schwabe married Gwendolen Rosamund (*b*. 1888/9), daughter of Herbert Jones; they had one daughter. Unable to serve in the First World War owing to frail health, Schwabe was appointed an official war artist; his drawings of the Women's Land Army at work are in the Imperial War Museum. After 1918 he taught at the Camberwell and Westminster schools of art and taught drawing at the Royal College of Art. In 1930 he succeeded Henry Tonks as Slade professor of fine art at University College, London, and as principal of the Slade School of Fine Art; there, despite his long illness, he remained until his death, although George Charlton took over the actual running of the school. He was a member of the New English Art Club and of the London Group, with whom he exhibited regularly. He collaborated with F. M. Kelly in *Historic Costume* (1925) and *A Short History of Costume and Armour* (1931), illustrated a number of other books, notably on ballet in association with the publisher C. W. Beaumont, and made designs for some theatrical productions.

Randolph Schwabe (1885–1948), by Francis Dodd, 1916

Schwabe had a remarkable amount of miscellaneous information on nearly all subjects, and a scholarly knowledge of some—acquired by very wide reading. A slight stammer never hindered his flow of entertaining conversation; he had a quick and subtle sense of humour. In appearance he resembled the stereotypical professor: bespectacled, with a large forehead and longish hair. He took the task of teaching very seriously and was said to be much respected by his students; his gentle, kindly manner never inspired the terror commanded by his predecessor, Henry Tonks.

Schwabe is best remembered as an architectural draughtsman but his subject matter also encompassed portraiture and figurative work, landscapes, still life, and nature studies, his usual signature being 'R. Schwabe'. His drawings and prints are not remarkable for their imagination but are beautifully precise and reasonable statements of fact. His style has often been described as intellectual, and his illustrations in particular tend to be utilitarian rather than highly original. Schwabe died at his home in Dunbartonshire—Auchenteil, 25 Suffolk Street, Helensburgh—on 19 September 1948, and was survived by his wife. STEPHEN BONE, *rev.* TERRY ANN RIGGS

Sources C. Tennyson, introduction, *Randolph Schwabe: memorial exhibition* (1951) [exhibition catalogue, Arts Council of Great Britain, London] · *The Times* (21 Sept 1948) · P. Skipwith, introduction, *Randolph Schwabe, 1885–1948* (1982) [exhibition catalogue, Fine Art Society, London, 2–19 Nov 1982, and The Gallery, Glasgow, 27 Nov – 21 Dec 1982] · A. Horne, *The dictionary of 20th century British book illustrators* (1994) · B. Peppin and L. Micklethwaite, *Dictionary of British book illustrators: the twentieth century* (1983) · *WWW*, 1941–50 · K. Parkes, 'The architectural drawings of Randolph Schwabe', *Artwork*, 1/3 (Feb–April 1925), 178–82 · G. M. Waters, *Dictionary of British artists, working 1900–1950* (1975) · M. Harries and S. Harries, *The war artists: British official war art of the twentieth century* (1983) · A. Windsor, ed., *Handbook of modern British painting and printmaking, 1900–1990*, 2nd edn (1998) · Bénézit, *Dict.*, 4th edn · R. H. Wilenski, *Draughtsmen Edna Clark Hall, Henry Rushbury, Randolph Schwabe, Leon Underwood* (1924) · b. cert. · m. cert. · d. cert.

Archives Man. City Gall., corresp. | Tate collection, Rothenstein corresp.

Likenesses F. Dodd, chalk drawing, 1916, Man. City Gall. · F. Dodd, two drypoints, 1916, NPG [*see illus.*] · R. Schwabe, self-portrait, pencil sketch, UCL

Schwabe, Salis (1800–1853), calico printer and philanthropist, was born in Oldenburg, northern Germany, and educated chiefly in Hanover. He had at least one brother. At the age of seventeen he left Germany to become a chemist at a calico printing works in Glasgow, where he later set up in business on his own account as a manufacturer and exporter of printed cottons. In or about 1832 Schwabe's factory was brought to a halt by a serious strike and, after he had sought to recruit alternative labour in Ireland, the building was set on fire by a riotous mob. He then moved on to Manchester, where, with the help of other German émigré industrialists, he quickly re-established himself as a merchant and calico printer. Schwabe's first home and warehouse were in Mosley Street in central Manchester, once a fashionable residential district but during the 1830s being rapidly converted to commercial purposes. There his neighbour, also a recent arrival in Manchester, was his fellow calico printer and an ambitious young Liberal politician, Richard Cobden.

Schwabe's mercantile interests developed rapidly, shifting focus from the continent to Britain's principal market in the Far East. In 1834 Sykes, Schwabe & Co. was opened in Liverpool and Boustead, Schwabe & Co. in Singapore. Bousteads also had branches in Shanghai and Singapore. To feed this rapidly growing export market, a partnership link was established with Broad Oak Calico Printing Works at Accrington, but evidently this was inadequate to meet the demand.

In 1839 or 1840, as his business prospered, Schwabe took over the small printing works of Daniel Burton in Rhodes, a village near Middleton, a mill town some 5½ miles north of the city. During the following decade it developed into the largest calico-printing complex in Britain, covering an area of 31 acres, famously boasting the tallest factory chimney in the industrial north (some said in Europe), and employing a labour force of more than 750. The commercial side of the business remained in the warehouse district of central Manchester, while in 1842 Schwabe moved his residence to Rusholme House in Chorlton-on-Medlock, on the fashionable southern side of the city.

Schwabe, for whom the Rhodes works was, according to his obituarist, 'a mine of almost princely wealth' (*Manchester Guardian*, 30 July 1853), was a model, if patriarchal, employer. He built a model school for the 'industrial village' of Rhodes, and at the time of his death he was planning a public reading room, supplied with books and newspapers, where men could meet in the evening for a cup of coffee. Frances von Bunsen, the wife of the Prussian ambassador, who visited Rhodes in 1849, admired 'the numberless arrangements' which Schwabe had made 'for the comfort and intellectual furtherance' of his workpeople (Aronsfeld, 6). There is certainly evidence of exceptionally close and cordial relations between Schwabe, his loyal manager, John Jones, and the workers in the factory. When, in 1852, the engravers held a banquet at the works, Schwabe was their guest of honour.

In 1837 Schwabe married a younger cousin, Julia *Schwabe (1818–1896), of Hamburg, whose brother, Adolf, he took on as a junior partner at Rhodes. In 1847 he moved with his wife and young family into Crumpsall House, a luxurious Georgian mansion set in its own extensive grounds with an ornamental lake, in Manchester's northern suburbs—an amazingly smart house, according to Elizabeth Gaskell, who was a frequent visitor. The Schwabes travelled widely and frequently for business and pleasure and kept a house in Paris and a magnificent 'marine villa', Glyn Garth, on the south coast of Anglesey, but Crumpsall House remained their main place of residence. During the 1840s, as the circle of the Schwabes's friends greatly widened, it became one important focus for the Liberal élite which then dominated Manchester politics and society.

Already converted from Judaism to Unitarianism in Glasgow—the result, it was said, 'of sincere and deliberate conviction' (*Manchester Guardian*, 30 July 1853)—in Manchester Schwabe joined the Upper Brook Street Chapel, then under the ministry of John James Tayler, which had proved attractive to other German settlers of Jewish origin. For those abandoning Judaism, for whatever reason, Unitarianism offered a form of Christianity which gave them shelter from the evangelical storm of early nineteenth-century Manchester. The Schwabes also became part of the close-knit, cultured, and influential Unitarian social circle which centred on the Cross Street Chapel and the house of its minister, William Gaskell, and his wife, Elizabeth, and which was one important constituent of the hegemonic Liberalism of Manchester in the 1840s. The Schwabes were frequent guests of the Gaskells, who themselves stayed on many occasions at Crumpsall House, Glyn Garth, the Schwabes's Parisian house, and the home in Heidelberg of Julia Schwabe's sister. Mrs Gaskell's correspondence portrays Julia (the 'Grace' of her letters) as one of her closest friends and confidantes, a person to whose tastes and opinions she frequently deferred.

For the Schwabes, as for other German-Jewish immigrants, the Gaskell household also provided a point of entry into the respectable political and philanthropic activities of middle-class Manchester. Among the many causes to which Schwabe contributed personally and financially during the 1840s were the elementary education of the working classes, the enlargement and improvement of the Manchester Royal Infirmary, the introduction of model lodging houses for the wayfaring poor, and the setting up of a reforming school for juvenile offenders. He was interested more generally in penal reform and encouraged and supported the work of rescue and rehabilitation initiated by the prison philanthropist Thomas Wright. He took a particular interest in a plan to remove mental patients from the city-centre infirmary to a more retired and salubrious situation in the Cheshire countryside. The result was Cheadle Royal Lunatic Asylum, for which he raised much of the initial £25,000 and of which he became treasurer for the rest of his life. Schwabe is said also to have engaged in a 'secret charity' which enabled young men of slender means to set up in business.

Schwabe was a generous patron of the arts in Manchester, and particularly of music. He made large donations to the new Manchester Athenaeum and to the nascent Manchester School of Art. At Crumpsall House his guests included Jenny Lind, Joseph Joachim, Jane Carlyle, and Clara Schumann. Chevalier Sigismund Neukomm, then considered to be one of Haydn's most brilliant pupils, lived there in the mid-1840s. Chopin stayed there briefly in the summer of 1848 when he played at one of the Gentlemen's Concerts arranged by the Schwabes to raise funds for the infirmary. He left with warm memories of his reception by 'the kind Schwabes' (Brookshaw, 10). Schwabe's patronage extended to the Hallé Orchestra, recently established through the agency of his friend and fellow calico printer Herman Leo.

In politics Schwabe was active in the Liberal cause. In 1848 he chaired a meeting of German residents in Manchester called to celebrate the liberal revolution in Prussia and to express solidarity with the Frankfurt assembly. He was an enthusiastic supporter, personally and financially, of the Anti-Corn Law League, in which he became a close friend of Cobden. He was an occasional guest at Cobden's London home and accompanied him on several of his European tours as guide, interpreter, and companion. He was a stern and outspoken critic of more 'extreme' political trends, particularly the emergence of socialism, to which he attributed the fate of his Glasgow factory, and the consequences of which he foresaw (in a letter written to Mrs Rich in 1850) as 'the wretchedness of the working-classes … ruin to the employers and … [the] total subversion of existing relations of society' (*Reminiscences*, ed. Schwabe, 92). His preference was for free competition and for the kind of mutuality of respect and unity of purpose between employer and employee which he believed he had achieved at Rhodes. It was the task of the business community to 'do all in our power … to make our people frugal, provident, truly religious' (ibid.). From public platforms in Middleton he urged thrift on his own workers as the best means of coping with the ups and downs of the cotton economy.

Schwabe himself was deeply devoted to Unitarian Christianity. At Crumpsall House and Glyn Garth, his servants were gathered for evening prayer meetings at which he read from the Bible and from the sermons of Unitarian divines.

Schwabe died after a short illness on 23 July 1853 at Glyn Garth of scarlet fever following an attack of cholera. His funeral in Manchester a week later was a lavish affair. A procession from the lodge gates at Crumpsall House to Harpurhey cemetery was made up of a 'numerous body of black-clad workers from Rhodes Works' (*Manchester Guardian*, 3 Aug 1853), prominent members of the German colony, including Charles Hallé and Dr Louis Borchardt, leaders of the local Jewish community, the lord mayor and bishop of Manchester, and such Liberal notables as Cobden and George Wilson. Many shops *en route* closed as a mark of respect. An epitaph by the local 'ballad-monger', Charles Swain, was printed in the *Manchester Guardian* (3 August 1853). Schwabe left a widow and seven young children, none of them old enough to take over Rhodes Works, which passed into the temporary control of his brother Adolf Schwabe and the Manchester cotton merchant James Reiss.

To the obituarist in the *Manchester Guardian*, the mouthpiece of Liberal Manchester, Schwabe was the epitome of all that was refined, benevolent, tolerant, and high-minded in the middle-class citizens of the New Athens. A surviving posthumous bust by the Manchester sculptor William Bally has him dressed in a Greek toga. For the historian, his life demonstrates the ease with which German businessmen (many of recent Jewish extraction) were allowed to move in the Liberal circles of Manchester's middle-class society. For their part, the local Liberal élite, by drawing men such as Schwabe into their midst, effectively linked the city with the civilized milieux of Paris, Berlin, and Vienna, so adding substance to their aspiration to convert the 'boom city' of Manchester into a centre of modern civilization. BILL WILLIAMS

Sources *Manchester Guardian* (30 July 1853) • *Manchester Guardian* (3 Aug 1853) • S. D. Chapman, *Merchant enterprise in Britain: from the industrial revolution to World War I* (1992), 147–8 • *The letters of Mrs Gaskell*, ed. J. A. V. Chapple and A. Pollard (1966) • J. Seed, 'The role of Unitarianism in the formation of liberal culture, 1775–1851', PhD diss., U. Hull, 1981 • J. S. Uglow, *Elizabeth Gaskell: a habit of stories* (1993) • *Reminiscences of Richard Cobden*, ed. J. Schwabe (1894) • J. Fielding, *Rural historical gleanings in south Lancashire* • S. Brookshaw, *Concerning Chopin in Manchester* (1937) • C. C. Aronsfeld, 'A pioneer in liberal education: the life of Julia Salis Schwabe', *Association of Jewish Refugees Information* (July 1977) • T. M. Endelman, *Radical assimilation in English Jewish history, 1656–1945* (1990) • B. Williams, *The making of Manchester Jewry, 1740–1875* (1976) • N. Roberts, *Cheadle Royal Hospital: a bicentenary history* (1967) • Manchester Central Library, *Proceedings on the occasion of the bicentenary of the Cross Street Chapel, June 24–25, 1894*

Archives Middleton Central Library, Lancashire, programme and report of speeches

Likenesses W. Bally, marble bust, Middleton Central Library, Middleton, Lancashire

Wealth at death under £180,000: will, 1853

Schwanfelder, Charles Henry (1774–1837), landscape and animal painter, was born on 11 January 1774 at the Headrow, Leeds, the son of John James Schwanfelder, a painter of clock dials, trays, snuff-box lids, and a landscape artist of limited ability, and his wife, Elisabeth Farrer. Schwanfelder learned the principles of painting from his father and quickly developed a skill in depicting animals, particularly horses and dogs. However, little is known of his early years until he described himself as a portrait painter and drawing master in a Leeds handbill in 1800. Schwanfelder came to notice as one of the founding contributors at the Northern Society for the Encouragement of the Fine Arts exhibition in 1809 when he provided twenty-two paintings in a total of 202 exhibits. The majority of his pictures were landscapes, which were generally praised, but the *Leeds Mercury* criticized his painting of a fox for the 'wooden appearance of his legs' (10 April 1809). The following year Schwanfelder was represented by fourteen works, including ten Yorkshire views which were again well received except by 'Maul Stick' of the *Mercury*, who suggested that Schwanfelder 'had better never meddle even with landscape except so far as it may serve as a background to his pictures of animal life' (26 May 1810). Perhaps it proved a blessing that for some reason the annual exhibitions were discontinued until 1822. Despite the strictures levelled at his work, his reputation grew and he attracted an increasing circle of patrons in Leeds and Yorkshire. On 26 November 1810 Schwanfelder married at Gainsborough, Lincolnshire, Elizabeth Wade, with whom he had a daughter, Caroline, baptized in York in 1816.

Schwanfelder's first picture to be hung at the Royal Academy was *Setter Dog* in 1809 followed by *Landscape Study from Nature* in 1811. At the academy in 1814 his portrait of a horse, *Malcolm, an Arabian, the Property of HRH the Prince Regent*, appears to have led to his appointment as animal painter to the prince the following year. Three horse portraits commissioned by the prince regent are in the Royal Collection. He was reappointed animal painter to George IV in 1821. Schwanfelder sporadically contributed a further eight animal and sporting paintings to the Royal Academy until 1835, and a total of six pictures to the British Institution between 1815 and 1819. By 1815 his enthusiasm for landscape had extended his painting tours to the Lake District, to north Wales, and finally to Scotland, each area providing settings for many of his animal portraits. At the resumption of the Northern Society exhibitions, Schwanfelder included a few portraits. In 1825 thirteen of the artist's fourteen pictures were sold, providing him with a comfortable income in excess of £300. In later years he exhibited paintings of Bible stories such as *Daniel in the Lions' Den* (1828) and *Balaam, the Ass and the Angel* (1834). Of the latter the waspish reviewer of the *Leeds Mercury* thought the 'ass is charming, the angel hideous' (28 June 1834). The specific nature of this local criticism over the years seems almost vindictive, but it is true to say that Schwanfelder's animal paintings often lack the elements of panache and animation found in pictures by his more cosmopolitan contemporaries. By 1835 his landscape expeditions were curtailed by asthma and he spent some of his time as a tutor to local young artists. His health deteriorated rapidly and, with the development of a disease to his windpipe, he sought help in London. He died there after an operation on his throat on 2 July 1837, and was buried at Leeds on 9 July. Twenty of his paintings can be seen at Leeds City Art Gallery, although of this number a few are merely attributed to Schwanfelder.

CHARLES LANE

Sources A. Budge, 'C. H. Schwanfelder: animal painter to the prince regent', *Leeds Art Calendar*, 85 (1979), 11–19 • *Leeds Mercury* (10 April 1809) • *Leeds Mercury* (26 May 1810) • *Leeds Mercury* (28 June 1834) • Graves, *RA exhibitors* • Graves, *Brit. Inst.* • S. Mitchell, *The dictionary of British equestrian artists* (1985) • M. H. Grant, *A chronological history of the old English landscape painters*, 3 vols. (1926–47), vol. 2, pp. 446–7 • W. H. Thorp, *John N. Rhodes: a Yorkshire painter, 1809–1842* (1904) • *Transcripts of Leeds parish church*, Thoresby Society, 25 (1923) • *IGI* • *DNB*

Likenesses W. Frederick, oils, 1825, Leeds City Art Gallery • C. H. Schwanfelder, self-portrait, oil on panel, Leeds City Art Gallery • C. H. Schwanfelder, self-portrait, oils, Leeds City Art Gallery

Schwartz, Christian Friedrich (1726–1798), missionary, was born on 22 October 1726 at Sonnenburg, in Neumark, Prussia (now Stronsk, near Gorzów, Poland), the son of George Schwartz, a baker and brewer, and Margaret Grundt (*d.* before 1731), widow of Hans Schönemann. A daughter, Maria Sophia, had been born three years earlier. Having earnestly, like Hannah of ancient Israel, prayed for a son, Margaret dedicated her youngest child to Christ and made her husband and pastor vow that the boy would be nurtured for the sacred service of God. Aged eight, Christian was sent to the grammar school in Sonnenburg, where, under the devout and effectual teaching of the local pastor, Helm, he learned the disciplines of daily worship, was confirmed in a personal pietistic faith, and partook of his first communion. In Küistrin (about 1740), where he came under the instruction of the syndic's daughter, he was profoundly influenced by heroic stories about the activities of the Royal Danish Mission (otherwise known as Danish-Halle-SPCK) in India, and by the writings of Professor Hermann August Francke, under whom his teacher had herself studied. Entering Halle University in 1746, he was given bed and board in the famous Weisenhaus (orphan house) that Francke had founded. Already a disciplined scholar and thinker, Schwartz now not only acquired a proficiency in Greek, Hebrew, Latin, and modern European languages, but also became thoroughly acquainted with the latest currents of Enlightenment thought (including advances in philosophy, theology, mathematics, and sciences, both applied and theoretical). Christian caught the eye of the veteran missionary Benjamin Schultz, who had recently returned from two decades in India, having worked first in Tranquebar and then in Madras. Schultz asked Schwartz to assist him in the production and printing of a new translation of the Tamil Bible. It was Schultz who suggested to Francke that Schwartz would make an ideal missionary. Francke readily agreed; and Schwartz's appointment was confirmed.

Ordination and passage to India Together with two other young missionaries (G. H. Conrad Hüttemann and David Poltzenhagen) who were also bound for India, Schwartz was ordained in Copenhagen on 17 September 1749. In London, which he reached on 8 December, he was invited to preach and did so several times, notably on Christmas day at the Chapel Royal. While in England, he became acquainted with the Calvinistic Methodist preacher George Whitefield. He departed on board the East Indiaman *Lynn* (29 January 1750) and landed in Cuddalore on 17 June. He arrived at the Danish trading settlement of Tranquebar a few days later.

Since their first arrival in 1706 Danish missionaries had shown themselves to be resourceful. Despite ordeals, they had mastered local languages, translated modern texts (both scriptural and scientific), established schools and printing presses, gathered congregations of Tamil Christian believers, and trained indigenous disciples as pastor-teachers (catechists) who, reflecting the latest in advanced and modern ideas of education developed at Halle, had become harbingers of radical change. Thus, even before Schwartz's arrival in India, an evangelical form of Tamil Christianity had already gained a firm foothold in south India, consisting of some six to eight European (mainly German) missionaries, dozens of local Tamil pastor-teachers, and some 1674 'confessing' believers (an accounting not now confirmable).

The south India which Schwartz entered in 1750—and, indeed, the entire Coromandel coast as well as the interior Carnatic—was embroiled in ceaseless wars. Clive's East India Company sepoy forces were engaged in battle campaigns against those of Dupleix, with the very survival of the English company at stake. Schwartz's reports conveyed heart-rending tales, horrific details, and insightful social analysis of the consequences of the fighting for village communities. While Danish territories such as Serampore and Tranquebar remained on the sidelines and were largely untouched by the rise of the English East India Company, Schwartz himself could not escape being drawn into these political events, an involvement born of his increasing engagement with peoples far beyond the Danish settlement at Tranquebar.

Yet, to begin with, this was not so. The young Schwartz worked with local Tranquebar congregations and schools during his first decade. Already proficient in European languages, he became no less fluent in local Indian languages, modern and classical: Tamil, Telugu, Sanskrit, Marathi, Dakhni-Urdu (southern Hindustani), Persian, and Portuguese (the coastal lingua franca). His reputation as a gifted teacher grew as he established a school in every local congregation (faithfully following the Halle philosophy and formula of trying to bring literacy in the mother tongue to every person). Eventually, he and his 'helpers' became responsible for all mission work south of the Kaveri River—a task which involved caring for congregations in such cities as Tanjore, Trichinopoly, and Tinnevelly. In 1760 he crossed the Palk Strait and travelled among Tamil villages of Dutch Ceylon.

While Schwartz was visiting Trichinopoly two years later, the company's garrison commander, Major A. Preston, implored him to assist following the deaths of many soldiers and sepoys in an explosion at the fort's powder magazine. The military base had no chaplain to comfort the sick and bury the dead, and Preston promised to build a 'prayer-school' hall for Tamil Christians if Schwartz agreed to stay. In 1764, when troops were ordered to march and besiege Madura, Preston again urged the missionary to act as his military chaplain. Schwartz's actions—ministering to sick and wounded sepoys and soldiers—seem to have been so appreciated that he was given an award of 900 pagodas by the nawab of the Carnatic (Arcot), the prince whose palace in Trichinopoly was then under company 'protection'. Schwartz used the funds for schools, adding a special 'orphan school' for offspring of European soldiers. After Preston's death in the Madura campaign Schwartz in turn provided help to Colonel Wood, who contributed to the building of a large and proper (*pakka*) stone church. This structure, seating 1500, was dedicated on 18 May 1766. Within its imposing compound, Christ Church, a large mission house and schools, both English and Tamil, flourished.

Chaplain for the East India Company This development, extraordinary and unforeseen, brought about a major shift in Schwartz's career. Much correspondence passed between authorities in London, Madras, Halle, and Copenhagen before new understandings were reached. Henceforth, while the old arrangement of transnational collaboration between Halle, London, and Tranquebar continued as before, Schwartz was to be more formally designated and supported as a special missionary of the Society for Promoting Christian Knowledge. In 1768 he also received a formal appointment from the East India Company gazetting him as its chaplain for Trichinopoly on an annual salary of £100—most of which continued to be ploughed into missionary outreach projects. His regular working station, both as a missionary and as a chaplain, was to be in Trichinopoly.

Schwartz proved to be singularly effective and successful in his new assignment. His knowledge of languages, together with his warmly engaging, genuinely caring, and gentle manner, enabled him to relate to many kinds of mercenary soldiers and sepoys: British, German, Portuguese, Maratha, Mughal, Telugu, and Tamil. Consistently cheerful, kind, and selfless, he won the hearts of officers and troopers alike. At the same time his missionary activity continued to expand, through the use of his 'helpers', whom Schwartz had trained and met each morning and evening, sometimes accompanying them on missionary forays to more distant places.

In 1773, however, war again ravaged the land. The storming of Tanjore by the nawab's forces brought suffering to people of that city. Schwartz organized a relief effort and helped local Tamil Christian congregations to rebuild their prayer and school halls. His efforts to bring help to the poor and suffering, Christian and non-Christian alike, brought him further fame, and after the raja's restoration he was asked to settle permanently in the city. On more than one occasion, when no grain could be obtained for the starving populace, his word became surety for the floating of huge loans, without which no stabilizing of the local market or purchase of food relief for masses who were dying from famine was possible. In 1778, after yet another personal invitation from the raja (the first having been in 1768), he moved to Tanjore. In doing so, he left his junior colleague Christian Joseph Pohle to carry on as missionary and chaplain in Trichinopoly. As a token of his appreciation, the raja of Tanjore contributed to the building of a new stone place of worship, seating 500, for the evangelical congregation in his city.

A few months later Schwartz was suddenly summoned to Madras. There he was asked to undertake a secret mission to Haidar Ali, ruler of Mysore, on behalf of the company. This request was made at the specific insistence of the Mysore ruler: no other emissary was deemed able to instil more trust among princes in south India, and none could combine this with such fluent knowledge of relevant languages. Schwartz reluctantly agreed to go, but only so long as it was clearly understood that he was going only as a missionary and an emissary of peace. During his eight-week journey he and his unarmed entourage of attendants took advantage of every opportunity to preach or teach. When he finally arrived at Seringapatam, he was ceremonially received, both in public durbar and in private audience, with great courtesy and respect. When Schwartz returned to Madras and personally reported his conversations to the governor of Madras (Fort St George), he handed over the prize purse of 300 rupees which Haidar Ali had given him; and when this was returned to him he made it the nucleus of a special fund for an English 'orphan school' in Tanjore. From neither government, Madras or Mysore, would he accept any personal payment beyond expenses for travel. However, in the process he did succeed in securing for Pohle a chaplain's salary of £100 a year, which he himself had previously received from the company. Schwartz's personal impressions of Haidar and of this whole episode are to be found in his letters to Europe. He was never convinced that his efforts had done much to avert the war which he saw coming.

In April 1780 work was completed on the church, St Peter's, at Tanjore. A house and compound in the village suburb of Vallam was converted into a prayer and school hall and other building work begun. But again all activities were interrupted by war. Haidar's armies, 'one-hundred-thousand strong', broke upon the Carnatic, destroying John Baillie's brigade near Kanchipuram and sweeping to the gates of Madras itself. Once more Schwartz found his hands full, tending the hungry, sick, wounded, and dying. Such was Haidar's esteem for Schwartz that he also allowed the missionary to pass unmolested among his own troops. Later, when peace negotiations commenced, Schwartz was again called to act as a go-between (*dubash*), and twice served in this capacity. Both attempts failed—the first because Tipu Sultan's pickets stopped him at the border (Haidar having died); and the second when he became so afflicted by boils ('eruptions') on his legs that he could not travel. Colonel William Fullarton, then commander of the Madras field forces, later wrote: 'The integrity of this irreproachable missionary has retrieved the character of Europeans from imputations of general depravity.'

Teacher, administrator, and guardian Schwartz's most notable achievements—in modern education and in government—still lay before him. He was the first to develop a scheme for a modern, government-subsidized 'public' system of schools in India. Initially begun under the rajas of Tanjore, Shivaganga, and Ramnad, his high schools so impressed the company's resident at Tanjore that he persuaded the company's directors in London and its government at Fort St George to subsidize the whole venture, even though none of the schools lay within company territory. The schools were filled by Maratha Brahman youths who would eventually take up positions on the higher rungs of the civil service within the entire Madras Presidency. The English curriculum, while utilizing biblical and Christian texts, also reflected the latest features of Enlightenment thinking.

At the same time Schwartz laid the foundations for what was to become the largest and strongest evangelical Christian community in India. As early as 1769 and 1771 word had come to him that Tamil Christians had settled in Tinnevelly. An affluent Brahman widow, residing with an English officer at the company's fort at Palamcottai, appealed to Schwartz for help. In 1778 Schwartz baptized her, christening her Rasa Clarinda. Later, after Rasa Clarinda had made a personal endowment of funds to pay for the construction of a proper prayer-school hall for the new congregation, Schwartz sent Satyanathan Pillai, one of his most gifted 'helpers', to serve as resident. In 1790, after rigorous examination in Tanjore, Satyanathan was formally ordained and, as the first Tamil evangelical missionary, commissioned for service in Tinnevelly. In 1799 Satyanathan and David Sundaranandam, a local convert and disciple who came from the then lowly Shanar community, inspired India's first mass movement of conversions to Christianity. Thousands turned to the new faith and suffered severe persecution for doing so.

Meanwhile, north of Tinnevelly, war again brought further devastation to Tanjore. This time distresses were further aggravated by the avarice and oppression of the raja's servants. Thousands fled the country and left it waste. Knowing his reputation, the company's resident at the Tanjore durbar recommended that Schwartz be made a member of a special committee of investigation. At Schwartz's plea, the raja dismissed corrupt officials and, without coercion, restored a modicum of justice to the people. Seven thousand returned to cultivate their fields on the faith of Schwartz's pledges. The British resident used his influence to have Schwartz appointed royal interpreter (on a salary of £100 a year). When the rapacity of the raja's servants again became intolerable, Schwartz drew up a state paper suggesting how the administration of justice might be reformed. As a consequence, he and his 'helpers' were put in charge of the courts. Then, in 1787, as Tulaji Raja lay dying, he adopted Serfoji, a ten-year-old cousin, as his heir, and begged Schwartz to serve as the boy's guardian. Schwartz hesitated, and initially declined. But, when the company set the boy aside and made Amir Singh raja in his place, and when Amir Singh's servants began to threaten the boy's life, refusing to allow Schwartz to continue his education, the missionary appealed to the Madras government and was formally recognized as the boy's guardian. Finally, in 1793, after Amir Singh's servants again made attempts on Serfoji's life, so that the boy had to be placed in a special house surrounded by armed sepoys, Schwartz journeyed to Madras in order to appeal personally for redress. He brought Serfoji with him, along with two widows of the late raja. The Madras governor in council heeded Schwartz's appeal to reconsider Serfoji's claim to the throne with the effect that Serfoji was restored to that position which the deceased raja had originally begged Schwartz to protect.

News of the approval of the East India Company's directors in London did not reach India until after Schwartz's death. But by then the raja, an enlightened and highly educated young man ruling in his own right, had come to think of the old missionary not only as his protector and regent, but as his father and friend. Indeed, the prince had imbibed so much learning from his teacher that he had built a special palace, which he dubbed Saraswati Mahal, expressly to contain a room of wonders (*Wunder Kammer*), replete with a modern library, microscopes, telescopes, and the latest in scientific apparatus and instruments. During his final illness Schwartz called Serfoji to his side and bestowed a special blessing upon him, exhorting the prince to rule all his subjects with even-handed justice, to protect his Tamil Christian subjects from persecution, and to submit himself to the grace and mercy of the one and true God who alone could give eternal peace.

Character and legacy Schwartz died at Tanjore on 13 February 1798 and was buried at St Peter's Church on the same day. Serfoji Maharaj composed heartfelt English verses and read them at the memorial service, and requested from England a marble sculpture, by John Flaxman, which now stands in St Peter's Church. It depicts the old man on his deathbed, surrounded by his beloved Tamil 'helpers' and holding the maharaja's hand. On a huge brass memorial in St Mary's at Fort St George the East India Company had Bacon inscribe a long eulogy of tribute. Except for something to his sister's family, Schwartz left all possessions, along with £1000, for the work to which he had given so many years.

In a world awash with corruption and injustice, both European and Indian, Schwartz's personal integrity was never questioned. He showed indifference to personal power or wealth. 'He was', Reginald Heber later wrote, 'one of the most active and fearless, as he was one of the most successful, missionaries since the Apostles' (Pearson, 2.419). Heber estimated that 6000 Tamils had come to faith directly because of Schwartz. In Tinnevelly many thousands more were converted after his death. Young missionaries were told to emulate

> that worthy man and labourer in Jesus Christ who established such a reputation of candour, integrity, and disinterestedness among both natives and Europeans, as cannot fail to recommend the cause of Christianity to men of every description who have ever heard his name. (*SPCK Report No. IV: some Account of the Society's Protestant Missions*, 1788, 119)

Their words could echo Joseph Jaenicke's confession: 'My connexion with Mr. Schwartz is another proof of [God's] good providence over me' (*Memoirs of … Jaenicke*, 28); or Paizold's anecdote of overhearing Brahmans at Tiruvallur solemnly declare, 'you are a holy man: if all your Christians thought, spoke, and lived as you do, we would, without delay, undergo the change and become Christians' (*SPCK Report*, 1797, 126–7). Simple folk 'thronged around their beloved Teacher, everyone trying to get near him'. Perhaps among all his Tamil followers, even including Satyanathan Pillai, Rasa Clarinda, and David Sundaranandam, none surpassed the cultural distinction of Vedanayagam Sastri, a schoolteacher and 'poet laureate' to Maharaja Serfoji, who left an enormous corpus of Tamil poetry and prose, both classical and modern.

Robert Eric Frykenberg

Sources *DNB* • E. Beyreuther, *Bartholomaeus Ziegenbalg: a biography of the first protestant missionary in India, 1682–1719*, trans. S. G. Lang and H. W. Gensichen (Madras, [1955]) • R. Caldwell, *Records of the early history of the Tinnevelly mission* (1881) • *Church of England missions, containing a sketch of the life of Schwartz and an account of the Church of England societies*, Church of England (1840), 12 • J. F. Fenger, *History of the Tranquebar mission* (1863), iv, 312–24 • W. Fullarton, *A view of the English interest in India; and an account of the military operations in the southern part of the peninsular during the campaigns of 1782, 1783, and 1784: in two letters* (1787) • J. Foster, 'The significance of A. W. Boehme's *The propagation of the gospel in the East*', *Oecumenia* (1968) • W. Germann, *Missionar Christian Schwartz: sein Leben und Wirken aus Briefen des Halleschen Missionsarchives* (Erlangen, 1870) • J. Hough, *History of Christianity in India*, 5 vols. (1845) • *Memoirs of the Rev. Joseph D. Jaenicke, a fellow labourer with Swartz at Tanjore* (1833) • D. Jeyaraj, *Inkulturation in Tranquebar: der Bertrag der frühen dänisch-halleschen Mission zum Werden einer indisch-einherimischen Kirche (1706–1730)* (Erlangen, 1996) • J. Kaye, *Christianity in India* (1955) • E. A. Lehmann, *Es begann in Tranquebar* (Berlin, 1955); abridged Eng. trans. as

It began in Tranquebar (Madras, 1956) • H. Liebau, 'German missionaries as research workers in India: their diaries as historical sources (Benjamin Schultze (1689–1760)—exception or norm?)', *Studies in History*, 11/1 (1995), 101–18 • J. Page, *Schwartz of Tanjore … with illustrations [incl. a portrait]* (1921) • C. F. Pascoe, *Two hundred years of the SPG*, rev. edn, 2 vols. (1901) • H. D. Pearson, *Memoir of the life and correspondence of the Reverend Christian Frederick Swartz to which is prefixed, a sketch of the history of Christianity in India*, 2 vols. (1835–9) • J. Richter, *Die deutsche Mission in Südindien* (Gütersloh, 1902) • J. Richter, *The history of missions in India* (1906) • T. Robinson, *The last days of Bishop Heber* (Madras, 1829) • W. Robinson, ed., *Ringeltaube, the Rishi: the pioneer missionary of the LMS in Travancore … letters and journals* (1902) • [C. F. Schwartz], *Defense of missions in India: a letter* (1796) • *Remains of the Rev. C. F. Schwartz, missionary in India: consisting of his letters and journals; with a sketch of his life*, 2nd edn (1826) • H. Sharp, *Selections from the educational records* (Calcutta, 1920), pt 1 (1811–39) • *An abstract of the annual reports and correspondence of the Society for Promoting Christian Knowledge, from … 1709, to the present day*, Society for Promoting Christian Knowledge (1814) • *Lives of missionaries in southern India*, SPCK (1863–5) • *Notices of Madras [and the coast of Coromandel] and Cuddalore in the last century, from the letters and journals of earlier missionaries of the Society for Promoting Christian Knowledge*, SPCK (1858) • J. Storz, 'Die Indienmaterialien der Franckeschen Stiftungen in Halle/Saale: ein Überblick', *Zum Indianbild in DDR* (Halle, 1983) • W. Taylor, *A memoir of the earliest protestant missions at Madras* (Madras, 1847) • R. Vorbaum, *Christian Friedrich Schwartz: Evangelischer Missionar in Trankebar, Triutschinapalli und Tanjour in Östindian—nach seinem Leben und Wirken dargestellt* (Düsseldorf, 1851) • M. Wilks, *Historical sketches of the south of India, in an attempt to trace the history of Mysoor*, 3 vols. (1810–17) • D. Wright, 'Swartz of Thanjavur: a missionary in politics', *South Asia*, new ser., 4 (Dec 1981), 94–105 • D. Wright, 'Swartz of Thanjavur: Raja Guru?', *Indian Church History Review*, 15 (Dec 1981), 123–44

Archives Archiv der Franckeschen Stiftungen, Franckeplatz 1 Haus 5, Halle/Saale, o-4020, Germany, letters • BL OIOC, home miscellaneous series, H/Misc/571; H/Misc/774; H/Misc/285A • BL OIOC, military, political and secret consultations, Madras/Fort St George • BL OIOC, political and secret corresp. with India, Fort St George, L/P&S/278/4; L/P&S/292 • Evangelisch-Lutherische Mission zu Leipzig, Missionshaus, Paul-List-Strasse 17–19, Leipzig o-7010, Germany • Trinity Church, Marylebone Road, London, Society for the Promotion of Christian Knowledge archives, extracts from the journals and manuscripts of the Revd John C. Kohlhoff • Universitäts-und Landesbibliothek Sachen-Anhalt, August-Bebel-Strasse, Halle/Saale, o-4020, Germany • register for each missionary, extracts from missionary letters, East India Mission correspondence books • annual reports and corresp. of the Society for Promoting Christian Knowledge, from the commencement of its missions [SPCK annual reports]

Likenesses line drawing, repro. in *Defense of missions in India, by the late venerable Mr. Swartz published by the Society for Promoting Christian Knowledge in the report for 1795* (1815)

Wealth at death bequest to sister's family; remainder (along with £1000) left for missionary work

Schwartz, George Leopold Adolf (1891–1983), economist and journalist, was born at 39 Temple Street, Brighton, on 10 February 1891, the elder son and eldest of four children of Adolph George Schwartz (Schwarz), an Austrian Jew who was a hotel waiter and later a wine merchant, and his wife, Antonia Held, who was Hungarian but not Jewish. George went to Varndean School in Brighton, and after studying at St Paul's Training College, Cheltenham, became a teacher in 1913 in a school under the aegis of the London county council. At this time he also studied at the London School of Economics (LSE) and became interested in economic problems. When the First World War broke out he enlisted in the army and served at Gallipoli.

After the war Schwartz graduated from the LSE, and in January 1924 was appointed secretary of the executive committee of the London and Cambridge Economics Service. His first publication, *Output, Employment and Wages in the United Kingdom, 1924*, which appeared in 1928, was mainly a statistical analysis not intended for the general reader. On 22 September 1927 he married Rodka (Rhoda) Lomax (1893/4–1966), who was born in Kovno, Russia, the daughter of Paul Getowitz; she had previously been married to Conrad Hope Lomax, an artist, from whom she obtained a divorce. They had no children. In August 1930 Schwartz became an Ernest Cassel lecturer in commerce at London University and, in collaboration with one of his colleagues, Frank W. Paish, published *Insurance Funds and their Investment* (1934).

During the early years of the Second World War Schwartz assisted Arnold Plant in the preparation of a wartime social survey intended to supply the government with information about the reaction of the public to rationing and other emergency measures. He resigned his post as lecturer in 1944 on appointment as deputy City editor of the *Sunday Times* and economic adviser to the Kemsley newspapers. Between 1945 and 1954 he was also editor of the *Bankers' Magazine*, which, when he took it over, was desperately in need of revival, as the war years had seriously affected its circulation. His energy and enthusiasm in this task were amply rewarded; as a result of his nine years' work the circulation of this periodical was materially increased and its reputation substantially enhanced. After retirement as an editor of the *Sunday Times* in 1961 at the age of seventy, he continued for another ten years to contribute to the paper a column on economic affairs.

Schwartz's attitude to politics and economics was summed up in his entry in *Who's Who*, where he described his recreation as 'detesting government'. In the foreword to *Bread and Circuses, 1945–1958* (1959), a selection of his newspaper articles, he wrote:

> My approach to economic and social problems is governed by the early training I received … at the London School of Economics, which a grand and apparently incorrigible popular delusion brands as a hotbed for disaffected unorthodoxy. The unorthodoxy escaped me. (*Bread and Circuses*, 7)

In one of his articles (30 April 1950) he reiterated his distaste for authority, saying: 'It is a persistent delusion of the human race that Government is composed of men who take a longer view of its destinies than do the governed themselves' (ibid., 53). If his ideas are compared with those of his contemporary economists he appears to be most nearly in sympathy with the views of Sir Dennis Robertson; at the other extreme he constantly lambasted the socialist dogma of those, such as Harold Laski and Hugh Dalton, who gave the LSE the reputation which, thought Schwartz, was undeserved.

Schwartz believed passionately in the freedom of the individual and was unsparing in his criticism of any opponent of capitalism, from William Temple, archbishop of Canterbury, to Richard Crossman, a controversial figure in the cabinet of Harold Wilson. The archbishop had claimed that capitalism 'doesn't even work'—Schwartz in reply wrote:

> Such allegations … do not emanate appositely from episcopal palaces which have had the milk delivered daily on the doorstep for centuries and into which the necessaries and minor luxuries consonant with plain living and high thinking have flowed uninterruptedly as a result of 'uncoordinated and planless human effort'. (*The Times*, 6 April 1983)

To Schwartz economics was never a dismal subject, dry as dust: to him it was a living, exciting subject to be explained not exclusively with theoretical dogma but with common sense and a pragmatic concern for the welfare of the individual. He succeeded in conveying his views to a wide circle of readers in simple, realistic prose. Little is known of his private life; his friends thought highly of his genial humour, spiced with sardonic wit, which he used in college common rooms or at the Reform Club, but clearly he kept his personal life private. Schwartz died at Colindale Hospital, London, on 2 April 1983. H. F. OXBURY

Sources *The Times* (6 April 1983) • staff records, London School of Economics • b. cert. • m. cert. • d. cert.
Archives BLPES, notes and papers mainly relating to Swaffham
Wealth at death £219,298: probate, 11 July 1983, *CGPLA Eng. & Wales*

Schwartz, Martin (*d.* 1487), mercenary, was born in Augsburg in the Holy Roman empire. A Swiss chronicle suggests that Schwartz left the trade of shoemaker to become a mercenary, first distinguishing himself with valour in 1475 at the siege of Neuss, Rhineland, where he was knighted. As a military entrepreneur commanding 200–500 Swiss, he made a name in the wars of the Low Countries. He gained a reputation for boldness but also for pitilessness. This brought him to the attention and into the service of Maximilian, king of the Romans (*d.* 1519). As a great drinker, addicted to showy jewellery, he was the butt of jokes by Maximilian's jester.

Schwartz and his Swiss pikemen formed part of the force sent from the Low Countries by Margaret, dowager duchess of Burgundy (*d.* 1503), to aid the Yorkist pretender Lambert Simnel in 1487. Having been joined by John de la Pole, earl of Lincoln, they arrived in Ireland on 5 May. Simnel was crowned king in Christ Church, Dublin, on 24 May, and Schwartz's army was joined by an Irish contingent under Sir Thomas Fitzgerald. They landed at Barrow, Lancashire, on 4 June and marched quickly south. On 16 June the army was routed by Henry VII at the battle of East Stoke, Nottinghamshire, in or after which Schwartz died. A recent tradition has his death as the result of a heroic but suicidal charge at the vanguard of Henry VII's army. In fact Schwartz's pikemen were totally overwhelmed by the superior English longbow. Both English and Swiss chronicles record Schwartz's accusation of betrayal, that he had been deluded about the degree of support available in England. His mercenary band was wiped out and the Burgundian chronicler Molinet suggests that he, like his soldiers, died of multiple arrow wounds. The Swiss describe him captured, much wounded, on the battlefield, and executed on a scaffold over a river. If this does not mean that his severed head was displayed on a bridge it might indicate execution at Newark.

The manner both of Schwartz's life and of his death secured him a place in folk tale and literature. At East Stoke the site of his death is identified at Willow Runnel. Here it is said he was buried with a willow stake through his body, and from this stake grew a willow grove. John Skelton immortalized him in his poem 'Agaynst a comely coystrowne' (*c.*1495–1497?), and William Wager referred to him in his interlude 'The longer thou livest' (*c.*1568). Henry VII's blind poet laureate, Bernard André, compared him to Diomedes, the king of Argos and friend of Odysseus. In reality he was one of a number of urban drifters who enjoyed the mercenary life of chances and easy, big, gains. The expedition of 1487 was too risky to fit comfortably into that frame, as Schwartz himself seems to have realized at the last moment. His part in it nevertheless earned him, perhaps surprisingly, a posthumous literary fame. IAN ARTHURSON

Sources *Die Berner-Chronik des Valerius Anshelm*, 5 (Bern, 1896) • 'Chronique d'Adrien de But', *Chroniques relatives à l'histoire de la Belgique sous la domination des ducs de Bourgogne … par … Kervyn de Lettenhove*, ed. K. de Lettenhove, 1 (1870), pt 1 • *Chroniques de Jean Molinet*, ed. G. Doutrepont and O. Jodogne, 3 vols. (1935–7) • F. Redlich, 'The German military enterpriser', *Vierteljahrschift fur sozial- und-Witschaftsgeschite*, 47 (1964), vol. 1 • R. P. Shilton, *The battle of Stoke-field, or, Burham fight* (1828) • *John Skelton: the complete English poems*, ed. J. Scattergood (1983) • A. H. Thomas and I. D. Thornley, eds., *The great chronicle of London* (1938) • *DNB*
Archives Archives Départementales du Nord, Lille

Schweickhardt, Heinrich Wilhelm (1746–1797), landscape painter and etcher, who is believed to have been of Dutch descent, was born in Brandenburg or in Hamm, Westphalia, the son of the engraver L. Schweickhardt. From 1755 he studied under Girolamo Lapis, an Italian painter, at The Hague; and lived there until the end of 1786, when troubles arose in the Low Countries, and he left for London. In Royal Academy catalogues after 1791 he is called 'Director of the Academy at The Hague' (Waterhouse, 335). He gained a considerable reputation for his landscapes, especially the winter scenes, in which he introduced cattle and figures in the tradition of Dutch seventeenth-century landscapes. He painted also seapieces and a few portraits, and made some excellent drawings in pen and ink, in bistre, and in chalk. He likewise etched some clever plates of animals. He dedicated a series of eight etchings of animals drawn from nature to Benjamin West (published by Boydell). He exhibited at the Royal Academy from 1786 to 1796, and at the Society of Artists in 1790. He lived at 13 Haymarket, 19 Mount Street, Grosvenor Square, and 7 Arabella Road, Pimlico, consecutively. Schweickhardt died in Belgrave Place, Pimlico, London, on 8 July 1797. His work is held in the Musée du Louvre, Paris, the National Gallery, London, Blackburn Museum and Art Gallery, and public collections in Hamburg and Vienna.

Schweickhardt left a son, Leonardus Schweickhardt (1783/4–1862), who engraved several plates, as well as many maps, among which were those for Eckhoff's *Atlas of Friesland*, published in 1850. He died at The Hague in January 1862, in his seventy-ninth year. Schweickhardt's daughter Katharina Wilhelmina, born in The Hague on 3 July 1777, possessed much talent as an artist, and still more as a poet. She became in 1797 the second wife of the Dutch poet Willem Bilderdijk. She died at Haarlem on 16 April 1830. R. E. GRAVES, *rev.* CHLOE JOHNSON

Sources Bryan, *Painters* • Bénézit, *Dict.*, 4th edn • Graves, *RA exhibitors* • Waterhouse, *18c painters*

Likenesses H. W. Schweickhardt, self-portrait, oils, Bilderdijk-Museum, Amsterdam

Schweppe, (Jean) Jacob (*bap.* 1740, *d.* 1821), artificial mineral water manufacturer, was baptized in the Liebfrauenkirche in Witzenhausen, Hesse, on 16 March 1740, the son of Conrad Schweppe, a peasant. Believing that their son lacked the strength for agricultural life his parents turned him over to a travelling tinker when he was only eleven or twelve years old. Before long the tinker brought him back, explaining that the boy was so adept at mending pots that he should be put to the silversmiths' craft; the same then occurred, the silversmith recommending that he learn the jewellers' craft. Schweppe soon moved to Geneva, a centre for this trade, was formally accepted as a resident of Geneva—the first step to naturalization—and on 4 October 1767 he married, in a protestant church, Eléonore (*d.* 1796), the daughter of Antoine Roget and his wife, Susanne Bertrand. Of their nine children only one daughter, Nicolarde (1777–1836), known as Colette, survived infancy.

For nine years from 1777 Schweppe was in partnership with Jean Louis Dunant, during which time he submitted his master-work and was admitted *maître-bijoutier* in the jewellers' guild of Geneva. He was an enthusiastic amateur scientist and a keen reader of the literature of physics, where he encountered the works of Joseph Priestley, who had been experimenting with mildly aerated waters. About 1780 Schweppe began developing apparatus for making artificial mineral water, and was the first to use a force pump to carbonate under pressure. He gave these waters to any whom the doctors thought would benefit from them. Demand grew and eventually he was persuaded to accept payment, thus by 1783 establishing a commercial enterprise. His continuing experiments to improve the pump brought him in touch with Nicolas Paul, son of Geneva's leading scientific instrument maker, and Henry Albert Gosse, a noted pharmacist. The three men entered into a nine-year partnership in 1790 and decided to establish a second factory in London, to be managed by Schweppe.

Schweppe arrived in London on 9 January 1792 with an introduction from Professor Marc-Auguste Pictet of Geneva, and established his factory in Drury Lane. Initially he found few customers, for mildly aerated waters were widely available. Business was so slow that the partners recalled him in December, but matters became confused by the political situation in France, which permeated adjacent parts of Switzerland, and came to a head when France declared war on Britain in February 1793. Schweppe feared that he and his daughter, who had now joined him, would be expelled, and appealed to the government to be allowed to remain in London. After considerable wrangling the partnership was dissolved in 1796; Schweppe traded his share of the Swiss partnership for the London business—his factory and home were now in Margaret Street. His wife died in Geneva in 1796 at a time when he and Colette were unable to travel there.

By this time Schweppe's assorted mineral waters were being drunk for their curative powers and as refreshing beverages, sometimes mixed with syrup or wine. Medical practitioners were impressed by their high carbonation and Erasmus Darwin specifically recommended Schweppe's waters in his treatise *Zoonomia* (1794–6). About 1796, in preparation for his retirement, Schweppe sold three-quarters of his interest to three Jerseymen, keeping one-eighth each for himself and Colette, later yielding half of this residue to their manager, Stephen DeMole, against his promise not to divulge the secrets of manufacture.

The French annexation of Geneva in 1798 meant that Schweppe found himself a French citizen when he returned about 1802; he settled near Geneva at Les Petits Crêts, in Bouchet, Petit Saconnex. Colette married in 1806 and lived in Geneva near her father. He occupied himself with gardening, agriculture, and mechanics. A skilled clockmaker, he constructed, in his eightieth year, a detailed and intricate orrery to replace an earlier one which annoyed him by the clicking of its wheels.

Two contemporary diarists recorded their impressions of Schweppe. Charles de Constant, cousin of the more famous Benjamin, French writer and politician, said of him in 1816, 'his great age, his white hair, contrast strongly with his vivacity and his energy; he has an originality of expression and a fire which belong only to genius'. Gilbert Elliot, second earl of Minto, while staying in Geneva in 1821, recorded an account of Schweppe given him by J. J. Huber, the blind Swiss naturalist, an old friend of Schweppe in Bouchet. Huber described him as a man of very great genius and originality; a man of learning but also of much modesty and simplicity of character. Schweppe had at that time suffered an apoplectic attack from which he died at Les Petits Crêts, on 18 November 1821. D. A. SIMMONS, *rev.* ANITA MCCONNELL

Sources D. A. Simmons, *Schweppes: the first 200 years* (1983) • Bibliothèque Publique et Universitaire, Geneva, MSS fr. 2633, 2649, 2651 (Gosse) • NL Scot., Minto MSS 11986–9

Likenesses oils ('from a description'), repro. in Simmons, *Schweppes*, frontispiece

Schwitters, Kurt (1887–1948), artist and poet, was born on 20 June 1887 in Veilchenstrasse, Hanover, Germany, the son of Eduard Schwitters (*d.* 1931) and his wife, Henriette (*d.* 1945); his parents had a women's outfitting shop in Theaterplatz, Hanover.

Although Kurt Schwitters was born in Germany, his last years were spent in Britain after he fled first from cultural anathema in Germany and then from the German invasion of Norway. In Britain Schwitters found a refuge, where he could work undisturbed and little recognized as one of the most influential figures in twentieth-century European art. The unpretentious lifestyle of his last years was characteristic of his independence of mind. He was in contact with many avant-garde groups during his life yet he carefully maintained an independent standpoint, creating his own one-man movement which he called Merz, a syllable of the name 'Kommerzbank', observed on a fragment of discarded and torn paper which he incorporated into a collage. Characteristically he worked with the discarded ephemera of daily life, collecting and assembling pieces of many materials into objects of beauty which now hang in many of the world's major museums.

A frail child, Schwitters grew up in the family home at 5 Waldhausenstrasse in the south part of Hanover, where he attended the *Realgymnasium* I. During a prolonged illness at the age of fourteen he wrote poetry and music, and in 1906 he began to paint. Subsequently he had a thorough art education at the Kunstgewerbeschule in Hanover and the Akademie der Bildenden Künste in Dresden. He married Helma Fischer (*d*. 1945) in Hanover in 1915; they had a son, Ernst Schwitters. Engaged in war service between March and June 1917, Schwitters was soon declared unfit and sent to work as a draughtsman in a factory near Hanover. Henceforth he complemented his naturally inventive creativity with a draughtsman's disciplined precision. He perfected a collage technique which he described in 1919:

> Merz-pictures are abstract works of art. What the word Merz essentially denotes is the combining of all conceivable materials for artistic purposes and the equal technical evaluation of the individual materials. Merz-painting makes use not just of paint, canvas, brush and palette but of all materials perceptible to the eye, and of all requisite implements. At the same time it is unimportant whether or not the material was already formed for some purpose or other. A perambulator wheel, wire netting, string and cotton wool are factors having equal rights with paint. The artist creates through choice, distribution, and disassociation of the materials. (Schmalenbach, 94)

On the other hand his work as a draughtsman in a factory made him aware of machinery and this precision is evident in his typographic designs.

The slaughter and suffering of war had shaken profoundly Schwitters's faith in the loyalties and cultural norms of his generation. Despairing soldiers returned to a defeated country on the brink of revolution. By 1917 Schwitters was committed to rebellious experiment in art, rejecting any return to the patronage and values of the age which plunged Europe into the First World War. The Russian revolutions of 1917 had demanded an art which was partisan, political, and public. But the failed revolution in Germany arose from dismay, poverty, and destruction. Political artists became ferocious social critics, particularly in Cologne and Berlin. There the Dada movement, an anarchic reversal of conventional values, attacked the very concept of art. Dada recognized no authority and made a method out of contradiction. Schwitters devised his own response, Merz, in the winter of 1918–19.

Schwitters maintained his independence by contacting many avant-garde groups throughout the 1920s, balancing them to establish a position of his own yet still remain visible as an artist. Dada was one such formation, as was De Stijl, the Dutch-based group of artists and designers which included Piet Mondrian, Theo van Doesburg, and others. Schwitters was attracted also to the new Bauhaus by its design principles, and to international constructivism from Germany and Russia. He exhibited at Der Sturm in Berlin, an expressionist stronghold. Through the activities of the Provinzialmuseum and the Kestner Gesellschaft in Hanover, he also knew of the peripatetic Russian artist and designer El Lissitzky, who was to have a profound effect on his typographic designs. In 1924 he formed his own publicity company, the Merzwerbezentrale, characterized by designs which were practical, effective, intelligent, and legible.

Typographic work was perhaps the least part of Merz, however. Schwitters made more and more collages from scraps of paper, photographs, and the detritus and ephemera of his surroundings. Fragments of the printed page introduced dramatic juxtapositions of scale, font, and colour to produce new effects, later to be used in design projects. But in his collages he specialized in fragmentation: his pieces of paper, wood, buttons, and cloth were rarely whole and their messages were never complete. With these fragments of daily life he turned discarded rubbish into harmonious, suggestive, and overtly beautiful compositions.

In Schwitters's hands collage ranged from formal compositions of proportion and colour, to visual juxtapositions with new meanings, like the contrast of elements in a poetic metaphor. In fact Schwitters remained active as an innovative poet throughout his career. His performances were often witty and outrageous; frequently they contained no words. One poem evoked a long-postponed sneeze and ended with the breaking of a plate. His most celebrated long poem was a wordless phonetic incantation, the 'Ursonata', declaimed by Schwitters on many occasions. Merz activities in Hanover grew to embrace a tall construction at his home. He called it the Merzbau, an accumulation which grew through the ceiling and into the room above. It incorporated display cases of objects assembled together and even housed a live guinea-pig.

With the rise of Hitler and national socialism in Germany, Schwitters became insecure. In 1937 four of his works were included in the Entartete Kunst ('Degenerate art') exhibition held in Munich. Thirteen other works were removed from German museums. He travelled abroad, settling in a self-imposed exile at Lysaker, near Oslo. Here he began another Merzbau. He never returned to Germany and when German forces attacked Norway he fled, arriving in Edinburgh in 1940, to spend the last seven and a half years of his life in Britain.

Schwitters was arrested and interned as an enemy alien at various places until he entered the detention camp in Hutchinson Square at Douglas on the Isle of Man. Such an experience was unintelligible to refugees antagonistic to Hitler, for whom Schwitters certainly had not the slightest sympathy. But at Douglas, without credit to British organizers, the camp contained so many professors, athletes, musicians, philosophers, and artists that it made a kind of university-in-exile. The Amadeus Quartet met there and an extensive programme of lectures was arranged. Schwitters performed his poems and painted portraits. Parts of the 'Ursonata' were used as greetings between initiate inmates at the camp. The apocalyptic German painter Ludwig Meidner was also there, as was Fred Uhlman, the novelist and collector of African carvings, whose portrait by Schwitters is in the Hatton Gallery at the University of Newcastle upon Tyne.

On his release Schwitters moved to London, where he was received by the critic Herbert Read and the artists Ben Nicholson and Barbara Hepworth. Here he heard of the death of his wife Helma in Hanover and the destruction of the Merzbau there. In 1945 he moved to Ambleside in the Lake District to live in peaceful seclusion with his friend Edith Thomas. At Little Langdale he began a last large construction in a stone barn, now known as the Elterwater Merzbarn. He cemented to the wall material and objects from the area to form the basis of a deep relief construction; a ceramic egg, part of a watering can, and a piece of string were caught up in a curving and colourful form suggestive of rebirth and growth in the landscape. But Schwitters died on 8 January 1948 in the hospital at Kendal without completing the project. He was buried on the 10th in Ambleside churchyard. The Abbot Hall Art Gallery at Kendal has several of his British works and in July 1965 the Merzbarn wall was moved to the Hatton Gallery at the University of Newcastle.

Schwitters is increasingly recognized as a profound influence in post-war attitudes to art. Every art movement involving the assemblage of discarded and used material probably owes a debt to him. Photographs which show him in his last years happy and relaxed, far from the international contacts which made him so influential, are deceptive, for he had in his pocket a cheque from the Museum of Modern Art in New York. He also wanted to found a new international periodical called *Pin* with the Dadaist Raoul Hausmann, then living in Limoges, and simultaneously he was working on a Merzbau construction which could have been the most ambitious of them all.

John Milner

Sources J. Elderfield, *Kurt Schwitters* (1985) • W. Schmalenbach, *Kurt Schwitters* (1967) • *Kurt Schwitters in exile: the late work, 1937–1948* (1981) [exhibition catalogue, Marlborough Fine Art, London] • S. Lemoine, ed., *Kurt Schwitters* (1994) [exhibition catalogue, Musée Nationale d'Art Moderne, Centre Georges Pompidou, Paris] • M. Dachy, ed., *Kurt Schwitters: Merz* (1990) • J.-C. Bailly, *Kurt Schwitters* (1993) • K. Trauman-Steinitz, *Kurt Schwitters: a portrait from life* (1968) • P. Kirkeby and others, *Schwitters: Norwegian landscapes, the zoological gardens lottery and more stories*, trans. W. Glyn Jones and J. Neugroschel (1995)

Archives NRA, priv. coll. | Tate collection, papers relating to him collected by Klaus Hinrichsen • Tate collection, corresp. and files of his partner Edith Thomas relating to him | SOUND South German Radio, Scherzo in Ursonate [recorded Frankfurt, 5 May 1932] • An Anna Blume: die Sonate in Urlauten, Lords Gallery, London [vinyl recording, 1958]

Likenesses photographs, repro. in Schmalenbach, *Kurt Schwitters*

Sciama, Dennis William (1926–1999), cosmologist, was born on 18 November 1926 in Manchester, the younger of the two sons of Abraham Frederick Sciama (1891–1969) and his wife, Nelly, *née* Adés (1902–1974). He was educated at Malvern College and then at Trinity College, Cambridge, where he read mathematics and physics, but widened his education by attending Wittgenstein's seminars, and obtained his BA in 1947. After a brief interlude studying solid-state physics, he became one of the few research students ever formally supervised by P. A. M. (Paul) Dirac. His prime intellectual mentors, however, were Hermann Bondi, Thomas Gold, and Fred Hoyle, the originators of steady-state cosmology. Sciama became enthusiastically committed to this theory, and to the concept known as Mach's principle, according to which the inertial frame—the frame of reference in which a gyroscope or pendulum stays fixed—is determined by the most distant galaxies. His PhD thesis gained him a research fellowship at Trinity College in 1952. This was a defining moment in his career: had he failed to obtain a fellowship he would have abandoned research and joined the family textile business.

After holding visiting fellowships at the Princeton Institute for Advanced Study (1954–5) and at Harvard (1955–6) Sciama was, during 1959–61, a research associate at King's College, London. The lively group at King's, led by Hermann Bondi and Felix Pirani, was spearheading a revival in the study of Einstein's general relativity—a theory that dated from 1916 but which had subsequently become sidelined from mainstream physics. Relativity's further resurgence in the 1960s owed a great deal to the novel insights and techniques introduced by Sir Roger Penrose. It was Sciama who inspired Penrose, originally a pure mathematician, to take up the subject. Sciama married Lidia Dina, an anthropologist, in Venice on 26 November 1959; they had two daughters, Susan (*b.* 1962) and Sonya (*b.* 1964).

In 1961 Sciama returned to Cambridge, becoming a lecturer in applied mathematics and (from 1963) fellow of Peterhouse. He derived little satisfaction from undergraduate teaching, even though he was a first-rate lecturer. However, he attracted exceptional research students and it was through his creative support of them that he made his prime contribution; among his first cohort several achieved subsequent distinction, the most prominent being Stephen Hawking.

Sciama eloquently defended the steady state almost to the last ditch. The idea that the universe could exist for ever, in a unique self-consistent state, had an intense aesthetic appeal to him—as he had spelt out in his first book, *The Unity of the Universe* (1959). But when unequivocal contrary evidence mounted up in the 1960s he recanted, and was thereafter a zealous advocate of the big bang. The 1960s were also a time of rapid advance in observational astronomy: cosmological theories could genuinely be tested, and black holes seemed actually to exist, rather than being merely exotic theoretical constructs. Sciama's 'school' was one of the three in the world which collectively transformed the new subject of relativistic astrophysics into one of the liveliest frontiers of science (the other two 'schools' were led by equally charismatic figures: Y. B. Zeldovich in the USSR and J. A. Wheeler in the USA). In 1969 Sciama published *The Physical Foundations of General Relativity*, and in 1971 *Modern Cosmology* (2nd edn, 1975).

In 1971 Sciama moved to Oxford as a senior research fellow of All Souls. He was one of the first scientists in that college, where his urbanity and engaging wit helped to allay concerns that these new disciplines might erode the traditional ethos. In Oxford he continued as a mentor of many outstanding students. During 1978–83 he also held a part-time professorship at the University of Texas. In 1983 he was invited to lead a research group at the International School of Advanced Studies (SISSA) in Trieste. He moved full-time to Italy (a country with which he had a strong affinity), but maintained a base in Oxford. His group maintained a fertile output. However, his main individual research effort during those years—a novel cosmological conjecture about subatomic particles called neutrinos—went the way of the steady-state theory. Sciama cajoled his colleagues to make the crucial measurements; the outcome disproved the theory. But even transient theories can be a stimulus, and Sciama revelled in boisterous debate irrespective of the final verdict.

At a conference celebrating Sciama's sixty-fifth birthday, a 'family tree' was prepared enumerating his research students and their own research students. The first two 'generations' comprised more than 200 names; Sciama's intellectual progeny—many themselves intellectual leaders—were by the time of his death even more numerous. It was an attraction of the Italian academic system that the retiring age was seventy-five, and Sciama continued working almost until his death from cancer, in Oxford, on 19 December 1999. He was buried three days later and was survived by his wife and two daughters. His last scientific papers appeared posthumously.

Sciama was highly articulate, with wide interests, especially in theatre and literature. His scientific strengths were his breadth, his feel for what was important, and his infectious enthusiasm. His pervasive contributions to research in cosmology and gravity extended over more than forty years. They stemmed not just from his own work but, even more, from the generations of young researchers he inspired and trained in Cambridge, Oxford, and Trieste. He achieved further influence through general lectures, books, and articles, and was a committed advocate of pure science and of international collaboration. He was elected a fellow of the Royal Society in 1982; he also had honorary membership of the American Philosophical Society (1981), the American Academy of Arts and Sciences (1982), and the Accademia dei Lincei of Rome (1984). He served as president of the International Society of General Relativity and Gravitation during 1980–84. MARTIN J. REES

Sources G. Ellis, A. Lanza, and J. Miller, eds., *The renaissance of general relativity and cosmology: a survey to celebrate the 65th birthday of Dennis Sciama* (1993) · *The Times* (23 Dec 1999) · *WWW* · personal knowledge (2004) · private information (2004)

Likenesses photograph, repro. in *The Times*

Wealth at death £453,128—net: probate, 10 Jan 2001, *CGPLA Eng. & Wales* · £457,724—gross: probate, 10 Jan 2001, *CGPLA Eng. & Wales*

Sclater, Edward (1623–1698x1700), clergyman and Roman Catholic convert, was born on 3 November 1623 in London, the son of Edward Sclater, probably a merchant tailor of London. Descended from a family from Slaughter in Gloucestershire, in the year after his birth he was entered on the books of Merchant Taylors' School, where he later studied. He matriculated from St John's College, Oxford, on 4 December 1640, graduating BA on 6 July 1644 and proceeding MA on 1 February 1648. He claimed that he served on garrison duty during the siege of Oxford and that he was later ejected from the university for refusing to take the solemn league and covenant. No one at Oxford was tendered the covenant and the parliamentary visitors' register confirms that, like many members of the university, he was actually removed (on 7 July 1648) for offering only an equivocal submission to their authority. After leaving Oxford he served as vicar of Fyfield in Berkshire, a living he had held since 1647 and which was in the gift of Richard Baylie, provost of St John's. Sclater claimed that he was persecuted for refusing to take the engagement of loyalty to the Commonwealth, but in 1653 he was still holding his benefice at Fyfield. He married his wife, Margery, in or before that year, in which a daughter, Rebecca, was baptized at the church. Sclater also alleged that he refused an offer of clerical promotion from the regicide Valentine Walton. This rebuff did not prevent the triers from installing him as vicar of Esher in Surrey in 1658. After the Restoration he presented a memorial to Charles II detailing his 'hardships' during the civil war and interregnum. The purpose was probably to confirm him in the living at Esher. In 1663 he was also made curate of St Mary's, Putney.

While curate of Putney Sclater appears to have been threatened with being turned out of his living. In a letter to William Sancroft, probably written some time between 1677 and 1682, Sclater claimed that he was harassed for suggesting the king should be given enough money to make his government 'easy and comfortable', that his parishioners should return members of parliament that were loyal to the king, and that the line of succession should not be altered (Bodl. Oxf., MS Tanner 290, fol. 228). In 1681 he was certainly preaching sermons to his parishioners denouncing the recently uncovered 'Presbyterian plot'.

After the accession of James II, Sclater converted to Catholicism, vindicating his actions in *Consensus veterum* (1686). He claimed that it was a fear of being outside the communion of the universal church and a growing belief in the real presence of Christ's body and blood in the eucharist which led him to abandon Anglicanism. He also argued that, unlike the Roman church, protestant churches could not claim foundation from St Peter's see. The tract generated replies from Edward Stillingfleet, Edward Gee, and Edward Pelling. *Nubes testium*, published in the same year, has also been attributed to Sclater but is probably by John Gother. On 3 May 1686 Sclater was granted a special dispensation by James II which meant that he could absent himself from his cures at Esher and Putney (but still receive the profits from them) while paying a curate to stand in for him, leaving him free to pursue his other career as a schoolmaster.

After the revolution of 1688 Sclater returned to the Anglican faith, making a public recantation on 5 May 1689, when Gilbert Burnet, bishop of Salisbury, preached in the Savoy chapel. It must have been a particularly humiliating experience as his critic, Edward Gee, under the supervision of Henry Compton, bishop of London, drafted the recantation. Sclater had to disown the views expressed in his book and acknowledge his sin in continuing to receive the profits from ecclesiastical livings which he was, by law, disqualified from holding. After this public abasement, Sclater retired from teaching and lived privately near Exeter Change in London. He died some time between 1698 and 1700, when his successor appeared at Putney. His son Edward (1655–1710) went on to be fellow and bursar of Merton College, as well as rector of Gamlingay, Cambridgeshire, from 1685, while another son, George, became rector of Hayes in 1688 and Westerham, Kent, in 1696. EDWARD VALLANCE

Sources *DNB* · *Walker rev.*, 34 · Bodl. Oxf., MS Tanner 290, fols. 227–8 · 'Walton, Valentine', *DNB* · A. Hornecle, *An account of Mr Edward Sclater* (1689) · *CSP dom.*, 1686–7, 101 · E. Sclater, *Consensus veterum* (1686) · E. Sclater, *A sermon preached in the church of Putney* (1681) · E. Gee, *Veteres vindicati* (1687) · M. Burrows, ed., *The register of the visitors of the University of Oxford, from AD 1647 to AD 1658*, CS, new ser., 29 (1881)
Archives BL, memorial, Add. MS 24064 | Bodl. Oxf., Tanner MS 290

Sclater, Philip Lutley (1829–1913), zoologist, was born on 4 November 1829 at Tangier Park, Hampshire, the second son of William Lutley Sclater (1789–1885) and Anna Maria, *née* Bowyer (*d.* 1879). He was educated at Winchester College (1842–5), whence he obtained a scholarship to Corpus Christi College, Oxford (1846–9). He received a first in mathematics in 1849 and remained at Oxford for a further two years, studying natural history and modern languages. In 1851 he entered Lincoln's Inn and practised on the western circuit for a number of years after his call to the bar.

Sclater was an accomplished ornithologist, and he published a number of articles in the journals of the Linnean and Zoological societies. His most important paper was 'On the general geographic distribution of the members of the class aves'. This paper identified six zoogeographic regions of the world according to their bird life. This concept was developed by subsequent writers and Sclater's terminology remains in use to this day. He was a frequent traveller to Europe and often stayed with the ornithologist Charles Lucien Bonaparte in Paris. His first visit to America was in 1856 when he travelled on foot and by birch-bark canoe as far as the Mississippi and met leading American naturalists. Subsequent journeys took him back to North America, to north and south Africa, and to Europe. He contributed four volumes to the *Catalogue of Birds at the British Museum*.

In 1850 Sclater became a fellow of the Zoological Society of London and in 1857 a member of its council. In 1859 he was elected secretary of the society. The financial and scientific affairs of the society were not in good order at that time. Sclater ensured that the *Transactions* and *Proceedings* were published at the due time, and that the library was greatly improved. In 1886 responsibility for the *Zoological Record* (founded in 1864) was assumed by the Zoological Society on his initiative. Other activities included the founding in 1858 of *Ibis*, the journal of the British Ornithologists' Union, which he edited (apart from the years 1865–77) until 1913.

In 1861 Sclater was elected a fellow of the Royal Society and in 1862 he married Jane Anne Eliza Hunter-Blair (*d.* 1915), daughter of Sir David Hunter-Blair, third baronet. They had one daughter and three sons, the eldest of whom, William Lutley (1863–1944), was also an ornithologist and succeeded his father as editor of *Ibis* (1913–30).

Sclater's elder brother, George Sclater-*Booth (later Lord Basing), was appointed president of the Local Government Board by Disraeli in 1874 and for two years Sclater acted as his private secretary. However he declined a permanent position as this would take him from his study of natural history. In 1892 he was elected chairman of the British Ornithologists' Club.

During Sclater's period as secretary, many new buildings were erected in the zoological gardens, but he was more anxious to secure that a rare species should be added to the official list than that it should be sedulously cared for. Before his retirement in 1902, his administration of the zoological gardens was subjected to mounting and justified criticism. He made a poor impression when giving evidence to the society's reorganization committee and although he persuaded the council to nominate his son William as secretary, he was not elected by the fellows.

Sclater was always very helpful to other zoologists, but this was marred by an arrogant and dictatorial manner. His retirement was spent in Hampshire where he was an active and by far the oldest member of the Hampshire hunt. He died at his home, Odiham Priory, as a result of a carriage accident on 27 June 1913. J. C. EDWARDS

Sources *Bulletin of the United States National Museum* (1896), ix–xix · *The Ibis*, 10th ser., 1 (1913), 642–9 · *Proceedings of the Linnean Society of London*
Archives NHM, ornithological papers | NHM, letters to Albert Gunther and R. W. T. Gunther · NHM, corresp. with Sir Richard Owen and William Clift · Oxf. U. Mus. NH, letters to Sir E. B. Poulton · U. Cam., department of zoology, letters to Alfred Newton
Likenesses photograph, *c.*1895, repro. in *Bulletin of the United States National Museum* · Maull & Fox, photograph, RS · photograph, repro. in *Ibis* · photograph, Zoological Society of London
Wealth at death £24,030 1*s.* 6*d.* gross; £17,741 12*s.* 4*d.* net: probate, 27 Aug 1913, *CGPLA Eng. & Wales*

Sclater, William (*bap.* 1575, *d.* 1627), Church of England clergyman, was baptized on 25 October 1575 at Leighton Buzzard, Bedfordshire, son of Anthony Sclater (1519/20–

1620), the rector there, and his wife, Margaret Loughborowe. From Eton College, William was admitted scholar of King's College, Cambridge, on 24 August 1593, and three years later became fellow. He graduated BA in 1598 and proceeded MA in 1601. Shortly after 1601 he began to preach at Walsall, Staffordshire, where he refused to wear the surplice, and on 4 September 1604 he was presented to the vicarage of Pitminster, near Taunton, Somerset, by John Coles. He was still in trouble with the courts for nonconformity in 1606, even while serving as rural dean, yet, he proceeded BD in 1608 and by the next year was urging other moderate puritans to conform. By 1609, too, he had married his first wife, whose name is unknown; William *Sclater (*bap.* 1609, *d.* 1661), the eldest of the two sons and five daughters of the marriage who survived their father, was born that year.

In 1617 Sclater proceeded DD. Bishop Arthur Lake so valued his preaching that he made him his chaplain and a prebendary of Bath and Wells in 1619. Sclater also enjoyed the patronage of Lord Stanhope of Harrington, a member of the privy council, whose chaplain he was, and Lady Elizabeth Poulett. The latter persuaded her husband, John, Lord Poulett, to prefer him to the valuable living of Lympsham, Somerset, in September 1619. He retained Pitminster, however, leaving the care of Lympsham to a curate. At some date in the 1620s Sclater married his second wife, Marie or Mary, who apparently came from Mells, Somerset; they had one daughter.

Sclater published several separate sermons and a treatise on justification, *The Key to the Key of Scripture* (1611). He defended tithes in *The Minister's Portion* (1612) and again in *The Question of Tithes* (1623), in which he attempted to refute John Selden. His friend Edward Kellett thought his arguments 'unanswerable' by 'sacrilegious church-robbers' (*Miscellanies of Divinity*, 1635, 1.83). Sclater's best-selling *Expositions* on 1 and 2 Thessalonians (1619, 1627) merited five more editions by 1638. His son William edited many of his works posthumously, including *Three Sermons* (1629) and *A Brief and Plain Commentary on the Prophecy of Malachy* (1650).

A staunch Calvinist, Sclater regarded the innovations of avant-garde conformists with horror. The refusal of some divines to identify the pope as Antichrist, together with James I's policy of moderation towards Romanists, caused him to wonder what had become of 'that ancient severity and strict hand over papists' (*A Three-Fold Preservative*, 1610, E1*r*). Sclater's godly sympathies are unmistakable. Since the main obstacle to further reformation was not 'our petite dissensions', but the presence of 'loytering, unlettered, [and] dissolute men amongst the clergy', he argued that authorities should connive at the nonconformity of peaceable and diligent pastors (ibid., E2*v*). Sclater was highly esteemed by leading west-country puritans such as Sir John Horner and Sir John Bampfield, and was one of the thirty-four godly ministers to whom Richard Bernard dedicated his influential clerical manual, *The Faithful Shepherd*, in 1621. His experience suggests that in Jacobean Somerset, where preaching was scarce, ceremonialists such as Lake and precisionists such as Sclater could work together in the interests of evangelization.

Sclater had suffered from the stone since at least 1618, when he wrote the epistle to his exposition on 1 Thessalonians. He died at Pitminster some time between 29 June 1627, when he made his will, and 22 October, when it was proved. Fuller pointed to his eminent piety to refute the charge that clergymen's sons 'too often embrace wild courses' (Fuller, 1.79). JIM BENEDICT

Sources Wood, *Ath. Oxon.*, new edn, 2.229 • T. Harwood, *Alumni Etonenses, or, A catalogue of the provosts and fellows of Eton College and King's College, Cambridge, from the foundation in 1443 to the year 1797* (1797), 200, 227 • K. Fincham, *Prelate as pastor: the episcopate of James I* (1990), 10, 193–4, 235–6, 260–61 • A. Milton, *Catholic and Reformed: the Roman and protestant churches in English protestant thought, 1600–1640* (1995), 26, 50–51, 54, 57, 111, 157–8, 213, 292, 462, 464 • PRO, PROB 11/152, fol. 280 • Fuller, *Worthies* (1840), 1.78–80 • *N&Q*, 5 (1852), 457–9, 518–20, 569 • G. Oliver, *Ecclesiastical antiquities in Devon*, 1 (1840), 114; 2 (1842) • Venn, *Alum. Cant.* • W. Sterry, ed., *The Eton College register, 1441–1698* (1943), 308 • *Fasti Angl.* (Hardy), 1.424 • M. Stieg, *Laud's laboratory: the diocese of Bath and Wells in the early seventeenth century* (1982), 322, 336, 347

Archives BL, extracts from Pitminster's minister's portion, Add. MS 4927, fols. 143, 148

Wealth at death at least £140, incl. £120 bequeathed to seven children; also £20 or 'Lease of a ground' at Mells to daughter: will, PRO, PROB 11/152, fol. 280

Sclater, William (*bap.* 1609, *d.* 1661), Church of England clergyman and religious writer, was baptized at Pitminster, Somerset, on 2 June 1609, the elder of two sons of William *Sclater (*bap.* 1575, *d.* 1627), rector of Pitminster, and his first wife, whose name is unknown. As a scholar from Eton College, on 26 June 1626 he was admitted to King's College, Cambridge, where he became a fellow. He graduated BA early in 1630 and about that time was ordained. Three years later he proceeded MA, but resigned his fellowship and in 1634 married Jane Beavys of Exeter. On 12 December 1636 he was instituted to the rectory of St Stephen's, Exeter. In 1640 he proceeded BD and published *Deaths Summons*, a sermon preached in the cathedral in January 1639 for Exeter citizen Peter Taylor. Appointed on 18 September 1641 to the prebend of Wedmore in Exeter, on 5 November he preached in the cathedral a memorial sermon for the Gunpowder Plot, published as *Papisto-mastix, or, Deborahs Prayer Against Gods Enemies* (1642). He was later in London to deliver the topical *The Remedie of Schisme, or, A Meane to Settle the Divisions of the Times* (1642).

In the upheavals following the outbreak of civil war, in 1644 Sclater was ejected from St Stephen's, but on 14 February 1645 he was instituted to the vicarage of Cullompton, the previous incumbent having died. John Walker recorded that there Sclater was in 'a manner persecuted' (*Walker rev.*, 124), although he was never formally sequestrated. There was no minister present in his parish on several Sundays in 1649, according to a return made the following year, which also claimed that Sclater had neglected his cure. In 1650 he took the engagement to the new regime; he also published a collection of his father's sermons on the book of Malachi. Presented on 11 February 1651 under the great seal to the rectory of St Peter-le-Poer in Broad Street, London, he seems to have regarded the parish as his home, but he regularly preached outside the city. In 1651 he returned to Cambridge to proceed DD; his *Concio ad clerum* (1651) was delivered on 17 June. Later he seems to have been active following the assize judges on the western circuit. His *Civil Magistracy by Divine Authority Asserted* (1652), which served as a statement of the *de facto* case for obeying the Commonwealth government, was preached at Winchester assizes on 4 March 1652 and repeated at Taunton on 22 August. *The Grand Assizes, or, The Doctrine of the Last General Judgement* (1653) was delivered at Winchester on 28 July 1652, while *A Divine Cordiall for the Devout Soule* (1653) was aired at Taunton on 4 April 1653, but he had returned to London by 25 September 1653, when he preached at St Botolph, Aldersgate, a funeral sermon for the orientalist and Anglo-Saxon scholar Abraham Wheelocke.

It was not until 1655 that Sclater was formally replaced at Cullompton, and even then he kept some connection with the west country. He retained St Peter-le-Poer at the Restoration, but following his death in London in 1661 the administration of his estate was granted at Exeter. He was survived by his son, also William *Sclater (1638–1727).

GLENN BURGESS

Sources Foster, *Alum. Oxon.* • *Walker rev.*, 124 • Wood, *Ath. Oxon.*, new edn, 3.227–9 • *DNB* • *ESTC* • parish register, Pitminster, Somerset, Som. ARS, 2 June 1609 [baptism]

Sclater, William (1638–1727), nonjuring Church of England clergyman, was born at Exeter on 22 November 1638, the only son of Dr William *Sclater (*bap.* 1609, *d.* 1661), sometime fellow of King's College, Cambridge, and at the time of his son's birth rector of Cullompton, Devon, and of St Stephen's, Exeter, and later a prebendary of Exeter Cathedral, and his wife, Jane Beavys. His late grandfather, also William *Sclater (*bap.* 1575, *d.* 1627), had been the moderate puritan rector of Pitminster, Somerset. Having suffered some measure of hardship as a result of their adherence to the cause of the Church of England during the 'Great Rebellion', the family moved to London following Dr Sclater's compliance with the new regime and appointment to the rectory of St Peter-le-Poer in 1650. After attending Merchant Taylors' School, where he was admitted in 1651, the younger Sclater matriculated at Pembroke College, Oxford, on 29 April 1659. He was appointed vicar of Brampford Speke in Devon in 1663.

Deprived as a nonjuror at the revolution Sclater lived in obscurity until 1717, when, writing anonymously as 'a Presbyter of the Church of England', he published the work for which he is best remembered: *An Original Draught of the Primitive Church*. This late venture into print, which quickly went into a second edition, was provoked by the appearance in 1713 of a second edition of *An Enquiry into the Constitution, Discipline, Unity and Worship of the Primitive Church*, first published in 1691 by Peter King, a prominent whig lawyer and erstwhile protégé of John Locke, who had been one of the managers for the prosecution in the trial of Dr Henry Sacheverell and later became first Baron King of Ockham and lord chancellor from 1725 to 1733. Sclater, who courteously declared his aversion for 'the unpleasant Paths of Controversy' (preface), displayed profound patristic learning, making particular use of the works of Cyprian, Irenaeus, Ignatius, and Tertullian, to disprove King's argument that the church in the earliest centuries of the Christian era had been governed in a congregational fashion by a presbyterian ministry, and that the separation of modern protestant dissenters from the episcopalian church could be justified.

Sclater died on 14 March 1727. His death was reported in the Jacobite newspaper, *Mist's Weekly Journal*, which gave him the character of

> a truly great Man in all Respects, whether we consider him as a Christian or a Scholar: In his single Character he obviated all the objections of a loose and free-thinking Age against the Clergy; he was learned without Pedantry, and pious without Affectation; he was an instance that the sincere Christian, the fine Gentleman, and the most seraphick Piety might consistently be together. (*Mist's Weekly Journal*, 25 March 1727)

RICHARD SHARP

Sources J. H. Overton, *The nonjurors: their lives, principles, and writings* (1902) • *GM*, 1st ser., 62 (1792), 910 • *DNB* • Foster, *Alum. Oxon.* • Venn, *Alum. Cant.* • *Mist's Weekly Journal* (25 March 1727) • W. Sterry, ed., *The Eton College register, 1441–1698* (1943) • *Walker rev.*

Scobell, Henry (*bap.* 1610, *d.* 1660), parliamentary official, is said to have been born in Cornwall, but his antecedents in fact lay in Plymouth, Devon, where he was baptized at St Andrews parish church on 16 December 1610, the tenth child and fifth son of William Scobell (*fl.* 1594–1610). By 1635 he was a deputy registrar in chancery, and from about 1649 was acting registrar, deputizing for Miles Corbet MP. He was admitted to Lincoln's Inn on 15 March 1639 at the request of John Herne, then reader of that society, and was called to the bar on 11 February 1647.

Scobell was active early on in the parliamentarian cause. He contributed significant sums towards the Irish adventure and the defence of his native Plymouth. By 1643 he would appear to have taken up employment as an under-clerk to the clerk of the Commons. The following year, he was serving as secretary to the commissioners for the parliamentarian great seal. On 6 January 1649 he was appointed clerk of the Commons in place of Henry Elsyng. On 14 May 1649 the Rump Parliament passed an act appointing him clerk of the parliament for life, a post to which he was reappointed by the Barebone's Parliament on 5 July 1653. Scobell combined his service in parliament with the publication of a series of works concerned with legislation and parliamentary procedure, first issued during the 1650s. He was the author of *Memorials of the Method and Manner of Proceedings of Parliament in Passing Bills* (1656, reissued in 1658, 1670, and in Dublin in 1692) and of *Remembrances of some Methods, Orders and Proceedings of the House of Lords* (1657; reprinted with *Priviledges of the Baronage of England*, collected by John Selden, in 1689). In addition he edited *A Collection of Several Acts of Parliament, 1648–1651* (1651) and *A Collection of Acts and Ordinances from 3 November 1640 to 17 September 1656* (2 parts, 1657–8). A tract, *The Power of Lords and Commons in Parliament in Points of Judicature* (1680), signed H. S., has been attributed to him. His appointment as clerk to the protectorate parliaments was disputed in 1654, when MPs questioned his presumption in taking up his post before receiving a call from the chair. Having received the protector's patent to be clerk of the parliaments in January 1658, a post which entailed service as clerk of the new upper chamber or 'other house', he was ousted from the Commons.

Scobell was increasingly viewed with suspicion by republican MPs and when the Rump Parliament was restored in 1659 a bill was ordered to repeal the act appointing him to the clerkship for life. When the Rump was restored for a second time later that year, his fall from favour was complete. He came under question for his behaviour at the expulsion of the Rump on 20 April 1653, when he had entered in the *Journal* of the house that 'this day his excellence the lord G[eneral] Cromwell dissolved this house'. Under examination, he admitted that he had had neither instruction nor permission to record any such thing. He excused himself by saying:

> that for the word 'dissolved', he never at that time did hear of any other term; and desired pardon if he would not dare to make a word himself what it was six years after, before they came themselves to call it an Interrupcion. (Pepys, *Diary*, 1.12–13)

Not satisfied with this answer, the Rump set up a committee to decide whether or not his offence came within the Act of Indemnity.

The high disdain now adopted by the house towards its erstwhile clerk clearly reflects the insecurity of its own position, but probably also Scobell's undoubtedly Cromwellian credentials. He seems to have been co-opted on to several sub-committees of the interim council of state set up in the wake of the Rump's 'interruption' in 1653. He certainly became very closely associated with the protectorate court, serving as secretary to the privy councils of both Oliver and Richard Cromwell on a salary of £500 per annum and with a suite of rooms at Whitehall formerly belonging to the board of greencloth. In his capacity as Westminster JP he personally conducted the civil marriage of two of the first lord protector's daughters. In 1659 he secured the second lord protector's grant and demise of a piece of ground in Old Palace Yard for the purpose of building a meeting-place for the Westminster church to which he belonged.

Scobell played a distinctive part in the religious policies of the protectorate. As secretary to the council he was closely involved in the relief of Piedmontese protestants. From 1655 he also co-ordinated a conciliar scheme designed to replace the lapsed commission for augmentation of clerical livings. There is evidence to suggest he had somewhat congregationalist leanings. About the time the first lord protector sought to have drawn up a common confession of faith by a gathering of congregational ministers at the Savoy in 1658, Scobell again co-ordinated arrangements, while appearing to have sought to influence proceedings, in particular by organizing the reinforcement of the doctrine of infant baptism. The Independent ministers John Rowe and Seth Wood were remembered in a codicil to his will, which was made on 22 July 1660 and proved on 29 September following. In it he disposed of the lease on a house in Westminster, as well as property in Hertfordshire. Clearly he had not done too badly out of his years in chancery and the public service, which had also included the office of registrar to the trustees for sale of deans' and chapters' lands, from which position he acquired church estate. He left a wife, Jane, who was still living in 1669, but mentioned no children.

Sean Kelsey

Sources G. E. Aylmer, *The state's servants: the civil service of the English republic, 1649–1660* (1973), 98, 256–8, 372 • W. P. Baildon, ed., *The records of the Honorable Society of Lincoln's Inn: admissions*, 1 (1896), 238 • W. P. Baildon, ed., *The records of the Honorable Society of Lincoln's Inn: the black books*, 2 (1898), 373 • K. S. Bottigheimer, *English money and Irish land* (1971), appx A • J. Hatsell, ed., *Precedents of proceedings in the House of Commons*, 4th edn, 2 (1818), 261–2 • W. R. McKay and J. C. Sainty, eds., *Clerks in the House of Commons, 1363–1989* (1989), 87 • T. Verax [C. Walker], *Anarchia Anglicana, or, The history of independency*, pt 2 (1649), 254 • F. Peck, ed., *Desiderata curiosa*, new edn, 2 vols. in 1 (1779), 491–512 • *JHC*, 6 (1648–51), 112, 209; 7 (1651–9), 281, 365, 581, 587, 659, 752, 767, 777, 805, 814 • *Diary of Thomas Burton*, ed. J. T. Rutt, 4 vols. (1828), vol. 1, pp. xx, 299; vol. 2, pp. 313, 316–17, 336, 348–50, 403–4; vol. 3, p. 2 • *The Clarke papers*, ed. C. H. Firth, 3, CS, new ser., 61 (1899), 132, 133–4n. • *CSP dom.*, *1648–9*; *1653–60* • New College, Oxford, MS 328, fol. 106 • PRO, PROB 11/301; PROB 12; PROB 6/44, fols. 366v–367; fols. 37, 43; fol. 73 • MS material in copies of H. Scobell, *Remembrances*, 1657, BL, Add. MS 36102; Hargrave MS 167; Harleian MSS 4879 and 6423 • volume of ordinances and acts, V&A NAL, Forster Library, no. 7770 • *IGI*

Likenesses T. Simon, gold medal, 1649, NPG • medal, *c.*1650, repro. in E. Hawkins, A. W. Franks, and A. Grueber, eds., *Medallic illustrations* (1885)

Wealth at death significant estate in Hertfordshire; several bequests over £100: will, PRO, PROB 11/301, fols. 366v–367

Scobie, Edward Vivian (1918–1996), journalist and historian, was born Edward Vivian George Scobie Dalrymple in Roseau, Dominica, British West Indies, the eldest child in the family of four sons and one daughter of Evan Harrington Eversley Scobie Dalrymple, a lawyer and the registrar of births and deaths for Dominica, and his wife, Maud, *née* Piper. He later recalled spending much time within hearing distance of his father conversing with friends over drinks; his father, a prominent local figure, played 'cricket and tennis at the club, and at weekends … always went swimming' (Scobie).

Scobie (who in adulthood initially hyphenated his last two names, as Scobie-Dalrymple, then dropped the name Dalrymple) was educated at Roseau Boys' School, then Dominica grammar school. A keen swimmer, he also played cricket and football, became a local table tennis champion, and won several poetry prizes. He first experienced New York while visiting an uncle in Harlem; during his stay he frequented venues such as the Savoy and Renaissance ballrooms. After returning to Dominica he played trumpet in a band, married, and had a son.

Following the outbreak of the Second World War, Scobie travelled to Britain to join the Royal Air Force. He stayed for twenty-three years. His early exposure in New York had prepared him well for after-hours RAF life in 1940s Britain. He soon discovered London nightclubs and other places where black people gathered. Following demobilization he started working as a general factotum for the drummer George Lionel 'Happy' Blake at his West End club and began writing for publications targeted at a black readership, such as the British *Checkers* (July 1948 – January 1949) and *Bronze* (published in the 1950s). Discovering a talent for journalism, he also became the London correspondent for several US publications, including *Ebony*, *Jet*, *Our World*, and the *Chicago Defender*, mainly covering visits by American performing artists—Billy Daniels, Sarah Vaughan, Billy Eckstine, and others—and writing about their British counterparts, such as Joe Harriott, Shake Keane, and Reginald Foresythe. He was one of the BBC reporters who covered the Notting Hill disturbances in September 1958.

From reporting at the BBC, Scobie moved on to writing scripts and broadcasting his own work. On the domestic service his programmes included *Come Along to Freedom* (an evocation of the American slave resistance movement, the underground railroad), a reconstruction of his father's wake for the Third Programme, and a profile of Ken 'Snakehips' Johnson for the Home Service. But he worked mainly for the Caribbean Service, creating programmes for *Calling the Caribbean* and *Caribbean Voices*, and other similar series on a variety of subjects. He profiled major historical black figures in Britain, among them Francis Barber and Ignatius Sancho. In a thirty-minute broadcast in 1960, he assessed the reigns of three African pontiffs, St Victor (189–199), St Miltiades (311–314), and St Gelasius (492–496); his research into the lives and times of these personalities was pioneering. So began his interest in the hidden contribution of black men and women to Western civilization, a subject which thereafter held his interest and which he pursued throughout the rest of his life.

A broadcasting career was now looking promising, as he read his own poems and interviewed show business guests, but Scobie was also taking an interest in magazine publishing. From March to December 1960 he edited *Tropic*, a magazine founded by the Jamaican publisher Charles Ross, then became editor-in-chief of *Flamingo* (1961–3), seemingly a well-resourced magazine with City of London connections. This was an ambitious project, and at one stage associate editors included the Ghanaian Ellis Komey, the British journalist John Harold, and Kenneth Campbell from Jamaica. Its stated mission was to publish a regional edition everywhere in the world where there was a significant community of Africans or African-descended people. At one stage the Ku Klux Klan sent Scobie a threatening letter from Waco, Texas; the magazine proprietors lodged a complaint with the US embassy in London, and sought police protection.

On 18 June 1960 Scobie married an English journalist, Molly Douglas (*b.* 1931/2); she was the daughter of Arthur Victor Douglas-Jones, an army officer, and by the time of their marriage was a divorcee and had changed her name to Scobie by deed poll. Living in Surrey, they had two daughters, and Scobie began writing his seminal book *Black Britannia: the History of Blacks in Britain*, which was eventually published by Johnson Publications of Chicago in 1972. In acknowledging those who co-operated in the development of the book, he thanked Molly Scobie for reading and typing the first six chapters of the manuscript. C. L. R. James was also named for reading it and making 'important suggestions which were incorporated'. Scobie said that the book was based on ten years of research and more than twenty years working as a writer in London. The dedication read: 'To my homeland Dominica and its people—both I love dearly'.

The *Flamingo* dream was not fully realized, although the British edition of the magazine was flourishing when Scobie's tenure was ended before his return to Dominica in 1964. Strains developed in his marriage, but the next eight years saw him actively engaged in politics in tandem with journalism. Twice mayor of Roseau, he also became vice-president of the Dominica Freedom Party, which he helped create in 1968, and he edited the weekly *Dominica Herald* newspaper. He also edited a small volume of short stories, articles, and poetry, entitled *Dies Dominica* (1965), to celebrate 3 November as Dominica day (a date that was previously marked as discovery day). His thinking at this time was revealed in a short poem, 'The return home', which he contributed to this publication:

> With adolescent speed I fled;
> Leaving the mountain-glowering Caribbean shores …
> Now I am home,
> Like Ulysses
> I shall no longer roam.

In his latter assertion Scobie was wrong. In 1972 he left Dominica to teach in the USA, first as associate professor at Rutgers University, then as visiting professor at Princeton University, and finally as professor of history at the City College of New York. His impact on and off campus was unmistakable. He entered a third marriage (to Florrie Green) and had two more daughters. Some of his most important scholarly articles and essays started appearing in the acclaimed *Journal of African Civilizations* and its special anthologies, edited by Dr Ivan Van Sertima. A selection of his writings, including contributions on African resistance to slavery and a re-examination of the Haitian revolution, were brought together in a book, *Global African Presence*, published posthumously in 2001.

Physically a big man, 6 feet 4 inches tall, with a gentle voice, Scobie was always sensitive towards other people's feelings. Even when railing against racism, his writing conveyed warmth mixed with conviction—qualities which earned him much respect and support. He suffered a stroke in early October 1996, but died from a heart attack on 14 November. Following a mass and cremation in New York, his remains were taken to Dominica for burial in the Anglican cemetery in Roseau, after a mass at the Roman Catholic cathedral. He was survived by his wife, Florrie, and by his five children living in Britain, France, and the USA.

KEN CAMPBELL

Sources E. Scobie, ed., *Dies Dominica* (1965) · *The Independent* [Dominica] (20 Nov 1996) · R. Rashidi, 'Dr Edward Scobie', www.saxakali.com, 20 Jan 2002 · R. Rashidi, 'Dr Edward Scobie—major authority on the presence of Africans in early Western Europe', www.caribvoice.com/Profiles/scobie, 20 June 2002 · personal

knowledge (2004) • private information (2004) [Aaron Dalrymple; Judge Ashton Piper; Val Wilmer] • m. cert. [Molly Scobie]
Likenesses portrait, repro. in I. Van Sertima, ed., *African presence in early Europe* (1986), frontispiece

Scobie, Sir Ronald Mackenzie (1893–1969), army officer, was born on 8 June 1893 in India, the son of Mackay John Scobie, a civil servant. Educated as a scholar at Cheltenham College and at the Royal Military Academy, Woolwich, he was commissioned into the Royal Engineers in February 1914. A man who excelled at all sports, shortly before the outbreak of war he played rugby for Scotland against England, Ireland, and Wales. He also played rugby for the army.

Scobie was sent out to France in October 1914. Though wounded shortly after his arrival, he recovered to fight in the trenches for the remainder of the war, being twice mentioned in dispatches and winning the Military Cross. Promoted captain in 1917, he received his brevet majority just two years later. In September 1920 he returned to England, where for four years he commanded a company at Woolwich. From 1927 to 1931 he was a staff captain, and later a brigade major, at Aldershot, before spending three years overseas as director of military artillery at the Royal Military Academy, Australia, during which he was promoted brevet lieutenant-colonel. On 9 February 1927 he married Joan Duncan (*b*. 1904/5), daughter of William Henry Sidebotham, a solicitor, of Farnham, Surrey. They had a daughter.

By 1939 Scobie was in London, as a full colonel and assistant adjutant-general at the War Office, and on the outbreak of war was made deputy director of mobilization, a role at which he excelled. In late spring 1940 he went out to the Middle East to serve as deputy adjutant-general on General Wavell's staff before being appointed, in August, as a brigadier, general staff, in the Sudan. There, under General Sir William Platt, he helped plan the northern arm of the massive pincer that broke Italian military power in east Africa. Scobie with Platt captured Agordat in February 1941, broke the kernel of Italian resistance at Keren in March 1941, and finally took the whole of Eritrea. In the opinion of General Sir Frank Messervy, a fellow officer and friend, it was Scobie, through his diplomatic handling of two quarrelling divisional commanders and his insistence on persevering with the attack, who saw the crucial battle of Keren through to its victorious end (Maule, 5).

In October 1941, a month before Sir Claude Auchinleck launched his 'Crusader' offensive against Rommel, Scobie, now a major-general, was appointed to succeed General Moreshead as commander of the garrison of Tobruk. After leading the 70th British division in by sea to relieve the Australian defenders, he and his men held the fortress in the face of furious enemy assault and even broke out from the town to make contact, if only for a few hours, with Auchinleck's advance troops. Besieged again, with only forty-eight hours of artillery ammunition left, Scobie kept attacking as the battle of Sidi Razegh raged to the south. The garrison held out for another two weeks before finally being relieved. For his efforts in Eritrea and at Tobruk he was appointed OBE in 1941 and CB in 1942.

From February to August 1942, for the duration of Rommel's counter-offensive, Scobie was once again on the staff as deputy adjutant-general. His next posting was as general officer commanding another beleaguered outpost, this time the island of Malta. There he remained, blockaded by sea and under attack from the air, until the siege was finally lifted with the conclusion of the north African campaign. He returned to Cairo in 1943 as chief of staff to General Sir Henry Maitland Wilson, commander-in-chief Middle East, where, among other tasks, he helped plan the invasion of Sicily and amphibious operations in the Aegean.

In the following year Scobie was given command of the British force due for dispatch to Greece to keep order, following the German withdrawal, until a constitutional administration could be established. When he and his force duly arrived in October 1944 they found the country in a state of complete disorder and on the verge of widespread civil war. Members of EAM, the communist-led movement of national liberation, and of its military wing, ELAS, were threatening to seize power and already occupied much of Athens and the surrounding countryside. Supported by the British government, Scobie declared publicly that all guerrilla groups must disband, that he would stand by the returned Greek government in exile, led by Georgeios Papandreou, until a legal armed force was behind it and free elections could be held, and that he would protect it against any *coup d'état*. EAM denied the charge that they were preparing a coup, but the crisis quickly reached boiling point.

In December 1944 heavy fighting broke out in Athens between ELAS and British troops. At one point British and Greek government forces seemed in danger of being overwhelmed. Reinforcements were sent, with a corps commander to take operational control, enabling Scobie to assume overall command. Only after a visit to Athens by Winston Churchill and Anthony Eden late in December did the civil strife there begin to draw to a close. Papandreou resigned, a regency was declared, and a new cabinet formed, more acceptable to EAM. But it took forty days of bitter fighting before Scobie and four ELAS delegates signed a military truce, on 11 January 1945, and disarmament of the guerrillas could start.

Scobie's fine efforts in Greece were recognized by his appointment to KBE in 1945. Most Greeks, too, held him in high esteem, perhaps unusually for a commander of foreign troops engaged as a temporary force of occupation, but their affection and respect were genuine. He received the freedom of Athens and the grand medal of the municipality, and was decorated with the grand cross of George I of Greece, and whenever in public was greeted by cheers and cries of 'Scobie! Scobie! Scobie!'. He remained in command in Greece until 1946.

Scobie was tall and lean, with a long, ruddy face, a slightly aquiline nose, and a small, military moustache.

Although his chestnut hair turned later to grey, he long retained his youthful looks. A quiet, modest, and softly spoken man, his determined and sincere manner inspired confidence and unfailingly commanded respect. 'Above all, he was such a very nice person', recalled General Eric Harrison, who had known Scobie since schooldays at Cheltenham: 'A man of complete integrity who disliked duplicity so much that he would be the right person to judge it' (Maule, 4). Sir Frank Messervy recorded of Scobie that he was 'absolutely straight and honest and you knew that, whenever it was, he would tell the absolute truth. He was … a first-class leader of men' (ibid., 5).

After retiring from the army in 1947, Scobie served as lieutenant of the Tower of London from 1951 to 1954 and as colonel commandant, Royal Engineers, from 1951 to 1958. He and his wife settled at the Old Toll Gate, Mattingley, Hampshire, and he maintained his interest in sport, being delighted in 1965 to be made vice-patron of the Army Rugby Union.

Scobie died in the Cottage Hospital, Odiham, Hampshire, of pneumonia brought on by influenza, on 23 February 1969. RODERICK BAILEY

Sources *Current biography* (1946) • *The Times* (25 Feb 1969) • H. Maule, *Scobie: hero of Greece* (1975) • m. cert. • d. cert.
Archives IWM, papers and diaries of commands in the Middle East, Malta, and Greece
Likenesses W. Stoneman, photograph, 1946, NPG

Scoffin, William (1654/5–1732), Presbyterian minister, was a self-taught man and a good mathematician. Nothing is known of his family or background. John Rastrick, the precariously conforming vicar of Kirton, Lincolnshire, appointed him curate of the chapelry of Brothertoft. There, on 3 July 1683, William Scoffin (presumably the curate himself and not one of his kin) married Ann Buttery. Scoffin resigned the curacy in August 1686, a year and a half before Rastrick also felt that he could no longer stay within the Church of England as it then was.

Following the passing of the Toleration Act in 1689 Scoffin became minister of a presbyterian congregation at Sleaford, Lincolnshire, where he preached for over forty years. He was poor, receiving several grants from the Common Fund between 1691 and 1696 and further grants in 1730 and (in ignorance of his death) in 1733, yet was noted for his charity. He may well have supplemented his income (then and earlier) by teaching. *A Help to True Spelling and Reading* (1705) was the product of his 'having spent some years in the exercise of teaching' and also contained 'some of the chief principles in religion, in a plain and easy metre' together with a catechism on the scriptures (Scoffin, foreword). Scoffin also published *The faithful souldier's reward … in two funeral sermons, occasioned by the death of Katherine Disney* (1692). He died in November 1732, aged seventy-seven, and was buried at Sleaford on 12 November. He was survived by his second wife, Elizabeth (*d*. 1738?), and in his will remembered the family of his old friend and mentor John Rastrick, leaving books to two of Rastrick's sons. CAROLINE L. LEACHMAN

Sources *Calamy rev.*, 429 • A. Gordon, ed., *Freedom after ejection: a review (1690–1692) of presbyterian and congregational nonconformity in England and Wales* (1917), 347 • *The nonconformist's memorial … originally written by … Edmund Calamy*, ed. S. Palmer, 2 (1775), 165 • E. Calamy, *A continuation of the account of the ministers … who were ejected and silenced after the Restoration in 1660*, 2 vols. (1727), vol. 2, p. 461 • *IGI* • W. Scoffin, *A help to true spelling and reading* (1705) • *DNB* • will, 16 Dec 1732, Lincs. Arch., Prebendal Court of Stafford
Wealth at death left books: will, 16 Dec 1732, Lincs. Arch., prebendal court of Stafford; *Calamy rev.*

Scogan [Scoggin], **Henry** (*c*.1361–1407), poet, of Norfolk, succeeded his brother John as lord of the manor of Haviles, near Great Rainham, in 1391. The suggestion in the *Dictionary of National Biography* that he studied at Oxford seems to have arisen from a confusion with John *Scoggin or Scogan. He was in the service of Richard II and at some time resided in London. He is almost certainly the Scogan who was a friend of Chaucer, who addressed to him a short poem, 'Lenvoy a Scogan', an entertaining verse epistle, rather Horatian in tone, probably in the later 1390s. It jestingly suggests that, since Scogan has not been faithful in an affair, Venus is weeping so copiously that all will be drowned by her tears and that Cupid will take revenge on all those 'that ben hoor [grey] and rounde of shap' (Chaucer, 'Lenvoy a Scogan', line 31). Scogan may say, 'Lo, olde Grisel [old grey horse?] lyst to ryme and playe' (ibid., line 35), but Chaucer is not able or willing to write verse. In the envoy Scogan, 'that knelest at the stremes hed Of grace' (ibid., line 43), is asked to remember his friend, and never defy love again. Whether the poem, which survives in three manuscripts and the editions of Caxton (1477–8) and Thynne (1532), has any ulterior purpose is not known. He was probably the Henri Scoggan who in 1390 had a loan (of 26*s*. 8*d*.) from the merchant Gilbert Maghfeld—like Chaucer and others associated with Chaucer. He was one of three persons bound as mainpernors for a detinue of 106*s*. 8*d*. on 7 September 1390, and this may have something to do with an apparent need of ready money. On 11 August 1394 he was granted protection for six months, and on 16 April 1399 for one year, on going to Ireland with the king.

Scogan was tutor to the four sons of Henry IV, who may well be the recipients of his *Moral Balade* addressed to 'my noble sones, and eek my lordes dere'. This poem, surviving in BL, Harley MS 2251, and Bodl. Oxf., MS Ashmole 59, found its way into the Chaucer editions of Caxton and Thynne (1542). In the Ashmole manuscript it is said by the scribe John Shirley to be to the princes, at a supper of a meeting of merchants in the Vintry, at the house of Lewis John; in the printed editions it is said to be addressed to the lords and gentlemen of the king's house. Scogan calls it a 'litel tretys', 'writen with myn owne hand full rudely' ('Scogan's Ballade', ll. 3–4). In age he laments that in his misspent youth he cherished vices rather than virtues: this 'complaint' is to warn them and to urge them to follow virtue, for lordship without virtue cannot endure. He cites Chaucer's views on true nobility and quotes his balade of *Gentilesse*. Lords nowadays do not wish to hear about virtue, and act like a ship without 'governaunce', but:

> vertuous noblesse
> Roted in youthe, and with good perseveraunce,
> Dryveth away al vyce and wrecchednesse.
> (ibid., ll. 158–60)

Tullius Hostilius and Julius 'the conquerour' rose from humble origins to high estate through virtue; Nero, Belshazzar, and Antiochus fell because of their vices. The poem, written after Chaucer's death in 1400, dates perhaps from 1406 or 1407. Scogan died in 1407 and was succeeded in his estates by his son Robert.

DOUGLAS GRAY

Sources Emden, *Oxf.*, 3.1656–6 · G. L. Kittredge, 'Henry Scogan', *Harvard Studies and Notes in Philology and Literature*, 1 (1892), 109–17 · E. Rickert, 'Extracts from a fourteenth-century account book', *Modern Philology*, 24 (1926–7), 111–19, 249–56 · M. N. Hallmundson, 'Chaucer's circle: Henry Scogan and his friends', *Medievalia & Humanistica*, 10 (1981), 29–34 · 'Scogan's Ballade', *Chaucerian and other pieces*, ed. W. W. Skeat (1897), [vol. 7] of *The complete works of Geoffrey Chaucer* (1894–7), 237–44 · *The Riverside Chaucer*, ed. L. D. Benson, 3rd edn (1989), 655 · F. Blomefield and C. Parkin, *An essay towards a topographical history of the county of Norfolk*, [2nd edn], 11 vols. (1805–10), vol. 7, p. 141

Scoggin [Scogan, Scogin, Skogyn], **John** (*supp. fl.* 1480), supposed court jester and author, was associated in the sixteenth and seventeenth centuries with the earlier Henry *Scogan (*c.*1361–1407), the friend of Chaucer; however, he may very well have been an entirely fictitious character, the 'author' of a jest book, which survives as *The iestes of Skogyn* (printed *c.*1570 by T. Colwell), and a jester at the court of Edward IV. The book is probably identifiable with the 'Skogan', which appears in the list of Captain Cox's books in Robert Langham's *A Letter* (1575) (where it occurs among other merry tales, such as the collection of 'Howleglas' (Till Eulenspiegel), and a couple of poems by Skelton). The earliest known print survives only in fragmentary form (*STC, 1475–1640*, 21850.3), but there is a copy of the edition of 1626 (by Francis Williams; *STC, 1475–1640*, 21850.7). Its title, *The First and Best Part of Scoggins Jests* probably alludes to a rival 'continuation' compiled from other sources (1613; *STC, 1475–1640*, 21851). There are later chapbook versions, and numerous references to it in the sixteenth and seventeenth centuries confirm its popularity. One similar collection, *Dobsons Drie Bobbes*, describes itself as 'son and heire to Scoggin'. The *Iests* are said to have been 'gathered' by Andrew Boorde (*d.* 1549), the physician who is reported as saying that he is publishing it to make men merry and to be an antidote to melancholy. It is not certain whether this is an unfounded attribution (*Merie Tales of the Mad Men of Gotam* was also attributed to him) or whether he was in fact the compiler, or the author.

The preface associates Scoggin with Oxford: 'I have heard say that Scogin did come of an honest stocke, or kindred, and his friends did set him to schoole at Oxford, where hee did continue untile the time he was made Master of Art' (*The First and Best Part*), and Oxford is the setting for several of the jests. According to the 'biography' embedded in the stories, he went to London, then for a time to Bury. He became a fool in the household of Sir William Neville (presumably the son of the first earl of Westmorland, who was made earl of Kent in 1461), who introduced him to court. The king, delighted by the jester's wit, gave him a house in Cheapside. However, because of his plain speaking, he fell from favour, and went to France—where the same pattern recurred. Returning to England, he was eventually pardoned by the king and queen. He died of a 'perilous cough' and was buried on the east side of Westminster Abbey (where later Henry VII's chapel was built). The connection with Oxford produced some later elaboration:

> as Scogan is described as repairing to St. Bartholomew's Hospital with other masters during an outbreak of the plague, it was reasonably inferred by Thomas Warton the younger that he was connected with Oriel College, the fellows of which were allowed to go there *pro peste evitanda* in 1519 and subsequent years. (Emden, *Oxf.*)

It may be the cause of the belief that Henry Scogan had studied at Oxford. The confusion of the two Scogans is implied in Shakespeare's *2 Henry IV*, where Falstaff is said to have broken Scoggin's head at the court gate (Shakespeare, *2 Henry IV*, III.ii), and is explicit in Jonson's *Fortunate Isles*, where Scoggin is described as

> a fine gentleman and a master of arts
> Of Henry the fourths times that made disguises
> for the kings sons and writ in ballad royall
> Daintily well.

As in the case of Skelton, who after his death became the supposed 'author' of a book of merry tales, and with whom Scoggin is often associated, or the Parson of Kalenborowe, Scoggin seems to fit a favourite pattern of a learned man who is at the same time a jester. His jests use traditional matter of the kind found in other jest books, and are reasonably 'merry'.

DOUGLAS GRAY

Sources Emden, *Oxf.*, 3.1656 · J. Wardroper, *Jest upon jest: a selection from the jestbooks and collections of merry tales published from the reign of Richard III to George III* (1970) · *DNB* · *The first and best part of Scoggins jests*, ed. A. Boord (1626)

Scoles, Joseph John (1798–1863), architect, was born in London on 27 June 1798, the son of Matthew Scoles, a joiner, formerly of Shirburn, Oxfordshire, and Elizabeth Sparling, who was descended from the Irelands of Crofton Hall, Yorkshire. His parents were Roman Catholic. Educated at the Franciscan school at Baddesley Green, Warwickshire, Joseph was apprenticed in 1812 for seven years to his kinsman Joseph Ireland, an architect largely employed by the Roman Catholic bishop Dr John Milner (1752–1826). During his apprenticeship his detailed drawings were revised by the architectural and antiquarian draughtsman John Carter (1748–1817), through Milner's influence, and he thus had his attention directed at an early period to medieval ecclesiastical art. Ireland, as was customary at that period, frequently acted as contractor as well as designer, and Scoles from 1816 to 1819 was resident at Hassop Hall, Derbyshire, and in Leicester, supervising the building of Roman Catholic chapels designed by Ireland. One was classical, the other Gothic. In 1819 he set up his own practice, having gained the commission from Thomas Roberts for a house (West End Lodge) at Esher, Surrey. On 15 January 1820 he was admitted to the Royal Academy Schools, when his age was recorded as twenty-four, and began to exhibit drawings at the academy.

In 1822 Scoles left Britain in company with Joseph Bonomi the younger for further study, and devoted himself to archaeological and architectural research in Rome, Sicily, Greece, Egypt, the Sudan, and Syria. In Sicily he assisted Samuel Angell and William Harris in their explorations. In Syria and Egypt Henry Parke and Frederick Catherwood were often his companions. He and Parke published in 1829 an engraved *Map of Nubia, Comprising the Country between the First and Second Cataracts of the Nile*, from a survey made jointly by them in 1824. Scoles also published a map of the city of Jerusalem. His plan of the church of the Holy Sepulchre, Jerusalem, with his drawings of the Jewish tombs in the valley of Jehoshaphat, was published by Professor Robert Willis in his monograph of 1849. The plan of the temple of Cadacchio, contributed by Scoles to the supplementary volume of *The Antiquities of Athens*, by J. Stuart and N. Revett, was published without acknowledgement. Two sheets of Greek and Roman details, drawn by Francis Arundale from sketches by Parke and Scoles in 1823, were published by A. C. Pugin in 1828. The illustrations to the article 'Catacomb' in the *Dictionary of the Architectural Publication Society* (1850) comprise plans of a catacomb in Alexandria drawn in 1823 by Scoles, Parke, and Catherwood. He was a founder and active member of the Syro-Egyptian Society. A watercolour drawing by John Hollins ARA, formerly in the possession of his son A. C. Scoles, shows Scoles in the local costume he adopted while in Syria.

Meanwhile in 1826 Scoles returned home and resumed his practice. In 1827–8 he planned and carried out the building of Gloucester Terrace, Regent's Park, for which John Nash supplied the general elevation. He showed his ingenuity by varying the internal arrangements behind Nash's elevation, and his independence by changing the proportions of Nash's details (and especially of the cornice), while preserving the contours of the mouldings. Nash passed the work with the observation that the parts looked larger than he expected. Gloucester Villa, at the entrance to the park, was solely due to Scoles. In 1828–9 he erected a suspension bridge over the River Bure at Great Yarmouth, which in 1845 gave way with fatal results, owing to concealed defects of workmanship in two of the suspending rods.

In 1831 Scoles married Harriott Cory, daughter of Robert Cory, a solicitor of Great Yarmouth. This brought him several further commissions in that town, including St Mary's Church of England Chapel, South Town (1831–2; enlarged later), St Peter's Church of England Church (1831–3; later St Spiridion's Greek Orthodox Church), and the repair of the tower of St Nicholas's Church (1834). Later he built St Mary's Roman Catholic Church and presbytery (1848–50), and was probably the architect of Britannia and Columbia Terraces (on Marine Parade and Apsley Road), built in 1848–55. Elsewhere, for the Church of England, he built St George's Church, Edgbaston, Birmingham (1836–8; later comprehensively enlarged), added a new aisle and fittings to St Peter and St Paul, Burgh Castle, Suffolk (1845–7), and restored St Mary's, Blundeston, Suffolk (1849–50). Otherwise, his ecclesiastical work was for the Roman Catholic church. His first important church was St Peter's collegiate church, Stonyhurst, Lancashire (1832–5). Like his Anglican churches, this was Gothic, in this case Perpendicular. A. W. N. Pugin was probably referring to it when he wrote to W. Osmond in January 1834, with reference to his impending conversion: 'A very good chapel is now building in the north and when compleat I certainly think I shall recant' (*The Collected Letters of A. W. N. Pugin*, ed. M. Belcher, 1, 2001, 24).

Scoles's other Roman Catholic churches include: St Winefride's, Holywell, Flintshire (classical, 1832–3; enlarged 1909–12); Our Lady's, St John's Wood, London (Early English Gothic, 1833–6); St Ignatius's, Preston, Lancashire (Perpendicular, 1833–6; enlarged 1858); St Mary's, Newport, Monmouthshire (Early English Gothic, 1838–42); St David's, Cardiff (Gothic, 1842; dem.); St John's, Islington, London (Norman, 1841–3); the Immaculate Conception, Farm Street, London (Decorated Gothic, 1844–9); St Francis Xavier's, Liverpool (Early English Gothic, 1845–9); the Immaculate Conception, Chelmsford, Essex (Early English Gothic, 1847); the Holy Family, Ince Blundell, Lancashire (classical, 1858–9); and Holy Cross, St Helen's, Lancashire (Decorated Gothic, 1860–62). Scoles's design of the church of St John, Islington, was severely censured by A. W. N. Pugin in an article in the *Dublin Review* for 1842 (reprinted in *The Present State of Ecclesiastical Architecture in England*, 1843, 109–10). Scoles was defended by J. A. Hansom in *The Builder* (1 April 1843).

Scoles also designed various church altars, schools, and convent buildings. For the London Oratory he designed the residence (1854), the temporary church (1854; enlarged 1856), and the Little Oratory, as well as a school in Macklin Street, Drury Lane (*c*.1852; dem.), and St Wilfrid's Convent, Cale Street, Chelsea (1859–60). For Prior Park College, Bath, Scoles designed St Mary's Church, in the classical style, to harmonize with the great Georgian house. It has an elegantly impressive Corinthian interior. It was begun in 1844, but completed only in 1871–82, according to his design, by his son A. J. C. Scoles.

Scoles's work shows a progression, characteristic of his time, from the Perpendicular Gothic of Stonyhurst (its outline based on King's College chapel, Cambridge), and the adaptation of the Norman style to a plan derived from the Gesù, Rome, at St John's, Islington, to the 'correct' Decorated of Farm Street. His stylistic versatility, although it did not endear him to the ecclesiologists, was well suited to the assorted needs of his Catholic clients.

Scoles was one of the founding fellows of the Royal Institute of British Architects in 1835, and was honorary secretary from May 1846 to May 1856, and vice-president in 1857–8. To the society's proceedings he contributed papers on monuments of Egypt, the Holy Land, Italy, Greece, and England. He died on 29 December 1863 at his residence, Crofton Lodge, Hammersmith, and was buried in St Thomas's cemetery, Fulham, London. He was survived by his wife, four sons, and eight daughters. Two of the sons—the Revd Ignatius Cory Scoles SJ (1834–1896) and the Revd Alexander Joseph Cory Scoles (1844–1920)—were trained as architects, and continued to practise as such after ordination as priests. Scoles's pupils included J. A. Cory, S. J. Nicholl, F. W. Tuach, G. J. Wigley, and T. J. Willson. He expressed the wish that his incomplete works should be finished by S. J. Nicholl, which Nicholl accomplished in partnership with T. J. Willson.

S. J. NICHOLL, *rev.* PETER HOWELL

Sources *Catholic Annual Register* (1850) • *The Builder*, 22 (1864), 41 • Gillow, *Lit. biog. hist.* • [W. Papworth], ed., *The dictionary of architecture*, 11 vols. (1853–92) • Graves, *RA exhibitors* • B. Little, *Catholic churches since 1623* (1966) • Stephen Welsh's notes, 1973, RIBA BAL • D. Evinson, *Pope's corner* (1980) • *Catalogue of the drawings collection of the R.I.B.A.* • *Dir. Brit. archs.* • Colvin, *Archs.* • D. Evinson, *Catholic churches of London* (1998) • R. O'Donnell, 'Roman Catholic church architecture in Great Britain and Ireland, 1829–1878', PhD diss., U. Cam., 1983 • W. R. Dawson and E. P. Uphill, *Who was who in Egyptology*, 3rd edn, rev. M. L. Bierbrier (1995), 382 • S. Tillett, *Egypt itself: the career of Robert Hay* (1984), 15, 17, 49–50, 74 • *CGPLA Eng. & Wales* (1864) • D. Evinson, *St Thomas's, Fulham* (1976) • S. C. Hutchison, 'The Royal Academy Schools, 1768–1830', *Walpole Society*, 38 (1960–62), 123–91, esp. 173 • private information [family papers]

Archives CUL, letters to Joseph Bonomi

Likenesses J. Hollins, watercolour drawing; in possession of A. C. Scoles

Wealth at death under £1000: probate, 16 Dec 1864, *CGPLA Eng. & Wales*

Scoloker, Anthony (*d.* 1593), translator and printer, established the first press at Ipswich, probably in 1547. Conceivably he may be identified as the Antony Scolacar who on 21 January 1542 was bound apprentice to the London grocer John Over but never made free of the company; the presumption of an apprenticeship at age sixteen, however, would mean that by age twenty-one Scoloker not only had mastered the craft of printing but also possessed a command of languages sufficient for the production of a handful of colourful translations from German, Dutch, and French. It is also possible that Scoloker learned to print on the continent, and he may have been associated in some way with the Ghent printer and typefounder Joos Lambrecht, from whom he obtained type and pictorial woodblocks.

The first appearance of Scoloker's name in print is on the title-page of *The Just Reckoning of the Years unto 1547*, 'translated out of the Germaine tonge into Englishe by Anthony Scoloker the 6. daye of July 1547'. This chronology of events from the creation onwards is part of a coherent group of six small tracts, all of them set in a distinctive black letter type but none giving information as to printer or place of printing. One of the six is dated 1548, and in that same year Anthony Scoloker of St Nicholas's parish, Ipswich, is named as printer in six other books. These use new types obtained from Lambrecht, but they share with the books of the first group a stock of woodcut initials from London, and like the earlier tracts they address the radical reform of the English protestant church. Two of the works issued over Scoloker's name were his own translations, a dialogue between a 'Christen Shomaker and a Popysshe Parson' from the German of Hans Sachs, and *The Ordinary for All Faithful Christians* from the Dutch original by Cornelius van der Heyden, first published by Lambrecht at Ghent in 1545; for the latter Scoloker made use of Lambrecht's set of sixty-five pictorial woodblocks, which include, among other scenes of common life, the earliest representation of a printing press to appear in an English book. Three further works name the Ipswich schoolmaster Richard Argentine as translator, and the sixth consists in part of a translation by Richard Rice, a local clergyman who also wrote one of the anonymously issued books that are now attributed to Scoloker's Ipswich press.

By June 1548 Scoloker had left Ipswich for London. In that month he is named, in partnership with William Seres, as printer of two books; one of these, an anti-mass tract by Jean Viret, also credits Scoloker with having translated the text from French. Eight other books are known from the partnership of Scoloker and Seres, all either dated 1548 or undated. Seven further undated works give Scoloker's name alone, with addresses in the parish of St Botolph, Aldersgate, and in the Savoy rents; four more, all of them printed in his distinctive Ghent types, have a false imprint or none at all. Some of Scoloker's type appeared again in a book issued around 1554, but no printer is named and Scoloker's connection with the book is uncertain. Later records suggest that the printer may have deserted his craft and turned merchant, for an Antony Scoloker or Skolokor, milliner, is named five times in a London port book of 1567–8 as receiving shipments of such small goods as razors and lute strings.

A Middlesex subsidy roll of 3 April 1549 lists one Hance Rycard, an alien, as dwelling with the Englishman Anthony Scolyca in the liberty of the duchy of Lancaster, which accords with the Savoy rents address, but neither name recurs in later rolls. Several entries in the burial registers of St Mary-le-Strand also presumably relate to Scoloker and his family: Judith Scoloker (probably a daughter) was buried on 5 September 1563; 'Anthony Scollinger sonne of Anthonie' on 12 May 1574; a servant of 'Jone Scollenger' on 31 May 1574; and 'Mistress Scoliker' on 21 August 1599. The same register records the burial of 'Anthony Skolykers' himself on 13 May 1593.

A different Anthony Scoloker is often named as the author of the long poem *Daiphantus, or, The Passions of Love* (1604), notable mainly for its allusions to Shakespeare. The title-page of *Daiphantus* identifies the author only as 'An. Sc.', which was expanded to 'Anthony Scoloker, a printer' by Francis Douce, the first modern writer to discuss the poem (F. Douce, *Illustrations of Shakespeare*, 1807, 2.265). However, despite its frequent repetition, there is no documentary support for Douce's conjecture.

JANET ING FREEMAN

Sources J. I. Freeman, 'Anthony Scoloker, the "*Just reckoning* printer", and the earliest Ipswich printing', *Transactions of the Cambridge Bibliographical Society*, 9 (1986–90), 476–96 • *STC, 1475–1640* • C. L. Oastler, *John Day, the Elizabethan printer* (1975) • R. E. G. Kirk and

E. F. Kirk, eds., *Returns of aliens dwelling in the city and suburbs of London, from the reign of Henry VIII to that of James I*, Huguenot Society of London, 10/1 (1900) • B. Dietz, ed., *The port and trade of early Elizabethan London: documents*, London RS, 8 (1972) • wardens' accounts of the Grocers' Company, GL, Guildhall MS 11,571/5, fol. 146 • J. A. Roberts, '*Daiphantus* (1604): a Jacobean perspective on Hamlet's madness', *Library Chronicle of the University of Pennsylvania*, 41 (1978), 128–37 • parish register, St Mary-le-Strand, 13 May 1593 [burial]

Scoloker, Anthony (*fl.* **1604**), poet, is assumed to be the full name of the 'An. Sc. Gentleman' who published a poem described on the title-page of the quarto as *Daiphantus, or, The Passions of Love* (1604). It is also assumed that a printer and translator of the 1540s with the same name was his ancestor. The quarto is the only publication extant by 'An. Sc.' and the only evidence so far discovered of his existence.

Daiphantus is a narrative poem of 942 lines whose eponymous hero improbably and hastily falls in love with four successive women. Rejected by all, he goes mad, but upon pledging that he will remain chaste, he is restored to sanity by the therapeutic employment of music. Tediously clever, over-elaborate, and pointless though it is, the poem does provide a unique description of a piece of stage action in *Hamlet*. Daiphantus in his madness:

> Puts off his cloathes; his shirt he onely weares,
> Much like mad *Hamlet*; thus as Passion teares.
> (Scoloker, sig. E4v)

But the main value of *Daiphantus* lies in its lively preface. According to Scoloker, a prefatory epistle:

> should be like the *Never-too-well read Arcadia*, where the *Prose* and *Verce* (*Matter* and *Words*) are like his [Sidney's] *Mistresses* eyes, one excelling another and without Corivall: or to come home to the vulgar['s] elements, like *Friendly Shakespeare's Tragedies*, where the *Commedian* rides, when the *Tragedian* stands on Tip-toe: Faith it should please all, like Prince *Hamlet*. (Scoloker, sig. E4v)

Whether or not Scoloker was, as some deduce, a friend of Shakespeare, this preface, according to Harold Jenkins ('*Hamlet* then till now', *Shakespeare Survey*, 18, 1965, 35), ranks as the earliest certain reference to Shakespeare's *Hamlet* (as opposed to earlier versions of the Hamlet story). It provides another piece of irrefutable evidence (since the anti-Stratfordians constantly require refutation) that someone named Shakespeare wrote *Hamlet* and other tragedies. And it is refreshing to hear that while *Hamlet* pleased 'all', the source of his popularity among the 'vulgar' was the willingness of friendly Shakespeare to give relief from the Tragedian's tiptoe arias by a ride with the Comedian. P. J. FINKELPEARL

Sources An. Sc. [A. Scoloker], *Daiphantus, or, The passions of love* (1604)

Scoones, Sir Reginald Lawrence (**1900–1991**), army officer, was born on 18 December 1900 at Hermitage, Sutton Heston, Brentford, Middlesex, the son of Major Fitzmaurice Thomas Le Fevre Scoones, of the Royal Fusiliers, and his wife, Florence (*née* Osborne). General Sir Geoffry Allen Percival Scoones (1893–1975), commander of the 4th army corps which defeated the Japanese at Imphal, Burma, in 1944, and subsequently commander-in-chief, central command, India (1945–6), and British high commissioner in New Zealand (1953–7) was an elder brother. He was educated at Wellington College, where he was captain of the rugby football fifteen, and at the Royal Military College, Sandhurst, and was commissioned into the Royal Fusiliers in 1920. He transferred to the Royal Tank Corps in 1923, and was posted to Sudan, where he was a machine-gun officer with the Sudan defence force from 1926 to 1934. While there he married, on 7 November 1933 in Khartoum, Isabella Bowie (Ella) Nisbet, daughter of John Nisbet, of the Isles of Cumbrae, Scotland. They had one daughter. After returning to England Scoones became adjutant of 1st Royal Tank regiment (RTR) in 1936 and was appointed to the staff of the experimental mobile division, as a GSO3, in 1938.

In 1939 Scoones was posted, as brigade major, to the cavalry brigade in Cairo and became a GSO2 in General Richard O'Connor's western desert force. At this time the art of desert exploration was in its early stages and the expertise of the long range desert group and Special Air Service lay in the future, but Scoones, who was not unfamiliar with the desert, was able to organize desert reconnaissance which proved invaluable when the Italians, with massive numerical and armour superiority, invaded Egypt in September 1940. Fortunately the quality of the British forces and the generalship of O'Connor proved much superior to the Italians when O'Connor counter-attacked in December 1940. Two British divisions destroyed ten Italian divisions, took 130,000 prisoners, 380 tanks, and 845 guns, while themselves sustaining 500 killed, 1373 wounded, and 55 missing. The final battle was at Beda Fomm, 50 miles south of Benghazi in February 1941. Scoones was immediately appointed OBE for his part in this success. His next posting was as second-in-command of the 42nd RTR, and on 18 November 1942, when the 'crusader' offensive was launched by General Sir Claude Auchinleck, there was a series of hard-fought battles around Sidi Rezegh, and 4th Indian division, which 42nd RTR was supporting, captured Sidi ʿUmar. During these battles Scoones was promoted to command 42nd RTR. By the end of this campaign he had accumulated enough experience of tank warfare to make him an expert on instructional needs and he was posted back to the War Office as deputy director of military training.

In 1943 Scoones was appointed to take over command of 254 tank brigade in Burma, where the British and Indian troops were planning to advance across the Chindwin River. There he joined his oldest brother, Geoffry, who was commanding 4th Indian corps. However, while the British were planning to drive the Japanese out of Burma, the Japanese were preparing to launch an invasion of India; they had some success in the initial stages of their attack when they threatened Imphal by occupying a hill at Nungshigum on the northern edge of the Imphal plain. This move put them within range of the Imphal petrol and ammunition dumps and the Kangla airfield. The Japanese did not believe that tanks could climb hills but learned their mistake when the British tanks supporting the Dogras crawled upwards, though sustaining heavy casualties among their tank commanders who were obliged to control the battle by standing up in open turrets and directing their drivers through thick vegetation which obscured their view. Nungshigum was captured but with heavy casualties on both sides. Scoones was appointed DSO for his skill and courage in commanding the brigade, which he continued to do until he was wounded near Mandalay.

After recovery Scoones returned to the War Office, once again as deputy director, military training. In 1947 he was offered the appointment of assistant kaid (commandant) of the Sudan defence force. Three years later he was appointed kaid, in the rank of major-general. Although he was extremely popular with all ranks and enjoyed his appointment very much, the post was not without its difficulties. With the approach of independence (Sudan became a sovereign independent state in 1955 and a republic in 1956) he had the task of preparing for the handover of military authority to Sudanese officers. His advice was not invariably heeded. He intimated that officers from the north should not be posted to units in the south. When this happened it contributed to triggering off the civil war, which led to several coups and a particularly bloody conflict that continued for many years, with external influences also contributing to instability.

Scoones retired from the army in 1954 and was then appointed chairman of the brewing industry's National Trade Development Association. He was director of the Brewers' Society from 1957 to 1969. He was made OBE in 1941 and DSO in 1945, and was appointed CB in 1951 and KBE in 1955. Cully Scoones commanded widespread respect for his integrity and reliability, complemented by a splendid sense of humour which enabled him to defuse an impending awkward situation with an appropriate witty remark. A modest man, he always made light of his own achievements which ranged over command tactics, forward planning, and diplomatic skills. He died of heart failure and prostate cancer at the Westminster Hospital, London, on 6 October 1991. PHILIP WARNER

Sources royal tank regiment archives, Royal Armoured Corps Museum, Bovington Camp, Wareham, Dorset • K. Chadwick, *The royal tank regiment* (1970) • D. Rooney, *Burma victory* (1992) • *WWW*, 1991–5 • citation for DSO, PRO • private information (2004) • *The Times* (14 Oct 1991) • b. cert. • d. cert. • *CGPLA Eng. & Wales* (1992)
Likenesses photograph, repro. in *The Times*
Wealth at death under £125,000: probate, 26 Feb 1992, *CGPLA Eng. & Wales*

Scorburgh, Sir Robert (*d.* 1339), justice, took his name from Scorborough in the East Riding of Yorkshire, a few miles north of Beverley. He was linked with the latter town all his life, though the chronology of his associations is not without problems. A man of his name was appointed attorney to the archbishop of York at a Newgate gaol delivery in 1301, to audit the receipts of a grant of pavage to Beverley in 1303, and to deliver Beverley gaol in 1304. In 1305 he received an oyer and terminer commission from the minster chapter, and in 1307 he represented the town in parliament. In 1311 Archbishop Greenfield appointed him to deliver Beverley gaol and take assizes there. Little is recorded of his career in the years immediately afterwards, but at Michaelmas 1318 either he or a namesake was made a serjeant and began to plead in the bench. Although it seems likely that there was only one man involved, and that Scorburgh, having already worked at Westminster, perhaps as an attorney, was now actively pursuing his career there, it remains possible that there were two men of his name, perhaps father and son or uncle and nephew, and that the gap after 1311 is one between generations.

From 1319 onwards Scorburgh was regularly appointed to commissions, nearly always in Yorkshire, and often in or near Beverley. He seems to have prospered, because he is also recorded as lending money, while in 1322 he bought the wardship of an heir with estates in Yorkshire and Lincolnshire. In 1329 he was made a justice on eyre for Nottinghamshire, and in the following year for Derbyshire. In 1331–2 he was a gaol delivery justice for Cumberland, Westmorland, and Yorkshire, and in 1333 was named as a justice for an abortive Durham eyre. On 7 January 1334 he was instructed to proceed with all haste to Flanders to investigate attacks upon one another by Englishmen and Flemings. On 2 November 1332 he was appointed a baron of the exchequer, and reappointed on 19 November 1333 and 7 January 1334, but although he was paid until Easter 1335 order was given for his replacement on 6 January 1335. This was probably because on 28 July 1334 he had been made chief baron of the Dublin exchequer. Continuing English commissions suggest that he was not always there; in November 1336, for instance, he was a member of an important Yorkshire commission reviewing crime and disorder in that county, one whose proceedings clashed with those of the bench which was then at York. Nevertheless on 28 July 1337 he was appointed a justice of the Dublin bench. Shortly afterwards his health seems to have begun to fail. On 11 March 1338 he was granted exemption from office holding, and by 20 October following a replacement had to be named to a commission to levy a subsidy in the East Riding 'in the room of Robert de Scorburgh, now too infirm to attend thereto' (*Calendar of the Fine Rolls*, 1337–47, 97). He died in 1339, some time before 30 November.

Knighted by Michaelmas 1335, in May 1336 Scorburgh paid 100 marks for the manor of Scoreby. He also came to hold property in Stamford Bridge, Etton, and Ravensthorpe as well as in Beverley, where in 1324 he was licensed to found a chantry 'in the chapel of Corpus Christi in his dwelling place' (*CPR*, 1321–4, 365). The name of his wife is unrecorded, but he had at least three sons. The eldest, Thomas, was an idiot, liable as such to become a royal ward, and Scorburgh tried to keep his estates out of crown hands by conveying them to his other sons, William and Roger. But although in January 1340 the lands were delivered to the latter for them to hold during pleasure, three months later they were entrusted to a royal nominee, signalling the failure of the judge's plans.

HENRY SUMMERSON

Sources *Chancery records* • W. P. Baildon, ed., *Feet of fines for the county of York, from 1327 to 1347, 1–20 Edward III*, 1, Yorkshire Archaeological Society, 42 (1910) • A. F. Leach, ed., *Memorials of Beverley Minster*, 2 vols., SurtS, 98, 108 (1898–1903) • *The register of William Greenfield, lord archbishop of York, 1306–1315*, ed. W. Brown and A. H. Thompson, 1, SurtS, 145 (1931) • *The register of Thomas of Corbridge, lord archbishop of York, 1300–1304*, 2, ed. A. H. Thompson, SurtS, 141 (1928) • *CIPM*, 8, no. 249 • *Calendar of inquisitions miscellaneous (chancery)*, PRO, 2 (1916) • F. Palgrave, ed., *The parliamentary writs and writs of military summons*, 1 (1827) • J. P. Collas and T. F. T. Plucknett, eds., *Year books of Edward II*, 23: *12 Edward II*, SeldS, 65 (1950) [1950 for 1946] • Sainty, *Judges* • D. Crook, *Records of the general eyre*, Public Record Office Handbooks, 20 (1982) • Baker, *Serjeants*, 154

Scoresby, William, senior (1760–1829), Arctic whaler and navigator, was the second child and elder son of eight children born to William Scoresby (1732–1816), a small farmer of Cropton, near Pickering, some 20 miles from Whitby, Yorkshire, and his first wife, Ann Harland (*d.* 1799), from the neighbouring parish of Salton. He was born on 3 May 1760 at Nutholme Farm, Cropton. After the boys at Cropton School played a trick on him which caused him to lose consciousness, he was kept away from school, being taught at home by his mother and working on local farms. Unhappy at a neighbouring farm, in 1779 he prepared to go to sea by studying navigation and sailed in 1780 as apprentice to the captain of the *Jane* which traded from Whitby to the Baltic. His navigational skills enabled him in 1781 to detect an error in reckoning and thereby prevent the loss of the ship, but for this he incurred the ill will of the officers whose incompetence he had exposed. He therefore left the ship at London in October 1781 and joined the *Speedwell* carrying stores to Gibraltar. The ship and her men were captured by the Spanish and the men imprisoned, but Scoresby managed to escape and, helped by peasant women, reached Cadiz, and, as a stowaway on an English ship, returned to England.

In England Scoresby returned to farm work during 1783–4, and in 1783 married Lady Mary (1765–1819), so named because she was born on Lady day, the eldest daughter of John Smith, a small farmer from Cropton. They had eleven children of whom six died in infancy. Three daughters and two sons survived, the elder son being William *Scoresby, Arctic scientist. Each summer from 1785 to 1790 Scoresby sailed on the *Henrietta* to the Greenland whale fishery, and each winter sailed on coastal vessels. When the *Henrietta*'s captain retired in 1790 he ensured that Scoresby took his place, preferring him to more experienced but less skilful men. A disastrous first season was followed by six extremely successful ones and in 1798 Scoresby accepted a very advantageous offer from Gale & Sons of London, although his wife was unwilling that he should leave Whitby. After further success in command of the Gales' ship *Dundee* he took command and one-eighth ownership of a new ship, *Resolution* of Whitby, in 1802. His successful command of the *Resolution* between 1803 and 1810 brought profits to the company of on average 25 per cent per annum. After the 1810 voyage he resigned command to his son William and himself took command of the *John* belonging to a Greenock whale-fishing company of which he was one of four partners. He commanded the *John* until after the 1814 voyage, when he resigned command to his daughter Arabella's husband, Thomas Jackson. After a year on shore in 1816 Scoresby took command of the *Mars* of Whitby and in 1817 bought the *Fame*. When his hopes that she might be used for a government sponsored voyage of discovery to the Arctic, commanded by his son, were dashed, he took her to the Greenland fishery. She sailed each year between 1819 and 1823, but in the last year was destroyed by fire in the Orkneys and Scoresby decided to retire since his considerable fortune was unlikely to be much augmented from further trips to the now over-exploited Greenland waters. William junior estimated his father's profits in his thirty years as a captain to be over £90,000, or more than 30 per cent per annum on the capital invested, a record exceeded by few. Scoresby retired to Whitby, and published a pamphlet about a scheme to provide work for the poor and improve Whitby harbour in 1826; he died in 1829.

Scoresby was a powerfully built, energetic man and an exceptional navigator and seaman. Although not trained as a scientist, he was an acute and systematic observer of the behaviour of sea, ice, and wind, and shrewd in the inferences he drew therefrom. His primary purpose was always commercial, but he combined commercial aims with scientific achievement, notably in May 1806 when he reached 81°30′ N, which, at just over 500 miles south of the north pole, long remained the highest latitude reached by a ship. He was always on the lookout for practical innovations which improved efficiency. Often, as with his protected crow's nest or his system of ballast loading to make ships more manoeuvrable, they simultaneously made his men's lives safer. He was a devout man, attending the Wesleyan chapel when on land and conducting regular Anglican services for his men when at sea. His innovations were taken up by many contemporary whalers, but his most enduring influence was in shaping the scientific and religious career of his son William.

J. K. Laughton, *rev.* Elizabeth Baigent

Sources W. Scoresby, *Memorials of the sea: my father* (1851) • C. Stamp, *The Scoresby family* (privately printed, Otley, 1989) • R. E. Scoresby-Jackson, *The life of William Scoresby* (1861) • T. Stamp and C. Stamp, *William Scoresby, Arctic scientist* (1975) • Explorers' Club of New York, *Seven logbooks concerning the Arctic voyages of Capt. William Scoresby, Snr, of Whitby, England* (1916–17) • T. Sheppard, *The Scoresbys, father and son, and the lost colonies in Greenland* (1939)

Archives Kendall Whaling Museum, Sharon, Massachusetts • Mystic Seaport Museum, Mystic, Connecticut, corresp. and papers

Likenesses H. Adlard, stipple, NPG • J. Thomson, stipple (after A. Wivell), BM, NPG; repro. in *Imperial Magazine*, 4 (1822) • engraving, repro. in Scoresby, *Memorials of the sea* (1851) • oils (as mature man), Hull Maritime Museum; repro. in Stamp and Stamp, *William Scoresby*, 15 • oils, priv. coll.; repro. in Stamp and Stamp, *William Scoresby*, 14

Scoresby, William, junior (1789–1857), Arctic scientist and divine, was born in Cropton, near Pickering, Yorkshire, on 5 October 1789. He was one of eleven children born to William *Scoresby (1760–1829), Arctic whaler and navigator, and his wife, Lady Mary Smith (1765–1819). Of

William Scoresby junior (1789–1857), by David Octavius Hill and Robert Adamson, *c*.1844

their five surviving children, he was the third, having two elder sisters and a younger brother and sister. His family moved to Whitby shortly after his birth and he made his first voyage to the Arctic with his father when only ten years old. In 1803 he was apprenticed to his father on the *Resolution* and in all but one year between 1803 and 1823 he sailed each summer to the Greenland whale fishery. In 1806 William and his father, respectively chief mate and master of the *Resolution*, took their ship to a record northing, reaching 81°30′. That autumn William junior enrolled at Edinburgh University where he spent the winters studying chemistry and natural philosophy. His teachers, themselves keen to learn about polar seas, urged him to plan and carry out specific researches in his summers in the Arctic. His friendship with Robert Jameson began thus and continued for many years, to their mutual benefit; Sir Joseph Banks suggested other lines of enquiry and provided some apparatus. Scoresby's research began in 1807 with his meteorological journals, and in 1809 he was elected to the Wernerian Society of Edinburgh, through whose journal he published several early papers. In 1810 he made his last voyage with his father who, when his son reached the age of twenty-one, resigned to him the command of the *Resolution*. On 25 September 1811 William junior married Mary Elizabeth Lockwood (1787–1822), daughter of a shipbroker in Whitby. They had three children, William (1812–1837), Frederick Richard Holloway (1818–1831), and Henry (born and died in 1820).

Between 1813 and 1817 Scoresby sailed to the Arctic in command of the newer and larger *Esk*, making many of his most important discoveries in Arctic geography, meteorology, and oceanography. During the winter of 1817–18 he corresponded at length with Banks on the possibility of a government-sponsored voyage of discovery to the Arctic, hoping that he might lead it. However, although the idea was taken up, a naval officer was to take command. This decision typified Scoresby's isolation from the naval and scientific establishment, which hampered his research. Despite this, he continued to write scientific papers and in 1819 was elected fellow of the Royal Society of Edinburgh. In the same year he moved with his family to Liverpool to supervise the building of a whaler, the *Baffin*, which he had designed and which proved very successful. In 1820, during his absence, his *Account of the Arctic Regions* (2 vols.) was published. Using vivid and detailed descriptions of equipment and hunting methods, he gave an account of early Arctic whale fishery and, using detailed statistics, described its economics. He reviewed the history of Arctic exploration and made far-sighted suggestions as to how it might be further advanced. The work attracted the notice of scientists throughout Europe, while also gaining a wide readership, including Mrs Gaskell, who used material from it in *Sylvia's Lovers* (1863). In 1822 Scoresby charted and named a large section of the east coast of Greenland, publishing the chart in *Journal of a Voyage to the Northern Whale-Fishery* (1823), which added to his considerable reputation as an Arctic scientist and scholar. It was at this time that he met Humphrey Davy, who showed great interest in his magnetic experiments.

In 1822 Scoresby returned from the summer voyage to learn of his wife's death. His deep religious convictions had been strengthened by hers, and he decided to enter the church. First, however, he made a brief visit to France, where his work aroused much interest among such scientists as Arago (with whom he corresponded for some years), Ampère, Cuvier, von Humboldt, and Gay-Lussac. He was elected fellow of the Royal Society in 1824 and corresponding member of the Institut de France in 1827. He made his last voyage to the Arctic in 1823 and in the following year entered Queens' College, Cambridge, as a 'ten year man', whereby, without being resident, he could proceed to a degree after ten years. He was ordained deacon in 1825 and from 1825 to 1827 was curate of Bessingby, near Bridlington Quay, Yorkshire, with a stipend of £40 a year, compared with his previous earnings of, on average, £800 a year. From 1827 to 1832 he was the first chaplain of the newly established Floating Church for Seamen in Liverpool. While in Liverpool, he married Elizabeth Fitzgerald (*d.* 1847) of Corkbegg, Ireland, in 1828, and was a founder member of the British Association for the Advancement of Science in York in 1831. For the rest of his life he regularly attended and contributed to meetings, and was puzzled as to why he was never called to high office in the association. From 1832 to 1837 he was chaplain in charge of Bedford Chapel, Exeter, where, despite his church duties and the tragic deaths of his two surviving sons, his work on magnetism continued and culminated in the publication of the first volume of *Magnetical Investigations*

(1839). He was made BD in 1834 and DD in 1839 while at Exeter.

Somewhat reluctantly, Scoresby accepted the appointment offered by the evangelical Simeon trustees, of vicar of Bradford, in 1838. This large, industrial, dissenting parish caused Scoresby constant anxiety and cost him his health. Before his breakdown, however, he had shown his vision and energy in social reform. He helped to establish model schools and to improve public health and factory working conditions. During his time at Bradford, despite his onerous duties, he sustained his scientific interest: by regular papers to the British Association; by the publication of the final volume of *Magnetical Investigations* (1843), in which he set out in full his trials and conclusion on the connection between the grade and dimensions of steel and its magnetic characteristics; and, in collaboration with the young Joule, by researches into electromagnetism. His first visit to the United States in 1844 did little to improve his own health but he was impressed by working conditions for women in the cotton mills of Lowell, Massachusetts, and on his return published *American Factories and their Female Operatives* (1845), and renewed his efforts to improve working conditions in Bradford before he resigned the living in 1846. He made a second tour of Canada and the United States in 1847–8, during which he received news of his second wife's death.

From 1846 to his death in 1857 Scoresby held no permanent appointment, but on his third marriage, in 1849 to Georgiana Ker or Kerr (*d.* 1910/12), he moved from Whitby to settle in her home town of Torquay, becoming an unpaid lecturer at Upton church. This was a very productive period for Scoresby. He wrote, advised, and lectured on the Franklin mystery, publishing his *Franklin Expedition* in 1850. In the same year he edited *The Whaleman's Adventures* and in 1851 published *Memorials of the Sea: my Father*, in which he recorded the contributions to Arctic navigation made by his father and by father and son together. He became interested in hypnotism and zoistic magnetism, trying to explain by scientific means phenomena which apparently depended on the pull of mysterious 'vital forces'. He was appointed in 1855 to the newly formed Liverpool Compass Committee which was charged with investigating the deviation of the compass in wooden and iron ships in response to losses at sea caused by compass errors and deviations. In connection with this inquiry he arranged to sail in 1856 with his wife on the maiden voyage of the *Royal Charter* to Australia and back, to make systematic observations on the magnetism of iron ships. This was his last and longest experiment and he was provided with equipment, although unfortunately not up-to-date charts. He was awarded an honorary MA degree of the University of Melbourne on this visit.

Scoresby was very pleased with his results which he communicated in person to the committee on his return; they were published in 1859, after his death. He was the first person to investigate ships' magnetism in an iron ship as it travelled from the northern to the southern hemisphere and his findings lent powerful support to warnings that attention to compass deviation must be unremitting if the safety of vessels was not to be compromised. Shortly after his return his health failed and he died in Torquay on 21 March 1857; he was buried at Upton church, Torquay. He was survived by his third wife, but his children, all from his first marriage, had predeceased him. He left his instruments, apparatus, books, and personal papers to the Whitby Literary and Philosophical Society, of which he was a founder member.

Scoresby wrote prolifically, publishing more than one hundred works on topics ranging from polar geography, oceanography, and natural history, to magnetism, religion, and social reform. He invented and constructed several pieces of apparatus for his experiments and was an active lecturer to both scientific and popular audiences. His outstanding work was in oceanography and magnetism. Using his 'marine diver', which carried down a self-registering thermometer, he established that Arctic waters, unlike temperate and tropical waters, were warmer at greater depths than at the surface. He did pioneering work in establishing Arctic currents and waves and his work on the Gulf Stream was particularly important. His systematic observations on Arctic meteorology were long without parallel and his detailed observations of ice influenced later glacial geomorphology, as well as being of considerable practical importance to Arctic mariners. His study of electromagnetism and his construction with Joule of an electromagnetic machine were important in a new field of magnetic science. His charts of the coasts and extent of ice in many polar regions, and his sketches of the coasts, were important in Arctic navigation. He was a skilful observer of flora and fauna and used his considerable artistic talent to record his findings. Some of Scoresby's work, particularly that on magnetic attraction, was similar to that being carried out elsewhere in Europe; but, cut off from much scientific discussion, he began his experiments anew and reacted angrily to suggestions that his work was not original. He worked in relative isolation, without government support, often with limited time and always with limited equipment. As a consequence, he had to break off promising work (such as that with Joule), to fulfil other obligations, and some of his work was poorly presented and received. His *Magnetical Investigations*, for example, contained a vast mass of undifferentiated material, only some of which bore publication, and in which many extreme results were due to impurities in the metal he was experimenting with. His best work was done when he was young: when men such as Jameson and Banks directed him to promising lines of enquiry; when his considerable skill in whaling provided the money and opportunity for research; and when other European powers were keenly interested in his results. However, despite later handicaps, Scoresby was a leading scientist in his day, whose reputation has endured since his death.

ELIZABETH BAIGENT

Sources R. E. Scoresby-Jackson, *The life of William Scoresby* (1861) · T. Stamp and C. Stamp, *William Scoresby, Arctic scientist* (1975) · A. McConnell, 'The scientific life of William Scoresby jnr with a catalogue of his instruments and apparatus in the Whitby

Museum', *Annals of Science*, 43 (1986), 257–86 • R. I. Murchison, *Journal of the Royal Geographical Society*, 28 (1858), 137–40 • B. Waites, 'William Scoresby, 1789–1857', *Geographers: biobibliographical studies*, 4, ed. T. W. Freeman and P. Pinchemel (1980), 139–47 • C. Stamp, *The Scoresby family* (privately printed, Otley, 1989) • *DNB* • F. L. Cross, ed., *The Oxford dictionary of the Christian church*, 2nd edn, ed. A. E. Livingstone (1974); repr. (1983)

Archives Mystic Seaport Museum, Mystic, Connecticut, corresp. and papers • Scott Polar RI, corresp. • Whitby Museum, Whitby Literary and Philosophical Society, journals and papers | NRA, corresp. with Sir Joseph Banks • U. Lpool L., letters to Elizabeth Rathbone

Likenesses E. Smith, line engravings, 1821 (after A. Mosses), BM, NPG; repro. in *Imperial Magazine*, 3 (1821) • J. S. Cotman, pencil drawing, 1824, V&A • D. O. Hill and R. Adamson, photograph, *c*.1844, Scot. NPG [*see illus.*] • E. Cockburn, oils, Whitby Museum • J. B. Hunt, stipple and line engraving (after photograph by M. Claudet), NPG • engraving, repro. in Stamp, *Scoresby family* • portrait, Hull Maritime Museum

Scory, John (*d.* 1585), bishop of Hereford, originated in Norfolk, and became a friar in the Dominican house at Cambridge about 1530. He signed the surrender of the house on its dissolution in 1538, and seems to have been a willing, indeed eager, convert to the Reformation. He quickly graduated into the orbit of Archbishop Thomas Cranmer of Canterbury, and in 1541 was one of the six preachers appointed by Cranmer to evangelize his diocese. In a group carefully balanced between conservatives and evangelicals, Scory soon identified himself as an outspoken reformer, and, not for the last time, his impetuosity sparked trouble for his patron. In May 1541 Scory's preaching was the subject of a formal complaint by two conservative prebendaries. In September 1543 three of the six preachers, including Scory, were temporarily imprisoned after mutually inflammatory sermons, a by-product of the prebendaries' plot, the most serious attempt to undermine Cranmer during Henry VIII's last, conservative years.

With the accession of Edward VI, Scory was not immediately called up to greater things; the delicate political circumstances of the early part of the reign called for more emollient qualities than Scory had thus far exhibited. Instead he was chosen, probably by Cranmer, for the difficult assignment of preaching at the execution of Joan Bocher. The case of this radical sectarian dissident was one that would come to haunt the regime, and frantic efforts were made to induce her to recant and save herself in the last days before her execution. But Bocher proved obdurate, and on 2 May 1550 died 'raging and railing' against the unfortunate preacher. This difficult service ultimately received its reward. About this time Scory was made examining chaplain to Nicholas Ridley in the diocese of London; shortly thereafter he was appointed bishop of Rochester (26 April 1551). Scory was also appointed one of the commissioners to revise the ecclesiastical laws (February 1552). In May 1552 he was translated to the diocese of Chichester.

The difficult circumstances following the death of Edward revealed once again the volatile and impetuous side of Scory's nature. In the eerie lull that followed Mary's accession the reformers were at first left undisturbed, though Scory was ousted from Chichester in August 1553 when the deprivation of his predecessor George Day was declared illegal. The uneasy calm was shattered in September 1553 when Archbishop Cranmer made a public declaration against the mass. Written some time in August but not immediately published, it seems to have been vented abroad on the personal initiative of Scory, who, visiting the archbishop at Canterbury, had asked Cranmer's leave to take a copy. The archbishop was unaware that Scory intended to print hundreds of copies for distribution, but faced with this *fait accompli*, boldly asserted his authorship and was immediately arrested.

This inadvertent role in Cranmer's downfall shortly after appeared in a far harsher light, for while his fellow evangelicals faced arrest or exile, Scory seems briefly to have flirted with conformity. According to several contemporary sources Scory renounced his wife and submitted to Bishop Bonner, being absolved and even, it is said, briefly allowed to officiate in London diocese. Within a very short time, however, Scory had thought better of this course; indeed, it is possible that the story of his recantation was a defamatory fiction invented by his many enemies. Scory is represented as having recanted before Bonner in July 1554, but in fact by the early summer of that year he had joined the exile and settled in Emden, becoming a citizen of the German town on 20 June 1554.

In exile Scory's chequered history seems not to have been held against him. The exiles were all too aware of the pressures on those who remained in England, and how many former protestants had drifted into conformity. They would doubtless have been relieved that the Marian church did not claim so prominent a backslider as Scory. Now he had joined the exile, Scory was in fact the senior ranking Edwardian bishop abroad, and his services were much in demand. In the summer of 1554 Edmund Grindal wrote to Scory in Emden to ask him to become minister of the English church in Frankfurt, though in the event the appointment went elsewhere, perhaps after opposition from within the community. In fact Scory was happy to settle in Emden. At one point (1556–7) he briefly journeyed south to assist the other exile congregations, but he returned to Emden and was there at the end of Mary's reign.

Scory quickly took up a position of leadership at Emden; in local records he is variously described as the church's minister, bishop, or superintendent, this latter designation reflecting the influence of John à Lasco's London church order on the Emden congregation's liturgy and organization. Scory was assisted in the government of the church by his fellow minister Thomas Young (later archbishop of York), six elders, and four deacons. Evidently Scory had no difficulties with adopting a form of church government that reflected the practice of the 'best Reformed churches' rather than those of the Edwardian prayer book. Sadly, the gift of controversy that had followed Scory throughout his career manifested itself again in Emden. Towards the end of the reign the leaders of the church found themselves under fire from within the congregation for having moved the place of worship without consultation as a result of a local outbreak of plague. Perhaps more serious than the original cause of complaint was the arbitrary way Scory and Young attempted to browbeat the complainant, denouncing him in open church before he had the chance to make his case. For this the two ministers were in effect censured by the local Emden town consistory.

A more constructive achievement was Scory's contribution to the literature of the exile. Emden became an important centre of English protestant printing; the choice of titles, including works by Cranmer and Ridley (both of whom Scory had served as chaplain), suggests that Scory played an important role in directing the publishing programme. His own personal contribution was not insignificant, including one original work, the *Epistle Written to All the Faithful that Be in England* (STC 21854), and translations of Cyprian and Augustine. Scory's purpose in rendering the latter works into English, as he explained in the preface to the Augustine translation, was to demonstrate that the church of Henry VIII and Edward VI was a true Catholic church, its doctrines and practice wholly consistent with that of the apostolic church and the early Christian centuries. But the subject matter of the sermons by Cyprian—endurance in the face of persecution—was also significant. In his own *Epistle* Scory addressed the theme that preoccupied the exiles, encouraging the faithful to remain true and admonishing backsliders. There was no reference to his own brush with temptation.

Perhaps Scory's most enduring achievement was not one of these smaller vernacular works but the new edition of Cranmer's *Defensio de verae doctrinae de sacramentis* (1557). One of the most important of Cranmer's doctrinal works, this had been published first in 1550, and then adapted and extended to respond to the criticism raised by the replies of Richard Smith and Stephen Gardiner. The Emden edition was bolstered by a copious range of marginal citations, and a dedication signed by most of the leading members of the exile. It became, in effect, the official doctrinal manifesto of the exile, and Scory's role in its production attests to his continuing and sincere devotion to the memory of his former patron.

On Mary's death Scory lost no time in returning to England. As one of the most experienced survivors of the Edwardian church he was guaranteed a prominent position in the new church, and he seems to have been marked out for high office from an early stage. He preached before the queen in Lent 1559, and took part in the staged disputation with the Catholic bishops (31 March 1559) designed to discredit them before the crucial meeting of parliament. Scory's role as supporter of the new regime may indeed have been more important than was once realized. A document discovered in the 1990s reveals that in April 1559 he was charged with drawing up a list of all the exile scholars who had been or still were abroad and presenting their names to the privy council. The writer speculated that this had something to do with the scandal caused by the recent publication of John Knox's infamous *First Blast*. Be this as it may, Scory's future was assured, and on 15 July 1559 he was appointed bishop of Hereford, one of the first bishops to be nominated by Elizabeth. The only hitch came when it appeared that Scory would take a recalcitrant line on the planned depredations of episcopal incomes projected under the 1559 Act of Exchanges. Brief consideration was given to switching him to Norwich, which was to be less affected by exchanges, but in the event the original appointment was confirmed (20 December). Scory was as good as his word, fighting a stubborn rearguard action to defend his income; the issue of exchanges in the case of Hereford was not finally settled until 1562.

Before leaving London, Scory preached the solemn service of commemoration for the dead French king, Henri II—a signal distinction which suggests that even in the talented group that made up Elizabeth's first bench of bishops Scory was much esteemed as a preacher. But as he prepared to leave the capital, few could have envied him his new position in the Welsh marches. The county and diocese of Hereford were one of England's backward corners, its inhabitants slow, conservative, and stubbornly resistant to change in matters of religion. When in 1564 the privy council ordered a general survey of opinion among the leaders of provincial society to test support and opposition to the new settlement, Scory's return was one of the longest and most depressing. The numbers deemed 'no favourers to this religion' were challenged only by those judged 'neuters' or indifferent. In Hereford itself, the mayor and all the members of the city council could be placed in one or other of these categories, 'so that on the holl Council or election ther is not on that is counted favourable to this religion' (Bateson, 15). Even in his own cathedral Scory found little comfort: all the prebendaries and almost the entire staff are denounced as 'rank papists'.

At the beginning of the reign at least Scory set himself conscientiously to the matter in hand, bombarding Secretary Cecil and Archbishop Parker with requests for reinforcement and assistance, not least the provision of active preaching ministers. The fact that for each part of his diocese Scory could in 1564 name a quorum of men suitable for appointment as JPs in place of those hostile to the settlement suggests that he had acquainted himself very fully with the local personalities. But the government turned a deaf ear to his entreaties; for all Scory's dire warnings, Hereford was hardly likely to prove a threat to the security of the realm, and in an era of harsh priorities its evangelism could be left to a later time.

Scory gradually accommodated himself to these realities. No longer the firebrand preacher, he occupied himself with the stewardship of his resources, though once again not without controversy. Scory proved one of the most aggressive and energetic estate managers among the bishops, felling timber at what the crown regarded as an unacceptable rate. He also attracted criticism for lending money at interest. The bishop indignantly denied the charge of usury, but certainly he died in possession of a comfortable fortune. In matters of policy he was dutifully compliant. He affirmed the articles of 1562, and in 1576 moved to suppress prophesying in his diocese. In old age his reputation suffered as his health and energy declined. His later years were further blighted by family unhappiness. His son, Sylvanus, a profligate wastrel, decamped to the Low Countries as a soldier rather than occupy the comfortable berth as a prebendary of Hereford Cathedral provided by his anxious father. The bishop died at Whitbourne on 25 June 1585. The unusually generous sum of £600 left by him to the poor represented a conscious abandonment of his troublesome progeny. Scory was survived by his wife, Elizabeth, who died on 8 March 1592.

ANDREW PETTEGREE

Sources C. H. Garrett, *The Marian exiles: a study in the origins of Elizabethan puritanism* (1938) • A. Pettegree, 'The English church at Emden', *Marian protestantism: six studies* (1996), 10–38 • E. J. Baskerville, *A chronological bibliography of propaganda and polemic published in English between 1553 and 1558* (1979) • D. MacCulloch, *Thomas Cranmer: a life* (1996) • B. Usher, 'Sitting on the "old school" bench: the episcopal appointments of 1559–1562 and the failure of William Cecil', unpublished manuscript • F. Heal, *Of prelates and princes: a study of the economic and social position of the Tudor episcopate* (1980) • M. Bateson, ed., 'A collection of original letters from the bishops to the privy council, 1564', *Camden miscellany, IX*, CS, new ser., 53 (1893) • P. Collinson, *The Elizabethan puritan movement* (1967) • *STC, 1475–1640*, nos. 921, 6152, 21854

Scot, Alexander (1560–1616), judge and writer, was born in Kininmouth, Aberdeenshire; his parents are unknown. After graduating MA from King's College, Aberdeen, he left for France, and studied first theology in Tournon and then, between about 1580 and 1584, law in Bourges. He obtained a doctorate in civil and canon law and, according to Barjavel, studied in Avignon under Jacques Cujas. In 1588 he published an edition of his *Apparatus Latinae elocutionis, ex Ciceronis libris collectus* at Lyons. His two-volume *Oraisons de Cicéron* appeared in 1588 and 1589, and a thousand-page grammar book, *Universa grammatica Graeca*, in 1593. While at Lyons he married Marie Pilhote.

In 1593 or 1594 Scot was appointed principal regent of the college of Carpentras, and to thank the administrators of the town for their warm welcome, sent them a copy of his grammar with a dedicatory epistle. He settled there on 31 May 1594, and was joined by his wife and at least one child. The couple had at least ten more children between 1599 and 1611; their son Horace (*b.* 1603) was the godson of Horace Capponi, bishop of Carpentras. A clever Hellenist, Scot attracted a considerable number of pupils, and when Cardinal Acquaviva, legate of Avignon, visited Carpentras, thirty-six of Scot's students welcomed him with a verse allocution at the town's gate. Scot was still principal in 1601 when he published a thesaurus for lawyers, *Vocabularium utriusque juris*, dedicated to William Chisholm.

By 1608 Scot had left the college and is attested as *juge mage* at the major court of Carpentras, a position which he still held in 1611. He was also advocate and general procurator of the episcopal revenue in Carpentras in 1609, 1611, and 1616. At this period he collected and brought to light the posthumous works of Jacques Cujas, publishing them in 1614 as *Opera priora et posthuma*. Scot lived at the château of Rocans, in the commune of Aubignan. He died in 1616. His son Jean, doctor in law at Carpentras, was admitted advocate at the court of the palais of Avignon in 1627; another son, Esprit, still owned a barn and some land at Aubignan in 1637.

MARIE-CLAUDE TUCKER

Sources M.-C. Bellot-Tucker, 'Maîtres et étudiants écossais à la faculté de droit de l'Université de Bourges aux XVIe et XVIIe siècles', PhD diss., University of Clermont-Ferrand, 1997, 1.283–5; 2.453–7 • Moulinas et Patin, 'Notes sur le collège de Carpentras', *Mémoires de l'Académie de Vaucluse* (1893), 269 • R. Barjavel, *Dictionnaire historique du département du Vaucluse* (1841), 397–8 • D. Irving, *Lives of Scotish writers*, 1 (1839), 210 • F. Michel, *Les écossais en France, les français en Écosse*, 2 vols. (1862), vol. 2, pt 2, 262 • Archives communales, Carpentras GG4

Scot, David (*c.*1770–1834), orientalist and writer, was born in Penicuik, near Edinburgh. He was the son of William Scot, a small farmer, who is said to have sold his cow to pay the expense of printing a theological pamphlet. Scot was educated at the parish school and Edinburgh University. He was licensed as a preacher by the presbytery of Edinburgh on 25 November 1795. He supported himself by private teaching, while he studied medicine, and graduated MD on 25 June 1812. He formed close friendships with Alexander Murray (1775–1813) and Dr John Leyden, and under their guidance he made himself master of many Asiatic tongues, at the same time acting as tutor to candidates for the Indian service.

In 1812 Scot was an unsuccessful candidate for the Hebrew chair at Edinburgh University; but, through the influence of Sir John Marjoribanks of Lees, he obtained the parish living of Corstorphine, near Edinburgh, to which he was presented on 22 August and ordained on 17 November 1814. On 15 November 1832 he married Helen Heugh, daughter of John Heugh of Gartcows. They had no children. After a ministry of nineteen years he was appointed in 1833 professor of Hebrew at St Mary's College, St Andrews. When on a visit to Edinburgh to attend a meeting of the British Association, he was seized with a dropsical complaint, and died on 18 September 1834. His wife survived him; she died on 18 August 1870.

Besides editing Murray's posthumous *History of the European Languages*, Scot was the author of *Essays on Various Subjects of Belles Letters* (1824), *Discourses on some Important Subjects of Natural and Revealed Religion* (1825), *Key to the Hebrew Pentateuch* (1826), and *Key to the Psalms, Proverbs, Ecclesiastes, and Song of Solomon* (1828). He also wrote a Hebrew grammar (1834) for the use of his class; it is said that he dictated it extempore to the printers.

GEORGE STRONACH, *rev.* C. A. CREFFIELD

Sources *Fasti Scot.* • Anderson, *Scot. nat.* • T. Murray, *Biographical annals of the parish of Colinton* (1863)

Scot [*née* Rutherford], **Elizabeth** (1729–1789), poet, was born at Hermiston Hall, her parents' country mansion near Edinburgh, on 17 July 1729, one of two daughters of David Rutherford (1690–1763) and Alice Watson. Her father, counsellor at Edinburgh, was the first son of Robert Rutherford and his first wife, Bethia Lidderdale. Robert Rutherford, a prosperous solicitor as well as the deputy receiver-general of supply for Scotland, was the proprietor of Fairnilee, a manor house in Selkirkshire. Elizabeth Rutherford was taught Latin and Greek at home, and showed a precocious interest in literature, writing poetry from the age of eleven.

The poet Allan Ramsay (1686–1758) fostered Rutherford's poetry writing, and she corresponded with the blind poet Thomas Blacklock (1721–1791), as well as with Helen Maria Williams (1762–1827). Her writing was also encouraged by her literary aunt Alison (Rutherford) Cockburn (1713–1794), who was her father's half-sister by Robert Rutherford's second marriage, to Alison Ker. Alison Cockburn held soirées in Edinburgh to which she invited important writers and philosophers such as Robert Burns (1759–1796) and David Hume (1711–1776), as well as her niece and her husband, Walter Scot of Wauchope, whom Elizabeth Rutherford married on 16 April 1768. Elizabeth Rutherford's first engagement had been cut short by her fiancé's drowning on a voyage from Ireland to Edinburgh. Her grief for her deceased fiancé is reflected in a few of her poems in her *Alonzo and Cora*, which was published posthumously by subscription in 1801.

Scot's diverse poems in quatrains or heroic couplets range from elegies ('The Lover's Complaint') to topical tales ('The Shipwreck, or, Melancholy Fate of Captain Pierce and his Two Daughters'), and to narratives based on contemporary works ('Alonzo and Cora' on Jean Marmontel's *The Incas* (1777)) or on Greek legend ('Leander and Hero'). *Alonzo and Cora* also includes the first publication of a verse letter by Elizabeth Scot to Robert Burns, and Robert Burns's poem in reply. In 1787 Alison Cockburn had lent Elizabeth Scot her copy of Robert Burns's *Poems, Chiefly in the Scottish Dialect* (1786), which instigated Scot's letter-poem to Burns in Scots English: 'The Guidwife of Waukhope-House to Robert Burns, the Air Shire Bard' (February, 1787). This poem, in rhyming couplets, praises Burns's humour and acknowledges him as a fellow poet:

> But be ye plughman, be ye peer,
> Ye are a funny blade, I swear …
> Yet proud I am to ca' ye brither.

Burns responded in hexameters, setting out his apologia to his sympathetic admirer. Yet, after visiting her and her husband at Wauchope House in May 1787, Burns satirized her in a prose letter: 'Mrs Scot has all the sense, task, intrepidity of face, and bold critical decision which usually distinguish female authors.' In comparing Elizabeth Scot to Mrs Dawson, Burns wrote, 'a certain air of self-importance and a duresse in the eye seem to indicate, as the Ayrshire wife observed of her cow, that "she had a mind of her ain"' (Rutherford, 191). But despite his satire of her demeanour, Burns recognized in Elizabeth Scot a fellow poet who supported him in his efforts to 'sweetly tune the Scottish lyre' ('The Answer', March 1787). Elizabeth Scot died in 1789, in Edinburgh, of dropsy complicated by asthma. She was survived by her husband.

JENNIFER BREEN

Sources E. Scot, 'Preface', *Alonzo and Cora, with other original poems* (1801) · parish register, Edinburgh [births], 17/7/1709 · *The poems and songs of Robert Burns*, ed. J. Kinsley, 1 (1968), 324–7; 3 (1968), 1225, 1229 · A. Rutherford [Cockburn], *Letters and memoirs of her own life*, ed. T. Craig-Brown (1900) · *The letters of Robert Burns*, ed. J. de Lancey Ferguson, 2nd edn, ed. G. Ross Roy, 2 vols. (1985), vol. 1, p. 104 · S. Tytler and J. L. Watson, *The songstresses of Scotland*, 1 (1871), 180–81

Scot, George, of Scotstarvit (*d.* 1685), writer, was the only son of Sir John *Scot, Lord Scotstarvit (1585–1670), of Scotstarvit Tower, Fife, and his second wife, Elizabeth, daughter of Sir James Melville of Halhill. Little is known of Scot's early life, but, given that his father was a noted benefactor, he may have been educated at St Andrews University. In 1663 he married Margaret (*d.* 1685?), daughter of William Rigg of Aithernie, an Edinburgh merchant. It seems likely that upon his marriage Scot was made laird of Pitlochie, Fife, and his children Euphaim and James were born there.

Scot and his wife, like their respective fathers, were covenanters, who remained unreconciled to the Episcopal church in Scotland which emerged after 1660. The more rigorous crackdown of presbyterians in Scotland in 1674 saw Scot and his wife fined £1000 on 25 June for attending conventicles in Fife. They were imprisoned in the Tolbooth in Edinburgh until their fine was paid on 23 July. According to one of Lauderdale's correspondents, Scot had on this occasion 'had a discourse well stuffed with impertinences' (*Laing MSS*, 1.394), including praise for the work of John Welch, a noted field preacher. On 20 July 1676 Scot and his wife were again accused of attending conventicles, including field conventicles, and of consorting with rebels and fugitives. Scot was himself declared a fugitive for failing to appear before the Scottish council on 1 February 1677. Having been apprehended in Edinburgh, he was considered 'a person of most pernicious and factious practices and altogether irreclaimable' (Mather, 268), and sent to Bass Rock in the Firth of Forth, a prison for such irreconcilables. He was freed on 5 October 1677 on condition he stayed on his own lands, and having posted bond for 10,000 merks. On 13 May 1679 he was brought before the council charged with 'keeping conventicles', and questioned about his contact with John Balfour, wanted in connection with the murder of Archbishop Sharp.

Scot was in London in 1679, where he met several prominent Scots interested in colonial ventures in North America. After a further bout of imprisonment he was released on 1 April 1684 after agreeing to go to the plantations together with his wife's cousin Archibald Riddell, an 'obnoxious preacher'. On 1 January 1685 he was issued with a permit allowing his emigration. To stimulate interest in this venture Scot wrote *The model of government of the province of East New Jersey, in America; and encouragement for such a design to be concerned there*, which was published in 1685 in Edinburgh. The book was dedicated to James Drummond, earl of Perth and lord chancellor of Scotland, and his brother John Drummond, Viscount Melfort, and was aimed at encouraging Scottish emigration to East New Jersey. Scot was rewarded for his literary efforts with a grant of 500 acres in East New Jersey on 28 July 1685, but he found difficulty in recruiting covenanters to a project associated with episcopal or Quaker proprietors. Eventually, he was given some of the covenanting rebels incarcerated in Dunnottar Castle, although the numbers (200) may have been exaggerated. Scot and his family sailed from Scotland at the end of July 1685 in the *Henry and Francis* of Newcastle, a ship of 350 tons. He never saw New Jersey as like many others on board he succumbed to a fever before its arrival at Perth Amboy on 7 December. His will of 31 October 1685 does not mention his wife, who presumably predeceased him of the same disease. He made his daughter, Euphaim, sole executor of his lands in America, and his goods and servants on board. His Scottish property he left to his son, James. STUART HANDLEY

Sources E. H. Mather, 'George Scot of Pitlochy', *Proceedings of the New Jersey Historical Society*, new ser., 7 (1922), 260–78 • W. A. Whitehead, *East Jersey under the proprietary governments*, 2nd edn (1875), 361–9 • N. C. Landsman, *Scotland and its first American colony, 1683–1765* (1985), 99–122 • J. E. Pomfret, *The province of East New Jersey, 1609–1702: the rebellious proprietary* (1962), 196–7 • W. Nelson, ed., *Calendar of New Jersey wills, 1670–1730*, Archives of the State of New Jersey, 1st ser., 23 (1901), 408 • *Report of the Laing manuscripts*, 1, HMC, 72 (1914), 394, 402–8 • W. Anderson, *The Scottish nation*, 3 (1868), 413 • Allibone, *Dict.* • I. B. Cowan, *The Scottish covenanters, 1660–88* (1976)

Scot, Sir John, of Scotstarvit, Lord Scotstarvit (1585–1670), judge and writer, was the son of Robert Scot the younger (*d.* 1588) of Knightspottie, Perthshire, and Margaret, daughter of Alexander Aitcheson of Gosford. After his father's death, his grandfather Robert Scot of Knightspottie resigned his office of directory of chancery in favour of a kinsman, William Scot of Ardross, on condition that he in turn resigned it to John when he reached the age of twenty-one. However, when John claimed the office after graduating from the University of St Andrews as a master of arts (probably in 1605) William refused to resign it, and was not persuaded to do so until 26 March 1611.

Scot married, probably in 1608, Anne Drummond (*d.* 1636), daughter of Sir John Drummond of Hawthornden and sister of the poet William Drummond. In 1611, having bought Tarvit and other lands in Fife, Scot assumed the designation of Scotstarvit. He was knighted in 1617, probably during James VI's visit to Scotland, which Scot celebrated in Latin verses published in 1619. In August that year he received permission to go to Flanders and other foreign parts for a year. This probably reflects a wish to pursue his scholarly and literary interests, and on his return in 1620 he endowed a chair of humanity (Latin) in St Leonard's College at St Andrews, and not only presented nine books to form the basis of a class library but also persuaded over fifty other Scots to donate one or two volumes each. He was admitted to the privy council of Scotland on 1 April 1622, and after the accession of Charles I in 1625 he became deeply involved in the faction fighting of the period. Scot was said to have suggested to the king changing feudal tenures in Scotland to increase royal revenues and free the gentry from domination by the nobility, and he was influential in the policy of removing nobles from the office of ordinary lord of session. Sir James Balfour commented: 'a bussie man in foule wether, and one quhosse [whose] covetousnesse far exceidit his honesty' (*Historical Works of Balfour*, 2.147), but Scot's diligence brought him reward. In January 1629 he was appointed an extraordinary lord of the court of session, and though he was replaced in November 1630 he became an ordinary lord of session on 28 July 1632.

Scot claimed that he was behind the rise to pre-eminence of the earl of Menteith, having been the first to suggest his appointment as a privy councillor, but the two men soon quarrelled, and the earl threatened that 'he s[h]ould breake his necke' (Scot, 'Trew relation', 11.285). Instead, however, Scot took a leading part in breaking his enemy. Menteith obtained a grant of the earldom of Strathearn, but fears were raised that this could indicate that he had a better claim to the throne than King Charles. Scot was zealous in pressing the argument, and in 1633 Menteith was stripped of the earldom and of all offices. At this point Scot seems to have decided to withdraw from political infighting and concentrate on his administrative duties: up to the end of 1632 he had been a very active member of the council, but thereafter he withdrew, and when a new council was appointed in 1641 he was omitted from it. The change no doubt partly reflected Scot's increasing absorption in the advancement of two major schemes of patriotic publication. The Amsterdam publisher Blaeu was producing a series of volumes devoted to the modern Latin verse of particular countries, and Scot recruited the Aberdeen poet Arthur Johnston to edit a Scottish contribution. Work began in the 1620s, and culminated in the two-volume *Delitiae poetarum Scotorum* (1637), which included some of Scot's own verse. Scot's commitment to the work was demonstrated by the fact that he visited Amsterdam to help see the work through the press, as well as paying the entire cost of printing. His lifelong love of Latin poetry was also reflected in his organization of publication of the works of Arthur Johnston at Middelburg in 1642.

From the 1620s Scot also pursued an ambitious cartographic project. Timothy Pont had compiled a remarkable series of manuscript maps of Scotland at the end of the sixteenth century, and in 1626 William Blaeu, who was planning an atlas and knew of Pont's work, asked Scot if he could supply maps of Scotland. Scot responded enthusiastically, and recruited Robert Gordon of Straloch to prepare the maps for publication and draft some new ones. It was, however, to be nearly thirty years before the maps were published.

When open opposition to Charles I's policies in Scotland emerged in 1637 Scot appears to have had no hesitation in joining the rebels, sharing the common grievances about misgovernment and changes in religion. He did not seek to play a public role in the covenanting movement, but he signed the national covenant in Ceres on 30 April 1638, and in November 1639 he was one of four lords of session who refused to sign the rival king's covenant. In 1641, when Charles reached a short-lived settlement with the covenanters, Scot obtained the king's favour for his cartographic work, and gained support from the general assembly for the compiling of written accounts of the Scottish counties to accompany the maps. After the defeat of the covenanters by the royalist marquess of Montrose at Kilsyth on 15 August 1645 Scot sailed to the Netherlands, 'being fled, as the most part of the well affected were constrained for a time to doe' (*Journal of Thomas Cunningham*, 130), though he had probably already been planning a visit, as he held talks in Amsterdam with the Blaeus to advance work on the atlas. In 1648, when controversy over the engagement (an agreement to help Charles I against his enemies in England) split the covenanters, he sided with those opposed to the treaty, and after the engagers, who included most of the nobility, were ousted from power he exploited the situation by taking up a cause he had first espoused over twenty years earlier, the freeing of the gentry from domination by the nobility through changes in feudal tenure. The legislation he sponsored brought him, he claimed, the 'deadly hatred' (Snoddy, 129) of the lords of erection (those nobles whose power rested on possession of former church lands), though the English conquest that swiftly followed meant it had no practical effects.

After the conquest Scot was deprived of his positions as directory of chancery and lord of session (1652). He campaigned to be restored to the chancery, combining this with seeking aid from the new regime for the atlas. In February 1654 Colonel Robert Lilburne, the English commander-in-chief in Scotland, wrote to Cromwell supporting Scot's request for copyright protection for the Blaeu maps of Scotland, which were now at last on the verge of publication. Lilburne commented: 'I finde the said mappes might bee very usefull to the army' (C. H. Firth, ed., *Scotland and the Protectorate*, 1899, 45). Helping a foreign army of occupation can hardly have been the first use that Scot had envisaged for his maps, but he was prepared to accept almost anything that aided publication, including the alteration of the dedication to Charles II to one to Cromwell. Scot himself proceeded to London in 1654 to advance his interests on several fronts. A number of petitions to Cromwell failed to get his chancery post restored to him, and the Act of Grace and Pardon of 1654 fined him £1500 sterling. The fine was cancelled in 1655, however, and in other ways the mid-1650s were years of success. Cromwell granted copyright for the maps, and they were published as the fifth volume of Blaeu's *Atlas novus* (1654; reissued in 1662 as vol. 6 of the *Atlas Major*). Further, Scot organized the publication in London of the works of William Drummond, who had died in 1649: the *History of Scotland* appeared in 1655, the *Poems* in 1656. Finally, he was 'an instrument in causing' the publication in 1655 of Sir Thomas Craig's *Jus feudale*, a work which Scot also translated into English (Scot, 'Trew relation', 11.190).

Deprivation from office led Scot to reflect on the instability of success, and he compiled *The Staggering State of Scottish Statesmen* describing the rise and fall of leading Scottish officials in the preceding century: 'staggering' not only provided pleasing alliteration but was central to his theme: men rose, staggered, and fell. He included himself as an example of this process, depicting himself as a 'doer of great services to the king and country, yet, by the power and malice of his enemies, he has been at last thrust out … in his old age' (Scot, *Staggering State*, 163). Thomas Carlyle described the work as 'a strange little book, not a satire but a Homily on Life's nothingness enforced by examples' (Snoddy, 206). But melancholy tendencies in Scot's outlook had been visible long before his personal misfortunes. One of his Latin poems, translated by William Drummond, had ended:

Who would not one of these two offers try—
Not to be born, or, being born, to die.
(Snoddy, 42, 222)

In 1660 Scot was provoked by a reference to him in a life of Charles I by Sir William Sanderson (1658) as being 'a busie person' or meddler (Snoddy, 73). Furious at the insult, Scot wrote his long 'Trew relation', emphasizing his services to the crown—and largely ignoring the years in which he had been a covenanter. Though Sanderson's jibe was the immediate pretext for Scot's relation, he also hoped that this selective record of service would help him regain the chancery, but instead of being restored to office he was fined £500 sterling by the Act of Indemnity of 1662 for his covenanting past.

Some years after the death of his first wife, Anne, in 1636, Scot had married Elizabeth, daughter of Sir James Melville of Halhill. There was one son of this marriage, the writer George *Scot. A third marriage followed, perhaps about 1647, to Eupham, daughter of John Monypenny of Pitmilly. Scot died in 1670, and in spite of his age a report in 1669 that he 'had great designes to have made a good fischer toune' on the island of Inchkeith (*Journals of Sir John Lauder*, 190–91) indicates that he remained active to the end.

Though Scot indignantly rejected the phrase, he may well be called a 'busy man', assiduous in his work in the chancery and (at times) in the council and in political controversy. He was also active as an elder in church courts, from kirk session to general assembly, though his argumentativeness sometimes made him tiresome. In pursuing a case before the assembly in 1641 he exasperated his audience with 'a world of mirrie tales … manie take him bot for a wrangler' (R. Baillie, *Letters and Journals*, ed. D. Laing, 3 vols., 1841–2, 370). His main claim to fame, however, is the literary and scholarly publications which he sponsored, outstanding given the general poverty of such patronage in Scotland in the period. The statement that learned men 'came to him from all quarters; so that his house [Scotstarvit Tower] was a kind of college' (Nisbet, vol. 2, appx, 282) is exaggerated, but Scot, with his contacts with a range of Dutch and other continental scholars and his close relationship with his brother-in-law and other Scottish poets, formed a sorely needed focus for cultural activity in the country. Moreover, his generous patronage was not confined to scholarly realms. The aftermath of a disastrous fire in Glasgow in 1652 aroused his sympathy, and he endowed a fund with land from his Fife estates to support six poor apprentices during their training. DAVID STEVENSON

Sources *DNB* • T. G. Snoddy, *Sir John Scot, Lord Scotstarvit* (1968) • J. Scot, *The staggering state of Scottish statesmen from 1550 to 1650*, ed.

C. Rogers (1872) • J. Scot, 'Scotstarvet's "Trew relation"', ed. G. Neilson, *SHR*, 11 (1913–14), 164–91, 284–96, 395–403; 12 (1914–15), 76–83, 174–83, 408–12; 13 (1915–16), 380–92; 14 (1916–17), 60–67 • D. G. Moir, 'A history of Scottish maps', in *The early maps of Scotland to 1850*, Royal Scottish Geographical Society, 3rd edn, ed. D. G. Moir, 1 (1973) • *The historical works of Sir James Balfour*, ed. J. Haig, 4 vols. (1824–5) • *Reg. PCS*, 1st ser. • *Reg. PCS*, 2nd ser. • *Reg. PCS*, 3rd ser. • A. Nisbet, *A system of heraldry*, 2 vols., 2nd edn (1816) • letters to J. Scot, NL Scot., Adv. MS 17.1.9 • R. V. Pringle, 'An early humanity class library: the gift of Sir John Scot and his friends to St. Leonard's College (1620)', *The Bibliotheck*, 7 (1974–5) • *Journal of Thomas Cuningham of Camprere*, ed. E. J. Courthope, Scottish History Society, 3rd ser., 11 (1928) • *Journals of Sir John Lauder*, ed. D. Crawford, Scottish History Society, 36 (1900)

Archives NL Scot., corresp. and poems

Scot [Scott], **Michael** (*d.* in or after **1235**), translator, philosopher, and astrologer, may have been a member of the Scott family of Balwearie, near Kirkcaldy, in Fife. His date of birth is unknown.

Life and career About 1210 Scot went to Toledo, where, with one Abuteus 'the Levite', he translated scientific and astrological texts from Arabic into Latin. In 1215 he accompanied Archbishop Rodrigo of Toledo to Rome for the fourth Lateran Council, in particular to discuss with the pope the designation of primacy for the archbishopric of Toledo. Following his return to Spain, Scot completed his translation of the *De motibus celorum* of al-Bitrugi (Alpetragius) on 18 August 1217; he refers to this when sending to Étienne de Provins his Latin version of Averroes's commentary on Aristotle's *De caelo et mundo*. This communication is significant because Étienne was a member of the commission at Paris appointed by Pope Gregory IX to censor Aristotle's writings on natural philosophy; it was through his contacts with Paris that Scot received the title 'magister'—Lynn Thorndike has suggested that he taught there in 1230, giving lessons on the *Tractatus de sphaera* of John de Sacrobosco.

In the autumn of 1220 Scot moved from Toledo to Bologna, where he worked on a compilation of gynaecological diagnoses. It was here that he met the philosopher Orlando da Cremona and also the emperor Frederick II, whose employment he was subsequently to enter, helping Frederick with researches into birds as well as acting as the emperor's astrologer and physician. About 1230 Scot translated at Frederick's court the *Abbreviatio Avicenne de animalibus*, which he dedicated to the emperor. The work is based upon Aristotle, several of whose works Scot translated, though conflicting attributions make it impossible to identify all of them with certainty. However, it would appear that he translated the *Historia animalium*, the *De caelo et mundo*, and the *De anima*, and perhaps also the *Physics*; the Graeco-Latin version of Aristotle's *Nicomachaean Ethics*, and the translation from Arabic into Latin of commentaries on Aristotle by Averroes have also been attributed to him. Such ascriptions are uncertain. The translation of Averroes's commentary on Aristotle's *De anima* contained in Paris, Bibliothèque Nationale, MS Lat. 14385, fols. 133–160v, is indeed there specifically ascribed to Scot, but here and elsewhere it remains possible that the work is that of a collaborator. Nevertheless, Scot has been claimed as one of the first exponents of the philosophy of Averroes in western Europe, despite the fact that there are few open references to the teachings of Averroes in his works, and that, indeed, Scot declared himself an opponent of the theory of the eternity of the world.

The fact that Scot was a scholar in the service of Frederick II did not affect his standing with the papacy. In January 1224 Pope Honorius III, describing Scot as one who 'flourishes among other men of learning with a singular gift of learning' (Thorndike, *Michael Scot*, 33), asked Archbishop Langton of Canterbury to give him a benefice, and later that year Scot was offered the archbishopric of Cashel in Ireland, though he declined it on the grounds that he did not know the language of that country. In 1225 he was licensed to hold an additional benefice in England and two in Scotland. In 1227 Gregory IX praised Scot's translations of Arabic and Hebrew texts into Latin. However, neither Albertus Magnus, who cast doubts upon Scot's understanding of Aristotle, nor Roger Bacon, writing towards the end of the thirteenth century, entirely shared the admiration expressed by successive popes, and Bacon declared that Scot had claimed translations as his own while having no knowledge of the languages or sciences in question. Bacon did, however, credit Scot with making known the works of Aristotle in the years around 1230.

Little else is known about the course of Scot's life, and his personality remains elusive, though an autobiographical element has been claimed for passages in his *Liber introductorius*, describing the man born under Mercury as a great reader and possessed of wide curiosity, who takes an interest in such things as painting and sculpture at the same time as he pursues wide-ranging studies in science and magic. There is also considerable uncertainty concerning the date of Michael Scot's death. The poet Henry of Avranches, writing early in 1236, refers to Scot (whom he describes as a second Apollo) as being lately dead; but this is contradicted by the Hebrew astrologer Juda ben Salomon ha-Cohen, who tells of his corresponding with Scot for ten years from 1233, thereby putting the date much later. Scot may have returned to England in 1235, accompanying Piero della Vigna on his mission to arrange the marriage of Henry III's sister Isabella to Frederick II. He has also been improbably identified with the Master Michael of Cornwall 'called Scot' who was chancellor to Jean and Mathilde de Chartres in 1252–3. An abridgement of Scot's *Liber introductorius*, which introduces astrological material from after the death of King Manfred in 1266 (Kues, Spitalbibliothek, MS 209), is attributed to one William Scot, and it is possible that an M could have been mistaken for a W.

Writings: the *Liber introductorius* and the nature of the universe At the centre of Scot's own work stands his *Liber introductorius*, written to serve as an introduction to the study of astrology, but also presenting its author's understanding of the relationship between microcosm and macrocosm. It has four interrelated sections: an introduction or 'Prohemium', followed successively by the *Liber* *introductorius* proper, in the form of a book of four 'distinctions', or divisions, said to have been composed at the emperor's request, the 'Liber particularis', also written at Frederick's request, and the *Liber phisionomie*, dedicated to Frederick II, and the only part of the work to have been printed. Later in the thirteenth century his writings influenced both Vincent of Beauvais's *Speculum doctrinale* (book I, chap. 1) and books III and IV of Bartholomew Anglicus's *De proprietatibus rerum*, which summarize Scot's reasoning on the soul. Indeed, the format of Scot's *Liber introductorius* was exactly followed by the latter author.

The 'Prohemium' of Scot's work includes questions previously discussed in the *Elucidarium* of Honorius Augustodunensis (Honorius of Autun) in the first half of the twelfth century: the causes of divine action; the disposition of heaven and earth; the role of animals and of man; the work of angels. Here, in addition, Scot elevates astrology to a position inferior only to theology. After this introduction, based largely on twelfth-century encyclopaedism, comes the 'Liber quattuor distinctionum', with its 'new' astrological and philosophical subjects. In the 'four parts' are, respectively: 1) the properties of the planets and their influence on man's actions; 2) a treatise on musical harmony; 3) an analysis of the problems involved in the use of astrology and suggested answers to questions put in consultations; 4) the nature and the qualities of the soul.

The universe as described by Scot is conceived in Aristotelian terms, as enclosed by the nine spheres and surrounded by the waters above the heavens; all creatures exist within this universe thanks to the First Cause, a thesis derived from the pseudo-Aristotelian *Liber de causis*. As the earth is the lowest part of the firmament, the constituents of which matter is made there are less noble; they are, in fact, called *elementata* or secondary elements, to distinguish them from the pure elements to be found in the higher spheres of the firmament.

The properties of nature may be used by all rational creatures: angels, devils, and the human soul. The angels provide the necessary link between macrocosm and microcosm, between man and God. The universe also contains evil spirits; the 'Liber quattuor distinctionum' relates the actions of the demons who love blood, both that of men and of their own kind. Those who practise necromancy are allied with these demons, and although this art is condemned, Scot admits that those who practise magic can use it for the purposes of good. However, he also warns that practising this science involves the risk of encountering those evil angels who cause famine, war, and pestilence, and who are summoned by the invocations of irreligious women. Set against these evil demons and their powers are the good angels, whose job it is to lead the human soul towards eternity, whether in hell, purgatory, or heaven.

The astrologer's art In the 'Liber quattuor distinctionum' Scot also expands on the twelfth-century Salerno school treatise, *De adventu medici ad egrotum*. He suggests that doctors should consider not only the colour of the patient's urine and his pulse rate, but also his occupation and the hygiene of his surroundings. In effect, the doctor should obtain a broad clinical picture of the patient, and consider whether the illness might be caused by an affective problem or financial loss. Moreover, since the doctor should do anything which might relieve suffering, he may advise the patient to turn to magicians. Since magical practices are condemned by philosophers and the church, Scot insists that they must only be advised when the doctor knows that the patient cannot be helped by the use of conventional medicine, and it must be with the sole aim of finding a relief for the suffering of the patient.

Scot is not always consistent on these subjects. Despite his enthusiasm for astrology, he makes a clear distinction between the influence of the stars on bodily generation and corruption, and the freedom of the human soul to make independent judgements uninfluenced by the stars. Elsewhere, he invites parents to consult the stars before sending their children to study, in order to choose the most suitable discipline for them. He advised Frederick II to consult sages only when the moon was waxing, since a waning moon fills men and beasts with sadness and they lose the means of reasoning. Doctors, too, must consider the moon; for instance, when the moon is in the Ram, the head, which is the part of the body subject to that sign, must not be treated.

These and other instructions appear in the section 'De notitia regiminis astrologi', where Scot extols the astrologer's craft as worthy of praise and honours since, through this doctrine, he draws nearer to God; the astrologer's services are also often required by rulers, thus attracting handsome rewards. However, Scot also warns that the study of the stars requires lengthy study and freedom from the need to earn a living; astrology is not an appropriate science for a poor man lacking the necessary books. Scot's own adherence to astrology was not without contradictions. More than once he stresses the church's intolerance of those who try to use the hidden powers of the stars for their own ends, while referring elsewhere to the church's approval of astrology; in fact, in the 'Liber particularis', Scot praises Abu Maʿshar (Albumasar), al-Qabisi (Alcabitius), and al-Farghani (Alfraganus), learned astronomers and experts in a science considered to be wholly respectable. Although he leaves the question of whether the stars have a soul to the theologians, Scot does maintain that the planets experience feelings and joy. These stars are governed by angels, as officers of heaven, and other guardians watch over animate and inanimate substances.

Macrocosm and microcosm In Scot's view, man is the noblest creature in the universe, superior to the angels and planets, and the human body is capable of all the virtues possessed by herbs, stones, flowers, and stars. In this completeness, the human intellect resembles the heavens, since it contains all things within itself. God being the cause of all things, Scot states that, as a servant is bound to his master, so every man is by his nature bound to honour the creator of the world. Man, however, is master of all earthly creatures, who must serve him as a vassal serves his lord.

In the 'Liber quattuor distinctionum', the relationship between macrocosm and microcosm appears to be one of a small scale replication in the tradition of the *Aratea* of Germanicus Julius Caesar. Scot drew his inspiration for these images from the Monte Cassino school, but also from Islamic sources, which provided many iconographical details—Medusa's bearded head, for instance, has been unequivocally identified with the demon Algol. Scot absorbed these Arabic figurative cycles into his work, which can be compared with Ovid's *Metamorphoses*, Aristophanes's *Thesmophoriazusae*, or Hyginus's *Poeticon astronomicon*, and thus radically altered the iconography of the planets; this new interpretation reappears in the Renaissance in the frescoes of the Cappellone degli Spagnoli in the church of Santa Maria Novella in Florence.

The 'Liber particularis' was designed to facilitate the study of astrology and make it more comprehensible. It contains the questions put to Scot by Frederick II on the structure of the earth, the location of hell, why sea water is salt, and volcanic activity. These questions are in the tradition of the *Salernitan Questions*, and there is an introduction in which Scot discusses with the emperor the misery of life on earth and the hope of divine redemption.

Science and religion This scientific and theological view of the world is accompanied in Scot's 'Liber particularis' by historical notes on the ancient Roman rulers: Caesar was mild, but ruthless in his imposition of tributes; only Octavian (Augustus) was of angelic beauty. In the same work, following Ovid's *Fasti* and Macrobius's *Saturnalia*, Scot pays tribute to the 'astronomer kings' Romulus and Numa Pompilius, 'inventors of the calendar'. But he condemns the folly of the rulers of old in putting forward the theory that blood originates from a union of Jupiter, Venus, and Mercury. He is equally scathing about pagan cults and the false Christians who believe in them; they not only worship those gods as the Saracens do, but at all times consult diviners and sorcerers. All Scot's works, like the discussions he had with the emperor, are marked by this interweaving of religion and science and this is also seen in the *Liber physionomie*, where Scot urges Frederick II to encourage the study of science and to hold disputations at his court at which the emperor could hear the diverse opinions of scholars and wise men. The invitations issued were apparently accepted. In fact, the Latin translation (sometimes attributed to Scot) of Maimonides's *Guide to the Perplexed* is prefaced by a discussion of parables and an analysis of Maimonides's work, a discourse which combines the arguments of John of Salisbury's *Policraticus* and the exegesis of the *Guide to the Perplexed*, with the aim of emphasizing the need to read Deuteronomy. This introduction to the *Guide* recalls the *Malmad ha-Talmidim* ('A spur for students'), in which Jacob Anatoli, a Jewish philosopher from Provence who worked with Scot, collected together the exegetic debates between Frederick II and Michael Scot as they discussed various biblical texts. It is here that Scot, commenting on Hosea 14: 10, notes that man is like the fir tree, whose evergreen branches, lifted heavenwards, symbolize the vitality of all the sciences.

In analysing Maimonides's work, Scot and Anatoli found themselves in conflict with Frederick II, who supported the neoplatonic idea of the existence of matter before the creation of the world. Scot notes, however, that the problem of the *yle*, or primordial chaos, has been the subject of cavilling definitions by philosophers and that there is no simple solution to the question.

The whole of the *Liber introductorius* is strongly influenced by theological studies; Scot observes that a knowledge of nature and of living creatures is one of the paths to a knowledge of the Creator, and that it is through astronomy that the many secrets of God can be understood. Nature is controlled by God, who can alter its laws by miraculous interventions, defined as everything which is contrary to nature.

Scot's sources and his use of them Influences on Scot can be traced to the commentary on the *Hexaëmeron* of Basil of Caesarea, as well as to Boethius, St Augustine, Isidore of Seville, Bede, Alcher de Clairvaux, Hugues de St Victor, Abelard, and William de Conches; references to Aristotle, Avicenna, and Averroes, however, are rare. The *Liber physionomie* shows the influence of the pseudo-Aristotelian *Secretum secretorum*, of the second book of Rhazes's *Liber Almansor*, of Constantine the African's *De coitu*, and of the *Liber nativitatum* of Abubacer. The latter describes how the physical and intellectual characteristics of the unborn child are influenced by the position of the planets as well as by the quality of the seed and the humour of the parents. Reflecting this influence, the *Liber physionomie* begins with a detailed description of the phases of conception and the development of the embryo. Scot considers embryology and neonatology essential for an understanding of those human characteristics indicated by physiognomic features. This science, which Scot describes as the intelligent understanding of nature, by means of which the virtues and vices of all creatures may be known, is presented as being of extreme utility for the 'scientist–emperor' Frederick II, in helping him to know and judge the intentions of his associates. Thus a man with red hair may be judged as envious, spiteful, haughty, and malevolent; a pallid complexion indicates not only poor health but also a malicious and lustful character, inclined to infidelity and unlawfulness.

The eclectic tendencies which Scot displays in his writing identify him as a Christian philosopher who took all the opportunities offered by the developments in natural sciences in the twelfth century. In addition to the ideas promulgated in the Sibylline books and works of magic, he refers to the *Liber ymaginum*, the *Testament of Solomon*, the *De secretis angelorum*, and the *Liber lune*, with their blend of Hermetic, Arabic, and Hebrew traditions and ideas. For Scot, this combination of doctrines constitutes the knowledge of hidden things which raises man among the mighty and brings him, while still in the body, almost to the gate of paradise.

Minor works Among Scot's works is a short commentary on the *Regulae urinarum* by Marius Salernitanus, leading to speculation that Scot belonged to the so-called Salerno medical school. In fact, Scot's leanings were quite different from those of that school; he did not use the medical anthology known as the *Articella*, which served as a manual in schools and universities, and he blended medical science and astrology, which the Salerno masters would never have accepted. Furthermore, he also compiled an *Ars alchemie* intended to rescue this science from the obscurity in which it had been deliberately shrouded by the philosophers of the time.

Afterlife in legend Scot's fame as an astrologer, reinforced by the notoriety of his employer, was such that many prophecies of the coming of Antichrist were attributed to him; however, several have an anti-Ghibelline stamp, and are consequently unlikely to have been his. In 1228 the Pisan mathematician Leonardo Fibonacci presented Scot, who had asked for a copy of his *Liber abaci*, with a revised text and invited him to amend it; Cardinal Raniero Capocci, learning of this correspondence between the two scholars, included some of the questions put by Frederick II to his astrologer in an anti-Ghibelline prophecy, in an attempt to circulate propaganda which would discredit the emperor. Against such a background, it is not surprising that Michael Scot soon came to have a reputation as a magician. The Franciscan chronicler Salimbene de Adam, writing well before the end of the thirteenth century, recounts among the superstitions which he attributes to Frederick II the emperor's asking Scot how far his palace was from the heavens, and then, when Scot had made a calculation, having the palace hall lowered and asking Scot for a second estimate. When Michael had declared that either heaven had risen or the earth had become lower, Frederick knew that he was dealing with a true astrologer. Elsewhere in his *Cronica* Salimbene refers to Michael Scot as a soothsayer and observes that much of what he had foretold had indeed come to pass.

Dante was less impressed; and in Canto 20 of the *Inferno* he places Scot in the circle of hell reserved for sorcerers, with a derogatory allusion both to his meagre flanks and to his acquaintance with magical trickery. To Boccaccio, in his *Decameron* of the middle of the fourteenth century, Scot was simply a great master of necromancy; and he was clearly seen in the same light by those who identified him, in the fresco painted between 1366 and 1388 by Andrea Bonaiuti in the Cappellone degli Spagnoli of Santa Maria Novella in Florence, as the philosopher in Jewish dress who tears up the scriptures in front of St Dominic, while the saint reprimands a group of heretics who include Arius and Averroes. Benvenuto da Imola, writing in the 1370s, tells how Scot was able to foretell the manner of his own death, from the falling of a stone on his head, and therefore always wore a metal skullcap, only to be killed when he took it off on entering a church, whereupon a stone duly fell on him. Benvenuto was, however, sceptical about many of the magical feats attributed to Scot, and in this he was followed by Scot's later compatriot Thomas Dempster. Although Dempster in his *Historia ecclesiastica gentis Scotorum* (1627) describes Scot as dying in 1291 in extreme old age, he also attributes to him an admirable knowledge of medicine (*physicarum rerum*). Dempster also reports that innumerable old wives' tales were still circulating among the populace in which Scot featured as a magician. Sir Walter Scott, in the second canto of *The Lay of the Last Minstrel* (1805), both in his verses and in his notes accompanying them, presents a wide-ranging sample of such stories, for instance that with his magic wand Scot could ring the bells of Notre Dame in Paris from his grotto in Salamanca. In more recent times the works of C. H. Haskins and Lynn Thorndike, in particular, while placing appropriate stress on Scot's position as Frederick II's astrologer, have also brought out the value of his work as a translator and philosopher. PIERO MORPURGO

Sources L. Thorndike, *Michael Scot* (1965) · J. Wood Brown, *The life and legend of Michael Scot* (1897) · M. Scot, *Liber phisionomie* (1477) · P. Morpurgo, 'Il capitolo de informacione medicorum del *Liber introductorius* di Michele Scoto', *Clio: Rivista Trimestrale di Studi Storici*, 20 (1984), 651–61 · P. Morpurgo, 'Il "Sermo suasionis in bono" di Michele Scoto a Federico II', *Rendiconti dell' Accademia Nazionale dei Lincei*, 38 (1983), 287–300 · P. Morpurgo, 'Federico II e la fine dei tempi nella profezia del cod. escorialense f.III.8', *Pluteus: Periodico Annuale di Filologia*, 1 (1983), 135–67 · P. Morpurgo, 'Note in margine a un poemetto astrologico presente nei codici del "Liber particularis" di Michele Scoto', *Pluteus: Periodico Annuale di Filologia*, 2 (1984), 5–14 [contains Scot's 'De notitia regiminis astrologi'] · S. H. Thomson, 'The texts of Michael Scot's *Ars alchemiae*', *Osiris*, 5 (1938), 523–59 · *'The sphere' of Sacrobosco and its commentators*, ed. L. Thorndike (1949), 247–342 · J. Carmody, ed., *Al-Bitruji: 'De motibus celorum': critical edition of the Latin translation of Michael Scot* (1952) · *Aristotle: De animalibus: Michael Scot's Arabic–Latin translation, books XV–XIX: 'On the generation of animals'*, ed. A. M. I. van Oppenraaij (1992) · U. Bauer, *Der 'Liber introductorius' des Michael Scotus in der Abschrift Clm 10268 der bayerischen Staatsbibliothek München: ein illustrierter astronomischer astrologischer Codex aus Padua, 14 Jahrhundert* (1983) · G. M. Edwards, 'The two redactions of Michael Scot's *Liber introductorius*', *Traditio*, 41 (1985), 329–40 · C. D. Fonseca, ed., *Federico II e l'Italia* (1995) · A. Graf, 'La leggenda di un filosofo: Michele Scotto', *Miti, leggende e superstizioni del medio evo* (1892–3), 293–320; repr. (1984) · C. H. Haskins, *Studies in the history of mediaeval science*, 2nd edn (1927), 242–98 · R. Manselli, 'La corte di Federico II e Michele Scoto', *L'Averroismo in Italia: Atti del convegno dell' Accademia Nazionale dei Lincei* [Rome 1977] (1979), 63–80; repr. in R. Manselli, *Scritti sul medioevo* (Rome, 1994), 183–208 · C. Sirat, 'Les traducteurs juifs a la cour des rois de Sicile et de Naples', *Traduction et traducteurs au moyen age*, ed. G. Contamine (1989), 169–91 · W. Tronzo, ed., *Intellectual life at the court of Frederick II Hohenstaufen* (1994), 241–8 · P. Toubert and A. Paravicini Bagliani, eds., *Federico II e le scienze* (1994) · 'Michael Scotus', *Medioevo Latino* · L. Minio Paluello, 'Michael, Scot', *DSB*, 9.361–5 · C. Vasoli, 'Michele Scoto', *Enciclopedia Dantesca*, ed. U. Bosco, 2nd edn, 6 vols. (1984), vol. 3 · M. S. Calo' Mariani and R. Cassano, eds., *Federico II: immagine e potere* (1995) · P. Morpurgo, 'Fonti di Michele Scoto', *Rendiconti dell' Accademia Nazionale dei Lincei*, 38 (1983), 59–71 · P. Morpurgo, 'Michele Scoto tra scienza dell'anima e astrologia', *Clio: Rivista Trimestrale di Studi Storici*, 19 (1983), 441–50 · P. Morpurgo, 'Il concetto di natura in Michele Scoto', *Clio: Rivista Trimestrale di Studi Storici*, 22 (1986), 5–21 · P. Morpurgo, 'Michele Scoto e Dante: una continuità di modelli culturali?', *Filosofia, scienza e astrologia nel trecento Europeo: Biagio Pelacani Parmense*, ed. G. Federici Vescovini and F. Barocelli (1992), 79–94 · P. Morpurgo, 'Michele Scoto e la circolazione dei manoscritti scientifici in Italia Meridionale: la dipendenza della Scuola Salernitana dalla Scuola Parigina di Petit Pont', *Atti del Congresso sulla diffusione delle Scienze Islamiche nel Medioevo Europeo (2–4 Ottobre 1984)* (1987), 167–91 · Y. V. O'Neill, 'Michael Scot and Mary of Bologna: a medieval gynecological puzzle', *Clio Medica*, 8 (1973), 87–111 · Y. V. O'Neill, 'Michael Scot and Mary of Bologna: an addendum', *Clio Medica*, 9 (1974), 125–9 · A. M. I. van Oppenraaij, 'Quelques particularités de la méthode de traduction de Michel

Scot', *Rencontres de cultures dans la philosophie médiévale: traductions et traducteurs de l'antiquité tardive au XIVe siècle*, ed. J. Hamesse and M. Fattori (1990), 121–9 • A. Paravicini Bagliani, ed., 'La crisi dell'alchimia', *Micrologus: Natura, Scienze e Società Medievali*, 3 (1995) • J. F. Rivera Recio, 'Personajes hispanos asistentes en 1215 al IV Concilio de Letràn', *Hispania Sacra*, 4 (1951), 335–58 • L. Thorndike, 'Manuscripts of Michael Scot's *Liber introductorius*', *Didascaliae: studies in honor of Anselm M. Albareda* (1961), 425–47 • D. Abulafia, *Frederick II: a medieval emperor* (1988) • P. Toynbee, *A dictionary of the proper names and notable matters in the works of Dante*, rev. C. S. Singleton (1968), 446–8 • [*Cronica fratris Salimbene de Adam ordinis Minorum*], ed. O. Holder-Egger, MGH Scriptores [folio], 32 (Hanover, 1905–13) • *Thomae Dempsteri Historia ecclesiastica gentis Scotorum, sive, De scriptoribus Scotis*, ed. D. Irving, rev. edn, 1, Bannatyne Club, 21 (1829), 494–5 • E. Menesto', ed., *Federico II e le nuove culture: atti del XXXI Convegno Storico Internazionale* [Todi 1994] (Spoleto, 1995)

Archives Bibliothèque Nationale, MS Lat. 14385, fols. 133–60v • Spitalbibliothek, Kues, MS 209 | Ambrosiana, Milan, MS L. 92 Sup. • Biblioteca Apostolica Vaticana, Vatican City, MSS Pal. lat. 1157, 1211, 1245, 1251, 1260, 1330, 1335; Vat. lat. 4440 • Biblioteca Apostolica Vaticana, Vatican City, MS Rossi 421 • Biblioteca Comunale, Palermo, MS 4.Qq.A.10 • Biblioteca del Real Monasterio, San Lorenzo del El Escorial, MS, e III 15 • Biblioteca del Real Monasterio, San Lorenzo del El Escorial, MS f. III. 8 • Biblioteca Nazionale, Naples, MS, XV.F.91 • Biblioteca Nazionale Centrale, Florence, MS, sez. Magliabechiana cl. xv, cod. 27 • Bibliothèque Nationale, Paris, MS nouv. acq. 1401 • BL, Add. MS 24068 • Bodl. Oxf., MS Bodley 266 • Bodl. Oxf., MS Canonici. misc. 555 • Staatsbibliothek, Munich, MS CLM 10268

Wealth at death held four ecclesiastical grants: Manselli, 'La corte di Federico II'

Scot, Patrick (*fl.* **1618–1625**), writer, followed James I from Scotland into England on his accession. In June 1618 he was engaged in the work of raising voluntary gifts for the supply of the king's exchequer by threatening various persons with prosecutions for usury (*CSP dom., 1611–18*). Six years later, on 11 August 1624, James I wrote a letter of recommendation on Scot's behalf (*CSP dom., 1623–5*). It would appear, from the general tone of his works, that Scot occasionally acted as tutor to Prince Charles. In 1621, for example, he printed *A table-booke for princes containing short remembrances for the government of themselves and their empire*, which was dedicated to Charles. A detailed celebration of the king's erudition and particular care in selecting 'godly and learned Tutors' is followed by chapters of advice covering the condition, duties, conduct, security, piety, and humility of princes. The value of education, its consonance with reason, and its role as a safeguard against the abuse of power and descent into chaos is a persistent theme: 'The due calling to mind that a prince is homo … ought to bridle his power, and the consideration that he is Deus, or, vice Dei, Gods vicegerent, ought to curb his will' (p. 68).

The thrust of this text is clearly comparable with Scot's earlier work, *Omnibus et singulis affording matter profitable for all men, necessarie for every man, alluding to a father's advice or last will to his sonne* (1619). Conceived in the confidence of the king's patronage it was dedicated to King James and to Prince Charles, and directed towards the improvement of society in general via emphasis on daily meditations, patience, and moderation. At the end are some verses, 'ad serenissimam Magnæ Britanniæ Annam reginam defunctam'. The work was reprinted in 1619 and was rearranged and revised as *A Father's Advice or Last Will to his Son* (1620).

Scot retained a deep interest in matters affecting the church in Scotland. Although he was evidently resident in Amsterdam in 1623 and 1625, observing the life of separatist churches, he still assumed the role of commentator and didactic authority for an English audience (Hanbury). In 1623 he produced *The tillage of light, or, A true discoverie of the philosophicall elixir commonly called the philosophers stone*, dedicated to John, marquess of Hamilton, a gentleman of the king's bedchamber. In this work, punctuated with warnings of succumbing to greed and temptation, Scot sought to establish sound theological and moral guidelines for the alchemist's quest: 'Man is the Microcosmos, or abridgement of the creation: the philosophers worke is the abridgement of mans Formation' (p. 41). Recognizing that curiosity and exploration are innate qualities of the human condition he nevertheless constructed definite boundaries around his subject: 'You see then that nature and art, either severally or joyntly are but the handmaids of divine providence which filleth, governeth and overspreadeth all things, and ruleth every part thereof with infallible councell and most certaine reasons' (pp. 7–8).

Two of Scot's texts focused directly on religious controversy. In the opening address to the reader of *Calderwood's recantation, or, A tripartite discourse directed to such of the ministrie and others in Scotland that refuse conformitie to the ordinances of the church* (1622) Scot confesses to past transgressions ('One favor I crave, That thou wilt not curiously enquire what I have beene, or pry into my former Errors … upon Earth, but consider with judgement what now I am, and how affected to the Truth' (sig. A2*r–v*), but attempted to justify his work by repenting his faults and expressing his commitment to the peace and unity of the church. He examines the causes and proliferation of heresy, incensed at its influence, and lists the various defence mechanisms (loyal preachers, royal clemency, and general assemblies) that had recently been deployed. In essence Scot's work was a rallying call for conformity; battling against anarchy and separatism he urged that faith and baptism should be central to the church's response: 'Whosoever then by contentious controversies in matters indifferent, unswaddle the Church of her Bonds of Peace, are in the right way of dividing the Unitie of Spirit, to open a Gap to all disorder and scandall' (p. 2).

Provoked by further sedition in 1625, Scot printed his final text, *Vox vera, or, Observations from Amsterdam examining the late insolencies of some pseudo-puritans separatists from the church of Great Britaine*. He denounced the activities of Andrew Melville and Scottish support of separatism, contrasting them with the unity and wisdom of both King James and his court: 'There is no possible way unto peace and quietnesse unlesse the probable voyce of every entire societie or body politike over-rule all private opinion of that same body' (p. 45). He concluded with a series of impassioned appeals to the bishops and ministers of Scotland, whom he believed to be the agents to bind and heal the church. W. A. SHAW, *rev.* ELIZABETH HARESNAPE

Sources *STC, 1475–1640* · *CSP dom., 1611–18*, p. 97, no. 42 (30 April 1618), p. 97, no. 52 (2 May 1618), p. 97, no. 99 (10 June 1618); *1623–5*, p. 171, no. 37 · B. Hanbury, *Historical memorials relating to the independents, or congregationalists*, 3 vols. (1839), 1.473

Scot [Scott], **William** (*c.*1558–1642), Church of Scotland minister and historian, was the son of Robert Scot (*d.* *c.*1605) from Mylndeane, Fife. He graduated MA from the University of St Andrews in 1586. By 1593 he was minister of Kennoway, Fife, and two years later he first attended the general assembly. The assembly of March 1596 appointed him a visitor in Dumfriesshire and in May Scot delivered a 'notable exhortation' to the synod of Fife concerning the general assembly's invocation to renew the covenant with God (Calderwood, 5.433). In February 1597 he was one of two ministers from Cupar presbytery chosen to meet representatives of the other presbyteries of Fife concerning questions from the king about ecclesiastical authority. In the autumn of 1600 he attended a conference of delegates from the synods with the king, at which the first Jacobean bishops were appointed, in the absence of the contingent from Fife. Having given him further commissions of visitation in 1600 and 1602, in the latter year the general assembly also appointed him 'to wait upon' the Catholic earl of Huntly to instruct him and his family (ibid., 6.166).

In 1604 Scot became minister of Cupar and became prominent in opposition to the king's episcopal policy. In April 1605, moderating the synod of Fife, he 'taught powerfullie against the corruptions' in the kirk (Calderwood, 6.276). Later that year he petitioned the king in favour of ministers imprisoned for holding an illegal general assembly at Aberdeen. In the summer of 1606 Scot and seven others, including Andrew and James Melville, were summoned to court. In July, after subscribing a written protest at the Scottish parliament against the restitution of bishops, the eight went south. Discussions at Hampton Court focused on the Aberdeen assembly of 1605 and Scot is recorded as having 'declairit his judgement solidlie in few wordis' (*Autobiography and Diary of … Melvill*, 660). In common with his colleagues he was warded with a bishop, in his case that of Peterborough. He remained in London until May 1607, and in the meantime various English nobles tried to engage him as their chaplain. Allowed to go home because his wife, Janet Smyth, was ill, he was then confined to his parish, although in the interim he had been appointed by the crown as 'constant moderator' of Cupar presbytery, an innovation to which he was opposed.

During 1608 and 1609 Scot corresponded with James Melville, his 'loving and deere Father' in exile in England (Calderwood, 6.785). In spite of his confinement he attended the general assembly in 1608 and a conference at Falkland in 1609 designed to resolve ecclesiastical disputes. In July 1614 his confinement was lifted, yet he did not return to the synod of Fife until 1622 in protest at its being presided over by the archbishop of St Andrews. In Edinburgh at the time of parliament in June 1617 he was one of fifty-five ministers to subscribe a declaration in favour of ecclesiastical independence. An attempt to have him appointed minister of Edinburgh was blocked by the crown because of his opposition to its ecclesiastical policy, which had led to the assumption that he had been the author of David Calderwood's *Perth Assemblie*, asserting the illegality of the general assembly of 1618.

Scot spent the rest of his life out of the political spotlight. In 1620 he erected the spire of Cupar parish church which is an enduring monument to his ministry there, as is the fine silver communion plate, commissioned in the same year and in regular use at the end of the twentieth century. In 1622 he published in the Netherlands *The Course of Conformitie*, a dialogue concerning the decayed state of the kirk. Three years later David Dalgleish became his assistant and went on to marry his daughter, Barbara. In his declining years Scot wrote *Apologetical narration of the state and government of the Kirk of Scotland since the Reformation*, which concentrated on the period between 1590 and 1633, recounting events from an anti-episcopalian and anti-Erastian standpoint. It was not published until 1846, although Calderwood used the manuscript. Scot died on 20 May 1642 aged about eighty-four and was buried beside the church he had served for over forty years. He was survived by his wife. ALAN R. MACDONALD

Sources W. Scot, *An apologetical narration of the state and government of the Kirk of Scotland since the Reformation*, ed. D. Laing, Wodrow Society, 19 (1846) · D. Calderwood, *The history of the Kirk of Scotland*, ed. T. Thomson and D. Laing, 8 vols., Wodrow Society, 7 (1842–9) · *Fasti Scot.*, new edn · *The autobiography and diary of Mr James Melvill*, ed. R. Pitcairn, Wodrow Society (1842) · T. Thomson, ed., *Acts and proceedings of the general assemblies of the Kirk of Scotland*, 3 pts, Bannatyne Club, 81 (1839–45) · J. Forbes, *Certaine records touching the estate of the kirk in the years MDCV & MDCVI*, ed. D. Laing and J. Anderson, Wodrow Society, 19 (1846) · record of the diocesan synod of St Andrews Benorth Forth, NA Scot., CH2/154/1 · *Reg. PCS*, 1st ser., vols. 7, 10 · A. R. Macdonald, *The Jacobean kirk, 1567–1625: sovereignty, polity and liturgy* (1998)

Scotland, James (1774–1849), newspaper proprietor and editor in the West Indies, was born at St John's, Antigua, on 4 May 1774, the eldest son of John Scotland (*d.* 1792), a merchant originally from Edinburgh but well established on that island by the second half of the eighteenth century. George Scotland (1782–1865) was his brother and chief justice of Trinidad from 1833 to 1849. Like many other progeny of the white élite of merchants and planters which controlled the British West Indies, James Scotland was sent to Britain to be educated, in his case at Wandsworth, Charterhouse School, and Trinity College, Cambridge. Progress must have been turbulent if judged by his expulsion from Charterhouse and failure to graduate from Trinity, yet despite these failings he was admitted to the Inner Temple on 5 July 1793. Any attempts he made to pursue a legal career in Britain seem to have foundered because he returned to Antigua around 1800. He married Esther (*d.* *c.*1805) and they had several children, including James junior, who achieved prominence as a barrister and member of the island assembly.

Despite his father's success James Scotland does not

appear to have thrived, and he undertook a variety of work between 1800 and 1830. Around 1805 he probably edited the *Antigua Journal*, between 1806 and 1810 he worked as a clerk, and in 1818 he was employed as a schoolmaster. By the late 1820s he was vestry clerk in St Mary's parish, but it was with the death of Robert Priest, editor of the *Antigua Free Press*, in September 1830 that Scotland finally found an opportunity.

Most West Indian journalists eked out a precarious living, surviving on meagre advertising revenues, circulations of a few hundred subscribers, and, occasionally, contracts to print government business. In these circumstances they could not afford to alienate readers, yet Scotland changed the paper's hitherto pro-slavery stance and began, cautiously at first, then with vigour, to argue for the immediate emancipation of the slaves and for the concession of civil and political rights to the free coloureds. Inevitably there were rumours that Scotland was in the pay of the abolitionist movement, but he seems to have been motivated by nothing more than genuine disgust—perhaps stemming from his Methodism—with the system of slavery upon which West Indian society had for so long been based.

The consequences of establishing an outpost of the abolitionist movement in Antigua were widespread. After years of editorial equivocation his fellow Antiguan journalist Henry Loving was inspired to take the *Weekly Register* in a similar direction, and for a time the island was in the unique position of having no editor prepared to defend the interests of the planters. The situation changed with the appearance of the *Antigua Herald*, founded by public subscription in response to the pro-abolition press hegemony which had been established by Scotland and Loving.

Not surprisingly both men became targets for white outrage during this period: Loving was horsewhipped in May 1831, and in October of that year Scotland was sentenced to six months in gaol and fined £200. Ostensibly for contempt of court, the attack was a reaction to the publication of writings which influential white observers had deemed dangerous to the stability of Antigua. In keeping with the practice of the times, however, Scotland was allowed to edit the paper from his cell and he remained defiant, aggravating the original offence to the extent that rumours surfaced of a plot to destroy his printing presses outright. With the governor deaf to Scotland's pleas for protection it took the intervention of the secretary of state to secure his release in January 1832.

From then on until the abolition of slavery in 1834 Scotland continued to write in favour of immediate abolition. By that point change of some sort had become inevitable and the British government devised a system of apprenticeship to smooth the transition to full freedom. A number of stipendiary magistrates were needed to administer the system and Scotland applied for a post. However, with the Antigua assembly voting to abolish slavery outright the need for these officials in the colony was obviated and Scotland slipped from prominence in the years that followed. He relinquished control of the *Free Press* early in 1835, and despite an attempt by Thomas Fowell Buxton to win the patronage of Lord Glenelg for him in 1837 Scotland failed to achieve a public appointment until he was made deputy postmaster-general of Antigua in 1840. He held the post until his death at St John's, Antigua, on 2 July 1849.

A. P. Lewis

Sources V. L. Oliver, *The history of the island of Antigua*, 3 vols. (1894–9) · Venn, *Alum. Cant.* · [R. L. Arrowsmith], ed., *Charterhouse register, June 1769–May 1872* (1964) · [Mrs Flannigan], *Antigua and the Antiguans: a full account of the colony and its inhabitants*, 2 vols. (1844) · R. Lowe, *The Codrington correspondence, 1743–1851: being a study of a recently discovered dossier of letters* (1951) · W. W. Rouse Ball and J. A. Venn, eds., *Admissions to Trinity College, Cambridge*, 5 vols. (1911–16) · D. Dobson, *Directory of Scottish settlers in North America*, 6 vols. (1984–6) · *Antigua Free Press* · *Weekly Register* [Antigua] · PRO, CO 10 · PRO, CO 393 · Boase, *Mod. Eng. biog.* · H. Pactor, *Colonial British Caribbean newspapers: a bibliography and directory* (1990) · Glos. RO, Codrington MSS, MF 351/10; 375

Archives PRO, CO 7 · PRO, blue books, CO 10 · PRO, CO 393 · PRO, CO 714

Scotson, James (1836–1911), headmaster, was born in Manchester, the son of Robert Scotson, a working man. From the age of seven he attended the New Jerusalem School, Peter Street, Manchester (founded for boys in 1827 and opened for girls in 1844). He was apprenticed as a pupil teacher at the school, then attracting some 600 pupils, in 1849 and appointed assistant master from 1854. Having been awarded a first-class teacher's certificate, he was appointed headmaster with effect from 1 January 1858. On 14 August 1857 he married Betsey (*b.* 1836/7), daughter of John Taylor, at the New Jerusalem Church, Bolton Street, Salford.

From 1862, under payment by results, reading, writing, and arithmetic were examined in six standards, but Scotson extended the curriculum and began to develop a specialist school for older pupils. In 1880 Peter Street was merged with the Lower Mosley Street British School as the Central School under the Manchester school board and consolidated into one of the first higher grade schools for pupils who had passed standards I–IV and wished to prolong their education. Scotson was appointed headmaster.

In 1884 the royal commission on technical education, chaired by Bernhard Samuelson, recorded the emergence of higher grade schools where additional subjects were taught more satisfactorily than in schools containing children of all ages and all stages of progress. Scotson's school was described as remarkable (Samuelson commission second report, 1.425). There were 320 boys and 200 girls taking mathematics, science, physical geography, and French. On 7 July 1884 a four-storey building, complete with two laboratories and a machine-drawing room, was opened in Deansgate by A. J. Mundella, the minister responsible for education. Bringing together picked intellects in higher schools from great towns and cities, he said, would stimulate all the elementary schools below them (*School Board Chronicle*, 41).

In December 1886 Scotson gave evidence to the Cross commission and urged that schools similar to his own should be set up in every town of from 10,000 to 15,000 inhabitants. In his view their purpose was either to form a connecting link between the ordinary elementary school and existing secondary schools, or where the latter were either inferior or did not exist at all, to take their place. Pupils could stay until they were sixteen; fees were 9*d*. per week. There were now 208 boys and 129 girls in standard VI, 215 boys and 103 girls in the new standard VII; also retained in the school were 300 boys and 50 girls who had passed standard VII who were assembled in a so-called organized science school under the auspices of the Department of Science and Art (South Kensington), which granted the school 10*s*. a year for every pupil who attended 250 times and passed its science examination. These pupils were also taught French, arithmetic, and composition; their day began with an hour's religious instruction. Twenty-five per cent of the boys left to go into engineering, chemical laboratories or architecture. Two-thirds of recent girl leavers went into teaching. By 1891 Scotson had 1400 pupils: 1000 boys and 400 girls. His staff consisted of sixteen masters and assistants; the headmistress had a staff of six and there were special teachers for science, engineering, French, German, and cookery. Two former pupils, one male, one female, had recently been awarded a BSc from Victoria University of Manchester; another had gained a double first at Oxford.

Though he was on the executive of the National Union of Elementary Teachers in the 1870s Scotson of Manchester, as he was known (Christian, 48), preferred not to rise further, but when twenty headmasters of higher grade and organized science schools met in Manchester on 5 November 1892 and set up an association he was elected first annual president. Two years later, answering a circular letter from the Bryce commission addressed to some twenty distinguished educationists, Scotson outlined his plans for connecting higher grade schools' boys' departments with grammar or secondary schools. Higher grade schools would have a lower part, into which former elementary pupils could enter having passed standard IV. If a boy wished to prepare for a profession he would complete standard V, then be prepared for the classical department of a secondary school. The majority would progress into the organized science school, most for a two-year course in science, mathematics, and modern languages, a few for three or four years to compete for national or county scholarships. The Bryce report, however, favoured a system in which the higher grade school would be an institution made distinct from grammar or secondary schools by the intended leaving age of its scholars. In 1897 a joint memorandum drawn up by the Association of Headmasters (representing the grammar schools) and the Association of Higher Grade Schools agreed this principle which was incorporated in the Board of Education's higher school minute of April 1900. Higher grade schools' function as a conduit by which able elementary school pupils could pass upwards without encountering a selective bar had ended: a few, including the Central School, were awarded secondary status.

Scotson, who had been awarded an MSc in 1902 by the Victoria University of Manchester, *honoris causa*, remained in charge of his school until the change took place. He retired in July 1904. Bearded, tall, and well built, with a thunderous voice, he was a genial man of powerful intellect, forcible yet sympathetic. In 1884 Mundella had provided him with a famous epitaph: 'When I want to point to some first-rate schoolmasters in England I generally begin with Mr Scotson. Mr Scotson I consider the prince of our elementary schoolmasters' (*School Board Chronicle*, 41). Scotson died at his home, 19 Wellington Road, Whalley Range, Manchester, on 4 June 1911. His remains were cremated two days later at Manchester crematorium.

ROBIN BETTS

Sources *The Schoolmaster* (14 Jan 1893), 88 • *The Schoolmaster* (23 July 1904), 166 • *The Schoolmaster* (10 June 1911), 1166 • *School Board Chronicle* (12 July 1884), 41–2 • *Manchester Guardian* (5 June 1911), 7 • *Manchester Guardian* (7 June 1911), 12 • Cross commission second report (1887), 261–80; 1017–18 • Samuelson commission second report (1884), 1.424–6; 4.157–61 • Bryce commission report (1895), 5.389–92, 421–6 • H. Lever and J. G. Birkby, *A short history of the Central High School for Boys, Manchester* (1935), 1–12 • R. J. Murphy, 'The development of the Manchester higher grade board schools, 1870–1890', PhD diss., University of Manchester, 1983 • G. A. Christian, *English education from within* (1922) • W. H. G. Armytage, *A. J. Mundella* (1951) • E. Eaglesham, *From school board to local authority* (1956) • *Practical Teacher*, 12/1 (1891), 23–9 • m. cert.

Likenesses photograph, repro. in Lever and Birkby, *Short history of the Central High School*, 16–17 • photograph, repro. in *The Schoolmaster* (23 July 1904)

Wealth at death £2955 1*s*. 5*d*.: probate, 13 July 1911, *CGPLA Eng. & Wales*

Scotstarvit. For this title name *see* Scot, Sir John, of Scotstarvit, Lord Scotstarvit (1585–1670).

Scott. *See also* Scot.

Scott [Scot] **family** (*per. c.*1400–*c.*1525), gentry, of Scot's Hall, Smeeth, Kent, is first represented in the fifteenth century by Sir Robert Scott, lieutenant of the Tower in 1424, whose daughter and sole heir, Alice, married William Kemp, nephew of John *Kemp, archbishop of York.

Sir Robert's brother **William** [i] **Scott** (*d.* 1434) was granted the manor of Combe in Brabourne, Kent, by Peter Combe in 1402. By 1409 he had married his first wife, Joan (*d.* in or before 1425), daughter of Sir John Orlestone (*d.* 1397), and sister of Margaret, wife of William Parker, with whom she became coheir to the Orlestone estate by 1419. The terms of William [i]'s settlement of 1425 with the Parkers suggest that he and Joan had children who did not survive: by this settlement William purchased Joan's moiety and the property of Richard, her deceased brother, thereby bringing to the Scotts the manors of Orlestone (with its advowson) and Capel, Kent, and Stonlink, Sussex. His second wife was Isabel (*d.* 1457?), the youngest daughter of Vincent Finch, or Herbert, of Netherfield, Sussex. William [i] may have fought at Agincourt. He was sheriff of Kent first in 1413; in 1419 he was among those granted the keeping of the temporalities of the see of Rochester, and from the following year he appears on other Kentish commissions; he was escheator for Kent and Middlesex in 1424–5, sheriff of Kent again in 1428 and MP in 1430–31. He was legal counsel to Robert, Lord Poynings. With his kinsman Archbishop Kemp he owned a deer park at Birling. In 1431 he was residing at Combe, with lands at Bircholt,

West Hythe, Eastbridge, Worth, Wilmington, Street, Hurst, and Estenhanger, with a total annual rental value well in excess of £23. He is credited with having rebuilt Scot's Hall, and probably also the chapel of the Holy Trinity in Brabourne church, where he directed he should be buried. He died on 5 February 1434. With Isabel he had a son and heir, **Sir John Scott** (1423–1485), and a younger son, William [ii] Scott (*d.* 1491), among other children.

The family rose to national prominence through Sir John's unshakeable commitment to the house of York. His career in Lancastrian service demonstrated his potential: he appeared on Kentish commissions from 1450, and together with John Fogge and Robert Horn he spent over £333 in suppressing Cade's uprising; king's esquire by 1456, he was frequently involved in Kentish musters and arrays. He first sat as a Kentish JP in 1458, and the following year he was appointed deputy to the earl of Shrewsbury as chief butler of Sandwich. But the turning point in his career came in June 1460, when, with Fogge and Horn, he gave support to the Yorkist earls that proved crucial to their success in Kent. Rich rewards followed within a year of Edward IV's accession, including annuities totalling £73 6*s.* 8*d.*, a knighthood, the offices of tronage and pesage in the port of London, joint chirographer of common pleas, deputy to Lord Wenlock as chief butler of Sandwich, the lieutenancy of Dover under the earl of Warwick, and the plum position of controller of the household. This did not exhaust a grateful king's largesse: in 1462 he was among those granted the custody of the lands of the attainted earl of Oxford, and of the bishop of Durham's temporalities; he was also made keeper of Higham, Buckinghamshire. The same year he was granted the reversion in fee simple of the castle and manor of Chilham and the manors of Wilderton and Molash with extensive lands: these were the jointure of Margory, widow of the attainted Thomas, Lord Ros of Helmsley (*d.* 1464). In 1464 the king granted him an interest in further Ros property at Chilham, Godmersham, and Throwley. He had to wait until 1478 for the remainder to fall in with Lady Ros's death, but in the meantime she had agreed that he could occupy the properties, and he was residing at Chilham Castle by 1476, when he had a grant of a weekly fair, annual market, free warren, and court of piepowder there. In 1463 he was granted in fee two thirds, with reversion of the remaining third, of the manors of Old Swinford (with its advowson) and Snodsbury in Worcestershire, in royal hands by the attainder of the earl of Wiltshire. The same year he was included in the group entrusted with the keeping of all the wardships, marriages, and ecclesiastical temporalities coming into royal hands, the profits to maintain the royal household. The following year he was to be reimbursed from the London tonnage and poundage the £256 3*s.* 6*d.* he had expended on ships for the Scottish expedition. His pension as controller was exempted from resumptions in 1463 and 1467, and in the latter year he was given the custody of the Kentish lands of Sir Robert Poynings (*d.* 1461), the marriage of whose son and heir, Edward *Poynings, he had purchased in 1466. He later married Edward to his daughter Isabella (*d.* 1528).

In addition to fulfilling his household duties, Sir John Scott served his king at home and abroad. He was appointed sheriff of Kent in September 1460, and thereafter was a ubiquitous commissioner in the county. He continued as a Kentish JP until his death, apart from the period of the readeption. He also sat on the Buckinghamshire bench between 1479 and 1484. He represented Kent in the parliament of 1467–8, and probably also in 1461–2, 1463–5, and the first parliament of 1483, as well as sitting for Appleby, Westmorland, in 1472–5.

In September 1467 Sir John helped negotiate the marriage between the king's sister Margaret and the duke of Burgundy, and he accompanied Margaret to her wedding the following year. He was at Brussels in November 1467 negotiating a commercial treaty with Burgundy, and from May 1469 to February 1470 he was involved in negotiations with the Hanse in Flanders. In April 1471 he succeeded the earl of Warwick as lieutenant of the Cinque Ports and by March 1472 was marshal of Calais. In 1473 and 1474 he was sent on diplomatic missions to Burgundy, Utrecht, and Bruges.

Sir John was busy in Edward IV's defence in the climactic years from 1468 to 1470, as a frequent commissioner of muster and array in Kent and Buckinghamshire. He almost certainly went into exile during the readeption, and returned to fight at Barnet and play an important part in the suppression of Fauconberg's rebellion in May 1471. His position as controller of the household was not renewed in 1471, perhaps because of his new commitments in Calais, but he continued to enjoy the king's trust: in February 1473 he was appointed as one of the tutors to the prince of Wales. Scott remained loyal to Richard III, at least until the end of 1484. In March 1485 he was bound in £1000 to appear before the king and council to answer concerning the matter of debt, so he too may have become alienated from the regime by then. He continued to draw his pension under Henry VII, until his death on 17 October 1485.

Sir John Scott married Agnes (*d.* 1486/7), daughter of William de Beaufitz of The Grange, Gillingham, Kent (and probably also citizen and fishmonger of London), with whom he had two daughters and a son and heir, William [iii]. Sir John and Agnes were buried in the north wall of Brabourne church. At his death he held lands in Calais, and the manors of St Cleres, Essex, 'la Moote', Sussex, in addition to his properties in Kent. Here he held the manor and advowson of Orlestone, and the manors of Capel, Hayton, Hall, and Mead. He also held the manor of Bournewood, near Orlestone, and land in Romney Marsh given to him by Sir John Cheyne in 1457 as satisfaction for a debt.

Sir John's younger brother **William** [ii] **Scott** (1428?–1491), was the founder of the Essex branch of the family. With his wife, Margery, an Essex heiress, he had his heir, John Scott (*b.* *c.*1456), five other sons—William [iv], Edward, John, George, and Hugh—and two daughters—Joan, wife of Hugh Fenne, and Elizabeth. He was MP for

Huntingdon in 1450–51, but he maintained links with his native county: he sat for Rochester in 1455–6, and was on Kentish commissions in the 1450s, as well as being commissioned to defend Winchelsea against the earl of Warwick in December 1459. After Edward IV's accession he was employed on royal service in Essex, while in 1462 he was commissioned to administer the Hungerford lands in the west, and in 1482 he joined Sir John Scott in arraying Kentish troops for the defence of Calais. He was an Essex commissioner under Richard III, and in 1489–90 a Kentish JP and commissioner of array.

William [ii] Scott lived at his wife's manor of Stapleford and also at Theydon Mount, both in Essex. In addition, at his death on 3 November 1491 he held the Essex manors of Wolfhampton, Ovesham Hall, Margate Guynge, and Great Fordham, and the manor of Woolstan, granted to him by Henry VII after the attainder of the duke of Norfolk.

Sir John Scott's son and heir, **Sir William** [iii] **Scott** (1459–1524), of Brabourne and Iden, Sussex, followed in his father's footsteps in much of his public life. He helped to suppress Buckingham's rebellion, being present at the siege of Bodiam Castle in October–November 1483, and was a commissioner of array for Sussex and Essex in 1484. His loyalty to Richard III was pardoned by Henry VII and by November 1489, when he was knighted with Prince Arthur, he had been appointed a member of the council and controller of the household. Sitting on numerous Kentish commissions of array, oyer and terminer, and gaol delivery, he was also appointed sheriff in 1490, 1501, and 1516, and JP from 1494 to 1506. He represented Kent in the parliament of 1495. Scott was appointed marshal of Calais in 1491 and the following year lieutenant of Dover. In 1501 he attended the reception of Katherine of Aragon, and in 1520 he was at the Field of Cloth of Gold. In May 1522 he was among those who received Charles V at Dover.

In 1495 Sir William [iii] Scott found himself the beneficiary of a settlement that his father had made thirty years earlier with Sir John and Joan Lewknor, whereby Sir John Scott and his heirs were granted a remainder interest in the manor of Brabourne in the event of the Lewknors' dying without surviving issue. The childless Joan was widowed at the battle of Tewkesbury and with her death twenty-four years later Sir William became lord of Brabourne.

William's wife was Sybil (*d.* 1528), daughter of Sir John Lewknor of Goring, Sussex. He died on 24 August 1524 and was buried in the chancel of Brabourne church. He was succeeded by his heir, John *Scott (*d.* 1533).

PETER FLEMING

Sources J. R. Scott, *Memorials of the family of Scott of Scott's Hall* (1876) • J. C. Wedgwood and A. D. Holt, *History of parliament*, 1: *Biographies of the members of the Commons house, 1439–1509* (1936) • H. Miller, 'Sir John Scott, *d.* 1533', HoP, *Commons, 1509–58* • *Chancery records* • *A descriptive catalogue of ancient deeds in the Public Record Office*, 6 vols. (1890–1915) • *Inquisitions and assessments relating to feudal aids*, 6 vols., PRO (1899–1921), 110, 134, 138 • *CIPM, Henry VII*, 1, nos. 110, 134, 138 [Sir John Scott]; no. 779 [William [ii] Scott]; 1078 [Sir William [iii] Scott] • wills, PRO, PROB 11/8, sig. 15; PROB 11/7, sig. 15; PROB 11/21, sig. 29 • P. Fleming, 'The character and private concerns of the gentry of Kent, 1422–1509', PhD diss., U. Wales, 1985 • *CIPM*, 18, nos. 53, 139

Archives PRO, PCC, 15 Milles [Agnes (*d.* 1488)] • PRO, PCC, 15 Logg [Sir John (*d.* 1485)] • PRO, PCC, 29 Bodfelde [Sir William (*d.* 1523/4)] • PRO, inquisitions post mortem, 18 Henry VI, 53 and 139

Likenesses memorials, Brabourne church, Kent

Wealth at death £23 p.a.; William [i] Scott: *Inquisitions* • over £115 p.a.; Sir John Scott: *CIPM*, Henry VII, 1, nos. 110, 134, 138 • over £50 p.a.; William [ii] Scott: *CIPM*, Henry VII, 1, no. 779 • manor of Brabourne valued at £40 p.a.; Sir William [iii] Scott: *CIPM*, Henry VII, 1, no. 1078

Scott, Captain [Scott of the Antarctic]. *See* Scott, Robert Falcon (1868–1912).

Scott, Adrian Gilbert (1882–1963). *See under* Scott, Sir Giles Gilbert (1880–1960).

Scott, Agnes Neill. *See* Muir, Wilhelmina Johnston (1890–1970).

Scott, Alexander (*c.*1520–1582/3), poet, has three poems attributed to him in the Bannatyne manuscript (1565–8, NL Scot., published in facsimile as *The Bannatyne Manuscript*, ed. D. Fox and W. A. Ringler, 1980), and two more are 'signed' internally with the same name. Thirty more poems in the same manuscript are ascribed to 'Scott' in their colophons. All thirty-five poems are usually attributed to one and the same author (other contemporary manuscripts merely yield a few alternative versions). Beyond this, nothing about Scott can be stated with certainty.

Convergences of poetry, time, place, and loyalties single out Alexander Scott, musician, prebendary of the Chapel Royal in Stirling, as the most likely author of these poems. His origins are unknown, but his career is linked closely to royal service and circles of royal supporters. On 28 February 1539 he received the Chapel Royal prebend of Ayr; he may be the Alexander Scott, fife player, who in Paris in June 1540 was contracted to play for the Basoche, the association of the guild of clerks of the palace of justice, well-known for their annual festivities, which included pageantry and plays. His two natural sons, John and Alexander, brothers german, were legitimated on 21 November 1549. No record of a marriage exists, but a colophon to one of his poems in the Bannatyne manuscript, 'quod Scott quhen his wyfe left him', carries some weight, considering Bannatyne's connections to the poet. It has been suggested that the son Alexander the younger was the poet; he was granted the Chapel Royal prebend of Coylton secundo in 1567, and died shortly before 27 March 1581, leaving a widow, Elizabeth Lindsay, and a son, Alexander. However, in a sonnet from the early 1580s Alexander Montgomerie refers to his fellow poet 'old Scott' as still alive. Considering the fact that the father survived the son, it is highly unlikely that the son was at any time referred to as 'old Scott'. Moreover, the few datable links that can be made between historical fact and the writer of the poems attributed to Alexander Scott clearly point towards an author who had reached maturity by the early 1540s.

On 12 July 1548 Alexander Scott, organist, was granted a canon's portion of Inchmahome Priory, in absence as well as in presence, by its commendator, John Erskine. This must be the same man as Alexander Scott, parson of Balmaclellan (a Chapel Royal prebend), who eleven days later was licensed to pass to France with his master, the same John Erskine. A colophon to one of Scott's lyrics claims it treats 'of the Maister off Erskyne', which suggests Erskine's servant is the poet. The Erskines were the customary guardians of royal offspring, and Scott's licence must have been in connection with the queen's departure on 7 August to France. It is unlikely Scott stayed in France—if indeed he went—for long; French servants soon replaced most of Mary's Scottish staff.

Erskine and the earl of Cassillis were appointed curators of Mary, queen of Scots, in August 1554. On 14 January 1555 Cassillis promised one Alexander Scott an annual pension for past services, with John Bellenden as surety. Cassillis, a prominent, pragmatic royalist, promised to pay an annual pension to Scott until the latter received a monk's portion of Crossraguel Abbey. Similar provisions regarding others who took care of the young queen, and the Bellendens' status as cultural patrons of the manuscript of their kinsman Bannatyne, strongly suggest that this Alexander Scott, servant to Cassillis, is the same trusted servant of John Erskine.

In 1556–8 Alexander Scott was paid by Edinburgh town council for singing in their choir and playing on the organs. His 'New Yeir Gift' to Mary (1562, Scott's only dated poem) proves he was considered a suitable spokesman to address the queen, newly returned from France. A mixture of advice to and support of Mary, it carefully balances criticism of Catholics and protestants in the interest of the 'common weill', a *via media* that presents Scott as a social reformer rather than a protestant. Scott's status also explains why his poems stand out, both in quantity and quality, from other contemporary poetry in the Bannatyne manuscript.

From 1559 to 1570, as pensioner of the bishopric of Galloway and the abbey of Inchaffray, Scott purchased lands in Fife and Perthshire. In 1573 his son Alexander was officer of the pantry in the English household of Mary; in April 1577 he received permission to travel to Scotland, but on arrival the privy council ordered Alexander Scott, son to Alexander Scott in Stirling, not to leave Scotland without the regent's licence or contact anyone abroad but behave himself as a dutiful subject of the king; indeed, in this period 'Alexander Scott's son' presented psalms 'in English' to James VI, possibly those his father wrote (Durkan, 79). Related to this surely is a letter sent by the regent from Edinburgh on 12 May to Alexander Scott in Stirling. On 11 October 1577 John Scott, son to Alexander Scott in Stirling and preparing to pass to England, is also told to behave himself. Cautioner and surety in these matters is John Robesoun, cutler burgess of Edinburgh, son of the musician's sister. Mary in vain repeatedly asked Walsingham to make good his promise that Alexander Scott, her groom of the pantry, would be returned to her.

The musician, therefore, in the 1570s resided in Stirling, close to the Chapel Royal and the royal nursery, and was apparently still a well-known figure in royal circles, while his sons' trips to England are highly suspect in the eyes of the protestant regent. All this suggests that Alexander Scott, servant to his majesty, who in Edinburgh in November 1573 witnessed an important legal transaction involving George Bannatyne, is the musician rather than his son, which again suggests the father is the poet. Likewise, Alexander Scott, pallbearer at James VI's entry into Edinburgh in 1579, is probably the father. A complicated sequence of documents proves that the musician died between 18 June 1582 and 30 July 1583. No other relatives than those listed above are mentioned in these documents.

Of Scott's extant poems, some twenty-five are short lyrics about love. Their exceptional metrical variety and vernacular directness underpin their fresh look at conventional literature. Written in a courtly plain style, they nevertheless reveal a musician's ear for rhythm and melody (the partly polyphonic music of four lyrics survives) and cover all aspects of human sexual relationships. They instance an understanding of lyric poetry as the rhetorical composition of a putative self rather than cathartic self-expression. These lyrics are generally metaphysical rather than Petrarchan, though Scott often mixes these two modes in order to set up dialogical patterns of introspection: compressed into conjunction, these discourses, normally considered contradictory, are yoked together to form challenging existential oxymorons, creating an unexpectedly modern psychology of self. Scott's protean lyrical persona seems particularly contemporary because of the poet's awareness—frequently passed on to the persona—that any 'self' is fictional and fissiparous. In this way Scott linked a medieval and Scots poetics to stimuli more typically associated with Renaissance and modern poetry, and thus almost single-handedly prepared the kind of argumentative yet introspective lyric that culminated in the poetry of Alexander Montgomerie and, later, Robert Ayton.

Scott's other, slightly longer, works include, apart from the 'New Yeir Gift' (with 224 lines his longest poem), two psalm translations (which may indicate reformist sympathies), a burlesque jousting poem, and half a dozen quite graphic satirical and moral poems which confront their audience with sexual love as a physically fulfilling, emotionally enriching, mentally challenging, and morally transgressing phenomenon. Because of its range, explicitness, and open-endedness, Scott's work has been described as ethically incoherent, but recent revisions of such essentialist readings have restored his multilayered texts as attractively complex poems, an appealing alternative to contemporary English poetry as anthologized in Tottel's *Miscellany* (1557). THEO VAN HEIJNSBERGEN

Sources J. MacQueen, ed., *Ballattis of luve: the Scottish courtly love lyric, 1400–1570* (1970) · J. Durkan, 'The library of Mary, queen of Scots', *Mary Stewart: queen in three kingdoms*, ed. M. Lynch (1988), 71–104 · register of deeds, NA Scot., RD1 · register of testaments, NA Scot., CC8 · privy council register, NA Scot., PC1 · register of acts and decreets, NA Scot., CS7 · calendar of charters, NA Scot., RH6 · charters, NL Scot., Ch.B.1876 · J. M. Thomson and others, eds., *Registrum magni sigilli regum Scotorum / The register of the great seal of Scotland*, 11 vols. (1882–1914) · M. Livingstone, D. Hay Fleming, and others, eds., *Registrum secreti sigilli regum Scotorum / The register of the privy seal of Scotland*, 8 vols. (1908–82) • J. D. Marwick, ed., *Extracts from the records of the burgh of Edinburgh, AD 1403–1589*, [1–2, 4], Scottish Burgh RS, 2–3, 5 (1869–82) • M. Wood and R. K. Hannay, eds., *Extracts from the records of the burgh of Edinburgh, AD 1589–1603*, [6] (1927) • R. Adam, ed., *Town treasurer's accounts, 1552–1567* (1899), vol. 2 of *Edinburgh records: the burgh accounts* • *CSP Scot.* • J. R. N. MacPhail, ed., *Papers from the collection of Sir William Fraser*, Scottish History Society, 3rd ser., 5 (1924), 223–4 • W. A. Lindsay, J. Dowden, and J. M. Thomson, eds., *Charters, bulls and other documents relating to the abbey of Inchaffray*, Scottish History Society, 56 (1908) • *Documents relative to the reception at Edinburgh of the kings and queens of Scotland, 1561–1650* (1822) • G. F. Warner, ed., 'The library of James VI, 1573–83', *Miscellany … I*, Scottish History Society, 15 (1893), xi–lxxv, 586–95 • A. Lang, 'The household of Mary queen of Scots in 1573', *SHR*, 2 (1904–5), 345–55 • T. van Heijnsbergen, 'The interaction between literature and history in Queen Mary's Edinburgh: the Bannatyne manuscript and its prosopographical context', *The Renaissance in Scotland: studies in literature, religion, history, and culture offered to John Durkan*, ed. A. A. MacDonald and others (1994), 183–225

Wealth at death was owed min. £700; in receipt of over £1000 shortly before death: register of deeds, NA Scot., RD1; register of testaments, NA Scot., CC8

Scott, Alexander (*fl.* 1793). *See under* Johnston, William (*fl.* 1792–1817).

Scott, Alexander John (1768–1840), naval chaplain, the son of Robert Scott, a retired naval lieutenant, and his wife, Jane, *née* Comyn, was born at Rotherhithe, London, on 23 July 1768. His father died in 1770, leaving the family in straitened circumstances, and in 1772 his uncle, later Rear-Admiral Alexander Scott, going out to the West Indies in command of the *Lynx*, took the boy with him. For the next four years, he lived principally with Lady Payne, wife of Sir Ralph Payne (afterwards Lord Lavington), governor of the Leeward Islands, who used to call him Little Toby. In 1776 his uncle was posted to the *Experiment* on the coast of North America, where, in the attack on Sullivan's Island on 28 June, he lost his left arm, and suffered other severe wounds, which compelled him to return to England and retire from active service. Alexander returned to England at about the same time, and was sent to school. In 1777 Payne procured for him a nomination to a foundation scholarship at Charterhouse School (admitted 5 August), from where he obtained a sizarship at St John's College, Cambridge, in 1786. He was of a convivial disposition, and ran into debt. A good classicist, he abhorred mathematics, but duly graduated BA in 1790 (MA 1806). In November 1790 he was ordained deacon to a small curacy in Sussex, and in November 1792 was ordained priest. However, still in debt from Cambridge, and with his uncle refusing assistance, in February 1793 he accepted the offer of the chaplaincy of the *Berwick* with Captain Sir John Collins, an old friend of his father.

The *Berwick* was one of the fleet that went to the Mediterranean with Lord Hood, and, by the time she arrived on the station, Scott, who had devoted himself to the study of Italian and Spanish, had acquired a competent knowledge of both. French he had previously mastered, so that he quickly became of special use to his captain in his relations with Italians and Spaniards. In March 1795 the *Berwick* was captured, but Scott happened to be on leave at

Alexander John Scott (1768–1840), by Siegfried Detlev Bendixen, 1840

Leghorn, and shortly afterwards was appointed by Sir Hyde Parker to be chaplain of his flagship, the *St George*. Parker developed a warm friendship for Scott, and employed him as a foreign secretary.

Scott accompanied Parker in the *Queen* to the West Indies where, as 'the only clergyman on the spot', he was obliged to attend the execution of the *Hermione* mutineers. At Jamaica, through Parker's influence with the governor, he was appointed to a living on the island, to the value of £500 a year, tenable with his chaplaincy. In 1800 Parker returned to England, and Scott went with him on leave of absence, joining him in the *Royal George*, when Parker was appointed second in command of the Channel Fleet, and subsequently in the *London* when Parker hoisted his flag as commander-in-chief of the fleet going to the Baltic. With his remarkable aptitude for languages, Scott, who already had a good knowledge of German, quickly picked up Danish, and was at work on Russian. After the battle of Copenhagen he was employed as secretary to the conferences on shore. Nelson, who had known him in the Mediterranean, made a special request to Parker for his assistance. In this role he drew up the articles of the convention of Copenhagen but declined to subscribe his name to the convention as secretary. Afterwards, when Parker was recalled, Scott also refused Nelson's invitation to come to the *St George*, saying that 'he could not bear to leave the old admiral at the very time when he stood most in need of his company'. However, he did promise Nelson that he would come to him when he could leave Sir Hyde.

In the last days of 1801 Scott learned that his living in Jamaica would be declared vacant if he did not return at once. He accordingly went out in the *Téméraire*, arriving at Port Royal on 5 April 1802, when he was appointed by Sir John Thomas Duckworth to be chaplain of the flagship *Leviathan*, and dispatched in the former prize *Topaze* to San Domingo to try and discover why the French had sent an army of 20,000 men to that island after peace had been concluded. He failed to solve the puzzle, but found that sickness had so disorganized the French ranks that nothing was to be feared from them. While Scott was returning to the admiral in the frigate *Topaze*, the ship was struck by lightning, and he was seriously injured. To physical trouble was added the worry of finding, on arrival at Kingston, that his living had been given away by the governor. In the meantime, however, the governors of the Charterhouse had presented him to the vicarage of Southminster in Essex, which he visited early in 1803, after his passage home.

During the brief peace of Amiens, while both were staying in London, Nelson visited Scott and persuaded him to act as his foreign secretary should he be appointed to a foreign station on the resumption of war. In May 1803 Nelson was appointed to the Mediterranean, for where Scott sailed in the *Amphion*, from which he was transferred, off Toulon, to the *Victory*. As secretary and interpreter, he was able to render Nelson efficient assistance in a private capacity. Officially he was chaplain of the *Victory*, and nothing else. The arrangement by which Nelson paid him £100 a year was entirely a private one. He was frequently sent, as though on leave, to Leghorn, Naples, Barcelona, or other places; the readiness with which he gained admission to fashionable society enabled him to bring back intelligence. He continued with Nelson on this footing for his whole time in the Mediterranean, during the chase to the West Indies, and until he landed at Portsmouth on 20 August 1805. Before the end of that month he joined Nelson at Merton, and on 15 September sailed with him once more in the *Victory*. On 21 October he attended Nelson during the admiral's final hours, receiving his last wishes. On the return of the *Victory* to England, he attended the coffin as it lay in state at Greenwich, and until it was finally laid in the crypt of St Paul's.

The only public recognition Scott received for his services was the degree of DD conferred on him in 1806 by Cambridge on the royal mandate. The Admiralty refused to acknowledge his unofficial services, and even stopped his time and pay as chaplain for the many weeks he had been absent from his ship on leave, though the stoppage was eventually withdrawn. On 9 July 1807 he married Mary Frances (1785–1811), daughter of Thomas Ryder, registrar of the Charterhouse; they had two daughters, the younger of whom was Margaret *Gatty (1809–1873), writer and artist.

Scott settled down as vicar of Southminster (from 1803 to 1840) on a narrow income, scantily extended by a small half pay. In 1816 Lord Liverpool presented him to the crown living of Catterick in Yorkshire (vicar 1816 to 1840, in plurality with his other living); at the same time he was appointed chaplain to the prince regent, which gave him the right to hold two livings. From then he lived mostly at Catterick, engaged in his professional duties and accumulating a large library, mostly of foreign books. Among them were represented forty different languages, though his knowledge of many of these was limited. He died at Catterick on 24 July 1840, and was buried in the churchyard of Ecclesfield, near Sheffield, on 31 July.

J. K. LAUGHTON, *rev.* ROGER MORRISS

Sources A. Gatty and M. Gatty, eds., *Recollections of the life of the Rev. A. J. Scott* (1842) · G. Taylor, *A history of the chaplains of the Royal Navy* (1928) · private information (1897) · P. Mackesy, *The war in the Mediterranean, 1803–1810* (1957) · Venn, *Alum. Cant.*

Archives NMM, corresp. and papers · Royal Naval Museum, Portsmouth, corresp. and papers as secretary to Lord Nelson, and secretary to Hyde Parker | BL, letters to Lady Hamilton and her mother, Egerton MS 3782 · BL, letters to Lord Nelson and Earl Nelson, Add. MSS 3932, 34939, 34992

Likenesses S. D. Bendixen, portrait, 1840, NMM [*see illus.*]

Scott, Alexander John [Sandy] (1805–1866), theological dissident and educationist, was born on 26 March 1805 at the Middle Parish manse, Greenock, the fifth of six children born to Dr John Scott (1763–1836), a Church of Scotland parish minister, and his wife, Susanna, daughter of Alexander Fisher of Dychmount. Sandy Scott, as he was called, was educated at the local grammar school in Greenock, and in October 1819 matriculated at Glasgow University, graduating MA in May 1824. From October 1823 to May 1827 he also studied theology at the Glasgow Divinity Hall, and on 27 September 1827 was licensed as a preacher in the Church of Scotland by the presbytery of Paisley. Within months of his licensing Scott began to express doubt concerning the traditional Calvinism of the Scottish church, specifically its doctrine of the love of God being limited to the elect. At about the same time he formed his lifelong friendships with Thomas Erskine of Linlathen and John McLeod Campbell of Row. By 1828 virulent opposition to Scott and his friends had developed from within the national church. In the summer of that year Scott joined Edward Irving in London, where he was promised theological freedom. He began his assistantship at the Scots Church, Regent Square, in the autumn of 1828, preaching daily to the poor of Westminster, and at the same time influencing Irving's theology. In return it was likely the latter who introduced Scott to Samuel Taylor Coleridge, Thomas Carlyle, and other literary figures in London. Coleridge he came to regard as the greatest single influence on his thinking.

It was during this time in London that Scott's theology developed a distinctive emphasis on the spirit. He was drawn to the vitality of the early church and its more organic rather than organizational form. In contrast to what he saw to be the rigid doctrine and ecclesiology of the nineteenth-century Scottish church he developed a theology that appealed to the authority of the spiritual conscience, an inner faculty capable of discerning spiritual truth. This in part led him to write and preach on the spiritual gifts of the New Testament church. Irving and others, some of whom were later to form the Catholic Apostolic church, were encouraged by Scott to believe that the gifts of the early church should characterize the church in every age. The charismatic outbursts of 1830, first in Port Glasgow and later in London, can be seen as directly related to Scott's teaching, as well as being the first appearance of modern pentecostalism. Scott, however, considered the phenomenon to be religious hallucination and immediately distanced himself from it. This eventually led to a painful parting with Irving.

Meanwhile Scott had received a call in January 1830 to the Scots Church, Woolwich, an event which ultimately was to lead to his heresy trials. The presbytery of London's examination of him, extending over most of the year, attracted press attention and public interest. Scott refused to accept the Westminster confession as an expression of his own faith, for it denied God's grace as being for all people. He objected also to the confession's sabbatarianism and to its understanding of ordination as limiting the work of the Holy Spirit to the church. Scott published at this time two works which further articulated the basis of his divergence from the church's official doctrine. In both *On the Divine Will* (1830) and *Hints for Meditation on Acquaintance with God* (1831), he stated that God's divinity is to be understood in terms of Christ's humanity, and that therefore the love that is seen in Christ is a reflection of God's love for all people. Also he questioned the confession's doctrine of total depravity, and, as proponents of the Celtic stream of spirituality in Scotland before him had done, asserted that humanity is made in the image and likeness of God.

In 1831 Scott's trial was taken up by his home presbytery in Scotland. On 4 May, with only one dissenting vote, the presbytery of Paisley declared that he could no longer be considered a licentiate of the Church of Scotland. Scott appealed to the highest ecclesiastical court in the land, the Church of Scotland's general assembly. There on 27 May 1831 he asked to be tried, not by the church's subordinate standard of faith, the seventeenth-century Westminster confession, but by the holy scriptures. The former, he said, contained doctrines that were contrary to the word of God. Such a direct assault upon the theology of the Kirk's confession was unprecedented, and it met with no sympathy in the assembly. He was unanimously deposed from the ministry, and all ministers were forbidden from employing him to preach in their pulpits.

In the midst of his heresy trials Scott married Ann (*d.* 1888), the third daughter of Alan Ker of Greenock, on 14 December 1830. Together they returned to Woolwich, where a large part of the Scots Church chose to form an independent congregation around Scott at Providence Chapel in New Road. In January 1839 they relocated to the Welsh Chapel on Parson's Hill, near Herbert Road. The Scotts lived in Plumstead Common, just below Shooter's Hill, overlooking the Thames. It was here that their two children were born, Susan Fisher and John Alexander (*d.* 1894).

For the first fifteen years after his deposition, Scott's base for teaching and preaching was his little Woolwich Chapel, but it was during these years that his sphere of influence expanded. Increasingly he translated his theology into philosophical and educational, as well as socio-political, concerns, and lectured widely on these subjects, especially in London and Edinburgh. His close friends now included Carlyle, J. C. Hare, Daniel Macmillan, and F. D. Maurice, all of whom spoke of his breadth of vision and his power of expression. He often lectured on the theme of the unity of truth, and especially the relationship between science and religion. At a time when many religious minds were beginning to react to the early evolutionary thought of Lyell and Darwin, Scott emphasized that there is only one ultimate source of truth, and that to truly understand is to find a unity in all things, both spiritual and material.

During the Woolwich years Scott travelled abroad, especially in Switzerland and France, and formed friendships with the Swiss theologian Alexandre Vinet, and the French painter Ary Scheffer, and particularly with Frédéric Chopin. Observing the socio-political situation in France he turned his attention to the reform of education in Britain, and in his *Social Systems of the Present Day* (1841) related the principles of Christianity to the political situation in Britain, in the conviction that the application of Christ's teaching was the key to social unity.

Late in 1846 the Scotts took up residence at 40 Gloucester Crescent, Regent's Park, which became a regular meeting place for many of his literary friends, now including Thackeray, Ruskin, Francis Newman, and the controversial actress Fanny Kemble. As well as his public lecturing throughout Britain, Scott was now writing for the *North British Review* and continued to pursue his commitment to the education of the working classes. In April 1848, along with Maurice, Hare, Charles Kingsley, and John Ludlow, he became one of the founders of Christian socialism and a contributor to *Politics for the People*, the twofold aim of which was the daring attempt in mid nineteenth-century Britain to Christianize socialism and to socialize Christianity.

Also in 1848, on 4 November, Scott was appointed to the professorship of English language and literature at University College, London, and in October of the following year became one of the founders and first professors of Bedford College in London, the first centre of higher education for women in Britain based on the principles of religious freedom. Two of his lectures were published as *Suggestions on Female Education* in 1849.

In October 1850 Scott became the first principal of Owens College, later Manchester University, as well as the professor of English language and literature and of moral and mental philosophy. Like University College, it also was established as a centre of higher education totally free from religious tests. Early in 1851 the Scotts took up residence at 2 Park Place, Halliwell Lane, in Manchester. During the critical and formative years of Owens College, Scott set the highest of academic standards, often in the face of pressure from the city to offer a more practically based education. Owing to failing health, however, and a lack of administrative ability, he resigned the principalship in May 1857, but his personal influence as a teacher continued to create a profound effect on many students. It was during these years that some of the future leaders of English nonconformity, such as James Baldwin Brown the younger and David Worthington Simon, came under his theological influence. Similarly, some of the later nineteenth-century Scottish reformers of theology, such as Norman Macleod, Robert Herbert Story, and John Tulloch, were influenced by him in their formative years. And it was during the Manchester period that perhaps his best known disciple, the novelist George MacDonald, was inspired by both his theology and the central place given in his thought to the use of the imagination. These members of a younger generation were inspired by his breadth of thought and largeness of soul. The extraordinary power of his extemporaneous speech, combined with his striking physical appearance, jet black hair and pale, massive features, created memorable impressions. Although his health increasingly failed him, Scott was determined to pursue the development of education for the working classes, and in 1858, along with others, he founded the Manchester Working Men's College in the mechanics' institute on David Street. During his final years he more and more needed to take time away from Manchester to regain strength. In the autumn of 1865 he travelled to Veytaux on the northern shore of Lake Geneva. There, on 12 January 1866, Scott died; he was buried in the cemetery at Clarens. J. PHILIP NEWELL

Sources J. P. Newell, 'A. J. Scott and his circle', PhD diss., U. Edin., 1981 • A. J. Scott, *Discourses* (1866) • J. P. Newell, *Listening for the heartbeat of God: a Celtic spirituality* (1997) • J. Finlayson, *Memoir of Rev. Alex. J. Scott, M.A.* (1886) • *The Scotsman* (19 Jan 1866) • *The Spectator* (3 Feb 1866) • *The Guardian* (20 Jan 1866) • W. Hanna, *Letters of Thomas Erskine* (1877) • G. MacDonald, *George MacDonald and his wife* (1924) • J. Hunter, 'Alexander Scott', *The Expositor*, 21 (1921) • 'Case of Mr Scott: heresy', *Caledonian Mercury* (28 May 1831) • *Testimonials to Alexander J. Scott, a candidate for the chair of logic and metaphysics in the University of Edinburgh*, 2 pts (1856) • *CGPLA Eng. & Wales* (1866) • NA Scot. • *Greenock Advertiser* (17 Dec 1830) • D. Campbell, *Memorials of J. M. Campbell* (1877), 2.125

Likenesses engraving (after bust by H. S. Leifchild, 1860), repro. in W. Shaw, *Manchester old and new*, 2 (1896), 93 • photograph, U. Edin., New Coll. L.; repro. in Scott, *Discourses* [attached inside front cover] • portrait, repro. in J. Hair, *Regent Square* (1899), 86

Wealth at death under £600: administration, 30 June 1866, *CGPLA Eng. & Wales*

Scott, Alexander MacCallum (1874–1928), politician and author, was born on 16 June 1874 at Boathouse, Blantyre, Lanarkshire, the first of three children of John Scott (1815–1888), a fruit grower and sometime shopkeeper, and his second wife, Rebecca MacCallum (*d.* in or after 1926). His father—a United Presbyterian church elder, temperance stalwart, and member of the local school board—left an enduring impression. Rebecca Scott, widowed with an income of £150 a year, was ambitious for her oldest child.

Educated at Polmont public school and Falkirk high school, Scott went to Glasgow University where he was a contemporary of John Buchan, W. M. R. Pringle, Robert Horne, and H. N. Brailsford. He was active in Liberal clubs and the students' representative council, and president of the union during 1896–7. Graduating in law in 1897 he ate his dinners at the Middle Temple, and from 1908 practised sporadically on the western circuit. Purposefully engaged in Liberal politics, he served as secretary of the League of Liberals against Aggression and Militarism (1900–03), becoming secretary of the New Reform Club and a Lewisham borough councillor (1903–6). In spite of these successes, he was beset with a sense of isolation. Social intimacy with clever radical contemporaries like Brailsford, Francis Hirst, and J. L. Hammond was tentative and transient.

Eager to supplement his income, and consolidate his credentials as a radical commentator, Scott published *The Truth about Tibet* in 1905. Extensive travel in Scandinavia and Russia resulted in two books in 1908, *Through Finland to St Petersburg* and *Licensing in Scandinavia*. *Beyond the Baltic* (1925) later recorded his observations, including meetings in Kaunas, Lithuania, with former ministers of the Belarusian Democratic Republic, and devoted a chapter to 'White Russia' (Belarus), a nation 'concealed behind the present colours of the map of Europe' (*Belarusian Chronicle*, no. 3, spring 1998). Planned books on democratic theory, architecture, and many other subjects were never written. But, believing that Winston Churchill was 'born to greatness', Scott turned a series of magazine articles into a biography whose proofs were read by Churchill before its publication in 1905. Over the next two decades he wrote political columns in *The Observer*, *The People's Journal*, and *Reynolds' News*.

Scott's appointment in 1909 as private secretary to the secretary for Scotland, John Sinclair, first Baron Pentland, helped open the door to a parliamentary career. The unexpected retirement of his friend James William Cleland created a vacancy in the safe Liberal seat of Glasgow Bridgeton. Scott entered the House of Commons in December 1910, having married Jessie, daughter of Dr John Hutchison, former rector of Glasgow high school, earlier in the year.

In the Commons Scott set out to overcome 'the frowning battlements of the Inner ring' (diary, 18 Dec 1912). His diary records a relentlessly self-critical and despondent back-bench existence. Always on the lookout for causes to make his own, he wore his radicalism conspicuously, advocating a minimum wage and reforms in housing, education, and the poor law. He was a vocal devolutionist, a founding executive member of the Liberal foreign affairs group in 1911, but most visible as a tirelessly immovable anti-suffragist. Philip Snowden, for one, did not think he went down well. Scott was, he recalled, 'a strange character. He always struck me as having the typical Scottish metaphysical mind. He spoke with great deliberation. He seemed as though he was laboriously dragging out his words, not from his head but from his chest' (Snowden, 1.313).

Disillusioned by Asquith's wartime leadership but never seduced by Lloyd George, Scott sensed that there might yet be a great role for Churchill. He produced *Winston Churchill in Peace and War* in spring 1916. Churchill read the proofs, telling his wife that the notes he had provided made him 'feel how important it is for me to put on record a full & complete account of this gt series of war events' (Gilbert, 1479). Scott had concluded that political adversity had taught his subject restraint and an understanding of the long game, a game that he too had long sought to play.

At Churchill's request Scott joined the back-bench malcontents of the Liberal war committee, and provided candid assistance in preparing the former first lord's evidence for the Dardanelles commission. Late in 1916 Scott was chosen as secretary by the Scottish unofficial Liberal members. He declined an invitation in January 1917 to become parliamentary private secretary to the new secretary for Scotland, Robert Munro. But on Churchill's return to office later that year he joined him as parliamentary private secretary at the Ministry of Munitions and followed him to the War Office. To the discomfort of both men, he severed the link with Churchill in 1919 as a blind alley he could not afford (diary, 20 Nov, 14 Dec 1919).

A vote against Asquith in the debate (9 May 1918) on the allegations by General Sir Frederick Maurice that Lloyd George had misled the Commons about the state of the army in France ensured Scott's return as a couponed Liberal in 1918. Twelve years of hope for office were finally rewarded in mid-1922 when at Churchill's suggestion Lloyd George made him the coalition government's Scottish whip. Churchill's proposal that Scott also become parliamentary secretary for the Scottish board of health was not taken up.

Scott had defeated James Maxton at the general election of 1918 but had no chance of repelling him in the Glasgow Labour surge of November 1922. As the reunited Liberal Party candidate for Glasgow Partick in December 1923 Scott ran a poor third after openly criticizing the Liberal leadership for offering only a 'blank negative to Socialism' (Lyman, 254). Persuaded that Labour, not a disintegrating Liberal Party, was where radicals now belonged, he joined the Labour Party, Independent Labour Party, and the Fabian Society late in 1924. Two years later he was adopted as prospective Labour candidate for East Aberdeenshire, the seat held by the colourful progressive tory Robert Boothby.

Both Scott—an early supporter of 'aeroplaning' (diary, 2 Jan 1912)—and his wife were killed in a plane crash into the Puget Sound while flying from Victoria, British Columbia, to Seattle on 25 August 1928. Their only child, a son, survived them. Assessing his own political career, Scott attributed his failure to penetrate the inner ring to his lack of wealth, powerful friends, personal magnetism, and 'intellectual power to force my way' (diary, 3 Dec 1921). He might fairly have added the misfortune of entering a parliament already replete with ambitious and abler men.

CAMERON HAZLEHURST

Sources A. M. Scott, diary, U. Glas. L. • *Dod's Parliamentary Companion* • 'Mr A. MacCallum Scott, MP', *Lloyd George Liberal Magazine*, 1/8 (May 1921), 456 • *WWW* • *WWBMP* • *Liberal yearbook* • private information (2004) [J. H. MacCallum Scott, son] • C. Hazlehurst, *Politicians at war, July 1914 to May 1915* (1971) • J. Adam Smith, *John Buchan* (1965) • I. G. C. Hutchison, *A political history of Scotland, 1832–1924* (1986) • A. J. Dorey, 'Radical liberal criticism of British foreign policy, 1906–1914', DPhil diss., U. Oxf., 1964 • A. J. A. Morris, *Radicalism against war, 1906–1914* (1972) • B. Harrison, *Separate spheres: the opposition to women's suffrage in Britain* (1978) • M. Gilbert, ed., *Winston S. Churchill*, companion vol., 3/2 (1972) • P. B. Johnson, *Land fit for heroes: the planning of British reconstruction, 1916–1919* (1968) • R. W. Lyman, *The first labour government, 1924* (1957) • C. Coote, *A companion of honour: the story of Walter Elliot* (1965) • T. Wilson, *The downfall of the liberal party, 1914–1935* (1966) • CAC Cam., Churchill papers • P. Snowden, *Autobiography* (1934)

Archives U. Glas. L., corresp., diaries, journals, and papers | CAC Cam., Churchill papers

Likenesses photograph, *c*.1921, repro. in 'Mr A. MacCallum Scott, MP', 456

Wealth at death £7921 18*s*. 9*d*.: confirmation, 24 May 1929, *CCI*

Scott, Alexander Mackie (1920–1989), poet and scholar of Scottish literature, was born on 28 November 1920 in a two-roomed cottage at 13 Western Road in the Woodside suburb of Aberdeen, the only child of Alexander Mackie Scott (1894–1976), a power-loom tuner, and his wife, Magdalina Cheyne (1895–1988), daughter of Robert Adams and his wife, Elizabeth. His parents were both Scottish; his forebears were craftsmen and farmers from the rural north-east of Scotland.

While Scott was at the Kittybrewster primary school in Aberdeen, he began to imitate stories he found in children's comic magazines. Between 1932 and 1935 this led to his creating in longhand his own weekly magazine, complete with serial stories and hand-drawn illustrations. In the tales he devised, fantasies of buccaneers, detectives, and 'redskins' were juxtaposed with versions of the English public-school life depicted by Frank Richards and others. These last retained their interest for him (he was working on a study of Richards before he died). He also wrote much verse in English following Romantic and Victorian models. 'The Red Planet Calling Red Circle' was his first publication, appearing in the *Hotspur* (13 July 1935) while he was at the Aberdeen central school. When he entered Aberdeen University in 1939, Scott was not only writing copious amounts of poetry but had attempted a novel, and was writing anti-war stories and dramatic sketches as well as material for school and undergraduate reviews. He started to read contemporary poetry while a first-year undergraduate, and discovered Burns during summer 1940.

In autumn 1939 Scott joined the Peace Pledge Union, but his pacificism crumbled in the crisis of Britain's isolation at the beginning of the Second World War; he was not called up until November 1941. He was commissioned in the Royal Artillery but transferred to the Gordon Highlanders. He landed on D-day with the 5th/7th Gordon Highlanders. Wounded at the battle of Falaise Gap in August 1944, he returned to duty and won the Military Cross for his conduct in leading a company attack during the battle of the Reichswald Forest on 8 February 1945. He married Catherine Goodall (*b.* 1920), a schoolteacher, on 10 May 1944. They had two sons, Crombie and Ewan.

After the war Scott returned to Aberdeen University to complete his degree in English language and literature, and graduated in 1947 with first-class honours. Scott's commitment to Scottish literature developed during the later years of the war: an unpublished poem suggests that he was reading Hugh MacDiarmid in barracks in Germany before being demobbed, and his concluding post-war years as an undergraduate consolidated his knowledge of Scottish verse through the ages. He began writing verse in Scots during the war, and thereafter wrote in both Scots and English; he claimed that the choice of language for a new poem was dictated by the language of the first line which came to him.

While completing his degree, Scott was briefly an editor of the *North-East Review*, an Aberdeen-based literary journal in which some of his earliest published poems appeared. This was the first of his several editorships of small magazines, a field in which his contribution was individual, important, and distinguished. He was offered, but refused, a scholarship to Merton College, Oxford. His first academic employment was as assistant lecturer in English at the University of Edinburgh (1947–8), but within a year he was a lecturer in Scottish literature at the University of Glasgow, and he lived in Glasgow for the rest of his life.

Scott's first collection of poetry, *The Latest in Elegies*, appeared in 1949, and thereafter he was seen as one of a group of poets sometimes referred to as the Lallans Makars, associated with MacDiarmid's programme for a nationalist literary revival. A brief *Selected Poems* followed in 1950. *Mouth Music* came out in 1954 but he wrote few poems in the mid-1950s, and apparently none at all between 1957 and 1965. His impulse to write was subject to hiatuses which he found distressing.

Much of Scott's creative energy in the 1950s was directed towards drama. The short comedy *The Last Time I Saw Paris* won a Festival of Britain award for verse drama in 1951, and several other plays gained him lesser awards in the 1950s. In all, seventeen plays can be traced, many written for radio. Most are in Scots, several in verse. Three are full-length stage plays and were produced by the Glasgow Citizens' Theatre. They include *Right Royal* (produced in 1954) with which he had a notable success. Later Citizens' productions of his work were less successful, though still attractive to popular audiences. He turned away from the stage, however, believing that commercial theatre in Scotland no longer provided sufficient encouragement for distinctively Scottish drama.

Scott returned to poetry from the mid-sixties until the early 1980s, when his poetry petered out again. His work from this period includes *Cantrips* (1968) and *Selected Poems, 1943–1974* (1975). One of his most frequently anthologized poems is 'Coronach', written in memory of fallen comrades on the second anniversary of D-day. It is characteristic of him in its use of Scots to combine terse, tough manliness with tender emotion. It is, however, uncharacteristic of him in being a war poem: this successful soldier wrote surprisingly few poems reflecting his wartime experiences, and allowed only a few of those poems to see print. Among his generation of Scottish poets he was one of the most craftsman-like, producing poems reflecting a care for traditional features of sound and form. He presents himself in many of his poems in Scots as a downright, plain-speaking common man who nevertheless is compassionate towards the follies and sufferings of humankind. He is also seen as placing a premium on intellectual and aesthetic values. His characteristic voice leans towards the satirical and the humorous, perhaps best exemplified in 'Scotched', the famous sequence of tersely hilarious two-line squibs evoking typical Scottish attitudes on a medley of topics, such as 'Scotch Passion'. Many of his best poems are satirical or critical responses to aspects of life and popular culture after the 1950s. On the other hand, he produced love poems of great tenderness. Most of his virtues as a poet are found in his long and subtle poem on his native city, 'Heart of Stone', the writing of which brought him a new creative impetus in the mid-1960s.

As an academic Scott contributed immensely to the emergence of Scottish literature as a subject in universities and schools (he was made the first head of the department of Scottish literature at Glasgow in 1971). His major contribution to research came early in his career. His work on the poet William Soutar was particularly important. He produced an edition of Soutar's diaries, *Diaries of a Dying Man* (1954), and a study of the poet, published in 1958. He also produced selected editions of the poems of his own sixteenth-century namesake (1952), and one of the poems of William Jeffrey (1951). He was a gifted anthologist, and at different stages in his career edited important small journals, including *The Scots Review* (1950–51) and *The Saltire Review* (1954–8). He was joint editor of *The Scottish Review* (1980–85) and *New Writing Scotland* (1983–6). He was skilled in spotting talent in emergent writers, and his encouragement and nurturing of these were not the least of his contributions to the literary life of Scotland. His vigorous-minded critical comment found regular outlet in the press and on radio. Above all, he was a memorable university teacher, inspiring generations of students, several of whom became academics in Scottish literature.

Alexander Scott was tall and striking in appearance, his strong features crowned by a profusion of long hair which he never lost. His forceful personality and strong opinions made him a powerful presence in committees, and his energy and commitment were decisive in establishing a number of fledgeling literary and academic projects throughout his career. His combativeness was both valuable and a drawback: in the small world of Scottish literary and cultural politics he made some enemies. It may also have contributed to his failure to be awarded a personal chair; his university rank was that of reader when he retired.

In 1977 Scott was diagnosed as suffering from emphysema, which gradually worsened; he retired as head of department in 1983. He died of lung cancer on 14 September 1989 at Stobhill Hospital in Glasgow, and was cremated at Maryhill on 16 September. He was survived by his wife. His ashes were scattered in the O'Dell Garden, King's College, Aberdeen, on 2 December. A large collection of poetry, 'Incantations: Poems and Diversions' was unpublished at his death; it was incorporated into the *Collected*

Poems (1994). Much unpublished and uncollected verse remains. Despite his intermittent career as a poet, he remains, nevertheless, one of the leading poets in Scotland to build on Hugh MacDiarmid's achievement.

DAVID ROBB

Sources personal knowledge (2004) · private information (2004) [Catherine Scott, widow] · autobiography, NL Scot. · A. Scott, 'Growing up with granite', *As I remember: ten Scottish authors recall how writing began for them*, ed. M. Lindsay (1979), 89–105 · b. cert. · b. cert. [Alexander Mackie Scott, father] · b. cert. [Magdalina Cheyne Adams, mother] · d. cert. [Alexander Mackie Scott, father] · d. cert. [Magdalina Cheyne Scott, mother]

Archives NL Scot., corresp. and MSS

Likenesses E. Coia, drawing, *c*.1975, priv. coll. · C. Scott, drawing, 1988, priv. coll. · K. Kynoch, oils, 1994, priv. coll. · A. Catlin, photograph, repro. in A. Catlin, *Natural light: portraits of Scottish writers* (1985)

Scott [*née* Spottiswoode], **Alicia Anne** (1810–1900), poet, was born on 24 June 1810 at Spottiswoode, East Lothian, the eldest child of John Spottiswoode (*c*.1779–1866) and Helen Wauchope (*d*. 1870), daughter of the laird of Niddrie, a veteran Jacobite who as a boy had met Prince Charles Edward Stuart before Culloden. Her two brothers became soldiers, and her sister married Sir Hugh Hume Campbell of Marchmont. She grew up, and lived all her life, in a close network of border family relationships.

Alicia was well educated. From her father she acquired a lifelong fascination with botany, geology, and archaeology. She was proficient in French and Italian. The landscape painter Peter DeWint taught her watercolour painting, a lifelong hobby, and Manuel Patricio Rodriguez García was her singing-master. She sang and played the harp to considerable effect. Her great-niece recalled that 'She was always making tunes, or recalling the old ones with which her memory was stored; and she would sing to herself for hours during those interminable drives, of which, in later life, she was so fond' (Scott, xvi). In childhood Alicia collected and wrote down the songs and stories heard in the Spottiswoode cottages.

Soon after her sister's marriage in 1834 Alicia was staying with her at Marchmont and found there Allan Cunningham's four-volume work of 1825, *Songs of Scotland, Ancient and Modern*. Cunningham had reprinted a song of two stanzas, 'Annie Laurie', from a little collection of ballads edited by Charles Kirkpatrick Sharpe. Sharpe in turn had taken down the words from the recitation of Miss Margaret Laurie of Maxwelton, his father's first cousin. The ardent author of the lyric was reputed to be William Douglas of Fingland (*b*. 1672) who had been attracted by Anna (1682–1764), the ninth and last child of Sir Robert Laurie, first baronet, of Maxwelton in Dumfriesshire. (Unromantically, William had gone on to marry the daughter of an Edinburgh merchant and Anna a nearby landowner, Alexander Fergusson of Craigdarroch.)

As Alicia told the story herself, she had in her head the tune she had made to 'an absurd ballad, originally Norwegian, I believe, called Kempie Kaye' (Scott, xxiii). She saw that the words of 'Annie Laurie' would fit it, but did not like the second stanza, so she altered that and added a third completely her own. Her sister and brother-in-law admired the result, and accordingly she wrote it down for them.

Alicia's work was tantamount to bowdlerization. While she hardly changed the first stanza, in the second, the lines

She's jimp about the middle,
Her waist you may weel span …
And she has a rolling eye …

—with their intimations of carnality—give way to vaguer adoration:

Her face it is the fairest
That ever sun shone on …
And dark blue is her e'e …

Thus rendered unexceptionable, the song passed into general circulation. British soldiers sang it during the Crimean War of 1853–6. Afterwards, the author gave 'Annie Laurie' and several other songs to Lonsdale to publish for a bazaar in aid of the widows and orphans of war casualties. 'Annie Laurie' travelled thereafter all over the world, from the parlours of Europe to the Antipodean outback, and eventually to the recording studios of London and New York.

On 16 March 1836 Alicia Spottiswoode married Lord John Scott (1809–1860), brother of the duke of Buccleuch. He had a public role in London as MP for Roxburghshire, and after a couple of years their chief residence was Cawston in Warwickshire, his property by inheritance. Fortunately, though, he was a keen fisherman, hunter, and yachtsman who did not baulk at his wife's preference for an outdoor life in Scotland whenever possible. They had no children and the landmarks in her life were mostly bereavements. Her sister died young; Lord John Scott died in 1860; both her brothers were dead before her father expired in 1866; and her mother's demise in 1870 left her quite alone as chatelaine of Spottiswoode and Cawston.

But Scott's zest for life was unabated. So was her passion for Scotland. She joked, 'I would rather live in a pigsty in Scotland than in a palace in England' (Scott, xxxix). Trim-figured, simply dressed, with a red shawl round her shoulders, her fine skin unblemished, her eyes still deep blue, the incessantly charitable 'Lady John' went far beyond the calls of *noblesse oblige*. She sympathized with the travelling people, and had a special concern for 'imbeciles' and people with physical deformities—her bailiff had to restrain her from offering a whole house to the famous Elephant Man Joseph Merrick. In the last three decades of her life she travelled every summer to Thurso, in the far north, where she bathed in the icy waters of the Pentland Firth and took great interest in local archaeological sites. While there she became aware of the oppression of the inhabitants of Fair Isle by the truck system, and bought them a schooner big enough to take their fish catch independently to market. Her youngest relatives found her fun. Her great-niece recalled that 'she had no small fidgets about torn clothes, wet feet, getting into mischief or being late for lessons' (ibid., xlii). She organized wild adventurous hunts for real 'treasure'. She was fit as a flea, and taking a great interest in the Second South African War, just before influenza swept her away on 12 March

1900. She was buried in a blinding snowstorm in the old kirk at Westruther on the sixty-fourth anniversary of her marriage.

After Scott's death her great-niece collected over sixty sets of verses by her. Alicia Scott was an accomplished practitioner of styles popular in her youth, when Scott, Campbell, and Byron had dominated taste. Much of her verse is in Scots. She wrote Jacobite songs and poems about landscape, elegiac verses, hymns, and imitation ballads. Though three of her poems were chosen by Catherine Kerrigan for her *Anthology of Scottish Women Poets* (1991), it is just one of these, 'Annie Laurie', which makes a large mark on history. As a product of oral tradition which came her way via two collectors it represents the complex processes by which favourite Scottish songs have been fabricated and transmitted. (Her claim to have written 'Annie Laurie' is actually rather stronger than Burns's *vis-à-vis* 'A red, red rose'.) As an aristocratic lady working in Scottish folk tradition, she is of a distinguished company which includes Jean Elliott, Lady Anne Lindsay, and Lady Nairne, all of whom wrote songs which became standards. ANGUS CALDER

Sources A. A. Scott, *Songs and verses*, ed. M. Warrender (1904) · G. Irving, *Annie Laurie: the romantic story of the song and its heroine* (1948) · A. Cunningham, ed., *The songs of Scotland, ancient and modern*, 4 vols. (1825)
Archives NL Scot., music MSS

Scott, Andrew (**1757–1839**), poet, was born at Bowden, Roxburghshire, on 19 April 1757, the son of John Scott (*d. c.*1769), day labourer, and his wife, Rachel, *née* Briggs. Educated at only a very basic level, Scott was for some time a cowherd, and then a farm-servant. At the age of nineteen he enlisted in the 80th regiment, with whom he served through five campaigns in the American War of Independence. He wrote original songs to entertain his comrades; most of this material was lost. After the surrender of Cornwallis at Yorktown on 19 October 1781 Scott was for some time a prisoner of war in Long Island. He returned to Scotland after the armistice of 4 January 1784, and settled at Bowden, where he married and had five children. He worked as a farm labourer to support his family, and was also encouraged by Walter Scott, John Gibson Lockhart, and others to continue writing poetry. He published several editions of verse entitled *Poems, Chiefly in the Scottish Dialect* (1811; 1821; 1826). He acted as a church officer for several years before his death at Bowden on 22 May 1839.
T. W. BAYNE, *rev.* SARAH COUPER

Sources A. Scott, *Poems, chiefly in the Scottish dialect* (1808), iii–v · J. C. Goodfellow, *Border biography* (1890), 56–60 · C. Rogers, *The modern Scottish minstrel, or, The songs of Scotland of the past half-century*, 1 (1855), 260–62 · Irving, *Scots.*
Likenesses R. Scott, engraving (after G. Watson), repro. in Scott, *Poems*

Scott, Anna [Anne], **duchess of Monmouth and *suo jure* duchess of Buccleuch** (**1651–1732**), noblewoman, was born in Dundee on 11 February 1651, the third daughter of Francis Scott, second earl of Buccleuch (1626–1651), and his wife, Margaret Leslie (*d.* 1688), daughter of John Leslie,

Anna Scott, duchess of Monmouth and *suo jure* duchess of Buccleuch (1651–1732), by Sir Godfrey Kneller, *c.*1688 [with her sons James Scott, earl of Dalkeith (left), and Henry Scott, earl of Deloraine (right)]

earl of Rothes, and widow of Alexander Leslie, Lord Balgonie. It was her father's early death, and more particularly the absence of a male heir and the nature of the entailing of the Buccleuch estate, that made Anna, following the premature deaths of her two elder sisters, Mary (in 1661) and Margaret (in 1652), so valuable a pawn in the family politics of Restoration Scotland, whence she progressed to the margins of the larger dynastic politics of later Stuart Britain.

The complex entail of the Buccleuch inheritance informed the objective of Anna's formidable mother, in partnership with her third husband, David, second earl of Wemyss, which was to prevent any attempted marriage to the Buccleuch heiresses by the heirs of John Hay, second earl of Tweeddale. The latter, an ambitious close kinsman and Buccleuch creditor, was married to Jean Scott, sister of Earl Francis and next heir to the Buccleuch inheritance after Francis's three daughters. To this end, eleven-year-old Mary was given in an illegal under-age marriage to another kinsman, fourteen-year-old Walter Scott, created earl of Tarras. The illegality was used to prevent Tarras's subsequently being able to claim the marriage settlement's extremely generous provision upon Mary's early death. Anna remained the Buccleuch heir, and the same anti-Tweeddale objectives would see Lady Wemyss approach Charles II in May 1661 with the plan for Anna's marriage to Charles's eldest bastard, James Crofts (1649–1685), later duke of Monmouth [*see* Scott, James]. The marriage contract would see Crofts adopt the Scott surname, but in its provision for him it violated both the original entail and the laws of Scotland, settling the inheritance upon Monmouth and his heir should Anna predecease him. Concern in the Scottish parliament was overridden and the contract ratified there.

The marriage of Anna and James Scott was celebrated at Whitehall on 20 April 1663 and consummated on 9 February 1665. It lasted in conjugal terms until 1679, and produced six children, of whom only two sons, including Henry *Scott, first earl of Deloraine, survived childhood. On the scaffold Monmouth remained professedly steady to his six-year attachment to Lady Henrietta Wentworth, his last but not his first infidelity. The Monmouths had in common only financial extravagance and a particular excellence in dancing, which was unhappily ended in May 1668 when Anna sustained a dislocated hip which lamed her for life. That she had no influence over the malleable 'Prince Perkin' was ultimately to her advantage. Her priority following her husband's 1685 rebellion was to protect the interests of her sons and more broadly the Buccleuch inheritance, with which she identified in a manner that echoed the determination and intelligence that had characterized her mother. Having spent the duration of Monmouth's rebellion in the Tower, and with the injured monarch, James II, predisposed in her favour, she finally secured her husband's confirmation that she had known 'nothing of his last design', thereby freeing her sons—and thus the Buccleuch inheritance—from the penalties of attainder. Attainder having forfeited Monmouth's English titles, the Buccleuch honours, now a dukedom, and estates were formally restored to Anna and thence her eldest son, restoring the original entail, on 17 November 1687.

There is no evidence of Anna's having been marked by the smallpox which she contracted in 1661, but contemporary commentators remark on wit rather than beauty. In character she was confessedly self-sufficient and reserved. Her career at court survived its Restoration and revolution incarnations, being sustained by her friendship with Queen Catherine, the then duke and duchess of York, and the future queens Mary and Anne, and extending to Princess, later Queen, Caroline. It was distinguished by a literary and artistic patronage, with roots in her pre-accident support of amateur theatricals at court, and including Dryden, Shadwell, and Kneller.

In 1688 Anna married Charles, third Baron Cornwallis (1655–1698), with whom she had a further three children, of whom one survived to adulthood; this happier marriage ended with Cornwallis's death in 1698, upon which she retired to Scotland. There she oversaw the lavish rebuilding of Dalkeith Castle and maintained a quasi-regal status, but returned to London upon the Hanoverian succession. She resisted all pressure to relinquish the Buccleuch title in her own lifetime in favour of her son, preferring to be 'a man in my own family'. She died in London in February 1732, short of her eighty-first birthday, and was buried at St Nicholas's Church, Dalkeith. Of Monmouth she would never speak, and there is no reference to him on the inscription of her coffin, though the fatal connection is commemorated in the Monmouth Room at Bowhill. EIRWEN E. C. NICHOLSON

Sources M. Lee, *The heiresses of Buccleuch: marriage, money, and politics in seventeenth-century Britain* (1996) • GEC, *Peerage*

Likenesses G. Kneller, group portrait, oils, *c.*1688 (with her sons), Drumlanrig Castle, Dumfriesshire [*see illus.*] • studio of P. Lely, oils, Buccleuch estates, Selkirk, Scotland • P. Schenk, mezzotint (after G. Kneller), BM • R. Williams, mezzotint (after W. Wissing), BM • attrib. W. Wissing, oils, Buccleuch estates, Selkirk • W. Wissing, oils, Buccleuch estates, Selkirk • oils, repro. in Lee, *Heiresses of Buccleuch*

Scott, Archibald (1837–1909), Church of Scotland minister, was born on 18 September 1837 at Bogton, in the parish of Cadder, Lanarkshire, the sixth and youngest son of James Scott, farmer, and his wife, Margaret Brown. He was educated at Cadder parish school and at Glasgow high school before entering Glasgow University at the age of fourteen. On graduating BA in 1855 he proceeded to the study of divinity and was licensed by the presbytery of Glasgow on 8 June 1859. After brief assistantships at St Matthew's Church, Glasgow, and at Clackmannan, he was ordained minister of the East Church, Perth, on 2 March 1860. On 4 June 1861 he married Isabella Greig (*d.* 1892) with whom he had six children, four of whom died in early childhood. A son and daughter outlived him.

Scott moved rapidly between charges. He was translated to Abernethy in Perthshire (29 January 1863) and thence to Maxwell church, Glasgow (1 June 1865), where he demonstrated his ability to build up a congregation. A brief sojourn in the quieter atmosphere of Linlithgow (23 September 1869) ended when he was called to Greenside in Edinburgh (21 September 1871), where he remained until translated to the prestigious charge of St George's, Edinburgh (29 January 1880). Such was his influence that a substantial number of his Greenside congregation followed him.

Scott's emergence as a leading figure in the church was both recognized and accelerated by his appointment as a trustee of the Baird Trust, established by James Baird for the benefit of the Church of Scotland. The fund and, by extension Scott, faced initial mistrust lest the money be used to further any particular tendency within the church, but the critics were soon disarmed. In 1876, although not distinguished by any scholarly achievement, Glasgow University conferred the degree of DD on him.

Scott's appointment as convener of the business committee of the general assembly in 1888, which gave him constant membership of that body, enabled him to be the effective leader of the church. Although he was less of a public figure, Scott occupied a position within the established church similar to that of Principal Robert Rainy in the Free Church. Scott led his church through his sensitivity to its mood, 'No man could better interpret the voiceless opinion of the Church than he' (*The Scotsman*, 19 April 1909). While Scott guided the course of numerous assemblies, his influence was mainly exercised in committees. At his death he was a member of twenty-seven, four of them as convener. Scott took the opportunity offered by the Scottish Churches Bill to insert a clause which allowed the Church of Scotland greater freedom in terms of subscription to the 'formula'. It was his overture in the presbytery of Edinburgh in 1907 which initiated the process of reunion with the United Free Church of Scotland. Much of the impetus for this was a result of his trip to South Africa in 1902 with representatives of the latter.

His other responsibilities left little room for scholarship, but Scott was Croall lecturer in 1889–90 and Baird lecturer in 1892–3. These lectures, which appeared as *Buddhism and Christianity* and *Sacrifice: its Prophecy and Fulfilment*, reflected his interest in comparative religion and were his only publications.

Scott married second, on 18 July 1894, Marion Elizabeth Rankine (*b.* 1854). There were no children of the marriage. At the end of 1908 Scott became ill and he died on 18 April 1909 at Tantallon Lodge, North Berwick. He was buried on 22 April in the Dean cemetery, Edinburgh.

LIONEL ALEXANDER RITCHIE

Sources Lord Sands, *Dr Archibald Scott of St George's, Edinburgh, and his times* (1919) • *Fasti Scot.* • *The Scotsman* (19 April 1909) • *Life and Work* (June 1909), 136–7 • A. L. Drummond and J. Bulloch, *The church in late Victorian Scotland* (1978), 202–4 • *WWW* • private information, 1912 • *DNB* • *CCI* (1909)

Likenesses three photographs, *c.*1857–1909, repro. in Sands, *Dr Archibald Scott* • G. Reid, oils, 1902, Church of Scotland, Edinburgh • J. P. Macgillivray, bronze bust, 1907, St George's Church, Edinburgh

Wealth at death £9049 13*s.* 11*d.*: confirmation, 17 June 1909, *CCI*

Scott, Benjamin (1788–1830). *See under* Scott, Thomas (1747–1821).

Scott, Benjamin (1814–1892), chamberlain of London, was born at Felix Place, Back Road, Islington, London, one of nine children of Benjamin Whinnell Scott (1782–1841), then junior, later chief, clerk to the chamberlain of London, and his wife, Susan, daughter of George and Elizabeth Saunders of Hemel Hempstead. Benjamin was schooled at Totteridge, Hertfordshire, before entering the chamberlain's office in 1827 at the tender age of thirteen. Two of his brothers later came into that office. In 1841 he succeeded his father as chief clerk. He married, in 1842, Kate (*d.* 1892), daughter of Captain Glegg of the dragoon guards. Four of their children survived him.

Scott held office under three chamberlains, and on the death of the third, Anthony Brown, early in 1853, he was himself nominated to stand for chamberlain—the City of London corporation's chief financial officer. The post was customarily held by past lord mayors, and Scott had for his opponent alderman Sir John Key, who had been twice lord mayor. Scott later estimated that he had laid out £3000 in the course of his campaign, of which £1000 had gone on refreshments, explaining, 'In a contested election the City people eat and drink, whether friend or foe, at your expense' (minutes of evidence, nos. 4638-59 and 5840-8).

Key was elected by the small majority of 224 votes. At the end of 1853, owing to the continued friction produced by the contest, Scott resigned his appointments under the corporation, and a year later became secretary of the new Bank of London, which he had taken part in establishing. In July 1858, on the death of Sir John Key, he was the only candidate, and when elected, was the youngest for a long time: even more unusually, most of his career had been with the corporation.

When Key died the ancient office of chamberlain was reviewed and modernized. The chamberlain was henceforth forbidden to undertake any other business or occupation. The salary was reduced by £1000 to £1500, and no longer included a share of the revenue, although Scott was later to receive generous gratuities. On assuming office, however, he was still required to give personal security of £30,000 and sureties of £15,000.

Scott's knowledge of finance made him especially useful to the corporation. On 'black Friday' 1866, through his judgement in investments, the corporation lost not a penny, although they had at the time £700,000 out on loan. In 1888 the common council acknowledged his financial services by a eulogistic resolution and the gift of £5000. The presentation addresses which he delivered when honorary freedoms were bestowed by the corporation were marked by dignity and eloquence. In 1884 he published for the corporation *London's Roll of Fame*, a collection of such addresses with the replies during the previous 127 years.

For many years he devoted much spare time to lecturing to the working classes, and in December 1851 was the chief promoter of the Working Men's Educational Union, which was formed to organize lectures for workmen. For this society he wrote and published three lectures. He was a fellow of the Royal Astronomical Society, and much interested in the study of astronomy and statistics. In 1867 he published his influential *Statistical Vindication of the City of London*. Scott continued the family tradition of holding clerkships in the Wheelwrights' Company and he did much to promote revival of the Glovers' Company, in which he was free by patrimony and served on the court of assistants.

Scott was a staunch nonconformist, temperance advocate, and social reformer; he campaigned for the abolition of church rates, the promotion of ragged schools, state education, and preservation of open spaces, being largely responsible for bringing Epping Forest into the corporation's ownership. Towards the endowment of the nonconformist church in Southwark in memory of the Pilgrim Fathers he contributed £2000. He worked hard to promote the passing of the Criminal Law Amendment Act of 1885, and published an account of his efforts in a pamphlet, *Six Years of Labour and Sorrow*.

The Scotts lived at Heath House, Weybridge, Surrey, for twenty years and in later years they had a town house at 12 Stanley Crescent, Notting Hill, London. Scott continued his official duties until December 1891, when he was taken ill with influenza and pneumonia. He died at Stanley Crescent on 17 January 1892, three days after his wife. They were buried together at Weybridge.

CHARLES WELCH, *rev.* ANITA MCCONNELL

Sources B. R. Masters, *The chamberlain of the City of London, 1237–1987* (1988), 72–86 · *City Press* (12 Dec 1891) · *City Press* (20 Jan 1892) · J. R. Scott, *Memorials of the Scott family of Scot's Hall* (1876), 243 · 'Royal commission to inquire into … the corporation of London', *Parl. papers* (1854), 26.405–6, 527–8, no. 1772 [minutes of evidence] · d. cert. · *CGPLA Eng. & Wales* (1892)

Wealth at death £16,668 9*s*. 2*d*.: probate, 24 Feb 1892, *CGPLA Eng. & Wales*

Scott [*née* Douglas], **Caroline Lucy**, **Lady Scott** (**1784–1857**), novelist, was born on 16 February 1784, the eldest child of Archibald James Edward *Douglas, first Baron Douglas (1748–1827), and his second wife, Frances Scott (1750–1817) [*see* Douglas, Frances], sister of Henry, third duke of Buccleuch. She had an elder half-sister by her father's first marriage as well as younger siblings. On 27 October 1810 she married Captain George Scott (1770–1841), who was eventually knighted and promoted to vice-admiral.

Scott published all three of her novels anonymously, perhaps contributing to the occasional confusion of her works with those of the novelist Harriet Anne *Scott, Lady Scott (1819–1894). Caroline Lucy Scott, however, did not begin her career as a writer until she was in her forties; her first novel, *A Marriage in High Life* (2 vols.), was published in 1828. According to the title-page, the book was edited by the author of *Flirtation*, Scott's distant cousin Lady Charlotte Bury. The plot, about an aristocrat who neglects his pious, middle-class wife and devotes himself to his mistress, is said to have been based on fact. Scott's two subsequent novels, *Trevelyan* (1833) and *The Old Grey Church* (1856), also explore the conflicts between pious individuals and their more fashionably self-indulgent friends or family. *Trevelyan* was fairly successful; the *Quarterly Review* thought it 'the best feminine novel … that has appeared since Miss Edgeworth's *Vivian*' (vol. 50, 429), and Lady Louisa Stuart reported that it was 'as much *blown* … as if the name were affixed to it' (Stuart, 246). George Eliot was less kind to Scott in her essay 'Silly Novels by Lady Novelists', describing *The Old Grey Church* as 'an Evangelical travesty of a fashionable novel' (Eliot, 212–13) and mocking its 'drivelling kind of dialogue, and equally drivelling narrative' (ibid., 214), but Scott remained sufficiently popular at mid-century to have her two earlier novels reprinted following the publication of *The Old Grey Church*. (*A Marriage in High Life* was reissued in 1857 and *Trevelyan* in 1860.)

In addition to her fiction, Scott wrote several educational works, which appeared under her own name: *Exposition of the Types and Antitypes of the Old and New Testament* (1856), *Incentives to Bible Study: Scripture Acrostics, a Sabbath Pastime for Young People* (1860), and *Acrostics, Historical, Geographical, and Biographical* (1863). The last two works, which were published posthumously, are collections of word games, in which young readers are given questions to test their religious and secular knowledge; as in her fiction, Scott evidently intended to instruct while amusing. Caroline Lucy Scott died at Petersham, Surrey, on 20 April 1857.

PAM PERKINS

Sources review of *Trevelyan*, *QR*, 50 (1833–4), 413–30 · G. Eliot, 'Silly novels by lady novelists', *Works*, 22 (1908) · Burke, *Peerage* · W. L. Clowes, *The Royal Navy: a history from the earliest times to the present*, 7 vols. (1897–1903) · L. Stuart, *Letters*, ed. R. B. Johnson (1926) · d. cert. · *DNB*

Archives BL, agreement with Richard Bentley (1856), Add. MS 46617, fol. 60

Likenesses W. Say, mezzotint (after C. L. Douglas), BM

Scott, Charles James Kennedy Osborne [*known as* Charles Kennedy Scott] (**1876–1965**), musician, was born on 16 November 1876 in Church Street, Romsey, Hampshire, the only child of William Scott (1819–1891), silk mercer, and his wife, Rosa (1852–1933), daughter of John Frederick Osborne JP, schoolmaster, of Osborne House, Romsey. His father was born at Allanbank, Dunblane, the son of James Scott of Greenloaning, Perthshire. Charles Kennedy Scott was educated at King Edward VI School, Southampton, and received musical instruction from a local teacher.

In October 1894 Scott entered the Brussels Conservatoire de Musique, where he studied the violin with Alexandre Cornélis. In 1895 he changed to the organ, for which he felt greater aptitude. His new professor, Alphonse Mailly, also gave instruction in plainchant, and Mailly's methods, especially his close attention to the rhythmic playing and expressive phrasing of Bach's organ music and the proper interpretation of plainchant, influenced Scott deeply. For counterpoint and composition he studied under Ferdinand Kufferath, and later under Edgar Tinel. In 1897 he was awarded the *premier prix avec distinction* and the Mailly prize for organ playing.

In 1898 Scott settled in London and became active as a teacher and as organist at the Carmelite priory in Kensington. In May 1899 he gave a concert at Steinway Hall, one of the singers being his cousin Mary Scott Donaldson (1873–1956), a fellow student and prizewinner at Brussels. She was the daughter of James Donaldson, merchant, of Glasgow. They were married on 5 April 1900, and had two sons and one daughter. The elder son, Charles W. A. Scott, came into prominence as an outstanding airman in 1931, when he lowered the record time for a solo flight from England to Australia held by Air Commodore Kingsford Smith, set up another record for the return flight, and was awarded the Air Force Cross for distinguished services to aviation (*The Times*, 6 May 1946).

Scott once remarked that the important steps in his life had taken place through the agency of other people. When visiting the London Library at the invitation of Frederick Cox, he observed some large volumes published by the Musical Antiquarian Society. Cox opened one of them: it was John Wilbye's *First Set of Madrigals* (1598). Scott's interest was immediately kindled; and he began to make scores of other fine works of the period, secular and sacred, from the British Museum partbooks.

One evening Thomas Beecham, who had made a special

study of Tudor music while a pupil of Charles Wood, happened to meet Scott, who, he wrote:

> had not long been back in London from Paris, Vincent d'Indy and the Schola Cantorum. He too was full of the subject of ancient choral music and thought it might be fun to collect about a dozen persons together, sit round a table and sing it for our own amusement. (Beecham, 52)

Before long a group of enthusiasts were meeting to sing madrigals and Tudor church music at each other's houses. After a few months Scott proposed that the group be increased to a size large enough for public concert appearance. The reconstituted body, originally named the English Madrigal Choir, became the renowned Oriana Madrigal Society. It was founded by Scott in the autumn of 1904, and gave the first of two private performances on 14 November that year at Leighton House. Its first public concert, when the strength of the choir was forty singers, took place at the Portman Rooms, Baker Street, on 4 July 1905. 'Under Scott's masterly direction', wrote Beecham, it acquired during the next few years 'a technical skill, an eloquence of expression and an insight into the music it was called upon to interpret that placed it an easy first among the small choirs of the kingdom' (ibid.).

In that year Scott began to issue his own editions of madrigals, choral ayres, and other music of the sixteenth and seventeenth centuries, under the title *Euterpe*. The fifteen volumes of this series appeared between 1905 and 1914. Almost all the seventy items were later reissued to the public in separate copies, and these performing editions offer valuable insights into the artistic methods of an outstanding interpreter.

Scott now wrote a manual for members of the Oriana Madrigal Society. *Madrigal Singing* (1907, 2nd edn 1931) dealt systematically with the study of madrigal music and contained an explanation of the modal system. It addressed the disputed question of whether crescendos, diminuendos, and other gradations of time and tone had a place in polyphonic music. Scott pointed out that the Romanian signs for such gradations, equivalent to the modern signs, were in use in the performance of Gregorian music in the eighth century, and concluded that the Elizabethans probably sang their music 'with a very fair degree of expression' (Scott, *Madrigal Singing*, 90–91).

In 1911 Scott became organist and musical director at the Ethical Church, Bayswater, the home of the West London Ethical Society. His mind turned to a new selection of canticles, hymns, responses, and anthems. The results of such thinking appeared in volume 2 of *Social Worship* (1913), to which, as music editor, he wrote an illuminating introduction. The professional choir of fourteen carefully chosen voices became celebrated.

The Oriana Madrigal Society was extending its range, introducing the carol in 1908 and works by Purcell and Bach in 1911. Balfour Gardiner was planning his series of concerts featuring British composers in 1912 and 1913. Through the good offices of Norman O'Neill, Gardiner invited Scott to conduct the Oriana, which now numbered sixty voices, in two programmes of both early and modern works. The fresh footing the choir thus gained was confirmed by its appearance at a Royal Philharmonic Society concert in November 1913.

In 1914 Scott assisted Rutland Boughton at the newly founded Glastonbury Festival. He conducted the first performance of Boughton's *The Immortal Hour* on 26 August, and the first performance with orchestra at the Bournemouth Winter Gardens on 7 January 1915. Boughton persuaded Scott, a number of whose vocal compositions had been published by 1913, to undertake a setting of the morality play *Everyman*. Scott's four-act music drama of 1916–17 was the culmination of his work as a composer. The vocal score of *Everyman* appeared in 1936, and the orchestration was revised in 1940–41. The première of this moving and original chamber opera was broadcast by BBC Radio 3 on 31 March 1977.

The coming of peace in 1918 brought the opportunity to apply Oriana standards to a chorus of 300 voices, the Philharmonic Choir, which Scott formed at Gardiner's suggestion in 1919. Its many first performances included that of Gustav Holst's *The Hymn of Jesus* in March 1920. Beecham wrote of the Philharmonic Choir that 'the genius of Kennedy Scott' had lifted it 'to a higher cultural level than any other in the kingdom' (Beecham, 66). Scott's interests were wide-ranging. With the Bach Cantata Club, which he formed in 1926 with the help of Hubert Foss, he played an important part in the Bach revival in London, performing over seventy of the cantatas with a choir of about thirty singers in St Margaret's, Westminster, where the reverberation time, in relation to the building's volume, corresponds to that of the Thomaskirche at Leipzig.

In 1929 Scott joined the staff of Trinity College of Music as conductor of the college choir, and introduced the study of plainsong, which lay outside the ordinary curriculum. He was appointed a teacher of singing in 1930. His two-volume book *Word and Tone* ('an English method of vocal technique for solo singers and choralists') appeared in 1933. In the Oriana Madrigal Society's jubilee year Scott published a book which summed up a lifetime's experience, *The Fundamentals of Singing* (1954). This 'inquiry into the mechanical and expressive aspects of the art' also illuminates some large issues of artistic philosophy.

The Oriana Madrigal Society's last concert took place a month after Scott's eighty-fifth birthday, in December 1961. In that year he was elected a fellow of the Royal College of Music; he had been awarded an honorary fellowship by Trinity College of Music some years earlier. It was a principle of his work to put words first, to 'make speech the basis of your song'. He once wrote: 'Can we conceive anything more perfect than a fugue of Bach or a sonnet of Shakespeare?' (Scott, *Fundamentals*, 95). When active musical work was no longer possible for reasons of health, he turned his attention in 1963 to recording his own readings of Shakespeare's sonnets. He completed these significant recordings, together with selected poems by Milton, Wordsworth, and Arnold, in 1964. Scott's last public appearance was in February 1965, when he spoke to the West London Humanist Society on 'The philosophical sonnets of Shakespeare'. He died in London at St Pancras Hospital on 2 July 1965, and was buried on 8 July beside his parents in Romsey cemetery.

Scott's choice of programmes for the Oriana in its first decade 'struck out new lines', wrote Gillies Whittaker, 'and gave fresh ideas to choral conductors all over the world' (Whittaker). This spirit of enterprise inspired all his choral work, and led to such notable premières as that of Arnold Bax's *Mater ora filium*. He was, in Harold Rutland's words, a man of great culture and charm, but could nevertheless be a stern taskmaster, since he expected all concerned to spare nothing to achieve the desired result (Rutland, 40). Scott's views on the partnership of word and tone ensured new standards of pronunciation and articulation. The sonority and variety of tone colour achieved by his choirs added a new dimension to the musical experience. Yet this was only the base from which the essence of his work took wings. As he once wrote: 'Mere notes, effected by a sort of standardized technique, are quite inadequate; such a process is pattern-making, not a revelation of spirit' (Scott, *Fundamentals*, 412).

MICHAEL POPE

Sources S. de B. Taylor, 'Charles Kennedy Scott', *MT*, 92 (1951), 492–6 · *The Times* (3 July 1965) · C. Cleall, *The Times* (7 July 1965) · P. Jennings, *The Times* (9 July 1965) · T. Beecham, *A mingled chime: leaves from an autobiography* (1944) · R. Elkin, *Queen's Hall, 1893–1941* (1944), 64–7 · C. K. Scott, 'Reminiscences', in P. Heseltine, *Frederick Delius*, 2nd edn, ed. H. Foss (1952), 157–70 · R. Peck, 'The Oriana Madrigal Society (1904–1954)', *MT*, 95 (1954), 537–9 · M. Hurd, *Immortal hour: the life and period of Rutland Boughton* (1962) · H. Rutland, *Trinity College of Music: the first hundred years* (1972) · S. Lloyd, *H. Balfour Gardiner* (1984) · W. G. Whittaker, 'Choral singing', *Encyclopaedia Britannica*, 13th edn (1926), vol. 1, pp. 630–31 · personal knowledge (2004) · private information (2004) [Michael Barron, husband of Rosemary Barron, *née* Scott (*d.* 1998), granddaughter] · b. cert. · m. cert. · d. cert. · C. K. Scott, *The fundamentals of singing* (1954) · C. K. Scott, *Madrigal singing*, 2nd edn (1931) · *Who's who in music*, 2nd edn (1937) · I. D. MacKillop, *The British ethical societies* (1986), 119–20 · *Sotoniensis* [magazine of King Edward VI School, Southampton] (summer 1899), 43

Archives SOUND priv. coll., Scott speaking sonnets of Shakespeare and other poems (recorded 1963–4)

Likenesses H. Bulman, portrait, 1909, Trinity College of Music, London · H. Lowery, photograph, after 1909, Trinity College of Music, London · portrait, after 1909, Trinity College of Music, London · G. C. Beresford, photograph, repro. in *MT* (Oct 1920) · bronze head, Trinity College of Music, London

Wealth at death £32,923: probate, 4 Nov 1965, *CGPLA Eng. & Wales*

Scott, Charles Prestwich (1846–1932), newspaper editor and proprietor, was born at Bath on 26 October 1846. He was the eighth child and fourth son of Russell Scott (1801–1880), a partner in a coal company, and his wife, Isabella Civil, daughter of Joseph Prestwich, wine merchant. Scott's upbringing was Unitarian. He attended Hove School, Sussex, run by a Unitarian minister, and Clapham grammar school. He also, for reasons of health, spent a period with a private tutor on the Isle of Wight, the Revd Arthur Watson. Despite religious obstacles, in 1865 he secured admission to Corpus Christi, Oxford, immersing himself in a full university life—including rowing and debating—and graduating BA in 1869 with a first class in

Charles Prestwich Scott (1846–1932), by Francis Dodd, 1916

literae humaniores. Thereafter, he habitually looked to Oxford for recruits to his staff.

Scott's choice of career was determined by three things: family connections, his evident literary skills, and his strongly directed personality. J. E. Taylor, his cousin (but many years his senior), owned the *Manchester Guardian*, which Taylor's father had founded. An organ both of the flourishing cotton trade and of religious and political dissent, it was the most valuable newspaper property outside London. Taylor offered Scott a position on the paper which he took up in 1871, and elevated him to the editorship in January 1872. Scott, aged only twenty-five, was many years junior to the more experienced of his colleagues, but this did not prove a difficulty. His piercing brown eyes, striking good looks, newly acquired beard, and authoritative manner left no doubt who was in charge. Scott remained editor for fifty-seven years.

Within a short time Scott was attracting to the newspaper highly distinguished writers on the arts and sciences, including such figures as A. W. Ward, James Bryce, C. E. Montague, and Arnold Toynbee. In politics the *Manchester Guardian* in 1872 was more whig than radical. Scott, for more than a decade, seemed content with this. But perhaps he began foreshadowing a change in political direction by the attention his paper began devoting to social questions. The *Guardian* carried well-documented accounts of conditions in the mining districts of northern England, of the indifferent housing of the poor, and of deficiencies in the medical services. Scott sent W. T. Arnold (grandson of Arnold of Rugby, and nephew of Matthew) to Ireland, from whence came reports of appalling social conditions and their connection with political discontents and political crime.

Hence the ground was not unprepared when, in 1886, W. E. Gladstone committed his party to Irish home rule (thereby splitting the Liberal Party). Scott embraced the cause. It proved a wide-ranging conversion, from which Scott emerged not just a home-ruler but a social radical. His newspaper in the next three decades opposed British imperialism in South Africa (and in particular Cecil Rhodes's exploitation of native labour), resisted large programmes of armaments, and gave devoted support to women's suffrage and the many schemes for social improvement embodied in what, with the Liberals restored to office from 1905, became the 'new Liberalism'.

In 1895, while remaining editor of the *Manchester Guardian*, Scott entered parliament for the Leigh division of Lancashire as a Liberal. He remained until 1905. It proved a stormy decade. The Second South African War not only divided the Liberals (again) but cost the *Manchester Guardian* readers and advertisers on account of its 'unpatriotic' attitude. What Scott particularly derived from his spell in parliament was personal attachments and antipathies. He never forgave H. H. Asquith his 'imperialist' position during the Second South African War, nor forgot Lloyd George's courage in taking a stand for the 'pro-Boer' line.

In 1905, following Taylor's death, Scott became proprietor as well as editor of the *Manchester Guardian*. Taylor's will left the fate of the paper unclear, and Scott had to raise £240,000 to secure it. It was not a reckless investment. Certainly, the *Guardian's* brand of responsible journalism could never capture the mass market conjured forth by Northcliffe, and it was already threatened by encroachment from the metropolis. But it rested on a powerful provincial base, and appealed well beyond Lancashire as the one quality newspaper espousing the radical cause.

With the Liberals in power from 1905, Scott found important figures eager to consult him and secure his good opinion. He travelled often to London to talk with them, and from 1911 occupied the return journey recording what had transpired. Unwittingly, he thereby compiled a body of documents providing penetrating insights into the contemporary thinking of men such as Lloyd George and Winston Churchill. Plainly they respected his opinion, even if they did not always act on it.

With the outbreak of war in 1914 Scott confronted painful and ambiguous issues. Hitherto influenced by the myopic R. T. Reid, Lord Loreburn (also an ally from his days in parliament), he had tended to discount the threat from Germany and to locate international troubles in the diplomatic system. But once Britain was committed to war, Scott took a determined line. The struggle, he judged, must be conducted with determination. Certainly, during 1915 and 1916 he argued against conscription, and deplored the ferocious suppression of the Easter rising in Dublin. But he did not doubt that the nation must dispense with Asquith's rather aloof leadership and accept the passionate commitment to the struggle of Lloyd George—even at the head of a mainly Conservative government.

Some of Lloyd George's actions after 1916, such as the enactment of female suffrage (1918) and the espousal of the cause of a Jewish national home in Palestine, gave Scott great satisfaction. (He had contributed directly to the latter outcome by introducing Chaim Weizmann, both Zionist and munitions chemist, to Lloyd George in 1915.) But Scott loathed other aspects of Lloyd George's wartime and post-war governments: military intervention against the Bolsheviks in Russia, the malevolent jingoism of the 1918 election campaign, and uncontrolled military repression in Ireland. On this last matter, for a year (1920–21) Scott severed relations with Lloyd George.

The post-war world was not a hopeful place for Scott. The decline of cotton threatened Manchester and its great newspaper. Hopes for the League of Nations dwindled when the United States rejected Woodrow Wilson. The Liberal Party was split again, and the rivalry of Labour towards it, with consequent dispersal of the anti-Conservative vote, ensured a succession of tory governments. During the 1920s Scott once more pinned his hopes on Lloyd George, and welcomed Labour's (brief) accessions to office. But neither cause prospered. Concerning his newspaper, he encouraged useful initiatives, such as film and radio reviews and the introduction of the *Manchester Guardian Commercial*. But by the time he resigned his editorship in 1929, he had somewhat outlived his usefulness.

During his lifetime, Scott was not without his critics. He could be stingy in remunerating valuable colleagues, and at close quarters he might seem authoritarian rather than noble-minded. Yet he was entitled to the high stature he acquired during his lifetime and has since retained. For, as another prominent editor put it, the *Manchester Guardian* became under him 'a newspaper with which the whole world had to reckon' (Hammond, 59).

On 20 May 1874 Scott married Rachel Susan Cook, daughter of the professor of ecclesiastical history at St Andrews University [*see* Scott, Rachel Susan (1848–1905)]. She was one of the original undergraduates at what was to become Girton College, and she regularly reviewed novels for the *Manchester Guardian* until her premature death in November 1905. Of their four children (three boys and one girl), one became manager of the newspaper and another, Edward Taylor *Scott, succeeded Scott as editor.

From 1882 until his death Scott lived at The Firs, Fallowfield, amid a large garden and noble trees. He took to making the journey to and from the *Manchester Guardian* offices by bicycle, involving travelling late at night, and he kept up the practice until beyond his eightieth birthday. His last recorded mishap ('I have a useful knack of falling without hurting myself') occurred less than a year before his death. In 1923 Scott was made an honorary fellow of his Oxford college, and in 1930 a freeman of the city of Manchester. He persistently declined offers of a peerage.

Scott died at The Firs on 1 January 1932. Manchester thereupon paid him a remarkable tribute: on a cold winter morning, huge numbers turned out to offer their last respects in what became an unofficial, unorchestrated, state funeral. Scott is best remembered for the dictum that the primary business of a newspaper is 'the gathering of news': 'Comment is free, but facts are sacred' (*Manchester Guardian*, 5 May 1921). Yet for him the real interest of a newspaper lay with the leading article, and with its power to mould and direct opinion. It was the elevated quality of the opinions he sought to propagate, and the measured way in which he advocated them, which gave his career in journalism its special distinction. TREVOR WILSON

Sources D. Ayerst, *Guardian: biography of a newspaper* (1971) • J. L. Hammond, *C. P. Scott of the Manchester Guardian* (1934) • *The political diaries of C. P. Scott, 1911–1928*, ed. T. Wilson (1970) • W. H. Mills, *The Manchester Guardian: a century of history* (1921) • [A. P. Wadsworth], ed., *C. P. Scott, 1846–1932: the making of the Manchester Guardian* (1946), 146–7 • *CGPLA Eng. & Wales* (1932)

Archives Balliol Oxf., corresp. • BL, corresp. and memoranda, Add. MSS 50901–50909 • Chaim Weizmann Archives, Rehevoth, Israel • JRL, corresp., diaries, and papers • Man. CL, Manchester Archives and Local Studies, articles, letters, and obituaries | BLPES, letters to the Courtneys • BLPES, corresp. with E. D. Morel • Bodl. Oxf., letters to J. L. L. B. Hammond and B. L. Hammond • CAC Cam., corresp. with Lord Fisher • HLRO, corresp. with David Lloyd George • HLRO, letters to David Soskice • TCD, corresp. with John Dillon • U. Birm. L., corresp. with W. H. Dawson

Likenesses F. Dodd, etching, 1916, NPG [*see illus.*] • J. Epstein, bronze bust, *c.*1926, Man. City Gall. • E. Kapp, drawing, 1931, Barber Institute of Fine Arts, Birmingham • T. C. Dugdale, oils, Manchester Press Club • photograph, repro. in *The Guardian*

Wealth at death £15,829 8*s.* 6*d.*: probate, 16 Feb 1932, *CGPLA Eng. & Wales*

Scott, Lord Charles Thomas Montagu-Douglas- (1839–1911), naval officer, born at Montagu House, Whitehall, London, on 20 October 1839, was the fourth son of Walter Francis Montagu-Douglas-*Scott, fifth duke of Buccleuch (1806–1884), and his wife, Lady Charlotte Anne Thynne (1811–1895), youngest daughter of Thomas Thynne, second marquess of Bath. After beginning his education at Radley College, he entered the navy on 1 May 1853 as a cadet on the *St Jean d'Acre*, then newly commissioned by Captain Henry Keppel. In her Scott took part in the Baltic campaign of 1854, being present at the capture of Bomarsund, and in 1855 saw further active service in the Black Sea. In November 1856 he followed Keppel into the *Raleigh*, going out to the China station, and after the ship was wrecked in April 1857, served in the tenders to which the officers and crew were transferred. He was thus present at the engagements at Escape Creek, Fatshan (Foshan) Creek, and other boat actions in the Canton River in June and July 1857. In July he was appointed to the *Pearl* (Captain E. S. Sotheby) which, with the *Shannon*, was ordered from Hong Kong to Calcutta on the outbreak of the Indian mutiny. Scott landed with the *Pearl*'s naval brigade in September 1857, and served ashore until invalided on 15 June 1858; the brigade formed part of the Gorakhpur field force during the operations in Oudh. He was twice mentioned in dispatches, for gallant conduct at Chandarpur on 17 February 1858, and again for having, with three others, captured and turned on the enemy one of their guns at the battle of Belwa on 5 March.

Having passed his examination on 21 May 1859, Scott was specially promoted lieutenant on 19 July. In that rank he served on board the *Forte*, Keppel's flagship, on the Cape of Good Hope station and the south-east coast of America, and in June 1861 was appointed to the frigate *Emerald*, attached to the channel squadron. From November 1863 until he was promoted commander on 12 September 1865, he was a lieutenant in the royal yacht. Early in 1868 he went out to the China station to take command of the sloop *Icarus*, and in November 1868 served as second in command of the naval brigade under Captain Algernon Heneage which was landed for the protection of British subjects at Yangchow (Yangzhou); in December he commanded a flotilla of boats which, with a naval brigade under Commodore Oliver Jones, destroyed three pirate villages near Swatow (Shantou). He returned home in 1871, and was promoted captain on 6 February 1872.

From 1875 to 1877 Scott commanded the *Narcissus*, flagship of the detached squadron, and in July 1879 commissioned the *Bacchante*, in which he had charge of the royal cadets, Albert Victor, duke of Clarence and Avondale, and his younger brother George (later King George V), who made their first cruise in her to the Mediterranean, West Indies, South America, Falklands, South Africa, Australia, Japan, China, Malaya, and home via the Mediterranean in 1882. For this he was created CB (civil). He married, on 23 February 1883, Ada Mary (*d.* 21 Nov 1943), daughter of Charles Ryan of Derriweit Heights, Macedon, Victoria, Australia; they had two sons.

In 1885 and 1886 Scott commanded the *Agincourt* in the channel, and in January 1887 became captain of the dockyard at Chatham. He was an aide-de-camp to Queen Victoria from June 1886 until promoted to his flag on 3 April 1888. In 1889 he served as umpire on the naval manoeuvres, then, for three years from September 1889, was commander-in-chief on the Australian station; on 10 March 1894 he was promoted vice-admiral, and in May 1898 was made a KCB (military). On 30 June 1899 he reached the rank of admiral, and in March 1900 was appointed commander-in-chief at Plymouth, where he remained for the customary three years.

Scott was advanced to GCB on 9 November 1902, and retired on 20 October 1904. In retirement Scott, along with many of his contemporaries, opposed Lord Fisher's Admiralty reforms. He died, after a long illness, on 21 August 1911 at his home, Boughton House, near Kettering, Northamptonshire. Scott's career was dominated by aristocratic and royal connections, being made by Henry Keppel, and furthered by the prince of Wales (later Edward VII). His real abilities, unlike his courage and resourcefulness, were never put to the test.

L. G. C. LAUGHTON, *rev.* ANDREW LAMBERT

Sources C. Penrose-Fitzgerald, *Sir George Tryon* (1898) • V. Stuart, *The beloved little admiral* (1967) • W. B. Rowbotham, ed., *The naval brigades in the Indian mutiny, 1857–58*, Navy RS, 87 (1947) • E. R. Fremantle, *The navy as I have known it* (1904) • D. Bonner-Smith and E. W. R. Lumby, eds., *The Second China War, 1856–1860*, Navy RS, 95 (1954) •

G. M. Bennett, *Charlie B: a biography of Admiral Lord Beresford of Metemmeh and Curraghmore* (1968) • Burke, *Peerage* • *CCI* (1911)
Archives Northants. RO, logbooks and papers | Beaulieu, Brockenhurst, letters to first Baron Montagu of Beaulieu
Likenesses F. Grant, oils, 1842, Buccleuch estates, Selkirk, Scotland • G. Richmond, chalk drawing, Buccleuch estates, Selkirk, Scotland
Wealth at death £2710 6*s*. 9*d*.: confirmation, 6 Nov 1911, *CCI*

Scott, Charlotte Angas (1858–1931), mathematician, was born in Lincoln on 8 June 1858, daughter of Caleb Scott (*d.* 1919) and his wife, Eliza Ann, *née* Exley. She came from a Congregational background, and moved with her family when she was seven to Manchester, where her father had become head of the Lancashire College. In 1876 she went to Girton College, Cambridge, on a scholarship funded by the Goldsmiths' Company. On 31 January 1880, to public acclaim, it emerged that she had done well enough in the final tripos to be the eighth wrangler (though women were not then ranked, nor were they eligible for a degree). The public excitement that attended a woman's superb achievement at mathematics was intense. *The Times* took it up, and in 1881 the senior members of Cambridge University voted 398 to 32 in favour of ranking women with the men in the tripos (although it was not to grant women degrees until 1948).

Charlotte Angas Scott (1858–1931), by unknown photographer, in or after 1885

Scott continued her studies at Cambridge, chiefly inspired by the lectures of Arthur Cayley, the Sadlerian professor, with whom she deepened her taste for geometry. In 1885 she took a London DSc, since Cambridge awarded no higher degrees to women, and for a time taught at Cambridge, though prospects were negligible. Then the new women's college of Bryn Mawr, Pennsylvania, which opened officially on 23 September 1885, offered her a position as associate professor. Scott was the only woman among the five associate professors, with a starting salary of $2000 a year. Her teaching was highly regarded, and earned her the college's first endowed professorship in 1909. Her lectures on projective geometry were published as a book, which remained in print throughout the century. She was active in the life of the college until isolated by increasing deafness, and she seems to have been regarded as one of those rare mathematicians whose capacity for logical thought extends beyond their subject and to embrace daily life. She was deeply principled, once, in 1898, rebuking the college president (Carey Thomas) for diluting women's education. Her personality seems to have been at once severe and vulnerable: severe in her decision never to marry but to pursue a career; severe in her personal appearance and in her dislike of women's smoking or using make-up; but patient with others if (but only if) they tried. The student song about her went:

S is for Scott
Superior Scott
She is kind in the main
If you have any brain
But if you have not
Superior Scott!

However, she enlivened her retirement by betting on the horses, to which she applied her grasp of mathematical statistics.

Scott's contributions to Bryn Mawr, and to the cause of women in mathematics, were remarkable. She was the dissertation adviser to seven women students, putting Bryn Mawr third behind Chicago and Cornell in the number of PhDs they granted to women. Thanks in part to Scott, 14 per cent of doctorates in mathematics awarded before 1940 went to women; in the 1950s this number declined to 5 per cent. She was influential from the start in the American Mathematical Society and was its vice-president in 1905–6, and for twenty-seven years from 1899 was a co-editor of the *American Journal of Mathematics*. The American Mathematical Society fêted Scott at its spring meeting in Bryn Mawr in 1922, when A. N. Whitehead was the main speaker. Unquestionably, she earned this influence principally through the quality of her research.

Scott had a sharp eye for rigour in her own subject, the theory of algebraic curves. This is a subject with a geometrical aspect and also deep roots in the theory of complex functions, and many nineteenth-century mathematicians worked on it. The theory of these curves was most difficult when the curves crossed themselves; to overcome such difficulties various techniques were available which replaced complicated self-intersections by a number of simpler ones, and Scott was a master of these. Her work did much to illuminate a problem which was to perplex everyone of her generation. The English mathematician F. S. Macaulay praised her as a propounder of new ideas and an interpreter of the work of others (notably, his own).

Another major result in the subject concerned the equations of curves that passed through all the intersection points of two curves whose equations were given. In 1899

Scott gave her account of this result. The theorem, due originally to two eminent German mathematicians, Brill and Noether, had recently been proved by David Hilbert in an algebraic way (it forms part of his famous *Nullstellensatz*) and was later to be proved by many people. For Scott the theorem called for a thorough-going geometrical proof, which she duly gave. In 1906 Scott's health worsened with an attack of rheumatoid arthritis, and her research almost stopped. She retired in 1925 and returned to Cambridge, where she died at her home, Carholme, 2 Storey Ways, on 10 November 1931. She was buried at St Giles's Church, Cambridge. J. J. GRAY

Sources P. C. Kenschafl, 'Charlotte Angas Scott, 1858–1931', *College Mathematics Journal*, 18 (1987), 98–110 · F. S. Macaulay, 'Dr. Charlotte Angas Scott', *Journal of the London Mathematical Society*, 7 (1932), 230–40 · E. Finch, *Carey Thomas of Bryn Mawr* (1947) · *CGPLA Eng. & Wales* (1932)

Archives Bryn Mawr College, Bryn Mawr, Pennsylvania, archives

Likenesses photograph, in or after 1885, Girton Cam. [*see illus.*]

Wealth at death £828 18*s*. 10*d*.: probate, 26 March 1932, *CGPLA Eng. & Wales*

Scott, Charlotte Anne Montagu-Douglas-, duchess of Buccleuch and Queensberry (1811–1895). *See under* Scott, Walter Francis Montagu-Douglas-, fifth duke of Buccleuch and seventh duke of Queensberry (1806–1884).

Scott, Clement William (1841–1904), theatre critic, was born in London on 6 October 1841, the son of William Scott, a parish curate, and his wife, Margaret, the daughter of William Beloe. Following education at a private school in London and at Marlborough College, he entered the War Office as a temporary clerk in May 1860, and in 1862 rose to the position of junior clerk. The position meant little to him, although he was to remain there until 1879. Nevertheless, a colleague at the War Office, Thomas Hood, was instrumental in launching Scott on his journalistic career by introducing him to Frederick Ledger, the editor of *The Era*, who asked him to write occasional critical pieces. From 1863 to 1865 Scott served as drama critic for the *Sunday Times*, a position he was asked to relinquish when actor–managers protested at the acerbity of his writing. Although this caustic intolerance would later cloud his judgement of new theatrical trends, at this stage in his career it was directed at what he took to be shoddy playwriting and the dramatic practices of second-rate theatre managements. Moreover, he was able to channel his wit into writing for *Fun*, where he was joined by the satirists H. J. Byron, F. C. Burnand, and W. S. Gilbert, and for the *London Figaro*, as its drama critic under the *nom de plume* Almaviva. During this time he became a convert to Roman Catholicism, undoubtedly influenced by his father, a fervent admirer of Newman, and married his first wife, Isabel Busson Du Maurier (*d.* 1890), the sister of George *Du Maurier, the artist and author of *Trilby*, on 30 April 1868 at Brompton Oratory.

In 1871 Scott began his long association with the *Daily Telegraph*. In 1878 he succeeded E. L. Blanchard as its principal drama critic, a position he held until the end of 1897. In this capacity he was to wield an extraordinary influence

Clement William Scott (1841–1904), by Walery, *c*.1890

as the champion of the new breed of actor–managers epitomized by his friends the Bancrofts and Henry Irving. At the same time he was no disinterested onlooker, as his involvement as editor of the monthly journal *The Theatre* from 1880 to 1889 demonstrates. The journal had been started by Irving as an unofficial organ of self-promotion. In 1879 he sold it to Scott for the nominal sum of £1000 ('I thought it might prove a valuable property to you', Irving was to write to Scott in 1888 when financially the journal was in great difficulty). Henceforward Scott used its columns to glorify Irving's achievements and to consolidate his own position as London's principal leader of dramatic taste and opinion.

Scott came to prominence at a time when theatre practitioners were consciously seeking a respected status comparable to that of other professions. To do so meant finding a voice, which Scott took it upon himself to provide. Actor–managers saw the advantages of cultivating his support and Scott was flattered by their attentions. His critical voice was characterized by either flamboyant and unequivocal praise or equally uncompromising denunciation. At the same time his position of authority can be measured by the fact that he was asked to advise Augustus Harris on managerial problems and Wilson Barrett on a title for *The Sign of the Cross*. In 1892 he even helped George Alexander persuade Oscar Wilde to modify the structure of *Lady Windermere's Fan* by suggesting its desirability in the columns of the *Daily Telegraph*, and influenced Pigott, the examiner of plays, on the extent to which Edward

Brandes's play *A Visit* should be censored (16 March 1892). Managers provided a box for Scott on opening nights, which confirmed in his own eyes that he had indeed reached the pinnacle in his profession, an opinion which many theatregoers shared. It is little wonder that he came to see himself as the spokesman for popular theatrical taste and the preserver of what he took to be Victorian verities epitomized by the achievements of the West End theatre. Nevertheless, Scott's career in journalism was eventful for his quarrels with those who accused him of venality. In 1882 he sued Henry Sampson of *The Referee* for libel, and won. When he was accused by the American actor Richard Mansfield in 1889 of being susceptible to managerial bribes, it required the intervention of Irving to avert what would have been an uncomfortable court appearance.

Scott was aware of the new French critical assault on the theatre, especially by Emile Zola, by the late 1870s, but was unprepared for the advent of Ibsen. He was appalled by the implications of plays such as *A Doll's House*, which he saw on 7 June 1889. It was a play of 'men without conscience and women without affection' (*The Theatre*, July 1889). Even more affronting were the productions of *Ghosts* (13 March 1891), which he characterized in a *Daily Telegraph* editorial as a 'loathsome sore unbandaged' (14 March 1891), and *Hedda Gabler* (20 April 1891), a study which 'justifies the most appalling selfishness' (*Daily Telegraph*, 21 April 1891). The plays suggested to him a personal and social scrutiny which Scott's paternalistic view of Victorian theatre could not accommodate. 'Give me pleasure houses for the people; not morgues, or dissecting rooms … or places where unhealthy, morbid subjects are introduced' (in Mrs Clement Scott, *Old Days in Bohemian London*, 7). He was equally out of step with the new criticism of William Archer and George Bernard Shaw. None the less Scott's ability to differentiate between performance and play did not desert him and he responded enthusiastically to performers such as Janet Achurch and Elizabeth Robins, however much he disapproved of their dramatic vehicles. His perspicuous understanding of performance values as distinct entities which demanded critical analysis of their components remained his enduring achievement in the late Victorian period.

Although primarily a theatre critic, Scott was a diverse journalist. He contributed travel essays to the *Daily Telegraph*, which he collected into the anthologies *Round about the Islands* (1873), *Poppy Land-Papers* (1886), and *Pictures Round the World* (1894), as well as poetry and short stories. At the end of his journalistic career he published collections of his Irving reviews and essays (*From 'The Bells' to 'King Arthur'*, 1896), reminiscences of the stage (*The Wheel of Life*, 1898), and a theatrical autobiography, which described the evolutionary progress of dramatic representation in England since the 1840s (*The Drama of Yesterday and Today*, 1899). He was also a skilful adapter of French plays, notably three plays by Sardou for the Bancrofts, the first two in association with B. C. Stephenson, under the pseudonyms Bolton and Saville Rowe: *Peril*, based on *Nos intimes* (Prince of Wales Theatre, 30 September 1876), *Diplomacy*, based on *Dora* (Prince of Wales, 12 January 1878), and *Odette* (Haymarket Theatre, 25 April 1882).

Scott's first wife died on 26 November 1890, and in April 1893 he married Constance Margaret Brandon, an actress, who survived him. In 1897 he was obliged to resign from the *Daily Telegraph*. In an interview with Raymond Blathwayt for *Great Thoughts* he was unwise enough to suggest that the acting profession was an inevitable source of female immorality. His self-importance had overreached itself, and Edward Lawson, the newspaper's proprietor, was forced to distance himself from the furore which the remarks provoked. Scott went to the United States and contributed occasional articles to the New York *Daily Herald*. Back in London in 1901 he founded a short-lived weekly paper, *The Free Lance*, but an accident in 1902 complicated by 'gouty neuritis' confined him to bed. He died at his home, 15 Woburn Square, London, on 25 June 1904, and was buried in the chapel of the Sisters of Nazareth, Southend. VICTOR EMELJANOW

Sources *The Times* (27 June 1904) • C. Scott, *The drama of yesterday and today*, 2 vols. (1899) • Mrs C. Scott, *Old days in bohemian London: recollections of Clement Scott* (1919) • L. Irving, *Henry Irving: the actor and his world* [1951] • *The life and reminiscences of E. L. Blanchard, with notes from the diary of Wm. Blanchard*, ed. C. W. Scott and C. Howard, 2 vols. (1891) • *DNB* • [S. Bancroft and M. E. Bancroft], *Mr and Mrs Bancroft on and off the stage: written by themselves*, 8th edn (1891) • Huntingdon Library, Irving–Scott letters • J. H. Kaplan, 'A puppet's power: George Alexander, Clement Scott and the replotting of *Lady Windermere's Fan*', *Theatre Notebook*, 46 (1992), 59–72 • m. cert. • d. cert.

Archives Hunt. L. • University of Rochester, New York, Rush Rhees Library, corresp. | Theatre Museum, London, letters to Lord Chamberlain's licensee

Likenesses Walery, photograph, c.1890, NPG [*see illus.*] • P. Naumann and R. Taylor & Co., group portrait, wood-engraving (*Our literary contributors—past and present*), BM, NPG; repro. in *ILN* (14 May 1892) • photograph, repro. in Scott, *Drama of yesterday and today*

Wealth at death £4484 17*s*. 2*d*.: probate, 4 Aug 1904, *CGPLA Eng. & Wales*

Scott, Cuthbert (*d.* 1565), bishop of Chester, appears to have been a Lancashire man. He studied at Christ's College, Cambridge, graduating BA in 1535 and proceeding MA in 1538; he was elected to a fellowship in the latter year. He proceeded to the degrees of BTh in 1544 and DTh in 1547 (incorporated DTh at Oxford in 1554). He seems to have been absent from his college, though not from Cambridge, on an unusually high number of occasions after his election as fellow. His concern about the religious changes of the times was reflected in a sermon he gave at Paul's Cross in 1544, and in his complaint in 1545 to Stephen Gardiner, then chancellor of the university, about the performance in his college of a play, *Pammachius*, which touched on Lenten fasting and the ceremonies of the church. He became a prebendary of the Sepulchre chapel in York Minster in 1546, and rector of Etton in Yorkshire in March 1547. Absent from Cambridge for the whole of the reign of Edward VI, in 1549 he became rector of Beeford, also in Yorkshire.

Having kept a low profile during Edward's reign, Scott returned to Cambridge after the accession of Queen Mary, and was appointed master of Christ's on 8 December 1553. He was collated to the prebend of Chamberlainwood in St Paul's, London, on 26 March 1554 (he relinquished this on 28 May 1558), and in that year took part in the public disputation at Oxford with Cranmer, Latimer, and Ridley. In 1554 and again in 1555 he was vice-chancellor of Cambridge University. Essentially conservative in matters of religion, he was nominated bishop of Chester in April 1556 and formally provided on 6 July; he had resigned his mastership by the end of the year. In January 1557 he returned to Cambridge, as head of a commission appointed by Cardinal Pole to carry out a visitation of the university, during which he caused the bones of the reformers Martin Bucer and Paul Fagius to be exhumed and burnt in the market square. But such absences seem to have been rare and Scott appears on the whole to have been a conscientious resident bishop who was also active in preaching. He was greatly concerned to repel recent protestant inroads in his diocese, and devoted much attention to improving standards of behaviour among his parochial clergy. He was also successful in adding substantially to the number of men taking orders, in ceremonies at which he usually presided in person—of nine conducted during his episcopate he missed only one, that of December 1558. He secured important financial assistance from the crown, adding some £200 p.a. to his revenues, while Queen Mary's grant to him of the right to present to the six prebendal stalls in Chester Cathedral added significantly to his patronage. He oversaw the refoundation of Manchester College with an establishment consisting of a warden, eight fellows, four clerks, and eight choristers, and used it as a spearhead for the restoration of Catholicism in Lancashire.

All these achievements were called in question after Queen Mary died on 17 November 1558. Scott was inevitably opposed to many of the changes of religion which were introduced in the early months of Elizabeth's reign. When the Uniformity Bill was passing through parliament in 1559 Scott spoke strongly against it in the Lords (perhaps on 27 or 28 April), drawing heavily on scripture, the fathers, and the councils of the church. He defended the mass and the Catholic priesthood, and argued against the whole idea of imposing faith by statute:

> And as for the certainty of our faith, whereof the story of the Church doth speak, it is a thing of all other most necessary, and if it shall hang upon an act of parliament we have but a weak staff to lean unto. (Strype, *Annals of the Reformation*, 1/2.439–40)

Offered the oath of supremacy, he refused to take it, with the result that on 26 June 1559 he was deprived of his bishopric and heavily fined. When he would not pay he was committed to the Fleet on 13 May 1560. He was released on bail some time in 1562 or 1563, and confined to a radius of 20 miles from the town of Finchingfield in Essex. From there he escaped to the continent in April or May 1563, making his way to Louvain, where he died on 9 October 1564 and was buried in the Franciscan church. A report of Nicholas Sander to Cardinal Moroni, dating from about 1561, describes Scott as 'equal to the rest [of the imprisoned bishops and others] in constancy, and superior to all in eloquence' (Pollen, 16, 39–40), a judgement which sums up well the conduct of his life.

Kenneth Carleton

Sources *Fasti Angl., 1541–1857*, [St Paul's, London] • W. M. Brady, *The episcopal succession in England, Scotland, and Ireland, AD 1400 to 1875*, 2 (1876) • Cooper, *Ath. Cantab.*, 1.233–5 • Venn, *Alum. Cant.*, 1/4.31 • J. Strype, *Annals of the Reformation and establishment of religion … during Queen Elizabeth's happy reign*, new edn, 1/2 (1824) • J. Peile, *Biographical register of Christ's College, 1505–1905, and of the earlier foundation, God's House, 1448–1505*, ed. [J. A. Venn], 1 (1910) • J. H. Pollen, ed., *Miscellanea, I*, Catholic RS, 1 (1905) • *The acts and monuments of John Foxe*, ed. S. R. Cattley, 8 vols. (1837–41) • C. Haigh, *English reformations: religion, politics, and society under the Tudors* (1993) • K. Carleton, *Bishops and reform in the English church, 1520–1559* (2001) • C. Haigh, *Reformation and resistance in Tudor Lancashire* (1975) • W. F. Irvine, ed., 'The earliest ordination book of the diocese of Chester, 1542–7 & 1555–8', *Miscellanies relating to Lancashire and Cheshire*, 4, Lancashire and Cheshire RS, 43 (1902), 25–126 • C. Scott, speech on the Uniformity Bill, Bodl. Oxf., MS Tanner 302; BL, Cotton MS Vespasian D XVIII; repr. in J. Strype, *Annals of the reformation and establishment of religion … during Queen Elizabeth's happy reign*, new edn, 1/2 (1824), 438–50; and in *Proceedings in the parliaments of Elizabeth I*, ed. T. E. Hartley, 1 (1981), 18–26 • 'Answer to the oration of John Stokys' (1557); and 'Oration at the condemnation of Bucer and Fagius', J. Foxe, *Acts and monuments*, ed. G. Townsend and S. R. Cattley (1837)

Scott, Cyril Meir (1879–1970), composer and writer on the occult, was born on 27 September 1879 in Oxton, Cheshire, the youngest of the three children of Henry Scott (1843–1918), businessman and amateur Greek scholar, and his Welsh wife, Mary Griffiths. Not a strong child, Scott was taught by a series of private tutors; his obvious musical talent led to his enrolment in 1891 at the Hoch Conservatorium, Frankfurt am Main, to learn the piano with Lazarro Uzielli and theory with Engelbert Humperdinck. In 1893 he came back to England, but he later returned to Frankfurt as a composition student of Iwan Knorr (1853–1916), remaining until 1898. The hopes of English music rested briefly in the 'Frankfurt group' of Scott and his fellow students Balfour Gardiner, Percy Grainger (a close friend), Roger Quilter, and Norman O'Neill.

In Germany, Scott became a friend of the poet Stefan George. His visual sensibilities were awakened by a friend of George, the stained-glass artist Melchior Lechter, who inspired both Scott's lifelong preference for a Gothic style of domestic surroundings and his youthfully picturesque appearance of 'overlong hair and curious ties' (Scott, *Bone of Contention*, 75). His other interests were equally unconventional. Though brought up as a low-church Anglican, he embraced the yoga teachings of the Swami Vivekananda in 1902 and the tenets of theosophy from 1907. He lived the rest of his personal and professional life according to his esoteric beliefs, and the guidance (via various mediums) of his 'master', Koot Hoomi. Thus in 1921 he was directed to work through karma from a relationship in a previous existence, by marrying Rose Laure Allatini (the novelist Eunice Buckley) (1890–1980), with whom he had a daughter, Vivien, and a son, Desmond. After an amicable separation from Rose in 1939, Scott settled in Sussex in 1943 with a companion, Marjorie Hartston (*d.* 1997), who acted as his medium; he lived in Sussex for the rest of his life.

Among Scott's considerable literary works were many poems, translations of Baudelaire and Stefan George, writings on natural remedies including some with such disconcerting titles as *Crude Black Molasses: Nature's Wonder Food* (1947), and two discursive but entertaining autobiographies, *My Years of Indiscretion* (1924) and *Bone of Contention* (1969). His most substantial writing is to be found in books on esoteric matters such as the trilogy *The Initiate* (3 vols., 1920–32), which remained popular long after his death, and *Music: its Secret Influence throughout the Ages* (1933); in the latter he describes the occult power of music in shaping the destiny of mankind.

Scott's compositions achieved early success, and were championed by Hans Richter, who conducted the *Heroic Suite* in 1900. Several Promenade Concert performances followed, including those of his first symphony (in 1903), the overture to *Princess Maleine* (in 1907), and *Two Poems for Orchestra* (in 1913), and Fritz Kreisler was impressed enough by the piano quartet to lead its first performance in 1901.

Scott was also a professional pianist. His idiomatic piano compositions range from the rhythmically complex cyclic-form piano sonata no. 1 (1909) to suites: his 'occult' suite *Egypt* (1913) was dedicated to 'my friend Mrs Marie Russak, that enlightened Seer, who brought back for me the memory of my past Egyptian lives'. He also wrote numerous small piano pieces, such as the popular 'Water Wagtail' and 'Lotusland'. Robert Elkin became Scott's enthusiastic publisher and promoter and pressured him into production of further charming and facile miniatures and songs, which were enthusiastically performed by musical amateurs both in Britain and abroad.

Unfortunately, the English musical establishment after 1918 was marching to the tune of English folk-song and the Tudor music revival, and Scott's cosmopolitan and occult interests were out of step. The disparaging music criticism of the mid-1930s, coupled with the BBC music department's dismissive attitude towards Scott's more serious compositions, illustrates the depths into which his once-proud reputation as a major English composer had disappeared by that time.

Yet Scott's music has undoubted strengths. Percy Grainger admired the 'magical power of Cyril's chord-skill' (Armstrong, 18), and claimed an influence on Scott's ground-breaking experimentation with irregular rhythms, which were inspired by the 'incessant flux' (Scott, 'Fragments of a lecture', 183) of universal natural forces. His orchestration is subtle, as in the brass-less piano concerto no. 1 (1915) and the Gallic sound-world of his *Aubade* (1911). Although he was dubbed 'the English Debussy' (Scott, *Bone of Contention*, 124), this was a similarity that was firmly denied by both him and the French composer. Nevertheless, French harmonic and textural influence is very clear in the piano quintet (1904–5), which in 1925 was belatedly awarded the Carnegie Trust prize, while the opening of the *Idyll* (1923) for voice and flute closely resembles that of Debussy's *Prélude à l'après-midi d'un faune* (1892–4).

As Scott became increasingly immersed in the esoteric, so his musical style changed. Early works were characterized by both impact and drive, as was his opera *The Alchemist* (1917), successfully produced in Essen in 1928 (but not without the aid of occult intervention from Master Koot Hoomi, who was persuaded during a rehearsal dispute to 'come in one of his subtle bodies and diffuse peace' (Scott, *Bone of Contention*, 188). Later works, such as *Summerland (Devachan)* (1935) and *The Hymn of Unity* (1947), were pervaded by an atmosphere of hypnotic calm, achieved through Scott's use of ostinati, pedal notes, and harmonic stasis, a style which may have evolved from his interest in meditation, breathing, and yoga techniques. Ironically, his oriental interests were condemned as spurious in 1932 by the writer and composer K. S. Sorabji, who described Scott's music as an 'astonishing production … which underneath its trumpery finery of ninths, elevenths, added sixths, joss sticks, papier-Asie Orientalism and pinchbeck Brummagem-Benares nick-nackery, oozes with glutinous commonplace' (Sorabji, 63).

Scott was unfairly considered a poseur rather than a composer, probably because of his occult beliefs, his flamboyant appearance, and his refusal to conform to current musical fashion. Yet his rueful analysis of his musical role seems accurate and honest:

> I had some forty years ago helped to extricate British music from the academic rut in which it had got fixed, and having performed that office, it might well be that *that* was all I was destined to do along musical lines in this particular incarnation! (Scott, *Bone of Contention*, 218)

Scott died at his home, Santosa, 53 Pashley Road, Eastbourne, on 31 December 1970; his ashes were interred at St Nicholas's Church, Pevensey, Sussex. DIANA SWANN

Sources C. Scott, *Bone of contention: life story and confessions* (1969) · C. Scott, *Music: its secret influence throughout the ages* (1933) · C. Scott, 'Fragments of a lecture delivered to the Fabian Society, summer 1913', *Monthly Musical Record*, 44 (1914), 89–91, 121–3, 147–8, 182–3 · K. S. Sorabji, *Around music* (1932) · T. Armstrong, *Delius centenary booklet* (1962) · *CGPLA Eng. & Wales* (1971) · M. Hurd, 'Scott, Cyril (Meir)', *New Grove* · private information (2004) [Desmond Scott, son; Marjorie Hartston-Scott]

Archives BBC WAC, files | BL, letters to Countess Ilse Scilern, Add. MS 54509 | SOUND BL NSA

Likenesses H. Lambert, photogravure, *c.*1922, NPG · G. Hall Neale, oils, exh. 1930, NPG

Wealth at death £45,108: probate, 18 May 1971, *CGPLA Eng. & Wales*

Scott, Daniel (1694–1759), theological writer and lexicographer, was born on 21 March 1694, the son of Daniel Scott, a London merchant, and his second wife, and the half-brother of Thomas Scott (*d.* 1746), Independent minister at Norwich, whose children included Joseph Nicol *Scott, Thomas *Scott (*d.* 1775), and Elizabeth *Scott. The family was probably a branch of the Scotts of Stapleford Tawney, Essex. Daniel was admitted to Merchant Taylors' School, London, on 10 March 1704 but, with the intention of entering the ministry, he left in 1710 to enter Samuel Jones's academy in Gloucester, which moved to Tewkesbury in 1712. There he continued his studies in Latin and

Greek and began to learn Hebrew, Chaldee, and Syriac; he also attended a course on Jewish antiquities. Among his fellow students were Thomas Secker, afterwards archbishop of Canterbury, and the philosopher Joseph Butler, a future bishop of Durham. From Jones's academy he entered the University of Leiden on 13 August 1714, as a student in theology. He appears again in the registers as a student of medicine on 20 June 1718. He graduated LLD from Leiden on 16 May 1719 and he is said to have graduated LLD at the University of Utrecht but his name is not in the Utrecht *Album studiosorum* (1886). While at Utrecht he became a Baptist and joined the Mennonite communion.

Scott returned to England in the early 1720s and probably went to live in Colchester. He was certainly living there when Philip Doddridge, who was to become a close friend, met him for the first time in June 1741. There is no record, however, of Scott having been a minister in Colchester. According to the memoir of his life, probably written by Job Orton and prefixed to the Sherborne edition of Scott's *Essay towards a Demonstration of the Scripture-Trinity* [1770?] his 'invincible diffidence and excessive modesty prevented him from entering the ministry though he was eminently qualified for it' (Orton, 'Memoir', 12). His main occupation was as a scholar and critic, in which capacity he gained a reputation for great learning, critical acumen, and exactness. Doddridge described him as 'one of the most extraordinary persons for learning, ability, candour and piety that I have ever met with' (Doddridge) and Job Orton, probably Scott's greatest admirer, acclaimed him as 'one of the devoutest as well as wisest man I know' (*Letters to Dissenting Ministers*, 1.28). Secker and Butler continued to honour him with their esteem, friendship, and correspondence, even though they did not share his views on the doctrine of the Trinity.

The most celebrated of Scott's theological works was his *Essay towards a Demonstration of the Scripture-Trinity*, first published anonymously in 1725 and for some time erroneously attributed to James Pierce of Exeter. This treatise, which reveals that Scott had come to embrace Arian views, seems to have been speedily bought up and suppressed. Scott was convinced that Edmund Gibson, bishop of London, was responsible for this. A second edition, with some additions, was published in 1738 but apparently suffered a similar fate. Not all, however, shared Gibson's fears. To Orton the *Essay* was a most valuable contribution to the debate on the doctrine of the Trinity and he recommended it to 'the unprejudiced and serious perusal of those who are desirous to know the truth' (Orton, 'Memoir', 19). A third edition was published in Sherborne in 1779, at a time when the arguments over the Trinity had been given extra impetus by Theophilus Lindsey and other Unitarian writers. In 1741 Scott published *A New Version of St Matthew's Gospel*, with critical notes and a review of John Mill's edition. This was followed in 1745 and 1746 by his *Appendix ad thesaurum Graecae-linguae*, in two volumes, dedicated respectively to Secker and Butler, which was heralded as a work of extraordinary critical skill and precision. The many years of close study spent by Scott on the *Appendix* broke his health and spirits, especially as he lost several hundred pounds by its publication, and brought a premature end to his literary career. He died, unmarried, at Cheshunt on 29 March 1759 and was buried in the churchyard there on 3 April.

ALEXANDER GORDON, *rev.* M. J. MERCER

Sources [J. Orton ?], 'Memoir', in D. Scott, *An essay towards a demonstration of the scripture-Trinity*, 3rd edn (1770?), 11–19 · *Letters to dissenting ministers and to students for the ministry from the Rev. Job Orton*, ed. S. Palmer, 2 vols. (1806), vol. 1, p. 28; vol. 2, pp. 247–8 · H. McLachlan, *English education under the Test Acts: being the history of the nonconformist academies, 1662–1820* (1931), 126–31 · Allibone, *Dict.* · A. Chalmers, ed., *The general biographical dictionary*, new edn, 27 (1816), 271–2 · C. Surman, index, DWL · P. Doddridge, letter to Mercy Doddridge, 10–11 July 1741, DWL, Reed MS 28

Scott, David (1746–1805), merchant and director of the East India Company, was born in 'the early weeks' of 1746 at the family residence, Dunninald House in Craig, Forfarshire, and was baptized on 27 February 1746 (Philips, 1.x n. 1; Anderson, 3.411). He was the tenth of thirteen children of Robert Scott (1705–1780), the progressive laird of Dunninald, and his wife, Ann, daughter of General John Middleton of Seton. David attended both school and university at St Andrews where he matriculated in 1759. At the age of seventeen, like many well-educated but impecunious Scots, he sought his fortune in India. Lacking a nomination in the East India Company service, he engaged in private trade as a ship's officer, entered into partnerships with Parsi businessmen and servants of the company, and founded the agency house of Scott, Tate, and Adamson at Bombay. Some of his capital came from his happy marriage to a rich widow, Louisa Jervis, *née* Delagard (*d.* 1803), with whom he had three daughters and a son.

It was the enterprise of private merchants like Scott, often in partnership with East India Company servants, which had slowly built up the trading connections of the British in western India. But the expansion of Bombay's trade was repeatedly threatened by the military power of Mysore and the Marathas, and by the oppressive government of local rulers. Scott and his associates concluded that Bombay had to control the ports and territory which were vital to its trade, and he helped to finance Bombay's military attempts to do this in the 1770s, which ended in defeat. In 1784 the Bombay government owed him nearly £200,000.

In 1786 Scott moved to London, where he directed the English business of his agency house and kept up close connections with his partners and friends in Bombay. Convinced that radical new policies were needed if Britain (and his fellow merchants) were to benefit fully from the company's new position in India, his aim was to expand its territorial power as a shield for the expansion of private British trade. He quickly won the confidence of Pitt, and the friendship of Henry Dundas, the head of the India Board of Control. Dundas helped Scott to become a director of the company in 1788, and to be elected MP for Forfarshire from 1790 until he was defeated in 1796. He was then elected for the Forfar burghs, a seat which he held until his death.

In the court of directors Scott was opposed by the shipping interest, which controlled the company's ships and was hostile to private traders who threatened their monopoly. In 1793 the shipping interest attacked Scott by banning directors from trading with India. Scott responded by vesting his son David, aged eleven, with control of his agency house. As deputy chairman he succeeded in 1795 in reforming the shipping system. In 1798 he proved how India-built ships could reduce the company's shipping costs, but his open support of private British traders alienated his fellow directors and this measure was defeated. The following year his enemies accused him of trading illicitly with the French.

Their hostility was sharpened by Scott's and Dundas's encouragement of the aggressive policy pursued by Wellesley in India, which had increased the company's territory while increasing its debt and threatening its financial survival. Scott had worked closely with Wellesley between 1795 and 1797, when the latter was a member of Dundas's India board, and he used this connection to support the independent expansionist policy of the Bombay government in which his own trading partners were influential. He persuaded Wellesley not to disband the presidency and to retain the pliant Jonathan Duncan as governor. But, with the fall of Pitt's government in 1801, Scott lost the crucial political support which Dundas had given him. Although he defended Wellesley loyally, he was unable to prevent the directors from recalling him in 1804. Fighting ill health and pain since 1796, Scott died exhausted in London on 4 October 1805, two years after his beloved wife, and was buried in St Marylebone burial-ground. He had spent much of his money as well as his health in fighting the monopolies which he saw as the enemies of the private enterprise which had built up British power in India. PAMELA NIGHTINGALE

Sources *The correspondence of David Scott, director and chairman of the East India Company, relating to Indian affairs, 1787–1805*, ed. C. H. Philips, CS, 3rd ser., 75–6 (1951) • P. Nightingale, *Trade and empire in western India, 1784–1806* (1970) • C. H. Philips, *The East India Company, 1784–1834* (1940) • H. Furber, *John Company at work* (1948) • bap. reg. Scot. • W. Anderson, *The Scottish nation*, 3 vols. (1866–77)
Archives BL OIOC, corresp. and papers relating to India • BL OIOC, corresp., MSS Eur. D 534; Eur. F 18; Eur. B 152; Eur. B 170; Eur. D 589 • NL Scot., corresp. | BL OIOC, home miscellaneous series of the India Office records, nos. 728–731A • Bucks. RLSS, letters to Lord Hobart • NA Scot., letters to Lord Melville • NL Scot., Laing MSS • NL Scot., corresp. with Lord Melville • NL Wales, corresp. with Lord Clive • PRO, letters to William Pitt, PRO 30/8
Likenesses Romney, oils, 1793–4, Forfar County Buildings, Angus

Scott, David (1806–1849), painter and poet, was born on 10 or 12 October 1806 at Parliament Square, High Street, Edinburgh, the fifth child of Robert *Scott (1777–1841), an engraver, and his wife, Ross Bell, whom he married in 1800. The deaths of his four elder brothers within a few days of each other in 1807 had a devastating and lasting effect on his deeply religious parents, who soon after moved to St Leonards, near Edinburgh, then relatively rural. David and his three younger siblings grew up in a household where 'a smile was a rare thing within the threshold and silence was enjoined as an act of wisdom' (Scott, 16). This sombre atmosphere, where long evenings were spent in silent reading and study, doubtless contributed to Scott's melancholic cast of mind. His health was never good and 'it was in his nature to be sad' (ibid., 32).

David Scott (1806–1849), by David Octavius Hill and Robert Adamson

Initially taught at home by his father, Scott attended the high school of Edinburgh between 1817 and 1821 before entering the Trustees' Academy, as his father's apprentice. He was compelled to follow the painstaking and boring work of a jobbing engraver when his father's health broke down in 1819, but was allowed to continue studies at the Trustees' Academy until 1825; there he formed friendships with, among others, John Steel, Daniel Macnee, and Alexander Fraser. In May 1827 he became a founder member of the Edinburgh Life Academy Association, and this enabled him to further study life drawing. In 1832 he briefly studied anatomy under Dr Monro and his travels in Italy between 1832 and 1833, and in particular the fifteen months spent in Rome, gave him further opportunities to advance his drawing technique in a series of anatomical drawings made in the Hospital of the Incurable, and 137 life drawings and oil studies. However, his draughtsmanship was often criticized even by those who most admired his painting.

Scott's first exhibited painting, characteristically entitled *The Hopes of Genius Dispelled by Death*, was exhibited at the Royal Institution in 1828. Throughout his career

Scott's choice of subject matter was frequently death, terror, or the supernatural. His themes were obscure and difficult for the general public to comprehend. His grand, imaginative, and heroic subjects were usually looked at from a subjective, melancholic standpoint. Although a prolific and ambitious painter, Scott rarely managed to sell his pictures or receive favourable reviews, for he did very little to make his pictures accessible. That a reasonable body of his work was thought worth preserving was due largely to the considerable efforts of his younger brother, the poet and painter William Bell *Scott, whose *Memoir* describes Scott's background, his uncertainties, and his lifetime efforts to gain recognition. William reveals Scott to be a lean, handsome, nervously energetic and essentially solitary figure, in spite of his several friends and admirers in Edinburgh; lacking the ability to empathize with others, full of self-preoccupations and religious doubt, growing gradually more dissatisfied and embittered but convinced that his painting should be judged 'by its sentiment by its mental bearing' (Scott, 34). In his writing David Scott consistently stressed that composition, colour, and technique must, in the last resort, be subordinated to the overriding importance of ideas in art.

Scott's fellow artists were sufficiently impressed by his huge picture *Lot and his Daughters Fleeing from the Cities of the Plain* together with *Fingal, or, The Spirit of Lodi* and *The Death of Sappho* to elect him a full academician of the Scottish Academy in 1829 at the age of twenty-three. In 1836 he was appointed a visitor to the Trustees' Academy, but was rejected for the post of master in 1843. He never received the public recognition he longed for and felt he deserved. His failure to win any prize in the competitions for the decoration of the new houses of parliament in 1843 was a bitter blow. Scott's poems, many of which, at his own request, were destroyed unread after his death, were published only posthumously. W. B. Scott devoted a chapter of his *Memoir* to his brother's poetry, reproducing several untitled pieces as well as 'A Dream', 'Dead Memories', and 'The Funeral of Nelson' (Scott, 301–16).

Scott's set of engravings, *The Monograms of Man*, influenced by William Blake and John Flaxman, were well received when published in 1831 but did not sell, while his highly imaginative and sympathetic illustrations of Coleridge's *Ancient Mariner* took six years to find a publisher. During his travels in France, Switzerland, and Italy between 1832 and 1834 Scott visited the usual artistic centres of the grand tour and was confirmed in his historical ambitions. He studied the old masters closely and kept a detailed diary, the basis of a later series of long articles in *Blackwood's Edinburgh Magazine* (1839–41). No marked changes in style were evident on his return to Edinburgh in the two large canvases *Sappho and Anacreon* (Glasgow Art Gallery and Museum) and *Discord*, which used the theme of filial rebellion to show the overthrow of the old order by the new. These works were exhibited at the Royal Scottish Academy in 1840 along with *Philoctetes Left on the Isle of Lemnos*, and all demonstrate Scott's admiration of William Etty. One painting executed in Rome, *The Vintager* (1833; Aberdeen Art Gallery) is unique in its subject matter, clarity, and bright colour. His style varies from picture to picture, so that there is no clear development—although certain strong characteristics are apparent and almost all his work had a historical, fictional, or spiritual basis. *Queen Elizabeth at the Globe Theatre* received no recognition in 1841 when exhibited at the Royal Academy and he avoided further rejection in London exhibitions. On the death of his father in 1841 he moved from Stockbridge to a large studio at Easter Dalry House, Edinburgh, where he produced several large canvases including *The Dead Rising after the Crucifixion* (exh. 1845) and the powerful *Traitor's Gate* (NG Scot.).

Scott's technique was 'one of sudden impulse and effort—a thing of the mood and the moment', wrote his late nineteenth-century biographer (Gray, 18) but D. G. Rossetti, introduced to his work by the artist's brother, described Scott as 'the painter most nearly fulfilling the highest requirement for historic art, both as a thinker and a colourist who has appeared among us from the time of Hogarth to his own' (ibid., 12). For the art historian J. L. Caw, 'an imaginative painter in a period of domestic and historical genre, a dreamer in an age of prose, David Scott was clearly out of place' (Caw, 128). Several more recent historians have placed his work firmly in the tradition of British Romantic painting while identifying Alexander Runciman's subject painting as a major influence. Certainly his largest picture, *Vasco de Gama Rounding Cape Horn*, purchased, just before his death, by public subscription and presented to Trinity House, Leith, owes much to Runciman's *Fingal and the Spirit of Loda*.

Scott died, unmarried, at his home, Easter Dalry House, Edinburgh, of 'internal inflammation and chronic dyspepsy' (Scott, 341) on 5 March 1849 and was buried in Edinburgh four days later. His works are in several public collections including the National Gallery of Scotland; Glasgow Art Gallery and Museum; Kirkcaldy Museum and Art Gallery; Aberdeen Art Gallery; and the Hunterian Art Gallery, University of Glasgow. JOHN MORRISON

Sources W. B. Scott, *Memoir of David Scott, RSA* (1850) · J. M. Gray, *David Scott, RSA, and his works* (1884) · J. L. Caw, *Scottish painting past and present, 1620–1908* (1908) · M. Campbell, *David Scott, 1806–1849* (1990) · D. Irwin and F. Irwin, *Scottish painters at home and abroad, 1700–1900* (1975) · R. Brydall, *Art in Scotland, its origin and progress* (1889) · D. Macmillan, *Scottish art, 1460–1990* (1990) · W. Hardie, *Scottish painting, 1837 to the present* (1990) · S. Cursiter, *Scottish art to the close of the 19th century* (1949) · C. B. de Laperriere, ed., *The Royal Scottish Academy exhibitors, 1826–1990*, 4 vols. (1991) · D. Macmillan, *Painting in Scotland: the golden age* (1986) [exhibition catalogue, U. Edin., Talbot Rice Gallery, and Tate Gallery, London, 1986] · E. Gordon, *The Royal Scottish Academy of painting, sculpture and architecture, 1826–1976* (1976)

Archives NG Scot., corresp. with the Trustees' Academy · NG Scot., albums and sketchbook · Royal Scot. Acad., letters | NL Scot., extracts from corresp., journals and memoranda, made by his brother

Likenesses D. Scott, self-portrait, oils, 1832, Scot. NPG · R. S. Lauder, oils, 1839, Scot. NPG · D. O. Hill and R. Adamson, calotype photograph, Scot. NPG [*see illus.*] · C. Lees, oils, Royal Scot. Acad. · W. B. Scott, etching (after D. Scott), BM; repro. in Scott, *Memoir* · W. B. Scott, etching (on his deathbed; after pencil sketch by

unknown artist), BM • J. Steell, marble bust, NG Scot. • J. Steell, plaster bust, Scot. NPG • woodcut, BM; repro. in *Art Journal* (1849)
Wealth at death £1384 17*s*. 6*d*.: confirmation, 1852, Scotland

Scott, Douglas William (1913–1990), industrial designer and educator, was born on 4 April 1913 at 4D Peabody Buildings, Southwark, London, the son of Edward Scott, a borough council meter inspector, and his wife, Lilian Eliza Grace Charlton. He grew up in south London, attending St Philip's Junior School, in Lambeth, followed by the nearby Archbishop Temple Grammar School. Aged thirteen he won a London County Council scholarship to the Central School of Arts and Crafts, where he trained as a silversmith in the department of metal studies from 1926 to 1929. His first employment was in Birmingham, at Osler and Farady, a long-established, traditional, and high-quality electric lighting company with established markets at home and abroad. He designed light fittings for cinemas, civic buildings, and other architectural settings in a variety of styles from the contemporary vogue for art deco to historical derivations from earlier periods. However, in 1933 he moved back to London as chief designer for GVD Illuminator, a firm which specialized in the fashionable field of concealed architectural lighting. After three years he joined the newly established London offices of Raymond Loewy Associates, thereby becoming one of the first professional British industrial designers. Loewy was a celebrated American industrial designer who had already enjoyed a considerable reputation in the United States working for a number of large-scale, high-profile corporate clients, although his direct involvement with the London office was limited. Scott worked alongside the British designer John Beresford Evans under the watchful eye of the American office manager, Carl Otto, a stylist who had previously worked for General Motors. During his period at Loewy Associates, Scott was influenced by the lessons of American commercial styling, blending it with the emphatically practical, common-sense approach that characterized his own design philosophy. Among the office's clients were Allied Ironfounders, for whom Scott redesigned the Aga cooker and designed the Rayburn cooker; Electrolux and the General Electric Company (GEC), for whom he designed domestic appliances and street lighting; and Rootes, the motor manufacturers, for whom he worked on the Hillman Minx car project. However, the office closed in November 1939, following the outbreak of war two months earlier. In that year he had married Katherine Tierney, with whom he had a son and a daughter.

During the war years Scott worked in the engine department of the aircraft manufacturers De Havilland, learning a good deal about materials and production engineering and enhancing his methodological inclinations. Despite an offer from Raymond Loewy to manage a new London office, after the war Scott took on a variety of freelance commissions, including luxury luggage for Papworth Industries (1947), coach design for London Transport (1946 and 1948), and radio cabinet and selector systems for Rediffusion (1946–7). Following a four-year stint teaching industrial design at the Central School of Arts and Crafts he formed a design consultancy with Fred Ashford in 1949—Scott–Ashford Associates—and gained design work for control and switch-gear in the electronics industry. Scott's relative standing in the design profession was demonstrated by the fact that the Council of Industrial Design, established under the Board of Trade in 1944 to improve standards of design in British industry, recommended him to the Scottish clock manufacturer Westclox, which was seeking to launch an economical, well-designed product for the mass market. Typically, in 1952 Scott produced a low-cost, practical, and elegant design solution which combined an understanding of materials, production processes, and aesthetics. Very important in this period was his work for London Transport, which included designs for the Regent type coach (RTC)—a luxury Green Line double-decker, the original prototype for which had been produced by Norbert Dutton and Ronald Ingles. Working closely with the London Transport design team he also designed the bodywork and interior for the new, streamlined Regal Four (RF) coach (1948), a heavily glazed sightseeing version of which went into service for visitors to the Festival of Britain in 1951. Scott was also closely involved with prototype work for the ubiquitous Routemaster bus (1952–4). This red double-decker became a symbol of London, having gone into production in 1959 and remained in service for more than forty years. It was the last bus that was custom-designed and built by London Transport; elegant and subtly curved, it was characterized by highly practical, easily maintained yet elegant interiors, with tartan moquette seat covering also designed by Scott. In 1955 he split from Fred Ashford, who had become increasingly committed to teaching rather than to their partnership, and established Douglas Scott Associates, retaining most of the Scott–Ashford client base.

Douglas Scott Associates produced a number of designs over the twenty-one years of its existence, including work for British Sound Recorders (tape recorders), the General Post Office (stamp-vending machines, payphones, and clocks), Prestige (kitchenware), Ideal-Standard (sanitaryware), Marconi (broadcasting equipment and mobile outside studios), and English Electric (electrical motor housings and computer control systems). The product range covered the entire scale—from slide viewers to heavy-duty, caterpillar-tracked excavators—and every level of technology from handwhisks to colour television cameras. One of his most widely known designs was the Roma washbasin for Ideal-Standard, which went into production in 1964 and sold several million worldwide. One of the reasons for its success stemmed directly from Scott's research into the materials and processes used in its manufacture, the ways in which it would be used in the home, and the practicalities of economic distribution. His diligent analysis was followed through in full-scale mock-ups that resulted in a lasting design solution, the understated elegance of which led to its acceptance in the permanent collection of the Museum of Modern Art in New York.

Scott also made an important contribution to design

education, establishing the industrial design curriculum at the Central School of Arts and Crafts, London, in 1945. Originally held in the evenings, the curriculum proved popular, and Scott became a full-time teacher in 1946. Following his pragmatic approach to design, students were encouraged to study materials and production techniques and to work to a tight budget, all of which geared them for subsequent work in the marketplace. However, such a business-like, practical approach to design led to tensions in the prevailing art school ethos, in which notions of creativity were paramount. Following criticism from the Ministry of Education inspectorate Scott resigned in 1949, although he continued to teach at the school, on and off, between 1952 and 1972, and established a postgraduate programme in 1966. His tutelage provided a fertile breeding ground for industrial design in Britain, influencing key figures like Martin Rowland, Bill Moggridge, and David Ogle. His approach and curriculum design was also admired by Ramon Torres, head of architecture at the Universidad Nacional Autonoma de Mexico (UNAM) in 1966, who sought to establish industrial design in his own institution. This eventually led to an invitation to Scott to be a visiting professor at UNAM in 1970. This in turn resulted in further visits, in 1973 and 1975, before he was made a full-time professor of industrial design from 1976. Having closed Douglas Scott Associates to accommodate this dramatic change he remained in Mexico for three years, instituting a tough educational regime. From then until his death, on 2 October 1990 at Lymington, Hampshire, he worked as a freelance lecturer and design consultant for a number of engineering companies.

Scott gained professional acknowledgement through three Design Council awards. In 1973 he won the Instituto Mexicano de Commercio Exterior's gold medal for design; he was made a royal designer for industry (RDI) in 1974; and the design medal of the Society of Industrial Artists and Designers was awarded to him in 1983. He was also elected for the Japan Design Foundation's second international design awards in Osaka in 1985. But while he may have been highly respected in professional circles he remained comparatively unknown to the general public. Scott was a quiet, unassuming man who eschewed publicity. His students at the Central School of Arts and Crafts generally viewed him as rather serious and somewhat austere, with a highly disciplined and business-like outlook; these personal qualities remained with him throughout his life. Jonathan Glancey, writing about him in his 1988 monograph, stated:

> he has sought no acclaim and has made little money from his half century as an industrial designer. He has, as he says, always been too busy to think about the money or possible fame. Yet his best designs rank among the British classics. But in this respect Scott is no different from the dozens of backroom engineers and draughtsmen who produced some of the most elegant machines and products of the [twentieth] century. (Glancey, 93)

Jonathan Woodham

Sources *The Independent* (12 Nov 1990) • *Design* (Nov 1990) • *Design Week* (16 Nov 1990) • J. Glancey, *Douglas Scott* (1988) • information file, V&A NAL • J. Pilditch and D. Scott, *The business of product design* (1965) • J. Woudhuysen, 'Route master', *Design*, 418 (Oct 1983), 58–61 • 'Design Centre awards 1963', *Design*, 174 (June 1963), 52–3 • *Central to design—central to industry*, Central School of Art and Design (1982) • F. MacCarthy, *All things bright and beautiful: design in Britain, 1830 to today* (1972) • 'European standards', *Design*, 129 (Sept 1959), 63 • *Designers in Britain*, 4 (1954) • *Designers in Britain*, 6 (1964) • J. Woudhuysen, 'The secret of Scott', *Design Week* (30 Sept 1988) • b. cert. • d. cert.

Scott, Dukinfield Henry (1854–1934), palaeobotanist, was born in London on 28 November 1854, the youngest of the five sons of the architect George Gilbert *Scott (1811–1878) and his wife, Caroline Oldrid (1811–1872). Scott was educated by tutors at home, and under the influence of his mother took to field botany before he was fourteen. After reading Griffith and Henfrey's *Micrographic Dictionary* (1854) he became interested in plant structure, the study of which eventually became his main occupation. However, despite his early interest in botany, he went up to Christ Church, Oxford, in 1872 to read classics and, after graduating in 1876, spent three years training as an engineer.

In the autumn of 1879 Scott's botanical interests stirred again and, at the suggestion of W. T. Thiselton-Dyer Scott decided to study the subject in Germany. From 1880 to 1882 he worked intermittently in the University of Würzburg under Julius von Sachs. On his return to England he became assistant to Daniel Oliver at University College, London. In 1885 he was transferred to the Normal School of Science, taking charge, under T. H. Huxley, of all the botanical work. Financially independent, Scott pursued his career of regular teaching for a decade only before becoming, in 1892, honorary director of the Jodrell Laboratory at Kew. When he left this post fourteen years later he retired to East Oakley House, near Basingstoke. He married, in 1887, one of his earliest students, Henderina Victoria (*d.* 1929), daughter of Hendericus Martinus Klaassen FGS, whose family was of Dutch extraction. They had three sons, the eldest of whom was killed in the First World War; the second died at school, and the third died in infancy; there were also four daughters.

In 1889 Scott met the palaeobotanist W. C. Williamson, professor of natural history at Manchester. A visit to Manchester opened Scott's eyes to the field that he was to make his own. In his words: 'my work, since I knew Williamson, owes its inspiration to him.' Following Williamson's move to London about 1892 the two men worked in concert until Williamson's death in 1895. Scott then continued alone the investigations into the structure and affinities of the fossil plants of the Palaeozoic rocks. The sections used by Williamson and Scott went to the British Museum (Natural History); the Scott collection includes more than 3000 slides of carboniferous plants.

In addition to research papers, Scott published books on broader lines, such as *Studies in Fossil Botany* (1900) and *Extinct Plants and Problems of Evolution* (1924). He also wrote an elementary textbook, *An Introduction to Structural Botany* (1894; 14th edn, 1948). All Scott's books were atypical for the period, avoiding dogmatic statement, and stressing what remains unknown as much as what is known. In everything he wrote Scott's attitude towards his problems was orientated to the Darwinian and phylogenetic outlook of his period; he stated explicitly in 1900 that 'the ultimate object of morphological inquiry is to build up the genealogical tree of the organic world'. Nevertheless, after a quarter of a century's further work, his modest conclusion was that 'we know a good deal about extinct plants, but not enough, as yet, to throw much light on the problems of their evolution'. Despite this modesty, Scott was outstanding as a structural palaeobotanist. His flair for divining the 'build' of a plant, his clear and succinct mode of presentation, his balanced judgement, and his readiness to sacrifice cherished ideas as soon as the evidence was shown to weigh against them combined to endow his work with lasting life.

Scott was elected FRS in 1894 and received a royal medal in 1906 and the Darwin medal in 1926. He was president of the Linnean Society (1908–12) and received the society's gold medal in 1921. He was president of the Royal Microscopical Society (1904–6), of the South-Eastern Union of Scientific Societies (1909), of section K (botany) of the British Association (1896 and 1921), and of the palaeobotanical section of the International Botanical Congress (1930). He received the Wollaston medal of the Geological Society in 1928. Honorary degrees were conferred upon him by the universities of Manchester and Aberdeen. Scott died at East Oakley House on 29 January 1934. AGNES ARBER, *rev.* ALEXANDER GOLDBLOOM

Sources *DSB* • H. N. Andrews, *The fossil hunters: in search of ancient plants* (1980), 97–101 • A. C. S., *Obits. FRS*, 1 (1932–5), 205–27 • *Annals of Botany*, 49 (1935) • *Journal of Botany, British and Foreign*, 72 (1934), 83–8 • *Nature*, 133 (1934), 317–19 • F. E. Weiss, *Proceedings of the Linnean Society of London*, 146th session (1933–4), 166–9 • *New Phytologist*, 24 (1925) • *New Phytologist*, 33 (1934) • *Current Science*, 2 (1934)

Archives Linn. Soc., autobiography • NHM | BL, corresp. with Macmillans, Add. MS 55222 • BL, corresp. with Marie Stopes, Add. MS 58472 • U. Glas., Archives and Business Record Centre, letters to Frederick Bower

Likenesses J. Kerr Lawson, oils, RBG Kew • Maull and Fox, photograph, RS • photograph, RS • portrait, Hunt. L.

Wealth at death £40,419 0s. 6d.: resworn probate, 9 April 1934, *CGPLA Eng. & Wales*

Scott, Edward Taylor (1883–1932), journalist, was born on 15 November 1883 at The Firs, Whitworth Lane, Rusholme, Manchester, the third and last son of Charles Prestwich *Scott (1846–1932), editor and owner of the *Manchester Guardian*, and his wife, Rachel Susan Cook [*see* Scott, Rachel Susan (1848–1905)]; the name Taylor acknowledged the Scotts' cousins, co-founders of the paper. He was educated at Rugby School and then at Corpus Christi College, Oxford, but left without a degree to study economics at the then new London School of Economics; in London he boarded with the family of the anti-imperialist writer John Atkinson Hobson. Again he left (in 1906) without a degree to become private secretary to Sydney Olivier, the Fabian socialist and newly appointed governor of Jamaica, but almost at once (1907) achieved a London BSc (Econ.) degree as an external student. Before going to Jamaica he married on 5 September 1907 Mabel Josephine Hobson (1886–1969), J. A. Hobson's daughter; they had four children.

Edward Taylor Scott (1883–1932), by Francis Dodd, 1920s

After two years (1907–9) in Jamaica, where he and his wife were intimate friends with the Olivier family, Scott became a financial journalist in the City office of the London *Daily News*; in 1913 he moved to Manchester as commercial editor of his father's newspaper. Early in 1915 he joined the Royal Field Artillery; taken prisoner in the German offensive of March 1918 and held at St Quentin, he was long posted missing, but was home by Christmas. His experiences in the First World War affected him deeply: during the 1919–21 period of labour unrest, when he was in charge of economic and social topics, his leaders 'always show a sympathy with men who might well have been gunners in his battery a year before. His views about cabinet ministers, company directors and trade union bosses often resemble a front line soldier's opinion of the staff' (Ayerst, 432).

Because foreign affairs in the 1920s so often turned on economics and finance—as over German inflation and reparations—Scott's expertise made him in effect the paper's chief foreign as well as home leader writer. He was now also its part proprietor: in 1914 his father had divided the bulk of his shares among his two surviving sons and his son-in-law, C. E. Montague. The elder brother, John Scott, kept to the management side; in 1925 Montague deliberately left the editorial staff to make room for Ted Scott, as he was known. In 1929 C. P. Scott formally retired and Ted became editor. The octogenarian father, however, as 'governing director' still came to the office every day and exerted an influence the son could not withstand. Scott achieved full autonomy only on his father's death on 1 January 1932, and then could exert it only for a few months. His colleague and devoted friend Malcolm Muggeridge later made the harassing father–son relationship the theme of a novel, *Picture Palace* (1934); the *Manchester Guardian*, however, got the publisher to withdraw it.

In the 1920s Scott broadened the paper's economic and financial coverage, launching the *Manchester Guardian Commercial* (later discontinued) and *Manchester Guardian Weekly*. The policy he followed was shaped both by his own radical, independent temperament and by the stress of the two great crises he lived through, the post-war boom and slump and the world depression that started in 1929. 'One can hardly doubt', he wrote in one leader, 'that [self-government in industry] will come, and resistance to it may be futile' (*Manchester Guardian*, 23 June 1921); in another, that to keep productive workers unemployed was 'the economics of the madhouse' (ibid., 23 Nov 1921; Ayerst, 432). He guided the paper in opposition to the 1926 general strike but also to parts of the Emergency Powers Act. In 1931 he led it gradually away from approval of the National Government (which, in his absence on holiday, his deputy W. P. Crozier had welcomed), criticizing its conduct of the election campaign and opposing the uniform cut in unemployment benefit; this led many business firms to cancel advertising—a severe loss of revenue. By 16 November 1931 he was writing to J. L. Hammond:

> it seems to me broadly that politics are getting into an ugly shape and that we shall be driven more and more to take an anti-property line. And that is fatal to a twopenny paper. I myself feel that I am getting more and more of a socialistic way of thinking (or rather feeling) but the more I look at the Socialist party the less I like it. (Ayerst, 471)

In overseas matters he shared the paper's sympathy with Weimar Germany and its suspicion of colonialism.

Where Scott might have led his 'twopenny paper' is unknowable: on 22 April 1932 he took his son Richard to Windermere for a boating weekend; while they were on the water, very cold at that season, a freak squall capsized the boat. Richard got on top. Scott tried to swim ashore, but the cold brought a seizure; he sank and drowned. His remains were cremated four days later at Manchester crematorium.

Scott cared more for ideas and argument than for style. A dark, well-built, handsome man of great charm, he was 'so reserved and so modest that the toughness of his mind and the independence of his character escaped the negligent eye. He was of all men the most sincere and the least prejudiced' (Martin, 186). He had started to innovate and, in newspaper history, remains a great might-have-been.

John Rosselli

Sources D. Ayerst, *Guardian: biography of a newspaper* (1971) • K. Martin, *Father figures* (1966) • *Manchester Guardian* (23 April 1932) • *The Times* (23 April 1932) • *The Times* (26 April 1932) • *WWW* • C. H. Rolph, *Kingsley: the life, letters and diaries of Kingsley Martin* (1973) • I. Hunter, *Malcolm Muggeridge* (1980) • F. R. Gannon, *The British press and Germany, 1936–1939* (1971) • *The political diaries of C. P. Scott, 1911–1928*, ed. T. Wilson (1970) • private information (2004) [assistant archivist, Special Collections, U. Lond. Library] • *CGPLA Eng. & Wales* (1932) • b. cert. • m. cert. • d. cert.

Archives JRL, archives of the *Manchester Guardian* | BLPES, letters to Edwin Cannan • Bodl. Oxf., letters to J. L. L. B. Hammond and B. L. Hammond

Likenesses F. Dodd, oils, 1920, priv. coll. • F. Dodd, pencil drawing, 1920–29, The Guardian, London [*see illus.*] • F. S. Schmidt, photograph, *c.*1930, priv. coll.; repro. in *Manchester Guardian*

Wealth at death £27,856 6*s.* 10*d.*: probate, 28 May 1932, *CGPLA Eng. & Wales*

Scott, Elisabeth Whitworth (1898–1972), architect, was born on 20 September 1898 at Hartington, Poole Road, Bournemouth, Hampshire, one of the ten children of Bernard Scott, surgeon, and his wife, Lydia Margaret, *née* Whitworth. Bernard Scott's father, Samuel King Scott, a Brighton doctor, was the younger brother of the architect Sir George Gilbert *Scott and his mother, Georgina, was the sister of that architect's first pupil, George Frederick *Bodley. Scott was educated at home until she was fourteen and then at Redmoor School, Canford Cliffs, Bournemouth. In 1919 she entered the Architectural Association Schools, where she gained her diploma in 1924. Scott then worked as an assistant to Niven and Wigglesworth, then in the office of Louis de Soissons at Welwyn Garden City, and then for Oliver Hill. She was working for Maurice Chesterton when she entered the open international competition to rebuild the Shakespeare Memorial Theatre at Stratford upon Avon, which had been destroyed by fire in 1926.

Scott's design was selected unanimously in 1928 by the Anglo-American assessors out of seventy-two entries. George Bernard Shaw remarked that her design was the only one that showed any theatre sense (*The Times*, 24 June 1972). Elisabeth Scott thus became the first woman ever to win a major architectural competition and to undertake a large public commission in Britain. She had been assisted in preparing the competition drawings by two fellow students at the Architectural Association, Alison Sleigh and J. C. Shepherd (who subsequently married), and the partnership of Scott, Chesterton, and Shepherd was formed in 1929 to carry out the commission, although Maurice Chesterton disclaimed 'any personal share whatever in the successful design' (*Daily Telegraph*, 6 Jan 1928). Sir Geoffrey Jellicoe (who had been in partnership with Shepherd) later recorded that 'in the partnership, Scott provided the initiative, Chesterton the administration and Shepherd the flair' (*Architects' Journal*, 12 July 1972, 68).

Scott's design, which gently adapted north European modern architecture to English conditions, was also remarkable for the sensitivity shown to scale and to the site by the River Avon. In execution the theatre was faced in brick rather than stone and the interior was redesigned after a tour of modern theatres in Germany insisted upon by William Bridges-Adams, the director of the Shakespeare Memorial Theatre. If the completed building was found to be inadequate in terms of its facilities and the narrowness of the proscenium arch, much of the fault lay in the competition brief and expert advice. However, most of the criticism the building received after its opening in 1932 stemmed from its conspicuous modernity; Sir

Edward Elgar, the composer, found it 'so unspeakably ugly and wrong' that he refused to go inside (S. Beauman, *The Royal Shakespeare Company: a History of Ten Decades*, 1982, 100).

Scott was later joined by John Breakwell—her firm became Scott, Shepherd, and Breakwell—and was responsible for the Fawcett Building at Newnham College, Cambridge. Completed in 1938, this is an austere design in a style which reflected the later work of Edwin Lutyens and which, perhaps, failed to fulfil the promise suggested by the Shakespeare Memorial Theatre—although, for Scott, it was an easier commission as she was happier in the company of intellectual women. Other buildings by the partnership included: alterations to the Marie Curie Hospital in Hampstead, London; an elementary school at Northallerton, Yorkshire (1941); the Homer farm school for infants at Henley (1936); houses at Gidea Park, Essex, Fludger's Wood, Oxfordshire, and Stoke Row at Henley; and a house for a doctor at Morden (1933) which was more modernist in character and attributed to Scott alone. After the Second World War she was in private practice and worked with Ronald Phillips & Partners on housing, hotels, and luxury flats in the Bournemouth area. She also worked for Bournemouth borough architects' department after 1962 and was responsible for rebuilding the pavilions on Bournemouth and Boscombe piers. Scott finally retired from practice in 1968, the year after completing a house in Swanage for her lifelong friend Sybil Clement Brown.

As a feminist, Scott was an active member of the Fawcett Society and employed young women architects to work on the Stratford project. 'Elisabeth Scott was representative of women architects of her generation', Lynne Walker has written; 'she was conscious that she would encounter discrimination' (L. Walker, 'Women and architecture', *A View from the Interior*, ed. J. Attfield and P. Kirkham, 1989, 102). She had to cope with the assumption that, as a woman, she could not really have been responsible for the Stratford theatre design; when a newspaper reporter wrote that he

> expected to meet a modern woman of the extreme type, as strong, direct and bold as the design. Instead I found a retiring, somewhat shy and very feminine woman … it seemed almost incredible that she could have produced something that was so extremely opposed to her own personality.

Scott retorted that generous provision had been made for tea on the terrace and 'was not that sufficiently feminine?' (*Daily News*, 4 and 6 Jan 1928). Geoffrey Jellicoe recalled that 'Elisabeth was gentle, unassuming, determined, and with a personal integrity that acknowledged her associates' help' (*Architects' Journal*, 12 July 1972, 68). Notwithstanding her architectural connections, it was Scott's design talent together with her determination that secured her the Stratford commission, and her competition win was a most important step in advancing the status of women in a male-dominated profession in the years after the First World War. Scott married George Richards in 1936 and died on 19 June 1972. GAVIN STAMP

Sources *The Times* (24 June 1972) • G. A. Jellicoe, *Architects' Journal* (12 July 1972) • fellowship nomination form, 1946, RIBA BAL • L. Walker, 'British women in architecture, 1671–1951', *Women architects: their work* (1984) • *ArchR*, 71 (June 1932) [Shakespeare Memorial Theatre issue] • 'Shakespeare Memorial Theatre, Stratford-on-Avon: result of competition', *RIBA Journal*, 35 (1927–8), 145–7 • A. Minett, 'One woman in architecture: the life and work of Elisabeth Scott, 1898–1972', BArch diss., U. Newcastle, 1988 • b. cert.

Scott [*married names* Williams, Smith], **Elizabeth** (**1707/8–1776**), hymn writer, was born at Hitchin, Hertfordshire, the daughter of Thomas Scott (1679/80–1746), Independent minister, and his wife. Joseph Nicoll *Scott (1702/3–1769) and Thomas *Scott (1705–1775) were her brothers. In 1709 the family moved to Norwich, where Elizabeth was probably educated at home by her father whom she idolized. The name and vital dates of her mother have not been traced.

Elizabeth's father described her to his friend and fellow minister Philip Doddridge in 1739 as one 'who devotes her self to doing Good a Protestant Nun' (Nuttall, no. 534). She was also a poet who, by 1740, had compiled a manuscript volume, dedicated to her father, containing some ninety of her hymns and lyrics (now at Yale University). Doddridge, who admired, read, and transcribed her hymns, enjoyed her company, finding 'hourly some new Discoveries' of 'the Fineness of her Genius' and 'the Extent of her Knowledge', not to mention her piety, filial affection, humility, generosity, and great sentiments (letter of 2 July 1744, Nuttall, no. 983). At the same time she was highly strung and depressive. Her father wrote to Doddridge in December 1744 of her nervous system being so disordered that she was taken with 'an Universal trembling'; in May 1745 she confessed to Doddridge 'a guilty, selfish, condemning conscience, a hard unbelieving heart, a frowning God, a withdrawn Spirit'; she 'renounced every pleasure' and was thought to be close to death until she was relieved by Doddridge's letters and 'repeated and unreserved conversations' (Nuttall, nos. 1022, 1062, 1072, 1074–6). She was plunged into further depression by the death of her father on 15 November 1746, particularly as his last years had been clouded by the Arianism of his son Joseph Nicoll.

In 1750 Elizabeth was living in London with her brother Daniel and family. It was probably there that she was courted by Elisha Williams (1694–1755), evangelical pastor, regimental colonel, and one-time rector of Yale College, who was visiting England to solicit funds for both college and regiment. As a man of devotion and action, with great physical and mental energy, he was a suitable mate for the woman Doddridge esteemed 'among the greatest Treasures of our Island or our World' (Nuttall, no. 1679). Elisha and Elizabeth were married at Norwich on 29 January 1751 and departed for Connecticut in August. Williams died on 24 July 1755 and Elizabeth married at an unknown date the Hon. William Smith (1697–1769), an associate justice of the supreme court of New York and a co-religionist of her late husband. Smith also predeceased her. In both cases Elizabeth was the second wife of a widower with grown-up children; she did not have children by either marriage. She died at Wethersfield, Connecticut, on 13 June 1776, aged sixty-eight. The terms of her will, made the day before she died, imply that Williams's family treated her better than Smith's did.

Elizabeth was probably uninvolved when her hymns were published from her friends' transcripts. The first to be printed were probably those in William Dodd's *Christian's Magazine* and the Unitarian *New Collection … for the Use of Protestant Dissenters in Liverpool* (both 1763). Others appeared in nineteenth-century collections for the use especially of Unitarians, Baptists, and evangelicals. According to the *Dictionary of National Biography* about fifteen were in use in the 1890s, but it seems that all had fallen out of use by the beginning of the twenty-first century. JAMES SAMBROOK

Sources *The correspondence and diary of Philip Doddridge*, ed. J. D. Humphreys, 5 vols. (1829–31) • *Calendar of the correspondence of Philip Doddridge*, ed. G. F. Nuttall, HMC, JP 26 (1979) • *DAB* • J. Browne, *A history of Congregationalism and memorials of the churches in Norfolk and Suffolk* (1877), 205, 267–9 • *IGI* • J. Julian, ed., *A dictionary of hymnology*, rev. edn (1907), 1019–20 • will, dated 12 June 1776, Yale U.

Archives DWL, London Congregational Library, letters to Philip Doddridge, Reed MS, 4–11 • Yale U., Beinecke L., personal corresp., business papers, and poems

Likenesses portrait, 1937, priv. coll.; photographic copy, Yale U.

Wealth at death over £500 cash; 1700 acres of land (probably in Hartford county, Connecticut); bonds and notes to an unknown amount; household goods, incl. books, silver, etc.

Scott [*née* Chalmers], **Elizabeth** (*d.* 1795), textile manufacturer, was a daughter of William Chalmers, sometime provost of Aberdeen, but little else is known about her family background. In October 1744 she married Archibald Scott (*c.*1700–1784), a surgeon in Musselburgh, Edinburgh. His earnings, barely sufficient to support a growing family, declined as he grew older, obliging Elizabeth to look for some means to supplement their income. She was able to enter the existing textile industry at Musselburgh and extend the manufacture of plain cloth; eventually she employed nearly 1200 people, selling her output to printers in England and in Scotland.

In 1761 Elizabeth Scott applied for a grant from the board of trustees for fisheries, manufactures and improvements, and by then she was manufacturing various grades and qualities of cloth. As the board was seeking to foster the linen trade in Scotland, it allowed her £40 for her linens and suggested that she apply to the Edinburgh Society for Encouraging Arts, Sciences, Manufactures, and Agriculture (established in 1755) for a grant for cottons. Later that year she again approached the board, wishing to purchase more looms for 'brown cottons', woven from a linen warp and a cotton weft, which she was sending directly to England. In addition she offered to employ women and children from the Musselburgh poorhouse as cotton spinners; her proposal was accepted, and apparatus, teachers, and supervisors were arranged, following existing practice in Edinburgh. Her output in 1762 reached 11,000 yards of cotton cloth, which encouraged her to apply to the board for a higher award. She continued to manufacture a variety of textiles, and probably also dyed yarns for weaving the checked fabrics which were in demand for export to the plantations.

An act of 1727 required all textiles containing linen to be stamped, as a guarantee of quantity and quality, small samples of cloth being taken to the nearest official, in this case at Edinburgh. Major manufacturers could summon the stampmaster to their works or were allowed their own stamp. In April 1766 Elizabeth Scott became the only woman to be issued with such a private stamp—testimony to the size of her business and to her status as a manufacturer. She continued to employ spinners at Musselburgh poorhouse, providing training and remuneration which was appreciated by the poorhouse directors, which included her husband; additional cotton yarn was bought in, mostly from Glasgow, and linen yarn was purchased from the staplery set up by the British Linen Company in Edinburgh.

Elizabeth Scott travelled to London in 1764–5 in company with Thomas Foggo, one of her bankers, to establish a market for her products. By 1766 she was selling materials at the newly opened Linen Hall in Edinburgh and was probably supplying James Stirling, a Glasgow bleacher and printer. She obtained further grants from the board in 1776 to set up a school for teaching the use of the new spinning jenny. These provided for apparatus, money to pay for a teacher, and subsistence for twelve students; a year later she had ten extra scholars, and though her grant ceased she was permitted to keep the apparatus. Also in 1776 two of the £10 prizes for the best Scottish goods offered for sale at the Linen Hall were awarded to her for twelve pieces of pillow fustian and twelve cotton dimities.

By the early 1780s water-powered mills operating on Scotland's west coast rendered Elizabeth Scott's products uncompetitive, and she gave up most of her manufacturing interests. The board nevertheless continued to consult her, and she successfully entered a few items for competitions; but on her own admission, thirty years' labour had brought its rewards. She had managed to oversee the education of her children, who were now established, and she and her husband could enjoy a comfortable retirement, albeit brief, as Archibald Scott died in 1784. Their elder son William became an Edinburgh banker, and a younger son Robert became a physician who later worked in London and Winchester.

Elizabeth Scott's later years were blighted by a protracted legal case for defamation of character, which ran from 1783 to 1794 and suggested that one of her children had been fathered by Mansfeldt de Cardonnel of Musselburgh, commissioner of customs. Her husband, despite his seniority and his reputation for high moral virtue, seems to have been untroubled by these accusations and left her as sole manager of his estate, much of which she was obliged to spend on the legal proceedings, until the property of her accuser was sequestered. She died in Inveresk, near Edinburgh, on 6 April 1795 and was buried there four days later. ANITA MCCONNELL

Sources V. Habib, 'An eighteenth-century cotton manufactory in Scotland: Elizabeth Scott in Musselburgh', *Scottish Industrial History*, 8/1 (1985), 2–19 • *Edinburgh Evening Courant* (11 April 1795)

Scott, Lord Francis George Montagu-Douglas- (1879–1952), politician in Kenya and army officer, was born at Dalkeith on 1 November 1879, the sixth and youngest son of William Henry Walter Montagu-Douglas-Scott, earl of Dalkeith (later sixth duke of Buccleuch and eighth duke of Queensberry; 1831–1914), and his wife, Lady Louisa Jane (*d.* 1912), third daughter of James *Hamilton, first duke of Abercorn (1811–1885). Scott was educated at Eton College, and from there entered Christ Church, Oxford. He did not, however, take a degree, leaving in 1899 to join the Grenadier Guards and participate in the Second South African War, in which he saw action in the Orange Free State and Transvaal.

From 1905 to 1910 Scott served as aide-de-camp to the viceroy of India, the earl of Minto, combining his duties with his two principal sporting interests, cricket and pig-sticking. In the early months of the outbreak of the First World War Scott was serving on loan to the Irish Guards, in the rank of captain commanding a company. He was severely wounded in the leg during the first battle of Ypres, a wound which caused him lasting pain, necessitating an amputation in 1933 and limiting his service for the rest of the war to commanding the Grenadier Guards depot battalion. He was mentioned in dispatches and made a companion of the DSO for his bravery at Ypres and finished his service in 1920 with the rank of lieutenant-colonel. In 1915 Scott married Lady Eileen Nina Evelyn Sibell (*d.* 1938), eldest daughter of the earl of Minto [*see* Kynynmound, Gilbert John Elliot Murray, fourth earl of Minto (1845–1914)]. His wife supported him fully in his later political career and ambitions. They had two daughters.

In 1924 Scott moved to Kenya where he bought a 3500 acre farm at Rongai from Lord Delamere, building himself a home on the estate. Shortly afterwards he entered Kenya's local politics, and in 1925 was elected a member of the colony's legislative council for the Ukamba constituency, the franchise being that of Europeans only, men and women. His political career developed in the early 1930s when in 1931 he was chosen by his fellow settler elected members to lead their delegation to represent their opposition to a possible 'Closer Union' of the three British east African colonies before a joint select committee of both houses of parliament. The settlers' fears were based on the apprehension that any form of closer union would subsume settler interests below the native African policies of the other territories. Scott and his colleagues hoped Kenya would advance to a self-governing colony status similar to Southern Rhodesia. Later in the year Scott succeeded Delamere both as leader of the European elected members and as member for the significantly more important Rift Valley constituency, the centre of Kenya's white settlement. In 1932, under the informal 'government by agreement' (with the settlers) policy under which colonial Kenya was governed at the time, Scott was appointed to the governor's executive council.

Scott's political views were centred on his belief in white settlement (preferably with squirearchy or military service backgrounds) and hopes for its increase together with criticism of the colonial government, focusing especially on the right of the settler community to be consulted on all policy matters. This belief led him into clashes with the governor, Sir Joseph Byrne, whose views were more critical of the settlers, the most serious clash occurring in 1936. Scott and the second 'unofficial' (that is, settler) member of the executive council resigned as a protest against Byrne's reservation to himself and his officials of policy concerning the organization of the colony's defence. Scott also consistently criticized the expenditure of the colonial government, seeking economies, and he opposed, ultimately unsuccessfully, the introduction of income tax on the settler community. Despite his championship of the settlers' cause he was sufficiently prescient to foresee a future in which indigenous educated Africans would, he argued, participate more successfully with local Europeans than with colonial officials. He did not, however, grasp the reality of Kenya's population increase in his advocacy of the removal of surplus resident labour from white settler farms. In 1937 Scott returned to the executive council. He had, through his influential connections in London, played a part both in securing the appointment of a new governor more acceptable to the settler community, and also in the reconstitution of the executive council to provide for increased unofficial membership, though not, as Scott had hoped, with ministerial office.

Despite his age and leg amputation, Scott rejoined the army in 1941; he took part in the Ethiopian campaign, being again mentioned in dispatches, and served on the staff of the general commanding east African forces. His absence on service and the gentlemanly moderation of his political expression was, however, resented by his constituents, a resentment leading to his resignation from the legislative council in 1944. After the end of the war he attempted in 1948 to regain his seat, but was defeated by Michael Blundell, to be the last political leader of Kenya's white settlers. His defeat marked the end of his political career, and a retirement which he at first found difficult to bear. He was, however, consoled by Blundell's acceptance of advice based on his own wide experience.

On a visit to Britain, Scott died suddenly after a heart attack at Paddington Station, London, on 26 July 1952. Scott was an influential and important settler politician in his time, the core colonial period; by 1948, however, that period was ending. As a man Scott was widely respected for his strong, clear sense of duty and decisive manner, though at times, as a result of his war wound, he could prove short-tempered. He was appointed KCMG in 1937, an unusual honour for an unofficial representative.

Anthony Clayton

Sources *The Times* (28 July 1952) · *DNB* · V. Harlow, E. M. Chilver, and A. Smith, eds., *History of East Africa*, 2 (1965) · A. Clayton and D. C. Savage, *Government and labour in Kenya, 1895–1963* (1974, [1975]) · R. Kipling, *The Irish guards in the Great War* (1923) · *CGPLA Eng. & Wales* (1953) · Burke, *Peerage* (1980) · E. Trzebinski, *The Kenya pioneers* (1991) · M. Blundell, *So rough a wind: the Kenya memoirs of Sir Michael Blundell* (1964)

Archives Bodl. RH, corresp. • Bodl. RH, diaries of travels in India, Kenya, and the Middle East • University of Nairobi, Kenya, corresp. and papers
Likenesses O. Birley, portrait; known to be at Deloraine in 1971
Wealth at death £4125 19*s.* 9*d.* in England: Kenyan probate sealed in England, 26 Aug 1953, *CGPLA Eng. & Wales*

Scott, Francis George (1880–1958), composer, was born on 25 January 1880 at 6 Oliver Crescent, Hawick, Roxburghshire, the second son and youngest of three children of George Scott (*d.* 1907), supplier of loom parts, and his second wife, Janet Greenwood (*d.* 1897). The boy was proud to share a birthday with Robert Burns. Educated at Hawick Academy and Brand's Teviot Grove Academy, Hawick, he took piano lessons until he began composing at fifteen, when his parents halted them, lest music should distract him from schoolwork.

In 1897 Scott went to read English at Edinburgh University and train as a teacher at Moray House college of education. He gave up his degree course in the second year, however, disliking the constraints of academic life. He taught English at schools in Hawick and Falkirk before Langholm Academy engaged him in 1903. Meanwhile he studied externally for a music degree from Durham University (1902–9).

Scott transferred to Dunoon grammar school in 1912, and there fell in love with a colleague named Burges Gray (*d.* 1967), who gave birth to their daughter, Francine, in Paris in 1914. They married at Fraserburgh on 4 September 1915 and rented a flat in the Langside area of Glasgow, where Scott worked at a succession of schools: Kelvinhaugh (1914–15), Kennedy Street (1915–19), and Townhead (1919–25). The couple had three more children, Lilias, George, and Malcolm, by 1927.

Marriage and fatherhood coincided with the musical metamorphosis of F. G. Scott. He had been writing songs in late Romantic style; a few featured in a concert at Greenock in 1912. When a listener said that they were as good as Richard Strauss's lieder, Scott recognized his unoriginality and determined to evolve a fresh musical idiom—not only for himself but for Scotland. Calvinism, poverty, and the absence of a royal court had historically stunted any native tradition of art music. He hoped to fill this gap in the national culture by deriving a distinctively Scottish style from folk-song, Scots poetry and speech rhythm, and pibroch (the ancient bagpipe music of the Gaels). His wife, a trained mezzo-soprano, made him aware of the subtleties of vocal writing. All his most important works are short solo songs with piano accompaniment, of which he composed over 200 and published 125 (largely at his own expense).

The earlier of the five volumes of Scott's *Scottish Lyrics Set to Music* (1922–39) provided new melodies for verses by Burns; they could not displace in public affection the genuine folk-tunes already associated with the words, though some literary figures praised their sensitivity. Scott mixed very little with other musicians but enjoyed discussing his work with the poet Edwin Muir and the French lecturer Denis Saurat. In public he came across as a formidable Edwardian schoolmaster, with watch-chain, bow tie, and a booming voice. Piercing blue eyes stared out from beneath a beetle-brow, whose height was enhanced by the brushing-back of his thick grey hair. The nose was sharp, the mouth tight-lipped, and he could be as fierce as he looked. But his private character had a mischievous streak, and friends could not tell whether his solemn exterior was the residue of a Presbyterian upbringing or something of a pose: a backdrop of 'respectability' to show off his iconoclastic opinions to more startling effect. Intellectual argument delighted 'FG', who sometimes defended outrageous views until he burst out laughing. The explosive vigour of the man was in contrast to the frequent delicacy of his music.

Scott learned in 1923 that the poet known as Hugh MacDiarmid was actually Christopher Murray Grieve, once his star pupil at Langholm. Their reunion gave rise to a creative partnership which aimed at saving Scotland from torpid Anglicized provincialism. By re-establishing Scots as a literary language and starting a ferment of poetry and music, they sought to initiate a 'Scottish Renaissance'. With his twenty-two MacDiarmid settings, Scott confounded those who might have dismissed him as a mere purveyor of pastiche folk-song. Here was music both recognizably Scottish and thoroughly contemporary, capturing the mood and meaning of the poems in ways which seemed strikingly expressive and spontaneous. The songs ranged from the dramatic and eerie to the lyrical or comic. Chief among them are 'Country Life' (1923), 'Crowdieknowe' (1924), 'The Eemis Stane' (1924), 'Moonstruck' (1929), and 'Milkwort and Bog-Cotton' (1932).

Echoes of Béla Bartók and Arnold Schoenberg in his harmonies testify to the fact that Scott was never a chauvinist. He scorned most British composers, admittedly, but saw Scottishness as his contribution to international music. In 1921 the French composer Jean Jules Roger-Ducasse had offered him free tuition in Paris; Scott felt unable to leave Glasgow. There was always tension between his absorption in art and his desire for a stable family life and steady income. In 1925 he became music lecturer at Jordanhill training college for teachers and moved to a terraced house in Munro Road, Glasgow.

Scott and Grieve drifted apart in the 1930s, as the poet became more political. FG was also a left-wing Scottish nationalist, yet he saw separatist agitation as premature. He tried his hand at orchestral pieces (clumsily perhaps) and obtained lyrics for new songs from William Soutar and the poems of the fifteenth-century bard Dunbar.

Scott's music was heard by only an infinitesimal public even in Scotland, as he made no concession to commercialism. Grieve and Kaikhosru Sorabji declared him the equal of Hugo Wolf or Gabriel Fauré; others disparaged him as the house composer of a cranky clique. Arguably, the enthusiasm of Scottish nationalists for his work narrowed its appeal. After 1945 performances did multiply, thanks in part to the Scottish Arts Council and the Saltire Society, which aided the publication of *Thirty-Five Scottish Lyrics and other Poems* (1949). Scott, who retired in 1946, was senile by 1957, when Glasgow University awarded him a doctorate. He died at his home, 44 Munro Road, Glasgow, on 6 November 1958 and was buried in Wellogate cemetery, Hawick.

The songs of F. G. Scott subsequently found favour with Scottish recitalists, though the Scots language still scared off English singers. A musical miniaturist of exceptional individuality, he remained much admired by a few and all but unknown to the rest. JASON TOMES

Sources M. Lindsay, *Francis George Scott and the Scottish Renaissance* (1980) · Grove, *Dict. mus.* (1954) · *New Grove*, 2nd edn · H. MacDiarmid, *Contemporary Scottish studies*, reprint (1995) · W. Muir, *Belonging* (1968) · E. Muir, *An autobiography* (1954) · H. MacDiarmid, *Francis George Scott—an essay on the occasion of his seventy-fifth birthday* (1955) · J. Purser, *Scotland's music* (1992) · K. Sorabji, *Mi contra fa* (1947)

Archives Scottish Music Information Centre, Glasgow, papers | U. Edin. L., C. M. Grieve (Hugh MacDiarmid) archive, letters and papers

Likenesses W. Johnstone, portrait, *c.*1932 · B. Schotz, bronze head, 1947 · portraits, repro. in 'Songs of Francis George Scott', Robertson Publications, 1980, front and back of album cover

Scott, Geoffrey (1884–1929), writer and architect, was born on 15 June 1884 in Hampstead, London, the fourth son and the youngest of seven children of Russell Scott (1837–1908) and his wife, Jessie Thurburn (1844–1921); he was the nephew of Charles Prestwich *Scott, the distinguished editor of the *Manchester Guardian*. His father was a flooring manufacturer whose success in business, along with family money, allowed him to provide a comfortable home for his wife and family. Scott spent his early childhood at home in Hampstead and attended local schools, including (for a year) the Highgate School. In 1898, he matriculated at Rugby School. There he distinguished himself among his classmates as someone who was interested in aesthetics. Success at Rugby led to New College, Oxford, which he entered in the autumn of 1902 after spending a year at St Andrews. He studied under the eminent classicist Gilbert Murray and gained some recognition by winning the Newdigate prize in 1906 and the chancellor's essay prize in 1908. The latter, entitled *The National Character of English Architecture* (1908), provided the groundwork for his later work, *The Architecture of Humanism*.

Scott's life changed in March 1906 when, accompanied by John Maynard Keynes, he visited the Villa I Tatti, the home outside Florence of the art connoisseurs Bernard and Mary Berenson. Scott quickly developed an intense relationship with Mary, nineteen years his senior, writing to her about his great enthusiasm for classicism and revealing to her the most intimate details of his life at Oxford, including his homosexual relationships. Mary fell in love with Scott and willingly supported him emotionally and even financially. She helped him at the beginning of his career when, having achieved only a second in Greats, he was unable to proceed with his plans to become a classical scholar. In 1907 she introduced him to the young architect Cecil Pinsent [*see below*]; after Scott worked with the American interior designer Ogden Codman on his uncompleted *catalogue raisonné* of French châteaux, Scott and Pinsent formed an architectural partnership in Florence. Scott's interest in and knowledge of architecture had begun at an early age, under his father's influence, and had developed during his extensive travels and study in Italy, especially with the Berensons. Scott had little formal architectural training, apart from a few months in 1907–8 at the Architectural Association School in London.

The first to commission Scott and Pinsent were the Berensons, who asked them to renovate the interior of the Villa I Tatti and to design its gardens. Soon their work was in demand among the many rich Anglo-Americans in Florence. Their first major project, completed in 1913, was the Villa Le Balze in Fiesole, designed in a Renaissance style for John D. Rockefeller's son-in-law, the American philosopher Charles Augustus Strong. At the same time he was designing buildings and gardens Scott was writing his architectural *magnum opus*, *The Architecture of Humanism*, published in August 1914. The book is often cited as one of the most important treatises on architecture of the twentieth century. A defence of Renaissance architecture as a standard for all architecture, Scott's book is also an attack on the many styles that had emerged during the nineteenth century. Beautifully constructed and original in many respects, it depends on previous work by Berenson, Vernon Lee, Adolf von Hildebrand, and Theodor Lipp.

Scott's emotional life before the First World War was as tumultuous and ill-defined as his career. After affairs with a number of women, Scott married Lady Sybil Marjorie Cutting (1879–1942) on 23 April 1918. Lady Sybil, the daughter of Hamilton Cuffe, fifth earl of Desart, was the rich Anglo-Irish widow of the American diplomat William Bayard Cutting and the mother of the historian Iris Origo. The marriage precipitated a rupture with Mary Berenson, who, as a result, had a nervous breakdown, and led to tension in his friendship with Edith Wharton. Scott himself was forced to spend the summer and autumn of 1919 in Lausanne under the care of the well-known psychologist Dr Roger Vittoz.

It was during this time in Switzerland that Scott began his biography of the eighteenth-century novelist Madame de Charrière. *The Portrait of Zélide* was his most celebrated book: considered by many to be among the most beautifully written of twentieth-century biographies, it reflects the influence of Lytton Strachey in its brevity and its appeal to a general reader. Because of his difficult home life, he took five years to complete this short biography. For several years after the war he also worked in the British embassy in Rome as the head of its press office. With the beginning of a most complicated love affair with Vita Sackville-*West (1892–1962) in October of 1923, which was as much a literary friendship as an emotional involvement, Scott was able to finish his book. It was published to much critical acclaim in 1924. When it won the James Tait Black memorial prize in 1926, Scott's reputation as a writer was firmly established.

The relationship with Vita Sackville-West precipitated Scott's divorce from Lady Sybil in 1926; she later married the writer Percy *Lubbock. Now Scott began his work for the American businessman Colonel Ralph Isham who had recently bought the Boswell papers, probably the most important literary discovery of the century, from Boswell's descendants. Scott went to America in October 1927 as the first editor of the Boswell papers and spent almost two years on Long Island working on them. He died suddenly of pneumonia on 14 August 1929 at the Rockefeller Institute, New York, after the publication of the first six volumes to much acclaim and the signing of a very lucrative contract with Houghton Mifflin to write a full-length biography of Boswell. His ashes were brought back to New College, Oxford, in the same year.

Scott was a polymath whose interests extended beyond his success as a biographer, aesthetician, architect, and editor. He wrote poetry, magazine articles, and book reviews, did numerous caricatures and some interior design (including a bed which is now at the Victoria and Albert Museum). His brilliant mind and superb classical education allowed him to excel in a variety of fields. He was, moreover, sought out by many for his conviviality: Mary Berenson, Edith Wharton, Gerald Wellesley (the future duke of Wellington), any number of other literary and artistic figures, American plutocrats, and European aristocrats all found him to be a delightful companion. He was known not only for his witty conversation and erudition but also for his temperamental behaviour and his snobbery. Today, Scott's work is remembered by a small group of serious readers who admire the elegance of *The Architecture of Humanism*, *The Portrait of Zélide*, his edition of the Boswell papers, and his unpublished letters.

Scott's architectural partner, **Cecil Pinsent** (1884–1963), was born in Montevideo, Uruguay, on 5 May 1884, the son of Adolphus Ross Pinsent (1851–1929), a businessman, and his wife, Alice Nuttall (1855–1901). Educated at Marlborough College (1897–1900), the Architectural Association School (1901–5) and the Royal Academy School of Architecture (1905–6), he began his career in England, but spent most of his life in Italy, especially in Tuscany, designing gardens and villas in the Renaissance style. Among his most important works, apart from the Villa I Tatti and the Villa Le Balze, are the gardens at La Foce, Chianciano, Siena (1924–36), for Antonio and Iris Origo, the Villa Gli Scafari, at Lerice (1932), for Lady Sybil and Percy Lubbock, the Villa Colletti-Perucca at Castiglioncello (1932), for Mrs Colletti-Perucca, and the Villa Le Sabine for Count Niccolo Antinori, at Bolgheri, Livorno (1935). He died in Hilterfingen, Thunersee, Switzerland, on 5 December 1963, and was buried there. RICHARD M. DUNN

Sources R. M. Dunn, *Geoffrey Scott and the Berenson circle* (1998) · correspondence, Villa I Tatti · correspondence, Yale U. · correspondence, priv. coll. · *Mary Berenson: a self-portrait from her letters and diaries*, ed. B. Strachey and J. Samuels (1983) · E. Samuels, *Bernard Berenson, the making of a legend* (1987) · N. Mariano, *Forty years with Berenson* (1966) · I. Origo, *Images and shadows: part of a life* (1970) · N. Nicolson, *Portrait of a marriage* (1973) · E. Wharton, *A backward glance* (1934) · M. Fantoni, H. Flores, and J. Pfordesher, eds., *Cecil Pinsent and his gardens in Tuscany* (1996) · *DNB* · *CGPLA Eng. & Wales* (1929) · *CGPLA Eng. & Wales* (1964) [Cecil Pinsent]

Archives Harvard University, near Florence, Italy, Center for Renaissance Studies · NRA, priv. coll., family papers | Indiana University, Bloomington, Lilly Library, Hannah Whitall Smith MSS · King's AC Cam., letters to John Maynard Keynes · Yale U., Beinecke L., Muriel Draper MSS

Likenesses photograph, *c.*1912, repro. in Dunn, *Geoffrey Scott and the Berenson circle*, frontispiece · N. Hamnet, pen-and-ink drawing, 1920–29, Richard Dunn Collection, 58 Copeces Lane, East Hampton, New York · W. Rothenstein, pen-and-ink drawing, 1920–29, priv. coll. · photograph, 1920–29, Yale U., Beinecke L., Max Ewing collection · photographs, Villa I Tatti, Settignano, Italy · photographs, priv. coll.

Wealth at death £12,436 16*s*. 0*d*.: administration, 25 Nov 1929, *CGPLA Eng. & Wales* · £29,439—Cecil Pinsent: probate, 1964, *CGPLA Eng. & Wales*

Scott, George. *See* Scot, George, of Scotstarvit (*d.* 1685).

Scott, Sir George Gilbert (1811–1878), architect, was born on 13 July 1811 at the parsonage house at Gawcott, Buckinghamshire, the third son of the Revd Thomas *Scott (1780–1835) [*see under* Scott, Thomas (1747–1821)], the first perpetual curate of that village and later the rector of Wappenham, Northamptonshire, and the grandson of the Revd Thomas *Scott (1747–1821), known as the Commentator, rector of Aston Sandford, Buckinghamshire. Scott's mother, Euphemia Lynch (1785–1853), was the only daughter of Dr Lynch of Antigua and connected with the Gilberts, a family of West Indian planters. In his *Personal and Professional Recollections*, written between 1864 and his death (one of the first autobiographies of an architect to be published), Scott was concerned to emphasize that his mother was 'well-born, of a good old family' and 'related to persons of good position', which somewhat undermined his intention to demonstrate how far he had risen from humble origins to professional success (Scott, 10).

Scott came from a large family and several brothers, cousins, and uncles were Anglican clergymen, from whose patronage he later would benefit in his extensive church work. In the village and county, however, Scott's father and family were ostracized for their strong connection with the evangelical wing of the Church of England, and his 'aunt Gilbert' had once been kissed by John Wesley, 'which she esteemed a great privilege' (Scott, 36).

Education and early works Scott was educated first at home and then, for a year, with his uncle, the Revd Samuel King, at Latimers, near Chesham, Buckinghamshire. Scott's father, who was an amateur architect responsible for building the parsonage and rebuilding the church at Gawcott, recognized in his son's love of sketching medieval churches a predilection for architecture. In 1827 Scott was articled in London to James Edmeston (1781–1867), who was more successful as a hymn writer than as an architect and wrote 'Lead us, heavenly father, lead us'. Edmeston's practice was not inspiring and he warned Scott's father that sketching medieval buildings was a waste of time. Scott finished his pupillage in 1831 and then worked for the contractors Grissell and Peto, gaining practical experience, in particular, from superintending the work at the Hungerford Market in London, designed by Charles Fowler. In 1832 Scott entered the office of the architect Henry Roberts (1803–1876), who was then working on the Fishmongers' Hall by London Bridge.

The sudden death of his father at the beginning of 1835 made Scott realize that 'I must adopt my course with

Sir George Gilbert Scott (1811–1878), by George Richmond, 1877

promtitude, or my chances in life were gone' (Scott, 78). He had already been invited to help his friend Sampson Kempthorne, architect to the poor-law commissioners, in the design for the new union workhouses proposed under the Poor Law Amendment Act of 1834; now Scott threw himself into this work to set up in practice on his own. He invited William Bonython Moffatt (1812–1887), the son of a builder from Cornwall whom he had met in Edmeston's office, to assist him and between them, living in 'constant turmoil', they secured a considerable number of commissions in the local competitions for workhouses. Most of the resulting buildings were severely utilitarian but some, such as the one, now a hospital, at Amersham, Buckinghamshire, in a Tudor style, exhibited a degree of architectural pretension. Scott entered into a formal partnership with Moffatt in 1838, and the firm of Scott and Moffatt also won competitions to design Reading gaol and the Infant Orphan Asylum at Wanstead, Essex, where Scott designed Elizabethan elevations to Moffatt's plan.

In 1838 Scott married his cousin Caroline Oldrid (1811–1872), the daughter of John Oldrid, draper, of Boston, Lincolnshire, who provided him with five sons and the domestic stability and support he needed with an increasingly hectic professional life. Mrs Scott soon became anxious to terminate her husband's partnership with Moffatt and 'was constantly pressing it upon my attention, but my courage failed me, and I could not muster pluck enough to broach it' (Scott, 130). In the event it was she who, in 1845, took matters into her own hands and went to see Moffatt when Scott was out of town. The consequence was that the partnership was formally terminated at the end of 1846. Scott has been criticized both for his vacillation and for abandoning his partner, but the original manuscript of his *Recollections* makes it clear that Moffatt was not only irresponsible and dangerously involved in railway speculation, but had also 'got into a sad way of offending employers … He was also extravagant, keeping four horses, and one thing with another all our practice led rather to debt than to laying by money' (ibid., 446). Later, in 1860, Moffatt was imprisoned for debt and Scott assisted with legal fees and, for the remainder of his life, continued to help his fallen partner, whose 'misfortunes in subsequent years have been a great sorrow to me. They have been the natural consequence of speculative practice and indeed of speculation wholly alien to his profession' (ibid.).

While in partnership with Moffatt, Scott was able to indulge his interest in medieval architecture and design new churches, although he was later ashamed of his first efforts with their short chancels and internal galleries as 'no idea of ecclesiastical arrangement, or ritual propriety, had then even crossed my mind' (Scott, 86). Gothic church design was, however, then being raised to new levels of stylistic and liturgical correctness by the polemics of the Cambridge Camden Society in its journal, *The Ecclesiologist*, and by those of the architect A. W. N. Pugin, and Scott was strongly influenced by both. He met Benjamin Webb and joined the society in 1842 and he later recalled how 'Pugin's articles excited me almost to fury' (ibid., 88) and how he was awakened by 'the thunder of Pugin's writings … I was from that moment a new man. Old things (in my practice) had passed away, and, behold, all things had become new, or rather modernism had passed away from me and every aspiration of my heart had become mediaeval' (ibid., 373). This was soon demonstrated in the design for the martyrs' memorial at Oxford and in that for the rebuilding of the church of St Giles's, Camberwell, London. In 1845 Scott won the international competition for rebuilding the St Nikolaikirche in Hamburg and his design was carried out (ruined in the Second World War) after he managed to defeat the German architect Gottfried Semper with the assistance of a local faction in favour of the Gothic. He was nevertheless condemned by *The Ecclesiologist* for designing a Lutheran church. Scott remained a broad-church Anglican and was never close to the Anglo-Catholic wing which was in the vanguard of church design; as he remarked, 'amongst Anglican architects, Carpenter and Butterfield were the apostles of the high church school—I, of the multitude' (ibid., 112).

Major works In consequence, Scott built up a large ecclesiastical practice but his church work was never innovative or as strongly influenced by continental Gothic as was that of his former pupils G. E. Street and G. F. Bodley; he would later criticize 'Ruskinism, such as would make Ruskin's very hair stand upon end; Butterfieldism gone mad with its endless stripings of red and black bricks' (Scott, 210). Scott was content to accept the orthodoxy of an English Geometrical Decorated Gothic or 'Middle

Pointed' as 'our agreed *point de départ*' or 'nucleus of development' (ibid., 208), although by the later 1850s he introduced French details into his work. After Scott's death, one obituarist observed that his architecture had

> the merit of being a thoroughly national revival of the Gothic style. In sentiment and in detail it neither offended by its violence nor sacrificed English to modern sympathies. If not remarkable for its originality, or its energy, it was always pleasing, moderate, and sensible. Indeed it had, in common with its author, a geniality that was eminently impressed upon everything he did. (*Building News*, 19 April 1878)

Scott considered that, 'on the whole, my best church' (Scott, 176) was All Souls', Haley Hill, Halifax, which was built in 1856–9 at the expense of Colonel Edward Akroyd MP. It is certainly representative, with its asymmetrically placed tower and spire, Decorated Gothic detail, richly carved sculptural detail, and figure sculpture inside and out, together with fine stained glass by the firm of Clayton and Bell, whose formation Scott was instrumental in encouraging. Other significant churches include: the parish church of Doncaster, rebuilt, typically, in Geometrical Decorated rather than Perpendicular Gothic after a fire in 1853; All Saints', Sherbourne, Warwickshire (1859–64); All Saints', Ryde, Isle of Wight (1866–82); St Mary Abbots, Kensington, London (1868–79); and St Mary's Episcopal Cathedral in Edinburgh, begun in 1874 and completed by his son J. O. Scott. Scott also worked in both ancient English universities and was responsible for the chapels at Exeter College, Oxford (1854–60), and St John's College, Cambridge (1862–9).

Scott followed Pugin in maintaining that Gothic was a universal style and showed more invention in his secular work. However, apart from vicarages, he did not design many houses; his most significant domestic works were Kelham Hall, outside Newark-on-Trent (1858–61), built for J. H. Manners Sutton, and Walton Hall, Warwickshire (1858–62), for Sir Charles Mordaunt, both of which were rather ponderous and unsuccessful compositions. In 1857 Scott published his *Remarks on Secular and Domestic Architecture, Present and Future*, which argued that 'our Gothic Renaissance' need not be constrained by the use of the pointed arch and that it could encompass modern improvements such as plate glass and cast iron; indeed, Scott insisted, 'these iron constructions are, if anything, more suited to Gothic than classic architecture' (p. 111). And, in considering the architecture of the future, Scott addressed the dilemma of his age, acute historical consciousness: in contrast to all former periods, 'we are acquainted with the history of art … This is amazingly interesting to us as a matter of amusement and erudition, but I fear is a hindrance rather than a help to us as artists' (ibid., 263–4). Writing this book coincided with the competition for new government offices in Whitehall which enabled Scott to demonstrate the utility of his theories in the designs he submitted. But although Scott eventually managed to secure the commission, this inaugurated the principal engagement in the contemporary 'battle of the styles' and it ended in defeat, compromise, and the undermining of his status as a leader in the Gothic crusade.

In the absurdly mismanaged triple competition announced in 1856, Scott produced an integrated scheme influenced by Italian Gothic for both the Foreign and War offices, but was only placed third for the building before the prime minister, Lord Palmerston, set the results aside. However, the short-lived Conservative government of Lord Derby was more favourably disposed to the Gothic and eventually, following intensive lobbying by the Gothic party, Scott was appointed architect for the Foreign Office in November 1858. By now the War Office had dropped out of the project and the India Office had come in (with its architect Matthew Digby Wyatt), but Scott's new Gothic design was rejected when Palmerston reassumed the premiership in May 1859 and demanded that he produce 'something more like modern architecture' (Scott, 194), that is, a classical design.

Public controversy raged throughout the year, with the opposition to Scott and the Gothic style being led by Professor T. L. Donaldson and by Charles Barry junior who, after all, had beaten Scott in the original competition for the Foreign Office. A threat by the prime minister to appoint a 'coadjutor' (in fact, Henry Garling, who had won the competition for the War Office) then made Scott produce an Italian–Byzantine compromise, but this did not meet with approval and Palmerston dismissed it as 'neither one thing nor t'other—a regular mongrel affair' (Scott, 197). Scott was then faced with a choice between resignation—which 'would be to give up a sort of property which Providence had placed in the hands of my family' (ibid., 191)—and working in a style which, in theory, he disapproved of. In the event, he did as he was told and produced an accomplished if unconventional Italian classical design with a picturesque front facing St James's Park. As he later admitted, Scott visited Paris for ideas, 'bought some costly books on Italian architecture, and set vigorously to work to rub up what, though I had once understood pretty intimately, I had allowed to grow rusty by twenty years' neglect' (ibid., 199). The new design was accepted by parliament in July 1861; work began in 1863 and, with the addition of the Home and Colonial offices to the east of the site, was completed in 1874, although the corner towers and *porte-cochère* Scott designed for the Parliament Street elevation were never executed. The staterooms, notably the ambassadors' staircase and the grand reception room, are of particular magnificence, and enabled the Foreign Office to become 'a kind of national palace, or drawing-room for the nation', as Scott's ally, A. J. B. Beresford Hope MP, later described it (Toplis, 164).

Scott was able to use the horizontally composed secular Gothic manner he had originally proposed for the Foreign Office in his winning design of 1865–6 for the Midland Grand Hotel at St Pancras Station, a building criticized for offending against the Victorian principle of propriety in architecture and which he himself admitted was 'possibly *too good* for its purpose' (Scott, 271). In the grand staircase Scott showed himself to be a master at handling both space and structure, while he also showed considerable skill in integrating his building with the vaults, retaining walls, and single span train shed already designed by the

Midland Railway's engineer W. H. Barlow, noting with pleasure that 'as if by anticipation its section was a pointed arch' (ibid.). Other important secular works carried out during the decade included the Albert Institute in Dundee, Leeds Infirmary, Preston town hall (dem.), and the University of Bombay. Scott also designed the new buildings for Glasgow University, a commission secured without competition, to the indignation of the Scottish architectural profession: Alexander Thomson remarked in 1866 that 'everybody knows that his establishment being the most fashionable in the metropolis, his business is so enormous that, to expect him to bestow more than the most casual consideration on the work which passes through his office, is altogether unreasonable' (G. Stamp, ed., *The Light of Truth and Beauty: the Lectures of Alexander 'Greek' Thomson, Architect*, 1999, 64). A disappointment came, however, when Scott failed to win the limited competition for the new Royal Courts of Justice in 1866, but by then he had been chosen to design the monument which is perhaps most representative of its age: that to Albert, prince consort, in Hyde Park.

The Albert memorial Scott was one of the architects invited by Sir Charles Eastlake to submit designs for a memorial to Prince Albert in 1862 following the abandonment of the scheme for a monolith obelisk. His Gothic design was chosen the following year. Scott recalled 'how long and painful was the effort before I struck out an idea which satisfied my mind' (Scott, 263), and it has been suggested that he was assisted by the publication in *The Builder* of Thomas Worthington's design for a Gothic shrine enclosing a statue proposed for the Albert memorial in Manchester. Another useful precedent was the Sir Walter Scott monument in Edinburgh designed by G. M. Kemp. What Scott proposed was 'the realization in an actual edifice, of the architectural designs furnished by the metal-work shrines of the middle ages' (ibid., 264). In this aim he required the assistance of sculptors, both to execute the flanking groups and for the continuous frieze around the base of the monument illustrating architects, painters, sculptors, poets, and musicians through history (in which, at the insistence of the queen, Scott himself was discreetly inserted between C. R. Cockerell and A. W. N. Pugin in the section by J. Birnie Philip). By uniting sculpture and architecture and by combining marble, stone, bronze, enamel, and metal, Scott succeeded in realizing the widest ideals of the Gothic revival. Upon completion of the structure in 1872, Scott was knighted by Queen Victoria at Osborne House—styling himself Sir Gilbert Scott. The memorial, however, did not meet with a universally favourable reception from critics, and Scott wrote that 'if this work is worthy of their contempt, I myself am equally deserving of it, for it is the result of my highest and most enthusiastic efforts' (ibid., 269). Scott's designs in both Gothic and Byzantine for the nearby Albert Hall were not acceptable to the South Kensington authorities.

Restoration work As with most Victorian church architects riding on the tide of the revival of the Church of England, much of Scott's practice consisted of the restoration of old churches, both medieval and of later date, in response to the need to make them conform to modern ideas of liturgical arrangement as well as reversing later alterations and dealing with the effects of years of neglect. Scott's first restoration was of Chesterfield church, which was soon followed by that of St Mary's, Stafford, where in 1842–5 he rebuilt the chancel roof with one of high pitch and replaced a large Perpendicular window with Early English lancets while retaining the low-pitched roof and Perpendicular clerestory of the nave. This restoration was praised by the historian Edward A. Freeman but criticized by the Revd J. L. Petit for 'not being sufficiently conservative' (Scott, 98).

In his *Plea for the Faithful Restoration of our Ancient Churches*, published in 1850 but written two years earlier, Scott ventured forward 'as a champion of conservatism' and claimed that, all too often, 'a restored church appears to lose all its truthfulness, and to become as little authentic, as an example of ancient art, as if it had been rebuilt on a new design' (p. 21). Scott, however, was often guilty of conjectural restoration so that, in its review of his book, *The Ecclesiologist* observed that 'he words his dogmas so very moderately, that in point of fact we can discover but little difference in him from that shade of the *Eclectic* theory of which we are the professors' (*The Ecclesiologist*, 11, new ser., 8, June 1850, 12–13). Scott certainly subscribed to the Ecclesiological Society's orthodoxy that Decorated Gothic was the best style and that Perpendicular was debased, so that later features in a church could be replaced by work in a better style, and in his archaeological investigations he often managed to find evidence which enabled him to reconstruct the design of long-lost features. The principal problem, however, with Scott's restorations of churches is that he carried out far too many of them.

Scott's first cathedral was Ely, where he was appointed surveyor in 1847. Others soon followed, and eventually Scott was involved with almost every medieval cathedral in England and Wales, whether advising on restoration or designing new furnishings. In 1849 he succeeded Edward Blore as surveyor to Westminster Abbey, 'a great and lasting source of delight' (Scott, 151). He published the results of his enthusiastic researches in the volume of *Gleanings from Westminster Abbey* which he edited (1861; expanded edn, 1863). At the abbey Scott prevented further decay of the internal stonework by indurating it with a solution of shellac dissolved in spirits of wine, a method which proved less successful when applied to the cloisters. He also recovered the original design of the triple portals of the north transept, although the incorrect rebuilding of the rest of the façade was carried out by his successor as surveyor, J. L. Pearson. Perhaps Scott's triumph at the abbey was the complete restoration of the much mutilated chapter house, which was 'a labour of love' which recovered many original features. He also designed the block of buildings at the entrance to Dean's Yard and the Crimean War memorial in front.

At Ely Cathedral Scott restored the original external design of the timber lantern of the octagon and moved the choir to the east of the crossing; he also designed new stalls, screen, organ, and a reredos, and erected a new nave ceiling which was painted by Henry Le Strange and Thomas Gambier Parry. Scott developed a profound understanding of medieval structures, and at Salisbury he strengthened the tower and spire with the assistance of the engineer Francis Sheilds. At Chichester Cathedral he reconstructed the central tower and spire after the original fabric collapsed in 1861. At Lichfield, as at Salisbury, much of Scott's work consisted of undoing the destructive alterations made earlier by James Wyatt, and he also restored the west front of the cathedral. At St Albans Abbey Scott strengthened the central tower, corrected the leaning of the south side of the nave and succeeded in reconstructing the shrine of St Alban from hundreds of fragments discovered during the restoration. Unfortunately, following the creation of the see of St Alban in 1877 and Scott's death, the cathedral was extensively rebuilt by Sir Edmund Beckett (later Lord Grimthorpe), whom Scott described in his *Recollections* as 'the leader among those who wish me to do what I ought not to do' (Scott, 357).

Scott also carried out extensive works at the cathedrals of Chester, Exeter, Hereford, Ripon, Rochester, Worcester, St David's, Bangor, and St Asaph. In these, and in others, much of Scott's work consisted of the design of new furnishings in response to the requirements of modern Anglican choral worship. In doing this, he sometimes had to tread a careful path between the demands of the deans and chapters and the need to respect historic fabric. In several cathedrals Scott introduced open screens to make a necessary liturgical division while satisfying the taste for an uninterrupted vista to the altar; sometimes these were of timber but at Salisbury, Lichfield, and Hereford, he designed screens of metal. Working with Francis Skidmore, of Coventry, Scott was an inventive and inspired designer of metalwork, and his cathedral screens were among his finest creations. At Hereford, however, he complained that Skidmore had 'followed my design, but somewhat aberrantly. It is a fine work, but too loud and self-asserting for an English church' (Scott, 291). But when this composition of wrought and cast iron, copper and brass, mosaic, semi-precious stones, and timber, all coloured and gilded, was exhibited at the 1862 International Exhibition in London, the *Illustrated London News* pronounced that it was 'the most noble work of modern times' and that it 'stands forth to the world as a monument to the surpassing skill of our land and our age' (*Illustrated London News*, 30 Aug 1862, 246). (The screen was removed from Hereford in 1967 and is now in the Victoria and Albert Museum, London.)

As the best-known and most prolific of restorers, Scott had to bear the brunt of criticism resulting from growing unease about the role of the architectural profession in this activity. In his presidential address to the Royal Institute of British Architects (RIBA) in 1873, Scott admitted that

> our old buildings, too often—nay, in a majority, I fear, of cases—fall into the hands of men who have neither knowledge nor respect for them, while, even among those who possess the requisite knowledge, there has been too often a lack of veneration, a disposition to sit in judgement on the work of their teachers, a rage for alteration to suit some system to which they had pledged themselves in their own works; and even the preposterous idea that the ancient examples they were called upon to repair were a fitting field for the display of their own originality! (*RIBA Transactions*, 28, 1878, 204)

But this did not prevent John Ruskin, who had condemned restoration as 'a Lie from beginning to end' in the *Seven Lamps of Architecture*, declining the gold medal of the RIBA the following year because of his opposition to both restoration and architectural professionalism. Scott, as president, took this rebuff personally.

Other critics of Scott's activities included the Revd W. J. Loftie and the architect J. J. Stevenson, who shocked many of his audience at the RIBA in 1877 by the vehemence of his condemnation of his former employer in his lecture on 'Architectural restoration: its principles and practice'. And in that same year William Morris founded the Society for the Protection of Ancient Buildings, announcing in *The Athenaeum* that he had been provoked by the resumption of Scott's restoration of Tewkesbury Abbey. Scott was greatly hurt by these attacks, and always defended himself at length. One of the last contributions to his *Recollections* was a discussion of 'The anti-restoration movement' dated October 1877. After Scott's death, his pupil J. T. Micklethwaite, who would later become surveyor to Westminster Abbey, observed with justice that

> he could restore a design from a few remains with a skill that ensured a very close resemblance to the original work, and that faculty may have tempted him to carry out the work of restoration to a greater degree than modern criticism approves of. On the other hand there are two or three things to be considered. In the first place, the custodians of a building on which Sir Gilbert was employed would not have allowed him to do anything else than restore it in the manner he did, and those restorations he treated as he did would, in all probability, have been done much worse if he had not done them, or if they had been done by men who did not possess his skill. (*RIBA Transactions*, 204)

Writings Scott's practice was so very busy that it is surprising that he found time to write anything, but, as he stated in his *Recollections*, 'pretty well all that I write is the product of my travelling hours' (Scott, 177). In addition to his books, Scott wrote lengthy reports on the ancient cathedrals and churches he was invited to restore as well as numerous published letters, articles, and lectures. From 1857 until 1873 he gave lectures at the Royal Academy, where he was appointed professor of architecture in 1868, and the results of his research and teaching were posthumously published in 1879 in two volumes as *Lectures on the Rise and Development of Mediaeval Architecture*. Scott was elected an associate of the Royal Academy in 1855 and Royal Academician in 1860. Earlier, he had been active in the establishment of the Architectural Museum, later absorbed by the South Kensington Museum.

Domestic and professional establishments Scott's industry and activity were legendary but his professional success was achieved at the cost of personal sacrifice. The death of his 'dearest Carry' in 1872 evoked deep feelings of guilt, with Scott admitting that 'she was so much alone, owing to my best hours being at business & on journeys that I have no doubt she frequently did feel melancholy & when I returned home jaded with work & often disturbed by severe anxiety and disappointment I fear I did little to enliven her spirits' (Scott, 463). At first, after their marriage, Scott and his wife lived above the office in Spring Gardens, Charing Cross; in 1844 they moved to Avenue Road, St John's Wood, and in 1856 to the Admiral's House at Hampstead. In 1864 Scott took the Manor House at Ham, Surrey, and in 1869 he rented Parkhurst at Leith Hill, Surrey, moving the following year to Rook's Nest, a large house at Godstone, Surrey, where, at the 1871 census, Scott and his wife were at home with their two youngest sons, his valet, John Pavings, and nine servants. In 1873, following the death of his wife, Scott moved back to Ham and in 1875, because of ill health and a declining practice, he returned to London to live with his second son, John Oldrid, at Courtfield House, Collingham Road, Kensington. For a man so concerned with family and status, it is perhaps curious that Scott never bought or built a country house for his family; perhaps there was no time.

In 1838 Scott had moved his office from Carlton Chambers in Regent Street to 20 (renumbered 31 in 1866) Spring Gardens, where it remained for the rest of his career. In this mid-Georgian house Scott ran what must have been the largest architectural practice in Europe at the time. When Sir Thomas Graham Jackson was a pupil in 1858–61, there was then a staff of twenty-seven, including pupils, salaried assistants, and clerks. 'Of Scott we saw but little', Jackson recalled.

> He was up to the eyes in engagements and it was hard to get him to look at our work. I have seen three or four men with drawings awaiting correction or approval grouped around his door. The door flew open and out he came. 'No time today!'; the cab was at the door and he was whirled away to some cathedral where he would spend a couple of hours and then fly off to some other great work at the other end of the kingdom. (*Recollections*, ed. Jackson, 58–9)

This incessant activity accounts for such apocryphal stories as Scott telegraphing Spring Gardens from a provincial railway station to ask, 'Why am I here?'

Nevertheless, Scott managed to keep control of his office with the help of trusted assistants such as John Burlison, and the output remained characteristic and even in style and quality. As Jackson recalled, 'Scott had a wonderful power of making rapid expressive sketches and from these his men were able to produce work which, curiously enough, did fall into something of a consistent style that passed for Gilbert Scott's' (*Recollections*, ed. Jackson, 59). Another old pupil, Ralph Neville, insisted that 'on all occasions every drawing and every single detail of work in his office went through his hands and was submitted to his judgement' (*RIBA Transactions*, 199). The 'Spring Gardens Academy' also attracted gifted young architects, and assistants or pupils who later achieved distinction included Robert Rowand Anderson, G. F. Bodley (Scott's first pupil), Somers Clarke junior, W. H. Crossland, C. Hodgson Fowler, Jackson, R. J. Johnston, J. T. Micklethwaite, William Niven, E. R. Robson, J. J. Stevenson, George Edmund Street, Hugh Thackeray Turner, and William White.

Later life After Scott fell dangerously ill at Chester in November 1870 with heart disease and bronchitis, his practice began to contract and he increasingly relied on his second son, John Oldrid. Although much of the office production now became rather mechanical, with Scott increasingly out of touch with architectural developments, he showed that he was still capable of fine things in such works as the Hook Memorial Church at Leeds (1876–1880) and St Mary's Homes at Godstone, Surrey (1872), where he was influenced by the half-timbered 'Old English' manner. Having declined the office in 1870, Scott served as president of the RIBA from 1873 until 1876; he had been awarded the institute's royal gold medal in 1859. Scott's last years were marred by declining health and by what he felt were unfair personal attacks on him. Acutely and unnecessarily sensitive to criticism, he was further saddened by the undermining of the Gothic cause by the advent of the eclectic free classical 'Queen Anne' style which was even taken up by his own architect sons. Scott's last entry in the notebooks containing his *Recollections*, dated January 1878, was a defence against this 'vexatious disturber of the Gothic movement' in which he argued that 'a so-called "Queen Anne" house is now more a revival of the past than a modern gothic house' (Scott, 375).

Sir Gilbert Scott died of heart failure on 27 March 1878 at Courtfield House. He was accorded the honour of being buried in Westminster Abbey and Queen Victoria sent a carriage to join the funeral procession from Kensington on 6 April. Scott's body is now covered by a brass designed by his old pupil G. E. Street, and his wife, Caroline, lies under a monument he designed in Tandridge churchyard in Surrey. Scott's will was proved on 11 April 1878 with a personal estate of under £120,000. This was largely divided between his four surviving sons. A fifth son, Albert Henry Scott, had died in 1865 at the age of twenty and Alwyne Gilbert Scott (1849–1878), a barrister, died eight months after his father. Scott's youngest son, Dukinfield Henry *Scott (1854–1934), became a palaeobotanist and professor of botany at the University of London. The two eldest, George Gilbert *Scott (1839–1897) and John Oldrid Scott (1841–1913), both trained under their father as architects and were left the practice, but, in the event it was the younger brother who inherited the office—and soon disposed of most of the drawings as well as personal papers, claiming to Scott's old clerk of works, J. T. Irvine, that 'the quantity was so enormous that it was quite necessary to thin them down' (J. O. Scott to J. T. Irvine, 22 April 1880, Royal Commission on the Ancient and Historical Monuments of Scotland).

In coming to terms with 'the most successful architectural career of modern times', Scott's obituarists were measured (*The Builder*, 6 April 1878). Although Scott had become a public figure, representative of the aspirations and confidence of the mid-Victorian architectural profession, E. W. Godwin hesitated

> to nominate Scott's works as those of a genius. If he had not the great gift he however possessed others which in these days are perhaps even more conducive to success. He was indefatigable in business and a fervent worker. No chance was ever missed, no opportunity neglected, and thus he obtained a somewhat unenviable notoriety among less energetic or less industrious architects, of being over anxious to obtain commissions. (*British Architect*, 155)

All agreed, however, about the sweetness of Scott's character. Godwin noted that 'he was one of those who spoke well of you behind your back, and, above all, one who, though he desired to be just in his estimate of men, could look kindly upon their shortcomings' (ibid.), while Beresford Hope spoke of how 'how truly modest he was. If anything, he carried that out to a fault. He was anxious; he was often hurt in his feelings by things which he could afford to laugh at. … with all his zeal, all his earnestness, and all his conviction, he never bore malice' (*RIBA Transactions*, 199).

In his funeral sermon Dean Stanley spoke of Scott's 'indefatigable industry, his childlike humility, his unvarying courtesy, his noble candour … his generous encouragement of the students of a rising generation' (Scott, 395). The following year, in his introduction to the published version of Scott's *Recollections*, the dean of Chichester wrote of 'the strength and ardour of those religious convictions which were with him an inheritance' and he mentioned that, when Scott's valet repeatedly asked why the underside of his arms were sore, he eventually admitted that 'when I am praying, especially for my sons, I feel I cannot do enough. I feel kneeling to be but little, and I prostrate myself on the floor' (ibid., xx) (a revelation which some reviewers of the book found distasteful). His eldest son, who edited the volume, elsewhere wrote that 'he was an *Anglican* essentially and in the best sense of the term' and was 'decidedly opposed to Roman practices on many points' (ibid., 492).

Scott was described in one obituary as being 'of middle height' with

> a fine head with a squarely formed chin, indicative of firmness of character; but his manner might be described in the epithets which Goldsmith described that of Sir Joshua Reynolds (also, it may be noted, a great worker), as 'gentle, complying, and bland'; and we remember often wondering how he could preserve a manner so quiet, easy and undisturbed in the midst of all the enormous amount of work he was doing. (*The Builder*, 6 April 1878)

A portrait of Scott in oils was executed by George Richmond for the RIBA in 1877. The chalk study for this was engraved as the frontispiece for Scott's *Recollections* (1879) and is now in the National Portrait Gallery, London, which also owns a sketch made in 1859 by C. B. Birch of Scott lecturing at the Royal Academy. Two further portraits by Richmond are at the Royal Academy and in the possession of Scott's descendants. Scott expressed regret that he never commissioned a portrait of his wife as 'we always talked of getting Richmond to do this but her constant absence from London interfered' (Scott, 466). In 1873 Scott edited a volume of *Family Prayers by the Late Mrs Geo. Gilbert Scott*.

Soon after his death an attempt was made by *The Builder* to catalogue Scott's vast professional output and the published list included 732 buildings or projects, but this was far from complete. A letter from Scott's assistant Charles R. Baker King to G. G. Scott junior, dated 27 May 1879, cited 541 executed works. For his *The Work of Sir Gilbert Scott* published in 1980, David Cole compiled a list of 879 works from these and other sources, but was not able to claim that it was definitive. The sheer scale of Scott's achievement continues to daunt historians of architecture.

GAVIN STAMP

Sources *CGPLA Eng. & Wales* (1878) • G. G. Scott, *Personal and professional recollections by the late Sir George Gilbert Scott, R.A.*, ed. G. Stamp (1995) • I. Toplis, *The foreign office: an architectural history* (1987) • *Recollections of Thomas Graham Jackson*, ed. B. H. Jackson (1950) • *Proceedings of the Society of Antiquaries of London*, 2nd ser., 7 (1876–8), 381–4 • *The Times* (8 April 1878) • *Transactions of the Royal Institute of British Architects* (1878–9), 193–208 • *The Builder*, 36 (1878), 339–43, 360; 37 (1879), 115–16, 140–43 [list of works] • *Building News*, 34 (1878), 309–10, 338–9, 385–6 • *British Architect*, 9 (1878), 155–6 • D. Cole, 'Some early works of George Gilbert Scott', *Architectural Association Journal*, 66 (1950), 98–108 • *Sir Gilbert Scott (1811–1878): architect of the Gothic revival* (1978) • D. Cole, *The work of Sir Gilbert Scott* (1980) • J. Heseltine, G. Fisher, G. Stamp, and others, eds., *Catalogue of the drawings collection of the Royal Institute of British Architects: the Scott family* (1981) • K. A. Morrison, 'The new-poor-law workhouses of George Gilbert Scott and William Bonython Moffatt', *Architectural History*, 40 (1997), 184–203 • C. Webster and J. Elliott, eds., *'A church as it should be': the Cambridge Camden Society and its influence* (2000)

Archives RIBA BAL, architectural sketchbooks and drawings • RIBA BAL, corresp. and papers • Royal Commission on the Ancient and Historical Monuments of Scotland, Edinburgh, National Monuments record of Scotland, architectural drawings, letters, and MS • Royal Commission on the Ancient and Historical Monuments of Scotland, Edinburgh, papers | Bath Central Library, papers relating to restoration of Bath Abbey • Berks. RO, corresp. relating to Berkshire churches • BL, corresp. with Sir A. H. Layard, Add. MSS 38993–38996 • Bodl. Oxf., corresp., sketches and estimates relating to rebuilding of Woolland church and Cattistock church • Ches. & Chester ALSS, letters relation to Rode church • Dorset RO, corresp. relating to Woolland House • Glos. RO, letters, plans, etc. relating to Sudeley Castle alteration • Glos. RO, papers relating to Cirencester church • Herefs. RO, letters to F. T. Havergal • Highclere Castle, Hampshire, Highclere church specification and accounts • JRL, letters to E. A. Freeman • RIBA, corresp. relating to St John's Cathedral, Newfoundland • Warks. CRO, letters to Miss Ryland relating to Sherbourne church • Worcs. RO, report on Worcester Cathedral choir restoration

Likenesses C. B. Birch, pencil drawing, 1859, NPG • photographs, 1860–79 • G. Richmond, oils, *c.*1870, RA • G. Richmond, coloured chalk drawing on paper, 1877, NPG • G. Richmond, oil study, 1877, RIBA [*see illus.*] • J. D. Miller, mezzotint, pubd 1880 (after W. B. Richmond), BM • G. G. Adams, medallion sculpture, exh. RA 1884, NPG • E. Edwards, photograph, NPG; repro. in L. Reeve, ed., *Portraits of men of eminence*, 1 (1863) • London Stereoscopic Co., carte-devisite, NPG • G. Richmond, drawing, priv. coll. • brass sculpture over tomb, Westminster Abbey • photograph, NPG • relief portrait on frieze, Albert Memorial, London • wood-engraving (after photograph by J. Watkins), NPG; repro. in *ILN* (23 Feb 1861) • wood-engraving (after photograph by Mr Dolamore), NPG; repro. in *ILN* (3 Aug 1872) • wood-engraving (after photograph by London Stereoscopic Co.), NPG; repro. in *ILN* (3 April 1878)

Wealth at death under £120,000: probate, 11 April 1878, *CGPLA Eng. & Wales*

Scott, George Gilbert (1839–1897), architect and scholar, was born on 8 October 1839 at 20 Spring Gardens, London, the eldest of the five sons of Sir George Gilbert *Scott (1811–1878), architect, and Caroline Oldrid (1811–1872), daughter of John Oldrid, draper, of Boston, Lincolnshire. Scott won a scholarship to Eton College in 1852. In 1857 he began a three-year articled pupillage in his father's office in Spring Gardens, after which he worked there as an assistant. Friends then persuaded him to enter Cambridge University and Scott went up to Jesus College in 1863 and in 1866 headed the first class in the moral sciences tripos. In 1868 Scott won the Burney prize for an essay published in 1870 as *The argument of the intellectual character of the first cause, as affected by recent investigations of physical science*. In 1872 he was elected a fellow of Jesus College, but was obliged to resign after four months owing to his marriage that year to Ellen King Sampson (1854–1953), daughter of William King Sampson, of Eastbourne, Sussex.

On his nomination form for election as a fellow of the Royal Institute of British Architects (declared void in 1878), Scott stated he was in independent architectural practice from 1863, but he had continued to assist his father, who passed on to him the restoration of Cheddleton church, Staffordshire (1863–6), and the restoration and enlargement of the hall and combination room at Peterhouse, Cambridge (1868–71), in both of which he used William Morris and his firm for decoration and stained glass. Scott's early career, however, is difficult to document, as all his papers and drawings were destroyed in a fire in 1870 in the house in Cecil Street, London, off the Strand, where he had rooms, a disaster that may have encouraged more freedom in designing but also affected his health. Scott subsequently opened an office at 7 Duke Street, Portland Place, while in 1872 he and his wife moved into 26 Church Row, Hampstead.

George Frederick Bodley, his father's former pupil, was the principal influence on Scott's own architecture. With Bodley and Thomas Garner, and J. D. Sedding, Scott was responsible for changing the direction of English church design in the 1870s by using English and late styles of Gothic instead of thirteenth-century and continental models, and he went further than his friend Bodley by defending the despised Perpendicular. This was evident in his cemetery chapel at Ramsgate, Kent (1869–71), and the additions to Cattistock church in Dorset (1872–6); but the building which became most influential was his masterpiece, the church of St Agnes, Kennington Park, London (1874–91; dem.). Designed for Anglo-Catholic worship and the English liturgy, the spare Late Gothic interior, with its characteristic arch mouldings disappearing into the piers, was filled with furnishings about which there was 'the mysterious but unmistakable smell of Renaissance that hung about his most Gothic details' (H. S. Goodhart-Rendel, 'The work of Temple Moore', *RIBA Journal*, 35, 26 May 1928, 478). St Mark's, New Milverton, Leamington Spa (1876–9), was designed in a similar style but All Hallows, Southwark (1879–92; dem.), was better-known and combined the refinement of Late Gothic with the toughness of the mid-Victorian urban church. Scott's other churches included that at Eastmoors, Yorkshire (1881–2), and what is now the Roman Catholic cathedral at Norwich (1882–1910), built by the fifteenth duke of Norfolk.

Scott was described by E. W. Godwin as 'a master and a leader in the "Queen Anne" revival' as he showed in his domestic architecture (*British Architect*, 9, 5 April 1878, 156). His only country house was Garboldisham Manor, Norfolk (*c.*1868–1873; dem.), but he designed a group of houses in Westbourne Park, Hull, and several vicarages. He also undertook work at Oxford and Cambridge. At Pembroke College, Cambridge, he built a new block (1879–93) in a Renaissance manner and enlarged Wren's chapel with rare tact and sensitivity at a time when few were prepared to defend classical work of the seventeenth and eighteenth centuries. Scott also designed wallpaper and furniture and, with Bodley and Garner, set up the firm of Watts & Co. *c.*1874 to produce their own designs. Scott moved in artistic circles: the architect Alexander Thomson met him at a dinner in 1871, when he 'made his appearance in black knee breeks black silk stockings high heeled shoes with large buckles, blue coat, yellow vest white neck cloth with stiffner and frilled shirt—he is one of the Queen Ann folks' (*Alexander Thomson Society Newsletter*, 11, October 1994, 11).

Scott's diffidence towards professional practice was encouraged by a large inheritance following Sir Gilbert Scott's death in 1878. He edited his father's *Personal and Professional Recollections* (1879), and in 1881 published his *Essay on the history of English church architecture prior to the separation from the Roman obedience*; the previous year he had shocked members of his family by becoming a Roman Catholic. Scott's later years were clouded by mental instability and scandal, and he gradually withdrew from practice. In 1883 his behaviour required him to be confined in the Bethlem Hospital, from which he escaped to Rouen. In 1884, following a public examination under the 1862 Lunacy Act resulting from a petition by his wife and brothers, he was found to be of unsound mind although, as he wrote to a friend,

> here in France I have been examined by the official medicals, and have been pronounced with equal certainty to be perfectly sane, and quite competent to manage both other people's affairs and my own. I am thus insane in the Kingdom of England and sane in the Republic of France. (Scott to Edward Walford, *The Times*, 12 May 1884, 14)

Scott returned to England in 1885, but he had to be confined in St Andrew's Hospital, Northampton, in 1888 and again in 1891–2. His loyal pupil and 'coadjutor' Temple Lushington Moore (1856–1920) finished Scott's outstanding jobs other than the Norwich church, which was completed by his brother John Oldrid Scott. His wife moved the children to Hollis Street Farm, Ninfield, Sussex, in 1889 and Scott spent his last years in rented accommodation in London. He died on 6 May 1897 from acute cirrhosis of the liver and heart disease while a permanent resident in the Midland Grand Hotel, St Pancras, designed by his father.

When admitted to St Andrew's Hospital in 1891, Scott was described as 'short of stout build, muscular and well nourished … Features regular, eyes grey, pupils equal. Hair bald on top, hair, beard, moustache and whiskers grey' (St Andrew's Hospital records). He was buried on 11 May 1897 in the Hampstead additional burial-ground in London. Of his six children, four survived infancy. One son was the radiologist Sebastian Gilbert Scott and the two other sons, Sir Giles Gilbert *Scott and Adrian Gilbert *Scott [*see under* Scott, Sir Giles Gilbert], achieved distinction as architects. GAVIN STAMP

Sources professional correspondence, notes, sketchbooks, RIBA BAL · Bethlem Hospital archives · St Andrew's Hospital archives, Northampton · Jesus College, Cambridge, archives · *The Architect*, 57 (14 May 1897), 311 · *British Architect* (14 May 1897), 341 · *British Architect* (11 June 1897), 413 · *Building News*, 72 (1897), 699 · *The Builder*, 72 (1897), 531 · W. Millard, 'Notes on some works of the late Geo. Gilbert Scott', *ArchR*, 5 (1898–9), 59–67, 124–32 · J. Heseltine, G. Fisher, G. Stamp, and others, eds., *Catalogue of the drawings collection of the Royal Institute of British Architects: the Scott family* (1981), 117–66 · G. Stamp, 'George Gilbert Scott, junior, architect 1839–1897', PhD diss., U. Cam., 1978 · G. Stamp, *An architect of promise: George Gilbert Scott junior (1839–1897) and the late Gothic revival* (2002) · *CGPLA Eng. & Wales* (1897) · *The Times* (2–5 April 1884) · *The Times* (8–10 April 1884) · *The Times* (15 April 1884) · *The Times* (12 May 1884) · *The Times* (16 June 1884) · *The Times* (23 June 1884)

Archives Norfolk RO, report relating to internal rearrangement of Norwich Cathedral · RIBA, architectural sketchbooks and drawings · RIBA, corresp. and papers · Royal Commission for the Ancient and Historical Monuments of Scotland, Edinburgh, letters

Likenesses double portrait, photograph (with his wife), priv. coll. · photographs, priv. coll.

Wealth at death £41,710: probate, 16 July 1897, *CGPLA Eng. & Wales*

Scott, George Herbert (1888–1930), airship commander, was born in Lewisham, London, on 25 May 1888, the eldest son of George Hall Scott, civil engineer, and his wife, Margaret Wilkinson. He was educated at Alton School, Plymouth, at Richmond School, Yorkshire, and at the Royal Naval Engineering College, Keyham. From 1908 onwards he was engaged in general engineering, and just before the First World War he was employed on building naval vessels in the yards of the Sociedad Española de Construcción, at Ferrol, Spain.

Soon after the outbreak of the First World War in 1914 Scott joined the Royal Naval Air Service as a flight sub-lieutenant and was sent for training to the airship stations at Farnborough and Kingsnorth, Kent. In May 1915 he was appointed to the airship station at Barrow in Furness, and remained there until October 1916, when he left in order to take command of the airship station at Anglesey. In March 1917 he was back at Barrow as captain of the Parseval airship P4.

In April 1917 the first British rigid airship to fly, no. 9, which had been built by Messrs Vickers at Barrow, was taken into service at Howden, Yorkshire, and Squadron Commander Scott was posted to Howden to take command of her. In July he took the ship on patrol off the north-east coast and was in the air for twenty-seven hours, a notable flight for a British rigid at the time. He subsequently commanded the same airship at Cranwell, Lincolnshire, and at Pulham, Norfolk, and it was while at the latter station that he developed the system—with which his name is associated—of mooring airships at the head of a mast or tower.

On the formation of the Royal Air Force in April 1918 Scott was gazetted to the rank of major. In November 1918, soon after the signing of the armistice, he went to Inchinnan, Renfrewshire, where Messrs William Beardmore were building the rigid R34, a copy of the Zeppelin airship L33 which had landed, owing to damage by anti-aircraft gunfire, near Mersea Island in September 1916. He was given command of the R34 on her completion, and received orders to prepare for a voyage to the United States of America. The journey was made in July 1919. The R34 left East Fortune, East Lothian, at 1.42 a.m. on 2 July and returned to Pulham, where she landed, at 6.57 a.m. on 13 July. The outward journey to Mineola, east of New York, during which mails were dropped at Newfoundland, was made in 108 hours 12 minutes, and the homeward journey, after circling New York, was completed in 75 hours 3 minutes. During her whole flight of some 6000 miles the R34 was in wireless touch with the Air Ministry in London. She encountered severe electrical storms, particularly off St John's, and she was much thrown about; but Scott's cool, alert, and expert handling brought the ship safely through. This was the first airship flight across the Atlantic, and the first aerial transatlantic round trip. For his achievement Scott was appointed CBE, a somewhat meagre recognition compared to the knighthoods awarded a month earlier to Alcock and Brown for their one-way transatlantic flight. He had already received the Air Force Cross in 1918 for his work on airships during the war.

Shortly before the R34 voyage Scott married Jessie Buchanan, the eldest daughter of Archibald Jack Campbell, senior manager at Beardmore's factory, where the airship was built, and his wife, Catherine, *née* Crawford. In October 1919 he retired from the Royal Air Force, but in 1920 he joined the technical staff of the Royal Airship Works at Cardington, Bedford. Airship development in England had been stimulated by the war, but began to languish in peacetime, and soon ceased altogether—although a nucleus staff, including Scott, was retained at Pulham. About 1924 the government once again took up the problem of the airship, and Scott was appointed to the Air Ministry as officer in charge of flying and training in the directorate of airship development. The project was to open up airship communications throughout the British empire, and in 1927 Scott visited Canada in order to advise the Canadian government on selecting a site for an airship base. As a result of his visit, a mooring tower was built at St Hubert, Montreal.

In January 1930 Scott was appointed assistant director for airship development with responsibility for all airship flying operations and for training airship crews. He was also responsible for the trials of the new British rigids, the R100 and R101. He made his second flight across the Atlantic, although not in command, in the R100, which left Cardington at 3.48 a.m. on 29 July 1930 and reached St Hubert, Montreal, at 2.25 a.m. on 1 August after a journey of 3364 miles. On 4 October 1930 he set out as a passenger in the

R101 on a flight to India, and he was among the forty-eight victims (who included the air minister, Christopher Birdwood Thomson) when the ship crashed and caught fire at 2 a.m. on 5 October at Allonne, near Beauvais, France. He was survived by his wife and their son and three daughters. Scott had been responsible with Lieutenant-Colonel V. C. Richmond, the designer of the R101, for the unbraced transverse frame, first used in that ship and regarded as one of the most important developments in airship construction.

Scott was a quiet, conscientious, and hard-working officer. A trained and experienced engineer, he had a firm belief in the future of the airship, and his life was devoted to the establishment of the airship as a safe and reliable form of transport. His pioneering efforts he regarded solely as incidental to this end, and in no sense as record-breaking achievements. He was, without doubt, the foremost British airship commander of his time.

H. A. JONES, *rev.* M. C. CURTHOYS

Sources personal knowledge (1937) • private information (1937) • E. M. Maitland, *The log of H.M.A. R34* (1920) • R. D. S. Higham, *The British rigid airship, 1908–1931: a study in weapons policy* (1961) • P. Abbott, *Airship: the story of R34* (1994) • B. Collier, *The airship: a history* (1974) • D. Beaty, *The water jump: the story of transatlantic flight* (1976) • m. cert.

Archives FILM BFI NFTVA, news footage

Likenesses photographs, 1919, repro. in Abbott, *Airship*

Wealth at death £438 3s. 1d.: administration, 22 Nov 1930, *CGPLA Eng. & Wales*

Scott, George Lewis (1708–1780), mathematician, was born at Hanover in May 1708, the eldest son of George Scott of Bristo in Scotland, and Marion Stewart, daughter of Sir James Stewart bt, of Coltness, lord advocate of Scotland. His father held diplomatic offices at various German courts, was envoy-extraordinary to Augustus I, king of Poland, in 1712, and was an especial friend of the elector of Hanover (afterwards George I), whose names Scott was given at baptism. Princess Sophia (1630–1714) was his godmother. At the close of 1726, after his father's death, his mother moved to Leiden for the education of her children.

Scott was called to the bar at the Middle Temple, became FSA on 3 June 1736, and FRS on 5 May 1737, and was a member in 1736 of the Society for Encouragement of Learning. At this date James Thomson, the poet, was one of his friends. In November 1750 Scott was made sub-preceptor to Prince George and his younger brothers, on the recommendation of Lord Bolingbroke through Lord Bathurst. Horace Walpole wrote with heavy irony, 'You may add that recommendation to the chapter of our wonderful politics' (*Letters*, 232). As Scott was considered a Jacobite, his appointment caused considerable stir through the belief that he would inculcate in his pupils the doctrine of the divine right of kings. By July 1752 the tutors were divided into factions, and the quarrel lasted all the year. In February 1758 Scott was made a commissioner of excise in London, and he held that post until his death. He also served the board of longitude.

Scott, who was a pupil of de Moivre, was celebrated for his knowledge of mathematics. On 7 May 1762 he sent a long letter to Gibbon on the books which he should study in analysis, geometry, and the physico-mathematical sciences, and Gibbon, on 19 October 1767, asked him to supply a survey of the physical and mathematical sciences in England, for insertion in the *Mémoires littéraires de la Grande-Bretagne* (1768–9) that he was preparing in conjunction with Georges Deyverdun. In December 1775 Gibbon sent for his perusal a part of the *Decline and Fall of the Roman Empire*. Robert Simson, the Scottish mathematician, corresponded with Scott about algebra and geometry. Charles Burney (1726–1814) described him as an excellent musician, and as performing on the harpsichord. He was an intimate friend of the composer J. C. Pepusch, whom he assisted in drawing up a paper for the Royal Society on the genera and systems of ancient Greek music. The materials which Ephraim Chambers left for a supplement to his dictionary of arts and sciences were committed to Scott's care for selection, revision, and expansion. The two volumes appeared in 1753, and he is said to have received £1500 for his services.

Scott was very tall, and big. Fanny Burney, who met him in 1769 at a party, found him 'very sociable and facetious too'. As they both disliked cards he entertained her 'extremely with droll anecdotes and stories among the Great and about the Court' (*Early Diary*, 1.155). He treated his great bulk with humour. According to one anecdote Dr Johnson was one day giving way to tears, when Scott, who was present, clapped him on the back and said, 'What's all this, my dear sir? Why, you and I and Hercules, you know, were all troubled with melancholy'. The doctor was 'so delighted at his odd sally that he suddenly embraced him' (*Johnsonian Miscellanies*, 50–51).

About 1752 Scott married Sarah Robinson [*see* Scott, Sarah] but they separated. Her friends condemned him for his bad treatment of her, and the rumour spread that he had tried to poison her. The veracity of these claims has, however, not been established. Scott died on 7 December 1780. Lord Brougham's judgement that he was 'perhaps the most accomplished of all amateur mathematicians who never gave their works to the world' (Brougham, 135–6) suggests the obscurity into which his writings fell.

W. P. COURTNEY, *rev.* ALAN YOSHIOKA

Sources *The early diary of Frances Burney, 1768–1778*, ed. A. R. Ellis, 2 vols. (1889) • A. Rees and others, *The cyclopaedia, or, Universal dictionary of arts, sciences, and literature*, 45 vols. (1819–20) • *The diaries and correspondence of the Right Hon. George Rose*, ed. L. V. V. Harcourt, 2 vols. (1860) • [W. Mure], ed., *Selections from the family papers preserved at Caldwell*, 3 vols., Maitland Club, 71 (1854) • *The miscellaneous works of Edward Gibbon*, ed. J. Holroyd [Lord Sheffield], 2nd edn, 1–2 (1814) • W. Trail, *Account of the life and writings of Robert Simson* (1812) • *GM*, 1st ser., 50 (1780), 590 • *GM*, 1st ser., 75 (1805), 218–19, 811–12 • J. Nichols, *Anecdotes, biographical and literary of the late Mr. William Bowyer, printer* (privately printed, London, 1778) • H. L. Piozzi, 'Anecdotes', in *Johnsonian miscellanies*, ed. G. B. Hill, 1 (1897), 147–351, esp. 228 • H. Brougham, *Lives of the philosophers of the time of George III* (1855) • *The letters of Horace Walpole, earl of Orford*, ed. P. Cunningham, 2 (1857); repr. (1891)

Scott, Sir Giles Gilbert (1880–1960), architect, was born on 9 November 1880 at 26 Church Row, Hampstead, London, the third son of George Gilbert *Scott (1839–1897)

Sir Giles Gilbert Scott (1880–1960), by Howard Coster, 1934

and the grandson of Sir George Gilbert *Scott (1811–1878), both architects. Scott's mother, Ellen King Sampson (1854–1953), was the daughter of William King Sampson, of a Sussex yeoman family. In 1889 her uncle George King-Sampson died and left Hollis Street Farm outside Ninfield to the young Giles Scott, with a life tenancy to his mother, which enabled her to take her children to Sussex and escape her sometimes violent husband who, in 1884, had been declared of unsound mind. The most direct influence of Scott's father on his upbringing was to choose his school, Beaumont College, Windsor, because he admired the buildings there designed by J. F. Bentley.

In Sussex Ellen Scott took her children 'steeplechasing' on bicycles to visit churches and she decided that her two youngest children, Giles and Adrian, should follow in their father's profession. In 1899 Scott was articled for three years to Temple Lushington Moore, his father's former pupil and 'coadjutor', but it was not a conventional pupillage as he saw little of Moore, who worked at home in Hampstead while his office in Staple Inn was run by P. B. Freeman. Although Scott hardly knew his father—he later recalled seeing him only twice—he became familiar with his architecture, and later remarked that 'I always think that my father was a genius. … He was a far better architect than my grandfather and yet look at the reputations of the two men!' (Scott to J. Betjeman, 19 Dec 1938, Betjeman papers, University of Victoria, British Columbia).

Cathedral and church commissions With the encouragement of Moore, Scott entered the second competition for a new Anglican cathedral in Liverpool in 1902 with a 'Design for a twentieth century cathedral', for which he prepared the drawings at home in Battersea in his spare time. To his surprise, this was one of five designs chosen to go forward to a second round, in preference to schemes by, among others, Temple Moore. In 1903 Scott's design was selected by the assessors, Norman Shaw and G. F. Bodley, but it was a choice which dismayed the Liverpool Cathedral committee on account of Scott's youth, lack of experience, and religion: he was still only twenty-two, and a Roman Catholic. In the event, the compromise was reached that Bodley should join Scott as joint architect for the project.

Although Bodley had been a close friend of Scott's father, this was not a happy collaboration, especially after the elder architect had acquired two more cathedrals in the United States to design; Scott complained that this 'has made the working partnership agreement more of a farce than ever, and to tell the truth my patience with the existing state of affairs is about exhausted' (Kennerley, 38). He was on the point of resignation when Bodley died in 1907. The separate lady chapel was then under construction and Scott promptly redesigned everything above the arcades, making the vault more continental in style with curvilinear ribs and the triptych reredos more elaborate. This first part of the cathedral was opened in 1910. In that same year the cathedral committee approved Scott's proposal completely to redesign the rest of the building: a remarkably brave decision, not least because it necessitated the demolition of stonework already executed. Scott had become increasingly unhappy with his winning design, which, for all its imagination, belonged essentially in the Gothic tradition established by his father, Bodley, and Temple Moore. With Bodley gone, 'I decided to start all over again' (Cotton, 29), and Scott made his new conception much more monumental, sublime, and, in its overall symmetry, almost classical in feeling: what John Summerson described as a 'sudden diversion of late Victorian Gothic into an equivalent of Edwardian Baroque' (Ford, 235). Instead of twin towers inspired by Durham Cathedral, Scott now proposed a single, central tower rising above pairs of transepts, which had the further advantage of providing the central space required but not supplied in the original competition design.

Scott also greatly simplified the elevations to create a masterly balance between massive bare walls of pink sandstone and concentrated detail. Writing later, he explained how 'at Liverpool I have endeavoured to combine the uplifting character imparted by vertical expression with the restful calm undoubtedly given by the judicious use of horizontals' (*Morning Post*, 19 July 1924). This, together with the rich sculptural feeling of the great reredos and other furnishings, may reflect the influence of Albi Cathedral, France (which, in fact, Scott never saw), as well as that of a visit to Spain made with Sir Frederick Ratcliffe, honorary treasurer and later chairman of the cathedral executive committee, who became a lifelong friend. Scott designed every detail in the building and the work of craftsmen and artists, such as the sculptor Edward Carter Preston and the stained-glass artist J. H. Hogan, had to conform to the architect's personal vision.

By adopting symmetry for the cathedral, Scott imposed an obligation on posterity which ensured its completion in a very different economic and social climate and he continually refined his design as the building rose. In 1922 the American architect Bertram Goodhue described it as 'the finest modern church building without a doubt' (*Daily Courier* [Liverpool], 5 Sept 1922, 5), while for H. S. Goodhart-Rendel it was

> a scenic prodigy, displaying the great imaginative power of its designer ... it has permanence as the memorial of long and arduous labour on the part of an architect exceptionally sensitive to the tastes and aspirations of his contemporaries, and permanence also as a memorial of the lofty aims of countless able artists who, in three generations, spent their efforts in the service of Romance. (Goodhart-Rendel, 252)

The choir and first pair of transepts were opened in 1924, the central tower was finished in 1942, and the first bay of the nave was opened a year after the architect's death, in 1961. The (liturgical) west end was finally completed to a revised and reduced design by his old assistant, Roger Pinckney, made for Scott's former partner Frederick G. Thomas.

The building of Liverpool Cathedral, an undertaking on a prodigious scale, dominated Scott's life, and it was in Liverpool that he met Louise Wallbank Hughes (1888–1949), whom he married in 1914. The daughter of Richard Hughes, she had been working as a receptionist in the Adelphi Hotel and was, to the distress of Scott's mother, a protestant. Despite his astonishing early success, Scott initially had little work other than the cathedral; his first complete church was the Annunciation at Bournemouth (1905–6), in which he used the high, flush transept idea he had initially proposed for Liverpool to make a sort of crossing tower at the end of a low nave. Another Roman Catholic church, at Sheringham, Norfolk (1909–14), revealed Scott's development towards simplifying Gothic forms, and the contemporary church at Ramsay on the Isle of Man (1909–12), with its rugged tower facing the sea, displays his acute sensitivity to site. At the church of Our Lady at Northfleet, Kent (1913–16), Scott's Gothic was made more monumental and unified with horizontal banding like classical rustication, and the modelling of the tower and shallow transepts makes the building seem like a prototype for Liverpool Cathedral. Similarly experimental is St Paul's, Stonycroft, in Liverpool (1913–16), where the wide vaulted interior is cleverly expressed externally in triple transepts.

Scott established himself as one of the most accomplished and sophisticated inter-war ecclesiastic designers in Britain in the several churches he designed for both Anglican and Roman Catholic parishes. In these buildings traditional styles were given a distinctive contemporary expression. He always took great care over building materials, and at St Andrew's, Luton (1931–2), long and streamlined behind a powerful squat west tower, interior transverse arches of reinforced concrete were expressed externally by buttresses faced in beautiful brickwork. At St Francis's, Terriers, High Wycombe (1928–30), a church of sophisticated simplicity faced in knapped flint, he demonstrated his masterly handling of natural light by omitting the west and clerestory windows so that dramatic illumination comes from the transepts and crossing tower placed towards the east. The Roman Catholic church at Ashford, Middlesex (1927–8), with its inward-sloping, self-buttressing walls, was a particular favourite of the architect.

Scott seldom repeated himself, and he experimented with different church plans. The Anglican church of St Alban, Golders Green, London (1932–3), is cruciform and built of special thin bricks, with pitched tiled roofs over the four arms and the low central tower. The Roman Catholic cathedral at Oban (1931–51) has a massive, rugged tower of pink granite facing the sea while the timber roof raised above tall, simple piers gives the interior a grandeur out of proportion to its actual size. A. S. G. Butler wrote how

> Oban cathedral is a notable example of a design most suitable to its site and, in every way, to its purpose. It was Scott's power to grasp clearly the practical object of a building and design it on that basis. Appearance followed from the expression of this more than from a preconceived idea of beauty. (*DNB*)

Scott also designed the church at Ampleforth College, Yorkshire, as well as boarding-houses for the school, and completed the nave of the church at Downside Abbey, Somerset. At St Alphege's, Bath (1927–30), and at the chapel for Lady Margaret Hall, Oxford (1931–2), he used a simplified Romanesque style instead of Gothic. Perhaps his finest chapel for an educational institution is that at Charterhouse, Godalming (1922–7), where a long, powerful mass like a fortress is articulated by a row of thin flush transepts which allow light to enter laterally as if from a hidden source.

Secular architecture Scott was far from being exclusively a church architect, and his success at Liverpool led to a series of large secular commissions after the First World War (in which he served as a major in the Royal Marines, supervising the construction of defences in the English Channel). The Memorial Court for Clare College, Cambridge (1922–32), was built on the west side of the River Cam in a refined neo-Georgian or 'neo-Grèc' manner in silver-grey brick. His own London house, Chester House, in Clarendon Place (1924–5), and Whitelands College at Putney (1929–31) were designed in a similar style. At Clare, a few years later, the dramatic central axis through the war memorial arched entrance was closed by the tall tower and massive wings of the new Cambridge University Library (1930–34), a building designed after study of American libraries in which windows between bookstacks were linked to leave the intervening brickwork to read as massive pilasters. The New Bodleian Library at Oxford University (1935–46), in its semi-traditional style with rounded corners, was perhaps less successful, but the technical achievement of keeping the building low in scale by building underground was considerable. More appropriate in Oxford was Longwall Quad at Magdalen College (1928–9), which continued St Swithun's Buildings by Bodley and Garner in a simplified Tudor manner.

As an established architect, knighted in 1924, Scott was in demand as consultant on new commercial building projects in London. He acted as 'associated architect' with Gordon and Viner on the William Booth Memorial Buildings at Denmark Hill in south London (1926), where his personal treatment of the tall brick tower is unmistakable. Scott's Gothic canopy proposed in 1939 for the King George V memorial close to Westminster Abbey met with opposition, however, particularly from the newly founded Georgian Group defending the buildings on the site, and his alternative, classical design, with a statue by William Reid Dick executed in 1946–7, is not characteristic. Equally untypical but much more successful was Scott's design for the Charing Cross Road façade of the Phoenix Theatre. He was also responsible for Cropthorne Court at Maida Vale (1928–9), where a clever diagonal zigzag plan was adopted to obviate light wells. American architects expressed surprise that Scott could handle so much work; in the 1920s, Roger Pinckney recalled,

> it was a small office, not more than 8 to 10 altogether, very informal and apparently unbusinesslike, but it was our pride never to have delayed a job from lack of drawings. Sir Giles designed everything himself, down to the smallest detail, but did not do a lot of visiting. (Pinckney to Stamp, 11 Sept 1974)

Other assistants included A. G. Crimp, the office manager, Lesslie K. Watson, and Arthur Gott.

A remarkable aspect of Scott's career was how he rose to the technological challenges of the twentieth century, for which his training as a church architect can hardly have prepared him. In 1924 he was one of three architects invited by the newly founded Royal Fine Arts Commission to design a standard telephone kiosk for the General Post Office. Scott proposed a classical design in cast iron surmounted by a Soanian dome which reflected the contemporary interest in Regency architecture (it may be significant that he became a trustee of Sir John Soane's Museum at this time). This was chosen the following year and went into production as the General Post Office's kiosk no. 2. Scott subsequently adapted his design for other kiosk types and a decade later reduced and refined it for mass production, giving the fenestration a more horizontal and modernistic character. This, the no. 6 or jubilee kiosk, was introduced in 1935 and soon became ubiquitous and a familiar aspect of the British landscape.

Scott's resourceful talent as an industrial designer was confirmed in 1930, when he was asked to act as consultant architect to the London Power Company for its electricity generating station in Battersea. This large and controversial structure had already been designed by J. Theo Halliday, of Halliday and Agate, and the engineer Sir Leonard Pearce. Scott's evident ability to handle huge awe-inspiring masses of masonry, to balance concentrated ornament against bare wall-surfaces, was put to good effect in such buildings; he chose the external bricks, detailed the walls with 'jazz modern' fluting to humanize the structure while not denying its scale or industrial character, and remodelled the four corner chimneys to resemble classical columns. After the first half of the Battersea power station was completed in 1933, it became one of the most admired as well as conspicuous modern buildings in London. 'Whatever criticisms have been levelled against it, it remains one of the first examples in England of frankly contemporary industrial architecture', concluded Nikolaus Pevsner in 1957 (Pevsner, *London*, 1957, 510).

Scott's success at Battersea resulted in similar industrial commissions, notably the Guinness brewery at Park Royal (1933–5), where he worked with the consulting engineers, Sir Alexander Gibb & Partners, on designing the several large brick-faced blocks; Scott wrote of such work that 'there is not nearly as much to do as might be anticipated from the size of the buildings' (Scott to H. Robertson, 17 Oct 1947, RIBA). In 1932 he was appointed by the London county council to design the controversial new Waterloo Bridge. Working with the engineers Rendel, Palmer, and Tritton and with Sir Pearson Frank, he proposed an austere and elegant structure of reinforced concrete with five shallow arches faced externally in Portland stone. After further controversy over the demolition of John Rennie's Greek Doric bridge, work on its replacement began in 1937 and it was formally opened in 1945, although without the railings or the sculptural groups at either end proposed by the architect.

Having demonstrated such versatility and openness to new ideas, Scott was an ideal choice for president when the Royal Institute of British Architects was celebrating its centenary. It was a time when the authority of historical styles was being undermined by the impact of ideas from the modern movement in Europe and, in his inaugural address, delivered in 1933, Scott announced that 'I hold no brief either for the extreme diehard Traditionalist or the extreme Modernist and it seems to me idle to compare styles and say that one is better than another.' Scott believed in 'a middle line' and was impatient of dogma, although happy to use new types of construction such as reinforced concrete when appropriate; his approach to design was intuitive rather than intellectual. He was not hostile to modernism, and recognized its 'negative quality of utter simplicity' as a healthy reaction against 'unintelligent Traditionalism'. But although he liked fast cars (and drove a Buick at the time), Scott believed that the machine aesthetic had been taken to extremes at the expense of the human element in architecture: 'I should feel happier about the future of architecture had the best ideas of Modernism been grafted upon the best traditions of the past, in other words, if Modernism had come by evolution rather than by revolution' (*RIBA Journal*, 11 Nov 1933, 5–14).

Scott's belief in compromise and in 'gradual evolution' was to be rejected in the changed architectural climate after the Second World War, but at first enemy bombs brought opportunities. He was appointed architect for the new Coventry Cathedral in 1942, following the destruction of the town centre, and prepared a scheme with a remarkable centralized plan around a free-standing baldachin. The arrival of a new bishop in 1943 obliged him to modernize the interior with unusual parabolic arches, but this scheme was criticized by the Royal Fine Arts Commission for its compromised character and in 1947 Scott resigned, commenting that

> it is unlikely that a modernist or a traditional design will ever meet the approval of both parties. … These differences of opinion, and the formation of numerous societies, committees and commissions etc. to give them expression, are characteristics of our time; they harass the unfortunate

artist and hamper the production of the work. (Scott to the provost of Coventry, 2 Jan 1947, RIBA)

Scott's scheme for rebuilding the House of Commons was less controversial. Following the decision by the wartime parliament to rebuild the chamber exactly the same size and shape as the old, a select committee sought the architect 'best qualified to provide plans in keeping with the Gothic style of the Palace' ('Select committee on the House of Commons', 4), so that Scott's appointment in 1944 now seems almost inevitable. Assisted by his younger brother Adrian and working with Dr Oscar Faber as consulting engineer, he succeeded in creating a new chamber in harmony with, but distinct from, the surrounding architecture by Barry and Pugin, while incorporating new technology and creating much more ancillary accommodation within the confined space. Scott described this as the most complex building with which he had ever been involved, and compared the new interior to that of a battleship. He followed Pugin in adapting Gothic to new purposes, but his was different, personal in style and characteristic of his time. 'Feeling as we do that modernist architecture in its present state is quite unsuitable for the rebuilding of the House of Commons', Scott wrote,

and bearing in mind that the Chamber forms only a small portion of an existing large building, we are strongly of the opinion that the style adopted should be in sympathy with the rest of the structure, even if it has to differ in some degree in order to achieve a better quality of design. ('Select committee on the House of Commons', 8)

Although when the new chamber was opened in 1950, few had a good word to say for Scott's unfashionable 'Neon Gothic,' both the tact and the cleverness of his approach have become evident over the intervening years.

Scott also rebuilt the war-damaged hall of London's Guildhall for the city corporation (1950–54), replacing Sir Horace Jones's Victorian timber roof with one with transverse stone arches which the medieval original probably possessed. In addition, he designed an office building to the north in his modernistic brick manner. But his greatest impact on the City of London was to rebuild Bankside power station on the south bank of the Thames opposite St Paul's Cathedral, even though the Royal Academy planning committee, which he had chaired after the death of Sir Edwin Lutyens, had advocated the removal of industrial buildings from such sites in 1944. Scott's design was published in 1947 and provoked controversy, with the architect lamely countering that 'power stations can be fine buildings, but it must be demonstrated' (*The Builder*, 23 May 1947, 494).

This Scott certainly did demonstrate in what was his supreme 'cathedral of power'. He disagreed with modernists by arguing that appropriate ornament had a purpose even in industrial buildings, and that 'contrast between plain surfaces and sparse well-placed ornament can produce a charming effect' (Stamp and Harte). At Bankside the brickwork is superb, achieving a monumentality that reflects Scott's generation's interest in the sublime monuments of the ancient world, and, in contrast to Battersea where he had never been happy with the upturned table configuration, he contrived to gather all the flues into one single chimney or campanile. Completed in 1960, the building had a short life as an oil-fired power station before becoming an art gallery, Tate Modern at Bankside, although in the conversion carried out in the 1990s by the Swiss architects Herzog and de Meuron, the symmetrical stepped profile of the principal elevation was removed.

Death, the work of his son and brother, and posthumous reputation Scott continued to design churches in the post-war years which, although superficially conservative, reveal a continuing interest in internal structural expression. In his new Carmelite church in Kensington (1954–9), which replaced another casualty of the Second World War, Scott used transverse concrete arches pierced by passage aisles to support a continuous clerestory as well as developing his favourite motif of flush transepts. The new Roman Catholic church in Preston (1954–9) is reminiscent of his pre-war church at Luton in its repetitive length. Scott's last church was the Roman Catholic church of Christ the King at Plymouth, and he was working on the preliminary details of the executed scheme in University College Hospital when he died there of lung cancer on 9 February 1960.

After a requiem mass at St James's, Spanish Place, London, Scott was buried by the Benedictine monks of Ampleforth outside the west end of his great cathedral at Liverpool next to his wife at a point which should have been enclosed by a *porte-cochère* had his final design of 1942 been carried out. The marriage had been singularly happy and they had three sons, of whom two survived infancy. The younger, Richard Gilbert Scott (*b.* 12 Dec 1923), trained as an architect and became a partner in the firm in 1952, before eventually completing several projects such as the Guildhall Library, London, but he resigned from Liverpool Cathedral rather than make further economies to his father's conception. The firm of Sir Giles Scott, Son & Partner was finally dissolved in 1986. Until 1934 Giles Scott practised from 7 Gray's Inn Square, where Bodley had had his office; he then worked in 3 Field Court, Gray's Inn, and in 1956 moved to 6 Gray's Inn Square. He shared these offices with his younger architect brother, Adrian.

Adrian Gilbert Scott (1882–1963) was born on 6 August 1882 and had also been articled to Temple Moore. He assisted his brother Giles in early domestic jobs such as Greystanes, Mill Hill (1907), and during the First World War served in the Royal Engineers at Gallipoli and Egypt and was awarded the Military Cross. His principal work was the Anglican cathedral in Cairo (1933–8; dem.), for which the first designs were made in 1918. Most of his other buildings were for the Roman Catholic church and are very similar in style to his brother's. Adrian Scott also designed his own house, Shepherd's Well, Frognal Way, Hampstead (1930), in a neo-Georgian manner. After the Second World War, during which he was deputy controller of military aircraft production, Adrian Scott rebuilt the Roman Catholic church of Sts Joseph and Mary in Lansbury, Poplar (1951–3), using a pyramidal cruciform plan similar to that earlier used for St James's Church,

Vancouver (1937). Mercifully, his simplified scheme for completing the Metropolitan Cathedral in Liverpool designed by Sir Edwin Lutyens was soon abandoned. A particular success was the rebuilding of St Leonard's Church, Hastings (1953–61), which is enlivened by nautical symbolism. Adrian Scott married Barbara Agnes, daughter of the marine painter Charles Napier Hemy. He died on 23 April 1963 and was buried alongside his wife and father in the Hampstead churchyard extension.

Of Giles Gilbert Scott, A. S. G. Butler recalled that 'this excellent architect was a man of medium height and, at first sight, not unduly impressive, in view of his high distinction. He was very modest and approachable, with a charming sense of humour' (*DNB*). Apart from architecture, Scott's passion was for golf. He lost most of his hair at an early age and John Summerson, who worked briefly in his office, was initially dismayed to find that the famous architect was a short man in an overcoat and bowler hat, with a newspaper under his arm, smoking a cigarette (he then smoked sixty a day): 'I was disappointed that the creator of so passionate a piece of architecture as Liverpool Cathedral could be so unpassioned in his person' (autobiography of Sir John Summerson). In many ways Scott had a very conventional outlook, and assistants were sometimes disconcerted by his golfing and business friends. 'He was a jovial, generous man who looked more like a cheerful naval officer than an architect' (*Birmingham Post*, 10 Feb 1960), recorded Sir John Betjeman. For Sir Hubert Worthington 'his was a singularly beautiful character, free of the jealousies that so often spoil the successful artist. He bore life's triumphs and life's trials with an unruffled serenity' (*RIBA Journal*, April 1960, 194).

Scott became a fellow of the Royal Institute of British Architects in 1912 and received the institute's royal gold medal in 1925. He was elected an associate of the Royal Academy in 1918 and a full academician in 1922, the youngest since Turner. He was knighted in 1924 after the consecration of the first portion of Liverpool Cathedral and was appointed to the Order of Merit in 1944. He was also made a knight of the order of St Olaf of Norway for his advice on the completion of Trondheim Cathedral.

GAVIN STAMP

Sources correspondence and drawings, RIBA BAL • H. Worthington, *RIBA Journal*, 67 (1959–60), 193–4 • N. Pevsner, *ArchR*, 127 (1960), 424–6 • *Architect and Building News* (20 April 1960), 511–16 • *The Builder*, 198 (1960), 345–6 • *The Times* (10 Feb 1960) • *Manchester Guardian* (10 Feb 1960) • J. Betjeman, *Birmingham Post* (10 Feb 1960) • *Liverpool Daily Post* (10 Feb 1960) • private information (2004) [Richard Gilbert Scott, son; colleagues] • family papers, priv. coll. • G. Scott, 'My life for one job', *Daily Herald* (12 Nov 1931) • C. H. Reilly, 'Sir Giles Gilbert Scott', *Building* (March 1929), 106–11 [repr. in *Representative British architects of today* (1931), 142–56] • G. G. Scott, *RIBA Journal*, 42 (1933), 5–14 • G. G. Scott, *The Builder* (23 May 1947) • G. Stamp and G. B. Harte, *Temples of power* (1979) • unpublished autobiography of Sir John Summerson • P. Kennerley, *The building of Liverpool Cathedral* (1991) • 'Profile: Giles Gilbert Scott', *The Observer* (29 Oct 1950) • G. Stamp, 'Giles Gilbert Scott: the problem of "Modernism"', *Britain in the Thirties: Architectural Design*, 49/10–11 (1979), 72–83 • J. Heseltine, G. Fisher, G. Stamp, and others, eds., *Catalogue of the drawings collection of the Royal Institute of British Architects: the Scott family* (1981) • V. E. Cotton, *The book of Liverpool Cathedral* (1964) • B. Ford, ed., *The Cambridge guide to the arts in Britain*, 8 (1989) • H. S. Goodhart-Rendel, *English architecture since the Regency* (1953) • *DNB* • *London: the cities of London and Westminster*, Pevsner (1957) • 'Select committee on the House of Commons', *Parl. papers* (1943–4), 2.591, no. 109 • C. Riding and J. Riding, *The houses of parliament: history, art, architecture* (2000) • G. Stamp, 'Giles Gilbert Scott and Bankside power station', *Building Tate Modern*, ed. R. Moore and R. Ryan (2000)

Archives CUL, notebook of memoranda, sketches, etc. • Pembroke Cam., letters • RIBA, professional corresp., drawings, sketchbooks | RIBA BAL, letters to W. W. Begley • St Deiniol's Library, Hawarden, corresp. with Henry N. Gladstone relating to Burton church

Likenesses W. Stoneman, two photographs, 1924–44, NPG • P. Evans, pen-and-ink drawing, 1927, NPG • H. Coster, photograph, 1934, NPG [*see illus.*] • R. G. Eves, oils, 1935, NPG • R. G. Eves, oils, 1935, RIBA • R. Guthrie, chalk drawing, 1937, NPG

Wealth at death £98,965 0s. 1d.: probate, 3 May 1960, *CGPLA Eng. & Wales*

Scott, Gregory (1532/3–1576), Church of England clergyman, was born at Sebergham, Cumberland, the son of Richard Scott. On 13 August 1550, at the age of seventeen, he was admitted at King's College, Cambridge, as a scholar from Eton College. He was fellow from 1553 to 1554, probably graduating BA during that period. He is not known to have gone into exile and perhaps prudently retired to Cumberland, since he cannot be traced for the rest of Mary's reign.

One of the first protestant ordinands of Elizabeth's reign, Scott was ordained by John Scory, bishop of Hereford, on 22 December 1559, as of Carlisle diocese, on behalf of Matthew Parker, archbishop of Canterbury. On 20 February 1560 he became only the second clergyman to be granted a diocesan preaching licence by the new bishop of London, Edmund Grindal. Grindal hailed from St Bees, about 20 miles from Sebergham, and the two men had probably long known each other.

Scott was granted letters patent by Nicholas Bacon, the lord keeper, for the crown living of Thimbleby, Lincolnshire, on 11 March 1560, and became a chaplain to Nicholas Bullingham, bishop of Lincoln. In December 1563 John Best, bishop of Carlisle, dispatched Scott to London with a letter asking Grindal to secure him a vacant prebend at Carlisle. Grindal sent him on to William Cecil with a letter of recommendation. He was the fittest candidate for the task of reforming the cathedral chapter, being 'well learned, and of good zeal and sincerity, as partly I know by mine own experience' (Nicholson, 285). Grindal further referred him to Bacon but doubted whether the presentation was in the crown's gift, 'being a prebend of the new erection'. Indeed on 2 May 1564 Scott was collated canon of the third stall in Carlisle Cathedral by Best himself. In that office he took strong action during 1567 and 1568 in suing for remedy against leases of cathedral lands made contrary to the statutes. Vicar of St Michael's, Appleby, from 1569, and also rector of Workington, Cumberland, he was chancellor and vicar-general of Carlisle diocese from 1570. In the latter year he wrote, in verse, *A briefe treatise agaynst certayne errors of the Romish church very plainly, notably and pleasantly confuting the same by scripture and auncient writers*. Although presumably a response to the northern uprising of 1569–70, it was not published until 1574.

On 19 December 1576 Thomas Burton was collated to Scott's cathedral stall following his death, and to St Michael's, Appleby, some days later. His undated will was probated on 10 June 1577. It contains bequests to his father and to five brothers. The bulk of his estate was divided between his two daughters Anne and Jane who, though not yet of marriageable age, were appointed joint executrices. They were left to the care of three overseers including Scott's 'brother' Thomas Risheworthe, to whom in the event probate was granted. Perhaps therefore Mrs Scott had been Risheworthe's sister.

On 24 October 1568 a contemporary of these names, described as 'professor of arts', was granted letters patent for the vicarage of Catterick, Yorkshire. He apparently held it until his death, some time before 14 July 1590. It was doubtless this man who compounded for the rectory of Kirklington, about 12 miles south of Catterick, in February 1575. BRETT USHER

Sources Venn, *Alum. Cant.*, 1/4.31 • *Registrum Matthei Parker, diocesis Cantuariensis, AD 1559–1575*, ed. W. H. Frere and E. M. Thompson, 1, CYS, 35 (1928), 338 • GL, manuscripts section, DL/C/331, fol. 327*v* • BL, Lansdowne MS 443, fol. 94*v* • W. Nicholson, ed., *The remains of Edmund Grindal*, Parker Society, 9 (1843) • state papers domestic, Elizabeth, PRO, SP12/44/6 and /48/4–5 • state papers domestic, supplementary series, PRO, SP46/14/13 • *Fasti Angl.* (Hardy), 3.251 • exchequer, first fruits and tenths office, composition books, PRO, E334/9, fol. 38*v* • *CPR, 1566–9*, no. 1196

Scott, Sir (Henry) Harold (1874–1956), pathologist and historian of tropical medicine, was born on 3 August 1874 at Spalding, Lincolnshire, the son of the Revd Dr Douglas Lee Scott (1846–1914), headmaster of the Mercers' School from 1876 to 1914, and Mary Anne Elizabeth, eldest daughter of Edward Rogers, of Cambridge. He was educated in London at the Mercers' and City of London schools, and afterwards at University College, London, and St Bartholomew's and St Thomas's hospitals, qualifying MRCS, LRCP, in 1897; he then became house physician at the latter hospital. In 1899 he married Harriette (*d.* 1933), daughter of the Revd d'Arcy Harrington Preston of Attleborough, Norfolk; they had one son, who died in 1922. In 1934 he married, secondly, Eileen Anne, daughter of the Revd R. P. Prichard, vicar of Wilburton, Isle of Ely.

Scott joined the Royal Army Medical Corps (RAMC) in 1900 and served with the rank of captain in the South African field force until 1902 (while there he discovered corynebacteria in veld sores); he received the queen's medal with five clasps. During his time in South Africa he contracted enteric fever. Then followed private practice at Ludlow, Shropshire, until in 1910, three years after becoming MD (London), he was appointed government pathologist in Jamaica. There he developed his lifelong interest in tropical medicine, and rightly attributed the local 'vomiting-sickness' to the ingestion of unripe ackee fruit (*Blighia sapida*), and a 'central neuritis' (later known as the Strachan–Scott syndrome) to a diet of sugar cane. During the First World War he returned to England, and again served with the RAMC as pathologist to the Cambridge Hospital, Aldershot. Following that he took a Milner research fellowship in comparative pathology at the London School of Hygiene and Tropical Medicine, and while there he elucidated (under the direction of R. T. Leiper) the life cycle of the small tapeworm *Hymenolepis nana*.

In 1922 Scott was appointed pathologist and bacteriologist at Hong Kong (his major research interest here lay in pulmonary tuberculosis); however, after a relatively short spell he developed acute tropical sprue and was invalided home. After his recovery he was appointed pathologist at the Zoological Society of London (where he continued his study of tuberculosis in animals). In 1928 he became secretary of the colonial medical research committee and wrote 'Memorandum on medical research in the colonies (protectorates and mandated territories), 1928–30'. In 1930 he was appointed assistant director of the Bureau of Hygiene and Tropical Diseases, and in 1935 he succeeded Sir Arthur Bagshawe as director; he edited the *Tropical Diseases Bulletin*, the *Bulletin of Hygiene*, and (for two years) the *Bulletin of War Medicine* for the Medical Research Council. After his retirement he continued to contribute to bureau publications.

Scott was a great medical and scientific writer; his works included *Post-Graduate Clinical Studies: for the General Practitioner* (1907); *Health Problems of the Empire* (with Andrew Balfour, 1924); *Some Notable Epidemics* (1934); and, what is generally regarded as his greatest work, *A History of Tropical Medicine* (2 vols., 1939); this was based on his two Fitzpatrick lectures to the Royal College of Physicians in 1937–8. He also wrote, jointly with D. T. Richardson, the *British Red Cross Manual of Tropical Hygiene* (1946).

Scott was additionally a lecturer on tropical disease at Westminster Hospital medical school, London, and was an examiner for the conjoint and Liverpool diplomas in tropical medicine and hygiene, and tropical hygiene, respectively. He was elected vice-president (1937–9) and president (1943–5) of the Royal Society of Tropical Medicine and Hygiene; his presidential address was entitled 'The influence of the slave-trade in the spread of tropical disease'. He also served as a member of the tropical subcommittee of the Royal Society, and chairman of the Anglo-Soviet Medical Committee. He had been elected FRSE (1917) and FRCP (1925), and was later appointed CMG (1936) and KCMG (1941).

Scott was of slight stature, a good-looking man, always immaculately dressed, who was conservative in outlook and deeply religious, being a devout member of the Church of England. He was above all a classical scholar. He had a keen sense of humour, but could not be described as a clubbable man. He was never pompous. His major relaxation was to be found in books (he read novels, biographies, histories, and travel books, and had a particular fascination with famous trials), though he was also fond of music; he took little exercise and did not play any sport. He read Greek and Latin, and studied Dutch in his seventh decade.

Scott retired from the Bureau of Hygiene and Tropical

Diseases in 1942 and lived quietly thereafter at Braintree, Essex, where he died at his home, Fox Meadows, Courtauld Road, after a long illness, on 6 August 1956.

G. C. Cook

Sources Munk, *Roll* • *The Lancet* (18 Aug 1956), 360–61 • *BMJ* (18 Aug 1956), 422–3 • *The Times* (8 Aug 1956), 11 • *Nature*, 178 (1956), 520 • *Transactions of the Royal Society of Tropical Medicine and Hygiene*, 50 (1956), 515–66 • *WWW* • Venn, *Alum. Cant.*

Likenesses photograph, repro. in *The Lancet*, 360 • photograph, repro. in *Transactions of the Royal Society*, facing p. 515

Wealth at death £29,667 5s. 1d.: probate, 7 Dec 1956, *CGPLA Eng. & Wales*

Scott, Sir Harold Richard (1887–1969), civil servant and commissioner of police, was born in Banbury on 24 December 1887, the youngest of three sons of Richard Scott, a skilled craftsman, and his wife, Hannah Hopecroft. The family moved to Taunton, and Scott won a scholarship to Sexey's School, Bruton. From there he went on to Jesus College, Cambridge, the first from his school to get a Cambridge scholarship. There he took three triposes in different subjects, securing a first in natural sciences (1907), a second in history (1908), and, after taking his BA, a first (with distinction) in modern languages (French) in 1909. In 1910 he took the first division examination for the civil service and secured a place in the Home Office, which he joined in 1911. Scott found that he and a contemporary were the only non-public-school boys in the administrative class in the department. He was soon caught up in the wartime expansion of government activity, being concerned mainly with the regulation of foreign trade. In 1916 he married Ethel Mary, daughter of James Golledge of Bruton, gentleman. They had a son and two daughters. After a brief spell in the newly created Ministry of Labour Scott returned to the Home Office in 1919.

There followed a period of ten years of overwork and stagnant promotion, but his career took off with his promotion first to assistant secretary and then as the chairman of the Prison Commission (1932–9). Scott threw himself with enthusiasm into this exacting assignment. He had already established a good personal relationship with Alexander Paterson, whose influence on penal reform in the post-war period was outstanding, and he stood firm in the face of some ministerial pressure in the difficult period of unrest following the recent Dartmoor mutiny. Scott extended the scope of prisoners' employment, established the first open prison camp, and set up the Imperial Training School for prison officers at Wakefield, a pioneer effort in public service training.

When Sir John Anderson, the former head of the Home Office, was put in charge of a hastily improvised London civil defence organization during the Munich crisis, he appointed Scott as his chief staff officer, and when Anderson became minister for civil defence he made Scott responsible for the urgent task of accelerating London's civil defence arrangements, with the title of chief administrative officer for the London civil defence region, as from February 1939. Although London was bound to be the main target for attack, its preparations were seriously inadequate. The next two years were probably the most

Sir Harold Richard Scott (1887–1969), by Bassano, 1947

fruitful of Scott's public life. With a small administrative and professional staff he quickly imposed his personality and capacity for decision on the chaotic scene of London's local government. With the support of Herbert Morrison, the leader of the London county council, he brought together the most influential councillors and officers. For operational purposes the ninety-five local authority control centres were co-ordinated through nine group centres, working through an efficient communications system to the London regional headquarters established in the Geological Museum in South Kensington.

By the time war broke out the civil defence machine was ready to operate, although there was still much ground to make up, and good use was made of the unexpected respite before bombing started a year later. When the raids died down after May 1941 Scott was moved to the Ministry of Home Security, first as deputy (1941–2) and then as permanent secretary (1942–3). He then served for nearly two years as permanent secretary of the Ministry of Aircraft Production (1943–5). At the end of 1944, most unexpectedly, Scott was asked by the home secretary, Herbert Morrison, to become commissioner of police of the metropolis.

Scott's years as commissioner (1945–53) were generally regarded as successful. There were no startling innovations, as Scott found that his main task had to be the adaptation of the wartime organization of the Metropolitan Police to meet peacetime conditions, and he was hampered throughout by a manpower shortage for which it seemed that no solution could be found. Scott had the disadvantage, as commissioner, of looking like a civil servant in uniform, although in fact, with his powers of quick decision, he had no use for bureaucracy. He was respected as a fair-minded chief and a humane disciplinarian. He dealt firmly with industrial disputes and efficiently with the problems created by Marshal Tito of Yugoslavia's state visit, as well as with the great occasion of the coronation. He retired to the west country in 1953 after eight years. He wrote a highly successful book, *Scotland Yard* (1954), and a memoir, *Your Obedient Servant* (1959). Scott was an honorary fellow of Jesus College, Cambridge. He was appointed CB in 1933, KBE in 1942, KCB in 1944, and GCVO in 1953.

Scott was good-humoured, approachable, and unflappable. Confronted with a problem he would reduce it to its essentials, get on with producing a solution, and see that it was put into effect. He died on 19 October 1969 in Minehead, Somerset. KENNETH PARKER, *rev.*

Sources *The Times* (20 Oct 1969) • H. R. Scott, *Scotland Yard* (1954) • private information (1993) • personal knowledge (1993) • H. R. Scott, *Your obedient servant* (1959) • *CGPLA Eng. & Wales* (1970)
Archives FILM BFI NFTVA, documentary footage • BFI NFTVA, news footage • BFI NFTVA, record footage
Likenesses W. Stoneman, photograph, 1945, NPG • Bassano, photograph, 1947, NPG [*see illus.*] • P. Greenham, portrait; at Scotland Yard, London, in 1993
Wealth at death £7946: probate, 5 Jan 1970, *CGPLA Eng. & Wales*

Scott, Harriet Anne, Lady Scott (1819–1894), novelist, was born in Bombay, the only daughter of Henry Shank of Castlerig and Gleniston, Fife. On 28 November 1844 she married Sir James Sibbald David *Scott, third baronet (1814–1885), with whom she had three sons and four daughters.

Lady Scott, a highly accomplished woman, who has sometimes been confused with another novelist, Caroline Lucy *Scott, Lady Scott (1784–1857), wrote eight novels of which the first four were published anonymously. Her books have been praised as using genuine powers of characterization to comment on gender and class. Their narrative style has been compared to that of Susan Ferrier. The titles include *The Henpecked Husband* (1847, reprinted in 1853 and 1865), *The Only Child: a Tale* (1852, reprinted 1865), and *The Skeleton in the Cupboard* (1860, printed in 1861). She also contributed to *The Queen* newspaper, and to various magazines, and published a small book entitled *Cottagers' Comforts, and other Recipes in Knitting and Crochet: by Grandmother* (1887).

Lady Scott died at her home, 18 Cornwall Gardens, Queen's Gate, London, on 8 April 1894.

G. C. BOASE, *rev.* SARAH COUPER

Sources Blain, Clements & Grundy, *Feminist comp.* • J. Foster, *The peerage, baronetage, and knightage of the British empire for 1883*, 2 [1883] • *N&Q*, 8th ser., 9 (1896), 448; 10 (1896), 186 • private information (1897) [Miss Henrietta Caroline Sibbald Scott, The Firs, Newbury, Berkshire]
Wealth at death £6234 5*s*. 7*d*.: probate, 30 July 1894, *CGPLA Eng. & Wales*

Scott, Helenus (*bap.* **1758**, *d.* **1821**), East India Company military surgeon, was born at Dundee and baptized on 28 August 1758 at Auchterhouse, Forfarshire, the son of David Scott, clergyman of Auchterhouse, and his wife, Mary Mitchell. He studied at Marischal College, Aberdeen, from 1773 to 1777 before studying medicine at Edinburgh from 1777 to 1779. He entered the service of the East India Company as a normal cadet, but, transferring to medical service, was commissioned as an assistant surgeon in January 1783, and served chiefly in the Bombay presidency. In 1787 the Bombay medical board chose him as apothecary to the hospitals of the region. On 19 March 1805 he was created MD by Marischal College. He became a member of the Bombay medical board in 1801 and was selected president in 1806. Scott retired from the East India Company in 1810.

After thirty years in India Scott returned to England, and after some time attending medical lectures, began practice at Bath. On 22 December 1815 he was admitted a licentiate of the Royal College of Physicians, and in 1817 he moved to London and began to practise as a physician in Russell Square. His extensive Indian connection and reputation in the treatment of hepatic disease soon gave him a large practice. In 1817 he contributed an interesting paper to the *Transactions* of the Medico-Chirurgical Society on the use in medicine of nitromuriatic acid, a substance he had tested by bathing in it daily for a week and assessing his own reaction to it. Scott used it in a wider range of diseases than was customary, but its frequent use in the treatment of enteric fever and other illnesses originated in his advocacy of its merits. He published no other medical works, but while in India wrote a novel, *The Adventures of a Rupee* (1782). He died on 16 November 1821 while on a voyage to New South Wales. PATRICK WALLIS

Sources Munk, *Roll* • D. G. Crawford, *A history of the Indian medical service, 1600–1913*, 2 vols. (1914) • H. Scott, 'On the internal and external use of the nitro-muriatic acid in the cure of diseases', *Medico-Chirurgical Transactions*, 8 (1817), 172–200 • *Fasti academiae Mariscallanae Aberdonensis: selections from the records of the Marischal College and University, MDXCIII–MDCCCLX*, 2, ed. P. J. Anderson, New Spalding Club, 18 (1898), 141, 346 • *DNB* • bap. reg. Scot.
Archives BL, corresp. with Sir Joseph Banks, Add. MSS 33979–33982, 35262

Scott, Henry, first earl of Deloraine (1676–1730), army officer, was the third but second surviving son of James *Scott, duke of Monmouth (1649–1685), and Anna *Scott, duchess of Buccleuch (1651–1732). In 1693 he married Anne Duncombe (*d.* 1720), daughter of William Duncombe of Batthesden in Bedfordshire. The marriage produced two sons, Francis (1710–1739), who became the second earl of Deloraine, and Henry, third earl (1712–1740). They also had a daughter, Anne, who never married. On 29 March 1706 Queen Anne created Scott earl of Deloraine, Viscount Hermitage, and Lord Goldielands; the main title was derived from the lands of Deloraine in the parish of Kirkhope, Selkirkshire. He was elected to the last Scottish parliament in October 1706, and voted in favour of the treaty of Union. At the general election of 1715, and again in 1722 and 1727, he was chosen one of the Scottish representative peers. In 1725 he was vested with the Order of the Bath, and appointed gentleman of the bedchamber to

George I. From the time of his accession to the peerage he served in the army. In 1707 Scott was appointed commander of an infantry regiment and on 1 June 1715 he was promoted to colonel of the 2nd troop, Horse Grenadier Guards. His military career continued with further promotions on 7 April 1724 to colonel of the 16th regiment and on 9 July 1730 to colonel of the 3rd cavalry regiment with the rank of major-general in the army.

Scott enjoyed a reputation for courtesy and politeness assumed by Edward Young to derive from his ancestors, who were of royal blood: 'Stanhope in wit, in breeding Deloraine' (*Night Thoughts*, 1742). His mother, however, took a different view. Her will reproached him with gracelessness and extravagance, and she left him only £5.

On 14 March 1726 he married his second wife, Mary [*see* Scott, Mary, countess of Deloraine (*bap.* 1703, *d.* 1744)], daughter of Charles Howard, grandson of the first earl of Berkshire; they had two daughters, Georgina Caroline and Elizabeth Henrietta. Lord Deloraine died suddenly on 25 December 1730 and was buried at Lidwell in Sandford St Martin, Oxfordshire. Lady Deloraine served as governess to the princesses Mary and Louisa, daughters of George II. In April 1734 she married William Wyndham of Ersham, Norfolk. She died on 12 November 1744 and was buried at Windsor.

T. F. HENDERSON, *rev.* PHILIP CARTER

Sources GEC, *Peerage*

Likenesses G. Kneller, group portrait, oils, *c.*1688 (with his mother and brother), Drumlanrig Castle, Dumfriesshire; *see illus. in* Scott, Anna, duchess of Monmouth and *suo jure* duchess of Buccleuch (1651–1732) • G. Kneller, group portrait, oils, *c.*1688 (with his family), Buccleuch estates, Selkirk, Scotland • W. Faithorne junior, mezzotint (after J. Closterman), BM • G. Kneller, double portrait, oils (as a boy; with his brother), Buccleuch estates, Selkirk, Scotland • oils (as a boy), Buccleuch estates, Selkirk, Scotland

Scott, Henry, third duke of Buccleuch and fifth duke of Queensberry (1746–1812), landowner and army officer, was born in London on 13 September 1746, the second but eldest surviving son of Francis Scott, styled earl of Dalkeith (1721–1750), and his wife, Caroline, Baroness Greenwich (1717–1794), eldest daughter of the second duke of Argyll. In 1751 he succeeded his grandfather, also Francis Scott, as duke of Buccleuch and as earl of Doncaster in the English peerage. His mother soon married the brilliant English politician Charles *Townshend in 1755. Townshend took great interest in the education of his stepchildren (including Buccleuch's brother Campbell Scott and his sister Frances, later Lady Frances *Douglas). Like his grandfathers, Buccleuch was sent to Eton College (from 1757). Unlike them, however, his stepfather arranged that he and his brother complete their education by having no less a figure than Adam Smith, the celebrated moral philosopher and later political economist, act as their tutor on a tour of Europe which began in 1764. In fact Smith and Buccleuch spent almost all their time in France, apart from two months in Geneva. The death of the duke's brother in Paris on 18 October 1766 precipitated Buccleuch's return to Britain with his tutor, who remained his friend for life. In 1790, two months before

Henry Scott, third duke of Buccleuch and fifth duke of Queensberry (1746–1812), by Thomas Gainsborough, *c.*1770

his tutor's death, Buccleuch still wrote to Smith in terms of warm affection: 'We have long lived in friendship, uninterrupted for one single moment since we first were acquainted' (*Correspondence of Adam Smith*, 323).

On his return to Britain Buccleuch assumed the responsibilities that he was destined to inherit. Even before he attained his majority in September, he married Lady Elizabeth Montagu (1743–1827) by special licence in a Church of England ceremony on 2 May 1767. Lady Elizabeth was the only daughter and heir of George, created duke of Montagu in 1766 (a title which had become extinct in 1749 with the death of his father-in-law, John, second duke of Montagu). In 1767 Buccleuch took his wife to the principal seat of the Buccleuch estate at Dalkeith Palace outside Edinburgh, where he learned of his stepfather's sudden death just before he formally entered into his inheritance on his twenty-first birthday (13 September). Scotland's greatest landowner had returned to live on an estate that had been abandoned by its owners for decades and he returned as the pupil of the man who even then was seen as one of Scotland's greatest modern philosophers. Many in the country looked to him for leadership at a time when other prominent members of the Scottish aristocracy, such as the third earl of Bute, had withdrawn from public life.

The young duke tried to respond by leading public campaigns to encourage Scottish manufactures, to build a Forth–Clyde canal linking Scotland's great rivers, to prevent government interference in Scottish elections, and, most notably, to galvanize the economy through the foundation of a new bank that would provide the credit crucial for Scottish economic development. Douglas, Heron &

Co., the so-called 'Ayr bank', was principally capitalized by the value of the Buccleuch and Queensberry estates, setting an example followed by the majority of the Scottish landowning class. When the bank failed in 1772 national ruin on the scale of the Darien disaster at the turn of the eighteenth century appeared imminent, but the Scottish banking system survived. The debt incurred by Buccleuch would remain for the rest of his life, but such was his prestige and the value of his estates in England as well as Scotland that the debt could be managed and serviced without destroying his inheritance. The misadventure would inform Adam Smith's meditations in the book he had been writing since parting from his pupil, *The Wealth of Nations* (1776), which led Buccleuch to secure Smith's appointment to a valuable place on the Scottish board of customs.

Another key attachment formed by Buccleuch when he came to Scotland was his friendship with the lawyer and politician Henry Dundas, four years his senior and already solicitor-general for Scotland from 1766, who owned land in Edinburghshire adjacent to the Buccleuch estate at Dalkeith. Dundas joined Buccleuch in many of his enterprises, including Douglas, Heron & Co. The two men were most closely associated in an attempt to secure the patronage of the city of Edinburgh, opposing Dundas's distant kinsman Sir Lawrence Dundas by insisting on the importance of established landed and legal leadership for Scotland's capital. Their campaign extended into opposing Sir Lawrence's influence in Scottish banking, which resulted in a revolution in the Royal Bank of Scotland that replaced Sir Lawrence as governor with the duke of Buccleuch in 1777; this marked the beginning of his recovery from previous financial disappointments.

Once France declared war on Britain in aid of the American congress in 1778, Buccleuch raised a regiment of fencibles, or volunteers, for home defence. It saw service the following year in an attempt to restore order in Edinburgh following the anti-popery riots that were directed against Henry Dundas's proposed bill for Roman Catholic relief in Scotland. Buccleuch held the rank of colonel during his service, and lavished a substantial amount of time, energy, and money on the regiment, which was disbanded at the end of the war. Buccleuch remained a leading supporter of Dundas and the younger Pitt in Scotland after the war, though he did not attend parliament frequently. His electoral interest in parliamentary matters was always at the disposal of the government, and was crucial in helping Dundas attain a position of outright domination of Scottish politics. By 1795 Buccleuch had even acquired interests in Launceston, Cornwall, in search of parliamentary representation that could be put at the service of the government. At the same time he continued to improve his estates both in Scotland and England. The latter were augmented when his wife inherited the Montagu estates, largely in Northamptonshire, in 1790. Their son Henry became Baron Montagu of Boughton (Northamptonshire) in succession to his grandfather.

With the outbreak of war with republican France in 1793 Buccleuch again became involved with Scottish affairs, and played a key role in advising Dundas and Pitt regarding the creation of a Scottish militia in 1797. In 1803 the city of Edinburgh appointed Buccleuch colonel of its 2nd and Royal Leith regiments in recognition of his primary role in Scottish defence. He had been made lord lieutenant of Midlothian and East Lothian in 1794 and became lord lieutenant of Roxburgh in 1804. Again he acted as a colonel with responsibilities for defence of Edinburgh, this time for the 10th Edinburgh regiment of militia.

There are indications that during the war years Buccleuch came to doubt the general goodness of enlightened improvement as taught to him by Smith. In 1797 Dundas had written to him that militia regiments would still be necessary after the war to maintain order among the emerging manufacturing areas cut off from traditional influences of landowner and church. By 1809 the duke is said to have believed that manufactures in general had been pushed too far in Britain, and that the development of textile mills on his estate at Langholm in Dumfriesshire had not raised the value of his land but rather rendered his residence there disagreeable, 'if not disgusting' (NA Scot., GD224/522/3/90).

Among Buccleuch's other honours were his membership of the Order of the Thistle in Scotland from December 1767, an honour he resigned on being made knight of the Garter on 28 May 1794. He was captain-general of the Royal Company of Archers in Scotland from 1778 until his death, and he was first president of the Royal Society of Edinburgh, from 1783 until his death. Together with his wife he was involved in charitable work such as the founding of Edinburgh's Royal Blind Asylum and School. On 23 December 1810, by the death of his cousin William, fourth duke of Queensberry, he succeeded to that title and the extensive estates in Dumfriesshire that went with it. He was undoubtedly the premier member of the Scottish nobility in his lifetime, a dedicated Briton with estates in England as well as Scotland that engaged his close attention. His death at Dalkeith Palace on 11 January 1812 (less than a year after that of his old friend Dundas) marked the end of an era of enlightened public leadership by the great nobility of Scotland. He was buried at Dalkeith Palace chapel. He was succeeded as fourth duke of Buccleuch by his second but eldest surviving son, Charles, styled earl of Dalkeith during the lifetime of his father. In addition to his younger son Henry mentioned above, he was also survived by his daughters Mary, Elizabeth, Caroline, and Harriet, all of whom married into aristocratic families in England and Scotland. ALEXANDER MURDOCH

Sources NA Scot., GD224 [Buccleuch MSS] · NA Scot., GD51 [Melville MSS] · NL Scot., Melville MSS · I. Ross, ed., 'Educating an eighteenth-century duke', *The Scottish tradition*, ed. G. W. S. Barrow (1974) · W. Fraser, *The Scotts of Buccleuch*, 2 vols. (1878) · D. J. Brown, 'Henry Dundas and the government of Scotland', PhD diss., U. Edin., 1989 · M. Fry, *The Dundas despotism* (1992) · J. Dwyer and A. Murdoch, 'Paradigms and politics: manners, morals and the rise of Henry Dundas, 1770–1784', *New perspectives on the politics and culture of early modern Scotland*, ed. J. Dwyer, R. A. Mason, and A. Murdoch (1982), 210–48 · A. Murdoch, 'The importance of being Edinburgh: management and opposition in Edinburgh politics, 1746–1784', *SHR*, 62 (1983), 1–16 · GEC, *Peerage*, new edn · *Scots peerage* ·

The correspondence of Adam Smith, ed. E. C. Mossner and I. S. Ross (1977), vol. 6 of *The Glasgow edition of the works and correspondence of Adam Smith* · J. E. Cookson, *The British armed nation, 1793–1815* (1997) · J. Ferguson, *The sixteen peers of Scotland: an account of the elections of the representative peers of Scotland, 1707–1959* (1960)

Archives NA Scot., corresp. and papers · NRA, priv. coll., corresp. and papers · Wilts. & Swindon RO, estate papers relating to Wiltshire property | NA Scot., letters to Henry Dundas, first Viscount Melville · NL Scot., Melville MSS · NL Scot., corresp. relating to volunteers · priv. coll., Montagu-Douglas-Scot MSS · Wilts. & Swindon RO, corresp. with George Herbert, eleventh earl of Pembroke

Likenesses J. Reynolds, oils, 1768, Buccleuch estates, Selkirk · T. Gainsborough, oils, *c*.1770, Buccleuch estates, Selkirk [*see illus.*] · M. F. Quadal, oils, 1780, Buccleuch estates, Selkirk · J. Downman, drawing, 1783, Buccleuch estates, Selkirk · H. P. Danloux, group portrait, 1798 (with his family), Buccleuch estates, Selkirk · R. B. Paul, group portrait, oils, 1892 (after J. Reynolds), Buccleuch estates, Selkirk · G. H. Every, mezzotint (after T. Gainsborough), BM · H. D. Hamilton, drawing, Beaulieu Abbey, Hampshire · H. Meyer, stipple (after T. Heaphy), BM · attrib. C. Read, oils, Buccleuch estates, Selkirk

Scott, Henry Young Darracott (1822–1883), inventor of selenitic cement and military engineer, second son of Edward Scott, a quarry owner, was born at Plymouth, Devon, on 2 January 1822. He was educated privately and entered the Royal Military Academy, Woolwich, in 1838. Commissioned as second lieutenant in 1840, early the next year Scott reported to the Royal Engineer Establishment at Brompton, Chatham, where he undertook further studies for some fifteen months. He was then stationed for a few months at Woolwich, and afterwards at Plymouth, and in 1843 was promoted first lieutenant and ordered to report to Gibraltar.

While engaged in the reconstruction of escarps at the fortress of Gibraltar, Scott noticed the quick decomposition of shale and speculated that it might prove a useful ingredient in cement making. This affected the course of his professional life, as he subsequently contributed to advances in building technology. In 1848 he was appointed assistant instructor in fieldworks at the Royal Military Academy, Woolwich. By then he had gained a reputation as a person possessed of an ingenious mind, gentle temperament, extraordinary social graces, and generosity of spirit. Scott also took up the study of chemistry at King's College, London. He soon began experiments in trying to make a cement from some specimens of shale which he had sent to him from Gibraltar.

Following his promotion as senior instructor at Woolwich in 1851, on 19 June that year Scott married Ellen Selena, youngest daughter of Major-General Bowes. Later that same year he was made second captain. As an offshoot of his work at the academy, Scott then began an optional course in applied chemistry at the Royal Engineer Establishment, Chatham. While engaged in this work at Chatham, Scott invented and patented 'Scott's patent cement' (1854 and 1855), which was known from the 1870s as selenitic cement. This new material was to become a rival to Portland cement as well as other patented cements, particularly for plaster and stucco work. Scott was the first to ascertain the action of sulphur compounds and sulphuric acid on quicklime, the process for producing selenitic cement. In 1855 he was appointed instructor

Henry Young Darracott Scott (1822–1883), by unknown engraver, pubd 1883

in surveying at the establishment and took charge of the chemical laboratory. The next year, he patented another method for making selenitic cement. It proved commercially viable and production was taken up by Lee, Son, and Smith, one of the most prominent of the Medway cement manufacturers. The new product was used in many public building projects and in some private sector construction. Scott's further experiments on selenitic cement served as a springboard for improving the knowledge and skill of the Royal Engineers in the use of cement and concrete. He wrote several articles for the *Professional Papers of the Corps of Royal Engineers* in conjunction with this work and contributed 'A short account of Scott's patent cement' to *Papers Read at the Institute of British Architects* (1857).

During his time at Chatham, Scott assisted the director, General Henry Drury Harness, in undertaking reform of the architectural and survey courses, in direct response to public criticism and parliamentary investigations following the débâcle of the Crimean War. Scott also developed an innovative method of topographical field-sketching using a system of hachures that was subsequently adopted for use at the Royal Military Academy and Sandhurst as well as at Chatham. Besides his military duties, he contributed much to the local community; he regenerated a young men's society by giving lectures in chemistry and other scientific subjects, advised a company on the siting and construction of the area's first waterworks, and offered talks in science to convicts in the Chatham prison.

In 1863 Scott was promoted brevet-major and then regimental lieutenant-colonel. The following year he was seconded to the civil service for the commissioners for the exhibition of 1851; he later served as the commission's secretary in 1873–82. Sir Henry Cole had secured his services to help run the Royal Horticultural Society's garden at South Kensington, and Scott was made an administrative officer in the government's Department of Science and Art. Following the death of Captain Francis Fowke RE, architect to the department, Scott was appointed his successor, early in 1866. Scott's title was director of works (later director of new buildings) whereas Fowke had been called architect and engineer. Scott was to turn his flair for science and organization to the task of joining innovative technology and Victorian taste, in new public buildings for South Kensington's cultural complex. At the same time, he continued his inventive genius and business ventures with cements.

In 1867 Scott began work as design and construction co-ordinator of the Albert Hall, the undertaking for which he is most remembered. He had to modify Captain Francis Fowke's original design concept and work out constructional details. Scott's architectural knowledge was rudimentary and he relied heavily on his draughtsman assistant, Gilbert R. Redgrave, architect James William Wild, and on decorative artists, structural engineers, and manufacturers.

Scott specified his patent cement throughout the Albert Hall and made innovative use of terracotta, a material that he helped bring into fashion. In 1868, Scott patented a process for treating sewage and making cement from the sludge; he set up a company two years later which proved not to be a commercial success. Even so, it was a notable attempt to join Victorian concern for sanitation to the introduction of new building materials. In 1871, Scott formed the Patent Selenitic Company Limited; it traded for fourteen years, being dissolved on the expiry of the patent. Many other firms made Scott's cement under licence. Scott was an indefatigable inventor and obtained some fifty-nine patents for cement and lime as well as for various types of kilns. It is likely that he was driven to pursue such ventures partly to help support his wife and their fifteen children.

Scott's elliptical iron roof for the Albert Hall, completed in 1871, was a triumph in state-of-the-art design for wide-span structures. Civil engineer Rowland Mason Ordish was probably the principal creative genius behind the design. The ironwork was fabricated by the engineering company of Sir William Fairbairn, and two of the ablest Victorian engineers, John Fowler and John Hawkshaw, advised Scott on the roof. The architectural treatment of the ceiling was greatly determined by a hanging cloth velarium, suggested by James William Wild, the practical function of which was to improve acoustics. Scott himself must be credited with orchestrating this collaborative achievement. Possibly because of the many predictions that the roof would fail, it is said that when the time arrived for removing the scaffolding which supported the roof, Scott sent everyone out of the building and himself knocked away the final support (*Royal Engineers Journal*).

Scott was promoted to brevet-colonel in 1871 and retired from the army that year as honorary major-general. A host of honours followed, including civil companion in the Order of the Bath (1871), associate of the Institution of Civil Engineers (1874), and fellow of the Royal Society (1875). He was extremely modest in acknowledging his own contributions, most often giving primary credit to others. Scott demonstrated this in his paper on the construction of the Albert Hall, published in *Royal Institute of British Architects Sessional Papers* (1872).

In 1880 Scott, together with G. R. Redgrave, won the prestigious Telford premium for a paper on the manufacture and testing of Portland cement, published in the *Proceedings of the Institution of Civil Engineers* (1880). They recommended Portland cement test standards that could be universally adopted in Britain; the first such standards in the world had been established in Germany only two years before. Early in 1882, the government decided to make the board of works responsible for buildings of the South Kensington museum and Scott's position as secretary was terminated without compensation. Apparently, the stress and anxiety brought on by this situation caused his health to fail and he died on 16 April 1883 at his home, Davenport House, Silverdale, Sydenham. Scott was buried in Highgate cemetery, Middlesex. After his death the 'Scott Memorial Fund' was set up by a group of his colleagues to benefit his widow and eight children who were still dependent. JOHN WEILER

Sources J. Weiler, 'Army architects: Royal Engineers and the development of building technology in the nineteenth century', PhD diss., University of York, 1987 • D. Cooke, 'General Henry Young Darracott Scott', *Royal Engineers Journal*, 13 (1883), 164–8 • *PICE*, 75 (1883–4), 319–22 • *DNB* • H. Y. D. Scott, 'Account of a new cement, and the experiments which led to its discovery', *Professional Papers of the Corps of Royal Engineers*, new ser., 6 (1857), 143–8 • H. Y. D. Scott, 'Account of the manufacture of a new cement invented by Captain H. Scott', *Professional Papers of the Corps of Royal Engineers*, new ser., 10 (1861), 132–58 • H. Y. D. Scott, 'On the construction of the Albert Hall', *Professional Papers of the Corps of Royal Engineers*, new ser., 21 (1873), 49–63 • H. Y. D. Scott, 'On the construction of the Albert Hall', *Sessional Papers of the Royal Institute of British Architects* (1871–2), 83–9 • H. Y. D. Scott, 'The Royal Albert Hall; part plan of roof', *Engineering* (20 Aug 1869), 117–18 • H. Y. D. Scott, 'Clean drains and improved mortars', *Sessional Papers of the Royal Institute of British Architects* (1871–2), 26–31 • G. R. Redgrave and C. Spackman, *Calcareous cements*, 2nd edn (1905) • H. Y. D. Scott and G. R. Redgrave, 'The manufacture and testing of Portland cement', *PICE*, 62 (1879–80), 67–86 • H. Y. D. Scott, 'Observations on limes and cements: their properties and employments', *Professional Papers of the Corps of Royal Engineers*, new ser., 11 (1862), 15–94 • *CGPLA Eng. & Wales* (1883) • Boase, *Mod. Eng. biog.*

Likenesses photograph, Royal Engineers Museum, Brompton Barracks, Chatham, Kent • wood-engraving, NPG; repro. in *ILN* (5 May 1883) [*see illus.*]

Wealth at death £775: probate, 8 June 1883, *CGPLA Eng. & Wales*

Scott, Hew (1791–1872), minister and annalist of the Church of Scotland, was born in Haddington on 5 February 1791, son of an excise officer, Robert Scott, and his wife, Catherine Dunbar. His father died while he was a boy and his family existed on the income from a small shop. Scott received his education at the local school before attending classes at Edinburgh University between the 1813–14 and 1819–20 sessions, with the intention of entering the ministry. He graduated MA from King's College, Aberdeen, in December 1816. Thomas Thomson, deputy clerk-register of Scotland, offered him employment with the records at Register House, Edinburgh, where he became known, facetiously, as the 'Peripatetic Index'.

Licensed by the presbytery of Haddington in 1820, Scott was slow to obtain preferment. However, by this time he had already conceived his life's work, which was to chronicle the succession of ministers in the Church of Scotland since the Reformation. His extended spell as a probationer allowed him time to pursue this goal, but frustration at his lack of advancement led him to accept a missionary post in Canada. To this end he was ordained by the presbytery of Haddington in 1829, but the timely intervention of David Laing, the antiquary, prevented his departure. Scott occupied a succession of assistantships at Garvald, Ladykirk, Cockpen, and Temple before he was offered the charge of Anstruther Wester in Fife, to which he was admitted on 12 June 1839.

While never neglectful of duty, Scott continued with the preparation of *Fasti ecclesiae Scoticanae*, which eventually appeared in three volumes of two parts each, between 1866 and 1871. The impression was limited to 250 copies, at 25*s.* per part. Sales, however, were a disappointment to the man whose superhuman efforts, in daunting circumstances, the work represented. Scott had visited all the presbyteries and about 760 parishes in order to examine original records. He preached in over 300 of the parishes he visited. The *Fasti* was compiled on letter-backs and Scott's correspondence was conducted using turned envelopes, a typically frugal practice. Charles Rogers, briefly his assistant, considered that 'he indulged a warm temper, was careless in his apparel, and a little too careful of his coin, but he was withal a kindly and obliging man and a faithful minister' (Rogers, 82). Scott married, on 3 February 1859, Sarah McDougall, *née* Kennedy (*d.* 1874), a schoolmaster's widow. This late marriage, together with his miserly habits, may have lain behind the apocryphal story of the minister who 'married the widow of the schoolmaster for the sake of the dead dominie's new coat' (Gourlay, 162).

Scott was honoured with the degree of DD from St Andrews University in 1867. His church recognized the significance of his life's work by carrying it on; a later editor concluded that 'By the triumphant realisation of his early dream, Hew Scott made not only the Church but the whole of Scotland his debtor' (Crockett, xii). He died at Anstruther on 12 July 1872.

LIONEL ALEXANDER RITCHIE

Sources W. S. Crockett, 'Biographical sketch of Hew Scott D.D.', *Fasti Scot.*, new edn, 1.xi–xvi • *Fasti Scot.*, new edn, 5.185 • G. Gourlay, *Anstruther* (1888), 159–63 • C. Rogers, *Leaves from my autobiography*, Grampian Club (1876), 81–2 • M. F. Conolly, *Biographical dictionary of eminent men of Fife* (1866), 395–6 • private information (1897) • *DNB*
Archives U. Edin. L., letters to David Laing
Likenesses portrait (in old age), repro. in Crockett, 'Biographical sketch', frontispiece
Wealth at death £4577 6*s.* 1*d.*: inventory, 9 Sept 1872, NA Scot., SC 20/50/44/1039 • £9000; plus a parcel of land at Pittenweem, Fife: *Fasti Scot.*; Gourlay, *Anstruther*

Scott, Hugh Stowell [*pseud.* Henry Seton Merriman] (**1862–1903**), novelist, was born at 16 Rye Hill, Elswick, Newcastle upon Tyne, on 9 May 1862, the son of Henry Scott, a shipowner, of Newcastle, and his wife, Mary Sweet, daughter of James Wilson Carmichael, marine painter. Hugh was educated at Loretto School, Musselburgh, and afterwards at Vevey and Wiesbaden. At eighteen he was placed by his father in an underwriter's office at Lloyd's in London, but he disliked the routine of commerce, and hoped to travel abroad and to study foreign nationalities. He was thus impelled to try his hand at the writing of romance. His first novel was *Young Mistley*, which he submitted to Bentley and published anonymously in 1888. In his next book, *The Phantom Future* (1889), he adopted the pseudonym Henry Seton Merriman in order to evade the disapproval of his family, and he used the same disguise throughout his literary career. *The Phantom Future* was followed by two other stories equally immature, *Suspense* (1890) and *Prisoners and Captives* (1891). Scott subsequently suppressed these three novels in Britain, but he failed to prevent their continued circulation in Canada and the United States. In 1892 he succeeded in interesting James Payn, then editor of *Cornhill*, in a well-constructed story of French and English life, *The Slave of the Lamp* (1892), which after running through the magazine was well received on its separate issue. Its successor, *From One Generation to Another* (1892), was welcomed so warmly as to justify Scott, whose means were always ample, in adopting exclusively the profession of novelist. In 1894 his west African story *With Edged Tools* caught the fancy of the public and gave him a prominent position among popular novelists of his day. There quickly followed *The Grey Lady* (1895), which dealt with seafaring life; some of its scenes were drawn from a visit to the Balearic Islands. Henceforth Merriman, as he was invariably called by the critics, lived a comparatively secluded life in the country, varied by foreign travel. On 19 June 1889 he had married Ethel Frances Hall. They had no children.

In conjunction with Stanley J. Weyman, a literary comrade who achieved a success parallel to his own, Scott studied the methods of Alexandre Dumas, and devoted all the time and money he could spare to the detailed *mise en scène* of a series of novels of modern nationalities. His most ambitious and, on the whole, most successful performance was the exciting Russian story which appeared in 1896 entitled *The Sowers*, which went through thirty editions in England alone, and was included in the Tauchnitz collection. It was followed at intervals of nearly eighteen months each by *Flotsam* (1896), a story of Delhi in mutiny days; *In Kedar's Tents* (1897), a tale of Spanish Carlist intrigue; *Roden's Corner* (1898), an Anglo-Dutch story embodying an attack on unprincipled company promoting; *Dross* (Toronto, 1899), which was not issued in volume form in Great Britain; *The Isle of Unrest* (1900), a story of Corsican vendetta somewhat in the Mérimée vein; *The Velvet Glove* (1901), in which, following the lead of *In Kedar's Tents*, he depicted a Spanish gentleman and put some of his best work; *Barlasch of the Guard* (1902), a story of Danzig in 1812 and of Borodino and after, one of his most successful attempts at historical presentation; *The Vultures* (1902), dealing with the abortive rising in Poland after the assassination of the Tsar Alexander in 1881; and *The Last Hope* (1904), a curious story of 1849 in which strands of Bourbon and Louis Napoleon romance are ingeniously mixed. The last work was issued posthumously. At his death Scott was one of the most effective and widely read novelists of his day. His success under a pseudonym had led several impostors to represent themselves as authors of his most widely circulated books. His faults were a growing tendency to a moralizing and sententious cynicism, a stereotyped repertory of characters—strong silent gentlemen, reserved and romance-loving maidens, and inflexibly trusty servants—and a progressive heightening of human faculties and idiosyncrasies at the expense of verisimilitude. His method did not suit either the short story or the essay, and his attempts in these directions, *Tomaso's Fortune and other Stories* (1904), remained deservedly obscure, although he had collaborated with his wife's sister, E. Beatrice Hall (S. G. Tallentyre), on two other volumes of short stories: *From Wisdom Court* (1893) and *The Money Spinner* (1896). Scott's success was exclusively literary, for he avoided all self-advertisement. Scott died prematurely, after an attack of appendicitis, on 19 November 1903, at his home, Long Spring, Melton, near Woodbridge, Suffolk, and was buried at Eltham, Kent. In August 1912 his wife remarried; her new husband was the Revd George Augustus Cobbold, perpetual curate of St Bartholomew's, Ipswich.

A memorial collected edition of fourteen of Scott's novels in as many volumes appeared in 1909–10.

THOMAS SECCOMBE, *rev.* REBECCA MILLS

Sources *WWW, 1897–1915*, 1.358 • *Men and women of the time* (1899), 982–3 • *The Times* (20 Nov 1903) • F. Swinnerton, 'Introduction', in H. S. Merriman [H. S. Scott], *Young Mistley* (1966), vii–xvii • b. cert.
Wealth at death £53,202 16*s.* 10*d.*: probate, 30 Jan 1904, *CGPLA Eng. & Wales*

Scott, Sir James, of Balwearie (*d.* 1607x13), landowner, was the eldest son and heir of Sir William Scott of Balwearie and Strathmiglo in Fife (*d.* in or before 1579) and Janet Lindsay, daughter of the laird of Dowhill. In 1579 he was served heir to his father and under him the family's lands reached their greatest extent, 'but with him the wealth and dignity of the family came to an end' (Leighton, 2.186) and, by the end of his life, most of the lands had been dissipated.

Scott appeared as one of the cautioners for the good behaviour of William Douglas of Lochleven in December 1583, when Douglas obtained licence to travel abroad. Soon after this the first evidence appears of Scott's association with Francis Stewart, first earl of Bothwell. In March 1588 he was summoned before the privy council for allowing certain prisoners, taken as surety for the peaceful behaviour of border criminals, to escape. In 1590, at the coronation of Anne of Denmark as James VI's queen, Scott was knighted but he was soon to fall from favour through his association with Bothwell and with the rebel Catholic earls of Huntly, Angus, and Erroll. He was 'repeatedly fined for real or alleged assistance' to Bothwell 'in his various mad attempts to gain possession of the king's person' (Leighton, 2.186). According to a number of sources he was with Bothwell in June 1592 when Bothwell assailed the king in Falkland Palace and he brought with him 'a reasonable nomber of inarmit [i.e. armed] horsemen' (*Historie … of King James*, 250). In November 1593 he attended a convention of the estates at Holyrood which passed an Act of Oblivion, giving the rebel Catholic earls until the end of January 1594 to prove their loyalty and obedience. At that convention a committee was appointed to receive their petitions for clemency and devise ways of dealing with them, and Scott was one of its number.

In desperation at their political marginalization, Bothwell and the Catholic earls were thrown together and in August 1594 they met at a tavern near the kirk of Menmuir in Fife where they subscribed a band for mutual aid. Scott 'wes in companie with thame' (Moysie, 121), witnessed the band, and was given it for safe keeping. In September he was with the Catholic earls at the battle of Glenlivet and fought against a royal force sent against them under the earl of Argyll as the king's lieutenant. He was subsequently captured and warded in Edinburgh Castle and then, on 23 January 1595, removed to the tolbooth of Edinburgh where he was held overnight. He 'produceit and delyverit' (*Reg. PCS*, 1st ser., 5.205) the band to the king and revealed that the four earls had planned to imprison James and crown Prince Henry king in his stead, as had happened to James and his mother in the summer of 1567. He was not held for much longer, however, receiving a remission under the great seal in return for a fine of £20,000. Some ministers meeting in Edinburgh argued over whether he should be excommunicated, in spite of his remission, but it was agreed that the matter should be passed to the general assembly and local church courts within whose jurisdiction he lived.

As well as having been involved with powerful people who were regarded by the crown as dangerous rebels, Scott also appears to have been repeatedly in trouble with the privy council over more trivial matters throughout his adult life. In August 1599 he was commanded to give caution in 5000 merks (£3333 6*s.* 8*d.* Scots) that he would keep the peace. On 5 November 1601 he was denounced by the privy council for having failed to answer for the alleged destruction of the crops of Patrick Pitcairn of Pitlour, and on 16 October 1602 he was compelled to find caution in 3000 merks (£2000 Scots) not to harm Pitlour.

Scott must have married before September 1600, at which time his son William was first recorded, being described as his heir apparent. His wife was Elizabeth Wardlaw, daughter of Andrew, laird of Torrie, and they had one other son, James, and a daughter, Janet, who married the laird of Balmuto. Scott of Balwearie's heirs were, however, left with almost nothing. To pay the numerous fines imposed on him, especially for his association with Bothwell and the Catholic earls, he was forced to sell off his lands bit by bit. The result was that by 1600 all that remained were the castle and village of Strathmiglo, and even those were lost to the family about the time of his death. A story survives of his unpleasant nature in later life, perhaps brought on by the ruin which he had brought upon his family. According to the story he was throwing some stale oatmeal out of his castle window when a beggar who happened to be passing asked if he could be allowed some, since it was being thrown out anyway. Scott is supposed to have refused, which provoked the beggar into cursing the miserly laird, saying that he would one day be glad to have such food. It is unknown whether or not Scott ever reached such a state of penury, for the date of his death is not recorded. The last reference to him in the registers of the privy council dates from 5 March 1607, although his son was still being described as 'apparent' (heir apparent) of Balwearie as late as January 1610 (*Reg. PCS*, 1st ser., 8.717). In February 1613 Scott appears in that register for the first time as 'the late' Sir James Scott of Balwearie (ibid., 9.554) and in February 1615 William first appears in the record as the laird of Balwearie. Owing to James's losses, his grandson was forced to enter military service on the continent 'having been deprived of any portion of the family estates' (Leighton, 2.187).

Alan R. MacDonald

Sources *DNB* • R. Douglas and others, *The baronage of Scotland* (1798) • J. M. Leighton, *History of the county of Fife*, 3 vols. (1840) • D. Calderwood, *The history of the Kirk of Scotland*, ed. T. Thomson and D. Laing, 8 vols., Wodrow Society, 7 (1842–9) • D. Moysie, *Memoirs of the affairs of Scotland, 1577–1603*, ed. J. Dennistoun, Bannatyne Club, 39 (1830) • *Reg. PCS*, 1st ser. • [T. Thomson], ed., *The historie and life of King James the Sext*, Bannatyne Club, 13 (1825) • *APS*, 1593–1625

Wealth at death died in poverty

Scott [*formerly* Crofts], **James, duke of Monmouth and first duke of Buccleuch (1649–1685)**, politician, was born on 9 April 1649 at Rotterdam, the illegitimate son of *Charles II (1630–1685) and Lucy *Walter (1630?–1658), daughter of William Walter (or Walters) of Roch Castle, near Haverfordwest, in Pembrokeshire, and his wife, Elizabeth Prothero. Charles met Lucy during a brief visit to The Hague in July 1648, when she was still under the protection of Colonel Robert Sidney (1628–1668), and it was during this time that Monmouth was evidently conceived. Lucy 'prov'd so soon with child and came so near in time' that some later questioned whether Charles was Monmouth's true father. Charles's brother, the duke of York (later James II), thought that when Monmouth reached manhood he bore a striking resemblance to Sidney, 'both in stature and in countenance, even to a wort in his face' (Clarke, 1.492), though York, of course, had his own reasons for casting aspersions about Monmouth's paternity. Charles always acknowledged Monmouth to be his son, and portraits of the two as adolescents show a clear family likeness.

Most biographers have assumed that Charles resumed his relationship with Lucy when he returned to the Netherlands in September 1648, although the historical record is obscure. When James was born, he was found a nurse at the house of a merchant named Claus Ghysen, in Schiedam, just outside Rotterdam, while Lucy took lodgings in Antwerp at the home of Mrs Harvey (mother of the celebrated Dr William Harvey, who discovered the circulation of the blood), and Charles left for France. John Evelyn later recalled meeting Lucy at St Germain-en-Laye in August 1649, where she had come to be introduced to Charles's mother, Henrietta Maria. However, that September Charles left for Jersey, so as to be in a better position to watch developments in Scotland and Ireland, and a year later he embarked for Scotland, in a last-ditch attempt to rescue the royalist cause. When he returned to France following the royalist defeat at Worcester in September 1651, he made no attempt to revive his affair with Lucy.

James Scott [Crofts], **duke of Monmouth and first duke of Buccleuch (1649–1685)**, by Sir Godfrey Kneller, 1678

Rumours were later to emerge that Charles and Lucy had married during their brief time together, though there is no firm evidence that they did, and it seems intrinsically unlikely. It is true that Charles's sister Mary, princess of Orange, made references to Charles's 'wife' in a couple of letters addressed to her brother in 1654, but she appears to have been using the term euphemistically and it is unclear whether she had Lucy in mind in any case. On her deathbed Lucy made a secret confession of her life to John Cosin, later bishop of Durham, which gave rise to the story that she had admitted having married Charles and had given her confessor a 'black box' containing the proof; when Cosin died in 1672, there was no one left to refute such talk. Some accounts hold that Charles and Lucy were secretly married in Liège; Buccleuch family legend has it that the third duke of Buccleuch (1746–1812) found the marriage certificate (or a copy of it) when he was going through some papers at Dalkeith, and decided to burn it. However, the fact that in 1654 Lucy sought Charles's leave to marry another suitor seems to imply that she did not think herself legally married to the king.

Early years James had what must have been a traumatic early childhood. He survived an attempt to kidnap him in 1650 (his mother suspected by Commonwealth agents), though he was missing for ten days before he was eventually found. For safety reasons Lucy decided to remove him from Schiedam, taking him first to Boxtel, near Breda, and then to Paris, where she became mistress to Viscount Taaffe, whose daughter she was to bear. In 1655, after the break-up of that relationship, Lucy moved with her two children to The Hague, where she became the mistress of

Thomas Howard, the earl of Suffolk's brother. At Charles's insistence they left the Netherlands in January 1656, setting up home in London above a barber's shop opposite Somerset House, but a nervous republican regime had them arrested and sent to the Tower at the end of June. The following month, by special order of the protector, they were shipped back to Flanders, and by August 1657 Lucy was in Brussels with her children, penniless, having now been abandoned by Howard. When she threatened Charles, who was now living at Bruges with his new mistress, Catherine Pegge, that she would make public his old letters to her if he did not pay her the annuity he had been promising for some time, Charles decided to have his son kidnapped. The first attempt, in December 1657, was bungled, but in March 1658 Thomas Ross, one of the king's spymasters, successfully seized the boy. Mother and son were separated for good; Lucy was to die before the end of the year, whereas young James was sent to Paris and placed in the care of Lord William Crofts, a gentleman of Charles's bedchamber, whose surname he now took.

James's education to date had been woefully neglected; at the age of nine he could neither read nor count. He now spent two years at a *petite école* and then briefly attended the academy of Familly. He also received some instruction in Catholicism at the hands of Father Goffe of the Oratorian College of Notre Dame des Verlus, although he never converted. After the Restoration his abductor, Ross, was appointed his tutor, but James underwent no further formal education. Neither reading nor writing came easy to him; as a fifteen-year-old, penning a letter would make him 'sigh and sweat' (*CSP dom.*, *1664–5*, 76), while even as an adult his handwriting was childlike and his spelling highly idiosyncratic. Intellectually, it has been said, he was 'very ill-equipped … to enter the world of Restoration politics' (Clifton, 82).

Life at court Charles saw little of James between the abduction of 1658 and the Restoration in 1660, and did not summon his son back to England until the summer of 1662. Once young James joined the royal court at Whitehall, however, he quickly won over his father's affections. Titles and honours followed. A marriage was arranged to the wealthy Scottish heiress Anna (Anne) *Scott, countess of Buccleuch (1651–1732), in anticipation of which James changed his last name to Scott (Anne's father had stipulated that any female heir had to marry someone who took the family name) and as such was knighted. On 10 November 1662 a warrant was issued granting Sir James Scott the titles of duke of Monmouth, earl of Doncaster, and baron of Fotheringay, though the last, because of its tragic associations with Charles's great-grandmother Mary, queen of Scots, was subsequently replaced by the title of Baron Scott of Tynedale. James was officially created on 14 February 1663, being given precedence over all dukes not of the blood royal, and on 28 March he was nominated to be a knight of the Garter (installed 23 April). His marriage took place on 20 April 1663, shortly after his fourteenth birthday (his bride was a mere twelve), on which day he was also created duke of Buccleuch, earl of Dalkeith, and Lord Scott of Whitchester and Eskdale.

Although the countess of Buccleuch was estimated to be worth some £10,000 p.a., Anne's mother, Lady Wemyss, had the money entailed out of Monmouth's grasp. However, Charles made sure his son was well provided for. In 1662 he granted Monmouth a patent for regulating the export of all new drapery for thirty-one years, which provided the duke with an annual income of £8000. Towards the end of the following year Charles gave him part of the new building constructed at the Cockpit for a town residence, and in March 1664 he bought him Sir John Ashburnham's house in Chiswick, 'with all that is in it', for £7000 (*CSP dom.*, *1663–4*, 539). In February 1665 Monmouth was granted a pension of £6000 p.a. (increased to £8000 p.a. in 1673), and in 1667 an additional allowance of £4000 p.a. to defray the cost of entertaining the king to suppers at his lodgings. In April 1670 the king bought Moor Park for Monmouth from the duke of Ormond at a cost of £13,200.

Monmouth enjoyed the typical recreational pursuits of a Restoration courtier: hunting, racing, gambling, dancing, and, as he entered adolescence, drinking and womanizing. Samuel Pepys thought the young duke spent 'his time the most viciously and idly of any man', and predicted that he would not 'be fit for any thing' (Pepys, 7.411, 16 Dec 1666). Such was Monmouth's extravagance that in April 1667 he had to be advanced £18,000 on his pension to cover his debts. Although his wife was to bear him four children, his relations with her were always formal and distant, and he had a succession of mistresses. In 1669 he had a daughter with Elizabeth Waller, the daughter of the old parliamentarian soldier Sir William Waller; in 1673 he was sharing the popular Moll Kirke with both his uncle and Lord Musgrave; and he later had four children with Eleanor Needham, whom he met in 1674. His last affair was to be with Henrietta Maria *Wentworth (1660–1686), whom he met in early 1680, and with whom he came to form a deep emotional attachment. There was also a violent side to Monmouth's personality. When the MP Sir John Coventry made a weak joke in the House of Commons about the king's fondness for actresses, Monmouth (possibly acting under orders from his father) sent some Life Guards to ambush Sir John as he made his way home late one night and slit his nose. Parliament responded by passing the Coventry Act (1671), banishing those responsible and making the cutting, maiming, or disfiguring of any man a felony without benefit of clergy and incapable of being pardoned by the king. In February 1671 Monmouth was involved in a drunken brawl in a brothel in Whetstones Park with Christopher Monck, the young duke of Albemarle, which resulted in a beadle being run through; it is not clear whether Albemarle or Monmouth drew the sword which killed the man, and both were given royal pardons to prevent the possibility of prosecution.

Military career and offices under the crown The University of Cambridge awarded Monmouth an honorary MA degree on 16 March 1663 (incorporated at Oxford on 28 September), and on 21 February 1665 he was admitted a member of the Middle Temple. However, he was destined for a career in the armed forces. On 24 March 1665 he joined the fleet which under his uncle the duke of York was to win the victory of Solebay on 3 June. At the end of June 1666 he received a commission as captain of a troop of horse, and on 16 September 1668 Charles made him captain of the Life Guards, in place of Lord Gerard of Brandon, who in compensation was given £8000 and allowed to purchase Monmouth's Chiswick residence, together with various other properties, at a knock-down price. On 29 April 1670 Monmouth was appointed to the privy council, and in October of that year a writ was issued calling him to the House of Peers. In 1672 he was placed in command of the British auxiliaries sent to France to assist Louis XIV against the Dutch, and in July 1673 he took part in the successful siege of Maastricht, which was to earn him an inflated reputation as a military leader. On 24 November 1672 a warrant was issued granting him the office of chief justice in eyre south of Trent, in place of the earl of Oxford, who was paid £5000 to surrender the position, and at the beginning of February 1673 Monmouth was appointed lord high chamberlain of Scotland for life. The passage of the Test Act in late March 1673, designed to remove Catholics from positions of authority under the crown, brought him further offices: in April he was appointed lord lieutenant of the East Riding of Yorkshire and governor and captain of Kingston upon Hull in place of the Catholic Lord Belasyse (Monmouth subsequently also became high steward of the town), and on 22 June he was made an Admiralty commissioner when his Catholic uncle, the duke of York, surrendered the office of lord high admiral. The next year he was appointed master of the horse (14 April), a privy counsellor in Scotland (18 May), chancellor of Cambridge University, and commissioner to conclude a treaty with Sweden (both August). In January 1675 he was made governor of Sutton's Hospital (the Charterhouse), and on 15 March 1677 lord lieutenant of Staffordshire and high steward of the town of Stafford.

Charles was by now schooling Monmouth to take over command of the armed forces. Upon the death in 1670 of the then commander-in-chief, George Monck, first duke of Albemarle, the army had been entrusted to a committee answerable directly to the king. In 1674, however, Charles established that all orders relating to the armed forces should be brought first to Monmouth for examination before being sent for royal approval and countersignature by the secretary of state. The job had no name and Monmouth no commission, but it was a way of 'initiating him into business', as Monmouth's secretary, James Vernon, put it (*CSP dom.*, *1673–5*, 119). Although the duke of York made appointments above the rank of captain, colonels of regiments were instructed to obey Monmouth's commands, and Monmouth took responsibility for the quartering and general duties of troops in billets, the relief of garrisons, the movement of troops across the country, and the suppression of riots (including the London weavers' riots of August 1675). During this time he also introduced a number of reforms into the army. In February 1678 he was sent at the head of a small force to protect Ostend against the French, and finally, in April 1678, he was appointed captain-general of all the land forces in England, Wales, and Berwick. Later that year Monmouth returned to Flanders in command of the English force to fight in the triple alliance against France.

Rumoured legitimacy and rivalry with the duke of York Charles tended to treat Monmouth as if he were a prince of Wales. Reference to being the king's natural son was deleted from Monmouth's marriage contract, and on being invested with the Order of the Garter Monmouth was empowered to assume a coat of arms resembling the royal, without the baton sinister denoting illegitimacy. When Charles saw Monmouth dancing with the queen 'with his hat in his hand' at the St George's feast at Windsor Castle in April 1663, he came and kissed him and made him put his hat on, signifying that he regarded the two as equals. In April 1667 a warrant was issued granting Monmouth the royal arms themselves, though now the baton sinister was added. Nevertheless, in the commission granting the captaincy of the Life Guards Charles referred to Monmouth simply as 'his beloved son' (*CSP dom.*, *1667–8*, 556); in subsequent official orders he used the style 'our dearest and most entirely beloved son' (*CSP dom.*, *1673–5*, 327–8; *1675–6*, 200).

Charles's self-evident fondness for his son fuelled speculation that he would declare Monmouth legitimate. As early as October 1662 Lord Sandwich told Pepys that it was being 'whispered' at court 'that young Crofts is lawful son to the king, the king being married to his mother' (Pepys, 3.238, 27 Oct 1662), and Charles's supposed plans 'to legitimate the Duke of Monmouth' continued to be 'much talked of' over the course of 1663 and early 1664 (Pepys, 4.376, 9 Nov 1663). Talk of legitimizing Monmouth resurfaced following the fall of the earl of Clarendon in 1667, the idea being particularly attractive to the former first minister's enemies, who felt they could not be safe unless they also brought down the duke of York, who was married to Clarendon's daughter. The duke of Buckingham tried to persuade the king 'to own a marriage with the duke of Monmouth's mother', while the earl of Carlisle offered to bring the matter before the House of Lords, and although Charles 'would not consent to this; yet he put it by in such a manner', Gilbert Burnet tells us, as made everyone conclude 'he wished it might be done, but did not know how to bring it about' (*Burnet's History*, 176; *CSP dom.*, *1667–8*, 165, 259). Monmouth himself firmly believed that his father and mother had been married. He had been told as much by his tutor, Ross, shortly after the Restoration; Ross had even tried to get Bishop Cosin of Durham to confirm the story and acknowledge that he had conducted the ceremony, though Cosin refused and informed the king, who temporarily removed Ross from Monmouth's presence. In February 1664 Pepys heard that Monmouth threatened 'he would be the death of any man that says the King was not married to his mother' (Pepys, 5.56, 22 Feb 1664).

The speculation about Monmouth's legitimacy and

Charles's continued doting upon his son clearly troubled the duke of York. In May 1663 Pepys expressed his suspicion that all was 'not kind between the King and the Duke, and that the King's fondness to the little Duke doth occasion it' (Pepys, 5.123, 4 May 1663). In November 1673 Monmouth turned down his father's offer to replace the duke of Lauderdale as commissioner in Scotland for fear 'that employment would draw upon him the envy of' his uncle (Christie, 2.72), while in 1677 York frustrated a design to get Monmouth appointed lord lieutenant of Ireland. However, York and Monmouth were as yet far from being bitter rivals. They dined and hunted together regularly throughout the 1670s, and those 'nere his Royal Highnesse', one correspondent wrote in July 1673, observed that he had 'a particular kindnesse and affection for his Grace' (ibid., 1.119). Indeed, in 1676 Monmouth became godfather to the daughter born to York's second wife, the duchess of Modena.

Despite his later alliance with the whigs, Monmouth was not linked to the opposition to the court that began to emerge from the mid-1670s. He first met the future country and whig spokesman Anthony Ashley Cooper (later earl of Shaftesbury) in 1665, when he and the king made a brief visit to Cooper's Dorset home after the court had been forced out of London because of the plague, but it was a long time before he and Shaftesbury came to be politically associated. It is perhaps significant that, following the passage of the 1673 Test Act, Shaftesbury and Monmouth took the Anglican sacrament together at St Clement Danes Church in the Strand, with Shaftesbury's secretary, John Locke, serving as witness to both, though it should be remembered that Shaftesbury, at this time, was still attached to the court (London Metropolitan Archive, MR/RS/2/217–218). When Shaftesbury moved into opposition, he and Monmouth became political adversaries. Monmouth joined York and the earl of Danby in urging the king not to accede to Shaftesbury's petition to be released from the Tower in 1677, where the earl had been imprisoned for questioning the legality of the recent fifteen-month prorogation of the Cavalier Parliament. When Shaftesbury drew up a list of the political sympathies of the lay peers later that year, identifying potential supporters with a 'w' for 'worthy' and opponents with a 'v' for 'vile', he gave Monmouth a triple 'v'.

Monmouth's falling-out with York occurred in April 1678, over the former's appointment as captain-general. York insisted that the style 'natural son' be used in Monmouth's commission; Monmouth, on discovering this, had his secretary cut the word 'natural' out of the document before it was presented to the king for signature. Charles signed the document without paying much attention, but when York drew the matter to the king's notice he cancelled the warrant by clipping a piece out of his own signature and had a new one drawn up which indicated Monmouth's illegitimacy. Monmouth resented the fact that his new honour had been smeared with the taint of bastardy; York, on the other hand, resented seeing his nephew promoted to such a height while he himself was fobbed off with the meaningless title of 'generalissimo'. In a vote on the army in the House of Lords the next month Monmouth sided with the country opposition for the first time and supported a motion to disband the new levies as speedily as possible.

The Popish Plot and exclusion crisis, 1678–1681 Monmouth returned to England from campaigning in Flanders in August 1678, just as the agitation over the Popish Plot was beginning to stir. Although initially sceptical of Titus Oates's story of an alleged Catholic conspiracy to kill the king, burn London, and massacre English protestants, as a privy counsellor and captain of the guards Monmouth was inevitably drawn into investigating the plot, which he began to take more seriously. By October it had emerged that he himself was supposedly on the conspirators' hit list. Later that month he delivered a report to the Lords from the committee set up to explore ways of providing for the king's safety and removing Catholics from the army, and by the end of the year he could report to the king in council that several Catholic officers had been dismissed and replaced by protestants. Although the idea of excluding the Catholic duke of York from the succession was not to be formally promoted in the Commons until the spring of 1679, Londoners were already beginning to think of Monmouth as a possible protestant successor in the autumn of 1678. When the king announced to both houses of parliament on 9 November 1678 that he would consent to any bills that would make them 'safe in the reign of my successor, so as they tend not to impeach the Right of Succession, nor the descent of the crown in the true line', his speech was reported in the streets as a resolution 'that the Duke of Monmouth was to succeed the King', prompting numerous bonfires to be lit throughout the capital in celebration (Cobbett, *Parl. hist.*, 8, 1678, 1035; *JHC*, 1667–87, 9.536; *Ormonde MSS*, new ser., 4.470). People presumably thought the king was hinting he would declare his son legitimate; indeed, the persistence of such rumours led Charles to make a statement before the privy council early in the new year affirming that the only wife he had ever married was Queen Catherine.

For the time being, however, Monmouth's allegiances remained with the court. In November 1678 he voted against the passage of the second Test Act, aimed at excluding Catholics from parliament (though he absented himself from the vote on the proviso exempting the duke of York, testifying to how deep the rift between him and his uncle had become), and in December he voted against the impeachment of Danby. When elections were held for a new parliament in the new year, Shaftesbury identified the two men returned on Monmouth's interest as supporters of the court. Shaftesbury and the earl of Essex did manage to persuade Monmouth to drop his support for Danby in March, and in April Monmouth played a key role in persuading the king to restructure his privy council so as to bring in members of the opposition in an attempt to rebuild national unity, though he did so as a royal adviser seeking ways to defuse the opposition challenge. There is no evidence that Monmouth harboured any pretensions to the throne at this stage or that any leading politicians thought he would be a suitable alternative to York. The court, and most members of the reformed privy council, backed the idea of limitations on a Catholic successor; Shaftesbury and his allies preferred exclusion, but the Exclusion Bill introduced into the Commons in May 1679 provided that the succession should pass to the 'next Lawful Heir', as if the 'Duke of York were actually dead' (*A Copy of the Bill Concerning the Duke of York*), implying York's daughter Mary, the wife of William of Orange.

When the Scottish covenanters rose in rebellion in the spring of 1679, in reaction to Lauderdale's policy of religious persecution, Charles appointed Monmouth general of all the forces in Scotland and dispatched him to put down the revolt. After defeating the rebel army at Bothwell Bridge on 22 June, Monmouth urged his father to adopt a policy of leniency as a way of soothing religious tensions north of the border. Charles issued an indulgence allowing Scottish presbyterians to meet in house conventicles, while most of those taken prisoner were eventually released under the terms of an indemnity granted in July. On 3 July Monmouth was presented with the freedom of the city of Edinburgh, and on 29 July, following Monmouth's return to England, Charles made him captain-general of all the forces in Scotland (Monmouth's original commission had only been for the duration of his stay in that kingdom).

With the Exclusion Bill having been frustrated by the peremptory dissolution of parliament in May, the opposition now began to look towards Monmouth, whose stature was growing all the time, and who was not only popular with the masses but also had an armed force under his command. By the summer it was being reported that Monmouth and Shaftesbury were meeting 'very often' (*Hastings MSS*, 2.388), while those close to Monmouth were beginning to agitate more actively on his behalf. Monmouth's client and army friend Sir Thomas Armstrong busied himself searching for the black box which supposedly contained the certificate of marriage between Charles and Lucy Walter, and in May he allegedly spoke to the earl of Oxford about endeavouring 'to get the succession to be on Monmouth', which the earl reported back to the king (*Seventh Report*, HMC, 472). With nothing having been resolved about the succession, the volatility of the situation was brought to a head when Charles suddenly fell ill on 21 August, and for a few days seemed on the verge of death: the duke of York was in Brussels, where the king had sent him into temporary exile earlier that year, Monmouth was urging his father on his visits to his sickbed to make sure he stayed there, and Monmouth's crony Armstrong was busy holding meetings with the London radical Francis Jenks 'and the rest of the gang in the City' (*CSP dom.*, 1679–80, 240). 'If the king had died', the earl of Sunderland was convinced, the duke of Monmouth 'would have made great troubles, either setting up for himself, or for a Commonwealth' (*Diary of … Sidney*, 176). Sunderland, together with Essex and the marquess of Halifax, urged York to return immediately to England; Charles recovered, and the crisis subsided; and Essex and Halifax convinced Charles that the best solution was to send both dukes into exile. Charles revoked Monmouth's commission as captain-general of the English army on 12 September, stripping him of his Scottish command the next day, and ordered him to leave the country. False reports of a last-minute change of heart prompted Londoners to light bonfires on the night of 17 September to drink the king and the duke's healths, but Monmouth, now being cried up by 'all the phanaticks and malecontents … as the great confessor for the protestant religion' (*Correspondence of Hatton*, 1.194), had to go. He left for Utrecht on the 24th.

By now, many in England were beginning to look to Monmouth as the obvious protestant alternative to York. In mid-October the *Appeal from the Country to the City* appeared, advocating Monmouth as the best person to succeed in the event of the king's untimely death, and claiming that 'He who hath the worst Title, ever makes the best King', because he has to make up for his lack of right by pleasing the people (Blount, 7–8). By the end of the following month Monmouth was back in England. Upset by the king's decision to recall York from Brussels and send him instead to head up the government in Scotland, he returned to London, uninvited, late on the night of 27 November. The news of Monmouth's arrival spread quickly; before dawn bonfires had been lit in several places, and on the night of the 28th there were allegedly more bonfires than had ever been seen 'since those for the restoration of his Majesty' (*Correspondence of Hatton*, 1.203). Charles was outraged, and on 1 December stripped Monmouth of most of his remaining offices (except those of master of the horse and chancellor of Cambridge University), and ordered him to return to exile. Monmouth refused to go.

Totally estranged from his uncle, and angry at the way he had been treated by his father, Monmouth allowed himself to get increasingly drawn into opposition intrigues. Speculation over the black box revived. By the spring of 1680 it was being said that the box had fallen into the possession of Lord Gerard of Brandon, and although Brandon publicly denied this and Charles reissued statements affirming that he had never married Lucy Walter, the topic generated a lively pamphlet debate. For some, however, whether a fully solemnized church marriage had taken place was not the issue. In 1680 William Lawrence published his *Marriage by the Morall Law of God*, in which he attacked the church's attempts to secure a monopoly over marriage, insisted on the legality of what we would call common law marriages, and claimed that it should be high treason to slander the king's eldest son with illegitimacy. Monmouth also began actively promoting himself. In February 1680 he made a brief progress to Chichester, where the local gentry, civic authorities, and townsfolk afforded him a warm reception. In the early summer he made a series of public appearances in London, dining with anything up to sixty whig nobles and gentry at a time, before setting out on a tour of the west country towards the end of July, making his way first to Bath and then to Shaftesbury's house in Dorset, before doing the rounds of the local whig gentry in Wiltshire, Somerset, and Devon. Everywhere he went huge numbers of people 'of all sorts, all sexes, all ages and degrees' came from miles around to greet him, shouting 'God bless our King Charles, and God bless the Protestant Duke' (*True Narrative of the Duke of Monmouth's Late Journey*, 2, 4); he even touched for the king's evil, thereby signifying his belief in his own royal dignity. On his return to London he made a brief visit to Oxford (16–18 September), where he was welcomed by the mayor and several aldermen amid cries of 'God bless the Protestant Duke' and 'No York, no bishops, no university', and on the following day was made a freeman of the city (*CSP dom., 1680–81*, 31). Once back in London Monmouth moved to a house in Bishopsgate Street (behind the Excise Office), in the heart of the City, and resumed his public dinners with whig magnates.

To accommodate the possibility of the succession being settled on Monmouth, the second Exclusion Bill, introduced into parliament in November 1680, simply provided for the exclusion of the Catholic heir without mentioning who should succeed instead; it was later modified in committee, however, to include the proviso that the crown should descend as if the duke of York were dead. The bill was defeated in the Lords on 15 November, and parliament dissolved early in the new year, but the whigs continued to promote Monmouth's candidacy. In February 1681 Monmouth made another trip to Chichester, where he was greeted by over 400 gentry and the city's two MPs, and treated to dinner by the whig peer Lord Grey of Warke, who lived nearby; the local inhabitants celebrated with the inevitable bonfires. A third Exclusion Bill, which once again left the question of the successor open, was introduced into the parliament which met at Oxford on 21 March, while Shaftesbury sought to circumvent the whole issue by inviting Charles to agree to the 'expedient' of settling the throne on Monmouth. Charles was outraged, and dissolved parliament after just eight days.

The Rye House intrigues As the court began its counter-offensive against the whigs following the dissolution of the Oxford parliament, Charles left the way open for a reconciliation with his son. He rewarded Monmouth's discretion in staying away from a whig dinner held in London in early April by giving him a gift of £4000 to pay his debts. Yet despite being urged by his own secretary, James Vernon, to approach the king, Monmouth decided to stand by his whig associates. He visited Shaftesbury in the Tower following the earl's arrest on treason charges that summer; was present at his court hearing in November, when a London grand jury threw out the bill against the earl; and stood bail for him upon his release from prison. As opinion in the country became increasingly polarized over the issue of exclusion, Monmouth's supporters out of doors started sporting blue ribbons, to distinguish themselves from the friends of the duke of York, who wore red ones. Monmouth witnessed the climax of the London pope-burning procession at Smithfield on 17 November 1681, when the huge crowd drank healths to him and his father 'conjunctively' (*Westmorland MSS*, 174). Crowds were again out in force in the capital on the evening of the 24th, following Shaftesbury's *ignoramus* verdict, celebrating at bonfires, looking to pick fights with local tories and supporters of the court, and roaming the streets chanting 'No Popish successor, no York, a Monmouth!' (*CSP dom., 1680–81*, 583). In reaction, Charles stripped Monmouth of his remaining English offices and banned him from court (1 December 1681). At the end of the year Monmouth was also removed from the Scottish privy council and stripped of his remaining Scottish offices for refusing to take the oath required by the Scottish Test Act of 1681: holding Monmouth accountable to the test was in itself intended to make a political statement, since the act had stipulated that 'the King's lawful Brothers and Sons' were the only ones to be exempt (*APS*, 8.244).

Following the king's decision to recall the duke of York and his return to England in the spring of 1682, Monmouth at last decided to see if he could effect a reconciliation with his father. He sent Major Abraham Holmes to meet with Charles in May, but Holmes made it clear that although Monmouth would kneel before the king, he would not do so before his uncle. Charles was indignant, and forbade anyone in his service henceforth to have any communication with Monmouth. When the king fell ill that month, Monmouth attended an emergency meeting convened at Shaftesbury's London residence, Thanet House, with Armstrong, Grey, William Lord Russell, and Major John Manley, where the group allegedly decided that if Charles should die they would launch a rebellion with the aim of summoning a parliament to determine the succession. Charles recovered, but plans for an uprising were revived following the tory success at the London shrieval elections that summer. Given that the sheriffs were responsible for empanelling juries for London and Middlesex, once the tory sheriffs were in place the whigs could no longer expect to escape the clutches of the law through *ignoramus* verdicts; for those who had reason to fear for their lives, the time for desperate measures had come. Shaftesbury, Grey, Armstrong, Russell, and Monmouth reconvened at Thanet House, probably some time in July, where Shaftesbury, Russell, and Monmouth allegedly argued for an insurrection. Several more meetings followed. Shaftesbury, it was decided, would be responsible for London; Russell was to sound out the west country; Grey to canvass Essex; while Monmouth was to make a progress to Cheshire, under the guise of attending the horse races at Wallasey, to gauge the level of support in the north-west and discuss options with the whig peers, lords Macclesfield and Delamere, and their sons, Lord Gerard of Brandon and Henry Booth.

Monmouth set off for the north-west in early September, passing through Coventry and Nantwich before reaching Chester on the 9th. He received a rapturous welcome wherever he went, was sumptuously dined by the local whig gentry, achieved victory in the horse races to boot, and was fêted by riotous crowds at bonfires shouting 'A Monmouth, a Monmouth' and even 'Let Monmouth reign' (*CSP dom., 1682*, 391, 406). At Liverpool he touched again for the king's evil. On his return home the government had Monmouth seized at Stafford and brought back to London under arrest, where he was released after posting a bond for his good behaviour. Shaftesbury wanted

Monmouth to return to Cheshire immediately to launch a rebellion, but Russell advised that things were not ready, and Monmouth declined to act. Shaftesbury was now beginning to lose patience with the duke, and started to discuss with other conspirators the possibility of assassinating Charles and James on their return from the races at Newmarket in October. Monmouth learned of the design through Robert Ferguson, whom he commissioned to act as an agent provocateur to infiltrate the conspiracy with the design of making sure it came to nothing. When the project collapsed, Shaftesbury decided to give Monmouth and the insurrection scheme one more chance. A date was set for the evening of 19 November, shortly after gunpowder treason day and the anniversary of Elizabeth's accession (the two days of anti-Catholic commemoration in the whig calendar), and a Sunday, when the shops would be shut and enough people on the streets to provide a cover for the comings and goings of the rebels. The mood of the capital seemed propitious; there were pro-Monmouth demonstrations in London on gunpowder treason day (commemorated that year on the 6th because the 5th fell on a Sunday), as whig crowds paraded through the streets chanting 'No York, a Monmouth, a Monmouth'. The scuffles that broke out with local tories, however, prompted the government to take extra security measures to prevent there being any bonfire celebrations on the 17th, and with the west still not ready, the conspirators decided to postpone their plans. Shaftesbury fled England on the 28th, and was to die in Amsterdam on 21 January 1683.

The idea of an uprising now came to be pursued by a newly formed 'council of six', comprising Monmouth, Russell, Essex, Lord Howard of Escrick, Algernon Sidney, and John Hampden. A separate group of conspirators, led by Robert West, decided to proceed with the assassination plot, planning to ambush the king and his brother on their return from the spring races at Newmarket at a house called the Rye, in Hertfordshire. The council of six decided to draw in the earl of Argyll and his Scottish supporters, with the idea of launching co-ordinated rebellions in London, the west country, Cheshire, and Scotland. They were fatally split, however, between those who favoured the establishment of a commonwealth (Essex, Sidney, and Hampden) and those who simply wanted to force the king to come to terms. As it turned out, the assassination plot was frustrated by a fire that broke at Newmarket on 22 March, which forced the royal brothers to depart several days earlier than anticipated. The council of six, however, pushed ahead with its planned uprising, and by mid-June had reportedly reached agreement on a draft manifesto, which provided for parliament's control of the militia, the right of counties to elect sheriffs, annual parliamentary elections, liberty of conscience, and the degrading of those nobles who had acted contrary to the interest of the people. Yet by now it was too late, as the conspiracy had already been betrayed to the government on 12 June. Monmouth went into hiding; on the 28th the government issued a proclamation offering a £500 reward for his apprehension, and on 12 July an indictment was brought against him for high treason.

After spending time first in Cheshire, Monmouth took refuge in Lady Wentworth's house, Toddington, Bedfordshire, while the government pursued its prosecution of the plot. Charles was distraught to learn of his beloved son's involvement. He also needed the information Monmouth could provide to help convict the other conspirators. Seeing an opportunity to bolster his own position at court, the marquess of Halifax endeavoured to broker a reconciliation between father and son. On 13 October he visited Monmouth at Toddington with a message from Charles that he would never believe he 'knew any thing of that part of the Plot that concern'd *Rye-House*', and persuaded him to crave the king's pardon (Welwood, 373). Monmouth wrote Charles a letter denying knowledge of the assassination plot though apologizing for having done many things that angered the court. Two clandestine meetings between father and son and a further conciliatory though vaguely worded letter from Monmouth followed, before he finally surrendered himself on 24 November, acknowledged his guilt before both Charles and York, and revealed all he knew of the conspiracy on the understanding that his confession would be kept secret. The next day Charles convened an extraordinary meeting of the council to announce that Monmouth had submitted, reporting that his son had 'shewed himself very sensible of his Crime in the late Conspiracy, making a full Declaration of it', and that at the duke of York's request he had decided to stop all further proceedings against him (*LondG*, no. 1880 22–6 Nov 1683). By the evening Monmouth was back at court, and on the 26th, the day that Algernon Sidney was sentenced to death for his role in the conspiracy, he received his pardon and a gift from his father of £4000. Monmouth was furious, however, when Charles's announcement to the council was published in the *Gazette*, and insisted to his friends he had 'confessed no plott, because he never knew any' (DWL, Roger Morrice Ent'ring Book, P.392). With the government's credibility at stake, Charles felt he had no choice but to secure a written confession. On 6 December Monmouth signed a vaguely worded document affirming that he had 'owned the late Conspiracy' and lamented his role in it (though 'not conscious of any designe' against the king's life), and promising never to act against the king again (ibid., p. 406; *State trials*, 9.1099). However, fearing this might be used to secure the conviction of his friend Hampden, Monmouth asked for it back the next day; Charles reluctantly complied, and ordered his son not to return to court. On 25 January 1684 the government issued subpoenas for Monmouth to give evidence at Hampden's trial, set for 6 February. Monmouth fled to the continent, and by April he was in Brussels.

The Monmouth rebellion, June–July 1685 For the time being Monmouth chose to keep his distance from the English and Scottish dissidents in exile in the Low Countries. He was able to live in comfort with his mistress, Lady Wentworth, having been granted an annuity of £6000 p.a. by the marqués de Grana, the governor of the Spanish Netherlands, and was appointed colonel of a Spanish regiment. He was also entertained by William of Orange at

The Hague, who bestowed further military honours upon him. Monmouth returned to England briefly in November 1684, to arrange the sale of a manor, and made one last attempt to be restored to his father's favour. At the end of December, now back at The Hague, he learned from Halifax that he would be allowed to return to Westminster in February, when the duke of York was due to be in Edinburgh for the meeting of the Scottish parliament. These schemes were brought to naught by Charles's sudden death on 6 February. James II immediately sent notice to William of Orange to have Monmouth arrested, but Orange tipped Monmouth off, who fled first to Rotterdam and then to Brussels. There he was told that Charles II of Spain had ordered his arrest, so he returned to the United Provinces, where he found refuge at Gouda.

Meanwhile, the Scots in exile, led by Argyll, had been continuing to plot insurrection during the latter months of 1684, and had already made plans to invade Scotland in the spring of 1685. In January 1685 the English exiles held a meeting in Utrecht to discuss ways of enlisting support in England for Argyll. Although Monmouth might have been ignorant of such developments—he was to write that he was 'so much in love with a retir'd Life' that he was 'never like to be fond of making a Bustle in the World again' (Welwood, 325)—he quickly resumed contact with exiled Scottish and English dissidents following his father's death. Around 23 February he went to Amsterdam to confer with the Scots, where he pledged his support for their enterprise and even offered assurances that he would not claim the crown for himself without taking their advice. At a meeting with Argyll on the 25th, it was decided that Monmouth should be responsible for raising England and most of Ireland, while Argyll would answer for Scotland and the north of Ireland. Soon Monmouth was sending emissaries to the radicals in England urging the need for speedy action, believing that the best time for an insurrection would be a day or two before parliament met on 19 May, when most of the lords lieutenant, militia officers, and tory peers would be in London. His friends in England were unconvinced that the timing was right; Monmouth learned from one of his emissaries, Robert Cragg, that 'he would not find such a disposition in the people of England at this time to give him that assistance which he might expect … People were cold' and there was 'a great backwardness in the gentlemen'. The duke replied that 'he could not nor would alter his resolution, for he had promised the Scots' and would not be 'false to them' (*House of Lords MSS*, 2.393–4), and so plans for co-ordinated rebellions pushed ahead. Argyll was to head for the Scottish highlands; Monmouth for the English west country, the site of his triumphant progress five years earlier; while London and Cheshire were expected to rise in support.

Argyll set sail from Amsterdam on 2 May. Monmouth's invasion force, comprising three ships and eighty-three men, was not ready to leave until 24 May, and then contrary winds held them up in the channel so that they were not to land at Lyme Regis, Dorset, until 11 June. At Lyme Monmouth issued a declaration (probably penned by Robert Ferguson), in which he alleged that the English government had been changed from a limited monarchy into an absolute tyranny; accused James II of poisoning the late king, usurping the throne, and ruling against the law; and demanded the repeal of all penal laws against protestant dissenters, annual parliaments, the appointment of judges on good behaviour rather than at royal pleasure, the restoration of corporate charters that had come under attack during the years of the tory reaction, and the repeal of the Corporation and Militia Acts. Although Monmouth believed himself to have a legitimate right to the crown, he did not 'insist upon his Title' at present, the declaration said, but would leave 'the determination thereof to the Wisdom, Justice, and Authority of Parliament, legally chosen and acting with Freedom' (*Declaration of James, Duke of Monmouth*). The declaration reached London on 13 June, and three days later a bill of attainder was issued against Monmouth and a price of £5000 placed upon his head.

The rebels spent their first few days at Lyme enlisting recruits and gathering supplies, though Monmouth was forced to dismiss his best officer, Andrew Fletcher of Saltoun, for killing his paymaster-general, Thomas Dare, in a squabble over a horse. On 15 June they left for Taunton, passing through Axminster, Chard, and Ilminster, and taking on new recruits along the way. Taunton, which they reached on the 18th, proved the most fertile recruiting ground. Even at its peak, however, the rebel army probably never exceeded 3000 men. The greater part of the rebels came from urban backgrounds, with a heavy concentration from the depressed west country cloth trades, though there were some farmers and village craftsmen and labourers. Many who enlisted were either dissenters or people who sympathized with their plight, though recent work has warned against exaggerating the nonconformist presence in Monmouth's army. Particularly worrying to the leadership was the failure to attract gentry backing. Ferguson urged that the only way to gain the support of the landed classes was for Monmouth to assume the title of king, and so on 20 June at the Taunton market cross a proclamation was read affirming that on the death of Charles the crown 'did legally descend and devolve upon … Monmouth' and declaring him 'our lawful and rightful sovereign and king, by the name of James the Second' ('Monmouth's Proclamation at Taunton', Watson, 278). The tactic failed: the gentry were not won over, and if anything Monmouth only managed to alienate some of his own supporters, who feared that, having sold out over the issue of the crown, he would next back down on his demands for political and religious reform.

On 21 June Monmouth and his army left Taunton for Bridgwater, whence they moved on to Glastonbury and Shepton Mallet, with the intention of marching on Bristol. Deflected by royalist troops at Keynsham, they turned towards Bath, which they were unable to capture, so they withdrew to Norton St Philip, where they survived a frontal attack by the royal army, before moving south to Frome. It was here that they learned the news of Argyll's defeat. With the collapse of the rebellion in Scotland, and with the anticipated risings in Cheshire and London having failed to materialize, Monmouth knew that the cause was lost. He convened a council of war and proposed abandoning the enterprise: the officers should flee to some seaport, while the rank-and-file could return home and take the benefit of James II's proclamation of pardon. Although there was much support for the suggestion, an impassioned speech by Lord Grey, in which he argued that for Monmouth to leave the army now would be an act 'so base that it could never be forgiven by the people' (Clifton, 191), persuaded Monmouth to go on. With the royalist army poised to cut the rebels off if they attempted to march east through Wiltshire on the road towards London, Monmouth decided to turn west back into Somerset, where he had been told that 'a great Club army' of some 10,000 men 'were up in the marshes' and ready to join the rebel forces (Dunning, 31). Monmouth re-entered Bridgwater on 3 July, but only about 160 new recruits came forward. Late on the night of the 5th Monmouth moved his army towards the king's forces encamped on nearby Sedgemoor in a bold attempt to take them by surprise, but Monmouth's men were routed in battle the next day and Monmouth himself took flight. He was found two days later hiding in a ditch in the woods just outside Ringwood.

Monmouth was taken back to London and imprisoned in the Tower on 12 July. The act of attainder already passed against him meant that no trial was necessary, and he was ordered to be executed on Tower Hill on 15 July. The day before, Monmouth wrote begging letters to James II and the queen, pleading for his life, but to no avail, though the king did allow his nephew to see his children one more time and agree that he should be beheaded instead of hanged. The bishops of Ely and Bath and Wells were sent to tend to Monmouth in his last hours, but they refused to administer him holy communion because he would not acknowledge that his cohabitation with Lady Wentworth had been a sin. Monmouth gave no speech from the scaffold, but instead produced a signed paper in which he disclaimed all title to the crown, acknowledged that Charles II had told him he had never married his mother, and implored the king to be kind to his wife and children. Despite being paid well by his victim, the executioner mangled the job. It took him five strokes of the axe to sever the head from Monmouth's body; after the first stroke Monmouth was purportedly seen to lift his head in anguish, and, according to Evelyn, the crowd of onlookers were so incensed that 'they would have torne' the executioner 'in pieces' if he had not been protected by a heavy guard (Evelyn, 4.455). Monmouth's remains were buried under the communion table of St Peter's Church in the Tower.

At the end of August a special commission of oyer and terminer, known to history as the 'bloody assizes', was set up under Judge Jeffreys to try some 1300 suspected rebels. The vast majority were found guilty and sentenced to death, though in the end only about 250 were executed, while 850 had their sentences commuted to transportation. A few score of the Monmouth rebels escaped to the continent, mainly the Low Countries. Rumours soon started circulating, throughout the kingdom, that Monmouth was not really dead and would soon rise again, someone else having supposedly been executed in his place—'an old man with a Beard', a husbandman from Lyme Regis thought (Dorset RO, DL/LR/A3/1, 20). One report from May 1686 claimed that Monmouth was alive and well and going 'about in womans Cloaths in Bristoll and Summersettsheer' (BL, Add. MS 41804, fol. 168). During that same spring the government received intelligence that a young gentleman posing as Monmouth's son was intriguing with exiled political dissidents in the Low Countries; in October a man claiming to be Monmouth himself was found concealed in a house some 10 miles outside London. Nevertheless, it is probably fair to say that at the time of the rebellion Monmouth's cause was not particularly popular in the nation at large. The years of tory reaction had seen public opinion turn against the whigs and rally behind the crown in defence of the existing legal establishment in church and state; hence why the rebels had such difficulty in gathering recruits, and why no other part of the country rose in sympathy as anticipated. Indeed, news of the defeat of rebellion was celebrated with bonfires in several places throughout the kingdom.

Monmouth's English titles were forfeited by his attainder, but the Scottish peerage, which his widow enjoyed by her own right, was left unaffected. The duchess of Buccleuch was to remarry in 1688 and live to the age of eighty-one, dying in 1732. Of his legitimate children, Monmouth was survived by two sons: James Scott, earl of Dalkeith, and Henry *Scott, created earl of Deloraine in 1706 (his first-born son, Charles, earl of Doncaster, had died as an infant in 1674). His daughter Lady Anne Scott, who had been taken hostage by the government at the time of the rebellion, died in the Tower in August 1685 at age ten, and was buried in Westminster Abbey. Lady Henrietta Wentworth returned to England in the autumn of 1685 and died on 23 April 1686, it was said of a broken heart; she was twenty-six. A child that she was said to have had with Monmouth was brought up in Paris by a close friend of the Wentworths, Colonel Smyth, and named James Wentworth Smyth Stuart. He took part in the Jacobite rebellions of 1715 and 1745, and took as his second wife Maria Julia Crofts, the daughter of James, a son of Monmouth and Eleanor Needham. Of Eleanor's other children with Monmouth, Henry died unmarried, Isabella died young, and Henrietta married the duke of Bolton. Monmouth's daughter with Elizabeth Waller married James de Cardonnel, secretary to the duke of Schomberg.

Monmouth's historical reputation has been the subject of considerable debate over the generations. He has been seen alternatively as a dupe and as a schemer: as a political puppet who was unscrupulously manipulated by others to promote their own agendas, or as an embittered royal bastard ruthlessly pursuing his own personal ambitions. In fact neither view really fits. The key to understanding Monmouth lies in his troubled childhood, spoiled youth, the complex nature of his relationships with both his mother and his father, and the personality traits and character flaws which his peculiar upbringing helped engender. He was undoubtedly emotionally unstable; as one biographer has put it, he was controlled, not by any one individual, but 'by violent emotions towards his father, mother, and uncle; and by pride, honour, and resentment' (Clifton, 288). Those who did try to use Monmouth often found to their frustration that he could not easily be pushed around. Yet in the end it was his own sense of honour which led him to launch a rebellion in 1685 when he had at last found peace in a retired life: as the son of a king whom (he believed) had been murdered, he felt he could not sit by and watch his hated uncle seize his inheritance; nor could he do nothing as Argyll went it alone in Scotland. It was also his sense of honour that led him to continue with his enterprise even when he knew the cause was lost. Although the rebellion was a disaster, most agree that Monmouth himself showed considerable skill as a military leader (much more so than Argyll, for example, or the man who led the Devon militia against Monmouth's army, Christopher Monck, duke of Albemarle). Some have argued that the ideals of the Monmouth rebels lived on, and were largely fulfilled at the time of the revolution of 1688. Yet the reforms demanded by the manifestos of both 1683 and 1685 were in fact much more far-reaching than those eventually enacted in 1689. Monmouth spearheaded a movement which, in the context of its time, was genuinely radical, and arguably too extreme to appeal to a broad enough cross-section of the population to stand a realistic chance of success.

TIM HARRIS

Sources GEC, *Peerage*, new edn, vol. 9 • R. Clifton, *The last popular rebellion: the western rising of 1685* (1984) • P. Ealre, *Monmouth's rebels: the road to Sedgemoor* (1977) • T. Harris, *London crowds in the reign of Charles II* (1987) • R. Dunning, *The Monmouth episode: a guide to the rebellion and bloody assizes* (1984) • J. N. P. Watson, *Captain-general and rebel chief: the life of James, duke of Monmouth* (1979) • J. Bevan, *James duke of Monmouth* (1973) • E. D'Oyley, *James, duke of Monmouth* (1938) • R. Ashcraft, *Revolutionary politics and Locke's two treatises of government* (1986) • R. L. Greaves, *Secrets of the kingdom: British radicals from the Popish Plot to the revolution of 1688–89* (1992) • Pepys, *Diary* • Evelyn, *Diary* • *The life of James the Second, king of England*, ed. J. S. Clarke, 2 vols. (1816) • J. Macpherson, ed., *Original papers: containing the secret history of Great Britain*, 2 vols. (1775), vol. 1 • T. Sprat, *A true account and declaration of the horrid conspiracy against the late king* (1685) • *Bishop Burnet's History of his own time*, new edn (1850) • *State trials*, vol. 11 • *CSP dom.*, 1660–85 • *A copy of the bill concerning the duke of York* (1679) • [C. Blount], *An appeal from the county to the city* (1679) • *True narrative of the duke of Monmouth's late journey* (1680) • *The declaration of James, duke of Monmouth* (1685) • J. Welwood, *Memoirs of the most memorial transactions* (1700) • *An historical account of the heroick life and magnanimous actions of the most illustrious protestant prince, James, duke of Monmouth* (1683) • *Seventh report*, HMC, 6 (1879) • *The manuscripts of the earl of Westmorland*, HMC, 13 (1885); repr. (1906) • *The manuscripts of the House of Lords*, 4 vols., HMC, 17 (1887–94), vol. 2 • *Report on the manuscripts of the late Reginald Rawdon Hastings*, 4 vols., HMC, 78 (1928–47), vol. 2 • *Diary of the times of Charles the Second by the Honourable Henry Sidney (afterwards earl of Romney)*, ed. R. W. Blencowe, 2 vols. (1843) • W. D. Christie, ed., *Letters addressed from London to Sir Joseph Williamson*, 2 vols., CS, new ser., 8–9 (1874) • E. M. Thompson, ed., *Correspondence of the family of Hatton*, 2 vols., CS, new ser., 22–3 (1878) • BL, Middleton MS, vol. 2, Add. MS 41804 • R. Morrice, Ent'ring Book, DWL [vol. P] • K. H. D. Haley, 'Shaftesbury's lists of the lay peers and members of the Commons, 1677–8', *BIHR*, 43 (1970), 86–105 • J. R. Jones, 'Shaftesbury's "worthy men": a whig view of the parliament of 1679', *BIHR*, 30 (1957), 232–41 • W. Lawrence, *Marriage by the morall law of God* (1680) • misdemeanour book, Lyme Regis, 1681–1751, Dorset RO, DL/LR/A3/1 • sacrament certificates, 1673, LMA, MR/RS/2/217–218 • *LondG* (1666–85) • *APS*, 1670–86 • J. Scott, duke of Monmouth, *An abridgement of the English military discipline* (1690) • *Calendar of the manuscripts of the marquess of Ormonde*, new ser., 8 vols., HMC, 36 (1902–20), vol. 4

Archives BL, letter-book during embassy to France and Low Countries, 66 • BL, memorandum book, Egerton MS 1527 • Buckminster Park, Grantham, corresp. | BL, letters to Lord Essex, Stowe MSS 200–210, *passim* • BL, letters and papers relating to his rebellion, Add. MSS 41803–41804, 41812–41820 • CUL, corresp. relating to University of Cambridge • NA Scot., curators and commissioners papers • NRA, priv. coll., letters to Sir Robert Atkyns

Likenesses S. Cooper, drawing, *c.*1660, Royal Collection • N. Dixon, miniature, *c.*1663, Buccleuch estates, Selkirk, Scotland • P. Lely, oils, *c.*1665–1675, Buccleuch estates, Selkirk, Scotland • P. Lely, oils, oval, *c.*1665–1675, Buccleuch estates, Selkirk, Scotland • G. Kneller, oils, 1678, Buccleuch estates, Selkirk, Scotland [*see illus.*] • G. Kneller, oils, 1679, Buccleuch estates, Selkirk, Scotland • attrib. G. Kneller, oils, 1680–89, Goodwood, West Sussex • W. Wissing, oils, 1680–89, Palace House, Hampshire; version, NPG • W. Wissing, oils, *c.*1683, Clarendon College; on loan to Palace of Westminster, London • R. Arondeaux, silver medal, Scot. NPG • C. Boit, watercolour on ivory, Scot. NPG • J. Huysmans, oils, Buccleuch estates, Selkirk, Scotland • J. vander Vaart, mezzotint (after W. Wissing, 1680–89), BM, NPG; repro. in Bevan, *James, duke of Monmouth*, 193

Scott, James (1733–1814), Church of England clergyman and writer, was born in Leeds, the son of James Scott, vicar of Bardsey, Yorkshire, and domestic chaplain to Frederick, prince of Wales, and Annabella, daughter of Henry, fifth son of Tobias Wickham, dean of York. He was educated at Bradford grammar school and from 1752 at St Catharine's College, Cambridge. He later moved to Trinity College, and graduated BA in 1757, whereupon he was elected fellow; he proceeded MA in 1760, BD in 1768, and DD in 1775. He won the Seatonian poetry prize on three occasions and was a frequent and admired preacher at the university church between 1760 and 1764 in which year he also began a part-time residence in London. He was lecturer at St John's, Leeds (1758–69), and curate of Edmonton (1760–61).

In 1765, under the inspiration of Lord Sandwich and using the pseudonym Anti-Sejanus, he contributed to the *Public Advertiser* a series of animated diatribes against Lord Bute which were reprinted in *A Collection of Interesting Letters* (1767). He was also the author of the pieces signed Philanglia which appeared in the same collection, and of others by Old Slyboots, collected in *Fugitive Political Essays* (1769). In 1771 he married Anne Scott, daughter of Henry Scott; they had three children, all of whom died in infancy. In the same year as his marriage he was presented through Lord Sandwich's interest to the rectory of Simonburn, Northumberland, where he spent twenty years and £10,000 in endeavouring to collect his tithes. Scott's prolonged litigation caused considerable hostility in the parish and led to an attempt on his life, prompting his move to London.

Besides his political *jeux d'esprit* and his Seatonian poems, 'Heaven', 'Purity of Heart: a Moral Epistle', and 'An

Hymn to Repentance', Scott was author of *Odes on Several Subjects* (1761), *The Redemption: a Monody* (1763–4), and *Every Man the Architect of his Own Fortune* (1763). He died at his home in Somerset Street, Portland Square, London, on 10 December 1814 and was survived by his wife. His death was marked by the publication of a lengthy obituary in the *Gentleman's Magazine* (December 1814) and a volume of his *Sermons on Interesting Subjects* (1816), together with a life by Samuel Clapham. J. M. Rigg, *rev.* Philip Carter

Sources 'Memoirs of the late Rev Dr James Scott', *GM*, 1st ser., 84/2 (1814), 601–3 · *GM*, 1st ser., 86/2 (1816), 527–31 · Nichols, *Lit. anecdotes* · Venn, *Alum. Cant.*

Scott, Sir James (1790?–1872), naval officer, son of Thomas Scott of Glenluce in Wigtownshire, and of Ham Common in Surrey, a cadet of the Scotts of Raeburn, was born in London on 18 June, probably in 1790. He entered the navy in August 1803 on the frigate *Phaeton* (Captain George Cockburn) and served in her for two years on the East India station. In February 1806 he joined the *Blanche* (46 guns, Captain Lavie) and was present at the capture of the French frigate *Guerrière* near the Färoe Islands on 19 July. In September 1806 he was entered on the *Captain* (74 guns), again with Cockburn; and in July 1807 in the *Achille* with Sir Richard King. In April 1808 he rejoined Cockburn in the *Pompée* and in her went out to the West Indies, where, in February 1809, he took part in the capture of Martinique. He came home with Cockburn in the *Belle Isle*, and under him commanded a gunboat in the capture of Flushing in July and August. On 16 November 1809 he was promoted lieutenant of *La Flèche* (14 guns), in the North Sea, and was in her when she was wrecked off the mouth of the River Elbe on 24 May 1810. In July he was appointed to the *Barfleur* on the Lisbon station, and in October he was moved into the sloop *Myrtle*, in which he served at the siege of Cadiz, and afterwards on the west coast of Africa until April 1812. He was then appointed to the *Grampus* (50 guns), again with Cockburn, whom in August he followed to the *Marlborough* (74 guns). In November she went out to the coast of North America, where Cockburn, with his flag in the *Marlborough* and afterwards in the *Sceptre* and *Albion* (both 74 guns), had command of the operations in Chesapeake Bay. Scott, closely following Cockburn, was constantly employed in landing parties and cutting-out expeditions, and he acted as Cockburn's aide-de-camp at Bladensburg, Washington, and Baltimore. In consequence of Cockburn's very strong recommendation, Scott was promoted commander on 19 October 1814. He married, on 3 May 1819, Caroline Anne (*bap.* 1798), the only child of Richard Donovan of Tibberton Court, Gloucestershire, and Caroline Elizabeth Yate. They had one son, the Revd Honywood Dobyns Yate Scott.

In May 1824 Scott commanded the bomb-vessel *Meteor* in the demonstration against Algiers, and in the following November he was appointed to the *Harlequin* (18 guns) in the West Indies. He was promoted captain on 8 January 1828. From 1834 to 1836 he commanded the *President* (50 guns) in the West Indies, as flag captain to Cockburn; and from 1837 to 1840 he was again in the *President*, in the Pacific, as flag captain to Rear-Admiral Ross. In 1840–41 he commanded the *Samarang* (26 guns) on the China station and had an active and important share in the operations on the Canton River, leading to the surrender of Canton. He was made a CB on 29 June 1841. He had no further service but was promoted in due course rear-admiral on 26 December 1854, vice-admiral on 4 June 1861, and admiral on 10 February 1865. On 10 November 1862 he was made a KCB. In accordance with the terms of the orders in council of 24 March 1866, as he had never hoisted his flag, he was put on the retired list. Against this and the retrospective action of the order he protested in vain. He wrote *Recollections of a Naval Life* (3 vols., 1834) and *Memorandum of Services of Sir James Scott* (1866). He died at Cheltenham, Gloucestershire, on 2 March 1872, having had a career made almost entirely by a single patron; he was a willing follower, rather than an initiator.

J. K. Laughton, *rev.* Andrew Lambert

Sources D. Syrett and R. L. DiNardo, *The commissioned sea officers of the Royal Navy, 1660–1815*, rev. edn, Occasional Publications of the Navy RS, 1 (1994) · *The Times* (9 March 1872) · O'Byrne, *Naval biog. dict.* · private information (1897) · *Memorandum of services of Sir James Scott* (1866) · E. Holt, *The opium wars in China* (1964) · J. Gray, *Rebellions and revolutions: China from the 1800s to the 1890s* (1990) · G. S. Graham, *The China station: war and diplomacy, 1830–1860* (1978) · Boase, *Mod. Eng. biog.* · *CGPLA Eng. & Wales* (1872) · *IGI*
Archives NMM, logbooks and papers
Wealth at death under £800: administration with will, 13 May 1872, *CGPLA Eng. & Wales*

Scott, Sir James George (1851–1935), administrator in Burma and author, was born at Dairsie, Fife, on 25 December 1851, the younger son of George Scott (*d.* 1861), minister of Dairsie, and his wife, Mary, daughter of Robert *Forsyth, writer and advocate. In 1864 George and his elder brother Robert Forsyth Scott, later master of St John's College, Cambridge, were taken by their widowed mother to school at Stuttgart for three years. Scott showed promise at King's College School, London, and at Edinburgh University, but, having narrowly missed a scholarship, left Lincoln College, Oxford, without taking a degree, owing to lack of means.

In 1875–6 Scott, as special correspondent of *The Standard*, accompanied an expedition sent to Perak, Malaya, to investigate the murder of the British resident, J. W. W. Birch, and to quell subsequent disturbances. From Malaya he went on to Lower Burma and taught at St John's College, an Anglican mission school, becoming headmaster in 1879. A keen sportsman, he played rugby for the Harlequins and London Scottish, and was responsible for introducing association football to Burma. In 1881 he returned home and read for the bar, but missed, by one place, the law scholarship at the Inner Temple which might have enabled him to practise. The publication of his first book, *The Burman: his Life and Notions* (2 vols., 1882), gave him an immediate reputation; it was widely recognized as a classic account of Burmese life and culture. In 1884 he returned to the East as war correspondent of *The Standard*, reporting on the French campaigns of 1884–5 in Annam (Vietnam): this resulted in his second book, *France and*

Tongking: a Narrative of the Campaign of 1884, and the Occupation of Further India (1885). Between campaigns he travelled to China and Hong Kong.

Invalided home, Scott was at the Inner Temple (by which he was eventually called to the bar in 1896) when the British annexation of Upper Burma on 1 January 1886 gave him his supreme chance. The senior cadre in Burma, hitherto drawn from the Indian Civil Service, had to be expanded at short notice and he was appointed in April 1886 to the newly formed Burma commission. After probationary postings in Mandalay, Meiktila, and Hlaingdet, he became in December 1886 assistant commissioner to the Shan States, where he was to spend his entire Burma career, quickly establishing himself as an authority on Shan affairs and language. An incessant writer and keen photographer, his output included articles, novels, and books on Burma, of which his massive compendium *Gazetteer of Upper Burma and the Shan States* (5 vols., 1900–01; repr. 1983) is still of value.

The three dozen Shan States, covering over 40,000 square miles, were then largely unexplored and undeveloped. Their hereditary chiefs (*sawbwa*) were engaged in intermittent warfare, some resenting the overthrow of their suzerain the king of Burma, others appealing to the British for help and protection. From 1886 to 1890 half a dozen civil and military officers escorted by small parties of troops mounted a series of expeditions through difficult territory to gain the hill tribes' recognition of British rule and to reassure the Shan chiefs that there would be no interference in their internal affairs provided peace was maintained, trade was unrestricted, and the administration was just and efficient. The peaceful success of this project was largely due to Scott. He had an iron physique, great energy, and a quick temper, but he also had a warm heart, and was a good commander who seldom failed to win people over. His diaries reveal him as a lively and humorous observer of the Burma scene, to whom marches of 25 miles, settling local disputes, writing innumerable official reports, and battling with malaria were all routine events.

Scott was appointed assistant superintendent, Shan States, in December 1888, and was concurrently deputed to serve on the Anglo-Siamese boundary commission of 1889–90 led by Ney Elias, and during this period explored the trans-Salween Karenni territory and secured the allegiance of the important eastern Shan state, Kengtung. In July 1892 his substantive appointment of 1891 as superintendent for the northern Shan States, with headquarters at Lashio, was confirmed. He served from late 1893 to 1894 as British chargé d'affaires at Bangkok, and as British commissioner on the Mekong (Anglo-French buffer state) commission of 1894–5, and on the Burma–China boundary commission of 1898–1900. Scott was appointed deputy commissioner, political department, in 1900, and in November of that year went to Peking (Beijing) for fifteen months to study Chinese. After travelling home on leave via Japan and America, he returned to Burma in 1902 to become superintendent and political officer of the southern Shan States, with headquarters at Taunggyi. He was appointed CIE in 1892 and KCIE in 1901. He retired in March 1910, and settled in London. He received a police medal for voluntary service as a special constable during the First World War, and revisited Burma in 1919.

Scott was married three times: first in 1890 to Elizabeth Dora (*d.* 1896), daughter of James Campbell Connolly, chaplain of Woolwich Dockyard; second on 23 November 1905 to Eleanor Sarah, only child of John William McCarthy, county court judge, with whom he had a daughter, Eleanor Mary Padômma (*b.* 1906), the marriage being dissolved in 1918; and third in 1920 to the author Geraldine Edith (*d.* 1955), fifth child of the Revd Henry Arthur Mitton, master of Sherburn House, Durham, who became his literary collaborator and biographer. His last years were spent at Thereaway, Graffham, near Petworth, Sussex, where he died on 4 April 1935.

Patricia M. Herbert

Sources G. E. Mitton, *Scott of the Shan hills: orders and impressions* (1936) • S. Saimong Mangrai, *The Shan States and the British annexation* (1965) • J. Falconer, introduction, in Shway Yoe [J. G. Scott], *The Burman: his life and notions* (1989) • *History of Services of Gazetted and Other Officers in Burma* (1909) • BL OIOC • *CGPLA Eng. & Wales* (1935) • A. Dalby, 'J. G. Scott (1851–1935): explorer of Burma's frontier', *Explorers of south-east Asia: six lives*, ed. V. T. King (1995)

Archives BL OIOC, articles, corresp., diaries, papers, press cutting albums, and other manuscripts, MS Eur. F 278 • CUL, corresp. and papers • Duke U., Perkins L., corresp. and papers • SOAS, letter-book | Mitchell L., NSW, letters to G. E. Morrison

Likenesses Lomer, portrait, 1892, repro. in Mitton, *Scott of the Shan hills*; formerly in possession of Lady Scott • photographs, BL OIOC; repro. in Mitton, *Scott of the Shan hills*

Wealth at death £1401 12*s.* 2*d.*: probate, 7 May 1935, *CGPLA Eng. & Wales*

Scott, James Robert Hope- (1812–1873), barrister, born on 15 July 1812 at Marlow, Buckinghamshire, was the third son of General Sir Alexander *Hope (1769–1837) of Rankeillour and Luffness, and grandson of John Hope, second earl of Hopetoun. His mother was Georgina Alicia (*d.* 1855), third and youngest daughter of George Brown of Ellerton, Roxburghshire. Hope's childhood, from 1813 to 1820, was spent at the Royal Military College, Sandhurst, of which his father was the founder and first governor. James Hope (as he then was) then joined his parents and a tutor, William Mills, of Magdalen College, Oxford, on a continental tour which took in Dresden, Lausanne, and Florence. After a year at Kepier grammar school, Houghton-le-Spring, under the Revd William Rawes (1823–4), he entered Eton College at Michaelmas 1825. There he was a pupil of the Revd Edward Coleridge. He left Eton in December 1828 and spent much of the following year in Paris as the guest of the duchesse de Gontaut, governess to the French royal family. He went into residence at Christ Church, Oxford, at Michaelmas 1829 and graduated BA in November 1832 with an honorary fourth class in classics. On 13 April 1833 he was elected a fellow of Merton College, and early in 1835 began legal studies at Lincoln's Inn under the eminent conveyancer John Hodgkin (1800–1875), a Quaker, and William Plunkett, conveyancer of the Temple.

A new era in Hope's life began in 1836 with the beginning of an intense friendship with W. E. *Gladstone, his slightly older contemporary at Eton and Christ Church, and with the lawyer Edward Badeley (1803–1868). He was now one of a group of devout young laymen practising a strict rule of life and dedicated to philanthropic activity on behalf of organizations such as the Society for the Propagation of the Gospel, the Society for Promoting Christian Knowledge, and the Children's Friend Society for Emigration. As fellow and bursar of Merton College he developed an interest in its early history, and in 1838 produced a report urging a return to the ideals of its founder as expressed in its statutes. His ideas on the religious reformation of the university in the spirit of Walter de Merton and William Waynflete were expanded in an article on the Magdalen College statutes which he wrote for the *British Critic* in 1840, at the request of J. H. Newman. His long friendship with Newman began in 1838.

Hope held Gladstone in thrall by the fascination of his personality, and exercised a strong influence on Gladstone's mind and actions over a period of fifteen years (1836–51). It was he who saw Gladstone's work on church-state relations through to publication in 1838. Between 1840 and 1843 he was closely involved with Gladstone and H. E. Manning in plans for the foundation at Glenalmond, Perthshire, of a college for the education of the Scottish Episcopalian clergy. On an Italian tour with Badeley, from September 1840 to May 1841, he made a close study of ecclesiastical education and developed an admiration of the Society of Jesus. He had designed Trinity College, Glenalmond, which opened in 1847, to be a seminary, but in the event it came to function primarily as a public school.

On 24 January 1838 Hope graduated BCL at Oxford, and two days later was called to the bar at the Inner Temple. In 1840 he was junior counsel on behalf of the deans and chapters petitioning against the Ecclesiastical Duties and Revenues Bill, and when on 24 July the bill came before the Lords on second reading he made his reputation by a masterly speech of three hours' duration before a full house. Gladstone later recalled it as the most impressive display of oratory he had heard in his lifetime. In August 1840 Hope was appointed chancellor of the diocese of Salisbury. It might have been expected that he would make his career as an ecclesiastical lawyer, but instead he chose the more neutral ground of the parliamentary bar, specializing in railway legislation. He rapidly built up an immensely lucrative practice, in due course becoming standing counsel to almost every railway company in the United Kingdom, and his representations to parliamentary committees largely helped to establish railway law. In one year alone he saw twenty-five bills through parliament for the London and North-Western Company. He achieved a notable triumph in 1857 as counsel for the corporation of Liverpool in their opposition to the Mersey Docks and Conservancy Bill. Here he indulged in an uncharacteristically florid encomium of Liverpool, enquiring whether it was to become 'forsooth, the Piraeus of such an Athens as Manchester' (*Memoirs*, 2.115). His manner in committee was normally imperturbable and brisk.

In the early 1840s Hope was closely identified with the Tractarian movement and became J. H. Newman's confidant. The establishment of the Anglo-Prussian see of Jerusalem in the winter of 1841 prompted him to publish a vigorous protest. On 10 February 1845 he resigned the chancellorship of Salisbury, but the process of his separation from the Church of England was long drawn out. The Gorham trial and judgment of 1849–50 and Newman's lectures on the difficulties of Anglicans in 1850 brought his religious crisis to a head. He was received into the Roman Catholic church at Farm Street, west London, along with his friend H. E. Manning, on 6 April 1851. His conversion was a grievous blow to Gladstone, who owned to feeling 'unmanned and unnerved' (Gladstone, *Diaries*, 4.325). Hope was dropped as Gladstone's executor, and the friendship never recovered its former intimacy.

On 19 August 1847 Hope married Charlotte Harriet Jane Lockhart (*d.* 1858), only daughter of John Gibson *Lockhart (1794–1854) and his wife, Sophia Scott (1799–1837), and granddaughter of Sir Walter Scott. She became a Catholic soon after his own conversion. In August 1848 he became the tenant of Abbotsford, which he rented from his wife's brother, Walter Lockhart Scott. At the latter's death on 10 January 1853 he became, by right of his wife, the owner of Abbotsford, and thereupon assumed the surname of Hope-Scott. He made substantial alterations to the house. In 1855 he purchased the estate of Dorlin, near Loch Shiel, in an area of the west highlands largely populated by Catholics, and built a house there. In all, he spent some £40,000 during the last thirteen years of his life on the building of Catholic churches and schools in Scotland.

Charlotte Hope-Scott died in childbed on 26 October 1858, and their new-born child on 3 December; Walter Michael, the infant son and heir (born on 2 June 1857), died eight days later. On 7 January 1861 Hope-Scott married again, his second wife being Lady Victoria Alexandrina (*d.* 1870), eldest daughter of Henry Granville Fitzalan-*Howard, fourteenth duke of Norfolk (1815–1860). The duke had died on 25 November 1860, leaving Hope-Scott guardian of his heir, who was still a minor. He and his friend Serjeant Edward Bellasis (1800–1873) were also joint trustees of Lord Edmund Howard, to whom the Alton Towers estates had been devised by Bertram Arthur Talbot, seventeenth earl of Shrewsbury. After much litigation, a considerable portion of the property was secured to Lord Edmund.

On 22 August 1867 Queen Victoria visited Abbotsford. In the same year Hope-Scott bought the Villa Madona at Hyères, in the south of France, where much of his later life was passed. In 1867 he wrote the magisterial statement which contributed to the repeal of the Ecclesiastical Titles Act. His second wife died in childbed on 20 December 1870, nine days after giving birth to a son, James Fitzalan: from this second blow Hope-Scott never recovered. He withdrew from his legal practice and his health declined. In his final years he occupied himself with an abridgement of Lockhart's *Life of Sir Walter Scott*, published in 1871 with a preface addressed to Gladstone. He died at his London home, 7 Hyde Park Place, on 29 April 1873.

Newman preached at the requiem at Farm Street on 5 May and the interment took place at St Margaret's Convent, Edinburgh, on 7 May.

Hope-Scott's only surviving child from his first marriage, Mary Monica (*b.* 1852), married in 1874 Joseph Constable Maxwell, third son of William, Lord Herries, who assumed the name of Scott in right of his wife as heir of Abbotsford. From his second marriage Hope-Scott left a son, James Fitzalan *Hope, later created Baron Rankeillour (1870–1949), and three daughters.

Strikingly handsome in appearance, fastidious and reserved in manner, decisive in the conduct of his profession, and possessed of a strong sense of duty, Hope-Scott was a man who preferred to exercise influence rather than power, and seemed detached from worldly success. It is a paradox that the disciple of Walter de Merton and Walter Scott should have made his fortune as the leading advocate of the railway age. Something of the spell which he cast in his youth can be felt in the posthumous tributes of his closest friends, Gladstone and Newman (*Memoirs*, 2.252–65, 2.273–87). G. MARTIN MURPHY

Sources *Memoirs of James Robert Hope-Scott, with selections from his correspondence*, ed. R. Ormsby, 2 vols. (1884) • Gillow, *Lit. biog. hist.* • *The letters and diaries of John Henry Newman*, ed. C. S. Dessain and others, [31 vols.] (1961–), vols. 6–26 • Gladstone, *Diaries* • H. C. G. Matthew, *Gladstone, 1809–1874* (1986) • *The Scotsman* (8 May 1873) • *Edinburgh Courant* (8 May 1873) • *The Tablet* (10 May 1873) • *Law Times* (10 May 1873) • *The Month*, 19 (1873), 274–91 • E. Bellasis, *Memorials of Mr Serjeant Bellasis* (1893) • H. Tristram, *Newman and his friends* (1933), 104–8 • *CGPLA Eng. & Wales* (1873) • G. H. Martin and J. R. L. Highfield, *A history of Merton College, Oxford* (1997), 280

Archives NL Scot., corresp., diaries, and other papers | Arundel Castle, West Sussex, corresp. with Newman and others • Birmingham Oratory, letters to J. H. Newman • BL, corresp. with W. E. Gladstone, Add. MS 44214 • Bodl. Oxf., letters to H. E. Manning • LPL, corresp. with bishop of St Andrews

Likenesses G. Richmond, watercolour drawing, 1842, Abbotsford House, Borders region, Scotland • G. Richmond, crayon, 1847, Scot. NPG • G. Richmond, oils, 1850, Abbotsford House, Borders region, Scotland • M. Noble, marble bust, 1873, Abbotsford House, Borders region, Scotland • G. Richmond, chalk drawing, Abbotsford House, Borders region, Scotland

Wealth at death under £20: probate, 1873, *CGPLA Eng. & Wales*

Scott, Sir James Sibbald David, third baronet (1814–1885), antiquary and army officer, born at Egham on 14 June 1814, was the eldest son of Sir David Scott, baronet (1782–1851), of Egham, nephew and successor of Sir James Sibbald of the East India Company's service, who was created a baronet in 1806. The mother of James Scott was Caroline (*d.* 25 Jan 1870), daughter of Benjamin Grindall, a descendant of Elizabeth I's archbishop.

Scott was educated at Christ Church, Oxford (matriculated December 1832, BA 1835), was a captain in the Royal Sussex militia artillery from 21 April 1846 to 22 January 1856, succeeded to the baronetcy in 1851, and was JP and deputy lieutenant for Sussex and Middlesex. He was a fellow of the Society of Antiquaries, and an active member of the Royal Archaeological Institute, to whose journal he contributed.

Sir James's chief work was *The British Army: its Origin, Progress, and Equipment* (2 vols., 1868; 3rd vol., 1880); it was copiously illustrated. In the summer of 1874 he visited Jamaica, and later published *To Jamaica and Back* (1876), which described Jamaica's military and naval history, and the 1865 disturbances.

Sir James's wife, whom he married on 28 November 1844, was Harriet Anne *Scott, *née* Shank (1819–1894), novelist. They had three sons and four daughters. He died on 28 June 1885 at Ayres Villa, Church Road, Upper Norwood, Surrey. E. M. LLOYD, *rev.* JAMES FALKNER

Sources *The Times* (30 June 1885) • Burke, *Peerage* • Militia lists • Foster, *Alum. Oxon.* • Boase, *Mod. Eng. biog.* • Kelly, *Handbk*

Wealth at death £2938 4*s.* 11*d.*: probate, 1 Aug 1885, *CGPLA Eng. & Wales*

Scott [*married name* Middleton], **Jane Margaret** (*bap.* **1779**, *d.* **1839**), theatre manager and actress, one of at least four children of John Scott (1752–1838) and his wife, Elizabeth (1750–1829), was baptized at St Martin-in-the-Fields, Westminster, on 6 June 1779. Her father was a prosperous London 'watercolour preparer' who also sold optical instruments at 417 Strand. She was educated in music, and began her working life giving singing lessons. In 1804 John Scott converted a warehouse behind his shop for the performances of her and her pupils, and then demolished twelve properties in an adjoining alley, Bailey's Court, to erect the Sans Pareil Theatre (which later became the Adelphi). Here Jane Scott, like Charles Dibdin at his Sans Souci Theatre, offered a solo entertainment, singing her own compositions to her own piano accompaniment, varied with her father's light shows. They soon gathered a theatrical company; in 1806 the theatre was licensed for entertainments, in 1807 for pantomime, and by 1809 for burletta.

Jane Scott's artistic ambition met the challenge of modern entertainment. She encouraged performers who went on to substantial careers, such as Caroline Giroux (Mrs Serle), George Davidge, and Richard Flexmore, and with her core company she participated in the development of new kinds of theatre. Almost the only personal information we have from a contemporary is that she was generous towards the work of others. She was artistic director, she performed leading roles, and she wrote prolifically: the bills often boasted that the whole evening's entertainment was written by her. In 1809 came her first burletta, *Mary the Maid of the Inn*, and in December 1810 a melodrama, *Disappointments*; in 1811 she produced her first farce, *The Animated Effigy*, and a comic operetta, *The Lowland Romp*. Between 1806 and 1819 she wrote more than fifty stage pieces, comic and serious, spectacular and simple. These included translations from the French (*The Conjuror*, 1815) and French-style vaudeville (*The Dinner of Madelon*, 1816), but also English farces (*Whackham and Windham*, 1814), adaptations from the fiction of Maria Edgeworth and Walter Scott (*The Row of Ballynavogue*, 1817; *The Fire Goblin*, 1819), history plays (*The Forest Knight*, 1813), fairy plays (*Fairy Legends*, 1818), topical plays (*The Fortunate Youth* 1818), and Gothic melodramas—one with a subplot for the dancer Giroux (*Asgard the Demon Hunter*, 1812), another with a leading role for herself (*Camilla the Amazon*,

1817)—and at least one pantomime each year, accommodating the skills of rope-walking monkeys and juvenile clog dancers. She wrote one melodrama, *The Old Oak Chest* (1816), that was printed and widely staged beyond her own theatre. This play, a story of oppressive rulers and heroic pirates, was popular in the illegal cheap theatres that sprang up to challenge the beleaguered theatres royal.

The Sans Pareil was itself politically significant: it was sanctioned by the lord chamberlain, Lord Dartmouth, and challenged the long-standing duopoly of the stage in London with new providers of entertainment. Jane Scott and her father, coming from outside the established theatrical networks, thus became participants in the battle for a 'free' stage. Jane Scott's theatre is also embedded in the artistic developments of her time, mediating Gothic and Romantic sensibility to pleasure-seekers in the nascent West End. She had her finger on the pulse of a new world of entertainment for all, and her management of the theatre she created is important for its responsive and intelligent reading of the new audiences and the provision of exciting work for them to enjoy.

It is indicative of her practical, self-sufficient relationship to her work that Jane Scott never appeared elsewhere than in her own theatre, and when she retired in April 1819 (her father having sold the theatre at a handsome profit) she never appeared again, nor published any of her writing. On 11 April 1822 she married a half-pay naval officer, John Davies Middleton (1790–1867), and by the terms of her settlement was able to retire on a comfortable personal income to her own house, Mole House, Hersham, Walton-on-Thames, Surrey. Her father went on to buy the Olympic Theatre and thus to invest, from 1830, in the managerial talents of another woman, Madame Vestris. When he died in 1838 he left the Olympic (and an inn in Hersham) to his daughter. Jane Scott had no children. She died of breast cancer on 6 December 1839 in Walton-on-Thames and was buried in the family vault in the parish church of St Mary with St John. Her legacy of a model of theatre work radically different from the pompous vacuities of the 'legitimate' stage was long either vilified or ignored by critics and historians, and only began to be recognized at the end of the twentieth century.

JACKY BRATTON

Sources A. L. Nelson and G. B. Cross, eds., *The Adelphi Theatre calendar, part I: The Sans Pareil Theatre, 1806–19, The Adelphi Theatre, 1819–50* (1988) [31 microfiches; Nottingham, Hallward Library, PN2596. L6.A3] • E. Fitzball, *Thirty-five years of a dramatic author's life*, 2 vols. (1859) • Theatre Museum, London, Adelphi records • O'Byrne, *Naval biog. dict.* • *IGI* • Westminster rate books • d. cert.

Scott, Jean [Janet], **Lady Ferniehirst** (*b.* *c.*1548, *d.* after 1593), landowner, was the eldest of the three daughters of Sir William Scott the younger of Buccleuch (1520–1552) and his wife, Grisel (*d.* after 1552), second daughter of John Betoun of Creich. Jean's grandfather had married as his second wife Janet, daughter of Andrew Kerr of Ferniehirst, but in spite of this close connection a violent feud erupted between the Scotts and the Kerrs, near neighbours on the border with England, and in 1552 the situation worsened still further when Jean's father was killed in a skirmish by the Kerrs. In 1565 both families decided on a reconciliation, and a complicated agreement was drawn up, involving various marriages between Scotts and Kerrs. Sir Thomas Kerr, now laird of Ferniehirst, was the only leading member of his family to refuse to take part in the pacification. Ironically, not one of the arranged marriages took place, but when Sir Thomas's first wife, Janet Kirkcaldy, died, leaving him with five small children, he married Jean Scott, daughter of the murdered Sir William. Their wedding in 1569 finally ended the feud, and Jean and Sir Thomas settled down happily together, although when her brother Sir Walter Scott died in 1574, £1000 of her dowry was still unpaid. From the time of her marriage she was known as Lady Ferniehirst as the laird's wife.

Sir Thomas Kerr was a man of integrity, but his principles resulted in great disruption to their family life. Long active in support of Mary, queen of Scots, he sheltered leaders of the English northern rising at his castle of Ferniehirst, near Jedburgh, in 1569, and as a result an invading English force demolished the building the following spring. He was forced to go into exile on the continent in 1573 after helping his former father-in-law, Sir William Kirkcaldy of Grange, in an ultimately unsuccessful attempt to hold Edinburgh Castle for Mary, and although he was allowed to return in 1581, he was back in France again in 1583. During the early 1580s Jean was a regular correspondent of Mary, queen of Scots, and in her role as an intermediary between James VI and his mother, did much to keep the exiled queen's cause alive in Scotland. She also ran her husband's estates for him, and on 15 January 1583 he granted her power of attorney to deal with his debts in both France and Scotland.

Jean's activities on her husband's behalf can be glimpsed in a letter she wrote to him from Falkland Palace on 1 September 1583 telling him that she had spent the past month at court trying to persuade James VI to allow him to return. Thanks to the support of the earl of Huntly, her efforts had finally been successful. Sir Thomas could now come back whenever he pleased, she said, and she signed herself in the conventional style of the time, 'Your humble and faythfull bedfallou till deith, Jene Scot' (NA Scot., GD 40, Lothian MSS, portfolio IX). Sir Thomas was restored to public life, but after an incident on the border in 1585, when the English warden's son-in-law Francis, Lord Russell, was killed, he was held partly responsible. He was imprisoned in Aberdeen Castle, where he died the following March, leaving Jean with three sons and a daughter. One of her sons was Robert *Carr, James I's favourite, who became earl of Somerset.

It is not known when Jean Scott died. She is last recorded in 1593, in the only surviving portrait of her, by an unknown artist, which shows her still in deepest mourning, gazing sorrowfully at the viewer. Her hair is concealed by a veil with a widow's peak, she has heavy ropes of pearls round her neck, and her spousing ring can clearly be seen on her right hand, which rests on a book. Above her head is the inscription 'Ubi amor, ibi fides' ('where there is love there is faith'). Like many women of her time, she had supported her husband in both public and private life, finding genuine love and contentment in her arranged marriage. ROSALIND K. MARSHALL

Sources W. Fraser, *The Scotts of Buccleuch*, 1 (1878) • letters of Jean Scott, NA Scot., Lothian MSS, GD 40, portfolio IX • R. K. Marshall, *Virgins and viragos: a history of women in Scotland, 1080–1980* (1983) • R. Grant, 'Politicking Jacobean women: Lady Ferniehirst, the countess of Arran and the countess of Huntly, c.1580–1603', *Women in Scotland, c.1100–c.1750*, ed. E. Ewan and M. M. Meikle (1999), 95–104, esp. 97 • *Scots peerage*, 2.230–31; 5.62–70

Likenesses oils, 1593, priv. coll.; repro. in Marshall, *Virgins and viragos*, facing p. 160

Scott, John. *See* Skot, John (*fl.* 1521–1537); Scot, Sir John, of Scotstarvit, Lord Scotstarvit (1585–1670); Waring, John Scott- (1747–1819).

Scott, Sir John (1423–1485). *See under* Scott family (*per.* c.1400–c.1525).

Scott, Sir John (*b.* in or before **1484**, *d.* **1533**), soldier, was the eldest son of Sir William *Scott (1459–1524) [*see under* Scott family (*per.* c.1400–c.1525)] of Scot's Hall, Smeeth, Kent, and Sybil (*d.* 1529), daughter of Sir Thomas Lewknor of Trotton, Sussex. Claiming descent from John Balliol, the Scott family was well established by the mid-fourteenth century, and by the reign of Henry VII was among the leading families of Kent. John Scott's immediate relatives included Thomas *Rotherham, archbishop of York, and Sir Edward *Poynings. It was under Poynings that he travelled to the Netherlands in July 1511 as part of a 1500-strong expeditionary force sent by Henry VIII to aid Margaret, regent of the Low Countries, against Charles, duke of Gueldres. The small army served with distinction, and as one of the senior captains Scott was knighted by the young Archduke Charles before his return to England in November. Henry VIII transmuted the honour into a knighthood of the body. Although it is unclear whether he took part in the campaigns against France launched in 1512 and 1513, he was certainly part of the force being gathered at Calais in 1514 when Anglo-French peace talks halted the war. He accompanied Henry to the Field of Cloth of Gold in June 1520 and took part in the duke of Suffolk's invasion of northern France in 1523.

At home Scott was active in local government. Chosen as MP for New Romney in 1512, it is probable that he was returned to parliament on several other occasions. He was appointed a commissioner of the subsidy for Sussex in 1514 and 1515 and for Kent in 1523 and 1524, the same county in which he served as sheriff in 1527 and 1528, and finally as a JP from 1531 until his death on 7 October 1533. He had married by 1507 Anne, daughter of Reginald Pympe of Nettlestead near Maidstone, with whom he at least five sons and six daughters. LUKE MACMAHON

Sources *LP Henry VIII* • HoP, *Commons, 1509–58*, 3.282–3 • J. R. Scott, *Memorials of the family of Scott of Scot's Hall in the county of Kent* (1876) • J. G. Nichols, ed., *The chronicle of Calais*, CS, 35 (1846) • *Hall's chronicle*, ed. H. Ellis (1809)

Scott, John (*fl.* **1539–1571**), printer, not to be confused with the London printer John *Skot, is first heard of in Edinburgh in June 1539, when he had the grant of two rooms with basement cellars in a house north of Edinburgh's Cowgate, adjacent to Borthwick's Close. He is there described as 'calligrapher' or 'impressor' (NA Scot., B22/1/11, fols. 105, 123*v*). However, he did not tarry there long, as on 19 December of that year he renounced this grant with the consent of his wife, Margaret Leis. This probably preceded his removal elsewhere, although he is not heard of again until 5 April 1547, this time in Dundee: for reasons unspecified, the privy council warned the constable of Dundee, then also its provost, to arrest Scott and present him before them in Edinburgh Castle. The explanation is probably that Scott was printing forbidden books and a parliamentary censorship statute of 1551 may have been in part prompted by his activities as he seems to have been the only printer active in Scotland at that time.

Scott next appears in St Andrews where in 1552 he printed the so-called *Catechisme* of Archbishop Hamilton, actually the work of the Catholic refugee and former Dominican prior at Newcastle Richard Marshall. The following year parliament proposed to publish its acts but, if Scott was commissioned to print them, no copy survives. Scott's next dated book was Patrick Cockburn's *In Dominicam orationem pia meditatio* (1555) followed by William Lauder's *Ane Compendious and Breve Tractate Concerning the Office of Kynges* (1556), a versified work. A defence of Catholic general councils, *Ane Compendius Tractive* by Quintin Kennedy, abbot of Crossraguell, followed in 1558. Probably between about 1554 and 1559, Scott produced a number of undated works. These included some works by David Lindsay of the Mount in which Scott alleged that the editions of Lindsay by 'Samuel Jascuy' were unreliable and had not been produced in Paris as their imprint claimed but in Rouen or London. From his own first edition of Lindsay, Scott made it clear that he produced the work at the expense of Johannes Machabeus (that is, the former Dominican prior of Perth, John Macalpine) of Copenhagen; Lindsay's works were reprinted several times again by Scott, the last time in 1571 at the expense of Henry Charteris. Probably in 1559, Scott printed *Ane Godlie Exhortation* on the eucharist, but this is now the sole survivor of other prints by him on baptism, extreme unction, and matrimony.

The confession of faith, professit and belevit, be the protestantes within the realme of Scotland (1561) followed, probably printed in Edinburgh, to where Scott had returned about this time. In 1562 there followed from his press two works by Ninian Winzet, a Catholic priest born in Renfrew, *Certane Tractatis* and *The Last Blast of the Trompet*. These were brought to the notice of the burgh authorities, apparently by Thomas Alexander who as bookseller ('mercator librorum') had recently been made burgess of the city (Borg Watson, 27): Scott's premises were raided by the city magistrates and the printer was imprisoned. With Scott confined to prison, the following year Alexander applied for but did not get Scott's printing materials. These were instead put into the keeping of the printer Thomas Bassandyne in March the following year, at whose order and expense *Ane Compendeus Buke of Godlye Psalms and Spirituall Songis* (1565) was printed, an edition of the work by the brothers Wedderburn better known as *The Gude and*

Godlie Ballatis. This work, the only surviving copy of which was recently discovered in Göttingen, was printed in Scott's types if not by Scott personally. Either way, Scott was out of custody by 1568 and was once again printing; the last work from his press, another edition of Lindsay, appeared in 1571. JOHN DURKAN

Sources R. Dickson and J. P. Edmond, *Annals of Scottish printing* (1890) · protocol book of Andrew Brownhill, NA Scot., B22/1/11, fols. 105, 123*v* · *Reg. PCS*, 1st ser., 1.69 · R. Pitcairn, ed., *Ancient criminal trials in Scotland*, 1, Bannatyne Club, 42 (1833), 161 · D. McRoberts, ed., *Essays on the Scottish Reformation, 1513–1625* (1962) · *STC, 1475–1640* · C. B. B. Watson, ed., *Roll of Edinburgh burgesses and guild-brethren, 1406–1700*, Scottish RS, 59 (1929), 27 · D. Patrick, ed., *Statutes of the Scottish church, 1225–1559*, Scottish History Society, 54 (1907), 175 · *APS, 1424–1567*, 488 · R. K. Hannay, ed., *Acts of the lords of council in public affairs, 1501–1554* (1932), 528 · A. J. Mann, *The Scottish book trade, 1500–1720* (2000)

Scott, Sir John (*d.* 1616). *See under* Scott, Sir Thomas (1534x6–1594).

Scott, John (1632?–1704), adventurer and spy, may have been born at Ashford, Kent, in 1632, the son of a royalist colonel, John Scott, but his origins and early life are uncertain. According to his own later account, having committed some misdemeanours against parliamentary soldiers Scott was transported to the Americas in 1643 under the care of Emmanuel Downing, father of Sir George Downing, first baronet. On his arrival Scott was bound out to Lawrence Southwick of Massachusetts and received a good education in the latter's home. Unfortunately his resentful temperament led him into several clashes with the law. In 1652 he went to sea, and he was later alleged to have spent some time in Tortuga among the buccaneers, also acquiring knowledge of Native American languages. Scott held various occupations in his early life: sailor, blacksmith, herdsman, trader, and attorney. In 1654 he went to Long Island, where he traded in land, furs, and goods. By 1657 he was a freeman and tax commissioner in Southampton, Long Island, and had purchased land and a house. He was, however, often in trouble, causing dissension among the colonists and frequently ending up in gaol. One contemporary noted that he was 'born to work mischief' (*CSP col.*, 337). In 1658 Scott married Deborah Raynor; the couple had two sons, John and Jeckomiah. Scott deserted, and then was divorced from, his wife about 1671, when he began a relationship with Deborah van Egmont. His first wife married again after the divorce but the pair may well have renewed their liaison in later life.

In 1660 Scott appeared in England as the representative of some respectable New Englanders who were petitioning the king over a land purchase. Thomas Chiffinch, page of the bedchamber and keeper of the king's closet, introduced him to Joseph Williamson, under-secretary of state, who took a keen interest in colonial matters and cartography, in which Scott claimed to be an expert. The two men subsequently struck up a friendly rapport. Scott returned to the Americas in 1663, but not before he had apparently perpetrated a confidence trick on a Quaker couple, Daniel and Dorothea *Gotherson. They gave him £2000 to invest in the colonies, as well as custody of their son, whom Scott was alleged to have afterwards sold to a New Haven innkeeper. Scott claimed to be a royal official, but mounting accusations by colonial authorities of dishonest land transactions, theft, and fomenting sedition forced him to leave for the West Indies in 1665; there he took a commission in Sir Thomas Bridge's regiment and saw action against the Dutch in Tobago in 1665–6. He was also involved in the expedition against St Kitts, where he was generally less successful and, it was said, had been thought a 'notorious coward' (Bodl. Oxf., MS Rawl. A 175, fol. 149*v*). Some evidence points to a court martial at Nevis in 1668 but Scott soon left for England where, in spite of his faults, Joseph Williamson took him up once more and introduced him to the earl of Arlington. The result of this patronage was a title, royal geographer, in August 1668. Thereafter he often styled himself 'Shield bearer and geographer to the King of Great Britaine' (Bodl. Oxf., MS Rawl. A 175, fol. 1). About this time he wrote a number of manuscript tracts describing the West Indies.

Scott, however, soon lost Williamson's friendship owing to a theft committed in the under-secretary's lodgings, and was imprisoned in the Gatehouse prison for debt. By 1669 he had disappeared from the London scene only to re-emerge in the Low Countries. His claim to have fled England after killing a page of the duke of York may possibly have been intended to cover his new role as a spy for the Stuart regime, but he had already made one notorious attack on the earl of Anglesey, whom he beat with a cudgel in the street. In the Netherlands Scott joined the Dutch army to recruit and train troops and apparently won over John de Witt with tales of his military prowess. Nevertheless, Scott's main business was espionage, and he was subsequently employed by the intelligence systems of three states, England, the United Provinces, and France. He made frequent trips to London and elsewhere and was involved in various scandals over money and recruits in this period. He deserted the Dutch army in March 1672, claiming that he could not serve against his own country in the forthcoming war. In that same month Joseph Williamson engaged Scott to gather covert information within Dutch territory. One Morainville's papers were later seized in London as a result of his activities, but this affair may have been a Dutch counter-intelligence game.

In June 1672 Scott was seen on the fringes of the joint Arlington and Buckingham peace mission to Europe, 'very magnificent in his habit' (Bodl. Oxf., MS Rawl. 188, fol. 262). Scott dined at Buckingham's table and began an association with the duke that he was to develop in later years. When Arlington provided Scott with an allowance to gather intelligence and placed him in Bruges for this purpose, he was chased out of the city. He also managed to betray three British spies to the Dutch. In 1673 Williamson heard that 'several complaints have been made of Coll. Scott in Flanders, [and he] does the king all the ill service his capacity will give him leave' (Christie, 1.85). Throughout this period, Scott, a capable mapmaker, frequently tried to sell charts and maps (some of which were stolen) to various governments. He also perpetrated a series of frauds to gain money and used a plethora of disguises, aliases, and military titles to increase his social standing and protect his real identity.

In the winter of 1673–4 Scott transferred his 'thousand chimerical projects' to Paris (PRO, SP 78/138, fol. 145). There he sought the support of the marquis de Seigneley in casting guns for the French king, but the business floundered in mutual recrimination and Scott soon returned to the espionage trade. During 1677–8 he crossed back and forth over the channel, visiting the entourage of Buckingham and other opposition leaders to Danby. Monsieur de Pélissary, the treasurer-general of the French navy, also engaged Scott to gather naval intelligence. He made several visits to see Buckingham in the Tower in 1677 and Buckingham paid some of his debts. Scott was allied with the Green Ribbon Club, and as the crisis progressed he expressed hopes of entering parliament and planned to marry Lady Frances Vane, flattering and besieging her in the manner befitting a soldier, much to her family's distress. Scott was obscurely linked with the death of Sir Edmund Godfrey in 1678 and was indeed behaving oddly when Godfrey went missing—abruptly leaving London two days before the body was discovered. Scott later claimed that he had fled because he had heard he was to be 'clapped up and starved' (Grey, 7.311). He had been observed travelling the coasts of Sussex and Kent and had stayed with Sir Francis Rolle, an MP who had taken money from the French. Samuel Pepys, who was informed of Scott's flight, made an attempt to stop him at the coast under the belief that Scott was a Jesuit priest. Scott took his revenge by joining Buckingham's associates in an attempt to destroy Pepys. He returned to England and was arrested, but deposed that he had seen charts, plans, and other intelligence from Pepys in the office of Pélissary. Scott also claimed to have discovered evidence that Pepys was a secret Roman Catholic. In the unsympathetic House of Commons of 1679, where any rumours of closet Catholicism were believed, Pepys was soon sent to the Tower where he turned his energies into undermining Scott's reputation by gathering unsavoury information about his opponent's past. Scott's violent temper eventually proved to be his undoing. In a drunken brawl in 1682 he murdered a coachman and was once again forced to flee the country.

An agent of the Stuart regime came across Scott in 1683 in Scandinavia, where Scott claimed he had numerous secrets about the whigs and others, but little came of this and Scott retired to Montserrat in the West Indies and lived there at least until 1694. In the following year he reappeared in Europe and promptly became involved in Jacobite intrigues, possibly as a spy for the regime of William III. He was in England in 1696 in 'pretty good habit and a bob wigg' and flourished a pardon for the murder of the coachman (*Private Correspondence … of Samuel Pepys*, 1.129). This visit reawakened the interest of Pepys in his former enemy's doings. Scott promptly left for the West Indies where he subsequently held various positions in local government. His death in 1704 in Bridgetown, Barbados, where he was subsequently buried, finally put an end to his life of restless wandering. ALAN MARSHALL

Sources *CSP col.*, vol. 5 • Bodl. Oxf., MSS Rawl. A. 175–188 • W. D. Christie, ed., *Letters addressed from London to Sir Joseph Williamson*, 2 vols., CS, new ser., 8–9 (1874) • PRO, SP 78/138 • A. Grey, ed., *Debates of the House of Commons, from the year 1667 to the year 1694*, 10 vols. (1763) • *Private correspondence and miscellaneous papers of Samuel Pepys, 1679–1703*, ed. J. R. Tanner, 2 vols. (1926) • W. C. Abbott, *Colonel John Scott of Long Island, (1634–1696)* (New Haven, 1918) • L. T. Mowrer, *The indomitable John Scott: citizen of Long Island, 1632–1704* (New York, 1960) • D. G. Greene, *Diaries of the Popish Plot* (New York, 1977) • A. Marshall, *Intelligence and espionage in the reign of Charles II, 1660–1685* (1994)

Archives Bodl. Oxf., MSS Rawl. A. 175–188 • PRO, state papers 29 Charles II • PRO, state papers 78 France • PRO, state papers 84 Holland

Scott, John (1638/9–1695), Church of England clergyman, was the son of Thomas Scott, a grazier of Chippenham, Wiltshire. He was apprenticed in London (very unwillingly, according to Anthony Wood), but after three years left his trade and matriculated as a commoner of New Inn Hall, Oxford, aged nineteen, on 13 December 1658. There he showed 'great proficiency in logicals and philosophicals', but left without graduating. He was ordained and rose through 'some mean employment', becoming successively minister of St Thomas's, Southwark, perpetual curate of Holy Trinity Minories, London, and, in 1678, rector of St Peter-le-Poer, London (Wood, *Ath. Oxon.*, 4.414). He was also lecturer of a church in Lombard Street, London. He was collated a prebendary of St Paul's in March 1685, the year that he proceeded BD and DD at Oxford.

According to Wood, Scott 'obtained a great name, and was much resorted to for his most admirable way of preaching' (Wood, *Ath. Oxon.*, 4.414). This reputation no doubt explains the string of sermons which he delivered to prominent City institutions and at the funerals of worthies over the course of the 1680s. Several of these show strong links with City toryism. In September 1680 he preached before the Honourable Artillery Company. However, his sermon, given that it was published at the height of the exclusion crisis, was surprisingly apolitical given its tory audience and focused on the virtue which should underpin the martial life. His sermon before the lord mayor and aldermen on 16 December 1683 took as its text: 'And meddle not with those that are given to change' ('Proverbs', 24: 21); in his epistle dedicatory he felt it both timely and 'an exceeding good Office to all, and particularly to the Dissenters and their Adherents (whose Discontents render them of all men most obnoxious to factious impressions) to warn them … of the manifold Mischiefs of Faction'; his targets were 'the Agitators and Patrons of Faction, whose Business it is, to Seduce the Simple and well meaning from their Duty and Safety' (J. Scott, *Sermon … 16 Dec. 1683*, 1684). In 1685 Scott was selected to deliver an impeccably loyalist sermon before the aldermanic bench on the day of thanksgiving for the defeat of Monmouth's rising, and again preached the duty of submission to lawful powers at the Essex assizes that summer.

By the following year the perceived threat posed to the Church of England by the policies of the Catholic James II was becoming very apparent to Scott. His funeral sermon recalled how in these years Scott stood firm against Romanism, having a 'resolute Adherence to well-chosen Principles' and maintaining 'an unspotted Fidelity to the Church' (*Works*, 2.569). His third published sermon before the lord mayor was delivered on the twentieth anniversary fast day of the great fire: a cry for moral reformation which strongly implied that a wrathful God might be provoked to deliver up a sinful people, 'baptized into the best Church, and educated in the purest Religion in the World' to popery (J. Scott, *A Sermon Preached … September the Second, 1686*, 28–9). In 1688 he published *The texts examined which papists cite out of the Bible to prove the supremacy of St Peter and of the pope over the whole church*. In 1689 Scott took the oaths to the new monarchs, and, Wood reports, 'might have soon after been a bishop, had not some scruples hindered him' (Wood, *Ath. Oxon.*, 4.414–15); perhaps he did not wish to step into the place of a bishop deprived for nonjuring. Nevertheless his basic sympathy for the Church of England of William III and its reforming aspirations is evident. He was chosen to preach the sermon at Fulham on 13 October 1689 at the consecration of Gilbert Ironside, Simon Patrick, and Edward Stillingfleet as, respectively, bishops of Bristol, Chichester, and Worcester. Scott held high expectations of the clergy: in the sermon he affirmed that pastors should be sent and commissioned by God, and instructed in God's mind and will, while their conversation should express the goodness and purity of their own doctrine. He resigned from St Peter-le-Poer in 1691 to be appointed by the king rector of St Giles-in-the-Fields.

Scott's importance lies in his legacy as a devotional writer whose works discussed godly living and prayer. His main work was *The Christian life from its beginning to its consummation in glory: together with the several means and instruments of Christianity conducing thereunto, with directions for private devotion and forms of prayer, fitted to the several states of Christians* (1681; expanded second edition 1683–7, two volumes each published in two parts; 9th edition 1729–30). His primary thesis was that happiness consists in 'a free and intimate Knowledge of God', and also in 'a free and undistracted choice of God' (*Works*, 1.4, 5), and the rest of the work expounded the means to these ends.

Scott's main engagement in controversy with nonconformists was a firm, measured statement of the spiritual case for the Anglican commitment to formal prayer, *Certain cases of conscience resolved, concerning the lawfulness of joyning with forms of prayer in publick worship* (2 parts, 1683–4). Countering nonconformist claims that words in public prayer should be spontaneous, Scott rejected even the desirability of a supposed 'Gift of Prayer', which had been alleged to enable the offering of words that had been divinely inspired. He insisted that it was impossible to distinguish between a supposed gift of prayer and natural, or acquired, fluency of speech, and sternly declared that the:

> seeming devotion that is raised in the minds of the People by the gingling of the Ministers words about their fancies, is generally false and counterfeit, for as words do naturally impress the fancy, so the fancy doth naturally excite the sensitive affections; so that when the affections are excited meerly by the art and musick of the words of Prayer, it is not Devotion but Mechanism. (Scott, *Certain Cases*, pt 1, p. 45)

By contrast Scott taught that the Holy Spirit 'enables us to offer up our Prayers to God with such ardent and devout affections as are in some measure sutable to the matter we pray for' (Scott, *Christian Life*, vol. 2, pt 2, p. 93). Scott wrote of prayer:

> there is no one duty whatsoever to the due performance of which our carnal affections are naturally more listless and averse; and therefore as herein we have most need of the Holy Spirit's assistance, so herein he more especially operates on our minds, exciting in us all those graces and affections which are proper to the several parts of our Prayer. (ibid., 94)

Scott was buried at St Giles-in-the-Fields on 15 March 1695, when his funeral sermon was preached by Zacheus Isham. His will, made on 12 December 1690, appointed his wife, Elizabeth, executor and sole beneficiary; she proved it three days after his funeral. RICHARD J. GINN

Sources *DNB* • Wood, *Ath. Oxon.*, new edn, 4.414–16 • Foster, *Alum. Oxon.* • *The works of the reverend and learned John Scott*, 2 vols. (1718) • J. Scott, *Certain cases of conscience resolved, concerning the lawfulness of joyning with forms of prayer in publick worship*, 2 pts (1683–4) • J. Scott, *The Christian life from its beginning to its consummation in glory*, 3rd edn, 2 vols. in 2 pts (1692) • will, PRO, PROB 11/424, sig. 40

Likenesses M. Vandergucht, line engraving, NPG; repro. in Scott, *Certain cases* • R. White, line engraving, BM, NPG; repro. in J. Scott, *Practical discourses*, 2nd edn (1701)

Scott, John (1730–1783), poet and writer, younger son of Samuel Scott, a linen draper and Quaker preacher, and his wife, Martha Wilkins, was born in Grange Walk, Bermondsey, London, on 9 January 1730. Scott began studying Latin under John Clarke, a local Scottish schoolmaster. To avoid smallpox, Scott's family moved to Amwell, Hertfordshire, about 1740—a move which ended Scott's formal classical education. About 1747 he began studying English poetry, mentored by Charles Frogley, a self-educated bricklayer whose daughter he later married.

From 1753 until 1758 Scott contributed verses to the *Gentleman's Magazine*. Edward Young praised his *Four Elegies Descriptive and Moral* (1760), which also received attention from Elizabeth Carter and Catherine Talbot. These poems explore the tension between a sense of loss and hard-won contentment, recognizing the inevitability of change but urging virtue as an antidote to political and moral decline. During a smallpox outbreak in 1761 Scott moved briefly to St Margaret's, about 2 miles from Amwell, where he met John Hoole, his biographer. After being successfully inoculated by Thomas Dimsdale in 1766 he began visiting London, where Hoole introduced him to Samuel Johnson and where he met James Beattie, William Jones, Lord Lyttelton, and Catharine Macaulay.

Scott's mother died in 1766, his father early in 1768. In 1767 he married Sarah Frogley, his mentor's daughter, who died in childbirth the following June. Following their child's death in August, Scott wrote a touching elegy to his wife (privately printed in 1769), describing the 'last, last parting, ere her spirit fled', but finally accepting affliction as virtue's 'minister of pain'. During this difficult period he supervised road-building between Ware and Hertford. He went on to attack Johnson's *False Alarm* and *Patriot* in anonymous pamphlets (1770 and 1775) defending liberty and the middle ranks of society.

Following his marriage to Maria De Horne on 1 November 1770, Scott moved back to the family house at Amwell, where Johnson visited him in 1773. The same year he published his *Observations on the Present State of the Parochial and Vagrant Poor*, arguing with energy and authority for less severe treatment of the indigent. Private charity should not be forbidden, Scott claims, for it may be 'a needful auxiliary … when [the law] can operate no farther'. He deplores the practices of farming out the operation of workhouses and breaking up families; and he advocates a more general and uniform system of taxation for equitable relief, administration by trustees drawn from a larger unit than the individual parish, available relief where paupers live (rather than only in their native parishes), healthier accommodation, educational resources for young people, and road works—badly needed, as he also emphasizes elsewhere—to employ discharged soldiers. The *Observations* were followed in 1776 by *A Prospect of Ware and the Country Adjacent* and by *Amwell, a Descriptive Poem*, a long poem in blank verse drawing on autobiographical reference and a very particular knowledge of local landscape and history, as well as on the literary tradition of the 'place poem'.

Scott participated in the debate about Thomas Chatterton's Rowley poems, defending Chatterton's genius while deploring his fraud (*GM*, 47, August 1777, 361–5). In 1778 he defended Beattie against the charge of failing to produce a promised sequel to his work on moral truth (*GM*, 48, March 1778, 112). The same year Scott published *A Digest of the Highway and General Turnpike Laws* and his *Moral Eclogues*, which combine classical pastoral conventions with his usual precise sense of natural history and his favourite themes of change, loss, and consolation in retirement. The versatility these works demonstrate characterizes Scott's work: maintaining a house at Ratcliff, he participated in the London-based literary world, the local affairs of Amwell and Hertfordshire, and broader political issues. His sympathies were wide-ranging and active, including occasionally hard-hitting social criticism that extended to government policy abroad as well as at home (as, for example, in one of his 'Oriental Eclogues', 'Serim, or, The artificial famine').

The Poetical Works of John Scott (1782), illustrated by a title-page portrait and other engravings (some by William Blake), was attacked in the *Critical Review* (July 1782) and defended in Scott's 'Letter to the critical reviewers' (1782). Before his *Critical Essays* were published Scott died of fever at Ratcliff, on 12 December 1783, and was buried in the Quaker burial-ground there on 18 December. In spite of their political and critical disagreements, Johnson agreed to write Scott's life. Following Johnson's death, Hoole took on this task, publishing 'An account of the life and writings of John Scott, esq.' in Scott's *Critical Essays on some of the Poems of Several English Poets* (1785). Scott was survived by his wife and his six-year-old daughter, Maria De Horne Scott.

Samuel Scott (1719–1788), John Scott's elder brother, born in Gracechurch Street, London, on 21 May 1719, moved to Amwell with his parents and brother in 1740. Unlike his brother, he had little interest in poetry or politics, believing that 'it becometh not the members of [the Society of Friends] to meddle much in those matters, or to be active in political disquisitions' (*Diary*, 1 Sept 1780). Having studied Quaker devotional writings, he entered the ministry in 1753. On 3 October 1754 he married and moved to Hertford.

Scott's *Diary* was published in 1809. His *Memoir of the Last Illness of John Scott* records the struggle between the active life his brother chose and the introspective spiritual tradition they shared. He died on 20 November 1788.

Anne McWhir

Sources L. D. Stewart, *John Scott of Amwell* (1956) • J. Hoole, 'An account of the life and writings of John Scott, esq.', in J. Scott, *Critical essays* (1785) • J. Scott, 'The life of Scott', *The poetical works of John Scott* (1795) • A. Chalmers, ed., *The general biographical dictionary*, new edn, 32 vols. (1812–17) • G. G. Cunningham, ed., *Lives of eminent and illustrious Englishmen*, 8 vols. (1836–8) • 'Review of the poetical works of John Scott with anecdotes of the author', *European Magazine and London Review*, 2 (1782), 193–7 • A. Chalmers, 'The life of John Scott', *The works of the English poets from Chaucer to Cowper*, ed. A. Chalmers, 17 (1810), 445–52 [incl. memoir of Scott's death, ascribed elsewhere to his brother, Samuel Scott]

Likenesses J. Hall, line engraving (after J. Townsend), BM, NPG; repro. in J. Scott, *The poetical works of John Scott* (1782)

Scott, John, first earl of Clonmell (1739–1798), judge and politician, was born on 8 June 1739, probably in co. Tipperary, the third son of Thomas Scott (*d.* 1763) of Urlings, co. Kilkenny, later of Modeshill and Mohubber, co. Tipperary, and of Rachel Prim (*d.* 1784?), eldest daughter of Mark Prim of Johnswell, co. Kilkenny. Earlier claims that Scott's father was called Michael and that his mother was a member of the Purcell family probably arose from Archdale's ambiguous statement, in his edition of John Lodge's *Peerage of Ireland* (1789), that Michael Scott, son of an English officer killed in the Williamite war, had married a Miss Purcell, by whom 'he had issue Thos. Scott of Mohobber in the county of Tipperary esq. deceased and John Lord Earlsford is one of his [Thomas's] younger sons' (Lodge, 7.242). Thomas Scott had an estate of 1400 acres in co. Tipperary. John Scott was educated in Clonmel under the Revd John Harwood and the Revd William Denis; he entered Trinity College, Dublin, on 16 April 1756 and graduated BA in 1760. After studying at the Middle Temple he was called to the Irish bar in 1765.

Parliamentary lists compiled for the Irish administration confirm the traditional version of Scott's entry into politics; at a time when the lord lieutenant, George, fourth Viscount Townshend, was trying to build up a new castle party in the Commons, George Forbes, fifth earl of Granard, placed his borough of Mullingar at the disposal of the government, and the lord chancellor, James Hewitt, first Viscount Lifford, recommended Scott, a rising young lawyer, as a suitable recruit. However, these sources are, perhaps significantly, silent on the associated claim that

John Scott, first earl of Clonmell (1739–1798), by Gilbert Stuart, *c.*1790

Scott had up to then been a militant patriot and a supporter of Charles Lucas. In the Commons, where he sat for Mullingar from 1769 to 1783 and for Portarlington from 1783 to 1784, he quickly established himself as one of the administration's most reliable and effective spokesmen. He was appointed counsel to the revenue board in 1772 and solicitor-general on 15 December 1774. His reputation for brazen effrontery in defending the most hopeless case, reflected in the nickname Copper-Faced Jack, appears to date mainly from this period. A particular task in his early years was apparently to 'stand up' to Henry Flood (Kelly, 150). The rivalry between the two continued even after Flood had accepted office; in November 1775 remarks by Scott reflecting on Flood's change of allegiance provoked talk of a duel.

On 1 November 1777 Scott was appointed to succeed the deceased attorney-general, Philip Tisdall. He was also sworn of the privy council, and the lord lieutenant, John Hobart, second earl of Buckinghamshire, seems to have expected him to replace Tisdall in leading for the administration in the Commons. By autumn 1779, however, Buckinghamshire and his chief secretary, Sir Richard Heron, had alienated Scott and his political ally John Beresford by courting popularity through pandering to former parliamentary opponents. Scott declined to take the lead in the forthcoming session, and with Beresford used private correspondence with English contacts to condemn what they considered to be Buckinghamshire's and Heron's disastrous policy. Scott was particularly indignant at the indulgence shown to what he called 'ministerial patriots', 'in the pay, but not the service, of government' (*Correspondence*, 1.100–01), and declared his resentment at being asked to oppose measures that were being backed by 'swarms of placemen and privy councillors' (ibid., 136–7). At the same time he emphasized the absolute necessity of removing the restrictions on Irish trade, warning that otherwise 'you will see this kingdom follow America step by step, until we are all undone' (ibid., 1.66).

Scott's public stance of unwavering support for the administration made him a particular target of public hostility. In the major riot of 15 November 1779 he narrowly escaped a hostile crowd, allegedly armed with swords and pistols, and the windows of his house were smashed. When Buckinghamshire was at last replaced in 1780 Scott quickly re-established a harmonious working relationship with his successor, Frederick Howard, fifth earl of Carlisle, and with the new chief secretary, William Eden. In November 1781 he scored his most famous parliamentary triumph when he mocked Henry Flood, now back in opposition, through the parable of Harry Plantagenet, a poacher temporarily turned royal huntsman, who found on returning to the forest that he had lost all influence there.

Following the fall of Lord North's ministry in March 1782 Scott was one of a number of Irish office holders dismissed by the marquess of Rockingham's new administration. The dismissal, coinciding with an attack of rheumatic fever, hit him hard; Beresford described him as sinking under his misfortunes, and as hopelessly torn between resentment and fear of jeopardizing a reversion that he still held. By late 1783, however, a new lord lieutenant, Robert Henley, second earl of Northington, was once again seeking efficient parliamentary managers, and Scott returned to office as prime serjeant (31 December 1783). Northington's successor, Charles Manners, fourth duke of Rutland, also valued his services highly; in November 1784 he reported to William Pitt the younger that he had discussed recent proposals for a reform of the Irish electoral system with Scott, 'whom I have on all occasions found most zealously and personally attached to me' (*Rutland MSS*, 3.148). Rutland's chief secretary, Thomas Orde, had a lower opinion of Scott, whom he described as unfit to be lord chancellor, attacking what he called his 'wantonness' and his overweening pretensions (ibid., 3.258, 361, 416). Under Rutland, Scott was appointed chief justice of the king's bench (20 May 1784) and took the title Baron Earlsfort of Lisson Earl.

In 1785 Earlsfort was part of the group charged with drawing up the bill to implement Pitt's plans to formalize Anglo-Irish commercial relationships but he advised against any attempt to force this through parliament once the scale of opposition became clear. Rutland's successor, George Temple-Nugent-Grenville, first marquess of Buckingham, was also initially close to Earlsfort. At the height of the regency crisis, however, Earlsfort threatened to withdraw his support unless he was allowed to exchange an office worth £500 per annum for one worth £800. Initially outraged at 'the treachery of one so near to me' (*Fortescue MSS*, 1.396–7), Buckingham reluctantly agreed but he subsequently regarded Earlsfort as 'slippery' (ibid., 1.469). In June 1789 he was obliged, under an engagement inherited from Rutland, to recommend Earlsfort for an earldom but he privately suggested that he should receive only a viscountcy, as 'the more favours his lordship has to expect, the more certain we shall be of his support' (ibid., 1.481). Earlsfort duly, but resentfully, accepted the title of Viscount Clonmell on 18 August 1789. He was promoted to the earldom of Clonmell on 6 December 1793.

During 1789–90 Clonmell became the centre of renewed controversy by issuing fiats under which the newspaper editor John Magee, then being sued for libel by Francis Higgins and others, could be held in prison indefinitely unless he found exceptionally high securities for the payment of any damages that might be awarded against him. Magee retaliated by organizing raucous public entertainments, including pig races, on a plot of ground adjoining Clonmell's house. A parliamentary debate on the matter, in May 1791, though formally inconclusive, was interpreted as implying a general repudiation of Clonmell's action.

Clonmell's career made him a figure of particular detestation to patriots. James Caulfeild, first earl of Charlemont, for example, described him as 'that tool of every minister, that degrading instrument of English usurpation, that impudent assertor of slavery' (*Charlemont MSS*, 1.64). Such verdicts have inevitably influenced later accounts. More recent historical writing, however, suggests that Clonmell is more appropriately assessed, like Beresford or Foster, as one of those office holders who saw themselves primarily as servants of government rather than as politicians. A memorable passage in his diary, comparing Ireland to southern Africa—with the common people 'divided, oppressed, pillaged and abused', as the Khoi-Khoi (Hottentots); English government as the Dutch planters; the followers of successive lords lieutenant as 'bushmen or spies and swindlers'; and the Anglo-Irish political magnates as lions and tigers (Fitzpatrick, 33)—suggests bitter realism but hardly either complacency or indifference. On 4 May 1782 he made a dramatic speech in the Commons, insisting that he had always believed that the British parliament had no right to impose laws on Ireland and that no official emolument would ever induce him to say otherwise (*Parliamentary Register*, 1.351–3). This, however, was when he already knew that he was to be removed from office. Later Clonmell seems to have opposed the brutal security measures adopted in the period leading up to the rising of 1798, complaining in his diary that the government 'are driving things to extremities; the country is disaffected and savage; the parliament corrupt and despised' (Fitzpatrick, 54). His views on the Catholic question were liberal; he supported Gardiner's Catholic Relief Bill in 1778. When, two years later, he wrote to James Butler, Roman Catholic archbishop of Cashel, warning of allegations that Butler had behaved aggressively towards protestants, he insisted that he did so 'only to put you upon your guard', and assured the archbishop that he did not 'find from any other quarter the least insinuation against the discretion, benevolence and becoming conduct which every man expects from you' (Renehan, 1.338–9).

Clonmell's personality is difficult to assess. His diary reveals a driven, privately insecure man. Repeated resolutions to work harder (including proposals to restrict himself to four hours' sleep per night), to eat and drink less, and to curb his natural tendency to levity are interspersed with maxims of breathtaking cynicism: 'Make every man your dupe by flattery'; 'Never be intimate with any man or woman but for the purpose of answering your purposes upon them' (Fitzpatrick, 25, 28). Yet it is difficult to know how far this self-created ideal of a manipulative and amoral schemer should be taken at face value. Sir Jonah Barrington acknowledged strength of character as well as self-interest:

> Courageous, vulgar, humorous, artificial, he knew the world well and he profited by that knowledge. He cultivated the powerful; he bullied the timid; he fought the brave; he flattered the vain; he duped the credulous; and he amused the convivial … Half liked, half reprobated, he was too high to be despised and too low to be respected. (Barrington, 1.313)

Assessment of Clonmell's character is further complicated by the uncertainty surrounding the origins of his wealth, estimated at the time of his death as bringing him an income of £25,000 a year (*Lord Shannon's Letters*, 104). In 1767 Scott, recently qualified as a barrister, married Catherine Maryanne, daughter of Thomas Mathew of Thomastown, co. Tipperary, and widow of Philip Roe, allegedly against the wishes of her family and in a clandestine ceremony. After her death on 19 March 1771 he was said to have claimed two separate sums of £6000 each as due to him, through his late wife, on the basis of Mathew family settlements, and in 1776 to have accepted 2000 acres of land, worth £1000 a year, in settlement of his claim. A separate allegation was that he had accepted from Mathew a lease on lands in co. Tipperary in trust for Mathew's mistress, Celia Robinson, a Catholic, but had appropriated the property for himself. Neither allegation, resting on documentation surviving from intricate family and legal disputes, can be tested with any certainty; one recent account points out that both are difficult to reconcile with Clonmell's long friendship with the Mathews' relative, Archbishop Charles Agar (Malcolmson, 70–71). Clonmell's second wife, whom he married on 23 June 1779, was Margaret Lawless (1762/3–1829), daughter and heir of Patrick Lawless, a Dublin banker. With Margaret he had a son, Thomas (1783–1838), who succeeded his father as second earl, and a daughter, Charlotte (1787–1846), who married John Pyndar, third Earl Beauchamp. Clonmell died at his home in Harcourt Street, Dublin, on 23 May 1798 and was buried in St Peter's Church. His widow died on 5 November 1829 in Portman Square, London. S. J. Connolly

Sources *The manuscripts and correspondence of James, first earl of Charlemont*, 2 vols., HMC, 28 (1891–4) • *The manuscripts of his grace the duke of Rutland*, 4 vols., HMC, 24 (1888–1905) • *The manuscripts of J. B. Fortescue*, 10 vols., HMC, 30 (1892–1927) • J. Porter, P. Byrne, and W. Porter, eds., *The parliamentary register, or, History of the proceedings and debates of the House of Commons of Ireland*, 2nd edn, 1 (1784) • J. Barrington, *Personal sketches of his own times*, 2nd edn, 2 vols.

(1830) • J. Lodge, *The peerage of Ireland*, rev. M. Archdall, rev. edn, 7 vols. (1789) • W. Hunt, ed., *The Irish parliament, 1775* (1907) • M. Bodkin, ed., 'Notes on the Irish parliament in 1773', *Proceedings of the Royal Irish Academy*, 48C (1942–3), 145–232 • P. W. Malcolmson, *Archbishop Charles Agar: churchmanship and politics in Ireland, 1760–1810* (2002) • J. Kelly, *Henry Flood: patriots and politics in eighteenth-century Ireland* (1998) • T. P. Power, *Land, politics, and society in eighteenth-century Tipperary* (1993) • *The correspondence of the Right Hon. John Beresford, illustrative of the last thirty years of the Irish parliament*, ed. W. Beresford, 2 vols. (1854) • W. J. Fitzpatrick, *Curious family history, or, Ireland before the union*, 6th edn (1880) • L. F. Renehan, *Collections on Irish church history*, ed. D. McCarthy, 2 vols. (1861–74) • *Lord Shannon's letters to his son*, ed. E. Hewitt (1982) • GEC, *Peerage*, new edn, vol. 3 [Clonmell] • F. E. Ball, *The judges in Ireland, 1221–1921*, 2 vols. (1926)

Archives BL, letters to William Eden, Add. MSS 34417–34429, 34461 • BL, corresp. with Charles Jenkinson, Add. MSS 38209–38210, 38222, 38306, 38309

Likenesses G. Stuart, portrait, *c*.1790; Sothebys, 24 Nov 1965, lot 71 [*see illus.*] • P. Condé, stipple and line engraving (after watercolour miniature by R. Cosway), BM, NG Ire. • stipple, NPG

Wealth at death £25,000 p.a.: Hewitt, ed., *Lord Shannon's letters*, 104

Scott, John, first earl of Eldon (1751–1838), lord chancellor, was born on 4 June 1751 in Love Lane, Newcastle upon Tyne, the third son and eighth of thirteen children of William Scott (1696/7–1776), a 'hoastman' or coal factor, and his second wife, Jane (*c*.1709–1800), the daughter of Henry Atkinson of Newcastle upon Tyne.

John Scott, first earl of Eldon (1751–1838), by Sir Thomas Lawrence, 1825

Family background and education Scott was the grandson of another William, described as yeoman, who was a clerk to a coal fitter (merchant) at Newcastle and who became a merchant in his own right and the owner of coal barges, or keels, operating in the east coast trade. His son William was apprenticed in 1716 to the same trade and prospered, becoming the owner of several keels and a public house, which was used to supply his workmen with liquor under the truck system of wages in kind. He also took up maritime insurance and became a prominent figure in Newcastle business circles. Industrious and frugal, he built up a moderate fortune, but he was a man of little education, and it was to his second wife, Jane, that his sons, William *Scott, later Baron Stowell (1745–1836), a notable maritime and international lawyer, Henry (1748–1799), who inherited his father's business, and John, owed their incentive to study. They were sent to the Royal Free Grammar School at Newcastle, where the master was the Revd Hugh Moises, a well-known teacher to whom Scott later attributed his training in habits of industry and his strong religious views. When he became lord chancellor he made Moises the first of his chaplains.

When he reached the age of fifteen, Scott was intended by his father to follow him into the coal trade, but his brother William, who was then a college tutor at Oxford, persuaded their father to send John there also, and on 15 May 1766 he matriculated from University College. His brother secured for him a fellowship restricted to men born in Northumberland, which he took up on 11 July 1767 when he was only sixteen. However, Scott showed little inclination for academic study, expecting to become no more than a country parson, in preparation for which career he developed a taste for port which never left him. He took his BA degree on 29 February 1770 and stayed to work for his MA, which he took on 13 February 1773. In June 1771 he entered for, and won, an English essay prize for a composition entitled 'The advantages and disadvantages of foreign travel', a rather stilted work in imitation of Dr Johnson and, not surprisingly in view of his complete lack of practical experience in the subject, lacking in original thought or imagination. As in some of his judgments later in his career, he attempted to balance all the arguments for and against his thesis and came only hesitantly to a conclusion.

Marriage and a change of course Scott's intended course of life was now shattered by his falling headlong in love with Elizabeth (1754–1831), the sixteen-year-old daughter of a fellow townsman, Aubone Surtees, a wealthy banker. They met in church one Sunday at Sedgefield and in a short time the young couple were in love. The difficulty was that the Surtees family were socially a cut above the son of a keelman and public-house keeper with career prospects no better than those of a country clergyman. They had to meet in secret while she was out riding, and when her parents put pressure on her to marry a more suitable bridegroom they decided to elope. The plan was carried out in the classic manner—the bride-to-be descended into her lover's arms down a ladder from a first-floor window of her parent's house—and they fled to Scotland, where on 19 November 1772 they were married according to the rites of the Church of England at Blackshiels, on the road to Edinburgh, by the Revd John Buchanan, a minister of the Scottish Episcopal church at

Haddington. On returning to Newcastle they were forgiven by Scott's father, but it was some weeks before the Surtees family were reconciled. The marriage was then resolemnized two months later, on 19 January 1773, at St Nicholas's Church, Newcastle, in the presence of the bride's father, who settled the sum of £1000 on the happy pair. Scott senior settled £2000 on them. They then left for Oxford, where John was to prepare for a new career.

Scott's marriage barred any prospect of a fellowship at Oxford, and it was unlikely that he would make any headway in the church without a college living. He therefore determined on the law, and he devoted the next few years to studying for the bar. He worked hard—he later said that a lawyer should live like a hermit and work like a horse, and he followed the second at least of these precepts. He was fortunate to secure a temporary post as vice-president of New Inn Hall during the absence of the principal in India, and he also took his place as vice-professor of law, which involved lecturing to the undergraduates, although he admitted that he knew no more than they did, and he could only read out his predecessor's lectures until he became more knowledgeable. He also took private pupils from University College, and in addition to his college stipend of £60 per annum he received a small allowance from his brother William, who constituted himself his protector. He was now able to devote his time to study. He gave up his fellowship on 19 November 1774, though he remained at New Inn Hall for a further year, and worked from four in the morning until late at night, sometimes with a wet towel round his head to keep him awake. In March 1774 his son John was born, and in summer 1775 the family moved to London in order for him to further his career at the bar. His studies had provided him with a wide knowledge of common law and equity, and he studied the law of real property under the eminent conveyancer Matthew Duane. He attended the courts at Westminster Hall with regularity, particularly the court of king's bench, then under Lord Mansfield at the height of his reputation. His extraordinary industry thus equipped him for a legal career of great future distinction. He had entered Middle Temple on 28 January 1773, and he was called to the bar on 9 February 1776.

Early years in the legal profession By his own account, Scott's first year or two at the bar were penurious. He claimed to have earned only 9*s.* in the first twelve months. When he went on to the northern circuit, however, he began to prosper. His first major case was as counsel before the House of Commons on an election committee which was judging the disputed Newcastle election in 1777, and he also acquired a general retainer from the city corporation. At the same time that he began to earn money, his father died (6 November 1776), leaving him £1000. Shortly afterwards Scott decided to settle in London rather than in the north-east, and in hope of greater business transferred to the court of chancery from king's bench, despite his inexperience of equity law. His hopes were not at first realized: business was slow to materialize, and for a time he considered returning to Newcastle to become a provincial attorney. But his involvement in the chancery case of *Ackroyd* v. *Smithson*, over a disputed will, made his reputation overnight when he pleaded successfully before Lord Thurlow, on 4 March 1780, in an appeal against the judgment of the master of the rolls. Further cases followed, including a case before the House of Lords in support of the duke of Northumberland and one before the Commons concerning a dispute over the Madras Council. On 4 June 1783—his thirty-second birthday—he took silk, having vindicated his claim to precedence over Erskine and Pigot, whose patents had been made out before his. This brought him again to the notice of Thurlow, who took him up and promoted his legal and political career. It was Thurlow who persuaded Lord Weymouth to return Scott for his pocket borough of Weobley in Herefordshire in 1783, and he supported the 'king's friends' in opposition to the Fox–North coalition despite the fact that Thurlow had remained chancellor. The position was clarified when Thurlow remained in office after George III had dismissed the coalition and turned to the younger Pitt. The chancellor and his protégé were henceforward staunch supporters of the king, rather than followers of the prime minister.

Political beginnings When the Fox–North India Bill came before the House of Commons Scott spoke against the measure, but his maiden speech on the first reading, on 20 November 1783, was badly received. He declared that he was 'attached to no party' and attempted to appear as an impartial onlooker who had not yet made up his mind, but concluded that the bill was 'of a dangerous tendency' (Cobbett, *Parl. hist.*, 23, 1783, 1239). When Fox pointed out the inconsistency, Scott determined to attack him, and on the third reading, on 8 December, attempted a witty and sarcastic riposte in the manner of Richard Brinsley Sheridan. Unfortunately he overdid it, packing his speech with feeble jokes culled from Joe Miller, the comedian, alluding to Sayers's cartoon depicting Fox as Carlo Khan riding to despoil the British Treasury, and reading several verses from the book of Revelation, comparing Fox's seven commissioners to be appointed to govern India to the biblical beast with seven heads. He concluded with allusions to Thucydides and to Shakespeare's *Othello*, leaving the house gasping at his jumble of allusions and flimsy attempts at humour. To make matters worse, Sheridan answered him with counter-quotations from the same sources, including the passage in Revelation where the seven-headed beast was replaced by 'seven angels clothed in pure and white linen' (Cobbett, *Parl. hist.*, 24, 1783–5, 33–7). The experience was salutary: Scott gave up the pursuit of satirical burlesque and in future confined his parliamentary speaking to plain and factual expression. He was never a brilliant orator, despite his practice in the courts, but made his impact through reasoned argument and legal authority, though his innate tendency to see all sides of any question sometimes made his speeches too involved to convince his audience.

For the next few years Scott attended the house as regularly as his legal business allowed and became known as a steadfast supporter of the government, although he was ready and able to disagree with Pitt on occasion. In March

1785 he spoke to condemn the attempt, in the Westminster scrutiny, to deprive Fox of the seat he had won, after a close and hard-fought struggle, on the grounds of improper electoral practices. The scrutiny by the high bailiff of Westminster of the votes cast in the election had dragged on for several months, and, the house having lost patience with what increasingly appeared to be a vindictive persecution of Fox, it had been resolved to terminate the process and instruct the high bailiff to confirm Fox's return. On 9 March Fox moved to expunge the proceedings respecting the scrutiny from the *Journals*, and despite the government's opposition to this motion Scott supported it on strictly legal grounds, declaring that it ought not to be permissible for ministers to use the process to keep constituencies unrepresented on the pretext of a scrutiny. His speech clearly showed that, as his biographer wrote, 'with him the wishes of his party, and of the minister who headed it, were of less weight than the considerations of principle and of constitutional law' (Twiss, 1.170). The speech gained him the respect of his hearers, including both the prime minister himself and Fox: Scott declared towards the end of his life that Fox 'never said an uncivil word to me during the whole time that I sat in the House of Commons', which he attributed to his speech on the Westminster scrutiny (ibid., 1.172).

For the remainder of the parliament Scott voted, and occasionally spoke, with the administration. On 24 May 1785 he defended Pitt's scheme for the regulation of commercial relations with Ireland, which was bitterly attacked by the whig opposition, and on 2 June 1786 on the Rohilla war charge against Warren Hastings he again took his stand on a constitutional principle, objecting to any attempt to pass a general resolution against Hastings without first hearing the specific charges against him. Once more Fox took occasion to remark that he had 'a very high respect … for the learned gentleman … whose great abilities and high character entitled him to the respect of every man' (Twiss, 1.174). However, Scott took little part in the debates on Hastings or in the eventual impeachment, devoting himself more to the business of the circuit and of his office of chancellor of the county palatine of Durham, to which he was appointed by Lord Thurlow's brother, the bishop of Durham, in 1787. In 1788 Scott and Erskine, among other lawyers, were consulted by Pitt on the interpretation of the India Act of 1784, and it was on Scott's advice that the minister introduced the controversial Declaratory Bill in 1788 which asserted the right of the government to order troops to India independently of the authority of the East India Company's board of directors. Scott successfully defended the bill in the Commons on 5 March 1788, when he was 'one of [Pitt's] most fervent and able supporters' (HoP, *Commons, 1754–90*, 416). His political future was assured.

Solicitor-general and the regency crisis, 1788–1793 Lord Mansfield's resignation as lord chief justice in June 1788 created a ladder of preferment among the law officers, and as a consequence Scott was appointed solicitor-general and (rather against his will) was knighted, according to custom, on 27 June. He was re-elected for Weobley on 7 July and resumed his seat in the house. A few weeks later George III suffered his first major attack of mental derangement, which presented the government with the problem, among others, of how to pass the necessary legislation to install a regent in the king's place when the king's incapacity made it impossible to secure the royal assent. It was Scott who suggested the solution adopted by Pitt, of securing the agreement of both houses to the use of the great seal to signify consent—a device ridiculed by the opposition as 'the phantom' but one which gave the proceedings a cloak of legality in an unprecedented situation. He justified the measure on the grounds of necessity: it also prevented the opposition whigs from succeeding in their tactic to make parliament appoint the prince of Wales as regent without parliamentary restrictions, which would have enabled him to give his friends a permanent lease of power. On 22 December Scott drew a firm distinction between a vacancy of the throne on the king's death and a temporary incapacity of a monarch who was still in possession of it, so justifying Pitt's tactic of placing parliamentary restrictions on a regency in order to keep the king's authority intact. George III did not forget, and acknowledged Scott's service soon after his recovery when he called him to Windsor to thank him personally 'for the affectionate fidelity with which he [had] adhered to him when so many had deserted him in his malady' (Twiss, 1.196).

Scott's fidelity was not matched by his political patron, Thurlow, who was suspected of having intrigued with the opposition whigs in the hope of keeping his place under a regency, but, loyal as ever, Scott always denied that Thurlow had acted out of self-interest rather than concern for the king in case of a change of ministers. Pitt took a different view, and from this time his relations with the lord chancellor became frostier, until he secured his dismissal in June 1792. Scott felt bound to offer his own resignation, but Thurlow dissuaded him, and he continued to hold his office until February 1793, when he succeeded Archibald Macdonald as attorney-general.

The French Revolution and the safety of the constitution In his new office Scott was primarily responsible for the prosecution of state prisoners accused of crimes against the constitution and the established government, a responsibility which suddenly became of great importance and relevance under the supposed threat to external safety and internal order posed by the French Revolution and by its sympathizers inside Britain. Pitt's policy of repression of political dissent was christened by his political opponents a 'reign of terror', akin to that of the revolutionaries in France, and the radicals, who were influenced by Thomas Paine's *Rights of Man* but mainly responded to long-standing English traditions of liberal thought, were driven underground or silenced in the name of a patriotic struggle against foreign conquest and the subversion of British liberties. Scott's prominence in this conflict gained him the reputation of 'the best hated man in England'. The notorious Traitorous Correspondence Act of 1793 and the Treasonable Practices and Seditious Meetings Acts of 1795, which struck at the hitherto constitutional right of free assembly and extended the crime of high treason to writing and speaking against the regime, were his handiwork. He defended in parliament the government's action in bringing foreign troops into the country and the severity of the Scottish judges in punishing the reformers Thomas Muir, Thomas Palmer, and others who had been indicted for sedition because of their participation in the Scottish reform movement. The success of these prosecutions encouraged the government to imitate them in England. A number of reforming activists, including Thomas Hardy, a master shoemaker and secretary of the London Corresponding Society, which had been set up to link together the various local reform groups, and the Revd John Horne Tooke, who had been an enthusiast for reform since the days of John Wilkes, were arrested and charged with high treason. Scott was instrumental in bringing this charge against them, rather than the lesser charge of sedition which did not necessarily carry the barbarous penalty prescribed for treason, and he led for the crown in the trials which followed in October and November 1794. His opening speech in Thomas Hardy's trial amounted to 100,000 words and lasted nine hours (*State trials*, 24.241–370). Thurlow caustically remarked on hearing the news: 'Nine hours. Then there is no treason, by God!', and the jury, which had been painstakingly selected to bring in a guilty verdict, agreed with him. Had the charge been sedition, it is certainly possible that the prosecution would have succeeded, though the brilliant defence by Thomas Erskine was also largely responsible. The charges against Horne Tooke and John Thelwall, which were led by the solicitor-general and Serjeant Adair respectively, were similarly unsuccessful, and the remaining prosecutions were dropped. Scott's insistence on the graver charge was blamed by critics in the Commons for this outcome, but it derived from his literal interpretation of the government's policy of branding all reformist activity in the circumstances of national emergency as designed to aid the enemy and overthrow the regime.

The setback did not deter Scott from pursuing political dissent. He had supported Pitt's suspension of habeas corpus in June 1794, and he himself moved its continuation in January 1795, alleging that it was necessary to counter a radical plan to subvert the constitution. He also made frequent use of the device of *ex officio* informations to suppress publications critical of the government by short-circuiting the normal processes of the law, and in April 1798 he introduced the Newspaper Proprietors' Registration Act to compel newspapers to disclose their owners so that they could be held to account for their contents. He claimed that his purpose was to attack not the liberty but the licentiousness of the press. He opposed Quaker relief on 6 March 1797, and in the aftermath of the naval mutinies of 1797 he introduced a bill to prevent the administration of illegal oaths. He prosecuted a number of United Irishmen after the rising of 1798, justified the renewed suspension of habeas corpus on 21 December 1798, and on 19 April 1799 defended additional measures to suppress seditious societies. He supported all Pitt's wartime legislation, spoke in favour of the introduction of income tax in December 1798, and denied opposition charges of ill treatment of political prisoners in that month and again in May 1799.

Scott was one of the busiest members of Pitt's administration, working long hours in the office, and in the House of Commons frequently taking a leading part in major debates. Charles Abbot, later speaker of the House of Commons, described his speeches at this time as:

> Argumentative and copious in his matter, but involved in his style; always qualifying his assertions to a degree which does away their force, and too much inclined to draw the whole debate into a question about the vindication of his own conduct.

He was listened to with respect on legal questions, but his complexity of style and his rigidly conservative views limited his effectiveness.

Scott retired from his seat at Weobley in 1796, and at the general election in May he was returned by the duke of Newcastle for Boroughbridge, ironically with Sir Francis Burdett, the future radical leader, as his fellow member. His active career was beginning to damage his health, and his colleague Sir John Mitford, the solicitor-general, warned Pitt that the law officers were overworked and could no longer cope with the load of business. Scott later wrote that he felt 'worn down with labour and fatigue' (*Anecdote Book*, 114), and he was relieved by his appointment, at his own solicitation, as lord chief justice of common pleas on 17 July 1799, to which Pitt agreed on condition that he took a peerage. He had bought an estate at Eldon, co. Durham, in 1792 for £22,000 and he adopted the title of Baron Eldon of Eldon. George III, who had been following Scott's career with approval, also made it a condition that he should accept the lord chancellorship 'when he might call upon me to accept it' (ibid., 115). That moment was to come sooner than either expected.

'My lord chancellor': Eldon and George III As lord chief justice, Eldon took little part in political affairs, and he declared himself happy in that office. In the meantime, Pitt had brought about the union with Ireland as a measure to strengthen Britain in face of the continuing threat from France, and to further this aim he proposed to the king that a measure of relief to the Irish Catholics would reconcile Ireland to the cause. George III, however, was inflexibly opposed to any change in the exclusive status of the Church of England as the national church, pleading the obligation in his coronation oath to preserve the status of the church unaltered. Pitt felt it incumbent on him to resign in February 1801 on the grounds that the king refused to take his advice, and his former colleagues divided on the Catholic question. Henry Addington, speaker of the House of Commons and a personal friend of Pitt, was a determined anti-Catholic, and the king turned to him to form a new administration to resist emancipation. The resignation of Loughborough, Pitt's lord chancellor, enabled the king to appoint Eldon in his place, and Eldon believed, as he said to a friend, that he could not do otherwise than fulfil his promise. The arrangements for the new administration were delayed, however, by another attack of the king's derangement, and it was not until 14 April 1801 that George delivered the great seal to him with a rather melodramatic gesture, drawing the seal from under his coat and saying that it came 'from my heart' (*Anecdote Book*, 5). Clearly the king was not fully recovered, but there was no doubt that he had a fondness for Eldon, to whom he often referred as '*my* lord chancellor'. The lord chancellor was already known as 'the keeper of the king's conscience', chiefly because it was one of his duties to advise the monarch on matters concerning the church and on ecclesiastical appointments, and a close relationship soon developed between them.

Eldon remained lord chief justice while holding the office of lord chancellor until 21 May 1801, owing to the need to complete the business of the Easter term. The king's complete recovery was not announced until June, although Eldon obtained his signature to a commission for passing bills on three occasions in April, giving rise to suspicions that the ministry was concealing the true state of his health in order to avoid a regency. George III himself, however, expressed his gratitude for Eldon's conduct and attachment immediately he was declared well.

Eldon was a loyal colleague to Addington, but he regarded himself, as George had expressed it, as 'the king's chancellor' rather than as a member of the prime minister's party. He was closely involved in the continuing difficulties arising from the relationship between the king and his eldest son. Early in 1802 the prince of Wales was seeking to relieve his financial predicament by claiming to be paid the arrears of the income of the duchy of Cornwall which had been paid into the Treasury during his minority, while George III was resolutely opposed to any further encouragement of what he considered his son's disgraceful extravagance. It was to Eldon that that prince's emissary, Lord Moira, went to open negotiations, but Eldon warned him that the king would not be persuaded, and the plan was abandoned. It was clear to Eldon that, in case of a regency, the prince would appoint Thurlow as his chancellor, and despite their continuing connection he was not disposed to co-operate willingly.

George III's return to normal health lasted only until the early weeks of 1804. On 9 February the duke of Kent told the prince of Wales that their father was showing repeated symptoms of mental instability, but the ministers made no public announcement. The political situation was delicate, as the renewal of war with France in May 1803 soon exposed Addington's deficiencies as a war minister and led to a demand for the return of Pitt. Henry Brougham believed that Eldon played a central role in the subsequent manoeuvres. In March 1804 he offered to persuade the king to get rid of Addington and reappoint Pitt as prime minister, and on 22 April 1804 he passed on to the king Pitt's letter giving him notice of his intention to join in Fox's proposed motion on the defence of the country, which was likely to force Addington's resignation. Eldon was criticized for apparently betraying the minister he had supported since his appointment, but in the current state of the House of Commons and of public opinion it was almost certain that Addington would be defeated. He had also to persuade the king to accept the inevitable, for George III had become attached to Addington, who was an easier man to deal with than the domineering Pitt. Eldon managed the king with skill, and the change of ministers was accomplished on 10 May 1804. A week later the king wrote to express his thanks 'to his excellent Lord Chancellor, whose conduct he most thoroughly approves', paying tribute to 'the uprightness of Lord Eldon's mind' which had 'borne him with credit and honour … through a most unpleasant labyrinth' (Twiss, 1.450).

George III's illness had broken out intermittently during these events, but the ministers refused to acknowledge his real state of health. Eldon declared in the Lords on 1 March 1804 that there was 'no suspension of the royal functions', and he obtained the king's assent to bills twice during March. The king's full recovery was announced at the end of March, but disturbing symptoms recurred throughout April and May and into June. On 2 June the prince of Wales complained that he had not been kept informed of his father's condition. He was still being regularly attended by his doctors, but the ministers persisted in declaring him to be fully competent to perform his duties. The prince's political allies claimed that ministers were concealing the king's condition in order to retain power by unconstitutional means. The prince demanded a full statement to the privy council of 'all material circumstances relative to the king's health and treatment' (prince of Wales to Eldon, 2 June 1804, *Correspondence of George, Prince of Wales*, 5.26). Eldon went to Carlton House and, according to Lord Grey, 'with great agitation, and occasionally with tears', acknowledged that the king 'had been in a very unpleasant way', but he asserted that the physicians were now satisfied of his recovery (Grey to Mrs Grey, 4 June 1804, Grey MSS, Durham University Library). The prince summoned the doctors to Carlton House and questioned them, and, on their admission that the king was still under medical supervision, protested to Eldon against 'a procedure so unconstitutional' (2 July 1804, *Correspondence of George, Prince of Wales*, 5.45–6). The king continued to behave eccentrically until the end of the summer, but ministers persisted in denying that he was incapable of performing his royal duties.

Eldon and the royal family Relations between the king and his eldest son were also beset by family difficulties. The king was fond of the prince's estranged wife, Caroline, and of their daughter, Princess Charlotte, but the prince was determined to prevent Caroline having any say in their daughter's education or any but occasional access to her. The king believed that his son's way of life was unsuitable for the bringing up of a young girl, and in 1804 he proposed that the princess, now eight years old, should come to reside with her grandparents at Windsor. Her father feared that her mother would have access to her and tried to make conditions to prevent it, but for the sake of reconciliation with the king he was prepared to contemplate the proposals. Eldon was employed by the king as a go-between in the negotiations, but the prince was convinced that Eldon was no neutral emissary and that he was doing his best to thwart him. When he heard, on the morning that he was due to travel to see his father after his supposed recovery from his illness, that the king had invited Charlotte and her mother to visit him first, he turned back and refused to go on with the proposed visit. Eldon did his best to soothe feelings on both sides, advising the prince against sending a disrespectful letter to his father, and that he should defer matters until the conclusion of the king's forthcoming visit to Weymouth for recuperation. When the king returned to Kew he received his son kindly, if distantly, but the scheme to allow Charlotte to live at Windsor was dropped.

Pitt's second administration ended with the minister's death in January 1806. It was replaced by the predominantly whig 'ministry of all the talents', which did not include Eldon. The king parted with him reluctantly and is said to have asked him to lay the seals on a sofa, 'for I *cannot*, and I *will not* take them from you' (Twiss, 1.512). During the following months Eldon acted as adviser to the princess of Wales during the delicate investigation by the ministry of her alleged adulterous affairs, which the prince hoped might turn up evidence on which he could base a divorce. The outcome was favourable to the princess, and her husband accordingly had another cause to resent Eldon's conduct.

When the opportunity arose to get rid of the new ministers because of their attempt to provide some minor relief to the Catholics, it was to Eldon that the king turned in March 1807. The circumstances are still not wholly clear, but the approaches to the duke of Portland to form a new version of the former Pittite administration certainly involved Eldon, though he later denied having done anything improper. He resumed the lord chancellorship on the appointment of the Portland ministry on 1 April, and he retained the post for a further twenty years. He fully supported the king's obduracy on the Catholic question: 'I cannot disobey my old and gracious master', he wrote on 31 March 1807, 'struggling for the established religion of my country' (Twiss, 2.31). His concern was more for the nature of the state than for the church: he wrote in 1825 that 'the Establishment is formed not for the purpose of making the Church political, but for the purpose of making the state religious' (ibid., 2, facing 538). Henceforward, Eldon was the leading advocate of resistance to demands for emancipation by the Catholics, and it became the central tenet of his political creed.

Old Bags: Eldon and George IV George, prince of Wales, became regent in 1811 when his father finally succumbed to his mental illness. It was generally expected that the old ministers would be replaced by the prince's friends, and in particular that Eldon would lose the chancellorship. He had supported Spencer Perceval's plan for a restricted regency which might prevent a change of government, but the regent failed to construct such a ministry, mainly because since Fox's death he had abandoned his support of the whigs and because he himself had altered his views on the Catholic issue. He first postponed any change of ministers on account of respect for his father and the desire not to impede any possible recovery by reversing his policy, but as time went on he grew accustomed to the existing ministers and to their views on the prosecution of the war and the maintenance of the protestant constitution. In Eldon's case, he told him, after reading the king's correspondence regarding his affairs in 1804, that he had discovered that the chancellor did not hate him, as he had assumed, but that he had been scrupulously fair towards his interests. Closer acquaintance confirmed the prince's respect and liking for his chancellor, whose convivial outlook was congenial, and he soon gave him the nickname Old Bags, in reference to the bag in which chancellors carried the great seal. It was to Eldon that the prince turned in 1812 to help him put pressure on his rebellious seventeen-year-old daughter, Princess Charlotte, to force her to accept her father's choice of attendants. The prince gave her a thorough telling-off in front of Eldon, who declared that if she were his daughter he would lock her up. Charlotte, in tears, told one of her aunts that she had been compared to 'a collier's daughter' (*Letters of George IV*, 1.216n.).

On 7 July 1821 George insisted on conferring on Eldon the earldom which he had previously refused, with the titles of Viscount Encombe (derived from the estate of Encombe in Dorset which he acquired in 1807) and earl of Eldon. For the remainder of the regency and until Eldon's retirement in 1827 they remained good friends and dinner companions, and George IV came to rely on his advice as his father had done.

Eldon led the tory section of the cabinets of Perceval and Lord Liverpool, and in the eyes of liberals he became the epitome of resistance to all reform, whether of the criminal law or of the electoral system. He was blamed for securing the defeat in the House of Lords of a number of humane reform measures, including the employment of climbing boy chimney sweeps, and, although he did not oppose outright the bill against child labour in cotton mills in 1819, he pointed out that there was already a remedy in common law against masters who overworked children. He opposed Samuel Romilly's campaign to reduce the number of capital statutes against trivial offences on the same grounds as his objections to the abolition of the slave trade in 1804 and 1806, as an unwarranted interference with the rights of property, and on 23 February 1823 he asserted that the slaves in the West Indies were better looked after by their masters than the poor in England were by their landlords. The same legalistic concern for propertied rights led him to oppose the punishment of the corrupt electors of Aylesbury in 1804 and to defend the close boroughs in the Reform Bill debates of 1831–2. He was constantly attacked in the press, and his house in Bedford Square was besieged by a mob in the corn-law riots of 1815. He defended the repressive legislation of the post-war years when radical agitation grew to its height; he regarded the Manchester radicals who met at 'Peterloo' as traitors to their country, and he introduced in the Lords the 'Six Acts' of 1819 which placed further restrictions on public meetings and reform propaganda. When George IV attempted to divorce his wife in 1820,

Eldon presided with acknowledged impartiality over what came to be called the queen's trial in the House of Lords and, though he considered her guilty, his summing-up at the end was equally judicious. However, he annoyed Liverpool by opposing the withdrawal of the bill of pains and penalties against her.

Eldon and the Catholic question Eldon was a powerful presence in the cabinet and exercised an ascendancy in the Lords, despite his lack of oratorical gifts. Brougham declared that he was the power that held Liverpool's cabinet together. Above all he came to symbolize resistance to Catholic emancipation. He opposed concessions to the Catholics in 1805 on the ground that they owed allegiance to a foreign power, but personal considerations also played a part. He had conceived a dislike of George Canning as far back as 1806, considering him overambitious, and that statesman's support of emancipation confirmed his opinion against it. Throughout the 1820s Eldon opposed all the attempts to remove the Catholic disabilities, although he maintained in 1827 that it was the protestant character of the House of Lords that was responsible and that 'no man in the kingdom was a greater friend to toleration than he was': he opposed emancipation only on political grounds, believing that the Catholics should 'have everything except power in a Protestant state', and in 1828 he also opposed the repeal of the Test and Corporation Acts, which gave protestant dissenters political equality with Anglicans.

In 1827, after Liverpool was disabled by a paralytic stroke, George IV commissioned Canning to form a government. Eldon, together with the duke of Wellington and the other high tories in the administration, resigned. It was the end of his official career: when Wellington became prime minister in 1828 the chancellorship went to Lyndhurst, and Eldon remained on the back benches. He supported Wellington in general, but he disliked the presence of four Canningites in the cabinet and blamed them for his exclusion, though he stressed that he had no desire for further office.

Legal career Eldon was not only a prominent political figure for over forty years but also the greatest lawyer of his time. Philip Francis described him as early as 1788 as 'the great luminary of the law' (*Memoirs of … Wraxall*, 5.75). His early studies and his conscientious industry at the bar and on the bench equipped him with a wide knowledge of the law, and he applied it with a conscientiousness and impartiality that would have made him a model judge, but for his excessive scrupulosity in coming to a decision between competing parties that was entirely correct. He was so anxious not to do an injustice that he could barely arrive at a conclusion without so many qualifications as to bewilder his hearers. This otherwise admirable quality was partly responsible for the long delays in giving justice that built up during his chancellorship. Another important factor was the great increase in the number of petitions and motions to the court of chancery, especially after the union with Ireland in 1800, when all Irish appeals were added to his workload.

Throughout the 1820s Eldon was frequently criticized for his extreme caution in reaching a judgment by whigs and radicals in parliament, notably Jeremy Bentham, who dubbed him Lord Endless. However, even those who taunted him recognized the importance of his decisions, which were seldom appealed from and hardly ever reversed. The *Legal Observer* in 1831 stated that 90 per cent of cases argued in equity referred to his decisions, and thus he had settled all the rules of equity. Along with Nottingham and Hardwicke, Eldon is regarded as one of the principal architects of equity jurisprudence. He staunchly defended equity as a distinct jurisdiction and tried hard to maintain a firm line between common law and equity, at a time when he believed that common-law judges were attempting to encroach on equity's domain.

Eldon was also perceived as the greatest obstacle to the reform of the chancery, which by the 1810s had been seen as the area of civil law most in need of reform. The appointment of a vice-chancellor in 1813 proved controversial: since he was an assistant to the chancellor, rather than an independent judge, his decisions generated a large number of appeals which then took up the lord chancellor's own time, thereby defeating the object of the exercise. However, Eldon saw all parliamentary motions on chancery reform as personal attacks on himself; a rather emotional man, he became very depressed by them and was often on the verge of resignation. He was shielded by Robert Peel from these attacks, and the main investigation into the chancery, the royal commission of 1824–6 (of which Eldon was the nominal head), avoided looking at the conduct of the chancellor and limited itself to technical matters. Though proponents of chancery reform such as Michael Angelo Taylor, John Williams, and Henry Brougham regarded this commission as a body of Eldon's cronies, designed to protect him, it did produce useful recommendations that were acted on for the next fifteen years.

Eldon's opponents also accused him of resisting reform for financial reasons: it was said that he wanted to keep the bankruptcy jurisdiction united to chancery on account of the high fees he earned from commissions in bankruptcy. He certainly made a large fortune from his earnings as lord chancellor, and his annual income generally exceeded £15,000. In addition, he had powerful patronage as lord chancellor, which he used to benefit his family, notably his son William Scott. Eldon's perceived avarice continued to be attacked by politicians and the press even after he left office, and he continued to defend his conduct in the House of Lords.

Last years in politics Canning's administration lasted only four months, and he made no move to carry Catholic emancipation, in deference to the king who was now strongly against it. On his premature death he was succeeded by the weak Viscount Goderich, whose tenure was also short, and in January 1828 the duke of Wellington took the reins. His touchstone was the national interest and the avoidance of public disorder, and when Daniel O'Connell secured his illegal election for co. Clare he decided that the concession of Catholic emancipation was the only way to avert civil war. George IV unwillingly gave way, despite the counter-pressure of his brother the duke of Cumberland, a rabid anti-Catholic, who enlisted Eldon's support and that of other high tories. Eldon obtained two private audiences with the king in March and April 1829 to urge him to withhold his consent to the Emancipation Bill, but the king realized that he could form no alternative government, the main opposition being even more in favour of it, and the bill became law on 13 April.

Eldon's last major parliamentary campaign was directed against the reform bills in 1831–2. He and Wellington led the resistance in the Lords, and in May 1831, when the king was under pressure to create sufficient whig peers to give the government a majority, he denounced the step as unconstitutional, but to no avail. When the king gave way and the passage of the bill became inevitable, he joined Wellington in withdrawing from the house to allow it to pass. It received the royal assent on 7 June 1832. During the remaining years of the whig ministries Eldon opposed their Irish church legislation and law reforms. He was venerated by the die-hard element in the tory party and was received with acclamation at the installation of Wellington as chancellor of Oxford University in 1834, although he had been defeated in the election for that office by the pro-Catholic Grenville in 1809. In 1864 his reputation as a reactionary drew down the censure of William Ewart Gladstone, who described him as 'the great champion of all that was most stupid in politics' (*Diary of Henry Greville*, 21 July 1864). Eldon's last years were saddened by the death of his wife on 28 June 1831 and that of his second but only surviving son, William Henry, on 6 July 1832. Eldon died at his London house in Hamilton Place on 13 January 1838 and was buried on 26 January beside his wife at Kingston, Dorset. His grandson John inherited his titles and estates.

Character Eldon was a handsome man, of middle height and build, a pleasant countenance, and a genial character. He was convivial enough to please George IV as a table companion, was a good judge of fine port, and possessed a fund of entertaining anecdotes. However, he had few intellectual interests, was not widely or well read, and was a poor sportsman: he was so bad a shot that his brother Lord Stowell declared that he killed nothing but time, and he gave up riding as a young man after a fall from a horse. He was a devoted husband, father, and grandfather, but a strict parent. He was not a regular churchgoer, and accepted the title of a buttress of the church—supporting it from outside—his concern for the maintenance of the Anglican establishment being motivated by political rather than religious convictions. He was a major figure in the political world of early nineteenth-century England.

E. A. Smith

Sources H. Twiss, *The public and private life of Lord Chancellor Eldon*, 3 vols. (1844) • J. Campbell, *Lives of the lord chancellors*, 8 vols. (1845–69) • *Lord Eldon's anecdote book*, ed. A. L. J. Lincoln and R. L. McEwen (1960) • H. Brougham, *Historical sketches of statesmen … in the time of George III*, 2nd ser. (1839), vol. 2 • *The later correspondence of George III*, ed. A. Aspinall, 5 vols. (1962–70) • *The correspondence of George, prince of Wales, 1770–1812*, ed. A. Aspinall, 8 vols. (1963–71) • *The letters of King George IV, 1812–1830*, ed. A. Aspinall, 3 vols. (1938) • Cobbett, *Parl. hist.* • *Hansard 1* • *State trials*, vols. 24–5 • *The diary and correspondence of Charles Abbot, Lord Colchester*, ed. Charles, Lord Colchester, 3 vols. (1861) • *The correspondence of Charles Arbuthnot*, ed. A. Aspinall, CS, 3rd ser., 65 (1941) • *The journal and correspondence of William, Lord Auckland*, ed. [G. Hogge], 4 vols. (1861–2) • J. E. Cookson, *Lord Liverpool's administration: the crucial years, 1815–22* (1975) • *Memorials and correspondence of Charles James Fox*, ed. J. Russell, 4 vols. (1853–7) • A. Goodwin, *The friends of liberty* (1979) • D. Gray, *Spencer Perceval* (1963) • *The Greville memoirs, 1814–1860*, ed. L. Strachey and R. Fulford, 8 vols. (1938) • Lady Enfield, memoir, in *Leaves from the diary of Henry Greville*, ed. A. H. F. Byng, countess of Strafford, 4 vols. (1883–1905) • W. Hinde, *Canning* (1973) • M. M. Drummond, 'Scott, John', HoP, *Commons, 1754–90* • W. Stokes, 'Scott, John', HoP, *Commons, 1790–1820* • D. Le Marchant, *Memoir of John Charles, Viscount Althorp, third Earl Spencer*, ed. H. D. Le Marchant (1876) • M. McCahill, *Order and equipoise: the peerage and the House of Lords, 1783–1806* (1978) • *Diaries and correspondence of James Harris, first earl of Malmesbury*, ed. third earl of Malmesbury [J. H. Harris], 4 vols. (1844) • G. Pellew, *The life and correspondence of … Henry Addington, first Viscount Sidmouth*, 3 vols. (1847) • E. Phipps, *Memoir of the political and literary life of Robert Plumer Ward*, 2 vols. (1850) • S. Romilly, *Memoirs of the life of Sir Samuel Romilly*, 3 vols. (1840) • *The diaries and correspondence of the Right Hon. George Rose*, ed. L. V. V. Harcourt, 2 vols. (1860) • A. S. Turberville, *The House of Lords in the age of reform, 1784–1837* (1958) • *The historical and the posthumous memoirs of Sir Nathaniel William Wraxall, 1772–1784*, ed. H. B. Wheatley, 5 vols. (1884) • GEC, *Peerage*

Archives BL, papers, dep. 10031 • Middle Temple, London, MSS • NRA priv. coll., corresp. and papers • Encombe, Dorset, MSS | BL, corresp. with first and second earls of Liverpool, Add. MSS 38243–38577 • BL, letters to Sir Robert Peel, Add. MS 40315 • CKS, letters to William Pitt • CUL, corresp. with Spencer Perceval • Cumbria AS, Carlisle, letters to first earl of Lonsdale • Devon RO, corresp. with Lord Sidmouth • Dorset RO, corresp. with William Bond • Exeter Cathedral, letters to Henry Phillpotts • Glos. RO, letters to Lord Redesdale • Gwynedd Archives, Dolgellau, letters to Richard Richards • Harrowby Manuscript Trust, Sandon Hall, Staffordshire, corresp. with Lord Harrowby • LPL, corresp. with Charles Manners-Sutton • NA Scot., corresp. with Lord Melville • Newcastle Central Library, letters, mainly to his cousin H. U. Reay • Niedersächsisches Hauptstaatsarchiv Hannover, Hanover, letters to duke of Cumberland • NL Scot., corresp. with Haldane family • NRA, priv. coll., corresp. with William Adam • NRA, priv. coll., corresp. with Spencer Perceval • NRA, priv. coll., letters to Lord Stowell • PRO, letters to William Pitt, PRO 30/8 • Royal Arch., letters to George III • U. Southampton L., letters to duke of Wellington • W. Sussex RO, letters to duke of Richmond • Winchester College, Hampshire, letters to H. D. Gabell

Likenesses T. Lawrence, oils, *c.*1795, Encombe, Dorset • W. Owen, oils, 1812, Guildhall, Newcastle upon Tyne; copies, Bodl. Oxf. and Hamilton Place • W. Owen, oils, exh. RA 1812, University College, Oxford • T. Lawrence, oils, 1824, Royal Collection; version, NPG • S. W. Reynolds and E. Scriven, mezzotint, pubd 1824 (after F. Stephanoff), BM; [for Sir G. Nayler's work on coronation of George IV] • T. Lawrence, 1825, priv. coll. [*see illus.*] • studio of T. Lawrence, oils, *c.*1828 (after portrait, 1824), NPG • etching, pubd 1829 (after unknown artist), NPG • F. Tatham, marble bust, 1830, NPG • H. W. Pickersgill, oils, 1832, Merchant Taylors' Hall, London • H. P. Briggs, oils, 1834, Middle Temple, London • M. L. Watson and G. Nelson, marble group, *c.*1843–1847, University College, Oxford • W. Behnes, bust, Inner Temple, London • J. Doyle, caricatures, BM • G. Hayter, group portrait, oils (*Trial of Queen Caroline, 1820*), NPG; sketches, NPG • W. Owen, oils, Convocation House, Oxford • Sievier, engravings, BM • portraits, repro. in Twiss, *Public and private life*

Wealth at death under £700,000: *DNB*

Scott, John (1774–1827), engraver, was born on 12 March 1774 at Newcastle upon Tyne, where his father, John Scott, worked in a brewery. At the age of twelve he was apprenticed to a tallow chandler named Greenwell in the city's old meat market, but he devoted all his spare time to the study of drawing and engraving. When he had finished his apprenticeship he was enabled to move to London through the generosity of his fellow townsman Robert Pollard, an engraver, who gave him two years' instruction, at the same time paying him for his work. On leaving Pollard he obtained employment from Wheble, the proprietor of the *Sporting Magazine*, and for many years he executed the portraits of racehorses published in that periodical. The next work upon which Scott was engaged was W. B. Daniel's well-known *British Rural Sports* (1801), many of the plates in which were both designed and engraved by him. He became the ablest of English animal engravers, and his *Sportsman's cabinet, or, A correct delineation of the various dogs used in the sports of the field*, 2 vols. (1803), *History and Delineation of the Horse* (1809), and *Sportsman's repository, comprising a series of engravings representing the horse and the dog in all their varieties, from paintings by Marshall, Reinagle, Gilpin, Stubbs, and Cooper* (1820), earned for him great celebrity. A pair of large plates, *Breaking Cover*, after Reinagle, and *Death of the Fox*, after Gilpin, issued in 1811, are regarded as his masterpieces. The recognition he received for his work as an animal engraver is clearly captured in a drawing of him by J. Jackson engraved by W. T. Fry, which shows him sitting in his studio, looking confidently towards the viewer, a painting of a dog behind him.

Scott also undertook much work for publications of a different kind, such as Tresham and Ottley's *British Gallery*, Ottley's *Stafford Gallery*, Britton's *Fine Arts of the English School*, Hakewill's *Tour in Italy*, and Coxe's *Social Day*, and he executed a single plate for both *Memoirs Illustrative of the Life and Writings of John Evelyn, Esq.* (1818) and *The History and Antiquities of Westminster Abbey* (1856). He laboured unceasingly at his profession until he suffered a stroke in 1821, which practically terminated his career; during the last years of his life he was assisted by the Artists' Benevolent Fund, of which he had been one of the originators. Scott never fully recovered from his stroke and later became ill again, and senile. He died at his residence in Chelsea on 24 December 1827, leaving a widow, several daughters, and one son, John R. Scott. The younger Scott also became an engraver and executed a few plates for the *Sporting Magazine* as well as a drawing of his father in red, black, and white chalk, now in the British Museum print room.

F. M. O'Donoghue, *rev.* Eleanor Tollfree

Sources Redgrave, *Artists*, 382 · *GM*, 1st ser., 98/1 (1828), 376 · *Engraved Brit. ports.*, 4.38 · L. Binyon, *Catalogue of drawings by British artists and artists of foreign origin working in Great Britain*, 4 (1907), 42

Likenesses W. T. Fry, stipple, pubd 1825 (after drawing by J. Jackson, 1823), BM, NPG · W. T. Fry, stipple, pubd 1826 (after drawing by J. Jackson, 1823), BM · J. R. Scott, red, black, and white chalk drawing, BM

Wealth at death *GM* · helped to set up (with eight other artists) the Artists' Fund for needy artists in 1809–10; later called upon fund himself for assistance, so cannot have been well off

Scott, John (1777–1834). *See under* Scott, Thomas (1747–1821).

Scott, John (1784–1821), journalist, was born the eldest son of Alexander Scott (*d.* 1818), an Aberdeen upholsterer, and his English wife, Catherine Young, on 24 October 1784 in Broadgate, Aberdeen. He was taught to read by his mother and at the age of eight was sent to Aberdeen grammar school, where Byron was a junior schoolfellow. In November 1796, soon after his twelfth birthday, he won a scholarship to Aberdeen's Marischal College but left after three years, possibly at the request of his father, who may have persuaded him to join the family business. In the winter of 1800–01, after a quarrel with his father, Scott left home for Edinburgh, then travelled to Glasgow, where he became a clerk in the Royal Bank. He moved to London after two years in this post and in July 1803 entered the War Office as a temporary assistant clerk, which job Leigh Hunt, whom he was later to befriend, did at about the same time. For a while Scott lodged in Fulham with the French engraver Jean-Marie Delattre and his family. He appears to have met William Hazlitt in 1805 and the two men later became firm friends.

In 1807 Scott's burgeoning friendship with Leigh Hunt led to his appointment as editor of *The Statesman*, a radical newspaper which Hunt had founded in the previous year. Scott may also have had dealings with *The News* at this time. Along with Hunt one of his chief mentors in this period was the veteran journalist James Perry, proprietor of the *Morning Chronicle*, who was also a former student of Marischal College. On 30 September 1807 at St Marylebone, Middlesex, Scott married Caroline Antoinette Colnaghi (1786–1874), daughter of the printseller Paul *Colnaghi [*see under* Colnaghi family]. At the end of the following year he left *The Statesman* to set up his own radical weekly, *The Censor*, which he edited until its collapse after only a few months.

Scott then changed tack, moving north to Lincolnshire in order to edit a new weekly newspaper, *Drakard's Stamford News*, the mouthpiece of a prosperous tradesman, John Drakard, who was waging war on local tories. With the editorial support of a radical Stamford grocer, councillor, and amateur poet, Octavius G. Gilchrist, Scott made the *Stamford News* into an influential voice of political liberalism, whose causes included electoral reform, the abolition of slavery, Catholic emancipation, and press freedom. As an advocate of reform Scott was a moderate and in his pamphlet of 1810, *The Necessity of Reform*, proposed that every man who paid taxes should have a vote. In 1812 he contributed to the debate on national education with another pamphlet. More controversial was his violent attack on military flogging, which resulted in a conviction for libel and a gaol sentence for John Drakard.

After three years in Stamford Scott returned to London in 1813 as owner and editor of *Drakard's Paper* (the London edition of the *Stamford News*). *Drakard's* was modelled on the Hunt brothers' *Examiner* and it was while visiting Leigh Hunt in gaol that Scott met again his old schoolfellow Byron, who apparently snubbed him. In 1814 Scott renamed his newspaper *The Champion* and began to publish literary criticism by Thomas Barnes, dramatic and art criticism by Hazlitt, and occasional pieces by Charles

Lamb. In October 1814 he visited Paris for the first time and afterwards recorded his impressions in *A Visit to Paris in 1814* (1815). He sent a copy of this work to Wordsworth and while visiting B. R. Haydon in his studio in April 1815 met the poet, who was sitting for his cast. The two men became close friends. After Waterloo, Scott took the opportunity of revisiting the French capital via the battlefield and Brussels.

On his return home Scott discovered *The Champion* in dire financial trouble. To save money he was forced to shed contributors and write much of the material himself, including the art criticism. Pricked by Haydon, he lent support to Lord Elgin over the Greek marbles, and it was also through Haydon that he met John Hamilton Reynolds, who was gradually to shoulder much of Scott's editorial workload. *Paris Revisited in 1815*, a sequel to his earlier work, appeared in 1816 and was widely acclaimed. Reginald Heber considered Scott 'the ablest of the weekly journalists' and an excellent 'French tourist' (Heber, 2.432). Walter Scott was an admirer too, and William Beckford made four pages of notes on the two works. Encouraged by his success Scott next tried his hand at epic poetry, for which he had little talent, but despite kind advice from Wordsworth a projected 1800-line celebration of Waterloo was never completed.

In April 1816 Scott's violent attack on Byron in *The Champion* over the poet's indelicacy in publishing details of his private life led to a final estrangement from Leigh Hunt, who was one of Byron's most loyal supporters. At this time Scott suffered one of his periodic bouts of what appears to have been consumption and in the following June he left with his family for the continent once again, ostensibly for his health. Illness dogged the travellers in France and in Paris tragedy struck with the death of Scott's eldest son, Paul, in November. A long verse tribute, *The House of Mourning*, was hastily composed but its publication did not advance Scott's reputation as a poet. Keats thought it 'vile'. By March 1817 Scott had disposed of *The Champion* and was no longer even a contributor to it. Instead he looked in other directions and for a while considered writing for the tory *Quarterly Review*.

In the summer of 1817 the Scotts moved for a short spell to the village of Thoméry, near Fontainebleau, and in September illness forced Caroline Scott to return to London, where she remained. By now her husband had moved back to Paris, from where he sent contributions to the *British Review*. His travels had for some while been partly financed by generous advances from his publisher Longman, who had commissioned him to write a three-volume account of his tour, but when the first two volumes failed to materialize the payments stopped. Scott was consequently driven to bully Robert Baldwin, publisher of the *British Review*, to guarantee payments for manuscripts submitted. Early in 1818 he left Paris, visiting Lyons, then Geneva, but from there was obliged to return to England following the death of his father on 24 March. By 23 November he was back in France and soon in Italy, where he spent five or six weeks in Milan before moving off to Venice. Here he was entertained by Byron, who forgave him for the *Champion* attack. He then travelled to Rome and afterwards visited Ischia.

While in Italy, Scott received a letter from Robert Baldwin inviting him to edit a new monthly magazine in London. He expressed an interest but soon afterwards received an invitation from Sir James Mackintosh to apply for a lucrative post as assistant in the East India Company, which he accepted. His absence abroad probably cost him the job, however, and it went instead to the novelist Thomas Love Peacock. By August 1819 Scott was back in London as editor of the projected *London Magazine*, which was to be a monthly miscellany with a pronounced literary bias and, in its political liberalism, an antidote to the rabid toryism of *Blackwood's Magazine*, which was edited in Edinburgh by J. G. Lockhart and John Wilson. The first issue appeared in January 1820 and contained contributions from, among others, Octavius Gilchrist, Horace Smith, B. W. Proctor, Bernard Barton, Hazlitt, and T. G. Wainewright. Charles Lamb joined these regular contributors in August with 'Recollections of the South Sea House', the first of his famous *Essays of Elia*. Scott himself was contracted to write a third of each issue, which he did anonymously and under a number of pseudonyms, including Edgeworth Benson.

In May 1820 appeared the first of Scott's many attacks on the writings of Z in *Blackwood's*, whose venom had been directed at the 'cockney school' of Keats, Cornelius Webbe, Hazlitt, and Leigh Hunt. He successfully provoked Lockhart, the main object of his assaults, into branding him a 'liar and a scoundrel', but a physical confrontation was averted until February 1821, when a provocative statement from Jonathan Henry Christie, Lockhart's agent in London, was interpreted by Scott as a slur on his character. Christie was challenged to a duel and on 16 February the pair met at Chalk Farm, between Camden Town and Hampstead, at about nine o'clock in the evening. Christie did not fire on the first occasion, but owing to a misunderstanding between the seconds was forced to fire on a second occasion in self-defence. Scott was hit in the lower abdomen and removed to a local tavern, where he lay, attended by family and friends, until his death in the evening of 27 February. He was buried on 9 March in St Martin-in-the-Fields. Christie and James Traill, his second, were tried on the charge of wilful murder, but acquitted. A subscription was opened for Scott's family. In April 1821 appeared his posthumous *Sketches of Manners, Scenery etc. in the French Provinces, Switzerland and Italy* (the second half put together by Horace Smith from Scott's notes). Scott also wrote the letterpress for *Picturesque Views of Paris and its Environs* (1820–23), for which Frederick Nash supplied the drawings. In appearance Scott was short in stature but handsome, with an aquiline nose, dark eyes, and dark, curly hair. R. M. HEALEY

Sources P. O. Leary, *Regency editor: life of John Scott* (1983) · J. Bauer, *The London Magazine, 1820–29* (1953) · L. M. Jones, 'The Scott–Christie Duel', *Texas Studies in Literature and Language*, 12/4 (1970–71), 605–29 · *Byron's letters and journals*, ed. L. A. Marchand, 4 (1975) · L. A. Marchand, *Byron: a biography*, 3 vols. (1957) · *The diary of Benjamin Robert Haydon*, ed. W. B. Pope, 5 vols. (1960–63) · L. M. Jones, *The life of John Hamilton Reynolds* (1984) · *The autobiography of Leigh Hunt, with* *reminiscences of friends and contemporaries*, new edn (1885) · Z, 'The cockney school of poetry', *Blackwood*, 3 (1818), 519–24 [Z probably John Gibson Lockhart and John Wilson] · J. Curling, *Janus Weathercock* (1938) · R. Heber, *Life* (1830) · parish register (burial), St Martin-in-the-Fields, London, 9 March 1821

Archives Harvard U. · NL Scot., corresp. and literary MSS · Wordsworth Trust, Dove Cottage, Grasmere | Beds. & Luton ARS, Samuel Whitbread collection · Princeton University, New Jersey, P. G. Patmore collection · U. Edin., John Murray archives · U. Reading, Longman archives

Likenesses J. Pastorini, miniature, 1804, priv. coll. · J. Boaden, oils, 1814, priv. coll. · S. Kirkup, pencil drawing, 1819, Scot. NPG, Edinburgh

Scott, John (1794–1871), racehorse trainer, was born at Chippenham, Cambridgeshire, near Newmarket, on 8 November 1794. His father was a jockey and a trainer, who became landlord of The Ship inn at Oxford, and died at Brighton in 1848, aged ninety-seven. At an early age John entered his father's stables, and at the age of thirteen he won a £50 plate at Blandford. He began as a lightweight jockey but soon put on weight, and after having to lose 2½ stone to ride in a £70 plate he was glad to give up riding races. In 1815 he and his younger brother William *Scott (1797–1848) moved north to the stable of James Croft at Middleham, Yorkshire, where John was put in charge of Filho da Puta, which won the St Leger that year. Shortly after this he was employed by Thomas Houldsworth of Rockhill in Sherwood Forest as private trainer, a position he held for eight years. He then trained for two years for the Hon. E. Petre at Mansfield, Nottinghamshire, and brought out Theodore, the winner of the St Leger in 1822. In 1825 he bought Whitewall House, Malton, Yorkshire, with training stables for a hundred horses, and he lived there for the rest of his life. He had many of the best horses in England under his charge, and became acclaimed as the Wizard of the North, a well-merited title as he trained forty-one classic winners, including the winners of sixteen St Legers, nine Oaks, and six Derbys. Prime among his successes was West Australian, which in 1853 became the first horse to win the triple crown of Two Thousand Guineas, Derby, and St Leger.

Scott was a dignified figure, with long white hair in his old age. He entertained nobles and villagers at his home, carving joints with a knife the handle of which was made from the shank bone of Rowton, his third St Leger winner. He was highly regarded by the owners who employed him, Sir Samuel Martin being one of his executors. His first wife, a Miss Baker, with whom he had a daughter, was the daughter of an innkeeper at Mansfield; his second wife, with whom he had a son, died in March 1891. On a foggy morning in August 1871, while watching his horses work out on Stockton racecourse, Scott caught a chill from which he never recovered, and he died at Whitewall House on 4 October 1871. He was buried on 9 October in Malton cemetery, where a monument was erected in his memory. A tablet in nearby Norton church was erected by public subscription. WRAY VAMPLEW

John Scott (1794–1871), by J. B. Hunt (after Harry Hall)

Sources The Druid [H. H. Dixon], *Scott and Sebright* (1862) · R. Mortimer, R. Onslow, and P. Willett, *Biographical encyclopedia of British flat racing* (1978) · W. Vamplew, *The turf: a social and economic history of horse racing* (1976) · J. B. Radcliffe, *Amongst the Yorkshire trainers* (1899) · G. Plumptre, *The fast set: the world of Edwardian racing* (1985) · J. Rice, *History of the British turf*, 2 vols. (1879) · *DNB*

Archives Durham RO, Bowes papers

Likenesses J. B. Hunt, line engraving (after H. Hall), NPG [*see illus.*] · portrait, repro. in *Sporting Review* (Sept 1855) · portrait, repro. in *ILN* (21 Oct 1871) · portrait, repro. in *Bailey's Magazine* (April 1862)

Wealth at death under £20,000: resworn probate, Dec 1872, *CGPLA Eng. & Wales* (1871)

Scott, John (1799–1846), surgeon, born in Bromley, Kent, on 20 February 1799, was the only son of James Scott MRCS (1770–1849), a general practitioner living at Clay Hill, Beckenham, Kent, and his wife, Mary. His father was particularly successful in the treatment of chronic ulcers and diseased joints. John Scott, educated at a private school in Sevenoaks and at Charterhouse School, London, became apprenticed to Sir William Blizard, senior surgeon to the London Hospital, Whitechapel, about 1816. He became LSA in 1819, MRCS in 1820, and one of the original 300 fellows of the Royal College of Surgeons in 1843. Scott practised with his father for a short time, but after marriage to Susannah Louisa, daughter of the Revd John St John, canon of Worcester, he moved to London, and was living in New Broad Street by 1824; in 1844 he purchased 17 Park Lane, Mayfair.

Scott was elected surgeon to the Ophthalmic Hospital in Moorfields in 1826 and assistant surgeon to the London Hospital in 1827; he became full surgeon in 1831 and resigned owing to ill health in 1845.

Benefiting from his father's experience, Scott gained wide recognition for alleviating diseased joints with an elaborate medicated bandage. In *Surgical observations on the treatment of chronic inflammation … as exemplified in the diseases of the joints* (1828), he specified: (i) wash the joint with soap and water, (ii) rub with camphorated spirits of wine, (iii) apply mercurial ointment on lint strips, (iv) encase in lead oxide plaster on calico, (v) cover with saponified plaster on leather, and (vi) bandage overall with calico; in the absence of complications, this was maintained for weeks or months. In effect the joint was totally immobilized, promoting resolution of pain and inflammation. Others found his directions too complex and pursued simpler methods of achieving joint rest. Nevertheless Scott's 'dressing' or strapping was recommended by adherents well into the twentieth century. Scott's 'ointment' refers to a compound formulation for the dressing, containing camphor, olive oil, mercury, and yellow wax. Scott treated chronic ulcers by his father's method of strapping the whole leg from the toes upwards, and he was opposed to Thomas Baynton's method of strapping for only a short distance above the ulcer. Constant practice is said to have rendered him the most skilful bandager in London.

In a monograph *Cataract and its Treatment* (1843), Scott described a sickle-shaped corneal knife designed to diminish rotation of the eyeball caused by inserting wedge-shaped blades; this sound innovation never came into general use. Scott and John Dalrymple, a colleague at Moorfields, commissioned and collected quality water-colour drawings of eye diseases; after Scott's death Dalrymple published these as a superb and now rare atlas, *Pathology of the Eye* (1852). Scott also wrote *Cases of Tic-douloureux and other Forms of Neuralgia* (1834). He was a bold, but not particularly brilliant, operator, and is said to have been the first surgeon in England (as opposed to Scotland) to remove the upper jaw.

Scott was of an uncertain and irritable temper, often harsh with patients and even friends. Antagonistic towards colleagues, he assumed a superior position and derived pleasure from any triumph in argument, regardless of wounded feelings. General practitioners rarely, if ever, called him in a second time. This unhappy temperament was aggravated by the onset of an insidious illness which debilitated him over several years, causing his death at the age of forty-seven, in Brighton, on 11 April 1846. He was buried at Bromley church, where a memorial tablet was erected to his memory. His wife and father survived him; there were no children. Scott had deep religious convictions and left the bulk of his estate to missionary, Bible, and related societies. JOHN KIRKUP

Sources S. D. Chippingdale, 'Some early members of the hospital staff, VIII', *London Hospital Gazette*, 19 (1912–13), 269–71 • *Medical Times and Gazette*, 14 (1846), 135–6 • V. G. Plarr, *Plarr's Lives of the fellows of the Royal College of Surgeons of England*, rev. D'A. Power, 2 (1930), 273–4 • E. T. Collins, *The history and traditions of the Moorfields Eye Hospital: one hundred years of ophthalmic discovery and development* (1929), 64–5; 77 • private information (1897)

Likenesses H. Howard, oils • S. W. Reynolds, engraving (after H. Howard), possibly Royal London Hospital Medical College • S. W. Reynolds, engraving (after H. Howard), repro. in Collins, *History and traditions of the Moorfields Eye Hospital*, pl. 8

Wealth at death house in Park Lane, Mayfair to his wife; annuity to sister; legacies to societies, incl. the Church Missionary Society, and the British and Foreign Bible Society: Chippingdale, 'Some early members'

Scott, John (1830–1903), shipbuilder and engineer, born at Greenock, Renfrewshire, on 5 September 1830, was the eldest son in a family of five sons and six daughters of Charles Cuningham Scott of Halkshill, Largs, Ayrshire, and his wife, Helen, daughter of John Rankin. His father was a member of Messrs Scott & Co., a leading firm of shipbuilders on the River Clyde, which was founded by an ancestor in 1710. After education at Edinburgh Academy and Glasgow University, John Scott served an apprenticeship to his father, and, on attaining his majority, was admitted to partnership in the firm. In 1868 he became its responsible head, in association with his brother, Robert Sinclair Scott, and directed its affairs for thirty-five years. The ships constructed in the Scott yard during his charge included many notable vessels for the mercantile marine as well as for the British navy; others, such as the battleships *Canopus* and *Prince of Wales*, were engined there.

Scott was closely connected with the development of the marine steam engine. At an early date he recognized the economy likely to result from the use of higher steam pressures, and about 1857 he built the *Thetis*, of 650 tons, which was fitted with a two-cylinder engine of his own design and with water-tube boilers of the Rowan type, the working pressure being 125 lb per square inch. The result was satisfactory so far as economy of fuel was concerned, though he encountered problems of internal corrosion. Scott later introduced the water-tube boiler into a corvette which his firm built for the French navy—the first French warship fitted with compound engines. Similar boilers and engines were proposed by him and accepted for a corvette for the British navy, but owing to the impossibility of complying with the requirement that the tops of the boilers should be at least 1 foot below the load-line, the adoption of the water-tube boiler was deferred. Further pursuit of the question of higher steam pressures led him to make the acquaintance of the engineer Samson Fox, with whom he was associated for many years in the development of the corrugated flue. He became chairman of the Leeds Forge Company, and carried out in conjunction with Fox the first effective tests of the strength of circular furnaces. In September 1864 he married Annie, eldest daughter of Robert Spalding of Kingston, Jamaica; they had two sons and a daughter.

Although his business claimed the greater part of his attention, Scott made three unsuccessful attempts to enter parliament as Conservative candidate for Greenock—in 1880, 1884, and 1885. For many years he was deputy chairman of the Greenock Harbour Trust, and for twenty-five years chairman of the local marine board. He was a lover of books and formed one of the finest private libraries in Scotland, reflecting his interest in Scotland and the Stuarts and containing some rare first editions and early manuscripts as well as literature relating to his own profession. An ardent yachtsman, he was a member of many Scottish yacht clubs and commodore of the Royal Clyde yacht club.

Scott also took an active interest in the volunteer movement, and in 1859 he raised two battalions of artillery volunteers. From 1862 to 1894 he was lieutenant-colonel of the Renfrew and Dumbarton artillery brigades, and on relinquishing active duty in the latter year he was made honorary colonel. For his services in connection with the movement he was made a CB in 1887.

Scott was one of the original members of the Institution of Naval Architects, established in 1860, and became a member of council in 1886 and a vice-president in 1903. In 1889 he contributed to the society's *Transactions* a paper entitled 'Experiments on endeavouring to burst a boiler shell made to Admiralty scantlings', which was the outcome of some tests made by him with boilers for the gunboats *Sparrow* and *Thrush* built by his firm for the British navy. He was elected a member of the Institution of Civil Engineers in 1888, and was also a member of the Institution of Engineers and Shipbuilders in Scotland, a fellow of the Royal Society of Edinburgh, and a fellow of the Society of Antiquaries in Scotland.

Scott died at his home, Halkshill, Largs, Ayrshire, on 19 May 1903 and was buried at Largs; his wife survived him. His library was sold at Sothebys from 27 March to 3 April 1905. W. F. Spear, *rev.* Anita McConnell

Sources *The Engineer* (22 May 1903) • *Engineering* (22 May 1903) • *Transactions of the Institution of Naval Architects*, 45 (1923), 335
Likenesses G. Reid, oils, 1885, priv. coll.; last known at Halkshill, 1912
Wealth at death £265,376 1*s*. 4*d*.: confirmation, 2 Dec 1903, *CCI* • 1*s*.: eik additional estate, 10 Oct 1906, *CCI*

Scott, John (1836–1880), botanist and gardener, was born on 5 April 1836 at Denholm, Roxburghshire, Scotland, the son of Robert Scott, a tenant farmer, and his wife, Helen Turnbull. He had one elder sister. At the age of four Scott became an orphan and was brought up by an aunt and educated at the parish school. During this time he developed an interest in botany, a passion which was encouraged by his cousin, the Revd James Duncan, a keen botanist. When he was fourteen Scott became an apprentice gardener, working in Jedburgh and Westmorland (not at Chatsworth as many sources state) before joining the staff of the Royal Botanic Garden, Edinburgh, under James McNab. He became foreman of the propagating department there in 1859. Scott was elected an associate of the Botanical Society of Edinburgh on 10 July 1862 and contributed three papers to that society's *Transactions*, one of which (on the fertilization of orchids) was particularly well received.

In 1862 he began a fruitful correspondence with Charles Darwin, who wrote that Scott's letters 'show remarkable talent, astonishing perseverance, much modesty, and what I admire, determined difference from me on many points' (*Life and Letters*, 3.300). In 1864 Scott became an associate of the Linnean Society of London at the invitation of George Bentham. He carried out a number of experiments on behalf of Darwin at this time, an association which apparently contributed to Scott's increasing alienation from James McNab. Not feeling that his abilities were receiving due recognition, Scott resigned his post at Edinburgh in March 1864 and sought employment elsewhere. Later in that year Darwin paid for Scott's passage to India where, through the patronage of Joseph Dalton Hooker, he became curator of the Royal Botanic Garden, Calcutta, under its superintendent, Thomas Anderson.

At Calcutta, despite being condemned to live in a house officially reported unfit for human habitation, Scott busied himself enthusiastically, mainly in repairing the damage caused to the garden by the cyclone of 1864. Later work included experiments with cotton cultivation and at least two trips to Sikkim. In February 1870 his major work, 'Notes on the tree ferns of British Sikkim', was read at the Linnean Society of London (and was published subsequently in its *Transactions* in 1874) and he was elected a fellow of that society in 1873. Scott also carried out more experimental work for Darwin, providing information for his *Expression* (1872). From November 1872 to September 1878 Scott was seconded by the government of India to the opium department, with orders to investigate the diseases that affected the opium crop and to improve its yield. This work resulted in his *Manual of Opium Husbandry of Behar and Benares* (1877). While at Darjeeling, where he was sent later to report on the disease of coffee plants, he developed a spleen complaint, and in 1879 this forced his return to Britain on two years' sick-leave. When he visited the Edinburgh Botanical Gardens in May of that year his former colleagues were shocked by his poor state of health. Scott died at the house of his sister, Agnes, at Garvald, East Lothian, on 11 June 1880. He never married.

Scott published over twenty papers, all on botanical or agrobiological subjects, including seven in the *Journal of the Agricultural and Horticultural Society of India* (1869–74). He was held in high regard as a botanist by his contemporaries. Sir George King described him as 'one of the most remarkable self-taught men I ever met' (*More Letters*, 1.218), and Darwin recorded that Scott was the best observer he had ever come across. However, Scott's career undoubtedly suffered from his shyness and an excessive modesty; King recorded that 'the condition of nervous tension in which he seemed to live was indicated by frequent nervous gestures with his hands and by the restless twisting of his long beard in which he continuously indulged' (ibid., 1.217). Andrew Grout

Sources W. Gorrie, *Transactions of the Botanical Society* [Edinburgh], 14 (1883), 160–61 • *More letters of Charles Darwin*, ed. F. Darwin and A. C. Seward, 2 vols. (1903) • *The life and letters of Charles Darwin*, ed. F. Darwin, 3rd edn, 3 vols. (1887) • *The correspondence of Charles Darwin*, ed. F. Burkhardt and S. Smith, 10 (1997) • *Annual Report of the Royal Botanic Garden, Calcutta, 1870–71* (1871) • *Annual Report of the Royal Botanic Garden, Calcutta, 1878–9* (1879) • F. A. Stafleu and R. S. Cowan, *Taxonomic literature: a selective guide*, 2nd edn, 6, Regnum Vegetabile, 115 (1986) • b. cert. • d. cert.
Archives Botanic Garden, Calcutta, India, herbarium • RBG Kew, specimens and letters

Wealth at death under £100: administration, 1880, *CGPLA Eng. & Wales*

Scott, Sir John (1841–1904), legal adviser, was born at Wigan, Lancashire, on 4 June 1841, the son of Edward Scott, a solicitor, and his first wife, Annie Glover. He had two brothers and a sister, as well as two half-brothers and two half-sisters from his father's second marriage, to Laura, *née* Hill. From 1852 to 1860 Scott was educated at Bruce Castle School, Tottenham; he then matriculated at Pembroke College, Oxford. He graduated BA in 1864 and proceeded MA in 1869. A fast left-hand bowler, he was captain of his college cricket team, and in 1863 played in a match between Oxford and Cambridge.

Scott was called to the bar by the Inner Temple on 17 November 1865 and then joined the northern circuit. He wrote on legal questions for *The Times*, the *Law Quarterly*, and other periodicals, and his *Bills of Exchange* (1869) became a widely read text-book. On 16 February 1867 he married Edgeworth Leonora, the daughter of Frederic *Hill (1803–1896), brother of Rowland Hill. They had four sons, including Leslie Frederic *Scott, who became an MP in 1910, and four daughters.

A chronic heart condition drove Scott to the Riviera for many months in 1871–2. While there he learned French and Italian and studied the French legal system. This information stood him in good stead when, on medical advice, he went to Alexandria towards the end of 1872, to pursue his profession there. In 1874, on the formation of a court of international appeal from the courts for foreign and native litigants, Scott was made, on the recommendation of the British agent and consul-general, the English judge, and in February 1881 was made vice-president of the court. G. J. Goschen, on his mission to Egypt in 1876, nominated Scott English commissioner of the public debt, but the khedive, Isma'il Pasha, would not release him from his post and the appointment went to Lord Cromer (then Major Baring). From 1873 onwards Scott's letters to *The Times* from Alexandria record Egyptian history of the period. He used his influence to suppress slavery and to improve the condition of the fellahin. In the Alexandria riots of June 1882 he narrowly escaped being killed, but remained at the court house day and night to assist in protecting the records.

In October 1882, when the khedive conferred on him the order of the Osmanie, Scott was appointed as puisne judge of the high court at Bombay. One of his judgments settled the law of partition among Hindus, and another defined the extent of Portuguese ecclesiastical jurisdiction over the Roman Catholics of western India. Scott continued to write on Egyptian affairs for the local and London press. His letter to the *Times of India* (26 December 1884), signed 'S', foreshadowed political transitions in India. For a year, from April 1890, he was seconded to Egypt to examine the whole system of Egyptian jurisprudence, and to propose amendments. Despite opposition from the Egyptian premier, Rıza Pasha, Lord Cromer persuaded the khedive to accept Scott's recommendations and to appoint him judicial adviser to the khedive; Rıza Pasha soon resigned (May 1891), pleading ill health.

Scott's impartiality and goodwill towards the Egyptians and his ability to reform, without destroying, existing institutions, helped him to create a sound judicial system in Egypt. He established circuits, comprising forty stations, in place of only three centres of justice, simplified and accelerated the procedure of the courts, organized a system of inspection and control, replaced incompetent judges, and established a school of law. Scott did much of the inspection himself, travelling throughout the country; his annual reports from 1892 to 1898 leave an interesting record of Egypt and of his achievement.

Scott, who was made KCMG in March 1894, retired in May 1898 for health and other reasons. The khedive conferred on him the order of the Mejidieh of the highest class. In June 1898 the University of Oxford awarded him an honorary DCL, and he became an honorary fellow of his old college, Pembroke. He was also elected a member of the Athenaeum, and Wigan conferred upon him the freedom of the city early in 1893. He was also made a vice-president of the International Law Association.

In 1898 Scott was appointed deputy judge advocate-general of the army, during the Second South African War. He joined other ex-judges of India in a memorial advocating the separation of judicial and executive functions in India, dated 1 July 1899. He died, after a long illness, at his residence, Ramleh, College Road, Norwood, London, on 1 March 1904 and was buried in St John's churchyard, Hampstead. F. H. BROWN, *rev.* LYNN MILNE

Sources J. Scott, reports as judicial adviser, 1892–8, PRO · *The Times* (5 March 1894) · *The Times* (11 May 1898) · *The Times* (3 March 1904) · *Oxford Magazine* (9 March 1904) · H. R. Fox Bourne, *Administration of justice in Egypt* (1909) · *Indian Magazine and Review* (April 1904) · earl of Cromer [E. Baring], *Modern Egypt*, 2 vols. (1908) · A. Milner, *England in Egypt* (1892) · private information (1912)

Likenesses E. G. Hill, chalk drawing, Pembroke College, Oxford · J. H. Lorimer, portrait, priv. coll.

Wealth at death £6967 10s. 6d.: probate, 21 April 1904, *CGPLA Eng. & Wales*

Scott, Sir John Arthur Guillum (1910–1983), ecclesiastical civil servant, was born in East Battersea, London, on 27 October 1910, the eldest of the three children and elder son of Guy Harden Guillum Scott, a barrister, and his wife, Anne Dorothea Fitzjohn. Scott's paternal grandfather, Sir Arthur Guillum Scott, was accountant-general of the India Office. Scott's father became in 1920 assistant secretary of the newly established church assembly and in 1939 secretary (jointly with L. G. Dibdin), and was also chancellor of the diocese of Oxford. Scott's brother was in government service in Nigeria and his sister, Judith, was from 1954 to 1971 secretary of the Council for the Care of Churches.

Scott was educated at King's School, Canterbury. In 1929, after a brief period in a City bank, he joined the staff of Queen Anne's Bounty. In the 1930s Scott was a member of the Inns of Court regiment (TA). He served in the Second World War, was wounded and mentioned in dispatches, and, when war ended, was on the Ceylon staff of Lord Louis Mountbatten. After demobilization Scott rejoined the Inns of Court regiment, in which he had a fierce pride, ending as lieutenant-colonel commanding, and being awarded the territorial decoration in 1945. There was much that was soldierly, in the best sense, in Scott's character and bearing; and as a bureaucrat he was always rather more the staff officer than the Whitehall mandarin. In 1938 he married (Muriel) Elizabeth, daughter of James Ross, departmental manager of Fownes, the well-known firm of glovers. They had one daughter.

In 1946 Scott replaced his father on the staff of the church assembly, serving for two years under L. G. Dibdin. In 1948 he succeeded to the secretaryship. His primary task was to service the thrice-yearly sessions of the assembly and its committees. But he was constantly on call to serve as secretary or assessor to a variety of committees dealing with the financial and administrative structures of the church, with the appointment, deployment, and payment of bishops and clergy, with liturgy, with relations with other churches, with church–state relations and much else. He did not see himself as a radical, but he was not against change if it was necessary or desirable. It was often he who, when others had agreed upon aspirations, would give expression to them in terms of positive proposals, leading to acceptable and practicable legislation.

Scott had close, trusting relationships with the two archbishops of Canterbury whom he served. G. F. Fisher appreciated the young staff officer who helped him to run the church assembly with dispatch. With A. Michael Ramsey the relationship was more complex. Each man seemed somewhat in awe of the other—Ramsey of the efficient man of business, and Scott of the archbishop whose intellect he found daunting. Recognition came from church (a Lambeth DCL in 1961, shortly before Fisher's retirement) and state (a knighthood in 1964). Church people sensed the depth of Scott's Christian commitment, though he did not wear his religion on his sleeve. He was a man of great personal charm; he was an excellent host; he had a remarkable memory for names and faces. No one enjoyed more the pomp and circumstance of the great church or state occasion. Yet there was a restraint about him which, as the years went by, acquired a touch of the Olympian, placed as he was literally and metaphorically above the battle and seemingly unmoved by it. People liked him, but not many felt that they knew him well. He was, indeed, a private person, on close terms outside his family with only a few, such as his secretaries, a close Church House aide of the 1960s, and his successor.

When the general synod came into being in 1970, replacing the church assembly, Scott was its first secretary-general. When it was decided that a younger man should succeed him after two years, he accepted with excellent grace, setting himself to groom his successor with all his own and his father's accumulated professional cunning, for between them they had served the church assembly for the whole of its fifty-year life.

The Scotts had lived in Buckinghamshire while he worked in London. On his retirement from the synod in 1972 Scott moved to Chichester, to become the first communar (lay administrator) of the cathedral. He and Lady Scott threw themselves with enthusiasm into the life of the cathedral and its close as he began to establish an administration to meet the pastoral and financial needs of the time, including the vastly increased number of visitors. He retired for a second time in 1979, continuing to live in Chichester. He died there on 6 May 1983.

Derek Pattinson, *rev.*

Sources *Church Times* (13 May 1983) · *The Times* (7 May 1983) · personal knowledge (1990) · *CGPLA Eng. & Wales* (1983)
Archives Bodl. Oxf., corresp. with third earl of Selborne
Wealth at death under £25,000: probate, 4 Aug 1983, *CGPLA Eng. & Wales*

Scott, John William Robertson (1866–1962), journalist, was born on 20 April 1866 at Wigton in Cumberland, the second of eight children (the first died in infancy) of David Young Crozier Scott, commercial traveller and temperance orator, and his wife, Janet, daughter of John Robertson. His border origins were wholly rural. He was educated at Quaker and grammar schools. His parents, who held broad and liberal views, welcomed many like-minded visitors of several nationalities to a home that was 'serious but not austere, of great affection and care'. Robertson Scott wrote of his father, as one who had much to do in setting the course of his life, that he was 'not only a teetotaller and a non-smoker, but a believer in cold baths and a disbeliever in bottles of medicine'. His parents were members of the Evangelical Union, but the family went to Quaker, Wesleyan, and Congregational services 'impartially'.

The family moved to Carlisle about 1876 and three or four years later to Birmingham, where Robertson Scott's father was summoned to take charge of the organization to which he had devoted already a disproportionate share of his time and energies: the Independent Order of Good Templars. One of Robertson Scott's first jobs was as secretary to Joseph Malins, head of the grand lodge of the Good Templars in England; but he had already decided on a career in journalism. His father died at the age of forty-three, when he was still in his teens. As the eldest surviving son he accepted the challenge and supported his mother, brother, and three sisters on meagre journalistic earnings. In retrospect he was grateful for 'a realizing sense of what poverty is'. The first payment had come from C. P. Scott of the *Manchester Guardian*, and he was contributing to several national journals when H. J. Palmer offered him a staff appointment on the *Birmingham Gazette*; but he had to leave when he stipulated that, as a Liberal, he should write nothing in support of the Conservative cause. He was working again as a freelance when, in 1887, he was invited by W. T. Stead to join him on the *Pall Mall Gazette*. He worked for six years on that paper under Stead and then Edward T. Cook. When Cook left to found the *Westminster Gazette* in 1893 Robertson Scott accompanied him and wrote a daily feature, 'Round the world'. In 1899 he transferred to the *Daily Chronicle* under H. W. Massingham, but resigned with him in November of that year on the issue of the Second South African War, with which the proprietors sympathized.

It was then that Robertson Scott decided to live and

write in the country. He acquired a cottage at Great Canfield in Essex and 'invented that pioneer in rural journalism and authorship, "Home Counties"'. In 1902 he was invited by J. St Loe Strachey to contribute farming articles to the *Country Gentleman*. In the next few years, using the same pseudonym, he was closely associated with the *World's Work* and *The Field*; he also wrote hundreds of articles and several books in a style peculiarly his own. They were for townspeople about farmers and smallholders, farm workers and landowners, how they lived and made a living, omitting the technicalities. He travelled the country and made frequent visits abroad, notably to the Netherlands and Denmark. His energy was prodigious, his journalistic output remarkable. In 1906 he married the talented Elspet (*d*. 1956), daughter of George Keith, of HM customs. They had no children. Together they contributed to the life of rural Essex, forming at Dunmow the Progressive Club for 'men and women of markedly different upbringings and associations, politics, denominations and incomes', and producing in Lady Warwick's big barn plays by Synge, Barrie, and Bensusan.

When war broke out in 1914 Robertson Scott was above military age. He paid two visits to the Netherlands, then sold his Essex property and went to Japan. Looking ahead to the period of post-war reconstruction, he had in mind two studies: one of the small-farming system and rural life in Japan, the other (never accomplished) of large-scale farming in the American mid-west. While in Japan, gathering material with characteristic penetration and vigour, he started and edited with official backing a monthly, the *New East*; he refused to adopt a propagandist approach and tried to explain Japan and the Japanese to the West and Western ideas to the East. In 1916 appeared, in both English and Japanese, his book *Japan, Great Britain and the World*; but it was not until 1922, a year after his return home by way of the United States, that his copious notes were published as *The Foundations of Japan*, long the standard work in English on the rural life and people of that country.

On his return Robertson Scott resumed his journalistic writing, became an enthusiastic adviser to the National Federation of Women's Institutes (he published, in 1925, *The Story of the Women's Institute Movement*), and was a hard-working member of the Liberal land committee which produced *The Land and the Nation* (1923–5). At this time he contributed to *The Nation* a series of four articles which grew to twenty-four and was published anonymously as *England's Green and Pleasant Land* (1925), his best-selling book. It described frankly and penetratingly, through the people and their talk about neighbours and themselves, the life of a contemporary village. *The Dying Peasant and the Future of his Sons* followed a year later.

In 1923 Robertson Scott had moved to the Cotswold hamlet of Idbury in Oxfordshire. Four years later, at the age of sixty-one, he founded the quarterly review, *The Countryman*. He and his wife were business and advertisement manager, editor, sub-editor, and principal contributors. Ignoring the advice of friends, and with never more than £500 capital, they made it the most successful venture in periodical publishing between the two world wars. Non-party, though firm enough in opinion, it was packed with rural life and character, placing before town, city, and country dwellers vividly and convincingly the facts, and strengthening the forces of rural progress; but to achieve its more serious purpose it needed also to entertain. Robertson Scott sold the magazine in 1943 and continued to edit it with full independence for a further four years.

Despite the demands of *The Countryman*, Robertson Scott was active in local government. Housing had been one of his most compelling interests since he contributed to the *Country Gentleman* a series of articles entitled 'In search of a £150 cottage'; this led to an exhibition at Letchworth opened by the duke of Devonshire. For ten years he chaired his district council housing committee, and served under four ministers of health on the Central Housing Advisory Committee. He became a JP and founded the Quorum Club, an educational society with a good library for magistrates. He set great store by the gatherings of 'village neighbours' in Idbury School to hear an invited speaker each Sunday afternoon. In 1947, on his retirement, Robertson Scott was made a Companion of Honour. Two years later he was awarded an honorary MA degree by Oxford University.

A self-styled agnostic, Robertson Scott had an infectious faith in humanity. He envisaged a future where ordinary men and women would grow in stature as their opportunities expanded. All his strivings, tremendous energy, knowledge, and journalistic skill were directed to extending these opportunities. He was always welcoming to people and causes. He was greatly helped by a devoted wife, herself a gifted writer, who provided him with a satisfying home background. He lived until his middle nineties with faculties undiminished, and died at home at Idbury Manor on 21 December 1962.

John Cripps, *rev.*

Sources J. W. R. Scott, *The day before yesterday* (1951) · J. Cripps, *The Countryman*, 60 (1963), 13–30 · personal knowledge (2004) · *CGPLA Eng. & Wales* (1963)

Archives BL, corresp. with Sir Sydney Cockerell, Add. MS 52752 · BL, corresp. with Society of Authors, Add. MSS 56801–56802 · BL, corresp. with Marie Stopes, Add. MS 58499 · JRL, letters to the *Manchester Guardian* · Mitchell L., NSW, letters to G. E. Morrisson

Likenesses A. van Anrooy, oils, *c*.1930–1939, offices of *The Countryman*, Burford, Oxfordshire · H. Coster, photograph, *c*.1930–1939, NPG

Wealth at death £38,933 6*s*.: probate, 19 Feb 1963, *CGPLA Eng. & Wales*

Scott, Jonathan (1735–1807), Independent minister, was born on 15 November 1735 at Shrewsbury, the second son of Captain Richard Scott of Scott's Hall in Kent and Mary, the daughter and heir of Jonathan Scott of Belton Grange, near Shrewsbury. After 'a polite education' (*Evangelical Magazine*, 15.489), he became a cornet at the age of seventeen and subsequently a captain-lieutenant in His Majesty's 7th regiment of dragoons, in which he served for seventeen years including several campaigns in Europe.

Intermittently religious from a young age, he was converted by the preaching at a Sussex country house of the leading London evangelical William Romaine, a close associate of the Calvinist Methodist leader Selina, countess of Huntingdon. Thereafter Scott began to preach, first to his own soldiers: in a letter to the religious controversialist Sir Richard Hill, he refers to 'the Lord extending his mercy and his grace' as he congregated his men twice daily in his lodgings from 1766 for prayer and Bible study. A year later, starting in Leicester, he began preaching wherever his regiment was posted, indoors or out, sometimes with violent opposition, so that he acquired the reputation of being 'an arrant methodist'. His correspondence reveals friendship with many evangelical leaders, especially Hill, John Fletcher of Madeley, John Newton, and Henry Venn (Macfadyen, 51–4).

In 1769, a year after his marriage on 1 June 1768 to Elizabeth Cley (*d.* 1799), a pious heiress of Wollerton in Shropshire, Scott was faced with an ultimatum from his superior officers to choose between his preaching and his military career. As a result he resigned his commission, though he continued to appear in the pulpit in uniform, and was widely known as Captain Scott. More than any other minister, Scott was responsible for the establishment of evangelical congregationalism in Staffordshire; some twenty-two churches trace their origins to his labours, not to mention five churches in Shropshire, six in Cheshire, four or five in Lancashire, and others in Derbyshire which were profoundly influenced or started by him. At Middlewich in Cheshire and Leek in Staffordshire congregations which had adopted Unitarianism were restored through his efforts to evangelical orthodoxy. Pressed to become pastor of the congregation at Lancaster, a position he would have found too restricting, he did consent to be ordained there in September 1776 as 'presbyter at large' (Urwick, 137).

From about 1776 Scott concentrated his work in the under-provided county of Staffordshire. Beginning in Newcastle under Lyme, where the baptismal registers of the chapel he founded date to 1777, he seven years later purchased land called the Marsh on which a new chapel was erected. The work was soon extended to the potteries where he preached in what he called 'his old cathedral', namely the streets. The 'Tabernacle' in Hanley, the fruit of his labours there, was opened in 1784 in self-conscious resemblance to George Whitefield's chapel in London, where Scott preached frequently for twenty years. Other Staffordshire towns which benefited from Scott's ministry include Lichfield, Stone, Uttoxeter, and Stafford. However, the military parson was not always well received; his preaching in Gnosall in mid-Staffordshire in 1778, with George Burder, provoked a 'formidable riot'. John Wesley, it appears, was also unhappy with some of Scott's activities. Recording the minister's presence at a sermon preached in Newcastle under Lyme in March 1781, Wesley—apparently laying some kind of proprietorial claim to missionary activity in north Staffordshire—wrote of how Scott and his preachers 'have lately begun to preach both here and at Burslem. If they would go and break up fresh ground we should rejoice, but we cannot commend them for breaking in upon our labours after we have borne the burden and the heat of the day' (*Journals*, 6.309). Scott, as part of the Calvinistic evangelical revival, was unprepared to leave the field to the Arminians, whose record historically he found unsatisfactory.

During the 1780s Scott entered into a partnership with the evangelical activist Willielma, Viscountess Glenorchy, who financed the training of suitable young men through the Oswestry and Newcastle under Lyme academy. In addition Lady Glenorchy provided funds for underpaid ministers and for the building of new churches, with Scott acting as her secretary, treasurer, and committee, exercising an authority which has been called 'more than episcopal'. On her death in July 1786 Glenorchy left a chapel and house at Matlock to Scott; this became his home and headquarters from 1794, though he preached on alternate Sundays at Matlock and Nantwich. Following the death of his first wife on 31 December 1799 he married in 1802 the widow of a Samuel Barrow of Nantwich. Scott himself died at Nantwich on 28 May 1807 and was buried at Queen Street Chapel, Chester, on 9 June. Commemorations of his life were generous towards a man who, while promoting religious diversity, had proved a loyal subject, marrying 'genuine patriotism with conscientious dissent from the established church'. Such commitment was also readily apparent to congregants appreciative of a minister who, if not blessed with special intellectual gifts, 'was an honest, resolute, autocratic man, with a considerable allowance of practical shrewdness, a warm heart and a complete devotion to the cause which he had espoused' (*Evangelical Magazine*, 15.546–7).

J. H. Y. Briggs

Sources *Evangelical Magazine*, 15 (1807), 489–96, 537–48; 16 (1808), 196–9 • D. Macfadyen, 'The apostolic labours of Captain Jonathan Scott', *Transactions of the Congregational Historical Society*, 3 (1907–8), 48–66 • A. G. Matthews, *The Congregational churches of Staffordshire* (1924) • five letters, DWL, Congregational Library • H. F. Burder, *Memoirs of the Revd George Burder* (1833) • B. Nightingale, *Lancashire nonconformity*, 6 vols. [1890–93], vol. 1, pp. 255–6 • F. J. Powicke, *A history of the Cheshire County Union of Congregational churches* (1907) • E. Elliot, *A history of Congregationalism in Shropshire* (1898) • W. Urwick, ed., *Historical sketches of nonconformity in the county palatine of Cheshire, by various ministers and laymen* (1864) • *The journals of John Wesley*, ed. N. Curnock, 9 vols. (1909–16)

Archives DWL, Congregational Library, five letters

Likenesses engraving, repro. in *Evangelical Magazine*, 434

Scott, Jonathan (1753–1829), orientalist, born at Shrewsbury on 8 March 1753, was the third son of Jonathan Scott of Betton, Shropshire, and Mary, daughter of Humphrey Sandford of the Isle of Rossall, Shropshire. Major John Scott [*see* Waring, John Scott- (1747–1819)] was his eldest brother. He was educated in Shrewsbury at the Royal Free Grammar School which he left in 1766 to travel to Bengal with his elder brothers, John and Richard. Jonathan entered East India Company service as a cadet in 1769, devoting his leisure to the study of Persian and Hindustani, and Indian history. He was posted ensign to the 29th battalion sepoys in 1772, made lieutenant in 1777, and finally captain in 1781. In 1779 he was appointed Persian interpreter to Major William Popham, under whom he saw action at the capture of Gwalior, and in quelling the rebellion of Chet Singh. He also served in the same capacity under Lieutenant-Colonel Jacob Camac in his expedition against the Marathas.

Governor-General Warren Hastings appointed Scott his private Persian translator in 1783, responsible for communications with the native powers judged too diplomatically sensitive to be trusted to an Indian secretary. Hastings also valued Scott's historical investigations which took their cue from Robert Orme's thesis that the reign of Aurangzeb and of his successors was the key epoch of Mughal Indian history. Scott consulted the best native authorities, and amassed materials collected by his brother Captain Richard Scott, and by Lieutenant-Colonel Henri Polier, concluding that a fuller understanding of recent history might be gained from an insight into the history of the Deccan.

Scott was elected to the Asiatic Society of Bengal soon after its inception in 1784, and established himself as a member of Hastings's intellectual circle to the extent that, the governor-general having been recalled, Scott resigned his commission on 28 January 1785 and sailed with him for England in the *Berrington* on 8 February as one of a select group of companions. On 15 December 1786 he married his cousin, Anne (*b.* 1750), the daughter of Daniel Austin, rector of Berrington, Shropshire. They had a son who died at a young age, and a daughter, Anna Dorothea, who was later to marry her cousin, William Richard Stokes of Shrewsbury.

In London in 1786, Scott published his first work, *A translation of the memoirs of Eradut Khan, a nobleman of Hindostan, containing interesting anecdotes of the Emperor Aulumgeer Aurungzebe, and of his successors, Shaw Aulum and Jehaundar Shaw*. His conclusions concerning the contemporary relevance of the demise of the Mughal empire were published in 1791 in *An Historical and Political View of the Decan, South of the Kistnah*, and an appendix to the second edition of 1798 included updated material concerning treaties with Tippoo Sultan. Meanwhile in Shrewsbury in 1794 he published at his own expense his two-volume *Ferishta's history of Dekkan from the first Mahummedan conquests, with a continuation from other native writers … to the reduction of its last monarchs by the emperor Aulumgeer Aurungzebe; also the reigns of his successors … to the present day; and the history of Bengal … to the year 1780*.

Despite the enthusiastic reception of these works, Scott was disappointed in his hopes of patronage from Hastings or the East India Company, and turned his hand to more popular literary orientalism. He published in London the *Bahar-Danush, or, Garden of knowledge: an oriental romance, translated from the Persic of Einaiut Oollah* (3 vols., 1799), and in Shrewsbury, *Tales, Anecdotes and Letters, Translated from the Arabic and Persian* (1800). The latter included several tales from a fragment of an *Arabian Nights* manuscript which James Anderson had obtained in Bengal.

Scott's scholarly bent was apparent in his plans to produce a new translation of the Edward Wortley Montagu manuscript of the *Arabian Nights*, and he provided a description of its contents in William Ouseley's *Oriental Collections* (1797). In the event he contented himself with a substantial revision of Antoine Galland's French translation (1704–17), making occasional corrections from the Arabic. In 1811 Scott published his *Arabian Nights Entertainment* in six volumes, the sixth volume entirely occupied by tales translated for the first time from the Montagu manuscript. This constituted the first literary translation of the *Arabian Nights*, providing a critical introduction and copious annotation of the Muslim religion and customs. Scott's version was reprinted in Philadelphia in 1826 (6 vols.), and in London in 1883 (4 vols.) and 1890 (4 vols.), being also widely used as a basis for pirated and bowdlerized editions.

In 1802 Scott was appointed professor of oriental languages at the Royal Military College, Marlow, and subsequently at the East India College, Haileybury, but he resigned company service in 1805, dissatisfied with the remuneration and status accorded him, publishing his *Observations on the Oriental Department of the Hon. Company's East India College at Hertford* in 1806. In 1809, regretting his rash resignation, he unsuccessfully applied to the court of directors for patronage to translate further Mughal historical works.

Scott received the honorary degrees of DCL from the University of Oxford in 1805 and LLD from Cambridge in 1808 for his services to oriental literature and history. Though somewhat isolated in Shrewsbury from academic colleagues, he encouraged the orientalist researches of his townsman Samuel Lee. He died on 11 February 1829 at his residence in St John's Row, Shrewsbury, and was buried in the church of his baptism, St Chad's. He was survived by his wife and daughter.

MICHAEL J. FRANKLIN

Sources BL OIOC, E 1/119, no. 220 · *Annual Register* (1829) · *GM*, 1st ser., 99/1 (1829), 470–71 · *Memoirs of the life of the Right Hon. Warren Hastings, first governor-general of Bengal*, ed. G. R. Gleig, 3 vols. (1841) · V. C. P. Hodson, *List of officers of the Bengal army, 1758–1834*, 4 (1947), 4, 37 · parish register, St Chad's, Shrewsbury · J. S. Grewal, *Muslim rule in India: the assessments of British historians* (1970), 34–6 · review, *Critical Review*, 3rd ser., 22 (1811) · review, *Critical Review*, [new ser.], 13 (1795) · review, *Analytical Review* (April 1795) · review, *British Critic*, 5 (1795), 209–18, 516–25 · Burke, *Gen. GB*

Archives BL OIOC, E 1/119, no. 220 | BL, letters to Warren Hastings and others, Add. MSS 29146–29190, *passim*

Wealth at death none: BL OIOC, E 1/119, no. 220

Scott, Joseph Nicol (1702/3–1769), Independent minister and physician, was born at Hitchin, Hertfordshire, where his father, Thomas Scott (1679/80–1746), was the minister of Back Street Chapel. He was the eldest of six children, who included his brother Thomas *Scott (1705–1775) and sister Elizabeth *Scott (1707/8–1776). He was born into a family with strong Independent connections: his paternal grandfather, Daniel, left a legacy to Isaac Watts, and Thomas's half-brother was Daniel *Scott (1694–1759), theological writer and lexicographer. On 13 October 1709 his father, who was a correspondent of Philip Doddridge, succeeded John Stackhouse as minister of a congregation that had separated from the Old Meeting, Norwich; when, by 1717, the split had been healed, he became minister of the Old Meeting. Joseph Scott spent his formative years in

Norwich. It is not known where he received his education, but his later writings show a familiarity with classical languages, and he published a translation of Homer in blank verse. About 1725 he became assistant to his father, who in 1726 published his only work, *An Attempt to Prove the Godhead of Christ*, the text of a sermon dealing with the divinity of Christ with a foreword by Isaac Watts. In 1737 or 1738 Joseph was dismissed from the Old Meeting for opinions tending toward Socinian or Arian views on the nature of Christ. This was a terrible blow to his father, whose nervous system became permanently unhinged; he died on 15 November 1746.

Scott was established by supporters in a Sunday lecture at the French church, St Mary-the-Less. At first a considerable success, support and finance apparently waned. Two volumes of discourses, *Sermons Preached in Defence of All Religion whether Natural or Revealed*, were published (1743); one sermon affirmed the annihilation of the wicked, anticipating the thought of Samuel Bourn of Norwich. By the date of publication Scott was studying medicine at Edinburgh, whence he graduated MD in 1744. He practised as a physician in Enfield, Middlesex, for some years, where his considerable learning found its fullest expression in *A New Universal Etymological English Dictionary* (1755), a greatly enlarged edition of Nathan Bailey's *Dictionarium Britannicum* (1730).

By his will of 1759 John Reynolds, a former high sheriff of Suffolk, left an estate in Felsham, Suffolk, to Scott. Scott died there, aged sixty-three, on 23 December 1769 and was buried at the Old Meeting in Norwich, where there is a monument. *The Gracious Warning* (1774) by George Wright alluded to Scott's uncanny premonition of his own death. Scott left a considerable estate to his wife, Martha Bell, and other relatives. His wife died at Aylsham, Norfolk, in 1799, aged eighty-seven.

Alexander Gordon, *rev.* S. L. Copson

Sources J. Browne, *A history of Congregationalism and memorials of the churches in Norfolk and Suffolk* (1877) • W. Urwick, *Nonconformity in Hertfordshire* (1884) • *Nomina eorum, qui gradum medicinae doctoris in academia Jacobi sexti Scotorum regis, quae Edinburgi est, adepti sunt, ab anno 1705 ad annum 1845*, University of Edinburgh (1846) • will of John Reynolds, esq., 1759, PRO, PROB 11/848, sig. 280 • [J. Chambers], *A general history of the county of Norfolk*, 2 vols. (1829) • *GM*, 1st ser., 69 (1799) • will, proved, 2 Jan 1770, PRO, PROB 11/954, sig. 29

Wealth at death £4900; plus property in Norwich and Suffolk: will, PRO, PROB 11/954, sig. 29

Scott [*née* Bruce], **(Edith Agnes) Kathleen**, **Lady Scott** [*other married name* (Edith Agnes) Kathleen Young, Lady Kennet; *known as* Kathleen Kennet] **(1878–1947)**, sculptor, was born at the rectory, Carlton in Lindrick, Nottinghamshire, on 27 March 1878, the youngest of the eleven children of Lloyd Stewart Bruce (1829–1886), a Church of England clergyman, and his first wife, Jane (Janie) Skene (*c.*1838–1880), an amateur artist. Kathleen was descended from Scottish royalty on her father's side and Phanariot aristocracy on her mother's. Orphaned at the age of eight, she was brought up in Edinburgh by her great-uncle, the historian William Forbes Skene, and was educated at two English boarding-schools. Her disciplined and restricted upbringing provoked a strong sense of independence

(Edith Agnes) Kathleen Scott, Lady Scott (1878–1947), by Charles Haslewood Shannon, 1907 [*The Sculptress*]

and, after rejecting the idea of teaching, she attended the Slade School of Fine Art, London (1900–02). The absence of adequate sculptural education there probably explained her decision to enrol at the Académie Colarossi, Paris.

Her memoirs, *Self-Portrait of an Artist* (1949) (published under the name Kathleen Kennet), vividly recount her bohemian life in Paris between 1902 and 1906. She had several notable admirers, including Edward Steichen, Rembrandt Bugatti, and Aleister Crowley. One of her flatmates, given the pseudonym Hermione, was the designer Eileen Gray. Kathleen was befriended by Auguste Rodin, whose influence was reflected in the fluid modelling of her earliest surviving works. These statuettes, all in private collections, reflect her obsession with motherhood and the baby as a miracle of creation. Her concern for babies born amid the Turkish atrocities in Macedonia led her to quit her studio in 1903 to assist with child relief there. In 1905 she again put sculpture on hold to tend her friend Isadora Duncan, during her pregnancy.

Kathleen's Parisian experiences prepared her for a triumphant entry into London's artistic and literary society, where her new friends included George Bernard Shaw, James Barrie, Max Beerbohm, and Henry James. In 1906, through the socialite Mabel Beardsley, she met Captain Robert Falcon *Scott (1868–1912). They were married on 2 September 1908 and their son, Sir Peter Markham *Scott, was born the following year. For Kathleen this fulfilled a romantic, Wagnerian quest for the right man to sire the son she had long desired. Her brief marriage was marked by lengthy separations from Scott due to his naval duties and, from 1910, his second Antarctic expedition. On her return voyage to New Zealand to meet him in 1913, she learned of his death the previous year.

Granted the rank of a widow of a knight commander in the Order of the Bath and known as Lady Scott, she aroused widespread admiration for the dignified and courageous manner in which she bore her loss and for her determination to give her son a happy childhood. Her regard for what she called Scott's 'gloriousness' is reflected in her best-known sculpture, a bronze statue of him (1915) in Waterloo Place, London. This rugged portrayal shows Scott staring into the distance with the determined smile recorded on newsreel films. The replica (1916–17), in Christchurch, New Zealand, benefits from being carved in marble, its whiteness poignantly evocative of the Antarctic. When not engaged on these statues, Kathleen undertook wartime work. After helping to establish an ambulance service in northern France, she worked in the Vickers factory in Erith, Kent, making electric coils, and in 1917 was private secretary to Sir Matthew Nathan, permanent under-secretary at the Ministry of Pensions. In 1918 she reconstructed faces of the war wounded, her models acting as a basis for the plastic surgery which followed. These achievements do not sit comfortably with her opposition to women's suffrage, which was founded partly on Victorian conservatism and partly on dislike of special pleading.

Kathleen's career as a sculptor peaked during the inter-war years. In all, she had six major exhibitions, regularly exhibited at the Royal Academy, became an associate member of the Société Nationale des Beaux-Arts (1923), was awarded a bronze medal at the salon of the Société des Artistes Français (1925), and was elected to the council of the Royal Society of British Sculptors (1937), followed nine years later by fellowship of the society. In 1937 the BBC's first television programme on sculpture focused on her portraits and working methods and in 1938 a book on her sculpture, *Homage*, was published with commentary by Stephen Gwynn. Her popular reputation was evident in numerous newspaper and women's magazine articles on her work and personality.

Kathleen Scott's works belong to two principal categories: portraits—mostly busts but also statues and statuettes, of her eminent male contemporaries—and ideal sculptures of youths. She outspokenly preferred males, both as company and as sitters. Rather than avoiding women as 'more difficult and less interesting to model', she was attracted to sculpting 'the heads of men whose features suggest high power or intellect … most artists like best to produce what they know best. What they know best is commonly what they love best' (*Weekly Dispatch*, 3 April 1927). She was uniquely placed to know—and love—men of power and intellect. Her friend James Lees-Milne observed that '[t]here seemed to be no public figure with whom she was not on intimate terms' (Lees-Milne, 2). Four of her models were prime ministers—Herbert Asquith, David Lloyd George, Stanley Baldwin, and Neville Chamberlain. Other friends included the explorer Fridtjof Nansen, T. E. Lawrence, E. M. Forster, J. B. Priestley, Malcolm Sargent, Hugh Walpole, and Woodrow Wilson's adviser, Edward M. House. The products of such friendships are vigorously modelled busts and statuettes which provide a valuable visual record of contemporary celebrities. Among her most successful are the bust of Chamberlain (1936, City of Birmingham Museum and Art Gallery), which casts a plausibly humane light on an often caricatured politician, and the half-length bronze portrait of George Bernard Shaw (1938, Russell-Cotes Art Gallery and Museum, Bournemouth), who poses, head between hands, as 'a serious and ascetic philosopher' (*Evening Standard*, 1 June 1939). Her work is widely represented in public collections, including the Tate collection, the National Portrait Gallery, and the Imperial War Museum.

Kathleen Scott's ideal sculptures usually portray lissom young men and sometimes double as memorials. Reactions to them vary from the adulatory Geoffrey Dearmer—'a classic economy relieved of austerity by a touch of romanticism' (*DNB*)—to the damning Lees-Milne: 'Their exclamatory gestures and striving towards the sublime are fairly commonplace … verging on … sentimentality' (Lees-Milne, 15–16). The latter verdict applies to the smiling, pre-adolescent, nude volunteer, entitled *Here am I, Send me* (1922, Oundle School, Northamptonshire). Yet this work, together with others such as *These had Most to Give* (1923–4, Scott Polar RI, Cambridge) and *Ad astra* (1938, Welwyn Garden City, Hertfordshire), are supple in modelling and elegant in silhouette, forming a strangely moving homage to the male body. Their poses are sometimes evocative of modern dance and hint at those struck by Isadora Duncan. Kathleen herself was an energetic, enthusiastic, and sure-footed dancer, particularly ballroom, and a highly capable ice-skater. She took both pride and amusement in teaching Bernard Shaw to dance, when the latter was aged sixty-one. By the end of Kathleen's life her output had slowed, and she appeared increasingly stylistically reactionary. Her unrelenting hostility towards the sculpture of Jacob Epstein, Frank Dobson, and Henry Moore compounded this view and helps to explain why her work has been accorded less art historical recognition than it deserves. While the comparison would not have appealed to either of them, Kathleen Scott was the most significant and prolific British woman sculptor before Barbara Hepworth. She died of leukaemia on 24 July 1947 at St Mary's Hospital, Paddington, London, having lived since 1927 at Leinster Corner, Lancaster Gate, London. She was cremated, and after her funeral service at West Overton church, Wiltshire, a commemorative plaque was placed there. She was survived by her son, Sir Peter Scott; by her second husband, the politician, journalist, and businessman (Edward) Hilton (Bill) *Young (1879–1960), whom she had married in 1922 and who had been knighted in 1927 and had been created Baron Kennet in 1935; and by their son, Wayland.

Kathleen Scott believed that 'she was an artist first; her work constantly called her from the distractions of family and social life' (Kennet, 10). The latter were, however, immensely important 'distractions' for her. It could be said that she 'sculpted' the personalities of both her first husband and their son. While she guarded the heroic status of the former, she took immense pride in the latter's development as an artist, naturalist, and pioneer conservationist. Socially she was held in high, indeed cloying, affection by her many celebrated friends. This came about through her loyalty, generosity, candour, and optimism. Her charisma was considerable, but so too was her discretion. Shaw, Barrie, and Nansen were ardent admirers and, as wartime prime minister, Asquith considered her a confidante, telling her that she had 'the best brain of any woman I know' (ibid., 156). MARK STOCKER

Sources L. Young, *A great task of happiness: the life of Kathleen Scott* (1995) • K. Kennet, *Self-portrait of an artist: from the diaries and memoirs of Lady Kennet, Kathleen, Lady Scott* (1949) • M. Stocker, '"My masculine models": the sculpture of Kathleen Scott', *Apollo*, 150 (Sept 1999), 47–54 • J. Lees-Milne, *Fourteen friends* (1996) • S. Gwynn, *Homage: a book of sculpture* (1938) • E. Huxley, *Scott of the Antarctic* (1978) • *DNB* • M. Stocker, '"Loving hands and an eye that knew": Kathleen Scott, sculptor and romantic', *Australasian Victorian Studies Journal*, 3 (1997), 52–9 • M. Stocker, '"Loving hands and an eye that knew": the Scott memorials in Christchurch and London', *Bulletin of New Zealand Art History*, 19 (1998), 55–65 • A. Garrihy, 'Scott, Kathleen', *Dictionary of Women Artists*, ed. D. Gaze (1997), 1253–5 • P. Attwood, 'Kathleen Scott: the sculptor as medallist', *British Numismatic Journal*, 60 (1990), 121–9 • F. Spufford, *I may be some time: ice and the English imagination* (1996) • *CGPLA Eng. & Wales* (1947)

Archives Birmingham Museums and Art Gallery • Bodl. Oxf., diary • CUL, MSS • IWM • NPG • NRA, priv. coll., MSS catalogue of sculpture • Russell-Cotes Art Gallery, Bournemouth • Scott Polar RI, corresp. • Tate collection | Bodl. Oxf., letters to Jack Lambert | SOUND BBC television programme on sculpture, 1937

Likenesses C. H. Shannon, oils, 1907, Musée d'Orsay, Paris [*see illus.*] • C. H. Shannon, oils, 1908, Johannesburg Art Gallery, South Africa • photographs, repro. in Kennet, *Self-portrait of an artist* • photographs, repro. in Young, *Great task of happiness* • photographs, CUL, Kennet MSS

Wealth at death £43,395 11*s*. 6*d*.: probate, 27 Nov 1947, *CGPLA Eng. & Wales*

Scott, Laurence Prestwich (1909–1983), newspaper publisher, was born on 10 June 1909 at 5 Carill Drive, Rusholme, Manchester, the eldest of five children of John Russell Scott (1879–1949), newspaper publisher, and his wife, Alice Olga (1883–1978), youngest child of Archibald Briggs, colliery owner, and his wife, Alice Sophia. He succeeded to the chairmanship of the Manchester Guardian and Evening News Ltd on the death of his father in 1949, and as a grandson of Charles Prestwich *Scott, editor of the *Manchester Guardian* from 1871 to 1932, was of the third and last generation of the family to preside over the fortunes of the paper and company.

Scott went to Rugby School and Trinity College, Cambridge, where he took a good degree in economics and was a half-blue at chess. His father, having himself lived under parental dominance, did not wish to presume upon his son's career, and it was left unspoken whether Laurence's future lay in the newspaper business. Accordingly he joined the London and North Eastern Railway as a traffic apprentice. On deciding that this could not be his career he secured management and editorial traineeships on the *News Chronicle* and the *Financial News*, and became circulation manager of the London evening paper *The Star*. It was not until the company in Cross Street, Manchester, felt the acute manpower shortage of the Second World War that negotiations with the Air Ministry secured Laurence's release from photographic intelligence in the RAF so that he should come to his father's aid and prepare to take over the company. He arrived in 1944, at the age of thirty-five.

It was soon apparent to Scott that although the *Manchester Guardian* had a national and international reputation it would not survive the rigours of post-war competition without at least three radical changes. These were to put news on the front page in place of classified advertising, to drop 'Manchester' from the title, and to print in London as well as Manchester (a notion which Lloyd George had urged on his grandfather C. P. Scott in 1914). The paper at that time had a much overworked editor, A. P. Wadsworth, who gave his entire energy to the quality of the paper's contents and procrastinated, to Scott's growing dismay, about the weighty managerial matters on Scott's mind. Thus it was September 1952 before front-page news appeared.

The Suez crisis of 1956 supervened before the next move could be made. During this crisis Scott gave full support to his new editor, Alastair *Hetherington, in his impassioned opposition to British involvement despite the fear, mistaken as it turned out, that the policy would bring about a collapse in circulation. Scott honoured scrupulously the distinction between the editor's and the manager's roles.

'Manchester' was dropped from the title in 1959, and in 1961 printing in London began. In the late 1940s Scott had encouraged his technical staff to experiment with facsimile transmission of pages from Manchester to London. This pioneering work was successful, and was soon used overseas, but Scott did not adopt it for fear of opposition (never articulated by them) from the typographical trade unions. Instead a complicated and expensive system of simultaneous 'tele-typesetting' in both printing centres was adopted, which was one cause of *The Guardian*'s unhappy early years in London. Another cause was the false assumption, not abandoned until 1964, that although printed in London the paper could still be run from Manchester. Preparations for the great leap forward had been inadequate, for which Scott's indulgence to senior managerial colleagues must be held largely responsible.

Unlike his father Scott was not the proprietor; he was chief executive acting on behalf of the Scott Trust to which his father, with his co-operation, had transferred the entire ownership of the company, making it unique in the newspaper world. In the mid-sixties Scott began negotiations with Gavin Astor, chairman of *The Times*, for a merger of the two papers. He pursued the notion in different guises over many months, but it was resisted by Hetherington and most of the editorial staff, and came to nothing. The failure of this endeavour led to a thorough restructuring of the company by the creation of operating boards of management of *The Guardian* and the *Manchester Evening News*. Scott became non-executive chairman of the parent company, but it was no longer a family concern.

'Scott of the Guardian' was a man of tall stature and natural dignity, with the handsome features of the family. He was liked and respected by the staff and by the reading public in Manchester. In his early London years he had done voluntary work at the youth centre at Toynbee Hall and half hankered after membership of the Hutterian

Bruderhof, a protestant order to which his sisters belonged. In the event he remained a nominal Unitarian. Scott's first wife was Constance Mary, daughter of William Fisher Black, textile agent; they married at a register office in London in 1939, and had two sons and a daughter. She died of cancer in September 1969.

Scott was a director from its inception of Anglia Television and became chairman of the Press Association and an active deputy chairman of the council of Manchester University. Throughout *The Guardian*'s travails he bore also the strain of his first wife's illness. On 14 February 1970 he married again. His second wife was his secretary, Jessica Mary Crowther Thompson, third child of Joseph Kenyon Thompson, lecturer and administrator in agriculture, and his wife, Sybil Crowther. They had one son. He retired in November 1973, and having left his house at Westow Lodge, Alderley Edge, devoted himself to a house and garden at Siddington, near Macclesfield. Scott died of a brain haemorrhage on 2 September 1983 at West Park General Hospital, Macclesfield, and was buried at Siddington parish church. GEOFFREY TAYLOR

Sources *The Guardian* (5 Sept 1983) • G. Taylor, *Changing faces: a history of The Guardian, 1956–1988* (1993) • D. Ayerst, *Guardian: biography of a newspaper* (1971) • private information (2004) • d. cert. • b. cert.
Archives Guardian Media Group plc, Manchester, corresp., memoranda, etc. • JRL, *Guardian* archives, general corresp. | FILM BBC Panorama, interview with James Mossman, 2 Jan 1967
Likenesses photograph, Guardian Media Group plc, Manchester • photograph, repro. in Taylor, *Changing faces*, facing p. 83
Wealth at death £163,214: probate, 16 Nov 1983, *CGPLA Eng. & Wales*

Scott, Leader. *See* Baxter, Lucy (1837–1902).

Scott, Sir Leslie Frederic (1869–1950), judge and politician, was born on 29 October 1869 at Hornsey, Middlesex, the eldest of the four sons in the eight children of Sir John *Scott (1841–1904), who became judicial adviser to the khedive, and his wife, Edgeworth Leonora, daughter of Frederic *Hill, inspector of prisons for Scotland. From Rugby School he won a classical exhibition at New College, Oxford (of which he became an honorary fellow in 1939), and was placed in the second class both in honour moderations (1890) and in *literae humaniores* (1892). In 1894 he was called to the bar by the Inner Temple, of which he was afterwards a bencher, and read in chambers with his cousin Maurice Hill and with Hugh Fenwick Boyd. In 1898 he married Ethel (*d*. 1954), daughter of Henry A. James, of Suffolk Hall, Cheltenham, Gloucestershire. They had no children.

Scott began his practice at Liverpool, chiefly in commercial and maritime cases. He was remembered there as 'profoundly industrious … He used to worry his cases as a terrier does a rat … he had no manner of use for "devils" or pupils, for he did every jot and tittle of work himself' (Campbell, 91). But of the many pupils that Scott did have, the most notable was F. E. Smith, later first earl of Birkenhead, to whom Scott remained close throughout his time in politics. He moved his chambers to London in 1906, became a KC in 1909, and in the following year began his political career as Conservative member of parliament for the Exchange division of Liverpool, a seat which he held until he resigned it in 1929.

Scott took a progressive line on social questions, striving to encourage class harmony. Before the First World War he was a member of the Unionist Social Reform Committee. During the debates on electoral reform in 1917 he supported proportional representation and was an advocate of women's suffrage. In parliament one of his most significant achievements was as chair of the inquiry, between 1917 and 1919, which laid the groundwork for the introduction of centralized land ownership registration, against the opposition of solicitors. Scott admitted that he had 'so packed the committee as to produce a unanimous report' (Campbell, 484). His aim was to broaden property ownership and thus to 'cut the ground from under the feet of the Bolshevists' (Waller, 305). The draft bill produced by the committee was shepherded through parliament by Birkenhead and was, said Scott, 'the biggest legal reform that has ever been put upon the Statute Book of this country' (Campbell, 485).

Scott was a member of Lloyd George's wartime reconstruction committee and from March to October 1922 was solicitor-general in the Lloyd George coalition government. He was knighted in that year. The fall of the coalition was a bitter blow to Scott, who said at a meeting with Birkenhead soon after that:

> He had been six months in office as Solicitor-General after twelve years in the House. If he had given the slightest sign of throwing over his colleagues, he could have secured the Attorney-Generalship in the new Administration. Instead he voted with Austen Chamberlain. (Campbell, 611)

Austen Chamberlain was replaced by Bonar Law as Conservative leader, with Bonar Law becoming the new prime minister. Scott was subsequently hurt when Baldwin passed him over for the attorney-generalship in 1924, and although he remained active in parliament in matters such as housing, town planning, factories, and the regulation of money-lending, he decided to return to his private legal practice. In 1927 he represented the Indian Princely States at the inquiry into how they might be affected by any move towards self-government in British India. In the same year he was sworn of the privy council.

In 1935, at the age of sixty-six, Scott was appointed direct to the Court of Appeal, becoming in 1940 the senior lord justice. He retired in 1948. His *Times* obituary noted that 'it could not be maintained that Scott was a great judge' (*The Times*, 6). It was said of him that he was inclined in seeking a solution of a legal problem to base himself upon over-wide generalizations; and some of his judgments were subsequently criticized, as in *Leachinsky* v. *Christie* (1945), criticized by Lord du Parcq in 1947, and in *Bonnington Castings, Ltd* v. *Wardlaw*, 1956, where the law lords had to correct a dictum of Scott's. Scott also provided a famous example of the degree to which judges could be divorced from the understandings of everyday life, when he admitted during a libel case in 1943 that he had had to be informed by a fellow judge that 'the word "pansy", as applied to a man, has a slang sense, often used, of an opprobrious character' (Pannick, 33).

Apart from that on land ownership, Scott was a member, and frequently chairman, of many government and other committees. He was chairman of the Agricultural Organisation Society (1917–22) and of the committee on ministers' powers (1929–32) after the resignation in 1931 of Lord Donoughmore, and was seconded from the Court of Appeal to sit upon the committee on land utilization in rural areas (1941–2), the report of which is usually called the Scott report. He was a founder member and on the executive of the Council for the Preservation of Rural England, and was chairman of its Berkshire branch, in which capacity he helped to preserve the amenities of the village of Letcombe Basset. In 1947 he was the first president of the National Association of Parish Councils, and from 1914 to 1947 was president and chairman of the Central Association for Mental Welfare. He was the British representative at four Brussels conferences on international maritime law.

Scott wrote several books: *The Effect of War on Contracts* (1914), *British Agriculture, the Nation's Opportunity* (in collaboration, 1917), *The Case of Requisition* (with A. Hildesley, 1920), and *The New Law of Property Acts Explained* (with B. B. Benas, 1925). He was also a painter in oils and exhibited at the New English Art Club and at the Royal Scottish Academy. He died at the Acland Nursing Home in Oxford on 19 May 1950. A riverside garden at Winchester was dedicated to him in 1952 in memory of his services to rural England. P. A. LANDON, *rev.* MARC BRODIE

Sources *The Times* (22 May 1950) · J. Campbell, *F. E. Smith, first earl of Birkenhead* (1983) · J. Foster, *Oxford men, 1880–1892: with a record of their schools, honours, and degrees* (1893) · D. Pannick, *Judges* (1987) · R. Blake, *The unknown prime minister: the life and times of Andrew Bonar Law* (1955) · Burke, *Peerage* · P. J. Waller, *Democracy and sectarianism: a political and social history of Liverpool, 1868–1939* (1981) · *CGPLA Eng. & Wales* (1950)

Archives U. Warwick Mod. RC, corresp. and papers | BL OIOC, letters to Lord Reading, MSS Eur. E 238, F 118 · HLRO, corresp. with Andrew Bonar Law · HLRO, letters to David Lloyd George · Welwyn Garden City Central Library, corresp. with Frederic Osborn

Likenesses W. Stoneman, photograph, 1927, NPG

Wealth at death £26,126 3*s.* 3*d.*: probate, 28 July 1950, *CGPLA Eng. & Wales*

Scott, Mackay Hugh Baillie (1865–1945), architect, was born at Beard's Hill, St Peter's, Broadstairs, Kent, on 23 October 1865, the first of the fourteen children of Mackay Hugh Baillie Scott, a Scot whose considerable wealth seems to have come mainly from sheep farms in Australia, and his wife, Martha Waters, who was English. While he was a child his family moved to Worthing in Sussex, where he went to school. From 1883 to 1885 he attended the Royal Agricultural College in Cirencester, with a view to managing his family's property in Australia. But shortly before he was due to leave for Australia Scott decided to become an architect, and from 1886 to 1889 he was articled to C. E. Davis of Bath. On 16 February 1889 he married Florence Kate Nash (1862–1939). They went to the Isle of Man for their honeymoon, and then settled there, in Douglas, where Scott got a job with a surveyor. A daughter was born in 1889 and a son in 1891, and in 1892–3 Scott

Mackay Hugh Baillie Scott (1865–1945), by unknown photographer, *c.*1906

built a house for his family in Douglas. He set up in practice there on his own and continued to work there until 1901. The Isle of Man probably did not offer great prospects to an architect of Scott's abilities, but he quite soon found a way of furthering his career without leaving the island.

In January 1895 Scott published an article entitled 'An ideal suburban house' in *The Studio*, the leading progressive art magazine of the day. It was followed by several others on the design of middle-class houses. He wrote about homeliness, the quality he saw in old cottages and farmhouses; about simplicity and the clearing away of genteel clutter; and about the fireplace as the focus of family life. His most radical idea was the 'houseplace', a single large room in middle-class houses, with alcoves off it for eating, reading, talking, and so on, instead of the several small rooms of middle-class propriety. He wrote in an easy, middlebrow way and the illustrations, from his own designs, showed gleaming hearths, timber-framed inglenooks, and ornament drawn from nature and romance: the home as refuge. In the articles he published between 1895 and about 1900 Scott found his subject matter and his way of operating professionally.

For the articles are interwoven with the development of

Scott's early houses on the mainland. Bexton Croft at Knutsford, Cheshire (1895–6), was published as 'An ideal suburban house', the subject of his first article, while Seven Gables, Cambridge (1897–8), appeared as 'A small country house' in *The Studio* for December 1897. Others, such as Blackwell, Windermere (1898–1900), and the White House, Helensburgh, near Glasgow (1899–1900), were more loosely related to the articles, but had the timber-framed, double-height halls, generous ingle-nooks, and rich natural ornament which clients had seen illustrated there. At Blackwell much of Scott's decoration in plaster, metal, wood, textiles, and glass survives, showing his unusual judgement in the combination of colours, the geometry which disciplines and invigorates his natural ornament, and the interplay of plain and decorated elements. The furniture he designed from the mid-1890s, much of it made by the firm of John P. White in Bedford, has these qualities: simple, sturdy pieces with plank-like members against which are set panels of concentrated natural ornament, painted or inlaid. With these houses and this furniture Scott's work reached its early maturity.

The Studio was widely read in Europe and America. Early in 1897 Scott was asked to decorate and furnish two rooms in the Neues Palais at Darmstadt, Germany, for the grand duke of Hesse and by Rhine, a grandson of Queen Victoria. This was followed, later in 1897, by tiny, fantasy-laden interiors in a tree house on the royal estates for Princess Marie of Romania, the grand duke's sister: Scott devised a decorative symbolism of sunflowers for the sitting-room, poppies for the bedroom, and lilies for the oratory. His 1901 competition design for a country house for a connoisseur, sponsored by the German magazine *Zeitschrift für Innendekoration*, won second prize when no first was awarded, principally because of his interiors, which glowed with ornament and hangings in pinks and blues and greens. Over the next decade Scott designed (and in most cases built) about a dozen houses and interiors in Europe and the United States, of which Landhaus Waldbühl at Uzwil in Switzerland (1907–11) was probably the most elaborate. It survives with its full complement of furniture and interiors. Probably no British architect working in the domestic field was better known in Europe before the First World War than Scott.

In 1901 Scott moved to Bedford, and converted two early nineteenth-century cottages just outside the town into a house for his family and an office. By now he had a considerable reputation, but he did not go to London, and chose not to move in architectural circles. He was an important figure within the arts and crafts movement, but he never became a member of the Art Workers' Guild, its principal London organization. He was a modest-looking moustachioed figure, gentle and often droll, but little is known about him as a man, because of the lack of documentary evidence. An assistant's recollections of his office at this time give a glimpse of him:

> a long, low cottage, pink washed, with a mossy tiled roof … At the rear facing an acre of orchard, projected at one end, Scott's office (originally the detached washhouse), smothered in ivy; at the other end a wooden wing housed the staff … Red turkey twill curtains hung at the windows, and the brick floor had strips of brightly coloured matting … Two or three times a day, Scott would stroll across slowly from his room to ours, generally with a cat in his arms. (Kornwolf, 250–51)

All the time he was keeping the architectural papers supplied with illustrations of his work, maintaining that combination of journalism and remoteness which he had discovered on the Isle of Man. In 1906 he published a book, *Houses and Gardens*, a detailed account of his ideas on house design and a fetchingly illustrated survey of his work. It seems to have brought him many clients.

Scott's houses in these years have strong, defining roofs, a clear disposition of parts, and a feeling for the texture of brick, stone, wood, and plaster. Of the groups of smaller houses he built in the new garden suburbs, those on the south-east corner of Meadway and Hampstead Way in Hampstead Garden Suburb (1908–9), or 36–38 Reed Pond Walk, Gidea Park, Essex (1910–11), are good and accessible examples. From about 1903 onwards he would often design a garden for a new house, laying it out as a series of compact outdoor rooms, along axes that run through the house as well. His interiors in these years generally took their cue from the forms and finishes of the exterior, and thus are plainer, more traditional, than those of the 1890s. The techniques and materials of English vernacular building were, increasingly, Scott's benchmark in design. Here was a language in which he could express his enduring ideal of homeliness without recourse to the extravagance of symbolism and elaborate decoration, a way of building that was ordinary and to hand. He worked in this way for the rest of his life.

In March 1911 Scott's house and office were almost completely destroyed by fire. For some years he wandered with his wife and family from place to place, running the office as best he could until he closed it down in 1914. The Scotts did not have a permanent home until 1921, when he bought Ockhams at Edenbridge, a Kentish farmhouse which he repaired and lived in for the next twenty-one years.

In 1919 he opened an office in partnership with A. E. Beresford, who had worked for him since 1905 and took care of the business side of the practice. Their office was in Holborn, so Scott was working in London for the first time. But he resisted its pressures. Beresford was always in the office punctually, Scott was often late. Sometimes he did not come in at all, but preferred to work among the fields of Kent. They took up where he had left off in 1914 (though commissions no longer came from Europe), and in the 1920s their output equalled that of the pre-war years. Their houses were mostly neo-Tudor in style, some in a free neo-Georgian, and all handled with the reverence for traditional building which Scott had absorbed in the Bedford years. Old ways of working were cultivated, old materials were reused; tiles were brought to the site with the lichen still on them. These houses have not been studied as closely as Scott's earlier work because they seem so traditional. But Diane Haigh's study of Church Rate Corner, a modest house in Cambridge of 1924, shows Scott's traditionalism as spare, refined and intelligent, a sensibility honed down to the pleasure of materials and the good sense of using familiar methods for familiar purposes.

From about 1935 Scott began to play less part in the practice. He was then aged seventy and near the end of a long and remarkably focused career. He had put up several hundred buildings, over almost fifty years. He had re-established his career after the First World War, which left many of his contemporaries adrift. The great majority of his buildings were detached, middle-class houses, and his whole career had been bound up with a building type typical of his time, the single family house within commuting distance of a city. Throughout his work he had concentrated on the expression of domesticity, and the criticism sometimes made, that his houses are sentimental, perhaps arises from this: they say 'Home sweet home' so sweetly. Scott, whose intellectual blandness was his strength, would have turned this criticism round, by pointing, as he did in all his writings, to the importance of feelings in the experience of houses. But one should also say that the reputation of his best work rests on other qualities besides, on skilful planning, and a handling of masses that is, remarkably, most effective in his smallest buildings.

Commuting, which combines participation in the city with emotional distance from it, is perhaps a good image for the whole strategy of Scott's career, for the consistency with which he kept personally aloof from the metropolitan centre of architecture while keeping his work always in the professional press. Between the wars he became a commuter himself. But when John Betjeman, who got to know him at this time, went to visit him at Edenbridge, he seemed like an 'unassuming countryman', not like an architect at all (Betjeman, 'Mackay Hugh Baillie Scott', 78).

In 1939 Scott's wife died. His partnership with Beresford came to a formal end with the outbreak of war. In 1942 he sold Ockhams. He was by now an invalid, looked after by a permanent nurse, and spent the next two years in nursing homes or rented cottages in Devon and Cornwall. He died on 10 February 1945 in Brighton Municipal Hospital, and was buried at Edenbridge. ALAN CRAWFORD

Sources J. B. Kornwolf, *M. H. Baillie Scott and the arts and crafts movement: pioneers of modern design* (1972) • D. Haigh, *Baillie Scott: the artistic house* (1995) • M. H. B. Scott, *Houses and gardens* (1906) • M. H. B. Scott and A. E. Beresford, *Houses and gardens* (1933) • J. Betjeman, 'Mackay Hugh Baillie Scott', *Journal of the Manx Museum*, 8 (1968), 77–80 • K. Medici-Mall, *Das Landhaus Waldbühl von M. H. Baillie Scott: ein Gesamtkunstwerk zwischen Neugotik und Jugendstil* (1979) • D. Haigh, 'M. H. Baillie Scott: 48 Storey's Way, Cambridge', *Architects' Journal* (22 July 1992) • G. Zelleke, 'Harmonizing form and function: Mackay Hugh Baillie Scott and the transformation of the upright piano', *The Art Institute of Chicago Museum Studies*, 19 (1993), 161–73 • *John Betjeman: coming home: an anthology of his prose, 1920–1977* (1998) • b. cert. • d. cert.

Archives Landhaus Waldbühl, Uzwil, Switzerland, architectural drawings and corresp. relating to the design and construction of the house • Manx Museum and National Heritage, Douglas, Isle of Man, letters to E. J. Graves

Likenesses photograph, *c*.1885, Manx Museum and National Heritage, Douglas, Isle of Man • photograph, *c*.1906, RIBA [*see illus.*]

Wealth at death £6672: probate, 14 Sept 1945, *CGPLA Eng. & Wales*

Scott, Margaret (*d.* 1692). *See under* Salem witches and their accusers (*act.* 1692).

Scott [*married name* Hamilton-Russell], **Lady Margaret Rachel (1874–1938)**, golfer, was born on 5 April 1874, the second daughter in the family of five sons and two daughters of John Scott, third earl of Eldon (1845–1926), and his wife, Henrietta Minna (*d.* 1921), eldest daughter of Captain Henry Turnor.

Lady Margaret grew up playing golf with her father and brothers on a private nine-hole course on the family estate, Stowell Park, in Gloucestershire. She became famous for winning the first three Ladies' Golf Union (LGU) championships, 1893–5, with a consummate ease that secured her reputation as the best woman player of her day. Within her family, however, she had to share golfing honours with her brother Michael, who in 1933, as a 55-year-old grandfather, became British amateur champion.

Women's golf was its infancy in Lady Margaret's day. The first women's clubs in Britain were founded in the 1860s, but the game made slow progress in the face of a litany of objections by men that typified male attitudes towards attempts by women to act independently. According to Mabel Stringer, the first female sports journalist, it was 'amazing women learned to play at all considering what they had to contend with and the little inducement there was for them to persevere and practise' (Stringer, *Golfing Reminiscences*, 14), and also considering the cumbersome clothing in which the dictates of fashion compelled them to play.

A watershed in the history of women's golf occurred in the spring of 1893 with the foundation of the LGU and the inauguration of the first annual championship. The competition was held at the Lytham and St Anne's club in Lancashire, 13–15 June; registration was open to members of any golf club, and play was by match over eighteen holes on a relatively short and easy nine-hole ladies' course. There were thirty-eight entrants from England, Ireland, and France, most unmarried and of limited skill. Lady Margaret was expected to win, and she did not disappoint, averaging 42 for nine holes, winning the majority of matches comfortably, and defeating Issette Pearson, the honorary secretary of the LGU, in the final round by 7 and 5. Her victory was a revelation to spectators to 'what pitch of perfection a lady golfer might rise' (Slaughter, 313). At the award presentation ceremony Lady Margaret's acceptance speech was delivered by her father, in keeping with the prohibitions of the day against ladies speaking in public. That the champion was beautiful, charming, and the daughter of a peer, and that her dress, demeanour, and style of play epitomized grace and femininity, helped to quash criticism about competitive golf being unbecoming for ladies and added a touch of glamour that contributed to making the game fashionable and respectable.

Lady Margaret Rachel Scott (1874–1938), by Messrs Hedges, 1893

The following year in the second championship, 29 May–1 June, Lady Margaret took on a stronger field of more than sixty at the Littlestone club in Kent. Play was from shortened tees on the men's eighteen-hole course 'that fairly bristled in sand bunkers, canals, rabbit holes, and endless traps' (Slaughter, 314). In the final Scott again defeated Issette Pearson 'without appearing to exert her powers to any extent' (Mackern and Boys, 25), confirming her reputation as 'a gowfer braw' (Stringer, *Golfing Reminiscences*, 40).

Lady Margaret earned her third consecutive title in May 1895, when she bested a field of eighty-four at the Royal Portrush club in Ireland over the rough and difficult men's course, which was only slightly altered for the occasion. This time she was harder pressed, being forced for once to play the final two holes in a close first-round match against Miss M. E. Phillips. In the semi-final against Mrs Ryder-Richardson she had to 'pull up wonderfully' (Hezlet, 111) after being four down at the turn, in order to move on to the final and victory over Miss E. Lythgoe. With her remarkable unbeaten record intact, Lady Margaret then resigned her golf club memberships and retired. Although she participated occasionally in club matches thereafter, she never played in public again.

By the unanimous consent of her contemporaries, Lady Margaret was in a class by herself among those who competed in the early ladies' championships. Photographs reveal a beautiful, fashionably dressed young woman with a full, easy, confident swing (overswing by later standards). Descriptions of her game as excellent, strong, and finished, and her style as perfect, supple, and powerful yet graceful abound. Neither an exceptional driver nor putter, her greatest strengths as a player were marvellous concentration, coolness, and self-possession, along with a strong, determined grip and easy use of clubs in any kind of lie and outstanding play through the green that was characterized by long, straight drives and crisp, deadly approach shots. Horace Hutchinson, the amateur champion and an eminent writer on golf, was amazed by her ability to 'pick the ball off an indifferent, unsympathetic lie with a brassy … and send it flying straight to the mark … better than any other lady' (Hutchinson, *Book of Golf*, 202; Hutchinson, *Fifty Years of Golf*, 163). The fine quality of Lady Margaret's play helped to alter the conception of the ladies' golf game among sceptical men and set a high standard for other women to emulate.

On 27 April 1897 Lady Margaret married the Hon. Frederick Gustavus Hamilton-Russell (*d.* 1941), third son of the eighth Viscount Boyne. There were no children. Lady Margaret died at their London home, 3 Cambridge Gate, Regent's Park, on 27 January 1938.

KATHLEEN E. MCCRONE

Sources H. G. Hutchinson and others, *The book of golf and golfers* (1899) · L. Mackern and M. Boys, eds., *Our lady of the green: a book of ladies' golf* (1899) · M. Hezlet, *Ladies' golf* (1904) · F. E. Slaughter, ed., *The sportswoman's library*, 1 (1898) · K. E. McCrone, *Sport and the physical emancipation of English women, 1870–1914* (1988) · M. Stringer, *Golfing reminiscences* (1924) · D. Steel and P. Ryde, eds., *The Shell international encyclopedia of golf* (1975) · H. G. Hutchinson, *Fifty years of golf* (1919) · B. Darwin and others, *A history of golf in Britain* (1952) · M. Stringer, 'Christmas golf twenty years ago', *Ladies Golf*, 2 (1913), 14 · *CGPLA Eng. & Wales* (1938)

Likenesses Messrs Hedges, photograph, 1893, NPG [*see illus.*] · portrait, repro. in N. Gibson, *A pictorial history of golf* (1968), 47 · portrait, repro. in Slaughter, ed., *Sportswoman's library*, 317 · portrait, repro. in Hutchinson and others, *Book of golf and golfers*, facing p. 198, 199 · portrait, repro. in Stringer, *Golfing reminiscences*, facing p. 36 · portrait, repro. in E. Wilson, *A gallery of women golfers* (1961), 15

Wealth at death £2541 9*s.* 11*d.*: administration, 1938

Scott, Marion Margaret (1877–1953), musicologist, was born on 16 July 1877 at 66 Longton Grove, Sydenham, London, one of the two daughters of Sydney Charles Scott (1850–1926), a solicitor, and his wife, Annie Prince (*d.* 1942). She grew up in Norwood, south-east London, and inspired perhaps by the concerts at the Crystal Palace decided to train as a violinist at the Royal College of Music, where she studied with Fernández Arbós from 1896 to 1901, gaining her ARCM in 1900. She published a book of poems, *Violin Verses*, in 1905. Until the late 1920s she pursued a career as a violinist, forming her own string quartet and organizing concerts of contemporary British music; she was leader of the Morley College orchestra when Gustav Holst was director of music. Her interest in contemporary music extended to that of Paul Hindemith, and she read a paper, 'Paul Hindemith: his music and its characteristics', to the Musical Association in 1930. During the war she published articles in the *Listener* on Michael Tippett (1943) and Holst (1944). She remained closely connected with the Royal College of Music all her life, and in 1906 helped to found the RCM Union, a society which enabled former students to keep in touch with each other and the college: she was joint honorary secretary from 1906 to 1937, when she became editor of the *R. C. M. Magazine*, until 1944. One of the founders of the Society of Women Musicians in 1911, she served as president from 1915 to 1916.

Marion Scott first met the poet and composer Ivor Gurney (1890–1937) in 1912, when he was a student at the

Royal College of Music, and despite the difference in their ages they became close friends. She encouraged him, and after he had enlisted in the army in 1915 corresponded with him at the front, and he sent her his poetry for safekeeping. She was instrumental in getting his first volume of poems, *Severn and Somme*, published in 1917, and championed his poetry in her presidential address to the Society of Women Musicians in December 1916, 'Contemporary British war-poetry, music, and patriotism', which was published in the *Musical Times* in March 1917. When Gurney was committed to the City of London Mental Hospital in Dartford in 1922 she remained in close touch, visiting him, and helping to pay his bills, and in 1923 she began to collect his manuscripts, including all that he was writing in the asylum, and persuaded his family to send her any music, poems, and letters in their possession. She began to make plans for publication, but although a few poems appeared in magazines, and *Lights Out*, Gurney's settings of six poems by Edward Thomas, was published privately in 1926, it was not until 1938 that the first two of five volumes of fifty of his songs were published, with prefaces by Scott. This was as a result of pressure over several years from Gurney's friend Gerald Finzi. Finzi had first suggested publication in 1925, but he found Scott difficult to deal with, guarding the manuscripts possessively, but too busy, or too inefficient, to make a selection and prepare them for publication. In the end most of the editing was done by Finzi, Herbert Howells, and Howard Ferguson, and they also did most of the work involved in preparing a symposium of articles on Gurney for the January 1938 edition of *Music and Letters*. Scott gained full control of Gurney's literary estate after his death in 1937, and she wrote the preface for the third volume of songs, which appeared in 1952. The two final volumes came out in 1959 and 1979.

In the 1930s Marion Scott became the leading British authority on the life and music of Haydn. Her first article—on the chronology of Haydn's string quartets, written at the request of the editor, A. H. Fox-Strangways—appeared in *Music and Letters* in 1930, and she went on to prepare an edition of the quartet she had established as the original op.1, no.1: in the introduction she wrote, 'Haydn did not *invent* the string quartet; he *made* it—an infinitely higher achievement'. Other scholarly articles followed, including two in 1932, the bicentenary of Haydn's birth, in *Music and Letters*, and the *Musical Quarterly*, on Haydn's visits to England. In 'Mi-Jo Haydn' (*Monthly Musical Record*, 1939), she analysed the arguments in a dispute over the authorship of a symphony attributed to Haydn's brother Michael, concluding that the first two movements were by Michael, and the finale by Joseph. In 'Haydn and folksong' (*Music and Letters*, 1950) she argued that Haydn used folk melodies because he was an early collector of folk song. She prepared an exhaustive catalogue of Haydn's works for the fifth edition of Grove's *Dictionary of Music and Musicians* (1954), but although she planned to publish a book on Haydn she had completed only three chapters by her death, and her only book was *Beethoven* (1934), in the Master Musicians series. From 1945 to 1952 she edited the proceedings of the Royal Musical Association. She also collected rare eighteenth-century Haydn editions, a collection which she left to Cambridge University Library.

Although she suffered from ill health for much of her life, and was a semi-invalid for many years following an accident when she was thrown out of a hansom cab in her youth, Scott had great determination. She lived with her parents until her mother's death in 1942, when she moved to Kensington. She died after a long illness on 24 December 1953 at her home, 4 Rutland House, Marloes Road, Kensington, London, and was cremated at Golders Green four days later. She was unmarried. At the time of her death, her election to a fellowship of the Royal College of Music had just been approved.

Anne Pimlott Baker

Sources R. Hughes, 'Marion Scott's contribution to musical scholarship', *R. C. M. Magazine*, 50/2 (1954), 39–42 • K. Dale, 'Memories of Marion Scott', *Music and Letters*, 35 (1954), 236–40 • M. Hurd, *The ordeal of Ivor Gurney* (1978) • *The Times* (29 Dec 1953) • *R. C. M. Magazine*, 50 (1954), 43–7 • *Music and Letters*, 35 (1954), 134–5 • *New Grove*, 2nd edn • b. cert. • *CGPLA Eng. & Wales* (1953)

Likenesses photograph, *c.*1922, repro. in Hughes, 'Marion Scott's contribution', facing p. 44

Wealth at death £30,401 2*s.* 11*d.*: probate, 22 March 1954, *CGPLA Eng. & Wales*

Scott [*née* Howard; *other married name* Wyndham], **Mary, countess of Deloraine** (*bap.* **1703**, *d.* **1744**), courtier and royal mistress, was baptized at Winchester Cathedral, Hampshire, on 28 February 1703, the daughter of Charles Howard (*b.* 1681), a naval officer, and his wife, Elizabeth Batten. Her father was a grandson of Thomas Howard, first earl of Berkshire, and a great-grandson of Thomas Howard, first earl of Suffolk. By 1723 she had become a maid of honour to Caroline, princess of Wales. She lost that post when, on 14 March 1726, she married Henry *Scott, first earl of Deloraine (1676–1730). They had two daughters, Georgia Caroline (*bap.* 1727), who married Sir James Peachey, master of the robes, and Elizabeth Henrietta (*bap.* 1729). At the time of their marriage her husband was lord of the bedchamber to George Augustus, prince of Wales [*see* George II (1683–1760)], and he continued in the prince's service as a gentleman of the bedchamber when the prince became king. It was probably following her husband's death that she was appointed governess to the king's youngest daughters, Mary and Louisa. She held the post on the condition that she did not marry again, but through negotiations with Queen Caroline and the older princesses, in April 1734 she was allowed to marry William Wyndham (*d.* 1743), of Ersham, Norfolk, eldest son of Colonel Thomas Wyndham. Wyndham was deputy governor to George II's youngest son, William Augustus, duke of Cumberland, and had formerly been the governor of Chelsea Hospital.

Lady Deloraine's likeness appears in William Hogarth's conversation piece *A Performance of 'The Indian Emperor, or, The Conquest of Mexico by the Spaniards'* (1732–5). She is depicted leaning forward, encouraging one of her children to pick up a fallen fan during a children's performance of John Dryden's play, at the home of John Conduitt, master of the Royal Mint. Her royal charges, Mary and Louisa, stand near her in front of the fireplace. Hogarth's intention may have been to suggest 'the tangle of passion, conquest and deception' (Uglow, 170) that the children in the painting will encounter in adult life. This tangle was evident in Lady Deloraine's career. For example, the nineteenth-century anecdotist, William Drogo Montagu, seventh duke of Manchester, repeated gossip that the countess of Deloraine, whom he described as the 'King's Concubine' (Manchester, 2.330), had poisoned Queen Caroline's maid of honour Mary McKenzie. The motive appears to have been jealousy as a Mr Price, for whom the countess was said to entertain a 'tendre', was in love with McKenzie. According to Manchester, McKenzie recovered and, the day before her marriage to Price, was persuaded by Queen Caroline to meet the countess at supper, as public proof either of the countess's innocence or of Mary's forgiveness of her.

In 1735 George II boasted to Lord Hervey that he had seduced Lady Deloraine the winter before, prompting Hervey to note that the king had made 'the governess of his two youngest daughters his whore and the guardian-director of his son's youth and morals his cuckold' (*Hervey's Memoirs*, 196). Lady Deloraine does not seem to have become a serious contender for the king's affections until the summer of 1737, when the king had become separated from his recognized mistress, Amalie von Wallmoden, who was living in Hanover. Then, she was denying to Charlotte Clayton, Lady Sundon, among others, that she had bowed to royal demands and was hinting to prime minister Sir Robert Walpole that if she did consent, she would be well paid for it. None the less, Hervey reported it as common knowledge that the king was 'tasting all the pleasures with Lady Deloraine which she was capable of bestowing' (ibid., 195). He noted that when Walpole questioned the paternity of her son, she teased that it was her husband's 'but I will not promise whose the next shall be' (ibid., 196). Walpole feared that with 'a lying tongue and a false heart' (Hardy, 84) Lady Deloraine might exert political influence: she had already boasted that she alone had kept the king from travelling abroad when the pleas of Walpole and the queen had failed.

Hervey recognized that she was politically harmless, regarding her as a vain and simple woman with a 'wretched head' (*Hervey's Memoirs*, 196). Following the death of Queen Caroline in November 1737, some ministers thought that Lady Deloraine could be used to help them influence the king as the queen had done, but both Walpole and Hervey recognized that the king regarded Lady Deloraine as a sexual conquest rather than companion, and Walpole arranged for Amalie von Wallmoden to be brought over from Hanover. Lady Deloraine, who had never been regarded highly by the princesses, was eclipsed as a royal favourite. She died in London on 12 November 1744 and was buried at Windsor. She left £8000 capital bank stock in trust for her daughters; her son with William Wyndham is not mentioned in the will, and must have predeceased her. BARBARA WHITE

Sources *DNB* · Duke of Manchester, *Court and society from Elizabeth to Anne, edited from the papers at Kimbolton*, 2 vols. (1864), 2.330 · GEC, *Peerage* · *GM*, 1st ser., 1 (1731), 24; 4 (1734), 217; 13 (1743), 443; 14 (1744), 619 · A. Hardy, *The king's mistresses* (1980) · *Lord Hervey's Memoirs*, ed. R. Sedgwick, rev. edn (1963); repr. (1984) · J. Uglow, *Hogarth: a life and a world* (1997) · J. Chamberlayne, *Magnae Britanniae notitia, or, The present state of Great Britain*, 28th edn (1727)

Likenesses W. Hogarth, portrait, 1732–5, priv. coll.; repro. in N. McWilliam, *Hogarth* (1993), 60

Wealth at death £8600 capital South Sea annuities, plus £2000 capital bank stock; subject asked that annuities be sold; fetched £6000 making £8000 total capital bank stock: will, 1744, PRO, PROB 11/736, sig. 252

Scott [*married name* Taylor]**, Mary** (**1751/2–1793**), poet, was born in Milborne Port, Somerset, the daughter of a linen merchant. Little is known of her before the publication, in her early twenties, of her poem *The Female Advocate* (1774). It seems that her life had been dominated by illness: in the poem's dedication she writes of her 'years of ill health', and in the poem itself of her 'languor, and unceasing pains'. *The Female Advocate* also contains clues to particular friendships. The 'Lady' to whom it is dedicated was evidently Anna Steele, who is also addressed as Theodosia, author of *Poems on Subjects Chiefly Devotional* (1760). Like Scott, Steele was both earnestly religious and an invalid. It is probably Scott whom Steele addresses as Myra in a poem first published in the posthumous second edition of her *Poems*, that speaks of a friend to whom she is 'In suffering and in sentiment allied'. Steele was the eldest daughter of a lay Baptist preacher and timber merchant, William Steele, who appears in *The Female Advocate* as Philander, a man who has encouraged her writing. Scott praises in the poem another male mentor and friend to 'the female cause'; according to a manuscript note by Sarah Froud, who in 1774 owned the copy now in the Huntington Library, this was Richard Pulteney. Pulteney (1730–1801) was a physician who, from 1765, lived in Blandford, Dorset, and wrote books on botany.

The title page of *The Female Advocate* declared it to be occasioned by reading John Duncombe's *The Feminead* (1754), a celebration of female learning and, in particular, of women poets. In rhyming couplets Scott supplemented Duncombe's verse catalogue, commending literary women omitted by him, and adding several more recent writers. Those with strong protestant inclinations were singled out for praise. She wrote that the poem, which appeared in a second edition in 1775, sprang from her 'indignation' at the disdain of many men for 'female education'.

Although Scott appears to have remained in Milborne Port, living with her parents, until she was in her late thirties, she clearly had contacts with a circle of intellectual protestant dissenters. *The Female Advocate* was published by Joseph Johnson, who would become well known as a publisher of writing by dissenters. Her brother, Russell Scott, was a Unitarian minister in Portsmouth and, in the early 1770s, she met John Taylor (1753–1817), first a student then a tutor at the Daventry Academy for Unitarians. Marriage to Taylor was opposed by her mother, an invalid for whom Scott cared until her death in 1787. Her father died the next year and shortly afterwards, in May 1788, she and Taylor, who had become minister of a chapel at Ilminster, Somerset, married.

In the 1770s Scott established an epistolary friendship with Anna Seward, whose published letters, seven of them written to Scott, are the main source of information about her. Seward's father, Thomas, had been praised in *The Female Advocate* for his poem 'The female right to literature', and this may have led to the correspondence between the two women. They wrote to each other mainly about literary topics and, according to a letter from Seward to William Hayley, met only once. Scott published 'Verses Addressed to Miss Seward, on the Publication of her Monody on Major André' in the *Gentleman's Magazine* in June 1783. Roger Lonsdale speculates about her being the Miss Scott whose two poems 'Dunotter Castle' and 'Verses, on a Day of Prayer, for Success in War', were included in *Poems by the most Eminent Ladies*, probably published in 1780. In the year of her marriage she published *The Messiah*, a blank verse epic with Christ as its hero (reviewed in the *Monthly Review*, 79, 1788, 277). This was her last known publication.

Scott gave birth to a daughter in 1789 and a son in 1791. The latter, John Edward *Taylor (1791–1844), would become founder and editor of the *Manchester Guardian*. Her husband became a Quaker by 1792, an alteration which, from the evidence of Anna Seward's correspondence, placed some strain upon her as he had earlier influenced her to adopt Unitarian beliefs. She continued to suffer from poor health and, three weeks before her third child was due to be born (according to a brief obituary in the *Gentleman's Magazine*), she died on 5 June 1793, aged forty-one, in Bristol. She was survived by her husband.

John Mullan

Sources R. Lonsdale, ed., *Eighteenth-century women poets: an Oxford anthology* (1989), 320–21 • M. Scott, *The female advocate*, ed. G. Holladay (1984) • *Letters of Anna Seward: written between the years 1784 and 1807*, ed. A. Constable, 6 vols. (1811) • A. Steele, *Poems on subjects chiefly devotional*, 3 vols. (1760) • *GM*, 1st ser., 63 (1793), 579

Scott, Michael. *See* Scot, Michael (*d.* in or after 1235).

Scott, Michael (1789–1835), planter in Jamaica and writer, was born on 28 October 1789 at Cowlairs, on the outskirts of Glasgow, the fifth and youngest son of Allan Scott, a Glasgow merchant, and owner of a small estate at Cowlairs, and his wife, Margaret, *née* Buchanan. Scott was sent to grammar school, as the Glasgow high school was then called, and matriculated at the university when he was only twelve years old, remaining there until 1805.

In 1806 Scott went to Jamaica, where he was taught to manage estates by George William Hamilton, a nephew of Robert Bogle of Gilmorehill, a Glasgow merchant and family friend. Besides being an independent trader, Hamilton also acted as an estate agent and trader for those West Indian landlords who preferred to enjoy the revenues of their estates in a non-tropical climate, such as England. Hamilton was to form the model for Aaron Bang, a vivid character in the book for which Scott is best known, *Tom Cringle's Log*. In 1810 Scott entered business in

Michael Scott (1789–1835), by Augustin Edouart

Kingston, and consequently travelled frequently, both by sea and road, experiences that he later drew on in his writing. In 1817 Scott returned to Scotland for a prolonged visit, and on 31 May 1818 he married Margaret Cathran Bogle, the daughter of Robert Bogle. He went back to Jamaica immediately afterwards, but left the island finally in 1822 and settled in Glasgow. There he entered business on his own account, and also became a partner in his father-in-law's firm, Bogle, Harris & Co., of Glasgow, and Bogle, Douglas & Co., of Maracaibo.

Scott began to publish stories based on his experiences in Jamaica in the September 1829 issue of *Blackwood's Magazine*. They soon became so popular that William Blackwood advised that they should be connected in order to make a continuous narrative, and so Scott prefixed the general title of 'Tom Cringle's Log' to what is now the eighth chapter in July 1832, and the serial was concluded in August 1833. The *Quarterly Review* had praised it as the most brilliant series of magazine papers of that time, and its 1834 volume publication was well received. Although Captain Marryat thought it melodramatic, Coleridge pronounced it to be 'most excellent', and thought that it came nearer to Smollett than anything he could remember. Both Scott and Smollett wrote travel narratives set in the West Indies; both were gifted story-tellers, and both were more adept at description than structure. One of the distinctive qualities of Scott's work, however, is its skilful rendering of Jamaican speech. There is some doubt as to where the chapters were written, and Anthony Trollope in *The West Indies and the Spanish Main* refers to a tradition that the work was written at Raymond Hall, the house which Scott occupied high up among the Blue Mountains, which are described in exquisite detail in *Tom Cringle's Log*.

Scott's second story, 'The Cruise of the Midge', appeared serially in *Blackwood's Magazine* between March 1834 and June 1835. In 1836 it too was printed anonymously in book form in Paris. Its effect is marred by melodrama and laboured humour, although the narrative is full of spirit and keen observation. Both works graphically depict the torment of slavery and the slave trade, but Scott chose not publicly to advocate social reform. Both works were reprinted in several languages.

Scott combined his writing activities with an active business career and the raising of a large family. He died in Glasgow on 7 November 1835, and was buried in the necropolis, where an unpretentious monument marks his grave. During his lifetime, Scott so successfully concealed his authorial identity that even Blackwood died without knowing his contributor's name; Scott's authorship was only revealed posthumously.

J. R. MacDonald, *rev.* Lucy Kelly Hayden

Sources M. Morris, 'Introduction', *Tom Cringle's log* (1895), vii–xviii • G. Douglas, 'Michael Scott', *The 'Blackwood' group* (1897), 134–50 • L. K. Hayden, 'The Caribbean presence in *Tom Cringle's log*: a commentary on Britain's involvement in slavery and the slave trade', *Journal of Caribbean Studies*, 6 (autumn 1989), 309–21 • A. Trollope, *The West Indies and the Spanish main* (1859) • D. E. Herdeck, ed., *Caribbean writers: a bio-bibliographical-critical encyclopedia* (1979) • bap. reg. Scot. • m. reg. Scot. • T. Royle, *The Macmillan companion to Scottish literature* (1983) • Allibone, *Dict.* • M. Drabble, ed., *The Oxford companion to English literature*, rev. edn (1995)

Archives NL Scot., letters to William Blackwood and Sons

Likenesses A. Edouart, silhouette, Scot. NPG [*see illus.*]

Scott, (Guthrie) Michael (1907–1983), Anglican clergyman and campaigner for racial equality, particularly in southern Africa, was born at Lowfield Heath, Sussex, on 30 July 1907, the third and youngest son (there were no daughters) of Perceval Caleb Scott, a clergyman in the high-church tradition, and his wife, Ethel Maud Burn. The misery of the Southampton slums surrounding his childhood home in Northam made a deep impression on him. He was educated at King's College, Taunton. In 1926 he went to Switzerland and then to South Africa to recuperate from tuberculosis. He studied at St Paul's Theological College in Grahamstown, South Africa. After returning to England, he went to Chichester Theological College in 1929. The bishop of Chichester, George Bell, ordained him as a deacon in 1930 (he became a priest in 1932). Scott's involvement with political issues began in 1934 when he was a curate at All Souls, Lower Clapton, London, at the time of the hunger marches. He had many contacts with communists during the 1930s.

From 1937 to 1939 Scott was in India, first as chaplain to the bishop of Bombay and later as chaplain in St Paul's Cathedral, Calcutta. At this time he was continuing to experiment with communist beliefs (which he later abandoned), and his moral and religious questioning led to an inner conflict. He returned to England and, after the outbreak of the Second World War, chose to enlist in the RAF in 1940, as aircrew rather than as a chaplain. In 1941 he was invalided out with Crohn's disease, which continued to trouble him throughout his life. In 1943 he again went to South Africa. Until 1946 he was assistant priest at St Alban's Coloured Mission on the outskirts of Johannesburg. Appalled by conditions of life for non-white people he worked for the Campaign for Right and Justice. In 1946 he was asked to observe Indian passive resistance in Durban against the Asiatic Land Tenure and Indian Representation Act. Volunteers, who stood on forbidden open land and were attacked by white hooligans, were joined by Scott, who was arrested and sent to prison. On release his parish licence was withdrawn by Bishop Geoffrey H. Clayton, who disapproved of his unauthorized absence from the parish and the extent of his political involvement.

From then on Scott was besieged with requests from oppressed groups who desperately wanted their case to be heard. At the request of African former soldiers, he lived in the gang-ruled shanty town called Tobruk outside Johannesburg and was prosecuted for living in a native urban area. He went to Bethal in the eastern Transvaal to investigate the conditions of near slavery in which white farmers held black labourers. His dedication and disregard for his own comfort became legendary. He was a loner but always drew on the help of devoted friends and supporters. His emaciated good looks, height, and shabby crumpled appearance, with pockets bulging with papers, made him conspicuous. He was a poor speaker. He struggled with self-doubt but, having reached a decision, was tenacious in spite of his diffidence. Invited to Bechuanaland by Tshekedi Khama, regent of the Ngwato people, he met the exiled chief of the Herero who asked him to go to see Chief Hosea Kutako and other chiefs in Windhoek. With them he drew up the Herero petition for the return of the Herero lands and against the incorporation of South-West Africa with South Africa; he was appointed their spokesman to the United Nations in 1947. In 1949 he was the first individual petitioner to be heard by the fourth (trusteeship) committee of the UN and asked for matters pertaining to South-West Africa to be referred to the International Court of Justice. He attended UN sessions for the next thirty years for the International League for Human Rights and kept South African race oppression on the agenda. In 1949 Scott's general licence was withdrawn by Bishop R. Ambrose Reeves on the grounds that he was out of the country. When Bishop George Bell heard of this he gave him a licence.

From 1950, having been refused entry to South Africa, Scott lived in London, initially as a guest of the Friends International Centre. When at UN sessions he lived in New York, often at the General Theological Seminary. He became honorary director of the non-party-political Africa Bureau which in 1952 started to focus attention on issues in British Africa. Scott also undertook projects outside the bureau's scope, identifying himself with passive resistance in Nyasaland against a central African federation. In 1959 he took part in the peace protests in the Sahara against the French atom bomb and he joined the World Peace Brigade in 1962. From the early 1960s he was associated with Bertrand Russell in the peace movement and became vice-president of the Committee of 100. Russell and he jointly published *Act or Perish* in 1961. Scott served two prison sentences as a result of these activities.

From 1958 representatives of the Naga people, who wanted independence from India, sought Scott's help. In 1962 he took A. Z. Phizo, president of the Naga national council, to London to expose the war in Nagaland. Scott consulted Jawaharlal Nehru about a proposal for a cease-fire. In 1964 he was invited by the Nagaland Church Council to be one of three members of a peace mission to the Nagas. Between 1964 and 1966 he made strenuous marches in Nagaland, meeting villagers and members of the underground movement. The Indian government deported him from Nagaland in May 1966.

In the 1970s many groups and individual refugees turned to Scott for help. In 1979 he initiated the organizations Rights and Justice and World Wide Research to focus attention on human rights. His great contributions were his identification with the oppressed and his prophetic Christian insights into the seeds of conflict and the need for peaceful change. Africa did not forget him. He was honoured by Zambia in 1968 and in 1975 was made an honorary canon of St George's Cathedral, Windhoek, Namibia. He died on 14 September 1983 at his home, 43 King Henry's Road in London. He never married.

TREVOR HUDDLESTON, *rev.*

Sources M. Scott, *A time to speak* (1958) • personal knowledge (1990) • *The Times* (16 Sept 1983) • *CGPLA Eng. & Wales* (1984) • *WWW*
Archives Bodl. RH, papers | Bodl. RH, Greenidge MSS • Bodl. RH, corresp. with Margery Perham and related papers
Wealth at death £65,394: probate, 26 Jan 1984, *CGPLA Eng. & Wales*

Scott, Patrick. *See* Scot, Patrick (*fl.* 1618–1625).

Scott, Paul Mark (1920–1978), novelist, was born at 130 Fox Lane in the north London suburb of Southgate on 25 March 1920, the younger of the two sons of Thomas Scott (1870–1958) and his wife, Frances Mark (1886–1969). Thomas Scott and his cousins George, Philip, and Gilbert Wright were Yorkshiremen: artists turning out up-market calendars, cards, and sporting pictures, who moved down as a clan from Headingley, Leeds, to London, where Paul's father specialized in the 1920s in drawing furs and lingerie for the fashion trade. Scott diagnosed a fundamental division in himself between the practical down-to-earth streak inherited from his father and the ruthless imaginative drive implanted in him by his mother, an ambitious and increasingly dissatisfied working girl from south London.

Scott was educated at Winchmore Hill collegiate school in Southgate, leaving suddenly without qualifications when his father's business came close to ruin in 1934. The shock reinforced what became a central split in Scott's life and work. He found a job at fourteen as an accountant's clerk, taking evening classes in bookkeeping, and tapping out poems in his lunch hour on the office typewriter. He said that the rigid class distinctions, the pretensions, aspirations, and ruthlessly enforced social codes of suburban Southgate meant that, when he first encountered British India, he understood in his bones how it worked.

Paul Mark Scott (1920–1978), by Mark Gerson, 1977

'Half close your eyes here', he said of the streets where he grew up, 'and you're in Mayapore' (Spurling, 9).

Scott's *Raj Quartet*—televised in 1983 as *The Jewel in the Crown*—would become a key literary and historical text in the evolution of Britain's relationship with India. But its author had no Indian background or family connections, and no particular interest in the raj until, having been called up as a private soldier on the outbreak of the Second World War, he found himself shipped out in 1943 as an officer cadet in the conscript army hastily assembled to repel the Japanese forces threatening to invade India after defeating the British in Burma the year before. Scott ended up a captain in the Indian Army Service Corps, organizing supply lines for the Fourteenth Army's unexpectedly successful reconquest of Burma. Like many of his civilian contemporaries, he had been initially appalled by what he found on the subcontinent—by the heat, dust, poverty, disease, and overcrowding, above all by the imperial attitudes of the British—but over the next three years he fell deeply in love with India.

While stationed in Torquay in 1941, Scott had met and, on 23 September of that year, married a nursing sister called Nancy Edith Avery (*b.* 1914), always known as Penny; she subsequently became a novelist herself. Back in north London after the war, he earned a living for himself, his wife, and daughters, Carol (*b.* 1947) and Sally (*b.* 1948), as an accountant responsible for the shaky finances of two small publishing houses, the Falcon and Grey Walls presses. In 1950 he joined the literary agency Pearn, Pollinger, and Higham (later David Higham Associates), where he was generally agreed to be, in the words of one of his authors, E. M. Almedingen, as 'a prince among agents'

(Spurling, 198). Satisfied customers included best-selling novelists like Morris West, M. M. Kaye, and Arthur C. Clarke, as well as young contemporaries whose careers he launched, such as John Braine (*Room at the Top*, 1957) and Muriel Spark (*Memento mori*, 1959).

Scott's own modest success with *Johnny Sahib* (1952) was followed by another five ambitious but uneven novels, all but one set in India or the Far East, mostly peopled by men in uniform, many of them probing the uneasy bond between two brothers or close male friends. In 1960, on the strength of *The Chinese Love Pavilion*, Scott left David Higham to take his chances as a full-time writer. *Birds of Paradise* (1962) taught him that he could not go on drawing for ever on the dwindling capital of his Indian memories. After two largely unsatisfactory experiments with other settings (*The Bender*, 1963, and *Corrida at San Feliu*, 1964), he flew back alone to India on a journey which he knew would make or break him as a writer.

Scott staked everything on this return, driven by a sense of having failed to fulfil his own hopes as a writer, by financial desperation, and by increasing bodily weakness, the effect of chronic amoebic dysentery originally contracted in India and kept at bay afterwards by alarming quantities of alcohol. Scott's reimmersion in India at the beginning of 1964 proved morally disturbing and physically disastrous. He survived thanks to a treatment for amoebiasis only marginally less deadly than the disease, was pronounced cured in May, and sat down in June to write the first paragraph of *The Jewel in the Crown*. Eventually published in 1966, it would become the first of four novels collectively known as the *Raj Quartet*. The others were *The Day of the Scorpion* (1968), *The Towers of Silence* (1971), and *The Division of the Spoils* (1975). All were set in India in 1942–7 against the background of political unrest leading up to the British departure and the slaughter that followed partition and independence. Scott said that for him the British raj was an extended metaphor: 'I don't think a writer chooses his metaphors. They choose him' (Spurling, 118).

At the core of Scott's quartet lay a confrontation—based initially on the two sides of his own deeply divided, bisexual nature—between the young Indian Hari Kumar and the police superintendent who pursues and torments him, Ronald Merrick. Kumar represented everything that had been bright, hopeful, and brutally crushed in the young Scott. Merrick—a repressed homosexual with illiberal, authoritarian instincts, fatally convinced of his own overriding racial superiority—provided the vehicle for a strange, searching, by no means unfeeling exploration of the darkest side of the British in India. The four novels collectively achieved an epic sweep and power rare in the English novel and quite unlike E. M. Forster's *Passage to India*, with which they were unfavourably compared by Scott's contemporaries.

Scott had always felt himself to be, in both literary and social terms, an outsider in his own country. Probably only an outsider could have commanded the long, lucid perspectives he brought to bear on the end of the British raj, exploring with passionate, concentrated attention a subject still generally treated as taboo, or fit only for historical romance and adventure stories. The *Raj Quartet* was received at the time with no great enthusiasm. Scott's only recognition in his lifetime came when he won the Booker prize for a pendant to the *Quartet*, *Staying on*, in November 1977. Too ill to attend the prize-giving, he died of cancer in the Middlesex Hospital, London, on 1 March 1978, his wife surviving him. Scott would have been amazed by the wave of nostalgia that swept Britain in the wake of the televised series based on his novels. But he might have been less surprised to find that history was on his side. Scott saw things other people would sooner not see, and he looked too close for comfort. His was a bleak, stern, prophetic vision and, like Forster's, it has come to seem steadily more accurate with time.

HILARY SPURLING

Sources H. Spurling, *Paul Scott: a life* (1990) · *DNB* · b. cert. · m. cert. · private information (2004)
Archives Georgetown University Library, Washington, DC, corresp. with Bruce Marshall
Likenesses M. Gerson, photograph, 1977, NPG [*see illus.*] · P. Cashmore, photograph, repro. in Spurling, *Paul Scott* · photographs, repro. in Spurling, *Paul Scott*
Wealth at death £48,597: probate, 21 April 1978, *CGPLA Eng. & Wales*

Scott, Sir Percy Moreton, first baronet (1853–1924), naval officer and engineer, was the son of Montagu Scott, a solicitor, and his wife, Laura Kezia Snelling. He was born in Canonbury, Middlesex, on 10 July 1853. He was educated at Eastman's naval academy, Southsea, and entered the cadet training ship HMS *Britannia* in September 1866.

Early career, 1867–1899 In December 1867 Scott was appointed to the frigate *Forte*, which became the flagship in the East Indies. In June 1868 he was rated as a midshipman, and returned to Britain in February 1872. After a year in the ironclad *Hercules*, and after being promoted sub-lieutenant in December, he joined the gunnery training ship *Excellent* to complete his examinations. Subsequently he volunteered for the Second Anglo-Asante War, and was appointed to the *Active*, flagship of Admiral Sir William Hewett. Although he arrived too late for active service, he remained in this ship until April 1877, taking part in minor operations on the west coast of Africa. He was promoted lieutenant in November 1875 for service on the River Congo. In September 1877 he returned to the *Excellent*, and after his course remained on the staff until July 1880.

Scott was then appointed gunnery lieutenant of the *Inconstant*, flagship of Admiral Lord Clanwilliam's squadron, for a round-the-world voyage. The squadron was detained at the Cape of Good Hope, but did not serve ashore in the First South African War. It ended the cruise going to Alexandria for the Egyptian campaign of 1882. Here Scott was noticed in dispatches for his skill in moving and handling three captured 7 ton guns for the army. In November 1882 he was appointed senior staff officer of the Devonport gunnery school HMS *Cambridge*, before

Sir Percy Moreton Scott, first baronet (1853–1924), by unknown photographer

returning to the *Excellent* in April 1883, to join Captain John Arbuthnot Fisher, and remained there until he was promoted commander in September 1886. Between September 1887 and February 1890 he served in the Mediterranean as commander of the battleship *Edinburgh*. He then returned to the *Excellent* for another three years, when he created the shore establishment on Whale Island which he had planned in 1884. Promoted captain in January 1893, Scott served on the ordnance committee at Woolwich for two and a half years. On 10 January 1893 he married Teresa Roma, eldest daughter of Sir Frederick D. Dixon-Hartland. They had three children. In May 1896 he took command of the small cruiser *Scylla* on the Mediterranean station, and remained in her until July 1899. During this commission he developed and introduced into service a number of critical inventions for increasing the rate and accuracy of naval gunfire, to exploit the new quick-firing guns, along with signal equipment. Scott recognized that competition and reward were the keys to gunnery improvement. The *Scylla* established new records for gunnery. His commander-in-chief, Admiral Sir John Hopkins, advised him to keep control of his patents.

South Africa, China, and fame, 1899–1902 In September 1899 Scott was appointed to command the largest cruiser afloat, *Terrible*, with orders to proceed to the China station. Once again he was detained at the Cape, until March 1900, by the Second South African War. This time he attracted notice by devising and building land service mountings for 4.7 inch guns from his ship, which played a critical role in the defence of Ladysmith. He also provided field mountings for 12-pounder, 4.7 inch, and 6 inch guns to serve with the naval brigade, which alleviated the army's lack of heavy artillery. For these services he was created CB. He also acted as military commandant of Durban, at a time when the city was threatened by the Boer advance. When the *Terrible* reached China, Scott landed further guns, for the operations against the Boxer uprising, including the relief of the Peking (Beijing) legations. Once the campaign was over Scott devoted his efforts to perfecting the gunnery of his ship, which reached new and unprecedented levels, and with the help of the flag-captain, John Rushworth Jellicoe, inspired the whole squadron. He also shared his enthusiasm with Lieutenant William S. Sims of the US Navy, who became the leader of modern American naval gunnery. When he returned home in 1902, Scott was already a celebrity and received a public welcome, and the CB and CVO from the king. From this time gunnery was a public issue, and Scott was not behindhand in encouraging the more intelligent journalists.

Gunnery development, profit, and controversy, 1903–1914 In 1904 Scott was awarded £8000 for his various inventions: by this time he had already entered into a royalties agreement with Vickers, who manufactured all his devices. Ultimately this netted him over £200,000 from sales to the Admiralty and various foreign governments. He was in the habit of taking his payment in handfuls of banknotes at Vickers's London office.

In April 1903 Scott was appointed captain of the *Excellent*, and he devoted the next two years to improving the gunnery of the service. When he reached the rank of rear-admiral, in 1905, Fisher created the post of inspector of target practice for him, and kept him employed in it until July 1907. By developing the gunlayer's test and the battle practice firing at a moored target Scott markedly improved the gunnery of the service. He was one of the key figures in Fisher's technical revolution. His methods enabled the navy to fire accurately, and to think about increasing the range at which actions were fought from 2000 yards to around 10,000. It was therefore fitting that on the occasion of the launch of the epochal all-big-gun battleship *Dreadnought* in 1906 the king should create him KCVO. In July 1907 Scott received his first, and only, admiral's command afloat. The 1st cruiser squadron, with his flag in *Good Hope*, formed part of Admiral Lord Charles Beresford's Channel Fleet. Within a year Scott's relationship with Beresford became critically strained. As part of Fisher's inner circle Scott was anathema to Beresford, who suspected him of being a spy for the first sea lord. At the same time Scott had a low opinion of Beresford, which on two occasions became public knowledge. On 4 November 1907 Scott, as senior officer at Portland, signalled one of his cruisers 'Paintwork appears to be more in demand than gunnery, so you had better come in in time to make yourself look pretty by the 8th'. The reference was to a planned inspection by the Kaiser. On the 8th Beresford, who had only heard about the signal that day, publicly berated Scott, and then issued a humiliating signal to the fleet. He was wrong, doubtless affected by ill health and hostility toward the Admiralty, then headed by Fisher. The following year, while under way, Beresford ordered Scott's squadron to carry out a manoeuvre that would have led to a collision. Scott wisely refrained from acknowledging it until it was cancelled. To prevent any further trouble while Beresford served out the remainder of his truncated command, Scott's squadron was detached for a mission to South Africa, in connection with the union there, followed by a cruise to promote British interests in South America. The former part of the mission was particularly successful. This was another part of Fisher's revolution, replacing the old system of weak ships on station with the occasional visit of large and powerful squadrons. Promoted vice-admiral in December 1908, he hauled down his flag in February 1909.

For the next four years Scott's efforts were devoted to the development of gunnery equipment, in particular the director firing system, which enabled all the guns of a ship to be laid onto a single target from a central aiming position. After early experimental installations aboard various ships from 1907 the system was put into production in 1913. It was crucial to the success of long-range gunfire under wartime conditions. In 1910 Scott was created KCB and awarded a further £2000 for his inventions. In 1911 he divorced his wife on the grounds of her adultery, and was awarded custody of their three children. In March 1913 he retired from the service. Having made many enemies, and being too intimately connected with Fisher's reforms, there had been no question of any further sea appointments. He had also earned considerable amounts of money in royalty payments from Vickers, which did nothing to make him popular with his fellow officers, even if it allowed him to accept a baronetcy in February 1913. On 23 March 1914 he married Fanny Vaughan Johnston, formerly the wife of Colonel A. P. Welman (from whom she obtained a divorce), third daughter of Thomas Ramsay Dinnis, although they separated soon afterwards.

First World War and after Shortly after the outbreak of war in 1914, Scott was recalled to the Admiralty by Fisher, and remained until May 1916. He began by fitting out sixteen merchant ships to resemble modern battleships, and continued to work on gunnery questions, before moving on to consider counter-measures against the submarine threat, which he, like Fisher, had prophesied before the war. When the first Zeppelin air raids on London began in September 1915 Balfour, then first lord of the Admiralty, appointed Scott to create a gun defence system for the capital, which he controlled until the army took over in the following February. His pioneering work played a large role in defeating this threat. His elder son was killed at the battle of Jutland, 31 May 1916, when the armoured cruiser *Defence* blew up.

Although closely consulted by Jellicoe's Admiralty board on post-Jutland gunnery reforms up to the end of 1917, Scott was ignored thereafter. He was also active on Fisher's board of invention and research, working on anti-aircraft gunnery. In 1920 he successfully sued Vickers over a unilateral change in the computation of his royalties. After the war Scott wrote a series of powerful letters to *The Times*, developing the view, which he had first advanced in April 1914, that the day of the battleship was over. In view of the performance of submarines and aeroplanes he argued that Britain should not build any more battleships, but rely on submarines and smaller craft. Coming from the father of modern heavy naval gunnery such opinions carried some weight, and would have been more seriously addressed if he had not earned a reputation for controversy. With the benefit of hindsight it is clear that his views were premature, although the effectiveness of the gas weapons he advocated was never tested in action. His memoirs, *Fifty Years in the Royal Navy*, were published in 1919; although controversial, they do not deal with many of the most interesting aspects of his career, and a chapter on his quarrel with Beresford was excised when Lord Charles died. Scott died of a heart attack at his home, 52 South Audley Street, London, on 18 October 1924. After a funeral service and cremation in London his ashes were committed to the sea at Spithead. He left an estate valued at £130,000 and two houses. His second son, Douglas Winchester Scott (*b.* 1907), succeeded to the title.

Scott was a small but strongly built and energetic man, dark-haired, and usually seen with a full naval beard. The dominating feature of his life was a powerful logical intellect that made him impatient of slower minds, and of complacent bureaucrats. Although he was a fine sea officer and an able squadron commander, Scott made his career as a gunnery specialist. His brief experience of high command demonstrated that he was better placed elsewhere. His character and habits of thought made subordination difficult, and once he had achieved a measure of financial independence he gave full rein to the harsh and judgemental side of his nature. Because he was impatient and critical of opposition it required a truly great man, Fisher, to appreciate his merits and exploit his services. He possessed a unique genius, one that could grasp practical problems and exploit existing technology to improve the performance of systems. His contribution to the naval renaissance associated with Fisher was immense. Scott provided the example, the methods, and important components of the equipment that brought naval gunnery into the twentieth century. He began by increasing the rate of fire of medium-calibre guns, and ended up with the director system that exploited the potential of Fisher's dreadnoughts. Abroad his methods were widely copied, and his equipment extensively purchased. Scott was one of the most important specialist contributors to the creation of the modern Royal Navy. If that process will always be associated with the name of Fisher, Scott must be accorded a prominent place among his supporters.

ANDREW LAMBERT

Sources P. Padfield, *Aim straight* (1966) · P. Scott, *Fifty years in the Royal Navy* (1919) · A. J. Marder, *From the Dreadnought to Scapa Flow: the Royal Navy in the Fisher era, 1904–1919*, 5 vols. (1961–70), vol. 1 · J. Brooks, 'Percy Scott and the director', *Warship '96: Fifth International Symposium on Naval Submarines* [London 1996] (1996), 150–70 · G. M. Bennett, *Charlie B: a biography of Admiral Lord Beresford of Metemmeh and Curraghmore* (1968) · J. G. Wells, *Whaley: the story of HMS Excellent, 1830 to 1980* (1980) · J. T. Sumida, *In defence of naval supremacy: finance, technology and British naval policy, 1889–1914* (1989) · Burke, *Peerage* (1924) · *DNB* · *CGPLA Eng. & Wales* (1924)

Archives NMM, corresp. with Sir Julian S. Corbett · PRO, admiralty archives · PRO NIre., corresp. with Edward Carson · Vickers archives

Likenesses J. Collier, oils, 1904, HMS *Excellent*, Portsmouth · Spy [L. Ward], caricature, watercolour study, NPG; repro. in *VF* (17 Sept 1903) · photograph, repro. in Scott, *Fifty years* [*see illus.*]

Wealth at death £129,671 15*s*. 5*d*.: probate, 17 Dec 1924, *CGPLA Eng. & Wales*

Scott, Peter Duncan (1914–1977), forensic psychiatrist, the second son of Walter Scott, a brewer, and his wife, Jennie (formerly Troop), was born at 37 Earlsbury Gardens, Handsworth, Birmingham, on 13 June 1914. He was educated at St Cuthbert's preparatory school in Great Malvern, at Bromsgrove School, and at St Catharine's College, Cambridge, followed by clinical training at the London Hospital. He qualified in 1939 and soon joined the Royal Naval Volunteer Reserve, in which he had originally intended to serve as a surgeon, but he had to become shore based because of unmanageable seasickness. On 25 October 1940 he married Lilian Ruth (*b*. 1912/13), daughter of Daniel John Lewis, a quarry owner. Following contact with E. W. Anderson (later professor of psychiatry at Manchester), Scott took up psychiatric work, obtained the diploma in psychological medicine in 1944 through a correspondence course, and became a neuropsychiatric specialist. After the war he was recommended to Sir Aubrey Lewis and became a registrar at the Maudsley Hospital, followed by a year at Runwell Hospital, Essex.

In 1948 Scott returned to the Maudsley to take charge of clinical forensic services, and remained in that post until his death; there were very few specialists in this aspect of psychiatry when the National Health Service began in that year. For the first fifteen years Scott was concerned mainly with juvenile delinquents, both at Stamford House remand home and at the Maudsley out-patient department. This experience influenced his later work with adult offenders, in that he always looked for the former child and adolescent that the adult had once been, in forming his opinion. Scott's reports were marked by their penetrating descriptions and accessible language. Subsequently he took up a joint appointment between the Maudsley and the prison medical service at Brixton prison, turning his attention to major offenders. He held two evening out-patient clinics every week, so that those attending would not have to miss work. He had urged that the medical work of prisons should be taken over by the National Health Service, but this view was rejected by the government. The joint appointment system, however, ultimately failed.

Scott's enormous clinical experience, together with his personal qualities of integrity, lucid thinking, and clear expression, caused his advice to be sought for many commissions and working parties, for example, on the special hospitals, on murders at Carstairs State Hospital, on the prison medical service, the home secretary's Advisory Council on the Penal System, and the Aarvold subcommittee on dangerous offenders. The only times that his name became known to the public, though, were when he advised the police in the Spaghetti House and Balcombe Street sieges in 1975—the origin of a new form of psychiatric skill. His advice to avoid any immediate use of force and play for time had successful results. He opposed the inauguration of a national programme of medium security units, believing that these would simply select out 'nice' patients, and continue to reject those who were most in need. His contribution to the public services was acknowledged by his appointment as CBE in 1974; he had been elected FRCP and FRCPsych. in 1971.

Although an editor of the *British Journal of Criminology*, Scott wrote relatively little himself, but his few publications were both original and influential. Together with Robert Mark he published *The Disease of Crime: Punishment or Treatment?* (1972). Though widely read, he considered theories and classifications no substitute for personal understanding of the patient—a quality he demonstrated to a special degree. As a result his teaching was based on the individual offender, from which he drew both unique and general lessons. Scott evolved his own diagnostic categories for forensic cases which were both original and expressed in non-technical language, but these, regrettably, never entered the published canon. He delighted in teaching and was very popular with specialist trainees, but he did not involve himself in formal research. He was chairman of the forensic psychiatry section of the Royal College of Psychiatrists, 1975–7.

As an individual, Scott was quiet and reserved, allowing few people to get on intimate terms with him. He was devoted to his wife, Lilian, and their two daughters. His greatest spare time interest was bird-watching, in which he was an expert, and he was accomplished in such do-it-yourself activities as carpentry and bricklaying.

Although there had been psychiatrists before who examined offenders, wrote about them, and gave evidence in courts, Scott was essentially the founder of forensic psychiatry as a recognized discipline in Britain. He did this particularly in association with his successor at the Maudsley, Professor T. C. N. Gibbens. Furthermore, on the world scale, British forensic psychiatry then attained a foremost position through his pupils, who undertook the research and writing that were not his own forte. Scott exercised enormous influence through his example, his individual teaching, and the impression made by his personal qualities on colleagues, administrators, judges, and politicians. Yet he did nothing to promote his own reputation or propagate his views; others constantly came to him for advice. He 'never deviated from his working attempts to improve the lot of patients who were otherwise despised and rejected' (J. C. G. in *The Lancet*), continuing to believe that the National Health Service had failed the disturbed offender:

> He was equally loyal to society in believing firmly that compassion did not mean sentimentality, and that the psychiatrist's role was to help the offender to come to terms with society as it is, and not as it should be. He was acknowledged as the foremost forensic psychiatrist of his time. (Munk, *Roll*)

Scott died at his home, 53 Park Road, Chiswick, London, on 6 August 1977 after a short illness. The Royal College of Psychiatrists subsequently established an annual lecture in his memory. HUGH FREEMAN

Sources Munk, *Roll* • *BMJ* (3 Sept 1977), 646 • *The Lancet* (20 Aug 1977), 415 • b. cert. • m. cert. • d. cert.
Wealth at death £323,908: probate, 28 Nov 1977, *CGPLA Eng. & Wales*

Scott, Sir Peter Markham (1909–1989), painter, ornithologist, and broadcaster, was born at 174 Buckingham Palace Road, London, on 14 September 1909, the only child of Captain Robert Falcon *Scott (1868–1912), Antarctic explorer, and his wife, (Edith Agnes) Kathleen *Scott (1878–1947), sculptor, daughter of Canon Lloyd Stewart Bruce. His father died in 1912 and in 1922 his mother married Edward Hilton *Young, who became first Baron Kennet. There was one son of this marriage. In his last message home before he died Scott had urged his wife to make his son interested in natural history, which was better than sport. In the event, Peter Scott came to excel at both. He was an energetic child, with a passion for natural history, who spent much time drawing and painting. He also shone at sports, ice-skating, and sailing in small boats. From his preparatory school, West Downs, he went to Oundle. He then studied at Trinity College, Cambridge, from 1927 to 1930, where he hoped to take the natural sciences tripos, but failed his part one in 1930. He stayed on for an extra term and obtained an ordinary degree in December 1930 (zoology, botany, and history of art). During his Cambridge days he took up wildfowling, and in 1929 *Country Life* magazine printed two articles on the sport written and illustrated by him.

From Cambridge Scott went to the Akademie der Bildenden Künste in Munich for a term, and then spent two years at the Royal Academy Schools in London. In 1933 he held his first one-man exhibition, which was a huge success, at Ackermann's Galleries in London. He was able to make his living as a painter of wildfowl, producing his first book (entitled *Morning Flight* and published by *Country Life*) in 1935. This was followed by *Wild Chorus* in 1938. Lavishly illustrated with his paintings, both books became very popular and ran to twelve editions.

Scott excelled at sailing and won a bronze medal in the 1936 Olympic games, for single-handed yachting. He also

Sir Peter Markham Scott (1909–1989), by Howard Coster, 1944

won the prestigious prince of Wales cup for international 14 foot dinghies in 1937, 1938, and 1946. In the late 1950s he developed a passion for gliding, and won the British gliding championships in 1963.

At the outbreak of war in 1939 Scott volunteered for the Royal Naval Volunteer Reserve. After training he spent two years in destroyers, mainly in HMS *Broke* in the western approaches, becoming a first lieutenant, and then he served in the coastal forces in steam gunboats. He became senior officer of the flotilla, was awarded a DSC (1943) and bar, and was thrice mentioned in dispatches. He also invented a night camouflage scheme for naval ships. His final appointment was the command of a new frigate, as a lieutenant-commander. With the war coming to a close, Scott was adopted as the Conservative candidate for Wembley North, but he failed to be elected by 435 votes, having had only two weeks to prepare for the election.

While visiting the River Severn at Slimbridge in Gloucestershire in 1945, in search of a rare goose among the wintering white-fronted geese, Scott decided to establish a research organization, which he had planned for many years, to study the swans, geese, and ducks of the world. The Severn Wildfowl Trust was set up at Slimbridge in 1946 and soon boasted the largest collection of wildfowl in the world. Later known as the Wildfowl and Wetlands Trust, it expanded into nine centres around Britain. Scott remained its honorary director until he died. Scientific research took him to Iceland in 1951 to study pink-footed geese on their breeding grounds, and to the Perry River region of northern Canada, where in 1949 he mapped this unknown area while in search of the breeding grounds of the Ross goose. Scott did more than any British contemporary to save wildlife species from extinction.

When the BBC founded a television centre in Bristol Scott helped to establish the natural history unit there, planning a programme on natural history called *Look*, which he hosted for seventeen years. Many of the early programmes contained his own film which he shot on his travels. He took part in *Nature Parliament*, a radio programme which ran for twenty-one years, and was the narrator in many other programmes.

In the early 1950s Scott became involved with the International Union for the Conservation of Nature and Natural Resources. He helped build up the species survival commission of the union and was chairman in 1962–81. With two friends, in 1961 he founded the World Wildlife Fund (later the World Wide Fund for Nature) to raise the money needed to finance nature conservation around the world. As its chairman from 1961, he designed its panda logo and invented the red data books listing endangered species. He travelled abroad extensively on behalf of the fund, establishing national appeals, advising on conservation issues and areas for reserves, lecturing, and fundraising. He was also involved in numerous other conservation and naturalist societies. He became as much of an expert on coral fish as he was on birds and his records have proved scientifically useful.

Scott's autobiography, *The Eye of the Wind*, was published in 1961 and was reprinted many times. He was a prolific author and illustrator, his final books being the three volumes of *Travel Diaries of a Naturalist* (1983–7).

Scott was elected rector of Aberdeen University, 1960–63, and appointed chancellor of Birmingham University, 1974–83. Appointed MBE in 1942 and CBE in 1953, he was knighted in 1973. In 1987 he became both CH and a fellow of the Royal Society. He had honorary degrees from the universities of Exeter, Aberdeen, Birmingham, Bristol, Liverpool, Bath, Guelph, and Ulster. He was also awarded numerous medals, prizes, and foreign honours.

Strongly built and of average height, Scott was warm and friendly, tackling everything with enthusiasm. He liked to paint every day. In 1942 he married the novelist Elizabeth Jane Howard, daughter of David Liddon Howard, timber merchant. They had a daughter. This marriage was dissolved in 1951 and in the same year he married (Felicity) Philippa, daughter of Commander Frederick William Talbot-Ponsonby, of the Royal Navy, and his wife, Hannah (*née* Findlay). They had a daughter and a son. Peter Scott died from a heart attack in hospital in Bristol on 29 August 1989. His remains were cremated, and the ashes were scattered at the Wildfowl and Wetlands Trust reserve at Slimbridge. Memorial services were held in St Paul's Cathedral, London, on 20 November 1989 and at the church of St John the Evangelist, Slimbridge, on 30 November.

Paul Walkden, *rev.*

Sources *The Times* (2 Sept 1989) • *The Independent* (21 Nov 1989) • P. Scott, *The eye of the wind* (1961) • J. Benington, *Sir Peter Scott at 80: a retrospective* (1989) • E. Huxley, *Peter Scott* (1993) • personal knowledge (1996) • *CGPLA Eng. & Wales* (1990)

Archives CUL, corresp. and papers • RGS, diaries | Bodl. Oxf., corresp. with Lord Monckton • Rice University, Houston, Texas, Woodson Research Center, corresp. with Sir Julian Huxley • University of Dundee, corresp. with Dr John Berry | FILM BBC archives, Caversham

Likenesses H. Coster, photograph, 1944, NPG [*see illus.*] • P. M. Scott, self-portrait, oils, Wildfowl and Wetlands Trust, Slimbridge, Gloucestershire • J. Shackleton, bronze busts, Wildlife and Wetlands Trust centres

Wealth at death £593,532: probate, 12 Jan 1990, *CGPLA Eng. & Wales*

Scott [*née* Cook], **Rachel Susan** (1848–1905), educationist and journalist, was born on 1 February 1848 at St Andrews, Fife, Scotland, the youngest of the five daughters of Revd John *Cook (1807–1869), minister of St Leonards, St Andrews and later professor of ecclesiastical history, University of St Andrews, and his wife, Rachel Susan Farquhar. She was educated at Madras College and then privately at home before becoming one of the first three students at Emily Davies's college at Hitchin, the forerunner of Girton College, where she studied from 1870 to 1873. Despite knowing no Latin or Greek until a few months before going to college, she was the first woman to attempt the classical tripos at Cambridge, gaining a second class in 1873. She served on the governing body of Girton College for several years.

On 20 May 1874 Rachel Cook married Charles Prestwich *Scott (1846–1932), editor of the *Manchester Guardian*, the leading Liberal newspaper. They lived at The Breeze, Kersal, from 1874 to 1881, where their three eldest children, Madeline (1876), Laurence Prestwich (1877), and John Russell (1879), were born. Edward Taylor (1883), their fourth child, was born at The Firs, Fallowfield, Manchester, where Rachel was to live until her death.

Through the auspices of the Manchester Association for Promoting the Education of Women, Rachel Scott spearheaded the campaign in the city to open the university to women. Between 1877 and 1883 she organized the Manchester and Salford College for Women, acting as its secretary. The association held classes in advanced subjects for women, taught and examined by professors of Owens College. In 1883 women were admitted to the newly federated Victoria University, and to its degrees, firstly on five years' probation and eventually permanently. Her successful campaign to open the university to women had been supported by her husband and advocated by the *Manchester Guardian*. She was also on the council of Ashburne House hall of residence for women students.

Rachel Scott became a member of the committee of Manchester High School for Girls in 1872, the year after its foundation, becoming honorary secretary of its preparatory school. She was also one of the founders of Withington Girls' School and took a keen interest in the progressive co-educational school Ladybarn House. As a hardworking member of Manchester's school board from 1890 to 1896, she was a supporter of free education for elementary school children before it became the policy of the board. Like Lydia Becker, her predecessor on the school board, she argued the case for women school board officers to be appointed. Her speeches on the hustings during school board elections were much admired and she headed the poll in 1890. She resigned her seat in order to spend part of each year in London in support of her husband, who had been elected to parliament in 1895.

Rachel Scott was very active politically and was a frequent speaker on social, educational, and political subjects. She was an ardent supporter of the Liberal Party and of the Women's Liberal Association, being the chair of the executive of the Lancashire and Cheshire Union of Women's Liberal Associations from its formation in 1893 and becoming its president in 1900. She continued in this post until 1903, when ill health resulted in her resignation. She was also an active supporter of women's suffrage. An eloquent public speaker, her voice was described as having 'filled the Free Trade Hall without perceptible effort' (*Manchester Guardian*, 29 Nov 1905). During her husband's electoral campaigns she was noted as having spoken at her very best when violent opposition was offered or threatened, as was the case at a meeting held in the Queen's Hall, London, when a mob rioted at the door. She was described by a contemporary as having 'spent herself for girls and women' (Burstall, 65) and by George Eliot as one of the most beautiful women she had ever met (*The Scotsman*, 1 Dec 1905).

Rachel Scott was a frequent contributor to the *Manchester Guardian* from 1873 and collaborated with her husband in editorial work. Her publications include an edition of Tacitus' *Agricola* with notes and translation, published anonymously in 1885. She was a contributor to Professor G. Saintsbury's English edition of the works of Honoré de Balzac and she translated *Une fille d'Ève* and *Mémoires de deux jeunes mariées*. She died at her home, The Firs, Fallowfield, Manchester, on 27 November 1905 and her funeral was held at the Manchester crematorium.

JOYCE GOODMAN

Sources K. T. Butler and H. I. McMorran, eds., *Girton College register, 1869–1946* (1948) • M. Tylecote, *The education of women at Manchester University, 1883–1933* (1941) • S. A. Burstall, *The story of the Manchester High School for Girls, 1871–1911* (1911) • S. Tooley, 'Ladies of Manchester', *The Woman at Home* (1897?) • *Manchester Guardian* (29 Nov 1905) • *Girton Review* (1905) • J. L. Hammond, *C. P. Scott of the Manchester Guardian* (1934) • D. Ayerst, *Guardian: biography of a newspaper* (1971) • *The Scotsman* (1 Dec 1905) • 'The funeral of Mrs C. P. Scott', *Manchester Guardian* (3 Dec 1905) • *Morning Post* (20 Nov 1905) • *Yorkshire Post* (20 Nov 1905) • parish register, Fife, St Leonards, 1 Feb 1848, 8 March 1848 [births and baptisms] • m. cert. • d. cert.

Likenesses photograph, repro. in Burstall, *Story of Manchester High School* • photograph, repro. in Tooley, 'Ladies of Manchester' • photograph, repro. in Hammond, *C. P. Scott of the Manchester Guardian*

Wealth at death £502 12*s*. 1*d*.: English administration endorsed in Scotland, 27 Nov 1908, *CCI*

Scott [Scot], **Reginald** (*d*. 1599), writer on witchcraft, was the first son of Richard Scott (*d*. before 1544), landowner, of Scott's Hall, Kent, and his wife, Mary (*d*. 1582), daughter of George Whetenall of Hextall's Place, Kent. After his father's death his mother married Fulk Onslow, clerk of parliament. She died on 8 October 1582. According to Anthony Wood, Scott was educated at the University of Oxford, probably at Hart Hall, but he did not obtain a degree. He married Jane, daughter of Thomas Cobbe of Aldington, Kent, on 11 October 1568 at Brabourne, Kent. They had one daughter, Elizabeth, who married Sackville Turnor of Tablehurst, Sussex. Scott later married Alice Collyar, who already had a daughter, Marie, by her former husband. He had close connections with his cousin Sir Thomas *Scott (1534x6–1594) of Scott's Hall, and tells us that he was financially dependent upon him.

For many years Scott was surveyor of flood defences on Romney Marshes, Kent. In 1583 he played a major role in building a dam in Dover Harbour, where he worked in association with Sir Thomas Scott and the mathematician Thomas Digges. Water released through a sluice in the dam was intended to scour silt out of the harbour, which had become inaccessible to shipping. This major project was the most important engineering feat of the Elizabethan period. In 1586 and 1587 he was collector of subsidies for the lathe of Shepway, Kent. In 1588 he served as a captain of foot-soldiers and 'trench-master' (or engineer) in the levies which his cousin encamped near Dover at the time of the Spanish Armada. He was elected MP for New Romney in 1589. He made his will on 15 September 1599 and died at Smeeth, Kent, on 9 October. Scott left his small properties about Brabourne, Aldington, and Romney Marsh to his widow. The last words of his will are: 'great is the trouble my poor wife hath had with me, and small is the comfort she hath received at my hands, whom if I had not matched withal I had not died worth one groat' (Scott, xxviii).

Three works by Scott survive (a life of Sir Thomas Scott once existed in the papers of Abraham Fleming, but is now lost). *A Perfite Platforme of a Hoppe Garden* was published in 1574 with reprints in 1576, 1578, 1640, 1654, and 1659. This is the first practical treatise on hop culture in English and appears to be based on direct knowledge of agricultural practices in the Low Countries. The first edition was dedicated to William Lovelace of Bethersden, Kent, serjeant-at-law. The book contains woodcut illustrations of the process.

The Discoverie of Witchcraft, his most important work, was published without licence in 1584 and reprinted in 1651, 1654, and 1665. The first modern edition was in 1886, and there were several in the twentieth century. A partial translation into Dutch appeared at Leiden in 1609 and was reprinted in 1637. Scott's objective was to refute the *Démonomanie* of Jean Bodin (1580) and to go well beyond the arguments of the most radical author on witchcraft known to him, Johann Weyer, whose *De praestigiis daemonum* (1566) had been attacked by Bodin. Scott made a number of remarkable claims. He maintained that there were no witches in contemporary England and that all those executed for witchcraft were innocent—he had tried to find anyone who would offer instruction in witchcraft without success. He asserted that none of the terms used in the Bible which had been translated as 'witch' had that meaning in the original languages, thereby undermining the claim that there was a biblical sanction for the execution of witches, and he is thus a significant figure in the history of biblical criticism. According to Scott, witchcraft was an impossible crime, because words could not work upon the world. His arguments thus implied a radical separation between mind and matter. He contended that where curses or spells were followed by unpleasant events the link between the two was entirely coincidental.

Scott went beyond a systematic attack on the intellectual foundations of the belief in witchcraft because he described witch accusations in England as resulting out of a particular type of social encounter: old women begging for food or other assistance would curse their neighbours when they were turned away empty handed; if something bad then happened—the death of a child, perhaps—the old woman would be taken to be a witch. Witchcraft accusations in England thus arose in the context of disagreements over expectations and obligations relating to charitable giving. This sociological account was persuasive to contemporaries and has been adopted by modern historians. As far as Scott was concerned, those who confessed to being witches were either deluded or the victims of torture, while much of what Bodin had taken to be evidence for the existence of witchcraft in different eras and diverse cultures Scott was prepared to dismiss as mere fable and fiction. His book was a remarkable triumph of erudition for an obscure country gentleman with little formal education: he listed 212 Latin and 23 English authors on whom he drew. He had clearly taken an interest in contemporary English trials, but there is no evidence to support the suggestion that he was a JP, beyond the fact that he claimed the title of esquire.

Scott bolstered his study of witchcraft with attacks on other forms of credulity and superstition, under which heading he included Catholicism and astrology. He dismissed alchemy as a type of confidence trick. He reproduced from a manuscript detailed procedures for conjuring up demons, presumably with the idea that his readers could demonstrate for themselves that such techniques were ineffective. And he set out to show how easy it was to confuse an observer. To this end he dedicated book 13 to the first significant account of how to perform conjuring tricks. The book, with some revisions, was republished as *The Art of Juggling* (1612; repr. 1614) by S. R., which was itself absorbed into *Hocus Pocus Junior* (1634); this had numerous editions in the seventeenth century (one calling itself the thirteenth edition appeared in 1697) and was the basis of later manuals on legerdemain which continued to appear into the twentieth century.

The *Discoverie* ended with a 'Discourse on devils and spirits' (which is unfortunately omitted from some modern reprints; the 1665 edition contains a spurious second discourse). Although this discourse avoided a full-frontal attack on orthodoxy, it appears from it that Scott was not a Trinitarian and did not believe that the account of the fall in the book of Genesis referred to a historical event. He seems to have held that the idea of good and evil spirits was simply a metaphor for internal promptings towards good and evil experienced by the individual and that the individual could overcome evil and become truly good. The discourse was incompatible with orthodox protestant Christianity, which stressed predestination, and it, together with Scott's association with Abraham Fleming (who worked with him on the *Discoverie* and published a familist prayer book in 1581), suggests that he may well have been a member of the Family of Love. Familists are known to have denied the reality of the devil. Thomas Basson, publisher of the Dutch translation of the *Discoverie*, published familist works. Yet Scott obviously believed he could call on the protection of leading figures in the kingdom: as well as to Sir Thomas Scott, the *Discoverie* is dedicated to Sir Roger Manwood, chief baron of the exchequer, to John Coldwell, dean of Rochester (afterwards bishop of Salisbury), and to William Redman, archdeacon of Canterbury (afterwards bishop of Norwich).

Scott was very widely read in the late sixteenth and early seventeenth centuries—Gabriel Harvey and Thomas Nashe refer to him, and William Shakespeare and Thomas Middleton were evidently familiar with the *Discoverie*. He was attacked at length by James VI of Scotland in his *Daemonology* (1597) and referred to by almost all the Tudor and early Stuart authors on witchcraft (Henry Holland in 1590, George Gifford in 1593, John Deacon and John Walker in 1601, William Perkins in 1608, John Cotta in 1616, and Richard Bernard in 1627). Thomas Ady's *Candle in the Dark* (1655) and John Webster's *Displaying of Supposed Witchcraft* (1677) were the first works to defend Scott's uncompromising scepticism directly, and he was still an indispensable reference point for Francis Hutchinson in his *Historical Essay Concerning Witchcraft* (1718). Scott also had a significant influence on Samuel Harsnett, later archbishop of York, and, through him, on two important witchcraft cases, in which the supposed victims were Mary Glover (1602) and Anne Gunter (1604). Both cases encouraged scepticism regarding claims of bewitchment. Ady thus seems justified in his claim that Scott made 'great impressions on the magistracy and clergy' (*DNB*). It is often asserted that James ordered that all copies of the *Discoverie* be burnt when he came to the English throne, but there is no contemporary evidence to support this story, which first appeared in 1659. Nicholas Gyer's *English Phlebotomy* (1592) is dedicated to Scott.

Scott is also the author of a lengthy account of the rebuilding of Dover Harbour in the second edition of Raphael Holinshed's *Chronicle* (1587), where it appears under the year 1586. This was based on his experience on the project. His expertise as an engineer is apparent from his account, which well exemplifies the social egalitarianism that characterizes all his work.

DAVID WOOTTON

Sources S. Anglo, 'Reginald Scot's *Discoverie of witchcraft*: scepticism and Sadduceeism', *The damned art: essays in the literature of witchcraft* (1977), 106–39 • E. H. Ash, '"A perfect and absolute work": expertise, authority and the rebuilding of Dover Harbor, 1579–1583', *Technology and Culture*, 41 (2000), 239–68 • L. Estes, 'Reginald Scot and his *Discoverie of witchcraft*', *Church History*, 52 (1983), 444–56 • S. J. Forrester, *The annotated discovery of witchcraft, booke xiii* (Calgary, AB, 2000) • HoP, *Commons, 1558–1603*, 3.355–8 • M. MacDonald,

Witchcraft and hysteria in Elizabethan London: Edward Jorden and the Mary Glover case (1991) • *DNB* • A. Patterson, *Reading Holinshed's 'Chronicles'* (1994) • F. Peck, ed., *Desiderata curiosa*, 1 (1732) • R. Scot, *The discoverie of witchcraft*, ed. B. Nicholson (1886); facs. edn (1973) • J. Sharpe, *The bewitching of Anne Gunter* (1999) • R. H. West, *Reginald Scot and Renaissance writings on magic* (Boston, Ma, 1984) • Wood, *Ath. Oxon.*, new edn, 1.679 • D. Wootton, 'Reginald Scot/Abraham Fletcher/the Family of Love', *Languages of witchcraft*, ed. S. Clark (2001), 119–38

Scott, Robert (*d.* 1631), army officer in the Swedish and Danish services and military inventor, is a man of whom nothing is known before 1623, when Gustavus Adolphus of Sweden granted the Scot James Spens, son of the Stuart ambassador in Stockholm, Sir James Spens, authority to levy a body of Scottish soldiers for Swedish service. In the same year Scott levied 200 men for the king of Sweden, presumably as part of Spens's recruitment drive. For the next five years Scott served in the Swedish army, eventually acting as the army's quartermaster-general. Scott was mentioned in royal correspondence to the Danish Court by Erik Krabbe, the Danish resident in Stockholm, in connection with Gustavus Adolphus's impending campaign in western Prussia in 1628. The Danes were interested in Scott because of his development of light artillery.

While in Swedish service Scott developed a type of leather-covered cannon, also known as the leather gun, in competition with one Melchoir von Wurmbrand. These cannon were revolutionary in that they were light enough to be carried by two men, they fired the same size shot as conventional cannon with half the powder, and they could fire up to a hundred times without having to be left to cool down. Scott used different proportions to Wurmbrand in the construction of his cannon. He also told the king that he had contrived a way of reloading his cannon ten times before a soldier could reload his musket once. Some Danish noblemen witnessed a demonstration of the leather cannon in Stockholm at which the Swedish king was said to have been suitably impressed. However, Scott wished payment of 20,000 Swedish riksdaler for his invention, a sum which Gustavus Adolphus refused to pay.

The Danes successfully recruited Scott from Swedish service in 1628 and he received his appointment as the master-general of artillery on 6 September. This appointment has caused some historical debate since such a military rank had not previously existed within the Danish army. None the less a record exists in the Copenhagen archive of Scott's appointment as 'General Artillerimeister' with a salary of 400 Danish rigsdaler per month, four times that of other officers of artillery. Scott's service for the Danish crown was short, and had ended by the time Denmark pulled out of the Thirty Years' War. Scott left the service of Christian IV to return to England. The exact date of his departure is unclear, some sources suggesting October or November 1628 and others placing his leaving some time after the treaty of Lübeck in 1629. He was certainly in Stuart service by September 1629. There he acted as a gentleman of the bedchamber to Charles I.

As part of his Stuart service Scott received new accommodation from the crown. Charles I wrote to Attorney-General Heath on 3 September 1629 ordering him to purchase a house in Lambeth, which came with 8 acres of land. For this purpose Heath was ordered to contract himself to the chancellor of the exchequer for the sum of £1400. Five months later, on 15 February 1630, Scott and his family were issued with a grant of denization. This document notes that Scott had a wife named Anne and two children, Charles and Anne, as well as a nephew also called Robert Scott. According to Sir James Balfour Paul (*Scots peerage*, 2.282), Scott's other nephew, James Wemyss, was also included in an act of denization issued to Scott in 1630, although no mention of this appears in the *Calendar of State Papers, Domestic*.

Within only a few days of the grant of denization being issued, on 20 February 1630, it was ordered that Scott should receive £600 per annum in wages. During this brief time in the service of Charles I, Scott managed to introduce the leather cannon into the British Isles, but he did not live to see the deployment of his weapon. He died in 1631 and was buried in St Mary, Lambeth, in Surrey where an epitaph to his artillery invention can be found.

The effectiveness of the leather cannon has been doubted (G. Parker, *The Military Revolution: Military Innovation and the Rise of the West, 1500–1800*, 1996, 33–35), but there is ample evidence of its being regarded as an excellent weapon during the wars in the three Stuart kingdoms between 1638 and 1651. It first saw service with the Scottish covenanters in the version developed by General Alexander Hamilton, known as 'Dear Sandy's stoup'. Later, leather cannon could be found in the English parliamentarian and Cromwellian service in the Scott model, as developed and refined by his nephew Wemyss. Many of these guns also ended up in royalist service after the capture of Wemyss and his artillery train in 1644.

STEVE MURDOCH

Sources O. Blom, 'Smaa bidrag til artilleriets historie under Kristian d. 4de', *Historiske Tidsskrift*, 3 (1900–02), 332–44 • *CSP dom.*, 1629–31 • L. W. Munthe, *Kungliga fortifikationens historia*, 1 (1902), 222 • T. Riis, *Should auld acquaintance be forgot … Scottish–Danish relations, c.1450–1707*, 2 (1988), 116 • *Scots peerage*, 2.282 • letter from King to Count James Spens, 23/9/1623, Swedish Riksarkiv • A. Grosjean, 'Scots and the Swedish state: diplomacy, military service and ennoblement, 1611–1660', PhD diss., U. Aberdeen, 1998

Scott, Robert (*b.* in or before 1632, *d.* 1709/10), bookseller, was the son of Arthur Scott, clerk of York. Nothing is known about his early childhood or his education, but on 10 January 1649 he was apprenticed to Daniel Frere, a London bookseller. After two years he was turned over to the bookseller William Wells, and freed of the Stationers' Company on 31 March 1656. His name appears in imprints rather infrequently from the year 1661 with the address *ad insignia Principis in vico Little Britain dicto*, or in English at the Prince's Armes in Little Britain, London, which was to remain his address throughout his career. He was made a liveryman of the Stationers' Company on 20 April 1664. At some point he married a daughter of William Wells; this may have been the Elizabeth (*d*. 1697) who was noted as Scott's wife in the marriage tax assessment for the London parish of St Botolph, Aldersgate, in 1695.

The 1670s and 1680s were the busiest years for Scott as a publisher, judging by the number of publications that carried his name, although his total output was never as large as that of some of his contemporaries. He frequently published works in association with other booksellers, in the early years often with William Wells, his former master. His publications range from solid theological or scientific volumes such as George Bull's *Harmonia apostolica* (1670) or Marcello Malpighi's *Opera omnia* (1686) to popular literature, such as *The Famous History of the Seven Champions* (1687) and *Don Quixote* (1675). He also published several works written by John Evelyn. After the death of William Wells in early 1673 Scott went into publishing partnership with his brother-in-law, George Wells, but Scott was first and foremost a bookseller, selling books to people such as Samuel Pepys and Robert Hooke. Scott was considered the major importer of scholarly books in Latin from the continent and made frequent trips abroad to supplement his stock and to fulfil commissions given him by cherished customers such as John Cosin, bishop of Durham. In 1674 he brought out his *Catalogus librorum ex variis Europae partibus advectorum* of well over 200 pages with about 6500 items. A large part of his stock (25,000 items in 8800 lots) was sold in 1688 in an auction organized by his former apprentice Benjamin Walford, but Scott retained a bookshop, possibly on a smaller scale, until at least 1692, when Pepys mentions to his friend John Evelyn that he has been in Scott's shop. An unwise association with Adiel Mill of Amen Corner, whom many considered to be a speculator, led to a substantial loss for Scott, who tried with several other of Mill's creditors to recoup some assets by selling off Mill's stock of books in 1691.

Scott was the London agent of the Oxford University Press, for whom he published William Beveridge's *Pandects*, and of the Bodleian Library, selling them the manuscripts that had belonged to Lord Christopher Hatton, which Scott had bought after Hatton's death in 1670. He was an active and leading member of the Stationers' Company. He was elected to its governing body in June 1681 and, over the remainder of his career, fined for all the offices, including that of master of the company in 1691, when reference was made to his considerable deafness. No publications carry his name after 1706 and his last attendance at a company meeting was in November 1708; he may have retired to the country. He was buried on 13 January 1710 in the parish of St Botolph, Aldersgate. His will, made on 4 February 1708 and proved on 17 January 1710, appointed as executors his eldest sons, Charles and Robert, and his daughter, Ann, who were to benefit equally from his estate; he also requested only a modest funeral. MARJA SMOLENAARS

Sources L. Rostenberg, 'Robert Scott, Restoration stationer and importer', *Papers of the Bibliographical Society of America*, 48 (1954), 49–76 • D. F. McKenzie, ed., *Stationers' Company apprentices*, [2]: *1641–1700* (1974), 60 • H. R. Plomer and others, *A dictionary of the printers and booksellers who were at work in England, Scotland, and Ireland from 1668 to 1725* (1922) • will, GL, MS 9171/55 • private information (2004) [M. Treadwell, Trent University, Canada]

Scott, Robert (1777–1841), engraver, the son of Robert Scott and his wife, Grizell, was born on 13 November 1777 at Lanark, Scotland, where his father was a skinner. He was educated at the grammar school in Musselburgh before being apprenticed to the engraver and printer Alexander Robertson in 1787 and training at the Trustees' Academy in Edinburgh under David Allan. Twenty-five red chalk drawings by Scott after Allan are contained in a bound volume in the National Gallery of Scotland, dated 1788. These drawings depict antique subjects, while the remainder of the volume comprises 203 engravings of portraits, landscapes, and book illustrations. Scott first became known by some plates in Dr James Anderson's periodical *The Bee* in 1792. The first engraving was of the French poet Jean Frissant; later contributions in 1793 and 1794 included portraits of William Tytler, vice-president of the Society of Scottish Antiquaries, and the painters John Brown and Gavin Hamilton. A watercolour portrait of Andrew Fletcher, Lord Milton, the lord justice-clerk, after Allan Ramsay, is in the Scottish National Portrait Gallery. About 1795 Scott drew a portrait of Caroline of Brunswick, queen consort of George IV; an engraving by Thomas Barrow of this drawing is held in the Victoria and Albert Museum.

Although he was a talented draughtsman, Scott 'cared little for his own art and looked upon anyone becoming a painter as a man throwing away his chances in life' (Minto, 1.18); he concentrated on engraving as a more lucrative career. In 1799 he set up his own business in Edinburgh, comprising a large engraving workshop, in Parliament Square. He retained these premises until they were destroyed by fire in 1824, when he re-established his business at 65 Princes Street. The output from his workshop was prolific and varied: he had the equipment for copperplate-engraving, etching, mezzotinting, aquatinting, and lithography and also introduced to Edinburgh the art of engraving on steel.

Scott is best remembered for his landscape engravings, such as *Views of Seats and Scenery Chiefly in the Environs of Edinburgh* (1795–6), from drawings by A. Carse and A. Wilson, and his illustrations to George Barry's *History of the Orkney Islands* (1805) and the 1808 edition of *Gentle Shepherd*. For twenty years he executed prints of Scottish country seats for the *Scots Magazine*. Scott is less well known for such singular engravings as *Glasgow Lunatic Asylum*, an impression of which is held in the Victoria and Albert Museum, and his illustrations for editions of the works of British poets and travel books. He capitalized on the Napoleonic wars by producing prints of military and naval figures, and he engraved a famous memorial celebrating Nelson's victory at Trafalgar on 21 October 1805. His workshop employed many assistants who produced plates for illustrated books, such as *Memorabilia of Perth* (1806), published by William Morison, and Morison's *Guide to the City and County of Perth* (4th edn, 1820). Scott also kept printing presses, his principal customer being the Gainsborough publisher Henry Mozley, for whose 1804 edition of James Thomson's *Seasons* he engraved four plates after designs by John Burnet. Burnet was trained as an engraver by Scott; other apprentices included John Horsburgh and James Stewart.

On 29 March 1800 Scott married Ross Bell, the daughter of Robert Bell, a Musselburgh mason. The family home from 1812 to 1827 was Hermits and Termits, St Leonards, Edinburgh, where two of their sons, the artists David *Scott (1806–1849) and William Bell *Scott (1811–1890), grew up. In 1807 four of their five sons had died within a few days of one another; the deaths had a profound effect on the couple and the domestic environment of their remaining children. A keen purchaser of the illustrated works of British poets and novelists, Scott also collected old plates and numbered among his collection originals by Guercino and Wenceslaus Hollar. Scott's last known work was a set of twenty views, *Scenery of Edinburgh and Midlothian* (1838), from drawings by his son W. B. Scott, whom he had trained as an engraver. He died in January 1841 in Edinburgh. The National Gallery of Scotland holds some of his engravings and drawings; engravings may also be found in the Victoria and Albert Museum; the City Art Centre, Edinburgh; the University of Edinburgh Library; Perth Museum and Art Gallery; and the British Museum, London. LUCY DIXON

Sources P. J. M. McEwan, *Dictionary of Scottish art and architecture* (1994) · Bryan, *Painters* (1886–9) · G. H. Bushnell, *Scottish engravers* (1949) · M. Campbell, *David Scott, 1806–1849* (1990) · W. B. Scott, *Memoir of David Scott, RSA* (1850) · *Autobiographical notes of the life of William Bell Scott: and notices of his artistic and poetic circle of friends, 1830 to 1882*, ed. W. Minto, 2 vols. (1892) · H. Smailes, *The concise catalogue of the Scottish National Portrait Gallery* (1990) · K. Andrews and J. R. Botchie, *National Gallery of Scotland Scottish drawings* (1960) · D. Irwin and F. Irwin, *Scottish painters at home and abroad, 1700–1900* (1975) · Edinburgh and Leith, postal directory, 1797–8 · Edinburgh and Leith, postal directory, 1840–41 · *Scots Magazine* (1800–20) · S. Lloyd, *Raeburn's rival: Archibald Skirving, 1749–1819* (1999) [exhibition catalogue, Scot. NPG, 22 Jan – 5 Apr 1999] · M. A. Balfour and A. Doughty, eds., *The Edinburgh scene: catalogue of prints and drawings in the Edinburgh Room, Central Public Library* (1951) · *DNB* · Canongate register of marriages, 1564–1800

Likenesses J. Arrowsmith, black chalk drawing, 1820, Scot. NPG · W. B. Scott, lithograph, 1831, BM · J. Le Conté, engraving (after D. Scott), Scot. NPG · W. B. Scott, lithograph, Scot. NPG

Scott, Robert (1811–1887), lexicographer and dean of Rochester, was born on 26 January 1811 at Bondleigh, Devon, the son of Alexander Scott (1781–1847), then rector there, and his wife, Agnes. His father moved to Egremont rectory, Cumberland, and Robert attended St Bees, and afterwards Shrewsbury School, then under Dr Samuel Butler, afterwards bishop of Lichfield. He entered Christ Church, Oxford (of which he was elected a junior student along with Henry George *Liddell), in January 1830. He was Craven scholar in 1830, Ireland scholar in 1833, and in the same year graduated BA with first class in the final classical school. In 1834 he won the Latin essay prize, and became fellow of Balliol in 1835, acting as tutor in that college (with Archibald Campbell Tait, afterwards archbishop of Canterbury) until 1840. He was ordained in 1835, and held the college living of Duloe, Cornwall, from 1840

Robert Scott (1811–1887), by Samuel Alexander Walker, 1874

to 1850. He was prebendary of Exeter from 1845 to 1866, and held the rectory of South Luffenham, Rutland, from 1850 to 1854, being select preacher at Oxford in 1853–4. He married, first, on 1 December 1840, Mary Harriet, daughter of Rear-Admiral Thomas Folliott Bough, who died on 5 December 1845, and, second, on 7 June 1849, Mary Jane Ann, daughter of Major Hugh Scott, who died on 6 January 1885.

In 1854 Scott was elected master of Balliol College, in succession to Dr Richard Jenkyns, and in opposition to Benjamin Jowett, whose orthodoxy was questioned. In the election, Scott was the victor by six votes to five, and 'for ten years he was an obstructive, wielding his numerical ascendancy to crush all Jowett's schemes of reform' (W. Tuckwell, *Reminiscences of Oxford*, 2nd edn 1907, 202). Outside the college he was an active but highly conservative delegate of the university press. Scott held the mastership until 1870, being also Dean Ireland's professor of exegesis from 1861 to 1870. Much of Balliol's success during his mastership must be ascribed to the efforts of Jowett, whose influence seems to have prompted Gladstone to make Scott dean of Rochester in 1870, the appointment in part timed so as to ensure Jowett's election as his successor in Balliol. Scott was again select preacher at Oxford in 1874–5. He died at the deanery, Rochester, on 2 December 1887.

Scott published two sets of sermons and a commentary on the epistle of James, but is best known as joint compiler (with H. G. Liddell, dean of Christ Church) of a Greek–English lexicon (usually referred to as 'Liddell and Scott'). Work was begun, on the basis of the Greek–German lexicon of Passow, in 1836, and the first edition was published by the university press in 1843. Six more editions, involving much correction and enlargement, appeared in Scott's lifetime, although Liddell, who was always the more active partner, was alone responsible for the seventh edition (1883). The lexicon was largely rewritten for the ninth edition of 1940 and supplements were published in 1968 and 1996.

HENRY CRAIK, *rev.* RICHARD SMAIL

Sources *The Times* (3 Dec 1887) • *The Guardian* (14 Dec 1887) • I. Elliott, ed., *The Balliol College register, 1833–1933*, 2nd edn (privately printed, Oxford, 1934) • G. Faber, *Jowett* (1957) • P. Sutcliffe, *The Oxford University Press: an informal history* (1978) • P. G. W. Glare, *Studies in lexicography*, ed. R. Burchfield (1987) • Gladstone, *Diaries* • Boase, *Mod. Eng. biog.* • *CGPLA Eng. & Wales* (1888)

Archives Pusey Oxf., corresp. and papers | Balliol Oxf., corresp. relating to affairs of Balliol College, Oxford • Balliol Oxf., letters to Richard Jenkyns • BL, corresp. with Samuel Butler, Add. MSS 34587–35068, *passim* • BL, corresp. with W. E. Gladstone, Add. MS 44295 • LPL, corresp. with A. C. Tait • NL Scot., corresp. and papers relating to Revised Version of Bible

Likenesses photograph, 1874, NPG [*see illus.*] • oils, Balliol Oxf. • wood-engraving (after photograph by S. A. Walker), NPG; repro. in *ILN* (17 Dec 1887)

Wealth at death £58,203 3*s*. 11*d*.—effects in England: probate, 14 Feb 1888, *CGPLA Eng. & Wales*

Scott, Robert Bisset (1774–1841), writer on military jurisprudence, was commissioned lieutenant in the Tower Hamlets militia on 9 November 1807. In 1810 he published anonymously his first work, *The military law of England (with all the principal authorities) adapted to the general use of the army in its various duties and relations, and the practice of courts-martial.* He also published *The Excellence of the British Military Code … Exemplified* (1811). He was himself brought to a court martial by his colonel on 19 December 1811 for neglect of orders, and for breaking his arrest; but the court practically acquitted him, and even the private admonition which they adjudged was remitted. They considered the facts adduced in support of the charges were of a vexatious nature.

Two years afterwards Scott's colonel, Mark Beaufoy, was tried by court martial, Scott being the prosecutor. The trial lasted from 26 October to 24 November 1813. The court acquitted Beaufoy of most of the numerous charges, but found him guilty of some irregularities in the enlistment of recruits, and of culpable neglect in not preventing illegal deductions from the men's pay. They sentenced him to be removed from the command of his regiment, which he had held since it was first raised in 1797, but they stated that, in the conduct of the prosecution, Scott had not been 'actuated by that regard for the service which alone ought to influence an officer upon such an occasion'. So, while the sentence was confirmed, Scott was informed that his further services would be dispensed with (22 January 1814).

Scott then started a weekly paper, the *Military Register*, and published in 1816 *The Stratagems of War*, a translation of Frontinus. He worked as a military advocate, 'with considerable success on various courts martial' (*GM*). In 1830 he went to Portugal to serve against Dom Miguel, and is said to have freed Sir John Milley Doyle from prison; but this was untrue as Doyle was freed two years before at the instance of Sir Frederick Lamb. Scott was twice married, 'and lost his second partner as he had his first, by death awfully sudden' (*GM*). In 1836, Scott's income having become inadequate and precarious, on the recommendation of Sir Herbert Taylor William IV made him a pensioner of the Charterhouse, near Smithfield, London, where he died on 22 October 1841. He was interred in the Charterhouse burial-ground on 3 November.

E. M. LLOYD, *rev.* ROGER T. STEARN

Sources *GM*, 2nd ser., 16 (1841), 657 • G. Hodder, *History of the 7th battalion rifle brigade* (1884) • reports of courts martial, Royal United Institute for Defence Studies, Whitehall

Scott, Robert Eden (1769–1811), philosopher, was born in Old Aberdeen on 13 April 1769. His mother was Elizabeth Scott, daughter of Thomas Gordon who was a professor of Greek at the University of Aberdeen. The Gordon family had been prominent in the university for over two centuries. His father was John Scott, rector of Durham, USA. He graduated MA at the University and King's College, Aberdeen, on 30 March 1785, was appointed regent on 8 May 1788, and, after holding in co-professoriate the chair of natural philosophy interchangeably with those of Greek, mathematics, and moral philosophy, held the last exclusively from 1800 until his death. He married in Old Aberdeen on 19 February 1797 Rachel Forbes of Thainstown. He died in Edinburgh, in January (probably on the 14th) 1811. Scott was author of *Elements of Rhetoric* (1802); *Elements of Intellectual Philosophy, or, An Analysis of the Powers of the Human Understanding* (1805); *Inquiry into the Limits and Peculiar Objects of Physical and Metaphysical Science* (1810). He belonged to the Scottish, or common-sense, school of philosophy.

J. M. RIGG, *rev.* C. A. CREFFIELD

Sources P. J. Anderson, ed., *Officers and graduates of University and King's College, Aberdeen, MVD–MDCCCLX*, New Spalding Club, 11 (1893) • *Scots Magazine*, 59 (1797), 143 • *Scots Magazine and Edinburgh Literary Miscellany*, 73 (1811), 159 • R. Blakey, *History of the philosophy of mind* (1848)

Archives U. Aberdeen, corresp. and papers

Likenesses portrait; last known at U. Aberdeen, 1897

Scott, Robert Falcon [*known as* Scott of the Antarctic] (1868–1912), naval officer and Antarctic explorer, was born on 6 June 1868 at Outlands, Milehouse, near Stoke Damerel, Devonport, the third of the six children of John Edward Scott (1830–1897), a brewer, and his wife, Hannah, the daughter of William Bennett Cuming, a Lloyd's surveyor.

Education and early career Invariably known as Con by his immediate family, Scott seemed destined from the start for a naval career. His paternal grandfather and the latter's three brothers were all naval officers, and his uncle Henry Cuming became a vice-admiral. As a very young child he was taught at home by governesses. At the age of eight he attended Exmouth House School, Stoke

Damerel, and later, aged eleven, was sent to Stubbington House, Fareham, to be crammed for the Royal Navy. When he was thirteen he joined the training ship HMS *Britannia*, and he passed out in 1883 with first-class certificates in mathematics and seamanship. Between 1883 and 1887 he served in turn aboard the *Boadicea*, the *Monarch*, and the *Rover*. In this last ship, while on the West Indies station, he was noted by Sir Clements Markham, secretary and later president of the Royal Geographical Society, as a likely candidate for the leadership of a future Antarctic expedition.

In 1887–8 Scott studied and qualified for his lieutenancy at the Royal Naval College, Greenwich, with high honours, and was then appointed sub-lieutenant in the *Spider*. In 1889 he was posted to the *Daphne* and then to the *Amphion* for service on the Pacific station at Esquimalt, British Columbia. In 1891 he returned to England to serve briefly in the *Caroline* in the Mediterranean, from which he transferred to the *Vernon* (shore establishment) to specialize in torpedo work. He qualified as torpedo lieutenant, first class, and in 1893 was appointed to the *Vulcan*. Aged twenty-five and an expert in his field, Scott was growing in confidence and keen for promotion; but a sequence of family crises put his prospects in jeopardy. His father's bankruptcy in 1894 obliged the family to move to Holcombe House, Shepton Mallet, Somerset. From 1895 to 1896 Scott served in the torpedo school *Defiance* and from 1896 to 1897 in the battleship *Empress of India*, where he again encountered Markham. His father's death in 1897, followed by that of his brother in 1898, left Scott as sole provider for his mother. Then in June 1899, while on leave from the *Majestic*, he again chanced on Markham and from him learned of maturing plans for a British national Antarctic expedition. Scott promptly applied for the command, despite, as he later put it, having 'no predilection for Polar exploration' (Scott, *Voyage*, 1.32). On 9 June 1900 a joint committee of the Royal Geographical Society and the Royal Society agreed to appoint Scott as leader. Shortly afterwards he was gazetted commander.

First Antarctic expedition, 1901–1904 At the time little was known of Antarctica, whose very continentality was then only conjectured. Scott's formal instructions were to explore to its eastern extremity the ice barrier discovered by Sir James Clark Ross in 1841 and to search for the land believed by Ross to lie to its east. Additionally he was to ascertain the extent of Victoria Land, penetrate its interior, and carry out an extensive programme of scientific research. Lacking all knowledge of the techniques of polar travel, Scott wisely sought advice from the experienced Arctic explorer Fridtjof Nansen. Within a year he had completed the recruiting and provisioning required to overwinter in Antarctica, and on 6 August 1901 set sail in the purpose-built, ice-strengthened vessel *Discovery*.

Scott's official narrative of the expedition, *The Voyage of the 'Discovery'* (1905), a classic of its genre, tells the story. The ship's officers were predominantly from the Royal Navy, an exception being Lieutenant Ernest Shackleton, an ex-merchant navy officer. The five civilian scientists included Dr Edward Adrian *Wilson, who was to achieve a reputation as surgeon, zoologist, and artist, and was to become Scott's close friend and confidant on this and his last expedition. The long voyage south enabled Scott to get to know his men and to take on the direction of the scientific work and to master its details. The *Discovery* entered the pack ice in January 1902 and sailed the length

Robert Falcon Scott (1868–1912), by Herbert George Ponting, 1911

of the Great Ice barrier (now Ross Ice shelf), Scott surmising correctly that this was no glacier but a floating ice mass of vast extent. To the east of the barrier the mountains of what was to be named Edward VII Land were discerned. Scott returned westward and established winter quarters off Hut Point, Ross Island. The *Discovery* was employed as a base from which to explore the adjacent barrier and mainland: exploration was to take the form of a series of probes, made by sledging parties, to the south and to the west. In the Antarctic spring of 1902 Scott, accompanied by Wilson and Shackleton, achieved the then record southerly latitude of 82°17′ S, but the failure of the sledge dogs, incipient signs of scurvy, and the physical collapse of Shackleton compelled Scott to turn back. They reached winter quarters with great difficulty. In January 1903 the *Discovery*, held fast by ice, was located by the relief ship *Morning* (Captain W. Colbeck), which enabled Scott to repatriate Shackleton and to continue the scientific work for a second season. Notable among the many sledge journeys made was an expedition to the western mountains, when Scott, accompanied by Petty Officer Edgar Evans and Leading Stoker William Lashly, ascended the Ferrar glacier to the polar plateau at an altitude of 9000 ft and explored the ice sheet in a westerly direction for some 200 miles, a record achievement for that time. In February 1904 the *Discovery* was finally freed from the ice and, accompanied by the relief ships *Morning* and *Terra Nova*, returned home in triumph. With twenty-eight sledge journeys accomplished, the ice sheet explored, and a comprehensive scientific programme completed, Scott, notwithstanding the failure of his dogs (a form of polar traction to which he was to remain sentimentally and steadfastly averse) and his lack of previous experience, had more than proved his abilities as a leader of the first scientific expedition to pass two consecutive winters in a high latitude of Antarctica. In addition, the first extensive land journeys into the interior of the continent had been accomplished.

A criticism levelled against Sir Clements Markham, Scott's mentor, that he erred in selecting a naval officer and non-scientist as leader of the *Discovery* expedition, whose prime objectives were scientific, seems in retrospect to be unjustified. In the course of his career Scott had demonstrated a keen interest and expertise in all matters technical. The historian Hugh Robert Mill wrote of him as 'a man not only born to command but sympathetic with every branch of scientific work' (Mill, *Siege of the South Pole*, 409). Scott's powers of leadership may be debated but those who served under him in a scientific capacity all spoke highly of his unfailing interest and encouragement in their work.

Naval career and marriage On his return to England Scott was fêted as a national hero; he lectured, he socialized, and he laboured at his book. The navy promoted him captain, which brought a welcome rise in pay. His numerous honours included appointment as a CVO, the award of the polar medal, and the patron's gold medal of the Royal Geographical Society, all in 1904. In 1905 he was awarded honorary degrees of DSc from the universities of Cambridge and Manchester. Other honours numbered the gold medal of the Scottish Geographical Society, membership of the French Légion d'honneur, and awards from Russia, Denmark, Sweden, and the USA.

In August 1906 Scott returned to active service, commanding in turn the *Victorious* (1906), the *Albemarle* (1907), the *Essex* (1908), and the *Bulwark* (1909). Finally in 1909 he secured a home posting, as naval assistant to the second sea lord. His professional career seemed assured, yet plans to return south to continue the work of the *Discovery* expedition, long dormant, were to be reactivated by rumours of rival expeditions, and more immediately by Shackleton's return to Ross Island in 1907 and his near attainment of the south pole in 1908. By then Scott had married, on 2 September 1908, the artist Kathleen Bruce (1878–1947) [*see* Scott, (Edith Agnes) Kathleen], the eleventh child of Revd Lloyd Steward Bruce, canon of York, and his wife, Janie, *née* Skene. Kathleen, like Scott, was a complex character. Their early courtship was tortured by mutual self-doubt, he thinking himself unworthy of her, she fearing that her own unconventional lifestyle would ill suit the structured routine of a naval officer. The birth on 14 September 1909 of a much desired son, Peter Markham *Scott, was to change everything, prompting Kathleen to observe that the happy event was the cause of her falling for the first time 'gloriously, passionately, wildly in love with my husband' (L. Young, 108). The diary which she later kept for Scott during his absence in the Antarctic provides convincing evidence for the strength of her feelings for him. She was an ardent supporter of his plans to return to Antarctica; the day before his son's birth he publicly announced his intention to plant the union flag at the south pole.

Scott's last expedition, 1910–1912 In contrast to the *Discovery* expedition, Scott's British Antarctic expedition was a private venture for which he alone was responsible. His reputation as an explorer attracted some 8000 volunteers, from whom he chose several former *Discovery* men, including Wilson, whom he appointed chief of a civilian staff of nine. While achieving the south pole, following Shackleton's uncompleted route, was a prerequisite of fund-raising, for Scott (who loathed begging for money) an ambitious programme of science was to be 'the rock foundation of all effort' (Scott, *Last Expedition*, 1.167). Desperately short of funds, the expedition left England on board the *Terra Nova* and reached Ross Island on 22 January 1911; winter quarters were established at Cape Evans. With the scientific programme under way and the *Terra Nova* sent east to land a party on King Edward VII Land, Scott set about the laying of One Ton Depot, a cache of fuel and food to be located on the barrier at lat. 80° S in preparation for the attempt on the pole. However, deteriorating weather and the failure of the pony transport compelled Scott to deposit supplies at lat. 79°29′ S. On the return route he received a message from Victor Campbell, then leading a geological party to Cape Adare, reporting the presence of Amundsen in the Bay of Whales preparing a raid on the south pole using dogs. Already aware of the Norwegian's intentions via a telegram received in Melbourne—'Beg leave inform you proceeding Antarctic, Amundsen' (Huxley, *Scott*, 600) and possibly interpreting the message as an intention to land on the opposite, Weddel Sea coast, Scott's immediate reaction was 'to go forward and do our best for the country without fear or panic' (Scott, *Scott's Last Expedition*, 1.186). Nevertheless, this news, following the loss of a number of his ponies, was a severe blow to morale.

The winter of 1911 was spent at Cape Evans, preparing equipment and laying plans for the forthcoming pole journey. A 'University of Antarctica' with specialist lectures was instituted, and Scott encouraged and contributed to the *South Polar Times*, an expedition magazine initiated on the *Discovery* expedition.

On 1 October 1911 Scott set out from Cape Evans at the head of the main pole party, preceded by two experimental motor sledges, both of which broke down in a matter of days. The first stage of the journey across the barrier was accomplished by a combination of dog and pony transport and man-hauling, depots being laid *en route* for the returning parties. All went well until the end of November, when snowstorms followed by blizzards at the approaches to the Beardmore glacier held up progress for several days, inducing in Scott one of his periodic bouts of depression. But, once on the Beardmore glacier with the last of the ponies shot for food and the dogs returned to base, Scott's favoured method of transport—man-hauling—could be indulged. Aged forty-three, and the oldest member of the party, Scott contrived ever to be in the lead. With the aid of skis the treacherous ascent to the polar plateau was accomplished without accident. On 22 December the first returning party was dispatched and the final stage of the pole journey commenced. By 30 December, cheered by the fact of having 'caught up Shackleton's dates' (Scott, *Last Expedition*, 1.525), Scott was mercifully unaware that only 100 miles away Amundsen's party was on the homeward trail. On 3 January Scott made the fateful decision that five rather than four men should go forward to the pole, namely Scott himself, Captain L. E. G. *Oates, Lieutenant H. R. Bowers, Wilson, and Petty Officer Edgar Evans. On 4 January the last supporting party was dismissed, and five days later Shackleton's farthest point south was passed, at lat. 88°25′ S. On 16 January Bowers observed one of Amundsen's black marker flags, silent witness to the victory of the Norwegians. Finally, on 17 or 18 January, the vicinity of the pole itself was observed. 'This is an awful place', wrote Scott in his journal, 'and terrible enough for us to have laboured to it without the reward of priority' (ibid., 1.544). Following the discovery of Amundsen's tent, with its note for Scott stating that he had achieved his objective on 14 December 1911, the dejected Britons began their return journey—'800 miles of solid dragging—and good-bye to most of the day-dreams' (ibid., 1.546).

Robbed of their victory, short of rations, and suffering progressively from the effects of exposure, for Scott and his companions the return proved indeed a *via dolorosa*. The Beardmore glacier was reached on 7 February and time found to collect 35 lb weight of fossil rocks, vital clues to the geological history of Antarctica. Then at the foot of the glacier Evans collapsed and died. Once back on the barrier, Scott, Wilson, Oates, and Bowers struggled on, physically deteriorating in the face of low temperatures, adverse winds, and shortages of food and fuel. On 16 March Captain Oates sacrificed his life for his companions. On 19 March the three survivors pitched their tent for the last time. With Scott incapacitated by a gangrenous foot Bowers and Wilson planned a forced march to One Ton Depot, only 11 miles distant, but never left their tent. With no fuel and only two days' food in hand the end was inevitable. On or about 29 March Scott, probably the last to die, ended his journal with these words:

> We shall stick it out to the end, but we are getting weaker, of course, and the end cannot be far. It seems a pity, but I do not think I can write more … For God's sake look after our people … (Scott, *Last Expedition*, 1.595)

It is a measure of Scott's vitality and strength of will that even *in extremis* he could maintain his journal, write twelve perfectly composed letters to family, friends, and next of kin, and leave a 'Message to the public' outlining the causes of the disaster. Here he blames inability to achieve the safety of One Ton Depot on the appalling weather without reference to his inability to locate it at lat. 80°S as previously planned. Nor is there mention of his last minute addition of a fifth man to the pole party. Both these factors must have contributed to the absence of any margin of safety in matters of food and fuel. It is of course easy to be judgemental; what captured and still captures the imagination of the public are the oft quoted words of the 'Last Message':

> Had we lived, I should have had a tale to tell of the hardihood, endurance and courage of my companions which would have stirred the heart of every Englishman. These rough notes and our dead bodies must tell the tale … (ibid., 1.607)

Aftermath and reputation Apsley Cherry-*Garrard, sent to relieve Scott, was held up by a blizzard at One Ton Depot and forced back to Cape Evans. Eight months later, on 12 November 1912, a search party led by Dr E. L. Atkinson, by some miracle, discovered the tent entombing the frozen corpses along with Scott's journals and papers and the precious rocks. The bodies were buried where they lay under a snow cairn at lat. 79°50′ S; a commemorative cross was later erected on Observation Hill, Ross Island.

News of the tragedy reached London in February 1913, and a memorial service was held in St Paul's Cathedral. Scott's widow was granted the rank, style, and precedence of the wife of a knight commander in the Order of the Bath. A memorial fund launched by the lord mayor of London raised £75,000, using which the Scott Polar Research Institute in Cambridge was founded and the scientific results of Scott's journey published.

Not perhaps a born leader, Scott nevertheless came to earn the friendship and loyalty of those closest to him. Loyalty characterizes the narrative accounts published in the aftermath of the *Terra Nova* expedition, such as E. R. G. R. Evans's *South with Scott* (1921), H. G. Ponting's *The*

Great White South (1921), and Griffith Taylor's *With Scott: the Silver Lining* (1916). A. Cherry-Garrard's classic narrative *The Worst Journey in the World* (1922), while staunchly upholding Scott's qualities as a leader, was openly critical of his organization. The first professional biography, Stephen Gwynn's *Captain Scott* (1929), is incomplete and essentially an act of hero-worship, perhaps intended to counterbalance J. Gordon Hayes's *Antarctica* (1928), which, while giving due praise to Scott's science, laid the blame for the pole disaster at the door of Scott's misplaced loyalty to outmoded naval tradition. A decade later George Seaver took up in detail the theme of Scott's personality in his *Scott of the Antarctic* (1940), using family papers and Scott's journals to demonstrate how the explorer came to recognize the flaws in his own nature and sought to remedy them in the testing environment of Antarctica.

With the death of Lady Scott (then Lady Kennet) in 1947 Scott's biographers had free rein. Reginald Pound's *Scott of the Antarctic* (1966), a full-length biography based on family and official papers, was distinguished by its completeness, accuracy, and balance. Two years later Scott's private journals were published in facsimile manuscript as *The Diaries of Captain Scott* (1968), exposing for all to read the full nature of his inner struggles. Elspeth Huxley's *Scott of the Antarctic* (1977) explored in more detail Scott's relationship with his wife, and portrayed him as a hero, albeit a reluctant one. Less charitable was Roland Huntford's controversial double biography *Scott and Amundsen* (1979), which sought to topple the Briton from his heroic plinth, charging him with incompetence and the perversion of his literary talent for the purpose of exculpating himself from blame for the disaster. This interpretation was hotly contested by Wayland Young in his article 'On the debunking of Captain Scott' (*Encounter*, May 1980, 8–19). A decade later Beryl Bainbridge's incisive novel *The Birthday Boys* (1991) suggested that, to the bitter end, Scott could command not merely the loyalty but also the love of his companions, and successfully restored the heroes to the status of human beings. In 2001 Susan Solomon used detailed, modern meteorological data to suggest that the polar party did indeed suffer abnormally severe weather on the return journey, as Scott himself had claimed, though this did not wholly account for their difficulties. She further suggested that Wilson and Bowers chose to remain and die with the badly frostbitten Scott rather than take advantage of the abating blizzard to reach One Ton Depot.

Cinema, stage, and the television screen have all reflected the ebb and flow of criticism. The Ealing Studios' film *Scott of the Antarctic* (1948), with magnificent music by Ralph Vaughan Williams, and with John Mills portraying Scott, was conventionally patriotic and stiff upper-lipped, in stark contrast to Trevor Griffith's screenplay for Central Television, *The Last Place on Earth* (1985), which, iconoclastic to a degree, was intent on demolishing heroic myth in the larger context of British imperial decay and national decadence. More convincing was the American playwright Ted Tally's *Terra Nova*, first staged in Britain in 1980, which portrayed Scott undergoing mental catharsis by means of imagined dialogues with his wife, Kathleen, and his *alter ego* Amundsen.

Of the many memorials erected to commemorate Scott, the statue by Kathleen Scott in Waterloo Place, London, is the best-known. Behind the heroic image which it portrays lay a complex and contradictory individual. Of medium height, not physically strong yet possessed of impressive stamina, Scott was by nature insecure and self-doubting, the victim of depressive moods and bouts of indolence. Yet he was ever alert to these disabilities and strove to triumph over them, supported by a deep-rooted sense of justice and a trust in the dispensations of providence.

Scott represented in his personality and in his prose an extreme form of the late-Victorian concept of the English gentleman: 'manly', straightforward, stubborn, unimaginative, and gentle. He sensed his iconic role, and his death in 1912 was soon felt strangely to have foreshadowed the fate of many of his class in the First World War. H. G. R. KING

Sources R. F. Scott, *The voyage of the 'Discovery'*, 2 vols. (1905) • R. F. Scott, *Scott's last expedition*, ed. L. Huxley, 2 vols. (1913) • R. F. Scott, *The diaries of Captain Robert Scott: a record of the second Antarctic expedition, 1910–1912*, 6 vols. (1968) • A. Cherry-Garrard, *The worst journey in the world*, 2 vols. (1922) • G. Seaver, *Scott of the Antarctic: a study in character* (1940) • R. Pound, *Scott of the Antarctic* (1966) • E. Huxley, *Scott of the Antarctic* (1977) • R. Huntford, *Scott and Amundsen* (1979) • W. Young, 'On the debunking of Captain Scott', *Encounter*, 54/5 (1980), 8–19 • D. James, *Scott of the Antarctic: the film and its production* (1948) • T. Tally, *Terra nova: a play* (1981) • B. Bainbridge, *The birthday boys* (1991) • G. Taylor, *With Scott: the silver lining* (1916) • E. R. G. R. Evans, *South with Scott* (1921) • H. G. Ponting, *The great white south* (1921) • J. G. Hayes, *Antarctica* (1928) • S. Gwynn, *Captain Scott* (1929) • T. Griffiths, *Judgement over the dead: the screenplay of 'The last place on earth'* (1986) • D. Preston, *A first rate tragedy: Captain Scott's Antarctic expeditions* (1997) • L. Young, *A great task of happiness: the life of Kathleen Scott* (1995) • H. R. Mill, *The siege of the south pole* (1905) • S. Solomon, *The coldest March: Scott's fatal Antarctic expedition* (2001)

Archives BL, diaries, Add. MSS 51024–51044 • British Columbia Archives and Records Service, corresp. • CUL, corresp. • NMM, corresp. and papers relating to his Antarctic expedition • PRO • RGS, diary • RS • Scott Polar RI, corresp., diaries, and papers • State Library of New South Wales, Sydney | Canterbury Museum, letters to Louis Charles Bernacchi • RGS, letters to Royal Geographical Society | FILM BFI NFTVA, 'Cardiff: the ship *Terra Nova* leaving harbour towards the south pole', Pathé Frères, 1 July 1910 • BFI NFTVA, 'British Antarctic expedition, 1910–1913', 1924 • BFI NFTVA, 'The great white silence', 1924 • BFI NFTVA, actuality footage • BFI NFTVA, documentary footage • BFI NFTVA, news footage

Likenesses E. A. Wilson, pencil drawing, 1901, Scott Polar RI • E. A. Wilson, silhouette, 1902?, Scott Polar RI • D. A. Wehrschmidt, oils, 1905, NPG • C. P. Small, oils, 1910, NPG • H. G. Ponting, photograph, 1911, NPG [*see illus.*] • L. Calkin, oils, 1913; last known at United Service Club, London [c/o Crown Commissioners] • J. C. Lawrence, oils, 1913, Scott Polar RI • Hester, mechanical reproduction, NPG; repro. in *VF* (19 Feb 1913) • H. Mann, oils (posthumous), RGS • H. G. Ponting and others, photographs, Scott Polar RI • K. Scott, bronze bust (posthumous), Scott Polar RI • K. Scott, bronze statue (posthumous), Waterloo Place, London • A. G. Walter, bronzed plaster group of statues, Scott Polar RI • E. A. Wilson, pencil drawing, Scott Polar RI • Carrara marble statue (after bronze statue by K. Scott), Christchurch, New Zealand • photographs, NPG

Wealth at death £5067 11*s.* 7*d.*: resworn probate, 13 May 1913, *CGPLA Eng. & Wales*

Scott, Sir Robert Heatlie (1905–1982), diplomatist and civil servant, was born in York Street, Peterhead, Aberdeenshire, on 20 September 1905, the second of four children and eldest of three sons of Thomas Henderson Scott, civil engineer, and his wife, Mary Agnes, *née* Dixon, teacher, both originally from Selkirk. The family moved to Trinidad when Scott's father was appointed city engineer of Port of Spain in 1915. There Scott completed, at Queen's Royal College, his schooling begun at Inverness Academy. He scored a precocious success by winning at the age of fifteen an 'island' scholarship to New College, Oxford. The college refused to accept him at that age and he taught at his school for two years before coming to England. At Oxford he realized he was not a mathematician (he obtained a third class in moderations in 1924) and switched to law (in which he gained a second class in 1926). While at Oxford he was secretary of the Oxford Union. He was called to the bar by Gray's Inn in 1927. He simultaneously sat the civil service examinations and gained third place in all departments. He chose the Far Eastern consular service as his first appointment, and was appointed a student interpreter in November 1927, vice-consul in January 1930, and acting consul in July 1935.

In China Scott met and on 11 October 1933 married another Scot, Rosamond Aeliz (*b.* 1911/12), daughter of Robert Nugent Dewar-Durie, banker, of the Imperial Bank of Persia. They had a son, Douglas (who died in 1955 on national service with the Royal Marines), and a daughter, Susan. Prior to 1939 Scott served in Peking, Manchuria, Chungking, Shanghai, Canton, Hong Kong, and Japan. His languages included Chinese, Japanese, German, Dutch, French, Latin, and some Russian. During his time in China his energy and inquisitiveness attracted the hostile attention of the Japanese authorities. At the outbreak of the Second World War he was posted to Japan to conduct British propaganda and was subsequently transferred in 1941 to Singapore to open a branch of the ministry of information—always equated by the Japanese with intelligence and spying.

As the crisis deepened in Singapore, Scott was appointed to the governor's war council which consisted of himself and the three service chiefs—a singular tribute to his talents. Contemporary reports indicate that he outshone his colleagues in spirit and imagination. When the city fell he attempted to get away on the last boat to leave (his wife had already gone on ahead to Australia). The boat was soon intercepted by a Japanese destroyer. He volunteered to row across to the warship with some others in an attempt to persuade the enemy captain to allow the refugee ship to proceed. The sea was rough and the Japanese captain impatiently opened fire on the refugee ship before the lifeboat could reach the destroyer. There were few survivors. Scott succeeded in reaching Sumatra where he was briefly in hiding until he was returned as a prisoner to Singapore.

After a period in solitary confinement Scott was put in Changi gaol with other civilian prisoners. He was already considered a marked man by the Japanese. However, he soon became a leading figure in the camp. The prisoners were slackly administered at first and were able to maintain contact with people outside and from time to time visited the city in the course of administering themselves. But towards the summer of 1943 the Japanese became uneasy; they were planning a surprise raid to impose stricter discipline in the camp when a remarkable event occurred. A commando force, daringly led by Captain Ivan Lyon, reached Singapore from Australia undetected and blew up Japanese tankers in the harbour. The Japanese authorities in Singapore mistakenly thought that the raiders had accomplices within the camp. Scott was assumed to be the ringleader. For weeks he was terribly beaten and tortured but no confession was ever obtained. He was put on trial and eventually sentenced to six years' imprisonment in Outram Road prison. Throughout his ordeal he conducted himself calmly and with self-assurance. Drawing on his previous experience of the Japanese, he successfully sought to establish a moral and intellectual ascendancy over his persecutors, who found his arguments and predictions most disturbing. During part of this period he was held in solitary confinement at the top of the prison tower where from time to time he could be observed by his fellow prisoners in the yard below. He became known throughout the camp and in the city as 'the man in the tower' and became a symbol for the British and Chinese of defiance and resistance. His wife in Australia was unaware of his fate and drew a widow's pension.

Following the Japanese surrender a controversial decision was taken to stage war crimes trials in Singapore. Scott was a principal but somewhat reluctant witness. His testimony was given without rancour and with such fairness that all were astonished—not least the accused. He never subsequently showed animosity towards the Japanese. Some years later, with the help of the British ambassador in Tokyo, he arranged to meet some of his former gaolers who had escaped execution. After a slow start the gathering proved a great success.

After Scott's release he returned to Britain; there, following convalescence, he resumed his duties with the Foreign Office. He was appointed CBE in 1946 and CMG in 1950, and from September 1950 to July 1953 was assistant under-secretary of state of the Foreign Office, with responsibility for Far Eastern affairs. This period included the Korean War and its problems. He then served as minister at the British embassy in Washington until October 1955, when he was sent to Singapore as commissioner general for the United Kingdom in south-east Asia, a regional post with civil and military responsibilities. His appointment was greeted with warm approval by the people of the area and by the British colonial officials and service chiefs with whom he worked in great harmony. He was an invaluable source of good advice locally and helped Whitehall to understand the changing attitudes of old and new countries. He travelled widely and constantly in the area, seeing old friends and making new ones among the post-war leaders. He was promoted GCMG in 1959, having been appointed KCMG in 1954.

Scott's war record and his unusual experience of both

civilian and service affairs encouraged the government to appoint him in January 1960 as the first civilian commandant of the Imperial Defence College. He was outstandingly successful and moved on to the Ministry of Defence in August 1961 as permanent secretary. This move proved to be something of a disappointment. The management of a huge civil service department did not suit his individualistic talents. It was also a period of bitter inter-service rivalry as the service chiefs tried to adjust themselves to necessary structural changes. Nevertheless those who served with him in Whitehall (like those who served with him overseas) were impressed by his modesty, originality, peace of mind, ease of manner, and preoccupation with essentials. All his business was conducted with a sense of fun, heightened by his habit of drafting directly and inexpertly on to a portable typewriter.

Scott retired in December 1963 and went to live near Peebles on the banks of the Tweed where he bought a disused railway station and built a new house across one of the platforms, called Lyne Station House. He received an honorary LLD from Dundee in 1972. His great energy and zest for life ensured that in his retirement in his beloved Scotland he remained active. Absorption with family and with British and foreign friends, counselling young offenders, salmon fishing, his duties as lord lieutenant of Tweeddale—all these and many other interests kept him constantly and happily occupied. He died at his home on 26 February 1982, of cancer. He was survived by his wife, and daughter. GREENHILL OF HARROW, *rev.* ALEX MAY

Sources *The Times* (6 June 1961) • *The Times* (2 March 1982) • Burke, *Peerage* • *WWW* • *FO List* (–1961) • personal knowledge (1990) • private information (1990) • b. cert. • m. cert. (consular record) • d. cert.

Archives BLPES, interview • NL Scot., corresp. and papers; further papers | FILM Bodl. Oxf.

Wealth at death £81,548.17: confirmation, 2 June 1982, *CCI*

Scott, Robert Henry (1833–1916), meteorologist, was born in Dublin on 28 January 1833, one of the six children (five sons and a daughter) of James Smyth Scott QC, a prominent Dublin lawyer, and his wife, Louisa, daughter of Charles Brodrick, archbishop of Cashel, and sister of the sixth and seventh viscounts Midleton. His elder brother Charles (*d.* 1894) was headmaster of Westminster School from 1855 to 1883. Scott was educated at Rugby School and Trinity College, Dublin, where he was classical scholar (1853), graduating senior moderator in experimental physics (1855), MA (1859), and honorary DSc (1898). He also obtained a diploma from Dublin School of Engineering. From 1856 to 1858 he studied chemistry, physics, mineralogy, and meteorology in Germany, working under Heinrich Dove in Berlin and Justus von Liebig in Munich.

Scott undertook the translation of Dove's famous book *Das Gesetz der Stürme*, which was published in Britain as *The Law of Storms* (1862). Dove dedicated the book to Admiral Robert FitzRoy, head of the meteorological department established under the Board of Trade in 1854, and FitzRoy ensured its acceptance within Britain by including it in his series of *Meteorological Papers*. FitzRoy died in 1865 and two years later the department was reconstituted as the Meteorological Office under a meteorological committee appointed by the Royal Society.

Scott had begun teaching in Dublin in 1859. He applied unsuccessfully for the chair of technology at Edinburgh, and in 1862 was appointed keeper of minerals to the Royal Dublin Society. He married Susan Louisa (1842/3–1901), daughter of the Hon. Walter George Stewart, island secretary of Jamaica, on 9 August 1865. There were no children.

Scott's meteorological output was confined to the translation of Dove's book but in 1866 he was approached by his intimate friend Edward Sabine, then at the height of his influence as president of the Royal Society and prospective chairman of the new meteorological committee, and was offered the directorship of the Meteorological Office. There were no other candidates and Scott was appointed director in January 1867. It was a clear case of personal patronage, but he was to remain executive head for thirty-three years. The office's constitution changed in 1877, control passing to a meteorological council. Scott's role and salary remained unaltered, although his designation became secretary to the council, a position he occupied until his retirement in 1900. He was succeeded by William Napier Shaw.

Scott was never a leading scientific thinker and probably owed his election as fellow of the Royal Society in 1870 to Sabine, but he was a capable administrator. His most important legacy to meteorology was as secretary of the international meteorological committee from its inception in 1873 until 1900. Meteorology is one of the most international of the sciences, and Scott played a significant part in establishing the tradition of co-operation between countries that became the norm. He retained an interest in mineralogy and served as president of the Mineralogical Society 1888–91. He joined the Meteorological Society in 1871 and was its foreign secretary from 1873 until his death, apart from 1880–81 when secretary and 1884–5 when president. Heavily bearded, Scott was a witty and apparently sociable man but became increasingly pedantic and intolerant of views divergent from his own. Doubtless this contributed to the personality problems within the British meteorological establishment during the later nineteenth century.

Scott published two books, *Weather Charts and Storm Warnings* (1876) and *Elementary Meteorology* (1883), the latter becoming a standard text and running into nine editions. He also contributed over eighty papers and articles to a diversity of publications. Scott died on 18 June 1916 at 6 Elm Park Gardens, Chelsea, London, and was buried at Peper Harow, Godalming, then the Surrey seat of the Brodrick family. JIM BURTON, *rev.*

Sources *The Meteorological Magazine*, 51 (1916), 81–3 • *Quarterly Journal of the Royal Meteorological Society*, 42 (1916), 301–4 • *Nature*, 97 (1916), 365–6 • CUL, Stokes collection • Berks. RO, Benyon MSS • Mineralogical Society, London, archives • m. cert. • d. cert. • RS

Archives Berks. RO, corresp. • Meteorological Office, Bracknell, corresp. as director • PRO, corresp. and papers, BJ1 | CUL, corresp. with Sir George Stokes

Likenesses photograph, repro. in *Meteorological Magazine*

Wealth at death £13,651 0s. 4d.: probate, 9 Sept 1916, *CGPLA Eng. & Wales*

Scott, Ronald [Ronnie] (**1927–1996**), jazz saxophonist and nightclub owner, was born at the Mothers' Home, 396 Commercial Road, Stepney, London, on 28 January 1927, the son of Joseph Schatt (also known as Jock Scott), a saxophonist and orchestra leader, and his wife, Sylvia (Cissie) Rosenbloom, a saleswoman who lived at 33 South Tenter Street, Aldgate. His father, 'an urbane, humorous, charismatic and hard-gambling man', abandoned the family when Scott was four years of age, leaving Ronnie to be brought up by his mother and grandmother (*The Guardian*). After unsuccessful attempts to play both the cornet and the soprano saxophone, Scott was given a tenor saxophone by Solomon Berger, his stepfather, and almost immediately showed an affinity for the instrument. He took lessons from the musician Jack Lewis, father-in-law of the singer Vera Lynn, and later from the bandleader Harry Gold.

At the age of sixteen Scott was sufficiently competent to play with ephemeral bands appearing at clubs in the Soho area of London, then in 1944 he joined the band of the Belgian trumpeter Johnnie Claes, with which he remained for a year. During this time the band appeared in the George Formby film *George in Civvy Street*, with Scott clearly visible on screen. At the end of 1945 he worked briefly in a band led by Dennis Rose, a musician whose fresh ideas were to have a great influence on Scott and a rising generation of young British jazz players. In February 1946 Scott joined the new and prestigious Ted Heath orchestra; he remained for a year, appearing on a number of Heath's recordings made for the Decca label.

After being dismissed by Heath, Scott and the drummer Tony Crombie made their first trip to the United States in order to hear the new jazz form, called bebop, played by its creators in New York clubs. A few months later Scott was back in the USA, this time as a member of the drummer Bobby Kevin's band aboard the newly refurbished liner *Queen Mary*. By now he had become a member of a group of like-minded British jazz musicians, including John Dankworth, Dennis Rose, and Tony Crombie, and after a short stay with the sextet of the piano-accordionist Tito Burns, Scott became a founder member of the Club Eleven, a co-operative jazz group which opened its own club in a rehearsal room on Great Windmill Street, London.

Club Eleven lasted from January 1949 until April 1950 and gave Scott his first experience of running a jazz club. He worked in the bands of Jack Nathan and Vic Lewis until the spring of 1951, when the drummer Jack Parnell formed his first orchestra and asked Scott and other leading jazz musicians to join. In January 1953 Scott and a number of others left Parnell and formed a successful nine-piece band under Scott's leadership. This band brought together some of the finest jazz players in Britain, made several recordings for the Esquire record label, and firmly established Scott as perhaps the most important figure in his field. But Scott's decision to enlarge the band led eventually to its breakup through lack of bookings. He then co-led another band with Tony Crombie before taking his own sextet on a tour of the USA.

Ronald [Ronnie] **Scott** (**1927–1996**), by Philip Sayer, pubd 1991

On his return to Britain at the beginning of 1957 Scott formed a quintet with the young tenor saxophonist Tubby Hayes and named it the Jazz Couriers. This was arguably one of the most important of all British jazz units, and the public responded by giving it considerable support. When it disbanded in August 1959 it was not for lack of musical success or popularity: Scott had decided to give up touring and open his own jazz club. 'Ronnie Scott's' opened its doors at 39 Gerrard Street, London, on 30 October 1959 and almost immediately became the focal point for jazz in the capital. The management of the club was handled by Scott's partner Pete King, a musician who had worked with him on many occasions, while Scott himself was responsible for its public image as well as frequently playing there with his own small group.

The club gave Scott the opportunity to display his natural talents as wit and raconteur as well as his unrivalled abilities as a first-class jazz improviser. For the first two years of the club's life the long-standing disagreement between the British and US musicians' unions was still in force, making it impossible for American musicians to work in Britain. Thanks to considerable negotiations by the manager Pete King, the American tenor saxophonist Zoot Sims was allowed to play at the club for four weeks in November 1961. Basing subsequent bookings on reciprocal exchange, the club played host to many famous soloists and bands over the succeeding years and, thanks in large part to Scott's and King's work, the union ban was eventually resolved. Among those who played at the club were Dizzy Gillespie, Dexter Gordon, Coleman Hawkins, and Stan Getz.

In December 1965 Ronnie Scott's moved to larger premises in Frith Street, London, and in October 1991 another branch was opened in Birmingham, but Scott, an inveterate Londoner, spent most of his time at Frith Street, where he had established a jazz club with an international reputation. Its clientele often included politicians, royalty, and prominent show-business personalities, all of whom found the relaxed atmosphere, plus Scott's policy of never capitalizing on their presence, to their liking. Scott was appointed OBE for his services to music in 1981. According to John Fordham, Scott could be 'dismissive, intimidating and self-preoccupied', and he could be generous, playful, and disarmingly modest. Indeed he 'had to be reminded of the remarkable role the [club] had played in the development of British jazz' (*The Guardian*). In 1979 he published *Some of my Best Friends are Blues*, written with Mike Hennessey.

In the final year of his life Scott suffered health problems including recurring dental difficulties, the bane of many musicians, saxophonists in particular. This resulted in his failing to appear at his club as a playing musician for most of 1995. A gum operation had resulted in the removal of all his teeth and in the fitting of a plate, which he hoped would enable him to perform again in public. He had planned to announce his return to work by playing at the club on Christmas eve 1996, but was found dead from barbiturate poisoning at his home, 21 Elm Park Mansions, Park Walk, London, on 23 December. An interdenominational service of remembrance for Scott was held at St Martin-in-the-Fields, London, on 7 April 1997 and attended by hundreds of friends and musicians. Scott never married but had a number of lengthy relationships, two of which produced a son, Nicholas, and a daughter, Rebecca. ALUN MORGAN

Sources J. Chilton, *Who's who of British jazz* (1997) · R. Scott and M. Hennessey, *Some of my best friends are blues* (1979) · *The Guardian* (27 Dec 1996) · *The Independent* (27 Dec 1996) · b. cert. · d. cert.
Likenesses P. Sayer, photograph, pubd 1991, priv. coll. [*see illus.*]

Scott, Sir Ronald Bodley (1906–1982), physician, was born in Bournemouth on 10 September 1906, the eldest of six sons (there were no daughters) of Maitland Bodley Scott, general practitioner in Bournemouth, and his wife, Alice Hilda Durancé George. He was educated at Marlborough College and Brasenose College, Oxford, where he obtained a degree in natural science in 1928. Bodley Scott completed his clinical training at St Bartholomew's Hospital, London, graduating BM, BCh in 1931. The same year he married (Edith) Daphne (*d.* 1977), daughter of Lieutenant-Colonel Edward McCarthy, of the Royal Marine Artillery.

Once qualified, Bodley Scott served a short period as house physician at St Bartholomew's and then left to join the family practice in Bournemouth. However, he had evidently made such an impression as a student and house physician that he was invited to return, first as chief assistant to A. E. Gow, and then as first assistant on the medical unit. This was a recognized route for those who were going on to consulting practice. During this time he obtained his MRCP (1933), and developed an interest in clinical haematology. He obtained his DM at Oxford in 1937, on the newly developed technique of bone marrow aspiration. His studies on the subject led to his describing with A. H. T. Robb-Smith the clinical entity of histiocytic medullary reticulosis in *The Lancet* in 1939.

In 1936 Bodley Scott became a consultant at the Woolwich Memorial Hospital, a post he filled until 1971. During the Second World War he entered the Royal Army Medical Corps, and in 1941 was sent to the Middle East, where he was responsible for the medical division in no. 63 and no. 43 general hospitals. He was elected FRCP in 1943. At the end of the war he returned to London. He was one of the first new assistant physicians to be appointed at St Bartholomew's (1946) and he rapidly became an internationally recognized figure in the management of leukaemia and lymphoma. He introduced drug treatment for these invariably fatal illnesses, and was one of the first in Britain to use nitrogen mustard and other chemotherapeutic agents. He remained a shrewd general physician, with a penetrating intelligence and great clinical skill.

In 1949 Bodley Scott was appointed physician to the household of King George VI and from 1952 to 1973 he was physician to Queen Elizabeth II. He was appointed KCVO in 1964 and GCVO in 1973. He was made consultant physician to British Railways (Eastern Region) in 1957; honorary consultant in haematology to the army from 1957; consultant physician to the Florence Nightingale Hospital in 1958; consultant physician to the King Edward VII Hospital for Officers in 1963; and in the same year honorary consultant to the Royal Navy. Two years later he became honorary consultant to the Ministry of Defence.

At the Royal College of Physicians, Bodley Scott was successively councillor (1963–6), censor (1970), and vice-president (1972). He was president of the Medical Society of London (1965–6), president of the British Society of Haematology (1966–7), president of the section of medicine of the Royal Society of Medicine (1967–8). He was made a member of the court of assistants of the Society of Apothecaries of London in 1964, and became master in 1974. He served as a member of council of the Imperial Cancer Research Fund from 1968, and the British Heart Foundation from 1975, eventually becoming chairman of the latter.

As a teacher Bodley Scott excelled in a postgraduate setting. His achievements in his speciality were acknowledged by invitations to give the Lettsomian lecture of the Medical Society of London in 1957, the Langdon-Brown lecture in 1957, the Croonian lecture in 1970, and the most prestigious lecture offered by the Royal College of Physicians, the Harveian oration, in 1976. To appreciate Bodley Scott's breadth of vision it is necessary to turn to his Lettsomian lecture on leukaemia. It must be remembered that at that time no adult patient survived acute leukaemia; but Bodley Scott insisted that 'although the outlook was bleak, the use of active drugs must be attempted in order to achieve a remission of the disease, for a nihilistic approach would create an impenetrable barrier against therapeutic advance'. As well as lecturing, Bodley Scott also achieved academic success with his edition of *Price's Textbook of Medicine* (12th edn, 1978), and with the *Medical Annual*, which he edited from 1979; both of these owed much to his encyclopaedic knowledge of medicine and his clear, concise style. He published his last book, *Cancer—the Facts*, in 1979.

Bodley Scott combined a remarkable ability in clinical medicine with a deep awareness of the need for innovation and experiment. He was a wise observer of humanity and behind his reserved, almost shy manner he appreciated people's foibles and commented on them with an astringent wit. Despite his reserve, however, he could speak forcibly and with effect.

Following the death in 1977 of his first wife, in 1980 Bodley Scott married Jessie, the widow of Alexander Page Gaston, of Sevenoaks, and daughter of Thomas Mutch, farmer in Aberdeenshire. She survived the car accident near Parma, Italy, on 12 May 1982, in which Bodley Scott died. J. S. MALPAS, *rev.*

Sources *The Lancet* (22 May 1982), 1195 • *BMJ* (22 May 1982), 1567 • *The Times* (13 May 1982) • V. C. Medvei and J. L. Thornton, eds., *The royal hospital of Saint Bartholomew, 1123–1973* (1974) • Munk, *Roll* • personal knowledge (1990)
Archives Wellcome L., diaries and papers
Likenesses photograph, repro. in Munk, *Roll*, vol. 7
Wealth at death £150,295: administration, 9 Nov 1982, *CGPLA Eng. & Wales*

Scott, Samuel (**1701/2–1772**), marine painter, was the son of Robert Scott (*d.* 1737), a barber-surgeon. From 1726 he produced seascapes and pictures of naval engagements. He married Ann Bolton (*d.* 1781) at St Mary's Church, Newington Butts, London, in 1723 and they had one daughter, Ann Sophia, who was baptized at St Paul's, Covent Garden, a year later. In London the Scotts lived at 4 Tavistock Row, moving in 1747 to 2 Henrietta Street, Covent Garden. Scott held an appointment as accountant clerk at £100 per annum in the stamp duty office, Lincoln's Inn.

After 1732 Scott started to paint in recognizable areas around Wapping and Limehouse in east London. By 1740 he had moved upstream to central London. With the exception of Covent Garden, where he collaborated with Sawrey Gilpin, his London scenes invariably show the Thames, the buildings serving only as backdrops to waterborne activity. His subjects were limited to Old London Bridge, the Tower of London, the Thames with Montagu House, the York Buildings Water Tower, the building of Westminster Bridge, Westminster from Lambeth, Westminster with neighbouring houses, and the arch of Westminster Bridge, each of which he painted several times. Scott moved to Twickenham in 1755, where he painted versions of Pope's villa and the Thames from Eel Pie Island. *The Five Days Peregrination*, a journal of a trip to Kent made with Hogarth, Thornhill, and others in 1732, which included four drawings by Scott, was published in 1782 with aquatints by R. Livesay. Elected a governor and custodian of the Foundling Hospital in 1746, Scott was also a member of the committee which proposed the foundation of the Royal Academy in 1755. He exhibited *A View of the Tower of London* at the Royal Academy in 1771, two works at the Society of Artists in 1761, another in 1764, and again in 1765. His portrait was painted by Thomas Hudson in 1731. His apprentices were Sawrey Gilpin, William Marlow, and Arthur Nelson, the first two of whom provided the references to Scott which are mentioned by Joseph Farington in his diary.

Scott's principal patrons for his sea battles were the Vernon, Anson, and Sandwich families. Contemporary letters and accounts show that he worked for the duke of Bedford, Viscount Folkestone, the earl of Montagu, the earl of Devon, Sir Edward Littleton, the St Quintin and Windham families, and the East India Company. Sir Robert Walpole was one of his earliest patrons; Edward Walpole, who acquired four of his pictures, was accustomed 'when in London to sup every Tuesday at Scott's house' (Farington, *Diary*, 2.625) and proposed elopement to Ann Scott in 'a very humorous letter', and Horace Walpole eulogized Scott in his *Journal*, *Anecdotes of Painting*, and notes on the exhibitions of the Society of Artists and the Free Society of Artists. He also encouraged his friends to buy Scott's pictures, of which he himself owned eight as well as several drawings.

From 1765 to 1769 Scott lived with his married daughter in Ludlow, Shropshire, where he painted the high street, the castle, and Ludford Bridge. Following his daughter's death he retired to Bath in 1769, and died in Walcot Street 'after a long and painful illness' on 12 October 1772; he was buried on 22 October in Walcot parish church. His collection of his own paintings was sold by Langfords in January 1773. RICHARD KINGZETT

Sources R. Kingzett, 'A catalogue of the works of Samuel Scott', *Walpole Society*, 48 (1980–82), 1–134 • G. Thompson, ed., *Samuel Scott bicentenary: paintings, drawings and engravings* (1972) [exhibition catalogue, Guildhall Art Gallery, London, 4 May – 3 June 1972] • H. Walpole, 'Horace Walpole's journals of visits to country seats', *Walpole Society*, 16 (1927–8), 9–80 • H. Gatty, 'Walpole's notes on exhibitions', *Walpole Society*, 27 (1938–9), 55–88 • H. Walpole, *Anecdotes of painting in England … collected by the late George Vertue, and now digested and published*, 2nd edn, 4 vols. (1765–71) • H. Walpole, *A description of Strawberry Hill* (1774) • Vertue, *Note books*, vol. 3 • Farington, *Diary*, 2.625; 3.765–6 • R. Livesay and T. Rowlandson, *Hogarth's tour* (1782)
Likenesses T. Hudson, oils, *c.*1730, NPG • J. Deacon, watercolour, 1750, BM • J. Deacon, pencil and wash, BM • oils, NPG

Scott, Samuel (**1719–1788**). *See under* Scott, John (1730–1783).

Scott [*née* Robinson], **Sarah** (**1720–1795**), novelist and historian, was born on 21 September 1720, one of twelve children of Matthew Robinson (1694–1778) of Edgeley and West Layton Hall in the parish of Hutton Magna, Yorkshire, and Elizabeth (*c.*1693–1746), daughter of Robert Drake, recorder of Cambridge.

Family and early years Sarah was the younger daughter and one of nine children who survived to adulthood. Matthew [*see* Morris, Matthew Robinson- (1713–1800)] inherited his mother's estate of Mount Morris, Kent, became an MP and political pamphleteer, and later second

Baron Rokeby. Thomas *Robinson studied law and published a legal text before his death at thirty-three. Morris, who was the sisters' favourite, also studied law, practised as a solicitor, and wrote a political pamphlet. Robert became a merchant ship captain and died in China in 1756. Elizabeth [*see* Montagu, Elizabeth (1718–1800)], married a significantly older and richer man, helped to manage his mining interests, and as a widow was a co-founder of the highly influential circle of intellectual upper-class men and women known as the bluestockings. William became a literary clergyman and a friend of the poet Thomas Gray. John seems to have suffered from mental illness. Charles first joined his brother Robert at sea and after being called to the bar was recorder for Canterbury, a bankruptcy commissioner, and MP for Canterbury.

Their maternal grandmother, Sarah Morris Drake, was widowed and then married the renowned Cambridge scholar and classical republican, Dr Conyers *Middleton. The Robinson children spent much time at Cambridge, where their step-grandfather took an interest in the intellectual development of the girls. The family resided mostly at Mrs Robinson's estate of Mount Morris. The Robinsons were a competitive and disputatious family, and, as frequent mediator, Mrs Robinson was called 'the Speaker', as in the House of Commons. The sisters were close, and remained so through life, with the occasional disagreement. Because they were said to be as alike as two peas in a pod, Sarah was nicknamed Pea; because of Elizabeth's restlessness she was known as Fidget, and Sarah was nick-named Bridget as a complement. In early letters Elizabeth often addressed Sarah as Sally, or Madam Sally. Throughout their lives Elizabeth was generally given pre-eminence, though she regarded Sarah as superior in certain respects, particularly intellectual and literary interests, in which she encouraged her.

The sisters' adult lives took different directions, however. In her mid-teens Elizabeth was befriended by Lady Margaret Harley, daughter of the earl of Oxford, remained her companion after Lady Margaret's marriage, and thereby enjoyed access to fashionable London society. Sarah spent much time by herself on the family estate, taking strenuous walks and reading a great deal. The sisters' letters from youth throughout life discuss a wide range of books in English and French, including romances, current novels such as *Tom Jones* and *Sir Charles Grandison*, history, travels, the major poets, essays and *belles lettres*, religious writing and moral philosophy. Never physically robust, Sarah suffered much from headaches. Nevertheless, her early letters exhibit a witty, satirical, and fastidious outlook on people, fashionable society, and courtship and marriage, a strong interest in handsome and intelligent men, and contempt for men who feared educated women, for women with no intellectual interests, and for unclean persons of either sex. In 1741 Sarah contracted smallpox, then regarded as destroying a woman's beauty and thus lowering her value in the marriage market. Just over a year later Elizabeth married the fifty-year-old Edward Montagu, grandson of the earl of Sandwich, amateur mathematician, and owner of coal-mines in Yorkshire. Sarah was left to tend their mother, who was dying of cancer, while their father took the housekeeper as mistress. After her mother's death in 1746 Sarah stayed with various friends and relations and, after a visit to Bath with her sister and her husband, she stayed on as companion of the invalid **Lady Barbara Montagu** (*c*.1722–1765), daughter of the earl of Halifax. In 1748 the two women pooled their limited resources to live together, participating in a larger circle of pious and charitable Anglican women, and with few intervals remained so until the death of Lady Bab (as she was called) in 1765.

Marriage and Lady Bab By the late 1740s, however, Sarah Robinson had an understanding with George Lewis *Scott (1708–1780), a long-time family friend from Canterbury. He was 'a tall, big man, very sociable and facetious, an accomplished musician' and mathematician (Climenson, 1.206), a dozen years older than Sarah. Though qualified for the bar, he lacked a profession. Since Sarah Robinson's dowry, like her sister's, was small, being just £1500, and publication of her first book, *The History of Cornelia* (1750), a novel, would make no difference, Robinson and Scott could not marry until, partly through her manipulation of the patronage system, he was appointed sub-preceptor to the young prince of Wales in 1750. The couple were married on 15 June 1751 and set up house in Leicester Square, near Leicester House, residence of George Scott's royal pupil. It was always understood that Lady Barbara would form part of their household—a not uncommon arrangement for that time. In April 1752 Sarah Scott was removed from the home by her father and brothers, for reasons never disclosed, but serious enough to warrant such action, to give rise to passing semi-public scandal, to obviate reconciliation, and to engender in Sarah Scott a lifelong bitterness towards her husband.

Such reasons could have ranged from spousal abuse by him, through disclosure of a prior marriage or illicit relationship on his part, to emphatic personal or sexual incompatibility between the couple. The decisiveness of her family's intervention on her behalf, with the circumstances already described, make it unlikely, though not impossible, that the cause was partly her relationship with Lady Barbara—or solely that—or the realization by Sarah Scott of her own personal or sexual aversion to conjugality, which a woman at that time would have been expected to overcome or endure. Later references in family letters do suggest that the marriage was never consummated. In any case, all parties had an interest in suppressing public scandal because Scott's income, and thus his ability to continue the £100 a year maintenance promised to his estranged wife, was dependent on holding his public office. Sarah Scott and Lady Barbara returned to Bath for a life of domesticity and practical piety, decorating their small house, cultivating their garden, and, with other devout women, assisting the poor, especially abandoned or vulnerable females, through organizing small-scale manufacture and retail. It is clear that they loved each other, and there is no unequivocal evidence that there was or was not a sexual dimension to that love.

From 1754 Scott and Lady Barbara spent summers at nearby Bath Easton, returning to Bath for the winters. They organized a small school of industry, teaching literacy, numeracy, and needlework to a dozen poor girls, and providing for the education of some poor boys. Scott returned to authorship to help out with their household and philanthropic expenses. She translated a moralistic French novel, *Le laideur aimable*, by Antoine, marquis de La Place, as *Agreeable Ugliness* (1754), published, like all her work, anonymously, and followed this with an original fiction, *A Journey through every Stage of Life* (1754), comprising tales told by a witty female servant to divert her mistress, a disgruntled princess exiled by her brother to clear his way to the throne. Scott's novels ignore the libertine fiction of earlier women writers such as Aphra Behn and Delarivier Manley and owe less to Samuel Richardson's 'revolution' in fictional representations of subjectivity than to the pious and moralistic fiction by women such as Elizabeth Rowe and Jane Barker. Educational writing was attracting increasing numbers of women writers, too, and in the late 1750s Scott and Lady Barbara planned sets of cards teaching children 'useful' subjects such as history and geography.

Millenium Hall and other writing Scott had a lifelong fascination with public affairs and the accession of George III in 1760 provided new stimulus to her writing. In 1761 she compiled *The History of Gustavus Ericson, King of Sweden*, promoting the figure of the 'patriot king', or selfless ruler in the broad national interest, idealized by classical republicans. In the same year she wrote a satirical letter on the public enthusiasm for the young king's bride, the princess of Mecklenburg, but she then exploited that interest with *The History of Mecklenburg, from the First Settlement of the Vandals in that Country to the Present Time* (1762). In 1762 she also published a utopian novel, *A Description of Millenium Hall and the Country Adjacent*, her most successful work, with four editions by 1778. Again based on the familiar eighteenth-century form of inset narratives in a frame story, it tells of a number of middle-class and upper-class women who manage through chance or choice to elude the system of courtship, marriage, and property that subordinated women to the interests of a landed society and economy. Together these women form a community devoted to religion, the arts, and philanthropy, redirecting agrarian capitalism to protection of the oppressed, marginalized, and victimized in society, from women like themselves to the poor, the disfigured, and the disabled.

Millenium Hall gives utopian fictional form to the Anglican social ideals of what by this time was known as the 'bluestocking circle'. This was a social and epistolary network of upper- and middle-class men and women formed in fashionable London society around 1750 and led by Scott's sister, Elizabeth Montagu, and a few other women of independent means. The group's nickname probably came from the blue worsted stockings worn by men in informal social gatherings and symbolizing the group's avoidance of courtly formality along with courtly sexism and courtly vices. The group promoted intellectual exchange and sociability between men and women in terms already set out by social philosophers such as David Hume and Adam Smith, promoting new models of civil society. The women in the group also engaged in literary and philanthropic patronage. Despite *Millenium Hall*'s sympathetic representation of bluestocking feminist values, however, it was thought to contain a critical portrait of Elizabeth Montagu, the so-called 'queen of the bluestockings', as the overly status-conscious and courtly Lady Brumpton. Scott and her sister did differ, in a friendly way, over the degree of involvement in fashionable society that was consistent with properly Christian values and practices, and Montagu seems often to have worried over the extent of her enjoyment of the good things that her wealth and status made available to her. The fictional Lady Brumpton is less an indication of serious difference in a central relationship of the sisters' lives than another instance of their ongoing and lifelong dialogue about important moral, ethical, social, and political questions, and how a committed Anglican should address them.

Soon, however, the other major relationship of Scott's life would draw to a close. Although Scott's and Lady Barbara's finances were much improved by the latter's receipt in 1763 of an annual pension of £300, Lady Barbara had long been in deteriorating health and died in August 1765. Scott turned again to writing and to practical philanthropy, enthusiastically encouraged by her sister. She published another utopian novel, *The History of Sir George Ellison* (1766), the devout and benevolent protagonist of which was seen as a version of Samuel Richardson's idealized Christian hero, Sir Charles Grandison. As a model for the social and economic reform of Britain on Christian principles, estate by estate, the novel continues the work of both *A Description of Millenium Hall* and her histories of 'patriot kings'. At the same time Scott was planning, with several women friends, to set up a version of Millenium Hall on a small estate at Hitcham in Buckinghamshire. Montagu was one of the four major shareholders and supplied the project with equipment, livestock, and staff support from her and her husband's estate at Sandleford in Berkshire. A number of problems, including a crisis in Scott's own health, caused the project's failure within months of its inauguration.

Scott continued to rely on authorship to supplement her small income, like most contemporary women writers working at the lower end of the literary order of her time. She again tried translation from French and projects for children's educational books; there is no record of these being published. She once again addressed public affairs, however, in the oblique form of biographical history. As early as 1762 Scott had noted with alarm: 'The lowest artificer thinks now of nothing but the constitution of the government' (Doran, 125). The emergence of urban working-class politics associated with John Wilkes in the 1760s had been considered obliquely by her sister in her anonymously published *Essay on … Shakspeare* (1768), with discussion of the dramatist's representation of the mob in plays such as *Coriolanus*. Montagu had also represented Shakespeare as the voice of English culture and political traditions against the denigration of Voltaire and his claims for the superiority of French literary culture under absolute monarchy. Scott addressed the new politics of patriotism, protestantism, and populism in *The Life of Theodore Agrippa d'Aubigné* (1772), which celebrates the French protestant hero of resistance to combined Catholic conspiracy, absolutist court monarchy, and plebeian violence.

Again tacitly linking public and private spheres, history and fiction, in the same year Scott published her last novel, *The test of filial duty; in a series of letters between Miss Emilia Leonard, and Miss Charlotte Arlington*. It takes up another major form of female fiction, the novel in letters, which tended to emphasize female friendship, often against the world and its male-dominated systems of property and patronage. It may also be partly a response to Tobias Smollett's *The Expedition of Humphry Clinker* (1770), which examines, among other things, the social and cultural disparateness of Britain, and the different stages of modernization reached in England, Scotland, and Wales. Scott restricts her comparison to England and Wales, but presents a similar theme of the over-civilization of England contrasted to the cultural backwardness yet also greater social vigour of Wales. Like many eighteenth-century novels Scott's also examines the problem of determining the proper balance between parental and especially paternal authority against children's rights to subjective autonomy in choosing a marriage partner, in face of the prevailing system of landed property and inheritance. Analogies between domestic and public issues were commonplace in fiction of the period, and Scott's novel participates in this important interest of the novel-reading public.

Later years Scott did not apparently publish again, perhaps because she no longer needed the money. The death of Edward Montagu in 1775 enabled his widow to assure her sister's financial security with an annuity of £200, and there was additional income after the death of the sisters' father in 1778. Scott moved about, staying with various friends and with her sister. Though her husband's death in 1780 reduced her income she was undismayed, later telling her sister: 'Experience shew'd me that by reducing my house rent, keeping a Maid less, & some other reductions, I cou'd go on very well, & be as comfortable as before' (28 Oct [1784], Montagu MSS). She continued to follow public affairs and society gossip with avidity, and the careers of her brothers with interest. Ill health continued to bother her, and when a stay at a Norwich clinic in 1784–5 seemed to relieve her lifelong headaches, she took a small house at nearby Catton in 1787, despite her sister's protests at the much greater difficulty of visiting from there. She found her frail health and relative isolation no hindrance to her lifelong passion for political news, telling her sister:

> However my body may be decay'd, & small & precarious as my interests in this World are I do not feel my public spirit diminished, & am as warm in my good wishes for my country, & as curious about the events which can effect it as if I were as strong as Hercules. (22 Jan [1788], ibid.)

Like many of her class and generation Scott was repelled and fascinated by the French Revolution, and wrote to her sister after the September massacres at Paris in 1792:

> tho' the accounts from France chill my blood, & make it boil alternately, yet I never before felt so much impatience for news papers. The horrible events they relate keep my mind in a ferment, & almost entirely possess it. (23 Sept [1792], Montagu MSS)

She relished the report that Tom Paine had been her husband's protégé when George Scott was a commissioner of excise, and she denounced the 'English Jacobins' of nearby Norwich as 'Presbyterians' and 'the very dregs of the people' (12 July [1794], ibid.; Blunt, 303). She took particular interest in the female supporters and victims of the Revolution. She imagined the revolutionaries degrading the French princess royal by forcing her to marry a *sans-culotte* (19 Nov [1793], Montagu MSS) and, like Burke, she denounced the Parisian women who marched on Versailles in October 1789 and dragged the king back to the capital. By 1795 she found herself so exhausted emotionally by reading of revolutionary horrors that she regretted reading the fictional horrors of Ann Radcliffe's *Mysteries of Udolpho*, telling her sister:

> it is the last series of horrors which I shall peruse, for I find them too much for my weak nerves; I shall endeavour to keep my imagination in sunshine. I am not equal to any thing affecting; a cool suspense from pleasure & from pain, is all my feeble frame will bear. (18 Feb [1795], ibid.)

Sarah Scott died on 3 November 1795 at Catton; on her instruction her papers were destroyed at her death. Her one work to have a lasting influence was *A Description of Millenium Hall*; echoes of it can be heard in a number of novels, including those of Mary Wollstonecraft. By the time of her death, however, she was forgotten, and *Millenium Hall* was attributed to other writers, such as Oliver Goldsmith. Renewed interest in Scott and her work is due to late twentieth-century feminist scholarship and criticism. GARY KELLY

Sources *Mrs Montagu, 'Queen of the Blues': her letters and friendships from 1762 to 1800*, ed. R. Blunt, 2 vols. (1923) • *Elizabeth Montagu, the queen of the blue-stockings: her correspondence from 1720 to 1761*, ed. E. J. Climenson, 2 vols. (1906) • J. Doran, *A lady of the last century (Mrs Elizabeth Montagu)* (1873) • G. Kelly, introduction, in S. Scott, *A description of Millennium Hall* (1995) • S. H. Myers, *The bluestocking circle: women, friendship, and the life of the mind in eighteenth-century England* (1990) • B. Rizzo, introduction, in S. Scott, *The history of Sir George Ellison*, ed. B. Rizzo (1996) • S. Scott, letters to Elizabeth Montagu, Hunt. L., Montagu papers

Archives Hunt. L., letters, mainly to Elizabeth Montagu

Likenesses E. Haytley, portrait (Sarah Scott?), repro. in Haytley, *Sandleford Park* • E. Haytley, portrait

Scott [*née* Hopkins], **Sheila Christine** (**1922–1988**), aviator, was born at 12 Park Avenue, Worcester, on 27 April 1922, the only child of Harold Reginald Hopkins (1896–1978), confectioner, and his wife, Edyth Mary, *née* Kenward. The parents' marriage, which took place in Birmingham on 1 January 1921, ended in 1925 when Edyth ran away with an actor whom she had met when his company was playing at the Worcester Playhouse. Sheila then went to live with her paternal grandparents and two aunts. In this solid middle-class family Edyth's defection and ultimate divorce were a terrible disgrace. All her photographs were removed. Her name was never mentioned and the Hopkins family behaved as if she had never existed. If her mother had tried to contact her, Sheila was never allowed to know. From kindergarten to sixth form she attended the Alice Ottley School for Girls in Worcester at which her great-grandmother had been a founder pupil.

When Sheila was ten her father remarried. His second wife, Aileen Harper, was a gentle, ladylike perfectionist with little idea of how to cope with the difficult teenager Sheila had become after the death of her grandparents. Her father had inherited the family baking and confectionery business and she felt he was more interested in his activities as an alderman and chairman of Worcester racecourse than in her. She became obsessed with finding her mother, and frequently played truant from school to do so. Inevitably she failed her school certificate, passing her matriculation at the second attempt after being kept locked in her room by Aileen.

Having volunteered to train as a nurse at Haslar Royal Naval Hospital, Portsmouth, Sheila Hopkins enjoyed the social life of a wartime naval base. Posted to London in 1943, she met film producer Alexander Korda. With his assistance she was taken on as understudy to Deborah Kerr and then decided on an acting career. She adopted the stage name Sheila Scott, by which she was known for the rest of her life. Her marriage, on 17 November 1945, to Rupert Leaman Bellamy (*b*. 1907/8), a well-to-do old Harrovian and acting lieutenant-colonel in the Royal Electrical and Mechanical Engineers (REME), did not last. When Rupert was posted away Sheila stayed on in their London home in Queen's Gate Mews in order to further her acting career. She took private drama tuition and enrolled on a Lucie Clayton modelling course. After divorce in 1950 Sheila's life became chaotic. She was strikingly beautiful, witty, and intelligent, and there was always a string of admirers around to indulge her craving for the excitement of social high life. There were, however, dark periods of drug and alcohol dependence necessitating psychiatric treatment.

Having failed in various careers and dissatisfied with her life, late in 1958 Sheila Scott went to Elstree airfield with the intention of learning to fly. Tense and a heavy smoker, she was not a promising pupil and having failed her driving test four times she found learning to fly just as difficult. Transferring to Thruxton airfield, Hampshire, it was nine months before she was ready to fly solo. What she lacked in aptitude she made up for in persistence and when she finally achieved her private pilot's licence she declared it was the proudest moment of her life. Among the flying fraternity she found the family she sought and she joined as many clubs as possible, including the Royal Aero Club, the Tiger Club, and the British Women Pilots' Association (BWPA).

Now the owner of a Thruxton Jackaroo, a converted Tiger Moth she christened *Myth*, Sheila Scott extended her horizons with non-radio flights to the Channel Islands; she won her first trophy, presented to her by Lady Brabazon, at the Jersey air rally. Encouraged by the engineers who had converted her little Jackaroo, and with just six months to learn the technique of flying at speed over a set course, she entered the 1960 national air races, gaining enough points to become air racing champion of her class. She was awarded the De Havilland national air racing trophy. Obsessive as ever, she entered all the races and attended as many rallies as possible while learning all about aviation. For her achievement in that year she was awarded the BWPA Jean Lennox Bird trophy. The next ten years were the happiest of her life. The Cessna Aircraft Company loaned her aircraft to show off in air races and paid her as a demonstrator. An invitation to America for Cessna sales week followed. Finding aviation considerably cheaper in the USA than in Britain, she obtained a commercial licence and instrument rating. Needing a more sophisticated aircraft, she sold the Jackaroo *Myth* and continued racing in a borrowed Piper Comanche 250.

Returning to America in 1964 Scott obtained commercial seaplane and helicopter ratings in three weeks. For this achievement she was awarded the Amelia Earhart trophy and election to the exclusive Whirly Girls Club. Competitive flying became an addiction. Discovering that fifteen light-aircraft records around Europe had not been attempted for several years she borrowed a single-engine Piper Comanche 400 and broke them all in thirty-six hours, covering 2300 miles in ten and a half hours of flying time.

Scott now set her sights on a round-the-world flight and poured all her money into buying a Piper Comanche she named *Myth Too*. Leaving London airport on 18 May 1966 she covered 32,000 miles in 184 flying hours, arriving back at Heathrow thirty-three days and three minutes later. She was awarded the prestigious American Harmon trophy for the year's most outstanding woman pilot and became the first woman recipient of the silver award of merit of the Guild of Air Pilots and Navigators. Amy Johnson's record between London and Cape Town was the next to be broken, in July 1967, followed by the north and south Atlantic records the same year. She was appointed OBE in 1968.

In 1971 Scott's flight over the north pole and one and a half times round the world was her most ambitious yet. Flying a specially modified twin-engine Piper Aztec (G-AYTO) christened *Mythre*, she co-operated with NASA in environmental and biomedical experiments and with the RAF Institute of Aviation Medicine in investigations into the sleep patterns and problems of long-distance pilots. Though successful she returned with debts of £20,000. Ambitious plans to circumnavigate both the north and the south pole had to be abandoned when *Mythre* was wrecked by Hurricane Agnes at the Piper airfield, Lockhaven, Pennsylvania.

Forced to sell *Myth Too* and without an aircraft, Sheila Scott's active flying life came to an end. During ten years she had taken 107 international records. She was awarded the BWPA Brabazon cup for three consecutive years in 1965–7 and the Royal Aero Club Britannia trophy in 1967. In 1971 she was presented with the Royal Aero Club gold medal and the BWPA Jean Lennox Bird trophy.

Living in reduced circumstances and without what she called the 'elixir which kept her alive', she found the 1970s and early 1980s difficult. There were depressive periods, a return to alcohol dependence, and suicide attempts necessitating stays in psychiatric clinics. However, she could always rise to the occasion when called upon to make a public appearance, looking still beautiful and immaculate as ever. Supported by loyal friends she completed her account of her flying career *On Top of the World* (1973) and also became involved in working with difficult teenagers. She continued to support aviation associations worldwide and was a founder and first governor of the British section of the American Ninety Nines Inc., an international association of women pilots.

In 1984, at Baden-Baden, Sheila Scott was elected president of the European Women Pilots' Association and presided over their annual meetings in 1985 in Geneva and 1986 in Vienna. That year, as European vice-president of the World Aerospace Education Organization, she attended the conference in Delhi inaugurated by Rajiv Gandhi. In 1987, diagnosed with inoperable cancer, she faced her final challenge with the same courage she had shown on her flights. She died on 20 October 1988, and was cremated at Golders Green; a year later her ashes were scattered over Thruxton airfield. ENID DEBOIS

Sources S. Scott, *I must fly* (1968) · S. Scott, *On top of the world* (1973) · British Women Pilots' Association Archives, Brooklands, near Weybridge, Surrey · private information (2004) [Rosemary Jones, cousin; Royal Aero Club] · *WWW* · b. cert. · m. cert.

Archives British Women Pilots' Association, Brooklands, near Weybridge, Surrey, archives, scrapbooks, and papers

Likenesses J. Mendoza, oils, 1968, priv. coll. · E. W. West, oils, 1968, Worcester Art Gallery · Z. Roboz, charcoal drawing, 1973, repro. in Scott, *On top of the world*, frontispiece · photographs, NPG

Scott, Sir Terence Charles Stuart Morrison- (1908–1991), zoologist and museum director, was born on 24 October 1908 in Paris, the only son of Lieutenant-Colonel Robert Charles Stuart Morrison-Scott (*d.* 1938), barrister, and his wife, Amy A. Mosselmans. After Eton College and Christ Church, Oxford, he entered the Royal College of Science, London, in 1931 to study zoology, where he graduated BSc with first-class honours in 1935 and proceeded MSc in 1939. For a short while he researched bird behaviour at London Zoo, and he was briefly an assistant master at Eton. He married on 19 December 1935 Rita Layton (*b.* 1905), daughter of Edwin James Layton; they had no children.

On 1 October 1936 Morrison-Scott was appointed to the scientific staff of the British Museum (Natural History), as assistant keeper (second class), and assigned to the mammal room. His scientific papers of 1937–9 reported on his work at the zoo, and subsequent studies on material in the museum's mammal collections. In pursuit of a detailed investigation of elephant molars, in March 1938 he visited the Zoological Museum, Berlin, where he measured some sixty African elephant skulls; he also observed curatorial and exhibition techniques there and at the Hamburg Museum.

Sir Terence Charles Stuart Morrison-Scott (1908–1991), by Walter Bird, 1966

With the outbreak of war, as an officer of the Royal Naval Volunteer Reserve, Morrison-Scott was called up on 6 October 1939. After leading a mixed fleet of private yachts hurriedly mustered to protect the Solent, he served two years as signals officer at Dartmouth. In 1944, with the rank of lieutenant-commander, he was given command of the 12th flotilla of tank landing craft. He was awarded the Distinguished Service Cross for gallantry during the invasion of Normandy.

In September 1945 the director of the British Museum (Natural History) made an urgent plea to the Admiralty for the return of Morrison-Scott to take charge of the mammal galleries. He was released on 24 December, initially as assistant keeper (first class), but was promoted to senior scientific officer on 1 January 1948 and to principal scientific officer on 1 November 1948. He became an active member of the Scientific Officers' Association, formed in 1949. His scientific productivity was now channelled into preparing three definitive reference works in collaboration with Sir John Reeves Ellerman, bt: first, the massive *Checklist of Palaearctic and Indian Mammals* (1951, second edition 1966), then *Southern African Mammals: a Reclassification* (1953), which also involved R. W. Hayman, a colleague at the museum, and finally *Supplement to F. N. Chasen (1940): Handlist of Malaysian Mammals* (1955). This taxonomic research concentrated his attention on the need for stability in systematic names. At the 1958 London meeting of the International Congress of Zoology, the successful ratification of the definitive text of the *International Rules of Zoological Nomenclature* was attributed to his perseverance as chairman of the relevant section. All but one of his fifteen scientific papers from 1954 to 1965 (his last) were devoted to nomenclatural issues.

Elected to the council of the Zoological Society of London in 1947, Morrison-Scott served as honorary treasurer from 1950 until 1976. During these years he also became a trustee of the Imperial War Museum (1956–60) and a governor of the Imperial College of Science and Technology (1956–72). In 1952 he was awarded the degree of DSc (London).

In May 1956, after the death of Frank Sherwood Taylor, director of the Science Museum, Morrison-Scott was chosen to succeed him. He carried forward existing plans to develop the new centre block, and to enhance education facilities for children. He managed to retain substantial financial support from industry, but struggled with the parsimony of government funding. Finally, in 1960, the annual purchase grant (static since 1945) was raised from £2000 to £8000, but Morrison-Scott was frustrated in his wish to improve the status (and pay) of skilled craftsmen at the museum.

In 1960, on the retirement of Sir Gavin de Beer, Morrison-Scott returned to the British Museum (Natural History) as director on 1 May. Here he faced entrenched compartmentalism, with each departmental keeper defending his own fief. In addition he inherited a staff disciplinary problem which became protracted and public, ultimately being debated on four separate occasions in parliament. His decision to dismiss the scientist in question was endorsed by all ministers concerned, including three successive chancellors of the exchequer. He also managed the complex legislative and administrative process, culminating in the British Museum Act of 1963, which finally severed the outmoded historic connection with Bloomsbury.

In 1963, for the guidance of the museum's trustees, Morrison-Scott presented a policy paper on the functions of the British Museum (Natural History)—he was adamant in retaining the name, which was later replaced by the name Natural History Museum. He recognized the significance of the museum's roles in education and exhibition, but placed greater weight on the science performed, unseen by the public. His highest priority was for new building to house the vast and increasing collections and to provide working space for staff and visitors. Over the next decade, this aspiration was progressively advanced. In 1965 he was knighted.

Initially the museum was in competition with the other national museums for Treasury funds allocated on the advice of the Museums and Galleries Commission. In 1966, however, Morrison-Scott obtained transfer to the Department of Education and Science, and comparability with the research councils. Thenceforward (until 1987) the council for scientific policy and its successors became the arbiter of the museum's objectives and the resources needed to achieve them. The construction of a new north-east tower within the South Kensington site was agreed (formally opened in 1973), as was the removal of the bird room to a purpose-built wing of the Rothschild Museum at Tring, Hertfordshire, completed in 1971. Thus, when Morrison-Scott retired at the end of November 1968, he had negotiated significant new resources for the attainment of the museum's scientific objectives.

A tall, handsome man, a natural leader and administrator, a lover of the classics, and a craftsman in stone (who learned lettering from David Gill), Morrison-Scott had been a successful oarsman at school and university, and he enjoyed sailing, skiing, shooting, and flying, achieving his solo licence in 1975. He was a deputy lieutenant for West Sussex, and was a fellow of the Zoological Society of London, the Linnean Society, and the Institute of Biology. In retirement he served on the Standing Commission on Museums and Galleries (1973–6), and as a National Trust council member (1968–83).

Morrison-Scott died at his home, Upperfold House, Fernhurst, Sussex, near Haslemere, on 25 November 1991, and was cremated at Chichester crematorium; his wife survived him. A circular plaque in the cloisters of Chichester Cathedral records the restoration of one bay in his memory; so, too, does a plaque on the restored console table in the Stone Hall of Uppark, a National Trust property.

CRANBROOK

Sources m. cert. • *WWW, 1991–5* • Lord Zuckerman, 'Sir Terence Morrison-Scott DSC, DSc', *Journal of Zoology*, 228 (1992), 1–4 • *The Times* (28 Nov 1991) • R. V. Melville, *The Times* (1 Jan 1992) • Lord Zuckerman, *The Times* (12 Dec 1991) • J. E. Hill, *The Independent* (10 Dec 1991) • W. T. Stearn, *The Natural History Museum at South Kensington: a history of the museum, 1735–1980* (1998) • personal files, 1936–9, NHM [reports on activities] • MSS record of staff publications, NHM, mammal section • introductions, *Annual Reports* [Science Museum, London] (1957–60) • private information (2004) [Lady Morrison-Scott, widow; Ms S. Snell, NHM] • d. cert. • *CGPLA Eng. & Wales* (1992)

Likenesses W. Bird, photograph, 1966, NPG [*see illus.*] • photograph, repro. in *The Independent* • photograph, repro. in *The Times* (28 Nov 1991)

Wealth at death £22,567: probate, 24 Jan 1992, *CGPLA Eng. & Wales*

Scott, Thomas, of Petgormo (*d.* **1541**). *See under* Scott, Sir William, of Balwearie (*d.* 1532).

Scott, Sir Thomas (**1534x6–1594**), landowner, was the eldest son of Sir Reginald Scott (*d.* 1555) of Scot's Hall, Smeeth, Kent, and his wife, Emmeline, daughter of Sir William Kempe of Olantigh by Wye, Kent, and his wife, Eleanor, daughter and coheir of Sir Robert Brown of Betchworth, Surrey. He was the grandson of Sir John *Scott (*b.* in or before 1484, *d.* 1533), while Reginald *Scott (Scot), the writer on witchcraft, was a cousin.

Scott was admitted to the Inner Temple in November 1554. He entered into his father's estates at his death the following year, inheriting thirty manors centred in the Medway valley and the Ashford area. His arranged marriage to Elizabeth, the daughter of his wealthiest neighbour, Sir John *Baker of Sissinghurst Castle, Cranbrook, and his wife, Elizabeth, daughter and heir of Thomas Dinley, only increased his riches. Related to Robert Dudley, earl of Leicester, and a correspondent of many aristocrats, Scott made lavish display of wealth and hospitality that caused his contemporaries in the county to view him 'like a reigning monarch' (Pickering and Hasler, 3.356). He rebuilt Scot's Hall into a magnificent mansion about 1580, and also extensively rebuilt Nettlestead Place, his house by the Medway. He was said to have entertained hundreds at a time, and his Christmas feasts were renowned. He was knighted in 1570.

With his first wife Scott had seventeen children, of whom at least eleven were boys, the eldest being Thomas (*c.*1563–1610) and John Scott (*d.* 1616) [*see below*]. Following his first wife's death Scott married twice more, both wives coming from within the ranks of the Kentish gentry. In 1583 he married Elizabeth, daughter of Ralph Hayman of Somerfield House, Sellinge, and his wife, Elizabeth, daughter of William Till. His third wife was the thrice-widowed Dorothy, daughter of John Bere of Horseman's Place, Dartford (and successively wife of John Heyes, Edward Scott, and George Fynche). No children survived from the last two marriages.

Scott was a JP in Kent from 1561, and of the *quorum* by 1571. He was a commissioner of piracy in 1565, of coastal defence in 1569, and of piracy in the Cinque Ports of Sussex in 1578, commissioner of grain by 1573, sheriff of Kent in 1576–7, and deputy lieutenant by 1582. He was superintendent of works in Dover harbour in 1580, and supervised the rebuilding of the harbour and the sea walls, and the draining and improving of Romney Marsh, in the 1580s. As colonel-general of Kent's forces during the Armada campaign, he commanded the camp at Northbourne. In 1591 he joined the earl of Essex's French expedition. Interested in horse breeding, he raised large horses and wrote a book on breeding that has not survived.

Scott had a brief parliamentary career, being elected county MP in 1571–2 and 1586. He served on at least forty-seven committees, and was active in many of them, especially on local government, religion, and matters pertaining to the queen. He spoke openly for the execution of Mary, queen of Scots, for the discovery and punishment of Jesuit priests, the sovereignty of the Netherlands, and the petitioning of Elizabeth to marry. Perhaps his career in parliament was brief because of his outspoken manner in a discreet forum.

Generous in his time, Scott did not leave much to charity at his death, preferring to confer his wealth on his wife, many sons, daughters' dowries, and grandchildren. He died on 30 December 1594, having lived 'nine & fifty years' as his epitaph declared, leaving considerable wealth in land, buildings, livestock, and plate, and no debts (J. R. Scott, *Memorials*, 197). The citizens of Ashford had offered his family free burial in a tomb in the chancel of their church. But he was buried in Brabourne church, though his body was apparently later moved to Scot's Hall chapel, probably after the desecration of his monument at Brabourne during the second civil war in 1648.

Scott established his second son, **Sir John Scott** (*d.* 1616), army officer and landowner, at Nettlestead Place, and in his will also left him £150. By the time of his father's death John had married his first wife, Elizabeth (1549/50–1599), daughter of Sir William Stafford of Blatherwick, Northamptonshire, and widow of Sir William Drury (1527–1579). She died on 6 February 1599. Scott's second wife was Catherine, daughter of the merchant and financier Thomas *Smythe (1522–1591) and widow of Sir Rowland *Hayward (*c.*1520–1593), merchant and lord mayor of London. Little is known of John Scott's early career, but he served in the Netherlands and France. He was knighted by Peregrine Bertie, Lord Willoughby de Eresby, English commander in the Netherlands, in 1588, though within two years relations had deteriorated between Scott and his commander so far that he challenged his commander to a duel. Willoughby spurned the challenge with aristocratic disdain, scorning to fight with a commoner and describing Scott as 'an ignorant and paltry fellow' (BL, Cotton Galba MS D.vii, fol. 111*r*). The cause of the dispute was Scott's disrespectful words about his senior officer Sir Thomas Wilsford, another Kentish gentleman. He captained a band of lancers under the earl of Essex on the Cadiz expedition in 1596, and was again in the Low Countries in 1597. A staunch friend of Essex, he was imprisoned in the Tower of London for his complicity in the earl's rebellion in 1601. He was saved from trial by Sir Robert Sidney and his kinsman the earl of Dorset. In Kent John Scott, rather than his elder brother, Thomas, seems to have wielded the local influence of his family. In 1600 he was one of those gentry in conflict with Henry Brooke, Lord Cobham, over the Medway navigation. At the county election of 1601 Scott was encouraged by Lord Buckhurst to stand for the county seat in opposition to the Cobham faction, though he stood down when Cobham came to terms over the division of the seats. In 1602 he was made a deputy lieutenant. Elected to the House of Commons for Kent in 1604–10, Scott is not recorded as participating in any business, though he was one of a group of MPs who had a secret meeting with Salisbury in 1610 to discuss his proposed great contract.

Scott's primary domestic occupation was in building works. He was preoccupied with building at Nettlestead, the expansion of his gardens there across the Medway, and construction of a new bridge across the river that was later pulled down. There is correspondence with Robert Cecil, earl of Salisbury, and Sir Robert Sidney (later earl of Leicester) in 1605–6 for service or loans to save his estate. Apparently he was still owed money by the crown for his services in the Low Countries. In 1611 Edward Wotton wrote offering him a command of lancers, both for his experience and to relieve his debts.

Scott died in his principal residence at Nettlestead Place about 28 December 1616, and was buried at the adjoining church, where his two wives were also buried. According to his will he hoped to be one of the 'elect'. He left most of the estate he could dispose of to his wife, Catherine, but his debts (uncatalogued) were so large that he offered her £500 in cash (if the executors could raise it) if she declined her dower and took her jointure as the latter had been heavily mortgaged. In the end his debts were too large for his estate, and later Nettlestead, inherited by his younger brother, Edward, was pulled down and sold for its materials.

Louis A. Knafla

Sources J. R. Scott, *Memorials of the family of Scott, of Scot's Hall, in the county of Kent* (1876) • M. R. Pickering and P. W. Hasler, 'Scott, Thomas', HoP, *Commons, 1558–1603* • E. Hasted, *The history and topographical survey of the county of Kent*, 2nd edn, 3 (1797), 355–8; 8 (1799), 3.355–8; 8.4–5 • will, PRO, PROB 11/85 [T. Scott] • will, PRO, PROB 11/131 [J. Scott] • BL, Harleian MS 474 [a book of JPs (1583) for T. Scott] • T. Scott's ceremonial duties in the Low Countries, 1581–2, BL, Cotton Galba MS D.vii, fols. 111–112 • indenture of T. Scott's estates at death, 1610, PRO, C142/322/178 • *Archaeologia Cantiana*, 10 (1876), 265–7 • J. R. Scott, 'Pay lists of the forces, raised in Kent, to resist the Spanish invasion, 1588', *Archaeologia Cantiana*, 11 (1877), 388–91 • N. H. MacMichael, 'The descent of the manor of Evegate in Smeeth with some account of the lords', *Archaeologia Cantiana*, 74 (1960), 1–43 • J. M. McGurk, 'Armada preparations in Kent and arrangements made after the defeat', *Archaeologia Cantiana*, 85 (1970), 71–93 • *CSP dom.*, *1565*; *1572*; *1580*; *1585*; *1588* • Cobbett, *Parl. hist.*, 1.973 • R. Scot, *The discoverie of witchcraft*, ed. B. Nicholson (1886), xxiii–xxiv • R. C. Stone, 'Calcombe, Ireland and the St Legers', *Archaeologia Cantiana*, 91 (1976), 114 • W. Notestein, *The House of Commons, 1604–1610* (1971), 562 • T. Scott, commission for Dover harbour, 1583, BL, Lansdowne MS 37 • T. Scott to earl of Leicester, correspondence, 1585, BL, Cotton Titus MS B.vii, fol. 67 • J. Scott, letter to T. Hayes, 1592, BL, Add. MS 33924, fol. 11 • *APC*, 1592–4 • T. Scott, letter to L. Bufkin, 1597, BL, Add. MS 33924, fol. 23 • J. Scott, letter to Lord Buckhurst, 1600, BL, Add. MS 34218, fols. 56–7 • T. Scott, correspondence with commissioners of sewers, 1600, BL, Add. MS 34218, fols. 57–8 • J. Scott and John Leveson, correspondence, 1600, BL, Add. MS 34218, fols. 41–3 • J. Scott, letter to Lord Essex, 1600, BL, Add. MS 33924, fol. 27 • J. Scott, letter to R. Twisden, 1605, BL, Add. MS 34175, fol. 9 • J. Scott, correspondence with Robert Cecil, Sir Robert Sidney, and Edward Wotton, 1605–11, Hatfield House, Salisbury MSS 114–115 • J. Scott to Edward Wotton, correspondence, 1611, BL, Cotton Julius MS C.iii, fol. 335 • P. Clark, *English provincial society from the Reformation to the revolution* (1977) • W. A. Shaw, *Knights of England*, 3 vols. (1906)

Likenesses S. De Wilde, etching, pubd 1803 (after unknown artist), BM, NPG • engraving (after painting by Zucchero), repro. in Scott, *Memorials*, 214

Scott, Thomas (*c.*1566–1635), landowner and politician, was the eldest in a family of four sons and two daughters of Charles Scott (*d.* 1596), a puritan landowner and justice of the peace, of Godmersham near Canterbury, and his wife Jane, daughter of Sir Thomas *Wyatt of Boxley, executed for rebellion in 1554. Scott's education is uncertain but it seems likely that he attended the cathedral school, Canterbury, and afterwards went to Cambridge University.

Scott inherited the family estate in 1596, the year in which he married his first wife, Elizabeth, the daughter of John Webbe, a prominent Canterbury merchant; they had one child, Jane. His second wife, whom he married in 1602, was Mary, the daughter of John Knatchbull of Mersham, a substantial Kentish landowner; they had a son, Thomas (who predeceased him), and three daughters.

From 1612 until towards the end of his life Scott lived for a good part of the year in Canterbury. In 1613–14 he was in conflict with Archdeacon Charles Fotherby over an amalgam of personal and religious issues. Increasingly involved in local politics, in 1614 he supported Sir Edwin Sandys as a candidate in the county elections to the Addled Parliament. In 1618 he obtained the freedom of the city of Canterbury and shortly after became a member of the common council, though he was soon removed, owing to the hostility of the corporation ruling group. A zealous though conformist puritan, Scott acquired a reputation in the early 1620s as an opponent of the city leaders and as a critic of royal policy.

In 1624 Scott was elected MP for Canterbury in a fierce campaign inflamed by anti-Catholicism. He also stood in the 1625 and 1626 elections, but was defeated by the corporation's candidates. He was re-elected as MP for Canterbury in 1628, with wide freeman and puritan support. Little is known about his activities in parliament, but in 1628 he opposed the billeting of troops and was summoned before the privy council; four years later he was in conflict with the authorities again over musters.

The principal evidence for Scott's radical opinions comes from his extensive diaries and other unpublished writings. In 1626 he wrote on the need for parliamentary reform, calling for the expulsion of non-resident borough MPs whom he regarded as illegally elected, and also for a major redistribution of seats in the House of Commons. In 1627 he produced a radical and wide-ranging indictment of royal policy, denouncing George Villiers, first duke of Buckingham, identifying Charles I as a tyrant, and espousing resistance theory.

Scott's life was dominated by an intense commitment to godly religion, which involved searing spiritual experiences and recurrent bouts of melancholic despair. But he also showed a striking interest in international developments, particularly the progress of the protestant cause in France and Germany during the Thirty Years' War. He was a passionate, combative, choleric, and difficult man, frequently embroiled in legal disputes. Thomas Scott died in Godmersham in May 1635. His heir was Dorothea Scott [*see* Gotherson, Dorothea], a friend of several of the regicides and a Quaker pamphleteer and preacher during the 1650s. PETER A. CLARK, *rev.*

Sources CKS, U951; Z9, 10, 15–17 • P. Clark, 'Thomas Scott and the growth of urban opposition to the early Stuart regime', *HJ*, 21 (1978), 1–26 • G. D. Scull, *Dorothea Scott, also Gotherson and Hogben* (1882); rev. edn (1883) • R. P. Cust, *The forced loan and English politics, 1626–1628* (1987)

Archives BL, Wyatt MSS, commonplace book, 4, 29, loan 15 • CKS, papers | BL, Harley MS 7018, fols. 89–90 • Bodl. Oxf., MS Ballard 61 • Bodl. Oxf., MS Rawl. A346, fols. 224–34*v*, 285–97*v* • Bodl. Oxf., MS Rawl. D911, fols. 186–7*v*

Scott, Thomas (*d.* 1626), protestant polemicist, was possibly the son of a Norfolk cleric of the same name, though he is equally likely to have been a Scot. On the strength of two sermons 'preached before the kings majestie' and published in 1616, it has been claimed that Scott was one of the chaplains to James VI and I. This has been disputed, however, since he is found matriculating in the theological faculty of the University of St Andrews in the autumn of 1618. Indeed, to judge from a remark made by Scott in 1623 about a previous life of sin and his personal redemption, it is possible that he had not made a decision to enter the ministry before 1618. This being so, he is possibly the author of a political libel published in 1616, *Phylomythie, or, Phylomythologie* by 'Thomas Scott, Gent.' Although it was principally concerned with the Essex

Thomas Scott (*d.* 1626), by Crispijn de Passe the elder, 1624

divorce scandal, several of its themes recur in the pamphlets of Scott the minister in the 1620s, notably his defence of the Anglo-Scottish union, posited on the common maintenance of true religion, and his disgust for 'church papists' in England who supported the Spanish cause in the Low Countries and denigrated the United Provinces, the stadholder, and the states general. The *Dictionary of National Biography* however, identified the author of *Phylomythie* as **Thomas Scott** (*fl.* 1602–1611), poet, who wrote *The Foure Paradoxes*, a series of six-line verses on the theme of art, law, war, and service. Published in 1602, this work carried a brief dedication to Helena Snackenborg, dowager marchioness of Northampton, in which the author noted that composition of his work had 'wasted much pretious time' (sig. A2*r*). The work was republished in 1611 with an identically worded dedication to Sir Thomas Gorges—presumably Helena's son rather than husband, who had died the year before. In 1620 the Thomas Scott who had matriculated at St Andrews was incorporated bachelor of divinity in the University of Cambridge as a member of Peterhouse. By the end of the year he was rector of St Saviour's, Norwich.

While in Edinburgh, in the first half of 1619, Scott had written the anonymous tract for which he is best-known, namely *Vox Populi, or, Newes from Spayne*. It was first published, probably in London, by mid-November 1620 at the latest, and quite possibly earlier. It purports to describe the report of the Spanish ambassador, Gondomar, to the council of state in Madrid on his return from his first embassy to England in 1618. The ambassador recounts the success of his efforts to subvert the English government, and describes with evident satisfaction the crowds that flocked to mass in his chapel in London. Relaxation of the recusancy laws, the banning of decent protestant preaching as 'puritan', and the distribution of popish propaganda, Gondomar claims, have all been obtained by bribery of courtiers and the king's ministers. Gleefully Gondomar also describes the failure of Ralegh's expedition and his subsequent destruction, connived at by the unholy alliance of greedy courtiers, personal enemies, and outright papists which the Spaniard boasts of orchestrating. He is congratulated by his political masters and praised for contributing so helpfully to the realization of Spanish ambitions for the establishment of that great bugbear of the age, both constitutional and commercial, a 'universal monarchy'.

Apparently taken for a piece of genuine reportage at a time of deep, and not entirely unjustified, religious paranoia, the anonymously published pamphlet caused a furore, and prompted an energetic hunt for its author. Its printers remained at work producing new editions, though they were evidently disturbed by the hue and cry—several of these editions 'are composed of assorted sheets of different impressions hastily bound together' (Adams, 'Captain Thomas Gainsford', 143). At some point the pamphlet was taken off the press, handed over to scriveners, and distributed in manuscript instead. The author's identity was discovered only at the beginning of February 1621. Scott had gone into hiding almost as soon as the storm broke, and he made his escape, 'having … fore-notice of the pursuivant', so it was said (*DNB*). Scott himself later claimed that this warning came to him in a dream, but it is probably an early indication of the kind of protection he would continue to enjoy for the rest of his career. He subsequently resurfaced in the Netherlands. In *Dictionary of National Biography* the author of *Vox populi* was mistaken for another Thomas Scott, minister from Ipswich, one of the third earl of Pembroke's chaplains (and probably the author of the 1616 sermons with which Scott of Norwich has been credited). Scott of Ipswich preached a sermon at Bury St Edmunds in 1622 which appeared in print under the same title as another published by Scott of Norwich a year later, *Vox Dei*. On these grounds it has been assumed, erroneously, that the author of *Vox populi* had returned to England in 1622. In fact, however, that year he became preacher to one of the English regiments in the Netherlands and a minister at Utrecht. He appears never to have returned to his homeland.

Given the scale of his polemical output in the years which followed, and his freedom from pursuit or punishment, it is reasonable to assume that Scott acted with some sort of backing. It has been suggested that he published *Vox populi* with the sponsorship of Achatius von Dohna, ambassador of Frederick, the elector palatine, and his agent Abraham Williams. On the other hand, it has been argued that Scott sought to state the premises of his own 'rabid' anti-popish zealotry with as much apparent moderation as possible in order to appropriate consensus to his own narrow purposes, and this may explain why *Vox populi* did not actually refer to Frederick, upon whose claims to the Bohemian throne the elector's father-in-law, James I, looked so doubtfully (Lake, 806). However, Scott was not principally concerned to spare the blushes of his king, and this tract stands as a powerful and excoriating criticism of the Hispanophile and pacific strands of Jacobean foreign policy. In particular Scott sought to damage irreparably the policy of 'the Spanish match'. By marrying his eldest surviving son, Charles, to the infanta of Spain, James I believed he might obtain some sort of influence over Spanish foreign policy. For many contemporaries, however, the price of this diplomatic solution to the crisis of international protestantism was far too high.

In *Vox populi*, as later in the tracts written on the continent, Scott articulated strong 'country' ideology, contrasting the honest patriotism of the ordinary people and their representatives in the Commons with the vogue for all things Spanish within the highest circles of government and society; in particular he advocated an ideal of active citizenship which has been described as quintessentially puritan, or else classical republican, but which could equally well be characterized as both. But rather than doing so in self-conscious opposition to the effete and corrupted 'court', he wrote with a very clear sense of the sinful corruption evident in both court and country. He regarded slothful justices, Catholic gentry, and impropriators of church livings in provincial society as just as prominent as decadent courtiers in the devilish plans hatched by Spain and Rome. Moreover, rather than being written in outright repudiation of the court and all its ways, Scott's efforts were conceived in full awareness of the impact of such opinions on the conduct of national politics at the highest level, which he sought most obviously to influence in his exaltation of parliament as the best guarantee that the king would not lack for honest and patriotic counsel. Although his sentiments were oftentimes avowedly populist, Scott was playing to numerous audiences, one of them as illustrious as those privy councillors (such as Archbishop Abbott and the third earl of Pembroke) known for their strong resentment of the prevailing policies at court. The sheer vigour of his argument in *Vox populi* appears to have earned Scott at least tacit support at the English court, probably including noted Hispanophobes like the earl of Pembroke and his clients in the House of Commons. More certainly, Scott received a warm and hospitable reception in the Netherlands—a large part of the reason why his would-be prosecutors in England, including Secretary Calvert, so comprehensively failed to get their man. His appointment to the responsible position of spiritual mentor to the English military establishment on the continent also testifies to the success with which he commended himself to his protectors on the continent. In 1621 Scott had written powerfully in defence of the resumption of the United Provinces' war of independence, and in advocacy of English support for the Dutch cause. He was also increasingly active as a propagandist on behalf of the elector palatine.

Scott clearly harboured radical ideas, some of which he evidently tempered out of consideration for the sensibilities of his sponsors. Hence he showed equal dislike for both precisians and conformists, whom he professed to consider just as careerist as each other: he who overlooked the deficiencies of the established church was no worse than he who criticized them in order that 'he may be a head of a faction and be thought somebody'. Scott warned the precisians that 'thou art bound to resist and breake thine own crooked and perverse will and subject it to the will of God who hath subjected thee to Caesar' (Lake, 808). It is clear from the pamphleteer's membership of the famous synod or classis set up by English divines in the Netherlands in 1621 that he obtained practical experience of the presbyterian system of church government, and that he considered it at least the equal of the episcopalian system pertaining in England. However, he appears to have held in check whatever desire he may have had to level attacks at the Church of England. His principal sponsors, the Bohemian faction, did not see their interests well served by any overt criticism of the established order, sensitive as they were to the charges of their Arminian and 'Hispaniolized' enemies, who equated support for the Dutch and Bohemian causes with antimonarchist insurrection.

By the end of 1623, with the failure of the trip to Madrid by Charles and Buckingham, and the coming of a 'blessed revolution' in English foreign policy, Scott's position was vindicated. His pamphlet *Vox Dei* (1623?) opened with thanks to the duke of Buckingham and the prince of Wales for having saved England from Spanish plots. While on the continent, Scott wrote consistently in defence of the protestant cause. He was an influential advocate of war with Spain in vindication of Frederick's rights and the defence of international, evangelical protestantism. He appears also to have had a hand in publishing the anti-Spanish propaganda of others—several of those tracts appearing in the 'collected works' volume of 1624 were clearly not entirely his own. The outpourings from his own pen are unmistakable, however. *Vox regis*, written in 1624 and published after the parliament, appeared with a frontispiece depicting the prince of Wales reuniting Frederick and Elizabeth with King James, 'the clergy offering their prayers, the Lords offering their swords and the Commons their hearts and money' (Adams, 'Protestant cause', 457). In 1624 he wrote *A Briefe Information of the Affaires of the Palatinate* in defence of the elector palatine's claims to the throne of Bohemia. *Certain Reasons and Arguments of Policie* in the same year returned to the theme of James's exploitation by the Spaniards and argued for the termination of the Anglo-Spanish treaties. In the *Second Part of Vox populi*, Scott explicitly acknowledged the closeness of his relationship with Maurice of Nassau and with Frederick and Elizabeth, to whom he dedicated the tract out of thanks for their 'respect … towards me' (ibid., 459). Scott was also a consistent advocate for the need for unity among the reformed churches of protestant Europe, as well as greater unity between England and the United Provinces.

After the failure of the Cadiz expedition, Scott wrote another pamphlet, called *Sir Walter Rawleigh's Ghost, or, England's Forewarner* (published in 1626), which aimed further blows at the Spanish faction in England. This tract may have appeared posthumously. The author of *Vox populi* was assassinated on 18 June 1626 by an English soldier called John Lambert, who thrust Scott through the belly with a rapier as the minister, accompanied by his brother William and his nephew, also Thomas Scott, passed on his way to the church of St Peter at Utrecht. He was buried in Utrecht. The assassin was tortured and eventually executed, but consistently denied acting at the instigation of priest or Jesuit; he appears to have been motivated either by some peculiarly intense spiritual derangement, or else a desire to avenge Scott's supposed obstruction of his career. SEAN KELSEY

Sources *A briefe and true relation of the murther of Mr. Thomas Scott* (1628) • S. R. Gardiner, *History of England*, 10 vols (1899–1901), 3.392–3 • *DNB* • S. L. Adams, 'The protestant cause: religious alliance with the west European Calvinist communities as a political issue in England, 1585–1630', DPhil diss., U. Oxf., 1973 • S. Adams, 'Captain Thomas Gainsford, the "Vox spiritus" and the *Vox populi*', *BIHR*, 49 (1976), 141–4 • P. G. Lake, 'Constitutional consensus and puritan opposition in the 1620s: Thomas Scott and the Spanish match', *HJ*, 25 (1982), 805–25 • *STC, 1475–1640* • Venn, *Alum. Cant.* • M. Peltonen, *Classical humanism and republicanism in English political thought, 1570–1640* (1995)

Likenesses C. van de Passe the elder, line engraving, 1624, BM, NPG [*see illus.*] • W. Marshall, line engraving (after C. Passe), BM, NPG

Scott, Thomas (*fl.* **1602–1611**). *See under* Scott, Thomas (*d.* 1626).

Scott [Scot], **Thomas** (*d.* **1660**), politician and regicide, is of uncertain parentage and background. One theory is that he was born in Little Marlow, Buckinghamshire, the son of Thomas Scott, a London brewer, and his wife, Mary Sutton; another is that he was descended from Thomas Scot, a Yorkshireman, who married Margaret, widow of Benedict Lee of Burston, Norfolk, and daughter of Robert Pakington. Contemporaries claimed he was educated at Westminster School and at Cambridge, but there is no clear evidence for his admission to, attendance at, or graduation from either institution. He is said to have practised as an attorney, but appears not to have entered any of the inns of court. In 1626 he married Alice Allinson of Chesterford, Essex, from whom he is said to have inherited a plentiful estate.

Political career, 1644–1658 On 27 June 1644 Scott's name appears in the list of the parliamentary committee for Buckinghamshire. In 1645 he was returned to the Long Parliament, in place of Sir Ralph Verney, for Aylesbury, where he later served as recorder. His election was secured through the influence of the county committee. By the end of 1645 he had taken the covenant, as required. But he showed little sympathy for presbyterian policies. He was one of those members of the Commons who joined the army and signed the engagement of 4 August 1647. In December 1648 he declared that presbyterian was the new name adopted by cunning papists. In the same year he is credited with ordering the destruction of the monument of Archbishop Parker at Lambeth and the disinterment and burial of his remains under a dunghill.

In January 1649 Scott urged the impeachment of those lords who opposed bringing the king to justice, and helped to formulate the declaration establishing the supremacy of the House of Commons. On 9 January 1649, however, he supported resuming communications with the upper house, and his support for constitutional revolution clearly did not extend to anything so sweeping as the *Agreement of the People* proposed by John Lilburne. Scott declined an invitation to finalize the Leveller manifesto in December 1648. He was appointed one of the commissioners for the trial of Charles I, signed the king's death warrant, and was only absent twice during the trial [*see also* Regicides]. He was elected a member of each of the five councils of state elected during the Commonwealth, and in the election to the fifth was seventh on the list, obtaining 93 votes out of 114. A prominent member of the new government, sometimes styled its secretary of state, Scott went to Edinburgh shortly after it fell to Cromwell late in 1650, and was witness to the battle of Worcester. He was a strong supporter of the war with the Dutch, and also sat on the committee responsible for establishing the union with Scotland. The accounts of the Spanish ambassador at the court of the English Commonwealth indicate that Scott was in receipt of a pension from the king of Spain at this time.

From the end of 1647 Scott had regularly handled information and intelligence of a sensitive nature. This role was now formalized. On 1 July 1649 the council of state appointed Scott to 'manage the intelligence both at home and abroad for the state', and granted him £800 a year for that object (*CSP dom.*, *1649–50*, 221). This involved the employment of spies and secret agents, both at foreign courts and among the exiled royalists, and gave Scott an important influence both in foreign and domestic policy. His papers have mostly perished, but in 1660 he drew up an account of his proceedings as an intelligencer which throws some light on the history of the Commonwealth. The post also brought him wealth. In addition to owning property at Little Marlow he bought an estate from Sir John Pakington at Heydon Hall, and was one of the purchasers of Lambeth House. Although he claimed that his official gains were small, he also made a minor purchase of church lands.

Scott was a vehement supporter of the Commonwealth, opposed Cromwell's dissolution of the Rump Parliament in 1653, and remained hostile to him throughout the Protectorate. In the protector's first parliament he represented Wycombe (though his election was disputed) and was, according to Edmund Ludlow, 'very instrumental in opening the eyes of many young members' on the question of the legality of the new constitution (*Memoirs*, 2.391). In consequence he was one of those members excluded from the house for refusing to sign the engagement of 12 September 1654, accepting the government as settled in a single person and parliament. In 1656 Scott was returned to Cromwell's second parliament as member for Aylesbury, but failed in the attempt also to be chosen at Wycombe. The council of state, however, kept out Scott and about ninety more republicans. All those excluded were, however, admitted in January 1658 at the opening of the second session. Scott at once proceeded to attack the 'other house', which had been established in accordance with the *Humble Petition and Advice*. On 29 January he made a long oration, reviewing the whole history of the civil war, justifying the execution of the king ('resorted unto as the last refuge') and the abolition of the Lords, and denouncing the attempt to put fetters upon the people of England by reviving a second chamber (*Diary of Thomas Burton*, 3.109). 'Shall I,' he said, 'that sat in a parliament that brought a king to the bar, and to the block, not speak my mind freely here?' (ibid., 2.382).

Political career, 1659–1660 In Richard Cromwell's parliament of 1659, Scott, who again sat for Wycombe, was equally prominent among the opposition. He pronounced a panegyric on the Long Parliament, attacked Oliver Cromwell's foreign policy, which ran counter to his own Hispanophile tendencies, opposed the admission of the members for Scotland, and spoke against the recognition of Richard Cromwell and the powers given the protector by the constitution. On the fall of Richard Cromwell and the restoration of the Rump, Scott became a person of great influence in the new government. He was appointed a member of the council of state on 14 May 1659, and again on 31 December of the same year. He was also one of the six members of the intelligence committee appointed on 24 May 1659, and was finally given the sole charge of the intelligence department on 10 January 1660.

When Lambert interrupted the sittings of the Rump in October 1659, Scott entered into correspondence with General Monck, and took an active part in opposing the army. In conjunction with Sir Anthony Ashley Cooper he made an unsuccessful attempt to seize the Tower. When the Rump was once more restored he was made secretary of state on 17 January 1660, and sent to meet Monck on his march from Scotland and congratulate him on his success. Monck's biographer claimed that the general found Scott's company very irksome, regarding him as a spy sent by parliament, but that he treated him with great civility and professed to be guided by his advice. After Monck's march into the City and his threatening letter to the Rump of 11 February, Scott was again sent as parliamentary commissioner to him, and his reception opened Monck's eyes to the fact that he had been deluded. Ludlow accused Scott and Heselrige of then making shift for themselves, applying to Monck 'rather out of hopes to get their own termes then to get any on behalfe of the Commonwealth' (Ludlow, *Voyce*, 89).

The readmission of the members of the Commons excluded in 1648 put an end to Scott's secretaryship and his power, but before the dissolution of the Long Parliament he took the opportunity to affirm the justice of the king's execution, saying that he desired no better epitaph than 'Here lies one who had a hand and a heart in the execution of Charles Stuart.' Ludlow and some of the late council of state hoped to raise money and troops for a last effort to prevent the restoration of Charles II, but Scott, who had promised his assistance, finding the scheme had no prospect of success and that his arrest was imminent, resolved to retire to the country. In April 1660, finding himself, as he said, in danger of assassination, he took ship for Flanders. In spite of his disguise he was recognized at Brussels in June 1660 and attempts were made to seize him. These were baffled by the intercession on his behalf of the Spanish diplomat Don Alonso de Cardenas 'whom [Scott] had obleiged when Embassadour in England' (Ludlow, *Voyce*, 241). In the end Scott was persuaded to surrender himself to Sir Henry de Vic, the king's resident at Brussels, in the hope of saving his life by thus obeying the royal proclamation for the surrender of the regicides. The credit of capturing him or persuading him to surrender was much disputed.

Trial and death Scott was returned to England and at once sent to the Tower, on 12 July 1660. The House of Commons had excepted him from pardon on 6 June, and the exception was maintained in the Act of Indemnity. Some promise of life appears to have been made to him if he would discover the agents from whom he had obtained information of the plans of Charles II during the time he was intelligencer. He drew up accordingly 'A confession and discovery of his transactions', to which he appended a petition for his life, apologizing for his 'rash and over-lavish' words in parliament, and pleading his constant opposition to Cromwell, but his revelations were not held sufficiently valuable; he was tried with the other regicides on 12 October 1660. Scott pleaded not guilty, argued that the authority of parliament justified his actions, and, when his words about the king's death were urged against him, claimed that they were covered by the privilege of parliament. He was condemned to death and executed by hanging, drawing, and quartering at Charing Cross on 17 October 1660. He behaved with great courage, and died protesting that he had engaged in 'a cause not to be repented of' (Ludlow, *Voyce*, 242).

Scott is thought to have married three times, although this may be erroneous. In addition to his first wife he is thought to have wed Grace (1622–1646), daughter of Sir Thomas Mauleverer of Yorkshire, in 1644. However, Grace's memorial inscription in Westminster Abbey records her marriage to Colonel Thomas Scott, not impossibly the MP of that name who sat for Aldburgh in Yorkshire, with whom the regicide is frequently confused. The alleged third spouse who petitioned to visit Scott in 1660 was called Alice, and it is perfectly possible that this was indeed the regicide's first and only wife. Scott's son William was made a fellow of All Souls by the parliamentary visitors of Oxford, and graduated BCL on 4 August 1648. In April 1666 William, who was then an exile in the Netherlands, was summoned by proclamation to return to England. He preferred to remain in the Netherlands as a spy for the English government, who secured him by means of his mistress, Aphra Behn. Another son, Colonel Thomas Scott, was arrested in Ireland in 1663 for a plot, turned king's evidence, and was expelled from the Irish parliament. Alice Scott, daughter of the regicide, married William Rowe, who was scoutmaster-general in 1650.

C. H. Firth, *rev.* Sean Kelsey

Sources [T. Scott?], *A pair of cristall spectacles* (1648) • *Mercurius Pragmaticus*, 40–41 (26 Dec 1648–9 Jan 1649) • *JHC*, 4–8 (1644–67) • *CSP dom.*, *1649–60* • *Diary of Thomas Burton*, ed. J. T. Rutt, 4 vols. (1828) • S. R. Gardiner, *History of the great civil war, 1642–1649*, 4 vols. (1893); repr. (1987), vol. 4, p. 268 • C. H. Firth, 'Thomas Scot's account of his actions as intelligencer during the Commonwealth', *EngHR*, 12 (1897), 116–26 • *The writings and speeches of Oliver Cromwell*, ed. W. C. Abbott and C. D. Crane, 2 (1939) • D. Underdown, *Pride's Purge: politics in the puritan revolution* (1971) • B. Worden, *The Rump Parliament, 1648–1653* (1974) • E. Ludlow, *A voyce from the watch tower*, ed. A. B. Worden, CS, 4th ser., 21 (1978) • J. H. Ohlmeyer, *Civil war and Restoration in the three Stuart kingdoms: the career of Randal MacDonnell, marquis of Antrim, 1609–1683* (1993) • G. S. S. Yule and R. Zaller, 'Scott, Thomas', Greaves & Zaller, *BDBR*, 3.149–50 • Venn, *Alum. Cant.* • *The memoirs of Edmund Ludlow*, ed. C. H. Firth, 2 vols. (1894) • A. Davies, *Dictionary of British portraiture*, 1 (1979) • J. L. Chester, ed., *The marriage, baptismal, and burial registers of the collegiate church or abbey of St Peter, Westminster*, Harleian Society, 10 (1876)

Archives Bodl. Oxf., MSS Rawl. • Bodl. Oxf., MSS Tanner

Likenesses G. P. Harding, line engraving, pubd 1809, NPG • group portrait, line engraving (*The regicides executed in 1660*), BM; repro. in *Rebels no saints* (1660) • line engraving, NPG

Scott, Thomas (1705–1775), poet and hymn writer, was the younger son of Thomas Scott (1679/80–1746), Independent minister at Norwich (previously at Hitchin). Daniel *Scott (1694–1759) was his uncle, Joseph Nicoll *Scott (1702/3–1769) his brother, and Elizabeth *Scott (1707/8–1776) his sister. He was born at Hitchin and educated for the ministry at Kibworth dissenters' academy in Leicestershire. One of his fellow pupils was Philip Doddridge, the hymn writer, who later became a close friend and admirer of Scott's father and sister: Doddridge said of the father, 'I believe he was one of the holiest & most benevolent Men upon Earth' (Humphreys, 4.515). Scott wrote poetry at the academy, but a subscription volume planned in 1723 and a poem printed in London in 1724 (Humphreys, 1.164, misdated 1722, and 440) have not been traced.

As a young man Scott took charge of a small boarding-school at Wortwell, Norfolk, and preached to the Independent congregation at Harleston. He revised the *Poems on Several Occasions* (1733) of Mary Masters and contributed six poems to the work. In 1733 he became minister of the congregation at Lowestoft, and in 1738 he succeeded Samuel Say as assistant to Samuel Baxter at St Nicholas Street Chapel, Ipswich. He preached the funeral sermon for Samuel Baxter (*d.* 13 July 1740), with the title *The Morality and Death of Good Ministers Improv'd*, published in Ipswich in the same year. In that sermon he said that he had known Baxter for two or three years only.

During his ministry at Ipswich, Scott published other sermons: *The Nature, Obligation and Advantage of National Fasts Consider'd* (1741; published 'at the Request of several of the Hearers'); *Great Britain's danger and remedy, in a discourse, delivered at Ipswich, on the day appointed for a general fast* (1757); and *The Reasonableness, Pleasure, and Benefit of National Thanksgiving* (1759; referring to the prosperity of the war with France, ascribed to 'the Blessing of Divine Providence').

Scott's poems include *England's Danger and Duty* (1745), on the Jacobite rising; *Reformation* (1746), a diatribe in heroic couplets against human wickedness, from Old Testament times to the Britain of Scott's day; and *A Father's Instructions to his Son* (1748), a poem dedicated to Arthur Onslow, speaker of the House of Commons, and full of Polonius-like advice to be careful in expenses, avoid drink and gambling, be modest and virtuous, and keep good acquaintance. These were followed in lighter mood by *The Anglers* (1758), eight dialogues about fishing, including one set locally on the River Orwell. The poems are enriched by comic notes, alluding usually to the state of eighteenth-century poetry.

In his own lifetime Scott was best known for *The Table of Cebes, or, The Picture of Human Life* (1754; reprinted in a modified version, without Scott's learned notes, in Dodsley's *Collection*, vol. 6, 1758), a kind of 'vanity of human wishes' poem; and *The Book of Job, in English Verse* (1771; 2nd edn 1773). The notes to both of these poems are laborious and detailed: indeed *Job* was said to be 'more valuable as a commentary than as a translation' (A. Chalmers, *General Biographical Dictionary*, 32 vols., 1812–17, 27.272).

Scott's poems and hymns appeared in his *Lyric Poems, Devotional and Moral* (1773), 'written in hope … of assisting well-disposed minds, in their noblest pleasures and improvements', and 'as a kind of little poetical system of piety and morals' (Preface). It contained hymns which were used in some eighteenth- and nineteenth-century hymn books, such as the Unitarian collection by Kippis and Rees of 1795. The best-known, according to Julian's *Dictionary of Hymnology* (1892, 1020) were 'Delay' ('Hasten, sinner, to be wise') and 'Persecution' ('Absurd and vain attempt! to bind / With iron chains the free-born mind'). Since Julian's entry of 1892, Scott's hymns have fallen completely out of use.

Scott remained as minister of the chapel at Ipswich until 1774, when he began to suffer from ill health. He was elected minister of an endowed chapel at Hapton, Norfolk. He died at Hapton in 1775, and is buried in the parish churchyard. His library was sold in 1777.

J. R. Watson

Sources J. Julian, ed., *A dictionary of hymnology* (1892) • *The correspondence and diary of Philip Doddridge*, ed. J. D. Humphreys, 5 vols. (1829–31) • *Calendar of the correspondence of Philip Doddridge*, ed. G. F. Nuttall, HMC, JP 26 (1979) • J. Browne, *A history of Congregationalism and memorials of the churches in Norfolk and Suffolk* (1877), 267–9, 288 • T. Scott, *The morality and death of good ministers* (1740) • Nichols, *Lit. anecdotes*, 3.672 • W. P. Courtenay, 'Mary Masters', *N&Q*, 10th ser., 3 (1905), 405 • *DNB*

Archives Congregational Library, London, corresp. • DWL, corresp. | Yale U., Osborn collection, corresp.

Scott, Thomas (1745–1842), army officer, was born on 25 December 1745, the second son of John Scott of Malleny, Midlothian, and his wife, Susan, the daughter of Lord William Hay of Newhall, the third son of John, second marquess of Tweeddale. The Scotts of Malleny were descended from John, the eldest son of Sir William Scott of Clerkington, appointed senator of the court of justice in 1642, by his second wife, Barbara, the daughter of Sir John Dalmahoy of that ilk.

Thomas Scott joined the 24th regiment of foot as an ensign on 20 May 1761 and in the following year served in Germany under the command of Ferdinand, duke of Brunswick. He was present at the battles of Wilhelmsthal and Fulda, where he carried the regimental colours. Between 1763 and 1769 he was stationed at Gibraltar, and on 7 June 1765 he obtained his lieutenancy. In 1776 he went from Ireland with his regiment to America. During the advance up Lake Champlain he distinguished himself with a party of natives with a surprise attack on a party of Americans who were cutting brushwood. He spent the winter at the native village of the lake of two mountains, securing the support of 100 warriors with whom he served in General Burgoyne's campaigns in 1777. He was promoted captain-lieutenant on 14 July before volunteering, in September, to make a perilous journey through the American lines disguised as a pedlar to open up communications between Burgoyne's army and New York. In his journal he recalled being betrayed by a guide and 'fired at by two sentinels at a distance of three or four yards from me' (Fonblanque, 288). The preceding messengers, who had attempted this journey, had been captured by the American troops and hanged. Scott reached Sir Henry Clinton on 8 October with details of Burgoyne's critical position at Saratoga, but by then the situation had deteriorated, and Burgoyne was forced to surrender on 17 October 1777. Promoted captain in the 53rd foot on 8 October 1777, Scott served on Sir John Johnson's two raids along the Mohawk River in 1780, then commanded for a year at Machilmackinac.

In 1788 Scott returned to Europe, and during the Nootka Sound crisis of 1790 he served as a marine in the fleet on HMS *Hannibal*. In March 1793 the 53rd left for the Netherlands under Sir Ralph Abercromby. Following service during the sieges of Valenciennes and Dunkirk, Scott was promoted major on 13 November for his exertions during the defence of Nieuport.

On 27 October 1794 Scott purchased the lieutenant-colonelcy of the Scotch brigade (2nd battalion, 94th regiment of foot); he served with his regiment at Gibraltar in 1795 before moving to the Cape of Good Hope. Having served in Cape Town in 1797–8 the Scotch brigade moved to India with General David Baird. Scott commanded a sepoy brigade at the storming of Seringapatam, the capital of Mysore, in 1799. In 1800 ill health compelled him to return home, but the East Indiaman in which he travelled was captured by a French privateer in the English channel; however, after some weeks in captivity he was exchanged. In January 1801 he was appointed brevet colonel, and in September 1802 he became inspecting officer of the Edinburgh recruiting district. In 1803 he was appointed deputy inspector-general of the recruiting service in north Britain and in August 1804 he was promoted brigadier-general. Scott became a major-general on 25 April 1808 and lieutenant-general on his retirement from the Scottish staff on 4 June 1813. During his fifty-two years of service he was never unemployed or placed on half pay. On 22 July 1830 he received the rank of general. In retirement he resided mainly at Malleny and was appointed deputy lieutenant for Midlothian. He died, unmarried, on 29 April 1842 at Malleny and was succeeded by his nephew Carteret George Scott.

E. I. Carlyle, *rev.* Alan Harfield

Sources J. Philippart, ed., *The military calendar*, 3rd edn, 5 vols. (1820) • Irving, *Scots.* • Burke, *Gen. GB* (1838) • R. Douglas and others, *The baronage of Scotland* (1798) • E. de Fonblanque, *Political and military episodes … derived from the life and correspondence of the Right Hon. John Burgoyne* (1876) • G. Paton, F. Glennie, and W. P. Symons, eds., *Historical records of the 24th regiment, from its formation, in 1689* (1892) • C. T. Atkinson, *The south Wales borderers, 24th foot, 1689–1937* (1937) • R. Cannon, ed., *Historical record of the fifty-third, or the Shropshire regiment of foot* (1849) • *Army List* (1762–1843)

Scott, Thomas (1747–1821), Church of England clergyman and biblical scholar, was born at Bratoft, Lincolnshire, on 4 February 1747, the son of John Scott (*d.* 1777), farmer, and his wife, Mary Wayet (*d.* 1777), the tenth of their thirteen children. He began his education as a day boy at burgh school and a year later at Benington School, near Boston, living with his brother and sister on one of his father's farms. At the age of ten he transferred to a school in Scorton, Yorkshire, and in September 1762 he was apprenticed to a surgeon in Alford but was dismissed after two months for some act of misconduct. After returning home he was sent by his father as a shepherd to a farm where he worked for nine years, only to find that his father intended to bequeath it to one of his brothers. In reaction, he took up again his Eton Greek grammar and his 'few torn Latin books' and in 1772 left home and enquired of a clergyman in Boston about taking orders. He so impressed this man and the archdeacon of Lincoln (Gordon) that he continued his studies and actually obtained a title to the curacy of Martin, near Horncastle. The bishop of Lincoln, John Green, however, rejected him, ostensibly for lack of his father's consent and supporting testimonials, but possibly also suspecting him of Methodism and objecting to his rustic manners and speech. Scott gained the necessary consent and testimonials and was duly ordained on 20 September 1772, being priested on 13 March 1773. He served only two weeks at Martin and was then appointed to the joint curacy of Stoke Goldington, where the rector was nephew by marriage to the bishop and also subdean of Lincoln, and Weston Underwood, Buckinghamshire, at £50 a year. He found the people of Stoke ignorant and ungodly, and those of Weston Roman Catholic, though 'A very pretty congregation comes constantly to church' (Scott, 36).

In 1775 Scott, perhaps not surprisingly, exchanged Stoke for Ravenstone, Buckinghamshire, where he lived for the next two years before moving to Weston Underwood. In the meantime on 5 December 1774 he had married Jane Kell (*d.* 1790) who originated from Hexham, Northumberland, and was at the time governess–companion in the household of Scott's friends, the Wrightes, in the nearby village of Gayhurst. Scott also continued his studies, especially in Hebrew, and had even entered his name shortly after ordination for the BD at Clare College, Cambridge, a course, however, which he did not pursue mainly on the grounds of expense. During these years John Newton, whom he at that time regarded as 'a methodist and an enthusiast', was ministering at Olney, close to the villages where Scott was curate (Scott, 41). He heard Newton preach and thought the sermon directed at himself. In January 1774 he felt guilty on learning that Newton

Thomas Scott (1747–1821), by Joseph Collyer the younger, pubd 1820 (after Laurence Joseph Cossé)

had visited two of his own dying parishioners. In May 1775 the two men met at a clergy visitation and engaged in a correspondence for the rest of that year, with Scott trying to stir controversy. It was also in that year that Scott found himself troubled by the Athanasian creed and the necessity of accepting it through article 8 of the Thirty-Nine Articles. This was in some degree the result of his Socinian views, possibly a legacy of his father's own espousal of such opinions. In 1777 however he experienced an evangelical conversion, doubtless the outcome of rigorous intellectual conviction, 'bringing his religious inquiries to a decisive result … upon the doctrines of the atonement, human depravity, the Trinity, justification, the work of the Holy Spirit and, finally, on that of personal election' (ibid., 77). In his new-found fervour he renounced cards and the theatre, and preached and lectured five times a week, his addresses often lasting for an hour. The story is told in his spiritual autobiography, *The Force of Truth*, which received stylistic polishing from the poet Cowper, also living in Olney at this time, and was published on 26 February 1779.

Scott himself moved to Olney on 25 March 1781, replacing the unsatisfactory successor to Newton who had left for London in 1780. It was a reluctant and in many ways unhappy move, not least because of the presence in the town of both Anglican and dissenting Calvinists of disputatious temperament and antinomian inclinations. Despite his own acceptance of the doctrines of personal election, there was always a strong moral and practical emphasis in Scott's teaching that led to accusations of Arminian leanings, criticism in no way mollified by his own scrupulous refusal to compromise in any way. It was at Olney indeed that Scott experienced another intellectual crisis about doctrine, this time as to the admissibility of infant baptism which, however, he resolved on the analogy with the Abrahamic covenant. Of his stay in Olney he wrote:'I am very unpopular in this town, and preach in general to small congregations' (Scott, 134), though he thought later that he had made a deeper and apparently more lasting impression than he had realized when he left in 1785.

In that year Scott was elected morning preacher and visiting chaplain to the patients at the Lock Hospital in London for reformed prostitutes. There were problems—the board was divided, there was a lot of hyper-Calvinism, and Scott, with his provincial roughness, compared ill alongside his polished colleague Charles Edward De Coetlogon. As so often, he complained of being more meanly rewarded financially than he felt he had been led to expect. Besides his position at the hospital, which yielded £80 a year, he was able in February 1790 to secure an afternoon lectureship at St Mildred's, Bread Street, producing £30 a year, and a preaching engagement on alternate Sunday mornings at six o'clock at St Margaret, Lothbury, involving a 3 mile walk in each direction and paying 7*s*. 6*d*. a time. His main difficulties, however, remained with the governors of the Lock Hospital and their attempts to make him accord with their own views, to which he responded with characteristic uncompromising firmness: 'Gentlemen … you possess authority sufficient to change me *for* another preacher, whenever you please, but you have no power to change me *into* another preacher. You cannot induce me to alter my method of preaching' (Scott, 156–7). Whatever may have been the views of the governors, Scott was popular with the inmates of the hospital, and in 1787 he was instrumental in setting up an asylum refuge for the women on their discharge, itself a prototype for similar institutions in Dublin, Bristol, Hull, and other cities.

After his wife's death in 1790 Scott married a lady by the name of Egerton in March or early April 1791. He remained in London for a further decade, but failing health compelled him to resign his work at St Margaret, Lothbury, in 1801, and on 22 July of that year he was instituted to the living of Aston Sandford, a village in Buckinghamshire, where with a stipend of less than £180 per year he found it necessary to build a parsonage house. He remained in the metropolis for a while, and indeed became sole chaplain at the Lock Hospital at £150 per year on 25 March 1802. A year later, however, he moved to Aston Sandford. There he undertook the training of missionaries for the Church Missionary Society, of which he was a founding father at the Eclectic Society meeting in March 1799, its first secretary (until 8 December 1802), and the preacher of its first anniversary sermon at St Ann Blackfriars on 26 May 1801. With age his lifelong asthma grew worse and he was increasingly afflicted with deafness. He died at Aston Sandford on 16 April 1821 and was buried there on 23 April, but his funeral sermon by Daniel

Wilson of Islington (later bishop of Calcutta) was preached in the parish church of Haddenham because that of Aston was too small for the occasion.

Scott was a prolific writer. His *Theological Works* (10 vols., 1823–5) was edited by his son John, as was his *Letters and Papers* (1824). During his lifetime Scott's principal works, in addition to *The Force of Truth* mentioned above, included *Essays on the most Important Subjects in Religion* (1794), *Sermons on Select Subjects* (1796), an annotated edition of *The Pilgrim's Progress* (1795), *Four Sermons on Repentance* (1802), *Remarks on the Bishop of Lincoln's Refutation of Calvinism* (1812), and *The Articles of the Synod of Dort* (1818). There was also a posthumous volume of *Village Discourses* (1825). His major work, however, for which he is now alone remembered, was his commentary on the Bible (4 vols., 1788–92). He agreed with the publisher Thomas Bellamy to produce 100 weekly numbers at a fee of 1 guinea a number. In the end it ran to 174 numbers, but its production had a history both chequered and costly. After fifteen numbers Scott was told that he himself would have to finance the continuance. Bellamy went bankrupt; Scott had lent him money and was now left with his own debts of about £500. In addition he became involved in chancery suits first with the printer who had followed Bellamy and then, having sold the copyright in 1810 for £2000, in a further suit about the publication of the third edition. In 1813 he still found himself in debt to the tune of £1200, but an appeal to Charles Simeon, who gave £590, and to other friends and sympathizers enabled him by 25 February 1814 to say that he had received at least £2000 in little more than two months.

Scott saw the Bible as inspired by the Holy Spirit, but he also claimed a divine–human encounter in which each writer contributed of his own individuality to what was written. He also stressed the need to read each part in that sense in which it is proposed as truth, recognizing the presence of differing genres in the various books. He sought to reinforce interpretation by confirmatory cross-reference and insisted on the primacy of doctrine and precept over fact. He accepted the role of reason in examining the text, understanding the language, and discerning the meaning. Nevertheless, as Sir James Stephen noted in his essay 'The evangelical succession', Scott lacked the intellectual equipment to elucidate adequately as well as the imagination to respond deeply; and, to compound these deficiencies, his literary style, though plain and lucid, was also monotonous and pedestrian. These same limitations appear also to have marked his preaching which was, however, perhaps a little incongruously described as being vigorous and inspiring. There is indeed much in his writing as well as in his estimates of his own unpopularity that suggests a critical, not to say querulous, spirit. He was severe and irascible, but at the same time candid, dedicated, and sincere. He had the approval of William Wilberforce, who did not think well of Scott's colleague at the Lock Hospital, De Coetlogon. In particular, Wilberforce appreciated Scott's 'strong sense, the extensive acquaintance with Scripture, the accurate knowledge of the human heart, and the vehement and powerful appeals to the conscience' (Pratt, 29). The moral element in his preaching often led to doubts about his Calvinism among those of an antinomian inclination, but Scott's rejection of the high Calvinistic doctrine of predestined damnation was one reason which commended him to the young John Henry Newman, who in his *Apologia* acknowledged Scott as 'the writer who made a deeper impression on my mind than any other, and to whom (humanly speaking) I almost owe my soul' (J. H. Newman, *Apologia pro vita sua*, ed. M. J. Svaglic, new edn, 1990, 18).

John Scott (1777–1834), eldest son and biographer of the above, born in April 1777 at Ravenstone and baptized on 7 July 1777 at Weston Underwood, was educated at Magdalene College, Cambridge, graduating BA in 1799 and MA in 1803. He became curate to Thomas Dykes at St John's, Hull in 1799 and was appointed master of Hull grammar school in 1800. He became lecturer at Holy Trinity, Hull, on 4 August 1801 and simultaneously vicar of North Ferriby, then in the gift of Wilberforce. He added the vicariate of St Mary Lowgate, Hull, in 1816, and was there succeeded in turn first by his son and then his grandson. He was prominent in the work of the Hull Tract Society and the local branches of the Bible Society and the Church Missionary Society, as well as promoting religious education and anti-slavery activity and opposing Catholic emancipation. He published *Five Sermons on Baptism* (1812) and continued Joseph Milner's *Church History* as well as defending it in his *Vindication* (1834) against H. J. Rose and other detractors. His *Life* of his father was first published in 1822.

Thomas Scott (1780–1835), the fourth son, born on 9 November 1780, was educated at Queens' College, Cambridge, graduating BA in 1805 and MA in 1808. He was curate of Emberton, Buckinghamshire, in 1805–6 and first perpetual curate of Wappenham, Northamptonshire (1806–33), where he had to build the vicarage which subsequently had to be demolished because of its poor construction. In 1806 he married Euphemia Lynch (1785–1853), only daughter of Dr Lynch of Antigua; they had thirteen children, including the architect Sir George Gilbert *Scott. In 1833 he became rector of Wappenham, where there had been no resident incumbent for more than a century and where Thomas, his eldest child, succeeded him after his death on 24 February 1835. His sermons with a memoir by his brother-in-law Samuel King (adapted from the original in the *Christian Observer*, April 1835) appeared in 1837.

Benjamin Scott (1788–1830), the youngest son, born on 29 April 1788, was also educated at Queens' College, Cambridge, graduating BA in 1810 and MA in 1813. He was curate to Edward Burn at Birmingham and subsequently vicar of Bidford and Salford Priors, Warwickshire (1826–30). He died on 30 August 1830 at Llandegley, Radnorshire, where he was buried. His *Sermons* (1831) was edited by his brother Thomas.

ARTHUR POLLARD

Sources J. Scott, *Life of the Rev. Thomas Scott*, 9th edn, revd (1836) • A. C. Downer, *Thomas Scott the commentator* (1909) • J. H. Pratt, ed., *The thought of the evangelical leaders: notes on the discussions of the Eclectic Society, London, during the years 1798–1814* (1856); facs. edn (1978) • J. Stephen, 'The evangelical succession', in J. Stephen, *Essays in ecclesiastical biography*, 4th edn, 2 (1860) • M. Seeley, *The later evangelical fathers* (1879) • A. Pollard, 'Anglican evangelical views of the

Bible, 1800–1850', *The Churchman*, new ser., 74 (1960), 166–74 • J. Lawson, *A town grammar school through six centuries: a history of Hull grammar school against its local background* (1963) • *DNB* • Venn, *Alum. Cant.*

Likenesses J. Collyer the younger, line engraving, *c*.1820, BM • J. Collyer the younger, line engraving, pubd 1820 (after L. J. Cossé), BM, NPG [*see illus.*] • J. Collyer the younger, line engraving, pubd 1820 (after L. J. Cossé), U. Birm. L., Church Missionary Society Archives • W. Bond, engraving, 1822 (after L. J. Cossé), repro. in Scott, *Life of the Rev. Thomas Scott* • H. Meyer, engraving (after L. J. Cossé), repro. in Scott, *Letters and papers*, ed. J. Scott (1824) • stipple, NPG; repro. in *New Baptist Magazine* (1826)

Scott, Thomas (1780–1835). *See under* Scott, Thomas (1747–1821).

Scott, Thomas (1808–1878), freethinker, was born on 28 April 1808 in France, where he was brought up as a Roman Catholic and became a page at the court of Charles X. Having an independent fortune, he travelled widely, and spent some time among North American Indians. About 1856 he grew dissatisfied with Christianity, and in 1862 he started issuing tracts advocating 'free enquiry and the free expression of opinion'. These were printed at his own expense, and given away mostly to the clergy and cultured classes. Between 1862 and 1877 he issued, first from Mount Pleasant, Ramsgate, afterwards from Norwood, upwards of 200 separate pamphlets and books, which were ultimately collected in sixteen volumes. Scott's range of contacts is shown by his writers, who included Unitarians such as F. W. Newman, M. D. Conway, and R. R. Suffield, Anglicans such as Bishop Samuel Hinds and E. V. Neale, theosophists such as Annie Besant, and others such as Dr G. G. Zerffi and J. A. Symonds. Scott also reprinted such works as Bentham's *Church of Englandism and its Catechism Examined* (1818) and David Hume's *Dialogues on Natural Religion*. His own contributions to the series were slight, but he suggested subjects, revised them, discussed all points raised, and made his house a salon for freethinkers. He corresponded quite frequently with Gladstone, who respected his work. Scott was a competent Hebrew scholar, and saw through the press J. W. Colenso's work on the Pentateuch and book of Joshua in the absence of the bishop from England. He also revised *Ancient Faiths Embodied in Ancient Names* by Thomas Inman. Scott put his name on *The English Life of Jesus* (1872), a work designed to do for English readers what Strauss and Renan had done for the French and Germans; but the work is said to have been written in part by the Revd Sir George W. Cox. Scott also wrote a number of pamphlets, mostly on aspects of Christian evidences. He became the patron of Charles Voysey, establishing a theistic church in 1870 and moving to Upper Norwood to be near it. Scott died at 11 The Terrace, Upper Norwood, London, on 30 December 1878. He was married, and his wife survived him.

J. M. Wheeler, *rev.* H. C. G. Matthew

Sources *National Reformer* (5 Jan 1879) • *The Times* (15 Jan 1879) • *The Freethinker* (24 March 1879) • Boase, *Mod. Eng. biog.* • A. Taylor, *Annie Besant: a biography* (1992) • Gladstone, *Diaries*

Archives BL, corresp. with W. E. Gladstone, Add. MSS 44434–44450 *passim*

Likenesses photograph, repro. in A. Besant, *An autobiography* (1893), 112 [*see illus.*]

Thomas Scott (1808–1878), by unknown photographer

Scott, Thomas McLaughlin [Tom] (1918–1995), poet and literary critic, was born on 6 June 1918 at 25 Newlands Drive, Partick, Glasgow, the son of William Kerr Scott, shipyard boilermaker, and Catherine Young Scott, *née* Baillie, shop assistant. He suffered a traumatic accident in early childhood: while reaching for a book on an upper shelf he upset a boiling kettle and was seriously scalded. Hospital treatment was long and painful, and in the course of it he contracted scarlet fever. In consequence he began his education, at Thornwood School in Glasgow, two years late.

In 1931 his father lost his job and the family was uprooted to St Andrews, where Scott senior became a building labourer in the employ of Tom's maternal grandfather, a master builder. Tom attended Madras College, St Andrews, until he was fifteen (1933), when he left school to become a butcher's message boy. D'Arcy Wentworth Thompson, professor of zoology at St Andrews University, noticed him on his bicycle round, looking intently at a bird. Thompson got chatting to him and was impressed by the intellectual curiosity of a working-class lad who knew nothing of the rarefied life of the official students. Scott often recorded his debt to Thompson's tutelage. The St Andrews years, variously inspiring and frustrating, were the making of his sequence of autobiographical poems in Scots, *Brand the Builder* (1975). This work laments the Anglicization of the ancient university and the condition of its cathedral, left in ruins after the depredations of the protestant reformers. The decline of St Andrews was for Scott symptomatic of the vandalization of Scottish culture since the Reformation and the union with England.

Scott considered poetry to be 'verse that sings', and for a time his ambition was to become a singer (*Agenda*, 42). A labouring job under his grandfather and his uncle ended acrimoniously, and with unemployment a course of singing lessons came to an end. When war broke out in 1939 he was posted to the pay corps, first in Perth and later in Manchester, where the bombing raids provoked 'Sea Dirge', his first published poem (*Poetry London*, 1941). He served in Lagos, Nigeria, from May 1941 to June 1943 and subsequently lived in London during the late 1940s and early

1950s; various jobs included a spell at Ealing Studios as an extra in such films as *Oliver Twist* (1948). He befriended the poets W. S. Graham and Dylan Thomas, and went through a phase as a poet of the New Apocalypse, a literary movement founded in the 1930s by Henry Treece and J. F. Hendry.

On 12 May 1951, in London, Scott married Bertha Elizabeth Lang, *née* Marks, a divorcée who was a dress designer, painter, and sculptor. The receipt of an Atlantic Award in literature enabled him to visit Italy and Sicily, where he discovered his Scots-language voice, especially in the poem 'Telemakhos'. With T. S. Eliot's encouragement and Hugh MacDiarmid's example he undertook his Scots translations *Seevin Poems o Maister Francis Villon* (1953). At the invitation of Edwin Muir, who was at that time its warden, he attended Newbattle Abbey College for working men, at Dalkeith, Midlothian; he subsequently took an MA and, with the aid of a Carnegie fellowship, a PhD in English and Scottish language and literature at the University of Edinburgh.

In 1956 Scott moved to St Vincent Street, Edinburgh; that year saw the publication of *An Ode ti New Jerusalem*, a testament to his ethical socialism. On 14 March 1959 he was divorced from Elizabeth. Nineteen sixty-three was the year of *The Ship and Ither Poems*, whose title-poem exemplifies his belief that only the long poem, not the short lyric, could express an expansive, integrated vision of life; it takes its cue from the sinking of the *Titanic* but the literal narrative is enriched by layers of symbolic evocation of man's ambivalent past and uncertain future. On 27 April 1963 he married a fellow student, (Margaret) Heather (*b.* 1934/5), daughter of Eric Cyril Fretwell, a civil servant, and his wife, Ivy Lillian, *née* Johnson. They had three children.

The monograph *Dunbar: a Critical Exposition of the Poems* (1966) is as much the work of a practising poet as of a scholar; here Scott analyses the supreme craftsmanship, typical of the medieval Scots 'makars', which he sought to emulate in his own creative output. He was a Scot of European mind, like his revered makars. In the course of his poetic career he translated Baudelaire and also Dante, whose 'polysemous allegory' he considered the noble precursor of the 'polysemous veritism' more appropriate to poets, like himself, who were working in a scientific age (T. Scott, 'Lament for the Great Music', *Agenda*, 5(4)–6(1), autumn–winter 1967–8, 20). His own poetry was in turn translated into Italian by Nat Scammacca, Enzo Bonventre, and Carla Sassi. He edited the anthologies *The Oxford Book of Scottish Verse* (with John Mac Queen, 1966) and *Late Medieval Scots Poetry* (1967). His anti-war poems included in *At the Shrine o the Unkent Sodger* (1968) paid tribute to Albert Schweitzer's 'reverence for life'.

In 1968 Scott moved with Heather to 3 Duddingston Park, Edinburgh, where he lived for the rest of his life. He briefly taught English literature for the Open University during the 1970s but mainly earned his living from freelance writing. His edition of the *Penguin Book of Scottish Verse* appeared in 1970. In the book-length poem on evolution, *The Tree* (1977), he maintained that human beings were 'not fallen angels' but 'rising animals'. Another anti-war volume, *The Dirty Business*, was published in 1986. His *Collected Shorter Poems* (1993) was supplemented by the posthumous collection *Pervigilium Scotiae* (1997), a volume shared with his fellow Scottish poets Sorley MacLean and Hamish Henderson. His book-length history of Scottish literature remains mostly unpublished.

Tall, formidable, outspoken, Scott despised theorizing academics; in his student days he had a physical contretemps with one of the lecturers. He satirized the careerist politicians and intellectuals who, in his opinion, had betrayed Scottish political and cultural values. In 1985 he was diagnosed with myeloma; typically he universalized his cancer as both symbol and symptom of a world despoiled by pollution and money values. He died on 7 August 1995, aged seventy-seven, at the Royal Infirmary, Edinburgh, and was cremated at the city's Warriston cemetery. TOM HUBBARD

Sources T. Scott, 'Autobiographical note', *Scotia Review*, 13–14 (Aug–Nov 1976), 32–8 • private information (2004) [H. Scott; S. G. Green] • T. Hubbard, 'Tom Scott: a voyager in verse', *The Herald* (8 Aug 1995) • T. Hubbard, 'Reintegrating Scots: the post-Macdiarmid makars', *The history of Scottish literature*, 4: *Twentieth century*, ed. C. Craig (1987), 179–93 • *Chapman Review*, 47–8 (spring 1987) • J. D. McClure, *Language, poetry and nationhood: Scots as a poetic language from 1878 to the present* (2000) • *Agenda*, 30/4–31/1 (1993) [*Tom Scott special issue*] • personal knowledge (2004) • b. cert. • m. cert. [Margaret Heather Fretwell] • d. cert.

Archives NL Scot., corresp. and papers • NL Scot., literary corresp. and papers • U. Edin. L., letters | U. Leeds, corresp. with George Barker | SOUND NL Scot., *Poems of Tom Scott read by Tom Scott et al.* (1995), 2 audiocassettes • Scottish Poetry Library, 'Tom Scott reads his poetry', unpublished audiocassette made for the Scottish Poetry Library by Tom Scott, (1986)

Likenesses J. A. Cairns, pencil drawing, repro. in *Chapman Review* • A. Gray, portrait, repro. in *Chapman Review* • double portrait, photograph (with David Morrison), repro. in Scott, 'Autobiographical note' • drawings, repro. in *Chapman Review* • photographs, repro. in *Agenda*

Wealth at death £124,404.12: confirmation, 27 Sept 1995, *CCI*

Scott, Sir Walter, of Buccleuch (*c.*1490–1552), border chieftain, was the eldest son of Sir Walter Scott of Buccleuch (*d.* 1504) and his wife, Elizabeth Ker of Cessford (*d.* 1548). He was married three times: first to Elizabeth Carmichael, with whom he had two sons, David and Sir William Scott of Kirkurd, both of whom died in the lifetime of their father; secondly to Janet Ker, widow of George Turnbull of Bedrule, from whom he was divorced; and thirdly, by June 1544, to Janet Beaton (*d.* 1569), widow of Sir James Crichton of Cranstoun Riddel and divorced wife of Simon Preston of Craigmillar, with whom he had two sons, Walter and David, and three daughters, Grisel, Janet, and Margaret. He also had an illegitimate son, Walter Scott of Goldielands. He is referred to in contemporary sources as either Sir Walter Scott of Buccleuch (in Rankilburn, in the south-east portion of the old shire of Selkirk), or else of Branxholme, his main residence, near Hawick in Teviotdale.

Buccleuch was a minor when his father died in 1504 and his affairs were consequently at first in the hands of a tutor, Walter Scott of Howpasley. He may have been knighted immediately before the battle of Flodden in

1513. He played a prominent part in the political struggles of the minority of James V, when various factions vied for control of the young king. He supported the regent Albany until the latter's final departure for France in 1524, and thereafter was associated with the powerful earl of Lennox. With the earls of Angus and Lennox and the master of Kilmaurs he made a night attack on Edinburgh in November 1524 in an unsuccessful coup. After the king had fallen into Angus's hands late in 1525 Buccleuch was foremost in opposing his erstwhile ally. On 25 July 1526 he led a force of Scotts, Kers, and Turnbulls against Angus at Darnwick, near Melrose, in an attempt to wrest the king from his clutches. He supported a further unsuccessful effort to rescue the king from Angus at Linlithgow the following September, when Lennox, its leader, was slain.

The historian Lindsay of Pitscottie, writing in the 1570s, is clear that Buccleuch had been encouraged by the king to appear in arms against him at Melrose. No doubt it was through the influence of the king that the worst Buccleuch would suffer for this apparent treason would be a period of exile in France. Once James assumed control of government in the summer of 1528 Buccleuch was absolved of any treasonable behaviour and was rewarded on 14 July 1528 with appointment as warden of the western portion of the middle march. It was reported in London at this time that he was one of a small group who ruled and advised the king. In 1529 he was given Angus's former lordship of Jedburgh Forest.

Buccleuch was often to the fore in outbreaks of Anglo-Scottish hostilities. Along with the Kers he mounted a devastating raid into the English middle march in the winter of 1532 with a force of 3000 men in retaliation for the ravaging of his own lands by the earl of Northumberland. The men of Teviotdale again raided Northumberland in December 1542, presumably either led by Buccleuch or with his connivance. However, in other respects Buccleuch does not appear to have been well fitted for a career in the service of James V, and he was to suffer several periods in ward in the 1530s, with good reason as far as royal authority was concerned. Thus in 1530 he was imprisoned for failing to keep order on the march, and in 1535 he was charged with assisting the English warden, William, Lord Dacre, in burning Cavers and Denholm in Roxburghshire during the winter of 1532–3. As this last instance shows, Buccleuch was like other leaders on both sides of the border in that his activities were not confined to raiding the other side, and he was even charged with lifting the late king's sheep from Melrose Abbey at the end of 1542. Presumably it was such activities which led to his being dubbed Wicked Wat in a late eighteenth-century history of his family.

After James V's death in 1542 the patronage of Cardinal David Beaton, a kinsman of his second wife, brought Buccleuch in 1543 the keepership of Newark Castle. Buccleuch is credited by Buchanan with an important part in the victory over the English at Ancrum Moor on 27 February 1545: he advised that the Scots should all fight on foot, and the English, thinking that the removal of their horses meant that the enemy was taking flight, made an ill-judged and disastrous attack. Buccleuch also fought at Pinkie on 10 September 1547. Despite being threatened and cajoled by the English, and suffering severe losses at their hands, he refused in the wars of the 1540s either to desert the Scottish cause or, unlike many of his neighbours, to take English assurance. In 1550 he was again entrusted with an important post, that of warden of half of the middle march, followed by the captaincy of Liddesdale in 1551.

Buccleuch had inherited significant landholdings in the middle march from his father. In 1519 he was appointed bailie of the lands of Melrose Abbey, a position which became hereditary in his family. He was also provost of the burgh of Selkirk in 1549. As the head of an important border kindred he might have been expected to have been relied on more by royal authority, but for most of his lifetime the services of his neighbours, the Kers, were preferred. Buccleuch had inherited a feud with the Kers which flared up intermittently between periods of apparent co-operation and *rapprochement*, as in 1530 when he married Janet Ker. But the Kers were often politically and militarily opposed to the Scotts in the wars of the 1540s, and relations must have been exacerbated when in June 1551 Buccleuch replaced Walter Ker of Cessford as warden of the middle march. When a party of Kers murdered Buccleuch on the high street of Edinburgh on the night of 4 October 1552, it is unlikely that they had forgotten that in 1526 Andrew Ker of Cessford had died at Melrose at the hands of one of their victim's servants. Buccleuch was succeeded by his grandson Walter, son of Sir William Scott of Kirkurd. DAVID H. CALDWELL

Sources W. Fraser, *The Scotts of Buccleuch*, 2 vols. (1878) • *LP Henry VIII* • J. Bain, ed., *The Hamilton papers: letters and papers illustrating the political relations of England and Scotland in the XVIth century*, 2 vols., Scottish RO, 12 (1890–92) • R. K. Hannay, ed., *Acts of the lords of council in public affairs, 1501–1554* (1932) • [G. Buchanan], *The history of Scotland translated from the Latin of George Buchanan*, ed. and trans. J. Aikman, 6 vols. (1827–9) • *The historie and cronicles of Scotland … by Robert Lindesay of Pitscottie*, ed. A. J. G. Mackay, 3 vols., STS, 42–3, 60 (1899–1911) • W. Scot, *A true history of several honourable families of the right honourable name of Scot*, 3rd edn (1786) • G. Burnett and others, eds., *The exchequer rolls of Scotland*, 15 (1895) • J. M. Thomson and others, eds., *Registrum magni sigilli regum Scotorum / The register of the great seal of Scotland*, 11 vols. (1882–1914), vol. 3 • *State papers published under … Henry VIII*, 11 vols. (1830–52) • *Scots peerage*, 2.228–30 • T. I. Rae, *The administration of the Scottish frontier, 1513–1603* (1966) • J. Cameron, *James V: the personal rule, 1528–1542*, ed. N. Macdougall (1998)

Scott, Walter, of Harden (*c.*1550–1629?), landowner and border reiver, also known as Wat o'Harden and Auld Wat Scott, was the son of William Scott of Todrig, who purchased the lands of Harden from Alexander, fifth Lord Home, about 1550. William Scott had died by 13 April 1563, when a *clare constat* was issued for Walter as his heir. On 22 June 1566, aged about sixteen, Walter Scott was officially seised in his Harden estates, and on 21 March 1567 he married Mary, daughter of John Scott of Dryhope, who was widely known as the flower of Yarrow for her exceptional beauty. They had seven children, William of Harden, Hugh of Greenhead, Walter of Essindean, Francis, Margaret, Esther, and Janet.

In the early 1590s Walter Scott was a supporter of Francis Stewart, first earl of Bothwell, and as such was pardoned, along with some of his kinsmen, on 4 September 1591. On 27 June 1592, however, Scott assisted the earl's raid upon Falkland Palace, and having ignored orders to attend the council afterwards was outlawed. His castle of Harden was destroyed by Walter Scott of Goldielands and Gideon Murray of Elibank. He remained active on Bothwell's behalf during the following winter, when with his brother William he led a well-organized attack on Drummelzier and Dreva and carried off 4000 sheep, 200 cattle, 40 horses, and goods valued at £2000.

Walter Scott features repeatedly in border ballads, and his name also makes several appearances in the more prosaic records of border crime, as both victim and perpetrator. In October 1580 his steadings were sacked by Martin Elliot of Bradley and the Armstrongs of Quhitlaugh, and eighty cattle and six horses were allegedly taken. Two months later, with Lady Margaret Douglas he laid a formal complaint against the Elliots, who were put to the horn after failing to appear before the privy council but who struck again against Scott on 15 December, plundering his lands in Hotscote. The events of the ballad 'Jamie Telfer' are thought to have occurred around this time: when the eponymous hero's cattle are lifted by English raiders, he secures the support of the entire Scott clan, including 'Wat o'Harden and his sons' (Fraser, *Scotts*, 179). When Walter Scott of Buccleuch organized the rescue of Kinmont Willie Armstrong from Carlisle Castle on 13 April 1596, the English warden Thomas, Lord Scrope, described Scott of Harden as 'the cheife man aboute Buclughe' (Bain, 2.120). Such exploits gave him an almost legendary reputation as a fighter and raider; it is claimed that his wife was in the habit of placing a pair of spurs before him when the larder was bare, as a signal that he must go reiving for his dinner, and Scott himself was said to have remarked of a haystack, 'Aye, if ye had fower legs ye wouldnae stand there lang' (Fraser, *Steel Bonnets*, 79).

His wife Mary having died, in 1598 Scott married Margaret Edgar of Wedderlie, widow of William Spottiswood of that ilk. They had a daughter, Margaret. Scott appeared a reformed man on 29 October 1602, when he subscribed a general band to control malefactors, but at the end of 1605 he was again in danger of outlawry, this time for poaching in the Northumbrian forest of Cheviot, Tynedale, and Redesdale. In 1611 a quarrel with the neighbouring Murrays of Elibank led to the imprisonment of his son William by Gideon Murray; to secure his release, according to the ballad 'Muckle-mouthed Meg' (later embellished by James Hogg and then Robert Browning), William was forced to marry Elibank's unattractive daughter Agnes, or 'Meg'. Two marriage contracts for the couple survive, the second attesting Walter's illiteracy, his name having been appended by a notary 'because I can nocht wryte' (Murray, 82).

On 13 June 1612 Scott was appointed a JP for Selkirkshire, though he continued to be involved in acts of disorder. In 1616 a quarrel with the Scotts of Bonnington over fishing rights in the River Ettrick led to the accidental death of his son Walter. In the years which followed, however, Scott of Harden emerged as a reliable local administrator, helping the earl of Buccleuch to clear his debts, continuing to act as JP, and even being considered as a possible sheriff of Selkirk in August 1621. Even so, he was still sometimes negligent. In January 1623 and July 1625 he failed to attend meetings to discuss Scottish wool exports to England, and on 18 January 1627 he was ordered to pay £200 to the treasurer-depute for failing to come to the Selkirk justice courts and quarter sessions on five occasions between 1623 and 1625. He is last recorded in April 1629, and probably died soon afterwards, though the exact date is unrecorded. J. R. M. SIZER

Sources W. Fraser, *Scotts of Buccleuch*, 1 (1878) • W. R. Carre, *Border memories: sketches of prominent men and women on the border*, ed. J. Tait (1876) • J. Bain, ed., *The border papers: calendar of letters and papers relating to the affairs of the borders of England and Scotland*, 2 vols. (1894–6), vol. 2 • *Scots peerage*, 7.73–7 • J. M. Thomson and others, eds., *Registrum magni sigilli regum Scotorum / The register of the great seal of Scotland*, 11 vols. (1882–1914), vol. 6 • G. M. Fraser, *The steel bonnets* (1971) • E. J. Cowan, ed., *The ballad in Scottish history* (2000) • A. C. Murray, *Memorials of Sir Gideon Murray of Elibank* (1932) • *Reg. PCS*, 1st ser., vols. 5, 8–14 • *Reg. PCS*, 2nd ser., vols. 1–2

Scott, Walter, of Buccleuch, first Lord Scott of Buccleuch (1565?–1611), landowner and border reiver, claimed to have been born in 1565 although it is possible that the actual date of his birth was several years later. He was the only son of Sir Walter Scott of Branxholm and Buccleuch (1549–1574) and Lady Margaret (*c.*1545–1640), eldest daughter of David Douglas, seventh earl of Angus, and subsequently wife of Francis *Stewart, first earl of Bothwell (1562–1612). Although a minor at his father's death, Walter received royal dispensation to disregard his minority and was retoured heir to the family estates on 3 July 1574. Margaret Douglas held the ward of her son but the main beneficiary of this action was James Douglas, earl of Morton, who was not only the regent who authorized the document but also the great-uncle and tutor of the recipient. Following the death of the previous laird, the Buccleuch estates were subject to intermittent reiving by both English and Scottish families such as the Kerrs, Armstrongs, Elliots, and Crosiers. Although Margaret Douglas tried to defend her son's lands by force of arms and by legal action, the reiving was an enduring feature of border life and continued uninterrupted until the early seventeenth century. Probably as a punishment for one such confrontation, in the early months of 1583 Scott, still a teenager, was warded in Blackness Castle. His subsequent escape and pardon by the king marked the start of a long and ambivalent series of dealings with his monarch.

In November 1585 Buccleuch raised the Scotts and marched with the earls of Angus, Mar, and Bothwell against the earl of Arran and James VI at Stirling Castle. Following Arran's departure from court, the laird returned to the border. The summer of 1586 was spent raiding English borderlands along with Bothwell and Lord Maxwell and, when these activities continued into the politically sensitive early months of 1587 (following

Queen Mary's execution), Buccleuch was warded in Edinburgh Castle (having previously appeared before the privy council 'touching good rule and quietness ... on the borders hereafter, under pain of treason' (*Reg. PCS*, 1st ser., 4.183). His disfavour was short-lived, however, and during the Armada crisis of 1588 the laird had a commission to protect Selkirkshire from the intrusion of strangers.

From an early age Buccleuch appears to have suffered from illness and in September 1590 he sought permission to travel to France to alleviate his gout. He spent the winter on the continent and made contacts in London, Paris, and Flanders. On his return and for much of 1590s he was a prominent figure at court. In May 1590 he had received recognition of royal favour when he was knighted at the coronation of Queen Anne. Initially, he had grown in influence at court and on the border with the assistance of his stepfather, the earl of Bothwell. However, following that earl's disgrace in mid-1591 Buccleuch was able to retain his authority, and indeed increase it. Although Buccleuch's allegiance to (and sympathy with) his stepfather was never entirely broken, he was prepared to consider his own best interests and disown the earl for political gain. In July 1591 he was rewarded with the office of keeper of Liddesdale. Shortly afterwards James reassessed the situation on the border and stripped Buccleuch of his new responsibilities and exiled him overseas (under penalty of £10,000 Scots). The exile was to have lasted for three years but within fifteen months (through the intervention of Queen Anne) the laird was granted permission to return home. At court Buccleuch was noted most often as being in the queen's favour—in 1595 she wished him to undertake guardianship of Prince Henry—and this protected him from the greater indignation of James VI. Somewhat surprisingly, Buccleuch also maintained an allegiance with Chancellor John Maitland, first Lord Maitland, until his death in 1595, and he made every effort to foster alliance with powerful courtiers such as Lord Hamilton, the earl of Mar, and the prior of Blantyre. Like his political allegiances, his religious inclinations were carefully cultivated. He was the hereditary patron of Rankilburn kirk and, in 1590, the possessor of a commission against Jesuits. While it is normally recognized that Buccleuch was a favourer of a general pro-English and protestant policy (to the extent that in 1599 James VI feared that Buccleuch was becoming too Anglicized), at least one contemporary, Lord Ralph Eure, suspected the laird of secretly favouring Catholicism.

Although Buccleuch's prominence at court meant more of his time was spent at his town house in Edinburgh, his family life remained firmly based on the border; his main residence remained Branxholm. It is likely that his sisters Mary and Margaret both married border lairds, and, on 1 October 1586, he had married Margaret Kerr, the sister of Sir Robert Kerr of Cesford (a long-time raiding partner). The marriage resulted in one son, Walter (*b.* *c.*1587), and three daughters, Margaret, Elizabeth, and Jean (Buccleuch also had two illegitimate offspring, John and Jean). Despite frequent absences, Buccleuch's stature on the border did not diminish and his involvement in cross-border raiding remained strong. To the English and Scottish government officials he was one of the greatest threats to peace on the border. In 1593 Buccleuch sided with the laird of Johnstone (his wife's cousin) against the laird of Maxwell in the feud that culminated in the battle of Dryfesdale Sands. Always one to keep his options open, several years later he sided with Maxwell against Johnstone. In 1594 Buccleuch was reappointed keeper of Liddesdale, having previously received more lands following the forfeiture of the earl of Angus and, on his eighth wedding anniversary, having received from the king a grant of his stepfather's comital lands. Since the earl's forfeiture these had belonged to Ludovick Stewart, duke of Lennox, and were only resigned by him three days after the king's grant. These estates added considerably to Buccleuch's wealth—although two years later Eure still reckoned 'his poverty great' (*Calendar of Border Papers*, 2, no. 283)—and helped counteract the fact that his mother continued to extract rent from her terce estates (whether legally or not). Acting as lord and keeper, he informed the unruly Liddesdale families that if any of them stepped out of line, he would hang them.

Buccleuch's most notorious escapade took place in 1596, when, under cover of darkness and with a group of eighty supporters, he removed 'Kinmont Willie' Armstrong from the prison of Carlisle Castle, to the distress of the garrison, the city, and the English court. The ultimate result, after considerable diplomatic pressure, was that in 1597 he was warded first in Edinburgh Castle and then in English custody at Berwick. By the mid-1590s it was thought that he had committed over twenty murders and he was considered 'the scourge of God [*flagellum Dei*] to his miserably distressed and oppressed neighbours' (*Calendar of Border Papers*, 2, no. 626). On 16 August 1599, when still in England, he was granted his traditional Scott lands as the newly erected barony of Branxholm. Before returning to Scotland he paid a nine-month visit to Paris for his health, where he was involved as a witness in a court case and revealed a complete inability with the language. Buccleuch would have been an obvious candidate to undertake more responsibility on the border after the union of the crowns, but in 1604 he was granted £6800 by the states general to fight in the Low Countries. He went himself and, as colonel and captain, headed a company of 200 borderers in the service of Prince Maurice of Nassau. Although he returned to Scotland following the truce of 1609, his troops remained on the continent and were still fighting (despite being unpaid) in 1611.

James VI considered that Buccleuch was 'a man of energy, prompt in counsel and action, powerful in fortune, force of arms and following' (Fraser, 1.231) and on 18 March 1606 issued a royal commission to the earl of Montrose to create Buccleuch, in the king's name, first Lord Scott of Buccleuch. This commission finally formalized the style of the laird family who for several generations had led a chameleon existence as lairds of Branxholm and Buccleuch. He continued to enjoy respect at court and on the border for the rest of his life and in February 1611 was appointed to the Scottish privy council. The appointment was of little practical value, however, as on 15 December 1611, at Branxholm, Scott—the Bold Buccleuch—died. He was buried at Hawick. His wife survived him.

ROB MACPHERSON

Sources W. Fraser, *The Scotts of Buccleuch*, 2 vols. (1878) • J. Bain, ed., *The border papers: calendar of letters and papers relating to the affairs of the borders of England and Scotland*, 2 vols. (1894–6) • *CSP Scot.* • G. Ridpath, *Border history of England and Scotland*, facsimile edn (1979) • *Reg. PCS*, 1st ser. • *Reg. PCS*, 2nd ser. • D. Calderwood, *The history of the Kirk of Scotland*, ed. T. Thomson and D. Laing, 8 vols., Wodrow Society, 7 (1842–9) • *Scots peerage* • [T. Thomson], ed., *The historie and life of King James the Sext*, Bannatyne Club, 13 (1825) • R. G. Macpherson, 'Francis Stewart, fifth Earl Bothwell, 1562–1612: lordship and politics in Jacobean Scotland', PhD diss., U. Edin., 1998
Archives NA Scot., GD 224

Scott, Walter, of Satchells (*b.* 1613, *d.* in or after 1688), soldier and genealogist, was the son of Robert Scott of Satchells, Roxburghshire, and his wife, Jean, daughter of Sir Robert Scott of Thirlestane, and the great-grandson of Walter Scott of Sinton and Margaret Riddell. The Satchells estate was so impoverished that he had to spend his youth herding cattle, but he ran away at sixteen to join the regiment which Walter Scott, earl of Buccleuch, took to the Netherlands in 1629. He was, by his own account, in active military service at home and abroad for fifty-seven years. He appears to have returned to Scotland before 1654, as his signature appears on a Scottish legal document of 12 September that year. He is said to have married and had a daughter called Gustava, in honour of King Gustavus Adolphus of Sweden.

At the advanced age of seventy-three Scott began his metrical *True history of several honourable families of the right honourable name of Scot, in the shires of Roxburgh, Selkirk, and others adjacent, gathered out of ancient chronicles, histories, and traditions of our fathers*. By his own admission he was illiterate, being barely able to sign his name, and so hired schoolboys to write to his dictation. He died some time after 1688, when his work was first printed. Four later editions appeared between 1776 and 1894. The work is often cited by genealogists of the Scott clan, and was highly valued by Satchells's namesake, Sir Walter Scott the novelist.

HENRY PATON, *rev.* ALEXANDER DU TOIT

Sources K. M. Scott, *Scott, 1118–1923* (1923), 56, 107 • W. Scott, *A true history of several honourable families of the right honourable name of Scot*, ed. J. G. Wenning (1894) • W. Fraser, *The Scotts of Buccleuch*, 1 (1878), xx–xxxi • J. G. Lockhart, *The life of Sir Walter Scott*, [new edn] (1896), 18–22
Wealth at death probably very little; 'no estate left except his designation', i.e. the by-name 'of Satchells': Sir Walter Scott, quoted in Fraser, *Scotts of Buccleuch*

Scott, Walter, earl of Tarras (1644–1693), nobleman, was born on 23 December 1644, the eldest son of Sir Gideon Scott of Highchester (*d.* 1676) and Margaret, daughter of Sir Patrick Hamilton of Preston and his wife, Elizabeth. On 9 February 1659, aged fourteen, he married, by special dispensation from the presbytery of Kirkcaldy, Mary, in her own right countess of Buccleuch (1647–1661), daughter of Francis Scott, second earl of Buccleuch (*d.* 1651) and his wife, Lady Margaret Leslie (*d.* 1688). She was eleven. The match was born out of the collusion of her mother, now countess of Wemyss, and his father, one of Mary's curators, to outmanoeuvre John Hay, second earl of Tweedale, Mary's uncle, whom they believed had designs on the Buccleuch estate. The couple were separated by the civil authorities until Mary reached her minority, when she ratified what had been done. Scott was not allowed to assume his wife's title, but on 4 September 1660 Charles II created him earl of Tarras, Lord Almoor and Campcastill for life. The countess died on 11 March 1661. After protracted legal proceedings, their marriage contract was reduced on the grounds of the countess's pupillarity at the time of the marriage; Tarras was refused the annuity promised him out of his wife's property. The Buccleuch title, meanwhile, passed to Mary's only surviving sister, Anne *Scott (1651–1732), who in 1663 married the king's son James Scott, duke of Monmouth.

From 1667 to 1671 Tarras travelled in France, Italy, and the Netherlands. Returning by the English court, he endeavoured in vain to move Charles II to grant him a provision out of the Buccleuch estates. On 31 December 1677 he married Helen, daughter of Thomas Hepburn of Humbie and granddaughter of Archibald *Johnston, Lord Wariston. They had five sons and five daughters. Toward the end of Charles's reign Tarras took part in the plots to exclude the duke of York from the throne. He was arrested in 1684 and, on his own confession, found guilty of complicity in Monmouth's treason and condemned to death on 5 January 1685. Owing, however, to his confession (urged by his wife and others), he obtained a remission, and was reinstated in his honours and lands by letters of rehabilitation on 28 June 1687. He died on 9 April 1693.

HENRY PATON, *rev.* DAVID MENARRY

Sources W. Fraser, *The Scotts of Buccleuch*, 1 (1878), 320–400 • *Scots peerage* • M. Lee, *The heiresses of Buccleuch* (1996) • *APS* • *Reg. PCS*, 1st ser. • *The diary of Mr John Lamont of Newton, 1649–1671*, ed. G. R. Kinloch, Maitland Club, 7 (1830), 141 • J. Nicoll, *A diary of public transactions and other occurrences, chiefly in Scotland, from January 1650 to June 1667*, ed. D. Laing, Bannatyne Club, 52 (1836), 248–9 • Buccleuch muniments from Dalkeith, NA Scot., GD 224 • NA Scot., Scott of Harden papers, GD 157 • M. D. Young, ed., *The parliaments of Scotland: burgh and shire commissioners*, 2 vols. (1992–3) • J. M. Thomson and others, eds., *Registrum magni sigilli regum Scotorum / The register of the great seal of Scotland*, 11 vols. (1882–1914), vol. 8, item 66, p. 21 • GEC, *Peerage*, new edn
Archives NA Scot., corresp. and papers • priv. coll. (NRA), corresp. and papers | NA Scot., Buccleuch muniments from Dalkeith, GD 224 • NA Scot., Lord Polwarth (Scott of Harden papers), GD 157
Likenesses portrait, repro. in Fraser, *Scotts of Buccleuch*

Scott, Sir Walter (1771–1832), poet and novelist, was born in College Wynd in the Old Town of Edinburgh on 15 August 1771, the tenth child of Walter Scott (1729–1799) and Anne Rutherford (1739?–1819). His father, son of Robert Scott (1699–1775), a prosperous border sheep farmer, and of Barbara Haliburton, became a writer to the signet in 1755, and had a successful career as a solicitor in Edinburgh. His mother was the daughter of Dr John Rutherford (1695–1779), professor of physiology in the University of Edinburgh, who had studied in Edinburgh, Rheims, and Leiden (under Boerhaave), and of his first wife, Jean Swinton. Scott's parents married in 1758, and had thirteen

Sir Walter Scott (1771–1832), by Sir Henry Raeburn, 1808

children: besides Walter, those who survived childhood were Robert (1767–1787), John (1769–1816), Anne (1772–1801), Thomas (1774–1823), and Daniel (1776?–1806).

Early years and education In 1932, and again in 1969 and 1970, Arthur Melville Clark argued that Scott was born in 1770, but his case was comprehensively destroyed by James C. Corson in 1970. Scott was indeed born on 15 August 1771. He seems to have been a healthy baby, but in the winter of 1772–3 he contracted what is now called poliomyelitis, and became permanently lame in his right leg. The best medical advice in Edinburgh was available; but there was, of course, neither diagnosis nor cure, and his maternal grandfather Rutherford advised that he be sent to his paternal grandfather's farm, Sandyknowe, near Smailholm in Berwickshire, to benefit from country air. Many attempts were made to cure Scott's disability (without success), and much (successful) effort over the years was given to improving the use of the leg. Throughout his life Scott was conscious of his lameness, but it seems to have caused no psychological damage. The physical feats of later life—like climbing the Castle Rock in Edinburgh (*Redgauntlet*, *Waverley Novels*, 1993–2004, 17.2–3), the fights in which he engaged after his return to Edinburgh (*Waverley Novels*, 1829–33, 1.xcii), the long walks he undertook in his late teens and twenties (Scott, 'Memoirs', 35–6), and his activity as a volunteer cavalryman—suggest that his lameness did not restrict him, but at least some of this physical activity, or perhaps even the reporting of physical activity, was deliberate overcompensation for his disability.

Scott lived at Sandyknowe from 1773 to 1778, apart from about a year spent in Bath where he was taken by his aunt Janet (or Jenny) Scott in the middle of 1775, a spell in 1776 with his family in their new home at 25 George Square, Edinburgh, and some weeks probably in 1778 at Prestonpans, near Edinburgh, where he went for sea bathing. In Sandyknowe he was in the company of adults and received much attention from his grandmother and aunt. In his 'Memoirs' he says that the earliest sources of the historical information that characterizes his work were 'the old songs and tales which then formed the amusement of a retired country family': his grandmother used to tell him 'many a tale of Wat of Harden, Wight Willie of Aikwood, Jamie Tellfer of the fair Dodhead, and other heroes, merrymen all of the persuasion and calling of Robin Hood and Little John' (Scott, 'Memoirs', 13). His uncles told him stories about the Jacobite rising of 1745 and the executions in Carlisle. His aunt Jenny read popular songs to him from works such as Allan Ramsay's *The Tea-Table Miscellany*, and he learned long passages off by heart from her reading. He was thus an active participant in a traditional oral culture, and at the same time was taking written literature back into the oral, in a reverse movement to his own later practice when he translated traditional into written narratives. Although he learned to read at a dame school in Bath in his fifth year, he was not unduly precocious as a reader; it was the narratives he learned from oral recitation that were crucial to his intellectual and imaginative development.

In 1778 Scott rejoined his own family in Edinburgh. At home he found he had siblings, two older brothers, a sister, and two younger brothers. He said he felt the change 'very severely', and talked of 'the agony which I internally experienced' (Scott, 'Memoirs', 19). Further, an anecdote presented long afterwards as fiction in 'My Aunt Margaret's Mirror' has the ring of personal experience:

> There is the stile at which I can recollect a cross child's-maid upbraiding me with my infirmity, as she lifted me coarsely and carelessly over the flinty steps, which my brothers traversed with shout and bound. I remember the suppressed bitterness of the moment, and, conscious of my inferiority, the feeling of envy with which I regarded the easy movements and elastic steps of my more happily formed brethren. (*Waverley Novels*, 1829–33, 41.298)

He took refuge in literature, and talks of 'reading aloud to my mother Pope's translation of Homer, which except a few traditionary ballads and the songs in Allan Ramsay's Evergreen was the first poetry which I perused' (Scott, 'Memoirs', 19). He continued to imbibe stories which later emerged in his novels: he first heard the story which forms the basis of *The Bride of Lammermoor* from his maternal great-aunt Margaret Swinton who died in 1780, and by the age of ten he had heard many tales of the Jacobite rising of 1745 from Alexander Stewart of Invernahyle, one of his father's favourite clients.

In 1779 Scott was sent to the high school of Edinburgh. He was a pupil there from 1779 to 1783, although Scott himself says that he was three years under Luke Fraser, and two under the rector, Dr Alexander Adam (Scott, 'Memoirs', 22). Latin dominated the curriculum, and while Fraser taught grammar, in which Scott did not do well, Adam was able to enthuse him with a love of literature. They read Caesar, Livy, Sallust, Virgil, Horace, and Terence; they were encouraged to translate the poets into English verse, and Scott's first such attempt, the description of Etna erupting in the third book of the *Aeneid*, was kept by his mother. Adam recognized a boy of ability and encouraged him; Scott responded and knew that he had 'a character for learning to maintain' (ibid., 23). The high school was important in a second respect. Many of those who later came to hold positions of power in Scotland were Scott's contemporaries: in 1809 he recalled how he 'first crept swinging my satchel through George's Square with Robert Dundas' (*Letters*, 2.261)—the Robert Dundas who was eldest son of Pitt's most formidable minister, Henry Dundas, first Viscount Melville, and himself a government minister almost continuously from 1807 to 1830. At the high school 'networking' began, and the connections formed there allowed Scott to benefit from the patronage system by which power was transmitted in Scotland. In addition these connections later constituted his primary audience: it was they whom he initially addressed, and it was they and their kind who bought his works.

In 1783 Scott had to leave the high school before the end of the session because of ill health, and he was sent to his Aunt Janet, who now lived in Kelso. He attended the Kelso grammar school under Lancelot Whale, where he continued his study of Latin, and also taught it to junior classes. Possibly the most notable development of his half-year in Kelso was the friendship he formed with one of his fellow pupils, James Ballantyne, later to be his printer, business partner, and literary adviser.

Although the schooling Scott received was acceptable for the period, it was limited (Latin was the only subject on the curriculum), and abbreviated by illness. Its deficiencies must have been obvious for in 1782 Scott's father employed a tutor, James Mitchell, to supplement his son's education. Scott does not report what Mitchell taught him, but their talk centred on the covenanters and seventeenth-century politics, thus beginning the generation of the knowledge deployed in *Minstrelsy of the Scottish Border*, and in novels like *Old Mortality*. His own reading was more important than formal instruction. He read poetry, including Shakespeare and Milton. He collected chapbooks. On the advice of the blind poet Thomas Blacklock he became 'intimate with Ossian and Spenser' (Scott, 'Memoirs', 26). He borrowed works of history from the library in the high school. At Kelso subscription and circulating libraries allowed him to start on Richardson, Fielding, Smollett, and Mackenzie, and he even read Tasso 'through the flat medium of Mr. Hole's translation' (ibid., 27). But by far the most important discovery was Thomas Percy's *Reliques of Ancient English Poetry*, which Scott read with almost physical pleasure in the garden in Kelso. Scott makes much of the unsystematic nature of his reading, but by any standards it was remarkable for a twelve-year-old boy.

In November 1783 Scott entered the University of Edinburgh. He studied Latin for a year after enrolling in both the junior and senior classes at the same time. The professor of Latin was incompetent and, Scott says, 'amid the riot of his class I speedily lost much of what I had learned under Adams and Whale'. Scott was no classicist, but he understates his own command of Latin for throughout his career he was able to quote accurately, and from memory, lines and passages from Roman authors, and to adjust them both verbally and grammatically to fit a new context. He studied Greek for two years (two years were necessary for graduation), but did so badly that he came to be known as the '*Greek Blockhead*' (Scott, 'Memoirs', 30). In his second year (1784–5) he took a class in logic and metaphysics under Professor John Bruce, in which he did well and was required to read an essay before the principal, William Robertson the historian. However, he became ill in the course of his second year at university, and although he registered for a third to continue study under Bruce, he was still (or perhaps again) ill and withdrew from the university early in 1786.

On 31 March 1786 Scott was indentured to his father for five years to train as a solicitor, and so entered 'upon the dry and barren wilderness of forms and conveyances' (Scott, 'Memoirs', 32). His work seems to have consisted mainly in copying legal documents, and from doing this he acquired an ability to write long and fast, and a scribal habit which he never lost: every recto of a manuscript of a Scott novel is filled with writing, the only white space being a narrow margin down the left-hand side. But he had a distaste for the job and detested the office. 'Never a being from my infancy upwards hated task-work as I hate it', he wrote in his journal in 1825; 'propose to me to do one thing and it is inconceivable the desire I have to do something else' (*Journal*, 23). Yet he did what was required of him in his father's office, because, he says, he loved his father, and because he liked to earn a little money to spend on the theatre or books from the circulating library. He already had enough French to read romances in the original and now paid for twice-weekly Italian lessons. He relieved the boredom of legal copying by surreptitiously reading works of imaginative literature buried under weightier books. He did read novels, although he found that it required 'the art of Burney or the feeling of Mackenzie' to get his attention. It was the 'adventurous and romantic' that really held his interest, and everything 'which touched on knight errantry was particularly acceptable' (Scott, 'Memoirs', 32–3).

In the early months of 1787 Scott suffered a bowel haemorrhage (it is not clear what exactly was wrong), and was so seriously ill that his life was threatened. It is probable that the regime prescribed made him worse: the weather was 'raw and cold', and yet he had to sleep under a single blanket; he was 'bled and blistered' until he 'scarcely had a pulse left'; he was given only enough food to stay alive; he was not allowed to talk (Scott, 'Memoirs', 34). Recovery was slow; there were relapses; and he was restricted to a vegetarian diet for some months. But Scott did recover, grew strong, and enjoyed remarkably good health for the next thirty years.

With the recovery of health Scott began to spend leisure

time on 'expeditions' with friends and acquaintances to such places as the field of the first battle of the Jacobite rising of 1745, 9 miles east of Edinburgh. His principal object, he said, was 'the pleasure of seeing romantic scenery', and, more importantly, 'the places which had been distinguished by remarkable historical events' (Scott, 'Memoirs', 37). However, in spite of what Lockhart said there is no evidence of Scott having visited the highlands in the 1780s, and Scott's own, undated, story about his going while still an apprentice to evict some highland tenants who were refusing to vacate a farm could have taken place at any point up to March 1791 when his apprenticeship terminated. He also began to renew friendships originally made in school, but which had lapsed over the period of his illnesses between 1785 and 1787, particularly that with Adam Ferguson, son of the Adam Ferguson who had written *An Essay on the History of Civil Society*. It was in Ferguson's house that Scott met Burns in 1787.

By 1789 Scott knew that he could not tolerate life as a solicitor, and no doubt he was stimulated to change direction by the renewal of friendship with young men who already intended to become advocates: the bar was 'the line of ambition and liberty' (Scott, 'Memoirs', 41). At some point he was offered a partnership by his father. Whether this was a matter of form (Scott's apprenticeship terminated in March 1791), kindness as Scott implies, or a desire to control an errant son as John Sutherland suggests, cannot be known, but in choosing the bar Scott makes out that he was acting in accordance with his father's wishes. That may be so, but Walter Scott senior was a narrow man quite out of sympathy with an imaginative son, and the way in which the independent Scott 'took off' in the 1790s indicates a rejection of much of what his father stood for.

In 1789 Scott returned to university, and this second period at college, unlike the first, was crucial to his intellectual development. He studied moral philosophy under Professor Dugald Stewart, found him an inspirational teacher, and absorbed Stewart's version of the philosophy of common sense. Further, Stewart ran a literary salon at which Scott was a frequent visitor both as a student and as a young advocate. In his first year he also studied universal history under Alexander Fraser Tytler. In 1790–91 he took civil law (which he did not enjoy but passed the examination set by the Faculty of Advocates) and Scots law, which he continued in the following session, 1791–2. The professor of Scots law, David Hume, nephew of the philosopher, and later (1811–22) one of Scott's colleagues as clerk to the court of session, had a formidable effect: 'I copied over his lectures twice with my own hand from notes taken in the class', Scott wrote, 'and when I have had occasion to consult them I can never sufficiently admire the penetration and clearness of conception which were necessary to the arrangement of the fabric of law' (Scott, 'Memoirs', 42). Hume made sense of Scots law, and Scott was enthused by the way in which law was simultaneously antiquarian and political, historical and contemporary.

In this second period at university Scott also participated in the clubs and societies which were such an important feature of the Edinburgh scene in the eighteenth century, and which formed an essential function in the preparation of young men for public life. In 1789 he co-founded the Literary Society. Over two years the society met every Friday evening in a masonic lodge in Carrubbers Close, and then, transforming into 'The Club', retired to an oyster bar, which was also frequented by some of Edinburgh's most distinguished thinkers—Adam Ferguson the philosopher, Joseph Black the chemist, and James Hutton the geologist. In December 1790 Scott was elected to the Speculative Society, which met weekly during the university session from November to April; he was appointed its librarian in January 1791 and its secretary-treasurer in November. Typically, the business consisted of an essay read by one of the members followed by a debate. Scott's first essay, read on 26 November 1791, was entitled 'The origin of the feudal system'. Commenting in a letter of 30 September 1790 to his uncle Robert Scott on an earlier version of the essay, Scott said that the feudal system 'proceeds upon principles common to all nations when placed in a certain situation' (*Letters*, 1.17). In other words, Scott had absorbed a fundamental position in Scottish Enlightenment historiography.

Scott did not take university examinations and did not formally graduate. Few men did. His aim was to qualify as an advocate, and on 6 July 1792 he passed the Scots law examination of the Faculty of Advocates and was admitted as an advocate on 11 July. His thesis, in Latin, on the prescribed topic 'De cadaveris damnatorum' ('About [the disposal of] the bodies of condemned criminals'), was dedicated to the lord justice clerk, Lord Braxfield, the senior criminal judge of Scotland.

Scott's own 'Memoirs' of his first twenty-one years constitute the principal source of information about his early life. Lockhart calls the work an 'autobiographical fragment'; it has also been called the 'Ashestiel fragment' after the house in which Scott wrote the first section. But it is not a fragment: it is a complete short work, covering the days of his youth and concluding naturally with his entry at the age of twenty-one into manhood and his profession. The 'Memoirs' were written in two stages, in 1808 and 1810–11, and they were extensively revised in 1826; when he wrote his autobiography he was already recognized as the editor of a great collection of ballads and as a famous poet, and so the narrative of his own life probably has a strong element of teleological self-construction.

Scott's narrative puts particular emphasis on the stories he heard and the books he read, yet he says remarkably little about writing. But the creative impulse began early. Pieces of school work were kept by his mother and by Alexander Adam. He told stories to other boys in the high school, and tells of his walks with John Irving in 1786 during which they invented stories 'in which the martial and the miraculous always predominated' (Scott, 'Memoirs', 33). Some of his poems to 'Jessie' in Kelso survived, and in an undated letter now thought to belong to 1792 he writes:

> I have made odes to nightingales so numerous they might suffice for all that ever were hatched, and as for elegies,

> ballads, and sonnets and other small ware, truly I can assert their name is legion, for they are many. But besides these I have dared to attempt something of a more imposing character—an epic poem of hundreds upon hundreds of lines—a chronicle in verse of the wondrous doings of some famous Knights whose names, even, I doubt much you have ever heard. (*Letters*, 1.3–4)

Even allowing for a considerable element of self-mockery, it is clear that Scott was writing.

Scott also says nothing about the French Revolution. The omission is striking, for it is impossible to believe that it was not a red-hot topic with his friends whose arguments 'sometimes plunged deeply into politics and metaphysics' (Scott, 'Memoirs', 40). What was discussed is not recorded, and none of the surviving letters of the period 1789–92 raises a political issue. However, he led in a debate in the Speculative Society on 1 March 1791 about whether putting Charles I to death was justifiable, which was carried in the affirmative (the vote was reversed on 18 December 1792 during the trial of Louis XVI). He and a few friends called themselves 'the mountain', the name of one of the more extreme parties in revolutionary France. And given that until 1792 it was the tories under Pitt who were the reforming party in the House of Commons, it is possible that the young Walter Scott had a sympathetic view of the Revolution, like his character Jonathan Oldbuck in *The Antiquary* (*Waverley Novels*, 1993–2004, 3.277–8). Scott later opposed all forms of political reform; what he thought in 1789 is not known, and can only be deduced. In the past that has been done by projecting his later views backwards, but that may not have been a satisfactory procedure.

1792–1797: the young advocate and marriage As an advocate Scott was not a failure, nor was he a success. He lost his first case, defending a drunken minister before the general assembly of the Church of Scotland in 1793, but had ten further cases in his first year. He earned £24 3*s*., £57 15*s*., and £105 in his first three years respectively. In his first ten years he appeared before the House of Lords, the court of session, the high court of justiciary, and various sheriff courts.

Scott did not have many cases to prepare, and legal terms were short: there was much time to fill in. He lived the life of a young man: he was a hard drinker in a hard-drinking age, and there are also hints of sexual exploits. There is some sexual banter in a letter to Clark of 1792 in which he talks of his 'chère adorable' without identifying the woman. On 4 March 1828 Scott met for the first time for thirty years David Erskine of Cardross, whom he described as 'my old friend and boon-companion with whom I shared the wars of Bacchus, Venus and sometimes of Mars' (*Journal*, 437). George Allan, Scott's first biographer, writing in 1832, claimed to possess 'undeniable evidence that Scott was concerned … in at least one illicit amour' (Allan, 181). In fact only two women with whom Scott was involved before he met his wife can be identified. The first is Jessie; no surname is known, but she belonged to Kelso and was the daughter of a tradesman. It appears that they first met in 1787 or 1788 while Scott was at Rosebank, his uncle's house in Kelso. James C. Corson has shown that the last of Scott's letters to her cannot have been written earlier than 1792. It was thus a four- or five-year relationship. The inference can be made that they were lovers, and that it was Scott who broke off the liaison.

The second woman was Williamina Belsches, daughter of Sir John Belsches and his wife, Lady Jane Leslie-Melville, of Fettercairn in Kincardineshire (now Aberdeenshire). Scott probably first met Williamina in 1790 when she was fourteen, but it seems improbable (on the grounds of age) that there was any relationship. The earliest indication of his love for her is in 1793, if he was right in saying in 1827 that he had carved her name 'in runic characters on the turf beside the castle gate' (*Journal*, 315) in St Andrews thirty-four years previously. He proposed marriage in August 1795 and considered her reply 'highly flattering and favourable' in spite of her asking him to wait (*Letters*, 1.40). However, over the winter of 1795–6 Williamina met William Forbes, son of one of Scotland's wealthiest bankers; her letters indicate her attraction to him and her mother favoured his suit. In April and May 1796 Scott made a three-week visit to the north-east; he extracted a reluctantly given invitation to Fettercairn House, but the visit was not a success. Williamina's engagement to Forbes was announced in October 1796. One of Scott's 'mountain' friends wrote: 'This is not good news. I always dreaded there was some self-deception on the part of our romantic friend, and I now shudder at the violence of his most irritable and ungovernable mind' (Lockhart, 1.242). Williamina married Forbes the following January.

In September 1797, eight months later, Scott met Margaret Charlotte Carpenter (1770–1826) at Gilsland, a spa in Cumberland; within three weeks he proposed to her; and they got married in Carlisle on 24 December. Biographers have tended to argue that Williamina was the great love of Scott's life, that he married Charlotte on the rebound, and that Charlotte was second best. Long afterwards in his *Journal* Scott himself said that he had been 'Broken-hearted for two years—My heart handsomely pieced again—but the crack will remain till my dying day' (*Journal*, 43), but this is a tribute to both Williamina and Charlotte. The Forbes marriage did not produce any kind of social dislocation, for Scott and Forbes were co-operating in February 1797 on the small committee which planned Edinburgh's volunteer cavalry regiment. And the correspondence of Walter and Charlotte in autumn 1797 is boisterous and teasing, and indicates strong physical attraction. Scott liked Charlotte's 'laughing Philosophy' (*Letters*, 1.79), and her responses to him verge on the racy. She was attractive, mature, and verbally sophisticated, and quite unlike Williamina.

In marrying Charlotte Scott took considerable risks. He made no enquiries about her, and could not answer his family's questions about her background. In fact, she was French, the daughter of Jean François Charpentier of Lyons and his wife, Élie Marguerite Volère, also known as Margaret Charlotte Volère (*d*. 1788), and had been brought up a Catholic, although she was baptized an Anglican in

1787. Her parents had separated about 1780, possibly after her mother had had an affair with a young Welshman. When precisely mother, daughter, and son came to England has not been determined, but it is known that Charlotte's mother returned to Paris in 1786, leaving behind her children who became the wards of the earl of Hillsborough, later marquess of Downshire. As the latter married in 1786 it has been presumed that Charlotte's mother had been his mistress, but there is no known evidence to support the presumption. When Scott proposed to Charlotte, he did not know all this. He got engaged before he told his parents anything about her; he did not report that she was French (Charlotte looked foreign and throughout her life spoke English with a strong French accent); he said that she had an annuity of £500 from her brother, when, in fact, she received an irregular allowance. Scott was marrying an 'unknown'; he was not marrying for social position; he was not marrying for property. He was marrying for love and he was marrying a woman to whom he was intensely attracted.

Scott's political views were by now firmly constitutional; after the terror began in September 1792, after Louis XVI was beheaded in January 1793, and after France declared war on Britain on 1 February 1793, he lost any sympathy he might have had. In April 1794 he got involved in a fight with some anti-royalist Irish students, and was bound over to keep the peace. In June he was one of the thousand gentlemen who volunteered their services as constables to prevent popular disturbances, and he wrote with approval of the Edinburgh volunteer regiment formed to oppose a French invasion. In September he attended the trials of Watt and Downie, who were accused of organizing a plot for a general rising and proclaiming a republican government, and in October he watched Watt's execution. He served with great enthusiasm in the Royal Edinburgh light dragoons from its formation in 1797, and acted as its secretary and quartermaster.

Scott's exploration of Scotland continued and became more adventurous. He now really did visit the highlands, or rather the fringes of the southern highlands. In 1793 he went with Adam Ferguson on a trip to Loch Katrine and the Trossachs. On another occasion he went with William Clerk to Craighall near Blairgowrie, then on to Patrick Murray's in Meigle, where they were joined by Adam Ferguson. From here they took trips to see Dunnottar Castle, near Stonehaven, where the Scottish regalia had been hidden during Cromwell's invasion of Scotland, and visited Glamis Castle, which in those days had not been 'improved', but was still a medieval fortress with a complex system of defensive ditches and walls. Such trips were productive for many of the places described in Scott's poems and novels were seen on holidays like these. But these places are not reproduced in a 'photographic' way: the Trossachs at large feature in *The Lady of the Lake* and *Rob Roy*, but the fictional Tully-Veolan of *Waverley* fuses aspects of different buildings, and brings together stories and incidents which appertain to a variety of places.

Scott's exploration of the borders was more thorough. On 26 August 1791 he wrote to William Clerk from Northumberland, reporting on what he made of the topography of Flodden and the locations of other battles; he was in Northumberland again in September 1792, talking of Hexham and of Hadrian's Wall. On his way back he visited Liddesdale, in the extreme south-west of Roxburghshire, in the company of Robert Shortreed, a Jedburgh lawyer. Seven more 'raids', as Scott called them, followed over seven years (normally in the autumn).

The Liddesdale raids reveal well the way in which Scott conducted research. He met (and drank with) a variety of farmers and from them heard many stories about characters and localities, and some songs and ballads. He visited the surgeon Dr John Elliot of Cleuchhead, who had a manuscript collection of ballads which he made available to Scott and who, having met Scott, looked for new ballads and further versions of known ballads—in 1794 he wanted Shortreed 'to refresh Dr. Elliots memory with regard to my Old Songs' (*Letters*, 1.33). Scott himself sought out ballad singers and mentally compared their versions with versions he already knew. He explored the historic remains of Hermitage Castle and in 1793 sent a guinea for 'carrying on our joint operations', that is for a 'dig' at Hermitage (ibid., 1.28). He collected historical artefacts. He later read relevant historical documents in Register House, and had friends transcribe relevant manuscripts in the British Museum. Scott's greatness as scholar and writer comes from his imaginative ability to synthesize these different kinds of historical evidence to create narratives in which detail is used to reveal the way in which people in the past construed their world and invested it with meaning. Shortreed later said that Scott was only doing it for 'the queerness and the fun', but also observed that 'He was *makin' himsell* a' the time' (Lockhart, 1.195–6). Scott's life in the nineties was a preparation for his life as a writer. There was certainly much merrymaking, but so deliberate was the seeking of historical materials that it is possible to infer an aim and a strategy, which culminated in *Minstrelsy of the Scottish Border*.

But Scott's self-training as cultural anthropologist did not make him a writer. The actual transformative experience seems to have been the encounter with German Romanticism. The Edinburgh interest in German literature began with Henry Mackenzie's 1788 lecture on German drama to the Royal Society of Edinburgh. In 1792 Alexander Fraser Tytler, Scott's history professor, published his translation of Schiller's *Die Räuber*; Scott bought his copy in July, and even in his 'Essay on imitations of the ancient ballad', written as late as 1830, the excitement of a new literature breaks through the formal prose as he hails the discovery of a race of poets who wished 'to spurn the flaming boundaries of the universe' (*Poetical Works*, 4.39). In the autumn of 1792 Scott and six or seven friends found themselves a teacher. As with Latin before, Scott paid less attention to grammatical precision than to meaning: he was 'in the practice of fighting his way to the knowledge of the German by his acquaintance with the Scottish and Anglo-Saxon dialects' (ibid., 4.42). In 1795 Anna Laetitia Aikin read an unpublished translation of Bürger's *Leonore* at one of Dugald Stewart's parties, and although Scott was not present he was stimulated to find his own copy of the German original. He met the Aberdonian James Skene of Rubislaw, who had lived in Saxony for some years and had a collection of German books. The poems in the German manner included within Matthew Lewis's *The Monk* (1796) were a further stimulus, and in April 1796 Scott tried his hand at translating *Leonore*. 'He began the task … after supper, and did not retire to bed until he had finished it, having by that time worked himself into a state of excitement which set sleep at defiance' (Lockhart, 1.235). So pleased was Scott with the reaction of his friends that he proceeded to translate another Bürger poem, *Der wilde Jäger*, and the two were published together anonymously as *The Chase and William and Helen: Two Ballads from the German of Gottfried Augustus Bürger* on 1 November 1796, priced 3s. 6*d*.

'I was German-mad', said Scott in a letter of 13 December 1827 (*Letters*, 10.331). The new enthusiasm liberated Scott from the constrictions of eighteenth-century English poetry. But in the long run what was of far greater importance to Scott was the German interest in national identity, folk culture, and medieval literature. Scott's sensitivity to the nationalist precedent afforded by late eighteenth-century German writing helps distinguish his poetic world from that of his Romantic contemporaries Wordsworth and Coleridge. When combined with the different varieties of literary nationalism embodied in Burns and Macpherson, the German example helped propel Scott towards his own attempt to repossess the special territory of Scotland's past.

1798–1802 and *Minstrelsy of the Scottish Border* After his marriage Scott set up house with Charlotte at 50 George Street, Edinburgh. In the summer of 1798 he and Charlotte rented a cottage at Lasswade, a village a few miles south of Edinburgh, and this was their summer home until 1803. While there he developed his literary and political contacts, and made a series of new ones; he was a visitor at Melville Castle, then the home of Robert Dundas, the lord advocate (the government's chief legal officer in Scotland), and at Dalkeith Palace, home of the earl of Dalkeith, his fellow dragoon in the volunteer regiment and heir to the dukedom of Buccleuch. Here he met Lady Douglas, sister of the duke of Buccleuch, and Lady Louisa Stuart, daughter of the former prime minister the earl of Bute, two in a series of aristocratic women with whom Scott later maintained a slightly flirtatious correspondence. Lady Louisa later became one of Scott's most acute critics, and a trusted friend.

On 14 October 1798 Charlotte gave birth to their first son, but the baby died the next day. Later that autumn the Scotts moved to a second house in Edinburgh's New Town, 19 Castle Street. In April 1799 Scott's father died. On 24 October Charlotte gave birth to a daughter, Charlotte Sophia Scott, and this time the baby survived. Their son Walter was born on 26 October 1801; their fourth and fifth children, Anne and Charles, were born on 2 February 1803 and 24 December 1805. In December 1801 they purchased and moved to their permanent Edinburgh address, 39 Castle Street.

Scott's work as an advocate was expanding, but his fee income was small (he earned only £135 9*s*. in 1798), and so when in November 1799 the sheriff-depute of Selkirkshire died, Scott sought the position. (Despite the name the sheriff-depute was the principal judge in a Scottish county.) Scott had now made himself a wholly suitable recipient of the rewards of the patronage system by which posts were filled and political support for the government maintained in Scotland in the eighteenth century: he had the required professional qualification for a sheriff (that is, he was an advocate), he professed the right political opinions, he was making a mark for himself as a scholar–poet, and above all he had established the right connections. No doubt Scott's friendships with the earl of Dalkeith and Robert Dundas were used as part of a process in which the duke of Buccleuch took up Scott's candidature with Henry Dundas, who controlled all political patronage in Scotland. Lockhart says that Scott always remembered with gratitude 'the strong intercession' of William Dundas, nephew of Henry Dundas, and himself a member of the government (Lockhart, 1.318). On 16 December 1799 Scott became the new sheriff-depute of Selkirkshire, at a salary of £300 per annum. As he could continue to practise at the bar, the appointment was an additional responsibility, and an additional source of income.

Scott remained sheriff of Selkirkshire until his death in 1832. By modern standards the appointment did not involve much work, but it was not a sinecure. Although the sheriff court could hear civil cases, its main work involved minor criminal offences. Most of the routine cases were handled by a local sheriff-substitute (Scott appointed the Melrose solicitor Charles Erskine in 1800), with Scott sitting in person only when cases were disputed, but the greater part of the criminal process was conducted in writing. Throughout his career Scott read the written statements of the arguments and the evidence, and determined the case in writing. In addition, the sheriff acted as police officer, searching for evidence and culprits, and had a series of administrative functions. He was also required to go to each sitting of the high court in Jedburgh when it was on circuit to hear serious criminal cases.

In October 1797 Scott had sent a copy of 'The Erl-King', his translation of Goethe's *Der Erlkönig*, to his aunt Christian Rutherford (*Letters*, 1.76–7), and on 1 March 1798 it was published in a revised form in the *Kelso Mail*. He was invited by Matthew Lewis, the notorious author of *The Monk*, who passed the winter of 1798–9 in Edinburgh, to contribute to *Tales of Wonder*, a new two-volume collection that Lewis was planning, but although Scott submitted the three poems he had promised ('The Fire-King', 'Glenfinlas', and 'Frederick and Alice') Monk repeatedly postponed publication, and it did not appear until November 1800. In the meantime Scott published the first English translation of Goethe's *Götz von Berlichingen* in London on 14 March 1799 (the translator was given as 'William Scott' on the title-page), and he wrote *The House of Aspen*, an imitation rather than a translation of *Die heilige Vehme* by Veit Weber (pseudonym of Georg Philip Ludwig Leonhard Wächter). Scott sent it to London in the hope of having it staged; John Kemble was interested but eventually decided that there was 'too much blood' (*Poetical Works*, 12.366)—and it remained unpublished until 1829.

But the great project was the preparation and publication of *Minstrelsy of the Scottish Border*. As the 'Memoirs' indicate, Scott as a child had heard and probably learned ballads from his grandmother. He was also a field collector. This is a view that has repeatedly been challenged, but, although none of the ballads that he heard on his Liddesdale raids has survived in a holograph manuscript, Scott had an extraordinary memory and could recite poems after hearing a single oral recitation; it seems inconceivable that he did not use that memory when collecting ballads in the field. Scott also searched manuscript collections, the two most important being those of Herd and Glenriddell. He belonged too to a circle of ballad collectors who swapped texts with each other: for instance in August 1800 he invited Robert Jamieson, whose *Popular Ballads and Songs* appeared in 1806, to visit him in Lasswade where they exchanged copies of ballads derived from two separate manuscripts recording the Aberdeenshire ballad corpus of Anna Gordon, or Brown. There is abundant evidence of his seeking out particular individuals to obtain ballads they knew or copies they possessed. He also made limited use of printed sources.

The first hint of the *Minstrelsy* is in a letter of 17 February 1796 to the Scottish antiquary George Chalmers, to whom Scott sent a selection of his ballads, but the real impulse to publish seems to have followed Scott's meeting Richard Heber and John Leyden in the autumn of 1799. Letters of 1800 to Heber, the Oxford bibliophile, who had passed the winter of 1799–1800 in Edinburgh, imply that Heber had been urging Scott to publish, and that Leyden, a borderer, a linguistic polymath, and an enthusiast for all things Scottish, had volunteered to help. By June 1800 Scott had agreed a contract with the London publishers Cadell and Davies for a two-volume collection, to be printed by James Ballantyne of Kelso, and to be ready for publication by Christmas 1801. He wrote to the duke of Buccleuch asking for permission to dedicate the collection to him. Work on the project accelerated in the autumn of 1800: on 19 October Scott told Heber that Leyden and he 'work hard at old Ballads during the forenoon & skirmish in the Evening upon the old disputes betwixt the Cameronians & their opponents' (*Letters*, 12.171–2). On 16 October he wrote to Thomas Percy asking for help in finding better versions of some of his fragments, and on 18 October to James Currie in Liverpool asking about possible ballads in Burns's manuscripts. On 27 March 1801 he told another correspondent, George Ellis, that his border ballads would see the light at the beginning of the year, and in April he was back on a field trip in Liddesdale and Ettrick Forest in search of additional materials. *Minstrelsy of the Scottish Border* was published in two volumes on 24 February 1802, priced 18*s*.

Most of the materials for the first edition were gathered by Scott. Leyden contributed only two ballad texts, but they wrote the 'Essay on the fairies of popular superstition' which heads the ballad 'The Young Tamlane' together. In 1802 the collection contained fifty-two items, of which twenty-two were classed as historical, twenty-six as romantic, and four (two by Scott and two by Leyden) as imitations. Of the forty-eight traditional items twenty-six had not previously appeared in print. A second edition was published in 1803; there were now eighty-six items, including traditional material collected by or from James Hogg, William Laidlaw, and Charles Kirkpatrick Sharpe, none of whom had contributed to the first edition. Scott did not 'steal' the work of others, as has been suggested—the new contributors were only too pleased to participate in an already successful project, and they were acknowledged. A good deal of reconstruction took place before the next edition of 1806, but only four new items were added. By 1812 the *Minstrelsy* had its final complement of ninety-six items, including three imitations passed off as traditional by the antiquary Robert Surtees; of the items added between 1803 and 1812 only fifteen traditional songs had not previously appeared in print.

In the most detailed examination of Scott's editorial method Keith W. Harry has demonstrated that Scott was indeed right when on 30 July 1801 he said to Currie: 'I have made it an invariable rule to attempt no improvements upon the genuine Ballads which I have been able to recover' (*Letters*, 1.120). Scott's method was to fuse versions of a single ballad story in order to create more coherent ballad texts. Of the ballads published in the first edition, five have no known source, and thirteen have a single source; the remainder are derived from two or more sources. The extant materials for the *Minstrelsy* show that Scott gathered a very large number of fragments, from which his creative editing produced complete songs. Harry further shows that the materials used by Scott were justified by tradition or by manuscript versions, and that, although Scott may have added occasional words or phrases to resolve a crux, the frequently repeated opinion that Scott wrote lines and even whole stanzas is simply wrong.

Scott's recreative methodology may have created excellent literary texts, but could not now be regarded as an acceptable editorial procedure. However, on 3 May 1825 in a letter to William Motherwell, Scott indicated that he thought his original methodology had been wrong, and advocated a new approach which was not only adopted by Motherwell but is now regarded as standard procedure:

> I think you should print it exactly as you have taken it down, and with a reference to the person by whom it is preserved so special as to enable any one to ascertain its authenticity … I think I did wrong myself in endeavouring to make the best possible set of an ancient ballad out of several copies obtained from different quarters … the singers or reciters by whom these ballads were preserved and handed down must, in general, have had a facility … of filling up verses which they had forgotten, or altering such as they might think they could improve. Passing through this process in different parts of the country, the ballads … became, in progress of

> time, totally different productions, so far as the tone and spirit of each is concerned. In such cases, perhaps, it is as well to keep them separate, as giving in their original state a more accurate idea of our ancient poetry, which is the point most important in such collections. (*Letters*, 9.100–02)

In his agreement with Cadell and Davies Scott must have stipulated that his friend James Ballantyne of Kelso should print the collection. It was, and is, unusual for an author to choose the printer; in doing so Scott showed his interest not just in content but in books as artefacts which would articulate the 'message', and make clear the social standing of its creators. Scott was an advocate, and Ballantyne a solicitor who in 1796 founded his own newspaper, the *Kelso Mail*. Their co-operation began in 1798 when 'The Erl-King' appeared in Ballantyne's columns, but in his letter of 22 April 1800 Scott outlined plans of some daring: he suggested that Ballantyne might move his business to Edinburgh, edit a newspaper, found a '"Monthly Magazine" and a "Caledonian Annual Register"', print papers for the court of session, 'the best paid work which a printer undertakes', and publish literary works, 'either ancient or modern'. He also suggested that Ballantyne, with his education, could improve on prevailing standards in both design and accuracy. In other words Scott laid out a business strategy for Ballantyne and, implicitly, himself, which was to be fulfilled over the following two decades. Ballantyne did not embark immediately on Scott's ventures (it was not until 1803 that he moved to Edinburgh), but this letter marks the beginning of a literary and business partnership which lasted the rest of their lives. It also shows that Scott's imagination encompassed the whole business of literature.

In the summer of 1802 Scott was visited by Thomas Longman, head of the London publishers Longman and Rees, who bought the copyright of the *Minstrelsy* for £500. From this he must have learned two things: first, that he could command very considerable fees for his literary work, and second that rivalry between publishers could boost what he could make from them. Longman's purchase necessitated a quick second edition, but in fact Scott created a substantially new work by expanding each department. The imitations included the first publication of three more poems by Scott, one of which, 'Cadyow Castle', is a 'vivid trailer', as Sutherland puts it (Sutherland, 90), for *The Lay of the Last Minstrel*. The second edition of the *Minstrelsy* appeared on 25 May 1803, in three volumes, priced £1 11*s*. 6*d*.

1802–1814: Scott as editor While working on the *Minstrelsy*, Scott was also preparing an edition of the version of the medieval romance *Sir Tristrem* to be found in the Auchinleck manuscript, owned by the Advocates' Library. About 1800 Joseph Ritson had suggested that the poem was the composition of Thomas the Rhymer, the poet and seer reputed to have belonged to Earlston, a village only 5 miles from Sandyknowe, and, motivated by their local and national patriotism, Leyden and Scott were eager to concur. Initially the work of transcription was undertaken by Leyden, and the annotation by Scott, but in 1801 Leyden withdrew (he is thought to have disapproved of the sexually explicit nature of some sections of the poem). Although the work was substantially complete by the end of 1802, it was not published until May 1804. The newly established firm of Archibald Constable & Co., Scott's leading publisher for the first time, clearly did not think it would succeed, for it printed only 150 copies and priced them at £2 2*s*., and it may have had moral objections. Scott himself had no qualms on this score: indeed he consistently opposed (not always successfully) the bowdlerization, or castration as he termed it, of literary works, including his own. But *Sir Tristrem* was not an editorial success. Scott did not have that knowledge of medieval English which would have enabled him to ascertain provenance, thus leaving him free to indulge his Scottish fantasy. He did not know enough about the cycles of Arthurian legend, and thus argued that the late version before him was the original Arthurian text. And he tried to assimilate the poem to the minstrels of the ballad tradition. However, medieval romance did offer him a model for his long narrative poems.

In a letter to George Ellis of 8 October 1808 after the publication of *Marmion* Scott said that editing 'may be considered as a green crop of turnips or peas, extremely useful for those whose circumstances do not admit of giving their farm a summer fallow' (*Letters*, 2.93). It is in this way that his editing has usually been seen, as recreation, providing both recuperation and materials for imaginative literature. Unquestionably, the works Scott edited were utilized in his long poems and novels, but they were also an extraordinary scholarly achievement in their own right. Between 1806 and 1814 works edited by Scott included: *Original Memoirs, Written during the Great Civil War* (1806), *The Works of John Dryden* (18 vols., 1808), *Memoirs of Robert Cary, Earl of Monmouth … and Fragmenta Regalia* (1808), *A Collection of Scarce and Valuable Tracts* (13 vols., 1809–15), *The Ancient British Drama* (3 vols., 1810), *The Memoirs of the Duke of Sully* (5 vols., 1810), *The Poetical Works of Anna Seward* (3 vols., 1810), *The Modern British Drama* (5 vols., 1811), *Secret History of the Court of James I* (2 vols., 1811), Sir Philip Warwick's *Memoirs of the Reign of King Charles the First* (1813), and *The Works of Jonathan Swift* (19 vols., 1814). Only three editions of significance came later: *Memorie of the Somervilles* (1816), *Memorials of the Haliburtons* (1820), and *Military Memoirs of the Great Civil War* (1822).

Scott edited historical documents and literary texts mainly of the seventeenth century, although his period stretches back into the late sixteenth century and forward to the death of Swift in 1745. In a sense his editing constitutes a single interlocking endeavour: he cites no fewer than nine of his editions in *A Collection of Scarce and Valuable Tracts*, and various editions were undertaken to reinforce work elsewhere. As editor Scott aimed to expand the materials then available. For instance, in *Original Memoirs* he included two brief lives from manuscript sources, and ten from seventeenth-century tracts. His Dryden was advertised as the first complete edition. *A Collection of Scarce and Valuable Tracts* was not the first selection from the tracts collected by Lord Somers (the title-page describes this as the second edition, and as 'revised and augmented'), but to the 882 tracts previously published he added a further 81. *Secret History of the Court of James I* contains five rare works, two of which he had previously cited in *Memoirs of Robert Cary* and described as 'scandalous'. In his Swift some 122 items (83 letters, 22 poems, and 17 pieces of prose) were added to the corpus.

Following the editorial practice of his time, Scott had no settled methods or principles for choosing or establishing a text. He used previous editions as copy texts wherever possible, and he seems to have done little to check the reliability of transcripts furnished by his correspondents. He adopted the notes of his predecessors, very often without acknowledgement. He also added introductions and notes of his own, and it is this new material that made his editions distinguished. Because he worked so much in the sub-literature of the seventeenth century he had an unrivalled knowledge and understanding of the period. He was not systematic—he added many notes to the first eight volumes of *A Collection of Scarce and Valuable Tracts* yet none to the next five—but he is always illuminating. And it may be taken that the epigraph on the title-page of that work—'The bent and genius of the age is best known in a free country, by the pamphlets and papers that come daily out, as the sense of parties, and sometimes the voice of the nation'—expresses his view of history: he is more concerned with the analysis of historical forces as evidenced in these ephemeral papers than with historical events as such. As a literary historian he was the first to relate literature to its social, political, and economic context, and in his edition and biography of Dryden, who above all poets was immersed in his times, Scott shows a powerful imaginative grasp of the interplay of the writer and his society. His edition of Swift was less successful (although he corrected some of the problems in the second edition of 1824) not because it was so dependent on the work of the previous editor, John Nichols, nor because he was less intellectually engaged in the project, but essentially because unlike Dryden Swift could not be successfully presented as a construction of his period.

Scott was the greatest editor of his age. Others were more precise, and more accurate, but they were more precise and more accurate about more limited areas. None had his ability to illuminate the past through the exercise of scholarship. None was such a perceptive critic of literature. In *Minstrelsy of the Scottish Border* he published the most exciting collection of ballads ever to appear. In his collections of historical documents he made more history available and related all its various materials and strands with more insight than any of his contemporaries. In *The Works of John Dryden*, in which his life of Dryden forms the first volume, he produced one of the great collected editions of an author's works. Finally Scott's skill and the tact in using literature as historical evidence, and recreating history as literature, has never been surpassed.

1802–1817: Scott as poet In Scott's letters and in the autobiographical essays which he wrote for his collected works there is a repeated, irritatingly deferential, acknowledgement of the part played by Scott's friends and coadjutors in the creative process. But it can be argued that Scott was uniquely indebted to others, writers past and present as well as friends, for phrases, stories, and ideas, to which 'the modifying colours of the imagination' (to use Coleridge's phrase) gave 'the interest of novelty'. He is the great transformer of inherited materials. *The Lay of the Last Minstrel* has the form of a medieval romance, and its metre was learned from Coleridge. Scott inset two songs in a modified ballad stanza, another in the Spenserian stanza, and an English version of the 'Dies irae'; he localized the action by an invocation of names in the manner of the raiding ballads; he drew on a period and technical vocabulary found in his reading of historical documents. There are at least 3000 allusions to other literary texts. The whole is an intertextual tissue. This transformative use of other materials recreates a sixteenth-century past which Scott then authenticates with explanatory notes. Scott was the editor of his own fiction, turning that fiction into a historical document 'intended to illustrate the customs and manners, which anciently prevailed on the Borders of England and Scotland' (*Poetical Works*, 6.37).

The *Lay* was written over an extended period. It is possible that the 'epic poem of hundreds upon hundreds of lines' which Scott mentioned to Jessie in 1792 was a rudimentary form of the poem. It is certain that in December 1802 he thought he would include a long poem of his own in the third volume of the *Minstrelsy*: it 'will be a kind of Romance of Border Chivalry in a Light Horseman sort of stanza' (*Letters*, 12.231), he told George Ellis. He heard the tale of Gilpin Horner in late January 1803; he read portions to Ellis in May; by 21 August 1804 Ballantyne had received the manuscript for typesetting. It was published in Edinburgh on 12 January 1805, with a run of 750 copies, priced £1 5*s*. Thus the statement that he wrote it 'a canto per week' (*Poetical Works*, 6.29) is highly misleading: Scott was never truthful about the length of the gestation period, nor about the amount of effort and thought he put into his creative work.

The *Lay* was greatly successful; a second edition of 1500 copies priced at 10*s*. 6*d*. appeared in October 1805, and in 1806 a third of 2000 in February, a fourth of 2250 in August, and a fifth of 2000 in November. The sixth edition in 1807 was of 3000 copies. In Scott's lifetime there were twenty-one British editions of the poem (sixteen separate and five in collected editions). The reviewers were more restrained than the readers. Although all wrote with approval, they were puzzled about genre. The *Lay* was recognized as a development of medieval romance, the ballad, or both, and it was praised as an improvement on both, but there was little sense of the excitement which might have greeted the inauguration of a new poetic genre. Placing a narrative back in time to create a temporal exoticism was not completely new: *The Ancient Mariner* had been published in 1798, and Scott had heard *Christabel* recited by a mutual friend in 1802 (it was not published until 1816). But the verse form was new. It is regrettable that Coleridge did not publish the first part of *Christabel* in 1798, nor the second in 1800, for he would then have been recognized in his own time as the 'inventor' of the new metrics. Scott undoubtedly learned from Coleridge, but it was not plagiarism, and overall the *Lay* exploits the fluidity of the verse form with extraordinary skill. As John Sutherland has said, 'Technically the *Lay* is, for 1805, a startlingly innovative poem' (Sutherland, 100). It was also innovative in its development of the framing narrative as a paradigm for the recovery of the past. The poem was written by Walter Scott and dedicated to the earl of Dalkeith, and in it the Minstrel in the 1690s tells Dalkeith's ancestor, the first duchess of Buccleuch, his tale of her ancestors in the mid-sixteenth century. It treats of a period when Scotland and England were still hereditary enemies, and it demonstrates how the ritualization of violence offers a means to contain and transcend it. The 'lesson' from history is unconvincing, but the poem offers unforgettable formulations of feeling:

Breathes there a man, with soul so dead,
Who never to himself hath said,
This is my own, my native land!
(*Poetical Works*, 6.187, canto 6.1)

Such patriotism is infectiously positive, and that which can be remembered has moral power.

Ballads and Lyrical Pieces, a collection of eight ballads and five songs, all previously published but not readily available, appeared in September 1806. *Marmion*, according to Lockhart, was begun in November 1806. On 13 January the following year Scott told Anna Seward that he had begun a poem on Flodden, the battle on 9 September 1513 in which James IV, king of Scots, was killed and the Scottish army annihilated. On 31 January 1807 he accepted Constable's offer of £1100 for the new poem. He sent a proof sheet of the first canto to Lady Abercorn on 11 February. On 15 May he expected to see the poem out by Christmas, but it was September before he sent Lady Abercorn the second canto. The third canto was completed in November, and on 19 January 1808 he told Lady Louisa Stuart that 'Marmion is, at this instant, gasping upon Flodden field' (*Letters*, 2.3). It was published on 22 February 1808, and proved even more popular than *The Lay of the Last Minstrel*: 8000 copies were sold in its first year.

Marmion is the most intellectually ambitious of Scott's long poems, and until the late twentieth century the least understood. The subject has repeatedly been found to be wanting in some way: from Jeffrey in the *Edinburgh Review* in 1808 to Sutherland in his 1995 biography, reviewers have asked why Scott built his poem round the greatest catastrophe in Scottish history. They have considered the long descriptions of buildings, feasts, and dress to be tediously antiquarian, have been puzzled about a villain as hero, and have found the epistles to Scott's various friends which introduce each of the six cantos to be 'digressive' (*Letters*, 1.347), to use Scott's own word. Scott himself said his plan was 'to exhibit ancient costume, diction, and manners' (ibid., 2.55), but this is another defensive statement which denies a much bolder aim. *Marmion* represents Flodden as the consequence of the personal moral corruption of James IV and of Lord Marmion (among others), whose hypocrisy undercuts the public virtues of the chivalric code. Neither is cleansed nor made heroic by war, and Marmion in particular remains in death a philanderer, murderer, and fraudster. In the epistles Scott tackles the problem of the relevance of his poetry. He laments the situation of Britain following the deaths of Pitt, Fox, and Nelson, and although the strongly elegiac tone suggests that change and decay are inevitable the counter-argument is that

on the ancient minstrel strain
Time lays his palsied hand in vain.

Scott works his way through to a realization that art whether written in the past or the present, and whether about the past or the present, can invigorate both the private and the public spheres.

In all Scott's long poems there are passages of sheer brilliance, and there are passages which seem inept (and *Marmion* is no exception). But there is a sense in which Scott's work is literature only because of the need for a medium, and that it is closer to performance, a permanent negotiation between tale teller and audience, in which the excitement of the moment takes both parties through to the end. However, the six epistles in *Marmion* are wholly different: they are Scott's personal meditations on who he is, and on the status of his art; they explore the Romantic themes of memory, consciousness, and identity. They are Scott's finest poems, yet when they appeared they were universally criticized. In later years Scott often discussed the nature of his fictions in framing narratives, using fictitious personae. Never again did he use his own voice; never again did he attempt to explore his own mind and personality in the genre most closely associated with Coleridge, the conversation poem.

The first hint of *The Lady of the Lake* comes in a letter of 9 June 1806 to Lady Abercorn in which Scott talks of 'a Highland romance of Love Magic and War', but although he considers it a distant prospect he had by 6 August written a bit. However, on 13 January 1807 he told Anna Seward that he had laid the project aside and taken up *Marmion* instead. When he resumed *The Lady of the Lake* is not known, but in August 1809 he went on a holiday to Loch Lomond and showed Lady Louisa Stuart (whom he met at Buchanan House) some of what he had written. But the poem did not seem to be developing in the normal way, for in a letter to Mrs Clephane of 27 October he seems to suggest that he had been writing some of the inset poems rather than the narrative. By 31 December, however, he had made 'considerable progress' (*Letters*, 2.274), and proofs of the first two cantos were sent to Lady Abercorn on 14 March 1810, and the third and fourth on 14 April. It was published on 8 May 1810, and more than 20,000 copies were sold before the end of the year. *The Lady of the Lake* was the most phenomenal success.

In *The Lady of the Lake* the romance form is employed as a structure, but there is no surprise: the reader recognizes the end at the beginning, and there is neither a journey of self-discovery nor a mysterious revelation. Indeed Coleridge complained that he could not remember a narrative poem in which the sense of progress was so languid. It is more obviously Arthurian in shape than the two previous poems, and because of this Scott uses audience expectation to maintain a momentum while the actual poem acts as a framework for an elaborate pattern of inset tales, separate lyrics and ballads, and descriptive set pieces. This is a poem in which the author–narrator exhibits his command, and consciously and obviously uses romance motifs (the stag hunt, the wild wood versus the court, the outlaw versus the king, prophecy and its fulfilment, the king's confrontation with the lady of the lake) to treat a theme that became much more pronounced in his novels, the conflict between contiguous societies in different stages of development.

Scott wrote two more long poems, *Rokeby* (1813) and *The Lord of the Isles* (1815), the first set in Yorkshire during the civil war in the seventeenth century, and the second concerning Robert the Bruce and his struggle to free Scotland that culminated in the battle of Bannockburn in 1314. In spite of large sales (more than 10,000 of *Rokeby* and 13,750 of *The Lord of the Isles*) in the first year, there was disappointment about their failure to achieve distributions comparable to those of *The Lady of the Lake*. Scott later accounted for the loss of his overwhelming popularity to a change in public taste: the first two cantos of *Childe Harold's Pilgrimage* appeared in 1812. But neither poem was as good as *The Lady of the Lake*.

Scott had lost interest. He did not say as much, but his experiments in the minor poetry, *The Vision of Don Roderick* (1811), *The Bridal of Triermain* (1813), and *Harold the Dauntless* (1817) suggest a need for the more complex narratorial strategies of *Marmion*, which he exercised in his novels. Scott did not stop writing poetry after 1817; he actually wrote a great deal but it was nearly all lyrical, and nearly all set within his prose fiction. Many of these poems are superb, although habitually neglected by anthologists of Romantic literature.

1802–1814: family life Under pressure from the lord lieutenant of Selkirkshire, who reminded him that a sheriff was required to have a residence in his shrievalty, Scott gave up his tenancy of the summer cottage in Lasswade and from 1804 rented Ashestiel, a house near Galashiels in Selkirkshire, from his cousin James Russell who was serving in India. Ashestiel was, in Scott's own words, 'a decent farm-house overhanging the Tweed, and situated in a wild pastoral country' (*Letters*, 1.220). It is difficult to determine exactly how much time he spent in Ashestiel, but it was considerable, and all the references in his letters imply that the Scotts were happy.

The marital relationship seems to have been close and affectionate. For instance, Scott begins his letters to Charlotte from London in 1807 with such salutations as 'My dearest love', 'My dear Charlotte', 'My dearest Mimi'; he then chats about whom he has been dining with, reports on legal and political business, asks about the children, and finishes by asking her to kiss them all, or telling her to 'seek out every way of amusing your widowhood' (*Letters*, 12.106). Thus his famous statement to Lady Abercorn in 1811 that their match 'was something short of love in all its forms which I suspect people only feel *once* in their lives' (ibid., 2.287, 12.487) must be taken as a statement about the state of feeling in 1811, not a judgement on the whole of marriage.

The letters give regular reports of his children's education. He considered Sophia to be bright: 'I am at pains with her education because you know "learning is better than house or land"' (*Letters*, 1.270). On returning from the visit to London of 1807 he told Lady Abercorn that he found all his 'little people in great health and spirits and beginning to talk a little French under their mother's instructions'. He continued:

> I am very anxious that my sons in particular shall be masters of the modern European languages an accomplishment which although much neglected in our common mode of education may be of the utmost use to them in future life. (ibid., 1.362)

Charles was thought to be the cleverest of the family. In due course the two boys were sent to the high school in Edinburgh, in 1809 and 1813 respectively, while the girls had instructors at home.

Scott, Charlotte, and their children were happy, but Scott's brothers posed considerable problems. His youngest brother, Daniel, seems to have misappropriated public money when working for the Edinburgh custom house in Edinburgh. Scott probably met the shortfall, and thanks to Ellis in 1804 found him a position in the West Indies. Daniel returned in disgrace in 1806 and drank himself to death, having had a liaison with a woman. A son was born posthumously. Scott refused to attend the funeral, but a sum of money was paid to the mother, and Scott paid for his nephew's education and apprenticeship and assisted with his emigration to Canada in 1831. His younger brother Thomas (Tom) became bankrupt in 1807, and fled the jurisdiction of Scotland. It emerged that Tom, a lawyer who had inherited his father's practice and was agent for the Duddingston estate of the marquess of Abercorn, had misapplied his client's funds. Scott eventually paid off the debts and through political influence found Tom a new post with a regiment in Canada. The dedication of *The Lady of the Lake* to the marquess shows that the cost of saving Tom was more than monetary.

Scott's circle of friends and relationships grew with fame. Preparations for the *Minstrelsy* and *Sir Tristrem* brought him into contact with Heber, Ellis, Ritson, Douce, and many other collectors and antiquaries. The Wordsworths visited in 1803, and the Scotts reciprocated in 1805. Southey visited in 1805. Campbell dined with Scott in 1803. On his visit to London in 1806 Scott met Joanna Baillie, and was 'taken up' by London society, found a patron in Lady Abercorn, dined with the princess of Wales, and met Canning.

From 1800 the Scotts had a regular income of more than £1000 per annum: the sheriffdom was worth £300, fees from advocacy came to about £200 and were rising, and Charlotte had an income of about £500 (although this later fell to about £300) from her brother in India. From about 1805 Scott sought a more lucrative crown appointment, and in 1806 concluded a complicated negotiation to succeed George Home as a principal clerk to the court of session. Home was deaf and incapable of performing his duties, but as there was no pension Scott agreed to Home retaining his salary until death, from which time Scott would be paid. Scott took up his duties in May 1806, and retired from advocacy. Home lived on; Scott occasionally grumbled, but in 1811 after the passing of a superannuation act Scott began to agitate for Home to be awarded his pension. Home proved awkward, but eventually in 1812 Scott began to receive his salary, now fixed at £1300 p.a. His job was not a sinecure, involving such matters as legal research and putting the decisions of the court into proper legal form; but as the hours were 10 a.m. to 1 or 2 p.m. from Tuesday to Saturday during legal terms, which lasted about twenty-two weeks per year, the remuneration was handsome, and it raised the Scotts' regular income to about £2000 a year.

There were also Scott's literary earnings. Scott earned royalties of £100 on the first edition of the *Minstrelsy* and £169 on the first edition of the *Lay*. Longmans bought the copyright of the *Minstrelsy* for £500 in 1802. They bought the *Lay* for £500 in November 1805, and at the same time they paid £167 in advance for the rights to *Ballads and Lyrical Pieces*. Constable paid £1100 for *Marmion* in 1807, and Miller £720 for Dryden. Constable then paid £1500 for Swift, £500 up front and £1000 on publication.

In addition, there was an income from Ballantyne's printing business. In 1802 Scott advanced Ballantyne £500 (possibly the money he received from Longmans for the copyright of the *Minstrelsy*) to help him set up business in Edinburgh. In 1804 he inherited £5600 from his uncle Robert Scott of Rosebank in Kelso, and when early in 1805 Ballantyne asked for a further loan, Scott suggested instead that he become a partner in the printing business. The £500 loan was capitalized; Scott added a further £1500. The partnership agreement was signed on 14 March 1805; a third of the profit of the company was to go to Ballantyne as salary, and the remaining two-thirds were to be split between the two partners. Scott promised to direct business in Ballantyne's direction, and in this he was supremely successful, for it was a condition in each publishing contract that his work had to be printed by James Ballantyne & Co. The business was highly profitable, but the firm was in continuous need of new capital to finance its growth, and the new capital came mainly from Walter Scott.

1806–1814: business and politics From 1806 Scott became more directly involved with politics. To some extent this was chance: the new whig government of 1806–7 had assented to Scott's arrangement with George Home, but early in 1807 it proposed to reform the court of session in a way which would have abolished the clerkships. Scott was appointed by his fellow clerks to negotiate compensation on their behalf, but as he arrived in London in March 1807 the government resigned and he found himself talking to new tory ministers. In 1808 Scott was made secretary to the parliamentary commission to inquire into the administration of justice in Scotland, which reported in 1810.

Then in April 1808 the *Edinburgh Review*, owned by Archibald Constable and edited by Francis Jeffrey, published Jeffrey's hostile review of *Marmion*. The review properly identified many issues for critical debate, but from a man who was regarded as a friend its manner and tone were unacceptable, and when in the October issue of the *Edinburgh Review* Jeffrey published an article against continuing the Peninsular War Scott (like many others) cancelled his subscription. In the midst of the public row about the *Edinburgh*'s defeatism, John Murray arrived in Edinburgh to discuss establishing a new tory periodical to advance the ministerial point of view, and Scott threw himself energetically into planning what was to become the *Quarterly Review*. Scott had broken with his Edinburgh publisher.

Constable was the most innovative publisher of his age. He paid large sums of money to secure best-selling authors, and he recouped his outlay by a marketing strategy which involved heavy advertising and the promotion of star names. It was he who recognized first the possibilities of a mass market for best-selling authors, and Scott's final edition had its birth in Constable's marketing ideas. Scott's break with Constable was disastrous for both parties. Indeed it can be argued that the seeds of the crash in 1826 were sown here, for Scott now established his own publishing company: on 19 July 1809 Scott, James, and John Ballantyne signed a deed of co-partnery which set up the publishing business John Ballantyne & Co.

While *The Lady of the Lake* and *Rokeby* were profitable, all other authors' works made losses. The *Edinburgh Annual Register*, a periodical which began publication in 1810, for all its intellectual interest (its first number included Scott's 'View of the changes proposed and adopted in the administration of justice in Scotland', his first reasoned exposition of a philosophic conservatism) lost £1000 per issue. Even worse, James Ballantyne & Co. ceased to be profitable as Constable & Co. withdrew its business.

By 1812 it had become apparent that John Ballantyne & Co. was making unsustainable losses. The national financial crisis of 1812–14 led to reduced orders for books from retailers, late payments, and the bankruptcy of many companies whose debts to John Ballantyne & Co. were either not paid or paid only in part. John Ballantyne & Co., being undercapitalized and relying too heavily on bank credit, found itself unable to meet its own bills and to repay bank loans on time, and *Rokeby* failed to generate enough ready money to meet obligations. Protracted negotiations with Constable in 1813 led to the purchase of Ballantyne stock on the condition that John Ballantyne & Co. ceased to be an active publisher, to the sale of a share in *Rokeby*, and later to the advance sale to Constable of rights for the publication of *The Lord of the Isles*. Scott had to ask the duke of Buccleuch to guarantee a bank loan of £4000, which he used to repurchase the copyright of *The Lady of the Lake* and *Rokeby* from John Ballantyne & Co., thus putting £4000 into the business to keep it solvent. Many friends lent small sums. All the personal loans were repaid in 1814, but it was not until Whit Sunday 1818 that the bond signed by the duke was returned to him. The business was eventually wound up profitably in 1817, but the results were less good for Archibald Constable & Co., which, to secure Scott as a Constable author by buying unsaleable stock, was effectively taking over the Ballantyne debts. But there was a reconciliation, and as part of the reconciliation Constable commissioned essays on chivalry and the drama for the supplement to the *Encyclopaedia Britannica* (published 1818 and 1819 respectively).

In 1811 Scott's lease of Ashestiel expired, and, needing a new place, he opened negotiations with Dr Douglas, the minister in Galashiels, for the purchase of Newarthaugh, a farm of about 100 acres on the south bank of the Tweed near Melrose. On 20 June Scott agreed to pay £4200, to take entry on Whit Sunday (15 May) 1812, and to pay £1500 then and the rest within five years. He at once began to think of what he would build, and by the time of their flitting in 1812 had renamed the estate Abbotsford. But it is a measure of the financial desperation of 1813 that nothing was undertaken to improve what was only a five-room cottage until 1814.

1814–1831: Scott the novelist *Waverley* was published on 7 July 1814 by Archibald Constable & Co. in Edinburgh, and by Longman, Rees, Orme, and Brown in London. As P. D. Garside has shown, the novel was probably begun in 1808 (the date '1st November, 1805' in the first chapter is part of the fiction), continued in 1810, and completed in 1813–14; it was first advertised in 1810, and again in January 1814. The early part (up to the beginning of chapter 5) was probably written in parallel with Scott's 'Memoirs' and with the *Marmion* epistles, and thus it may be seen as a third attempt in authorial self-exploration in 1808.

Although *Waverley* was anonymous, Scott was being identified in reviews before the end of 1814. Yet his novels were always published anonymously, and nothing he said by way of explanation—that it was an experiment (it was, and at first his friends did not like it), that a person employed in the supreme civil court of Scotland should not write novels, that Lord Byron had displaced him as the public's favourite poet—is wholly convincing. It had been a custom to publish novels anonymously, as a poet he had been gradually overcrowded with social admirers, he liked being mysterious, it was a good sales gimmick—each of these has been cited as a reason for maintaining anonymity. However, between 1814 and 1827, when he publicly acknowledged his authorship, Scott maintained the fiction that it was the author of *Waverley* and not Walter Scott who wrote the Waverley novels, and no title-page ever bore his name.

Between 1814 and his death in 1832 Scott published twenty-three works of fiction, four of which contain two tales: *Waverley* (1814); *Guy Mannering* (1815); *The Antiquary* (1816); *Tales of My Landlord* (1816), containing *The Black Dwarf* and *Old Mortality*; *Rob Roy* (1817); *Tales of my Landlord*, second series (1818), containing *The Heart of Mid-Lothian*; *Tales of my Landlord*, third series (1819), containing *The Bride of Lammermoor* and *A Legend of Montrose*; *Ivanhoe* (1819); *The Monastery* (1820); *The Abbot* (1820); *Kenilworth* (1821); *The Pirate* (1821); *The Fortunes of Nigel* (1822); *Peveril of the Peak* (1823); *Quentin Durward* (1823); *Saint Ronan's Well* (1823); *Redgauntlet* (1824); *Tales of the Crusaders* (1825), containing *The Betrothed* and *The Talisman*; *Woodstock* (1826); *Chronicles of the Canongate* (1827); *The Fair Maid of Perth* (1828); *Anne of Geierstein* (1829); and *Tales of my Landlord*, fourth series (1831), containing *Count Robert of Paris* and *Castle Dangerous*.

It appears that Scott was writing a novel every nine months, but the speed of production was in fact uneven: there was a gap of fifteen months between *Guy Mannering* and *The Antiquary*, but *Tales of my Landlord* was published only six months later. Following the publication of the third series of *Tales of my Landlord* in June 1819 he completed four novels in the next eighteen months. After *Woodstock* in 1826 his production of fiction diminished, partly because he grew more interested in writing history. The intellectual foundations of his fiction were laid long in the past, and the gestation period for a novel was usually over a year and sometimes considerably longer. When he finished one novel an interval of about two months would normally elapse before he started on the next. The initial writing could be comparatively slow as he would reread key sources, but once into volumes 2 and 3 Scott speeded up, and with typesetting taking place just as soon as each section of copy was received, and with proofs going back to him as soon as each sheet was ready, publication followed within a few weeks of his completing the manuscript.

Scott wrote on one side of quarto sheets of paper; he made corrections as he wrote, and used the opposing versos for larger changes and expansions. The next morning he reread what he had written, correcting, adding, and developing ideas. So that his handwriting should not be seen in the printing house, thus maintaining the pretence of anonymity, Scott's original manuscripts were copied, and it was the copies which were sent to the compositors. The compositors set the text before them and also supplied punctuation, normalized spelling, and corrected minor errors. Proofs were read in-house against the copies, and were used to improve the punctuation supplied. When the initial corrections had been made, a new set of proofs was drawn and sent to James Ballantyne. He acted as Scott's 'common reader' and his editor. He sent the annotated proofs to Scott, who usually accepted his suggestions but sometimes rejected them. Scott made many more changes; he cut out redundant words, and substituted the vivid for the pedestrian; he refined the punctuation; from time to time he reworked and revised passages extensively, and in so doing made the proofs a stage in the composition of the novels. Scott's corrections and revisions were copied by Ballantyne on to a clean set of proofs, the changes were made and the next proofreading was normally done in-house, and then the sheets were printed off: Scott received revises only occasionally. Thus the printing of sheets was going on as Scott was still writing, and Scott was using his proofs as direction markers for the development of his plots. The novels were normally published in three volumes (the 'Tales' were in four), and Scott fitted his fictions to this tripartite structure.

The title 'the Waverley novels', which was used in reviews, and which was adopted as the collective name for Scott's last edition, has tended to make readers and critics consider them as a single *œuvre*. However, this homogenizing effect distorts an understanding of Scott as novelist. Scott's novels (in the plural) do not attempt to show that heroic action is neither heroic nor useful, although that might be said of *Waverley*; they are varied in period, in subject, and in technique. Indeed, Scott could be said to be a novelist who constantly explores new problems and uses new fictional structures to do so.

Of Scott's twenty-three novels, only three (*Guy Mannering*, *The Antiquary*, and *Saint Ronan's Well*) are set in his own lifetime. The other twenty are set in the past, and each is set in a different period. Some critics have tried to read the novels in their historical order, but this approach does not work as there are different kinds of history in different novels. *Waverley* constitutes a valid interpretation of 1745–6. It is justified as historical analysis by the wealth of precise period detail and Scott's understanding of the political, economic, social, and cultural basis of the Jacobite rising of 1745. *Waverley* is a *Bildungsroman*, a novel about a young man's moral development; its originality consists in the test of his maturity being his ability to recognize the outcome of history. But *Ivanhoe* is not a valid interpretation of 1194: it is an eclectic work drawing on material from pre-conquest times through to the fourteenth century. *Ivanhoe* is essentially a moral work. It is an intense consideration of misogyny and racial oppression, in which the attempted rape of Rebecca the Jewess by the dominant figure of the Norman master race, Brian de Bois-Guilbert, is a powerful symbol of the themes of the novel. *Ivanhoe* may be set in a distant period, but it has a political modernity which makes it one of the most remarkable novels of the nineteenth century.

Scott was interested in periods of conflict, particularly conflict arising from the competition of societies and cultures in different stages of development, but there is no single 'take' on the subject. *Quentin Durward*, set in 1465–8, is a study of the first modern state in the process of destroying the feudal system. *Old Mortality* is a study of a civil war in which the two sides are divided by religion, political ideology, and class. In *The Bride of Lammermoor*, set in the first edition in 1703–5, two factions in the Scottish parliament fight for supremacy, and use power to enrich themselves and despoil the other side; in that conflict Edgar and Lucy, a pair of Romeo and Juliet lovers, are destroyed. In Scott's greatest and most profound novel, *The Heart of Mid-Lothian*, set in the main in 1736–7, the protagonist who at the beginning is ruled by her clear conception of conscience gradually finds her conscience politicized as she realizes that justice is deeply compromised by expediency and the political context. In the conscience of Jeanie Deans one can see Scott's belief that human beings were products of society, and could be described in terms of social function and class, personal and national history, and language. *Guy Mannering*, set in 1781–2, offers no simple opposition: the Scotland represented in the novel is at once backward and advanced, traditional and modern—it is a country in varied stages of progression in which there are many social subsets, each with its own laws and customs. And if the subject matter is varied, so too is the 'mood'. *The Antiquary* is an optimistic comedy in which the action is resolved by a coming together of all classes in defence of the country; *Kenilworth* is a tragedy; *Chronicles of the Canongate* is a compendium of three tragic tales held together by the commentary of the embittered narrator.

Scott was an experimental novelist. *Waverley* is a third-person narrative, in which the narrator is in full control of the information given to the reader; but in *Guy Mannering*, the next novel, the authority of the narrator is undercut by direct speech, by inset letters, by the letters and journal entries of several characters, by the epigraphs heading each chapter which are not part of the narration but give a different perspective, by prophecies made by characters, all in all a narrative in which the social subsets mentioned above get a chance to articulate their own way of seeing things. In *Old Mortality* the nominal author, Peter Pattieson, uses his first chapter to describe the way in which he gathers and deploys the information on which his history of 1679–89 is based. *Rob Roy* is the first first-person retrospective narration in which the narrator is convincingly wiser than he was in the days of his youth. Scott's restless exploration of the possibilities of different kinds of narrative reaches its highest development in *Redgauntlet*. The first volume consists of a series of letters between two friends, Darsie Latimer and Alan Fairford, while volumes 2 and 3 consist of Darsie's journal and third-person narrative, interwoven with each other by an unidentified editor. All three volumes include a series of inset tales nominally recorded by Darsie and Alan. Scott's formal *mélange* was new in 1824, but each of the different forms is in some way characteristic of the 1760s, and appropriate to a novel much of which was purportedly written in 1765. In addition to their historical typicality, the movement between literary kinds generates shifts in perspective, and so keeps the reader aware that the perception of 'truth' is at least in part determined by narrative mode. *Redgauntlet* is a metafictional novel, repeatedly drawing attention to its language and its shifting forms, and in the process demonstrating that the past is not a *donné* but is created by tale-telling.

Scott is credited with inventing the historical novel. Novels about the past such as Jane Porter's *The Scottish Chiefs* (1810) were published before *Waverley*, but Scott was right to claim in a comment on his imitators in 1826: 'They may do their fooling with better grace but I like Sir Andrew Aguecheek do it more natural' (*Journal*, 214). Scott did not just use formal expository prose in his analysis of the past, but also a variety of dramatic languages to represent different ideologies and different class perspectives on the movements of history. He did not impose a single view of the past by representing everything in the narrator's ideolect, but allowed his characters to use a variety of geographic and social dialects to speak for themselves. In addition, his knowledge of the literature of the past in all its forms gave him an unrivalled sense of appropriate period diction, and his use of direct quotation, and of incidents and tales found in the literature of the period, allowed the past to speak in its own language.

Waverley was published on 7 July 1814 in an edition of

1000 copies. A second edition of 2000 copies appeared in August, a third of 1000 in October. In Scott's lifetime there were eight separate editions, and the novel also appeared in six collections. The initial imprint for *Guy Mannering* was 2000 copies; for *The Antiquary* 6000 copies; for *Rob Roy* 10,000 copies. Thereafter the number of copies in the first edition of each novel was usually about 10,000; even in 1829 8500 copies of *Anne of Geierstein* were printed. As the size of the initial imprint rose, the number of editions fell, and so unit manufacturing costs dropped. At the same time the price was pushed up: *Waverley* cost £1 1*s*., *The Antiquary* £1 4*s*., and *Ivanhoe* (which was better printed and on better paper) £1 10*s*., until the final price for a three-volume novel was reached with *Kenilworth* at £1 11*s*. 6*d*. in 1821. The publishing of Scott's novels was organized to improve their profitability.

Scott's agreement with his publishers normally licensed them to sell a stated number of copies of a novel manufactured by James Ballantyne & Co., and stipulated that the author should have a half share in the profits, the profits being the publisher's receipts, less the cost of manufacturing and marketing, and that a certain amount of old John Ballantyne stock should be purchased. Later both James and John Ballantyne were given a sixth share in the profits.

In negotiating with publishers, Scott employed John Ballantyne until his death in 1821 as his literary agent, but as John was not trusted James would sometimes substitute for him. Scott was the first writer to have an agent, and used him to play one publisher off against another. In 1817 he instructed James to negotiate a deal for *Tales of my Landlord* with the Edinburgh publisher William Blackwood and his London correspondent John Murray instead of the usual Constable. Scott preferred Constable to all other publishers, but by trying another publisher he created an auction for his work. What Scott achieved by such manoeuvres was not an increase in the author's profits, but more contracts for as yet unwritten works, which were paid for by promissory bills payable at stated intervals in the future. The publisher expected to be able to pay these as the cash came in from the sales of the work, while Scott usually took them to the bank and sold them for ready money at a discount on their face value. The publisher then owed the money to the bank, not the author.

The profits from the publication of Scott's fiction were enormous, and enriched all parties: from the first edition of *The Antiquary* Scott made about £1682, and from the imprint of 10,000 of the second series of *Tales* he expected to make up to £4000. But even greater sums came from the sale of his copyrights; with the exception of Murray's quarter share in *Marmion* which he had been unable to buy back, Scott sold all his copyrights to Constable for £12,000 in 1819. Further sales of his copyright in new novels followed in 1821 and 1823.

1802–1831: Scott as critic Scott contributed reviews to the *Edinburgh Review* from 1802 to 1808, to the *Quarterly* from the first number in 1809, and to *Blackwood's Edinburgh Magazine* from 1818. He returned to the *Edinburgh Review* in the same year, and wrote for the *Foreign Quarterly Review* from 1827. By modern standards reviews of the period are wordy, and involve numerous extracts which offer the reader the chance of a real sampling of the work reviewed. In spite of the expansive manner Scott has insight, and his discussion goes to the central issues in critical debate. He objects to Currie's niceness in excluding poems by Burns which might be considered morally offensive, for he considers 'The Jolly Beggars' Burns's most brilliant work and describes 'Holy Willie's Prayer' as 'exquisitely severe' (*Prose Works*, 17.247). He reviewed both the third and fourth cantos of *Childe Harold's Pilgrimage*, and remarked 'Childe Harold may not be, nor do we believe he is, Lord Byron's very self, but he is Lord Byron's picture, sketched by Lord Byron himself' (ibid., 17.341); there has never been a better formulation of the relationship between Byron and his fictional character. His review of Jane Austen's *Emma* is simply the best piece of contemporary criticism on her work. He shows a cunning awareness of the ways in which the diarist reveals himself in his review of the first edition of Pepys, and immediately applied that awareness to himself in his *Journal*. He wrote on many contemporaries—Godwin, Croker, Southey, Campbell, Maturin, Mary Shelley, Galt, Hoffmann—as well as many books of contemporary scholarship on a wide variety of subjects including Ellis's *Specimens of Early English Poetry*, Todd's edition of Spenser, Ossian, Ritson's *Annals of the Caledonians*, tree planting, and Pitcairn's *Trials*. He also reviewed his own *Tales of my Landlord* in the *Quarterly* as a joke but showed an insight into his own fiction unequalled by any other critic.

Scott nowhere wrote a theory of literature, but in his reviews, his 'Lives of the novelists', his essays, debates such as that in the 'Introductory Epistle' to *The Fortunes of Nigel*, his introductions to his collected poetry and prose, and his remarks scattered through his letters, a comprehensive interpretation of literature can be seen. He is a Romantic in relating literature to the expression of the imagination, in emphasizing originality, but he has a sociologist's awareness of the social function of literature. In his 'Essay on romance' every major development in literary form is linked to changes in social conditions, and, conversely, he also sees literature as historical evidence which can be used to diagnose the condition of society. Scott is never as subtle in his detailed verbal commentary as Coleridge. It is argument which distinguishes his general literary discussion, and in his arguments he can be recognized as the first true theorist of fiction.

1812–1825: Abbotsford On moving to Abbotsford in 1812 Scott commissioned a plan for a new cottage from William Stark. But in 1813 Scott could only afford to prettify, Stark died, and the plan was abandoned in 1814. Scott extended the estate by purchasing Kaeside for about £3000 in November 1815, part of Abbotslee in January 1816, Dick's Cleugh (which he renamed the Rhymer's Glen to locate True Thomas's meeting with the Queen of Fairies on his own estate) in December 1816, Toftfield (which he renamed Huntlyburn) in September 1817, and Broomilees in 1820. His principal interest was not in the farms but in woodlands, and by March 1818 he estimated that he had planted a million trees.

In 1816 Scott began planning a new house, and commissioned plans from William Atkinson, a London architect. Building commenced in 1817 and continued into 1819, and resulted in what is now the dining-room, the armoury, and the breakfast parlour (initially Scott's study) of the present house. Old stones came from other buildings such as the Edinburgh Tolbooth and Lindean church, and were incorporated into the new structure. The old farmhouse was demolished in January 1822, and the second part of the new house consisting of the present entrance hall, the study, the library, and the sitting-room was built between 1822 and 1825.

Abbotsford has often been derided. Many might have spent wealth such as Scott's on another object, but Scott chose to spend his own money in creating an estate and building a house. In its day it was a modern dwelling, using up-to-date technology such as gas lighting. It was laid out in a way convenient for a scholar who needed ready access to books, but who was also obliged to do much entertaining. His library, described in the late and as yet unpublished work 'Reliquiae Trotcosienses', was for use, not display, and is distinguished for its collection of works on popular superstitions. Abbotsford remains a house full of interest and curiosity, and, taken with its contents, constitutes a material history of Scotland from the days before museums.

1812–1826: public life Scott's friendship with the princess of Wales precluded, he thought, friendship with the prince, so in 1812 it was a surprise to learn that in a conversation with Byron the prince had talked of his delight in Scott's poetry. An offer of the poet laureateship followed in 1813, but Scott refused, as he thought the office ridiculous. In April 1815 Scott was invited to dine with the prince, found him an excellent companion, and was allowed to look at Jacobite papers in the prince's library. In January 1817 he was instructed to prepare a warrant to open the chest in Edinburgh Castle in which the Scottish crown jewels, which had not been seen since 1707, were thought to be, and on 4 February 1818 the box was broken open and the regalia were found. It seems that immediately afterwards William Adam, a recent friend of Scott but an old friend of the prince regent, suggested that Scott might be made a baronet, a suggestion which ruffled a few ministerial tempers as they wished to maintain their complete control of patronage in Scotland, but which resulted in the award being announced in December 1818.

After the war, hard times, political discontent, and a rebirth of republican sentiments such as had not been articulated in Scotland since 1792–4 regenerated the radical movement. From August 1819 numerous meetings were held in Glasgow and Lanarkshire to demand universal suffrage and annual parliaments. On 16 August the meeting of 80,000 people at St Peter's Fields in Manchester was broken up; 11 people were killed and 421 injured. Scott supported the magistrates in print. Additional troops were sent to disaffected areas, and Scott became extremely active and vociferous in re-establishing the volunteer corps which had been raised during the wars with France. In December he contributed three letters against radicalism to the *Edinburgh Weekly Journal* (edited by James Ballantyne); on 1 January 1820 they were published in pamphlet form as *The Visionary*.

To students of Scott his behaviour during the 'radical war' is deeply embarrassing, for his response to events was hysterical. There is no straightforward explanation. In 1817 and more seriously in the middle of 1819 Scott was ill with gallstones; in June 1819 he was thought to be dying. It is possible that the psychological effect of critical illness disturbed his judgement for a time. In turning himself into one of the landed gentry, with a title, he may have misjudged his political role and significance. It is significant too that his elder son Walter had decided on an army career, that Scott had to purchase a commission in the cavalry for £735 in June, that the uniform and kit proved extremely expensive, that his uncle, his aunt, and then his mother—three members of one family—died in December, and that his daughter Sophia became engaged to John Gibson Lockhart in January 1820, and that they married on 29 April 1820, fifteen days after the culmination of the 'radical war'. This was a period of high stress.

Honours, with their corresponding responsibilities, were thrust on him. He was elected president of the Royal Society of Edinburgh in December 1820. In July 1822 the king announced a visit to Scotland and the organization was imposed on Scott. He had two weeks to arrange festivities and ceremonials suitable to welcome the first monarch to visit Scotland since Charles II was crowned in 1651, and he had to fill in a fortnight, 14–29 August 1822. He turned it into a fancy-dress party, insisting that all gentlemen should appear in kilts. Every commentator points out that highland dress was inappropriate for lowlanders, but Scott was making Scotland different, breaking tribal identities by equipping all Scotland with visible symbols of Scottishness, and freeing Scotland from the kind of inhibitions that prevented his father from enjoying himself. This was Scotland's greatest party: there was a ceremonial landing in Leith, followed by processions through the city, balls, a grand review, a display of the honours of Scotland, dinners, a gathering of the clans, and a command performance of Daniel Terry's dramatic version of *Rob Roy*. The visit and the *brouhaha* did not please everyone, and many wrote down their cynical, detached observations, and yet in writing as they did about the absurdity of it all they testify to its success: it could not be ignored.

The king's visit exhausted Scott. His closest friend, William Erskine, died the day the king arrived. It took Scott two months to recover, and to begin work again on the second half of *Peveril of the Peak*. In 1823 he became involved with planning the creation of the Edinburgh Academy, and proposed that the curriculum should include English and Scottish history and literature. He purchased promotions to lieutenant (1823) and captain (1824) for his son Walter. He became chairman of the Edinburgh Oil Gas Company in 1824. He became governor of the Scottish Union, and an extraordinary director of the

Edinburgh Life Assurance Company. He negotiated Walter's marriage to the heiress Jane Jobson in 1825. Scott was a public servant, a public figure, a landowner, and a man of business, as well as being the great author.

1826: the crash On Sunday 20 November 1825 Scott began his *Journal*. Reviewing the first edition of Pepys's diaries just a month later, he remarked that 'in this species of self-intercourse we put many tricks upon our actual and our moral self', and so even although he recognized that his journal would one day be published, he vowed not to change any entry retrospectively. Later interference with the daily record is indeed minimal. The *Journal* fulfils the nursery rhyme motto he put at its head:

> As I walked by myself
> I talkd to my self
> And thus my self said to me
> (*Journal*, xlviii)

Scott is always aware of the way in which literary form tends to fix meaning, and so he tries to ensure that the *Journal* is undistorted by method. He is endlessly interesting; he records what he had been doing; he comments acutely on what goes on around him; he works out intellectual positions; he analyses himself; he lays himself out on the page. The *Journal* is a superb work, but its greatness is ultimately due to an accident of timing. It opens with Scott at the height of his fame and prosperity. Within six months he was ruined and his wife was dead. He undertook to repay all his debts, and the *Journal* records how a heroic decision to do right and to act well gradually destroyed him mentally and physically.

The system under which the publishers Archibald Constable & Co., their author, and their printers did business with each other was unsophisticated. There was no limited liability; companies were governed by partnership law in which all business and personal assets are at risk. Neither business had sufficient working capital and both relied on bank borrowing to provide it. Payments were usually made by promissory bills. In addition, there were accommodation bills in which Archibald Constable & Co. and James Ballantyne & Co. effectively guaranteed each other's bank loans. It was a recognized system of trade, but it was expensive and risky. The winter of 1825–6 was a period of severe economic recession, and the funds coming into the publishers were insufficient to pay off their debts as these became due. In November and December Scott raised £15,000, but neither Hurst, Robinson (the London publishers) nor Constable were able to raise new loans, and so when Hurst, Robinson were unable to retire a bill on the due date, and the banks tried to get back the money which Constable had received from them but which Hurst, Robinson had been due to pay, there followed the insolvency of all the companies and all their partners.

The total indebtedness of Scott and Ballantyne, the partners in James Ballantyne & Co., proved to be over £126,000. Of this £20,000 was Scott's private debt. Some £15,000 consisted of bills drawn by Scott and accepted by James Ballantyne & Co.; this was effectively borrowed money put into the printing business by Scott. Scott's private indebtedness was thus £35,000. The trading debts of the company came to about £13,000; in addition it had borrowed £29,000 on bills guaranteed by Constable, making the debts of James Ballantyne & Co. £42,000. In addition Scott had provided guarantees to Constable for £9000 of Constable's borrowings, and James Ballantyne & Co. had guaranteed £30,000 of Constable's borrowings, giving a total of £39,000, which consisted of the debts of others but for which Scott and Ballantyne were legally liable. Finally, there was a mortgage on Abbotsford of £10,000 which Scott raised in December 1825 to assist Constable.

There were various ways of dealing with insolvency. Archibald Constable and his partner Robert Cadell chose sequestration: all their private assets and all the assets of the company were sold for the benefit of creditors, but in the end only 2*s.* 9*d.* in the pound was available. Scott and Ballantyne chose to sign a trust deed in favour of their creditors. The aim was to repay the debts in full, but the advantage of a trust was that the terms on which repayment was to take place were a matter of agreement. The trustees chose to sell 39 Castle Street. They were unable to sell Abbotsford as Scott, as part of young Walter's marriage settlement in January 1825, had entailed Abbotsford on Walter and his heirs male, but they allowed Scott to retain his life rent of Abbotsford, and the use of his library and furnishings. It took time to settle the ownership of literary property contracted for, but not yet delivered, but in December 1827 Lord Newton allocated ownership of *Woodstock* and *The Life of Napoleon* to Scott's trustees. However, the most important aspect of the trust was Scott's promise to allocate future literary earnings to it. Scott was the only one of those involved in the crash able to generate a large income, and he thus became responsible for paying not just his own debts, but also all those of James Ballantyne & Co. (for which James was equally liable), and some £39,000 of the debts of Constable and Cadell.

From the publication of Lockhart's *Memoirs of the Life of Sir Walter Scott* in 1837–8 there has been bitter controversy about responsibility for the crash of 1826, but the debate has always been naïve. Bankruptcy is not a moral issue. The recession of 1825–6 bankrupted some banks, and thousands of businesses and individuals, as well as Sir Walter Scott. Economic conditions and structural faults in the economic system were the primary causes of failure: had there been limited liability only the printing and publishing companies would have fallen. But notwithstanding the mess in 1826 Ballantyne, Constable, and Scott had developed a new industry in Edinburgh. Constable had broken London's dominance in book publishing, and whereas in 1803 Ballantyne had bought all his printing supplies in London, in 1826 much of his paper was produced in Penicuik, the types were manufactured in Edinburgh and Glasgow, the ink was home-made, and at its greatest in 1823 James Ballantyne & Co. operated twenty-three presses.

In February 1826 there may have been a degree of calculation in Scott's entering the debate on a government measure introduced to deal with the economic crisis which would have restricted the rights of the Scottish banks to issue their own notes, but Scott represented it as a nationalist issue, 'the late disposition to change every thing in Scotland to an English model' (*Journal*, 94). In February and March he wrote three letters to the editor of the *Edinburgh Weekly Journal* in which he used the currency issue as an exemplum for the larger tendency. The letters caused a sensation. Ministerial friends were very angry, but withdrew the measure. The banks were grateful; taking a lead from his old rival in love, William Forbes, they agreed to the creation of a trust for the settling of Scott's debts, and *The Letters of Malachi Malagrowther*, as the letters are now known, is recognized as a classic in political argument.

The first dividend of 6*s*. in the pound for Scott's creditors was agreed in December 1827, the second in July 1830. In recognition of what had been achieved the creditors agreed on 17 December 1830 to give Scott his library, furniture, curiosities, and household goods. In 1833 the creditors received a final dividend: in all, 18*s*. in the pound was paid, the other 2*s*. being represented by the creditors' gift to Scott. It was an extraordinary achievement. It was based primarily on Scott's own literary output. *Woodstock* (1826), *The Life of Napoleon Buonaparte* (1827), *The Fair Maid of Perth* (1828), *Anne of Geierstein* (1829), and the fourth series of *Tales of my Landlord* (1831) generated large sums for the trust. Scott also wrote for himself, and in so doing irritated his trustees, but he found he could not live on his official salaries while maintaining an appropriate style of life at Abbotsford and travelling to Paris in October and November 1826 to conduct research for *Napoleon*. So he applied to his own needs the income from *Chronicles of the Canongate* (1827), four series of *Tales of a Grandfather* (his histories of Scotland and France written for his eldest grandson), the *History of Scotland* (1829–30), written for Lardner's *Cabinet Cyclopaedia*, and *Letters on Demonology and Witchcraft* (1830). But by far the biggest project was what is familiarly known as the 'Magnum opus', Scott's own edition of his novels. The full story has been told by Jane Millgate in *Scott's Last Edition* (1987), but, in short, this was not just a literary undertaking but a large commercial project. The trustees had to purchase the copyrights when auctioned by Constable's trustees on 20 December 1827. Scott wrote introductions to each work, and new notes, and corrected the text in a sporadic way. Two engravings were ordered for each volume. Above all, the project required an astute manager, and for this the trustees used Robert Cadell, even although he was formally still an undischarged bankrupt. Publication began on 1 June 1829, and for four years a volume was issued monthly, priced 5*s*. The project was a phenomenal success, with sales reaching over 30,000 a month. By Scott's death £51,128 had been repaid. Life insurance (£22,000), the purchase of all the copyrights from Scott's heirs by Cadell for £24,500, and the undistributed income of £12,179 led to the complete payment of the debts in 1833.

1826–1832: final years After Lady Scott's death on 14 May 1826 Scott wrote to his daughter Sophia: 'Whatever were her failings they hurt only herself and arose out of bodily illness' (*Letters*, 10.39). It is not clear what was wrong. From 1823 Scott's letters repeatedly mention asthma, but the term may only indicate difficulty in breathing. Oedema and a blotchy discoloration of her face noticed by some visitors suggest partial heart failure. At the end of her life she was taking digitalis. However, she was in great pain (was it cancer?), and took so much laudanum that it is probable that James Hogg was right in saying that Charlotte became addicted. Although expecting the end for two years Scott found her death difficult. He preferred to go to Edinburgh to fulfil his duty in court rather than watch her die, and his commentary in the *Journal* on his response to her death is the most moving section of the whole. On 11 June he wrote:

> Bad dreams about poor Charlotte—woke thinking my old and inseparable friend beside me and it was only when I was fully awake that I could persuade myself that she was dark low and distant—and that my bed was widowd. (*Journal*, 157)

As a result of the crash and Charlotte's death Scott began to commit whole days to writing. It is not surprising that he complained about headaches. Nor is it surprising, given his life of unceasing labour and the death of Charlotte, that he was frequently depressed. From January 1827 he complained more frequently about his lameness, and of pain in his leg (he was probably suffering from post-polio syndrome). The *Journal* is full of reports of ailments.

On 15 February 1830 Scott suffered his first stroke. He retired as principal clerk to the court of session on 12 November with a pension of £864, and soon afterwards suffered a second, damaging stroke which affected his ability to write and to express himself clearly, but he again recovered. The following month he presided in the sheriff court, and began a pamphlet advocating the reintroduction of the income tax rather than reform of the House of Commons. The paper remains unpublished, as in the ferment for reform all Scott's advisers thought it would damage sales, but the idea that social justice requires the redistribution of wealth rather more than the extension of voting rights has, over the last two centuries, had formidable intellectual and political support. In April 1831 he had a third stroke, but over the summer worked on the fourth series of *Tales of my Landlord*, and on a fifth series of *Tales of a Grandfather* (the second on the history of France), which remained unpublished until 1996. He worked too on further notes for the 'Magnum opus'. In July he reluctantly agreed to go to the Mediterranean for the sake of his health. The original idea was for an overland journey, but William IV made a royal command that Scott be given a passage on a man-of-war, and in October he embarked on HMS *Barham* for the Mediterranean, Malta, and Naples. He moved on to Rome, and on 11 May 1832 began the overland journey home, via Florence, Venice, Verona, the Brenner Pass, Augsburg, Mainz, and down the Rhine. In Nijmegen he had a fourth stroke. He spent three weeks in London before travelling north by steamboat to Edinburgh. He reached Abbotsford on 11 July, and died there on 21 September 1832. He was buried on 26 September beside his wife in Dryburgh Abbey, Berwickshire.

Abbotsford had been settled on Walter and his heirs male. Scott's only possessions were his library, the museum pieces, and the household goods at Abbotsford (valued at £12,000 by the trustees), and his copyrights. His will, dated 4 February 1831, left everything in Abbotsford to Walter, who was to pay Sophia £1000 (she had already received £1000 on her marriage), and £2000 to each of Anne and Charles. Scott stipulated that his literary property should be divided between all four children. It included those works which had not been assigned to the trustees, and the copyright to everything else which would revert to the family when the creditors were paid and the trust wound up.

Scott's children did not enjoy the fruits of his success. In selling the copyrights to Cadell they were cheated. The large legacy left to their mother by her brother benefited only later generations, as Charles Carpenter's widow, who had the life rent of the estate, lived until 1862. Anne Scott died in 1833, and Sophia in 1837; Charles lived until 1841, dying unmarried in Tehran, and Walter died without issue in 1847.

Scott's reputation Scott was the most successful writer of his day. Not only did he sell more books, but he was the author most generally admired. His books sold right through the nineteenth century, and he retained his reputation until the 1890s. Of course other writers created space for themselves by distancing themselves from Scott and his achievement (such is the anxiety of influence), but for the most part they did not deny the greatness of that achievement. In the 1890s school editions of his works began to appear, and thereafter his popularity declined, reaching its nadir in the 1950s and 1960s. Scott suffered from enforced reading, but changes in critical taste and theory were also a major factor. The model of the well-wrought urn will not fit Scott. Late twentieth-century theory in its wariness of inherent meaning, and its recognition of the artificiality of literary form, worked in Scott's favour. In addition, the first critical edition of his novels, the Edinburgh Edition of the Waverley novels (1993–2004), has shown an even more sophisticated use of linguistic polyphony than has ever previously been recognized.

Scott was subject to sustained twentieth-century hostility because he was a unionist and a tory, and allegedly responsible for all popular myths about Scotland, and for tartanry, tourism, and kitsch culture. But the objections are misconceived: what later generations have made of his work is not the fault of an author. Scott's creative impact on Scotland was to define Scottishness in cultural rather than political terms, and so to maintain the idea of nationhood in a country which for the following two centuries was without independent political institutions. That in itself has been a subject of attack by theorists of nationalism. Scott has no myths about national origins, founding fathers, iconic events, or an organic past. His theoretical interest in the writing of history prevented his works from ever providing a basis for a political programme.

In Europe, however, the impact was the reverse. Scott had been inspired by the German interest in national identity, folk culture, and medieval literature, but it was he more than anyone else who in his poetry and his novels created the means of dramatizing the past. Scott's life work was the propagation and preservation of the cultural difference of a national community in opposition to the hegemonic tendencies of the British state, but throughout Europe similar materials became the vehicle for political action. There has been little study of the conditions in which a desire to preserve the past is transformed into an active claim to the right of self-determination, but it is probable that Scott's images of nationhood were more powerful than even Rousseau's thinking.

Scott's impact on other arts is less contentious because so obvious. He was a radical inventor of literary forms, and he turned the novel into an expressive medium for a variety of period, class, and regional experience. All British, American, and European novelists of the nineteenth century learned from his ways of writing. He was the great inventor in opera too. The librettos of some ninety operas are based on Scott's poems and novels, including those of Rossini's *La donna del lago* (1819), Bellini's *I puritani* (1835), Donizetti's *Lucia di Lammermoor* (1839), Bizet's *La jolie fille de Perth* (1867), and Sullivan's *Ivanhoe* (1891). Such composers recognized that the extraordinarily varied texture of Scott's novels, which combined narrative, dialogue, poetry, and song, in a medley of languages and dialects, could be successfully represented in music. More plays have been adapted from his works than those of any other writer. Pictures of scenes from Scott abound, and after the duke of Wellington he was the person most frequently painted, and whose image was most widely distributed in the first half of the nineteenth century. In *Portraits of Sir Walter Scott* (1987) Francis Russell records 233 separate representations.

Scott has always been considered collectable. His literary manuscripts were given to Archibald Constable by Scott in 1823. They were sold by Constable's trustees, re-collected by Robert Cadell, who added manuscripts from the post-1823 era, only to be dispersed once more in the 1860s. John Pierpont Morgan began collecting Scott manuscripts in the late nineteenth century, and his great collection is now found at the institution which bears his name, the Pierpont Morgan Library, New York. In addition to letters and literary manuscripts, the National Library of Scotland possesses Scott's 'interleaved set', the interleaved, printed editions of his novels, on which he corrected the text and added notes, and in which are bound the manuscript introductions for the 'Magnum opus', Scott's own collection of the Waverley novels, published in 48 volumes 1829–33. Literary manuscripts are also widely dispersed throughout Britain and the United States.

As a man Scott was worldly. He had no religious beliefs. He was brought up in the Church of Scotland, came to hate the narrowness of the Presbyterian tradition he had experienced, and although he became an elder in Duddingston kirk he seldom attended church. The pew in his name in St John's Episcopal Church in Princes Street in Edinburgh was occupied by Charlotte. He was a most generous man, as his support of his brothers' sons and all the small gifts he made to indigent poets testify. He had a streak of the ruthlessness of the successful businessman: he found that the Revd Edward Forster had begun work on an edition of Dryden, suggested they join forces, and then pushed him out. He was selfish in the way that creative men are selfish: for all his sociability and his capacity to make other people laugh, he offered others very little intimacy. But what does this matter? Walter Scott changed the world's understanding of history.

DAVID HEWITT

Sources *The letters of Sir Walter Scott*, ed. H. J. C. Grierson and others, centenary edn, 12 vols. (1932–79) • J. C. Corson, *Notes and index to Sir Herbert Grierson's edition of the letters of Sir Walter Scott* (1979) • J. G. Lockhart, *Memoirs of the life of Sir Walter Scott*, 7 vols. (1837–8) • W. Scott, 'Memoirs', *Scott on himself*, ed. D. Hewitt (1981) • *The journal of Sir Walter Scott*, ed. W. E. K. Anderson (1972) • W. B. Todd and A. Bowden, *Sir Walter Scott: a bibliographical history* (1998) • W. Scott, *Waverley novels*, 48 vols. (1829–33) • *The poetical works of Sir Walter Scott, bart.*, ed. J. G. Lockhart, 12 vols. (1833–4) • W. Scott, *Waverley novels*, ed. D. Hewitt and others, Edinburgh edition, 30 vols. (1993–2004) • W. Scott and others, correspondence, NL Scot. • *The prose works of Sir Walter Scott, bart.*, 28 vols. (1834–6) • J. Millgate, *Scott's last edition* (1987) • E. Johnson, *Sir Walter Scott: the great unknown*, 2 vols. (1970) • J. Sutherland, *The life of Sir Walter Scott* (1995) • P. D. Garside, 'Dating *Waverley*'s early chapters', *The Bibliotheck*, 13 (1986), 61–81 • J. C. Corson, 'Birth of the last minstrel: vital year in debate', *Weekend Scotsman* (26 Dec 1970), 1–2 • A. Melville Clark, *Sir Walter Scott: the formative years* (1969) • H. Grierson, *Sir Walter Scott, bart.* (1938) • K. W. Harry, 'The sources and treatment of traditional ballad texts in Sir Walter Scott's *Minstrelsy of the Scottish border* and Robert Jamieson's *Popular ballads and songs*', PhD diss., U. Aberdeen, 1975 • F. Russell, *Portraits of Sir Walter Scott* (1987) • H. P. Bolton, *Scott dramatized* (1992) • J. Mitchell, *More Scott operas* (1996) • T. P. MacDonald, 'Sir Walter Scott's fee book', *Juridical Review*, 62 (1950), 288–316 • D. A. Low, 'Walter Scott and Williamina Belsches', *TLS* (23 July 1971), 865–6 • P. Garside, 'Patriotism and patronage: new light on Scott's baronetcy', *Modern Language Review*, 77 (1982), 16–28 • G. Allan, *The life of Sir Walter Scott, baronet* (1834) • J. Hogg, *Anecdotes of Sir W. Scott*, ed. D. S. Mack (1983)

Archives NL Scot., corresp., business papers, and accounts | BL, corresp. with Sir T. D. Lauder, M/615 [copies] • BL, corresp. with Sir Robert Peel, Add. MSS 40350–40399 • BL, letters to A. Seward, Add. MS 37425, fols. 97–116 • BL, letters to G. Thomson, Add. MSS 35263–35265, *passim* • Bodl. Oxf., letters to Lord Byron and Lady Byron • Bodl. Oxf., letters to Mary, Thomas, and William Somerville • Bodl. Oxf., letters to Lady Louisa Stuart [copies] • Castle Ashby, Northamptonshire, letters to Lady Northampton • Cork City Library, letters to Thomas Crofton Croker • DWL, letters to William Wordsworth • Hornel Library, Broughton House, Kirkcudbright, letters to Charles Kirkpatrick Sharpe • Hunt L., letters to John Wilson Croker and Thomas Scott • John Murray, London, letters to Sir William Knighton • Mitchell L., Glas., Glasgow City Archives, letters to Sir Ilay Campbell • Morgan L., letters to Lady Abercorn, George Ellis, John Gibson, Sir William Knighton, Robert Southey, and Daniel Terry • NA Scot., letters to third, fourth, and fifth dukes of Buccleuch • NA Scot., letters to William Clerk and Sir George Clerk • NA Scot., letters to General Fairfax • NA Scot., letters to marquesses of Lothian • NA Scot., letters to first and second Viscounts Melville • NA Scot., letters to Lord Montagu • NA Scot., letters to John Taylor • NA Scot., corresp. with Hugh Scott and Harriet Scott • New York Public Library, letters to John Gibson and Sir Robert Peel • New York University, letters to second and third Viscounts Melville • NL Scot., letters to James Ballantyne • NL Scot., letters to John Ballantyne • NL Scot., letters to Blackwoods • NL Scot., letters to Edward Blore • NL Scot., letters to Robert Cadell • NL Scot., letters to Archibald Constable • NL Scot., letters to George Craig • NL Scot., letters to John Wilson Croker • NL Scot., letters to Thomas Crofton Croker • NL Scot., letters to Maria Edgeworth • NL Scot., letters to Charles Erskine • NL Scot., letters to Adam Ferguson • NL Scot., letters to Sir William Forbes • NL Scot., letters to Matthew Weld Hartstonge • NL Scot., letters to Benjamin Robert Haydon • NL Scot., letters to Richard Heber • NL Scot., letters to Rachel Jobson and others [copies] • NL Scot., letters to Sir William Knighton [copies] • NL Scot., letters to William Laidlaw • NL Scot., corresp. with Lady Anne Lindsay • NL Scot., corresp. with J. G. Lockhart • NL Scot., letters to Longman & Rees • NL Scot., corresp. with Henry Mackenzie • NL Scot., letters to first and second Viscounts Melville • NL Scot., letters to Lord Minto • NL Scot., letters to J. B. S. Morritt • NL Scot., letters, mostly to Patrick Murray [copies] • NL Scot., letters to Charlotte Champion Pascoe, Robert Pitcairn, and others • NL Scot., letters to Sir Robert Peel • NL Scot., letters to John Richardson • NL Scot., corresp. with his wife, Charlotte Scott • NL Scot., letters to Sophia, Walter, Anne, and Charles Scott • NL Scot., letters to William Scott • NL Scot., letters to Anna Seward • NL Scot., letters to Shortreed family • NL Scot., letters, mostly to James Skene • NL Scot., letters to Robert Southey • NL Scot., letters to Lady Louisa Stuart • NL Scot., letters to Robert Surtees • NL Scot., letters to Lady Sutherland • NL Scot., letters to Daniel Terry • NL Scot., letters to Thomas Thomson • NL Scot., letters to Joseph Train • NRA, priv. coll., letters to William Adam • NRA, priv. coll., letters to James Ballantyne • NRA, priv. coll., letters to Buchanan and Edmonston families • NRA, priv. coll., letters to Mrs Clephanes, Miss Clephanes, and the marchioness of Northampton • NRA, priv. coll., letters to John Scott of Gala • NRA, priv. coll., letters to Sir John Sinclair • NRA, priv. coll., corresp. with Lady Louisa Stuart • Princeton University, New Jersey, letters to Maria Edgeworth and Robert Southey • PRO NIre., letters to Lady Abercorn • RCS Eng., corresp. with Joanna Baillie • Royal Arch., letters to Sir William Knighton • Signet Library, Edinburgh, letters to James Ballantyne and David Laing • Trinity College, Hartford, Connecticut, letters to Lady Frances Douglas • U. Aberdeen, letters to Thomas Crofton Croker • U. Edin. L., letters to Maria Edgeworth and Sir Robert Peel • U. Leeds, letters to John Wilson Croker and Sir William Knighton • U. Leeds, letters to Maria Edgeworth, Robert Southey, and Daniel Terry • U. Reading L., Longman Archive, corresp. • University of Texas, Austin, letters to Robert Maturin • Wordsworth Trust, Dove Cottage, Grasmere, Cumbria, letters to Robert Southey and William Wordsworth • Yale U., letters to John Wilson Croker, Maria Edgeworth, John Gibson, Richard Heber, and Richard Polwhele

Likenesses J. Saxon, oils, *c.*1805, Scot. NPG • H. Raeburn, oils, 1808, priv. coll. [*see illus.*] • H. Raeburn, oils, 1809, priv. coll. • A. Geddes, oils, 1818, Scot. NPG • E. Landseer, oils, 1824, NPG

Wealth at death £12,000—and reversion of copyrights

Scott, Sir Walter (1826–1910), civil engineer and publisher, was born on 17 August 1826 in The Wheatsheaf inn, Abbey Town, Cumberland, the second of six children of Samuel Scott (1791–1833), innkeeper and farmer, and his wife Mary, *née* Martin (*d.* 1877). Walter's parents were poor and after his father died, when Walter was seven years old, his education was minimal. At fourteen he was apprenticed to a mason and then found work on the Caledonian Railway. Railway work took him to Newcastle upon Tyne where in 1849 he established his own business as a builder and contractor. He specialized in large-scale contracts, mainly railway and dock construction. On 17 November

1853 he married Ann Brough (1825–1890), the daughter of John Brough, a husbandman. They had six children.

Scott was engaged to build a printing factory for the Tyne Publishing Company, but the business failed in January 1882. Although Scott had no experience of printing or publishing, in August he appears to have taken over the business in lieu of payment for the factory. He appointed David Gordon, a bookbinder already working for Tyne Publishing, as general manager. Gordon was an excellent choice and gradually extended the publication programme. Tyne's list (mostly giftbooks, but also including a few biographies, a Bible, and miscellaneous titles) was kept in print, and a series of reprints of standard texts was introduced. Then came a series of selected editions, the Canterbury Poets, and the Camelot series of prose works with Ernest Rhys as general editor. Original publications followed, including works by Bernard Shaw, W. B. Yeats, and George Moore. The first English translations of Ibsen began to appear in 1888.

Building and contracting continued, with railway work still the mainstay. Scott built the first 'tube' underground railway in London, opened on 4 November 1890 by Edward, prince of Wales. The line ran from King William Street under the Thames to Stockwell. His business interests widened and before he died he had a seat on boards of at least eighteen companies including steelworks, coalmines, and shipyards. His first wife having died in 1890, on 11 January 1892 he married a widow, Helen Meikle (*c.*1850–1923), the daughter of John Dykes, a farmer. Scott was a Conservative councillor in Newcastle from 1881 to 1890 and a JP for Northumberland. He was made a baronet in the king's birthday honours of 1907. He died on holiday at Hôtel du Cap Martin, Menton, France, on 8 April 1910 and was buried in Menton on 11 April. He left just over £1,424,000, one of only fifteen truly self-made millionaires in Britain before 1939. JOHN R. TURNER

Sources priv. coll. • J. R. Turner, 'Sir Walter Scott (1826–1910), civil engineering contractor', *Transactions* [Newcomen Society], 64 (1992–3), 1–19 • J. R. Turner, 'A history of the Walter Scott publishing house', PhD diss., U. Wales, Aberystwyth, 1995 • J. R. Turner, *The Walter Scott publishing company: a bibliography* (1997) • m. certs. • W. D. Rubenstein, *Men of property: the very wealthy in Britain since the Industrial Revolution* (1981), 125–6 • *CGPLA Eng. & Wales* (1910)
Archives priv. coll.
Likenesses engraving, repro. in *Newcastle Weekly Chronicle* (2 Dec 1899), 7 • photographs, priv. coll. • portraits, priv. coll.
Wealth at death £1,424,130 3*s.* 6*d.*: English probate endorsed in Scotland, 26 Sept 1910, *CCI*

Scott, Walter Francis Montagu-Douglas-, **fifth duke of Buccleuch and seventh duke of Queensberry** (1806–1884), magnate and politician, born at Dalkeith House, Midlothian, Scotland, on 25 November 1806, was the second, but eldest surviving, son of Charles William Henry Montagu-Scott, fourth duke of Buccleuch (1772–1819) and the Hon. Harriet Catherine Townshend (1773–1814). He was thirteen when he succeeded to the dukedom, and sixteen when he entertained George IV for a fortnight at Dalkeith House during his ceremonial visit to Scotland in

Walter Francis Montagu-Douglas-Scott, fifth duke of Buccleuch and seventh duke of Queensberry (1806–1884), by George Richmond, 1864

1822. He was educated at Eton College and at St John's College, Cambridge, graduating MA in 1827. On 13 August 1829 he married Lady Charlotte Anne Thynne [*see below*], youngest daughter of Thomas Thynne, second marquess of Bath, and the Hon. Isabella Elizabeth Byng (*d.* 1830), third daughter of the fourth Viscount Torrington; they had three daughters and four sons, the youngest of whom was Lord Charles Thomas Montagu-Douglas-*Scott. Buccleuch was created knight of the Garter in 1835. He entertained Victoria and Albert at Dalkeith in 1842, in which year he was sworn of the privy council. A staunch Conservative, he was lord privy seal in Peel's ministry from February 1842 to January 1846, and lord president of the council from January to July 1846, reluctantly accepting repeal of the corn laws.

As the owner of the largest and wealthiest estates in Britain, Buccleuch exercised an almost feudal control over his many tenants, with a reputation for evicting those who did not vote in accordance with his wishes. Gladstone's opponent in the Midlothian campaign of 1879 was Buccleuch's eldest son, the earl of Dalkeith, who was defeated in spite of the extensive creation of 'faggot votes' by the duke's agents. Buccleuch was president of the Highland Agricultural Society in 1831–5 and 1866–9. Between 1835 and 1842, he built at his own expense a pier and breakwater at Granton, forming a harbour which was developed as a port on the Firth of Forth. He was president of the Society of Antiquaries from 1862 to 1873 and of the British Association in 1867; and he was elected chancellor of Glasgow University in 1877. He died at Bowhill, Selkirk, on 16 April 1884, and was buried on 23 April in St Mary's Chapel, Dalkeith.

Charlotte Anne Montagu-Douglas-Scott, duchess of Buccleuch and Queensberry (1811–1895), was mistress of the robes to Queen Victoria in 1841–6, and used her connections with Peel's ministry to secure patronage for her brothers. Her hospitality, exercised at the many Buccleuch houses in Scotland and at Montagu House in London, was often remarked upon by contemporaries. Under the influence of Henry Manning and Cecil, Lady Lothian, she converted to Roman Catholicism in 1860, after struggling with her conscience for many years over the distress it would cause her Presbyterian husband. After the death of the duke in 1884, she made her home at Ditton Park, Slough, Buckinghamshire, where she died on 28 March 1895; she was buried at Dalkeith. The family connections with the court were maintained by her daughter-in-law Louisa Jane, wife of the sixth duke, who served as mistress of the robes in 1886–92 and 1895–1901.

K. D. Reynolds

Sources GEC, *Peerage* • R. Kelley, 'Midlothian: a study in politics and ideas', *Victorian Studies*, 4 (1960–61), 118–40 • R. R. James, *Rosebery: a biography of Archibald Philip, fifth earl of Rosebery* (1963) • R. Stewart, *The politics of protection: Lord Derby and the protectionist party, 1841–1852* (1971) • W. A. Lindsay, *The royal household* (1898) • *CGPLA Eng. & Wales* (1895) [Charlotte Anne Montagu-Douglas-Scott] • K. D. Reynolds, *Aristocratic women and political society in Victorian Britain* (1998)

Archives NA Scot., corresp. • NRA, priv. coll., corresp. and papers | Beaulieu archives, John Montagu Building, Beaulieu, Brockenhurst, corresp. with Lord Montagu of Beaulieu • BL, corresp. with Lord Aberdeen, Add. MS 43201 • BL, corresp. with W. E. Gladstone, Add. MSS 44361–44460 *passim* • BL, corresp. with Sir Robert Peel, Add. MSS 40406–40598 *passim* • Bodl. Oxf., Manning MSS • Devon RO, letters to Sir Thomas Dyke Acland • NA Scot., letters to Lords Lothian • NL Scot., corresp. with Walter Scott • NRA Scotland, priv. coll., letters to J. J. Hope Johnstone • NRA, priv. coll., letters to A. R. Drummond • St. Deiniol's Library, Hawarden, letters to Sir John Gladstone; letters to Sir Thomas Gladstone • U. Edin. L., letters to David Laing • U. Southampton L., letters to duke of Wellington • UCL, corresp. with Sir Edwin Chadwick • W. Sussex RO, letters to fifth duke of Richmond; letters to sixth duke of Richmond

Likenesses W. Ingalton, double portrait, oils, 1822 (with Lord Scott), Buccleuch estates, Selkirk • T. Campbell, bust, 1835, Boughton House, Northamptonshire • F. Grant, group portrait, oils, *c*.1841 (*A hill run with the duke of Buccleuch's hounds*), Buccleuch estates, Selkirk • G. Hayter, group portrait, oils, 1842 (*The christening of the prince of Wales*), Royal Collection • J. Watson-Gordon, two oil paintings, 1842, Buccleuch estates, Selkirk, Scotland • F. Grant, oils, *c*.1861, Archer's Hall, Edinburgh • H. Weeks, bust, 1861, Boughton House, Northamptonshire • G. Richmond, drawing, 1864, Beaulieu, Hampshire [*see illus.*] • D. Macnee, oils, 1877, Buccleuch estates, Selkirk • K. Warren, oils, 1884, Buccleuch estates, Selkirk • K. Warren, oils, 1884, Beaulieu, Hampshire • attrib. J. Jackson, oils, Eton • G. Richmond, chalk drawing, Buccleuch estates, Selkirk • F. R. Say, oils, Scot. NPG • Window & Bridge, two cartes-de-visite, NPG • cartoon, repro. in *Punch*, 77 (6 Dec 1879), 259 • oils, Beaulieu, Hampshire • portrait (Charlotte Ann Montagu-Douglas-Scott), Royal Collection

Wealth at death £475,050 0*s*. 1*d*.: probate, 30 Oct 1884, *CGPLA Eng. & Wales* • £435,318 11*s*. 3*d*.: confirmation, 12 Aug 1884, *CCI* • £4014 10*s*. 4*d*.—Charlotte Anne Montagu-Douglas-Scott: probate, 27 June 1895, *CGPLA Eng. & Wales*

Scott, Sir William (*d*. 1352x6), justice, is usually said to have been a native of Kent, but in fact originated in Yorkshire, probably at Birthwaite in the parish of Kexbrough, in the part of the West Riding around Barnsley where he afterwards accumulated an estate. Without much doubt he owed his early advancement to the patronage of his fellow Yorkshireman Robert Bardelby. He is first recorded in 1319 witnessing a grant of lands near Barnsley to Bardelby, who was later commemorated in a chantry founded by Scott in Monk Bretton Priory. After receiving a legal training he was made a serjeant in October 1329 and began to plead in the bench. In 1334 he became a king's serjeant, and thereafter his ascent was rapid. Knighted in 1336, he was made a justice of the common pleas on 18 March 1337, and of king's bench on 2 May 1339. At the same time he was acting over much of England as a justice of assize and gaol delivery and as a commissioner, while from 1334 he was often among the lawyers and justices summoned to parliament.

On 8 January 1341 Scott was appointed chief justice of king's bench, succeeding Sir Robert Parning, and on the 13th he was named to a commission to try William de la Pole and other royal ministers and justices dismissed in the previous year's purge. He was already hearing allegations of ill doing against the king's agents in several counties. In the following year his own salary was increased by £40, no doubt as a safeguard against corruption. A trier of petitions in nearly every parliament between 1340 and 1346, Scott was also very active in the localities. King's bench held sessions under his presidency at York in 1343 and in East Anglia in 1344, he continued to take assizes and gaol deliveries, the latter at Newgate as well as in a number of southern counties, and he was appointed to many commissions. Although the latter were mostly concerned with commonplace allegations of dishonesty and violence, they sometimes involved important people, including the king, Queen Philippa, the earl of Suffolk, the bishop of Ely, and the abbot of Westminster, and also weighty matters. In March 1344, for instance, he headed a commission to examine the sensitive issue of unlicensed wool exports from London, and in November that year was appointed to investigate people who were taking royal pleas out of the realm, above all to the papal court at Avignon.

Scott continued to receive commissions until 10 September 1346, but on 16 November he was replaced as chief justice by Sir William Thorp. There is no evidence that he was disgraced, and he received a very few further commissions, the last on 14 February 1348. The likeliest explanation of the sudden end of his judicial career is a breakdown of health, quite possibly resulting from the demands of his employment. In 1344, for instance, not only did he accompany king's bench to Norfolk and Suffolk, and attend parliament at Westminster in April, but he was also appointed to commissions in London, Yorkshire (in February, May, and August), Lincolnshire, Nottinghamshire, Surrey, and Essex. It may be significant that on 31 December 1345 he and his wife had been licensed to choose a confessor who could give them plenary remission at the hour of death. Scott retired to Yorkshire, where he attended to the consolidation of his estate, which came to include the manors of Great Houghton and Ardsley, lands at Barugh, Darfield, Billingley, and Brierly, and the advowsons of several churches. He also made provision for his chantry at Monk Bretton. He was still alive on 10 March 1352, when he gave the advowson of Hickleton to the priory, but was certainly dead by 11 May 1356, and probably by 1354. With his wife, Alice Lisle, whom he had married by 1333 and who had died by 1351, he had at least two sons, John and William, and a daughter, Elizabeth. It was John Scott who in 1385 completed the foundation of the Scott chantry. HENRY SUMMERSON

Sources *Chancery records* • *RotP*, vol. 2 • *CEPR letters*, vol. 3 • G. O. Sayles, ed., *Select cases in the court of king's bench*, 7 vols., SeldS, 55, 57–8, 74, 76, 82, 88 (1936–71), vols. 4–6 • *Reports … touching the dignity of a peer of the realm*, House of Lords, 4 (1829) • W. P. Baildon, ed., *Feet of fines for the county of York, from 1327 to 1347, 1–20 Edward III*, 1, Yorkshire Archaeological Society, 42 (1910) • W. P. Baildon, ed., *Feet of fines for the county of York, from 1347 to 1377, 21–51 Edward III*, 2, Yorkshire Archaeological Society, 52 (1915) [for 1914] • J. W. Walker, ed., *Abstracts of the chartularies of the priory of Monkbretton*, Yorkshire Archaeological Society, 56 (1924) • A. H. Thompson and C. T. Clay, eds., *Fasti parochiales*, 1, Yorkshire Archaeological Society, Record Ser., 85 (1933) • M. J. Stanley Price, ed., *Yorkshire deeds*, 10, Yorkshire Archaeological Society, 120 (1955) • J. Hunter, *South Yorkshire: the history and topography of the deanery of Doncaster*, 2 (1831) • Baker, *Serjeants*, 155, 536 • Sainty, *Judges*

Scott, William (*d.* 1434). *See under* Scott family (*per. c.*1400–*c.*1525).

Scott, William (1428?–1491). *See under* Scott family (*per. c.*1400–*c.*1525).

Scott, Sir William (1459–1524). *See under* Scott family (*per. c.*1400–*c.*1525).

Scott, Sir William, of Balwearie (*d.* 1532), lawyer and diplomat, was the eldest son of William Scott of Balwearie, judge. He had a brother, David. Scott was married twice: first, by October 1484, to Elizabeth Moncrieff, and second, by September 1495, to Janet Lundy. These marriages produced at least three sons, William, Thomas [*see below*], and John. The designation Mr William Scott of Flawcraig, under which he appears in 1489, shows that by then Scott was a graduate. His legal career had begun by October 1490, when he first appeared as a procurator before the lords of council. From 1493 he acted as royal chamberlain of Fife, and may already have been keeper of Falkland Palace, an office he certainly held in May 1497.

Scott first appeared as a lord of council on 25 August 1495 and by November 1497 he had been knighted. His judicial career was soon busy; between 1497 and 1504 he appeared on almost two-thirds of the recorded sederunts of the lords of council dealing with judicial matters, and thereafter he appeared consistently on such sederunts. Taken prisoner at Flodden (1513), he was redeemed from English captivity with funds obtained from the provost and canons of St Salvator's College in the University of St Andrews, to whom in return he disponed in 1515 lands in his barony of Strathmiglo. In January 1523 Scott was made a justice-depute by the justice-general, the third earl of Argyll; a year later he was involved as an adviser in restructuring the administration of criminal justice in order to promote the punishment of serious crimes. The surviving record between 1526 and 1531 shows him acting regularly as justice-depute. In September 1514 he was one of those deputed to meet Queen Margaret Tudor to discuss matters concerning the king's authority.

In April 1516 Scott was granted a protection for himself and his friends for an embassy to England, but his major diplomatic efforts were made in the 1520s. In September 1524 he was one of the commissioners sent to negotiate a truce with England, and in 1525 he was one of the parliamentary lords of the articles deputed to meet English ambassadors. In July 1528 he was instructed by James V to compose a letter of state to the king of England and later that year was one of the commissioners to make peace with England, this time drafting his own instructions with Adam Otterburn, a fellow commissioner. The negotiations resulted in the treaty of Berwick. Scott acted as a commissioner to obtain redress in the borders in September 1531 and October 1532, on both occasions with his son Thomas.

By 1492 Scott had received the fee of Pitscottie in Fife, with his father retaining the liferent, and in 1495 he was granted a lease of the lands and mill of Strathmiglo in Fife. The king incorporated Strathmiglo into a free barony in 1510 and granted it to Scott, who in 1527 founded a collegiate kirk there. Scott also held a tenement in the High Street, Edinburgh. In 1529, with his sons William and Thomas, he successfully petitioned the lords of council to annul a decreet arbitral in favour of the abbey of Balmerino concerning the lands of Petgormo in Fife which he had apprised from Hugh Moncreif; he thereby vindicated his right to the lands which later passed to his son Thomas. On 6 June 1531 Scott was one of the lawyers appointed to a 'secret council' set up to deal with business arising from the Western Isles. At the foundation of the college of justice in May 1532 he was nominated as the first lord on the temporal side, but he died before 7 November that year.

On 20 November 1532 Scott's son **Thomas Scott of Petgormo** (*d.* 1541) was admitted to his place as a lord of session. Thomas was married to Agnes Moncreiff and was succeeded by a son, also called Thomas. He had received lands in Roxburgh from the king in 1516 for good service, and in 1529 was made one of the king's squires and gentlemen. In February 1531 he was named as one of those who had a vote on the session. He was one of several advocates who acted as king's advocate in the absence of Adam Otterburn, doing so in May 1530 and in July 1532. In 1536 Scott succeeded Nicol Crawford as lord justice-clerk, and in January 1540 he was a commissioner sent to the borders to extradite rebels from England. He died before 9 March 1541. JOHN FINLAY

Sources manuscript acts of the lords of council, NA Scot., C.S.5; Crawford Priory Collection, GD 20 • [T. Thomson], ed., *The acts of the lords auditors of causes and complaints,* AD *1466–*AD *1494*, RC, 40 (1839) • [T. Thomson], ed., *The acts of the lords of council in civil causes, 1478–*

1495, 1, RC, 41 (1839) • G. Neilson and H. Paton, eds., *Acts of the lords of council in civil causes, 1496–1501*, 2 (1918) • A. B. Calderwood, ed., *Acts of the lords of council, 1501–1503*, 3 (1993) • R. K. Hannay, ed., *Acts of the lords of council in public affairs, 1501–1554* (1932) • Rymer, *Foedera*, 1st edn, vol. 11 • J. M. Thomson and others, eds., *Registrum magni sigilli regum Scotorum / The register of the great seal of Scotland*, 11 vols. (1882–1914), vols. 2–3 • M. Livingstone, D. Hay Fleming, and others, eds., *Registrum secreti sigilli regum Scotorum / The register of the privy seal of Scotland*, 1–2 (1908–21) • T. Dickson, ed., *Compota thesaurariorum regum Scotorum / Accounts of the lord high treasurer of Scotland*, 1 (1877) • G. Brunton and D. Haig, *An historical account of the senators of the college of justice, from its institution in MDXXXII* (1832) • J. Finlay, 'Professional men of law before the lords of council, *c.*1500–*c.*1550', PhD diss., U. Edin., 1997 • J. Cameron, *James V: the personal rule, 1528–1542*, ed. N. Macdougall (1998)

Scott, Sir William, of Clerkington, Lord Clerkington (*d.* **1656**), judge, was the eldest son of Laurence Scott of Harprig (*d.* 1637?), advocate, clerk of session, clerk of the privy council, and clerk of parliament. He succeeded his father in December 1637 and was knighted by Charles I in November 1641. He was a member of the committee of war in 1644, 1646, 1647, and 1649 and, after the enactment of the Act of Classes (1649), barring from office those involved in the engagement with Charles I, was appointed an ordinary lord of session on 7 June 1649, taking the title Lord Clerkington. He was a member of the committee of estates (1649, 1651), and a commissioner to parliament for the shire of Edinburgh in 1650–51. He joined Argyll in March 1651 in unsuccessfully opposing moves to admit some of those excluded from civil office since 1649 to the committee to manage the army. He was a commissioner of supply in 1655. Contemporaries considered him competent, and he was described by Nicoll as 'a verry guid judge' (Nicoll, 188).

Scott and his first wife, Catherine, daughter of Morison of Prestongrange, whom he married on 4 October 1621, had three children: Laurence, his heir, William, and Catherine, who married Hugh Montgomerie of Bridgend. By his second marriage, to Barbara, daughter of Sir John Dalmahoy, bt, he had four sons and three daughters: Barbara, Agnes, John of Malleny, Frances, Alexander, James of Scotsloch, and Robert, dean of Hamilton. He died of apoplexy in Edinburgh on 23 December 1656.

T. F. HENDERSON, *rev.* ALISON G. MUIR

Sources M. D. Young, ed., *The parliaments of Scotland: burgh and shire commissioners*, 2 (1993), 611 • *APS*, *1643–51* • G. Brunton and D. Haig, *An historical account of the senators of the college of justice, from its institution in MDXXXII* (1832), 341 • Anderson, *Scot. nat.* • J. Nicoll, *A diary of public transactions and other occurrences, chiefly in Scotland, from January 1650 to June 1667*, ed. D. Laing, Bannatyne Club, 52 (1836), 188 • *The letters and journals of Robert Baillie*, ed. D. Laing, 3 vols., Bannatyne Club, 73 (1841–2), vol. 3 • J. R. Young, *The Scottish parliament, 1639–1661: a political and constitutional analysis* (1996)

Scott, Sir William, second baronet (*c.*1670–1725), poet, was born in Selkirkshire, the son of Sir Francis Scott, first baronet (1645–1712), and Henrietta Ker (*d.* 1741). Sir William was the last member of the Scott family of Thirlestane in Selkirkshire to retain the name of Scott. On 15 December 1699 he married Elizabeth, only surviving child of Margaret, Baroness Napier, and John Brisbane; they had three daughters and a son, Francis, who became the third Lord Napier. Elizabeth died in 1705, and Scott married Jean, daughter of Sir John Nisbet of Dirleton, and widow of Sir William Scott of Harden, on 30 June 1710. A graduate of the University of Edinburgh, Scott was admitted into the Faculty of Advocates on 25 February 1702.

In 1702 Scott published a brief legal prose work, *Disputatio juridica*, dedicated to the Buccleuch branch of the Scott family, but it is as a neo-Latin poet that he has secured a minor literary reputation. A moderately substantial collection of poems appeared in a volume of Archibald Pitcairne's *Selecta poemata*, published in Edinburgh in 1727, to which Thomas Kincaid also contributed. This single collaborative venture suggests that Scott belonged in some way to this significant intellectual, cultural, and artistic circle in late seventeenth- and early eighteenth-century Scotland. The evidence of a considerable number of dedicatory, personal, and occasional verses (those dated refer to the 1720s) suggests the likely circle or coterie of the volume's reception. There are epistolary addresses, or verse epistles, and a poem on Allan Ramsay, 'Poëtae Scoti'. The dominant poetic form is the ode, especially Horatian, and there is a small body of amatory poems.

Scott's literary canon may also be extended by inclusion of the song lyric which periodically has been attributed to him, 'The Blithesome Bridal' or 'Come, fy! Let us a' to the wedding'. Authorship of this text, the poetic celebration of a convivial rural wedding, is shared with the early seventeenth-century Scottish writer Francis Sempill of Beltrees. The attribution to Scott is based on a commonly attested family tradition (Napier, 239). The poem's most recent editor, MacLaine, decides in favour of its being an anonymous composition with neither the Sempill nor Scott attribution secure (though, historically, editors have preferred Sempill to Scott). This gently carnivalesque song proved popular, being printed (anonymously) in James Johnston's *Scots Musical Museum*, Watson's *Choice Collection*, and in Allan Ramsay's *Tea-Table Miscellany* (though one might assume that here authorship would have been credited to Scott).

Scott's work attests the persistence of Scottish neo-Latin traditions in this period, and implicitly echoes the intellectual and aesthetic impulses of Edinburgh's influential episcopalian and Jacobite circle. Scott died on 8 October 1725; six years earlier he had executed a deed of entail of his Thirlestane estate. He was survived by his wife.

S. M. DUNNIGAN

Sources Anderson, *Scot. nat.* • M. Napier, *History of the partition of Lennox* (1835) • W. Fraser, *The Scotts of Buccleuch*, 2 vols. (1878) • *Scots peerage* • D. Laing, ed., *A catalogue of the graduates … of the University of Edinburgh*, Bannatyne Club, 106 (1858) • A. H. MacLaine, ed., *The Christis Kirk tradition: Scots poems of folk festivity* (1996) • A. Cunningham, ed., *The songs of Scotland, ancient and modern*, 4 vols. (1825) • R. Burns and others, *The Scots musical museum*, ed. J. Johnson and W. Stenhouse, new edn, 4 vols. (1853) • J. Watson, *A choice collection of comic and serious Scots poems both ancient and modern; by several hands*, pts 1–3 (1706–11) • A. Ramsay, *The tea-table miscellany: a collection of choice songs, Scots and English* (1775) • T. F. Henderson, *Scottish vernacular literature: a succinct history*, 3rd edn (1910)

Scott, William, **Baron Stowell** (1745–1836), judge and politician, was born on 17 October 1745 at Heworth, co. Durham, the fourth child and eldest son of William Scott (1696/7–1776) and his second wife, Jane Atkinson (1709–1800). Both the Scott and the Atkinson families were engaged in the coal transport trade in Newcastle upon Tyne as 'fitters', middlemen who bought from the colliery owners and sold to shippers on the Tyneside docks. Anxiety over the progress of Jacobite forces in the autumn of 1745, however, caused Jane Scott to flee Newcastle to the comparative quiet of a family property a few miles south of the city, where she gave birth to William and his twin sister, Barbara. The Scotts had three further children who survived infancy, including John *Scott, who became the first earl of Eldon.

The accident of his birth in co. Durham had important consequences for William Scott's education and early career. On the advice of the Revd Hugh Moises, his master at the Royal Grammar School in Newcastle, Scott sought and obtained a scholarship for Durham natives at Corpus Christi College, Oxford. He matriculated on 3 March 1761, and following the receipt of his undergraduate degree in the autumn of 1764 he was elected to a Durham fellowship at University College. The academic life beckoned, and Scott's progress during the next ten years suggests that he was not deaf to its call. As tutor and then senior tutor at his college he gained a reputation as an excellent teacher. His university lectures, following his election in 1773 as Camden reader in ancient history, were also highly regarded. He contributed both time and money to expanding the collection of the Bodleian Library, and he convinced his father that John, the youngest Scott brother, had sufficient intellectual promise to join him at University College. Throughout his life Scott would retain a fondness for Oxford and the convivial, intellectual society he first encountered in the college senior common room.

Progress as a civil lawyer Almost from the start of his time at Oxford, however, Scott's attention was partly focused on the law. In 1762 he was admitted as a student at the Middle Temple, and after he obtained his MA in 1767 his university training also took a legal turn. In 1772 he completed the bachelor's degree in civil law. An inheritance resulting from his father's death may have provided Scott with the financial security to change his profession. In 1776 he resigned his tutorship, and early in 1777 he moved to London and took chambers in the temple. In 1780 he was called to the bar. While important, this qualification was of lesser significance than receipt of his doctorate in civil law and his admission to the Faculty of Advocates at Doctors' Commons in the previous year. These enabled him to appear in the courts whose practice was based on the civil or Roman law, rather than the English common law. While not a stranger to the common law, Scott would make his reputation as an advocate and judge in the Admiralty and ecclesiastical courts.

In determining why Scott chose this area of practice, commentators have pointed to three factors as likely to have been persuasive. First, while they may not have

William Scott, Baron Stowell (1745–1836), by Thomas Phillips, 1827

equipped him for the rough and ready advocacy of the circuit, where most common lawyers cut their professional teeth, his academic achievements provided an ideal foundation for success in tribunals where knowledge of the learned law of ancient Rome, the Roman Catholic church and the Church of England, and the universities of continental Europe was essential. Second, the civilian bar was much smaller than the common law or equity bars, so that competition for the ambitious newcomer was less keen. Finally, the American war was bringing an increased business to one branch of civilian practice, namely the Admiralty court's jurisdiction over questions of prize, thus making the career of the civilian advocate more financially attractive.

Scott achieved professional success almost from the outset. He became a leading advocate, despite his early unwillingness to depart from written speeches by which he would address the bench. Further achievements, moreover, were not long in coming. In 1782 he was appointed advocate-general to the Admiralty, and in 1788 he became king's advocate-general and was knighted. As advocate-general he was the senior crown law officer, the government's chief adviser on matters of civil, canon, and maritime law, and the Foreign Office's standing officer on international law. In addition to drafting legal opinions and appearing for the crown in litigation during his ten-year period of office, Scott served briefly on the prosecution team in the Warren Hastings impeachment. 1788, however, also marked his elevation to the bench of the consistory court of the diocese of London, the most important English matrimonial court. Although the

Church of England could not grant a legal divorce, it had the power to separate a married couple, and it could determine that a supposed marriage was invalid. Scott's decisions in matrimonial cases, therefore, concerned such matters as the nature of the marriage contract, the conduct sufficient to justify separation on the grounds of cruelty or adultery, and the defence of recrimination. Beyond the matrimonial sphere his judicial attention was given to matters of ecclesiastical law as diverse as defamation, burials, and brawling in church.

A hesitant parliamentarian Scott's parliamentary career did not begin until 1790, when he was returned for Downton in Wiltshire. Competition between the borough's patrons had resulted in Scott's defeat on a petition in 1784. He had also failed to win a seat for Oxford University in 1780. This latter result was turned around in 1801, and he continued to represent his university for the next twenty years, until his elevation to the Lords. Scott was a steady, if unspectacular, supporter of the successive Pittite and tory governments of this period. He approved of the orders in council to blockade French-controlled ports, he advised Spencer Perceval when corruption charges were levelled against Frederick, duke of York, and he supported ministers throughout the debates on the Regency Bill in 1810–11. He did not, however, become an effective parliamentary speaker. More than one observer described him as unimpressive, and his early efforts tended to be ignored by William Cobbett's *Parliamentary History*. Neither did he look out for opportunities to address the house. On matters with which he had either professional expertise or personal interest, however, he played his part. He brought in four bills dealing with practice in the prize courts and the distribution of prize money, as well as the 39 Geo. III c. 37 (1799) on the prosecution of non-capital offences at sea. He also defended his court from the attacks of Thomas, Lord Cochrane (later tenth earl of Dundonald), and he resisted attempts to reform the office of Admiralty registrar. Scott was also a reluctant reformer of the ecclesiastical courts. During the progress of his Reform Bill in 1813, he fended off attempts to abolish the sanction of excommunication, and he downplayed stories of unfairness in defamation cases. Moreover, as an MP whose constituency had a large proportion of Church of England clergymen, Scott felt obliged to give particular attention to matters affecting church interests. He was responsible for the 43 Geo. III c. 84 (1803) and the 57 Geo. III c. 99 (1817), which relaxed the restrictions on clerical non-residency, trading, and farming, and regulated the payment of curates. He opposed, by contrast, all measures to restrict liability for tithes and, after initial uncertainty, he spoke in favour of the divorce bill of George Eden, second Baron Auckland. He did not consider refugee monastic communities sufficiently dangerous to justify their restriction, but he was hostile to both Catholic emancipation and repeal of the Test and Corporation Acts.

Judge of the Admiralty court In 1798 Scott was appointed judge of the high court of Admiralty and sworn of the privy council. He fulfilled this judicial office for thirty years and achieved a reputation to rival Lord Mansfield's. The Admiralty court had jurisdiction in three general areas: crimes committed on the high seas, civil disputes of a specifically maritime character, and prize, which concerned the seizure of enemy property at sea and the rights of its captors to a portion of the proceeds. The statutory limitations on the court's criminal jurisdiction provided few opportunities for the Admiralty judge to do other than apply the principles of the common law. Scott's impact, therefore, was made elsewhere. The civil, or instance, jurisdiction had for centuries been restricted by statute and the jealous supervision of the common-law courts, and when Scott came to the bench it was still extremely narrow. Nevertheless, Scott's decisions established or confirmed important principles relating, *inter alia*, to salvage, seamen's wages, and hypothecation—a master's right to pledge cargo to pay for necessary repairs to his ship. Moreover, although one commentator describes Scott as having 'an intense fear' (Wiswall, 33) of prohibition—the common-law writ that stopped proceedings in rival tribunals—the tendency of his judgments was to expand the jurisdiction of his own court. This coincided with a period of statutory expansion and quiescence by the common-law courts, which resulted in a wider Admiralty jurisdiction later in the century. Scott's most important work on the Admiralty bench, however, was in the area of prize. The long war with France, and the dominance of the British navy during that conflict, resulted in a steady stream of cases. In resolving whether claims of prize were justified, Scott discussed such issues as contraband, blockade, nationality, and national commercial character, and the respective rights of belligerents and neutrals. The number, range, and quality of his decisions meant that Scott laid foundations for the international law of war which remained important into the twentieth century.

Scott's judicial reputation Scott's judicial opinions have been praised as learned, lucid, and creative. As to the first quality, there can be no doubt. Scott knew and quoted the works of Hugo Grotius, Samuel Pufendorf, and other civilian writers, and the breadth of his knowledge is illustrated in *Gilbert* v. *Buzzard* (1821), where he cited Cicero, Sir Henry Spelman, and Sir Thomas Browne's *Urne Buriall*. His ability to marshal the facts and relevant authorities to produce clear, well-reasoned judgments won the admiration of critics as distinct as Samuel Taylor Coleridge and Henry Brougham. The latter affirmed that Scott's

> vast superiority was apparent when, as from an eminence, he was called to survey the whole field of dispute, and to marshal the variegated facts, disentangle the intricate mazes, and array the conflicting reasons which were calculated to distract or suspend men's judgement. (Brougham, 2.73–4)

How far Scott was creative, however, is less certain. Commentators such as Sir William Holdsworth and E. S. Roscoe have presented Scott as a lawgiver. They have pointed to the absence of printed case reports as freeing Scott from the constraints of prior decisions. Henry Bourguignon, however, has shown that in the Admiralty context, at least, this assessment of Scott's judicial conduct is misconceived. By bringing to light the surviving manuscript cases, legal opinions, and advocates' notebooks, Bourguignon has demonstrated that Scott did not 'hover like the Spirit of the Creator over a primordial void' (Bourguignon, 244), but profited from the collective wisdom of the civilian legal community. This qualification does not taint Scott's achievement, which was to state clearly the unpublished tradition, and to provide thoughtful, persuasive reasoning to justify that tradition to future scholars and practitioners. And in some areas, such as the law of blockade and the doctrine of continuous voyage, Scott did demonstrate considerable creative ability. His own decisions, moreover, were reported by Sir Christopher Robinson, Thomas Edwards, Sir John Dodson, and John Haggard, and he took considerable care over their production to ensure that both form and substance were accurately preserved. If not a lawgiver in the absolute sense, Scott did provide, through the publication of his decisions, an important practical basis for modern English Admirality law and the international law of war. It was, as Holdsworth has noted, 'a happy accident that the first appearance of regular reports should coincide with the judicial career of the greatest civilian whom this country has ever produced' (Holdsworth, *Eng. law*, *Some Makers of English Law*, 227).

Scott's independence as a judge has also been questioned. At the outset of his career on the Admiralty bench he affirmed that a prize court should apply international law, and that even during a war in which Britain was fundamentally engaged, the court must 'administer with indifference that justice which the law of nations holds out to independent states, some happening to be neutral and some belligerent' (C. Robinson, *Reports of Cases Argued and Determined in the High Court of Admiralty*, 1799–1808, 1.349–50). Americans, however, whose ships carried the lion's share of neutral trade during the Napoleonic period, felt that Scott did not always afford sufficient protection to the rights of neutrals, and this view has some merit. His willingness to depart from the rule that only an effective, and not a paper, blockade was lawful, and his dictum that an order in council could alter an established rule of international law, suggested a certain degree of partiality in such cases as *The Fox and others* (1811), and *The Snipe and others* (1812). To conclude that Scott's professional conduct was tainted by political concerns, however, would grossly overstate the evidence, and his career included important instances in which he did not shrink from legal decisions that contravened his political views. Unlike his brother John, then lord chancellor, who assured his colleagues in the summer of 1815 that some means would be found to justify Napoleon's incarceration on St Helena, Scott felt that incarceration by the allies would violate the law of nations, and that therefore he could provide little assistance to the government. Similarly, his decision in *The slave Grace* case (1827), that a slave who became free on arrival in England resumed her unfree status when she returned to Antigua, where slavery was legal, reflected his understanding of international law and not his attitude towards slavery. He wrote to the American supreme court justice, Joseph Story:

> I was not deciding the question of the lawfulness of the slave trade, upon which I am rather a stern abolitionist, but only the narrow question whether … our new execution of the slave code … was a new suspension of it as regarded England, but left it in full operation with regard to the Colonies. (Sankey, 340)

Moreover, following the termination of hostilities between Britain and America, American judicial and academic opinion mellowed, and Scott's views on matters of international law were highly influential in American legal thought throughout the nineteenth century.

Personal life Scott's professional responsibilities sat lightly upon him. Election to Samuel Johnson's literary club in 1778 had introduced him to London artistic and intellectual circles, and thereafter he liked to spend convivial evenings at one or other of his clubs, or among his legal colleagues at the Middle Temple. Society hostesses too found Scott's polished wit and gentlemanly manners, if not his somewhat unkempt appearance, an attractive addition to their table. His brother waggishly observed that Scott 'never had fewer than 365 good dinners, in any one year' (Townsend, 360), and that his only exercise was 'the exercise of eating and drinking' (ibid., 362). The latter, at least, was not strictly true, as Scott was also a great London sightseer. He took pleasure in puppet shows, prize fights, and the curiosities on display at arcades and showrooms. He seems particularly to have patronized those amusements that could be enjoyed for little or no expense, and indeed he had a reputation for thrift that contrasted sharply with his very considerable wealth. Anna Maria Bagnall (*bap.* 1755, *d.* 1809), whom he married at St Marylebone on 7 April 1781, was an heiress, and the combination of his judicial salary and the fees associated with several Admiralty and ecclesiastical sinecures made him a wealthy man. In 1807 Joseph Farington estimated his annual income at £17,000.

William Scott's career is inevitably compared with that of his brother John. They served together as law officers, and the younger served as lord chancellor for almost as long as the elder presided in the Admiralty court. Their political outlook was also similar, and if he played a less vocal role in parliament, William's suspicion of change was equal to John's. Only in the matter of a peerage did William trail significantly, and given John's political prominence and William's regular support of the government, this is somewhat surprising. Rumours of a peerage were frequent from 1802 onwards, and the honour was certainly not unwanted, but it was not until 1821 that the elder Scott became Baron Stowell of Stowell Park. He took his title from an estate in Gloucestershire he had purchased in 1811. Lord Stowell did not become a regular attendant in the upper house, and *Hansard* records only a few speeches during the debates in 1822 and 1823 to amend the law on clandestine marriages. His proxy, however, was generally at the government's service. The Scott brothers also maintained a close personal friendship, which was expressed in regular, if not daily, communication and in consultation on matters of personal or professional concern. John dissuaded William from resigning his Admiralty judgeship in 1808 in favour of a higher-ranking but less important appointment in the ecclesiastical courts.

William Scott was less fortunate in his other domestic relations. His first wife died on 4 September 1809, and two of their four children died in infancy. Their surviving son died unmarried of alcoholism at the age of forty-one. On 10 April 1813 Scott was married a second time, to Louisa Catherine (1767–1817), the widow of John Browne, first marquess of Sligo, and youngest daughter of Richard *Howe, Earl Howe. They had met when her son, the marquess, came before Scott on a charge of encouraging sailors to desert their posts in order to serve on his yacht. Scott's brother considered the marriage ill-advised, and his judgment proved sound. The couple were ill matched as regarded age, temperament, and lifestyle. Lady Sligo did convince Scott to give up his accommodation in Doctors' Commons for grander quarters in Grafton Street and then in Cleveland Row. He returned to her house in Grafton Street after her death at Amsterdam on 20 August 1817.

Scott resigned from the consistory court in 1820, but continued to serve on the Admiralty bench until 1828. During his last few years in office, however, his physical health was beginning to fail. Poor eyesight and a faltering voice obliged him to ask counsel to recite his judgments. He spent his last years largely at Earley Court, his first wife's Berkshire estate, where he received visits from his brother and his daughter Marianne (1782/3–1842), who had become Lady Sidmouth on her marriage to Henry Addington, first Viscount Sidmouth. He died there on 28 January 1836, and was buried on 3 February at Sonning, Berkshire. He left an estate sworn at under £250,000 in personalty. Senility in Lord Stowell's last few years shielded him from knowledge of the death of his son William (*b.* 1794) on 26 November 1835, so the will in the latter's favour was not altered. R. A. MELIKAN

Sources H. J. Bourguignon, *Sir William Scott, Lord Stowell* (1987) • W. C. Townsend, *Twelve eminent judges* (1846) • F. L. Wiswall, *The development of admiralty jurisdiction and practice since 1800* (1970) • R. G. Thorne, 'Scott, Sir William', HoP, *Commons, 1790–1820* • *The Farington diary*, ed. J. Greig, 8 vols. (1922–8) • Holdsworth, *Eng. law* • Baron Brougham and Vaux [H. Brougham], *Works of Henry, Lord Brougham*, 4 vols. (1872) • W. S. Holdsworth, *Some makers of English law* (1938) • E. S. Roscoe, *Lord Stowell: his life and the development of English prize law* (1916) • W. E. Surtees, *A sketch of the lives of Lords Stowell and Eldon* (1846) • Viscount Sankey [J. Sankey], 'Lord Stowell', *Law Quarterly Review*, 52 (1936), 327–44 • Foster, *Alum. Oxon.* • A. W. B. Simpson, ed., *Biographical dictionary of the common law* (1984) • *GM*, 2nd ser., 5 (1836), 427–30 • GEC, *Peerage* • *The public and private life of Lord Chancellor Eldon, with selections from his correspondence*, ed. H. Twiss, 3 vols. (1844)

Archives Inner Temple, London, consistory court sentences • MHS Oxf., notes taken during scientific lectures at Oxford • Office of the Registrar of the Admiralty, Stowell notebook • U. Oxf., student notebook | BL, corresp. with Robert Peel, Add. MSS 40270–40397 *passim* • CKS, letters to William Pitt • Encombe House, Dorset, Eldon papers • Glos. RO, Freeman-Mitford papers, letters to Lord Redesdale • Inner Temple, London, Mitford legal MS • LPL, Fulham papers • U. Nott. L., letters to third duke of Portland • Warks. CRO, letters incl. to Sir Roger Newdigate and Lady Sophia Newdigate • Yale U., Beinecke L., corresp. with James Boswell

Likenesses G. Dance, pencil drawing, 1803, NPG • J. Hoppner, oils, *c.*1806, University College, Oxford • W. Owen, oils, *c.*1811–1816, Convocation House, Oxford • W. Behnes, marble bust, 1824, NPG • T. Phillips, painting, 1827, Middle Temple [*see illus.*] • M. L. Watson and G. Nelson, group portrait, marble sculpture, *c.*1843–1847, University College, Oxford • G. Hayter, group portrait, oils (*The trial of Queen Caroline, 1820*), NPG • T. Phillips, oils, CCC Oxf.

Wealth at death less than £250,000 personalty: *GM*, 427–30; will, PRO, PROB 11/1859, sig. 190

Scott, William (1797–1848), jockey, brother of the trainer John *Scott (1794–1871), was born at Chippenham, near Newmarket, and was first employed in the stables of his father (*d.* 1848), a former jockey and trainer who kept The Ship inn, Oxford. In 1815 he received further instruction from the trainer James Croft, of Middleham, Yorkshire, and was then employed by Thomas Houldsworth of Rockhill in Sherwood Forest until 1823. As a partner with his brother in the Whitewall House training stables at Malton, Yorkshire, from 1825, he had the opportunity of riding many good horses and soon became one of the best-known and most successful jockeys of his day. His victories included three Two Thousand Guineas, an equal number of Oaks, four Derbys, and nine St Legers. In 1836 he married a daughter of Mr Richardson, a prosperous draper from Beverley. She died in 1844, leaving a son and a daughter.

Like many jockeys, Scott developed a drinking problem. Too much brandy on the morning of the race allegedly cost him a Derby—and a triple crown—on Sir Tatton Sykes in 1846. Coarse in both character and riding style, he verbally intimidated other jockeys during races. So aggressive was his riding that his career was interrupted by a number of injuries resulting from falls. After quarrelling with his brother, he set up training stables on his own at his home, Highfield House, near Malton, but by then on the verge of alcoholism, he was not successful. His last mount was Christopher in the Derby of 1847. Scott died at Highfield House on 26 September 1848, and was buried on 2 October at Meaux, near Malton. WRAY VAMPLEW

Sources R. Mortimer, R. Onslow, and P. Willett, *Biographical encyclopedia of British flat racing* (1978) • M. Tanner and G. Cranham, *Great jockeys of the flat* (1992) • W. Vamplew, *The turf: a social and economic history of horse racing* (1976) • Nimrod [C. J. Apperley], *The turf* (1901) • The Druid [H. H. Dixon], *Scott and Sebright* (1862) • *Bell's Life in London* (1 Oct 1848), 3 • *DNB*

Likenesses H. Hall, oils, Yale U. CBA • J. F. Herring, oils, Yale U. CBA • portraits, repro. in *Sporting Review* (Oct 1842)

Scott, William (1813–1872), Church of England clergyman, was born in London on 2 May 1813, the second son of Thomas Scott, a merchant, of Clement's Lane and Newington, Surrey, and his wife, Lucy. In October 1826 he was admitted to Merchant Taylors' School, London, and on 14 June 1831 he matriculated at Queen's College, Oxford, as Michel exhibitioner. He was Michel scholar in 1834–8, and graduated BA in 1835 and MA in 1839. He was elected a fellow of Queen's in 1835 but resigned soon after, on his marriage to Margaret Louisa Harriet Beloe, granddaughter of

William Beloe (1758–1817). Ordained deacon in 1836 and priest in 1837, he held three curacies, the last of which was under William Dodsworth (1798–1861) at Christ Church, Albany Street, London. In 1839 Scott became perpetual curate of Christ Church, Hoxton, London, where he remained until 1860. Widely known as Scott of Hoxton, he transformed the life of the parish, particularly with regard to the reordering of liturgy and ceremonial within his church, which he carried out despite die-hard protestant opposition. His detractors accused him of placing candles on the altar, crossing himself, robing the choir in surplices, and embracing a variety of other practices which were widely regarded as extreme and ritualistic in the context of the 1840s. This opposition to his attempt to apply Tractarian principles to the worship offered by the Church of England culminated in an incident at another east London church, St Andrew's, Well Street, on 30 November 1850, when he was threatened by an anti-ritualist mob in the course of a service there. In 1860 he was appointed by Lord Chancellor Campbell as vicar of the City living of St Olave Jewry with St Martin Pomeroy.

Scott was energetic in the wider promotion of high-church principles, and in 1841, when the *Christian Remembrancer* was established for this purpose, he was made co-editor with Francis Garden (1810–1884). In 1844, when the paper became a quarterly, James Bowling Mozley (1813–1878) succeeded Garden for a short time, but for most of its existence (it ceased publication in 1868) Scott was sole editor. He felt deeply the conversion to Roman Catholicism of J. H. Newman: although never intimate with him, he wrote of Newman to J. B. Mozley that he had 'lived upon him, made him my better and other nature' (*Letters of the Rev. J. B. Mozley*, 168–9).

Scott took a leading part in the controversy following the Gorham judgment. His *Letter to the Rev. Daniel Wilson* (1850), a reply to Wilson's bitter attack on the Tractarians, *Our Protestant Faith in Danger*, published earlier that year, passed through four editions. In 1846 he had joined E. B. Pusey and his associates in their efforts to prevent the ordination at St Paul's of Samuel Gobat, the Lutheran bishop-elect of Jerusalem. The projected ordination provoked fierce—but ultimately unsuccessful—opposition from high-churchmen. Some were opposed to the Anglo-Prussian scheme of a Jerusalem bishopric, which they believed would threaten the maintenance of Anglican order and doctrine, while others had doubts about Gobat's personal orthodoxy. Ten years later, with Pusey, Keble, and others, Scott was one of the eighteen clergy who signed the protest against Archbishop Sumner's condemnation of G. A. Denison's eucharistic doctrine. Scott's advice was much sought by Henry Phillpotts (1778–1869), bishop of Exeter, and by Walter Kerr Hamilton (1808–1869), bishop of Salisbury. He was among the founders of the *Saturday Review*, the most influential weekly periodical of the time dealing with contemporary and other intellectual issues, to which he frequently contributed. He was also a leading member of W. E. Gladstone's election committees at Oxford, voting for him at his last candidature in 1865. His strength lay in his abilities as an organizer and as an adviser to, and publicist for, the different causes with which he was involved.

In London, Scott's influence was especially strong: he was one of the prime movers in the formation in 1848 of the London Union on Church Matters, and from 1859 onwards was chairman of committees of the Ecclesiological Society. He was also one of the chief advisers of deans Milman and Mansel in the work of restoration at St Paul's Cathedral, acting for some time as honorary secretary of the restoration committee. In 1858 he was elected president of Sion College, then undergoing reform, and in the next year he published a continuation of the *Account* of that foundation by John Russell (1787–1863). His other works included an edition of R. Laurence's *Lay Baptism Invalid* (1841) and two of the seven volumes of the works of Archbishop Laud for the Library of Anglo-Catholic Theology (1847). Several of Scott's sermons appeared in Alexander Watson's collections (1845–7). His *Plain Words for Plain People* (1844), attacked the Society for Promoting Christian Knowledge for distorting theological works in its attempts to produce popular religious literature.

Scott died of spinal disease and cirrhosis of the liver on 11 January 1872 at his home, 56 Albany Street, Regent's Park, London, and was buried in Highgate cemetery on 17 January. His wife, together with three sons and two daughters, survived him.

G. Le G. Norgate, *rev.* N. W. James

Sources *The Guardian* (17 Jan 1872) • Foster, *Alum. Oxon.* • Crockford (1870) • C. J. Robinson, ed., *A register of the scholars admitted into Merchant Taylors' School, from AD 1562 to 1874*, 2 vols. (1882–3) • R. W. Church, *The Oxford Movement: twelve years, 1833–1845* (1891), 351 • *Letters of the Rev. J. B. Mozley*, ed. A. Mozley (1885), 150, 155, 168–9, 321–2 • *Letters and correspondence of John Henry Newman during his life in the English church*, ed. A. Mozley, 2 vols. (1891), vol. 2, pp. 396, 436 • H. P. Liddon, *The life of Edward Bouverie Pusey*, ed. J. O. Johnston and others, 4 vols. (1893–7), vol. 3, pp. 70–78, 442 • *Report of the Ecclesiological late Cambridge Camden Society* (1847–8) • *CGPLA Eng. & Wales* (1872)

Archives LPL, corresp. and papers

Likenesses photograph, *c.*1870, LPL

Wealth at death under £7000: probate, 4 March 1872, *CGPLA Eng. & Wales*

Scott, William Alphonsus (1871–1921), architect, was born on 1 September 1871 in Dublin, the eldest of the four sons and four daughters of Anthony Scott (*c.*1845–1919), architect, and his wife, Catherine Hayes (*d.* 1904). He was educated at the classical school, Manorhamilton, co. Leitrim, St Finian's Seminary, Navan, Meath, and the Metropolitan School of Art in Dublin. He received his early professional training from his father in Drogheda, co. Louth, from 1887 to 1890, before being articled for three years to Sir Thomas Newenham Deane & Son (Sir Thomas Manly Deane). In 1893 he returned to his father's office, where he worked for six years as an assistant. Their most notable achievement together, as A. Scott & Son, was Enniskillen town hall, co. Fermanagh (1897–1901), won in competition; William was responsible for the design, which was in a conventional Renaissance revival style.

In 1899 Scott left his father's office and went to London to gain wider experience, working in several offices but most significantly in that of the superintending architect's department of the London county council, a hotbed of progressive architectural ideals at that time. There he was engaged for two years, his most notable personal contribution being the design and supervision of the new fire station at West Hampstead (1900–02), in which he adopted the domestic style of the famous English architect C. F. A. Voysey. During his period in London he returned briefly to Enniskillen in 1900 to marry Catherine, daughter of the MP Patrick Crumley, with whom he had one child. In 1902 he resigned his position with the London county council and returned to Ireland to establish his own practice in Dublin, where he settled for the rest of his life.

Scott's practice was extensive and varied, and combined his new-found interest in English-inspired arts and crafts design with a long-standing devotion to early Irish architecture. In ecclesiastical and allied work, exclusively for the Roman Catholic church, his own denomination, he usually tended toward the revival of Irish forms, principally Celtic or Romanesque, as in the church at Spiddal, co. Galway (1903–7) and the O'Growney memorial tomb at Maynooth College, co. Kildare (1903–5), but he often introduced a strong Byzantine element—as at Enniskillen convent Chapel (1905–6) and the large pilgrimage church St Patrick's Basilica at Lough Derg, co. Donegal (designed in 1919; built 1926–31). Other church work included important Celtic-ornamented furnishings for Loughrea Cathedral, co. Galway (1903–10), and for the Honan Chapel, Cork (1916).

Scott's domestic architecture was of an arts and crafts vernacular-revival type, as at Killyhevlin House, co. Fermanagh of 1903 (now much altered), and the 'garden village' at Talbot's Inch, Kilkenny (1906), where his cottages were originally roofed with thatch. A personal predilection for cubic massing and simple forms—a kind of protomodernism—was evident in some of his other work, principally the town hall at Cavan (1907–10), and St Mary's College, Galway (1910–12), in which contemporaries saw the germs of a modern national style. His hostel for pilgrims at Lough Derg (1910–11), meanwhile, was built entirely of reinforced concrete.

Scott was a member and silver medallist of the Society of Architects, London, an associate of the Royal Institute of British Architects, and a fellow of the Royal Institute of Architects of Ireland. He was also an associate member of the Royal Hibernian Academy, a president of the Architectural Association of Ireland, and a member of council of the Arts and Crafts Society of Ireland. Following the death of Sir Thomas Drew he was appointed professor of architecture at the National University of Ireland, from 1911 until his death.

Scott was famously described as 'that late drunken genius Scott' by the renowned Irish poet W. B. Yeats, for whom he restored and furnished in 1917–19 a medieval tower house, Thoor Ballylee in co. Galway (M. Hanley and L. Miller, *Thoor Ballylee, Home of William Butler Yeats*, rev. 2nd edn, 1976, 21). Scott appears to have been a popular and genial member of the architectural profession in Ireland, which clearly held him in high regard, but an early death cut short his career as the most significant Irish architect of his generation. Prone to pneumonia, he suffered two serious attacks, in 1913 and 1914, before eventually succumbing to a third, in 1921, which apparently developed from a chill caught while attending the funeral of Dr William J. Walsh, the Roman Catholic archbishop of Dublin. He died on 23 April 1921, at his home, Idrone Terrace, Blackrock, Dublin, and was buried three days later in Glasnevin cemetery, Dublin. His wife survived him. Three years before his death Scott had had the unusual experience of reading his own obituary when he was confused in the Dublin press with an English architect of the same name, who died at Cannes in April 1918, a mistake repeated by *The Times* and *The Builder*, and perpetuated by *Who Was Who*. PAUL LARMOUR

Sources *Irish Builder*, 63 (1921), 326 • *WWW*, *1916–28* • P. Larmour, 'The drunken man of genius: W. A. Scott (1871–1921)', *Irish Architectural Review*, 3 (2001), 28–41 • S. Rothery, *Ireland and the new architecture* (1991) • J. Sheehy, *The rediscovery of Ireland's past: the Celtic revival, 1830–1930* (1980) • *The Builder*, 114 (1918), 252 [three years before his death] • *Freeman's Journal* [Dublin] (25 April 1921) • nomination form, 1898, RIBA BAL • R. Elliott, *Art and Ireland* [1906] • *Thom's directory: Dublin* (1902–21)

Likenesses F. O'Donohue, crayon drawing, *c.*1911, repro. in *Irish Architect and Craftsman* (15 April 1911) • photograph, *c.*1911, repro. in *Irish Builder* (13 May 1911), 302 • Lafayette, photograph, repro. in *Freeman's Journal*

Scott, William Bell (1811–1890), poet and painter, was the son of an Edinburgh engraver, Robert *Scott (1777–1841) and his wife, Ross, daughter of Robert Bell, mason. He was the younger brother of the painter and poet David *Scott (1806–1849). William Bell Scott had five older brothers, but four of them had died in an epidemic in 1807, leaving David Scott the only survivor of the 'older family', as Scott came to regard it. His parents never recovered from their loss and his mother would often call William by the name of one or other of the children who had died. Like his father and his brother, Scott did not go to Edinburgh University but instead trained in fine art at the Trustees' Academy. With his brother David he was among a group of remarkable painters including William Dyce (with whom he later became friendly), Robert Scott Lauder, William Leighton Leitch, and Daniel Macnee. Robert Scott admired Blake's engravings and such works as Henry Fuseli's illustrations to Milton, and David and William were set to copy these works every evening; it was a quiet, serious, industrious household. Again through his father and brother Scott had access to literary circles in Edinburgh, and he met Walter Scott (who gave advice on one of his early poems, and to whom he believed he was distantly related); John Wilson (Christopher North), the celebrated conservative critic; Thomas De Quincey, whom he greatly admired; and the chemist, Dr Samuel Brown (subject of one of David Scott's most successful portraits), who became a close friend both of Scott and of his most valued patron, Lady Trevelyan. The first fruits of William Bell Scott's talents appeared in 1831 when he published his first poem, 'In Memory of P. B. Shelley', in *Tait's Edinburgh Magazine* (edited by John Wilson), and showed two small paintings at the Trustees' Academy. In 1834 he exhibited

William Bell Scott (1811–1890), by Frederick Bacon Barwell, 1877

his first picture at the Royal Scottish Academy (a subject from Coleridge's *The Ancient Mariner*) and with a friend he edited the *Edinburgh University Souvenir*.

Move to London Scott moved from Edinburgh to London in 1837 in order to establish himself as a painter. His first major painting, *The Old English Ballad Singer*, was exhibited at the British Institution in 1839. The painting has a typically learned and serious source. He was prompted by Sir Philip Sidney's praise for 'the old song of Percy and Douglas' in *Apology for Poetry* to imagine the singer of what was popularly known as the ballad of Chevy Chase, recording the battle of Otterburn (1388). (Scott would return to this subject for his decorative paintings at Wallington Hall in the 1860s.) The first painting that he had accepted for exhibition at the Royal Academy was *Chaucer, John of Gaunt and their Wives* (1842). Scott's London circle included an older generation—Leigh Hunt, Benjamin Haydon, and Carlyle—and painters making good commercial careers, such as W. P. Frith and Augustus Egg, and he met Tennyson and Browning. He is thought to be the inspiration for the unknown ambitious painter in Browning's poem 'Pictor ignotus'. Leigh Hunt helpfully promoted Scott as a poet and introduced him to younger literary men including G. H. Lewes, later George Eliot's partner. Among the younger artists and sculptors he knew Ford Madox Brown, Holman Hunt, J. E. Millais, Alexander Munro, and Thomas Woolner. He recalled making friends with Richard Dadd shortly before that brilliant and unstable painter murdered his father and was shut away in an asylum.

Scott's most intimate contact in London was with the Rossetti family. When D. G. Rossetti, Millais, and Holman Hunt formed themselves into the Pre-Raphaelite Brotherhood (PRB), William Bell Scott was closely associated with them. Some of his poems, including 'Rosabell' (a narrative poem based on his meeting with an Edinburgh prostitute) and 'A Dream of Love' were published by Leigh Hunt in the *Monthly Respository* in 1846, and D. G. Rossetti was prompted by the poems to make contact with him. Rossetti sought his advice about his own poetry (including 'The Blessed Damozel' and 'My Sister's Sleep') and invited Scott to contribute poems to the PRB's journal, *The Germ*. Two of his poems appeared: 'Morning Sleep' and 'Early Aspirations'. The latter, a sonnet, is a very personal meditation on ambition and failure, themes with which Scott would be obsessed for much of his life. The young PRB members were initially mocked by the critics, but in 1851 they were powerfully defended by John Ruskin, the most influential art critic in the country, and for the young men the tide turned. Scott was left out; his own work, like that of Ford Madox Brown, was never praised, or indeed mentioned, by Ruskin, and both painters felt, with good reason, that their careers in London in the 1840s were blighted by the care with which Ruskin distanced himself from their work.

Dante Gabriel and William Michael Rossetti were for some years loyal champions of Scott's work, and Christina Rossetti was a close friend (although there is no evidence for the story that she and Scott were in love for a time). All the Rossettis in due course visited Scott in Newcastle, where he lived first in St Thomas's Street, later in St Thomas's Crescent, very close to his School of Design (the houses in which he lived still stand). Through Scott the Rossettis met Lady Trevelyan, who in turn bought some of D. G. Rossetti's work. As a young man William Bell Scott was tall, good-looking, and had an appealing Scottish accent, and D. G. Rossetti dubbed him a 'stunner' (a term Rossetti normally reserved for astonishingly beautiful women such as Lizzie Siddall and Jane Burden—Mrs William Morris—the artists' models who in due course became Rossetti's wife and mistress respectively). Scott's closeness to the Rossettis led to a plan for an Italian tour in summer 1862 with Dante Gabriel and William Michael Rossetti; in the event Dante Gabriel was unable to travel following the death of his wife, Lizzie Siddall, earlier in the year, and Scott and W. M. Rossetti went to Italy without him. This tour was brief but of lasting importance for Scott because of his first hand exposure to Italian Renaissance painting.

On 31 October 1839 Scott married Letitia Margery Norquoy, a woman considerably older than himself who was regarded by all his friends as a shrill, neurotic, demanding, and difficult person. The marriage was clearly unhappy, it was childless, and may have been unconsummated (like the Ruskins'), but Scott and his wife never formally separated. In 1843 Scott submitted a cartoon for a large decorative painting in the competition for the adornment of the new houses of parliament. He was unsuccessful, but his painting caused him to be appointed in November 1843 as the first master of the School of Design, as it was then called, at Newcastle upon Tyne (it was later part of the national art school system established by Henry Cole for the improvement of manufacturing design). He took an enlightened attitude to his job, seeing it as a way of discovering talent among working-class men (all the students were men). His teaching was in tension with the general scheme of the schools of design, and later (after 1851) with Henry Cole's overarching scheme: Scott was happy to give individual tuition, to have his students study from the human figure, and to allow them to aspire beyond industrial design, none of which was approved by the London authorities running the scheme.

The Wallington scheme The tide turned for William Bell Scott when he made friends with the most generous and visionary of his patrons, Sir Walter and Lady Trevelyan of Wallington Hall, Northumberland. Pauline Trevelyan (1806–1866) initially became interested in him when she was invited to review his *Memoir of David Scott* (1850). She was a close friend of John Ruskin, and with Ruskin's general guidance she commissioned a decorative scheme for the central hall of Wallington, which she had had enclosed by John Dobson, the celebrated Newcastle architect. Between 1855 and 1861 Scott painted eight scenes of Northumbrian history, starting with the building of Hadrian's Wall and ending with a scene showing contemporary Newcastle industry by the Tyne. This last painting, called *Iron and Coal, the Nineteenth Century*, is Scott's most important single achievement. It celebrates progress and the dignity of the labourer much in the manner of Ford Madox Brown's *Work*, in which heroically sturdy young road builders are admired and applauded by F. D. Maurice (founder of the Working Men's College) and Thomas Carlyle. (Brown had started work on his painting in 1852, and although it was not finished until later than *Iron and Coal* it is likely that it influenced Scott.) Road building is not manufacture, of course, and Scott's painting has the distinction of being the only Pre-Raphaelite painting which records an industrial process.

Iron and Coal closes an alternating sequence of subjects: there are four paintings of notable figures (Cuthbert, Bede, Gilpin, and Grace Darling) and four of historical periods (the Roman, the Viking, the border wars, and the nineteenth century). Scott continued to work on the Wallington scheme with a mural of the battle of Chevy Chase on the upper walls of the central saloon. He hoped to be commissioned to complete the scheme with a ceiling design, but after Pauline's death in 1866 the motive force for the decoration of Wallington had gone. Sir Walter Trevelyan married again and the second Lady Trevelyan (formerly Laura Capell Lofft, a close friend of Pauline Trevelyan) disliked Scott and terminated the commission.

The Wallington decorative scheme brought fame to William Bell Scott and the Trevelyans and transformed the reputation of the arts in the north-east. In 1855, the year in which Pauline conceived the Wallington scheme, a local journalist wrote in despair that the 'fine arts in Newcastle appear literally to be dead and buried', and that with the growing prosperity of the people of Newcastle and Sunderland came a growing ignorance of art and a preference for 'champagne and claret' (Quinn, 53). By 1862 that had been significantly changed. The Wallington scheme was recognized as an innovation of national as well as regional significance, and it was widely reviewed in the national press. The paintings were exhibited in London before finally being hung in Wallington. The only comparable recent decorative scheme was the frescoes of Arthurian subjects painted by Rossetti, Edward Burne-Jones, Morris, Val Prinsep, and others in Thomas Deane's and Benjamin Woodward's new Gothic Oxford Union building in 1857. Scott's Wallington paintings prompted similar decorative schemes elsewhere in the country, such as the cycle of twelve historical paintings for Manchester town hall (depicting episodes in the history of Manchester from Roman times to the recent past) undertaken by Ford Madox Brown in the 1870s, and the later decorative scheme commissioned for the Scottish National Portrait Gallery.

Relations with Ruskin Scott's abiding resentment against Ruskin was brought into sharp focus by jealousy. As the famous critic was one of Lady Trevelyan's closest friends, Scott inevitably felt himself in unequal rivalry for her attention. When Ruskin had earlier befriended and patronized D. G. Rossetti, Scott had felt that one of his closest male friends in effect was being stolen. The froideur with Ruskin did Scott damage. He found it necessary to disparage J. M. W. Turner only because Ruskin had championed that painter, and although Scott was studiously Pre-Raphaelite in his methods he mocked and condemned Ruskin's teaching techniques at the Working Men's College in London from 1854 onwards. (Ruskin's teaching involved faithful observation of natural forms, the central doctrine of the Pre-Raphaelites.) After Ruskin's wife, Effie, left him for J. E. Millais, Scott wrote that Lady Trevelyan had seen that Millais and Effie were in love when they stayed at Wallington in 1853, and had tried to persuade Sir Walter to warn Ruskin of this. There is no evidence for this, and Lady Trevelyan's diary makes it clear that this story of Scott's is just an invention, a product of his immovable dislike of Ruskin.

Ménage à trois In 1859 William Bell Scott met Alice Boyd, of Penkill Castle, Ayrshire, when she came to study art in Newcastle. He used her as a model (she figures prominently in the foreground of Scott's own favourite among his sea paintings, *Grace Darling*, at Wallington Hall). The relationship became very close. Scott's wife, Letitia, accepted the situation—presumably she had little choice—and from the 1860s Scott lived with Alice Boyd and with Letitia in a *ménage à trois* in Scotland and London until the end of his life. His relationship with Alice Boyd led to Scott's second commission for another important decorative scheme. After the death of her brother in 1865 Alice became the owner of Penkill and over several years in the 1860s Scott painted there a series of frescoes illustrating James I's poem *The King's Quair*.

In 1862 the national management of art schools had changed again, and Scott, appointed under the previous system, was offered redundancy (with a pension) which he took after some hesitation in 1863. At about this date he suffered a disorder which caused him to become totally bald, and he took to wearing a wig. He went back to London and thereafter divided his time between the metropolis and Penkill. He was commissioned by Henry Cole to design stained-glass windows for the South Kensington Museum (now the Victorian and Albert Museum) in London; he worked as an examiner in the London art schools during this period and edited literary texts. In 1870 he was able to buy a substantial property in London: Bellevue House, 92 Cheyne Walk, Chelsea. For the last eight years of his life he was disabled by angina, and was nursed by Alice Boyd until his death at Penkill on 22 November 1890.

Reputation At his best William Bell Scott was a distinguished painter. *Iron and Coal* and *Grace Darling* are major achievements. Among Scott's many good portraits are his remarkably vivid study of Swinburne (Balliol College, Oxford) and his beautiful and affectionate profile portrait of Lady Trevelyan which hangs with his more formal portrait of Sir Walter Trevelyan at Wallington. His big, ambitious painting of the building of the New Castle (the medieval structure which gives Newcastle its name) was commissioned by subscription to mark his retirement from the Newcastle post in 1863, was completed in 1865, and is now in the Newcastle Literary and Philosophical Society's collection.

Scott was also a serious and versatile poet, and saw himself in competition with his friend D. G. Rossetti as a master of the twin arts of poetry and painting. (He was perhaps more industrious in both these arts than was Rossetti.) He took the view that his 'fallen woman' poem, 'Rosabell' (about an Edinburgh prostitute) was the inspiration both for Rossetti's poem 'Jenny' and for his painting *Found*. *Found* was never finished, but at one point it was commissioned by the Newcastle patron James Leathart, who was introduced to Rossetti by Scott. In his lifetime Leathart, often with Scott's help, built up one of the most important collections of Pre-Raphaelite paintings in the country, but his business failed and the collection had to be sold.

William Bell Scott's philosophical poetry includes *Hades and the Progress of the Mind* (1838), and the long and grandiose *The Year of the World* (1846). His lyric and narrative poetry, often very attractive, is found at its best in the small collection *Poems* (better known as *Poems by a Painter*) (1854) and the larger *Poems by William Bell Scott* (illustrated by Scott and Sir Lawrence Alma Tadema, 1875) and *A Poet's Harvest Home* (1882).

The most important of Scott's prose works is his biography of his brother, *Memoir of David Scott* (1850), the book which made William Bell Scott into a familiar name. Scott was deeply distressed by his brother's early death in 1849, and the biography is a moving and well written but also clear-sighted account. He also published a great number of books arising directly from his work as a teacher—a large volume of half-hour lectures on the whole history of European art, for example—and many introductions to edited texts, which in his later life made a substantial part of his literary income.

William Bell Scott wrote an autobiography in the 1850s which he seems to have abandoned and partly destroyed about 1855, and then returned to and completed in the 1870s. It was published posthumously in 1892 as *Autobiographical Notes*, edited by a friend, Professor W. Minto of Aberdeen. The book betrays some bitterness and disappointment, and a tendency to bolster his own reputation by seeking to belittle the talents of his friends, including D. G. Rossetti, Holman Hunt, and Woolner. Swinburne, who was much younger than Scott, had received great kindness from him and had been very fond of him (they met initially because the Swinburne family were neighbours of Lady Trevelyan in Northumberland). Scott had advised and helped him with his poetry and Swinburne had affectionately dedicated *Poems and Ballads III* to Scott, and wrote a moving and substantial verse tribute to him which was published in *The Athenaeum* shortly after Scott's death in November 1890. In his autobiography, though, Scott tends to treat Swinburne as a delinquent schoolboy. Swinburne responded in 1892 with a piece in the *Fortnightly Review* which is regularly quoted in accounts of Scott's life. It is tantrum prose, in which Swinburne calls the now dead Scott 'imbecile, doting, malignant, mangy' (Walker, 240–41). The anger stirred up in Swinburne and others by Scott's *Autobiographical Notes* has tended to affect subsequent judgements of the book, and to obscure the fact that it is an indispensable memoir of the early Pre-Raphaelites and of the subsequent lives of the Rossettis, Hunt, Swinburne, Woolner, Munro, and others, and also that it is the central source for an understanding of Lady Trevelyan's princely commission for him to paint the Northumbrian history cycle for Wallington Hall.

JOHN BATCHELOR

Sources *Autobiographical notes of William Bell Scott*, ed. W. Minto, 2 vols. (1892) · W. B. Scott, *Memoir of David Scott, R.S.A.* (1850) · W. E. Fredeman, 'The letters of Pictor ignotus: William Bell Scott's correspondence with Alice Boyd, 1859–1884', *Bulletin of the John Rylands Library*, 58 (1975), 66–111 · W. E. Fredeman, 'The letters of Pictor ignotus: William Bell Scott's correspondence with Alice Boyd, 1859–1884, part 2', *Bulletin of the John Rylands Library*, 58 (1976), 306–52 · R. Trevelyan, *A Pre-Raphaelite circle* (1978) · P. Trevelyan, diary, 44 vols., University of Kansas, Lawrence, Kenneth Spencer Research Library [microfilm held at U. Newcastle] · W. B. Scott, letters to Sir Walter and Lady Trevelyan, U. Newcastle, Robinson L., special collections · W. B. Scott and W. M. Rossetti, correspondence, U. Durham L., archives and special collections · V. Walker, 'The life and work of William Bell Scott, 1811–1890', PhD diss., U. Durham, 1951 · *Literary and artistic remains of Paulina Jermyn Trevelyan*, ed. D. Wooster (1879) · P. J. Quinn, 'Picturing locality: art and regional identity in the north-east of England, 1822–1900', PhD diss., University of Sunderland, 1997 · *Reflections of a friendship: John Ruskin's letters to Pauline Trevelyan, 1848–66*, ed. V. Surtees (1979) · C. Trevelyan, *Wallington* (1947) · R. Trevelyan, *Wallington* (1994) · *DNB* · *CGPLA Eng. & Wales* (1891)

Archives Bodl. Oxf., diaries [copies] · NL Scot., corresp. and literary MSS · U. Leeds, Brotherton L., papers · University of British Columbia Library, Vancouver, diaries and literary MSS | BL, letters to Royal Literary Fund, loan 96 · BL, letters to W. T. Watts-Dunton, Ashley MS 1482 · Bodl. Oxf., letters to D. G. Rossetti [copies] · Bodl. Oxf., letters to W. M. Rossetti [copies] · Cornell University, Ithaca, New York, Olin Library, letters to Margaret Raine Hunt · JRL, letters to Alice Boyd · LUL, letters to Austin Dobson · National Gallery, London, letters to Ralph Nicholson Wornum · TCD, letters to Edward Dowden · U. Durham L., corresp. with W. M.

Rossetti, letters • U. Leeds, Brotherton L., letters to Edmund Gosse • U. Newcastle, Robinson L., corresp. with Sir Walter Trevelyan and Lady Trevelyan • University of British Columbia Library, Vancouver, letters to William Holman Hunt • University of British Columbia Library, Vancouver, letters to James Leathart • University of Chicago Library, letters to Arthur Munby, NUC MS 64-59

Likenesses D. Scott, oils, *c.*1832, Scot. NPG • W. & D. Downey, group portrait, photograph, carte-de-visite, 1863 (with D. G. Rossetti and John Ruskin), NPG • W. B. Scott, self-portrait, 1867, Scot. NPG • W. B. Scott, etching, 1875 (after A. Boyd), BM • F. B. Barwell, oils, 1877, NPG [*see illus.*] • W. B. Scott, self-portrait, etching (aged twenty), BM • W. B. Scott, self-portraits, etchings, BM • T. Sibson, pen-and-ink drawing, V&A

Wealth at death no value given: confirmation, sealed, 29 May 1891, *CGPLA Eng. & Wales*

Scott, William George (1913–1989), painter and printmaker, was born on 15 February 1913 in Greenock, Renfrewshire, the third of eleven children and eldest son of William John Scott, a signwriter and house decorator from Enniskillen in co. Fermanagh, northern Ireland, and his Scottish wife, Agnes Murray. The family moved to Enniskillen in 1924, where he attended Enniskillen Technical School and, encouraged by his father, enrolled in evening classes in art. In 1928 he entered Belfast College of Art with a local scholarship. From 1931 to 1935 Scott studied at the Royal Academy Schools in London, where he won the silver medal for sculpture in 1933, the Landseer scholarship in painting (1934), and a Leverhulme travelling scholarship in 1935. Once freed from the restrictions of academic training, he sought alternatives to both English landscape painting and to the surrealist and abstract modes of the day.

In 1937 Scott married (Hilda) Mary, daughter of William Lucas, a paint manufacturer of Bristol. She was a sculptor, and a fellow student at the Academy Schools. They were to have two sons. For the next two years they travelled in Italy and the south of France, and taught during the summers at a painting school at Pont Aven in Brittany. It was there that Scott did his first mature paintings. They prefigure his later work in their modesty of subject matter (the single figure, still life, and landscape), a deliberate simplicity in composition, a painterly touch, and rich tonality. Cézanne was an important influence, and Scott was also affected by other French painters, notably Bonnard and Matisse. In November 1938 he exhibited at the Salon d'Automne, and was elected sociétaire.

At the outbreak of war in September 1939 the Scotts moved to Dublin, where their elder son, Robert, was born in January 1940. After a few months in London, in 1941 they took a cottage at Hallatrow in Somerset, where Scott created a market garden and taught part-time at Bath Academy of Art. James, his second son, was born in July 1941. In 1942, shortly before his first one-man exhibition at the Leger Gallery, London, Scott volunteered for the armed forces, and joined the Royal Engineers. As an ordnance map maker he learned lithography, and in north Wales made watercolour landscapes in the pervasive English Romantic mode of the time. These were shown in London in 1944 and 1945.

In September 1946 Scott painted the seminal *The Frying Pan*, his first table-top still life, featuring a frying pan, bowl, and toasting-fork, props that with a number of other simple kitchen objects (such as saucepans, spoons, eggs, beans, and fish) were to recur as motifs in his work. Scott invested these simple things with multivalent symbolic significance, first as attributes of the elemental life of the simple poor; later they seem to be the components of obscure sexual encounters in what Scott referred to as 'the secret in the picture'. This intensity of regard for domestic objects was derived from a French tradition of still-life painting (variously exemplified by J. B. S. Chardin, Paul Cézanne, and Georges Braque), with which Scott felt a particular affinity.

In 1946 Scott had returned to Hallatrow, and was appointed senior painting master at Bath Academy of Art, now at Corsham Court in Wiltshire. He taught there, highly regarded by staff and students, until 1956. During the late 1940s he made fruitful contacts with many of those St Ives artists associated with Ben Nicholson, who were moving towards a simplifying abstraction of forms. These artists, among them Roger Hilton, Terry Frost, Peter Lanyon, Bryan Winter, Patrick Heron, and Adrian Heath, formed the nucleus of a British school of abstract painting, within which Scott was to be a prime mover and major influence throughout the 1950s.

Scott maintained an individual creative course, the momentum and direction of which was determined by his own predilections towards a reductive simplification of forms and an evocative richness of surface texture. In 1953 in New York he was the first British painter to meet the abstract expressionists at first hand, and was impressed by the expansive scale and confidence of their work. The effect was to confirm his sense of identity as essentially a European painter, whose abstraction was derived from first-hand experience of the world of familiar objects and phenomena. He returned to the painterly evocation of figurative subjects, freed from direct description but never absolutely free of reference. In the mid-1960s Scott experimented with an even-surfaced decorative abstraction, but the flattened outlines of domestic utensils and ambiguous fruit and vegetable forms invariably found their way back into his work. These formal and symbolic elements of the pictorial drama are unmistakably personal in origin, and resolutely modern in their deployment on the flat surface of the canvas.

William Scott was widely recognized as an artist of international standing. He represented Britain at the twenty-ninth Venice Biennale in 1958, and at the sixth Bienal, São Paulo, in 1961. He was appointed CBE in 1966. He received honorary doctorates from the Royal College of Art (1975), Queen's University in Belfast (1976), and Trinity College, Dublin (1977). The Tate mounted a major retrospective in 1972. He was elected ARA in 1977 and RA in 1984. Scott was unostentatious in appearance; but his emphatic dark brows and small beard were expressive of an intense temperament. Small and wiry, and compact of energy, he was quick and precise in his gestures, and deliberate in manner. He died in Coleford, Somerset, on 28 December 1989, after suffering from Alzheimer's disease for several years. Scott's work is represented in many public collections, in Britain and abroad, including the Tate collection, the Ulster Museum, the Scottish National Gallery of Modern Art, and the Guggenheim Museum, New York. MEL GOODING, *rev.*

Sources R. Alley, *William Scott* (1963) • A. Bowness, *William Scott paintings* (1964) • A. Bowness, *William Scott* (1972) • N. Lynton, *William Scott* (1990) • A. Bowness, *William Scott: paintings, drawings and gouaches, 1938–71* (1972) [exhibition catalogue, Tate Gallery, London, 19 April – 29 May 1972] • William Scott Foundation archives, London • *The Times* (30 Dec 1989) • *The Independent* (2 Jan 1990) • *CGPLA Eng. & Wales* (1990)

Archives William Scott Foundation, 13 Edith Terrace, London, archives | Tate collection, transcript of an interview for TV South West

Wealth at death £198,565: probate, 11 Dec 1990, *CGPLA Eng. & Wales*

Scottish colourists (*act.* **1900–1935**), painters, were a loose association of four painters, from Edinburgh and the west of Scotland, whose work during the first three decades of the twentieth century revitalized painting in Scotland through their awareness of new developments in painting in France before 1914. Their response to the innovative use of colour and painterly handling in paintings by Henri Matisse and his followers provided a conduit for such new work to reach Britain and, particularly, Scotland in the first half of the twentieth century. It was not a movement that produced leaders and followers, and although all four artists knew each other they rarely worked together in more than pairs, and never as a group of four.

John Duncan Fergusson (1874–1961) was born in Leith, Edinburgh, on 9 March 1874, the son of John Ferguson and his wife, Christina Fergusson. He always maintained that he enrolled at Edinburgh University to study medicine, although there is no record of his enrolment there, and then transferred to art classes at the Trustees' Academy, Edinburgh *c.*1893. The curriculum there did not suit him and he left, whereafter he was largely self-taught with occasional terms at various academies and ateliers in Paris. The work of the Glasgow Boys and James McNeill Whistler were major influences on his early paintings (see *Dieppe, 14 July 1905: Night*; Scottish National Gallery of Modern Art, Edinburgh), as was the work of French artists seen on his regular visits to Paris and northern France between 1895 and 1906. After a successful exhibition in London, Fergusson decided to settle in Paris, where he lived until 1913, when he moved to the Mediterranean coast. In Paris he became part of the artistic café society of Montparnasse, meeting Picasso and other leading artists, becoming a sociétaire of the Salon d'Automne, and absorbing much of the excitement and advances in painting that characterized Paris before 1914. Paintings such as *Rhythm* (1911; University of Stirling) and *Les Eus* (1911–13; Hunterian Art Gallery, University of Glasgow) show his assimilation of French avant-garde artistic and philosophical alliances.

The outbreak of war forced Fergusson's return to Edinburgh, where Peploe also was living, but by 1918 he was living in London, with the dancer Margaret *Morris (1891–1980). He soon became an integral part of the Chelsea art world and also of the summer schools that Morris arranged for her growing number of pupils in the Margaret Morris Movement. He returned to France with Morris and her dance classes until forced, again by the outbreak of war, to return to Scotland, to Glasgow, in 1939. There, with Morris, he established an alternative artistic environment in the city, separate from the established worlds of the Glasgow School of Art and the Glasgow Art Club. He remained in the city until his death, at his home, 4 Clouston Street, on 30 January 1961.

Samuel John Peploe (1871–1935) was born at 39 Manor Place, Edinburgh, on 27 January 1871, the son of Robert Luff Peploe, secretary of the Commercial Bank, Edinburgh, and his second wife, Anne Watson. After the death of his father in 1884 Peploe was encouraged by his guardians to follow a career in the army; his refusal led him to enter a law firm, but in 1893 he persuaded the guardians to allow him to enrol in the Trustees' Academy, in Edinburgh. Like Fergusson he was unhappy with the teaching and left for Paris, where he attended classes at various academies and ateliers. He was quick to absorb the influence of Manet, and on his return to Edinburgh *c.*1897 he embarked on a successful career as a landscape, figure, and still life painter. He then met Fergusson, and the two painters formed an immediate rapport based as much on personal liking as on their mutual admiration for Whistler, the Glasgow Boys, and post-impressionist French painting. They were the first of the Scottish colourists to work together, and broadly formulated the principles on which all four artists would concentrate until the mid-1930s. In 1910, using the proceeds from a successful exhibition in 1909, and following his marriage in that year to Margaret MacKay (1874–1958), Peploe joined Fergusson in Paris, where his artistic education was completed and his mature style emerged. Together they began to explore Brittany and the west coast of France before Fergusson determined to follow in the footsteps of van Gogh and Gauguin by moving to Antibes.

Peploe's innate conservatism and his devotion to his growing family prevented him from settling in the south of France with Fergusson, and he again returned to Edinburgh. Although his new paintings, such as *Still Life* (*c.*1913; Scottish National Gallery of Modern Art), did not meet with the approval of his dealer Peploe gradually achieved success and remained in Edinburgh for the rest of his life, with brief excursions to the south of France (see *Landscape at Cassis*, 1924; Scottish National Gallery of Modern Art) and annual holidays in the Western Isles, principally Iona. In 1927 he was made a full member of the Royal Scottish Academy and in 1933 he began to teach part-time at Edinburgh College of Art. He died in Edinburgh, at 35 Drumsheugh Gardens, on 11 October 1935.

Peploe was introduced to Iona by **Francis Campbell Boileau Cadell** (1883–1937), who was born in Edinburgh on 12 April 1883, the first child of Francis Cadell, a surgeon, and Mary Hamilton Boileau. His request to attend art school was supported by his liberal parents, encouraged by a family friend, Arthur Melville. He enrolled at the Royal Scottish Academy life school but, like Peploe and

Fergusson at the Trustees' Academy, was disillusioned by the teaching. With his mother he moved to Paris in 1899, to enrol in the Académie Julian, and returned to Edinburgh in 1903; in 1906 his family moved to Munich, to return to Edinburgh in 1908. In his early life, therefore, he was well-travelled, and through family connections he met many of the future patrons who were to sustain him through the commercial vicissitudes of his career. One such figure was Sir Patrick Ford, who financed a visit to Venice in 1910, following Cadell's unsuccessful first solo show in Edinburgh in 1909. In Venice, Cadell began to paint in a manner similar to Peploe, whose work he had seen in Edinburgh, and he returned to Scotland with a group of paintings showing a clear grasp of impressionism and the effects of light on colour. He soon established a niche in Edinburgh, painting portraits, figure subjects, and still lifes that reflected the douce, middle-class milieu of the New Town. His studios at 130 George Street (1909–20) and 6 Ainslie Place (1920–32) were usually as much the subject of his paintings as the sitters themselves (see *The Black Hat*, 1914; Edinburgh City Art Centre, and *The Orange Blind*; Glasgow Museums and Art Galleries).

In 1915 Cadell enlisted as a private soldier in the Royal Scots, 9th battalion, resisting a commission until 1918, when he was transferred to the Argyll and Sutherland Highlanders, 8th battalion, as a second lieutenant. Peace brought with it an uncertain future for him; changing social mores, his own extravagant lifestyle and personal life, and an unpredictable commercial demand for paintings brought an inexorable decline in his wealth, health, and output. He survived the 1920s with the support of consistent patrons such as W. G. Service and Ion Harrison, and with the friendship and encouragement of Peploe, with whom he holidayed frequently on Iona and occasionally in the south of France. Cadell had discovered Iona *c.*1913 and it was to become an important subject for him. In 1935 he was elected a full member of the Royal Scottish Academy but he was by then in considerable financial and physical distress. He died, of cancer, in Edinburgh on 6 December 1937. He never married.

The fourth member of the group, **(George) Leslie Hunter** (1877–1931), was not associated with Edinburgh. He was born on 7 August 1877 in Rothesay, on the island of Bute, the son of William Hunter, a pharmacist, and his wife, Jeannie. In 1892, after the deaths of two of his sons from tuberculosis, William Hunter took his family to California, where he bought an orange grove. In 1899 he and his wife returned to Scotland, but Leslie and an elder brother decided to stay in California, moving north from Los Angeles to San Francisco. Hunter enjoyed the cosmopolitan freedom of the city and taught himself to draw and paint, earning a living as a book and newspaper illustrator. He seems to have returned to Scotland some time between 1903 and 1905 and also visited Paris with a group of American artists. It is not known whether at this time he encountered the work of Fergusson and Peploe, which was regularly on show in dealers' galleries and public exhibitions in Scotland, or whether he saw any of the great exhibitions of the work of the post-impressionists. Hunter returned to San Francisco via New York in 1905. His association with authors such as Bret Harte and Jack London, for both of whom he illustrated novels, probably helped him to secure an exhibition in a San Francisco gallery. Unfortunately both the gallery and all Hunter's work in it were destroyed by the great earthquake of 1906.

Hunter returned to Scotland to live with his mother in Glasgow, earning a living again from newspaper illustration. He moved to London and then to Paris, and began to paint more seriously, studying the work of Dutch and French still life painters of the seventeenth and eighteenth centuries. He returned to Scotland after the outbreak of war, and worked as a labourer on an uncle's farm in Lanarkshire. He continued to paint, and exhibited with Alexander Reid in Glasgow in 1916, as a result of which he acquired a nucleus of collectors who helped to sustain his erratic way of life over the next decade or so. He had further success with Reid after the war, and with the proceeds of these sales visited Paris, Florence, and Venice in 1922 and 1923. A friend, John Ressich, introduced him to Fergusson, through whom he met Peploe, and with Reid's involvement he exhibited with the other three painters in London and Paris in the mid-1920s.

Hunter began to suffer from both mental and physical illness, and his unpredictable behaviour isolated him from fellow painters and from all but the most dedicated patrons. In 1926 he set out for the south of France, where he encountered both Fergusson and Peploe, but his paintings found no market in Scotland and Reid was forced to terminate the stipend that he had been paying him. Undeterred, Hunter arranged an exhibition in New York, which had some success, perhaps more in the renewal of old friendships than financially, and in 1929 he returned to France, where he settled in St Paul de Vence. Illness forced his return to Scotland, where he began to paint on the shores of Loch Lomond, followed by some months in London, where a new patron, the impresario C. B. Cochran, commissioned him to make sketches of one of his productions. He returned to Glasgow, where he again fell ill, and was admitted to hospital for emergency surgery. There it was found that he was beyond cure, and he died on 7 December 1931. He was unmarried.

The consistent link between the Scottish colourists is a love of paint and its particular qualities, and an understanding of the power of colour and design in painting. From an early interest in *plein-air* painting through to the immediacy of fauvist painting the colourists never lost sight of the painterly qualities that they inherited from their study of the Glasgow Boys. Scottish painters from the middle of the eighteenth century had expressed their fascination with fluid handling, bold compositions, and clear colour—qualities that the four colourists reinforced through their association with French painting.

The Scottish colourists brought to British painting an awareness, gained principally at first hand, of the developments made in Paris by Picasso and, particularly, Matisse and the Fauves in the first decade of the century. Roger Fry's post-impressionist exhibitions had sent English painting in search of 'significant form', and Fry had not included the work of the Scots in his shows. The four Scottish colourists responded more to the vitality, both painterly and emotional, of the gestural handling and brilliant colour of Gauguin, van Gogh, and Matisse. Despite their successes in showing in London in the 1920s they did little to divert avant-garde English painters from the impact of surrealism, constructivism, and the work of German refugees such as Naum Gabo, Antoine Pevsner, and Kurt Schwitters. Their success and influence lay with English painters such as Matthew Smith and David Bomberg, who shared their knowledge of, and interest in, French pre-war painting, and with a younger generation of artists in Scotland who, throughout the 1940s and 1950s, saw in the work of the colourists a direct link with Picasso and Matisse and all that had come to be seen as pivotal in the development of painting in the twentieth century. The work of the colourists epitomized that aspect of the Scottish character in which a sense of responsibility, caution, and respect for convention is balanced by an element of irresponsibility, rebelliousness, and even aggression. The colourists harnessed this underlying aspect of their nature, and through it involved British painting in the mainstream of European art of the twentieth century. ROGER BILLCLIFFE

Sources R. Billcliffe, *The Scottish colourists* (1989) • G. Peploe, *S. J. Peploe, 1871–1935* (2000) • K. Simister, *A living paint: J. D. Fergusson, 1874–1961* (2001) • P. Long and E. Lumming, *The Scottish colourists, 1900–1930* (2000) [exhibition catalogue, NG Scot.] • T. J. Honeyman, *Three Scottish colourists* (1950) • T. Hewlett, *Cadell: the life and works of a Scottish colourist, 1883–1937* (1988) • T. J. Honeyman, *Introducing Leslie Hunter* (1937) • d. cert. [Samuel John Peploe] • private information (2004) [grandson of Samuel John Peploe]

Archives Fergusson Gallery, Perth, corresp., sketchbooks, drawings, etc. [John Duncan Fergusson] • NL Scot., T. J. Honeyman Archive, Hunter papers • NL Scot., corresp. and papers [Francis Campbell Boileau Cadell] • Scottish National Gallery of Modern Art, corresp. [John Duncan Fergusson]

Likenesses photographs, repro. in R. Billcliffe, *Scottish colourists* (1989) • photographs, repro. in Long and Lumming, *Scottish colourists, 1900–1930* (2000)

Scottow [Scotto], **Joshua** (**1618–1698**), merchant and author in America, is presumed to have been born in Suffolk of a maritime family. He migrated to Boston, Massachusetts, in 1634 with his widowed mother, Thomasine, and an elder brother, Thomas (*b.* 1612). His mother was admitted to the Boston church that year. The brothers joined the same congregation in 1639 and were granted land along Muddy River (now Brookline). By 1640 Scottow had a wife, Lydia (*d.* 1707). In 1641 the first of the couple's seven children was born, four of whom survived him.

Scottow was a merchant, dealing in farm lands and waterfront lots in and around Boston. In 1653 the Massachusetts general court, the colony's legislature, granted him and John Leverett a special licence to trade with the French in Acadia. In 1661 pursuit of this commerce led to his being accused of violating the newly passed parliamentary Navigation Acts for his role in the purchase and resale of a condemned cargo, a charge repeated in 1665 during the royal commission's investigation of New England's role in the emerging empire. The issue was never resolved at law. During these years Scottow also began acquiring land in what is now Maine, to which he moved about 1671. He remained until King Philip's War (1675–6) devastated the region's frontier, then returned to Boston. Despite his age he was then elected captain of horse in the colony's militia, as much an honorary and political post as a military one.

Unlike some other New England entrepreneurs, Scottow was a staunch supporter of puritan orthodoxy and of Massachusetts's relative autonomy. He was a rather cosmopolitan figure, as suggested by his Acadian trade. These interests and commitments were reflected in his literary activities. In 1649, as he began to prosper, he donated an expensive four-volume Greek thesaurus to Harvard College with the stipulation that he and his family had priority on its use, which suggests academic, if not clerical, ambition. Indeed, his son Thomas graduated from Harvard in 1677.

In 1668, in response to a controversy over the toleration of Baptists, he published in Boston his translation of a late sixteenth-century French history of the Anabaptist movement, which indicates not only a command of the French language but also some familiarity with Huguenot polemics. Late in his life he wrote two other works, *Old Men's Tears for their Own Declensions* (1691) and *A Narrative of the Planting of the Massachusetts Colony anno 1628* (1694). Both were responses to Massachusetts's loss of its charter and closer incorporation into the empire during and after the revolution of 1688. The first is a lament for his and his generation's moral and religious lapses. The second is an account of the colony's founding as a puritan reform experiment.

Joshua Scottow died in Boston in January 1698. He was survived by his wife, who lived until 1707, and three daughters and one son. He was an articulate pioneer in the development of New England's distinctive regional colonial economy and culture. RICHARD P. GILDRIE

Sources J. A. Levernier and D. R. Wilmes, eds., *American writers before 1800: a biographical and critical dictionary*, 3 vols. (1983) • 'Sketch of Captain Joshua Scottow', *Publications of the Colonial Society of Massachusetts*, 10 (1906), 370–78 • B. Bailyn, *The New England merchants in the seventeenth century* (1955) • D. B. Rutman, *Winthrop's Boston: a portrait of a puritan town, 1630–1649* (1965) • *The diary of Samuel Sewall, 1674–1729: newly edited from the manuscript at the Massachusetts Historical Society*, ed. M. H. Thomas, 2 vols. (1973) • *DNB* • T. G. Wright, *Literary culture in early New England, 1620–1730* (New York, 1966) • J. G. Reid, *Acadia, Maine, and New Scotland: marginal colonies in the seventeenth century* (1981)

Scotus, John. *See* John Scottus (*fl.* *c.*845–*c.*870).

Scougal, Henry (**1650–1678**), Church of Scotland minister, is believed to have been born at Leuchars, Fife, in June 1650, the second son of Patrick *Scougal (1607–1682), minister of Saltoun and later bishop of Aberdeen, and of his first wife, Margaret (or Jean) Wemyss (*d.* before 1660). As a young child he was allowed by his father to 'stay in the Room, when Clergymen, or Scholars, or others, from whom any Thing might be learn'd were with him', in order to nurture 'an early Disposition of judging right of both Men and Things' (Cockburn, 29). In 1664 he entered King's College, Aberdeen, where he was subsequently 'made constant president' of the regular meetings held among the student body to discuss philosophical and religious issues (Gairden, 265). After graduating MA on 9 July 1668, Scougal was subsequently appointed a regent, or lecturer, at King's, where his father was by then chancellor. As a regent, he was remembered for being 'the first in this corner of the land' to structure his philosophy teaching according to Cartesian principles to discourage his students from acquiring 'a disputing humour and vanity in hard words and distinctions', while remaining concerned to 'guard them against the debauched sentiments' to be found in Thomas Hobbes's *Leviathan* (1651) (ibid., 267).

In the summer of 1673 Scougal was ordained and appointed minister of Auchterless, Aberdeenshire, in which capacity he also served as precentor in the cathedral church, Old Aberdeen. At Auchterless he insisted on being present during all church services, thus abandoning customary practice whereby the minister joined the congregation just before the sermon and allowed the first part of the service to be conducted by the reader. In a sermon preached before the synod of Aberdeen, he later described the considerable challenges confronting a rural minister, including, for example, the duty of catechizing, which involved telling 'the same things a thousand times to some dull and ignorant people, who perhaps, shall know little when we have done' (*Works*, 231). On 12 August 1674, however, the synod appointed Scougal professor of divinity at King's College, following his successful defence of a set of theses entitled *Positiones aliquot theologicae, de objecto cultus religiosi*. As professor he continued to dissuade his students from developing 'an itching curiosity about questions and strifes of words, which minister to vanity and contention', while spending his summer vacations purchasing books and conversing with clerical colleagues in England and France (Gairden, 295).

In 1677 Scougal consented to the anonymous publication of his manual of personal devotion entitled *The Life of God in the Soul of Man* in which he characterized 'true Religion' as a 'Union of the Soul with God, a real participation of the Divine Nature, the very Image of God drawn upon the Soul' (*Life of God*, 5). The following year, however, he became increasingly ill with consumption and died, unmarried, on 13 June 1678, aged twenty-eight. He was buried in King's College chapel. Following his father's death in 1682, over a thousand volumes from the Scougals' shared collection was bequeathed to King's College Library, together with a sum of 5000 merks to augment the professor of divinity's salary. A copy of the morning and evening service forms which Scougal devised for the cathedral church was published in 1791. Entrenched antipathy towards liturgical forms within the Scottish kirk ensured that their regular use was, however, quickly abandoned following the re-establishment of presbyterianism in the revolution of 1688–9.

By contrast, Scougal's *Life of God* quickly attained the status of an enduring religious classic. Its latitudinarian theology, mystical piety, and intense spiritualism bore close affinity to works produced by Cambridge Platonists, such as John Smith and Jeremy Taylor. After Gilbert Burnet published a second edition of the work in 1691, over a dozen subsequent editions appeared in the century following Scougal's death. While John Wesley reprinted the work in 1744, George Whitefield later ascribed his own conversion experience to having read a copy of the *Life of God* which had been lent to him by Charles Wesley a decade earlier. As Whitefield recalled 'I never knew what religion was, till God sent me that excellent treatise' (Whitefield, 46–7). Elsewhere, a French translation appeared at The Hague in 1722, followed by a German version in 1755, and a Welsh edition in 1779. In 1756 Benjamin Franklin printed another German version which he distributed among the German-speaking settlers in Pennsylvania where it 'proved most acceptable at this Time' (*Papers*, 6.535). During the eighteenth century there also appeared several editions of Scougal's collected works, which comprised his sermons, together with several *Private Reflexions and Occasional Meditations* composed while he was a student in the 1660s, a set of *Divine and Moral Essays* and the sermon preached by George Gairden at Scougal's funeral in 1678.

CLARE JACKSON

Sources G. Gairden, 'A sermon preached at the funeral of the Revd. Henry Scougal', in *The works of the Revd. Mr Henry Scougal* (1765) • D. Butler, *Henry Scougal and the Oxford Methodists* (1899) • G. D. Henderson, 'Henry Scougall', *The burning bush: studies in Scottish church history* (1957), 94–119 • G. Burnet, ed., 'Preface', in H. Scougal, *The life of God in the soul of man*, 2nd edn (1691) • P. J. Anderson, ed., *Officers and graduates of University and King's College, Aberdeen, MVD–MDCCCLX*, New Spalding Club, 11 (1893) • G. D. Henderson, 'Henry Scougall at Auchterless', *Scottish Notes and Queries*, 3rd ser., 11 (1933), 149 • [J. Cockburn], *A specimen of some free and impartial remarks on public affairs* (1724) • G. Whitefield, *Journals*, ed. Banner of Truth Trust (1960) • *The papers of Benjamin Franklin*, 6, ed. L. W. Labaree and R. L. Ketcham (1963) • W. Orem, *A description of the chanonry, cathedral and King's College of Old Aberdeen in the years 1724 and 1735* (1791) • J. Pinkerton, *Iconographia Scotica, or, Portraits of illustrious persons of Scotland* (1797)

Archives NL Scot., devotional manual, MS 5405 • U. Aberdeen L., lecture notes, MSS K157, K159, and 1026 • U. Aberdeen L., sermon notes, MS 2612

Likenesses J. Scougal?, portrait, U. Aberdeen, King's College • T. Trotter, line engraving, BM, NPG; repro. in Pinkerton, *Iconographia Scotica*

Scougal [Scougall], **Patrick** (**1607–1682**), bishop of Aberdeen, was the son of John Scougal of that ilk, Haddingtonshire. He graduated MA at Edinburgh in 1624. Twelve years later he became minister of Dairsie, near St Andrews, where the church had been rebuilt by Archbishop John Spottiswood as his 'private chapel' in a style 'determined by the archbishop's beliefs about the role of churches as houses for the kind of worship he thought was seemly' (Ash, 131). On 5 October 1641 Scougal reported to the provincial assembly 'that there was sindrie crosses in there kirk at Darsie', although he conceded that they 'be some wes not thoght to be superstitious'. He was a leader in purging his church of these popish vestiges, and 'earnestly desired' the assembly to appoint visitors (*Ecclesiastical Records, Synod of Fife*, 127).

In 1640 Scougal was on the leet to be chosen preacher to an army regiment under the command of Robert Balfour,

Lord Balfour of Burleigh. He was admitted to another Fife parish, Leuchars, on 25 March or 2 April 1645 after presentation by King Charles I in December 1644. He attended the general assembly in 1648, and became involved in affairs outside his own parish. On 16 August 1649 he preached the sermon at the admission of the minister of Elie. In March 1650 he sat on a committee appointed to consider a problem of access to a parish church; in July he raised £100 for a regiment of horse to fight against the invading English; and in October and November 1650 he was one of those who presented a letter to Charles II about his siding with the 'malignants'. In April 1654 he moderated the provincial assembly at St Andrews.

At some point during these years, possibly as early as 1645, Scougal married Margaret (or Jean) Wemyss. They had three sons and two daughters—John, later commissar of the diocese of Aberdeen and provost of Old Aberdeen; Henry *Scougal (1650–1678); James, Lord Whitehill of Session (*d.* 1702); Catherine, who later married first William Scrogie, bishop of Argyll, second, Patrick Forbes, bishop of Caithness, and third, Roderick Mackenzie of Kinchullardrum; and Jane (or Joanna) who later married Patrick Sibbald, professor of divinity at Marischal College, Aberdeen. According to Robert Baillie, in 1658 Scougal was a candidate for the faculty of St Andrews University. Instead, apparently with his brother John's help, he went to Saltoun, east of Edinburgh, where he was admitted on 29 January 1659, though he was not replaced at Leuchars until 1661 and retained some connection with Fife. Following his first wife's death, on 6 January 1660 he married Anne Congalton (*d.* 1696).

On 3 February 1661 Scougal preached to the Scottish parliament, 'honestly' (*Life of Robert Blair*, 376), and on 28 May he received a parliamentary commission to try witches in Samuelstown, as part of the last great Scottish witch-hunt. In the autumn James Sharp, future archbishop of St Andrews, made efforts in Fife to persuade some, including Scougal, to avail themselves personally of the benefits of episcopacy. Some of his neighbours at Saltoun were already conforming. On 5 December 1662 Scougal was elected professor of divinity at the University of Edinburgh, but he refused the honour. By late 1663 his future path had clarified. On 14 January 1664 he was provided to the bishopric of Aberdeen; he was appointed to the see by the king on 25 February, and consecrated at St Andrews on 11 April by Archbishop James Sharp, Alexander Burnet, archbishop of Glasgow, and one other. John Lamont noted that the see's annual income was about 9000 or 10,000 merks. It is scarcely imaginable that Scougal's migration into the episcopalian camp did not generate controversy and hostility, though this is not highly visible in contemporary sources, perhaps because of his solid reputation of probity and piety.

In his first synod as bishop in October 1664, Scougal manifested his interest in the affairs of students. He and the synod appointed a general parochial collection for the support of two needy young Polish students living in Aberdeen, 'who left their awin cuntry, being troubled for ther professione of the true protestant religione', requesting every minister 'to add their awin charitie' to the appeal (*Synod of Aberdeen*, 275–6). Scougal also encouraged poorly paid ministers to seek augmentation. His competing desires of conformity and leniency in matters of religion resulted in synodal action against the Quakers of the north-east and other dissenters. Although Scougal initially showed his moderation in his dealing with Alexander Jaffray, who had been punished with house arrest by the high commission in 1665, on 11 September 1668 he had him imprisoned in the gaol in Banff; Jaffray wrote to Scougal that 'this present imprisonment, and the usage I am meeting with, may very warrantably be termed, cruel severity and oppression' (*Diary of Alexander Jaffray*, 282).

In 1664 Scougal also became chancellor of King's College, Aberdeen, where eight years later he had to fight the burgh council's claim to jurisdiction over students. Yet a letter of 1674 concerning his refusal to countenance the transfer of one of the ministers of St Machar's Cathedral reveals both a firmness of purpose and also a strong desire to get along with the burgh authorities. Both episcopal and academic office sometimes demanded he make unpopular decisions, however; in 1680 a regent at King's accused the bishop of having exercised undue influence over the election of a new principal. The privy council determined that he had done no wrong, and was merely exercising his legitimate powers. The same year he was party to the rigorous, if short-lived, prosecution of James Gordon, parson of Banchory-Devenick and author of the critical *The Reformed Bishop* (1679), a work which advocated more 'catholic' doctrines. According to Robert Wodrow, Scougal had a hand in the Aberdeen ministers' statement of opposition to the 1681 Test Act, a draconian and incoherent statement of the royal supremacy in the church.

Scougal died of asthma on 16 February 1682 in Aberdeen and was buried in his cathedral. His wife, who survived him by nearly fifteen years, subsequently remarried and became Lady Gunsgreen. According to his epitaph Scougal bequeathed money to St Machar's Cathedral, King's College Library, and the public hospital of Old Aberdeen. The same source claimed that he was 'a man deserving all praise, as being piously peaceable, modestly prudent, the honour and pattern of learned probity; neither morosely sullen, nor proudly learned; while he lived, a present sanctuary to the needy' (Monteith, 82). John Lauder of Fountainhall described him 'a moderat man, and but half Episcopall in his judgement' (Lauder, *Historical Observes*, 61), and when Robert Blair wrote of the three episcopal consecrations which had taken place in 1664 he described two as 'prelates', but referred only to 'Mr Patrick Scougal of Aberdeen' (*Life of Robert Blair*, 467), avoiding the pejorative. Bishop Gilbert Burnet, in the preface to his *Life of William Bedell*, wrote of Scougal's 'endearing gentleness … to all that differed from him, his great strictness in giving [holy] orders, his most unaffected humility and contempt of the world'. He was especially concerned for younger men, 'so that a set of men grew up under his labors, that carry still on them clear characters of his spirit and temper'. In his famous *History* Burnet again praised Scougal, though 'I thought he was too much under Sharp's conduct, and was at least too easy to him' (*Bishop Burnet's History*, ed. Burnet and Burnet, 1.217). Alexander Brodie was less sanguine, writing in 1678 that Henry Scougal had 'vented' various unorthodox doctrines, including the equal authority of Plato and Seneca with Peter and Paul, and that Bishop Patrick 'does not disclaim or discountenanc it' (Brodie, 404).

DAVID GEORGE MULLAN

Sources L. B. Taylor, ed., *Aberdeen council letters*, 6 vols. (1957), 5.159 • *APS*, 1661–9, appx, 76 • M. Ash, 'Dairsie and Archbishop Spottiswoode', *Records of the Scottish Church History Society*, 19 (1975–7), 125–32 • *The letters and journals of Robert Baillie*, ed. D. Laing, 3 vols., Bannatyne Club, 73 (1841–2), 3.365 • *Diary of Alexander Jaffray*, ed. J. Barclay, 2nd edn (1834), 282 • G. Burnet, *The story of Quakerism in Scotland, 1650–1850* (1952), 54–5, 65, 66 • *Bishop Burnet's History of his own time*, 1, ed. G. Burnet and T. Burnet (1724), 217 • G. Burnet, *The life of William Bedell, D.D. Bishop of Kilmore in Ireland* (1685) • A. Dalzel, *History of the University of Edinburgh*, 2 (1862), 189, 334 • A. Brodie, *The diary of Alexander Brodie of Brodie*, ed. D. Laing (1863), 404 • J. Dowden, *The bishops of Scotland … prior to the Reformation*, ed. J. M. Thomson (1912), 402 • *Ecclesiastical records: selections from the minutes of the presbyteries of St Andrews and Cupar, 1641–1698* (1837), 52, 57, 125 • *Ecclesiastical records: selections from the minutes of the synod of Fife* (1837), 123, 127, 130, 133, 156, 164, 171, 177, 210, 221 • *Fasti Scot.*, new edn, 1.392; 5.148, 222; 7.331, 383 • G. Grub, *An ecclesiastical history of Scotland*, 4 vols. (1861), 3.266–75 • R. Keith and J. Spottiswoode, *An historical catalogue of the Scottish bishops, down to the year 1688*, new edn, ed. M. Russel [M. Russell] (1824), 133 • J. Lamont, *The chronicle of Fife; being the diary of J. L. of Newton, from 1649 to 1672*, ed. A. Constable (1830), 8, 67, 111, 148, 167 • *Historical notices of Scotish affairs, selected from the manuscripts of Sir John Lauder of Fountainhall*, ed. D. Laing, 1, Bannatyne Club, 87 (1848), 133, 167, 250, 260 • J. Lauder, *Historical observes of memorable occurrents in church and state, from October 1680 to April 1686*, ed. A. Urquhart and D. Laing, Bannatyne Club, 66 (1840) • *The Lauderdale papers*, ed. O. Airy, 3 vols., CS, new ser., 34, 36, 38 (1884–5); repr. (New York, 1965), vol. 1, p.198 • B. P. Levack, 'The great Scottish witch hunt of 1661–1662', *Journal of British Studies*, 20 (1980), 90–108 • *The life of Mr Robert Blair … containing his autobiography*, ed. T. M'Crie, Wodrow Society, 11 (1848) • R. Monteith, *An theater of mortality, or, A further collection of funeral-inscriptions over Scotland*, 8 vols. (1713) • J. Nicoll, *A diary of public transactions and other occurrences, chiefly in Scotland, from January 1650 to June 1667*, ed. D. Laing, Bannatyne Club, 52 (1836), 409 • P. J. Anderson, ed., *Officers and graduates of University and King's College, Aberdeen, MVD–MDCCCLX*, New Spalding Club, 11 (1893) • J. Stuart, ed., *Selections from the records of the kirk session, presbytery, and synod of Aberdeen*, Spalding Club, 15 (1846), 274 • R. Wodrow, *The history of the sufferings of the Church of Scotland from the Restoration to the revolution*, ed. R. Burns, 3 (1829), 304, 308

Likenesses T. Trotter, line engraving, BM, NPG; repro. in J. Pinkerton, *Iconographia Scotia* (1797) • portrait, U. Aberdeen

Scougall [Scougal] **family** (*per.* *c.*1650–*c.*1740), portrait painters, worked in Edinburgh in succession to George Jamesone (1590–1644). With the passage of time the work of David, John, and George Scougall has become inextricably intermingled and their biographical details remain noticeably incomplete. **David Scougall** (*fl.* 1654–1682), the eldest of the dynasty, was born to unknown parents at an unknown date. He first comes before us with the portrait (Scot. NPG) of Lady Jean Campbell, marchioness of Lothian (*d.* 1700), inscribed in a seventeenth-century hand with his name and the date 1654. It is the earliest of many paintings given to him, and from the surviving accounts for his work it appears that he was as much in demand as a copyist as for his original compositions. On 10 March 1668, for instance, he was charging John, second earl of Tweeddale, for two copies of Tweeddale's picture, five copies of portraits of Lady Tweeddale, 'the 2 children's pictures', and various gilded frames (MS 14636, Yester papers, 10 March 1668, NL Scot.).

If the '2 children's pictures' were those of Lord David and Lady Jean Hay in a private Scottish collection, then Tweeddale must have been well pleased, for they are charming, sympathetic, and accomplished renderings of the small sitters in their elaborate costume. At its best David Scougall's work is as elegant as it is sensitive, but other paintings ascribed to him are astonishingly variable in quality and some of the compositions are highly derivative. His picture of William, first earl of Annandale, three-quarter length, in armour (priv. coll.) is an exact copy of the 1682 painting by Kneller of the earl's uncle, William, third duke of Hamilton (priv. coll.), apart from the head. At least half a dozen of Scougall's other known works follow Kneller very closely, while his full-length of William, third earl of Lothian, in armour (priv. coll.) has its background copied from Van Dyck's full-length of James, first duke of Hamilton, in armour (priv. coll.).

It remains difficult, if not impossible, to distinguish his pictures from the work of **John Scougall** (*c.*1645–1737?), born in Leith, Scotland, to unknown parents but probably a cousin of Patrick Scougall, archbishop of Aberdeen. On 22 April 1680 the archbishop granted him a licence to marry Margaret, daughter of James Gordon of Seaton, in St Machar's Church, Aberdeen. Where John had learned the art of portraiture remains unknown, but it is tempting to assume that he had studied in Edinburgh with David Scougall. Certainly by 1682 he had established his own practice and in December of that year charged Lord Panmure £9 4*s*. for his picture and several frames (Dalhousie muniments, GD45/18/977, NA Scot.). By the 1690s his aristocratic patrons included Lady Wemyss, the laird of Dundas, and George, first earl of Melville, who brought the painter John Medina to Edinburgh.

The poll tax records for 1694 (E70/4/4, NA Scot.) show that Scougall was then living in New Kirk parish, Edinburgh, with his wife, three children, two servants, and an apprentice, George Scougall. His poll tax valuation of 10,000 merks Scots (£555 sterling) put him in the same category as the wealthiest merchants of the capital, and he apparently owned the lowest house on the east side of Advocates' Close, adding an upper storey to it and fitting out one entire floor as a picture gallery. That same year he and his wife purchased her father's half net's salmon fishing on the River Don, Aberdeenshire, paying 8500 merks for it (register of deeds Dur, lxxxii, p. 191, NA Scot.), and two years after that Scougall subscribed £200 sterling to the Darien scheme.

His links with the north make it likely that John was the 'Mr Scougall' employed in 1706 to copy the heads of portraits of Sir William Dunbar of Hempriggs, his wife, and son (-in-law?) for use as models for three effigies Sir William was having made for a monument he was erecting at Gordonstoun, where his widowed daughter lived (Dunbar correspondence, RH9/18/18/25, NA Scot.). In 1711 Scougall was copying pictures at Alloa House (Stanley Cursiter MS notebook, Scot. NPG) and the year after that the magistrates and town council of Glasgow bought two full-length portraits of King William and Queen Mary from 'Mr Scougall' at a cost of £27 sterling. The following August their treasurer paid 'John Scougall, elder' £15 for a portrait of Queen Anne, which they hung in Glasgow council house (Renwick, 422, 482).

How long the artist lived is uncertain. A John Scougall died at Prestonpans in 1737 and his testament was later registered in Edinburgh commissary court on 13 January 1744. The inventory lists the contents of a substantial house and includes among the furnishings a number of history pictures, sea pieces, and still lifes, with six sketches of 'women's postures'. Much longer is the list of books, many of them theological, but also comprising history and travel. However, the portrait painter born about 1645 would have been ninety-two by the time this John Scougall died. It seems far more likely that the testament registered in 1744 was that of a John Scougall the younger who has somehow been merged with the artist.

John Scougall's work certainly did not equal that of his presumed kinsman David Scougall, although it is in most cases superior to the youngest member of the trio, **George Scougall** (*fl.* 1694–1737). Once again, little is known of George's background. He is presumably the apprentice to John Scougall noted in the 1694 poll tax and according to Sir George Chalmers was indeed John's son (Caw, 17). At any rate, he too was soon producing portraits of stern ladies in low-necked chemises and billowing draperies, their baleful spouses clad in the armour that they would never have worn in real life. In 1696 George Scougall branched out to design the title-page for *The Parfait Mareschal, or, Compleat Farrier*, Sir William Hope of Balcomie's translation of Jacques de Solleysell's famous treatise on equitation and farriery. It is competent, if not inspired. Two horsemen flank a solid arch from which a horse's head gazes down benevolently, while through the archway may be glimpsed various other mounted figures performing equestrian exercises. John Sturt's name appears in one corner as the engraver, with George Scougall acknowledged in the opposite corner as the artist.

Like his supposed father, George worked in Glasgow. In 1715 the Merchant's House commissioned him to paint one of their benefactors, James Govane, and two years later Hutcheson's Hospital, Glasgow, employed him to copy portraits of their founders, George and Thomas Hutcheson. Also in 1717 Glasgow Trades House asked him to produce a picture of their deceased benefactor, James Thomson, tanner. For this he was paid £54. Thus encouraged, he was by 1723 renting a property in Glasgow which belonged to the Trades House but in 1737 he owed six years' rent. Since the debt was now considered by the authorities to be 'desperate', it was cancelled (Lumsden, 241) and with that George Scougall vanishes from the records. His kinsmen had made their fortunes by supplying the Scottish gentry, professional middle class, and aristocracy with portraits at a time when other artists were not available in Scotland. George Scougall was far less successful, but his paintings hang along with theirs in the serried ranks of grim-faced seventeenth-century men and their plain wives adorning the walls of Scottish country houses to this day. ROSALIND K. MARSHALL

Sources artists' files, Scot. NPG • M. Apted and S. Hannabus, eds., *Painters in Scotland, 1302–1700* (1978), 84–8 • A. M. Munro, ed., *Records of Old Aberdeen* (1899–1909), 1.277, 2.155 • H. Paton, ed., *Register of interments in the Greyfriars burying-ground, Edinburgh, 1658–1700* (1902), 579 • J. Stuart, ed., *List of pollable persons within the shire of Aberdeen, 1696* (1844), 2.563 • NA Scot., Dalhousie muniments, GD45/18/977 • register of deeds, NA Scot., Dur, lxxxii, p. 191 • poll tax records, NA Scot., E70/4/4 • NA Scot., Leven and Melville papers, GD26/6/155/1 • typescript of Stanley Cursiter notebook, Scot. NPG • D. Wilson, *Memorials of old Edinburgh* (1891), 2.12 • R. Renwick, ed., *Extracts from the records of the burgh of Glasgow*, 4 (1908), 422, 482 • H. Lumsden, ed., *Records of Trades House of Glasgow, 1713–77* (1934) • Edinburgh register of testaments, NA Scot., 13 Jan 1744 • *The Darien papers* (1849), 379 • J. L. Caw, *Scottish painting past and present, 1620–1908* (1908)

Scougall, David (*fl.* 1654–1682). *See under* Scougall family (*per. c.*1650–*c.*1740).

Scougall, George (*fl.* 1694–1737). *See under* Scougall family (*per. c.*1650–*c.*1740).

Scougall, John (*c.*1645–1737?). *See under* Scougall family (*per. c.*1650–*c.*1740).

Scouler, John (1804–1871), naturalist, was born on 31 December 1804 in Glasgow, the son of a calico printer. Educated privately in Kilbrachan, he went on to study medicine at the University of Glasgow. At that time William Hooker (1785–1865) was professor of botany and the city's botanical garden was an important centre for floristic botany. Scouler was attracted to natural history and Hooker identified him as a promising student. Upon completion of his medical course in 1823 Scouler undertook further study of human and comparative anatomy in Paris.

On Hooker's recommendation, Scouler was appointed as a ship's surgeon and naturalist by the Hudson's Bay Company. In July 1824 he sailed, with David Douglas (1799–1834), on the *William and Ann*, bound for the Columbia River on America's Pacific north-west coast. The activities of the two naturalists during the expedition were typical of early nineteenth-century scientific travellers. They collected zoological specimens while at sea and made botanical and mineralogical investigations during their landfalls in Madeira, Brazil, Juan Fernandez, and the Galápagos. Scouler and Douglas were the first naturalists to explore Oregon Country, where Scouler combined plant hunting with ethnography, later publishing a vivid account of his travels in the *Edinburgh Journal of Science* (1826–7). Shortly afterwards, Scouler made another voyage as a ship's surgeon, collecting plants in the Cape of Good Hope and several locations in the Indian Ocean.

In 1827 Scouler graduated MD. He practised medicine in Glasgow, and helped establish the *Glasgow Medical Journal*. Ultimately more interested in natural history than medicine, Scouler was, in 1829, elected fellow of the Linnean Society and appointed professor of natural history and museum curator at Anderson's University. In 1833 he became professor of mineralogy to the Royal Society, Dublin, soon extending his brief to include geology and zoology. He retained his Scottish connections and was very influential in the development of palaeontology in the west of Scotland as well as in Ireland. He prepared the geological exhibition for the Glasgow meeting of the British Association (1840) and in 1850 Glasgow University granted him an honorary LLD.

In 1853 Scouler returned to Glasgow. His retirement was spent travelling, collecting, and working informally in the Andersonian Museum. The author of more than twenty papers on natural history, Scouler was also a considerable linguist and classical scholar. A devout Christian, he was a critic of the evolutionary theories of Robert Chambers and Charles Darwin, defending the doctrine of final causes. Several species of plant and fossil were named for him, as well as a mineral. His herbarium is now owned by Strathclyde University and his fine book collection is in the Mitchell Library. Scouler died at his home at 108 Woodlands Road, Glasgow, on 13 November 1871 and was buried at Kilbrachan. He had a wife and child, although nothing is known about them save that they both predeceased him by many years.

Malcolm Nicolson

Sources W. Keddie, 'Biographical notice of the late John Scouler, MD, LLD, FLS', *Transactions of the Geological Society of Glasgow*, 4 (1872), 194–205 · B. Lloyd, 'John Scouler, MD, LLD, FLS (1804–1871)', *Glasgow Naturalist*, 18 (1962), 210–12 · *Glasgow Herald* (15 Nov 1871) · Desmond, *Botanists*, rev. edn · *Glasgow Herald* (18 Nov 1871) · NA Scot., SC 36/48/67/472–474

Archives Mitchell L., Glas., papers

Wealth at death £1338 14*s*. 5*d*.: confirmation, 30 Dec 1871, NA Scot., SC 36/48/67/472–474

Scovell, Edith Joy (1907–1999), poet, was born at Sheffield on 9 April 1907, the daughter of Canon Frederick George Scovell (1870–*c*.1951), vicar of St Andrew's Church, Sharrow, Sheffield, and his wife, Edith Anne, *née* Holl (*c*.1875–*c*.1964). She had seven brothers and sisters, and remained in close touch with them all her life, though she did not continue as a member of the Anglican—or any—church. She was a boarder at Casterton School in Westmorland (where the Brontës had been pupils), and went from there in 1928 as a scholar to Somerville College, Oxford, where she read first classical moderations and then English. She did not do well in her finals, but edited the Somerville literary paper *The Fritillary*, and contributed poems to university periodicals and to Basil Blackwell's annual anthologies.

Joy Scovell then maintained herself as a secretary in London (while writing poetry and publishing occasionally in periodicals) until on 1 December 1937 she married Charles Sutherland *Elton (1900–1991), reader in ecology at the University of Oxford. They set up house in Oxford, first in a flat in Banbury Road, and then at 61 Park Town, a pleasant crescent with a central garden for the residents, which Charles and Joy helped to tend. They had two children.

Joy Scovell's first collection of poems, *Shadows of Chrysanthemums*, was published by Routledge during the Second World War (1944), and attracted praise from fellow poets Stephen Spender and, notably, Geoffrey Grigson, who singled her out as 'the purest of our women poets'. Her next book, *A Midsummer Meadow*, followed after only two years, and then came *The River Steamer* in 1956, but after that she published no collection for a quarter of a century, chiefly because of a fear, as she put it, 'of writing a fake mystical poem', covering territory of the imagination which she had already explored. Learning to read Italian and visiting Italy gave her a new poetic experience during this time, and she translated some of the poems of Giovanni Pascoli, publishing them in Michael Schmidt's *Poetry Nation Review*. Other sources of inspiration for her later poetry were the birth of her grandchildren, her visit to her daughter in Montserrat, and her work as field assistant to her husband in the rain forests of Central and South America.

Delight in the natural world is the mainspring of Joy Scovell's poetry: her verse conveys a sense of the holiness of all creation, thanks to an intensity of gaze which seems to bring the reader face to face with the mystery of being. Her imagery is visual rather than auditory, and her epithets new-minted: the 'magnolia-flowering swan', whose feet are like 'ridged and bitter ivy'; the 'Michaelmas breast' of a pigeon; the 'bemused and under-water dance' of infant hands. She was not interested in technical experiment for its own sake, yet the chosen form always seemed right for its subject matter, and her ear was impeccable. For a time she thought of herself as a pantheist, but later 'settled down as an agnostic'. In her fine poem 'Agnostic' she describes this sense of mystery in creation and addresses those who possess belief in God:

> You with religious faith, to whom
> Life speaks in words you understand,
> Believe I also with my dumb
> Stranger have made a marriage bond
> As strong and deep and torturing and fond.

The Space Between appeared in 1982, published by the Cresset Press on the advice of John Hayward, and a pamphlet, *Listening to Collared Doves*, followed from the Mandeville Press. Finally Michael Schmidt's Carcanet Press issued Joy Scovell's *Collected Poems*, which included her translations, in 1988. She pursued her course undistracted by any search for popularity—joined no groups, gave no poetry readings (until once at the very end of her life)—but in her final years was glad to be 'discovered' by some young poets and students.

Slender and of medium height and gentle-voiced, Scovell took a lively interest in the work of her contemporaries. The Eltons' marriage was described as a 'true conversation'. Their interests complemented each other, and each respected the other's privacy. As Joy Scovell wrote in 'Any Traveller's Apology':

> If you were gone I could never in fact or dream
> Set out, for dread of coming home.

That solitary state she did have to endure in her old age, for Charles Elton died in 1991. Still living in Oxford and facing with great courage her increasing deafness, Joy Scovell died on 19 October 1999 at St Luke's Home, Oxford. She was cremated in Oxford on 30 October.

ANNE RIDLER

Sources personal knowledge (2004) • private information (2004) [Robert A. Elton, son] • *The Times* (26 Oct 1999) • *The Independent* (12 Nov 1999) • *Daily Telegraph* (Nov 1999) • P. Scupham, *Poetry Nation Review*, 131

Scovell, Sir George (1774–1861), army officer, the son of George Scovell of Cirencester, was born in London on 21 March 1774. He was commissioned as cornet and adjutant in the 4th Queen's Own dragoons on 5 April 1798, became lieutenant on 4 May 1800, and captain on 10 March 1804. He exchanged to the 57th foot on 12 March 1807.

Sent to the Peninsula in the following year, Scovell was employed in the quartermaster-general's department throughout the war, taking a particularly prominent part in the deciphering of encoded messages which had been captured from French troops and agents. He also witnessed Corunna, the passage of the Douro, Talavera, Busaco, Fuentes d'Oñoro, Ciudad Rodrigo, Badajoz, Salamanca, Burgos, Vitoria, the Pyrenees, Nivelle, Nive, the passage of the Adour, and Toulouse. He commanded the corps of guides and was in charge of the postal service and the communications of the army until 1813, when he was appointed (on 15 June) to the command of the staff corps of cavalry. He had been made brevet major on 30 May 1811, and lieutenant-colonel on 17 August 1812, having been mentioned in Wellington's Salamanca dispatch. On 2 January 1815 he was made KCB.

Scovell was in the Waterloo campaign as assistant quartermaster-general, and in command of the cavalry's staff corps. During the subsequent occupation of France, he was often entrusted with the responsibility of preventing confrontation between the troops and the people. He received the Waterloo medal and the Russian order of St Vladimir (fourth class).

On 25 December 1818 Scovell was placed on half pay, and on 23 March 1820 he was appointed to the command of the royal wagon train. He became colonel in the army on 27 May 1825, major-general on 10 January 1837, lieutenant-general on 9 November 1846, and general on 20 June 1854. He was lieutenant-governor of the Royal Military College, Sandhurst, from 25 April 1829 to 2 February 1837, and governor from then to 31 March 1856. He was made colonel of his old regiment, the 4th dragoons, on 18 December 1847, and received the GCB on 18 May 1860. He died at his residence, Henley Park, Guildford, Surrey, on 17 January 1861.

E. M. LLOYD, *rev.* DAVID GATES

Sources C. W. C. Oman, *A history of the Peninsular War*, 5 (1914), 317, 611–18; 6 (1922), 2, 37 • *GM*, 3rd ser., 10 (1861), 349 • *Supplementary despatches (correspondence) and memoranda of Field Marshal Arthur, duke of Wellington*, ed. A. R. Wellesley, second duke of Wellington, 15 vols. (1858–72), vols. 1–11 • J. Philippart, ed., *The royal military calendar*, 3rd edn, 5 vols. (1820) • Boase, *Mod. Eng. biog.* • *CGPLA Eng. & Wales* (1861)

Archives PRO, corresp. and papers, WO37 | Royal Military College, Camberley, letters to General Le Marchant and Dennis Le Marchant

Sir George Scovell (1774–1861), by William Salter, 1834–40

Likenesses W. Salter, oils, 1834–40, NPG [*see illus.*] • T. Heaphy, watercolour drawing, NPG • W. Salter, group portrait, oils (*Waterloo banquet at Apsley House*), Wellington Museum, Apsley House, London

Wealth at death under £70,000: probate, 27 Feb 1861, *CGPLA Eng. & Wales*

Scrafton, Luke (1732–1770?), East India Company servant, was born on 22 March 1732 in the City of London, the son of Richard Scrafton, surgeon, and his wife Susannah (*d.* 1771/2). He was appointed a writer in the East India Company's Bengal service in March 1746 and was made an assistant at the Dacca factory on 20 October 1749. In 1751 he was promoted to the rank of factor and joined the council at Dacca, where he remained until 1756 when the nawab of Bengal, Siraj ud-Daula, turned against the company. The factory surrendered to his forces and Scrafton and other company servants were held for a period as prisoners. The nawab's capture of Calcutta was reversed by Robert Clive in January 1757, and in the following month Scrafton acted as one of two emissaries to the nawab; two months later he was, at Clive's request, sent to the durbar, the nawab's court, at Murshidabad, to assist William Watts (who was later briefly president of the council in Bengal). Scrafton's knowledge of Persian and his diplomatic skills were put to good use in the conspiracy against Siraj ud-Daula, and he was present when Siraj ud-Daula was defeated by Clive at Plassey in June 1757. After Plassey, Scrafton succeeded Watts at the durbar and found himself at the heart of the changed political environment in which the new nawab, Mir Jafar, and the British found themselves. In addition to his official activities (and having reaped a substantial financial reward from the change of nawab), he became involved in revenue farming under fictitious names and made loans to *zamindars* at high rates. His departure from the durbar in August 1758 coincided with a particularly demanding visit to Calcutta by the nawab, during which Scrafton acted as interpreter; in the months that followed, however, he ceased to be involved in mainstream affairs and was critical of Clive. In 1759 he left Calcutta for Madras on account of ill health, and eventually returned to England.

In England, Scrafton engaged in intellectual pursuits and corresponded with the historian Robert Orme, from whom he sought advice. In 1763 he published *Reflections on the government, etc of Indostan; with a short sketch of the history of Bengal, from the year 1739 to 1756; and an account of the English affairs to 1758*. This work, praised by Voltaire, was one of several such works which appeared in this period and which served to bring events in India to the attention of a wider audience than hitherto. In the same year Scrafton toured Europe, but the politics of the East India Company increasingly occupied him. Although he was not on close personal terms with Clive he supported Clive's cause, and served as a director of the company between 1765 and 1768; for most of this period Clive was in Bengal and Scrafton was an important representative of his interest within the court of directors. He also defended Clive against accusations made by Henry Vansittart—a former governor of Bengal with whom Scrafton apparently once almost fought a duel—in *Observations on Mr Vansittart's Narrative*, published in 1766. His skills as a propagandist seem also to have been utilized by the directors in the periodical the *East India Observer*, in the same year.

In September 1769 Scrafton sailed for India as Clive's representative on a supervisory commission designed to improve the administration of the company's affairs. The *Aurora*, which carried the supervisors (among them Henry Vansittart), was not heard from again after it left the Cape of Good Hope on 27 December, and it would appear that the ship foundered in heavy seas following a decision by the captain to navigate the Mozambique Channel in bad weather. D. L. Prior

Sources Dacca factory minutes, court minutes, East India Company records, BL OIOC • BL, Warren Hastings MSS • BL OIOC, MS Eur. Orme • BL OIOC, Sutton Court MSS, MS Eur. F 128 • K. K. Datta and others, eds., *Fort William–India House correspondence*, 1–2 (1957–8) • J. G. Parker, 'The directors of the East India Company, 1754–1790', PhD diss., U. Edin., 1977 • W. B. Bannerman and W. B. Bannerman, jun., eds., *The registers of St Stephen's, Walbrook, and of St Benet Sherehog, London*, 1, Harleian Society, register section, 49 (1919) • A. M. Khan, *The transition in Bengal, 1756–1775: a study of Saiyid Muhammad Reza Khan* (1969) • P. J. Marshall, *East Indian fortunes: the British in Bengal in the eighteenth century* (1976) • P. J. Marshall, *The British discovery of Hinduism in the eighteenth century* (1970) • M. Bence-Jones, *Clive of India* (1974) • *GM*, 1st ser., 41 (1771), 190, 237
Archives BL OIOC, corresp., MS Eur. Orme | BL, Hastings MSS • BL OIOC, Clive MSS • BL OIOC, Sutton Court collection
Wealth at death see will, PRO, PROB 11/971, 389

Scragg, Thomas (1804–1886), drainpipe-machine manufacturer, was born in Monks Coppenhall, Cheshire. Scragg was a common family name in Monks Coppenhall in the early nineteenth century, and two such named families had a son baptized Thomas in 1804 (on 17 June and 23 September). The husbands in both families were recorded as working in agriculture, as a farmer, and as a farm labourer. Thomas Scragg similarly found employment in agriculture, and by 1841 was bailiff for the Calveley part of the Davenport estate in Cheshire. By that time he lived in Calveley, 6 miles west of his birthplace, and was married to Mary (1806–1884), from nearby Wardle. Employed at Calveley by Edward Davenport, Scragg developed his drainpipe-making machine in the early 1840s. In its ability to mass-produce cylindrical drainpipes, the most reliable of fills for under-drains, Scragg's invention made possible a reduction in the cost of under-draining and an improvement in its permanence and effectiveness. The machine became integral to the large-scale under-draining of waterlogged farmland that occurred in the second half of the nineteenth century and was one of the major technical advances in English agriculture between 1700 and 1900.

Waterlogging presented considerable difficulties for the effective use of agricultural land, and contemporary estimates of the area needing draining—10 to 16.5 million acres—indicated the scale of the problem. From the 1830s coherent systems of drain layout (known as deep thorough draining) were devised, initially by James Smith of Deanston but modified by Josiah Parkes, which were applicable to most conditions of soil wetness. Yet the full benefits of these draining systems were dependent on the use of a durable drain fill. Of available fills bushes, straw, and other vegetative material possessed but a limited life; stones and semi-circular, handmade tiles laid on soles, though more durable were subject to blockage and dislodgement. The cylindrical drainpipe represented a technical advance over other fills: easier to handle, with less likelihood of stoppage and displacement, and with great durability, they brought longevity, if not permanence, to the new draining systems.

Handmade but expensive drainpipes had been reported from various parts of the country at the end of the eighteenth century: John Read recorded making 3 inch diameter drainpipes in Kent in 1795. Several simple machines producing limited numbers of pipes were noted by 1840 in Suffolk, Essex, Kent, and Sussex. To facilitate the widespread use of drainpipes, these early machines had to be redesigned to provide standardization of form and to increase output, thereby reducing costs.

The first of these improved machines was credited to Scragg. In 1842 his machine was demonstrated to Parkes by Davenport at Capesthorne. The machine was exhibited to a wider audience at the 1845 Shrewsbury meeting of the Royal Agricultural Society of England, where it was awarded the prize for the best drainpipe-making machine. Although Scragg's invention was followed swiftly by many others, Philip Pusey could report in 1851 that Scragg's machine had come to dominate, along with those of Henry Clayton and John Whitehead. Scragg continued to exhibit his machine at the Royal Agricultural Society's annual meetings until 1859, being awarded prizes in 1846, 1849, 1852, and 1856, and at the Great Exhibition in 1851.

With its ability to make 2500–3000 pipes per day, the machine brought considerable price reductions: in 1845, 1 inch and 2 inch diameter pipes cost respectively 12*s.* and £1 5*s.* per 1000. At these prices waterlogged land could be drained with the new draining systems at about £5 per acre, permanent under-draining being obtainable at nearly the same cost as traditional methods. The effective under-draining of wet agricultural land in England was now possible.

Scragg made little attempt to develop other aspects of farm technology. Instead he diversified his occupational interests at Calveley, where he remained for the rest of his life. He added coal agency and drainpipe-machine manufacturing to land stewardship in the 1850s. After 1860 he concentrated on his commercial interests and from a 5 acre holding was described variously until 1878 as a coal merchant, a brick and tile maker and dealer, and a drainpipe manufacturer. He died on 6 November 1886 at the age of eighty-two at Edleston, in the adjacent parish of Acton. A. D. M. Phillips

Sources census returns for Calveley, 1841, PRO, HO 107/96; 1851, HO 107/2170; 1861, RG 9/2620; 1871, RG 10/3714; 1881, RG 11/3549 · parish register, Monks Coppenhall, 17 June 1804, Ches. & Chester ALSS, PI9/1/4 [baptism] · parish register, Monks Coppenhall, 23 Sept 1804, Ches. & Chester ALSS, PI9/1/4 [baptism] · d. cert. · d. cert. [Mary Scragg] · A. D. M. Phillips, *The underdraining of farmland in England during the nineteenth century* (1989), 27–30, 158–61 · J. Parkes, 'Report of the exhibition of implements at the Shrewsbury meeting in 1845', *Journal of the Royal Agricultural Society of England*, 6 (1845), 303–23 · P. Pusey, 'Report to HRH the president of the commission for the exhibition of the works of industry of all nations', *Journal of the Royal Agricultural Society of England*, 12 (1851), 587–648 · S. Bagshaw, *History, gazetteer, and directory of the county palatine of Chester* (1850), 600 · *The Post Office directory of Cheshire* (1857), 62; (1878), 94 · *History, gazetteer, and directory of Cheshire*, F. White and Co. (1860), 236 · *Morris and Co.'s commercial directory and gazetteer of Cheshire*, 1 (1874), 225

Scratchley, Sir Peter Henry (1835–1885), military engineer and colonial administrator, was born on 24 August 1835 in Paris, the thirteenth child of Dr James Scratchley of the Royal Artillery, and his wife, Maria, the daughter of Colonel Roberts. After a private education in Paris he entered the Royal Military Academy at Woolwich under the patronage of his father's schoolfriend Lord Palmerston. Despite indifferent health he passed out first in his class in February 1854 and was commissioned first lieutenant in the Royal Engineers the same year.

After studying at Chatham, Scratchley was sent to Dover, whence, on 24 July 1855, he went to the Crimea. He was present at the fall of Sevastopol, and took part in the expedition to capture Kinburn on the Black Sea. For his services he received the Crimean and Turkish war medals.

On his return to England in July 1856 Scratchley was stationed successively at Aldershot and Portsmouth. From October 1857 to 1860 he served in India, where during the mutiny he was three times mentioned in dispatches. He received the Indian war medal with clasp for Lucknow; some of his Indian experiences are recorded in *Professional Papers of the Corps of Royal Engineers* (1858).

On 1 October 1859 Scratchley was promoted second captain, and in 1860 was given command of a detachment of Royal Engineers, with whom he arrived at Melbourne in June. He was employed by the Victorian government to design defence works and to superintend their construction, and was also appointed colonial engineer and military storekeeper. An enthusiast for the volunteer movement, he was a founder and later honorary lieutenant-colonel of the Victorian artillery and engineers' volunteers. In September 1863, after the colonial legislature failed to provide funds for the defence works, Scratchley resigned. At St John's Church, Heidelberg, Melbourne, on 13 November 1862, he married Laura Lilias Brown, later Browne (*d.* 1917), the daughter of Sylvester John Brown, later Browne, a shipmaster, and his wife, Elizabeth Angell, *née* Alexander, and the sister of the novelist T. A. Browne (Rolf Boldrewood).

Scratchley arrived in England in 1863. On 15 March 1864 he was promoted brevet major for his war services and stationed at Portsmouth until October, when he was appointed assistant inspector of works for the manufacturing department of the War Office; he later became inspector of works. He retained his interest in Australian defences and in 1865 wrote a report on the defence of South Australia.

Scratchley was promoted first captain in 1866, regimental major in 1872, and brevet lieutenant-colonel in 1874, and in 1877 was selected to accompany Lieutenant-General Sir William Jervois on a mission to the Australian colonies to advise as to their defences. It was in accordance with their able report that the defence works of Sydney harbour, Port Phillip, Adelaide, and Brisbane were mainly constructed. In 1878 Scratchley was appointed commissioner of defences for the five eastern Australian colonies and New Zealand. His plans were largely implemented, so that by 1885 he was satisfied that the Australian colonies at least were 'fairly well prepared'. His views on defence were clearly stated in the evidence he gave to the 1881 commission on New South Wales defences, of which he was vice-president and chairman of the military subcommittee. He retained his earlier belief that, because of British sea power, threats to Australia would be limited. He advocated land defence works near key ports, torpedoes, and submarine mines for defence, and at sea floating batteries and unarmoured gunboats with heavy guns. He advocated a paid volunteer force with able officers 'to meet the contingency of the naval defences not meeting the enemy at sea'.

Scratchley was promoted brevet colonel on 20 February 1879, and in May was made a companion of St Michael and St George for his services in Australia. He retired from active military service on 1 October 1882, with the honorary rank of major-general, but continued in his employment under the Colonial Office. In April 1883 he visited England to consult the War Office as to the general plan of defences for the colonies of Australasia.

In November 1884 the imperial government, having

repudiated the action of the Queensland government in annexing the whole of New Guinea, decided to declare a protectorate over the south-eastern part, and on 22 November Scratchley was gazetted her majesty's special high commissioner for this territory. He arrived at Melbourne on 5 January 1885. The colonies were angry that the delay in dealing with New Guinea had allowed other powers to annex parts of it, and this irritation was increased by their having to find £15,000 a year for the maintenance of the government of the new protectorate. Scratchley's first duty was to visit each colony to arrange its quota of the contribution. On 6 June 1885 he was created KCMG. On 28 August, Scratchley reached Port Moresby, where he established his seat of government. Faced with problems caused by the incursions of white explorers and a suspicious and hostile native population, he soon found himself on the side of the natives. He believed they had been maltreated and that this justified their murder of several European adventurers, and, convinced that 'New Guinea must be governed for the natives and by the natives', he planned to appoint chiefs to represent British authority. He also tried to protect native land rights. On an expedition to the north coast he contracted malaria and died at sea between Cooktown and Townsville on 2 December 1885. He was survived by his wife, son, and two daughters; he was buried on 16 December in St Kilda cemetery, Melbourne, with public honours, but on 30 April 1886 he was reburied in the Old Charlton cemetery, Woolwich, England.

Reserved in nature, short, with a long, waxed military moustache, Scratchley gained universal respect in Australia; he resisted the formation of a military caste and his enlightened attitude towards the natives of New Guinea was in advance of his time. Fort Scratchley at Newcastle, New South Wales, and Mount Scratchley in the Owen Stanley range in New Guinea commemorate his name.

R. H. VETCH, *rev.* GERALD WALSH

Sources *AusDB*, 6.98–9 · C. K. Cooke, *Australian defences and New Guinea* (1887) · *Votes and proceedings*, Victoria Legislative Assembly (1860–61) · New South Wales Parliament, Legislative Council, *Journal* (1881) · *Votes and proceedings*, Queensland Legislative Assembly (1886) · H. Jackman, 'Sir Peter Scratchley: her majesty's special commissioner for New Guinea', *Journal of the Papua and New Guinea Society*, 3 (1969), 46–56 · *Sydney Morning Herald* (2 Dec 1885) · *Sydney Morning Herald* (3 Dec 1885) · *The Times* (4 Dec 1885) · m. cert. · P. Scratchley, 'Report on demolition of nawab's fort, Furruckbad, 1858', *Professional Papers of the Corps of Royal Engineers*, new ser., 8 (1858), 44 · P. Scratchley, 'Notes on forts and entrenchments of Kussia Rampoor, in Oudh', *Professional Papers of the Corps of Royal Engineers*, new ser., 8 (1858), 93

Archives NRA, priv. coll., journals and papers | Mitchell L., NSW, R. Towns & Co. MSS

Likenesses photograph, repro. in Cooke, *Australian defences*, frontispiece · photograph, Government House, Sydney, Australia · wood-engraving, NPG; repro. in *ILN* (12 Dec 1885)

Wealth at death £14,979: will and probate, Victoria, Australia, no. 32/96 · £4179 14*s*. 9*d*.: probate, 6 April 1886, *CGPLA Eng. & Wales*

Scrimgeour [Scrymgeour], **Henry** (1505?–1572), diplomat and book collector, was born in Dundee, most likely in 1505 but possibly in 1508 or 1509, since Andrew Melville gives Scrimgeour's age at death as sixty-three. His parents were James Scrimgeour, burgess, who had died by 23 May 1525, and his wife, Jonet, who was still alive in June 1552. Henry's sister Margaret married John Young, father to Sir Peter Young, later royal librarian to James VI, while another sister, Isobel, married Richard Melville of Baldovie, and was mother to the presbyterian reformer James Melville. Having first attended Dundee grammar school, Henry Scrimgeour then went to St Salvator's College, St Andrews, in 1532. He determined as a bachelor in 1533, and won first place in the examination for licence the following year. Some time later he proceeded to Paris where he studied under Guillaume Budé and Pierre Ramus. The name 'Henricus Scrymgeour' appears twice in the rector's register, on 23 March and 22 June 1538. He incepted under the Scot William Cranston, and shortly afterwards went to Bourges to study civil law for four years under Éguinaire Baron and François Douaren. While in Bourges, he formed an acquaintance with Jacques Amyot, professor of Greek, and succeeded the Hellenist in becoming preceptor to the sons of Guillaume Bochetel, the secretary of state, probably for three or four years. In February 1547 he returned to Scotland for a short stay and Bochetel recommended him in a letter to Mary of Guise as an 'homme de honneste vie, de vertu et de grand sçavoir tant en lettres grecques que latines' ('a man of honourable life, integrity, and great learning in both Greek and Latin literature'; M. Wood, ed., *Balcarres Papers*, Scottish History Society, 7, 1925, 201).

Back in France in 1548, Scrimgeour accompanied his pupil Bernardin Bochetel to Padua. Although a Catholic, he was plunged into the controversies of the Italian Reformation when he visited a young lawyer of Cittadella, Francesco Spiera, who was slowly dying of despair, having adopted the new opinions and then been forced to recant. Scrimgeour wrote an essay on piety, published at Geneva (under the name of Henricus Scotus) by Jean Gerard and with a preface by Calvin dated December 1549, entitled *Exemplum memorabile desperationis in Francisco Spera, propter abiuratam fidei confessionem* (1550). The tract was republished the same year in Basel. None the less, it was some years before Scrimgeour would openly show his adherence to protestantism, and his second publication was a law book, an edition of the *Novellae*, printed by Estienne in Geneva in May 1558 and subsidized by Ulrich Fugger, entitled: *Impp. Justiniani, Justini, Leonis novellae constitutiones*. The *Novellae* were fundamental to the teaching of law on the continent at this time, and a new edition was badly needed. Scrimgeour used his contacts with the French ambassador to Venice to gain access to the important Bessarian codex there, and his edition was well received by contemporary lawyers. The period between 1558 and his last visit to Italy in 1564 represents the most energetic part of Scrimgeour's activity in another capacity, that of book collector; it is accepted that the greatest part of the Greek, Latin, and Hebrew manuscripts of the Fugger collection were gathered by Scrimgeour, who frequently travelled between Augsburg and Italy. It is today the core of the Vatican Palatine collection. Scrimgeour also acted as agent in buying books for Otto-Heinrich, the elector palatine.

Scrimgeour kept his benefices in Scotland all his life, but he also enjoyed an income in France—there exists an authorization given to him in 1556 by King Henri II to hold and receive benefices in his country of adoption. The Scot had remained close to Bernardin Bochetel, now abbot of St Laurent des Aubats (Pouilly-sur-Loire, near Cosne), and he now engaged on a diplomatic career, travelling to Padua, Venice, Florence, Rome, Milan, Mantua, and Bologna, and also to Bourges, where he tried unsuccessfully to set up a printing press. Bochetel had several times invited him to Vienna, and he finally went there in November 1560. Bochetel may have wanted his diplomatic services at this time to help him in difficult negotiations with the German Lutheran princes, or with the colloquy of Poissy of 1561 between French reformers and Catholics, or with the Council of Trent, which after a ten-year interval had resumed its sessions in January 1562. However, Scrimgeour's stay in Vienna was brief, for by the end of 1561 he was in Geneva. It may be that events in Scotland and the failure of the colloquy of Poissy forced an irrevocable decision upon him. Moreover, Ulrich Fugger, now a Lutheran, had a plan for a public library in Geneva in order to secure his large and important collection of rare books, and Scrimgeour was associated with this project. At the same time, on 30 December, he was honoured by the magistrates of Geneva who received him as a burgess, three years after John Knox, and thanks to Calvin he soon became involved in the city's public life.

On 18 April 1562, with Calvin's blessing, Scrimgeour married Françoise de Saussure (*b.* 1542/3) in the Genevan church of St Pierre. His wife came from a family of religious refugees from Lorraine, which they had left in 1552, and her father Antoine de Saussure, lord of Dommartin, settled in Lausanne. However, Françoise soon died, on 1 February 1568, aged twenty-five, leaving a three-year old daughter, Marie. In 1563 the Genevan pastors appointed Scrimgeour reader in philosophy, and the same year he was admitted to the town's council of two hundred. Later he started giving lessons in civil law. He was neither an assiduous teacher nor a good one: 'il lit inutilement' wrote Theodore Beza (Borgeaud, 92 n. 4). Moreover he was often away from Geneva, for instance in Padua where 'D. Henricus Schrenzer scottus' is recorded in July 1564 as counsellor to the Scottish nation of jurists. When Calvin died in the spring of 1564 Scrimgeour was witness to his will. About this time he acquired the old castle called Villette, outside Geneva, but his house burnt down and by 1569 Bochetel had caused the French treasury to pay him 200 crowns in assistance. On 3 January 1570 Scrimgeour joined the council of sixty at Geneva, and on 11 May he remarried. His second wife was Catherine de Veillet, daughter of Aubert Veillet, *maitre des comptes* (chief financial officer) at Chambéry. At this time two regents—the earls of Moray and Mar—and also George Buchanan tried to attract Scrimgeour back to Scotland to assist in the education of the young James VI, but he regretfully declined, arguing his age and the instability of Scotland. Henry Scrimgeour died in Geneva on 23 September 1572.

MARIE-CLAUDE TUCKER

Sources F. de Borch-Bonger, 'Un ami de Jacques Amyot: Henry Scringer', *Mélanges offerts à Abel Lefranc* (Paris, 1936), 362–73 • J. Durkan, 'Henry Scrimgeour, Renaissance bookman', *Edinburgh Bibliographical Society Transactions*, 5/1 (1971–87), 1–31 • M. C. Bellot-Tucker, 'Maîtres et étudiants écossais à la faculté de droit de l'Université de Bourges aux XVIème & XVIIème siècles', doctoral diss., University of Clermont-Ferrand, 1997, 1.263–8, 336–7, 354; 2.424–34 • [T. de Bèze], *Correspondance de Théodore de Bèze*, ed. H. Aubert, 7 (Geneva, 1973), 24, 82–3, 251–2, 346–9 • J. M. Anderson, ed., *Early records of the University of St Andrews*, Scottish History Society, 3rd ser., 8 (1926), 128, 132, 321 • C. Borgeaud, *L'académie de Genève* (1900) • W. A. McNeill, 'Scottish entries in the *Acta rectoria universitatis Parisiensis*, 1519 to *c*.1633', *SHR*, 43 (1964), 66–86, esp. 80 • E. H. Kaden, 'Ulrich Fugger et son projet de créer à Genève une 'librairie' publique', *Geneva* (1959) • A. L. Covelle, *Le livre des bourgeois de l'ancienne république de Genève* (1897), 270 • A. Andrich, *De natione Anglica et Scota iuristarum Universitatis Patavinae* (1892), 92 • Bodl. Oxf., MS Cherry 5 • E. C. St Pierre, 1553–71, Archives de Genève, B.M. 2

Scriven, Edward (1775–1841), engraver, was born, according to a note he wrote to his fellow engraver John Pye, at Alcester, near Stratford upon Avon, Warwickshire. His interest in art was encouraged by his parents, and with the support of his friend William Courand of Evesham he became the pupil of the engraver Robert Thew, at Northall, Hertfordshire, with whom he resided for seven or eight years. 'And that continual, anxious, unproductive struggle, which is the pursuit of engraving … followed' (Pye, 314). Master and pupil were employed by John Boydell in producing stipple engravings for his *Shakspeare Gallery*. Scriven engraved *Brutus's Tent, in the Camp near Sardis* after Richard Westall to illustrate *Julius Caesar* in the folio-size *A Collection of Prints from Pictures Painted for the Purpose of Illustrating the Dramatic Works of Shakspeare, by the Artists of Great Britain* (2 vols., 1802, with a dedication of 1805, 2, no. 30). In his diary entry for 15 August 1797 Joseph Farington mentions that Scriven had boarded at Weymouth, when his terms were '25 shillings a week for breakfast & dinner & supper—but you find the tea & sugar' (Farington, *Diary*, 3.884). When Thew died in 1802, Scriven succeeded him as engraver to the prince of Wales.

By 1809 Scriven was living in Somers Town, Middlesex, and from 1813 until his death he lived there at 46 Clarendon Square. That year he was awarded the lesser gold medal of the Society of Arts for his engraving of a self-portrait by Gerrit Dou. In 1815 he gained the gold Isis medal for five stipple engravings in the crayon manner after Benjamin West's studies of heads for his *Christ Rejected*. One of these, entitled *The Scoffer*, is remarkable for the vigour with which it conveys West's arresting close-up portrayal of the wide-eyed, dishevelled, broken-toothed mocking head of the subject. The powerful emotions portrayed in this and his lithograph *St John*, from West's *St John Baptizing Christ*, are absent in the rest of Scriven's work, which consisted for the most part of elegant portraits and antiquarian subjects. In 1820 Scriven was a mourner at West's funeral.

Scriven contributed to several expensively illustrated books and series of engravings, notably *The British Gallery of Contemporary Portraits* (1809–17), William Jerdan's *National Portrait Gallery* (1830–34), and Anna Jameson's

Beauties of the Court of Charles II (1833). Of the more than 200 portrait engravings by Scriven listed in Freeman O'Donoghue's *Catalogue of Engraved British Portraits Preserved in the … British Museum* (6 vols., 1908–25), those after portraits of artists, including Hogarth, Henry Fuseli, James Barry, and Thomas Girtin, for the *Library of the Fine Arts*, and those of historical subjects, including Shakespeare, Thomas Bodley, and Anne Boleyn, for Edmund Lodge's *Portraits of Illustrious Personages of Great Britain* (1821–34), are notable. Scriven also contributed engravings to works published by the Society of Dilettanti, among them *Ancient Marbles in the British Museum* (1814), H. Tresham and W. Y. Ottley's *British Gallery of Pictures* (1818), and T. Dibdin's *Aedes Althorpianae* (1822). From about 1816 he had two pupils, Benjamin Phelps Gibbon and Robert William Sievier; the latter went on to become a sculptor.

In 1820 Scriven engraved for Byron's publisher, John Murray, a drawing of Byron made in Venice in 1818 by G. H. Harlow. Of only fifty impressions taken from the first state of the plate (artist's proof, BM) one was acquired by Benjamin Disraeli and remains at Hughendon Manor, Buckinghamshire. Scriven engraved on copper and on steel. In a letter of 8 April 1829 he explained to Murray why his charge for four steel plates, 'the Buonaparte portraits', was higher than for engravings on copper:

> the difference of time-taking is so considerable between *copper* and *steel*, that what may appear as a heavy charge upon the latter, but too frequently pays the Engraver far less for his labour, than what would seem moderate on copper. (Hunnisett, *Steel Engraved Book Illustration*, 167)

Working with 'taste and skill and extreme industry' (*DNB*), Scriven became eminent in his profession. The most sumptuous publication to which he contributed was *The Coronation of his most Sacred Majesty King George IV*, prepared by Sir George Nayler and published in 1837. The copy in the British Museum includes hand-coloured plates after drawings by James and Philip Stephanoff. These record the appearance and costume of those who took part in the coronation, intended by the prince regent to outdo in its magnificence that of Napoleon. Many of these illustrations were previously published by G. B. Whittaker, among them Scriven's *The King in his Royal Robes* (1826). Several of Scriven's plates are lettered 'E. Scriven Historical Engraver To His Majesty Sculp.'.

Pye recorded how, after visiting the impoverished and sick engraver Thomas Tagg in 1809, Scriven became the prime mover and general secretary in the founding on 1 February 1810 of the Artists' Fund of Provident Care (generally known as the Artists' Annuity Fund or the Artists' Fund). The Society of Artists, who contributed to the fund, also founded a benevolent fund for the protection of artists' widows and children. A portrait of Scriven by A. Morton, *c*.1840, engraved by Scriven's pupil Gibbon for Pye's *Patronage and British Art*, sensitively records his gentle, bespectacled appearance and is inscribed below: 'He used to wend his way across the busy City, alone & unheeded to solace affliction—Hence arose the Artist's Incorporated Fund.' Following his death, at his home on 23 August 1841, Scriven was buried in Kensal Green cemetery. He was survived by his wife, Joanna Elizabeth, whom he had married before 1802, and five children. Members of the Artists' Fund raised a memorial stone to Scriven 'to record their sense of the services he rendered to humanity, and to the national character of British artists, by his zeal on behalf of the constitution of that society' (Pye, 314).

Annette Peach

Sources J. Pye, *Patronage of British art: an historical sketch* (1845) · F. L. Colvile, *The worthies of Warwickshire who lived between 1500 and 1800* [1870] · *Engraved Brit. ports.* · B. Hunnisett, *An illustrated dictionary of British steel engravers*, new edn (1989) · E. Scriven, prints, BM, department of prints and drawings · will, PRO, PROB 11/1954, sig. 771 · A. Peach, 'Portraits of Byron', *Walpole Society*, 62 (2000), 1–144, esp. 91–2 · H. Meller, *London cemeteries*, 3rd edn (1994), 203 · B. Hunnisett, *Steel engraved book illustration in England* (1980), 167

Likenesses A. Morton, portrait, *c*.1840 · B. P. Gibbon, etching (after W. Mulready), repro. in Pye, *Patronage*, 314 · B. P. Gibbon, line engraving (after A. Morton), BM, NPG · W. Mulready, drawing, V&A

Wealth at death all to wife: will, PRO, PROB 11/1954, sig. 771

Scrivener, Frederick Henry Ambrose (1813–1891), biblical scholar, son of Ambrose Scrivener (1790–1853), a stationer, and his wife, Harriet Shoel (1791–1844), was born at Bermondsey, London, on 29 September 1813. He was educated at St Olave's School, Southwark, from 1820 to 1831, when he was admitted at Trinity College, Cambridge. He was elected scholar on 3 April 1834, and he graduated BA as a junior optime in 1835, and MA in 1838. In 1835 he became an assistant master at Sherborne School. On 21 July 1840, he married Anne (*d.* 1877), daughter of George and Sarah Blofeld. They had at least two children.

From 1838 to 1845 Scrivener was curate of Sandford Orcas, Somerset, and from 1846 to 1856 he was headmaster of Falmouth School. He also held the perpetual curacy of Penwerris, which he retained until 1861. He became rector of St Gerrans, Cornwall, in 1862, and prebendary of Exeter in 1874.

Scrivener's scholarly devotion was to the text of the New Testament. His first important publication was *A full and exact collation of about twenty Greek manuscripts of the holy gospels (hitherto unexamined)*, in 1853. *An Exact Transcript of the Codex Augiensis* (with collations of fifty other manuscripts) was published in 1859. The introduction to this volume was also published separately as *Contributions to the Criticism of the Greek New Testament*. Scrivener published two collations of Codex Sinaiticus: one in Wordsworth's New Testament (1856), the other on its own in 1864. A transcription of Codex Bezae Cantabrigiensis appeared in 1864, and transcription of the Chad gospels (with a collation of Codex Amiatinus) was published in 1887. *Adversaria critica sacra* (which consisted principally of studies and collations of ten more manuscripts) was published posthumously in 1893. His *Plain Introduction to the Criticism of the New Testament* first appeared in 1861, with a second edition in 1874.

Scrivener's achievement did not go unnoticed: on 3 January 1872, he was granted a civil-list pension of £100 in recognition of his services in connection with biblical criticism and in aid of the publication of his works. He was created LLD of St Andrews in the same year, and DCL of Oxford in 1876. He took an important part in the revision of the English version of the New Testament (1870–82).

In 1876 Scrivener became vicar of Hendon, Middlesex. Soon after this appointment, he began to find it difficult to keep pace with the advance of criticism, and the strain of preparing the third edition of his *Plain Introduction* (1883) led to a paralytic stroke in 1884. Nevertheless he continued to prepare a fourth edition, which was completed by the Revd E. Miller after the author's death. Scrivener died at the vicarage, Hendon, on 26 October 1891. Scrivener's *Plain Introduction* continued to be useful for its information on the history of the printed editions, and more rarely for its material on manuscripts. In addition Scrivener produced several useful editions of the *textus receptus*. Other works include *Six Lectures on the Text of the New Testament* (given to a general audience) and his studies on the Authorized Version.

Scrivener held reactionary views on the history of the New Testament text. He inclined towards J. W. Burgon against B. F. Westcott and F. J. A. Hort in favouring the *textus receptus*. His abilities lay not in the field of theory but in his remarkable accuracy as a transcriber and collator. It is on this that his reputation rests today. His transcriptions of the codices Bezae and Augiensis continue to be of particular importance, and his collations are also still of value. Living in an age when many new manuscripts were being discovered, he played an important role in showing his contemporaries and successors how many interesting readings were to be found.

E. C. MARCHANT, *rev.* D. C. PARKER

Sources Autobiography, BL, 4908.d.8 [unpublished proof sheets] • Boase & Courtney, *Bibl. Corn.*, 2.639–41, 3.1334 • K. Lake, review of 4th edition of *A plain introduction*, *Classical Review*, 10 (1896), 263–5 • *CGPLA Eng. & Wales* (1891)
Archives BL, 4908.d.8
Likenesses portrait, repro. in *The Graphic*, 10/41 (1875)
Wealth at death £5081 7*s*. 0*d*.: probate, 26 Nov 1891, *CGPLA Eng. & Wales*

Scrivener, Matthew (1622?–1688), Church of England clergyman, was probably born at Sibton, Suffolk, one of at least three younger sons of John Scrivener of Sibton, and Elizabeth Walsingham. He matriculated at St Catharine's College, Cambridge, in 1639, graduated BA in 1643–4, and proceeded MA in 1647.

In 1666 Scrivener became vicar of Haslingfield, 5 miles south-west of Cambridge. He published *Apologia pro s. ecclesiae patribus adversus Joannem Dallaeum De usu patrum &c: accedit Apologia pro Ecclesia Anglicana adversus nuperum schisma* (1672), to which a dissenter, Henry Hickman, replied with *The Nonconformists' Vindication* (1679). In 1674 he published *A course of divinity, or, An introduction to the knowledge of the true Catholic religion, especially as professed by the Church of England*. His final published work was *A treatise against drunkenness described in its nature, kindes, effects, and causes, especially that of drinking healths* (1685).

Scrivener made his will on 4 March 1688, leaving bequests to his housekeeper, Mary Meriton, his 'honoured friend' Lettice Wendy, the widow of Sir Thomas Wendy of Haslingfield, his brother Ralph, and a host of nieces and nephews. The poor were also remembered and £50 each left to the university library and towards a new college chapel at St Catharine's. The college also benefited from a bequest of various lands and tenements. He had died by 5 May 1688, when his will was proved, and was buried at Haslingfield.

STUART HANDLEY

Sources Venn, *Alum. Cant.* • will, PRO, PROB 11/391, sig. 68, fols. 189*r*–190 • will, PRO, PROB 11/324, fols. 317–318*v* [Thomas Scrivener, brother] • E. Carter, *The history of the University of Cambridge* (1753), 358 • *IGI* • *East Anglian miscellany* (1929), 2 • Wood, *Ath. Oxon.*, new edn, 4.370

Scroggs, Sir William (*c*.1623–1683), judge, the son of William Scroggs (*d*. 1647) and his wife, Elizabeth (*d*. 1651), was probably born in Rainham, near Stifford, Essex, where his father lived. He was not the William Scroggs born in Deddington, Oxfordshire, recorded at Oriel College, Oxford. He was descended from a family which had held the manor of Patmore Hall, Hertfordshire, since the sixteenth century. His grandfather, also William, held property in Suffolk and became a wool merchant in London. Scroggs took an interest in his ancestry, as correspondence in 1670 reveals (Dunlop, 49–50). Sir William Dugdale, who bore him a personal grudge, asserted that Scroggs's father was a 'one-ey'd butcher' and described his mother as a 'big fat woman with a red face like an alewife'. Anthony Wood cautioned the reader to 'suspend … belief' in this characterization (Wood, *Ath. Oxon.*, 4.119). However, it was widely reported, and as Scroggs became politically controversial he suffered ridicule and derision because of his alleged lowly social origins.

Education, marriage, and family Scroggs probably entered Pembroke College, Oxford, in 1639 at the age of sixteen. Under the tutelage of a 'noted tutor' he 'became master of a good Latin stile, and a considerable disputant' and graduated BA on 23 January 1640 (Wood, *Ath. Oxon.*, 4.115). When the civil war broke out he took up arms for the king, but 'had so much time allowed him' that he proceeded MA on 26 June 1643. Aspiring to a career in the church for his son, Scroggs's father bought 'the reversion of a good parsonage' for him (ibid., 4.116) but Scroggs chose the law instead and entered Gray's Inn on 22 February 1641. The civil war disrupted his legal studies; he rose to the rank of captain of a foot company, took part in engagements in Kent, Essex, and Colchester in 1648, and suffered wounds, claiming later that his injuries disabled him from walking before the lord mayor of London on ceremonial occasions, as required of his position as a city counsel. He was called to the bar on 27 June 1653; his name did not appear in the *Reports* until 1658.

About 1643 Scroggs married Anne (*d*. 1689), daughter of Edmund Fettiplace, of Berkshire. Described as a 'matronly, good woman' (North, *Lives*, 1.197), Anne was also a woman of spirit who in 1681 was 'very pressing about her annuity' (*Ormonde MSS*, 4.73). Her brothers became close friends of Scroggs: Alexander was executor of his will, and Christopher was living with him when he died. Anne Scroggs had at least four children, an only son, Sir William Scroggs [*see below*], and three daughters: Mary

Sir William Scroggs (*c*.1623–1683), after John Michael Wright?, 1678

died unmarried in 1675; Elizabeth (1644–1724) married first Anthony Gilby of London, a barrister, with whom she had three sons, and after his death in 1676 the Hon. Charles Hatton, the younger brother of Christopher, Viscount Hatton. She was buried in Lincoln Cathedral. Another daughter, Anne (*d.* 1692), married in 1681 as his third wife Sir Robert *Wright, the lord chief justice of the court of king's bench; they had a son and three daughters. Scroggs predeceased his wife—North errs in saying that she 'died long before him' (North, *Lives*, 1.197). Scroggs had a house in Essex Street in the 'Essex Buildings near the Temple' in London and a country estate, Weald Hall, near Brentwood in Essex, purchased in 1667, where it was said 'every day … was [a] holyday' (ibid.; *VCH Essex*, 2.530). This purchase drew him into a law suit over repayment of a debt owed by the previous owner. Scroggs held other properties in Essex and was granted the right to keep two fairs every year, his request suggesting some interest in country living.

Early legal career to 1678 Scroggs's early legal career prospered thanks to his talents, political principles, and connections. He wrote well and was 'valued for readiness in speaking', both desirable qualities in a lawyer (*Bishop Burnet's History*, 2.196). He won admiration, even from Roger North, a detractor, for his 'Wit' and 'Boldness', his 'fluent Expression and many good Turn of Thought and Language' (North, *Examen*, 568). Scroggs came to the notice of the court and received a knighthood, probably in 1664. In 1667 he argued before the House of Lords the duke of Buckingham's claim to the barony of De Ros, winning praise from Samuel Pepys as an 'excellent' man (Pepys, 8.22). He won appointment as counsel for Sir William Penn in 1668, but the case was dropped. The year 1669 marked steady advance: Scroggs was elected a bencher of Gray's Inn in June, awarded the coif in October, made a king's serjeant in November, and appointed counsel to the City of London. In the early 1670s (if not before) he handled the legal affairs of Christopher, Lord Hatton, with whom he developed a lifelong friendship. These moves owed nothing to court favour, even a nineteenth-century detractor admitted (Foss, *Judges*, 7.167).

Scroggs, however, owed his advancement to the highest legal posts to the patronage of Thomas Osborne, earl of Danby, the lord treasurer. In 1676, at Danby's insistence, he was appointed to the court of common pleas. To avoid the appearance that the appointment was to 'better serve a turn', Scroggs urged the king to elevate him before parliament rose (Thompson, 1.164). Already there were whispers of corruption: pranksters posted papers about town saying that judgeships were up for sale and young lawyers might apply to the lord treasurer (*Seventh Report*, HMC, appx 1, 484a). Scroggs's commitment to the royal prerogative also recommended him, North reporting that he was 'preferred for professing loyalty' (North, *Lives*, 1.196). His address upon his appointment to the court of common pleas won extravagant praise. An admirer told the king that this 'excellent' speech taught the people more loyalty to the crown than all the sermons printed since the Restoration (*The Correspondence of Henry Hyde, Earl of Clarendon and of his Brother Laurence Hyde, Earl of Rochester*, 2 vols., 1828, 1.2). In it Scroggs expressed abhorrence of corruption and popular favour, saying that he sought 'Reputation and a Good Name' by doing his 'Duty' and not otherwise (*A Speech Made by Sir William Scrogg*, 5–7). Two years later, in 1678, Scroggs became lord chief justice of the court of king's bench. In a speech later printed Scroggs declared that loyalty to the king was the 'Heart and Life' of the legal profession, that the crown must be 'guarded by lawyers as well as Laws', and that in his court lawyers could expect favour to be 'measured to them by their Loyalty' (*The Lord Chief Justice Scroggs his Speech*). Soon afterwards Danby's impeachment and removal deprived him of a friend and left him exposed as a protégé of a discredited minister.

The Popish Plot Scroggs's position as lord chief justice brought him to the centre of affairs during the Popish Plot. That crisis erupted in early September 1678 when Titus Oates and William Bedloe revealed to the king and others that there was a Jesuit plot afoot to murder Charles II and place his Roman Catholic brother, James, duke of York, on the throne. With hysteria spreading throughout the nation, parliament summoned Oates and sent for Scroggs on 24 October to be present while Oates was testifying. Announcing himself as fearing 'the face of noe man where his king and countrie were concerned' and, accepting Oates's claims without hesitation, Scroggs 'issued out at one tyme, 40 or 50 warrants against noblemen and others' and 'with so much frankness and expedition that he received the public thanks' (*Kenyon MSS*, 107; *Ormonde MSS*, 4.462). Insensitive to the scepticism of the king and some privy councillors regarding Oates's testimony,

Scroggs went with the tide of a frightened public, allying himself with the House of Commons. Formal proceedings against the accused began almost immediately and continued at a furious pace; from November 1678 to June 1679 Scroggs sent fourteen men to their death. Only one man brought to trial, Samuel Atkins, was acquitted. The record of these trials belies the usual picture of Scroggs as a judge of little legal learning, no conscience, and entire willingness to defer to Oates and Bedloe in the proceedings.

The first trial on 21 November 1678 concerned William Staley, a young Catholic banker, who was overheard in a tavern threatening to kill the king. His words, readily proved by men with whom he talked, were treason at law. Scroggs permitted the defendant to call two witnesses (as was proper) and instructed the jury not to be swept along by 'the disorders of the times' in a 'case of a man's life'. But he also ridiculed Staley's weak defence and intemperately addressed the jury. When a guilty verdict was returned, he mockingly remarked to Staley, 'Now you may die a Roman catholic, and when you come to die, I doubt [not] you will be found a priest too'. Scroggs further revealed a coarse and brutal streak when, upon hearing of the elaborate burial that Staley's family and friends had arranged, ordered his body exhumed and his quarters set over the city gates. Within a week, on 27 November, there followed the trial of Edward Coleman, secretary to the duke and duchess of York, on a charge of high treason for conspiring to murder the king. Scroggs sharply questioned Oates about his testimony before the privy council, told Bedloe not to read his testimony from his notes and then questioned him, and, in conformity with legal procedures, allowed Coleman to question his accusers, assuring him that the court would hear any witnesses he brought in. Coleman's letters, rather than the testimony of Oates and Bedloe, which Scroggs downplayed, convicted the prisoner. In his summation, Scroggs delivered a little homily on contrition and confession. Describing himself as a Christian, Scroggs condemned the Catholic church for using 'blood and violence' in propagating religion and altering governments in its interest, and expressed incredulity that anyone 'of understanding' could accept Catholicism. Showing a gentler side, Scroggs allowed Coleman private visits by his wife and friends (*State trials*, 7.1–78; Kenyon, 'Acquittal', 115–25).

The trial of the Catholic priests Thomas White, alias Whitbread, William Ireland, John Fenwick, Thomas Pickering, and John Grove, on a charge of treason for conspiring to murder the king that took place on 17 December hastened to counter the allegation that the government was trying to smother the plot. In conformity with the legal principle that two witnesses were required for conviction in a treason trial and because Bedloe was unable to corroborate Oates's testimony, Scroggs returned Whitbread and Fenwick to prison until more proof arrived. He was technically correct in ruling inadmissible evidence to be brought from St Omer to England to prove that Oates was there when he claimed otherwise. The other justices concurred. However, he had no legal basis for disallowing certain evidence about Ireland's whereabouts at a critical time in Oates's narrative or in counterbalancing witnesses to that same point to invalidate Ireland's position. In the absence of compelling evidence from Oates and Bedloe, Scroggs focused his summation on the reality of the plot and his contempt of Catholicism. With unseemly rhetorical extravagance he declared: 'They eat their God, they kill their king and saint the murderer'. The guilty verdict met with Scroggs's enthusiastic approval (*State trials*, 7.79–142).

Two months later, on 10 February 1679, Robert Green and Lawrence Hill, Catholic labourers, and Henry Berry, a protestant hand, were brought to trial at king's bench on a charge of murdering Sir Edmund Godfrey. Miles Prance, a Catholic silversmith, who turned state's evidence after two recantations, testified against the accused. Oates and Bedloe played but little part. The defence was inconsequential. In a lengthy review of the evidence, Scroggs concluded that he found 'nothing incoherent' in Prance's account and again dilated on the evilness of Catholicism, expressing wonder that 'any man should be of that persuasion and keep his reason' (*State trials*, 7.219). But Scroggs directed the jury in moderate terms: 'We would not add blood to innocent blood', he began, adding that if jurors found the evidence compelling, 'then the land is defiled unless this be satisfied' (ibid., 7.213). When the jury returned a guilty verdict, he expressed his entire agreement with them, his words provoking a 'great shout of applause' from observers (ibid., 7.221).

The next day Samuel Atkins, a clerk in the Admiralty office and a protestant, was charged as an accessory to the murder of Godfrey on grounds of Bedloe's identifying him. Atkins had a strong alibi and Bedloe confessed himself uncertain that Atkins was truly the man he had seen. This admission compromised Bedloe and the attorney-general sought assurance that thereby the 'king's evidence was not disproved'. 'Not a tittle', replied Scroggs, defending Bedloe. At the verdict of not guilty the lord chief justice counselled the defendant and his star witness to 'go you and drink a bottle' together. This was the only jovial note in any Popish Plot trial.

During the spring public hysteria mounted, the first Exclusion Bill, disabling the Catholic duke of York from his place in the succession to the throne, passed the House of Commons on 15 May 1679, and the king prorogued parliament. Against this background, on 13 June five Jesuit priests, the high-placed Thomas Whitbread (provincial of the Jesuits in England), William Harcourt (rector of London), and John Fenwick (procurator), and also John Gavan and Anthony Turner, were tried at the Old Bailey. Other legal officers joined Scroggs and king's bench judges, a testimony to the importance of this trial to the government. Scroggs, supported by 'all the judges of England', overruled Whitbread's contention that since he had been before the bench in February he could not according to law be tried twice for the same cause. Oates, as in previous trials, bungled his testimony, prompting Scroggs to observe, 'I perceive your memory is not good', although he administered no further rebuke. Gavan discomfited

Oates by his defence and Whitbread brought out inconsistencies in Oates's writing and testimony without provoking comment from Scroggs. Stephen Dugdale, whose presence Scroggs much admired, and Prance, testified for the prosecution, and with Scroggs's help they strengthened the crown's case. Scroggs discredited the testimony of Catholic defence witnesses by implying that it was 'instructed' by the church. In his summation Scroggs expressed entire satisfaction with Dugdale's evidence, defended Oates as a 'good' man who had done England 'good' in revealing the plot, and declared that the murder of Godfrey was only a 'handsel' for the murder of the king (*State trials*, 7.416). The jury returned a guilty verdict.

The next day, on 14 June, Richard Langhorne, a Catholic lawyer, was tried at the Old Bailey for high treason for plotting the murder of the king and the subversion of the government. Oates and Bedloe embellished what they had said and/or written before about Langhorne, Bedloe linking Langhorne to Coleman, a relationship which one justice declared 'rivets the whole'. In his summary statement Scroggs declared that the 'Plot is proved as plain as the day, and that by Oates'. As he had done before, the lord chief justice mingled cautions against shedding innocent blood with the reminder that 'all our lives are at stake'. He ended with the hope that God would defend the nation against popish plots and 'from all the bloody principles of papists' and instructed the jury to 'follow your consciences; do wisely, do honestly' (*State trials*, 7.418–91).

The acquittal of Sir George Wakeman On 18 July 1679 Sir George Wakeman, the queen's Catholic physician, and three Benedictine monks, William Marshal, William Rumley, and James Corker, were tried before Scroggs at the Old Bailey on a charge of high treason for conspiring to poison the king. From the outset Scroggs was tougher on the prosecution witnesses than he had ever been before. Closely questioning Bedloe on his testimony, Scroggs concluded that he found in it nothing 'material' against the accused. He reminded Bedloe to stick to the truth: 'I would be loth to keep out popery by [methods] they would bring it in, that is, by blood or violence. I would have all things very fair'. When Oates's testimony respecting a letter allegedly written by Wakeman and said to prove his intention to murder Charles for a price collapsed in the face of counter-evidence, Scroggs did nothing to save it. Wakeman's chief witness, Sir Philip Lloyd, a clerk of the council, to whom the court had given permission to testify, deposed that at the council meeting on 30 September 1678 Oates had not pressed charges against Wakeman and had specifically refused an opportunity to do so. Oates's excuse that he was tired out met with a tirade of disbelief and scorn from Scroggs. As the trial proceeded, Oates became so discomfited that he declared he was ill and requested permission to retire, which request Scroggs denied. In his summation, Scroggs spoke, for the first time in these trials, in favour of the accused; he advised the jury to discharge Rumley because there was but one witness, stressed Oates's confusion over Wakeman's handwriting and his failure to identify Wakeman before the council, and raised doubts that words Wakeman uttered, according to Bedloe, were 'plain enough' for conviction. 'These men's bloods are at stake, and your souls and mine. … Therefore, never care what the world say, follow your consciences', he counselled. As he was leaving the court, Bedloe cried out 'My lord, my evidence is not right summed up'. 'I know not', said Scroggs, 'by what authority this man speaks'. Such exchanges lay at the heart of later charges that Scroggs had harassed Oates and Bedloe (*State trials*, 7.591–688).

The acquittal of Wakeman and the three monks was a defining moment in Scroggs's life and career. The verdict met with a firestorm of outrage, directed mostly at the lord chief justice: 'All people now rail extremely at Scroggs', it was said (*Seventh Report*, HMC, appx, 474a; *Le Fleming MSS*, 160). One has only to compare his handling of previous trials to his management of Wakeman's to see the difference, advised a contemporary (Luttrell, 1.18). At a meeting of the council in early August, Shaftesbury declared that Scroggs was 'no longer fit to serve either King or nation' (*Ormonde MSS*, 4.533). Scroggs suffered further damage from an impolitic courtesy visit that the Portuguese ambassador paid him to thank him for sparing the queen embarrassment or worse (*Bishop Burnet's History*, 2.232). Rumours that the ambassador had left bags of gold at his house, that the jurors had also accepted bribes, and that Scroggs had received instructions from the court to assure an acquittal, flew about London (Luttrell, 1.17–18). There is no proof of these charges nor of North's story that Scroggs changed course after Sir Francis North had assured him privately that Shaftesbury had lost influence at court (North, *Examen*, 568). Scroggs did not need instructions. This trial posed an obviously serious and delicate problem for the court; the accusation came perilously close to the queen. The court itself assisted Wakeman to make his defence, which Scroggs, no doubt, knew. The king had also signalled a new willingness to resist Shaftesbury and the House of Commons by dissolving parliament on 10 July. A guilty verdict would have been a catastrophe for the government.

Wakeman's acquittal precipitated a vicious campaign in the press against Scroggs. Such a campaign was possible because the Licensing Act of 1662 which had controlled the press for seventeen years had lapsed with the dissolution of parliament. Henry Care was first to denounce Scroggs in the 1 August issue of his popular *Weekly Pacquet of Advice from Rome*. Care announced the discovery of a marvellous medicine with the power to make 'Justice deaf as well as blinde', remove 'spots of deepest treason', and induce people to 'behold nothing but Innocence in the blackest Malefactors'. Other scurrilous pieces followed. *Satyr Against Injustice, or, Sc——gs upon Sc——gs* provided six triplets of abuse of Scroggs, one saying, 'Our Judge to Mercy's not inclin'd / Unless Gold change Conscience and Mind'; Jane Curtis was tried for publishing this piece. Francis Smith, a well-known bookseller, was charged with publishing another offensive tract, *Some Observations upon the Late Trial of Sir George Wakeman*, which observed that Scroggs suffered from Clodpate's disease, that is 'to sham up an evidence' according to who was with him that morning. Scurrilous efforts were made to make the name Clodpate stick to the lord chief justice. *A New Year's Gift* so offended Scroggs that he committed Francis Smith jun. for selling it to a coffee house; this piece accused Scroggs of bribery and added a postscript about judges under Edward III and Richard II who were sentenced to death for taking bribes. So extensive was the press campaign that insinuations about Scroggs's role spread far beyond London. While on circuit in August, Scroggs suffered terrible indignities, including having a half-dead dog tossed into his carriage and his sleep disturbed as he was driven along by a man rapping on the top of his coach and calling out 'A Wakeman, A Wakeman' (Luttrell, 1.19–20; *Memoirs of the Verney Family*, 2.321). At the Hereford assizes on 4 August Scroggs presided over proceedings against a popish priest, Charles Kerne, who was acquitted because of inadequate evidence. At the Stafford assizes, where two other priests, Andrew Bromwich and William Atkins, were tried, Scroggs intemperately told the jury that they 'had better be rid of one priest than three felons'; the accused were condemned to death (*State trials*, 7.715–30). Report had it that Scroggs had 'mauled and knocked down all the priests and Papists' to recover his position (*Ormonde MSS*, 4.535). Scroggs was warmly welcomed when he visited Windsor on 29 August 1680. Charles, recuperating from a serious illness, 'was very extraordinarily favourable to him'. Remarking upon how ill he had been used, the king declared, 'But they have used me worse, and I am resolv'd we will stand and fall together'. Scroggs replied in his witty way that he hoped they should stand and not fall (Thompson, 1.192).

Scroggs defended himself in a powerful speech before the court of king's bench on 23 October 1679. Insisting that he had conducted the trial 'without fear, favour, or reward; without the gift of one shilling', Scroggs lashed out at 'hireling Scriblers … who write to Eat, and Lye for Bread', warning them that there was a law now to 'punish a Libellous and Licentious Press' and that he intended to use it (*The Lord Chief Justice Scroggs his Speech*). The 'law' that Scroggs had in mind was a ruling by the judges that held that the king might seize libels against the government or individuals and gaol the persons responsible pending trial. The court, which felt keenly the absence of the Printing Act, followed with a royal proclamation on 31 October announcing the points in the ruling. To critics the judges' ruling and the resulting proclamation made law without parliament's involvement and were reasons for intense anxiety about the legislative role of parliament.

Scroggs implemented his threat against the press in ways that were questionable at law. Defying regular legal procedures, he used his warrant to call in Henry Care on 23 October 1679 and subsequently summoned Francis Smith and Jane Curtis. His summons of Curtis created a special legal problem because, as a *femme couverte*, she could not be legally prosecuted. Scroggs, in effect, adopted the pretence that she was a feme sole, thereby opening himself to criticism. Upbraiding all these press persons in coarse language, Scroggs thundered that he would 'fill all the Gaols in England with [them] and pile them up as Men do Faggots' and that he would 'shew no more Mercy than they could expect from a Wolf that came to devour them' (*JHC*, 9.688–9, 690). Refusing to accept bail, Scroggs remanded the defendants to gaol to force them to the expense of buying a writ of habeas corpus, a move also subject to censure.

Scroggs's continuing rage over the charge of corruption further undermined his position. In mid-December he encountered Shaftesbury and a group of political leaders at the lord mayor's dinner and conversation about the recent trials ensued. When Scroggs proposed a toast to the duke of York, a fracas erupted. Scroggs, now much in his cups, indignantly declared his innocence in the Wakeman matter. Shaftesbury was conciliatory, conceding that Scroggs had taken no money, and after two or three hours Scroggs left, mollified. Nevertheless, hostility between Shaftesbury and Scroggs remained, for the acquittal of Wakeman was a serious set-back for Shaftesbury and the enmity between the two men was personal and long-standing, ante-dating the Popish Plot. On 21 January 1680 Oates and Bedloe presented to the privy council thirteen articles of high misdemeanours against Scroggs, a move they had had underway since August 1679. The substance of the articles was similar and in some cases identical to the ones used later to impeach Scroggs. In an aside Oates boldly asserted that he thought he could prove that Scroggs had danced naked. The council, with the king present, heard the charges and Scroggs's defence (which he had six days to prepare) and dismissed the case, leaving legal redress to Scroggs. Scroggs, however, did not take them to court, a measure of their power and his weakness.

Scroggs carried on his active role as lord chief justice. He continued to preside over trials associated with the Popish Plot frenzy, among them that on 3 February 1680 of John Tasborough and Anne Price, who were charged with trying to suborn Stephen Dugdale. The trial is notable for Scroggs's probing insistence that the evidence be clear and applicable to the accused. Scroggs involved himself closely in interrogating witnesses, remarking that he would 'shew you all very fair play'. He excused himself before the end of the trial to attend to business in the exchequer chamber. The accused were judged guilty and fined (*State trials*, 7.882–926). On 11 June the popish midwife Elizabeth Cellier was tried before Scroggs in king's bench on a charge of treason for conspiring to kill the king and introduce Catholicism. The point at issue was the testimony of the notorious Thomas Dangerfield, whom Cellier challenged as a convicted felon. Scroggs insisted that she 'produce the record'; satisfied, he dismissed Dangerfield, shouting 'I wonder at your impudence, that you dare look a court of justice in the face'. Scroggs instructed the jury that the case was plain, for there was but one witness, and that indirect, to an act of treason. The verdict was not guilty (ibid., 7.1043–55). Two weeks later, on 23 June, Roger Palmer, earl of Castlemaine, was tried on a charge of treason for conspiring to murder the king and alter the government. Scroggs pressed Oates closely on the details of his account, reluctantly accepted Dangerfield as a witness after protracted disagreement, and cited his conscience, duty, and oath in reminding the jury of Dangerfield's criminal past. He warned them that two credible witnesses were required to convict; the jury, accepting his guidance, returned a not guilty verdict. Moreover, three days later Scroggs and other justices took part in the peremptory dismissal of the Middlesex grand jury before the end of its terms. By dismissing the jury the judges scuttled a scheme, orchestrated by the radical whig leadership, to indict the duke of York as a popish recusant. All the judges concurred in the dismissal, but Scroggs took the brunt of the blame. The incident highlighted the bench's use of legal powers that seemed arbitrary and unjust to court critics and figured in the attempt to impeach Scroggs.

Scroggs also played a central role in the government's effort to restrain the press. Responding to the crown's request, a majority of the bench (newly reconstituted in February 1680), with Scroggs in the lead, handed down additional rulings: one, on 5 May, declared that the king may 'by Law prohibit the printing & publishing all [unlicensed] News Bookes & Pamphletts of News', a position that violated law (PRO, PC/68, 496). A royal proclamation followed and Scroggs promptly issued warrants to implement the proclamation. Another ruling, issued on 28 May, specifically targeted Care's *Weekly Pacquet*, forbidding anyone whatsoever from printing it. Even loyalists admitted that this ruling was an arbitrary use of legal power. These rulings enlarged the fear that Scroggs, as leader of the bench, was usurping the law-making power of parliament.

Scroggs presided over two of the four trials of press persons: one, that of Benjamin Harris on 5 February for printing the notorious tract, *An Appeal from the Country to the City*, attracted huge crowds which indulged in 'halloos' and 'hems'. Such antics deeply disturbed Scroggs who described the 'hummers' as 'enemies to the government'. He railed against booksellers for selling seditious material that compromised the peace of the nation just to make money. He attempted to plea-bargain with Harris to discover the name of the author, but failing, he treated the defendant severely. He also rebuked the jury for their verdict, which judged Harris guilty of selling the book, but not of a malicious design. The second press trial concerned Henry Care, who was tried on 2 July for comments in the 2 August 1679 issue of the *Weekly Pacquet*. Scroggs expressed incredulity over the popularity of the press and renewed anger over the presence of huge crowds, but he admitted that Care's authorship of the offending passage was 'not plain' and indulged himself in a lengthy statement about probable and conjectural evidence. The jury returned a guilty verdict but in October, when Care appeared before the court to be sentenced, the case was dismissed, Scroggs no doubt wanting to avoid renewed protests against the government.

Impeachment and removal from office On 23 November 1680, eight days after the defeat of the second Exclusion Bill, whig members of the House of Commons turned their disappointment against the judges at Westminster and appointed a committee to examine the proceedings of the justices. A month later, on 23 December, the Commons received the committee's report and ordered it to prepare impeachment charges against four justices: Scroggs, Sir Thomas Jones (a justice of the court of king's bench), Sir Richard Weston (a baron of the court of exchequer), and Sir Francis North, lord chief justice of the court of common pleas. On 5 January 1681 the lower house accepted the eight articles of impeachment that the committee had prepared against Scroggs alone, agreed to designate the charges as 'High Treason and other great Crimes and Misdemeanours', and instructed the committee to draw up an impeachment against the other justices, a step the committee never took. The eight articles of impeachment against Scroggs condemned his political and legal activities and personal behaviour. Article one accused him of 'traiterously' attempting to 'subvert the Fundamental Laws and Establisht Religion and Government' of the nation with the aim of introducing 'Popery and Arbitrary and Tyrannical Government against Law'. Cast in language reminiscent of that used in the civil-war impeachments of Archbishop William Laud and Thomas, earl of Strafford, the charge conveyed the fear that Scroggs by his judicial rulings in the matter of the press threatened parliament's control of legislation. Article two focused on Scroggs and the other justices' handling of the Middlesex grand jury in June 1680. Scroggs's enemies saw in that episode another subversion of law, normal legal processes, and parliament, a reinforcement of article one.

The next four, closely related, articles concerned Scroggs's handling of the press in ways detrimental to the legal rights of the press, the nation's law and legal processes, and the legislative role of parliament. Article three cited the ruling by Scroggs and the other judges of the court of king's bench that banned Care's *Weekly Pacquet of Advice from Rome*. Article four charged the lord chief justice and his colleagues with unfair levying of fines to the disadvantage of protestant publishers. Article five condemned Scroggs alone for refusing legitimate and sufficient bail, for imprisoning writers and booksellers, and for verbally abusing them; it charged that Scroggs refused bail 'onely to put them to Charges'. Article six complained that Scroggs had used general warrants for 'attaching the Persons and seizing the Goods' of the king's subjects. The warrants the committee identified in its report related to the press. Article seven addressed Scrogg's 'defaming' and 'disparaging' the evidence of witnesses, thereby encouraging the Popish Plot, a silent reference to his handling of Oates and Bedloe in Wakeman's trial. Article eight was an *ad hominen* attack on Scroggs charging him with 'frequent and notorious Excesses and Debaucheries'.

These eight articles were read in the House of Lords on 7 January with Scroggs standing at his place. A majority of peers, including all the lords spiritual and peers who favoured Danby, took steps to protect him. They refused to commit Scroggs, granted him bail (contrary to precedent on a treason charge), permitted him to draw bail sureties from among the lords themselves (ignoring the awkwardness of having men who would be his judges serve as his sureties), gave him a copy of the articles of impeachment and an opportunity to answer them in writing, and allowed him to remain on the bench until his trial, 'trusting his modesty' (*Autobiography*, 181; Luttrell, 1.62). The Lords' actions provoked two protests from whigs in the house, one at the vote against committing Scroggs, the other at permitting him to remain on the bench pending trial. The Lords' actions also prompted bitter denunciation by whigs in the House of Commons, who saw them as a violation of precedent and law respecting a person under impeachment for high treason.

Scroggs was saved by the king. Charles dissolved the second Exclusion Parliament on 20 January 1681, called for new elections, and summoned the next parliament to meet in Oxford on 21 March, thereby interrupting the proceedings. But when Hilary term began Scroggs did not take his place on the bench, because, rumour had it, the king had commanded him to absent himself. On 24 March, Scroggs's reply to the indictment, denying that the charges were treason, and his petition for a speedy trial were presented to the House of Lords. These papers were sent to the lower house, which responded by asking that Scroggs's bail be discharged and he himself committed. Within the week, however, Charles dissolved the Oxford parliament, which aborted the impeachment proceedings. The dissolution was, Roger North thought, lucky for Scroggs, for parliament would have pursued his impeachment with a resulting 'embroil … not easy to conjecture' (North, *Examen*, 568).

Although Scroggs escaped a legal judgment, he did not escape a political decision. On 11 April, much to his surprise (it was said), the king removed him as lord chief justice, but softened the disgrace by giving him a handsome pension of £1500 per annum and appointing his son to the rank of king's counsel and knighting him. Also, coincidentally or otherwise, Sir William Wright, who had married Scroggs's daughter Anne just the week before, was appointed one of the judges for Wales. There was even talk thereafter of a possible comeback of Scroggs, but that did not happen. He lived privately at Weald Hall attending to his affairs, which he described in his will as 'in agitation'. The will, dated 3 June 1683, reveals a man of considerable wealth, with properties in Essex, London, and Norfolk and other monetary resources, who relished his family and friends and left bequests to many individuals, including the poor of South Weald. He provided for his 'loveing wife' through trusts and enjoined his son to be 'extraordinarie kind and obedient' to her. To his son he left Weald Hall and, upon the death of his wife, the remainder of all his properties and rents.

Appearance and character Scroggs was a tall, handsome man of ample size. His portrait painted in 1678, probably to celebrate his elevation to the post of lord chief justice, shows a commanding figure exuding self-confidence with dark brown eyes under heavy brows, a strong chin, and a full, clean-shaven face. Said by his political enemies to be the companion of 'high court rakes', Scroggs had a reputation for debauchery, loose living, and love of drink (North, *Examen*, 567; North, *Lives*, 1.196; *Bishop Burnet's History*, 2.196). He admitted candidly to his friend Lord Hatton that there was nothing he liked more than wine, the stronger the better and preferably claret, and intimated that he preferred it to women. He suffered from gout, but was fit enough at the age of forty-eight to strip off his gown and coif, vault over the bar in Westminster Hall, and flee, with other justices following, from a mad cow which was disrupting business in the hall. His exuberant personality led him into unseemly episodes, including an assault and battery incident early in his career that brought him the enmity of Justice Matthew Hale, and an undignified verbal assault on the female plaintiff in the law suit regarding Weald Hall. In mid-life he was careful with money, keeping himself 'very poor', and refusing to pay the fees due to the College of Arms upon his knighthood, a move that dashed Dugdale's expectations and provoked his animosity. After winning high office, however, Scroggs lived well and 'feathered his nest' (North, *Lives*, 1.197). He augmented his fortune by selling to booksellers the exclusive right of publishing the Popish Plot trials over which he presided. Popish Plot hysteria, partisan political infighting, personal vendetta, and a libellous press destroyed his reputation. His personal weaknesses—ambition, pride, love of drink, and unrestrained tongue and behaviour—also helped to bring him down. The negative contemporary assessment prevailed with later whiggish historians and others, like Sir Walter Scott and Swift; only a few historians, such as Sir James Stephen, Sir John Pollock, and J. P. Kenyon, have dissented. The trial records and his *Practice of Courts-Leet and Courts-Baron*, published after his death in 1701 with four editions, the last in 1728, disprove the charge of legal incompetence. His handling of the Popish Plot trials reflects his initial acceptance of the reality of the plot, alarm for the safety of government and religion, and abhorrence of Roman Catholicism, all popular attitudes. As a judge whose office drew him into the highest counsels, he also had the interests of the court at heart. He strained the law in the Popish Plot trials; he violated it in dealing with the press. His attempted impeachment is notable for the prominent role of press people and judicial rulings respecting the press. Underlying the proceedings was the fear that the bench, under Scroggs's leadership, was usurping the role of parliament as the law-making body of the nation.

Scroggs died of a heart attack on 25 October 1683 at his house in Essex Street, London. He was buried in the parish church at South Weald on 29 October 1683. Political circumstances were now different; an elegy immediately appeared praising him as one who stood firm 'when Torrent Faction rag'd' and as an 'Oracle of Law' who could not be bought (*An Elegy in Commemoration of the Right Worshipful Sir William Scroggs*).

Sir William Scroggs (1652?–1695), lawyer, Scroggs's only son, was born at Stifford, Essex. He matriculated at Magdalen College, Oxford on 26 March 1669, was a chorister from 1669 to 1673, and received the BA degree on 4

March 1673. Admitted to Gray's Inn on 2 February 1669, he was called to the bar on 27 October 1676. In 1684 Scroggs married Mary (1663–1684), daughter of Sir John Churchill, master of the rolls, who died childless a few months later. The next year, on 1 December 1685, Scroggs married Anne Bluck, aged twenty-one, daughter of Matthew Bluck, usher of the rolls, and one of six clerks in chancery. They had five boys, one born posthumously, and two girls.

Scroggs's interests were advanced by his father's influence. In January 1679 Sir Joseph Williamson, secretary of state, acting on orders from the king, asked the duke of Albemarle to support Scroggs for election to the House of Commons as member for Maldon. Scroggs, however, did not stand. Also in 1679 the earl of Sackville suspected that Scroggs senior had promoted Titus Oates's accusation against him to 'introduce his son' (*Fourth Report*, HMC, appx, 298). To soften the blow of removing his father from office, the king knighted young Scroggs on 16 April 1681 and appointed him a king's counsel.

On 18 June 1681, with others from Gray's Inn, Scroggs attended the king at Windsor and presented him an address of thanks for his declaration explaining why he had dissolved the Oxford Parliament. Intemperate in nature, Scroggs assaulted a fellow counsellor at the Bury assizes in July 1681 for refusing an oath. By September 1681 he was prominent enough among crown supporters for Shaftesbury to mention him as one who would replace the incumbent justices and 'carry the prerogative higher' (*CSP dom.*, *1680–81*, 457). In November 1682 he served as counsel to the Hilton brothers, notorious informers, in a trial before Sir Francis North at the Guildhall. He suffered from scurrilities in lampoons over the rumour that his grandfather was a butcher: he was said to be of the race of Kill Mad Ox (*Le Neve's Pedigrees*, 346). At his father's death in 1683 Scroggs inherited Weald Hall and all his father's lands in Essex. He sold Weald Hall in 1685. In 1691–9 the law suit against his father concerning the property was settled in Scroggs's favour. At his mother's death in 1689 he inherited the remainder of his father's estate, including properties in London. When James II came to the throne in 1685 Scroggs was reappointed king's counsel, and he enjoyed further recognition in serving Gray's Inn as treasurer from November 1687 to November 1688. He died at St Clement Danes on 24 January 1695. North said that he was a 'sufferer in the wars of amour', implying that the cause was a venereal disease (North, *Lives*, 1.197). His death was apparently unexpected; his will was made orally on his death bed 'immediately before death' and signed by persons in attendance. Scroggs left his widow his entire estate and made her his executor. His place of burial is unknown. Lady Scroggs died on 23 April 1746 at the age of eighty-one and was buried at Chute in Wiltshire.

Lois G. Schwoerer

Sources L. G. Schwoerer, 'The attempted impeachment of Sir William Scroggs', *HJ*, 38 (1995), 843–73 • J. P. Kenyon, 'The acquittal of Sir George Wakeman: 18 July 1679', *HJ*, 14 (1971), 693–708 • J. Kenyon, *The Popish Plot* (1972) • J. R. Dunlop, *The family of Scroggs* (1929) • *State trials*, vols. 6–8 • *First report*, HMC, 1/1 (1870); repr. (1874) • *Fourth report*, HMC, 3 (1874) • *Seventh report*, HMC, 6 (1879) • *Eleventh report*, HMC (1887) • *Thirteenth report*, HMC (1892) • *The manuscripts of S. H. Le Fleming*, HMC, 25 (1890) • *The manuscripts of Lord Kenyon*, HMC, 35 (1894) • *The manuscripts of the House of Lords*, new ser., 12 vols. (1900–77), vol. 8 • *Calendar of the manuscripts of the marquess of Ormonde*, new ser., 8 vols., HMC, 36 (1902–20), vols. 4–6 • *JHC*, 9 (1667–87) • *JHL*, 13 (1675–81) • A. Grey, ed., *Debates of the House of Commons, from the year 1667 to the year 1694*, 10 vols. (1763) • *CSP dom.*, *1664–5*; *1677–82* • E. M. Thompson, ed., *Correspondence of the family of Hatton*, 2 vols., CS, new ser., 22–3 (1878) • R. North, *The lives of … Francis North … Dudley North … and … John North*, ed. A. Jessopp, 1 (1890) • R. North, *Examen, or, An enquiry into the credit and veracity of a pretended complete history* (1740) • *Bishop Burnet's History* • Wood, *Ath. Oxon.*, new edn, 2.469; 4.11 • *DNB* • Pepys, *Diary*, 8.22 • *The lord chief justice Scroggs his speech to the lord chancellour* (1678) • *A speech made by Sir William Scrogg … at his admission to … the court of common pleas* (1676) • R. Morrice, 'Ent'ring book, being an historical register of occurrences from April, anno 1677 to April 1691', DWL • Newdigate newsletter, Folger, L.c.998 • N. Luttrell, *A brief historical relation of state affairs from September 1678 to April 1714*, 1 (1857) • K. H. D. Haley, *The first earl of Shaftesbury* (1968) • F. P. Verney and M. M. Verney, *Memoirs of the Verney family during the seventeenth century*, 2nd edn, 4 vols. in 2 (1907) • L. G. Schwoerer, 'Liberty of the press and public opinion, 1660–1695', *Liberty secured? Britain before and after 1688*, ed. J. R. Jones (1991), 213–19 • *Articles of high misdemeanours, humbly offered and presented to the consideration of his most sacred majesty, and his most honourable privy council, against Sir William Scrogs … together with his lordships answer thereunto* (1680) • *The autobiography of Sir John Bramston*, ed. [Lord Braybrooke], CS, 32 (1845) • J. Haydn, *The book of dignities: containing lists of the official personages of the British empire*, ed. H. Ockerby, 3rd edn (1894); repr. as *Haydn's book of dignities* (1969) • *Le Neve's Pedigrees of the knights*, ed. G. W. Marshall, Harleian Society, 8 (1873) • Foster, *Alum. Oxon.* • *An elegy in commemoration of the right worshipful Sir William Scroggs* (1683) • will, PRO, PROB 11/374, fols. 322*r*–323*r* • will, PRO, PROB 11/424, fol. 250*r*–*v*

Archives BL, Add. MSS 28053, fol. 114; 29549, fols. 62, 64, 68–75; 29565, fol. 108

Likenesses mezzotint, 1678 (after unknown artist), NPG • oils, 1678 (after J. M. Wright?), NPG [*see illus.*]

Wealth at death properties in Essex, London, and Norfolk; £200 p.a. for his wife out of certain properties held in trust; bequests to members of extended family, friends, and the poor of South Weald; Weald Hall to son, along with other properties in Essex, and everything else upon his widow's death

Scroggs, Sir William (1652?–1695). *See under* Scroggs, Sir William (*c*.1623–1683).

Scroope, Sir Adrian (1614/15–1667). *See under* Scrope, Adrian (1601–1660).

Scrope, Adrian (1601–1660), army officer and regicide, was born at Wormsley Hall in Oxfordshire, the son of Robert Scrope and Margaret Cornwall, daughter of Richard Cornwall of London; he was baptized at Lewknor on 12 January 1601. Scrope was educated at Hart Hall, Oxford (where he matriculated on 7 November 1617), and the Middle Temple (which he entered in February 1619). In November 1624 he married Mary Waller, daughter of Robert Waller of Beaconsfield, cousin of the poet Edmund Waller, and Anne (*née* Hampden), who was John Hampden's aunt. They had four children, Edmund (who became a fellow of All Souls College, Oxford, and keeper of the privy seal in Scotland), Robert (who became a fellow of Lincoln College, Oxford), Margaret, and Anne.

Scrope gave his enthusiastic support to parliament on the outbreak of the civil war, raising a troop of horse in October 1642 to serve as captain under the earl of Essex. He subsequently fought in Sir Robert Pye's regiment of

Adrian Scrope (1601–1660), by or after Robert Walker

horse (1644), before accepting a commission in the New Model Army (April or May 1645) as major in the cavalry regiment of Sir Robert Graves. He was probably present, therefore, when the regiment fulfilled three important duties in the early months of 1647—to transport money to Newcastle for paying off the Scottish army and to escort Charles I from Newcastle to Holmby House in Northamptonshire (both in January) and to guard the king there under house arrest (February to May). He supported the army in its quarrel with parliament and subsequent mutiny over disbandment (May), before succeeding Graves as colonel of the regiment (June or July).

At the start of the second civil war in March 1648 Scrope was based with half his regiment in Dorset, where he maintained the garrisons and suppressed a riotous demonstration near Blandford. He was then ordered to assist in putting down the royalist rising in Kent led by the earl of Norwich (May), check the danger from Lord Goring's forces in Essex (June), and join Fairfax at the start of the siege of Colchester (also in June). Soon afterwards he was detached from the siege, first to give chase to the earl of Holland, whom he routed and captured at St Neots on 10 July, and later to reinforce the town of Yarmouth against an expected landing there by Prince Charles. Having returned to London by the autumn of 1648 he was closely involved in the deliberations of the council of the army, which led to the *Remonstrance of the Army* (20 November) and Pride's Purge (6 December). On 15 January 1649 he was made a member of the committee charged with the detailed organization of the trial, the custody of the king, and the security of the court. Republican in sympathy, he willingly accepted his appointment as one of the commissioners to try the king in the high court of justice (6 January 1649); he attended the sittings with great regularity (20–27 January) and signed the death warrant [*see also* Regicides].

In the spring of 1649 Scrope's cavalry regiment mutinied. Selected by lot to join Cromwell's army in Ireland, the soldiers voted (1 May) against either redeployment or disbandment (which was the other option), publishing instead *The Resolutions of the Private Soldiery of Colonel Scroope's Regiment of Horse* … (1649). In this document, which was strongly influenced by Leveller ideas, they demanded the restoration of the elected army council of 1647 and the implementation of the democratic programme outlined in *An Agreement of the People* (1647). Only eighty officers and men stayed loyal to Scrope. The mutineers, based at Salisbury, seized the colours, elected fresh officers, rejected Scrope's attempts at pacification, and marched eventually to Burford, having been joined by others from the regiments of both Ireton and Harrison (making a total force of some 900 men). There they were routed in a midnight attack by Fairfax's forces, who, outnumbering the rebels by two to one, captured 340 prisoners and dispersed the rest (15 May). Four of the ringleaders were sentenced to death by court martial, though one of these was later pardoned. Scrope's regiment was disbanded and his own military career effectively ended. Unpopular with the vast majority of his troops, he had proved himself to be a heavy-handed commander and an insensitive negotiator.

Scrope was, however, appointed governor of Bristol Castle in succession to Major-General Philip Skippon (4 October 1649), a position he held until the demolition of the fortifications there in 1655. In May of that year he was made a member of the council established by Cromwell for the government of Scotland, at a salary of £600 per annum. According to Ludlow, the Protector's decision was based on his concern over the ambitions of Lieutenant-General Monck, whom he had appointed as commander-in-chief: '… that he might balance him with some of another temper, who might guard upon his actions, he sent Colonel Adrian Scroope …' (*Memoirs of Edmund Ludlow*, 1.394). Although Scrope remained in Scotland until July 1658, when he was granted three months' leave of absence, his heart was not in administration. A man of little personal ambition, he played no part in the political manoeuvres which took place after Cromwell's death.

At the restoration of Charles II, Scrope surrendered himself (along with eighteen other regicides) in accordance with the royal proclamation (4 June 1660). The Commons, however, voted to permit his inclusion under the terms of the Act of Indemnity on payment of a fine equivalent to the yearly value of his estates (9 June). Although he was consequently released on parole (20 June), the Lords countered this move not only by ordering the arrest of all regicides, but also by specifically excepting Scrope from pardon (23 July). After a further attempt to support Scrope's case (13 August) the Commons finally yielded to sustained pressure from the Lords (28 August). Scrope regarded this as a serious breach of faith, because his surrender had been based on a belief that indemnity would be granted. Arrested in August, he was eventually brought to trial at the Old Bailey (12 October), where he pleaded 'not guilty' to the charge of 'imagining and compassing the death of the king'. Crucial evidence against him was given by Major-General Richard Brown, the mayor elect of London, who recalled a conversation after the Restoration in which Scrope had seemingly justified the king's execution and failed to denounce it as murder.

In his own defence Scrope pleaded that, in error, he had acted as a member of the court on the orders of parliament. 'I hope an error of judgment shall not be accounted malice or an error of the will; truly, I never went to work with a malitious heart'. Although the president of the court (Sir Orlando Bridgeman) rejected his arguments, he nevertheless concluded: 'Mr Scroope (to give him his right) was not a person as some of the rest, but he was unhappily engaged in that bloody business, I hope mistakenly' (Noble, 2.221, 222, 226). He was duly sentenced to death and executed at Charing Cross on 17 October. Eyewitnesses noted the dignity, courage, and cheerfulness with which he conducted himself at both his trial and his execution—behaviour which aroused a great deal of compassion in others.

Scrope is sometimes confused with his distant relative, **Sir Adrian Scroope** [Scrope] (1614/15–1667), son of Sir Gervase Scroope of Cockerington in Lincolnshire (*d.* 1655), who commanded a regiment for the king in the civil war and was seriously wounded at Edgehill (23 October 1642). Sir Adrian married Mary Carr (1631–1685), daughter of Sir Robert Carr of Sleaford, and was the father of Sir Carr *Scrope (1649–1680), the courtier and poet. He fought for the king in the civil war, was fined heavily for his delinquency, and was knighted at the coronation of Charles II (23 April 1661). He died in 1667. JOHN WROUGHTON

Sources Greaves & Zaller, *BDBR* • C. H. Firth and G. Davies, *The regimental history of Cromwell's army*, 2 vols. (1940) • M. Noble, *The lives of the English regicides*, 2 (1798) • S. Barber, *Regicides and republicans* (1998) • I. Gentles, *The New Model Army in England, Ireland, and Scotland, 1645–1653* (1992) • *DNB* • *The memoirs of Edmund Ludlow*, ed. C. H. Firth, 2 vols. (1894), vol. 1 • *The Clarke papers*, ed. C. H. Firth, 4 vols., CS, new ser., 49, 54, 61–2 (1891–1901) • *A declaration of the proceedings of his excellency, the Lord General Fairfax* (1649) • *JHC*, 8 (1660–67) • *JHL*, 11 (1660–66) • *CSP dom.*, 1648–9; 1658–9

Likenesses C. Townley, etching, pubd 1801 (after portrait by or after Walker), BM, NPG • by or after R. Walker, oils, NPG [*see illus.*]

Wealth at death see will, PRO, PROB 11/327, sig. 97

Scrope, Sir Carr, baronet (1649–1680), poet, was born on 20 September 1649 in Aswardby, Lincolnshire, the eldest son of Sir Adrian *Scroope or Scrope (1614/15–1667) [*see under* Scrope, Adrian], of Cockerington, Lincolnshire, and Mary, Lady Scrope (1631–1685), daughter of Sir Robert Carr of Sleaford, Lincolnshire. He attended Wadham College, Oxford, from 1664 to 1667, was awarded the MA in February 1667, and was created a baronet in January 1667. His father died in debt, and administration of Sir Adrian's estate was granted on 5 September 1667 to the principal creditor.

In 1675 Scrope's younger brother Gervase was killed by Sir Thomas Armstrong in a duel at Dorset Garden playhouse, occasioning the duke of Buckingham's bitter satiric lines

> His brother murder'd and his mother whor'd,
> His mistress lost, yet still his pen's his sword.
> (Lord and others, 331)

The 'mistress' referred to in these lines from the 'Familiar epistle to Mr. Julian' (1677), an extended satiric lampoon attacking Scrope's 'hideous' physical appearance and poetic pretensions, is Cary Frazier, celebrated for her beauty and extravagance. In 1676 Scrope gave up his pursuit of Cary Frazier, commenting that 'his estate will scarce maintain her in clothes' (*Rutland MSS*, 31). Scrope's mother, Lady Scrope, a Roman Catholic and a 'great Witt' (Evelyn, 4.345), was at this time the mistress of Henry Savile.

A Restoration wit and man of fashion (though perhaps more of a Sir Fopling Flutter than a Dorimant), Scrope was the object of a number of satires and lampoons, by the earl of Rochester, Buckingham, and others. One of the few contemporary authors to characterize Scrope in favourable terms was Aphra Behn, who cited the 'natural softness' of 'those little chance things' of Sir Carr as exemplifying 'that unstudied, and undesigned way of writing … used by a Courtier who has Wit' (Behn, sig. 1*v*). He contributed a prologue and a song ('As Amoret with Phillis sat') to George Etherege's *Man of Mode* (1676), a prologue to Nathaniel Lee's *Rival Queens* (1677), and a song ('One night when all the village slept') to Lee's *Mithridates King of Pontus* (1679). His song 'I cannot change as others do', which was circulated widely in manuscript miscellanies, was savagely parodied by Rochester as 'I swive as well as others do' (Vieth, 231–8). Scrope contributed a translation of Ovid's 'Sapho to Phaon' to *Ovid's Epistles* (1680) and two translations, one from Ovid's *Amores* and one from Jorge de Montemayor's *Diana*, to the Dryden–Tonson *Miscellany Poems* (1684). Of his satires, the longest and most ambitious is 'In Defense of Satire' (1677) which argues the conventional line that satire is 'virtue's friend', didactic in intent; it was answered by Rochester's 'On the Supposed Author of a Late Poem *In Defense of Satyr*' (1677), to which Scrope responded in the same year with an epigram 'The Author's Reply' ('Rail on, poor feeble scribbler'). In 1677 Scrope and Katherine Sedley quarrelled in the queen's drawing-room about 'some lampoon made of her that she judged him the author' (*Rutland MSS*, 37); this may well be one of several satiric and lyric poems by Scrope, no longer extant, which according to Anthony Wood continued to be passed 'from hand to hand' for some time after his death (Wood, *Ath. Oxon.*: *Fasti*, 2.294).

In addition to the 'Familiar Epistle to Mr. Julian' and 'On the Supposed Author', other satiric attacks on Scrope include Rochester's 'On Poet Ninny' (1677) and scornful lines on 'the purblind knight / Who squints more in his judgment than his sight' in Rochester's 'An Allusion to Horace' (1675). 'Advice to Apollo' (1677–8) lists Sir Carr, 'that Knight o' th' wither'd face', first among the unworthy pretenders to the bays, while the Mulgrave–Dryden 'Essay upon satire' (1679) treats Scrope as the quintessential fop. Scrope's short stature, his squint, his ugly, 'hard-favor'd' appearance, and his relentless, unsuccessful pursuit of the women of the court are repeated motifs in 'A Satyr' ('Of all the wonders since the world began'), 'On the Supposed Author', and 'A Familiar Epistle':

Still he loves on, yet still as sure to miss …
What fate unhappy Strephon does attend,
Never to get a mistress or a friend?
('Familiar Epistle', Lord, 390)

In August 1680 Scrope was reported to be 'in no good condition' at Tunbridge Wells and in considerable pain, having 'carried a physician of his own' with him (Cartwright, 289). He died in the parish of St Martin-in-the-Fields, Westminster, and was buried in the parish church in November 1680; at his death the baronetcy became extinct, and the family estate devolved on his only surviving brother, Robert Scrope esquire.

WARREN CHERNAIK

Sources D. Vieth, *Attribution in Restoration poetry* (1963) • 'The session of the poets (1666)', *Poems on affairs of state: Augustan satirical verse, 1660–1714*, ed. G. de F. Lord and others, 1 (1963), 327–37 • J. Wilson, *The court wits of the Restoration* (1948) • *The poems of John Wilmot, earl of Rochester*, ed. K. Walker (1984) • Wood, *Ath. Oxon.: Fasti* (1820) • *The manuscripts of his grace the duke of Rutland*, 4 vols., HMC, 24 (1888–1905), vol. 2, pp. 31, 37 • J. Cartwright, *Sacharissa* (1893) • *DNB* • *Ovid's epistles* (1680) • [J. Dryden], *Miscellany poems* (1684) • [A. Behn], *Miscellany* (1685) • *Poems on affairs of state … by the greatest wits of the age* (1697) • *State poems, continued* (1697) • G. Etherege, *Dramatic works*, ed. H. Brett-Smith (1927) • N. Lee, *Works* (1713) • Foster, *Alum. Oxon.*, *1500–1714* • Evelyn, *Diary* • B. Burke, *A genealogical history of the dormant, abeyant, forfeited and extinct peerages of the British empire*, new edn (1866) • *CSP dom.*, *1666–7* • A. R. Maddison, ed., *Lincolnshire pedigrees*, 4 vols., Harleian Society, 50–52, 55 (1902–6) • M. Thormählen, *Rochester: the poems in context* (1993) • *The letters of John Wilmot earl of Rochester*, ed. J. Treglown (1980) • N. Fisher, ed., *That second bottle: essays on John Wilmot, earl of Rochester* (2000)

Archives Bodl. Oxf., MSS • Yale U., MSS | BL, Add. MS 73540 • BL, Egerton MS 2623 • BL, Sloane MS 1458

Wealth at death see administrations, PRO, PROB 6/58, fol. 138*v*; PRO, PROB 6/55, fol. 175*v*; PRO, PROB 6/72

Scrope, Emanuel, earl of Sunderland (1584–1630), nobleman, was the only child and heir of Thomas Scrope, tenth Baron Scrope (*c*.1567–1609), and his wife, Philadelphia (*d*. 1627), lady-in-waiting to Queen Anne and daughter of Henry *Carey, first Baron Hunsdon, a cousin of Queen Elizabeth I. He was born probably in Hunsdon, Hertfordshire, on 1 August 1584, matriculated from Queen's College, Oxford, on 25 June 1596, and succeeded his father as eleventh baron, and as steward of the royal honour of Richmondshire, in 1609. The Scropes owned extensive estates in Wensleydale (whose value had been increased in the late sixteenth century by mineral exploitation) and at Langar in Nottinghamshire. Scrope was much more the courtier than his father had been—a participant in court masques and festivities and notorious as a gamester, burdened with large gambling debts. He had Catholic sympathies, however, and came to be regarded in the north as a patron of recusants. As a result, in January 1619, during one of the pro-Spanish phases of James I's foreign policy, he was appointed lord president of the council in the north, replacing Edmund, third Baron Sheffield, lately a persecutor of Catholics, probably at the prompting of the Spanish ambassador, Gondomar.

Scrope now headed an institution already discredited by the involvement of its late president, Sheffield, and secretary, Sir Arthur Ingram, in the hated alum monopoly, regarded as responsible for the depression in the West Riding clothing industry. His pro-recusant policies increased the council's unpopularity, particularly among the puritan clothiers, whose formidable leader was the late parliamentary oppositionist, Sir John Savile. The lord president tried to attract support by embarking on a reform of the council, particularly by a reduction in its fees, but could make little progress against the obstructionism of Secretary Ingram, who had the backing at court of the lord treasurer, Lionel Cranfield. Scrope relied almost exclusively on George Villiers, first duke of Buckingham, but consequently had to adapt himself to the tergiversations of the latter's policies. By 1627 Buckingham's pro-Catholic foreign policy had collapsed and he was bent on a French war; the need now was for the service of men with enough local influence to raise money for this purpose. Sir John Savile, Scrope's principal opponent, was therefore introduced into the council as its vice-president but effective head, Scrope's presidency retaining only a titular significance. He was compensated by being raised, on 19 June 1627, to the earldom of Sunderland. However, this arrangement too collapsed when the assassination of Buckingham in August 1628 led Charles I to call a parliament. In this Sir Thomas Wentworth, Savile's old Yorkshire enemy and rival, played a leading role in the House of Commons. There charges of corruption were successfully brought against the vice-president, and in November 1629 his resignation from the office was forced. Scrope followed suit in December, receiving £3000 for his office, and Sir Thomas Wentworth succeeded him as lord president.

Irrespective of his merits, the weakness in Scrope's position made success in his office unlikely. He was hampered by his Catholic sympathies, his inadequate local following, and his lack of independent political weight at court. He was already in poor health at the time of his resignation, and he did not long survive it; he died on 30 May 1630 and was buried at Langar on 6 June. He left no children from his marriage to Lady Elizabeth Manners (*d*. 1654), daughter of John, fourth earl of Rutland. The barony of Scrope devolved on the representative of his niece Mary but was not taken up; the earldom of Sunderland became extinct. Scrope had a liaison with his servant Martha Jeanes, with whom he had a natural son and three daughters. John, the son, became a fellow-commoner of Trinity College, Oxford, and died unmarried. Two of the daughters, Mary and Annabella, eventually inherited the Scrope estates. A third daughter, Elizabeth, married Thomas Savage, Earl Rivers.

MERVYN JAMES, *rev.*

Sources *CSP dom.*, *1619–31* • *Report on manuscripts in various collections*, 8 vols., HMC, 55 (1901–14), vol. 8 • *Report on the manuscripts of the late Reginald Rawdon Hastings*, 4 vols., HMC, 78 (1928–47), vol. 4 • G. Radcliffe, *The earl of Strafforde's letters and dispatches, with an essay towards his life*, ed. W. Knowler, 2 vols. (1739) • T. D. Whitaker, ed., *The life and original correspondence of Sir George Radcliffe* (1810) • R. R. Reid, *The king's council in the north* (1921) • GEC, *Peerage*

Scrope, Sir Geoffrey (*d.* 1340), justice and administrator, was probably born in the early 1280s, the son of Sir William Scrope (*b.* in or before 1259, *d.* in or before 1312), the earl of Richmond's bailiff in Richmondshire, and his wife, Constance, most likely the daughter of Thomas, son of Gille (or Gilde) of Newsham. William's administrative functions would have required at least a rudimentary legal knowledge, and perhaps this encouraged him to have his two sons trained as lawyers. The legal career of Geoffrey's elder brother, Sir Henry *Scrope (*b.* in or before 1268, *d.* 1336), was already established in 1292, when he was a pleader in the common bench at Westminster, and would culminate in his becoming chief justice of king's bench in 1317. It is likely that his brother's success, and the presence of the bench at York between 1298 and 1304, were of considerable advantage to Geoffrey, who is first referred to in a legal context in 1306, when he was appointed attorney to Thomas Meynill. He became a serjeant at Michaelmas 1309, and about Easter 1315 he was appointed one of the king's serjeants. From 1317 he was regularly summoned to councils and parliaments among the justices.

Although in 1313–14 he was among the lawyers retained by Thomas, earl of Lancaster, Scrope's political sympathies seem always to have been with the crown, as he showed at the London eyre of 1321, when his aggressive conduct of royal business, in his capacity of king's counsel, and above all his repeated challenges to the city's traditional liberties, earned him intense unpopularity. In the following year he took part in the proceedings which condemned Thomas of Lancaster and others of the king's enemies, and he was involved in the trial of Andrew Harclay, earl of Carlisle, convicted of treason on 3 March 1323. So closely did he become identified with the regime of Edward II and the Despensers that later in 1323 he was one of those whom the Mortimers planned to murder. Nevertheless he continued to prosper, being appointed a justice of the common pleas on 27 September 1323, and chief justice of king's bench on 21 March 1324. In between these promotions, probably on 2 October 1323, he was knighted. He was also nominated to numerous judicial commissions, but no less important, in the context of Scrope's career as a whole, was his work as a diplomat. In 1319 he took part in negotiations with the Scots at Berwick, and was one of the commissioners who on 30 May 1323 concluded a thirteen-year truce at Bishopthorpe. In the following year he took part in abortive efforts to make a lasting Anglo-Scottish peace.

When Edward II was overthrown in the autumn of 1326, Scrope went in danger of his life. But although the Londoners pillaged his city house, he showed a capacity for survival to match his instinct for power. On about 13 October, when Bishop Stapledon was murdered by the London mob, Scrope managed to switch his allegiance to Queen Isabella, thereby retaining his chief justiceship, and in January 1327 was a member of the delegation that received Edward II's abdication. In July–August 1327 he took part in the unsuccessful Stanhope Park campaign against the Scots, and was subsequently one of the commissioners who on 17 March 1328 negotiated the treaty of Edinburgh conceding Scottish independence. At the same time he took an important part in the new government's efforts to restore order after Edward II's fall. How far Scrope was an initiator of policy is uncertain, and some of the claims made for him in this respect may have been exaggerated. But as a chief justice he would certainly have been involved in the preparation of the important Statute of Northampton of May 1328, and in the consequent decision to act against lawlessness through a revival of the general eyre. Scrope himself presided at the 1329–30 Northamptonshire eyre, and at its opening made a speech explaining its programme, 'that the peace of the land might be preserved and kept and the said misdeeds and offences be redressed' (Sutherland, 1.5–6).

When Roger Mortimer was in his turn overthrown in the autumn of 1330, Scrope once more made a smooth transfer of his allegiances, becoming one of the young Edward III's principal counsellors. In 1332 he made a series of important speeches in successive parliaments, dealing with relations with Scotland and France as well as with law enforcement at home: much of what he said on the latter issue in the March parliament was included in the commissions sent to the newly appointed keepers of the counties immediately afterwards, and he was himself appointed to a commission to deal with disturbers of the peace in fourteen midland counties. He remained a chief justice, but was always liable to be distracted by his continued employment as a diplomat, especially in the early 1330s. In 1330 he was sent to treat with Philippe VI of France concerning a crusade to the Holy Land and disputes over the Agenais and the duchy of Aquitaine, and took part in negotiations at Paris in 1333–4. Perhaps he found so much travelling burdensome, for in 1334 the king granted that he should not be 'constrained or urged to go overseas against his will' (Stones, 8), but his diplomatic services continued to be in demand, and in 1338 he went to treat with Ludwig IV of Germany, and to negotiate with the French at Arras. In 1340 he took part in unsuccessful negotiations with the Scots for a final peace.

Scrope also had a reputation as a jouster and soldier, one which his last years suggest was well deserved. Having retired as chief justice at Easter 1338, he accompanied Edward III to Flanders later that year, and in 1339 took part in the stand-off with the French army at La Capelle on 23 October. Earlier that month a would-be mediator, Cardinal Bertrand de Montfavence, was terrorized into a state of collapse by Scrope, who gloatingly displayed to him the appalling effects of English devastation in the countryside of Picardy. Scrope returned to England, and probably assisted in the drafting of legislation in 1340 before rejoining the king in Flanders. With good reason did Edward III on 3 May grant him an annual pension of 200 marks, 'for willing and valuable services many times rendered' (Rymer, *Foedera*, 2/2.1123). To the end of his life Scrope was a partisan for the authority of the crown. His counsel was said to have been behind Edward III's dramatic return to England at the end of November 1340, to take action against Archbishop Stratford and other ministers whom the king believed had betrayed him, and when he died at Ghent, probably on 2 December, the archbishop's supporters saw his death as a providential deliverance. Scrope's body was brought back to England for burial in Coverham Abbey, Yorkshire.

Scrope ended his days a rich man—six ships were needed to carry his horses and retinue to Flanders in 1340. But the sources of his wealth are unclear. Although he received pensions from Westminster Abbey and Durham Priory, and probably others, it has none the less been estimated that his services to the crown and other patrons brought him only about £80 per annum. This excludes his private practice as a lawyer, which was probably considerable; at the London eyre of 1321 he acted for forty-two clients as well as the king, and won most of his cases. His landed inheritance is unlikely to have been substantial, but Scrope's political success certainly helped him to build up an estate. In the 1320s and later he received grants of forfeited lands; after the fall of Roger Mortimer, for instance, he was given or confirmed in manors in Kent and Yorkshire. He may also have exploited the economic difficulties created for his neighbours by Scottish raids, by advancing them money on the security of their property, and then foreclosing when they could not repay their debts. Most of his acquisitions were in Yorkshire, in the North and East Ridings, and in York itself. But he also acquired properties in the midlands and south, especially the Leicestershire manors of Great Bowden and Market Harborough. Although his descendants were later to be associated with Masham, Scrope's principal Yorkshire residence was at Clifton-on-Ure, which he was licensed to crenellate on 23 September 1317; he also resided at Burton Constable, obtained from Sir Roald Richmond before 1321, and imparked and crenellated in 1338.

Scrope made a number of grants to religious houses. He gave a messuage in York to Fountains Abbey in 1318, rights to fishing and wood and the advowson of the church in Wharram Percy to Haltemprice Abbey in 1327, and a further grant of moorland to Haltemprice in 1331. In 1329 he endowed a chantry at Patrick Brompton for the souls of himself and his wife; her name was Ivetta, and it is likely, though incapable of conclusive demonstration, that she was the daughter of William Roos of Ingmanthorpe, and that she predeceased her husband. They had five sons, of whom the eldest, Henry *Scrope (1312?–1392), became first Lord Scrope of Masham. Of their other sons, Geoffrey became a canon of Lincoln Cathedral, and William was active as a soldier in France, but little is recorded of Thomas and Stephen. Their daughters, Beatrice and Constance, married into the Luttrell family of Lincolnshire.

Brigette Vale

Sources B. Vale, 'The Scropes of Bolton and Masham, *c*.1300–*c*.1450: a study of a northern noble family', PhD diss., University of York, 1987 • E. L. G. Stones, 'Sir Geoffrey le Scrope (*c*.1285–1340), chief justice of the king's bench', *EngHR*, 69 (1954), 1–17 • GEC, *Peerage*, new edn, 11.554–61 • B. Vale, 'The profits of the law and the 'rise' of the Scropes: Henry Scrope (*d*. 1336) and Geoffrey Scrope (*d*. 1340), chief justices to Edward II and Edward III', *Profit, piety and the professions in later medieval England*, ed. M. Hicks (1990), 91–102 • *Chancery records* • H. M. Cam, ed., *The eyre of London, 14 Edward II, AD 1321*, 2 vols., SeldS, 85–6 (1968–9) • D. W. Sutherland, ed., *The eyre of Northamptonshire: 3–4 Edward III, AD 1329–1330*, 1, SeldS, 97 (1983) • D. Crook, 'The later eyres', *EngHR*, 97 (1982), 241–68 • N. Denholm-Young, *The country gentry in the fourteenth century* (1969) • A. Musson, *Public order and law enforcement: the local administration of criminal justice, 1294–1350* (1996) • H. G. Richardson and G. O. Sayles, 'The king's ministers in parliament, 1272–1377 [pts 2–3]', *EngHR*, 47 (1932), 194–203, 377–97 • J. R. Maddicott, *Thomas of Lancaster, 1307–1322: a study in the reign of Edward II* (1970) • J. Taylor, *English historical literature in the fourteenth century* (1987) • J. Sumption, *The Hundred Years War*, 1 (1990) • Rymer, *Foedera*, new edn, 2/2.1123

Scrope, George Poulett [*formerly* George Julius Thomson] (**1797–1876**), geologist and political economist, was born on 10 March 1797. Baptized George Julius Thomson, he was the second son of the Russia merchant John Thomson of Waverley Abbey, Wimbledon, and his wife, Charlotte, daughter of Dr John Jacob of Salisbury. He was educated at Harrow School, and in 1815 entered Pembroke College, Oxford. The following year, however, he migrated to St John's College, Cambridge, probably in search of more scientific studies. (It was at this time he replaced his second name Julius with Poulett, which his father had recently adopted from an earlier and aristocratic branch of his family.) He spent the winter of 1817–18 with his parents in Naples, where he explored Vesuvius and the surrounding volcanic region. This experience first aroused his lifelong fascination with volcanoes, and he returned to Italy in the next two years to extend his fieldwork. His scientific interests were fostered at Cambridge by Edward Daniel Clarke, the professor of mineralogy, who had visited several volcanic regions during his extensive travels, and by Adam Sedgwick, the then recently elected professor of geology.

On 14 April 1821 he married Emma Phipps Scrope (*d*. 1866), the only child and heir of William *Scrope of Castle Combe, Wiltshire. Shortly before, he formally adopted his bride's surname in place of his own, presumably as a part of the marriage settlement. For the rest of his life he styled himself consistently George Poulett Scrope, generally using his two adopted ancient surnames together.

Early geological researches Graduating BA in 1821, Scrope embarked on two years' geological fieldwork on the continent, financed by his now ample private wealth. He first spent six months exploring the extinct volcanoes of central France—particularly in Auvergne. He then travelled through Italy, and was in Naples to witness the great 1822 eruption of Vesuvius. The violence of the eruption made a deep impression on him and he extended his earlier studies of the area and also of other volcanic regions in Italy. On his way back to England he travelled through Germany, visiting the extinct volcanoes of the Eifel region. He returned to England in the autumn of 1823 with greater first-hand knowledge of volcanoes and volcanic regions than anyone then active in the Geological Society in London. The following year he was elected a fellow of that body; less than a year later he joined his contemporary Charles Lyell as one of its secretaries. In 1826 he was elected a fellow of the Royal Society.

George Poulett Scrope (1797–1876), by John Samuelson Templeton, pubd 1848 (after Eden Upton Eddis)

Scrope's first substantial published work in geology was his *Considerations on Volcanos* (1825), in which volcanic processes were treated as crucial evidence for a general causal model of the earth. Scrope adopted the hypothesis, then coming back into favour among geologists, that the earth had begun as a hot fluid body and had cooled gradually over vast spans of time. He argued that the intensity of tectonic movements of the earth's crust and of volcanic activity had declined progressively to their present levels. He held that present volcanoes, for example, were reliable guides to the past in qualitative terms, but quantitatively they might have been dwarfed by those in earlier periods of the earth's history. Like other geologists, Scrope also inferred that the slow cooling of the earth's surface could account for the fossil record of apparently tropical plants and animals in some of the earlier rock formations.

In making such inferences, Scrope, like many geologists on the continent, argued that 'actual' or 'modern causes' (processes directly observable in the present world) such as volcanoes should be used as far as possible to interpret the past history of the earth; but he also conceded that that history had included occasional events on a larger scale than any known from human observations or records. For example, like James Hall a decade earlier, Scrope suggested that a sudden elevation of a land mass or mountain range might have generated a series of huge tsunamis or tidal waves, analogous to those known in human history but on a far larger scale; and that they in turn could have produced the striking topographical and depositional features that William Buckland had recently defined as 'diluvial'. Scrope was opposed to Buckland's use of this 'geological deluge' to reinforce the historicity of the biblical flood, but he was far from denying the reality of catastrophic events, particularly in the more remote past. He criticized the use of 'catastrophes' and 'deluges' in geological explanation, but only when such putative events were not related to observable modern causes. His approach to these methodological issues was closely similar to that adopted by his friend Lyell a few years later.

Scrope's attempt to formulate a 'theory of the earth' was not well received by other geologists, among whom such high-level speculative theorizing was regarded either as an outmoded genre in the style of James Hutton, or as grossly premature. However, in 1827 Scrope published his *Geology of Central France*, based on his fieldwork there, explicitly to display some of the detailed evidence for his 'theory'. The accompanying album of panoramic landscapes, engraved from his own sketches, made vividly real to British armchair travellers a region that Nicholas Desmarest (1725–1815) had first made famous half a century earlier, and that other French naturalists had since described in detail. Scrope's text and images gave persuasive force to his argument, adopted from Desmarest, that over vast spans of time occasional volcanic activity had punctuated the continuous erosion of the valleys by the streams that still flow in them: the younger lavas flowed down the present valleys, but the older ones had been left high and dry by subsequent erosion, and now capped the surrounding hills in more or less fragmentary form.

However, Scrope strengthened Desmarest's theory by denying that there were two distinct 'epochs' of lava flows, ancient and modern. He plotted the longitudinal profiles of the lavas against an accurate scale of altitude, and claimed that they formed an unbroken continuum, from the most highly eroded remnants of basalt on the highest hilltops, down to the recent flows in the present valleys, many of them still connected to well-preserved cratered cones of loose volcanic ash. Scrope therefore argued that the occasional lavas formed a 'natural scale' on which the continuous process of erosion could be plotted: contrary to claims made by Buckland's Oxford colleague Charles Daubeny, there was no sign of any recent violent 'deluge' in Auvergne.

Scrope also attempted to calibrate his natural scale. He argued that even the most recent cones and lavas, which were as well preserved as the historically dated ones he had seen in Italy, must have been prehistoric, since human records back to Roman times contained no hint of any volcanic activity in central France. That suggested a rough calibration by which the still older eruptions would have to be of almost unimaginable antiquity. It made a convincing case for his claim that what was needed for more effective geological interpretation was simply 'Time! Time! Time!' (*Geology of Central France*, 165). That conclusion was far from novel, but Scrope's evidence for it was persuasively concrete; and his argument was promptly given much wider circulation, at least in Britain, when Lyell reviewed the book enthusiastically in the *Quarterly Review*.

Scrope's claim for the explanatory potential of a vast time-scale was expressed in terms of a vivid metaphor, which soon became a cliché among geologists: they needed, he argued, 'to make almost unlimited drafts upon antiquity' (*Geology of Central France*, 165). The metaphor made particular sense in relation to Scrope's anti-bullionist views on the banking system, as first expressed in public in his booklet *On Credit-Currency* (1830). Geological time was like the wholly paper-based currency that he advocated in place of the precious metals. Just as the supply of paper money could and should be kept level with the demand, so geologists could and should invoke as much time as was necessary to explain the observed effects.

Political views and activities Scrope had become increasingly concerned with economic and social affairs since his return to England in 1823. Settling at Castle Combe, which his father-in-law had vacated, Scrope's duties as a magistrate made him acutely aware of the social problems of rural poverty, and he became a forceful critic of the poor laws. At the same time, he was well aware of current economic issues: he was close to his younger brother Charles Poulett *Thomson (later Lord Sydenham), who worked in the family business before becoming an MP (and later president of the Board of Trade). In 1831 Scrope himself stood for two 'rotten' Wiltshire seats, urging the cause of reform as a bulwark against revolution. Defeated, he turned to the nearby manufacturing borough of Stroud in Gloucestershire. He was narrowly defeated there in the general election of 1832, but that result was overturned on grounds of malpractice, and Scrope was elected unopposed in 1833. He remained MP for Stroud until he resigned the seat in 1867.

Scrope spoke only rarely in parliament: 'a parliamentary reputation is like a woman's', he once said; 'it must be exposed as little as possible' (Sturges, 25, n. 26). He preferred to make his points in essays for the *Quarterly Review* and in brief pamphlets, the profusion of which earned him his nickname of Pamphlet Scrope. His earlier pamphlets exposed the iniquities of the poor laws in England; later, he vehemently criticized government and absentee landlords for the still worse problems of Irish poverty. On the local level he was, in the aristocratic manner, an enlightened landlord and a compassionate magistrate; on the national level, a vehement critic of the poor laws and of Malthusian doctrines. In his *Principles of Political Economy* (1833), his most substantial publication on such issues, he argued that the proper aim of the economist was to promote social welfare, using the generation of wealth as a means to that end. He advocated emigration to the colonies as the best solution to the problems of poverty and over-population; indeed he was criticized for treating emigration as a panacea for all social ills. Scrope's liberal and somewhat idiosyncratic views did not fit easily into any party mould, and unlike his brother he never held office.

Later geological interests Scrope's active political life soon withdrew him from the centre of British geology, but he wrote important essays for the *Quarterly Review*, on the work of Lyell (1830, 1835), Buckland (1836), and Roderick Murchison (1839). In these essays Scrope reinforced his earlier theoretical arguments, for example strongly approving Lyell's use of modern causes as a key to the geological past, but rejecting his scepticism about the broadly directional character of the earth's history. In 1856 Lyell asked for Scrope's help in his renewed attack on the theory of 'craters of elevation', by which some larger volcanic cones were attributed to sudden crustal upheaval rather than the slow accumulation of lava flows. This brought Scrope out of geological retirement: he read an important paper on the subject to the Geological Society (1856); he revisited central France in 1857 and 1858; he revised his book on that region (1858), though in more turgid prose and with much less impressive illustrations; and he rewrote his more theoretical book as *Volcanos* (1862). Translations made his work well known throughout Europe, and in 1867 he received the Wollaston medal, the Geological Society's highest award.

In addition to his geology and his politics, Scrope was also active in local history: he published a fine history of Castle Combe (1852), and in 1853 he became the first president of the Wiltshire Archaeological and Natural History Society, writing many papers for its magazine.

Personal life and later years Scrope's wife had been disabled by a riding accident soon after their marriage; there were no children. However, for many years he kept the actress Mrs Grey in grand style in London, and about 1838 they had a son, known as Arthur Hamilton. Scrope sent him to Eton College and Christ Church, Oxford, and later purchased a commission for him; in 1856 (after the death of Scrope's father-in-law) he and his wife formally adopted Hamilton. After his wife died in 1866, Scrope sold Castle Combe, moved to Fairlawn in Cobham, Surrey, and in 1867 resigned his parliamentary seat. The same year he married the 26-year-old Margaret Elizabeth Savage, who survived him. Scrope died at home on 19 January 1876 and was buried at Stoke d'Abernon, Surrey. He left his papers to his nephew Hugh Hammersley, but they were later apparently lost or destroyed. MARTIN RUDWICK

Sources G. P. Scrope, *Memoir on the geology of central France*, 2 vols. (1827) [2nd edn, 1858] • P. Sturges, *A bibliography of George Poulett Scrope: geologist, economist, and local historian* (1984) [incl. biography] • G. P. Scrope, *Considerations on volcanos* (1825); 2nd edn as *Volcanos* (1862) • G. P. Scrope, *Principles of political economy* (1833) • G. P. Scrope, *On credit-currency and its superiority to coin* (1830) • [G. P. Scrope], review, *QR*, 43 (1830), 411–69 • [G. P. Scrope], review, *QR*, 53 (1835), 406–48 • [G. P. Scrope], review, *QR*, 56 (1836), 31–64 • [G. P. Scrope], review, *QR*, 64 (1839), 102–20 • G. P. Scrope, 'On the formation of craters and the nature of the liquidity of lavas', *Quarterly Journal of the Geological Society*, 12 (1856), 326–50 • [G. P. Scrope], 'Dr Chalmers on political economy', *Westminster Review*, 17 (1832), 1–33 • G. P. Scrope, *History of the ancient manor and barony of Castle Combe* (1852) • M. J. S. Rudwick, 'Poulett Scrope on the volcanos of Auvergne: Lyellian time and political economy', *British Journal for the History of Science*, 7 (1974), 205–42 • R. Opie, 'A neglected English economist: George Poulett Scrope', *Quarterly Journal of Economics*, 44 (1929), 101–37 • S. Rashid, 'Political economy and geology in the early nineteenth century: similarities and contrasts', *History of Political Economy*, 13 (1981), 726–44

Archives BL, genealogical papers, Add. MSS 28205–28206 | American Philosophical Society, Philadelphia, Lyell papers • Bodl. Oxf., corresp. with Sir Thomas Phillipps • GS Lond., letters to Sir Archibald Geikie • GS Lond., letters to Sir R. I. Murchison

Likenesses J. S. Templeton, lithograph, pubd 1848 (after E. U. Eddis), BM [*see illus.*] • portrait, repro. in A. Geikie, *Life of Sir Roderick I. Murchison*, 2 (1875), 108

Wealth at death approx. £180,000: Sturges, *A bibliography*

Scrope, Sir Henry (*b*. in or before **1268**, *d*. **1336**), justice, was the eldest son of Sir William Scrope (*b*. in or before 1259, *d*. in or before 1312) of Bolton in Wensleydale, in the North Riding of Yorkshire; his younger brother, Sir Geoffrey *Scrope, was also to become a noted justice and royal servant. The two men appear to have been on close terms throughout their lives, with Geoffrey's early advancement perhaps helped by his elder brother's support. Their mother, Constance, was almost certainly the daughter of Thomas, son of Gille (or Gilde) of Newsham. Their father, a man of small estate who was bailiff of Richmondshire in 1294, and was knighted at the battle of Falkirk in 1298, came of a family who had established themselves in the East Riding and in North Lincolnshire and whose name is said to derive from a nickname of old Norse origin meaning 'crab': a crab was the family crest.

Henry Scrope was put to study the law by his parents, and was a countor of the bench (or advocate) not later than 1292. In 1306, 1307, and 1308 he received various judicial commissions, and on 27 November 1308 he was appointed a justice of the common pleas. He may have been helped in his legal career by his friendship with Henry de Lacy, earl of Lincoln: he worked for the earl in the 1290s, acted as his executor in 1311, and in 1334 requested prayers for his soul. The earl allowed Scrope to augment his arms with the Lacy armorial bearing of a lion rampant.

Scrope became a supporter of Edward II, and in May 1311 was attendant upon Gilbert de Clare, earl of Gloucester, who was Edward's lieutenant in England during the king's absence in Scotland. In September that year he withdrew from parliament, in response to restraints placed upon the king by the magnates, but was peremptorily ordered by Edward to return. In March 1312 Edward commissioned Scrope to treat with a provincial council of lay and ecclesiastical magnates about those parts of the ordinances that were hurtful or prejudicial to the king. In March 1314 Edward entrusted him with a mission to Wales, to investigate the bitter dispute between Gruffudd de la Pole and John Charlton over the lordship of Powys, and on 15 June 1317, having shaken off the control of the magnates, promoted him to be chief justice of king's bench. It was during Scrope's tenure of this office, in Hilary term 1319, that matters affecting the interests of the crown were first enrolled on separate membranes of the king's bench rolls, forming what were thereafter known as their *Rex* sections. In 1322 Scrope received a share of the estates forfeited by supporters of Thomas, earl of Lancaster (from whom in 1318–19 he had been in receipt of robes), to which early in 1323 Edward added the Swaledale lands of Andrew Harclay. But in July that year, for some unexplained reason (possibly connected with earlier oyer and terminer proceedings), he was replaced as chief justice. However, on 10 September he was appointed justice (or keeper) of the forests north of Trent, he received summonses with the justices to the parliaments intended to be held in 1324 and 1325, and in March 1326 he was trying Yorkshire offenders by special commission.

On 5 February 1327, following Edward III's accession, Scrope was restored to judicial office as 'second justice' (the title was new) of the common pleas, his old post being occupied by his brother; it was stated by the crown that this was because Henry Scrope was no longer equal to such labours as before, 'and for no other reason' (*CPR, 1327–30*, 25). From 28 October 1329 to 19 December 1330 he took the place of his brother, who was then abroad, as chief justice of king's bench. On the latter date he was made chief baron of the exchequer, a post he held until his death, though momentarily in November transferred to be chief justice of the common pleas—perhaps by clerical error, for within twenty-four hours he received a new patent restoring him to his old place. Henry Scrope had been knighted by February 1311, and, like his brother, he also acted as a knight-banneret. He died on 7 September 1336, and was buried in the Premonstratensian abbey of St Agatha at Easby, close to Richmond, the patronage of which, with Burton Constable and other lands, he had purchased in 1333 from the descendant of its founder.

Sir Henry Scrope built up considerable estates, including twenty-one manors, principally in Yorkshire, but also in Middlesex, Bedfordshire, Hertfordshire, and Rutland. With his wife, Margaret, perhaps the daughter of either Lord Ros or Lord Fitzwalter, he had three sons, all under age at his death. William, born about 1320, distinguished himself in the French and Scottish wars, and died on 17 November 1344, of a wound received two years earlier at the battle of Morlaix in Brittany. He left no issue, and his next brother, Stephen, having predeceased him, the estates passed to Richard *Scrope, first Lord Scrope of Bolton and chancellor of England. Sir Henry's widow married Sir Hugh Mortimer of Chelmarsh, Shropshire, and lived until 1357. JAMES TAIT, *rev.* NIGEL RAMSAY

Sources N. H. Nicolas, ed., *The Scrope and Grosvenor controversy*, 2 vols. (privately printed, London, 1832) • GEC, *Peerage* • Baker, *Serjeants*, 146, 536 • *CIPM*, 8, no. 43 • G. O. Sayles, ed., *Select cases in the court of king's bench*, 7 vols., SeldS, 55, 57–8, 74, 76, 82, 88 (1936–71), vol. 4, pp. lix–lxi, 110 • N. Neilson, 'The forests', *The English government at work, 1327–1336*, ed. J. F. Willard and W. A. Morris, 1 (1940), 394–467, esp. 403 • *Chancery records* • E. L. G. Stones, 'Sir Geoffrey le Scrope (*c*.1285–1340)', PhD diss., U. Glas., 1950 • J. R. Maddicott, *Thomas of Lancaster, 1307–1322: a study in the reign of Edward II* (1970) • H. M. Colvin, *The white canons in England* (1951)

Wealth at death see *CIPM*

Scrope, Henry, first Baron Scrope of Masham (**1312?–1392**), soldier and administrator, was born on 29 September, probably in 1312 (the inquisitions taken after his father's death give his age variously, between twenty-five and twenty-eight 'and more'). He was the eldest son of Geoffrey *Scrope and his first wife, Ivetta, most likely the daughter of William Roos. He was first armed in the

Scottish campaign of 1333; he was knighted before Berwick, and fought at Halidon Hill. He served in Scotland again in 1335, and in 1340 took part in the sea battle at Sluys. His father died in that year, and he obtained livery of his inheritance in March 1341. In 1342 he was in Brittany, and was present at the sieges of Vannes and Morlaix. During the justiciarship of Ralph Ufford (1344–6) he saw service in Ireland. He was in Flanders, with Edward III in 1345, and in 1346 (according to depositions at the *Scrope* v. *Grosvenor* trial in 1386) he fought as a banneret both at Crécy (26 August) and at Nevilles Cross (17 October). In 1347 he was at the siege of Calais; and in 1350 he fought in the great sea battle off Winchelsea, known as Espagnols-sur-mer.

In November 1350 Henry Scrope was for the first time summoned individually to parliament as Lord Scrope (the designation 'of Masham' appears after 1371, when his cousin Richard *Scrope of Bolton was summoned, to distinguish the branches of the family). After this his position became more prominent. In 1354 he was one of the ambassadors to Innocent VI seeking to arbitrate between England and France. He served on Edward III's Picard expedition in 1355, and at the siege of Berwick in 1357; and in August 1357 he was a member of the commission to treat with the Scots for the liberation of David II, king of Scots, and for a truce. In 1359 he served under John of Gaunt in the great *chevauchée* toward Rheims, and in 1360 he was appointed to the important post of warden of Calais and Guînes, which he seems to have held, officially, until 1370. He also served on a number of important diplomatic missions, including those which treated (unsuccessfully) for a marriage between Edmund of Langley, Edward III's fifth son, and Margaret, daughter of the count of Flanders (1362 and 1364). In 1369 he served, at the reopening of the war, under John of Gaunt in France; and in 1370–71 he was for a year warden of the western march towards Scotland. From January to November 1371 he was also steward of the king's household. During the Good Parliament of 1376 he was one of the peers on the committee that the Commons requested to advise and 'intercommune' with them (*RotP*, 2.322). In October 1377 he was named in parliament as a member of the first 'continual' council of Richard II's minority. He served at this period on a number of significant commissions in Yorkshire and Northumberland, the last important ones being those to preserve the peace and put down rebels in Yorkshire (14 December 1381 and 8 March 1382). His later years seem to have been spent in retirement on his estates; although Gilbert Talbot in his deposition in *Scrope* v. *Grosvenor* alleged that he served in Scotland in 1383 and 1385, this is unconfirmed, and probably arises from a confusion with his cousin Richard Scrope. He died on 31 July 1392.

Henry Scrope enjoyed a high reputation as a warrior, as a tourneyer, and later as a councillor and administrator. In his early years his principal connection seems to have been with William de Bohun, earl of Northampton, in whose retinue he served in 1333, 1340, 1342, 1346, 1347, and 1355. Later his most important connection seems to have been with John of Gaunt, under whom he served in 1359 and 1369, though he was less intimately associated with him than his contemporary and cousin Richard Scrope of Bolton. As arms he bore the famous family coat, azure a bend or, with a label of three points argent for a difference. He was married twice, first to Agnes and second to Joan; the surnames in both cases are uncertain. With Joan he had five sons; Geoffrey, who was killed on crusade in Prussia (1362); William, who fought against the Turks at Satalia (1361) and died in the East; Stephen, who likewise went on crusade and who ultimately succeeded him; Richard *Scrope, who rose to be archbishop of York and was executed in 1405; and John. He had two daughters, Joan, who married Henry, Lord Fitzhugh, and Isabel, who married Sir Robert *Plumpton (1341–1407) of Plumpton [*see under* Plumpton family (*per.* *c.*1165–*c.*1550)].

M. H. Keen

Sources N. H. Nicolas, ed., *The Scrope and Grosvenor controversy*, 2 vols. (privately printed, London, 1832) • GEC, *Peerage* • Rymer, *Foedera*, vols. 5–6 • *RotP*, vols. 2–3 • *CPR*, *1361–7*; *1381–5* • *Calendar of the fine rolls*, PRO, 5 (1915) • C. D. Ross, 'The Yorkshire baronage, 1399–1435', DPhil diss., U. Oxf., 1950, 177, 447 • *CIPM*, 8, no. 281 • [J. Raine], ed., *Testamenta Eboracensia*, 3, SurtS, 45 (1865), 32 • B. P. Vale, 'The Scrope of Bolton and of Masham, *c.* 1300 - *c.* 1450', DPhil diss., University of York, 1988 • W. P. Baildon, ed., *Feet of fines for the county of York, from 1327 to 1347, 1–20 Edward III*, 1, Yorkshire Archaeological Society, 42 (1910), 170 (no. 136)

Wealth at death £637—value of his estates p.a. in 1406 • £754—value of his estates p.a. in 1413

Scrope, Henry, third Baron Scrope of Masham (*c.*1376–1415), soldier and administrator, was the eldest son of Stephen, second Baron Scrope of Masham (*d.* 1406), and Margery, widow of John, Lord Huntingfield. Little is known of his career before the accession of Henry IV. During his youth he gained some military experience overseas, receiving payment of £20 from Richard II in 1390 for his expenses in serving in Barbary. In August 1397 he was in receipt of an annuity of £40 from Richard II, an award immediately continued by Henry IV following the deposition of Richard II. The transition to the new regime was a smooth one for Scrope, who may have sympathized with the opponents of Richard II, since in his will of 1415 he asked that masses be said for the soul of Thomas, duke of Gloucester (*d.* 1397), and bequeathed to the bishop of Winchester a small breviary given to Scrope by the duke.

Scrope's commitment to the new regime was obvious by 1403, when he was styled 'king's knight' and went on active military service in Wales. Given custody of Laugharne Castle in Carmarthenshire, he helped to defeat the rebels at the battle of Shrewsbury in 1403, and received a share of their forfeited possessions. He was still serving in Wales in 1406, when he came into his inheritance on the death of his father, while from 1408 he was employed on diplomatic service to the crown. In that year Scrope accompanied the king's daughter Philippa to Denmark for her marriage, and in 1409 he travelled to Paris for negotiations with French ambassadors. He was made knight of the Garter in 1410.

In January 1410 Scrope was appointed treasurer of England, an office he held until December 1411. Since this office was normally held by individuals with substantial personal means, the appointment is an indicator of Scrope's political reliability and of his wealth, a wealth that enabled him to make large loans to the crown. Scrope's political standing is shown by his being granted the towns of Hampstead and Hendon in July 1411 for the lodging of his men, servants, and horses during his attendance at parliament and at the king's council, a grant confirmed on 23 May 1413 by Henry V. The accession of Henry V made no obvious alteration to Scrope's position. In 1413 he was sent on diplomatic missions to Paris, Leulinghem, and Calais, and in 1414 he was involved in negotiating the crucial alliance with the Burgundians. In February 1415 he attended the council meeting at which the arrangements for Henry V's forthcoming expedition to France were discussed, though he absented himself from the council meeting of 27 May 1415 for no apparent reason.

Henry Scrope's career in royal service ended unexpectedly on 6 August 1415 when he was executed for high treason in Southampton on the eve of Henry V's Agincourt campaign. His head was dispatched to York and displayed on Micklegate Bar, a particular humiliation since the family held property on Micklegate. Scrope's involvement in the 'Southampton plot' has never been fully explained. There were no obvious signs of disaffection towards Henry V, and no evidence that the king was neglecting him. Earlier in 1415 Scrope had made an indenture to serve with the king in France, and in his will he bequeathed to the king an image of the Virgin and asked him to be a good lord to his mother, his wife, and his heir. Scrope's implication in the plot is most likely to have been the result of his close family and financial ties with the other plotters, *Richard, earl of Cambridge, Edmund (V) *Mortimer, earl of March, and Sir Thomas Grey. Once the plot was discovered he claimed that he had intended to reveal it, but had not done so by the time the earl of March himself betrayed the conspirators to the king. He may, however, have felt that his prospects might improve if the younger and more easily influenced earl of March were on the throne.

Scrope had made a will before his anticipated departure for France which is revealing both in its religious sentiments and as evidence of his wealth. The austere tone of its preamble was probably due less to Lollard sympathies, for which there is no evidence, than to the serious nature of his religious commitments. As well as works by the Yorkshire mystic Richard Rolle—the *Incendium amoris* and *Judice me Deus*—he owned copies of the *Revelations of St Bridget*, the *Prick of Conscience*, and a primer with the matins of the Blessed Virgin Mary in English. Ownership of such books placed Scrope in the van of contemporary tastes. He was extremely generous in his gifts to religious houses, and especially to hermits and anchorites. His bequests to St Bridlington Priory may have been partly a family tradition, but are likely to have been stimulated by the new cult of St John of Bridlington (*d.* 1379), who had been canonized in 1401 largely through the efforts of Scrope's uncle Archbishop Richard Scrope (*d.* 1405). Scrope himself had anticipated burial in an alabaster tomb in York Minster, where members of his family were afterwards buried.

Precise estimates of Scrope's wealth are difficult to make, but it is revealing that he should have tried to settle £2000 on his second wife, Joan, in lieu of her claim on his estate, while in 1413 he claimed to have been robbed of goods to the value of £5000. In his will he made numerous cash gifts to religious houses, relatives, and members of his household, while the inventory of his goods enumerates hundreds of ecclesiastical vestments.

Henry Scrope married twice, first, by 1399, Philippa Brian (*d.* 1406), and second, by July 1411, Joan (*d.* 1434), the widow successively of Edmund, duke of York (*d.* 1402), and William, Lord Willoughby (*d.* 1409). There were no children of either marriage, and Scrope's heir was the third of his four brothers, John (*d.* 1455), who had succeeded to the barony by 1426. Nevertheless, Scrope's execution in 1415 effectively destroyed the economic and territorial power base of his family. His estates were forfeit to the crown, and were rapidly granted to Henry V's more loyal supporters. The North Riding estates were granted to Lord Fitzhugh, but there was some doubt as to whether they had been entailed or not, and it was on this basis that John Scrope commenced a lengthy lawsuit for their recovery in 1424. Although the sentence of forfeiture for treason was never reversed, John Scrope finally obtained the permanent recovery of the lands in 1442, when he paid William Fitzhugh £1000 in return for them. BRIGETTE VALE

Sources *Chancery records* • PRO, E 403/E 404 • Rymer, *Foedera*, 1st edn, vol. 4 • C. L. Kingsford, 'Two forfeitures in the year of Agincourt', *Archaeologia*, 70 (1920), 71–100 • T. B. Pugh, 'The Southampton plot of 1415', *Kings and nobles in the later middle ages*, ed. R. A. Griffiths and J. Sherborne (1986) • *Report of the Deputy Keeper of the Public Records*, 43 (1882), appx 1 • B. P. Vale, 'The Scropes of Bolton and of Masham, c.1300–c.1450', PhD diss., University of York, 1987 • *CPR, 1413–16*, 328, 409 • *CClR, 1396–9*, 77, 376 • *Calendar of the fine rolls*, PRO, 13 (1933), 79, 211 • Inquisition post mortem of father Stephen Scrope

Wealth at death approx. £6000: Rymer, *Foedera* 4.131

Scrope, Henry, ninth Baron Scrope of Bolton (**1533/4–1592**), soldier, was the second, but eldest surviving, son of John Scrope, eighth Baron Scrope (*d.* 1549), and Lady Katherine Clifford (*d.* 1598), eldest daughter of Henry *Clifford, first earl of Cumberland. His father took part in the Pilgrimage of Grace, but in 1548 was serving in Protector Somerset's army in Scotland in command of 200 foot. His son may have accompanied the expedition, but there is no other evidence of early military service. He married, first, Mary North (*d.* 1558), daughter of Edward *North, first Baron North, with whom he had a daughter Mary, who herself married William Bowes of Streatlam, near Barnard Castle. His second wife, whom he married before 10 September 1565, was Lady Margaret Howard (*d.* 1591), daughter of the poet Henry *Howard, styled earl of Surrey. They had two sons, Thomas and Henry.

The ninth baron was summoned to parliament from 1555 to 1589. In 1556 he was instructed to assist the president of the council of the north, the earl of Shrewsbury. In March 1560 he became marshal of the army sent by Elizabeth to assist the anti-regent Scots in the siege of Leith.

The English intervention resulted in the French evacuation of Scotland by the treaty of Leith (6 July), leaving the field open for the triumph of the Scottish protestants. By 20 January 1561 Scrope had been appointed to the council of the north, and remained a member until his death. In 1562 he became captain of Carlisle Castle (salary of £221 per annum), where he conducted building work, and warden of the west marches (salary of £424 annually), holding these positions until his death. That he occasionally attended court is suggested by his presence at Shane O'Neill's submission to the queen on 6 January 1562.

In September 1563 Scrope and other English commissioners negotiated a border treaty with the Scots. As warden, he rejected the Scottish offer of Hermitage Castle in exchange for an English alliance in 1564. In October 1565 he provided sanctuary to James Stewart, earl of Moray, following his defeat by his half-sister Mary, queen of Scots, in the chaseabout raid. In 1568, when news of Mary's arrival in Carlisle reached London, the privy council ordered Scrope and Sir Francis Knollys north to take charge of the charming refugee. The baron spent 20 marks weekly on his foreign guest. On 15 June he accompanied her outside Carlisle Castle to attend a football match. However, the proximity of Carlisle to Scotland, and the constant flocking of English Catholic nobles and gentry to the exiled queen, necessitated a move to Scrope's castle at Bolton in Wensleydale, Yorkshire, on 13 July. Lady Scrope conveyed messages from her brother the duke of Norfolk, encouraging Mary and probably making the first suggestion of a match between the queen and Norfolk. Her husband, however, warned London in November about the plans by Lord John Hamilton, commendator of Arbroath Abbey, to rescue the queen. Suspicious of his wife's communications with Mary, he moved Lady Scrope to a house 2 miles away from Bolton. Worries about the short distance (60 miles in a straight route) to Scotland and the prevalence of Catholicism among the local gentry led to Mary's move further south to Tutbury on 26 February 1569, allowing Scrope to return to his duties to the border.

While Scrope attended a hawking party hosted by the duke of Norfolk at Tattershall in June 1569, his loyalty to Queen Elizabeth was unquestioned. When the earls of Northumberland and Westmorland rebelled later that year, he forwarded Westmorland's appeal to his sister-in-law Lady Scrope to Cecil. He took active measures to repress the rebellion, but failed to prevent the earls' escape to Scotland. He preserved order in Cumberland during Leonard Dacre's uprising in February 1570, and in March he had a commission to assess treason fines against the supporters of the northern earls. In April he received a reinforcement of 500 foot and 100 horse with which to raid the defeated Dacre's Scottish allies. Although he burnt Ecclefechan and several villages in Eskdale and Annandale, Scrope's forces met significant Scottish resistance and wreaked less havoc than in the middle and east marches. Nevertheless, Scottish raiding ceased for a time as a result of the incursion.

Scrope maintained good relations with his Scottish counterparts (lords Maxwell and Herries and the earl of Angus) between 1573 and 1579; such partnerships were essential for maintaining good order in the borders. By February 1581, however, the situation had deteriorated and he requested a reinforcement of 100 foot and 100 horse. That June he gave refuge to followers (including Angus) of the recently deposed regent Morton in Carlisle. In company with the warden of the middle march he invaded Liddesdale in November. By July 1582 Scrope was refusing to meet the Scottish middle warden on account of his failure to redress the slaughters committed in Bewcastle Dale and Gillsland by Liddesdale Scots, although he remained willing to meet the western warden. The breakdown in order led him to suggest that the government provide 450 men to defend the borders, action which would force all the raids north. In 1585 he served as a commissioner inquiring into the murder of Francis, Lord Russell. The lack of co-operation in Scrope's area continued until March 1586 when James VI allowed him to raid north against Scottish outlaws. However, in August he complained to the privy council about the failure of the Scottish warden Lord Maxwell to provide justice against the Grahams of Esk. When an English party under Scrope's orders captured three Grahams, Maxwell's brother attacked them. Meanwhile the queen had nominated Scrope for the Garter, and he was installed by proxy on 15 April 1585. By October 1590 he had established good relations with Sir John Carmichael, Scottish west warden. A year later he reiterated his complaints about the constantly unruly Liddesdale men; the Scottish middle march warden Sir Robert Kerr failed to subdue them, and the grievance remained unresolved.

Scrope died in Carlisle on 13 June 1592 and was buried in the cathedral there on 22 August. Queen Elizabeth commented, 'we have great cause to be sorry in respect of the honourable service he has long time done us in that office' (*CSP dom., addenda, 1580–1625*, 332). George MacDonald Fraser considered him 'one of the best Wardens in Border history' (Fraser, 248). He was succeeded as tenth baron by his son Thomas (*d.* 1609). Thomas's son Emmanuel Scrope became earl of Sunderland on 19 June 1627 and died on 30 May 1630, the last of his line. EDWARD M. FURGOL

Sources GEC, *Peerage*, new edn, 11.548–9 • *CSP dom., addenda, 1580–1625* • *CSP Scot.* • G. M. Fraser, *The steel bonnets: the story of the Anglo-Scottish border reivers* (1971) • G. R. Hewitt, *Scotland under Morton, 1572–80* (1982) • *The Warrender papers*, ed. A. I. Cameron, 1, Scottish History Society, 3rd ser., 18 (1931) • J. A. Froude, *The reign of Elizabeth*, 5 vols. (1911) • J. Bain, ed., *The border papers: calendar of letters and papers relating to the affairs of the borders of England and Scotland*, 2 vols. (1894–6) • M. R. McCarthy, H. R. T. Summerson, and R. G. Annis, *Carlisle Castle: a survey and documentary history* (1990), 177–87

Archives BL, corresp. and papers, Cotton MSS

Likenesses oils; at Bolton Hall, Yorkshire, in 1897

Scrope, John, fifth Baron Scrope of Bolton (1437/8–1498), soldier, was the eldest of the three sons of Henry, fourth Baron Scrope (1418–1459), and Elizabeth (*d.* in or after 1498), daughter of his kinsman, John, fourth Baron Scrope of Masham, and Elizabeth, daughter of Sir Thomas Chaworth of Wiverton, Nottinghamshire. He was born on 22 July 1437 or 1438. He was first summoned to parliament from July 1460, the year following his father's death, and regularly thereafter, and was knighted at about the same time. Scrope was a supporter of the earl of Salisbury from the very early 1450s, supported his son the earl of Warwick at the battle of Northampton in 1460, and fought for Edward IV at Towton in March 1461, where he was seriously hurt. He then took part in the reduction of the northern Lancastrian strongholds. In 1462–3 he was admitted, with his first wife, Joan, to the Guild of Corpus Christi in York. He was made knight of the Garter before April 1463, captain of Newcastle from December 1463, and was probably at the battle of Hexham in May 1464. He was regularly on the commission of the peace for Cambridgeshire (in which county he held lands) from 1461 until 1484 and frequently on that for the North Riding of Yorkshire.

However, by March 1469 Scrope was supporting the earl of Warwick and was fomenting a rising in Richmondshire on Warwick's behalf. On the collapse of this he submitted to Edward IV and was pardoned, although he again supported Warwick during the short Lancastrian restoration, helping to raise troops in the eastern counties. He seems not to have fought at the battles of Barnet or Tewkesbury though, and to have been quickly forgiven by Edward because on 11 May 1471, that is only a week after Tewkesbury, he was reappointed to the commission of the peace for Cambridge. On 3 July 1471 he was one of those who swore allegiance to Edward, son of Edward IV. In 1474 he was one of the commissioners to negotiate a marriage between the king's youngest daughter, Cecily, with James, son and heir of James III, king of Scots, and stood proxy for her at the betrothal in October of that year. In 1475 he accompanied the king to France with 20 men-at-arms and 200 archers, although before he went he was ordered in May to abstain from using the arms of the Isle of Man for the duration of the expedition, without prejudice to his right to use them, if any. As heir of the attainted William Scrope, earl of Wiltshire, his great-great-uncle, he claimed these arms, which were used by Thomas, Lord Stanley, as the current Lord of Man.

In 1475–6 Scrope went on a mission to Milan and Rome with Earl Rivers. He continued to be appointed to various commissions, for example as commissioner of oyer and terminer in Middlesex in 1477 and of array in the North Riding of Yorkshire in 1480. He was one of the commanders in the army of Richard, duke of Gloucester, invading Scotland in July 1482, leading the van with the earl of Northumberland, and was one of the commissioners who treated with the ambassadors of Alexander, duke of Albany, brother of James III of Scots, in London in February 1483.

Scrope had been a councillor of Richard of Gloucester since at least 1475, and continued in that role after the duke's accession as Richard III. He attended the coronation on 6 July 1483, receiving velvet as a special gift from the king for the queen's coronation and on 24 July was made chamberlain of the duchy of Lancaster for life. In November 1483 he was appointed to a commission of array to resist the rebels and a commission to arrest them. Although he had no previous connection with the area, in December 1484 he was granted a number of manors in the western counties and made constable of Exeter Castle for life, thus becoming one of the northern supporters planted by Richard III in parts of the south to help control them. He was also responsible for the defence of the western coast. He was regularly appointed to the commissions of the peace in Devon and Cornwall in Richard's reign as well as to those of Cambridgeshire and the North Riding of Yorkshire as he had been in previous years, although not after the death of Richard III. He was at sea in March 1484 for the defence of the realm, but was almost certainly with Richard at the battle of Bosworth, although he was not attainted afterwards and he was allowed to attend the Garter banquet in York in April 1486. Scrope supported Lambert Simnel in June 1487, attacking York with his cousin Thomas, Lord Scrope of Masham. After this he was imprisoned in Windsor Castle, and received a pardon in February 1488, although even by July 1489 he was still not allowed to go further north than the River Trent. By 1492 however Scrope was apparently completely rehabilitated and in May 1492 he was retained to go abroad with Henry VII in his invasion of France, and was appointed to the commission of the peace in Norfolk from 1494 until he died. In August 1497 he assisted the earl of Surrey in raising the siege by the Scots of Norham Castle.

Scrope married three times. His first wife, whom he married after 22 November 1447, was Joan, daughter of William, fourth Lord Fitzhugh (*d.* 1452), and Margery, daughter of William, Lord Willoughby. With her he had one child, his heir, Henry. She died before 1470 and he married second, before 10 December 1471, Elizabeth, daughter of Oliver St John and Margaret Beauchamp, daughter and heir of Sir John Beauchamp of Bletsoe, and widow of William, fifth Baron Zouche. She was living in 1489 and died before 3 July 1494. They had one child, Mary, who married Sir William *Conyers (1467/8–1524) of Hornby [*see under* Conyers family]. Scrope married third, after 9 February 1491, Anne, daughter and heir of Sir Robert Harling of East Harling, Norfolk, and Jane, daughter and heir of Edmund Gunville, and widow of Sir William Chamberlaine and Sir Robert Wingfield. They had no children and Scrope died, possibly at East Harling, on 17 August 1498. In his will, dated 3 July 1494 and 8 August 1498 (proved on 5 November 1498 at York), he asked to be buried in St Agatha's Abbey, Easby (as had several of his ancestors), or in the Dominican priory at Thetford, depending on where he died. He left a printed Bible and a volume of chronicles (also printed) to St Agatha's. As his executor he named his wife, who survived him for only a short time, dying on 18 September 1498.

P. W. Hammond

Sources GEC, *Peerage* • [J. Raine], ed., *Testamenta Eboracensia*, 4, SurtS, 53 (1869), 94–7 • *CPR, 1461–1509* • R. Horrox, *Richard III, a study of service*, Cambridge Studies in Medieval Life and Thought, 4th ser., 11 (1989) • A. J. Pollard, *North-eastern England during the Wars of the Roses: lay society, war and politics, 1450–1500* (1990) • *Recueil des croniques … par Jehan de Waurin*, ed. W. Hardy and E. L. C. P. Hardy, 5 vols., Rolls Series, 39 (1864–91), vol. 5 • R. Somerville, *History of the duchy of Lancaster, 1265–1603* (1953) • M. J. Bennett, *The battle of Bosworth* (1985) • A. F. Sutton and P. W. Hammond, eds., *The coronation* *of Richard III: the extant documents* (1983) • inquisition post mortem, Henry VII, vol. 2

Scrope, John (*c.*1662–1752), judge and politician, was the only son of Thomas Scrope (*d.* 1704), a merchant of Small Street, Bristol, and his wife, Mary, daughter of Thomas Hooke, also a Bristol merchant. He was the grandson of Adrian Scrope, MP and regicide. Scrope's upbringing in Bristol took place against the background of radical whig activity in the city where his father was among the leaders of the 'exclusion' campaign to debar the duke of York from succession to the throne; and Scrope himself participated in 1685 with other Bristolians in the Monmouth rebellion. In 1686, the year of his entry to the Middle Temple, he published at Utrecht a personal attack on the pro-Catholic policies of James II in the form of a tract against papal authority entitled *Exercitatio politica de cive in republica pontificia*. He appears to have continued his underground activities for a while longer, acting as an agent between the whigs and the prince of Orange, and on one journey to the Netherlands was supposed to have disguised himself as a woman. In 1693 Scrope received his call to the bar and in the course of the next decade established himself as a successful member of his profession. His wealth was augmented in 1704 on inheriting his father's estates at Wormsley, Buckinghamhire.

In May 1708 Scrope was appointed by the Godolphin ministry, probably on Lord Chancellor Cowper's recommendation, as one of the five barons of the newly reconstituted court of exchequer in Scotland. His duties as an exchequer baron at Edinburgh were primarily concerned with the judicial and administrative supervision of the Scottish revenue system and, largely because of his readiness to travel regularly, he soon became the chief, and most influential, instrument of liaison with the Treasury in London. The salary of £500 a year was soon doubled to compensate for his having given up a lucrative barrister's practice, and was further increased in February 1710 to £1500 to keep pace with the expense of journeying between London and Edinburgh. His administrative flair and a sharp nose for financial complexity made him one of the central figures in Scottish administration in the years that followed the union. It was fortunate that he had long been on terms of friendship with Robert Harley, and after coming to power in 1710 Harley treated Scrope as one of his chief Scottish advisers. Scrope acted briefly as a commissioner of the great seal during September and October 1710, and in December 1716 served as a judge at the trial of Jacobite rebels at Carlisle. He retained office at the Hanoverian accession in 1714, and in 1722 was elected to parliament for Ripon. When William Lowndes, the distinguished and long-serving secretary to the Treasury, died on 20 January 1724 Scrope was immediately appointed to succeed, and surrendered his Scottish post on 25 March. At some point, though it is not clear when, he was joint author, with his fellow baron Sir John Clerk of Penecuik, of *A Historical View of the Forms and Powers of the Court of Exchequer in Scotland*; however, this was not published until 1820.

Now past the age of sixty, Scrope took charge of the Treasury at Whitehall under the direction of its first lord, Robert Walpole, and was responsible for all detailed arrangements and transactions relating to the government's finances. With Walpole leading the government in the Commons, the demands on Scrope in presenting and defending the government's 'ways and means' measures in parliament were not great, though he was noted for his mastery of factual detail. After his election for Bristol in 1727, in which he obtained a huge majority, he was prompted to give attention to matters of wider fiscal concern bearing on the city's economic interests. These included the Africa Company's attempt to monopolize the slave trade, which he helped to block, and the Bristol-led complaints about the illegal export of Irish wool, on which he chaired a major select committee in 1731. However, his espousal of Walpole's unpopular excise scheme in 1733, contrary to the corporation's instructions, cost him his Bristol seat in the election the following year, and in 1735 he was relieved of the city recordership, which he had held since 1728. He was returned instead for Lyme Regis, Dorset, which he continued to represent until his death.

Following Walpole's fall from power early in 1742 Scrope was summoned in June as a key witness to the committee of secrecy investigating the administration, but resolutely refused to divulge any information on Walpole's use of 'secret service money' on the grounds that it was accounted for to the king only. Horace Walpole described him on this occasion as 'a most testy little old gentleman', reporting that Scrope had told the committee that:

> he was forescore years old and did not care if he spent the few months he has to live in the Tower or not; that the last thing he would do should be to betray the King and next to him the earl of Orford. (Walpole)

A few weeks later William Pulteney, the former 'patriot' whig leader now in office, was forced to admit the impracticality of dismissing Scrope from the Treasury as some had urged:

> Mr Scrope is the only man I know that thoroughly understands the business of the Treasury and is versed in drawing money bills. On this foundation he stands secure and is immovable as a rock; besides I really take him for an exceeding honest man. (*Correspondence of John, Fourth Duke of Bedford*)

Thus Scrope remained in office until his death on 9 April 1752. To his nephew and heir Francis Fane, an MP and a lord commissioner of trade, he left a 'vast fortune' comprising his 'mansion' in Small Street, Bristol, and property in Oxfordshire and Buckinghamshire. He was buried in Lewknor parish church, Oxfordshire. A. A. HANHAM

Sources HoP, *Commons, 1715–54*, 2.413–14 • will, 1752, PRO, PROB 11/794/108 • J. Latimer, *The annals of Bristol in the seventeenth century* (1900), 418 • J. Latimer, *The annals of Bristol in the eighteenth century* (1893), 160, 166, 188, 354 • P. W. J. Riley, *The English ministers and Scotland, 1707–1727* (1964), 79, 162–6 • Walpole, *Corr.*, 17.458–9 • *Correspondence of John, fourth duke of Bedford*, ed. J. Russell, 3 vols. (1842–6) • H. A. C. Sturgess, ed., *Register of admissions to the Honourable Society of the Middle Temple, from the fifteenth century to the year 1944*, 1 (1949), 218

Archives BL, letters to Lord Hardwicke, Add. MSS 35585–36139 • Hunt. L., letters to Edmund Herbert • NA Scot., letters to John

Clerk • NL Scot., corresp. with Robert Arbuthnott • NL Scot., corresp. with Duncan Forbes • Northants. RO, paper as secretary to Treasury • PRO, Treasury, working MSS

Likenesses attrib. G. Kneller, oils, Bristol City Museum and Art Gallery • portrait, Gov. Art Coll.

Wealth at death according to Henry Pelham, £2000 p.a. (probably fairly accurate) plus £100,000 'in money' (probably over-inflated); Lord Chancellor Hardwicke said Scrope's wealth smaller than supposed: HoP, *Commons*, 1715–54, 2.414; will, 1752, PRO, PROB 11/794/108

Scrope, Richard, **first Baron Scrope of Bolton** (*c*.1327–1403), soldier and administrator, was the third son of Sir Henry *Scrope (*b*. in or before 1268, *d*. 1336), a lawyer who acquired a considerable estate in north Yorkshire, and his wife, Margaret, who was probably the daughter of either Lord Ros or Lord Fitzwalter. Active as a soldier at an early age, in 1346 he fought successively at Crécy (26 August) and Nevilles Cross (17 October), being knighted after the latter battle; he then took part in Edward III's siege of Calais, concluded on 3 August 1347. On 29 August 1350 he fought in the sea battle off Winchelsea, and late in 1355 he campaigned in France, before returning to England with the king for the relief of Berwick Castle in January 1356. Up to this point he had served under a number of captains, under Henry, Lord Percy, at Nevilles Cross, under either the earl of Warwick or the earl of Northampton at Winchelsea. But he now became increasingly closely connected with the young John of Gaunt, a connection certainly strengthened by the latter's being earl of Richmond. It was in Gaunt's retinue that with five other members of the Scrope family Richard took part in Edward III's French campaign of 1359–60, and he served abroad under Gaunt, in France, Spain, and Scotland, on a further five occasions, in 1367, 1369, 1373–4, 1384, and 1385. On 8 November 1367 he was formally retained by Gaunt, with an annuity of £40 per annum. He also enjoyed the favour of the king, and at his death was able to bequeath to his son Stephen a sword which had belonged to Edward III.

During the 1360s Scrope was active in domestic affairs, locally and nationally, being appointed to nine commissions of oyer and terminer and of the peace, almost exclusively in the North Riding of Yorkshire, which he also represented in parliament in 1365. Military service had probably helped to make him wealthy—in the 1360s he was active in buying lands, especially in Wensleydale and Swaledale—and it is not surprising that on 8 January 1371 he should have received a personal summons to parliament, thereby becoming Baron Scrope of Bolton. Further promotion followed, doubtless owing much to Gaunt's influence, when on 27 March 1371 Scrope was appointed treasurer of England. The demands of the French war had created acute financial difficulties. Scrope's treasurership saw serious attempts at retrenchment, as well as the appointment of a special treasurer at war. For a while order was restored, but it is unlikely that Scrope had any specialized financial skills, and the private dealings with London financiers of William, Lord Latimer, and Richard Lyons, apparently undertaken without the treasurer's knowledge to raise loans for the king, at considerable expense to the latter, led to renewed fiscal confusion, and in 1376 did much to discredit the whole government. But by then Scrope was no longer in office, having resigned on 26 September 1375.

Scrope showed both integrity and independence during the Good Parliament of 1376. Questioned about the loans made to the king, he refused at first to answer unless he was released from his councillor's vow of secrecy, but once he had been licensed to speak, he gave evidence damning to Latimer and Lyons. His conduct earned him widespread respect, yet did nothing to lose him the favour of John of Gaunt, and following the death of Edward III he was appointed steward of the household to the young Richard II. On 29 October 1378 he resigned this office to become chancellor of England. In spite of considerable difficulties, Scrope showed great skill in office, especially as a spokesman for the government in parliament, delivering a series of speeches to the Commons which have been described as 'models of their kind. They combined firmness with flexibility, and frankness with the occasional but necessary half-truth' (Saul, 50). But continuous failures in the war with France eventually led to the government's collapse, and Scrope resigned on 30 January 1380. At the end of the year he was appointed a warden of the west march, an office he held at first jointly, but later alone, until 14 March 1382, and in which he directed important works on the gatehouse of Carlisle Castle, supplying lead from his own Wensleydale mines.

Scrope did not remain away from the centre of affairs for long. Following the disasters of the peasants' revolt, on 4 December 1381 he was reappointed chancellor, according to Walsingham, 'at the petition of all the magnates and commons' (*Historia Anglicana*, 2.49). But he soon found that popular approval was no substitute for royal favour. His efforts to control Richard II's extravagance were resented, and when he refused to seal charters giving control of the Mortimer inheritance to royal favourites, the king dismissed him, on 11 July 1382. According to Walsingham, Scrope told Richard he would never hold office under him again. This did not prevent Scrope's serving as a warden of the west march from February to July 1384, and in fact he became involved in government on several further occasions, though hardly in the king's interest. In 1385 he was a member of a committee of nine appointed to investigate royal revenues and expenditure, and in November 1386 he was named to the continual committee set up by the Wonderful Parliament to oversee and direct the workings of government in the following year. It is true that in that parliament Scrope spoke in defence of the chancellor, Michael de la Pole, but this was probably on strictly personal grounds—de la Pole was his brother-in-law. In November 1387 Scrope acted as a spokesman for the lords appellant in their dealings with the king, and at the end of the Merciless Parliament he was one of a committee appointed to watch over the king's actions. Following the Cambridge parliament of September 1388 he became one of a small group of councillors who shared responsibility for government until the king's resumption of power in May 1389.

Scrope may not have been as totally disaffected from the king as his actions in the late 1380s might suggest; certainly his eldest son, William *Scrope, would become one of Richard II's principal supporters, executed as such in 1399. But though he was summoned to a council in London in April 1390 to discuss a proposed embassy to France, Scrope was usually only tangentially involved in government after 1389, for instance being employed in negotiations with the Scots in 1393 and 1394, and acting regularly as a trier of petitions in parliament until 1397. He was, however, active in promoting the welfare of his own soul, being licensed in 1393 to found a chantry of six chaplains in Bolton Castle, and to endow Easby Abbey with the means to maintain first six and ultimately ten additional canons, along with two secular chaplains and twenty-two poor men. Piety was accompanied, for Scrope, by an evident concern for his standing in the eyes of society, lastingly demonstrated by his great castle at Bolton in Wensleydale. Designed by the Durham architect John Lewyn, under an indenture of 14 September 1378, it comprised eight major residential suites, and is said to have cost about £12,000 over twenty years—evidence, it may be, for the profits of government office as well as of war, since Scrope's landed income, even after he had added substantially to his estates, was only about £600 per annum.

Equally compelling evidence for Scrope's concern for his rights and status is provided by the famous lawsuit which he initiated in 1385 against the Cheshire knight Sir Robert Grosvenor, over the right to the arms azure a bend or. Referred to the court of chivalry, the action lasted for five years, and heard depositions from 397 witnesses, 246 of whom appeared for Scrope. Drawn predominantly, though not exclusively, from the north of England, the latter included the dukes of Lancaster and York, the earls of Arundel, Derby, Devon, and Northumberland, lords Basset, Clifford, Dacre, and Neville, the heads of many northern monasteries, and large numbers of knights and esquires, including the poet Geoffrey Chaucer. Their testimony provided abundant evidence for the respect which Scrope enjoyed in landowning society, as well as vindicating his claim to the disputed coat of arms. The fact that he was appointed to be one of their executors by the second earl of Arundel, William Ufford, earl of Suffolk, and Archbishop Thoresby of York, and was an attorney for the duke of Gloucester in 1395, similarly shows that he was widely trusted among the aristocracy. In 1399, however, the overthrow of Richard II, and particularly the execution of Scrope's eldest son, seemed to threaten the future of his whole family. Lord Scrope gave his support in parliament to Richard's deposition, and then made an emotional appeal, 'with great humility and bitter weeping', that the judgment on his son should not be used to justify his own and his other children's disinheritance. Henry IV was merciful, reassuring Scrope that he 'regarded him as a loyal knight, and had always regarded him as such' (*RotP*, 3.453).

Scrope served as a councillor in 1401, and attended parliament in 1402, but his commitment to the new regime was never fully tested, since he died on 30 May 1403, and was buried in Easby Abbey. He seems to have spent his later years mostly at his manor of Pishiobury, Hertfordshire, which he bought in 1394, and where he drew up his will on 2 August 1400. As well as showing that Scrope died a very wealthy man, the will also sheds a good deal of light on his personality and preoccupations. The latter centred upon his family. In 1344 or 1345 he had married Blanche, daughter of William de la Pole, who predeceased him, dying some time after 1378; with her he had four sons, William, Roger, Stephen, and Richard. Roger and Stephen he married to two of the three daughters and coheirs of Robert, third Lord Tybotot, having purchased their wardship and marriage. But he showed himself concerned to endow his descendants with a common memory as well as with worldly goods. Thus he bequeathed to Roger, his eldest surviving son, a rosary which had belonged to Scrope's own father, and the missal and breviary that he had himself used to say his morning and evening prayers, and left to him pieces of plate which had belonged to the earls of Arundel and Suffolk, along with instructions that these were to become heirlooms in memory of the earls. His family was the object of his affections as well as of his dynastic ambitions. He left a blessing along with an estate to Roger, as his 'dearest' eldest son, and addressed his namesake, godson, and nephew, Richard *Scrope, archbishop of York, as 'my most dear father and son'. But his benevolence extended beyond his immediate family circle, to members of his household, each of whom seems to have been remembered, including every servant in the kitchen of Bolton Castle.

Scrope showed his religious devotion in his bequests to a wide range of northern monasteries and friaries, as well as in a gift of £40 to the work then in progress on York Minster. The same motive doubtless lay behind the concern he expressed for the poor of Richmondshire, for instance his bequest of £20 to be distributed among his poor tenants there. The residue of his estate was to go to the hospice for the poor and its associated college which he had founded at Wensley. This last project came to nothing, but his lands and title descended in his posterity until 1630.

Brigette Vale

Sources B. Vale, 'The Scropes of Bolton and Masham, *c.*1300–*c.*1450: a study of a northern noble family', PhD diss., University of York, 1987 · GEC, *Peerage*, new edn, 11.539–41 · *Chancery records* · N. H. Nicolas, ed., *The Scrope and Grosvenor controversy*, 2 vols. (privately printed, London, 1832) · *RotP*, vol. 3 · L. C. Hector and B. F. Harvey, eds. and trans., *The Westminster chronicle, 1381–1394*, OMT (1982) · V. H. Galbraith, ed., *The Anonimalle chronicle, 1333 to 1381* (1927) · [J. Raine], ed., *Testamenta Eboracensia*, 1, SurtS, 4 (1836), 272–8 · A. Tuck, *Richard II and the English nobility* (1973) · N. Saul, *Richard II* (1997) · W. M. Ormrod, *The reign of Edward III* (1990) · G. Holmes, *The Good Parliament* (1975) · *Thomae Walsingham, quondam monachi S. Albani, historia Anglicana*, ed. H. T. Riley, 2 vols., pt 1 of *Chronica monasterii S. Albani*, Rolls Series, 28 (1863–4) · S. Walker, *The Lancastrian affinity, 1361–1399* (1990) · A. Goodman, *The loyal conspiracy: the lords appellant under Richard II* (1971) · A. Goodman, *John of Gaunt: the exercise of princely power in fourteenth-century Europe* (1992) · C. Given-Wilson, *The English nobility in the late middle ages* (1987) · Tout, *Admin. hist.*, vol. 3 · J. Hughes, *Pastors and visionaries: religion and secular life in late medieval Yorkshire* (1988) · R. L. Storey, 'The wardens of the marches of England towards Scotland, 1377–1489', *EngHR*, 72 (1957), 593–615 · R. L. Storey, 'Liveries and commissions of the peace, 1388–1390', *The reign of Richard II: essays in honour of May McKisack*, ed. F. R. H. Du Boulay and C. M. Barron (1971), 131–52

Wealth at death very wealthy; approx. £600 in income from land p.a.: Given-Wilson, *The English nobility*, 157

Scrope, Richard (*c.*1350–1405), archbishop of York, was the third son of Henry *Scrope, first Baron Scrope of Masham (1312?–1392), soldier, and his wife, Joan.

Family background and early advancement Henry Scrope's distinguished military career had been followed by diligent service to the crown in parliament and council, and family influence probably played a greater part than any spiritual qualities in launching Richard's successful career in the church. His first preferment, as rector of Ainderby Steeple, near Northallerton, in 1368, was at the presentation of his uncle Richard *Scrope, Baron Scrope of Bolton. This was followed in 1371 by a Lancastrian connection in the form of a grant of the wardenship of the free chapel of the castle of Tickhill, which belonged to John of Gaunt, duke of Lancaster. Scrope was still not even an acolyte when he was appointed official to Thomas Arundel, bishop of Ely (*d.* 1414), his future archiepiscopal colleague, in 1375. He was ordained deacon on 20 September 1376 by his brother-in-law, Archbishop Alexander Neville of York (*d.* 1392), and priest on 14 March 1377 by Arundel. In the meantime he had studied arts at Oxford before embarking on the study of law, probably at Cambridge, which was where he presumably became licentiate in civil law by 1375 and a doctor of canon and civil law by 1383. He was chancellor of the university in 1378. From 1382 to 1386 he appears to have been based primarily at Rome, where he served as a papal chaplain and an auditor of the curia. In 1382 he was instituted as dean of Chichester, and in September 1385 he was elected bishop of that see, only for the combined wishes of pope and canons to be thwarted by Richard II's insistence on the advancement of his own confessor, Thomas Rushook, bishop of Llandaff. Compensation followed swiftly with Scrope's provision as bishop of Coventry and Lichfield on 18 August 1386, and consecration by the pope at Genoa on the following day. He had returned to England by 15 November and took up his diocesan duties from 22 May 1387.

In common with many of his fellow prelates, Scrope combined a significant involvement in secular affairs with his spiritual obligations. As befitted a member of a northern baronial family, he acted as an envoy to Scotland in 1378 and 1392, and served as a conservator of the truce in 1394. In 1397 he was dispatched on a mission to Rome, probably because of his familiarity with the curia, to promote Richard II's scheme for the canonization of Edward II. It may have been in recognition of recent efforts on the king's behalf, as well as of his good standing with the pope, that he was translated to the archbishopric of York on 15 March 1398, while still at Rome.

Archbishop of York Until 1399 there is no evidence that Scrope participated directly in the factional strife that punctuated Richard II's reign. In that year, however, he was compelled to respond to the coup that led to Richard's deposition and the accession of Henry IV. In view of certain procedural similarities between the deposition of

Richard Scrope (*c.*1350–1405), manuscript painting [standing, right]

Richard and that of the emperor Frederick II by the pope in 1245, it was more probably as a distinguished canon lawyer than as a political partisan that Scrope, with his fellow lawyer John Trefnant, bishop of Hereford (*d.* 1404), was chosen to head the commission appointed to receive the captive king's 'voluntary' abdication on 29 September; and it was he who announced it in a quasi-parliamentary assembly that met on the following day. His prominent role continued when he joined his fellow archbishop, the newly restored Thomas Arundel, in escorting Henry of Lancaster to the vacant throne, although the actual crowning was to be performed a fortnight later by his senior colleague.

Attempts to assess the nature and development of Scrope's personal affiliations in the turbulent early years of Henry IV's reign tend to be tainted with hindsight. He remained in his diocese except in times of parliaments and great councils. The dominance of Henry Percy, earl of Northumberland (*d.* 1408), and his family and affinity, in northern England, and the Percys' crucial role in helping to put Henry IV on the throne, meant that any archbishop of York was almost certain to become involved with them at the local and national level. Thus in 1400 Scrope headed a commission to collect a loan to help to pay for the expedition to Scotland that Henry had undertaken, it may be assumed, under pressure from his powerful northern allies. Scrope's younger brother John was married to Elizabeth, widow of Northumberland's second son, Thomas, and one of the archbishop's sisters, Isabel, had married Sir Robert Plumpton, who had strong connections with the Percys. However, against any suggestion that these and other relationships had already made Scrope an adherent of the Percys must be set the fact that, at least up to the end of 1402, any personal or professional association with that family was quite compatible with unequivocal loyalty and good service to the crown.

Involvement in rebellion Nevertheless, when the Percys revolted in the summer of 1403, choices had to be made. The chronicler John Hardyng, himself a Percy retainer, claimed that Scrope was among those who encouraged the Percys in their rebellion, but there is no hint in official sources that he came under suspicion, even though Archbishop Arundel, a firm supporter of Henry IV throughout his reign, found it necessary to declare his own innocence. Thus while rebellion in the Percy cause in the summer of 1405 represented a plausible course of action for almost any member of the clerical or lay establishment in the north, there seems to have been no suspicion that Scrope was about to take that momentous step.

The problem of accounting for Scrope's decision to rebel is compounded by an absence of convincing motives. Sympathetic clerical writers alleged that Scrope's rebellion was inspired primarily by his growing disapproval of Henry IV's oppression of the church. Although the charges against the king appear to lack any real substance, they were perhaps foreseeable in any attempt to justify the taking up of arms by an archbishop. Scrope's only recorded gesture against a political threat to the church was his predictable support in October 1404 for Arundel's spirited resistance to proposals in parliament at Coventry for the confiscation of ecclesiastical property. Attempts to explain Scrope's rebellion have focused on the manifesto by which he incited the people of York to rise with him. The most plausible version of this document, as reproduced by the chronicler Thomas Walsingham, includes complaints of abuse of church and clergy; excessive taxation of the laity; misappropriation of much of this revenue by unspecified individuals; and unfair treatment of members of the nobility. The latter charge was probably tailored to the grievances of the young Thomas Mowbray, earl marshal, who held lands in Yorkshire, and whose involvement in the rebellion perhaps represented a filial reaction to the disastrous quarrel between his father, Thomas (I) Mowbray, first duke of Norfolk (*d.* 1399), and Henry of Lancaster in 1398, which had resulted in his father's death in exile. The general tone of the manifesto had much in common with the calls for better government, in the shape of greater financial and even political accountability, made by the Commons in Henry's parliaments. This line of 'responsible' sedition contrasted markedly with the Percys' uncompromising attempts to overthrow a king who had ceased to serve their purposes.

However, it is highly unlikely that Scrope's action at the same time as Northumberland's renewed rebellion was coincidental, and this assumption seems reinforced by the military shortcomings of Scrope's following at York. While it seems agreed that the archbishop marched out of York dressed for combat, the eight or nine thousand townsmen and country-folk who rallied behind his banner had little claim to be regarded as a fighting force. Nevertheless, their militancy virtually destroyed any possibility that they might convince the king of the justness of their cause by peaceful persuasion, yet Scrope and his supporters had no realistic hope of imposing their will by force. The likeliest supposition is that their rising was part of a broader movement in which Northumberland's more militant Yorkshire levies were to have the dominant role. The plan of campaign seems to have been that the earl should make his way down from Northumberland, concentrating recruitment in the Percy strongholds of Cleveland and Topcliffe to the north of York, and those of Tadcaster and Spofforth not far from the city. York was probably designated as the rallying-point for all the Percy forces, which would then march south, inspired by the archbishop's claims on their behalf to the moral high ground against the king.

The relationship between Northumberland and Scrope remains a matter for speculation: was Scrope a straightforward ally of the earl, cynically using his position to mislead people as to the true purpose of the rising; an unworldly cleric deceived as to Northumberland's intentions; or a naive idealist hoping that he could divert the rebellion into more moderate constitutional channels? But one thing is clear. By lending his respected name to the insurrection, Scrope almost single-handedly transformed its image from that of a conflict between the king and an 'overmighty subject' to that of a 'crusade' for good government.

Failure and execution All the same, defeat was guaranteed almost from the start by the failure of Northumberland's attempt to capture Ralph Neville, first earl of Westmorland (*d.* 1425), the mainstay of royal authority in the north, as an essential prelude to the rising, and by his subsequent northward flight abandoning the gathering rebels to their fate. The three days that Scrope, Mowbray, and Sir Robert Plumpton's son, William, spent with their followers on Shipton Moor, a few miles outside York, represented a desperate period of waiting for reinforcements that never came. On 29 May they were instead confronted by Westmorland and the king's son John, who had already dispersed the leaderless Topcliffe rebels. Scrope's 'army' was almost certainly incapable of effective resistance, and he had little alternative but to put himself at Westmorland's mercy. While he may simply have surrendered unconditionally in the hope that he might salvage something from the collapse of the rising, several chroniclers claimed that Westmorland deceived him into disbanding his men in exchange for a promise of favourable consideration of his programme of reform. Even when Westmorland arrested Scrope and his chief lieutenants, the archbishop may have hoped that his ecclesiastical eminence would at least save his life. However, Henry IV soon showed that he was determined to make an example of the rebel archbishop. When the king arrived at Pontefract, where Westmorland had imprisoned Scrope, on 3 June, he refused the archbishop's request for an interview, and the king's half-brother Sir Thomas Beaufort (*d.* 1427) was sent to seize Scrope's crozier—his symbol of office—a mission only accomplished after a protracted struggle.

With his resolve possibly strengthened by the anticlericalism of certain of his household knights, the king seems to have decided at an early stage that Scrope must die. It was probably reports of Henry's intentions that prompted Archbishop Arundel to ride day and night from London, in a desperate attempt to forestall the king—an attempt in which insistence on the physical inviolability of an archbishop and counsels of political expediency were perhaps subtly interwoven. His arrival, however, seems to have impelled Henry to strike before reasoned opposition to his resolve had time to develop. On the morning of 8 June, while Henry was reassuring the exhausted Arundel at Scrope's official residence of Bishopthorpe that he would not act rashly, a hastily convened commission headed by Thomas Fitzalan, earl of Arundel (*d.* 1415) (nephew of the archbishop), and Sir Thomas Beaufort, deputizing for the king's son John and for Westmorland as constable and marshal of England respectively, was sitting in judgment on Scrope and his fellow insurgents in another room of the same building. Since the chief justice, Sir William Gascoigne (*d.* 1419), had refused to participate in irregular proceedings against Scrope, the minor lawyer Sir William Fulthorpe was assigned the task of condemning him to death for treason. Accepting his fate, according to the chroniclers, with edifying piety and dignity, the archbishop was led through the streets of York to Clementhorpe, just outside the city. Here he was beheaded, it was said, by five blows of the axe representing the five wounds of Christ. He was the first English prelate to suffer judicial execution.

Cult and reputation Scrope's body was taken to York Minster to be buried, with the king's consent. Henry's conciliatory gesture in allowing the archbishop to be buried amid his recent supporters soon led to claims that miracles had occurred at his tomb, and a cult of martyr-worship arose that prompted a series of official reactions culminating in September 1406 in the cordoning-off of the tomb with high barriers. Although this popular veneration, with its attendant myth that Henry's execution of Scrope had caused him to be stricken with leprosy, did not develop into a serious threat to the king, it survived to secure official toleration as a more devotional and less seditious cult as part of Henry V's attempts at political conciliation. In the 1450s the promotion of the claim to the throne of Richard, duke of York (*d.* 1460), led to the representation of Scrope as an early martyr in the cause of Yorkist legitimacy, and an attempt to secure his canonization in 1462, in the wake of Edward IV's accession, was to mark the climax of a political cult, which thereafter seems to have been rendered superfluous by its supporters' success.

A potentially much greater problem for Henry IV was the sentence of excommunication imposed by Pope Innocent VII (*r.* 1404–6) upon everyone involved in Scrope's execution. However, this solemn edict was reduced to a minor embarrassment when Archbishop Arundel put political stability before clerical outrage and neglected to publish it in England. In 1407 persistent diplomatic efforts combined, according to hostile sources, with generous bribery at the curia, secured Henry a pardon from Innocent's successor Gregory XII (*r.* 1406–15). Benefiting from the fact that Scrope was at least technically guilty of armed insurrection, Henry had suffered few repercussions from a hasty decision regarded by many contemporaries as sacrilegious and scandalous.

After a long and conventionally successful career in the church, Scrope failed completely both as political reformer and military leader. However, while treating sceptically the chroniclers' simplistic image of the archbishop as a great churchman sacrificed to a noble cause that was essentially his own, historians have tended to give him the benefit of the doubt in suggesting that his motives in 1405 may have been more honourable than those of the self-seeking lords with whom he misguidedly decided to make common cause. PETER MCNIVEN

Sources P. McNiven, 'The betrayal of Archbishop Scrope', *Bulletin of the John Rylands University Library*, 54 (1971–2), 173–213 · 'Annales … Henrici quarti', *Johannis de Trokelowe et Henrici de Blaneforde … chronica et annales*, ed. H. T. Riley, pt 3 of *Chronica monasterii S. Albani*, Rolls Series, 28 (1866), 280–420, esp. 391–3, 400, 402–10 · *Thomae Walsingham, quondam monachi S. Albani, historia Anglicana*, ed. H. T. Riley, 2 vols., pt 1 of *Chronica monasterii S. Albani*, Rolls Series, 28 (1863–4), vol. 2, pp. 269–71 · J. Raine, ed., *The historians of the church of York and its archbishops*, 2, Rolls Series, 71 (1886), 306–10, 4287–333; 3 (1894), 288–94 · J. H. Wylie, *History of England under Henry the Fourth*, 4 vols. (1884–98), esp. vol. 2, pp. 192–244, 339–58 · Emden, *Oxf.* · F. S. Haydon, ed., *Eulogium historiarum sive temporis*, 3 vols., Rolls Series, 9 (1858–63), vol. 3, pp. 405–8 · J. A. Giles, ed., *Incerti scriptoris chronicon Angliae de regnis trium regum Lancastrensium* (1848), 43–9 · *The chronicle of John Hardyng*, ed. H. Ellis (1812), 351, 362–3 · *RotP*, 3.604–5 · J. W. McKenna, 'Popular canonisation as political propaganda: the cult of Archbishop Scrope', *Speculum*, 45 (1970), 608–23 · R. N. Swanson, ed., *A calendar of the register of Richard Scrope, archbishop of York, 1398–1405*, 2 vols. (1981–5) · G. E. Caspary, 'The deposition of Richard II and the canon law', *Proceedings of the second international congress of medieval canon law, Boston College, 12–16 August 1963*, ed. S. Kuttner and J. J. Ryan (1965), 189–201

Archives Borth. Inst., archiepiscopal registers, register, 1398–1404, R.1.16

Likenesses manuscript painting, York Minster [*see illus.*] · stained-glass window, York Minster

Scrope, Stephen (1397–1472), author and translator, was the grandson of Richard *Scrope, first Baron Scrope of Bolton (*c.*1327–1403), and the eldest son of Sir Stephen Scrope, several time deputy in Ireland under Henry IV, and the Tiptoft heiress, Millicent (*d.* 1446). Stephen's father died of plague in 1408, and in 1409 his mother married her husband's butler, John *Fastolf, giving her new husband a life interest in all her estates. Fastolf sold Stephen's wardship in 1411 to Chief Justice William Gascoigne for 500 marks and Scrope was sent to Gawthorpe near Leeds; he returned unhappy to his mother and stepfather in 1413, suffering a disfiguring illness that incapacitated him for active military service. Nevertheless his later adolescence was spent in secretarial service for Fastolf in Normandy, an experience that would serve him well when he began his activities as a translator of French literature.

Scrope finally returned to England to live with his mother in 1428; a marriage was arranged in 1432–3 to Margaret Doreward which Scrope was to describe later as a disaster. Moreover he was required by Fastolf to pay the bulk of the 500 marks for the wardship, and consequently forced to sign away his claims to his mother's estates during Fastolf's lifetime. After his wife's death, some time between 1445 and 1449, Scrope fell heavily into debt, and he returned to Fastolf's new residence, Caister. His mother died in 1446, and Scrope remained with his stepfather until 1456, when he married Joan, daughter of another chief justice, Sir Richard Bingham. Scrope finally entered his parents' Yorkshire and west-country inheritance in 1461, when Fastolf died, though he received none of his stepfather's own lands in East Anglia. Debts forced him to sell most of his Yorkshire lands, and in 1467 he even gave up his life interest in his father's estates at Castle Combe, Wiltshire. Nevertheless, it was at Castle Combe that Scrope died in 1472. He was survived by his wife and his only son, John, who succeeded to what remained of his father's lands in 1481.

Such a life, viewed in terms of the chivalric traditions of the Scropes of Bolton, was a failure; but Scrope and Fastolf's secretary, William Worcester, formulated an educational programme that provided members of their master's household with military and heroic ethics based on French translations and adaptations of the literature of ancient Rome. Originally in the library of Charles VI, the books used had been purchased by Fastolf's employer, John, duke of Bedford, and some found their way into Fastolf's library. In 1440 Scrope translated Christine de Pisan's 'Epistle of Othea' from French into English and addressed it to Fastolf (St John's College, MS H.5). Worcester similarly dedicated his 'Boke of noblesse' to Fastolf and Scrope contributed to this work reminiscences of Fastolf's military activities in France (BL, Royal MS B.xxii). In both works Fastolf, though retired, is seen as the focus of hopes for the reconquest of Normandy and the realization of a Roman imperial ideal. This was to be achieved through a redefinition and rejuvenation of English chivalry through cultivation of the four cardinal virtues, especially prudence, Fastolf's main virtue (according to Worcester) as a commander in Normandy, and of the military and moral discipline of the ancient Romans.

In 1450 Scrope translated for Fastolf a compilation of the wisdom of ancient philosophers, 'The dicts and sayings of the philosophers' (Cambridge, Emmanuel College, MS I.2.10; CUL, MS Dd.9.18). This work, and Worcester's translations of Cicero, 'Old age' and 'Friendship', which were also dedicated to Fastolf, represent a programme of popularizing classical philosophy. 'The dicts and sayings of the philosophers' provides succinct biographies of leading Greek and Roman statesmen, philosophical quotations, and aphorisms, including exhortations to lead a prudent, pragmatic, and rational life that would have appealed to a self-made man such as Fastolf.

Scrope's emphasis on reason went beyond observation of behaviour, like Worcester he was interested in physical and mental health: he loaned Worcester a book providing instructions on the treatment of hernias, and supplied him with medical notes which were incorporated in Worcester's medical notebook (BL, Sloane MS 4, fols. 38*v*, 57*v*). 'The epistle of Othea' reveals an interest in astrology and the humours; and in his prologue Scrope explains how the Greek myths are glossed in a way that they can be used to confront emotional turbulence and misfortune with prudence. 'The dicts and sayings of the philosophers' similarly explores happiness and depression, and provides advice, specifically intended for Fastolf, on how to achieve detachment in the face of old age. Scrope and Worcester integrated classical myths with Christian morality, transmitting a view of Christianity that emphasized free will and a rational attitude towards death and guilt, and a code of ethics that embraced curiosity about human behaviour and the emotions.

Such curiosity was applied by Scrope to his own moods. His friend Worcester described him as moody, sensitive, and aloof, and he engaged in an acrimonious correspondence with Fastolf over a long period; but he genuinely tried to get close to his stepfather, and in 1452 addressed a complaint to him about his disturbed childhood. Scrope pointed out that Fastolf in the first year of his mother's remarriage 'sold me—through whiche sale I tooke sekenesses that kept me 13 of 14 yere swyng, whereby I am disfigured in my persone and shall be whilest I lyve'. This illness recurred whenever the issue of leaving Fastolf's household arose, and Scrope brought charges against the Pastons representing Fastolf's estate, for the emotional and physical damage he suffered from one 'who bought me and sold me as a beste, ayens al ryght and lawe, to myn hurt'. Protesting that 'I had the soor and felte the hurte', he levelled recriminations at both stepfather and his mother: 'mesemeth that neyther he ne she had noon auctorite to selle me; wherefor I conceyve that I was wrongfully doon to' (BL, Add. MS 28209, fols. 21–2). Scrope's complaint constitutes an eloquent criticism of the system of wardship (the basis of the education of the English aristocracy), and the emotional damage it inflicted on children. JONATHAN HUGHES

Sources J. Hughes, 'Stephen Scrope and the circle of Sir John Fastolf: moral and intellectual outlooks', *Medieval knighthood*, 4, ed. C. Harper-Bill and R. Harvey (1990), 109–46 • K. B. McFarlane, 'William Worcester, a preliminary survey', *England in the fifteenth century: collected essays* (1981), 199–225 • C. F. Bühler, ed., *The dicts and sayings of the philosophers: the translations*, trans. S. Scrope, W. Worcester, and others, EETS, 211 (1941) • C. de Pisan, *The epistle of Othea*, ed. C. F. Bühler, trans. S. Scrope, EETS, 264 (1970) • N. Davis, ed., *Paston letters and papers of the fifteenth century*, 2 vols. (1971–6) • G. P. Scrope, *History of the manor and ancient barony of Castle Combe, in the county of Wilts.* (1852) • BL, Add. MS 28209 • J. G. Nichols, ed., *The boke of noblesse: addressed to King Edward the Fourth on his invasion of France in 1475*, Roxburghe Club (1860)

Archives CUL, MS Dd.9.18 • Emmanuel College, Cambridge, MS I.2.10 • St John Cam., MS H.5 | BL, Add. MS 28209, fols. 21–2 • BL, Royal MS B.xxii • BL, Sloane MS 4, fols. 38*v*, 57*v*

Wealth at death annuity of £34 2*s.* 4*d.* during 1467–72 from estates at Castle Combe and Oxendon, inherited from mother: BL, Add. MS 28209, fol. 23*v*

Scrope [Bradley], **Thomas** (*d.* **1492**), bishop of Dromore, was probably born at Bradley in the parish of Medbourne, Leicestershire, a member of the Scrope family, who were prominent landowners there. As his name does not occur in the records, James Tait suggested that he was perhaps an illegitimate offspring of one of the two sons of Richard *Scrope, first Baron Scrope of Bolton (*c.*1327–1403). Thomas Scrope joined the Carmelites in Norwich, and after completing his studies there, began travelling the countryside preaching repentance, and announcing that 'the new Jerusalem, the bride of the Lamb, was about to come down from heaven' (Bale, *Cat.*, 1.630). Thomas Netter (*d.* 1430), the Carmelite provincial, wrote a letter of complaint to the prior of Norwich, ordering that Scrope be restrained. He retired to a hermitage in the Carmelite house, and contemporary documents in the 1440s refer to 'Friar Thomas, the recluse' there. In the 1430s Scrope translated Philip Ribot's 'The institute of first monks', a classic Carmelite text, into English for his prior, Cyril Garland. On 5 May 1441 he was given a papal indult to choose his own confessor, and on 3 December 1441, at the prompting of his relations, he wrote a short treatise on the Carmelite order, which he dedicated and sent to Pope Eugenius IV (*r.* 1431–47).

During his time as a hermit, Scrope wrote two further historical works on the Carmelites and probably a life of St Brocard, an early prior-general of the Carmelites, attributed to him and published by Daniel a Virgine Maria in 1680.

Possibly as a result of further family influence Scrope travelled to Rome, and on 12 January 1450 he was appointed bishop of Dromore in Ireland and consecrated in Rome on 1 February. Bale preserves the text of a letter from the provincial, Nicholas Kenton, written during the summer of 1450 (dated erroneously by Bale to 1448) to the Irish bishops, recommending Scrope and mentioning that he was coming to Ireland. However, any visit there must have been very short as Scrope was given permission to officiate in the Norwich diocese on 12 September 1450, and he was performing ordinations there regularly from this date onwards. On 24 November 1454 he was admitted as rector of Sparham, Norfolk. On 29 July 1457 Richard Misyn, another Carmelite, was appointed bishop of Dromore although Scrope continued to use the title.

On 3 June 1466 Scrope was admitted rector of Trowse, but he is absent from the diocesan records during the three years following. It is probably during this period that the tradition of his appointment as papal legate to Rhodes by Pope Paul II should be dated. Little is known about his mission except that John Leland records that he met a Franciscan friar there, a convert Jew from Jerusalem, with whom he had frequent talks. Sir James Ware, writing in the seventeenth century, claims that Scrope came into conflict soon after his arrival with the local clergy and people because he failed to learn their language. Scrope reappears in English records on 25 February 1469 when he performed ordinations in Maidstone and again on 1 April in Canterbury. He was back in the Norwich diocese on 17 March 1470 and continued to serve there from then on. In 1477 he consecrated the new Carmelite church in Ipswich. On 21 March 1478 Scrope performed his last ordinations in Norwich diocese, and on 27 May 1478 he was admitted rector of Lowestoft where he appears to have retired. Bale records that in his later years Scrope walked barefoot through the countryside, teaching the commandments to the people and giving away his possessions. He died on 15 January 1492, when he was said to be nearly 100, and was buried in the parish church of St Margaret, Lowestoft. Bale, a fellow Carmelite from Norwich, regarded him as a saintly man and wrote an epitaph for him in 1526.

Scrope's translation of 'The institute of first monks' survives in Lambeth Palace Library, MS 192. In all he wrote four historical works on his order, three while a hermit and a later one, probably during the 1450s, addressed to Cyril, archdeacon of Dromore. Three of them, severely edited, are printed in the *Speculum Carmelitanum* (1680). A list of Carmelite saints, noted by Bale, is part of one of these works, but copied by Scrope from an earlier source. His other works, including some sermons on the ten commandments, are lost although a manuscript of liturgical offices, prayers, and other spiritual works which once belonged to him survive as BL, Harley MS 211.

Scrope's historical compositions are somewhat repetitive, consisting of the same quotations from other authors without any particular literary style or inventiveness. However, they were well known in the order and helped to perpetuate the idea that the Carmelites could trace their origins back to Elijah the Prophet. Scrope's reputation for holiness, though, was more well-founded, and he deserves an honoured place among the mystics of fifteenth-century England. RICHARD COPSEY

Sources J. Bale, Bodl. Oxf., MS Bodley 73 (SC 27635), fol. i (3) v, 2, 12*v*, 17, 25*v*, 51*v*, 108*v*, 120*v*, 131*v*–132, 135*v*, 186, 195*v* • J. Bale, Harley MS 1819, fols. 196*v*–197, 198*v* • J. Bale, BL, Harley MS 3838 [fols. 40, 107*v*–108*v*, 219–219*v*] • Bale, *Cat.*, 1.629–30 • R. Copsey, 'Thomas Scrope', *Dictionnaire de spiritualité ascétique et mystique: doctrine et histoire*, ed. M. Viller and others (1937–95) • T. Winship, 'Thomas Scrope; Carmelite and bishop', *Aylesford Review* (autumn 1957), ii, 1, 22–5 • Daniel a Virgine Maria, ed., *Speculum Carmelitanum*, 2 vols. (Antwerp, 1680) [minor references] • J. Bale, Bodl. Oxf., MS Selden supra 41, fols. 87, 164, 180*v* • E. Gillingwater, *An historical account of the ancient town of Lowestoft, in the county of Suffolk* (1790), 294–5, 340–42 • *Commentarii de scriptoribus Britannicis, auctore Joanne Lelando*, ed. A. Hall, 2 (1709), 472–3 • G. Mesters, 'Thomas Scrope', *Lexikon für Theologie und Kirche* (1965), 10.147 • F. O'Briain, 'Bradley, Thomas de', *Dictionnaire d'histoire et de géographie ecclésiastiques*, ed. A. Baudrillart and others, 10 (Paris, 1938) • J. Pits, *Relationum historicarum de rebus Anglicis*, ed. [W. Bishop] (Paris, 1619), 681–2 • *The whole works of Sir James Ware concerning Ireland*, ed. and trans. W. Harris, rev. edn, 1 (1764), 261–2; 2 (1764), 324 • J. Weever, *Ancient funerall monuments* (1631), 768–9 • register of Bishop Lyhert, Norfolk RO, xii, fols. 214–15

Archives Bayerische Staatsbibliothek, Munich, Clm 8180, fols. 117–140*v*, 192–220*v* • Bibliothèque Nationale, Paris, MS Lat. 5615, fols. 92–106 • CUL, MS 6.11 • LPL, MS 192 • Stadtarchiv, Frankfurt, Carmeliterbücher C46, fols. 70–86 • Stadtarchiv, Cologne, MS W203, fols. 303–41

Scrope, William, **earl of Wiltshire** (**1351?–1399**), soldier, administrator, and courtier, was the eldest son of Richard *Scrope, first Baron Scrope of Bolton (*c.*1327–1403), and Blanche de la Pole, sister of Michael, earl of Suffolk. He followed in the footsteps of his father in entering the service of John of Gaunt, duke of Lancaster, joining the latter in expeditions to France in 1369 and 1373, and subsequently serving as Gaunt's lieutenant in Gascony in 1390–93. Even as late as 1398 Gaunt appointed William Scrope and Thomas Percy as his executors. Scrope's military experience is also said to have included campaigns in Italy and Prussia. There is no evidence that he held any part of the Scrope of Bolton estates during his lifetime. Instead, to an increasing extent, he made his career in the service of the crown, and the list of grants and annuities made to him from 1384 until his death indicate both his military and administrative skills and the reliance placed on him by *Richard II. In 1384 Scrope received £800 as steward of Aquitaine; in March 1385 he received £500 for the stewardship of Calais; in April 1386 he was keeper of Cherbourg; in November 1389 he was keeper of Brest. After 1389 Scrope was more involved in events at home. In February 1389 he was granted the custody of Bamburgh Castle, later given to his brother Stephen Scrope. In April 1392 he bought the Isle of Man from the earl of Salisbury, and in July 1393 he was given Marlborough Castle for life in lieu of an annuity of 200 marks.

In February 1393 Scrope had begun a more intimate association with Richard II's administration, when he was appointed under-chamberlain of the king's household, and from February 1394 onwards he was given a number of major appointments connected with the Welsh borders and also with the pacification of Ireland, which was one of Richard's objectives in the latter part of his reign. He accompanied Richard II on his Irish expedition of 1394, and became the key official in the crown lands in the west. In February 1394 he was given the keepership of Beaumaris Castle and in March 1394, as under-chamberlain, he was required to examine the castles in north Wales and Chester. In the same year he became a knight of the Garter. In February 1395 he was appointed keeper of the lordship of Uriell, keeper of Drogheda, and keeper of Conwy Castle for £40 per annum. In April 1396 he was appointed justice of Ireland, constable of Queensburgh Castle, joint keeper of Caernarfon Castle, and keeper of Pembroke Castle. In 1397 he was appointed keeper of the castle and town of Barnard Castle which was subsequently granted to him in tail male. He was also appointed keeper of Dublin Castle and of the castle at Painscastle in Wales. In 1398 he was keeper of Richmond Castle in the North Riding of Yorkshire and of the new forest of Richmond. He was appointed surveyor of forests in Cheshire, was given the constableship of Castle Lyons Castle, and appointed life justice of north Wales at £100 per annum.

By this time Scrope was also keeper for life of the Isle of Anglesey, and held a dominant position in north Wales, built up in association with Richard II's plans to create a power base for himself in the region based on the palatinate of Chester, which in 1397 had been elevated into a principality. It was partly to the same end that Scrope benefited considerably from the forfeitures of the magnates hostile to Richard II. In 1397 he was granted the Welsh estates of the disgraced earl of Warwick, and in March 1398 Daliley Castle and Wellington Haye, Shropshire, forfeited by the earl of Arundel; he also became justice of the Arundel marcher lordships. He was given the wardship of the Mortimer lands in north Wales in August 1398. In March 1399 he was given Pickering Castle and the following month was made constable of Knaresborough Castle, both appointments from estates forfeited by Henry Bolingbroke.

William Scrope had become an invaluable servant to Richard II and he was among the members of a new nobility created by Richard who were closely identified with the king personally. On 29 September 1397 he was created earl of Wiltshire, the highest rank ever achieved by the Scrope family, and he was among those who appealed Gloucester, Warwick, and Arundel of treason in that year. He was subsequently given custody of Warwick on the Isle of Man and was accused of treating him cruelly. In the final years of Richard II's reign Scrope was deeply involved in the day-to-day administration of government. He had been appointed treasurer on 17 September 1398 and, together with a small group of other officers, oversaw most government business, including the retrospective fining of those who had sued for pardon for the events of 1387–8. The events of 1399, when Richard II left for Ireland and Bolingbroke invaded England during his absence, with the resulting collapse of support for the crown, are well known. William Scrope fled to Bristol, but Bolingbroke captured him there and had him beheaded, on 29 July. His head was displayed on London Bridge until November 1400.

The contemporary view of William Scrope was almost universally hostile. The poem 'Richard the Redeless' of *c.*1399, which puns on the names of the king's favourites, Scrope's among them, and describes them as 'kytes' battening on the resources of the crown, shows that he was regarded as one of those courtiers to whom the profits of government in the last years of Richard II's reign were almost entirely confined. According to Thomas Walsingham a more wicked or cruel man would not easily be found. Even allowing for Lancastrian bias, Scrope was clearly a man who aroused particular antagonism. In 1389 William Scrope and his brother Stephen were bound over for 10,000 marks to do no harm to Walter Skirlaw, bishop of Durham (*d.* 1406), and on 24 January 1390 William offered a jewel worth £500 to the shrine of St Cuthbert for trespasses done by him and his people in Durham. After Scrope's death several of those who had suffered at his hands appealed against his decisions, including the bailiffs of the exchequer, who had had their allowances of £100 cut to £7 by him.

The earldom of Wiltshire was a political creation which could not survive the deaths of the holder and his patron. The surviving members of the family did not have the means to sustain such an honour, and it was not until the nineteenth century that any attempt was made to restore it. There were no children from William Scrope's marriage with Isabel, daughter of Sir Maurice Russell of Kingston Russell in Dorset. William predeceased his father, and was survived by his brothers Roger, second Lord Scrope of Bolton (*d.* 1403), and Stephen (*d.* 1409).

BRIGETTE VALE

Sources *Chancery records* • B. P. Vale, 'The Scropes of Bolton and of Masham, c.1300–c.1450', PhD diss., University of York, 1987 • N. H. Nicolas, ed., *The Scrope and Grosvenor controversy*, 2 vols. (privately printed, London, 1832) • J. Coleman, *English literature in history, 1350–1400* (1981) • R. R. Davies, 'Richard II and the principality of Chester, 1397–9', *The reign of Richard II: essays in honour of May McKisack*, ed. F. R. H. Du Boulay and C. M. Barron (1971), 256–79 • *DNB* • B. Williams, ed., *Chronicque de la traïson et mort de Richart Deux, roy Dengleterre*, EHS, 9 (1846) • C. Given-Wilson, *The royal household and the king's affinity: service, politics and finance in England, 1360–1413* (1986)

Scrope, William (1772–1852), artist and writer, was second son of Richard Scrope DD (1729?–1787), and his wife, Anne, daughter of Edmund Lambert of Boyton, Wiltshire. He was a direct descendant of Richard, first Baron Scrope of Bolton, lord treasurer to Edward III, and succeeded to the property of the Scropes of Castle Combe, Wiltshire, on the death of his father in 1787. In 1795 the Scrope estates of Cockerington, Lincolnshire, also passed to him. On 4 January 1794 he married Emma, daughter of Charles Long of Grittleton, Wiltshire.

Scrope was an excellent classical scholar, a keen sportsman, and one of the ablest amateur artists of his time. He painted views in Scotland, Italy, Sicily, and elsewhere, and exhibited occasionally from 1808 at the Royal Academy, and later at the British Institution, of which he was one of the most active directors. He was frequently assisted in his work by William Simson. None the less, Scrope perhaps achieved more general acclaim for his two well-known books, *The Art of Deerstalking* (1838) and *Days and Nights of Salmon-Fishing in the Tweed* (1843), each illustrated with plates after Edwin and Charles Landseer, David Wilkie, W. Simson, and others, and each reprinted thrice, up to 1894 and 1921 respectively. Scrope rented a place near Melrose, where he lived on terms of great intimacy with Sir Walter Scott. He was a member of the Accademia di San Luca at Rome, and a fellow of the Linnean Society.

Scrope died at his home, 13 Belgrave Square, London, on 20 July 1852. He was the last male representative of his family. His only daughter and heir, Emma Phipps, married, in 1821, George Poulett Thomson, who then assumed the name and arms of Scrope [*see* Scrope, George Poulett].

F. M. O'DONOGHUE, *rev.* JULIAN LOCK

Sources *GM*, 2nd ser., 38 (1852), 201 • *The Athenaeum* (24 July 1852), 800 • Boase, *Mod. Eng. biog.* • *The journal of Sir Walter Scott*, ed. W. E. K. Anderson (1972) • Graves, *Artists*, 3rd edn • Burke, *Gen. GB* • *GM*, 1st ser., 57 (1787), 643–4 • *GM*, 1st ser., 64 (1794), 88
Archives BL, family papers, Add. MSS 28205–28213

Scrots [Stretes], **Guillim** (*fl.* 1537–1553), portrait painter, described as a 'Dutchman' (BL, Add. MS 30198, fol. 22*v*), was probably a native of the southern Netherlands; his name is spelt Stretes in some sources. Nothing is known of his early life, training, or parentage. The first part of his career appears to have been spent at the Habsburg court in Bruges, where he was appointed painter to Mary of Hungary, regent of the Netherlands, on 1 September 1537, at a salary of 6 sous per day. During his employment with her he is documented as having produced portraits of the Habsburg emperor Charles V and the empress Isabella. These are not known to survive. Surviving portraits of the young archdukes Maximilian (later Emperor Maximilian II) and Ferdinand (both Kunsthistorisches Museum, Schloss Ambras, Innsbruck) are convincingly attributed to Scrots on the basis of stylistic comparison with his English work, and may have been painted at the diet of Speyer in 1544. They are three-quarter length oil portraits on panel, with a typically Netherlandish attention to surface detail and pattern, and the illusionistic rendition of texture, a sympathetic if not penetrating approach to the characterization of his sitters, and a striking colour scheme: both boys are shown in black and gold costumes against a bright green background. Scrots is last recorded in the Low Countries as a witness to a deposition on 24 October 1544, in which all the other witnesses are citizens of Antwerp, and so it is assumed that he was in Antwerp at that time.

Scrots went to England to take up a position as a painter at the court of Henry VIII probably in the second half of 1545. Here he was paid the very substantial annual salary of £62 10*s*. from at least Michaelmas that year, making him the highest paid artist at the English court at the time. He was presumably regarded as the successor to Hans Holbein the younger, who had died in 1543, but who had been paid a much lower salary of £30 in his position as king's painter. It is likely that Scrots's previous court employment enabled him to command this high salary, whereas Holbein had not worked at a court before going to England.

Various portraits produced in England after Holbein's death, of greatly varying quality and style, have been attributed in the past to Scrots, but there is little secure evidence linking him to specific paintings. The only documentary evidence of his work in England is a payment from the king and council in March 1551 for three full-length portraits, two of Edward VI for Sir Philip Hoby and Sir John Mason and one of Henry Howard, earl of Surrey (1517?–1547). Sir Philip Hoby and Sir John Mason were both ambassadors, Hoby having been appointed ambassador to the court of Charles V in April 1548 and Mason to the court of Henry II of France in 1550. Both men were involved in negotiations for a marriage between Edward VI and Princess Elizabeth of France, which came to a head in May 1551, and it seems most likely that the portraits of the young king painted for these men were produced in connection with these negotiations. A group of surviving portraits of Edward VI, in oil on panel, is probably correctly associated with Scrots and his studio on the basis of this payment. Five of these are full lengths, the most accomplished being those now at Hampton Court Palace and the Musée du Louvre, Paris. The approach to the modelling of the young king's face in the Louvre portrait is particularly close to that of Archduke Ferdinand in the portrait at Schloss Ambras.

The portrait of the earl of Surrey, who had been charged with treason and executed in January 1547, has proved more elusive. It is described in the 1551 payment as 'a picture of the late earle of Surrey attainted and by the counsailes comanndement fetched from the said Gwillms howse' (Royal MS, 18, 124, fol. 69*v*, BL). It has been suggested that it may correspond to a large full-length portrait on canvas that was in the collection of Surrey's descendants, the dukes of Norfolk (now belonging to the National Portrait Gallery, but still at Arundel Castle). However the latter painting is perhaps more likely to have been produced by an Italian artist working in the style of Giovanni Battista Moroni. A portrait on panel, showing the head only, but probably a fragment of a larger painting (NPG), may be a better candidate for all that remains of Scrots's portrait of Surrey; Netherlandish in style, like the portraits at Schloss Ambras it has a plain bright green background and the modelling of the face is sophisticated and sensitive.

Perhaps the most remarkable work attributed to Scrots is a portrait in distorted perspective of Edward VI (NPG). This type of 'anamorphic' portrait was popular in the Habsburg courts in the early sixteenth century; designed to amaze the viewer and display the artist's skills, the distorted image appears unintelligible at first glance, but viewed from the correct angle, or using a special viewing device, the perspective is corrected and the portrait resolves itself into legibility. The antiquarian George Vertue recorded in the early eighteenth century seeing the signature 'Guihelmus pingebat' on the original frame (Vertue, *Note Books*, 1.54) and the conjunction of the name, date, royal sitter and Habsburg court associations suggests strongly that Scrots should be identified as the artist.

As far as can be judged by his small surviving *œuvre*, Scrots's contribution to English art was to bring the glamorous Habsburg court style briefly to the court of Henry VIII, and then to that of Edward VI, forming a link between the sophisticated portraiture of Hans Holbein and the flatter, more abstracted Anglo-Netherlandish style that characterized the painting of the Elizabethan court. He adopted the pose of Hans Holbein's full-length mural portrait of Henry VIII at Whitehall Palace for his paintings of the young Edward VI, but Scrots's strong lighting and simple but striking colour schemes give his portraits a flatter appearance, emphasizing their decorative surfaces. His work in turn influenced that of Hans Eworth, the Netherlandish artist who was most dominant in England immediately after Scrots; in its approach to modelling the face, for example, Eworth's portrait of Lord Darnley (1555; Scot. NPG) is particularly comparable to Scrots's portrait of Edward VI in the Louvre.

It is not known why Scrots disappears from the court records after 1553; his last salary payment in England was made for a period ending in June of that year. The termination of his court employment may of course be connected with the succession of Mary I to the throne, but there is currently no evidence as to whether he left the country for good, or remained until his death at some later date. No paintings post-dating the reign of Edward VI have been convincingly attributed to him.

CATHARINE MACLEOD

Sources C. MacLeod, 'Guillim Scrots in England', MA diss., Courtauld Inst., 1990 • E. Auerbach, *Tudor artists* (1954) • G. Heinz, 'Das Porträtbuch des Hieronymus Beck von Leopoldsdorf', *Jahrbuch der Kunsthistorischen Sammlungen in Wien*, 71/35 (1975), 165–310 • R. Strong, *Tudor and Jacobean portraits [in the National Portrait Gallery]* (1969) • H. Nellis, *Chambre des Comptes de Lille: catalogue des chartes du sceau de l'audience* (Brussels, 1915) • A. Pinchart, 'Tableaux et sculptures de Marie d'Autriche reine douarière de Hongrie', *Revue Universelle des Arts*, 3 (1856), 127–46 • E. Auerbach, 'Holbein's followers in England', *Burlington Magazine*, 93 (1951), 44–51 • E. Auerbach, 'Notes on some northern mannerist painters', *Burlington Magazine*, 91 (1949), 218–22 • G. Heinz and K. Schütz, *Porträtgalerie zur Geschichte Österreichs von 1400 bis 1800* (Vienna, 1976) • J. Baltrusaitis, *Anamorphoses, ou, Perspectives curieuses* (Paris, 1955) • Conseil d'État et Audience, '1640' or '1630', National State Archives, Brussels • Redenkamer/Chambre des comptes, National State Archives, Brussels, nr. 48, fol.41*r* • payment record, BL, MS Royal 18, 124, fol. 69*v* • Court of Augmentations and Predecessors and Successors: miscellaneous books, PRO, E 315/236, fol. 183*r*; E 315/245, fol. 67*v*; E 315/255, fol. 94; E 315/220, fol. 44 • Court of Augmentations: treasurers' accounts, PRO, E 323/3, m. 89; E 323/4, m. 37; E 323/5, m. 36; E 323/6, m. 21; E 323/7, m. 23*v*; E 323/8, m. 39 • records assembled by the State Paper Office, PRO, SP 4/1, no. 99

Scrutton, Sir Thomas Edward (1856–1934), judge, was born on 28 August 1856 in East India Dock Road, Poplar, London, the elder son of Thomas Urquhart Scrutton, a prosperous shipowner, later of Buckhurst Hill, Essex, and his wife, Mary, daughter of the Revd Edward Hickman. The Scruttons had for several generations run a shipping line, originally under sail, between the United Kingdom and the West Indies. Scrutton's father was a Congregationalist in the days when the Society for the Liberation of Religion from State Patronage and Control was a political force, and Scrutton was sent to Mill Hill School to be educated.

Scrutton's industriousness showed itself from an early age. At London University he took the degrees of BA, MA, and LLB (1882), with honours. He also won a scholarship at Trinity College, Cambridge, obtained a first class in the moral sciences tripos, and was awarded the senior Whewell scholarship for international law in 1879, and was placed first in the first class of the law tripos of 1880. He won the Barstow scholarship of the inns of court in 1882. Finally, he won the University of Cambridge's Yorke prize for a legal essay in 1882, 1884, 1885, and 1886, the first to win the distinction more than three times.

Although he probably hoped to be elected to a fellowship at Trinity, Scrutton was deemed by some of the fellows there, though intelligent and immensely hardworking, not to be 'original'. Furthermore, he was lanky and rather uncouth and was thought to have been the only Englishman of his time who never shaved in his life. A photograph of him as president of the Cambridge Union in 1880 shows him with a downy beard. One of the few diversions which he allowed himself from his study was to ride an old-fashioned high bicycle, a daredevil sport contested between rival cyclists from Oxford and Cambridge. While still an undergraduate he became engaged to Mary, the daughter of Samuel Crickmer Burton, a solicitor from Great Yarmouth.

Scrutton was called to the bar by the Middle Temple in 1882, and formally joined the south-eastern circuit: but he never went on it again. In 1884 he and Mary got married, and moved to Westcombe Park, a suburb near Blackheath. They had four sons and a daughter; their youngest son was killed in the First World War. Scrutton became a KC in 1901 and a bencher of his inn in 1908, after which the family moved to a flat at 134 Piccadilly. Scrutton never took much part in the social life, or in the business, of the inn, and did not hold office.

Scrutton read in chambers with Sir A. L. Smith and was at the same time professor of constitutional law and legal history at University College, London. After leaving Smith, he had chambers for a time in Essex Court, and when his practice began to grow moved to a large set of chambers at 3 Temple Gardens. The growth of his commercial practice was helped by the publication in 1886 of his book *The Contract of Affreightment as Expressed in Charter Parties and Bills of Lading*, which became a leading textbook on the subject, the fourteenth edition appearing in 1939. He also turned his essay on the laws of copyright, with which he won the Yorke prize in 1882, into a textbook, *The Laws of Copyright* (1883), and generated another considerable and lucrative sideline to his law practice.

In 1892 a highly technical case about general average came before Mr Justice J. C. Lawrence in the non-jury list. That unlearned judge (one of the political promotions of Lord Halsbury) was so obviously unfit for the task that it led to the establishment of a commercial court in 1895 under Sir J. C. Mathew. For some fifteen years Scrutton and his great rival, J. A. Hamilton (afterwards Viscount Sumner), were among its busiest practitioners.

In those years Scrutton got through an immense amount of work, spending his time either in the courts, or in the hideous room which he occupied in the hideous block called Temple Gardens, and in which a Spartan rigour reigned. Scrutton sat on a windsor chair, without a cushion, at a battered writing-table, to the side of which was a table, loaded with papers, that had come out of one of his father's ships; a rough piece of wood filled the hole that had enclosed the mast. When darkness set in, the only source of light was a Victorian chandelier with fish-tail gas burners. The other two rooms were filled with 'devils' and pupils, including, at various times, the future Lord Atkin, Lord Wright, Lord Justice MacKinnon, Mr Justice Fraser, and Mr Justice Henn Collins. At 4.15 p.m. the group met together for some repulsive tea and dry Bath Oliver biscuits. Scrutton, silently absorbed in thinking about his work, would stride about the room until, almost daily, the top of his head crashed into the knob of the chandelier that hung from the ceiling.

In February 1909 Scrutton's rival, Hamilton, was promoted to the bench. Soon afterwards Scrutton was sent as special commissioner on the north-eastern circuit. In April 1910, on the recommendation of Lord Loreburn, he was appointed a judge of the King's Bench Division, on the resignation of Mr Justice Sutton. He received a knighthood in the same year.

Scrutton soon proved himself a very efficient judge, though not a popular one. He had never had good manners and he indulged in petulant rudeness to counsel, and to solicitors' clerks on summonses. Eventually all the chief City solicitors, his former clients, gave a joint retainer to Alfred Chaytor, then a leading junior who took silk in 1914, to make a protest to the judge in court. Chaytor discharged his task with firmness. Scrutton listened without comment, but proved his contrition by his subsequent conduct.

For six years Scrutton was a successful judge of first instance in London (often in the commercial court), and on circuit. He was very efficient in trying prisoners, although he had had no such experience at the bar. In 1915, at the Old Bailey, he had to try a notorious murderer, George Joseph Smith, in the sensational 'brides in the bath' case, and popular opinion concurred with the professional view that he was a great judge.

In October 1916, on the resignation of Lord Justice Phillimore, Scrutton was promoted to the Court of Appeal, and became a member of the privy council. During eighteen years in that court he displayed ever-increasing judicial powers, and when for the last seven years he presided over one of its divisions, he had had few, if any, superiors in that position. When at the bar, he had been hampered, if anything, by an immense knowledge of case law. Towards the end of his career he came to see the wood rather than the trees, and developed a mastery of legal principles. Indeed he achieved a good deal of that originality which had seemed lacking in his Cambridge days. Scrutton mellowed with age. Although he continued never to shave, in his later years he cut his beard in an Elizabethan style. On one occasion in 1932 he behaved in a manner reminiscent of his youth, when he responded with great rudeness to an appeal from H. A. McCardie (whom he probably despised intellectually). McCardie, however, was even more injudicious, and unjudicial, in his protest in court by way of rejoinder. In May 1936 an American professor, K. N. Llewellyn, was rich in his praises of Scrutton in an article about him in the *Columbia Law Review*, declaring him 'a matchless commercial lawyer', 'among the noblest of the judicial bench', 'a greater commercial judge than Mansfield', and 'the greatest English-speaking judge of a century'.

Scrutton's numerous published writings included *The Elements of Mercantile Law* (1891); an annotated version of *The Merchant Shipping Act, 1894* (1895); and an article entitled 'The work of the commercial courts' (*Cambridge Law Journal*, 1, 1921). He also had published his three remaining Yorke prize essays which appeared as *The Influence of the Roman Law on the Law of England* (1885), *Land in Fetters* (1886), and *Commons and Common Fields* (1887).

Apart from the law, Scrutton was interested in poetry, travel, music, and church architecture. With his wife he regularly attended orchestral concerts at Covent Garden, and in his travels in Germany his lodestar was the music at Bayreuth and Munich. He was a member of the Reform

Club and, when a judge, of the Athenaeum, but he was rarely seen in either place: if he had any spare time he spent it at home. In 1886 he made his only attempt to take part in national politics when he stood unsuccessfully as a Liberal candidate for the Limehouse division.

Scrutton, who had always enjoyed cycling and was a keen watcher of rugby, cricket, and athletics, was an enthusiastic, if not a very skilful, golfer. He presented the Scrutton cup for an annual competition between the inns of court. It was in the course of a golfing holiday at Sheringham in the summer vacation of 1934 that he was found to be suffering from a hernia. He was taken to hospital at Norwich where he died on 18 August. He was buried in the Rosary cemetery at Norwich.

F. D. MACKINNON, *rev.* HUGH MOONEY

Sources *The Times* (21 Aug 1934) • *The Times* (1 Sept 1934) • *The Times* (3 Oct 1934) • *Manchester Guardian* (21 Aug 1934) • K. M. Llewellyn, 'On warranty of equality, and society', *Columbia Law Review*, 36 (1936), 699–744 • *CGPLA Eng. & Wales* (1934)

Likenesses W. Stoneman, photograph, 1917, NPG • Ape Junior, caricature, Hentschel-Colourtype, NPG; repro. in *VF* (28 June 1911) • O. Edis, two photographs, NPG • photograph, repro. in T. E. Scrutton, *Charter parties and bills of lading*, 14th edn, frontispiece

Wealth at death £105,180 4*s*. 7*d*.: resworn probate, 7 Nov 1934, *CGPLA Eng. & Wales*

Scrymgeour, Edwin (1866–1947), prohibitionist and politician, was born on 28 July 1866 at 25 Nethergate, Dundee, the fifth of the eight children of James Scrymgeour (1821–1887), temperance and charity worker, and his wife, Jeanette (1837–1925), daughter of David Calman, superintendent of the graving dock in Dundee. Scrymgeour inherited from his father a vigorous Wesleyan Methodist religious belief, a conviction that drink was evil, and a compassion for the poor. He did not inherit his father's toryism. Edwin Scrymgeour wanted the world transformed by the socialism that only a sober people could bring about.

After attending West End Academy in Dundee, Scrymgeour worked as a clerk, initially in London for a textile manufacturing company owned by his elder brothers, George and Charles. After this company failed he was employed in Dundee by the Caledonian Railway Company and later by a firm of iron and steel merchants. On 14 June 1892 he married Margaret (1866–1947), daughter of Thomas Croston, telegraphic superintendent. The marriage was childless. Scrymgeour followed his father into active membership of the Independent Order of Good Templars, a semi-masonic anti-drink organization popular across Scotland in the late nineteenth century. In 1895 he was elected to the parish council, the body in charge of Dundee's poorhouses and poor relief, as an Independent Labour Party (ILP) candidate. For some years he combined work and politics until, in 1901, his commercial career came to an end when the vehemence with which he pursued his political activities caused annoyance to his employer.

Scrymgeour's connection with the ILP also ended in 1901 when he became a founder member of, and the leading force in, the Scottish Prohibition Party (SPP). From 1904 he was the paid organizer of the party, a post he later combined with editing the *Scottish Prohibitionist*, the party's weekly paper. It was as a member of the SPP that he was elected to Dundee town council in 1905. His style on the council was stormy and uncompromising, on one occasion provoking physical attack from another member, on others suspension. His first parliamentary contest as an SPP candidate was against Winston Churchill at a by-election in Dundee in 1908. On that occasion he was unsuccessful, as he was at four later attempts: 1910 (twice), 1917, and 1918. He took a pacifist position during the war, but managed to increase his vote. In 1922 he caused surprise by topping the poll in the two-member seat, defeating Churchill. It was as a socialist, rather than as a prohibitionist, that he was elected—Dundee showed no inclination to vote dry when offered the chance at the veto polls held in the early 1920s. He described himself as prohibitionist and Labour, and made it clear that the abolition of drink would, of itself, solve nothing. Thirty thousand Dundonians and a band gathered at the railway station to see him off to parliament, as the members of the SPP danced with abandon on the platform.

Once at Westminster, Scrymgeour allied himself with the Scottish ILP members, many of whom he had previously worked with in anti-war activities, though he never rejoined the party. If he had done so he would not have been particularly unusual in his extremism, his attitude to drink, his support for a Scottish parliament, or in his strong religious belief. The labour movement in Scotland was overwhelmingly 'dry', and had two clergymen among its MPs in the 1920s. Ten of the fourteen supporters of his Liquor Traffic Prohibition Bill, first moved as a private member's bill in 1923, which would have introduced complete prohibition, were Scottish Labour MPs. The bill was moved a second time in 1931. By then drink was taken far less seriously as a political issue, and his support came from scattered eccentrics across the house.

Scrymgeour was defeated in the anti-Labour landslide at the 1931 general election. His faith in politics was shattered. He became convinced that his time would be better devoted to religion, and he worked for the rest of his life as a hospital chaplain. The prohibition party was wound up in 1934. He died at his home, 2 Errol Terrace, 92 Victoria Road, Dundee, on 1 February 1947, and was buried at the eastern cemetery, Dundee.

JOHN KEMP

Sources Dundee Reference Library, Dundee, Scrymgeour MSS • W. M. Walker, *Juteopolis*, 1st edn (1979) • W. M. Walker, 'Dundee's disenchantment with Churchill', *SHR*, 49 (1970), 85–108 • W. M. Walker, 'The Scottish Prohibition Party and the millennium', *International Review of Social History*, 18 (1973), 353–79 • Dundee Reference Library, Lamb collection, Scrymgeour family MSS, 421 (71) • W. Knox, ed., *Scottish labour leaders, 1918–39: a biographical dictionary* (1984) • W. Norrie, *The life of James Scrymgeour of Dundee* (1887) • *WWW*, 1941–50 • m. cert.

Archives Dundee Central Library, papers | FILM BFI NFTVA, documentary footage

Likenesses J. D. Revel, oils, 1926, Dundee city council

Wealth at death £1524 3*s*. 9*d*.: confirmation, 9 April 1947, *CCI*

Scrymgeour, Henry. *See* Scrimgeour, Henry (1505?–1572).

Scrymgeour, Sir James, of Dudhope (*c*.1550–1612), administrator, was the eldest son of John Scrymgeour of Dudhope (*d*. 1568) and his wife, a member of the family of

Campbell of Auchinbreck. On his father's death in November 1568 Scrymgeour succeeded to the hereditary offices of constable of nearby Dundee and standard-bearer of Scotland. The latter office was ratified to him by the privy council in 1592, and by parliament in 1594 and 1600.

During the Marian civil war Scrymgeour supported the king's party. From at least the early 1570s to the early 1590s he was linked to the Lyon family, which was powerful in Angus (Forfarshire), and he also supported the Ruthven raiders. Consequently on 23 January 1584 he was ordered into exile, and on 21 April following he was one of the rebel leaders charged to surrender Stirling Castle to the king. However, once King James took personal control of the government in 1585, Scrymgeour, like many others, turned to royal service. He had been charged with several crimes in the late 1570s and 1580s, but his conduct did not go beyond what was generally regarded as acceptable, and his reputation for violence has been exaggerated by some historians. Moreover, the very fact that the king employed him from the mid-1580s suggests a greater degree of self-restraint, since incurably violent nobles were increasingly excluded from power. As early as 1587 Scrymgeour received a grant for good service. In 1589 he held Fintry Castle against the Brig o' Dee rebels, acted as a commissioner to the general assembly of the kirk, and was sent to Denmark to help arrange James's marriage, witnessing the subsequent contract. For such services he won the king's trust, and about 1590 he was knighted. Scrymgeour's reliability and solid protestant credentials brought him many other appointments. He was at various times a collector of taxes, a commissioner against Jesuits, an overseer of parliamentary elections, a commissioner to hold parliament, and a juror at important state trials. He helped bear the pall at Prince Henry's baptism in 1594. In 1597 he was again a commissioner to the general assembly. A commissioner for the union in 1604, between 1605 and 1612 he frequently attended the privy council.

Scrymgeour was also a figure of considerable local importance in Angus, thanks to his estates there and his office of constable of Dundee, and he devoted much effort to maintaining and enhancing his position. He was admitted a burgess of Dundee in 1576 and from 1588 was frequently provost of the burgh, in which position he actively supported both the interests of individual burgesses and those of the city as a whole. For example, he took a prominent part in defending Dundee's rights against the burgh of Perth in their battle for control of the trade of the Water of Tay. His local power also involved him in burgh politics, as when in 1604 he successfully disputed a burgh election on the ground that it was illegal.

Scrymgeour married twice. His first marriage (for which there is a contract of 13 June 1565) was to Margaret Carnegie (*d.* 1576), a daughter of Sir Robert Carnegie of Kinnaird. She was the mother of all Scrymgeour's children—Elspeth, Margaret, John, and Catherine. She died on 9 January 1576, and he was contracted on 23 August 1576 to Magdalene Livingstone, daughter of Alexander, fifth Lord Livingstone, and married her in 1577; she outlived her husband. Sir James Scrymgeour died at Holyroodhouse Abbey, Edinburgh, on 13 July 1612.

His only son and heir, **John Scrymgeour**, first Viscount Dudhope (*d.* 1643), was a resolute royalist from the very beginning of the covenanters' revolution. He attended every parliament until the covenanting rebellion, and was a lord of the articles in three out of four of them—in 1612, 1621, and 1633. King James stayed at his house on 20 May 1617 during his visit to Scotland, and Scrymgeour was knighted by 1620. In 1630 and 1631 he was appointed a commissioner for surveying the laws of Scotland, and in 1634 he was appointed to the high commission. On 1 May 1627 he was charged with sheltering James Seton, a Jesuit priest. It is not clear if Scrymgeour was a lifelong Roman Catholic, but some of his actions are consistent with this possibility. In the 1621 parliament he voted in favour of the five articles of Perth and on 1 February 1639 he refused to sign the covenant. One of the 'resolutes' who supported the king in 1639, Scrymgeour was created Viscount Dudhope when Charles I visited Scotland in 1641. In September 1596 he married Margaret, daughter of Sir David Seton of Parbroath, formerly comptroller of Scotland, with whom he had nine children. He died on 7 March 1643. His eldest son, **James Scrymgeour**, second Viscount Dudhope (*d.* 1644), covenanter and military leader, served in parliament and was appointed to the committee of estates in 1643, and when the covenanters decided to support the English parliamentarians he was appointed a colonel of the Forfarshire foot. On 2 July 1644 he fought at Marston Moor and received a wound from which he died three weeks later. Scrymgeour was admitted a burgess of Dundee on 9 July 1619. He inherited from his father a quarrel with the city of Dundee over his family's rights to hold the first fair of Dundee (first granted in 1384), and over other issues ranging from his contributions to the minister's salary to his attempts to establish a burgh of barony that would challenge the city's trading and industrial privileges. He married (contract, 4 August 1618) Isabella Ker, daughter of Robert, first earl of Roxburghe, with whom he had five children. He died on 23 July 1644, and his widow died after 29 September 1659.

Their eldest son, **John Scrymgeour**, first earl of Dundee (*d.* 1668), became a royalist leader and supporter of Charles II. But after his father's death he remained a covenanter until the engagement between the Scots and Charles I in 1648, after which he served as a colonel of horse in the army that was defeated by Cromwell at Preston. He was treated as a 'malignant' in 1649, and in 1650 became a royalist, with an important role in an aborted royalist coup in October 1650. He fought for Charles II at Worcester in 1651 and escaped, then fought again in Middleton's rising in 1654 and was captured. In 1659 he was still a prisoner in Scotland. At the Restoration he was made a privy councillor, and was created earl of Dundee on 8 September 1660. His lands were recovered from the forfeited estates of the marquess of Argyll, but in 1666 both his lands and offices, including the constableship of

Dundee, were seized for debt. In 1644 Lord Dudhope married Anna Ramsay, daughter of William, first earl of Dalhousie; they had no children. He died on 23 June 1668. In the absence of direct male heirs his lands reverted to the crown and his titles lapsed: they were successfully claimed in 1952 (Dudhope) and 1953 (Dundee). His widow survived him and remarried on 13 October 1670.

MICHAEL WASSER

Sources *Scots peerage*, vols. 3, 5, 9 • *Reg. PCS*, 1st ser., vols. 2–13 • *Reg. PCS*, 2nd ser., vols. 1–8 • *APS*, 1567–1686 • *DNB* • J. M. Thomson and others, eds., *Registrum magni sigilli regum Scotorum / The register of the great seal of Scotland*, 11 vols. (1882–1914), vols. 4–11 • M. Livingstone, D. Hay Fleming, and others, eds., *Registrum secreti sigilli regum Scotorum / The register of the privy seal of Scotland*, 6–8 (1963–82) • A. H. Millar, ed., *The compt buik of David Wedderburne, merchant of Dundee, 1587–1630*, Scottish History Society, old ser. 28 (1898) • commissariot court of Edinburgh, NA Scot., CC8/8/20, fols. 85v–86v • D. Calderwood, *The history of the Kirk of Scotland*, ed. T. Thomson and D. Laing, 8 vols., Wodrow Society, 7 (1842–9), vols. 4–6 • *CSP Scot.*, 1589–97 • T. Thomson, ed., *Acts and proceedings of the general assemblies of the Kirk of Scotland*, 3 pts, Bannatyne Club, 81 (1839–45), pts 2–3 • N. Tranter, *The fortified house in Scotland* (1966), vol. 4 • F. D. Bardgett, *Scotland reformed: the Reformation in Angus and the Mearns* (1989) • Burke, *Peerage* • A. Nicoll, *The first history of Dundee, 1776*, ed. A. H. Millar (1923) • P. Donald, *An uncounselled king: Charles I and the Scottish troubles, 1637–1641* (1990) • F. D. Dow, *Cromwellian Scotland, 1651–1660* (1979) [cog 24969] • D. Stevenson, *Revolution and counter-revolution in Scotland, 1644–1651*, Royal Historical Society Studies in History, 4 (1977) [cog 24969] • GEC, *Peerage*, new edn, 4.477–9
Archives NA Scot.

Scrymgeour, James, second Viscount Dudhope (*d.* **1644**). *See under* Scrymgeour, Sir James, of Dudhope (*c.*1550–1612).

Scrymgeour, John, first Viscount Dudhope (*d.* **1643**). *See under* Scrymgeour, Sir James, of Dudhope (*c.*1550–1612).

Scrymgeour, John, first earl of Dundee (*d.* **1668**). *See under* Scrymgeour, Sir James, of Dudhope (*c.*1550–1612).

Scudamore family (*per.* **1500–1820**), gentry, in Herefordshire and the southern marches of Wales, were descended from a Norman family which settled at Upton Scudamore in Wiltshire before the conquest. A cadet branch of the family had moved by the early 1380s to Holme Lacy, 5 miles south-east of Hereford on the west bank of the River Wye, but until the early sixteenth century they were overshadowed by their cousins the Scudamores or Skydmores (the latter being the more usual spelling until the sixteenth century) of Kentchurch, Herefordshire.

Foundations in country and court The founder of the fortunes of the Holme Lacy branch was **John Scudamore** (*c.*1486–1571), the son of William Skydmore, or Scudamore (1464–*c.*1520), and his wife, Alice Mynors (*d.* 1558), who rose to prominence through service at court, where he was a gentleman usher by 1515, and through his friendship with Thomas Cromwell. He used his positions to amass local office and influence: he was variously sheriff of Merioneth and Herefordshire, steward of the city of Hereford, MP for Herefordshire in 1529, JP in Herefordshire, Worcestershire, Shropshire, and Gloucestershire, *custos rotulorum* of Herefordshire by 1561, steward of several duchy of Lancaster manors, and, from 1553, a member of the council of Wales. Appointed in 1536 a receiver of the court of augmentations for Herefordshire, Shropshire, Staffordshire, and Worcestershire, he built up the family estates from the spoils of the dissolved monasteries, especially the lands of Dore Abbey in western Herefordshire. His new wealth was reflected in his rebuilding of Holme Lacy House in brick in the 1540s. He maintained his local power under Elizabeth, despite his religious conservatism (he made a decidedly Catholic will), and, it was noted in 1570, was one of those local governors who had 'woon unto them … the hartes of theire cowntrie' (Atherton, 26).

John Scudamore married twice. His first wife, Sybil Vaughan (*d.* 1559), whom he married by a licence dated 10 May 1511, was the mother of all nine of his recorded children. Following her death and in or before 1564 he married Joan Rudhall, widow of Richard Reade of Oddington; she appears to have predeceased him. He died at Holme Lacy on 25 September 1571. Scudamore had arranged court offices for two of his younger sons, Richard (*d.* 1586), who was in the late 1540s and early 1550s London agent to Sir Philip Hoby, ambassador at the court of the holy Roman emperor Charles V (his letters to Hoby were published by the Camden Society in 1990), and Philip (*d.* 1602), but his eldest son, William, who had married Ursula Pakington (*d.* 1558), predeceased him in 1560. The wardship of William's eldest son, **Sir John Scudamore** (1542–1623), who was born on 1 February 1542, was granted to Sir James Croft of Croft Castle, Herefordshire, a noted local magnate and courtier. By 1563 Croft had arranged the marriage of his ward to his daughter, Eleanor, and he developed a strong friendship with his son-in-law which survived Eleanor's death late in 1569. Scudamore entered the Inner Temple in November 1569. When Croft was made comptroller of the household in 1570 it was natural that Scudamore should turn courtier. By early 1572 he had been made a gentleman pensioner; he was knighted in 1592 and was made standard-bearer of the gentlemen pensioners in 1599.

Although his court office helped bolster his power, the principal prop of Sir John Scudamore's influence was his second wife, Mary (*d.* 1603), daughter of Sir John Shelton of Norfolk and a member of the queen's privy chamber, whom he married in January 1574. She was more important at court than her husband for she had the queen's ear, and could control the access of suitors to the queen; to her enemies, thus, she was 'a barbarous, brazen-faced woman', but to her friends she formed, with Lady Blanch Parry and the countess of Warwick, 'A Trinity of Ladies able to worke miracles' (Atherton, 28). Bolstered further by friendship with the seventh earl of Shrewsbury and his countess, John rose as a local magnate in Herefordshire: *custos rotulorum* in 1574, deputy lieutenant in 1575, sheriff in 1581, and MP for the shire in the 1570s and 1580s. He stood adroitly apart from the bitter feud for power within Herefordshire between Croft and Sir Thomas Coningsby, but saw some of his local power wane after Croft's death in 1590 and the intervention of the second earl of Essex on Coningsby's side.

Sir John, however, weathered the storms and used his son **Sir James Scudamore** (*bap.* 1568, *d.* 1619) as a means of keeping a channel open to the Essex interest. James was baptized at Holme Lacy on 10 June 1568 and possibly entered Gray's Inn in March 1595. He had attached himself first to Sir Philip Sidney (he bore the pennon of arms at Sidney's funeral in 1587) and then, in the mid-1590s, emerged as one of the great courtier knights at Elizabethan tilts, bearing the motto 'L'escu d'amour' as a pun on his name. His portrait shows him in his best Greenwich suit of armour (parts of which are now in the Metropolitan Museum of Art in New York); he was probably the model for Spenser's Sir Scudamour in the *Faerie Queene*; and he accompanied Essex on the attack on Cadiz in 1596 (where he was knighted) and the Islands voyage the following year. Sir James married Mary Houghton, daughter and coheir of Peter Houghton, a London alderman, on 21 March 1597, and after her death in August 1598 married, shortly before 28 June 1599, Mary (*d.* 1632), widow of another of Essex's captains, Sir Thomas Baskervile, and daughter of Sir Thomas Throckmorton of Gloucestershire. Sir James retired from tilting in 1600 and Sir John lost his court offices on the death of Elizabeth in 1603, but both maintained the chivalric tradition at Holme Lacy, where they trained war horses. Holme Lacy seemed at that time, it was said, 'not onely an Academy, but even the very Court of a Prince' (Atherton, 30). The interests of father and son, indeed, ranged more widely than military service: they were patrons of the Bodleian Library, and friends with Bodley himself, John Dee, and Thomas Allen. Sir John died at Holme Lacy on 14 April 1623 and was buried there next day.

Ennoblement Sir James Scudamore's second marriage turned sour after 1604 and he repudiated Mary finally in 1608. No formal divorce was ever arranged, and Mary, with her son from her first marriage, spent the next two decades seeking relief from any quarter she hoped might look upon her favourably, from the bishop of London and the privy council to the courts of chancery and the arches, and even parliament, all with very little success. Mary's treatment at the hands of Sir John and Sir James did not, however, spoil their reputations and so Sir James's eldest son, John *Scudamore (1601–1671), was able to step into the family's power, prestige, and offices in the early 1620s relatively unchallenged. With him the family reached its apogee: he was made a baronet in 1620, a year after his father's death, on 13 April 1619, was ennobled as first Viscount Scudamore of Sligo, Ireland, in 1628, and was Charles I's ambassador in France from 1635 to 1639. In Herefordshire he was the only resident peer and probably the wealthiest inhabitant, his estates having been augmented through his marriage in 1615 to Elizabeth Porter, who brought him lands worth around £600 per annum centred upon the former monastic site of Llanthony Secunda near Gloucester. The first viscount's political power in the southern marches, together with his learning, cultivation of cider apples, breeding of cattle, and especially his piety (his gifts to the church and to ministers, and his re-edification of churches, particularly Abbey Dore), ensured that his reputation as 'the Glory of our Countrey' (Atherton, 264) would remain unsurpassed in his lifetime or throughout the eighteenth century. The honour accorded to the viscount was easily sufficient to protect the family name from the reputation for treachery to the royalist cause accorded to his youngest brother, Sir Barnabas *Scudamore (*bap.* 1609, *d.* 1651/2). The imputation was most certainly groundless, however, and Sir Barnabas continued a zealous supporter of the king until his death.

The first viscount's son **James Scudamore** (1624–1668) failed to follow in his father's pious footsteps. He was born on 26 June 1624 and went to St John's College, Oxford, from 1640 to 1641. He spent much of the 1650s either recklessly gambling away his fortune or fleeing his creditors. He diced his way across France where, it was said, he lived like a madman, a 'monster' whom 'the suburbs of hell can scarse yield the like', owing money to people 'from the President to the Cobler' (Atherton, 160). He escaped his victims and pursuers by travelling further east, first to Italy, then around the eastern Mediterranean, where his adventures over five years took him to the Egyptian pyramids, incarceration in a pest house on the island of Zante, and battles with Turks, Spaniards, Neapolitans, and pirates. His father, meanwhile, tried to repair the ruins of James's estate and, after he returned to England in 1661, sought to oversee his introduction to power, engineering his election as MP for Herefordshire that year. James may also have served with the fleet in the Second Anglo-Dutch War.

Decline James Scudamore predeceased his father—he died on 18 June 1668—and after the latter's death in 1671 the family's political position in Herefordshire was gradually eclipsed, particularly by the Somersets, dukes of Beaufort, and the Brydges family, lords Chandos. The Scudamores' wealth, by contrast, increased through profitable if not always well-judged marriages.

John Scudamore, second Viscount Scudamore (*bap.* 1649, *d.* 1697), the son of James Scudamore's marriage, on 14 September 1648, to Jane Bennett (1628/9–1700) of Kew, was baptized at St Andrew's, Holborn, on 19 October 1649. He was educated at Westminster School from 1661 to 1665, then at Christ Church, Oxford, from 1666. He took his MA degree in 1667. He succeeded his grandfather as second viscount in 1671 and in June the following year married Lady Frances Cecil (*d.* 1694), daughter of John, fourth earl of Exeter, 'one of the impedents women as ever was knowne or heard of' (*Rutland MSS*, 2.56). He then set about rebuilding Holme Lacy House in a French style, with Hugh May as the architect. MP for Hereford in 1673 and for Herefordshire in the three Exclusion Parliaments he was initially close to the whigs and supported exclusion in 1680 and 1681, but two events in that latter year served to distance himself from them. First, on the dissolution of the Oxford Parliament the earl of Shaftesbury apparently offered Scudamore a colonel's commission in Herefordshire in a proposed revolutionary army, but the viscount, taking fright at the implications of armed resistance, allegedly exclaimed that he would never fight against the laws of the land; other Herefordshire whigs thereupon rounded on Scudamore as both 'timorous' and 'a person of poor or low spirit' (*CSP dom.*, *1682*, 291, 425–6). Later in 1681 the viscountess eloped with Thomas Coningsby (later Lord Coningsby), another of the Herefordshire whigs, causing consternation in the whig camp.

Lord Scudamore took his wife back but for the rest of the 1680s was much more circumspect in his politics, declining to stand for parliament. He promised to advance £100 to William of Orange in 1688 but ultimately failed to do so, and in the 1690s moved even further from his former allies, leading to accusations that he had basely deserted the whigs. His chaplain and several other of his family and associates all became nonjurors and their influence on him was probably telling, for he refused the oaths to the new regime and lost all his offices in 1695. His sister Mary Prince, *née* Scudamore (1650–1718) was also a nonjuror. She was known in her widowhood as Lady Prince and regarded as a 'very whimsical Woman', but Thomas Hearne (yet another nonjuror) considered her 'a worthy Lady, very honest & charitable, & did much good' (*Remarks*, 6.262–3).

On the second viscount's death on 2 June 1697 the title and lands passed to his eldest surviving son, **James Scudamore**, third Viscount Scudamore (*bap.* 1684, *d.* 1716), who was born at Shannon Park, Ireland, and was baptized on 16 July 1684 at Holme Lacy. He was educated at Gloucester Hall, Oxford, from 1695. When his father died James was still a minor, which meant a further diminution of the family's local influence. He spent much of the next six years travelling on the continent, mainly in Italy, accompanied by Theophilus Downes, a nonjuring former fellow of Balliol College, Oxford. After returning to England in 1703 and reconciling himself to the government he married Frances (1684–1729), only daughter of Simon, fourth Baron Digby, on 5 March 1706. Lord Scudamore sustained a bad fall from his horse in 1710 which almost killed him and this was said to have impaired his understanding thereafter, but his handicap prevented neither his re-election as tory MP nor the award of the degree of DCL by Oxford University in 1712. He died aged only thirty-two on 2 December 1716 leaving an only daughter. His widow went on to be a celebrated patron of literary men including Alexander Pope, John Gay, and Thomas Southerne, the dramatist, all of whom visited Holme Lacy. Her death from smallpox on 3 May 1729 occasioned Pope's comment 'and Scud'more ends her name' (*Works*, 2.436), for the title had become extinct on the third viscount's death, but the Holme Lacy estate in fact perpetuated the family name for another century.

Scandal and extinction **Frances Fitzroy-Scudamore** [Frances Scudamore, duchess of Beaufort] (1711–1750), only child of the third viscount and his wife, was born on 14 August 1711. She was accounted a great prize, for the substantial Scudamore estates had been significantly increased by the acquisition in 1704 of all the lands of the Scudamores of Ballingham, neighbouring cousins and for most of the seventeenth century close allies of the Holme Lacy family. On 28 June 1729 Frances married Henry Somerset, third duke of Beaufort (1707–1745), who took the name Scudamore by act of parliament the following year. In spring 1740 Frances began an affair with William, Lord Talbot of Hensol (1710–1782), which occasioned the separation of the duke and duchess in June; Frances received back all the Scudamore estates. In September 1741 she and Talbot had an illegitimate daughter who was baptized as Fanny Matthews, but who died shortly afterwards. The affair became notorious, and public interest in the case heightened when in 1742 the duke began proceedings in the church court against the duchess for adultery, and she launched a counter suit alleging the duke's impotence. He demonstrated the falsity of her claim by undergoing a test of his virility before six witnesses (Stone, 133). The duke's eventual triumph was capped by a divorce granted by a private act of parliament in March 1744. The affair fizzled out soon afterwards, and on 17 July 1748 Frances married Colonel Charles Fitzroy (1713?–1782), presumably a love match for he was but the illegitimate son of the second duke of Grafton. The following year Fitzroy assumed the additional surname of Scudamore. The marriage proved short-lived, for Frances died on 15 February 1750, only five days after giving birth to a daughter.

That daughter, **Frances Fitzroy-Scudamore** [*married name* Frances Howard, duchess of Norfolk] (1750–1820), inherited the Holme Lacy estates and married (as his second wife) Charles *Howard, later eleventh duke of Norfolk (1746–1815), on 2 April 1771, but is said to have had a fit of hysterics on the church steps immediately after the ceremony and soon succumbed to progressive mental illness. George III repeatedly refused the duke's requests for an annulment; since Norfolk was known as the 'Drunken Duke', prone to debauchery and averse to soap, water, and new clothes, the marriage cannot have been much comfort for the duchess either, and the couple had no children. After the duke's death a complex series of chancery cases began for the inheritance of the Holme Lacy estate, estimated to be worth £30,000 a year. On the duchess's death, on 22 October 1820, the direct descendants of the first Lord Scudamore became extinct and the legal proceedings intensified. The vaults of Holme Lacy church were dug up in a vain search for evidence, and the final legal complications were not settled until May 1829 with the order that the estate should be divided among the descendants of the first viscount's eldest sister.

IAN ATHERTON

Sources W. Skidmore, *Thirty generations of the Scudamore/Skidmore family in England and America* (Akron, 1991) • I. J. Atherton, *Ambition and failure in Stuart England: the career of John, first Viscount Scudamore* (1999) • L. Stone, *Broken lives: separation and divorce in England, 1660–1857* (1993), chap. 6 • N. E. Key, 'Politics beyond parliament: unity and party in the Herefordshire region during the Restoration period', PhD diss., University of Cornell, 1989 • *The manuscripts of his grace the duke of Portland*, 10 vols., HMC, 29 (1891–1931) • *The manuscripts of his grace the duke of Rutland*, 4 vols., HMC, 24 (1888–1905), vol. 2, pp. 56–7 • *CSP dom.*, *1682*, 290–92, 424–6 • *Remarks and collections of Thomas Hearne*, ed. C. E. Doble and others, 11 vols., OHS, 2, 7, 13, 34, 42–3, 48, 50, 65, 67, 72 (1885–1921) • HoP, *Commons*, *1715–54*, vol. 2 • *The correspondence of Alexander Pope*, ed. G. Sherburn, 5 vols. (1956) • *The works of Alexander Pope*, ed. W. Elwin and W. J.

Courthope, 10 vols. (1871–89), vol. 2, p. 436 • *The correspondence of Jonathan Swift*, ed. F. E. Ball, 6 vols. (1910–14), vol. 4, p. 37 • J. H. Overton, *The nonjurors: their lives, principles, and writings* (1902) • W. J. Tighe, 'Country into court, court into country: John Scudamore of Holme Lacy (*c*.1542–1623) and his circles', *Tudor political culture*, ed. D. Hoak (1995), 157–78 • 'The letters of Richard Scudamore to Sir Philip Holby, September 1549 – March 1555', ed. M. Dowling, *Camden miscellany, XXX*, CS, 4th ser., 39 (1990) • GEC, *Peerage* • will, PRO, PROB 11/53, fols. 314–15 [John Scudamore, *d*. 1571] • HoP, *Commons, 1660–90*, 3.407–8

Archives BL, charters, Add. Chs. 1308–1349, 1351–1357, 1359–1371, 1813–1973 • BL, papers, Add. MSS 11041–11059, 11689–11690, 11816, 35097, 36307, 45140–45148 • BL, papers, Add. Rolls 1350, 1358 • Bodl. Oxf., travel diary of third viscount, 1698–1700, MS Eng. 2 2018 • Folger, papers, Vb2–3 • Hereford Cathedral Archives, accounts, 1632, 6417 • Hereford Cathedral Archives, accounts, 1635–1638, 1640–1644, 1661–1662, L. C. 647.1 • Hereford City Library, accounts 1667–1668, 631.16 • Hereford City Library, volumes of third viscount's travel diaries, 1701, L. C. 920 Scud • PRO, papers, C 115 • PRO, state papers, foreign: France, dispatches as ambassador, SP 78/97–107 | Arundel Castle Archives, Howard letters and papers, incl. letters of first Viscount Scudamore

Likenesses oils, *c*.1595–1600 (Sir James Scudamore), Kentchurch Court, Herefordshire; repro. in R. C. Strong, *The cult of Elizabeth: Elizabethan portraiture and chivalry* (1977) • oils, in or after 1599 (Sir John Scudamore), Kentchurch Court, Herefordshire • oils (Sir John Scudamore), Kentchurch Court, Herefordshire • portrait (Frances Scudamore), repro. in Stone, *Broken lives*; photograph, Yale U. CBA

Scudamore, Sir Barnabas (*bap*. **1609**, *d*. **1651/2**), royalist army officer, was baptized on 2 April 1609 at Timsbury, Somerset, the ninth and youngest child of Sir James *Scudamore (*bap*. 1568, *d*. 1619) [*see under* Scudamore family], and his second wife, Mary, *née* Throckmorton (*d*. 1632), widow of Sir Thomas Baskervile. His parents' marriage had been strained for several years and shortly after his baptism Sir James permanently repudiated his wife, although they were never legally divorced.

Scudamore slipped into the obscurity and comparative poverty of Stuart younger sons. With an income of only about £50 per annum (his eldest brother Sir John *Scudamore, from 1628 first Viscount Scudamore, had inherited the bulk of the family's wealth and position) he was forced to seek his own way in the world, and he was later described as 'a man of noe fortune' (BL, Harleian MS 6868, fol. 100). He may have been in the earl of Cork's service in Ireland in the summer of 1631, and in December that year he sailed to the Netherlands to enlist as a soldier. He was back in England by March 1636 and in the service of Cork, travelling as an attendant with the earl's two sons to France.

Only as the king's fortunes declined did Scudamore's rise. A captain in the English forces sent against the Scots in 1640, he joined the royalist army promptly on the outbreak of the English civil war and was wounded at Coventry on 20 August 1642, and at Edgehill on 23 October 1642. By the spring of 1643 he was sergeant-major to Colonel Henry Hastings in the midlands, seeing action at Hopton Heath and Lichfield. By May 1644 he had returned to his native Herefordshire where he was major-general to Nicholas Mynne, whom he succeeded as governor of Hereford on 10 September 1644. It was hoped that he would unite soldiers and civilians, and he had the backing of a number of the leading citizens of Hereford where his brother Viscount Scudamore was high steward. Scudamore's zeal in raising men and contributions, and his high-handedness in ignoring due process of law against tax defaulters, however, helped to provoke a club-men rising in March 1645 which was only suppressed with the assistance of Prince Rupert.

As a commander Scudamore was resourceful and resolute. He developed a siege tower which he unsuccessfully used against Canon Frome in November 1645, and in the summer of 1645 he held Hereford for five weeks against a besieging Scottish army. In gratitude the king knighted him and, if a persistent rumour can be credited, would have raised him to a barony had Scudamore been able to afford the creation fees. However, Scudamore also had a fatal flaw—a predilection for arguing. He quarrelled with two of his deputy governors in succession, with disastrous consequences: in revenge one killed his cousin and brother-in-law, Sir John Scudamore of Ballingham; the other later denounced Scudamore to the king as a traitor. Disputes with other junior officers and with the inhabitants of the city led directly to the fall of Hereford to a dawn raid on 18 December 1645.

Scudamore escaped as the city fell and fled to Worcester, but allegations (certainly groundless) that he had betrayed Hereford in return for a large bribe led to his imprisonment on a charge of treachery. He languished in gaol for six months and was only released at the surrender of Worcester in July 1646. Unable to clear his name in a court of war he published his own *Defence* in 1646 but many remained convinced that he had sold Hereford to the parliament. On the outbreak of the second civil war he may have been active for the king in Kent in May 1648, and he was certainly trying to raise troops in Newmarket where he was captured in June. On 15 November 1648 he married Katharine Saunders, who appears to have predeceased him. He may previously have been married to a woman with the maiden name Brydges. He was arrested on suspicion of royalist plotting in the summer of 1651, and though soon released, he was in desperate financial straits; he died in London some time between 9 December 1651 (when he wrote to a cousin) and 11 March 1652 when Lord Scudamore wrote of his death. IAN ATHERTON

Sources *Sir Barnabas Scudamore's defence*, ed. I. J. Atherton (1992) • BL, Harleian MS 6868 • E. Walker, *Historical discourses upon several occasions* (1705) • parish register, Timsbury, Som. ARS, D/P/Tims 2/1/1 [baptism] • W. Skidmore, *Thirty generations of the Scudamore/Skidmore family in England and America* (1992) • Herefs. RO, B56/1 • parish register, London, St Bartholomew-the-Less, GL, MS Challen 52 [marriage] • PRO, PROB 6/27, fols. 117*v*–119*r* • BL, Add. MS 11043 • PRO, SP 23/12 • PRO, SP 23/116 • PRO, SP 23/222

Archives BL, papers, Add. MS 11043 • PRO, papers, C 115/I2/5613–60

Wealth at death value of estate £50 p.a.; in debt £1000: PRO, SP 23/222, pp. 677, 681

Scudamore, Sir Charles (**1779–1849**), physician, third son of William Scudamore, a surgeon, and his wife, Elizabeth

Rolfe, was born at Wye, Kent, where his father was in practice. His grandfather and great-grandfather were surgeons at Canterbury, and were descendants of a family from Ballingham, Herefordshire. Frank Ives Scudmore (1823–1884) was his nephew. He was educated at Wye grammar school and began his medical education as apprentice to his father. He continued his studies at Guy's and St Thomas's hospitals in London, for three years, after which he settled in practice as a surgeon at Highgate, where he remained for ten years. He married, on 24 June 1811, Georgiana Johnson; they had no children.

Scudamore next undertook further medical study at Edinburgh, from 1813, and graduated MD at Glasgow on 6 May 1814; his thesis was entitled *De arthritide*. He was admitted a licentiate of the Royal College of Physicians, in London, on 30 September 1814, and began practice as a physician in Holles Street, London. He had some knowledge of chemistry, and in 1816 published *An Analysis of the Mineral Water of Tunbridge Wells*, the first of his several works on mineral waters. In the same year he published the book which established his reputation as an expert on gout, *A Treatise on the Nature and Cure of Gout*; this was based on his observation of about a hundred cases of gout, and contains one of the first contributions to the study of the distribution of gouty changes throughout the body. Among other observations, he mentions that there were in 1814 only five hackney carriages and less than twenty private carriages in Glasgow, and he attributes the rarity of gout there to the constant walking even of the rich citizens. Scudamore was the first English author to mention the frequent presence of a circular chest, instead of an elliptical one, in persons subject to gout. He showed little capacity for observing disease at the bedside, but had some knowledge of morbid anatomy.

In 1820 Scudamore was appointed physician to Prince Leopold of Saxe-Gotha-Altenburg. During the following decade he wrote prolifically on a variety of medical subjects, and in 1827 published *A Treatise on Rheumatism*, which paints an interesting picture of the period when rheumatic fever was beginning to be separated in medical writings from chronic rheumatism. Scudamore treated rheumatic fever by bleeding, purgatives, colchicum, tartar emetic, opium, and quinine. He went to Ireland, in March 1829, as physician to the duke of Northumberland, then appointed lord lieutenant, who knighted him at Dublin on 30 September 1829. He was also admitted an honorary member of Trinity College, Dublin, during his stay in Ireland.

Scudamore also spent part of every year at Buxton, and was physician to the Bath Charity there. He published *An Analysis of the Tepid Springs of Buxton* in 1820. In April and May 1843 he visited Gräfenberg, and on his return he published a small book on the water-cure treatment being used there. Scudamore died in his London house, 6 Wimpole Street, of heart disease, on 4 August 1849.

NORMAN MOORE, *rev.* PATRICK WALLIS

Sources Munk, *Roll* • *Medical Times*, 20 (1849), 168 • *The Lancet* (25 Aug 1849), 214 • *GM*, 2nd ser., 32 (1849), 425–6

Scudamore, Frances Fitzroy- (1711–1750). *See under* Scudamore family (*per.* 1500–1820).

Scudamore, Frances Fitzroy- (1750–1820). *See under* Scudamore family (*per.* 1500–1820).

Scudamore, Frank Ives (1823–1884), writer and Post Office administrator, was born in February 1823 in Eltham, Kent, the son of John Scudamore, a solicitor from a prominent Herefordshire family, and his wife, Charlotte, daughter of Colonel Francis Downman. Educated at Christ's Hospital, he married, in 1851, Jane Ellen Moore Sherwin, daughter of a Greenwich surgeon.

An individual with a great appetite for work, Scudamore pursued two careers simultaneously. The first was as a writer of light pieces for *Punch*, the *Comic Times*, and other magazines as well as more serious works ranging from orthography to the Eastern question. But it was his second career as an activist civil servant, urging the expansion of the government into areas and pursuits previously considered neither ideologically acceptable nor fiscally appropriate for state action, which was the great cause of his life and the foundation of his historical significance. Scudamore joined the Post Office in 1840, the year of Rowland Hill's penny post, and the beginning of a fundamental reorientation of the department's role in Victorian society. Although Scudamore never served as a departmental surveyor and, therefore, was considered by some of his colleagues to lack necessary field experience, he advanced rapidly. By 1864 he had risen to the position of assistant secretary, having been chosen over his rival, Anthony Trollope, who had more years of service in the department. In 1868 he was named second secretary of the Post Office, and appeared well positioned for future promotions. But it was less his official job titles than the projects which he sponsored which made Scudamore arguably the most important civil servant in the entire government by the late 1860s.

The first of these projects was government-operated savings banks. Although Scudamore did not conceive the original idea for such a system, he became its most persuasive proponent. The banks, established in 1861 under Post Office direction, offered safe, efficient service and grew rapidly. By 1862 there were 180,000 accounts, and the system ultimately surpassed the Trustee Savings Banks in attracting deposits from the working and lower middle classes, its natural clientele. For Scudamore such results only confirmed his belief that government, in certain instances, could provide economic services more effectively than private initiative. This led him next to advocate the sale of life insurance and annuities through the Post Office. However, in this case the programme, instituted in 1864, never fulfilled Scudamore's projections. Fewer than 25,000 policies were sold between 1865 and 1884. In part this outcome resulted from the fact that certain schemes which Scudamore advocated for bringing the programme to the public's attention, such as government-organized lectures on the advantages of the department's system, were never implemented. In part, however, the programme failed because Scudamore underestimated the

Frank Ives Scudamore (1823–1884), by unknown engraver

strength of competing alternatives offered by friendly societies and private firms.

Characteristically Scudamore did not waver in his faith in what he termed the 'co-operative society', in which technocrats such as himself would plan and control bureaucracies to ensure social harmony through low prices and efficient management. In 1865 Lord Stanley of Alderley, the postmaster-general, commissioned him to study the condition of the privately owned telegraph companies, and to consider the possible results of nationalization. Over the course of the next five years Scudamore became the great advocate of state take-over of the industry. He made detailed estimates of likely purchase costs and financial results. He lobbied leading politicians, such as W. E. Gladstone, on the wisdom of nationalization, and he formed alliances with Edward Taylor of *The Guardian* and Edwin Chadwick to rally public support. These efforts bore fruit in 1869 when parliament allocated £7 million for telegraph purchase costs and capital improvements.

The next year Scudamore assumed direction of the Post Office telegraphs, and moved quickly to expand the system, now charging lower tariffs than under private management. In many ways Scudamore's optimistic predictions of the results of a nationalized system proved to be accurate. The average price of a telegram fell by 6*d*. to 1*s*. 1*d*. During the first year of government management, the number of telegrams sent increased by 3 million to almost 10 million. The public was without question pleased with the quality of service provided by Scudamore's department. However, certain problems arose to cloud the picture. For one, the system never fulfilled Scudamore's hopes for savings under centralized management. Wage costs escalated, as more employees at higher salaries than under the pre-1870 system were hired. Accordingly, the system also failed to meet Scudamore's net revenue (profit) projections, and usually incurred large losses. Neither was it clear that government management avoided the pitfalls of employee strife and maladministration, as Scudamore had claimed that it would. In 1871 a telegraphists' strike broke out, which although swiftly crushed still soured labour relations. More seriously, in 1873 it was revealed that Scudamore, in haste to expand a system which he regarded as virtually his own, had spent over £800,000 without Treasury or parliamentary approval. In a crisis which disrupted Gladstone's government and which helped to establish the concept of ministerial responsibility, William Monsell, the postmaster-general, was forced to resign. Scudamore remained in office, but chafed under new restrictions on his independence until his resignation in 1875.

Scudamore then began a new life when he accepted the offer of the Ottoman government to reorganize the Turkish post office; and in 1877 the order of the Mejidiye was conferred on him. Not surprisingly, he found the pace of improvement in Turkey so slow that he retired, and then occupied his time writing. He died in Therapia in the Ottoman empire on 8 February 1884 and was buried in the English cemetery at Scutari, in the country where he had taken up a self-imposed exile. C. R. PERRY

Sources C. R. Perry, *The Victorian Post Office: the growth of a bureaucracy*, Royal Historical Society Studies in History, 64 (1992) • M. J. Daunton, *Royal Mail: the Post Office since 1840* (1985) • J. Kieve, *The electric telegraph: a social and economic history* (1973) • A. Clinton, *Post Office workers: a trade union and social history* (1984) • C. R. Perry, 'Scudamore, Frank Ives', *DBB* • *CGPLA Eng. & Wales* (1884) • d. cert. • will, proved, Britannic Majesty's Supreme Consular Court, Constantinople, Turkey, 3 March 1884

Archives Royal Mail Heritage, London, postmaster general minutes, Post 30 • Royal Mail Heritage, London, telegraph records, Post 82–3 | UCL, corresp. with E. Chadwick

Likenesses engraving, repro. in Daunton, *Royal Mail* [*see illus.*]

Wealth at death £5150: administration with will, 23 July 1884, *CGPLA Eng. & Wales*

Scudamore, Sir James (*bap.* **1568**, *d.* **1619**). *See under* Scudamore family (*per.* 1500–1820).

Scudamore, James (**1624–1668**). *See under* Scudamore family (*per.* 1500–1820).

Scudamore, James, **third Viscount Scudamore** (*bap.* **1684**, *d.* **1716**). *See under* Scudamore family (*per.* 1500–1820).

Scudamore, John (*c.***1486–1571**). *See under* Scudamore family (*per.* 1500–1820).

Scudamore, Sir John (**1542–1623**). *See under* Scudamore family (*per.* 1500–1820).

Scudamore, John, **first Viscount Scudamore** (**1601–1671**), diplomat and politician, was born on 24 or 28 February 1601 at Holme Lacy, Herefordshire, the eldest son of Sir James *Scudamore (*bap.* 1568, *d.* 1619) [*see under* Scudamore family] and his second wife, Mary (*d.* 1632), widow of

Sir Thomas Baskervile (*d.* 1597) and daughter of Sir Thomas Throckmorton of Gloucestershire, and his wife, Elizabeth; Barnabas *Scudamore (*bap.* 1609, *d.* 1651/2) was his younger brother. His parents' marriage soured, and his father finally repudiated his mother in 1608. John Scudamore married, on 12 March 1615, Elizabeth (*bap.* 1600, *d.* 1651), daughter and heir of Sir Arthur Porter of Llanthony, Monmouthshire, and Hempsted, Gloucestershire, and his wife, Anne; the marriage brought substantial estates, power, and connections to the Holme Lacy Scudamores. After the marriage John continued his studies, matriculating at Magdalen College, Oxford, in November 1616 before being admitted at the Middle Temple in December 1617; in November 1618 he left England for France with a licence to travel for three years.

Social and political preferment Scudamore's travels were cut short by the early death of his father in April 1619; he returned to England where his grandfather, old Sir John Scudamore (1542–1623), oversaw his preferment. His grandfather bought John a baronetcy in June 1620, immediately promoting him to the place of precedence in Herefordshire, a county with no resident peer, and over the next three years old Sir John, with the assistance of the lord lieutenant, the earl of Northampton, and a neighbour, Sir Walter Pye, ensured the smooth transition of the family's power in the southern marches to the baronet. Young Sir John assumed the captaincy of the Herefordshire county troop of horse which his father had previously held, was elected senior knight of the shire for Herefordshire to the 1621 parliament, was appointed to the commission of the peace for Herefordshire in February 1622 and *custos rotulorum* in May, and in the same year was made a deputy lieutenant in the county. By the time his grandfather died, in April 1623, the still youthful Sir John Scudamore was the most powerful magnate in Herefordshire, witnessed by his appointment to the council in the marches of Wales (under the jurisdiction of which both Herefordshire and Gloucestershire fell) in August 1623 and his election once again as the senior knight of the shire to the 1624 parliament.

Scudamore was ambitious, however, for further preferment from the king. Using his contacts at court, especially Sir Roger Palmer, cupbearer to Charles I, he pressed his claims to have agitated for royal policies among MPs, to have been zealous in the collection of the subsidy, and to have perfected the trained bands in Herefordshire. The historical record is silent on the first claim, while modern research has shown the slender basis for the second (Atherton, chap. 4), but in the mid-1620s Scudamore was an active local governor and particularly zealous as a deputy lieutenant. He worked hard to fashion an image of martial prowess to follow in the footsteps of his grandfather, a gentleman pensioner to Queen Elizabeth, and father, one of the foremost tilters at court in the 1590s, casting himself as the agent through which the county horse would be improved and trained, and organizing his household servants and retainers into a horse troop. While the king was said to have a 'good opinion' of Scudamore (PRO, C115/M24/7758), his appeals fell on deaf ears and his position in Herefordshire began to be eclipsed by the rise of others, notably Pye and Sir Roger Harley, both of whom had attached themselves to the favourite the duke of Buckingham. Scudamore was returned to parliament in 1625 for the city of Hereford rather than the shire, and did not stand in 1626. In addition, he faced two further crises in the mid-1620s: financial problems as he tried to raise the money to pay the marriage portions of four of his sisters and the debts of his uncle and mother; and personal tragedy, with the early deaths of his first three children.

Religious conversion and friendship with Laud Scudamore was rescued from his troubles by a religious conversion and the patronage of the favourite. By 1622 he had established a warm friendship with William Laud. When the friendship began is not known, though it may have been when Laud was dean of Gloucester between 1616 and 1621. Laud acted almost as a proxy father to Scudamore, fussing over his health and that of his wife, and warning him to beware of the January cold; he was also a friend at court, a divinity tutor, and a spiritual friend to the young baronet. The two men met at Holme Lacy, as Laud travelled between London and diocesan responsibilities (Laud preached at Holme Lacy on Sunday 20 November 1625, for example), and in London when Scudamore's affairs took him there. In January 1627 Scudamore asked Laud's advice for a way out of his problems: could he sell some of his impropriations to pay his debts? Laud's reply, that a layman had no right to possess what belonged to the clergy by divine law, set the baronet on a course of restoring impropriations and avoiding sacrilege that was to dominate the rest of his life. Scudamore found other estates to sell to ease his financial worries.

Scudamore had identified himself as one of the handful of lay Laudians. He was about to join another select set—the Buckinghamites—to restore his political fortunes. He seems to have attached himself to the favourite in 1626, proving his mettle in the efficient administration of the forced loan in Herefordshire in 1627 and vigorously, if ineffectually, defending the duke in the 1628 parliament (in which Scudamore was again MP for Hereford). His reward came in July 1628, when (like so many others that year) he was raised to the Irish peerage, as Baron Dromore and Viscount Scudamore of Sligo, even though, like the others, he had neither estates in nor connections with Ireland.

Buckingham's death was a severe personal blow—Scudamore sent an early account of the duke's assassination to Laud—and according to a later family tradition he attended the favourite's funeral, but he did not, as earlier accounts have suggested, retire from affairs. True, he did not attend the 1629 session of parliament; none the less, when later that year, after sustained complaints from the English nobility about Englishmen like Scudamore with Irish titles but no estates in Ireland, the king removed the Irish viscounts from all commissions in England, Scudamore was retained by Charles I on the Herefordshire commission of the peace, a signal mark of royal favour. In the early 1630s he was added to further commissions in Herefordshire: those for knighthood fines and for raising contributions for the repair of St Paul's Cathedral. On these he was an active commissioner.

Scudamore also spent the early 1630s restoring the church at Dore in Herefordshire. The estates of the former Cistercian abbey had come to the Scudamores after the dissolution but by the early seventeenth century the abbey church, which formed the parish church of Dore, was badly in need of repair. Between 1632 and 1635 Scudamore restored the building, forming the parish church from the crossing and choir of the abbey; he added a new roof, south porch, tower, belfry, a new bell, and a churchyard wall. The church was also fitted out in full Laudian style with an altar, new woodwork (rails, screen, pulpit, reading desk, and pews), and stained glass. The total cost was more than £425. In addition, he endowed it with the impropriate rectory and all the tithes from the hitherto exempt site and demesne of the abbey, and gave the manor house to the rector to live in (when this later proved liable to flooding he had it pulled down and rebuilt). The restored church was a model of the viscount's high-church or Laudian beliefs, stressing the beauty of holiness, the central place of the eucharist, and the role of ceremonious worship, points all reinforced by the day-long service of consecration on 22 March 1635. Nor was Dore the only church to benefit from Scudamore's piety and fear of committing sacrilege. He built stone parsonages for the ministers of Holme Lacy and Hempsted; he repaired Holme Lacy church and twice gave it a new set of plate; he endowed Hempsted and two other churches with impropriate tithes; and he contributed to the repairs of three cathedrals—Hereford (of which he was high steward), St Paul's, and Bristol. In his lifetime Scudamore was held up as 'a Worthy Copy for others to write after' and praised for his restoration of church lands and protection of the clergy (W. Carpenter, *Jura cleri, or, An Apology for the Rights of the Long-Despised Clergy*, 1661, 11).

Embassy to France Early in 1635 Scudamore was appointed as Charles's ambassador to France, though his departure was delayed until August. Lacking diplomatic experience, he was chosen at Laud's behest to uphold the rights of the Church of England abroad, for in 1635 Charles was uninterested in pursuing a French alliance, preferring to seek after Spain and the Habsburgs instead. Shortly after his arrival Scudamore's embassy chapel, furnished with all Laudian trappings and ritual, caused considerable controversy on both sides of the channel. It was later alleged that it was 'adorned according to the newe devise, so that manie Papists there said they were at the English masse' (R. N. Worth, ed., *The Buller Papers*, 1895, 128), but Scudamore received the full backing of both Charles and Laud.

Scudamore did not, however, have the support of Henrietta Maria, and in April 1636 his mission was seconded by the appointment of the staunchly protestant earl of Leicester as extraordinary ambassador. Immediately the two fell to quarrelling: they could agree on nothing, neither religion (the earl inclining to the Huguenots whom, it was believed, felt snubbed by Scudamore's Laudianism), nor English policy in Europe (the earl wanting an Anglo-French alliance, the viscount supporting the king's pro-Spanish peace). Leicester, a more adroit politician with greater support at the English court, soon triumphed and the remainder of Scudamore's embassy saw his exclusion from negotiations and gradual eclipse in all his other duties by Leicester, who lost no opportunity to ridicule him to the English court as an incompetent, pro-Spanish dullard with no respect in France.

Nevertheless, others had a higher opinion of Scudamore's intellectual and political abilities. In his native Herefordshire his reputation and power remained undiminished. His reputation for learning in divinity and philosophy earned him the friendship of the philosophers Thomas Hobbes, Sir Kenelm Digby, and others in the circle of Marin Mersenne in Paris, and in particular with Hugo Grotius (the Swedish ambassador to France), with whom he discussed plans for a union of the English and Scandinavian churches.

Political eclipse and royalism Frustrated by the negotiations with the French, humiliated by the triumph of Leicester, and dispirited by the absence of his wife (who had returned to England in September 1638), in November 1638 Scudamore asked for his recall and returned to the English court in March 1639. Though from 1640 he took a house in Petty France, Westminster, to be near the court, no further honours were granted him, despite a tradition that returning ambassadors were generally preferred. The opposition of Henrietta Maria and the king's preoccupation with the rebellion in Scotland counted against him. He apparently spent most of the next three-and-a-half years in Westminster, and was relatively aloof from affairs in Herefordshire, intervening directly only infrequently, such as to sign a pro-episcopacy petition in January 1642, or to secure the election of his son James (1624–1668) as MP for Hereford at a by-election in the spring of that year. In his absence the royalist party in the county formed around others, with Fitzwilliam Coningsby (*c.*1595–1666) securing its leadership. While Scudamore's younger brother Barnabas had joined the king's army by August 1642, the viscount lay low during both the summer (even though he was appointed a commissioner of array in Herefordshire) and the occupation of Hereford by parliamentarian forces (September–December 1642). The resumption of royalist control in Hereford, however, saw a major struggle between Scudamore and Coningsby for leadership of the royalist party. By the end of March 1643 Scudamore, with his better connections in the king's court at Oxford and traditional power base in Hereford (of which he had been high steward since 1630), had won, but only by starving Coningsby's regiment of men, money, and supplies until it was, Coningsby claimed, 'rather like a Constables watch then a Garrison' (Bodl. Oxf., MS Tanner 303, fol. 115*v*). The confusion sown in Hereford by the struggle between Scudamore and Coningsby, and the lack of leadership provided by the former, was matched by the incompetence of Lord Herbert of Cherbury, the king's commander in south Wales and the southern marches. Thus it was that when Sir William Waller appeared before

Hereford with a small force on 25 April 1643 Scudamore and the royalist garrison promptly surrendered with barely a shot fired in anger. Scudamore was sent to London as a delinquent and placed under house arrest; he was not released until 20 March 1647. He estimated his losses at £22,190, including his composition fine, the plunder of his houses at Holme Lacy and Petty France, and the destruction of two houses at Llanthony at the time of the siege of Gloucester.

Scholarly, religious, and agricultural pursuits For the remainder of the 1640s and 1650s Scudamore lived peaceably at Holme Lacy and Petty France, devoting himself to agriculture, divinity, and charity. A noted agricultural improver throughout his life, he discovered, grafted, and developed the redstreak apple which became celebrated as the best cider crab in the seventeenth century. It was famed as the 'Scudamore crab' and its cider, for which Holme Lacy became famous, as the 'vin de Scudamore' (Bodl. Oxf., MS Don. f. 5, fols. 36–7; *Portland MSS*, 2.292). Scudamore is also credited with introducing from the Low Countries the ancestors of the renowned white-faced Hereford cattle.

In 1648 Samuel Hartlib thought Scudamore 'a great schollar' who was 'studying hard continually', while in 1663 the Herefordshire clergyman, philosopher, and horticulturist John Beale called him 'a person learned and greate fautor of sound learning' (Sheffield University, Hartlib papers, 31/22/19B; H. Oldenburg, *Correspondence*, ed. A. R. Hall and M. B. Hall, 13 vols., 1965–86, 2.11). In 1656 Peter Gunning turned down his offer of a £40 annuity to live in his household and tutor him in philosophy. Undaunted, Scudamore secured the guidance of Henry Hammond for his reading. On his wife's death in December 1651 he insisted on tithing his extra-parochial estates at Llanthony. From then until 1662, when he secured a private act uniting Llanthony to the parish of Hempsted, he applied both the accruing tithes and their arrears to the relief of distressed orthodox divines. By 1662 he had dispensed more than £1650 to about eighty clerics, some of them obscure country ministers, others nationally renowned figures, including Matthew Wren, with whom he was close friends, Richard Sterne, Robert Herrick, and John Bramhall.

Last years At the Restoration Scudamore returned to his former local offices and power, and sought the preferment of his son James. A wayward character and inveterate gambler who had spent the later 1650s hiding first in France and then in the eastern Mediterranean to escape his creditors, James was elected MP for Herefordshire in 1661, but his father's hopes were dashed by James's death on 18 June 1668. The viscount died on 19 May 1671, probably at Petty France, and was buried on 8 June at Holme Lacy. He was succeeded by his grandson, John Scudamore, the second viscount (1649–1697). IAN ATHERTON

Sources I. J. Atherton, *Ambition and failure in Stuart England: the career of John, first Viscount Scudamore* (1999) • PRO, duchess of Norfolk deeds, C115 • M. Gibson, *A view of the ancient and present state of the churches of Door, Home-Lacy, and Hempsted; endow'd by the right honourable John, Lord Viscount Scudamore. With some memoirs of that ancient family; and an appendix of records and letters relating to the same subject* (1727) • W. Skidmore, *Thirty generations of the Scudamore/Skidmore family in England and America* (Akron, 1991) • parish register, Holme Lacy, 1561–1727, Herefs. RO, AL 17/1 [baptism, burial] • *Letters of the Lady Brilliana Harley*, ed. T. T. Lewis, CS, 58 (1854), 245–6 • *Diary of the marches of the royal army during the great civil war, kept by Richard Symonds*, ed. C. E. Long, CS, old ser., 74 (1859), 195 • GEC, *Peerage*, new edn • *The manuscripts of his grace the duke of Portland*, 10 vols., HMC, 29 (1891–1931), vol. 2

Archives Arundel Castle archives, West Sussex, corresp. and papers • BL, charters, additional charters 1308–1349, 1351–1357, 1359–1371, 1813–1973 • BL, charters, additional rolls 1350, 1358 • BL, papers, Add. MSS 11041–11059, 11407, 11689–11690, 11816, 35097, 45140–45148 • Folger, papers, Vb 2–3 • Hereford Cathedral Library, accounts, MS 6417 • Hereford City Library, accounts and papers • Hereford City Library, dissertation on wars in Germany and Netherlands | PRO, duchess of Norfolk deeds, C 115

Likenesses E. Bower, oils, 1642, Kentchurch Court, Herefordshire; repro. in J. Webb, *Memorials of the civil war between King Charles and the parliament of England as it affected Herefordshire and the adjacent counties*, ed. T. W. Webb, 1 (1879), frontispiece

Wealth at death estate valued at approx. £4000 p.a.: Symonds, *Diary of the marches*, 195

Scudamore, John, second Viscount Scudamore (*bap.* **1649**, *d.* **1697**). *See under* Scudamore family (*per.* 1500–1820).

Scudamore, William Edward (1813–1881), Church of England clergyman and devotional writer, only son of Dr Edward Scudamore and nephew of the physician Sir Charles Scudamore MD (1779–1849), was born at Wye, Kent, on 24 July 1813. Having been educated at a school in Brussels, at Edinburgh high school, and then at Lichfield Cathedral school, he entered St John's College, Cambridge, as a sizar on 6 July 1831, and graduated BA as ninth wrangler in 1835. He was on 14 March 1837 admitted a fellow of St John's, whence he proceeded MA in 1838. After a short time as assistant master at Oakham School, he went to Minto, Roxburghshire, as tutor in the family of Gilbert Elliot, second earl of Minto. Scudamore was ordained priest in 1839, and in March of that year was presented to the living of Ditchingham in Norfolk, then restricted to fellows of St John's. On 20 October 1840 he married Albina (1815/16–7 June 1898), daughter of John King.

Scudamore's views were largely influenced by the Oxford Movement as expounded at Cambridge by John Fuller Russell. As the first resident rector at Ditchingham for almost a century, he restored the parish church, built a school, and raised subscriptions for a chapel of ease in an outlying portion of the parish. In 1854 he assisted Lavinia Crosse in the foundation at nearby Shipmeadow of a sisterhood and small penitentiary. In 1859 the community, named the Society of All Hallows, was moved to Ditchingham where it flourished under Scudamore's wardenship and took on responsibility for an orphanage and hospital. Scudamore devoted his leisure to patristic and liturgiological studies, which bore fruit in *Notitia eucharistica* (1872). He was influenced by the works of Richard Hooker and high-churchmen of the seventeenth century, but rejected the ritualist extremism of the English Church Union, with which he engaged in controversy (1872–3).

Scudamore was most widely known for his devotional works, especially *Steps to the Altar* (1846), which had gone into sixty-seven editions by 1887, though his personal profit from its worldwide success amounted to only £40. Scarcely less popular was his *Words to Take with Us* (1859). In addition to other works on church history and controversy he contributed some lengthy articles to Smith's and Cheetham's *Dictionary of Christian Antiquities* (1875–80). Scudamore died at Ditchingham rectory on 31 January 1881, and was buried in the parish cemetery. He and his wife, who outlived him by seventeen years, were survived by two sons and a daughter.

THOMAS SECCOMBE, *rev.* G. MARTIN MURPHY

Sources Venn, *Alum. Cant.* • Boase, *Mod. Eng. biog.* • A. T. Cameron, *Religious communities of the Church of England* (1918) • *The Guardian* (2 Feb 1881) • *The Guardian* (9 March 1881) • *Church Times* (11 Feb 1881) • *The Times* (7 Feb 1881)

Archives U. Newcastle, Robinson L., letters to Sir Walter Trevelyan

Wealth at death under £5000: probate, 16 March 1881, *CGPLA Eng. & Wales*

Scudder, Henry (*d.* 1652), Church of England clergyman and author, was probably born in Horton Kirby, Kent, in the mid-1580s, one of at least three sons of Henry Scudder and his wife, Elizabeth. Having been admitted to Christ's College, Cambridge, he probably graduated BA early in 1603; he proceeded MA in 1606. A near-contemporary at college was William Whately, who became lecturer and from 1610 vicar of Banbury, Oxfordshire. On 7 June 1608 Scudder married, at Banbury, Whately's sister-in-law Bridgett, daughter of George Hunt (1551/2–1633), rector of Collingbourne Ducis, Wiltshire. At some date he acquired the living of Drayton, Oxfordshire; he had resigned it by 22 September 1619. He had joined the local combination of ministers led by John Dod, whose members included Whately, Robert Cleaver, and Robert Harris, and it was perhaps through it, and its lay patrons, that he managed to survive without a parish. His first publication, *A Key of Heaven* (1620), an application of the Lord's prayer, was dedicated to Thomas Crewe of Steane, the godly lawyer and Northamptonshire gentleman, in thankfulness for 'the many kindnesses you have shewed me' (sig. A4).

Following the death of his father-in-law, on 28 May 1633 Scudder was presented by the king to the rectory of Collingbourne Ducis. His most celebrated work, *The Christians Daily Walk with God*, had first appeared two years previously. In 1635 it reached its sixth edition, which contained an epistle written by the leading minister John Davenport. A German translation by Theodore Haak appeared in Frankfurt in 1636. There were at least nine further editions; the recommendations by John Owen and Richard Baxter in the 1674 edition are testimonies to the importance of this book to the religious and devotional life of the protestant community and its appeal to a broad range of presbyterian and congregational readers. As Baxter observed, the book is 'so prudent and spiritual, apt and savory the Directions, and all so fully suited to our ordinary cases and conditions, that I heartily wish no family might be without it' (Scudder, *The Christians Daily Walk in Holy Security and Peace*, 1674 edn, A4v).

As a literary executor with Edward Leigh to Whately, who died in 1639, Scudder brought to publication Whately's *Prototypes, or, The Primarie Presidents out of the Book of Genesis* (1640), and wrote the accompanying life of the author. On 5 May 1642 he was sanctioned by parliament as a lecturer for Warminster and in June of that year he joined the Westminster assembly. He was an active participant in its affairs, reviewing the proofs of the Westminster confession of faith and acting as a member of the committee for scriptures. His name appears at regular intervals in the minutes, but he was often recorded as absent. Preaching before parliament in October 1644 a sermon published as *Gods Warning to England by the Voyce of his Rod* (1644), Scudder called on members to repent their sins and lead a strictly devotional life to avert God's impending judgments on the nation. That year he also published an edition of Caleb Grantham's *The Godly Mans Choice*, a manual on marriage to which Scudder added his own 'profitable directions how persons should live as becometh Christians in the married state'.

On 10 May 1645 Scudder was admitted as interim rector of St Mildred Poultry, London, and from there signed that year the petition addressed to the common council of the City by ministers who were dissatisfied with the proposed presbyterian organization of London parishes. By 1647 he had spent a brief period at St Andrew by the Wardrobe, but within a short time he seems to have returned to Wiltshire. He was at Collingbourne Ducis when he drew up his will on 12 February 1652. By this time his first wife had died and he had married Joyce, whose other name is unknown. Evidently a fairly prosperous man, he left land in Hurstbourne Tarrant, Hampshire and in Horton Kirby to his three married daughters—Jane, wife of Richard Russell, Martha, wife of Thomas Jacob, and Bridgett, wife of John *Grayle (1613/14–1651/2) (who may have ministered at Collingbourne Ducis during Scudder's absence in London before moving to Tidworth in the same county). Legacies also went to his granddaughter Elizabeth, daughter of Elizabeth Scudder and John *Tombes (1602–1676), the anti-paedobaptist minister, and to a number of relatives who had moved to New England, including his brother Thomas. He lived long enough to make a codicil on 20 March 1652, but died before 31 May when his will was proved, and was buried at Collingbourne.

KENNETH GIBSON

Sources A. F. Mitchell and J. Struthers, eds., *Minutes of the sessions of the Westminster assembly of divines* (1874) • A. Argent, 'Aspects of the ecclesiastical history of the parishes of the City of London, 1640–49, with special reference to the parish clergy', PhD diss., U. Lond., 1983 • W. A. Shaw, *A history of the English church during the civil wars and under the Commonwealth, 1640–1660*, 2 vols. (1900) • B. Williams, ed., *The subscription book of bishops Townson and Davenant 1620–1640*, Wilts RS, 32 (1977) • E. J. Bodington, 'The church survey in Wiltshire, 1649–1650', *Wiltshire Archaeological and Natural History Magazine*, 40 (1919), 297–317 • Venn, *Alum. Cant.* • J. S. W. Gibson, ed., *Marriage register of Banbury*, 1: 1558–1724, Banbury Historical Society, 2 (1960), 42 • will, PRO, PROB 11/223, sig. 195 • *Calamy rev.*, 568g • *Walker rev.*, 52–3 • W. J. Oldfield, 'Index to the clergy whose ordination, institution, resignation, licence or death is recorded in the diocesan registers of the diocese of Oxford … 1542–1908', 1915, Bodl. Oxf., MS Top. Oxon. c. 250 • Foster, *Alum. Oxon.* • private information (2004) [S. J. Skudder]

Likenesses W. Sherwin, line engraving, BM, NPG; repro. in H. Scudder, *The Christians daily walk*, 11th edn (1674)

Wealth at death see will, PRO, PROB 11/223, sig. 195

Scully, Denys (1773–1830), barrister and political activist, was the eldest surviving son (with three brothers and two sisters) of James Scully (1738–1816), a prosperous grazier of Kilfeacle, co. Tipperary, and Catherine Lyons (1739–1818) of Croom, co. Limerick. He was born at Kilfeacle on 4 May 1773. After schooling at the Kilkenny Academy (1785–6) he was destined for a commercial career but switched to the law when an act of 1792 admitted Catholics to the Irish bar, to which he was called from the Middle Temple in 1796 after concurrently completing his education at Trinity College, Cambridge. On 25 November 1801 he married Mary (*d.* 1806), eldest daughter of Ferdinand Huddleston of Sawston Hall near Cambridge. Her family were neighbours of the lord lieutenant, Philip Yorke, third earl of Hardwicke, and brought Scully an introduction to the viceregal court. On the renewal of the war with France in 1803 he published a pamphlet urging his countrymen not to side with the French and was seen for a time as a 'Castle Catholic'. When a new Catholic committee was formed in the autumn of 1804, however, he took the lead in thwarting the viceroy's efforts to get a petition suppressed and was a member of a delegation which was received by Pitt on 12 March 1805 and on his refusal of support turned to the opposition.

During the next three years, marked by the ascendancy of John Keogh, Scully stood aside from the committee. His first wife died without children on 17 April 1806, and on 8 September 1808 he married Catherine (*d.* 1843), daughter of Vincent Eyre of Sheffield Park, who brought him a dowry of £14,000 and with whom he had nine children. The youngest son, William Francis John *Scully, made his fortune in land speculation. From 1809 on Scully and Daniel O'Connell were leaders of the popular party, opposed to any form of government veto on the nomination of bishops. While O'Connell steadily established his ascendancy, Scully, a poor speaker and temperamentally inclined to manipulate others, worked mainly behind the scenes. Only in 1811–12 did he achieve momentary fame with his *Penal Laws*, published at the height of an agitation which he himself had fomented by convoking an assembly of elected delegates to test the 1793 Convention Act in the courts. Discouraged by repeated failure at Westminster, and distracted by family litigation over his father's will, he became less active after 1817. Fat as a young man, Scully was 'fully as broad as he is long' when he was felled by a stroke in May 1823. In a pamphlet of 1824 he criticized O'Connell for taking up grievances that were not specifically Catholic ones. After another stroke he died at Kilfeacle on 25 October 1830, and was buried in the Scully plot on the Rock of Cashel.

Scully's second son, **Vincent Scully** (1810–1871), barrister, was born on 8 September 1810. He rose to be a QC. He sat as a Liberal for Cork in the parliament of 1852–7, showing a special interest in free trade in land. In 1856 his reputation suffered from the Tipperary Bank crash, as he was a nominal director and a cousin of the swindler John Sadleir. In 1859, however, he was re-elected, and sat until 1865. He married Susanna Grogan (*d.* 1874) on 6 September 1841 and died at Grove End, London, on 4 June 1871. He was credited with a punning sense of humour, an example of which is perhaps to be found in the motto inscribed on Scully's Cross, erected by him beside his father's tomb on the Rock of Cashel: *In hoc signo vincent* ('In this sign shall they conquer'). B. C. MacDermot

Sources B. C. MacDermot, ed., *The Catholic question in Ireland and England, 1798–1822: the papers of Denys Scully* (1988) • B. C. MacDermot, ed., *The Irish Catholic petition of 1805: the diary of Denys Scully* (1992) • *The correspondence of Daniel O'Connell*, ed. M. R. O'Connell, 1–2, IMC (1972) • T. Wyse, *A history of the late Catholic Association* (1829) • R. L. Sheil, *Sketches, legal and political*, ed. M. W. Savage, 2 vols. (1855) • J. D. White, *A guide to the Rock of Cashel*, 3rd edn (1888) • S. M. Hussey, *Reminiscences of an Irish land agent* (1904) • Burke, *Gen. Ire.* • *Freeman's Journal* [Dublin] (3 Nov 1830)

Archives NL Ire., corresp. and papers | BL, Hardwicke and Holland House MSS • Cambs. AS, Huddleston MSS • NL Ire., Callanan MSS • Warks. CRO, Throckmorton MSS

Wealth at death under £40,000—Vincent Scully

Scully, Vincent (1810–1871). *See under* Scully, Denys (1773–1830).

Scully, William Francis John (1821–1906), land speculator, was born on 23 November 1821 at Kilfeacle House, co. Tipperary, Ireland, the youngest child of Denys *Scully (1773–1830), barrister and political activist, and his wife, Catherine Eyre (*d.* 1843). One of his brothers was Vincent *Scully (1810–1871) [*see under* Scully, Denys]. William Scully was born into a dynasty founded on command of the law, the assertion of Catholic claims, and commercial exploitation of land. He was sent to the Jesuit school at Stonyhurst, Lancashire, when aged fourteen, and he remained there for one school year. He was then apprenticed to a Dublin solicitor but did not proceed into the profession.

Scully devoted himself instead to the acquisition and management of land. The share of the family's landed holdings available for him was greatly increased with the death in 1842 of his eldest brother, James, who was brutally assassinated, apparently in revenge for harsh behaviour towards tenants. This did little to diminish the robustness of Scully's behaviour as a landlord. His passion for the use of advanced agricultural techniques, of which he had a thorough grasp, was an additional source of friction with his tenants. In August 1865 at Kilkenny crown court he was given a sentence of twelve months' imprisonment (which he may not have served), for striking the head of the wife of a tenant resisting the service of an eviction writ. In August 1868 he attempted to serve eviction notices on the tenants of Ballycohey, co. Tipperary, a recently acquired townland whose inhabitants had refused to accept new, highly restrictive leases. On 14 August, in a carefully planned ambush, two of Scully's party were killed and he himself received gunshot wounds. The affair was reported in sensational terms throughout Ireland and Britain. Even the most fervent upholders of landlord rights tended to agree that Scully's behaviour was insupportable, not least because of his personal participation in what convention saw as work proper to subordinates. The Ballycohey affray had a significant impact on Gladstone's perception of the Irish land question, and so on the genesis of the Land Act of 1870. Scully continued to be an Irish landlord almost to the end of his life but in 1870 he took up residence in London.

Starting in 1850 Scully also acquired land in Illinois, USA. From 1866 onwards this investment yielded profit and already by 1870 Scully was a dollar millionaire. Huge acquisitions that year in Kansas and Nebraska were added to subsequently. From his home in Holland Park, London, Scully methodically organized and managed a transatlantic landed empire which relied on systematic drainage, scientific soil improvement, a distinctive 'cash rent' lease (the 'Scully lease'), paternalistic estate regulation, a talented hand-picked management team, and intensive three-month visits every other year by Scully himself. By 1896 his American landholdings amounted to 250,000 acres. In October 1902 Scully was granted USA citizenship. He had been living in Washington, DC since 1900, but he returned to London later in 1902.

In 1851 Scully married Margaret Mary Sweetman of Dublin; they had three daughters before her death in 1861. On 10 February 1876 he married Enriqueta Angela Chynoweth (1849–1932), of London, and they had three sons and one daughter. John Scully (1849–1885) was the child from an earlier liaison of Scully's. His mother's name is not known, and he attended Rugby School at his father's expense and was later employed on the Scully estates in the USA. In his will (dated 1901, at Washington) William Scully explicitly disinherited the children of his first marriage for reasons that are unknown. An imperious response to anything or anyone that thwarted him was characteristic. In 1867 or 1868 he had reacted to a parish priest's criticism from the altar by becoming an Anglican, to the distress of his siblings, two of whom were nuns. He died at his home at 12 Holland Park, London, on 17 October 1906, and was buried at Kensal Green cemetery. He was survived by his second wife. Estimates of his wealth ranged between 10 and 50 million dollars.

R. V. COMERFORD

Sources H. E. Socolofsky, *Landlord William Scully* (c.1979) • W. E. Vaughan, 'Ireland c.1870', *A new history of Ireland*, ed. T. W. Moody and others, 5: *Ireland under the Union, 1801–1870* (1989), 726–800 • E. D. Steele, *Irish and British politics: tenant right and nationality, 1865–1870* (1974)
Archives priv. coll., business records
Likenesses portrait, repro. in Socolofsky, *Landlord William Scully*, frontispiece
Wealth at death est. $10,000,000–$50,000,000

Scupham, John (1904–1990), educationist and broadcaster, was born on 7 September 1904 in Market Rasen, Lincolnshire, the younger son and third of five children of Roger Scupham, master builder and monumental mason, and his wife, Kate, daughter of Thomas Hulme Whittingham, proprietor of the *Rasen Mail* and bookseller. He was educated at Market Rasen grammar school and then became a scholar of Emmanuel College, Cambridge, gaining first-class honours in part one of the history tripos (1925) and in English (1926).

Scupham was a polymath, who would have been a scientist had his school been able to provide the grounding. His wide reading, together with an intense interest in people of all kinds, no doubt contributed to his success as a teacher. From 1927 to 1946 his experience was unusually varied, with teaching in grammar schools in Newcastle, Liverpool, and Derby, Workers' Educational Association tutoring in forces education, and running the department of liberal studies and adult education at Cambridge Technical College. He prided himself on the fact that he had done everything from teaching apprentices to write a few lines of literate English to examining open scholarships in history at a group of Cambridge colleges. In 1932 he married Dorothy Lacey (*d*. 1987), daughter of Fred Clark, a Lincolnshire draper, and their happy marriage produced a son and a daughter.

From 1946 to 1965 Scupham worked in educational broadcasting at the BBC. Starting as an education officer with the Schools' Broadcasting Council, a body representing the educational world within the corporation, he progressed rapidly to become assistant head of school broadcasting and in 1954 was made head of educational broadcasting. His work with the council, visiting schools and colleges, and meeting other educationists, enabled him to guide the production departments in what was needed. His profound understanding of the issues involved in teaching and learning through broadcasts made him a formidable head of the complete production machine and in 1963 he was made the first controller, educational broadcasting. This enhanced role reflected the expansion that had occurred under his aegis as head.

The expansion, which Scupham promoted with considerable energy and fortitude, was mainly exemplified by the creation of a school television department in 1959 and a further education department in 1965, which, when added to the two equivalent radio departments, constituted a large output 'empire'. This was resented by a number of very senior managers in the television service. It took them some time to realize that Scupham's small yet precise physique, his quiet, reasonable negotiating style, and his absolute moral integrity concealed a steely will. He believed passionately in the importance of disseminating knowledge widely and saw broadcasting as a new, powerful medium through which to achieve this both at home and abroad. Like John Reith, the BBC's first director-general, he worked tirelessly in the arena of international broadcasting and, as he revealed in his books *Broadcasting and the Community* (1967) and *The Revolution in Communications* (1970), believed that mass media have important social purposes. He was appointed OBE in 1961.

Towards the end of his BBC career Scupham helped to

devise plans for a College of the Air, but when the more ambitious Open University project emerged he worked assiduously and diplomatically to see that the BBC played a vital role. After retiring from the BBC in 1965 he sat on the ministerial committee to advise on the setting up of the university, and from 1969 to 1978 was a member of its council. He was awarded an Open University honorary doctorate in 1975. Among his many other activities were participation in the inquiry undertaken by John Newsom in 1961–3, which championed the educational needs of less able children, and in the Church of England board of education (1960–72), as well as the presidency of the educational section of the British Association (1965–6).

Scupham was a lifelong, but not uncritical, member of the Church of England, a proud provincial, who combined a sense of life's mysteries with an extensive knowledge of modern thinking. Like Matthew Arnold, he thought that 'the men of culture are the true apostles of equality', but was wise enough at the end of his life to see that times were changing. Scupham died on 10 January 1990 in Norwich, near to his daughter, having lived much of his married life in Harpenden, Hertfordshire.

JOHN CAIN, *rev.*

Sources *The Times* (12 Jan 1990) · *The Independent* (15 Jan 1990) · recorded interview with John Scupham, 1984, BBC archives, BBC Oral History Project · BBC WAC · personal knowledge (1996) · private information (1996) · *CGPLA Eng. & Wales* (1990)
Archives BBC WAC | SOUND BBC archives, London, BBC Oral History Project, recorded interview with John Scupham, 1984
Likenesses photographs, BBC WAC
Wealth at death £220,623: probate, 23 March 1990, *CGPLA Eng. & Wales*

Scurr, John (1876–1932), politician, was born in Brisbane, Queensland, Australia, on 6 April 1876, the son of Louis James Rennie of Poplar, London, a captain in the merchant navy. His mother, sister of Captain John Scurr of Poplar, died shortly after his birth and at six months of age he was adopted by his maternal uncle, also a captain in the merchant navy, and took the family name. He grew up as a Roman Catholic in the East End of London and was educated at George Green's school in Poplar, of which in later life he became chairman of governors, and at King's College School.

Scurr's early employment history was mundane enough, encompassing minor clerical posts and the running of his own hardware retail business, but a keen political awareness developed and he became attracted to opportunities for social reform. From 1897 he was a member of the Poplar Labour League and was active on the Poplar Trades and Labour Representation Council, of which he became president in 1911. For some time he was on the executive of the United Irish League, a member of the Social Democratic Federation, where he was associated with George Lansbury (who secured him employment with the *Daily Herald*), and a member of the Independent Labour Party. Fired by the example in his teenage years of Cardinal Manning's successful intervention in the dockers' strike of 1889, Scurr was a keen advocate of improving work conditions for casual dock labourers; in 1910–11, during a year of industrial strife, he was an impressive district chairman of the dockers' union.

In 1910 Scurr married Julia O'Sullivan (*d.* 1927), daughter of John O'Sullivan from co. Cork. She shared his religious, social, and political ties and had been an active member of the Poplar board of guardians since 1907, a local councillor, and like Scurr, a suffragette enthusiast. The couple had two sons and a daughter.

As a prominent figure in local government, a member of the Poplar borough council (of which he became an alderman in 1919), and chairman of the Stepney board of guardians, Scurr was outspoken in arguing for the welfare of the disadvantaged. He supported the policy of 'Poplarism' which envisaged an increase in provision for outdoor relief and the establishment of a rates equalization fund. In 1921 he was imprisoned for six weeks, along with a number of other council members including his wife, for refusing to collect the rates in protest against burdens facing poor boroughs. On his release from Brixton his 'martyrdom' did not lessen his popularity, and he was elected mayor of Poplar in 1922 and appointed chairman of the metropolitan boroughs standing joint committee. From 1925 to 1929 he was an alderman of the London county council. His pacifism and sympathy for conscientious objectors in the First World War, his anti-colonialist attitudes in regard to Ireland and India, and his vociferous opposition to the working conditions of Indian employees under the British raj marked him out as a fearless man of integrity and outspoken zeal.

Conscious that a parliamentary seat would give wider currency to his views, Scurr made several attempts to secure election. On a socialist ticket he unsuccessfully contested by-elections at South-West Bethnal Green in July 1911, Chesterfield in August 1913, Bethnal Green again in February 1914, and Ipswich in May 1914. At general elections, standing as a Labour candidate, he was unsuccessful at Buckingham in 1918 and Stepney Mile End in 1922. In 1923, however, he was elected at Stepney Mile End and increased his majority there in 1924 and 1929.

Never robust in health, Scurr did not achieve in parliament the prominence he had attained in local government. He was chairman, however, of the Independent Labour Party's parliamentary group in 1925 and helped to frame a *modus vivendi* between it and the Labour Party. He resigned from the Independent Labour Party three years later because of its shift to the left and consequent hostility to some policies of the Labour government. Scurr was outspoken in the house on matters of enduring interest to him, especially in 1924 in introducing a bill to amend the constitution of the Port of London Authority and in matters relating to local rating, poor relief, and economic exploitation. In his writings in 1924 and 1925 as editor of the *Socialist Review*, he emphasized 'the duty of a working class political party is to challenge the fundamental basis on which our social system is based' (*Socialist Review*, Sept 1925).

Scurr's personal commitment to reform was challenged in 1931, when his religious beliefs influenced his political actions. The president of the Board of Education, Sir Charles Trevelyan, was unable to convince Ramsay MacDonald of the need to make adequate provision for voluntary schools in a bill to raise compulsory school leaving age from fourteen to fifteen. Scurr thought the failure to provide for the costs of the measure in terms of added classroom space, teacher provision, and equipment was, in essence, an attack on the method of appointment of teachers in denominational schools. He introduced an amendment requiring financial aid to be made available to voluntary schools before the proposed bill should come into operation. He spoke with sincerity, earnestness, and dignity of 'times and occasions when all party ties have to go in obedience to what one considers to be a higher claim', for 'if the Bill passes without giving financial assistance to non-provided schools, a large number of children will suffer by reason of the deficiencies which must result' (*Hansard 5C*, 21 Jan 1931). Scurr's amendment was supported by thirty-five defectors from the Labour Party and was passed. Subsequently the bill itself was defeated in the Lords and Trevelyan resigned. The gratitude of the Catholic body to Scurr was manifested in June 1932, after his defeat in the general election of 1931, when an appeal in *The Times* for financial support during his final critical illness was made by Father Bernard Whelan of Westminster Cathedral. He died in Manor House Hospital, Golders Green, London, on 10 July 1932 and was buried on 13 July in St Patrick's cemetery, Leytonstone, after a requiem mass at St Joseph's Church, Highgate Hill, London. His wife predeceased him in 1927.

V. A. McCLELLAND

Sources 'Scurr, John', *DLB*, vol. 4 • *The Times* (11 July 1932) • *Hansard 5C* (1931), 247.193–8 • *The Times* (18 June 1932) • L. MacNeill Weir, *The tragedy of Ramsay MacDonald* (1938), 249 • R. J. A. Skidelsky, *Politicians and the slump: the labour government of 1921–31* (1967), 322–33 • B. Saeks, *Ramsay Macdonald: in thought and action* (New Mexico, USA, 1952), 189–90 • P. S. Gupta, 'British labour and the Indian left, 1919–1939', *Socialism in India*, ed. B. R. Nanda (1972), 69–121 • *The Labour who's who* (1927) • *Socialist Review* (Sept 1925) • R. Barker, *Education and politics, 1900–1951: a study of the labour party* (1972) • A. J. A. Morris, *C. P. Trevelyan: portrait of a radical* (1977) • N. Branson, *Poplarism, 1919–1925: George Lansbury and the councillors' revolt* (1979)

Wealth at death £233 4s.: administration, 28 Oct 1932, *CGPLA Eng. & Wales*

Seabury, Samuel (1729–1796), first bishop of the Protestant Episcopal church in the United States of America, was born on 30 November 1729 at Groton, Connecticut, the son of Samuel Seabury (1706–1764) and Abigail Mumford. His father was a missionary, under the jurisdiction of the bishop of London, working for the Society for the Propagation of the Gospel (SPG). The young Seabury attended Yale College (1745–8), where he studied ten subjects and subscribed to penal laws which forbade him 'to play at swords (nor) go into any tavern' (Dexter, 2.7). Having graduated BA (and later proceeded MA), he worked as a catechist before going to Edinburgh University (1752) to study medicine for one year—regarded as a basic necessity for one proposing to become a missionary. He was examined by the SPG and ordained deacon and priest in 1753 with the hope that he would 'prove a very diligent and useful missionary' (SPG, abstract of proceedings, 1753–4, 57, Bodl. RH).

After returning to the colonies Seabury was successively rector of New Brunswick, New Jersey, of Jamaica, of Long Island, and of Westchester, New York, where he served until 1776. On 12 October 1756 he married Mary (1736–1780), the daughter of Edward Hicks of New York, with whom he had six children. He reported regularly to the SPG in London, expressing, among other things, his concern 'that Quakerism is the seat of Infidelity' (SPG, letters, 1759, 114, Bodl. RH) and noting 'the differences encountered by the number of Deists' (ibid., 1762, 160). As a result of his experience at Westchester he pleaded for an episcopate in the colonies to confirm communicants and sustain the work of the American mission. His letters also show his awareness of colonial resentment of Britain's policy of imperial taxation, though he remained totally loyal; in 1766—the year of the Declaratory Act—he was one of 312 signators 'determined to support the Constitution at the hazard of lives and property' (Beardsley, 23). Seabury's convictions were put to the test when he was briefly imprisoned in 1775 by the revolutionary forces in Connecticut, following the publication of a series of pamphlets attacking patriot institutions including the continental congress. In a long letter to the SPG he reported that he had closed his church. 'There would be neither prayer nor sermon' until he could pray for George III, he wrote, while assuring the society (which paid him £50 a year) that he would not leave his mission 'so long as it was practical to stay' (SPG New York Letters B2 and 3, 29 Dec 1776, Bodl. RH). This, and subsequent letters, give a graphic account of troop movements while conceding that both revolutionaries and loyalists plundered and foraged. Seabury accepted an appointment as a chaplain to the king's forces under General William Hume and spent much of the war in New York. His loyalty and piety were rewarded with an honorary doctorate of divinity from the University of Oxford (1777). The SPG, 'sensible of his great worth' (annual report, 1777, 46), continued to pay his stipend until a change of policy as late as 1785; thereafter friends in Britain ensured him an income for the rest of his life.

In early 1783 Seabury was invited by a group of ten Connecticut clergymen led by the Revd John Rutgers Marshall to become the first bishop of a national episcopal church in the United States. In July 1783 he travelled to England to seek consecration as their bishop. The stumbling-block, however, was the obligation to take an oath to the crown, to which Seabury, now a citizen of the United States, could not subscribe. Moreover, an Erastian church could not justify consecration without the consent of the state of Connecticut. Instead Seabury, recalling his Scottish links of thirty years earlier, approached the Scottish nonjuring bishops, the descendants of ministers who had refused to swear the oath of allegiance to William and Mary. At first they too were reluctant to grant Seabury's request until they received assurance that Britain recognized the United States. The Scottish bishops also received the implicit support of the archbishop of Canterbury, who asked that the Scottish prelates 'would not send the suppliant away empty-handed' (letter of 20 Nov 1783, Wilberforce, 205). Delays continued throughout 1784. Seabury wrote home that 'the expense of continuing another winter is greater than will suit my purse' (letter to Myles Cooper, 1 Aug 1784, Beardsley, 114), while the nonjuring Bishop John Skinner noted that he did not want it to be thought 'we always fished in troubled waters' (Beardsley, 107). It was not until 14 November that Seabury was consecrated as bishop of Connecticut in a discreet ceremony at a house in Aberdeen in the presence of three of the four Scottish bishops.

An agreement, known as the Concordat, was signed acknowledging full communion between the episcopalians of Scotland and Connecticut. In particular, the new bishop—the first protestant bishop on American soil—agreed to recommend that the form of communion service to be followed in the United States should be closer in style and theology to the Scottish office of 1746 than to the English Book of Common Prayer (1662). 'By gentle methods of argument and persuasion to introduce it by degrees into practice' (Concordat, article 5, GD 530/571/14, NA Scot.), was the guidance. Bishop Skinner wrote to the archbishop of Canterbury that Seabury seemed 'a truly pious, prudent and well-principled man' (*Scottish Guardian*, 25 Nov 1884).

Finally, in May 1785 Seabury returned home to New London, Connecticut. Two years later William White and Samuel Provoost were able to be consecrated in London, after an act of parliament (1786) had allowed such consecrations of men from outside the British dominions. Skinner wrote to Seabury hoping that there would 'be no occasion for two separate communions among the episcopalians' (Skinner to Seabury, 20 June 1787, Skinner, 67). He had no need to fear. Seabury, by 'gentle methods', brought 'a harmonious conclusion' (Wilberforce, 215) between the English and Scottish traditions when the prayer book and constitution of the Protestant Episcopal church in the United States were approved in 1790. Seabury was appointed the first presiding bishop and also assumed the see of Rhode Island.

Seabury spent the remainder of his life in the quiet pastoral care of his scattered flock. A contemporary saw him as someone to whom 'theological niceties were (an) aversion' (Abraham Jarvis, 5 May 1796, Beardsley, 361). He remained a poor man on his meagre £50 a year, and it was as a friend and physician to the deprived that he was remembered. Yet he had an awareness of the dignity of his office with a modesty of manner. To the question, 'How old are you, bishop?', he replied 'Old enough to be better than I am' (Beardsley, 365). He was robust in appearance, with a clear, sonorous voice, and it was at the end of a four-week journey of 134 miles on horseback through his two dioceses that he died, of apoplexy, on 25 February 1796 in New London. He was buried three days later in the public burial-ground there. The links he established with the Episcopal church in Scotland are commemorated in the enlargement, in 1948, of St Andrew's Cathedral in Aberdeen and in the consecration, in 1956, of a new bishop of Aberdeen by the then bishop of Connecticut.

GERALD M. D. HOWAT

Sources E. E. Beardsley, *Life of Samuel Seabury* (1884) · C. F. Pascoe, *Two hundred years of the SPG*, rev. edn, 2 vols. (1901) · S. Wilberforce, *A history of the Protestant Episcopal church in America* (1856) · J. Skinner, *Annals of Scottish episcopacy* (1818) · W. J. Seabury, *Memoir of Bishop Seabury* (1909) · B. E. Steiner, *Samuel Seabury* (1971) · *Seabury centenary handbook* (1884) · G. J. C. Douglas, 'Scottish liturgy', *Pan-Anglican*, 8/1 (1957), 26–9 · *Scottish Guardian* (25 Nov 1884) · F. B. Dexter, *Biographical sketches of the graduates of Yale College*, 6 vols. (1885–1912) · D. S. Armentrout, 'Seabury, Samuel', *ANB* · *IGI*

Archives Bodl. RH, annual report · Bodl. RH, United Society for the Propagation of the Gospel New York, letters, B2 · Bodl. RH, United Society for the Propagation of the Gospel journals, 21, 23, 25 · NA Scot., concordat, GD 530/571/14; CH 12/12; CH 12/14 · U. Aberdeen, diocesan archives, MS 3320 · Yale U., papers, diary | NL Scot., Fettercairn papers, ACC 4796

Likenesses portrait, repro. in Beardsley, *Life of Samuel Seabury*, frontispiece

Seacole [*née* Grant]**, Mary Jane** (**1805–1881**), nurse, was born Mary Jane Grant in Kingston, Jamaica, one of at least two daughters and one son of a Scottish soldier and the mixed-race proprietress of a boarding-house for officers and their families. Much of Mary Grant's early life remains obscure; from her mother she acquired nursing skills and an understanding of the Creole medical tradition, based on herbal treatment, and she is known to have made two voyages to London in the early 1820s. On 10 November 1836 she married, in Kingston, one of her mother's resident guests, Edwin Horatio Seacole, a godson of Lord Nelson, but she was soon widowed. With her sister, Louisa, she ran the family boarding-house for several years, supervising its reconstruction after Kingston's great fire in 1843. She nursed cases of cholera and yellow fever in Jamaica and at Las Cruces in Panama where, for more than two years, she helped her brother manage a hotel. On returning to Jamaica she was briefly nursing superintendent at Up-Park military camp.

The coming of war with Russia in 1854 prompted Mary Seacole to sail to England, but when she tried to join Florence Nightingale's vanguard of nursing sisters she met a rebuff. At her own expense she took ship to the Crimea, arriving in February 1855 at Balaklava, where her husband's kinsman, Thomas Day, was employed on shipping business. By late April 'Seacole and Day' had opened the British Hotel, near the village of Kadikoi, halfway between the harbour and British headquarters. The hotel housed an officers' club and a good, clean canteen for the troops. While Thomas Day remained at Balaklava, Mrs Seacole managed its facilities. Her independent status ensured a freedom of movement denied the formal nursing service; by June she was a familiar figure at the battlefront, riding forward with two mules in attendance, one carrying medicaments and the other food and wine. She brought medical comfort to the maimed and dying after the assault on the Redan, in which a quarter of the British force was killed or wounded, and she tended Italian, French, and Russian casualties at the Chernaya two

Mary Jane Seacole (**1805–1881**), by Count Victor Gleichen, 1871

months later. Yet, on the day after the Chernaya battle, she could supply 'a capital lunch on the ground' for a cricket match between the guards division and other regiments (Astley, 268). When allied troops entered Sevastopol on 9 September Mrs Seacole obtained a special pass to go forward with her mule-train, becoming the first woman to enter the burning city: 'Every step had a score of dangers', she later wrote, 'and yet curiosity and excitement carried us on and on. I was often stopped to give refreshments to officers and men, who had been fasting for hours' (Seacole, 210).

Mary Seacole remained in the Crimea until July 1856. By then she was in financial difficulties, for the armistice found her and Day with surplus stocks of food and equipment, and outstanding bills to pay. On returning to England she opened a canteen at Aldershot, a venture that failed through lack of funds. By November she was bankrupt. From July 1855, however, William Howard Russell and other war correspondents had made her name familiar to British newspaper readers, and both *The Times* and *Punch* supported appeals to reimburse Mary Seacole for her losses in the Crimea. She was encouraged to write an autobiography, published by Blackwood in July 1857 as the *Wonderful Adventures of Mrs Seacole in Many Lands*: it sold well. Her disinterested services to 'the Army, Navy and British Nation' were recognized by a Seacole fund, approved by the queen and under the patronage of the prince of Wales and two royal dukes. She survived in some comfort until 14 May 1881, when she died of 'apoplexy', at her home, 3 Cambridge Street, Paddington. Her grave at Kensal Green Roman Catholic cemetery, reconsecrated on the initiative of Jamaican nurses in 1973, honours her 'care for the sick and wounded in the West Indies, Panama and on the battlefields of the Crimea'. ALAN PALMER

Sources M. Seacole, *Wonderful adventures of Mrs Seacole in many lands*, ed. Z. Alexander and A. Dewjee (1984) · W. Simpson, *The autobiography of William Simpson*, ed. G. Eyre-Todd (1903) · J. D. Astley, *Fifty years of my life in the world of sport*, 1 (1894), 268 · A. B. Soyer, *Soyer's culinary campaign: being historical reminiscences of the late war* (1857) · A. W. Palmer, *The banner of battle: the story of the Crimean War* (1987) · tombstone, St Mary's Roman Catholic cemetery, Kensal Rise, London

Likenesses V. Gleichen, terracotta bust, 1871, Institute of Jamaica, Kingston [*see illus.*] · drawings (contemporary), repro. in Seacole, *Wonderful adventures*

Wealth at death £2615 11s. 7d.: probate, 11 July 1881, *CGPLA Eng. & Wales*

Seafield. For this title name *see* Ogilvy, James, fourth earl of Findlater and first earl of Seafield (1663–1730); Ogilvy, James, sixth earl of Findlater and third earl of Seafield (*c*.1714–1770).

Seaford. For this title name *see* Ellis, Charles Rose, first Baron Seaford (1771–1845); Ellis, Charles Augustus, sixth Baron Howard de Walden and second Baron Seaford (1799–1868).

Seaforth. For this title name *see* Mackenzie, Colin, of Kintail, first earl of Seaforth (*c*.1597–1633); Mackenzie, George, second earl of Seaforth (*d*. 1651); Mackenzie, Kenneth, third earl of Seaforth (1635–1678) [*see under* Mackenzie, George, second earl of Seaforth (*d*. 1651)]; Mackenzie, Kenneth, fourth earl of Seaforth and Jacobite first marquess of Seaforth (*bap*. 1661, *d*. 1701); Mackenzie, William, fifth earl of Seaforth (*d*. 1740).

Seaforth and Mackenzie. For this title name *see* Mackenzie, Francis Humberston, Baron Seaforth and Mackenzie of Kintail (1754–1815).

Seagar, John (*d*. **1656**), Church of England clergyman, was a member of the family of Seagar or Segar of Broadclyst, Devon. He attended Wadham College, Oxford, and was listed on 10 July 1613 as a pupil of a Devon fellow, Matthew Osborne (*d*. 1661). He matriculated on 3 June 1614 and graduated BA as of Wadham on 23 May 1617, proceeding MA from St Mary Hall on 28 June 1620. By 1628 Seagar had returned to Devon, acquiring the vicarage of Lamerton in that year; on 16 July 1631, following the death of Robert Stennings, he was instituted to the rectory of Broadclyst on the presentation of a kinsman, William Seagar.

During the civil wars, as Seagar reminded his parishioners, there were 'three years of which time I was forced by the violence of soldiers to absent my self from you' (Seagar, preface). But it was as minister of Broadclyst that in June 1648 he signed *The Joint-Testimonie of the Ministers of Devon*, one of a series of tracts issued about that time in which the authors urged the imposition of a presbyterian system and protested that 'a toleration of all blasphemous heresies by a law, is diametrically opposed to the grace and duty of zeal' (*Joint-Testimonie*, 32). A few months later, on 19 January 1650, *A Discoverie of the World to Come According to the Scriptures* (1650) was licensed by Joseph Caryl and signed by Seagar, again as minister of Broadclyst, recalling in the preface the eighteen years of his service in that cure. He published this work 'being desirous before my death to leave among you some token and testimonie of my love towards you' and he expected that the second coming of Christ in the flesh was also imminent. Seagar was not quite right in either prediction. He survived until 13 April 1656 and was buried at Pitminster, Somerset. His will, which left 719 acres of land in co. Tipperary to his nephews William and George Seagar, significant sums to other kin, and £5 to the poor of Broadclyst, was proved by his widow, Dorothie, on 14 May. STEPHEN WRIGHT

Sources R. B. Gardiner, ed., *The registers of Wadham College, Oxford*, 1 (1889) · Wood, *Ath. Oxon.*, new edn · J. Seagar, *A discoverie of the world to come according to the scriptures* (1650) · will, PRO, PROB 11/254, fol. 348

Seager, Charles (1808–1878), orientalist, was the son of John Seager (1776–1849), of Evesbatch, Worcestershire, rector of Welsh Bicknor, Monmouthshire, from 1808 until his death on 27 May 1849. John Seager was the translator of several works on Greek grammar and prosody, and published a supplement to Johnson's *Dictionary* in 1819. Seager matriculated at Magdalen Hall, Oxford, on 30 November 1832 and in 1834 he was elected a scholar of Worcester College. In that year he published an ode in Hebrew to mark the inauguration of the duke of Wellington as chancellor of the university, and in 1836 he gained the Kennicott Hebrew scholarship. He graduated BA on 25 May 1836 (MA, 1839) and was ordained priest in May 1837. From 1839 to 1843 he was an assistant lecturer in Hebrew, under E. B. Pusey. Closely associated with the Tractarian party he, along with Mark Pattison and J. B. Mozley, lived from 1838 at the house for young writers established in St Aldates, Oxford, by Pusey and J. H. Newman. He was one of the earliest Tractarian converts to the Roman Catholic church. In January 1842 Pusey wrote to Newman asking him to correct Seager's romanizing tendencies, but although Newman made the attempt, Seager was received into the Catholic church on 12 October 1843 at St Mary's College, Oscott. His secession caused Pusey much pain and embarrassment. His wife, Anna (*d.* 1893), whom he had married in 1839, converted in 1844.

Having spent many years as an independent scholar, when the Catholic University College was established at Kensington by Cardinal Manning in 1875 Seager was appointed to the chair of Hebrew and comparative philology. His knowledge of oriental languages was extensive, but Hebrew, Arabic, and Syriac were his specialities. During the latter part of his life, however, he turned his attention to the languages of Assyria and Egypt, and he regularly attended the classes instituted by the Society of Biblical Archaeology under A. H. Sayce and P. Le Page Renouf. He was an active member of the council of the society. Shortly before his death he was readmitted a member of the University of Oxford, from which he had been expelled on his secession to Catholicism. A decree was passed enabling him to replace his name on the books without payment of the usual fees. He died suddenly at the Hôtel de la Ville, Florence, while attending a congress of orientalists, on 18 September 1878, and was buried in Oxford. His widow died at Ramsgate on 27 March 1893. One of his sons, Ignatius, was ordained priest in 1869 and died in 1870. Another, Osmund (1843–1920), educated at the Jesuit college at Metz and at Newman's University in Dublin, later became an assistant principal at the Admiralty. In addition to his contributions to the *Transactions* of the Society of Biblical Archaeology, Seager published some eleven works on philology, liturgy, apologetics, and politics, as well as a book of travels in the Rhineland, *The Female Jesuit Abroad* (1853).

THOMPSON COOPER, *rev.* G. MARTIN MURPHY

Sources Gillow, *Lit. biog. hist.*, 5.488–9 · *The Athenaeum* (21 Sept 1878), 372 · *The Athenaeum* (28 Sept 1878), 403 · H. P. Liddon, *The life of Edward Bouverie Pusey*, ed. J. O. Johnston and others, 4 vols. (1893–7), vol. 2, pp. 229–30, 377 · *The letters and diaries of John Henry Newman*, ed. C. S. Dessain and others, [31 vols.] (1961–), vols. 6, 22 · *The Times* (23 Sept 1878), 9 · J. Gondon, *Motifs de conversion de dix ministres anglicains* (1847), 191–202 · J. B. Mozley, *Letters* (1885), 85–6 · W. J. Oldfield, 'Index to the clergy whose ordination, institution, resignation, licence or death is recorded in the diocesan registers of the diocese of Oxford … 1542–1908', 1915, Bodl. Oxf., MS Top. Oxon. c. 250 · *The Tablet* (21–8 Sept 1878), 368, 377, 400, 402, 408 · *CGPLA Eng. & Wales* (1878)

Wealth at death under £3000: probate, 14 Nov 1878, *CGPLA Eng. & Wales*

Seager, Edward (1812–1883), army officer, was born on 11 June 1812 and, after serving in the ranks for nine years and 188 days from 1832, became a cornet of the 8th light dragoons on 17 September 1841. He was adjutant from 5 October 1841 to 25 October 1854, being gazetted lieutenant on 29 June 1843, captain on 26 October 1851, and major on 31 January 1858. He served with his regiment in the Crimean War of 1854, and up to February 1855, and was present at the battles of Alma, Balaklava (where he was wounded in the charge of the light brigade), Inkerman, and the siege of Sevastopol. On 28 June 1855 he was appointed assistant military secretary to Major-General Lord William Paulet, commanding on the Bosphorus, and he continued in the same office under Sir Henry Knight Storks until the end of the war, when he was awarded the Mejidiye (fifth class). He subsequently served in central India, 1858–9, was present at the action of Boordah, and was mentioned in the dispatches.

From 5 August 1859 to 5 August 1864 Seager was lieutenant-colonel of his regiment, and was then gazetted a brevet colonel in the army. From 3 November 1864 to 31 January 1870 he was acting quartermaster-general in the Dublin district, and from 1 April 1873 to 3 April 1878 inspecting officer of yeomanry cavalry at York. On 15 January 1870 he became a major-general, and on 1 July 1881 was placed on the retired list with the rank of lieutenant-general. On 10 May 1872 he received a reward for 'distinguished and meritorious services', and on 2 June 1877 he was gazetted CB.

Seager was married and had a daughter. He was noted as a devoted family man, of firm Christian conviction. He died at his home, Sion House, Scarborough, on 30 March 1883. G. C. BOASE, *rev.* JAMES FALKNER

Sources *Army List* • *The Times* (2 April 1883) • *Hart's Army List* • F. W. Lummis, *Honour the Light Brigade* (1972) • *Letters of Edward Seager* • J. Harris, *The gallant six hundred* (1973) • *British Army Review* (1960) • Boase, *Mod. Eng. biog.*

Likenesses photograph, *c.*1854, repro. in *British Army Review*; copy, priv. coll.

Wealth at death £24,699 0s. 7*d.*: probate, 21 May 1883, *CGPLA Eng. & Wales*

Seager [Segar], **Francis** (*fl.* **1549–1563**), translator and poet, was born and raised in a yeoman family in Devon. He began his literary career at the time of the explosion of protestant publication during the reign of Edward VI. In 1549 the London printers John Day and William Seres published *A brefe declaration of the great, and innumerable myseries, [and] wretchednesses used in courte*. This tract constitutes a new edition and expansion by Seager of William Caxton's translation of Alain Chartier's *Curial* from the original French. Seager's *Certayne psalmes select out of the psalter of David, and drawen into Englyshe metre, wyth notes to every psalme*, printed twice by Whitchurch in 1549, by Harrington in 1549 and 1550, and by William Seres in 1553, marks the beginning of a collaborative relationship with Robert Crowley, an important protestant poet, publisher, bookseller, and editor. Dedicated to Francis Russell, son of the earl of Bedford, this work is a metrical translation of nineteen psalms, together with a poem in the same ballad metre, entitled 'A Description of the Life of Man, the World and Vanities Thereof'. Crowley assimilated Seager's versifications into his compilation of the first complete metrical psalter in English, which aimed to recover the lyricism of biblical song in the vernacular. He may have been the 'Fraunces Nycholson *Alias* Seager' who was made free of the Stationers' Company on 24 September 1557.

During the reign of Mary I, Seager again turned to Seres to publish his *Schoole of Vertue, and booke of good nourture for chyldren, and youth to learne theyer dutie by* (1557). This popular work consists of twelve chapters of simple, irregular rhyme, each describing a particular 'duty' and the 'degrees' necessary for its achievement. An acrostic that spells out the author's name provides a preface. Amid a flurry of moralistic attacks on poetry Crowley issued a new edition of the *School of Vertue* in 1582, arguing that poetry plays an important role in the moral education of both children and adults, and is a powerful didactic tool. To Seager's work Crowley added his own metrical 'Prayers and Graces'. The popularity of Crowley's edition among a humble readership is suggested by a comment claiming that this book was 'commonly sold at the stalls of ballad-singers'. An abridged version of *School of Vertue* also appears in Robert Weste's *Booke of Demeanor* of 1619, reprinted in 1817, and again in 1868, by the Early English Text Society, as *The Babees Book*.

Seager contributed a moralistic poem of forty-four rhyme royal stanzas entitled 'How Richard Plantagenet, duke of Gloucester, murdered his brother's children, usurping the crowne' to the 1563 edition of the *Mirror for Magistrates*. He found ample evidence of political corruption and tyranny in the story of Richard III and hoped that his history would provide a model of vice that contemporary civil servants might avoid. A prose colloquy appended to the poem acknowledges the irregularity of Seager's rhyme royal but claims that it observes decorum in complementing Richard's unsavoury character. Scholars assume that William Shakespeare incorporated minor details from Seager's poem into *The Tragedy of Richard III* (*c.*1592).

Francis Seager is remembered as a versatile man of letters, important in bringing the humanist impetus of much popular poetry of the day into the service of the Reformation. JOHN N. KING

Sources *DNB* • *STC, 1475–1640* • J. N. King, *English Reformation literature: the Tudor origins of the protestant tradition* (1982) • M. Radick, 'Two notes on Surrey's Psalms: i, Francis Seager's Psalms; ii, the text of Surrey's psalm 88', *N&Q*, 220 (1975), 291–4 • Arber, *Regs. Stationers*, 1.69

Seago, Edward Brian [Ted] (**1910–1974**), landscape painter and writer, was born on 31 March 1910 at 13 Christchurch Road, Norwich, the younger son and second child of Francis Brian Seago (1881–1959), a coal merchant, and his wife, Mabel Reeve Woodroffe (1878–1962) from Beccles, Suffolk, and a governess before her marriage. A severe heart complaint (paroxysmal tachycardia) meant that he was able to have little formal education, though he attended schools in Lowestoft and Norwich (1918–23). From childhood he determined to be a painter despite lack of parental encouragement, and from the age of thirteen he studied with Bertram Priestman, who had a holiday home near by.

Seago's self-discipline meant that, confined to bed during repeated convalescences, he spent his days making studies of the skies annotated with the weather conditions, just as John Constable had a century before. Other influences on him included John Crome, John Sell Cotman, Arnesby Brown, and Alfred Munnings, from whom he sought advice. He studied anatomy, became a keen horseman, and, at the Maddermarket Theatre in Norwich, painted scenery and acted, determined, as far as possible, to lead a normal life. He toured England, Ireland, and France with a travelling circus, carried out pre-war espionage in Europe, and formed a deep relationship with a young performer whose tragic death was a precursor of the deaths of two other young men he loved. He wrote and illustrated his circus travels in *Circus Company* (1933), *Sons of Sawdust* (1934), and *Caravan* (1937).

With his friend John Masefield, the poet laureate, he produced *The Country Scene* (1937), *Tribute to Ballet* (1938), and *A Generation Risen* (1942)—all combinations of poems and paintings. The ballet world succeeded the circus as a theme and, under the patronage of the businessman and collector Henry Melchett, he met celebrities including H. G. Wells, Winston Churchill, and Augustus John.

During wartime Seago concealed his heart trouble to become a camouflage officer when his friends and painting companions were his commanding officers Field Marshal Sir Claude Auchinleck and Lieutenant-General Sir Harold Alexander (later Field Marshal Earl Alexander of Tunis). He learned to fly 'to see the other side of the clouds'

(Goodman, 157), designed the insignia for the airborne forces, and wrote *Peace in War* in 1943 and *High Endeavour* in 1944, the year he was invalided out of the army. Alexander then invited him to join him for the final stages of the Italian campaign and to paint. The results were a book, *With the Allied Armies in Italy* (1945), and a London exhibition of his wartime Italian paintings.

After the war Seago settled by the Norfolk broads and had his own boat, equipped as a studio, which he himself sailed on painting excursions in the Netherlands, France, Spain, and Portugal. He also travelled to Italy, Burma, Bangkok, Greece, Morocco, and Turkey, and to Sardinia where he had a holiday home. When he was in Hong Kong his self-appointed guide was a Chinese boy, Edward Tsui, whom he adopted and brought to England to be educated. By this time he tended only to make painting sketches out of doors and rely on his photographic memory, which gave him total recall of any subject for at least ten years, to complete the pictures in his studios. He was a prolific and extremely fast painter but, despite phenomenal popularity, he received little critical acclaim. In 1952 he was one of twelve artists officially invited to paint the coronation of Elizabeth II, and he exhibited regularly in Canada, the USA, and South Africa. In 1956 he was invited by Prince Philip, duke of Edinburgh, to visit Antarctica with him on the royal yacht *Britannia*. The result of the trip was sixty Antarctic paintings, which Seago gave to Prince Philip to form part of a very extensive royal collection of his work.

Prince Charles, from childhood, was surrounded by Seago's paintings and often visited him at his home near Sandringham. He was 'powerfully influenced', he said, 'and totally captivated by the unique way in which he could convey atmosphere on canvas and by the living texture of his pictures' (Goodman, foreword). When the prince started painting in watercolour, Seago, who never gave lessons and regarded watercolour painting as 'a very private affair', agreed to talk him through a picture of a broadland scene while he explained his technique. 'It was one of the most impressive demonstrations of sheer creativity I have ever seen … I went away inspired', Prince Charles recalled (ibid., 236).

Seago painted portraits of George VI and Queen Elizabeth, Elizabeth II, Prince Philip, and Princess Margaret, while the many personalities he portrayed who became his friends included the actors Noël Coward, Donald Sinden, Peter Cushing, Michael Denison, and Dulcie Gray. They testify to the many facets of a painter who lived life to the full but whose greatest passion was to paint the East Anglian landscape in all its moods. He was elected to the Royal Society of British Artists in 1946, and was made an associate of the Royal Society of Painters in Water Colours in 1957 and a full member in 1959.

Edward Seago died, unmarried, in London on 19 January 1974 after an operation in Sardinia for a brain tumour. He was cremated, and Peter Seymour, his friend and helpmate for the last twenty-eight years of his life, scattered his ashes over the Norfolk marshes he loved to paint.

Jean Goodman

Sources *DNB* • J. Goodman, *Edward Seago: the other side of the canvas* (1978) • H. Shipp, *Edward Seago: painter in the English tradition* (1952) • F. W. Hawcroft, *Edward Seago: a review of the years 1953–1964* (1965) • *The Times* (21 Jan 1974) • *Edward Seago, 1910–1974: memorial exhibition* (1974) [exhibition catalogue, Marlborough Fine Art Gallery, London, Dec 1974] • J. Goodman, *Seago — a wider canvas* (2002)

Archives CAC Cam., papers | FILM BBC, Norwich, Light out of the sky, TV documentary

Likenesses photograph, 1938, Hult. Arch. • G. Anthony, photograph, *c.*1950, Hult. Arch. • photographs, repro. in Goodman, *Edward Seago*

Wealth at death £333,222: probate, 22 Dec 1975, *CGPLA Eng. & Wales*

Seagrave [Segrave], **Sir Gilbert of** (*d.* 1254), administrator and justice, was the second son of Stephen of *Seagrave (*d.* 1241) of Seagrave, Leicestershire, and Rohesia, daughter of Thomas Despenser. His elder brother, John, having died, Gilbert succeeded to his father's estates in Leicestershire, Worcestershire, Warwickshire, Nottinghamshire, and Derbyshire on his father's death in 1241.

The door to royal service was no doubt opened for Seagrave by his father, the justiciar. He was in Brittany before 1232, probably during Henry III's campaign of 1230–31, and in 1233 he escorted from Northampton to Gloucester the proceeds of the fortieth from Cambridgeshire and Huntingdonshire. As part of the distribution of spoils on the death of Ranulf (III), earl of Chester, Seagrave received custody of the manor and castle of Newcastle under Lyme in December 1232, and in 1233 was granted Burton and part of Horncastle for his maintenance in the king's service. But when the father fell, so did the son; he had to surrender Newcastle and answer proceedings against him in June 1234. Although Stephen of Seagrave was back in the king's favour by 1236, Gilbert seems to have remained outside the favoured circle until after his father's death, when he was pardoned the relief due on his father's lands. He was appointed justice of the forests south of the Trent in May 1242 and governor of Kenilworth Castle from 1242 to 1244. There is no record that Gilbert acted as justice of the forest after October 1245. In 1248 he paid the king 100 marks to be quit of all claims arising from tenure of that office.

In 1251 Seagrave emerged again from obscurity, sitting as a justice in king's bench and as one of the justices to hear pleas in the city of London. In August 1253 he accompanied the king to Gascony where he continued to act as a justice, and in the following January he was sent home by the king as one of his messengers to ask for money from a parliament. He later rejoined the king, and was in Gascony on 16 June, and at Bordeaux as late as 7 September. Very soon afterwards, on a mission with Simon de Montfort to persuade Alexander III, king of Scots, to support Henry III's Sicilian enterprise, he started home through Poitou in the company of John de Plessis, earl of Warwick, and other nobles. Despite a safe conduct from Louis IX, the party was treacherously seized by the citizens of Pons in Poitou, where Seagrave fell ill, and died in prison before 8 October. On 12 October his wardships, and the wardship of his own lands during his son's minority, were granted to the king's son Edward.

By 30 September 1231 Seagrave had married Amabilia, daughter and heir of Robert of Chalcombe; she was still living in 1282. They had two children, Nicholas of *Seagrave, who became first Lord Seagrave, and Alice, wife of William Mauduit, earl of Warwick. Matthew Paris describes him as 'a man noble and rich and of fine character' (Paris, *Chron.*, 5.463). JOHN M. TODD

Sources *Chancery records* • Paris, *Chron.* • *Ann. mon.*, 3 • PRO, King's bench records (curia regis rolls), KB 26 • GEC, *Peerage*, new edn, 11.601–3 • J. Nichols, *The history and antiquities of the county of Leicester*, 2/1 (1795), appx, pp. 108–20; 3/1 (1800), 407–9 • F. M. Powicke, *King Henry III and the Lord Edward: the community of the realm in the thirteenth century*, 2 vols. (1947) • N. Vincent, *Peter des Roches: an alien in English politics, 1205–38*, Cambridge Studies in Medieval Life and Thought, 4th ser., 31 (1996), 321, 334, 444–5 • A. A. M. Duncan, *Scotland: the making of the kingdom* (1975), vol. 1 of *The Edinburgh history of Scotland*, ed. G. Donaldson (1965–75), 564 • *CIPM*, 1, no. 334 • *A descriptive catalogue of ancient deeds in the Public Record Office*, 6 vols. (1890–1915), vol. 2, p. 351

Wealth at death see *CIPM*

Seagrave [Segrave], **Gilbert** (*b.* before **1258**, *d.* **1316**), bishop of London, was the son of Nicholas of *Seagrave, first Lord Seagrave (1238?–1295), and his wife, Maud (Matilda). His date of birth is not recorded, although he seems to have been born in the mid-thirteenth century: he received his first benefice in 1279 and if he was then at least twenty-one, as canon law decreed, he can have been born no later than 1258. He received a university education, since he is called *magister* by the London chronicler describing his enthronement; it is not known where, but Cambridge must be a possibility, since he was chancellor of that university, probably in 1292–3.

Seagrave's first known benefice was the rectory of Kegworth, Leicestershire, to which he was presented by his father in 1279 when he is described as subdeacon. He was also rector of Aylestone, Leicestershire, from 1293 to 1296. In the early fourteenth century he obtained prebends in the cathedral churches of London, Hereford, and Lincoln, holding the prebend of Portpool at London in 1301, the prebend of Hunderton at Hereford from some time after 1304, and the prebend of St Martin's in Durnstall at Lincoln from 12 August 1302. By 2 June 1306 he was precentor of St Paul's, London, while still retaining his prebends, and the rectory of Fenstanton, Huntingdonshire. A papal letter of 4 June 1306 gives permission for Seagrave to keep the precentorship, which he had obtained without papal dispensation, while retaining the prebends and church mentioned above.

On 16 or 17 August 1313, perhaps with the benefit of the influence of his brother John *Seagrave, Lord Seagrave, Gilbert Seagrave was elected bishop of London. Royal assent was granted on 22 August, the temporalities were restored on 28 September, he was confirmed on 17 September by the chapter of Christ Church, Canterbury, the see of Canterbury being vacant, and was consecrated by Henry Woodlock, bishop of Winchester, on 25 November, on the same day laying the foundation stone for the shrine of St Earconwald. He is reported to have been on bad terms with Archbishop Walter Reynold, but otherwise little is known of his brief episcopate, although he seems to have been conscientious in carrying out his episcopal duties. On 18 April 1314 he began a visitation of his cathedral church and on 26 May of the same year he attended convocation at Blackfriars, London. The extant names of canons of St Paul's during his episcopate do not suggest that he practised nepotism: although two other Seagraves occur, neither was appointed until after the bishop's death. He is known to have kept an episcopal register which would, no doubt, have provided a clearer picture of his activities. However, only a fragment survives, containing an indulgence for those giving towards repairs to the fabric of St Paul's Cathedral and a letter requesting his help in obtaining for Cardinal Raimond de Fargis, a papal appointee, the fruits of his benefice within the diocese.

The new bishop had little time to exercise his diocesan authority. Seagrave died on 18 December 1316, and was buried on the 30th; the site of his grave is unrecorded. PHILIPPA HOSKIN

Sources *Fasti Angl., 1300–1541*, [St Paul's, London] • *Fasti Angl., 1300–1541*, [Lincoln] • *Fasti Angl., 1300–1541*, [Hereford] • W. Stubbs, ed., *Chronicles of the reigns of Edward I and Edward II*, 2 vols., Rolls Series, 76 (1882–3) • *CEPR letters*, vol. 2 • Emden, *Cam.*, 516 • GEC, *Peerage*, new edn, 11.603–5

Seagrave [Segrave], **Gilbert** (*c.*1260–1312), theologian, was probably a member of the Leicestershire baronial family of Seagrave, and if so was possibly a younger son of Nicholas of *Seagrave, first Lord Seagrave (1238?–1295). He must have read arts at Oxford from about 1280, and was admitted rector of Harlaxton, Lincolnshire, on 20 November 1282. While studying and teaching at Oxford he was maintained by additional benefices, which he was dispensed to hold on 3 February 1291: he became a canon of Lincoln, with the prebend of Milton Ecclesia, on 8 February 1297; sacrist of the chapel of St Mary and the Holy Angels, York, on 2 August 1303 (but resigned it under royal pressure in 1304); and archdeacon of Oxford on 10 December 1303. By then he had probably left Oxford and was in the service of Thomas Corbridge, archbishop of York (*d.* 1304), as his seneschal (1303) and proctor in parliament (1301). He went overseas, perhaps to represent the crown at the coronation of Pope Clement V, in October 1305; he was certainly at the papal curia at the Château St Symphorien d'Ozon near Lyons in 1312, where he died and was probably buried.

Seagrave's theological *quaestiones* and quodlibets were said by Leland to be preserved in most Oxford libraries. If so, there is no trace of them now, and they were even unknown to Bale. All that remains of his work is a disputed question with its magisterial determination, and a response to the question of another master, the Cistercian Thomas Kirkeby, in the first quire of the Worcester collection of disputed questions (Worcester Cathedral, MS Q.99). In these debates, which probably took place about 1297, he was associated with Richard Clive, Thomas Sutton, and William of Macclesfield, three luminaries of the brilliant Oxford generation of theologians who included Duns Scotus (*d.* 1308). Seagrave's question, whether the emanation of the Word in divine beings should precede the distinction of ideas, is a characteristically abstract topic of its time. JEREMY CATTO

Sources 'Quaestiones', Worcester Cathedral, MS Q.99, fols. 1–8v • R. M. T. Hill, ed., *The rolls and register of Bishop Oliver Sutton*, 1, Lincoln RS, 39 (1948), 33 • R. M. T. Hill, ed., *The rolls and register of Bishop Oliver Sutton*, 3, Lincoln RS, 48 (1954), 139 • episcopal register II, Reg. Dalderby, Lincs. Arch., Lincoln diocesan archives, fols. 46v, 277v • *The register of Thomas of Corbridge, lord archbishop of York, 1300–1304*, 2, ed. A. H. Thompson, SurtS, 141 (1928), 27, 130 • *CEPR letters*, 1.524, 602, 625; 2.4, 104, 214 • *CPR, 1301–7*, 383, 397, 435 • *Snappe's formulary and other records*, ed. H. E. Salter, OHS, 80 (1924), 53 • *Joannis Lelandi antiquarii de rebus Britannicis collectanea*, ed. T. Hearne, 6 vols. (1715), vol. 4, p. 152 • A. G. Little and F. Pelster, *Oxford theology and theologians*, OHS, 96 (1934), 279–81, 287–91 • Emden, *Oxf.*, 3.1663–4
Archives Worcester Cathedral, MS Q.99, fols. 1–8v

Seagrave [Segrave]**, Sir Hugh** (*d.* **1387**), administrator and courtier, was, on the evidence of his arms, a junior or bastard member of the baronial Seagrave family, which became extinct in its main line in 1353. He may be the Hugh who was squire to Queen Philippa in 1369, and seneschal of the household to John of Gaunt, duke of Lancaster, in Gascony before 4 November 1372. He emerges as Sir Hugh Seagrave, knight, negotiating peace with Flanders at Calais in March 1371. On 8 October 1372 he became steward of the lands of Edward, prince of Wales (the Black Prince), whom he served until the prince died in 1376, when Seagrave became one of his master's executors. Confirmed on 6 July as steward of all the lands in England and Wales which the prince had held, he then served the prince's widow, Joan. Following Edward III's death in June 1377, he became steward of the household of Richard II and on 20 July 1377 was appointed to what was effectively a council of regency, serving until 30 October 1378. His pay indicates that he attended the council almost daily. His reward was confirmation of the late prince's grant (made on 8 October 1372) of £100 a year, with 150 marks more from Richard II. In addition to his domestic duties, Seagrave took part in negotiations with France from 1378 to 1380. These proved fruitless; in 1381 he treated more successfully for Richard II's marriage to Anne of Bohemia.

During the peasants' revolt of 1381, following the murders of Simon Sudbury, the chancellor, and Sir Robert Hale, the treasurer, on 14 June, the king gave the great seal to Seagrave on 16 June, though without the title chancellor. Seagrave advised the abbot of St Albans to concede all that the abbot's people asked; though this gave the appearance of moderation, Seagrave knew that the concessions would not stand. In July the king came to St Albans and harshly judged the rebels. On 10 August Seagrave surrendered the great seal (and the stewardship) to become treasurer; in November he advocated parliament's revocation of the peasants' charters.

Seagrave held the great seal again, with others, between 11 July and 20 August 1382, after the king had dismissed Richard Scrope as chancellor. When Richard II had a friendlier chancellor, Michael de la Pole, in 1385, Seagrave sat with a commission that fined John Cavendish for defaming de la Pole. Seagrave resigned as treasurer on 17 January 1386, and died on 4 February 1387. He may have had a wife, Isabel, but neither she nor a child is mentioned in sources relating to his death. JOHN L. LELAND

Sources *Chancery records* • PRO, Issue Rolls, E 403 • *Thomae Walsingham, quondam monachi S. Albani, historia Anglicana*, ed. H. T. Riley, 2 vols., pt 1 of *Chronica monasterii S. Albani*, Rolls Series, 28 (1863–4) • Tout, *Admin. hist.* • *RotP*, vol. 3 • N. Saul, *Richard II* (1997) • A. B. Steel, *Richard II* (1941); repr. (1962) • A. Goodman, *John of Gaunt: the exercise of princely power in fourteenth-century Europe* (1992) • S. Justice, *Writing and rebellion: England in 1381* (1994) • R. B. Dobson, ed., *The peasants' revolt of 1381* (1970) • J. Campbell, *Lives of the lord chancellors*, 5th edn, 10 vols. (1868) • R. H. Ellis, ed., *Catalogue of seals in the Public Record Office: personal seals*, 1 (1978) • R. R. Sharpe, ed., *Calendar of letter-books preserved in the archives of the corporation of the City of London*, [12 vols.] (1899–1912), vol. H • *John of Gaunt's register*, ed. S. Armitage-Smith, 2 vols., CS, 3rd ser., 20–21 (1911) • *CPR, 1370–74*, 404 • *CIPM*, 16, no. 155
Archives PRO, E 403
Wealth at death manor of Somerford, Wiltshire, held for life: *CIPM*, 16, no. 155

Seagrave [Segrave]**, John, second Lord Seagrave** (**1256–1325**), soldier and baron, was the eldest son of Nicholas *Seagrave, first Lord Seagrave (1238?–1295), and his wife, Matilda, who was probably a Lucy. In 1270 John married Christiana, daughter of Hugh de Plessis, and granddaughter of John de *Plessis, earl of Warwick. Although his family had been on the side of Simon de Montfort during the civil war of the 1260s, John Seagrave had established links with the future Edward I by way of the crusade. He served in the Welsh campaigns of 1277 and 1282–3, in Ireland in 1287, and in Scotland in 1291. He was summoned to serve in Gascony in 1297 (although he did not go), and was actively employed against the Scots from that year until 1322, during which time he held positions of strategic and military importance. Following the death of his father he was summoned to parliament as a peer from 26 August 1296 to 8 May 1325.

In 1297 John Seagrave entered into an indenture with Roger (IV) Bigod, earl of Norfolk and the earl marshal, to provide Bigod in time of war with sixteen or, as the occasion demanded it, twenty cavalry. If Seagrave was required in peacetime, his party would receive *bouche a court* (food and drink), and he, as a banneret, and his knights would be provided with robes equal to any of their rank in the earl's household. As part of the agreement Bigod enfeoffed Seagrave with the manor and advowson of Lodden in Norfolk for the duration of his service. Later that year Seagrave offered Edward I the earl's excuses—he had been ill—for not attending in person to serve with the king in Flanders. On 22 August 1297 Seagrave accompanied Roger (IV) Bigod and Humphrey (VI) de Bohun, earl of Hereford, to the exchequer, where they delivered a letter protesting at the levy of an eighth procured by Edward I and complaining of the burdensome nature and unconstitutionality of the king's extension of the traditional obligations of taxation. But Seagrave did homage to Edward I at Carlisle on 30 June 1300 and on 12 February 1301 set his seal to the barons' letter of complaint to the pope. In the same year, following an inquiry and discussion concerning the role of the marshal of England, Seagrave, who had acted as deputy marshal on the

Scottish campaign after Bigod's withdrawal in 1298, was paid £100 in place of the customary perquisites of the office, usually an entitlement to booty. This agreement was only reached by the inclusion of a proviso that this would not create a precedent, and that neither the marshal nor his deputy would be regarded as having failed in their duties.

In August 1302 Seagrave was made constable of the castle of Berwick, and in November became the king's lieutenant in Scotland (positions he held until 1305). With the ending of the truce with the Scots in late September he was ordered to make a mounted foray past Stirling as far up as Kirkintilloch, assisted by various northern lords. In February of the following year he organized a raid through Scottish territory, and was ambushed near Maid's Castle, wounded, and captured, but later rescued. He continued to mount raids against the Scots during the winter of 1303–4, and having taken care to avoid infiltration by Scottish spies, managed to rout a force led by William Wallace and Simon Fraser. Although they escaped capture, Seagrave worked closely with Robert Bruce in tracking them down, and was encouraged by Edward I proverbially to make good the hood as well as they had made the cloak. Wallace was eventually handed over into Seagrave's custody in the summer of 1305, escorted to London, and tried at a special commission of gaol delivery. Seagrave was one of the justices. Following Wallace's conviction and execution Seagrave was given the task of escorting the quarters of the dead man's body north to their final destinations (Newcastle, Berwick, Stirling, and Perth), for which he received 15*s.* in remuneration. In 1306, in consideration of the labours and troubles suffered by his wife, Christiana, in living in Scotland while her husband was there in the king's service, they were granted a scutage of 40*s.* for each fee held of the inheritance of her late father for the regnal year 1302–3.

In January 1308 Seagrave was summoned to attend Edward II's coronation, and in March of the same year was appointed constable of Nottingham Castle and justice (or keeper) of the forest north of the Trent. However, he was forced to resign the latter office in favour of Piers Gaveston on 1 October 1310 (for this he was given pecuniary compensation), but he was restored to it for life on 4 September 1312. He was also appointed keeper of Scotland either side of the Forth in 1309, and, four years later, keeper of the marches in Cumberland. In June 1311 Seagrave was warned not to become embroiled in a quarrel between Walter Birmingham and his own brother, Henry Seagrave, who had been sheriff of Norfolk and Suffolk and constable of Norwich Castle, and was besieged in Norwich. In 1315 John Seagrave appears to have suffered a similar fate, since he complained that the townsfolk of Nottingham had rung the common bell, broken down the gates of the castle, assaulted his men, and besieged him there for eight days without allowing access for provisions. In August 1318 he was appointed to the continual council set up under the treaty of Leake, which was required to give assent to Edward II's actions outside parliament.

Two years later Seagrave was made a keeper of the peace in Warwickshire. With the disintegration of relations between Edward II and Thomas of Lancaster, Seagrave was urged in January and April 1321 to avoid illegal or treasonable gatherings, and in November not to attend a meeting of peers. In the same month he was required to muster both cavalry and infantry in the counties of Warwickshire, Leicestershire, and Staffordshire against the rebel forces. In February 1322 he was ordered to raise as many foot soldiers and men-at-arms as possible, and as constable of Nottingham Castle he was to ensure the castle was provisioned and defended. Later in the same year he was commanded to array his men and tenants to appear at York. After the civil war Seagrave's attention was refocused on Scotland, and in late 1322 and early 1323 he was ordered to array men in Nottinghamshire and Derbyshire in preparation for an invasion. In July 1324 he went to Aquitaine as captain of the forces for the duchy, and in November of the same year was summoned to fight in Gascony.

Over the course of his life John Seagrave acquired numerous lands and perquisites. According to the dictum of Kenilworth the Seagrave lands had an annual value of 500 marks (£330) per annum, which was a figure about the middle of the spectrum for baronial landholding. In a charter dated 4 July 1270 John and Christiana were granted the manor of Stottesdon in Shropshire by Hugh de Plessis 'in free marriage'; it was to be held by Seagrave of the king for one knight's fee. In 1281 Roger of Kingswood conveyed to John and Christiana all the lands held of them in Kingswood in Shropshire in exchange for lands and woods at Cherle and the watermill there. Before receiving livery of his father's lands in 1295 Seagrave held a quarter of a knight's fee at Calvedon in Warwickshire in 1275, one knight's fee in Atterton and Witherley in Lincolnshire in 1282, the manor of Penn in Buckinghamshire in 1289, and Blyborough in Lincolnshire in 1289. Some of these grants may have come from Nicholas Seagrave himself. Royal grants included the right to free warren at Penn in 1296 and at Alconbury in Huntingdonshire six years later.

In the general eyre of 1299–1300 at Cambridge John Seagrave was required to answer to the *quo warranto* inquiries concerning his claim to hold view of frankpledge and the assize of bread and ale in Connington, Boxworth, and Fen Drayton. In 1300 he was given twelve oaks for timber from Cannock Forest, and ten oaks from Whittlewood Forest, for the construction of a chapel at Chalcombe Manor. In 1301 he paid £800 for custody of the lands of his wife's father, Hugh de Plessis, together with the marriage of Hugh's heirs. In the same year he was given licence to crenellate his dwelling at Bretby in Derbyshire and, four years later, his manor at Calvedon. In 1305 Seagrave was also given permission to hold fairs and markets at Woodweston in Huntingdonshire, which was extended to his manor at Fenstanton in the same county in 1315, and to Aspel in Warwickshire in 1318. In September 1312 he was given the choice of lands to the value of £100 yearly (for him and his heirs) or the grant of £1000 to buy such lands.

Four years later, in the survey known as the *Nomina villarum*, he was described as lord of Newbury, Berkshire, Connington, Boxworth, and Fen Drayton, Cambridgeshire, Repton, Derbyshire, Alconbury, Weston, Stanton, and Hilton, Huntingdonshire, Stottesdon, Shropshire, and Chalcombe, Northamptonshire. In 1318 Seagrave received the lands of his younger brother Henry, which through a reversion clause had passed to him on the latter's death. In 1323 he was allowed to alienate a messuage at Fenstanton near the parsonage there to allow the parson, Thomas Seagrave, and his successors to enlarge the house.

John Seagrave died some time before 4 October 1325. An account for funeral expenses was rendered by John Grey on 23 November 1325. He was buried at Chalcombe Priory. Christiana survived him, and was still alive in 1331. His brother Nicholas *Seagrave was also summoned as a peer from 1295 until his death in 1321, while another brother, Gilbert *Seagrave (*d.* 1316), was bishop of London. John's eldest son, Stephen, who became the third baron, married Alice Arundel, but died some time before 12 December 1325, and was similarly buried at Chalcombe. His younger son and namesake married Juliana, daughter and heir of John Sandwich. The title was inherited by Stephen's ten-year-old son, John, whose wardship and marriage were entrusted to *Thomas of Brotherton, earl of Norfolk. John in due course married Margaret *Brotherton, the earl's daughter and sole heir, consolidating the family's status and territorial position, but died in 1353, leaving a daughter, Elizabeth (*b.* 1338), who at the age of eleven married John (III) Mowbray (*d.* 1368). A. J. MUSSON

Sources *Chancery records* • GEC, *Peerage*, new edn, 9.384; 11.605–12 • C. Moor, ed., *Knights of Edward I*, 4, Harleian Society, 83 (1931), 236–8 • J. Stevenson, ed., *Documents illustrative of the history of Scotland*, 2 (1870) • *CDS*, vol. 2 • K. B. McFarlane, 'An indenture of agreement between two English knights for mutual aid and counsel in peace and war', *BIHR*, 38 (1965), 200–10, esp. 201–8 • M. Prestwich, *Edward I* (1988) • M. Prestwich, *War, politics, and finance under Edward I* (1972) • S. Letters, 'The history of the Segrave family from *c.*1160–1295, with an edition of the calendar of the Seagrave cartulary', PhD diss., U. Lond., 1997

Archives BL, Add. MS 37671 • BL, Harley MS 4748

Wealth at death manors and lands in Oxfordshire, Shropshire, Hampshire, Buckinghamshire, Northamptonshire, Nottinghamshire, Derbyshire, Warwickshire, and Leicestershire

Seagrave [Segrave], **Nicholas of, first Lord Seagrave (1238?–1295)**, baron, was the son of the justice Gilbert of *Seagrave (*d.* 1254) and his wife, Amabilia, ultimately the sole heir of Robert of Chalcombe, and grandson of the justiciar Stephen of Seagrave. Following Gilbert's death in 1254 his lands were granted to Henry III's son Edward, allowing provision for the widow's dower; Nicholas, the heir, was described as sixteen or seventeen years old. On 2 March 1257 Seagrave, described as the king's squire (*valettus*), was ill at Windsor with two other squires, and the king's bailiff was instructed to have necessaries supplied to them until they were well. In July Seagrave was described as receiving allowances in the royal household for three horses and three boys and their shoe money, and for meat, fish, wine, and candles. Still described as squire, he made a fine of 300 marks (£200) to gain seisin of his father's lands and tenements on 18 April 1258, and performed homage.

Too young and inexperienced for prominence in the struggle between Henry III and the reformers during 1258–9, Seagrave had protection while on pilgrimage to Pontigny in the spring of 1259, and on 28 October protection while crossing with the king to France; protection was renewed until midsummer on 28 December 1259, when he was described as having gone to Pontigny. On 31 March 1260 he was one of over a hundred barons and tenants-in-chief summoned to London three weeks after Easter, and on 16 September 1261 swore to serve the king faithfully. The following month he was summoned with horses and arms. Since he was principally a Leicestershire landowner, perhaps it is not surprising that Seagrave should have chosen to align himself with the supporters of Simon de Montfort, earl of Leicester, whose following was largely drawn from the midlands, or that on 7 December 1261 he should have been required, along with Montfort, Earl Warenne, Hugh Despenser, and others, to put his seal within fifteen days to the peace made at Kingston between the barons and the king.

The chronicler Thomas Wykes lists Seagrave among the young lords who were prominent among Montfort's supporters in the spring of 1263; he was involved in the attack on the bishop of Hereford, Peter d'Aigueblanche, on 7 June. Ordered on 25 May 1263 to go to the king at Worcester in August, there to receive knighthood, and join the Welsh expedition, in December that year he was among the barons who agreed to refer their dispute with Henry III to the arbitration of Louis IX. When the French king's award, favourable to Henry, was followed by the outbreak of civil war, Seagrave fought at Lewes in May 1264, where he led the London contingent which was routed by the Lord Edward. From 17 June 1264 until 21 April 1265 Seagrave had custody of the castle of Rockingham and the forests between the bridges of Oxford and Stamford. He was summoned to Montfort's Hilary parliament of 1265. A would-be participant in a tournament at Dunstable planned for 17 February 1265, but prohibited because of its likely threat to public order, he took part in negotiations with the king for the release of the Lord Edward. He fought at Evesham in August 1265 and was taken prisoner. Henry III, describing Seagrave as 'the king's enemy', then gave his lands to his own younger son Edmund. Seagrave must either have escaped or secured his release, for he had a safe conduct to treat for peace in September 1266. Nevertheless, in 1267 he was among the rebels still holding out at Ely, and there was some suspicion that either he or his mother (who had married the royalist Roger de Somery, one of the counsellors responsible for the dictum of Kenilworth) had some responsibility for its fall. Seagrave was one of the rebels admitted to Southwark in April, and had a safe conduct in the summer of 1267 for those whom he would bring to court to make peace. He was finally pardoned on 1 July 1267. The disinherited rebels were allowed to redeem their lands on a sliding scale according to their level of participation in the civil wars, and Seagrave was among those charged five years' annual value. His debt to Edmund on this score was only settled shortly after his death in 1295.

Once pardoned, Seagrave was rapidly taken into royal favour. In May 1270 he had protection for four years as a crusader, and in January 1271 had four years' exemption from summonses to eyres, and was licensed to appoint attorneys. From 1277 until his death in 1295 he regularly received military summonses, against the Welsh in 1277, 1282, and 1294, and to accompany Edmund in Gascony in 1295; he was also summoned to a military council at Gloucester in 1287 and to parliament in 1283 and 1295. Letters of protection in 1285 covering his going overseas with the king, and his appointing attorneys later that year when 'gone to Ireland', testify to a life of vigorous activity. One reward that came his way was the grant, for 100 marks, of custody of lands of William de Ferrers on 18 May 1288.

By the late 1280s the distinction was sometimes being made between Nicholas of Seagrave the elder and Nicholas of Seagrave the younger, giving rise to ambiguity in contemporary documentation offering no such identification. The elder Nicholas, who was close to Edward I himself in age, was summoned to parliament and to military service in the latter half of 1295, so it must be assumed that he was thought fit for action until close to his death. T. F. Tout believed that it was the younger Nicholas who probably received the castles of Dumbarton and Ayr from James, the steward of Scotland, in 1291, but the elder was involved in the Scottish Great Cause, and it seems on balance likely that, whichever was involved, it was the same Nicholas who both received the castles from James, and sat with him and the bishop of Glasgow at Ayr receiving Scottish fealties in 1291. On 6 July 1291 Nicholas of Seagrave and Henry son of Nicholas of Seagrave had protection staying in Scotland on the king's service, and the elder Nicholas (named as such) similarly in April 1292. In the procedural discussions of the Great Cause, Seagrave's name is given among those recommending recourse to English rather than imperial law, and the superiority of primogeniture over proximity as a claim. On 20 June 1294 Nicholas of Seagrave was appointed, along with the bishop of Durham, the archbishop of Dublin, and Hugh Despenser, to negotiate with the German king and the archbishop of Cologne. Less strenuous appointments in 1290–92 were to various judicial commissions including investigation of maladministration in the Isle of Man, and to inquire into weirs on the Trent.

Seagrave's wife, Matilda, was probably a member of the Lucy family. On 26 August 1288 a commission of oyer and terminer was appointed to hear the complaint of Nicholas of Seagrave the elder and Matilda his wife that forty-six named persons of both sexes had assaulted Matilda at Exhall, Warwickshire, thrown her out of her carriage, and taken away her long cart laden with victuals and other goods. The *Song of Caerlaverock* attributes five sons to Seagrave; the eldest of these was John *Seagrave, variously described as over thirty and (more reliably) thirty-nine at his father's death. The second son was Nicholas *Seagrave, lord of Stowe. The elder Nicholas had died by 12 November 1295, and John had done homage for his father's lands by 10 December 1295. The terms of a grant on 14 July 1292 of a market and fair at Mountsorrel, Leicestershire, and of free warren on his demesnes, along with the particulars of his inquisition post mortem, show that the estates of the elder Nicholas of Seagrave were concentrated in Derbyshire, Warwickshire, Huntingdonshire, Leicestershire, and Northamptonshire. He was buried at Chacombe Priory, Northamptonshire. At an unknown date before his death Seagrave had relinquished the arms previously borne by his family, and had adopted instead the arms, sable a lion argent rampant crowned or.

HELEN M. JEWELL

Sources *Chancery records* • *CClR* • *Calendar of the fine rolls*, 22 vols., PRO (1911–62) • *Calendar of the charter rolls*, 6 vols., PRO (1903–27) • *CIPM* • H. S. Sweetman and G. F. Handcock, eds., *Calendar of documents relating to Ireland*, 5 vols., PRO (1875–86) • F. Palgrave, ed., *The parliamentary writs and writs of military summons*, 1 (1827), 832 • *VCH Warwickshire*, 3.213; 4.150; 5.105; 8.121 • *VCH Leicestershire*, 2.88 • E. L. G. Stones and G. G. Simpson, eds., *Edward I and the throne of Scotland, 1290–1296*, 2 (1978), 105–7, 112, 122–3, 213, 217 • P. Chaplais, ed., *Treaty rolls preserved in the Public Record Office*, 1 (1955), no. 212 • [Walter of Exeter?], *The siege of Carlaverock … with a translation, a history of the castle and memoirs of the personages commemorated by the poet*, ed. and trans. N. H. Nicolas (1828), 12, 123 • *Ann. mon.*, 2.365; 3.222, 246; 4.133, 207 • H. R. Luard, ed., *Flores historiarum*, 3 vols., Rolls Series, 95 (1890), vol. 3, p. 6 • R. F. Treharne and I. J. Sanders, eds., *Documents of the baronial movement of reform and rebellion, 1258–1267* (1973), 284–5 • R. F. Treharne, *The baronial plan of reform, 1258–1263*, [new edn] (1971), 273, 302, 323, 335 • J. R. Maddicott, *Simon de Montfort* (1994), 68–70 • F. M. Powicke, *King Henry III and the Lord Edward: the community of the realm in the thirteenth century*, 1 (1947); repr. (1966), 554 • *CIPM*, 1, nos. 334, 679; 3, no. 297 • *CPR, 1258–1266*, 468 • *Close rolls of the reign of Henry III*, 12, PRO (1936), 306

Wealth at death *CIPM*, 3, no. 297 • over £120 p.a. from lands in 1260s: Maddicott, *Simon de Montfort*, 70

Seagrave [Segrave], **Nicholas** (*d.* 1321), administrator and soldier, lord of Stowe, Northamptonshire, was the second son of Nicholas of *Seagrave, first Lord Seagrave (1238?–1295), and his wife, Matilda de Lucy. He was born later than 1256, the probable year of birth of his elder brother, John *Seagrave, second Lord Seagrave. It was probably he, rather than his father, who served as castellan of Dumbarton and Ayr castles in 1291–2. He was first summoned to parliament, as 'Nicholas de Seagrave, junior', in August 1295, and continued to be so summoned until 1321. He was present at Falkirk in 1298, and at the siege of Caerlaverock in 1300, where he served in the retinue of the earl of Hereford. On 12 February 1301 he sealed the barons' letter of grievances to the pope as 'Nicholas de Seagrave, lord of Stow'.

In 1301 Seagrave was involved in a dispute over the manor of Chrishall, Essex, with Walter Langton, bishop of Lichfield, which was eventually settled before the king at Evesham. In the same year he and his wife, Alice, were accused along with numerous others of breaking houses of Ralph de Monthermer, earl of Gloucester and Hertford, near Kingston, Berkshire. During the Scottish campaign of 1303–4 Seagrave became involved in a heated dispute with John Cromwell. When Edward I refused to allow Seagrave's challenge to trial by combat, he deserted the king's army in order to travel to France, there to seek trial by battle. He managed to cross to France despite the efforts of Robert de Burghersh, warden of the Cinque Ports and constable of Dover, but was arrested at Dover upon his return. Although he was rescued by twenty-one barons of Dover and returned to his manor of Stowe, he was summoned from there by the sheriff of Northampton in January 1305 to appear before parliament at Westminster. He submitted himself to the king's judgment in parliament. He was apparently sentenced to death, but was sent to the Tower of London instead, and later released on the security of his own letters patent and seven mainpernors. He was quickly restored to the favour of Edward I, and he served with the king on his final Scottish campaign in 1307. On 23 February 1308 he was released from his obligations by Edward II.

Seagrave was one of Edward II's staunchest supporters at the outset of the reign. In the crisis of March 1308 he was appointed custodian of Northampton Castle, and even after the banishment of Piers Gaveston, he was one of four royal councillors singled out to be removed from the court by the Northampton parliament of August 1308. Despite this, there is little evidence that Seagrave played a major role at court. He is very rarely found among the witnesses to royal charters before 1312, and his vilification in 1308 may have had more to do with his adherence to Thomas, earl of Lancaster, still loyal to the king at this time, than to his own activities.

On 12 March 1308 Seagrave had been appointed marshal of England, although his right to this office was challenged unsuccessfully by William le Mareschal. Indeed, in July 1311 the king forbade both to come to parliament armed, in consequence of their dispute. Seagrave's tenure of this office may also have been the occasion of one early conflict between the earl of Lancaster and the king. As marshal, Seagrave was entitled to appoint the marshal of the exchequer. His first appointee, Elias de Pouger, died in September 1310 and was replaced by Jocelin Brankescombe. Seagrave was in Scotland at the time, but later confirmed the appointment. At Michaelmas 1311, however, the king replaced Brankescombe with Arnald de Tilly, a Gascon associated with Gaveston, who was soon thereafter singled out for banishment in the supplement to the ordinances. The barons of the exchequer were ordered to accept Seagrave's nominee as marshal of the exchequer once again. Although Seagrave himself hardly seems to have been a central player in this drama as reported in the *Vita Edwardi secundi*, it may well have affected his relationship with the king over time. On 20 September 1312, in the tense atmosphere prevailing after the execution of Piers Gaveston by the baronial opposition, Seagrave was part of a delegation including the earl of Pembroke, the elder Despenser, Edmund Mauley, and John Cromwell, that went to the Guildhall in London to ask for increased security in defending the city against the king's enemies. On 20 December he acted on behalf of the king along with the earl of Pembroke and the elder Despenser in witnessing the treaty between Edward II and his barons. He continues to appear occasionally as a witness in the charter rolls in 1313 and 1314, but after 6 December 1314 his name appears only once more, on 20 May 1319 at York. Presumably his continuing service to the earl of Lancaster, whose retainer he remained throughout the reign until his death, made his early position at court increasingly untenable.

In 1316 Seagrave was deprived of the marshalship, which was granted to Edward II's half-brother, Thomas of Brotherton. In 1317 the king issued orders for Seagrave's apprehension and the seizure of his lands, along with similar orders for other of Lancaster's adherents, but these orders were cancelled on 24 September of the same year. In 1318 he was one of Lancaster's retainers pardoned for all offences committed before 7 August, and he was also named to a committee to set the agenda for the upcoming parliament. In 1318–19 he served with the earl of Lancaster in Scotland with four knights and ten men and was present at the siege of Berwick. He attended the Westminster parliament of October 1320 on behalf of the earl of Lancaster. In January 1321 he was named as one of the magnates empowered to meet with Robert Bruce. On 21 April 1321 he was one of several magnates ordered not to attend illegal assemblies, and on 12 November of the same year was forbidden to attend the meeting of the 'good Peers'. He died on 25 November 1321.

Seagrave held considerable lands in Northamptonshire, Suffolk, and Essex. He obtained the manor of Stowe through his marriage to Alice, daughter of Geoffrey of Armenters and widow of Gerard Lisle, and the castle at Barton Seagrave. His heir was his daughter Maud, aged twenty-five and more at the time of his death, who married Edmund de Bohun of Church Brampton, Northamptonshire. Seagrave is described in *The Siege of Carlaverock* as one 'whom nature had adorned in body and enriched in heart'.

J. S. Hamilton

Sources *CIPM*, 3, no. 297; 6, no. 322 · *CCIR* · *CPR, 1301–7*, 184 · PRO, charter rolls, C 53 · W. Stubbs, ed., *Chronicles of the reigns of Edward I and Edward II*, 2 vols., Rolls Series, 76 (1882–3) · H. R. Luard, ed., *Flores historiarum*, 3 vols., Rolls Series, 95 (1890) · J. R. Maddicott, *Thomas of Lancaster, 1307–1322: a study in the reign of Edward II* (1970) · GEC, *Peerage* · [Walter of Exeter?], *The siege of Carlaverock … with a translation, a history of the castle and memoirs of the personages commemorated by the poet*, ed. and trans. N. H. Nicolas (1828)

Wealth at death see *CIPM*, 6, no. 322

Seagrave, Robert (*b.* **1693**, *d.* in or after **1755**), Church of England clergyman and writer, was born on 22 November 1693 at Twyford, Leicestershire, second son of Robert Seagrave, vicar of Twyford from 1687 to 1720, and his wife, Mary (*née* Moore), of Morton, Nottinghamshire. He was educated at Oakham School, Rutland—where 'Orator' Henley (the eccentric London preacher John Henley) was two years his senior—and matriculated at Cambridge in 1711, having entered as sub-sizar and Leeds scholar at Clare College on 8 November 1710, the year in which he was also a Johnson exhibitioner. He became BA in 1714 and MA in 1718. Seagrave was made deacon on the title of Loseby, Leicestershire, in the diocese of Lincoln, on 26 February 1716; and it is known that from 1720 to 1726 one

Robert Seagrave, himself or possibly his father, was rector of Cold Overton, Leicestershire.

Thus Seagrave was already ordained well before the eighteenth-century evangelical movement had effectively started. In 1731 he began publishing tracts (at least ten by 1755) advocating evangelical beliefs, the first of which won the appreciation of William Grimshaw in Yorkshire soon after his conversion. By 1731 Seagrave had apparently moved to London, and by 1738 he is said to have withdrawn from the established church; but like John Wesley and other leaders better known, he may well not have done so. He became, however, a supporter of George Whitefield, and when Dr Joseph Trapp, vicar of Christ Church Greyfriars, London, preached against Whitefield, on the undesirability of being righteous overmuch, in 1739 Seagrave published an *Answer*, to which Trapp replied, an exchange of views noticed at some length in the *Gentleman's Magazine* (*GM*, 9.418–20, 476).

In the same year Seagrave began to officiate at regular Sunday evening preaching in Loriners' Hall, London Wall, Basinghall Street, London, later adding Tuesday and Thursday lectures, and 'for some years preached with much success' (Tyerman, 1.212). It was now that his aptitude for writing hymns came to the fore. Seagrave's *Hymns for Christian Worship* (1742; 4th edn, 1748) included thirty of his own. Two of these, 'Now may the Spirit's holy fire' and 'Rise my soul and stretch thy wings', were still in use in 1892. Seagrave was also among those associated with the erection of Whitefield's Tabernacle (1741); and in 1744 he took charge during the temporary absence of its regular ministers. John Griffith, subsequently an independent minister, was converted (*c*.1743) by Seagrave's preaching at Loriners' Hall. Seagrave was apparently associated with a small body of English Calvinistic methodists about whose activities there is relatively little record.

In 1749 Seagrave gave up his ministry at Loriners' Hall. In 1751 a fourth edition of his tract addressed to the University of Cambridge appeared. By 1753 he was preaching at a chapel in Bull and Mouth Street, off St Martin's-le-Grand, London, and he contributed to Whitefield's *Hymns for Social Worship* (1753). His last tract was published in 1755. No reference to later activities has been found; but Seagrave was still remembered with appreciation 100 years later. In 1860 Daniel Sedgwick appealed in *Notes and Queries* for additional information. A biographical introduction to Sedgwick's edition of Seagrave's hymns appeared without further details. In 1884 an American author, E. F. Hatfield, included Seagrave in his *Poets of the Church*, published both in New York and in London, but with little more detail. An anonymous writer in the *Evangelical Magazine* said of Seagrave 'He was a good minister of Jesus Christ, a workman who needed not to be ashamed. He was a man of eminent piety, great humility, and remarkable zeal and diligence' (1814, 304). It is not known whether or not he married. J. S. REYNOLDS

Sources *IGI* · W. L. Sargant, ed., *The book of Oakham School, with register* (1906) · Venn, *Alum. Cant.* · W. J. Harrison and A. H. Lloyd, *Notes on the masters, fellows, scholars and exhibitioners of Clare College, Cambridge* (1953) · *GM*, 1st ser., 9 (1739), 418–20, 476 · H. Venn, *Funeral sermon and sketch of … Grimshaw* (1763), 32 · W. Wilson, *The history and antiquities of the dissenting churches and meeting houses in London, Westminster and Southwark*, 4 vols. (1808–14), vol. 2, p. 559; vol. 3, p. 315 · 'Memoir of the late Rev. Benjamin Ingham', *Evangelical Magazine and Missionary Chronicle*, 22 (1814), 301–8, esp. 304 · [A. C. H. Seymour], *The life and times of Selina, countess of Huntingdon*, 1 (1839), 198 · *N&Q*, 2nd ser., 9 (1860), 142, 250, 314 · D. Sedgwick, *Hymns and spiritual songs by R. Seagrave* (1860) [with biographical sketch] · J. Miller, *Singers and songs of the church* (1869), 152–4 · L. Tyerman, *The life of the Rev. George Whitefield*, 2 vols. (1876–7), vol. 1, pp. 212, 278, 285; vol. 2, p. 294 · E. F. Hatfield, *The poets of the church: a series of biographical sketches of hymn writers* (1884) [extracts on fiche, Bodl. Oxf.] · T. Wright, *Lives of the British hymnwriters*, vol. 3 (1914), 152–4, 266 · E. Welch, ed., *Two Calvinistic Methodist chapels*, London RS, 11 (1975), 5

Seagrave [Segrave], **Sir Stephen of** (*d.* 1241), justice and administrator, was son of Gilbert of Seagrave, who held lands at Seagrave in Leicestershire and in 1166 held Brailes in Warwickshire as a fourth part of a knight's fee, under William, earl of Warwick. Gilbert was an under-sheriff of Warwickshire and Leicestershire during Richard I's reign and acted as a justice itinerant in Lincolnshire and Leicestershire in 1195. Out of regard for Hugh Despenser, Stephen of Seagrave's brother-in-law, King John in 1208 remitted half a debt of 112 marks that, as his father's heir, Seagrave owed the crown. Remaining faithful to the king, he received from him in 1216 custody of the lands of the rebel Stephen de Gant in Lincolnshire and Leicestershire, and the manor of Kineton in Warwickshire in fee, at a yearly rent. Seagrave married first Rohesia, daughter of Thomas and sister of Hugh Despenser, and second Ida, also called Ela, sister of Henry Hastings, who in 1247 was fined £500 for an unlicensed second marriage with Hugh Pecche. He had three sons: John (*d.* 1231), the eldest, who married Emma, daughter and heir of Roger de Caux; Gilbert of *Seagrave (*d.* 1254), who succeeded him; and Stephen; he also had a daughter, Eleanor.

After the accession of Henry III Seagrave's importance and offices rapidly increased. From 1217 onwards he was prominent as a justice; he sat at Westminster in 1218 and later, and was constantly employed on eyre. In 1219 he was one of the king's proctors at Norham before the papal legate for the hearing of a dispute with the Scottish king. In 1220 he was given the custody of Sauvey Castle, Leicestershire, and received a grant from the king of the manor of Alconbury in Huntingdonshire. He was sheriff of Essex and Hertfordshire from 1220 to 1224, and of Lincolnshire from 1221 to 1223. From 1228 to 1234 he was sheriff of Buckinghamshire, Bedfordshire, and Northamptonshire and from 1229 to 1234 of Warwickshire and Leicestershire. Seagrave's wealth increased, and he purchased lands; and when Henry departed for Brittany in 1230 he was appointed one of the regents. In 1232 he was granted the profits, other than the farms paid into the exchequer, of the counties of Bedford, Buckingham, Warwick, and Leicester for life. On the fall of Hubert de Burgh in that year, the king appointed Seagrave chief justiciar, though he was only a knight, having previously given him custody of the castles of Dover, Rochester, Canterbury, Windsor, Odiham, Hertford, and Colchester. He was violently hostile to de Burgh, and pressed the king to imprison him, and even to put him to death as a traitor.

Seagrave as chief justiciar became closely associated with the royal favourite Peter des Roches, and in conjunction with him counselled Henry to resist Richard Marshal, earl of Pembroke, Gilbert Basset, and other lords who in 1233 were associated against the government. The bishops in October threatened to excommunicate him and others of the party by name for giving the king evil counsel, but finally pronounced only a general sentence against those who turned the king's heart against his natural-born subjects. He accompanied the king's army to Grosmont in November, and lost his baggage when Marshal's adherents surprised the royal camp. The king having made an offer to Marshal in December, provided that he would surrender to his mercy, Seagrave ensured that the earl should be informed that he advised him to do so. In the first days of 1234 Richard Siward, at the head of a company of outlaws, ravaged Seagrave, burnt his fine houses, oxen, and stores of grain, and carried off many valuable horses and rich spoil. Later the same band ravaged Alconbury, and burnt his buildings there. He was much hated, and it was believed that he was concerned in the treachery by which Richard Marshal lost his life in April. When in May the king was reconciled to his lords, Seagrave was dismissed from his offices, and on 14 June was deprived of five of his manors, and was called upon to give an account of his receipts and expenditure. He took shelter in the abbey of St Mary des Prés, near Leicester, where it is said that he resumed clerical tonsure: this may mean that he had taken minor clerical orders early in his career (though he had been knighted by 1219 at the latest). On 14 July he appeared before the king at Westminster, under the protection of the archbishop of Canterbury. Henry called him a foul traitor for having evilly advised him against Hubert de Burgh and his other lords, and demanded his accounts, but, at the archbishop's request, gave him until Michaelmas to make them up. He is said to have attempted to excuse himself by laying the blame on Peter des Roches and Walter Mauclerk. In February 1235 he is said to have paid a fine of 1000 marks to be reconciled with the king, but was not subsequently taken back into favour as he had hoped.

In June 1236 Seagrave was fully restored to favour, and in 1237 was reconciled by the legate Otto to the lords whom he had offended. He was appointed justice of Chester in June 1237. Henry seems to have again made him one of his trusted counsellors, and it was perhaps because he was on specially confidential terms with the king that, in common with Richard, earl of Cornwall, and the queen, he was exempted by name from the excommunication pronounced by the archbishop of Canterbury in 1239 against certain of the king's advisers. In February 1239 he became a justice of the court *coram rege*, and when William of Raleigh was elected bishop of Norwich in April of that year became senior justice of that court. In the last two years of his life, according to Matthew Paris, he held a dominant position in the administration, though his direction of affairs seems to have been unadventurous. Shortly before his death he entered the Augustinian abbey of St Mary des Prés, where he died probably on 11 October 1241.

Paris says that Seagrave was easily led by others, that he owed his rise from a humble station to great wealth and high office to his own exertions, that he cared more for his own interest than the public good, but that he did some things that merited the happy end of life that he made. Certain of Seagrave's opinions on points of law are cited with respect by the author of *De legibus et consuetudinibus Angliae*. He was a benefactor to the abbey of St Mary des Prés, and to the priory of Stoneleigh, and the Cistercian abbey of Combe, both in Warwickshire. His shield, as given by Paris, was blazoned sable, three garbs or, banded gules. William Hunt, *rev.* Paul Brand

Sources GEC, *Peerage* • R. V. Turner, *Men raised from the dust: administrative service and upward mobility in Angevin England* (1988), chap. 7 • *Chancery records* • R. C. Stacey, *Politics, policy and finance under Henry III, 1216–1245* (1987) • Paris, *Chron.*, vols. 3–4 • *Curia regis rolls preserved in the Public Record Office* (1922–), vol. 16, p. 23

Seagrave [Segrave], **Stephen** (*d.* **1333**), archbishop of Armagh, was a member of the important Leicestershire house of Seagrave. He studied at Cambridge, became doctor in canon law before 1306, and served as chancellor of the university between 1303 and 1306. In this capacity he witnessed in Bordeaux on 17 June 1306 the settlement of the statute controversy between the university and the friars. From May 1296 he was rector of Aylestone, near Leicester, within the sphere of the family interest, and from 1300 to 1318 he was rector of Stowe, Northamptonshire, the chief seat of his kinsman Nicholas *Seagrave (*d.* 1321), whose son Gilbert had preceded Seagrave as chancellor of the University of Cambridge *c.*1292–1293.

The position of his kinsman John *Seagrave as warden of Scotland for Edward I and Edward II probably secured for Stephen Seagrave substantial preferment in that country, though he secured the promise rather than the enjoyment of the Scottish revenues. In August 1307 he became dean of Glasgow and in 1309 acquired a canonry in Dunkeld with prebend of Rattray. Robert Wishart, bishop of Glasgow, was one of the heads of resistance to the English. Accordingly on 10 January 1309 Edward II requested Pope Clement V and the cardinals to remove Wishart from his bishopric, and appoint Seagrave in his place, describing him as his 'familiar clerk, of noble birth and sound morals' (Rymer, *Foedera*, 3rd edn, 1, pt 4, 135). Seagrave did not secure the nomination to Glasgow, but on 27 December of the same year he received licence from the pope to hold two more benefices in plurality, as his present preferment had been reduced in value by reason of the war between the English and the Scots. The success of Robert I must soon have deprived Seagrave of all hope of Scottish bishoprics or deaneries. He was forced to borrow largely, owing in 1310 £80 to William Upton, a London citizen, and in 1311 £60 to another. On 29 January 1315 Seagrave was appointed archdeacon of Essex. He was admitted in 1315 to the living of Stepney, near London. Before 1319 he was canon of St Paul's, London, and had resigned his archdeaconry. He was involved in a controversy with Robert

Baldock, bishop of London, with regard to his rights over the manor of Drayton. Before April 1318 he was also canon of Lincoln and by 5 December 1320 dean of Lichfield.

On 16 March 1323 Seagrave was provided by Pope John XXII to the archbishopric of Armagh, vacant since the resignation of the non-resident Roland Jorz, who had been suspended for various offences. His consecration was postponed by the pope for a year. On 31 July 1323 the temporalities were restored. On 28 April 1324 he was ordered by the pope to leave Avignon, and devote himself to his diocese. He had already been consecrated bishop by Raynaldus (Reginaldus) de Porta, cardinal-bishop of Ostia. Previously there had been a rumour in England that Seagrave had resigned his archbishopric to the pope, retaining only the honour of the bishop's office, without its duties or emoluments. On 25 June 1325 he informed the pope from Armagh that he and his suffragan bishops had promulgated the papal condemnation of the excommunicate king of the Romans, Ludwig of Bavaria, in both the English and Irish languages. In July 1328 Seagrave went to the papal curia, with a commendation from Edward II to the pope and permission to cross the sea from Dover with his horses and equipment. On 15 October 1330 he received permission from the pope to hold as a non-resident benefices worth £100 a year. He appears to have made little impact in Ireland, though a number of letters printed by Theiner (*Vetera monumenta*) reflect papal recognition of his authority beyond the boundaries of the ecclesiastical province of Armagh. Seagrave died in England on 27 October 1333. T. F. TOUT, *rev.* KATHERINE WALSH

Sources *CEPR letters*, 2.28, 68, 172, 229, 239–41, 244, 337 • A. Theiner, *Vetera monumenta Hibernorum et Scotorum historiam illustrantia* (Rome, 1864), 228–30, 233–7, 249f., 263 (nos. 453, 454, 456, 462, 463, 465, 468, 492, 517) • Rymer, *Foedera*, 3rd edn, 1/4.135; 2/2.81; 3.5 • *CClR, 1307–13*, 330, 445; *1327–36*, 403 • *CPR, 1313–17*, 214; *1317–21*, 555 • *Fasti Angl., 1300–1541*, [Lincoln], 561 • *Fasti Angl., 1300–1541*, [Hereford], 334 • *Fasti Angl., 1300–1541*, [Salisbury], 597 • *Fasti Angl., 1300–1541*, [St Paul's, London], 9, 23 • *Fasti Angl., 1300–1541*, [Coventry], 5, 29 • J. B. Sheppard, ed., *Literae Cantuarienses: the letter books of the monastery of Christ Church, Canterbury*, 2, Rolls Series, 85 (1888), 108 • *Adae Murimuth continuatio chronicarum. Robertus de Avesbury de gestis mirabilibus regis Edwardi tertii*, ed. E. M. Thompson, Rolls Series, 93 (1889), 28 • R. Newcourt, *Repertorium ecclesiasticum parochiale Londinense*, 1 (1708), 71 • *The whole works of Sir James Ware concerning Ireland*, ed. and trans. W. Harris, 1 (1739), 81 • C. Eubel and others, eds., *Hierarchia Catholica medii et recentioris aevi*, 2nd edn, 1 (Münster, 1913), 109 • N. Cantalupus and R. Parker, *The history and antiquities of the University of Cambridge* (1721), 190 [citing BL, Cotton MS Faustina C.iii, fol. 84r (for S. as chancellor)] • A. G. Little, 'The friars v. the University of Cambridge', *EngHR*, 50 (1935), 686–96, esp. 688–90 • Emden, *Cam.*, 516 • M. B. Hackett, *The original statutes of Cambridge University* (1970), 244

Seale, Morris Sigel (1896–1993). *See under* Porter, Dorothea Noelle Naomi (1927–2000).

Seally, John (1741/2–1795), writer, born in Somerset, was educated at Bristol grammar school, with a view to ordination. He may possibly be identical with the John Sealy, son of John Sealy of Bridgwater, Somerset, who matriculated from Hertford College, Oxford, on 22 May 1760, aged eighteen, and graduated BA in 1764. The death of his uncle and patron obliged him to enter a solicitor's office, which he soon left to learn the business of a merchant under Malachy Postlethwayt. He so disliked his master's strictness, however, that, with some assistance from his mother, he took up authorship and journalism as a means of livelihood. During a visit to Manchester he persuaded a wealthy heiress to elope with him, but was overtaken by the father at Worcester. The lady is said to have died broken-hearted, and Seally consoled himself by marrying, in 1766, a reputedly rich widow of double his age, named Ann Soley Lewis (*b. c.*1728), only to find, some years later, that she had no money and a husband (the Revd William Lewis) still living. In the meantime Seally sought occupation as a writing master and accountant. About 1767 he established a school in Bridgwater Square, Westminster, and after some years' successful tuition took holy orders. After his separation from Mrs Lewis, about 1773, he married Mary Ann, eldest daughter of Joseph Humphreys, rector of Ellisfield, Hampshire, and of North Stoke, Somerset, who survived him. In 1790 he was presented to the vicarage of East Meon with Froxfield and Steep, Hampshire.

Seally was elected fellow of the Royal Society on 30 June 1791. During a trip to Rome in 1774 he obtained admission to the Roman Academy (Arcadia) by a eulogy on Maria Maddelana Fernandez Corilla, poet laureate of Italy. He was also MA and LLD.

Seally contributed occasional verses to various magazines, projected a short-lived political paper signed 'Britannicus', conducted for some time the *Universal Museum* and the *Freeholder's Magazine*, and was involved in the *St James's Magazine*, edited by Robert Lloyd. He likewise published several novels, poems, and encyclopaedias, including: *The Loves of Calisto and Emira, or, The Fatal Legacy* (1776), of which a French translation was published, at Paris, in 1778; *Moral Tales, after the Eastern Manner* (1780?); *The Marriage of Sir Gawaine* (1782), an opera; *A Complete Geographical Dictionary* in two volumes (1787); and *The Lady's Encyclopedia* in three volumes (1788). Seally's career also involved producing educational books and handbooks such as: *The Accountant's Companion, or, Schoolmaster's New Assistant to Practical Arithmetic* (1770); *New Running Hand Copies, Designed for the Use of Schools* (1770?); and *A Specimen of Writing, in the Modern Ornamental Hands of Great Britain* (1794). Seally died in Queen Square, Westminster, in March 1795. GORDON GOODWIN, *rev.* GRANT P. CERNY

Sources will, PRO, PROB 11/1260, sig. 280 • Foster, *Alum. Oxon.* • T. Thomson, *History of the Royal Society from its institution to the end of the eighteenth century* (1812), appx 4, p. lxii • *N&Q*, 7th ser., 11 (1891), 287, 395 • D. E. Baker, *Biographia dramatica, or, A companion to the playhouse*, rev. I. Reed, new edn, rev. S. Jones, 1/2 (1812), 637 • Watt, *Bibl. Brit.* • private information (1897) [the vicar of East Meon]

Seaman, Lazarus (*d.* 1675), clergyman and ejected minister, was born in Leicester. In 1624 he was admitted sizar at Emmanuel College, Cambridge, where he graduated BA in 1628 and proceeded MA in 1631. He appears to have come from a poor family, for Calamy stated that 'as he came in mean Circumstances to the College, so he was forc'd soon to leave it; and to teach School for a Livelyhood' (Calamy,

Abridgement, 2.16). A contemporary pamphlet also asserted that in the early years of his career Seaman had been 'a country Pedagogue' (Hotham, *Corporations Vindicated*, 58–9). Seaman was ordained deacon on 12 February 1628. He is probably the Lazarus Seaman who married Elizabeth Glasier at Burwash, Sussex, on 26 October 1630, an identification which, by suggesting a possible link with the puritan networks of that county, may help explain why Seaman was later to appear as chaplain to the earl of Northumberland. Elizabeth Seaman died in 1648.

An occasional sermon at the parish church of St Martin Ludgate, London, procured Seaman a lectureship there in 1634 but in 1638, if not earlier, he was chosen lecturer by the parish of All Hallows, Bread Street, which was in the early seventeenth century a wealthy parochial community in the City. In the latter year, probably at the request of Philip Nye, Seaman edited and published Richard Sibbes's *A Glance of Heaven*. 'Having some care committed to me by Mr. P. N. whom this businesse chiefly concerned', Seaman wrote in his prefatory epistle to the Christian reader, 'I could doe no lesse then let you understand, here is one rich piece of Spirituall Workmanship, and wrought by a Master-builder, very usefull for building up, and beautifying of Gods Temples'. In spite of this clear indication of his association with the puritan brotherhood there are no known confrontations between Seaman and the ecclesiastical authorities during this period of the Laudian rule in the church.

Early in September 1642, when the rector of All Hallows, John Lawson, was dying, a group of thirty-six parishioners, some of whom, such as John Venn, Maurice Gethin, Tempest Milner, and William Kendall, were important civic leaders in civil-war London, petitioned the House of Lords to request Archbishop Laud, 'in whose care petitioners cannot confide' (*Fifth Report*, HMC, 47), to appoint Seaman to the living. An order was accordingly issued on 9 September. Laud, now in the Tower, still believed that he had 'six months respite by law' and procrastinated, though in the meantime he promised the earl of Northumberland that he 'would give this, out of my respects to his Lp., to Mr. Seaman his chaplain' (*Works*, 3.248; 4.14–15). However, on 6 January 1643 the Lords simply ordered Seaman to be the minister of All Hallows. Later in the year he was appointed by a parliamentary ordinance to sit in the Westminster assembly of divines, and in early April 1644 he was chosen by the earl of Manchester as master of Peterhouse, Cambridge, to replace John Cosin, who had been ejected the month before. Seaman had become an eminent presbyterian minister in the City.

In the following years Seaman played an active role in the Westminster assembly. He sat on several committees and took part in debates over important religious issues such as ministerial ordination, administration of the sacrament, and, above all, the form of church government. He was considered by Robert Baillie to be one of the English divines in the assembly who supported the Scottish position. Indeed, on 25 September 1644, when he was invited to preach a fast sermon before the House of Commons, Seaman reminded the house that 'we have a Covenant' and 'the publique faith of the Kingdome is engaged in it'. And he further admonished that 'it is *Holy, Just* and *Good. Urge it, Renew it*, but above all, *Keepe it*' (Seaman, *Solomons Choice*, 45). He was probably also involved in the concerted agitation in 1645 among the lay and clerical presbyterians in the City for a strong presbyterian church government, though his name was conspicuously absent from the signatories who presented the 'desires' of the City ministers to the common council on 28 November. Four parishioners of All Hallows, Bread Street, signed two citizens' petitions. In any case, later in the year Seaman, as one of the deans of Sion College, London, participated in what a contemporary pamphleteer called 'that Syon-College-conspiracy' (*Divine Observations*, 3); according to William Walwyn, this produced the London ministers' letter against the Independents and toleration 'seasonably, and purposely to meet with the Letter from Scotland' (*Writings*, 172). Indeed, both the letter from the Scottish kirk and the London ministers' letter were presented to the Westminster assembly on 1 January 1646. On 27 January 1647, when he was invited to preach a fast sermon before the House of Lords, Seaman complained that:

> we are neither so cold as by publique indulgence to tolerate all opinions, nor so hot as to suppresse one Sect. Not so cold as not to admit of Presbyteriall government upon triall, and in part; nor so hot as to receive it wholly in the power, and practice … (Seaman, *The Head of the Church*, 29)

When the sermon was published he told the House of Lords in his epistle dedicatory that their task now was to disband the army, to dismantle the garrisons, to settle the militia in safe hands, and 'for this *the Vowes of God are upon you* to bring the three Kingdomes unto the neerest conjunction and uniformity in Religion'.

When the London provincial assembly was eventually convened in May 1647 Seaman, who had been appointed trier by several ordinances, was a delegate from the first classis. A faithful member, he was twice to serve as moderator of the assembly, and to attend its very last meeting on 15 August 1660. In September 1648 he was one of the ministers sent by the parliament to discuss church government with Charles I on the Isle of Wight, 'where his Majesty took particular Notice of the Doctor's singular Ability in the Debates' (Calamy, *Abridgement*, 2.16). In January 1649 Seaman signed the *Vindication* of the London ministers against the trial of the king. Later in the year he proceeded DD at Cambridge. 'This Degree', said William Jenkyn in Seaman's funeral sermon, 'he took by performing his Exercises appointed by the Statutes of the University'. And according to Jenkyn the thesis Seaman defended in the 'Divinity-Act' was 'to assert the Providence of God in disposing of Political Government' (Jenkyn, 52). This was, indeed, a timely subject in that year of political crisis, and it probably resolved doubts in Seaman's own mind. In any case he was one of the few presbyterian ministers who in future years openly preached submission to and acceptance of the Commonwealth at Cambridge as well as in

London, for which he was pitilessly attacked by a pamphlet entitled *Lazarus's Sores Licked* (1650).

In the 1650s Seaman enjoyed the trust of the successive governments under the Commonwealth and the protectorate. He was president of Sion College in 1651 and 1652, and vice-chancellor of Cambridge University in 1653 and 1654. In the latter year he was also appointed assistant to the commissioners for London and Cambridgeshire under the new ecclesiastical system of triers. At the same time he was able to speak for the national ministry and in defence of tithes, as in his sermon before the City magistrates at Mercers' Chapel in 1650 or in his testimony before a committee of Barebone's Parliament in 1653. However, troubles arose at Peterhouse. First there was the quarrel in 1651 with Charles Hotham, a senior fellow at Peterhouse, over Seaman's refusal to accept the election of Tobias Conyers to a fellowship. Conyers was to become an Arminian and an associate of John Goodwin's gathered church in London, and his unorthodox views had been known at Cambridge. But Hotham, Conyers's tutor, complained first to a parliamentary committee and then publicly in pamphlets. He spoke against Seaman's single negative voice and absenteeism. According to Hotham, Seaman never resided at Peterhouse and his occasional visits 'will not amount to one of the whole seven years of his employment of that Mastership'. And Hotham observed that 'the Mastership of the Colledge was not intended as … Augmentation to a London Ministers Parsonage' (Hotham, *Corporations Vindicated*, 50). Afterwards, in 1658 and 1659, Seaman encountered strong opposition from the senior fellows of Peterhouse when he gave one of the fellowships to his own son, Joseph. In this case he appears to have gained the favour of both Cromwells. In the unsettling situation of 1659, Seaman was also prominent among the presbyterians who tried to co-operate with the Independents and Baptists in London.

In 1660, after the return of Charles II, Seaman became 'a little estranged' from his presbyterian brethren who attempted to achieve some agreement with the episcopalians for the future religious settlement. According to Richard Baxter, this was because the court gave him 'no encouragement' and he was 'hardlier spoken of at Court' (*Reliquiae Baxterianae*, 229). Perhaps his earlier close relationship with the Commonwealth and the protectorate put him now in an unfavourable light in the eyes of the royalists. He was ejected from his mastership of Peterhouse in August 1660 and two years later from the ministry of All Hallows, Bread Street. In his farewell sermon he spoke of peace, especially 'that *inward* peace that we enjoy, if our Conscience hath been troubled with terrors of sin, wrath, &c' (*The Second and Last Collection*, 4). Perhaps in the same spirit, he persuaded Baxter to refrain from publishing a statement against taking the oath under the Five Mile Act in 1665. He lived mostly at Hammersmith, Middlesex, where he was licensed as presbyterian in 1672. He later built a chapel in Meeting-House Yard, Wood Street, Holborn. He died at his home in Warwick Court, Warwick Lane, Newgate Street, on 3 September 1675 and was buried at All Hallows, Bread Street, four days later. Seaman was a learned man, and William Jenkyn praised him emphatically for his 'Casuitical' theology 'both for directing and easing of Conscience' (Jenkyn, 53). In his will, made in the parish of Christ Church, London, on 2 June 1675, Seaman put his library of over 5000 volumes in trust and laid down stipulations for its sale. It was the first to be sold by public auction in England. He was survived by a daughter, Elizabeth Seaman, and a brother, Caleb Seaman, in Dublin. TAI LIU

Sources L. Seaman, *Solomons choice, or, A president for kings and princes, and all that are in authority* (1644) • L. Seaman, *The head of the church, the judge of the world* (1647) • L. Seaman, *The diatribē proved to be paradiatribē* (1647) • L. Seaman, *The glasse for the times* (1650) • R. Sibbes, *A glance of heaven* (1638) • W. Jenkyn, *Exodus, or, The decease of the holy men and ministers* (1675) • E. Calamy, ed., *An abridgement of Mr. Baxter's history of his life and times, with an account of the ministers, &c., who were ejected after the Restauration of King Charles II*, 2nd edn, 2 vols. (1713) • *The second and last collection of the late London ministers farewel sermons* (1663) • *Catalogus variorum & insignium librorum instuctissimae bibliothecae* (1676) • will, 21 June 1676, PRO, PROB 11/351, sig. 72 • C. Hotham, *A true state of the case of Mr. Hotham* (1651) • C. Hotham, *Corporations vindicated in their fundamental liberties* (1651) • *The works of the most reverend father in God, William Laud*, ed. J. Bliss and W. Scott, 7 vols. (1847–60) • *The writings of William Walwyn*, ed. J. R. McMichael and B. Taft (1966) • *Reliquiae Baxterianae, or, Mr Richard Baxter's narrative of the most memorable passages of his life and times*, ed. M. Sylvester, 1 vol. in 3 pts (1696) • *Calamy rev.* • A. F. Mitchell and J. Struthers, eds., *Minutes of the sessions of the Westminster assembly of divines* (1874) • C. E. Surman, ed., 'The records of the provincial assembly of London, 1647–1660', DWL [2 vols.] • J. Twigg, *The University of Cambridge and the English Revolution, 1625–1688* (1990) • Tai Liu, *Discord in Zion: the puritan divines and the puritan revolution, 1640–1660* (1973) • *Divine observations upon the London ministers' letter against toleration* (1646) • *Fifth report*, HMC, 4 (1876) • *IGI*

Archives Bodl. Oxf., letters to Lord Wharton, Rawlinson letters, 50.22, 25; 53.73, 76

Wealth at death library of over 5000 volumes sold by public auction

Seaman, Sir Owen, baronet (1861–1936), journal editor and satirist, was born on 18 September 1861 above his father's artificial-flower shop at 199 Sloane Street, Chelsea, London, the second of the three children and only son of William Mantle Seaman (1838–1893) of Suffolk, a nonconformist and a successful dressmaker and businessman, and his wife, Sarah Ann Balls (*d.* 1907), the daughter of John Balls, a Suffolk farmer. Seaman was sent to Mill Hill School, and at seventeen his academic and athletic talents enabled him to secure a scholarship into the sixth form at Shrewsbury School, where he was selected as head boy. He went to Clare College, Cambridge, in 1880 on a scholarship. In 1882 he captained the Clare boats and was university Porson prizeman in Greek iambics and then graduated first class in part one of the classical tripos of 1883, going on to take the BA in 1884 and the MA in 1887. Meanwhile he had come under the stylistic influence of the so-called Cambridge wits, especially C. S. Calverley and J. S. Stephen, 'masters' of satirical light verse, based on the shared sensibilities of those schooled in classical languages. He began to compose light verse and parodies, some of which were published in the *Cambridge Review* and the *Oxford Magazine*.

Seaman was a schoolmaster at Rossall School, Fleetwood, Lancashire (1884–6), Magdalen College School, Oxford (1887), and lecturer and a professor in classics at the Durham College of Science, Newcastle upon Tyne, from 1888 to 1893. He also taught for the Cambridge University Extension Society, and lectured on Browning in the summer of 1892 at Chautauqua in New York. His father's death in 1893 freed him from schoolmastering.

Seaman returned to London and lived with his mother—who died in 1907—at Tower House, 77 West Hill, on Putney Heath. He stayed there until about 1913, when he moved to a flat, 2 Whitehall Court, off Horseguards Avenue, Westminster. He lived an active and ordered social life, and had mistresses, but never married. The novelist Pearl Craigie (with whom he had a relationship about the turn of the century) asserted that Seaman was the model for Densher, the 'weak, smug Englishman' in Henry James's *The Wings of the Dove* (Prager, 175).

Seaman rapidly established his reputation as a satirist with verses, skits, and burlesques in *Granta*, the *National Observer*, *The World*, and *Punch*. *Horace at Cambridge* (1895), described by Evoe (E. V. Knox), his successor at *Punch*, as 'a brilliant undergraduate exercise in parody' (*DNB*), was followed by parodies of elder and contemporary poets which Knox thought enlivened the 1890s interregnum in the poet laureateship. John Lane at the Bodley Head issued collections of his verses, which were also published in New York. Called to the bar in 1897, Seaman never practised. That same year his skills at parody led to an invitation to join the *Punch* table. There he continued to write and publish parodies, especially of Tennyson and George Meredith, but much of his verse took a Conservative political tone influenced by his views of the Second South African War, the embarrassments of the Liberal Party over home rule, free trade, and the pretensions of Wilhelmine Germany.

In 1902 Seaman became assistant editor of *Punch*, and in 1906 the editor. The schoolmasterish Seaman disciplined its writing and organization and assembled a staff of able writers, including Evoe, E. V. Lucas, and A. A. Milne, and edited them over-assiduously. Supported by the proprietors, Lawrence Bradbury and Philip Agnew, and the business manager, Herbert Heather, he tightened up *Punch*, which he felt was a national institution, and made it an expression of conservative values and a financial success. Above all he wanted lucidity, regularity, intelligibility, and 'soundness'—that is, a Conservative political reliability. What he got was a self-satisfied, stodgy, increasingly right-wing, and sometimes unfunny weekly. During the First World War his memorial pieces and verses made him a poetic spokesman of the patriotic mood.

In the 1920s Seaman's *Punch* was increasingly out of sympathy with the times; it appeared to many to be 'written by the half-witted and proud of it' (Price, 227). Exceptions were A. P. Herbert's *Misleading Cases*, Milne's whimsical poems about Christopher Robin and Winnie the Pooh which were illustrated by E. H. Shepard, and W. C. Sellar and R. J. Yeatman's burlesque history text, *1066 and All That*. Seaman's last years at *Punch* were redeemed by the cartoons of H. M. Bateman, Fougasse (Kenneth Bird), Bert Thomas, Lewis Baumer, George Belcher, and Arthur Watts. Little direct competition meant that *Punch* attracted up-market advertisers and it became a 'shop window' for the advertising industry. It increased in size and weekly circulation to over 150,000, with some colour illustrations. Seaman having had a bout of ill health, the *Punch* proprietors finally persuaded him to retire at the end of 1932, though he confessed that he'd 'have liked to die in harness' (Seaman to P. Agnew, 7 Jan 1932, London, *Punch* Library and Archives).

Despite Seaman's accomplishments as editor of what was then a national institution, and as a wit and raconteur and a considerable social success, his life was always shadowed by shame over his family origins. He was oversensitive to social slights and latterly a 'sometimes fantastic' snob (Price, 179). No satirist can have been less bohemian—'in later life the most hysterically genteel *Punch* man since Leech' (ibid.). In 1914 he was knighted, and when the king remarked, 'I have often been tempted to send you a good joke', Seaman replied, 'I'd have loved to post your majesty one of our rejection notices.' He was elected an honorary fellow of Clare College in 1909, and received honorary degrees from Durham (1906), Edinburgh (1924), and Oxford (1933). His autobiographical *Interludes of an Editor* was published in 1929. When he was created a baronet in January 1933, he wrote a couplet to friends who congratulated him:

I thank you from a swelling heart,
for being glad that I'm a Bart.

He died of pneumonia, after a heart attack, in his flat at 2 Whitehall Court, on 2 February 1936 and was buried three days later at Putney Vale cemetery, where his parents lay. That same day a memorial service was held for him at St Martin-in-the-Fields. PETER MELLINI

Sources J. Adlard, *Owen Seaman: his life and work* (1977) · R. G. G. Price, *A history of Punch* (1957) · A. A. Milne, *Autobiography* (New York, [1939]) · *DNB* · *Punch* Library and Archives, London, Owen Seaman MSS · *'Punch'* letter book, 1931–43, *Punch* Library and Archives, London · P. Fitzgerald, *The Knox brothers* (1977) · A. Prager, *The mahogany tree: an informal history of 'Punch'* (1979) · C. L. G. [C. L. Graves], 'Punch centenary volume', in C. L. Graves, *Mr Punch's history of the Great War* (1919) [pts I–X] · O. Seaman, *Horace at Cambridge* (1895) · O. Seaman, *The battle of the bays* (1896) · O. Seaman, *Borrowed plumes* (1902) · O. Seaman, *Interludes of an editor* (1929) · R. B. Ince, *Calverley and some Cambridge wits of the nineteenth century* (1929), 75–116 · C. S. Calverley, *Verses and translations* (1905) [introduction by O. Seaman] · *The Times* (3 Feb 1936) · *CGPLA Eng. & Wales* (1936)

Archives *Punch* Library and Archives, London, papers · NRA, corresp. and papers | BL, letters to T. A. Guthrie, Add. MSS 54264–54267, *passim*, 54272 · BL, corresp. with Society of Authors, Add. MS 56803 · Cheltenham College, letters to Charles Turley · CUL, letters to E. C. Bentley · CUL, letters to Margaret Sharp · NL Scot., corresp. with Lord Rosebery · Ransom HRC, corresp. with John Lane · U. Leeds, Brotherton L., letters to Sir Edmund Gosse and others · U. Leeds, Brotherton L., letters to Clement Shorter · W. Sussex RO, corresp. with Oswald Barron

Likenesses A. L. Coburn, photograph, 1914, NPG · H. Coster, photographs, 1930–39, NPG · H. A. Oliver, oils, *Punch* offices, London · photographs, *Punch* offices, London, Owen Seaman file · photographs, repro. in Adlard, *Owen Seaman*

Wealth at death £46,336 4*s.* 9*d.*: resworn probate, 13 March 1936, *CGPLA Eng. & Wales*

Seaman, William (1606/7–1680), orientalist, was probably born at Upton Scudamore, near Warminster in Wiltshire, the son of William Seaman, 'gentleman' (*d.* 1660), who rented the manor farm, known as Acres Farm, in the same year, and bought the lease in 1636. Seaman matriculated at Balliol College, Oxford, on 7 February 1624, aged seventeen, graduating BA at the same time, and proceeded MA on 6 July 1626. In 1628 he was appointed rector of Upton Scudamore, a living which afforded him about £100 a year. Shortly after his institution he went to Constantinople in the service of Sir Peter Wyche, English ambassador from 1628 to 1639. He there learned Turkish and possibly also Arabic. There is no information about the date or the length of his stay, but it cannot have been very long since he was officiating at Upton Scudamore in 1628 and, it would seem from the bishops' transcripts, from 1631 onwards. On 24 October 1634 he married Mary Hollimar (*d.* 1671) from Ashton Gifford in Codford St Peter. The couple had at least one son.

Seaman gradually obtained a reputation as a Turkish expert—his position in the republic of letters was confirmed by his correspondence with the French scholar Louis Picques—while he proved his capabilities as an Arabist with his translation of the index of a codex on Islam, entitled in English the 'Splendour of the exhorter', in the archbishop of Canterbury's library at St Martin's (BL, Add. MS 24858). His first publication in the domain of Turkish studies was his translation into English of a historical work, the initial part of Sadettin Hoca's *Tac üt-tevarih* ('The crown of histories') published as *The Reign of Sultan Orchan, Second King of the Turks* (1652). Here, as in his other works, he stressed the utility of Turkish for historians. The translation was dedicated to Jane, Lady Merick, formerly the widow of Sir Peter Wyche, to whose family he remained devoted after Sir Peter's death in 1643.

In December 1655 Seaman was appointed secretary of the trade committee (which met at Westminster) at a yearly salary of £100. Some years later he became involved in an international project of evangelization of the Levant, originating in the circle of Samuel Hartlib, whose millenarian convictions included belief in the imminent conversion to Christianity of the Muslims and a determination to hasten the process. In England the plan was fostered by Hartlib himself, Henry Oldenburg, John Dury, and above all Robert Boyle, with Edward Pococke and John Worthington taking a marginal role. It obtained even more support in the Netherlands, thanks mainly to the Bohemian scholar Jan Amos Comenius and the French refugee Petrus Serrarius. A fundamental role was to be played by the translation of the Bible into Turkish. The Dutch, who relied on a Polish convert to Islam in Constantinople, were slow, however, and only the Old Testament was completed. Boyle then turned to Seaman, who had already translated the Johannine epistles into Turkish in 1659, asking him to translate the entire New Testament. By 1664 Seaman had done so and two years later his translation was published at Boyle's expense in Oxford, making Seaman the first European to publish a Turkish translation of the New Testament. In the meantime, also at the instigation of Boyle, Seaman had translated into Turkish John Ball's *Short Catechisme*. It was published in 1660, the first Turkish work to be issued at Oxford. Copies were distributed by Robert Huntington, chaplain to the Levant Company in Aleppo.

In 1670 Seaman published his *Grammatica linguae Turcicae*. Boyle undertook to buy £20 worth of copies, and Sir Cyril Wyche (Sir Peter's youngest son) also contributed. Seaman had hoped to publish a Turkish–Latin lexicon on which he had been working for some years (and on which he continued to work until the year of his death), but the dictionary remained in manuscript (Bodl. Oxf. MS Rawl. Or. 58). He did, however, assist Edmund Castell in assimilating the contents of Ni'matullâh's Persian–Turkish dictionary in the *Lexicon heptaglotton* published in 1669. In his study of Turkish, Seaman was a pioneer in England. He was the first Englishman to produce a grammar, but not the first European. In contrast to Seaman's, however, few other Turkish grammars were printed in Ottoman characters.

The quality of Seaman's work was widely criticized, at the time and later. Jacobus Golius, professor of Arabic at Leiden and with a sound knowledge of Turkish, reported the devastating judgement of Seaman's New Testament by the Armenian Shahin Kandy. There was little point in circulating the translation in the Ottoman empire, he said, since it would probably be considered incomprehensible, so 'artificial' were 'the nature and the use of the language' (Kleerkoper and Stockum, 1243). The grammar hardly fared better. It lacks any form of systematic approach to Turkish, contains numerous errors, and includes a thoroughly unreliable guide to the pronunciation of the language. Less than forty years later Thomas Vaughan could truthfully say of his own Turkish grammar that, although it could not compete with the lexicographical work of the imperial interpreter Meninski (which was published in 1680 and remained unsurpassed until the nineteenth century), at least it was 'an Improvement of Mr Seaman's'. But he nevertheless acknowledged his debt to a predecessor to whom his grammar owed 'its Form, and well-nigh all the Substance too' (Vaughan, xvi). Seaman had also had trouble with his Latin, and had applied to Samuel Clarke, the architypographus of the Oxford University Press, and to Clarke's master, Edward Pococke, to improve his style and correct his preface.

Seaman, whom Edward Pococke's biographer Leonard Twells described as a moderate nonconformist and 'a sober, discreet, and modest man' (Twells, 276), was profoundly committed to the conversion of the Muslims and the propagation of protestantism in the Levant. He spent much of his time in London, where he owned a house in Whitecross Alley, Moorfields, and consorted with the 'Turkie merchants' and members of the Levant Company who provided numerous subscribers to his Turkish New Testament and saw to the distribution of his translations in the Ottoman empire. Yet he appears to have been a conscientious rector of his living. He died at his London house on 7 November 1680, and was buried two days later at Upton Scudamore at his church of St Mary the Virgin.

ALASTAIR HAMILTON

Sources [M. Daly], *The Turkish legacy: an exhibition of books and manuscripts to mark the fiftieth anniversary of the death of the founder of the Turkish republic Mustafa Kemal Atatürk* (1988) • E. G. E. van der Wall, *De mystieke chiliast Petrus Serrarius (1606–1669) en zijn wereld* (1987) • *The correspondence of Robert Boyle*, ed. M. Hunter, A. Clericuzio, and L. M. Principe (2001), vols. 2 and 5 • L. Twells and S. Burdy, *The lives of Dr Edward Pocock … Dr Zachary Pearce … Dr Thomas Newton … and of the Rev Philip Skelton*, 2 vols. (1816) • *VCH Wiltshire*, vol. 8 • bishops' transcripts, Wilts. & Swindon RO, Upton Scudamore bundle 1 • F. Babinger, 'Die türkischen Studien in Europa bis zum Auftreten Josef von Hammer-Purgstalls', *Die Welt des Islam*, 7 (1919), 103–29 • M. M. Kleerkoper and W. P. van Stockum, *De boekhandel te Amsterdam, voornamelijk in de 17de eeuw*, 2 (The Hague, 1916) • Foster, *Alum. Oxon.* • T. Vaughan, *A grammar of the Turkish language* (1709) • Bodl. Oxf., MS Pococke 428, fols. 3–4, 129–30 • parish registers, Upton Scudamore, Wilts. & Swindon RO • *DNB* • Boyle papers, 4, fols. 148v–149r • E. Castell, *Lexicon Heptaglotton* (1669), vol. 1 • *CSP dom.*, 1655–6 • Bodl. Oxf., MS Rawl. Or. 58

Archives Bodl. Oxf., interleaved dictionary, MS Bodl. Or. 203 • Bodl. Oxf., preface to Turkish grammar, MS Pococke 428, fols. 3–4, 129–30 | BL, letters to S. Clarke, Add. MS 22905, fols. 91–3

Seán Mac an tSaor. *See* Carpenter, John (1729–1786).

Searchfield, Rowland (1564/5–1622), bishop of Bristol, was probably born in London. He was educated at Merchant Taylors' School, London, from 1575 to 1582, when, aged seventeen, he went to St John's College, Oxford, of which he was later made a fellow. He graduated BA on 11 October 1586 and proceeded MA on 2 June 1590.

Granted leave of absence by his college in February 1594 to preach in London, Searchfield reportedly delivered about twenty sermons, including one at Paul's Cross. On his return to Oxford he became university proctor in April 1596 and gained his BD degree on 30 June the same year. John Manningham described him, while at Oxford in 1602/3, as 'a dissembled Christian, like an intemperate patient which can gladly heare his physicion discourse of his dyet and remedy, but will not endure to obserue them' (11). However, when Searchfield resigned his fellowship on 26 November 1606 St John's granted him £10 'in consideration that he hath taken great pains in writing of many things for the college, and done many good and commendable services for the college' (Stevenson and Salter, 362). In his thesis for his DD degree, gained on 1 June 1608, Searchfield argued that various forms of religion were incompatible with unity of faith, that no one could be saved by the faith of another, and that heretics should be compelled to conform outwardly.

In 1600 Searchfield had become rector of Eastleach Martin, Gloucestershire, an incumbency he held for the rest of his life. On 3 December 1600 he was also presented to the living of Emly, but resigned ten months later in 1601 and became vicar of Evenley, Northamptonshire, and rector of Burthrop, Gloucestershire. The distractions of Oxford no doubt underlie an indictment for prolonged absence from his parish during Bishop Thomas Ravis's 1605 visitation of Gloucester diocese. In 1606 Searchfield became vicar of Charlbury, Oxfordshire, where he was made a JP. Having been earlier unsuccessful in an attempt to gain appointment as a chaplain to the new archbishop, Richard Bancroft, he became a chaplain-in-ordinary to James I before whom he preached Lenten sermons on 8 April 1617 and 17 March 1622.

Searchfield was nominated bishop of Bristol on 12 March 1619 and consecrated on 9 May. During his primary episcopal visitation, on Holy Cross day 1619, he consecrated the chapel of Chantmarle Manor near Cattistock, Dorset, 'where he confirmed five hundred people, young and old, until he was so weary that he left some unconfirmed, and escaped to his bed at Melbury' (Fincham, 128). Searchfield supported his clergy's ultimately unsuccessful attempt to increase their inadequate stipends by appealing to the citizens of Bristol for a contribution towards their maintenance. With his wife, Anne, daughter of Ralph and Mary Hutchinson of Oxfordshire, Searchfield had a son, also Rowland, who later became a prominent Bristol citizen. Searchfield died on 11 October 1622, probably in Bristol, and was buried in the sanctuary of Bristol Cathedral. Following renovations there in the 1680s, a memorial stone to him was placed in the north transept wall.

M. DORMAN

Sources Foster, *Alum. Oxon.* • *Diary of John Manningham*, ed. J. Bruce, CS, old ser., 99 (1868) • *DNB* • W. H. Stevenson and H. E. Salter, *The early history of St John's College, Oxford*, OHS, new ser., 1 (1939) • J. Hutchins, *The history and antiquities of the county of Dorset*, 3rd edn, ed. W. Shipp and J. W. Hodson, 4 (1874), 416 • J. Latimer, *The annals of Bristol in the seventeenth century* (1900), 75–6 • K. Fincham, *Prelate as pastor: the episcopate of James I* (1990), 125, 128, 134, 313 • C. J. Robinson, ed., *A register of the scholars admitted into Merchant Taylors' School, from AD 1562 to 1874*, 1 (1882), 22 • PRO, SP 14/9/65, 14/90/101, 14/109/20, 14/134/2 • R. C. Latham, ed., *Bristol charters, 1509–1899*, Bristol RS, 12 (1947), 181, 203 • P. McGrath, ed., *Merchants and merchandise in seventeenth-century Bristol*, Bristol RS, 19 (1955), 256, 268 • Wood, *Ath. Oxon.*, new edn, 2.261 • Wood, *Ath. Oxon.: Fasti* • *The letters of John Chamberlain*, ed. N. E. McClure, 2 (1939), 236 • R. Bigland, *Historical, monumental and genealogical collections, relative to the county of Gloucester*, ed. B. Frith, 3 (1992) • C. M. Clode, ed., *Memorials of the Guild of Merchant Taylors of the fraternity of St John the Baptist* (1875), 665 • E. B. Fryde and others, eds., *Handbook of British chronology*, 3rd edn, Royal Historical Society Guides and Handbooks, 2 (1986), 231, 237, 264

Archives PRO, SP 14/9/65, 14/90/101, 14/109/20, 14/134/2 • Westminster Abbey, muniment book 15

Searle, Frank (1875–1948), transport entrepreneur, was born at 43 High Street, Worthing, on 15 July 1875, the son of George Searle, an iron-founder, and his wife, Charlotte (*née* Knight). Searle was originally trained as a locomotive engineer but, displaying early commercial sense, realized that road transport, which began to be mechanized with money-making possibilities from the later 1890s, offered more rewarding prospects, especially as steam power was an obvious early contender. Searle came to realize, however, that the petrol engine, then being developed in France with earlier German patents, offered a much more favourable power-to-weight ratio. He set about mastering the new technology, and courageously set up on his own as a consulting engineer in the West End of London.

In 1905 Searle went to Paris, and arranged to represent

Turgan and Lacoste-Battman, several of whose chassis he was able to sell to the London and District Motor Omnibus Company, one of the stock exchange speculations of the time, which ran the Arrow fleet of vehicles. They kept breaking down, however, and the final part of the order had to be cancelled. Thus Searle was obliged to abandon his consultancy; but such was his reputation as a motor engineer that Arrow engaged him as an employee to keep their other vehicles on the road.

None of these early motor buses was sturdy enough to withstand the constant jolting in London traffic. All the moving parts worked loose, and horse buses were able to withstand the new competition, even though the rivalry was soon so severe that few businesses made any profit. In these circumstances the older established, and better funded, London General Omnibus Company (known as the General), which experimented very cautiously with the new motors, managed to maintain a sounder financial position.

The General appointed Searle superintendent of its Mortlake garage at £350 a year in early 1907. Within three months he was transferred to the chief garage at Cricklewood in place of the manager of the motor department, an electrical engineer and former tramway man, who was unable to cope with the twenty-five different models then being tried out from there. On 18 May 1907 Searle was chosen from a shortlist of five as the General's chief motor engineer at a salary of £450 a year, raised to £500 a year at the beginning of 1908. So fierce had competition become by then that other companies fell into the General's grasp, and Searle found himself in charge of a motley collection of about 600 vehicles, none of which could survive the punishment of operating for long in London traffic. He persuaded the General to allow him to design and build a motor chassis which would survive.

'We cribbed shamelessly', Searle later recalled as he remembered the way in which they incorporated the best features of all the existing models. The result was known as the X-type, the prototype of which was completed on 12 August 1909, but given a police licence to run in service only just before Christmas. The real winner was a lighter, 3½ ton vehicle. This, the vastly improved B-type, was first produced on 7 October 1910, and quickly licensed for service a mere eleven days later. By the end of October 1911 the General had replaced all its 343 horse buses. The B-type enabled it to regain its unchallenged dominance over all upstart rivals.

There were, however, other manufacturers who had, by then, developed more satisfactory motor buses, and they were anxious to acquire a share, however small, of Britain's main motor bus market. Notable among them was the midlands firm of BSA–Daimler. It launched the Premier Motor Bus Company with this objective and, at the beginning of May 1911, it was rumoured that Searle had been offered a senior management position with Premier. The General reacted strongly. Searle was ordered to appear before the directors. His salary was increased from £1000 to £1250 a year, subject to his undertaking to devote his whole time to the company's service and not to make reports, or do any other service, for any other person or company. He asked for time to consider these new arrangements. When he appeared before the board again, on 4 May 1911, his salary was increased to £2000 provided he immediately signed a new contract. This he refused to do on the spot. He was thereupon curtly dismissed, given three months' salary in lieu of notice, and went to work for Daimler. During the First World War he served in the tank corps and was mentioned in dispatches. He received the DSO in 1918 and CBE the following year.

Searle returned to Daimler after the war in charge of its hire-car division. When BSA bought into Air Transport and Travel in 1920 he became managing director and in 1922 took the same role with Daimler Airways, which flew first to Paris, then to Amsterdam instead, and eventually on to Berlin; an internal route was also developed between London and Manchester. In April 1924, when Daimler and the two other British companies were merged to form the Imperial Air Transport Company (later Imperial Airways) with a tapered, ten year, £1 million government subsidy, Searle became managing director.

Frank Searle was married, and he and his wife, Alice, had at least one son. Searle died at his home, 6 Dunbar Road, Bournemouth, on 4 April 1948, and was cremated in Bournemouth crematorium four days later. His death went almost unnoticed by *The Times*, which after reporting the deaths of a former chief inspector of lifeboats, and a prominent figure in South African shipping, added rather as an afterthought: 'We also announce with regret the death of Colonel Frank Searle, CBE, DSO' (*The Times*, 6 April 1948). THEO BARKER

Sources T. C. Barker and M. Robbins, *A history of London Transport*, 2 (1974), 131–2, 167–8, 172–3, 177–8 · C. E. Lee, 'A chapter in London bus history', *The Omnibus*, ed. J. Hibbs (1971), 181–90 · E. Birkhead, 'The Daimler Airway: April 1922 – March 1924', *Journal of Transport History*, 3 (1957–8), 195–200 · A. J. Quin-Harkin, 'Imperial Airways, 1924–40', *Journal of Transport History*, 1 (1953–4), 197–215 · *The Times* (6 April 1948) · *WW* · R. E. G. Davies, *History of the world's airlines* (1964) · b. cert. · d. cert. · *CGPLA Eng. & Wales* (1948)

Likenesses portrait, repro. in Barker and Robbins, *History of London Transport*, pl. 77

Wealth at death £44,732 3s. 3d.: probate, 14 Dec 1948, *CGPLA Eng. & Wales*

Searle, George Frederick Charles (1864–1954), physicist, was born on 3 December 1864 at Oakington, Cambridgeshire, eldest of the three sons and two daughters of William George Searle (1829–1913), vicar of Oakington, and his wife, Harriet Susan, formerly Theobald. Searle attended the village school for only six days. After this his father, a former mathematician and linguist, took over his son's education in the usual subjects, plus the Hebrew language. Searle early developed a passion for mechanics, teaching himself the use of tools and building himself a dynamo. He was fourteen when his father took him round the Cavendish Laboratory in Cambridge, a visit which greatly impressed him and turned his mind to physics. After eighteen months of private coaching Searle won a foundation scholarship to Peterhouse, Cambridge, where he read mathematics. The following year, 1888, he obtained a second-class degree in the natural sciences tripos and began research at the Cavendish Laboratory under J. J. Thomson. He was to be associated with the laboratory for the rest of his life.

Searle's first research, in collaboration with Thomson, concerned the ratio between electrostatic and electromagnetic units of electricity and was published in the Royal Society's *Philosophical Transactions* (181A, 1890, 583–621). It was followed by the publication of many independent projects, mostly dealing with magnetic measurements or electromagnetic theory, but occasionally with properties of matter or heat. The Royal Society elected him FRS in 1905. He married, on 3 September 1904, a widow, Alice Mary Parsons, daughter of Thomas Edwards, solicitor, who survived him; there were no children. In 1911, convalescing from illness, he and his wife visited the West Indies and Canada.

In 1890 Searle was appointed university demonstrator and in 1900 university lecturer. 'Searle's class', as it was known, was intended for the increasing numbers of undergraduates reading for part one of the natural sciences tripos, and during the Michaelmas and Lent terms about a hundred students attended three times a week. Most of Searle's time and effort were spent devising ingenious and original experiments, for which he worked out and wrote up the theory and experimental details with great thoroughness, leading Thomson to comment that Searle 'has done more than anyone for the teaching of practical physics at Cambridge … He has taken infinite pains and thought to improve the course and replace old experiments with others of greater educational value' (Thomson, 114–15).

John Ashworth Ratcliffe took over from Searle in 1935, but it took a whole term to get him out of the classroom. During the war Searle officially resumed teaching, and when Ratcliffe returned he had again to get Searle, then aged eighty, out of his classroom. Searle was capable of a dry humour that amused his students but when in brusque mood could reduce those from Newnham and Girton to tears. Within the Cavendish he was regarded with a mixture of awe, amusement, and affection, able to boast in later years that he had taught both father and mother of the then holder of the Cavendish chair, and to have had more Nobel prizewinners as his pupils than any other man.

When young, Searle had developed an interest in the history of the church and he did for a while lecture locally on the subject. Religion held an important place in his life: he held strong beliefs on the influence of religion on mind, and of mind on body, extending this to spiritual healing. He was for many years a lay reader in the Church of England. Within university circles he was known to hold strong views opposing vivisection and experiments on animals. At a tea party given at the Cavendish in honour of his ninetieth birthday he spoke movingly of his experiences in physics and religion. He died at his home, 170 Hills Road, on 16 December 1954.

ANITA MCCONNELL

Sources G. Thomson, *Memoirs FRS*, 1 (1955), 247–52 • F. Horton, *Nature*, 175 (1955), 282–3 • J. J. Thomson, *Recollections and reflections* (1936) • J. G. Crowther, *The Cavendish Laboratory, 1874–1974* (1974) • b. cert. • m. cert. • d. cert. • *CGPLA Eng. & Wales* (1955)

Archives CUL, papers | U. Reading L., letters to Robert Ditchburn

Likenesses photograph, repro. in Thomson, *Memoirs FRS*

Wealth at death £15,616 1s. 1d.: probate, 17 March 1955, *CGPLA Eng. & Wales*

Searle, Humphrey (1915–1982), composer and writer on music, was born on 26 August 1915 at Oxford, the eldest of the three sons (there were no daughters) of Humphrey Frederic Searle (1887–1965), of Oxford, a commissioner in the Indian Civil Service, and his wife, Charlotte Mathilde Mary (May; 1889–1973), daughter of Sir William *Schlich, the pioneer of forestry studies at Oxford. He was educated at Winchester College (1928–33) and at New College, Oxford, where he obtained a second class in classical honour moderations (1935) and a third in *literae humaniores* (1937). In 1937 he became Octavia scholar at the Royal College of Music (his teachers were John Ireland, Gordon Jacob, and R. O. Morris), and went to study at the Vienna Conservatorium (1937–8). In Vienna he took private lessons from Anton Webern.

In 1938 Searle joined the BBC music staff. From 1940 to 1946 he served with the Gloucestershire regiment, intelligence corps, and general list, and after the war, when still in Germany, he assisted Hugh Trevor-Roper in research for *The Last Days of Hitler* (1947). He resumed producing at the BBC, leaving in 1948 to work freelance. An enthusiast for promoting new music, he was general secretary of the International Society for Contemporary Music (1947–9). In 1951–7 he served as music adviser to Sadler's Wells Ballet.

A distinguished Liszt scholar, Searle was generous in imparting knowledge to colleagues. He compiled a new catalogue of Liszt's works (incorporated in *Grove*, 1954 edn; updated in *New Grove*, 1980), and wrote a seminal book, *The Music of Liszt* (1954). He founded the Liszt Society along with his friends Constant Lambert, William Walton, Sacheverell Sitwell, and others, and was its first honorary secretary (1950–62). Other books included *Twentieth Century Counterpoint* (1954), *Ballet Music* (1958), and *20th Century Composers: Britain, Scandinavia and the Netherlands* (1972). He also edited Schoenberg's *Structural Functions of Harmony* (1977), and translated Josef Rufer's textbook on twelve-note composition (1954) and a selection of Berlioz's letters (1966).

Searle's compositions show the influence of Liszt, Webern, and Schoenberg. This radical continental outlook encouraged a style not then fashionable in Britain, and Searle remained an unfashionable though vigorous, independent, and prolific composer. The neglect of his large output of colourful, powerfully emotional works, written in strongly personal idiom and with a predilection for unusual forms, never seemed to daunt him. *Night Music* (for Webern's sixtieth birthday, 1943) closely approached twelve-note technique. His first truly serial work, *Intermezzo for 11 Instruments* (1946), was written in memory of Webern. Almost all his subsequent compositions use the twelve-note method. His finesse in instrumental detail

Humphrey Searle (1915–1982), by Michael Ayrton, 1965

and subtle nuance is the legacy of Webern; his natural Romanticism has affinities with the Romantic Schoenberg; his fascination with Liszt is seen in the metamorphosis of themes in his piano sonata (1951).

A powerful trilogy for speakers, chorus, and orchestra (1949–51) set texts by Edith Sitwell and, as centrepiece, *The Riverrun* by James Joyce. Between 1953 and 1964 Searle produced five symphonies, the piano concerto no. 2, three ballets, and two operas: *The Diary of a Madman* (after Gogol; premièred at the Berlin festival of 1958 and awarded the UNESCO radio critics' prize) and *The Photo of the Colonel* (1964, after Ionesco). He also wrote much other chamber, orchestral, vocal, and incidental music. A BBC production, *The Foundling*, for which he wrote the music, won the Italia prize. His final opera was *Hamlet* (Hamburg, 1968; Covent Garden, London, 1969). Many of these works richly deserve revival. In 1949 Searle married Margaret Gillen (Lesley; 1904–1957), daughter of John Gray, a cartage contractor. In 1960, three years after her death, he married an actress, Fiona Elizabeth Anne (*b.* 1933), daughter of John Wilfred Nicholson CIE, a forest officer in the service of the Indian government who had studied under Sir William Schlich. There were no children of either marriage.

A shy man, Searle displayed an integrity and a cosmopolitan outlook which won respect among his students. He was composer in residence at Stanford University, California (1964–5); professor of composition at the Royal College of Music from 1965; guest composer at the Aspen Music Festival, Colorado (1967); and guest professor at the Staatliche Hochschule für Musik, Karlsruhe (1968–72), and at the University of Southern California, Los Angeles (1976–7).

Searle's deep interest in the spiritual nature of humankind is reflected in his later choral–orchestral works: *Jerusalem*, *Kubla Khan*, *Dr Faustus*, and *Oresteia*. Colour and his love of adventure permeate orchestral works like *Labyrinth* (1971) and *Tamesis* (1979). His humour is seen in splendid settings of Edward Lear's *The Owl and the Pussy Cat* and T. S. Eliot's 'Skimbleshanks the Railway Cat'. For all his reserve and professional detachment he loved conviviality, and the memoirs (as yet unpublished) of this fine writer and friend of Cecil Gray, Dylan Thomas, Constant Lambert, and the Sitwells are a fascinating record of his times.

Searle was appointed CBE in 1968; honorary FRCM in 1969; and an honorary professorial fellow, University College of Wales, Aberystwyth, in 1977. Searle died on 12 May 1982 in London and was cremated at Golders Green crematorium five days later. DEREK WATSON

Sources personal knowledge (2004) • private information (1990) • C. Mason and H. Cole, 'Searle, Humphrey', *New Grove* • *The Times* (13 May 1982) • *CGPLA Eng. & Wales* (1982) • b. cert.

Archives BL, corresp. and musical MSS, Add. MSS 71721–71862 | FILM BFI NFTVA, documentary footage | SOUND BBC WAC • BL NSA, current affairs recordings • BL NSA, oral history interview • BL NSA, performance recording • BL NSA, 'Tribute to Humphrey Searle', 29 June 1982, NP6235BW / TR1 C1

Likenesses E. Auerbach, photograph, *c.*1950, Hult. Arch. • E. Auerbach, photograph, 1955, Hult. Arch. • M. Ayrton, pencil drawing, 1965, NPG [*see illus.*]

Wealth at death £14,235: probate, 4 Nov 1982, *CGPLA Eng. & Wales*

Searle, January. *See* Phillips, George Searle (1816–1889).

Searle, John (*d.* 1746), gardener, is of unknown parentage; he was literate but relatively uneducated. About 1724 he became the gardener at Alexander Pope's villa in Twickenham, a position he held until Pope's death in 1744. Searle married Sarah Scott (*b.* 1692/3) on 18 August 1729 at St Anne's, Soho; three children born to them between 1730 and 1737 were baptized at St Mary the Virgin Church, Twickenham. Sarah Searle became Pope's housekeeper.

Pope's letters refer affectionately to Searle as an oracle of pineapples and a hortulan philosopher. He is famously the trusty porter at the opening of Pope's *Epistle to Arbuthnot* (1735). In his will Pope made Searle executor of his legacy to the poor of Twickenham, and left him £100 over and above a year's wages to himself and his wife.

Searle contributed plans of the garden and grotto and a perspective view of the grotto to a little miscellany, *A Plan of Mr. Pope's Garden* (1745). A description of the grotto by the anonymous compiler of this volume (probably Robert Dodsley, who published it) may be based on information from Searle, who regularly guided garden visitors.

During Pope's lifetime Searle worked occasionally for Ralph Allen: he was in Allen's employ after Pope's death and named Allen as a trustee in his will, but his own death (of smallpox) was at Twickenham, where he was buried at St Mary the Virgin Church on 21 February 1746. His wife, Sarah, was alive in 1783, aged ninety.

JAMES SAMBROOK

Sources J. Serle, *A plan of Mr. Pope's garden* (1982) [with introduction by M. Brownell, Augustan Reprint Society no. 211] • *The correspondence of Alexander Pope*, ed. G. Sherburn, 4 (1956) • W. K. Wimsatt, *Portraits of Alexander Pope* (1965), 120 • P. Martin, *Pursuing innocent pleasures: the gardening world of Alexander Pope* (1984) • A. J. Sambrook, 'The shape and size of Pope's garden', *Eighteenth-Century Studies*, 5 (1971–2), 450–55 • M. Mack, *The garden and the city* (1969), appx D • will, LMA, X7416, 1093–1095 • *IGI* • *St James's Chronicle* (13 Dec 1783) • parish register, Twickenham, St Mary the Virgin, 1730–37 [baptism] • parish register, Twickenham, St Mary the Virgin, 21 Feb 1746 [burial]

Searle, Thomas (1777–1849), naval officer, son of James Searle of Staddlescombe, Devon, was born in Devon on 29 May 1777. He entered the navy in November 1789; served on the Mediterranean, home, and Newfoundland stations; and in 1796 was in the *Royal George*, flagship of Lord Bridport, by whose interest he was made lieutenant, on 19 August, in the fireship *Incendiary*. In November 1796 he married, at an early age, Ann, daughter of Joseph Maddock of Plymouth Dock and Tamerton Foliot, Devon. They had a large family: eight daughters survived their father.

In 1797 Searle was in the *Prince*, flagship of Sir Roger Curtis; in 1798 he was in the frigate *Nemesis*, on the North American station; and in 1799 he commanded the cutter *Courier* (12 guns) in the North Sea. On 22 November 1799 he was made commander on the recommendation of Lord Duncan, who was greatly pleased with his activity during the year, and especially with his gallant capture of a large French privateer on 23 November. From June 1800 to October 1802 he was employed in the transport service, and from July 1803 to April 1804 with the Portsmouth division of sea fencibles. From 1804 to 1806 he commanded various small vessels off Boulogne and the north coast of France, and in December 1806 was appointed to the brig *Grasshopper* (18 guns) for service in the Mediterranean. His service in the *Grasshopper* was marked, even in that age, 'as dashing in the extreme'. On 11 December 1807, off Cape Palos, he engaged a heavily armed Spanish brig of war with two settees (Mediterranean lateen-sailed vessels) in company; he captured the brig and drove the settees to seek safety in flight. Lord Collingwood officially reported the affair as 'an instance of the zeal and enterprise which marked Searle's general conduct' (O'Byrne, *Naval biog. dict.*). On 4 April 1808, in company with the frigates *Alceste* and *Mercury*, he assisted in destroying or capturing a convoy of merchant vessels at Rota, near Cadiz, after dispersing or sinking the gunboats that escorted them, and silencing the batteries of Rota, which protected them. This last service was performed by the brig alone

> by the extraordinary gallantry and good conduct of Captain Searle, who kept in upon the shoal to the southward of the town so near as to drive the enemy from their guns with grape from his carronades, and at the same time kept in check a division of the gunboats that had come out from Cadiz to assist the others engaged by the *Alceste* and *Mercury*. It was a general cry in both ships: 'Only look how nobly the brig behaves'. (Murray Maxwell to the secretary of the Admiralty, *LondG*, 23–26 April 1808, 570)

Following Maxwell's letter Searle was advanced to post rank on 25 April 1808, though the promotion did not reach him until July. Meanwhile, on 23 April, in company with the brig *Rapid* on the south coast of Portugal, he fell in with two richly laden Spanish vessels from South America, under convoy of four gunboats. The merchant ships ran in under the batteries of Faeroe, by which they were protected. However, the brigs, having captured two of the gunboats, driven the other two on shore, and silenced the batteries, brought off the ships which were carrying cargoes of the value of £60,000.

On leaving the *Grasshopper*, Searle was presented by the crew with an 80 guinea sword and, shortly after, by Lloyd's with a piece of plate worth 100 guineas. In 1809 he commanded the *Frederickstein* (32 guns) in the Mediterranean, in 1810–11 the *Elizabeth* (74 guns) in the North Sea and at Lisbon, and in 1811–12 the frigate *Druid* in the Mediterranean. On 4 June 1815 he was made a CB.

From 1818 to 1821 he commanded the frigate *Hyperion* (42 guns) in the channel (in attendance on George IV) and in a voyage to South America, from which he brought back specie worth half a million sterling. From 1836 to 1839 he was captain of the *Victory* (104 guns), at that time guardship at Portsmouth; and on 9 November 1847 he was promoted rear-admiral. He died at his home, Kingston House, Portsea, Hampshire, on 18 March 1849 and was buried at the garrison chapel in Portsmouth. Searle, a handsome, strongly built man of middle height, with black hair and dark complexion, had a remarkable career, made by exceptional skill and courage.

J. K. LAUGHTON, *rev.* ANDREW LAMBERT

Sources D. Syrett and R. L. DiNardo, *The commissioned sea officers of the Royal Navy, 1660–1815*, rev. edn, Occasional Publications of the Navy RS, 1 (1994) • O'Byrne, *Naval biog. dict.* • J. Marshall, *Royal naval biography*, suppl. 1 (1827), 309 • W. James, *The naval history of Great Britain, from the declaration of war by France, in February 1793, to the accession of George IV, in January 1820*, [2nd edn], 6 vols. (1826), vol. 2, pp. 379–80, 382, 413–14; vol. 4, pp. 270–71, 326, 329–30 • private information (1897) • P. Mackesy, *The war in the Mediterranean, 1803–1810* (1957)

Sears, Isaac (*c.*1730–1786), revolutionary politician in America, was born in New England to Joshua Sears, an oyster fisherman, and Mary, *née* Thatcher. Different sources list the Cape Cod towns of West Brewster and Harwich, Massachusetts, as well as both Norwalk and Norwich, Connecticut, as his place of birth. His parents were Congregationalists of long standing but in adult life Sears embraced Anglicanism and joined the élite Trinity Church in New York city.

Whatever the place of his birth or the scene of his childhood Sears was identified with New York city for most of his adult life; he moved there on his own late in his youth. He went to sea in the intercolonial coasting trade and rose rapidly to command of his own vessel. He turned to privateering during the Seven Years' War and he acquired enough capital from his voyages to establish himself as a merchant at the war's end. Despite the trading depression that set in with the cessation of war contracts Sears prospered. Most of his business was coastal and with the West Indies but he did undertake trade across the Atlantic to Britain. He was starting to rise in the world.

Sears also married. His bride was Sarah Drake, whose father ran a waterfront tavern frequented by seafarers and shore workers. Despite his growing wealth these people formed Sears's natural milieu and provided the base for the political career that he was about to begin; unquestionably this drew on his cultivation of latent class tensions within New York society. His wartime success notwithstanding Sears remained a parvenu, with no entry to New York's merchant élite. He was distinguished enough after the war to merit a title but this was captain, to reflect his command at sea, rather than the more honorific 'Mr' or 'Gent'. In this regard he was very much like Alexander McDougall, who also moved from command of a privateer to radical leadership via mercantile trade.

Sears allied himself in New York's turbulent, faction-riven politics with the Livingston family—Hudson Valley landlords who controlled the provincial assembly and who gave a lead in resisting the Stamp Act in 1765. Sears may have been their liaison with street politics; New York saw disturbance after disturbance in the winter of 1765–6 and the observant army captain John Montresor credited him with being able to raise a mob when he chose, for which he was dubbed King Sears.

Between 1765 and 1775 Sears moved from organizing sporadic uprisings to helping to organize a revolutionary movement. He was a founder of the Sons of Liberty, the impromptu network of militant writers and street leaders who turned high-principled opposition to British policies into the direct resistance that made those policies impossible to enforce. One of their first successes was preventing the distribution of stamps and stamped paper in November 1765 by forcing the resignation of the colony's stamp distributor. New York Sons of Liberty also forced Maryland's distributor to resign when he passed through their province. Sears personally joined the team that negotiated agreements between the Sons in New York and similar groups elsewhere at the end of 1765.

Sears continued to be active in opposition to the Townshend taxes and the New York Restraining Act (1767) but radical politics fell into a lull when Townshend's measures were repealed in 1770. None the less Sears helped with the establishment of a Committee of Mechanics in 1773, just before the destruction at Boston of East India Company tea. He joined the committees of Fifty-One, Sixty, and One Hundred men that led New York resistance to British policy during the next two years. He personally led the crowd that opened the city arsenal and seized firearms after fighting broke out in Massachusetts in April 1775.

Sears then left for Connecticut, which he used as a base for raids against loyalists, both in New York city and on Long Island. In 1776, when the British abandoned Boston but took control of New York, he settled in the Massachusetts capital. He spent the war years there, organizing privateering voyages and trading supplies to the American forces. He also involved himself in efforts to control spiralling wartime inflation by the sort of street politics that had served so well in resisting Britain after 1765. Price controls proved useless, however, and at the end of the war Sears himself was a rich man. He returned to New York late in 1783 and proudly occupied the pew in Trinity Church that had belonged to a prominent loyalist, now exiled. He was elected to the state legislature in 1784. His election signalled the ascendancy of people who never could have occupied high office in the colonial order; it also promised continuing bitterness between the victorious revolutionaries and the former loyalists. He served in the seventh legislative session, which took up the task of organizing the peace in 1784, but not in its successor.

Late in 1785 New York city voters elected Sears to the legislature again, after a partisan battle between men of his sort and people of more conservative mind. By that time, however, he had apparently lost interest in politics and was returning to thoughts of commerce. He helped to organize the voyage of the *Empress of China*, the first New York vessel to engage in direct oriental trade, and he joined the ship's company himself. It proved to be his final adventure. He died on the *Empress of China* on 28 October 1786, of an unspecified disease that he had contracted at sea. He was interred near Canton (Guangzhou).

Sears's life exemplifies a major dimension of the American revolutionary story. Ambitious even before the war of independence he found in the movement the opportunity for considerable fame, for wealth, and for political power. The coming to prominence of his kind of person marked a major transformation in American public life. Unquestionably their emergence and ascendancy bothered others, who saw them as dangerous, irresponsible demagogues. Driving such men from power was one reason for the counter-movement that led to the United States constitution in 1787. Sears, however, was dead by then. Even had he been alive he probably would not have been drinking with seafarers and stevedores in waterfront taverns. EDWARD COUNTRYMAN

Sources C. L. Becker, *The history of political parties in the province of New York, 1760–1776* (1909) • R. J. Christen, '"King Sears": politician and patriot in a decade of revolution', PhD diss., Columbia University, 1968 • E. Countryman, *A people in revolution: the American revolution and political society in New York, 1760–1790* (1981) • P. Maier, 'Isaac Sears and the business of revolution', in P. Maier, *The old revolutionaries: political lives in the age of Samuel Adams* (1980)

Sears, John George (1870–1916), shoe manufacturer and retailer, was born on 6 February 1870 in Northampton, the eldest child of James Sears, leather seller and shoe manufacturer, and Amelia (*née* Cushion), both of Northampton. After attending a local elementary school Sears was apprenticed in the shoe trade, working for the Manfield company in Northampton. In 1891 he began a business with his younger brother William Thomas Sears, under the name J. Sears & Co. Production was initially small-scale with the company able to take outwork for the strike-bound Manfields during the great shoe dispute of

1895. A year later, with his business prospering, Sears married Caroline Wooding, of Northampton, with whom he had one daughter and two sons.

The company soon began to make a bigger mark. According to an obituarist,

> it was not alone in the manufacture of boots and shoes that Mr. Sears won his way. … He was the pioneer of the modern multiple business which caters for the middle class man and makes specialities lines at fixed prices. (*Northampton Daily Chronicle*, 19 Feb 1916)

In 1897 Sears opened his first branch shop, and in 1900 a branch in Fleet Street, London. By 1912 the company had eighty branches, forty-seven of which were in the London area. Production was continually expanded with moves to bigger works and then extensions to a purpose-built factory. In January 1912 the company was floated as a public company under the name J. Sears & Co. (Trueform Boot Company) Ltd. In 1913 it took over another local manufacturing company run by Frank Panther who joined the Sears board. The war brought further prosperity from government orders and when Sears died the company was employing some 1000 workers in production and 1000 in retailing.

Sears was renowned for his capacity for work, and some felt that overwork contributed to his early death at the age of forty-six. However, the company success was the result of a team effort, including that of his brother, Frank Panther, and others, and for this reason the firm continued to prosper after his death. Sears's own flair lay in the retailing side, especially in selecting sites for high-street shops that would prove attractive to middle-class customers, and in overseeing the development of the retailing strategy.

It was expected that local manufacturers would play a role in the regulation of the shoe industry, and Sears served on the clicking arbitration board. In 1913 he also became president of the Northampton Shoe Manufacturers Association. However, the ill health that was to dog his last years and lead to his early death forced him to step down. This perhaps also prevented him from playing a more prominent political role. He was a Liberal in politics but refused to stand for local office. Like other manufacturers he supported local philanthropic causes. His ill health was such that he finally withdrew from real influence on the business in the last year of his life.

During his lifetime Sears rose from being a humble 'clicker' (or leather cutter) in the shoe industry to the position of a great manufacturer and retailer. As he became more prominent, his lifestyle inevitably changed. He had been born into a Congregationalist family, but later switched to the Church of England. In 1913–14 he bought and extended Collingtree Grange in Northamptonshire, the former estate of a prominent local brewer, and there he spent his last years collecting books and works of art, and taking an interest in breeding pedigree cattle. He was a prominent mason and served as a provincial grand master.

Sears died on 19 February 1916 at Collingtree Grange, survived by his wife; he was buried at St Columba's Church, Collingtree, on 23 February. The firm which he and his brother founded was to experience dramatic growth in the early twentieth century. It eventually became Sears plc, a conglomerate which played a major role in the retailing of shoes and clothing in the UK in the second half of the twentieth century.

MICHAEL HAYNES

Sources *Northampton Daily Chronicle* (19 Feb 1916) • *Northampton Daily Chronicle* (24 Feb 1916) • *Northampton Daily Echo* (19 Feb 1916) • *Shoe Trades Journal* (25 Feb 1916) • *Shoe and Leather Record* (25 Feb 1916) • *Illustrated biographic directory of British shoe and leather traders* (c.1916–c.1919) • K. Brooker, 'Sears, John George', *DBB* • W. E. Burnham, 'A century of shoemaking, 1844–1944', Northampton Public Library • J. Swan, 'Sears plc', *International directory of business histories*, 5 (1992), 177–9 • A. V. Eason, *'Saint Crispin's men', a history of Northamptonshire's shoemakers* (1994) • d. cert.

Likenesses photograph, repro. in *Northampton Daily Chronicle* (19 Feb 1916) • photograph (as a young man), repro. in Eason, *'Saint Crispin's men'*

Wealth at death £400,718 17s. 4d.: probate, 26 April 1916, *CGPLA Eng. & Wales*

Season, Henry (1693–1775), almanac writer and medical practitioner, was born on 23 January 1693, in the village of Broomham (now Bromham), near Chippenham in Wiltshire. His mother died in childbirth, and he was raised by his maternal grandmother, who also provided his early education. By the age of five he was reading the Bible, but he was not able to enter into full-time education, being obliged to earn a living early on. By the age of eleven he was employed in 'a mechanick business' (*Speculum Anni*, 1734, A2r), spending his spare time reading in divinity, history, and philosophy, and writing poetry. At seventeen he joined his father in London for four months, working as an assistant funeral undertaker. However, he disliked metropolitan life and soon returned to settle in Bones Lane, Broomham. By now, encouraged by the local squire, John Nicholson, he was studying physic and astronomy, to which he then added astrology.

Season described himself as a 'licenced Physician and surgeon' (*Speculum Anni*, 1751, title-page). It seems that about 1721 he agreed (though not without initial misgivings) to take over from the deceased local physician. He found that it suited him, and maintained for the rest of his life an evidently successful medical practice which included the sale of various powders, tinctures, and remedies. For purposes of both diagnosis and prescription, he availed himself of the ancient tradition of medical, herbal, and humoral astrology, thus integrating his studies of astronomy and cosmology with those of physic. Of more recent authorities, he drew some comfort and sanction from the theories of Richard Mead concerning planetary effects, via the earth's atmosphere, on disease.

Season combined his medical practice with that of straightforward judicial astrologer, giving astral advice on personal problems. In that role he was respected and feared by the village commoners as a cunning- or wiseman, or 'conjurer'—an appellation that irritated Season, who saw his astrology as perfectly consistent with Anglican Christianity and reason. While admitting that the superstition of both some astrologers and their clients had resulted in casting magic spells and the like—while many others 'do ridicule an Art they are entirely ignorant of'—he stoutly maintained that 'The ancient Astrology is a Branch of natural Philosophy, no way inconsistent or impugned by Scripture' (*Speculum Anni*, 1774, C2r–3r). He thus rejected the more openly divinatory and inexplicable practices such as elections (choosing the most propitious time to begin an enterprise) and horary judgements (answering a query on the basis of the planetary positions at the time of its asking, or reception by the astrologer), and derided overly precise predictions as crude and illegitimate. Thanks to such degeneracy, he complained, astrologers now were 'scarce ever half so much rewarded or regarded as a French Cook, Italian Songster, or even an English Dapper-witted Dancing-master' (*Speculum Anni*, 1751, A2).

In 1732 Season was offered the editorship of an annual almanac, hitherto produced by Thomas Lane, called *Speculum Anni*. He accepted, and from his first issue (for 1733) until his last (for 1774) stamped his own distinctive personality on a frequently bland and repetitive medium in a way that is the reason why he still has, and deserves, our attention. It certainly seems to have received that of his contemporaries, including the back-handed compliment of an abusive attack on 'Nostradamus Season', as 'an illiterate scurrilous Quack', in the 1756 edition of the anti-astrological almanac *Poor Robin*.

The typical *Speculum Anni* consisted principally of a rather idiosyncratic chronology, from ancient times until the present; an 'Enigma', challenging readers for its resolution, with successful answers to be carried the next year; a section in which the astronomical and astrological phenomena for each day of the year were presented, and their implications, whether social or natural, briefly discussed; and a few pages devoted to a topic of Season's choice. The whole was leavened with his forceful reflections and assertions. In religion, he was vigorously Anglican. This adherence entailed no contradiction with his astrology: 'All Eclipses, great Conjunctions, Comets and Configurations of Planets, are all Oracles of Divine Providence; which, whosoever despiseth, contemneth the Admonitions of God', he wrote (*Speculum Anni*, 1774, C3r). His Anglicanism also overlapped with a firm conviction of English national superiority. He thus lashed out at papists, Jews, and atheists as corrupting foreign influences, and bewailed the corruption of morals resulting from the decline in attendance at church and observation of the Sabbath.

Season also repeatedly denounced the vices of smoking, snuff, and gambling, and especially the availability of cheap liquor. This low opinion of people's natural probity applied equally to their intelligence. On non-compliers with the new-style calendar, for example, who felt that they were being cheated of eleven days, Season remarked contemptuously that 'some such Apes we have in my own Parish, who are altogether incorrigible, and whose Understanding is scarce a degree above that of a Hottentot' (*Speculum Anni*, 1761, 2–3). (His opinion of other races may also be inferred.)

Nevertheless, Season could not afford entirely to do without the rural poor. Indeed, in one year, in an effort to render his almanac more readily comprehensible to his semi-literate readers, he replaced the symbols of moon's signs with drawings of the corresponding parts of the body (the head for Aries, and so on). His contempt coexisted, however paradoxically, with a genuine concern for their welfare, just as his patriotism was of the progressive kind. His radical politics, evident in his constant urging of reforms to help the common people and criticizing the government for its corruption, was a dominant theme in his almanac. He was a friend of the earl of Shelburne, the radical whig leader, and of Sir Edward Holt, MP for Chippenham. He extolled Shelburne, Pitt, and especially John Wilkes for championing English liberty and justice.

Season died on 10 November 1775. There is a plaque on the wall of the parish church of St Nicholas, Bromham, commemorating him. Thomas Wright, in Leicestershire, took over editing the *Speculum Anni* with the issue of 1775, but failed to maintain its interest. PATRICK CURRY

Sources *Speculum Anni* (1773) · *Speculum Anni* (1774) · B. S. Capp, *Astrology and the popular press: English almanacs, 1500–1800* (1979) · P. Curry, *Prophecy and power: astrology in early modern England* (1989), 126–7 · commemorative plaque, St Nicholas's Church, Bromham, Wiltshire · *Poor Robin* (1756)

Seaton. For this title name *see* Colborne, John, first Baron Seaton (1778–1863).

Seaton, Edward Cator (1815–1880), public health administrator, was born at Rochester, Kent, the son of an ex-naval surgeon. His early medical career followed the classic pattern of the ambitious young medical practitioner. He received his initial medical training from his father, took his MD at Edinburgh University in 1837, and briefly studied in Paris. He then joined his father in practice in Rochester, supplementing his income by working as a poor-law surgeon in the north Aylesford area. In 1841 he purchased a small practice and moved to Sloane Street, London. In addition to his private practice Seaton held posts at the Chelsea, Brompton, and Belgrave dispensaries. He was active in a number of medical societies and was a founding member of both the Western Medical Society and, in 1850, the Epidemiological Society; later he held the president's post in each. He was also a member of the London Pathological Society.

Seaton owed his career in public health to his membership of the Epidemiological Society, then the foremost forum for the discussion of public health matters; its members acted as *ex officio* advisers to government. In 1850 Seaton was appointed secretary to its committee on smallpox and vaccination. The committee's report was drawn up by Seaton and presented to parliament in 1852 (*Parl. papers*, 1852–3, 101, no. 434, and 1854–5, 45, no. 88). It recommended that voluntary vaccination be replaced with a compulsory system. The report proved highly influential, its appearance coinciding with the introduction of a bill to make vaccination compulsory; the report was consequently greeted as timely expert advice on the subject. A number of its suggestions were subsequently incorporated into the Compulsory Vaccination Act of 1853.

The report established Seaton as an authority on vaccination and began his lifelong collaboration with John Simon, a fellow member of the Epidemiological Society and medical officer to the General Board of Health and later to the privy council. Both men were eager to expand the government's role in public health and to bring public health under expert supervision. Seaton's career mirrored the development of this central government role. In 1858 Seaton was appointed as one of the first medical staff at the privy council. As a temporary inspector (paid 5 guineas per day) Seaton investigated rates of vaccination in London. The following year this local study was expanded and it became a national survey, providing Seaton with sufficient work to allow him to give up private practice. The study concluded that much public vaccination practice was incompetent—a finding used to justify the creation of a permanent inspectorate to supervise the work of vaccinators. Seaton was appointed as one of the four inspectors and given a salary. Over the next few years, in addition to his routine inspection work, he produced a *Handbook of Vaccination* (1868) as well as reports on the viability of calf-lymph (1870) and on the 1871–3 smallpox epidemic (1875). He was probably involved in drafting the Vaccination Bill of 1871, and he also conducted inspections into the sanitary state of various towns and cities. With the dissolution of the medical office of the privy council in 1871, Seaton moved to the Local Government Board and became assistant medical officer under Simon. In June 1876 he succeeded Simon as medical officer. Seaton was noted for his administrative abilities—his meticulous eye for detail, his capacity for work, and his sound judgement—qualities which balanced John Simon's more visionary character.

Seaton's career brought professional honours and increasing wealth. In 1872 he was made a fellow of the Royal College of Physicians. He moved to Surbiton in 1862 and to Gordon Square, London, in 1877. Seaton was the father of four sons and four daughters, one of whom became the second wife of Sir George Buchanan (1831–1895). Seaton became ill in 1878 and was greatly affected by the death of his favourite son in the same year. He suffered a stroke in late 1879, and died at his son-in-law's house, 48 Ladbroke Grove, Notting Hill, London, on 21 January 1880; he was buried at Kensal Green cemetery.

DEBORAH BRUNTON

Sources *Medical Times and Gazette* (31 Jan 1880), 137–8 • *BMJ* (31 Jan 1880), 188 • *BMJ* (24 Jan 1880), 140 • *Transactions of the Epidemiological Society*, 4 (1875–80), 430–31 • Munk, *Roll* • *Medical Register* (1864–80) • course file on medical graduates, U. Edin. L., special collections division • R. Lambert, *Sir John Simon, 1816–1904, and English social administration* (1963) • *DNB* • *The Lancet* (31 Jan 1880), 188–9 • d. cert.

Wealth at death under £9000: probate, 9 March 1880, *CGPLA Eng. & Wales*

Seaton, John Thomas. *See* Seton, John Thomas (*b. c.*1735, *d.* in or after 1806).

Seaton, Roger of (*c.*1230–*c.*1280), justice, belonged to a family that took its name from Seaton in Rutland. The fact that he is first recorded as an attorney *c.*1253 suggests that he was born about 1230, possibly at Seaton. Later evidence suggests that he may have studied canon law at Oxford; by 1258 he was styled *magister*. By 1260 he was utilizing his knowledge of canon law in service as the official and commissary-general of Walter of Kirkham, bishop of Durham (*d.* 1260), in all matters delegated to the bishop by the Holy See. He was also in the service of Kirkham's successor, Robert of Stichill (*d.* 1274). He may have been his chancellor, and was later one of his executors.

In 1268, in what looks like a major change of career, Seaton switched from a world where his training in canon law was of immediate practical use to one where it was only of limited relevance, by entering the king's service as one of the justices of the common-law courts. His first period as a justice of the common bench started in Hilary term 1268. He left the court after Hilary term 1271 to lead an eyre circuit that visited the counties of south-eastern and eastern England. Although the circuit was brought to a premature end in mid-November 1272, with the death of Henry III, Seaton was immediately reappointed to the common bench, and on the death of Gilbert of Preston became the court's chief justice as from the beginning of Hilary term 1274. He served as chief justice of the court until the end of Trinity term 1278. The few surviving law reports from this period indicate that what he said was thought worth recording, but provide too little material to allow any real estimate of his professional abilities. During this period Seaton also acted as the justice of an assize circuit in 1273–4 and headed the eyres held in Middlesex in 1274 and in London and in Bedfordshire in 1276. He was also nominal sheriff of Northamptonshire from late 1272 to October 1274, and gave a speech on the king's behalf to the autumn parliament of 1275, explaining the king's need for money.

It was probably soon after his retirement from the common bench that Seaton suffered a stroke. He entered the Augustinian house at Thornton in Lincolnshire in 1279, having already appointed executors who were allowed to collect his debts and pay his debtors as though he were dead. They included Master Oliver Sutton, later bishop of Lincoln, who is known to have studied canon and civil law at Oxford, and Master Nicholas of Higham who may also have studied at Oxford. Seaton probably died not long after his entry into Thornton; his brother, Richard of Seaton, was his heir.

Roger of Seaton held a number of valuable ecclesiastical livings, many of which he seems to have held simultaneously. One of his earliest livings was at Wicken in Northamptonshire to which he was presented by John Fitzalan of Wolverton, who seems to have been an early patron. He also held the living of Seaton and the Northamptonshire churches of Maidwell and Earls Barton, the Yorkshire church of Rowley, the Durham church of Egglescliffe, the Cambridgeshire church of Over, and the Sussex church of Broadwater. In addition he had prebends in York Minster and Lincoln Cathedral, and was master of the hospital of Sherburn, co. Durham.

PAUL BRAND

Sources P. A. Brand, *The earliest English law reports*, 1, SeldS, 111 (1995), cxxv–cxlii

Seaton, Thomas (1684–1741), Church of England clergyman and religious writer, was born at Stamford, Lincolnshire. He was probably the Thomas Seaton who was baptized there on 2 October 1684, the son of John and Dorothy Seaton. He was admitted a sizar of Clare College, Cambridge, on 6 May 1701, under the tuition of Mr Clarke, bedel of the university. He graduated BA in 1705; he was elected a fellow of his college in the following year, and proceeded MA in 1708. Having been ordained deacon on 9 March 1707 and priest on 29 September 1709 he was appointed chaplain to Daniel Finch, second earl of Nottingham. He became vicar of Madingley, Cambridgeshire, in 1713 and was presented, by Nottingham, to the vicarage of Ravenstone, Buckinghamshire, on 9 November 1721, whereupon he resigned his fellowship.

By his will Seaton bequeathed his estate at Kislingbury, Northamptonshire, to the University of Cambridge, on condition that out of the rents a prize should be annually awarded to a master of arts of that university who had composed the best poem in English on the attributes of the supreme being or some other sacred subject. The prize would be judged by the vice-chancellor, the master of Clare College, and the professor of Greek. Publication of the winning poem has continued since the first was printed, in 1750, apart from 1766, 1769, and 1771. Many of these compositions are collected in *Musae Seatonianæ*.

Seaton published a number of religious writings. He contributed to the theological controversy provoked by William Whiston's heterodox views on the Trinity and prophecies, publishing his first work, *The Divinity of our Saviour Proved*, in 1719. He continued his defence of orthodoxy in *The defects of the objections against the New Testament application of the prophecies in the Old, exposed* (1726) and *A Compendious View of the Grounds of Religion, both Natural and Revealed* (1729). His other works addressed moral and devotional issues; in *The Conduct of Servants in Great Families* (1720), dedicated to his patron, Nottingham, he advised householders to hold family prayers and closely supervise the moral conduct of their servants.

Seaton, who was unmarried, died on 18 August 1741 at Ravenstone, where he was buried on 23 August. A large tombstone with a Latin inscription was erected to his memory in the churchyard.

Thompson Cooper, *rev.* S. J. Skedd

Sources Venn, *Alum. Cant.* • will, PRO, PROB 11/713, sig. 280 • E. Carter, *The history of the University of Cambridge* (1753) • C. H. Cooper and J. W. Cooper, *Annals of Cambridge*, 5 vols. (1842–1908), vol. 4, p. 243 • *Camden's Britannia*, ed. R. Gough, 3 vols. (1789), vol. 2, p. 177 • *N&Q*, 3rd ser., 2 (1862), 506 • *IGI*

Seaton, Sir Thomas (*bap.* 1806, *d.* 1876), army officer in the East India Company, was baptized on 28 May 1806, the eldest son of John Fox Seaton of Pontefract and his wife, Anne. In 1822 he obtained a cadetship in the East India Company's service, and on 4 February 1823 he was commissioned as ensign in the 10th Bengal native infantry. In July he was transferred to the 2nd battalion of the 17th native infantry, stationed at Ludhiana in the Punjab. This battalion was soon afterwards converted into the 35th Bengal native infantry. He served with the 1st battalion (which had become the 34th) from October 1824 until July 1825, then returned to the 35th, and remained in it until 1857. His commission as lieutenant was dated 1 May 1824. He took part in the siege of Bharatpur, and was afterwards stationed at Meerut and in the Lower Provinces, where, at Barrackpore on 21 August 1831, he married Caroline, fourth daughter of J. Corfield of Knowle Lodge, Taunton, Somerset. On 2 April 1834 he was promoted captain. In 1836, his wife having died on 14 November 1835, he went to England on furlough for three years. He married, on 27 July 1838 at Edinburgh, Elizabeth, daughter of John Harriman of Whitehaven, Cumberland. She died on 12 November 1872.

Seaton returned to India in 1839. His regiment was serving in the First Anglo-Afghan War, and he hastened to join it. After crossing with a convoy the Shikarpur Desert to Bagh in the intense heat of June, he rejoined his regiment at Kabul on 8 September 1839. He remained there two years, except for a short expedition to Bamian. In October 1841, when the regiment was about to return to India as part of Sale's brigade, the Afghan rising erupted. The brigade fought through the Khurd Kabul Pass, and to Jalalabad, reaching it on 12 November, then held it.

During the defence of Jalalabad Seaton showed his resourcefulness. Sent to destroy an outlying fort which might give cover to the enemy, he diverted a stream to it, and so demolished it. In the first two months of the defence the wine and spirits were all consumed, but Seaton made a still with some washermen's pots and a matchlock barrel, and supplied his mess with spirits as long as there was sugar left. After the siege he was made CB. He was given the local rank of major on 4 October 1842.

From 1842 to 1851 Seaton was brigade-major at Agra. In November 1852 he was promoted major, and in June 1854 brevet lieutenant-colonel. After three years' furlough in England he took command of his regiment at Sialkot on 31 January 1855. In May 1857 he went to Simla on account of his health, but within a week he was sent to Ambala to take command of the 60th native infantry. On 10 June the regiment mutinied, drove away its officers, and marched to join the mutineers in Delhi. The officers went to the British camp, where there was much surprise at their safe arrival.

Seaton served as a field officer during the earlier part of the siege. On 23 July he was dangerously wounded, and after the fall of Delhi he was sent up to Simla. In November he was again fit for duty, and was made lieutenant-colonel of the 1st Bengal (European) fusiliers, his commission dated 27 June. He was promoted brevet colonel on 13 October. With a force of 2300 men, including his own regiment, he escorted a large convoy from Delhi through the Doab, to join the commander-in-chief. He fought the mutineers near Bibrahan, at Patiali, and at Mainpuri, defeating them by skilful tactics with little loss.

Seaton joined Sir Colin Campbell at Fatehgarh on 7 January 1858, and was left in command there as brigadier during the siege of Lucknow. He had only a small force, but finding that the mutineers were gathering in large numbers in the neighbourhood, he marched out on the night of 6 April, attacked a force of them at Kanker, and routed them, capturing their guns and baggage, so that the main road to the north-west was no longer in danger.

In June Seaton was sent to Shahjahanpur, and on 8 October he surprised and defeated the Oudh mutineers at Buragaon. In the following spring, as the fighting was at an end, his brigade was broken up.

In March 1858 he was made KCB, and in June 1859 he retired with the rank of major-general. He published his two-volume autobiography, *From Cadet to Colonel*, in 1866, and *A Manual of Fret Cutting and Wood Carving* in 1875. After several years in England he settled in France on account of the milder climate, and he died at Chatou, Paris, on 11 September 1876. E. M. Lloyd, *rev.* James Lunt

Sources T. Seaton, *From cadet to colonel: the record of a life of active service*, 2 vols. (1866); repr. in 1 vol. (1877) • *Annual Register* (1876) • *ILN* (23 Sept 1876) • J. H. Stocqueler, *Memoirs and correspondence of Major-General Sir William Nott*, 2 vols. (1854) • J. C. Pollock, *Way to glory: the life of Havelock of Lucknow* (1957) • Lady Sale, *A journal of the disasters in Affghanistan* (1843) • J. W. Kaye and G. B. Malleson, *Kaye's and Malleson's History of the Indian mutiny of 1857–8*, new edn, 6 vols. (1897–8) • P. Macrory, *Signal catastrophe: the story of a disastrous retreat from Kabul, 1842* (1966) • *Hart's Army List* • Burke, *Gen. GB* (1894) • V. C. P. Hodson, *List of officers of the Bengal army, 1758–1834*, 4 (1947) • *CGPLA Eng. & Wales* (1876)

Archives BL OIOC, Alice Massy corresp., MS Eur. B 181

Wealth at death under £1500: probate, 22 Nov 1876, *CGPLA Eng. & Wales*

Seaward, John (1786–1858), civil engineer, was born at Lambeth, London, in January 1786, the son of a builder. After studying classics and mathematics with equal proficiency, he began working with his father as a surveyor and architect. He was afterwards engaged by Grillier & Co. to supervise the erection of Vauxhall Bridge, one of the first to be built with cement.

This position brought Seaward the acquaintance of Jeremy Bentham and the engineers Ralph and James Walker. He then managed some lead-mines in Wales, acquired a knowledge of chemistry, and became friendly with Arthur Woolf, Richard Trevithick, and other mechanical engineers. On his return to London he superintended the construction of Gordon's, Dowson's, and other docks on the Thames, and became agent for the Gospel Oak ironworks in Staffordshire. He was also connected with the Imperial and Continental Gas Company, which introduced gas lighting into several towns in France, Belgium, and the Netherlands. In 1823 he made drawings for a new London Bridge and published a treatise on suspension bridges, which gained the attention of Sir Humphrey Davy and other scientists. In 1824 he established the Canal ironworks, Millwall, Poplar, for the construction of machinery. He joined the Institution of Civil Engineers as a member in 1826, and frequently attended its meetings.

A younger brother, **Samuel Seaward** (1800–1842), joined John in 1825. He had sailed to Bombay and China in the service of the East India Company, and completed an apprenticeship with the Maudslay ironworks in London. He published a *Description of an improved gauge for ascertaining the pressure of highly compressed steam, gases, and fluid bodies* (1824), and was elected fellow of the Royal Society on 10 June 1841. He also joined the Institution of Civil Engineers, serving as member of council.

In 1825 the Seawards patented a mechanism for propelling steam carriages on common roads, but thereafter concentrated on marine engines. They produced machinery for every part of the world, and made the name of Seaward widely known. Their first vessel, the *Royal George*, was intended to run between Dover and Calais. In 1829 they helped to form the Diamond Steam Packet Company, and built the engines for the boats which ran between Gravesend and London. Of these, the Ruby and the Sapphire were types for speed and for accommodation.

In 1836 the Seaward brothers brought out the direct-acting engines for the *Gorgon* and *Cyclops*, known as Seaward's engines, nearly dispensing with the heavy side-beam engines which up to that period were in general use. Their success was complete, and the saving obtained in the consumption of fuel by the double-slide valve, for both the steam and the exhaust, with other improvements, caused the government to entrust the Seawards with the building of twenty-four steamboats and some smaller vessels. They also adapted their engines to the vessels of the East India Company, the steam navigation companies, and the ships of foreign governments. They early advocated the use of auxiliary steam power for East India sailing vessels, and experimented with the *Vernon* in 1839 and 1840 with great success. They also designed large swing-bridges, dredging machines, cranes, and other dock apparatus, besides machinery for lead, saw, and sugar mills. Among the improvements and inventions for which the Seawards were personally responsible were the tubular boilers, which became standard in the Royal Navy, the detachable cranks for paddle-wheel engines, the telescopic funnel, the self-acting nozzles for feeding and for regulating the saturation of the water in marine boilers, the double passages in cylinders for both steam and eduction, and the cheese-couplings used to connect and disconnect the screw propeller to and from the engines.

John Seaward published treatises on bridge construction and high-pressure steam engines, and with Samuel wrote *Observations on the advantages and possibility of successfully employing steam power in navigating ships between this country and the East Indies* (1829). For *The Steam Engine*, published by Thomas Tredgold in 1850, he contributed articles on 'Steam navigation', 'Vessels of iron and wood', 'The steam engine', and 'Screw propulsion'.

The death of Samuel Seaward at 13 Endsleigh Street, London, on 11 May 1842 threw upon John Seaward the entire management of the Canal ironworks, yet with the assistance of his former apprentices he persevered. Among his most perfect works were the engines of the *Amazon*, 800 horsepower, which he believed would be a lasting monument to his fame. The vessel unfortunately was destroyed by fire on her first passage to the West Indies on 4 January 1852. After an extended illness, John Seaward died of bronchitis at his home, 20 Brecknock Crescent, Camden, London, on 26 March 1858. He was survived by his wife, Mary Elizabeth Seaward.

G. C. Boase, *rev.* D. H. Porter

Sources *PICE*, 18 (1858–9), 199–202 • *PICE*, 2 (1843), 11–12 [obit. of Samuel Seaward] • A. Gordon, *A treatise on locomotion* (1836), 47, 51 • Repertory of Patent Inventions, 1825 • *GM*, 3rd ser., 4 (1858), 566 • Boase, *Mod. Eng. biog.* • d. cert. • d. cert. [Samuel Seaward] • *CGPLA Eng. & Wales* (1858)
Archives Inst. CE
Wealth at death under £25,000: probate, 20 April 1858, *CGPLA Eng. & Wales*

Seaward, Samuel (**1800–1842**). *See under* Seaward, John (1786–1858).

Seaxburh [Sexburga] (*d.* **674?**), queen of the Gewisse, was the wife of *Cenwalh, king of the Gewisse, and has the distinction of being the only woman to appear in an Anglo-Saxon regnal list. Her reign is said to have begun in 672 after the death of her husband and to have lasted a year, though she may actually have ruled slightly longer than twelve months, as the next reign recorded in the Anglo-Saxon Chronicle is entered under 674. However, Bede characterizes the period after Cenwalh's death as a confused time when 'subkings took upon themselves the government of the kingdom' (Bede, *Hist. eccl.*, 4.12) and the chronicle compilers may have tidied up what was in reality a much more complex situation. In other cases where Anglo-Saxon widows are known to have exercised royal power they did so on behalf and in the name of their sons. Such regnal information that exists implies that Seaxburh ruled in her own right and it is not impossible that she was herself a descendant of the West Saxon royal house. On the other hand, the form of her name could suggest that she belonged to the East Saxon royal line, many of whose members bore names compounded with *Seax*, which does not seem to have been a name element favoured by descendants of Cerdic.

Barbara Yorke

Sources *ASC*, s.a. 672 • D. N. Dumville, 'The West Saxon genealogical regnal list and the chronology of early Wessex', *Peritia*, 4 (1985), 21–66 • Bede, *Hist. eccl.*, 4.12 • B. Yorke, *Wessex in the early middle ages* (1995)

Seaxburh [St Seaxburh, Sexburga] (*b.* in or before **655**, *d. c.***700**), queen of Kent, consort of King Eorcenberht, and abbess of Ely, is described by Bede in his *Historia ecclesiastica* as the eldest daughter of *Anna, king of the East Angles (*d.* 654?), wife of King *Eorcenberht of Kent, and mother of Eorcengota (who subsequently became a saintly inmate of the Gaulish abbey of Faremoutiers-en-Brie) and also of King Hlothhere of Kent. The same writer notes that Seaxburh succeeded her sister Æthelthryth as abbess of Ely and that she arranged for the translation and enshrinement of Æthelthryth's undecayed body sixteen years after her death, in a white marble coffin from the ruined Roman site of Grantchester. Given Bede's proximity in time to Seaxburh's life and his knowledge of the history of Ely, his information can be accepted as reliable. More difficult to evaluate is the information provided by a series of related hagiographical texts, concerned with Kentish royal saints and St Mildrith in particular, and ranging in date from possibly as early as the eighth century to the end of the eleventh, with derivative texts from later centuries. Certain of these texts describe Seaxburh as the mother not only of Eorcengota and *Hlothhere, but also of King Ecgberht and of Eormenhild, who is said to have been the wife of King Wulfhere of Mercia. It is not possible to corroborate this information but it is not implausible. The fullest account of Seaxburh is to be found in one of this series of texts, which is preserved in fragmentary form in London, Lambeth Palace, MS 427, fol. 211. According to this, Seaxburh and her daughter Eormenhild became nuns at Milton Regis, Kent, of which the Isle of Sheppey was a dependency. At this latter place Seaxburh built a monastery, presumably Minster in Sheppey, which took her thirty years to construct. She had been acting as regent for her son King Hlothhere, also for thirty years, and at the end of this term she is said to have bought his share of the district from him for the use of Minster in Sheppey (although it is not entirely clear what is meant by this), and to have obtained a blessing from Rome for the inmates of it. This text cannot be earlier than the viking period, since it alludes to viking attacks as prophesied by Seaxburh, and it may be as late as the eleventh century. Its information is therefore not especially trustworthy, and its character is markedly hagiographical. It was taken up by hagiographers at Ely, who seem to have drawn on it in the twelfth century to compose a Latin life of Seaxburh, in which the son on whose behalf she held the kingdom of Kent is named as Egbert (that is, Ecgberht) and not Hlothhere. Eormenhild is said to have become abbess of Ely in her turn; she is also said to have received the veil at Minster in Sheppey from Archbishop Theodore. The only firm dates which can be assigned to Seaxburh's life are 680, or possibly 679, when she succeeded Æthelthryth as abbess and 695 or 696 when she translated the latter's remains. Her husband Eorcenberht was king from 640 to 664 and her marriage to him cannot have been later than *c.*650 if it is true that Ecgberht, who succeeded him, was her son. The year of her death is unknown, but as she was the eldest daughter of a father who died in 654 a date of *c.*700 is not implausible. Seaxburh became an important saint at Ely, although of lesser importance than Æthelthryth. According to the twelfth-century *Liber Eliensis*, which may not be reliable on this point, her remains were translated to a new tomb at Ely by Bishop Æthelwold. It is certain that they were translated into the new abbey church there in 1106. Her feast day was 6 July; the feast of her translation was 17 October.

David Rollason

Sources S. J. Ridyard, *The royal saints of Anglo-Saxon England*, Cambridge Studies in Medieval Life and Thought, 4th ser., 9 (1988) • D. W. Rollason, *The Mildrith legend: a study in early medieval hagiography in England* (1982) • M. J. Swanton, 'A fragmentary life of St Mildred and other Kentish royal saints', *Archaeologia Cantiana*, 91 (1975), 15–27 • E. O. Blake, ed., *Liber Eliensis*, CS, 3rd ser., 92 (1962)

Seaxred (*d.* in or after **617**). *See under* East Saxons, kings of the (*act.* late 6th cent.–*c.*820).

Seaxwulf [Saxulf] (*d.* c.692), abbot of Peterborough and bishop of Lichfield, is described by Bede as the builder ('*constructor*') of Medeshamstede (as the first abbey at Peterborough was called) and in twelfth-century Peterborough traditions as 'a most powerful man' and 'a most energetic and religious man, most learned in both worldly and ecclesiastical affairs' (*Chronicle of Hugh Candidus*, 8–9). The same late traditions state that he began the foundation with the help of Peada, sub-king of the Middle Angles from 653 to 656 or 657, completing and endowing it with that of Wulfhere, king of the Mercians from 658 or 659 until 675, and that he also founded the hermitage of Thorney. It seems likely that Seaxwulf was a layman of high rank who adopted the religious life and used his worldly wealth to found a monastery for himself, in the mould of his near-contemporary Benedict Biscop. Peterborough was the principal monastery in the folk-territory of the Gyrwe, and it is a reasonable conjecture that Seaxwulf was either a leading member or a supplanter of that people.

In or shortly before 675, Bishop Wynfrith was expelled from the Mercian see of Lichfield (probably for opposing its division) and Seaxwulf succeeded him. Bede says that his diocese comprised both Mercia and Middle Anglia, as well as Lindsey during the period when it was under Mercian rule; during c.675–680 it lost the sub-kingdoms of the Hwicce and Magonsæte, which Archbishop Theodore made into separate sees. Nothing else is known of Seaxwulf's episcopate beyond Bede's statement that he gave refuge to Bishop Putta of Rochester in 676, but Peterborough memoranda suggest that he continued to take an interest in the fortunes of his monastery. The C text of the Anglo-Saxon Chronicle notes his death in 705, but this is certainly wrong: Stephanus records that in 691 or 692 Wilfrid succeeded to 'that bishopric which the most reverend Bishop Seaxwulf had formerly ruled before his death' (Stephanus, 92). JOHN BLAIR

Sources Bede, *Historia ecclesiastica gentis Anglorum*, ed. C. Plummer, 3 vols. (1896), vol. 1, pp. 218, 228–9; vol. 2, pp. 215–16 · E. Stephanus, *The life of Bishop Wilfrid*, ed. and trans. B. Colgrave (1927), 92 · J. Earle, ed., *Two of the Saxon chronicles parallel: with supplementary extracts from the others*, rev. C. Plummer, 1 (1892), 29–32, 35–7 [early 12th cent. Peterborough addenda to the ASC text] · *The chronicle of Hugh Candidus, a monk of Peterborough*, ed. W. T. Mellows (1949), 7–10, 12, 43, 159–61 · S. Keynes, *The councils of Clofesho* (1994), 33–4 and n. 141 · P. Sims-Williams, *Religion and literature in western England, 600–800* (1990), 87–8 · F. M. Stenton, *Preparatory to 'Anglo-Saxon England': being the collected papers of Frank Merry Stenton*, ed. D. M. Stenton (1970), 182–3

Sebright. For this title name *see* Mackenzie, Georgina Mary Muir [Georgina Mary Sebright, Lady Sebright] (1833–1874).

Sebright, Sir John Saunders, seventh baronet (**1767–1846**), politician and agriculturist, was born in Sackville Street, Westminster, London, on 23 May 1767, the elder son of Sir John Sebright, sixth baronet (*bap.* 1725, *d.* 1794), MP for Bath (1761–80), and Sarah (*d.* 1812/13), daughter of Edward Knight of Wolverley, Worcestershire. The family, originally from Essex, had settled in Worcestershire in the

Sir John Saunders Sebright, seventh baronet (1767–1846), by Samuel William Reynolds senior, pubd 1834 (after P. Boileau)

fourteenth century, and the baronetcy was conferred on Edward Sebright of Besford, Worcestershire, in 1626. From the late seventeenth century, when Sir Edward Sebright, third baronet, married Anne Saunders, the heir of Beechwood, near Hemel Hempstead, their main residence and sphere of influence shifted to Hertfordshire.

After attending Westminster School, Sebright entered the army in 1785, but retired, as a lieutenant in the Grenadier Guards, on succeeding his father in the title and estates in February 1794. On 6 August 1793 he had married Harriet (*d.* 1826), the daughter and heir of Robert Croftes of Harling, Norfolk; they had one son, Thomas Gage Saunders Sebright (1802–1864), Sebright's successor as eighth baronet, and eight daughters, of whom five died in their father's lifetime.

Nothing came of a notion of Sebright's standing for parliament at Bath in 1789. At the general election of 1807 he stood for Hertfordshire, which his uncle Sir Thomas Saunders Sebright, fourth baronet, had represented from 1715 to 1736. He came in unopposed, as he did at the next six general elections. At the seventh, in 1832, when he was persuaded to defer his intended retirement, he was returned at the head of the poll. He retired at the dissolution in 1834. In seeking Lord Spencer's support in 1807 he declared that he was 'not devoted to any party' and would 'always consider myself at liberty to act as I may think proper' (Sebright to Earl Spencer, 26 April 1807, HoP, *Commons, 1790–1820*, 5.117). He mostly acted up to these professions in the Commons, where he was a frequent and sometimes tiresome speaker, fond of proclaiming his virtuous independence. As a sincere and steady supporter of religious toleration, particularly Catholic emancipation, and of parliamentary reform, and a critic of excesses in public expenditure, he more often than not sided with the Foxite whig opposition until late 1830, but they could not take his support for granted, especially on questions of law and order, on which he could be an alarmist. He favoured relaxation but not drastic revision of the corn laws, and was a consistent advocate of reform of the game and usury laws. In a deliberate departure from his usual practice of studied neutrality, he declared his support for Canning's ministry in May 1827; but a year later, with typical perversity, he voted against the financial provision for Canning's widow and family. On 1 March 1831 he broke the 'dead silence' which had fallen on a stunned house at the close of Lord John Russell's speech detailing the Grey ministry's Reform Bill by seconding the motion for leave to introduce it and giving it his personal blessing (Aspinall, 13). Both inside and outside parliament he was a zealous supporter of reform during the following fifteen months, although later in March 1831 he published a short letter entitled *County Reform*, in which he expressed misgivings about the effect of enfranchising tenants with short leases. He had similar anxieties about the susceptibility to landlord influence of the tenants-at-will enfranchised by the Chandos amendment, but he accepted that the enactment of reform was the paramount consideration. On 4 February 1832 he belatedly joined Brooks's Club, thereby signifying his final adherence to the whigs. An improving agriculturist, with a deep interest in and love of animals, he published works entitled *The Art of Improving the Breeds of Domestic Animals* (1809), *Observations upon Hawking* (1826), and *Observations upon the Instincts of Animals* (1836). Sebright, who built and endowed a school at Cheverell's Green and erected almshouses at Flamstead, Hertfordshire, died at Turnham Green, Middlesex, on 15 April 1846.

Sebright's oddness and bluntness made him one of the minor celebrities of the Commons. Although Brougham, nettled by his support for repressive legislation in 1818, cursed him as 'Jack Gabble' (Brougham to Lambton, HoP, *Commons, 1790–1820*, 5.119), Le Marchant referred to him in 1831 as 'a sagacious, hardheaded man', whose 'opinion is generally esteemed of much weight' (Aspinall, 168). Frances Calvert, wife of his Hertfordshire parliamentary colleague Nicolson Calvert, wrote that he had 'some good qualities' but 'also a great many disagreeable ones', including 'a violent temper' (Blake, 20). Maria Edgeworth, who described his eyebrows as 'prodigious natural curiosities', stayed at Beechwood in 1822:

> Sir John Sebright is one of the most entertaining characters I ever saw. He is very clever, very vain, very odd, full of fancies and paradoxes and with abilities to defend them all … notwithstanding his philosophical tenderness principles about dogs and horses … he has been violent with his children … his daughters … all look under abject awe of him … They all have dogs faces … They do not seem to live happily together and in the midst of luxuries and fine house and park this perception chills their guests. (*Letters from England*, 325–6)

D. R. Fisher

Sources R. G. Thorne, 'Sebright, Sir John Saunders', HoP, *Commons, 1790–1820* • D. R. Fisher, HoP, *Commons, 1820–32* [draft] • *Maria Edgeworth: letters from England, 1813–1844*, ed. C. Colvin (1971), 320–32 • A. Aspinall, ed., *Three early nineteenth-century diaries* (1952), 13, 168 [extracts from Le Marchant, E. J. Littleton, Baron Hatherton, and E. Law, earl of Ellenborough] • W. Blake, *An Irish beauty of the Regency* (1911), 20 • *VCH Hertfordshire*, 2.196, 200 • *Old Westminsters* • *GM*, 2nd ser., 26 (1846), 93

Archives Herts. ALS, estate records

Likenesses S. W. Reynolds senior, mezzotint, pubd 1834 (after P. Boileau), NPG, BM [*see illus.*] • G. Hayter, group portrait, oils (*The House of Commons, 1833*), NPG

Wealth at death under £90,000: PRO, death duty registers, IR 26/1753/483

Seccheville, John de [John Dritton] (*d.* in or after **1292**), natural philosopher, was born at Exeter into a Devon landowning family. He had become a master of arts before 1245, probably at the University of Oxford. In 1248 Richard, earl of Cornwall, petitioned for a papal dispensation on behalf of Master John, clerk of Exeter, to enable him to hold several benefices simultaneously. Indeed, during his life Seccheville came to hold many benefices, thanks to his close links to the earls of Cornwall and of Gloucester and to the bishops of Exeter. Like many scholars at that time he went to Paris. He is mentioned as a teacher in the university's faculty of arts, and also as its rector, in 1256, when he was involved in the controversy between the secular and mendicant masters. In August 1256 the University of Paris sent a delegation to the pope to ask for the lifting of the excommunication of Guillaume de St Amour and other secular masters. The faculty of arts sent its rector, John de Seccheville (or John Dritton, as he was also known), and the philosopher Jean Belin. However, the rector remained in the background and was able to keep his name out of the pope's sentence, which mainly affected the secular masters of the faculty of theology.

By 1258 Master John was back in England as secretary of the earl of Gloucester, Richard de Clare. On 30 July 1259 Henry III sent Seccheville as an envoy to King Louis IX of France, carrying letters on the subject of peace. On 7 May 1262 a Master John was a witness of the charter in which Richard de Clare confirmed dispositions made by Walter of Merton for the support of scholars at Oxford. There is no evidence, however, that John de Seccheville was a member of Merton College; he is not mentioned in the earliest sources for the college. In 1263 Seccheville was back in Paris while Oxford was involved in the barons' war, with the university closed and the masters and students dispersed. But from 1265 onwards he stayed permanently in England, and may have become a member of the *familia* of Walter of Bronescombe, bishop of Exeter. Seccheville was involved *c.*1275 in legal proceedings as the principal executor for Richard de Clare, who had died in 1262. He is mentioned in charters until 1292.

Seccheville's major work is *De principiis naturae*, written about 1263–5 and published in 1956 in an edition by R. M. Giguère, based on Paris, Bibliothèque Nationale, MS Lat. 6552, fols. 4*r*–25*v*. Other manuscripts used are BL, Royal MS 12 E.xxv, fols. 32*r*–59*v*, and Oxford, Merton College, MS 292, fols. 70*r*–85*r* (incomplete text). This treatise is one of the first expositions of the natural philosophy being taught in the middle of the thirteenth century. Strongly shaped by Aristotelian dialectic, it is influenced by the Arab philosophers, and especially by the commentaries of Averroes. Seccheville was undoubtedly affected by the heterodox Aristotelianism that was favoured in the Parisian faculty of arts. But his *De principiis* was almost certainly written before the condemnation of Averroism in 1270, for the treatise was not condemned. On the contrary, *De principiis* was put on the list of teaching texts of the University of Paris (mentioned in a list of 1286, valued at 7 deniers and in another one of 1304, valued at 10 deniers). It was divided into fourteen *peciae*, or gatherings. The *Tractatus de excellentia philosophiae* (Oxford, Merton College, MS 292, 85*r*–87*v*) is a kind of continuation of the former work.

Other treatises have been attributed to Seccheville because his name is mentioned in the incipit or colophon, but their authorship is disputable. *Commoditates super relationem* (Oxford, Merton College, MS 292, fols. 87*v*–95*v*) was most probably written by Robert Kilwardby. And the commentary on *De generatione et corruptione* (Philadelphia, Free Library, MS Lewis European 53, fols. 65*r*–70*v*) was almost certainly written by Adam of Bockenfield, an Oxford graduate and colleague at Paris of Seccheville, whose alleged activity as a commentator on Aristotle's scientific corpus has no foundation in fact. On the other hand, a commentary on the *De interpretatione* (Cambridge, Peterhouse, MS 205, fol. 20*r*), commonly thought to be by Robert Kilwardby, may perhaps be by John de Seccheville.

Seccheville can be placed within the group of English, and more specifically Oxford, scholars who achieved a reputation as writers on logic and as commentators on natural philosophy and metaphysics. Some of them had also studied or taught in the Parisian faculty of arts, as Seccheville did. Alongside the better known Robert Grosseteste, Robert Kilwardby, William Sherwood, and Simon Faversham, less eminent but still notable scholars like John de Seccheville were forerunners of the prominence which Oxford attained in the fields of logic and mathematics in the fourteenth century.

Hilde De Ridder-Symoens

Sources J. de Sècheville, *De principiis naturae*, ed. R. M. Giguère, 14 (Montréal, 1956) · Emden, *Oxf.*, 3.1661–2 · P. Glorieux, *La faculté des arts et ses maîtres au XIIIe siècle*, Études de Philosophie Médiévale, 59 (1971), 238, no. 272 · J. C. Russell, *Dictionary of writers of thirteenth century England*, rev. edn (1967), 76–7 · R. J. Long, 'Adam of Buckfield and John Sackville: some notes on Philadelphia Free Library MS Lewis European 53', *Traditio*, 45 (1989–90), 364–7 · H. Denifle and A. Chatelain, eds., *Chartularium universitatis Parisiensis*, 4 vols. (Paris, 1889–97), vol. 1, s.a. 1286, no. 530, pp. 644, 649; vol. 2, s.a. 1304, no. 642, pp. 107, 112 · M.-M. Dufeil, *Guillaume de Saint-Amour et la polémique universitaire parisienne, 1250–1259* (1972), 251, 283 · J. A. Weisheipl, 'Science in the thirteenth century', *Hist. U. Oxf.* 1: *Early Oxf. schools*, 435–69, esp. 466 · P. S. Allen and H. W. Garrod, eds., *Merton muniments*, OHS, 86 (1928) · Paris, *Chron.*, 5.599 · M. Crevier, *Histoire de l'Université de Paris, depuis son origine jusqu'en l'année 1600*, 7 vols. (1761), 1.440 · G. Lacombe and others, eds., *Aristoteles latinus: codices*, 3 vols. (Rome, 1939–61), vol. 1, p. 522, no. 589 · F. M. Powicke, *The medieval books of Merton College* (1931), 154 · S. de Ricci, *Census of medieval and Renaissance manuscripts in the United States and Canada*, 3 vols. (1937), vol. 2, no. 2056 · J. A. Rodriguez, 'El averroismo de Juan de Secheville', *Logos* [Mexico], 18 (1990), 9–31 · J. A. Rodriguez, 'El aristotelismo de Juan de Secheville', *Logos* [Mexico], 17 (1989), 55–69 · J. A. Rodriguez, 'La unidad de la materia y el problema de los universales en Juan de Secheville', *Logos* [Mexico], 14 (1986), 11–26

Archives Bibliothèque Nationale, Paris, MS Lat. 6552, fols. 4*r*–25*v* · BL, Royal MS 12 E.xxv, fols. 32*r*–59*v* · Merton Oxf., MS 292, fols. 70*r*–85*r*, MS 292, fols. 85*r*–87*v* · Peterhouse, Cambridge, MS 205, fol. 20*r*

Seccombe, Lawrence Henry (1877–1954), banker and bill broker, was born on 1 June 1877 at Terrington Lodge, Terrington St Clement, Norfolk, the second son of Dr John Thomas Seccombe (1834–1895), a country doctor, and his second wife, Ellen (1848–1943), daughter of Henry Bates, a Terrington farmer. He was descended from an ancient Devon family. Lawrence was educated at St Edmund's School, Hunstanton, until he was thirteen and then at King Edward VI's School, Birmingham, to the age of eighteen. In 1895 he went straight from school to join Lyon and Tucker, a small firm of bill dealers in the City. By 1917, when he left for war service, Seccombe was a salaried partner in the discount house of Ryder & Co. He served as a second lieutenant (and acting captain from 30 April 1918), initially in the technical stores branch of the Royal Flying Corps and, subsequently, in the RAF and at the Air Ministry.

After returning to the City of London in the spring of 1919, Seccombe set up on his own account, taking into partnership S. R. Marshall and C. A. G. Campion. Money was borrowed from banks with surplus funds and invested in bills and bonds. Part of the starting capital came through a family connection of S. R. Marshall, and for this reason the new firm traded under the auspices of M. W. Marshall & Son. Montagu Norman, the governor of the Bank of England, was at this time keen to exercise a closer supervision of the money market. Needing to replace the bank's agent or 'special buyer' in the bill market, Norman turned to Lawrence Seccombe, who had in a short space of time developed a thriving bill business at Marshalls.

Seccombe's appointment in April 1922 had nothing officially to do with the company, but it necessitated a reorganization of his activities. The discount side of the firm in consequence became independent of M. W. Marshall & Son and henceforth it traded as Seccombe, Marshall, and Campion, with Seccombe as senior partner. Nevertheless, in keeping with Norman's obsession with secrecy, Seccombe received no official appointment as special buyer, merely a verbal agreement. Official dealings were, moreover, to be done confidentially and it was entirely appropriate that operations designed to restore market liquidity should come to be known as 'doing good by stealth' and the special buyer himself referred to as 'the Hidden Hand'.

The firm's bill-broking business, which had been growing rapidly, was now swollen by transactions on behalf of the Bank of England—mainly purchases and sales of Treasury bills designed to regulate financial conditions in line with national economic policy. The success or otherwise of these operations depended critically on the skill and tact of the special buyer, who was expected both to assess market conditions as the basis for official intervention and to secure the willing compliance of the discount houses with the bank's requirements. Seccombe also supervised the purchases of sample commercial bills in order to assess the quality of the transactions. In 1947 the firm became a private company with Seccombe as chairman, but it remained the smallest house in the market. Because of its unique role Seccombes escaped the process of amalgamation that occurred in the market generally in the 1930s and 1940s.

Seccombe was an outstanding figure among his contemporaries in the City of London. The complete man of business, he was always immaculately dressed, courteous, and gracious. Inclined to be hasty and impulsive, his judgement was amazingly good and his integrity never questioned. Above all, perhaps, Seccombe possessed a quality that Norman himself greatly admired and cultivated to an extraordinary degree: that of discretion, and of appearing inscrutable when necessary—so much so that Kenneth Peppiatt, the Bank of England's market expert, with whom Seccombe fished for several weeks annually on the Scottish Dee, would find it impossible to guess, when meeting him in the money market, what scale of business he was seeking to transact. Discretion also proved a sure defence. When, on one occasion, Seccombe was absent and the partner deputed to act failed to satisfy the bank, Norman recommended the latter's dismissal. Seccombe, however, played his strongest card: he said nothing; and did nothing.

Seccombe held the office of special buyer for thirty-two years. His tenure paralleled closely that of Montagu Norman as governor of the Bank of England, and the two worked closely together to maintain stability in the money market in years of great monetary crisis and upheaval. Such was the importance ascribed to the role of Seccombe's firm that, on the outbreak of the Second World War, the firm was moved into the secure basement of the Bank of England.

Seccombe married on 11 February 1915 Norah (1885/6–1959), daughter of Thomas Wood, a mine owner and mining engineer, and his wife, Ellen. They had two sons. Seccombe served as an urban district councillor for Weybridge in the 1920s and for Chertsey in the 1930s. In 1946 he was appointed high sheriff of the county of Surrey, and in 1952 he was appointed CBE for services to the City. He was very good with young people and devoted much time to youth schemes, including, during the war years, the sea cadets and the Air Training Corps. Most outdoor pursuits appealed to him, but he also enjoyed antiques and, latterly, foreign travel.

Seccombe died from a brain tumour at University College Hospital, London, on 28 November 1954. He was cremated on 2 December, and his funeral was held the same day at Pyrford church, Surrey, his ashes being later buried in the church walls. He was survived by his wife, and his second son, Hugh, succeeded him as chairman of the company. GORDON FLETCHER

Sources G. A. Fletcher, 'Seccombe, Lawrence Henry', *DBB* • R. S. Sayers, *The Bank of England, 1891–1944*, 3 vols. (1976) • A. Boyle, *Montagu Norman* (1967) • H. Clay, *Lord Norman* (1957) • J. Fforde, *The Bank of England and public policy, 1941–1958* (1992) • *CGPLA Eng. & Wales* (1955) • private information (2004) • b. cert. • m. cert. • d. cert.

Likenesses M. Mackinlay, oils, *c.*1930, priv. coll. • photograph (after M. Mackinlay), repro. in Fletcher, 'Seccombe, Lawrence Henry'

Wealth at death £53,642 18*s.* 8*d.*: probate, 29 Jan 1955, *CGPLA Eng. & Wales*

Seccombe, Thomas (1866–1923), literary scholar and biographer, born at Terrington St Clement, near King's Lynn, Norfolk, on 18 June 1866, was the eldest son of John Thomas Seccombe, a country doctor, and his wife, Elizabeth Margaret, daughter of Thomas Clout of Lambeth, London. His paternal grandfather was Sir Thomas Lawrence Seccombe, of the India Office. He was educated at Felsted School, and proceeded to Balliol College, Oxford, in October 1885, where he won the Stanhope prize in 1887 with an essay 'Political satire in England in the eighteenth century', and obtained a first class in modern history in 1889. He married Elizabeth Jane Goddard, the daughter of Henry Goddard, a Hampshire farmer, in 1896. They had two daughters and a son.

In 1891 Sidney Lee, who had just succeeded Leslie Stephen as editor of the *Dictionary of National Biography*, chose Seccombe as assistant editor, and he held that position until the editorial staff was disbanded on 31 December 1900 on the completion of the main work. In this post his kindliness and courtesy made him a favourite with the contributors and assisted materially to maintain those friendly relations among editors and contributors which characterized the whole period of publication. He contributed to the *Dictionary of National Biography* over 500 biographies, mainly of eighteenth-century writers, and also of sportsmen and athletes. Of particular note were his articles on Tobias Smollett and Sir John Vanbrugh. Later he wrote a number of articles for the 1901–11 supplement to the dictionary, including a memoir of George Meredith, an example of his best work.

After giving up his post on the dictionary, Seccombe devoted most of his time to literary work. He acted for many years as literary adviser to Constable & Co., and in this capacity urged the first publication in book form of George Gissing's *The Private Papers of Henry Ryecroft* (1903). He had already edited *The Lives of Twelve Bad Men* in 1894, but became best-known for his *The Age of Johnson* (1900), a study of the literature of the later eighteenth century, which ran to six editions during his lifetime. He continued this success by writing *The Age of Shakespeare* (1903) with J. W. Allen, which was similarly well received. After 1901 he collaborated for some time with William Robertson Nicoll on the *'Bookman' History of English Literature*, which appeared in 1905 and 1906. He edited, with introductory prefaces, many reprints of well-known authors, including James Boswell, George Borrow, Gissing, Elizabeth Gaskell, Apuleius, Oliver Goldsmith, and Smollett.

Seccombe was a dedicated teacher, and from 1907 lectured in modern history at the East London College of the

University of London. In 1912 he became professor of English at the Royal Military College, Sandhurst, leaving in 1919 to take up the post of lecturer in English language and literature at Oxford. In 1921 he accepted the chair of English literature at Queen's University, Kingston, Ontario. Illness compelled him to resign this post in the spring of 1923 and to return to England. He died at the Kistor Private Hotel in Torquay, Devon, on 20 June, within a month of his return. His wife survived him.

E. I. CARLYLE, *rev.* KATHERINE MULLIN

Sources *The Times* (21 June 1923) • J. Foster, *Oxford men, 1880–1892: with a record of their schools, honours, and degrees* (1893) • *WWW, 1929–40* • *The Bookman*, 64 (1923), 195–6 • P. Coustillas, 'Thomas Seccombe writes the Gissing entry in the DNB', *Gissing Newsletter*, 13 (1977), 1–18, 18–34 • G. Fenwick, *The contributors' index to the Dictionary of National Biography, 1885–1901* (1989) • personal knowledge (1937) • private information (1937) • *CGPLA Eng. & Wales* (1923)

Likenesses A. Barr, pencil drawing, *c.*1921, repro. in *The Bookman*

Wealth at death £16,768 5*s.* 11*d.*: probate, 22 Nov 1923, *CGPLA Eng. & Wales*

Sechnall mac Restitiúit (*fl.* 5th cent.). *See under* Meath, saints of (*act. c.*400–*c.*900).

Sechnassach mac Blathmaic (*d.* 671), high-king of Ireland, was a member of the Síl nÁeda Sláine dynasty of the Uí Néill. He was one of four known sons of *Blaímac (or Blathmac) mac Áeda Sláine, who was king of Tara (the title of the high-kings of Ireland) together with Sechnassach's uncle, Diarmait mac Áeda Sláine. Sechnassach himself became king of Tara some time after 665, when Diarmait, and perhaps Blaímac, died of the plague which lasted into 668. Little is known of Sechnassach's reign. He seems to have had close relations with the Leinstermen, for one of his daughters, Bé Fáil (*d.* 741), married *Cellach Cualann, king of Leinster (*d.* 715), and Sechnassach was married to Findelb ingen Chellaig, who may well have been the daughter of this same Cellach Cualann. Early Irish kings were polygynous, so even if he and Cellach were mutually fathers-in-law, this arrangement need not imply incest. Sechnassach's other daughters were Murgal and Mumain; no sons are mentioned in the sources. Sechnassach was killed in November 671, by the king of the minor southern Uí Néill dynasty of Cenél Coirpri, and was succeeded by his brother, *Cenn Fáelad mac Blathmaic.

PHILIP IRWIN

Sources *Ann. Ulster* • M. C. Dobbs, ed. and trans., 'The Banshenchus [pt 2]', *Revue Celtique*, 48 (1931), 163–234, esp. 185, 223

Secker, Martin [*formerly* Percy Martin Secker Klingender] (**1882–1978**), publisher, was born on 6 April 1882 at 24 Holland Road, Kensington, London, the only son of Edward Henry Klingender (*b.* 1853) and Julia Clark (1856–1906). A legacy of £1000 enabled him to enter publishing under James Eveleigh Nash in 1908. Nash employed him as a reader until 1910, when Klingender established himself as a publisher in the Adelphi, London. On 12 July 1910 he changed his name to Martin Secker by deed poll. He limited himself to non-fiction in his first year of business; the first novel he published, *The Passionate Elopement* (1911), was also the first by its author, Compton Mackenzie. It had been refused by Nash and others, but went on to sell over 9000 copies in eight years, and Mackenzie later enjoyed further success through Secker with *Carnival* (1912) and *Sinister Street* (1913–14). In his *Notes on Novelists* (1914) Henry James singled out Mackenzie, Hugh Walpole, and Gilbert Cannan as the most promising of the younger practitioners, and Secker published all of them. Sir Rupert Hart-Davis said he had 'fine taste in book design' and that the improvement in the design of general books had its origin with Secker before the First World War. In 1916 the novelist Rafael Sabatini became a partner in the business, which was known as Martin Secker Ltd from 1917. After the First World War Sabatini was replaced by Percival Presland Howe, who remained with Secker until the end.

By the end of his first decade Secker had also published novels by Oliver Onions (who had previously been published by Nash), Viola Meynell, Francis Brett Young, Norman Douglas, Frank Swinnerton, Arthur Machen, and Rafael Sabatini, and poetry by D. H. Lawrence, Ford Madox Hueffer (later Ford), Emily Dickinson, James Elroy Flecker, T. W. H. Crosland, and Maurice Baring. The first titles to appear in Secker's Critical Studies series were Arthur Ransome's *Edgar Allan Poe* and *Oscar Wilde*. Shortly afterwards Ransome transferred his rights in his published books to Charles Granville, and the next day Lord Alfred Douglas caused writs to be issued in respect of Wilde on Ransome and Secker; he later withdrew the writ against Secker, and the two remained friends. Some time in 1911 or 1912 Secker paid two advances to Douglas for a book to be called 'The Wilde myth': the text was set up in type, but the book was never published.

After Secker had read D. H. Lawrence's *The White Peacock* in 1911 he approached Lawrence for a collection of short stories. He became his British publisher in 1918 with *New Poems* (a 'decidedly false title' according to Lawrence), and he took on *The Rainbow*, which Methuen had had to suppress in 1915. Secker continued as Lawrence's publisher until Lawrence's death in 1930. Despite Lawrence's occasional exasperation at Secker's timidity (over, for example, *Lady Chatterley's Lover*), the relationship was friendly enough, extending to shared holidays in Italy, but never close. Secker may have sensed the distrust which Lawrence expressed in letters to his friends, but not, it has to be hoped, the opinion revealed in such epithets as 'scurvy little swine', 'of course … another Jew', and 'a shifty dog, as they [publishers] all are'.

After Viola Meynell broke off their engagement in 1919, Secker married Caterina Maria Capellero (1896–1968) on 30 August 1921; they had one son, Adrian, born in 1924. By the mid-1920s Secker was the pre-eminent British publisher of European work in translation of his time, with novels by Thomas Mann (*Buddenbrooks*), Hermann Hesse (*Steppenwolf*), Arnold Zweig (*Sergeant Grischa*), Franz Kafka (*The Castle*), and Leon Feuchtwanger's *Jew Süss*, Secker's greatest financial success, published against Lawrence's advice. Although there were many successes, Secker's credit was overstretched by 1935 and he filed for bankruptcy. In 1936 his company was bought for £3100 by Frederic Warburg and Roger Senhouse; the new company took the name Secker and Warburg, and Secker stayed on for two years in charge of production. Ironically, Secker had signed up the new firm's success, Gabriel Chevallier's *Clochemerle*, before the take-over, and if he could have survived for another six months it would have saved him. Secker then created the Unicorn Press, which published Arthur Symons's book on Aubrey Beardsley, Robert Hichens's *The Green Carnation*, and a collected edition of Oscar Wilde. He bought the Richards Press in 1937, formerly run by Grant Richards, his only close friend in British publishing; among his publications for this press were works by Richard Le Gallienne, James Elroy Flecker, A. E. Housman, and (rather surprisingly) Enid Blyton's Noddy series (jointly with Sampson, Low, Marston). He continued to publish until 1962, when he sold the business to John Baker.

Secker's first marriage was dissolved in 1938 and on 17 February 1955 he married Sylvia Hope Broadbent (*née* Gibsone) (1916–1999), a writer. Secker was short, dark, quiet, and invariably cheerful (despite the onset of total blindness in 1971). He died on 6 April 1978 at Bridgefoot, Iver, Buckinghamshire, which had been his home since 1912; his ashes were scattered at Bridgefoot.

JOHN TREVITT

Sources D. W. Collins, 'Martin Secker', *British literary publishing houses, 1881–1965*, ed. J. Rose and P. J. Anderson, DLitB, 112 (1991) • private information (2004) • *WWW, 1971–80* • *The letters of D. H. Lawrence*, ed. J. T. Boulton and others, vols. 1–7 (1979–93) • M. Horder, 'Conversations with Martin Secker', *TLS* (10 Dec 1976), 1565–6 • M. Horder, 'More conversations with Martin Secker', *London Magazine* (Dec 1978–Jan 1979), 93–104 • M. Horder, 'Martin Secker', *Blackwood*, 325 (1979), 126–31 • M. Secker, 'Publisher's progress', *Cornhill Magazine* (summer 1973), 20–32; (spring 1974), 256–63 • F. Warburg, *An occupation for gentlemen* (1959)

Archives U. Reading L., Martin Secker Ltd archives | Mitchell L., Glas., corresp. with R. D. Macleod • U. Birm. L., corresp. with F. Brett Young • Washington State University Libraries, Pullman, Washington, corresp. and papers relating to Richard Blake Brown

Likenesses E. O. Hoppé, photograph, priv. coll.; repro. in Collins, 'Martin Secker' • A. Secker, double portrait, photograph (with D. H. Lawrence), priv. coll.; repro. in *WWW*, vol. 5 • M. Secker, photograph, priv. coll.; repro. in *WWW*, vol. 1 • group portrait, photograph (aged ninety; with friends), priv. coll.; repro. in Horder, 'Conversations with Martin Secker' • photograph, repro. in Warburg, *Occupation for gentlemen*

Wealth at death £28,326: *The Times* (Aug 1978)

Secker, Thomas (1693–1768), archbishop of Canterbury, was born at Sibthorp, a small village in the Vale of Belvoir, in Nottinghamshire, on 21 September 1693; he was the second of three children of Thomas Secker (*bap.* 1631, *d.* 1700)—son of Leonard Secker, a butcher from Marston, Lincolnshire—and his third wife, Abigail (1665/6–1707), daughter of George Brough, a gentleman farmer from Shelton in Nottinghamshire. His father's elder brother William, in an interesting anticipation of the career of his more famous nephew, conformed to the Church of England and became vicar of All Hallows-the-Less, London, in 1663, and in 1667 rector of Lee, Essex, where he died in 1681. Secker's father was a nonconformist with a small income that enabled him to get by without pursuing any regular employment. The names of his first and second wives remain unknown. With his second wife he had a

Thomas Secker (1693–1768), by Sir Joshua Reynolds, 1764

daughter, Elizabeth, who married Richard Milnes, a member of a well-established Chesterfield family. With his third wife, whom he married in 1685, his eldest child was Abigail-Anna, born in 1690, and his youngest, George, born in 1696. Having acquired a young family to support at a relatively late age he rented a farm at Sibthorp from John Holles, duke of Newcastle, for £100 p.a., which led him to be designated a yeoman in contemporary records; he died at Sibthorp in 1700. According to Secker his father had been 'a pious & virtuous & sensible man' (*Autobiography*, fol. 3), who, although he had resisted becoming a dissenting minister, had had high hopes that his son Thomas would do so. Later commentators indeed discerned that something of the archbishop's dissenting background and upbringing remained with him for the rest of his life, finding a perceived 'shyness in his behaviour' and an 'affected quaintness in the tone of his voice' (Hasted, 12.511), which they associated with his nonconformist roots. After his father's death his mother married William Allen and continued to manage the Sibthorp farm until she died in 1707, aged forty-one.

Early years and education In 1699 Secker was sent to live with his half-sister Elizabeth and her husband, Richard Milnes, in Chesterfield. He went to the free school there, where the master, Richard Brown, was a staunch supporter of the Church of England. An almost certainly apocryphal story recounts how, after Secker had done well in his lessons, Brown had congratulated him, saying 'If thou wouldst but come over to the Church, I am sure thou wouldst be a bishop' (*GM*, 38.451). At the age of fifteen Secker was sent in 1708 to a dissenting academy at Attercliffe, near Sheffield, which was run by Timothy Jolly, an

Independent minister; this was because, as he later recalled, 'some of my Acquaintance entic[ed] me, sometimes to drink, & sometimes to go to Church' (*Autobiography*, fol. 4). By then he had acquired a competent knowledge of Greek and Latin. He was, however, unhappy at Attercliffe, which was not a particularly scholarly establishment, and he noted tartly:

> I lost much of this Learning there, & acquired but little instead of it. For only the old Philosophy of the Schools was taught there: and that neither ably nor diligently. The morals also of many of the young Men were bad. I spent my time there idly & ill. (ibid.)

He left after about eighteen months.

To offset this unprofitable educational experience Secker, while at Attercliffe, had become acquainted with Henry Etough, who would later conform to the Church of England; Matthew Leesom, later a dissenting minister at Thame; and Joseph Sills, afterwards an Independent minister at Henley. More importantly he became friendly with John Bowes, a future lord chancellor of Ireland. In 1710 he went to lodge in Bowes's father's house in London and there he learned geometry, conick sections, algebra, and French, and he studied Locke's *Essay Concerning Human Understanding* (1690). He met the celebrated nonconformist divine and hymn-writer Isaac Watts, who also boarded at the Bowes's house. Watts advised Secker to go to an academy in Gloucester in the house of Joseph Wintle, a distiller, which was run by Samuel Jones, a dissenting layman. Jones had studied at Leiden and was a distinguished orientalist; under his tuition Secker soon regained his knowledge of Greek and Latin, and added to it Hebrew, Chaldee, and Syriac, which stood him in good stead in later life in his studies of the Old Testament and early church history. He was also taught Jewish antiquities, logic, and mathematics. His fellow students at Jones's academy included several who would later be influential in eighteenth-century religious circles: Joseph Butler and Isaac Maddox, who like Secker later conformed to the Church of England and became bishops; and Samuel Chandler, Daniel Scott, and Jeremiah Jones, who became leading nonconformist divines. In 1713 Jones moved his academy to Tewkesbury, borrowing £200 from Secker to do so, but he soon took to drink and his teaching suffered as a result. Both Butler (February 1714) and Secker (June 1714) left the academy. While at Tewkesbury, Secker was privy to the correspondence between Butler and the influential latitudinarian Church of England clergyman Samuel Clarke about the latter's *A Demonstration of the Being and Attributes of God* (1705). To make sure that no one else knew of the correspondence Secker acted as a go-between, delivering Butler's letters by hand to the post office at Gloucester and bringing back Clarke's replies.

Having left Jones's academy Secker returned to Chesterfield. During the winter of 1714–15 he was living at Nottingham with his sister Abigail-Anna when his brother-in-law, Samuel Wildboare, died; Secker helped to put her affairs in order. He was by now having serious reservations about being a dissenter. During this period he read up about various theological subjects, such as the doctrine of the Trinity, on which for the time being he agreed with Clarke's liberal and decidedly Arian views; the inspiration of scripture, where he was influenced by Richard Simon's *Sentiment de quelques théologiens d'Hollande sur l'histoire critique du Vieux Testament* (1685), which questioned the historicity of parts of the Old Testament; and subscription to the Thirty-Nine Articles, about which he corresponded with Butler, who was now studying at Oriel College, Oxford. Secker also read the principal writers on lay and ministerial conformity, and he went through the New Testament in the original Greek, with the help of commentaries. By the autumn of 1715 he was living in London, where he studied various theological works, particularly those concerning the primitive church, including the apostolic fathers, Eusebius's *Ecclesiastical History*, and William Whiston's *Primitive Christianity Revived* (1711), all of which were central to the debates between conformity and dissent.

Medical training Secker now found himself accepting conformity to the Church of England as a layman but he was as yet unsure whether he could be ordained within the church. Because he needed more time to think matters through he began to apply himself to the subject of medicine, explaining his decision as 'a small change in my studies … from the spirit to the flesh' (Secker to John Fox, October 1716, in *Monthly Repository of Theology and General Literature*, 16.569). During the winter of 1716–17 he took some anatomy courses with the leading surgeon William Cheselden. According to Secker, Cheselden was 'occasionally much given to irreligious talk' (*Autobiography*, fol. 5). Mixing in such company allowed later opponents of the archbishop to criticize him for mocking religion in his youth. He was keen to stress in his autobiography—which he wrote to ensure that 'Some Facts and dates may prevent certain Falsehoods, & perhaps injurious falsehoods, from being spred concerning me hereafter' (ibid., fol. 1)—that he had not shared his mentor's views, although letters from 1716 to 1718, which were printed in volume 16 of the *Monthly Repository* (1821), do indicate a certain irreverent tone. Secker then went to live with a Mr Bakewell, an apothecary who had a house in King Street in Cheapside and who taught the future archbishop the rudiments of medical prescriptions and practice.

In January 1718 Secker left for Paris, where he lodged with the renowned anatomist Jacques-Bénigne Winslow. Secker also learned dissection at the Salpêtrière—a hospital that specialized in the care of poor patients and prostitutes. That an archbishop of the Church of England had dissected bodies was not mentioned by his future chaplain and biographer, Beilby Porteus, probably because this was considered an unseemly career path for one who had reached the highest position in the church. Secker's critics, on the other hand, made great play of this period in his life, accusing him of having received an unsuitable early training for an archbishop. While with Winslow, Secker worked at the Hotel Dieu Hospital and studied with J. F. A. Gregoire, the man-midwife and founder of the first obstetrics clinic. During his stay in France he also met Bernard-Sigefroi Albinus, professor at Leiden; Father

Montfauçon, the patristic scholar; and Martin Benson, his future brother-in-law and, later, bishop of Gloucester.

Though primarily studying medicine Secker continued to read theology and kept up his correspondence with Joseph Butler, who had by then taken orders with the Church of England. Butler's close friend was Edward Talbot, archdeacon of Berkshire and son of the bishop of Salisbury, and Talbot thought that Secker should be persuaded to be ordained within the Church of England. He assured Butler that if Secker took orders his father, the bishop, who himself had had liberal theological opinions, would find him a living. Butler let Secker know of this scheme and Secker contemplated it for two months. His theological scruples about becoming ordained had in any case grown weaker following the Salters' Hall dispute of 1719, which had split the dissenting camp, and, as he admitted in his autobiography, he was increasingly concerned about the financial risks of taking on a medical career. In August 1720 he returned to England; he met Edward Talbot and they got on well. In December Talbot unfortunately died of smallpox but, true to his promise, he had recommended his friends to his father. Secker was advised by Thomas Rundle, another theological liberal and at the time chaplain to Bishop Talbot, that he should take an Oxford degree before proceeding to holy orders and that this would be made easier if he first took the degree of doctor of physic at Leiden. Secker graduated MD from Leiden in 1721 and his thesis, 'De medicina statica', was printed there later in the same year; it was reprinted by Haller in 1748 as part of his *Disputationum anatomicarum selectarum*, volume 3. The thesis was a critical study of the pioneering metabolic work of the Italian physician Santorio Sanctorius, and in it Secker demonstrated Sanctorius's dependence on previous authorities and challenged his experimental method for not being rigorous enough.

Oxford, ordination, and marriage Secker returned to England and on 1 April 1721 entered Exeter College, Oxford, as a gentleman-commoner. Martin Benson, his friend from France, was a student of Christ Church; Rundle introduced him to John Conybeare, then a fellow of Exeter and later its rector and bishop of Bristol, who became Secker's 'nominal tutor' (*Autobiography*, fol. 11); he also became acquainted with Arthur Charlett, master of University College, and William Delaune, president of St John's College. Secker soon became aware of the tory bias of the university: 'I soon found, that the Whigs could procure me no Academical Favour, & therefore cultivated the Tories, particularly Dr Delaune' (ibid.). He also moved in non-juring circles for a time, mixing with the likes of Samuel Jebb, Thomas Carte, Sir John St Aubyn, and John King; in later years he was anxious to assert his loyalty to the government, claiming that though they did drink to the duke of Ormond they never drank the Pretender's health.

Secker lived in Oxford only as long as was needed to fulfil the residence requirements and was introduced to London society by Samuel Clarke, by then rector of St James's, Piccadilly, and George Berkeley, who became a close lifelong friend. There he spent much of his time at the houses of Bishop Talbot and of Mary Talbot, the widow of Edward. She had given birth to a daughter, Catherine, five months after her husband's death and lived with her companion, Catherine Benson, the sister of Secker's friend Martin. On 6 July 1722 Secker was admitted to the degree of BA as a result of a letter of recommendation from the chancellor. Talbot, now bishop of Durham, ordained Secker as deacon in St James's, Piccadilly, on 23 December 1722. On reviewing his relationship with the Church of England at the time of his ordination Secker stated in his autobiography that he had never officiated as a dissenting minister nor ever put himself forward as a candidate for the dissenting ministry, nor had he taken communion as a dissenter, and that he had constantly attended Anglican services since his return from France in 1720. Quite when Secker actually left dissent is not clear. Francis Blackburne later thought that the future archbishop gave up on nonconformity when he matriculated at Exeter College in 1721, because this necessitated subscription to the Thirty-Nine Articles; Secker's brother, George, however, suggested that he conformed when he was about seventeen. Secker's odyssey from dissent to conformity, and even the taking of orders within the Church of England, was common among nonconformists of his generation. In any case it may be misleading to draw too hard and fast a line between nonconformity and conformity in this period, given that it was not unusual to attend both the nonconformist meeting-house and the parish church. Even after his ordination it is likely that Secker retained his former liberal theological opinions and only slowly became a staunch defender of orthodox views. His ordination to the priesthood followed on 10 March 1723, again by Talbot in St James's, and it was here that he preached his first sermon, on 28 March. In July he went to Durham as joint chaplain to Bishop Talbot with Thomas Rundle, and preached the assize sermon at Newcastle upon Tyne. He was appointed to the valuable rectory of Houghton-le-Spring, near Durham, to which he was instituted on 12 February 1724, having first taken his MA at Oxford on 4 February. During the same year he helped his friend Joseph Butler to prepare for publication the sermons that he had earlier delivered at the Rolls chapel.

Secker's thoughts now turned to marriage. He proposed to Catherine Benson in April 1725—her mother died from consumption shortly after the announcement—and Bishop Talbot officiated at their marriage on 28 October in King Street Chapel, London. Though now married Catherine Secker did not want to stop sharing a house with Bishop Talbot's widowed daughter-in-law and her child, and so the two families lived together, both in the lodgings in Dover Street, London, and also at Houghton-le-Spring, where Secker was proving to be a hard-working rural incumbent. His medical knowledge came in handy in his northern parish and he regularly visited his sick parishioners, but Houghton was damp and Mrs Secker's health soon deteriorated; a plan was drawn up whereby Secker gave up Houghton for the more salubrious and prestigious rectory of Ryton, near Newcastle upon Tyne, where Dr Finney, the rector, was infirm and about to relinquish the living. For some reason the scheme was blocked by Thomas Rundle, whom Secker had for some time suspected to be 'selfish' and 'jealous' (*Autobiography*, fol. 13), and he advised the bishop to give Ryton to someone else. In the end the exchange went through and on 3 June 1727 Secker was instituted at Ryton and to the third prebend of Durham. He now lived mainly at Durham but went over every weekend to officiate at Ryton and spent three months there in the summer.

Mrs Secker's ill health continued to cause her husband concern and Secker took her first to London and then to Bath, where they stayed until 8 April 1728. There Secker met Ralph Allen and was present at the deathbed of George Stanhope, a leading high-church figure in Queen Anne's reign; he also cemented his friendship with George Berkeley and his wife. On returning to Durham, Secker was responsible, with Benson, for organizing the books and deeds of the cathedral; he paid methodical attention to ecclesiastical records throughout his career. Bishop Talbot died on 10 October 1730 and Secker preached the sermon at his funeral. He was now becoming well known as a preacher and, not unexpectedly, he was appointed a royal chaplain on 28 May 1732, on the recommendation of both Thomas Sherlock, bishop of Bangor, who had heard him preach in Bath, and Benson, who was also a chaplain to George II. This was to prove an important step in Secker's career, as his preaching abilities reached a wider circle, and he gained an increasing reputation; on 27 August he preached before Queen Caroline at St James's Chapel Royal. She was impressed by his performance and later invited him to attend her 'philosophical parties'. In July 1733 he was invited to preach the Act sermon at Oxford, entitled 'On the advantages and duties of an academical education', before taking the degree of doctor of civil law. This otherwise well-regarded sermon was later attacked in print by William Webster, clerical editor of the *Weekly Miscellany*, for not including enough scriptural quotations, although Secker later gave Webster some support.

St James's, Piccadilly, and the bishoprics of Oxford and Bristol

Secker's career as a prominent cleric was confirmed on 18 May 1733, when he was instituted as rector of St James's, Piccadilly, through the influence of Edmund Gibson, bishop of London. Secker continued to keep Ryton, and appointed a curate there. His methodical approach to work, his concern for accuracy and for keeping records in good order, and his evident business ability were soon seen at St James's, where immediately after his arrival he took vestry business in hand. He stopped the habit of spending money on treats for the parish and examined all the accounts of the officers, putting them in order and making rules for their use in the future. Not all the parishioners, however, were enamoured of Secker's business acumen and attention to detail. In his autobiography he noted that this became a running sore throughout his incumbency; in particular he remembered the trouble caused by Henry Fane, a wealthy parishioner, and Thomas Bonney, an assistant preacher in the parish, when he attempted to rent out part of the land belonging to the rectory to make the churchyard larger. He preached usually three Sundays a month at the parish church and, on the fourth, at each of the chapels of ease.

In December 1734 Secker unexpectedly received a letter from Bishop Gibson, informing him that George II had 'pitched' on him for the bishopric of Bristol. 'I had made no Application for it to any Person,' he later claimed, 'as indeed I never did for any thing, either before or afterwards' (*Autobiography*, fol. 21). He was consecrated at Lambeth Palace on 19 January 1735. As was to be characteristic of Secker on obtaining a new appointment he immediately investigated the diocese's records, and discovered that those for the county of Dorset housed at Blandford had been destroyed by fire. A new diocesan survey was needed and he immediately undertook a visitation of his see. He began the visitation at Shaftesbury and confirmed in fifteen places, reaching Bristol on 10 September, where he gave 20 guineas for the erection of a statue of William III in Queen Square. He also contributed to church building in the diocese. The speculum, or diocesan book, that emerged from his visitation was used by his successors until the early nineteenth century.

In 1737 Secker was offered the bishopric of Oxford, which at first he refused because accepting it would, he felt, have been financially disadvantageous. He finally agreed to accept after being told that he would get a handsome sum of money for a life lease for lands at Hook Norton on account of the death of Lord Chancellor Talbot. At Oxford he proved as diligent and hard-working as at Bristol. His first major task was to organize a visitation of the diocese, which he undertook in 1738; the answers to his queries have been published in a modern edition and are an invaluable window into church life in the period. Secker collected information pertaining to the see and he composed, as he had done at Bristol and as he would do at Canterbury, a speculum of the diocese, which unfortunately is now lost. His letters to the clergy while bishop of Oxford, many of which survive, reveal him to have been a conscientious pastor—a stickler for standards who demanded that clergy should give the best pastoral provision possible and who reproved clergy who did not live up to these ideals. The editor of his letters concludes that 'his approach as diocesan was generally vigilant, exacting and authoritarian, indeed severe to backsliders' (*Correspondence*, xx). Secker insisted that as far as possible clergy should perform 'full duty'—that is, give both morning and evening services on Sundays—and he encouraged residence in the parish. He held five visitations during his time at Oxford (1738, 1741, 1749, 1750, and 1753). The charges to his clergy that he delivered on these occasions gave advice on all manner of topics, ranging from study, ordination, relations with dissent, preaching, the importance of holy communion, and the importance of keeping up church fabric to the perils of having an unsupervised church choir. To a certain extent the charges demonstrate his reflections on issues and problems raised by the clergy in their day-to-day business. Secker paid particular attention to the ways in which confirmation was administered and began the practice of issuing confirmation tickets in order to help make these events more orderly. He was also keen to make sure that his clergy received a suitable income—supporting applications to Queen Anne's Bounty and urging his clergy to defend their rights to the full monetary worth of their livings. In the summer he resided at the bishop's palace at Cuddesdon, where he preached on Sundays, read lectures on the catechism, and held a public dinner every Thursday. He spent about £600 on the house and gardens, £180 on the chancel, and nearly £30 on the chancel of Wheatley chapel during his time as bishop. At Oxford he had frequent contact with members of the university, which, as a stronghold of high-churchmanship, regarded the whig bishop with some suspicion; he did well to avoid falling out with some of its members. One of his unofficial roles was to keep an eye on the politics of the university, which was rather ironic given that the ministry during the 1740s had some cause to doubt his loyalty. He was also brought into close contact with Sarah, duchess of Marlborough, as Blenheim Palace was within the diocese. Secker frequently visited her there and was made one of her executors. He officiated at her funeral service in 1744 and she left him money in her will.

Though successively bishop of Bristol and Oxford, Secker continued to hold both his prebend at Durham and the rectory of St James's *in commendam* until 1750, on the grounds that both Bristol and Oxford were rated as poor bishoprics financially. But he did not neglect his parish, spending most of the year in London, where he was a frequent preacher in the parish church, and employing a curate, Charles Linde, so that he could reside during the summer months in his dioceses. It was, for instance, while rector of St James's that Secker wrote his thirty-nine 'Lectures on the church catechism' for the use of his parishioners (published after his death in 1769 in two volumes). It was here too that he delivered some of his most influential sermons, such as the 1750 sermon following the London earthquake, where Secker accused Londoners of being degenerate and in need of moral reformation. In his own estimation at least he was a model cleric in the parish. During the harsh winter of 1739–40 he played a large part in the distribution of poor relief in the parish. He improved the parsonage house (spending over £500 in repairing it), instructed children in the catechism, gave out religious tracts, paid his curate a satisfactory wage, and paid for the reading of early-morning and late-evening prayers. He also helped obtain the Watch Act for the parish in 1735, despite initial opposition from some of the parishioners.

As rector of St James's, Secker's most illustrious parishioner was Frederick, prince of Wales, particularly after the prince had left the court, following the rift with his father, George II, in 1737 and had come to live at Norfolk House, which was within the parish boundaries. Secker had impressed the king with his sermon on the death of Queen Caroline in that year and he realized that the king had hoped that he could have done more to improve relations with his son. Secker, however, felt that he had little influence over the prince. Indeed he asked Robert Walpole whether he should visit the prince whenever he resided in the parish, as he did with every other person of rank, but Walpole advised him against doing so, even though Francis Ayscough, the prince's clerk of the closet, invited him to pay his respects. The first time that the prince came to St James's Church, Thomas Bonney, the assistant preacher, began the service with the scriptural quotation 'I will arise and go to my Father' (Luke 15: 18–19), which was taken in London gossip circles to be a direct hint to the prince, and it was also inaccurately rumoured that Secker himself had preached at the same service on the fifth commandment ('Honour thy Father and thy Mother'). According to Secker's own testimony his relations with the prince were cordial but not close. He did bow to the prince in church and he even altered the time of morning prayer from 10.30 to 11 for his convenience. In return the prince always gave an Easter offering of £21 and Secker baptized seven of the prince's nine children. At the baptism of the future George III in 1738 the prince gave Secker a gold snuffbox with his portrait in it. Yet Secker felt that it was because of his failure to do much to patch up relations between father and son, and because he sometimes voted against the court, that George II did not speak to him for several years. It was widely believed that his bad relations with the king ensured that he had a 'protracted tenure' of the relatively poor dioceses of Bristol and Oxford (Sykes, 64). His voting against the court was, he claimed, also a reason why his friend and now fellow bishop Joseph Butler became more reserved towards him during the late 1730s and early 1740s.

Politics Secker's position in the House of Lords illustrates that eighteenth-century bishops were not simply ministerial voting fodder. From his appointment to the bishopric of Bristol in 1735 until the late 1740s he regularly attended debates within the Lords, making notes (later used by William Cobbett as a source for his *Parliamentary History*), using the shorthand that he also used on other occasions, particularly when he wanted to keep information private (BL, Add. MS 6043 has Secker's reports on debates, 1735–42). On several major pieces of legislation he did vote against the government. His first protest at government policy was to vote, with Edmund Gibson and other bishops, against the Quaker Tithe Bill of 1736, which would have relieved Quakers from some of the pains of non-payment of tithes and which was regarded as an attack on church interests. His opposition to ministerial policy seemed confirmed when, on Easter Monday 1738, he preached the Spital sermon and praised Sir John Barnard, lord mayor of London, who had voted against the ministry on a number of occasions. He next voted against the government in 1739, after the Lords debate about the Pardo convention with Spain, in which the ministry appeared to sacrifice British to Spanish interests. But something of Secker's ambivalent attitude towards outright opposition can be seen when on 13 February 1741 he and Benson voted against the proposal in the House of

Lords to ask the king to remove Sir Robert Walpole 'from his presence and counsels for ever'. Yet they also voted against the motion for censuring this proposal. On 28 January 1742 Secker voted with 'formed opposition' in favour of a secret committee to enquire into the conduct of the war with Spain, especially into the alleged lack of reinforcements for Admiral Vernon's expedition. His criticism of the ministry was also demonstrated in 1741 and 1742, when Secker (with other bishops) voted for a Pension Bill that would make it compulsory for MPs to declare whether they had government pensions, and a place bill, which sought to bar MPs from having a court office. In the same year he abstained from voting on the second reading of the bill for indemnifying people who should make discoveries concerning Walpole's conduct. His next anti-government move was to vote against the Spirituous Liquors Bill of 1743, which would have reduced the duty payable on gin. Secker called the bill evil: 'the most unchristian bill that was ever brought in by any government; and therefore I think it incumbent on me as a Christian bishop to give my testimony against it in the most open and express manner I can' (Taylor, 'Church and state in England', 174–5). To counter this oppositional stance, on other occasions Secker could be a reliable supporter of the government. In 1744 he made a powerful speech in defence of 'an act to make it Treason to hold correspondence with the sons of the Pretender to the Crown, and for attainting them of High Treason in case they should land or attempt to land in Great Britain'. Early in 1745 his support for the government was also seen in the anti-Jacobite sermon that he preached at St James's in both February and October and that was later published. Nevertheless his pro-Hanoverian stance could be softened by his compassion for fellow clergy. In November 1743 he received a letter asking for his support for the Scottish clergy widows and children in their attempt to have a bill passed for their maintenance. His autobiography reveals some co-ordination of church policy on this issue; he remembered that 'No Bp opposed [it] … And we took Care that a Bp shd be present at each of its 3 readings in the House of Lords' (*Autobiography*, fol. 32). In 1748 Scottish Episcopal clergy protested against their persecution in the wake of the repressive legislation following the rising of 1745–6; Secker spoke in their defence. In 1753 he expressed reservations about Lord Hardwicke's Marriage Act, which he pressured Hardwicke to amend. His last major parliamentary intervention came in 1754. In the previous year he had supported the government's Jewish Naturalization Bill, although he did speak for a clause to disable Jews from being patrons of livings. But after the public clamour that followed the passing of the act, the duke of Newcastle was anxious to have it repealed and Secker was chosen as the bishop who would second the motion. His speech was very well received, though so moderate and judicious were his comments that some thought he was still supporting the bill. Staunch whig that he was Secker could also transcend party politics, as can be seen in his suggestion to Lord Hardwicke (probably in 1740) that it might be prudent, in forming a new ministry, to bring in some of the 'better' tories (ibid., 29).

Dean of St Paul's By 1750 Secker was on better terms with George II, and on 11 December he was promoted to the deanery of St Paul's. The king had been convinced that Secker had renounced his links with any oppositional tendencies: he 'has acted like a gentleman, and I know has declared it to the opposition themselves. He has told Lord Limerick that he would never be for a secret committee again as long as he lived' (Newcastle to Pelham, 23 Aug 1750, BL, Add. MS 32722, fol. 223). Having been made dean Secker recalled that the king did occasionally speak to him, although 'never with any Mark of Distinction' (*Autobiography*, fol. 49). On account of his promotion Secker resigned both his Durham prebend and the rectory of St James's, and when he preached his farewell sermon at the latter the congregation is said to have dissolved into tears. As dean he was extremely hard-working and went to St Paul's twice a day. Characteristically one of his first major tasks was to sort out the records and finances of the cathedral. During 1753–4 he examined the accounts of the surplus that had been left unspent after the cathedral had been rebuilt in the late seventeenth and early eighteenth centuries and that was meant to have been reserved for repairs; he was concerned that the principal was being diminished and he made sure that it would be safeguarded in future. He had the documents about the cathedral put in order and personally indexed and corrected a copy of the statute book, and examined the registers and chapter books, extracting from them useful material for his successors. He was also instrumental in the repair programme, which put the cathedral in a better condition.

During the 1750s Secker was involved in some of the intellectual debates of the time, and a number of writers on behalf of the church sought his opinion of their work. His grounding in early Christian history was put to use in 1749–50 in helping Thomas Church in his controversy with Conyers Middleton over the existence of miracles after the time of the apostles, and in 1755 he commented on Church's *Analysis of the Philosophical Works of the Late Viscount Bolingbroke*. Secker was also a promoter of the work of Benjamin Kennicott (whom he made vicar of Culham, in the diocese of Oxford, in 1753), encouraging him in efforts to collect and collate Hebrew manuscripts and defending his scholarly methods against the critiques of the Hutchinsonians. He also read through Thomas Sharp's drafts in his disputes with the Hutchinsonians, and from 1749 he had encouraged the bluestocking Elizabeth Carter, daughter of the rector of Deal and an intimate of Catherine Talbot, in her edition of *Epictetus*, which was finally published in 1757.

Archbishop of Canterbury On 19 March 1758 Archbishop Matthew Hutton died and the duke of Newcastle proposed that Secker should succeed him. George II apparently asked whether Secker had been connected with the Leicester House opposition and the duke assured the king that he had not. The king consented to the appointment on 22 March and Secker was confirmed archbishop at Bow church on 21 April. Later that summer the University of Oxford presented an address to George II and, given the king's former suspicion of the university, Secker intervened to make sure that he received it kindly. Secker's warmer relations with the monarchy were cemented in 1760, when George III (whom he had baptized) succeeded his grandfather. Horace Walpole sniped that at the young king's accession Secker attempted to make himself 'first minister in a court that hoisted the standard of religion' (Walpole, 1.16) and tried to elbow out leading aristocratic families. There is little evidence of this, although Secker did hope that the new court would set a standard for religious practice. As archbishop he presided over George's coronation in 1761, revising the coronation service, and officiated at the marriage ceremony between George and Charlotte of Mecklenburg-Strelitz earlier in the same year.

Secker's archiepiscopate has claims to be one of the most, if not the most, distinguished in the eighteenth century. As archbishop he continued to be as hard-working as he had been in his former posts in the church, and he aimed to have a detailed grasp not only of diocesan business but also of the wider role that his post demanded. If there is a central feature about his occupation of the see it was perhaps his near obsession with paperwork in trying to keep up with developments on all fronts. The headquarters of his administrative machine was Lambeth Palace, which, being near the court and parliament—and in the absence of convocation—was the hub of national church life. Secker used Lambeth as a meeting place for bishops and also for interviewing and entertaining Kentish gentry and clergymen in his diocese. This could be costly and household expenses took over half his income, accounting for £4692 6*s.* 2*d.* in 1767. Testimony to the importance of Lambeth in Secker's archiepiscopate is the large archive that he amassed at Lambeth Palace Library. With his encouragement there was a thorough re-ordering of the archival and printed collections of his predecessors, and their act books, by the Lambeth librarian, Andrew Coltée Ducarel.

As archbishop Secker made some attempt to create a national policy. He worked particularly closely with his fellow archbishop Robert Hay Drummond of York to co-ordinate responses to problems facing the church, and they acted together over the administration of Queen Anne's Bounty. His concerns for the well-being of the national church were, however, tempered by the existence of what he considered to be a laity suspicious of clerical power. In 1761 he warned against the opening of convocation to do any real business, since 'in whatever way we act, we will excite great offence' (Taylor, 'Bishop Edmund Gibson's proposals', 185). During the last decade of his life Secker had to prioritize his engagements and cut down on his public appearances. He was no longer so involved in parliament as previously. This was partly because since 1754 he had been a supporter of the duke of Newcastle; in his new role he was consulted by successive ministries on promotions and he did not want to suggest that his previous connections indicated disloyalty to governments that did not include Newcastle or his circle. Furthermore by the time of his appointment to the archbishopric he found the long days and the heat of the upper chamber too much. One of his last parliamentary interventions was to speak, on 8 May 1765, opposing repeal of the Marriage Act and the passing of a new Marriage Bill; in 1767 he ceased attending the Lords altogether. He had been one of the most popular preachers of the day, and from the mid-1730s he could be found speaking on all manner of occasions and at all kinds of fund-raising meetings for the church. He himself noted that he had preached 'about' fifty-six charity sermons alone in and around London. He decided therefore, in 1760, not to accept any more requests to preach at similar events.

A hallmark of Secker's archiepiscopate was his attempt to strengthen links with foreign protestants. His own concern for the plight of persecuted protestants living in continental Europe reflected his belief that England, as the leading protestant nation, should look after its protestant brethren abroad. Even before he had become archbishop Secker was known to sympathize with their cause. In 1757 the congregation of the protestant church at Thorn, in Prussia, many members of which had been massacred by neighbouring Catholics, successfully petitioned Secker for help to publicize their cause in England in their attempt to rebuild their church. As archbishop Secker secured relief for the Vaudois community in 1767–8 and launched a national brief for their support. He seems to have particularly favoured financial aid to Hungarian protestants, giving £10 p.a. to the professors of Debreczen and to Johannes Uri, a Hungarian specialist in oriental languages. A related issue was the position of foreign protestants who now lived in England. At least as early as 1752 Secker had contributed to the maintenance of Huguenots living in London; as archbishop he was also keen to establish links with French Huguenot congregations and corresponded with John James Majendie, especially over financial aid. He also used his position to try to persuade Huguenots to conform to the Church of England, and he promoted several of those who took orders to Canterbury livings.

One issue that did become important during Secker's archiepiscopate was the question of a bishop for the American colonies. As early as 1741 he had stressed in a sermon to the Society for the Propagation of the Gospel in Foreign Parts that it was essential to have a resident bishop in North America, and in 1749 he was involved with drafting a petition for a bishopric in Nova Scotia. In 1751 he wrote a letter to Horace Walpole (which he did not want published until after his death), which replied to an earlier letter of Walpole's to Bishop Thomas Sherlock attacking such a scheme as being against the colonists' wishes. Secker put forward the view—much influenced by his correspondence with Samuel Johnson, president of King's College, New York—that the colonists wanted bishops of their own and that a bishop (or bishops) would be essential to the maintenance of the church in North America. Not surprisingly the issue of the plans for an

American bishopric was used by some of Secker's opponents in the 1760s. Thomas Hollis had formerly been an admirer of Secker, even presenting him with a head of Socrates made from green jasper at the time of his promotion to the bishopric of Oxford, but seems to have fallen out with Secker after the 1741 sermon. Hollis co-ordinated opposition on both sides of the Atlantic to what were considered to be Anglican encroachments and he encouraged the Boston congregationalist Jonathan Mayhew to write a polemic against the designs of the Society for the Propagation of the Gospel in Foreign Parts in 1763. In response Secker tried to put the case, as firmly and as judiciously as possible, for the creation of a bishopric in his *An answer to Dr Mayhew's observations on the charter and conduct of the Society for the Propagation of the Gospel in Foreign Parts* (1764).

Secker's views on the need for an American bishopric aroused criticism from within the ranks of his own clergy. In 1766 Francis Blackburne, archdeacon of Cleveland and a vigorous low-churchman, published *The Confessional*; it appeared anonymously and was part of a wider attack on the requirement that Church of England clergy should subscribe to the Thirty-Nine Articles. Blackburne argued for a further reformation of what he considered to be popish elements within the church; not only did he accuse Secker's predecessor, Archbishop William Wake, of foregoing protestant principles in his talks with the Gallican church but he criticized Secker's aims to create an episcopate in the colonies as being evidence of the popery that remained within the church, going so far as to compare Secker to Archbishop Laud. Secker found out who was behind the publication and encouraged Gloster Ridley to write against it in *Three Letters to the Author of the Confessional* (1768), providing much of the text for it himself and defending Ridley in the press. The archbishop tried to clear his predecessor of the charges that Blackburne had made against him, carefully going through Wake's papers in Oxford and elsewhere to prove him innocent. As part of his attempt to clear the Church of England's hierarchy from the imputation of popery, a year earlier Secker had written an article to the press under the pseudonym Misopsuedes, refuting the charge that Bishop Butler had been a closet papist.

At the diocesan level Secker was an energetic archbishop. True to form his first major task was to set out on his primary visitation from 10 to 27 July 1758. He followed this up with visitations in 1762 and 1766 but he needed to be convinced that archbishops of Canterbury were only required to visit their diocese once every four years rather than triennially. The charges delivered on these occasions continued his policy at Oxford of advising his clergy on pressing pastoral difficulties. The returns to his queries from the first visitation, with information added from the later visitations, were digested by him in his speculum. He was the first archbishop since the early part of the century to undertake a thorough visitation of the peculiars and, as at Bristol and at Oxford, he took especial care to regulate the organization of confirmations and encouraged the taking of communion. He was keen to be candid and was generous and benevolent when he felt that his clergy were trying their best but he could be quite sharp with clergy whom he considered were not fulfilling their pastoral duties. Some clergy seem to have resented the new archbishop's obsession with detail and his attempt to tighten up pastoral care in the diocese, seeing this as undue interference.

Secker paid particular interest in those ordained to a Canterbury title and refused to ordain those whom he thought lacked satisfactory theological knowledge; it was said that he had a black book containing the names of those whom he would not ordain or promote. He took a particular interest in those who acted as curates in the diocese. During his time as archbishop very few clergy were dismissed for misconduct, though he frowned on beneficed clergy who fell below his ideal of clerical behaviour. Only Samuel Bickley, vicar of Bapchild, was deprived by Secker; this was in 1764, on a charge of attempting to commit sodomy (though characteristically the archbishop gave Bickley some money in recompense).

One of the most time-consuming aspects of diocesan administration was the management of the archiepiscopal estates. A particular concern for Secker was the estate that had belonged to St Gregory's Priory, with the earls of Chesterfield as tenants. He tried (unsuccessfully) to get the tenants to pay pensions to the curates, and this may explain the fourth earl's much quoted assertion that Secker 'signs his own name, when he writes "Thomas Cant."' (*GM*, 53/2.1032n.). In the end Secker paid the pensions himself. He took care to monitor, and if needs be to take a firm line with, estate officials who might bring the name of the church into disrepute. Likewise he took care over the woodland owned by the archbishopric and lands owned by the three hospitals for the poor in the diocese. The wealth of clergy was an especial concern of his and he urged incumbents to preserve, and if necessary regain, their financial rights of the church but at the same time not to appear contentious. During his archiepiscopate Sir Philip Boteler was encouraged by Secker to augment thirty-eight parishes in the diocese through Queen Anne's Bounty.

During Secker's archiepiscopate Methodism made a slow but significant impact on the diocese. As one reared among dissenters Secker realized that the Anglican clergy might learn much from the Methodists. He was aware that Methodism might divide the church but thought that the best way to curb its growth was for the clergy to emulate its best features. In his charge of 1762 he told the clergy of his diocese that 'a chief reason why we have so little hold on our people is that we do not converse with them'. He pointed out that continental protestants, Catholics, and 'both the Old Dissenters from our Church and those who are forming new separations, gain and preserve a surprising influence amongst their followers by personal religious intercourse' (*Eight Charges*, 285). He recognized that there was some truth in the Methodists' criticisms; in his attempts to improve the pastoral performance of the clergy it could be argued that he had ends in view similar to those of the early Methodist leaders. In a proposed article of 1759 he exhorted his clergy to 'preach diligently the doctrines of justification by faith in Christ; warning against the abuses of that doctrine and of separating themselves from the Church to follow unauthorised teachers' (LPL, MS Secker 7, fol. 99*v*). Secker was aware of the tendency for rationalistic sermons yet he wondered whether the Methodists did not exaggerate the wrongs of the Anglican clergy. He realized that one reason why they did well was because leaders like Wesley could portray Methodism as a movement from within the church. He understood the aversion of many Methodists to separatism and told the vicar of St John's, Thanet, in 1765 that if the Methodists in his parish had a place where they met they ought to be licensed as dissenters:

> yet possibly some of them may be unwilling to call themselves Dissenters, and to be esteemed such by other persons. And in that case, it may be worthwhile to try what effect the fear of law will have upon them. (Secker to Harrison, 11 Oct 1765, LPL, MS Secker 3, fol. 242)

Secker suffered from ill health for much of his life, which makes his commitment to hard work even more impressive. Montagu Pennington, nephew of Secker's protégé Elizabeth Carter, later observed that 'Dr Secker's manners were not usually considered as prepossessing (one satisfactory apology for which may be found in his constant bad health)' (Pennington, 1.161). Secker recorded his various bouts of illness in his autobiography. The entry for 1724 (the first time that he noted his state of health) recalled that he had 'for some Years had a very troublesome Cough in the Winter: & felt a Weakness and Pain in my Breast, on speaking much or loud' (*Autobiography*, fol. 14). In July of that year he went to the Hot Well in Bristol and stayed there until September. The only remedy that seemed to have any effect was to discharge blood from an opening in his arm, which he left open until the end of his life. From the early 1740s he also suffered from the stone and tried various remedies, including Mrs Stephen's medicine, first in liquid and then in solid form. From 1761 to 1764 he suffered from 'dangerous fits of the stone' but these seem to have been cured by soap pills. An increasingly frequent and serious illness was gout (probably related to the hearty quantities of wine that he bought), from which he first suffered in 1742. This was always exacerbated when he was tired or under pressure, and he had an attack every two years or so. In the 1760s the condition became particularly severe. In 1762 he was so afflicted with it that he could not visit the diocese in person and delegated the responsibility to John Green, bishop of Lincoln. From 1764 onwards, he had especially long periods of gout, and in that year had a fainting fit when resident in Canterbury for the deprivation of Samuel Bickley.

Last illness and will The last year of Secker's life was acutely painful. He was suffering from a cancerous thigh bone and arthritis but continued to discharge much business as well as furthering schemes for the relief of foreign protestants and writing against those who criticized his archiepiscopate. On Easter Tuesday 1768 all the bishops, as usual, dined at Lambeth and Secker encouraged them to make lists of those clergy in their dioceses who were resident and non-resident, which illustrates how he wanted to improve the pastoral provision of the church as a whole. He died at Lambeth Palace, of a caries of the femur, on 3 August. He was buried in a covered passage leading from the palace to the north door of Lambeth church, and in his will he requested that his remains should have neither a monument nor an epitaph erected over them.

Secker's will—which named Mrs Talbot and John Burton, an Oxford associate, as executors—was characteristically well thought out, and his bequests rewarded people and causes with whom he had long been connected. Mrs Talbot and her daughter, Catherine, with whom he had lived since 1725 and who had effectively kept house for him since his wife's death, were given £13,000 in consols, to be managed by his chaplains and to be distributed to charities when they died. He left £1000 to the Society for the Propagation of the Gospel in Foreign Parts for general purposes and another £1000 to help establish a bishopric in North America. The Society for Promoting Christian Knowledge was left £500. Secker had earlier given handsome donations to both these bodies. He also left £500 to the corporation of the sons of the clergy (and £200 to the corporation's society of stewards) and £500 to the Irish protestant working schools. His early medical training was reflected in the £500 each that he left to the hospitals of Croydon; St John, Canterbury; St Nicholas, Harbeldown; to St George's, London, to the Lying-in Hospital, and to the incurables of St Luke's Hospital. It was reflected too in the £400 that he left to the asylum at Lambeth, and in the £300 each that went to the Magdalen, the Lock, the Smallpox, and the Inoculation hospitals. He donated £2000 to help rebuild and repair houses belonging to the poorer parishes in the diocese of Canterbury and £500 to Bromley College, Kent. £1000 was to be given out to his servants and £200 to people who had helped him. He left all his personal books and papers, as well as his manuscripts, to Lambeth Palace Library. His literary executors were his chaplains Beilby Porteus and George Stinton.

Secker had earlier made substantial gifts to his relatives and particularly to his nephews John Frost (who died in 1765) and George Secker, both of whom received preferment in addition to substantial financial assistance. He was also generous to the children of friends, including George Berkeley, son of the philosopher bishop. If anything Secker's family connections and ties of friendship appear to have grown stronger with age. Perhaps one reason why he clung to his extended family is that his close friends and fellow bishops Benson, Berkeley, and Butler, as well as his wife, Kitty, who died in 1748, departed this life within five years of each other. Secker's account book shows that apart from these gifts he dispersed a considerable amount of his income in charity to the poor and needy.

Secker was a tall man with an imposing presence. Several contemporary portraits of him convey something of his commanding personality, most notably that by Sir Joshua Reynolds, which was completed in 1764 and which was placed in the gallery at Lambeth, a copy of which can be found at St Edmund Hall, Oxford. In addition to his autobiography Secker left a voluminous correspondence, as well as the specula and account books already mentioned. Besides the charges he published a large number of sermons, which, together with his 'Lectures on the catechism', the 'Oratio, quam coram synodo provinciae Cantuariensis anno 1761 convocata habendam scripserat, sed morbo praepeditus non habuit, archiepiscopus', and his 'Instructions given to candidates for orders', were collected and printed after his death. He did not publish any major piece of scholarship, although manuscripts at Lambeth Palace Library show detailed work on the book of Daniel, which demonstrates his potential as an Old Testament scholar.

Secker's life illustrates some of the salient features of the Church of England during the eighteenth century. The very fact than an erstwhile dissenter from a relatively unpromising social background rose to the highest position within the church's hierarchy indicates the generally open nature of the church in this period. His time as a Church of England cleric and as a member of the church's hierarchy challenges some of the adverse judgements surrounding the church at this time. As a pastor, preacher, and administrator he was exemplary, and for these qualities he was revered by both contemporaries and successors. His charges, widely read both in his lifetime and later, went some way to make up for the lack of pastoral training in the period before the 1830s; they covered a wide range of topics, from how to deliver a sermon to the ways in which clergy should deal with refractory parishioners. They articulated the central tension in the clergy's role as Secker envisaged it: the need to win the support of society without sacrificing clerical ideals. He nevertheless received some criticism for what were perceived to be his strong views and authoritarian nature. Yet despite the accusations of popery and high-handedness already quoted others saw him as an example of moderation in the mould of Archbishop Tillotson. Secker himself highly regarded his predecessor Thomas Tenison. Secker's churchmanship is not easily characterized, and in any case reflects an eighteenth-century meshing of what are sometimes called high-church and low-church views. Though he came to be seen as a high-churchman and a defender of orthodoxy his dissenting background and his former religious liberalism endeared him to a wider range of views and people. Something of the range of his qualities, which could be used to support both high-church and evangelical positions, was listed by George Huntingford, bishop of Hereford, in 1828: 'I have always admired Arch-bishop Secker for his learning, his piety, his vigilance, his firmness, his mildness, his moderation, his discretion' (Huntingford to Howley, 1 Aug 1828, LPL, Howley papers). Secker certainly seems to have been able to retain contact with people whose views he did not share, such as Philip Doddridge, Isaac Watts, John Leland, Nathaniel Lardner, and Samuel Chandler. If in the nineteenth and early twentieth centuries he was well thought of both by high-churchmen and by evangelicals, in the late twentieth century he was increasingly admired for his aptitude for administration, sheer hard work, and managerial abilities. JEREMY GREGORY

Sources *The autobiography of Thomas Secker, archbishop of Canterbury*, ed. J. S. Macauley and R. W. Greaves (Lawrence, Kansas, 1988) · *The correspondence of Bishop Secker*, ed. A. P. Jenkins, Oxfordshire RS, 57 (1991) · *The speculum of Archbishop Thomas Secker*, ed. J. Gregory, Church of England Record Society, 2 (1995) · H. A. Lloyd-Jukes, ed., *Articles of enquiry addressed to the clergy of the diocese of Oxford at the primary visitation of Dr Thomas Secker*, Oxfordshire RS, 38 (1957) · E. Ralph, ed., 'Bishop Secker's diocese book', *A Bristol miscellany*, ed. P. McGrath, Bristol RS, 37 (1982), 23–69 · T. Secker, *Eight charges delivered to the clergy of the dioceses of Oxford and Canterbury* (1769) · T. Secker, *Lectures on the catechism of the Church of England with a discourse on confirmation*, 2 vols. (1769) · *The works of Thomas Secker LLD, late lord archbishop of Canterbury. To which is prefixed, a review of his grace's life and character, by Beilby Porteus, late lord bishop of London*, 6 vols. (1811) · L. W. Barnard, *Thomas Secker: an eighteenth-century primate* (1998) · E. Hasted, *The history and topographical survey of the county of Kent*, 2nd edn, 12 vols. (1797–1801) · *Monthly Repository*, 16 (1821), 506–7, 569–74, 633–5, 722 · F. Blackburne, *Works*, 1 (1805) · F. Blackburne, *Memoirs of Thomas Hollis* (1980) · *GM*, 1st ser., 38 (1768) · *GM*, 1st ser., 53 (1783) · N. Sykes, *Church and state in England in the XVIII century* (1934) · J. Gregory, *Restoration, reformation, and reform, 1660–1828: archbishops of Canterbury and their diocese* (2000) · *Public characters*, 10 vols. (1799–1809), vol. 1 · J. R. Guy, 'Archbishop Secker as physician', *The church and healing*, ed. W. J. Sheils, SCH, 19 (1982), 127–35 · J. R. Guy, 'De medicina statica. Archbishop Thomas Secker, a forgotten English iatromechanist', *XXVIIIth International Congress for the History of Medicine* (Paris, 1982), 134–7 · H. Walpole, *Memoirs of the reign of King George the Third*, ed. G. F. R. Barker, 4 vols. (1894); repr. (1970) · M. Pennington, *Memoirs of the life of Mrs Elizabeth Carter*, 2 vols. (1825) · S. J. C. Taylor, 'Church and state in England in the mid-eighteenth century: the Newcastle years, 1742–1762', PhD diss., U. Cam., 1987 · LPL, Howley papers · Bodl. Oxf., MS Add. 269 · LPL, MS Secker · S. Taylor, 'Bishop Edmund Gibson's proposals for church reform', *From Cranmer to Davidson: a Church of England miscellany*, ed. S. Taylor (1999), 169–202

Archives BL, corresp. and papers, Add. MSS 39311, 39315 · Bodl. Oxf., personal account book · LPL, autobiography, papers, and writings; corresp. and papers | BL, letters to Thomas Birch, Add. MS 4318 · BL, corresp. with earls of Hardwicke and Charles Yorke, Add. MSS 35586–35695 · BL, corresp. with duke of Newcastle, Add. MSS 32722–46688 · Sheff. Arch., letters to brother and sister, Bagshawe C 330 [copies] · Wesley College, Bristol, corresp. with Charles Wesley and John Wesley (as John Smith) · Yale U., Beinecke L., Osborn collection, diary of his housekeeper

Likenesses J. Vandebank, portrait, *c*.1730–1739, probably LPL · C. Phillips, oils, 1740, Oxford diocese · J. Macardell, mezzotint, 1747 (after J. Wills), BM, NPG · attrib. T. Hudson, oils, *c*.1747–1758, St James's Church, Piccadilly, London · attrib. J. Reynolds, oils, *c*.1758, LPL; version, NPG · attrib. A. Ramsay, oils, *c*.1760, LPL · J. Reynolds, portrait, 1764, LPL [*see illus.*] · J. Reynolds, portrait, second version, St Edmund Hall, Oxford

Wealth at death see will, *GM*, 38, 451

Secker, William (*d*. 1681?), Church of England clergyman and religious writer, of whose parentage and education nothing is known, does not appear in the published admission records of either Oxford or Cambridge.

In 1658 (or possibly early 1659; George Thomason marked his copy as acquired on 24 March and so immediately on the eve of the change of year in old style dating) Secker published a wedding sermon that he had delivered at Edmonton, Middlesex, as *A Wedding Ring Fit for the Finger, or, The Salve of Divinity on the Sore of Humanity*. A second publication, *The nonsuch professor in his meridian splendour, or, The singular actions of sanctified Christians*, based on seven sermons which he had given at All Hallows, London Wall, followed in 1660: George Thomason acquired his copy in October. Secker dedicated the book to Sir Edward Barkham of Tottenham, Middlesex, and his wife, Dame Frances, praising their godliness, their constancy to true religion, 'when others have sailed with every wind of Doctrine', and their loyalty to the king:

> you cast more propicious aspects upon Religion, then ever to think it a friend unto Rebellion, & lookt upon Fear God, and honour the King, as a couple that God had joyned together, and that no man might put asunder. (Secker, *Nonsuch*, sigs. A4r, A3v)

Both these works of practical divinity were published by the presbyterian Thomas Parkhurst, and *The Nonsuch Professor* at least has a Calvinist tone. Both books were reprinted many times well into the nineteenth century in Britain and America, sometimes together in one volume. *A Wedding Ring* had gone through ten editions by 1730, and was later translated into Welsh and German.

The religious writer is very possibly the William Secker who was admitted to the rectory of Leigh (now Leigh-on-Sea) in Essex on 30 August 1667 upon the presentation of Charles Rich, earl of Warwick. Circumstantial evidence lends plausibility to the suggestion that the writer and the incumbent are the same men. Neither seems to have possessed university degrees, while the puritan piety displayed in the books is in line with that patronized by Warwick's wife, Mary. Secker's successor was admitted to the living, made vacant by his death, on 12 November 1681.

H. R. FRENCH

Sources R. Newcourt, *Repertorium ecclesiasticum parochiale Londinense*, 2 vols. (1708–10), 2.384 • W. Secker, *A wedding ring fit for the finger, or, The salve of divinity on the sore of humanity* (1658) [Thomason tracts, BL, E 1648/4] • W. Secker, *The nonsuch professor in his meridian splendour, or, The singular actions of sanctified Christians* (1660) [Thomason tract, BL, E 1750/1] • I. Green, *Print and protestantism in early modern England* (2000), 206, 656

Seckford, Sir Henry (*d*. 1610), merchant and courtier, was the sixth of the ten children of Thomas Seckford (1495–1575) of Bealings, Suffolk, and his wife, Margaret (*d*. 1557), the daughter of Sir John Wingfield of Letheringham, Suffolk. Seckford Hall, near Woodbridge, Suffolk, was his childhood home. He was probably apprenticed as a grocer, for he was later a member of the Grocers' Company. He married three times. His first wife, a widow, Alice Karvile, the daughter of Sir Henry Bedingfield, brought a son, Henry, who became Seckford's ward on 18 July 1560. Alice must have died by 3 December 1583, as it is recorded that Seckford married Helen Bird (Burd) at St James's Church in Clerkenwell, Middlesex, on that date. It seems Seckford lived in Clerkenwell until 1596 at least, as two of his servants, Hans and Philip Christian, were buried in that church. Helen Bird may well have belonged to the rich merchant family of that name, and she certainly brought him land in Clapham, Surrey, as part of her dowry. On 6 June 1594 Helen was buried in St Matthew's Church, Ipswich, Suffolk. Some time after this date Henry married his third wife, Rebecca, the widow of John Rowe (and granddaughter of Sir Thomas Rowe, Lord Mayor of London in 1568). This too would have been a marriage linking mercantile interests. Henry was outlived by Rebecca, who still occupied their home in Clerkenwell in 1619. Henry never had any children.

Seckford (the name appears in a variety of spellings) is first heard of as a merchant and the owner of an 80 ton vessel known both as the *Anne Sackford* and the *Anne Frances*, of Ipswich. In 1557 an unnamed merchant bought a half-share in her for £120, and the vessel was regularly chartered for Spain, carrying grain, cloth, and, in 1568, raisins and Spanish skins. With a 200 ton ship, the *Harry Sackford*, ordered from Woodbridge shipyard in 1563, Seckford opened a new trading route to south-eastern Spain, but the Spaniards seized her on her return and sent her crew to the Spanish galleys. Seckford also imported wine from Bordeaux, using the *Anne Sackford* and chartering other vessels, but this traffic was disrupted through internal French politics, leading to the arrest of some of his ships.

Efforts to protect his Iberian trade by membership of the Spanish Company at its inception in 1577 and on its revival in 1605 were futile. In 1578 William Pett of Limehouse built for Seckford the 100 ton *Seabright*; while sailing illegally to Spain she was detained in Lisbon, losing him another £600. The Anglo-Spanish conflict of 1585 rendered trade virtually impossible, driving Seckford to pursue less lucrative sources of income. From 1573 to 1582 he and his brother Thomas jointly held the appointment of victualler of the realm of Ireland. His ships transported foodstuffs from East Anglia and the south-west, together with ordnance from the queen's arsenal, to provision the English soldiers stationed in Ireland. Elizabeth also paid for his pinnace to carry the admiral of the Irish fleet from Bristol in 1579.

With legitimate business yielding small profits and tardy payment, Seckford turned increasingly to privateering, in which he was involved for about twenty years. He captured several French vessels, which he managed to bring into home ports, but his attack in 1579 on the Danish *Maiden*, spoiling her cargo of sugar and cast iron, provoked a charge of piracy, not dropped for many years. His pinnaces *Discharge* and *Return* were his most successful privateering ships. In 1590 the *Discharge* and other privateers took part in an English assault on two Italian ships off Cape St Vincent, and brought them, with their rich cargoes, into English ports. In the face of strong Italian protest the ships and cargoes were impounded by order of the privy council, pending a court case, which in 1593 found one ship fair prize and required the other cargo to be divided between captors and owners. Seckford retained about £10,000-worth of goods but was fined £12,000 for pillaging one of the ships.

This severe blow to his finances came when Seckford was mourning the death of his wife, Alice, and his brother Humphrey. As Humphrey's executor he was attempting to clear debts of £2000, but Humphrey's assets proved insufficient and led to litigation. It is uncertain whether

Seckford continued privateering after 1590. He was, however, approached to construct ships for the navy in the late 1590s, and received the queen's bounty of 5s. per ton over 100 tons. The bill for timber used in their construction was still outstanding in 1603, showing him to be a slow payer, and perhaps also short-tempered, for the would-be recipient was given a 'beating and kicking … in grievous sort' (letter re suit of *Campion* v. *Seckford*, BL, Lansdowne MSS, 156.75, fol. 324).

Seckford took an interest in voyages of discovery. He unwisely invested £25 in Martin Frobisher's second voyage to North America, and hoped to profit from all three of Thomas Cavendish's voyages of 1585, 1586, and 1591, by acting as victualler and assisting Cavendish to raise money by mortgaging his lands. He and Humphrey were Cavendish's land agents from 1585 to 1589, overseeing estates in Suffolk and Lincolnshire. Seckford bought a third share in several Lincolnshire manors in 1573, and in 1585 Cavendish sold the brothers a lease to his Lincolnshire estates 'for diverse great somes of money and for and in consideration of diverse bondes and other encumbrances entered into by Henry and Humphrey Sackford esquires' (PRO, chancery proceedings, James I, c2/CC7/42; PRO, REQ 2/26/21). In the following year they sold it all conditionally to George Ognell, a rich London merchant, for the £1000 needed for Cavendish to build two new ships. The 1591 voyage was badly organized and provisioned, the crew mutinied, and Cavendish died. Before leaving he had written to Tristram Gorges, his executor, that Seckford was 'an hungry man and one that will seeke muche, use your discretion with him; he can clayme nothinge but as a parte vitler' (D. Quinn, *The Last Voyage of Thomas Cavendish*, 1976, 34).

Queen Elizabeth made Seckford one of her grooms of the privy chamber in 1558, with an annual fee of £20, supplemented by a rich gift in 1562 for his services. Following the death in 1559 of Sir Thomas Cawarden, master of the tents and revels, Seckford became master of the tents, hales, and pavillions by royal patent of 1560, with an annual fee of £30 and accommodation in part of the former hospital of St John of Jerusalem in Clerkenwell, a post he held until Elizabeth's death. Seckford's duties required him to make, store, and keep in repair the canvas hales (open shelters) and tents which housed horses and grooms on Elizabeth's progresses round England. More elaborate canvas structures were made to accommodate the entertainments performed for Elizabeth over Christmas. Seckford incurred heavy debts on these duties, which the queen was slow to honour. From 1570 he was also keeper of the privy purse, in charge of the queen's private expenses. He was master of the toyles (hunting nets), in effect from 1576 but officially from 1585, giving him responsibility for the royal deer. Benefiting from the indirect rewards available to crown servants, he was appointed guardian to minors and rented lands in Shropshire from the queen. In recognition of his loyal service to Elizabeth, James I knighted him at Clerkenwell on 11 May 1603.

Seckford died at his home in Clerkenwell, and was buried on 15 October 1610, in accordance with his will, in St James's, Clerkenwell, as close to his brother Humphrey as possible. Apart from 40s. to the poor of the parish, everything went to his widow, Rebecca, who was also his executrix. Seckford left debts of £3509 in connection with his royal service. His will is surprisingly brief for such an important merchant and royal servant, suggesting that there may originally have been an inventory.

SUSAN M. MAXWELL

Sources S. M. Maxwell, 'Henry Seckford: Elizabethan courtier, merchant and privateer', *Mariner's Mirror*, 82 (1996), 387–97 • S. M. Maxwell, 'The various exploits of Thomas, Henry and Humphrey Seckford, 16th century merchants', 1991 [unpublished paper] • P. Croft, 'English trade with Elizabethan Spain', DPhil diss., U. Oxf., 1969 • K. R. Andrews, 'The economic aspects of Elizabethan privateering', PhD diss., U. Lond., 1951 • A. Feuillerat, ed., *Documents relating to the office of the revels in the time of Queen Elizabeth* (1908); repr. (1963), 46–9 • N. Williams, 'The master of the royal tents and his records', *Prisca munimenta: studies in archival & administrative history presented to Dr. A. E. J. Hollaender*, ed. F. Ranger (1973), 162–8 • B. Dietz, ed., *The port and trade of early Elizabethan London: documents*, London RS, 8 (1972), 17–18 • K. R. Andrews, ed., *English privateering voyages to the West Indies, 1588–1595*, Hakluyt Society, 2nd ser., 111 (1959), 143, 151, 156, 163 • C. L'Estrange Ewen, 'Organised piracy round England in the sixteenth century', *Mariner's Mirror*, 35 (1949), 29–42, esp. 34 • N. J. Williams, 'The maritime trade of the east coast ports, 1550–1590', DPhil diss., U. Oxf., 1952, 146–7, 248 • J. P. Malcolm, *Londinium redivivum, or, An antient history and modern description of London*, 4 vols. (1802–7), vol. 3, p. 220 • PRO, HCA 14/19, 21, 22 • PRO, HCA 1/41 • PRO, HCA 3/18 • BL, Lansdowne MSS, 156/75, fol. 324 • PRO, REQ 2/50/38 • *CSP dom.*, 1566–79, 309 • V. B. Redstone, 'The Seckfords of Seckford Hall', *Proceedings of the Suffolk Institute of Archaeology and Natural History*, 9 (1895–7), 359–69 • *CPR*, 1558–1560, 35, 338; 1560–63 • augmentation office leases, PRO, E310 • BL, Lansdowne MS 167, fol. 295 • Suffolk RO, Ipswich, ESRO MD 7643/3/3 • will, PRO, PROB 11/116, sig. 95

Archives BL, Add. MS 5754, fol. 200 • BL, Add. MS 5017, art. 4 • BL, Davy's Suffolk collection, vol. 72, Add. MS 19148, fols. 200, 248*v*, 251*r* • BL, Harley MS 598 • BL, Burghley papers, Lansdowne MS 29 • BL, Caesar papers, Lansdowne MS 145, fol. 253 • BL, Caesar papers, Lansdowne MS 157, fols. 69–70, 290–91 • BL, Lansdowne MS 44/78, fol. 407 • BL, Lansdowne MS 133, fol. 23 • BL, Lansdowne MS 140, fols. 26, 38, 85, 91 • BL, Lansdowne MS 143, fol. 43 • BL, Lansdowne MS 144, fol. 368 • BL, Lansdowne MS 156, fol. 315 • BL, Lansdowne MS 167, fol. 295 • BL, miscellaneous papers, 22,115 • BL, Stowe MSS, 150 [fols. 21–4] • LPL, Carew papers (Ireland) • PRO, Court of Request papers, REQ 2/44/66 • PRO, Court of Request papers, REQ 2/50/38 • PRO, Court of Request papers, REQ 2/94/20 • PRO, Court of Request papers, REQ 2/101/7 • PRO, Court of Request papers, REQ 2/102/3 • PRO, Court of Request papers, REQ 2/113/39 • PRO, Court of Request papers, REQ 2/126/47

Wealth at death owed crown £3509: BL, Lansdowne MS 167, fol. 295

Seckford, Thomas (1515/16–1587), lawyer and administrator, was the second son of Thomas Seckford (*c*.1495–1575), of Great Bealings in Suffolk, and Margaret, daughter of Sir John Wingfield of Letheringham in the same county. A monument erected by him to his parents at Great Bealings reveals his age as sixty-seven in 1583. The Seckfords had been lords of the manor of Great Bealings since the fourteenth century, and the elder Thomas rebuilt Seckford Hall there. The son was admitted to Gray's Inn in 1540, at the same time as William Cecil (later

Lord Burghley), perhaps after a spell at Cambridge and an inn of chancery. Although he was called to the bar, and in 1556 delivered a reading and became a bencher, little is known of his legal practice save that he is mentioned as counsel in the court of requests in the 1550s. He became a member of parliament in 1554 and served (for four different constituencies) in seven parliaments between then and 1572. On 6 September 1558 he was appointed deputy chief steward of the duchy of Lancaster, for the northern parts, and on 9 December 1558 the new queen appointed him a master of requests, which was followed by the stewardship of the Marshalsea. At about the same time he was added to the commissions of the peace for Middlesex and Suffolk, and he was also put on the high commission for ecclesiastical causes. Indeed, he became an indefatigable administrator, arbitrator, interrogator, and commissioner in all kinds of business.

Rather late in life, in 1567, Seckford married Elizabeth, daughter of Thomas Harlow and widow successively of William Billingsley and Sir Martin Bowes (*d.* 1566); she predeceased him in 1586. In 1579 he acquired another lucrative office, as general surveyor of the court of wards and liveries under Burghley's mastership. In that capacity he became involved with the cartographer Christopher Saxton, whom he employed at his own expense to prepare between 1573 and 1579 the celebrated county maps, which bear Seckford's arms. They were the first of their kind. He also assisted William Harrison in his description of Britain, and Harrison dedicated to him his 'Description of Scotland' in Holinshed's *Chronicles*. It was no doubt through his offices and his land dealings that he acquired his considerable fortune, which he used in building the Great House (or Seckford House) in St Matthew's parish, Ipswich, and two houses in Clerkenwell, Middlesex, one of them next to St John's Priory. He bought the dissolved priory of Felixstowe, and owned various manors and lands in Suffolk. After his wife's death, without children, he made the plans for founding the Seckford Almshouse for thirteen poor men at Woodbridge, Suffolk, which was supported by the revenue from the Clerkenwell properties; the trustees were, in addition, to make grants to Woodbridge School. Seckford was also responsible, as steward of the liberty of St Etheldreda, for building the new sessions house in Woodbridge, which is now part of the shire hall and still displays his arms. He died at Clerkenwell on 19 December 1587 and, after a temporary burial at Clerkenwell, was reinterred in the family vault at Woodbridge. The plain tomb, without inscription, which he had built before his death in the north aisle, was broken up in 1839. J. H. BAKER

Sources HoP, *Commons, 1558–1603*, 3.362–4 • A. D. Briscoe, *A Tudor worthy: Thomas Seckford of Woodbridge* (1979) • V. B. Redstone, 'The Seckfords of Seckford Hall', *Proceedings of the Suffolk Institute of Archaeology and Natural History*, 9 (1895–7), 359–69 • HoP, *Commons, 1509–58*, 3.286 • Cooper, *Ath. Cantab.*, 2.18–19 • W. Hervey, *The visitation of Suffolk, 1561*, ed. J. Corder, 1, Harleian Society, new ser., 2 (1981), 199–201 • *The ancient state, authoritie, and proceedings of the court of requests by Sir Julius Caesar*, ed. L. M. Hill (1975), 159, 180 • J. L. Chester and G. J. Armytage, eds., *Allegations for marriage licences issued by the bishop of London*, 1, Harleian Society, 25 (1887), 35 • family monument, Great Bealings, Suffolk

Likenesses engraving, 18th cent. (after copy of Seckford? figure) • S. Lowell, line engraving, pubd 1792 (after T. Johnson), BM, NPG • group portrait, oils (Thomas Seckford?), Goodwood House, West Sussex; oil copy of Seckford? figure, eighteenth century, Seckford's Almshouse, Woodbridge, Suffolk

Wealth at death possessed considerable fortune; incl. various manors and lands in Suffolk and elsewhere

Secord [*née* Ingersoll], **Laura** (1775–1868), United Empire loyalist and heroine, was born on 13 September 1775 in Main Street, Great Barrington, Massachusetts, the first child of Thomas Ingersoll (1749–1812), merchant, and Elizabeth Dewey (1758–1784). Although he fought as a patriot during the American War of Independence and was later promoted to major in the militia, Thomas Ingersoll decided in 1785 to seek his fortune in the British colony of Upper Canada. Laura moved with her family to Queenston, near her father's lands in present-day Ingersoll, Ontario. There Thomas for a time ran a tavern, and Laura met her future husband, James Secord (1773–1841). He was of impeccable United Empire loyalist pedigree. Descended from French Huguenot stock, his father and two elder brothers fought on the British side during the American War of Independence (two of them as officers) in Butler's rangers. James and Laura were married, probably in 1797, and had six daughters and one son. They lived in the St David's-Queenston area until James became collector of customs at Chippawa in 1835. It was there that Laura ended her days, dying on 17 October 1868.

Laura Secord's life has become famous because of her role in conveying intelligence of a planned surprise attack by the Americans to Lieutenant James Fitzgibbon during the Anglo-American War, resulting in a decisive victory for the British at the battle of Beaver Dams. Americans may have Paul Revere's ride: Canadians have Laura Secord's walk. Her story has been much embellished over time, and begins with the heroic rescue of her husband, then a sergeant in the 1st Lincoln militia, from the battlefield at Queenston Heights. Reportedly she threw her body upon his wounded frame, challenging the enemy to kill her first. How she later learned of the planned attack is unknown, but tradition has it that some American officers demanded a meal at her house, then fell to discussing strategy loudly. Obviously James Secord was incapacitated, so Laura, although, according to Fitzgibbon, 'of slender and delicate frame', departed on the morning of 22 June 1813 to warn the British. She made a trek of upwards of 20 miles through fields and woods, avoiding the open road. As night fell she happened upon a Canadian Indian encampment, and its chief led her the rest of the way. One early chronicler, W. F. Coffin, wholly invented the tale of her taking a cow and pretending to milk it when accosted by American sentries. This association with wholesome dairy products doubtless contributed to her being adopted in 1913 by Canadian senator Frank O'Connor as the figurehead for his chain of chocolate candy shops, which continued throughout the century.

In her own time Laura Secord's heroism was largely

unrecognized. Neither Fitzgibbon, who received honours and a promotion, nor any of the other officers involved, acknowledged her in their official reports of the battle. James Secord, debilitated by his war injuries, received a small pension, but he and Laura struggled in poverty until he was appointed registrar in 1828 and then, in 1833, judge of the surrogate court of the Niagara district. Their repeated petitions to government, supported by certificates from Fitzgibbon, were unsuccessful. After James died on 22 February 1841 Laura returned to a state of poverty.

The first recognition of Laura Secord's heroism came from the prince of Wales in 1860 after a visit to Canada, when he awarded her £100. Some twenty years after her death she was taken up as a cause by early feminists who, glossing over the Ingersoll rebels in favour of the Secord loyalists, aspired to set her on 'a pedestal of equality … upon the roll of Canadian heroes' (Curzon, Preface) as an example of stalwart white pioneer womanhood. They mounted a campaign, appealing to Canadian women and children to contribute 10 cents and 1 penny respectively, and in 1901 raised a monument at her grave in Drummond Hill cemetery, Lundy's Lane, Chippawa, topped by a bronze bust by Mildred Peel, who also painted Laura's portrait in 1905 for the Ontario legislature. This was followed by a monument placed at Queenston Heights in 1910 by the Canadian government and a memorial hall in the Laura Secord School at Queenston.

Since then, some historians have mocked Laura Secord's popular image and contended that her famous walk did not contribute to the defeat of the Americans. Setting aside the many romantic embellishments of her story, most today would agree that the evidence shows that Laura Secord did warn Fitzgibbon in a timely fashion. As such she deserves to be remembered by posterity as the heroine of Beaver Dams. KATHERINE M. J. MCKENNA

Sources R. McKenzie, *Laura Secord: the legend and the lady* (1971) • C. Morgan, '"Of slender frame and delicate appearance": the placing of Laura Secord in the narratives of Canadian loyalist history', *Journal of the Canadian Historical Association*, 2nd ser., 5 (1994), 195–212 • L. Secord, 'A history of the war between Britain and the United States of America, during the years 1812, 1813 and 1814', *Anglo-American Magazine*, 3 (1853), 467 • C. B. Secord, *The Church* (18 April 1845) • *Niagara Mail* (27 March 1861) • *Niagara Mail* (3 April 1861) • *Niagara Mail* (17 Oct 1868) • W. S. Wallace, *The story of Laura Secord: a study in historical evidence* (1932) • W. F. Coffin, *1812, the war and its moral: a Canadian chronicle* (1864), 146–53 • E. A. Currie, *The story of Laura Secord and Canadian reminiscences* (1913) • G. Ingram, 'The story of Laura Secord revisited', *Ontario History*, 57 (1965), 85–97 • S. A. Curzon, *Laura Secord, the heroine of 1812: a drama; and other poems* (1887) • J. Carnochan, 'Laura Secord monument at Lundy's Lane', *Transactions of the Niagara Historical Society* (1913), 11–8

Archives NA Canada

Likenesses M. Peel, bronze bust, 1901, Drummond Hill cemetery, Lundy's Lane, Niagara Falls, Ontario, Canada • M. Peel, oils, 1905, Government of Ontario Legislature • bronze effigy on monument medallion, 1910, Queenston Heights, Ontario, Canada • portrait, repro. in S. A. Curzon, *The story of Laura Secord: a heroine of 1913*, 2nd edn (1898), title page • portrait, repro. in Currie, *Story of Laura Secord*, frontispiece • portraits, repro. in McKenzie, *Laura Secord* • woodcut, NA Canada

Wealth at death died in poverty

Secundinus. *See* Sechnall mac Restitiúit (*fl.* 5th cent.) *under* Meath, saints of (*act. c.*400–*c.*900).

Securis [Hatchett], **John** (*fl.* 1550–1580), physician, was born in Salisbury. His name was a latinized version of the English surname Hatchett. Securis was educated at Winchester College, and studied at the University of Paris for two years about 1550, while still very young. He attended and admired the lectures of Jacobus Sylvius, and studied pharmacy in the shops of several apothecaries. He afterwards studied at Oxford, although not at New College as was stated by Wood (*Ath. Oxon*, 1.458), and in 1554 published his first book. Entitled *A gret galley lately com into England out of terra nova laden with phisitions, poticaries, and surgions*, it is a dialogue attacking foolish and misguided physicians.

Securis returned to live in Salisbury, and seems to have been licensed to practise medicine by the bishop, to whom he presented a memorial on the granting of episcopal medical diplomas. It contained seven proposals: that every one who wished to practise in the diocese, and was not a graduate of a university, should only do so on receipt of a diploma from the bishop or his chancellor; that surgeons should be required to show that they could read and write; that apothecaries should not prescribe medicines; that no unlicensed person should practise; that no one should assume a university degree which he did not lawfully possess; that midwives should be sworn before the bishop; and that apothecaries' shops should be inspected from time to time by physicians. He mentions the College of Physicians in this memorial with great respect.

In 1561, and perhaps earlier, Securis began to publish *A Prognostication* for the year, a small black-letter book, containing definitions of legal terms, advice on suitable times for letting blood, weather forecasts, and suchlike information. He seems to have continued these until 1580.

In 1566 Securis published *A Detection and Querimonie of the Daily Enormities and Abuses Committed in Physick*, a small book in an idiomatic, informal style. It discusses physicians, surgeons, and apothecaries, laying down rules for the education and conduct of each. Securis expresses his belief in the power of the royal touch of the kings of England and of France. The book contains a Latin dedication to the universities of Oxford and Cambridge. It was reprinted in 1651, together with Robert Record's *The Urinal of Physick*.

The date of Securis's death is unknown. **Michael Securis** [Hatchett] (*fl.* 1545), a physician who lived in the 'new borough of Sarum', was author of 'Libri septem de antiquitate ac illustri medicinae origine', extant in Digbt MS 202 in the Bodleian Library, Oxford, together with some other medical opuscula by the same author.

NORMAN MOORE, *rev.* SARAH BAKEWELL

Sources Foster, *Alum. Oxon.* • T. F. Kirby, *Winchester scholars: a list of the wardens, fellows, and scholars of … Winchester College* (1888), 126 • J. Aikin, *Biographical memoirs of medicine in Great Britain: from the revival of literature to the time of Harvey* (1780)

Securis, Michael (*fl.* 1545). *See under* Securis, John (*fl.* 1550–1580).

Sedbergh, Adam (*c.*1502–1537), abbot of Jervaulx, was, as a Cistercian monk, ordained subdeacon at York on 22 September 1526, deacon on 6 April 1527, and priest on 15 June. These dates suggest that he was born about 1502. When still a young man, in or about 1533, he succeeded Robert Thornton as abbot, and almost immediately found himself involved in high politics. On the visit of Sir Francis Bigod and Dr Thomas Garret to the abbey, on 11 July 1535, George Lasynby interrupted Garret's sermon in justification of the royal supremacy to assert that the headship of the church belonged to the pope alone. Sedbergh joined with Bigod in denouncing Lasynby to Cromwell, and the monk was subsequently tried for treason at the York assizes in August and executed.

Sedbergh emerged unscathed from this encounter, only to succumb the following year. On 11 October 1536, soon after the outbreak of the Pilgrimage of Grace in the East Riding, insurgents arrived at Jervaulx demanding to see him. With his own father and a boy, Sedbergh fled to Witton Fell and remained there for four days. In his absence the rebels tried to persuade the convent to elect a new abbot, and in this extremity the monks prevailed upon him to return. Threatened with death by the rebels, Sedbergh took their oath and went with them to the great muster at Darlington where he spoke in favour of the rising. While the royal pardon might have extended to the abbot's behaviour in the first half of the pilgrimage, it could not save him from his actions early in the new year, when in February local agitators tried again to raise the commons and came to Jervaulx for a second time. On this occasion, before seeking refuge in Bolton Castle he gave them money for drink, and passed them on for a further reward to the quondam abbot of Fountains, then resident in the abbey. Once he had defeated the rebels Norfolk dispatched Sedbergh and the quondam of Fountains to London, where they were tried on a charge of treason, condemned, and put to death on 26 May 1537. On account of the abbot's attainder, Jervaulx Abbey and all its possessions reverted to the crown. CLAIRE CROSS

Sources *LP Henry VIII*, vols. 8–9, 12 · Borth. Inst., Abp. reg. 27, fols. 211r, 212v, 213v · A. G. Dickens, *Lollards and protestants in the diocese of York, 1509–1558* (1959) · L. E. Whatmore, 'George Lazenby, monk of Jervaulx: a forgotten martyr?', *Downside Review*, 60 (1942), 325–8 · G. W. O. Woodward, *The dissolution of the monasteries* (1966) · D. Knowles [M. C. Knowles], *The religious orders in England*, 3 (1959) · C. Cross and N. Vickers, eds., *Monks, friars and nuns in sixteenth century Yorkshire*, Yorkshire Archaeological Society, 150 (1995) · *VCH Yorkshire*, vol. 3

Wealth at death attainted

Sedding, Edmund (1836–1868), architect and musician, was born on 20 June 1836, the son of Richard and Peninnah Sedding of Summerstown, near Okehampton, Devon. John Dando *Sedding (1838–1891) was his younger brother. At an early age he displayed antiquarian tastes, which led to his visiting cathedrals, abbeys, and churches in England and France. In 1853 he entered the office of George Edmund Street, where he devoted himself to the study of Gothic architecture. For some time he resided as an architect in Bristol, and, after again spending a period in London, moved about 1862 to practise in Penzance. He married, on 18 August 1862, Jessie, daughter of John Proctor, chemist, of Penzance; they had four children, one of whom, Edmund Harold (1863–1921), was articled to J. D. Sedding and set up an independent practice in Plymouth in 1891. In Cornwall, Sedding rebuilt or restored the churches of Gwithian, Wendron, Altarnun, North Hill, Ruan, St Peter, Newlyn, and St Stephen by Launceston, while he had in progress at the time of his death a new church at Low Marple, Cheshire, a rectory, and two churches in Wales, the restoration of Bigbury church, Devon, and a mansion at Hayle, Cornwall, for W. J. Rawlings.

Sedding was a performer on the harmonium and organ, and an admirer of ancient church music. He was closely involved with two leading ritualistic churches, being for a time cantor of the church of St Raphael, Bristol, and organist of St Mary the Virgin, Soho. He greatly exerted himself in the revival of carol singing, and his books of Christmas carols were very popular. His chief musical compositions included: *A Collection of Nine Ancient Christmas Carols for Four Voices* (1860), which ran to six editions; *Jerusalem the Golden: a Hymn* (1861); and *Seven Ancient Carols for Four Voices* (1863). To F. G. Lees's revisions of J. Purchas's *Directorium Anglicanum* (2nd edn, 1865) he supplied fifteen quarto pages of illustrations. In 1865 Sedding's health failed, and he died at Penzance on 11 June 1868. He was buried in Madron churchyard on 16 June. His wife survived him. G. C. BOASE, *rev.* DONALD FINDLAY

Sources *DNB*

Archives Bodl. Oxf., letters

Sedding, John Dando (1838–1891), architect, was born on 13 April 1838 at Eton, the second son of Richard and Peninnah Sedding. In 1858 he joined his elder brother Edmund *Sedding (1836–1868) in the office of G. E. Street, where William Morris, Philip Webb, and Richard Norman Shaw were also pupils. All reacted against Street's hard-edged style in favour of later, more gentle idioms. After leaving Street's office in 1863 Sedding inclined towards decorative work, concentrating on the study and design of embroidery, wallpapers, and metalwork. From 1865 he worked with Edmund in Penzance, then moved to Bristol after Edmund's death in 1868 and to London in 1874; there he established himself at 18 Charlotte Street before transferring in 1880 to 447 Oxford Street, next door to Morris & Co.

In 1872 Sedding married a kindred spirit, Rose Catherine Tinling (*d.* 1891), daughter of Edward Douglas Tinling, canon of Gloucester, and through her brother the Revd G. D. Tinling came his first major commission, for St Clement's Church, Bournemouth. After his move to London, and with his wife's support, the architectural side of his practice, hitherto limited to schemes for hypothetical houses, began to develop steadily. He had learned much

John Dando Sedding (1838–1891), by Hayman Selig Mendelssohn [detail]

about building texture by copying plates in Ruskin's books, and in 1876 he submitted sketches to Ruskin, who encouraged him, saying that 'if you would be a real architect, you must always have either pencil or chisel in hand' (*The Works of John Ruskin*, ed. E. T. Cook and A. Wedderburn, 1903–12, 37.199). Believing architecture to be, not a commercial venture, but a divinely inspired art inseparable from handicraft, he formed a school of masons, carvers, and modellers from nature, and exerted a powerful influence over them by his friendly enthusiasm and close working knowledge of their craft.

Sedding's church restoration work, principally in and around London and in Somerset, Devon, and Cornwall, drew on his understanding of the organic nature of old churches acquired during his time in Cornwall. There too he had developed a response to the spirit of place, made clear in three new churches: Holy Redeemer, Clerkenwell (1887–95), for the Italian quarter, is in the Renaissance style; at Holy Trinity, Chelsea (1888–90), for an artistic locality, he attempted to create a synthesis of furnishings by leading artists; and for St Peter's, Earling (1889; built by Wilson in 1892–3), for a prosperous suburb, he devised a broad open chamber lit by a large west window with flowing Perpendicular tracery. Nor did he shun modern materials: Clerkenwell has concrete columns enclosing steel girders. His Catholic churchmanship (he was sidesman and later churchwarden at St Alban the Martyr, Holborn, from 1878) ensured that his church plans are focused on a prominent altar. His other principal new churches were St Dyfrig's, Cardiff (1885–93; dem. 1961), St Edward's, Netley (1886), St Elwyn's, Hayle, (1886–90), All Saints', Falmouth (1887–90); and St Augustine's, Highgate (1885–8).

Sedding's church furnishings, especially silversmith's work, embroidery, and woodwork, were ornamented, not with conventional symbolic devices, but with details drawn from nature: animals and birds enliven lush foliage on screens, doors and reredoses in churches such as Meavy (1884), Holbeton (1887), and Ermington (1889) in Devon, all restored for the Mildmay family, for whom he designed a lodge at Flete, a rare secular commission. Other examples are found in four silver pastoral staves designed around 1890.

Although elected FRIBA in 1874 and appointed diocesan architect for Bath and Wells, Sedding showed little interest in architectural politics and held few formal appointments; but he joined the committee of the Art Workers' Guild at its founding in 1884 and became its second master (1886–7). His influence was exercised through training his pupils, including the jeweller John Paul Cooper, the cabinet-makers Ernest Barnsley and Ernest Gimson, and the ceramicist Alfred Powell, as well as the architect C. A. Nicholson. His chief assistant was Henry Wilson (1864–1934), who after Sedding's death completed several of his works, adding towers at Bournemouth and Clerkenwell.

In 1888 Sedding moved to West Wickham, Kent, and developed his affection for the old English style of gardening, with formal plans and clipped yew hedges, which he championed in *Garden-Craft Old and New* (1891). After his death was published *Art and Handicraft* (1893), embodying views on architecture originally formulated in a paper read before the Edinburgh Art Congress in 1889.

Sedding was a simple, impulsive, warm-hearted man with a sense of fun, who inspired undying devotion in his friends and pupils. His published writings show the spontaneity and freshness of his thought, and are characterized by elegance and feeling. He died suddenly at Winsford vicarage, Somerset, where he was engaged on the restoration of the church, on 7 April 1891 and was buried in West Wickham churchyard with his wife, who died (probably of grief) a few days later. They had four sons, but his practice was inherited by Edmund Harold Sedding (1863–1921), son of his brother Edmund, who practised in Plymouth, carrying out church building and restoration in Devon and Cornwall, and published *Norman Architecture in Cornwall: a Handbook to Old Cornish Ecclesiastical Architecture* (1909). The nephew's new churches of St Peter, Shaldon (1893–1902), and St Mary, Newton Abbot (1904–8), show how thoroughly he had absorbed his uncle's ecclesiastical style, just as his care for craftsmanship is mirrored in his repairing of the chancel screens at St Buryan and St Winnow and the exuberant naturalistic woodwork at Crantock, by Pinwill of Exeter.

THOMAS SECCOMBE, *rev.* DONALD FINDLAY

Sources H. Wilson, *A memorial of the late J. D. Sedding … with a short sketch of his life* (1892) • J. P. Cooper and G. H. Wilson, 'The work of John D. Sedding, architect', *ArchR*, 3 (1897–8), 35–41, 69–77, 125–33, 188–94, 235–44 • E. F. Russell, 'Memorial notice', in J. D. Sedding, *Garden-craft old and new* (1891) • H. Wilson, 'John D. Sedding: his life & work', *British Architect*, 37 (1892), 15–18, 25–6, 35 • *The Builder*, 60 (1891), 298 [with list of works] • W. R. Lethaby, 'A note on the artistic life and work of John D Sedding', *The Builder*, 61 (1891), 270–71 • *The Times* (10 April 1891) • *Building News* (7 March 1890) • *Journal of Proceedings of the Royal Institute of British Architects*, new ser., 7 (1890–91), 264 • E. F. Russell, 'The late John Sedding', *Journal of Proceedings of the Royal Institute of British Architects*, new ser., 8 (1891–2), 109–10 • *Victorian church art* (1971) [exhibition catalogue, V&A, Nov 1971 – Jan 1972] • *CGPLA Eng. & Wales* (1891)

Archives RIBA BAL, sketchbooks

Likenesses H. R. Hope Pinker, bust, Art Workers' Guild, London • H. S. Mendelssohn, photograph, RIBA BAL [*see illus.*] • two photographs, repro. in Wilson, *Memorial of the late J. D. Sedding*, frontispiece

Wealth at death £5279 17*s.* 6*d.*: resworn administration with will, Jan 1893, *CGPLA Eng. & Wales* (1891)

Seddon family (*per. c.*1750–1864), furniture makers, apparently hailed from Lancashire. According to his great-grandson the architect John Pollard Seddon, **George** [i] **Seddon** (*c.*1727–1801) is thought to have gone to London about 1750. On his arrival there he established a cabinet-making firm that was to become the largest in the metropolis during the last quarter of the eighteenth century. George [i] Seddon has been identified as the cabinet-maker who, in 1754, purchased his freedom of the London Joiners' Company.

By 1753, when he took on his first apprentice, George [i] Seddon had acquired a 2 acre site in Aldersgate Street including London House (the former residence of the bishop of London), which remained the location of the firm's workshops until 1850. With his wife, Lydia, *née* Oldham (*d.* 1788), whom he had married by licence (she being over twenty-one) on 14 June 1759 at Holy Sepulchre without Newgate, George [i] Seddon had at least ten children who were baptized in the church of St Botolph, Aldersgate: John (*bap.* 26 Sept 1760); Thomas [i] [*see below*]; Robert (*bap.* 26 Sept 1762); George [ii] [*see below*]; Mary (*bap.* 4 Oct 1764, *d.* 1 Dec 1818); Catherine (*bap.* 12 March 1766); Elizabeth (*bap.* 26 April 1767); Lydia (*bap.* 5 June 1768, *d.* 13 July 1833); Esther (*bap.* 22 Dec 1771); and Dorothy (*bap.* 17 April 1774, *d.* 1799). The firm expanded quite quickly during the 1760s; by 1768 100 journeymen were employed and in a fire that year 'upwards of eighty chests of tools were destroyed' (Beard and Gilbert, 793). When in 1783 there was a further fire, the firm enjoyed the services of nearly 300 'of the most capital hands' in London (ibid., 794). The value of stock and household goods insured increased from £3300 in 1768 to £13,000 in 1787, for the business alone.

A remarkable contemporary description of George [i] Seddon's workshop by Sophie von La Roche provides a vivid picture of his business. In 1786, during her journey through England and Holland, she visited:

> Mr Seddon's, a cabinet-maker … who employs four hundred journeymen in all sorts of tasks, which are necessary for the proper furnishing of any house: cabinet-makers, wood-carvers, gilders, mirror-workers, upholsterers, brass-founders—who make the fine bronze into ornaments—and locksmiths. All this is carried out in a building with six wings. In the basement mirrors are cast and polished. In one of the other departments nothing is produced but chairs, sofas and stools of all kinds … One large room is absolutely full up with finished articles in this line, while more rooms are occupied by writing-tables, cupboards, chests-of-drawers. (Gilbert and Wood, 30–34)

The visitor also admired 'A thousand articles of straw-coloured satinwood, charming and quite perfectly made … Chinz, silk and wool fabrics for curtains and bed hangings' (ibid.).

Of the proprietor, Sophie von La Roche wrote:

> Seddon seemed to me a respectable man, as foster-father to four hundred employees, and a man of genius, who understands the requirements both of the needy and the affluent, and who knows how to please them with the products of nature and of other manufactories' artistry; who has made himself master of the qualities of wood from all parts of the world, and has the chemical knowledge how to colour them … and who has both the managerial ability to appraise the time and trouble spent by all his employees, and the creative talent to keep on devising new forms. (ibid.)

A portrait of George [i] Seddon (V&A), painted towards the end of his life, shows a kindly and respectable-looking man, intelligent and unostentatious in manner. This suggests that Sophie von La Roche observed him accurately during her London visit. In his entrepreneurial skills, George [i] Seddon had something in common with the Birmingham manufacturer Matthew Boulton, with whom he had dealings and corresponded. Seddon was also connected to the enterprising Josiah Wedgwood, from whom he purchased medallions which were inserted into his furniture; Wedgwood was also one of his customers.

For a firm of its size, it is perhaps surprising that little surviving eighteenth-century furniture has been identified. There is, however, archival evidence for some major commissions and important patrons: these include Charles Townley for Towneley Hall, Lancashire; Catherine the Great, empress of Russia; Sir Thomas Egerton for Heaton Hall, Yorkshire; the fifth duke of Beaufort for Badminton House, Gloucestershire; the fifth duke of Bedford for Woburn Abbey, Bedfordshire; and the second Lord Mansfield for Kenwood House, Middlesex. Perhaps the most extraordinary creation of the firm was the painted and carved satinwood cabinet fitted as a writing and dressing table, dated 1793, ordered for Charles V of Spain, but not delivered; this piece survived until about 1910, when it was broken up.

Thomas [i] **Seddon** (*bap.* 1761, *d.* 1804) was baptized on 21 June 1761 and bound apprentice in the Joiners' Company in 1775. **George** [ii] **Seddon** (*bap.* 1763, *d.* 1815) was baptized on 16 October 1763, and bound apprentice in 1777; he trained as an upholsterer. As liveryman in 1757 and later master, their father was influential in the Joiners' Company. In 1785 George [i] Seddon took both sons into partnership, and from about 1790 or 1791 they were joined by the upholsterer Thomas Shackleton, who had married their sister Mary. Some of the furniture supplied by Seddon, Sons and Shackleton survives in private collections and gives a good indication of their finest late eighteenth-century creations. Among the pieces the partnership delivered to D. Tupper of Hauteville House, St Peter Port, Guernsey, described in M. Harris & Sons, *Old English Furniture* (1935, 62–3), and for R. Clarke of Bridwell House, Dorset, some of which was sold at auction at Bearnes, Torquay, Devon, on 14 October 1992, was elegant satinwood furniture with painted decoration.

It is not known how the Seddon house style was created, but it appears that the firm followed the latest fashions, even if their own creative talents were somewhat limited and conservative. George [i] Seddon subscribed to Thomas Chippendale's *Director* (1754), Thomas [i] Seddon subscribed to Thomas Sheraton's *Drawing Book* (1792) and, in

1826, Thomas [ii] Seddon and George [iii] Seddon [*see below*] signed a prefatory recommendation to *Practical Cabinet Maker* by P. Nicholson and M. A. Nicholson. Much of Seddons late eighteenth-century production, in mahogany or satinwood, is of a type familiar from the publications of George Hepplewhite and Thomas Sheraton. In common with other late eighteenth- and early nineteenth-century cabinet-makers, Seddons were alive to the commercial prospects of patent and mechanical furniture. About 1780 Seddons invented a writing-table and filing cabinet for Sir Herbert Croft known as a Croft; in 1798 they produced a desk with a rising section of drawers and pigeon-holes controlled by a mechanism patented by Day Gunby; and, at the same period, a patent architect's table.

When George [i] Seddon retired in 1798, the firm passed to his two sons, Thomas [i] Seddon and George [ii] Seddon, with financial provision being made for himself and his three daughters. After his wife, Lydia, had died on 27 March 1788, George [i] Seddon married Jane and he provided in his will for her, his sons, and his daughters. He died at Hampstead on 25 November 1801 and was buried there the following day in the old churchyard. The firm did not prosper, but none the less struggled on during the next two decades, despite a period of bankruptcy. In 1804, the year that Thomas [i] Seddon died, the brothers both served as officers in the volunteer army—Thomas as a lieutenant-colonel and George as a captain of the London (Loyal) 11th regiment. On 26 May 1787 Thomas [i] Seddon had married Mary, daughter of John Pollard, who had earlier lent George [i] Seddon £10,000 to invest in his business. Thomas and Mary had at least eight children, including **Thomas** [ii] **Seddon** (*bap.* 1793, *d.* 1864), who was baptized on 8 January 1793 and apprenticed to his uncle George [ii] Seddon from 1806 to 1813. In 1815 Thomas [ii] Seddon took over the firm and was joined two years later by his brother, **George** [iii] **Seddon** (*bap.* 1797, *d.* 1857), who was baptized on 5 February 1797. By the time of his death, aged fifty-two, in September 1815, George [ii] Seddon had married, but had no children. He was buried on 20 September 1815 at St Botolph, Aldersgate. On 18 August 1820 Thomas [ii] Seddon married at St Martin Orgar with St Clement, Eastcheap, London, Frances Nelson, *née* Thomas, with whom he had at least eleven children.

Not much is known of the firm from 1815 until 1827 when George [iii] Seddon entered a partnership with Nicholas Morel to supply furniture for George IV at Windsor Castle. The partnership of Morel and Seddon gave its address as 13 Great Marlborough Street, but the manufactory remained in Aldersgate Street. At this date, for the first time, the firm became associated with the manufacture of furniture by named designers. They employed P. Bogaerts, J.-J. Boileau, F.-H.-G. Jacob-Desmalter (in the neo-classical style), and A. W. N. Pugin (in the Gothic style). About 1830 the same partnership supplied furniture to the marquess of Stafford for Stafford House. Much work from these two commissions survives, or can be identified in late nineteenth-century photographs.

The Morel and Seddon partnership appears to have ended by 1831, but Thomas [ii] Seddon and George [iii] Seddon, who received a royal warrant in 1832, continued into the 1850s. After a fire in 1830, when 100 tool chests were destroyed, the firm moved to new premises designed by J. B. Papworth in Gray's Inn Road. Regency-style furniture made during the second quarter of the nineteenth century can sometimes be identified by the firm's paper label attached to the undersides, for example, of tables and cabinets. The artistic and technical quality of surviving furniture by the Seddon family, together with knowledge of the size of their workshops, have ensured that their firms enjoy a high reputation in the history of English furniture making. George [iii] Seddon died, apparently unmarried, at Boulogne, France, on 3 August 1857, and Thomas [ii] Seddon died at his home, 27 Grove Terrace, Kentish Town, London, on 13 September 1864. In the later nineteenth century the family's reputation was enhanced by two of Thomas [ii] Seddon's sons, the Gothic revival architect John Pollard *Seddon (1827–1906), and the landscape painter and furniture designer Thomas *Seddon (1821–1856). MARTIN LEVY

Sources J. P. Seddon, *Memoirs and letters of the late Thomas Seddon artist* (1858) · G. Beard and C. Gilbert, eds., *Dictionary of English furniture makers, 1660–1840* (1986) · C. Gilbert, 'Seddon, Sons & Shackleton', *Furniture History*, 33 (1997), 1–29 · C. Gilbert and L. Wood, 'Sophie von La Roche at Seddon's', *Furniture History*, 33 (1997), 30–34 · C. Gilbert, 'A few Seddon gleanings', *Furniture History*, 34 (1998), 226–37 · Birm. CL, Boulton papers · Keele University, Wedgwood archive, Ledger 6; 21050–21111, fols. 31 and 407 · *CGPLA Eng. & Wales* (1864) · private information (2004) [Society of Genealogists] · *IGI* · PRO, PROB 11/1369 [will of George [i] Seddon], fols. 45*v*–49*v* · G. B. Hughes, 'George Seddon of London House', *Apollo*, 65 (1957), 177–81 · British Consulate Register · H. Roberts, *For the king's pleasure. The furnishing and decoration of George IV's apartments at Windsor Castle* (2001)

Archives Keele University, Wedgwood archive, ledger 6 · Lancs. RO, bank deposit and account books for Heaton Hall · priv. coll., Charles Townley account book · priv. coll., Badminton papers

Likenesses portrait, *c*.1795 (George [i] Seddon), V&A; repro. in R. Edwards and M. Jourdain, *Georgian cabinet-makers*, rev. edn (1955), p. 211, fig. 172

Wealth at death under £2000—Thomas [ii] Seddon: resworn probate, 31 Oct 1864, *CGPLA Eng. & Wales*

Seddon, Felix John Vaughan (1798–1865), orientalist, was a younger son among the fourteen children of William Seddon (1756/7–1808), attorney in Manchester, and his wife, Penelope, *née* Watson. He was probably born at his parents' residence in Pendleton, and was educated at Manchester grammar school from 1806. In 1815 he went to India in the service of the East India Company, and while there devoted himself to the study of oriental languages, particularly Persian and Hindustani. After passing the revenue board examinations he was in 1820 appointed registrar of Rangpur, Bengal, where he familiarized himself with Bengali and Sanskrit. At the outbreak of the First Anglo-Burmese War, in 1824, he accompanied the army to Assam as translator and accountant to the governor-general's agent on the north-eastern frontier. He was chosen because of his ability, through the medium of Sanskrit, to acquire the local languages, especially Manipuri, which he was the first European to learn. He translated the articles of war and artillery exercise for use of the

Manipuri levy, and prepared a grammar and dictionary of Assamese. In 1830 failing health forced him to return to England and abandon his work on a comparative dictionary of Manipuri, Thai, and Burmese.

On 12 July 1833 Seddon was elected professor of oriental languages at King's College, London, and in 1835 published *An Address Delivered in King's College … on the Languages and Literature of Asia*. He also assisted in translating the Bible into some Eastern languages. In 1837 he returned to India, intending to found a college at Lucknow, with the support of William IV, but when he arrived there he found that the king of Oudh was dead, and his successor was opposed to the plan. This and other difficulties obliged him to abandon the undertaking. He was afterwards appointed preceptor to the titular nawab of Bengal. The latter part of his life was spent at Murshidabad, Bengal, where he died, unmarried, on 25 November 1865.

C. W. SUTTON, *rev.* R. S. SIMPSON

Sources J. F. Smith, ed., *The admission register of the Manchester School, with some notes of the more distinguished scholars*, 2, Chetham Society, 73 (1868), 166, 244–5

Seddon, George (*c*.1727–1801). *See under* Seddon family (*per. c*.1750–1864).

Seddon, George (*bap.* 1763, *d.* 1815). *See under* Seddon family (*per. c*.1750–1864).

Seddon, George (*bap.* 1797, *d.* 1857). *See under* Seddon family (*per. c*.1750–1864).

Seddon, John (1643/4–1700), writing-master, was probably born in London but nothing is known of his early life or parentage. During his lifetime he was much admired for a level of ornamental penmanship which was notable for its enormous flourishes produced with one continuous stroke of the pen. Indeed, Seddon's calligraphy was characterized by the unusually imaginative monsters and dragons with which he embellished his compositions and it was for this reason that he gained a reputation as a virtuoso penman. He published a number of copy-books, but the first was a modest production entitled *The Ingenious Youth's Companion* (1690) and engraved by J. Sturt. 'It contains an alphabet of two-lines copies, in a small round hand, with great variety of flourishes, which … were performed *à la volée*' (Massey, 2.129), that is without pencilled guide lines. This was followed by *The Penman's Paradise* (1695) and the posthumously published *The Penman's Magazine* (1705), both of which contained such highly ornamented writing and were, according to both William Massey's and Mark Noble's interpretations, viewed more as a form of art than as exercises for students to copy. He became master of Sir John Johnson's Free Writing School in Priest's Court, Foster Lane, Cheapside, a post he held until his death. Though the circumstances remain unknown John Seddon died on 12 April 1700 at the age of fifty-six.

THOMPSON COOPER, *rev.* LUCY PELTZ

Sources A. Heal, *The English writing-masters and their copy-books, 1570–1800* (1931) • W. Massey, *The origin and progress of letters: an essay in two parts* (1763) • *Engraved Brit. ports.* • 'Calligraphy', *N&Q*, 3rd ser., 11 (1867), 291 • *A biographical history of England, from the revolution to the end of George I's reign: being a continuation of the Rev. J. Granger's work*, ed. M. Noble, 3 vols. (1806) • Thieme & Becker, *Allgemeines Lexikon* • J. I. Whalley, *English handwriting, 1540–1853* (1969)

Likenesses J. Sturt, line engraving (after W. Faithorne), BM, NPG; repro. in *Penman's paradise both pleasant and profitable* (1695)

Seddon, John (1719–1769), dissenting minister and religious controversialist, was born at Lomax Fold, Little Lever, near Bolton, Lancashire, the son of Peter Seddon (1689–1731), dissenting minister at Penrith, Cumberland (1717–19), and later at Cockey Moor, in the parish of Middleton, Lancashire (1719–31). On his father's death Seddon's education was undertaken by the congregation of Cross Street, Manchester. He attended Stand grammar school under William Walker from 1731 to 1733 and subsequently Caleb Rotheram's academy at Kendal, where in 1733 he was one of the first three students to be admitted. He remained there at least until Christmas 1738 before completing his education at Glasgow University, whence he matriculated in 1739, but there is no evidence of him being awarded the MA degree with which he is often credited.

On leaving Glasgow, Seddon became assistant at Cross Street to Joseph Mottershead, and was ordained there on 22 October 1742. In 1743 he married Mottershead's eldest daughter, Elizabeth (*d.* 1765). He was a preacher of facility and power and was the first minister of Cross Street to preach Socinianism instead of, then the prevalent form of anti-Trinitarianism, Arianism. Joseph Priestley, when a tutor at Warrington Academy (1761–8), spoke of Seddon as 'the only Socinian in the neighbourhood', adding, 'we all wondered at him' (Rutt, 1.59). He embodied his views in a series of six sermons, of which the first was preached on 27 May 1761. In these he declared that the New Testament provided no foundation for a belief in the Trinity. His utterances caused a good deal of excitement, but while his outspokenness may have won him increased respect it gained him few converts. The sermons were not published until 1793, by which time they were out of date, but they are noteworthy for their time as anticipating the historical argument advanced by Priestley.

Seddon, despite his heterodox views, lived on good terms with neighbouring clergy, especially with John Clayton (1709–1773), the Jacobite fellow of Manchester collegiate church, and with his colleague and father-in-law, Joseph Mottershead. His amiable disposition and charity to the poor made him a popular preacher. He was not, however, a prolific writer, and the sermons mentioned above and a preface to Thomas Dixon's *The Sovereignty of Divine Administration* (1766) seem to have been his only publications.

After a long illness Seddon died in Manchester on 22 November 1769, and was buried in Cross Street Chapel. His library was sold on 26 February 1770.

ALEXANDER GORDON, *rev.* M. J. MERCER

Sources C. Surman, index, DWL • B. Nightingale, *Lancashire nonconformity*, 6 vols. [1890–93], vol. 5 • F. Nicholson and E. Axon, *The older nonconformity in Kendal* (1915) • W. D. Jeremy, *The Presbyterian Fund and Dr Daniel Williams's Trust* (1885) • *Life and correspondence of Joseph Priestley*, ed. J. T. Rutt, 2 vols. (1831–2) • G. E. Evans, *Vestiges of protestant dissent* (1897) • 'A list of the divinity students educated at

Dr Rotheram's Academy, Kendal', *Monthly Repository*, 5 (1810), 321–7, esp. 322–3 • list of students at Kendal, DWL, N.C.A., L54/2/11
Archives DWL, corresp. • Harris Man. Oxf., corresp. and papers

Seddon, John (1724–1770), dissenting minister and tutor, was born at Hereford on 8 December 1724, the son of Peter Seddon (*d.* 1760), dissenting minister successively at Ormskirk and Hereford, and his wife, Elizabeth Eckley. He was a second cousin of John Seddon (1719–1769), minister at Cross Street, Manchester, with whom he has often been confused. In 1742 he was admitted to Kendal dissenting academy, under Caleb Rotheram, and in 1744 he matriculated from Glasgow University, where he was a favourite pupil of Francis Hutcheson and William Leechman. On finishing his studies he succeeded Charles Owen as minister of Cairo Street Chapel, Warrington, and was ordained there on 8 December 1747. He proved to be a popular minister and soon attracted the attendance of the Percival family, who left the established church and later engaged him as private tutor to Thomas Percival (1740–1804). Percival later wrote of Seddon 'As a gentleman, a scholar, a preacher, a companion and a friend, he was almost without an equal' (*Monthly Repository*, 1810, 430).

Following the closure of the dissenting academies at Kendal in 1753 and Findern, Derbyshire, in 1754, a project was launched in July 1754 to establish by subscription a dissenting academy in the north of England, primarily to educate candidates for the ministry. Seddon was a prime mover in the scheme and his skill and perseverance at drumming up support from local merchants no doubt contributed to the trustees' decision to locate the school in Warrington rather than Ormskirk. On 30 June 1757 he was elected secretary and Hugh Willoughby of Parham accepted the invitation to become president of the academy. When the academy opened on 20 October, Seddon was appointed librarian; his former pupil Thomas Percival was the first student to be enrolled. In addition to divinity students Warrington also took fee-paying private pupils, who were offered an education that would prepare them for a professional or commercial career. On 19 July that year Seddon married Sarah Hoskins at St Philip's, Birmingham; according to Job Orton she was the daughter of a deceased equerry to Frederick, prince of Wales. They had no children.

Seddon soon fell out with John Taylor, professor of divinity and moral philosophy at Warrington, whose prickly character was such that he took offence at what he saw as Seddon's interference. As secretary, Seddon liaised between the tutors and the management committee and sat in on the tutors' meetings; and as librarian he approved every book purchase. Moreover Taylor did not share the high opinion of Hutchesonian metaphysics that Seddon had acquired at Glasgow and they took opposing sides in a local controversy respecting forms of prayer. On 3 July 1750 a group of dissenting ministers from the north-west met at Warrington to consider introducing set forms into dissenting worship and a subsequent meeting at Preston on 10 September 1751 declared in favour of 'a proper variety of public devotional offices'.

The following year the provincial assembly set up a committee to decide the matter and a long controversy ensued. When on 16 October 1760 a number of dissenters in Liverpool, led by the porcelain manufacturer Thomas Bentley, decided to build a chapel for liturgical worship and invited several dissenting ministers to prepare a prayer book, Taylor declined and Seddon accepted. On 6 January 1762 at a meeting at the Merchants' Coffee House in Liverpool, Seddon submitted 'the new liturgy', which was published as *A form of prayer and a new collection of psalms, for the use of a congregation of protestant dissenters in Liverpool* (1763). Edited by Seddon, the new liturgy was written by Philip Holland and Richard Godwin (1722–1787), minister at Gateacre, near Liverpool, and was used in the Octagon Chapel, Liverpool, which opened in 1763. Seddon declined to become minister at the Octagon Chapel and chose not to use the liturgy in his own ministry, preferring extempore prayer.

Seddon regarded Warrington Academy as 'his favourite child' and Taylor's complaints about his interference may have been justified for, according to William Turner, Seddon was 'somewhat too meddling, and perhaps occasionally assuming, in his intercourse with the Tutors' (*Monthly Repository*, 8.190). However, his dynamic influence on the academy was a crucial factor in maintaining its success. In 1762 he toured the major cities in England, visiting dissenting congregations, in an attempt to encourage subscriptions and to recruit more fee-paying pupils. His carefully kept accounts and minutes show that the academy's fortunes revived, albeit temporarily, and he turned his attention to another problem. Discipline was always a difficulty at the academy and in 1767 he was appointed to the newly created office of 'rector academiae'. One of his new duties was to take a weekly register of the students in order to encourage regular attendance. At the same time he succeeded Joseph Priestley in the chair of belles lettres, with a salary of £100 plus the fees from private pupils attending his lectures. Despite his own financial problems (he had lost his wife's fortune by investing it in a calico-printing works at Stockport) Seddon accepted only half of the salary as he was aware that the academy could little afford to pay the full salary. An excellent orator, he lectured on language, oratory, theology, and philosophy.

Outside the academy Seddon was a co-founder and the first president of Warrington Public Library (1758) and the first secretary of the Lancashire and Cheshire Widows' Fund (1764). He died suddenly after suffering a seizure while out riding at Warrington on 23 January 1770 and was buried in Cairo Street Chapel; he was survived by his wife. ALEXANDER GORDON, *rev.* S. J. SKEDD

Sources P. Holland, 'A funeral sermon for the Rev. Mr Seddon of Warrington', *Sermons on practical subjects*, 2 vols. (1792), 2.197–224 • R. B. Aspland, 'Brief memoir', *Christian Reformer*, 10 (1854), 224ff. • 'Letters and papers of the Rev. John Seddon', *Christian Reformer*, 10–11 (1854–5), 224–358, 613; 365–75 • A. Holt, ed., 'The Seddon letters', *Transactions of the Unitarian Historical Society*, 7 (1941–2), 226–38, 269–89 • H. McLachlan, *Warrington Academy: its history and influence*, Chetham Society, 107, new ser. (1943) • H. McLachlan, *English education under the Test Acts: being the history of the nonconformist academies,*

1662–1820 (1931) • V. F. [W. Turner], 'Historical account of Warrington Academy', *Monthly Repository*, 8 (1813) • *GM*, 1st ser., 27 (1757), 338 • B. Nightingale, *Lancashire nonconformity*, 6 vols. [1890–93], vol. 2 • *IGI*

Archives DWL, corresp. • Harris Man. Oxf., corresp. and papers

Likenesses silhouette, repro. in J. Kendrick, *Profiles of Warrington worthies*, 2nd edn (1854)

Seddon, John Pollard (1827–1906), architect, was born on 19 September 1827 at London House, 150 Aldersgate Street, London, the third child of Thomas *Seddon (*bap.* 1793, *d.* 1864) [*see under* Seddon family] and Frances Nelson, *née* Thomas (1800–1880) and great-grandson of George *Seddon (*c.*1727–1801), furniture maker [*see under* Seddon family]. His elder brother was the landscape painter Thomas *Seddon (1821–1856), whose friendships with W. H. Hunt and F. M. Brown prompted Seddon's collaboration with Pre-Raphaelites on a variety of works in the 1850s and 1860s, for example Rossetti's reredos for Llandaff Cathedral. After attending Bedford grammar school Seddon was articled in 1847 to T. L. Donaldson, and in the same year joined the Architectural Association as a founder member; he served as honorary secretary in 1850–51. Despite Donaldson's neo-classicism Seddon was seduced in 1849 by Ruskin's *Seven Lamps of Architecture*, and was quickly converted to the philosophy of the Gothic revival, staunchly maintaining throughout his long career that Gothic was the only true Christian art, 'most scientific and beautiful, and most in accordance with common sense' ('Ancient and modern ornament contrasted', *Building News*, 29 Jan 1858, 109–12). In 1852, while building a small hotel in Southerndown, Glamorgan, he met John Prichard, diocesan architect of Llandaff, who offered him a partnership in 1853. The arrangement lasted until 1863, with Seddon largely responsible for the Monmouthshire jobs. Following an acclaimed competitive entry for the War and Foreign offices, Seddon established in 1858 the partnership's Whitehall office, through which he gained greater individual exposure. He was elected fellow of the Royal Institute of British Architects (RIBA) on 5 March 1860, and repeatedly elected honorary secretary between 1862 and 1871. On 12 May 1864 he married Margaret Barber (1836–1910) of Brighouse, Yorkshire, with whom he had three children, Maud, Hugh, and Katherine.

Seddon's architectural practice flourished in the 1860s and early 1870s. Significant secular designs included University College, Aberystwyth (1864–86), an entry in a law courts competition (1866), and the speculative bungalow development of Birchington-on-Sea, Kent (1880–82). But Seddon was essentially an ecclesiastical architect, and he built churches at Chigwell Row, Essex (1865–7), Great Yarmouth (St James's, 1869–78), Ullenhall, Warwickshire, and Ayot St Peter, Hertfordshire (1874–5), and Hoarwithy, Herefordshire (*c.*1872–85). He restored many medieval churches, notably St Nicholas's, Great Yarmouth (1863–77), Llanbadarn Fawr, Cardiganshire (1867–80), and Grosmont, Monmouthshire (1869–75), but disdained the sentimentality of the Society for the Protection of Ancient Buildings. In 1884 he took John Coates Carter into partnership, and continued to work in his later years, primarily on ecclesiastical commissions, and greatly assisted by Carter; the Stroud School of Art and Sciences (1890–99), with W. M. C. Fisher, was an important exception. Seddon designed numerous church fittings, including some for Llandaff, and several splendid pieces were made by the family firm for the 1862 International Exhibition. He was also a prolific designer of stained glass and mosaic, the east window of Sunningwell church, Berkshire (1877), and the pulpit at Betchworth, Surrey (1885), being notable examples. Seddon wrote numerous articles and gave frequent lectures. His incisive wit was notorious: he once publicly ridiculed some of his contemporaries as creators of the *hair-stand-on-end-style* ('Sundry notes upon some miscellaneous subjects', *RIBA Transactions*, 1863–4, xxiii). He published several books, including *Progress in Art and Architecture with Precedents for Ornament* (1852), *Memoir and Letters of the Late Thomas Seddon, Artist* (1858), and *Rambles in the Rhine Provinces* (1867). Seddon died in St Thomas's Nursing Home, London, on 1 February 1906 and was buried four days later in Fulham cemetery. His wife survived him.

TYE R. BLACKSHAW

Sources M. Darby, *John Pollard Seddon* (1983) • *The Architect* (9 Feb 1906) • *The Builder*, 90 (1906), 150 • *Building News*, 90 (1906), 203 • index of births, marriages, and deaths in *The Times*, GL • biography file, RIBA BAL • *Memoir and letters of the late Thomas Seddon, artist* (1858) ['memoir' by J. P. Seddon] • W. Burges, 'The International Exhibition', *GM*, 3rd ser., 12 (1862), 663–76 • W. Burges, 'The International Exhibition', *GM*, 3rd ser., 13 (1862), 3–12 • *The Builder*, 49 (1885), 179–80 [obit. of T. L. Donaldson] • E. A. Grüning, 'Memoir of the late Professor Donaldson', *Transactions of the Royal Institute of British Architects*, new ser., 2 (1885–6), 89–95 • *CGPLA Eng. & Wales* (1906)

Archives Cardiff PRO • JRL, letters • NL Wales | LPL, Incorporated Church Building Society records • LPL, corresp. with A. C. Tait relating to stained glass in Broadstairs • Norfolk RO, copy report relating to west front of Norwich Cathedral

Likenesses Architectural Photographic Association, photograph, 1867, Courtauld Inst., Conway Library • photograph, repro. in *Church Bells and Illustrated Church News* (17 Jan 1902), 142 • portrait, repro. in *Building News*, 58 (17 Jan 1890), 115 • portrait, University College, Aberystwyth

Wealth at death £6294 7*s.* 2*d.*: probate, 26 March 1906, *CGPLA Eng. & Wales*

Seddon, Richard John (1845–1906), prime minister of New Zealand, was born at School Brow, Eccleston, St Helens, Lancashire, on 22 June 1845. His father was Thomas Seddon, the son of a farmer at Bickerstaffe, near St Helens, and headmaster of Eccleston Hill grammar school; his mother, Jane Lindsay, was a Scot from Annan, Dumfriesshire, and the teacher at the local denominational school.

Early years Seddon seems to have been a difficult pupil. The only subject which interested him at school was mechanical drawing. After being removed from Eccleston School at the age of twelve, he worked for two years on his grandfather's farm at Barrow Nook and then embarked on an apprenticeship at the workshops of Daglish & Co., engineers and ironfounders of St Helens. After five years there and at the Vauxhall Iron Foundry in Liverpool, he

Richard John Seddon (1845–1906), by unknown photographer

obtained a Board of Trade engineer's certificate. He then decided to emigrate to Australia, probably with the aim of trying his luck on the goldfields, and in 1863 worked his passage to Melbourne on the *Star of England*.

After working at the government railway workshops at Williamstown, Seddon prospected on the Bendigo goldfields, with, it seems, little success. In February 1866 he sailed for Hokitika on the west coast of the South Island of New Zealand, where there had been a recent major gold rush. He went to the Old Six Mile diggings at Waimea and joined an uncle, Nathan Seddon, who had written urging him to come. Although continuing to enjoy little success as a prospector, he put his knowledge of engineering to good use in constructing reservoirs and water-races. He invested the money which he earned in opening stores. Having prospered, he was able to return to Melbourne at the end of 1868 and, on 13 January 1869, to marry his fiancée of three years, Louisa Jane (1851–1931), the daughter of John Stuart Spotswood, a ferryman, of Williamstown, Victoria. The couple returned to live on the west coast of the South Island.

Entry into public life Seddon gradually became involved in public life. As a miners' advocate or lay litigant he represented miners in cases before the goldfields warden. In 1870 he was elected to the Arahura road board and served several terms as its chairman. In 1874 he was elected to the Westland provincial council for Arahura on a platform of advocacy of a better water supply for the goldfields. He was elected chairman of committees on the council. In 1876, after the abolition of the provinces, he was elected to the Westland county council.

In the winter of 1876 Seddon staked a claim on a newly discovered goldfield at Kumara and went to live there, transferring his publican's licence from Big Dam, and establishing the Queen's Hotel at Kumara. In 1877 he was elected the first mayor of Kumara. In 1875 he stood unsuccessfully for the Hokitika seat in the house of representatives. He studied *Hansard* and works on parliamentary procedure, such as those by Erskine May, which he came to know almost by heart. In 1879 he was elected for Hokitika as a supporter of Sir George Grey. He represented Kumara from 1881 to 1890 and Westland from 1890 until his death in 1906. In the house in the 1880s he saw himself as primarily a miners' and west coast representative, and he concentrated on issues of a parochial nature rather than larger colonial issues and party politics. However, he became a leading authority on mining legislation and served as chairman of the goldfields committee in 1887 and 1888.

When the Liberals took office under John Ballance in January 1891, Seddon was appointed minister of public works, mines, defence, and marine. As minister of public works he was noted for his promotion of a co-operative contract system for road-making and other projects. He was attacked by his political opponents for his lack of refined political manners, but this served only to reinforce his appeal to the common people in this new age of democratic politics (New Zealand had universal adult suffrage from 1893). He developed a populist style of leadership. His political philosophy was simple: 'It is the rich and the poor; it is the wealthy people and the landowners against the middle classes and the labouring classes' (cited in Drummond, 70). He toured the country constantly, addressing meetings and banquets, meeting innumerable deputations, and mastering the art of giving away very little while flattering his audiences.

When Ballance became ill in late 1892, Seddon was a logical choice to become premier, largely because of his mastery of parliamentary procedure. Ballance wanted a former premier, Sir Robert Stout, to be his successor, but illness set in too rapidly for him to arrange an orderly transfer of the leadership to Stout before his death at the end of April 1893. On 1 May the cabinet agreed that Seddon would serve as caretaker premier and that the party would be asked to settle the matter of the leadership when parliament reassembled. The expectation was that the Liberal caucus would then choose between Seddon and Stout. But Seddon was determined to hold on to the position and manoeuvred to ensure that such a vote did not take place. He led the government to victory in the general election at the end of 1893 and claimed this as the people's verdict on who should lead the party and the country. Seddon completely out-manoeuvred his rival, Stout, by playing on the Liberal members' fears that, if a leadership dispute dragged on, the party would become divided, faction-ridden, and paralysed at a crucial stage in the implementation of many of the principal reforms on which it had embarked. Seddon led his party to victory at five successive general elections—1893, 1896, 1899, 1902, and 1905—a feat which has not been matched since by any New Zealand party leader.

Seddon as premier Although the leader of New Zealand's first party government, Seddon kept the extra-parliamentary Liberal Party organization in a subordinate position. In 1898 he had a new organization formed to establish Liberalism in the country: the Liberal and Labour Federation. As its title suggests, one of its principal purposes was to ensure the continued integration of Labour into Liberal politics. It was given only a very carefully controlled influence over the choosing of candidates and minimal impact on the making of policy, which Seddon wanted retained firmly under the control of the parliamentary party.

Seddon was a cautious politician with a keen instinct for the limits of public willingness to accept change. His main political aim was to consolidate the major achievements of 1891–4, and in this he was notably successful. When he became premier in 1893 many major reforms had already been or were in the process of being enacted. These included the Advances to Settlers Act and the Industrial Conciliation and Arbitration Act (both 1894). Long an opponent of votes for women, he was obliged to accept this reform when it was passed by the legislative council in 1893. The reform that became most closely identified with him personally was that of old-age pensions (1898), partly because of the determined fight which he maintained over several years to get it enacted against strenuous opposition, and partly because underlying his interest in it was his long-standing concern for the welfare of ex-miners on the west coast. In June 1896 he replaced Joseph Ward as colonial treasurer, a position he held until his death. He was a very cautious financier who budgeted for surpluses, maintained the spirit of 'self-reliance', and made a carefully calculated and restrained return to borrowing first for advances to settlers and then for public works.

Seddon held numerous portfolios during his premiership. In January 1896 he replaced William Pember Reeves as minister of labour, another post he held until his death. The path-breaking industrial arbitration and conciliation system had been introduced in 1894. Seddon established a close and effective relationship with the secretary of labour, Edward Tregear, in implementing the scheme, which appeared to be largely responsible for the industrial peace of the era 1896–1906. He was also minister of education from June 1903 until his death and minister of immigration for the same period, when he promoted legislation to prevent any further Chinese migration to New Zealand. For much of his career he manifested a deep-seated prejudice against the Chinese, an attitude that derived from his time on the goldfields. When his opponents wanted to wound him, they accused him of having been an associate of Chinese. In addition, Seddon was minister of public works from January 1891 to March 1896 and minister of defence from January 1891 to June 1896 and again from January 1900. He became minister of native affairs in September 1893 and held this post until the end of 1899. His attitude to the Maori, while sympathetic, was basically paternalistic. He made frequent visits to Maori tribes and very successfully used his powers of persuasion to obtain their consent to the selling of land.

Seddon, who was nicknamed 'King Dick', dominated all aspects of the work of his government and concentrated a large proportion of the most important portfolios in his own hands. He had a zest for politics and was not easily depressed or thrown off course. He sometimes behaved outrageously, flouting the conventions, but he had a very acute sense as to when he could get away with so doing, and he almost invariably did. Numerous political scandals erupted during his premiership. He survived them all, and even attracted public sympathy when he accused his critics of harassing him in order to undermine the government and its reform programme. The most celebrated scandal erupted in 1905, when allegations were made of an unauthorized payment to one of Seddon's sons. These were proved to be totally without foundation. Sympathy for Seddon undoubtedly helped him to win his fifth successive election victory in 1905.

Imperial interests Seddon became known both in New Zealand and in Britain as an active and vociferous imperialist. He put pressure on the Colonial Office to annex Samoa, with the idea that New Zealand would then administer it on Britain's behalf. He also sought the incorporation of Fiji into New Zealand. He was very critical of Britain's caution in the Pacific at a time when other powers were expanding their control over territories there. He was especially upset at Britain's acquiescence in the acquisition of the Hawaiian Islands by the United States in 1897, and made his feelings known directly to President McKinley on a visit to Washington. He did succeed in persuading the Colonial Office to permit New Zealand to annex the Cook Islands in 1900. Seddon played a prominent role in the affairs of empire from 1897 on. Under the cloak of his imperialism he energetically promoted New Zealand's interests. His aim was to acquire for the colonies greater influence over British imperial policy. For example, at the 1897 colonial conference he proposed a consultative council of colonial representatives to advise the British government. His extrovert behaviour made him into something of a celebrity when he attended the diamond jubilee celebrations in 1897 and the coronation of Edward VII in 1902. In 1897 he was made a privy councillor and awarded an honorary LLD by Cambridge University. He attracted much publicity through his outspokenness concerning the Second South African War: at the end of 1899 he was to the forefront among the colonial leaders in offering soldiers for the war, and in all 6700 soldiers were sent to South Africa in nine contingents. He visited South Africa in 1902 at Kitchener's invitation. At home he aroused and exploited popular nationalistic enthusiasm.

The later years of the premiership From about 1897 the state of Seddon's health gave increasing cause for concern. He was a large man, just under 6 feet in height and weighing nearly 20 stone in later life. He was totally committed to politics and worked very long hours, allowing himself few diversions. But the long hours of work began to take their toll, and he developed a heart condition. Rumours began to circulate that he would have to resign, perhaps to go to London as agent-general. The political situation was destabilized by the manoeuvring that always precedes transitions to a new leader. From 1900 on Seddon was under pressure to reconstruct the cabinet and get rid of some of the less competent ministers. He had always been loyal to those who were loyal to him and had sheltered some mediocre politicians in his cabinet, receiving their loyalty in return. By contrast, dissident Liberal members were often denied political advancement. He evaded calls for change, not wanting to dismiss his loyal colleagues, and seeing advantages in keeping the prospect of reconstruction perpetually dangling before back-benchers. There were even plots to engineer his retirement, but these all came to nothing because of the unwillingness of Joseph Ward, the obvious successor, to take a lead in forcing the issue. Seddon did indicate that he would retire from the premiership when he returned to New Zealand after attending the premiers' conference in London in April 1907, but he died on 10 June 1906, on board the *Oswestry Grange*, while returning to Auckland from a visit to Australia. He was buried on 21 June on Observatory Hill in the Wellington cemetery adjacent to the botanic gardens. His wife survived him.

Seddon was not himself an ardent reformer, but his political skill and mastery of the arts of gaining and holding the support of the New Zealand electorate proved invaluable in entrenching the major changes in land, labour, taxation, and other areas of policy which the Liberal government of the 1890s enacted. His party lost office six years after his death as his successors were unable to maintain the close links which he had forged with the people. For this he must bear some of the blame: his strong, at times autocratic, style of leadership was beneficial in holding the government together and on course, but it frustrated the growth of a vigorous, independent Liberal Party in the country. DAVID HAMER

Sources R. M. Burdon, *King Dick: a biography of Richard John Seddon* (1955) • D. Hamer, *The New Zealand liberals: the years of power* (1988) • J. Drummond, *The life and work of Richard John Seddon* (1906) • T. E. Y. Seddon, *The Seddons: an autobiography* (1968)

Archives Archives New Zealand, Wellington • NL NZ, Turnbull L.

Likenesses photographs, 1861–1904, repro. in Drummond, *Life and work of Richard John Seddon*, frontispiece, 6, 22, 32, 352 • two photographs, *c*.1895–1904, repro. in Hamer, *New Zealand liberals*, 144, 256 • Gunn & Stuart, photogravure, NPG • E. Von Mayern, oils, City of Auckland Art Gallery, New Zealand • chromolithograph caricature, NPG; repro. in *VF* (17 April 1902) • memorial bust, St Paul's Cathedral, London • photograph, NL NZ, Turnbull L. [*see illus.*] • two photographs (as a young man; in middle age), repro. in Burdon, *King Dick*, 16, 49

Seddon, Thomas (1753–1795/6), Church of England clergyman and author, was born at Acres Barn, Pendleton, Lancashire, the son of John Seddon, farmer, of Pendleton. He received his early education at a number of local schools, including the Manchester grammar school. He was intended by his father for the medical profession and at the age of seventeen was entered for training at the Manchester Infirmary. His own aspirations, however, lay towards the church and while still at the infirmary he received an education in the classics under the tutorship of the Revd John Clayton of the collegiate church in Manchester. Encouraged by a promise of preferment from a certain baronet, he entered Magdalen Hall, Oxford, as a gentleman commoner, matriculating in 1776. He does not seem to have taken any degree and according to his own account was not much benefited by an academic education but he obtained a testimonial and without difficulty was ordained a deacon in 1777 and priest in 1778. The original promise of preferment was not fulfilled, and a combination of improvidence and the expense of his education left Seddon in debt. He sought to resolve his financial difficulties by making an advantageous marriage and on 2 October 1777 married Margaret Sidebottom, a young lady of good family near Manchester. The marriage seems to have proved a disappointment to both parties—there were no children—and seems effectively to have terminated by separation before 1786.

Seddon's early career in the church was also a disappointment. In 1779 he was licensed as incumbent of Stretford, a small living in which he had served as curate since 1778, and in 1781 was also offered the new living of St George's, Wigan. However, his living at Stretford was sequestered for debt after he had been there two or three years, while opposition from an influential group of parishioners in Wigan obliged him to give up St George's. His reputation was further damaged by his publication in 1779 of *Characteristic strictures, or, Remarks on upwards of one hundred portraits, of the most eminent persons in the counties of Lancaster and Chester: particularly in the town and neighbourhood of Manchester*. This work, penned under the influence of multiple disappointments and published anonymously, consisted in a number of satirical and libellous sketches of local notables and gave great offence.

After the sequestration of Stretford, Seddon appears to have sought to supplement his income by writing and by serving as chaplain to the earl of Lonsdale. In 1786 he published his most significant work, *Letters written to an officer in the army on various subjects, religious, moral, and political, with a view to the manners, accomplishments, and proper conduct of young gentlemen*, in two octavo volumes. This work, probably addressed to his brother the future Lieutenant-General Daniel Seddon, together with his other published output (a number of sermons and a volume of 1780 entitled *Impartial and Free Thoughts on a Free Trade to the Kingdom of Ireland*) reveal him generally to have been a man of conventional high-church tory views.

Although in the autobiographical introduction to the *Letters* Seddon described himself as retired from all professional engagements and without hope of succeeding to any, his career seems to have revived in 1788, when he was nominated to the perpetual curacy of St Anne's Lydgate in Saddleworth, which he held in plurality with Stretford. The living was poor, however, and his debts continued to increase. In the 1790s he was prominent in co-ordinating anti-radical activity in the area and in 1794 he became chaplain to the 104th regiment of foot, the Royal Manchester volunteers, before leaving in 1795 to join the regiment at Belfast. He met his death by drowning, possibly with men from the regiment who had been transferred to an expeditionary force to the West Indies and whose transport was lost in a gale on 18 November 1795 near Portland. No notification of his death, however, reached Manchester before May 1796, and its precise date remains uncertain. MARK SMITH

Sources T. Seddon, *Letters written to an officer in the army on various subjects* (1786) • C. C. W. Airne, *St Anne's Lydgate: the story of a Pennine parish, 1788–1988* (1988) • F. R. Raines, 'Catalogue of incumbents of Lydgate', Chetham College Library, Raines MSS, 15.57 • J. F. Smith, ed., *The admission register of the Manchester School, with some notices of the more distinguished scholars*, 1, Chetham Society, 69 (1866) • J. Bailey, *Old Stretford* (1878)

Wealth at death probably in debt: Airne, *St Anne's Lydgate*

Seddon, Thomas (*bap.* 1761, *d.* 1804). *See under* Seddon family (*per.* c.1750–1864).

Seddon, Thomas (*bap.* 1793, *d.* 1864). *See under* Seddon family (*per.* c.1750–1864).

Seddon, Thomas (1821–1856), landscape painter, was born on 28 August 1821 at 150 Aldersgate Street, London, the eldest of the nine children of Thomas *Seddon (*bap.* 1793, *d.* 1864), cabinet-maker [*see under* Seddon family], and his wife, Frances Nelson, *née* Thomas (1800–1880). After indulging his passion for drawing at a boarding-school in Epsom, Surrey (later removed to Stanmore, Middlesex), which he attended from 1828 for about ten years, parental opposition to the professional pursuit of fine art led him to enter his father's firm, Seddon & Sons; in 1841–2 he studied ornamental art in Paris. He returned to Seddon & Sons and began to design furniture, and to attend life classes at Charles Lucy's studios at Tudor Lodge in Mornington Crescent, London; there he met Ford Madox Brown, who was to become his artistic mentor. From about 1848 to about 1852 he took classes at the Artists' Society in Clipstone Street.

Seddon's first landscape sketches date from the summer of 1849, during a visit to Betws-y-coed in Caernarvonshire, Wales, where he was already asserting the value of painstakingly transcribing nature. In 1852, a year after taking up painting professionally, his first oil, *Penelope* (priv. coll.), was shown at the Royal Academy. The earliest of his landscapes to be traced, *Léhon, from Mont Parnasse* (exh. RA, 1854; Museo de Arte de Ponce, Ponce, Puerto Rico), was executed in Brittany in the summer of 1853. By this date Seddon and William Holman Hunt—an equally devout Christian—were planning a trip to the East.

Seddon landed in Egypt on 6 December 1853, met the explorer Richard Burton, and executed a watercolour of him, *An Arab Shakyh in his Travelling Dress* (exh. Art Gallery and Museum, Brighton, 1983; priv. coll.). Hunt arrived in January 1854; although reliant on Seddon's gifts as a linguist, he took exception to his adoption of Arab costume and propensity for practical jokes. In the following month the artists encamped close to the pyramids, which Seddon painted at sunset (retouched 1855; exh. 14 Berners Street, London, 1855, and the Fine Art Society, London, 1978; priv. coll.). Their first sight of Jerusalem, on 3 June 1854, was, for both artists, a deeply moving religious experience: Seddon camped at Aceldama and for five months worked on *Jerusalem and the Valley of Jehoshaphat from the Hill of Evil Counsel* (1854–5; exh. 14 Berners Street, London, 1855; Tate collection).

On 19 October 1854 Seddon left Syria for Dinan in France, where he became engaged to Emmeline Bulford; they married in Paris on 30 June 1855, and a daughter was born to them in 1856. On his return to London in January 1855, Madox Brown observed that Seddon's pictures 'present quantities of drawing and truthfulness seldom surpassed but no beauty, nothing to make the bosom tingle. Could I but have seen them in progress—I will do all I can to make him improve them yet' (*Diary*, 117). From 17 March to 3 June nine of these works were exhibited at Seddon's studio at 14 Berners Street, including *Dromedary and Arab at the City of the Dead, Cairo* (priv. coll.) and the watercolours *The Great Sphinx at the Pyramids of Gizeh* (Ashmolean Museum, Oxford) and *Interior of a Deewan, Formerly Belonging to the Copt Patriarch, Near the Esbekeeyah, Cairo* (also exh. RA, 1856; priv. coll.), all of which are dated 1854. A larger one-man show was held at 52 Conduit Street in May and June of 1856.

Although Seddon completed many of his orientalist pictures in Europe, where he also painted replicas and new compositions such as *Arabs Return to their Tents on the Border of the Egyptian Desert* (exh. Society of Arts, 1857; priv. coll.), which was commissioned by William Marshall of Preston in 1856 and which was Seddon's last finished painting, he was passionately committed to painting in the East and thus returned to Cairo in October 1856. He died there of dysentery on 23 November and was interred in the protestant burial-ground in the city. His tragic demise galvanized the Pre-Raphaelites into organizing a subscription to buy *Jerusalem* for presentation to the National Gallery. It formed the centrepiece of an exhibition of over one hundred of Seddon's works at the Society of Arts in London on 6 May 1857, which John Ruskin opened with a memorable speech sealing the artist's reputation as the quintessential 'prosaic' Pre-Raphaelite, committed to faithful transcription of historic landscape (*Journal of the Society of Arts*, 360–62). JUDITH BRONKHURST

Sources *Memoir and letters of the late Thomas Seddon, artist* (1858), 'Memoir' by J. P. Seddon • A. Staley, *The Pre-Raphaelite landscape* (1973), 96–106; 2nd edn (2001), 128–40 • *The diary of Ford Madox Brown*, ed. V. Surtees (1981), 66, 117, 165, 171 • *Journal of the Society of Arts*, 5 (1856–7), 360–62 [speech of 6 May 1857 by John Ruskin on Thomas Seddon] • G. P. Landow, 'William Holman Hunt's letters to Thomas Seddon', *Bulletin of the John Rylands University Library*, 66 (1983–4), 139–72 • P. Conner, ed., *The inspiration of Egypt* (1983), 133 • A. Bowness, ed., *The Pre-Raphaelites* (1984), 37, 151–3, 270 • M. A. Stevens, ed., *The orientalists: Delacroix to Matisse* (1984), 227 [exhibition catalogue, RA, London, 24 March – 27 May 1984] • T. Newman and R. Watkinson, *Ford Madox Brown and the Pre-Raphaelite circle* (1991), 35 • [W. M. Rossetti], 'Fine arts: oriental pictures by Mr Seddon', *The Spectator* (14 April 1855), 392 • *List of works by the late Thomas Seddon, on view at the Society of Arts* (1857) • 'Letters from Sir John Everett Millais (1829–1896) and William Holman Hunt (1827–1910) in the

Henry E. Huntington Library, San Marino, California', ed. M. Lutyens, *Walpole Society*, 44 (1972–4), 1–93, esp. 58–9, pl. 10b · *Eastern encounters: orientalist painters of the nineteenth century* (1978), nos. 57–9 [exhibition catalogue, Fine Art Society, London, 26 June – 28 July 1978] · *The Post Office London directory* (1822), 316 · private information (2004)

Archives JRL, letters to his family relating to his visit to Jerusalem

Likenesses photograph, *c.*1853, priv. coll.; repro. in J. S. Maas, *The Victorian art world in photographs* (1984), 116 · W. H. Hunt, pen-and-ink caricature, Hunt. L., letter to D. G. Rossetti, 12 March 1854, HM 12963; repro. in Lutyens, ed., 'Letters from Sir John Everett Millais', pl. 10b · T. Seddon, self-portraits, pen-and-ink, repro. in *Memoir and letters*, 39 and 63 · lithograph (after detail of photograph, *c.*1853), repro. in *Memoir and letters*, frontispiece

Sedgwick, Adam (1785–1873), geologist, was born on 22 March 1785 in the vicarage at Dent, Yorkshire, the third of seven children of Richard Sedgwick (1736–1828), the local vicar, and his second wife and cousin, Margaret (*née* Sturgis). From an early age Sedgwick attended the grammar school at Dent, between the ages of eight and sixteen under the instruction of his father. In 1801 he was sent to the grammar school at Sedbergh conducted by the Revd William Stevens.

The Cambridge student In 1804, after a summer of tutoring from the self-taught mathematician John Dawson, Sedgwick entered Trinity College, Cambridge, as a sizar, a position which allowed poorer students to pay reduced fees in exchange for doing menial duties. Unsophisticated, untravelled, and uncouth, Sedgwick gradually began to make an impression at Cambridge, despite a near-fatal attack of typhoid in 1805. He was elected to a college scholarship in 1807, and graduated fifth wrangler in the following year. He took private pupils and read for a Trinity fellowship, which he finally obtained in 1810. Overworked in preparing for the position and dissatisfied with its duties, in 1813 he burst a blood vessel and his health broke down completely. Sedgwick recovered during the next few years, but suffered thereafter intermittently from poor health. He became an assistant tutor in mathematics at Trinity in 1815, and was ordained a year later, when he also travelled for several months on the continent.

Early years as Woodwardian professor In 1818 Sedgwick was elected to the Woodwardian professorship of geology at the University of Cambridge, a post which he was to hold with great distinction for the next fifty-five years. He had previously attended the mineralogical lectures of Edward Daniel Clarke and read a few works on the subject, but he was elected on the strength of his character, connections, and general ability. The new appointment galvanized Sedgwick into action. He undertook his first geological excursion in that summer and became a fellow of the Geological Society of London. In 1819 he delivered his first course of lectures, and joined with John Stevens Henslow and others to encourage scientific pursuits within the university by founding the Cambridge Philosophical Society.

Sedgwick's most immediate concern after taking up his chair was to build up the geological collections of the university. He collected rocks and fossils during systematic tours in the British Isles and elsewhere in Europe, and he

Adam Sedgwick (1785–1873), by Thomas Phillips, 1832

also purchased rare specimens, either with his own funds or through public appeals. The collection quickly outgrew its original accommodation, and in 1841 spacious new quarters were at last made available. By this time the Woodwardian had a reputation as one of Europe's outstanding geological museums.

Early field studies In connection with his summer collecting tours, Sedgwick became an accomplished field geologist, learning much from Henslow and William Daniel Conybeare. His earliest papers, read in 1820 before the Cambridge Philosophical Society, discussed the structure of the ancient rocks of Devon and Cornwall. An important monograph published in the Geological Society *Transactions* in 1829 used the Magnesian Limestone as a key for working out the structure of New Red Sandstone of north-east England. Sedgwick correlated the rocks with their counterparts in Germany, showing that these strata formed an uninterrupted succession from the Lias down to the Coal Measures.

In 1828 Sedgwick accompanied the wealthier but less experienced Roderick Murchison, whom he had met at the Geological Society, on a tour of Scotland. Opposing the work of John MacCulloch, they concluded that the ancient sandstones of the north-west highlands could be correlated with the Old Red Sandstone to the east, a finding which geologists abandoned in the second half of the century after much controversy. The two men became close friends, and during the following summer travelled in the eastern Alps, aiming to find a continuous succession to bridge the notorious gap between the fossil faunas of the Secondary and Tertiary strata.

As these early papers show, Sedgwick believed that the

remaining 'lost pages' in the record of the rocks would be found, and that geologists could hope to obtain a comprehensive picture of earth history. Two eloquent presidential addresses to the Geological Society in 1830 and 1831 expressed his theoretical views. Discussing Charles Lyell's recently published *Principles of Geology* (1830–33), Sedgwick agreed that geologists had demonstrated the need for a vastly expanded time-scale. He abjured his support for fellow cleric William Buckland's attempt to find empirical evidence for a universal flood, and attacked those, like Andrew Ure and William Cockburn, who interpreted geology in the light of scripture. However, Sedgwick rejected what he saw as Lyell's gratuitous assumption that geological processes had been uniform in intensity throughout all time. He argued that the empirical record of the strata bore witness to catastrophic events without parallel in forces currently shaping the face of the earth.

Below the Old Red Sandstone From the late 1820s, Sedgwick's chief goal in geology was to complete a big book on the strata below the Old Red Sandstone. Most of his papers over the next two decades were progress reports on this project, as Sedgwick toured the Lake District, Wales, and the southern uplands of Scotland to add to his knowledge of the older rocks. In 1831 he entered north Wales with the young Charles Darwin, who thereby gained his first training in the field. Sedgwick, with his thorough grounding in mathematics, had an unrivalled ability to work out the complex geological structures characteristic of these strata. Particularly important was a distinction, which he emphasized from the late 1820s, between stratification, jointing, and slaty cleavage. Sedgwick was also guided by Leonce Elie de Beaumont's theory of the elevation of mountain chains, which he believed would provide a key to unravelling the older rocks.

The Cambrian While Sedgwick was in north Wales, Murchison independently began examining the younger and more fossiliferous strata of south Wales and the Welsh borders. Together, their work provided the foundations for a new classification of the oldest rocks with fossils: Sedgwick's strata were called the Cambrian, while Murchison's became the Silurian. This amicable arrangement was threatened when Henry De la Beche discovered Coal plants in rocks which appeared to be of the same age as those which the two friends had been studying. The resulting controversy, in which the two friends collaborated closely, bore fruit in their 1839 announcement of the Devonian system as a distinctive period in earth history.

The creation of the Devonian, however, also effectively removed any distinctive fauna from Sedgwick's Cambrian. The problem was exacerbated when John Eddowes Bowman, Daniel Sharpe, and finally the official Geological Survey extended its work into Sedgwick's territory during the early 1840s; most of the strata which had been identified as being older than the Silurian proved to be of the same age. Almost all geologists followed Murchison in wiping the Cambrian off the map, ignoring Sedgwick's attempts to create alternatives to what he condemned as a grossly over-extended Silurian. Sedgwick believed that the question involved nothing less than the foundations of proper scientific method. Strata classifications required a secure understanding of geological structure; only then could fossils take their rightful place in establishing correlations. For Sedgwick, the issue was one of first principles.

By the 1850s, with his book on the older rocks scarcely begun, Sedgwick argued the case for the Cambrian in increasingly intemperate language. He cut off links not only with Murchison, but also with the Geological Society and the metropolitan geological community more generally. The controversy was settled only after Sedgwick's death. The discovery of a fauna below that of Murchison's oldest Silurians—first in Bohemia and then in Wales—became the basis for a redefined Cambrian. The uppermost strata of Murchison's expanded system were called Silurian, and the strata in between were termed Ordovician.

Thoughts on evolution Throughout his life, Sedgwick was an eloquent advocate of the moral basis of scientific enquiry, which he saw as a bulwark against the chilling influence of unbelief. His *Discourse on the Studies of the University* (1832), originally delivered as a sermon in Trinity College chapel, argued for the place of geology within natural theology, opposing what he condemned as the misuse of the science by scriptural literalists. The sermon reserved its strongest fire for the utilitarian philosophy of John Locke and William Paley, eliciting a savage reply from John Stuart Mill in the *Westminster Review*.

Sedgwick passionately opposed all attempts to explain the origin of new species through natural laws. He was particularly concerned about Robert Chambers's anonymous best-seller, *Vestiges of the Natural History of Creation* (1844), which introduced an evolutionary cosmology to a wide public. Such views threatened to undermine the moral and spiritual basis of Christian society, and Sedgwick condemned them in a long review for the *Edinburgh Review* and in even longer additions to the bloated fifth edition of his *Discourse* (1850). By the time Darwin sent him a copy of the *Origin of Species* in 1859, Sedgwick's reaction was predictably one of dismay:

> You have *deserted*—after a start in that tram-road of all solid physical truth—the true method of induction, and started off in machinery as wild, I think, as Bishop Wilkins's locomotive that was to sail with us to the moon. (Clark and Hughes, 2.357)

That Darwin, a former student, should fall from grace was especially shocking. Sedgwick's lectures, like all those in the natural sciences at Cambridge in the first half of the century, were extracurricular and aimed to make geology an appropriate study for the Christian gentleman. 'I cannot teach you all geology', he told his class, 'I can only fire your imaginations' (Clark and Hughes, 2.489). Nevertheless, he must have hoped they would follow his advocacy of proper reasoning: when Sedgwick set his first examination questions in 1851 after the introduction of the natural sciences tripos, he asked students to show that the fossil evidence does not support evolution.

The educator and administrator Sedgwick was a major performer at the British Association for the Advancement of Science, serving as president at its third meeting in 1833 at Cambridge. In this capacity he voiced his belief that science should be extended to working-class audiences. He gave vivid and widely reported lectures throughout the country, serving as an example of the compatibility of truths of religion and science. In 1820 he became a fellow of the Royal Society of London, which awarded him its Copley medal in 1863 as part of an anti-Darwinian campaign.

Sedgwick was active in university politics and administration. He was appointed senior proctor in 1827, and in 1847 he served as secretary to Prince Albert in his capacity as university chancellor. In politics a firm whig, Sedgwick strongly supported reform of the ancient universities and the abolition of religious tests, and for two years from 1850 he sat on the royal commission appointed to investigate the affairs of the university. His relatively modest income from his chair was supplemented by his college fellowship at Trinity and by his appointment in 1825 to the vicarage of Shudy Camps, Cambridgeshire. In 1832 the whig government offered Sedgwick the valuable living of East Farleigh, which he turned down. Two years later he accepted a prebendal stall at Norwich, which required absence from Cambridge for only two months of each year. Much influenced by the sermons of Robert Hall, Sedgwick had strong evangelical views and opposed innovations in Anglican ritual.

Final years Sedgwick never married, nor could he have done so without giving up the Woodwardian chair, which stipulated that its holder must remain a bachelor. Contemporaries admired his erratic brilliance, while regretting his inability to produce a sustained argument in prose. He was animated, generous, disorganized, hospitable, and prone to procrastination and hypochondria. By the end of his life he was increasingly lonely and isolated at Cambridge, although he received visitors and maintained a wide correspondence, especially with his nieces. He retained a lifelong connection with his home village of Dent, recalled in autobiographical pamphlets issued in 1868 and 1870. Sedgwick died in his rooms at Trinity College on 27 January 1873, and was buried in the college chapel on 1 February. The Sedgwick Museum in Cambridge was established by his successor, Thomas McKenny Hughes, as a memorial to house the collections he had done so much to bring together. He is also memorialized in the Sedgwick prize, given at Cambridge for a student essay; the Sedgwick Club, the undergraduate geological society; and by a granite memorial fountain in Dent.

J. A. Secord

Sources J. W. Clark and T. M. Hughes, *The life and letters of the Reverend Adam Sedgwick*, 2 vols. (1890) • M. J. S. Rudwick, *The great Devonian controversy: the shaping of scientific knowledge among gentlemanly specialists* (1985) • J. A. Secord, *Controversy in Victorian geology: the Cambrian–Silurian dispute* (1986) • M. Ruse, *The Darwinian revolution* (1979) • C. Speakman, *Adam Sedgwick: geologist and dalesman, 1785–1873* (1982) • *CGPLA Eng. & Wales* (1873) • J. A. Secord, *Victorian sensation: the extraordinary publication, reception, and secret authorship of 'Vestiges of the natural history of creation'* (2000)

Archives CUL, letters and biographical MSS • GS Lond., account of tour through France; papers relating to work on magnesian limestone north of the Tees • Trinity Cam., corresp. • U. Cam., Sedgwick Museum of Earth Sciences, corresp., field notebooks, geological collection, and MSS | Bath Royal Literary and Scientific Institution, letters to Leonard Blomefield • BL, corresp. with Charles Babbage, Add. MSS 37182–37199, *passim* • BL, letters to McVey Napier, Add. MS 34625 • CUL, corresp. with Sir George Airy • CUL, corresp. with William Whewell • GS Lond., letters to Roderick Impey Murchison • NHM, corresp. with Sir Richard Owen and William Clift • Oxf. U. Mus. NH, letters to John Phillips • RS, letters to Sir John Herschel • U. Durham, letters to General Charles Grey • UCL, letters to Lord Brougham

Likenesses A. Edouart, silhouette, 1828, NPG; version, U. Cam., Sedgwick Museum of Earth Sciences • T. Phillips, oils, 1832, U. Cam., Sedgwick Museum of Earth Sciences [*see illus.*] • S. Cousins, mezzotint, pubd 1833 (after T. Phillips), BM, NPG • S. Laurence, oils, *c.*1844, Department of Geology, Cambridge • H. Weekes, marble bust, 1846, GS Lond. • T. H. Maguire, lithograph, 1850, BM, NPG; repro. in T. H. Maguire, *Portraits of honorary members of the Ipswich Museum* (1850) • W. Boxall, oils, 1851, Trinity Cam. • T. Woolner, marble bust, 1860, Trinity Cam.; related plaster cast, NPG • L. Dickinson, chalk drawing, 1867, U. Cam., Sedgwick Museum of Earth Sciences • R. B. Farren, oils, 1870, Department of Geology, Cambridge • H. W. Jukes, pencil drawing (as a young man), Department of Geology, Cambridge

Wealth at death under £4000: probate, 3 April 1873, *CGPLA Eng. & Wales*

Sedgwick, Adam (1854–1913), zoologist, was born on 28 September 1854 at Norwich, Norfolk, the eldest son of Richard Sedgwick, vicar of Dent, Yorkshire, and his wife, Mary Jane, daughter of John Woodhouse of Bolton-le-Moors, Lancashire. Educated at Marlborough College, he spent a short time at King's College, London, before entering Trinity College, Cambridge, in 1874. There Sedgwick was influenced by the physiologist Michael Foster and the embryologist Francis Maitland Balfour, whose lectures and practical classes attracted him and won him over to a career in zoology rather than medicine.

In 1877 Sedgwick obtained first-class honours in the natural sciences tripos and in 1878 became foundation scholar of Trinity and demonstrator to Balfour. In the latter year he published his first research, with Balfour, on the head-kidney in the embryo chick, a full account appearing in 1879. Independent papers followed, related to kidney development in other organisms, including the marine free-living mollusc *Chiton*.

In May 1882 Cambridge created a professorship in animal morphology for Balfour and allocated funds for new lecture rooms and laboratory facilities. Two months later, however, these arrangements were threatened when Balfour lost his life in a climbing accident in Switzerland. Under difficult circumstances Sedgwick was asked to assume Balfour's teaching duties, and Trinity appointed him to the college lectureship Balfour previously held. In 1884 he was appointed university lecturer in animal morphology with a stipend of £100; in 1890 he became reader. He married Laura Helen Elizabeth Robinson, daughter of Captain Robinson, of Armagh, in 1892 and they had two sons and a daughter. In 1897 he accepted the post of tutor at Trinity College, which he held until 1907.

Sedgwick headed a vibrant school of zoology at Cambridge. He supervised elementary biology (required for medical students) and elementary and advanced classes in animal morphology, and directed the work of research students. In the university he, along with Foster, continued Balfour's efforts to increase university support for the life sciences; yet he was unfriendly to the movement to give women full access to the university and its scientific institutions.

Sedgwick's major research work stemmed from Balfour's earlier study of the aberrant terrestrial tracheate arthropod *Peripatus* (Onychophora), which attracted interest by exhibiting characters of both annelids (segmented worms) and metamerically segmented arthropods (insects, arachnids, and crustaceans). In 1883 Sedgwick travelled to South Africa, collecting over 300 live specimens of *P. capensis*. He published a series of papers on the embryology and systematics of this transitional form. Collected together in 1889, they are exemplars of classical zoology, combining careful anatomical and embryological descriptions with considerations of leading theoretical questions. After his research ceased in the mid-1890s Sedgwick returned to these questions in a number of general articles. In these he launched an attack on such core biological concepts as cell theory, recapitulation, the biogenetic law, and germ-layer theory, and challenged current views of the evolution of multicellular organisms from protozoans, and the nature of variation and heredity. His attacks on orthodoxy provoked controversy and criticism. Yet his views found a following among his students and future leading figures in British zoology, including Gavin De Beer, C. Clifford Dobell, James Gray, Ernest William MacBride, Edward Stuart Russell, and D'Arcy Wentworth Thompson.

Sedgwick was the author of the influential *Student's Text-book of Zoology* (3 vols., 1898–1909). Elected fellow of the Royal Society in 1886, he twice served on its council. He was active in the British Association for the Advancement of Science and in the Cambridge Philosophical Society, serving as president in 1908. In 1898 he was a secretary to the fourth international congress of zoology held at Cambridge, editing its *Proceedings*. For many years he helped edit the *Quarterly Journal of Microscopical Science*.

After serving twenty-five years as *de facto* professor of animal morphology (the position having lapsed on Balfour's death), without the title or the remuneration, Sedgwick was elected, following Alfred Newton's death in 1907, to the vacant professorship of zoology and comparative anatomy. In 1909, however, he resigned to become professor of zoology at the newly constituted Imperial College of Science and Technology. Although it has been suggested that Sedgwick accepted this position out of a sense of duty, he was also distressed by Cambridge ordinances instituted in 1908, placing restrictions on the professor's control of the museum. In London he devoted himself to reorganizing the department and courses in economic zoology, and in the reform of the British Museum (Natural History). However, his health began to fail in 1911 owing to a pulmonary ailment, and after eighteen months of decline, and despite a winter in the Canaries, he died at his home, 2 Summer Place, South Kensington, London, on 27 February 1913. In appearance, Sedgwick was of medium height with a ruddy complexion. Known for his quick temper, he nevertheless inspired the affection of pupils and friends.

MARSHA L. RICHMOND

Sources E. W. M. [E. W. MacBride], *PRS*, 86B (1913), xxiv–xxix • J. S. Gardiner, *The Zoologist*, 4th ser., 17 (1913), 110–16 • *Nature*, 91 (1913), 14–15 • *The Times* (28 Feb 1913) • W. Bateson, correspondence, CUL
Archives ICL, corresp. • Trinity Cam., letters | CUL, corresp. with A. C. Seward and William Bateson
Likenesses photograph, 1908?, U. Cam., department of zoology • W. Strang, chalk drawing, 1909, U. Cam., department of zoology • W. Strang, portrait, 1909, ICL
Wealth at death £15,277 15*s*. 5*d*.: probate, 9 May 1913, *CGPLA Eng. & Wales*

Sedgwick, Amy [*real name* Sarah Gardiner] (**1835–1897**), actress, was born in Bristol on 27 October 1835, the daughter of William Gardiner. After acting as an amateur in London in 1852, apparently under the name of Mortimer, she appeared at Richmond Theatre in 1853 as Julia in *The Hunchback* by Sheridan Knowles, when she took Amy Sedgwick as her professional name. She then went to Bristol to play Mrs White in the farce of that name, but owing to a misunderstanding with the lessee appeared only for one night. She then went to Cardiff, where she took the part of Pauline in Bulwer-Lytton's *The Lady of Lyons*. Later she played on Moseley's Yorkshire circuit, and then went to Manchester, where she was employed by John Knowles for three seasons and became a great favourite.

Amy Sedgwick's first professional London appearance was at the Haymarket, under J. B. Buckstone, on 5 October 1857, again playing Pauline. On 7 November she was the first Hester Grazebrook in Tom Taylor's *Unequal Match*, the part with which her name long remained associated. On 16 October 1858 she married Dr W. B. Parkes, who died in 1863. She remained at the Haymarket until 1860, her roles including Beatrice in *Much Ado about Nothing*, Lady Teazle, Rosalind, and Peg Woffington. Among her creations at this period were Kate Robertson in J. Palgrave Simpson's *The World and the Stage*, Una in Edmund Falconer's *Family Secret*, and Lady Blanche in Taylor's *Babes in the Wood*.

In June 1861 Sedgwick was at the Olympic, where she was the first Mrs Bloomly in Horace Wigan's *A Charming Woman*, and in February 1863 she played Orelia in Lewis Filmore's *The Winning Suit*. In 1866 she managed the Haymarket during the summer season, and on 2 October played Lady Macbeth to Barry Sullivan's Macbeth at Drury Lane. Back at the Haymarket, she was the first Blanche de Raincourt in Mead's adaptation *The Coquette*. On 10 October 1868 she opened the Marylebone, renamed the Royal Alfred, as director (under H. B. Lacy), with *Pindee Singh* by C. H. Stephenson, in which she played the title role. Despite the presence at the opening of the duke of Edinburgh, the play (and Sedgwick's directorship) was not a success. Another original part followed at the Haymarket: Ida Fitzherbert in Le Thière's *All for Money* (July 1869). On 27 May 1873 Sedgwick married a Liverpool solicitor, Charles

Pemberton (*d.* 1875). Her last appearance in London was as Constance in Knowles's *The Love Chase* at the Haymarket in May 1877. Thereafter she took pupils and gave recitals and readings in London and the provinces, more than once reading before Queen Victoria. She married Charles Goostry on 3 August 1878, and lived in Brighton for some years, before finally moving to Hill View, Haywards Heath, where she died on 7 November 1897. She was buried in the churchyard there. A capable actress, she failed to reach the first rank. JOSEPH KNIGHT, *rev.* J. GILLILAND

Sources *Daily Telegraph* (9 Nov 1897) • C. E. Pascoe, ed., *The dramatic list* (1879) • H. Morley, *The journal of a London playgoer from 1851 to 1866* (1866) • F. Hays, *Women of the day: a biographical dictionary of notable contemporaries* (1885) • *The Athenaeum* (13 Nov 1897), 682 • *The Athenaeum* (20 Nov 1897), 718 [correction] • *A dictionary of contemporary biography* (1861) • *Men of the time* (1875) • *The life and reminiscences of E. L. Blanchard, with notes from the diary of Wm. Blanchard*, ed. C. W. Scott and C. Howard, 2 vols. (1891) • Hall, *Dramatic ports.* • Boase, *Mod. Eng. biog.*
Archives Theatre Museum, London, letters
Likenesses H. Watkins, albumen print, 1855–9, NPG • W. Goodman, pastels, Garr. Club • D. J. Pound, stipple and line engraving (as Hester in Taylor's *An unequal match*; after photograph by Juliane), BM, NPG; repro. in *Illustrated News of the World* [supplement] • marble bust, Brighton Art Gallery • portrait, Brighton Art Gallery • portrait, Harvard TC • two cartes-de-visite, NPG • woodcut, Harvard TC; repro. in *Ballou's pictorial annual gift book* (1858)

Sedgwick, Daniel (1814–1879), hymnologist, was born on 26 November 1814 in Leadenhall Street, London, the son of William Sedgwick and his wife, Frances. He was baptized at St Katharine Cree, London, on 25 December 1814. After serving an apprenticeship, he became a shoemaker. In 1839 he married, and joined the Strict Baptist congregation at Providence Chapel, Grosvenor Street, Commercial Road. In 1837 he had given up shoemaking to deal in secondhand books. He gradually worked up a connection among collectors, mainly of theological literature. His shop was at 81 Sun Street, Bishopsgate.

In 1840 Sedgwick taught himself writing, and acquired a neat and clear hand, but never gained any facility in literary composition. In 1859 he commenced publishing reprints of works by the rarer hymn writers of the seventeenth and eighteenth centuries, under the general title of Library of Spiritual Song. Pursuing his studies in hymnology, he produced in 1860 *A Comprehensive Index of Many of the Original Authors and Translators of Psalms and Hymns*, with the dates of their various works, chiefly collected from the original publications; an enlarged second edition appeared in 1863. After this he was recognized as the foremost living hymnologist. He was consulted by men of all opinions—by Charles Haddon Spurgeon, when compiling *Our Own Hymn-Book* (1866), and Josiah Miller, when writing *Singers and Songs of the Church* (1869). When Sir Roundell Palmer was compiling his *Book of Praise* in 1862 the sheets were submitted to Sedgwick's inspection; he identified the majority of the compositions. In fact, hardly a hymnbook appeared in his later days in which his aid was not acknowledged. Ironically, 'the hymn-books in use in every religious denomination' during Sedgwick's career 'were directly indebted to … a man whom many people would have been ashamed to speak to in the streets on account of his seedy appearance' (*N&Q*, 409). His manuscripts were used in J. Julian's *Dictionary of Hymnology*. Sedgwick died of heart disease at 93 Sun Street on 10 March 1879, and was buried in Abney Park cemetery. His wife, Hannah, survived him; they had had no children.

G. C. BOASE, *rev.* MEGAN A. STEPHAN

Sources *N&Q*, 8th ser., 2 (1892), 409, 451 • J. Julian, ed., *A dictionary of hymnology* (1892), 1036–7 • R. Palmer, *The book of praise* (1863), v • *The Bookseller* (2 May 1879), 424 • C. H. Spurgeon, *Our own hymn-book* (1870), vi–vii • Allibone, *Dict.* • *Earthen Vessel* (July 1879), 199
Wealth at death under £200: probate, 5 May 1879, *CGPLA Eng. & Wales*

Sedgwick, James (1775–1851), author, son of James Sedgwick of Westminster, was born in London. He matriculated from Pembroke College, Oxford, on 30 October 1797, but did not graduate. He was called to the bar at the Middle Temple on 23 January 1801. At this time he published several legal works, including *Remarks on the Commentaries of Sir William Blackstone* (1800), and edited the sixth edition of Sir Geoffrey Gilbert's *Law of Evidence* (1801). He wrote for the *Oxford Review* anonymously in 1807 and 1808. In 1809 he was appointed a commissioner of excise at Edinburgh, and in 1811 chairman of the excise board. In 1815 he was nominated by the Treasury to a seat on the London excise board, but this appointment was cancelled in consequence of the prince regent's having promised the marchioness of Hertford that Colonel Sir Francis Hastings Doyle should have the first vacancy. By way of compensation Sedgwick was appointed examiner of the droits of Admiralty accounts, at his previous salary of £1500 a year. He was promoted on 25 August 1817 to chairman of the board of stamps. At the beginning of 1818 he undertook an inquiry into the conduct of the stamp revenue in Scotland, and discovered great abuses. His effort to secure the permanent dismissal of the officer to whom the disorder was attributable proved, to his irritation, unsuccessful. At the same time he offended Lord Liverpool and the government by publishing *Observations* and writing on the inquiry in the *Morning Chronicle*. His fourteen letters were reissued in the form of three pamphlets. When, in 1826, the board of stamps was dissolved, he was the only member denied a pension. In 1828, however, he received a small retiring allowance of £400 a year.

Sedgwick thus had a grievance, and the greater part of the rest of his life was spent in memorializing successive administrations or petitioning parliament. In 1845 he published a further series of aggrieved letters, including one attacking Sir John Easthope, proprietor of the *Morning Chronicle*, for it had ceased to print his complaints. He was a director of the county fire office. Sedgwick died on 26 January 1851 at his house, 3 Church Street, Kensington, London, from the effects of a fall in Queen Street, Bloomsbury. He was married, and left one daughter.

G. C. BOASE, *rev.* H. C. G. MATTHEW

Sources *GM*, 2nd ser., 35 (1851), 436–7 • *The Times* (30 Jan 1851) • *Law Times* (8 Feb 1851)

Sedgwick, John (1600/01–1643). *See under* Sedgwick, Obadiah (1599/1600–1658).

Sedgwick, Obadiah (1599/1600–1658), Church of England clergyman, was born in the parish of St Peter, Marlborough, Wiltshire, son of Joseph Sedgwick, the vicar there. With two younger brothers, John [*see below*] and Joseph, he was said to share the characteristic of only 'four fingers on a hand' (Wood, *Ath. Oxon.*, 3.66). He matriculated at Queen's College, Oxford, on 18 June 1619, aged nineteen, but migrated to Magdalen Hall and graduated BA on 5 May 1620, proceeding MA on 23 January 1623. In 1626 he was tutor to Matthew Hale. After ordination he served as chaplain to Horace, Lord Vere of Tilbury, in the Low Countries, in 1628–9. While there he corresponded with John Davenport and was part of a network of reform-minded clergy. He proceeded BD at Oxford on 16 January 1630, and in the same year became curate and lecturer at St Mildred, Bread Street, London, where he attracted a large following. Censured and suspended by Bishop Juxon in 1637, Sedgwick took refuge at Leez, the earl of Warwick's house in Essex. In 1638 he preached a sermon subsequently published as *Military Discipline for the Christian Souldier* (1639) to the London artillery company. In 1639 Warwick presented him to the vicarage of Coggeshall, Essex, worth £110 per annum; Sedgwick was to remain Warwick's friend and an habitué of Leez.

After the opening of the Long Parliament, Sedgwick returned to St Mildred's where, in royalist eyes, he confirmed his reputation as a 'scandalous and seditious minister' (Wood, *Ath. Oxon.*, 3.441). In 1642 he was one of the six 'loving friends' to whom Warwick transferred control of his many Essex advowsons; his fellow trustees included John Pym, Edmund Calamy, and Stephen Marshall. Sedgwick's place in opposition councils was already established. On 25 May 1642 he preached his first fast sermon before the House of Commons, and later that year he was briefly chaplain to the regiment of Colonel Denzil Holles and was present at Edgehill. Nehemiah Wharton approved his 'heavenly sermons' to the army (*CSP dom.*, 1641–2, 391).

In 1643 Sedgwick was appointed one of the licensers of divinity books, and he was an original and assiduous member of the Westminster assembly. His sympathies lay with the presbyterians but his views were not rigid. He favoured a Scottish alliance, belonged to a London classis, urged ministerial authority in an orderly church, and deplored the rise of sects: 'every Sectary', he said in 1644, 'makes an Arke of his owne fancie' (*An Arke Against a Deluge*, 1644, 19). In 1645 he resigned Coggeshall to become rector of St Andrew's, Holborn, London, and in 1646 he moved to St Paul's, Covent Garden.

Between 1642 and 1648 Sedgwick preached some fourteen or fifteen sermons to one or other of the houses of parliament. From 1642 to 1644 these sermons served the interests of his old political and religious allies, for example, *Haman's Vanity* (1643) on the discovery of Waller's plot, *An Arke Against a Deluge* (1644) making the best of defeat at Lostwithiel, and an unpublished sermon of 18 December 1644 supporting the self-denying ordinance. Thereafter new preachers and new issues took centre stage, and only one of his later parliamentary sermons was published (*The Nature and Danger of Heresies*, 1647). In the same year his *A Short Catechisme* appeared.

Sedgwick was a successful preacher who reputedly in hot weather 'unbutton[ed] his doublet in the pulpit, that his breath might be longer, and his voice more audible to rail against the king's party' (Wood, *Ath. Oxon.*, 3.442). The style of his printed sermons is clear and easy, less bloodthirsty than that of many of his contemporaries, but marked by vivid images: God's special providence, he said, 'clasps the Church, as the fethers of the hen doth the chicken' (*Haman's Vanity*, 1643, 15–16). In person he appears to have possessed the sociability that Warwick valued in his clerical friends. He was uxorious—though very little is known of his wife, Priscilla—and, in the judgement of his enemies, 'a sensuall and voluptuous man' (*De L'Isle and Dudley MSS*, 6.561–2). He opposed episcopacy and believed that the causes of the church and of parliament were interdependent. Despite later disappointment at 'the Crossenesse of events' (*The Shepherd of Israel*, 1658, 377), Sedgwick's commitment to the cause he espoused in the early 1640s seems never to have wavered.

In 1651 Sedgwick urged leniency for Christopher Love, in 1653 he was appointed a trier, and in 1654 an assistant to the ejectors of unsatisfactory ministers, but the sermons published posthumously by literary executors who included his old allies Stephen Marshall and Edmund Calamy suggest that in these years he turned increasingly to the pastoral care of his flock. In 1656, as his health failed, he retired to Marlborough, where 'he died very wealthy' in January 1658 (Wood, *Ath. Oxon.*, 3.444). He was buried at Ogbourne St Andrew, Wiltshire, beside his father. By his will, dated 17 March 1654, his eldest son inherited land, money, books and plate 'which the King and Queene of Bohemia gave unto mee'. His younger children, Frances, Joseph, Susan, and Priscilla, received a total of £2800, and the 'godly poor' of Covent Garden £20.

John Sedgwick (1600/01–1643) matriculated (aged eighteen) at Queen's College, Oxford, on the same day as his elder brother, Obadiah, and graduated BA from Magdalen Hall on 6 December 1622, proceeding MA on 7 July 1625 and BD on 9 November 1633. He was vicar of Bisley, Gloucestershire, between 1625 and 1638 but was deprived after accusations of simony. He married Anne Buttery, his second wife (nothing is known of the first), in 1632. He became vicar of Clavering, Essex, and in 1641 rector of St Alfege, London Wall. His earlier success as lecturer at St Giles Cripplegate had angered the incumbent, William Fuller, and divided the parish.

Between 1624 and 1643 John Sedgwick published four sermons and *Antinomianisme Anatomized, or, A Glasse for the Lawlesse* (1643), a work criticizing those who denied Christians were under 'morall law'. As chaplain in Essex's army his 'famous sermons' impressed soldiers and civilians alike (*CSP dom.*, *1641–2*, 388, 400). In 1643, turning combatant, he lead a regimental assault on Launceston. He died in October 1643 and was buried at St Alfege on 15 October.

BARBARA DONAGAN

Sources Wood, *Ath. Oxon.*, new edn • Foster, *Alum. Oxon.* • J. F. Wilson, *Pulpit in parliament: puritanism during the English civil wars, 1640–1648* (1969) • A. Laurence, *Parliamentary army chaplains, 1642–1651*, Royal Historical Society Studies in History, 59 (1990) • *Report on the manuscripts of Lord De L'Isle and Dudley*, 6, HMC, 77 (1966) • BL, Add. MS 4275, fols. 158–64 • B. Donagan, 'The clerical patronage of Robert Rich, second earl of Warwick, 1619–1642', *Proceedings of the American Philosophical Society*, 120 (1976), 388–419 • *CSP dom.*, *1641–2*, 388, 391–7, 400 • *Mercurius Rusticus* (1647), 212–13 • *JHC*, 3 (1642–4), 138 • will, PRO, PROB 11/272, sig. 20 • Greaves & Zaller, *BDBR* • R. Newcourt, *Repertorium ecclesiasticum parochiale Londinense*, 2 vols. (1708–10) [John Sedgwick] • B. Brook, *The lives of the puritans*, 2 (1813) [John Sedgwick] • *STC*, *1475–1640*, nos. 22149–50a, 23829, 25023.5 • Wing, *STC* [John Sedgwick]

Archives BL, MS notes and sermons [copies] • BL, sermons, Harley MS 1198

Likenesses T. Athow, line engraving, pubd 1792 (after an unknown artist), BM, NPG • W. Richardson, engraving • portrait, oils, priv. coll.

Sedgwick, Robert (*bap.* **1613**, *d.* **1656**), merchant and army officer, was baptized on 6 May 1613 in Woburn, Bedfordshire, the son of William Sedgwick (*d.* 1632) and his wife, Elizabeth Howe, and brother of William *Sedgwick (*bap.* 1609, *d.* 1663/4). He emigrated to Boston, Massachusetts, in 1635, and then to Charlestown, Massachusetts, in 1637; was made a freeman of the colony. He was elected captain of Charlestown's militia and deputy to the general court, the colony's legislature, in 1636, 1638–44, 1648, and 1649. He also served as commander of Massachusetts's artillery company, which he had helped to found, in 1641, 1645, and 1648. In 1645 he commanded Castle Isle, the key to Boston harbour. In 1652 he was chosen major-general of Massachusetts.

Sedgwick was equally prominent in the colonial economy. Beginning as an importer, especially of cloth, he helped to organize the fisheries. He became a leading dealer in fish, his brother-in-law, London financier Robert Houghton, providing links to London importers. Working through partnerships, Sedgwick invested in the establishment of the famed Saugus Iron Works as well as the building of ships, wharves, and warehouses in the towns around Boston harbour. He also owned the Tide Mill at Charlestown, another of the colony's early major industrial projects. Inevitably involved in land development, he aided in the creation of the town of Woburn in 1642. His commercial and military interests gave him a sophisticated sense of England's imperial opportunities in the Americas. In 1644, for instance, he participated in a company to tap into the Great Lakes fur trade by flanking Dutch New Netherland by way of the Delaware valley. The scheme was thwarted by mismanagement and Dutch counter-measures. He also resisted the colony's isolationist impulses by petitioning in 1643 to repeal laws against Baptists and by protesting a 1645 law restricting residence of strangers to three weeks.

In 1653 Sedgwick returned to England to lobby for an American offensive against the Dutch during the First Anglo-Dutch War. In February 1654 Cromwell gave him four ships, 200 troops, and permission to raise local militia for an assault on New Netherland. Cromwell wished to impress New England with the protectorate's authority and intention to expand English power in America. In June 1654 the fleet arrived in Boston and soon 700 men were recruited. However, word arrived of the treaty of Westminster, ending hostilities, and though Sedgwick wished to continue the campaign, the New England governments refused and reopened commerce with the Dutch.

Instead, Sedgwick led his forces against the French in Acadia. From July to early September 1654 the expedition captured and garrisoned French posts at St John, Port Royal, and Pentagoet on the Penobscot, thus ending French penetration of the region for the next thirteen years. Sedgwick, working through his son-in-law John Leverett, then gathered a cargo of masts and sailed back to England.

Impressed, Cromwell, in June 1655, gave Sedgwick twelve ships and 800 soldiers to reinforce the Western Design, an expedition against the Spanish Caribbean. He found the demoralized army occupying Jamaica after its catastrophic defeat at Hispaniola. Although he lived less than a year from his arrival, Sedgwick, appointed one of the commissioners for civil government of the island, played a major role in laying the foundation for the eventual success of the new colony. He inaugurated the commerce between New England and Jamaica, essential to the future prosperity of both. He discouraged piracy, even against the Spanish, and sought instead permanent agricultural settlers. He failed to recruit New Englanders, but in March 1656 some 1400 planters from Nevis, led by their governor, migrated to Jamaica.

Nevertheless, Sedgwick was oppressed by a sense of failure, and, soon after receiving word of his appointment as commander-in-chief of English forces in America, he died in Jamaica on 24 May 1656. His secretary claimed the new responsibilities had hastened his death. 'There is so much expected of me', he said, 'and I, conscious of my own disabilities, having besides so untoward a people to deal with, am able to performe soe little, that I shall never overcome it; it will breake my heart' (Thurloe, *State papers*, 5.155). He left a widow, Johanna Blake, and five children in London.

RICHARD P. GILDRIE

Sources H. D. Sedgwick, 'Robert Sedgwick', *Publications of the Colonial Society of Massachusetts*, 3 (1900), 156–74 • R. L. Jones, 'Sedgwick, Robert', *DAB* • S. S. Webb, *The governors-general: the English army and the definition of the empire, 1569–1681* (1979) • B. Bailyn, *The New England merchants in the seventeenth century* (1955) • J. G. Reid, *Acadia, Maine, and New Scotland: marginal colonies in the seventeenth century* (1981) • *DNB* • R. S. Dunn, *Puritans and Yankees: the Winthrop dynasty of New England, 1630–1717* (1962)

Sedgwick, Thomas (*d.* **1573**), Roman Catholic theologian, seems to have been a member of the Sedgwick family of north Yorkshire and co. Durham. His university career began at Peterhouse, Cambridge, where he graduated BA in 1530. Admitted a fellow of the college on 2 June 1531, he graduated MA in 1533, was ordained deacon in Lincoln on

22 December 1537, and graduated BTh in 1545. Sedgwick was one of the original fellows of Trinity College, Cambridge, being nominated by Henry VIII in December 1546. In June 1550 he publicly disputed with Bucer in Cambridge on justification by faith, defending the orthodox Catholic position. He was instituted to the rectory of Erwarton, Suffolk, in 1552.

In the following year Stephen Gardiner, the new lord chancellor, recommended both Sedgwick and Andrew Perne for the mastership of Peterhouse, and both were nominated by the fellows, the bishop of Ely selecting Perne for the position. In 1554 Sedgwick graduated DTh and was elected Lady Margaret professor of divinity, holding the chair until 1558, and was one of the team of Cambridge theologians deputed to Oxford to dispute with Thomas Cranmer, Hugh Latimer, and Nicholas Ridley on the nature of the mass in April of that year. In Oxford he was incorporated DTh, and on his return to Cambridge was elected vice-master of Trinity. On 12 March 1556 he was instituted to the vicarage of Enfield, Middlesex, on the presentation of the master and fellows of his college, but resigned it later that year. On 30 May 1556 he was admitted to the rectory of Toft, Cambridgeshire. He was one of the commissioners for religion and the examination of heretical books, and took an active part in the visitation of the university by Cardinal Pole's delegates in 1556 and 1557.

In 1557 Sedgwick was appointed regius professor of divinity, and in 1558 was collated to the rectory of Stanhope, Durham, by Bishop Cuthbert Tunstall, and was instituted vicar of nearby Gainford on the presentation of the master and fellows of Trinity. On 21 September 1559 he appeared before Elizabeth's royal visitors at Bishop Auckland, co. Durham, where he refused to subscribe to the oath of supremacy. He was thereupon remanded under sureties for four days, and then deprived of his livings. In 1561 he was removed from his professorship and confined to within 10 miles of the town of Richmond, Yorkshire. In 1567 George Neville, master of the hospital at Well, bequeathed him £4. After the northern uprising of 1569 Sedgwick was incarcerated in York Castle, where he died in 1573. Considered very learned by contemporaries (though with the reservation that he was not very wise), he left no known writings. PAUL ARBLASTER

Sources Cooper, *Ath. Cantab.*, 1.213, 553 · A. Forster, 'Bishop Tunstall's priests', *Recusant History*, 9 (1967–8), 175–204, esp. 192 · T. A. Walker, *A biographical register of Peterhouse men*, 1 (1927), 127 · J. Venn and J. A. Venn, eds., *The book of matriculations and degrees … in the University of Cambridge from 1544 to 1659* (1913), 596 · *Reg. Oxf.*, vol. 1 · C. Cross, 'Oxford and the Tudor state', *Hist. U. Oxf.* 3: *Colleg. univ.*, 117–49 · H. Gee, *The Elizabethan clergy and the settlement of religion, 1558–1564* (1898), 179

Sedgwick, William (*bap.* 1609, *d.* 1663/4), religious and political controversialist, was baptized at Woburn, Bedfordshire, on 17 August 1609, the son of William Sedgwick (*d.* 1632), gentleman, of London, and his wife, Elizabeth Howe. His brother was Robert *Sedgwick (*bap.* 1613, *d.* 1656), merchant and army officer.

Sedgwick entered Pembroke College, Oxford, in 1624 and studied under George Hughes, who instructed Sedgwick in the tenets of Calvinism. He matriculated on 2 December 1625, graduated BA on 21 June 1628, and proceeded MA on 4 May 1631. In 1635 he was incorporated at Cambridge. Sedgwick was married, but his wife's name and the date of their marriage are unknown. They appear to have had several children, of whom only three, William, Susan, and Mary, were listed in his will.

Sedgwick was rector of Farnham, Essex, from 5 February 1635 until 1643. He deplored the advance of Laudian innovation: 'idolatrous, superstitious Arminians carry the ball before them, they have prevailed lamentably these 7 yeares' (Webster, 262). Along with his old tutor Hughes, he promoted puritan ideals and sought spiritual solace in the mid-1630s by leading and participating in weekly fasts with fellow Essex godly ministers such as Thomas Parker, Samuel Rogers, and Nicholas and Thomas Noyes. Sedgwick's willingness to promote worthy religious causes brought him to the attention of John Dury, who was seeking assistance in his plan to effect a theological common ground between Lutherans and Calvinists.

On 29 June 1642 Sedgwick preached a fast sermon at St Margaret's, Westminster. Entitled *Zions Deliverance, her Friends Duty* (1642), this sermon established his pattern of using allegorical interpretations of the Bible to explain England's problems. In this respect, Sedgwick was not unlike parliament's more prominent ministers Stephen Marshall and Cornelius Burges; indeed, in reading Hebrew history as an analogue to the English protestant experience he was drawing on a theme commonplace since at least the Geneva Bible. Defining Jerusalem as the church of the Gentiles, he compared the impending war to Israel's deliverance from Egypt. As in ancient Israel during the rebuilding of the Temple, the king had been seduced by 'evill counsell' and the 'Reformation counted Rebellion', but parliament should not be afraid to rise up because 'God hath no more than he gets by conquest' (Sedgwick, *Zions Deliverance*, 7). The Lord would assist in accomplishing the Reformation, but the saints must help by employing qualified servants who valued public service above personal interest. Sedgwick preached another fast sermon in 1643, *Scripture a Perfect Rule for Church Government* (December 1643), which supported the effort to establish a presbyterian polity in the church.

Around March 1643 Sedgwick placed a curate in charge of the church at Farnham and served as an army chaplain in the regiment of Sir William Constable until May of that year. From July to December 1644 he was the chaplain at Wisbech garrison, Cambridgeshire, and he may have acted as a courier for Colonel Thomas Ayloffe. Sedgwick was the minister for the cathedral church of Ely from 1645 to 1649, a position to which he was appointed by Edward Montagu, earl of Manchester. His evangelical work there gained him the title the Apostle of the Isle of Ely, and impressed Cromwell, who wrote to the isle's sequestrators that Sedgwick 'fully deserve[d]' the pay owed him despite the committee's financial difficulties (Abbott, 1.325).

The question of Sedgwick's sanity has been raised by

contemporaries and historians alike. Reports vary as to whether he earned the nickname Doomsday Sedgwick after telling some gentlemen at Sir Francis Russell's house in Cambridge that the world would end in one week, or after prophesying in London that the world would end in fourteen days. The story of his London prophecies appeared in a newsletter dated 30 March 1647, which recorded that some ministers were sent to examine him. Sedgwick met with the preachers but refused to discuss his statements, and the paper's report that some thought he was 'distempered in minde', while others observed that 'he talks very sencibly', summarizes the confusing impression one gets when reading Sedgwick's pamphlets (*Clarke Papers*, 1.4).

Wood wrote that Sedgwick 'was a conceited whimsical person', but he displayed a keen sense of objectivity in faulting parliament and the king for the outbreak of the war, and in pointing out the army's errors in 1647 and 1648 (Wood, *Ath. Oxon.*, 2.335). The equitable distribution of blame appears in most of his pamphlets from 1647 onwards, beginning with *The Leaves of the Tree of Life* (August 1648). In this tract Sedgwick displayed an ardent nationalism. He acknowledged that the English had human faults, but described them as 'indeed a Race and seed of heavenly Lords', who had created a government that represented 'the highest and perfectest glory of God' (Sedgwick, *Leaves of the Tree of Life*, 3). He urged the powerful interests in the country to include the king in the peace settlement, and condemned the *Agreement of the People* as a 'covenant with hell' (ibid., 46). Contemporaries disagree as to whether Sedgwick showed this pamphlet to Charles at the Isle of Wight in 1647 or 1648, but according to Wood the king read only part of it before remarking that the author 'stands in some need of sleep' (Wood, *Ath. Oxon.*, 2.336). This treatise and Sedgwick's subsequent pamphlets demonstrate fervid spiritual feeling, but they do not exhibit the disorganization or pathos evident in Lady Eleanor Douglass's writings.

In late 1648 Sedgwick engaged in a polemical debate, during which he lambasted the army for bringing the king to judgment, and charged that the officers were politicians bent on forwarding their own interests. Recognizing his own notoriety, there was undoubtedly a hint of sarcasm in the title of *The Spiritual Madman* (20 December 1648), which began by arguing that England was under a military dictatorship, but deteriorated into a confused diatribe in which Sedgwick displayed sympathy for the Levellers' demand for an extended franchise, but advocated restoring the king and establishing some sort of mystical commonwealth wherein property would be shared by all. Support for the king led to accusations that Sedgwick was a royalist, and he refrained from publishing between 1648 and 1656 to disprove the charge. He maintained a lifelong friendship with Joshua Sprigge despite differences with the army, which Sedgwick blamed for the king's execution.

In *Some Flashes of Lightnings of the Sonne of Man* (1648) Sedgwick foretold the coming of the kingdom of God, but explained that it was within individuals. This pamphlet demonstrated more spiritual emotion than his preceding tracts, and it perhaps explains his later sympathy with Quakers and Muggletonians. He corresponded with John Reeve from 1652 to 1657 and visited James Nayler in prison in 1656. Sedgwick's name also arose during the committee debates to determine whether Nayler was guilty of blasphemy: Major-General Whalley clearly believed that Sedgwick and Nayler were both suffering from a similar insanity. He recalled an encounter with Sedgwick in which the minister's 'frenzy' caused him to claim that he was God and 'divers horrid things'; later Sedgwick had conceded that he was 'but a man' (*Diary of Thomas Burton*, 1.103–4).

With one exception, Sedgwick refrained from political discourse during the protectorate (1654–60). In *Animadversions upon a Letter* (January 1656), he castigated Vavasor Powell and the Welsh signatories of *A Word for God* (December 1655) for threatening the peace of the kingdom. Retaining his old even-handedness, he elucidated the strengths and weaknesses of the treatise and of the current government, but reminded the Welshmen that Cromwell was 'a great Man', who had been 'a main pillar of … strength' in all the upheavals since 1642 (Sedgwick, *Animadversions upon a Letter*, 20). Sedgwick also accepted the Restoration, and his support of Charles I in 1648 may partially explain why he was not ejected after 1660.

In 1661 Sedgwick set out his reflections on the preceding years of upheaval in *Animadversions upon a Book entitled Inquisition for the Blood of our Late Sovereign*, which elucidates and expounds a work he had published the year before. Stung by criticisms from both royalists and parliamentarians, Sedgwick admitted that he had been 'foolish' for anonymously publishing his earlier tract, but had decided at that time to 'own it' if it became controversial (Sedgwick, 1, 2). Consistent with his earlier pamphlets that blamed both sides for the war, Sedgwick indicted the army for executing the king, and commended the protectorate as the only stable Commonwealth government, although it was no more than the 'dressed up … carkase of King, Lords and Commons' (ibid., 61). He condemned the 'Saints' (the army) as a 'confused heap' who mistakenly associated the Good Old Cause with God's cause based on a partial and misunderstood reading of Revelation; God's cause, he scolded, did not include continuous warfare and political strife (ibid., 84, 108). Vilified by royalists and parliamentarians as a 'Fanatick' and 'Courtier', Sedgwick's claim that he had always acted as a mediator (but neither side would compromise, especially on the issue of religion) is perhaps true in light of the recommendation of him to Dury as a suitable collaborator in the 1630s. Believing that good existed in all people and all things, Sedgwick was optimistic that the restoration of Charles II and the monarchy were positive events, and that the former enemies should work towards accommodation.

Following the Restoration, Sedgwick may have held a living in Lewisham, Kent, where he died between the end of November 1663 and late February 1664. Anthony Wood reported that a 'Dr. S. C.' of Gr[eenwich?], Kent, had reneged on his promise to furnish an account of Sedgwick's death (Wood, *Ath. Oxon.*, 2.336). Sedgwick's will, dated 28 November 1663, indicates that he owned property at Great and Little Sampford, Essex. It also records the names of four sons-in-law, Nicholas Ashton, Timothy van Vleteren, Nathaniel James, and Francis Commins, of whom nothing further is known.

JOYCE SAMPSON

Sources *The writings and speeches of Oliver Cromwell*, ed. W. C. Abbott and C. D. Crane, 4 vols. (1937–47) • *CSP dom., 1644; addenda, 1625–49* • *The Clarke papers*, ed. C. H. Firth, 4 vols., CS, new ser., 49, 54, 61–2 (1891–1901) • *DNB* • Foster, *Alum. Oxon.* • R. L. Greaves and R. Zaller, eds., *Biographical dictionary of British radicals in the seventeenth century*, 3 vols. (1982–4), vol. 3 • *Report on the manuscripts of his grace the duke of Buccleuch and Queensberry … preserved at Montagu House*, 3 vols. in 4, HMC, 45 (1899–1926), vol. 1 • *Fifth report*, HMC, 4 (1876) • *JHC*, 2 (1640–42), 591a, 648a • *JHC*, 4 (1644–6), 487a • A. Laurence, *Parliamentary army chaplains, 1642–1651* (1990) • *Calamy rev.* • T. Webster, *Godly clergy in early Stuart England: the Caroline puritan movement, c.1620–1643* (1997) • *Diary of Thomas Burton*, ed. J. T. Rutt, 4 vols. (1828), vol. 1, pp. 103–4 • *IGI* • C. Hill, *The experience of defeat: Milton and some contemporaries* (1984) • *VCH Bedfordshire*, vol. 3 • W. Sedgwick, *Animadversions upon a book entitled Inquisition for the blood of our late sovereign* (1661) • Venn, *Alum. Cant.*, 1/4 • Wood, *Ath. Oxon.*, 1st edn

Archives BL, corresp. and papers, Add. MS 34253 • BL, John Reeve papers, Add. MSS 60168–60256 • Cambridgeshire County RO, Huntingdon, Edward Montagu, earl of Manchester letters and papers • Queen's University, Belfast, diary of Samuel Rogers, Percy MS 7 • RS Friends, Lond., James Nayler corresp. and papers

Wealth at death owned property at Great Sampford and Little Sampford, Essex: will, PRO, PROB 11/313–15 (26 Feb 1664); *Calamy rev.*, 432

Sedley, Catharine, *suo jure* **countess of Dorchester, and countess of Portmore** (**1657–1717**), royal mistress, born on 21 December 1657 at Great Queen Street, London, and baptized eight days later at St Giles-in-the-Fields, was the only child of Sir Charles *Sedley (*bap.* 1639, *d.* 1701) and his wife, Lady Catherine Savage (*d.* 1707), daughter of John Savage, Earl Rivers. As early as June 1673 Evelyn spoke of Catherine Sedley as 'none of the virtuous, but a wit' (Evelyn, *Diary*, 4.13). The Countess Cowper later thought that 'Lady Dorchester's Wit makes Amends for her Ugliness' (*Diary*, 74). The earl of Dorset, on the other hand, in one of his four poems about her, would dismiss her 'false pretence to wit and parts' (*Poems of Charles Sackville*, 44). Her plain appearance was widely reported, but may have been exaggerated, as some of those who commented on it, including Charles II, did so to belittle *James II (1633–1701). In 1676 Sir Winston and Lady Churchill were anxious for a match between their eldest son, John Churchill (afterwards first duke of Marlborough), and Catharine, his distant kinswoman, but these negotiations were soon broken off. Two years later she obtained a position at court as one of the maids of honour to the duchess of York and thus came to the attention of the duke. Before long she had supplanted Arabella Churchill as James's principal mistress. Persistent rumours also linked her to James's keeper of the privy purse, James *Grahme (1650–1730), and Grahme himself is said to have believed that he was the real father of the children she claimed were the duke's (Walpole, *Corr.*, 18.193). On becoming king in 1685 James broke off the affair as a moral example to the court, doing

Catharine Sedley, *suo jure* countess of Dorchester, and countess of Portmore (1657–1717), by Isaac Beckett (after Sir Godfrey Kneller, 1685)

the decent thing by setting her up with her own house in St James's Square (no. 21, the house formerly occupied by Arabella Churchill). Three months later two of the leading Anglican courtiers, the earls of Rochester and Dartmouth, contrived her return to favour, in the hope that she would be a protestant counterweight to the king's Catholic advisers. Grahme, as keeper of the privy buckhounds, was able to arrange secret assignations for the king while he was supposedly out hunting (E. Campana de Cavelli, *Les derniers Stuarts*, 2 vols., 1871, 2.75, 89). This ploy met with little success, except that James, by a patent of 20 January 1686, created her baroness of Darlington and countess of Dorchester for life. The queen was appalled and made her distress obvious when she next appeared in public. The Catholic advisers, led by the king's chaplain, Bonaventure Giffard, took the hint and demanded that the countess be banished. James almost immediately gave way. Withdrawing first to St James's Square, she refused to go abroad and, as a compromise, agreed to go into internal exile in Ireland. As a generous pay-off, she was granted an annual pension of £3000 to last until 1691, when she was promised quit-rents worth £5000 per annum from extensive estates in Ireland. On arrival in Dublin she found it 'intolerable' and the Irish 'mallincoly' (De Sola Pinto, 346). In August 1686 she returned to England, on the pretext of taking the waters at Tunbridge Wells (*CSP dom.*, *1686–7*, 253), whereupon the king discreetly resumed their affair. Following James's overthrow, her friendship with the Grahmes, Dartmouth, and the Hydes linked her to the most important group of Jacobite conspirators in London.

The countess certainly made no secret of her lack of respect for the new king and queen. Presented at court in April 1689, she offended Queen Mary by telling her that 'If I have broke one commandement, you have another; and what I did wase more naturall' (*Correspondence of the Family of Hatton*, ed. E. M. Thompson, 2 vols., 1878, 2.128–9). A remark made to the earl of Ailesbury at about the same time implied that she wanted William III assassinated (*Memoirs of … Ailesbury*, 1.254–5). In July 1690 she was called in for questioning by the government and remained a major suspect. Despite this, she successfully claimed part of her pension, and in 1703 the Irish parliament confirmed her right to her Irish rents. It helped that in August 1696 she had married one of William III's army officers, Sir David *Colyear, second baronet (*c.*1656–1730), who was created a baron in 1699 and earl of Portmore in the Scottish peerage four years later. Dorchester retained her caustic wit to the end, for, encountering both the duchess of Portsmouth and the countess of Orkney, mistresses to Charles II and William III, at court during the reign of George I, she famously quipped, 'God! who would have thought that we three royal whores should meet here!' (Walpole, *Corr.*, 18.193). She died at Bath, Somerset, on 26 October 1717, and was buried there. Twelve years later her body was transferred to the new Portmore vault in the church at Weybridge, Surrey, where she had owned a house since the late 1680s.

With her husband, the earl of Portmore, who survived until 2 January 1730, she had two sons—David, Viscount Melsington (*d.* 1729), and Charles Colyear, second earl of Portmore (1700–1785). With the duke of York (afterwards James II) she seems to have had several children who died young. The only child who lived to maturity was Lady Catherine Darnley; she married, on 28 October 1699, James Annesley, third earl of Anglesey, from whom, on account of alleged cruelty on his part, she was separated by act of parliament on 12 June 1701 (*Westmorland MSS*, 336). After his death, in January 1702, she married, secondly, on 16 March 1706, John *Sheffield, first duke of Normanby and Buckingham; she died on 13 March 1743, and was interred, with almost regal pomp, in Westminster Abbey. With her first husband she had an only daughter, Catherine, who married William, son of Sir Constantine Phipps, lord chancellor of Ireland. With her second husband she had a son, Edmund, who succeeded to the title and estates, but, dying unmarried during his mother's lifetime, bequeathed to her all the Mulgrave and Normanby property. These estates she left by will to her grandson, Constantine Phipps, first Baron Mulgrave, whose grandson, Constantine Henry Phipps, on his elevation to the marquessate, assumed the title of Normanby.

Andrew Barclay

Sources V. De Sola Pinto, *Sir Charles Sedley, 1639–1701* (1927) • *Report on the manuscripts of Allan George Finch*, 5 vols., HMC, 71 (1913–2003), vols. 2–4 • W. A. Shaw, ed., *Calendar of treasury books*, 8, PRO (1923), 548–71 • *Bishop Burnet's History*, 3.120, 245 • *The manuscripts of his grace the duke of Rutland*, 4 vols., HMC, 24 (1888–1905), vol. 2, pp. 37, 42–4, 50, 99, 101–3 • *The correspondence of Henry Hyde, earl of Clarendon, and of his brother Laurence Hyde, earl of Rochester*, ed. S. W. Singer, 2 vols. (1828), vol. 1, pp. 544, 552; vol. 2, p. 279 • *Memoirs of Thomas, earl of Ailesbury*, ed. W. E. Buckley, 1, Roxburghe Club, 122 (1890), 246, 254–5, 258–9, 277 • G. Agar-Ellis, ed., *The Ellis correspondence: letters written during the years 1686, 1687, 1688, and addressed to John Ellis*, 2 vols. (1829), vol. 1, pp. 23–4, 32, 35, 38, 42, 92 • *Diary of Mary, Countess Cowper*, ed. [S. Cowper] (1864), 5, 29, 70–1, 74 • E. Lloyd, 'Weybridge parish registers', *Surrey Archaeological Collections*, 17 (1902), 41–69, esp. 57–9 • Walpole, *Corr.*, 18.193 • *The poems of Charles Sackville, sixth earl of Dorset*, ed. B. Harris (New York, 1979), 41–6 • *The manuscripts of the earl of Westmorland*, HMC, 13 (1885); repr. (1906)

Archives BL, music book which belonged to her, Add. MS 30382 • Leics. RO, Finch MSS

Likenesses studio of P. Lely, oils, 1675, NPG • attrib. G. Kneller, oils, 1676–7, Althorp House, Northamptonshire, Spencer collection • studio of G. Kneller, oils, 1684, Ranger's House, London • L. Crosse, miniature, watercolour on vellum, *c.*1685–1690, NPG • I. Beckett, mezzotint (after G. Kneller, 1685), BM, NPG [*see illus.*] • E. Byng, pen and brown ink drawing (after G. Kneller), BM • R. Thompson, mezzotint (after studio of P. Lely), BM, NPG • R. Williams, mezzotint (after W. Wissing), BM, NPG

Wealth at death probably retained at least £5000 p.a. from Irish lands granted in 1686: *Calendar of treasury books, 1685–1689*, vol. 2, pp. 548–71; *Calendar of treasury books, 1689–1692*, vol. 4, pp. 1518–19; *Calendar of treasury books, 1556/7–1696*, 163, 273, 561

Sedley, Sir Charles, fifth baronet (*bap.* **1639**, *d.* **1701**), writer and politician, was baptized on 5 March 1639 at St Clement Danes in the Strand, London. His place of birth was probably his wealthy family's town house in Shire Lane near by. He was the youngest of nine children of Sir John Sedley, second baronet (*c.*1594–1638), of Southfleet, Kent, who had died on 13 August 1638, and Elizabeth (*b. c.*1595, *d.* after 1651), daughter and heir of Sir Henry *Savile, provost of Eton College. On 22 March 1656, after a private education, he entered Wadham College, Oxford, where his tutor was the poet and epicurean wit Walter Pope. Sedley succeeded to the family title in April 1656 on the death from measles of his brother William, having survived the same malady himself.

On 9 February 1657 Sedley married Catherine Savage (*c.*1640–1705), daughter of John Savage, second Earl Rivers, and sister to the widow of Sedley's brother Henry, third baronet (*d.* 1641). The couple set up house in Great Queen Street. On 7 March 1660 Sedley was appointed one of the (royalist) commissioners to reconstitute the militia in Kent and in October became a captain of the Kent volunteer horse. Aged twenty-one at the Restoration, Sedley took enthusiastically to the pleasures of the court and town, often in the company of Charles Sackville, Lord Buckhurst, later sixth earl of Dorset. His witty conversation and the fact that he 'never asked the king for any thing' made him a favourite drinking companion of Charles II. On 16 June 1663 Sedley, Buckhurst, and Sir Thomas Ogle provoked a riot through their drunken antics on the balcony of The Cock tavern in Bow Street. Sedley confessed to 'showing himself naked on a balcony, and throwing down bottles (pissed in) *vi et armis* among the people': second-hand accounts add further enormities (Keble, 1.168; Wood, *Ath. Oxon.*, 1099). For this he was briefly imprisoned and heavily fined. Gossip recorded by Pepys and references to Sedley in the fugitive satire of the

Sir Charles Sedley, fifth baronet (***bap.*** **1639,** ***d.*** **1701**), attrib. John Riley

time consistently represent him as a debauchee; however, he was also respected as a wit and man of fashion. On at least two occasions Pepys found his chatter in the theatre audience more entertaining than what was taking place on the stage (*Diary*, 4 Oct 1664, 18 Feb 1667). Dryden in dedicating *The Assignation* (1672) to Sedley is at pains to present him as a civilized advocate of '*erudita voluptas*' with no resemblance to the wild wit of legend. Sedley's rhymed oath for the 'ballers', reports of whose libertine behaviour so horrified Pepys, is a relatively temperate document, enjoining fidelity in love 'when one proves truly kind' and avoidance of those 'that know not to say no'. He appears to have liked dancing but not music and was a keen player of royal tennis.

In 1663 Sedley, Buckhurst, Waller, Sidney Godolphin, and Sir Edward Filmer contributed an act each to a translation in rhyme of Corneille's *La mort de Pompée*, which after a showing at court was given by the Duke's company at Lincoln's Inn Fields during the winter of 1663–4. He may also have contributed to a lost translation of the same dramatist's *Heraclius*. Three subsequent plays written for the professional stage, *The Mulberry Garden* (1668), *Antony and Cleopatra* (1677), and *Bellamira* (1687), show him to have been a gifted dramatist, though not of the first rank. Sedley's verse of the early Restoration years, written for manuscript circulation, has not survived in any quantity. The satire 'Timon', usually ascribed to Rochester, is given to him in several manuscript sources. The indecent lyric 'In the fields of Lincoln's Inn' is more likely to be by him than by Rochester. Some song lyrics and love poems appear in the printed miscellanies of the 1670s. Sedley's high standing as a critic was acknowledged when Dryden introduced him anagramatically as 'Lisideius', the champion of contemporary French drama, in the dialogue *Of Dramatic Poesy* (1668). He is named with Buckhurst in Rochester's 'An Allusion to Horace' (1675) as one of an inner circle of trusted literary judges. He was a friend and patron of Shadwell who acknowledged his revising hand in *A True Widow* (1678).

In the late 1660s Catherine Sedley, after showing symptoms of insanity, was consigned to a convent at Ghent where she remained until her death in 1705. The daughter of the marriage, the witty Catharine *Sedley (1657–1717), became the mistress of the duke of York, who, in 1686, created her countess of Dorchester. In April 1672 Sedley went through a form of bigamous marriage with Ann Ayscough (*d.* 1708), and moved house to Bloomsbury Square. The character Medley in his friend Etherege's comedy *The Man of Mode* (1676) represents him in his prime as a man of wit and pleasure. A satiric view from two or three years later is more patronizing:

> Expecting supper is his great delight,
> He toils all day but to be drunk at night;
> Then o'er his cups this chirping nightbird sits
> Till he takes Hewitt and Jack Howe for wits.
> (*Poems on Affairs of State*, 1.411)

The first line quoted is clarified by Carlos (probably another portrait) in *A True Widow*: 'I hate a dinner, 'tis a good meal for a dull plodding fellow of business … but the supper is the meal of pleasure and enjoyment' (*Complete Works of Thomas Shadwell*, 3.293).

Sedley was turned to more serious courses by being injured in the collapse of a tennis court in January 1681 and a major illness in 1686. He seems to have been reconciled with the church at this time, and to have written a now lost poem on the Trinity. A later panegyric of marriage, 'The Happy Pair', may be regarded as penance for his errors of the flesh. It is from this period too that he becomes actively engaged in politics.

The circle of court wits which included Sedley, Buckhurst, and Rochester were all under the spell of George Villiers, second duke of Buckingham. Sedley and Buckhurst accompanied him on his splendid embassy to Louis XIV in 1670. They followed Buckingham into opposition in 1673 after the fall of the Cabal ministry and were anti-Yorkists at the time of the Exclusion Bill crisis. In February 1677 Sedley was listed by Shaftesbury as 'doubly worthy'. In 1678 he assisted in the translation of Coleman's letters, then regarded as the principal documentary evidence for the alleged Popish Plot (Pinto, 310–11). In 1681 he was the dedicatee of John Crowne's anti-Catholic *Henry the Sixth: the First Part*. Shadwell's dedication to him of *The Tenth Satire of Juvenal* (1687) was also a whig political gesture. Sedley had entered the House of Commons in May 1668 as one of two members for New Romney, Kent, and sat in every subsequent parliament during his lifetime with the exception of that of James II (when he declined to stand) and the first of William and Mary. A supporter of the revolution but a whig of the 'anti-court' variety, he spoke with good sense and moderation in the parliaments after 1688. A speech against placemen and heavy war taxation delivered on 31 March 1690 was widely circulated in printed form. Having asked Charles II for nothing he maintained his principled independence under William except in the matter of procuring a knighthood for his son, Charles, with Ann Ayscough. This young man, to whom Sedley was deeply attached, was active in 1695 in opposing press-ganging for William's armies in Flanders.

Sedley's best writing is found in his lyrical and satirical verse, much of which is of great distinction. His translation of Horace's *Carmina*, 2.8 has been much admired. The love lyrics, which include the much anthologized 'Love still has something of the sea', are consistently inventive and well turned. He shared Dorset's admiration for the power and simplicity of the popular ballad, and could write well in the ballad manner himself. The sombre 'Ballad to the Tune of Bateman', narrating the murder of the whig lawyer John Hoyle, demonstrates how political satire can become more effective through restraint. It is likely that verse written against James II and his court remains unidentified in the manuscript miscellanies of the time. Although Dryden compared him with Tibullus, the strongest classical influence on his writing was that of Martial, whom Sedley imitated and translated with great flair. His sure touch as an epigrammist is apparent from the following distich: 'Thou swearst thou'lt drink no more: kind heaven send / Me such a cook or coachman, but no friend.' His later verse and a few speeches are preserved in the 1702 *Miscellaneous Works* and its enlarged reprint of 1707.

Sedley died at Hampstead on 20 August 1701 'like a philosopher without fear or superstition' (*Buccleugh MSS*, 2.793), and was buried at Southfleet church, Kent, on 26 August. By the time of his death, high living and generosity had left his estate encumbered with mortgages. He never acquired his daughter's art of pillaging the public purse, though a late letter to Dorset quoted by Pinto (pp. 207–8) shows him making an attempt. However, his heirs were able to repair much of the damage. He had descendants through his illegitimate son, Charles (*d.* 1701), who narrowly predeceased him, and the children of the countess of Dorchester. William Oldys claimed to have seen a settlement relating to two illegitimate daughters with the surname Charlot. The eldest of Dorchester's children, Lady Catherine Darnley, later duchess of Buckinghamshire (1679–1743), was acknowledged by James II but may have been the child of Colonel James Grahme. Her other surviving child, Charles, was the issue of her marriage to David Colyear, earl of Portmore. The family tree printed by Pinto (pp. x–xi) shows a remarkable array of distinguished and talented descendants, among them the eugenicist Sir Francis Galton, who would no doubt have seen more than chance in the matter. HAROLD LOVE

Sources V. De Sola Pinto, *Sir Charles Sedley, 1639–1701* (1927) • *The political and dramatic works of Sir Charles Sedley*, ed. V. De Sola Pinto, 2 vols. (1928) • J. H. Wilson, *The court wits of the Restoration: an introduction* (1948) • HoP, *Commons, 1660–90*, 3.409–10 • G. de F. Lord and others, eds., *Poems on affairs of state: Augustan satirical verse, 1660–1714*, 7 vols. (1963–75) • P. A. Hopkins, 'Aphra Behn and John Hoyle', *N&Q*, 239 (1994), 176–85 • D. M. Vieth, 'Sir Charles Sedley and the baller's oath', *Scriblerian*, 12 (1979), 47–8 • *The complete works of Thomas Shadwell*, ed. M. Summers, 5 vols. (1927) • J. Keble, ed., *Reports in the court of King's Bench … from the XII to the XXX year of the reign of … Charles II*, 3 vols. (1685) • Wood, *Ath. Oxon.*, 2nd edn • P. Beal and others, *Index of English literary manuscripts*, ed. P. J. Croft and others, [4 vols. in 11 pts] (1980–), vol. 1, pt 2, pp. 299–322 • *Report on the manuscripts of his grace the duke of Buccleuch and Queensberry … preserved at Montagu House*, 3 vols. in 4, HMC, 45 (1899–1926), vol. 2

Archives Bodl. Oxf., report of his speech in House of Commons

Likenesses attrib. J. Riley, oils, Knole, Kent [*see illus.*] • M. Vandergucht, line engraving, BM, NPG; repro. in *Works* (1722)

Wealth at death considerable, but heavily mortgaged: Pinto, *Sir Charles Sedley*

Sedulius [Sedulius senior] (*fl.* **7th–8th cent.**), religious writer, was probably an Irish exegete who wrote a commentary on Matthew's gospel, of which only a fragment survives. It has been postulated that he existed as a separate individual, earlier than—and distinct from—*Sedulius Scottus, who flourished on the continent *c.*850 and also wrote a commentary on Matthew. This earlier Sedulius is known only from a brief citation from his *Tractatus Mathei*, concerning the fig tree cursed by Jesus. He identified the fig as the tree from which Adam and Eve had eaten the forbidden fruit. There is no proof that this earlier Sedulius was an Irishman, but that is likely: the same identification of the fig tree as that from which Adam ate occurs in other insular texts, and the extant fragment is quoted in a Genesis commentary, which itself is of probable Irish authorship. In addition, Sedulius appears to have been a popular name among the Irish at this period: the annals of the four masters (a seventeenth-century compilation from earlier sources) give the obits of six Irish churchmen named Siadhal—presumably a Hibernicized form of the Latin Sedulius—between 752 and 855.

There are two reasons for regarding Sedulius 'senior' as being distinct from the better-known Sedulius Scottus. First, his commentary on Matthew is quoted by a Genesis commentary which itself has been handed down in a manuscript copied on the continent around the turn of the eighth and ninth centuries. Even if the manuscript is dated as late as possible, it would still be exceedingly unlikely that the fragment's author is identifiable with Sedulius Scottus, who was active in Francia *c.*850. This chronological point led Bernhard Bischoff to dub the Matthew commentator 'Sedulius senior', though care must be taken to distinguish him not only from Sedulius Scottus of the mid-ninth century, but also from the fifth-century continental Sedulius who composed a versified account of Christ's life. A second reason for regarding Sedulius 'senior' as distinct from Sedulius Scottus is that the latter does not identify the forbidden tree from which Adam and Eve ate as a fig tree in his commentary on Matthew. The citation in the Genesis commentary must therefore be from a different work, probably by a different author.

The case for two separate Sedulii is not absolutely watertight. However, the notion that there could have been a single, long-lived individual who composed two commentaries on Matthew, one in Ireland and one on the continent, is highly implausible. Given the evidence for the popularity of the name among the Irish, combined with that for a significant quantity of biblical commentaries being composed by Irishmen at the time, the suggestion that there were two separate individuals is probably right. The floruit of Sedulius 'senior' probably fell in the seventh or eighth century, the heyday of Irish biblical exegesis: the manuscript of the Genesis commentary provides a definite *terminus ad quem*. There is no evidence that he was ever a *peregrinus* ('pilgrim') to the continent.

An Irish Sedulius who was a bishop somewhere in Britain took part in a synod held at Rome under Pope Gregory II in 721. But there is no more reason to identify the author of the Matthew commentary with him than with any of the other Sedulii named in the annals of the four masters. CLARE STANCLIFFE

Sources B. Bischoff, 'Wendepunkte in der Geschichte der lateinischen Exegese im Frühmittelalter', *Sacris Erudiri*, 6 (1954), 189–281, 246–7 • C. D. Wright, 'Apocryphal lore and insular tradition in St Gall, Stiftsbibliothek MS 908', *Irland und die Christenheit: Bibelstudien und Mission*, ed. P. Ní Chatháin and M. Richter (1987), 124–45 • *AFM* • J. D. Mansi, *Sacrorum conciliorum nova, et amplissima collectio*, 12 (Florence, 1766) • M. Lapidge and R. Sharpe, *A bibliography of Celtic-Latin literature, 400–1200* (1985), 169 • J. F. Kelly, 'A catalogue of early medieval Hiberno-Latin biblical commentaries (II)', *Traditio*, 45 (1989–90), 393–434, esp. 405–6

Sedulius Scottus (*fl.* 840x51–860x74), poet and scholar, was an Irishman who spent most of his life in Francia. Little is known of his career apart from the evidence implicit in his own writings. He probably came from Leinster, in south-east Ireland, a notable home of Irish panegyric to kings. His date of birth is unknown. In Francia he was not at the forefront of public affairs, although his patrons were leading political figures. All that is known of Sedulius's status is his description of himself as *presbyter* ('priest'). He arrived on the continent some time between 840, when Louis the Pious died and his patron, Hartgar, became bishop at Liège, and 851, when the empress Irmingard died. It has been suggested that he arrived in 848, the date of the Irish delegation to Charles the Bald (*r.* 840–77). Sedulius disappears from the written record between 860 and 874. On the continent his main sphere of activity was in the Rhine–Flanders area, at Liège on the Meuse. He is believed to have been at the centre of a circle of Irish intellectuals and he and his Irish companions had contacts with Cologne, Metz, Laon, Soissons, St Amand, and Milan. He was associated not only with the bishops of Liège but also with those of the neighbouring dioceses of Cologne, Munster, and Metz. Marginalia in the manuscript Berne, Stadtbibliothek, MS 363, associated with Sedulius, mention Irishmen whose names occur in contemporary Irish annals, suggesting that Sedulius also retained his links with Ireland. His writings include eighty-three poems written for both lay and ecclesiastical patrons, grammatical and exegetical works, as well as a 'mirror for princes' (a text prescribing conduct appropriate for rulers).

Sedulius's poems take the form of court panegyric, religious poetry, nature poetry, and inscriptions. It has been argued that they show the influence of Irish vernacular poetry. He sang to some of the greatest in Francia: the emperor Lothar (*d.* 855) and his three sons, Charles (*d.* 863), Louis (*d.* 875), and Lothar II (*d.* 869); the empress Irmingard; Eberhard, count of Friuli; Hartgar, bishop of Liège; Gunthar, archbishop of Cologne; and to Irish friends. Sedulius is also credited with the authorship of nine poems in the Berne manuscript 363 which belong to a north Italian milieu, although it is not known whether he visited Italy. Berne 363 contains extracts from Dioscorides, Servius's commentary on the works of Virgil, the *Rhetoric* of Fortunatianus, the *Dialectic* and *Rhetoric* of Augustine, the *Ars rhetorica Clodiani de statibus*, the *Carmina* of Horace, extracts from Ovid's *Metamorphoses*, a fragment of Bede's *Historia ecclesiastica*, and an extract from Priscian. Sedulius's style is sophisticated and he uses numerous classical adornments of speech in his poetry. His poems contain allusions to works by Virgil, Ovid, and Venantius Fortunatus. The poetry is also remarkable for its human detail, humour, and awareness of contemporary events. In perhaps the earliest of his surviving poems, he describes his journey through the winter storms with his two companions to the palace of the kindly Bishop Hartgar. Another poem, written in mock heroic vein, describes the death of a ram which had been given to him as a gift. Elsewhere he describes the defeat of the Norsemen by an army which included Hartgar.

Sedulius's biblical scholarship is attested in diverse ways. A ninth-century Greek psalter (Paris, Bibliothèque de l'Arsenal, MS 8407) in Sedulius's hand has an interlinear Latin translation. The palaeography of this manuscript is very similar to that of a St Gallen manuscript of the gospels and that of a Dresden manuscript of the Pauline epistles, both of which are also bilingual. Sedulius wrote commentaries on St Paul, the *Collectanea in omnes beati Pauli Epistolas* (which relied heavily on Pelagius while omitting any heretical Pelagian material), and on Matthew, the *Collectaneum in Mattheum*, and explanations of prefaces to the gospels, the *Explanationes in canones et argumenta evangeliorum*. His exegesis reflects a grammarian's interest in points of language and he is almost unique for his time in citing his authorities.

The range of Sedulius's reading is illustrated by his florilegium, the *Collectaneum*, a preparatory notebook for his mirror for princes, the *De rectoribus Christianis*. The *Collectaneum* consists chiefly of historical, poetical, and rhetorical extracts, and includes excerpts from Cicero, Macrobius's *Somnium Scipionis*, Vegetius, Frontinus, the *Scriptores historiae Augustae*, Lactantius, Seneca, Fastidius, Terence, Porphyry, Caecilius Balbus, Publilius Syrus, Aurelius Victor, Orosius, Cassiodorus, Valerius Maximus, Rufinus, and Jerome, as well as the Irish texts *De duodecim abusiuis saeculi*, the *Proverbia Graecorum*, and the *Collectio canonum Hibernensis*.

The *De rectoribus Christianis* was written in prosimetrum form, alternating prose and verse, following the model of Boethius's *De consolatione philosophiae*. The themes stressed by Sedulius in the mirror are the derivation of the ruler's power from God, the importance of self-rule, the royal virtues of clemency, wisdom, and piety, respect for the ecclesiastical sphere, the importance of good advisers, and of God's aid in war. This work differs from other Carolingian mirrors for princes in the frequency with which it uses ancient and late antique authors—particularly unusual sources were the Christian military manual *De re militari*, by Flavius Vegetius Renatus and the *Scriptores historiae Augustae*, a text which describes the life and careers of the later Roman emperors. Although source scholars have identified Lothar II as the dedicatee of the *De rectoribus Christianis*, the most recent opinion favours Charles the Bald. Not only did Sedulius dedicate more poems to Charles than to any other ruler, but the political theories expressed in the mirror also correspond with the events of Charles's reign, and it contains parallels with the writings of Hincmar, archbishop of Rheims and adviser of Charles the Bald.

Like many of his Irish contemporaries, Sedulius showed an interest in language and grammar. He wrote grammatical commentaries on Eutyches (the *Commentum in Eutychem*), Priscian (the *Commentum super Priscianum*), and Donatus (the *Commentum in maiorem Donatum Grammaticum*). The commentaries of Sedulius, Muiredach, and the Anonymous of Lorsch all depend on an archetypal text belonging to an earlier Irish master.

Sedulius stands out among his Carolingian contemporaries for his knowledge of classical authors, although it is unknown whether he gained this learning in Ireland or on the continent. He was noted in Francia for the wealth of his scholarship and the standard of his Latin. The number of surviving manuscripts of Sedulius's works suggest that his Carolingian contemporaries most valued his work as a grammarian and exegete, in contrast to modern historians who have paid more attention to his poems and to his mirror for princes. LUNED MAIR DAVIES

Sources L. Traube, *O Roma nobilis: Philologische Untersuchungen aus dem Mittelalter*, Abhandlungen der Königliche Bayrische Akademie der Wissenschaften München, Philosophische-Philologische Klasse, 19/2 (1891) • H. Pirenne, *Sedulius de Liège*, Mémoires Couronnés et Autres Mémoires Publ. par l'Académie de Belgique, 33 (1882) • R. Düchting, *Sedulius Scottus: seine Dichtungen* (1968) • F. Brunhölzl, *Geschichte der lateinischen Literatur des Mittelalters, 1: Von Cassiodor bis zum Ausklang der karolingischen Erneuerung* (1975) • L. J. Rayner, 'The poetry of Sedulius Scottus and the vernacular poetic tradition of Ireland', PhD diss., U. Birm., 1986 • N. Staubach, *Rex Christianus: Hofkultur und Herrschaftspropaganda im Reich Karls des Kahlen, 2: Die Grundlegung der 'religion royale'* (1993) • L. Traube, ed., *Poetae Latini aevi Carolini*, MGH Poetae Latini Medii Aevi, 3 (Berlin, 1886–96)

Archives Bibliothèque de l'Arsenal, Paris, MS 8407 • Stadtbibliothek, Berne, MS 363

See, Sir John (1845–1907), businessman and politician in Australia, was born at Yelling, Huntingdonshire, on 14 November 1845, the son of Joseph See, a farm labourer, and his wife, Mary Ann, *née* Bailey. The family migrated in 1852 and began farming at Hinton on the Hunter River in New South Wales, where See attended school for three years and worked on the family farm until the age of sixteen. He and his brother then took up their own farm on the Clarence River, but the devastating floods of 1863 set him on a new career in commerce, initially as a produce merchant and commission agent in Sydney in partnership with George Nipper.

See's prodigious appetite for work and administrative ability ensured the success of his business interests. Shipping was added to the activities of Nipper and See in the 1860s and, seven years after the dissolution of the partnership in 1884, See's fleet was amalgamated with that of a larger enterprise to become the North Coast Steam Navigation Company Ltd, for which he received £70,000 and the joint managing directorship. John See & Co. continued to prosper as a produce firm, having opened a branch in Melbourne in 1869. With directorships in a number of insurance companies, as well as firms such as Washington, H. Soul Pattinson & Co., the Newcastle and Hunter River Steam Navigation Company, and the Australian Newspaper Company Ltd, and with trusteeships in the Savings Bank of New South Wales, Kurnell and National Parks, and the Sydney cricket ground, See was acknowledged as New South Wales's leading pluralist. His personal investments, particularly in mining and property, consolidated his reputation as a shrewd businessman. Other interests ranged from the Royal Agricultural Society (president, 1891–1907) to the Sydney Liedertafel, which sang with 'touching effect' at his funeral.

Surprisingly, See also found time for politics and parenthood. On 15 March 1876 he married Charlotte Mary (*d.* 1904), the daughter of Samuel Matthews of Devon, at Randwick, Sydney, where he built Urara, a 'lavish mansion', which was to accommodate their ten children. He was an alderman on Randwick council from 1877 to 1888, and mayor in 1880, 1881, and 1886. From 1880 to 1904 he sat for Grafton in the legislative assembly. His platform was 'progress', which at the local level meant 'roads, bridges, railways, post offices, and court houses' and protection of local agriculture. He held office under George Dibbs in 1885 and again in 1891–4, when he was colonial treasurer and minister for railways. Although See secured the passage of protectionist tariff legislation, he was less successful with his budgets as the economy worsened and the free trade interests targeted his policies. In opposition he supported federation on pragmatic grounds—it would aid 'progress'—and campaigned strongly for the referendums on the constitution in 1898 and 1899. With the Protectionists (progressives) again in government in 1899, William Lyne appointed him colonial secretary, and he became premier in March 1901. The Protectionists, with the support of the emergent Labor Party, retained office following the July elections and enacted important social legislation in the fields of industrial arbitration and female suffrage; but the onset of a severe drought and economic recession curtailed an ambitious public works programme. By early 1904 criticism of his ministry became more strident; on 16 March his wife died and his own health began to fail. Three months later See resigned, although he accepted appointment to the legislative council, where he remained a member until his death at his Randwick home from heart disease on 31 January 1907. He was buried the next day in the Anglican section of Waverley cemetery, Sydney, and was survived by four sons and three daughters, to whom he left an estate of £167,372.

Despite a large, muscular frame and a visage with deep-set, dark eyes and a black beard which gave him something of a saturnine appearance, See was an undemonstrative man and unimpressive speaker whose forte was administration rather than politics. Perhaps for these reasons he has been judged rather harshly as having contributed little to Australian political life. Yet See encapsulated two of the crucial characteristics of late nineteenth-century Australia: social mobility on the basis of merit—from the ploughshare to the premiership and to a KCMG in 1902—and a policy of 'socialism without doctrines', a pragmatic approach to the provision of infrastructure, particularly for the sparse, rural population. His political success was complemented by success in business to make him an archetypical Australian self-made man.

ROSS CURNOW

Sources *AusDB* · H. V. Evatt, *Australian labour leader* (1942) · W. G. McMinn, *George Reid* (1989) · G. N. Hawker, *The parliament of New South Wales, 1856–1965* (1971) · *Sydney Morning Herald* (1 Feb 1907) · *The Times* (1 Feb 1907)

Wealth at death £167,372—in Australia

Seear, (Beatrice) Nancy, Baroness Seear (1913–1997), politician, was born on 7 August 1913 at Rosebank, The Downs, Epsom, Surrey, the daughter of Herbert Charles Seear, mining engineer, and his wife, Beatrice Maud, *née* Catchpole. She was educated at Croydon High School for Girls and Newnham College, Cambridge. Having obtained a first-class degree in history in 1935, she joined the Quaker shoe firm of C. and J. Clark in Somerset (who were very accommodating, especially in terms of equal opportunities) as a personnel officer, one of the few professional roles in industry then open to women. It was not until she left that firm that she recognized how extensive was discrimination against women. She was seconded for a time during the war to the production efficiency board of the department of aircraft production. In 1946 she became lecturer in personnel management at the London School of Economics, where she remained until her retirement in 1978 (although continuing as visiting professor at the City University from 1980 to 1987); she was subsequently elected an honorary fellow in 1980. Her students described her as a stimulating and provocative teacher. She co-authored *Married Women Working* (1962) and *A Career for Women in Industry?* (1964), and independently wrote a succession of other publications, including *Industrial Social Services* (1964), *The Position of Women in Industry* (1967), and *The Re-Entry of Women into Employment* (1971).

Seear was a lifelong Liberal, joining the party in 1933 in the week Hitler dissolved the Reichstag, and fought seven parliamentary elections from 1950 to 1970 as well as a European election. She became president of the Liberal Party in 1965. Appointed a life peer in 1971, she left her most enduring mark on the country's legislation by sponsoring the Sex Discrimination Act of 1973, which had earlier been talked out in the Commons, but which she persisted in reintroducing in the Lords, forcing the government and the Commons to think again. On the death of Lord Byres in 1984 she was elected leader of the Liberal peers, a post she voluntarily relinquished in 1988 on the merger of the Liberals with the Social Democratic Party, nominating Roy Jenkins as leader of the new Liberal Democrat peers. In an age when prime ministers and leaders of the opposition emerge in their early forties and late thirties, it was Seear's unique achievement that she impacted on the British public only after what she called her 'sell-by date' of three score years and ten. This came about because the House of Lords agreed to the televising of their proceedings in 1985, four years before the Commons. The broadcasting authorities rightly judged that good coverage of their lordships' proceedings would influence the Commons to follow suit. Seear spoke in the very first televised debate—and stole the show with a typical noteless and forceful fifteen-minute speech. Because she had the wonderful knack of translating complex subjects into understandable prose with total clarity, in breathless and vigorous tones, she became a regular in the news bulletin coverage of parliamentary proceedings. This led to many invitations to appear on *Question Time* and *Any Questions*, where she delighted audiences with her masterly but good-humoured put-downs of chancellors of exchequer and other lesser ministers. On one such programme she memorably told John Prescott, 'Do shut up'—and he did. So she became known throughout the land as 'that liberal lady'.

All her life Seear devoted herself to the twin issues of women's rights and employment. She was prominent in the work of the top salaries' review body, the National Association for the Care and Rehabilitation of Offenders, the Industrial Society, and the Hansard Society commission on electoral reform and population services. She was president of the Institute of Personnel Management, the National Carers Association, the council of the Tavistock Institute, the Fawcett Society, and the British Standards Institution; she took the chair for the House of Lords select committee on unemployment, the archbishop of Canterbury's committee on the laws of affinity, and Morley College. Nevertheless, she did not like to be addressed as 'chair', being a stickler for the proper use of the English language. 'I am *not* a piece of furniture', she admonished (*Daily Telegraph*, 25 April 1997).

Seear was a committed but not narrowly doctrinaire Christian. One of the organizations she headed had a somewhat ineffectual treasurer, who amid a financial crisis raised his hands and declared 'God will provide'. 'Possibly', responded Nancy crisply; 'but God helps those who help themselves', and proceeded to direct just how they could get out of their problems (private information). Her former vicar from St John's Wood recalled at her funeral service that he went to visit her towards the end of her long battle with cancer. He had not seen her for some time and she was very weak. She fixed him with a steady eye as he entered her room and said: 'You *did* come right in the end on women priests, didn't you?' (personal knowledge). Seear was a woman of remarkably clear mind, lively opinions, and boundless energy, distinctively individual without being eccentric, faithful to her radical convictions without being dogmatic. She died in London of cancer on 23 April 1997. She never married.

STEEL OF AIKWOOD

Sources personal knowledge (2004) · private information (2004) · *The Times* (24 April 1997) · *The Independent* (24 April 1997) · *The Scotsman* (24 April 1997) · *Daily Telegraph* (25 April 1997) · *The Guardian* (25 April 1997) · *The Herald* (26 April 1997) · *WWW* · b. cert. · D. Brack and M. Baines, eds., *Dictionary of liberal biography* (1998)

Archives BLPES, papers · Women's Library, London, parliamentary papers, incl. submissions relating to equal opportunities, pay, and sex discrimination; further papers, incl. records relating to equal opportunities in employment | CUL, letters to her family

Likenesses photograph, repro. in *The Times* · photograph, repro. in *The Independent* · photograph, repro. in *Daily Telegraph*

Wealth at death £135,148: probate, 24 June 1997, *CGPLA Eng. & Wales*

Seebohm, Frederic (1833–1912), historian and banker, was born at Hillside House, Bradford, on 23 November 1833. His father was Benjamin Seebohm (1798–1871), a wool merchant and a prominent and active minister of the Society of Friends, who had come to Bradford from Friedensthal, in the principality of Waldeck-Pyrmont, as a boy of sixteen; his mother, Esther Wheeler, of Hitchin (1798–1864), was also a minister of the society. Both parents belonged to the society's evangelical wing. His elder brother was Henry *Seebohm, the ornithologist, and Frederic too took a keen interest in natural history as a boy. In his youth he also witnessed the destitution and unrest of the handloom weavers of the West Riding consequent upon the introduction of machinery. After attending Bootham School, York, from 1845 to 1849—a remarkable series of letters to his father gives a clear account of his life there—he tried out several possible careers, by working first in his uncle's grocery business at Huddersfield, then as an actuary for the Friends' Provident Institute at Bradford. While there he began to read for the bar at the Middle Temple, before moving to Hitchin in 1855; the lectures given by the jurist Henry J. S. Maine, which he now attended, had a lasting influence. He was called to the bar in 1856. On 29 July 1857 he married Mary Ann Exton (1833–1904), whose father, William Exton (*d.* 1851), had been a founding partner of a bank, Sharples & Co., at Hitchin; Seebohm himself became a partner in 1859 and when, in 1896, the bank became part of Barclay & Co. Ltd he was made a member of their board. The Seebohms lived in Hitchin, from their marriage to their deaths, in a house, The Hermitage, which had belonged to the Extons and which stood on a large central site. They had five daughters and one son. Seebohm was an efficient and successful banker and became president of the Institute of Bankers, but his energy and range of interests enabled him to pursue spare-time activities with vigour and originality. His interests—Christian, political and civic, and historical—informed one another, and achieved together a natural coherence. His publications, besides books, included articles and letters in all three spheres, especially in the *Fortnightly Review*, *Nineteenth Century*, and *The Spectator*.

Seebohm and his wife were fully committed members of the Society of Friends; his pamphlet on *The Crisis of Emancipation in America* (1865) was written in support of Quaker aid to freedmen. His personal beliefs appear in

Frederic Seebohm (1833–1912), by Elliott & Fry

two books, *The Facts of the Four Gospels* (1861) and *The Christian Hypothesis* (privately printed 1876; published posthumously, 1916, as *The Spirit of Christianity*). No theology was needed, in his view—only 'simple knowledge of an actual Deliverer' (F. Seebohm, *The Facts of the Four Gospels*, 8); faith and prayer would bring deliverance. He held that Christianity had 'nothing to lose from free inquiry' (ibid., v), and, indeed, scientific knowledge would save it from superstition; the Bible is evidence of God's work but was not divinely written. Christianity, he believed, should be seen as a progressive religion, a moral force moving society ever nearer the Christian ideal.

A Liberal in politics, Seebohm took particular interest in popular education—he was a friend of William Edward Forster, the MP for Bradford and later architect of the 1870 Education Act—and in the land question in England and Ireland. In 1877 he declined an invitation to succeed Walter Bagehot as editor of *The Economist*. He wished to stand for parliament in 1884, but his partners at the bank considered he could not be spared; his daughter wrote of this as 'a dreadful disappointment to him and to all of us' (Glendinning, 41). From 1886, following the Liberal Party's split over Irish home rule, he became a free-trade supporter of the Liberal Unionists. He was a member of the Welsh land commission of 1893–6, and wrote the historical introduction to its report. In Hertfordshire he was a justice of the peace and a member of the county council's education committee (1892–1912), and at Hitchin he was a member of the local board of guardians (1877–94) but was particularly concerned with education, as a governor of the grammar schools and president of the adult school. He was a considerable local benefactor, and gave land for a road which cut across the grounds of the family home (1878) and for the site of the high school for girls (1889).

Seebohm's first historical work originated with a long-standing interest in Thomas More; he contracted for his first article on the subject while on honeymoon in Edinburgh. He was also a collector of Erasmus's works. He looked more broadly, however, at the transition in thought and in society from the western Christendom of the Middle Ages to the post-Reformation period. In *The Oxford Reformers* (1867; 3rd edn, 1887) he examined the work of Colet, Erasmus, and More, and argued that if the reforms they advocated had been carried out the revolutionary crisis of the Reformation might have been avoided. *The Era of the Protestant Revolution* (1874) sketched the main lines of the conflict in the sixteenth century. In both works he is little concerned with theology, as narrowly understood, but rather with the intellectual and social implications of change.

If Seebohm's early historical work can be associated with his Christianity, his later work—which constitutes his principal contribution to historical studies—reflects his interest in land questions and in Maine's enquiries into early law and custom. His best-known and most innovative book is *The English Village Community* (1883; 4th edn, 1890). Taking as his starting point the open fields of early nineteenth-century Hitchin, he examined agrarian organization as underlying the social structure of the English medieval manor, and traced this structure—and thus the origin of the manor—back to the villas of the Roman period and beyond. In Wales, Scotland, and Ireland, however, the contrasting 'tribal system' continued into the middle ages. He then compared what he found in the British Isles with analogous development on the continent, both in areas of Roman rule and in Germany. The book includes maps of local field systems. *The Tribal System in Wales* (1895; 2nd edn, 1904) is a detailed investigation of what was covered in a single chapter of the earlier work, an extensive study of the Welsh kindred, its ramifications, its pastoral and agricultural peculiarities. It includes a substantial series of texts of the thirteenth- and fourteenth-century estate surveys in which he found evidence of ancient tribal structure. *Tribal Custom in Anglo-Saxon Law* (1902) is specifically 'supplemental' to the two earlier books; it examines traces of tribal organization not only in Anglo-Saxon, Welsh, and Irish laws, but also among early medieval Germanic peoples on the continent. Implicit in much of the work for these books were questions of measuring land, and Seebohm's last book was *Customary Acres and their Historical Importance*, published posthumously in 1914. Unfinished, but substantially complete, it presents a mass of evidence on the measures used for land throughout Europe, though most fully for the British Isles and north-west France.

Seebohm's analysis of medieval rural society had an immediate impact. It challenged comprehensively the accepted view that the English medieval manor, with its unfree tenants rendering labour services to their lord, had developed only in the late Anglo-Saxon period from scarcely structured communities of free Germanic settlers. In looking to continuity with the Roman villa, and to great estates as the key to medieval rural society, Seebohm paralleled the work of N. D. Fustel de Coulanges in France and of A. Dopsch in Germany. By the time of his death, however, the orthodox view had reasserted itself among English historians; in 1912 F. M. Stenton, while stressing Seebohm's importance in the development of current ideas, was able to write that 'very much of *The English Village Community* is now obsolete' (Stenton, 18). It was not until the 1950s that the work of, in particular, T. H. Aston and H. P. R. Finberg led to general recognition that Seebohm's model is the more correct. However, two aspects of Seebohm's work suffered no eclipse. He introduced to British historians what had been already recognized in Germany, the importance of field systems, of the way land was held and cultivated, as evidence of early social structure and historical origins—although the exact significance of this evidence is still debated. Secondly, he demonstrated that the Celtic areas of the British Isles had a distinctive pattern of landholding and a distinctive social structure in the middle ages. Both these aspects of Seebohm's work were the starting points for continuing research.

Surviving papers throw some light on Seebohm's working methods. Certainly in youth, probably throughout life, he read regularly and systematically on the subjects that interested him. He could not read Greek, but his knowledge of German began at an early age within the family. His wife wrote in 1868 of 'his pleasant visit to Cambridge looking over MSS in the University Library—so to his task hunting up any mention of Sir Thos More; Colet or Erasmus—dining in the evening with Maurice, Lightfoot &c' (journal, 30 July 1868, Herts. ALS, D/ESe/F11/14), and his son, Hugh Exton Seebohm, wrote after his death that for his earlier books 'the actual writing was done after the main work of the day was over, often in the midst of his family, sometimes with a child on his knee' (H. E. Seebohm, vii). For much of his work on medieval economic history he had transcripts made from documents at the British Museum, Public Record Office, and elsewhere. When on holiday in Britain or abroad he lost no opportunity of enquiring about local landholding and customs and of inspecting relevant records, and he had many and varied correspondents from whom he sought detailed information. He seems to have written his later books in discrete sections, brought together at a late stage of composition. As one might expect of the banker, he was fully at home with figures, and his surviving notes include many calculations.

The style of Seebohm's published writings, precise and lucid, reveals little of his personality. However, his personal letters show that he was earnest, immensely self-disciplined and hard-working, self-assured but of a sincerely modest and calm temperament; they suggest strongly that the picture, given in an obituary, of a man who was 'cheerful and equable in the home which he ruled by love' was not a merely conventional one (*Hertfordshire Express*, 10 Feb 1912). He was described as 'a powerful speaker, with a most incisive style of delivery' (ibid.) and one listener wrote that 'I have never seen a hostile audience handled so beautifully …; he ended his speech amid general cheering, for his fairness and manliness took them by storm' (Robert Marsh to Lady Godlee, 15 Dec 1912: papers in family possession). He read aloud, in literary evenings of the Young Men's Christian Association at Hitchin, and also within his family; his son records 'the peculiarly reverent and gentle tone' in which he read a passage from James Nayler on the spirit of Christianity, and 'the eager look with which he sought the sympathetic response of his listener at the close' (H. E. Seebohm, ix). Some pieces of his own verse survive, and he also drew—at least one picture in *The English Village Community*, of the Severn near Tidenham, is from his own sketch. When aged twelve, he wrote a charming and interesting account of a four-week visit to Germany; in later life his holiday travels included Scotland and Ireland, Brittany, Switzerland, Italy, Scandinavia, and Egypt. He had a wide circle of acquaintance, and Thomas Hodgkin (1831–1913) and Paul Vinogradoff were among his closest friends; other friends included C. M. Andrews, W. J. Corbett, Thomas Hughes (1822–1896), and Edward Burnett Tylor.

Seebohm received honorary degrees from the universities of Edinburgh (LLD, 1890), Cambridge (LittD, 1902), and Oxford (DLitt, 1908). He died at his home, The Hermitage, Hitchin, on 6 February 1912 after three years' illness and was buried at Hitchin. His daughter Esther Margaret Seebohm subsequently sorted his papers, selecting what was to be preserved and destroying the rest; she also painstakingly assembled many of his letters, written throughout his life to members of the family and to friends, and made careful copies, which survive. His son edited *Customary Acres* for publication, as well as the posthumous editions of *The Oxford Reformers* (1914) and *The Spirit of Christianity*, and gave his working papers to the Institute of Historical Research at London University; his books on economic history were given to the Maitland Library, Oxford, and some other books to the Bodleian Library, Oxford, and the British Museum. Other family papers were deposited in the Hertfordshire Record Office (Herts. ALS) in 1954 and 1983. P. D. A. Harvey

Sources Seebohm family papers, Herts. ALS · unpublished account of Seebohm family by Richard Seebohm · papers of Frederic Seebohm, U. Lond. · personal papers, priv. coll. · V. Glendinning, *A suppressed cry: life and death of a Quaker daughter* (1969) · H. E. Seebohm, preface, in F. Seebohm, *The spirit of Christianity* (1916) · *The Times* (7 Feb 1912) · *Hertfordshire Express* (10 Feb 1912) · *The Friend* (23 Feb 1912) · F. M. Stenton, 'Frederic Seebohm', *Reading University College Review*, 4 (1912); repr. in F. M. Stenton, *Preparatory to Anglo-Saxon England* (1970), 16–22 · *DNB*

Archives Herts. ALS, schoolbooks, journal, family corresp., D/ESe · LUL, corresp., notes, transcripts, paleography room, MS 924/1–52, /164 · priv. coll., corresp. and papers

Likenesses Elliott & Fry, photograph, priv. coll. [*see illus.*] · photograph (in early middle age), repro. in Glendinning, *A suppressed cry*, facing p. 21 · photograph (in middle age), priv. coll. · portrait (in old age), priv. coll.

Wealth at death £124,299 14*s*. 3*d*.: resworn probate, 30 April 1912, *CGPLA Eng. & Wales*

Seebohm, Frederic, Baron Seebohm (1909–1990), banker and philanthropist, was born on 18 January 1909 at Poynder's End, Hitchin, Hertfordshire, the second in the family of three sons and one daughter of Hugh Exton Seebohm, banker, of Poynder's End, and his wife, Leslie, daughter of George James Gribble. He was the grandson of the historian Frederic *Seebohm. The Seebohm family had emigrated from Germany to Yorkshire in the mid-nineteenth century, and subsequently had been for three generations Quakers and bankers at Hitchin; their bank had been one of the constituents of Barclays Bank on its formation in 1896. Seebohm was educated at the Dragon School, Oxford, at Leighton Park School in Reading, and then at Trinity College, Cambridge, where he read economics but left after two years (having achieved a third class in part one in 1929) to enter Barclays Bank, Cambridge, in 1929. He spent most of the next twenty-five years first in Sheffield, where he was posted in 1932, and after the war in York and Birmingham, as a local director. During this time he developed his interest in social services as treasurer of the Sheffield Council of Social Service, chairman of the community council in York, and a member of the Joseph Rowntree Memorial Trust. The Seebohms were related to the Rowntree family.

In 1938 Seebohm joined the Territorial Army and in 1939 was commissioned in the Royal Artillery. After attending the Staff College in 1944, he was posted to Supreme Headquarters Allied Expeditionary Force, as a lieutenant-colonel (GSO1). In 1945 he was mentioned in dispatches and awarded the bronze star of America.

Seebohm was appointed a director of Barclays Bank Ltd in 1947 and in 1951 of Barclays Bank (Dominion, Colonial and Overseas—DCO). In 1957 he moved to London in a full-time executive position in Barclays Bank DCO, becoming a deputy chairman in 1959 and chairman in 1965. Seebohm developed DCO from a federation of retail banks in the former colonies and South Africa into an international bank operating on a worldwide basis.

In spite of constant travelling overseas Seebohm continued to extend his interests in the City as chairman of Friends' Provident Life Office (1962–8), the Export Guarantees Advisory Council (1967–72), and Barclays Bank Ltd, where he became deputy chairman in 1968. In 1966–8 he was president of the Institute of Bankers. He was knighted in 1970. In 1972 he retired as chairman of DCO, which, as part of his international strategy, had been taken over by Barclays Bank Ltd in 1971 and renamed Barclays Bank International. He remained deputy chairman of Barclays until 1974 but, although he remained on the board until 1979, his interests were increasingly elsewhere. From 1974 to 1979 he was chairman of Finance for Industry, which had been set up by the banks in the aftermath of the Second World War to assist in the development of industry, a subject close to his heart.

Seebohm's wider reputation came from his other great interest, social service. His earlier experience made him a natural choice to head the government's inquiry (1965–8)

into local authority and allied personal social services, which led to the Seebohm report (1968). The far-reaching conclusions, most of which were embodied in the Local Authority (Social Services) Act of 1970, owed much to his strong personal convictions, skilled chairmanship, and vigorous advocacy. He was made a life peer in 1972. From the House of Lords, where he sat as an independent, he maintained a close interest in subsequent developments in the social services, as well as in financial matters, and served as chairman of the Joseph Rowntree Memorial Trust, and president of Age Concern, the National Institute of Social Work, the Royal Africa Society, and the Overseas Development Institute. He was asked by the government to report on naval welfare (1974) and the British Council (1980). He was high sheriff of Hertfordshire in 1970–71. He received honorary degrees of LLD from Nottingham in 1970 and DSc from Aston in 1976.

Seebohm's rather military bearing, conciseness of speech, and formidable powers of chairmanship, combined with a very direct approach and strong, sometimes unconventional, views, won him respect and affection in the many fields to which he contributed. In later years he became a member of the Society of Friends, which his father had left on 'marrying out'. He was a keen shot, played real tennis, and was later a skilled gardener and competent watercolour painter. He became an honorary member of the Royal Society of Painters in Water Colours.

In 1932 he married Evangeline, daughter of Sir Gerald Hurst QC; they had two daughters (one of them the writer Victoria Glendinning) and one son. Lady Seebohm died thirteen days after her husband as a result of a motor accident near Sutton Scotney in Hampshire. Seebohm died in the accident, on 15 December 1990. A memorial service was held in St Margaret's, Westminster, London, on 13 March 1991. PETER LESLIE, *rev.*

Sources Barclays Bank • *The Times* (17 Dec 1990) • *The Times* (14 March 1991) • private information (1996) • *CGPLA Eng. & Wales* (1991)

Likenesses J. Gunn?, portrait, Barclays Bank, Lombard Street, London

Wealth at death £407,812: probate, 18 April 1991, *CGPLA Eng. & Wales*

Seebohm, Henry (1832–1895), ornithologist, was born on 12 July 1832 at Horton Grange, Bradford, the eldest of four children of Benjamin Seebohm (1798–1871), a wool merchant from near Bad Pyrmont in Germany, and his wife, Esther Wheeler (1798–1864), of Hitchin, Hertfordshire, a granddaughter of William Tuke and a niece of Sarah Hustler. On marrying, his parents settled on a small farm, Horton Grange, near Bradford, where they remained for several years before moving to Bradford. Seebohm's siblings included Frederic *Seebohm (1833–1912), the historian, and Julia Eliza Seebohm (*d.* 1863), who married the cocoa manufacturer, Joseph Rowntree (1836–1925).

Both Seebohm's parents were active in the Society of Friends, and he was educated at the Friends' school, in York, where he developed a taste for natural history. His father started him early in life as a grocer's shop boy, but ultimately Seebohm settled at Sheffield where he became a manufacturer of steel. On 19 January 1859 he married Maria (*b.* 1839/40), daughter of George John Healey, merchant, of Moss Side, Manchester.

Seebohm's spare time was devoted to natural history, especially ornithology, and he made a number of journeys to the Netherlands, Greece, Asia Minor, Scandinavia, Germany, and Siberia to collect and study birds in their native haunts. One of his most successful expeditions was in 1875 to the lower Pechora River valley in Russia, with the zoologist John Alexander Harvie-Brown, when the eggs of the grey plover and of many rare species of birds were obtained. The account of this voyage, as well as that to Heligoland, where he went to study bird migration at the house of the ornithologist Heinrich Gätke, was given in his *Siberia in Europe* (1880). In 1877 Seebohm accompanied the Arctic explorer and merchant navy officer Joseph Wiggins (1832–1905) on a journey to Siberia. They travelled along the Yenisey River, where they made further important ornithological discoveries, recorded in Seebohm's *Siberia in Asia* (1882). On that voyage, Wiggins's ship was wrecked shortly after reaching the Kureyka, a tributary of the Yenisey. Later Seebohm visited southern Europe and South Africa to study European birds in their winter quarters, and to collect materials for *The Geographical Distribution of the Family Charadriidæ* (1887).

Seebohm was also author of several other works, including *Catalogue of Birds in the British Museum, vol. 5, Turdidæ* (1881), *A History of British Birds with Coloured Illustrations of their Eggs* (1882–5), *Classification of Birds* (1890), to which a supplement was issued in 1895, *The Birds of the Japanese Empire* (1890), *Geographical Distribution of British Birds* (1893), and *Address to the Yorkshire Naturalists' Union* (1893). He also contributed upwards of eighty papers, chiefly on ornithological subjects, between 1877 and 1895, to the *Proceedings of the Zoological Society*, *Ibis*, and other scientific publications. He left unfinished *The Eggs of British Birds* and *Thrushes*. His two Siberian expedition narratives were published together as *The Birds of Siberia* in 1901.

Seebohm joined the British Ornithologists' Union and the Zoological Society in 1873; he was elected a fellow of the Royal Geographical Society in 1878, and was one of the secretaries from June 1890 until his death. He was elected a fellow of the Linnean Society in December 1879. He was also a liberal contributor of ornithological specimens to the British Museum. He gave the museum his impressive collection of eggs, and compiled the fifth volume of the bird catalogue, published by the trustees in 1881.

In later years Seebohm resided at South Kensington, London, and Maidenhead, Berkshire. He died on 26 November 1895, following an attack of influenza, at his home, 22 Courtfield Gardens, South Kensington. He was survived by his wife but predeceased by his only son, Ted, who died in New York in unexplained circumstances in 1888. Seebohm's extensive ornithological collections of more than 16,000 bird skins and 235 skeletons were presented to the British Museum (Natural History).

B. B. WOODWARD, *rev.* YOLANDA FOOTE

Sources *The Times* (28 Nov 1895) • *Nature*, 53 (1895–6), 105 • *The Athenaeum* (7 Dec 1895), 794 • *The Ibis*, 7th ser., 2 (1896), 159–62 • private information (1897) [F. Seebohm] • B. B. Woodward and others, eds., *Catalogue of the books, manuscripts, maps, and drawings in the British Museum (Natural History)*, 8 vols. (1903–40) • *Catalogue of scientific papers*, Royal Society • *Zoological Record* • *Biographical catalogue: being an account of the lives of Friends and others whose portraits are in the London Friends' Institute*, Society of Friends (1888) • *The Ornithologist*, 1/1 (March 1896), 16–17 • V. Glendinning, *A suppressed cry: life and death of a Quaker daughter* (1969)

Archives CUL, diaries, journals, notebook • Herts. ALS, family corresp., schoolbooks • NHM, travel diaries | NHM, bird skins, skeletons

Likenesses portrait, repro. in *The Ornithologist*, 16

Wealth at death £102,479 11*s*. 3*d*.: probate, 11 Jan 1896, *CGPLA Eng. & Wales*

Seed, Jeremiah (*bap.* 1699?, *d.* 1747), Church of England clergyman and writer, was born at Clifton, Cumberland, and was probably baptized at Askham, Westmorland, the son of Jeremiah Seed (*d.* 1722), who graduated BA from Jesus College, Cambridge, in 1682, and was rector of Clifton from 1707 until his death.

Seed was educated first at Lowther grammar school, Westmorland, and matriculated on 7 November 1716 at Queen's College, Oxford. He was awarded a BA on 13 February 1722 and an MA in 1725. Having been elected a fellow of Queen's College in 1732, Seed gave eight lectures on the truth of Christianity, human nature, redemption, and the Trinity for the Lady Moyer lectureship at St Paul's Cathedral, London, in 1732–3. From 1732 to 1741 he served as curate to Daniel Waterland, vicar of Twickenham, Middlesex; he preached Waterland's funeral sermon on 4 January 1741. He was also rector of Ridge, Hertfordshire, from 1736 to 1738. Queen's College presented him in 1741 to the living of Knight's Enham, Hampshire, which he held until his death, along with that of Church Oakley, Northamptonshire.

Contemporaries greatly admired Seed's preaching. Samuel Johnson described his sermons as having 'a very fine style', but added 'he is not very theological' (Boswell, *Life*, 3.248). Towards the end of the nineteenth century the sermons were described as ranking 'among the most elegant productions of the British press, both with respect to their diction and imagery', and as abounding 'in sound argument and in just remarks on human life' (Allibone, *Dict.*, 2.1990). His published works were the *Discourses on Several Important Subjects* (2 vols., 1743), which included the text of his lectures at St Paul's, and also *The Posthumous Works* (2 vols., 1750), consisting of sermons, essays and letters. Seed died at Knight's Enham on 10 December 1747. He was survived by his wife, about whom no details are known.

CHARLOTTE FELL-SMITH, *rev.* ROBERT D. CORNWALL

Sources Venn, *Alum. Cant.*, 1/4.41 • Foster, *Alum. Oxon.* • A. Chalmers, ed., *The general biographical dictionary*, new edn, 32 vols. (1812–17) • Allibone, *Dict.* • *GM*, 1st ser., 17 (1747), 592 • J. Nicolson and R. Burn, *The history and antiquities of the counties of Westmorland and Cumberland*, 1 (1777); repr. (1976), 414 • W. F. Hook, *An ecclesiastical biography*, 8 vols. (1845–52), vol. 8, p. 311 • Boswell, *Life*, 3.248 • *London Magazine*, 16 (1747), 581 • *Calendar of the correspondence of Philip Doddridge*, ed. G. F. Nuttall, HMC, JP 26 (1979)

Likenesses S. F. Ravenet, line engraving (after F. Hayman), BM, NPG; repro. in J. Seed, *Posthumous works* (1750)

Seedo, Maria. *See* Manina, Maria (*fl.* 1712–1736).

Seeley, Harry Govier (1839–1909), palaeontologist and geologist, was born on 18 February 1839 in London, the second son of Richard Hovill Seeley (*b.* 1799/1800?) and his second wife, Mary Govier. The bookseller Robert Benton Seeley was his uncle; the historian John Robert Seeley (1834–1895) was his cousin. Although the family had been financially secure, Seeley's father, a goldsmith, had been declared bankrupt and was disowned by his family, having 'ruined himself with scientific experiments' (Seeley to Sedgwick, 17 Sept 1866, CUL). Thus, at the age of two, Seeley was sent to live with pianoforte makers. Between the ages of eleven and fourteen he went to a day school, before spending two years learning to make pianos. From the age of eleven he attended lectures at the Russell and London institutions, and later at the Royal School of Mines by T. H. Huxley, Edward Forbes, and others. Although in 1855 his uncle John Seeley paid to have him trained for the bar, Seeley felt uneasy as 'one of the "great unwashed"' (Seeley to Sedgwick, 7 Sept 1866). He abandoned legal studies, planning instead to become an actuary. He studied English and mathematics in the late 1850s at the Working Men's College founded by F. D. Maurice and the Christian socialists, and became secretary to the college's museum. Seeley supported himself by copying documents in the library of the British Museum, where Samuel Pickworth Woodward encouraged him to study geology.

In 1859 Seeley entered Sidney Sussex College, Cambridge, and was soon hired by Adam Sedgwick as an assistant in the Woodwardian Museum. Seeley lectured, arranged the collection, catalogued fossils, began field studies on the geology of the Cambridge Greensand, and took his place, as he saw it, 'not as a working man, but as a man' (Seeley to Sedgwick, 7 Sept 1866). He migrated to St John's in 1868, but never took a degree.

Despite a mental breakdown in the mid-1860s, in Cambridge, Seeley published important papers and two catalogues of pterodactyl fossils. In 1864 he reached the unexpected conclusion that pterodactyls were not reptiles, but a new subclass allied to the birds. His work was profoundly anti-evolutionary, advocating an idealist morphology that drew on Edward Forbes's platonic metaphysics. Throughout his life Seeley was combative and controversial, never afraid to defend unfashionable views. Three papers from 1866 to 1882 revived the widely dismissed theory of the vertebral origin of the skull and limbs. His division of dinosaurs into 'bird-hipped' and 'lizard-hipped' forms became the basis for most later classifications. Although often reinterpreted in Darwinian terms, this conclusion originated in an approach antithetical to tracing descent. Seeley's work on fossil reptiles culminated in a ten-part series in the *Philosophical Transactions* from 1888 to 1896. Anti-evolutionary concerns also underpinned his studies of theriodonts or mammal-like reptiles, which he travelled to Moscow and South Africa to see in 1889.

Harry Govier Seeley (1839–1909), by Bassano, *c.*1900

In 1872 Seeley married Eleanora Jane, the only daughter of William Mitchell (*d.* 1871), baker and corn factor, of St George's Lodge, Bath. They moved to London, where Seeley earned an income from literary work, private tutition, and lecturing; Eleanora assisted him, becoming a skilled cataloguer and natural-history artist. They raised four daughters, the eldest of whom, Maud, married Arthur Smith Woodward of the British Museum in 1894. In 1876 Seeley was appointed professor of geography and geology in Queen's College, London, and five years later he became dean. In 1876 he also became professor of geography and lecturer on geology at King's College, and in 1896 he succeeded to the chair of geology and mineralogy.

Seeley advocated the expansion of opportunities in higher education, especially for women, and aspired 'to be to the people of England in Science what Cobden was to his Country in procuring the adoption of free trade' (Seeley to Sedgwick, 7 Sept 1866). He taught for some years at Bedford College. For many years after 1880 he conducted field classes for the London Society for the Extension of University Teaching, and from 1890 he was lecturer on geology and mineralogy at the Royal Indian Engineering College at Cooper's Hill. He contributed regularly to the *Educational Times* and published several popular books, including *Story of the Earth in Past Ages* (1895) and *Dragons of the Air* (1901). On behalf of the Gilchrist Trust, Seeley spoke to large audiences throughout the British Isles using chalk diagrams and lantern slides of spectacular extinct reptiles. Seeley died at his home at 3 Holland Park Court in Kensington on 8 January 1909, and was buried in Brookwood cemetery. He was survived by his wife.

J. A. Secord

Sources A. S. W. [A. S. Woodward], *PRS*, 83B (1911), xv–xvii · 'Eminent living geologists: Professor H. G. Seeley', *Geological Magazine*, new ser., 5th decade, 4 (1907), 241–53 [incl. bibliography] · H. G. Seeley, letters to A. Sedgwick, 7–24 Sept 1866, CUL, Add. MS 7652.II GG.2–5 · W. E. Swinton, 'Harry Govier Seeley and the Karroo reptiles', *Bulletin of the British Museum (Natural History)* [Historical Series], 3 (1962–9), 1–39 · A. Desmond, *Archetypes and ancestors: palaeontology in Victorian London, 1850–1875* (1982) · W. J. Sollas, *Quarterly Journal of the Geological Society*, 65 (1909), lxx–lxxii · *CGPLA Eng. & Wales* (1909) · *DNB*

Archives King's Lond., Liddell Hart C., corresp. and notebooks · NHM, MSS · NHM, fossil collections | NHM, corresp. with Daniel Kannemeyer · NHM, letters to Sir Arthur Woodward · NRA, priv. coll., letters to his wife · U. Cam., Sedgwick MSS

Likenesses Bassano, photograph, *c.*1900, GS Lond. [*see illus.*] · photograph, 1907, repro. in 'Eminent living geologists', pl. XII · photograph, repro. in W. E. Swinton, 'Harry Govier Seeley', frontispiece

Wealth at death £474 18*s*. 5*d*.: probate, 6 Feb 1909, *CGPLA Eng. & Wales*

Seeley, Sir John Robert (1834–1895), historian, was born in London on 10 September 1834, third son of Robert Benton *Seeley (1798–1886), publisher and prominent evangelical, and Mary Anne, *née* Jackson (1809–1868), also an evangelical of a publishing family. After preparatory school at Stanmore, Seeley went to the City of London School under Dr G. F. W. Mortimer. A naturally bookish and eager scholar, he made rapid progress, entering the sixth form before his thirteenth year. Of 'slender nervous alert frame', 'small, spare, quick in his movements' (Wormell, 8), his health suffered, and his life's pattern began of intermittent periods of enforced withdrawal from studies.

Education and formation of religious views In 1852 Seeley entered Christ's College, Cambridge, as a scholar. At a time when modern literature did not figure in educational curricula, his already wide command of the English writers was thought remarkable in one who was becoming an accomplished classicist. A vacation in Dresden to become well-found in German began a lifelong admiration of Germany and things German. By temperament austere, Seeley none the less made his mark in the society of his college contemporaries, who included Walter Skeat, John Hales, Walter Besant, C. S. Calverley, John Peile, and Walter Sendall; and in the university at large he was known through his brother Leonard to Henry Sidgwick and Frederic Farrar. G. W. Prothero, his later colleague in the history faculty, judged Seeley 'one of the ablest of an able set' (*DNB*). Despite being again impeded by nervous illness, Seeley graduated brilliantly in 1857 among the candidates at the top of the classical tripos, and his pre-eminence was marked by the award of the senior chancellor's medal. Christ's promptly elected him to a fellowship, where for the next two years he tutored

Sir John Robert Seeley (1834–1895), by W. & D. Downey

and lectured in classics. In 1859 he returned to the City of London School as chief classical assistant master; from there in 1863 he went to University College, London (UCL), as professor of Latin.

Seeley's deep reading in modern English and European literatures (he published anonymously verses and translations in 1859) tended to make him impatient of much of the exclusive claims made for the Greek and Latin disciplines. His distaste for the system of competitive examinations had also by now become a distinctive trait; and UCL, he felt, was too much imbued with the examination-factory ethos then prevalent in the London colleges. All this meant that Seeley's tenure of the London chair would be likely to lead in directions diverging from his formal responsibilities to Latin and Roman studies. His edition of Livy eventually confirmed in 1871 his credentials in conventional classical scholarship; but his most characteristic production at London remained his inaugural lecture, *Classical Studies as an Introduction to the Moral Sciences* (1864). Here he argued that the educational dominance of Greek and Latin was simply a fact of life, which one perforce had to make the best of.

Certain trends in his thinking also contributed in these years to a fundamental shift in Seeley's intellectual outlook. The hold of his family evangelical tradition weakened under the influences of Carlyle and the 'Germano-Coleridgean' broad-church school. His scientific colleagues at UCL impressed him by their confidence in the claims for a commanding future role for positivist principles and experimental science. Seeley took an interest in F. D. Maurice's London Working Men's College, where Christian socialists and Comtean positivists led by Edward Beesly were in uneasy alliance, striving to rescue the working classes from the temptations of communism and commercialism. Their shared idealism of a co-operatively based social order at the expense of both competitive disorder and class war appealed greatly to Seeley. His outlook on politics likewise took on a profound distaste for the 'interminable scurrilous brawl' of political parties competing for office. The years of agitation and debate preparing for the second Reform Bill in 1866 and 1867 led Seeley to conclude that critical analysis of Britain's social predicaments pointed to the need for a more disciplined, coherent national morale, wherein a revitalized spirituality would imbue the material components of civic life in the light of a new 'science of politics'. Seeley's professional career would be a quest to determine the necessary religious and intellectual underpinnings of such a science.

***Ecce homo* (1865) and its reception** In 1865 appeared, anonymously, *Ecce homo: a Survey of the Life and Work of Jesus Christ*. Seeley's authorship was known within the circles familiar with the direction and development of his interests. He preferred anonymity for the wider world on the grounds that he judged his enterprise 'audacious and perilous' in the offence it might give both to orthodox Christians and to heterodox non-Christians; and especially to the evangelical piety of his family. His purpose was to suggest by analogy that just as 'the drama of ancient society had been played out', and its traditions and morals and civic values had become obsolete, so too with fretful and distempered modern society. What, he asked, had been 'Christ's object in founding the society which is called after his name', and how was it 'adapted to attain that object?' Seeley concluded that a reconsideration of 'the speculative commonwealth of Christ' would 'add a new chapter to the science of politics'; with implications unmistakably bearing upon the needs of the present. His reconsideration of that commonwealth utilized the new methods of historical and scientific criticism: he confined himself strictly to what the 'facts themselves, critically weighed', appeared to warrant, independently of what the doctors of the church, or even the apostles, had 'sealed with their authority'. He concluded, on this methodological premise, that Christ's object, as a new Moses, founder, legislator, and judge, was to constitute a state in which his laws contained not merely practical rules of life but declarations concerning the nature of God and man's relation to Him; wherein Christianity would begin to mean not mere fidelity or loyalty to Christ's person, but practical obedience to his rules of life and unquestioning acceptance of his theological teaching. Such Christianity would encompass liberally a universal ethic of positive morality and the 'enthusiasm of humanity'; it would encompass also the 'blessed light of science, a light yet far from its meridian and dispersing every day some noxious superstition, some cowardice of the human spirit' (J. R. Seeley, *Ecce homo*, 1866, 33–40, 50, 80, 328).

Twentieth-century commentators, remote from its world of 'audacity and peril', have drawn attention to the thorough topicality of *Ecce homo*, its sociological subtext, its being 'really an attempt to define the social role of elites' (Rothblatt, 157). Others have pointed to Seeley's seeking to 'reconcile the Positivist faith in science and the conception of a Church of Humanity with Christianity seen as an international ethical society' (Wormell, 22). Seeley himself disclaimed any controversial intent, avowing that the work was a 'fragment' and that a properly theological treatment would be the subject of a further volume. These disclaimers availed little. Christians and secularists alike found cause for offence. Lord Shaftesbury, the evangelical leader, notoriously denounced *Ecce homo* as a 'pestilential' book, fit to have been 'vomited from the jaws of hell'. Pusey, Newman, and Sidgwick in their different ways found Seeley's treatment objectionable. Public furore was undoubtedly stimulated by the anonymity of the author. W. E. Gladstone, however, had some 'cordial words' to say for it, for which Seeley was grateful. Later, in 1868, Gladstone gave an extensive notice of *Ecce homo* in *Good Words*, granting Seeley's good faith as a 'most honourable writer'.

Rather bruised by his ordeal, but nothing daunted as far as his general enterprise was concerned, Seeley shifted the spearhead of his advance towards his goal of a science of politics. Although he developed some of the features set out in *Ecce homo* (later published in collected form in *Natural Religion*, 1882), Seeley abandoned ethical universalism and positivist scientism as the central thrust of his strategy and regrouped his intellectual forces on decidedly national and historical lines. The writing of *Ecce homo* had impressed on him the extent to which a valid science of politics was only attainable with the assistance of 'a well-trained historical imagination, active and yet calm'. The intellectual discipline he found lacking in the moral sciences would be supplied by a scientific approach to history. In this Seeley was inspired by the achievements of the German school of critical history, and by the Prussian achievements both of an idealized state and of consequent military prowess. More direct inspiration came from the Coleridgean national church tradition. 'The church as a teacher of morality' was Seeley's contribution to a collection of essays edited by W. L. Clay and published in 1868, *Essays in Church Policy*, designed to examine the nature and future role of the Church of England as a national church.

Seeley's premise here was that the province of religion was much more national and political, and much less personal, than was commonly supposed. State and church belonged together, and the link between them was nationality. Morals could not be severed from society. Morality made religion, not religion morality. A higher, ideal, view of service both to the state and from the state must be propagated. If society was to be redeemed from demoralization and political malaise, morality must be taught by a trained élite: a version of Coleridgean clerisy, adept not in theology but history. 'Patriotism should be inculcated, national history closely connected with morality, and civil duties carefully explained.' The clergy were better positioned than any other profession for such a duty:

> Carlyle has said that every nation's true Bible is its history. If the Hebrew history be a cosmopolitan Bible, or rather the first part of one, I think there should be national Bibles also, and I can imagine no more proper and nobler task for a clergy than the perpetual shaping and elaborating of such a national monument. (Shannon, 242–6)

There was still the positivist touch: 'We should form, as it were, a national calendar, consecrate our ancestors—keep their images near us' (ibid.).

History at Cambridge From a twentieth-century academic viewpoint, Seeley's scheme for a national clerisy seems far more 'audacious and perilous' than *Ecce homo*. It is a tribute, in its way, to his unabashed directness of mind. The contrast with the mannered archness of Matthew Arnold's *Culture and Anarchy* of 1867 could hardly be more marked. It is probable that Gladstone was aware of Seeley's exalted vision of history as a national medium of social morality when, in 1869, on Charles Kingsley's resignation of the regius chair of modern history at Cambridge, the question of replacing him came before the prime minister. That question had come to take to itself a new kind of professional urgency and portent. At Oxford, Stubbs's ambition was to found a historical school in England. His surrogate and eventual successor in the Oxford regius chair, E. A. Freeman, had persecuted Kingsley as an amateur and a romancer. Gladstone was confronted with the task of finding for Cambridge a professor of Stubbsian seriousness of professional purpose. Freeman himself proposed such a person, Adolphus Ward; but Gladstone's principal adviser, Connop Thirlwall, bishop of St David's, had never heard of him. Maurice and Kingsley, both notably Coleridgean churchmen, favoured Seeley; but it was not until Charles Merivale, James Spedding, and Aldis Wright had all declined Gladstone's offers that Seeley's name topped the list of possibles. He was by no means a Stubbs; but a kind of Stubbs might be made out of him. Gladstone assured Maurice that 'Of Mr. Seeley's qualities I think very highly' (Wormell, 42).

Seeley meanwhile had married on 17 August 1869 Mary Agnes, *née* Phillott (*d*. 1921), of Unitarian provenance and a relative of Seeley's mathematical colleague at UCL, Augustus De Morgan. It was while on honeymoon vacation at Geneva in September 1869 that Seeley received Gladstone's offer of the regius chair. In accepting he told Gladstone: 'I believe there is no position in the world in which I could do so much good' (Wormell, 42).

Seeley lost little time in communicating to Cambridge his new evangel. In his inaugural lecture in February 1870,

'The teaching of politics', he was ready for direct, aggressive confrontation with the academic establishment. Education, he declared, was in its transition state in Britain. An 'artificial value' had for too long been given to classics and mathematics at Cambridge. There had been an illegitimate 'protection of particular studies and prohibition of others', by which 'cultivation' had been preferred to 'knowledge'. The 'old simple routine of Classics and Mathematics' had stifled the claims of those who 'make observations and try experiments', in short, the sciences. Seeley was wholly a believer in Freeman's dictum that 'history is past politics and politics present history'. But more than Freeman he wanted to emancipate historical study from the past. It was time that claims should be made for contemporary history. 'To turn history away from the past to the present is in fact to give it the interest of an experimental study.' Cambridge was a 'great seminary of politicians'. For them history could be made 'the school of statesmanship'. The present consisted of 'problems which still await their solution, questions which the time is still struggling to answer, controversies in which we are called on to take a side'. Condemning what he called 'the Waverley view of other times', Seeley emphasized the pedagogic capacity of historical science to 'study tendencies before they have reached their limit, predict the growth of power not yet mature, or calculate the stages of its decline' (Rein, 101–2, 105, 116–18).

As the startled classical dons reeled in ribald shock out of the Senate House, their spokesman, Montagu Butler, headmaster of Harrow and later master of Trinity, is credited with what Sir Geoffrey Elton called 'the finest double anti-compliment ever uttered' when he confessed his astonishment 'that we should so soon have been regretting poor Kingsley'.

It was Seeley's initial duty at Cambridge to guide the emancipation of history from its despised subsidiary place in the law tripos. History had been ejected from the moral sciences tripos in 1867 and divorce from the law tripos was looming. This was effected in 1873 and the history tripos commenced its small and struggling independent existence. Seeley would have preferred its being entitled the politics tripos, in accordance with his oft-proclaimed doctrine that history was best studied as the foundation of a science of politics. But he was not an effective academic politician. His dislike of the examination system integral to the tripos led to his taking a somewhat Olympian position in relation to the debates and wrangles of the faculty. Seeley was unfortunate in that the don most sympathetic to his prescription of a 'Historico-Political Tripos', both practical and scientific, was Oscar Browning, whose idiosyncrasies made it difficult for him to be taken seriously; while the proponents of 'pure' history, of 'history for history's sake', Adolphus Ward, George Prothero, and F. W. Maitland, were all men of acumen. The academic battlelines were drawn, it was said, between Seeley's 'thought without facts' and Ward's 'facts without thought'. Tripos reform in 1885 led to a decisive shift toward purism. Nor were the Seeleys advantageously at the centre of an agreeable social circle: he lacked anything in the way of lightness of touch; Mrs Seeley was notoriously a scold; and they entertained badly. Seeley's meagre professorial salary in his early years in his chair meant, moreover, that he had to devote much time to supplementing it by extra-mural lecturing. The Seeleys did not move house from London to Cambridge until 1880, after extra endowment for the chair was provided in 1879 by Henry Sidgwick.

***Stein* (1878)** All these academic disadvantages would perhaps have counted for less had Seeley made the intellectual impact he intended with his first, if belated, major published production of a historical study avowedly both practical as to end and scientific as to means, *The Life and Times of Stein, or, Germany and Prussia in the Napoleonic Age*, which appeared in three volumes from the Cambridge Press in 1878. With *Stein*, Seeley aimed at pulling all the salient lines of his thinking into coherent form. Having established the moral and ethical foundations of a disciplined, patriotic society and an idealized state, he wanted to offer a model of the statesmanship appropriate to such a polity. His anti-models were, precisely, what was currently on offer in Britain: Disraeli, exponent of bankrupt Palmerstonian Turcophilia, grappling unintelligently with Gladstone, hysterical fomentor of populist sentimentality.

Seeley lamented the passing in England of 'a national discipline which formed a firm, strongly marked national character'. The old aristocracy had made a virtue of and taken pride in a 'cool contempt for sentimentalism and fine phrases'. Now, instead of this 'massive strength approaching to brutality', a 'masculine grasp of reality', Englishmen had acquired all the contrary qualities: 'loquacity, sentimentalism, helpless confusion and inaccuracy of thought, hysterical weakness, and the habit of thinking in crowds' (Shannon, 249). *Stein*, Seeley hoped, would diffuse a salutary corrective influence. The reconstructor of the Prussian state after its collapse in 1806 was, in his own way, a kind of new Moses. He embodied both an ideal and a moral conception of the state in his resistance to the immorality and lawlessness of the Napoleonic-Jacobinical universal monarchy. Spain and Prussia, the 'immortal ideas of 1808 and 1813', gave the Europe of nations its correct cue; not the so-called 'immortal ideas of 1789'. For Seeley also, a vehement and consistent foe of the papal monarchy, the Prussia of the *Kulturkampf* was an essential aspect of its ideality. As the Prussia reconstructed by Stein represented the ideal moral state, so her wars were necessarily ideal moral wars: they had 'in a manner reconciled the modern world to war, for they have exhibited it as a civilizing agent and a kind of teacher of morals' (Seeley, *Stein*, 2.96).

What might be defined as, in Seeley's view, both the Mosaic legation of Stein and its bearing on the priestly attributes of the true historian was exposed in its most unabashed form in an exchange recorded by Lady Caroline Jebb in her biography of her husband, R. C. Jebb, the classical scholar. Jebb asked Seeley whether he intended to fulfil his undertaking in *Ecce homo* to write a study of Christ's divinity:

> The answer, most unexpected, was to the effect that he had fulfilled this intention already. On being pressed for an explanation, he said that he meant his Life of Stein! His questioner's comment on this ... was that if he had heard this statement attributed to Seeley, he would have scouted it as incredible. (Shannon, 248)

Possibly this reflected on Seeley's part defiance of a public which had failed to rise to the intellectual occasion and grasp the point of *Stein*. It was not, as Prothero remarked, 'one of his most successful productions'. This was all the more irritating to Seeley in that he had taken trouble to ingratiate himself by condescending to the biographical mode. He would have preferred, as a scientist of politics, to have written 'philosophical history', but had elected for 'educative purposes' to engage thereby the English mind (Shannon, 249). It does not seem to have occurred to Seeley that, as Prothero put it, 'the character of Stein hardly lends itself to attractive biographical treatment' (*DNB*).

The Expansion of England (1883) It was, however, when, as a scientist of politics, Seeley sketched out a programme for a future English Stein that he achieved plenary engagement with the English mind. *The Expansion of England*, two sets of his lectures delivered in Cambridge, published in 1883, proved an immediate and long-lasting success. (It did not go out of print until 1956: the year, appropriately, as has been pointed out, of the Suez fiasco.) With *Expansion*, Seeley combined brilliantly philosophical history with a winningly epigrammatic and stimulating style. In these lectures he followed the logic he had set out in his 1870 inaugural of studying tendencies with a view to prediction and calculation about the future. This capacity was the essence of the practical object for which scientific method was the means. As he had earlier challenged the classicists, so now Seeley challenged popular historians for whom, he considered, English history was gratification of curiosity about the past by means of a celebration of liberty and democracy. But 'since the future grows out of the past, the history of the past of England ought to give rise to a prophecy concerning her future'. What prophecy could the historians of liberty and democracy offer? All that 'Wilkes and general warrants' could offer was a sense of England's history winding down. Seeley insisted that the

> history of England ought to end with something that might be called a moral. Some large conclusion ought to arise out of it; it ought to exhibit the general tendency of English affairs in such a way as to set us thinking about the future and divining the destiny which is reserved for us. (J. R. Seeley, *The Expansion of England*, ed. J. Gross, 1971, 7)

That general tendency Seeley exhibited as the expansion of the English state as a power in the world; that destiny Seeley divined as being reserved was the gathering together of the imperial components into a coherent entity, a 'Greater Britain', which might, as a 'World Venice' founded on sea power, preserve Britain's role as a world power in the twentieth century, on a par with the other destined world powers, the United States and Russia. 'We seem', as he put it in a famous sentence, 'as it were, to have conquered and peopled half the world in a fit of absence of mind' (J. R. Seeley, *The Expansion of England*, ed. J. Gross, 1971, 12). For Seeley the great imperative was that 'mind' should be henceforth at the centre of Britain's policy.

Thus Seeley's lesson for the 'school of statesmanship'. Hitherto, Seeley had said many big things on direct, simple grounds. At last, with *Expansion*, the message made the big, direct, simple impact. Seeley had provided a generation disillusioned alike with Disraelian and Gladstonian politics, and puzzled by Britain's drifting uncertainly in a seemingly incoherent world, with fresh bearings both as to the explanatory shape of the past and to the predictive shape of the future. His last major (and posthumous) publications, especially *The Growth of English Policy* (1895), were developments and variations of these Rankean themes of states and powers. Two great statesmen would emerge as claimants for the Mosaic vocation of the Stein of Greater Britain: Chamberlain and Rosebery. Almost the first thing Rosebery did on becoming prime minister in 1894 was to confer a knighthood in the Order of St Michael and St George upon Seeley.

Death and reputation Seeley did not live long to enjoy his honour. He died of cancer at 7 St Peter's Terrace, Cambridge, on 13 January 1895. His health had never been sound. The 'slender nervous alert frame' of his youth declined into 'a somewhat lethargic exterior' to which 'ill-health had brought an almost excessive gravity of deportment and bearing which at first sight might almost be mistaken for hesitation or inertness' (Wormell, 8). His wife, it was generally agreed, was no great helpmate; and for domestic comfort he depended increasingly upon their one child, Frances Seeley. In 1882, under new statutes providing for quotas of professorial fellows in colleges, Seeley was elected to a fellowship in Gonville and Caius College, whose amenities he valued greatly. The history faculty he served honestly within his lights. He watched it grow from academic infancy to successful maturity, though he failed to imprint upon it his own vision as to its higher vocation. He was always an acclaimed and popular lecturer, and took an important initiative in establishing a seminar for advanced students. Seeley offended the young George Macaulay Trevelyan by dismissing Trevelyan's revered great-uncle as a charlatan and a littérateur. Yet it would be Trevelyan who would, with his *English Social History* (1944), write the next great best-seller of the Cambridge school. Trevelyan characterized Seeley as a 'fine old Victorian of a fighting, dogmatic breed' (G. M. Trevelyan, *An Autobiography and Other Essays*, 1949, 17). Certainly Seeley fought for the cause of imperial federation and against the cause of Irish home rule. Certainly he was dogmatic in his conviction as to historical means to political ends. And certainly he was Victorian in the sense that he handed on no professional intellectual legacy to the post-Victorian world other than the abiding popularity of his *Expansion of England*; which in any case came to be seen as something like the British empire itself, left over from the Victorian era, increasingly disembodied in time and space. By a kind of fatal irony, Seeley failed to predict that his admired Germany would insist on claiming its own destiny in *Weltpolitik*; that Providence had not ordered the future for the exclusive convenience of Greater Britain. It is Seeley's ironic fate to be of interest now to historians on grounds he would have repudiated as 'curiosity' or 'purism'. Yet it is by no means curiously anomalous that the history faculty library at Cambridge is named in his memory. As one of his most distinguished successors in the regius chair, Sir Geoffrey Elton, pointed out, Sir John Seeley was Cambridge's first truly notable regius professor of modern history. R. T. SHANNON

Sources D. Wormell, *Sir John Seeley and the uses of history* (1980) • *DNB* • S. Rothblatt, *The revolution of the dons: Cambridge and society in Victorian England* (1968) • J. R. Seeley, *The expansion of England*, ed. J. Gross (1971) • R. T. Shannon, 'Sir John Seeley and the idea of a national church', *Ideas and institutions of Victorian England*, ed. R. Robson (1967) • G. S. R. Kitson Clark, 'A hundred years of the teaching of history at Cambridge, 1873–1973', *HJ*, 16 (1973), 535–53 • G. A. Rein, *Sir John Robert Seeley*, ed. and trans. J. L. Herkless (1987) • T. W. Heyck, *The transformation of intellectual life in Victorian England* (1982) • S. Collini, D. Winch, and J. Burrow, *That noble science of politics* (1983) • G. R. Elton, *Return to essentials* (1991) • m. cert. • *CGPLA Eng. & Wales* (1895)

Archives LUL, corresp. and papers | BL, corresp. with Macmillans, Add. MS 55074 • CUL, letters to R. H. Quick • Girton Cam., letters to Emily Davies • King's AC Cam., letters to Oscar Browning • Trinity Cam., letters to Henry Sidgwick • U. Newcastle, Robinson L., letters to R. S. Watson

Likenesses C. Ewald, oils, 1896, U. Cam., Divinity School; version, Christ's College, Cambridge; version, Gon. & Caius Cam. • Crellin, carte-de-visite, NPG • W. & D. Downey, carte-de-visite, NPG [*see illus.*] • Elliott & Fry, carte-de-visite, NPG • G. Milner Gibson, ink caricature, Christ's College, Cambridge • photograph, Christ's College, Cambridge

Wealth at death £2340 0s. 4*d*.: probate, 18 Feb 1895, *CGPLA Eng. & Wales*

Seeley, Leonard Benton (1831–1893). *See under* Seeley, Robert Benton (1798–1886).

Seeley, Robert Benton (1798–1886), publisher and author, was born in Ave Maria Lane, London, and baptized on 30 March 1798 at St Faith's under St Paul's. He was the third of the twelve children of Leonard Benton Seeley, bookseller and publisher, and his wife, Harriet. His parents had come from Buckingham, where his grandfather had sold books since at least 1744. Leonard Benton Seeley's London business, established in 1784, acted as agent for the British and Foreign Bible Society in its early days, and served the more general literary demands of the evangelical community. Robert Seeley entered the business as a child, and continued the family religious tradition when he took control of the Crane Court shop in 1826 in partnership with William Burnside, later moving the business to Fleet Street. About 1830 he married Mary Anne Jackson (1809–1868), also 'an earnest evangelical' (Wormell, 5), whose brother John Henry Jackson was one of the partners in Seeley, Jackson and Halliday; they had four daughters and six sons. The firm established a reputation for 'taste and elegance' (*Publishers' Circular*, 15 June 1886, 601–2; Seeley was among the founders of that periodical). Both Daniel and Alexander Macmillan worked for him and Burnside during the 1830s, before starting their own firm. The *Christian Guardian* and the publications of the Church Missionary Society, as well as numerous theological books, appeared under their imprint.

Seeley's theology was a premillenarian eschatology and his church party evangelical; his party politics were tory. His authorship centred on history and theology. In 1834 *Essays on the Church by a Layman* argued that scriptural authority justified the established church: 'As [God] gave [England] a pure and scriptural church at first; gave he also wealth, and power, and prosperity, as a closely-connected consequence' (cited in Lewis, *Lighten their Darkness*, 22). Other works were evangelical biographies, such as his lives of Hannah More (1838), John Newton (1843), and Henry Martyn (1855). A leading figure in the Christian Influence Society in the 1830s and 1840s, he helped found the Church Pastoral Aid Society in 1837 and the Society for Improving the Condition of the Labouring Classes in 1844, and supported Shaftesbury's campaign for factory acts. Seeley opposed economic liberal ideas such as *laissez-faire*: he believed they impugned the character of God.

Seeley remained active in the publishing business until 1857, when it was taken over by his second son, Richmond Seeley. Robert Benton Seeley then embarked on an unsuccessful venture as newspaper proprietor in partnership with his eldest son, Leonard Benton Seeley [*see below*]. Also during these retirement years he wrote a popular history of the life and reign of Edward I, *The Greatest of All the Plantagenets* (1860; rev. edn, 1872), a work that, with his biographical writing, may have influenced his third son, the historian Sir John Robert *Seeley (1834–1895). His influence has also been traced to John Ruskin's knowledge of the 'condition of England question' (Harris, 13). Robert Benton Seeley died at his home, 59 Hilldrop Crescent, Camden Road, London, on 31 May 1886.

Leonard Benton Seeley (1831–1893), barrister and writer, was Robert Benton Seeley's eldest son. He was educated at City of London School and at Trinity College, Cambridge, where he graduated BA in 1852 and MA in 1855. He was elected fellow of Trinity College in 1854 and called to the bar at Lincoln's Inn in the following year. He practised as a conveyancer and equity draftsman, and in addition from 1862 to 1869 he was professor of modern history at Bedford College for Women, London. He wrote a number of popular biographies including *Horace Walpole and his Works* (1884), *Fanny Burney and her Friends* (1890), and *Mrs Thrale, afterwards Mrs Piozzi: a sketch of her life and passages from her diaries, letters & other writings* (1891). He died of a heart attack in the open street across from Chancery Lane, London, on 30 October 1893, leaving a widow, Caroline Blackwell Seeley. LESLIE HOWSAM

Sources D. M. Lewis, *Lighten their darkness: the evangelical mission to working-class London, 1828–1860* (1986) • D. Wormell, *Sir John Seeley and the uses of history* (1980) • *Publishers' Circular* (15 June 1886), 601–2 • D. M. Lewis, 'Leonard Benton Seeley', *The Blackwell dictionary of evangelical biography, 1730–1860*, ed. D. M. Lewis (1995) • F. A. Mumby, *Publishing and bookselling: a history from the earliest times to the present day*, rev. edn (1949) • M. J. Tuke, *A history of Bedford College for Women, 1849–1937* (1939) • *DNB* • *CGPLA Eng. & Wales* (1886) • *CGPLA Eng. &*

Wales (1893) [Leonard Benton Seeley] • J. Harris, 'Ruskin and social reform', *Ruskin and the dawn of the modern*, ed. D. Birch (1999)

Likenesses portrait, repro. in *Publishers' Circular*, 601

Wealth at death £1545 15s. 10d.: probate, 25 Aug 1886, *CGPLA Eng. & Wales* • £53 12s. 0d.—Leonard Benton Seeley: probate, 14 Dec 1893, *CGPLA Eng. & Wales*

Seely, John Edward Bernard, first Baron Mottistone (1868–1947), politician and soldier, was born at Brookhill Hall, between Derby and Nottingham, on 31 May 1868, the fourth son and seventh child of Sir Charles Seely, first baronet (1833–1915), and his wife, Emily (*d*. 1894), daughter of William Evans, of Crumpsall Grange, Lancashire. His family were wealthy colliery owners in the midlands, and his grandfather Charles Seely (1803–1887), for many years member of parliament for Lincoln, was a noted radical, who won notoriety by entertaining Garibaldi at his home on the Isle of Wight.

Education and early political career Seely was brought up in Nottinghamshire but spent most of his holidays on the Isle of Wight, where he passed his days sailing, shooting, climbing, and riding to hounds, displaying in youth the great energy and sense of adventure that would be his hallmarks as a man. He retained a constant affection for the Isle of Wight and it was from his Tudor manor there that he was eventually to take his title. He was educated at Harrow School (where he fagged for Stanley Baldwin) and from 1887 to 1890 at Trinity College, Cambridge. He graduated in 1890 and was called to the bar by the Inner Temple in 1897. On 9 July 1895 he married Emily Florence (*d*. 1913), daughter of Henry George Louis Crichton; they had three sons and four daughters.

While an undergraduate Seely joined the Hampshire yeomanry and when the Second South African War broke out he succeeded in arranging private but immediate transport to South Africa for his squadron, with the assistance of his uncle Sir Francis Evans, chairman of the Union Castle Line. He served against the Boers for eighteen months and his remarkable courage, although it occasionally brought him into conflict with authority, won him distinction and several decorations: he was appointed to the DSO in 1900.

During his absence in South Africa, Seely was elected, in May 1900, Conservative member for the Isle of Wight. In parliament his handsome appearance, friendliness, incisive speech, and ebullient unorthodoxy quickly singled him out as a coming man. With some of the younger Conservatives, in particular Winston Churchill and Lord Hugh Cecil, Jack Seely maintained a sustained attack on the Balfour government's administration of the army. He left the Conservative Party in March 1904 on the combined issues of protection and 'Chinese slavery', and, after resigning his seat, was re-elected without opposition at a by-election. In 1906 he was narrowly elected as a Liberal for the Abercromby division of Liverpool. When Campbell-Bannerman formed his government, Seely was 'left outside', but when Asquith became prime minister in 1908 he was appointed under-secretary to the Colonial Office and in 1909 was sworn of the privy council.

Since his chief at the Colonial Office, Lord Crewe, was in

John Edward Bernard Seely, first Baron Mottistone (1868–1947), by Walter Stoneman, 1924

the Lords, important work fell to Seely as under-secretary, and in particular the introduction of the measure which brought about the union of South Africa. In 1911 he transferred to the War Office, where in 1912, at the suggestion of Churchill, he succeeded Lord Haldane as secretary of state, a logical choice given his knowledge of army matters and his experience on the committee of imperial defence. He worked in close accord with the chief of the Imperial General Staff, Sir John French, whom he always held in affectionate admiration, and together they were responsible for the invitation to Foch to attend the British manoeuvres in 1912. Seely was active in preparing the army for the war with Germany that he believed was inevitable, and he gave special attention to the mobility of the proposed expeditionary force and the development of a flying corps.

The Curragh mutiny Seely and his advisers, however, had more immediate anxieties nearer home. During the later months of 1913 there was some discussion in the army—and a great deal more outside—about the position of the armed forces should the government be obliged to impose the policy of home rule for Ireland by force. In view of the speculation on this topic Seely summoned to the War Office on 16 December the general officers of the six army commands in the United Kingdom, to reassure them about the government's intentions and at the same time remind them of their obligations to uphold the civil power. It was an ambiguous message, obliquely delivered, and it failed in its objective of easing the tension that was growing in the army. On 14 March 1914 a cabinet committee of which Seely was a member decided to inform Sir Arthur Paget, commanding in Ireland, of the need to reinforce arms depots in the north against possible attack from Ulster Volunteers. Paget replied that he was reluctant to move troops for fear of precipitating a crisis in the country. He was again summoned to London, where by this time Churchill and Seely had persuaded themselves and the cabinet that trouble was imminent, a view which the dramatic departure of Sir Edward Carson for Belfast on the 19th did nothing to dispel. Certain movements of troops in Ireland were agreed and Paget was also instructed that Ulster-domiciled officers might 'disappear', in the event of their regiments' being employed in Ulster, without prejudice to their careers, but that other officers, who for conscientious reasons were not prepared to carry out their duty as ordered, were to say so at once and be dismissed the service.

No doubt Seely is to be blamed for agreeing to an arrangement that gave officers the opportunity of pronouncing judgement on orders which might be issued to them, but throughout the affair he sought to maintain the unity of the army. He was therefore overly anxious to meet the wishes of Paget and his own leading military advisers. The consequences of his meeting with Paget, though, were serious. Despite the gravity of the situation, Paget was not given written instructions, and when he got back to Dublin his observations gave rise to the mistaken impression that the government contemplated immediate coercive action against Ulster. As a result Brigadier-General Hubert Gough and fifty-seven of his officers in the 3rd cavalry brigade stationed at the Curragh made it known that they 'preferred dismissal if ordered north'. Paget relayed this news to London and Gough was accordingly relieved of his command, and ordered to report to the War Office with his commanding officers.

On Monday morning, 23 March, Seely, in the presence of Paget, French, and the adjutant-general, Sir Spencer Ewart, reassured Gough about the proposed troop movements and agreed to provide written confirmation which Gough might show to his officers. Later that day the cabinet, in Seely's absence, agreed a statement authorizing Gough to inform his commanders that there had been a misunderstanding, and that all that Paget had sought to do by his remarks was to assure himself that 'lawful commands' would be obeyed. Seely, who had been giving an account of events to the king, arrived as his colleagues were departing. Realizing that their statement would not satisfy Gough, he proceeded to amend it, 'off his own bat' as Ewart would later observe (Beckett, 193), by adding two paragraphs, one of which asserted that the government had no intention of using the forces of the crown 'to crush political opposition to the policy or principles of the Home Rule Bill'. Lord Morley, who was to answer for the government in the Lords that afternoon, assisted with 'the necessary literary graces' (*Inside Asquith's Cabinet*, 166). The revised memorandum, initialled by Seely himself, and by French and Ewart, was then handed to Gough. The latter, though, remained unsatisfied, and on the prompting of Henry Wilson, who was in close touch with the opposition, sought still further clarification from French: in effect a guarantee that his men would not be ordered to Ulster. Without informing Seely, French obliged, and Gough returned to his command.

The result of what Asquith called 'Paget's tactless blundering, and Seely's clumsy phrases' was a political débâcle for the government (*Letters to Venetia Stanley*, 60). The opposition suspected that a plot to coerce Ulster had been lately discovered and derailed, while supporters of home rule faced the prospect of substantial army opposition to the proposed legislation. In the House of Commons on 25 March, Seely took the blame, in an effort to avoid the resignations of the chief of the Imperial General Staff and the adjutant-general. Asquith, while repudiating what Balfour called the two 'peccant paragraphs' of the memorandum, and making it clear that he thought the secretary of state had made an error of judgement, declined to accept Seely's resignation. By 30 March, however, he had reluctantly concluded that the government 'could not possibly survive any recognition, express or implied, of the Gough treaty' (Stewart, 172), and that French and Ewart would therefore resign. 'Poor Seely', Asquith noted, was 'bound to follow suit', and it is a measure of the seriousness of the situation that Asquith himself took over at the War Office (*Letters to Venetia Stanley*, 62). The 'Curragh incident' thus cost Seely his portfolio, although he remained a member of the committee of imperial defence. He had shown considerable naïvety in his dealings with Paget and Gough and had become implicated in what, in his own words, 'looked like a private bargain with a few rebellious officers' (Seely, *Adventure*, 170).

War service and post-war politics The question whether Seely would have speedily returned to office was overtaken by the outbreak of war, and to one of his active disposition it was perhaps fortunate that he was now free to join the fighting. He was given a place on French's staff and left London on 11 August 1914; he was to remain in France with scarcely a break until 1918. Early in 1915 he was promoted temporary brigadier-general and given command of the Canadian cavalry brigade. Despite the reservations of some observers, Seely proved a success in France, and with his horse Warrior (about which he later wrote an engaging book), was conspicuous in many actions. His zest for adventure and many narrow escapes led to his being described as 'the luckiest man in the army', and he was never reticent about his exploits, of which there are many apocryphal stories. According to one of these he was reputed to have recommended his soldier servant for the Victoria Cross, 'Standing, as he was, never more than twenty yards behind me throughout the engagement' (Colville, 82).

Seely's first wife died in August 1913 and on 31 July 1917 he married Evelyn Izmé (*b.* 1886), the widow of his friend Captain George Crosfield Norris Nicholson of the Royal Flying Corps, and daughter of Montolieu Fox Oliphant Murray, first Viscount Elibank. There was one son of the marriage. Seely was appointed CB in 1916, CMG in 1918, and was five times mentioned in dispatches. In 1918 he was gassed and retired from active service with the rank of major-general. He became parliamentary under-secretary and deputy minister of munitions, and moved as under-secretary to the Air Ministry in January 1919. In November he resigned over the prime minister's refusal to give the Air Ministry a separate secretary of state.

Seely was member for the Ilkeston division of Derbyshire from a by-election in 1910 (after an earlier defeat in the same year at Abercromby) until 1922, when, in common with many Coalition Liberals, he was defeated. He was elected as a Liberal for the Isle of Wight in 1923 but was defeated in the following year. He devoted the rest of his life to the savings movement—he was chairman of the national committee (1926–43), and an active vice-chairman until his death—and to country pursuits. From 1918 he was lord lieutenant of Hampshire and the Isle of Wight. Ships and the sea were always his principal recreation and for much of his life he was coxswain of the Brook lifeboat. He was created a peer in June 1933.

House of Lords As Lord Mottistone, Seely regularly attended the House of Lords and took a special interest in the debates on British foreign policy, becoming a consistent advocate of appeasement. He visited Berlin in 1933, as chairman of the Air League, the guest of von Ribbentrop, and in summer 1935 returned to Germany on board his boat, *Mayflower.* His book *Mayflower Seeks the Truth*, published in Germany in 1937, became a vehicle for Nazi propaganda and the planned publication in Britain in 1938 was never executed. In May 1935 he informed the Lords that his 'many interviews with Herr Hitler … this remarkable man' had convinced him that the German leader was 'absolutely truthful, sincere and unselfish' in seeking peaceful accommodation with Britain (*Hansard 5L*, 96, 1044). He remained committed to this belief long after others had abandoned it, declaring himself in June 1939 'an unrepentant believer in … the policy of appeasement' (*Hansard 5L*, 113, 388). He later changed tack and in 1941, in articles in the *Sunday Times* and *Evening Standard*, denounced the brutality of 'Hitlerism'. This could not, however, dispel the lasting impression that he had been, as one historian observed, 'a considerable apologist for Nazi Germany' (Griffiths, 137).

Throughout his strenuous life Seely was conspicuous for a cheerful and brave bearing, not commonly found at Westminster. This sometimes left him open to ridicule and when he assumed his title of Mottistone parliamentary wags dubbed him Lord Modest One. But his sheer irrepressibility and optimism won for him friends on both sides of the house. He was the author of two books of autobiography which, even in their titles—*Adventure* and *Fear, and be Slain*—faithfully revealed the tang of his personality. Nor were his exciting experiences diminished in their telling. In his introduction to *Adventure* Lord Birkenhead wrote of his friend: 'few men of our day have experienced so many and various adventures; none, I think, can ever have displayed so much gusto in their telling'.

Seely died at 37 Tufton Court, Tufton Street, Westminster, on 7 November 1947. His second wife survived him. His eldest son was killed at Arras in April 1917 and the second son, Henry John Alexander (1899–1963), succeeded as second baron. ROGER FULFORD, *rev.* MARK POTTLE

Sources *The Times* (8 Nov 1947) • *The Times* (15 Nov 1947) • *The Times* (17 Nov 1947) • B. Scott, *Galloper Jack: a grandson's search for a forgotten hero* (2003) • A. P. Ryan, *Mutiny at the Curragh* (1956) • A. T. Q. Stewart, *The Ulster crisis* (1967) • R. Jenkins, *Asquith* (1964) • J. Fergusson, *The Curragh incident* (1964) • J. Colville, *Footprints in time* (1976), 82 • *H. H. Asquith: letters to Venetia Stanley*, ed. M. Brock and E. Brock (1982) • *Inside Asquith's cabinet: from the diaries of Charles Hobhouse*, ed. E. David (1977) • *WWBMP* • J. Seely, *Paths of happiness* (1938) • J. E. B. Seely, *Adventure* (1930) • Baron Mottistone, *My horse Warrior* (1934) • J. E. B. Seely, *For ever England* (1932) • I. F. W. Beckett, ed., *The army and the Curragh incident, 1914* (1986) • Burke, *Peerage* • R. Griffiths, *Fellow travellers of the right: British enthusiasts for Nazi Germany, 1933–9*, pbk edn (1983)

Archives Nuffield Oxf., corresp. and papers | Bodl. Oxf., corresp. with Herbert Asquith • CUL, corresp. with Lord Hardinge • HLRO, corresp. with Andrew Bonar Law • HLRO, corresp. with St Loe Strachey • U. Newcastle, corresp. with Walter Runciman | FILM BFI NFTVA, news footage

Likenesses W. Orpen, oils, 1918, IWM • W. Stoneman, photograph, 1924, NPG [*see illus.*] • A. J. Munnings, oils, National Gallery of Canada, Ottawa • Spy [L. Ward], watercolour caricature, NPG; repro. in *VF* (23 Feb 1905)

Wealth at death £9212 12*s.* 4*d.*—save and except settled land: probate, 6 May 1948, *CGPLA Eng. & Wales* • £5500—limited to settled land: probate, 27 Oct 1948, *CGPLA Eng. & Wales*

Seeman [Zeeman], **Enoch** (1689/90–1744), portrait painter, was born at Danzig in Germany, where his father, of Flemish origin, Enoch Seeman (*b. c.*1661), was settled as a painter. It is possible that the famous German virtuoso painter Balthasar Denner, who received some of his early instruction in painting at Danzig, may have been a pupil of Seeman's father, for some of Seeman's early paintings were executed in imitation of Denner's highly detailed style, including a self-portrait at the age of nineteen. In 1704 Seeman was taken by his father to London, and practised there as a portrait painter with great success. He resided in St Martin's Lane, and at first styled himself Enoch Seeman, junior. His earliest known portrait, *Colonel Bissett and his Family* (Forbes Castle, Aberdeenshire), inscribed 'Enoch Seeman pinx. AE 18½ 1708' (Allen, 352) was painted by more than one hand. He was probably helped in its execution by members of his family. Seeman's portraits or portrait groups were sometimes on a very large scale, such as the family group *Lady Cust and Nine Children* (1743) at Belton House, Grantham, his last recorded work. Seeman frequently painted his own portrait. An example of 1716 is in the British Museum, and was engraved by J. G. Schmidt. Another, with his daughter in boys' clothes, was at Strawberry Hill, Twickenham. A portrait by him of Sir Isaac Newton, formerly in the possession of Thomas Hollis FSA, was engraved in mezzotint by J. MacArdell. From 1717 Seeman received royal patronage, and painted a full-length portrait of George I (Middle Temple, London). He also painted George II and other members of the royal family. He died suddenly in St Martin's Lane, London, in March 1744. His son, Paul Seeman, painted portraits and still life, and his three brothers were all painters, one of whom, Isaac Seeman, died in London on 4 April 1751. The name is sometimes, but erroneously, spelt Zeeman. Further works by Seeman are in the National Portrait Gallery, London; Yale University Art Gallery, New Haven, Connecticut; the Metropolitan Museum of Art, New York; Dunham Massey, Cheshire; Belton House, Lincolnshire; and Dalkeith House, near Edinburgh.

L. H. CUST, *rev.* SARAH HERRING

Sources E. Allen, 'Seeman, Enoch', *The dictionary of art*, ed. J. Turner (1996) • Waterhouse, *18c painters*, 337 • O. Millar, *The Tudor, Stuart and early Georgian pictures in the collection of her majesty the queen*, 2 vols. (1963), vol. 1, pp. 26, 29n. 85, 144, 150, 153, 172, 173; vol. 2, nos. 508–13, 196 • J. Kerslake, *National Portrait Gallery: early Georgian portraits*, 1 (1977), 9, 35, 63, 89, 93, 100, 141, 282 • E. Einberg, *Manners and morals: Hogarth and British painting, 1700–1760* (1987), 34, 246 [exhibition catalogue, Tate Gallery, London, 15 Oct 1987 – 3 Jan 1988] • Vertue, *Note books*, 2.25, 75; 3.1, 4, 6, 13, 15–16, 54, 89, 125, 143, 155 • H. Walpole, *Anecdotes of painting in England: with some account of the principal artists*, ed. J. Dallaway, [rev. and enl. edn], 4 (1827), 56–7 • B. Stewart and M. Cutten, *The dictionary of portrait painters in Britain up to 1920* (1997) • Redgrave, *Artists* • A. F. Steuart, *Catalogue of the pictures at Dalkeith House, Dalkeith* (1890), 4

Likenesses E. Seeman, self-portrait, oils, 1716, BM • J. Faber junior, mezzotint, 1727 (after E. Seeman), BM, NPG • T. Chambers, engraving (after E. Seeman), BM • J. G. Schmidt, engraving (after E. Seeman), BM

Berthold Carl Seemann (1825–1871), by Maull & Polyblank, 1855

Seemann, Berthold Carl (1825–1871), botanist and traveller, was born on 28 February 1825 at Hanover, the son of a clarinettist at the Court Theatre, and his wife, Caroline. From October 1835 until September 1838 he was educated at the *Lyceum* at Hanover, then under Georg Friedrich Grotefend, the philologist, from whose son he received his first botanical teaching. At Easter 1839 Seemann became an apprentice gardener at the royal kitchen garden at Linden but apparently found little satisfaction in his work. From 1842 until March 1845 he served as assistant to the master gardener, Wendland, at the royal hill garden.

Seemann's first botanical paper was written when he was just seventeen. In 1844 he moved to the Royal Botanic Gardens, Kew, and worked under John Smith, the curator, in order to train himself as a plant collector. In 1846 Sir William Jackson Hooker procured Seemann's appointment as naturalist to HMS *Herald*, then engaged on a hydrographical survey of the Pacific. Seemann left England in August 1846 to join the *Herald* in Panama. Finding that the ship had not returned from Vancouver he explored the isthmus, finding many new plants, besides hieroglyphics at Veraguas, which he described in a paper read before the Archaeological Institute. He joined the *Herald* on 17 January 1847, and remained with her until June 1851. Almost all the west coast of America was explored, and three cruises were made into Arctic seas. In Peru and Ecuador, Seemann travelled with Bedford Pim from Payta, Peru, through the desert and over the Andes to Guayaquil, Ecuador; in Mexico he went from Mazatlán over the Sierra Madre to Durango and Chihuahua, narrowly escaping hostile Comanches and Apaches.

In 1848 the *Herald* was ordered to the Bering Strait to search for the Arctic explorer Sir John Franklin. Herald Island was discovered, and a higher latitude than any previously attained in that region was reached, while Seemann collected many plants and anthropological specimens relating to the Inuit, visited Kamtchatka and the Sandwich Islands several times, and finally returned home by Hong Kong, Singapore, the Cape, St Helena, and Ascension Island. *The Botany of the Voyage*, which was published between 1852 and 1857, with analyses by Hooker and 100 plates by W. H. Fitch, comprises the floras of Panama, north-west Mexico, 'West Esquimaux-land' (Alaska), and Hong Kong. Seemann's *Narrative of the Voyage* was published in two volumes in English in 1853, the same year that he was made doctor of philosophy of Göttingen, and was elected a member of the Imperial Academy Naturae Curiosorum (later the Leopoldine Academy) under the cognomen 'Bonpland'. Also in 1853 he began, in conjunction with his brother Wilhelm, to edit a German journal of botany entitled *Bonplandia*, of which ten volumes were published at Hanover between 1853 and 1862. Finding himself increasingly Anglicized, he gave up the issue of this journal, and in 1863 began the publication of the *Journal of Botany, British and Foreign*, in the editing of which, from 1869, he was assisted by Henry Trimen and John Gilbert Baker. In 1857 he went to Montreal, representing the Linnean Society at the meeting of the American Association for the Advancement of Science, and took the opportunity to visit the United States.

In early 1860 Seemann was commissioned by the Colonial Office, with Colonel Smythe, to report on the Fiji Islands, before the British government accepted their cession. In Fiji he made the ascent of Mount Voma and Mbuke Levu. His report was published in 1862 as *Viti: an Account of a Government Mission to the Vitian or Fijian Islands*. The appendix contained a catalogue of previously described plants of the islands, and some new species were described in *Bonplandia*. In the same year he contributed an essay, 'Fiji and its inhabitants', to Francis Galton's *Vacation Tourists*. In 1865 he began at his own expense the issue of a *Flora Vitiensis*, in ten parts with 100 plates, mostly by Fitch. Of this, nine parts, mainly written by himself, were published before his death. It was about this time that Seemann married an Englishwoman; she died about 1870. They had one daughter, Hildegarde Carolina Seemann, who survived him.

Partly in order to fund the publication of his *Flora Vitiensis*, in 1864 Seemann accepted a commission from the firm of Alexander Mendel at Amsterdam to report on the resources of Venezuela. There, near the Tocuyo River, he discovered a valuable bed of anthracite. From March to August 1866, and during 1867, he accompanied Bedford Pim to Nicaragua for the Central American Association. Seemann's letters to the *Athenaeum* and to the *Panama Star and Herald* were reprinted in 1869 as *Dottings on the Roadside in Panama, Nicaragua, and Mosquito*. One result of these journeys was the purchase by English entrepreneurs of the Javali goldmine, Chontales, Nicaragua, of which Seemann was appointed managing director. He had also the management of a large sugar estate near Panama.

Seemann became a fellow of the Linnean Society in 1852, and was a vice-president of the Anthropological Society and a fellow of the Royal Geographical Society. In botany he made a special study of the genus *Camellia* (which includes the tea plant), of which he published a synopsis in the *Transactions of the Linnean Society* (1859), and of the ivy family (*Hederaceae*), his account of which was reprinted from the *Journal of Botany* in 1868. He introduced into cultivation the cannibal tomato, once eaten with human flesh in the Fiji Islands, the candle-tree (*Parmentiera cerifera*), and several handsome species of palm. E. Regel dedicated to him the genus *Seemannia*, gesneriads, perennial plants native to the Andes.

Seemann was a versatile and prolific writer. Besides the works already mentioned, he was the author of several scientific treatises, the most important of which were perhaps his *Die Volksnamen der amerikanischen Pflanzen* (1851), *Popular History of the Palms* (1856), and *The British Ferns at One View* (1860), a coloured chart. He also wrote numerous articles in periodicals in English, German, and other languages. The Royal Society *Catalogue* lists ninety-eight of those relating to science alone. He was also a composer of music, and was author of three short German plays: *Wahl macht Qual*, *Der Wohlthäter wider Willen*, and *Die gelben Rosen*, all published in 1867 at Hanover where they enjoyed some popularity.

In 1871, at Javali in Nicaragua, Seemann's health failed, and after three weeks' illness he died there of fever with possible cardiac complications on 10 October 1871. He was buried the following day close to his house at the mine.

G. S. Boulger, *rev.* Andrew Grout

Sources H. G. Reichenbach, *Botanische Zeitung*, 30 (1872), 503–10 • *Journal of Botany, British and Foreign*, 10 (1872), 1–7 • F. A. Stafleu and R. S. Cowan, *Taxonomic literature: a selective guide*, 2nd edn, 6, Regnum Vegetabile, 115 (1986) • *Gardeners' Chronicle* (30 Dec 1871), 1678–9 • A. C. Smith, *Flora Vitiensis Nova*, 1 (1979), 43–7 • J. W. Parham, *Plants of the Fiji Islands*, rev. edn (1972), 2–3 • G. Sarton, *Sarton on the history of science* (1962), 262–4 • *Catalogue of scientific papers*, Royal Society, 5 (1871), 622–3 • *Catalogue of scientific papers*, Royal Society, 8 (1879), 926–7 • E. Edwards, *Portraits of men of eminence in literature, science and the arts, with biographical memoirs*, ed. L. Reeve and E. Walford, 6 vols. (1863–7) • *Proceedings of the Linnean Society of London* (1871–2), lxxiv–lxxix • J. G. Wilson and J. Fiske, eds., *Appleton's cyclopaedia of American biography*, 5 (1888), 453 • *CGPLA Eng. & Wales* (1872)

Archives Linn. Soc., papers • NHM, specimens • RBG Kew, corresp. and papers; specimens | RBG Kew, corresp. with George Bentham • RBG Kew, letters to Sir William Hooker

Likenesses Maull & Polyblank, albumen print, 1855, NPG [*see illus.*] • E. Edwards, photograph, 1863, repro. in Reeve, *Portraits of men of eminence* • V. Brooks, lithograph, NPG • lithograph (after photograph by E. Edwards, 1863), repro. in B. Seemann, *Flora Vitiensis* (1865–73), frontispiece

Wealth at death under £450: administration, 11 May 1872, *CGPLA Eng. & Wales*

Seffrid (II) (*d.* 1204), bishop of Chichester, is of unknown origins but, given the unusual name, is likely to have been related to Seffrid (I), bishop of Chichester from 1125 to 1145. Indeed while Seffrid (II) was bishop a nephew, also called Seffrid, became successively canon, treasurer, and dean of Chichester Cathedral, predeceasing his uncle. A Seffrid, possibly Seffrid (II) in his youth, witnessed a charter of Hilary, bishop of Chichester, shortly before 1157. Seffrid (II) studied law at Bologna, the greatest international centre of legal learning in his time, if, as is probable, he is the 'Seffrid the Englishman' whose mother Matilda was commemorated with an annual *obit*, according to a twelfth-century necrology of St Saviour, Bologna, a hostel specially favoured by English scholars. Later, Pope Celestine III referred to Godfrey de Lucy, bishop of Winchester, and Seffrid (II) as 'wise in the law' (*iuri sapientes*).

Seffrid first appears in English sources in 1172–3 when, as Master Seffrid (the title indicating an extended period of study at a major centre of learning), he became at once both a royal itinerant justice, as recorded in the pipe roll, and also archdeacon of Chichester. He obtained at about this time the rectorship of Westminster Abbey's church at Bloxham in Oxfordshire, which seems to have been reserved for men with good royal connections. He thus provides an example of the expanding opportunities of the time in ecclesiastical and secular administration for Englishmen who had studied abroad, and of the growing tendency to combine posts in both administrations, to which the distinguished canonist Pope Alexander III objected in 1179. It is possible that Seffrid took this objection to heart, for in his few years as dean of Chichester (1176/1178–1180), and in his near quarter-century (from 1180 until his death) as bishop, there is no evidence of his taking any part in royal administration, nor of his playing any but the purely formal role expected of a bishop in politics (for example, attendance at royal coronations, or acting in a minor way as peacemaker between the archbishops and monks of Canterbury). Rather the bishop appears from his charters as an assiduous diocesan, ensuring where possible endowments of vicarages for the material support of priests resident in parish churches, arranging alms for hospitals, regulating the prebendal system of his cathedral, and, not least, throwing himself into its building works. The cathedral suffered a fire in 1187, but was rebuilt and rededicated by Seffrid in 1199, and he also built the hall and chapel of the bishop's palace at Chichester and engaged in work on the episcopal castle at Amberley and the church of St Andrew on his manor of Bishopstone, both in Sussex. He died on 17 March 1204.

HENRY MAYR-HARTING

Sources H. Mayr-Harting, *The bishops of Chichester, 1075–1207: biographical notes and problems* (1963) • H. Mayr-Harting, ed., *The acta of the bishops of Chichester, 1075–1207*, CYS, 56 (1964)

Segal, Walter (1907–1985), architect, was born in Ascona, Switzerland, on 15 May 1907, to parents of Romanian origin: he was the son of the painter Arthur Segal (*b.* 1875) and his artist wife, Ernestine Chavas (*b.* 1879). His early life was spent at the centre of progressive social and artistic communities in Ascona and Berlin; his parents knew many of the Dadaists, as well as avant-garde architects and designers such as Walter Gropius, Laszlo Moholy-Nagy, and Mies van der Rohe. This liberal background was one against which the young Segal would react: 'if you did try to escape from this milieu', he said, 'it would engulf you' (Segal, 'Timber framed housing', 287). As a schoolboy, he showed a precocious talent for mimicking the forms of the new architecture, but, when it came to training for his chosen career, he passed up the opportunity to study at the Bauhaus, opting instead for 'an ordinary education' in which he would 'learn to build first' (Segal, 'Into the '20s', 36). He studied with the conservative architect M. J. Granpré-Molière in Delft, and at the Technischen Hochschulen in Berlin-Charlottenberg and Zürich (1929–32). Nevertheless, he found himself as disillusioned with the nostrums of the traditionalists as with those of the modernists; neither offered a route to his ambition to translate traditional craft methods to contemporary forms and usages, to build 'what I believed … was just simply a natural building' (McKean, 42).

Konrad Wachsmann's book *Holzhausbau* (1930)—which explained American balloon framing—and Segal's independent studies of joinery supplied him with a way out of his apparent impasse. His first opportunity to put his ideas into practice came in 1932, with a commission from Bernhard Meyer, his father's lifelong patron, for a small house in Ascona. Compactly planned, the single-storey frame-built wooden house was built about three weeks. Segal saw its unpretentious character and warm-toned interiors as marking a distance (which is less evident in retrospect) between himself and orthodox modernists: 'I tried to make this building as insignificant as I could. It was deliberately background achitecture … very different to the interiors I had known' (McKean, 40–42). The theme of providing an appropriate but unostentatious background to conviviality would recur throughout his later work. Segal's approach to the Ascona commission—in particular his use of a lightweight frame and 'transparent' constructional system—would inform much of his later, mostly domestic, work. It was followed by a handful of small buildings in Ascona and, later, Majorca, Spain. In Majorca he found his approach further vindicated by the example of domestic buildings which he found exemplary: 'without pretence … yet their sense of proportion and clarity, cannot be contested' (McKean, 56).

Hitler's accession to power in 1933 prevented Segal from returning to practise in Berlin. He accepted a temporary post (1934–5) as an excavation architect in Egypt, making detailed studies of dynastic Egyptian chairs, mainly from Tutankhamun's tomb. A project to write a monograph on the subject took him to museums in Italy and Britain and, in 1936, he decided to settle in London. Here he met Eva Bradt (1914/15–1950), daughter of Gustav Bradt, a doctor; she later became his wife on 21 September 1940 and also his architectural partner. Opportunities for independent architectural practice were limited at this time, and Segal made a modest living from commissions for interior and furniture design (the latter for Gordon Russell and Heals, among others). During the war Segal worked on the design of air raid shelters and, for the Ministry of Supply, on the design of hostels for munitions and other workers displaced from urban centres. Anticipating the need for large-scale, low-cost housing in the post-war years, he also began to develop a series of studies of designs for small houses. He put forward his ideas about housing, planning, and the environment in an exhibition, in articles, and in books such as *Planning and Transport* (1945) and *Home and Environment* (1946). His aim was, like Alvar Aalto, to create standardization with a human dimension. But although his ideas were influential within the architectural profession, commissions for local authority housing eluded him in the early post-war years.

Towards the end of the war Segal began to teach, combining this with a small-scale independent architectural practice. From 1944 to 1948 he taught at the Architectural Association; in 1973 he was Banister Fletcher professor at the Bartlett school of architecture, University College, London; and from 1976 he taught at the Thames Polytechnic. Students and colleagues valued him increasingly, as a 'live' link with the 'heroic period' of modernism, as well as for his cheerful iconoclasm in the face of bureaucratic planning constraints, and persuasive ideas about contemporary architecture and planning concerns. From the 1950s Segal's architectural practice picked up, although it remained modest in scale; he designed several private houses, some small-scale housing schemes and blocks of flats, offices, and a factory. But it was only in the late 1970s, as ideas of community architecture and self-help began to take root, that he saw some of his most cherished ideas about housing and conviviality begin to bear fruit, albeit on a small scale, in a self-build scheme in Lewisham in south-east London: here, far from being merely an architects' architect, he became definitively a people's architect.

Segal's first wife, with whom he had one son, died suddenly in 1950. He married Mary Moran Scott, who had five children, in 1962. Segal was of striking appearance, diminutive and bald, with a bushy white fringe. He was notoriously stubborn in pursuit of his architectural ideas;

compensatingly, he drew 'like an angel' and, with wide-ranging and scholarly interests, was excellent company. He died in London on 27 October 1985. His second wife survived him. CHARLOTTE BENTON

Sources J. McKean, *Learning from Segal* (1989) • *Architects' Journal* (4 May 1988) • W. Segal, 'Into the '20s', *ArchR*, 155 (1974), 31–8 • M. Emanuel, ed., *Contemporary architects*, 3rd edn (1994) • *The Times* (2 Nov 1985) • *An architecture of understanding … Walter Segal, 1907–85* (1988) [exhibition pamphlet] • W. Segal, 'Timber framed housing', *RIBA Journal*, 84 (1977), 284–95 • W. Segal, 'View from a lifetime', *Transactions of the Royal Institute of British Architects*, 91–1 (1981–2), 7–14 • m. cert.
Archives priv. coll.
Likenesses photographs, RIBA

Segar, Francis. *See* Seager, Francis (*fl.* 1549–1563).

Segar, Simon (*fl.* **1656–1712**). *See under* Segar, Sir William (*b.* in or before 1564, *d.* 1633).

Segar, Sir William (*b.* in or before **1564**, *d.* **1633**), herald, was probably the son either of Francis Segar and Anne Sherard, or of Nicholas Segar, brother of Sir Francis Segar, gentleman of the bedchamber to Maurice, landgrave of Hesse, and Eleanor Crakenthorpe (Noble, 230); the Segars were of Dutch origin. Trained as a scrivener, Segar was employed by Sir Thomas Heneage, who introduced him to the College of Arms. Created Portcullis pursuivant on 10 June 1585, he attended the earl of Leicester's splendid festival of St George, at Utrecht on 23 April 1586, of which he wrote an account. He became Somerset herald on 4 February 1589, and Norroy king of arms on 23 October 1597, although the patent was not signed until 2 June 1602 (Noble, 172).

At this time, Robert Cooke, Clarenceux king of arms, was encroaching on the traditional privileges of Garter king of arms. In 1595 Segar sided with Sir William Dethick, Garter, criticizing Cooke for his inability to write clearly and for making many grants of arms to 'base and unworthy persons for his private gaine onely' (Wagner, 207). In 1596 he continued to uphold Garter's rights against Cooke's successor, Richard Lee. Segar was appointed deputy Garter in place of the unpopular Dethick to invest Christian IV of Denmark with the Garter in June 1603. In 1604 he proclaimed the Anglo-Spanish peace in London. He was appointed as Garter by a signet bill in January 1604, although Dethick did not resign until December 1606. Segar obtained a great seal patent, confirming him as Garter, on 17 January 1607. In 1612 he invested Maurice, prince of Orange, with the Garter, and the same year was himself granted arms (BL, Harl. MS 1441, fol. 154b). He was knighted on 5 November 1616.

By 1584 Segar had married first Helen Somers (*d.* 1593x6) of Kent, and had three sons, Jacob, Giles (*d.* 1649), and Anthony (*b.* 1586), and three daughters, Catherine (*b.* 1585), Elizabeth (*b.* 1592), and Penelope, who married first Nicholas Charles (*d.* 1613), Lancaster herald, and then Timothy Cartwright of Marshbone, Gloucestershire, with whom she had Timothy Cartwright, builder of the Royal Exchange. By 1596 Segar had married Maria, daughter of Robert Browne of Evington, Herefordshire, and had four sons, John (*b.* 1596), who died in Virginia, Frederick (*b.*

Sir William Segar (*b.* in or before 1564, *d.* 1633), by Francis Delaram

1599), William, and Thomas (1609–1670), later Bluemantle pursuivant of arms, and three daughters, Ann, later wife of Lewis Latham of Ellonstow, Bedfordshire, Sarah (*b.* 1601), and Alice (*b.* 1603). In December 1616 Segar's rival Ralph Brooke, York herald, tricked him into confirming a concoction of foreign royal arms to Gregory Brandon, the common hangman of London who was masquerading as a gentleman about to embark for the continent. Brooke then reported him to James I, who imprisoned both Brooke and Segar in Marshalsea prison on 30 December 1616. They were released a few days later, the lord chamberlain hoping the experience would make the former more honest and the latter more wise (Wagner, 219–20).

On 1 March 1617 Segar was admitted to Gray's Inn. On 5 April, James I added £10 to the existing £50 paid to his office of Garter. The same year, he and William Camden conducted the heraldic visitation of Northamptonshire. On 16 November 1618 Segar became one of the commissioners to inquire into the condition of Lincoln's Inn Fields. In 1624 he was among those recommended by Edmond Bolton to be members of the projected Academy Royal. In 1627, accompanied by two of his sons, he and Dudley, Lord Carleton, visited The Hague to invest Henry

Frederick, prince of Orange, with the Garter. He was represented by Henry St George for the investment of Gustavus Adolphus of Sweden the same year, and by Phillipot for the investment of the elector Charles Louis of the Palatine in 1633.

Segar is known to have been author of thirteen manuscript and printed works, including *Honor, Military and Civill* (1602), verse praising James I, and on such subjects as the arms of the Garter knights, the office of earl marshal, the origins of the princely orders of collars, and the heraldry and genealogy of the English royal family and peerage. 'Segar's Roll' of armorial bearings (BL, Add. MS 8933), a treatise on heraldry, is so called because it was in his custody in 1605; *The Cities Great Concern* (1629), sometimes attributed to him, was really by Edmond Bolton. Segar was a conscientious herald and a formidable scholar yet, like many other Tudor genealogists, he authorized many pedigrees giving most improbable descents from fabulous ancestors. His long reign gave the college respite from the jealous controversies over the prerogatives of the three kings of arms.

Segar wrote his will on 10 December 1633, describing himself as being of Richmond, Surrey, and appointing Sir John Parsons his overseer. He died the same day and was buried the next in the chancel of Richmond parish church, Surrey. His will was proved on 21 January 1634 by his widow and executor, Maria. On 3 June 1649 administration of the estate was granted to his son Thomas, after Maria's death.

Segar's great-grandson was **Simon Segar** (*fl.* 1656–1712), author and librarian, the son of Thomas Segar of St Giles-in-the-Fields, Middlesex, and grandson of Thomas Segar, Bluemantle pursuivant of arms. He entered Gray's Inn in 1656, becoming library keeper (1674) and chief butler (1676). He wrote a manuscript peerage and published catalogues of peerage titles—*Honores Anglicani* (1712)—and of entrants, benchers, and treasurers of Gray's Inn, and *Aspidora Segariana*, an account of Sir William Segar's grants and confirmations of arms.

ANTHONY R. J. S. ADOLPH

Sources A. Wagner, *Heralds of England: a history of the office and College of Arms* (1967) • *DNB* • M. Noble, *A history of the College of Arms* (1805) • W. C. Metcalfe, *A book of knights banneret, knights of the Bath and knights bachelor* (1885) • J. Anstis, ed., *The register of the most noble order of the Garter*, 2 vols. (1724) • E. Ashmole, *The history of the most noble order of the Garter* (1715) • Rymer, *Foedera*, 1st edn, vols. 17–18 • will, proved 21 Jan 1634 • J. Weever, *Antient funeral monuments*, ed. W. Tooke (1767), 682 • J. Foster, preface, *The register of admissions to Gray's Inn, 1521–1889, together with the register of marriages in Gray's Inn chapel, 1695–1754*, ed. J. Foster (privately printed, London, 1889) • BL, Harley MS 1441, fol. 154b [Segar's grant of arms]

Archives NL Scot., heraldic MSS, Adv. MSS 31.4.5, 31.7.11 | Coll. Arms, College of Arms MSS, heraldic MSS, series L14, *passim* • Coll. Arms, Harley MSS

Likenesses F. Delaram, line engraving, BM, NPG [*see illus.*]

Ségéne mac Fiachna (*d.* 652). *See under* Iona, abbots of (*act.* 563–927).

Segrave, Gilbert de. *See* Seagrave, Sir Gilbert of (*d.* 1254); Seagrave, Gilbert (*b.* before 1258, *d.* 1316); Seagrave, Gilbert (*c.*1260–1312).

Segrave, Sir Henry O'Neal de Hane (1896–1930), land and water speed record-holder, was born in Baltimore, Maryland, on 22 December 1896, the only child of Charles William Segrave, Anglo-Irish landowner of co. Wicklow, later of co. Tipperary, and his first wife, Mary Lucy, daughter of James Kemp Harwood, officer in the US Navy; she died in 1898. Educated, unremarkably, at Eton College and, briefly, at the Royal Military College, Sandhurst, Segrave was commissioned into the Royal Warwickshire regiment. Wounded in France in May 1915, he transferred to the Royal Flying Corps (RFC) in October, and gained his wings in January. Twice shot down, wounded, and now a captain, he was grounded first at the War Office, later with the RFC headquarters in France, and finally at the Air Council before a posting to Washington (now a major) with the British aviation mission in June 1918. On 4 October 1917 he married Doris Mary, a comedy actress, daughter of George Stocker. There were no children.

A keen owner of fast motor cycles and cars since he was fifteen, Segrave set out after the war to be a racing driver. On his showing at the Brooklands circuit with a pre-war 4½ litre Opel and by persistent importuning, he was accepted, in 1921, as a team driver by Louis Hervé Coatalen, designer and racing manager to Sunbeam (soon to be the Anglo-French concern Sunbeam-Talbot-Darracq), the only British competitor in international events. That year Segrave won the Brooklands 200 mile race from his teammates Kenelm Lee Guinness and Malcolm Campbell. In 1923 he became, at Tours, the only Briton until 1938 (and Sunbeam the only British car until 1957) to win a European grand prix. He raced successfully with Sunbeam, preferring roads to track, and winning three further grands prix, until the end of 1927, when he retired, believing that

> owing to the near state of perfection which the automobile has reached … the need for carrying out experiments along unorthodox lines has diminished. Therefore the need for constructing specialized cars will automatically diminish also … the curve of what is physically possible will intersect the curve of what is practically worthwhile. (H. O. D. Segrave, *The Lure of Speed*, 1928, 24, 262)

The proper place for fast engines would, in the future, be where they operated most efficiently—in the air.

Segrave then took to record-breaking. Already, briefly, holder of the world's flying-start kilometre (152.33 m.p.h. on Southport Sands in 1926), he was the first person to travel at 200 m.p.h. over the mile: on 29 March 1927 at Daytona Beach, Florida, driving the huge chain-driven Sunbeam, powered by two First World War Matabele 22½ litre aero-engines, designed by Coatalen, he averaged 203.988 m.p.h. over the mile. Two years later, again at Daytona, on 11 March 1929, he recaptured the record from the American Ray Keech at 231.362 m.p.h. in *Golden Arrow*, designed by Captain J. S. Irving with a 900 hp aero-engine hired from Napier and originally designed for the Schneider trophy-winner Supermarine seaplane. For this feat he was received by President Herbert Hoover and knighted by George V.

In May 1927 Segrave had started racing boats. After

limited success with *Miss England I* in America, he returned to the challenge in 1930 in *Miss England II*, using two Rolls-Royce racing aero-engines. On Windermere on Friday 13 June 1930, he took the world mile record at 98.76 m.p.h., beating the record of the American holder, Commodore Garfield Wood, by 6 m.p.h. On a third run, the boat hit a floating object, capsized at speed, drowning a mechanic and mortally wounding Segrave, who died at Belle Grange, near Hawkshead, hours later, the holder of both land and sea records.

Though of independent means, Segrave worked first with KLG sparking plugs in 1920, as competition manager, then for Sunbeam from 1924, as head of their London sales department. In 1927 he joined the Portland Cement Company, who denied him car-racing rights but went on to be a sponsor for *Golden Arrow*. In 1927 and 1929 he designed stylish bodies for the Hillman 12 hp and then Straight Eight chassis; as technical adviser to the Aircraft Investment Corporation, which he joined in 1929, he shared in the design of the Segrave Meteor, an advanced four-seater, twin-engined monoplane.

Serious-minded and highly practical, Segrave trained hard for everything he did. Cool foresight and a quick mind enabled him to react swiftly in an emergency. He never crashed a car while racing—a rare distinction. Handsome and articulate, a keen patriot, he was greatly liked on both sides of the Atlantic. Brave, adventurous, single-minded, he died a national hero. As a *Times* leader put it: 'A man of genius in his own field, he must be counted among those who have deserved well of their kind, and his name will be remembered in honour' (*The Times*, 13). After cremation at Golders Green crematorium his ashes were scattered over Eton playing fields from his own plane. His wife survived him. H. G. Pitt, *rev.*

Sources *The Times* (14 June 1930), 13–14 · C. Posthumus, *Sir Henry Segrave* (1961) · C. Posthumus, *Land speed record* (1971) · m. cert.

Archives FILM BFI NFTVA, 'Another success for Segrave', Gaumont Graphic, 21 March 1929 · BFI NFTVA, 'Fastest man in the world', Topical Budget, 14 March 1929 · BFI NFTVA, 'Florida: all British motoring triumph', Topical Budget, 31 March 1927 · BFI NFTVA, 'Golden arrow, a record of Major Segrave's triumphant recovery of the Wakefield trophy', 1929 · BFI NFTVA, 'Segrave drives auto 231–36 miles an hour new world special mark', MGM News, 25 March 1929 · BFI NFTVA, 'Segrave record breaking attempt and death', 1930 · BFI NFTVA, 'Windermere — victory and death', British Screen News, 13 June 1930

Likenesses K. Collings, drawing, repro. in H. O. de H. Segrave, *The lure of speed* (1928), frontispiece · photograph, repro. in H. O. de H. Segrave, *The lure of speed* (1928) · photographs, repro. in Posthumus, *Sir Henry Segrave*

Wealth at death £17,868 4*s.* 2*d.*: probate, 22 July 1930, *CGPLA Eng. & Wales*

Segrave, Sir Hugh. *See* Seagrave, Sir Hugh (*d.* 1387).

Segrave, John de. *See* Seagrave, John, second Lord Seagrave (1256–1325).

Segrave, Nicholas de. *See* Seagrave, Nicholas of, first Lord Seagrave (1238?–1295); Seagrave, Nicholas (*d.* 1321).

Segrave, Stephen de. *See* Seagrave, Sir Stephen of (*d.* 1241); Seagrave, Stephen (*d.* 1333).

Seguarde, John. *See* Seward, John (1364/5–1435/6).

Seguier, John (1785–1856). *See under* Seguier, William (1772–1843).

Seguier, Margaret (*fl.* 1837–1870). *See under* Stewart, Anthony (1773–1846).

Seguier, William (1772–1843), picture dealer and art functionary, was born in the parish of St Martin-in-the-Fields, London, on 9 November 1772, one of the eldest of nine children of David Seguier, dealer in pictures and prints, and his wife, Elizabeth Thwaites. The Seguiers were descended from Huguenot refugees, one of whom had reputedly made a fortune as a chocolate manufacturer in Soho; one of David's brothers was a topographical and technical printseller in St Giles's between 1777 and 1809, where he went under the name of John Seago; another, Peter, a sculptor who had been apprenticed to Richard Hayward (1728–1800), appears to have practised in Rugby in the late 1780s, and to have had a son of the same name who worked from Coventry between 1816 and 1830. Both sculptors sign their monuments as 'Seager', which is also evidently the way in which David and William pronounced their name.

Like his younger brother John [*see below*], William Seguier was trained as an artist, reputedly by George Morland, and even—perhaps as an engraver—by William Blake. His original pictures were topographical views of London, but he may also have followed his father as a *pasticheur*: the posthumous sale of his pictures at Christies on 4 May 1844 included a work entitled *A Woody Scene with Trees, Near a Pool of Water*, 'admirably painted in the manner of Ruysdael'. According to his nephew, it was Seguier's marriage on 17 February 1797 to a wealthy fellow Huguenot, Anne Magdalene Clowden, with whom he had several daughters, which prompted him to give up painting. No doubt her money enabled him to set up independently of his father, officially as a picture restorer, but in fact primarily as a dealer and agent, early in the new century, initially at 32 Coventry Street, but from the latter half of the 1830s, in partnership with John, at 3 Russell Court, Cleveland Row. His earliest clients included the banker–collectors Henry Hope, John Dent, and Samuel Rogers, but by 1808 he was bidding at auction on behalf of one of the most prodigious buyers of the first third of the century, the commissioner of excise, George Watson (Taylor). In 1806 he was acting for Lord Grosvenor (later first marquess of Westminster) in his purchase of the Agar collection; from then on he steadily acquired a more aristocratic and influential clientele, beginning with the key figure of Sir George Beaumont, who had originally been advised by his father, but going on to act for Sir Charles Long (later Lord Farnborough), the earls of Darnley and Mulgrave, Sir Abraham Hume, Sir Robert Peel, and the duke of Wellington.

From about 1805—with Beaumont, Grosvenor, Mulgrave, the latter's brother General Edmund Phipps, David Wilkie, John Jackson, and Benjamin Robert Haydon—Seguier came to be part of a convivial group of artists and connoisseurs known to one another as 'the clique'.

Haydon's friendship has been unfortunate for Seguier's subsequent reputation, for the prickly painter convinced himself that Seguier had persuaded George IV not to buy his *Punch, or, May Day* in 1829, and his paranoia broadened this into the conviction that Seguier was the evil genius who had diverted a whole generation of connoisseurs from extending any significant patronage to contemporary British artists. Contrary to Haydon's dark imaginings, however, Seguier seems to have had no agenda of his own, but only the urge to make himself indispensable. Nor do the modest sums realized by the posthumous sales of his collections at Christies in April–May 1844—although his Rembrandt prints were remarkable—suggest that he was venal.

It was Seguier's private clients who helped him to his official career. Beginning as superintendent of the newly founded British Institution in 1805, he successively and concurrently became surveyor of the king's pictures in 1820, and keeper of the new National Gallery in 1824. Haydon alleged that 'His King does nothing without Mr. Seguier's advice' (*Diary*, ed. Pope, 3.455), but this would seem to have been restricted to practical matters of the kind that George IV had consulted him on at Carlton House and Kensington Palace while prince regent. Seguier was continued in the post of surveyor by William IV and Queen Victoria, hanging and publishing a summary catalogue of George IV's pictures in the picture gallery at Buckingham Palace after his death, and, with much less success, re-hanging many of the pictures from Kensington Palace at Hampton Court. At the National Gallery, too, his duties were those of a subordinate of the trustees. Surprisingly perhaps, in view of his original profession, his interpretation of 'attending to the preservation of pictures' never extended to anything more than surface cleaning of them. However, he did re-varnish, and mix the mastic varnish with oil, to combat 'blooming', thus leading to a slow but steady darkening; his brother's removal of the varnish from some pictures after Seguier's death gave rise to the first of many cleaning controversies in which the National Gallery has been embroiled. As keeper of the National Gallery, Seguier was, as his title suggests, an essentially eighteenth-century figure; in striking contrast to the *Kunstgeschichte*-inspired directorate of his ultimate successor, Sir Charles Eastlake. Seguier died on 5 November 1843 at 92 King's Road, Brighton, Sussex.

John Seguier (1785–1856), younger brother and partner of William Seguier, was his successor as superintendent of the British Institution. Born in London in 1785 he attended the Royal Academy Schools from 1807, and he too first practised as a topographical painter; a pair of views of Watson Taylor's house in Cavendish Square was bought back by William at the Erlestoke Park sale in 1832, and *Excavating the Regent's Canal* is in the Yale Center for British Art, New Haven, Connecticut. In his brother's lifetime he carried on the picture-restoring business, but also advised his own clients, notably Daniel Mesman (whose collection was left to the Fitzwilliam Museum, Cambridge, in 1834); after William's death he continued to serve the queen and Sir Robert Peel. His son with Margaret *Seguier [*see under* Stewart, Anthony (1773–1846)], elder daughter of the miniature-painter Anthony Stewart and herself a miniaturist, Frederick Peter (*d.* 1902), was continued in his father's post as picture-restorer in ordinary to the queen, and compiled the idiosyncratic *A Critical and Commercial Dictionary of the Works of Painters* (1870). John Seguier died on 7 June 1856 at 1 Camden Terrace, Camden New Town. ALASTAIR D. LAING

Sources *DNB* · J. Egerton, 'John Jackson RA *William Seguier* (NG6022)', *The British school* (1998), 388–98 · A. Laing, 'William Seguier and advice to picture collectors', *Studies in the history of painting restoration*, ed. C. Sitwell and S. Staniforth (1998), 97–120 · L. Cust, 'William Seguier, first keeper of the National Gallery', *Proceedings of the Huguenot Society*, 8 (1909–11), 157–64 · F. P. Seguier, 'Dictionary of monograms and identified paintings', BL, Add. MS 38799, vol. 45, fol. 42ff · F. P. Seguier, *A critical and commercial dictionary of the works of painters* (1870), 190 · *The diary of Benjamin Robert Haydon*, ed. W. B. Pope, 5 vols. (1960–63), vol. 1, pp. 11, 37, 64, 203–4; vol. 2, pp. 459–60; vol. 3, pp. 12–13, 70–71, 78–9, 93, 163–4, 187, 269–72, 324, 402, 426–31, 453–61, 598, 643–6; vol. 5, pp. 107, 327 · 'Select committee on arts and principles of design and their connexion with manufacturers', *Parl. papers* (1836), 9.284–94, no. 568 · 'Select committee on national monuments and works of art', *Parl. papers* (1841), session 1, 6.127–32, no. 416 · 'Select committee on … the National Gallery', *Parl. papers* (1852–3), 35.viii, 24, 28–9, 90–96, 331–4, 673–5, no. 867 · W. T. Whitley, *Art in England, 1821–1837* (1930), 68–76, 92–3, 103–5, 119–23, 206, 220–23, 270–71 · O. Millar, *The queen's pictures* (1977), 128, 141, 148, 156–62, 188–9, 199 · *The Times* (15 Nov 1843), 3 · *The Athenaeum* (18 Dec 1843), 1028 · *GM*, 2nd ser., 21 (1844), 97–8 · d. cert. · d. cert. [John Seguier]

Likenesses P. Wonder, oils, *c.*1826, priv. coll. · J. Jackson, oils, 1830, National Gallery, London; [painted for George Watson Taylor] · E. H. Baily, marble bust; [lost] · attrib. J. Jackson, oils, NPG · H. W. Pickersgill, kit-cat, priv. coll. · Miss Turner, lithograph (after E. H. Baily), BM

Seguin, Ann Childe (1809x14–1888). *See under* Seguin, Arthur Edward Shelden (1809–1852).

Seguin, Arthur Edward Shelden (1809–1852), singer, was born on 7 April 1809 in London, the son of Arthur Seguin, who was secretary at Her Majesty's Theatre for over fifty years. He was of Irish descent. He was educated at the Royal Academy of Music, from which he narrowly escaped dismissal in 1827 for some breaches of discipline. In that year he attracted attention with his fine singing at a students' public concert in the Hanover Square Rooms. He first appeared in opera as Basilio in Rossini's *The Barber of Seville* at the first dramatic performance of the Royal Academy on 8 December 1828. He sang at the Exeter festival in 1829. On 6 November 1830 he took the part of Ismael in Lord Burghersh's opera *Catherine*, Ann Childe [*see below*], who subsequently became his wife, filling the title role. In 1831 he sang Polyphemus in Handel's *Acis and Galatea* at the Queen's Theatre, Tottenham Street, under the management of George Macfarren, the elder. The following year Seguin was engaged at Drury Lane, where he appeared as Count Rodolfo in *La sonnambula* with Maria Malibran. He sang at Covent Garden (1833–4, 1835–7), and was extremely successful with his performance of Masetto in the revival of Mozart's *Don Giovanni* in February 1833. From 1835 to 1838 he appeared at the King's Theatre and at Drury Lane. On 13 August 1838 he created the part of the Baron in George Macfarren's *The Devil's Opera* at the English Opera House.

Immediately afterwards Seguin left England for America, where he made his début as the Count in W. M. Rooke's *Amilie* on 15 October at the Old National Theatre, New York. In America he formed an opera company, the Seguin Troupe, which toured successfully in both the United States and Canada. Seguin is said to have been elected a chief by an Indian tribe, and given a name meaning 'the man with a deep mellow voice'. He died in White Street, New York on 6 December 1852.

Seguin's wife, **Ann Childe Seguin** (1809x14–1888), was born in London. She was his fellow pupil, and subsequently a sub-professor at the Royal Academy of Music. The couple were married about 1831. They sang together at the Westminster Abbey festival in 1834. She made her Covent Garden début in 1835 as Marcellina in *Fidelio*, supporting Malibran. She was second principal soprano at the King's Theatre for two or three seasons, and in 1837 she sang the part of Donna Anna at Drury Lane in the English version of *Don Giovanni*. In America she continued to perform until her husband's death. After that she devoted herself to teaching music in New York, where she died in August 1888. R. H. LEGGE, *rev.* ANNE PIMLOTT BAKER

Sources *New Grove* • Boase, *Mod. Eng. biog.* • H. Rosenthal, *Two centuries of opera at Covent Garden* (1958) • Grove, *Dict. mus.* • *Overture*, 129 (Dec 1891)

Likenesses woodcut, 1838 • J. H. Bufford, lithograph? (after daguerreotype by Southworth & Hawes) • Fleetwood, lithograph (Ann Childe Seguin) • C. Parsons, lithograph (as Devilshoof in Balf's *The Bohemian Girl*) • Rosenthal, caricature, lithograph (*C-Bass*) • S. N., woodcut bust • bust (Ann Childe Seguin; as Norma) • etching on India paper (Ann Childe Seguin) • lithograph (Ann Childe Seguin) • lithograph (Ann Childe Seguin as the Gypsy Queen) • portrait, repro. in *The Era* (2 Jan 1853), 11 • woodcut (after J. H. Bufford; after Southworth & Hawes)

Seiber, Mátyás György (1905–1960), composer and teacher of music, was born on 4 May 1905 to a musical family in Budapest; his father, Michael Seiber, was a civil engineer, and his mother a piano teacher. In his teens he studied the cello at the Budapest Academy of Music with Adolf Shiffer and composition there with Zoltan Kodály—who was later to defend publicly the music of his young pupil—as, indeed, did Béla Bartók. In his early twenties Seiber was based in Frankfurt am Main, where he started his teaching career and took a class in jazz, the first of its kind, at the Hoch Conservatorium; he also conducted in musical theatres and was cellist of the Lenjewski quartet. At one stage he joined a ship's orchestra as a cellist. With the advent of Hitler, Seiber left Frankfurt in the autumn of 1933 and returned to Budapest; he visited Russia, but went in 1935 to England, where he was to live for the rest of his life. On 12 April 1946 he married a dancing teacher, Lilla Levy (*b.* 1912/13), daughter of Emil Bauer, an architect, and they had a daughter. In 1948 he settled in Caterham, Surrey.

The freelance pattern of Seiber's various activities continued in England. He wrote a ten-volume accordion tutor; he lectured on jazz; and he composed music for cartoon films. In 1942 his central involvement with the English musical scene began when Michael Tippett invited him to teach at Morley College, London; this distinguished and lively evening institute became the focus of his activities for the next fifteen years. He created and directed the Dorian Singers during this time. The première by the Morley College choir and orchestra of Seiber's cantata *Ulysses* in 1949 was not only to make his own name widely known, but it gave the first taste for many English audiences of continental modernism. He remained in closer touch with continental musical life than most of his English contemporaries. He attended the international Bartók festival at Budapest in 1948, and frequently thereafter went abroad for the festivals of the International Society for Contemporary Music, which often included performances of his own music. On a visit to Budapest just before the 1956 uprising he met and befriended the young György Ligeti, whose *Atmosphères* (1961) is dedicated to Seiber's memory.

In 1943 Seiber had helped Francis Chagrin to found the Committee (later Society) for the Promotion of New Music, which was to assist in moulding and encouraging a whole generation of young English composers. After the war he became the best-known—and undoubtedly the best—teacher of composition in England: his pupils included Peter Racine Fricker, Don Banks, Anthony Milner, Ingvar Lidholm, Peter Schat, Hugh Wood, and Anthony Gilbert. His teaching (to quote his own words about Kodály) had 'that curiously compulsive and suggestive power of drawing out from his pupils all their latent ability' (Wood, 110). He would strengthen a pupil's musical logic by continually asking 'why?', and enrich both his culture and technique by referring to a very wide range of music past and present.

Seiber's own music covered a wide range. He wrote a popular song in 1956 which not only was successful but won an award; he wrote film music and incidental music to radio plays; and, on the other hand, he wrote chamber, orchestral, and choral music of high calibre and permanent worth. His lifelong studies in folk-song, his interest in jazz, the abiding influence of his teacher Kodály were all meaningful elements in a mature style which owed much to the absorption and successful synthesis of Bartók and Arnold Schoenberg: his second string quartet and, in particular, his happily Bergian third string quartet bear eloquent witness of this. His small output of orchestral music is mainly for various solo instruments and orchestra: all of it is marked by the high standards of craftsmanship which his music invariably possessed.

Seiber's cantata *Ulysses* is quite rightly his best-known and most widely admired work; his poetic response to James Joyce's marvellous text, his sure feeling (gained through much practical experience) for choral writing, and a gift for glitteringly effective orchestration are here masterfully combined. A later Joyce setting, *Three Fragments* (using a text from *Portrait of the Artist as a Young Man*), is one of a late group of works in which he turned to stricter, more individual methods of organization. Outstanding among these are two works for violin and piano: the powerful *Concert Piece* of 1954 and the violin sonata of 1960. This fine work proved to be his last, and over it hangs the question mark posed by the untimely death of any creative artist. In 1960 Seiber was invited to lecture to South African universities, and it was during this visit that he was killed in a car crash in the Kruger National Park on 24 September. HUGH WOOD

Sources H. Wood, 'Seiber, Mátyás (György)', *New Grove* • *The Times* (27 Sept 1960) • *CGPLA Eng. & Wales* (1960) • m. cert.
Archives SOUND BL NSA, *Mining the archive*, 1995, H6226/2 • BL NSA, performance recordings
Wealth at death £21,517 13*s.* 2*d.*: probate, 21 Nov 1960, *CGPLA Eng. & Wales*

Seilern und Aspang, Count Antoine Edward (**1901–1978**), art historian and collector, was born at Frensham Place, Farnham, Surrey, on 17 September 1901, the youngest of three sons of Count Carl Seilern und Aspang (1866–1940) and his American-born wife, Antoinette, *née* Woerishoffer (1875–1901), who died five days after his birth. Brought up by his adored grandmother Anna Woerishoffer (1850–1931) in New York and Vienna, Seilern was educated at the third district Realgymnasium, Vienna (1912–20), and at the Wiener Handelsakademie (1920–21); he studied engineering at the Technische Hochschule (1922–4). He later worked in the timber industry in Yugoslavia and at banking in Vienna. As a wealthy young nobleman, he was a keen horseman, racehorse owner and breeder, and became a qualified air pilot. He went big game hunting in Africa, Mongolia, Indo-China, and Yukon between 1930 and 1933, and made a world tour in 1930–31.

At the suggestion of his father and his stepmother, Countess Ilse, he enrolled at Vienna University (1933–9) to study principally art history; an art historian family friend, Count Karl Wilczek, recommended him to Johannes Wilde for private tuition, thus beginning a lifelong friendship. His university teachers were Karl Swoboda, Julius Schlosser, and Hans Sedelmayr; but his interest in collecting was prompted by Count Karl Lanckoronski, himself a noted collector. Seilern's doctoral thesis on the Venetian influences on Rubens's ceiling paintings was accepted on 9 June 1939. Like his father and brothers Seilern had dual Austrian and British nationality, but he renounced his Austrian citizenship after the First World War, and was thus able to remove his collection and library (and that of Wilde) from 6 Brahmsplatz, Vienna, to London, in the summer of 1939. Seilern enlisted in the British army, becoming a private in the Pioneer Corps before volunteering for the Russo-Finnish campaign in March–April 1940. After escaping from occupied Norway to Sweden, Seilern joined the Royal Artillery and was eventually commissioned as an interpreter. During the war he acquired the lease of 56 Prince's Gate, South Kensington, London, a gloomy Victorian mansion which was to remain his London home for the rest of his life; he had bought a farm near Chesham, Buckinghamshire, in 1939.

Count Antoine Edward Seilern und Aspang (**1901–1978**), by unknown photographer

On his grandmother's death in 1931 Seilern inherited his share of a large fortune made from railways and the liberal German-language newspaper *New Yorker Staats-Zeitung*. He had begun collecting in the late 1920s, his taste shaped by the collections of the Kunsthistorisches Museum, Vienna, and by his growing interest in Rubens. Guided by Ludwig Burchard and Wilde, to whom he constantly turned for advice, Seilern had by 1939 built up a substantial collection of paintings and drawings: these included the Rubens *Landscape by Moonlight* (which Sir Joshua Reynolds once owned), Rubens's *modelli* for the wings of the Antwerp *Descent from the Cross*; and four *modelli* for the Jesuit church at Aranjuez by his other great love, Giovanni Battista Tiepolo. He eventually owned thirty-two paintings and twenty-two drawings by Rubens, and twelve paintings and twenty-nine drawings by Tiepolo. Superb drawings by Giovanni Bellini, Brueghel, Dürer, Hugo van der Goes, Michelangelo, Rembrandt, Watteau, Degas, Picasso, and Cézanne, as well as by contemporary Austrian artists, indicate the range of his taste, which also extended to Chinese bronzes. His greatest coup was the purchase, in 1942, of *The Entombment with Donor and the Resurrection* by the Master of Flémalle, which had been wrongly auctioned as by Adriaen Isenbrandt; rivalling this in splendour is Bernardo Daddi's *Virgin and Child with Saints*, 1338, which he bought in 1956 from the Collalto family, the only major Florentine work in the collection. In 1950 he commissioned Oskar Kokoschka to paint the three *Prometheus* panels for the ceiling of the anteroom in his Prince's Gate house. Seilern was a very generous benefactor to the museums, notably the National Gallery, London, and the British Museum, but insisted his gifts remain anonymous. He shunned publicity and abhorred dealers, the exception being James Byam Shaw of Colnaghi's, whose scholarship, judgement, and integrity he trusted. Through his friendship with Wilde, by 1948 deputy director of the Courtauld Institute, Seilern decided to bequeath his magnificent collection of 127 paintings and some 300 drawings to the Courtauld, and in deference to his wishes that it was not to bear his name, it is now known as the Prince's Gate collection. Between 1955 and 1971 he privately published a catalogue of his collection in seven volumes.

Of medium height and square-built, Seilern could be, by turns, an ebullient Viennese aristocrat at ease in society and charming to women, or a reclusive, serious scholar, eager to discuss art with other students and scholars, to whom he was generous in showing his 'little collection', as he called it. He amassed his treasures with a keen eye for quality, but was also deeply aware of the historical significance of the works he acquired. He never married, and died of heart disease at 56 Prince's Gate on 6 July 1978. He was buried in Frensham churchyard on 13 July but later exhumed and removed to the family vault at Aspang, south of Vienna. DENNIS FARR

Sources private information (2004) • personal knowledge (2004) • J. B. Shaw, *Burlington Magazine*, 120 (1978), 760–62 • A. Blunt, 'Antoine Seilern: connoisseur in the grand tradition', *Apollo*, 109 (1979), 10–23 • H. Braham, 'Introduction', *The Princes Gate collection* (1981), vii–xv • personal MSS, memorabilia, Courtauld Inst. • S. Hodgart, 'Wonderful windfall', *Sunday Times Magazine* (7 June 1981), 32–9

Archives Courtauld Inst., personal MSS, passports, photographs, and memorabilia

Likenesses photographs, Courtauld Inst., personal MSS [*see illus.*]

Wealth at death £30,836,261: probate, 19 April 1979, *CGPLA Eng. & Wales*

Seiriol [St Seiriol] (*fl.* **6th cent.**), holy man, is the patron of the churches at Penmon (on Anglesey) and Priestholm (an island off the east of Anglesey). His feast is celebrated on 1 February. According to the Welsh saints' genealogies, he was the son of Owain Danwyn, and thereby of local royal stock, and was numbered among the Seven Cousins (notable saints, said to be related). His cult is restricted to Anglesey; and since there is no surviving life (*vita*) or vernacular *buchedd* for Seiriol, information about him is limited to a series of much later traditions of even less reliability than medieval hagiography. These include the tradition, doubtless fictional, that Seiriol held daily meetings with St Cybi of Holyhead at Clorach, which is roughly midway between their respective churches. Accordingly, Seiriol is said to have faced westwards in the morning and eastwards in the afternoon in order to retain his fair complexion, while Cybi would face in the opposite directions to darken his complexion. Hence they became known as 'Seiriol Wyn a Chybi Felyn' ('White Seiriol and Yellow Cybi'). Of equally dubious historical value is the claim, preserved in material from the early seventeenth century, that Seiriol had a causeway built between his hermitage on Priestholm to Penmaen-mawr on the opposite shore on the mainland, and that he cut a passage through the rock at Dwygyfylchi to Llanfairfechan which became known as the King's Highway. It is also difficult to reconstruct a picture of Seiriol by referring to his two main church sites. Indeed, if the tradition that the church at Penmon was founded by the sixth-century king Maelgwn Gwynedd is rejected, then there is no historical record of the site until 971, when it was sacked by vikings. The surviving archaeological record also begins in the tenth century, with three decorated crosses (one now lost) probably constructed *c.*950–1000, and a font from the late tenth or early eleventh century (though this is not definitely associated with Penmon). The holy well at Penmon is probably of a later date and the earliest remaining church-buildings are in twelfth-century Romanesque style. The evidence for Priestholm is even slighter, the earliest reference being that by Gerald of Wales (*d.* 1220x23), stating that it was 'a small island inhabited by hermits' (Gerald of Wales, 190). The main church here is again Romanesque, but there is evidence of an earlier chancel (incorporating a long-cist burial) and a monastic enclosure with two phases of huts or cells. DAVID E. THORNTON

Sources P. C. Bartrum, ed., *Early Welsh genealogical tracts* (1966) • E. Hencken, *Traditions of the Welsh saints* (1987) • P. C. Bartrum, *A Welsh classical dictionary: people in history and legend up to about AD 1000* (1993) • Gerald of Wales, *'The journey through Wales' and 'The description of Wales'*, trans. L. Thorpe (1978)

Selbach (*d.* **730**). *See under* Dál Riata, kings of (*act. c.*500–*c.*850).

Selbie, William Boothby (**1862–1944**), college head and theologian, was born on 24 December 1862 at Chesterfield, the eldest son of Robert William Selbie (1825–1893), Congregational minister, and his wife, Harriet Raine Boothby. He was educated at Manchester grammar school and Brasenose College, Oxford (1882–6), before entering the newly founded Mansfield College as one of its first students in 1886. Here he studied theology under Andrew Martin Fairbairn, whose biography he eventually wrote. He was a contemporary and friend of Silvester Horne, whose biography he also later wrote. After finishing his course in 1889 he remained at the college for a further year as Hebrew tutor.

In 1890 Selbie began pastoral ministry at Highgate Congregational Church in London, where his gifts and power as a preacher began to mature. In 1902 he moved to Cambridge to succeed P. T. Forsyth as minister of Emmanuel Congregational Church, combining this ministry for some years with the teaching of homiletics and pastoral theology at Cheshunt College. From 1899 until 1909 he was also the editor of *The Examiner* (later the *British Congregationalist*).

In 1909 Selbie entered on his most important life's work as principal of Mansfield College, Oxford, in succession to Fairbairn, and remained there for the next twenty-three years. He regarded it as his prime task to educate future preachers, and his frequent comment on student sermons, 'that would not save the soul of a tomtit', was legendary. Though small in stature, his power as a preacher in the pulpit drew large congregations (not confined to nonconformists) from throughout the university and beyond to Sunday morning services in the college chapel, especially in the decade following the end of the First World War. His sermons were marked by forthrightness and common sense as well as by a profound theological and pastoral understanding. His skill as a counsellor and pastor was well known, and a wide variety of people sought his help.

In the college Selbie taught dogmatic and pastoral theology, and for many years his colleague as New Testament professor was C. H. Dodd. His own theological position was and always remained that of a liberal evangelical, but he loved to discuss new developments in theological thinking throughout his life. In 1926 he wrote of the need to 'preach the Christian message in terms which modern man can receive and understand, and yet retain all its saving and sanctifying power' (*Congregational Quarterly*, 1926, 359).

Selbie's reputation in Oxford was such that when divinity degrees were at last opened to non-Anglicans in 1920, for the first time since the seventeenth century, he was the first nonconformist to be honoured with the DD by decree. He served on the university's board of theology, and from 1921 to 1924 was Wilde lecturer, resulting in the publication of his most substantial book, *The Psychology of Religion* (1924), a pioneering study. In 1924 he was the first nonconformist theologian to be appointed an examiner in the university's school of theology. In 1926 he was elected as an honorary fellow of his old college, Brasenose.

Selbie's position at Mansfield College gave him considerable influence within his denomination, an influence which was to increase as he became well known through his preaching and his contributions to the *Christian World*. In 1910 he attended the Edinburgh Missionary Conference, and the following year he organized and edited for publication a series of lectures originally delivered in Mansfield College, entitled *Evangelical Christianity: its History and Witness* (1911). In 1914 he was elected chairman of the Congregational Union of England and Wales and delivered an outstanding address to the assembly in May of that year on the theme 'The church of the redeemed'. He urged his fellow Congregationalists to take the responsibilities of church membership, particularly attendance at church meetings, more seriously, and to understand more clearly what they stood for.

Selbie's participation in the ecumenical movement involved taking the churchmanship of his tradition seriously, and urging others to do the same. In 1921, in the wake of the Lambeth conference of 1920 and its 'appeal to all Christian people', he was chairman of the committee which produced a free church response, and continued in dialogue with Anglican representatives at Lambeth Palace. In 1913 he admitted the first female student to Mansfield, who four years later was the first woman to be ordained to the Christian ministry in Britain (Constance Coltman). He continued to support and encourage such women, and was elected a vice-president of the Society for the Ministry of Women. For some years after 1919 he served on the council of Somerville College.

Selbie's first major publication was *Schleiermacher: a Critical and Historical Study* in 1913. In addition to his work on the psychology of religion, he wrote a number of works on Congregationalism and free church principles, and was a regular contributor to the *Congregational Quarterly*.

In 1890 Selbie had married Mildred Mary Thompson (*b.* 1864, *d.* in or after 1964) of Wilmslow, a woman of powerful personality who presided over the principal's lodgings at Mansfield with great style. They had three sons (the eldest of whom was killed at Ypres in 1916) and one daughter. Selbie retired in 1932 but continued to live in Oxford, where he died at his home, 174 Banbury Road, on 28 April 1944. His funeral was held in the college chapel on 1 May; afterwards he was cremated and his ashes were placed in the college chapel. His wife outlived him for more than twenty years. ELAINE KAYE

Sources *Mansfield College (Oxford) Magazine* (Aug 1944) • E. Kaye, *Mansfield College, Oxford: its origin, history and significance* (1996) • *The Times* (29 April 1944) • *Congregational Quarterly* (1926) • *Congregational Quarterly* (1944) • *Congregational Year Book* (1894) • *Congregational Year Book* (1915) • *Congregational Year Book* (1945) • N. Micklem, *The box and the puppets* (1957) • Mansfield College annual reports, 1886–90 • Mansfield College annual reports, 1910–32 • E. Kaye, *C. J. Cadoux: theologian, scholar and pacifist* (1988) • Cheshunt College, Cambridge, calendar, 1905 • *CGPLA Eng. & Wales* (1944)

Archives Mansfield College, Oxford, archive

Likenesses John Russell & Sons, photograph, *c.*1917, NPG • E. Moore, oils, Mansfield College, Oxford

Wealth at death £1021 2*s.*: probate, 22 Sept 1944, *CGPLA Eng. & Wales*

Selborne. For this title name *see* Palmer, Roundell, first earl of Selborne (1812–1895); Palmer, (Beatrix) Maud, countess of Selborne (1858–1950); Palmer, William Waldegrave, second earl of Selborne (1859–1942); Palmer, Roundell Cecil, third earl of Selborne (1887–1971).

Selby. For this title name *see* Gully, William Court, first Viscount Selby (1835–1909).

Selby family (*per. c.*1520–1646), gentry, probably took their name from denizens of Selby in Yorkshire who migrated northwards to co. Durham and Northumberland in the middle ages. By 1603 there were at least sixteen branches of the family, of which the most notable was that associated successively with Branxton, Twizel, and Berwick. This branch was already established at Branxton, a few miles south-east of Coldstream, when about 1520 William Heron of Ford leased Twizel in Norhamshire (north Durham) to William Selby. At that time Twizel was occupied by John Selby of Grindonrig, a member of another branch of the family. William bought the property in 1525. He was the father of **John Selby of Twizel** (*d.* 1565), whose namesake and son **Sir John Selby** (*d.* 1595) laid the foundations for his family's prosperity. He amassed substantial property in north Durham, Northumberland, and Berwick upon Tweed, at his death holding lands in Berwick itself, Branxton, Shotton, Moneylaws, Pawston, Thornton, Emmothills, Twizel, Tindalhouse, and Wooler, as well as several fisheries in the Tweed, leases of tithes, and half the forest of Cheviot. His descendants held on to these properties during the seventeenth century, but did not accumulate further estates as Sir John had done.

The elder John Selby held the office of gentleman porter of the garrison town of Berwick from 1551 to 1556 and from 1557 to 1565, while his son held it from 1573 to 1595. This was a prestigious office in the borough and enabled the Selbys to control access to the town, though the actual functions of the office were left to deputies. The office was usually granted for life with a salary of £20 per annum and profits from borough revenues. The friendships of the Selbys with neighbouring Scots benefited Anglo-Scottish relations locally, but it also led to John Selby's temporary dismissal from the office of gentleman porter in 1556–7. He was summoned before the council of the north, but the charge was politically motivated and he was later reinstated. The root cause of his difficulties was John's sanctioning of the marriage, in 1556, of his elder son to Margaret Douglas, illegitimate daughter of the Scottish laird George Douglas of Parkhead. Margaret had been staying in Berwick while her father found it politically expedient to be out of Scotland. Nevertheless, cross border marriages were forbidden by border law, and as a senior office-holder upon the English border Selby was seen to be setting a bad example. In truth many flouted this law at lower levels of society, but Selby's rank marked him out for punishment. By all accounts this was a love match and proved to be a very successful marriage in the long term. The new kinship of the Selbys with the powerful Douglas family did them no harm in Scottish circles either. They had seven children, of whom the eldest was Sir William Selby junior [*see below*].

To emphasize their growing importance in the north the Selby coat of arms was listed in the Elizabethan roll of northern heraldry. John Selby was deputy warden of the English east march during 1560–64, while his son held that office 1568–95. Sir John often had to take command of the east march during the long absences of the warden, Henry Carey, Baron Hunsdon. Sir John was frequently a commissioner for the exchequer in local inquiries and sat at many bailiff courts in Berwick. He was also a fully commissioned captain in the Berwick garrison, for which he received £110 per annum. At one time he was captain of the Norham branch of the garrison, but was more usually stationed in Berwick. A JP for north Durham, he was sometimes a special messenger to English ambassadors resident in Scotland, as his safe passage to Edinburgh was always secured by his Scottish friendships.

Sir John Selby went beyond his father's achievements by giving longer service on the frontier, for which he received larger rewards. For example in 1582 he was awarded a lease of lands in Durham forfeited by the sixth earl of Westmorland, and was knighted. His alliances with powerful courtiers like Sir Francis Walsingham and Lord Burghley undoubtedly helped his ascent. When he died in 1595 Sir John left an inventory with goods valued at £374 9*s.*—a large amount for Berwick, though it would not have marked him as a wealthy gentleman in the south of England. In fact in his pursuit of power he was outshone by his younger brother **Sir William Selby senior** (*d.* 1612), first of Shoreswood and later Ightham Mote, Kent. To avoid confusion he was known as William senior when his nephew **Sir William Selby junior** (*c.*1556–1638) came of age. The two Williams held the office of gentleman porter of Berwick jointly after the death of Sir John in 1595 until the union of the crowns led to the abolition of the office in 1603. As a younger son William senior first amassed less property than his elder brother, but instead accumulated short-term leases of tithes in north Durham from the dean and chapter of Durham; these were lucrative in an inflationary era. He also collected rents on behalf of the dean and chapter as one of their local attorneys, and in that capacity was given a lease of Shoreswood manor, tithe corn, and mines in 1584. He bought the rights to other tithes in Northumberland at Humbleton, Earle, and Middleton Hall in 1590, and added those of Berrington and Kyloe in 1601, when he was also appointed keeper of Etal Castle by Queen Elizabeth. He followed Sir John in frequently acting as an exchequer commissioner in local inquiries and was also an active JP.

William Selby senior had a successful military career, first within the Berwick garrison, where he was a captain commanding 100 men, and then further afield in Ireland in the 1570s and the Low Countries in the 1580s. He was knighted by the earl of Leicester during the 1586 expedition to the Low Countries. By 1591 the influence he had gained from his family's associations with Lord Burghley enabled him to gain the mortgage of the lucrative estate of Ightham Mote in Kent from George Aleyn, and a year later he bought Ightham Mote outright, together with Aleyn's debts, for £4000. William went on to acquire further lands in Kent while still maintaining a presence in the borders as comptroller of the office of ordnance in the north parts. In addition he was master of the ordnance at Berwick and a captain pensioner at the rate of 5*s.* per day for his long service, which was not, however, always without controversy. In 1597 as part of a long-standing bloodfeud between the Selbys and the Grays he personally came to blows with Edward Gray of Morpeth (the deputy warden of the middle march) in a churchyard, during a brawl in which a man was killed. Nevertheless he was MP for Berwick in 1588, 1601, and 1604; the fact that he held lands near to London must have made it easier for him to perform his parliamentary duties. He never married and died at Ightham in 1612, to be succeeded by his nephew, William junior.

As uncle and nephew, William Selby senior and William Selby junior worked as an effective team in Berwick after the death of Sir John in 1595. When William senior was absent William junior continued to run the office of gentleman porter of the garrison and reported events to his influential uncle. And he too became MP for Berwick, being returned in 1593, 1597, and 1614. He went on to become sheriff of Northumberland in 1603–4, 1606–7, and 1616–17. It was not surprising that he should have been knighted by King James VI and I at Berwick on the latter's journey south to London in 1603, a fitting reward, it might seem, for the exemplary service which the Selbys had given on the Anglo-Scottish frontier. The fact that William junior had personally delivered the keys of Berwick to the king at Holyroodhouse on 27 March 1603 doubtless also helped. William junior married Dorothy Bonham of Kent and died on 14 February 1638 at Ightham, Kent, where he was buried.

The end of the frontier did not diminish the power of the Selbys, as they remained major landowners within north Durham. Even William junior's younger brothers Sir Ralph Selby and Sir John Selby made their mark by obtaining important offices after 1603. Sir Ralph was sheriff of Northumberland during 1613–14 and mayor of Berwick in 1631. Sir John's career had a shaky start for, much to the horror of his siblings, he joined the second earl of Essex's rebellion in 1601, apparently because he was infatuated with a lady close to Essex. But thanks to the intervention of his kin and their political allies John's sentence of execution was commuted to a 100 mark fine. His pardon was complete when he was knighted at Greenwich in 1604. He later served in the army of the king's brother-in-law, Christian IV of Denmark, before returning to Berwick, for which he was MP in 1621 and 1625.

The Berwick line overshadowed all the other branches of the Selby family outside Newcastle. Of these the most important were those of Biddlestone and Grindonrig. The former held one moiety of Biddlestone by the early sixteenth century, purchasing the other half from the Delavals of Seaton Delaval in 1576. They also bought and sold property at Newton in Alwinton over several generations. But though Selbys of Biddlestone were listed as jurors for inquisitions post mortem in 1546 and 1598, the fact that they were recusants probably prevented their holding local office of any consequence, and they did not advance beyond the status of gentlemen. The Selbys of Grindonrig had only a little tower there in 1541, and were forced to mortgage half of Grindonrig to their kinsman John Selby of Twizel in 1554, though presumably they later redeemed it. The William Selby who was an overseer of east march enclosures in 1561 was a member of this family. Grindonrig eventually passed to the Strothers of Kirknewton, through the marriage to John Strother in 1612 of Elizabeth, the likely sister and eventual heir of George Selby (*d.* 1646). MAUREEN M. MEIKLE

Sources PRO, patent rolls C66; chancery inquisitions post mortem series II, C142; state papers domestic: addenda, SP15; state papers borders, SP 59 · BL, Cotton MS Caligula C · CKS, Selby MS U947 · *Calendar of the manuscripts of the most hon. the marquis of Salisbury*, 24 vols., HMC, 9 (1883–1976) · *CSP Scot.*, *1547–1603* · J. Bain, ed., *Calendar of letters and papers relating to the affairs of the borders of England and Scotland*, 2 vols. (1894–6) · *CSP dom.*, 1547–1625 · *CSP for.*, 1558–89 · M. M. Meikle, 'Lairds and gentlemen: a study of the landed families of the Eastern Anglo-Scottish Borders, *c.*1540–1603', PhD diss., U. Edin., 1989 · E. Bateson and others, eds., *A history of Northumberland*, 15 vols. (1893–1940) · parish registers, Berwick and Holy Island, Northumbd RO, 647 · Northumbd RO, Delavel (Horsley) papers, 1DE · Berwick RO, guild minute books, B1/1; enrolment memoranda books, B6 · U. Durham L., archives and special collections, Durham probate records, wills, 1551–7, 1560–69, 1588, 1595; Mickelton and Spearman MS, vol. 6 · [J. Raine, W. Greenwell, and others], eds., *Wills and inventories from the registry at Durham*, 4 pts, SurtS, 2, 38, 112, 142 (1835–1929) · J. Anderson, ed., *Calendar of the Laing charters, AD 854–1837* (1899) · *LP Henry VIII*, vols. 1–21 · *The state papers and letters of Sir Ralph Sadler*, ed. A. Clifford, 2 vols. (1809) · *APC*, *1542–1604* · S. J. Watts, *From border to middle shire: Northumberland, 1586–1625* (1975) · J. Raine, *The history and antiquities of north Durham* (1852), 315, 338 · D. Home, *A history of the house and race of Douglas and Angus* (1657) · *Heraldic visitation of the northern counties in 1530, by Thomas Tonge*, ed. W. H. D. Longstaffe, SurtS, 41 (1863) · A. Hughes, *List of sheriffs for England and Wales: from the earliest times to AD 1831*, PRO (1898) · HoP, *Commons*, *1558–1603* · *CPR*, *1558–93* · dean and chapter registers, Durham Cath. CL, vols. 1–6

Archives Northumbd RO, deeds and estate papers · W. Yorks. AS, deeds and other papers

Wealth at death Sir John Selby (*d.*1595) left goods valued at £374 9*s.*: U. Durham L., Durham probate records wills, 1595

Selby, Charles [*real name* George Henry Wilson] (*c.*1802–1863), actor and playwright, was in 1832, as Charles Selby, a member of the company at the Strand Theatre, and two years later produced a farce, *The Unfinished Gentleman*, at the Adelphi. He worked out the idea of this piece in a series of papers which appeared in the *Sunday Times* and were reprinted with illustrations by Thomas Onwhyn in 1841 as *Maximums and Speciments of William Muggins, Natural Philosopher and Man of the World*. From the quasi-autobiographical revelations in this work (which is in the main a dull and unskilful imitation of the earlier style of Charles Dickens) it appears that Selby was self-educated, had visited Barbados, and had some nautical experience. He worked with his wife, Clara (1796/7–1873)—whose real name was Sarah Susannah—under W. C. Macready at Drury Lane during the 1841–2 season.

During his thirty years as an actor and playwright Selby performed principally character parts and supplied a long series of plays, mainly farces and burlettas—about ninety in all, according to Allardyce Nicoll—many of which were adapted from the French. Among his most successful pieces were *Robert Macaire* (1836), a three-act melodrama which had a long life on the stage and became one of Henry Irving's stock pieces. *Barnaby Rudge* (1841) was a dramatization of Dickens's novel, put on the stage midway through the novel's serial publication; Dickens was irritated by this, but wrote to Selby that 'if I could give you a patent for dramatizing my productions I would gladly do so; inasmuch as if they *must* be done at all, I would rather have them done by gentlemanly hands' (*Letters of Charles Dickens*, 2.333). Most of Selby's dramatic output consisted of one-act pieces of a light and pleasant nature, and several were included in Duncombe's, Webster's, and Lacy's collections of plays. In works such as *The Valet de Sham* (1838), *Powder and Ball! or, St Tibb's Eve!* (1845, a 'terpsichorean burletta'), *Taken in and done for* (1849), and *The Pirates of Putney* (1863, a 'nautical extravaganza'), Selby provided a considerable number of successful vehicles for himself and his fellow actors, including Frederick Yates, Edward Wright, Henry Compton, Robert and Mary Ann Keeley, Louisa Nisbett, and Harriet Waylett. He was a useful actor, with a good stage presence. He also published a school textbook, *Events to be Remembered in the History of England* (1851), which ran through many editions, and a skit, *The Dinner Question, by Tabitha Tickletooth* (1860). He died of dropsy and ague at his home, 17 Henrietta Street, Covent Garden, on 21 March 1863, and was buried in Kensal Green cemetery.

Selby was survived by his wife, a competent actress who specialized in middle-aged and elderly characters. After Selby's death she took pupils who wanted to go on the stage: they included Ada Cavendish. Clara Selby died on 8 February 1873.

JOSEPH KNIGHT, *rev.* KLAUS STIERSTORFER

Sources *N&Q*, 8th ser., 9 (1896), 211–12 • *The life and reminiscences of E. L. Blanchard, with notes from the diary of Wm. Blanchard*, ed. C. W. Scott and C. Howard, 2 vols. (1891) • *The Era* (22 March 1863) • *Era Almanack and Annual* [various] • Hall, *Dramatic ports.* • A. Nicoll, *A history of English drama, 1660–1900*, 6 vols. (1923–59) • *The letters of Charles Dickens*, ed. M. House, G. Storey, and others, 2 (1969) • *CGPLA Eng. & Wales* (1863)

Likenesses H. Watkins, albumen print, 1855–9, NPG

Wealth at death under £600: probate, 15 April 1863, *CGPLA Eng. & Wales*

Selby, John, of Twizel (*d.* 1565). *See under* Selby family (*per.* *c.*1520–1646).

Selby, Sir John (*d.* 1595). *See under* Selby family (*per.* *c.*1520–1646).

Selby, Prideaux John (1788–1867), naturalist, was born in Bondgate Street, Alnwick, Northumberland, on 23 July 1788, the eldest son of George Selby (*d.* 1804) of Beal and Twizell House, Northumberland, and Margaret, the second daughter of John Cook, a captain in the mercantile marine. The Selby family settled at Beal in 1588 and took a prominent part in the life of Northumberland and the borders.

Selby showed a great interest in ornithology from an early age and made his own notes and careful, coloured drawings of the birds in his district. He attended Durham grammar school, and was prepared, by private tuition, for University College, Oxford. He matriculated on 3 May 1806, but left after a few terms. He went to live at Twizell House, near Belford, Northumberland, in 1809. The following year, on 17 December, at Morpeth, he married Lewis Tabitha (1782–1859), the third daughter of Bertram and Tabitha Mitford of Mitford Manor; they had three daughters.

Selby took an active part in the social and political life of Northumberland. He served as a magistrate, as deputy lieutenant in 1817, and in 1823 as high sheriff for his county. He unsuccessfully contested Berwick at the general election, as a reformer, in 1812. However, his main interests were ornithology, forestry, and entomology. He was a skilful fisherman and an excellent shot. Selby's major work, *Illustrations of British Ornithology*, was published in nineteen parts between 1821 and 1833. It contained some 222 plates etched by Selby (mostly after his own drawings) with the assistance of his brother-in-law Admiral Robert Mitford. In 1819 Mitford was taught to etch by Thomas Bewick in Newcastle; he then taught Selby at Twizell House. Two volumes of text appeared, *Land Birds* in 1825 (revised in 1833) and *Water Birds* in 1833. The specimens on which the figures were based were nearly all collected and set up by Selby, aided by his butler, Richard Moffitt.

From 1825 until 1841 Selby assisted his friend Sir William Jardine (1800–1874) with the descriptions, drawings, and etchings for their joint publication, *Illustrations of Ornithology* (1836–43). During this period, in 1835 and 1836 respectively, he also wrote the volumes *Pigeons* and *Parrots* for Jardine's Naturalist's Library. Together, in conjunction with George Johnston, Selby and Jardine founded the *Magazine of Zoology and Botany* in 1836, which was widened in scope in 1838 when the name was changed to *Annals of Natural History*. Selby remained an editor until his death, contributing notes and articles up to 1841. He joined the Berwickshire Naturalists' Club soon after it was founded in 1831 and served as its president in 1834 and again in 1844. Between 1832 and 1859 he contributed many papers to the *History of the Berwickshire Naturalists' Club*. Further papers were published in other journals between 1823 and 1838.

In 1833 Selby joined a numerous party of students, led by Robert Graham and Robert Kaye Greville, on a tour through Sutherland. The following year he encouraged Jardine and his brother John, Greville, and James Wilson of Edinburgh to go to Sutherland in order to make a more extensive study of the fauna and flora of this largely unknown region. Selby kept detailed records of the fishes, insects, birds, and mammals seen on the tour, and painted some of the fishes in oils.

Selby also made contributions to entomology from the mid-1830s. He promoted the use of trees and straw bee skeps brushed over with sugar solutions in order to attract insects for collection. Selby collected lepidoptera, coleoptera, and hymenoptera—the last group then little studied.

Selby exhibited several paintings at the Royal Scottish Academy, of which he was elected an honorary member in 1827. He became a fellow of the Linnean Society in 1826 and intermittently attended meetings of the British Association for the Advancement of Science from 1833 onwards. In 1839 the University of Durham conferred on him the honorary degree of master of arts.

Selby's knowledge of botany and particularly of arboriculture was extensive. His practical experience in planting up hundreds of acres of ground at Twizell House with many varieties of trees, often recently imported, resulted in his being asked by Van Voorst to write a treatise on the subject, published as *A History of British Forest Trees Indigenous and Introduced* (1841–2).

Selby died at Twizell House on 27 March 1867, and was buried in Bamburgh churchyard. His family regularly attended St Aidan's Church, where there is a memorial window to Selby and his wife, donated by Frances Margaret Antrobus. Selby's collection of coleoptera, hymenoptera, aculeata, and lepidoptera was presented to the University of Cambridge. His collections of 1400 foreign bird skins, including several type specimens, and eggs, were also presented to the university. His collection of British birds was purchased by A. H. Browne of Callaly Castle, but has not survived. CHRISTINE E. JACKSON

Sources C. E. Jackson, *Prideaux John Selby: a gentleman naturalist* (1992) • L. Jenyns, *Reminiscences of Prideaux John Selby and Twizell House* (1885) • *Proceedings of the Linnean Society of London* (1867), xxvii • R. Embleton, 'Memoir of P. J. Selby', *History of the Berwickshire Naturalists' Club*, 5 (1868), 336–8 • *GM*, 3rd ser., 6 (1859), 548

Archives Bath Royal Literary and Scientific Institution, letters to Leonard Blomefield • Linn. Soc., letters • Northumbd RO, Newcastle upon Tyne, MSS • U. Newcastle, fauna of Twizell | CUL, corresp. with Sir William Jardine

Likenesses E. Hastings, oils, *c.*1810, Marshall Hall • T. H. Maguire, lithograph, *c.*1850, BM, NPG; repro. in T. H. Maguire, *Portraits of honorary members of the Ipswich Museum* (1852) • J. Moffat, photograph, *c.*1860, repro. in Jackson, *Prideaux John Selby* • engraving, RS

Wealth at death under £6000: probate, 21 May 1867, *CGPLA Eng. & Wales*

Selby [Salesby], **Robert of** (*fl.* **1137–1151**), administrator, was an Englishman who became chancellor of the newly founded Norman kingdom of Sicily. He was said by John of Hexham to have originated from 'Salesbia', which has sometimes been understood to indicate Salisbury, but more often Selby in Yorkshire. The case for the former is weakened by the lack of interest shown in a common origin by John of Salisbury, who knew Robert personally, and all authorities since Kehr, Caspar, and Chalandon, in the early years of the twentieth century, have called him Robert of Selby. John of Hexham and John of Salisbury noted his wealth, power, and generosity within Roger II's entourage. Several other Englishmen were employed at the Norman Sicilian court, most notably Thomas Brown, mentioned in the *Dialogus de Scaccario* (who may have been a protégé of Robert).

According to John of Hexham, Robert of Selby gave his help to William Fitzherbert, archbishop of York, in 1147, when his fellow Yorkshireman was in Italy hoping to rebuild his chaotic ecclesiastical career. He had taken over the office of chancellor from Guarinus, who died on 21 January 1137, during the joint German–Pisan invasion of southern Italy, assuming with some success Guarinus's role in the defence of Salerno and Campania against the invaders. By surrendering the city but not the castle of Salerno to the enemy he lured the Pisans into a truce with Roger II that served their commercial interests.

Assisted by a *magister capellanus* (who might eventually aspire to the chancellorship), the chancellor headed the office producing royal privileges, particularly those few that were issued in Latin. A particular concern of Guarinus and of Selby may have been the integration of the old Lombard writing office on the mainland into the largely Greek and Arabic secretariat based in Palermo. By 28 April 1140 Selby was functioning in Palermo as chancellor; later charters of Roger II show him moving northwards to Chieti (August 1140) and to Ariano (July 1142): after this he accompanied the king into Marsia and other disputed lands in central Italy. In late 1143 Selby responded to complaints that the Marsian lords were impinging on the rights of local communities; nevertheless, he tricked the Beneventans into the surrender of a charter securing them royal protection, and the archbishop of Benevento, on his way to complain at the papal curia, was taken captive by his agents; by March 1144 Selby was back in Palermo. He was responsible for the document in which the king provided the cathedral of Cefalù with two sarcophagi in 1145, but he was often away from Palermo; in November 1147 he was at Salerno and at Terracina, in the king's entourage, where he remained until at least 1149, to judge from Roger II's charters and other evidence. He appears to have exercised particular authority on the mainland. In 1149 he commanded troops that were instrumental in securing the return of Pope Eugenius III to St John Lateran, and presided over a great parliament at Melfi.

John of Salisbury tells how Selby tricked three simoniac priests into making bids for the see of Avellino, but arranged for the election instead of a poor monk; the priests were still forced to pay, and the profit went to the crown. More generally, John of Salisbury portrays him as a clever-witted, shrewd figure, able with words and most capable of earning respect for his skills, and J. J. Norwich has built on this to suggest that he was a cheerful and extrovert character, whose greatest achievement was the silence of the chronicles while he steadily built up royal control across the kingdom, and strengthened the administration. He also lived lavishly, accumulating great wealth which he was not averse to spending. His tolerance for alcohol seems far to have exceeded that of John of Salisbury, who later regretted his frequent drinking bouts with Selby. The date of his death is uncertain. Takayama and Matthew consider that he died in 1151, and it is generally argued that Maio di Bari, the next chancellor, was in position before Roger II died in February 1154.

D. S. H. ABULAFIA

Sources C. R. Brühl, ed., *Rogerii II regis diplomata Latina* (1987) • *Alexandri Telesini abbatis Ystoria Rogerii regis Sicilie Calabrie atque Apulie*, ed. D. Clementi and L. De Nava (1991) • *Romualdi Salernitani chronicon*, ed. C. A. Garufi, 1 (Città di Castello, 1914) • John of Hexham, 'Chron. Haugustaldensibus', *Gesta Federici I. imperatoris in Lombardia*, ed. O. Holder-Egger, MGH Scriptores Rerum Germanicarum, [27] (Hanover, 1892), 15 • *Ioannis Saresberiensis episcopi Carnotensis policratici, sive, de nugis curialium et vestigiis philosophorum libri VIII*, ed. C. C. J. Webb, 2 (1909), 173–4, 270–71 • *The letters of John of Salisbury*, ed. and trans. H. E. Butler and W. J. Millor, rev. C. N. L. Brooke, OMT, 1: *The early years, 1153–1161* (1986), 57–8, 255

[Lat. orig. with parallel Eng. text] • K. A. Kehr, *Urkunden der normannisch-sizilischen Könige* (1902), 49, 75–7 • E. Caspar, *Roger II* (1904) • F. Chalandon, *Histoire de la domination normande en Italie*, 2 (1907), 74, 112, 638 • M. Caravale, *Il regno normanno di Sicilia* (1966) • D. J. A. Matthew, *The Norman kingdom of Sicily* (1992), 210 • L. J. A. Loewenthal, 'For the biography of Walter Ophamil, archbishop of Palermo', *EngHR*, 87 (1972), 75–82 • H. Takayama, *The administration of the Norman kingdom of Sicily* (1993) • J. J. Norwich, *The kingdom in the sun* (1970), 52–3, 108–9, 146, 170

Selby, Thomas Gunn (1846–1910), missionary in China, born at New Radford near Nottingham on 5 June 1846, was the son of William Selby, who was engaged in the lace trade, and his wife, Mary Gunn. He was educated at private schools at Nottingham and Derby. At the age of sixteen he preached his first sermon, and in 1865 he became a student at the Wesleyan Methodist Richmond College.

In 1867 Selby entered the Wesleyan ministry, and in the following year he left England to become a missionary in China. He remained there for the greater part of fifteen years. Until 1876 he was in charge of the Wesleyan mission at Fatshan (Foshan), Canton (Guangzhou) province, a centre of anti-European hostility, which delayed the establishment of a mission. Selby attempted to introduce a rigid system of itinerancy, abandoned in the face of other missionaries' opposition. After returning to Britain for eighteen months, he began in 1878 the North River Mission at Shiukwan, inland from Canton. He travelled extensively, seeking to extend missionary activity inland. He once had to spend a month on the island of Hainan disguised as a native. Selby also travelled in India, Palestine, and Egypt. He made a close study of the Chinese language and wrote a 'Life of Christ' (about 1890) in Chinese, which was used for many years as a textbook in missionary colleges. Selby was a combative and non-conciliatory missionary, and 'often gave rise to great vexation of spirit' (Findlay and Holdsworth, 5.452).

After returning to Britain in 1882, Selby was a pastor in various circuits: at Liverpool (1883), Hull (1886), Greenock (1889), Liverpool (1892), and Dulwich (1895–8). He was a successful preacher and sermon writer, many of his sermons being published. *The Holy Writ and Christian Privilege* (1894) was accorded in many circles the rank of a Christian classic. Selby also published in 1895 some translations of Chinese stories, entitled *The Chinaman in his Own Stories*. His work was recognized in the Wesleyan ministry by his election to the legal hundred in 1891 and his appointment as Fernley lecturer in 1896.

In 1898 Selby became a 'minister without pastoral charge'. Living at Bromley, in Kent, he devoted himself to preaching and writing, and in his *Chinamen at Home* (1900) and *As the Chinese See Us* (1901) showed much insight and local knowledge. He was for twenty-five years a member of the Anti-Opium Society and a zealous advocate of the temperance cause.

Selby married, in 1885, Catharine, youngest daughter of William Lawson, of Otley, in Wharfedale, Yorkshire. They had one son and five daughters. Selby died at his residence, Basil House, 22 Oaklands Road, Bromley, Kent, on 12 December 1910, his wife surviving him.

S. E. Fryer, *rev.* H. C. G. Matthew

Sources *The Times* (15 Dec 1910) • *WWW* • G. G. Findlay and W. W. Holdsworth, *The history of the Wesleyan Methodist Missionary Society*, 5 vols. (1921–4) • *CGPLA Eng. & Wales* (1911)

Wealth at death £1533 3*s*. 7*d*.: probate, 6 March 1911, *CGPLA Eng. & Wales*

Selby, Walford Dakin (1845–1889), archivist and historian, was born at home on 16 June 1845, the eldest son of Thomas Selby of Whitley and Wimbush Hall, Essex, and his wife, Elizabeth, youngest daughter and coheir of Ralph Foster of Holderness, Yorkshire. His great-great-grandfather had taken the name Selby by royal licence in 1783, but the family name was originally Browne, and they claimed descent from the Brownes, viscounts Montagu. Selby once pursued a claim to that dormant peerage, but abandoned it as he was unable to prove a marriage on which the claim rested. He was educated successively at Brighton College, Tonbridge School, and with Dr Stromberg at Bonn, where he studied German and French.

In 1867 Selby became a junior clerk in the Public Record Office, where he ultimately became superintendent of the literary search-room. In 1882 his standing in the antiquarian world was recognized by a pay rise of £50 a year. In 1883, in conjunction with his friend James Greenstreet, he founded the Pipe Roll Society, of which he was director-in-chief and honorary treasurer until his death. At the Public Record Office he was known for his courtesy and a minute knowledge of the records under his charge. From 1884 to April 1889 he edited *The Genealogist*, and he was a frequent contributor to *The Athenaeum*, *The Academy*, *The Antiquary*, *Antiquarian Magazine*, and other periodicals. His papers on *The Robbery of Chaucer at Hatcham* and *Chaucer as Forester of North Petherton* (1886) were published in a series of *Life-Records of Chaucer*, which he edited for the Chaucer Society from 1875. He compiled *The Jubilee Date Book* (1887) and edited *Lancashire and Cheshire Records*, (2 pts, 1882–3), and *Norfolk Records*, with Walter Rye (1886). In 1875 he published a second edition of the *Book of Rules and Tables for Verifying Dates* by his colleague John Bond. At the time of his death he was preparing a new edition of the Red Book of the Exchequer, which was completed by Hubert Hall, an edition of Queen Elizabeth's manuscript translation of Boethius's *De consolatione philosophiae*, and a new index to the *Inquisitiones post mortem*. He contracted typhoid fever in November 1888 and died at his home, 9 Clyde Street, Redcliffe Gardens, South Kensington, on 3 August 1889. It was suggested that the fever had been caused by poor sanitary conditions at the Public Record Office. He was buried on 8 August 1889 at Kensal Green cemetery.

A. F. Pollard, *rev.* G. H. Martin

Sources *The Athenaeum* (1894), 194, 224 • L. T. Smith, *The Academy* (17 Aug 1889), 103 • E. Walford, 'The late Mr Walford D. Selby', *The Genealogist*, new ser., 6 (1889–90), 65–8 • J. D. Cantwell, *The Public Record Office, 1838–1958* (1991)

Archives U. Edin. L., corresp. with James Halliwell-Phillipps

Wealth at death £1453 2*s*. 7*d*.: resworn probate, March 1890, *CGPLA Eng. & Wales* (1889)

Selby, Sir Walford Harmood Montague (1881–1965), diplomatist and author, was born at 18 Alfred Place, Kensington, London, on 19 May 1881, the elder son of Charles

Edward Montague Selby, of 48 Sussex Square, Brighton, and his wife, Ellen Maria, *née* Banner. He was educated at Charterhouse School and at Christ Church, Oxford, where he passed a preliminary examination in jurisprudence but failed to take a degree. His contemporaries at Christ Church included two future secretaries of state for foreign affairs, Lord Halifax and Sir Samuel Hoare.

Selby entered the diplomatic service as an attaché in May 1904, but moved shortly afterwards to the Foreign Office as a clerk. He reverted to the diplomatic service once more to serve as third secretary in Berlin and then The Hague. On his return to the Foreign Office in April 1908 he became secretary to the Government Hospitality Fund. During 1910–11 he held the important post of secretary to George V's coronation committee, thus beginning a close association with the royal family which lasted throughout his career. He served as gold staff officer at the coronation of George V in 1911, receiving as a consequence the Coronation Medal and appointment as MVO.

In July 1911 Selby was appointed assistant private secretary to the foreign secretary, Sir Edward Grey. On 17 September 1912 he married, at St Paul's Church, Knightsbridge, Dorothy Orme (*b*. 1889/90), daughter of William Orme Carter, of The Lodge, Hurst Green, Sussex. They had two sons and one daughter. The elder son, Ralph Walford Selby, was also to join the diplomatic service.

When war broke out in 1914 Selby was anxious to leave the Foreign Office and join the army but he was not allowed to do so. From October 1917 to July 1918 he served as private secretary to Lord Robert Cecil, parliamentary under-secretary at the Foreign Office and minister of blockade. The Foreign Office's reluctance to allow its trained diplomats to leave the service was understandable, but ultimately Selby was allowed to join the Grenadier Guards as a second lieutenant, although by August 1918 there was little time left for him to see active service.

During his absence in the army Selby had been promoted to be an assistant clerk, and in November 1919 he became first secretary and head of chancery at the Cairo residency. He remained in this post until January 1922 when he began a new and important phase of his career on his return to the Foreign Office.

Selby was now well thought of, and in February 1924 he was selected to be private secretary to the first Labour prime minister, Ramsay MacDonald, who acted as his own foreign secretary. He continued to serve as private secretary to the foreign secretary until October 1932. He was one of those in the Foreign Office who advised Austen Chamberlain about the Locarno agreement in 1925, and was earmarked for promotion. He was made a CVO in November 1924, a CB in January 1926, and a KCMG in June 1931, but he never received a major embassy after his eight-year stint as principal private secretary, and a major memorandum he wrote in 1931 about Anglo-German relations was ignored by the Foreign Office.

In July 1933 Selby was appointed minister in Vienna, an obvious disappointment, as it was not one of the major embassies. But he was a success there as a doughty defender of Austrian independence who did his best to warn the British cabinet against allowing Austria's absorption by Nazi Germany. It was while he was posted to Vienna that Selby renewed his close acquaintance with the royal family, for it was to that city that the duke of Windsor went after his abdication. Selby met the duke at Vienna station and reported him as 'looking less tired than I had expected after the terrific strain through which he must have passed' (Selby to Godfrey Thomas, cited in Ziegler, 338). The duke then stayed with the Rothschilds, and Selby was advised to stay away from his wedding when it took place in Paris. Lady Selby did, however, attend.

Selby's posting in Vienna ended in December 1937 and he was then sent as ambassador to Lisbon. He remained in Portugal until December 1940 and his retirement from the service. Yet again his path crossed that of the duke of Windsor, who fled to Lisbon in 1940 after being forced to leave France by the German invasion. Selby did all he could to make the party welcome, but was undoubtedly embarrassed by rumours that the duke was about to launch a unilateral peace initiative. Robust diplomacy by Winston Churchill then forced the Windsors to leave for the Bahamas.

Selby remained embittered into retirement. His memoir, *Diplomatic Twilight* (1953), was arguably the most controversial written by a diplomatist in the post-war era. His main claim was that after 1931 'the Diplomatic Service lost its position. To all intents and purposes, it was never consulted' (Selby, 138). This, Selby claimed, was because the permanent under-secretary at the Treasury, Warren Fisher, influenced diplomatic appointments and exercised an unhealthy influence. As a result British foreign policy in the 1930s was misconceived, and Selby accused Lord Vansittart, the former permanent under-secretary at the Foreign Office from 1930 to 1937, of condoning the *Anschluss*, and encouraging the Sudeten leader Konrad Henlein to believe that Britain and France would never intervene to help Czechoslovakia. An infuriated Vansittart threatened to sue Selby for libel, and a parliamentary question in the House of Commons resulted in Vansittart's being exonerated from the charges in Selby's book. It was a sad end to a distinguished career. Selby, who had emigrated to Southern Rhodesia after the war, died in Salisbury, Southern Rhodesia, on 7 August 1965.

PETER NEVILLE

Sources W. Selby, *Diplomatic twilight, 1930–1940* (1953) • P. Ziegler, *King Edward VIII: the official biography* (1990) • E. L. Woodward and others, eds., *Documents on British foreign policy, 1919–1939*, 2nd ser., 18 (1980) • B. McKercher, 'Old diplomacy and new', *Diplomacy and world power*, ed. M. Dockrill and B. McKercher (1996) • N. Henderson, *Water under the bridges* (1945) • PRO, N. Henderson, personal file, FO 794/10 • M. Gilbert, *Sir Horace Rumbold* (1973) • Lord Vansittart [R. G. Vansittart], *The mist procession: the autobiography of Lord Vansittart* (1958) • CAC Cam., Vansittart MSS, VNST II/1/50 • *The Times* (9 Aug 1965) • b. cert. • m. cert. • Burke, *Peerage*

Archives Bodl. Oxf., corresp. and papers | BL, corresp. with Lord Cecil, Add. MS 51090 • CAC Cam., Vansittart MSS, VNST II/1/50 • HLRO, corresp. with Viscount Davidson • PRO, Nevile Henderson MSS, FO 800 265/266/267/268 • PRO NIre., letters to Lord Londonderry • U. Leeds, Brotherton L., corresp. with Sir Henry Legge-Bourke

Likenesses W. Stoneman, photograph, 1938, NPG

Selby, Sir William, senior (*d.* 1612). *See under* Selby family (*per. c.*1520–1646).

Selby, Sir William, junior (*c.*1556–1638). *See under* Selby family (*per. c.*1520–1646).

Selden, John (1584–1654), lawyer and historical and linguistic scholar, was born on 16 December 1584 and baptized on 20 December at West Tarring, Sussex, the eldest son of John Selden of Salvington in the same county, musician and yeoman, and of Margaret, only daughter and heir of Thomas Baker of Rustington, Kent, gentleman. He had two brothers who died in infancy and a sister, Mary. In 1609 his father held over 80 acres with an annual value of £23 5*s*.

Early career, friends, and publications After attending the prebendal free school in Chichester, on 24 October 1600 Selden matriculated from Hart Hall, Oxford. He was admitted to Clifford's Inn in 1602 and to the Inner Temple in November 1603. Doubtless helped by the 'humanity, courtesy and affability' of his courtly manners, on which the earl of Clarendon later remarked (Clarendon, 1759, 1.31), Selden made a number of important friends and became well connected in London antiquarian and literary circles. His first close friend was Edward Heyward of Reepham, Norfolk, admitted to the Inner Temple a year later than he. By about 1610 Heyward had erected a row of sixteen chambers, and he and Selden shared rooms on the top storey until 1620, when Selden took over the whole suite. Adjoining the Inner Temple grounds was Whitefriars, the London house of his earliest patrons, Sir Henry Grey (1583–1639), and his wife, Lady Elizabeth Grey (1582–1651) [*see* Grey, Elizabeth, countess of Kent], sister-in-law of another patron, Thomas Howard, earl of Arundel. Selden also formed an early and lasting friendship with Sir Robert Bruce Cotton, more than a decade his senior, for whom he acted as a copyist and to whose extensive library he had access. Others of his circle included John Donne, Edward Herbert, Lord Herbert of Cherbury, Samuel Daniel, the herald Augustine Vincent, and the travel writer Samuel Purchas.

Even as Selden engaged in the study of common law, he began scholarly research and writing in other fields. According to Anthony Wood, it was in London rather than in Oxford that Selden acquired his formidable linguistic competence: French, German, Spanish, Italian, Latin, Greek, Old English, Hebrew, Chaldean, Samaritan, Aramaic, Arabic, Persian, and Ethiopic were all cited in his published works. He soon made the acquaintance of Lancelot Andrewes, dean of Westminster from 1601 to 1605 and a long-term promoter of the study of oriental languages, and Andrewes's most notable pupil, William Bedwell, became a friend. Selden claimed to have assembled in 1605 the book on the gods of the ancient Middle East eventually published as *De dis Syris* (1617), and the dedication (to Cotton) of his work on the governance of England under the Britons, Saxons, and early Normans, *Analecton Anglobrittanicon* (1615), is dated 1607; probably

John Selden (1584–1654), by Sir Peter Lely?, *c.*1650

both had undergone considerable additions and revisions in the meantime. By 1609 he had drawn together a collection of sources and comments on early English governance that appeared long after his death as *Englands epinomis* (1681).

In the following year Selden's first books appeared. *The duello, or, Single Combat* (1610) was a brief work on the history of the single combat, especially as a medieval means of proof. *Jani Anglorum facies altera* (1610) was a much more substantial Latin treatise on the ancient laws of England, dedicated to Robert Cecil, earl of Salisbury. It provided the first relatively systematic and detailed account of the ancient Britons and Anglo-Saxons. It portrayed their constitutions as sharing sovereignty among the monarchs, nobles, clergy (first the druids and later Christian bishops and abbots), and freemen, and stressed the centrality of assemblies as places for the making, remembering, and interpreting of laws. 'These Assemblies do now sit in great State, which with a wonderful harmony of the Three Estates, the *King*, the *Lords*, and the *Commons*, or Deputies of the People ["Trium Ordinum, Regis, Magnatum, remque plebis procurantium harmoniâ"], are joyned together to a most firm security of the publick'. While ambiguous about the impact of the Norman conquest, sometimes arguing in favour of a major change in the laws of tenure by the conqueror and sometimes stressing the continuity of Saxon institutions and laws, Selden portrayed the parliaments of the early Norman kings as continuing under a new name the witenagemots or micel synods of the Saxons until, 'At length we borrowed of the *French* the name of *Parliaments*' (J. Selden, 'The reverse or back face of the English Janus' in his *Tracts*, trans.

R. Westcot [A. Littleton], 1683, 94; *Jani Anglorum*, 126). *Jani Anglorum* first put forward his interpretation of the English constitution as a mixed monarchy that continued to shape most of Selden's relevant writings for the rest of his life.

Historical and legal projects, 1612–1617 Called to the bar on 14 June 1612, Selden worked throughout his life as a barrister in London. His legal career stimulated rather than impeded his other interests. He had a great love of poetry, and his own compositions were sufficiently regarded in his lifetime for John Suckling to include him in his poem 'A session of poets' of 1637, but little of his verse survives. In 1610 he and Heyward provided commendatory verses for the collected poems of their friend Michael Drayton. In 1612 Selden's 'illustrations' of the historical poems in Drayton's *Poly-Olbion* brought the research already carried out for *Jani Anglorum* and *Analecton Anglobritannicon* to a new, wider, English-language audience. Drawing upon a humanist historical method, these notes first articulated Selden's historical method by stressing the importance of 'Synchronisme', the using as primary sources documents from as close as possible to the historical events under analysis (M. Drayton, *Poly-Olbion*, 1612, sig. A2*r*). His scholarly potential had begun to flower as he pursued simultaneous projects. Five years in a row substantial volumes in English and Latin came off the presses, starting with *Titles of Honor* (1614). In addition Selden wrote three short treatises and the first draft of *Mare clausum* for King James VI and I. Several of the works published during this decade displayed an extraordinary breadth and depth of learning, and two of them created a highly sophisticated new style of historical works published in the English language.

In *Titles of Honor* Selden acknowledged the contribution of his friends to his scholarly endeavour and personal life. He paid tribute to his 'beloved friend that singular Poet M. Ben: Jonson', while Jonson reciprocated with praise for 'his honord friend' in a commendatory verse:

> *Monarch*, in *Letters!*
> 'Mongst thy *Titles* showne,
> Of others *Honors*; thus, enioy thine owne
> (sig. B1*r*, 2*r*, d1*r*)

Selden also gave thanks for 'the Bounteous humanity and advise of theat learned Phisician Doctor Robert Floyd' [Fludd] in helping him overcome a 'dangerous and tedious sicknesse' (sig. A3*r*). The first edition of the work dealt historically with such European honorific titles as king, duke, count, baron, and knight, and also included special chapters entitled '*The beginning of* feuds' and 'Turkish *dignities*'. Breaking away from the genealogical concerns of most heralds and kings of arms, it derived honour from virtue, portrayed all civil honours as granted by the sovereign, and dismissed any claim to a hereditary nobility independent of the state (including the mystique of blood so favoured by some renaissance nobles). Each chapter opened with a discussion of the derivation of a particular title and then detailed its history and variations within a comparative European context, usually beginning with the Roman empire and coming up to the fringes of his own day. Those on dukes and counts observed that under the Romans: '*Dux* then properly was at first the *Generall of an Armie* under the Emperor' (pp. 182–3). Constantine the Great created the rival office of count by sending out important men from the imperial court to govern in the provinces. Not 'long after *Constantine*', these two offices became 'equall' in status (p. 184). The successor jurisdictions in France, Italy, and Spain continued to use duke and count as titles for offices until under the Carolingians they became attached to particular territories held by feudal military tenure and inheritable. With the collapse of royal power in France, dukes and counts usurped most of the marks of sovereignty, until strong kings of France claimed back those lost powers in the late middle ages.

In Saxon England, 'dux' and 'comes' translated the officiary and honorary title of earl, while comes also translated the officiary title of ealdorman. After the Norman conquest, through the introduction of continental laws the new king transformed the nature of an earldom from personal or officiary, 'making it feudall, and hereditarie' (p. 229). Building upon the scholarship of François Hotman, Selden represented the inheritable military tenure of the feudal law as originating in the Frankish empire and spreading to Germany and Italy by conquest and elsewhere in western Europe by imitation. Although the Saxons had military tenures, as seen in the laws of King Cnut, 'Those kind of Militarie Fiefs or Fees as wee now haue, were not till the Normans' (p. 301). *Titles of Honor* displayed a mature and almost unparalleled grasp of continental evidence and scholarship (including works on provincial as well as national history), and an acquaintance with English evidence (including manuscripts); it also reflected on the nature of law itself.

The project of comparative legal history also informed Selden's notes to Sir John Fortescue's *De laudibus legum Angliae* in an edition published in 1616. He faced more squarely than most common lawyers the legal consequences of the Roman conquest of Britain, noting that native Britons not only 'affected, we see, Roman language, Rhetorique, Roman habit, Roman pleasures, diet, and the like' but 'were not backward in affecting those laws, for which the languages and rhetorique was most usefull' (notes, 11–12). The normal adjustments of time combined with the succeeding conquests of the Saxons, Danes, and Normans to alter both the society and its laws: 'As succeeding ages, so new nations (comming in by a Conquest …) bring alwaies some alteration' (ibid., 9). This combination of continuity and change deliberately deconstructed Fortescue's seamless web of law, stretching unbroken from the Britons to his own day, into a suitable series of historical events, marked by such collections as the laws of King Cnut, King Edward, and King William. Within this new historical interpretation, the Norman conquest now seemed like just one more conquest that kept old customs and added new ones—not an unobtrusive or a catastrophic event.

Selden's notes to *De laudibus* also articulated a new vision of the English 'state' as grounded in a particular limitation of the laws of nature made at the foundation of the organized society that succeeded Roman rule. The common law of England began when 'naturall laws [were] limited for the conveniencie of civill societie here'. Thereafter those limitations 'have been … increased, altered, interpreted', and became like 'the ship, that by often mending had no piece of the first materialls', but 'yet (by the Civill law) is to be accounted the same still' (notes, 19). This provided a historical model for interpreting the laws of any independent jurisdiction. From the ancient past to the present, societies changed individual laws within the context of an ongoing distribution of powers made at their foundation, but as new laws helped each society to adjust to ever-changing needs, the shape of the 'state' remained the same. In England, this was a mixed monarchy in which the king, nobility, clergy, and freemen had always shared in lawmaking by custom and statute.

Between two famous English works appeared Selden's *De dis Syris*, a substantial treatise on the gods of the people surrounding the ancient Jews mentioned in the Pentateuch and the prophets, and their relationship to the gods of the ancient Greeks and Romans. In his lengthy prolegomenon he took a remarkably open approach to the belief in multiple gods of the ancients and their instruments of worship. He drew both on the writings of the ancient Jews, Greeks, and Romans (including some inscriptions), and on such medieval Jewish grammarians and commentators as Abraham ibn Ezra, Levi ben Gershon (Gershonides), Benjamin ben Jona, David Kimchi, Moses of Copucy, Solomon Iarchi (Rashi), and Moses ben Maimon (Maimonides). This marked a significant shift in attitude, for in 1610 he had dismissed '*Talmudical* Traditions' as 'Poetick Fictions taken upon trust' ('English Janus', 8).

In response to an enquiry from Ben Jonson about scriptural arguments adduced against cross-dressing, Selden wrote on 28 February 1616 a learned letter which disclosed several of the novel interpretations developed at length in *De dis Syris*, including the derivation of ancient European gods and goddesses from Asian deities, the report that 'Men did honor and invoke Venus in women's attire, and women the like to Mars in men's armour', the startling theory that 'the greatest names in the Eastern theologie of the Gentiles, were expressly noted by both sexes, and according to that mysterie of community of sexes, were worshipt', the conclusion that 'The self same was in Europe, where nothing of that kind was, if not traduced out of Asia', and the foundation of the origin of Mars and Venus in 'the masculin-foeminin or generative power supposed in the Sunne, or the Sunne and Moon, which were the first creatures idolatrously worshipt' (Rosenblatt and Schleiner, 66–70). No wonder this imaginative and controversial study of comparative religion won accolades from continental scholars.

The Historie of Tithes The most celebrated of Selden's treatises from this decade, *The Historie of Tithes* (1618), marked a major refinement in his theory and practice of history. Dedicated to Sir Robert Cotton, it praised his 'inestimable Library', which assured 'a curious Diligence in search after the inmost, least known and most usefull parts of Historicall Truth' (sig. A 2*r*). The preface recommended the scrutinizing of earlier interpretations and of all evidence with a searching, but moderate philosophical scepticism, which helped to clear away unsound interpretations and to promote soundly based truth. Selden also encouraged other scholars to verify his own representations of the past. Also key to his method was his great respect for 'true *Philologie*' and 'her two Hand-maids *Curious Diligence* and *Watchfull Industrie*' who discover 'many hidden Truths' not really accessible to 'any one restraind Profession' (pp. xii, xix). Marginal notes and a full bibliography of manuscript sources provided readers with access to the evidence presented in the text.

The Historie of Tithes offered political advice on an issue of burning contemporary relevance. Between 1605 and 1613 George Carleton (who became successively bishop of Llandaff and of Chichester), Thomas Ridley (a prominent civil and canon lawyer), and Foulke Robarts (a Norwich divine) had drawn upon the interpretation of medieval canon lawyers and some historical evidence to make strident attacks upon the lay ownership of tithes. Selden detected no link between ancient Jewish tithes and those of medieval Christian Europe. During its first four centuries, voluntary charity funded the Christian church. During the next four centuries, pious laymen started to offer perpetual endowments, including tithes, to particular monasteries and churches, but retained control of the patronage of the resulting livings. With careful philological readings of contemporary primary sources Selden deconstructed the long-standing assertions that tithes had existed by the law of nature and that parish clergy had collected tithes by divine right during the first 800 years of Christianity.

During the next 400 years, Selden explained, laymen began to dedicate tithes more frequently to particular churches or monasteries. The foundation and endowment of parish churches by laymen and the attachment to them of earlier gifts previously paid into a common diocesan fund created a parochial structure. During this era the clergy began to preach that tithes belonged by divine right to parish churches and to use this theory in an aggressive attempt to extend ecclesiastical power. Secular laws proclaimed by Charlemagne marked the first recorded attempt to create a legal right to tithes in western Europe. The four centuries from 1200 to 1600 witnessed the spread of enforced tithes over the whole of western Europe, the triumph in canon law of an argument for their parochial right, and the suppression of evidence for earlier, voluntary gifts in various repositories of ecclesiastical records. So successful was this clerical campaign for compulsory parochial tithes by divine right that secular laws began to enforce the collection of tithes within their jurisdictions.

In Anglo-Saxon England parishes came into existence largely as foundations by laymen who endowed them, and the argument that tithes had always belonged by divine right to the parish priest was anachronistic nonsense. Listing many references to lay consecrations of property and income to the church found in early manuscripts, Selden concluded that before the reign of King John lay tithing was voluntary, and thus many of the so-called appropriated tithes traced their 'chief originall from these arbitrarie Consecrations' (pp. 290–91). This brilliant reading of manuscript sources creatively reinterpreted the meaning of parishes in the early English church and stressed the positive role of laymen in the endowment of the church.

Selden also discovered that the general enforcement of divine-right tithes had spread across the face of western Europe as the result of a well-planned and executed programme of legal innovation. Starting in earnest about the year 1200, the enterprise reached a climax under Pope Innocent III and accompanied the climb of the papacy to the zenith of its political power in western Europe, including the England of King John. However, English common law, like the secular laws of other states in western Europe, came to enforce customary payments of cash in composition for crops and of fixed quantities other than a tenth; it also adjudicated any disputes over the rights of ownership of appropriated tithes. The aggressive clerical invasion of the property rights was eventually met by the statutes of the sixteenth century that controlled tithes and dissolved monasteries. As always for Selden, the law of God applied only as enforced through the laws of particular states. Underlying the occasionally flaming heat of the *Historie of Tithes* stood a profoundly protestant version of Christianity which envisaged a church governed by the prince and parliaments, integrated into society, and enriched by the creative talents of laymen, as well as those of the clergy.

A 'Review' at the end of the *Historie of Tithes* provided a brief history of the Roman law to show how it could not rightly claim to have ruled even western Europe in an unbroken sequence and pictured William I, his barons, and those 'learned in the laws' (identified as 'the common Lawiers of that time, as *Godric* and *Alfwin*') gathering together as a parliament in the fourth year of the conquest to hear and confirm the 'former Laws of the Kingdome' (p. 482). This vivid image of the historical triumph of the king-in-parliament appeared just in time for Selden's political career of the following decade. King James and his favourite, the marquess of Buckingham, forced Selden to withdraw *Historie of Tithes* from circulation, apologize to the privy council for the mistake of its publication, and endure in silence the attacks on it made by his critics. However, he would neither admit that it presented false evidence or interpretations nor retreat from the central thesis that the law of God found enforcement only in the laws of particular jurisdictions.

Legal historian and scholar, 1621–1628 In 1621 Selden received an opportunity to put his historical and constitutional ideas into action when employed as an expert legal historian by the House of Lords. This produced two concrete results, a draft roll of standing orders produced with Henry Elsyng, the clerk of parliament, and a lengthy report on the privileges of the Lords, including a section on the judicature, entitled 'The priviledges of the baronage in England' (HLRO). The latter used historical evidence to establish such 'speciall rights' as proxies, freedom from lawsuits during the sitting of parliament, and the power of judicature, and such 'private' privileges as trial by peers and giving evidence by a protestation upon honour instead of upon oath (fols. 2*v*, 98*r*). Although the treatise vested judicature in the Lords, Selden was imprisoned, ironically, on suspicion of vesting it in the Commons. The intervention of Lancelot Andrewes, bishop of Winchester, and the newly appointed lord keeper, John Williams, dean of Westminster and bishop of Lincoln, obtained a fairly quick release.

In 1621 Selden also acted as a legal consultant and a researcher for Francis Bacon, Viscount St Albans, gathering sources for the latter's history of Henry VII. His fullest statement on method appeared as a preface to Augustine Vincent's *A Discoverie of Errours* (1622). Selden commended Vincent for his diligent reading not only of published work but also of 'the more abstruse parts of *History*, which ly hid either in privat *Manuscripts*, or else in the publique *Records* of the Kingdome' (sig. A1*r*). Selden privileged those 'Acts of the State' preserved in the public records as the most extensive and reliable historical sources available. To sceptical critical analysis of sources he now added a quantitative imperative: the more contemporary and complete the sources, the more truthful the historical account.

During the 1620s Selden became involved in an impressive number of scholarly enterprises. On 24 May 1621 he wrote to James Ussher, then bishop of Meath, that a new edition of *Titles of Honour* was in the press. It probably drew upon a large number of studies, manuscripts, and printed public records. Selden's correspondence with Ussher from the 1620s dealt with an incredible range of scholarly topics, including the siting of churches in antiquity, the Samaritan Pentateuch (especially interesting for its chronology in comparison with those contained in the Hebrew and Greek versions), and British historical materials; in addition, they exchanged books and manuscripts, including many from Cotton's library. Selden's knowledge of Anglo-Saxon had improved to the degree that Ussher could suggest, when returning Cotton's 'two Saxon Annales' in August or September 1625, that Selden would earn the gratitude of antiquaries if he produced a composite Anglo-Saxon chronicle, but this came to nothing.

In 1623 Selden published a critical edition of the history *Eadmeri monachi Cantuariensis, historia novorum … sub Guilielmis I et II et Henrico I Angliae regibus*. Dedicated to Bishop John Williams, it included an edition of the 'laws of William I' (these displayed a striking similarity to the *Leges Edwardi Confessoris* printed by William Lambarde and provided evidence for a strong continuity across the potential break of the Norman conquest) and extracts from the Lichfield chronicle and the history of the pseudo-Ingulf, sources cited often in his early works. Selden saw Eadmer's text as an authentic contemporary voice that spoke vividly about the greedy exploitation of the revenues of the church by William II and the powerful political will of such churchmen as archbishops Lanfranc and Anselm. Since he had already singled out this period as one that had witnessed the powerful intrusion of popes and other clerics in secular affairs, he hardly accepted the theory of ecclesiastical independence from secular power supported by Eadmer. Five years later he published *Marmora Arundeliana* (1628), an edition of the classical inscriptions in Greek from the marbles collected from Asia Minor by Thomas Howard, earl of Arundel, with an introduction and notes. It contained the text of a treaty and a major chronology of considerable importance to European classical scholars, as well as a philological discussion of the word '*nomos*' that explored the relationship of music, poetry, and law among the ancient Greeks.

MP in the 1620s In 1623 Selden's old friend and patron Henry Grey succeeded to the earldom of Kent and engaged the lawyer as the manager of his estates. The following year Selden was returned as MP for Lancaster, perhaps through the help of the earl of Pembroke, the lord chamberlain and brother-in-law of the countess of Kent. He became an effective new member of the Commons, searching precedents for the actions of the house and serving on committees but speaking only occasionally. In 1626 he sat for Great Bedwyn, Wiltshire, most probably as a client of the earl of Hertford. Selden shared a number of goals with members of the Seymour network, including a strong dislike of the duke of Buckingham, support for constitutional monarchy, and a belief in reformed religion. He played a leading role in attacks made upon Buckingham, obtaining admission into the house for Sir Robert Howard, who lived openly with the countess of Purbeck (the wife of Buckingham's brother John), and working with Sir John Eliot, Sir Dudley Digges, and others on what became the attempted impeachment of the duke. Selden spoke forcefully, sat on the subcommittees that assembled the charges, dug up precedents for the procedures adopted, and was one of eight managers who presented the accusations against Buckingham to the Lords on 8 May. Actions against the duke failed with the dissolution of this parliament, but Selden helped to transform the transgressions of royal servants into a perceived threat to the ancient constitution.

Failure to obtain funding in parliament forced the privy council to raise money, troops, and supplies by other means to continue the war against Spain and the empire, and extend it to France. When five knights imprisoned for refusing to lend money to the king sought bail through a writ of habeas corpus, Selden became one of the counsel for the defence. Most of his legal work involved property law; this was the only high-profile case with criminal implications that he ever handled, and one of only two of his cases for which copious evidence has survived. In this hearing with wide-ranging constitutional ramifications he approached his argument as an advocate but also as a historian. When Sir Robert Heath, the attorney-general, defended the royal prerogative to act without normal restraints during a time of crisis, Selden argued that the crown must follow recognized procedures, 'without which we have nothing', or else jeopardize the ancient liberties of freeborn Englishmen: 'no man can be justly imprisoned by either of them [the king or the privy council], without a cause of the commitment expressed in the return' (*State trials*, 3.17). Using an expert contextual reading of Magna Carta chapter 29, Selden argued that if 'due process of the law' meant 'according to the laws' in general, as suggested by attorney-general Heath, then 'the freeman shall have no privilege above the villain' an obviously preposterous position for people who lived in early thirteenth-century England (ibid., col. 18). Selden's humanist interpretation, however, did not obtain bail for his client, as the judges remanded the prisoners back to gaol, with the lord chief justice, Sir Nicholas Hyde, noting that the precedents cited in the case told against them.

Discretionary imprisonment, the billeting of troops, imposition of martial law in England, and extra-parliamentary taxation or loans all became leading grievances when the next parliament assembled in March 1628. Selden sat for Ludgershall, Wiltshire, again as a client of the earl of Hertford. Named to fifty-seven committees and six subcommittees, he ranked among the top five committeemen in this session. In addition, his ninety-eight recorded speeches in the house and committee of the whole and twenty-six in the conference of 16 and 17 April helped to elevate him into a position of leadership. Drawing upon his wide learning Selden led the attack against discretionary imprisonment and martial law. His interpretation of the English constitution as a mixed monarchy from the very beginning helped to shape strongly felt grievances into resolutions and to collect them into a bill to uphold the traditional liberties of free Englishmen. However, Selden could not agree with the move made by Sir Edward Coke, supported by Sir Francis Seymour, to change from a bill to a petition of right on the grounds that it had less force, but he played a prominent, if somewhat diminished role in the debates which led to the passage of the petition.

In the session of 1629 Selden retained his position of leadership, strongly attacking the printing of the petition of right with the king's first answer (the one unacceptable to the Lords and Commons), passionately defending the parliamentary privilege of John Rolle, whose goods were seized for his refusal to pay tonnage and poundage, gratuitously insulting Secretary Sir John Coke (the primary spokesman for the crown in the Commons), and, in general, helping to polarize differences between royal servants and their critics. On the last day of the session Selden not only supported a vote on the resolutions moved by Sir John Eliot, but commanded the speaker (as the servant of the house) to put the question on pain of being replaced. Ironically, these actions subverted Selden's own ideal, which depended upon the co-operative working together of the king, Lords, and Commons. They also helped to make King Charles out of love with parliaments.

Imprisonment and publications of the 1630s Shortly after dissolution Selden and eight other members of the Commons came under the careful scrutiny of the privy council. Questioned about his part in the events of the last day of the session, Selden lost his will to resist and provided less than truthful answers. On the night before the justices were to deliver their decision on bail King Charles moved the prisoners to the Tower, where they rested outside the jurisdiction of the king's bench. From 24 June 1629 until the summer of 1630 Selden suffered close imprisonment, although he soon got access to his books and papers and moved in and out of the Tower from 1631 onwards. Only an apology made to the king in 1634 brought a final release without bail. These years of enforced leisure allowed Selden to finish two scholarly projects and start new ones.

A monument to the wide-ranging mastery of medieval continental and English sources and studies, the weighty second edition of *Titles of Honor* (1631) drew its evidence widely. As well as providing a model for a true history based upon many primary sources, this edition also sought to establish a solid foundation for a new philosophy of politics that would emulate the revolution in astronomy brought about by 'Copernicus, Tycho, Galileus, Kepler' (sig. ¶2*r*), although Selden's political advice remained more than a little obscured by the details of his analytical narrative.

Attempting to chart the origin and development of the titles of monarchy, nobility, and gentility in western Europe from the end of the Roman empire to the present, this new edition dissolved the unitary feudal law interpretation espoused in the first edition into various national, provincial, or local feudal laws. Selden portrayed these jurisdictions as a series of ancient constitutions, each having its own 'state' or 'frame of government' and its own feudal customs. Only the titles of emperor and king received a fully comparative treatment, with those of duke, count, baron, and knight unfolding country by country as rulers carried out their own adaptation of northern European customs to Roman offices. The Gothic king Theodoric, whose chancellor Cassiodor was a Goth 'bred up in the learning of the Romans', marked a key transition in linking Roman titles and northern tenures (p. 302). Selden's astute awareness of variation over time and space combined with his sophisticated representation of fealty, homage, service, and investiture with land to verify the overall interpretation.

Like their continental counterparts, the Anglo-Saxon kings of England shaped a new 'frame of government', using as their 'subordinate Titles of Temporall Honour' those 'of *Etheling*, *Ealdorman*, and *Thane* or *Thegn*' (p. 603). Selden's deepened understanding of Anglo-Saxon sources allowed him to provide a much more sophisticated analytic and chronological representation of these titles. Anglo-Saxon charters and Domesday Book showed that the Saxons had established the feudal holding of land by military service, and the Normans had taken it over and reshaped it. Since twenty years could not create a custom, Selden argued, historians could trust such manuscripts as Domesday Book as detailed guides to the military and fiscal obligations due from across the realm under the late Anglo-Saxon kings. Considerable evidence also showed how the highest officers in the land, ealdormen and earls, along with high-ranking churchmen and thegns, governed the realm through presiding over shire courts or witnessing royal charters. Occasionally the great men of the realm gathered together as a witenagemot or a micel synod 'which afterward was from the *Romance* Dialect stiled a Parliament' (p. 613). These assemblies advised in matters of state and made and interpreted laws, exercising both deliberative and judicial power. Here lay the origins for the Norman gatherings of tenants-in-chief of the crown and for later parliaments.

The Norman conquest brought few changes to patterns of landholding and governance, but replaced Saxon feudal thegns by Norman barons. Selden discussed at great length the feudal and military character of the early Norman baronage, the nature of the knight's fee as a grant of land designed to provide the service of a professional warrior, and the transformation of a baronage by tenure into one defined by receiving an individual summons to parliaments. These interpretations represented a major scholarly accomplishment, and they made the conquest of 1066 look like just one of many moments of innovation, one additional adjustment of northern customs to Latin offices, carried out through an assembly of notables. Indeed, the second edition of *Titles of Honor* provided sophisticated historical support for Selden's interpretation of the mixed monarchy of England, not least by placing it in a plausible, equally well-supported context of European ancient constitutions. It portrayed the continual calling of parliaments as a necessary part of English governance.

In the 1630s Charles I was looking for more acceptable advice, so Selden, encouraged by courtiers, presented a peace offering, *Mare clausum* (1635), which defended British sovereignty over a wide expanse of sea. First written about 1619 and then revised to take account of the minimalist theory of natural law contained in Hugo Grotius's *De jure belli ac pacis* (1625), it combined a lengthy, sophisticated theoretical discussion of law with a partisan and reasonably well-documented history of the exercise of maritime dominion. Book 1 argued: 'That the Sea, by the Law of Nature or Nations, is … capable of private Dominion or proprietie as well as Land', and book 2: 'That the King of *Great Britain* is Lord of the Sea flowing about, as an inseparable and perpetual Appendant of the British Empire'. The structure reflected Selden's view of the link between theory and history, law and fact: the capability of dominion arose to a significant extent from the evidence of dominion exercised over the sea in the past (J. Selden, *Of the Dominion, or, Ownership of the Sea*, trans. M. Nedham, 1652, 2).

In order to challenge the assumptions of those who had supported free trade on open waters, *Mare clausum* started with definitions of 'sea' (which included the oceans and seas nearly surrounded by land) and 'dominion', and discussion of the nature of 'law' ('Jus'). The binding law of nations and the law of God as revealed in scripture, although 'reputed by men to bee unchangable', became enforceable only through '*Additions* or Inlargements', which included the interpretations of judges and commentators (p. 13). Positive laws (customs, statutes, contracts, or treaties) transformed the universal laws of God and nature into enforceable laws with concrete penalties. Most existing legal systems fit into the categories of '*Civil*' law (the laws of particular societies) or the '*Common Law of divers Nations*' (laws jointly accepted by more than one state), but some occupied a third category, the '*Law of som* or *divers Nations, Civil* or *Domestick*' (international law accepted as binding by one or more states; p. 14). The last of these opened a place for the exercise of dominion over the sea.

Selden then turned to communal and private dominion. The parcelling of lands and goods derived not from the laws of God or nature, which were neutral on the subject, but from a covenant involving the 'consent of the whole bodie or universalitie of mankinde (by the mediation of something like a compact, which might binde their posteritie)' (p. 21). Even before they formed societies, occupiers could establish a preponderant use over a particular piece of land previously uninhabited. As abundant theory and practice demonstrated, explicit or implicit contracts turned the lands that they occupied into dominion, made it capable of allocation or inheritance, and established distinct local property laws. Dominion over the sea, however, had not remained uncontested. Through a careful examination of the practice of 'the more civilized and more eminent Nations of the past and present Age', whose laws and treaties showed that claims over adjoining seas 'hath been received into Custom, as a thing very usual, and agreeable to Law' (pp. 45, 53), Selden provided copious evidence to support the exercise of maritime dominion in general and of ancient and modern British dominion over the surrounding seas. These detailed discussions of ancient and medieval military and diplomatic affairs paid equal attention to the royal appointment of admirals and to parliamentary statutes and, while revealing fissures beneath the surface of the text, sugared the pill of mixed monarchy for Charles I with the sweetness of royal maritime sovereignty. Written in Latin for an international audience, *Mare clausum* constituted a classic defence for the extreme position that states could legitimately claim and exercise extensive sovereignty over the high seas.

Although relatively brief, Selden's two studies of ancient Jewish society demonstrated his new mastery of the Talmud and provided the first taste of a passion for Jewish studies that dominated his scholarship for the last two decades of his life. On 4 August 1625 Selden wrote to Archbishop James Ussher asking about the differences between the Samaritan and Hebrew versions of the Torah. On 2 November 1627 Ussher replied with corrections to Scaliger's Samaritan chronology and discussed the related problems that fascinated both scholars. Ussher knew that Selden read Arabic, Greek, and Hebrew and assumed that he also read Aramaic; another correspondent thought in 1634 that Selden was translating the 'Alcoran' (Bodl. Oxf., Selden MS, supra 108, fol. 52*r*). Instead, he had honed his skill in Aramaic and Hebrew and plunged deeply into a series of works based strongly upon the Torah, the Talmud, and Jewish commentaries.

The extent of this shift appeared in Selden's dedication of the joint printing of *De successionibus in bona defuncti* and *De successione in pontificatum Ebraeorum* (1636) to Archbishop William Laud. In the parliamentary session of 1629 Selden had attacked Laud, then bishop of London, for licensing bad books and refusing to license attacks on Arminianism or popery. With the shift in Selden's research during the 1630s, Laud's library proved very useful and the two men formed a friendship. Laud sent Hebrew books to Selden to settle the question of their authorship and also helped to negotiate his reconciliation with King Charles. In the dedication of 1636, Selden assured '*Antistes*' Laud that he was not one of those Hebraists who deserted to the other side, like the extreme sabbatarians, but explored Jewish wisdom in order to improve Christianity. He praised Laud for his 'incomparable' gift of a voluminous quantity of oriental manuscripts to the library of Oxford (sig. A1*r*). However, Selden had not accepted the archbishop's tendency to identify the Christian church with its clergy and to assert clerical independence from any secular power below the monarch. Although admitting that both the Babylonian and Jerusalem Talmuds contained fables and follies (especially about Jesus and the Virgin Mary), Selden gave them the sceptical, critical reading already practised on the sources used in his earlier histories. Carefully interpreted, the traditional wisdom, judicial decisions, and modes of scriptural exegesis that had accumulated from the days of Moses on Sinai to the diaspora and beyond provided the key for understanding the teachings and practices of the ancient Jews and early Christians.

The potentially more explosive of these two treatises was that on priestly succession, for it dealt with the sensitive issue of the divine origin of priesthood in 1636, when William Prynne published anonymously in Amsterdam his attack upon the biblical origins of episcopacy, *The Unbishoping of Timothy and Titus*. Selden noted how the customs and traditions of the Jews (like unwritten English common law) guided both the succession of the priests and their powers. Book 1 surveyed the history of the Jewish priesthood from Aaron to the destruction of the second temple, showing how high priests held sacred office through their lineage from Aaron. Book 2 explored the legal requirements of eligibility for ancient Jewish priesthood, and it also discussed priestly consecration, vestments, and sacrifices, and the differences between the first and second temples. Finally it portrayed priests as having authority in judgment and interpretation of law by virtue of their scholarly understanding of oral traditions, and the Great Sanhedrin as having the power to settle all such issues, including disputes over priestly succession. However, Selden did not fully define the membership of the Sanhedrin. Together these studies also carried into another historical setting his link between the binding laws of God and nature and the laws of particular societies, this time with the 'additions and enlargements' of the ancient Jews.

Rehabilitation and *De jure naturali* During the 1630s Selden received recognition and expanded his social life into new circles, including the court. In November 1632 he was elected a bencher of the Inner Temple; he and Sir Edward Herbert were among representatives from the inns of court who staged the masque *The Triumph of Peace* before the king and queen at the Banqueting House in February 1634 and again at the Merchant Taylors' Hall. As the court connections of the countess of Kent strengthened, Selden entered into a mentoring relationship with George Digby (the scholarly eldest son of the earl of Bristol), lending books, purchasing volumes, and enjoying his company. In February 1638 the courtier, connoisseur, and diplomat Sir Kenelm Digby wrote from Paris thanking Selden 'for the kind favour you did me in sending me your Mare Clausum and other workes' and reciprocated with a book in a fine French binding (Bodl. Oxf., Selden MS, supra 108, fol. 78*r*). Following the death of the earl of Kent in 1639 Selden took up permanent residence at White Friars, the home of the countess. There was clearly a widely circulating rumour that he married her, and the countess's description of herself in her will as 'late wife' rather than as 'widow' of Kent gives it some credence. John Aubrey asserted it as a truth, adding that Selden had had sexual relations with her during Kent's lifetime and with his knowledge; Selden inherited the countess's property after her death.

In his weighty treatise *De jure naturali et gentium, juxta disciplinam Ebrorum* (1640) Selden built upon both Grotius and rabbinic traditions, reducing the minimal moral duties of humans to seven laws imposed by God first upon Adam and later upon Noah and his descendants. He listed these as 'the prohibitions of idolatry and blasphemy, the injunction to establish a legal system, commandments against bloodshed, sexual sins, and theft, and a seventh law … added after the flood … forbidding anyone to eat flesh cut from a living animal' (Rosenblatt, 126). For an early seventeenth-century European they also provided the earliest possible starting point for discussion because these laws were 'given to the human race at its very creation' and 'revealed and made manifest, like principles or theorems in demonstrative matters, to every man whose mind was not depraved, who was not corrupted, and who intuited rightly and diligently enough' (*De jure naturali*, 109, as translated in Sommerville, 440). By invoking divine sanction, Selden clearly abandoned the move by Grotius to use only basic principles based upon human relationships.

Selden probably found the position of Grotius too vulnerable to sceptical subversion and used a story from Herodotus to argue 'that there were clearly no common principles of morality accessible to all men by the light of their natural reason' (Tuck, *Philosophy and Government*, 215). Earlier he had argued that each society limited the law of nature in its own way owing to particular context and to the diversity of opinion which arose from the weakness of human reason, and each had its unique *nomos*, the different 'state' or 'frame of government' that reflected and upheld its social arrangements. By 1640, however, unaided human reason and custom no longer fully satisfied Selden. The commands of God, continually upheld by an 'active intellect' through which the human mind perceived the truth, now provided a firmer foundation for natural law. Although most of Noah's descendants had to some extent lost sight of the original principles, the descendants of Schem and particularly the Jews remained especially open to the active intellect and best preserved them. This guaranteed that the rabbinic account of natural law stood closer to God's original commands than the fallible human traditions of other societies. The additions and enlargements of the laws of nature spelled out in the 'civil laws' of each society also stood rooted in another divine command: '*You must abide by contracts and forms of government agreed on by the citizens, and you must keep your word* or some such decree' (*De jure naturali*, 107, as translated in Tuck, *Philosophy and Government*, 216–17). The honouring of 'contracts' and 'frames of government' remained fundamental to social and political life, as in the second edition of *Titles of Honor* and *Mare clausum*. Although the first book of *De jure naturali* addressed general issues, the succeeding ones dealt with one (or two) of the Noachide laws, exhausting the meaning and implications of each with a plenitude of detail. Combining theory with historical evidence, Selden provided a divine sanction for the polity and laws of nations from the ancient Jews to early modern Europeans. This search for the expression of God's commands in human customs and jurisprudence characterized most of his future works.

The 1640s: public office, social circle, and the history of the church In the 1640s Selden served as a member of the Long Parliament (until excluded by Pride's Purge), acted as a lay member of the Westminster assembly, and continued extensive scholarly research and writing. His election as MP for Oxford University perhaps had the blessing of its chancellor, Laud, who tried to enlist Selden's help to relieve pressure for extensive religious reform by withdrawing the canons of 1640. Selden sat on fewer committees, spoke only infrequently in debates, and swayed the Commons far less often than in 1628–9. On 10 March 1641 he argued that since 'ancientlie Bishops in Saxon times had voices in making lawes' before voting for removal of clerical participation 'wee would give the clergie some other voices' (*The Journal of Sir Simonds D'Ewes*, ed. W. Notestein, 1923, 468 and n. 10). Against his advice the house initiated a bill to remove the bishops from parliament. For Selden this represented a serious subversion of the English 'frame of government'. A few months later he also spoke and voted against the attainder of Thomas Wentworth, earl of Strafford.

When Charles I began to gather supporters in the summer of 1642 the marquess of Hertford invited Selden to join him in royal service in York. In reply, Selden excused himself on grounds of illness, but also professed that his 'loyal and humble affections to his majestie and his service are and shall now be as great and as hearty as any mans' (Bodl. Oxf., Selden MS supra 123, fol. 159*r*). Ironically, his theory of mixed monarchy formed the basis for

His Majesties Answer to the XIX Propositions (1642). Selden collected printed material on the royal commissions of array and drafted a treatise debating whether such commissions were 'warrantable' by the common law and statute (Bodl. Oxf., Selden MS supra 124, fol. 1). An examination of the history of raising troops in England, especially 'knights service' concluded that 'the obligations that are made by homage and fealty are such as bind only in honor or conscience, but [subject] the party not to any punishment at the common law' (supra 124, 14–15). The military actions of royal servants had to be 'warranted by immemorial Custome or by act of Parlament, and not at all by arguments drawn simply from mischeif or convenience or inconvenience', or else they would violate the ancient 'frame of government' of England (supra 124, p. 18). Commissions of array had no foundation in custom or statute. Drawing upon many of his arguments from the debates over the militia in the session of 1628, he showed that mixed monarchy could defend the parliamentary as well as the royalist cause.

Some of Selden's scholarship in the 1640s offered advice less hidden than most of his earlier works. His translation from Arabic into Latin of the early section of a history of the Christian church in Alexandria, *Eutychii Aegyptii, patriarchae orthodoxorum Alexandrini* (1642), portrayed its author, Eutychius (877–940), as the Egyptian Bede, a reliable historian of his own people, and related how the evangelist Mark chose a shoemaker, Hananias, as the first patriarch of the city and established a council of twelve presbyters to choose and consecrate his successor from among their number. This ancient 'frame of government' for one of the earliest Christian churches was not unlike the modified episcopacy advocated by Archbishop Ussher and spoke to the arguments over divine-right episcopacy and presbyterianism that had started to rage openly in London in 1641. Eutychius charted the rise of bishops within the Alexandrine church, intruding themselves between the patriarch and the other clergy, and the loss by presbyters of their exclusive privilege of electing and ordaining the patriarch. In his commentary Selden used his understanding of ancient Jewish practices to shed light on the ecclesiastical offices mentioned in the New Testament and other early Christian sources. The consecration of especially studious Jews as 'presbyters' and the laying on of hands that initiated the most learned of them into the Great Sanhedrin indicated that the early Christianity portrayed by Eutychius had Jewish roots. Another section of his commentary attempted to find a middle way through the equally contentious issue of extemporaneous versus fixed or liturgical prayer sparked off by attacks upon the Book of Common Prayer in the early 1640s. Clearly he wanted the reforms of the present to incorporate the good practices of the past, a difficult position during an age of accelerated reformation.

From July 1643 onwards Selden participated in the often heated debates of the Westminster assembly, appointed by parliament to reform the Church of England. The vast majority of members were ordained clergy who strongly desired reforms in ecclesiastical governance, worship, and discipline, and a codification of doctrine. Many found it difficult to deal with a layman who questioned their readings of scripture and displayed greater expertise on a variety of issues than any of the clergy. Selden's best-known and, for the Scots, most vexing contributions came during the debates over excommunication. Robert Baillie, one of the Scottish clerical commissioners, characterized him as 'the head of the Erastians; his glory is most in the Jewish learning; he avows everywhere that the Jewish State and Church were all one, and that so in England it must be, that the Parliament is the Church' (*Letters and Journals of Robert Baillie*, 2.266). This downplayed Selden's deep knowledge and use of British history, including that of the church, but accurately summarized his interpretation. On 4 January 1644, when a committee report suggested that pastors and teachers had 'the power to inquire and judge who are fit to be admitted to the sacraments, or be kept from them; and also who are to be excommunicated or absolved from that censure', Selden responded by suggesting:

> that, in this kingdom, ever since it was a kingdom, Christian excommunication hath ever been by a temporal power; as in the Pope's rule here, his own excommunication could not be brought in hither, but by permission of the secular power. (*Whole Works of … Lightfoot*, 13.106)

In other debates he applied his rabbinic learning against compulsive readings of 1 Corinthians 5: 4 and Matthew 18: 15–17 favoured by the presbyterians. These clashes led to sharp rejoinders around Selden's table: 'presbiters have the greatest power of any Clergie in the World, and gull the Laytie the most' (Selden, *Table Talk*, 113). While unsuccessful in persuading a majority of the divines in the Westminster assembly, Selden and other lay delegates did persuade parliament to adopt more flexible policies on governance and excommunication than those supported by the presbyterians.

Collected mostly in the 1640s by his clerical amanuensis, Richard Milward, and published posthumously in 1689 with a dedication to his executors, Selden's 'table talk' reflected his concerns from this decade. Its contents, arranged alphabetically in short sections, were devoted mainly to issues of religion, morality, and politics. That on translations of the Bible demonstrated both his feeling of scholarly community and his common sense. In translating from French to English, he observed, one did not translate word for word but phrase by phrase: 'I say it is cold, not, it makes cold'; in the Bible, however, 'the Hebraisms are kept … which is well enough so long as scholars have to do with it; but when it comes among the common people, Lord, what gear do they make of it' (Selden, *Table Talk*, 6–7). He was not afraid to make fun of the clergy, but considered that the bishops had the same right to sit in the Lords as did the peerage, namely that of precedent. As in the common law, custom ruled. The section headed 'Jewes' summed up succinctly the basic interpretation put forward in his weighty Judaic studies:

> God att the first gave laws to all Mankind, but afterwards hee gave peculiar laws, to the Jewes which they only were to observe, Just as we have the Comon Law for all England, and

> yet ye have some Corporations, that besides that, have peculier lawes and priviledges to themselves. (ibid., 54)

This made the jurisprudence of the Jews look like the 'civil laws' of other societies, without the upholding power of the active intellect posited in *De jure naturali*. Glimpses of Selden's sardonic wit appeared occasionally in his published works and between the lines of letters from his correspondents, but characterized much of the conversational tone recorded by Milward, as seen in his account of the 'person of quality' who arrived at his chambers 'and told me he had two devils in his head (I wondered what he meant)' (ibid., 46).

During the 1640s Selden also received a number of rewards, made new friendships, and helped old friends. Parliament appointed him keeper of the records in the Tower in 1643 and named him one of the twelve commissioners for the Admiralty in 1644. In 1646 he was voted £5000 in compensation for his prosecution and imprisonment by the crown in 1629–31, but found it difficult to collect. He used his influence to save several libraries from pillage and disbursal, including the royal collection, that at Lambeth Palace, and that of Archbishop Ussher. He received wonderful letters of praise, such as that in 1647 from young Ralph Cudworth, the future Cambridge Platonist, accompanied by a 'pamphlet' on religion, a 'small expression of my great Respects to you' (Bodl. Oxf., Selden MS supra 108, fol. 1*r*). Other younger scholars, such as the very learned Dr Gerard Langbaine, provost of Queen's College, Oxford, sought Selden's protection from overzealous visitors in 1648. Working in Westminster, he helped many caught up in the tribulations of the civil wars.

Jewish and legal publications, 1644–1655 Selden's Jewish studies flourished in the 1640s and 1650s, spurred on by contemporary debates. Building upon his earlier interest in chronology, he published *De anno civili et calendario veteris ecclesiae seu reipublicae Judaicae, dissertatio* (1644). The reconciliation of the lunar and the solar years shaped the rituals and annual festivals of the Jews (and, through them, those of Christians), but Selden called it a 'civil' calendar because the application of the law of God in a workable manner was a human responsibility. The preface argued that Jewish traditions of interpretation could help Christians better to understand passages in the New Testament. A dialogical approach shaped much of the text, with Selden detailing the 'Talmudic and Scripturalist' interpretations of chronology as it related to a wide range of activity. The latter belonged to the Karaites, who traced their heritage back to the Sadducees, but derived from Anan ben David, who lived in the middle of the eighth century; 'Selden may be regarded as the first modern western scholar, Jew or gentile, to analyse the practices of this Jewish sect' (*John Selden on Jewish Marriage law: the Uxor Hebraica*, trans. J. R. Ziskind, 1991, 16). Instead of determining the new moon that marked the beginning of the month for the Jewish lunar calendar by mathematical calculation, the Karaites used visual observation. This could make the crucial difference of a day for the start of rituals. Although portraying the Karaites as having the deepest understanding of lunar time, Selden also saw Talmudic scholars as providing the foundations of the ordinary traditions of interpretation upon which even the Karaites had to rely. With their dialogical approach, great variety of voices and schools, and zeal for the word of God, Jewish scholars had become for Selden, perhaps ironically, the best model for Christians to move beyond their factional conflicts.

Selden's *Uxor Ebraica* (1646), written by the early 1640s, provided the scholarly basis for many of the interpretations in the controversial tract by John Milton, *The Doctrine and Discipline of Divorce* (1643). Selden's 622-page treatise exhaustively examined the nature of marriage and divorce as discussed in the Torah, the Talmud, and commentaries of a host of Jewish scholars. Book 1 opened by noting that while the 'civil laws' of other societies came from natural law (the Noachide laws), the 'civil law' of the Hebrews was 'partly Sacred Law' commanded in the Torah 'and partly ancestral custom and sanctions added by those who were in charge of such matters' (*Uxor Ebraica*, 33). It then discussed unions forbidden on the grounds of consanguinity and affinity, the Karaites, the marriages of high priests and kings, and the practice of polygamy (including that of Muslims). Book 2 dealt largely with betrothal, dowry, and marriage ceremonies among the Jews and gentiles, including the ancient Romans. After showing how Jewish and pagan customs of betrothal and marriage 'passed into Christianity', Selden turned to the practices of Greek and Latin Christians, and then to those in England, including the medieval ceremony of the Salisbury rite and the reformed one of the Book of Common Prayer. This led to the conclusion that Christian and Jewish marriage customs, while 'not often exactly the same' were 'analogous and similar' (p. 284).

Book 3 dealt with the nature of marriage and divorce. Jewish marriage involved mutual obligations between husband and wife, including the 'conjugal obligation' of regular sexual intercourse; these obligations provided a framework for judging its failure. Through careful philological comparison of key texts in New Testament Greek with the Aramaic of the rabbinic schools' teachings on the Deuteronomic grounds for divorce, Selden finally concluded that while Jesus's teachings initially seemed within the school of Shammai, which permitted divorce only for fornication, they were actually not very far from the permissiveness of the school of Hillel which allowed it for any reasonable cause. Natural law allowed spouses to marry and divorce 'by mutual consent', and this position shaped the interpretations of Jewish rabbis, the early Christians, and Greek and Russian Christians. Only the highly restrictive teachings and canon laws of western Christians were portrayed as unusual and unprecedented. An open-minded reader, Selden concluded, would know what changes to make to the English law of divorce. Although less directly, this political advice advocated reforms not unlike those already proclaimed by Milton.

In the 1640s Selden also revisited his earlier passion for the history of law in Europe, writing an introduction for his edition of *Fleta* (1647), an early treatise on English law from the reign of Edward I. Though badly printed, as he himself appreciated, it spelt out with greater subtlety and detail the history of the Roman law after the collapse of the empire in the West and of its interaction with the English common law briefly sketched in the 'Review' at the end of the *Historie of Tithes*. After providing an account of the usage and study of the Theodosian and Justinian codes in western and southern Europe from the fall of the Roman empire to the revival of learning in the twelfth century, Selden turned to Britain. The 'Anglo-Saxon invaders of England' used 'only their native Germanic customs' the 'laws of the Mercians, of the East Saxons and later of the Danes' (*Joannis Seldeni ad Fletam dissertatio*, trans. D. Ogg, 1925, 105). As in other parts of Europe, the Roman law reappeared in Britain in the twelfth century when 'the two Codes were introduced into England together in order that the most complete manuals of the Roman law extant in Latin might be available' (ibid., 109).

Under the early Normans the study of 'old English customs and laws as affecting public administration' by the learned monks of Abingdon helped to preserve them (*Joannis Seldeni ad Fletam dissertatio*, trans. D. Ogg, 1925, 129). This remained the law of the land, although 'archbishops and bishops who had studied civil and canon law as well as English law were frequently appointed His Majesty's judges and exercised full jurisdiction' (ibid., 143). These clerics helped to spread knowledge of the Roman and canon laws, and encouraged lawyers to use 'the very words and maxims of the civil law' in their 'pleadings before the king's judges' (ibid., 149), partly explaining the familiarity and use of the Roman law 'by Bracton, Thornton and the author of *Fleta* and in the Year Books of Edward II', but this expertise did not continue into the reign of Edward III (ibid., 159). Although many English lawyers and experts made use of Roman law 'in their studies, writings and debates' during the period from Stephen to Edward III, it did not become the law of the land, because of 'the unconcealed aversion which our ancestors had to' Roman law and 'the remarkable esteem in which the English or common law was held' (ibid., 161, 165). This history served both to introduce the reader to *Fleta* (which Selden discussed at some length at the end of this essay) and, perhaps more importantly, to inoculate England against any universalist claims of Roman or civil lawyers, one of the aims of so many of his earlier histories.

The last and most detailed of Selden's Judaic studies, *De synedriis et praefecturis juridicis veterum Ebraeorum* (1650–55), dealt with the ruling assembly, the Great Sanhedrin, and other judicial bodies of the ancient Hebrews. The last volume appeared posthumously and unfinished; all three together extended to 1841 pages in the edition of 1655. Although Selden had begun to research this topic during the 1630s, the pressures and debates of the following decade added relevance to the project. With its portrayal of the integration of the sacred and secular in ancient Jewish society, *De synedriis* may well have offered an indirect plea for England to return to a mixed government in which clergy sat in parliament. Jewish practices provided patterns not only for the early Christians, but for more recent reformers, as Selden had argued more than once in the Westminster assembly. The power of excommunication claimed by divine right by Roman Catholics, episcopalians, and presbyterians came under extended scrutiny in *De synedriis* and was attributed to human invention. The overarching power that resided in the Great Sanhedrin in Jerusalem provided Selden with the key for understanding the allusive and tantalizing New Testament texts upon which the Latin church had erected its claims for spiritual jurisdiction and its elaborate system of church courts. Containing both lawyers or teachers and priests learned in the law, the Great Sanhedrin handled both spiritual and secular questions and helped to maintain stability in ancient Jewish society.

The first volume of *De synedriis* dealt largely with the issue and history of excommunication. Among the ancient Jews and early Christians, it was exercised by magistrates, while priests, clergy, and lay teachers (rabbis) who dealt with spiritual matters did not exercise penal jurisdiction *ex officio* but only in their capacity as men wise in the law invited or elected to the civil task of judgment. Among the Jews, sinners excommunicated for breaking the law continued to participate in the whole range of ritual activities, even teaching, unless they also had some ritual uncleanness. Among the early Christians, the image of the spiritual sword ('gladium spiritalem') did not represent some independent coercive jurisdiction, but acted as a metaphor for the duties of preaching, praying, teaching, and administering the sacraments (vol. 1, p. 271). Only under the emperor Constantine did Christian clergy briefly act as judges.

The second volume concentrated upon the institutions of justice, where they derived their power, and who made up their membership, including the qualities of members of the Great Sanhedrin. It included a section on the qualifications of Jewish 'presbyters' and how they received their authority and ordination by human law, not divine right. The third volume dealt with the overarching power of the Great Sanhedrin, how it decided such unpriestly issues as war and peace, distinguished between prophets and pseudo-prophets, and supported and oversaw the high priest. With all its complexities and lengthy asides, this great work again showed that for Selden, political advice derived both from laws commanded by God and from the experience of humans in interpreting them. Jewish rabbis remained his most privileged interpreters and offered much wisdom to those Christians prepared to master their writings and style of exegesis.

Last months and legacy As he neared the end of his seventh decade Selden's precarious health declined. His long-time companion, the countess of Kent, died on 7 December 1651 and left him her property. Two years later he updated his will, appointing his 'beloved friends' Edward Heyward, John Vaughan, Matthew Hale, and Rowland Jewks the elder, as the heirs in trust of his lands and estate, and leaving only £100 each to the two sons of his sister, Mary, and her husband, John Bernard of Goring, Sussex, as country folk unused to riches; Aubrey thought he had at least one illegitimate daughter, but had considered such offspring unworthy heirs. Among many minor legatees were William Seymour, marquess of Hertford, 'Mr Grey Longueville', and Sir Thomas Cotton. Continuing to correspond with friends and scholars, Selden answered in October 1653 an enquiry from Archbishop Ussher about the identity of Gallio in the book of Acts, concluding—after examining works by Caesar Baronius, Grotius, and Justus Lipsius—that he may well have been Seneca's brother. By this time he was ill—'of a dropsey', according to Aubrey (*Brief Lives*, 274). In November 1654 he conversed with Ussher and Langbaine, which supports Anthony Wood's repetition of Sir Matthew Hale's comment that he died 'a resolved serious Christian' (Wood, *Ath. Oxon.*, 3rd edn, 1813–20, 3.376), rather than Aubrey's story that Thomas Hobbes persuaded Selden to turn away clergymen who came to pray with him. Following Selden's death at White Friars on 30 November, the aged archbishop of Armagh preached on 14 December at Selden's well-attended public funeral at the Temple Church; he was buried in the Temple Church on the same day.

During a lifetime of scholarship, legal practice, and public service, Selden amassed an extensive collection of books and manuscripts. A story circulated that he had revoked an original intention to bequeath these to the Bodleian Library, Oxford, but this was false. By the terms of his will the library was to receive his collection of Greek and Oriental manuscripts, selected Latin manuscripts, and his remaining Talmudic and rabbinical books. Most of these were forwarded by his executors to the Bodleian in 1659, although in the interim some had been lost. Among the 8000 volumes which arrived safely, some had belonged to Jonson, Donne, and Cotton; they remain there today. Selden's greatest legacy, however, was not the expensive hat band studded with diamonds that he left to Hertford but his extensive European and Jewish studies and his advocacy of a mixed monarchy. His histories on European and British topics displayed a meticulous application of continental humanist methods and a masterful reading of English and continental sources and commentaries in imaginative, detailed narratives of great complexity. The meticulous results of his plunge into the complex realm of Jewish studies showed great respect for the integrity of rabbinic interpretations and an unparalleled understanding of Jewish texts, traditions, and history, all conveyed in subtle, empathetic studies that used the wisdom of the Jews to teach a Christian audience. How fitting for one praised by the earl of Clarendon for 'his good nature, charity, and delight in doing good' (Clarendon, 1.31) and noted by Wood as 'the glory of the English nation, as Hugo Grotius worthily stiles him' (Wood, *Ath. Oxon.*, 3rd edn, 1813–20, 3.366). His contribution to scholarship was commemorated through the giving of his name to the Selden Society, founded to publish the significant documents of English legal history; volumes have appeared regularly since 1888. PAUL CHRISTIANSON

Sources Bodl. Oxf., MS Selden supra 108, 109, 123, 124 • J. Selden, *Opera omnia*, ed. D. Wilkins, 3 vols. in 6 (1726) • [J. Selden], *Table talk of John Selden*, ed. F. Pollock (1927); see also earlier edn (1808) • 'To my singular good Friend, Mr. *Augustine Vincent*', A. Vincent, *A discoverie of errours* (1622) • *Fleta*, 4, ed. G. O. Sayles, SeldS, 99 (1983) • *State trials* • R. C. Johnson and others, eds., *Proceedings in parliament, 1628*, 6 vols. (1977–83) • W. Notestein and F. H. Relf, eds., *Commons debates for 1629* (1921) • J. P. Rosenblatt and W. Schleiner, 'John Selden's letter to Ben Jonson on cross-dressing and bisexual gods', *English Literary Renaissance*, 29 (1999), 44–74 [includes Selden's text] • *The whole works of … James Ussher*, ed. C. R. Elrington and J. H. Todd, 17 vols. (1847–64) • D. R. Woolf, 'John Selden, John Borough and Francis Bacon's *History of Henry VII*, 1621', *Huntington Library Quarterly* (1984), 47–53 • D. S. Berkowitz, *John Selden's formative years: politics and society in early seventeenth-century England* (1988) • P. Christianson, *Discourse on history, law, and governance in the public career of John Selden, 1610–1635* (1996) • G. Parry, *The trophies of time* (1995) • J. P. Sommerville, 'John Selden, the law of nature, and the origins of government', *HJ*, 27 (1984), 437–47 • J. P. Rosenblatt, *Torah and law in 'Paradise lost'* (1994) • W. H. Cooke, ed., *Students admitted to the Inner Temple, 1547–1660* [1878] • *Aubrey's Brief lives*, ed. O. L. Dick (1949) • *The letters and journals of Robert Baillie*, ed. D. Laing, 3 vols. (1841–2) • H. Grotius, *De jure belli ac pacis* (1625) • *The whole works of the Rev. John Lightfoot*, ed. J. R. Pitman, 13 vols. (1822–5) • W. Prynne, *The unbishoping of Timothy and Titus* (1636) • Wood, *Ath. Oxon.*, new edn, 3.366–81 • *The diary of Bulstrode Whitelocke, 1605–1675*, ed. R. Spalding, British Academy, Records of Social and Economic History, new ser., 13 (1990) • GEC, *Peerage* • M. Feingold, 'John Selden and the nature of seventeenth-century science', *In the presence of the past: essays in honour of Frank Manuel*, ed. R. T. Bienvenu and M. Feingold (1991), 55–78 • R. Tuck, '"The ancient law of freedom": John Selden and the civil war', *Reactions to the English civil war, 1642–1649*, ed. J. Morrill (1982), 137–61 • R. Tuck, *Natural rights theories: their origin and development* (1979) • R. Tuck, *Philosophy and government, 1572–1651* (1993) • W. D. Macray, *Annals of the Bodleian Library, Oxford*, 2nd edn (1890), 110–11 • *The life of Edward, earl of Clarendon … written by himself*, 3 vols. (1759)

Archives BL, letters, MSS, and papers • Bodl. Oxf., corresp. and papers • Inner Temple, London, papers • LPL, papers | CUL, Littleton's notes for his speech for bail hearing of Selden with Selden's comments, MS Mm.6.63(4) • Lincoln's Inn, London, commonplace book, notes, papers, and MSS collections, Hale MSS 11, 12, 86 • U. Cal., Los Angeles, William Andrews Clark Memorial Library, notes and collections, Hale MS

Likenesses P. Lely?, oils, *c*.1650, Yale U., law library [*see illus.*] • J. Chantry, line engraving, 1661, BM, NPG; repro. in J. Selden, *God made man* (1661) • G. L., engraving, repro. in E. Pococke, *Contestio Gemmarum, sive Eutychii*, 2 vols. (1654–6), frontispiece • studio of P. Lely, oils (after type, *c*.1650), Clarendon collection; on loan to Plymouth Art Gallery, 1979; version, NPG • attrib. P. Lely, portrait, AM Oxf. • Van Hove, engraving (after bust by R. White, 1682), repro. in J. Selden, *The reverse or back-face of the English Janus* (1682) • R. White, line engraving, BM, NPG • oils, NPG • oils, AM Oxf. • oils (after unknown artist), NPG • portrait, Exeter College, Oxford

Select Society (*act.* 1754–1764), an Edinburgh debating club for gifted and socially prominent members of the city's intellectual élite, was the brainchild of the portrait painter Allan *Ramsay, who in the winter of 1754 gathered fifteen friends to form a discussion club.

Membership This initial society was composed, like the later membership, of Edinburgh's leading lawyers, churchmen, and academics, including the Revd John *Jardine, Francis *Home, Adam *Smith, John *Anderson, Alexander *Wedderburn, Simon *Fraser, James *Burnett, later Lord Monboddo, the Revd Alexander *Carlyle, Sir William *Pulteney (formerly Johnstone), David *Hume, and John *Swinton. Also among this original group was the physician **Alexander Stevenson** (*c*.1725–1791), who graduated MD from Glasgow University in 1749. Resident in Edinburgh from the early 1750s, Stevenson was a member not only of the Select Society but also of Edinburgh's Philosophical Society and Glasgow's Literary Society and Hodge-Podge Club. In 1766 he was appointed professor of medicine at Glasgow, where he remained until 1788 when he resigned, only to be reappointed with his nephew, Thomas Charles *Hope, as his assistant and the beneficiary of a reversionary interest. Stevenson's nephew was the son of his sister Juliana and her husband, the botanist John *Hope, who joined the Select Society in May 1755. During the 1780s Stevenson was an active land reformer, establishing a planned village at Sorn (Dalgain), Ayrshire. He died on 29 May 1791.

Alongside Stevenson's brother-in-law, John Hope, May 1755 saw a further sixteen lesser but still distinguished men join the society. Again the professional coverage was broad, including historians and writers such as the Revd John *Home and William *Robertson, the politicians Sir Gilbert *Elliot, third baronet, and Sir Henry *Erskine, and the advocate David *Dalrymple, as well as the future Edinburgh professors Hugh *Blair and James *Russell. By then the society had become a debating forum officially limited to about fifty members (from 2 May). However, the new limit of sixty was reached on 19 June and rose again to seventy-six at the end of December 1755, if one also counts the society's clerk, Walter *Goodall. Of the new recruits in this period, the most eminent were the future politician Andrew *Stuart and George *Dempster MP, the economist the Revd Robert *Wallace, the poet and later professor of natural philosophy at St Andrews the Revd William *Wilkie, the physicians Alexander *Monro *primus*, Robert *Whytt, and Sir Alexander *Dick (formerly Cunyngham), and the lawyers and legal scholars John *Dalrymple of Cousland, George Clerk-*Maxwell, Robert *Dundas, and Henry *Home, Lord Kames.

This group also contained several prominent merchants and bankers, including William *Tod and **Adam Fairholm** (*c.*1722–1764), the eldest son of an established Edinburgh corn merchant, Thomas Fairholm of Greenhill. Adam joined the family business in the early 1740s and became a leading figure in local financial, political, and commercial circles. By 1748 he had become a director of the Bank of Scotland, and twelve years later served in a similar capacity with the Royal Bank of Scotland. Three times elected to the town council, he was also a commissioner for the improvement of Leith harbour, and an active member in one of the great enterprises of mid-eighteenth-century Scotland, the Carron Iron Company, at the time the largest and most modern in Europe. However, in the early 1760s over-speculation brought financial difficulties for himself and his partners, including the architect and contractor John *Adam. The Fairholms were forced to give up their holdings in the Carron company and went into bankruptcy in March 1764. Thinking he was being pursued by bailiffs while fleeing to the continent, Adam Fairholm jumped from his ship and drowned in 1764. A slightly more successful career was had by another business member of the society, **Robert Arbuthnot of Haddo** (1728–1803), who was born in Peterhead, Aberdeenshire, where he established himself as a merchant and agent for the British Linen Bank, of which he later became a director (1767–70). Arbuthnot probably moved to Edinburgh about the time he joined the Select Society. However, like Fairholm, his business collapsed with the failure of the Ayr Bank in 1772. Through the efforts of friends he became secretary to the board of trustees for the Society of Arts, Manufactures and Fisheries, a post he held from 1779 to 1803. In addition to his participation in the Select Society, Arbuthnot was also a member of the Edinburgh Musical Society and the Highland Society of Scotland, of which he was director in 1784, and was a fellow of the Royal Society of Edinburgh from the following year. A patron of the music publisher George Thomson, Arbuthnot was also a long-term correspondent of his fellow Select Society member James *Beattie. He died in 1803.

By mid-1755 the society was clearly a desirable club to enter, one which had no trouble rejecting peers and gentry in favour of men of talent. With the limit now raised to 100, candidates continued to be admitted, including newcomers to the city such as the Revd Adam *Ferguson, William *Cullen, and the Revd John *Walker. By 1759 the names on the published members' list ran to 133. And at the very end of its life, the society could still recruit James *Boswell, Thomas *Erskine (a notable composer as well as the sixth earl of Kellie), and the soldier–diplomat Sir Robert Murray *Keith. Numbers, however, did not ensure success. Meetings were thin by December to mid-January 1756–7. In 1757–8 a committee was struck to revive the society and was temporarily successful. The 100-member club was revived again in early 1758, before going into another period of decline and revival in the following year. However, by the end of 1758 many of the new members were of no intellectual distinction and very likely had little commitment to the society which, as Alexander Carlyle wrote, 'was intended for philosophical inquiry and the improvement of the members in the art of publick speaking' (*Collected Works of Dugald Stewart*, 7.88). By 1760 another revival was needed. The society lingered in some disarray after 1761; by 1762–3 its great days were past and it ended during the winter of 1763–4. During its final years the club suffered a fate common to many similar bodies in relatively small capital cities. Most of its members were still in their thirties and were busy making careers. Some left Edinburgh to pursue their work; others fell behind in their dues and failed to attend, or to speak if they went to meetings. Others, having attained the cachet of membership, tended not to go to meetings. As a result the running of the society devolved upon a small number of its most assiduous members, who must have found their duties onerous, given its somewhat cumbersome structure and the formality of its procedures.

Organization and aims The society met on Wednesdays from 12 November to 12 August, first in the Advocates' Library, then the Masons' Hall (Mary's Chapel) in Niddry Wynd, and later at another hall used by St Giles Lodge. Members elected six presidents who were to officiate in turn over the debates on questions submitted to a committee struck annually from 1754. The president of the session was responsible for picking approved questions a week before they were discussed. Prominent members of the questions committee included James Burnett, Sir William Pulteney, William Robertson, Alexander Monro, and the writer to the signet **Alexander Tait** (*d.* 1781). The son of an Edinburgh merchant, and a student at the university (*c.*1735–1737), Tait was a cultured young man whose friends, including Francis Home, David Dalrymple, James *Edgar [*see under* Poker Club], and Francis *Garden, later Lord Gardenstone, would later join him as members of the Select Society. In 1744 he was made under- or substitute keeper of the signet, a place worth £40–50 p.a., which he retained until 1762. Tait's political connections were keenly whig; he was apprenticed to George Balfour, writer to the signet, in the wake of the Jacobite rising of 1745, and he or his father had earlier joined the Revolution Club about 1740. His connection with the Friendly Insurance Company of Edinburgh, together with his work as an agent of fire and insurance companies, and later as secretary to the Edinburgh Insurance, suggests an interest in innovation and improvement before he joined the society in 1754. Like many fellow members he combined improving interests with banking activities, becoming a director of the Bank of Scotland in 1762. Two years earlier he had been appointed principal clerk of session and was clerk to the processes of Scotland from 1779. He died on 8 July 1781.

The society's debates began with two or more members reading short statements or giving extempore speeches for or against the evening's question. This was followed by open discussion and concluded with a vote on which side had prevailed. The rules prohibited the discussion of religious issues and Jacobitism, but otherwise allowed formal and sometimes heated debate on a wide range of issues, which touched on art, literature, eloquence, the theatre, economics, politics and public policy, manners, and national improvement. Particular attention was paid to farming since many members were landholders. The essays of Lord Shaftesbury, Joseph Addison, and David Hume provided a fruitful source of subject matter, as did current affairs; in 1760, for example, the society debated and condemned the then vexatious issue of giving vales (the tipping of servants). The final question list numbered 158, of which 97 were considered in at least 155 debates held between 1754 and January 1763. The most popular question—debated six times in 1755–6—was the formation of a Scottish militia, though economic and social questions dominated the meetings as a whole.

During the 1750s the Select Society's activities produced two spin-off groups dedicated to aims shared by the parent body. From early 1755 members sponsored the Edinburgh Society for the Encouragement of Arts first proposed by Colonel (James) Adolphus Dickenson *Oughton. Instituted 'to ENCOURAGE genius, to reward industry [and] to cultivate the arts of peace', the society included all Select Society members as well as subscribers to the Edinburgh Society. Prominent managers from the society included Adam Fairholm, Alexander Tait, William Cullen, Robert Whytt, and Alexander Monro, chairman of its committee. All were among the judges of items submitted for debate, as were additional Select members, including Hugh Blair, David Hume, John Hope, and Alexander *Boswell, later Lord Auchinleck. Between 1755 and 1764 the society advertised 1111 premiums for such items as rugs, clover seed, beer, new looms, and good stallions, as well as finely printed and bound books. In 1759, probably its best year, the society offered 141 prizes worth about £590, though the actual amount presented is difficult to calculate. Within five years the society's activities had declined markedly to just 80 premiums in 1764, owing in part to falling subscription rates and a growing tendency to withhold awards or offer reduced prize money. A second spin-off group—the Select Society for Promoting the Reading and Speaking of the English Language in Scotland (1761–5)—stemmed from members' shared interest in elocution and good communication in debate. The founding resolution—which called for Englishmen 'duly qualified to instruct gentlemen in the knowledge of the English tongue' to open schools in Edinburgh—led in August 1761 to the foundation of the society to recruit teachers and supervise institutions. Select members on the society's board included Alexander Monro, William Cullen, Adam Fairholm, Sir Alexander Dick, and Lord Kames.

In their appreciation of the place of good English for personal and national improvement, the directors, together with fellow members of the main society, exhibited many of the interests and concerns of enlightened mid-century Scots. With its focus on contemporary issues, the Select Society provided a focal point for debates on socio-economic subjects developed in the writing of members such as David Hume, Adam Ferguson, Robert Wallace, James Burnett, and Sir John Dalrymple, and in the political pamphlets of Alexander Carlyle and Ilay *Campbell. This said, the Select Society, weighted towards a non-scientific literary membership, equally failed to address other leading areas of Enlightenment study. Key areas on which it seldom touched were the sceptical and common-sense philosophy of Hume, Thomas Reid, or George Campbell, the scientific work of Colin Maclaurin, Joseph Black, and James Hutton, and the university's medical research, despite physicians being the best-represented profession among its membership after lawyers. Likewise the society devoted little time to artistic achievement or how to understand it. For that one needs to look at other groups such as the Rankenian Club (*c.*1716–1774), the Edinburgh Medical Society (1731–5), the Philosophical Society of Edinburgh (1737–83), and later the Royal Society of Edinburgh (from 1783). Select Society members tended to continue their club life in smaller, exclusive groups, such as the *Poker Club, which were given to discussing serious, improving matters in convivial circumstances. The very exclusiveness of such clubs made them somewhat unstable, for it was their members who were often the most mobile and, despite the keen patriotic agenda, the ones least likely to stay in Scotland. Those who did stay in

Edinburgh bore a disproportionate share of club management and often struggled to maintain membership and secure adequate funding. ROGER L. EMERSON

Sources minutes of the Select Society, NL Scot., Adv. 23.1.1; MS 98/70 • *Caledonian Mercury* (1755–65) • *The autobiography of Dr. Alexander Carlyle of Inveresk, 1722–1805*, ed. J. Hill Burton (1910) • E. L. Cloyd, *James Burnett, Lord Monboddo* (1972) • R. L. Emerson, 'The social composition of Enlightened Edinburgh: the Select Society of Edinburgh, 1754–1764', *Studies on Voltaire and the Eighteenth Century*, 114 (1973), 291–329 • R. L. Emerson, 'The Enlightenment and social structures', *City and society in the 18th century*, ed. P. Fritz and D. Williams, Publications of the McMaster University Association for 18th Century Studies, 3 (1974), 99–124 • H. D. Erlam, 'Alexander Monro, *primus*', *University of Edinburgh Journal*, 17 (1953–5), 77–105 • B. Hillyard, 'The Edinburgh Society's silver medals for printing', *Papers of the Bibliographical Society of America*, 78 (1984), 295–319 • W. S. Howell, *Eighteenth-century British logic and rhetoric* (1971) • D. McElroy, 'The literary clubs and societies of eighteenth-century Edinburgh', PhD diss., U. Edin., 1952 • D. D. McElroy, *Scotland's age of improvement* (1969) • E. C. Mossner, *The life of David Hume* (1954) • N. Phillipson, 'Culture and society in the 18th century province: the case of Edinburgh and the Scottish Enlightenment', *The university in society*, ed. L. Stone, 2 (1974), 444–8 • J. Ramsay of Ochtertyre, *Scotland and Scotsmen in the eighteenth century*, ed. A. Allardyce, 2 vols. (1888) • J. Robertson, *The Scottish Enlightenment and the militia issue* (1985) • *Collected works of Dugald Stewart*, ed. W. Hamilton, 11 vols. (1854–60), vol. 7, pp. 88–92 • *Universal Scots Almanack* (1762–5) • A. Monro and others, 'Rules and orders of the Edinburgh Society for the Encouragement of Arts, Sciences, Manufacturers and Agriculture', 1755, NL Scot. • P. Clark, *British clubs and societies, 1580–1800* (2000), 2, 86, 120

Archives NL Scot., minutes of the Select Society, MS Adv.23.1.1 and MS 98/70 • NL Scot., Beattie MSS, Fettercairn Acc. 4796, boxes 91–8 [Robert Arbuthnot of Haddo] • NL Scot., Saltoun MSS, MS SMisc. 59 | NL Scot., Erskine Murray MSS, 5075–5076 [Alexander Tait] • U. Aberdeen L., letters to James Beattie, MS 30/2/1–150 [Robert Arbuthnot of Haddo] • U. Edin. L., Laing MSS, R. Wallace, 'Of the naturalizing of foreign protestants', La.II 620.26 • U. Glas. L., Cullen papers, W. Cullen, 'An essay on the construction of the plow', box 7

Selered (*d.* 746). *See under* East Saxons, kings of the (*act.* late 6th cent.–*c.*820).

Selfridge, Harry Gordon (1858–1947), department store owner, was born on 11 January 1858 at Ripon, Wisconsin, USA, the only son of Robert Oliver Selfridge (*d.* 1873) and his wife, Lois Frances Baxter (*d.* 1924). Robert Selfridge owned a small retail business in Ripon and from 1861 he served with the 3rd Michigan cavalry until 1865 when he resigned, having risen to the rank of major and assistant adjutant-general. He never returned home and died in an accident eight years later. Harry was brought up by his mother at Jackson, Michigan, where she was a teacher. After leaving school at the age of fourteen he became a bank clerk, with ambitions to join the navy. These were dashed when his application to the Annapolis naval academy was rejected on the grounds that he was slightly too small. His career changed when in 1879 he joined the department store and mail-order firm of Field, Leiter & Co. (later Marshall, Field & Co.) as a clerk. Through hard work and ability he rose to become manager of the retail department by 1886. In 1890 he married Rosalie Bickingham (*d.* 1918) of Chicago; they had three daughters and a son.

Selfridge proved to be a dynamic force at Marshall Fields

Harry Gordon Selfridge (1858–1947), by Sir William Orpen, 1927

in Chicago and travelled extensively for the organization, picking up new ideas wherever he went. After trips to London and Paris, Selfridge attempted to persuade Field to establish a department store in London similar to his successful Chicago business. In 1904, when Field would not agree to the venture, Selfridge decided to break with the firm that had made him a junior partner fourteen years earlier. He left Marshall Fields with a fortune of £300,000 and bought the Chicago firm of Schlesinger and Mayer, which he sold quickly for a profit of £50,000.

In 1906, after almost two years of unsatisfying experiences in Chicago and in European travel, Selfridge arrived in London, taking up residence in Arlington Street. He quickly assessed the commercial scene and returned to his idea of opening a large department store that would embody the latest ideas in retailing. Despite a relatively difficult economic climate Selfridge adhered to his scheme and found a site for his new store at the western end of Oxford Street. He engaged the Waring-White company to erect the building, based on the plans of the Chicago architect Daniel Burnham. Selfridge always thought big and his new store, opened in 1909, reflected this. He engaged the best buyers from Britain and America, offering high salaries to attract them. Many weeks before the store opened Selfridge had engaged some 1200 employees. He brought Marshall Fields' chief window-dresser, Goldsman, from Chicago to impress Londoners with exciting new window displays. Britain's top artists and designers were hired to produce new advertisements announcing the store's policies. In total £36,000 was spent on advertising the store's opening.

Selfridge's new store was not only large, containing

some 130 different retail departments; it introduced a range of customer services as well as offering improved working conditions for the staff. The store aimed at covering all normal requirements and provided new services such as a library, rest-rooms, and a free information bureau. All this was backed by masterly, persistent advertising, and the introduction of new methods of staff training. Selfridge made his presence felt as he passed through the store on his daily tours of inspection, always formally dressed with his top hat, for he had a critical eye for detail. His methods were an important transforming influence on London's retail scene and British retailing in general.

After the First World War Selfridge expanded his interests by acquiring control of a number of other department stores, all of which were allowed to retain their own character. During the 1920s he was in a difficult financial position and through the influence of Jimmy Wight, a large company promoter of the period, was persuaded to form the Gordon Selfridge Trust and Selfridge Provincial Stores Ltd with a registered capital of £5 million. The stock issues were oversubscribed and Selfridge received £2 million in exchange for his interest in the company. While Selfridge was a master in the art of obtaining credit and raising money, in the latter part of his life he managed to fritter away much of his fortune. Losses mounted throughout the 1930s, and the board eventually presented him with an ultimatum: to pay his debts or retire. In 1939 he resigned from the board with the honorary title of president and a modest salary of £6000. In January 1941 he was obliged to surrender this last link with his business.

It was Selfridge's love of the theatre and the people who made it sparkle that was to cause him problems in later life. After the death of his wife in 1918, Selfridge began a series of relationships with well-known stars, such as Gaby Deslys, whom he provided with a house. Later, in 1926, he became involved with Jenny Dolly and during eight years of extravagance at French casino resorts Selfridge ran through his entire fortune. For all his failings in later life Selfridge was a successful retailer and a man of highly optimistic temperament and agreeable manner. He was a great social entertainer, holding many functions for distinguished personalities at Lansdowne House or his country residence, Highcliffe Castle, Hampshire.

Selfridge became a naturalized British subject in 1937. He died propertyless at 2 Ross Court, Putney Heath, where he lived with his daughter Rosalie, on 8 May 1947, and was buried at Highcliffe churchyard alongside his wife and mother. GARETH SHAW

Sources *The Times* (9 May 1947), 7 · T. C. Bridges and H. H. Tiltman, *Kings of commerce* [1928] · J. W. Leonard, *The book of Chicagoans* (1905) · R. Pound, *Selfridge: a biography* (1960) · M. Pasdermadjian, *The department store* (1954) · J. W. Ferry, *A history of the department store* (1960) · A. Adburgham, *Shops and shopping, 1800–1914: where, and in what manner the well-dressed Englishwoman bought her clothes*, 2nd edn (1981) · d. cert.

Archives HL · JRL, Guardian Archives

Likenesses P. Evans, ink and watercolour, 1924, NPG · W. Orpen, oils, 1927, Selfridges, London [*see illus.*] · E. Kapp, drawing, 1928, Barber Institute of Fine Arts, Birmingham · A. P. F. Ritchie, chromolithograph caricature, NPG; repro. in *VF* (6 Dec 1911) · R. S. Sherriffs, ink and pencil caricature, NPG

Wealth at death believed to have owned no property: *DBB*

Seligman, Brenda Zara (1883–1965). *See under* Seligman, Charles Gabriel (1873–1940).

Seligman, Charles Gabriel (1873–1940), ethnologist, was born in London on 24 December 1873, the only child of Hermann Seligmann (1835–1889)—the final 'n' of the family name was dropped in 1914—a rich wine merchant, and his wife, Olivia Mendez da Costa. After uncongenial schooldays at St Paul's School, London, he won a scholarship to St Thomas's Hospital, where he took his first medical qualification in 1896, winning the Bristowe medal in pathology and becoming house physician a year later. He published papers on tropical diseases and on the heredity of hair and eye colour in 1896 and 1898. Through his friend and medical colleague C. S. Myers, who had been recruited as a medical member of the Cambridge anthropological expedition to the Torres Strait, he persuaded its leader, the marine zoologist A. C. Haddon, to take him also. This was in spite of Haddon's concerns that with Myers, William McDougall, and their former teacher W. H. R. Rivers already on board, Seligman's inclusion would medically overweight his party.

Seligman arrived in the Torres Strait from Australia in April 1898, spending most of May on the island of Mer, then stayed for two months with Haddon on the mainland of British New Guinea before returning to Mer. He visited the other islands of Mabuiag, Saibai, Thursday Island, Yam, and Nagir in September, and Cape York Peninsula, Australia, in November, before returning to England via Sarawak. His original intention had been to study plants and native medicine, but he extended his observations to associated rituals and their terminology, as well as pathology, in particular the testing of native colour perception, and incidentally making a contribution to ethnographic photography. Influenced by Rivers, he became interested in classificatory kinship studied by the 'genealogical method'. In the expedition's *Reports*, published in an odd chronology, he wrote in the second (1901) 'The vision of natives of British New Guinea'; in the fifth (1904) 'Birth and childhood customs', 'Women's puberty customs', and, with Haddon, 'Magic and religion'; in the third (1907) 'Gesture language of the western islanders' and, with Haddon, 'Fire signals in Torres Strait' and on the vocabulary of the Otat language at Cape Grenville.

Although Seligman returned to pathology as Salters' Company research fellow at St Thomas's Hospital, in 1901, where he became superintendent of the clinical laboratory, MRCP, and in 1906 MD, his real interest had become ethnology. In 1903 a chance meeting with the American Major Cooke-Daniels facilitated an expedition to New Guinea, in 1904, with Seligman as scientific director. He collected material in the Mekeo, Roro, and Massim areas of Papua (as British New Guinea was now renamed under Australian control), and this, together with his notes from 1898, provided the material for his book *The Melanesians of British New Guinea*, published in 1910, the year in which he

Charles Gabriel Seligman (1873–1940), by Sir William Rothenstein

was appointed to a lectureship in ethnology. In 1911 he also became FRCP.

On 4 July 1905 he married Brenda Zara [**Brenda Zara Seligman** (1883–1965)], who had been born in London at 20 Pembridge Crescent, Kensington, on 26 June 1883, the youngest of the fourteen children (seven sons, seven daughters) of Sarah and Myer Salaman, a well-to-do merchant; a brother was Redcliffe Nathan *Salaman. After attending Roedean School Brenda began pre-medical biology at Bedford College, London, before her marriage, but became her husband's co-worker in ethnology. In 1906, after an invitation from the government of Ceylon, she assisted him in the study of the aboriginal Vedda people, becoming an anthropologist in her own right. Their book *The Veddas* appeared in 1911. With funding from the government of Anglo-Egyptian Sudan, the Seligmans undertook a survey of the pagan Nilotic tribes (1909–10, 1911–12); the results were published as *Pagan Tribes of the Nilotic Sudan* (1932).

Seligman became part-time professor of ethnology at the London School of Economics (LSE) in 1913 and held the chair until 1934. In 1914 the Seligmans travelled with Haddon, Rivers, and R. R. Marett to the British Association for the Advancement of Science meeting in Australia. With them was B. M. Malinowski, a protégé of Seligman's then acting as Marett's secretary; as an Austrian subject under restrictions during the war, Malinowski remained to undertake field work in Papua (with Seligman's support in 1923 he became a colleague at the LSE, deliberately designating his post 'social anthropology' as distinct from ethnology). Elected FRS in 1919, Seligman was Hunterian professor, Arris and Gale lecturer of the Royal College of Surgeons, and Lloyd Roberts lecturer of the Royal College of Physicians in 1935. He had been president of Section H (anthropology) of the British Association for the Advancement of Science in 1915 and from 1923 to 1925 served as president of the Royal Anthropological Institute, of which he was Rivers medallist in 1925 and Huxley memorial lecturer and medallist in 1932. He became a foundation council member of the International African Institute when set up in 1926 (as the International Institute of African Languages and Cultures) to sponsor and fund research and fieldwork through a fellowship scheme, which from 1931 was supported by the Rockefeller Foundation. His pupil E. E. Evans-Pritchard, who followed up the Seligmans' work in Sudan, was, however, never a beneficiary, for the institute and the LSE had become embroiled, apart from personal animosities, in Malinowski's disagreement with Seligman over the nature of anthropology. A natural scientist, like Haddon, Seligman shared Haddon's view of 1898 that the urgent task was to observe and record indigenous society before it disappeared under the impact of the modern world, not to theorize. He collected and classified the 'facts', as he understood scientific enquiry to require, using genealogical methods developed by Rivers to conduct surveys of several groups through the medium of interpreters—rather than by the intensive study of one group through the mastery of its language: the field method perforce developed by Malinowski in the Trobriand Islands of Papua, and then taught by him at the LSE.

Seligman, however, during war service as a captain in the Royal Army Medical Corps treating shell-shock, became interested in the relationship between psychology and anthropology, an interest more particularly developed by Brenda, who was deeply influenced by Rivers's psychiatric work during the First World War in army hospitals. Both she and her husband wrote on the relevance of psychology to social organization. Nevertheless, the Seligmans' pre-war fieldwork was distinguished rather by careful, systematic recording and classification of observed phenomena, not psychological or social explanations of them. And Malinowski's condemnation of this kind of general, as distinct from intensive, fieldwork was a factor, apart from ill health, in Seligman's retirement from his chair in 1934 to live at Court Leys, Toot Baldon, in Oxfordshire. Here a number of younger anthropologists, but notably Evans-Pritchard, paid summer court, while others went to Malinowski at Sopra Bolzano. Seligman died at the Acland Nursing Home, Oxford, from infective endocarditis on 19 September 1940. Brenda went on to make a distinctive contribution as a specialist in kinship and social organization, and edited the sixth and last (1951) edition of *Notes and Queries in Anthropology*. She died at 22 Ilchester Place, Kensington, London, on 2 January 1965. Their thirteen-year-old daughter had died in 1919; a son survived them.

Although the Seligmans, affectionately known as the Sligs or the Sliggers, as 'ethnologists' seemed overtaken by Malinowskian 'social anthropology', their field observation was broad, accurate, thorough; and an innovation in what had hitherto been the 'armchair' anthropology of classicists like J. G. Frazer. Their breadth of interest, as well as their private means, were reflected in their fine collection of Chinese, Central Asian, and Lurestan bronzes, Chinese jade and sculptures, and Chinese and Korean ceramics exhibited by the Arts Council of Great Britain in 1966, now in the British Museum.

F. J. West

Sources Seligman papers; Malinowski papers, BLPES · CUL, Seligman MSS · CUL, Haddon MSS · Royal Anthropological Institute, Seligman MSS · C. S. Myers, *Obits. FRS*, 3 (1939–41), 627–46 · Trinity Cam., J. G. Frazer MSS · m. cert. · b. cert. [Brenda Seligman] · d. cert. [Brenda Seligman] · G. Stocking, *After Tylor: British social anthropology, 1888–1951* (1995) · *Man*, 65 (1965), 177–81 · *DNB*
Archives BLPES, papers · BLPES, personal and professional corresp. and papers, incl. field notebooks, diaries, journals, notes, lecture and research papers · CUL, papers · Royal Anthropological Institute, London, notes, mainly relating to art and anthropology of the Massim · Royal Anthropological Institute, London, photographic archive, photographs · SOAS, linguistic notes · U. Oxf., Griffith Institute, drawings of Meriotic subjects | BLPES, B. M. Malinowski papers · Bodl. Oxf., corresp. with J. L. Myers · CUL, corresp. with Meyer Fortes · CUL, corresp. with A. C. Haddon and notes relating to Mekeo · Trinity Cam., J. G. Frazer papers, corresp.
Likenesses W. Stoneman, photograph, 1933, NPG · W. Rothenstein, pencil drawing, NPG [*see illus.*] · photographs, Cambridge Museum of Anthropology and Archaeology · photographs, repro. in A. Herle and S. Rouse, eds., *Cambridge and the Torres Strait* (1998) · photographs, repro. in A. H. Quiggin, *Haddon, the headhunter: a short sketch of the life of A. C. Haddon* (1942)
Wealth at death £13,854 17*s*.—in England: probate, 1 Jan 1941, *CGPLA Eng. & Wales*

Seligman, Gerald Abraham (1886–1973), glaciologist, was born on 26 March 1886 at Clapham Park, London, the seventh and youngest child of Isaac Seligman (1834–1928), merchant banker, and his wife, Lina Messel (1851–1925), of Darmstadt, Germany. Both his parents were of German-Jewish origin. From 1900 to 1903, he was educated at Harrow School, whence he entered the South-eastern Agricultural College. In 1905 he went up to Trinity Hall, Cambridge, graduating in 1908 with second-class honours in natural sciences, with strength in chemistry and geology.

On holidays in the Alps and in Norway, Seligman had shown ability as a skier and, in 1907, he became an early member of the Ski Club of Great Britain. His skiing enthusiasm was to set the course of his later career but on first leaving Cambridge, he joined his brother Richard's new company, Aluminium Plant and Vessel (APV), manufacturing specialized process plant and containers. On 5 June 1915 he married Ursula Goode (1891–1982). The couple later had one daughter.

A scientist by inclination, Seligman was not satisfied with the life of a businessman. Although he remained a director of APV until 1959, in 1931 he ceased working full-time, thenceforth devoting himself to the study of snow and ice. He had valuable contacts in this field for, since 1921, he had edited and contributed extensively to *Ski Notes and Queries*, the journal of the Ski Club of Great Britain. He remained editor until 1935 and was president of the club from 1927 to 1929.

Seligman's early research centred on the structure of snow, with an examination of falling snow and avalanches. Following research in Cambridge, he published his classic work *Snow Structure and Ski Fields* (1936; repr., 1962). He moved on to consider the metamorphosis of snow into glacier ice and for this purpose organized expeditions to the Jungfraujoch, Switzerland, in 1937 and 1938. His personality and standing drew leading chemists and physicists into his parties. As a result of the work, many seminal papers in glaciology were published, presaging a new style in such research.

In 1936, Seligman was invited to form a British group reporting to the International Commission of Snow and Ice (ICSI). He responded by forming the Association for the Study of Snow and Ice. After war service with the Meteorological Office, he transformed his association into the British Glaciological Society, at the same time launching the *Journal of Glaciology*. He served as president of the society (later the International Glaciological Society) until 1963, and was co-editor of the journal until 1968. He was president of the ICSI from 1951 to 1954.

Following the dissolution of his first marriage in 1951, Seligman married (Pamela) Loris Arnould (*b.* 1917) on 21 August 1952, and they settled at Biddenden, Kent, where many glaciologists enjoyed the warm hospitality of their Tudor house. From here Seligman edited his journal, with an acute eye for style, content, and accuracy, assisted by equally rigorous academic colleagues. In 1968, his health forced a move to Folkestone, where he died, at his home, 46 New Metropole, from bronchopneumonia on 21 February 1973. He was cremated at Charing.

Seligman's work had been recognized by the award in 1933 of the Pery medal from the Ski Club of Great Britain for distinguished services to skiing, of the Back grant in 1940 and the Victoria medal in 1959 from the Royal Geographical Society for glaciological research, of an honorary doctorate in 1965 from the University of Innsbruck, and by the first award of the Seligman crystal in 1965 from his society. More importantly, he left an active and flourishing society with over a thousand members in thirty-three countries.

G. Hattersley-Smith

Sources J. W. Glen, 'Gerald Seligman: 1886–1973', *Journal of Glaciology*, 12/65 (1973), 169–71 · B. B. Roberts, 'Gerald Seligman', *Polar Record*, 16 (1972–3), 883–5 · J. Seligman, 'Gerald Seligman 26 March 1886–21 February 1973', unpublished MS, March 1973 · private information (2004) · personal knowledge (2004) · *CGPLA Eng. & Wales* (1973) · L. Herz, *Geschichte der familie Seligman* (1935) · Harrow School archives
Archives Scott Polar RI, MSS
Likenesses P. L. Arnould (later Seligman), portrait, 1947, priv. coll.; repro. in Roberts, 'Gerald Seligman', facing p. 884 · photograph, 1947, priv. coll.; repro. in *Journal of Glaciology*, 169
Wealth at death £43,884: probate, 16 Oct 1973, *CGPLA Eng. & Wales*

Selincourt, Agnes De (1872–1917), missionary and college administrator, was born at Alverstoke, Leigham Court Road, Streatham, London, on 4 September 1872, the eldest daughter and fourth child of Charles Alexandre De Sélincourt, merchant, and his wife, Theodora Bruce, *née* Bendall; her father was of French origin, possibly of Huguenot descent. From a private school in Dover she went in 1889 to the sixth form of Notting Hill high school, run by the Girls' Public Day School Company (GPDSC), and from there in 1891 to Girton College, Cambridge, where in 1894 she achieved first-class honours in the medieval and modern languages tripos. She next taught for one year at Sheffield high school (GPDSC), but having resolved as a student to devote her life to missionary work in India, she spent the following year (1895–6) at Somerville College, Oxford, studying oriental languages. With two Cambridge contemporaries, and with the blessing of the Student Volunteer Missionary Union (SVMU), she departed as planned for India, to set up in Bombay a centre where 'women of our own universities' could live together while engaging in work, chiefly educational or medical, of an evangelistic nature.

In 1901 Agnes De Selincourt was obliged for reasons of health to leave the Bombay settlement, but after a year of recuperation in England felt strong enough to accept appointment from January 1903 as the first principal of the Lady Muir Memorial College, Allahabad, founded under the auspices of the Zenana Bible and Medical Mission to train educated Indian women who were already Christians for work in schools, villages, and in the segregated women's quarters (zenanas) of high-caste families. Defeated once more by failing health, her own and her mother's, she returned to England in 1909, still hoping to go back to India but pleased meanwhile to make contact as an officer of the SVMU (now part of the Student Christian Movement, SCM) with the rising generation of women students.

In September 1913, just turned forty-one, Agnes De Selincourt became principal of Westfield College, Hampstead, University of London, in succession to Constance Maynard, who had been mistress (the title was not passed on) since its inception in 1882. The new principal, forward-looking, energetic (although still in delicate health), and indisputably a scholar, gave the college a fresh impetus that was badly needed. With the aim of bringing in more students, desirable on both educational and financial grounds, she publicized Westfield's academic achievements and produced the first illustrated prospectus. She brought distinguished people, Dr W. R. Inge, dean of St Paul's, for example, to the college to deliver lectures open to the public, and converted the annual garden party, hitherto a purely social occasion, into a formal commemoration day.

Agnes De Selincourt's management of the college was a wellnigh perfect example of the professionalism that could now be expected of women principals. She delegated household management to a qualified domestic bursar, a new appointment which more than proved its worth in the straitened circumstances of wartime. Effortlessly, it would seem, she gained the confidence of key members of the academic staff, some of them by many years her senior; she improved the lot of visiting staff by lending them her own room, 'tasteful and softly lit', for private interviews with students. Her own encounters with students (on whom she received regular reports) were mostly informal—at mealtimes, in Sunday evening discussion groups, when she often spoke to them of India, and in a literary society she took in hand—except for her weekly divinity lecture, attendance at which was obligatory. Based, like her predecessor's Bible classes, on study of the scriptures, they were intellectually more demanding, and were occasionally supplemented by courses from professional theologians, among them William Temple, a valued friend she had first met in SCM circles and who at her prompting was invited in 1914 to join the college council; in 1916 he became chairman.

Leadership of the college during wartime brought additional burdens and responsibilities: student bereavements, parents in financial difficulties, and a cleavage of opinion, which found Agnes De Selincourt on the side of the pacifists, over the righteousness or otherwise of the war itself. The college nevertheless remained full, and room for the expansion she had consistently advocated suddenly became vital. The problem was solved by the parent of a current student, Sir Joseph Maclay, from whom she secured a handsome benefaction which was applied to the purchase early in 1917 of a commodious house directly opposite the main buildings. But she realized that a college on the scale she envisaged would not be viable without considerable support from public funds, for which Westfield, because of the exclusively Anglican composition of its governing council, was ineligible. With Temple's backing, she persuaded the council (of which, unlike her predecessor, she was a member *ex officio*) to seek legal authorization for the required alterations. The matter was still not concluded when on 31 August 1917 she died at a nursing home in Whitby following a bicycling accident near the cottage she owned at Robin Hood's Bay in Yorkshire.

By all accounts a compelling personality, Agnes De Selincourt was small, dark, well dressed, sometimes vivacious in manner, sometimes abstracted. She was an accomplished public speaker, poised and incisive, and in more private debate a skilful and at times fiery opponent. Her religious faith, arrived at through prolonged study and meditation, was clearly the mainspring of her existence. Principal to only two complete generations of Westfield students, she had scant opportunity to realize her aspiration of raising up leaders for schools and colleges in India and the Far East, although a start was made when a student from China, Pao Swen Tseng, returned home to found a girls' school in Changsha. Agnes De Selincourt's commitments outside Westfield included membership of the university's board of oriental studies and of the organizing committee for the Lambeth diploma of student in theology.

Agnes De Selincourt's ashes were buried in the family grave at Brompton cemetery. Westfield's memorial service for her, at St Luke's Church, Hampstead, was held on 11 October, the day she had designated for the official opening of Maclay Hall, in the event named Selincourt as her memorial. 'To maintain connection with the family' her brother Professor Ernest De *Selincourt (1870–1943) was immediately elected to the Westfield council and served until 1937. JANET SONDHEIMER

Sources E. M. Carus-Wilson, ed., *Westfield College, 1882–1932* (1932) • J. Sondheimer, *Castle Adamant in Hampstead: a history of Westfield College, 1882–1982* (1983) • T. Tatlow, *The story of the Student Christian Movement* (1933) • *Church Times* (7 Sept 1917) • *Girton Review*, Michaelmas term (1917) • K. T. Butler and H. I. McMorran, eds., *Girton College register, 1869–1946* (1948) • A. De Selincourt, *Girton Review* (Oct 1903) • M. Thresher, *A venture of faith: history of the Lambeth diploma* (1989) • b. cert.

Likenesses J. Trevor, tinted photograph, 1921 (after pencil drawing; after photographs by A. de Biden Footner), Queen Mary and Westfield College

Wealth at death £5829 16s. 5d.: probate, 12 Dec 1917, *CGPLA Eng. & Wales*

Selincourt, Ernest De (1870–1943), literary scholar and university teacher, was born in Streatham on 24 September 1870, the third son of the four sons and three daughters of Charles Alexandre De Sélincourt, a clothing manufacturer, and his wife, Theodora Bruce Bendall. Agnes De *Selincourt was his sister. He was educated first at Huddersfield College and then in 1885 went to Dulwich College, where he played rugby and acquired a taste for the poetry of Wordsworth. He matriculated at University College, Oxford, in 1890, moving in a circle of friends which included John Shawcross, who was the future editor of the first modern edition of Coleridge's *Biographia literaria*.

De Selincourt flourished at Oxford, winning in 1893 a prize in English offered by University College. He was placed in the second class in honours moderations and also in *literae humaniores*, and was 'proxime' for the chancellor's prize for English essay. De Selincourt then spent two years studying Anglo-Saxon with Arthur Sampson Napier, lecturing at Bedford College, and giving tutorials at Oxford. On 19 December 1896 De Selincourt married Ethel Shawcross (1866/7–1931), daughter of William Tuer Shawcross, mill owner, of Rochdale; she and Ernest had two sons and two daughters. In the same year as his marriage De Selincourt was appointed lecturer in English literature at University College, and in 1899, university lecturer in modern English literature, the first such appointments at Oxford. In the subsequent years of his tenure at Oxford, De Selincourt's energy and thoroughness in lecturing, tuition, and developing the curriculum of the honour school of English language and literature were unparalleled.

In December 1908 De Selincourt was elected to the chair of English literature at Birmingham University and began the long process of shaping the institution's mission, particularly with respect to the humanities. De Selincourt's vision of higher education was progressive, interdisciplinary, and populistic. In his official capacities on a number of educational boards and councils in Birmingham, he advocated adult and popular education and the accessibility of the arts, and he also championed the education of women. Although he could be a formidable opponent in debate, he was admired by colleagues and students alike for his erudition, his insistence on high standards of

Ernest De Selincourt (1870–1943), by Walter Stoneman, 1930

scholarship, and above all, for his inspirational love of literature. De Selincourt, who by 1919 had become dean of the faculty of arts, and in 1931 vice-principal, retired from Birmingham University in 1935 leaving behind an institution transformed by his guidance which combined practical insight with an idealistic vision.

During his years at Birmingham University, other institutions conferred honours on De Selincourt: in 1927 he was elected fellow of the British Academy; from 1928 to 1933 he was Oxford professor of poetry (an honour he prized above all others); in 1929 he was made honorary LLD of Edinburgh, and in 1930, honorary fellow of University College. He also spent the years 1927 to 1931 touring and lecturing at prestigious universities in France, Germany, and the United States. He was president of the English Association in 1935–6.

De Selincourt's scholarship encompassed a wide range of British literature from Chaucer to his own day. His critical works and lectures exhibit an admirable balance between scholarly erudition and an aesthetic sensitivity for his subject. His criticism effectively wedded interpretation with evaluation through a carefully constructed aesthetic based on the poets he loved most, the Romantics. De Selincourt's authoritative solutions to difficult problems of the dating and provenance of various works are exemplary of the highest order of literary scholarship. He used this sound historical approach to produce editions of works of Keats (1905), Spenser (1912), W. S. Landor (1915), and Walt Whitman (1920); but his greatest contribution was to the study of William and Dorothy Wordsworth.

In 1906 De Selincourt published an edition of Wordsworth's *Guide to the Lakes*, which represented the beginning of a life's work in the editing of Wordsworth, and in 1926 he published a new edition of *The Prelude* from early manuscripts, with textual and critical notes. This pioneering edition of an early (*c*.1805) manuscript version of *The Prelude* printed page by page opposite the 1850 text became the blueprint for later editors of Wordsworth's most highly acclaimed poem, and also set the stage for the debate about intermediate stages of its composition and the relative merits of each of the versions. In 1933 De Selincourt published a biography of Dorothy Wordsworth assembled from family papers put at his disposal by Gordon Wordsworth, the poet's grandson, and in subsequent years came out with editions of Dorothy's writings, including her journals. On his retirement to Grasmere in 1935, De Selincourt had the opportunity to devote more time to the cataloguing of Wordsworth's manuscripts, which Gordon Wordsworth had given to the Dove Cottage Trust. De Selincourt served as chairman of the Dove Cottage trustees, and helped to found the Dove Cottage Wordsworth Library, which still houses the majority of Wordsworth's important manuscripts. His next project was a thorough revision and expansion of William Knight's edition of the letters of William and Dorothy Wordsworth; De Selincourt's edition, published in three parts and six volumes over the years 1935 to 1939, have since been revised in a second edition by various hands, and are second in importance to Wordsworth scholars only to the poetic texts themselves. These he edited in the masterly five-volume edition of *The Poetical Works of William Wordsworth*, which appeared over the years 1940 to 1949. All except for the first volume were published posthumously under the expert guidance of De Selincourt's colleague and friend Helen Darbishire. De Selincourt's edition of Wordsworth, though being superseded as instalments of the Cornell Wordsworth series issue from the presses, is still valuable to the Wordsworth scholar and stands as a monument of modern scholarship. De Selincourt died of heart failure after a short illness at the Olrig Nursing Home, Kendal, on 22 May 1943.

DAVID KALOUSTIAN

Sources H. Darbishire, 'Ernest De Selincourt', *PBA*, 29 (1943), 392–409 · *The Times* (25 May 1943) · *The poetical works of William Wordsworth*, ed. E. De Selincourt and H. Darbishire, 5 vols. (1940–49); 2nd edn (1950–59) [with prefaces] · *DNB* · *The letters of William and Dorothy Wordsworth*, ed. E. De Selincourt, 2nd edn, rev. C. L. Shaver, M. Moorman, and A. G. Hill, 8 vols. (1967–93) · F. Jordan, *The English Romantic poets: a review of research and criticism*, 4th edn (1985) · E. De Selincourt, *Oxford lectures on poetry* (1934) · E. De Selincourt, *Wordsworthian and other studies* (1947) · m. cert. · d. cert.

Archives Dove Cottage Library, Grasmere | Bodl. Oxf., letters to Gilbert Murray · U. Birm. L., special collections department, corresp. with Francis Brett Young

Likenesses W. Stoneman, photograph, 1930, NPG [*see illus.*] · G. Spencer, portrait, *c*.1943, Ladywood, Grasmere, Cumbria · F. Yates, oils, U. Birm., department of English · photograph, repro. in Darbishire, 'Ernest De Selincourt', 392

Wealth at death £24,412 5*s*. 0*d*.: probate, 17 July 1943, *CGPLA Eng. & Wales*

Selkirk. For this title name *see* Douglas, Thomas, fifth earl of Selkirk (1771–1820); Hamilton, George Nigel Douglas-, tenth earl of Selkirk (1906–1994).

Selkirk, Alexander (1676–1721), mariner, castaway, and probable source of inspiration for the character Robinson Crusoe, was born in Lower Largo, Fife, the seventh son of John Selcraig, shoemaker, and Euphan Mackie. He received schooling in Largo. His wilful nature manifested itself at an early age in his determination to go to sea against his father's wishes. In August 1695 a summons by the kirk session for 'indecent carriage' in church precipitated his departure. He had left for sea by 27 August, before he could be dealt with, and he did not reappear in Largo until 1701. After his return from sea he fell foul of the parish authorities again, this time on account of his behaviour during a domestic dispute. His brother Andrew set down a can of salt water from which Alexander mistakenly drank. Incensed at the mirth this caused, Alexander lashed out at his brother and had to be restrained from taking a pistol to him. For this he was rebuked before the parish congregation.

In May 1703, as Alexander Selkirk, he was appointed master of the privateer *Cinque Ports* (Captain Charles Pickering, commander). The *Cinque Ports* and her consort, the *George*, commanded by William Dampier, left Kinsale on 11 September bound for the South Sea. Pickering died on the coast of Brazil and was succeeded by Captain Thomas Stradling. Selkirk's seamanship is attested by his passage round the Horn in mid-February 1704, but his loyalty to Stradling is not so certain. At Juan Fernandez (Mas á Tierra), where the two vessels put in for refreshment, forty-two of the sixty or so men on board the *Cinque Ports* mutinied. Selkirk may have been among them. An engagement with a French ship soon afterwards seemed to galvanize the crew, and both ships then proceeded along the mainland coast towards Callao in search of prizes. By the end of May disappointing pickings and Dampier's persistent indecision caused such friction between the two commanders that they decided to part company. Selkirk elected to remain with Stradling.

The *Cinque Ports* now cruised independently on the coast of Central and South America until August. During this time Selkirk grew resentful of Stradling. A hurried refit at Juan Fernandez in September convinced Selkirk that the vessel was unseaworthy and he declared he would leave the ship rather than sail in her. Disembarking with 'his Clothes and Bedding, with a Firelock, some Powder, Bullets, and Tobacco, a Hatchet, a Knife, a Kettle, a Bible, some practical Pieces, and his Mathematical Instruments and Books' (Rogers, 126), Selkirk bid the boat's crew a hearty farewell but the moment they pulled away from the shore he experienced an immediate change of heart. Stradling, who may have anticipated a volte-face, had taken it upon himself to supervise Selkirk's transfer personally, and he steadfastly refused Selkirk's pleas to be taken up again.

For eight months or so Selkirk went about distracted 'and had much ado to bear up against melancholy, and the Terror of being left alone in such a desolate place' (Rogers,

126). However, the onset of winter forced him to build two huts, and faced with the challenge of survival he gradually reconciled himself to his predicament. He studied the Bible and began to embark upon a routine of daily religious exercises which included singing psalms and reading the scriptures aloud to retain the use of his speech. To distinguish the sabbath he kept a calendar. He bred cats for company and they preserved him from the rats which gnawed at his feet and clothes as he slept. His chief amusement was to hunt goats, and after exhausting his powder he relied on fleetness of foot to capture them. He tamed the kids to ensure a continual source of food for his old age when he might not be able to overtake them. In accounting for the time he spent on the island, Selkirk stressed the importance of two incidents. The first occurred when he was out hunting. Having stalked a goat to an unfamiliar part of the island, he lunged to catch the animal and his momentum carried him over the edge of an unseen precipice. The fall knocked him unconscious for at least a day and when he recovered his senses he discovered the goat dead beneath him. Second, he was very nearly captured by Spaniards who arrived at the island in two vessels. Anxious to ascertain the vessels' nationality, Selkirk inadvertently showed himself to observers in the ships. A landing party was dispatched to apprehend him and several shots were fired in his direction. Selkirk's agility allowed him to hide in the branches of a tree, at the foot of which his pursuers made water.

On 1 February 1709 two Bristol privateers, the *Duke* and *Duchess*, touched at the island for water. The *Duke* was commanded by Captain Woodes Rogers with Dampier on board as pilot. After dark a light was discerned ashore and the next day, sighting no ships, Rogers sent two boats to investigate. Towards evening the pinnace returned with 'a Man cloth'd in Goat-Skins, who look'd wilder than the first Owners of them [who] had so much forgot his Language for want of Use, that we could scarce understand him, for he seem'd to speak his words by halves' (Rogers, 125–9). Selkirk had been on the island for four years and four months. Dampier recommended Selkirk as having been the best man in the *Cinque Ports* and Rogers duly appointed Selkirk to be mate in the *Duke*.

Both ships sailed on 13 February to scour the coast of Chile for prizes. On 26 March a prize taken near the Isle of Lobos was renamed the *Increase* and Selkirk was appointed master. On 25 April, as part of the assault on Guayaquil, Selkirk formed part of a detachment under Lieutenant Connoly tasked with exploiting areas beyond the town. After the withdrawal from the town on 28 April Selkirk continued in command of the *Increase*, forming part of a screen to intercept vessels in transit between Panama and Lima. In the middle of September Rogers led his ships to the Galápagos for refitting before taking up stations off Cape St Lucas in November to await the arrival of the Manila galleon bound for Acapulco. By 20 December their quarry had yet to appear. Low on bread, and with worm penetrating their vessels' sheathing, the decision was taken to sail for the Ladrones [Mariana Islands]. As they were about to weigh anchor a sail was sighted, and on 22 December Rogers seized the richly laden *Nuestra Señora de la Encarnación*.

On 10 January 1710 Rogers set out to cross the Pacific, a voyage of over 6000 miles. The *Duke* was accompanied by the *Duchess*, and two prizes. The *Nuestra Señora* had been renamed the *Bachelor*, and Selkirk was appointed master on board under Captain Thomas Dover. They reached Guam on 11 March and departed within ten days for Batavia where they arrived in late June. Here they shared out a quantity of booty, Selkirk acting as a commissioner in this transaction. His own share was eighty pieces of eight. After refitting at Horn Island, they sailed for the Cape of Good Hope where they stayed for over three months. On 6 April they sailed in a convoy of twenty-five Dutch and English ships, arriving off the Shetlands on 15 July. After a final delay at the Texel Selkirk arrived in the Thames on 14 October 1711. His extraordinary circumnavigation had taken over eight years, more than half of which had been spent in total isolation.

Selkirk's conduct on the island won him universal admiration after the account of him given by Rogers in *A Cruising Voyage Round the World* (1712). His rehabilitation in Britain, however, proved less successful. The records of the court of queen's bench contain a process against 'Alexander Selkirke' of the parish of St Stephen, Bristol, for an assault on Richard Nettle, shipwright, on 23 September 1713 (Hart, 246). At some indeterminate date Selkirk returned to Largo where he lived for a while the life of a recluse, constructing a cave in his father's garden for the purpose of meditation. He became infatuated with a girl named Sophia Bruce, with whom he seems to have eloped to London. They may even have married. In a will, drawn up and signed in Wapping on 13 January 1718, Selkirk referred to Sophia as 'his loveing and well beloved friend Sophia Bruce of Pellmell London Spinster', and appointed her executrix and heir (*Scots Magazine*, 67, 1805, 673). These arrangements were concluded on the eve of Selkirk's return to sea.

On 20 October 1720 Selkirk embarked in HMS *Weymouth* as master's mate. On 12 December he married a widow named Frances Candis, in St Andrew's Church, Plymouth, signing a new will on the same day and leaving everything to his new bride. His address was given as Oarston (Oreston), Plymstock, Devon. By the end of March 1721 Selkirk was involved in operations against pirates and interlopers on the Guinea coast and it was here, during a period of unusually high mortality among the crew, that he probably contracted a fatal disease. The *Weymouth*'s log records Selkirk's death on 13 December 1721. Sophia Bruce's suit to prove Selkirk's first will in the prerogative court of Canterbury the following year led to a legal battle over the estate with Frances and her new husband. Sophia was unsuccessful, and failed to secure an injunction against her rival when the second will was proved on 5 December 1723. Sophia's fortunes eventually sank so low that she was forced to apply for alms from Revd Say, a dissenting minister of Westminster.

A tablet in honour of Selkirk was placed near his lookout on Juan Fernandez by Commodore Powell and the officers of HMS *Topaz* in 1866, and a bronze statue, erected in 1885, stands on the site of his former home in Largo. His sea chest, and a coconut shell cup, which may have been in use on the island, are preserved in the national museums of Scotland. The best evidence for the years Selkirk spent on Juan Fernandez is contained in Woodes Rogers's *Cruising Voyage*, of which a second edition was published in 1718. Selkirk's best memorial, however, is Daniel Defoe's immortal portrait of the castaway in *Robinson Crusoe*, which appeared the following year. There is some evidence that Defoe and Selkirk may have met, but stories that Defoe callously plundered Selkirk's journal for material, while telling its author it would never sell, are likely to be apocryphal. Sir Richard Steele's claim to have held frequent conversations with Selkirk in London is similarly unreliable. His moralizing account of Selkirk in *The Englishman* appears to have been a fabrication based on details furnished by Rogers. Nevertheless Steele's report that Selkirk had told him 'I am now worth 800 Pounds, but shall never be so happy, as when I was not worth a Farthing', when they met in the street, aptly sums up what seems to have been true during Selkirk's last years.

JAMES WILLIAM KELLY

Sources E. Cooke, *A voyage to the South Sea and round the world perform'd in the years 1708, 1709, 1710, and 1711*, 2 vols. (1712) • W. Rogers, *A cruising voyage round the world* (1712) • W. Funnel, *A voyage round the world, containing an account of Captain Dampier's expedition into the South-seas in the ship St George, in the years 1703 and 1704* (1707) • R. Steele, *The Englishman*, 25 (1–3 Dec 1713) • HMS *Weymouth*'s log, PRO, ADM 52/316 • kirk session minutes for Largo for the period 1691–1708, St Andrews University, MS CH2/960/2 • will, dated 12 Dec 1720, PRO, PROB 11/594 • Chancery proceedings, 1724–1758, PRO, C 11/52/31, C 11/297/61 • I. James, *Providence displayed, or, The remarkable adventures of Alexander Selkirk of Largo, in Scotland* (1800) • J. Howell, *The life and adventures of Alexander Selkirk: containing the real incidents upon which the romance of Robinson Crusoe is founded* (1829) • 'Providence displayed', *The Harleian miscellany*, ed. W. Oldys, 5 (1745), 402–6 • *History of Alexander Selkirk, mariner* (1780) • R. H. C. Adams, *The original Robinson Crusoe* (1877) • G. A. Aitken, *The life of Sir Richard Steele*, 2 vols. (1889) • R. L. Mégroz, *The real Robinson Crusoe, being the life and surprising adventures of Alexander Selkirk of Largo, Fife, mariner* (1939) • 'Say papers, no. 20: "Sophia Selchrig's petition to Mr. Say for relief"', *Monthly Repository*, 5 (1810), 531 • R. W. Lovett, 'Sir Richard Steele's "frequent conversations" with Alexander Selkirk', *English Language Notes*, 25/1 (1987), 46–50 • C. Wells, 'Defoe and Selkirk at Bristol', *The Academy* (30 Dec 1905), 1357–8 • W. H. Hart, 'Alexander Selkirk', *N&Q*, 2nd ser., 11 (1861), 246

Archives U. St Andr., kirk session minutes for Largo

Likenesses bronze statue, *c*.1885, on site of Selkirk's former house, Largo, Fife

Wealth at death £800 in 1713; £40 wages owed to him by Royal Navy: HMS *Weymouth*'s log, PRO, Admiralty records 52/316; Steele, *The Englishman*

Sellar, Alexander Craig (1835–1890). *See under* Sellar, Patrick (1780–1851).

Sellar, Patrick (1780–1851), sheep farmer and agent of highland clearances, was born on 5 December 1780 in Elgin, Moray, the only son of Thomas Sellar (1754–1817), solicitor, and his wife, Jean Plenderleath, daughter of the minister of college church in Edinburgh. His father, originally from Banffshire, practised successfully in Elgin, served the needs of local landowners, and entered their ranks when he bought the estate of Westfield in 1808. Patrick Sellar was educated at Edinburgh University for a legal career and he entered his father's business in 1803. His father joined a consortium for the reconstruction of harbour facilities at Burghead, in Moray, in 1805. Another partner was William Young, a local farmer and improvement entrepreneur.

In 1809 Sellar and Young began to give advice to Lady Stafford (Elizabeth Leveson-Gower), who was already embarked upon ambitious plans for the improvement of her vast highland estates in Sutherland. In 1810 they were appointed to manage the estate; Sellar was mainly responsible for rent collection and removals. Their policies entailed the massive rearrangement of the population and the land use, emptying extensive inland areas for sheep farms and creating a new coastal economy of crofters. These plans required the eviction of many thousands of small tenants, who resented the changes. Sellar acquired first a large arable farm and then complicated his role by bidding successfully for a large new sheep farm in Strathnaver.

Already responsible for removals in 1812, Sellar himself became the target of fierce hostility following particularly severe removals in Strathnaver in the middle of 1814. Over the following eighteen months various allegations emerged against him and he was eventually tried, in sensational circumstances, for acts of gross inhumanity, including culpable homicide, at Inverness in April 1816. He was alleged to have caused the deaths of several small tenants by setting fire to their houses in the course of the 1814 clearances. He was tried by a jury of landowners from outside Sutherland under Judge Pitmilly, and was completely exonerated. He routed his accusers and the removals were later completed under James Loch and Francis Suther. However, the controversy did not abate.

Sellar's employers, who regarded him as undiplomatic and harsh in his dealings with the people of Sutherland, soon eased him out of the Sutherland management. Sellar remained as their most reliable, but also their most disputatious, tenant and one of the greatest sheep farmers in the highlands. His house in Morvich was the centre of his activities. He was widely respected as an agricultural adviser and an expert on sheep. He was influential in establishing wool and sheep markets in the northern highlands, and in the formation of the Sutherland Association of Farmers. In 1819 he married Anne, daughter of Thomas Craig of Barmuckty, Elgin; they had nine children. Members of his large family were successful in several fields of Victorian society, and they conducted business in England, Australia, and the United States.

Between 1838 and 1844 Sellar bought the estates of Ardtornish and Acharn in Morvern in Argyll, paying £29,850 for 21,575 acres. He evicted 230 people and stocked the lands with Cheviot sheep from Sutherland. He thus established himself as a laird in his own right but, argumentative and combative by nature, he soon quarrelled with his new neighbours. His family played host at Morvern to Francis Palgrave, Alfred Tennyson, Herbert Spencer, Benjamin Jowett, and George Eliot. To the continuing fury of his family, his reputation and his memory were repeatedly sullied, especially by recurrent claims that he had been guilty of the charges unsuccessfully levelled against him in 1816.

Sellar came to personify the entire process of the highland clearances. He was always severely critical of the old highland ways and thought the highlanders should emigrate for everybody's sake. He advocated the suppression of Gaelic and the compulsory teaching of English. He had an exceptionally sharp turn of phrase and a caustic intelligence. After a long illness he died on 20 October 1851 at Park Place, Elgin, and was buried in the churchyard of Elgin Cathedral on 1 November.

The third son of Patrick and Anne Sellar was William Young *Sellar, professor of Latin in Edinburgh University. Their seventh son was **Alexander Craig Sellar** (1835–1890), advocate and politician. He was educated at Rugby School and graduated from Balliol College, Oxford, in 1859; he joined the Scottish bar in 1862. In June 1870 he married Gertrude Joanna, daughter of Octavius Smith of Ardtornish. He was appointed assistant commissioner to the education (Scotland) commission in 1864, and was legal secretary to the lord advocate of Scotland from 1870 to 1874. He was MP in the Liberal interest for the Haddington burghs from 1882 to 1885, before which he had been unsuccessful candidate for Devonport. He was an energetic party organizer but split from Gladstone over Ireland. In 1885 he was elected for the Partick division of Lanarkshire, whose electorate he regarded as somewhat turbulent, and was re-elected in 1886. He joined the Liberal Unionist Party in 1886 and was party whip from 1886 to 1888. He wrote on parliamentary reform, but his promising career was abbreviated by his early death, on 16 January 1890 at Parham Park, Pulborough, Sussex; his wife survived him. He was buried in Elgin Cathedral.

ERIC RICHARDS

Sources P. Gaskell, *Morvern Transformed* (1968) • E. M. Sellar, *Recollections and impressions* (1907) • T. Sellar, *The Sutherland evictions of 1814* (1883) • I. Grimble, *The trial of Patrick Sellar* (1962) • A. Mackenzie, *A history of the highland clearances* (1882) • E. Richards, *A history of the highland clearances: agrarian transformation and the evictions, 1746–1886*, 2 vols. (1982–5) • R. J. Adam, ed., *Papers on Sutherland estate management, 1802–1816*, 2 vols., Scottish History Society, 4th ser., 8–9 (1972) • *WWBMP* • *CGPLA Eng. & Wales* (1890) [Alexander Craig Sellar] • d. cert. • b. cert. [Alexander Craig Sellar] • d. cert. [Alexander Craig Sellar] • *DNB*

Archives NA Scot., Loch Muniments • Staffs. RO, Sutherland Collection | NA Scot., Ross MSS

Likenesses MacNee, portrait, repro. in Sellar, *Recollections and impressions* • double portrait (with his wife), Bettyhill Museum, Sutherland, Scotland • portrait, priv. coll.

Wealth at death £11,596 15*s.* 6*d.*—Alexander Craig Sellar: probate, resworn, Dec 1890, *CGPLA Eng. & Wales*

Sellar, Walter Carruthers (1898–1951), schoolmaster and humorous writer, was born at Golspie, Sutherland, on 27 December 1898, the second son of Patrick Sellar, a farmer, and his wife, Janet Anne Carruthers (*d.* 1914). He was a descendant of the Patrick Sellar notorious for his role in the highland clearances. In 1912 he won an entrance scholarship to Fettes College, Edinburgh. In 1914 he suffered a personal tragedy when his elder brother, Patrick, died at school, followed a few days later by their mother. The experience may well have induced the melancholy streak later noticed in Sellar but did not prevent his enjoying a successful career at Fettes, and he left as head boy in 1917. He then went into the army, commissioned as a second lieutenant in the King's Own Scottish Borderers, and served in France and Germany, suffering wounds that, though not severe, helped to undermine health that was never robust. On 29 April 1919 he matriculated from Oriel College, Oxford, reading modern history, but due to illness took only an aegrotat degree in 1922.

While at Oxford Sellar met the friend with whose name his own has become inseparably linked. **Robert Julian Yeatman** (1897–1968) was born in London, at 82 Ashley Gardens, Westminster, on 15 July 1897, the second son of Harry Oswald Yeatman (1856–1919), a London portshipper, and his wife, Benedicta Katherine Page. From 1911 he was educated at Marlborough College, where he succeeded alike as scholar, athlete, and musician, before leaving in 1914 to join the Royal Field Artillery. Commissioned lieutenant in 1915, he was awarded the MC a year later. He also suffered very severe wounds, described as having left him 'perforated like a colander' (Sherrin, xvi). In 1919 Yeatman (who pronounced his name Yetman) matriculated from Oriel College on the same day as Sellar, and took a second in modern history in 1922. At this point his and Sellar's paths diverged, for Sellar returned to Fettes as a schoolmaster, remaining there until 1928, while Yeatman after a spell in journalism became advertising manager for Kodak Ltd. Both men had literary ambitions. Sellar contributed short humorous articles to a number of journals and above all to *Punch*, which published three of them in 1925; in 1926 Yeatman too began to contribute to that journal.

In 1928 Sellar left Fettes and seems to have tried to make a career as a full-time writer, living in a cottage at Marlow. About the same time he married (Mary Dorothy) Hope Carruthers, an athlete who played hockey for England. They had two daughters, and it was probably the need for a secure income following his marriage that brought Sellar's literary experiment to an end, for in September 1929 he became a schoolmaster at Canford School, Dorset. He stayed there until he moved in July 1932 to Charterhouse School, Godalming, Surrey, where he remained for the rest of his life. There is no evidence on when his literary collaboration with Yeatman began but it was very likely during his year away from teaching, for on 10 September 1930 *Punch* began to publish extracts from their most famous book, *1066 and All That*, the last of them appearing on the day before it was published. It was an instant success, although so little was known about its authors that rumour credited it to the much better-known A. P. Herbert. Three further joint ventures followed: *And Now All This* (1932), *Horse Nonsense* (1933), and *Garden Rubbish* (1936), the first and last also receiving advance publication in

Punch. All sold well but without receiving the popular success of *1066*, which in 1934 provided the basis for a musical comedy with book and lyrics by Reginald Arkell and music by Alfred Reynolds.

At Charterhouse Sellar taught history at first but later became senior English master. In January 1939 he became housemaster of Daviesites and fulfilled his responsibilities with great conscientiousness, increasing the capacity of his house despite the outbreak of war. He was very popular with the boys, and not only because he mitigated the effects of rationing by buying extra food for them at his own expense. His health remained poor, however, and he died at St Thomas Hospital, Hambledon, Surrey, on 11 June 1951. A road at Charterhouse was afterwards named after him.

Meanwhile Yeatman had by 1937 married Eleanor May Simmonds, a gifted actress, with whom he had a son. He rejoined the army in 1940, serving as a captain in the Royal Artillery until in 1943 he was released to the Ministry of Information, where he worked until 1949. Afterwards he was employed as a copywriter, first by Haddons and then by S. L. Benson Ltd, from which he retired in 1962. He died in London, at 39/41 Royal Avenue, Chelsea, on 13 July 1968.

Sellar and Yeatman were temperamentally very different. Sellar was somewhat reclusive and inward-looking, with a religious cast of mind that found expression in some of his (unpublished) poetry, although like many shy people he enjoyed acting. Yeatman by contrast was very sociable, with a wide range of friends that included Clark Gable, W. H. Auden, and Christopher Isherwood. Each had a strong sense of humour but its quality differed, as can be seen in the two books that were ostensibly written by both men but were each in fact essentially the work of only one of them. *Horse Nonsense*, almost entirely by Yeatman, contains much wittily satirical comment on the mores and clichés associated with horses and riders: 'The Best People are still horse-conscious—neigh, animal-minded. In their eyes, persons who betray Blank Ignorance of The Horse, or, worse still, downright brutish Indifference to The Noble Animal, are definitely *beyond the pail*.' *Garden Rubbish*, largely written by Sellar and gentler in tone, is notable for a series of exuberant puns ('Greta Garbo—"I want to be a lawn"') and for the addition of the 'Unpleasaunce' to the traditional stock of garden amenities: 'Every fair-sized garden has one … they differ only in the number and variety of Depressing Things they harbour.' *And Now All This*, a genuine collaboration, is presented as a guide to 'Absolutely General Knowledge', and perhaps for that reason lacks cohesion. It scores a number of bull's-eyes, for instance an account of an Indian official's day (recycled by Yeatman from a contribution to *Punch* in 1926)—'after a hurried bath (*wallah*) dresses himself (*collah*) is down at a quarter to eight for breakfast (*swallah*)'—but is ultimately too diffuse to be wholly successful.

No such charge could be laid against Sellar's and Yeatman's first and most famous effort. The unity of *1066 and All That* comes primarily from the idea that does most to give the book its unique quality: that history consists less of what actually happened than of what can be remembered, or more often misremembered, as having happened. But hardly less inspired than the idea itself is the way it is exploited. Many of the garblings of names and facts serve simply to amuse, but many, too, constitute comments both shrewd and witty on the events described. Thus the definition of Poynings' law, of 1494, as an act 'by which the Irish could have a Parliament of their own, but the English were to pass all the Acts in it', is simultaneously an amusing conceit, the sort of misreading a careless schoolboy might plausibly perpetrate, and a pointed summary of the historical event.

It may be surmised that the theme of history as memory came from Sellar, whose unpublished essay on nonsense suggests that he had a penchant for general ideas and whose experience as a schoolmaster would certainly have familiarized him with the sort of textbook whose particular qualities *1066* lampoons. In its terms of reference *1066* pays a paradoxical tribute to the education it makes fun of. The reader who hopes to spot every joke will have to know the whole history of England from Roman times to 1918 and to have read widely in English literature as well; it refers directly to nearly all Shakespeare's history plays and also to writings by Milton (through a typographical joke), Pope, Gray, Keats, Tennyson, and Newbolt. More generally it is a book of its time in sharing the inter-war trend, found for instance in the humorous writings of J. B. Morton ('Beachcomber'), towards a less reverential attitude to the national past and especially to the Victorian tendency to perceive that past in terms of a glorious and imperial destiny.

The tone of *1066 and All That* is set by its preface, which acknowledges the authors' debt to 'the Great British People without whose self-sacrificing determination to become top Nation there would have been no (memorable) history', after which the reader is taken into a world of rigid moral judgements in which kings and ministers, all emphatically either good or bad, are regularly confounded by an unanswerable 'Irish Question', in which England is bound to become 'C of E', where patterns are established by waves—whether of invaders, pretenders, or even beards—and where all barons are wicked barons. In spite of the preface's tribute to the 'British' people the focus of the book is totally Anglocentric, ludicrously so: the Scots 'come right into History' in the thirteenth century, while Indian history begins only in the eighteenth, just before American history ends.

The satirical quality of *1066* was most likely Yeatman's essential contribution; probably his were the sharp comments on events like Queen Victoria's wars, which are reliably reported to have made Donald Soper a pacifist: '*War against Zulus*. Cause: the Zulus. Zulus exterminated. Peace with Zulus'. But equally important to *1066*'s success is an element of sheer fantasy, where history breaks almost entirely loose from its moorings, as in the account of Charles I and ship money: 'This so upset Charles that he went back to Westminster, and after cinquing several ports burst into the House of Commons and asked in a very royal way for some birds which he said were in there'.

This and a continuously inspired misrepresentation of names, sometimes satirical (Viscount Slaughterhouse, Sir Robert Repeel), sometimes purely comic (Harold Harebrush, the Elector Pantomime), which culminates in an uproarious confusion of Lambert Simnel and Perkin Warbeck (Warmnel, Perbeck, Wimneck …), was probably largely Sellar's contribution.

Their differences of personality notwithstanding, in *1066 and All That* Sellar and Yeatman achieved a perfect unity of theme and style. They were also fortunate in their illustrator. The drawings of John Patrick Reynolds (1909–1935) are as sharp and economical as the accompanying text, and no one who has seen his pictures of King John losing his clothes in the wash or Morton applying his fork is ever likely to forget them. Moreover by representing the jokes rather than the incidents from which they derive the illustrations have helped *1066* to transcend its time. The title defers to Robert Graves's autobiography, *Goodbye to All That* (1929), but with none of the latter's resentment. Indeed despite its sharp-eyed mockery and its wholesale slaughter of sacred cows the spirit that it conveys is overwhelmingly one of comic exuberance, which in turn has done much to justify its authors' claim to memorability. Sellar and Yeatman have contributed many phrases to the common stock, their comparison of the Cavaliers ('Wrong but Wromantic') with the Roundheads ('Right but Repulsive') being only the most famous. At the opening of the twenty-first century opinion remains consistent that the authors and their book constitute a thoroughly Good Thing. HENRY SUMMERSON

Sources N. Sherrin, introduction, in W. C. Sellar and R. J. Yeatman, *1066 and all that* (1990) • F. Muir, introduction, in W. C. Sellar and R. J. Yeatman, *1066 and all that* (1993) • W. C. Sellar, 'Poems and prose', Bodl. Oxf., 270d.230 • *Punch* (1925–36) • H. G. Newman, *Fettes College register, 1870–1953* (1954) • C. A. Lillingston, *Canford School register, 1923–1935*, 2nd edn (1936) • *Marlborough College register, 1843–1933* (1936) • *The Carthusian*, 20 (1951), 405–8 • *The Times* (13 June 1951) • *The Times* (17 July 1968) • private information (2004) • b. cert. • d. cert. • b. cert. [Robert Yeatman] • d. cert. [Robert Yeatman] • R. Samuel, 'One in the eye: 1066 and all that', *Theatres of memory*, 2 (1998), 208–13

Wealth at death no value given: confirmation, 24 Aug 1951, *CGPLA Eng. & Wales* • £20,911—R. J. Yeatman: probate, 1968, *CGPLA Eng. & Wales*

Sellar, William Young (1825–1890), classical scholar, was born at Morvich, Sutherland, on 22 February 1825, the third son of the seven boys and two girls of Patrick *Sellar (1780–1851), who was notorious as factor to the duke of Sutherland during the highland clearances, and his wife, Anne Craig. At the early age of seven he joined the youngest class in the Edinburgh Academy, then under its first headmaster, John Williams. At the age of fourteen he was dux, or head boy, of the school. From there he went to Glasgow University (1839–42), where Edmund Law Lushington was professor of Greek and William Ramsay (1806–1865) was professor of Latin. Under these teachers and friends Sellar advanced in classical learning. He gained a Snell exhibition and a Balliol scholarship, matriculating on 1 December 1842, and was a contemporary of his friends Matthew Arnold and Principal Shairp, and a pupil and friend of Benjamin Jowett. After taking a first class in *literae humaniores*, and graduating BA in 1847 (MA in 1850), Sellar was elected to a fellowship at Oriel in 1848, which he held until his marriage (1 June 1852) to Eleanor Mary (*b.* 1829), daughter of Alex Dennistoun, a Glasgow merchant and radical MP for Dunbartonshire (1835–7).

After teaching for a short time in the University of Durham (1850–51) Sellar went to assist Professor Ramsay in the Latin chair at Glasgow (1851–3). From 1853 to 1859 he was assistant professor of Greek at St Andrews. From 1859 to 1863 he held the Greek chair in that university, where his nephew Andrew Lang was a pupil, and from 1863 until his death was professor of Latin in the University of Edinburgh. He took a keen interest in politics as a Liberal and then, opposing Irish home rule, a staunch unionist. Shortsightedness contributed to a rather distant manner. Sellar died at Kenbank, Dalry, Kirkcudbrightshire, on 12 October 1890, and was buried in the churchyard at Dalry. His widow and their children survived him.

The least permanent, though perhaps the most important, part of Sellar's work was academic. A sound though not, in his own judgement, a brilliant, scholar, his appreciation of classical literature was keen and contagious. His modesty, humour, and generous sentiments aroused the affection of his pupils, many of whom had distinguished careers, while his learning secured their respect. He contributed the essays 'Lucretius' and 'Characteristics of Thucydides' to *Oxford Essays* (1855, 1857). His other works were *The Roman Poets of the Republic* (1863), *The Roman Poets of the Augustan Age: Virgil* (1877), and *Horace and the Elegiac Poets*, edited by W. P. Ker (1892). These were all remarkable examples of sound and sensitive literary criticism.

ANDREW LANG, *rev.* M. C. CURTHOYS

Sources A. Lang, 'Memoir', in W. Y. Sellar, *The Roman poets of the Augustan age* (1892) • L. Campbell, *Classical Review*, 4 (1890), 428–30 • E. M. Sellar, *Recollections and impressions* (1907) • private information (1897) • *Wellesley index*

Archives U. Edin., MSS | NL Scot., Fraser MSS

Likenesses Rodger of St Andrews, photograph, 1854, repro. in Sellar, *Recollections and impressions*, facing p. 56 • J. Faed, engraving, 1890, repro. in Sellar, *Recollections and impressions*, facing p. 322 • W. Hole, etching, NPG; repro. in W. Hole, *Quasi cursores* (1884) • R. T., wood-engraving, NPG; repro. in *ILN* (25 Oct 1890)

Wealth at death £15,890 19*s.* 2*d.*: confirmation, 13 March 1891, *CCI*

Seller, Abednego (1646/7–1705), nonjuring Church of England clergyman and religious writer, was the son of Richard Seller, of Plymouth. He matriculated at Lincoln College, Oxford, on 26 April 1662, aged fifteen. He did not take a degree, possibly because of poverty, but was ordained deacon on 11 March 1665 by Bishop Seth Ward of Exeter. He married Mary Persons on 2 December 1668 at Abbotsham, near Bideford, Devon. On 22 December 1672 he was ordained priest by Bishop Anthony Sparrow in Exeter Cathedral.

Seller's first publication appears to have been *An Infallible Way to Contentment* (1679). On 29 March 1682 he was installed as rector of Combeinteignhead, Devon, following presentation by Thomas Grey, earl of Stamford. While in that post he wrote *The Devout Communicant*. Published in

1686, it had reached its sixth edition by 1695 and it proved his most successful practical work, being republished with additions in 1704 as *The Good Man's Preparation for Receiving of the Blessed Sacrament*. Several other tracts of an anti-papist character followed. At this time Seller was also helping William Cave with his *Historia literaria* (1688). On 8 September 1686 Seller was installed vicar of St Charles, Plymouth. He did not appear at the bishop's visitation on 20 August 1689, but he still suffered deprivation for his failure to take the oaths to William and Mary.

Seller's response to the dilemma faced by the Church of England following the revolution of 1688 was to publish *The History of Passive Obedience* (1689). This argued against taking the oaths to the new monarchs, and brought forth refutations from divines such as Edward Stillingfleet. It was followed by *How far the clergy and other members of the Church of England ought to communicate with the non-swearing bishops* (1690), published anonymously, in which Seller's answer was an emphatic assertion that obedience was still owed to the nonjuring bishops, who had been deprived both schismatically and unlawfully. George Smalridge, the future bishop, wrote in November 1696 that 'Seller had the reputation of a scholar, though not of a good man, before he was a non-juror' (Nichols, *Illustrations*, 3.253). In that year Seller had published *The Antiquities of Palmyra*. In January 1700 Narcissus Luttrell reported that a fire in Red Lion Square had burnt down Mr Knightley's house where Seller's library 'with a great number of choice and scarce manuscripts were consumed' (Luttrell, 4.605).

Seller was resident in St Andrew's, Holborn, Middlesex, when he wrote his will on 9 July 1704. He left his manuscript of William of Malmesbury's 'De gestis pontificum' to the Bodleian Library; his Byzantine histories to Lincoln College; and a manuscript written by Lord Herbert to John Woodward, professor of physic at Gresham College. His other main concern was the maintenance and education of his two younger grandchildren, the daughters of his deceased daughter Margaret Bowen. The eldest granddaughter was to be placed with her uncle, Matthew Bowen. His wife received £20. In a codicil of 9 March 1705 he ordered 'all my papers, sermons, adversaria and manuscripts (except such manuscripts as are fairly transcribed from other copies) to be privately burnt'. His executors proved his will on 9 July 1705, and by the end of the month the manuscript promised to the Bodleian had arrived in Oxford. In October Thomas Hearne noted that a catalogue had revealed that Seller had owned 'a vast number' of books and almost 200 coins (*Remarks*, 1.53–4).

STUART HANDLEY

Sources Foster, *Alum. Oxon.* • J. Ingle Dredge, *Abednego Seller* (1886) • will, PRO, PROB 11/482, sig. 124 (fols. 292v–293v) • Nichols, *Illustrations*, 3.253 • N. Luttrell, *A brief historical relation of state affairs from September 1678 to April 1714*, 4 (1857), 605 • *Remarks and collections of Thomas Hearne*, ed. C. E. Doble and others, 11 vols., OHS, 2, 7, 13, 34, 42–3, 48, 50, 65, 67, 72 (1885–1921), vol. 1, pp. 9–10, 21, 53–4; vol. 4, pp. 605 • J. H. Overton, *The nonjurors: their lives, principles, and writings* (1902), 219–20, 492

Archives CUL, extracts from various books and MSS relating to Greek and Latin • CUL, MS notes on his *Antiquities of Palmyra* • CUL, MS notes on Gerard John Vossius's *De poetis Graecis et Latinis* • CUL, Sylloge Epistolarum | Bodl. Oxf., letters to Sir William Boothby [copies]

Seller, John (*bap.* **1632**, *d.* **1697**), maker of navigational instruments and chart and map seller, was baptized in London at St Katharine by the Tower on 29 December 1632, the son of Henry Seller(s), a cordwainer. Further family circumstance remains untraced, except that an elder sister was baptized at the same church in 1629. Seller was apprenticed to Edward Lowe in 1644 and became a freeman of the Merchant Taylors' Company in 1654. He further became a brother of the Clockmakers' Company in 1667 and served as warden of that company in 1692. His trade was originally that of a compass maker and so he is described, with a note that he also sold navigational instruments, in Timothy Gadbury's *The Young Sea-Mans Guide* (1659).

Seller's career was dramatically interrupted by his arrest for high treason in 1662, accused of involvement in a plot led by Thomas Tonge. The trial at the Old Bailey on 11 December 1662 revealed no connection between Seller and the other defendants: he had almost certainly done no more than repeat a rumour about a cache of arms, but this was enough for the jury to convict him. Tonge and others, all of whom admitted some degree of complicity, were executed, but Seller, after imprisonment in Newgate and a succession of petitions, was eventually pardoned. It was perhaps this incident that first brought Seller to the notice of the authorities: if so, it was a notice that was eventually to prove advantageous. The trade in printed maritime atlases and charts had previously been wholly dominated by the Dutch. In terms of national mercantile aspiration this was clearly unsatisfactory—as Seller himself put it in the dedication to *The English Pilot* (1671), 'we must see no further than their books direct us'—and when he proposed to produce English-printed maritime atlases he was soon given a royal licence, granted a virtual monopoly, and appointed hydrographer to the king in March 1671.

In the event, Seller was forced, whether by financial constraint, by lack of source material, or by the size of the task, to use as the core of his atlases a quantity of disused Dutch printing plates, originally engraved some fifty years earlier and said to have been acquired as scrap metal. These he 'refreshed in several places and used them in his pretended new work' (*Tangier Papers of Samuel Pepys*, 107). However that may be, Seller produced what he had promised, with the handsome first volume of *The English Pilot* appearing in 1671, dedicated to the duke of York, to whom he had earlier addressed his pleas from prison. Further instalments soon followed and to these were added *The Coasting Pilot* (1672) and the *Atlas maritimus* (1675). The publications may not have had their anticipated success and when a further volume of *The English Pilot*, covering the Mediterranean, was published in 1677 it was with additional partners, two of whom, John Thornton and William Fisher, were soon to take over the whole project.

Seller had meanwhile moved on to another enterprise no less ambitious, a new survey of the whole of England and Wales to be published in the form of a large-scale county atlas, the 'Atlas Anglicanus'. In association with John Oliver and the engraver Richard Palmer, Seller published fresh surveys of six counties between 1675 and 1681, as well as Oliver's map of London, but there the project ended. For the remainder of his career, Seller's output concentrated on less financially challenging material, in particular the production of miniature compendia and atlases of the type exemplified by the undated *Atlas minimus* and the *Atlas caelestis* (1680), the earliest British celestial atlas.

Seller never abandoned his original career as an instrument maker and some idea of the breadth of his activity is given in a lengthy catalogue of instruments preserved in the British Library copy of the *Atlas maritimus* (BL Maps C.8.d.5). In 1672 he successfully petitioned for a contract to supply the Chatham Dockyard with compasses and glasses. Aside from this practical work, to which must be added the occasional production of manuscript charts, Seller also taught on navigation, mathematics, surveying, gunnery, and fortification. He appears as a correspondent on the topic of magnetic variation in the *Philosophical Transactions* of the Royal Society in 1667. He wrote several textbooks, including the popular *Practical Navigation* (1669), outlining the mathematical basis of navigation through worked examples. Within the limits of contemporary practice his description of the various instruments and their use at sea is of exemplary clarity. He was further responsible for a large number of nautical almanacs, many relating to American waters. His other works include the very early set of London views, *A Prospect of London* (*c*.1680).

Seller operated throughout his documented career from premises at the Hermitage Stairs in Wapping, but for a number of years maintained additional retail premises in and about the Royal Exchange. Little is recorded of his private life. He is perhaps the John Seller granted licences for various Baptist meeting-houses in Kent in 1672, an identification made more likely by his connections with Chatham as well as his long professional association with the elder John Darby, a printer of known nonconformist affiliations. A court case over poor relief disbursed by Seller and not refunded reveals him to have been chapelwarden of Wapping Hamlet in 1688.

Seller has long had his detractors: his contemporary Robert Morden referred to him as an 'upstart Hydrographer who never did, nor ever knew how to project or draw a map or sea-chart' (*An Introduction to Astronomy*, 1702, pt 2, 32). Pepys, on the other hand, while aware of his limitations, still made use of Seller and understood the strategic importance of his activities: 'till Seller fell into it we had very few draughts, even of our own coasts, printed in England' (Pepys, *Naval Minutes*, 238). The extent to which he relied on earlier Dutch work has often been overstated and, by the only means perhaps available, he was successful in establishing a trade in London-printed charts, a trade further developed by Thornton and Fisher. It has perhaps been too little appreciated that he was also, by a line of descent through his apprentice Charles Price (1679?–1733), the founding figure of the school of map makers who came to dominate eighteenth-century British cartography, a group that included John Senex, Emanuel Bowen, Thomas Kitchin, and Thomas Jefferys. Judgement of Seller has likewise been prejudiced by the low survival rate of his work: not a single example of a large wall-map of the world is known to survive. Perhaps the best epitaph is the anagram of his name sometimes appended to his works, 'John Seller: Here's no ill'.

Seller and his wife, Elizabeth (*d.* 1711), baptized daughters Elizabeth (1655), Thomasin (1656), and Priscilla (1659). Their sons John and Jeremiah, apprenticed to Seller in 1681 and 1687 respectively, both briefly followed their father's career. Seller died of dropsy between 19 and 31 May 1697 and was buried at the church of St John-at-Wapping that month. His will noted an earlier advance of £500 to John junior and left the remainder of his estate, including his stock, to his widow and to Jeremiah, who subsequently formed a partnership with Charles Price.

LAURENCE WORMS

Sources *BL cat.* • *British Library map library catalogue* (1998) [CD-ROM] • S. Tyacke, *London map-sellers, 1660–1720* (1978) • C. Verner, 'John Seller and the chart trade in seventeenth-century England', *The compleat plattmaker: essays on chart, map, and globe making in England*, ed. N. J. W. Thrower (1978), 127–57 • *A briefe narrative of that stupendious tragedie late intended to be acted by the satanical saints* (1662) • R. A. Skelton, *County atlases of the British Isles, 1579–1830: a bibliography* (1970) • S. Pepys, *Naval minutes*, ed. J. R. Tanner, Navy RS, 60 (1926) • *The Tangier papers of Samuel Pepys*, ed. E. Chappell, Navy RS, 73 (1935) • records, Merchant Taylors' Company; Clockmakers' Company • parish register, London, St Katharine by the Tower; St John-at-Wapping • A. H. W. Robinson, *Marine cartography in Britain: a history of the sea chart to 1855* (1962) • will, PRO, PROB 11/438, fols. 119–20 • *CSP dom.*, 1672

Archives BL • NMM

Wealth at death approx. £1000: will, 1697, PRO, PROB 11/438, fols. 119–20

Sellers, James Henry (1861–1954). *See under* Wood, Edgar (1860–1935).

Sellers, Peter [*real name* Richard Henry Sellers] (**1925–1980**), comedian, was born in Portsmouth on 8 September 1925, the only child of William Sellers, a pianist of modest ability, and his wife, Agnes (Peg) Marks, who was one of the Ray Sisters entertainers and the great-granddaughter of Daniel Mendoza the pugilist. Although his mother was Jewish he was primarily educated at St Aloysius College in Hornsey Lane, Highgate, a Roman Catholic school run by the Brothers of Our Lady of Mercy. He left school at fourteen and entered the theatre world, doing most backstage jobs. He then developed a desire to play drums in a dance band. At this he became very proficient and, but for his ability at mimicry, might well have stayed a jazz drummer.

Called up into the RAF during the war, despite his mother's desperate efforts to have him disqualified on medical grounds, he finally ended up in its entertainment section in India, Ceylon, and Burma with Ralph Reader's gang show. Within a short time of leaving the services in 1947, such was his confidence and his ability as an impressionist that he duped a BBC producer, Roy Speer, by using

Peter Sellers (1925–1980), by Rex Coleman for Baron Studios, 1962

the voice of Kenneth Horne. The producer was duly impressed and gave him a small part in a comedy show.

In a short space of time Sellers appeared in several radio series—*Petticoat Lane*, *Ray's a Laugh*, *Variety Bandbox*, *Workers' Playtime*, *Third Division* (the first comedy show on the erudite Third Programme), finally reaching the highest acclaim in the revolutionary *The Goon Show*, which began in 1951 and ran for nine years. During this period he also appeared in variety, including the royal command performance. There were a few second-rate films: *Penny Points to Paradise* (1951), *Orders are Orders* (1954), *John and Julie* (1955), and *The Smallest Show on Earth* (1957). Then came a strangely original short film written and directed by Spike Milligan, entitled *The Running Jumping Standing Still Film* (1957–8), which won numerous awards because of its innovatory ideas. Sellers's big commercial break came with *The Ladykillers* (1955), but he received world acclaim for his outstanding performance in *I'm All Right Jack* (1959).

There followed a series of quality films, some successful and some not, including *The Millionairess* (1960), in which Sellers played opposite Sophia Loren, and *Waltz of the Toreadors* (1962), and one produced and directed by himself, *Mr. Topaze* (1961). He soared to new heights in his multi-character *Dr. Strangelove*. He did some black comedy films, one being *What's new Pussycat?* (1965), with Peter O'Toole and Woody Allen, but the watershed in his career was his portrayal of Inspector Clouseau in *The Pink Panther* (1963). This was followed by a period of indifference, and it would appear at one time that his career might have come to a conclusion. However, there followed *The Return of the Pink Panther* (1974) and *The Pink Panther Strikes Again* (1976), which renovated his career and made him a millionaire.

To summarize Sellers it could be said that he had one of the most glittering comic talents of his age, but what few people knew was that he never reached or was allowed to perform the levels of comedy that he delighted in most: the nonsense school. To his dying day he said his happiest days were performing in the Goon shows. He made a desperate attempt to recreate their atmosphere by making the film *The Fiendish Plot of Dr. Fu Manchu* (1980), which he co-wrote. But the fact that he never was a writer, or ever would be, and the collaboration with Americans, who had no like sense of humour, made the film a failure. However, most extraordinarily, he gave his finest performance in his last-but-one film, *Being there* (1979), which showed his incredible ability to recreate a character in which Peter Sellers himself seemed to be totally excluded. His last wry contribution to comedy was having Glenn Miller's 'In the Mood' played at his cremation.

Sellers was appointed CBE in 1966. He won many awards: best actor for 1959 (British Film Academy award); the Golden Gate award, 1959; the San Sebastian film award for the best British actor, 1962; best actor award, Tehran Film Festival, 1973; and the *Evening News* best actor of the year award, 1975.

Sellers suffered from a heart condition for his last fifteen years which made life difficult for him and had a debilitating effect on his personality. None of his marriages lasted long. His first one, in 1951 to Anne Howe, produced two children, Michael and Sarah, but was terminated in 1964. In the same year, after a whirlwind romance, he married the starlet Britt Ekland. There was one daughter of this marriage, Victoria, but the marriage was dissolved in 1969. In 1970 he married Miranda, daughter of Richard St John Quarry and Lady Mancroft; the childless marriage was dissolved in 1974. His last marriage, in 1977, to Lynne Frederick (*d.* 1994), also underwent emotional undulations, and all the signs point to a marriage that had failed; they had no children. Sellers died in the Middlesex Hospital, London, on 24 July 1980. Among the many who attended a later service of thanksgiving in London were Spike Milligan, Harry Secombe, and Michael Bentine, his former colleagues on *The Goon Show*.

SPIKE MILLIGAN, *rev.*

Sources P. Evans, *The mask behind the mask: a life of Peter Sellers* (1969) · A. Walker, *Peter Sellers* (1981) · M. Sellers, S. Sellers, and V. Sellers, *P.S. I love you* (1981) · *The Times* (25 July 1980) · personal knowledge (1986) · R. Lewis, *The life and death of Peter Sellers* (1994)

Archives BFI, personal scrapbooks | FILM BFI NFTVA, *Arena*, BBC 2, 11 Feb 1995 · BFI NFTVA, *Parkinson: the interviews*, BBC 1, 9 Aug 1996 · BFI NFTVA, 'The unknown Peter Sellers', ITV, 5 Aug 2000 · BFI NFTVA, current affairs footage · BFI NFTVA, documentary footage · BFI NFTVA, news footage | SOUND BL NSA, documentary footage · BL NSA, performance footage

Likenesses photographs, *c.*1955–1975, Hult. Arch. · R. Coleman for Baron Studios, photograph, 1962, NPG [*see illus.*]

Selling [Celling, Tyll], **William** (*c.*1430–1494), humanist scholar and prior of Christ Church, Canterbury, was almost certainly born about 1430 at Selling, 8 miles west of Canterbury. Selling was to be his name in religion, but his parents were William and Agnes Tyll, both of whom were eventually to enjoy the exceptional privilege of burial near Thomas Becket's tomb in Canterbury Cathedral. A Richard Tyll recorded as being supported by Prior Selling between 1475 and 1482 as a scholar at Canterbury College, Oxford, was specified as the prior's nephew. Presumably William Selling was taught initially at the Benedictine school of Christ Church, Canterbury, since by 17 February 1448, when ordained acolyte, he had already professed at the priory on 25 January. Thereafter he was ordained subdeacon (1449), deacon (1450), and on 18 September 1456 priest, celebrating his first mass at Canterbury eight days later.

By 18 April 1454 Selling was studying at Canterbury College, Oxford, which would be his principal residence for another decade. He must have been there for several years already, for on 7 February 1458, on the grounds of eight years' study of philosophy, with six of theology, he purchased a grace to supplicate for the bachelor of theology degree. His interest at Oxford in the *studia humanitatis* is substantiated by an autograph note that he was tutored in Latin eloquence by Stefano Surigone; this interest was lifelong, for example his letter of about 1470 to an Italian in London, wherein he presented William Worcester (otherwise William Botoner), who sought permission to see a manuscript of Livy's *Decades* with a view to purchase. On 26 September 1464 he received his prior's permission to study abroad for three years, and probably was admitted to his doctorate in theology at Bologna University on 22 March 1466. Leland wrote that Selling had learnt Greek at Bologna, hence supposedly from Andronicus Callistus, the university's professor of Greek. In the autumn of 1466 he was joined abroad by William Hadley, another Christ Church monk; the two visited Padua, probably briefly, receiving hospitality from the English widow of a Venetian citizen. Selling, at least, went to Rome, perhaps on priory matters, meeting the canon lawyer Pietro Mellini.

Selling had returned to his priory by 31 August 1468, when he preached before the archbishop and the community of some eighty monks on the eve of the election of a new prior, his theme being Judges 1: 1. He remained at the priory teaching; the future physician Thomas Linacre, perhaps a relative, was most likely one of his students. On 19 March 1469 he publicly charged a repentant Lollard opposed to the cult of St Thomas of Canterbury. By the following 3 October he had been chosen, with his fellow monk Reginald Goldstone, for a delicate mission to supplicate at Rome for plenary indulgences for all pilgrims to Becket's shrine on the jubilee of the saint's martyrdom, 29 December 1470. Selling bore the community's letter to Mellini, who lodged the brothers in Rome. Mellini's brother, bishop of Urbino, was datary, an official with the favour of the pope and authority in the curia, and he promoted the petition; the requisite bull, dated 4 June 1470, was undoubtedly taken home immediately. Further evidence of Selling's standing in his community was his appointment in 1470 as a chancellor, or prior's chaplain, with legal responsibilities for a prior's election; the community's register of 1471 is in a fine humanistic hand, almost certainly Selling's.

Following the death of Prior John Oxney on 2 July 1471, Selling supervised the election of his successor, William Petham. On the testimony of William Worcester about this time Selling gave basic Greek instruction to Dr Usk (probably Philip) of London. Following Petham's premature demise Selling was himself chosen prior, on 10 September 1472. This office, according to Johann Burckard valued at some 7000 ducats annually, he filled with distinction until his death, although it involved a shift from scholarship to administration of the largest monastery in Britain. Even so he fostered scholarship, for instance early in his priorate he procured a master for the grammar school at Canterbury, and in 1481 donated books to Canterbury College, Oxford. His particular concern was learning within his own community. He had built a study over the entrance to Green Court, 'Selling gate', for the prior's use; he glazed the south aisle of the cloisters, fitting it with carrels for studious brothers; he adorned with an ornamental ceiling the room over the prior's chapel which was to house Latin and Greek manuscripts acquired by him; this library was partially destroyed by fire in Henry VIII's reign. His investment in building reflects Italian Renaissance influences. He restored that portion of the city's wall bordering the cathedral which in 1492 the mayor and commonalty of Canterbury surrendered. Selling's programme for the cathedral's fabric included the 'Bell Harry steeple', brought to half its present height by the time of his death. In the case of the north-west transept, the work of enhancement was carried on in conjunction with Edward IV, who donated the 'royal window', completed in 1482.

As a mitred prior, Selling had the obligations of a spiritual lord to king and to convocation. In the interim from Bishop Waynflete's death on 11 August 1486 until late January 1487 when Henry VII confirmed Peter Courtenay as his successor, Selling administered the see of Winchester, the richest in England. His skills in classical rhetoric ensured his place on the impressive mission under Thomas Millyng, bishop of Hereford, which was sent by Henry VII to thank the pope for his marriage dispensation, a document that had also asserted that Henry was the rightful monarch. Shortly after the party reached Rome, on 8 May 1487, Selling delivered the oration of royal obedience; he took the opportunity to obtain confirmation of the prior's jurisdiction, and of Christ Church's exemption from attending black monk chapters. In 1490 the king, involved in Brittany, sent a delegation under Richard Fox, bishop of Exeter, to try to negotiate peace with the king of France. The embassy, which included Selling, reached Tours in May, agreeing a seven-month truce; the mission's authority was renewed in October 1490 and February 1491. The humanist Robert Gaguin, with the French party at Tours, entered into a personal correspondence with Selling, on 22 June 1492 sending two of his treatises in manuscript as a gift. Selling persuaded Louis XI to renew the annual gift of French wine for the Canterbury brethren, known as the 'wine of St Thomas' from its having been originally given by Louis VII following Becket's murder, and wrote to Louis to inform him that in gratitude the chapter had elected him to full confraternity. However, there seems to be no truth in the claim that Selling subsequently entertained King Charles VIII (*r.* 1483–98) at Canterbury.

Selling's scholarly output was limited to a translation into Latin of a Greek sermon by St John Chrysostom, completed in 1486; it provides evidence for the remarkable knowledge of Greek recorded in both his tomb inscription and the priory's obituary book. Information concerning his Greek terminations and pronunciation of Greek vowels written in his own hand survives in William Worcester's notebooks (BL, Cotton MS Julius F.vii, fol. 118). A number of his Latin orations, some of them in his italic hand, are extant (BL, Cotton MS Cleopatra E.iii), revealing his skill in Italian Renaissance oratory. Particularly notable is the speech he prepared for the cancelled convocation of 19 April 1483. Linacre benefited from Selling's patronage and accompanied him to Italy in 1487. Leland's claim that Selling first met the famous Florentine scholar and poet Angelo Poliziano in Bologna in the 1460s is erroneous, but possibly he did introduce Linacre to Poliziano at a later date. Selling died on 29 December 1494, and received the appropriate honour of burial in the 'martyrdom transept', directly before the altar. He is not to be confused with two namesakes, one of them associated with Canterbury College *c.*1504–17, the other abbot of St Augustine's, Canterbury, at his death in 1480.

CECIL H. CLOUGH

Sources Emden, *Oxf.*, 3.1666–7 · J. Greatrex, *Biographical register of the English cathedral priories of the province of Canterbury* (1997), 282–4 · B. Dobson, 'William Selling, prior of Canterbury Cathedral, 1472–94', *Canterbury Cathedral Chronicle*, 89 (March 1995), 15–21 · R. Weiss, *Humanism in England during the fifteenth century*, 3rd edn (1967), 150, 152–9, 188–9 · U. Balzani, 'Un ambasciata inglese a Roma', *Archivio della R. Società Romana di Storia Patria*, 3 (1879), 175–211 · C. Woodruff and W. W. Danks, *Memorials of the cathedral and priory of Christ in Canterbury* (1912), 207–8 · F. Woodman, *The architectural history of Canterbury Cathedral* (1981), 203, 205–8 · R. Weiss, 'Humanism in Oxford', *TLS* (9 Jan 1937), 28 · M. R. James, *The ancient libraries of Canterbury and Dover* (1903), l–li · R. Gaguin, *Epistolae et orationes*, ed. L. Thuasne, 2 vols. (1904), 1.95, 383–4 · *Commentarii de scriptoribus Britannicis, auctore Joanne Lelando*, ed. A. Hall, 2 (1709), 482–3 · W. A. Pantin, *Canterbury College, Oxford*, 4 vols., OHS, new ser., 6–8, 30 (1947–85) · obituary book, Canterbury Cathedral Archives · J. W. Bennett, 'John Morer's will: Thomas Linacre and Prior Selling's Greek teaching', *Studies in the Renaissance*, 15 (1968), 70–91 · [A. C. de la Mare and R. W. Hunt], eds., *Duke Humfrey and English humanism in the fifteenth century* (1970), 58 [exhibition catalogue, Bodl. Oxf.]

Archives BL, Cotton MS Cleopatra E.iii · BL, Cotton MS Julius F.vii | Canterbury Cathedral, archives, register S, obituary book, Cawston MS

Sellon, Baker John (1762–1835), serjeant-at-law, was born in London on 14 March 1762, the second son of William Sellon (*d.* 1790), perpetual curate of St James's, Clerkenwell. He was admitted into Merchant Taylors' School on 2 November 1773, and entered St John's College, Oxford, on 11 June 1779. He graduated BCL on 24 October 1785. On 24 January 1788 he married Charlotte (*d.* 1832), daughter of Rivers Dickinson of St John Street, Clerkenwell; they had a large family, of whom three daughters and one son survived infancy. Their second daughter, Maria Ann, married John James Hall, and their third daughter, Anne, married Sir Benjamin Collins Brodie.

Sellon wished to become a clergyman, but, at his father's request, he studied law, and was called to the bar from the Inner Temple on 10 February 1792. While at the Inner Temple, Sellon published his *Analysis of the practice of the courts of king's bench and common pleas, with some observations on the mode of passing fines and suffering recoveries* (1789). On being admitted to the bar, he worked on *The Practice of the Courts of King's Bench and Common Pleas* (2 vols., 1792–6). He also wrote *A Treatise on the Deity and the Trinity*, which was published posthumously in 1847 and edited by W. Marsh.

After practising for several years with distinction, Sellon was admitted a serjeant-at-law in the Easter term of 1798, and he later became leader of the Norfolk circuit. Increasing deafness, however, obliged him to refuse a judgeship, and finally to retire from the bar. In 1814, at his own request (he was apparently short of money), Henry Addington, Viscount Sidmouth, appointed him police magistrate at Union Hall; in January 1819 he was transferred to the Hatton Garden office. There he continued to act until his retirement in 1834. He died at his home in Hampstead, after a period of paralysis, on 19 August 1835.

GORDON GOODWIN, *rev.* JOANNE POTIER

Sources *GM*, 2nd ser., 4 (1835), 651–3 · Allibone, *Dict.* · Watt, *Bibl. Brit.*, 2.843 · *GM*, 1st ser., 60 (1790), 673, 763 · Foster, *Alum. Oxon.* · R. H. Hadden, ed., *Reminiscences of William Rogers, rector of St Botolph, Bishopsgate* (1888) · H. W. Woolrych, *Lives of eminent serjeants-at-law of the English bar*, 2 vols. (1869) · A. Polson, *Law and lawyers, or, Sketches and illustrations of legal history and biography*, 2 vols. (1840)

Sellon, (Priscilla) Lydia (1821–1876), founder of the Society of the Most Holy Trinity, was born on 21 March 1821 in Hampstead, Middlesex, but brought up at the family country house, Port-y-seal, in Grosmont, Monmouthshire. Her father, William Richard Baker Smith (1791–1860), son of Thomas Smith, receiver-general to the dean and chapter of St Paul's Cathedral, entered the Royal Navy in 1801 (lieutenant 1807), served in the Napoleonic wars, retired with the rank of commander, and on inheriting the property of his maternal aunt Sophia Sellon, assumed in January 1847 the name and arms of his mother's family. Priscilla Lydia Sellon, known as Lydia, was the third surviving child of his first wife, Priscilla Lydia White (*d.* 13 May 1823), who died when Lydia was little more than two. She grew up in a large family as her father married again and had eleven more children. She was educated at home by a Scottish Presbyterian governess. A lively and spirited young woman, she was allowed an unusual amount of independence by her father. When, in 1848, she wanted to go and work in appalling conditions among the poor in Plymouth and Devonport in response to an appeal by the bishop of Exeter, Henry Phillpotts, he gave her his support.

Lydia Sellon arrived in Devonport with only one helper, Catherine Chambers, the sister of a friend of her father, but quickly won the agreement of the bishop to start the

Devonport Sisters of Mercy. For the rest of her life Miss Chambers self-effacingly devoted herself to assisting Miss Sellon, dealing with her correspondence and, as 'Mother Eldress', with the routine administration of the order. They wore plain black dresses with black wooden crosses. Theirs was not the first sisterhood in the Church of England. The Park Village Sisterhood in London, the Sisterhood of the Holy Cross, was founded in 1845, but it was absorbed into the Devonport sisterhood in 1856 and the united sisterhood took the name the Society of the Most Holy Trinity. Lydia Sellon was first known as the Lady Superior or simply Mother within the community. Later—probably from 1852 when St Dunstan's Abbey, Plymouth, was built, largely at her own expense, as the society's main house—she was known as the abbess and on occasion used a pastoral staff.

From the beginning Lydia Sellon was advised and guided by Edward Bouverie Pusey whom she had probably met through the Chambers family. He was her spiritual director, spent much time in her company, and went overseas with her on more than one occasion. He heard the confessions of many of the sisters and was a generous benefactor of the community. So close was their relationship that it led to gossip, and her brother eventually published a formal denial of any engagement between them. Pusey was an enormous influence on her, but she undoubtedly influenced him too. It was, for example, she who introduced him to Joseph Leycester Lyne, later known as Father Ignatius, and persuaded Pusey to take an interest in him. One of the sisters said Lydia was like a mother to Pusey. Another, however, who left to become a Roman Catholic nun, alleged Pusey 'had an infatuation for Miss Sellon which was very little short of mania. The woman had laid a spell on him' (Gill, 155).

Lydia Sellon's plans for the society were ambitious and invariably exceeded its resources. Within two years of its foundation she had established in and around Devonport an orphanage, a home for delinquent boys, two refuges for training girls for domestic service, an industrial school, six model lodging houses for poor families, five ragged schools, a soup kitchen, a home for old sailors, and a naval training school, as well as working among female emigrants. She later set up soup kitchens, almshouses, a nurses' home, and a convalescent hospital. One of her most imaginative projects was setting up a printing press to provide work for young women who might otherwise have been forced into prostitution. Mother Lydia had early seen the possibilities of a press as employment for women and had herself learned printing. The society's activities extended beyond Devonport and Plymouth. Houses were set up in London, Bristol, Manchester, Bradford-on-Avon, Norwich, Carnmenellis, and Ascot but some of the experiments were very short-lived. In 1864 Mother Lydia was able to realize a possibility for which she had made provision in the statutes of the society, that of the sisters' becoming involved in mission work abroad. A few were sent out to the Sandwich Islands to establish a school. In 1867 Mother Lydia herself made the arduous journey to Honolulu with three more sisters to choose a site for a permanent mission station. It was the first time any Anglican sisterhood had ventured into work overseas.

All the early sisterhoods were viewed with suspicion and hostility, because they seemed to threaten the family and because mistakes were inevitably made, given that there was no tradition of the religious life in the Church of England to draw on. The very name stirred fears of 'popery'. The festivities for the laying of the foundation stone of St Dunstan's Abbey in 1850 were disrupted by a mob which pelted the sisters and clergy with potatoes and plates. The Society of the Most Holy Trinity drew more criticism than most, partly because of its association with Pusey and partly because of Mother Lydia's authoritarianism, exaggerated by gossip and rumour and by the allegations of one or two disaffected sisters and associates. Bishop Phillpotts was obliged to hold a public inquiry in February 1849 and, although he spoke warmly of Miss Sellon's work and character, in 1852 he withdrew from his role as visitor to the society. Bishop Blomfield of London tried to exclude her and the society from his diocese. Some of the clergy who might have been expected to support her, such as John Mason Neale, William John Butler, and Arthur Stanton, were in fact critical of her, especially of her independence of the parish clergy and her reputed ambition to become superior-general of all religious communities in England.

Lydia Sellon undoubtedly asserted her authority over the sisters and it is probably true that there were no formal chapters or elections of novices in her lifetime. The oldest sister at Ascot Priory stated, 'We are a despotic monarchy without a Parliament' (Gill, 153). Nevertheless it was no small achievement to establish the sisterhood and to organize and direct its many works in the face of a barrage of criticism and in an atmosphere of such mistrust. In 1852 pamphlets were published for and against her. She refused to defend herself in print but her father, who never wavered in his support of her, published in 1852 *Miss Sellon and the Sisters of Mercy: a contradiction of the alleged acts of cruelty exercised by Miss Sellon*, a full refutation of the allegations against her. A surprising tribute was paid to her by Wordsworth, who dedicated one of his last sonnets to her at the time of the bishop's public inquiry.

Much of the society's work was unseen and done for people who could not make their gratitude public. The work which received most recognition was the sisters' heroic nursing. A few sisters were sent to work under Florence Nightingale during the Crimean War but they had already distinguished themselves during a serious outbreak of cholera in Plymouth in 1849 which lasted almost six months. Mother Lydia immediately volunteered the help of her sisters, stating that 'the proper place for Sisters of Mercy is amongst the sick and dying' (Liddon, 199). One of the local papers acknowledged 'Nothing can exceed the zeal and devotion of this lady and the other Sisters' (Williams, 52). Another cholera epidemic in the East End of London in 1866 prompted her to write to *The Times* appealing for funds to establish an emergency hospital there. She took over an empty warehouse and staffed it with her own sisters and sisters from other communities. Father Ignatius and two of his Benedictine novices also helped. Mother Kate of St Saviour's Priory, Haggerston, met Mother Lydia at this time and described her as 'a most striking person, with commanding gestures, and a peculiarly imperative wave of a very well shaped white hand' (Warburton, 85). In 1870, when smallpox broke out in east London, Mother Lydia again sent sisters to help with nursing and the convalescent hospital at Ascot Priory came into its own. There were so many patients that some had to be accommodated in tents in the grounds. Mother Lydia was largely responsible for planning and directing everything although she was at the time threatened with blindness and so weak that she had to be carried about in a chair.

Lydia Sellon's health seems never to have been very strong. She had a stroke in 1861 which partially paralysed her for a time, and another in 1872 which left her right arm permanently paralysed. A third stroke when she was staying at Osborne House, West Malvern, Worcestershire, made her unable to swallow. She died there on 20 November 1876. Her body was taken to Ascot Priory, near Bracknell, Berkshire, and on 29 November she was buried in the graveyard there. PETER G. COBB

Sources T. J. Williams, *Priscilla Lydia Sellon*, rev. edn (1965) • S. Gill, 'The power of Christian ladyhood: Priscilla Lydia Sellon and the creation of Anglican sisterhoods', *Modern religious rebels: presented to John Kent*, ed. S. Mews (1993), 144–65 • A. M. Allchin, *The silent rebellion* (1958) • [K. E. Warburton], *Memories of Mother Kate* (1925) • J. S. Sellon, ed., *Sisters of Mercy: memos relating to the Society of the Holy Trinity* (1907) • H. P. Liddon, *The life of Edward Bouverie Pusey*, ed. J. O. Johnston and others, 4 vols. (1893–7), vol. 3 • O'Byrne, *Naval biog. dict.* • Boase, *Mod. Eng. biog.*

Archives Society of the Most Holy Trinity, Ascot Priory, Ascot, corresp. and papers [copies, Pusey Oxf.] | LPL, corresp. with Charles Blomfield • Pusey Oxf., letters to Lord Halifax and related papers

Likenesses crayon drawing, *c.*1848, Ascot Priory, Berkshire; repro. in Williams, *Priscilla Lydia Sellon* • photograph, *c.*1865, New Mill, Penzance; repro. in Williams, *Priscilla Lydia Sellon*

Wealth at death under £4000: probate, 29 Dec 1876, *CGPLA Eng. & Wales*

Sellors, Sir Thomas Holmes (1902–1987), cardiothoracic surgeon, was born on 7 April 1902 in Wandsworth, London, the only son and younger child of Thomas Blanchard Sellors, a general medical practitioner, and his wife, Anne Oliver McSparron. His father later practised at Westcliff-on-Sea, where Tom, as he was always known, was educated at Alleyn Court School. He then went to Loretto School, Musselburgh, and Oriel College, Oxford, where he received a second class in physiology (1923). He secured an entrance scholarship to the Middlesex Hospital, London, qualifying BM, ChB and MRCS, LRCP in 1926 before holding resident and surgical registrar appointments there. After a thorough grounding in general surgery, including a year in Scandinavia as recipient of the first G. H. Hunt award by Oxford University in 1928, he decided to specialize in chest work, which was then a rather limited field. He became FRCS in 1930.

In 1934 Sellors was appointed to the London Chest Hospital and then to various London county council hospitals and sanatoria, for some 90 per cent of thoracic surgery was then concerned with pulmonary tuberculosis. In 1933 he surprised many of his seniors with the publication of *Surgery of the Thorax*, and during the 1930s he started chest surgery units at the Radcliffe Infirmary, Oxford, and Leicester Royal Infirmary, which entailed even more travelling and a heavy workload. He became DM in 1933.

On the outbreak of the Second World War Sellors became adviser in thoracic surgery to the north-west metropolitan region of the Emergency Medical Service, based at Harefield Hospital, Middlesex. In the next few years, in addition to his tuberculosis work, he did an increasing number of resections for lung and gullet cancer, while the nascent field of heart surgery slowly demanded more of his time and interest. On appointment as thoracic surgeon to the Middlesex Hospital in 1947 he enjoyed close and cordial relationships with the cardiologists D. Evan Bedford and Walter Somerville which were to prove vital to the development of more complex heart surgery. He was responsible for the creation of three cardiac surgical units—at Harefield (which remained his first love), the Middlesex, and finally, in 1957, the National Heart Hospital.

Sellors showed a healthy conservatism in avoiding frankly experimental procedures, but was quick to utilize the significant advances of his contemporaries. Before there was a practicable heart–lung machine for open heart surgery he learned his hypothermic technique from Henry Swann in the United States and closed some 500 atrial septal defects with overall results which were unrivalled at that time. He and his team then acquired the early cardiopulmonary bypass technique from John Kirklin at the Mayo Clinic. Sellors became FRCP in 1963.

Ever courteous in the operation room, and never known to raise his voice (the fiercest reaction to an inept assistant was no more than his favourite admonition 'Juggins!'), Sellors was a superb craftsman, a master of sharp dissection. He did the first successful direct operation on the pulmonary heart valve for the relief of valvular stenosis, but, characteristically, was not the first to publish this success. He had retired from practice before coronary artery surgery was established and later frankly admitted that he had wrongly believed the successful and lasting anastomosis of such small vessels to be impracticable.

From the inception of the National Health Service Sellors was active in the medico-political field. Having been chairman of his regional consultants' and specialists' committee for some years, he was an inaugural member of the central committee and its chairman for five years. In 1958 he became chairman of the Joint Consultants' Committee, which linked the British Medical Association with the various royal colleges, an arduous task which he undertook for nine years. For this work and his services to surgery he was knighted in 1963. A Hunterian professor of the Royal College of Surgeons in 1944, he was elected to its council in 1957, and was vice-president in 1968–9 and president in 1969–72. He was president of the British Medical Association in 1972–3 and was awarded its gold medal in 1979. Throughout his busy surgical life he travelled widely abroad, lecturing and demonstrating. He was awarded honorary fellowships of the American (1971) and South African surgical colleges, as well as those of Edinburgh (1972) and the Royal College of Surgeons in Ireland (1975). He had honorary degrees from Groningen (1964), Liverpool (1970), and Southampton (1972), and was an honorary fellow of Oriel College, Oxford (1973).

Well after his retirement from surgical practice Sellors laboured for many good causes. Apart from his early textbook he wrote a number of surgical papers and edited several cardiothoracic works. Outside his professional work he had a capacity for gracious living. He was a keen gardener, a fine draftsman, and a competent painter in watercolours. He had great sympathy and kindness, and a quiet wit.

Sellors was of medium height and portly build, with a fine Churchillian head; his reading spectacles were generally perched near the end of his nose. He was thrice married and thrice widowed. His first wife, Brenda Lyell, died of acute appendicitis a few weeks after their marriage in 1928. She was the daughter of William Darling Lyell, advocate and sheriff-substitute of Lanark. In 1932 he married (Dorothy) Elizabeth, daughter of John Chesshire, businessman. They had a son, Patrick, who became surgeon oculist to the queen, and a daughter. Elizabeth died in 1953 and in 1955 Sellors married his secretary, Marie Hobson, who died in 1985. She was the daughter of Martin Greenwall or Grunwald, aeronautical engineer. Sellors lived latterly at Spring Coppice Farm, Speen, Aylesbury, Buckinghamshire, and died on 12 September 1987 in Parkside Hospital, Wimbledon, London, of carcinoma of the colon and chronic prostatic obstruction.

REGINALD MURLEY, *rev.*

Sources *The Times* (16 Sept 1987) · Munk, *Roll*, vol. 8 · personal knowledge (1996) · private information (1996) · *CGPLA Eng. & Wales* (1987)

Wealth at death £504,303: probate, 17 Dec 1987, *CGPLA Eng. & Wales*

Sellyng, Richard (*d.* 1467), poet, wrote a poem entitled 'Evidens to be ware and Gode Counsayle', followed by 'An Vocation til Oure Lady', which exist uniquely in BL, Harley MS 7333, folio 36a.

These rhyme-royal poems Sellyng claims to have written 'when age was come' and he submits the work in a conclusion of six couplets to John Shirley 'for to amende where it is a-misse' (Baugh, 179–81). Shirley's introduction describes him as 'that honourable squier', and a Richard Sellyng, esquire, figures in the records of the period. He may be identified with the Richard Sellyng who before 1432 was resident in Baconsthorpe, Norfolk, with his wife, Joanna, the widow of Sir William Bardolf. This Richard Sellyng conveyed Bernham's manor and the manor of Drayton to Sir John Fastolf, and Fastolf speaks of him in the Paston letters. Sellyng is recorded as the executor of Joanna's will in 1435, and through her he acquired the castle and lordship of Sangatte near Calais; she may have died some years earlier, however, for by 1429–30 a Richard Sellyng was married to Alice, widow of Sir John Wiltshire. He was probably also the Richard Sellyng, esquire, who took military service at Calais between 1434 and 1436; if true, this may have been where he first met John Shirley. By the latter part of the decade Sellyng was probably in Kent, where he appears as the husband of a third wife, Elizabeth Brockhill, only daughter and heir of Thomas Brockhill, in 1438. The couple had one son, John, born *c.*1441. Long 'broken with age and totally blind' (*CPR, 1452–61*, 242), Sellyng died on 16 May 1467. An edition of 'Evidens to be ware' was published in 1940 by A. C. Baugh.

CORINNE R. BERG

Sources A. C. Baugh, 'Richard Sellyng', *Essays and studies in honour of Carleton Brown* (1940), 167–81 · *The Paston letters, 1422–1509 AD*, ed. J. Gairdner, new edn, 3 vols. (1872–5) · C. Brown and R. H. Robbins, *The index of Middle English verse* (1943), item 4074 · F. Blomefield and C. Parkin, *An essay towards a topographical history of the county of Norfolk*, [2nd edn], 11 vols. (1805–10) · A. I. Doyle, 'More light on John Shirley', *Medium Aevum*, 30 (1961), 93–101

Archives BL, Harley MS 7333

Selous, Edmund (1857–1934), ornithologist and author, was born on 14 August 1857 in London, at Holgate Lodge, Gloucester Road, Regent's Park, the younger son in the family of two surviving sons and three daughters of Frederick Lokes Slous (or Selous), a wealthy stockbroker, and his third wife, Ann Holgate Sherborn, daughter of John Sherborn. He was the brother of Frederick Courteney *Selous, the hunter and African explorer, and the nephew of the artist Henry Courtney Selous and the dramatist Angiolo Robson Selous. Educated privately, he matriculated at Pembroke College, Cambridge, in 1877 (leaving without a degree); he was admitted to the Middle Temple in 1878 and called to the bar in 1881. After trips to southern Africa and India he practised briefly as a barrister and settled down to the life of a gentleman, pursuing the two great passions of his life: the study of natural history and that of great literature (French, German, and Spanish, all read in the original languages, as well as English). In 1886 he married Fanny, daughter of John Maxwell, publisher, and his wife, the novelist Mary Elizabeth *Braddon. They had a son (Gerald Holgate Selous, diplomat and Arabist) and twin daughters.

A conventional Victorian naturalist at first, Selous developed an aversion to blood sports and to all forms of scientific collecting involving cruelty to animals, against which, as a self-styled 'life-loving naturalist', he campaigned for the rest of his life, earning the enmity of certain important figures in the ornithological establishment of the day. In 1898 he began observing the habits of wild birds in earnest, making detailed notes on the spot; he became a key pioneer (as observer and interpreter) in the ethological study of bird behaviour, introducing the words 'bird-watcher' and 'bird-watching' into the language and producing a large output of influential scientific papers and books. The latter included *Bird Watching* (1901), *The Bird Watcher in the Shetlands* (1905), *Bird Life Glimpses* (1905), *Realities of Bird Life* (1927), *Thought-*

Transference—or what?—in Birds (1931), and *Evolution of Habit in Birds* (1933), as well as many essays (mostly in the *Saturday Review*), and several other books on popular natural history and for children.

Most of Selous's observations were made within walking or cycling distance of his various homes in England and abroad, but he also visited the Shetlands, Sweden, the Netherlands, and Iceland. Bird display was his speciality and he made a number of seminal studies. He was one of the first to seek evidence in the field for the concept of natural selection held by Charles Darwin, maintaining (then heretically) that a species' behaviour was as characteristic of it as any morphological feature.

Selous also championed the Darwinian idea of sexual selection, once more against the tide of contemporary scientific opinion. He obtained evidence of female choice in two species (the ruff and the black grouse) in which mate-selection is made communally, thus earning the later approbation of the distinguished geneticist Sir R. A. Fisher. Also obsessed by the problem of the co-ordinated flight manoeuvres of flocking birds, Selous sought the explanation in some form of extrasensory facility such as telepathy. Selous went on bird-watching and writing nearly to the end of his life and died at his home in Weymouth, Lydwell, Buxton Road, on 25 March 1934.

K. E. L. SIMMONS, *rev.*

Sources Venn, *Alum. Cant.* • U. Oxf., Edward Grey Institute of Field Ornithology, Edmund Selous collection • b. cert. • *CGPLA Eng. & Wales* (1934)
Archives U. Oxf., Edward Grey Institute | BL, corresp. with Society of Authors, Add. MS 56803
Wealth at death £16,217 13*s.* 11*d.*: probate, 26 June 1934, *CGPLA Eng. & Wales*

Selous, Frederick Courteney (1851–1917), hunter and explorer, was born at Regent's Park, London, on 31 December 1851, the son of Frederick Lokes Selous, of Huguenot descent, chairman of the stock exchange, and his wife, Ann Holgate Sherborn. He was the brother of Edmund *Selous the ornithologist. He was sent to Bruce Castle School, Tottenham, and subsequently, in 1866, to Rugby School, where he distinguished himself principally for his proficiency in games and his interest in wild bird life.

On leaving Rugby in 1868 Selous went abroad to learn French and German before entering on a medical career. That career, however, had no attractions for him, and, deciding to take his chance, he went to South Africa in 1871, determined upon the open-air life of a sportsman. The next ten years of his life as a hunter and ivory trader were years of strenuous effort, adventures, privation, and anxiety for the future. In quest of game he traversed the interior of South Africa from east to west and penetrated as far north as Zambia.

During a short visit to England in 1881, Selous wrote his first book, *A Hunter's Wanderings in Africa*, which secured him commissions from museums and dealers for trophies of big game; and since the ivory trade was by that time declining in southern Africa, he devoted the next few years to fulfilling those orders and acting as guide to hunting and prospecting parties. During this period his explorations resulted in some interesting discoveries, which were published in 1888 by the Royal Geographical Society. Other memoirs followed, and the society aided him with grants, and in 1892 awarded him the founder's gold medal. His activities during these years he subsequently described in *Travel and Adventure in South-East Africa* (1893).

Frederick Courteney Selous (1851–1917), by James Russell & Sons

When speculators began to take an interest in the potential mineral wealth of territories controlled by Ndebele (Matabele) and Shona chiefs Selous sensed an opportunity for the riches that had eluded him as a hunter. His literary skills, family connections, and detailed knowledge of Africa made him a formidable competitor in the scramble for concessions. On behalf of his 'Selous exploration syndicate' he announced an agreement with the Korekore people of north-east Mashonaland in defiance of Portuguese claims in the region. Cecil Rhodes, realizing that the alleged concession conflicted with his own designs on that territory, persuaded Selous to withdraw and accept a position in the British South Africa Company. He served, with the rank of captain, as guide and chief of intelligence to the 1890 pioneer column which occupied Mashonaland and founded Fort Salisbury. He left the company's service in 1892, but joined it again in 1893 when the Matabele campaign began. At its close he returned to England, bought a house at Worplesdon, Surrey, and married, on 4 April 1894, Marie Catherine Gladys, daughter of Canon Henry William Maddy, vicar of Down Hatherley, Gloucestershire; they had two sons. He was again in Matabeleland in 1895 and helped to subdue the Matabele uprising. In *Sunshine and Storm in Rhodesia* (1896) he gave an account of this campaign. He subsequently embarked upon a new career as an expert guide for European and American hunters 'on safari' in Africa. Through this work and his previous writings he attracted the attention of President Theodore Roosevelt of America, whom he accompanied on a shooting expedition to east Africa in 1909. This trip strengthened his growing conviction that the age of unrestricted big-game hunting had come to an end and that measures should be taken to conserve African wildlife for the enjoyment of generations to come.

When the First World War broke out in 1914, Selous immediately offered himself for active service; persevering, despite repeated rejections on account of his age, he was ultimately accepted for duty in German East Africa, and left England with a commission in the 25th Royal Fusiliers (the Legion of Frontiersmen) in the spring of 1915. He received his captaincy in the following August, and was awarded the DSO in September 1916. He was killed in action at the head of his company, near Kisaki, close to the Rufiji River, Tanganyika, on 4 January 1917, aged sixty-five, and was buried in Tanganyika within the boundaries of the game park that now bears his name.

The dramatic circumstances of his death, and the part he played in the establishment of colonial Rhodesia, conferred lasting fame on Selous. Though celebrated as a hunter, he was the first to deprecate his reputation as the 'Mighty Nimrod'. Many had shot more beasts with greater skill; his prowess consisted in his ability to translate his adventures into prose eagerly consumed by late-Victorian readers. For later generations of white Rhodesians Selous epitomized their pioneer virtues and in the 1970s anti-guerrilla war the élite Selous scouts were named after him. Yet his own opinions were hardly conventional. One of his first acts as an explorer was to name a Mount Cromwell in 'honour of him whom I consider the greatest of England's rulers' (Selous, *A Hunter's Wanderings*). His companion on several expeditions was an African woman who became the mother of two of his children (the later history of this family is shrouded in obscurity). Despite his association with the British South Africa Company, Selous condemned the Jameson raid of 1895 as a blunder and spoke up for the Transvaal Boers during the Second South African War of 1899–1902. After his death a scholarship was founded in his name at Rugby, and his collection of trophies, including heads and skins of big game, was bequeathed to the trustees of the British Museum (Natural History). Selous Street in Harlesden, north London, was named after him.

R. I. Pocock, *rev.* Norman Etherington

Sources J. G. Millais, *Life of Frederick Courteney Selous, D.S.O.*, 2 vols. (1919) • S. Taylor, *The mighty Nimrod: a life of Frederick Courteney Selous* (1989) • F. C. Selous, *A hunter's wanderings in Africa* (1881) • F. C. Selous, *Travel and adventure in south-east Africa* (1893) • F. C. Selous, *Sunshine and storm in Rhodesia* (1896) • F. C. Selous, *African nature notes and reminiscences* (1908) • J. S. Galbraith, *Crown and charter: the early years of the British South Africa Company* (1974) • J. M. Mackenzie, *The empire of nature, hunting, conservation and British imperialism* (1988) • *CGPLA Eng. & Wales* (1917)

Archives Brenthurst Library, Johannesburg, corresp. • National Archives of Zimbabwe, corresp., diaries, papers

Likenesses W. R. Colton, memorial bronze bust, exh. RA 1919, BM • O. M. Bryden, pastel drawing, 1935, NPG • J. Russell & Sons, photograph, repro. in Millais, *Life*, frontispiece [*see illus.*] • chromolithograph, NPG; repro. in *VF* (26 April 1894) • silhouette, NPG

Wealth at death £333,441 0s. 2*d*.: resworn probate, 24 March 1917, *CGPLA Eng. & Wales*

Selvon, Samuel Dickson [Sam] (**1923–1994**), novelist and short-story writer, was born on 20 May 1923 at 42–44 Mount Moriah Road, San Fernando, Trinidad, West Indies, the sixth of seven children of Bertwyn Fraser Selvon (1889–1951), cocoa merchant, and his wife, Daisy Irene Dickson (*c*.1887–1951). Bertwyn was of Madrasi Indian stock. Daisy Irene was of mixed race, the fourth of six children born to a Scotsman, George Van Buren Dickson, and Keasoo (later Laura), a woman of Indian origin. Selvon spent his childhood in a middle-class family home at 42–44 Mount Moriah Road in San Fernando close to the canelands (worked by descendants of Indians) and oilfields (worked by descendants of Africans), the two mainstays of the island's economy. His early schooling was at Miss Douglin's primary school, in Mount Moriah Road, and at the Vistabella Canadian Mission primary school, San Fernando. He completed his primary education at the San Fernando Canadian Mission school in 1937 and entered Naparima College, where he wrote impressive English compositions, but left in 1938, without taking the school certificate examination. In 1939 he enlisted in the Trinidad Royal Naval Reserve and became a wireless operator.

From 1945 to 1950 Selvon worked in Port of Spain and lived on its outskirts in Barataria. He edited the *Sunday Guardian*'s literary magazine, and wrote regular columns of a social and philosophical nature in the *Evening News* under the pseudonyms Ack-Ack, Denmar Cosel, Michael Wentworth, Esses, and the Big Buffer. Similar material appeared in the near-autobiographical *An Island is a World* (1955) and the collection *Foreday Morning: Selected Prose, 1946–1986* (1989).

The tall, handsome, light-skinned young man married Draupadi Persaud (1915–1972) from Essequibo, British Guiana, on 2 August 1947 at Susumachar Presbyterian Church in San Fernando. They lived in Barataria up to 1950 when Selvon led the post-war movement of West Indian writers that made London the West Indian literary capital for most of the fifties, sixties, and seventies. Draupadi joined him in London in 1951 and their only child, Shelley Sarojini, was born there on 4 February 1952. The couple divorced in 1962.

On 6 January 1963 Selvon married a Eurasian woman, Althea Nesta Daroux (born in Bhopal, India, in 1931), prototype of the girl immortalized in one of his finest short stories, 'My Girl and the City' and the family's breadwinner for many years. They had three children: Michael Dickson, Leslie Gordon, and Debra Jane. On 14 March

1978, after twenty-eight years in England, Selvon migrated to Canada, where his wife had relatives. The family settled in Calgary, Alberta. Selvon was held in high regard by those interested in West Indian literature and he still had many friends in Britain, but a growing dissatisfaction with life in the mother country prompted him to leave, never to return.

Selvon's familiarity with people of all classes and ethnicities fostered his notion of the Trinidadian person as 'a creature born of all the peoples in the world' (Selvon, *An Island is a World*, 1955, 257): all ethnic groups are projected in his writings and they are seen primarily as people in the complex process of becoming creole or 'of the island'. Some of his stories, however, notably 'Cane is Bitter' and the novels *A Brighter Sun* (1951), *Turn Again Tiger* (1958), and *The Plains of Caroni* (1972), give face and voice to Indians who form half the population of Trinidad but were regarded until recently as a minority needing to prove their allegiance to Trinidad. Outstanding among these works is *A Brighter Sun*, set during the war years and introducing Tiger, a peasant at war with himself as he seeks knowledge, experience, and identity. The novel also addresses the political issue of African–Indian relations.

The travails and the ebullient spirit of the first wave of West Indian migrants to London are depicted with humour and pathos in *The Housing Lark* (1965), in some of the stories in *Ways of Sunlight* (1957), and in Selvon's most celebrated novel, *The Lonely Londoners* (1956), which is the first of three books with a central character called Moses. In these works he used dialect for both narration and dialogue; and narrative structure and tone openly proclaim the symbiotic relationship between popular and literary, folktale and fiction, oral and scribal, that makes Selvon an original, the country's calypsonian in prose.

Although Selvon wrote poems and plays, it was his short stories and novels that restored a sense of self-worth to the descendants of enslaved Africans and indentured Indians, reflecting them in fiction as main characters and full human beings. He released dialect from its stereotyping as comic or pathetic, and united West Indian writing and orality, enabling writing to own up to the West Indian tone of voice and thus shake off its imitative character. The popular creator of characters like Tiger and Moses was generous but never far from poverty, was outwardly happy-go-lucky but often morose and introspective.

Selvon held a fellowship in creative writing at Dundee University in 1975–7; he became the first writer-in-residence at the University of the West Indies in 1982; and he took up writer-in-residence appointments at the universities of Victoria, Winnipeg, Alberta, and Calgary, where incidentally he had worked for a while as a janitor on first arriving in Canada. He was awarded an honorary doctorate by Warwick University (1989). He was also awarded the honorary degree of DLitt by the University of the West Indies in 1985 and, for achievement in literature, the country bestowed upon him two of its highest awards in 1969 and 1994.

A lifelong smoker not averse to the bottle, Selvon returned to Trinidad in late 1993. He died of respiratory failure due to extensive bronchopneumonia and chronic lung disease on 16 April 1994 at Piarco international airport, Trinidad. After cremation at St James crematorium, Trinidad, on 19 April his ashes were interred in the University of the West Indies cemetery, St Augustine, Trinidad.

KENNETH RAMCHAND

Sources *Trinidad Guardian* (1946–50) · *Evening News* (1946–50) [Port of Spain, Trinidad] · S. Nasta, ed., *Critical perspectives on Sam Selvon* (Three Continents Press, 1988) · S. Nasta and A. Rutherford, eds., *Tiger's triumph: celebrating Sam Selvon* (Dangaroo Press, 1995) · *Foreday morning: selected prose, 1946–1986*, ed. K. Ramchand and S. Nasta (1989) [includes bibliography] · A. Clarke, *A passage back home: a personal reminiscence of Samuel Selvon* (Toronto, 1994) · personal knowledge (2004) · private information (2004)

Archives Ransom HRC, MSS · University of the West Indies, St Augustine, Trinidad | SOUND BBC Radio Library, London, radio play scripts

Wealth at death four-bedroom house, 4031 Charlesworth Drive, Calgary, Alberta, Canada T2L 2E1: personal knowledge (2004)

Selwyn, Alfred Richard Cecil (1824–1902), geologist, was born on 28 July 1824 in Kilmington, Somerset, the son of Townshend Selwyn, canon of Gloucester, and his wife, Charlotte Sophia Murray, daughter of Lord George *Murray, bishop of St David's. His great-uncle was John Murray, fourth duke of Atholl, who had encouraged John Hutton's geology in the late eighteenth century.

Selwyn was tutored privately before formal schooling in Switzerland. There, he developed a love of geology and gained his mountaineering skills. When he returned to England in 1845 he was appointed to the geological survey where he joined a pioneering contingent of stratigraphers in mapping Britain's geological structures. Andrew Crombie Ramsay, the survey's local director, valued Selwyn's maps of complex Silurian formations in north Wales and western England as 'the perfection of beauty' (*Ottawa Naturalist*, 172). In 1848 Selwyn was duly promoted to geologist with an annual salary of £200.

In 1852 Selwyn married his cousin Matilda Charlotte Selwyn; they had nine children. In the same year the Colonial Office appointed Selwyn to direct the geological survey of Victoria, Australia. For seventeen years he assessed gold and fossil deposits in the state's Silurian strata, as well as assessing coal- and goldfields in Tasmania and South Australia, and overseeing production of sixty-one geological maps issued between 1853 and 1869. In reporting workable gold deposits below the Silurian, Selwyn corrected geological doctrine promulgated by Sir Roderick Murchison, director-general of the British Geological Survey, that the precious metal was never formed in older strata. He served on Victoria's commission of mines (1856), board of science (1858), and board of agriculture (1859). He was a commissioner for the Victorian Exhibition of 1861 and the London International Exhibition of 1862, and was involved with others at Dublin (in 1865), and Paris (1866).

In 1869 Victoria's legislature discontinued funding for the geological survey. Shortly thereafter, Selwyn was appointed director of the geological survey of Canada, succeeding W. E. Logan. The position, which he took up in December 1869, brought him many difficulties. His main challenge was to oversee the survey's complex transformation from a colonial to a modern national institution. However, in these efforts, the legacy of Logan's independent wealth, social status, political acumen, and international scientific reputation often overshadowed Selwyn's dedication, training, and experience. He found himself an outsider among colleagues who themselves coveted the directorship. Nevertheless, he soon became sufficiently proficient in Canadian geology to supervise detailed investigations, no mean feat with the dominion's expansion to include Manitoba and British Columbia only two years after his arrival. During his first decade as director, he criss-crossed the country to help plan the route of the proposed Canadian Pacific Railway. In reviewing Logan's analysis of the Quebec Group, which was being contested by the survey's former chemist, Thomas Sterry Hunt, Selwyn also systematized these Archaean formations, classifying them as anticlinal rather than synclinal structures.

Selwyn worked to shift the survey's efforts from broader strokes of general reconnaissance to finer details of mapping in selected type areas. In 1881 he standardized the legends and colour schemes of Canadian geological maps. After serving on the organizing committee of the International Geological Congress in 1878, he joined his American counterparts to develop common nomenclature and mapping schemes by 1889.

Federal legislation meanwhile altered the conditions under which the survey operated. After five years of increased funding from 1872, the act of 1877 subsumed the survey under the department of the interior, subjecting it once again to annual grants. The new scheme created four assistant directorships and defined new responsibilities in natural history and ethnology, necessitating the addition of a botanist, a zoologist, and a taxidermist. By 1881 the survey was transferred from Montreal to Ottawa, where Selwyn had to fight for adequate facilities. His increasingly specialized professional staff were integrated into the civil service by 1883. By then, his staff included civil and mining engineers employed to construct base maps and develop a mining section. In 1890 further legislation again reorganized the survey, reinstating a separate geological department under the ministry of the interior, tightening staff qualifications, and requiring Selwyn to provide statistics on Canadian mineral production.

Selwyn organized Canadian exhibits abroad, at Philadelphia (1876), Paris (1878), London (1886), and Chicago (1893). When the British Association for the Advancement of Science met in Montreal in 1884, its field trip to British Columbia narrowly escaped a rockslide triggered by Selwyn's own hammer.

Selwyn's designation of George Mercer Dawson as acting director during his absences ignited the burning resentments of Robert Bell and others who aspired to his position. Selwyn's personality no doubt exacerbated these difficulties: his firm convictions allegedly combined with a 'hasty temper' to transform virtues of discipline and orderliness into a stern and officious demeanour toward subordinates. Intense animosities were aired publicly during a government inquiry in 1884; it resolved little, and the bitterness continued.

In 1894, after returning from leave in England, Selwyn was surprised to find himself superannuated and succeeded by Dawson. In 1896, as president of the Royal Society of Canada (of which he had been a charter member since 1883), he capped his career with an important address on the origin and evolution of Archaean rocks. Other honours included election as FRS in 1874, the Murchison medal of the Geological Society of London in 1876, an LLD from McGill University in 1881, and a CMG (1886).

Selwyn's generation contributed greatly to geology as an imperial science. While he emphasized both economic and theoretical considerations, he was less successful than either Logan or Dawson were in forging links between these geological activities. He retired to Vancouver, where he died of a stroke on 19 October 1902.

SUZANNE ZELLER

Sources H. W. [H. Woodward], 'Eminent living geologists: Alfred Richard Cecil Selwyn', *Geological Magazine*, new ser., 4th decade, 6 (1899), 49–55 • A. E. B., 'Dr. Alfred Selwyn', *Ottawa Naturalist* (Dec 1902), 170–77 • *Proceedings and Transactions of the Royal Society of Canada*, 2nd ser., 9 (1903), viii–ix • H. M. Ami, 'Memorial or sketch of the life of the late Dr A. R. C. Selwyn', *Proceedings and Transactions of the Royal Society of Canada*, 2nd ser., 10 (1904), section 4, pp. 173–205 • H. M. Ami, 'Sketch of the life and work of the late Dr. A. R. C. Selwyn', *American Geologist* (Jan 1903), 1–21 • *Canada: the printed record* (1990) [microfiche] • R. A. Richardson and B. H. MacDonald, *Science and technology in Canadian history: a bibliography of primary sources to 1914* (1987) • H. M. A. and H. W., 'Alfred Charles [*sic*] Cecil Selwyn', *Quarterly Journal of the Geological Society*, 59 (1903), lxi–lxiii • R. A. Stafford, 'The long arm of London: Sir Roderick Murchison and imperial science in Australia', *Australian science in the making*, ed. R. W. Home (1988), 84–6 • M. Zaslow, *Reading the rocks: the story of the geological survey of Canada* (1975) • W. Waiser, *The field naturalist* (1989)

Archives Geological Survey of Canada, Ottawa, director's letter-books | ICL, Geological Survey of Great Britain, director-general's papers, De La Beche and Murchison papers, and papers of A. C. Ramsay • McGill University, Montreal, Dawson family collections

Likenesses photograph, repro. in A. E. B., 'Dr. Alfred Selwyn', 170 • photograph, repro. in Ami, 'Sketch of the life and work', pl. 1 • photograph, repro. in Ami, 'Memorial or sketch', 172

Selwyn, Sir Charles Jasper (1813–1869), judge, was the fourth and youngest son of William *Selwyn (1775–1855), legal writer, and his wife, Laetitia Frances, *née* Kynaston (*d.* 1842). The brother of George Augustus *Selwyn (1809–1878) and William *Selwyn (1806–1875), he was born at Church Row, Hampstead, Middlesex, on 13 October 1813. He was educated at Ealing, at Eton College, and at Trinity College, Cambridge, of which he was successively scholar and fellow. He graduated BA (1836), MA (1839), and LLD (1862). He was called to the bar at Lincoln's Inn on 27 January 1840, practised chiefly before the master of the rolls, and amassed a large fortune. As a counsel he was not very brilliant, but he got up his cases with singular accuracy and was listened to with great attention by the court. He served as commissary to the University of Cambridge from 1855 to 1858, took silk on 7 April 1856, and in the same year was made a bencher of his inn. He entered parliament as member for Cambridge University in April 1859, and sat for that constituency until 1868. He was a staunch Conservative and a committed churchman, remarkable for polished elocution and a firm but conciliatory tone. He spoke on a variety of subjects, notably opposing the Ecclesiastical Commission Bill on 6 June 1860. Selwyn became solicitor-general in Lord Derby's administration on 18 July 1867, and was knighted on 3 August. Disraeli appointed him a lord justice of appeal on 8 February 1868, and he was named a privy councillor on 28 March. As a judge, he proved himself considerate and patient.

Selwyn was twice married: first, in 1856, to Hester, fifth daughter of J. G. Ravenshaw, chairman of the East India Company, and widow of Thomas Dowler MD; second, on 2 April 1869, to Catherine Rosalie, daughter of Colonel Godfrey T. Greene and widow of the Revd Henry Dupuis, vicar of Richmond. His two marriages produced a son and two daughters. Selwyn, in conjunction with L. F. Selwyn, wrote in 1847 *Annals of the Diocese of New Zealand*. He died at Pagoda House, Richmond, Surrey, on 11 August 1869, and was buried in Nunhead cemetery.

G. C. Boase, *rev.* H. C. G. Matthew

Sources *Pen and ink sketches in chancery … by a lounger in the courts*, 1 [1866] • Boase, *Mod. Eng. biog.* • *Men of the time* (1868) • *Law Times* (14 Aug 1869); (18 Sept 1869) • *Eton portrait gallery* (1876) • *ILN* (24 Aug 1867), 200

Archives Surrey HC, estate, family, and legal MSS

Likenesses Mayland, double portrait, carte-de-visite (with Canon Selwyn), NPG • wood-engraving, NPG; repro. in *ILN*, 200

Wealth at death under £120,000: probate, 1 Sept 1869, *CGPLA Eng. & Wales*

Selwyn, George Augustus (1719–1791), wit and politician, was born on 11 August 1719 and baptized at Chislehurst, Kent, on 25 August, the second son of the three children of John Selwyn (1688–1751) of Matson, near Gloucester, and Mary (1690/91–1777), daughter of General Thomas Farrington of Chislehurst. Selwyn's father was the son of William Selwyn, governor of Jamaica (1703–4), and served as the aide-de-camp to the duke of Marlborough, MP for Gloucester between 1734 and 1751 and as treasurer of Queen Caroline's pensions before his death on 6 November 1751. His mother, who also served the queen as a woman of the bedchamber, was described by Lord Hervey as 'a simple cunning woman … the only … about the Court who loved Sir Robert Walpole' (J. Hervey, *Memoirs*, ed. R. S. Sedgwick, 1952, 196). It was at her house at Cleveland Court, St James's, Westminster, that Walpole and his secretary of state, Viscount Townshend, had earlier come to blows in a contest satirized in act II, scene X of John Gay's *The Beggar's Opera*. Mary Selwyn died on 6 November 1777 aged eighty-six.

In 1732 Selwyn entered Eton College, where his contemporaries included several lifelong friends, the politician Richard, second Baron Edgcumbe, the poet Thomas Grey, and the memoirist Horace Walpole. He matriculated at Hart Hall, Oxford, on 1 December 1739 but left the university to undertake a European tour during 1742–3 before

George Augustus Selwyn (1719–1791), by Sir Joshua Reynolds, 1766

returning to Oxford in late 1744 or early 1745. An offensive gesture in a tavern, which observers interpreted as mocking the holy communion, prompted the end of his university career soon after. By then, however, Selwyn's financial security was assured. Five years earlier he had received the first of several lucrative sinecures, the office of clerk of the irons and surveyor of the meltings of the mint, worth, together with his father's allowance, £220 per annum. The early death of his elder brother John, MP for Whitchurch, in June 1751 followed by that of his father in November led to Selwyn's inheritance of the family estate at Matson and a parliamentary interest which allowed him to nominate both members for Ludgershall, Wiltshire. From 1747 he himself occupied one of these seats until he took over as MP for Gloucester at the general election of 1754. For the next twenty-four years he offered, at a price, the Ludgershall seats to each incoming administration until his defeat at Gloucester in 1780 led to a return to his former constituency. Further income was obtained from the acquisition of three additional lifelong sinecures—the posts of registrar of court of chancery in Barbados (from 1753), paymaster of the board of works (from 1755 until its abolition in 1782), and two years later the surveyor-generalship of crown lands.

Selwyn's parliamentary performance proved remarkable only for its non-existence. During his forty-four years in the house he did not speak on a single occasion. At best a detached observer of parliamentary affairs, he was otherwise a sleeping partner, prone to slumber while in the chamber. As a result, his sporadic displays of political energy were used by more active members as an indication of the severity or urgency of a particular issue, notably the fate of Barbados during the American War of Independence. But as this example shows, self-interest was never far behind any cause for which Selwyn roused himself. His political companions included a number of individuals, among them James Hare, Charles James Fox, and the fifth earl of Carlisle, who also made up a social circle in which he proved far more lively. Selwyn himself declared that his only political master was the king, at whose disposal he claimed to lay his parliamentary interest, and whose lead he followed when, voting against Fox's East India Bill in November 1783, he offered his one and only act of defiance against the ministry of the day.

Selwyn came to life in London club society, in which he was a noted conversationalist, a dedicated gambler, and a celebrated humorist. Commenting during the last decade of Selwyn's life the memoirist Nathaniel Wraxall spoke of him possessing 'an infinite wit. He had indeed succeeded to Philip, earl of Chesterfield's reputation for *bon-mots*'. The key to Selwyn's success appears to have been the droll manner of his delivery. Horace Walpole remarked on the effective contrast between his 'demure' demeanour and biting witticisms (Walpole, *Corr.*, 35.170). For Wraxall the impact of his comments was 'greatly augmented by the listless and drowsy manner in which he uttered them, for he always seemed half asleep' (H. B. Wheatley, ed., *Historical and Posthumous Memoirs of his Own Time by Sir Nathaniel William Wraxhall*, 5 vols., 1884, 2.289). Certainly, lists of his most celebrated comments (see Jesse, 1.16–22), the majority of which have not stood the test of time, suggest that Selwyn's wit owed more to its performance than to its content. Rival wags rewarded his efforts with one further specious sinecure: receiver-general of waif and stray jokes.

Less light-hearted was Selwyn's interest in executions, at which he was a regular attender. In 1757, for example, he went to Paris to watch the dismemberment of the would-be royal assassin Damiens. His fascination with the moment of death and the resultant corpse was widely commented on within his circle. 'The next time Mr Selwyn calls shew him up', commented Henry, first Baron Holland, on his deathbed: 'if I am alive I shall be delighted to see him, and if I am dead he will be delighted to see me' (Jesse, 1.5). After his own death, Selwyn's peculiar pastime was vigorously debated by his friends in the *Gentleman's Magazine*; the biographer Philip Thicknesse, for instance, downplayed Selwyn's association with the macabre, which he attributed to gossip by Sir Charles Hanbury Williams and Lord Chesterfield (*GM*, 299, 705).

In later life Selwyn suffered from gout and dropsy, and he died from a 'violent urinary complaint' (*GM*, 61.94–5) on 25 January 1791 at his Westminster home in Cleveland Court, St James's. Though unmarried, he was the adopted father of Maria Emily Fagnani, later Maria Emily Seymour-*Conway, marchioness of Hertford (1770/71–1856) [*see under* Conway, Francis Ingram-Seymour-, second marquess of Hertford], the daughter of the Marchesa Fagnani. Rumours circulated as to whether Selwyn was the child's natural father, though it is now widely accepted that the father was one of Selwyn's closest friends, the rakish William Douglas, fourth duke of Queensberry. Certainly contemporaries like Lady Louisa Stuart were sceptical as to Selwyn's ability to enter a relationship: 'George Selwyn in love, George Selwyn gallant, were thoughts that never entered any one's head' (Cannon, 3.421). As well as to Maria (known as Mie-Mie), who later married Francis, marquess of Hertford, Selwyn developed a fierce attachment to several other children, including offspring of the earls of Coventry and Carlisle. In his will he left £30,000 and a house in Piccadilly to his adopted daughter; other bequests of 100 guineas each went to his nephews, Charles Townshend and Ebrow Woodcock. Following his death Selwyn was praised and defended by friends like Walpole—who wrote of the 'goodness of his heart and nature' (ibid.)—while the Revd Dr John Warner complimented a 'Social wit which, never kindling strife, Blazed in the small sweet courtesies of life'. On reflection, however, theirs are views with which it is difficult to agree. Narcissistic, self-serving, indolent, and prone to once barbed and now flat commentaries, Selwyn was a man of his day whose reputation has, deservedly, dated and withered over time. PHILIP CARTER

Sources DNB • J. H. Jesse, *George Selwyn and his contemporaries, with memoirs and notes*, 4 vols. (1843–4) • S. P. Kerr, *George Selwyn and the wits* (1909) • E. S. Roscoe and H. Clergue, eds., *George Selwyn, his letters and his life* (1899) • *GM*, 1st ser., 61 (1791), 94–5 • *GM*, 1st ser., 61 (1791), 299 • *GM*, 1st ser., 61 (1791), 705 • J. A. Cannon, 'Selwyn, George Augustus', HoP, *Commons*, 1754–90, 3.420–21 • P. Watson, 'Selwyn, Thomas', HoP, *Commons*, 1715–54 • GEC, *Peerage* • will, PRO, PROB 11/1202, fols. 53v–57v

Archives Hertford College, Oxford • S. Antiquaries, Lond., corresp. | BL, corresp., etc., relating to Mlle Fagnani, Egerton MSS 3257–3259 • Castle Howard, North Yorkshire, papers, letters to Lord and Lady Carlisle

Likenesses J. Reynolds, group portrait, oils, 1759–61 (*A conversation piece*), City Museum and Art Gallery, Bristol; *see illus. in* Williams, George James (1719–1805) • J. Reynolds, portrait, 1766, priv. coll. [*see illus.*] • H. D. Hamilton, pastel drawing, 1770, Castle Howard, North Yorkshire • J. Reynolds, double portrait, oils, *c*.1770 (with Frederick, fifth earl of Carlisle), Castle Howard, North Yorkshire

Wealth at death over £30,000; plus property in London and at Matson, Gloucestershire.

Selwyn, George Augustus (1809–1878), bishop of New Zealand and bishop of Lichfield, was born on 5 April 1809 at Church Row, Hampstead, Middlesex. He was the second of the four sons of William *Selwyn (1775–1855), barrister, and Laetitia Frances Kynaston (*d*. 1842), and brother of Sir Charles Jasper *Selwyn (1813–1869) and of William *Selwyn (1806–1875). He went when aged seven to Dr Nicholas's Preparatory School in Ealing, where J. H. Newman (the future cardinal) and his brother Francis were fellow pupils. Selwyn then went to Eton College, where he acquired a reputation both as a scholar and as an athlete, and in 1827 he proceeded as a scholar to St John's College, Cambridge. A rowing blue in 1829, he took his BA in 1831, coming second in the classical tripos, and his MA in 1834, and was elected a fellow of his college.

After Cambridge, Selwyn taught at Eton while employed as private tutor to two sons of the earl of Powys.

George Augustus Selwyn (1809–1878), by Mason & Co.

Ordained deacon in June 1833 he was briefly honorary curate at Boveney; ordained priest a year later, likewise on Trinity Sunday and at St George's, Hanover Square, London, he settled as curate to the vicar of Windsor, Isaac Gossett. He broke off his engagement to Anna, daughter of Eton's headmaster John Keate, and subsequently married Sarah Harriet (*d*. 1907), daughter of Sir John *Richardson, on 25 June 1839. Of their four children, only the two eldest sons survived, William and John Richardson *Selwyn.

At Windsor Selwyn's practical talent for organizing church life and his preoccupation with church order began to show. Highly critical of whig plans for reforming the Church of England and taking his cue from W. E. Gladstone, he circulated privately in 1838 his pamphlet *Are Cathedral Institutions Useless?* He argued against disendowment and for the revision of cathedral statutes based on his knowledge of Ely. He wanted the reinvigoration of cathedrals under episcopal leadership, in order to create diocesan centres for training ministers, teaching, providing for diocesan councils or synods, organizing missionary work, and assisting the poor. Reflecting the influence of the early Oxford Movement, these principles guided him subsequently in both New Zealand and Lichfield.

At this time the need for more colonial bishoprics was acutely felt by church leaders concerned to combat the global spread of nonconformity and Roman Catholicism. With the establishment of British rule in 1840 and the likely rapid expansion of white settlement, New Zealand's requirement was rated most highly. Although his brother William refused the new diocese, George Selwyn accepted readily and was consecrated at Lambeth on 17 October 1841; he took his Cambridge DD degree the following week, and sailed from Plymouth on Boxing day.

In New Zealand resources never permitted Selwyn to build the Norman-style cathedral which the Camden Society at Cambridge had advised him was appropriate to Maori understanding. But his foundation of St John's College, with its school 'to be conducted upon the plan (*mutatis mutandis*) of Eton' and its provision for training clergy, first at Waimate and from 1844 at Auckland, gave expression for a decade to his wish for an active diocesan centre. Selwyn spent five years becoming familiar with New Zealand. An imposing, energetic man, he travelled extensively, appointed archdeacons to help him, and convened synods of his clergy in 1844 and 1847. At the latter gathering, he issued his primary charge defining the principal issues facing his diocese.

Selwyn was convinced that missions should be proper church institutions under episcopal leadership, rather than societies of lay enthusiasts, and he supported the Tractarian ideal of the 'missionary bishop'. If this made his relationship with the Church Missionary Society (CMS) sometimes difficult, those problems were exacerbated by misunderstanding and difficulties of communication with England. He was soon in dispute with the society at home over questions of missionary placements and ordination. Locally he was drawn into a bitter wrangle with some CMS missionaries, which culminated in the society's dismissal of Henry Williams. Selwyn's part arose less from differences over authority than from his thoughtlessness, and from a concept of missionary work and desire for volunteers which led him to support Governor Grey's wish to reduce missionaries' private landholdings.

> The position of a Missionary in New Zealand requires his undivided attention to the natives … very little benefit has resulted from the combination of Agriculture with Missionary duties. … It is seldom that much good results in England from the union in the same person of the office of Clergyman and Landlord. (Evans, 38–9)

Selwyn's anti-Erastianism also showed itself in his persistent search both for the funds and for the endowments which would make the New Zealand church self-sufficient and for ways of increasing its powers of self-government. His discovery in 1854 that no legal obstacles prevented the holding of diocesan synods in colonial sees opened the way, in the absence of resistance from the imperial government, for colonial clergy and laity to meet and to regulate the affairs of their churches. Having seized the opportunity, Selwyn finally completed a draft constitution for the Church of New Zealand in 1857 and secured its adoption at the first general synod in 1859. Although he was opposed to disestablishment in Britain, by the late 1860s this movement in New Zealand had accomplished the final separation of church and state. Not only did other colonial churches follow this example, but support for Selwyn's practice from bishops in Australia, Canada, and

South Africa contributed much to the subsequent development of the church both in England and throughout the Anglican communion.

The same relentless activity characterized Selwyn's approach to the indigenous peoples of New Zealand and the western Pacific. Committed to a fundamental racial equality, Selwyn insisted on a liberal interpretation of the treaty of Waitangi, under which British authority had been acquired, and he was from the beginning a staunch defender of Maori rights, especially those of land sale and tenure. For this he was frequently attacked by settlers and their supporters in Britain such as Joseph Hume and J. A. Roebuck, especially from the time of the northern war of 1845–6. Nevertheless he constantly mediated in both inter-Maori disputes and conflicts between Maori and white settlers (Pakeha). Requiring all his clergy to learn Maori, as he had done on his first voyage from England, Selwyn was responsible for the revision of the Maori Bible and prayer book. Although criticized by some for delaying the ordination of Maori converts, in consequence of his expectations of the same standards for them as for European candidates in matters of behaviour and scholarship, there is little ground for doubting his conviction of the urgent necessity for a native ministry. That ministry began to emerge early in the 1860s but, along with Selwyn's attempts to promote Maori welfare, rights, and education, it was scarcely strong enough to survive the impact of the wars of the 1860s. This left the church's work among the Maori in ruins, though in many places Selwyn's personal reputation was only enhanced by his unselfish assistance of the wars' victims.

Selwyn's work with the Pacific islanders rested on the regular voyages he began in 1847. Exploiting an error in his letters patent, which extended his diocese as far as latitude 34° N, he systematically visited the islands and brought young islanders to St John's for schooling, returning them at regular intervals to instruct their own people. He gained support from the Australasian bishops' conference in 1850 for his oversight of the Melanesian mission, raised £10,000 as an endowment for a bishopric during his visit to Britain in 1854, and finally secured the consecration of his friend J. C. Patteson as bishop of Melanesia in 1861. There, as in New Zealand itself, persuading English church leaders and the Society for the Propagation of the Gospel (SPG) of the need for the subdivision of his huge see went hand in hand with Selwyn's attempts to secure the leadership of the infant church in the hands of like-minded friends. His success was reflected in the appointment of bishops C. J. Abraham, Henry Harper, and Edmund Hobhouse. Towards nonconformists he was civil and co-operative—for instance, in negotiating missionary spheres of activity with the presbyterians and the London Missionary Society. But his sympathy was limited by what he saw as their rejection of Anglicanism's comprehensiveness and the opportunity it offered for Christian unity.

At the first Lambeth conference, summoned in September 1867 to address colonial issues, Selwyn played a leading role in asserting the freedom of colonial churches to link themselves voluntarily with the Church of England. While in Britain he was admitted honorary DCL by Oxford University and, mindful of his own insistence on the principle of clerical obedience to ecclesiastical superiors, he very reluctantly accepted episcopal appointment to the diocese of Lichfield. Enthroned on 9 January 1868 he returned to New Zealand for a brief farewell.

At Lichfield the mark of the missionary bishop was soon made. The cathedral's statutes were revised and the laity further involved in diocesan affairs, and the theological college's work was expanded. Closer relations with the Canadian and American churches were fostered by Selwyn's visits in 1871 and 1874, and home missions as well as interest in overseas missionaries were greatly encouraged as a stimulus to the life of the whole church. With no more time for middle-class comforts or conventions than for finer points in theological debate, Selwyn was ever the active reformer and invigorator. He died on 11 April 1878 at the bishop's palace, Lichfield. For Gladstone, who attended his burial in the grounds of Lichfield Cathedral both as a lifelong friend and as godfather to his eldest son, he was 'one of the band of great Bishops' (Gladstone, *Diaries*, 16 April 1878). Selwyn College, Cambridge, was erected by subscription in his memory. ANDREW PORTER

Sources H. W. Tucker, *Memoir of the life and episcopate of George Augustus Selwyn*, 2 vols. (1879) • J. H. Evans, *Churchman militant: George Augustus Selwyn, bishop of New Zealand and Lichfield* (1964) • W. E. Limbrick, ed., *Bishop Selwyn in New Zealand, 1841–68* (1983) • W. E. Limbrick, 'Selwyn, George Augustus', *DNZB*, vol. 1 • T. E. Yates, *Venn and Victorian bishops abroad: the missionary policies of Henry Venn and their repercussions upon the Anglican episcopate of the colonial period, 1841–1872* (1978) • A. M. G. Stephenson, *The first Lambeth conference, 1867* (1967) • V. Martineau, *Recollections of Sophia Lonsdale* (1936) • Gladstone, *Diaries* • W. D. McIntyre, ed., *The journal of Henry Sewell, 1853–1857*, 2 vols. (1980)

Archives Bodl. RH, journals • Canterbury Museum, New Zealand, corresp. and papers • NL NZ, Turnbull L., corresp. • Selwyn College, Cambridge, corresp. and papers • Surrey HC, estate, family, and legal papers • University of Waikato Library, New Zealand, corresp. and papers | Auckland Public Library, letters to Sir George Grey • BL, corresp. with W. E. Gladstone, Add. MS 44299 • Bodl. Oxf., letters to W. C. Cotton • Bodl. Oxf., letters to Samuel Wilberforce • Devon RO, letters to Sir Thomas Dyke Acland • LPL, corresp. with A. C. Tait • U. Birm., letters to Church Missionary Society

Likenesses S. Cousins, mezzotint, pubd 1842 (after G. Richmond), BM, NPG • G. Richmond, oils, 1855, St John Cam. • oils, *c*.1867 (over photograph by Mason & Co.), NPG • Mason & Co., carte-de-visite, NPG [*see illus.*] • carte-de-visite, NPG • prints (after photographs), BM, NPG • wood-engraving, NPG; repro. in *ILN* (14 Dec 1867)

Wealth at death under £16,000: probate, 17 May 1878, *CGPLA Eng. & Wales*

Selwyn, John Richardson (1844–1898), bishop of Melanesia, the younger son of George Augustus *Selwyn (1809–1878), first bishop of New Zealand, and Sarah Harriet (*d*. 1907), daughter of Sir John Richardson, was born on 20 May 1844 at the Waimaté, in the Bay of Islands, New Zealand. He went to England in 1854, and was educated at Eton College and at Trinity College, Cambridge. A noted oarsman but a mediocre scholar, he graduated BA with a third class in the classical tripos in 1866; he proceeded MA in 1870. In 1867 he visited his father in New Zealand, intending to enter the legal profession after his return;

but his father's example and the influence of Bishop John Coleridge Patteson decided him to seek ordination in the English church. He was ordained deacon on Trinity Sunday 1869 by his father, who was then bishop of Lichfield. His first curacy was at nearby Alrewas, where he remained for a year and a half. He then acted as curate-in-charge at St George's, Wolverhampton, where the vicar was absent, having quarrelled with his parishioners. Selwyn's tact and energy resulted in his becoming vicar of St George's, but on hearing of Bishop Patteson's death in 1871 he offered himself as a missionary to the Melanesian mission. He married Clara Long, *née* Innes, on 16 January 1872. In February 1873 they set sail for Melanesia, and reached Norfolk Island in October 1873. An attack of rheumatism *en route* was Selwyn's first warning of the debilitating illness he would suffer in later life.

Selwyn's demonstrated ability, family legacy, and education made him an obvious choice to succeed Bishop Patteson. On 18 February 1877 he was consecrated bishop of Melanesia at Nelson, New Zealand. In December 1877 his wife, who had rejoined him after a visit to England, died in childbirth, and in the next year he lost his father. Despite these blows Selwyn persevered in developing the Melanesian mission along the lines pioneered by his father. Well-educated young gentlemen of pronounced high-church principles formed the backbone of his missionary force. Close ties were maintained with Eton, Oxford, and Cambridge. The centrepiece of the mission was its college on Norfolk Island to which young Melanesian islanders were carried on the mission schooner, *Southern Cross*, for short periods of instruction. Although it was not Selwyn's express policy to encourage British territorial annexations in the south Pacific, his links to influential circles inevitably gave his mission a quasi-political character which differentiated it from other evangelical operations in the region.

While visiting England, Selwyn made a second marriage, to Annie Catherine, *née* Mort, daughter of Thomas Sutcliffe *Mort, merchant, on 11 August 1885, and they returned to his diocese. In 1889, however, his continuing rheumatic afflictions compelled him to return again to England, and he arrived home in 1890. Surgery on his right leg left him permanently disabled, which forced him to give up his work in Melanesia. After recovering his health he was asked to become master of Selwyn College, Cambridge, a position he held until his death at Cambridge on 12 February 1898.

It was largely through Selwyn's influence that the home mission named Cambridge House was started in London. Selwyn was also unusually successful in encouraging Cambridge undergraduates to take up missionary work, both in England and overseas.

RONALD BAYNE, *rev.* NORMAN ETHERINGTON

Sources F. D. How, *Bishop John Selwyn: a memoir* (1899) • G. H. Curteis, *Bishop Selwyn of New Zealand* (1889) • D. Hilliard, *God's gentlemen: a history of the Melanesian mission, 1849–1942* (1978) • J. Garrett, *To live among the stars* (1982) • D. Hilliard, 'Colonialism and Christianity: the Melanesian mission in the Solomon Islands', *Journal of Pacific History*, 9 (1974), 93–116 • R. Ross, 'Evolution of the Melanesian bishopric', *New Zealand Journal of History*, 16 (1982), 122–45 • m. certs. • W. R. Brock and P. H. M. Cooper, *Selwyn College, a history* (1994)

Archives Bodl. RH, United Society for the Propagation of the Gospel, archives • LPL, corresp. on misconduct of the Revd. A. Brittain • Selwyn College, Cambridge, letters

Likenesses oils, Selwyn College, Cambridge

Wealth at death £25,432 13*s.* 3*d.*: probate, 21 May 1898, *CGPLA Eng. & Wales*

Selwyn, William (1775–1855), legal writer, was the second son of William Selwyn KC (*d.* 1817), treasurer of Lincoln's Inn in 1793, and Frances Elizabeth, daughter of Dr John Dod of Woodford, Essex. George Augustus Selwyn, the wit, was his father's first cousin. William was educated at Eton College and St John's and Trinity colleges, Cambridge, where he graduated BA in 1797, being first chancellor's medallist in classics and senior optime in the mathematical tripos; he proceeded MA in 1800. He married, in 1801, Laetitia Frances (*d.* 1842), youngest daughter of Thomas Kynaston of Witham, Essex. They had six children: William *Selwyn (1806–1875); George Augustus *Selwyn (1809–1878); Thomas Kynaston Selwyn (1812–1834) who, educated at Eton and Trinity College, Cambridge, was author of *Eton in 1829–1830: a Diary of Boating and other Events, Written in Greek*, edited with a memoir by Dr Edmond Warre (1903); Sir Charles Jasper *Selwyn (1813–1869); Laetitia Frances Selwyn; and Frances Elizabeth Selwyn, who married George Peacock, dean of Ely.

Selwyn was admitted a student at Lincoln's Inn in 1797, and called to the bar on 24 November 1807; he was elected treasurer in 1840. He joined the western circuit, was recorder of Portsmouth from 1819 to 1829, and took silk in Trinity vacation 1827. Soon after the marriage of Queen Victoria he was chosen to assist the prince consort in his legal studies. Selwyn was most noted for his famous *Abridgment of the Law of Nisi prius* (3 vols., 1806–8), a clear and well-arranged summary of the principal topics of private law, which reached a thirteenth edition in 1869. He also collaborated with George Maule in *Reports of Cases Argued and Determined in the Court of King's Bench* (2 vols., 1814).

In later life Selwyn became a chronic valetudinarian, and lived in retirement at Pagoda House, Kew Road, Richmond, Surrey, an estate inherited from his father in 1817. He died on 25 July 1855 while on a visit to Tunbridge Wells, and was buried near there in the churchyard of Rusthall.

J. M. RIGG, *rev.* JONATHAN HARRIS

Sources *GM*, 2nd ser., 44 (1855), 320–21 • Venn, *Alum. Cant.* • H. W. Tucker, *Memoir of the life and episcopate of George Augustus Selwyn*, 1 (1879), 5, 69; 2 (1879), 55 • C. Grey, *The early years of his royal highness the prince consort* (1867), 361–3 • Holdsworth, *Eng. law*, 8.32, 38; 13.460

Archives Surrey HC

Selwyn, William (1806–1875), Church of England clergyman, eldest son of William *Selwyn (1775–1855) and Laetitia Frances (*d.* 1842), youngest daughter of Thomas Kynaston of Witham, Essex, was born on 19 February 1806. George Augustus *Selwyn (1809–1878) and Sir Charles Jasper *Selwyn (1813–1869) were his brothers. He was educated under Keate at Eton College from 1823 and entered

St John's College, Cambridge, in October 1824. In the following three years in succession he gained Sir William Browne's medal for a Greek ode, and in 1826 carried off all the Browne medals. In the same year he was Craven scholar. He graduated in 1828 as sixth wrangler, and also senior classic and first chancellor's medallist. His subsequent degrees were MA in 1831, BD in 1850, and DD in 1864.

In March 1829 Selwyn was made a fellow of St John's, and in the same year gained the Norrisian prize. He was ordained deacon by the bishop of Ely in 1829 and priest by the bishop of Rochester in 1831. In 1831 he was presented by the duke of Rutland to the rectory of Branstone, Leicestershire. He married on 22 August 1832 Juliana Elizabeth, eldest daughter of George Cooke of Carr House, Doncaster. In 1846 he exchanged Branstone for the vicarage of Melbourne, Cambridgeshire, in the gift of the dean and chapter of Ely. He held Melbourne until 1853. In 1833 he was made a canon residentiary of Ely, an office which he retained until his death. When his brother-in-law Dean Peacock died he was offered the deanery of Ely. He declined it as it would have involved the resignation of the Lady Margaret professorship to which he was elected in 1855, having beaten his chief competitor, Harold Browne, by the casting vote of the chairman. 'It is Harold the conqueror this time, not William,' was his remark to his opponent, under the impression that the election had gone the other way. He insisted on setting apart out of his own income the yearly sum of £700 for the better endowment of the Norrisian professorship during Harold Browne's tenure of it, and after that for furthering the study of theology in Cambridge. Selwyn lived to see the new divinity school erected with the funds thus raised. In 1857 he was appointed Ramsden preacher and in 1859 was chaplain-in-ordinary to the queen. He served on the committee to revise the Authorized Version of the Old Testament. He was a fellow of the Royal Society from 1866, honorary joint curator of Lambeth Library from 1872, and president of the Cambridge Philosophical Society in 1867.

Selwyn had a strong interest in church–state relations, taking legal action to try to prevent Irish disestablishment. His major concern was the position of the cathedral in the church. He questioned the centralizing tendency of the ecclesiastical commission, and its emphasis upon the parish, publishing a pamphlet in 1840 entitled *An Attempt to investigate the True Principles of Cathedral Reform*. He believed in the capability of the church to reform itself through its councils, notably the chapter, when elevated to a role of bishops' council. In 1852 he was named a member of the cathedrals commission, and the report of 1854 was understood to be largely his work. He was also the moving cause of the rebuilding of his own college chapel, for which purpose funds had been accumulating under the bequest of a late master.

In appearance Selwyn was tall and spare, having been a keen oarsman in his youth. In Michaelmas term 1866, when riding along the Trumpington Road, he was thrown from his horse, owing to the carelessness, it was said, of an undergraduate who was riding on the wrong side of the road. In a copy of Latin elegiacs, dated 20 November, which appeared in *The Times* of 15 December 1866, the sufferer apostrophized the 'juvenum rapidissime' in lines of mingled humour and pathos. He never wholly recovered from the effects of the fall and died at Vine Cottage, Cambridge, on 24 April 1875, being buried at Ely on 29 April. He left a widow but no children. Selwyn published letters, speeches, sermons, and works on Old Testament criticism. J. H. LUPTON, *rev.* ELLIE CLEWLOW

Sources J. S. Wood, 'William Selwyn', *The Eagle*, 9 (1875), 298–322 • P. Barrett, *Barchester: English cathedral life in the nineteenth century* (1993) • Venn, *Alum. Cant.* • O. Chadwick, *The Victorian church*, pbk edn, 2 vols. (1987) • *The Guardian* (28 April 1875) • Boase, *Mod. Eng. biog.* • *GM*, 1st ser., 102/2 (1832), 263

Archives Surrey HC, family, legal, and estate papers, NRA 14087 Selwyn | BL, correspondence with W. E. Gladstone [1837–74] • Durham Cath. CL, letters to J. B. Lightfoot [1860–71] • LPL, letters to A. C. Tait and related papers [1862–74] • LPL, letters to C. Wordsworth [1836–66]

Likenesses A. B. Joy, marble bust, 1878, U. Cam., Divinity School

Wealth at death under £60,000: probate, 15 July 1875, *CGPLA Eng. & Wales*

Selwyn-Lloyd. For this title name *see* Lloyd, (John) Selwyn Brooke, Baron Selwyn-Lloyd (1904–1978).

Selyf ap Cynan [*called* Selyf Sarffgadau] (*d.* **613x16**), king of Powys, was the son of *Cynan Garwyn of Powys (*fl.* *c.*550–*c.*600). Known later as Sarffgadau (Serpent of Battles) and as one of the three *aeruetawc* ('battle leaders') of the Britons, Selyf was king of Powys, in north-east Wales, in the early decades of the seventh century. He was a descendant of Cadell Ddyrnllug of Powys and thereby a member of the main dynasty of that kingdom. He probably succeeded his father, Cynan Garwyn ap Brochfael Ysgithrog, who ruled that kingdom in the late sixth century. Selyf is notable as the main Welsh leader at the battle of Chester against Æthelfrith of Northumbria in 613x16, at which he was slain. It is not clear whether this implies he was dominant among the Welsh at that time or whether it merely reflects the strategic importance of Chester (then possibly in Powys) for Selyf's kingdom. The Irish chronicles call him 'rex Brittonum'('king of the Britons'). One of his allies at Chester may have been Gwion, brother of Cynddylan ap Cyndrwyn, a ruler of more southerly Powysian territories. Bede related an incident said to have occurred shortly before the battle. Many Welsh priests, mostly monks from nearby Bangor Is-coed, are said to have assembled at a safe distance to pray for a Welsh victory; they were under the guard of one Brochfael (possibly a kinsman of Selyf, though not mentioned in the genealogies). The pagan Æthelfrith, taking this pious act as one of aggression against his cause, ordered his men to kill these clerics, which they did, after Brochfael and his men had fled. The fortunes of Selyf's dynasty in the period immediately after his death are not known, though it is possible that ascendancy within Powys then passed briefly to the dynasty of Cynddylan ap Cyndrwyn. Selyf is conflated with his brother Eiludd in some genealogies and sometimes rendered as Eiludd's father; he would thereby be ancestor of the later kings of Powys, which is not certain. His sons would include Beli, Dona, Mael Mynan, and Eiludd, though most of these are probably unreliable.

DAVID E. THORNTON

Sources J. Williams ab Ithel, ed., *Annales Cambriae*, Rolls Series, 20 (1860) • P. C. Bartrum, ed., *Early Welsh genealogical tracts* (1966) • I. Williams, ed., *Canu Llywarch Hen* (1935); pbk edn (1978) • A. W. Wade-Evans, ed. and trans., *Vitae sanctorum Britanniae et genealogiae* (1944) • Bede, *Hist. eccl.*, 2.2 • *Ann. Ulster* • R. Bromwich, ed. and trans., *Trioedd ynys Prydein: the Welsh triads*, 2nd edn (1978) • J. E. Lloyd, *A history of Wales from the earliest times to the Edwardian conquest*, 3rd edn, 2 vols. (1939); repr. (1988) • D. P. Kirby, 'The bards and the Welsh border', *Mercian studies*, ed. A. Dornier (1977), 31–42

Semon, Sir Felix (1849–1921), laryngologist, was born on 8 December 1849 at Danzig, Germany, the elder son of Simon Joseph Semon, stockbroker, of Berlin, and his wife, Henrietta, *née* Aschenheim. His medical studies began at Heidelberg, but were interrupted by the Franco-Prussian War (1870–71), in which he served as a volunteer in the 2nd uhlans of the Prussian guard and was awarded the war medal with five clasps. After the war he returned to Berlin, proceeded MD in 1873, and took the *Staatsexamen* in 1874. He studied in Vienna and Paris, and then went to London with an introduction to Morell Mackenzie, who received him with kindness and in 1875 appointed him clinical assistant at the Hospital for Diseases of the Throat, Golden Square, London (in 1877 he was elected to the honorary staff). His reason for leaving Berlin and settling in London was that, being a Jew, he had little chance of promotion to professor in ordinary. He was sickened by antisemitism. At this time Semon translated Mackenzie's *Diseases of the Throat and Nose* into German and added his own footnotes.

No doubt using his mother's friendship with Richard Liebreich, a fellow German Jew who was ophthalmologist at St Thomas's Hospital, Semon in 1882 persuaded the hospital board to appoint him as physician to the throat department; he thus became the first laryngologist to be appointed to a general hospital. As he was not allowed to operate externally he was fortunate to enlist the skills of Sir Henry Butlin (1843–1912), who shared an interest in diseases of the throat. Their initial experience with laryngofissure for cancer of the larynx was disappointing, but better patient selection later improved their results.

Semon was an industrious worker, who carried out experimental research into the central motor innervation of the larynx with Victor Horsley (1857–1916) at the Brown Institution (University of London) in the Wandsworth Road. Their presentation on 19 June 1890 demonstrated that in all progressive organic lesions of the centres and trunks of the motor laryngeal nerves the abductor muscles of the larynx were affected before the adductors. This became known as 'Semon's law'. In 1887 he was appointed laryngologist to the National Hospital for the Relief and Cure of the Paralysed and Epileptic, Queen Square, London, where Horsley had been appointed surgeon a year earlier. Semon shared with Horsley an interest in the thyroid gland and demonstrated that cretinism, myxoedema, and post-thyroidectomy cachexia were one

Sir Felix Semon (1849–1921), by Sir Hubert von Herkomer, 1906

and the same. Later, in 1906, Semon was one of the first to emphasize the importance of vocal rest in tuberculosis of the larynx.

In 1876 Semon was admitted a member of the Royal College of Physicians (becoming fellow in 1885). He was instrumental in establishing the subsection of laryngology at the International Medical Congress in London in 1881, and in 1893 he helped to found the Laryngological Society of London (president, 1894–6). He was twice president of the section of laryngology of the British Medical Association. In 1884 Semon founded the *Internationales Centralblatt für Laryngologie und Rhinologie*, and was for twenty-five years its editor. In 1912 he published *Forschungen und Erfahrungen, 1880–1910*, a collection, in two volumes, of his numerous contributions to medical literature.

Semon received many distinctions. At Queen Victoria's diamond jubilee (1897) he was knighted; in 1901 he was appointed physician-extraordinary to King Edward VII, and in the same year became naturalized as a British subject. In 1902 he was created CVO (promoted KCVO in 1905). In 1889 Kaiser Wilhelm II awarded him the order of the Red Eagle (third class), for what Semon described in his autobiography as his part in the tragic illness of Crown Prince Frederick (later Frederick III), a part that was 'played behind the scenes', and was no doubt encouraged by his lifelong friendship with the sons of Bismarck, one of whom became German ambassador to the United Kingdom and the other foreign minister of the German empire. In 1894 the Kaiser conferred on Semon the title of royal Prussian professor.

Semon was a man with many artistic and social gifts, who excelled in whatever he took up. He was a fine pianist and composer, and at the end of the Franco-Prussian War his regiment entered Berlin to the strains of a march which he had composed when encamped outside Paris in the winter of 1870–71. He was a brilliant conversationalist and raconteur, and also fond of hunting, shooting, and fishing. He enjoyed his friendship with Edward VII, and played an important role in the establishment of the King Edward VII Sanatorium at Midhurst, Sussex.

In 1911, at the zenith of his professional career, Semon retired. In recognition of his services to medicine he was entertained at a banquet presided over by Sir Henry Butlin. The sum of £1040 was subscribed as a testimonial of esteem and appreciation, and at Semon's request the money was presented to the University of London to establish a Semon lectureship in laryngology. After a year's voyage round the world Semon retired to the house which he had built on the Chilterns above Great Missenden.

The First World War was a particularly unhappy time for Semon; as a naturalized subject of German origin he was in a difficult position and was eventually forced to publish a condemnation of his fatherland in *The Times*. This led to the loss of all his German and Austrian honours, together with the removal of his name from the frontispiece of the *Centralblatt für Laryngologie*.

Semon spent his retirement in writing his autobiography: when it was published, five years after his death, by his son Dr Henry Semon, it revealed some rather unhappy aspects of the father's character. Semon undoubtedly played a significant part in the development of laryngology, but his book was a litany of self-aggrandizement. He had few good words for Morell Mackenzie, to whom he owed so much of his earlier success, and suggested that if Mackenzie's most famous patient, the German crown prince, had come to him instead, his life would have been saved.

Semon married in 1879 Augusta Louise Dorette, daughter of Heinrich Redeker, wholesale furniture dealer, of Cloppenburg, Oldenburg; they had three sons. Semon died of heart failure at his home, Rignalls, Great Missenden, Buckinghamshire, on 1 March 1921 and was buried at Golders Green. His headstone bears the inscription 'Monumentum ejus incrementum scientiae'. His wife survived him.

F. DE H. HALL, *rev.* NEIL WEIR

Sources N. Weir, *Otolaryngology: an illustrated history* (1990) • P. McBride, 'The Semon lectures 1913', *Journal of Laryngology, Rhinology and Otology*, 28 (1913), 113–29, 169–87 • *Journal of Laryngology*, 36 (1921), 161–2 • *The Lancet* (12 March 1921), 561 • *BMJ* (12 March 1921), 404–5 • *The autobiography of Sir Felix Semon*, ed. H. C. Semon and T. A. McIntyre (1926) • *CGPLA Eng. & Wales* (1921) • personal knowledge (1927)

Archives RS | Wellcome L., laboratory book with Sir Victor Horsley

Likenesses H. von Herkomer, oils, 1906, Royal Society of Medicine, London [*see illus.*] • Spy [L. Ward], chromolithograph caricature, NPG, Wellcome L.; repro. in *VF* (1 May 1902)

Wealth at death £31,185 13*s*.: probate, 13 June 1921, *CGPLA Eng. & Wales*

Sempill, Francis, of Beltrees (*c.*1617–1682), poet and wit, the son of Robert Sempill of Beltrees, Lochwinnoch, Renfrewshire, and his wife, Mary, daughter of Sir Thomas Lyon of Auldbar, was the descendant of a family closely connected with the Stuart kings and with letters. He married his cousin Jean Campbell of Ardkinglas at Lochgoilhead, Argyll, on 3 April 1655, and succeeded his father at some time between 1660 (when Robert witnessed a baptism) and 1669, when Francis is found acting as laird of Beltrees. In 1677 he was appointed sheriff-depute of Renfrewshire, from which it may be deduced that, like his father, he had studied law. In the course of his duties he arrested a Walter Scott, 'a noted leader of conventicles and such-like disorders' (Wodrow, 2, appx, 8), and in the ensuing tumult was seriously wounded.

Francis is believed to have inherited the Beltrees estate embarrassed, as a result of his father's participation in the civil war. In keeping with the family motto, 'In loyaltie', he supported the Stuarts enthusiastically but was increasingly forced to alienate land, his financial problems having been (in his own view) exacerbated by the indemnity granted to the whig rebels after the Bothwell Bridge rising (1679), which prevented him from being compensated for his part in suppressing the revolt. By 1678 the superiority of Beltrees was sold to Thomas Crawfurd of Cartsburn, and in 1680 Sempill and his wife resigned their liferent of the remaining lands of Thridpairt to their son Robert, who undertook to pay his father's debts of 800 merks and £800 Scots. This presumably cleared the embarrassments which had forced Francis to take refuge in the debtors' sanctuary of the palace of Holyrood, Edinburgh, whence he was rescued in 1680 by James, duke of Albany (later James VII and II), an episode celebrated in 'The Banishment of Poverty' (1680).

Sempill's poems were not (as far as is known) published in his own lifetime, and most of those attributed to him appeared first as anonymous broadsheets. Family tradition credits him with an early talent for improvisation. Motherwell, in his introduction to *The Harp of Renfrewshire* (1819), writes, 'It is to be regretted that the manuscripts of Francis Sempill are irretrievably lost. They fell into hands which knew not their value, and it is to be feared out of them they will never be recovered' (Motherwell, xx). Some loose sheets containing poems attributed to him were given to James Paterson, editor of *The Poems of the Sempills of Beltrees* (1849), by H. G. Gardner, a descendant of the Beltrees family: it is presumably on the authority of these that Paterson ascribed to him 'The Blythsome Wedding' (also claimed on poor evidence for Sir William Scott of Thirlestane), 'A Discourse between Law and Conscience', an early version of 'Auld Lang Syne', 'She Raise and Loot Me In' (also attributed to Thomas D'Urfey), and 'Maggie Lauder', among others.

James Johnson attributed the dissemination of

Sempill's ballads in England to his friendship with one of Cromwell's officers in Glasgow, but the story, though charming, is unnecessary. Sempill, like other poets of his time, was writing in a pan-British culture in which songs and their settings moved easily across the border in both directions (it is noticeable that 'The Banishment of Poverty', probably the only poem of which his authorship has not been challenged, is set to an English tune, 'The Last Good Night'). The poems ascribed to him give evidence of wit, lightness of touch, and sense of rhythm.

Sempill died suddenly in his house in Paisley on 12 March 1682. The only physical description we have of him is his reference in 'July the Nine-and-Twenty Day' to his own 'glied eye and crooked snout'.

HARRIET HARVEY WOOD

Sources J. Paterson, *The poems of the Sempills of Beltrees, now first collected, with notes and biographical notices of their lives* (1849) • *James Watson's Choice collection of comic and serious Scots poems*, ed. H. H. Wood, 2 vols., STS, 4th ser., 10, 20 (1977–91) [incl. index: repr. of 1869 edn] • W. Motherwell, *The harp of Renfrewshire: a collection of songs and other poetical pieces* (1819) • R. Law, *Memorialls, or, The memorable things that fell out within this island of Brittain from 1638 to 1684*, ed. C. K. Sharpe (1818) • R. Burns and others, *The Scots musical museum*, ed. J. Johnson and W. Stenhouse, new edn, 4 vols. (1853) • R. Wodrow, *The history of the sufferings of the Church of Scotland from the Restauration to the revolution*, 2 (1722) • H. H. Wood, 'Burns and Watson's *Choice collection*', *Studies in Scottish Literature*, 30 (1998), 19–30

Sempill, Francis, Jacobite second Lord Sempill (*d.* **1748**), Jacobite agent, was born in France, the eldest son of Robert Sempill (1672–1737), army officer in the French service, who had been created a Jacobite peer by James Stuart, the Pretender, in 1712, and Elizabeth, *née* Abercromby (*d.* in or after 1737). Francis Sempill claimed descent from the old Renfrewshire family which had been raised to the peerage of Scotland in the fifteenth century, but there is no record of his ever having visited Scotland. He was educated at the Scots College, Douai (1706), spoke fluent French, became conversant with the ways of the French court, and was a practising Christian.

In the late 1730s William MacGregor (known as Drummond of Balhaldy) was sent to Paris to work with Sempill on behalf of an association of Scottish Jacobites. With Balhaldy and John Murray of Broughton, Sempill became a principal link to followers of the Stuart cause in Scotland and England. He exaggerated Jacobite strength and lied to win French support, and as a result made enemies among both French and Jacobites. The Pretender did not improve matters by setting up a second agent in Paris, Daniel O'Brien (later Jacobite earl of Lismore).

After the death of Cardinal Fleury, Sempill sent Louis XV a memoir requesting support for a restoration of the Stuart line, and a full-scale invasion of Britain was planned towards the end of 1743. This resulted in Prince Charles Edward's travelling to Paris, where he stayed at Sempill's house on the rue de l'Estrapade. Jacobites in France now divided into two factions: King James's party, comprising Sempill, Balhaldy, and O'Brien, and the prince's party, made up of Thomas Sheridan, his old governor, Earl Marischal, and Father George Kelly, who became Charles's evil genius. While Sempill and O'Brien quarrelled over who really spoke for the king, Sempill damaged his own cause by continuing to exaggerate potential support in Scotland for the invasion. Outmanoeuvred by Kelly, Sempill worked hard to retain James's confidence because of his financial dependence on Rome. James was probably aware of his agent's exaggeration, but it suited him to allow Louis to believe that support in Britain was greater than it actually was. The planned French expedition was abandoned in the summer of 1744, by which time Prince Charles had lost trust in Sempill. He complained that 'after making such a nois [*sic*] of his being able to do a great deal, he does nothing' (Miller, 317), forbade him contact with the French court, and scathingly called him Lord Simple (Kybett, 85). Like the French, Sempill knew nothing of the prince's planned rising in Scotland.

Sempill worked to persuade Louis to mount an invasion during the rising of 1745. Early in the following year he was at Ostend, acting as intermediary to English followers and ready to sail, but the battle of Culloden and a French desire for peace destroyed that hope. By now Sempill's criticism had infuriated the French and annoyed King James. He probably had a hand in the preparation of a lengthy 'Mémoire d'un Ecossais' (now in the foreign ministry archives, Paris), inspired by Cameron of Lochiel, which was sent to Louis XV in April 1747 in the hope of rekindling interest. The memoir was ignored, bringing to an end Sempill's career in which intense loyalty to Jacobitism had lured him into a life built around wild rumour and lies. His wife was Mary, daughter of Kenneth *Mackenzie, fourth earl of Seaforth, and widow of John Caryll of Harting. She died on 3 April 1740 and he died on 9 December 1748. He was buried at St Andrew's, Chartres.

HUGH DOUGLAS

Sources *Calendar of the Stuart papers belonging to his majesty the king, preserved at Windsor Castle*, 7 vols., HMC, 56 (1902–23) • F. McLynn, *France and the Jacobite rising of 1745* (1981) • J. S. Gibson, *Lochiel of the '45* (1994) • E. Cruickshanks, *Political untouchables: the tories and the '45* (1979) • C. Petrie, *The Jacobite movement*, 3rd edn (1959) • P. Miller, *James* (1971) • F. McLynn, *Charles Edward Stuart: a tragedy in many acts* (1988) • A. Lang, *Pickle the Spy* (1897) • *Memorials of John Murray of Broughton*, ed. R. F. Bell, Scottish History Society, 27 (1898) • GEC, *Peerage* • S. M. Kybett, *Bonnie Prince Charlie: a biography* (1988) • *Scots peerage*

Archives Achnacarry, Inverness-shire, Lochiel papers • NL Scot., John Murray papers

Wealth at death likely to have been very small; depended on grants from James Stuart and King Louis XV

Sempill, Hew, twelfth Lord Sempill (**1688–1746**), army officer, was born after 16 May 1688, probably at Castle Sempill, Renfrewshire, the fifth son of Francis Abercromby (1654–1703) of Fetterneir, Aberdeenshire, who was created Lord Glasfoord for life on 5 July 1685, and his wife, Anne, *suo jure* Lady Sempill (*d.* 1695), ninth holder of the title. The children of the marriage (five sons and a daughter) all carried their mother's surname.

Sempill entered the army as an adjutant in the 26th regiment of foot (the Cameronians) on 1 December 1708. He was made an ensign in July 1709 and served at the battle of Malplaquet that year. He was promoted captain on 12 July 1712, and placed on half pay in 1713, but he returned to active service by a supplementary commission of 26 September 1715 as captain of a newly raised company in his old regiment.

Sempill was promoted major on 5 April 1718 and in Manchester on 13 May 1718 he married Sarah (*d.* 1749), coheir and daughter of Nathaniel Gaskell of Manchester. They had five sons and six daughters. Although he succeeded to the peerage on the death of his brother John, eleventh Lord Sempill, in February 1727 he remained in the army. After twenty-three years' service with the Cameronians he transferred to the 19th regiment of foot (the Green Howards) as lieutenant-colonel on 12 July 1731. Lord Sempill sold the estates of Eliotstoun and Castle Sempill in 1727 and in 1741 bought the estate of North Bar, also in Renfrewshire.

On 14 January 1741 Sempill succeeded John Lindsay, twentieth earl of Crawford, as colonel of the Black Watch, then the 43rd foot. In 1743 the regiment, originally raised to keep watch in the highlands, received orders to proceed south to England; and when a rumour reached the soldiers in London that they were to be sent to the West Indies, they immediately began to return to Scotland, but were overtaken and compelled to turn back. Their destination was Flanders, and there, under Lord Sempill, they specially distinguished themselves in the defence of the town of Aeth when it was besieged by the French.

On 25 April 1745 Sempill was appointed colonel of the 25th foot (the King's Own Scottish Borderers); he was present at Fontenoy later that summer. At the battle of Culloden on 16 April 1746 his regiment occupied a place in the second line on the left wing where it was heavily engaged in repulsing the charge of the Jacobite army. He was appointed governor of Barbados in 1746 but did not take office.

Sempill died (following an operation on his arm) at Aberdeen on 25 November 1746, while in command of the troops stationed there. He was buried in West Church, Aberdeen, on 1 December. His eldest son, John (*d.* 1782), succeeded to the peerage.

T. F. HENDERSON, *rev.* JONATHAN SPAIN

Sources GEC, *Peerage* · *Scots peerage* · C. Dalton, *George the First's army, 1714–1727*, 2 vols. (1910–12) · C. Dalton, ed., *English army lists and commission registers, 1661–1714*, 6 (1904), 1707–14 · H. D. MacWilliam, ed., *The official records of the mutiny in the Black Watch: a London incident of the year 1743* (1910)

Likenesses portrait, Finlay House, Aberdeenshire; repro. in MacWilliam, ed., *Official records*

Sempill, Hugh (1596–1654), mathematician, born in Craigevar in Scotland, was a nephew of Colonel William Sempill, soldier of fortune and political agent. He entered the Society of Jesus and was assigned to Toledo in 1615. Later he moved to Madrid, where he became the rector of the Scots College. In 1635 he wrote a mathematics treatise or, rather, a reference book, for use in the Imperial College, Madrid, and dedicated it to Philip IV: 'De mathematicis disciplinis, libri duodecim ad Philippum IV, Hispaniarum et Indiarum regem catholicum'. The book was published in Antwerp; errata were corrected in 1640 for pages 148–9. This is possibly Sempill's most important work; it is divided into twelve chapters, the first two being the most interesting. In chapter one he discusses the position of pure mathematics in relation to science. He gives a short historical account, with references to contemporary mathematicians, and then contrasts the views of Aristotle (which he follows) with more contemporaneous authors who cast doubts on the possibility of fitting mathematics as a science into the cadre of knowledge. In the second chapter he discusses mathematics from the aspect of its various applications. In the remaining chapters he considers: geometry and arithmetic, which are dealt with briefly; optics; statics, in which a variety of mechanical topics including pyrotechnics and automata are considered; music; cosmography; geography, in which he includes a discussion on the Americas, using Spanish as well as Latin in the heading of a table concerning rents of metropolitan churches and cathedrals; hydrography, air, atmosphere, the sunset, meteorites, volcanoes, and comets; astronomy, in which a reference is made to Copernicus's astronomical observations; astrology, in which he discusses licit and illicit astrology, and reproduces the papal bull of Sixtus V refuting astrology; and, in the last chapter, the calendar. The book ends with a large index, of over sixty pages. This section of the book may be a preliminary version of a 'Dictionarium mathematicum' of his, which was never published.

In 1642 Sempill published, in Madrid, *Experientia mathematica de compositione numerorum, linearum, quadratorum, &c.*, in which he discusses basic algebra. Madrid's National Library possesses four more of his works in manuscript: 'Historia de Regimine Philippi IV'; 'Parecer sobre el riego de los prados de Aranjuéz y lugares vecinos en tiempos de Felipe IV'; 'Parecer sobre las señales que se vieron en el cielo, año 1637'; and 'Discurso contra los ministros codiciosos'. Sempill's significance lay in the scope of his desire to promote the application of mathematics to science. He died in Madrid on 29 September 1654.

EDUARDO L. ORTIZ

Sources *DNB* · A. de Backer and A. de Backer, *La bibliothèque des écrivains de la Compagnie de Jésus*, ed. C. Sommervogel, new edn, 3 vols. (Liège and Paris, 1869–76), vol. 2, p. 755 · 'Scotch and Irish authors', *Catholic Miscellany*, 9 (1828), 40–41 · H. Foley, ed., *Records of the English province of the Society of Jesus*, 7/2 (1883), 697 · L. Thorndike, *A history of magic and experimental science*, 8 vols. (1923–58), vols. 1–6

Archives Biblioteca Nacional, Madrid · Harvard U., Houghton Libary

Sempill, Sir James (1566?–1626), courtier and religious controversialist, was the eldest son of John Sempill (*d.* 1579) and his wife, Mary *Livingston [*see under* Queen's Maries (*act.* 1548–1567)], daughter of Alexander, fifth Lord Livingstone, and grandson of Robert *Sempill, third Lord Sempill (*c.*1505–1573x6). Both John and Mary Sempill were favourites of Mary, queen of Scots, from whom they received on 9 May 1565 the lands of Auchtermuchty in Fife and various properties in Ayrshire. In 1577 John Sempill confessed to, and was convicted of, participation in the conspiracy to assassinate the regent, the earl of Morton, in

January that year. He was sentenced to death but was reprieved and imprisoned in Edinburgh; he died on 25 April 1579, soon after his release. James Sempill was named after the future James VI and I, who, though an infant, was named as his godfather. The two children were educated together under George Buchanan. Half a century later Sempill recalled that James was:

> the king of my birth, the master of my service, the father of my name, framer of my nature, and the Gamaliel of my education, at whose feet (no, at whose elbow and from whose mouth) I confess I have suckt the best of whatsoever may be thought good in me. (Sempill, sig. A2*v*)

After this privileged start he completed his education at the University of St Andrews.

In 1594 Sempill married Geillis (*d.* 1618), daughter of George Elphinstone of Blythswood. They had five daughters, of whom Marion, Geillis, and Isobel were alive in 1618, and three sons, Robert, George, and William. When King James visited Paisley Abbey in 1617 Sempill prepared an oration which William, then aged nine, delivered before him in the great hall of the earl of Abercorn. But the boy was dead by September 1618, and George too died young. Sempill assisted James VI in preparing for the press his *Basilikon Doron* (1599), and was presented with one of the seven copies printed; this he showed to the presbyterian minister Andrew Melville, who disliked the views on church policy expressed there and saw to it that they were the subject of public discussion. In 1599 Sempill was resident in London as an agent of James VI; shortly after his return in February 1600 he was made knight bachelor, and in October 1601 he was sent on an embassy to France, travelling through England, and onwards by way of Dover. In February 1603 the king, in token of his services, presented him with 'a jewel of great beauty and value', which had belonged to Mary, queen of Scots (*Reg. PCS*, 6.533–4).

After his return from France Sempill seems to have been often at the court of King James in London. When Andrew Melville was imprisoned in 1606 he looked to Sempill as the man to effect his release. Melville remained in the Tower of London but his conditions improved. In 1610 he sought Sempill's advice as to how to further advance his case, revealing his intention to offer his services as tutor to the young Prince Henry, and confiding to his nephew James Melville that Sempill:

> takes a warm interest in my studies as well as in the welfare of my person, and what is more, I am persuaded that he takes a warm interest in the cause. The court does not contain a more religious man, one who unites greater modesty with greater genius, and a more matured judgment with more splendid accomplishments. In procuring for me a mitigation of my imprisonment, he has shewn, both by words and deeds, a constancy truly worthy of a Christian … thank him on my account; for he will not rest satisfied until he has effected my complete liberation. (McCrie, 410)

This may have overestimated Sempill's influence, but he was certainly a committed Calvinist. In 1618 he published at Middelburg *Cassandra Scoticana to Cassander Anglicanus*. In 1619 he provided a defence of the divine ordination of tithes in *Sacrilege Sacredly Handled*, which included prefatory verses by Melville. The work, Sempill claimed, was twenty years old. Its publication was evidently occasioned by John Selden's *History of Tithes*, published in the same year, and Sempill countered the arguments of Selden and Joseph Scaliger. In 1622, at Melville's suggestion, he published a work against Tilenus, a former colleague of Melville at Sedan, who had become an Arminian. He translated from the Dutch a highly partisan anti-Catholic poem, *The Pack-Mans Pater noster, or, A Dialogue betwixt a Chapman and a Priest* (1624). Sempill acquired property in Renfrewshire and Bute, and in Ireland, where he was granted the barony of Carbery, co. Cork, which passed to his eldest son. He died at his house at the Cross of Paisley in February 1626.

Sir James's son **Robert Sempill** (*d.* 1660x69), poet, was educated at Glasgow University, where he matriculated in March 1613. He married Marie Lyon, daughter of Sir Thomas *Lyon of Auldbar, and they had a son, Francis *Sempill, and a daughter, Elizabeth. Sempill expanded his father's satire as *A Pick-Tooth for the Pope, or, The Pack-Mans Pater noster* (1669), but his most notable work was the elegy *The Life and Death of the Pyper of Kilbarchen, or, The Epitaph of Habbie Simpson*, probably composed about 1640 but not published until about 1700. In this he pioneered the use of the verse form later dubbed the 'standard Habbie', which was used to such effect by Robert Burns. Sempill is also credited with the authorship of the epitaph on 'Sawny Briggs, nephew to Habbie Simson and brother to the Laird of Kilbarchan', and may have written other poems. He served as a royalist officer in the civil war. The Irish lands which his father had acquired were confiscated by the Cromwellian authorities, and though Robert was active in the Restoration, they were not returned. He died between September 1660 and June 1669. STEPHEN WRIGHT

Sources J. Paterson, *Poems of the Sempills of Beltrees* (1849) · T. M'Crie, *The life of Andrew Melville*, 2 vols. (1819) · J. Sempill, *Sacrilege sacredly handled, that is, according to Scripture only* (1619) · C. Craig, ed., *The history of Scottish literature*, 1: *Origins to 1660*, ed. R. D. S. Jack (1988) · D. Calderwood, *The history of the Kirk of Scotland*, ed. T. Thomson and D. Laing, 8 vols., Wodrow Society, 7 (1842–9) · *Reg. PCS*, 1st ser., vol. 6 · *Scots peerage*

Wealth at death substantially in land

Sempill, John, first Lord Sempill (*d.* 1513), landowner and administrator, was the eldest son and heir of Sir Thomas Sempill of Elliston in Renfrewshire and Elizabeth, daughter of John, first Lord Ross. Sir Thomas died at the battle of Sauchieburn (11 June 1488), fighting for James III. John retained his father's lands, but lost the sheriffdom of Renfrew to his local rivals Robert, first Lord Lyle (with whom Thomas Sempill had been at feud in 1483), John Stewart, earl of Lennox (*d.* 1495), and Lennox's son Matthew (*d.* 1513). These three, dissatisfied with their share of the spoils after James III's death, were among the rebels of 1489–90 and used their shrieval jurisdiction to attack the lands of former supporters of James III, including Sempill. Consequently, on 13 September 1489 Sempill received a lieutenancy as sheriff of Renfrew from James IV's regime so that he could act against the rebellious Lord Lyle and

Matthew Stewart, master of Lennox. Sempill had reduced Lyle's castle of Duchal with the king's artillery by July 1489, but the 1489–90 rebellion ended in political compromise, with Lyle restored to the government, and on 16 March 1491 James IV obliged Sempill and the Lennox Stewarts to end their feud.

However, Sempill continued to enjoy royal favour. He was styled knight on 20 June 1492, but was a lord of parliament by 1493, probably as a regional counterbalance to Lyle and the Lennox Stewarts on the crown's behalf. In 1492 he was among the ambassadors to England, and personally received £20 from Henry VII. He was given royal conveyances of Lochwinnoch (1501), Henderstoun Wester (1502), and Eliotstoun, Southannan, Glassford, Cassiltoun, and other lands (1503–5) in Renfrewshire and Ayrshire, which were confirmed by James IV in 1505–6 and 1508. By 1505 he was bailie of Cunningham, and he had a royal grant of Paidyeauch in Ayrshire on 8 June 1512. On 21 April 1504 he founded a collegiate church at Lochwinnoch.

By 9 September 1501 Sempill was married to Margaret (*d.* before 21 April 1504), daughter of Sir Robert Colville of Ochiltree, Ayrshire. They had three sons and two daughters, including the eldest, William, who became second Lord Sempill and before 1517 married Margaret, daughter of Hugh Montgomery, first earl of Eglintoun. John Sempill had remarried by 16 February 1506; he and his second wife, Margaret, daughter of James Crichton of Ruthvendenny, had no children. He was killed at the battle of Flodden on 9 September 1513, and it seems likely that he was buried in the church he had founded at Lochwinnoch.

MICHAEL A. PENMAN

Sources J. M. Thomson and others, eds., *Registrum magni sigilli regum Scotorum / The register of the great seal of Scotland*, 11 vols. (1882–1914), vol. 2 · G. Burnett and others, eds., *The exchequer rolls of Scotland*, 9–12 (1886–9) · *APS*, 1424–1567 · T. Dickson and J. B. Paul, eds., *Compota thesaurariorum regum Scotorum / Accounts of the lord high treasurer of Scotland*, 1–4 (1877–1902) · [T. Thomson] and others, eds., *The acts of the lords of council in civil causes, 1478–1503*, 3 vols. (1839–1993) · [T. Thomson], ed., *The acts of the lords auditors of causes and complaints, AD 1466–AD 1494*, RC, 40 (1839) · A. Gardner, ed., *Archaeological and historical collections relating to the county of Renfrew*, 2 vols. (1885–90) · *Scots peerage* · N. Macdougall, *James III: a political study* (1982) · N. Macdougall, *James IV* (1989) · *CDS*, vol. 4

Likenesses monument, collegiate church, Lochwinnoch, Sempill, Renfrewshire; repro. in Gardner, ed., *Archaeological and historical collections*

Sempill, Robert, **third Lord Sempill** (*c.*1505–1573x6), nobleman, was the elder son of William Sempill, second Lord Sempill (*d.* 1552), and his first wife, Lady Margaret (*d.* before February 1523), eldest daughter of Hugh Montgomery, first earl of Eglinton. The family lands formed the barony of Sempill in Renfrewshire, and in 1544, while Robert was still master of Sempill, his father granted him a charter of the office of sheriff of Renfrew. The following year he was rewarded with the bailiary of Paisley Abbey, after supporting its monks in a dispute with heretics. Captured by the English at the battle of Pinkie in 1547, he returned to Scotland on his release and became embroiled in a series of personal quarrels. He had a long-standing feud with the protestant Alexander Cunningham, fourth earl of Glencairn; on 9 April 1549 John Mure of Caldwell and several accomplices tried to assassinate him; and on 11 June that same year he killed William, Lord Crichton of Sanquhar, in the Edinburgh lodgings of James Hamilton, second earl of Arran, lord governor of Scotland and head of the house of Hamilton. Arrested and imprisoned in Edinburgh Castle, Sempill would have been executed, but managed to extricate himself because one of his daughters was the mistress of the influential John Hamilton, archbishop of St Andrews, Arran's half-brother.

In the 1550s Sempill was a loyal supporter of Mary of Guise, queen dowager and from 1554 to 1560 regent of Scotland, in her struggle against the protestant lords of the congregation. By now feuding with Arran, Sempill attacked him in 1560, and as a result the lords of the west besieged and captured Castle Sempill. Sempill himself, however, had managed to escape to the safety of Dunbar Castle, which was garrisoned by the French force sent to help Mary of Guise. When Mary, queen of Scots, returned to Scotland in 1561 he gave her his support, and in the autumn of 1565 was one of the commanders of her army when she and her husband, Lord Darnley, rode against the rebellious earl of Moray and his forces in the chaseabout raid.

Sempill was present at the baptism of Mary and Darnley's son, the future James VI, on 17 December 1566, and one of his own sons married Mary Livingston, one of the queen's four Maries. After the murder of Darnley in 1567, Sempill allied himself with the dead man's father, Matthew Stewart, thirteenth earl of Lennox, and saved the earl's life when he was the victim of an attack in Glasgow. Sempill's hatred of the Hamiltons provided a thread of continuity in his career which predisposed him to sympathize with Lennox, their hereditary enemy. As a conservative Roman Catholic he presumably disapproved of Mary's willingness to tolerate protestantism, and of her increasing involvement with the protestant James Hepburn, fourth earl of Bothwell, the man generally believed to be responsible for Darnley's death. On 12 April 1567 Sempill was a member of the assize which tried Bothwell for Darnley's murder, and on 15 June he commanded the vanguard of the army which opposed the queen at Carberry Hill.

Sempill was one of the signatories of the act authorizing Mary's imprisonment at Lochleven, and when she escaped in 1568 he fought against her at the battle of Langside on 13 May. The following year, he and his old adversary Glencairn became lieutenants of the western parts, with instructions to crush all support for the queen, and in recognition of his efforts he received the gift of the abbey of Paisley. Still pursuing his feud with the earl of Arran, in 1570 he attacked and set fire to Arran's castle at Hamilton. Seized by some of the earl's men, he was imprisoned at Draffen and then in Argyll, but he was freed in 1571 and sat in parliament and on the privy council. On 2 July 1572 he was made lieutenant-general and justiciar of the sheriffdoms of Lanark and Renfrew.

The following year Sempill became involved in an ecclesiastical dispute, when he tried to intrude Sir John Hamilton, a Roman Catholic priest, into the vicarage of Eastwood, and as a result he was both outlawed and excommunicated. He died between 1 August 1573 and 17 January 1576. With his first wife, Isabel, daughter of Sir William Hamilton of Sanquhar, he had four sons and two daughters, and with his second wife, Elizabeth Carlyle, he had another son. Sir William *Sempill was probably his illegitimate son. His complicated career combined old-style personal feuding with public office, and his conservative support of the Roman Catholic church earned him the condemnation of John Knox, who called him 'a man sold under sin, an enemy to God' (*Works*, 1.339).

ROSALIND K. MARSHALL

Sources *Scots peerage*, 7.538–43 · G. Donaldson, *All the queen's men* (1983) · *CSP Scot.*, *1595–7* · *The works of John Knox*, ed. D. Laing, 6 vols., Bannatyne Club, 112 (1846–64), vol. 1 · R. Douglas, *The peerage of Scotland*, 2nd edn, ed. J. P. Wood, 2 vols. (1813)

Sempill, Robert (*d.* 1595?), poet and protestant controversialist, was active during the early years of James VI's reign. Sempill's birth date is unknown; his allusion (in *Satirical Poems*, no. 45) to 'Epistle 25' of Clément Marot (1495–1544) prompted the mistaken notion that he knew Marot personally, and was born *c.*1530. Sempill's parentage is also unknown. Attempts to identify him with Robert, fourth Lord Sempill (1563–1611), who was a devout Catholic, are unconvincing. Sempill, styled in 1582 'burgess of Dumbartan, callit utherwys the makar' (register of deeds, NA Scot., 23, fol. 59), was probably not of noble birth.

Sempill devised plays and other entertainments for the court, but no texts survive. On 17 January 1568 'a play was made by Robert Semple, and played befor the Lord Regent and divers uthers of the nobilitie' ('Diary of Robert Birrel', 14); the expenses for this were met, in part, by Edinburgh council. Between April 1567 and March 1573 the *Accounts of the Treasurer*, which record the expenses of the royal household, note various payments to Sempill for clothing and other unspecified services, possibly related to entertainments. On 20 September 1581 he was paid for producing 'a pastyme' for King James in Dumbarton. The man styled 'capitane Sempill' in March 1573 may possibly be the poet (McInnes, 340). Many details in Sempill's poetry suggest that he had military experience; he either witnessed or participated in the sieges of Leith and Edinburgh Castle, which he describes with vividness and accuracy (*Satirical Poems*, nos. 39 and 43).

Sempill is most famous for his satires and invectives, largely composed between 1567 and 1584, a time of great turbulence in Scotland. The poems vigorously support the reformers, and display hostility to Mary, queen of Scots. There is outrage at the St Bartholomew's day massacre (1572); a lament for the assassinated Regent Moray (1570); an attack on Archbishop Hamilton, executed in 1571; and a scurrilous but amusing lampoon, *The Legend of the Bishop of St Andrew's Life* (1584). Several poems are signed openly; others hint at their authorship covertly, by an acrostic on the 'first letters of everie verse' (*Satirical Poems*, no. 8), or punning references to Sempill's name, used as a symbol for the simple, plain-speaking man. Another favourite satirical persona is 'Maddie of the Caill mercat', who signifies the opinion of the ordinary citizen. Three bawdy poems on women are ascribed to Sempill in the Bannatyne manuscript (1568). Some critics have also attributed to him the comedy *Philotus* and, more plausibly, the satirical work known as *Rob Stene's Dream*.

Sempill's poems circulated widely, both in manuscript and print; many were published as broadsides by the protestant printer Robert Lekprevik. English envoys sent several to their government in London (where they are preserved in the Public Record Office and the British Library). James Melvill, minister of Kilrenny, records that in 1570, as a child in Montrose, he much enjoyed Sempill's verses: from them he learned both of the state of the country, and also 'of the missours [measures] and cullors [rhetorical ornaments] of Scottes ryme' (*Autobiography and Diary*, 22–3). Although dismissed by some critics as crude and bigoted, Sempill's poems are metrically varied and rhetorically accomplished. Their pungent, combative style owes much to the 'flyting' tradition of earlier Scottish poets, such as William Dunbar and Sir David Lindsay.

On 9 June 1582 Sir Patrick Waus (Vans) was informed that Robert Sempill, 'the poyet' had been taken by 'men of weir' from Edinburgh to Dalkeith (*Correspondence of Sir Patrick Waus*, 247). Other accounts of this violent incident indicate that Sempill was imprisoned for several months by James, earl of Arran, who, with Esmé Stewart, duke of Lennox, had enormous influence over the young king. Sempill was variously accused of corresponding with Archibald, eighth earl of Angus, an extreme protestant, or of trafficking with the English in Berwick (Calderwood, 221; register of deeds, fols. 59 and 68*v*). Sempill survived this imprisonment, but the precise date of his death is uncertain. According to Thomas Dempster, an unreliable historian, he died in 1595 (*Historia ecclesiastica*, 602–3).

PRISCILLA J. BAWCUTT

Sources J. Cranstoun, ed., *Satirical poems of the time of the Reformation*, 2 vols. in 4 pts, STS, 20, 24, 28, 30 (1891–3) [incl. poems attributed to Sempill and biographical information] · register of deeds, NA Scot., vol. 23 · 'The diary of Robert Birrel … 1532 … to 1605', *Fragments of Scottish history* (1798) · A. J. Mill, *Mediaeval plays in Scotland* (1927), 106, 191–2 · C. R. Livingston, *British broadside ballads of the sixteenth century* (1991) · C. T. McInnes, ed., *Accounts of the treasurer of Scotland*, 12 (1970), 20, 51, 98, 140, 340 · J. D. Marwick, ed., *Extracts from the records of the burgh of Glasgow*, AD *1573–1642*, 1, Scottish Burgh RS, 11 (1876) · *The autobiography and diary of Mr James Melvill*, ed. R. Pitcairn, Wodrow Society (1842) · *Correspondence of Sir Patrick Waus of Barnbarroch, knight, 1540–1584*, ed. R. V. Agnew (1887) · D. Calderwood, *The history of the Kirk of Scotland*, ed. T. Thomson and D. Laing, 8 vols., Wodrow Society, 7 (1842–9), vol. 8 · *Thomae Dempsteri Historia ecclesiastica gentis Scotorum, sive, De scriptoribus Scotis*, ed. D. Irving, rev. edn, 1, Bannatyne Club, 21 (1829), 602–3 · *The Sempill ballates*, ed. T. G. Stevenson (1872)

Sempill, Robert (*d.* 1660x69). *See under* Sempill, Sir James (1566?–1626).

Sempill, Sir William (1546–1633), soldier, was probably the illegitimate son of Robert *Sempill, third Lord Sempill (*c.*1505–1573x6), nobleman. He spent most of his adult life in exile in Spain. Much of the information about his career comes from memorials that he gave to the Spanish government which deliberately shrouded or exaggerated his activities. Even his relationship to the Sempill family is unclear. He was certainly the uncle of Hugh *Sempill (1596–1654), the mathematician. Sempill may have been brought up in his father's native county, Renfrewshire.

Sempill began his career in the household of Mary, queen of Scots, and after her flight to England in 1568 offered his services to the Spanish government, apparently at her insistence. By 1573 he was well known in Spanish military circles but his petitions for military command probably met with rejection. He was an infantry captain fighting against Spain in the Low Countries by the early 1580s. On 25 March 1582 he took command of a Scottish company in Lier, a small but strategically important town between Antwerp and Brussels. He may have already decided to betray the Dutch when he took the commission. He was given a secret audience by Alexander Farnese, governor of the Low Countries, shortly before he did so. On the night of 1 August he joined Farnese's troops and led them into the town. With the element of surprise, it was quickly taken. Farnese rewarded Sempill with a grant of 1000 ducats and a gold chain. The capture of Lier was a small but significant step in the preparation for Farnese's brilliant successes in 1583–5, since it drove a wedge between Antwerp and Brussels.

Sempill was sent to Spain by Farnese in 1582 with a strong recommendation to the government. In Madrid he busied himself as an adviser on British and Dutch affairs, beginning a torrent of memorials advising the government on how to conduct its wars in the north. In 1587 he argued against sending the Armada, urging Philip II to wage economic warfare rather than take the risks involved in sending his great fleet. The king would not change his mind but recognized the force of Sempill's personality and decided to send him to Scotland to secure the neutrality or support of James VI.

Philip sent Sempill to the redoubtable Bernardino de Mendoza, ambassador in Paris and formerly ambassador in London, describing him as one of 'my Scottish servants' but warning that he needed to be closely supervised (Philip II to B. de Mendoza, 27 Nov 1587; *CSP Spain*, 1587–1603, no. 175, p. 171). Philip's senior adviser on foreign affairs, Juan de Idiáquez, confidently described Sempill as 'a man who may be trusted' (ibid., no. 194, p. 188). Sempill arrived in Paris at the beginning of December 1587 and impressed the ambassador with his 'zeal and steadfastness' (ibid., no. 259, p. 255). Mendoza sent him on to the Low Countries, where Farnese, now duke of Parma, recognized that Sempill could usefully serve a number of purposes. Most immediately he could provide an assessment of the numbers and strength of the Scottish Catholics. Parma hoped that, as a former servant of Mary, Sempill would be listened to when he urged the king to seek vengeance for his mother's blood. Parma also allowed himself to hope that Sempill would be able to raise a force of Catholic Scots to provide a diversion on the Anglo-Scottish frontier as he himself crossed the channel. Philip had the same expectation.

Sempill sailed from Dunkirk with Archibald Douglas, eighth earl of Angus and fifth earl of Morton, on 16 April 1588. They landed at Leith four days later. Sempill soon found that James was much more committed to the presbyterians than he had believed and that there was no hope of winning him to the Spanish side. His activities were watched carefully by both Scottish and English governments and he was arrested. He was released, apparently through the intercession of Catholic friends, but was almost immediately rearrested and placed under house arrest in Edinburgh. Parma received reports that he had been executed. Perhaps his presence was an embarrassment to James; at all events, Sempill once again escaped with suspicious ease. He made an attempt to meet the Armada as it sailed north—the only man, apparently, who voluntarily tried to board it as it headed off on its dreadful journey round the British Isles. Unsuccessful, he made his way back to the Low Countries, where he informed Parma that he had been waiting with a force of 2000 men in a suitable port for the Armada to arrive. No confirmation of this claim exists and it was probably significant that Parma refused to give Sempill further funding for his Scottish adventures.

Parma once again dispatched Sempill to Spain, where he settled down on the south coast, advising government officers on how to uncover the contraband activities of northern seamen in Andalusian ports. In 1593 he married María (*d.* 1646), daughter of Juan de Ledesma and his wife. The Ledesmas were an important family in the Spanish administration. Juan de Ledesma worked in the secretarial offices of the council of inquisition. The family had a reputation for bending the rules where profit was to be made and Sempill's marriage gave him good access to governmental circles. In 1597 he travelled to Madrid, where he urged the government to investigate rigorously the English, Irish, and French protestant captains who were trading in Spain under the guise of being Catholics, recommending that a few death penalties would bring a rapid end to such activities. The council of state acknowledged the seriousness of the problem and issued the first licences to search all English ships in order to find protestants trading as Catholics. Sempill himself was given authority to search ships along the entire southern coast and was assigned a salary, although he does not seem to have been given a formal position. A number of arrests were made on his authority.

In 1598 Sempill's stock rose still further at court when his cousin Robert Sempill, fourth Lord Sempill, was appointed as James's ambassador in Madrid. The two men worked closely together. Sempill's work also brought him into contact with the agents of the duke of Lerma, favourite of Philip III from his accession in 1598, and the owner of lucrative trading concessions on the southern coast. Sempill had access now to the very highest circles of government. In deciding whom to investigate and whom to arrest, he also had the right to decide which captains should go free, and he seems to have discreetly helped some of his compatriots. Perhaps here he was seeking favour with James, who was now all but certain to become the next king of England. If so, Sempill was playing both sides, for in June 1601 he strongly urged Philip III and the council of state to prevent James from winning the English throne. This was advice that the belligerent young king wanted to hear. Encouraged, Sempill flooded the government with proposals; he advised marriage between the Stewarts and the house of Savoy; he urged Philip to wage economic warfare; and he argued that the Dutch should be stopped from trading with Spain. In 1602 he was commissioned to go to the Low Countries to find out what he could about the intrigues for the English succession; nothing came of it, perhaps because he was too well known, perhaps because memories of the promptness with which he had been apprehended in 1588 raised doubts about his effectiveness. In 1603 Lerma personally authorized payment of Sempill's expenses.

With the coming of peace with England in 1604 Sempill's influence waned. He lived well enough in Madrid. In 1613 Philip gave him a house in recognition of his services to the crown; Sempill used it to endow a college for Catholic missionaries who were to be trained to return to Britain. The fall of Lerma in 1618 and the death of Philip in 1621 marked the end of his influence at court. He continued to bombard the government with projects—his last extant letter to the government dates from 1629—but he was too closely associated with the Lerma regime to win favour under Gasparo de Guzman, count-duke of Olivares, and was ignored. He died on 1 March 1633. His wife survived him by thirteen years; it is not known whether they had any children. PATRICK WILLIAMS

Sources Archivo General de Simancas, estado, 176, 624, 2029, 2034, 2035, 2138, 2144, 2224/2, 2234, 2309; 177, 178, 181, 182, 183, 186, 191, 840, 1734, 2764 · *CSP Spain, 1587–1603* · Real Academia de Historia, Madrid, D 34, fol. 148 · 'Pedro de Ledesma', 1625, Archivo Histórico Nacional ordenes militares, Madrid, Santiago 4409 · BL, Add. MS 28345, fol. 142r · G. Bentivollo, *Las guerras de Flandes desde la muerte del emperador Carlos V hasta la conclusión de la tregua de los doce años* (Antwerp, 1587), 244–5 · A. Carnero, *Historia de las guerras civiles, que ha avido en los estados de Flandes desdel año 1559 hasta el de 1609, y las causas de la rebelión de dichos estados* (Brussels, 1625), 173 · M. Alcocer y Martínez, *Consultas del consejo de estado 1600–06*, 2 vols. (Valladolid, 1930–32), vol. 1, pp. 161, 199 · D. Mathew and A. Mathew, 'William Semple's reports on Scotland in 1588 and 1610', *EngHR*, 41 (1926), 579–83 · A. J. Loomie, 'William Semple and Bristol's Andalucian trade, 1597–1598', *Spain and the early Stuarts, 1585–1655* (1996) · guerra antigua, 88, Archivo General de Simancas · N. Kamen, *Philip of Spain* (1997) · P. C. Allen, *Philip III and the pax hispanica, 1598–1621: the failure of the grand strategy* (2000)
Archives Scottish Catholic Archives, Edinburgh, letters and papers

Sempill, William Francis Forbes-, nineteenth Lord Sempill (1893–1965), engineer and aviator, was born on 24 September 1893 at Devonport, the eldest in the family of two sons and two daughters of John Forbes-Sempill, ninth baronet and eighteenth Lord Sempill (1863–1934), a soldier and landowner of Craigievar Castle, Aberdeen, and his wife, Gwendolen Emily Mary (*d.* 1944), the elder daughter of Herbert ap Roger of Kington St Michael, Wiltshire. He was educated at Eton College (E. W. Stone's house) and then from 1910 to 1913 served an engineering apprenticeship in the workshops of Rolls-Royce Ltd at Derby.

When war was declared in August 1914 Sempill—who held the courtesy title master of Sempill but was always known as Bill to his friends—joined the Royal Flying Corps (RFC) as an engineer second-lieutenant at Farnborough, and learned to fly at the Central Flying School at Upavon. He obtained the Royal Aero Club aviator certificate no. 922 on 9 September 1914. Combining engineering with flying duties, he transferred from the RFC to the Royal Naval Air Service in January 1916 with the rank of flight commander, and on 1 April 1918 to the newly formed Royal Air Force as a lieutenant-colonel. He was then promoted colonel. He retired from the RAF in June 1919.

In June 1918, when Sir Sefton Brancker led a two-man royal aircraft commission of Great Britain to the United States with Sir Henry Fowler, chief of munitions production, to advise on aircraft development and production, Sempill went as personal assistant and technical adviser. He learned much about America and even more about how to conduct a mission—which stood him in good stead when, in 1921, he was invited to lead a technical mission to Japan to set up an imperial Japanese naval air service. As a result the Japanese were equipped with British aircraft, trained by British pilots, and an aircraft factory was built, initially staffed by British design and production teams. Ironically it laid the foundations for Japanese naval air operations twenty years later. Sempill's success in Japan led to his being invited to head similar missions successively to Greece, Sweden, Norway, Chile, Brazil, and Argentina and to be awarded numerous foreign decorations.

Back in England in 1924 Sempill began twelve years of enthusiastic flying as an unofficial ambassador for British aviation at home and overseas. Flying a succession of light aeroplanes he competed—without success—in the king's cup air races of every year from 1924 to 1930. He used light aeroplanes consistently to make weekend visits to friends, in 1925 flew himself to Berlin to lecture, and in 1926 flew in eight hours fourteen minutes from Land's End to John o' Groats in a De Havilland Moth.

Sempill had joined the Royal Aeronautical Society in 1917; in 1926 he was elected chairman of its council, and from 1927 until 1930 he was the society's president. His successor, Richard Fairey, said of him in October 1930: 'Of all the presidents I have served Sempill must stand out as one of the greatest. Thanks to his vigour the society is now immensely stronger than when he first took over.' Out of 137 meetings during his term of office he presided over 135.

Sempill was active in numerous other aeronautical interests—on the Aeronautical Research Council, on the councils of the Air League and the Navy League, as deputy chairman, and then chairman, of the London chamber of commerce between 1931 and 1935, as president of the British Gliding Association from 1933 to 1942, and as president of the Institution of Production Engineers from 1935 to 1937. In 1930, 1931, and 1932 he arranged for the German airship *Graf Zeppelin* to fly to England to pick up passengers, first at Cardington and then at Hanworth for air cruises. Among his flights abroad were Stag Lane to Dublin and back just before Christmas 1925, Norway to Aberdeen in 1930, Australia and back in his Puss Moth G-ABJU in 1934, and in 1936 non-stop from Croydon to Berlin in eleven hours in a British Aircraft Corporation Drone ultralight aeroplane—and non-stop on the return in nine hours with a tail wind.

Through all of this Sempill lived an active social life centred around the Royal Aeronautical Society and its leading lights of the 1920s and 1930s—Lord Wakefield, Sir Sefton Brancker, Richard Fairey, Frederick Handley Page, and Peter Ackland.

Sempill succeeded his father as Lord Sempill on 28 February 1934, and was a representative peer for Scotland from 1935 to 1963. On 20 February 1919 he married Eileen Marion (*d.* 1935), the only daughter of Sir John Lavery, RA, and formerly the wife of Sir James Dickinson. They had two daughters, Ann and June, the latter being killed while driving an ambulance in Kensington during an air raid in 1941. After fighting tuberculosis for many years Lady Sempill died on 18 July 1935. On 1 February 1941 Sempill married Cecilia Alice (*d.* 1984), the elder daughter of Bertram Edward Dunbar-Kilburn, of Sandford St Martin, Oxfordshire, with whom he had three daughters. Sempill rejoined the naval air service in 1939 and retired in 1941. He died in Edinburgh on 30 December 1965 and was succeeded by his eldest daughter, Ann Moira (1920–1995).

A very Scottish, thick-set figure of medium height—he always wore full Scottish evening dress on all suitable occasions—practical, stubborn, and convivial, Sempill was an enthusiastic propagandist for aviation and 'flying for fun'. He was a sound engineer, an excellent cook who, whenever possible, baked his own bread, and a successful amateur farmer at Dedham in Essex and Craigievar Castle, Aberdeen. Sempill was excellent company and made a host of friends throughout his life. Among his publications was *The Air and the Plain Man* (1931).

PETER G. MASEFIELD, *rev.*

Sources J. L. Pritchard, *Journal of the Royal Aeronautical Society*, 70 (1966), 543–4 • *The Times* (31 Dec 1965) • personal knowledge (1981) • Burke, *Peerage* (1959) • Burke, *Peerage* (1999) • *CCI* (1967)
Archives Sci. Mus., papers, corresp., and photographs
Likenesses portrait, Royal Aeronautical Society, London
Wealth at death £24,379 8*s*.: confirmation, 7 Dec 1967, *CCI*

Semple, David (1808–1878), antiquary, was born at Townhead, Paisley, on 21 August 1808. Educated in the local grammar school, he trained in a lawyer's office before settling in business on his own account in Paisley, and was considered an able conveyancer. He was long the agent for the Liberals of the burgh. He was elected a fellow of the Society of Antiquaries of Scotland. He died at Paisley on 23 December 1878.

Semple's chief works—mainly dealing with local history—are: *Poll-Tax Rolls of Renfrewshire of 1695* (1862), *St Mirin* (1872), and *Barons and Barony of Renfrewshire* (1876). He also prepared a complete edition of Tannahill's *Poems*, with a memoir and notes (1870).

T. W. BAYNE, *rev.* H. C. G. MATTHEW

Sources Irving, *Scots.* • R. Brown, *Paisley poets: with brief memoirs of them and selections from their poetry*, 2 vols. (1889–90)
Wealth at death £13,258 17*s*. 6*d*.: confirmation, 6 Aug 1879, *CCI*

Semple, George (*c.*1700–1782), architect and engineer, claimed to have had modest origins—'my father … was a workman about the year 1675' (Semple, 79)—and little formal education, but he seems to have been descended from a well-connected line of Ulster-Scottish clergymen. He served an apprenticeship as a bricklayer, and was admitted a freeman of Dublin in 1735. By 1743—when transacting property business in Armagh—he was describing himself as an architect. He had at least two brothers: Edward (*d.* 1787), who was apprenticed to him, became a plasterer and architect, while John (*d.* 1784), also a plasterer, turned to brick and stone contracting.

Semple must have been married by 1740, but his wife's name has not been traced. In 1754 he acquired a site on Queen Street in the Oxmantown area of Dublin, where he built a number of houses, including his own residence. Semple also built three houses on Capel Street: a pair for Dr Edward Leigh, constructed next to the old mansion of the Conolly family in 1751–2, and another for Arthur Newburgh. Leigh was treasurer of St Patrick's Cathedral, where Semple designed and erected the 103 foot steeple in 1749. In the same year Semple built Newbridge, a country house at Donabate, co. Dublin, for the archbishop of Dublin, Charles Cobbe. His other country houses included Ramsfort, co. Wexford, for Colonel Abel Ram (1751; des. 1798) and Headfort, co. Meath, for the first earl of Bective (from 1760), a property which could boast interiors completed by Robert Adam in the 1770s. He also designed and built St Patrick's Hospital, Dublin (1749–57), erected with a legacy of Dean Swift.

Semple's best-known work was Essex Bridge (1753–5; replaced 1872–5) across the Liffey, which although visually similar to Labelye's Westminster Bridge (1739–50), was constructed by the coffer-dam method rather than the more usual caissons. The government awarded him £500 for his services after he lodged a petition in 1761. Semple described and illustrated the project in his expansive *Treatise on Building in Water* (1776), which he later reissued in 1780 with an appended paper entitled 'Hibernia's free trade, or, A plan for the general improvement of Ireland'. Throughout his career Semple attempted to interest public authorities in unsolicited projects, some stillborn examples of which he published. His proposal for a replacement for Ormonde Bridge in Dublin in 1776 was grounded on necessity, but other schemes were grandiose and impractical, such as the realignment of the mouth of the Liffey (1755), which he submitted to the ballast office in 1762, his plans for a 'spacious and commodious harbour for the Downs in England', and a system of 120 foot wide roads running the length and breadth of Ireland.

Semple died at Queen Street in April 1782. The principal beneficiaries of his estate were his daughter Elizabeth, widow of Thomas Keating, a member of a Clonmel brewing family, and her children. The architectural succession passed in time to John Semple's son John (1763–1840), who started out as a bricklayer and builder, and grandson John (1801–1882), who together as John Semple & Son were architects to the board of first fruits for the province of Dublin (1824–32), in which capacity they designed a number of quirky and inventive churches. John, a member of Dublin corporation, served as its unsalaried architect from 1823 to 1829, when he was succeeded by his son, who left office in 1832. FREDERICK O'DWYER

Sources G. Semple, *A treatise on building in water* (1776) • [W. Papworth], ed., *The dictionary of architecture*, 11 vols. (1853–92) • E. Harris and N. Savage, *British architectural books and writers, 1556–1785* (1990) • T. Ruddock, *Arch bridges and their builders, 1735–1835* (1979) • G. Daly, 'George Semple's charts of Dublin Bay, 1762', *Proceedings of the Royal Irish Academy*, 93C (1993), 81–105 • C. Allen, 'The church architecture of John Semple and Son', MArchSc diss., University College, Dublin, 1995 • J. W. De Courcy, *The Liffey in Dublin* (Dublin, 1996) • P. O'Keefe and T. Simington, *Irish stone bridges: history and heritage* (1991) • J. Harris, *Headfort House and Robert Adam: drawings from the collection of Mr. and Mrs. Paul Mellon* (1973) [exhibition catalogue, Heinz Gallery of the Royal Institute of British Architects, London, 2 April – 1 June 1973] • memorials of deeds, Registry of Deeds, Dublin • J. B. Leslie, ed., 'Index of clergy', typescript, Representative Church Body Library, Dublin • Betham's abstracts of wills, NA Ire. • R. Lascelles, ed., *Liber munerum publicorum Hiberniae … or, The establishments of Ireland*, 2 vols. [1824–30], 57 • *Faulkner's Dublin Journal* (13–16 April 1782)

Semple, James George (*b.* 1759, *d.* in or after 1799), adventurer, who also passed under the names Semple-Lisle, Maxwell, Harrod, and Grant, was born at Irvine, Ayrshire. He was the son of James Semple, formerly an exciseman, who eventually laid claim to the extinct title of Viscount Lisle. In 1776 he was serving in America, where he was taken prisoner, but was released in 1777 and returned to England. He then became involved with the novelist Mrs Eliza Gooch. Marrying a goddaughter of the notorious Elizabeth Chudleigh, duchess of Kingston, he accompanied the latter to the continent. There he claims to have accompanied Frederick the Great during his campaign of 1778, to have been introduced to the Empress Catherine of Russia, to have accompanied Prince Potyomkin to the Crimea, and to have designed a uniform for the Russian army. Upon returning to England in 1784 he was arrested for obtaining goods by false pretences, and on 2 September 1786 was sentenced to seven years' transportation. Released on condition of quitting England, he moved to Paris, where he passed himself off as a member of General Berruyer's staff, and as witnessing in that capacity the execution of Louis XVI. He returned to England in time to avoid arrest, and on 18 February 1795 was again sentenced to transportation, this time for defrauding tradesmen. Disappointed in his hopes of pardon, he stabbed himself in Newgate in December 1796, when about to be shipped for Botany Bay, and subsequently tried to starve himself to death. He recovered, and in 1797 was dispatched in the *Lady Jane Shore* bound for Australia. On 21 August 1797 a mutiny broke out, the captain having disregarded Semple's warning of impending riot. Semple, with several others, was allowed to leave the ship in a boat. He eventually landed in South America, and, after many adventures, reached Tangier, where he surrendered, and was sent back to England. He was committed to Tothill Fields prison, and at the time of publishing his autobiography, *The Life of Major J. G. Semple-Lisle*, in 1799, was still confined there. Nothing further is known of him.

J. G. ALGER, *rev.* HEATHER SHORE

Sources J. G. Semple, *The life of Major J. G. Semple-Lisle: containing a faithful narrative of his alternative vicissitudes of splendour and misfortune* (1799) • *Memoirs of the northern imposter, or Prince of Swindlers: being a faithful narrative of the adventures and deceptions of James George Semple* (1786) • *The northern hero: being a faithful narrative of the life, adventures and deceptions of James George Semple*, new edn (1786) • A. de E. Taunay, *Visitantes do Brasil colonial* (1933) • E. S. Gooch, *The life of Mrs. Gooch, written by herself*, 3 vols. in 1 (1792) • *Annual Register* (1796), 46–7 • *Annual Register* (1798), 60 • *GM*, 1st ser., 66 (1796), 1112
Archives NL Scot., Minto MSS, letters to Hugh Elliott • Yale U., Beinecke L., letters to James Boswell and others
Likenesses Harding, stipple, pubd 1799, NPG • Barlow, engraving (after portrait; mentioned by Bromley) • engraving (after drawing, taken when on trial at the Old Bailey, 2 Sept 1786), repro. in *The northern hero*

Semple, Robert (1777–1816), traveller and governor of the Hudson's Bay Company, the son of Robert Semple and Anne Greenlaw, was born at Boston, Massachusetts, on 26 February 1777. His parents were loyalists and returned to England about the time of the American War of Independence. He became a merchant for London firms and travelled widely, recording his impressions and adventures in short plain narratives which were well received. He was in Cape Colony in 1802, and published an account of his travels in 1803. In 1803 he was back in London, and on 26 June 1805 he left for a journey through Spain and Italy to Naples and thence to Smyrna and Constantinople, of which an account was published in 1807. In 1808 and 1809 he made a second journey in Portugal and Spain, eventually going to Gibraltar and Tangier; this he recorded in a book of 1810. That year he travelled in the West Indies and Brazil, and in a book of 1812 described Caracas, Venezuela, at the beginning of the rebellion against Spain. His adventurous journey in the rear of the allied armies from Hamburg by Berlin to Göteborg, in the course of which he was taken for an American spy by Lord Cathcart and arrested, was described in 1814.

In 1815 Semple was appointed governor of the Hudson's Bay Company territories through the influence of Lord Selkirk, although it is not clear what recommended him for the post. After leaving England in June 1815 he arrived at the Red River settlement in November to find that it had been destroyed by the North West Company. Both companies were trying to destroy the supply lines of the other and win the support of the local métis (mixed-race) population. The cause of the Hudson's Bay Company was not helped by disagreement between Semple and Colin Robertson, an experienced Hudson's Bay Company man, which resulted in Robertson's leaving the area in June 1816. Without Robertson's advice, Semple misjudged an encounter on 19 June 1816 at Seven Oaks between himself and a party of Hudson's Bay Company men on the one hand and a party of métis traders on the other. Having realized too late the need for heavy arms, Semple and about twenty others of his party were killed in a skirmish. The North West Company was later shown to have rewarded some of those involved in the killings. The massacre demonstrated the need for firm action to halt the feud and ultimately led to the amalgamation of the two companies in 1821. Semple's death was due in large measure to his appointment to a post for which he was unqualified. C. A. HARRIS, *rev.* ELIZABETH BAIGENT

Sources *DCB*, vol. 5 • J. M. Gray, *Lord Selkirk of Red River* (1963) • C. Martin, *Lord Selkirk's work in Canada* (1916) • *GM*, 1st ser., 86/2 (1816), 454 • A. Amos, ed., *Report of trials … relative to the destruction of the earl of Selkirk's settlement on the Red River* (1820)
Archives NA Canada

Sempringham, Gilbert of. *See* Gilbert of Sempringham (1083–1189).

Semprini, (Fernando Riccardo) Alberto (1908–1990), pianist and conductor, was born on 27 March 1908 in Bath, the second of three sons (there were no daughters) of Arturo Riccardo Fernando Semprini, musician, from Rimini, Italy, and his wife, Elizabeth Tilley, opera singer, from Dudley, Worcestershire. The family settled in Bath until Alberto was nine, when his father, a horn player, was appointed librarian to La Scala opera house, Milan. The boy was intensely musical and won a state scholarship to the Conservatorio Verdi to study piano, composition, and conducting. When he was only sixteen Arturo Toscanini, chief conductor of La Scala, auditioned him for the fiendishly difficult orchestral piano part in Igor Stravinsky's ballet *Petrushka* and gave him the job.

On his vacations Semprini played the piano on transatlantic liners, and while in New York was enthralled by jazz groups and the popular concert orchestra of André Kostelanetz. He discovered he could play this sort of repertoire far better than most classically trained pianists, and this seems to have proved a decisive influence in shaping his career. Another consideration was his marriage in Italy in 1931 to Brunilde Regarbagnati and the birth of three sons.

Semprini left the Conservatorio in 1929 with a doctorate of music and, though he occasionally conducted at La Scala and elsewhere, the piano was his first love. In the 1930s he and another Italian pianist, Bormioli, toured Europe as a popular piano duo, and later he formed his own rhythm orchestra in Italy, with which he made records, broadcasted, and played in a number of musical films. The outbreak of war in 1939 halted his career. He had angered the fascist authorities by playing western music against their orders; and though he had dual Italian and British citizenship, both passports were confiscated, obliging the family to keep a low profile. When eventually the allies advanced into southern Italy he managed to get to Rome, where he volunteered for the Entertainments National Service Association (ENSA), and gave many front-line concerts, his piano on the back of an army truck.

Among Semprini's troop audiences was the actor Michael Brennan, who offered to be his manager if he ever came to England. But immediately after the war he went to work and study in Spain, where he fell in love with a young Spanish dancer, María de la Concepción Consuelo García Cardoso, daughter of Generoso José García Inglesias, house painter. Sadly his first marriage had not survived the stresses of a musician's peripatetic life. He took Consuelo to England in 1949 and after his divorce in 1952 married her in the same year. There were two sons of this happy and enduring union.

(Fernando Riccardo) Alberto Semprini (1908–1990), by unknown photographer

When they arrived in England Brennan secured Semprini a BBC audition. He was immediately engaged to play in a series of fifteen-minute programmes in the style of the recently deceased Charlie Kunz, a popular pianist whose German name had caused public resentment. The style of Semprini quickly took over, pleased the listeners, and led to a short programme with orchestra, for which he chose, arranged, and orchestrated all the music. It was entitled *Semprini Serenade*, and was a subtle blend of classical pieces interspersed with selections from theatre and film music and the work of popular composers such as George Gershwin, impeccably performed and introduced quietly and economically from the piano. Soon the programme stretched to an hour; it remained on the air for twenty-five years.

Semprini appeared rarely on television, but was a great favourite from 1952 in the surviving variety theatres, sharing the bill with rising stars such as Peter Sellers and Harry Secombe, and touring the country in a caravan, pulled by an ancient ambulance, that contained a piano and a long table on which he worked out his orchestrations. Later he gave many concerts with a more classical content both in Britain and abroad. Whenever possible he drove his beloved Jaguar home through the night to *L'Espérance*, a sailing ship converted into a houseboat at West Mersea, Essex, where the family lived happily for many years.

Some critics regretted that Semprini did not pursue a more serious musical career. Certainly he could have performed at the very top of his profession, but he was master of his genre and millions of radio listeners and concert-goers loved his music. In 1972 he was made an officer of the order of St John and he was appointed OBE in 1983—both recognitions of his considerable efforts for charity. He was a tall, dark, dignified man with fine features, always immaculately dressed, but his gravity was often dispelled by a strong sense of humour and a charming smile. He looked Italian, but he was an Englishman at heart. He died in Brixham, Devon (where his home was 18 Windmill Close), from Alzheimer's disease, on 19 January 1990, and was survived by his second wife. His remains were cremated at Colchester, Essex, and his ashes were scattered in the sea off West Mersea.

IAN WALLACE, *rev.*

Sources *The Times* (20 Jan 1990) · *The Independent* (22 Jan 1990) · personal knowledge (1996) · private information (1996) [family; K. Davey] · *CGPLA Eng. & Wales* (1990)
Archives SOUND BL NSA
Likenesses photograph, Camera Press Ltd, London [*see illus.*]
Wealth at death under £100,000: probate, 9 July 1990, *CGPLA Eng. & Wales*

Sen, Keshub Chunder (1838–1884), religious reformer, second son of Pyarimohan (*d.* 1848/9) and Saradasundari (*née* Das) Sen, was born in Calcutta on 19 November 1838. His grandfather, Ramkamal Sen, *diwan* of both the Bengal Bank and the mint at Calcutta, was among the luminaries of the nineteenth-century Bengal renaissance. Pyarimohan, his second son, succeeded him at the mint. Keshub's father died when the boy was ten, but the family was prosperous and he grew up in the lap of luxury. An early influence which shaped his spiritual development was the deep devotionalism of his family environment.

He was educated at the Hindoo College as well as at the Metropolitan College. When the former was reorganized as Hindu School and Presidency College, Keshub went to Presidency College, where he studied until 1858. There he was the chief organizer of the British India Society, a very influential discussion group where he learned his first lessons in oratory for which he was later to become famous. The young men of the Sen family also set up in 1856 the Colootola Branch School, where children from less fortunate homes were provided with regular instruction free of charge. Also in 1856 he married Jaganmohini, the nine-year-old daughter of Chandranath Majumdar. He entered the married state in a puritanical mood, committed to self-restraint. His spiritual aspirations were first expressed in the founding of the Goodwill Fraternity, in which a few friends got together to discuss matters of the spirit. This led to the next step, in which he lost faith in the

Keshub Chunder Sen (1838–1884), by London Stereoscopic Co.

idolatrous rituals of his ancestral faith, and joined the theistic Brahmo Samaj, revived and reorganized by Debendranath Tagore. He left the family home with his wife and they went to live with the Tagores for some time in 1859. Debendranath set up the Calcutta Brahmo Samaj on an independent footing and Sen became one of its secretaries. He gave up his job at the Bank of Bengal in 1861 to devote himself to the work of the Samaj on a full-time basis.

Welfare activities became a new plank in the Samaj's programme under his leadership. Relief work during the malaria epidemic of 1861–2, finance to the famine stricken in north-western India, propaganda in favour of women's education, and the founding of a model educational institution, the Calcutta College, were among his major initiatives at this time. He also became the managing editor and in 1865 the proprietor of the Brahmo mouthpiece, the *Indian Mirror*. He started going out on tours of religious propaganda from 1861 onwards. In 1864 he went to Madras and Bombay, where he met Dadabhai Naoroji. The Maharashtrian leader M. G. Ranade helped to found the Prarthana Samaj ('prayer society') inspired by Sen's preaching. Sen's tours were inspired by a pan-Indian ideology and he paved the way for political initiatives inspired by the same ideal.

His reformist zeal, especially his attempt to establish an association of Brahmo representatives from all parts of India, Pratinidhi-Sabha, to run the society on a democratic basis, created tensions with Tagore. Eventually Sen and his friends left the organization and set up the Brahmo Samaj of India (Bharatvarshiya Brahmosamaj) in 1866. This emphasis on a pan-Indian identity became a hallmark of all his activities. He went on a propaganda tour of northern India in 1867 and on his return talked of the need to institute a system of active co-operation among educated Indians of all presidencies and provinces, nearly twenty years before the founding of the Indian National Congress. The Bharatvarshiya Brahmomandir ('Brahmo temple of India') was established in 1869 and it recognized the equal rights of men and women. Sen's efforts to legalize inter-caste marriage and the Brahmo marriage ritual, which avoided idolatrous elements, led to the Marriage Act of 1872.

Sen went to England in 1870 with five of his brethren in faith. There he established extensive contacts with scholars, religious leaders, and politicians, including W. E. Gladstone. He was also received by Queen Victoria, and returned to India full of enthusiasm for British rule in India and an emotional loyalty towards the queen. He was also keen to secure for India some of the benefits of the modern civilization he had witnessed in England, and set up the Indian Reform Association with this end in view. It had a five-fold agenda which emphasized education for women, craft schools, the education of the working classes, cheap periodicals for the poor, and agitation to fight the widespread evil of alcohol, and also raised funds to assist people in need. People from all communities assisted in the effort. Mary Carpenter, who went to India in 1866, and Annette Ackroyd (later Mrs Beveridge) helped in the attempt to spread education. The Bengal Social Science Association, partly inspired by Ackroyd, became a forum for propaganda in favour of women's rights. A journal for women, *Bamabodhini Patrika*, was one of the products of Sen's efforts. His loyalist concerns led to the foundation of the Albert Institute and Albert Hall on College Street, Calcutta, in 1876: its object was to counteract the growing animosity between the ruler and the ruled.

In 1872 he met Swami Dayananda Saraswati, the revivalist preacher, and his friendship with the mystic Ramakrishna Paramahansa from 1875 onwards profoundly influenced his spiritual development. His growing inclination towards an eclectic faith was partly induced by these encounters. But his conservatism and somewhat dictatorial ways led to tensions with his younger followers like Sibnath Shastri, who wanted to run the Samaj on truly democratic lines, and who had views on women's freedom more advanced than those of Sen. The crunch came when Sen agreed to give the elder of his two daughters, then aged thirteen, in marriage to the prince of Cooch Behar, in violation of the Samaj's principles. A section of his followers seceded and formed a new sect, Sadharan Brahmo Samaj. Sen moved more and more in the direction of an eclectic and emotional mysticism, eventually founding a new movement called Nababidhan ('new dispensation').

His public speeches had for many years been an important influence on the youth of Calcutta, but towards the closing years of his life he lost much of his appeal, in part because his credibility had been damaged by the Cooch Behar marriage. But there were more important reasons. His emphasis on loyalty to the British was ceasing to provide an acceptable ideology for the educated young, who were moving towards a more radical outlook and the ideal of independence. Keshub Chunder Sen died in Calcutta on 8 January 1884, by which time he had few followers left.

TAPAN RAYCHAUDHURI

Sources P. C. Mazoomdar, *Life of Keshab Chunder Sen* (1930) · B. Bandyopadhyay, *Keshabchandra Sen* (1958) · S. Sengupta and A. Basu, eds., *Samsad Bangali charitabhidhan* (1975)
Archives Office of Nababidham, Calcutta, India
Likenesses London Stereoscopic Co., photograph, NPG [*see illus.*] · portrait, National Library of India, Calcutta

Senán mac Geirrcinn (*fl.* 6th cent.). *See under* Munster, saints of (*act. c.*450–*c.*700).

Senanayake, Don Stephen (1884–1952), prime minister of Ceylon, was born in Colombo, Ceylon, on 20 October 1884, the youngest of the three sons of Mudaliyar Don Spater Senanayake and his wife, Elizabeth Catherine. His eldest brother was groomed for public life and sent to an English university. Senanayake was to manage the family's estates and attended St Thomas's College, Colombo. There he made his mark, not as a scholar but as a keen sportsman and ardent cricketer. He remained a loyal supporter of his old school and became a member of its governing body. After a short period as a clerk in the surveyor-general's office he left to manage the family coconut and rubber estates and their interests in plumbago mines. His energy in jungle clearing earned him the nickname Jungle John. In 1909 he married Emily Maud Dunuwille (*d.* 1964), with whom he had two sons.

In 1912 his brother F. R. Senanayake was active in organizing a temperance campaign in which D. S. Senanayake made his first appearance as a public speaker. He is reported as having no great command of either Sinhalese or English at that time. In the riots of 1915 he was placed under arrest for a few weeks. The aftermath of the riots led to the formation in 1917 of the Ceylon Reform League which in 1919 was merged in the Ceylon National Congress, of which Senanayake was a founder member. Pressure for constitutional reform in 1924 culminated in the grant of an unofficial majority in the legislative council, and in that year Senanayake was returned unopposed as one of three members representing the Western Province. As secretary to the unofficial members he gained much practical experience of the working of the government machine. In 1928 the report of the constitutional commission under Lord Donoughmore received a very mixed reception in Ceylon. Sir Herbert Stanley, the governor, was lukewarm; the professional politicians were indignant. Many of them had been to English universities and were looking for constitutional advance on the Westminster model. Instead they felt they were being fobbed off with a London county council form of administration. They also felt that the introduction of universal suffrage, sponsored by Drummond Shiels, would lead to gross abuses. Senanayake, with his shrewd common sense and much courage, took the line that half a loaf was better

Don Stephen Senanayake (1884–1952), by Vandyk, 1949

than no bread. At the end of 1929 the legislative council accepted the report by a majority of only two, Senanayake and Baron Jayatilake voting for it. In 1931 Senanayake was elected unopposed as member for Minuwangoda, unanimously elected chairman of the executive committee of agriculture, and appointed minister of agriculture. He was thus in a position to give practical proof of his determination to raise the standard of living of the Ceylon peasant, whose interests he had passionately at heart. He had big ideas and was in a hurry to carry them out. He was apt to be suspicious of criticism of his schemes, but once he was satisfied that it was intended to be constructive and not obstructive it left no abiding rancour. He was no respecter of persons, but the civil servant who won his confidence could count on his support. The Land Development Act and the irrigation schemes which he revived or initiated were a lasting tribute to his achievements.

A clash in 1940 between the governor and the board of ministers over the action of the inspector-general of police in challenging the orders of Jayatilake, home minister, resulted in the ministers, led by Senanayake, resigning from office. Although the breach was subsequently healed, the entry of Japan into the war in December 1941 brought Ceylon within the danger zone. In these circumstances Admiral Sir Geoffrey Layton was appointed commander-in-chief with responsibility for defence, while Sir Andrew Caldecott remained titular governor in charge of the civil administration. A war council was established under the presidency of the commander-in-chief, of which the governor, all the ministers, and the civil defence commissioner, Oliver Goonetilleke, were members. Jayatilake became Ceylon representative in India and was succeeded in the leadership of the state council (1942) by the more forceful Senanayake.

The demand for dominion status continued unabated, and in 1943 the British government issued a statement that the post-war re-examination of the constitution would be 'directed towards the grant to Ceylon of full responsible government under the Crown in all matters of internal civil administration'. This declaration, while it was regarded as a personal triumph for Senanayake, became the subject of much controversy, but on the strength of it the ministers, with the assistance of Ivor Jennings, prepared a draft order in council and submitted it to the British government in February 1944, urging that it should be considered at once and not await the end of the war. The government appointed another commission under Lord Soulbury; but the ministers decided officially to boycott it and withdraw their own draft. Thanks to the wisdom of Senanayake and the wiles of Sir Oliver Goonetilleke, however, the commission was courteously received and enabled to obtain a reasonable cross-section of local opinion. Senanayake was then invited to London to discuss the commission's report. His position was delicate. He had co-operated with the commission in Ceylon, but as its recommendations fell short of full dominion status he knew that they would be bitterly attacked by his political opponents, and he might even lose the support of some of his own party. He therefore continued to press officially for dominion status, while being personally prepared to accept something less if he could satisfy his critics that he had done his best. This was reflected in the terms of the motion which he moved in the council in November 1945. It accepted the Soulbury report by fifty-one votes to three. But the motion was very nearly never tabled at all, for in London Senanayake had gained the impression, rightly or wrongly, that the new Labour government was prepared to grant full dominion status. He felt he had been duped and returned to Ceylon a very angry man.

When at the end of 1946 Burma was offered independence inside or outside the Commonwealth Senanayake returned to the attack. In the light of the new situation the governor, Sir Henry Moore, gave his wholehearted support. Sir Oliver Goonetilleke was chosen to press Ceylon's claims in London; eventually the British government bowed to the inevitable and on 4 February 1948 Ceylon became independent. Senanayake, who had been sworn in as prime minister of the colonial state council, was resworn as the first prime minister of independent Ceylon and minister of defence and external affairs.

His tenure as prime minister was short, for he died in Galle Face Green, Colombo, on 22 March 1952 as the result of a fall from his horse. However, he established the political party that emerged from the Ceylon National Congress, the United National Party, as a major force in Sri Lankan politics. He also was crucial in making policy decisions which would set precedents for future governments. One of his personal projects was the colonization of the dry zone of eastern and central Ceylon. He oversaw the establishment of the first colonization scheme, the Gal Oya project in Amparai district. His vision was to build irrigation tanks that would allow settlers to farm the largely uninhabited jungles. Later governments would expand on his modest scheme and resettle more than 1 million Sri Lankans.

Senanayake inspired popular confidence by his personal integrity and powers of leadership. He was a big man, both physically and in his approach to the problems which confronted him. Although a devout Buddhist he was tolerant of the religious susceptibilities of others. No one suggested that he coveted power for his own personal aggrandizement: he wanted it for the accomplishment of the schemes which were so near his heart. He hoped to build up the United Party as representative of a Ceylonese nationhood working for the improvement of local conditions regardless of caste, creed, or race. Although he could castigate his opponents in debate, they bore him no ill will, as he would meet them on the most friendly terms outside the chamber and was always ready to listen to complaints. Perhaps one of the best tributes to his memory was made by one of his most implacable political opponents: 'I have differed from him bitterly and even violently on most political issues. But never once had I an occasion to falter in my regard and respect for him. He was indeed a political foe worthy of our steel.'

The elder of Senanayake's two sons, Dudley Shelton, after serving under his father as minister of agriculture, succeeded him for a short time as prime minister (1952–3) and returned to office again in March–April 1960 and in 1965. Senanayake's wife survived him.

HENRY MOORE, *rev.* R. C. OBERST

Sources I. Jennings, *The constitution of Ceylon* (1949) · C. J. Jeffries, *Ceylon: the path to independence* (1962) · J. Jupp, *Sri Lanka: Third World democracy* (1978) · C. R. De Silva, *Sri Lanka: a history* (New York, 1988) · private information (1971) · personal knowledge (1971)
Archives University of Peradeniya, Sri Lanka | FILM BFI NFTVA, current affairs footage · BFI NFTVA, news footage · IWM FVA, actuality footage
Likenesses Vandyk, photograph, 1949, NPG [*see illus.*]

Senatus Bravonius. *See* Worcester, Senatus of (*d.* 1207).

Senchán Torpéist (*fl.* 6th–7th cent.), Gaelic poet, is not commemorated by a contemporary annalistic reference. However, he is associated with Guaire Aidne (*d.* 663), Uí Fhiachrach king of Connacht, and many historians have imagined that he might have had genuine links with that king's court. Furthermore, it has been argued that an early Leinster genealogical poem, ascribed to him, may be his work. The evidence for his career is otherwise non-existent.

Despite this, Senchán is an important literary figure, alleged to have been chief poet of Ireland. He appears as the main protagonist in the various stories associated with the finding of the Irish epic, *Táin bó Cuailnge* ('cattle-Raid of Cuailnge'). The earlier, possibly originally ninth-century, versions describe how Senchán, on his own initiative or on the insistence of Guaire, calls the poets of Ireland together to recite the *Táin*. The poets only know scraps, however, for the *Táin* has been exchanged for knowledge of the *Culmen*, an Irish name for the *Etymologiae* of Isidore of Seville (570–636). In one version Senchán's son, Muirgein, makes an incantation at the grave of the dead pagan hero Fergus mac Róig. Fergus duly appears and recites the *Táin*, giving an eye-witness account. Another version describes how Senchán fasts against the dead saints, Brendan of Clonfert (*d.* 577?) and Ciarán of Clonmacnoise (*d.* 549?). Ciarán advises him, through a clerical proxy, to visit Fergus's grave and recite a poem there. Senchán does this, with the same result as in the first account.

These stories proved popular and by the eleventh century had been considerably expanded to incorporate the relationship of Guaire to his uterine brother, the saintly hermit Marbán. The poet–collector Senchán was transformed into the leader of a *tromdám*, 'a burdensome company', of poets, who make inroads into Guaire's legendary hospitality. Marbán's revenge is to impel Senchán to seek the *Táin* in reparation for his behaviour. This narrative reached its height with the late Middle Irish tale, *Tromdám Guaire*. Senchán's retinue is described in loving detail and Marbán's role is expanded, as is Senchán's quest for the *Táin*, which takes him to Scotland before he returns to Ireland.

Senchán's trip to Scotland in *Tromdám Guaire* may have been inspired by an anecdote related in the late ninth- or early tenth-century 'Cormac's glossary' under the word *prúll*. Here, Senchán visits the Isle of Man and, in the company of the spirit of poetry, brings back to Ireland a female poet, belonging to a minor branch of the Múscraige living among the Uí Fhidgeinte (modern co. Limerick).

However, Senchán's other literary associations are with Guaire. In an anecdote, 'Mac Dá Cherda and Cuimmíne Fota', which may date from the ninth century, the holy fool Mac Dá Cherda (*d.* 645?) proves himself to be the true chief poet of Ireland. Furthermore, Cuimmíne Fota (*d.* 661?), the saint and abbot of Clonfert, defeats Senchán in a poetic duel. The former's gospel lessons overcome Senchán's poetic compositions.

This, less than complimentary, view of Senchán seems to dominate the ninth-century *Scéla Cano meic Gartnáin*. It is Senchán's jealousy of Guaire's hospitality to the young hero Cano mac Gartnáin (*d.* 688?) which causes Cano to depart Guaire's court. But Senchán's behaviour is not completely reprehensible. An episode in *Scéla Cano* describes how Senchán sends two poems to the high-king, Diarmait, son of Áed Sláine (*d.* 665/8). He is insulted by the king, but, showing a forbearance much at odds with his picture in *Tromdám Guaire*, does not satirize him. He sends two more poems and is well rewarded by Diarmait.

The evidence for Senchán's association with the *Táin* is unhistorical and far too flimsy to treat seriously. The same can be said for the claim that Senchán compiled the earliest stratum of the genealogies. Clearly, the historical figure of Senchán attracted a series of legends. In these, Senchán is a representative of the poets. The narratives in which he appears emphasize the value of poets as tale-tellers or criticize the economic burden they place on the nobility. ELVA JOHNSTON

Sources R. I. Best and others, eds., *The Book of Leinster, formerly Lebar na Núachongbála*, 6 vols. (1954–83) • D. A. Binchy, ed., *Scéla Cano meic Gartnáin*, Medieval and Modern Irish Series, 18 (1963) • M. Joynt, ed., *Tromdámh Guaire*, Medieval and Modern Irish Series, 2 (1941) • S. Mac Airt, ed. and trans., *The annals of Inisfallen* (1951) • *Ann. Ulster* • Cormac mac Cuilennáin, *Sanas Cormaic: an old-Irish glossary*, ed. K. Meyer (1912), vol. 4 of *Anecdota from Irish manuscripts*, ed. O. J. Bergin and others (1907–13) • M. A. O'Brien, ed., *Corpus genealogiarum Hiberniae* (Dublin, 1962) • J. G. O'Keefe, ed., 'Mac Dá Cherda and Cummaine Foda', *Ériu*, 5 (1911), 18–44 • C. O'Rahilly, ed., *'Táin bó Cuailnge' from the Book of Leinster* (1967) • J. Carney, *Studies in Irish literature and history* (1955); repr. (1979) • J. Carney, 'Three Old Irish accentual poems', *Ériu*, 22 (1971), 28–80 • J. F. Nagy, 'Close encounters of the traditional kind in medieval Irish literature', *Celtic folklore and Christianity: studies in memory of William W. Heist* (1983), 129–49 • T. Ó Cathasaigh, 'The rhetoric of *Scéla Cano meic Gartnáin*', *Sages, saints and storytellers: Celtic studies in honour of Professor James Carney*, ed. D. Ó Corráin and others (1989), 233–50 • S. Ó Coileáin, 'The structure of a literary cycle', *Ériu*, 25 (1974), 88–125 • T. Ó Máille, 'The authorship of the Culmen', *Ériu*, 9 (1921–3), 71–6 • R. Thurneysen, *Die irische Helden- und Königsage* (1921) • R. Thurneysen, 'Colmán mac Lénéni und Senchán Torpéist', *Zeitschrift für Celtische Philologie*, 19 (1931–3), 193–209

Sendall, Sir Walter Joseph (1832–1904), colonial governor, born on 24 December 1832 at Langham Hall, Suffolk, was the youngest son of Simon Sendall (*d.* 1871), a Church of England clergyman, and his wife, Alice Wilkinson. A delicate boy, he attended the grammar school at Bury St Edmunds, and in 1854 proceeded to Christ's College, Cambridge, where he was a contemporary and friend of Walter Besant, John Peile (afterwards master), and above all Charles Stuart Calverley, whose sister Elizabeth Sophia (their father was vicar of South Stoke and prebendary of Wells Cathedral) he married in 1870. They had no children. Sendall graduated BA in 1858 and MA in 1867.

In 1859 Sendall joined the educational branch of the civil service in Ceylon, and the following year became inspector of schools there. He rose to be director of education (1870), but the climate and work told on his health, and in 1872, when on leave in England, he resigned.

In 1873 Sendall became assistant poor law inspector in the Oxfordshire district, but this appointment was abolished in 1875 and for six months, while unemployed, he devoted himself to studying and reporting on the Dutch poor laws. In 1876 he became a poor law inspector in Yorkshire under the Local Government Board, and in 1878 he was appointed an assistant secretary of the board. Ambitious to follow the career of a colonial administrator, in 1882 he accepted an offer of the lieutenant-governorship of Natal, but the politicians of that colony declined to approve the choice of a little-known candidate and the nomination was withdrawn.

In 1885 Sendall became the first governor of the Windward Islands on their separation from Barbados. Here he organized the new administration, living on Grenada, the chief island of the group. In 1889 he was transferred to Barbados, and in 1892 he became high commissioner of Cyprus and champion of its progress. He received the jubilee medal in 1897 and at the end of his term the following year he was transferred as governor to British Guiana, where he arrived on 23 March. The boundary with Venezuela, long a matter of dispute, was arbitrated in 1899, but Sendall was not directly involved in the negotiations. He left the colony on retirement on 1 August 1901. The following year he represented the West Indian colonies, Bermuda, and the Falkland Islands at the coronation of Edward VII and received the Coronation Medal.

Sendall appeared detached and reserved, but his sound judgement and integrity won him great confidence in his capacity as governor. He was made CMG in 1887, KCMG in 1889, and GCMG in 1899, and he received an honorary LLD from Edinburgh University. In his retirement he found recreation in literary work, as well as in the microscope, mechanics, and the lathe. He was a fellow of the Linnean, Royal Microscopical, and other scientific societies, as well as of the Hellenic Society. He was also chairman of the Charity Organization Society. He edited *The Literary Remains of C. S. Calverley*, with a memoir, in 1885.

Sendall died at his home, 91 Cornwall Gardens, South Kensington, London, on 16 March 1904, survived by his wife. His remains were cremated and interred at Golders Green. A memorial bronze is in the chapel of St Michael and St George, St Paul's Cathedral.

C. A. HARRIS, *rev.* LYNN MILNE

Sources *WWW, 1897–1915* • *The Times* (17 March 1904) • *Colonial Office List* (1903) • private information (1912) • personal knowledge (1912) • D. P. Henige, *Colonial governors from the fifteenth century to the present* (1970)
Archives Bodl. Oxf., Wodehouse MSS
Likenesses E. Lantéri, marble bust, NPG • memorial bronze, St Paul's Cathedral, London, chapel of St Michael and St George
Wealth at death £8420 9*s.* 3*d.*: probate, 12 May 1904, *CGPLA Eng. & Wales*

Senex, John (*bap.* 1678, *d.* 1740), publisher and maker of maps and globes, was baptized on 24 November 1678 at Ludlow, Shropshire, the son of John Senex, gentleman, and his wife, Marie. The family does not appear to have been native to that county. In 1695 Senex was apprenticed to the London bookseller Robert Clavell. Commencing business on his own account in 1702, first from premises opposite the south portico of St Clement Danes, Strand, and then next to the Fleece tavern, Cornhill, between 1703 and 1706, Senex formed an early partnership with the map makers Jeremiah Seller and Charles Price, the successors of John Seller, a partnership also involving the manufacture and sale of navigational instruments. He continued in partnership with Price at Whites Alley, Coleman Street, from 1707 to 1710, and then moved to Fleet Street, where he remained for the rest of his life, first at premises at the Globe in Salisbury Court (initially in partnership with John Maxwell) and from 1721 at the same sign opposite the church of St Dunstan-in-the-West.

One of Senex's earliest publications was the first edition in English of a major treatise by Edmond Halley, *A Synopsis of the Astronomy of Comets* (1705), an auspicious beginning to a career that saw Senex develop into one of the most distinguished London scientific publishers of the period. Often working with William Taylor (*d.* 1724)—the original publisher of Daniel Defoe's *Robinson Crusoe* (1719)—his publications included original works, reprints of valuable earlier works (often handsomely illustrated), and translations of the leading European writers on mathematics, perspective, chemistry, optics, anatomy, and architecture. He published, *inter alia*, *The Motion of Water and other Fluids* (1718), translated by John Theophilus Desaguliers from the work of Edmé Mariotte; an augmented edition of Francis Hauksbee's *Physico-Mechanical Experiments on Various Subjects* with the additional experiments demonstrating 'several surprizing phaenomena touching light and electricity' (1719); Sir Isaac Newton's *Universal Arithmetic* (1720); Henry Wilson's *Trigonometry Improv'd* (1720); *A Treatise of Painting by Leonardo da Vinci* (1721); Giovanni Maria Lancisi's *Anatomy Improv'd and Illustrated* (1723); Nicolas Bion's *The Construction and Principal Uses of Mathematical Instruments* (1723), a work augmented by Edmund Stone and one that displays Senex's own neat style of engraving to particular advantage in his depictions of the various instruments; William Whiston's *The Calculation of Solar Eclipses without Parallaxes* (1724); Edmund Stone's *A New Mathematical Dictionary* (1726); George Shelvocke's *A Voyage Round the World* (1726); and Thomas Wright's *The Use of Globes* (1740).

In tandem with bookselling, Senex was long concerned in the production of maps and atlases. Between 1707 and 1711 he worked with Price (and later Maxwell) on a large atlas series, issuing in 1707 broadside 'Proposals for a new sett of correct mapps' advertising the partners as 'Geographers to the Queen' and promising work that 'shall in correctness, and all other particulars, far exceed any yet done'. Senex and Price subsequently went their separate ways but Senex at length produced (with Maxwell) an augmented version of these maps as *The English Atlas* (1714), the bulk of the work engraved by himself. His portable version of the road maps of John Ogilby, published as *An Actual Survey of All the Principal Roads of England and Wales* in 1719, was a popular success, staying in print for many years, while his *A New General Atlas* (1721) remains the most elegant English world atlas of the time. The *Atlas maritimus & commercialis* (1728), a work to which Halley lent his assistance and the text for which is said to have been written by Defoe, featured maps drawn on a new 'globular' projection patented in 1721, which Senex had himself devised in association with John Harris and Henry Wilson. Individual maps of particular note included Halley's 'A description of the passage of the shadow of the moon over England' of 1715, the first printed solar eclipse map and one of the earliest scientific thematic maps. Senex produced special 'smoak'd glasses' for observing this eclipse (*Daily Courant*, 9 April 1715) and later published similar material not only by Halley but also by Whiston and Wright. He was also involved in the production of some of the earliest large-scale county maps, including Richard Budgen's 'An actual survey of the county of Sussex' (1723) and his own 'A new map of the county of Surrey laid down from an actual survey' (1729–30). The latter, published in association with the surveyor Richard Cushee (an apprentice of Charles Price), was surveyed in part by a novel method of releasing a nightly ball of flame from the summit of Box Hill in the autumn of 1721 and taking bearings from rockets set off at staggered intervals from surrounding hills. His large map of the British Isles in nine sheets is known only in one surviving example (Newberry Library, Chicago).

Above all Senex was esteemed for his globes. In 1706 Senex and Price announced a pair of 12 inch globes, the celestial one based on Halley's observations and showing nineteen new constellations 'never before printed on any globe' (*London Gazette*, 6–9 May 1706). In 1708 the partners advertised similar 16 inch globes and by the time of his death Senex was providing a range, of international reputation, varying from 3 to 28 inches in diameter at prices from 10*s.* to 25 guineas. One of his largest examples is depicted in the portrait by Richard Wilson of George III as a boy with his brother and their tutor.

A man of broad and enquiring mind, whose name is found on the subscription lists of many of the principal technical works of the period, Senex numbered among his apprentices not only the map engravers Samuel Parker and Thomas Hutchinson, but also the encyclopaedist Ephraim Chambers. In 1728 he was elected a fellow of the Royal Society and read there on 4 May 1738 a paper concerning improvements to the utility of celestial globes. His wide circle of acquaintance and connection encompassed most of the leading men of science of the day, many of whom he published. His connection with Desaguliers extended not merely to publishing his works and translations but into the world of eighteenth-century freemasonry: when Desaguliers was deputy grand master of that organization Senex published (with John Hooke) James Anderson's *The Constitutions of the Free-Masons* (1723), the earliest such compilation, the text revealing Senex at that time to have been a warden of one of the London lodges.

In the same year Senex married Mary Wilcox at St Margaret's, Westminster, on 27 August. The only recorded child of the marriage, Elizabeth Maria (*b.* 1730), married in 1752 Fitz Foy of Duntish Court, and later Castle Hill, in Dorset. Senex died on 30 December 1740 and was buried in the new vault of St Dunstan-in-the-West, Fleet Street, on 4 January 1741, remembered in a contemporary obituary as 'a sincere, worthy, honest man, and greatly valued by men of learning' (*Hooker's Weekly Miscellany*, 3 Jan 1741). His will left his entire estate to his widow, who continued the business in Fleet Street until 1755. LAURENCE WORMS

Sources *BL cat.* · *British Library map library catalogue* (1998) [CD-ROM] · S. Tyacke, *London map-sellers, 1660–1720* (1978) · R. V. Wallis and P. J. Wallis, eds., *Biobibliography of British mathematics and its applications*, 2 (1986) · E. G. R. Taylor, *The mathematical practitioners of Hanoverian England, 1714–1840* (1966) · G. Clifton, *Directory of British scientific instrument makers, 1550–1851*, ed. G. L'E. Turner (1995) · newspaper advertisements, Donald Hodson collection [*Daily Courant* (25 March 1708, 24 March 1711, 12 July 1711); *Tatler* (29 April – 2 May 1710); *The Spectator* (1 Oct 1711); *Post Boy* (4–7 July 1719; 15–18 April 1721; 12–15 Aug 1721); *Weekly Journal* (22 July 1721); *Evening Post* (23–5 Nov 1721); *Daily Journal* (10 March 1730)] · *IGI* [parish registers, London, St Margaret's, Westminster, St Dunstan-in-the-

West, and St George's, Hanover Square] • M. Senex, *A catalogue of globes, maps, &c. made by the late John Senex, FRS* (1741?) • D. F. McKenzie, ed., *Stationers' Company apprentices*, [3]: *1701–1800* (1978) • R. W. Shirley, *Printed maps of the British Isles, 1650–1750* (1988) • *GM*, 1st ser., 11 (1741) • will, PRO, PROB 11/708, sig. 52

Archives BL

Wealth at death thought to be substantial: will, PRO, PROB 11/708, sig. 52

Sengham, William (*fl.* 1252), Augustinian friar, is likely to have come from the village of Sengham in Norfolk. However, there is no contemporary evidence for his life and activities. Sengham is mentioned in John Bale's *Scriptorum catalogus*, but even this information was not obtained at first hand, being derived from the writings of the early fifteenth-century Carmelite Thomas Colby. According to Colby, William Sengham came from a humble social background and was educated in the arts as well as theology. Probably after the end of his formal training he went to northern Italy, where he joined the Johnbonites, one of several loosely organized groups of hermits who—largely owing to the initiative of Cardinal Ricardo Annibaldi—were merged into the order of hermit friars of St Augustine in 1256. According to Bale, Sengham had already returned to England in 1252, obeying the command of the Johnbonites' prior-general, Lanfranc, who wanted his order to extend into England. It is likely that Sengham was one of the first representatives of the Johnbonites, and later of the Augustinian friars, in England. A reference to 'Guilhelmus Sengham', one of those 'saints and doctors who extended the order into England in the thirteenth century' by Pamphilus (Pamphilus, 25*v*), who published a history of the Augustinian friars in Rome in 1581, may refer to Bale's work (published at Basel in 1557), but could equally be an independent corroboration.

Sengham is credited with the authorship of four treatises whose titles are known (*De fide et legibus*, *De claustro animae*, *De professione novitiorum*, and *De tentationum remediis*) but whose texts are lost. According to Roth, the author of the first treatise is unknown, and Sengham probably only wrote an index to the book.

Jens Röhrkasten

Sources F. X. Roth, *The English Austin friars, 1249–1538*, 2 vols. (1961–6) • Bale, *Cat.* • J. Pamphilus, *Chronica ordinis eremitarum S. Augustini* (1581) • T. de Herrera, *Alphabetum Augustinianum* (1644)

Senhouse, Humphrey (1705–1770), landowner and port founder, was born on 2 July 1705 at Millom Castle, Cumberland, the fourth child of Humphrey Senhouse (*d.* 1738) and his wife, Eleanor, daughter of William Kirkby of Ashlack, Lancashire. Humphrey Senhouse senior was a scion of an old gentry family in west Cumberland and had his roots in Whitehaven. He was agent at Millom Castle for his aunt until her death in 1715. The following year he moved his wife and children to the family property at Netherhall and Ellenborough, on the west Cumberland coast north of Workington, which he had purchased from his brother's heirs. His son subsequently built his town here and thus gained his reputation.

Senhouse was educated at a school at Lowther, Westmorland, from 1720 to 1723, and went to Queen's College, Oxford, in 1724. He returned home to Netherhall on the death of his younger brother in 1727. On 16 February 1731 at Carlisle Cathedral he married Mary, daughter and ultimately coheir of Sir George *Fleming of Rydal, Westmorland, dean (and later bishop) of Carlisle, a marriage which strengthened his standing and eased his entry into the close-knit hub of county society at Carlisle. They had three sons and a daughter. Their eldest son, Humphrey (1731–1814), confirmed the family's ascent into the cluster of gentry dynasties which dominated political life in Cumberland by serving as MP first for Cockermouth and then for the county.

His elder brother also having died young, Senhouse inherited the estate at Netherhall and Ellenborough on his father's death in 1738. He was soon to transform the trade of the northern part of the west Cumberland coalfield by founding a new town and port on his property. In the early eighteenth century there was a small harbour at Ellenfoot, from which coal was shipped, and in 1740 a Whitehaven merchant named Walter Lutwidge proposed the establishment of a new industrial settlement there. In 1749 Senhouse promoted a parliamentary bill to improve the harbour at Ellenfoot, with a view to obtaining a share of the coal trade, at that time dominated by Whitehaven and the Lowther family. Harbour work commenced in May 1749 and by the middle of the following year the new harbour was handling thirteen or fourteen ships at any one time.

From the very beginning Senhouse had planned to develop a new town at Ellenfoot, which he renamed 'Mary Port' in honour of his wife. More than one hundred rectangular plots in the town were sold between 1749 and 1769, almost half of the sales being in the years 1752 to 1754. Nearly all the purchasers were local. By the mid-1770s Maryport contained about 340 families and the port was home to 70–80 vessels, engaged principally in shipping coal to Ireland and the Isle of Man, but also in trading with the Baltic. Unlike Whitehaven, Maryport was not heavily involved in trade with North America. An iron furnace, established in 1754 on Senhouse's property beside the River Ellen by a consortium of Whitehaven merchants, provided for a secondary trade to supplement the export of coal. By the time of Senhouse's death, the port and town at Maryport yielded an annual return of over £150, out of a total rental income of over £600.

Senhouse retained a close personal interest in Maryport, playing the leading role in founding the town's church, St Mary's, which was consecrated in 1763. Although he and his family continued to worship at the parish church at Crosscanonby, he bore most of the expense of establishing the new church, providing all the stone for the building and the churchyard wall, paying for the furnishings, and negotiating a contribution to the curate's salary from the governors of Queen Anne's bounty. Patronage of the church was vested in Senhouse and his successors and a measure of independence from the mother church at Crosscanonby was achieved in 1766, when the churchwardens agreed no longer to collect contributions for communion wine from the inhabitants of Maryport.

Senhouse also took an active part in developing the coalmining industry on which his new port depended. In 1736 his father had agreed with Sir James Lowther of Whitehaven to refrain from mining, but Senhouse obtained a relaxation of that constraint and, in 1755, took a lease of Broughton colliery with his neighbour, John Christian of Ewanrigg, and four other partners, a move which helped to prevent Lowther from securing a monopoly over the west Cumberland coal trade. A waggonway, built across Senhouse's estate, carried coals from Broughton to the harbour at Maryport.

Humphrey Senhouse died at Bath in late June or early July 1770 and was buried in the family vault at Crosscanonby church on 26 July. The words on his monument in Maryport church, written by one of his sons, record his foremost achievement: 'the town of Maryport founded and flourishing through his auspicious patronage'.

ANGUS J. L. WINCHESTER

Sources E. Hughes, *North country life in the eighteenth century*, 2 (1965) • E. Hughes, 'The founding of Maryport', *Transactions of the Cumberland and Westmorland Antiquarian and Archaeological Society*, new ser., 64 (1964), 306–18 • J. V. Beckett, *Coal and tobacco: the Lowthers and the economic development of west Cumberland, 1660–1760* (1981) • Cumbria AS, Carlisle, PR 66/2, PR 47/1 • Cumbria AS, Barrow, BPR/10 • Cumbria AS, Carlisle, Senhouse papers, D/Sen

Archives Cumbria AS, Carlisle

Wealth at death over £600 income from properties, Aug 1769: Hughes, *North country life*, 82

Senhouse, Sir Humphrey Fleming (*bap.* 1781, *d.* 1841), naval officer, born in Barbados and baptized there on 6 June 1781, was the third son of Lieutenant William Senhouse RN (1741–1800), surveyor-general of Barbados and the Leeward Islands, and his wife, Elizabeth, daughter of Samson Wood, speaker of the Barbados assembly. His grandfather Humphrey Senhouse of Netherhall, Cumberland, had married Mary, daughter and coheir of Sir George Fleming, bishop of Carlisle.

Senhouse entered the navy in January 1797 on the *Prince of Wales*, flagship of Rear-Admiral Henry Harvey, in the West Indies. In November 1797 he was moved into the brig *Requin*, in which he first came to England towards the close of 1799. From March 1800 to April 1802 he served in the *Fisgard* under Captain Thomas Byam Martin and Captain Michael Seymour. On 9 April 1802 he was promoted lieutenant of the *Galgo*, and in May 1803 was appointed to the *Conqueror* (Captain Thomas Louis). With Israel Pellew, who relieved Louis in April 1804, he served in the Mediterranean, in the voyage to the West Indies, and in the battle of Trafalgar, until January 1806. He then went out to the West Indies in the *Elephant*, was put on board the *Northumberland*, flagship of Sir Alexander Forrester Inglis Cochrane, and in September 1806 was appointed to command the *Express* on the Spanish main and among the Leeward Islands until March 1808, when he joined the *Belleisle* as flag lieutenant to Cochrane. In July of that year he was sent home by Cochrane with dispatches. On 26 January 1809 he rejoined the admiral, now in the *Neptune*, and served through the capture of Martinique. For this, on 7 March, he was promoted to the *Wolverene*, commanding it, and afterwards the *Ringdove* and *Supérieure*, in the West Indies until December. In 1810 he married Elizabeth, daughter of Vice-Admiral John Manley; they had two daughters. In 1810–12 he commanded the brig-sloop *Recruit* (18 guns) at Gibraltar, Newfoundland, and Halifax, Nova Scotia; and in 1812–14 the *Martin* (18 guns) on the Halifax station, serving with distinction in the Anglo-American War.

On 12 October 1814 Senhouse was advanced to post rank, and from April to September 1815 commanded the *Superb* (74 guns), on the coast of France, as flag captain to Sir Henry Hotham. He was again with Hotham in the Mediterranean, as flag captain in the *St Vincent* (120 guns), which he commanded from 1831 to 1834. On 13 April 1832 he was made a KCH, and he was knighted again on 5 June 1834. In April 1839 he commissioned the *Blenheim* (72 guns), which he took out to China; he died on the ship on 14 June 1841, of fever contracted by fatigue and exposure during the operations at Canton (Guangzhou). He was buried at Macau (Macao). Fifteen days after his death he was nominated a CB.

J. K. LAUGHTON, *rev.* ANDREW LAMBERT

Sources G. S. Graham, *The China station: war and diplomacy, 1830–1860* (1978) • *GM*, 2nd ser., 16 (1841), 654 • J. Marshall, *Royal naval biography*, suppl. 3 (1829), 405 • *The Times* (8 Oct 1841) • *The Times* (9 Oct 1841) • O'Byrne, *Naval biog. dict.*

Archives Devon RO, letters to wife

Senhouse, Richard (*d.* 1626), bishop of Carlisle, was born at Nether Hall (or Alneburgh Hall), Cumberland, the third surviving son of John Senhouse (*d.* 1604) of Nether Hall, antiquary, and his wife, Anne Ponsonby (*d.* 1606); he was the great-great-nephew of William Senhouse (*d.* 1505), bishop of Carlisle from 1495 and of Durham from 1502. Senhouse matriculated pensioner at Trinity College, Cambridge, about 1592 and graduated BA in 1595. He was elected fellow of St John's and proceeded MA in 1598, was ordained deacon and priest at London on 4 October 1604, and proceeded BD in 1606. At Cambridge he was a famous preacher.

The king presented Senhouse to the royal livings of Steeple Bumstead, Essex, in 1606, and Cheam, Surrey, in 1608. Senhouse served the duke of Bedford as chaplain, and composed verses on the death of Prince Henry. By 1616, the year he first appears among the preachers at court during Lent, he had been appointed chaplain to Prince Charles. He preached in the prophetic, anti-Catholic vein common to Prince Charles's other chaplains; John Gauden noted that his 'eloquent tongue and honest heart were capable to *over-awe a Court*' (Gauden, 614).

On 21 November 1621 Senhouse was presented by the king to the deanery of Gloucester, and he was installed by proxy on 13 December. Having proceeded DD in 1622, on 26 September 1624 he was made bishop of Carlisle; there he took up residence out of parliament time. Charles I chose Senhouse to preach his coronation sermon; only the peroration of allegories on 'the crown of life' (Revelation 2: 10) survives in a manuscript Latin translation. Senhouse fell from his horse and died, intestate, on 6 May 1626, and was buried on 7 May in Carlisle Cathedral; his funeral sermon was preached by Lancelot Davies. Four court sermons, probably Jacobean, were published in 1627. P. E. McCullough

Sources R. Ley, 'Festa Britannica', BL, MS Stowe 76, fol. 248a–b · J. Gauden, *Ecclesia Anglicana suspiria* (1659), 614 · W. Hutchinson, *The history of the county of Cumberland*, 2 (1794), 266–70 · C. R. Hudleston and R. S. Boumphrey, *Cumberland families and heraldry*, Cumberland and Westmorland Antiquarian and Archaeological Society, extra ser., 23 (1978), 301–2 · J. Foster, ed., *Pedigrees recorded at the herald's visitations of the counties of Cumberland and Westmorland* (1891), 122 · Venn, *Alum. Cant.* · W. Whellan, ed., *The history and topography of the counties of Cumberland and Westmoreland* (1860), 110 · *Fasti Angl., 1541–1857*, [Bristol], 41 · PRO, E334/14, fol. 58a · PRO, E334/16, fol. 81b · PRO, E334/17, fol. 26a · *CSP dom., 1623–5*, 304, 353, 339 · K. Fincham, *Prelate as pastor: the episcopate of James I* (1990) · P. E. McCullough, *Sermons at court: politics and religion in Elizabethan and Jacobean preaching* (1998) [incl. CD-ROM]

Archives Cumbria AS, Carlisle, MSS | Carlisle Diocesan Archive, episcopal registers, DRC 1/3 [general register 1561–1643 (includes Richard Senhouse's register)]

Senhouse, William. *See* Sever, William (*d.* 1505).

Senior [*née* Hughes], **Jane Elizabeth** (1828–1877), workhouse and school inspector and philanthropist, was born on 10 December 1828 at Donnington Priory, Berkshire, the only daughter of seven children of John *Hughes (1790–1857), author, and his second wife, Margaret Elizabeth (1797–1887), second daughter of the Wilkinsons of Stokesley Hall, Yorkshire. Known as Jeannie, she had long blonde curly hair and blue eyes. On 10 August 1848 she married Nassau John Senior (1822–1891), son of Nassau William *Senior (1790–1864), the distinguished economist. Although admired by her husband's siblings (one described her as 'the brightest ornament in our house') it is unlikely that she was close to her father-in-law, who virtually cut John Senior out of his will and who held views on the relationship between the state and the poor far removed from those of Jane Senior. Her own brother, Thomas *Hughes (1822–1896), author of *Tom Brown's Schooldays* (1857), was a Christian socialist who promoted working men's associations, and while there is no evidence of Jane Senior's involvement with these activities, her own work does display a belief not only in charitable work but also in a more active role for the state.

As part of cultured London society Jane Senior was well connected and, like many middle-class women of her time, heavily involved in charitable work; Octavia Hill (1838–1912) and Louisa Twining (1820–1912) were both her friends. Her views accorded well with those of Twining: both were keen to promote women's work, not only in a voluntary capacity but also in state welfare work with the poor. During the Crimean War Senior worked as part of a team sending supplies to soldiers; later, during the 1870–71 Franco-Prussian War, she worked in the London office of the Red Cross, for which she was awarded a Red Cross medal. She was also an active workhouse visitor with a special interest in the fate of young girls when they left the workhouse; in 1875 she founded the Metropolitan Association for Befriending Young Servants. Her organizational and workhouse experience led to her appointment as the first woman government inspector, and it is for this that she is remembered.

On 18 February 1873 James Stansfeld (1820–1898), president of the Local Government Board and a renowned radical campaigner, in a move to receive 'a woman's point of view', appointed Jane Senior senior inspector of workhouses and of workhouse pauper schools with a brief to produce a report on the effect on girls of education in pauper schools. Both her appointment and report were controversial. The appointment of a woman was unpopular with other civil servants who, as Stansfeld later recalled, hated having a woman imposed on them.

Since the early nineteenth century there had been campaigns for middle-class women to exercise greater influence over poor-law policy and the running of the workhouses. It was argued that women would bring their 'domestic economy' skills to the work; indeed, the absence of women's influence was seen as a reason for the development of huge poor-law institutions, so beloved of official experts and decried by campaigners. From 1834 pauper children had been contained either in large London district institutions, in ordinary workhouses, or in separate schools. Intense debate peaked in the 1860s over the appropriate institutions for these children; although all were agreed that the type of institutions in which the children were placed was crucial to their future development and 'usefulness' to society, the issue remained unresolved. Non-official attitudes emphasized the importance of a family, or at least a vicarious family, for children, especially girls, who needed training in domestic skills to fit them for future work as domestic servants, their most likely destination on leaving the control of the poor-law authorities. In the 1860s the huge district schools of London were brought into disrepute by scandalous revelations of mismanagement, disease, and overcrowding, and this strengthened the case for the 'family' system.

Senior's 1874 report recommended dividing large schools into: cottage homes with about thirty children in each; 'scattered homes', where about thirty children would all live under one roof but attend the local schools; and the more piecemeal, but ultimately more widely adopted suggestion, that orphans should be individually boarded out in working-class homes with foster parents who would receive reimbursement from the poor rates. Her report has been hailed as a landmark in the history of official policy, although in fact attitudes among officials towards pauper children had already begun to change. It was not so much the views that were novel as the manner of their presentation—by a woman in an official capacity. Senior's ill health, which led to her resignation, and Stansfeld's short-term tenure of his post meant that while the policy advocated by Senior was acted upon, Stansfeld's example of appointing a woman to a senior post was not emulated for many years to come.

Jane Senior died on 24 March 1877 at her home, 98

Cheyne Walk, London; she was buried two days later at Brookwood cemetery, Woking. Her appointment as the first woman government inspector did not herald the arrival in Whitehall of women in high-profile and senior positions or break down prejudice against women in senior civil service posts; but her report did contribute to the development of the system of fostering of orphans in England. HELEN JONES

Sources *The Times* (29 March 1877) · *Englishwoman's Review* (14 April 1877) · F. D. How, *Noble women of our time* (1901) · F. Duke, 'Pauper education', *The new poor law in the nineteenth century*, ed. D. Fraser (1976), 67–86 · F. Driver, *Power and pauperism: the workhouse system, 1834–1884* (1993) · J. L. Hammond and B. Hammond, *James Stansfeld: a Victorian champion of sexual equality* (1932) · J. Packer, *Women and welfare: the Victorian women in public social service* (1988) · L. Twining, *Recollections of workhouse visiting and management* (1880) · m. cert. · d. cert. · S. L. Levy, *Nassau W. Senior, 1790–1864* (1970) · L. Twining, *On the supervision and training of workhouse girls* (1859/60?) · L. Twining, *Our poor laws and our workhouses* (1862)
Likenesses G. F. Watts, portrait; in possession of family in 1897
Wealth at death under £20: administration, 8 June 1877, *CGPLA Eng. & Wales*

Senior, Nassau William (1790–1864), political economist, was probably born on 26 September 1790 at Compton Beauchamp, Berkshire, although one source has it that he was born on 23 September 1790 at Uffington, Berkshire. He was the eldest of ten children of John Raven Senior (1764–1824), son of a merchant trading overseas, and his wife, Mary, daughter of Henry Duke, solicitor-general of Barbados. Before entering Eton College in July 1803, Nassau was taught at home by his father (a graduate of Merton College, Oxford), who became vicar of Durnford, Wiltshire, in 1791. At the age of sixteen the boy went as a demy to Magdalen College, Oxford, where—stung by failure at his first appearance in the schools—he hired an outstanding coach, Richard Whately, only three years his senior, in whom he found a lifelong friend. After getting a first in classics in 1811, Senior became a probationary fellow of Magdalen in 1812. His ambitions were then focused on a career in the law. He had already entered Lincoln's Inn in November 1810 and in 1813 the award of the Oxford University Vinerian scholarship enabled him to dedicate himself to legal studies. As pupil to Edward Sugden, later lord chancellor, he became a certificated conveyancer and was introduced to an influential section of London society. In 1817 after Sugden had become master of chancery, Senior took over the thriving practice in which he had been trained. By the time he was called to the bar in 1819 he was already earning a comfortably rising income. In April 1821 he married Mary Charlotte Mair (1791–1883), daughter of John Mair of Iron Acton, Gloucestershire, and they set up their first London home at 32 Kensington Square. A few years later Senior built a larger house at 13 Hyde Park Gate. There they entertained a cosmopolitan variety of intellectually lively friends from 1827 until 1864.

The first published evidence of Senior's interest in political economy was an article discussing a recent parliamentary report on the state of agriculture, in the *Quarterly Review* of July 1821 (he had already written several reviews

Nassau William Senior (1790–1864), by unknown engraver

on legal or literary subjects for the journal). The article attracted favourable notice from leading economists such as Ricardo, who wrote to H. Trower expressing satisfaction at having 'got so good an ally for what I think the correct principles' (*Works and Correspondence*, 9.120), and James Mill, who early in 1823 recommended Senior as a member of the recently formed Political Economy Club. For most of the next four decades Senior participated actively at the club's meetings, where current problems of economic theory and policy were regularly debated by prominent economists, bankers, businessmen, civil servants, and parliamentarians. By 1825 his credentials were sufficiently well attested for him to be appointed as the first incumbent of the Drummond chair of political economy at Oxford. It was during his 1825–30 tenure of the professorship that he won wide respect as a lucid exponent of what was still an infant discipline. Most of the lectures he then delivered were subsequently published as pamphlets, or embodied in his first book, *Outline of the Science of Political Economy* (1836). He also provided an appendix defining 'Ambiguous terms in political economy' for Richard Whately's *Elements of Logic* (1826). For several years he was an examiner in political economy at London University, which elected him to a fellowship in 1836.

By the age of forty Senior had acquired an enviable reputation in London society as a successful lawyer and economist whose judgement was considered basically sound by leading members of the Political Economy Club. Accordingly, in 1830, when Lord Melbourne became secretary of state for home affairs, he invited Senior to prepare a report on the laws relating to strikes and trade combinations. Characteristically, Senior responded by first systematically ascertaining the facts. Aided by a colleague expert in the common law, he circulated questionnaires and examined witnesses before presenting a carefully argued opinion. His report lay unpublished in Home Office files until 1841, when he embodied extracts from it in a parliamentary *Report on the Condition of the Handloom Weavers* (1841). Over thirty years later he reproduced it in full in the first volume of his *Historical and Philosophical Essays* (posthumously published in 1865)—on the grounds that the law affecting trade unions remained as defective as ever.

Senior said in his introductory professorial lecture (1827) that his interest in political economy was largely motivated by humanitarian concern for the poor, and by a conviction that understanding the causes of poverty was an essential preliminary to relieving it. His earliest research in this area was provoked by Lord Howick's suggestion that he should examine the voluminous material published on the poor in Ireland. The most striking feature of his conclusions was that he advocated a positive economic role for government, going far beyond *ad hoc* measures designed to relieve the worst social distress. He suggested, for example, that chronic poverty in Ireland called for government intervention to make capital available for productive investment in roads, railways, harbours, docks, and canals, as well as to encourage consolidation of farms into more efficient units of operation and to subsidize emigration. These were highly unorthodox views in the current climate of economic opinion. He also scandalized Anglican opinion by advocating the confiscation and transfer to the Roman Catholic church (to which the majority of Irish people belonged) of a substantial proportion of the income of the established episcopalian church—a recommendation so heretical that it is said to have forced his resignation from the chair of political economy at King's College, London, in 1830.

Senior continued to write on the Irish poverty problem, partly because frequent visits to his friend Whately (who was appointed archbishop of Dublin in 1831) kept his interest fresh and informed. However, in 1832 his attention was sharply focused on English poverty when he was appointed to the royal commission for inquiring into the administration and practical operation of the poor laws. In this case Senior's influence on the outcome was crucially important. Apart from Edwin Chadwick, he was the main driving force throughout the inquiry, from drafting the questionnaires circulated to all English parishes and identifying the relevant facts to be gathered by the twenty-six assistant (regional) commissioners for England and certain other countries (for purposes of international comparison), to writing the final report, published in 1834. Senior then acted as midwife to the Poor Law Amendment Act by careful explication and justification of the commission's recommendations to the lord chancellor and other cabinet ministers, and by continuously advising on the details of the consequent legislation as the bill went through parliament. He refused both a knighthood and the sum of £500 as reward for his public services. Later he refused the offer of a Canadian governorship and the position of legal member of the Indian council. He also turned down a place on the new poor-law board. However, he accepted gratefully the appointment in 1836 as one of the twelve masters of chancery, a post that gave him an annual lifetime salary of £2500 for duties which were more ceremonial than intellectually demanding and allowed him leisure to offer further uncompensated services to successive governments. In 1836, for example, he was consulted by the then home secretary, Lord John Russell, on Irish poor law reform; in 1837 he published *Letters on the Factory Act as it Affects the Cotton Manufacture*, addressed to the president of the Board of Trade, and was appointed to another royal commission—this time on the condition of the unemployed handweavers. Again the inquiry began with a painstaking assembly of facts by a team of assistant commissioners, and again the final report was largely Senior's work. It offered a comprehensive and sympathetic account of the handweavers' plight, but suggested no practical remedies and gave rise to no subsequent legislation.

In 1847 Senior was re-elected to the Drummond chair for a second five-year stint, during which he planned to digest his many economic articles, lectures, pamphlets, letters of advice to ministers, and parliamentary reports into a single 'great book'. He did not complete this project, no doubt partly because he failed to be elected for a further professorial term. Perhaps he was unable to achieve a sufficiently coherent analytical view of the subject. It is notable, for example, that when he reviewed J. S. Mill's magisterial *Principles of Political Economy* (1848) in the *Edinburgh Review* (October 1848), Senior was devastatingly sceptical both about the validity of what he called the 'science of political economy' and about the practical utility for policy purposes of the associated 'art of political economy'. Perhaps the completion of his 'great book' was also hindered by the fact that he was constantly in demand as one of the most luminous and perceptive government advisers of his era; in 1857, for example, he was again appointed to a royal commission, this time on another of his favourite remedies for poverty—popular education.

On the other hand, it is evident that during the last two decades of his life Senior's interests broadened considerably and that he spent an increasing amount of time talking and listening to the many European intellectuals and statesmen with whom he had developed close and enduring friendships. He had (since the early 1830s) been accustomed to spend the legal vacations travelling, often with his wife and two children, in England, Ireland, Belgium, France, or Italy—where they were entertained by a multitude of friends who had already stayed at 13 Hyde Park Gate. Senior's company was as much in demand as his advice, because he had the most sociable and outgoing of personalities, and a talent for attracting, as well as delivering, stimulating conversation and correspondence. Lord Overstone, for example, who had accompanied him on a tour of Lancashire cotton factories in 1837, referred to his 'very acute and intelligent mind united with other qualities which render him a very desirable travelling companion' (O'Brien, 222). His lifelong friendships with Alexis de Tocqueville and Comte Cavour began on their first visits to London (in 1833 and 1836), but it was not until Senior's 1848 visit to Paris that he began to write detailed reports of his interviews with prominent Europeans, and eventually to fill a series of journals with firsthand accounts of revolutionary events described by informed observers. He published selections from his interchanges with French statesmen (such as Thiers and Guizot) in the *Fortnightly Review* and the *Cornhill Magazine*; the most interesting of the conversations were subsequently edited by his daughter and published posthumously in book form.

Nassau Senior retired from the professorship in 1862 and died at 13 Hyde Park Gate on 4 June 1864, after a short illness. He was buried at Kensal Green cemetery. He was survived by his wife and his two children: Mary Charlotte Mair Simpson, to whom he willed full jurisdiction over his manuscripts, books, and pamphlets, and Nassau John Senior, a lawyer. His daughter-in-law, Jane Elizabeth Senior, became the first woman to be appointed an inspector of workhouses and pauper schools.

PHYLLIS DEANE

Sources M. Bowley, *Nassau Senior and classical economics* (1937) · M. C. M. Simpson, *Many memories of many people* (1898) · S. L. Levy, *Nassau William Senior* (1970) · *EdinR*, 88 (1848), 293–339 · *The works and correspondence of David Ricardo*, ed. P. Sraffa and M. H. Dobb, 11 vols. (1951–73), vol. 9 · *The correspondence of Lord Overstone*, ed. D. P. O'Brien, 1 (1971) · *DNB* · M. C. M. Simpson, ed., *Correspondence and conversations of Alexis de Tocqueville with N. W. Senior, 1834–59*, 2 vols. (1872) · M. C. M. Simpson, *Nassau Senior: conversations with M. Thiers, M. Guizot, etc.*, 2 vols. (1878) · A. I. T., 'The end of a long day's work', *Cornhill Magazine*, 10 (Aug 1864), 253–6

Archives Bodl. Oxf. · Bristol University Library · LUL · NL Wales · Trinity Cam. · U. Wales, Bangor | BL, corresp. with Lord Holland, Add. MS 52021 · BL, letters to Marvey Napier, Add. MSS 34621–34626 · Derbys. RO, Wilmot-Horton MSS · Devon RO, Fortescue MSS · NL Scot., Fraser MSS · Royal Library of Belgium, Brussels, letters to Adolphe Quetelet · UCL, letters to Lord Brougham · UCL, Chadwick MSS

Likenesses W. Drummond, lithograph, 1836 (after W. Behnes), BM; repro. in *Athenaeum portraits* (1836) · engraving, NPG [*see illus.*] · print, BM

Wealth at death under £18,000: resworn probate, April 1866, *CGPLA Eng. & Wales* (1864)

Senior, William (1861–1937), lawyer and author, was born on 17 December 1861 at Bond Street, Wakefield, Yorkshire, the son (there was also a daughter) of Thomas Senior (*d.* 1892), solicitor, and his wife, Lucy Ellen Winter. He was admitted to Clare College, Cambridge, in 1879, and graduated BA in 1883. Admitted a solicitor in 1886, he practised law alone in Wakefield.

In 1891 Senior published *Tutor and Pupils: Talks about Twelve Law Maxims*. He was a member of the Yorkshire Archaeological Society, and in 1894 published *The Old Wakefield Theatre*, a historical account. In 1895, following the death of his father, with whom he had lately been in partnership, he gave up his Yorkshire practice and moved to London. Resigning from the roll of solicitors, he was called to the bar at the Middle Temple on 29 April 1896, though the nature of his subsequent law practice remains obscure.

From 1902 to 1908 Senior wrote frequent articles for *Cornhill Magazine* and *Punch*; he is to be distinguished from the William Senior (*d.* 1920) who was editor of *The Field* during this period. He contributed regularly to the *Mariner's Mirror* from its inception in 1911 until 1913; from 1913 to 1919, he belonged to its editorial committee. He was a member of the council of the Society for Nautical Research from 1912 to 1927.

Senior was particularly interested in questions of maritime law, but he also wrote on general problems relating to the navy and the merchant marine. Much of his research was done at the Public Record Office; his articles, most of which appeared in the *Mariner's Mirror* and the *Law Quarterly Review*, dealt with the maritime courts, their judges and lawyers, and the trials there. His *Doctors' Commons* (1922) is anecdotal legal history for the layman, based upon a wide range of sources. The collection of old maritime cases which he published in *Naval History in the Law Courts* (1927) is of interest for the examples of situations involving common seamen.

His interest in English maritime courts and naval matters led Senior to maritime law in general. From 1930 until his death in 1937, Senior wrote an average of one article a year for the *Law Quarterly Review*. These eight articles are short pieces about various European jurists and their contacts with medieval England.

Senior died of a heart attack on 28 January 1937, at his home, 13 Alexandra Mansions, Chelsea, London. He had never married, and his residuary legatee was Clare College, Cambridge, which received approximately £46,000 'for the furtherance of the studies of legal history and comparative law'.

W. H. BRYSON

Sources W. H. Bryson, 'William Senior (1862–1937), legal historian', *American Journal of Legal History*, 16 (1972), 252–9 · *The Times* (1 Feb 1937), 1 · *Wakefield Express* (6 Feb 1937), 16 · *Law List* (1886–96) · *Kelly's directory of the West Riding of Yorkshire* (1893), 866, 886 · *Yorkshire Archaeological Journal*, 12 (1892–3), xii · H. A. C. Sturgess, ed., *Register of admissions to the Honourable Society of the Middle Temple, from the fifteenth century to the year 1944*, 2 (1949), 706 · Venn, *Alum. Cant.* · b. cert. · d. cert.

Wealth at death £63,186 4*s.* 4*d.*: probate, 1 April 1937, *CGPLA Eng. & Wales*

Senlis, Adam de [Adam of Evesham] (*d.* 1189), abbot of Evesham and canon lawyer, was probably related to the lords of Chantilly and the earls of Northampton. He entered the Cluniac priory of La Charité-sur-Loire and on 6 June 1157 became prior of Bermondsey, for which house he obtained privileges from Henry II. Adam left Bermondsey on 16 April 1161, having been elected abbot of Evesham. He often served as a papal judge-delegate, and in 1162 was one of the commissioners sent to Pope Alexander III (*r.* 1159–81) to obtain Thomas Becket's pallium, persuading the pope to confer it free of the usual charges. Adam reformed Evesham Abbey on Cluniac lines and seems to have been the first to exclude the laity from the abbey church. He finished the cloister and the nave, and with his own hands translated the relics of St Ecgwine (*d.* 717) to a new shrine in 1183. In 1189 he obtained a privilege of Pope

Clement III (*r.* 1187–91) granting the abbots of Evesham the use of the pontificalia (except the gloves and the ring, already used) and exemption from the bishop of Worcester's jurisdiction.

Among Adam's literary correspondents were Gerald of Wales, John of Salisbury, and Peter of Blois; his own writings, now lost, included *De miraculo sancte eucharistie, ad Rainaldum, Oratio exhortatoria ad sanctimoniales de Godstow, Sermones et homelie*, and *Epistole ad diversos*. Of his letters five survive in Jesus College, Oxford (MS 11, fols. [i], 2v, 130, 134v, and 140). Four of them are personal, the fifth is a report to Alexander III, edited by K. Christensen in *The Two Laws: Studies in Medieval Legal History Dedicated to Stephan Kuttner* (ed. L. Mayali and S. A. J. Tibbetts, 1990, 40–54). Adam's sermon on St Vincent, mentioned in one of the letters, may be represented in the same manuscript on folio 134. He died on 12 November 1189, presumably at Evesham Abbey, where he would also have been buried.

D. C. Cox

Sources W. D. Macray, ed., *Chronicon abbatiae de Evesham, ad annum 1418*, Rolls Series, 29 (1863), 100–02, 178 · J. Pits, *Relationum historicarum de rebus Anglicis*, ed. [W. Bishop] (Paris, 1619), 225 · *Ann. mon.*, 1.49, 53; 3.440–41; 4.385 · G. de Pont-Sainte-Maxence, *La vie de Saint Thomas le martyr*, ed. E. Walberg (Lund, 1922), 22–4 · D. Knowles, *The monastic order in England*, 2nd edn (1963), 331n · *Letters and charters of Gilbert Foliot*, ed. A. Morey and others (1967), 178 · 'De spiritualibus Anglie', BL, Harley MS 229, fol. 25 · *The letters of John of Salisbury*, ed. and trans. H. E. Butler and W. J. Millor, rev. C. N. L. Brooke, OMT, 2: *The later letters, 1163–1180* (1979), 286–9 [Lat. orig. with parallel Eng. text] · *Gir. Camb. opera*, 1.229–37 · 'Petri Blesensis epistolae', *Patrologia Latina*, 207 (1855), 304–6

Archives Jesus College, Oxford, MS 11, fols. [i], 2v, 130, 134v, 140

Likenesses seal, Westminster Abbey, attached to muniment 2857

Senlis, Simon (I) de [Simon de St Liz], **earl of Northampton and earl of Huntingdon** (*d.* **1111x13**), magnate, was the third son of Landri de Senlis, lord of Chantilly and Ermenonville, and a lady Ermengarde. The derivation St Liz (*de sancto Licio*) appears to be an attempted etymology for Senlis (*Silva necta*). His elder brother Guy de Senlis (*d.* 1124), a generous benefactor to Notre Dame de Senlis and St Martin des Champs, inherited the patrimony, his sons becoming prominent supporters of the Capetian kings, with three in succession holding the title of grand butler of France. Another brother, Hubert, became a canon of Notre Dame, Paris. Both the foundation charter of Sawtry Abbey, founded by his son Simon (II) de *Senlis (*d.* 1153), and the late register of St Andrew's Priory, Northampton, believed Simon (I) to have come to England in 1066 and to have been patronized by William I; but his absence from Domesday Book (1086) suggests that his arrival, or at least his endowment, took place under William Rufus.

Little is known about the career of Simon de Senlis, and it is unknown whether he aided Rufus during the serious baronial insurrections of 1088 in favour of his brother Robert Curthose. Nevertheless, he was distinguished enough to receive in marriage *Maud (or Matilda) (*d.* 1131) [*see under* David I], daughter of Earl *Waltheof and Countess Judith, niece of William the Conqueror, and was granted, probably in right of his wife, the earldoms of Northampton and Huntingdon, in or before 1090. The semi-legendary tract about the Countess Judith, *De comitissa*, written in the later years of Henry II's reign and incorporated into the account of the life and martyrdom of Waltheof compiled at Crowland *c.*1219, records an implausible tradition that the king had initially wished to give the widowed Judith and her lands to Simon, son of Ranulf the Rich, who had come with his elder brother Garnier (in fact Simon (I)'s uncle) and forty knights. Refusing Simon on account of his lameness, however, Judith and her daughters fled from the king's anger into the Ely marshes.

According to the *De comitissa*, Simon de Senlis made a successful pilgrimage to Jerusalem. This was almost certainly after the first crusade, for Suger notes that Simon was captured during William Rufus's Vexin campaign of 1098 against the Capetian heir-apparent, Louis, and subsequently ransomed. Earl Simon witnessed Henry I's charter of liberties issued at his coronation on 5 August 1100 and may have accompanied Henry on his campaign against Robert de Bellême's castle at Tickhill in 1102. He attests royal charters in England from 1100 to 1103, in 1106 and 1107, and in 1109 and 1110.

At Northampton Earl Simon probably constructed the first castle and walled the considerable settlement that had expanded beyond the earlier defences. Although the earliest surviving fabric of the round church of the Holy Sepulchre in Northampton dates to the second quarter of the twelfth century, it is possible that its foundation was inspired by Simon's pilgrimage. Here he also founded the church of All Saints and the Cluniac priory of St Andrew (between 1093 and 1100) as a dependency of La Charité-sur-Loire. When Hugh of Leicester, steward of Countess Maud, established monks of La Charité at Preston Capes (*c.*1090) in emulation of his lord, Earl Simon granted them the endowments of the secular college at Daventry to which they subsequently moved (between 1107 and 1108). The earl also made grants to Lincoln Cathedral.

Simon de Senlis embarked on a second journey east, but died at La Charité, 'the eldest daughter of Cluny', and was buried there in the great new priory church. It is possible that his body was subsequently moved to the priory of St Neots, which he had patronized. The date of his death is uncertain. He attests a grant of Henry I to Bath Abbey on 8 August 1111 at Bishop's Waltham, as the king was crossing to Normandy, and this may mark the earl's own outward voyage. By midsummer 1113, however, David of Scotland was recognized as earl of Huntingdon, marrying Simon's widow, Maud, although the earldom of Northampton reverted to the crown.

Simon de Senlis had three known children: Simon (II), *Waldef, who became abbot of Melrose (1148–59), and Matilda, who married Robert fitz Richard of Tonbridge. Countess Maud's younger sister Judith (or Alice) married Ralph de Tosny in 1103.

Matthew Strickland

Sources F. Michel, ed., 'Vita et passio Waldevi comitis', *Chroniques anglo-normandes: recueil d'extraits et d'écrits relatifs à l'histoire de Normandie et d'Angleterre*, 2 (Rouen, 1836) · *Reg. RAN*, vol. 2 · R. M. Serjeantson, 'Origin and history of the de Senlis family', *Associated*

Architectural Societies' Reports and Papers, 31 (1911–13), 504–17 • GEC, *Peerage*, new edn, 6.640–42 • *VCH Northamptonshire*, 3.2–5 • *An inventory of the historical monuments in the county of Northampton*, Royal Commission on Historical Monuments (England), 5 (1985) • M. J. Franklin, ed., *The cartulary of Daventry Priory*, Northamptonshire RS (1988)

Senlis, Simon (II) de, earl of Northampton and earl of Huntingdon (*d.* **1153**), magnate, was the elder son of Simon (I) de *Senlis. His career was complicated by rivalry with the Scottish royal house over the honour of Huntingdon, the inheritance of his mother, *Maud [*see under* David I]. He was a minor when his father died between 1111 and 1113, and custody of the estate, with the rank of earl, passed to Maud's second husband, David, future king of Scots. Following Maud's death in 1131, by which date Senlis had reached his majority, King David remained in control, despite Senlis's demands for justice. King Stephen then recognized Henry, son of David and Maud, as earl of Huntingdon in 1136 and again in 1139; and although Senlis had probably held the honour and earldom during Henry's temporary forfeiture (January 1138–April 1139), it was only on the final collapse of Stephen's Scottish diplomacy in the summer of 1141 that his claims were fully realized. His comital standing remains a source of much confusion. The argument that in 1136 Northampton was 'detached from the earldom of Huntingdon and made a separate earldom for Simon' (Davis, 129) is difficult to accept. (Some modern authorities have even seen him as an earl of Northumberland—he was never such.) His earliest known appearance as earl of Northampton occurs in 1138 or early in 1139; and the evidence suggests that 'Northampton' and 'Huntingdon' were alternative names for the same earldom, which normally, though not invariably, also embraced Bedfordshire and Cambridgeshire. One of Stephen's foremost adherents, Senlis fought at the battle of Lincoln on 2 February 1141, and was a commander of the victorious royalist army at Winchester the following September. His comital authority extended over Northamptonshire, Huntingdonshire, and Bedfordshire, and within the first two shires he exercised regalian rights and assumed full responsibility for county government, clearly at Stephen's bidding. Jocelin of Furness's life of Abbot *Waldef of Melrose, Senlis's younger brother, contains important information on his career and character. Henry of Huntingdon believed that he and Eustace, Stephen's eldest son, were the most uncompromising opponents of Henry Plantagenet in 1153, and that peace was possible only because of their sudden deaths. He was a major benefactor of numerous religious institutions, and founded a Cistercian abbey at Sawtry in 1146–7, as well as a Cluniac nunnery, Delapré Abbey. He married Isabella, or Elizabeth, daughter of *Robert, earl of Leicester, and was Leicester's named ally in his famous treaty with the earl of Chester *c.*1150. He and his wife, who as a widow married Gervase Paynel (*d.* 1194) of Dudley, had a son and at least one daughter: Simon (III) de Senlis (*d.* 1184), the last Senlis holder of the earldoms of Northampton and of Huntingdon, and Isabel, who married William Mauduit (*d.* 1194) of Hanslope. Simon (II) de Senlis died in August 1153 in Northampton and was buried in St Andrew's Priory, Northampton. KEITH STRINGER

Sources K. J. Stringer, 'A Cistercian archive: the earliest charters of Sawtry Abbey', *Journal of the Society of Archivists*, 6 (1978–81), 325–34 • cartularies of the Cluniac priory of St Andrew, Northampton, BL, Cotton MS Vespasian E.xvii; Royal MS 2.B.ix • *Reg. RAN*, vol. 3 • Henry, archdeacon of Huntingdon, *Historia Anglorum*, ed. D. E. Greenway, OMT (1996) • H. E. Salter, ed., *Eynsham cartulary*, 1, OHS, 49 (1907) • Jocelin of Furness, 'Vita sancti Waldeni', *Acta sanctorum: Augustus*, 1 (Antwerp, 1733), 241–77 • K. J. Stringer, 'An alleged medieval earl of Northumberland', *Archaeologia Aeliana*, 5th ser., 1 (1973), 133–6 • R. H. C. Davis, *King Stephen*, 3rd edn (1990) • GEC, *Peerage*, new edn • W. Farrer, *Honors and knights' fees … from the eleventh to the fourteenth century*, 2 (1924)

Archives BL, cartularies of the Cluniac priory of St Andrew, Northampton, Cotton MS Vesp. E.xvii; Royal MS 2.B.ix • BL, cartulary of the Augustinian priory of St James, Northampton, Cotton MS Tib. E.v • CUL, cartulary of the Benedictine abbey of Thorney, Add. MS 3020

Likenesses seal, BL

Sennett, (Alice) Maud Mary Arncliffe [*née* (Alice) Maud Mary Sparagnapane] (**1862–1936**), women's suffrage activist, was born on 4 February 1862 at 142 Bishopsgate Street Without, London, the elder daughter of Gaudente Sparagnapane (*c.*1816–1877), an Italian immigrant wholesale confectioner, and his wife, Aurelia Williams (*c.*1832–1915). Nothing is known of her education. Of striking, dark appearance, she became an actress, using the stage name Mary Kingsley. She played at theatres throughout England and Scotland and, for a year, in Australia. She married Henry Robert Arncliffe Sennett (1863/4–1944) at the church of Holy Trinity, St Giles, London, on 9 July 1898, put the stage behind her, and, with her husband, ran her family firm of 'G. Sparagnapane & Co., The Oldest Established Manufacturers of Christmas Crackers and Wedding Cake Ornaments', which had its premises on the borders of Clerkenwell and the City. There were no children of the marriage.

In 1906 Maud Arncliffe Sennett became interested in the women's suffrage movement which, for the next fifteen years, dominated her life. Between 1906 and 1913 she belonged, both consecutively and in parallel, to the constitutional and militant wings of the movement, being at some time a member of the constitutional London Society for Women's Suffrage as well as a member of the executive committees of the Women's Freedom League, the Hampstead branch of the Women's Social and Political Union (WSPU), and the Actresses' Franchise League. Her experience as an actress made her a most effective speaker; she did not undervalue her own worth in this respect. In November 1911 she was found guilty of using threatening behaviour after breaking a window in the office of the *Daily Mail*, protesting against the paper's policy of ignoring the fund-raising success of the WSPU. At her trial she is reported as saying:

> I am an employee of male labour, and the men who earn their living through the power of my poor brain, the men whose children I pay to educate, whose members of Parliament I pay for, and to whose old-age pensions I contribute—these are allowed a vote, while I am voteless. (*Votes for Women*, 24 Nov 1911, 126)

(Alice) **Maud Mary Arncliffe Sennett** (1862–1936), by Lena Connell, *c.*1908

Her subsequent fine was paid by Lord Northcliffe.

In 1913, inspired by the spectacle and emotion surrounding the funeral of Emily Wilding Davison and encouraged by Alexander Orr, an Edinburgh businessman she met there, who felt that men were keen to press for women's suffrage, Maud Arncliffe Sennett founded the Northern Men's Federation for Women's Suffrage (NMF). It was composed mainly of Scottish councillors and baillies, and she determined to send, in support of women's suffrage, a deputation of these worthies to Prime Minister Asquith, who was equally determined not to receive them. The NMF did, however, receive considerable press coverage and continued its campaign, generously funded by Maud Arncliffe Sennett, during the First World War. She, in turn, was accorded a singular deference by the members of the NMF, who were referred to as her 'bairns'. In 1916 she wrote a *Manifesto on Venereal Disease* and for the remainder of the war campaigned vigorously against the Contagious Disease Acts that were included in the Defence of the Realm Act. With the granting of a limited measure of enfranchisement to women in 1918 support for the NMF dwindled, despite Maud Arncliffe Sennett's renaming it the Northern Men's Federation for Women's Suffrage and Land Reform and drafting a 'Land Charter'. Although she kept in touch with some of her fellow suffragists, in the ensuing years she does not appear to have been involved in the continuing feminist campaigns but to have devoted her energies to her new foundation, the Midhurst–Haselmere Anti-Vivisection Society. She died from tuberculosis on 15 September 1936 at her home, Eversheds, Midhurst, Sussex. Her devoted husband then arranged the publication of her autobiography and gave to the British Museum the scrapbooks she had compiled during the suffrage campaign, thereby ensuring her the measure of immortality that she undoubtedly desired. In 1937 he married Johanna Olsen (*d.* 1939).

ELIZABETH CRAWFORD

Sources M. A. Sennett, *The child* [n.d., *c.*1938] • C. Eustance, 'Citizens, Scotsmen, "bairns": manly politics and women's suffrage in the Northern Men's Federation, 1913–20', *The men's share? Masculinities, male support and women's suffrage in Britain, 1890–1920*, ed. A. V. John and C. Eustance (1997), 182–205 • L. Leneman, *A guid cause: the women's suffrage movement in Scotland* (1995) • E. Crawford, *The women's suffrage movement: a reference guide, 1866–1928* (1999) • d. cert. • m. cert. • b. cert. • BL, Arncliffe Sennett MSS

Archives BL, MSS

Likenesses L. Connell, photograph, *c.*1908, Women's Library, London [*see illus.*] • G. Pownall, oils, 1913, Swan Theatre Gallery, Stratford upon Avon, Warwickshire

Wealth at death £5354 12*s.* 11*d.*: resworn probate, 14 Oct 1936, *CGPLA Eng. & Wales*

Seppings, Sir Robert (1767–1840), naval architect, was born at Fakenham, the fourth child of Robert Seppings and his wife, Lydia, the daughter of John Milligen, a linen draper at Harleston. His father was a cattle salesman but was not very successful and the young Robert had to work as a messenger, carrying letters on a mule. Lydia's brother John Milligen, a retired naval captain living at Plymouth and childless, adopted Robert Seppings and also two daughters of his brother Thomas. One of these girls, Charlotte, later married Robert Seppings while the other married Sir Richard Dacres.

Apprenticeship and innovation, 1782–1803 In 1782 Seppings was accepted as a personal apprentice by John Henslow, the master shipwright at Plymouth. Because of his co-ordinating role, the master shipwright may be seen as the equivalent of today's general manager, and even to be accepted as apprentice by such a man was a mark of distinction. Seppings completed his apprenticeship in 1787 and, helped by wartime expansion, rose rapidly through the ranks of shipwright, quarterman, and foreman to become assistant master shipwright at Plymouth Dock in 1797. His former master, Henslow, was now the surveyor and, aware of Seppings's merit, may quite properly have influenced the rapid rise of his former pupil.

Seppings became concerned over the time and manpower needed to lift a ship onto dock blocks for the examination of the keel area. He devised a block consisting of three wedges which could be removed in two-thirds of the time and with far fewer men. This invention was tried in the docking of the *San Joseph* in September 1800 and adopted at Plymouth in 1801 and was so successful that the Navy Board awarded him a bonus of £1000, a very large sum equivalent to about four years' salary, while the Royal Society of Arts awarded him its gold medal in 1803. The

Sir Robert Seppings (1767–1840), by William Bradley, 1833

Navy Board estimated that this improvement saved £11,000 over three years at Plymouth alone.

Chatham, 1804–1813 Seppings was further encouraged by appointment as master shipwright at Chatham in 1804, aged thirty-seven, very young for such a senior post. In this post he set to work to devise a systematic series of changes to the structure of warships to overcome the main problems of traditional frame-built ships. These were excessive deflection in a seaway leading to early rot, shortage of long timbers, and the weakness of the bow and stern against raking gunfire. The first of these problems was the most serious and cost large sums of money in repair bills.

The unequal forces of weight and buoyancy as the ship passed through waves would cause it to bend with the planks in the side sliding over each other, so that rectangular sections of the side changed in shape to lozenges. Seppings was later to describe this behaviour as like a five-bar gate without the diagonal. This deflection in shear—known as 'breakage'—disturbed the caulking and allowed sea water to seep in between the planks, which would rot quickly, further weakening the structure. Seppings's answer was to arrange diagonal frames on the sides of his ships, later further strengthened by packing the bottom solid with timbers, supporting the deck beams on continuous shelves rather than on individual knees, and arranging the deck planking on the diagonal. His scheme was developed and tried in stages. Some of his early ideas may have been used during the refit of the 36-gun frigate *Glenmore* in 1800 but details are obscure.

The Navy Board was, as usual, quick to act and in 1805 approved a limited use of Seppings's ideas for the repair of the *Kent*. This was further developed the following year in repairs to two other ships and the full diagonal system was first fitted to the *Tremendous* in 1810; in 1811 the *Albion* incorporated the complete system. The speed with which these changes were adopted is impressive; the navy needed every ship at sea in wartime and time in dock was severely limited but the Navy Board, and presumably the Admiralty, saw Seppings's work as so important that it was worth accepting that ships were out of service for a longer time while they were strengthened.

Measurements taken when *Tremendous* floated out of dock showed that the breakage with Seppings's modifications was negligible. In November 1811 John Barrow, the progressive second secretary (senior permanent civil servant), called a meeting of eminent scientists to consider Seppings's work. This meeting led to Thomas Young being asked to carry out a mathematical study of the loading and strains on a ship in a seaway. His study used fluxions (as opposed to calculus) and was almost incomprehensible but generally supported Seppings. Details of the meeting reached Napoleon a few days later and he commissioned the French mathematician Dupin to study Seppings's scheme. Dupin's analysis was both more enthusiastic and clearer than that of Young. Not for the first time—or the last—engineering design was well ahead of theoretical explanation.

Seppings presented a paper on his scheme to the Royal Society in 1814, as a result of which he was elected a fellow and later, in 1818, received their Copley medal. There was some hostility to Seppings on two grounds, the first being plagiarism. Other people had, indeed, tried diagonal stiffening but without success. Gabriel Snodgrass had been very successful in using diagonals to stiffen the ship in the transverse plane but did not expand his approach to the sides. Seppings himself said that the only external influence on his thinking was the design of the covered bridge over the Rhine at Schaffhausen. It was also alleged then, and has been alleged even recently, that Seppings's work was not 'scientific'. This is based on a fallacious equation between mathematics and science. Seppings's logical thought progression from loading by the sea to strains and hence to the alignment of structural members was truly scientific, confirmed as it was by measurement. There also seems to have been a contemporary belief that hydrodynamics was scientific while structural design was not.

An even more convincing proof of Seppings's scheme was provided in 1817, when the old 74-gun ship *Justicia* was used for trials before being broken up. A paper to the Royal Society showed that the breakage on undocking, measured with and without diagonals, was reduced by about a half by the stiffeners. It is interesting that in the original scheme the diagonals were in tension while those in *Justicia* were in compression, and Seppings was to claim that his original method was superior. The problem with wood construction is the strength of joints, and for this reason a modern designer would probably use the diagonals in compression. However, Seppings's approach worked well. A further paper in 1820 showed how the diagonal system could be used in merchant ships. Few merchant ships seem to have been built in this style, the conspicuous exception being I. K. Brunel's *Great Western*: Brunel acknowledged Admiralty assistance in planning her structure.

Surveyor, 1813–1832 Seppings was rewarded for his work by appointment as surveyor in 1813, the mid-forties being a typical age for appointment to this creative post. By 1815 his system was standard practice; the 120-gun *Howe* was probably the first new ship designed using Seppings's fully developed scheme.

Seppings was concerned over the damage and casualties at Trafalgar during Nelson's end-on approach, as the weak beak bulkhead provided little protection from raking fire. When *Namur* was razed in 1805 Seppings retained the heavy bow planking up to the upper gun deck and later developed this into the round bow which also became a standard feature, providing some protection against raking fire and permitting up to twelve guns to fire ahead. His round stern was less popular, mainly on aesthetic grounds, though there were a few practical problems such as the siting of the officers' 'heads'. He was knighted on 17 August 1819 on board the royal yacht *Royal George*, while under sail and with the royal standard flying. He was to receive gifts marking his achievements from the sovereigns of Russia, Denmark, and the Netherlands.

The end of the war meant that few new ships were designed and Seppings had few opportunities to demonstrate his skills as a designer. The later two-deckers of the *Canopus* class, such as *Ganges*, had Seppings's structure and are best seen as a new design. They were followed by the even bigger, 90-gun, ships of the *Rodney* class, which had a long and successful life. They were seen as particularly good in head seas and rolled little. *Nile* was fitted with engines in 1852–4 and later served as the famous training ship *Conway* before being destroyed by fire in 1956.

Seppings produced a modified version of his scheme using iron diagonals for frigates, as may be seen in the frigate *Unicorn* at Dundee. This was further developed in the 1830s by Lang and Edye for use in ships of the line. As surveyor, Seppings established a model room at the Admiralty showing developments in design; many of the models from this collection survive in the Science Museum and National Maritime Museum. Seppings was a keen supporter of the Admiralty School of Naval Architecture (established in 1811), even though his own son failed the entry examination.

It is sometimes argued that Seppings's ships were heavy, which may have been true when stiffening was added to an existing ship but should not have been the case in a new design, where the stronger ship should have been lighter. Seppings claimed that there was a considerable reduction in the number of trees required to build a ship when his methods were used, which must have equated to weight reduction. Perhaps more important, it was possible to build using shorter lengths of timber rather than the long pieces which were in short supply.

In the early post-war years there were many 'experimental sailings' in which ships by different designers were raced against each other; identical ships achieved very different results. Great importance was attached at the time to the results, but analysis shows that the skill of the captain, not just in sailing but also in adjusting the trim and the rigging was all important. In 1832 a joint sailing competition was held with the French, who were particularly impressed with the way that *Donegal*, a French-built prize, was much faster after British modifications.

One of the most successful captains in experimental sailings was Captain William Symonds, whose successes were achieved in ships of his own design. It should, however, be noted that Seppings's frigate *Castor* was consistently fast during the late 1830s. As a result of his political contacts Symonds was appointed as surveyor to replace Seppings in 1832, the first amateur to hold that professional post. In 1836 the University of Oxford conferred the degree of DCL on Seppings.

Achievement and death The vast increase in the size and gun power of wooden warships in the last decades from 1815 was only possible as a result of the introduction of diagonally framed ships. In 1819 the House of Commons finance committee drew attention to the savings from the greater durability of Seppings's ships. A final compliment came at the great naval exhibition of 1891, when the gallery showing progress in naval architecture was named the Seppings Gallery.

After his retirement Seppings lived at Taunton until his death there on 25 September 1840; he was buried in St Mary's Church, Taunton, where there is a tablet to his memory in the chancel which briefly records his achievements. Lady Seppings died at Taunton in 1834. His eldest son, John Milligen Seppings, was for twenty years the inspector of shipping for the East India Company at Calcutta. Another son, Captain Edward Seppings, together with his wife and two children, was killed at Cawnpore during the Indian mutiny. DAVID K. BROWN

Sources *DNB* • T. Wright, 'Thomas Young and Robert Seppings: science and ship construction in the early 19th century', *Royal Institution* (1981), 55–71 • D. K. Brown, *Before the ironclad* (1990) • R. Morriss, *The royal dockyards during the revolutionary and Napoleonic wars* (1983) • D. K. Brown, 'The structural improvement to wooden ships instigated by Robert Seppings', *Naval Architect* (May 1979) • B. Lavery, *The ship of the line*, 2 vols. (1983–4)
Archives NMM, corresp. [microfilm]
Likenesses W. Bradley, oils, 1833, NMM [*see illus.*]

Septimius Severus, Lucius (145/6–211), Roman emperor, was the founder of the Severan dynasty and passed his last four years in Britain directing military operations against peoples beyond the northern frontier of the Roman province. A ruthless reformer and efficient administrator, his reign ranks only after those of Augustus and Hadrian in the evolution of the empire. Severus was born on 11 April 145 or 146 at Lepcis Magna in Tripolitania (Libya), a prosperous Phoenician city on the north coast of Africa; his mother was Fulvia Pia, but the name of his father is not recorded. The Septimii may have been of local Punic origin who chose to assume the Italian family name. At seventeen Severus spoke in public and then departed for

Lucius Septimius Severus (145/6–211), bronze bust

Rome, retaining, it is recorded, an 'African accent' for the rest of his life (Magie, 19.9).

Having entered the Roman senate in 169, Severus rose steadily through the succession of traditional magistracies at Rome and imperial appointments in the provinces. His first wife was Paccia Marciana; she died at some time before 185, when, during a tour of duty in Syria, he married his second wife, Julia Domna. She belonged to the priestly dynasty of Emesa in Syria and as empress became a powerful figure in her own right. Severus achieved the consulship *c.*190 and was appointed governor of Upper Pannonia (Hungary and northern Croatia), a major command over three legions on the Danube frontier. The murder of Pertinax (28 March 193) triggered off a competition for power between three major provincial armies: that in Britain under Decimus Clodius Albinus, the Pannonian under Severus, and the Syrian under Gaius Pescennius Niger. It was Severus who made the first and, as it proved, decisive move: proclaimed emperor by his troops on 9 April, he was ruling in Rome by the end of May. To Albinus, Severus offered the novel title 'Caesar' with its implied promise of the succession and the consulship of the following year. In 196 Albinus, who was gaining popularity among the upper classes of the west, was declared a public enemy by the senate and replaced as Caesar by Caracalla [*see below*], Severus's elder son (he was raised to Augustus in 198). Severus's Danube legions defeated the weaker army of Albinus near Lugdunum (Lyons) on 19 February 197 amid scenes of horrific carnage. Harsh measures against adherents of Albinus resulted in confiscations of property and may even have caused a disruption of the commerce in wine and olive oil between Spain and Britain.

Cassius Dio informs us of the state of affairs on the northern frontier of Britain (*Dio's Roman History*, 75.5.4): the Caledonii, inhabitants of the Scottish highlands, had broken their pledge not to aid the Maeatae of central Scotland and, since Severus was busy with the Parthians, in order to ward off trouble, the new governor, Virius Lupus, could do no more than offer a large subsidy in exchange for a few prisoners. The same historian records a destructive invasion by peoples beyond the northern frontier around fifteen years before (*Dio's Roman History*, 72.8.2–6); yet there is no conclusive evidence for a major attack from the north in 197. Repair and rebuilding of the northern forts continued. An allusion in Cassius Dio to victories won in Britain and the dedication of an altar at Benwell (Collingwood and Wright, RIB 1337) on Hadrian's Wall to celebrate imperial victories may indicate that no major catastrophe brought Severus to Britain in 208. Yet there is the testimony of Herodian that a message came from the governor in Britain that 'the barbarians there were in a state of rebellion and were causing great damage, looting and wrecking virtually everything' (Herodian, 3.14.1). Both Cassius Dio and Herodian in fact give greater prominence to Severus's concern that his sons and the army needed the harsh discipline of war (*Dio's Roman History*, 76.11.1; Herodian, 3.14.2).

The imperial expedition to Britain in 208 was undertaken with characteristic vigour. Although coins of that year bearing the legend PROF[ECTIO] AUG[USTORUM] depict Severus riding on horseback (*Coins of the Roman Empire*, 568, 854) he was now suffering from a crippling disease (gout or arthritis) which caused him to be carried everywhere in a litter but 'in spirit he was tougher than any youth' (Herodian, 3.14.2). Accompanied by the empress, his sons, and senior military advisers (who included Papinian, prefect of the praetorian guard and the most distinguished jurist of the time), Severus crossed into the province with a large military force and a vast sum of money. The record of his British campaigns is deficient in many respects (*Dio's Roman History*, 16.12.1–5; Herodian, 3.14.6–8). There are no topographical details but only the outline of a guerrilla war in which the enemy harassed an army 'cutting down forests, levelling hills, filling up swamps and bridging rivers' (*Dio's Roman History*, 6.13.1). Operations continued during the following years, first against the Caledonii and subsequently against the Maeatae. By 210 Severus and both his sons had formally assumed the triumphal title Britannicus (*Coins*, 25, 34, 47, 49). Severus persisted with the effort until, having almost reached the extremity of the island, the Britons were forced to a settlement and to cede a great part of their territory. The victory was not conclusive and Severus was preparing to lead another attack on the Caledonii when he died at Eboracum (York) on 4 February 211.

The direction and scope of Severus's campaigns remain little known. A great deal of movement appears to have taken place by sea, for which a special combined command was created of the British, Rhine, and Danube fleets (coins of 209–11 bear images of Neptune and Oceanus). In Scotland only Cramond on the Forth and Carpow near Abernethy on the Tay can be linked with these campaigns: the former is a stone fort of normal auxiliary size (about 6 acres), the latter a purpose-built legionary base (about 24 acres). A rare coin of Caracalla showing a bridge of boats and the legend TRAIECTUS (*Coins*, p. 353) may depict the Tay crossing at Carpow where remains of large temporary enclosures have been found on both banks. Severus died in his sixty-sixth year in the eighteenth year of his reign. For all his unconcealed dislike of the regime, Cassius Dio offers what seems an authentic portrait:

> Small in stature but powerful until he grew weak from his illness his mind was sharp and very active. He was eager for more education than he had actually received. He was a man of few words but many ideas. He was considerate to friends, unforgiving towards opponents, single-minded in achieving his aims but caring nothing for his reputation. He raised money from every source but without killing anyone in the process, while for his part he paid out what was due without hesitation. (*Dio's Roman History*, 76.16.1–3)

Caracalla [Marcus Aurelius Antoninus] (188–217), Roman emperor, was Severus's elder son, who was born Septimius Bassianus on 4 April 188. He was known by his common nickname, which derived from his favourite dress, the Gallic cloak or *caracullus*. He succeeded Severus in 211, along with his brother Publius Septimius Geta. Despite the efforts of their mother, the brothers ignored their father's advice to work together, until Geta was murdered in the palace at Rome the following year, after which Caracalla ruled alone for a further five years, until his death on 8 April 217. On becoming emperor Caracalla immediately gave up the effort against the Britons: 'he made a settlement with the enemy, withdrew from their territory and evacuated the forts' (*Dio's Roman History*, 77.1.1) and with his brother rapidly headed back to Rome with the army 'as if they were returning as conquerors of Britain' (Herodian, 3.15.8). Nevertheless, Caracalla may have completed the campaign his father had planned for 211, while an inscription set over the east gate at Carpow seems to belong to the period when he was ruling alone. The division of Britain into two separate provinces, which Severus may have decided upon in 197, was now carried into effect, with the larger Upper Britain (Britannia Superior) in the south under a consular governor with two legions and in the north the smaller Lower Britain (Britannia Inferior) containing the remaining legion based at Eboracum. In the event, Caracalla's settlement proved lasting. The reconstruction of Hadrian's Wall defined permanently the northern limit of the Roman province, though effective control extended further north to roughly the line of the later England–Scotland border.

JOHN WILKES

Sources *Dio's Roman history*, ed. and trans. E. Cary, 9 vols. (1914–27) • Herodian, *History*, trans. C. R. Whittaker, 1 (1969) • D. Magie, ed. and trans., 'Life of Septimius Severus', *Scriptores historiae Augustae*, 1 (1921) • [Eutropius], *Eutropi Breviarium ab urbe condita*, ed. H. Droysen, MGH Auctores Antiquissimi, 2 (Berlin, 1879) • *Sexti Aurelii Victoris liber de caesaribus*, ed. F. Pichlmayr (Leipzig, 1911), 20 • *Pauli Orosii Historiarum adversus paganos*, ed. K. F. W. Zangemeister, 7 (Leipzig, 1889), 17 • A. R. Birley, *The African emperor, Septimius Severus* (1988) • S. S. Frere, *Britannia: a history of Roman Britain*, 3rd edn (1987), 154–70 • R. G. Collingwood and R. P. Wright, eds., *The Roman inscriptions of Britain*, 2 vols. (1965), RIB 1337 • *Coins of the Roman empire in the British Museum*, British Museum, Department of Coins and Medals, 1 (1923)

Likenesses bronze bust, BM [*see illus.*] • coins, repro. in H. Mattingly and E. A. Sydenham, *The Roman imperial coinage*, 4. 1 (1936), 54–206, 212–308 • portraits, repro. in A. M. McCann, *The Portraits of Septimius Severus, AD 193–211* (1968) • portraits, repro. in J. D. Breckenridge, 'Roman imperial portraiture from Augustus to Gallienus', *Aufstieg und Niedergang der römischen Welt*, II/12/2 (1981), 477–512

Séquard, Charles Édouard Brown- (1817–1894), physiologist and neurologist, was born on 8 April 1817 in Port Louis, Mauritius, the only son of Edward Brown (1784–1817), captain in the United States merchant service, and Charlotte Perrine Henriette, *née* Séquard (1788–1842). His mother was widowed during pregnancy and could not afford more than a rudimentary education for her son, whom she brought up with the help of her father, an emigrant from Marseilles. In 1838 Brown emigrated with his mother to Paris, to fulfil an ambition to become a novelist. He was devoted to his mother and honoured her after her death by adopting her former surname to make a double-barrelled name. He was generally regarded as a Frenchman, although Mauritius was then part of the British empire. He could have claimed citizenship of France or the United States of America through his parents, but he did not adopt French citizenship until the age of sixty-one.

Within a few months of arriving in Paris, Brown-Séquard's career plans changed, and he enrolled in the Faculté de Médecine, one of the leading medical institutions of the day. He graduated in 1846 with an MD thesis based on studies of nervous reflexes and sensory pathways in the spinal cord. This work provided a foundation for his demonstration that sensory nerve fibres cross in the spinal cord before ascending to the brain. This discovery aided the diagnosis of spinal damage and became known as the 'Brown-Séquard effect'. He presented his results in a paper to the Académie des Sciences in 1850. This early work led to further research on body temperature and the respiratory mechanism. In 1849 Brown-Séquard became auxiliary physician under Baron Larrey at the military hospital at Gros-Caillon, during an outbreak of cholera.

After practising and teaching medicine in Paris, Brown-Séquard, an ardent republican, left France following the coup d'état of 1851 and travelled to the USA, where he worked in Philadelphia, New York, and Boston, eventually becoming professor of physiology at the Medical College of Virginia (1854–5), where his outspoken opposition to slavery brought him into conflict with many of his colleagues. His peripatetic career continued for another twenty-three years. He lived in the USA, France, England, and Switzerland, holding appointments as physician to

Charles Édouard Brown-Séquard (1817–1894), by unknown engraver, pubd 1894 (after Serendat de Belzim)

the National Hospital for the Paralysed and Epileptic at Queen Square, London (1860–63), where he continued his experiments on rigor mortis, epilepsy, and sectioning the spinal cord; as professor of physiology at Harvard University (1863–8); as professor of comparative and experimental pathology in the Faculté de Médecine in Paris (1869–72); and as professor of physiology at the University of Geneva (1877–88).

Brown-Séquard married three times: first, in 1853, Ellen Fletcher (*d.* 1864); secondly, in 1872, Maria Rebecca Carlisle (*d.* 1874); and thirdly, in 1877, Elizabeth Emma Dakin (*d.* 1894). The marriages produced three children.

In 1856 Brown-Séquard demonstrated that removal of the adrenal glands was rapidly fatal to guinea-pigs, which confirmed observations of human adrenal disease reported the previous year by Thomas Addison. Attempts to reverse the effects of adrenalectomy by administering glandular extracts to animals were unsuccessful, but he kept in mind the idea of restoring active substances to the body, and this strategy later became a cornerstone of endocrinology research. Supposing that ageing was caused by a loss of 'invigorating substances' produced by the testicles, Brown-Séquard embarked on his best-known self-experiment in 1889, at the age of seventy-two. With the help of his assistant, Arsène d'Arsonval (1851–1940), he injected himself repeatedly with fresh extracts of animal testes—and claimed to feel younger and to have regained some of his former strength. Announcement of the results at the Société de Biologie in Paris on 1 June stimulated worldwide interest in 'organotherapy'. Many other doctors tested 'Brown-Séquard's elixir' on their patients, with mixed results. He distributed samples of the organ extracts gratis, to guarantee authenticity and quality and to thwart quacks who hoped to profit from his discovery. Not for the first time in his career, though, he had reached a conclusion too hastily; and, although aware of the dangers, had not been sufficiently cautious to exclude auto-suggestion as the explanation. Nevertheless, this was a fruitful error, as it set a lasting principle for treating endocrine disorders and stimulated interest in hormones.

As Brown-Séquard's reputation grew, he was in demand as a lecturer and travelled even more widely. He was said to have crossed the Atlantic Ocean at least sixty times, which was a slow and arduous business in those days. Affection for his native Mauritius drew him home on several occasions. During a visit in 1854 he helped the islanders during a severe cholera epidemic, which eventually claimed 12,000 lives. Believing that laudanum was superior to conventional treatments, he was said to have swallowed the vomit of victims to induce cholera symptoms, so that he could prove his theory to a hidebound medical establishment. The population was so thankful for his services that they awarded him a gold medal before he left for America. After leaving Virginia he spent another period in Paris and in 1858 gave a series of lectures at Edinburgh, Dublin, and Glasgow. His series of six lectures to the Royal College of Surgeons in London were later published as *Course of Lectures on the Physiology and Pathology of the Nervous System* (1860). Despite holding an appointment at the National Hospital, and building a lucrative practice in Wimpole Street, he left for the USA in 1863. In 1878 he returned to Paris for the last time, to take up the chair of experimental medicine at the Collège de France which had fallen vacant after the death of Claude Bernard. By this time he was laden with honours and prizes from many countries. He had been elected to the scientific academies of France and the USA. In Great Britain he was elected FRS and FRCP in 1860. In 1861 he gave the Royal Society's Croonian lecture and the Goulstonian lecture of the Royal College of Physicians. He was awarded an honorary LLD by Cambridge University (1880) and the Baly medal of the Royal College of Physicians of London (1883), and appointed chevalier of the Légion d'honneur in France (1880). Above all, he took pride in being a founder member in 1848 of the Société de Biologie, of which he was elected president in 1887.

Brown-Séquard made numerous important contributions to experimental physiology and pathology, and he quickly gained a worldwide reputation which rivalled even that of his friend Claude Bernard (1813–1878). During a long career he published 577 scientific works, including nine books, and helped to found several journals and learned societies. His productiveness was due to his very long working hours, abstemious lifestyle, and unswerving dedication to science. A nervous breakdown in 1851 was the price he paid for such dedication. He spurned lucrative private medical practice and never became a wealthy man. Brown-Séquard was regarded as unorthodox by his scientific peers because he tended to think intuitively and work impulsively, though this style may have helped him to stumble on important discoveries. His chief contributions were to knowledge of the nervous system and what were called 'internal secretions' before the word 'hormone' had been coined. He was a pioneer of experimental physiology and a staunch advocate of animal experimentation, which antagonized the growing antivivisectionist movement in Victorian Britain. But not all of his experiments depended on animals; and he sometimes performed on himself trials that were unpleasant or even painful.

Brown-Séquard died of a stroke in Paris on 1 April 1894,

at the age of seventy-seven, and was buried at Montparnasse cemetery. Despite his having been ridiculed for claiming to have found the secret of extended life, contemporaries praised his earlier achievements and were reluctant to dismiss his more imaginative theories. Writing in 1901, his biographer for the *Dictionary of National Biography* declared that 'he was much interested in the internal secretion of certain glands and, though his conclusions are not generally accepted, it seems probable that they will some day be found to contain the germ of further advances in physiology'. Those were prophetic words, because a few years later a number of new hormones was discovered. Indeed, he is often credited with being the father of endocrinology and hormone replacement therapy. ROGER G. GOSDEN

Sources M. J. Aminoff, *Brown-Séquard — a visionary of science* (1993) • J. M. D. Olmsted, *Charles-Édouard Brown-Séquard: a nineteenth century neurologist and endocrinologist* (1946) • J. D. Wilson, 'Charles-Édouard Brown-Séquard and the centennial of endocrinology', *Journal of Clinical Endocrinology and Metabolism*, 71 (1990), 1403–9 • *Nature*, 49 (1893–4), 556–7 • *The Lancet* (14 April 1894), 975–7 • *BMJ* (7 April 1894), 776 • *DNB* • M. Borell, 'Organotherapy and the emergence of reproductive endocrinology', *Journal of the History of Biology*, 18 (1985), 1–30 • M. Borell, 'Brown-Séquard's organotherapy and its appearance in America at the end of the nineteenth century', *Bulletin of the History of Medicine*, 50 (1976), 309–20 • V. C. Medvei, *A history of endocrinology* (1982) • L. A. P. Bestion, 'Le suc ovarien', MD diss., University of Bordeaux, 1898

Archives Collège de France, Paris • RCP Lond., papers • RS

Likenesses engraving, 1860, RS • engraving, pubd 1894 (after S. de Belzim), NPG [*see illus.*] • photograph (after engraving, 1860), repro. in Olmsted, *Charles-Édouard Brown-Séquard*

Sequeira, Abraham Israel. *See* Rodrigues, Gomes (*d.* 1678), *under* Rodrigues, Alphonso (*d.* 1716).

Sequeira, Isaac Israel. *See* Rodrigues, Alphonso (*d.* 1716).

Sequeira, James Harry (1865–1948), dermatologist specializing in the treatment of venereal diseases, was born on 2 October 1865 at 34 Leman Street, Whitechapel, London, the son of James Scott Sequeira, a surgeon, and his wife, Maria Rosina Rackwitz. His forebears were said to have been physicians for six generations originating in Portugal, probably of Sephardic ancestry. His father was for many years medical officer to the Spanish and Portuguese Jewish congregation, and his great-grandfather was physician to the Portuguese embassy in London. Sequeira was educated at King's College School, and entered the London Hospital with a scholarship in 1884, qualifying MRCS and LRCP in 1889 and MB BS with honours in medicine and obstetrics in 1890. He obtained his MD in 1891 and FRCS in 1893, winning also the Hutchinson prize, and was elected FRCP in 1905.

After junior appointments at the London Hospital and in the locality, failing to make a career in surgery, and influenced by Sir Stephen MacKenzie, a London Hospital enthusiast for specialization, Sequeira embarked on a career in dermatology. He visited Vienna, where L. Freund and Schiff were investigating therapeutic possibilities of X-rays. He then studied under Niels Finsen in Copenhagen, a Nobel prizewinner in 1903 and the originator of the Finsen lamp. This was a carbon arc lamp of high amperage producing ultraviolet radiation originally used in the treatment of lupus vulgaris, but later used for several dermatological conditions such as ringworm, dermatitis, and even warts, as photo-therapy. In 1900 the first Finsen lamp, a gift from Queen Alexandra, was installed at the London Hospital; in 1901 Sequeira translated Finsen's *Phototherapy*, and in 1902 he was elected assistant physician to the London Hospital in charge of the light therapy and skin departments. On 16 July 1903 he married Nellie Adams (*b.* 1881/2), daughter of James Adams, of Kenilworth, Warwickshire; they adopted two children, a boy and a girl.

Sequeira rapidly built a reputation as a dermatologist. Apart from being an early expert in photo-therapy, not only for lupus vulgaris, but for rodent ulcer, dermatitis, ringworm, and other conditions, he, like many of his contemporaries, was an expert syphilologist, being especially interested in congenital syphilis and serology. In the earlier part of the twentieth century, most European dermatologists also practised as syphilologists, syphilis still being a commonly seen disease with manifold skin manifestations. Very few physicians practised solely in venereology in Britain until the advent of the National Health Service in 1948. Sequeira was an astute diagnostician, with the ability to inspire junior colleagues and to teach medical students. Among his most celebrated pupils were William O'Donovan, London Hospital, John Ingram, Leeds General Infirmary and later Royal Victoria Infirmary and first professor of dermatology, Newcastle upon Tyne, Reginald Brain, Royal Free Hospital, and John Wigley, Charing Cross Hospital.

In 1902 Sequeira began a course of lectures at the London Hospital. In 1911 he published *Diseases of the Skin*, which reached a fifth edition in 1947, and was translated into Spanish. Between 1911 and 1915 he edited the *British Journal of Dermatology*. Like most physicians at that time, his practice was spent between his teaching hospital and private patients, who were seen later in the day at 63 Harley Street (from 1905), or at 8A Manchester Square (from 1913). He was remembered by Reginald Brain as a dynamic but diminutive person with a sympathetic nature, reminiscent of Mr Punch, with a head of thick white hair, a grand sense of humour, and a twinkle in his wide blue eyes.

During the First World War, Sequeira was consultant in dermatology to military hospitals in London. He was president of the section of dermatology of the Royal Society of Medicine (1925–7), and also, in the year of his retirement from the London Hospital, 1927, a councillor to the Royal College of Physicians. At one time he had been chairman of the executive committee of the Society for the Prevention of Venereal Disease, and a member of the Trevethin committee on venereal disease (1922–4). After his retirement Sequeira went to live in Kenya, where he took an interest in leprosy, became chairman of the Kenya branch of the British Medical Association and edited the *East African Medical Journal* for ten years. In 1932, he delivered the Chadwick lecture in London, in which he was somewhat critical of the administration of the colonial services, putting forward the view that officers whose main experience was in south-east Asia were not always at their best when transferred to Africa. Early in 1944, suffering from glaucoma, Sequeira unveiled a memorial at the London Hospital to four early technicians in the X-ray department who had died of carcinoma, Messrs Harnach, Suggers, Blackhall, and Wilson. Sequeira, too, suffered from the effects of radiation.

Sequeira returned to Kenya where he died at N'Dera of coronary artery disease after a short illness on 25 November 1948. He was one of a distinguished line of British dermatologists whose science and art was demonstrated in the excellence of their clinical achievements.

W. J. O'DONOVAN, *rev.* MICHAEL ANTHONY WAUGH

Sources *British Journal of Dermatology and Syphilis*, 61 (1949) • *The Lancet* (4 Dec 1948) • L. C. Parish and others, Bibliography of secondary sources on the history of dermatology, obits and biographies before 1973, *Archives of Dermatology*, 3 (1975), 1036–48, 1188–99 • J. Walton, P. Beeson, and R. Bodley Scott, eds., *Oxford companion to medicine* (1986) • A. E. Clark-Kennedy, *The London: a study in the voluntary hospital system*, 2 (1963) • Munk, *Roll* • A. W. Williams, *An epitomised index of dermatological literature* (1910) • *WW* • *Medical Directory* (1902) • b. cert. • m. cert.

Likenesses black and white photograph, repro. in *British Journal of Dermatology and Syphilology*, facing p. 17

Wealth at death £3133 11*s*. 2*d*.—in England: Kenyan probate sealed in England, 26 Aug 1949, *CGPLA Eng. & Wales*

Serbati, Antonio Rosmini- [*known as* Antonio Rosmini] (1797–1855), Roman Catholic philosopher and theologian, and founder of the Institute of Charity, was born on 24 March 1797 at Rovereto, then in the Austrian Trentino, the second of four children of a nobleman, Pier Modesto Rosmini-Serbati (1745–1820), and Giovanna (1757–1842), daughter of Count Formenti of Riva. He studied at home in Rovereto under the tuition of Don Pietro Orsi for the Liceo Imperiale at Trent. At the age of eighteen he discovered the basis for his philosophical system in the idea of being, and in 1819 began a translation of the works of St Thomas Aquinas, hoping through a study of ancient and modern authors to renew philosophy. In 1814 he decided to become a priest, and between 1816 and 1819 studied at Padua University, where he befriended the future lexicographer and revolutionary nationalist Niccolò Tommaseo (1802–1874). Rosmini received minor orders in May 1818, and was ordained deacon in 1820 and priest on 21 April 1821. In 1819 he wrote the statutes for a Catholic Society of Friends. As the elder son, he inherited a fortune on his father's death in 1820. After a visit to Rome in 1823 he devoted himself to the development of 'a system of truth'—critical of modern German, French, and English philosophies, Romantic, materialist, and sensationalist—which enabled him to pour out a flood of works on every philosophical subject during the last three decades of his life.

Another early friend was the great Italian novelist Alessandro Manzoni (1785–1873), who was to pay tribute to Rosmini in his *Dialogi dell'invenzione* (1850) and to kiss his feet as he lay dying. In 1828 Rosmini, inspired by St (the Marchesa) Maddalena di Canossa, founder in 1808 of the

Antonio Rosmini-Serbati (1797–1855), by Luigi Ceroni? (after Francesco Hayez)

Canossian Daughters of Charity, established in the sanctuary of Calvario of the town of Domodossola in Piedmont the Institute of Charity, a congregation of priests and brothers whose constitutions were approved by his friend Pope Gregory XVI in 1838. His early spiritual teaching is summed up in his *Maxims of Christian Perfection* (1830) and his early philosophical understanding in his *New Essay on the Origin of Ideas* (1830).

In 1835 Rosmini sent Luigi Gentili and two companions on a mission to England, at first to teach at Prior Park for the vicar apostolic of the western district, Peter Augustine Baines. The rapid growth of the institute in England owed much to Rosmini's direction of the impetuous Gentili, especially in urging the adaptation of the institute to the English character and conditions. Six members of the institute in England took their vows to it on Lady day 1838, while twenty priests took the same vows in Italy. An early English member was Newman's disciple William Lockhart (1820–1892). Rosmini wrote to Edward Bouverie Pusey after Newman's conversion to Roman Catholicism in 1845. He remodelled a recently founded order of women religious, a branch of the Sisters of Providence, in 1833. Its first English house was established by Lady Mary Arundel in 1843, the first English superior being a niece of the earl of Shrewsbury.

The Institute of Charity was at first bedevilled by the difficulty of movement between Austrian territory and Piedmont, and by the rigid Josephinist state control of the church under Austrian rule in northern Italy, one reason for Rosmini's dislike of state domination of the church. His years at the Rosminian novitiate at Stresa on Lake Maggiore between 1841 and 1848 saw the peaceful growth of his order. He wrote extensively about education, notably in his *Unity of Education* (1827) and *Freedom to Teach* (1854). His critique of probabilism in his *Treatise on Conscience* (1839) earned him the persistent hostility of many Jesuits, notably Antonio Ballerini, though the subsequent controversy was silenced by Gregory in 1843.

In the revolutionary year of 1848 Rosmini published his *Constitution According to Social Justice* and *Five Wounds of the Church* (written in 1832–3), and carried to Pope Pius IX a Piedmontese proposal for the creation of an Italian confederation. He resigned his Piedmontese commission, was told to prepare for the cardinalate, and fled with the pope to Gaeta, but in the conservative and pro-Austrian reaction after the fall of the Roman republic the *Constitution* and *Five Wounds* in 1849 were placed on the index of prohibited books, despite the affection for him felt by Pope Pius IX. After a comprehensive examination of his writings, Rome dismissed the charges against him in 1854. His friendships with certain leaders of the Risorgimento also aroused Catholic suspicion. He died at Stresa, probably from a cancerous gastric ulcer, on 1 July 1855 and was buried there at the church of the Crucified. New books by him continued to appear after his death, but a Holy Office decree in 1887 condemned forty propositions taken from his works. His collected writings occupy more than eighty volumes, while his nine thousand published letters fill thirteen volumes. SHERIDAN GILLEY

Sources C. Leetham, *Rosmini: priest and philosopher* (1982) · G. B. Pagani, *Life of Antonio Rosmini-Serbati* (1907) · D. Cleary, *Antonio Rosmini: introduction to his life and teaching* (1992) · D. Cleary, 'Rosmini-Serbati, Antonio', *New Catholic encyclopedia* (1967–89)
Archives Stresa, Italy
Likenesses L. Ceroni? (after F. Hayez) [*see illus.*] · F. Hayez, portrait, Galleria dell'Arte Moderna, Milan, Italy

Serena, Arthur (1852/3–1922), financier and benefactor, was born in Antwerp, Belgium; he was twenty-eight at the time of the 1881 census. He was the son of the exiled Venetian patriot Chevalier Leone Serena (*d.* 1885), a wealthy shipping and insurance broker who at one time worked closely with Daniele Manin for an independent Venetian republic, and his Belgian wife, Carla (*d.* 1884). Following the heroic five-month defence of the republic against the Austrians (1848–9) and the subsequent suppression of the uprising, Leone Serena, along with thirty-nine other revolutionaries, was denied the general amnesty and forced into exile. He was accompanied by Carla, whom he had married in 1847, and after temporary sojourns in Marseilles, Paris, and Antwerp the family finally settled in London in the mid-1850s; there Leone took up again the profession he had practised successfully in Venice. Carla Serena developed a career of her own in journalism, leading a peripatetic life which took her away from the family for some seven years, during which she also wrote successful travel books, including the still oft-quoted *Hommes et choses dans Perse* (Paris, 1883). She died in Greece in 1884 while researching for another book.

The details of Arthur Serena's education are sketchy: his entry in *Who's Who* mentions schooling at University College School and in Bonn. He inherited his father's business interests and during the 1880s joined the underwriting firm of Galbraith, Pembroke & Co. as the second senior partner; in 1898, after the firm's restructuring, he became one of three directors, and, after November 1911, senior partner. A corporate profile of the still-flourishing company from the early twenty-first century played down his role as a financial magnate, but suggested that the most evident trait of Arthur Serena as a man was his humanity, citing his many public offices and services. This list is confirmed by a brief curriculum vitae attached to his proposal in 1918 for founding a chair of Italian at Oxford University, which catalogues his many honorary appointments: a keen supporter of Anglo-Italian trade, he was elected honorary vice-president of the Italian Chamber of commerce; he also held appointments as chairman of the London Savings Bank, and as vice-chairman and treasurer of the London chamber of commerce. He played a role in public life after 1895 as a London justice of the peace, as a member of the Military Appeal Tribunal, and, for eighteen years, as visiting justice of Holloway prison. He also served on the management committee of the Royal Academy of Music. In 1892, as Liberal candidate, he unsuccessfully contested the parliamentary seat of Penryn and Falmouth. In the Anglo-Italian diplomatic sphere he became honorary consul-general for San Marino (and was proud to attend the coronation of George V as envoy-extraordinary and minister-plenipotentiary), British commissioner for the Milan Exhibition, and president of the committee for the Garibaldi centenary. He held the grand cross of the Crown of Italy, and was honoured as commendatore of the royal order of San Maurizio and San Lazzaro.

Arthur Serena's most lasting legacy is his financial support for the foundation of four major chairs of Italian at English universities. Concerning this, he wrote in September 1918 to ask the advice of Edward Hutton, the writer and literary critic and founding editor of the *Anglo-Italian Review*. Following Hutton's counsel, Serena agreed to provide £20,000 to create chairs of Italian at Cambridge and at Oxford; by autumn 1919 both posts had been filled. Serena later endowed similar chairs at Manchester and Birmingham. Favourable reports in *The Times* of 3 October 1918 accompany an equally eulogistic leading article on his donation, and a further article entitled 'Mr Serena's Gifts' (5 October) encapsulated the cordial atmosphere of the Anglo-Italian entente of the time. On 13 November 1918 *The Times* celebrated another donation by Serena—of funds for an annual gold medal for Italian studies, now in the gift of the British Academy. In Italy, unspecified chairs of English were also founded with Arthur Serena's financial help. In his will he left £385,000, distributed partly to his company's staff (who each received the equivalent of 10 per cent of their annual salaries) and partly to hospitals and benevolent societies.

Serena, who lived at 36 York Terrace, Regent's Park, London, and was unmarried, died of septicaemia on 31 March 1922. J. R. WOODHOUSE

Sources 1918–19, U. Oxf., archives • *WW* (1916–22) • *The Times* (1 April 1922) • U. Limentani, 'The Cambridge chair of Italian, 1919–1934', *Britain and Italy from Romanticism to modernism*, ed. M. McLaughlin (2000), 154–77 [Festschrift for Peter Brand] • www.galbraiths.co.uk/profile/history.htm [Galbraith, Pembroke & Co. website], 29 Nov 2001 • d. cert. • *CGPLA Eng. & Wales* (1922) • census returns, 1881 • census returns, 1901

Likenesses photograph, U. Oxf., Taylor Institution

Wealth at death £385,000: www.galbraiths.co.uk/profile/history.htm • £384,371 14*s*. 5*d*.: probate, 16 Aug 1922, *CGPLA Eng. & Wales*

Seres, William (*d*. 1578x80), printer and bookseller, was possibly of alien origin, as he was listed as a 'stranger' in the parish of St Gregory in lay subsidies of 1564 and 1577 for the Castle Baynard ward in London. There is some confusion over the pronunciation of his name on account of the several forms in which it appears across extant records. It is often pronounced as one syllable, but as his patron William Cecil always spelt it Seress it is likely that it was pronounced with two syllables, like the name of the harvest goddess—as indicated by the common variant spelling of his name Ceres. This is suggested also by the unusual spelling Searese, found in lay subsidies for 1577. The earliest books known to be published by Seres date to 1548, when he was in partnership with Anthony Scoloker (with whom he produced a number of reformist texts, including John Bale's *A Brefe Chronycle*) and also with John Day. His first imprint places him as a resident in Ely Rents in Holborn. Seres collaborated with Day on many works, among them Tyndale's New Testament (1548), Edmund Becke's Bible (1549), and Sir John Cheke's *Hurt of Sedicion* (1549). In 1548 Day's and Seres's joint production of Luke Shepherd's poem *John Bon and Mast Person* was said to have offended the Catholic aldermen of the city of London, and Day, if not Seres himself, appears to have been threatened with imprisonment. Seres also published some works with William Hill. He seems rarely to have worked alone and had many assigns, such as John Case, Nicholas Hill, William Powell, William Harford, William Copland, and Henry Denham.

Seres was made free of the city of London as a member of the Stationers' Company by redemption on 18 September 1548. As he is known to have been Cecil's servant by late 1548, Seres's freedom may have been due to Cecil's influence. In February, Cecil and one of his Lincolnshire neighbours, Lawrence Eresby, had sought to acquire the premises of a former chantry in London, but in order for the sale to go through someone had to take possession of the property. This was done by Seres and Cecil's clerk, Roger Alford, in November. The building in question was known as Peter College, part of which was to become Stationers' Hall in 1554. Seres himself also took possession of part of the property, and for the next two years imprints describe him as dwelling at Peter College. The lay subsidies for 1549 list him as a resident in the parish, and a lease for the property was granted formally to him on Lady day 1549. Seres had evidently been married for some time, as this lease stated that he could not sell any part of the college to his wife or children, but that he could at any time purchase the fee simple during the next decade. By 1551 his premises were described in imprints as The Hedgehog. A 25-year lease was granted to him in 1556.

On 11 March 1553 Cecil procured for Seres the patent to print all primers and psalters. However, on the accession of Mary a few months later the patent was revoked and, at some point during the reign, Seres was imprisoned. When in 1553, the duke of Northumberland's plots threatened to put Cecil himself in danger, the latter transferred some of his goods to Seres's household for safe keeping. Seres performed many further duties for Cecil during the rest of Mary's reign, principally that of rent collecting. During these years Roger Alford (Seres's earlier co-tenant) collected rents in Lincolnshire, where John Day (Seres's former printing partner) was housed on Cecil's land. Seres may have been aware of his former partner's surreptitious press there, and both men returned to London at approximately the same time in 1556 (Cecil paid Seres his discharge of £40 there on 29 September 1556, shortly after Day's return from Lincolnshire in July). Both Seres and Day worked as assigns for John Wayland (the printer of Marian primers), although it is not known how early this began: Seres is named as an assign for Wayland in 1559, but the erstwhile partners, having both been assisted by Cecil, probably returned to publishing at the same time upon their return to London.

Following the accession of Elizabeth, Seres was granted on 3 July 1559 an enhanced privilege for life to print psalters and primers in both Latin and English, and on 2 October he brought a suit against Day for issuing 'a quartron of psalmes with notes … without lycense and contrary to the orders' (Arber, *Regs. Stationers*, 1.124). Day was fined 12*s*. but received his own lucrative patent to print metrical psalms forty days later. In May 1560 the high commission ordered the Stationers' Company to punish anyone who infringed Seres's privilege, a sign of both the value of the privileges and Seres's own importance. In 1571 he received a further privilege for 'all manner of booke and bookes of private prayers primers psalters and psalmes bothe in greate volumes and small in Englishe or latine' for the lifetimes of both himself and his son William (Blayney, 25). However, the wide terms of this patent proved controversial. On 20 October 1578, in an attempt 'to avoid all contentions … and to thintente that a perfecte amitie and frindship … maie be had and contynued' (London, Stationers' Hall, Liber A, fol. 36), the company drew up an agreement between the two Sereses and a number of other members of the company (including John and Richard Day), clarifying precisely which rights belonged to which individuals. By this point, however, Seres the elder had already assigned his privilege to Henry Denham for an annual fee. Among Seres's publications after 1558 were translations by Arthur Golding—*The Eyght Bookes of Caius Julius Caesar Conteyning his Martiall Exploytes in Gallia* (1565) and *The .xv. Bookes of P. Ovidus Naso, Entytuled Metamorphosis* (1567)—as well as Thomas Blundeville's *The Fower Chiefyst Offices*

Belongyng to Horsemanshippe (1565–6) and Sir Geoffrey Fenton's *Monophylo* (1572).

Seres took an active role in the life of the Stationers' Company. Listed twenty-first in the company's charter of incorporation in 1557, and already a relatively senior member, he served as master no fewer than five times between 1570 and 1578. He died at some point between 9 December 1578, when he signed a company petition, and 18 January 1580, when he was noted as deceased by the company's governing body. The administration of his estate was granted to his widow, named as Agniti Seres, on 9 July 1580. After Seres's death, Denham and William Seres the younger signed a document whereby they handed John and Richard Day the sole rights for the printing of psalms; however, it was followed by a protracted dispute between Seres's widow and Denham. In 1582 Seres the younger petitioned Cecil for his assistance in protecting the 1571 patent against the infringements of John Wolfe and others: 'W[ch] priviledge … by the further helpe & goodnes of your honor was … graunted to hym [Seres the elder] & to me' (Blayney, 26). Seres the younger (who was elected to the livery of the Stationers' Company in 1578) carried on his father's business until 1603 but assigned much of the work to others. The Seres patent was incorporated into the Stationers' Company's joint-stock venture, the English stock, in 1603.

ELIZABETH EVENDEN

Sources P. Blayney, 'William Cecil and the stationers', *The Stationers' Company and the book trade, 1550–1990*, ed. R. Myers and M. Harris, St Paul's Bibliographies (1997), 11–34 · PRO, E 179/145/174, 219, 252 · PRO, C 82/1234 · BL, Lansdowne MS 118 · BL, Lansdowne MS 48/80, fol. 184*r* · PRO, SP 11/9, no. 34 · A. F. Pollard, ed., *Tudor tracts, 1532–1588* (1903), 195 · J. Ames, T. F. Dibdin, and W. Herbert, eds., *Typographical antiquities, or, The history of printing in England, Scotland and Ireland*, 4 vols. (1810–19), vol. 4, 194–5 · C. H. Timperley, *Typographical encyclopaedia* (1842), 362–3 · E. Evenden, 'The Michael Wood mystery: the Lincolnshire printing of John Day', *Sixteenth Century Journal* [forthcoming] · E. G. Duff, *A century of the English book trade* (1948), 147–8 · Hatfield House, Hertfordshire, Cecil MS 143, fol. 191 · *STC, 1475–1640* · Stationers' Hall, London, Liber A · Arber, *Regs. Stationers* · J. P. Collier, ed., *The Egerton papers*, CS, 12 (1840) · *CPR, 1569–72*, no. 2126 · B. P. Davis, 'William Seres', *The British literary book trade, 1475–1700*, ed. J. K. Bracken and J. Silver, DLitB, 170 (1996), 231–8 · administration, PRO, PROB 6/2, fol. 202*v* · D. W. Krummel, *English music printing, 1553–1700* (1975), 12–13

Archives BL, Lansdowne MSS 118, 48/80, fol. 184*r* · PRO, CP 143/191 · PRO, E 179/145/174, 219, 252 · PRO, SP 11/9 no. 34

Sergeant, (Emily Frances) Adeline (1851–1904), novelist, born at Ashbourne, Derbyshire, on 4 July 1851, was the second daughter of Richard Sergeant (1814–1870), a Wesleyan Methodist minister who studied with Jabez Bunting, and his wife, Jane, daughter of Thomas Hall, a Wesleyan Methodist minister. Jane Hall was well known in religious circles as the writer of various evangelical short stories under the pseudonym Adeline Hall. The Halls spent some time in Jamaica, on which they both published. Sergeant grew up in a climate of much literary and spiritual activity. At first educated by her mother, she was sent at thirteen to a school at Weston-super-Mare. At fifteen she published *Poems* (1866), with an introduction by her mother under her pseudonym Adeline; it was reviewed favourably in Wesleyan periodicals. From Lalcham, the nonconformist school at Clapham, Sergeant won a scholarship to Queen's College, London, with a presentation from the Governesses' Benevolent Institution. She then went to Cambridge, where she took a first-class honours certificate in the women's examinations.

After her father's death in 1870, Sergeant joined the Church of England and dedicated herself to teaching, writing, and philanthropic work. For the greater part of ten years she was employed as a governess at Riverhead, Kent. After some initial setbacks—her first novel was never published—in 1882 she won a prize of £100, offered by the *People's Friend* of Dundee, for *Jacobi's Wife*, a novel she wrote while visiting Egypt with friends. The work was serialized in the paper and was published in London in 1887. In 1885 she moved to Dundee and accepted a post on the staff of the *People's Friend*, where she stayed for two years. She was a regular contributor until her death, giving the firm for a time exclusive serial rights to her stories, and two or three of her novels ran serially every year.

In 1887 Sergeant moved to women's chambers at 14 Chenies Street, Bloomsbury, London, where, while working on her fiction, she joined the Fabian Society, taught at an organization for adult education, and travelled widely, spending the spring of 1899 in Palestine. A passionate supporter of women's suffrage, she sat on the committee of the Somerville Club for Women. Feeling solidarity with women of all classes, she particularly concerned herself with the lives and welfare of working-class girls, helping to run girls' clubs and becoming involved in rescue work. Her religious convictions fluctuated, and her novel *No Saint* (1886) reflects a phase of agnosticism. From 1893 she associated herself with the extreme ritualists at St Alban the Martyr, Holborn, and on 23 October 1899 was received into the Roman Catholic church. The processes of thought she described in *Roads to Rome, being Personal Records of some … Converts*, with an introduction by Cardinal Vaughan (1901).

Sergeant wrote over ninety novels and tales. Six appeared annually from 1901 to 1903, and eight in her last year, while fourteen were published posthumously, and she often made an income of over £1000 a year. This prodigious rate of production meant that the greater part of her work, the sensational type of novel which sold so well, was not taken seriously by critics. However, she was considered most successful in depicting the middle-class, provincial, nonconformist home, and the party autobiographical *Esther Denison* (1889) won comparisons with the work of Mrs Oliphant and George Eliot. In 1901 Adeline Sergeant moved to Bournemouth; she died there at her home, Agincourt, Albert Road, on 4 December 1904. She was unmarried.

CHARLOTTE FELL-SMITH, *rev.* KATHERINE MULLIN

Sources A. T. C. Pratt, ed., *People of the period: being a collection of the biographies of upwards of six thousand living celebrities*, 2 vols. (1897) · *Men and women of the time* (1899) · H. C. Black, *Notable women authors of the day* (1893) · Blain, Clements & Grundy, *Feminist comp.* · P. Schlueter and J. Schlueter, eds., *An encyclopedia of British women* *writers*, rev. edn (1998) • J. Shattock, *The Oxford guide to British women writers* (1993) • W. Stephens, *The life of Adeline Sergeant* (1905) • A. Sergeant, *Roads to Rome, being personal records of some … converts* (1901) • *The Athenaeum* (10 Dec 1904), 807–8 • personal knowledge (1912) • *CGPLA Eng. & Wales* (1905)

Likenesses Mendelssohn, photograph, repro. in Stephens, *Life of Adeline Sergeant* • photograph, repro. in Black, *Notable women authors*, 156

Wealth at death £294 16*s*. 9*d*.: probate, 25 Feb 1905, *CGPLA Eng. & Wales*

Sergeant, John (1623–1707), Roman Catholic controversialist and philosopher, was born on 2 February 1623 in Barrow upon Humber, Lincolnshire, the son of a respectable yeoman there, William Sergeant. After an early education under one Mr Rawson at school in the neighbouring village of Barton he was admitted as sizar to St John's College, Cambridge, in 1639. With his BA degree gained in 1643 and a recommendation from the master and fellows of his college he was appointed secretary to Thomas Morton, bishop of Durham. That employment introduced him to what he perceived as the devious misuse of texts and quotations in theological arguments; and with his protestant faith thereby undermined he was converted by George Gage to Catholicism. To avoid any danger from his erstwhile friends he was sent under the alias Holland (another being Smith) to the English College in Lisbon. A letter (in the Lisbon collection at Ushaw College) written apparently to his mother at this time refers apologetically to his abandonment of her after 'the great charges you had bestowed upon my education at Cambridge', but hints that 'some small allowance' would still be useful. He arrived at Lisbon on 4 November 1643 and after some eight months of devotional exercises was admitted as a student in June 1644. Finally ordained on 12 March 1649 he taught classics and theology, acted as procurator, and then as prefect of studies. Returning to England for some months in 1653 he successfully converted his parents and others to Catholicism and then resumed his academic duties in Lisbon until being sent to represent the college's interest at a meeting of the English chapter in London in 1655. He was appointed as secretary to that body on 19 December, and was to retain that laborious but influential post until ousted by John Leyburn as Rome's replacement late in 1667.

It was while acting as secretary to the chapter that Sergeant made his enduring reputation as a Catholic controversialist, engaging in long-running debates on the rule of faith with such eminent protestant adversaries as John Bramhall, Jeremy Taylor, Henry Hammond, Méric Casaubon, John Tillotson, and Edward Stillingfleet. The best known of his numerous theological works (some of which appeared under the initials S. W.) were produced in this context. *Schism Disarm'd* (1655) and *Schism Dispatcht* (1657) were responses to Hammond—an antagonist for whose diminished book sales and even for whose death these attacks were later held responsible; Bishop Richard Russell recalled reports of how the 'beardless' Catholic champion so battered Hammond's 'inflated ego that shame made him catch a fatal disease' (Sharratt, 175). In *Sure-Footing in Christianity* (1665) and *Faith Vindicated from Possibility of Falsehood* (1667), and later in his *Six Catholick Letters* (1687, 1688), Sergeant continued with the vehemence of a convert to urge the superiority of an oral and practical Catholic tradition over protestant resort to the scriptures as a certain ground of faith. His self-confident belief in the validity of his own position and procedures led to charges of arrogance and incivility, and he provoked not only reasoned rejoinders but also personal abuse and threats. Even friendly assessors, while stressing moral excellence and the diverting nature of his conversation, conceded some warmth of temper and impetuosity, and in his autobiographical apologia entitled (when published in 1816) 'Literary life' (dated 1700), Sergeant himself recalled how he had been described as 'an ill natur'd, absurd fellow, in perpetuall squibbles with everyone', as well as 'a great Drunkard, seldom out of a Tavern, or Alehouse' (Sergeant, 55). Protestants even accused him of throwing fireballs to stoke up the great fire of London, and he describes how he exonerated himself only by pleading physical incapacity; having looked after friends during the previous year's plague he had become so sick that he survived only as 'a mere Skeleton, nothing but Skin and bones' (ibid., 64). Recovered from that condition by 1673 he was able to evade the arrest allegedly planned, after an anti-Catholic proclamation, by Tillotson and Stillingfleet by fleeing to France at an hour's notice. But while abroad he suffered attack from yet another quarter. His erstwhile friend Peter Talbot, the exiled archbishop of Dublin and a notorious trouble-maker, denounced him (under the pseudonym Lominus) as heretical in *Blakloanae haeresis confutatio* (1675), and tried unsuccessfully to procure his censure by an assembly in Paris before approaching the authorities in Rome.

For Talbot, Sergeant's sin was to be a Blackloist, or follower of Thomas White (alias Blacklo), under whose intellectual influence he had come in Lisbon. The perennially hostile and paranoid George Leyburn, too, recalled 'the great zeal he had shown at Lisbon towards Mr Blacklow's new notions of philosophy', and was convinced that it was through White's patronage that Sergeant had been appointed to his post as secretary of a chapter which consisted of 'a pack of Mr Blacloes friends' (G. Leyburn, *Doctor Leyburn's Encyclical Answer*, 1661, 86, 16). It was indeed widely accepted that Sergeant 'put himself entirely into the hands of White … to be trained and taught by him' (Warner, 230), and Russell described how, 'with White's demonstrations … always on his lips and White's books in his hands, he gloried in being his disciple' (Sharratt, 175). This is not to say that the two did not have disagreements. Having visited White for two months in Rotterdam, at the time of the printing of *Statera morum* in 1660, Sergeant believed that even his mentor had gone too far towards encouraging moral laxity, and he published his own critical response as *Statera appensa* in 1661. Nevertheless, Robert Pugh was justified in generally implicating Sergeant in White's machinations in his edited collection of letters published as *Blacklo's Cabal* (1680); and since Blackloism implied not least the sacrifice of Jesuits in return for religious toleration, the Jesuit Pugh unsurprisingly described

Sergeant there as one 'of evil reputation' (R. Pugh, *Blacklo's Cabal*, 1680, 'Epistle').

That reputation was confirmed when, following White's death in 1676, Sergeant not only continued to keep Blackloism alive, but was also, after his return to England in 1678, suspected of implication in the Popish Plot. It is this problematic episode which laid him open to charges of being at best temporarily deranged, at worst an informer against the Jesuits. By June 1679 he had withdrawn to Amsterdam with the intention, he claimed, of learning Hebrew. Two months later he was in Brussels, and then in October he returned to London to give information to the privy council (*The Informations of John Sergeant*, 1681). He denied any personal knowledge of a plot, but his evidence seemed further to incriminate John Gavan, one of the priests already executed in the previous June. Following his deposition Sergeant himself was officially exonerated, licensed to live in the capital, and even granted a pension; but he paid a heavy personal and historiographical price, for he never overcame the suspicion and hostility of many fellow Catholics.

Sergeant continued, however, to engage in both theological and philosophical controversy. At a time of sceptical inroads in both those areas he persisted with a typically Blackloist insistence on 'beating down scepticism' (*The Method to Science*, 1696, preface) and establishing what he believed were secure intellectual foundations. His early interest in that matter is attested by a discussion on moral certainty which he had with John Wilkins, whom he met in Oxford during the protectorate; and that it remained of paramount concern is shown in the philosophical writings of his later years, including, most importantly, *The Method to Science* and *Solid Philosophy Asserted Against the Fancies of the Ideists* (1697). Fanciful ideists included such formidable proponents as Descartes and John Locke; but basing his own work on essentially Aristotelian foundations Sergeant utilized the earlier syntheses of Thomas White and Kenelm Digby to argue against those modern theorists and against any pragmatic replacement of certainty by probability as philosophy's goal. In this respect Sergeant can be seen as having tried to stem the tide of mainstream modern thought: his repudiation of compromise, his insistence on the need for absolute certainty, and his self-assured confidence in his own ability to attain it put him out of step with his contemporaries, and contributed further to his subsequent neglect; and despite being sometimes claimed as an intellectual precursor of Berkeley he has seldom appeared in histories of philosophy. His *Method to Science* provoked a response from the Cartesian Antoine Le Grand, and Locke's heavily annotated copy of *Solid Philosophy* survives, but Sergeant himself, while claiming that his critique had 'sunke Mr Locke's credit very much', disconsolately noted that 'he never reply'd one word' (Sergeant, 174).

Sergeant's other late works include *Ideae Cartesianae* (1698), a rejoinder to Le Grand; *Raillery Defeated* (1699), another response to Talbot; *Transnatural Philosophy* (1700), which warranted a second edition six years later; and his personal *Account of the Chapter* (1706). Such writings, together with extremely acrimonious correspondence in which he was engaged only weeks before his death, confirm Dodd's judgement that in 1707 he died, as a surviving portrait (now at Ushaw College, Durham) shows him living, with pen still poised in hand. His reputation as a controversialist lived on: as late as 1714 a resolution was unanimously passed at the chapter of the English secular clergy that, for the sake of harmony, his provocative books 'containing sharp and severe reflections upon his brethren of the chapter … be suppressed and destroyed' (Gillow, *Lit. biog. hist.*, 3.619). But by then that 'troublesome spirit' (as Russell described him) had himself finally been laid to rest in St Pancras churchyard on 20 October 1707.

BEVERLEY SOUTHGATE

Sources G. Anstruther, *The seminary priests*, 2 (1975) • D. Krook, *John Sergeant and his circle*, ed. B. C. Southgate (1993) • M. Sharratt, ed., *Lisbon College register, 1628–1813*, Catholic RS, 72 (1991) • J. Sergeant, 'Literary life', 1700, St John Cam.; printed in *Catholicon*, 2, 3 (1816) • Ushaw College, Durham, Lisbon Archives, Russell MSS • Westm. DA, Old Brotherhood archives, vol. 2 • Westm. DA, Westminster archives, vol. 39 • C. Dodd [H. Tootell], *The church history of England, from the year 1500, to the year 1688*, 3 (1742) • J. Warner, *The history of English persecution of Catholics and the presbyterian plot*, ed. T. A. Birrell, trans. J. Bligh, 2 vols., Catholic RS, 47–8 (1953) • Gillow, *Lit. biog. hist.* • Venn, *Alum. Cant.* • N. C. Bradish, *John Sergeant: a forgotten critic of Descartes and Locke* (1929)

Archives Ushaw College, Durham, Lisbon Archives, Russell MSS • Westm. DA, Old Brotherhood archives • Westm. DA, Westminster archives

Likenesses oils, Ushaw College, Durham

Sergeant, Lewis (1841–1902), journalist and author, the son of John Sergeant, a schoolmaster, and his wife, Mary Anne, daughter of George Lewis, was born at Barrow-on-Humber, Lincolnshire, on 10 November 1841; Adeline Sergeant, the novelist, was his first cousin. Sergeant, after education under a private tutor, matriculated at St Catharine's College, Cambridge, in 1861, graduating BA with mathematical honours in 1865. At the union he was an ardent Liberal and supporter of W. E. Gladstone. On 12 April 1871 he married Emma Louisa, daughter of James Robertson of Cheltenham.

After a period as a schoolmaster Sergeant entered journalism, becoming editor, in succession, of *An Anti-Game Law Journal*, *The Examiner*, and the *Hereford Times*. He was subsequently long connected with *The Athenaeum* and with the *London Daily Chronicle and Clerkenwell News* as leader writer. Meanwhile, he became a recognized authority on education, was elected to the council of the College of Preceptors, and edited the *Educational Times* from 1895 to 1902. Deeply interested in modern Greece, he supported Greek interests enthusiastically. From 1878 onwards he acted as honorary secretary of the Greek committee in London. He published *New Greece* in the same year (republished 1879), and *Greece* in 1880. In 1897 there followed *Greece in the Nineteenth Century: a Record of Hellenic Emancipation and Progress, 1821–1897*. He also wrote several popular histories, and some novels. King George of Greece bestowed on him the order of the Redeemer in October 1878. Sergeant died at

South Lodge, Poole Road, Bournemouth, on 2 February 1902; he left, with other children, an elder son, Philip Walsingham Sergeant, author of historical biographies.

CHARLOTTE FELL-SMITH, *rev.* JOSEPH COOHILL

Sources *The Times* (4 Feb 1902) • *WW* • *The Athenaeum* (8 Feb 1902), 179 • *The Sphere* (8 Feb 1902) • *CGPLA Eng. & Wales* (1902)
Likenesses portrait, repro. in *The Sphere*
Wealth at death £818 5*s*. 9*d*.: administration, 18 April 1902, *CGPLA Eng. & Wales*

Sergison, Charles (1654–1732), naval administrator, was born in London. The exact date of his birth and the names of his parents are not known, but he had at least two siblings: an elder brother, Michael, and a sister, Sarah, later the wife of Thomas Gibson of Darlington, co. Durham.

In July 1671 Sergison became a clerk at Chatham Dockyard. From 25 December 1675 he was a temporary clerk examining pursers' and victuallers' accounts under the Navy Board's chief clerk for victualling accounts, John Godwin. While employed in this work he married Anne Crawley (*b*. 1657) on 15 June 1676 at St Peter-le-Poer, London. She was a relation, possibly the daughter, of John Crawley, who too served as a Navy Board clerk from 1680 to 1717.

On 26 March 1677 Sergison was promoted to fill the place previously held by Richard Gibson as one of two clerks serving the clerks of the acts, Thomas Hayter and James Sotherne. Sergison remained in this post until 1686, when James II and the Admiralty secretary Samuel Pepys began to make administrative initiatives to reverse the decline in fleet efficiency and to rectify the administrative backlog that had resulted from the naval retrenchment during the last years of Charles II's reign. As part of this, the Navy Board's traditional organization was temporarily set aside. Five special commissioners for current business were appointed for three years. These new commissioners appointed Sergison as their secretary at a salary of £300 and assigned him the duties of keeping their minutes and maintaining records.

In August 1688 the commissioners reported their work complete, and in October the commission was dissolved, at which time many of the traditional offices of the Navy Board were revived, including that of clerk of the acts. On its revival Sergison at first retained the title of secretary, but in July 1689 he was named assistant clerk of the acts, while continuing to earn the same salary. In January 1690 James Sotherne, who had alone been clerk of the acts since 1679, left the Navy Board to become Admiralty secretary, and in his place Sergison was promoted. Sergison was the longest-serving of any clerk of the acts, holding office for more than twenty-nine years, from 6 February 1690 to 21 May 1719. For most of this period he held the office alone, though Samuel Atkins served jointly with him for four years from 11 February 1702 until Atkins's death in August 1706.

Following William III's death Sergison's patent was renewed on 28 August 1702 as a joint appointment, and again as an individual appointment on 26 August 1706, 6 October 1707, and 16 November 1714. Throughout this period, which included the entire Nine Years' War (1688–97), the War of the Spanish Succession (1702–13), and the naval war with Spain in 1718–19, Sergison, as clerk of the acts, was fourth in seniority at the Navy Board (after the treasurer, controller, and surveyor of the navy) but the principal civil servant in charge of its daily business. In this he acted as its collective secretary, directly responsible for drawing up contracts and drafts of letters on such matters as finance, victualling, contracts, stores, dockyard management, sick and wounded, and ship maintenance and construction. All this took place at the board's office, located in a building erected after its smaller predecessor had burnt in 1673, but still at the angle between Seething Lane and Crutched Friars, Tower Hill.

Sergison was granted arms in 1691, and in 1693 he bought the mortgage on a country house which he eventually purchased: Cuckfield Park, an Elizabethan structure originally built by the ironmaster Henry Bowyer in 1573 at the village of Cuckfield, Sussex. In later years Sergison enlarged Cuckfield Park by acquiring the nearby manors of Bentley Park (1697), Legh (1707), and Slaugham (1727). Throughout his career he appears to have been an extremely hard-working and diligent civil servant, who placed great emphasis on implementing modern administrative procedures. In addition to his work as clerk of the acts Sergison was elected MP for Shoreham in 1698 and retained that seat in the government's interest until defeated in 1702.

Despite, or more likely because of, his diligent work Sergison did not enjoy good health. During 1699 Samuel Pepys, a previous clerk of the acts, mentioned him among several of his friends who were ill, naming Sergison as one who was having a distressingly difficult time. On 24 May 1699, in an audience with William III on the state of the navy, Sergison repeatedly requested retirement, as he believed his health required a country life. The king reportedly replied, 'I can not part with you; I have more need of you now than ever' (Merriman, *Sergison Papers*, 9). The king authorized him to go to the country temporarily, if his health required it, but not permanently. Sergison made similar requests in 1701, which probably led to Atkins's joint appointment, a request that Sergison repeated after Atkins's death, but to no avail. Having reached the age of sixty-five, Sergison finally retired to Cuckfield Park in 1719, where he lived until his death on 26 November 1732. He was buried in Cuckfield parish church.

Typically for his time, Sergison took home with him on retirement the records of his office as well as a large collection of Navy Board ship models. His wife had died before him, and there were no children of the marriage; Sergison left Cuckfield Park and his naval collections to his elder brother's grandson. He also left a tenement in Leadenhall Street, London, named the King's Arms, and another in Chailey, Sussex, along with fifty cash bequests ranging from £10 to £5000, totalling nearly £28,000, to a wide range of relatives; to his household servants, who included at least one black servant; and to the poor of Cuckfield parish church, St Olave, Hart Street, London, and Christ's Hospital, London. Thomas Adley's wall monument to Sergison in the north aisle of Cuckfield parish church may well express Sergison's ideal of a civil servant. On it the figure of Truth is seated on a sarcophagus, holding a medallion portrait of Sergison, supported by a cherub. JOHN B. HATTENDORF

Sources J. M. Collinge, *Navy Board officials, 1660–1832* (1978) • *The Sergison papers*, ed. R. D. Merriman, Navy RS, 89 (1950) • R. D. Merriman, ed., *Queen Anne's navy* (1961) • *VCH Sussex*, 7.149–151, 161 • J. Ehrman, *The navy in the war of William III, 1689–1697* (1953) • *Private correspondence and miscellaneous papers of Samuel Pepys, 1679–1703*, ed. J. R. Tanner (1926), 1.194, 234, 248, 258, 266 • *Sussex Archaeological Collections*, 25 (1873), 62–84 • parish register, London, St Peter-le-Poer, GL [marriage] • will, PRO, PROB 11/655, sig. 296 • *IGI*

Archives NMM, corresp. and papers | US Naval Academy Museum, Annapolis, Maryland, H. H. Rogers ship model collection

Likenesses T. Adye, medallion, 1732, Cuckfield parish church, West Sussex • oils, 1950, repro. in Merriman, ed., *Sergison papers*; priv. coll.

Wealth at death land in Sussex; King's Arms, Leadenhall Street, London; plus fifty bequests totalling almost £28,000: will, PRO, PROB 11/655, sig. 296

Series, George William (1920–1995), spectroscopist, was born on 22 February 1920 at Otway Cottage Garage, Bushey Heath, Hertfordshire, the eldest of the four children of William Series (1892–1959), chauffeur to the marquess of Douro (the eldest son of the duke of Wellington) and his wife, Alice (1889–1976), *née* Crosthwaite. His two brothers died in infancy, and he was brought up with his sister in a cottage in the park of Stratfield Saye House, the home of the dukes of Wellington, near Reading. Series's antecedents had lived for many years in the village of Stratfield Saye, Hampshire, and he always felt his roots were there; his ashes were eventually interred at the village church.

At the early age of ten Series won a scholarship from the local village school to Queen Mary's Grammar School, Basingstoke. He immediately became fascinated with science, particularly chemistry, which opened up to him a world of equations and formulae. He set up his own laboratory in an empty (and often very cold) cottage adjoining his home, experimenting with chemicals 'borrowed' from school. At first he found physics much less interesting. When he was fourteen, however, his family moved a few miles to the village of Swallowfield and Series transferred to Reading School. Here the mathematical basis of physics was stressed, appealing to Series's instinct for a quantitative description of phenomena, and he soon developed a strong affinity for the subject.

In 1938 Series was awarded an open scholarship to read physics at St John's College, Oxford, but in 1940 his studies were interrupted by the war. A convinced pacifist at school, he became a conscientious objector. He spent two years in West Ham on air-raid relief work, and then served with the Friends' Ambulance Unit in Egypt, Italy, and Yugoslavia, where he set up a pathology laboratory at Derventa. He delayed his return until 1946 so that he could finish this work, and then resumed his studies, taking first class honours in 1947. At Oxford he met his future wife, Annette, daughter of John Edward Pepper, a retired civil servant; she was studying modern languages at St Hilda's.

George William Series (1920–1995), by Brian Petley, 1988

They married on 21 December 1948, and had a daughter (Caroline) and three sons: Robert, John, and Hugh.

Series remained at Oxford, carrying out research on the structure of the hydrogen atom at the Clarendon Laboratory under H. G. Kuhn FRS, for whom he developed a lifelong admiration and affection. Hydrogen, the simplest of all atoms, always fascinated Series, and he became a leading authority, writing one book on the subject and editing another. He took his MA and DPhil in 1950, and became a university lecturer in 1951 and a fellow of St Edmund Hall in 1954. He soon achieved distinction in a new area. Alfred Kastler's group in Paris had found an ingenious way to combine radio-frequency and optical techniques to study Zeeman and hyperfine splittings in atoms. Series saw the power of this approach and exploited it, but he also realized that the radiation from a coherent superposition of excited states would display interference effects. These 'quantum beats', demonstrated by Series's group in 1959, are of great practical importance because of the information they carry about the atoms and their environment, but they are also a phenomenon of great beauty. Their investigation and their successful interpretation were the subject of a series of seminal papers from Series's group, which brought him international recognition and became part of the spectroscopist's standard tool kit.

A recurring theme in Series's later work was the search for a way of accounting for spontaneous emission of radiation without quantization of the radiation field; he found quantum electrodynamics unpalatable because he felt that the underlying physics was being obscured by the mathematics. Though unsuccessful, his efforts gave him a unique insight into the physical basis of the interaction of radiation and matter which underpinned a variety of experimental and theoretical studies. These are characterized by a readiness to challenge conventional lines of thought, and many were work done jointly with distinguished overseas visitors. In 1968 Series accepted a chair at Reading University, where he stayed until his retirement in 1982.

Series had special links with New Zealand and India. J. N. Dodd came to Oxford in 1959 and began a long association between the Clarendon and the physics department at Otago. Series went to Otago as a William Evans visiting professor in 1972. His connection with India was stimulated by his admiration for the work of S. Pancharatnam. Series went there as a Raman visiting professor in 1982, and was made an honorary fellow of the Indian Academy of Sciences in 1984. In the same year the academy published a collection of his papers, *Laser Spectroscopy and Other Topics* (1985).

Series edited two journals, the *European Journal of Physics* (1980–85) and the *Journal of Physics B* (1975–80), and chaired and served on Research Council and Institute of Physics committees. In 1968 he helped to found the European Group for Atomic Spectroscopy, an association which broke new ground in fostering links between European laboratories. He was elected to the Royal Society in 1971, became a fellow of the Royal Astronomical Society in 1972, and received the Meggers award and the medal of the Optical Society of America in 1982.

Series's two passions were science and his family. He was a man of great sensitivity and deeply held convictions, but also courteous, kind, and considerate, with a sometimes impish sense of humour. When he lectured, whether to students or at an international conference, he held his audience enthralled as much by his intensity and missionary zeal as by the lucidity of his exposition. A scientific discussion with Series was an education, not simply because of the clarity of his thought, but because making progress even on the most mundane of problems brought him such obvious delight—to him the intellectual adventure was an end in itself. His wish to share this delight made him an outstanding teacher. He died at Sobell House, Oxford Radcliffe Hospital, on 2 January 1995. DEREK STACEY

Sources B. Bleaney, *Memoirs FRS*, 42 (1996), 387–98 • *WWW*, 1991–5 • personal knowledge (2004) • private information (2004) • *The Times* (16 Jan 1995) • *The Independent* (11 Jan 1995) • m. cert. • d. cert.
Archives U. Reading L., corresp. and papers; research papers, editorial corresp., autobiographical notes
Likenesses two photographs, 1971–88, repro. in Bleaney, *Memoirs FRS*, 386, 395 • B. Petley, photograph, 1988, priv. coll. [*see illus.*]

Serjeant, Robert Bertram (1915–1993), Arabic scholar, was born just before midnight on 22 March 1915 (he habitually gave his date of birth as 23 March), at 5 Cambridge Street, Edinburgh, the elder of the two children of Robert Thomas Riley Serjeant, customs and excise official, and his wife, Agnes Beatson, *née* Blair, a schoolteacher. He was educated at George Watson's College, Edinburgh, and entered the University of Edinburgh in 1932, where he read Semitic languages (Arabic and Hebrew). He obtained a first-class degree in 1936 and, in that same year, made a short visit to Syria, his first to the Middle East. On his return he took up a scholarship at Trinity College, Cambridge, in 1936, where he began research on the history of Islamic textiles. He was awarded the PhD degree in 1939. In 1940 he won a scholarship at the School of Oriental and African Studies (SOAS) in the University of London to travel to southern Arabia to undertake dialect studies there. These were interrupted, however, by the Italian threat from Ethiopia across the Red Sea to British Arabian possessions, and Serjeant was given a governor's commission in the Aden government guards. He returned to SOAS in 1941, and on 6 September of the same year married Marion Keith Robertson (*b*. 1917), an Edinburgh-trained medical doctor, and daughter of William Mitchell Robertson, an executive officer in the Scottish health department. Serjeant's academic career at SOAS was put on hold when, as part of the war effort, he was summoned in 1942 to the BBC and appointed editor of the *Arabic Listener*. In 1947 he spent a year carrying out fieldwork in the Hadhramaut on a colonial research fellowship. He was made reader at SOAS in 1948 and was appointed to the chair of modern Arabic there in 1955. In 1964 he returned to Cambridge with a lectureship in Islamic history and was appointed director of the Middle East Centre there. In 1966 he was made reader and in 1970 was elected to the Sir Thomas Adams's chair of Arabic in the University of Cambridge, in which position he remained until his retirement in 1982, when he moved to a country cottage in Scotland—Summerhill Cottage, Denhead, near St Andrews, Fife—where he lived for the rest of his life. He retained close contact in his retirement with his alma mater, the University of Edinburgh, and was awarded the degree of DLitt (*honoris causa*) there in 1985. In 1986 he was elected a fellow of the British Academy.

Serjeant's scholarly output was vast. His collected articles filled more than four volumes in the Variorum Collected Studies series: *Studies in Arabian History and Civilisation* (1981), *Customary and Shari'ah Law in Arabian Society* (1991), *Farmers and Fishermen in Arabia* (1995), and *Society and Trade in South Arabia* (1996). He published twelve monographs, of which the most important were: his thesis, first published between the years 1942 and 1948 in the journal *Ars Islamica*, and later as a monograph in Beirut in 1972 under the title *Islamic Textiles*; *South Arabian Poetry I: Prose and Poetry from Hadramawt* (1951), a major study of the colloquial poetry of south Arabia that incidentally contained much on Hadrami society; *The Portuguese off the South Arabian Coast: Hadrami Chronicles* (1963), in which the texts were translated and copiously annotated, and which contained several invaluable appendices; and *Ṣanʿāʾ, an Arabian Islamic City* (1983), composed by a team of Yemen specialists, but edited by Serjeant and Ronald Lewcock and very largely written by Serjeant himself—this book achieved worldwide recognition as the definitive work on the ancient capital of Yemen. The hallmarks of all his research were his meticulousness and the marriage between his work in the field and that in his library. He travelled often and extremely widely in the Middle East, especially the Arabian peninsula, and in Africa, India, and south-east Asia.

Serjeant was a man of heavy build and he cut a rather formidable figure. Despite his physical conformation, however, it was often said that he could compete with any mountain goat in agility if the goal happened to have some worthwhile scholarly benefit. He had a wonderful though subtle sense of humour (and a distinctive chuckle to go with it), which often manifested itself in some *extempore* doggerel to suit the occasion. The academic demands he made as a teacher and supervisor were high. He was generous with his time, the scholarly resources at his disposal, and his warm hospitality. He died after a heart attack at his home in Denhead on 29 April 1993 and was cremated on 4 May at Kirkcaldy. He was survived by his wife and their son and daughter. G. REX SMITH

Sources G. R. Smith, 'Robert Bertram Serjeant, 1915–1993', *PBA*, 87 (1995), 439–52 • *WW* (1993) • *The Times* (6 May 1993) • *The Independent* (12 May 1993) • private information (2004) [M. K. Serjeant] • b. cert. • m. cert.
Archives U. Edin.
Likenesses photograph, *c.*1990–1991, repro. in R. B. Serjeant, *Society and trade in South Arabia* (1996) • photograph, repro. in *The Times*
Wealth at death £164,996.02: confirmation, 18 Aug 1993, *CCI*

Serle, Ambrose (1742–1812), colonial official and religious writer, was born on 30 August 1742 and may have been the Ambrose Serle baptized on 17 September 1742 at St Giles, Reading, son of Ambrose and Ann Serle. He entered the navy. In 1764, while living in or near London, Serle became a friend of William Romaine. Like Romaine he was an evangelical within the Church of England and other friends included John Thornton, John Newton, Augustus Toplady, and Legh Richmond. A series of letters from Romaine shows the deep affection and sympathy in religious matters which subsisted between him and Serle.

When William Legge, second earl of Dartmouth, became secretary of state for the colonies in 1772, Serle was appointed one of his under-secretaries, and in January 1776 he was made clerk of reports. He went to America in 1774, accompanied the British army from 1776 to 1778, and during part of that time had control of the press in New York. Serle argued against the American War of Independence on religious grounds in his *Americans Against Liberty* (1775); his correspondence is rich in information on American affairs. On returning from America in 1780 he settled at Heckfield, Hampshire. In 1795, by which time he had attained the rank of captain in the navy, Serle was a commissioner of the transport service and the care of prisoners of war; he was reappointed in 1803 and 1809. Serle was a prolific devotional writer, and most of his works went into several editions; Romaine circulated Serle's *Horae solitariae* (1776) and *Christian Remembrancer* (1787). He was married, probably to Martha Woodrooffe who married an Ambrose Serle at St Pancras Old Church on 29 October 1774. He died on 1 August 1812 and was buried in the churchyard at Broadwater, near Worthing. In his will he left over £20,000, in addition to his property, to his wife and the five children mentioned in the will. Another daughter, Jane (1780–1792), was Mrs Romaine's goddaughter. H. L. BENNETT, *rev.* EMMA MAJOR

Sources J. C. D. Clark, *The language of liberty, 1660–1832: political discourse and social dynamics in the Anglo-American world* (1994) • *GM*, 1st ser., 82/2 (1812), 193 • *ESTC* • D. M. Lewis, ed., *The Blackwell dictionary of evangelical biography, 1730–1860*, 2 vols. (1995) • W. Roberts, *Memoirs of the life and correspondence of Hannah More*, 3rd edn, 4 vols. (1835) • *Annual Register* (1795) • will, PRO, PROB 11/1536, fols. 296–7 • *IGI*
Archives Hunt. L., military journal | BL, letters to Lord Nelson, Add. MSS 34919–34933 • NMM, letters to Lord Barham • NMM, letters to Lord Nelson
Wealth at death over £20,000; plus property: will, PRO, PROB 11/1536, fols. 296–7

Serlo (*fl.* **late 10th cent.**). *See under* Serlo (*b. c.*1108, *d.* after 1206).

Serlo (*d.* **1104**), abbot of Gloucester, was a canon at Avranches and a Benedictine monk at Mont-St Michel, in Normandy, before being appointed to the abbacy of St Peter's, Gloucester, in 1072. Before the conquest Gloucester Abbey would not have been singled out as one of the leading English monasteries, having only two monks and eight novices, but by the end of Serlo's life there were 100 monks and it stood out as a model house. As far as architectural history can be reconstructed from written sources, it seems that the extensions made to the Old Minster at Gloucester in 1058 by Ealdred, archbishop of York, had been intended to provide a suitable setting for royal crown-wearing ceremonies rather than for meeting the monks' needs. Ealdred had also been able to transfer some of the abbey's most valuable estates to the archbishopric of York because the abbot of Gloucester was his kinsman.

The opportunity for a transformation in the abbey's fortunes came in 1088 when baronial rebels, intent on ensuring that William II would not be able to organize crown-wearing ceremonies at Gloucester after the example of his father, attacked and seriously damaged the abbey during the civil war of royal succession. The attack formed part of a wider aristocratic reaction against the church in western England. William II's response was to help Gloucester Abbey in every way possible during the rest of his reign. He and eighteen of his barons donated a substantial number of estates to the abbey, and the monks were never again the victims of aristocratic unrest during the Anglo-Norman period. In 1089 the bishop of Hereford laid the foundation stone of the great new church at Gloucester and became the abbey's patron. In 1095 the archbishop of York was forced to return the disputed estates which Ealdred had taken over, after resisting royal writs and orders of restitution for twenty-five years. William II granted Serlo and the monks of Gloucester a privilege that gave them the whole of each sturgeon caught in their fisheries across the realm. Serlo was once able to persuade Wulfstan, bishop of Worcester, to honour the brethren's refectory by staying for dinner, and the wealth of the food led one young layman to mock the gluttony of the bishop and his hosts.

Under Serlo's leadership the abbey became a centre of spirituality and the scene of great ecclesiastical events. On 6 March 1093 Anselm was proclaimed as the new archbishop of Canterbury in Gloucester Abbey, and the bishop of Worcester and the abbot of Shrewsbury preached sermons and baptized people there. On these visits to Gloucester, Wulfstan performed two miracles and the abbot prophesied the demise of William II on the day before the latter's death. Miracles were performed more frequently at the abbey church than might be expected, perhaps because holy men in western England wanted regularly to visit Serlo and the new Norman-style church. The new building was eventually consecrated on 15 July 1100.

William of Malmesbury commented that Serlo of Gloucester was one of the three great abbots whose spirituality and rule over their abbeys distinguished them from all other ecclesiastics in England after the conquest, and Godfrey of Winchester noted in a poem that Serlo 'pleased the very princes whom he reproved' (Wright, 2.154). Serlo died on 3 or 4 March 1104 after more than thirty years as abbot. His achievement was to provide Gloucester Abbey with monumental architecture and an impressive monastic reputation, which enabled it successfully to replace its earlier role as a royal ceremonial church.

Serlo (*d.* 1147x9), abbot of Cirencester, also had connections in Gloucestershire, but should not be confused with the abbot of Gloucester of that name. He was the son of Sired the blacksmith and Leoflæd. He may have joined the monastic chapter at Salisbury Cathedral as a novice, and some time between 1111 and 1125 he became dean of the chapter. By 1125 he had moved to join the new Augustinian foundation at Merton in Surrey. Roger, bishop of Salisbury, had persuaded Henry I to grant Merton special privileges, and Serlo probably represented Roger's interests there. In 1129 Serlo and his mother sold the land which they owned in Gloucester to St Peter's Abbey with the agreement of Serlo's son, Bartholomew. The involvement of both mother and son in the sale raises the possibility that family land was being disposed of, and that Serlo may have had local connections in Gloucestershire. If so, it may have been a factor in his promotion to Cirencester. John of Worcester records that Cirencester College in Gloucestershire was refounded as an Augustinian abbey by Henry I in 1117, and Serlo was consecrated as the first abbot in 1131. The lands of the priest Regenbald, the chaplain of Edward the Confessor, were given by the king to the community in 1133. Bishop Roger of Salisbury may have played an important role in securing this gift for Cirencester, since he retained a life interest over the properties of Regenbald. Thanks to the patronage of the bishop of Salisbury, when Serlo died, on 30 January some time between 1147 and 1149, the community at Cirencester had a very secure endowment. It may be that Roger had also taken a personal interest in furthering the career of Serlo, who rose from being the son of an Anglo-Saxon blacksmith to become the ruler of one of the foremost centres of twelfth-century monasticism.

A. F. WAREHAM

Sources W. H. Hart, ed., *Historia et cartularium monasterii Sancti Petri Gloucestriae*, 3 vols., Rolls Series, 33 (1863–7) • *Willelmi Malmesbiriensis monachi de gestis regum Anglorum*, ed. W. Stubbs, 2 vols., Rolls Series (1887–9), vol. 2, p. 511 • *William of Malmesbury's life of Saint Wulstan: bishop of Worcester*, trans. J. H. F. Peile (1934) [trans. of *Vita Wulfstani*] • Ordericus Vitalis, *Eccl. hist.*, vol. 5 • M. Hare, *The two Anglo-Saxon minsters of Gloucester* (1993) • *Reg. RAN*, 1.445 • T. Wright, ed., *The Anglo-Latin satirical poets and epigrammatists of the twelfth century*, 2 vols., Rolls Series, 59 (1872) • C. D. Ross and M. Devine, eds., *The cartulary of Cirencester Abbey, Gloucestershire*, 3 vols. (1964–77) • W. St Clair Baddeley, *A history of Cirencester* (1924) • BL, MS Cotton Vesp A.n.f. 196 vi

Serlo (*d.* **1147x9**). *See under* Serlo (*d.* 1104).

Serlo (*b. c.***1108**, *d.* after **1206**), Cistercian monk, a member successively of the communities of Fountains (*c.*1137) and Kirkstall (1147), where he probably died, appears only in Hugh of Kirkstall's history (*Narratio*) of Fountains, written *c.*1205/6–1226. Hugh was commissioned by John of York, abbot of Fountains (1203–11), and instructed to use the recollections of the near centenarian Serlo as the basis of his account. In the circumstances of its turbulent foundation in late 1132 from St Mary's, York, Fountains would seem, retrospectively, an English Cîteaux, and the reformers at St Mary's the first Cistercians reborn. Serlo remarks in Hugh's *Narratio* that he was an eyewitness of the events of 1132, knew the reformers by name and in person, came from their region, was related to some of them, and was brought up (*nutritus*) with them: the word used suggests that he was an oblate at St Mary's. If so, he did not continue as a professed monk after the age of fifteen (*c.*1123): when he entered Fountains *c.*1137 he twice remarks that he did so 'from the world'. Serlo did not identify his relatives, nor is there any indication elsewhere. This might suggest that they were humbler members of the reforming party, who did not achieve abbatial office, but 'died as monks'. This accords with what is not known about Serlo himself: he may have been in Archbishop Thurstan's party which catalytically visited St Mary's in October 1132, but he is not named then or later as a member of the archiepiscopal household—he is not to be confused with the canon of York, Serlo, who was with Thurstan, and became one of the first important recruits to Fountains shortly before Serlo's own entry. He was not, as sometimes asserted, the brother of Abbot Ralph of Louth Park; he was not the author of poems on the battle of the Standard (1138) and the death of Somerled in an early Fountains manuscript; he is Gramaticus (*sic*) only in a sixteenth-century note on the reverse of the sole surviving medieval fifteenth-century manuscript of the *Narratio* which refers to John Bale's *Scriptores* (1559). His recollection of early Fountains is slight, and his ghosted centenarian memoirs had been prefigured at Byland by those of Roger, second abbot of that house.

Serlo (*fl.* late 10th cent.), monk, of St Augustine's, Canterbury, himself a shadowy figure of uncertain career, achievement, and reputation, is the most far-fetched of namesakes who have been associated with Serlo solely on the basis of his illusory literary output.

DEREK BAKER

Sources J. R. Walbran, ed., *Memorials of the abbey of St Mary of Fountains*, 1, SurtS, 42 (1863) • Dugdale, *Monasticon*, new edn • E. K. Clarke, *Fundacio abbathie de Kyrkestall*, Thoresby Society, 4 (1895) • D. Baker, 'The genesis of English Cistercian chronicles: the foundation history of Fountains Abbey', *Analecta Cisterciensia*, 25 (1969), 14–41; 31 (1976), 179–212 • L. G. D. Baker, 'The foundation of Fountains Abbey', *Northern History*, 4 (1969), 29–43 • D. Knowles, *The* *monastic order in England*, 2nd edn (1963) • M. Brett, *The English church under Henry I* (1975)

Archives Leeds Central Library, MS VR 5383 | BL, Arundel, Lansdowne MSS • Bodl. Oxf., Dodsworth, Add. MSS, Leland Collectanea 3, Top. Gen. C. 3 • Trinity Cam., Gale MSS

Sermon, William (*bap.* 1629, *d.* 1680), physician and inventor of medicines, was almost certainly the William, son of John Surman, who was baptized on 8 November 1629 at Eldersfield, Worcestershire. He had a brother John, and was a near relative of Edmund, son of Edmund and Jane Surman, baptized in 1644 at Naunton Beauchamp, Worcestershire, and of Edmund Sermon (*d. c.*1680), MA of St Mary's Hall, Oxford.

Sermon apparently decided at the age of fourteen to study medicine, having observed (from behind a hedge, while out hare-shooting) a young woman giving birth alone in a wood. He served for many years in the parliamentary forces under George Monck, and after the Restoration established a fashionable practice in London.

In 1661 Sermon was consulted by a patient suffering from dropsy; by the following year he had devised a pill which he successfully tried out on a friend. His pills must have contained aloes, as they were purgatives. In large doses (and strong men were recommended to take three at a time) they acted as emetics. To induce sweating he also offered a liquid medicine, presumably with an antimony base. Since the pills expelled all harmful humours and purified the blood, they were also reckoned to be effective against scurvy, venereal swellings, and jaundice.

Once Sermon had—by his own account—achieved some noteworthy cures in London during the great plague, early in 1666 he was invited by the mayor to Bristol, when the plague erupted there. In three months Sermon claimed to have cured all those who had followed his directions. With a thriving practice he stayed in Bristol until June 1669, when he was summoned to New Hall, Essex, to treat his old commander, Monck, by then first duke of Albemarle, who was gravely ill with dropsy. Sermon restored him to health in twenty-eight days, with nineteen pills. Monck, as Sermon later unblushingly wrote, evacuated by stool no fewer than 12 gallons of water; the patient also took Sermon's liquid drink infused in wine. On Sermon's departure in July the grateful Monck gave him a glowing testimonial; he died six months later, but not, Sermon defiantly maintained, of dropsy.

Sermon's career as a physician was now secure. A few weeks later Charles II requested the University of Cambridge to award him a doctorate of medicine. Sermon then moved to London and advertised his removal in the *London Gazette*, his address being East Harding Street, near Goldsmiths' Hall, Fetter Lane. Awarded his MD in 1670, and claiming to be physician-in-ordinary to the king, Sermon published his *Advertisement* (1670) concerning his 'most famous and safe cathartique and diuretique Pills'; it ran to eleven editions by 1675. It was issued by the bookseller Edward Thomas, at the Adam and Eve, Little Britain, also the sole agent for the pills, which by 1672 had no fewer than seventy-eight retail outlets throughout Britain, twenty-four in London, one in Edinburgh, and one in Dublin. They sold at the high price of 4*s.* for twenty pills, no reduction being given for quantity.

In 1671 Sermon produced *The Ladies Companion, or, The English Midwife*. Its frontispiece, drawn and engraved by William Sherwin, portrays the author at the age of forty-two as dark-eyed, bewigged, and in a doctor's gown, with a round face, and a slightly disdainful smile; the antiquary Anthony Wood called Sermon 'forward, vain and conceited'. Having declaimed in the preface about the 'black-mouth'd envy, that barks but cannot bite' excited by his successes, and having warned against worthless imitations of his pills, Sermon went on to cover obstetric subjects in plain and straightforward language. He demonstrated the empirical nature of medicine in his day by prescribing herbal remedies for various ailments, and stated that a woman was most likely to conceive a few days after menstruation ceased, particularly if she hung wild carrot seed over her left arm above the elbow. An interesting pregnancy test was to mix thoroughly equal quantities of white wine and the woman's urine; if the concoction resembled bean broth, she was with child. Sixteen rather imaginative copperplate illustrations showed the positions of full-term infants in the womb.

Sermon's third work, *A Friend to the Sick* (1673), narrated the most remarkable cures achieved by the pills. Prefaced by a sequence of laudatory verses by Payne Fisher, Edward Cocker, and William Winstanley, among others, it is of interest for being punctuated by a variety of rambling reminiscences. He was determined that what he called his great arcanum should not die with him, and he wrote out the formula on a large piece of parchment, sealed it, and entrusted it to his wife. She was the daughter of Thomas Saunders of Bristol, but nothing further is known about her, except that she died in her husband's lifetime without surviving children. On 15 October 1678 he married the twenty-year-old Edith Davis, of St Margaret's Lothbury; almost forty-nine, he gave his age as about forty-five. They had a son, George. Sermon died just over a year later: six days after making his will, he was buried at St Bride's, Fleet Street, on 9 January 1680. His wife was sole executor, but he referred affectionately to his first father-in-law, Thomas Saunders, asking him to oversee the will. Despite Sermon's efforts to ensure the survival of his pills, they vanished without trace, not being included in the list of patent medicines in the *Gentleman's Magazine* (1748, 346–50). T. A. B. Corley

Sources W. Sermon, *Advertisement concerning those most famous and safe cathartique and diuretique pills* (1670) • W. Sermon, *The ladies companion, or, The English midwife* (1671) • W. Sermon, *A friend to the sick, or, The honest man's preservative* (1673) • T. Gumble, *The life of General Monck, duke of Albemarle* (1671), 453–5 • Wood, *Ath. Oxon.* • *CSP dom.*, 1669, 441, 486; 1670, *with addenda 1660–70*, 732 • J. L. Chester and G. J. Armytage, eds., *Allegations for marriage licences issued by the dean and chapter of Westminster, 1558 to 1699; also, for those issued by the vicar-general of the archbishop of Canterbury, 1660 to 1679*, Harleian Society, 23 (1886), 286 • E. Arber, ed., *The term catalogues, 1668–1709*, 3 vols. (privately printed, London, 1903–6), vol. 1, p. 63 • Wing, *STC* • Venn, *Alum. Cant.* • will, PRO, PROB 11/302/76

Likenesses T. Cross, line engraving (aged forty-two), BM • T. Cross, line engraving (after his earlier work), BM, NPG • W. Sherwin, line engraving, BM, NPG; repro. in Sermon, *The ladies companion*
Wealth at death see will, PRO, PROB 11/302/76

Serocold, Claude Pearce (1875–1959), stockbroker, was born in Taplow, Buckinghamshire, on 5 July 1875, the fourth son of Charles Pearce-Serocold (1827–1904) of Taplow, and his wife, Marie Emilie Grenfell, daughter of Colonel George St Leger Grenfell. His father was then the senior partner at Reid's brewery, which he had joined as a young man. Serocold was educated at Eton College, where he coxed the Eton crew for three successive years and was president of Pop. He went up to New College, Oxford, and coxed the winning boat race crew in 1895 but he spent only a year there, coming down without a degree. His father gave him £10,000 to start his business career and he joined Rowe and Pitman, and became a member of the stock exchange in 1901. Two years later he moved to Cazenove and Akroyds.

Before the First World War, Serocold made little impact in the City of London. He was considered by his family to be something of a playboy, and a rather raffish one at that, because of his interests in music (he played the piano) and art and his love of France (particularly Cannes), and of the French language, which he spoke well. He nevertheless had a passion for the sea and was a member of the Royal Yacht Squadron. During the war he joined naval intelligence and, as one of Captain Reginald Hall's two personal assistants from 1915, was intimately involved in the codebreaking activities which contributed so much to the defeat of the Germans. After 'moving in a rare and mysterious world' (Beesly, 315) he returned to the firm a different man and soon became much more of a figure—and a well-respected one—in the City.

During the inter-war years Serocold and Charles Micklem—in a partnership described by Lionel Fraser as the ideal one—dominated Cazenove and Akroyds and made the firm a force in the City: 'One [Serocold] shrewd and charming, opened the door, and the other [Micklem] detailed and able, did the work' (Fraser, 207). Physically rather small, always neat and well-dressed, and generous and entertaining, Serocold was, however, more than just an opener of doors. A reliable confidant and a born diplomat, he re-established and cultivated the firm's link with Baring Brothers, and acted as personal broker to Lord Revelstoke in the 1920s. He developed useful connections with other merchant banks, including Schroders and Morgan Grenfell, and his family connections with the Smiths, a ubiquitous banking family, meant that he had cousins at Morgan Grenfell, Hambros, and other City institutions. His elder brother, Oswald Pearce-Serocold (1865–1951), had joined their father in the brewing business, which by merger in 1898 became Watney, Combe, Reid & Co., and in 1932 he became its chairman.

Serocold's social contacts brought new business to Cazenove and Akroyds, and he attracted significant clients such as Major M. E. W. Pope, a wealthy coalmine owner, and Sir Connop Guthrie, a Suffolk landowner. The firm could depend upon both Pope and Guthrie to invest if asked. His friends included the opera promoter and hotelier Richard D'Oyly Carte, and he often played bridge with the investment manager of the Prudential Insurance Company. From 1921 he served as a director of the Savoy Hotel, and he was also treasurer of King's College Hospital.

By the late 1930s, when he was in his early sixties, Serocold began to wind down his business life and spend less time on the firm's affairs, though he remained its senior partner until 1947. A great Francophile, he spent more and more time at his home in the south of France and thus found himself, in 1940, trapped in the German-occupied part of the country from where he was, with considerable drama, rescued. At the end of the Second World War he sold his London house in Hyde Park Gate to Winston Churchill, and in 1947, when he retired from the firm, he went to live in Monaco. He died there, in hospital, on 17 June 1959. JUDY SLINN

Sources D. Kynaston, *Cazenove & Co.: a history* (1991) • H. H. Janes, *The red barrel: a history of Watney Mann* [1963] • R. Roberts, *Schroders: merchants and bankers* (1992) • W. L. Fraser, *All to the good* (1963) • *CGPLA Eng. & Wales* (1959) • P. Beesly, *Room 40: British naval intelligence, 1914–18* (1982) • Venn, *Alum. Cant.* • *WWW* • b. cert.
Likenesses photographs, Cazenove & Co., London • portrait, Cazenove & Co., London
Wealth at death £128,449 8*s*. 7*d*.—in England: probate, 22 Dec 1959, *CGPLA Eng. & Wales*

Serraillier, Ian Lucien (1912–1994), writer, schoolmaster, and editor of books for children, was born on 24 September 1912 at Kandar, Dawlish Road, London, the eldest son of Lucien Serraillier (1886–1919) and Mary Kirkland Rodger (1883–1940). His father was an engineering company manager of French descent who died in the 1919 influenza epidemic leaving four children under seven. Serraillier's mother subsequently spent much of her time in Switzerland for her health, and the experience of taking responsibility for his young siblings as they journeyed from England to join her in the summer contributed one element to the book for which Serraillier is best known—*The Silver Sword*, a classic children's story about the aftermath of the Second World War.

Serraillier was educated at Brighton College, then at St Edmund Hall, Oxford, where he initially read classics, then changed to English. After graduating in 1935 he became a teacher, first in private schools. From 1940 until he became a full-time writer and editor in 1961 he taught in state grammar schools, and he became committed to making the best literature available and attractively presented to all children.

His mother brought up her family as Christian Scientists but in 1939 Serraillier joined the Society of Friends, and his Quaker beliefs led to his being registered in 1940 as a conscientious objector, assigned to teaching and civil defence. On 2 August 1944 he married Anne Margaret Rogers (*b*. 1923), the daughter of the deputy headteacher at the school in Dudley where he then worked, and their three daughters and son were born between 1946 and 1955.

Serraillier's poetry was first published in 1942 in a volume called *Three New Poets*, in which he set out his characteristic themes, derived from the experience of mountain climbing and the reworking of myth and legend. His poems appeared in many of the main poetry periodicals of the time and a further collection, *The Weaver Birds*, was published by Macmillan in 1944. His first adventure story for children, *They Raced for Treasure*, appeared in 1946. In 1948 the literary critic Robert Gittings introduced Serraillier, who was by now at Midhurst grammar school in Sussex, to Alan Hill, the founder of the educational books division of the London publisher William Heinemann. Alan Hill was keen to supply books for what, in his 1988 memoir *In Pursuit of Publishing*, he described as the destiny he saw for English: 'in the hands of a new generation of teachers … set fair to become the main cultural and humanistic focus of secondary education' (Hill). But Hill's visits to state grammar and secondary modern schools left him depressed by the sight of sets of class readers of long nineteenth-century texts, with no twentieth-century novels of any kind. He therefore determined to publish books 'without notes or introductions, which the kids will recognise as a real book'. In Serraillier he found his ideal series editor, who combined idealism and scholarship with a shrewd attitude to finance. The New Windmill series, named after the Heinemann colophon, depended on other publishers leasing their copyright of profitable titles, having accepted that the new series was going to be hardback but cheap, sold specifically to schools, and so reach a new market, rather than be in competition with their own sales. From the start the series aimed to be artistically and socially enlarging; its early titles ranged from the work of the contemporary poet C. Day Lewis to stories with working-class urban settings and modern American classics. It later became more widely international, introducing Camus, Colette, Hemingway, and Solzhenitsyn, and the publishers had an especial commitment to Commonwealth writers. Serraillier also broke new ground by publishing for schools unbowdlerized, unabridged editions of contemporary books that were elsewhere published for adult readers. In 1956 Serraillier's wife joined him as co-editor, and over the whole period the series was a considerable financial as well as critical success.

Serraillier compiled and wrote books for the New Windmill series himself, but also published outside the series a considerable number of original stories, poems, and prose and verse reworkings of traditional stories and classics. He contributed substantially to the BBC's *Children's Hour* and schools broadcasts, and wrote *Everest Climbed*, a tribute to the 1953 ascent, for which the leader of the team, Sir John Hunt, penned the introduction. He found poetry easier to work on during the school term than fiction, and sustained a considerable output, throughout his career, of original poems and verse retellings, many of which were selected for anthologies for children. But his continuing reputation rests largely on one novel. He had written one adventure story with a central European wartime setting, *There's No Escape* (1950), before researching and writing, over five years from 1951, the novel which stands out in style and achievement from all his other prose work. *The Silver Sword* (1956) tells the story of the children of a Polish schoolmaster imprisoned in the Nazi occupation; on his release at the end of the war the father returns to the family home to find it destroyed, the only occupant a street urchin to whom he gives the silver sword, a paperknife, hoping for help in tracing his children. The book is a morally subtle tale of journey and reunion, and it became a huge and lasting success, adapted for television and stage, and cited frequently throughout the succeeding decades in the literature of teaching as particularly effective for forming a bridge between the child's and the young adult's reading matter. It also stood the test of time outside the school context and continues in print.

Serraillier impressed those who met or worked with him as gentle, considerate, and courteous in manner, a conscientious, humane, and humorous teacher, and a spell-binding teller of tales to children. His style was informal: he hated suits, and his shapeless brown teaching jacket earned him the nickname of Sack at Midhurst school; his wife was Sackess and his children the 'little paper bags'. To his editor at Heinemann, Tony Beal, he seemed to have an innocence of nature—even, Beal wrote, 'a somewhat naïve attitude to life which seemed to go with a shrewd concern over money. He put me in mind of such Quakers as the Frys, Cadburys, etc.—why should good works not be profitable?'

Serraillier was tall, thin, and vigorous from daily walking; he had a lifelong love of mountains and the sea, and a particular commitment to the Sussex downs where he was settled from 1946 until his death. His graphic ability allowed him to illustrate some of his own early publications, and to become a keen photographer of the landscapes he loved. His last books were illustrated celebrations of the history of the villages around his home.

Ian Serraillier died of pneumonia, after suffering from Alzheimer's disease for some years, on 28 November 1994, in Woldhurst retirement home, Runcton, Chichester, and was cremated at Chichester on 2 December. He was survived by his wife. MARI PRICHARD

Sources A. Hill, *In pursuit of publishing* (1988) • I. Serraillier, 'Something about the author', *Gale Research Co, USA* (1987) [autobiographical article] • private information (2004) [Anne Serraillier, wife; Jane Serraillier Grossfeld, daughter; T. Beal] • B. Price, *Southern Arts Magazine* (Oct 1971) • T. Beal, *The Guardian* (6 Dec 1994) • *The Times* (5 Dec 1994) • J. Serraillier Grossfeld, afterword, *The silver sword*, Puffin Modern Classics (1993)

Archives priv. coll., papers, etc. • U. Reading | SOUND BBC

Likenesses B. Price, photograph, repro. in Price, *Southern Arts Magazine* • photographs, repro. in Serraillier, 'Something about the author'

Wealth at death £177,272: probate, 1995, *CGPLA Eng. & Wales*

Serres, Dominic (1722–1793), marine painter, was born at Auch in Gascony, France, and was educated at the famous Benedictine school at Douai. He is said to have been nephew of the archbishop of Rheims. His parents intended him for the church, but he ran away from his native town, and made his way on foot into Spain. He

Dominic Serres (1722–1793), by Philip Jean, 1788

there shipped on board a vessel for South America as a common sailor, and eventually became master of a trading vessel to Havana, Cuba, where he was taken prisoner by a British frigate and brought to England in the 1750s. After his release he married and lived for a time in Northamptonshire before moving to London. There he met the gifted marine artist Charles Brooking and was much influenced by his work. He shows the same concern for light and shadow on the surface of the water and his drawing of waves is never stereotyped.

In 1765 Serres became a member of the Incorporated Society of Artists, with which he exhibited for two years. On the establishment of the Royal Academy in 1768 he was chosen one of the foundation members, and was a constant contributor up to the time of his death. Between 1761 and 1793 he exhibited eight works at the Society of Artists, twenty-one at the Free Society, and 105 at the Royal Academy. Redgrave noted that Serres spoke English with fluency, was a good Latin and Italian scholar, and also spoke Spanish and Portuguese. These accomplishments, together with his competence as a painter and his undoubted charm, secured him royal favour and numerous commissions. In 1784 his friend and neighbour Paul Sandby wrote: 'But Dom is grown a very great man, has been to Paris, dined with the King's architect and is going to paint the Grand Monarque' (Sandby, 167). In 1792 he succeeded Joseph Wilton as librarian to the academy. He was also appointed marine painter to George III, but he did not long hold these offices.

Serres died on 6 November 1793, and was buried at St Marylebone Old Church. He had two sons, who followed his profession, John Thomas *Serres and Dominic, and four daughters, two of whom were honorary exhibitors at the Royal Academy. A miniature portrait of the artist by Philip Jean (National Portrait Gallery, London) shows the artist in his sixties, seated at his easel and putting the finishing touches to a painting of ships.

Forty-five paintings by Serres in the National Maritime Museum, Greenwich, include a fine ship portrait *HMS Royal George in the English Channel*, numerous sea battles, and a series of eleven paintings illustrating the capture of Havana in 1762 based on information and sketches supplied by Lieutenant Durnsford, who served in the campaign. Engravings of the series were published by Durnsford during 1764–5. Other paintings and drawings are in the Royal Collection and the Victoria and Albert Museum, London.

W. C. MONKHOUSE, *rev.* DAVID CORDINGLY

Sources E. H. H. Archibald, *Dictionary of sea painters*, 2nd edn (1989) • D. Cordingly, *Marine painting in England, 1700–1900* (1974) • R. Quarm and S. Wilcox, *Masters of the sea* (1987) • *Concise catalogue of oil paintings in the National Maritime Museum* (1988) • O. Meslay, 'Dominique Serres, peintre de marine du roi George III d'Angleterre', *Société Archéologique et Historique du Gers*, 3e trimestre (1997), 288–321 • Redgrave, *Artists* • E. Edwards, *Anecdotes of painters* (1808); facs. edn (1970) • W. Sandby, *Thomas and Paul Sandby* (1892) • *Memoir of J. T. Serres* (1826), 7 • *GM*, 1st ser., 63 (1793), 1058

Likenesses P. Jean, miniature, 1788, NPG [*see illus.*] • pencil and wash drawing, 1792, NPG • G. Dance, drawing, 1793, RA • D. Turner, etching (after O. Humphry), BM, NPG • J. Zoffany, group portrait, oils (*Royal Academicians, 1772*), Royal Collection

Serres, John Thomas (1759–1825), marine painter, was born in December 1759, the elder son of Dominic *Serres (1722–1793), also a marine painter. Serres was trained by his father, a founding Royal Academician, and himself taught painting and marine draughtsmanship all his life. At the age of seventeen he was sufficiently accomplished to exhibit at the Royal Academy; his first teaching post was at the short-lived (1779–87) Maritime School in Paradise Row, Chelsea, London. Though it has not been established whether Serres was patronized by the second earl of Warwick, it is certain that Serres met a house painter in Warwick's employ, Robert Wilmot, whose artistically precocious daughter, Olivia, became his pupil, and with whom he fell in love [*see* Serres, Olivia]. Serres made a continental expedition, to France (where he witnessed the fall of the Bastille in Paris in July 1789) and Italy where, perhaps through his father, he had been afforded certain introductions by Sir Joshua Reynolds. If the date 1790 on the most distinguished of Serres's paintings *The Thames at Limehouse* (Royal Collection) is accepted, he returned to England before the end of that year. After some delay he married Olivia Wilmot (1772–1835) on 1 September 1791 at Barton on the Heath, Warwickshire, where her uncle was the incumbent. The bride's unstable temperament gave rise to some misgivings about the match among the families of both parties.

On the death of his father in 1793 Serres succeeded him

as marine painter to George III and to the duke of Clarence. His marriage was under strain but nevertheless produced various offspring, of which perhaps only two children, both daughters, survived infancy. As an official draughtsman to the Admiralty Serres was frequently absent from home, for as much as six months in 1800 when he was actually on sea service. He made 'drawings in the form of elevations' of the coasts of France and Spain, a selection of which were published in *The Little Sea Torch* (1801) (Archibald, 197). He taught drawing at the Chelsea Naval School and in 1805 published, under joint authorship with his father, *Liber nauticus, and Instructor in the Art of Marine Drawing*, a work intended to assist his students which contained plates after his own work and that of his father. In his absence, his wife committed numerous infidelities, and several frauds, which included forging her husband's name on bank drafts to the extent that Serres became a declared bankrupt. In 1802 a separation was mutually agreed, trusteeship for the daughters being invested, *inter alia*, in Olivia's current lover. In 1804 Serres abducted one of the daughters, for which he was charged by the trustees with breaching the trust and consigned to prison. Olivia evidently pursued her artist's career, since in 1806, two years before Serres's release from prison, she was appointed landscape painter to the prince of Wales.

On his release, Serres sought better fortune in Edinburgh, but his wife pursued him there and he was again committed. On release Serres ventured into theatre investment, becoming, in 1817, one of the proprietors of the Coburg Theatre and later its scenic director. This project lost him what money he had made during the closing years of the war. The collection of old master and contemporary drawings Serres had inherited from his father were dispersed at about this time. His financial adversities were further compounded by the refusal in 1822 of George IV (who as prince of Wales had patronized his wife) to continue the patronage his father had shown Serres. Though refused permission to act as the king's official draughtsman on his royal visit to Scotland in 1822, Serres nevertheless produced 'a set of large and well-crafted watercolours recording the event' (Deuchar, 482) (National Maritime Museum, London). Again imprisoned for debt, the artist was released on grounds of health in December 1825, but required to live within the rules of the king's bench. Serres died on 28 December 1825.

Serres worked skilfully in various media but, while his accuracy in ship depiction was akin to that of his father, John Thomas Serres was inclined to overdramatize weather conditions, as in, for example, his painting of George III's yacht *Royal Sovereign* (1804; National Maritime Museum, London). He is, however, more extensively represented at the National Maritime Museum than his father. Though his early triumph with *The Thames at Limehouse* (which gained the approbation of George III) was perhaps unequalled by his later work, despite his disastrous marriage, Serres continued to produce work of sensitivity in its depiction of Thames-side life.

D. D. Aldridge

Sources *Memoir of J. T. Serres late marine painter to his majesty by a friend* (1826) • D. Cordingly, *Marine painting in England, 1700–1900* (1974), 84–5 • I. O. Williams, *Early English watercolours and some cognate drawings by artists born not later than 1785* (1952); repr. (1970), 199 • O. Millar, *The later Georgian pictures in the collection of her majesty the queen*, 1 (1969), 115–16 • E. H. H. Archibald, *Dictionary of sea painters* (1980) • S. Deuchar, 'Serres, John Thomas', *The dictionary of art*, ed. J. Turner (1996) • *IGI*

Serres [*née* Wilmot], **Olivia** [*alias* Princess Olive of Cumberland] (**1772–1835**), royal impostor, was born in Warwick on 3 April 1772, daughter of Robert Wilmot, house painter, and his wife, Anna Maria Brunton. She was baptized on 15 April 1772 at St Nicholas's Church, Warwick. Her father having embezzled the county rates, her parents subsequently moved to London, and Olivia spent much of her youth in the house of her uncle, Dr James *Wilmot, fellow of Trinity College, Oxford, and rector of Barton on the Heath, Warwickshire. In 1790, two men were hanged for burglary on her evidence. She married, on 1 September 1791, at Barton on the Heath, John Thomas *Serres (1759–1825) who had been her drawing master in London and who in 1793 was appointed marine painter to the king. She was at this time under age, and the marriage was conducted by special licence, her father having sworn an affidavit to their relationship and consenting to the marriage. The marriage was unhappy, and the couple separated in 1802, having had two daughters and at least one son.

Olivia Serres supported herself by painting and teaching, exhibiting landscapes at the Royal Academy between 1793 and 1808, and at the British Institution from 1806 to 1811; her work has been accounted competent. In 1806 she was appointed landscape painter to the prince of Wales, whom she subsequently plagued with an incoherent correspondence. During this period she also produced a number of romantic literary works, including a novel, *St Julian* (1805), *Flights of Fancy: Poems* (1806), and an opera, *The Castle of Avola* (1805). She came into the public eye in 1813, when she published a memoir of her uncle, Dr Wilmot, who had died in 1807, under the title *The Life of the Author of Junius's Letters, the Revd James Wilmot, DD*, claiming that she had documents to prove that he was the anonymous author of the controversial letters of the 1770s. A lengthy and heated argument in the pages of the *Gentleman's Magazine* ensued, which demonstrated the absurdity of Mrs Serres's assertions. The correspondence revealed a deep sense of paranoia: she wrote that 'I have, too, *political enemies—powerful ones*, whose characters and transactions, … have subjected me to much secret oppression' (*GM*, 1813, 414). In a pamphlet in 1817, she sought to re-establish the authenticity of her case, on the basis of the handwriting in the documents which were assumed by everyone else to be forged.

In 1817, the imposture escalated. Olivia Serres made her first claim to being the daughter of *Henry Frederick, duke of Cumberland, brother of George III. In a petition to the prince regent in 1818 she alleged that she was the daughter of the duke and a Mrs Payne, a sister of Dr Wilmot, and wife of a captain in the Royal Navy. Following the death of George III, her delusions of grandeur

Olivia Serres (1772–1835), by Sir Joshua Reynolds, 1790

increased. Now she claimed to be the *legitimate* daughter of the duke: she styled herself the Princess Olive of Cumberland, placed the royal arms on a coach she had hired, and dressed her servants in the royal livery. According to her fantasy, Dr Wilmot was married secretly to the Princess Poniatouski, sister of King Stanislaus of Poland, from which marriage a daughter was born. This daughter, who was brought up by Wilmot's sister, Mrs Payne, came to the attention of the duke of Cumberland who married her on 4 March 1767. Mrs Serres claimed to be the daughter of this marriage, and to have been substituted for a stillborn daughter of the Robert Wilmots, who were subsequently reputed to be her parents. She offered a large quantity of documents as corroborative evidence, including papers apparently written or witnessed by the earl of Warwick, who had died in 1816.

In July 1821 Olivia Serres was arrested for debt, but she moved that the proceedings be stayed on grounds that as a member of the royal family she was exempt from arrest in civil cases. She had herself rechristened in September 1821 at Islington as Olive, daughter of the duke of Cumberland and his first wife, Olive, but the privilege was denied, on grounds that she had already put in bail. At this point she produced what purported to be an early will by George III, leaving £15,000 to 'Olive, the daughter of our brother of Cumberland', and in 1822 applied through the courts to see George III's will. This was also denied, on grounds that the courts had no jurisdiction over royal wills.

Mrs Serres was not without supporters. The *British Luminary* took up her cause, and the genealogist Henry Nugent Bell was said to have reported favourably on it. More importantly, Sir Gerald Noel presented a petition to parliament in 1823, and in June moved that it be referred to a select committee, which motion was seconded by the radical Joseph Hume. Sir Robert Peel refuted her claims on the floor of the house by proving that her documents were fabricated, and caused much mirth by pointing out that if her English claims were rejected, 'the lady had two strings to her bow', for she had also claimed to be a legitimate descendant of the kings of Poland (*GM*, 1823, 637–8). The motion was rejected without a division.

The estranged husband of Olivia Serres, John Thomas Serres, who had been cast out of royal favour on account of his wife's pretensions, died in poverty in the rules of the king's bench on 28 December 1825, and in his will repudiated any belief in Olivia's claims. She herself died in the rules of the king's bench, in Trinity Square, Southwark, on 21 November 1835 and was buried in St James's Church, Piccadilly, on 3 December, under the name of Olive Cumberland. In her will, which was sworn at under £20, she left 1*s*. to each of 'my cousins of the Royal House of Guelph … to enable them to purchase a prayer for to teach them repentence for their past cruelties and injuries to myself, their legitimate and lawful cousin' (Pendered and Mallett, 266–7). In addition to the works published under her own name, she wrote much anonymously, and was probably responsible for the publication of the *Secret History of the Court of England* which appeared under Lady Anne Hamilton's name in 1828.

Lavinia Janetta Horton Ryves (1797–1871) was the elder daughter and eldest surviving child of Olivia and John Thomas Serres. Born in Liverpool in 1797, her childhood was disrupted by the disputes of her parents, and throughout her life she had divided loyalties. In 1822 she married the portrait painter Anthony Thomas Ryves (*d.* 1873?), with whom she had six children before divorcing him for cruelty and misconduct, in 1841. Her father opposed the marriage, and cut her out of his will in favour of her younger sister, Britannia. Following her mother's death in 1835, she styled herself Princess Lavinia of Cumberland and duchess of Lancaster, and asserted the legitimacy of her mother's claims. Sir Gerald Noel again took up the case, forming a committee of supporters, and attempts were made in 1842 and 1844 to claim the £15,000 supposedly left to Mrs Serres by George III. The claim failed, the court of chancery maintaining again that it had no jurisdiction over royal wills. In 1858 she published *An appeal for royalty: a letter to her most gracious majesty Queen Victoria from Lavinia, princess of Cumberland and duchess of Lancaster*, in which were published all the documents in the case, including those relating to a supposed marriage between George III and Hannah Lightfoot. In 1861 she obtained a declaration of the validity of her parents' marriage under the Legitimacy Declaration Act, and in 1866 brought a further case (with her son, William Henry Ryves) seeking a declaration that the duke of Cumberland and Olive Wilmot were lawfully married, and that Olive (Olivia), later Mrs Serres, was their legitimate child. The attorney-general, Sir Roundell Palmer, opposed their petition, and the jury found unanimously that the documents were forgeries. Following the rejection of her claims, Lavinia Ryves published a pamphlet, *Ryves v. the Attorney-General: was Justice Done?* in 1868. She died on 7 December 1871 at Haverstock Hill, London. K. D. REYNOLDS

Sources M. Shepard, *Princess Olive* (1984) · M. Pendered and J. Mallett, *Princess or pretender?* (1939) · *GM*, 1st ser., 83/2 (1813), 99, 154, 314, 414, 415, 545, 656 · *GM*, 1st ser., 84/1 (1814), 213, 344, 450, 535 · *GM*, 1st ser., 84/2 (1814), 6, 24, 363 · *GM*, 1st ser., 92/1 (1822), 33–8 · *GM*, 1st ser., 93/1 (1823), 560, 637–8 · *GM*, 1st ser., 96/1 (1826), 280–81 · *GM*, 2nd ser., 4 (1835), 93–4 · Waterhouse, *18c painters* · *DNB*
Archives priv. coll., Eldon MSS
Likenesses J. Reynolds, drawing, 1790, priv. coll. [*see illus.*] · Mackenzie, stipple, pubd 1805 (after G. F. Joseph), BM · portrait, repro. in O. Serras, *Flights of Fancy* (1804), frontispiece · two portraits, repro. in Pendered and Mallett, *Princess or pretender?* · two portraits (Lavinia Janetta Horton Ryves), repro. in Pendered and Mallett, *Princess or pretender?*
Wealth at death under £20: will, 1840, Pendered and Mallett, *Princess*, 266–7

Seru Epenisa Cakobau (1817?–1883), chief of Bau and king of Fiji, was born on the island of Bau in Fiji, a son of Tanoa Visawaqa (*d.* 1852) and Savusavu. His earliest known name was Seru; he later became known as Cakobau (pronounced Thakombau), and took the name Epenisa after conversion to Christianity.

Cakobau received the traditional upbringing of a Fijian chief and first came to notice in 1832 when his father, who had succeeded to the title of vunivalu (root of war) or ruling war chief of Bau, was deposed in a coup and forced to flee. Seru was spared the usual massacre, and led a counter-coup in 1837, returning his father to his former dignity. From this time Seru was known as Cakobau and evinced an unusual aptitude for managing the convoluted politics of kinship which governed inter-tribal politics and warfare in Fiji.

After consolidating his position at home, Cakobau proceeded to intervene in the internal politics of neighbouring chieftaincies, usually with a view to installing chiefs friendly to himself. By this means the power of Bau was increased to the point that a trial of strength with its neighbour and former ally, Rewa, became inevitable. Fuelled by personal animosities, war between the two chiefdoms broke out in 1843 and continued on and off until 1855. This war and its proxy campaigns were the central preoccupation of Fijian affairs in the mid-nineteenth century.

Wesleyan missionaries had been working in Fiji since 1835, and Cakobau's wars were a major obstacle to them. Cakobau was indifferent to, rather than opposed to, Christianity, being more concerned with its possibly corrosive effects on his authority than with its eschatology. He was forced to reconsider when his political alliances collapsed in 1853 and he was faced not merely with defeat but with personal annihilation and probably the obliteration of his chiefdom. After much soul-searching and consultation he converted on 30 April 1854 and underwent radical personal reform. His baptism did not take place until the missionaries were convinced of his personal piety and steadfastness, and was performed on 11 January 1857. Cakobau's political situation remained insecure until his enemies were defeated by a force of Tongans under the command of Tupou I, king of Tonga, at the battle of Kaba on 7 April 1855.

Cakobau succeeded his father as vunivalu (war chief) of Bau after the latter's death, which took place on 8 December 1852. His investiture took place on 26 July 1853. Since the early 1840s Cakobau had occasionally called himself Tui Viti or king of Fiji, a title which had not hitherto existed. This was probably intended to impress European traders, but it also signalled the extent of his ambition. It proved, however, to be a source of weakness because enemies among the small number of European resident traders exploited the name to hold him responsible for losses which they suffered at the hands of Fijians in those turbulent years. By 1855 these largely groundless claims by Americans, mainly the United States commercial agent John Brown Williams, amounted to $45,000. The commanders of US naval vessels which visited during the 1850s insisted on his taking responsibility for the claims, which he was unable to pay.

A further problem for Cakobau was the encroachment of Tongan colonists under the direction of the Tongan chief Ma'afu. He was offered a possible escape from both threats in 1858 by the suggestion of the first British consul in Fiji, William Thomas Pritchard, that he cede the islands to Britain. Britain's rejection in 1862 left Cakobau in a worse situation than before, as by then settlers were beginning to buy land in Fiji to establish cotton and coconut plantations, compounding the potential for further difficulties with foreign governments.

In 1865 the British consul, Henry Michael Jones, advised the creation of a confederation of chiefs which could establish common practices for dealing with such matters as land sales, and generally co-ordinate affairs. Cakobau, whose prestige was greatest among the chiefs, was elected its first president. The confederation never functioned, and settlers with Cakobau's passive compliance instituted a constitutional government of Bau and its supposed dependencies and with Cakobau as its king. A ceremony of coronation was conducted in May 1867. The government was a failure and Cakobau's predicament was aggravated by the resurrection of the American debt. A way out was offered in 1868 by a consortium of Melbourne capitalists (the Polynesia Company) who would pay the debt in exchange for 200,000 acres of land together with comprehensive and exclusive rights of commerce and government. Cakobau agreed, signing away rights that he did not possess. The company paid off the American debts and introduced settlers, but the project otherwise failed. Further attempts at government followed in the next few years, in each case Cakobau being acknowledged as the supreme chief whose permission and supporting authority were necessary, but the initiative was entirely with the settlers. The situation was exacerbated by the 1870 'great Fiji rush' when accelerated immigration increased the white population to nearly 2000. A moderately successful government finally emerged in 1871. A new constitution reserved for the king extensive powers, which in practice were exercised by his European advisers.

When the government of Fiji opened negotiations for annexation by Britain in 1874, Cakobau was fully involved, but wavered between seeking annexation and resisting it. In the end he acknowledged its inevitability, admitting that it was impossible to deal with settler opposition and the other problems caused by the establishment of a plantation economy. The new colonial regime instituted in 1874 was the prototype for indirect rule and local administration was conducted through chief-officials. Cakobau stood apart from any such role, living in retirement on a pension. He was consulted by successive governors on matters to do with native Fijian affairs until his death in February 1883.

Those who knew Cakobau in his later years described him as wise, just and loyal, dignified and courteous. During his days as an ambitious chief he had been ruthless, cunning, and a consummate dissembler. A master of the arts of war and intrigue in pre-European times, he was very much out of his depth in dealing with the challenges posed by European settlement, and showed no aptitude for either politics or administration in the new order. In this he contrasts with his rival, the Tongan Heneli Ma'afu, and even with his counterpart, Tupou I of Tonga. He had been the pacemaker in the turbulent 1840s but after the end of the Rewa war in 1855 he was hostage to his own eminence, unable ever to take control of events but also unable to react effectively to the initiatives of others, whether Tongan, Fijian, or European.

After his baptism Cakobau married one of his former wives, Samanunu (who took the baptismal name Litia), on 11 February 1857. With his various wives before his conversion he had five children, none of them with Litia. While several of them were eminent under the colonial regime, none succeeded to his titles of vunivalu of Bau or king of Fiji. His descendants are considered Fiji's most chiefly or royal family. I. C. Campbell

Sources D. Scarr, 'Cakobau and Ma'afu: contenders for pre-eminence in Fiji', *Pacific islands portraits*, ed. J. W. Davidson and D. Scarr (1970) • R. A. Derrick, *A history of Fiji* (1950) • D. Routledge, *Matanitu: the struggle for power in Fiji* (1985) • J. D. Legge, *Britain in Fiji* (1958)

Servat, William (*d.* 1318/19), merchant, was a native of Cahors in southern France; he was the last, and perhaps the wealthiest, of the prominent merchants from that city to engage in English trade and finance. He chose London as the base from which to operate a business extending from Montpellier to Bergen and with some connection to Paris. He was probably one of a group of 'men of Bordeaux' at Southampton in 1272, and was occasionally described as a merchant of Gascony. From 1273 onwards he was often named as a merchant of London, of which he had become a citizen by 1281. To the Sienese he was 'a Provençal dwelling in London' (Bigwood, 1, no. 28).

The supply of Gascon wine to the north was one source of Servat's prosperity and, like other merchants from Cahors and its region, he also transmitted spices and silk obtained in Provence. In Britain the main axis of his trade was along the east coast, where he was a major exporter of wool to Flanders, above all through Boston, but also through Hull and London. With other Cahorsins he contracted to manage the wool crop of Pipewell Abbey, Northamptonshire, from 1288 onwards. Wool deals perhaps underlay his relations with leading clergymen and others, but he also provided purely financial services. His interests in shipping enabled him to organize an extensive distributive trade from London. In 1305, for example, he chartered a ship to take wine from London to Aberdeen, returning with coal from Newcastle to London or Southampton. North Sea trade drew him into diplomacy: he delivered the king's loan (supplied by his Riccardi bankers) to the king of Norway's agent at Yarmouth in 1286, and accompanied the bishop of Durham's missions to Norway in 1290 (when he provided the ship) and in 1294. He sold wine and sugar to Durham Priory. Perhaps associated with the coinage in 1281, he ran the bishop of Durham's mint in 1300–02. In London he was a dealer in bonds, and supplied spices to a pepperer and silk to a tailor; a dyer and a Cheapside vintner were heavily in his debt.

Servat was already lending to the king by 1283, and helped finance the defence of Gascony after the fall of the Riccardi in 1294. By 1302 he had a lucrative contract to supply the royal wardrobe with spices, linen, cloth, and furs, and in that year, with partners from Montpellier and Provence, met almost a quarter of the wardrobe's demand for spices. In 1302–3 Flemish pirates in the channel seized his twelve-year-old son and a cargo of spices destined for the wardrobe, both in the care of his servant returning from Provence, and then seized another of his cargoes that was bound for Scotland. In 1303/4 Servat supplied wax to the wardrobe and contracted to supply 300 tuns of wine. In 1309 he agreed to supply 300 quintals of wax annually for five years, for which in 1312 an equivalent value of cloth was substituted. In 1311–12 he helped organize money and soldiers in London for the Scottish campaign, and in 1313 again supplied wine to the king. These debts were to be repaid out of the customs receipts at Marmande, in Gascony, and at several English provincial ports. At dates between 1305 and 1315 he had joint charge of the London customs and other royal interests in the city.

These years marked the peak of Servat's career. In or shortly before 1302 he moved from Cordwainer ward to take over the former headquarters of the Riccardi in Bucklersbury, the heart of London's financial district. In 1305 he obtained licence to crenellate the house and to build a stone tower above its gateway, a notable symbol of success. Alderman for Walbrook from 1308 until his death, he represented the city in parliament in 1309 and 1313. The scale of Servat's dealings with the crown, however, did not match that of the leading Italians with whom he sometimes did business. Eventually he was eclipsed by Edward II's ambitious Genoese banker, Antonio Pessagno, who early in 1313 was rumoured to have purchased his tower; the deal was in fact completed by 1315. In the summer of that year, which perhaps marked Servat's effective retirement from business, the king's outstanding debts to him amounted to £2246. Almost half that sum had been contracted under Edward I, and in December 1318 a third of it was still due. William Servat died in London between 7 December 1318 and 18 January 1319.

Servat had conducted his business through a kaleidoscopic network of servants, attorneys, merchants retained on contract, and partners. Those who traded while lodging at his London houses may also have been commercial associates. His connections with some of these individuals lasted for three or four decades. He spent his last years back in Cordwainer ward, at a house in a neighbourhood favoured by pepperers and Gascon wine merchants. There his chaplain received his income from the customs, traded in spices on his behalf, and tried to defraud him. Neither his wife, identified as Alice or (Alison) in 1302 and for whom a diamond ring had been purchased in 1305, nor his son is recorded as having been still with him. Despite his civic office, Servat seems to have identified himself primarily as the London-based member of a loose group of Gascon and Provençal partners for which, as a citizen of London, he provided crucial services. Thus his fortune, if he left one, may have been repatriated to Gascony, where the Servat family (its relationship to William is not proven) was soon to be prominent in the Agenais. In London his one memorial was 'Servat's tower', still renowned 250 years after his death.

DEREK KEENE

Sources I. F. Arens, 'Wilhelm Servat von Cahors als Kaufmann zu London, 1273–1320', *Vierteljahrschrift für Sozial- und Wirtschaftsgeschichte*, 11 (1913), 477–514 • N. Denholm-Young, 'The merchants of Cahors', *Collected papers of N. Denholm-Young* (1969), 290–99 • T. H. Lloyd, *Alien merchants in England in the high middle ages* (1982), 94–7 • T. H. Lloyd, *The English wool trade in the middle ages* (1977), 296–7 • G. A. Williams, *Medieval London: from commune to capital* (1963), 142–3 • P. Nightingale, *A medieval mercantile community: the Grocers' Company and the politics and trade of London, 1000–1485* (1995), 91–2, 104–5, 118–22 • G. Bigwood, *Les livres des comptes des Gallerani*, ed. A. Grunzweig, 2 vols. (Brussels, 1961–2) • D. Keene, 'Summary report on the Walbrook study: appendix', typescript, U. Lond., Institute of Historical Research, no. 156/12 • R. W. Kaeuper, 'The Frescobaldi of Florence and the English crown', *Studies in Medieval and Renaissance History*, 10 (1973), 41–95 • R. W. Kaeuper, *Bankers to the crown: the Riccardi of Lucca and Edward I* (1973) • A. H. Thomas, ed., *Calendar of early mayor's court rolls preserved among the archives of the corporation of the City of London at the Guildhall, AD 1298–1307* (1924) • CLRO, Miscellaneous Roll CC, m. 26 • PRO, E 368/72, rot. ISd • PRO, JUST 1/226, m. 1

Archives PRO, letter concerning the Flemish pirates in 1303, SC 1/28/55A

Service, James (1823–1899), politician and businessman in Australia, was born on 27 November 1823 at Kilwinning, Ayrshire, the son of Robert Service (1794–1883), a sewing agent and lay preacher, and his wife, Agnes, *née* Niven. He was educated at Kilwinning and at Glasgow College and opened a school at Saltcoats, but had to abandon it when he contracted tuberculosis. In 1846 he joined the tea and coffee business of Thomas Corbett & Co. in Glasgow, and became a partner. About 1850 he married Marian Allan; they had two daughters, but the marriage broke down in the 1850s.

James Service (1823–1899), by Freeman and Co., pubd 1899

Service emigrated to Victoria, Australia, in 1853. His parents soon followed and his father, a staunch 'moral force' Chartist, became prominent in the Churches of Christ and the temperance movement. James Service founded an importing house specializing in Robur tea, was a founder of the Commercial Bank of Australia in 1866 and chairman of directors from 1871 to 1881, and became an active chairman of the Alfred Hospital's board (1871–86). Soon known as a 'red-hot' Chartist, he gained political experience as chairman of the Emerald Hill 'model municipality'. He was elected to the legislative assembly in 1857 and joined William Nicholson's ministry as president of the board of land and works (27 October 1859 – 3 September 1860); supporting the populist land convention, he carried a radical bill designed to wipe out the 'social evil' of land monopoly. The legislative council returned it with some 250 amendments and, when Nicholson caved in, Service resigned from the ministry. He brought about provision for state aid to the Jewish religion, helped to force through the Common Schools Act of 1862, and carried the (Sir Robert Richard) Torrens reform of land transfer.

After two years in Europe, Service returned in 1865 but was not re-elected until 1874, when he became treasurer (31 July 1874–7 August 1875) in G. B. Kerferd's ministry. His bold budget, which attempted to systematize the tariff and introduce direct taxation, led to the ministry's downfall. In 1877 the radical protectionist Graham Berry came to power. After 'black Wednesday'—8 January 1878—when judges and civil servants were dismissed, Service soon became leader of the opposition and brought Berry down, but his scheme for reforming relations between the two houses was unpopular and his five months' premiership (5 March–3 August 1880) was unproductive. He resigned his seat and again set out on a long excursion to Europe.

In the Victorian context, protectionists were usually called 'liberals' and free-traders 'conservatives'. Service was a free-trader who did not 'go conservative' and was prepared to compromise sensibly over the tariff: as he said of himself, in a speech in 1883, he was 'a liberal of the Gladstone stamp'. He had strong egalitarian sympathies and supported the rights of trade unions but stressed the mutual interests of the classes; he gave bonuses, pegged to the firm's profits, to his own employees.

On his return from Europe Service formed a coalition with Berry (8 March 1883–18 February 1886). It was a triumph. He reformed the civil service and the railways, and abolished patronage; the public service board and the railways commission were established in 1883. As treasurer, he did not allow the boom to get out of control. Alfred Deakin revered Service as a model premier conducting a cabinet in which nothing was muddled.

Service's main contribution was to encourage the Australian colonies onto the international stage and to originate a sustained campaign for federal union. He backed Queensland's attempt to annex New Guinea and used the French threat to annex the New Hebrides to force a federal 'convention' in November 1883. He won agreement to confederate and form a federal council, but New South Wales and South Australia refused to co-operate; the council was hamstrung from the start, though it continued to meet into the 1890s. Colonial Office officials saw Service as disloyal and ignorant, but modified their views after German annexation of north-eastern New Guinea and French occupation of the New Hebrides. Believing in the empire's civilizing mission and in Australia's destiny as a nation, however unwisely enthusiastic, Service was a harbinger of new imperial expansion and definition of Australian regional interests. His contribution to the federal movement has never been adequately recognized.

On urgent medical advice, Service resigned the premiership in February 1886 and went overseas again. While away, he was a vigorous Victorian delegate to the 1887 colonial conference. He rejected the offer of a privy counsellorship as he had earlier a knighthood. He joined the legislative council in 1888, but resisted all efforts to recall him to prominence. In 1889 he persuaded the Melbourne chamber of commerce to contribute £500 to the striking London dockers. At the Melbourne banquet to the intercolonial conference members in 1890 he made the famous reference to the tariff being 'the lion in the way' to federation, and was a leading conciliator during the major strikes of 1890–91. In his last years he devoted himself, chairman once again, to rescuing the Commercial Bank from its parlous condition.

Service was a lean, sprightly, tallish man, balding with a full grey beard. Courteous and sociable, he bore few grudges and did not resort to personalities. He had no trace of snobbishness. His honesty was patent and, while adept at compromise, he was no trimmer. He was not an orator, but, as Deakin wrote, his 'strength lay in the lucidity of his thought and the singularity of his language, his skill in marshalling masses of facts or figures' (*Review of Reviews*, Australasian edn, November 1892). He was highly cultivated and well read, reminding J. A. Froude of a philosopher or an Anglican bishop. He had been a sceptic since his youth but retained an interest in religious questions. Most extraordinary of all in Victorian Melbourne—having separated from his wife, about 1860 he took another 'wife', Louisa Hoseason Forty, lived down the gossip, and won wide affection as a public figure.

Service died in East St Kilda, Melbourne, on 12 April 1899 and was buried in Melbourne general cemetery on the 14th. He was survived by Louisa Forty and their daughters. GEOFFREY SERLE

Sources newspaper cuttings book, State Library of Victoria, Melbourne, La Trobe Library • Service newspaper cuttings book, Royal Historical Society of Victoria • *AusDB* • G. Serle, *The rush to be rich* (1971) • *The Times* (13 April 1899) • *The Argus* [Melbourne] (13 April 1899) • J. A. La Nauze, *Alfred Deakin: a biography*, 2 vols. (1965) • R. C. Thompson, 'James Service: father of Australian foreign policy?', *Historical Studies: Australia and New Zealand*, 16 (1974–5), 258–76 • G. Davison, *The rise and fall of marvellous Melbourne* (1978) • J. A. Froude, *Oceana, or, England and her colonies* (1886) • d. cert.

Likenesses G. F. Folingsby, oils, 1880–89, State Library of Victoria • Freeman & Co., photograph, pubd 1899, NPG [*see illus.*]

Wealth at death £284,000: probate, *CGPLA Eng. & Wales*

Service, John (1833–1884), Church of Scotland minister and writer, was born at Campsie, Stirlingshire, on 26 February 1833, son of John Service, print engraver, and his wife, Elizabeth, *née* Clachar. Robert Dalglish MP, the owner of the calico works at which Service's father worked, took an interest in the development of the promising youngster who moved on from Campsie parish school to Glasgow University, where he studied for the ministry. While there he was much influenced by the astronomer John Pringle Nichol. Service worked as editor of the *Dumbarton Herald* (1857), and from 1858 to 1862 he was sub-editor of Mackenzie's *Imperial Dictionary of Universal Biography*. On 29 April 1859 he married Jessie, daughter of James Bayne, a Glasgow music teacher, with whom he had seven children.

Licensed by the presbytery of Glasgow on 12 January 1861, Service was ordained as missionary in the parish of Hamilton, Lanarkshire, in 1862. After ten months his health broke down and he moved to Australia. He was on the point of returning to Scotland when he was persuaded instead to go to Tasmania, where he became minister of St John's Presbyterian Church, Hobart Town. He remained there from 1866 to 1869, before returning to Scotland in May 1870. He was briefly assistant to Charles Strong at Anderston, Glasgow, until he was presented to the parish of Inch, Wigtownshire, where he was admitted on 11 April 1872. Service drew on his Australian experiences in writing a novel, *Lady Hetty* (1875), which initially appeared in *Good Words* as *Novantia*. He attracted attention through a volume of sermons, *Salvation Here and Hereafter* (1877), which revealed him as a thoughtful churchman, unusually well attuned to changing popular beliefs. The attention thus aroused led to his translation to the charge of Hyndland, in the west end of Glasgow, to which he was admitted in December 1878. He had been recognized by Glasgow University in the previous year, with the degree of DD. In his time at Hyndland, Service confirmed his growing reputation: as his obituary stated 'Though he never attracted great crowds, there was not in all Scotland so fascinating a preacher for a cultured audience' (*Glasgow Herald*, 17 March 1884).

Service was not prominent in church courts or in any other public role but exerted influence through numerous articles in magazines and newspapers, particularly the *Glasgow Herald*. He was a contributor to the controversial edition of *Scotch Sermons* (1880), and wrote an essay on Robert Burns for T. H. Ward's *English Poets*. Service died at his home, 6 Spring Gardens, Kelvinside, Glasgow, on 15 March 1884. His wife survived him.

LIONEL ALEXANDER RITCHIE

Sources J. Service, *Sermons* (1884) • *Fasti Scot.* • *Glasgow Herald* (17 March 1884) • *Glasgow Herald* (18 March 1884) • *The Scotsman* (17 March 1884) • *The Bailie* (18 April 1883) • *DNB* • *CGPLA Eng. & Wales* (1884)

Likenesses caricature, repro. in *The Bailie* • photograph, repro. in Service, *Sermons*

Wealth at death £760 10s. 5d.: confirmation, 13 June 1884, *CCI*

Service, Robert William (1874–1958), writer, was born on 16 January 1874 at 4 Christian Road, Preston, Lancashire, the eldest in a family of seven boys and three girls of Robert Service (*d.* 1908), a Scottish bank clerk, and his wife, Sarah Emily, *née* Parker (*d.* 1939), daughter of an English wholesale merchant and grocer who also owned a cotton spinning mill. When Robert was four, his father moved the family back to Scotland, and from 1878 to 1883 Robert and a younger brother were brought up by grandparents and aunts in Kilwinning, an industrial Ayrshire town, while the rest of the family settled in Glasgow. At this early age Robert acquired the character of a self-conscious loner and a disposition to make rhyming verses. Reclaimed by his parents, Robert was drawn into the shabby gentility which his feckless father struggled to maintain. He attended the well-regarded Hillhead high school, but he left at fourteen, worked in the Commercial Bank of Scotland, and essentially educated himself, though he did attend a few classes in English language and literature at Glasgow University. Meanwhile he published verses in Glasgow journals.

In April 1896 Service emigrated across the Atlantic and proceeded to British Columbia, where he worked on a farm held by Scottish immigrants in the Cowichan valley, then on the scruffier holding of an old Welshman almost in the wilderness. Seized by wanderlust, he worked his way up and down the Pacific coast, as far as Mexico, becoming, as he said, 'half a hobo'. But the other half of him retained Scots canniness. Service, the loner by choice, with a passion for solitary rambling, was, in slums and bar rooms, an observer rather than participant. He did not gamble and for long periods, now and throughout his life, avoided alcohol. Personally diffident and sexually prudish, he had an ear for popular speech and strove to 'feel and know' life in its raw and dangerous aspects while he guarded a detachment which had isolated him even from his immediate family.

Robert William Service (1874–1958), by unknown photographer, 1935

A steady position, taken when he was twenty-nine, directly led to his extraordinary success as the 'Canadian Kipling' (a misnomer, since he had neither the technical virtuosity nor the complexity of attitude found in the work of the great English poet). The Canadian Bank of Commerce moved him through branches at Victoria and Kamloops in British Columbia to Whitehorse and Dawson in the Yukon, almost in the Canadian Arctic. From 1904 to 1912, as a bank clerk and then as a freelance writer, he watched the decline of the Klondyke gold rush which had reached its peak in 1898. Unexpectedly, he made his fortune with 'The Shooting of Dan McGrew'—verses which would be recited over and over again throughout the English-speaking world and would inspire a film and even a ballet—and 'The Cremation of Sam McGee', which ultimately, in 1976, featured on a Canadian postage stamp.

These and other verses were published in 1907 in Toronto as *Songs of a Sourdough* and in New York as *The Spell of the Yukon*. The collection, often reprinted, sold more than 3 million copies by the mid-1950s. A sequel, *Ballads of a Cheechako*, appeared in 1909. 'Sourdough' and 'cheechako' became household words for 'prospector' and 'newcomer'. Service had a simple, alliterative power of phrasing and his verse was above all memorable. It created a new version of pastoral and made the Yukon a legendary land. When he turned to fiction his prose style was effective, if undistinguished. His novel *The Trail of '98* (1910) was flimsy, but lovers of his verse were again gratified by his unassuming eloquence and his virility in *Rhymes of a Rolling Stone* (1912). Service left Canada that year to report the Balkan war for the *Toronto Star*.

In 1913 Service married Germaine Bourgoin, daughter of Constant Bourgoin, owner of a distillery near Paris. They had a daughter, Iris. For the rest of his life Service had homes in France but remained a British subject. During the war he served with an American volunteer ambulance unit, then with Canadian army intelligence. His experiences of the horrors of the western front yielded a very popular book, *Rhymes of a Red Cross Man* (1916). When the war was over, he resumed life in the Latin quarter (see *The Pretender*, a novel, 1914), adopted a monocle, travelled to Hollywood (1921–2), indulged in a trip to Tahiti, and returned to explore the Parisian slums.

Verse had made Service wealthy (though his lifestyle remained thrifty, sometimes miserly). He had variable success with more melodramatic romances, *The Poisoned Paradise* (1922), *The Roughneck* (1923), *The Master of the Microbe* (1926), and *The House of Fear* (1927). In these years his avowed programme for a good life took shape: to enjoy in health and leisure the large income he had gained until he was 100 years old (see *Why Not Grow Young? Keeping Fit at Fifty*, 1928). No reader would have recognized this quiet, handsome, rosy-hued little gentleman, with his soft Scottish accent, as the 'roughneck poet'. 'I was not my type', he said, though he turned back to low-life verse with *Ballads of a Bohemian* (1921) and *Bar-Room Ballads* (1940).

When another war began, shortly after Service's second trip to the Soviet Union (though temperamentally sympathetic to socialism he was not deceived), he and his family found refuge in Hollywood, where he appeared as his own younger self in a feature film about the gold rush, accosted by Marlene Dietrich as he is writing 'Dan McGrew' in a saloon: even in Tinseltown he was a major celebrity. In 1945 he went back to his homes in Brittany and Nice, then purchased a villa in Monte Carlo. He published two volumes of autobiography, *Ploughman of the Moon* (1945) and *Harper of Heaven* (1948), but his main aim became to publish a thousand poems. Eight more books of verse appeared between 1949 and 1958. Three volumes of collected verse, the last posthumous, ran to more than 2000 pages. Though he was widely and deeply read in poetry, Service never claimed to be more than a versifier rhyming for 'lowbrows'. Few literary critics have taken his work seriously, even in his Scottish homeland, though he recognizably stands in the tradition of the medieval 'makars', Robert Burns, and R. L. Stevenson. Bard and story-teller, he writes with demotic humour and pathos on behalf of the deviant and the underdog, with a passion against war and a scorn for rank and privilege. Granted that he was sentimental, his sentiment is generous and humane. Memorials in Scotland and Canada testify to the impact he made. Service died on 11 September 1958 at Dream Haven, his summer home in Lancieux, Brittany, where he was buried. He was survived by his wife.

C. F. Klinck, *rev.* Angus Calder

Sources J. Mackay, *Vagabond of verse* (1995)
Archives Mitchell L., Glas., poems, photograph albums, misc. corresp. • priv. coll., MSS
Likenesses photograph, 1935, repro. in Mackay, *Vagabond* [*see illus.*] • photographs, repro. in Mackay, *Vagabond*
Wealth at death £1962 12*s.* 5*d.*—in England: administration with will, 24 Nov 1959, *CGPLA Eng. & Wales*

Sesay, al-Hajj Shaikh Jibril [*known as* Shaikh Gibril Sesay] (**1903–1988**), political leader, was born in the village of Mabayla in Sanda Tenraren chiefdom, Bomboli district, Sierra Leone. His father, Abu Bakari Lomeh Sesay (*b. c.*1879), was a Muslim scholar and wealthy merchant whose export-import business was based in Port Loko, an important economic and political centre. His mother was Yenoh Sesay, who helped to support the family with a thriving cloth dyeing business. Abu Bakari exported cloth, palm kernels, and kola nuts to Dakar, Senegal, where he maintained a residence, and he imported Islamic gowns and horses to Sierra Leone. Shaikh Jibril's grandfather, Pa Kemeh Sesay, was a powerful military leader in Sanda Romocolong during the mid-nineteenth century, and his uncle, Bakar Sesay, was town chief (*alimami*) of Rokukuna and often carried out the duties of paramount chief. As a member of such a prominent and wealthy family, Shaikh Jibril was expected to excel in public affairs.

After studying for several years with local Muslim scholars, Shaikh Jibril went to Freetown, Sierra Leone, about 1921 for further education. He pursued education in English at the Bethel day school and the African Methodist Episcopal Seminary. He continued his Islamic studies at Madrasa Islamiya, a government-recognized Muslim school, and privately with *alfa* Uthman Deen, who specialized in theology. After mastering English and Arabic his father sent him for advanced Islamic studies in the Gambia and Senegal, where Abu Bakari had close ties with the family of Malik Sy, who was the head of the Tijaniyya Sufi order. Shaikh Jibril studied from 1933 to 1938 with various master teachers in Banjul (Bathurst) and founded Mukarimeen, a scholars' organization. Next he travelled to Dakar for theological studies. Also he was initiated into the Tijaniyya order by ʿAbd al-Aziz Sy, the son of Malik Sy.

Shaikh Jibril returned to Freetown in 1942 and in that year was married to Zakia Bomporah, a daughter of Santigi Shaka Koroma, the *alimami* of the Temne ethnic group in Freetown. With another prominent young Temne he founded Ambas Geda, an organization for Temne youth, but he withdrew because he claimed that it did not promote orthodox Islam. In 1943 he founded the al-Imaniya Literary and Cultural Society, which generated funds for the purchase of land upon which he erected a school, Madrasa Imaniya, to strengthen Islam among the Temne. Shaikh Jibril was making an impact on Temne affairs in Freetown, and he next followed a path that would make him a prominent Muslim leader in Sierra Leone.

From 1946 to 1952 Shaikh Jibril studied Islamic law, theology, and Arabic at al-Azhar University in Cairo and received advanced degrees in these subjects. While at university he made his first pilgrimage to Mecca in 1949. Upon his return to Freetown he reorganized al-Imaniya and actively promoted other Muslim associations: the Sierra Leone Muslim Reformation Society, the Sierra Leone Muslim Pilgrims' Association, the Muslim Brotherhood, and the Sierra Leone Muslim Congress, of which he was secretary-general from 1953 to 1964. He was also the headmaster of Madrasa Imaniya and assistant imam, and subsequently imam, of Jami al-Jalil, the central Temne mosque in Freetown. His activities and responsibilities were instrumental in guiding Islamic affairs for the next three decades.

In 1957 Shaikh Jibril's political importance was recognized by the British governor of Sierra Leone, who appointed him to the Freetown city council along with Siaka Stevens, another Sierra Leonean born in the interior. On 9 July 1960 Shaikh Jibril hosted Siaka Stevens and fifteen others in discussions on the formation of a new political party and in calling for a general election before independence was granted by the United Kingdom. The All Peoples' Congress was formed under the leadership of Siaka Stevens, and the party dominated Sierra Leone politics from 1967 until 1992. In 1970 Shaikh Jibril was appointed Sierra Leone's ambassador to Cairo, and he resigned as imam. He remained in Cairo until 1976, and represented Sierra Leone's interests there and in Saudi Arabia. His close ties with al-Azhar University and with the Egyptian Cultural Centre in Freetown afforded him opportunities to enhance Islamic education and missionary work in Sierra Leone. He convinced the Egyptian government to fund several Arab teachers in Sierra Leone schools, and he worked with the al-Azhar missionaries who came to strengthen orthodox Islam.

After his return to Freetown in 1976, Shaikh Jibril's contacts with Egypt and Saudi Arabia provided him with the means to expand his educational and missionary work. He became chairman of the board of imams for the Sierra Leone Muslim Congress and an adviser to the Supreme Islamic Council. He continued to be active in national political issues as a member of the central committee of the All Peoples' Congress and in Temne political affairs, where his influence was formidable. He was appointed a justice of the peace and honoured with membership in the order of the Rokel, reserved for the most highly regarded Sierra Leoneans.

In his later years Shaikh Jibril travelled to Islamic conferences and raised funds to send more than 500 Sierra Leoneans to study in Cairo. In order to promote Sunni Islam in Sierra Leone he arranged for annual three-month courses for imams from all over the country. In recognition of his prominent role as a missionary he was appointed assistant secretary of the Muslim World League for the west African region. In 1985 he became chief Islamic judge (mufti) for Temne Muslims. In 1987 he was a founder and *ex officio* member of the national executive committee of the Federation of Sierra Leone Muslim Organisations, a government project to co-ordinate Muslim educational and missionary activities.

On 22 April 1988 Shaikh Jibril was elected to the position of national mufti under the auspices of the ministry of social welfare and rural development, which regulated national religious affairs. The choice was made by an electorate composed of 10 imams and 104 representatives of Islamic organizations. Shaikh Jibril was unable to take up the responsibilities of mufti, as shortly after the election he fell ill and was hospitalized. He died on 2 September 1988 at 11 Haruna Street, Freetown, survived by his four wives, twelve children, twenty-two grandchildren, and seven great-grandchildren. He was honoured by a public ceremony at the Freetown City Hall on 4 September. After services the same day at Jami al-Jalil he was buried at the Kissy Road cemetery. The funeral was attended by the president of Sierra Leone, the two vice-presidents, the city council chairman, many other government and civic leaders, diplomats, and hundreds of Muslim and Christian dignitaries. He was acclaimed as the most notable Muslim leader in Sierra Leone during the second half of the twentieth century. DAVID E. SKINNER

Sources D. E. Skinner, interview with al-Hajj Shaikh Jibril Sesay, Freetown, Sierra Leone, 12 April 1969 · D. E. Skinner, interview with al-Hajj Shaikh Jibril Sesay, 28 Aug 1985 · D. E. Skinner, interview with al-Hajj Shaikh Jibril Sesay, 31 May 1987 · D. E. Skinner, programme for funeral proceedings for al-Hajj Shaikh Jibril Sesay, 4 Sept 1988 · B. E. Harrell-Bond and others, *Community leadership and the transformation of Freetown, 1801–1976* (1978) · private information (2004)

Likenesses Skinner, photographs, 1969–87, priv. coll. · portraits, priv. coll.

Wealth at death well off; several properties

Setchel, Sarah (1813–1894), watercolour painter, was born in London, and baptized on 4 June 1813 at St Paul's, Covent Garden, the younger of the two daughters of John Frederick Setchel (*d.* 1846), bookseller in King Street, Covent Garden, and his wife, Mary. Her father collected art books, and wanted his daughters to become artists, but Sarah Setchel did not show any interest in drawing until after she left school, when she began copying in the British Museum and the National Gallery; she also took lessons in miniature painting on ivory from Louisa Sharpe. She exhibited six portraits at the Royal Academy between 1832 and 1845, and also exhibited fifteen pictures at the Society of British Artists in Suffolk Street until 1840. At first her subjects were usually children, but from 1834 she also included literary subjects, scenes from Shakespeare and Scott. Scenes of humble life and cottagers in particular appealed to her.

In 1841 Sarah Setchel was elected a member of the New Society of Painters in Water Colours, and in 1842 exhibited what came to be known as *The Momentous Question*, which established her reputation and led to many commissions. The subject matter was taken from George Crabbe's *Tales of the Hall* (1819), and when it was first exhibited the painting appeared with a long quotation from Crabbe. Depicting a prison interior, with a girl visiting a young man under threat of death, it became very popular as an engraving by Samuel Bellin. Her next exhibit was a miniature of her father (exh. New Society of Painters in Water Colours, 1845); it was much admired by the art critic of *The Athenaeum*, who said that it placed her 'at the head of all lady miniature painters' (*The Athenaeum*, 26 April 1845).

However, Sarah Setchel's eyesight was deteriorating, and she began to paint and exhibit less. After the death of her father in 1846 she gave lessons in watercolour painting to Mary Ann Criddle, who also suffered from poor eyesight and had given up painting in oils. She exhibited a few times at the New Society of Painters in Water Colours between 1848 and 1856, and two of her literary paintings were engraved: *And Ye shall Walk in Silk Attire* (exh. 1848), and *The Heart's Resolve* (exh. 1850), from Crabbe's tale of *Jessie and Colin* (engraved by Bellin). In 1860 Sarah Setchel went to Switzerland, where she consulted a German eye specialist in Graeforth, but her eyes continued to get worse. She moved to Sudbury, near Harrow, Middlesex, to live with her sister, and only exhibited two more paintings, in the 1866–8 winter exhibitions of the New Society of Painters in Water Colours; she resigned from the society in 1886. Sarah Setchel died unmarried on 9 January 1894 at 3 Lyon Villas, Sudbury. Two of her watercolours, one of which is *The Momentous Question*, are held in the Victoria and Albert Museum. ANNE PIMLOTT BAKER

Sources C. Yeldham, *Women artists in nineteenth-century France and England*, 1 (1984), 276–8; 2 (1984), 85 · E. C. Clayton, *English female artists*, 2 (1876), 124–9 · L. Lambourne and J. Hamilton, eds., *British watercolours in the Victoria and Albert Museum* (1980) · *DNB* · Mallalieu, *Watercolour artists* · Wood, *Vic. painters*, 3rd edn · census returns, 1881 · *IGI* · d. cert. · Graves, *RA exhibitors*

Wealth at death £69 9s. 9d.: administration, 5 March 1894, *CGPLA Eng. & Wales*

Seton family (*per.* c.1300–c.1510), nobility, had its territorial base in Lothian, where Seton and Winton, east of Edinburgh, were united with Winchburgh, on the west of the town, by William the Lion to make one knight's fee for Philip of Seton. The position of the family was later enhanced through service to Robert I, although this was hardly unwavering, as **Sir Alexander Seton** (*d.* c.1348), who made a bond in 1308 with two other Bruce adherents to defend Robert I and the realm of Scotland, was nevertheless in English service from 1309 until 1314. Personal considerations, probably concerning the security of his Lothian lands, may have led to this inconsistency, but his defection to the Scottish side on the eve of Bannockburn, reputedly bringing crucial intelligence of the poor morale in the English camp, led to Seton's rapid rehabilitation. He became one of a small group of trusted counsellors at the heart of royal service, attending the king regularly and holding the position of steward of Robert I's household in 1317, and steward to the king's infant son David from August 1328.

Seton was employed as an envoy in truce negotiations between 1317 and 1320, and his name appears on the declaration of Arbroath. He held Tranent, Myles, Elphinstone, and Falside in Haddingtonshire, in addition to land at Barns and the nearby east mill beside Haddington, these last being given by King Robert for services in Ireland as well as Scotland. As a further mark of favour, his lands of Seton were erected into a free barony, with the town of Seton achieving burghal status. By January 1328 he was governor of the town of Berwick, then a place of considerable military activity. His sons Alexander and William were killed fighting for David II in 1332–3, while during the siege of Berwick by Edward III in 1333, a third son, Thomas, was reputedly hanged on Edward's orders in sight of the town's garrison. After the battle of Halidon Hill in the same year, Seton accepted the need to maintain his position by working with the English victors, and attended Edward Balliol's parliament in 1334, but he was willing to swear allegiance to David II as soon as the Scottish side proved triumphant. Seton died c.1348, having been predeceased by all his sons.

Margaret Seton (*fl.* 1347) was her grandfather's heir. The chronicler Andrew Wyntoun relates the story of Margaret Seton's forcible abduction in 1347 by Alan Wyntoun (an ancestor of his), who may have been her distant relative as the Setons held the lands of Winton; and Bower embellishes the story with the consequent complaint brought before the king's court by her relatives, in settlement of which David II offered Margaret the choice of marrying Wyntoun or having him executed. Although Margaret chose marriage, her husband took the cross not long afterwards, according to Andrew Wyntoun in response to the continuing hostility of the Seton family, and died in the Holy Land. Their son, William, bore the name of Seton, being recorded as such on a charter of c.1367. According to Bower, he also went on crusade, but had returned to Scotland by 14 September 1402, when he fought at the battle of Homildon Hill, following which he was captured and imprisoned. He married Janet Fleming, elder daughter of Sir David Fleming of Biggar, with whom he had John, Alexander, and Janet. In 1408 his second son, Alexander *Seton [*see under* Seton, Alexander, first earl of Huntly (*d.* 1470)], married Elizabeth, the daughter and heir of Adam, lord of Gordon, from whom the earls of Huntly were descended [*see* Gordon family].

John Seton had succeeded his father by 1407, serving in that year as a hostage for the return from English captivity of Archibald, fourth earl of Douglas. On 24 March 1411 he received a charter from Robert Stewart, duke of Albany, the governor of Scotland, confirming him in the baronies of Seton and Tranent, and the lands of Winchburgh. He was appointed a commissioner to treat for the release of James I, and served briefly as a hostage for the king in 1424, his estates being valued at 600 marks, although he was released from his obligation in March 1424 as one of the men exchanged for other hostages. His subsequent service in the king's council underlines the reliance placed by James I at this time on support from prominent members of the Douglas affinity. Seton was dead by 1434. His son William had been killed at the battle of Verneuil in 1424, and so he was succeeded by his grandson.

George Seton, first Lord Seton (*d.* 1478), was a minor when he inherited, his lands and possessions, including a colliery at Tranent, being held in ward to the crown. He attained his majority by November 1437, and embarked on a career of court service which may have owed much to his family's Douglas connections during the minority of James II, possibly leading to his becoming a lord of parliament as early as 1445, although the style George, Lord Seton, indicating royal sanction, appears in official records only by 1451. In 1448 he travelled to France with the chancellor Lord Crichton, on an embassy to Flanders, France, and Burgundy to seek a foreign marriage for James II, and he returned to Flanders in 1449 or 1450 with Thomas Spens and other ambassadors, as part of a diplomatic mission connected with the downfall of the Livingston family. Notwithstanding the Setons' Douglas connections, political pragmatism seems to have determined George Seton's loyalty to the king, and he sat in parliament as Lord Seton on 14 June 1452, when James II sought to explain the murder of the eighth earl of Douglas to the three estates. He attended the king's council held at Dunfermline on 11 July 1458, and sat on the assize which condemned Robert, first Lord Boyd, and his son Thomas, earl of Arran, on 22 November 1469. He served as an ambassador to England in 1472–3. He died in 1478, and was buried at the church of the Black Friars in Edinburgh. He had married Margaret Stewart, daughter of John, earl of Buchan. They had a son, John, who died in 1476, having married Christian, daughter of John *Lindsay, Lord Lindsay of the Byres [*see under* Lindsay family of the Byres], with whom he had a son.

George Seton, second Lord Seton (*d.* 1507/8), succeeded his grandfather. He had studied at the universities of St Andrews and Paris, and undertook diplomatic duties in 1497 and 1499. In addition to his political and administrative activities, there is evidence that he engaged in trade, the Edinburgh customs returns for 1486–7 showing that he exported salt. In response to a plea for assistance from King Hans of Denmark, James IV attempted a naval expedition in 1502, for which Seton offered his ship, the *Eagle*. The royal treasury paid him an advance of £400 to have the ship ready for sea by 8 May 1502, but work on it was still going on at Inverkeithing when the king came to check on progress on 27 May. On 9 September the lords of council censured Seton for defaulting on his commitment, and he was ordered to repay the king's outlay on the ship, amounting to £1853 13*s.* 10*d.*, and to forfeit the *Eagle*. A final settlement, agreed on 17 September, allowed for the restoration of the ship to Seton in return for payment of £952. Sir Richard Maitland of Lethington, in his history of the Seton family, describes the second lord as well educated and an accomplished musician, and draws a flamboyant character sketch of him. He certainly employed a minstrel, whom he sent to entertain the king in 1502 during strained relations over the preparation of the *Eagle*, but Maitland none the less censures Seton for having been overly given to the pursuit of pleasure and bad company. He died between June 1507 and April 1508, and was buried in Seton church, originally parochial, but erected into a college by papal sanction granted on 22 December 1492 in response to Lord Seton's petition. By 23 April 1475 Seton had married Marion, daughter of Colin *Campbell, first earl of Argyll, and they had a son, George, subsequently third Lord Seton. C. A. McGladdery

Sources *Scots peerage*, 8.559–80 · G. W. S. Barrow, *Robert Bruce and the community of the realm of Scotland*, 3rd edn (1988) · N. Macdougall, *James IV* (1989) · *CDS*, vol. 4 · A. Grant, 'The development of the Scottish peerage', *SHR*, 57 (1978), 1–27 · GEC, *Peerage*, 11.633–4 · G. W. S. Barrow and others, eds., *Regesta regum Scottorum*, 5, ed. A. A. M. Duncan (1988) · R. Maitland of Lethington, *The history of the house of Seytoun to the year MDLIX*, ed. J. Fullarton, Maitland Club, 1 (1829)

Seton, Sir Alexander (*d. c.*1348). *See under* Seton family (*per. c.*1300–*c.*1510).

Seton, Sir Alexander (*d.* 1440/41). *See under* Seton, Alexander, first earl of Huntly (*d.* 1470).

Seton [*later* Gordon], **Alexander, first earl of Huntly** (*d.* 1470), magnate, was the eldest son of **Sir Alexander Seton** (*d.* 1440/41), son of William Seton and Janet Fleming. His mother was Elizabeth Gordon (*d.* 1439), daughter and heir of Sir Adam *Gordon, lord of Gordon, who died at Homildon Hill on 14 September 1402. When Alexander senior married Elizabeth Gordon in 1408, she brought with her the Berwickshire baronies of Gordon and Fogo, but also the lordship of Strathbogie in the heart of the north-east, largely neglected by the Gordons throughout the fourteenth century. Alexander had an elder brother, John Seton, who was already reasonably prominent in the borders, and so he seems to have taken the decision to develop his own sphere of influence, moving his base to the northern estates. Over the next two decades he gradually built up a network of support and alliances which included Alexander Stewart, earl of Mar (*d.* 1435), the most powerful magnate in the region, and also members of prominent local families, such as the Forbeses, Ogilvys, and Irvines of Drum.

More importantly, however, Seton also became involved in the negotiations to release James I from his long period of captivity in England. Knighted by 1419, he visited James while the king was with Henry V in France in 1422 and took part in talks held in England in 1423 and 1424. This not only brought him royal favour, it also brought him into contact with leading figures at court, among them William Crichton, who was to become chancellor of Scotland during the minority of James II. Seton never became a major political figure, but he remained on the fringes of the political scene both at the centre and in the north-east, a position that his eldest son was able to build on. In or about 1440 he left Scotland on pilgrimage, possibly carrying the heart of James I. He died on his journey between 31 August 1440 and 3 April 1441, probably in Rhodes, from where James's heart was returned to Scotland in 1444.

The early successes of Seton's son were based on the relationship Seton had developed with William Crichton, chancellor from 1439. In 1438 the younger Alexander divorced his first wife, Egidia Hay (*d.* 1441), in order to marry Crichton's elder daughter, Elizabeth (*d.* 1479), disinheriting his own eldest son in the process. Even at this early stage the younger Seton's territorial ambitions were evident, since he forced Egidia to resign into his hands the liferent of her family estates. So desirable was the union with Elizabeth Crichton that Seton was prepared to obtain his divorce from Egidia fraudulently, denying that he had received a papal dispensation for the marriage in 1426 and concealing the offending document 'with malicious intent in his own house' (Seton, 277). This deception came to light only in 1441, after the death of Egidia Hay, when Seton asked for, and was given, absolution for his transgressions. With the benefit of Crichton's support Seton set about establishing the family in the north-east, the two men working together to frustrate the claims of Robert, Lord Erskine (*d.* 1452), to the vacant earldom of Mar, effectively allowing Seton to step into the vacuum created.

Seton was knighted in 1439 or 1440 and most probably promoted to earl of Huntly in June 1445, as part of the settlement between the warring Crichton and Douglas-Livingston factions. In 1446, however, he and his supporters were heavily defeated in battle at Arbroath, when the new earl travelled south to aid his Ogilvy allies in their struggle with the Lindsays over the office of justiciar of Arbroath Abbey. As a result he was forced to retire to Strathbogie and concentrate on consolidating his regional position. His re-emergence onto the political stage came with James II's personal entry into politics in 1449. The young king chose to use Huntly as his principal northern ally during the struggles with the earls of Douglas, Crawford, and Ross that dominated the 1450s. Huntly was granted the lordship of Badenoch and castle of Ruthven in 1451, but proved unable to stand against the MacDonalds at this stage; Ruthven was destroyed by Ross's men. In 1452 Huntly achieved greater success when he marched south to confront the earl of Crawford, defeating him at Brechin despite the loss of two of his own brothers. The victory was fundamental in securing James II's position, and the contemporary Auchinleck chronicle suggests that at the time Huntly was operating in an official capacity as royal lieutenant. The chronicle states that 'thair was with the erll of huntlie fer ma [men] than was with the erll of craufurd becaus he displayit the kingis banere and said it was the kingis actioun and he was his luftennend' (McGladdery, 173). For Huntly, however, the opportunity to avenge his defeat at the hands of the Lindsays in 1446 and further establish his regional dominance was possibly just as important as any desire to secure royal authority.

Huntly's opportunism was again highlighted by his swift reaction to the final defeat of the Douglas faction at Arkinholm in 1455. Within seventeen days he had arranged the marriage of his teenage son and heir, George, to the widow of Archibald Douglas, earl of Moray (who fell in the battle), in an attempt to add that earldom to the family estates. On this occasion, though, James II reacted equally swiftly, proceeding to forfeit the earldom rather than allow the Setons to gain total dominance in the north-east. Huntly had some consolation when George was allowed to marry the king's sister Annabella after his divorce from the unfortunate countess of Moray.

In or about 1457 Huntly changed the family name to Gordon to try to secure the succession of George, his eldest son by his second marriage. In 1460 he was present at the siege of Roxburgh when James II was killed by the bursting of one of his own cannon. He has been described as a councillor in the early minority government of James III, but if this is true he seems to have taken little interest in his duties, preferring to remain in the north-east. After 1465 he apparently played a much more limited role in the family's concerns, allowing his son George to direct affairs. He and his first wife, Egidia Hay, the daughter of Sir John Hay of Tullibody, whom he married in 1427, had a son, Sir Alexander Seton, ancestor of the Setons of Touch, Stirlingshire. His second marriage, to Elizabeth Crichton, produced four sons and at least four daughters: George *Gordon, the eldest, succeeded him as the second earl of Huntly, and the second son, Sir Alexander Gordon of Midmar, was the ancestor of the Gordons of Midmar. Alexander Gordon, first earl of Huntly, died on 15 July 1470 at Huntly Castle and was buried in the cathedral church of Elgin. By the time of his death he had effectively established the Setons of Gordon as the most powerful family in the north of Scotland. SIMON C. APPLEYARD

Sources Gordon Castle muniments, NA Scot., GD44 • J. M. Thomson and others, eds., *Registrum magni sigilli regum Scotorum / The register of the great seal of Scotland*, 11 vols. (1882–1914), vol. 2 • *APS*, 1424–1567 • C. McGladdery, 'Auckinleck Chronicle', *James II* (1990), 160–73 • J. Robertson and G. Grub, eds., *Collections for a history of the shires of Aberdeen and Banff*, 5 vols., Spalding Club, 9, 17, 29, 32, 37 (1843–69) • B. Seton, 'The distaff side: a study in matrimonial adventure in the fifteenth and sixteenth centuries', *SHR*, 17 (1919–20), 272–82 • T. Innes, 'The Gordon peerage', *Juridical Review*, 42 (1930), 323–52; 43 (1931), 58–95 • J. Ferrerius, 'Historiae compendium de origine et incremento Gordoniae familiae', *The house of Gordon*, ed. J. M. Bulloch, 2, Third Spalding Club, 33 (1907) • J. Lesley, *The history of Scotland*, ed. T. Thomson, Bannatyne Club, 38 (1830)
Archives NA Scot., Gordon Castle muniments, GD 44 | NA Scot., Aboyne muniments, GD 181

Seton, Alexander (*d.* 1542), Dominican friar and evangelical reformer, was unusual among Scottish Dominicans in having noble parentage, being the son of Sir Alexander Seton of Touch and Tullibody and Elizabeth Erskine, daughter of Thomas, earl of Mar. He was not so unusual in his education, being recorded in the university rolls of St Andrews as becoming bachelor and licentiate in 1516 and 1518 respectively. He may also be identified with the 'Alexander de Scotia', who was given permission to study in Paris by the Dominican chapter-general in 1525. From 1530 to 1533 he was mainly in residence at St Andrews, acting as the prior of the Dominican convent there. Books survive which were in his use in the convent, some with his subscription. His next recorded appearance was in 1536, when he gave a series of Lenten sermons in St Andrews. In these he argued that it was not possible for man to satisfy for his sins and that redemption lay in faith alone. His teaching has been likened to that of John Macalpine (Maccabeus) with whom he was familiar. Once the series of sermons was over and Seton had left the town, another preacher denounced his teachings and his omissions, since he had not mentioned purgatory, pardons, pilgrimages, or prayers to saints, all of which were presumably counted by Seton as futile 'works'. The latter speedily returned, rang the church bell, and preached a sermon in his own defence.

Even at this point there is no suggestion that Seton felt his beliefs were in sufficient conflict with the church for him to need to leave his order. Indeed, he signed, with his name, order, and house, a copy of the works of Origen in 1536, and so was presumably in the convent in St Andrews at that time. In his sermon in reply, however, he attacked the bishops of Scotland, especially for failing to preach, which he argued was essential to their office. This was a point to be raised in the provincial councils of the Scottish church in the years after Seton's death, but it was not an issue to which Archbishop James Beaton warmed. Calderwood's claims of Seton's popularity with the people may have a tint of exaggeration, but it does seem fairly certain that he was liked by the king and had an accustomed place as royal confessor at court. This post was more normally held by a Franciscan, however, and so it is not surprising that the archbishop stirred up the traditional rivalries between the orders, thereby making life so uncomfortable for Seton that he left Scotland. From Berwick he wrote a letter to James V which is a curious mixture of self-defence, bitter recrimination, and accusations that his enemies were blinding the king's judgement.

Once in England, Seton became a trouble to the Henrician church authorities. By July 1539, when he was presented to the rectory of Fulbeck, Lincolnshire, he enjoyed the patronage of Charles Brandon, duke of Suffolk, who obtained denization for him and whose chaplain he became. In November 1539 he was reported to have preached in London that 'faith only did justify and that works were not helping nor profitable to any man but only to declare and testify our faith' (*LP Henry VIII*, Addenda, 1/2 no. 1463 (18)). At this moment he may have been hoping for Thomas Cromwell's support, but on 20 April following Cromwell dissociated himself from Seton, who nevertheless continued to receive support from Suffolk, or perhaps from the duke's evangelically minded wife, for in September 1542 he was presented to a second rectory in Lincolnshire. A sermon he delivered in St Antholin's, London, on 13 November 1541 led to his becoming embroiled in a dispute concerning free will and justification, although the charge that he had preached without episcopal licence may have seemed to the authorities just as serious an issue. His recantation on 18 December cannot have been brought about simply by the illness which caused his death late in 1542, in Suffolk's London house, for it seems that Seton had always had a strong regard for self-preservation. Despite his refusal to stand trial in Scotland and his recantation at Paul's Cross, he was remembered and revered by the reformers as a good preacher, and an account of his travails in 1541 was included by Foxe in the *Acts and Monuments*.

JANET P. FOGGIE

Sources *The works of John Knox*, ed. D. Laing, 6 vols., Woodrow Society (1985) • D. Calderwood, *The history of the Kirk of Scotland*, ed. T. Thomson and D. Laing, 8 vols., Wodrow Society, 7 (1842–9) • D. McRoberts, ed., *Essays on the Scottish Reformation, 1513–1625* (1962) • J. P. Foggie, 'The Dominicans in Scotland: 1450–1560', PhD diss., U. Edin., 1997 • J. Durkan and A. Ross, *Early Scottish libraries* (1977) • J. M. Anderson, ed., *Early records of the University of St Andrews*, Scottish History Society, 3rd ser., 8 (1926) • *The acts and monuments of John Foxe*, ed. S. R. Cattley, 8 vols. (1837–41), vol. 5, pp. 449–51 • S. Brigden, *London and the Reformation* (1989) • S. J. Gunn, *Charles Brandon, duke of Suffolk, c.1484–1545* (1988)

Seton, Alexander, first earl of Dunfermline (1556–1622), lord chancellor of Scotland, was the fourth son of George *Seton, fifth Lord Seton (*c.*1530–1586), and Isabel Hamilton (1529–1604), daughter of Sir William Hamilton of Sanquhar.

Early years Seton's fervently Catholic father destined him, as a younger son, for the church. Mary, queen of Scots, his godmother, gave him the temporalities of the priory of Pluscarden as a godchild's gift; he received the title of prior when aged nine. In 1571, when he was about fifteen, he became a student at the Jesuit-run German College in Rome, where he acquired an excellent classical education and an enthusiasm for books. According to his kinsman Alexander Seton, Viscount Kingston (*d.* 1691), he was 'a great humanist in prose and poesie, Greek and Latine; well versed in the mathematics and great skill in architecture and herauldrie' (Maitland, 63). How long he stayed in Italy is not clear, but there is no evidence that he took holy orders. From Italy he went to France, where he studied law. During his absence he was deprived of Pluscarden for failure to conform to the established protestant church.

Alexander Seton, first earl of Dunfermline (1556–1622), by Marcus Gheeraerts the younger, 1610

By late 1580 Seton was back in Scotland, where the political climate had improved for him with the overthrow of the regime of the regent, James Douglas, fourth earl of Morton. In 1581 he recovered Pluscarden. He narrowly avoided serious trouble in 1583 when a Jesuit, William Holt, who had been staying at the family house at Seton, was seized as he was about to depart for France. Holt was carrying a letter from Seton to his old schoolmaster in Rome expressing the hope that the true faith might be restored. Seton underwent an interrogation, but avoided real unpleasantness when the ultra-protestant regime of the Ruthven raiders lost its grip on power in June 1583.

When James VI began his personal rule in November 1585 with the overthrow of the regime of James Stewart, fourth earl of Arran, Seton was well positioned for a political career. He had acquired legal expertise, he had supported the coalition that overthrew Arran, and he and his family had been loyal supporters of Queen Mary and had suffered for it. James always set great store by men who, like Seton, had been loyal to his mother and then transferred that loyalty to himself. So in December 1585 Seton became a privy councillor, and on 27 January 1586 an extraordinary lord of session. He served on the committee of the articles in the parliament of 1587, which enacted the legislative programme drawn up by the king and his principal adviser, Sir John Maitland, later first Lord Thirlestane, and was rewarded when the lands of Pluscarden were exempted from the Act of Annexation of Kirk Lands to the Crown which this parliament enacted. These lands, and those of Urquhart, were combined in a barony which he received in that year.

Religious problems In February 1588 Seton had to make a personal decision of great importance. The king named him an ordinary lord of session; his colleagues were suspicious about his religious views and insisted that he commit himself to the established church by taking communion and subscribing its confession of faith. He did so, and for the rest of his life conformed outwardly to the official church; he was what the English called a church papist. This was perfectly satisfactory to the king, who, like Queen Elizabeth, was not interested in making windows into men's souls. As long as Seton conformed outwardly, James was not concerned about his private beliefs. To two Scottish Jesuits who visited him clandestinely in 1605 Seton professed his loyalty to the ancient faith, but explained that the time for an attempt to restore it had not yet come. 'He is now all-powerful in Scotland, but he will attempt nothing until he sees a solid foundation of hope', they concluded. 'Meanwhile he takes his portion in this life, though at the risk of that which is eternal' (Forbes-Leith, 187).

Seton's career continued to flourish despite the suspicions of the dominant presbyterian wing of the kirk, which were not allayed by his marriage in 1592, at the age of thirty-six, to Lilias Drummond (*d.* 1601), the teenaged daughter of the third Lord Drummond, an unpolitical and conformist family. In 1593 Seton became president of the court of session and chairman of a committee to manage the property of Queen Anne, James's equally young wife, whose favourite lady-in-waiting, Jean Drummond, was Lilias's sister. Anne became his patron, and in 1596, in her capacity as lady of Dunfermline, conferred on him the office of hereditary bailie and justiciar of the regality of Dunfermline, which was worth about £20,000 Scots a year. Seton's committee was so successful in managing the queen's finances that in January 1596 James made it the nucleus of an eight-man group to manage the royal finances, which were in a chaotic state. The membership of this committee, dubbed the Octavians, was alarming to the kirk: they were, in the words of a contemporary, 'all almost either Papists known or inclining to Popery or malignancy' (Row, 163). Seton deepened the kirk's suspicions by speaking in favour of the return from exile of the Catholic George Gordon, sixth earl of Huntly. The result was a religious riot in Edinburgh in December 1596, directed principally at Seton, 'that Romanist president, a shaveling and a priest' (Calderwood, 5.548). The riot failed to intimidate James, but he concluded that the Octavians, particularly Seton, were more of a political liability than a fiscal asset. He in effect abolished the committee by transferring its power to its most impeccably protestant member, Lord Treasurer Blantyre.

Political doldrums Seton did not lose the king's favour despite this set-back. On 4 March 1598 James made him a lord of parliament as Lord Fyvie, and in the same year forced his election as provost of Edinburgh, an office he held for ten years. Seton looked after the capital's interests so well that he became genuinely popular with its merchant élite. Among other things he publicly opposed a tax the king wanted to be levied in 1600 in order to raise an army to make good by force his claim to the English throne. Seton also mended his fences with the kirk by resisting the king's demand that the court of session reverse its decision upholding the claim of the Edinburgh minister Robert Bruce, whom the king disliked, to a pension out of the revenues of the abbey of Arbroath. If James overrode the court, said Seton, he and all the other judges would resign; James backed down.

On 8 May 1601 Seton's young wife died, and on 27 October that year he married his step-niece Grizel Leslie, daughter of the master of Rothes, now married to Lilias's sister Catherine. The Leslies were an impeccably protestant family. Seton's remarriage made it possible for him to be appointed guardian to the future Charles I, who was born at Dunfermline on 19 November 1600; he held this position until the summer of 1604. When Grizel died on 6 September 1606 Seton married into another protestant family. His new wife, whom he married aged fifty-one on 30 November 1607, was Margaret Hay (1592–1659), aged fifteen, daughter of the seventh Lord Yester, whose son and heir was to marry one of Seton's daughters from his second marriage. Seton's fence-mending succeeded. The kirk became less suspicious, as did George Nicolson, the English agent in Edinburgh, who in 1599 described Seton as an 'honest councillor' (*CSP Scot.*, *1597–1603*, 542).

The union of the crowns in 1603 gave Seton another chance at the real political power he wanted. He was the most highly placed man of law in the Scottish government; so in 1604 James made him the chief Scottish negotiator for the proposed Anglo-Scottish union. Seton suppressed his doubts about the union's desirability, conducted the negotiations with great skill, and made a valuable friend of the chief English commissioner, Sir Robert Cecil, the future earl of Salisbury. The union did not materialize, but Seton received his reward. On 13 December 1604 he became lord chancellor, an office he had coveted for a decade, and on 4 March 1605 earl of Dunfermline. He was now the highest-ranking official in the king's government, but real power eluded him owing to his mishandling of an act of defiance of the king on the part of a group of ministers in 1605.

The principal item now on James's domestic agenda was the restoration of episcopal authority in the church. Dunfermline had reservations because of his fear of the political ambitions of James's principal ecclesiastical adviser, Archbishop John Spottiswoode, who, he knew, distrusted him as a dangerous concealed papist. When in 1605 the king postponed the annual meeting of the general assembly of the church for the third year in a row, some of the ministers, who believed that the king had no legal right unilaterally to prevent the meeting, resolved none the less to convene at the scheduled time and place. Dunfermline allowed them to do so, provided that they promptly dispersed, which they did. James was very angry at what he perceived as a violation of his instructions. Six of the ministers were found guilty of treason in January 1606 by a packed jury which, even so, had to be threatened with a charge of wilful error before it would vote to convict.

After the trial Spottiswoode and the lord treasurer, George Home, earl of Dunbar, set out 'to procure the Chancellor his disgrace, as suspected to be an enemy to the estate of bishops' (Forbes, 406). The king was almost persuaded, but finally concluded that Dunfermline had acted mistakenly rather than disloyally. So Dunfermline stayed in office, but for the next five years Dunbar, not he, was James's principal adviser and agent in Scottish affairs. Dunfermline kept his position by loyally co-operating with Dunbar on a number of issues, notably the ending of free trade between England and Scotland in 1610, placing no obstacle in the way of Dunbar's high-handed reimposition of the authority of bishops in the church, and assuring the king of the wisdom of his policy and the efficiency of Dunbar in carrying it out, in a series of obsequious and flattering letters written in a prolix style, full of Latin tags and classical references, designed to appeal to his learned master. Dunbar's base was at court; in those matters with which he did not directly concern himself, highland policy for example, Dunfermline and his colleagues in Edinburgh were able to operate with considerable latitude.

Head of government Dunbar's sudden death on 20 January 1611 came at precisely the right time for Dunfermline. He had carefully cultivated all the important individuals and groups in Scottish politics save the irreconcilable Spottiswoode. Paradoxically, his troubles over the abortive general assembly made the presbyterian wing of the church look more kindly on him. They disliked the archbishop even more than they did him, and after 1606 attacks on him as a papist were rare. The fact that the power of bishops in the church had been so recently re-established doomed Spottiswoode's hopes of succeeding to Dunbar's place with James; the king well knew that to give an ecclesiastic political power at this juncture would cause a severe aristocratic backlash. After Dunbar's confrontational regime a period of consolidation was needed, for which Dunfermline's conciliatory methods were ideally suited. So in 1611 Dunfermline succeeded Dunbar as the king's principal adviser and agent in Scottish affairs, and as keeper for life of the palace and park of Holyroodhouse; he remained in power until his death.

Dunfermline's success was all the more remarkable in that he remained in Edinburgh, far from the king's court and the king's ear. His method was to create consensus in the privy council, which gradually filled with his former colleagues on the court of session, and to keep in touch with the king by letters sent either directly to him or to one of the Scots at court—usually either John Murray, first earl of Annandale, the keeper of the privy purse, or Thomas Erskine, first earl of Kellie, the captain of the guard, whose eldest son married one of Dunfermline's daughters. If James issued an order that the councillors thought unwise, they normally delayed executing it until they could make their case to the king. As the lord treasurer, John Erskine, nineteenth earl of Mar, later put it to Charles I, 'A hundred times your worthy Father has sent down directions unto us which we have stayed, and he has given us thanks for it when we have informed him of the truth' (*Mar and Kellie MSS*, 146).

The first years of Dunfermline's administration saw the consolidation and extension of the changes made during the Dunbar regime. Dunfermline served as royal commissioner at the parliament of 1612, which ratified the restoration of the power of bishops in the church, which Dunbar had forced through the general assembly in 1610. Parliament also approved a tax to help pay for Princess Elizabeth's wedding. Dunbar's successful efforts to maintain order on the borders were continued by a commission of which Dunfermline's brother Sir William Seton was a prominent member. The most conspicuous victim was the lawless eighth Lord Maxwell, beheaded in 1612, an indication that noble blood would no longer protect a malefactor from the executioner's axe. An even more prominent victim of the law and order campaign was the king's cousin Patrick Stewart, earl of Orkney, who had been in ward in Edinburgh since 1609 on charges of oppression of his tenants. In 1612 parliament annexed the earldom to the crown. Dunfermline's government began to negotiate with the earl over the terms on which he would formally surrender his rights. Instead Orkney authorized his bastard son to raise a rebellion. It failed; father and son were both executed early in 1615, and the earldom remained in the hands of the crown. In the south-western highlands the law and order campaign was equally successful, though the king's decision to entrust the Campbells with the task of subduing the rebellious MacDonalds and MacGregors did not please Dunfermline, who feared the aggrandizement of this ambitious family. Though trouble spots remained, the pacification of the highlands was, on the whole, very successful.

The welfare of the landed classes, and the maintenance of their local pre-eminence provided that they obeyed the king, was the guiding principle of Dunfermline's administration. He discouraged Archbishop Spottiswoode's effort to get rid of hereditary sheriffs. Dunbar's last parliament had authorized the creation of justices of the peace on the English model. Dunfermline implemented the statute very cautiously, and made no effort to limit the judicial rights of holders of regalities. The privy council looked after the interests of grain growers, sheep raisers, and mine owners; only in times of acute food shortage did the council adopt policies favouring the consumer rather than the aristocratic producer. Dunfermline made no effort to alter the archaic tax structure, and usually discouraged the voting of taxes. The peace and prosperity of these years made taxation less necessary in any event.

The last phase Dunfermline was responsible for the logistics of King James's only visit to his native land, in 1617, and on the whole it went well. James's principal public purpose was to arrange for changes in the Scottish church to bring its practices closer to those of the Church of England. The upshot was the so-called five articles of Perth, which, to James's surprise and irritation, met with considerable resistance as being 'popish' in nature. They failed to secure adoption in a general assembly held after his departure, and were pushed through only with difficulty at the assembly held at Perth in 1618. Dunfermline bears some responsibility for all this. On account of the political problems he had had in the past owing to the widespread belief that he was a concealed papist, he had carefully avoided religious issues in his reports to the king, though it is unlikely that he was unaware of how unpopular the five articles would prove to be. The long-range consequences for the monarchy were serious. In the face of popular resistance James eventually drew back and did not insist on the enforcement of the articles. What the episode demonstrated was that the power of the crown, greatly enhanced though it was after 1603, nevertheless had its limits.

James did not blame Dunfermline for the difficulties his religious policies encountered, and the chancellor's grip on power continued. The years following James's visit saw considerable governmental activity on behalf of various manufacturing interests: glass making, leather tanning, soap. In 1620 the war in central Europe began to affect Scotland. In 1621 parliament voted a large tax for the war, including, for the first time, a 5 per cent levy on annual rents, a significant broadening of the direct-tax base which remained in place after the short-lived British involvement in the war ended. It was Dunfermline's last major service to King James; he died on 16 June 1622 at home at Pinkie House, Musselburgh, aged sixty-six. On 9 July he was buried at Dalgety, Fife, where he had acquired a property in 1593; both Lilias and Grizel were buried there, and so in due course was his widow, who died on 30 December 1659. He left behind him cash and moveables worth about £44,000 Scots and over £11,000 Scots in debts owing to him, as well as his land. He died a rich man.

Dunfermline's success as a consensus builder and a political moderate was remarkable. He even defused his potentially explosive religious stance. Calderwood in recording his death could write, 'Howsoever he was Popishly disposed in his religion, yet he condemned many abuses … in the kirk of Rome. He was a good justiciar, courteous and humane … but no good friend to the bishops' (Calderwood, 7.549). His political rival Archbishop Spottiswoode wrote that 'He exercised his place with great moderation, and above all things studied to maintain peace and quietness' (*History of the Church*, 3.263). Dunfermline also left behind monuments to his aesthetic taste in his two notable houses, Fyvie Castle in Aberdeenshire, and Pinkie House in Musselburgh. His heir was his only surviving son Charles *Seton, born of his third marriage in 1615. His portrait, painted in 1610, hangs in the Scottish National Portrait Gallery.

MAURICE LEE JUN.

Sources M. Lee, *Government by pen: Scotland under James VI and I* (1980) • G. Donaldson, *Scotland: James V to James VII* (1965), vol. 3 of *The Edinburgh history of Scotland* (1965–75) • J. Wormald, *Court, kirk, and community: Scotland, 1470–1625* (1981) • *CSP Scot.*, 1597–1603 • *Reg. PCS*, 1st ser. • *Reg. PCS*, 2nd ser. • *Calendar of the manuscripts of the most hon. the marquis of Salisbury*, 24 vols., HMC, 9 (1883–1976) • *APS*, 1424–1625 • *Report on the manuscripts of the earl of Mar and Kellie*, HMC, 60 (1904) • H. Paton, ed., *Supplementary report on the manuscripts of the earl of Mar and Kellie*, HMC, 60 (1930) • D. Calderwood, *The history of the Kirk of Scotland*, ed. T. Thomson and D. Laing, 8 vols., Wodrow Society, 7 (1842–9) • J. Spottiswood, *The history of the Church of Scotland*, ed. M. Napier and M. Russell, 3 vols., Bannatyne Club, 93 (1850) • *The autobiography and diary of Mr James Melvill*, ed. R. Pitcairn, Wodrow Society (1842) • *State papers and miscellaneous correspondence of Thomas, earl of Melros*, ed. J. Maidment, 2 vols., Abbotsford Club, 9 (1837) • J. Maidment, ed., *Letters and state papers during the reign of King James the Sixth*, Abbotsford Club, 13 (1838) • R. Maitland, *The historie of the house of Seytoun … with the continuation, by Alexander Viscount Kingston*, ed. J. Fullarton, Bannatyne Club, 31 (1829) • J. Row, *The history of the Kirk of Scotland, from the year 1558 to August 1637*, ed. D. Laing, Wodrow Society, 4 (1842) • W. Forbes-Leith, ed., *Narratives of Scottish Catholics under Mary Stuart and James VI* (1885) • J. Forbes, *Certaine records touching the estate of the kirk in the years MDCV & MDCVI*, ed. D. Laing and J. Anderson, Wodrow Society, 19 (1846) • GEC, *Peerage*, 4.532

Likenesses M. Gheeraerts the younger, oils, 1610, Scot. NPG [*see illus.*]

Wealth at death cash and moveables approx. £44,000 Scots; debts owing over £11,000 Scots; landed estates

Seton, Alexander. *See* Montgomery, Alexander (1588–1661).

Seton, Alexander (*fl.* 1626–1649), army officer in the Danish and Norwegian services, is of uncertain origins. Family historians have identified him variously as Alexander Seton of Lathrisk and as the son of George Seton of Cariston (1554?–1620) and his wife, Margaret, daughter of Sir John Aytoun of that ilk, but the case for the former is inconclusive, while the latter is no more than a hypothesis. Nor is it known whether Seton married.

On 8 April 1626 Seton was appointed captain of a company of 500 English foot in Denmark, the same day that the king of Denmark wrote to Charles I asking him to authorize the recruiting of 1000 men by Seton and Francis Hammond. The Scottish privy council authorized Seton to levy 500 men in Scotland on 30 June. By 24 August he was in command of a *frifœnnike* (a unit attached to no regiment) as captain. His activities in the autumn of 1626 are not known, but on 28 February 1627 he was promoted lieutenant-colonel. Probably his unit was to become part of a new regiment with himself as second-in-command.

Seton was wounded in the action at Oldenburg Pass, in the duchy of Holstein, in September 1627, when the Danish forces tried to cover the embarkation of the forces of Bernard of Saxe-Weimar from the superior numbers of the general of the Catholic League, Tilly. Seton joined Sir Donald Mackay's regiment either in the autumn of 1627 or in 1628. Since his company had been ruined by heavy losses he asked about this time for 3000 rixdollars to levy a company of 500 men. He appears to have fought with the regiment at Stralsund in the summer of 1628, when Denmark's Scottish veterans played a major part in breaking the imperial siege of the Hanseatic port. Not wishing to transfer to Swedish service with the regiment when it was reformed in the autumn of 1628, Seton sold the commission for his company to his former lieutenant, Andrew Stuart, and left with the rank of colonel (his reckoning dated 4 October).

Seton seems to have transferred to the Norwegian army, where he is mentioned as a captain of foot in 1628. However, no more is known of his activities until 1645, when he held the rank of colonel in the Norwegian army and navy. In that year he is known to have commanded a squadron of dragoons between May and September, and to have been appointed admiral of a force of eight ships. He is last certainly known of listed as a colonel in Norwegian service on 19 April 1649. THOMAS RIIS

Sources S. Murdoch and A. Grosjean, 'Scotland, Scandinavia and Northern Europe, 1580–1707', www.abdn.ac.uk/ssne/ • T. Riis, *Should auld acquaintance be forgot … Scottish–Danish relations, c.1450–1707*, 2 vols. (1988), vol. 1, p. 96; vol. 2, pp. 119–20 • B. G. Seton, *The house of Seton: a study of lost causes*, 2 vols. (1939–41), 1.262, 366 • R. Seton, *An old family, or, The Setons in Scotland and America* (New York, 1899), 205

Seton, Alexander, first Viscount Kingston (1621–1691), nobleman and soldier, was born at Seton Palace, Haddingtonshire, the fourth but second surviving son of George *Seton, third earl of Winton (1584–1650), and his first wife, Lady Anne Hay (*d.* 1623x5), eldest daughter of Francis Hay, ninth earl of Erroll. On the visit of Charles I to Seton Palace in 1633, as a boy of twelve, he welcomed the king at the iron gate of Seton with a Latin oration and was knighted on the completion of his discourse. In 1636 he commenced a two-year period of study at the Jesuit college of La Flèche in France where he successfully defended his thesis and had it printed on satin and sent home to his father, to whom it was dedicated. Afterwards he made a tour through a great part of Italy, Spain, and France. He returned via England to Scotland in 1640, carrying with him letters of encouragement from Charles I to Catholic loyalists such as George Gordon, second marquess of Huntly, Robert Maxwell, first earl of Nithsdale, and his own father, the earl of Winton; he himself probably continued to embrace Catholicism. To avoid subscribing the solemn league and covenant, he went in 1643 to the Netherlands and on returning to Scotland some eight months later was excommunicated in Tranent church on 8 October 1644.

Shortly thereafter Seton crossed to France, where he remained in attendance on the young Prince Charles for three years. Late in 1647 he returned to England and carried messages back from the king to his wife, Henrietta Maria, and to the prince. According to his continuation of Sir Richard Maitland's history of his family, published as *History of the House of Seton* (1829), Seton carried word of the engagement to the queen at St Germain, telling her that a large Scottish army would invade England in the summer of 1648 and restore the king to his dignity. In August of that year he was a lieutenant-colonel of horse in the army of the engagement that was defeated by Oliver Cromwell at Preston.

Three days after the coronation of Charles II at Scone on 1 January 1651, Seton was created, by patent dated at Perth, Viscount Kingston and Lord Craigiehall, possibly the new king's first creation. By this time he had married Jean, daughter of Sir Andrew Fletcher, who had been a gentleman of the privy chamber to Charles I; their eldest child, Jean (or Anne), was born in April 1651, and there followed Charles (1653–1682), George (1654–1678), Alexander (1655–1676), and Isobel (1656–1677). Viscountess Jean died in the later 1650s. Barbara (1659–1679) may have been the daughter of Kingston's second wife, Elizabeth (1635/6–1668), daughter of Sir Archibald Douglas of Whittingehame, Haddingtonshire; they had three other children, Archibald (1661–1714), James (1667–1743), and Elizabeth (*b.* 1668), before Viscountess Elizabeth also died.

After the Restoration, Kingston held various military positions and commanded the militia troop of Haddingtonshire at the defeat of the covenanters on the Pentland Hills on 28 November 1666. He also served at his own expense under the duke of Monmouth, and played a part in the victory over the covenanters at Bothwell Bridge on 22 June 1679. On 28 July 1681 Kingston was one of the signatories to a declaration stating that it was unlawful under all circumstances to take up arms against the king, and that the national covenant and the solemn league and covenant were against the 'fundamental laws and liberties' of the kingdom (*Reg. PCS*, 7.705).

Kingston married again, first Elizabeth, daughter of John Hamilton, first Lord Belhaven, and then, on 3 August 1686, Lady Margaret (1651–1692), daughter of Archibald *Douglas, styled earl of Angus (*c.*1609–1655), and sister of James Douglas, second marquess of Douglas, and Archibald Douglas, first earl of Forfar. There were no children from either marriage. Kingston died on 21 October 1691 and was buried in the family vault at Seton Palace. Most of his children having predeceased him, his sons Archibald and James became successively second and third Viscount Kingston. The latter was attainted in the aftermath of the 1715 Jacobite rising, and the title became extinct.

JOHN J. SCALLY

Sources *APS* • *Reg. PCS*, 1st ser. • *Reg. PCS*, 2nd ser. • *The historical works of Sir James Balfour*, ed. J. Haig, 4 vols. (1824–5) • *Scots peerage* • GEC, *Peerage*, new edn • [W. C. Chambers], *Story of the Setons* (1874) • R. Maitland, *The historie of the house of Seytoun … with the continuation, by Alexander Viscount Kingston*, ed. J. Fullarton, Bannatyne Club, 31 (1829) • R. Douglas, *The peerage of Scotland*, 2nd edn, ed. J. P. Wood, 2 vols. (1813)
Archives NL Scot., MSS in legal case against him and his debts

Seton, Sir Alexander, of Pitmedden, first baronet, Lord Pitmedden (1639?–1719), judge, was the younger son of Sir John Seton of Pitmedden, third baronet (*d.* 1639), and his wife, Elizabeth, daughter of Sir Samuel Johnston of Elphinstone. Following his father's death commanding a royalist detachment at the battle of the Bridge of Dee on 18 June 1639, Alexander and his older brother, James, were raised as wards of their father's kinsman the entrepreneurial George Seton, third earl of Winton. In 1650 Seton matriculated at Marischal College, Aberdeen, and graduated in 1654. On 10 December 1661 he was admitted as an advocate of the Scottish bar and was knighted by Charles II in 1664. When his brother died serving the Royal Navy in 1667, Seton inherited the estate of Pitmedden, where in 1675 he began designing the formal terraced garden, later known as the 'Great Garden of Pitmedden'.

Following the demise of Sir Richard Maitland of Pittrichie, Seton was nominated an ordinary lord of the court of session on 31 October 1677 and took his seat as Lord Pitmedden on 13 November of that year. On the promotion of Lord President Falconer, he was subsequently admitted a lord of justiciary on 5 July 1682 and created baronet of Nova Scotia on 15 January 1684. Regarded as 'the touns deir frind Pitmedden', Seton represented the county of Aberdeen in the parliaments of 1681, 1685, and 1686 (Taylor, 4.320). Resolutely opposed to the attempts of James VII and II to secure the repeal of the test and penal laws, Pitmedden was, however, the only one of nine judges sitting in parliament who openly opposed the royal will. His consequent removal from office, by a royal letter dated 12 May 1686, and the dismissal of several other recalcitrant state officers were collectively judged to be 'warning shots … to terrify and divert other Members of Parliament from their opposition' (*Historical Notices*, 2.723). Having retired into private life thereafter, he declined reappointment as a judge after the revolution, deeming it inconsistent with the oath of allegiance he had previously sworn to James. A Latin panegyric of his life was composed by William Black in 1690.

As an appendix to the second edition of Sir George Mackenzie's *Laws and Customs of Scotland in Matters Criminal*, in 1699 Seton published 'A treatise of mutilation and demembration', examining how punishment for these crimes had evolved from strict adherence to the *lex talionis* to the imposition of arbitrary pecuniary damages. He was also the author of the posthumously published 'Explication of the XXXIX chapter of the statutes of King William', which defended the legal right of minors to be exempt from actions against their property. In or before 1673 he married Margaret (*d.* 1723), daughter of William Lauder, one of the clerks of session. They had five sons, including Sir William *Seton, and five daughters. Following Seton's death in 1719, his extensive library of over 3000 titles was sold by auction in 1720.

George Stronach, *rev.* Clare Jackson

Sources R. Douglas and others, *The baronage of Scotland* (1798) · *Historical notices of Scotish affairs, selected from the manuscripts of Sir John Lauder of Fountainhall*, ed. D. Laing, 2 vols., Bannatyne Club, 87 (1848) · L. B. Taylor, ed., *Aberdeen council letters*, 6 vols. (1942–61) · G. Brunton and D. Haig, *An historical account of the senators of the college of justice of Scotland, from its institution in 1532* (1849) · D. Dalrymple, Lord Hailes, 'A catalogue of the lords of session from the institution of the college of justice, in the year 1532', *Tracts relative to the history and antiquities of Scotland* (1900) · R. J. Prentice, *Pitmedden and its Great Garden* (1964) · *A catalogue of valuable books in several languages and faculties … being the library which belong'd to Sir Alexander Seaton of Pitmedden, baronet, etc.* (1719) · P. J. Anderson and J. F. K. Johnstone, eds., *Fasti academiae Mariscallanae Aberdonensis: selections from the records of the Marischal College and University, MDXCIII–MDCCCLX*, 3 vols., New Spalding Club, 4, 18–19 (1889–98) · W. Black, *Illustrissimo ac perhonorifico domino D. Alexandro Seton* (1690)

Seton, Alexander (1814–1852), army officer, born at Mounie in Aberdeenshire on 4 October 1814, was the second but eldest surviving son of Alexander Seton of Mounie and Janet Skene, his wife, daughter of Skene Ogilvy, minister of Old Machar, Aberdeenshire. He was descended from Sir Alexander *Seton, Lord Pitmedden. Alexander was educated at home until the age of fifteen, and then studied mathematics and chemistry for some months under Ferdinando Foggi at Pisa.

On 23 November 1832 Seton was gazetted second lieutenant in the 21st Royal North British Fusiliers, and the following year was sent with part of his regiment to Australia. He returned to Scotland on leave in 1838, and was promoted first lieutenant on 2 March. He rejoined his regiment in India, and received a company on 14 January 1842. Shortly after he exchanged into the 74th highlanders and was stationed at Chatham. There he studied for two years in the senior department of the Royal Military College, and in November 1847 received a first-class certificate. In 1849 he went to Ireland as assistant deputy quartermaster-general of the forces there. He held this post until 24 May 1850, when he was promoted major.

On 7 November 1851 Seton obtained the rank of lieutenant-colonel, and shortly afterwards was ordered to take command of the drafts destined for the Cape of Good Hope, where his regiment was engaged in the Cape Frontier War. He sailed in the steam troopship *Birkenhead*, which on the morning of 26 February 1852 struck a rock in False Bay, 20 miles south of Cape Town, and foundered in little more than ten minutes. Despite the suddenness of the catastrophe, Seton issued his orders with perfect calmness, ensuring that women and children got the few places in the boats. The scene was said by an eye-witness to have resembled a normal embarkation, but with less confusion. Out of 638 persons, 445 were lost, Seton himself being killed by the fall of part of the wreck. He died unmarried, and his property descended to his younger brother, David. The heroism displayed by Seton and the rest of those on the *Birkenhead* was commemorated by Sir Francis Doyle in his poem 'The Loss of the Birkenhead' in *The Return of the Guards and other Poems* (1866).

E. I. Carlyle, *rev.* James Falkner

Sources *Army List* · *Annual Register* (1852), 470–72 · *Hart's Army List* · Burke, *Gen. GB* · F. Maurice, 'The wreck of the *Birkenhead*', *Cornhill Magazine*, [3rd] ser., 2 (1897), 147–61 · Boase, *Mod. Eng. biog.*

Archives U. Aberdeen

Likenesses lithograph, *c.*1840 (as young man), priv. coll.

Seton, Charles, second earl of Dunfermline (1615–1672), politician and army officer, was born in Scotland towards the end of 1615 (probably late in November), the son of Alexander *Seton, first earl of Dunfermline (1556–1622), and his third wife, Margaret Hay (1592–1659), the sister of John Hay, first earl of Tweeddale. He succeeded his father on 16 June 1622. In 1633 his mother contracted herself in marriage to James *Livingston, first earl of Callendar. Dunfermline was incorporated in St Salvator's College, St Andrews, in 1629. He married Lady Mary Douglas (*d. c.*1659), the third daughter of William *Douglas, seventh earl of Morton, and his wife, Anne Keith, daughter of George *Keith, Earl Marischal. Contracts for the marriage were dated 29 March, 2 April, and 9 November 1632.

Dunfermline was a gentleman of the bedchamber of Charles I. He became an active supporter of the covenant, though he has been seen as one who from the beginning sought common ground with the king (C. Russell, *The Fall of the British Monarchies, 1637–1642*, 1991, 522). In May 1639 he led an infantry regiment in Fife in the army of Montrose which occupied the royalist burgh of Aberdeen. In June 1639 he was one of the leaders of the Scottish covenanting army which took up a position on Duns Law to bar the progress of Charles northwards, and on 6 June he presented a petition to the king in his camp that he would appoint commissioners to treat in regard of the matters in dispute. He was one of those who signed the articles of pacification, as well as a paper of submission to the king. In November he and John Campbell, earl of Loudoun, were sent to London to report to the king the proceedings of the assembly of the kirk and the parliament for ratification; but the king refused to receive them and forbade them to approach within 8 miles of the court. Dunfermline was also again sent to the king early in 1640, and on account of the discovery of the letter of the Scots to the king of France, was, with Loudoun and the other commissioners, detained for a time in custody.

Dunfermline was colonel of a regiment raised in western Fife in the Scottish army which, under Alexander Leslie, crossed the Tweed in August 1640. Following the covenanter victory at Newburn and the capture of Newcastle, the earl was appointed Scottish governor of Durham. In October he was appointed one of the eight Scottish commissioners for the treaty of Ripon, and he was also one of the subcommittee appointed for the final conclusion of the treaty in London. While in London he received from the king a lease of the abbey of Dunfermline for fifty-seven years. In August 1641 the estates appointed him a commissioner to the English parliament during the king's trip north. In September he was nominated a member of the Scottish privy council, an appointment confirmed in November. In 1642, as a man who had been partly won over by the royal concessions of 1641, Dunfermline was appointed the king's commissioner to the general assembly of the kirk of Scotland, which met on 27 July. As the English parliament and king presented the general assembly with their rival declarations, Dunfermline conveyed the king's good intentions while urging it not to reply to parliament without royal permission, but 'his weeping could not obtain it' (D. Stevenson, *The Scottish Revolution, 1637–1644: the Triumph of the Covenanters*, 1973, 250). Afterwards Dunfermline went to England, presumably on state business; he returned to Scotland in mid-September.

On 26 August 1643 the convention of estates nominated Dunfermline a colonel of Fife foot for the army being prepared to assist the English parliamentarians. The earl chose mercenaries as lieutenant-colonel and major. The regiment was raised from the presbyteries of Kirkcaldy and Dunfermline. Between January and July 1644 it served in the north-east of England, at the siege of York and at the battle of Marston Moor. In August it joined the forces besieging Newcastle. Dunfermline led his men in storming the town in October. Afterwards the regiment was divided, part remaining in England serving in garrisons and at the siege of Newark, while the remainder returned to Scotland to help suppress the royalists.

In January 1646 Dunfermline was chosen as a member of the committee of estates. The estates named him to the committee with the army in England on 3 February; the earl attended it periodically from July to November. After the surrender of Charles to the Scots at Newark in May, he was sent, along with Argyll and others, to treat with him, and accompanied Argyll to London to lay the king's case before parliament. Simultaneously his loyalty to the king's opponents became suspect. In August suspicions connected him with the French ambassador in a plot on the king's behalf. In January 1647 fears about him deepened, and Leven, the lord general, forbade Dunfermline and one other colonel access to the king.

On 4 May 1648 the estates named Dunfermline a colonel of horse in the engager army. Having supported the engagement for the attempted rescue of the king in 1648, he was debarred by the Act of Classes from holding any office of public trust. He went to the continent in April 1649 and took part in the negotiations at Breda in connection with the recall of Charles II, whom he accompanied to Scotland in June 1650. In July he entertained the king at Dunfermline. When in October the king left Perth and joined the northern loyalists, Dunfermline was one of the commissioners sent to arrange matters with him. On 29 October he was on petition freed from the disabilities imposed on him by the Act of Classes, and permitted to take his seat in parliament, following public repentance in late November. Shortly afterwards he was appointed one of the committee of estates for managing the affairs of the army, and he was in frequent attendance on the king during his stay in Scotland. In the army raised for the invasion of England his regiment (raised after 9 January 1651, mainly from the presbytery of Dunfermline) formed part of the 2nd brigade of horse. The regiment subsequently served in the Worcester campaign.

At the Restoration, Dunfermline was reinstated as a privy councillor on 13 February 1661 and sworn in on 22 September 1664. On 2 November 1667 he was appointed an extraordinary lord of session. He regularly attended the parliaments of the 1660s and served as a lord of the articles in 1669. In 1671 he was appointed lord privy seal. He died on or about 11 May 1672 at his home, Seton House, and was buried at Dalgety. He and his wife had had one daughter and three sons. The eldest son, Charles, was killed in a sea-fight with the Dutch shortly before his father's death; Alexander, the third earl, died in 1677; and

James, the fourth and last earl, in 1689 commanded a troop of horse under Dundee at Killiecrankie, and, being forfaulted, went to France, where he died childless in 1699. T. F. HENDERSON, *rev.* EDWARD M. FURGOL

Sources J. Balfour, *Works*, 4 vols. (1823–5) • E. M. Furgol, *A regimental history of the covenanting armies, 1639–1651* (1990) • J. Spalding, *Memorialls of the trubles in Scotland and in England, AD 1624 – AD 1645*, ed. J. Stuart, 2 vols., Spalding Club, [21, 23] (1850–51) • H. W. Meikle, ed., *Correspondence of the Scots commissioners in London, 1644–1646*, Roxburghe Club, 160 (1917) • *Scots peerage* • A. F. Mitchell and J. Christie, eds., *The records of the commissions of the general assemblies of the Church of Scotland*, 3 vols., Scottish History Society, 11, 25, 58 (1892–1909) • *Diary of the public correspondence of Sir Thomas Hope*, ed. [T. Thomson], Bannatyne Club, 76 (1843) • *The memoirs of Henry Guthry, late bishop*, ed. G. Crawford, 2nd edn (1748) • *The manuscripts of the duke of Hamilton*, HMC, 21 (1887) • GEC, *Peerage*
Archives NL Scot., deeds and family papers
Likenesses A. Simon, silver and lead metal sculpture, 1646, BM • attrib. A. Van Dyck, oils, Scot. NPG • plaster cast (after A. Simon), Scot. NPG

Seton, Sir Christopher (*c.*1278–1306), landowner, seems to have been of a family which took its name from Seton in Cleveland, North Riding of Yorkshire, and served the senior Brus family there until the male line failed in 1272. He was not related to the Setons of Lothian. His father, Sir John of Seton, died in 1299, before 7 July, when Christopher, said to be twenty-one, inherited Yorkshire lands and property in Cumberland bought by his father from a coheir of Richard Levington. Robert (V) de Brus (*d.* 1295) also acquired an active interest in Cumberland through his second marriage, to Christina of Ireby, between 1270 and 1275, and Sir John, who was described as Brus's knight in 1285, had demised lands there to Robert and Christina; these reverted to Christopher on Christina's death in 1305. Sir John was with Robert (VI) de Brus (*d.* 1304) in the king's service in Galloway in July 1296. Thus Seton had served Brus long before the marriage of Christopher to Christian *Bruce (*d.* 1356), daughter of Robert (VI) de Brus and sister of Robert Bruce, a marriage which had taken place by 1305. A simple explanation may be found in Christopher's service under John de Botetourt in the garrison of Lochmaben at least from April 1303 to March 1304, when he could have been thrown into the lady's company.

In February 1306 Seton faced a critical challenge. He and his younger brothers, Sir John Seton, who had served Edward I in Scotland in 1301, and Humphrey, were present at the murder of John Comyn in Dumfries after Robert Bruce had wounded him. The whole family was compromised and threw in its lot with Bruce, soon to be king. Christopher was left in charge of the Brus castle of Loch Doon, a modest stone octagon on a loch island in Ayrshire, while John was given command of Richard Siward's castle of Tibbers, which Bruce had seized; Christian stayed with her brother and was taken prisoner at Tain, Ross-shire, in 1306. Loch Doon and Tibbers held out even after that disastrous defeat. Loch Doon was besieged in early August and had fallen by the 16th, Tibbers perhaps a little later. Both brothers were quickly executed on Edward I's orders. Later Robert I endowed a chapel at Dumfries for Christopher's soul; evidently he was gibbeted there. He left no children. A. A. M. DUNCAN

Sources G. W. S. Barrow, *Robert Bruce and the community of the realm of Scotland*, 3rd edn (1988) • *CDS*, vol. 2, nos. 995, 1091, 1102, 1195, 1205, 1223, 1464, 1690, 1697, 1776, 1841; vol. 5, no. 472 • *CIPM*, 1, no. 800; 3, nos. 502, 583; 4, no. 280 • W. Farrer and others, eds., *Early Yorkshire charters*, 12 vols. (1914–65), vol. 2, no. 26 • H. R. Luard, ed., *Flores historiarum*, 3 vols., Rolls Series, 95 (1890), vol. 3, p. 134

Seton, George, first Lord Seton (*d.* **1478**). *See under* Seton family (*per. c.*1300–*c.*1510).

Seton, George, second Lord Seton (*d.* **1507/8**). *See under* Seton family (*per. c.*1300–*c.*1510).

Seton, George, fourth Lord Seton (*c.***1508–1549**), nobleman, was the second surviving son of George, third Lord Seton (*d.* 1513), and Janet Hepburn (*d.* 1558), eldest daughter of Patrick *Hepburn, first earl of Bothwell. Seton's elder brother, also named George, died in infancy. He succeeded, aged about five years, to the family lands and titles on the death of his father at the battle of Flodden (9 September 1513), and was served heir in Seton, Wintoun, and Tranent in Haddingtonshire and in Winchburgh, Binning, Hartshead, and Clents in Linlithgowshire.

On account of his youth Seton played little part in the turbulent politics of the minority of James V, and he entered public life only in 1526 when nominated a member of the *pro judicibus* committee in parliament. In July 1528 he aligned with the king against Archibald Douglas, sixth earl of Angus, and accompanied James from Stirling to Edinburgh as he moved against the earl. As a crown supporter he was named among the session of the lords of council convened by James on 6 July. In October 1528, together with other crown adherents in Haddingtonshire, Seton was charged with clearing Lothian of Angus and his supporters, and with ensuring that Angus's castle of Tantallon was isolated from supply in preparation for a royal siege.

Seton's subsequent public career under James V was unspectacular, being characterized by consistent loyal service for which he received a steady flow of royal patronage. This included the erection of his Linlithgowshire properties into the free barony of West Niddrie in 1541 and the erection of his town of Tranent into a burgh of barony in 1542. Following James's death in December 1542 Seton was associated closely with the regime of the regent, James Hamilton, second earl of Arran. In January 1543 Arran entrusted him with the custody of Cardinal David Beaton, who was confined briefly in Seton Castle. Seton's importance in Arran's government was underlined in March 1543 when he was nominated to the privy council, and he supported the regent in his negotiations for the marriage of Queen Mary to Edward, prince of Wales, formalized in the treaty of Greenwich. Seton subsequently followed Arran into his association with Cardinal Beaton and the pro-French party, for which his lands and castle at Seton were burned during the earl of Hertford's invasion of Scotland in 1544. Despite this Seton remained firm in his adherence to the pro-French party, a stance possibly strengthened by Beaton's feuing to him of valuable church properties in Linlithgowshire, and on 26 June 1545 he signed a band confirming Scotland's alliance with France.

Seton married twice. His first marriage, contracted on 10 April 1527, was to Elizabeth Hay, daughter of John, first Lord Hay of Yester, and his first wife, Elizabeth, eldest daughter of George Douglas, master of Angus. Their sons were George *Seton, who succeeded as fifth Lord Seton, and John and James; and their daughters were Jean, Marion, Margaret, Beatrix, and Eleanor. Elizabeth Hay was dead before February 1539, when Seton was betrothed to Marie Pieris, a Frenchwoman in the retinue of Mary of Guise, second queen of James V. They had two sons, Robert and James, and a daughter, Mary *Seton [*see under* Queen's Maries (*act.* 1548–1567)], who in 1548 accompanied Queen Mary to France and served her as one of the four Marys. Seton died on 17 July 1549 at Culross in Perthshire and was buried there, but his remains were later reinterred in the choir of his family's collegiate church at Seton. Among contemporaries he had the reputation of an excellent falconer. Marie Pieris survived him, and married before October 1554, Pierre de Clovis, seigneur de Bryante; she died around 1576. RICHARD D. ORAM

Sources *Scots peerage*, 8.580–85 · J. M. Thomson and others, eds., *Registrum magni sigilli regum Scotorum / The register of the great seal of Scotland*, 11 vols. (1882–1914), vols. 3–4 · *Reg. PCS*, 1st ser. · *APS*, 1424–1567 · T. Thomson, ed., *A diurnal of remarkable occurrents that have passed within the country of Scotland*, Bannatyne Club, 43 (1833) · J. Cameron, *James V: the personal rule, 1528–1542*, ed. N. Macdougall (1998) · A. Fraser, *Mary, queen of Scots* (1969) · GEC, *Peerage*, new edn, 11.635

Seton, George, fifth Lord Seton (*c.*1530–1586), politician, was the eldest son of George *Seton, fourth Lord Seton (*c.*1508–1549), and his first wife, Elizabeth (*d.* in or before 1539), daughter of John Hay, Lord Hay of Yester. In 1542 he went to the University of Paris in the company of William Maitland of Lethington, whose family lived nearby. He was first served heir to his father on 19 May 1550, and by contract dated 2 August that year he married Isabel (*c.*1529–1604), daughter of Sir William Hamilton of Sanquhar, high treasurer and lord provost of Edinburgh. They had one daughter and five sons.

Although all other evidence strongly suggests that Seton remained a staunch Catholic, Adam Wallace's arrest for heresy while at Seton's house at Winton in Haddingtonshire in 1550 and Seton's own exposure to the teachings of John Willock after the latter returned to Scotland from Emden in the autumn of 1558 may be the basis for John Knox's claim that Seton was an apostate. His personal connections at this time, however, all suggest a close attachment to the monarchy and the established religion. His aunt Katherine was prioress of the Dominican nunnery of St Catherine of Siena, on the outskirts of Edinburgh; his sister Marion was a maid of honour in the entourage of the regent, Mary of Guise; his stepmother, Marie Pieris, was a lady-in-waiting to the regent; his half-sister Mary *Seton [*see under* Queen's Maries] accompanied Queen Mary to France in 1548. He was one of the eight

George Seton, fifth Lord Seton (*c.*1530–1586), by Frans Pourbus the elder, 1572 [with his family]

commissioners chosen by parliament on 17 December 1557 to conclude the agreement with France, for the marriage of Queen Mary to the dauphin in April the following year.

In October 1557 Seton had been appointed lord provost of Edinburgh in succession to Archibald Douglas of Kilspindie. During his absence in France a number of presidents acted in his stead, including his friend Sir Richard Maitland of Lethington, father of William Maitland. Seton's reappointment as provost in October 1558 took place against a background of growing resentment among the burgh's merchants of the fiscal demands made by the regent. The next twelve months saw a series of conflicts between the town council and its provost, including the imprisonment of two bailies and the town clerk. These episodes seem to have been caused by a clash of personalities rather than religious differences, but by May 1559 they had come to a head with the prediction by the council of civil disorder and the counter-threat of Seton that he would impose order with his 'kin friends' (*Records of the Burgh of Edinburgh*, 3.38). But the hard-line provost was accused by the council of abandoning his post when the burgh's two friaries were sacked in mid-June 1559. In the unfolding crisis Seton found it difficult to serve two masters—the capital and the queen regent. When faced with the prospect of the town being sacked by the army of the lords of the congregation, the council, one-third of whom had protestant sympathies, adopted a policy marked by ambiguity and conciliation. Seton acted as the regent's agent when sent with the earl of Huntly on 29 July to negotiate a truce with the protestant lords. The regent's proposals included the offer of a religious referendum in the town, a prospect which neither the protestant minority nor the council, anxious to defend its liberties, welcomed.

During the next two months, with Knox installed as protestant minister in the burgh church of St Giles but with the Catholic mass still being said elsewhere, and the forces of the congregation withdrawn, the council met frequently, but Seton attended only once. At the time of the next election, at Michaelmas 1559, the regent resorted to a leet imposing Seton and a loyalist set of office holders on the town. Three weeks later, shortly after they deposed Mary of Guise as regent, the protestant lords used this leet as a pretext for dismissing the Seton-led council and imposing one of their own, led by the protestant laird of Kilspindie. The Kilspindie council was in turn thrown out of office and the Seton regime restored when the congregation withdrew from the burgh on 6 November. But the strength of support for the regent was much depleted: one report of 10 November described only Seton, James Hepburn, earl of Bothwell, and Borthwick as unambiguously loyal. In the capital Seton found it difficult to restore normality after the damage caused by coup and countercoup, although the mass was restored and St Giles's reconsecrated. The Seton council was again dismissed when an English army entered the town in April 1560; the regent retreated into Edinburgh Castle, and Seton joined the French troops defending the heavily fortified citadel of Leith.

Shortly after the death of Mary of Guise on 11 June 1560 but before the conclusion of the treaty of Edinburgh on 6 July and the evacuation of French forces some nine days later, Seton left for France. He arrived in Paris on 3 July. On 1 October, however, he obtained a passport to return to Scotland, via England. It is likely that he was engaged on an unofficial mission on Queen Mary's behalf and that the explanation he offered Nicholas Throckmorton, English ambassador in Paris, that he wanted, despite the fact that he had been 'evilly used' in Scotland, to 'go home and live and die a good Scotchman' was spurious (*CSP for.*, *1560–61*, no. 666). In April 1561, at Joinville, the queen conferred pensions on three of his sons.

Seton accompanied the queen on her return to Scotland in August 1561. He was quickly appointed to the privy council. Early in October 1561, in the face of a series of provocations from the hard-line protestant town council of Edinburgh, Mary tried to impose a leet of loyalists to replace Kilspindie as provost. Seton, still highly unpopular in the town, was on it. Given his previous record as provost, Knox's charge that Seton was 'a man most unworthy of any regiment' (Knox, 1.242) had some substance. In the event, a compromise was reached and Seton never again reached burgh office or was proposed for it by the queen. His future role lay rather in the royal court.

Yet here, too, there were difficulties. Efforts were made to effect a reconciliation between Seton and his powerful East Lothian neighbour Bothwell: on 10 November 1561 in the presence of the queen they concluded a bond to end a long-running feud. This feud, the threats he had made to his fellow Edinburgh councillors in 1558–9, and a heated quarrel between Seton and William Maitland of Lethington on the High Street of Edinburgh in October 1564, which led Mary to conclude that he should leave the country for a time, together suggest that Seton had an uncontrollable temper. They give some credence to Knox's jibe that he was 'a man without God, without honesty and oftentimes without reason' (Knox, 1.192).

None the less, Mary's first new year home was spent at Seton, and it is likely that it was then that the poem 'New year gift' of Alexander Scott, an elegant but ambiguous appeal for religious and other reform, was first performed. The close links between the queen and her volatile Catholic courtier were confirmed in 1563, when Seton was made master of the royal household. The appointment underlined the division within the royal administration between the household, which was French in tone, largely Catholic, and drawn mostly from families of middling rank, such as the Setons, and the privy council, the active part of which was solidly protestant and mostly of higher status. Yet Mary's court remains an intriguing enigma, and Seton's role in it unexplained. Certainly, the portrait which Seton commissioned about 1577, showing him elaborately dressed and wielding his staff of office, with his family coat of arms, complete with its royal or double tressure, and knight's armour prominently displayed, reveals an ambitious courtier, risen to prominence through royal service. Also revealing of the ambitions of this middling family was the elaborate 'armorial', a pictorial history of both the Seton and royal dynasties, and the family house at Seton itself, which was among the earliest private dwellings in Scotland to claim the status of a palace.

In the crisis years of 1567–73 Seton was one of the queen's most committed supporters. Mary's and Bothwell's army spent the night at Seton House before the confrontation at Carberry on 15 June 1567, and Seton fled north with the disgraced Bothwell before abandoning him. He was involved in the intrigue for Mary's escape from Lochleven on 2 May 1568, welcoming her at the lochside and taking her to his house at Niddrie. He was captured at Langside on 13 May. Imprisoned in Edinburgh Castle, he gained his liberty early in 1570 on the defection of the keeper, Sir William Kirkcaldy, to the Marian cause. In August the queen's party sent him from Aberdeen on a major embassy to win continental support (accompanied by the refugee earl of Westmorland and countess of Northumberland). For the next two years he pursued wide-ranging negotiations with Mary herself, the duke of Alba in the Netherlands, Philip II, Catherine dei' Medici, and the English Catholic party. One of the conditions which he tried to impose on Alba was that no council of blood would be set up in Scotland, as it had been in the Netherlands. He rebuked Catherine in 1571 for siding with England and abandoning the Franco-Scottish alliance that had stood 'sen Charles Mannis dais' (*CSP Scot.*, 3.592), but was himself eager for Spanish support and may well have been involved in the Ridolfi plot. He intrigued daringly with the Scottish troops in Dutch service in the hope of winning them over to Alba's side. He gained Spanish subsidies and endeavoured to persuade the queen's party that its best hopes lay with Spain.

Although nominally forfeited in August 1571, Seton retained effective possession of Niddrie. However, during 1572 the king's party gained the upper hand in the civil wars. Seton was a diehard 'queen's man' who stayed aloof from the submission of most leading Marians on 23 February 1573 in the pacification of Perth, but he eventually submitted in April and even professed protestantism. Evidently, however, he intended to continue the struggle by other means. He kept in touch with Mary (who retained his sister Mary Seton in her service until 1583), and visited the continent from time to time on her behalf. In 1574 Seton's daughter Margaret married Lord Claud Hamilton, the leading supporter of the Catholic interest among the Hamilton family. Seton was in the minority who voted against the earl of Morton's restoration as regent in May 1578, and was discomfited by the Hamiltons' downfall in 1579.

Seton's fortunes revived with Morton's overthrow. In February 1581 the new regime proposed sending him as an ambassador to England in February 1581, an appointment the English angrily rejected in view of his record. He sat on the assize that condemned Morton on 1 June. He was close to the royal favourite Esmé Stewart, duke of Lennox (though not to his associate James Stewart, earl of Arran), and was briefly admiral of Scotland. He intrigued with the French ambassador against the Ruthven regime that overthrew Lennox in 1582. In January 1584, after the Ruthven lords' downfall, he was sent as Scottish ambassador to France, officially for the re-establishment there of the Scots guard; he hoped to have his son Sir John *Seton (c.1553–1594) appointed to its command. He renewed his contacts with English Catholics on the way and assured Mary that he would use the mission to her best advantage, but his efforts achieved little. He was one of those captured at Stirling when the pro-English lords overthrew Arran on 2 November 1585.

Seton died on 8 January 1586, aged about fifty-five. He was survived by his wife, Isabel, who died on 13 November 1604, aged about seventy-five. She, like him, was buried in Seton church. Their eldest son, George, master of Seton, had died in March 1562; their second son, Robert (c.1552–1603), succeeded as sixth Lord Seton, was a favourite of James VI, and became earl of Winton in 1600. Of the three younger sons, Sir John Seton became Lord Barns; Alexander was prior of Pluscardine and later earl of Dunfermline; and Sir William Seton of Kyllismore, sheriff of Edinburghshire and postmaster-general of Scotland. Like their father, each of the surviving sons profited through royal service.

MICHAEL LYNCH

Sources G. Donaldson, *'All the queen's men': power and politics in Mary Stewart's Scotland* (1983) • *The lord provosts of Edinburgh, 1296–1932*, ed. M. Wood (1931) • R. Maitland, *The historie of the house of Seytoun … with the continuation, by Alexander Viscount Kingston*, ed. J. Fullarton, Bannatyne Club, 31 (1829) • *Scots peerage*, vol. 8 • M. Lynch, *Edinburgh and the Reformation* (1981) • J. D. Marwick, M. Wood, and H. Armet, eds., *Extracts from the records of the burgh of Edinburgh*, 14 vols., Scottish Burgh RS (1869–1967), vols. 2–3 • J. Knox, *The history of the Reformation of religion within the realm of Scotland*, ed. D. Buchanan, [another edn], 2 vols. (1816) • D. Calderwood, *The history of the Kirk of Scotland*, ed. T. Thomson and D. Laing, 8 vols., Wodrow Society, 7 (1842–9), vols. 1–4 • *Memoirs of his own life by Sir James Melville of Halhill*, ed. T. Thomson, Bannatyne Club, 18 (1827) • Lord Herries [John Maxwell], *Historical memoirs of the reign of Mary queen of Scots*, ed. R. Pitcairn, Abbotsford Club, 6 (1836) • *Register of the privy council*, vols. 1–3 • *CSP Scot.*, *1547–86* • W. A. McNeill, 'Scottish entries in the *Acta rectoria universitatis Parisiensis*, 1519 to c.1633', *SHR*, 43 (1964), 66–86

Likenesses oil on panel, 1570–79, Scot. NPG; on loan from NG Scot. • F. Pourbus the elder, group portrait, oil on panel, 1572, Scot. NPG; on loan from NG Scot. [*see illus.*] • group portrait, oils (after F. Pourbus), Scot. NPG

Seton, George, third earl of Winton (1584–1650), nobleman and politician, was born in December 1584, the second son of Robert Seton, first earl of Winton (*d.* 1603), and his wife, Lady Margaret (*d.* 1624), daughter of Hugh Montgomerie, third earl of Eglinton. He was educated in France—probably, following the tradition of his Roman Catholic family, at the Jesuit college of La Flèche. He returned to Scotland before 18 August 1602, since on that date he appeared with his elder brother Robert (*d.* in or after 1636) before the Haddington presbytery and promised to be a 'diligent hearer of the Word'. Following the death of their father, George was from 1604 styled master of Winton, but, after Robert's confinement for insanity and resignation of the peerage, he succeeded as third earl on 12 May 1607. Four years later his younger brother Alexander (1588–1661) succeeded to the estates of their maternal grandfather, taking the name Alexander *Montgomery, sixth earl of Eglinton. Winton married, on 26 April 1609, Lady Anne (*d.* 1623x5), eldest daughter of Francis Hay, ninth earl of Erroll; they had four surviving children, George (1613–1648), Alexander *Seton (1621–1691), Margaret, and Elizabeth. Anna died some time between May 1623 and February 1625, and in or before 1628 Winton married Elizabeth (*d.* in or after 1664), daughter of John Maxwell, sixth Lord Herries, and his wife, Elizabeth Maxwell; they had twelve children, including Sir John Seton of Garleton and Sir Robert Seton (*d.* 1671).

Winton was sworn of the Scottish privy council on 30 July 1607, and attended thereafter about one in three meetings until the Scottish troubles commenced in 1638. He attended parliament in 1608. He was made justice general of St Andrews (south of the Forth) on 9 March 1608; he was appointed a justice of the peace for Haddingtonshire in 1612; he became a burgess of Glasgow on 11 July 1618; and he was appointed to the standing committee on manufactures on 17 July 1623. In 1620 he erected the additional residence of Winton Castle in the parish of Pencaitland, Haddingtonshire, an original and remarkably striking modification of Tudor architecture after Inigo Jones. He also extended and improved the principal residence at Seton Palace. In Cockenzie he built twelve saltpans and a great harbour, the latter of which was destroyed in a storm in 1635. During his lifetime he acquired lands in Longniddry, Athelstaneford, and Garleton, which he gave to his eldest son by his second marriage, John Seton of Garleton, who was created a baronet on 9 December 1664.

Winton's involvement in local and national issues increased in the reign of Charles I. He was particularly active in the privy council between 1625 and 1630 where, for example, in the period 1629–30 he attended seventy-six out of 127 meetings. The high point occurred when he was made temporary president of the privy council from December 1625 to March 1626. He was made a commissioner of the exchequer on 8 March 1626 and in July of the same year was appointed to the commission for surrenders and teinds, a group established to oversee the king's controversial revocation scheme. His membership of other privy council committees included that for creating baronets in Nova Scotia, to investigate the office of high constable, and the debasement of the coinage. Winton was also appointed to the committee of council to prepare for Charles's coronation visit to Scotland in 1633, and was chosen one of the lords of the articles in the Coronation Parliament of that year. As he had done in 1617 during James VI and I's visit to Scotland, he twice entertained at his own expense Charles I and all of his court at Seton Palace.

Winton was referred to in 1638 by John Maxwell, bishop of Ross, as 'popishly affected' (*Historical Works of Balfour*, 2.263), and on the commencement of the first bishops' war in 1639 his estate was sequestrated after he left Scotland to wait on the king. For his support of Charles I he was forced to pay a fine of 36,000 merks in 1643 and had to pay a ransom of £40,000 Scots to the covenanters after his son Lord George Seton was captured on 13 September 1645 following the defeat of the marquess of Montrose at Philiphaugh. Despite this, he was a commissioner of war in Haddington in 1644 and 1646, and was appointed a commissioner for the accounts of Sir Adam Hepburn, treasurer of the army, on 11 November 1646. Two years later Winton fully supported the engagement intended to rescue Charles I from his imprisonment in England. During the mobilization, he was a colonel of horse and foot for the county of Haddington, and a commissioner of war in the counties of Haddington and Linlithgow. He also gave £1000 sterling in free gift for his equipage to James, duke of Hamilton, general of the Scottish army authorized by the Scottish parliament to invade England. When Charles II arrived in Scotland in 1650 Winton constantly attended the young king, but in November returned to his palace in Haddingtonshire to prepare for the coronation at Scone on 1 January 1651. However, he fell sick shortly after arriving home and died at Seton of a palsy on 15 December 1650, aged sixty-five. JOHN J. SCALLY

Sources *APS* · *The historical works of Sir James Balfour*, ed. J. Haig, 4 vols. (1824–5) · *Scots peerage* · GEC, *Peerage*, new edn · [W. C. Chambers], *Story of the Setons* (1874) · R. Douglas, *The peerage of Scotland*, 2nd edn, ed. J. P. Wood, 2 vols. (1813) · J. Gordon, *History of Scots affairs from 1637–1641*, ed. J. Robertson and G. Grub, 3 vols., Spalding Club, 1, 3, 5 (1841) · R. Maitland, *The historie of the house of Seytoun … with the continuation, by Alexander Viscount Kingston*, ed. J. Fullarton, Bannatyne Club, 31 (1829) · *Reg. PCS*, 1st ser. · *Reg. PCS*, 2nd ser. · J. Spalding, *Memorialls of the trubles in Scotland and in England, AD 1624 – AD 1645*, ed. J. Stuart, 2 vols., Spalding Club, [21, 23] (1850–51)

Likenesses oils, 1628, Traquair House, Scottish Borders

Seton, George, fifth earl of Winton (*b.* before **1679**, *d.* **1749**), Jacobite army officer, was born at Seton, the first and only surviving son of George Seton, fourth earl of Winton (1642–1704), and Christian (*d.* 1703), daughter of John Hepburn of Alderston. Raised in the Episcopal Church of Scotland, he succeeded to the title on the death of his father on 6 March 1704, but having gone abroad in June 1700 after a family quarrel did not return to Scotland until 1 November 1707. The issue of the succession was not a straightforward one as Seton had been born before the marriage of his parents. The marriage was established as lawful and Seton legitimated by the court of session in 1710. That declaration defeated any claim by the second Viscount Kingston, who had intruded himself into the Seton estates in 1705.

Winton showed his family's traditional loyalty to the Stuarts when, in 1715, he raised a troop of 300 horse and on 11 October joined Viscount Kenmure at Moffat in support of the Jacobite rising. During the campaign he advised Kenmure to move to the west of Scotland with a view to opening communication with the forces of the earl of Mar. This advice was in contrast to that proffered by Northumberland supporters of the Pretender (James Stuart), who advised marching into England. Despite this advice, Winton was persuaded to take part in the march into England and was captured at Preston on 14 November 1715. He was taken to London together with William, earl of Nithsdale, Robert, earl of Carnwath, William, Viscount Kenmure, and William, Lord Nairne. They were impeached before parliament in January 1716, and when Winton replied to the articles of impeachment he alone pleaded not guilty. At his trial, which took place in Westminster Hall in March 1716, he was found guilty of high treason and condemned to be hanged, drawn, and quartered, and his titles and lands to be forfeited. Three years later his estates would be sold to the York Buildings Company for £50,300. Winton's sentence came in spite of an able defence conducted by Sir Constantine Phipps, who 'advised him, as the only plea he had, to act the madman, and … he performed it to the life' (L. Inese to the duke of Mar, 3 Oct 1716, *Stuart Papers*, 3.15). The sentence of death was never carried out because, according to one account, Seton escaped from the Tower of London in a hamper (Seton, 1.272). From London he travelled to Calais, arriving on 18 September 1716. On joining the Pretender at Avignon in January 1717 he was granted a pension of 2000 livres a month, which was paid to him until his death. He moved to Rome and was admitted to the masonic lodge there on 16 August 1735. He became grand master in April 1736, holding office until the suppression of the lodge by Clement XII in August 1737.

There is no evidence that Seton was ever married to Margaret Maclear (Seton, 2.1006–9), but they had a son, Charles, who was born in 1711 and died in 1781. Seton died, aged over seventy, in Rome on 19 December 1749, and was buried near the Porta del Popolo. ROGER TURNER

Sources *DNB* · G. Seton, *A history of the family of Seton during eight centuries*, 1 (1896), 250–80; 2 (1896), 1006–9 · GEC, *Peerage*, new edn, 12/2.820–22 · *Calendar of the Stuart papers belonging to his majesty the king, preserved at Windsor Castle*, 7 vols., HMC, 56 (1902–23), vol. 3, p.15 · *State trials*, 15.805–98 · W. J. Hughan, ed., *The Jacobite lodge at Rome, 1735–7* (1910) · *Report on the manuscripts of the earl of Mar and Kellie*, HMC, 60 (1904), 419
Likenesses portraits, repro. in Seton, *History of the family*
Wealth at death all property was forfeited in 1716

Seton, George (1822–1908), genealogist and historian, only son of George Seton of the East India Company and Margaret, daughter of James Hunter of Seaside, was born in Perth, Scotland, on 25 June 1822. He was the heir of a line of Mary Seton, one of the 'four Maries' of the queen of Scots. Brought up by his widowed mother, he attended Edinburgh high school and the University of Edinburgh, and entered Exeter College, Oxford, in 1841, graduating in 1845. He was called to the Scottish bar in 1846, but did not practice. In 1849 he married Sarah Elizabeth (*d.* 1883), second daughter of James Hunter of Thurston, with whom he had a surviving son, George, a tea merchant in Calcutta and London, and three daughters, of whom two predeceased him.

In 1854 Seton was appointed secretary to the registrar-general for Scotland in Edinburgh, and in 1862 superintendent of the civil service examinations in Scotland; he held both offices until 1889. He was one of the founders of the St Andrews boat club (Edinburgh) in 1846, the first vice-chairman of the Society for Improving the Condition of the Poor, a fellow of the Royal Society of Edinburgh and of the Society of Antiquaries of Scotland. Over 6 feet 5 inches in height, he was of fine athletic build, lithe and active to an advanced age, and served in the royal bodyguard of Scottish archers. In 1859 he raised a company of forty volunteer grenadier artillerymen (Midlothian Coast artillery), all over 6 feet tall. St Bennet's, the house he built in Morningside, and where he lived from 1856 to 1890, became the residence of the Roman Catholic archbishop of Edinburgh. He died at his home, 9 Atholl Crescent, Edinburgh, on 14 November 1908.

Seton wrote widely on Scottish genealogy and social history, his most notable works being *The Law and Practice of Heraldry in Scotland* (1863) and a minutely learned history of the Seton family (2 vols., 1896), lavishly printed at his own expense. He also contributed various papers to the *Transactions* of the Edinburgh Royal Society and the Scottish Society of Antiquaries.

T. F. Henderson, *rev.* G. Martin Murphy

Sources *The Times* (16 Nov 1908) · *The Scotsman* (16 Nov 1908) · G. Seton, *A history of the family of Seton during eight centuries*, 2 (1896), 615 · C. J. Smith, *Historic South Edinburgh*, 2 (1979), 460 · *CCI* (1909)
Likenesses T. Duncan, portrait, 1832 · T. C. Hamilton, pencil drawing, 1890, Scot. NPG · W. S. Cumming, portrait, priv. coll. · Kay-Robertson, portrait
Wealth at death £22,244 1*s*. 4*d*.: confirmation, 21 Jan 1909, *CCI*

Seton, John (1508/9–1567), Roman Catholic priest and writer on logic, is of unknown origins and parentage. Although his tombstone in Rome recorded that he died in 1567 at the age of seventy, he himself testified in 1551 that he was forty-two years of age. This accords better with the fact that he graduated BA from St John's College, Cambridge, in 1528. He was elected a fellow of the college on Bishop Fisher's foundation shortly afterwards and commenced MA in 1532. He gained a high reputation as a tutor. After ordination he became a chaplain to Bishop Fisher, attending him in the Tower. In 1542 he was one of the college fellows who signed an appeal to the visitor against John Taylor, the master of the college and afterwards bishop of Lincoln. In 1544 Seton proceeded DTh and about that time became a domestic chaplain to another conservative clergyman, Stephen Gardiner, bishop of Winchester, the master of Trinity Hall, and chancellor of the university, who rewarded him with the rectory of Hinton Ampner, Hampshire.

Under Edward VI, Seton's religious convictions brought him to greater prominence as the Catholic wing of the English church was increasingly threatened. In 1550 he attended Peter Martyr's disputation in Oxford, and the following year he testified at Gardiner's trial about the bishop's denial of papal authority and his acceptance of the royal supremacy. To illustrate this he recounted how Gardiner had ordered him to welcome two of the boy king's chaplains, the protestants Roger Tonge and Giles Ayer, as new canons of Winchester Cathedral. A dinner was held in their honour on 5 April 1548. Later that evening Seton, along with another of the bishop's chaplains, Thomas Watson, escorted the new canons to the inns where they were staying, 'and there made them good cheer'. This was, so he deposed, the first time in four years that he had taken a drink in any of Winchester's public houses!

In return for his loyalty to Catholicism, Seton was presented by Queen Mary with a canonry of his own at Winchester in March 1554. On 14 April 1554 he incorporated DTh in Oxford after being sent by Gardiner, now lord chancellor, to take part in the disputation with Cranmer, Ridley, and Latimer. He visited in prison the London radical priest John Bradford to try to persuade him to conform to the Marian church, and did the same, equally unsuccessfully, in 1558 with Thomas Benbridge. Seton suffered for his beliefs in the early years of Elizabeth's reign and he was deprived of his canonry in June 1559. His name was included in a 1561 list of 'papistical clergy': he was described as learned but settled in his papistry, and was ordered to go no further than 20 miles from London. After imprisonment and further persecution he fled to Rome. He was buried in the cemetery of the English College in Rome, where a memorial recorded that he died on 20 July 1567.

As a Catholic polemicist Seton wrote a panegyric to celebrate Mary's coronation in 1553, as well as contributing Latin verses to Alban Langdale's *Catholica confutatio Nic. Ridlei*, published in Paris in 1556. However, he was most famous as a logician. His *Dialectica* was first printed in 1545. Dedicated to Gardiner as chancellor of Cambridge, he claimed that his colleagues John Cheke and Thomas Watson persuaded him to publish what has been called 'virtually the last major document in the history of scholastic logic in England' (Howell, 50–60). Nevertheless it remained the standard textbook for over a century, especially after the publication of an annotated edition in 1572, which was last reprinted in 1639. Such was its popularity among students that it was said to have circulated in manuscript before it was published. Even the Bodleian Library's printed copy of 1577 was shared among friends, being inscribed, 'Sum liber francisci Tred: et amicorum' ('I am the book of Francis Tred: and friends'; Bodl. Oxf., 70 c. 79). GLYN REDWORTH

Sources *The acts and monuments of John Foxe*, ed. S. R. Cattley, 8 vols. (1837–41), vol. 6 • T. Baker, *History of the college of St John the Evangelist, Cambridge*, ed. J. E. B. Mayor, 1 (1869) • *GM*, 1st ser., 93/1 (1823), 218 • Foster, *Alum. Oxon.* • *Fasti Angl., 1541–1857*, [Canterbury] • J. Strype, *Annals of the Reformation and establishment of religion … during Queen Elizabeth's happy reign*, new edn, 1 (1824) • W. S. Howell, *Logic and rhetoric in England, 1500–1700* (1956) • J. Seton, *Dialectica*, ed. P. Carter, 1572, Bodl. Oxf., 70 c. 79

Seton, Sir John, Lord Barns (*c.*1553–1594), judge, was the third son of George *Seton, fifth Lord Seton (*c.*1530–1586), and his wife, Isabel (*c.*1529–1604), daughter of Sir William Hamilton of Sanquhar. His father was a Catholic, and John Seton, despite acknowledging the government of James VI in April 1573, also continued to be associated with the Catholic interest and was excommunicated by the kirk. During the mid-1570s he visited the court of Philip II of Spain, where he was made a knight of the royal order of Santiago and a gentleman of the king's chamber.

Seton returned to Scotland in 1579 and suffered imprisonment at the hands of the earl of Morton's government. On Morton's fall at the end of 1580, Seton found favour with King James. He was sent to complain to Elizabeth I about her interfering on Morton's behalf, but was refused entry into England. On 9 May 1581 he was formally appointed by James VI as 'principall maister of all his hienes horsis and stabillis, cure, reull and ordour thairof' for life (Donaldson, 45). He opposed the ultra-protestant Ruthven raid in 1582, and in 1583 was employed as an envoy to Spain; in December that year he was included in royal letters of protection. His father granted him a charter for the barony of Barns on 10 May 1583.

In the late 1580s Seton's promotion was rapid: James VI made him on 3 January 1587 first master of the king's household, as well as admitting him on 27 January to membership of the privy council, and, in March of that year he was nominated ambassador to Spain. On 17 February 1588 he was appointed an extraordinary lord of session, with the title Lord Barns, replacing his brother Alexander *Seton, afterwards first earl of Dunfermline. Sir John married Anne, youngest daughter of William, seventh Lord Forbes, on 10 September 1588, at the house of Lord Ogilvie, an occasion attended by a number of Catholic lords. He died on 25 May 1594. His son and heir, Sir John Seton, became a gentleman of the privy chamber to Charles I; he also left an illegitimate son, Hannibal. DAVIE HORSBURGH

Sources M. Livingstone, D. Hay Fleming, and others, eds., *Registrum secreti sigilli regum Scotorum / The register of the privy seal of Scotland*, 8 (1982) • *Reg. PCS*, 1st ser. • G. Seton, *A history of the family of Seton during eight centuries*, 2 vols. (1896) • B. G. Seton, *The house of Seton: a study of lost causes*, 1 (1939) • J. M. Thomson and others, eds., *Registrum magni sigilli regum Scotorum / The register of the great seal of Scotland*, 11 vols. (1882–1914), vol. 5 • *Scots peerage*, 8.588–9 • G. Donaldson, *Scotland: James V to James VII* (1965), vol. 3 of *The Edinburgh history of Scotland* (1965–75) • *DNB*

Seton [Seaton], **John Thomas** (*b.* *c.*1735, *d.* in or after **1806**), portrait painter, was born in Scotland, the son of Christopher Seton (*d.* 1768), a gem engraver, who was a pupil of Charles Christian Reisen. Christopher Seton practised in London, became a director of the Society of Artists in 1765, and died on 6 October 1768. John Thomas Seton was a pupil of Francis Hayman and studied at the St Martin's Lane Academy in London. He was in Rome in 1758–9 and helped to buy pictures for Lord Bute's collection. In 1759 he is 'listed in the *Stato delle Anime* for the Parish of S. Lorenzo in Lucina as living in the Strada della Croce near the Piazza di Spagna (Archivio del Vicariato of the Vatican)' (Ford, 74 n. 12). On 3 March 1759 Richard Dalton wrote: 'Young Seaton and one Navy mind their studys much and hope will succeed in the portraits very well' (ibid., 68 n. 6).

Seton exhibited paintings at the Society of Artists in London between 1761 and 1772, and was elected a fellow of the society in 1769. His conversation pieces, painted about this time, are similar in style to Johan Zoffany's. His painting of the Chambers family (exh. Society of Artists, 1763) was sold at Sothebys on 13 March 1985 (lot 56). Walpole's description of it as 'A young lady sitting at a harpsichord, but talking, the mother sitting knotting, and a young lad standing at the other end of the harpsichord' (Graves, *Soc. Artists*, 229) leaves out the figure on the right, Sir Robert Chambers, chief justice of Bengal, and on the left, his brother Richard, mayor of Newcastle. Seton lived for some time in Bath, but was in Edinburgh between 1772 and 1774. In 1772 he painted an informal portrait of Elizabeth, countess of Leven, with her great-granddaughter Lady Anne Hope (priv. coll.). Another good example of his work is his portrait of John Carmichael, fourth earl of Hyndford (1773; priv. coll.). In 1774, when he exhibited three half-length portraits of ladies at the Royal Academy, his address was listed as St Andrew's Street, New Town, Edinburgh.

In 1773 Seton painted William Fullerton of Carstairs, East India Company surgeon in Bengal, and Captain Ninian Lowis (NG Scot.) in a work that:

> is perhaps indicative of the robust but somewhat stolid and banal style with which he was later to render his sitters in Bengal. Characteristic are the diagonal shadows which slant down from the top left, a rectangular mass of darkness on the right hand side, strong highlights … careful skill in depicting features and a puritanical relish for sparse, unorganised settings. (Archer, 109)

K. E. Maison noted that Seton's work 'shows a few invariable particularities: his sitter's eyes are always wide open and painted very minutely, but their gaze is nearly always oblique. Whenever possible, a dog … is introduced into the picture', and his figures 'are somewhat wooden and inactive' (Maison, 59).

In 1775 Seton applied to the East India Company and on 22 November was granted permission to go to Bengal to practise portrait painting. He arrived in Calcutta, probably on the *Lioness*, at the end of August 1776. He was in Bengal for nine years, and 'returned to England after an easy time … with twelve thousand pounds in his pocket' (Williamson, 142). In 1777 he exhibited a *Portrait of a Gentleman*, painted in Calcutta, at the Society of Artists. Seton bought a house in the avenue behind the residence of the governor-general of Bengal, Warren Hastings, for 33,000 rupees in October 1783 (Foster, 67). By that time his reputation was growing, and he was commissioned to paint the commander-in-chief, Lieutenant-General Sir Eyre Coote (1783; BL OIOC), and the governor-general, Hastings (1784; Victoria Memorial Hall, Calcutta; replica the basis for the mezzotint engraving by John Jones, 1785).

Seton subsequently returned to Edinburgh, where he practised with repute as a portrait painter, and was living in 1806; it is presumed that he died there. Portraits by Seton are in the Scottish National Portrait Gallery and the National Gallery of Scotland, Edinburgh. A portrait of Sir David Dalrymple, Lord Hailes (*c*.1766–7), which was thought to be a companion piece to Seton's portrait of Dalrymple's second wife, Helen Fergusson (both Newhailes collection, National Trust for Scotland), has been reattributed to Allan Ramsay. ARIANNE BURNETTE

Sources M. Archer, *India and British portraiture, 1770–1825* (1979) • W. Foster, 'British artists in India, 1760–1820', *Walpole Society*, 19 (1930–31), 1–88 • G. C. Williamson, *Life and works of Ozias Humphry RA* (1918) • B. Ford, 'The letters of Jonathan Skelton written from Rome and Tivoli in 1758 together with correspondence relating to his death on 19 January 1759', *Walpole Society*, 36 (1960), 23–84 • K. E. Maison, 'John Thomas Seton', *Apollo* (Sept 1941), 59–60, 79 • J. Ingamells, ed., *A dictionary of British and Irish travellers in Italy, 1701–1800* (1997) • Graves, *Soc. Artists* • Graves, *RA exhibitors* • E. Cotton, 'Victoria Memorial Hall, a new portrait of Warren Hastings', *Bengal: Past and Present*, 47 (April–June 1934), 106–10 • A. Smart, *Allan Ramsay: a complete catalogue of his paintings*, ed. J. Ingamells (1999) • Redgrave, *Artists* • P. J. M. McEwan, *Dictionary of Scottish art and architecture* (1994) • D. Irwin and F. Irwin, *Scottish painters at home and abroad, 1700–1900* (1975) • D. Macmillan, *Scottish art, 1460–2000* (1990) • artists' boxes, NPG, Heinz Archive and Library • artist's boxes, Courtauld Inst., Witt Library

Archives Mount Stuart Trust, Isle of Bute, Bute MSS, Dalton to Bute • Paul Mellon Centre for Studies in British Art, London, Brinsley Ford archive

Seton, Margaret (*fl.* 1347). *See under* Seton family (*per. c*.1300–*c*.1510).

Seton, Mary (*b. c*.1541, *d.* after 1615). *See under* Queen's Maries (*act.* 1548–1567).

Seton, Sir Reginald Macdonald Steuart-, second baronet (1778–1838). *See under* Steuart, Sir Henry Seton, first baronet (1759–1836).

Seton, Thomas (*d.* 1359/60), justice, probably came from one of the northern counties where the place name Seton or Seaton is common, and where much of his legal work was done. Though his origins and private life remain obscure, it is known that his wife was called Isabel and that they had a son called William. First recorded in 1340 as serving on an oyer and terminer commission investigating official misconduct in Cumberland and Westmorland, from Michaelmas term 1342 Seton appears as a serjeant-at-law in both the year-books and the records of the common bench. He held the office of king's serjeant from 1343 to 1345, and in June 1345 appeared before the king's council on behalf of the commonalty of the bishopric of Durham, asking for the remission of an eyre in return for a payment of 600 marks. A record from 1351 terms him Sir Thomas, but there is no firm evidence that he was knighted.

He was appointed a justice of the king's bench at Easter 1354, but on 12 October of the following year was moved to the common bench (having, however, enjoyed the higher salary paid to justices of the latter court even while on the king's bench). He served on the common bench until Trinity 1359, and on 5 July 1357, he was made a justice of the king's bench again, 'for this turn'. Just before his death he was said to be a member of the king's secret council. Edward, the Black Prince, also employed him in a legal capacity as a serjeant-pleader, and also as a member of his council. Periodic evidence of this service appears between 1347 and 1358, and he received robes and 50*s.* annually from the prince.

Seton sat on scores of oyer and terminer commissions and commissions of the peace. Many of these commissions involved issues of public order in the northern counties (Yorkshire, Northumberland, and Cumberland), such as the conflict between the garrison and civil administration at Carlisle in 1345, an assault on the warden of the Scottish march in October 1351, and in the winter of 1352 trespasses in the towns of Kingston upon Hull and Beverley (where he and his associates quickly filled the gaol and then delivered the prisoners under separate commission).

Seton evidently had enemies. While he was on his way to a council meeting in the exchequer in November 1357, a woman named Lucy, the wife of Robert Cokeside, loudly denounced him as a faithless traitor who deserved to be drawn and hanged. Seton secured her conviction and won damages of 100 marks. Yet only a few years later, in the summer of 1359, his enemies—'satellites of the devil' the court termed them (*CPR, 1358–61*, 280)—hired a chaplain, Thomas Nesebit, who gained entrance to Seton's dwelling on Fleet Street and then stuck a knife into his belly. Seton had died by May 1360, almost certainly as a consequence of this assault. RICHARD W. KAEUPER

Sources *Chancery records* • G. O. Sayles, ed., *Select cases in the court of king's bench*, 7 vols., SeldS, 55, 57–8, 74, 76, 82, 88 (1936–71), vols. 3, 6 • M. C. B. Dawes, ed., *Register of Edward, the Black Prince*, 4 vols., PRO (1930–33) • Baker, *Serjeants* • S. E. Thorne and J. H. Baker, eds., *Readings and moots at the inns of court in the fifteenth century*, 2, SeldS, 105 (1990) • *CPR, 1358–61*, 280, 361

Seton, Sir William, of Pitmedden, second baronet (*bap.* 1673, *d.* 1744), politician and writer, was baptized on 6 March 1673, the eldest son of Alexander *Seton of Pitmedden (1639?–1719), first baronet and lord of the court of session as Lord Pitmedden, and his wife, Margaret (*d.* 1723), daughter of William Lauder, one of the clerks of session. Throughout the troubles of the seventeenth century the Setons had proved loyal to the Stuarts, though Lord Pitmedden had found himself unable to accept either James

VII's policy of toleration or his subsequent deposition. Unlike his father, William embraced both toleration and the principles of the revolution of 1688, though without breaking definitively from his cavalier heritage. Exposure to his father's magnificent library (though this was sold on Lord Pitmedden's death) and to the precepts of an excellent tutor, William Smith, who in 1693 went on to become a regent at Marischal College, Aberdeen, may account for the erudition and political sophistication of Seton's later pamphleteering.

In the early part of his political career Seton adopted a 'country' oppositionist stance, and won immediate notoriety as a reformist pamphleteer of dubious loyalty. His anonymous *Memorial to the Members of Parliament of the Court Party* (1700) earned him imprisonment in the tollbooth of Edinburgh, and was burnt by the public hangman on 16 November 1700 for its 'high reflections' (*APS*, 10.210–11) on the king's majesty, the proceedings of parliament, and the government of the church. Apologizing to the parliamentary committee which had authorized his detention, Seton denied any 'sinistruous or bad designe' (ibid., 10.214) and won a prompt release. The *Memorial*, written in the traumatic aftermath of the Darien fiasco, advocated various plans for the regeneration of Scotland, criticized the union of the crowns for failing Scotland's interests, and, imprudently, urged suspension of judgement on King William's Scottish church policy 'till we have the Honour of seeing him here' (*Memorial*, 4).

Of more substance was *The Interest of Scotland in Three Essays* (1700, with a second edition in 1702), in which Seton set out a political programme whose central planks were to survive his later switch from oppositionist to placeman. Seton had already identified an incorporating union as the best solution to Scotland's ills, though his proposals for full integration of churches and laws as well as parliaments in *The Interest of Scotland* went much further than the treaty of union which Seton would help negotiate in 1706. Seton also displayed a commitment to mixed government and to the values of civil liberty and the protection of property rights, which played central roles in his unionist vision of a Scotland liberated within a united Britain from its turbulent magnates. These 'whiggish' positions sat awkwardly with his cavalier connections. Yet Seton was a sceptical whig: his Commonwealth-style constitutionalism stood at some remove from uncritical Williamite cheerleading, and his advocacy of presbyterian church government was far from unequivocal.

In *The Interest of Scotland* Seton continued the distinctive eirenic ecclesiology associated in the north-east with the Aberdeen doctors. Unconvinced by claims made for the divine right status of any particular form of ecclesiastical polity, Seton wondered which would best conform to the post-revolution constitution. Identifying episcopal hierarchy as a pillar of absolute monarchy, Seton concluded that, were England and Scotland to unite, as he believed they should, their liberties would be best protected by an Erastian union of their churches under either superintendency or presbytery.

The amphibious latitude which Seton displayed in both his politics and churchmanship bewildered his contemporaries as well as historians. In 1706 a Jacobite agent included Seton, elected to the Scottish parliament in 1702, in a list of the 'loyal and honest men' returned for Aberdeenshire (Macpherson, 2.17). On the other hand, Daniel Defoe pigeon-holed him as 'an honest whig' (*Letters*, 179). Despite his whiggish political philosophy, Seton's parliamentary career, which included a spell as a commissioner for public accounts in 1703–4, suggests a continuing adherence to the Episcopalian–Jacobite values of his family and region.

Seton endorsed the cavalier campaign for the toleration of Episcopalians in *A continuation of a few brief and modest reflexions persuading a just indulgence to be granted to the episcopal clergy and people in Scotland* (1703). In July 1704 he moved a patriot overture in parliament that there be no nomination of a successor to the crown in that session; consideration should be given instead to rectification of Scotland's government. The suspicion of Jacobitism is reinforced by Seton's support at this stage for the programme of the duke of Hamilton. Nevertheless, Seton's position bears some affinity with the scheme of limitations espoused by Andrew Fletcher of Saltoun, a salutary reminder of the shared inspiration of Commonwealth politics which explains the surprisingly narrow gap between Seton's commitment to incorporating union and Fletcher's celebrated anti-unionist patriotism. After all, in 1700 Seton had perceived 'a necessity for Scotland, either to unite with England, or separate from it' (W. Seton, *The Interest of Scotland*, 1700, 110). But patriotic trouble-making in pre-union Scottish politics was also often the first step to being bought off with office, and Seton's own brand was not without its price. In November 1704 the earl of Seafield, a leading courtier, received this message:

> Pittmeden younger pretends a great keyndnes to your Lo., and sayes most serieouslie to me that if your Lo. will obtain him a pension of one houndreth pound per annum, he will be your servant and give you a sutable returne. He would have the first termes payment at Candlemas nixt. (*Correspondence*, 382)

Nationalist historians have used this evidence of opportunism to discount the principled conviction behind Seton's subsequent activities to promote the union. Although his partisanship was weak and he enjoyed the rewards of office as a courtier, having become a collector of bishops' rents in 1705 (until 1714) and a commissioner for union in 1706, Seton was a long-standing supporter of incorporating union. He was described as a zealous supporter of union in Sir John Clerk of Penicuik's Latin history of the Union of 1707. Clerk also remarked that Seton was not renowned for eloquence, though he made a number of important parliamentary interventions in the Union debates. His speech of 2 November 1706 on the first article of union was published as a pamphlet, and his speech of 18 November on the third article is given at length in Defoe's *History of the Union*. Seton also published *Scotland's Great Advantages by an Union with England* (1706). Here Seton set out the easy choice facing Scotland between 'Union with Peace and Plenty, or Dis-Union with

Slavery and Poverty' (*Advantages*, 8), warned Jacobites not to aim at advancing 'the Interest of any Prince, to the disadvantage of their Country' (ibid., 9), and chided patriots for spouting empty rhetoric about the loss of Scottish nationhood: Scotland's 'Sovereignty and Independency' would be asserted to greater effect within the Union than for 'a long time' (ibid., 11).

Seton sat in the British parliament in 1707–8, and sat on the equivalent commission between 1707 and 1717. However, his active political and literary career culminated in the Union. He was described by his friend William Nicolson, bishop of Carlisle, as 'an ingenious Gentleman' (*London Diaries*, 451). He married Catherine (*d.* 1749), daughter of Sir Thomas Burnett of Leys, and they had four sons and five daughters. Seton died in 1744. COLIN KIDD

Sources G. Chalmers, 'Notes on Scottish writers', U. Edin. L., Seton bundle, MS Laing II 451 (2), fols. 414–23 • B. G. Seton, *The house of Seton: a study of lost causes*, 2 vols. (1939–41), 2.610–11 • G. Seton, *A history of the family of Seton during eight centuries*, 1 (1896), 477–9 • *APS*, 1696–1701, 210–11, 214 • D. Hume, *A diary of the proceedings in parliament and the privy council of Scotland, May 21, 1700 – March 7, 1707*, Bannatyne Club, 27 (1828), 17, 19–20, 139 • *Correspondence of James, fourth earl of Findlater and first earl of Seafield*, ed. J. Grant, Scottish History Society (1912), 382 • J. Clerk, *History of the union of Scotland and England*, ed. and trans. D. Duncan, Scottish History Society, 5th ser., 6 (1993), 86, 108 • *The letters of Daniel Defoe*, ed. G. H. Healey (1955), 179 • J. Macpherson, ed., *Original papers: containing the secret history of Great Britain*, 2 vols. (1775), vol. 2, p. 17 • *The London diaries of William Nicolson, bishop of Carlisle, 1702–1718*, ed. C. Jones and G. Holmes (1985), 451, 455 • J. Allardyce, ed., *The family of Burnett of Leys: with collateral branches*, New Spalding Club, 22 (1901) • D. Hayton, 'Seton, William', HoP, *Commons, 1690–1715* [draft] • D. Defoe, 'An abstract of the proceedings on the treaty of union within the parliament of Scotland', *The history of the Union of Great Britain* (1709), 28–32, 76–80 • R. L. Emerson, *Professors, patronage, and politics: the Aberdeen universities in the eighteenth century* (1992), 30 • J. Robertson, ed., *A union for empire: political thought and the Union of 1707* (1995), 83–8, 112, 151, 207–8, 220–22 • J. Robertson, 'Andrew Fletcher's vision of union', *Scotland and England, 1286–1815*, ed. R. A. Mason (1987), 208–11 • W. Ferguson, *Scotland's relations with England: a survey to 1707* (1977), 178, 191, 221, 234, 241, 244, 258, 262–3 • P. H. Scott, *Andrew Fletcher and the treaty of union* (1992), 110–11, 119, 147, 191 • GEC, *Baronetage*

Archives U. Aberdeen L., corresp. with Alexander Anderson Seton

Settle, Elkanah (1648–1724), playwright, was born on 1 February 1648 at Dunstable in Hertfordshire, the eldest of five children of Josias Settle (*d.* 1666), a barber and innkeeper, and his wife, Sarah.

Education and early works Settle was educated in the Dunstable area, and then at Westminster School, where he was a king's scholar. His education seems to have been financed by his uncle, also called Elkanah Settle, who later left him his estate. In 1666 Settle's first published work appeared, a patriotic poem on the Second Anglo-Dutch War, entitled *Mare clausum, or, A Ransack for the Dutch*. In the same year he left Westminster for Trinity College, Oxford, from where he matriculated on 13 July 1666. Shortly after he arrived in Oxford he began writing his first play, a heroic tragedy called *Cambyses*, on which he may have collaborated with a fellow undergraduate, William Butler Fyfe. The play was completed by December 1666, and was then accepted and performed by the Duke's Company managed by William Davenant, at its theatre in Lincoln's Inn Fields. It was a success, running for six days with a full house and earning Settle the patronage of Anne, duchess of Buccleuch and Monmouth, to whom the published version was subsequently dedicated.

***The Empress of Morocco* and the feud with Dryden** By the spring of 1667 Settle had left Oxford, without finishing his degree, and moved to London, where he became acquainted with the earl of Norwich, the earl of Rochester, and the earl of Mulgrave, probably through the influence of the duchess of Buccleuch and Monmouth. Within two years he had written another two plays, *The Conquest of China* and *The Empress of Morocco*, and a poem on the fire of London. *The Conquest of China* was not a great success, but *The Empress of Morocco* was enthusiastically received, and marked both the high point of Settle's literary career and the source of his literary feud with John Dryden. The play, a heroic tragedy in rhyming couplets, was selected for presentation at the court in Whitehall, where it was performed several times, to great admiration, in late 1672 or early 1673. In this amateur production the characters were played by courtiers, and both the earl of Mulgrave and the earl of Rochester contributed prologues for the performances, which were spoken by Lady Elizabeth Howard. At this time Settle held a post at court, having been appointed steward in 1672, probably through the influence of Rochester and Mulgrave. The court performances of *The Empress of Morocco* were followed on 3 July 1673 by the play's first public performance, by the Duke's Company, at Dorset Garden, where it was said to have run for a whole month. The play capitalized on the current fashion for bombastic rhymed drama set in exotic locations, and it was plotted around conflicts of love and honour in the royal house of Morocco. One of the chief attractions of the tragedy was undoubtedly its spectacular staging, and its elaborate palace scenes, fleets of ships, imprisoned princesses, and violent assassinations. The new playhouse at Dorset Garden was well suited to such a performance, having been recently equipped with the latest stage machinery and scenery. The King's Company, unable to compete with the visual splendour of the production, responded in December 1673 with *The Empress of Morocco: a Farce*, a burlesque of Settle's tragedy by Thomas Duffett.

The Empress of Morocco was published in 1673, advertising Settle on its title-page as 'Servant to his Majesty'. The play was accompanied by an epistle dedicatory to the earl of Norwich, the prologues by Rochester and Mulgrave, and six engravings. It was this prestigious edition of the play that seems to have riled Settle's older contemporary John Dryden, who joined forces in 1674 with Thomas Shadwell and John Crowne to mount an attack on Settle and his work, entitled *Notes and Observations on 'The Empress of Morocco'*. The group as a whole seems to have been motivated by jealousy of the young playwright's position at the court, and Dryden in particular was angered by Settle's references in the dedication to the laureate's attempts to gain patronage from the court wits with his latest play, *The Assignation* (1673). The collaborative *Notes and Observations* took the form of a lengthy critique of Settle's tragedy, which attacked the author for his low birth and lack of learning, parodied the bombast of the play, and questioned its elevated poetic language. Settle responded in the same year with his own *Notes and Observations on 'The Empress of Morocco' Revised* in which he defended his use of simile and metaphor, and applied the charges of bombast and high-flown language to Dryden's own recent heroic tragedy, *The Conquest of Granada*. It was during this controversy that Settle married Mary Warner, on 28 February 1674, in the parish church of St Andrew, Holborn. His wife seems to have died not long afterwards, and left no children.

Drama and politics, 1676–1688 Following the success of *The Empress of Morocco*, Settle put on a series of plays, including the early *Conquest of China* and an adaptation of William Heminge's tragedy *The Fatal Contract* (1653), which was renamed *Love and Revenge*. But he was no longer the court favourite, as he acknowledged in the prologue to the later, and more successful, heroic drama *Ibrahim*, produced in 1676:

> Applause is grown a strange Coy Mrs. Now;
> Courted by All, and yet obtained by few.
> (prologue)

Ibrahim was a dramatization of Madeleine de Scudery's *Ibrahim, or, The Illustrious Bassa*, which had been translated by Henry Cogan in 1652. It was followed in the same year by another romance adaptation, *Pastor fido, or, The Faithful Shepherd*, a play based on Richard Fanshawe's 1648 translation of Battista Guarini's pastoral *Il pastor fido*. Although Settle's play was again written in rhymed heroic verse, its epilogue announced its author's intention to abandon drama in rhyme, and in 1680 Settle's first venture in blank verse appeared, a tragedy called *Fatal Love, or, The Forced Inconstancy*, which was based on Achilles Tatius's Greek romance *Leucippe and Clitiphon*. With its anti-Catholic satire on priests and nuns, *Fatal Love* also marked the beginnings of the playwright's engagement with the politics of the exclusion crisis.

Between 1679 and 1683 Settle devoted much of his energy to political propaganda, writing on behalf of the whig exclusionists. In addition to producing pamphlets and satires, he seems to have been engaged by the earl of Shaftesbury, on behalf of the emergent whig party, to devise and manage the performance of the whigs' popular anti-Catholic pope-burning pageants in the City of London. The pageant that he created in 1680 was said to have been the most lavish on record, costing £1000 to produce. In the same year Settle also wrote his virulently anti-Catholic play *The Female Prelate*, an attack on the hypocrisy and licentiousness of the Roman church, which was acted at the Theatre Royal in the autumn of 1680 and published almost immediately afterwards, with a dedication to the earl of Shaftesbury. During the same period, just before the third Exclusion Parliament of March 1681, Settle also wrote, possibly commissioned by Shaftesbury, a pamphlet entitled *The Character of a Popish Successour, and what England may Expect from Such A One*. In it the playwright attempted to influence the outcome of the forthcoming parliament by demonstrating the need for legislation to avoid a Catholic succession, and he charged James, duke of York, with trying to alienate the affections of the English people from their king. The *Character* provoked a number of replies from tory propagandists, to which Settle in turn responded later in 1681 with *A Vindication of 'The Character of a Popish Successor'*.

Having established himself as a defender of whig arguments, Settle then went on to write a reply to John Dryden's attack on the whigs in his mock-biblical satire *Absalom and Achitophel*. Settle's answer to the poem, entitled *Absalom Senior, or, Achitophel Transpros'd*, appeared anonymously in April 1682. It began with a lengthy attack on the pope, and then went on to satirize the duke of York as Absalom and the marquess of Halifax as Achitophel, and to eulogize the earl of Shaftesbury and the duke of Monmouth as Barzillai and Ithream. The poem ended with an ironic prophecy on the glories of James's future reign. Settle's commitment to the whigs also involved him in another literary feud at this time, with the playwright Thomas Otway. In his poem *The Poet's Complaint of his Muse* (1680) Otway had satirized Rochester, Settle, and Shadwell, and Settle is said subsequently to have challenged Otway to a duel.

Changes in political allegiance, 1682–1689 Settle had consistently aligned himself with the whigs up until 1682. However, the earl of Shaftesbury's departure for the Netherlands, and the effective defeat of the exclusionist agenda at the end of 1682, brought about a shift in his political allegiances, and he began to write tory propaganda. In 1683 he published a pamphlet entitled *A Narrative*, in which he offered a series of explanations for his recantation. In the same piece he also exonerated the duke of York from any involvement in the plot, and attacked Titus Oates's *Narrative of the Popish Plot*, demonstrating that Oates's evidence was flawed and contradictory. Although Settle's political conversion was met with ridicule and scepticism by many of his contemporaries, he went on to publish a series of tory works, including *A Panegyrick on the Loyal and Honourable Sir George Jefferies* (1683), *Animadversions on the Last Speech and Confession of the Late William, Lord Russell* (also 1683), and *An Heroick Poem on the Coronation of James II* (1685). He also entered James's army on Hounslow Heath, where he is unlikely to have seen any active service, and during 1688 he took over the editing of the pro-government publication, *Pacquet of Advice from Rome*, formerly edited by Henry Care. He continued his support of James II right up until the invasion of William of Orange, publishing an attack on the Dutch, entitled *Insignia Bataviae, or, The Dutch Trophies Display'd*, in 1688. However, again he was supporting a losing side, and following the accession of William and Mary he changed allegiances, and published the Williamite Pindaric ode *A View of the Times, with Britain's Address to the Prince of Orange* in 1689.

Drama and poetry, 1688–1718 Settle's first major work after the revolution was a tragedy, *Distress'd Innocence, or, The Princess of Persia* (1691), on which he collaborated with Thomas Betterton and William Mountfort. In the preface to the play he declared his intention to leave political engagement for drama, and he went on to write a series of works that capitalized on the contemporary vogue for opera and semi-opera. In 1692 he produced *The Fairy Queen: an Opera*, based on Shakespeare's *A Midsummer Night's Dream* and set to music by Henry Purcell, which was performed at the Queen's Theatre, where it met with an enthusiastic response. It was followed in 1695 by *Philaster, or, Love Lies Bleeding*, an adaptation of the tragicomedy *Philaster* by Beaumont and Fletcher (published 1620). In 1697 he presented a comedy-opera, *The World in the Moon*, again complete with elaborate singing and dancing scenes, which was published with a dedication claiming that it was the most elaborate dramatic production ever performed on the English stage. In 1701 there was another highly extravagant visual display, in Settle's tragic opera *The Virgin Prophetess, or, The Fate of Troy*, a play set during the siege of Troy, which centred on the figure of Cassandra, and maximized its location with a series of spectacular scenes involving prospects of Troy in flames, and Helen leaping into the fire from the top of a turret. Following this opera Settle produced *The City-Ramble, or, A Play-House Wedding* in 1711, a comedy in blank verse and prose, which combined elements of two plays by Beaumont and Fletcher, *The Knight of the Burning Pestle* and *The Coxcomb*. However, he seems to have abandoned operatic drama until 1718, when he produced *The Lady's Triumph*, a domestic comedy centring on an intrigue between the young bride of an old alderman and her suitor.

At the same time as writing these works for the stage, in 1691 Settle took up a position as city poet, following the death of the previous incumbent, Matthew Taubman. His role in this capacity was to devise the annual pageants for the lord mayor's show, a task for which he was well qualified both through his experience in producing spectacular effects in the theatre, and in co-ordinating the pope-burning pageants of the exclusion crisis. It is uncertain for how long he held the post: he produced pageants in 1691–5, 1698–1702, and 1708, and though he wrote no pageants after 1708, he continued to be referred to as 'city poet' by contemporaries. He was also involved in the popular entertainments at Bartholomew fair. Printed attacks on Settle from 1683 onwards had associated him with the fair, but his first recorded presentation for the venue was *The Siege of Troy*, an adaptation of his earlier play *The Virgin Prophetess* (1701). It was performed at Bartholomew fair in 1707 and at Southwark fair in 1715 and 1716, and the preface to later editions of the play asserts that Settle was employed by the show-woman Mrs Mynn during this time. He is also said to have acted at Mrs Mynn's booth at Bartholomew fair, reputedly dressing up in a costume of green leather to play the dragon in a droll entitled 'St George for England', a performance which earned him the mockery of many of his adversaries.

In addition to these popular spectacles, from 1699 up until the time of his death, Settle produced an increasing number of commendatory poems. Most of them were written in rhymed heroic verse, and some reworked similar lines for a range of occasions. Many of the poems were funeral and marriage tributes, while others addressed contemporary affairs of state. Settle's verse was directed to both ends of the political spectrum, and his choice of subject matter does not seem to have been governed by any particular political allegiance. Thus under Anne's reign he both celebrated the future Hanoverian succession in *Eusebia triumphans* (1702), and then in 1706 contributed to the tory outpouring on the Anglican 'Church in danger' campaign with a poem entitled *Fears and Dangers, Fairly Display'd*.

In 1718 Settle entered the Charterhouse, where he continued to write panegyrics, and is also said to have been working on a tragedy entitled 'The Expulsion of the Danes'. However, the play, which has now been lost, did not appear on the stage, owing to its author's death, at the Charterhouse, on 12 February 1724. The whereabouts of Settle's will and place of burial are not known. The notice of his death, which appeared in the *True Briton* on 19 February 1724, describes the poet's appearance as a man 'of tall stature, red face, short black hair'.

Reputation Elkanah Settle's literary reputation has been dominated by his contemporary opponents' attacks on him. In the second part of *Absalom and Achitophel* (1682) Dryden described his writing as:

> free from all meaning, whether good or bad,
> And, in one word, heroically mad.
> (ll. 416–17)

while in Alexander Pope's *Dunciad* he is satirized for his changes of political allegiance and for his performance in costume at Bartholomew fair, 'reduc'd at last to hiss in my own dragon' (A. Pope, *The Dunciad*, 1743, 3.286). Yet although these writers have presented an influential image of the writer as a talentless hack, it is clear that much of Settle's drama was very popular in its own time, as the quarrel with Dryden over the success of *The Empress of Morocco* reveals. Settle was undoubtedly a central figure in the Restoration theatre, his talent for producing spectacular and elaborately staged plays being particularly well suited to the contemporary vogue for heroic and operatic drama. ABIGAIL WILLIAMS

Sources F. C. Brown, *Elkanah Settle: his life and works* (1910) [incl. comprehensive bibliography] · E. G. Fletcher, 'Bibliography of Elkanah Settle', *N&Q*, 164 (1933), 114 · M. E. Novack, ed., *'The empress of Morocco' and its critics: Settle, Dryden, Shadwell, Crowne, Duffet* (1968) · A. T. Doyle, ed., *Elkanah Settle's 'The empress of Morocco' and the controversy surrounding it: a critical edition* (1987) · E. Boswell, *The Restoration court stage (1660–1702): with a particular account of the production of 'Calisto'* (1932) · T. P. Haviland, 'Elkanah Settle and the least heroic romance', *Modern Language Quarterly* (June 1954), 118–24 · R. J. Ham, 'Otway's duels with Churchill and Settle', *Modern Language Notes*, 41 (1926), 73–89 · M. E. Novak, 'Elkanah Settle's attacks on Thomas Shadwell and the authorship of the *Operatic tempest*', *N&Q*, 213 (1968), 263–5 · *DNB*

Archives BL, Add. MSS 61360, 4253 · Bodl. Oxf., Eng. MS Poet. E.4 · Christ Church Oxf. · GL, Settle 1, 42a | BL, Sloane MS 4060 · Bodl. Oxf., Montagu MS d.1 · Trinity Cam., Rothschild Library catalogue no. 1825

Settle, Thomas (1555–1622), Church of England clergyman and separatist, was born to unknown parents. Nothing is known of his early life before he matriculated as a pensioner from Queens' College, Cambridge, at Michaelmas 1575. He left Cambridge about 1579 without a degree. On 1 March 1580 Edmund Freake, bishop of Norwich, ordained him to the ministry and instituted him rector of Westfield, Norfolk. He resigned Westfield on 7 October 1585. Even before that time, he seems to have been serving as curate to Robert Waller, vicar of Mildenhall, Suffolk. Mildenhall soon felt the force of Settle's godly zeal. To supplement his preaching and teaching he prepared *A Catechisme* [1587] for the inhabitants, and annexed to it 'A fardle of Christian duties'.

In 1584, however, Settle demonstrated his discontent with Archbishop Whitgift's religious policy. He signed a petition refusing subscription to the three articles, Whitgift's shibboleth of conformity, and began holding night-time conventicles in Mildenhall. Such activities did not go unnoticed. According to depositions taken on 22 April 1585 Waller and others accused Settle of not following the prayer book, and Settle stated that he disliked 'the order of the government of the church'. Furthermore, he characterized Archbishop Whitgift as 'a very enemy to the church and a Tirant and worse than ever [Bishop] Bonner was' (Lambeth Palace Library, carte antique et miscellanee XII, item 19, fols. 2*r* and 3*r*).

During part of 1585 and early 1586 Settle evidently preached at Boxted, Suffolk. Then, in May 1586, he was summoned before Archbishop Whitgift. According to Settle's account, this interview was a stormy one. The archbishop accused him of several irregularities, such as failing to use the ring in marriage and the sign of the cross in baptism. Settle replied that he taught nothing but what was in the word of God and the best theologians. He also refused to sign the three articles. Enraged, Whitgift ordered that he be imprisoned in the Gatehouse.

Settle next attracted the attention of George Carleton, a prominent Northamptonshire MP and puritan activist. After his release from gaol Settle went to Northamptonshire. There he became deeply involved in the presbyterian classis movement, and served as a delegate to its general conference in London during February 1589. His Northamptonshire sojourn ended in April 1589, when the privy council summoned both him and Carleton to appear as part of its Martin Marprelate investigation. By January 1590 Settle was once again confined in the Gatehouse.

The collapse of the classis movement led Settle to espouse more radical opinions. By April 1590 he had stopped taking communion with the established church, and by April 1592 he had become a full-fledged separatist. Later, in September, he became a charter member of the newly organized London separatist congregation which had Francis Johnson as its pastor, and helped officiate at several of the congregation's illegal services. He was again arrested, imprisoned, and examined by the authorities in late 1592 and early 1593. A transcript of his 6 April 1593 interrogation shows him still defiant.

However, quarrels among the separatists soon undermined Settle's zeal. Chief among these was the contention that broke out in early 1594 between Francis Johnson and his brother George over Francis's wife's dress and deportment. Settle at first opposed Francis, but later, because of Francis's subtle reasoning, he became confused and despondent. Eventually Settle agreed to conform. He was released from prison and travelled to Norfolk, where on 10 March 1596 he was licensed to preach and administer the sacraments at Barningham Winter and Matlaske. He was instituted to the livings of Barningham Winter and Matlaske on 2 May and 20 May 1601 respectively. A record of Settle's subscription to the three articles, dated 1 October 1600, survives at Lambeth Palace.

Settle relinquished Barningham Winter on 3 November 1614, but retained Matlaske. He was buried there on 13 December 1622. References to a 'Mrs. Settle' from the early 1590s suggest that he was married, but conclusive evidence is lacking. MICHAEL E. MOODY

Sources institution book of Bishop Freke, Norfolk RO, REG 14/20, fol. 46*r* · Rymer, *Foedera*, 2nd edn, 15.788 · institution book of Bishop Scambler, Norfolk RO, REG 14/20, fol. 129*v* · depositions, carte antique et miscellanee, XII, LPL, item 19, fols. 1*r*–3*v* · A. Peel, ed., *The seconde parte of a register*, 2 vols. (1915), vol. 1, p. 244; vol. 2, pp. 38–9, 262 · [T. Settle], *A catechisme* [1587] · *APC*, 1589, 131 · P. Collinson, 'Carleton, George (1529–90)', HoP, *Commons*, 1558–1603, 1.552–4 · *The writings of John Greenwood and Henry Barrow, 1591–1593*, ed. L. H. Carlson (1970), 299, 307, 364–5 · G. Johnson, *A discourse of some troubles and excommunications in the banished English church at Amsterdam* (1603), 98–101 · bishop of Norwich act books, 10 March 1596, Norfolk RO, ACT 31/34d · *The Registrum vagum of Anthony Harison*, ed. T. F. Barton, 1, Norfolk RS, 32 (1963), 212 · three articles subscription lists, carte antique et miscellanee, XIII, LPL, item 61, membrane xiv · parish registers, Matlaske, Norfolk RO, PD 229/2 · J. Craig, *Reformation, politics and polemics: the growth of protestantism in East Anglian market towns, 1500–1610* (2001), 56–8, 107–9 · Tanner's index to the bishop of Norwich's institution books, Suffolk RO, Bury St Edmunds, microfilm J510/1, J510/2, under 'Barningham Winter'

Seumas a'Ghlinne. *See* Stewart, James, of the Glen (*b.* before 1700, *d.* 1752).

Sevenoak [Sevenoke], **William** (*d.* in or after **1432**), merchant and mayor of London, was the son, or foster son, of William Rumschedde of Sevenoaks in Kent. There is no evidence to substantiate the legend that Rumschedde rescued him from abandonment in infancy. It was not unusual for London apprentices to assume the name of their birthplace, and the legend seems to have grown up from Sevenoak's own concern for the poor of his native town. He became a freeman of London in 1394 after an apprenticeship to an ironmonger, but he was readmitted to citizenship as a grocer in 1397, almost certainly under pressure from the Grocers' Company because he was engaged in their trade. He paid the substantial fine of £10 to join the Grocers' livery, and this fact, combined with his remarkably swift commercial rise in a difficult period for trade, must mean that he was well endowed with capital. By 1401 he was advancing credit of £100 to a grocer, and three years later he owned a ship which attacked Prussian ships between England and Zeeland. His foreign trade was diverse and included shipments of cloth, wool, and salt to Flanders and Zeeland and imports of wine in return. In 1409 he transported wheat from Yorkshire to relieve the dearth in London, and he also invested widely in London property, including a quay by the Tower of London. Although he advanced £100 in 1417—one of the highest contributions—towards Henry V's second expedition to France, he generally avoided government finance.

Sevenoak was warden of the Grocers' Company in 1404–5 and gave £26 13*s*. 4*d*. towards the building of its hall. After serving as a warden of London Bridge in 1404, he was elected alderman in 1411, sheriff in 1412, and a member of the Commons for London in 1417. In that decade of economic distress his responsibility for collecting the taxes of his ward may well explain the outburst of a fellow grocer, Thomas Mayneld, who threatened Sevenoak with hanging if he did not 'conduct himself well and honestly' (Sharpe, *Calendar of Letter-Books*, I, 132). When Mayneld was sentenced for his behaviour Sevenoak successfully interceded with the mayor for him, but there was a rigorous side to his character: when he was mayor himself in 1418 he tried to suppress Christmas mummings in London. However his piety and integrity are evident from the permission he obtained to use a portable altar, and from his appointment as a trustee of Whittington's charity. In his own wills were many bequests to churches, chantries, and the poor, and he provided for the foundation of almshouses and a grammar school in Sevenoaks. There is no mention in his wills of a wife or children. He died in or after July 1432 and may have been buried at St Martin Ludgate, London. PAMELA NIGHTINGALE

Sources R. R. Sharpe, ed., *Calendar of letter-books preserved in the archives of the corporation of the City of London*, [12 vols.] (1899–1912), vol. H–I • R. R. Sharpe, ed., *Calendar of wills proved and enrolled in the court of husting, London, AD 1258 – AD 1688*, 2 (1890) • J. A. Kingdon, ed., *Facsimile of first volume of MS archives of the Worshipful Company of Grocers of the city of London, AD 1345–1463* (1883) • *CClR, 1399–1429* • *CPR, 1401–5, 1422–9, 1429–36* • CLRO, Husting rolls • J. Stow, *A survay of London*, rev. edn (1603); repr. with introduction by C. L. Kingsford as *A survey of London*, 2 vols. (1908); repr. with addns (1971) • Chancery, certificates of statute merchant and statute staple, PRO, C 241/192/105

Sever, Henry (*d.* **1471**), college head, came from the diocese of Winchester, but his family background is obscure. First recorded in 1419, when he entered Merton as founder's kin, he was successively a bachelor fellow (admitted *c*.1420) and fellow (1423–37). He had graduated BA by 1422; he subsequently became a master of arts and was awarded a doctorate in theology before 1438. In the meantime he had been ordained deacon and priest in 1430, and subsequently entered the service of the crown, being appointed a chaplain to the king in 1437. Two years earlier, on 12 May 1435, he had become a canon of the collegiate church of St Mary Magdalene at Bridgnorth, Shropshire, which was a royal peculiar, and he later held a number of other important benefices, many of them as the result of royal patronage; these included a canonry in St Stephen's Chapel, Westminster, a prebend in St Paul's, London, where he eventually became chancellor, the deanery of Bridgnorth, and the wardenship of the king's free chapel in Tickhill Castle, Yorkshire.

Sever plainly stood high in the king's favour, for on 11 October 1440, in his charter of incorporation, Henry VI appointed him to be the first provost of the new royal foundation of Eton College, a post he held until 1442. He may have left the king's service in some disfavour, however, for in the following year Oxford University, whose chancellor he had become about October 1442, asked Pope Eugenius IV (*r*. 1431–47) to write to Henry VI in terms that would advance Sever in the king's favour. The appeal may have been effective, for by 1448 Sever had become the king's almoner, a post he still held in 1454—when the king's stables were reduced in that year, Sever was given fifteen of the king's horses.

Sever had been an unsuccessful candidate for the wardenship of Merton College in 1437, but he was elected to this position on 19 February 1456. His learned theological disputations were highly regarded by his Oxford contemporaries. He acted for the university to receive donations, especially books, for the library founded by Humphrey, duke of Gloucester (*d*. 1447), and he himself built up a substantial working theological library, which between 1466 and 1468 he presented to Merton College. His gifts to the college have led to some authors describing Sever as Merton's 'second founder', though building works on the Holywell tower and warden's lodgings attributed to him would appear to have been completed before and after his wardenship respectively. He died on 6 July 1471 in Oxford and was buried in the choir of Merton College chapel before the warden's stall; the monumental brass depicting him has since been moved to the south side of the chapel. Sever's will, dated 4 July 1471, was proved on 27 July. His bequests to Merton included a moiety of a tenement in Fleet Street, London, a house in West Tilbury, Essex, and a silver jug with six goblets. VIRGINIA DAVIS

Sources Emden, *Oxf.* • [J. Raine], ed., *Testamenta Eboracensia*, 3, SurtS, 45 (1865) • H. C. Maxwell Lyte, *A history of Eton College, 1440–1898*, 3rd edn (1899) • *Memorials of the reign of Henry VI: official correspondence of Thomas Bekynton, secretary to King Henry VI and bishop of Bath and Wells*, ed. G. Williams, 2 vols., Rolls Series, 56 (1872) • H. Anstey, ed., *Epistolae academicae Oxon.*, 2 vols., OHS, 35–6 (1898) • P. S. Allen and H. W. Garrod, eds., *Merton muniments*, OHS, 86 (1928) • A. T. Bannister, ed., *Registrum Thome Spofford … AD MCCCCXXII–MCCCCXLVIII*, CYS, 23 (1919) • *CPR* • *CClR* • *CEPR letters* • H. E. Salter, ed., *Registrum cancellarii Oxoniensis, 1434–1469*, 2 vols., OHS, 93–4 (1932) • B. Wolffe, *Henry VI* (1981)

Likenesses brass effigy, Merton Oxf.

Wealth at death property and personal goods: will, Raine, ed., *Testamenta*

Sever [Senhouse], **William** (*d.* **1505**), bishop of Durham, was born at Shincliffe, near Durham, but was probably a member of the Cumbrian family of Senhouse of Seascale; Sever was one of a number of contemporary variants of that family name. Ordained subdeacon on 11 March 1468 he became a monk of the Benedictine abbey of St Mary, York, and it may have been from there (so it was later claimed) that he went to study in Oxford—at either Gloucester or Durham College (both were Benedictine establishments). Elected abbot of St Mary's in April 1485, he was a leading subordinate of Thomas Howard, earl of Surrey, the king's lieutenant north of the Trent, who presided over a council that governed Yorkshire much as

Richard III's council had done. From 1486 Sever was justice of the Forest of Galtres, and JP in each of the three Yorkshire ridings. Letters in the *Plumpton Correspondence* show him receiving bills of complaint, examining witnesses, and advising arbitration, while in 1493 he and Sir Richard Cholmley settled a dispute between the weavers and cordwainers of York, disregarding the liberties of the city in the process.

On 4 September 1495 Sever was provided to the see of Carlisle; the temporalities were restored on 11 December, and he was consecrated in 1496. His immediate predecessor at Carlisle, Richard Bell, had also been a monk before becoming a bishop; but whereas Bell, who had previously been prior of Durham, failed in his efforts to hold the priorate *in commendam*, Sever was able to remain abbot of St Mary's. Almost nothing is known of his episcopate, since his register does not survive, though he once arbitrated in a dispute involving one of his kinsmen. But in May 1496 he served on a commission appointed (unsuccessfully, at this time) to arrange for the marriage of the king's daughter Margaret with James IV, king of Scots, and for a treaty between the two realms, while in 1499 he was made a conservator of the Anglo-Scottish truce. In the latter year he came to play an important role in the extension of royal authority into northern England, being given special authority in the north in matters pertaining to the king's prerogative; appointed to be receiver and surveyor of wardships, marriages, and other rights belonging to the crown, he was expressly charged with the discovery of concealments. In this position Sever set a precedent for the establishment in 1508 of the office of surveyor of the king's prerogative.

On 27 June 1502 Sever was translated to the far wealthier see of Durham; the temporalities were restored on 15 October, and he now resigned his abbacy of St Mary's. As bishop of Durham he continued to work in the king's interest—in a letter to Sir Reginald Bray, dated 7 December 1502, he reports a dispute over a woman (perhaps a wardship), and promises to tell Bray 'what I mean herein for the king's advantage' (Pollard, 390–91). He died on an unknown day in 1505, and was buried in St Mary's Abbey at York. JONATHAN HUGHES

Sources C. M. L. Bouch, *Prelates and people of the lake counties: a history of the diocese of Carlisle, 1133–1933* (1948) • W. C. Richardson, 'The surveyor of the king's prerogative', *EngHR*, 56 (1941), 52–75 • R. R. Reid, *The king's council in the north* (1921); facs. edn (1975) • Emden, *Oxf.*, 3.1669 • S. B. Chrimes, *Henry VII* (1972) • A. J. Pollard, *North-eastern England during the Wars of the Roses: lay society, war and politics, 1450–1500* (1990) • T. Stapleton, ed., *Plumpton correspondence*, CS, 4 (1839)

Severn, Joseph (1793–1879), painter, was born on 7 December 1793 at Hoxton, the eldest of the six children of James Severn, a musician whose family originally settled on the banks of the Severn River in Gloucestershire, and his wife, whose maiden name was Littel, and whose family were descended from Huguenots. Severn's parents were a study in contrast: his mother, whom Severn idolized all through his life, often calling her his 'angel mother' (Birkenhead, 2), had an even disposition, while his father was often irascible and demanding. His quick temper notwithstanding, it was reportedly his father who discovered and encouraged in his eldest and favourite son a talent for pictorial art after seeing a profile of himself drawn by the precocious five-year-old. When Joseph turned fourteen his father, in order to encourage further his talent and bolster his professional prospects, had him apprenticed to William Bond, an engraver who offered favourable terms for the apprenticeship. Although initially delighted with the prospect, when it became apparent to the novice that he was no longer progressing in his knowledge or artistic technique, Joseph became bored and resentful towards his master. Much to the consternation of his father, who argued for the worthiness of the engraver's profession, the maturing young Severn often complained bitterly about his situation and often threatened to quit. As Severn was nearing his majority, Bond, fearing the defection of his able apprentice, relented and allowed him more personal time. Severn enrolled in evening art classes at the Royal Academy Schools in 1813, where he later studied under Fuseli. Severn threw himself into his studies of art and literature and painted miniature portraits on the side for small commissions.

Joseph Severn (1793–1879), self-portrait, *c*.1820

Friendship with Keats It was towards the end of his bondage to Bond—no later than the late summer or early autumn of 1816—that Severn was introduced to Keats, probably by William Haslam. Severn was welcomed into the Keats circle, attended the 'immortal dinner' at Benjamin Robert Haydon's in 1817, and in 1818 painted portraits of all three of the Keats brothers, as well as of Haslam and John Hamilton Reynolds. He was especially drawn to Keats and, though somewhat shy about it, and feeling his inferior, often sought his company. Keats encouraged Severn in his oil painting 'The Cave of Despair', which depicted a scene from Spenser's *Faerie Queene* (book 1, canto 10). This was just his second attempt in the medium of oils, but Severn intended to enter the picture in the Royal Academy's student competition for the gold medal in painting, a prize that had not been awarded for over a decade because the submissions were poor. Though hampered in his efforts by miserable lodgings, and otherwise occupied with the miniatures he painted for money, Severn laboured long and hard and finally submitted his painting on 31 October 1819. To the astonishment of everyone, including himself, Severn won the prize on 10 December 1819. Besides the gold medal, the award brought with it not only excellent publicity in Severn's case for his budding business in miniatures but also entitlement to compete for the coveted travelling scholarship. But Severn's next decision, a momentous one, was to throw all of this into jeopardy—or so it seemed.

Severn had consoled Keats when he found out in the autumn of 1818 that Keats's brother Tom was dying of consumption (tuberculosis) and even offered to relieve Keats at Tom's bedside. After Tom's death on 1 December 1818, Severn and Keats spent more time together when Keats was in London. Keats's *annus mirabilis* (beginning in autumn 1818) was also something of a breakthrough year for Severn. But in 1820 things took a turn for the worse. Severn's winning the Royal Academy prize not only brought no new commissions but also aroused such intense jealousy from his fellow students at the academy that Severn discontinued his art classes there. Then, in February 1820, Keats, whose health had been indifferent for some time, discovered the unmistakable sign of his having contracted tuberculosis. He resolved, on doctor's advice, to go to Italy in hopes of convalescing in the favourable climate. The only problem was, as Haslam explained to Severn, that no one could be found to go with Keats. George Keats was in America, Charles Brown was on a walking tour and could not be contacted, and everyone else, including Haslam, whose wife was pregnant, had other obligations. When, on 12 September 1820, Haslam asked Severn if he would go, Severn impulsively agreed to accompany Keats and hurriedly made arrangements to depart on the *Maria Crowther* bound for Italy on 17 September. After hearing of his son's decision, Severn's father was so enraged that he knocked Joseph to the ground and attempted to bar him from leaving. Severn persisted in his resolution to accompany his friend, however, and it is solely from him, as a result, that there exists an account of Keats's last days. (It must be noted, though, that Severn was a notoriously unreliable source; the three separate 'reminiscences' that he wrote over the course of his life, as well as diary entries, letters, and testimonials related in the 1840s to Monckton Milnes, Keats's biographer, are often inconsistent and even contradictory.)

The passage to Italy on the small *Maria Crowther* was a trying one for the young men, as they had to endure five weeks of cramped quarters, poor provisions, a fellow passenger apparently dying of consumption, and stormy weather before they finally arrived on 21 October at the Bay of Naples, where they were forced to undergo a further debilitating ten-day quarantine. The pair left for Rome on 8 November and took up residence at 26 piazza di Spagna (now the Keats–Shelley House). The English physician Dr James Clark, whose services had been requested by Taylor and Hessey, Keats's publishers, had arranged for the rooms for the young men. It was there that Keats, faithfully attended by Severn, lived out the one hundred days remaining to him.

Once in Rome, Keats began to feel a little better and encouraged Severn to take advantage of the respite by availing himself of the city's magnificent artworks, which Severn did with great relish. He also began to work on his entry for the academy's travelling scholarship. The terms of entry included that the work had to be on a historical subject, and so Severn decided to paint 'The Death of Alcibiades'. But Keats had another relapse in mid-December and Severn was forced to abandon his painting and attend to him day and night. Keats had another period of better health at the end of the year and into January, so that Severn actually wrote to Mrs Brawne in a letter postmarked 11 January 1821 that he hoped that Keats would be able to come back to England with him that spring. But that was wishful thinking, for it was also on this date that Severn made his famous deathbed sketch of Keats, and it became apparent within a few days' time that Keats was not going to recover. Severn's accounts of Keats's final days emphasize the great suffering of his friend until the very end was imminent, at which point, avers Severn, Keats seemed to find peace. Keats died in Severn's arms on 23 February 1821. James Clark saw to most of the details of Keats's funeral and burial in the protestant cemetery because Severn was too exhausted from his ordeal of helping Keats into 'easeful Death'. It was another two years before Severn had erected at his own expense Keats's headstone with the famous epitaph that Keats had requested him to have inscribed: 'Here lies one whose name was writ in water'. Severn meant to honour Keats's dying wish with respect to his epitaph, but unfortunately, in consultation with Brown, he ended up diluting the sublime simplicity of this statement with a clumsy explanatory preamble meant to soften its intended cynicism.

While modern opinion is divided as to the purity of Severn's motives in accompanying Keats to Rome, Severn's contemporaries seemed convinced of his overall altruism in the matter, and Victorian sentiment inclined in this direction as well. Despite their argument about Christianity at Leigh Hunt's early in 1818, Shelley (whose funeral about a year and a half after Keats's Severn also attended) bestowed the highest praise on Severn in the preface to *Adonais* (1821), concluding his notice of Severn's aid to

Keats with the following: 'His conduct is a golden augury of the success of his future career—may the unextinguished Spirit of his illustrious friend animate the creations of his pencil, and plead against Oblivion for his name'. Some later commentators of a more demythologizing propensity, however, suggest that Severn might have been from the outset more self-interested in accompanying Keats to Rome than he wished to appear to posterity. They suggest that Severn was a social climber who intended to augment his own prestige through his association with Keats as well as to make connections in the flourishing art scene in Rome. While it is true that Severn profited from his friendship with Keats and that he tended to exaggerate his own importance in the chronicle of this period, his faithful devotion to Keats in the last days of the poet's life is not to be doubted, nor is it much sullied by his later efforts at self-promotion.

Artistic career and marriage After Keats's death, Severn, who really had no prospects for income and who had become saddled with paying back the costs of Keats's final illness, including the cost of room furnishings, which authorities had burnt (fearing contagion), moved to less expensive quarters at 18 via di San Isodoro, not too far from the piazza di Spagna. There, still grieving for Keats, he reverted his attention to his painting for the Royal Academy fellowship, the deadline of which was fast approaching. By mid-March a steady stream of well-wishers who had heard of his selfless nursing of Keats began to pay him visits. Thus his association with Keats helped him into artistic and genteel coteries, and since a number of his visitors were in a position to help Severn with commissions for portraits and other work, his professional prospects rose as well.

Severn finished 'The Death of Alcibiades' for all intents and purposes by the end of May 1821, put some finishing touches to it over the next few months, and sent it off to the Royal Academy in August. He experienced no little anxiety as the painting went missing for months, but it was finally discovered to have been mislaid at the Royal Academy itself. Severn, who had no competitors, was duly awarded the travelling pension of £130 p.a. for three years and also received £80 for his travelling expenses to Italy.

In September 1821 Severn, who was rapidly becoming known in English circles in Rome both for his painting and his exuberant and winning personality, was introduced to Lady Westmorland, who became his patroness of sorts. It was through her that Severn met his future wife at the end of 1824. Elizabeth Montgomerie (*d.* 1862), daughter of General Lord Archibald Montgomerie (*d.* 1814), was the ward of Lady Westmorland, but was unhappy in that situation because of Lady Westmorland's tyrannical ways. Anticipating that Lady Westmorland would oppose their union, the two kept their growing intimacy secret from her and revealed their wedding plans only at the last minute. Joseph Severn and Elizabeth Montgomerie were married on 5 October 1828 in Florence, and though she did give the bride away, Lady Westmorland severed all relations with the couple thereafter.

The first three years of marriage were clouded by a fraudulent lawsuit (it was eventually dismissed) that forced Severn to expend rather large sums of money. Although Severn had been industrious over the previous six years and had built up for himself a steady clientele for his pictures, and despite the fact that his wife had an allowance from her half-brother Lord Eglinton, the money just seemed to slip away, and so the couple were forced to delay their return to England. Children also began appearing on the scene. In summer 1829 Claudia, the first of six children, was born, followed by Walter *Severn, Ann Mary [*see* Newton, (Ann) Mary], and Henry Augustus. Although Severn was a highly respected and sought after artist in Rome, the family moved back to England in March 1841, ostensibly for the education of the children. They moved into an accommodating old house at 21 James Street at Buckingham Gate, and in the following August Elizabeth had twins—Arthur and Eleanor. Three of the Severn children (Walter, Arthur, and Ann Mary) became artists, and eventually Ann Mary's reputation as a painter eclipsed her father's.

Severn did not find it as easy to make a living in London. He entered a cartoon competition sponsored by Westminster Hall in 1843, but his was not selected to be one of those executed in fresco. He tried his hand at various other media (including decorative arts and magazine illustrations) and even thought about returning to his trade in miniatures, but they were out of vogue. So he turned to other projects. During the 1840s he helped Monckton Milnes (later Lord Houghton) on his biography of Keats and even tried his own hand at writing. He wrote essays—one on Keats appeared in the *Atlantic Monthly*—short stories, a historical romance, and there is even supposedly a lost novel on Titian using Keats as the model for the artist-protagonist, but writing was not his forte. Although the Severn family managed to get by on Elizabeth's allowance despite the relative scarcity of new commissions of any type, it became apparent that they could no longer afford the house at Buckingham Gate and so they moved to a more affordable house off Belgrave Road.

British consul at Rome In 1860 Charles Thomas Newton, who married Severn's daughter Ann Mary in 1861, resigned the consulship at Rome, and, probably at his suggestion, Severn applied for the position. Despite being a sprightly sixty-seven, Severn was in legal terms too old for the position, but thanks to the support of William Gladstone, Lord Houghton, John Ruskin, and especially Baron von Bunsen, as well as the concealment as far as possible of his real age, he was elected to the post anyway. He assumed the consulate in 1861; his wife, who was to conclude the family's affairs in London and then follow Joseph to Rome, died in transit, at Marseilles, in April 1862.

Despite the death of his wife, Severn was once again in his element in Rome. He revisited the grave of his poet friend and wrote that he was flooded with bittersweet memories every time he walked the steps of the piazza di Spagna. In his post as British consul he became something of a crusader against papal injustices, and despite his sometimes overestimating his own importance and straying into matters better left to ambassadorial compass, his overall goodwill often had a salutary effect in mediations on behalf of both English and Italians who had run afoul of papal law. Although Odo Russell, the unofficial British minister to the Vatican, characterized Severn soon after his arrival at Rome as a 'good natured goose, utterly unfit and unqualified for his post', some ten years later he wrote to Lord Granville that 'Patiently listened to, judiciously advised, kindly treated and carefully managed, Severn became a willing, useful and even energetic agent during the ten years we worked together in Rome' (Blakiston, 330). Severn resigned his consulship in 1872, receiving for his troubles a pension of £80 and a further £60 from the civil fund. He continued painting until almost the end of his life, often taking Keatsiana for his subjects, and though his fame as a painter has not stood the test of time, his many depictions of Keats and his circle continue to be widely viewed. In his later years he also planned, but never executed, a folio edition of Shelley's *Adonais*, to be illustrated by himself and his sons Walter and Arthur. He attended the unveiling of the memorial tablet on the Keats House in February 1879, and was there eulogized by Sir Vincent Eyre.

Severn died in Rome of natural causes on 3 August 1879 and was buried the next day in the new protestant cemetery, but at the intercession of Sir Vincent Eyre, Lord Houghton, and others, his remains were exhumed two years later and fittingly reinterred beside those of Keats. Though many were the suggestions submitted for his epitaph (including ones by Rossetti and Tennyson) it was Lord Houghton's that was chosen; the inscription begins, 'To the Memory of Joseph Severn, Devoted Friend and Death-bed Companion of John Keats, Whom He Lived to See Numbered Among the Immortal Poets of England' (Birkenhead, 280). DAVID KALOUSTIAN

Sources W. Sharp, *The life and letters of Joseph Severn* (1892); repr. (New York, 1973) • S. Birkenhead, *Illustrious friends: the story of Joseph Severn and his son Arthur* (1965) • H. E. Rollins, *The Keats circle*, 2nd edn, 2 vols. (Cambridge, Mass., 1965) • W. J. Bate, *John Keats* (Cambridge, Mass., 1963) • A. Ward, *John Keats: the making of a poet*, rev. edn (New York, 1986) • R. Gitting, *John Keats* (1968) • J. Ruskin, *Praeterita* (1990) • N. Blakiston, 'Joseph Severn, consul in Rome, 1861–1871', *History Today*, 18 (May 1968), 329–36, 68 • M. Pointon, 'Keats, Joseph Severn and William Hilton: notes on a dispute', *N&Q*, 218 (1973), 49–54 • C. A. Brown, *Life of John Keats*, ed. D. H. Bodurtha and W. B. Pope (1937) • J. Richardson, *Keats and his circle: an album of portraits* (1980) • W. Sharp, 'The portraits of Keats; with special reference to those painted by Severn', *Century Magazine*, 71/4 (Feb 1906), 535–51 • J. E. Walsh, *Darkling I listen: the last days and death of John Keats* (New York, 1999) • Bryan, *Painters* (1927) • W. H. Bond, L. Morriss, and H. Vendler, *John Keats, 1795–1995, with a catalogue of the Harvard Keats collection* (1995) • Lord Brock [R. Claude, Baron Brock], *John Keats and Joseph Severn: the tragedy of the last illness*, Keats and Shelley Memorial Association (1973) • J. Keats, *The Keats letters, papers and other relics* (1972) • A. Severn, *The professor: Arthur Severn's memoir of John Ruskin* (1967) • A. Lowell, *John Keats*, 2 vols. (Boston and New York, 1925) • R. M. Milnes [Lord Houghton], *Life, letters, and literary remains of John Keats* (New York, 1848) • *Letters of John Keats to Fanny Brawne*, ed. H. B. Forman (1878)

Archives Harvard U., Houghton L., corresp., drawings, and papers • Princeton University, New Jersey | BL, corresp. with W. E. Gladstone, Add. MSS 44356–44527, *passim* • Keats House, Hampstead, London, letters to family members, incl. some relating to paintings at Keats House • PRO, corresp. with Odo Russell, FO 918 • V&A NAL, letters to C. R. Leslie

Likenesses J. Severn, self-portrait, pencil drawing, *c.*1820, NPG [*see illus.*] • S. Kirkup, pencil drawing, 1822, repro. in Sharp, *Life and letters*, title-page • J. Severn, self-portrait, pencil drawing, *c.*1822, repro. in Richardson, *Keats*, 104 • J. Partridge, pencil drawing, 1825, NPG; repro. in Richardson, *Keats*, 104 • photograph, 1872, repro. in Richardson, *Keats*, 106 • J. Severn, self-portrait, oils?, 1876?, repro. in Richardson, *Keats*, 107

Severn, Merlyn (*d.* 1970), photographer, is of unknown origins. She left an autobiographical account of her photographic career, *Double Exposure* (1956), that deliberately omitted all personal details; she constructed an impression of a life that was designed to authenticate her identity as a photographer and an artist. We are invited to judge her only by her work, her attitudes, her career, and her self-perception. Most remarkable is the diversity of her photographic record, which reflects her extraordinary respect for humanity, animals, and nature. She was a pioneering photojournalist in many aspects, but especially in dance photography.

In January 1936, after a brief and unsuccessful career as a sculptor, Severn left Cheltenham to settle in London. She taught herself photography and, with the help of the aesthetic theorist Arnold Haskell, was given the freedom to photograph the dancers of Michel Fokine's Blum Company opening their season at the Alhambra Theatre in June 1936. Later that year she published *Ballet in Action*, the first serious study of choreography and dancing ever produced in Britain. Severn, labelled by Haskell as the first photographic critic of the ballet, not only contributed to the elevation of ballet in Britain as an art form and produced a valuable record of its history but also developed innovative approaches to dance photography. The success of *Ballet in Action* was followed by her equally successful one-person show at the Batsford Gallery in North Audley Street from 9 to 16 July 1937. Six of her photographs from the 'Ballet in action' series were accepted by the London Salon of Photography in 1937.

Severn was not only the first to photograph ballet 'in performance', starting the trend of action dance photographs, but also contributed numerous photographs of ballets and valuable technical photographic advice. Her technical judgement and her ability to capture the suggestion of movement in her photographs were revolutionary in dance photography; all previous photography of dance in Britain remained limited to poses. Severn's technical and stylistic skills enabled her to photograph dancers successfully during the performance, something previously thought impossible due to the difficulties of lighting.

Severn had planned to travel as a freelancer to Java in the East Indies to photograph Javanese dancers but was prevented from doing so because of war. During the Second World War she worked for the WAAF in 'special duties', or 'radar', and later spent a long internment on Guernsey under German occupation. After the war she returned to photographing the ballet, but this time she encountered many bureaucratic difficulties and faced increasing sensitivities towards copyright issues. She published her second book, *Sadler's Wells Ballet at Covent Garden*, in March 1946.

Severn was employed by *Picture Post* from 1945 to 1947 as a full-time staff photographer and continued to freelance for the magazine for the following nine years. Her work exemplifies the diverse contexts in which photography was used in journalism between 1930 and 1960, as well as the artistic techniques and developments of the medium. Her representation of the art of photography and self-presentation reveal her resistance to the prevailing stereotypes of the time. While *Picture Post* employed many freelance women journalists and photographers, Severn was the only one to be a salaried full-time employee. The extensive freedom that she experienced as a woman photojournalist set her apart from many other women working in the field. She was unique in her individuality and resistance to conformity, and often fought against being assigned stories that were thought fit for women to cover. She not only managed to avoid such stereotypical reportage but also often refused stories that she felt had no photographic potential. Her full-time status enabled her to participate in the *Picture Post* tradition of allowing its photojournalists to suggest stories of their own—a custom of which she took full advantage. On average she seems to have contributed four to five stories per year.

Severn's work at *Picture Post* eventually led her to cover a series of successful stories in the Belgian Congo and Ruanda-Urundi. In Africa she worked as a freelancer for *Picture Post*, received a commission from the South African Tourist Corporation to photograph lions, and collaborated with Hugh Tracey on a book, *African Dances of the Witwatersrand Gold Mines*, published by the African Music Society. Her touristic account, *Congo Pilgrim* (1952), and her autobiography, *Double Exposure*, leave records of her personal and artistic development during her seven years in Africa. Her recollections of that continent reveal her intense fascination with the ways in which her subjects, whether human or animal, expressed themselves and her genuine desire to understand the meanings attached to their methods of expression. She was strikingly perceptive and sympathetic to the situation of the colonized African. In Africa she found a world in which dance and culture were intimately connected—a relationship she found absent in the dance that she photographed in England. She found also an atmosphere within which she could freely work and a culture with which she felt comfortable. She returned to dance photography and became absorbed in the signification of dance in African culture.

Severn's photographic aims set her apart from the prevailing trends of photojournalism and appear more compatible with those of the artist. Her individuality as a photojournalist manifested itself in her approach to photography—one based on an apolitical stance and a reliance on intuition and 'unconsciousness' in order to capture a sense of naturalism in her work. Her perspective on photography, her artistic approaches, and her reliance on inspiration, instinct, and empathy for her subjects remained constant throughout her life. Such an identity as a photographer surfaces through her distinctive narrative photography and the very visual language that she developed in her writing.

Severn's photographic and literary legacy reveals her transference in different media of artistic and personal expressions—first through sculpture, then through the camera, and ultimately through words. She had a need to understand the subject that she photographed; her sustained interest in dance was fundamental to her life and photographic career, and her sensitivity to the cultural role of dance is apparent in both her writings and her photographs. She understood European ballet as an aesthetic and impersonal style of dance, one which offered great potential for photographic experimentation. Therefore she chose to detach herself from the dancers, deeming their own personalities irrelevant to their performance roles, and appreciated ballet purely for its aesthetic and theatrical qualities. In Africa she found dance and life united. She understood African dance as 'an authentic example of that cosmic reality which makes men dance together for the joy of dancing and for the proof of living' (Severn, *Double Exposure*, 180). She affirmed her commitment to Africa by returning to live in Salisbury, Southern Rhodesia, about 1956. She died in Africa in 1970.

ILYANA KARTHAS

Sources I. Karthas, 'Merlyn Severn: photographer—photojournalist—artist', MSt diss., U. Oxf., 1997 · M. Severn, *Ballet in action* (1936) · M. Severn, *Sadler's Wells Ballet at Covent Garden: a book of photographs* (1947) · M. Severn, *Congo pilgrim* (1952) · M. Severn, *Double exposure: a photographer's recollections* (1956) · [D. Hussey], 'Apologists of the ballet', *TLS* (16 July 1938), 481 · T. Hopkinson, 'How *Picture Post* began', *Picture Post* (2 Oct 1948), 13 · V. Williams, *The other observers: women photographers in Britain, 1900 to the present* (1886); repr. (1991) · J. Gardiner, *Picture Post women* (1993)

Severn, Walter (1830–1904), watercolour painter, was born on 12 October 1830 at Frascati, near Rome, one of six children and the eldest son of Joseph *Severn (1793–1879), painter, and his wife, Elizabeth (*d.* 1862), daughter of Archibald, Lord Montgomerie, and granddaughter of the twelfth earl of Eglinton. It is recorded that Joseph regretted not naming his son Walter Keats Severn, in memory of his friend John Keats. Walter's brother Arthur Severn (1842–1931) became a well-established marine watercolour painter, who in 1871 married Joan Agnew, a cousin of John Ruskin. Walter's sister Ann Mary (1832–1866) was a portrait painter. In 1841 the family returned to England and Walter Severn attended Westminster School (1843–7). While at Westminster he boxed and rowed, and on his boyhood visits to Eglinton Castle, Ayrshire, he developed an interest in country sports. It is reported that on these visits he sketched the ladies skating or playing croquet, but preferred to draw stags.

In 1847 Severn became a clerk in the Privy Council Office, where he apparently first appeared sporting black eyes from a school boxing match. He became a career civil servant, but continued to pursue an interest in the visual and applied arts. In 1857 he is reputed to have started collaborating with Charles Locke Eastlake in the making of art furniture, wallpaper, and textiles. It is also recorded that in 1865 he made a vigorous effort to revive what in the 1870s became known as art needlework. On 28 December 1866 Severn married Mary Dalrymple, daughter of Sir James Dalrymple Fergusson; they had six children. He was still able to devote some of his leisure time to watercolour painting and book illustration. It is reported that he exhibited fifty watercolours at Agnews in 1874, and in an undated letter, attributed to that year, Ruskin wrote to Severn to congratulate him on selling his pictures. In a further letter of 26 March 1875 from Brantwood, Ruskin gave Severn typically generous praise for his ability to sketch from nature: 'I have never myself seen anything so wonderful, in its way, as your power of obtaining true and complete effects in limited time' (*Works*). However, the rather weak drawing and brushwork of, for example, *A Scotch Loch* (V&A) did not readily translate any such power to an exhibition watercolour, and indicates the lack of a formal art training.

In December 1879, at the London Institution, Severn gave a lecture, *On the Art of Sketching from Nature in Water Colours*, concentrating on technique and materials. In 1887 he contributed a letter to a correspondence in *The Times*, making bold claims for the permanence of modern watercolour paints. Severn was writing as president of the Dudley Gallery Art Society, which he had helped to found in 1865 in reaction to the more exclusive art societies of the time, and which held annual exhibitions in London at the Egyptian Hall, Piccadilly. Among the books Severn illustrated were *The Golden Calendar* (*c.*1864), with country scenes illustrating contemporary poetry, and *The Order for Morning and Evening Prayer* (1873), with decorative, floral borders reminiscent of embroidery, of which Ruskin might have approved. On Joseph Severn's death in 1879, he was disappointed not to be left his father's paintings or his manuscripts by Keats. Walter Severn died of chronic enteritis at his home, 9 Earls Court Square, London, on 22 September 1904.

F. W. GIBSON, *rev.* MICHAEL SPENDER

Sources private information (1912, 2004) • E. O. Gordon, *The life and correspondence of William Buckland* (1894) • W. Sharp, *The life and letters of Joseph Severn* (1892) • *The Times* (23 Sept 1904) • S. Birkenhead, *Against oblivion: the life of Joseph Severn* (1943) • *The works of John Ruskin on CD-ROM*, ed. E. T. Cook and E. Wedderburn (1996) [CD-ROM] • J. C. Robinson and others, *Light and water-colours: letters to The Times* (1887) • *WWW*, *1897–1915* • d. cert. • m. cert.

Archives Harvard U., Houghton L., corresp., drawings, and MSS

Likenesses C. E. Perugini, portrait

Wealth at death £828 11*s.* 8*d.*: probate, 26 Oct 1904, *CGPLA Eng. & Wales*

Sewall de Bovill. *See* Bovill, Sewal de (*d.* 1257).

Sewall, Samuel (1652–1730), judge and diarist in America, was born on 28 March 1652 at Bishop Stoke, Hampshire, the second child of Henry Sewall (*c.*1615–1700) and Jane (1627–1701), daughter of Stephen and Alice (*née* Archer) Dummer. The Sewall and Dummer families had earlier emigrated to Newbury, Massachusetts, in 1634–5 and 1638 respectively. Out of 'dislike to the English Hierarchy' Samuel's paternal grandfather had sent his only child

Samuel Sewall (1652–1730), by John Smibert, 1729

ahead of him to New England, 'with Net Cattel and Provisions sutable for a new Plantation'. Henry and Jane were married in 1646, but the following winter, 'the Climat being not agreeable' to Jane's parents, the young couple returned with them to England (Thomas, xxix–xxx). Henry Sewall travelled to New England in 1659, two years after his father's death, to secure his estate. Although he had planned to return home to his pastorate at North Baddesley, Hampshire, the Restoration made it prudent for him to remain in Newbury and send for his wife and five children, who arrived in 1661. Jane bore three more children in Newbury.

Samuel Sewall attended Romsey grammar school in Hampshire, and shortly after his arrival in Newbury became a student of Thomas Parker, who prepared him to enter Harvard College in 1667. Sewall graduated BA in 1671, became a resident fellow and tutor in 1673, and graduated MA in 1674; he was later an overseer of the college. On 28 February 1676 he married Hannah (1658–1717), the only living child of John Hull, the wealthy and influential merchant, silversmith, and mint-master of the Massachusetts Bay Colony. Now Sewall put aside any plans for the ministry, and began to learn 'the manner of the Merchants' (Thomas, 1.18). The couple lived in the Hulls' Boston home. Sewall became a member of the Third (South) Church in 1677, just before the birth of the first of his fourteen children, of whom only six lived to maturity.

Sewall became a freeman of the colony in 1678, and the following year joined the ancient and honorable artillery company, receiving the rank of captain in 1701. He managed the Boston printing press from 1681 to 1684. With John Hull's death in 1683 Sewall took over his father-in-law's merchant business and property interests, and assumed many of his civic and political roles. At the end of 1683 he became a (non-resident) deputy to the general court from Westfield, and was elected to Hull's place as captain of the south company of militia, though he resigned the command on religious grounds in 1686 because of an order to put the cross in the militia's colours. Each year from 1684 to 1686 he was elected to the seat Hull left vacant on the court of assistants.

Matters related to the abrogation of the Massachusetts Bay charter in 1684 and the establishment of the royal government in 1686 caused Sewall to travel to England in November 1688. The journal he kept during his year-long trip describes his attendance to his family's property interests, visits to relatives, sightseeing, and efforts to support Increase Mather, minister of Boston's Second (North) Church, in his appeals for the restoration of the colony's privileges. Thus Sewall was absent from New England during the revolt against Governor Edmund Andros, which was an extension of the revolution of 1688, and the provisional re-establishment of the old government in the spring of 1689. When Sewall returned, he resumed his place on the court of assistants. He was named to the governor's council under the new province charter of 1691, and re-elected annually until his retirement in 1725. In May 1692 he was appointed commissioner of oyer and terminer for the Salem witchcraft proceedings. In December that year, despite the disfavour into which the witchcraft court had fallen, Sewall was made a justice of the superior court of judicature, and he became chief justice in 1718, a position he retained until his resignation in 1728. Alone among the witchcraft judges Sewall publicly recanted, standing in the South Church on 14 January 1697, a fast day, while the minister read on his behalf a bill in which he assumed the 'Blame and Shame' for his part in the trials (Thomas, 1.366–7). From 1699 to his death he was a commissioner (and for much of the time secretary and treasurer) of the Company for the Propagation of the Gospel in New England and Parts Adjacent. His published writings include an anti-slavery tract, *The Selling of Joseph: a Memorial* (1700), and other religious works and poetry. He was judge of probate for Suffolk County from 1715 to 1728, and held numerous municipal offices.

The diary Sewall kept from December 1673 to October 1729 is a rich source of social history and his most enduring legacy. Sewall reveals himself to have been an affectionate and engaged father. The birth, illness, and death of his children moved him profoundly. He tells of his son Samuel's difficulties as a student and apprentice, and of his troubled marriage to Rebeckah, daughter of Governor Joseph Dudley; daughter Elizabeth's religious fears; daughter Hannah's life as an invalid; son Joseph's rise to the ministry of the South Church; daughter Mary's death in childbed; and daughter Judith's marriage to William Cooper, minister of the Brattle Street Church. Though Sewall was deeply religious and constant to puritan ways (he abhorred periwigs and Christmas-keeping), his diary entries extend far beyond spiritual soul-searching, providing a remarkable record of his everyday interactions with notable and ordinary New Englanders. He rode the arduous court circuit until he was seventy-six; watched with the sick and bore the dead to their graves; and took into his home several children, including an American Indian boy, whom he prepared for Harvard.

Sewall's wife, Hannah, died on 19 October 1717. His often dispiriting pursuit of eligible widows thereafter is candidly documented in his diary. He married Abigail Woodmansey Tilley, *née* Melyen (*c*.1666–1720) on 29 October 1719, but she died within months. On 29 March 1722 he married Mary Gibbs, *née* Shrimpton (1667–1746), who survived him. Samuel Sewall died on 1 January 1730 and was buried in the Hull–Sewall tomb in Boston's Granary burying-ground. JUDITH S. GRAHAM

Sources *The diary of Samuel Sewall, 1674–1729: newly edited from the manuscript at the Massachusetts Historical Society*, ed. M. H. Thomas, 2 vols. (1973) • *Collections of the Massachusetts Historical Society*, 6th ser., 1–2 (1886–8) [*Letter-book of Samuel Sewall*, vols. 1–2] • J. S. Graham, *Puritan family life: the diary of Samuel Sewall* (Boston, MA, 2000) • T. B. Strandness, *Samuel Sewall: a puritan portrait* (1967) • D. D. Hall, 'The mental world of Samuel Sewall', *Worlds of wonder, days of judgment: popular religious belief in early New England* (1989) • O. E. Winslow, *Samuel Sewall of Boston* (1964) • C. K. Shipton, *Sibley's Harvard graduates: biographical sketches of graduates of Harvard University*, 17 vols. (1873–1975), vol. 2 • E. Howe, 'The abode of John Hull and Samuel Sewall', *Proceedings of the Massachusetts Historical Society*, 2nd ser., 1 (1884–5), 312–26

Archives Mass. Hist. Soc., papers

Likenesses N. Emmons, oils, 1728, Mass. Hist. Soc. • J. Smibert, oils, 1729, Museum of Fine Arts, Boston [*see illus.*]

Wealth at death see Strandness, *Samuel Sewall*, 47–53, 195; Howe, 'The abode of John Hull and Samuel Sewall'; 'Samuel Sewall Jr's memoranda', *Collections of the Massachusetts Historical Society*, 6th ser., 2

Seward, Sir Albert Charles (1863–1941), botanist and geologist, was born at West Place, Lancaster on 9 October 1863, the sixth child (and only son to survive childhood) of Abram Seward, who owned an ironmonger's business but devoted much of his time to local administration and religious work, and was mayor of Lancaster in 1877, and his wife, Marian Smith. From Lancaster grammar school Seward entered St John's College, Cambridge, where he obtained a first class in each part of the natural sciences tripos (1885, 1886), and became a scholar of his college (1885). In 1886 he began to study palaeobotany, working for a year in Manchester under William Crawford Williamson and afterwards visiting the principal museums of the continent to study the fossil plants in their collections. In 1888 he gained the Harkness scholarship and in 1890 was appointed university lecturer in botany at Cambridge. His essay *Fossil Plants as Tests of Climate* won the Sedgwick prize, and was published in 1892; the books and papers on fossil plants which followed led to fellowship of the Royal Society in 1898. He became a fellow of St John's in 1899 but resigned soon afterwards on appointment as fellow and tutor of Emmanuel College.

In 1906 Seward succeeded Harry Marshall Ward as professor of botany at Cambridge and relinquished his tutorship. He held the chair for thirty years and contributed greatly to the progress of the Cambridge botany school as

Sir Albert Charles Seward (1863–1941), by Harold Knight, 1937

a place of study and research. Like his predecessor he possessed great ability as a lecturer to undergraduates, and attracted many students to the study of plants. He was assisted by an able staff of lecturers and demonstrators, among whom was his close friend Frederick Frost Blackman, the eminent plant physiologist. The number of students working in the botany school considerably increased, and research students came from other universities at home and abroad, so that the building, which seemed so large when it was built in 1904, became much overcrowded until it was extended in 1934 with the financial help of the Rockefeller trustees.

Throughout his scientific career Seward was an indefatigable research worker and encouraged original investigation in many areas. Even when weighed down with administrative work he found time for the study of the collections of fossil plants which were sent to him from all parts of the world. He produced ten books and over a hundred original scientific papers. His textbook *Fossil Plants for Students of Botany and Geology* was begun in 1897 and four volumes appeared at varying intervals between 1898 and 1919. It gave a concise summary of the state of knowledge about the plants of past ages, covering all groups save the flowering plants. Its illustrations and long lists of references add to its permanent value. Another important book, published in 1931, was *Plant Life through the Ages*, which dealt with the more general biological and geological problems arising from the study of fossil plants. These included a valuable study of the geographical distribution of plants in the world in former times, a subject in which the author had long been interested. The value of his contributions to science was recognized by the award of a royal medal (1925) and the Darwin medal (1934) by the Royal Society, and Murchison (1908) and Wollaston medals (1930) by the Geological Society. His eminence as a botanist led to his appointment as president of the botany section of the British Association in 1903 and 1929. In 1930 he was president of the fifth International Botanical Congress; in the next year president of the International Union of Biological Sciences; and in 1939 president of the British Association.

In 1915 Seward was elected master of Downing College. The college had passed through many vicissitudes since its foundation in 1800; its endowments were small as compared with those of other colleges, and, owing to the war, its future seemed uncertain. During the twenty-one years of his mastership Downing attained a position and reputation higher than it had ever before possessed. Its numbers increased considerably, its buildings were improved by the addition of two handsome blocks designed by Sir Herbert Baker, its members took a prominent part in the life of the university, and a corporate unity was established which had not previously existed. In all of this the master took a leading part; his lodge became the centre of college life, he knew personally every undergraduate, he took an active interest in college clubs and societies, and he was very popular. He was interested in the improvement of amenities and administration in the college, but he always expected a high standard of intellectual endeavour from all its resident members. In 1924 he became vice-chancellor of the university, a post he held for the customary two years. He had previously served on the council of the senate and on many boards and syndicates, and now again displayed the same administrative ability which he had shown in his laboratory and his college.

From 1922 to 1924 Seward was president of the Geological Society of London and helped to guide the affairs of the society at a critical period. From his schooldays he had been intensely interested in geology, through the influence of his old friend John Edward Marr, and he contributed many papers to the *Quarterly Journal of the Geological Society*. On the day before his death he completed a popular book on geology in which the fascination of this branch of knowledge is admirably displayed. Seward served on the council of the Royal Society for two periods and in 1934 became its foreign secretary. In his later years he was the recipient of honorary degrees from the universities of Oxford, Dublin, Geneva, Manchester, Cape Town, Toronto, Edinburgh, Birmingham, Glasgow, and St Andrews, and honorary memberships of many foreign learned societies including the Royal Swedish Academy, the American Academy of Arts and Sciences, the Norwegian Academy, the New York Academy of Sciences, the geological societies of South Africa and Belgium, and the Palaeontological Society of Russia. In 1936 he was knighted.

When the new statutes at Cambridge came into operation Seward chose to come under them, and consequently, on reaching the retiring age in 1936, he relinquished his professorship and mastership and moved to London. He maintained connections with Cambridge, however, for he had been elected to honorary fellowships at each of his former colleges. He now devoted much of his time to the affairs of the Royal Society, the advisory council of the Department of Scientific and Industrial Research, and the standing commission on museums and art galleries. In 1938 he became a trustee of the British Museum. His free time was spent in research at the British Museum, where he was studying the early tertiary floras of Mull and the adjacent islands, a subject which formed the topic of his presidential address to the British Association in 1939. On the outbreak of war he returned to Cambridge for a time and then went to live in Oxford.

During a life of intense intellectual and administrative activity Seward regarded as a duty the work of making known to the public the discoveries of botanists and geologists. He wrote several popular books and many magazine articles on subjects which he found interesting, and was very generous in giving lectures to local scientific societies. He was joint editor with Francis Darwin of *More Letters of Charles Darwin* (1903), edited *Darwin and Modern Science* (1909) and *Science and the Nation* (1917), and was general editor of the Cambridge Botanical Handbooks.

Seward was twice married: first, on 1 July 1891 to Marion (1861/2–1924), daughter of Robert Brewis, shipbuilder, of Hartlepool, with whom he raised four daughters. To her he owed much when he was making his way in the scientific world, for she brought financial aid, and, in devotion to his interests, she relieved him of most of the duties which normally fall to the head of a family. She was an accomplished painter in watercolours and assisted him in the illustration of his books and papers. His second marriage, in 1927, was to Mary Adelia, daughter of James Henry Bogart, of New York city; she outlived him. Both marriages were exceptionally happy in the sharing of a common interest in his work, and in the help given by his wives as he carried out the social duties attaching to his position. Seward died at his home in Oxford, 14 Northmoor Road, on 11 April 1941.

H. H. Thomas, *rev.* Anita McConnell

Sources H. H. Thomas, *Obits. FRS*, 3 (1939–41), 867–80 • H. H. Thomas, 'Sir Albert Seward', *Nature*, 147 (1941), 667–8 • W. N. Edwards, *Quarterly Journal of the Geological Society of London*, 98 (1942), lxxviii–lxxxi • personal knowledge (1959) • private information (1959) • S. M. Walters, *The shaping of Cambridge botany* (1981) • b. cert. • m. cert., 1891 • d. cert. • *CGPLA Eng. & Wales* (1941)

Archives NHM, MSS • U. Cam., department of plant sciences, notebooks | BGS, letters to F. L. Kitchin • CUL, corresp. relating to Darwin and modern science • U. Glas., corresp. with Frederick Bower

Likenesses J. Gunn, oils, 1933, Downing College, Cambridge • H. Knight, oils, 1937, U. Cam., department of botany [*see illus.*] • O. Gelis, photograph, NPG

Wealth at death £34,247 5*s.*: resworn probate, 19 June 1941, *CGPLA Eng. & Wales*

Seward, Anna [*called* the Swan of Lichfield] (**1742–1809**), poet and correspondent, was born on 12 December 1742 in Eyam, Derbyshire, the first of two surviving children of Thomas *Seward (1708–1790), rector of Eyam, Derbyshire, later canon residentiary of Lichfield, Staffordshire, and his wife, Elizabeth Hunter (*d.* 1780), daughter of John Hunter, the headmaster of Lichfield grammar school

Anna Seward (1742–1809), by Tilly Kettle, 1762

whose most famous pupil was Samuel Johnson. Only one of Anna's siblings, Sarah (1744–1764), survived infancy, but she died in her twentieth year, just before she was to marry Joseph Porter, a merchant of Leghorn, the brother of Lucy Porter and the stepson of Samuel Johnson.

Early years and literary ambitions Apart from her first seven years in Eyam, Anna Seward lived all her life in Lichfield, from the age of thirteen on, in the same house, the bishop's palace in the grounds of Lichfield Cathedral. According to Seward, her adolescent years in Lichfield were Edenic; the sisters wandered in the cathedral close or did needlework and read to each other in the open air.

When Anna was fourteen, five-year-old Honora Sneyd, whose mother had just died, was adopted by the Seward family. Following the sudden death of Sarah in 1764, the friendship between Seward and Sneyd became intense; for the next six years, they had the daily pleasure of each other's company. Much to Seward's regret, in 1771, Honora Sneyd returned to her father's house after living for fourteen years with the Sewards. The beautiful and accomplished Honora Sneyd had several suitors, including Major John André and Thomas Day. In 1773 she became the second wife of Richard Lovell Edgeworth and the stepmother of four children, including Maria Edgeworth, but died young, of consumption, in 1780. Seward grieved the loss of Honora Sneyd throughout her life. Among the recurrent themes of Seward's best known poetry are Honora's beauty, the mutual joys of the Seward–Sneyd friendship, their alienation after Sneyd's marriage, and an enduring sense of loss. Seward's long-lived love for Sneyd and for her sister is inscribed on the very landscape of Lichfield in such poems as 'The Anniversary', 'Time Past', and 'Epistle to Miss Honora Sneyd …

from the grave of a Suicide'. Judging by the satirical comments Seward makes on married couples and her praise of the achievements of unmarried women, she came to value highly the independence of the single life. During her twenties, however, she had several proposals and was courted by at least two suitors: Cornet Vyse of Lichfield and a Colonel Taylor. Vyse married one of Seward's intimate friends, whose early death is the subject of a Seward monody. The strange correspondence that took place between Seward and Colonel Taylor's wife in 1796 reveals that the colonel continued, for decades, to be infatuated with Seward much to the chagrin of Mrs Taylor and to the surprise of Seward.

Although it is not known who dubbed Seward 'the Swan of Lichfield', her literary ambitions were stimulated by the early support of her father, who taught the precocious girl to read Shakespeare, Milton, and Pope at three, and to recite the first three books of *Paradise Lost* by the time she was nine. Canon Seward himself achieved some literary reputation by publishing poetry, including 'The female right to literature' (1748) in Dodsley's *Collection of Poems by Several Hands* (2.295–302); and by editing (with Lewis Theobald and Samuel Sympson) *The Works of Beaumont and Fletcher*, in ten volumes (1750). During the 1770s the Seward residence became the centre for an important local literary circle, which included Lichfield physician Erasmus Darwin and at times visitors such as Thomas Day and Richard Lovell Edgeworth. As an adolescent, Seward was encouraged to write by Dr Darwin whose own florid poetical style is said, unfortunately, to have influenced her own. Later, her budding talent was recognized at the poetical amusements organized by Lady Anna Miller at her Batheaston villa from 1775 to 1781. In *Poem to the Memory of Lady Miller* (1782) Seward expresses her gratitude for Miller's 'gentle ordeal' by which verses were put into an Etruscan vase, and then read aloud by a gentleman to the gathering at Batheaston. The best verses, including some of Seward's earliest publications, were chosen as prize poems and collected in Batheaston's annual volume of poetry.

Seward and Dr Johnson Seward's vexed relationship with Lichfield's celebrated native son Samuel Johnson is well known. On a personal level, as a close friend of Lucy Porter, she resented Johnson's marriage to Tetty Porter (Lucy's mother) and blamed him for Tetty's impoverished life in a writer's garret in London, after he had lost her widow's portion. It added fuel to the fire that Lucy Porter herself adored her stepfather as a deity. While Johnson was alive, Seward feared the sting of his mocking wit, as shown, for example, in his cruel stories about her maternal grandfather, his schoolmaster, of whom Johnson claimed that he never taught the boys, but whipped and they learned. Johnson later joked that, because of Anna Seward's strong resemblance to her grandfather, he trembled at the very sight of her. Seward also took umbrage at Johnson's dismissal of Lichfield as a cultural backwater because she felt his contempt slighted the literary endeavours of her father and his circle. Anna Seward's chagrin at the success of Johnson was also grounded in her own sense of thwarted ambition, given that she was acutely aware that the youthful talents of both Garrick and the uncouth Johnson had been cultivated by the most accomplished citizen of Lichfield, Gilbert Walmesley, in the very house, the bishop's palace, in which Seward grew up. Yet, though she might inhabit the very room of their studies, as a girl, she could find no Walmesley to sponsor her high intellectual and literary ambitions. Despite everything, Seward's personal connections with Johnson were such that she was invited by Johnson himself to make visits to him while he was on his deathbed in Lichfield during the autumn of 1784. Only after his death did Seward venture to publish, along with her praise of Johnson's literary achievements, her objections to his social bullying, his gloomy misanthropy, and his depreciation of the poetic merits of Thomas Gray, Ossian, and Chatterton, and other poets, whom she admired. She wrote against the 'old literary Colossus' even though she knew she would be ridiculed as 'an unlearned female entering the lists of criticism against the mighty Johnson' (*Letters*, 3.352). The letters she wrote, signing herself 'Benvolio', in the *Gentleman's Magazine* in 1786 and 1787 reveal that she became increasingly incensed by what she saw as the servile adulation granted to Johnson, especially by Boswell. For a brief time, in 1784, Boswell and Seward had been on very friendly terms. Their confidential correspondence indicates that he was in 'a flutter' over their conversations and desired to have 'a lock of that charming auburn hair I admired so much the delicious morning I was last with you' (Heiland, 386). Rejecting the 'voluptuous inclination' suggested in Boswell's request, Seward eventually sent him the lock of hair on her own terms of a chaste friendship (ibid., 387). After the publication of Boswell's *Life of Johnson*, however, an acrimonious public quarrel developed between Boswell and Seward, who argued that Boswell's idolatry of Johnson led him to suppress evidence of Johnson's despotic behaviour and its vicious effects, including Seward's minutes, which she obligingly supplied to Boswell at his request, detailing Johnson's public mortification of a young woman, Jane Harry, for converting to Quakerism. Seward's assessments of Johnson and her controversy with Boswell form only a small part of her accomplishments as a critic. To date, her extensive body of critical writings remains scattered in her letters, in her *Memoirs of the Life of Dr. Darwin*, and in various periodicals, waiting to be studied systematically and appreciated as an important and distinctive contribution to eighteenth-century criticism.

Literary recognition Throughout her life, Seward's main occupations were managing the family household, keeping up a wide correspondence with both famous and ordinary people, and writing poetry and criticism, when time allowed. As the only surviving child of invalid parents, Seward decided that she was required to care first for her ailing mother, who died in 1780, and then for her beloved father, whose increasingly diminished capacities of body and mind required, she claimed, that she develop stationary habits and limited ambitions. When her father died in 1790, he left her an independent income of £400 annually, and by special dispensation of her episcopal landlord she was permitted to remain living in the bishop's palace until her death. It was during the 1780s, while caring for her father, that she began to win acclaim for her poetry. Her *Elegy on Captain Cook* (1780), was very popular at the time, but when, in 1791, the Royal Society struck a medal to honour Cook, Seward was hurt that, while those who directed 'their attention to the moths, butterflies, and curry-combs of that voyage' were given medals, she whose poetry celebrated Cook's achievement was overlooked (*Letters*, 3.59). Among Honora Sneyd's suitors, Seward had favoured John André, whose romantic and noble qualities are memorialized in *Monody on Major Andrè* (1781), a timely poem protesting at André's court martial and hanging at Tappan by the Americans who condemned him as a British spy after the plans for the fortress at West Point were delivered to him by Benedict Arnold. Seward's denunciation of George Washington for his part in the affair was so fierce that Washington sent an emissary to Seward with evidence demonstrating that his role was limited. In 1784 she published *Louisa: a Poetical Novel, in Four Epistles*, which experiments with a hybrid form she calls a 'poetical novel', and which she considered to be her best work. *Louisa* went through four editions in 1784 and a fifth edition in 1785. Her *Original Sonnets on Various Subjects; and Odes Paraphrased from Horace* (1799) collects poems dated from the 1770s to 1799, some of which had already been published in periodicals. In the preface she defends the sonnet form against contempt of Johnson and other critics as a 'highly valuable species of verse'; and later, in a long footnote, justifies her poetic 'translations' of Horace, though she knew little Latin, by claiming that a literal prose translation is not as true to the 'essence' of Horace as the 'freedom of unimitative numbers' (167–9n.).

As the wit and good judgement of her letters show, Seward took the maintenance of her very large correspondence as a serious literary pursuit; she once quipped that an unanswered letter resembled 'an unexpiated sin' (*Letters*, 4.30). Her circle of friends and correspondents included a variety of celebrated figures of the late eighteenth century of whom only a few can be mentioned. During the early 1780s poet William Hayley wrote to praise her *Elegy on Captain Cook* and then visited Lichfield to pay her court, after which they became mutual admirers of each other's poetry. In 1788 Josiah Wedgewood wrote to enlist her pen against slavery, but she declined, claiming that Thomas Day and Hannah More had done a better job than she could do on the topic. In 1791, in a letter to Humphry Repton, whose theories on landscape improvement advocated turning England into a huge picturesque park, Seward recorded the practical achievements of her oldest friend, Mrs Mompesson whose lifelong industry and good taste led her to transform her ancestral estate into a highly desirable country retreat. In 1793 Seward found the sympathetic first-hand accounts of the French Revolution sent to her by her young friend Helen Maria Williams naïve; according to Seward, revolutionary France was 'a whole nation of Macbeths!' (ibid., 3.339). In a letter of 1803 to Walter Scott she greeted him with a high compliment for a woman of her sensibilities—'You Salvator! You Claude!'—which flattered his young ambitions and which eventually led to his visiting her in Lichfield (ibid., 6.91).

Erasmus Darwin and Seward's *Memoir* Seward's friendship with Dr Erasmus Darwin started during her adolescence when he was her neighbour and endured in spite of the literary abuses of which she accuses him. In one case she asserts that verses she wrote in his garden in 1779 were reproduced as his own, with a few additional lines, as the Exordium of his *Botanic Garden* (1791). This was done without the permission or knowledge of their author, even though the verses had already been published as her work in the *Gentleman's Magazine* (May 1783). In another case, Darwin wrote three poems and appended them to Francis Mundy's *Needwood Forest* (1776); he signed his name to the best one, his son's name to the second, and, without her knowledge, Seward's name to the third and worst poem. When Seward confronted him, 'he laught it off in a manner peculiar to himself, and with which he carries all his points of despotism' (*Letters*, 3.154). Such incidents did not deter Seward from publishing, in 1804, *Memoirs of the Life of Dr. Darwin*, a biography of Darwin's early life in Lichfield (from 1756 to 1781), that reveals her indulgent fondness for his idiosyncratic genius as a doctor, inventor, and writer. Her critical explication of Darwin's poetry and her comparisons of his work with that of other poets reveal not only her keen appreciation of Darwin's playful, voluptuous style, but also her own extensive knowledge of English poetry. At the same time, she uses the Darwin biography to write about her own life and to further her critical views. She reconstructs, in order to honour, the vibrant intellectual life of the Lichfield circle of which Darwin, her father and, eventually, Seward herself were the leading figures. In the interest of women's education, she defends Darwin's books on the sexual reproduction of plants against the charge that they are unfit reading for the fair sex: 'do not suppose that a virtuous girl, or young married woman, could be induced, by reading the Botanic Garden, to imitate the involuntary libertinism of a fungus or a flower' (ibid., 6.144–145). At times Seward is a vigorous critic of Darwin's errors, as when she censors his misrepresentation of the venerable Mary Delany in *The Love of the Plants* (the second part of *Botanic Garden*, published in 1789), as a mere artificial flower maker. Although Darwin refused to change future editions, Seward's *Memoirs of the Life of Dr Darwin* corrects the record by pointing out that Delany's ten folio volumes of paper cuttings of plants and flowers represent a brilliant achievement in art and science:

> She employed no material but paper, which she herself, from her knowledge of chemistry, was enabled to dye of all hues, and in every shade of each; no implement but her scissors, not once her pencil; yet never did painting present a

more exact representation of flowers of every colour, size, and cultivation, from the simple hedge and field-flower. (Seward, *Darwin*, 315–16)

Later years Over the course of her life Seward had many close friendships and dear correspondents, but she mentions four people as her deepest attachments: her sister, her father, Honora Sneyd, and finally John Saville, the vicar choral of Lichfield Cathedral, who had been a long-time friend of the Seward family. After her father's death in 1790, Saville, who was living, separate from his wife, in a small house in the cathedral close, became Seward's daily companion, her beloved 'Giovanni', with whom she shared many interests, ranging from their affection for her dog Sappho to their devotion to the music of Handel. After Saville's death in 1803, she paid his debts, supported his family, and had a monument built to his memory just outside the cathedral. During the last two decades of her life, Seward travelled regularly, looking for healthy retreats at Buxton, at Matlock, and in Wales, where she befriended the famous ladies of Llangollen, Lady Eleanor Butler and Sarah Ponsonby. The title poem of *Llangollen Vale with other Poems* (1796) honours the home and garden of Butler and Ponsonby that attracted so many celebrities to the site; their intelligent labour had 'converted a cottage, in two acres and a half of turnip ground, to a fairy-palace, amid the bowers of Calypso' (*Letters*, 4.99).

According to her own account, Anna Seward had agreeable features, a clear animated complexion, and tolerably good manners. While still a young woman, she began to grow plump, and, in 1768, she fell and fractured her knee-cap, causing an incurable limp that worsened as she aged. Yet, by all accounts, she remained a striking and majestic presence in Lichfield. She was a brilliant conversationalist, according to Edgeworth who met her in the 1770s; and throughout her life, she had a magnificent voice and gave pleasurable recitals of poetry and dramatic readings from Shakespeare's plays. Walter Scott, who met her late in her life, said that her 'great command of the literary anecdote' made her delightful company (Scott, xxiii). Over the years, Seward's body was assaulted by a multitude of rheumatic and other mysterious ailments. In 1794 she exacerbated her lung problems one evening when she read all the principal scenes in *Macbeth* to company in Nottingham with so much energetic exertion that '[I] have never breathed freely since' (*Letters*, 3.385). Increasing difficulties with her breathing led to an acute sensitivity to air quality, as her wry comments on the environment of Birmingham and other polluted places attest. Her two poems on Colebrook Dale, 'The lake, or, Modern improvement in landscape', as well as other poems present prescient criticisms of environmental degradation. Among their various themes, Seward's *Letters* are a rare treasury of grim observations on health; she often mentions particular cases, besides her own, assessing which treatment would be effective, as for example, when she considers whether amputation is an appropriate treatment for breast cancer. During the severe winters of the mid-1790s, she suffered from whitlows; all her finger-nails, then all her toe-nails, fell off one by one 'imprisoning me to my chair or couch during a fortnight, at three different periods … so much for bodily egotism' (ibid., 4.164). No wonder, by 1796, blighted by disease, she considered middle age detestable, and resolved not to sit for a portrait again until, and if, she reached a venerable old age. Yet her appearance remained impressive even as late as 1807, when her intelligent face, melodious voice, and attractive auburn hair and eyes were noticed by Walter Scott.

As her own health declined, Seward recognized her inability to finish projected collections of her poetry and letters, so she enlisted Scott as her literary executor. During her last days Seward was attended by women friends, as she had been all her life; her cousin Susan Seward and a Miss Fern read to her in the evenings as she lay dying of scorbutic fever. She died at her home on 25 March 1809 and was buried alone in the choir of Lichfield Cathedral on 2 April, and not, as she had requested, in the tomb either of her father or of John Saville.

The year following her death, Scott edited a three-volume set of Seward's poems, which he prefaced with a short biography (1810), but he declined to edit her letters. From a bequest of twelve volumes of copies and parts of manuscript correspondence, dated from 1784 to 1809, the Edinburgh publisher Archibald Constable produced an expurgated edition of six volumes of Seward's letters in 1811.

SYLVIA BOWERBANK

Sources *Letters of Anna Seward: written between the years 1784 and 1807*, ed. A. Constable, 6 vols. (1811) · A. Seward, *Memoirs of the life of Dr Darwin* (1804) · W. Scott, biographical preface, in *The poetical works of Anna Seward*, ed. W. Scott, 3 vols. (1810) · *GM*, 1st ser., 79 (1809), 379 · M. Ashmun, *The singing swan: an account of Anna Seward and her acquaintance with Dr. Johnson, Boswell, & others of their time* (1931) · D. Heiland, 'Swan songs: the correspondence of Anna Seward and James Boswell', *Modern Philology*, 90 (1992–3), 381–91 · *European Magazine and London Review*, 1 (1782) · R. L. Edgeworth and M. Edgeworth, *Memoirs of Richard Lovell Edgeworth*, 3rd edn (1844) · E. V. Lucas, *A swan and her friends* (1907) · *The Swan of Lichfield. Being a selection from the correspondence of Anna Seward. Ed. with a short biography and preface by Hesketh Pearson*, ed. H. Pearson (1936) · W. J. Bate, *Samuel Johnson* (1977); repr. (New York, 1979) · A. Seward, *Poem to the memory of Lady Miller* (1782) · J. L. Clifford, 'The authenticity of Anna Seward's published correspondence', *Modern Philology*, 39 (1941–2)

Archives BL, poems and letter-books, RP4112 [copies] · FM Cam., letters · Hunt. L., letters; literary MSS · NL Scot., literary MSS and papers [copies] · Samuel Johnson Birthplace Museum, Lichfield, corresp. and literary MSS · Staffs. RO, corresp. · U. Birm. L., letters | BL, letters to Anne Parry Price, Add. MS 46400 · JRL, letters to Hester Lynch Piozzi · NL Scot., corresp. with Sir Walter Scott · Samuel Johnson Birthplace Museum, Lichfield, letters to John Nichols · U. Birm. L., letters to the Dowdeswell family · Yale U., Beinecke L., corresp. with James Boswell; letters to Sophia Pennington

Likenesses T. Kettle, oils, 1762, NPG [*see illus.*] · J. Romney, portrait, *c*.1786, repro. in Lucas, *A swan and her friends* · A. Cardon, stipple, pubd 1811 (after T. Kettle), NPG · A. Cardon, engraving, Samuel Johnson Birthplace Museum, Lichfield · J. Chapman, stipple, BM, NPG; repro. in *Lady's Monthly Museum* (1821) · H. Landseer, stipple (after J. Downman), NPG · W. Ridley, stipple (after G. Romney), BM, NPG; repro. in *Monthly Mirror* (1797)

Wealth at death rich; left many annuities: will, detailed Ashmun, *Singing swan*, 266–70

Seward [Seguarde], **John** (1364/5–1435/6), schoolmaster, grammarian, and poet, appears to have originated in the north of England and to have been educated there, perhaps at Norham, Northumberland, and Guisborough in the North Riding of Yorkshire, before studying at Oxford University of which he called himself 'an unworthy subject'; he also wrote respectfully of John Leland (*d.* 1428), the leading Oxford schoolmaster of his day. Seward first occurs in 1404 in London as a schoolmaster and described himself as such until his death. His school was in Cornhill and seems to have been a private establishment for teaching Latin grammar, since it was not one of the authorized public schools of the capital. The Tudor bibliographer John Bale says that Seward at one time kept a school in Norwich, but this has not been substantiated and may have arisen because Seward dedicated one of his works to the local bishop, Richard Courtenay. His will, made on 5 June 1435 and proved in the following January, reveals that he had a brother and sister, a wife called Matilda, whose maiden name may have been Broke, and a married daughter, Sybil Scholdyng. The will does not prescribe a place of burial.

Seward had a good knowledge of classical Latin literature. He refers in his writings to Cicero, Horace, Ovid, Seneca, and Virgil, among others, and both echoes their style and alludes to their contents. He was also fond of Boethius. His works, which survive in three manuscripts, fall into two groups. His grammatical writings included a *Compendium super modis significandi* on speculative grammar, and five tracts on metre: *Hisagoga metrica*, *Mamilla*, *Somnium*, *Metristencheridion*, and *Cathametron*, the last of which has been lost. *Somnium* (written about 1403) is cast in the form of a dream in which the author meets Lady Philosophy (a Boethian figure) who opens to him the secrets of grammar and metre. He also wrote several poems: *Arpyilogus* and *Brachilexis sancte Arpyle*, moralizations of the story of the Harpies; *Antelopologia*, a description of the properties of the antelope addressed to Prince Henry of Wales, later Henry V, whose badge it was; and *Ludicra*, *Invectivae*, and epigrams. These last three works are poems, often humorous, exchanged with a group of like-minded men in London and sometimes concerned with discussing metrical topics. The group included William Relyk, master of a private grammar school at the Cardinal's Hat in Lombard Street, and some local clergy. Seward may also have written two epigrams in Oxford, Magdalen College, MS Lat. 15, fol. 128. In 1426 he compiled the cartulary of the guild of St Peter Cornhill. Such dates as occur in his works suggest that they were mostly written between about 1400 and 1420, and the names of people to whom they were addressed imply that Seward had contacts outside London, including John Eyton, canon of Repton, Simon Southerey, prior of St Albans, and William Swan, proctor of the Roman curia. He also dedicated or rededicated works to some important figures: Prince Henry, Edward, duke of York, Bishop Courtenay, Robert Hallum, bishop of Salisbury, Philip Repyndon, bishop of Lincoln, and Paul, bishop of Brindisi. Altogether Seward emerges as a man widely read and connected, but it is not clear whether his works ever gained him patronage, and he seems to have spent and ended his days in modest circumstances. NICHOLAS ORME

Sources V. H. Galbraith, *Kings and chroniclers: essays in English medieval history* (1982), section 7 • Emden, *Oxf.*, vol. 3 • U. Edin. L., MS La 148 • J. G. Clark, 'Intellectual life at the abbey of St Albans and the nature of monastic learning in England, *c.*1350–*c.*1440', DPhil diss., U. Oxf., 1997

Wealth at death modest: Galbraith, *Kings and chroniclers*

Seward, Thomas (1708–1790), Church of England clergyman, was one of at least three sons of John Seward of Badsey, Worcestershire, steward of Lord Windsor, and his wife, Mary. He was admitted a foundation scholar of Westminster School in February 1719. He was elected by the school to scholarships at Christ Church, Oxford, and Trinity College, Cambridge, in 1727, but upon his rejection by both he became a pensioner of St John's College, Cambridge, where he graduated BA in 1731 and proceeded MA in 1734.

Seward was ordained priest on 20 May 1732 at Rochester, and served as rector of Llan-maes, Glamorgan (1733–40). He was also a travelling tutor to Lord Charles Fitzroy, third son of the duke of Grafton, who died while on the tour in Italy in 1739. The duke of Grafton subsequently promised some preferment for Seward. He became rector of Eyam, Derbyshire, on 22 March 1740, and also of Kingsley, Staffordshire, on 2 April 1747 (having been presented by Lord and Lady Burlington); and on 30 April 1755 he was collated to the prebend of Pipa Parva in Lichfield Cathedral. In addition Seward was installed in the prebend of Lyme and Halstock in Salisbury Cathedral on 5 June 1755.

Seward had become a resident of the cathedral close at Lichfield in 1754, and he was acquainted with Dr Johnson, whom he used to entertain on his visits to Lichfield. Boswell described him as 'a genteel, well-bred, dignified clergyman, who had lived much in the great world' (Ashmun, 188); and he was recalled by another as 'a lovely man, of fine person and frank communicative spirit' (ibid., 189). He had active literary interests and four of his poems were printed anonymously in Robert Dodsley's *A Collection of Poems* (1748). Seward was the joint editor of an edition of the works of Beaumont and Fletcher which appeared in ten volumes in 1750. This did not meet with the later approbation of S. T. Coleridge, however, who wrote in his lectures on Shakespeare: 'Mr Seward! Mr Seward! You may be, and I trust you are, an angel, but you were an ass!' (Ashmun, 189). In 1779 Seward was portrayed as the canon in the novel *Columella* by Richard Graves.

Writing to Mrs Thrale in 1783 Dr Johnson commented that 'Seward called on me yesterday. He is going … to Paris and then to Flanders to contemplate the pictures of Claude Lorrain, and he asked me if that was not as good a way as any of spending time' (*Letters*, ed. Piozzi, 2.263). Mrs Thrale replied, 'I see no harm in his resolution … though the manner of expressing it was likely to offend you: yet he is not a man whom anyone can reproach with neglect of duty; he does more good than almost any person of twice his fortune' (ibid., 2.265). He was indeed assiduous in the performance of his prebendal duties.

Seward married Elizabeth (*d.* 1780), daughter of the Revd John Hunter, headmaster of Lichfield grammar school, on 27 October 1741. They had a son and several daughters, but only Anna and Sarah survived infancy. Their eldest daughter, Anna *Seward (1742–1809), 'the swan of Lichfield', was especially precocious, and her father declared that she could repeat passages from Milton's *L'Allegro* before she was three. Anna's poetic talent was nurtured by the literary milieu in which she grew up. Erasmus Darwin, for example, was a friend of the family. After her mother's death in 1780 Anna devoted herself to the care of her father.

In Boswell's *Life of Johnson* (1791), Johnson described Seward as a man who not only had an ambition to be 'a fine talker', but was a 'valetudinarian', adding, 'I do not know a more disagreeable character than a valetudinarian' (Ashmun, 189). Anna Seward took issue with this view of her deceased father, and secured a more favourable notice of his life in the *Gentleman's Magazine* for October 1794. In her own obituary in that magazine it was said that 'Mr Seward had graceful manners, great hilarity of spirits, and active benevolence' (ibid., 190). However, some of the lack of appreciation of Seward by his contemporaries, like Johnson and Horace Walpole, probably sprang from a certain lightness of touch. He once said of two young men concerning his daughter: 'If she can be in danger from — — she must be infinitely more seducible to escape by any possible restraints parental prudence can impose' (*Letters of Anna Seward*, 1.267).

Thomas Seward died at the bishop's palace, Lichfield, on 4 March 1790 and was buried in the cathedral close. His daughter erected a monument in memory of her parent, in Lichfield Cathedral; the verses which formed part of the epitaph were composed by Sir Walter Scott.

THOMPSON COOPER, *rev.* PAT BANCROFT

Sources M. A. Ashmun, *The singing swan: an account of Anna Seward and her acquaintance with Dr Johnson, Boswell and others of their time* (1931) • *Letters of Anna Seward: written between the years 1784 and 1807*, ed. A. Constable, 1 (1811) • *Letters to and from … Samuel Johnson*, ed. H. L. Piozzi, 2 vols. (1788) • Boswell, *Life* • *GM*, 1st ser., 60 (1790), 236, 280 • *GM*, 1st ser., 64 (1794) • *Fasti Angl.* (Hardy) • Nichols, *Illustrations* • *Old Westminsters*, vol. 2 • Venn, *Alum. Cant.* • chapter act book, 1700–1800, Lichfield Cathedral Library archives • *IGI*

Archives Yale U., Beinecke L., journal of tour in France

Likenesses R. H. Cromek, line engraving, pubd 1811 (after J. Wright), BM; repro. in Constable, ed., *Letters of Anna Seward*, vol. 2, frontispiece

Seward, William (1711–1740), promoter of Methodism and friend of George Whitefield, was born into a family of independent landed means at Badsey, a hamlet near Evesham, Worcestershire. Of his brothers, Thomas became a clergyman of the Church of England, and was in Genoa when William accompanied the Calvinistic Methodist leader George Whitefield to Georgia; a second brother, Henry, married a Baptist and became a strong opponent of Methodism; a third, Benjamin, enjoyed a Cambridge education, was converted by William in 1739, and occasionally wrote hymns. William himself succeeded in business as a stockbroker sufficiently well to enable him to devote himself to the evangelical movement to which he was exposed through active work for the London charity schools in the late 1720s, raising an income of £150 per annum for the Hackney school despite opposition from the parish's minister, churchwardens and vestrymen. Whitefield told Seward later that his 'nine years round of duties were no effects of the new birth at all', being merely '*preparation* for conversion itself' (*Letters of George Whitefield*, 180); Charles Wesley also took a modest view of his spiritual maturity, assessing him on 13 November 1738 as a 'zealous soul knowing only the baptism of John' (*Journal of the Rev. Charles Wesley*, 1.135). A week later, however, he noted that 'Mr Seward testified faith', and in January 1739 was present at a conference of Oxford Methodists.

Seward now began to travel with Whitefield, and joined him on his first and most triumphant American tour, in August 1739. There he acted as Whitefield's publicist, providing newspapers and booksellers with extracts of Whitefield's own writing as well as a series of partly fabricated stories which, blurring the boundary between news reporting and advertisement, did much to enhance the apparent impact of the tour. Not least he also supported Whitefield generously from his own pocket, a liberality which incensed his brother Henry. The latter now 'fell upon' Charles Wesley with accusations:

> I was the downfall of his brother, had picked his pocket, ruined his family, come now to get more money, was a scoundrel, rascal and so forth and deserved to have my gown stripped over my ears. He concluded with threatening how he would beat me, if he could but catch me on Bengeworth Common. (*Journal of the Rev. Charles Wesley*, 15 March 1740, 1.195)

And he did in fact have him forcibly removed from the neighbourhood.

Three months later William, who had given Whitefield valuable service in America by securing the advance contacts he needed to make his tours a success, was back in England on Whitefield's instructions, partly to mend family relations but still more to further urgent Georgia business. He was to bring out John Hutchings, one of the Oxford Methodists, to manage Whitefield's orphan house in Georgia; to persuade the Georgia trustees that their colony would not succeed without negro slavery, allowing a title to lands there and an independent magistracy; to collect money for a negro school in Pennsylvania; and to bring over money already in the hands of trustees for building a church at Savannah. Seward had already bought Whitefield 5000 acres on the forks of the Delaware to establish an evangelical refuge in the style of Herrnhut, and a negro school. Moreover Seward was a widower, and he wished to remove his daughter's education from a governess, and complete it at the orphan house. His arrival increased the theological tension between Whitefield and the Wesley brothers, who did not care for Seward's *Journal of a Voyage from Savannah … to England*, published in 1740. Falling under Baptist influence, Seward now quarrelled bitterly with Charles Wesley. These disputes were, however, overshadowed by Seward's sad fate. While accompanying Howell Harris on Whitefield's begging mission in south Wales, he lost his sight in a fracas at Caerleon and then, on 22 October 1740, was killed by a blow on the head, perhaps not intended to be fatal, at Hay. Charles Wesley was shocked. The Seward family disappeared from evangelical history. W. R. WARD

Sources W. Seward, *Journal of a voyage from Savannah to Philadelphia, and from Philadelphia to England* (1740) • A. Dallimore, *George Whitefield* (1970–80) • *The journal of the Rev. Charles Wesley*, ed. T. Jackson, 2 vols. [1849] • *George Whitefield's journals*, new edn (1960) • *Letters of George Whitefield, for the period 1734–1742* (1976) • L. Tyerman, *The life of the Revd George Whitefield*, 2 vols. (1876–7); 2nd edn (1890)
Archives Chetham's Library, Manchester, diary • JRL, journal • Moravian Church House, London, MS corresp. • U. Wales, Bangor, journal

Seward, William (1747–1799), anecdotist, the only son of eminent London brewer William Seward, was born in January 1747, probably in London. He began his schooling at a small seminary near Cripplegate, and in 1757 moved to Harrow School. For a time he attended Charterhouse School and matriculated at Oriel College, Oxford, on 4 June 1764 at the age of seventeen. On quitting university, Seward travelled on the continent, particularly in Italy, where he was inspired with a passionate interest in art and literature.

Possessing considerable property but with no taste for business, on his father's death Seward sold his interest in the brewery to pursue a literary life. His conversation and cultured tastes gained him entry to London's foremost literary circles. He became a 'great favourite' of the Thrales at Streatham and was godfather to their daughter Cecilia (*Letters of Samuel Johnson*, 3.35). In 1776 Seward introduced Charles Burney to the Thrales, and Fanny Burney later declared that she 'always retained a true esteem for him' (*Diary and Letters*, 3.175). Seward was an intimate friend of Samuel Johnson, and became a member of the Essex Club founded by him early in 1784. He was also a member of the Eumélean Club that met at the Blenheim tavern in Bond Street. Inspired by Johnson's highland tour of Scotland, Seward made a similar journey in 1777, travelling first to Edinburgh with letters of introduction from Johnson to James Boswell and James Beattie. He was among the friends who attended Johnson's funeral, and he assisted in the composition of his epitaph. He was elected FRS on 11 February 1779—which he once quipped stood for 'Fellow Remarkably Stupid'—and FSA on 25 March 1779 (*Journals and Letters of Fanny Burney*, 9.143). In June 1783 Seward's interest in art took him to Paris and Flanders, where he studied the pictures of Claude Lorrain. His wide circle of acquaintance in England included Tom Paine as well as the poet Anna Seward, who was no relation.

In an effort to dispel his habitual ennui, Seward began collecting anecdotes of celebrated personalities in a commonplace book. He contributed many of these, along with literary discoveries and other articles, to periodicals including the *European Magazine* and Cadell's *Repository*. The *Whitehall Evening Post* printed his series 'Reminiscentia'. His 'Drossiana' appeared in the *European Magazine* beginning in October 1789 and later formed the basis for his five-volume *Anecdotes of some Distinguished Persons* (1795–7), which passed into a fifth edition in 1804. This was followed in 1799 by two volumes of *Biographiana*. These volumes were deservedly popular, and Seward was praised for his 'felicity … in hitting off the leading features of his subject' (*GM*, 440). Seward's efforts as an anecdotist earned him the posthumous epithet of the 'publick bagman for scraps', from Thomas Mathias, in the *Pursuits of Literature* (Mathias, dialogue 2, ll. 61–2).

Among his close acquaintances, Seward had the 'Character of a Hypocondriack' (*Thraliana*, 1.358). In August 1781 he made the 'western tour' in England and returned having consulted 'a doctor, apothecary, or chemist, belonging to every town at which he had stopped', adding that this was also his method of gathering information about a place and its surroundings (*Diary and Letters*, 1.219). In 1788 Seward appears to have been temporarily confined in a strait-jacket as a result of insanity. Four years earlier Hester Thrale had written of being 'plagued … with a Visit from Seward, who I think is going out of his Senses by the oddity of his Behaviour' (*Thraliana*, 1.595–6, n. 4). In his later years Seward habitually spent the winter in London and the summer in the country. Seward's portrait was painted by George Dance on 5 May 1793, and engraved by William Daniell. A second portrait of him, by J. G. Wood, was engraved by Holl, and published on 3 June 1799. Despite his declared intention never to marry, Hester Thrale alludes to his having proposed to her shortly after her husband's death in 1781. Having now grown very corpulent, Seward died of a dropsy at his lodgings in Dean Street, Soho, on 24 April 1799, and was buried in the family vault at Finchley on 1 May.

Although Seward was said to be 'fond of his joke, and would sometimes indulge it at the expence of his good-nature', he was also praised for his liberality to writers and artists (*GM*, 440). Fanny Burney, for whose *Camilla* Seward helped raise subscriptions, wrote of him that 'his mind is all solid benevolence and worth'. She was struck by his 'singularities and affectation of affectation', but believed that this was 'mere quizziness' (*Diary and Letters*, 3.175). He subscribed 10 guineas toward purchasing an annuity for Richard Porson, and Charles Burney recounted Seward's 'good natured plan' for lessening the debt of an insolvent bookseller (*Letters*, ed. Ribeiro, 1.262). In an elegy to Seward's memory, Ann Hunter praised his 'kindly mild affections' and 'warm benevolence' (Hunter, 71). Hester Thrale succinctly observed of Seward's character that he was:

> beneficent tho' frigid, and amiable though he does not even wish to be beloved: yet his Moral & Literary Character inspire so much respect, and his perpetual ill Health so much Tenderness, that one loves him in spite both of one's self and him. (*Thraliana*, 1.220–21)

CATHERINE DILLE

Sources *The letters of Samuel Johnson*, ed. B. Redford, 3 (1992), 31; 4 (1994), 147, 241 • *The diary and letters of Madame D'Arblay*, ed. W. C. Ward, 1 (1892), 77–8, 89–90, 109–10, 132, 137, 142–5, 212–15, 218–22, 272; 2 (1892), 167, 170, 173, 411; 3 (1892), 174–5, 183 • *Thraliana: the diary of Mrs. Hester Lynch Thrale (later Mrs. Piozzi), 1776–1809*, ed. K. C. Balderston, 2nd edn, 2 vols. (1951), vol. 1, pp. 136, 220–21, 224, 319, 356, 358, 378, 535, 567, 576, 580, 595 (n. 4); vol. 2, pp. 770, 994 • *The letters of Dr Charles Burney*, ed. A. Ribeiro, 1 (1991), 262 • *DNB* • *GM*, 1st ser., 69 (1799), 439–40 • *The journals and letters of Fanny Burney*

(*Madame D'Arblay*), ed. J. Hemlow and others, 12 vols. (1972–84), vol. 2, pp. 110, 119; vol. 4, pp. 284–5; vol. 9, p. 143 • Nichols, *Lit. anecdotes*, vol. 2 (1812), 553; vol. 9 (1815), 467 • J. S. Watson, *The life of Richard Porson* (1861), 99 • A. Hunter, *Poems* (1802), 71–2 • T. J. Mathias, *Pursuits of literature: a satirical poem in four dialogues*, 2nd edn (1797), pt 2, lines 61–2 • R. L. Arrowsmith, ed., *Charterhouse register, 1769–1872* (1974), 445 • W. Gun, *Harrow School register* (1934), 24 • Foster, *Alum. Oxon.* • *Signatures in the first journal-book and the charter-book of the Royal Society* (1912), 34 • *Letters of Anna Seward: written between the years 1784 and 1807*, ed. A. Constable, 4 (1811), 265–6 • *European Magazine and London Review*, 36 (1799), 219–20 • *The early journals and letters of Fanny Burney*, ed. L. E. Troide, 2: 1774–1777 (1990), 223–4

Likenesses G. Dance, drawing, 1793, NPG • W. Holl, stipple, pubd 1799 (after J. G. Wood), BM, NPG • engraving, Bodl. Oxf.; repro. in *European Magazine and London Review*

Seward, William Wenman (*d.* 1805/6), writer on Irish politics and topography, may have been born in Dublin. He entered King's Inns, Dublin, and was admitted as an attorney in May 1776. He practised in the Irish court of common pleas from an address in Prussia Street, Dublin, from 1781 until 1804. Briefly, in 1805, he shared premises at 151 James's Street. His death—which probably occurred in Dublin—was reported in *Walker's Hibernian Magazine* for February 1806.

Seward was the author of a pamphlet, *The rights of the people asserted and the necessity of a more equal representation in parliament stated and proved* (1783), which extolled the Irish volunteer movement (to which he belonged) and advocated parliamentary reform in Ireland. His second publication, *The Hibernian gazetteer; being a description of the … towns in Ireland alphabetically arranged* (1789), was a compilation of information on the towns and villages of Ireland derived from other published sources (among them the studies of certain Irish counties by Charles Smith). It was novel for its alphabetical arrangement of place names. Such was its success that Seward revised and expanded it into a quarto volume containing some 6000 entries: *Topographia Hibernica, or, The topography of Ireland ancient and modern giving a complete view of the civil and ecclesiastical state of that kingdom* (1795; repr., 1797). The new work included entries on lakes, canals, harbours, caves, heaths, and so on, and, like its predecessor, was remarkable for its thoroughness and precision. An interleaved copy in the British Library has extensive manuscript notes by the author. Seward wrote his final work, a contemporary history entitled *Collectanea politica, or, The political transactions of Ireland from the accession of his majesty King George the III* (3 vols., 1801–4), at a time of strong passions and prejudices in Ireland engendered by the rebellion of 1798. Largely a compilation of contemporary documents, it was remarkable for the author's unwillingness to be judgemental and was justifiably described by Seward as 'a plain and impartial narrative'.

Nothing is known for certain of William Wenman Seward's lineage, but it seems likely that he belonged to the same family as John Seward, the Dublin mathematical instrument maker, who was born about 1701 and was still flourishing about 1750. He was presumably the father, or an uncle, of Thomas Seward, the attorney with whom he shared premises in 1805, whose name appeared in the Dublin directories from 1800 until 1846, and who acted as the duke of Devonshire's Irish law agent in 1816. He is not to be confused with William *Seward (1747–1799) FRS.

C. J. Woods

Sources *Wilson's Dublin directory* (1780–1806) • E. Keane, P. Beryl Phair, and T. U. Sadleir, eds., *King's Inns admission papers, 1607–1867*, IMC (1982) • private information • *Walker's Hibernian Magazine* (Feb 1806)

Sewel, Willem (1653–1720), translator, lexicographer, and historian of Quakerism, was born in the Netherlands on 19 April 1653 at Angeliers Gracht, Amsterdam, probably the only child of Jakob Willemszoon Zewel (*d.* 1658/9), a surgeon, and his wife, Judith (*c.*1631–1664), daughter of Conrad Zinspenning and his wife, Catherine. His paternal grandfather, William Sewel, was English. Sewel's parents, once prominent Mennonites, converted to Quakerism when he was four years old, and his birthplace became one of the earliest Quaker meeting places in Amsterdam. His mother became a notable Quaker minister and writer, and was probably the first Dutch female Quaker preacher. His early recollections of Quakerism in Amsterdam were to be incorporated in his later historical work. After his mother's death he lived with a maternal uncle and learnt Latin; there is no record of a formal education, and he was apprenticed to a weaver. In 1668 he made his only visit to England, lasting ten months: with other Dutch Friends he visited the Quaker leader Steven Crisp in prison in Ipswich and attended the funeral of Josiah Cole. On 19 February 1681 he married Jacomina (1661–1703), daughter of Willem and Jannitze Boekenoogen of Alkmar; they had three daughters and one son.

Sewel's literary activities began at the end of his apprenticeship, by which time he had a working knowledge of English, French, German, and Latin. His translations, journalism, and editorial work for other authors were his main means of livelihood from the mid-1670s. He also did some teaching and acted from time to time as interpreter for visiting English Friends. He appears to have produced twenty-eight Dutch or Latin translations, of works in English, Flemish, French, German, Italian, and Latin; eight of these were Quaker publications. Apart from Quaker writings, Sewel translated works by Robert Boyle, Gilbert Burnett, William Congreve, Edmund Ludlow, Henry Sacheverell, William Sherlock, and Sir William Temple. He contributed to the Dutch translation of Sir Thomas Browne's collected works. He also edited a Dutch edition of his own mother's writings in 1684. Sewel's correspondence with William Penn shows him to have been a thoughtful and critical translator, willing to engage with the author on the content of the work. His translations and summaries of foreign news for *De Amsterdamsche Courant* from 1690 was followed by contributions to the *Nederlansche Courant*, and from 1702 to 1705 to *Tweemandelijke Uittreksels van alle eerst uytkomende Boeken* of Rotterdam and its successor, *Boekzaal der Geleerde Wereld*, which published his portrait in 1705.

Sewel's importance today rests on his linguistic and historical work. His *New Dictionary English and Dutch*, [*or*,] *Nieuw woordenboek der Nederduytsche en Engelsche taale*, published

Willem Sewel (1653–1720), by Jacob de Later, 1705 (after Gerrit Rademaker)

in Amsterdam in 1691 (revised in 1708), represents the second most important English and Dutch dictionary to be published in the period. It emerged from his extensive experience as a translator, alongside guides to the English and Dutch languages, a tract defending his own spelling system, and a Dutch grammar. Sewel worked largely from an English–Latin dictionary, translating the Latin to Dutch, and from a Dutch–French dictionary, translating the French to English. The dictionary gained from Sewel's need in his translating work to include specialist terminology of a learned, legal, and ecclesiastical nature, where there might be no obvious Dutch equivalent words. The 1708 revised edition took about four years to prepare: the English–Dutch part was revised and supplemented on the basis of his recent translating work and the availability of a better English dictionary, while the Dutch–English part was more thoroughly revised. The revised dictionary remained the standard throughout the eighteenth century and formed the basis of John Holtrop's dictionary of 1789.

Sewel was an active Friend, translating Quaker texts, engaging in defensive correspondence with anti-Quaker writers, and interpreting and participating in the general work of Dutch Friends. He began a correspondence in Latin with English Friends when he was twenty-three. In 1696 he declined an invitation from Penn to move to Bristol and take charge of a Friends' school there. His principal and enduring achievement for the Society of Friends was the substantial *Histori van de opkomste, annwas, en voortgang der Christenen, bekend by den naam van Quakers*, first published in Amsterdam in 1717 and then revised and translated by him as *The History of the Rise, Increase and Progress of the Christian People called Quakers* (1722). Sewel had been much involved with supplying material to Gerard Croese for his *Historia Quakeriana* (1695), but continued to collect on a wider scale for his own work. His correspondence with Croese makes clear his disappointment at the latter's numerous misinterpretations, and this may have been a catalyst for his own writing.

Sewel based his work on notes compiled over a long period, on the published sources he collected, and on correspondence with English Friends. The London yearly meeting appears to have gathered historical material to assist him once the English version was in prospect. His history attempted to set down, more comprehensively than previous accounts, an accurate record of the history of the Friends, and his use of George Fox's *Journal* may have had more influence in the eighteenth century than direct reading of the *Journal*. Material was added to, removed from, and edited, in the English version of the *History*, taking account of the views of the meeting for sufferings in London and playing down Sewel's original accounts of some of the extreme or eccentric behaviour by occasional early Friends. Regularly reprinted, his *History* remained a standard source until the early twentieth century, despite the publication of several other works in the intervening period.

Sewel died on 13 March 1720, probably in Amsterdam. Records of efforts by other Friends to help his children suggest that his estate was modest. His books, including the printed sources for the *History*, were left by his son to Friends in Amsterdam. DAVID J. HALL

Sources W. I. Hull, *Willem Sewel of Amsterdam, 1653–1720* (1933) · N. E. Osselton, *The dumb linguists: a study of the earliest English and Dutch dictionaries* (1973) · *DNB* · J. Nickalls, *Some Quaker portraits certain and uncertain* (1958)

Archives RS Friends, Lond., MS vol. of his Latin letters [copies]

Likenesses J. de Later, engraving, 1705 (after G. Rademaker), Rijksmuseum, Amsterdam [*see illus.*] · J. Casper Philips, engraving (after G. Rademaker, 1705), repro. in W. Sewel, *Nederduytscke spraakkonst* (Amsterdam, 1733) · J. de Later, engraving (after G. Rademaker, 1705), repro. in Osselton, *The dumb linguists* · engravings, Riksprenten Cabinet, Amsterdam

Wealth at death presumed modest: Quaker records

Sewell, Anna (1820–1878), author, was born on 30 March 1820 at 26 Church Plain, Yarmouth, Norfolk, the elder of the two children of Isaac Sewell (1793–1878), draper, and his wife, Mary *Sewell (1797–1884), writer, daughter of John Wright and his wife, Ann. Her parents were both from old Norfolk Quaker families and she was raised in the Quaker faith. Sewell's life began and ended in Norfolk but in between was slightly peripatetic. A move to London soon after her birth culminated in her father's business failure in 1822, the year Anna's brother, Philip, was born.

Anna Sewell (1820–1878), by unknown photographer

Her father's succeeding positions, including travelling in Nottingham lace and many years in banking, contributed to further moves the family made. London homes in Dalston (1822–32) and Stoke Newington (1832–6) were followed by a period in Brighton (1837–45) and a series of homes in Sussex: in Lancing (1845–9), Haywards Heath (1849–53), and Graylingwell, near Chichester (1853–8). The Sewells moved to Abson, near Wick in Gloucestershire, in 1858 and to Bath in 1864. Sewell's last years (1867–78) were spent in the White House, Old Catton, near Norwich.

Sewell was educated at home by her mother until she was about twelve, when she began attending a day school in Stoke Newington. She had an early interest in natural history and a talent for drawing, and her mother schooled her in independence, obedience, and self-denial. Her school education ended and what her mother called her 'life of constant frustration' (Mrs Bayly, 71) began when, aged about fourteen, she slipped and fell while running home from school in the rain, injuring both her ankles. Possibly mismanaged in its treatment, the injury to her ankles led to a lameness which, although varying in its severity, was permanent and meant that at times she could not walk outside or stand for very long. She also suffered from a debilitating invalidism which varied in its intensity but remained with her for life characterized at times by pains in her chest, loss of strength in her back, and a 'weakness' in her head leading to periods of 'enforced idleness' (Mrs Bayly, 245). Cures were sought, including hydropathic treatment, in England and abroad.

Sewell never married or had children and, apart from periods at spas or visiting relatives on a family farm in Norfolk, she always lived with her parents. It was in Norfolk that she learned to ride and drive the horses upon which her lameness made her reliant. She and her mother were extremely close. Both were heavily involved in practical charity to help the poor and became involved with the temperance movement. Anna taught Sunday school as her health permitted and founded a working men's evening institute in Wick at which she and her mother taught. In her sixties, Mary Sewell achieved some literary fame on publication of a series of didactic ballads and prose works for workers and children. Anna read and edited her mother's work before publication and was regarded as 'a very severe critic' (Mrs Bayly, 248). Her niece described Anna as 'no mean artist'. 'Practical, critical, and far-seeing', with 'a very high moral standard', she was 'mercilessly honest' and 'quite fearless', skilled at driving horses and indignantly vocal when she saw cruelty to animals (M. Sewell, 2–5).

Sewell was above all deeply religious. Retaining many Quaker-influenced beliefs throughout her life, she left the Quakers at the age of eighteen. After 1836, when physically able to, she joined her mother in attending, without joining, various protestant denominations. She suffered periods of religious doubt and at times struggled with her faith but those who knew her regarded her as a remarkably patient and uncomplaining sufferer whose physical pain was concealed under a face radiant with faith: 'in her presence one had a feeling of being on holy ground' (Mrs Bayly, 255–6).

Sewell's only publication was *Black Beauty*, written intermittently from 1871 to 1877 at a time when her health further declined, and she was confined to the house and her sofa. In the early period of writing the novel she dictated to her mother from the sofa on which she lay; in 1876 she was able to write in pencil on slips of paper which her mother transcribed. The novel was sold to her mother's publishers, Jarrold & Sons, for an outright payment of £40 and published as *Black Beauty: his grooms and companions; the autobiography of a horse*, 'Translated from the Original Equine, by Anna Sewell', on 24 November 1877 when Anna was fifty-seven. Now a children's classic, the novel was originally written for those who worked with horses, 'its special aim', Sewell wrote, 'being to induce kindness, sympathy, and an understanding treatment of horses' (Mrs Bayly, 272). It has been seen as instrumental in leading to the abolition of the bearing-rein.

Anna Sewell has been neglected by history. In ironic contrast, her only book has achieved phenomenal success. Pirated in America in 1890, its sales broke publishing records. It is said to be 'the sixth best seller in the English language' (Chitty in Wells and Grimshaw, x). Sewell lived just long enough to know of her novel's early success. She died at the White House of hepatitis or phthisis on 25 April 1878 just five months after its publication. She was buried on 30 April 1878 in the Quaker burial-ground in Lammas near Norwich. ADRIENNE E. GAVIN

Sources A. Gavin, *A dark horse: the life of Anna Sewell* (2004) · S. Chitty, *The woman who wrote 'Black Beauty'* (1971) · Mrs Bayly, *The life and letters of Mrs Sewell* (1889) [biography of mother] · M. Sewell, 'Recollections of Anna Sewell by her niece', in A. Sewell, *Black Beauty* (1935), 1–6 · A. A. Dent, 'Miss Sewell of Norfolk', *East Anglian Magazine*, 15 (1955–6), 542–7 · M. J. Baker, *Anna Sewell and 'Black Beauty'* (1956) · E. B. Wells and A. Grimshaw, *The annotated 'Black Beauty'* (1989) · A. Sewell, *Black Beauty*, ed. P. Hollindale, new edn (1992) · R. Engen, 'Afterword', in A. Sewell, *Black Beauty* (1986), 214–29 · W. T. F. Jarrold, 'Appreciation and life of author', in A. Sewell, *Black Beauty* (1912), 1–12 · V. Starrett, '*Black Beauty* and its author', *Buried Caesars: essays in literary appreciation* (1923), 205–23 · E. B. Bayly, 'Memoir', in M. Sewell, *Poems and ballads* (1886), vii–xxvi · d. cert.

Archives Norfolk RO, corresp.

Likenesses J. Beer, oils, 1894?, repro. in Dent, 'Miss Sewell of Norfolk' · oils, repro. in A. Sewell, *Black Beauty*, new edn (1935) · photograph, repro. in Bayly, *Life and letters*, facing p. 244 [*see illus.*] · photograph (with her mother), repro. in Chitty, *The woman who wrote 'Black Beauty'* · photograph, repro. in Dent, 'Miss Sewell of Norfolk', following p. 542 · photographs and oils, repro. in Gavin, *A dark horse*

Wealth at death under £2000: probate, 9 Aug 1878, *CGPLA Eng. & Wales*

Sewell, Elizabeth Missing (1815–1906), writer, was born at High Street, Newport, Isle of Wight, on 19 February 1815, the third daughter in a family of seven sons and five daughters of Thomas Sewell (1775–1842), solicitor, and his wife, Jane, *née* Edwards (1773/4–1848). Elizabeth's brothers were Richard Clarke *Sewell (*bap.* 1803, *d.* 1864), lawyer; William *Sewell (1804–1874), tutor and scholar; Henry *Sewell (1807–1879), lawyer and politician in New Zealand; and James Edwards *Sewell (1810–1903), warden of New College, Oxford. Elizabeth Sewell was sent at the age of four to Miss Crooke's school at Newport and then, at thirteen, to the Misses Aldridge's school at Bath, where she was 'not taught well' (*Autobiography*, 33). At fifteen she returned home to help her older sister Ellen educate her two young sisters, Emma and Janetta. This was the beginning of Sewell's lifelong interest in the moral and academic education of middle-class girls.

Initially, however, the strongest influence on Sewell's career was her older brother, William, through whom she met the leading members of the Oxford Movement as well as Charlotte Mary Yonge. William's name appeared as editor on the title-page of her early novels and stories. Her first publication, *Stories, Illustrative of the Lord's Prayer*, appeared in 1840, having been originally printed in *The Cottager's Monthly Visitor*. Encouraged by William, she continued to write didactic fiction, and her earnings were an essential means of financial support for her family. Following two bank failures, her father lost over £3000 and died in debt in 1842.

Sewell's emotional response to the Oxford Movement was the impulse behind one of her most successful novels, *Amy Herbert* (1844), in which high-church views and religious values are staunchly espoused. Her novels, which were intended for a female readership, and examined the spiritual and domestic anxieties of young girls, were extremely popular in America as well as in Britain. *Laneton Parsonage* (1846–8) was intended to impress on children the need to guard against 'small sins' and understand the significance of their baptismal promises. The scrupulous observance of moral principle was Sewell's main interest, although she was also influenced by the religious fashions and controversies of the day. These included the 'rage for church building' (*Autobiography*, 81) in *Gertrude* (1845) and the temptations of secession to Rome in *Margaret Percival* (1847).

Although Sewell's home remained the Isle of Wight, she was well travelled and met the literary celebrities of the day. In 1849 she accompanied her Bonchurch neighbours, Captain and Lady Jane Swinburne and their son Algernon, the future poet, then a boy of twelve, to the Lake District where they visited Wordsworth at Rydal Mount. Tennyson was a neighbour on the Isle of Wight and Sewell later met Browning at a London dinner party. In 1851 she visited Paris and travelled extensively in Germany, Switzerland, northern Italy, and the Tyrol, returning regularly to Germany throughout the 1850s.

In 1852 Sewell and two of her sisters, in order to support a growing family of dependent nephews and nieces, opened a school at their home, Ashcliffe, in Bonchurch. Her nieces were the first pupils and, though they were joined by a handful of other pupils, all the girls called their teachers Aunt.

Increasingly, Sewell based her writing on her own experiences. *The Experience of Life* (1853) reflected on remaining unmarried, *Katharine Ashton* (1854) drew on her memories of Miss Crooke's school, while *Ursula* (1858) was inspired by her devotion to her brother William.

Throughout her writings on girls' education, which included *Principles of education drawn from nature and revelation, and applied to female education in the upper classes* (1865), Sewell stressed the need for middle-class girls to be taught by women and to be given a clear moral training in Church of England principles. In 1866 she began a new venture, St Boniface's School in Ventnor, which she described in her article 'An experiment in middle-class education', published in *Macmillan's Magazine* in 1872. In an article of 1888 for *Nineteenth Century*, 'The reign of pedantry in girls' schools', she attacked the new emphasis on examination-driven learning. While she acknowledged that her views were old-fashioned, she argued that girls should be prepared for a useful home life rather than a career. She also believed that children should have a broad historical grounding and she wrote several school textbooks, including *Historical selections: a series of readings from the best authorities on English and European history* (1868), on which she collaborated with her friend Charlotte Yonge. Sewell also contributed numerous articles to Yonge's journal, *The Monthly Packet*.

In 1869 Sewell visited the Institute for Protestant Deaconesses at Kaiserworth, Germany, twice reporting on the experience in *Macmillan's Magazine* (1870 and 1872). She was in Germany again during the Franco-Prussian War of 1870 and took her final trip abroad (to Switzerland) in 1872.

With the publication in 1891 of her final novel, *Home and after Life* (abridged from two earlier works), Sewell acknowledged that she was 'no longer a recognised popular authoress' (*Autobiography*, 202). Her books were indeed very much products of her day, when young women were excited by religious developments and unsure of their social role. Sewell hoped she would be the last of her sisters to die so that she would always be able to provide for them. This was indeed what happened: her gradual decline began with the shock of her sister Emma's death in 1897. She was supported in her old age by an annuity from her grateful pupils and by an award of £300 from the Royal Literary Fund.

Elizabeth Sewell died at her home, Ashcliffe, Bonchurch, on 17 August 1906 and was buried in the churchyard there on 22 August. Her *Autobiography*, edited by her niece Eleanor L. Sewell, was published in 1907. The photograph reprinted as the frontispiece shows a small and rather stout woman with a prominent nose and lips. One of her pupils, the novelist Mary Crawford (Mrs Hugh) Fraser, recalled 'her narrow, but staunch religious belief' and 'decorous lawfulness in every detail of the conduct of life' (Fraser, 1.223–4). VALERIE SANDERS

Sources *The autobiography of Elizabeth M. Sewell*, ed. E. L. Sewell (1907) • *DNB* • J. Shattock, ed., *New Cambridge bibliography*, 4 (1999) • *The Times* (18 Aug 1906) • Mrs H. Fraser [M. C. Fraser], *A diplomatist's life in many lands* (1910) • M. C. Owen, *The Sewells of the Isle of Wight* (privately printed, Manchester, 1906) • *The Athenaeum* (25 Aug 1906), p. 214 • *CGPLA Eng. & Wales* (1906)

Likenesses Hughes & Mullins, photographs, repro. in Sewell, ed., *Autobiography*, frontispiece

Wealth at death £7860 0s. 2d.: probate, 7 Sept 1906, *CGPLA Eng. & Wales*

Sewell, George (*bap.* **1687**, *d.* **1726**), author and physician, the eldest son of John Sewell, treasurer and chapter clerk to the dean and canons of Windsor, was baptized on 2 June 1687 at St George's Chapel, Windsor. He was educated at Eton College, being admitted as a king's scholar on 7 August 1699. Reminiscences of his schooldays were included in his poem 'The Favourite, a Simile'. He was admitted to Peterhouse, Cambridge, on 25 June 1706, where he graduated BA in 1709. For a time he studied medicine under Hermann Boerhaave at the University of Leiden, and about July 1725 he took the degree of MD at Edinburgh University. Sewell practised at first in London for some years, but without success. He then moved to Hampstead, where he met with better fortune, until competition ruined his practice. Necessity forced him to become a booksellers' hack, publishing numerous poems, translations, and political and other pamphlets.

As a young man Sewell inclined to toryism, and was a bitter critic of Bishop Burnet, whom he attacked in five pamphlets published between 1713 and 1715. He also wrote two pro-tory essays, in which he criticized the arguments of Sir Richard Steele. However, by 1718 he had attached himself to the cause of Sir Robert Walpole.

Sewell's best-known production remains his markedly anti-Spanish play the *Tragedy of Sir Walter Raleigh* (1719), first performed at the Lincoln's Inn Fields Theatre and later revived at Drury Lane in 1789. A man 'of amiable disposition', and possessing 'a very considerable genius' (Cibber, 4.191), Sewell contrived to link his name with some of the most distinguished writers of this period, including Joseph Addison, Matthew Prior, John Phillips, and Alexander Pope, adding a seventh volume to the latter's 1725 edition of Shakespeare. It was perhaps as a result of this unsolicited contribution that Pope, in the first edition of his 'Epistle to Dr. Arbuthnot', wrote of 'Sanguine Sew—'. Sewell revived his former interest in medicine with an account of Archibald Pitcairne (whose 'medical dissertation' he translated in 1717), which was posthumously attached to George Cheyne's *History of himself* (1743). Sewell died of consumption at Hampstead, in great poverty, on 8 February 1726 and was given a pauper's funeral on 12 February.

W. P. COURTNEY, *rev.* M. E. CLAYTON

Sources R. Shiels, *The lives of the poets of Great Britain and Ireland*, ed. T. Cibber, 4 (1753), 188–91 • [G. Jacob], *The poetical register, or, The lives and characters of all the English poets*, 2 (1723), 177–8 • H. J. Rose, *A new general biographical dictionary*, ed. H. J. Rose and T. Wright, 12 vols. (1853) • Venn, *Alum. Cant.* • J. J. Park, *The topography and natural history of Hampstead* (1844) • *IGI*

Sewell, Henry (**1807–1879**), lawyer and premier of New Zealand, was born at Newport, Isle of Wight, on 7 September 1807, the fourth son of Thomas Sewell (1775–1842), a leading solicitor of Newport, and his wife, Jane (1773/4–1848), the youngest daughter of John Edwards, a curate of Newport. His brothers were Richard Clarke *Sewell, James Edwards *Sewell, and William *Sewell, and his sister was Elizabeth Missing *Sewell. Henry was educated at Hyde Abbey School, near Winchester. He qualified as a solicitor and joined the family firm in 1826. His father died in 1842, leaving an estate encumbered with large debts. Rather than declare insolvency, the family undertook to repay the creditors, a task which took thirty years and overshadowed Sewell's career.

This crisis was followed by the death on 28 July 1844 of Sewell's first wife, Lucinda Marianne, the eldest daughter of General William Nedham of Mount Olive, Jamaica, and Widcombe, Bath, whom he had married on 15 May 1834. Their six children were brought up by Sewell's sister, and Sewell himself moved to London, where he joined the Canterbury Association, which was planning a Church of England colony in New Zealand. He became salaried deputy chairman in 1851 and two years later was sent out to New Zealand to wind up the association's affairs, having on 23 January 1850 married Elizabeth (1819–1880), the second daughter of Captain Edward Kittoe RN of Deal. Sewell arrived in February 1853 with Edward Gibbon Wakefield, and settled at Lyttelton. His successful disposal of the association's liabilities and assets included the creation of a substantial land endowment for the diocese of Christchurch.

Sewell lived in New Zealand for seventeen years, in three periods—1853–6, 1859–66, and 1870–76. He was a prominent figure in the first generation of colonial politicians, among whom he had the reputation of a lettered wit and an independent man of business. He represented Lyttelton on the Canterbury provincial council in 1855–6. He was a member of the house of representatives (1854–6, 1860, 1865–6) and sat in the nominated legislative council (1861–5 and 1870–73).

Sewell served in eight different ministries, starting with the 'mixed ministry' of officials and politicians under James Edward FitzGerald (14 June – 2 August 1854). When responsible government began he became the first premier (18 April – 20 May 1856), but could not retain a majority in the house. As treasurer, he was virtually deputy premier in the first stable ministry, led by Edward Stafford (2 June – 4 November 1856). Later he was negotiator on behalf of the colony in Australia and England (1857–9).

After returning to New Zealand in February 1859 Sewell soon left the ministry. Having written a pamphlet in 1846 advocating a system of land transfer by simple registration of title, he was a suitable appointee as first registrar-general of lands in 1861. In 1863 he inaugurated the first land registry under the Torrens system of land transfer. He served as attorney-general in three ministries between 1861 and 1865. After another four-year break in England, he was briefly minister of justice in 1870–71 and colonial secretary for a month in 1872.

Sewell finally left New Zealand in 1876 because of his wife's health and went to Romford, Essex, where his eldest son was curate. He later moved to 4 Salisbury Villas, Station Road, Cambridge, where he died on 14 May 1879. He was buried at Waresley, Huntingdonshire, where his wife's brother-in-law was vicar; Elizabeth was later buried beside her husband. Sewell recouped his finances in New Zealand by some modest suburban land dealings, but he was not really a colonist. Nor was he a successful politician. Contemporaries remarked on his 'dodgy lawyer-like way' and his ability to argue a case rather than enunciate a policy. He was a drafter of memoranda and back-up man rather than leader. He wrote ten pamphlets on legal, ecclesiastical, political and race-relations topics; his *Journal*, written first as a newsletter to family and associates (and copied out by Elizabeth), provides the fullest private account of persons and places in early Canterbury and the beginnings of self-government in New Zealand.

W. David McIntyre

Sources H. Sewell, *The journal of Henry Sewell, 1853–7*, ed. W. D. McIntyre, 2 vols. (1980) • G. H. Scholefield, ed., *A dictionary of New Zealand biography*, 2 vols. (1940) • W. D. McIntyre, 'Sewell, Henry', *DNZB*, vol. 1 • M. C. Owen, *The Sewells of the Isle of Wight: with an account of some of the families connected with them by marriage* (privately printed, Manchester, 1906) • G. H. Scholefield, ed., *New Zealand parliamentary record, 1840–1949* (1950)

Archives Canterbury Museum Library, Christchurch | Archives New Zealand, Wellington, New Zealand company directors' minute books • Canterbury Museum Library, Christchurch, letters to fourth Baron Lyttelton • Canterbury Museum Library, Christchurch, Selfe MSS • Canterbury Museum Library, Christchurch, Wakefield MSS • Diocesan Archives, Christchurch, Canterbury Association MSS • Diocesan Archives, Christchurch, Committee on Church Matters MSS • Diocesan Archives, Christchurch, Trusts MSS • NL NZ, Turnbull L., Canterbury Association letter-books • U. Durham, corresp. with third Earl Grey

Likenesses A. C. Barker, double portrait, photograph, 1850–1859? (with Tancred), repro. in W. J. Gardner, *A history of Canterbury*, vol. III (1971), following p. 144; priv. coll. • portrait, in or after 1856, Canterbury Museum, New Zealand • A. C. Barker, photograph, 1856–9, Canterbury Museum, New Zealand • photograph, 1860 (*Members of the house of parliament*), repro. in Sewell, *Journal of Henry Sewell*, vol. 2, following p. 256 • photograph, 1870–74 (Christchurch Club), Canterbury Museum, New Zealand

Wealth at death under £450: probate, 3 June 1879, *CGPLA Eng. & Wales*

Sewell, James Edwards (1810–1903), college head, was born at Newport, Isle of Wight, on 25 December 1810, seventh child and sixth son of Thomas Sewell (1775–1842), solicitor, of Newport, and his wife, Jane (1773/4–1848), daughter of the Revd John Edwards, curate of Newport. He was one of a family of twelve, which included Richard Clarke *Sewell, legal writer, William *Sewell, a Church of England priest Henry *Sewell, first premier of New Zealand, and Elizabeth Missing *Sewell, author. Admitted a scholar of Winchester College in 1821, James Sewell became a probationary fellow of New College, Oxford, in 1827, and a full fellow in 1829. He graduated BA in 1832, proceeding MA in 1835, and BD and DD in 1860, and was ordained deacon in 1834 and priest in 1836. Except for a few months in 1834–5, when he was curate at Hursley, Hampshire, he resided in New College from 1827 to his death in 1903. He filled successively every office in the college, and in 1860 he was elected warden. He took a large part in university affairs: he was the first secretary of the Oxford local examinations delegacy, and from 1874 to 1878 was vice-chancellor of the university. He actively aided the preservation and arrangement of the manuscript records in the library of New College.

During Sewell's long wardenship New College was transformed from a small foundation, limited to former pupils of Winchester College, to one of the largest colleges in the university. The chief responsibility for this growth is to be attributed to his colleagues, but Sewell, a conservative by instinct, loyally accepted changes which did not commend themselves to his own judgement. It was largely owing to him that there was no break in the continuity of college tradition and feeling, and that older generations of Wykehamists were reconciled to the reforms made by successive commissions and by the college itself. Sewell died unmarried in the warden's lodgings, New College, on 29 January 1903, and was buried in the cloisters of the college.

R. S. Rait, *rev.* M. C. Curthoys

Sources M. C. Owen, *The Sewells of the Isle of Wight: with an account of some of the families connected with them by marriage* (privately printed, Manchester, 1906) • H. B. George, *New College, 1856–1906* (1906) • *The Times* (30 Jan 1903) • *CGPLA Eng. & Wales* (1903) • J. Foster, *Oxford men and their colleges* (1893)

Archives New College, Oxford

Likenesses H. von Herkomer, oils, 1886, New College, Oxford • Spy [L. Ward], chromolithograph caricature, NPG; repro. in *VF* (5 April 1894) • etching (after H. von Herkomer), BM

Wealth at death £3697 11*s*. 2*d*.: probate, 2 March 1903, *CGPLA Eng. & Wales*

Sewell, Jonathan (*bap.* 1766, *d.* 1839), jurist in Canada, the son of Jonathan Sewall (1728–1796), the last British attorney-general of Massachusetts, and Esther Quincy, was baptized on 6 June 1766 at Cambridge, Massachusetts. He moved to England in 1775 with his loyalist parents, and was educated at Bristol grammar school and Brasenose College, Oxford. In 1785 he emigrated to New Brunswick and studied law, then in 1789 went to Quebec, where he was called to the bar on 30 October 1789. In 1793 he became solicitor-general, and in 1795 attorney-general and advocate-general. On 24 September 1796 he married Henrietta, known as Harriet, the daughter of William Smith, former chief justice of New York and Lower Canada. They had sixteen children, of whom twelve survived infancy. In 1797 Sewell entered the house of assembly as member for William Henry, for which he sat through three parliaments, until in 1808 he became chief justice of Lower Canada, an office he filled for thirty years. Shortly afterwards he was named speaker of the legislative council and president of the executive council. He resigned from the second in 1830 but held the speakership until his death.

As attorney-general Sewell prosecuted David McLane, an American undercover agent working for revolutionary France, on a charge of high treason (1797). While building a persuasive case, he was also a party to dubious transactions which ensured that the accused would be convicted and serve as a dramatic example. McLane was hanged, disembowelled, and beheaded before a huge throng of spectators in Quebec City.

Like most of the tiny English élite in the 1790s and early 1800s, Sewell was an alarmist who assumed that, if France invaded, the French-speaking Canadian majority would rise in supportive rebellion, with English heads targeted for local 'Jacobin' pikes. One political conclusion Sewell and others drew was the imperative need to anglify the Canadians, a viewpoint dropped during the Anglo-American War of 1812–14, when he realized the United States, not faraway France, had become the major external threat to the colony. Sewell's previous attempts at anglification had embittered relations between the Canadians and the English.

Sir James Henry Craig (1748–1812), governor from 1807 to 1811, quickly absorbed the garrison mentality of the English minority and acted on it in 1810 by imprisoning, without bail or trial, three leaders of the constitutionally liberal opposition *parti canadien*. These men—members of the provincial parliament and editors of their party's strident newspaper, *Le Canadien*—were charged with 'treasonable practices', the meaning of which was unknown on both sides of the Atlantic. With others of the executive council Sewell had advised Craig to do this, on the grounds that the three were in league with Napoleon through his ambassador to Washington. Sewell presided at a habeas corpus hearing of one prisoner, refusing the writ on the debatable basis that no parliamentary privilege existed. The British attorney-general later concluded the arrests had been illegal, as there was no proof whatever of treasonable practices.

One of Sewell's earliest acts as chief justice produced a remarkable episode in Canadian history. In 1809 he issued rules of practice for the Quebec king's bench and another set for the provincial court of appeals. In 1814 they were attacked by the assembly, under the leadership of James Stuart (1780–1853), as a usurpation of the law-making authority of the legislature and as affecting the liberty of the subject. Sewell was impeached for subverting the constitution and charged with malicious influence over the governor, leading to various specified acts which covered the whole range of conflict between the house and the government under Craig, including the incarceration of the *parti canadien* leaders. James Monk, chief justice of Montreal, was joined in the indictment, but only for issuing his own rules of practice. Like Sewell's they followed Westminster precedents very closely. Sewell defended himself in England, where the colonial secretary, Lord Bathurst, dismissed the political charges as a matter of constitutional principle, the governor alone being responsible for executive decisions. This undermined the *parti canadien*'s notion of a local ministry accountable in cases of serious misbehaviour to the assembly. The privy council found nothing wrong with the various rules of practice.

From 1793 Sewell exercised considerable influence over virtually every governor, reaching the pinnacle twice as 'prime minister': under Craig and Lord Dalhousie (1820–28). He successfully advised the latter to take a hard line—to the point of rejecting the assembly's choice of speaker (1827)—in the prolonged dispute over control of public appropriations. Not surprisingly the chief justice exploited his position to gain lucrative government patronage for himself and his family.

In the legislative council Sewell pursued an extreme tory line, for instance initiating the legally questionable imprisonment for libel of two *patriote* newspaper editors for attacking the upper house. He was also one of the pioneers of cultural development, and was a founder (1824) and later president (1830–31) of the Quebec Literary and Historical Society. He gave the first paper in 1824, *An essay on the juridical history of France, so far as it relates to the law of the province of Lower-Canada*. His other notable publications dealt in constitutional issues: expounding parliamentary procedure (1792) and advocating federation of the British North American colonies (1814, 1824).

Sewell died on 11 November 1839 and was buried four days later from the Anglican cathedral in Quebec City. He was survived by his wife. His judgments, particularly on French civil law, were remarkable for clarity, articulation of general principle, and profound scholarship. His main shortcoming as a judge was to find that law which suited the political interests of the executive. He was awarded an honorary LLD by Harvard University in 1832. At the end of the twentieth century he is recognized by Canadian legal historians as one of Canada's most accomplished jurists.

C. A. Harris, *rev.* F. Murray Greenwood

Sources NA Canada, Jonathan Sewell and family collection, MG23-GII10 · F. M. Greenwood and J. H. Lambert, 'Sewell, Jonathan', *DCB*, vol. 7 · F. M. Greenwood, *Legacies of fear: law and politics in Quebec in the era of the French Revolution* (1993) · E. Kolish, *Nationalismes et conflits de droits: le débat du droit privé au Québec, 1760–1840* (1994) · NA Canada, CO 42 series, MG 11, 1789–1839 · NA Canada, S series, RG4-A1, 1789–1839 · McGill University, Montreal, Herman Ryland MSS · G. O. Stuart, ed., *Reports of cases argued and determined in the courts of King's Bench and in the provincial Court of Appeals of Lower Canada* (1834)

Archives Archives Nationales, Quebec · Mass. Hist. Soc. · NA Canada, corresp., journals, and MSS | NA Canada, CO 42 and S series · NL Scot., corresp. with Lord Dalhousie

Likenesses oils, Canadian Senate; copy, NA Canada, C111156

Wealth at death £39,209: Greenwood and Lambert, 'Sewell, Jonathan'

Sewell [*née* Wright], **Mary** (**1797–1884**), writer and poet, was born on 6 April 1797 at Sutton in Suffolk, the third of the seven children of John Wright (*c*.1770–1854), farmer, and his wife, Ann (*c*.1772–1856), daughter of John Holmes, farmer, of Tivetshall in Norfolk. Her parents were both from Norfolk Quaker families and her upbringing was based on Quaker principles. Before she was two, the family moved to a farm at Felthorpe in Norfolk where she spent most of her childhood. When she was twelve the farm was sold and the family moved to Yarmouth where her father entered business with a shipowner. Early education at a dame-school was followed by tuition at home under a series of governesses. At fourteen her formal education was completed by a year at a Quaker boarding-school in Tottenham. She read poetry avidly, particularly Scott, Southey, Moore, and Byron. As a result of her father's financial ruin in 1817, she became a governess at a school in Essex; it was, she wrote, 'a great descent in the social scale' (Mrs Bayly, 48).

On 15 June 1819 Mary Wright married Isaac Sewell (1793–1878), whose parents were elders in the Friends' meeting at Yarmouth. The couple settled in a small house at 26 Church Plain, Yarmouth, where their first child, Anna *Sewell (1820–1878), was born. Shortly after Anna's birth they moved to London where business difficulties resulted in Isaac's financial failure. In 1822, after the birth of their son Philip, they moved to Dalston, and Isaac became a commercial traveller selling Nottingham lace. Sewell taught her children at home: subjects including natural history and science, as well as values such as independence, obedience, faith in God, and charity. To purchase books for their education, she wrote and sold her first work, *Walks with Mamma*, a book written in words of one syllable. In 1832 the family moved to Stoke Newington where both children attended school and Anna was lamed by a fall. Over the following years Mary sought unsuccessfully for a cure for her daughter and nursed her during the periods of invalidism which recurred throughout Anna's life. Mother and daughter were always extremely close, savouring 'the never-ceasing joy of each other's lives' (E. B. Bayly, xxii).

Deeply religious, Sewell experienced a spiritual crisis in her late thirties that resulted in her leaving the Quakers and being baptized. Over the following years she experimented with various protestant denominations. In later life she wrote: 'If I ever joined any religious body again … it would be the Friends—though I've left them' (Mrs Bayly, 84).

In 1836 the Sewell family moved to Brighton, where Isaac took a post as a bank manager. His future positions led to a series of homes in Sussex: in Lancing (1845–9), Haywards Heath (1849–53), and Graylingwell, near Chichester (1853–8). 1858 saw a move to Abson, near Wick in Gloucestershire, where Sewell's writing career began. Her writing was inextricably connected to the practical and active charity work she did throughout her life. Known for being plain-spoken and having 'a profound appreciation … of the miseries of others' (Mrs Bayly, 169), she visited the poor and was concerned with the plight of working women and with the moral education of children. She was involved in the anti-slavery movement, mothers' meetings, prison visiting, and the temperance movement. Together with Anna she founded a Working Men's Evening Institute in Wick at which they both taught.

It was not until Sewell's sixtieth year that she began writing for the public: 'I have a knack of a rough sort of rhyming that serves my purpose', she wrote (Mrs Bayly, 136). Her literary works, aimed at children and the working classes, were didactic, and often used pathos to teach faith in God, good behaviour, appreciation of nature, kindness, and temperance. In 1858 *Homely Ballads for the Working Man's Fireside*, a collection of verse written in simple language, appeared. *The Children of Summerbrook* (1859), a story in verse for children, followed and in 1861 *Stories in Verse for the Street and Lane* was published. Her best-seller *Mother's Last Words* (1860), recounting two young boys' obedience to their mother's dying words, 'had a sale unprecedented in the history of ballads' (Mrs Bayly, 146). *Our Father's Care* (1861), a poem about a young watercress girl, was, like other examples of her verse, read aloud at Sunday schools, in prisons, hospitals, and on ships. Her prose works included *Patience Hart's First Experience in Service* (1862), the story of a virtuous servant girl written in the form of letters to her mother, and *Thy Poor Brother* (1863) a work advising on poor visiting. Well-known during her writing career, her work has since been neglected, its didacticism and rhyming having fallen out of fashion.

In 1864 Sewell moved to Bath and in 1867, after her daughter-in-law's death, to Old Catton near Norwich to be near her son and his seven children. When approaching eighty she nursed her daughter through her final, painful seven-year illness which confined her to her sofa, during which time Mary transcribed and took dictation of Anna's only novel, the enduring classic *Black Beauty*. Her husband, increasingly feeble, also at this time became mentally ill. In 1878 her daughter, then her husband, died. Sewell remained active and involved in charity work until her own death from senile decay and congestion of the lungs on 10 June 1884 at her home, the White House, Old Catton. She was buried in the Quaker burial-ground at Lammas near Norwich. ADRIENNE E. GAVIN

Sources A. Gavin, *A dark horse: the life of Anna Sewell* (2004) • Mrs Bayly, *The life and letters of Mrs Sewell* (1889) [incl. autobiography by Mary Sewell] • E. B. Bayly, 'Memoir', in M. Sewell, *Poems and ballads* (1886), vii–xxvi • S. Chitty, *The woman who wrote 'Black Beauty'* (1971) • M. Nugent, 'Grandmother to Black Beauty', *London Mercury*, 26 (1932), 52–60 • M. J. Baker, *Anna Sewell and 'Black Beauty'* (1956) • J. Shattock, ed., *The Cambridge bibliography of English literature*, 3rd edn, 4 (1999) • *DNB* • *IGI* • d. cert. • register of births, quarterly meeting of Suffolk Society of Friends

Archives Norfolk RO, family and personal corresp.

Likenesses Burgess and Grimwood, photograph, 1872, Norfolk RO • photograph, repro. in Bayly, *Life and letters* • photographs, repro. in Gavin, *A dark horse* • photographs, repro. in Chitty, *The woman who wrote 'Black Beauty'*

Wealth at death £6223 18s. 5d.: probate, 15 July 1884, *CGPLA Eng. & Wales*

Sewell, Richard Clarke (*bap.* 1803, *d.* 1864), lawyer, was the eldest son of Thomas Sewell (1775–1842), a solicitor, of Newport, Isle of Wight, and his wife, Jane Edwards (1773/4–1848). Among his eleven siblings were James Edwards *Sewell, warden of New College, Oxford, Henry *Sewell, first premier of New Zealand, William *Sewell, a Church of England clergyman, and the novelist Elizabeth Missing *Sewell. He was baptized at Newport on 6 February 1803, and entered Winchester College in 1818. He matriculated from Magdalen College, Oxford, on 26 July 1821, was a demy of his college from 1821 until 1837, and a fellow from 1837 to 1856. He served as senior dean of arts in 1838, as bursar in 1840, and was vice-president and praelector of natural philosophy in 1842. He graduated with a second class in *literae humaniores*, BA 1826, and proceeded MA 1829, and DCL 1840. He was awarded the Newdigate prize for poetry in 1825. On 25 June 1830 he was called to the bar at the Middle Temple, became known as a special pleader, and took business on the western circuit and at the Hampshire sessions.

Tragedy overtook the family in 1842 when Sewell's father died, leaving large debts which the family undertook to clear. This may have influenced Sewell's decision to go to Australia towards the end of 1855. On 7 February 1856 he was admitted to the Victorian bar, where he gained considerable eminence, chiefly in criminal cases, including his leading the prosecution of one of the murderers of John Price, the notorious inspector-general of prisons, in April 1857. From May to August 1856 he edited the *Victorian Law Times and Legal Observer*, and from February 1857 he was reader in law at the new University of Melbourne, but the demands of his practice forced him to resign in July.

Sewell published extensively in Britain and Australia. His writings were mainly on legal subjects, but, like his brother William, he was also interested in the rights and constitutional position of the Anglican church, on which he published a work in 1848. For the English Historical Society, Sewell edited *Gesta Stephani* (1846). Making available this invaluable source on the reign of King Stephen was helpful, but the source itself was incomplete until missing parts were discovered in the latter half of the twentieth century, which discovery made earlier editions redundant.

Sewell died unmarried on 7 November 1864 in Melbourne and was buried the following day in Melbourne general cemetery.

G. C. Boase, *rev.* Elizabeth Baigent

Sources M. C. Owen, *The Sewells of the Isle of Wight: with an account of some of the families connected with them by marriage* (privately printed, Manchester, 1906) • W. D. McIntyre, 'Sewell, Henry', *DNZB*, vol. 1 • Foster, *Alum. Oxon.* • J. R. Bloxam, *A register of the presidents, fellows … of Saint Mary Magdalen College*, 8 vols. (1853–85) • *GM*, 3rd ser., 18 (1865), 386 [date of death is incorrect] • *The Argus* [Melbourne] (9 Nov 1864) • J. L. Forde, *The story of the bar of Victoria, 1839–1891* [1915] • J. V. Barry, *The life and death of John Price* (1964) • G. Blainey, *A centenary history of the University of Melbourne* (1957)

Sewell, Robert Beresford Seymour (1880–1964), zoologist, was born on 5 March 1880 at Leamington Spa, Warwickshire, the second son of the Revd Arthur Sewell, schoolmaster and chaplain to the order of St John of Jerusalem, and his wife, Mary Lee, daughter of Henry Franks Waring, a solicitor in Lyme Regis, Dorset. Both sides of the family were of Wessex stock; during Sewell's childhood the family moved to Weymouth, where he attended Weymouth College. He obtained an exhibition to Christ's College, Cambridge, in 1898, but before going up he studied zoology for six months at University College, London.

At Cambridge, Sewell obtained a double first in 1903; after two years as a junior demonstrator he entered St Bartholomew's Hospital, London, and qualified MRCS and LRCP in 1907. In 1908 he joined the Indian Medical Service, beginning an association which was to last more than twenty-five years. He was initially appointed a medical officer attached to the 67th and 84th Punjabi regiments, but in 1910 he became surgeon-naturalist to the marine survey of India and assistant superintendent in the Indian Museum in Calcutta, allowing his love of zoology to blossom.

Sewell's job was to look after the health of all on board the RIMS vessel *Investigator* during five or six months at sea each year. However, since the medical workload was generally very light, he spent most of his time studying marine biology—particularly the copepods—and oceanography. From 1911 to 1913 he was also seconded to the Calcutta Medical College as professor of biology.

On 5 August 1914, the day after the declaration of war, Sewell married Dorothy (*d.* 1931), daughter of William and Matilda Dean of Chichester, Sussex. He was almost immediately dispatched on military duty, serving as port health officer in Aden from 1914 to 1916 and thereafter in Sinai and in Palestine with Allenby.

After the war Sewell returned to India as superintendent of the zoological survey, but from time to time resumed seagoing duties as surgeon-naturalist on the *Investigator*. In 1925 he was appointed director of the zoological survey and head of the Indian Museum in Calcutta, finally retiring from the Indian Medical Service with the rank of lieutenant-colonel in 1933.

During home leave in England in 1932 Sewell was involved in the planning of a deep-sea expedition to the western Indian Ocean, to be funded from a bequest by Sir John Murray. He was ultimately appointed leader of the expedition in the Egyptian coast guard and fishery research vessel HEMS *Mabahiss*, lent by the Egyptian government and with a mixed British and Egyptian crew and scientific complement. The *Mabahiss* sailed from Alexandria on 3 September 1933 and returned on 26 May 1934. In the meantime almost 200 'stations', many in the deep sea, had been worked from the Gulf of Oman in the north to the Seychelles and Zanzibar in the south, and from the east coast of Africa to Ceylon. The scientific results, including biology, geology, and seawater chemistry (which included the discovery of an oxygen-depleted layer), were published by the British Museum (Natural History) in seventeen volumes between 1935 and 1967. However, Sewell was unable to find a publisher for his own narrative of the cruise, which was finally published by UNESCO in 1986.

Following the expedition Sewell was elected in 1934 to the fellowship of the Royal Society and retired to Cambridge. He continued to work in the zoology department, busy not only with the expedition reports and his own taxonomic work, but also with the editorship of the *Fauna of British India*, which he continued until the year before his death. In 1946 he spent four months in India at the government's invitation to advise on the reconstruction of the zoological survey and on the formation of the anthropological survey and the Central Fisheries Research Institute. The respect in which he was held in India was reflected in the presidency of the Asiatic Society of Bengal (1931–3), the Barclay memorial medal (1931), the Annandale memorial medal (1947), and honorary fellowships of the Indian Academy of Sciences, Bangalore and the Zoological Society of India (both in 1949). In the UK he also held the presidency of the Linnean Society (1952–5) and the Ray Society (1950–53).

Sewell's seventy or so scientific contributions, published between 1903 and 1958, include papers on the physical oceanography and geography of the Indian Ocean region, taxonomic and ecological studies of a wide range of animal groups from the Cnidaria to the fishes, and even anthropology. But from about 1912 his main interest lay in the taxonomy and distribution of the Copepoda, on which he published several major works, including those based on the collections made from the *Mabahiss*; these are still highly respected.

Sewell was a dedicated and enthusiastic freemason. He was initiated into the Concordia Lodge in Calcutta in 1912, joined the two university lodges in Cambridge after his retirement and was a founder member of the new Thirkill Lodge in 1953. Having been elected to various senior offices, in 1958 he was finally given the rank of past grand deacon in the grand lodge of England. On a personal level he was, according to C. F. A. Pantin (author of his obituary in *Memoirs FRS*), a well-loved figure in Cambridge, but at the same time a somewhat private man, rather difficult to get to know well. Pantin attributed this to the absence of old friends who could have shared the memories of his Indian days, rather than to a lack of social qualities. But the tone of Sewell's John Murray expedition narrative suggests that his background and experiences as part of the raj in British India had made him a rather formal man, acutely aware of protocol and status. This formality may have made him seem somewhat distant, particularly to the younger generation. Sewell died in the Evelyn Nursing Home in Cambridge on 11 February 1964, survived by two daughters. A. L. Rice

Sources C. F. A. Pantin, *Memoirs FRS*, 11 (1965), 147–55 · A. L. Rice, ed., *Deep-sea challenge: the John Murray/Mabahiss expedition to the Indian Ocean, 1933–34* (1986) · *DNB* · *CGPLA Eng. & Wales* (1964)
Archives Indian Museum, Calcutta · NHM, logbooks, papers, and station records
Likenesses photograph, repro. in Pantin, *Memoirs FRS* · photographs, NHM
Wealth at death £7222: probate, 1 May 1964, *CGPLA Eng. & Wales*

Sewell, Sir Thomas (*c.*1710–1784), judge, was the son of Thomas Sewell of West Ham, Essex, but nothing else is known of his background or origins. He was admitted a member of the Middle Temple on 6 June 1729 and called to the bar on 24 May 1734. He practised at the chancery bar where he worked hard and acquired 'a considerable practice' (Foss, *Judges*, 366), apparently receiving numerous briefs from dissenters. He took silk after twenty years' practice, being appointed on 4 April 1754, and was elected a bencher of the Middle Temple on 3 May of the same year. He was appointed Lent reader of his inn in 1762, and treasurer in 1765.

Having established himself in legal practice, Sewell embarked on an unremarkable political career. He unsuccessfully contested Wallingford, encouraged by Henry Pelham, in the general election of 1754, and subsequently sought the duke of Newcastle's nomination at Seaford (June 1755), Dover (April 1756), and Okehampton (October 1758), all without success. On 29 December 1758 he finally procured Newcastle's interest at Harwich, which he represented until the dissolution of March 1761—Newcastle subsequently assigned the seat to John Roberts. In spite of Newcastle's support, Sewell was badly defeated at Exeter in the general election of 1761, but he was returned on the government interest for Winchelsea at a by-election on 4 December 1761. He remained MP for Winchelsea until his defeat in 1768 and did not stand for parliament thereafter. Sewell 'made no mark in the House' (Namier, 422), rarely taking part in debates and confining his infrequent observations mostly to technical points. In December 1761 he was considered for the solicitor-generalship, but in the end Newcastle recommended Fletcher Norton.

Sewell's foray into politics was not at the expense of his legal practice. As a king's counsel he was 'in full business' (Namier, 422) at the chancery bar and reputed to be earning £3000 or £4000 per annum.

Sewell's elevation to the bench was unsolicited and unexpected. Sir Thomas Clarke, master of the rolls, died in November 1764, and Fletcher Norton (then attorney-general) was expected to succeed him. However, the lord chancellor, Robert Henley, first earl of Northington, vetoed the appointment and he and William Murray, Baron Mansfield, offered the mastership of the rolls to Sewell. The offer 'surprised every one exceedingly, and I am told no one more than Sewell himself, who had never applied for it, and who had no idea that he was in the contemplation of the Government' (W. G. Hamilton to John Calcraft, *Correspondence of William Pitt, earl of Chatham*, ed. W. S. Taylor and J. H. Pringle, 1838–40, 2.298n.). Despite the considerable drop in salary (the master of the rolls received £2500 a year) Sewell accepted the offer, partly, perhaps, because his very considerable chancery practice was beginning to tax his constitution. He was knighted on 30 November 1764, appointed master of the rolls on 4 December, and sworn of the privy council on 12 December.

Sewell was offered the Irish lord chancellorship in 1767, but he refused the offer and went on to preside over the rolls court for more than nineteen years. Although the master of the rolls was at the time the inferior equity judge, Sewell enjoyed greater influence than might ordinarily have been afforded by his office. During the chancellorship of Henry, second Earl Bathurst, that 'obviously inadequate' (Holdsworth, *Eng. law*, 12.314) judge 'leaned constantly' (Campbell, 7.132) on Sewell, whose assistance and influence were nowhere more clearly acknowledged than in *Palmer* v. *Mure* (1773). In that case, Lord Bathurst said, 'at first I differed in opinion with his Honour [Sewell], but he hath now convinced me … and I am first to thank him for the great pains he hath taken upon the occasion.' Sewell did not enjoy such a degree of influence over Lord Chancellor Thurlow, but the latter often handed over heavy, important cases to be dealt with by his deputy, thereby once more allowing to Sewell greater influence than he might otherwise have been expected to enjoy.

The eighteenth-century equity judge might not have been expected to encounter many *causes célèbres* in the execution of his office, but Sewell was involved in the well-publicized case of *Tothill* v. *Pitt* (1766). The elder Pitt was bequeathed a considerable amount of real and personal property by Sir William Pynsent and Sewell, at first instance, applying well established principles, held that the bequest was valid. Six years later his decision was reversed by the lords commissioners of the great seal, the reversal causing a 'burst of surprise' and attracting 'particular … censure' (Campbell, 130). Sewell's ruling was subsequently affirmed by the House of Lords.

Sewell's tenure of the mastership of the rolls was undoubtedly a success. Holdsworth described him as 'a very capable judge' and 'very experienced' (Holdsworth, *Eng. law*, 12.314, 327), and Campbell considered him 'a very eminent Equity judge' (Campbell, 7.130). Despite their great age, a number of his decisions are still good law, perhaps the greatest testament to judicial ability. Probably the most important of these is his judgment in *Fletcher* v. *Ashburner* (1779), still considered the *locus classicus* of the equitable doctrine of conversion.

Sewell was twice married. His first wife, whom he married at All Hallows, London Wall, on 8 April 1740, was Catherine, daughter of Thomas Heath of Stansted Mountfitchet, sometime MP for Harwich. They had four sons and three daughters, the third of whom, Frances Maria, was the mother of the novelist Matthew Gregory ('Monk') *Lewis. Catherine Sewell died on 17 January 1769 and on 20 March 1773 Sewell married his second wife Mary Elizabeth (*bap.* 16 Nov 1743), daughter of Dr Humphrey Sibthorp (1713?–1797), professor of botany at Oxford, and sister of John *Sibthorp. They had one daughter, who died in infancy.

In his later years on the bench, Sewell suffered a good deal from ill health, perhaps exacerbated by the heavy workload deputed to him by Thurlow. He made numerous offers of resignation, but his terms were always too high to be acceptable. Sewell died in office on 6 March 1784, and was buried in the Rolls Chapel. He was succeeded by Lloyd Kenyon (afterwards lord chief justice and first Baron Kenyon). Sewell died intestate, and his eldest son Thomas Bailey Heath Sewell (*d.* 1803) succeeded to his estate, including his country residence at Ottershaw Park, Surrey. NATHAN WELLS

Sources L. B. Namier, 'Sewell, Thomas', HoP, *Commons, 1754–90* · Foss, *Judges*, vol. 8 · J. Campbell, *Lives of the lord chancellors*, 4th edn, 10 vols. (1856–7), vol. 7 · Holdsworth, *Eng. law*, vol. 12 · J. Hutchinson, ed., *A catalogue of notable Middle Templars: with brief biographical notices* (1902) · Sainty, *Judges* · Sainty, *King's counsel* · H. Walpole, *Memoirs of the reign of King George III*, ed. D. Jarrett, 4 vols. (2000) · *IGI*

Sewell, William (1781/2–1853), veterinary surgeon, was born of Quaker parents, possibly William and Elizabeth Sewell, resident in Essex. He was possibly baptized on 10 February 1782. He was apprenticed at about sixteen years of age to Edward Coleman (1764?–1839), the second professor of the London Veterinary College, and at Coleman's request Sewell was appointed his assistant at the college on obtaining his diploma in 1799. According to the college minute books, Sewell was appointed assistant surgeon on 6 March 1799, but it is recorded in the register of pupils held by the college that he did not pass his examination until 30 March 1799. This contradicts J. B. Simonds, who states that it was not until after Sewell had passed his examination, on 30 March, that Professor Coleman applied to the college governors to appoint Sewell as his assistant surgeon. In 1803 Sewell became assistant professor at the college.

Sewell first came into prominence in connection with his supposed discovery in 1803 of a canal pervading the medulla spinalis, which he demonstrated in the horse, ox, sheep, hog, and dog. His opinions on this point were erroneous, but he has been credited with being on the brink of the great discoveries made many years subsequently by Sir Charles Bell. In July 1805 Sewell was appointed veterinary surgeon to the London and Westminster light horse volunteers; he maintained this role until 1850. In 1815 he made a tour of France, visiting the veterinary establishments at Lyons and Paris; in 1816 he made a similar tour of inspection through Germany by way of Vienna, Prague, Berlin, and Hanover. A report of this tour was submitted to the governors of the London Veterinary College in 1818; however, it was described by William Hunting, at a later date, as reading like an auctioneer's catalogue and containing not one single observation of value.

Also in 1818 an extremely important discovery, or rather rediscovery, that of neurotomy, was published in a paper presented by Sewell to the governors of the London Veterinary College. In 1823 a fuller and more detailed account was published in the *Elementary Lectures on the Veterinary Art* by William Percivall, who attributed to Sewell the chief credit for the discovery. However, in an article in the *Veterinary Record* for 31 March 1894, the author indicates that William Moorcroft had anticipated a cure for lameness in horses some years before Sewell presented his paper. Sewell also practised a new method of treating splints, considering the use of the firing iron as barbarous and cruel. In addition he claimed to have discovered a cure for glanders, in the use of sulphate of copper; this was looked upon with considerable distrust by his colleagues. He similarly incurred the displeasure of certain of his fellow veterinarians for having reported to the Royal College of Physicians rather than to the veterinary profession his finding of a case of vesicular calculus in the horse; details of an operation for lithotomy; and illustrations of glanders. Sir Frederick Smith records that Sewell was a 'very reserved man, unsociable, of few words, hesitating, unpopular with the students and unpopular with the profession'. Criticism of Sewell's teaching abilities is discussed at length in articles in *The Farrier and Naturalist* in 1828–9.

In 1828 the London Veterinary Medical Society was formed, and shortly after its formation Sewell became president, a post he occupied for several years. In 1836 there was some dissension among the members of the society and it was disbanded. It was later reformed as the Veterinary Medical Society. Edward Coleman became its patron, and Sewell its president. On the death of Coleman in 1839, Sewell was appointed to succeed him as principal of the Royal Veterinary College and he delivered his inaugural lecture on 18 November. Considerable disapproval was, however, shown at his decision to lecture on cattle pathology, a subject in which he was not considered to be sufficiently qualified, his speciality being rather that of surgery (however in 1842 J. B. Simonds was appointed to lecture on the diseases of cattle, sheep, and pigs). In 1840, during the prevalence of an epidemic of what was later named foot-and-mouth disease, the Royal Agricultural Society of England issued a circular to its members detailing full particulars as to the treatment of the disease according to the method recommended by Sewell. He was subsequently attacked by his colleagues, who claimed that his circular had spoilt their practice. In 1841 Sewell reported to the Royal Agricultural Society on the epidemic.

Coleman's death placed Sewell in many respects at the head of his profession, and his position received further recognition in 1852 by his election as third president of the Royal College of Veterinary Surgeons, which had received its royal charter in 1844. Sewell wrote two essays for the Veterinary Medical Association and presented two case histories to the Royal College of Physicians, and he made a few contributions to the veterinary and medical periodicals of the time. He also completed a report of his visit to the principal veterinary schools on the continent. Both his skill as an operator and his efficiency as a lecturer have been disputed, but he appears nevertheless to have achieved, eventually, a considerable success in both, and under his direction the Royal Veterinary College began to expand and improve its teaching facilities. Sewell was also instrumental in the fight for the royal charter for the profession and by 1852 had bridged the gap between veterinary education and veterinary practice.

Sewell married late in life; his wife, Mary *née* Wilkinson (1783/4–1841), died not long after his appointment as principal of the Royal Veterinary College. Towards the end of his life, owing to his advanced age and occasional illness, Sewell confined his attention to the administration of the college, the actual duties of lecturing falling chiefly on younger men such as William Spooner and J. B. Simonds. Sewell died in London at the college on 8 June 1853 at the age of seventy-one, and was buried at Highgate cemetery. He left no family.

Ernest Clarke, *rev.* Linda Warden

Sources J. B. Simonds, *The origin and progress of the Royal Veterinary College, 1791–1871* (1897) • F. Smith, *The early history of veterinary literature and its British development*, 4 vols. (1919–33); repr. (1976) • 'William Sewell, 1781–1853', *Veterinary Record* (31 March 1894), 573 • E. Cotchin, *The Royal Veterinary College, London: a bicentenary history* (1990) • I. Pattison, *The British veterinary profession, 1741–1948*, [another edn] (1984) • R. H. Dunlop and D. J. Williams, *Veterinary medicine: an illustrated history* (1996) • *The Farrier and Naturalist*, 1–2 (1828–9) • *The Veterinarian*, 2–14 (1829–41) • *The Veterinarian*, 26 (1853) • minute books, 1793–1867, Royal Veterinary College, London • 'Communications', Royal Veterinary College, London • essays of the VMA, 1836–7, Veterinary Medical Society, London • essays of the VMA, 1840–44, Veterinary Medical Society, London • register of pupils, 1794–1907, Royal Veterinary College, London • d. cert. • d. cert. [wife, Mary Sewell] • *IGI*

Archives RCP Lond., MSS 109/104–107 • Royal Veterinary College, London, 'Communications'

Likenesses pastels?, Royal Veterinary College, London

Sewell, William (1804–1874), clergyman and author, was born on 23 January 1804 and baptized on 13 January 1807 at Newport, Isle of Wight. He was the second son of Thomas Sewell (1775–1842), a prominent solicitor of Newport, variously recorder of the borough, twice its mayor, steward and deputy governor of the island, and of his wife and also first cousin, Jane (1773/4–1848), youngest daughter of the Revd John Edwards, curate of Newport. William Sewell had five brothers and six sisters, among them his elder brother Richard Clarke *Sewell (*bap.* 1803, *d.* 1864), a legal writer, and his younger siblings Henry *Sewell (1807–1879), first premier of New Zealand, the Revd Dr James Edwards *Sewell (1810–1903), warden of New College, Oxford, from 1860 until 1903, and the novelist Elizabeth Missing *Sewell (1815–1906). William Sewell attended Winchester College as a commoner from 1819 to 1822, and on 4 November 1822 matriculated at Merton College, Oxford, where he held a postmastership until 1827. He took first-class honours in *literae humaniores*, graduating BA on 2 June 1827, MA on 2 July 1829, and subsequently BD on 17 June 1841, and DD on 20 May 1857.

On 30 June 1827 Sewell was elected Petrean fellow of Exeter College, Oxford, winning the chancellor's prize for the English essay in 1828 and for the Latin essay in 1829. Ordained deacon by the bishop of Bristol in 1831 and priest by the bishop of Winchester in 1832, he served as curate at Whippingham, 3 miles from his home on the Isle of Wight, before his appointment on 10 July 1831 as perpetual curate of St Nicholas in Carisbrooke Castle, a moderate sinecure which he retained until his death. He returned to Oxford in 1831 as tutor at Exeter College, where he remained until 1853, serving as librarian from 1833, sub-rector and divinity reader from 1835, and dean from 1839. In 1832–3 he was an examiner in the classical schools, and from 1836 to 1841 Whyte's professor of moral philosophy, his exposition of Platonism doing much to break down the dominance of the Aristotelian tradition in the Oxford school. His professorial lectures were revised and published as *Christian Morals* and *Christian Politics*, both of which appeared in The Englishman's Library series in 1840, while *An Introduction to the Dialogues of Plato*, based on articles in the *British Critic* and the *Quarterly Review*, appeared in 1841. Sewell also established a moral philosophy club which met in its members' college rooms.

Sewell's steadfast high-churchmanship brought him into natural sympathy with the emerging Oxford Movement. The subscription controversy of 1834 provoked his earliest polemical writing, in pamphlets such as *The Attack upon the University of Oxford, in a Letter to Earl Grey* (1834), *Thoughts on the Admission of Dissenters to the University of Oxford* (1834), and his *Postscript to Thoughts on Subscription* (1835), while a prominent article of 1839 in the *Quarterly Review* on 'Oxford theology' warmly commended the writers of the Tracts for the Times. Sewell always steered an independent line, however, due partly to his idiosyncratic character, partly to his 'fearing the creation of a party' (W. Sewell, *A Letter to the Rev. E. B. Pusey, D.D.*, 1841, 10), but principally to his vehement anti-Catholicism. He therefore abhorred Newman's Tract 90 of 1841, explaining his position in a succession of pronouncements such as the published letter to Pusey, a notable article in the *Quarterly Review* (March 1842), 'The divines of the seventeenth century', and sermons such as *The Duty of Young Men in Times of Controversy* (1843), intended to counter tractarianism's Romeward direction. Sewell's anxiety at this trend was memorialized in the well-known pun on his name, Suillus (the Latin diminutive for *sus*, a pig), 'because he would not go the whole hog' (Stride, *Exeter College*, 159), attributed variously to Sydney Smith, Sewell's Exeter contemporary J. B. Morris, and (Sewell's own suspect) Richard Whately.

'Sewell of Exeter' gained the highest reputation as a tutor in these years (A. Quiller-Couch, *Reminiscences of Oxford by Oxford Men*, 351), and if his lectures were considered too discursive and eclectic for the purist, his intellectual range, trenchant opinions, and sheer unpredictability, made them magnetic to a broader undergraduate audience. It was therefore widely reported, and even interpreted as an expression of the university's official censure, when on 27 February 1849 Sewell, finding that an undergraduate had brought a copy of J. A. Froude's *The Nemesis of Faith* into a lecture, flung the book into the fire in Exeter hall. Despite his fixity of views Sewell was almost single-handedly responsible for improving the college's then unintellectual tone. His devoted pedagogy was the personification of his wider arguments for university reform, expressed in such satirical material as his anonymous *The University Commission, or, Lord John Russell's Postbag*, which appeared in four instalments in 1850, and published sermons such as his *Collegiate Reform* of 1853. Sewell took the typically singular position that Oxford's colleges should reform themselves by throwing open their closed scholarships and fellowships, but that the government had no right to intervene if they did not, the University Reform Act (1854) therefore representing a defeat for his vision. He was, moreover, one of the earliest advocates of what came to be known as university extension; his public paper to the vice-chancellor, *Suggestions for the Extension of the University* (1850) urged a federation of local professoriates giving instruction under the direct authority of Oxford and Cambridge, though the proposal foundered on its cost and university extension was ultimately felt rather through the system of local examinations.

The most important expression of Sewell's educational vision, however, was his conviction of the need to establish schools which could serve as nurseries of sound religion, a project begun in Ireland, where the church seemed most obviously in danger. Lord Adare, an Irish landowner and MP, and an active high-church layman, visited Sewell in Oxford in the spring of 1839, and after Sewell had twice visited Ireland in 1840 he collaborated with Adare's friend, near neighbour, and brother-in-law, the MP for co. Limerick William Monsell, and James Henthorn Todd, Adare's former tutor at Trinity College, Dublin, in order to found St Columba's College, which was opened on 25 April 1843 at Stackallan, co. Meath, before settling at Rathfarnham, near Dublin, in 1849. The college was intended to promote high-church principles and to aid the conversion of Irish Catholics through the use of the Irish language, and to furnish the gentry of Ireland with a school on the model of Winchester or Eton, though its Anglican proselytism and teaching of Irish did not survive the 1840s. Sewell initially contemplated serving as warden of St Columba's, but was deterred by worries over family responsibilities arising from his father's illness and then death in 1842, and his immersion in university politics. In December 1845 Sewell, Adare, and Monsell resigned as governors, and a new constitution was put in place; Sewell severed all ties with the college in support of its first warden, the Revd R. C. Singleton, who resigned in June 1846 in protest at the relaxation of rules requiring observance of the fasts of the church.

The principle on which Sewell apparently quit St Columba's, his albeit ephemeral association with tractarianism, and the later secession of Adare and Monsell to Rome, aroused some suspicion of his activities, though undaunted he immediately embarked on an analogous initiative on returning to England. He published his account of the experience, *Journal of a Residence at the College of St Columba, in Ireland*, in the spring of 1847, in order to prepare the way for St Peter's College (now Radley College) at Radley, just outside Oxford, which opened on 18 August 1847. Its motto, 'Sicut serpentes, Sicut columbae', underlined the continuities of approach, Sewell's churchmanship reflected in the school's observation of the fasts of the church and of full morning and evening service in the chapel. Singleton followed Sewell to Radley and served as its first warden, though he came to resent Sewell's constant interference in its affairs and resigned in 1851. Amid falling pupil numbers and deepening debt, Sewell himself served as warden between 1853 and 1861, assisted by his brother Robert. Sewell's hopeless disregard for financial matters only exacerbated Radley's plight, and its debts of £40,000 were paid off only when, after his desperate *Appeal for the Permanent Security and Foundation of St Peter's College, Radley* (1861), the merchant John Gellibrand Hubbard, later Lord Addington, MP for the City of London, lent that sum to the college and improved management was put in place, Sewell leaving the school.

Although Arnold of Rugby was the pioneer of the reform of public schools, Sewell was the first to give this development a high-church direction, and was unusual in his insistence on the collegiate rather than authoritarian model.

Sewell served as preacher at Whitehall in 1850, and select preacher at Oxford in 1852. In addition to numerous published single sermons he issued a number of collections, such as *Sermons on the Application of Christianity to the Human Heart* (1831), *Parochial Sermons on Particular Occasions* (1832), *Sermons Addressed to Young Men* (1835), and *The Character of Pilate and the Spirit of the Age* (1850). A miscellany of Sewell's school sermons appeared as *A Year's Sermons to Boys, Preached in the Chapel of St Peter's College, Radley* (1854), with a second volume of *Sermons to Boys* appearing in 1859, and a collection of *Sermons Preached in the Chapel of St Peter's College, Radley* in 1864. If these collections are repetitive and unremarkable, Sewell's classical scholarship, which included *Hora philologica, or Conjectures on the Structure of the Greek Language* (1830), and translations of *The Georgics* (1846), *The Agamemnon* (1846), and *The Odes and Epodes of Horace* (1850), was mostly derided by contemporaries.

Sewell came to far wider public notice, albeit anonymously, as a prolific reviewer for the *Quarterly Review*, contributing fifteen articles between February 1837 and September 1845 before his diversions in Ireland. Sewell's range and vigour were especially suited to periodical writing, though his articles were pungent rather than original: the *Review*'s editor J. G. Lockhart remarked of his pieces that 'They tell one nothing, they mean nothing, they are nothing, but they go down like bottled velvet' (James, 53). Equally noteworthy was Sewell's activity in the rapidly expanding field of religious fiction. His anonymous *Hawkstone: a Tale of and for England in 184—* (2 vols., 1845), which ran through numerous editions, is chiefly remembered for the wildly sensationalist tone of its emphasis on the church's lost social functions, its hostility to manufacturing and the commercial spirit, and its hysterical anti-Jesuitism. Sewell also anonymously issued *Uncle Peter's Fairy Tales* (1844), *Uncle Peter's Tale for the Nineteenth Century* (1868), and *The Giant: a Fairy Tale* (1870). Having introduced his sister Elizabeth to Keble and Newman among others, Sewell encouraged her to start writing in order both to promulgate church principles and to alleviate the heavy family debts left by their father. Her *Amy Herbert* (2 vols., 1844) and *Gertrude* (2 vols., 1846) duly embodied high-church views, while *Laneton Parsonage: a Tale for Children* (3 vols., 1846–9) was intended to encourage the use of the catechism, and was followed by the anti-secessionist *Margaret Percival* (2 vols., 1847), her voluminous early novels appearing without attribution but as 'edited by' her brother. Sewell himself also issued a volume of poetry, *A Clergyman's Recreation, or, Sacred Thoughts, in Verse* (1831), written mostly during his curacy at Whippingham and inspired by Keble's *Christian Year*.

Sewell's health, as well as his finances, had been broken by his years as warden of Radley, and after his resignation in 1861, with his fellowship at Exeter sequestrated, he moved about for several years, principally between Bonchurch on the Isle of Wight, where three of his sisters had opened a school, and London. He later travelled throughout Germany, Belgium, and Luxembourg, before in 1866 taking up residence at Deutz, on the Rhine opposite Cologne, where he worked on new translations of the *Iliad* and the *Odyssey*, and a new metrical version of the Psalms, which were left unpublished at his death, though *The Microscope of the New Testament*, the principal fruit of these years, appeared posthumously in 1878 edited by Sewell's friend the Revd W. J. Crichton. In 1870 Sewell was driven home by the Franco-Prussian War, and spent his last four years chiefly on the Isle of Wight. He died peacefully at the residence of his nephew the Revd Arthur Sewell, at Litchford Hall, near Manchester, on 14 November 1874, and was buried in St Andrew's churchyard, Blackley, Manchester. There is a window inscribed to his memory in the chapel at Exeter College, Oxford.

The very diversity of his interests has left posterity with little sense of Sewell's considerable contemporary reputation. At his death contemporaries agreed that he had dissipated his intellectual energies over too wide a range of subjects. Thomas Mozley reflected that 'Had he thought a little more he might have written to more purpose; and had he tried for less he might have obtained more' (T. Mozley, *Reminiscences*, 1882, 2.23–4). Garrulous and opinionated, he was perhaps easier company as an author or lecturer than in person. S. A. Skinner

Sources L. James, *A forgotten genius: Sewell of St Columba's and Radley* (1945) • E. M. Sewell, *Some last words of the Rev. W. Sewell, being a brief review of certain convoluted religious questions. With a prefatory notice by his sister* (1876) • C. W. Boase, ed., *Registrum Collegii Exoniensis*, new edn, OHS, 27 (1894) • W. K. Stride, *Exeter College* (1900) • *The Times* (16 Nov 1874) • *The Guardian* (18 Nov 1874) • *The Guardian* (2 Dec 1874) • *The Guardian* (9 Dec 1874) • G. K. White, *A history of St Columba's College, 1843–1974* (1980) • P. W. Jackson and N. Falkiner, *A portrait of St Columba's College, 1843–1993* (1993) • C. Hibbert, *No ordinary place: Radley College and the public school system* (1997) • E. Bryans, *Sicut columbae: a history of S. Peter's College, Radley, 1847–1924, being a continuation of the Rev. T. D. Raikes's 'Fifty years of Radley'* [1925] • *The recollections of the Very Rev. G. D. Boyle, dean of Salisbury* (1895) • W. Sewell, *Journal of a residence at the College of St Columba, in Ireland. With a preface* (1847) • W. Sewell, *An appeal for the permanent security and foundation of St Peter's College, Radley* (1861) • W. Sewell, *The microscope of the New Testament, edited by the Rev. W. J. Crichton, MA* (1878)

Archives Bodl. Oxf., family corresp. • Pusey Oxf., journal relating to foundation of St Columba • Radley College, Abingdon, corresp. and papers • St Columba's College, Rathfarnham, co. Dublin, corresp. | BL, letters to W. E. Gladstone, Add. MSS 443556–443587, *passim*

Likenesses sketch, *c*.1835, AM Oxf., Hope collection; repro. in James, *A forgotten genius* • attrib. G. Cruickshank, sketch, 1841, AM Oxf., Hope collection; repro. in James, *A forgotten genius* • J. Drummond, oils, 1857–8, Radley College, Oxfordshire

Wealth at death under £600: probate, 5 Dec 1874, *CGPLA Eng. & Wales*

Sexburga. *See* Seaxburh (*d.* 674?); Seaxburh (*b.* in or before 655, *d.* *c*.700).

Sexby, Edward (*c*.1616–1658), parliamentarian army officer and conspirator, described speculatively as the son of Marcus Sexby, alias Saxbie, of London, gentleman, was probably born about 1616, if the identification is correct, for in 1632, one Edward Sexby was apprenticed to Edward Price of the Grocers' Company, London. Sexby would later claim that his origins lay in Suffolk, but this is not inconsistent with his father's being a Londoner by the time Edward himself embarked on professional life.

Sexby entered Oliver Cromwell's double regiment of 'Ironsides' in 1643. At the foundation of the New Model Army Sexby was a trooper in the horse regiment of Lord General Thomas Fairfax. He went on to be 'the most radical of the original agitators' (Woolrych, 41), although doubt has been cast on the claim that he was a close associate of John Lilburne. On 30 April 1647 Sexby was interrogated at the bar of the House of Commons for his part in drafting, circulating, and presenting to the commander-in-chief an *Apologie of the Common Soldiers*, a key text in the radicalization of the parliamentary army, the first manifesto drawn up by the elective representatives of the ordinary soldiery. That summer, Sexby helped organize and maintain the solidarity of the army, acquiring with money provided by the senior officers, a printing press for the army and also acting as treasurer, reimbursing the expenses of the agitators of the regiments as they moved around the country and came to meetings of the general council of the army. He may have had a hand in seizing the king at Holdenby House. He was certainly among the twelve sent by Fairfax to lay charges against the eleven members on 16 July 1647. When the counsels of the military began to fracture in the autumn, Sexby performed the function of intermediary between the general council of officers and agitators and the overlapping organization comprising the so-called 'new agents', the radical cavalrymen who sought a republican constitution and the introduction of a very wide franchise indeed. It has been strongly argued that Sexby was at least part author of *The Case of the Armie Truly Stated*, the manifesto of the new agents.

At those sessions of the Putney debates inspired by *The Case*, and by the *Agreement of the People*, Sexby vigorously opposed the actions of his superiors in seeking to negotiate a peace with the king. Against those such as Henry Ireton who insisted that political enfranchisement depended on having a material stake in the life of the nation, Sexby championed the rights of ordinary soldiers to have a say in the future settlement of England irrespective of property ownership, and insisted that manhood suffrage 'was the ground that wee tooke uppe armes', a view for which he was roundly rebuked by Cromwell among others (Woolrych, 238–9). Although it has been argued that Sexby was instrumental in forestalling the even more radical agenda at Putney, represented by the *Agreement of the People*, at the close of the momentous debates in November 1647 he openly avowed his anti-monarchical loyalties. He signed the *Copy of a Letter Sent by the Agents of Severall Regiments*, which was printed and distributed around 11 or 12 November 1647, calling on the regiments of the army to disobey the order for three separate rendezvous, and to join together to resist the grandees of the general command. However, his own regiment had evidently ceased heeding him, and took no part in the fleeting insurrection which happened at Ware.

Sexby appears to have left the army at the close of 1647, but he happened to be at the battle of Preston and was entrusted with a dispatch to the speaker of the House of Commons from Cromwell announcing the parliamentary victory there. MPs rewarded this service with a gift to Sexby of £100. In February 1649 Sexby 'acted promptly', and apparently without any direct order from either parliament or council of state, in seizing the Scottish commissioners in England as they were about to take ship for home after roundly condemning the execution of Charles I. Sexby was briefly engaged thereafter in searching the posts at Dover and occasionally apprehending individuals suspected of threatening the security of the Commonwealth.

While John Lilburne and his associates languished in prison for their excoriating attacks on the tyranny of the free state, and Sexby's former radical cohort in the ranks of the army launched the mutiny which came to grief at Burford, the agitator Sexby himself became a prized trophy of the new regime, taking up a commission as a captain of foot and governor of Portland Castle. In June 1650 he was commissioned first as lieutenant-colonel, then as colonel, to command a regiment raised originally for service in Ireland, but subsequently diverted to Scotland. Sexby and his regiment headed north late in 1651. Certain 'miscarriages' dogged their progress, principally caused by the indiscipline of the men, brought on by a lack of pay. The regiment took part at the siege of Tantallon Castle in February 1651. In the following June Sexby was charged by a court martial with a host of irregularities, including false musters and the execution of a soldier contrary to justice. Given his attitude in 1647, it is ironic that Sexby was eventually cashiered from his command for withholding the pay of several Portland soldiers who had refused to serve under him when he was originally bound for Ireland.

A few months after the loss of his commission, Sexby was chosen by the council of state as an unofficial envoy to the Frondeurs, with a view to fanning the flames of revolt in south-west France. Based at Bordeaux, his activities were regarded with grave suspicion by many among the supporters of the prince of Condé. However, Sexby was able to commend to the republican Ormée faction some of those radical ideas which he had effectively abandoned when he entered the service of the English Commonwealth. In the spring of 1653 he even had a hand in drawing up a manifesto entitled *L'Accord du peuple*, a hastily edited version of the English Levellers' *Agreement of the People*, rather inappropriately applied to French conditions, as well as another text designed to appeal more specifically to the sensibilities of the Huguenots of rural Guyenne. This *Manifeste* called for land reform, religious toleration, and the establishment of godly government modelled on the puritan regime in England. This enthused some of the French rebels sufficiently to send a deputation to Westminster on an ill-fated quest for formal

English assistance in their struggle with Cardinal Mazarin and the young Louis XIV. But the revolt was finally crushed in August 1653, and Sexby himself fled back to England, where he continued to sponsor Anglo-Huguenot amity. It was rumoured in the following spring that he was to command a combined force of English troops and Irish levies in an invasion of Guyenne.

Meanwhile, Sexby spent much time and energy seeking to recoup his losses in the service of the state. After a year of lobbying for the settlement of his debts, a personal appeal to Cromwell eventually obtained a protectoral ordinance for payment of £1000 out of excise receipts. The betrayal of Sexby's once passionate belief in the sovereignty of the people would appear to have been complete. However, Sexby was by no means at peace with the new order in England, where the interests of protestant France were increasingly spurned in the quest for an alliance with Louis XIV. Sexby now threw in his lot with the enemies of the protectorate. Feared for his continued associations within the ranks of the army, steps were taken to arrest him in February 1655. But the party sent to apprehend him at Portland were themselves arrested by the mayor of the town and governor of the castle, on the grounds that 'they were attempting to deprive an Englishman of his liberty without being able to show a warrant' (Gardiner, 3.270). Sexby escaped to Flanders.

At Antwerp, Sexby made contact with royalists to whom he asserted that, if proper security were given for popular liberties, he would be happy to see Charles II restored. He also obtained an interview with the governor of the Spanish Netherlands, Count Fuensaldanha, soliciting military and financial assistance for a rising in England. In June the count sent Sexby to Spain to make his proposals before the council of state at Madrid, and the Englishman returned in December with supplies of money and conditional promises of support. Father Peter Talbot, who acted as interpreter in Sexby's dealings with Fuensaldanha, communicated his proposals to Charles II, urging the king to come to an agreement with Spain, and to utilize Sexby and his party. A year later, Sexby was still trying to raise an insurrection in England under Spanish auspices. The royalists were to assist, but he stipulated 'that no mention be made of the king before such time as Cromwell be destroyed, and till then the royalists that shall take arms shall speak of nothing but the liberty of the country, according to the declaration whereof I have spoken with the king of England's ministers' (Ogle and others, 3.315). Cromwell revealed details of the plot in dramatic fashion at the opening of his second parliament. An essential component was to have been the lord protector's assassination, to which end Sexby and his fellow conspirators demonstrated remarkable ingenuity. But all their plans failed, and in January 1657 an attempt to set fire to Whitehall led to the arrest of Miles Sindercombe. A few months later, about May 1657, there arrived in England copies of an apology for tyrannicide, entitled *Killing Noe Murder*, published by Sexby in Holland, evidently with the assistance of Silius Titus, under the name of Sexby's former fellow agitator William Allen. Sexby argued that Cromwell was a tyrant on a par with Caligula and Nero. However stable, his reign was an abrogation of law which constituted the enslavement of the English people and threatened the outright corruption of English society. In such circumstances the private citizen was perfectly within his rights in seeking to exact the punishment for which responsibility ought normally to rest with God and the magistrate. Tyranny being the suspension of the normal course of law, tyrannicide could not be regarded as an act of murder. In June 1657 Sexby himself crossed back over to England to promote fresh conspiracies against the Cromwellian regime. On 24 July, as he was embarking for Flanders, dressed 'in a mean habit disguised as a countryman', he was arrested (*DNB*). It was during imprisonment in the Tower that he confessed his authorship of *Killing Noe Murder*, although after the Restoration it would be attributed wholly to Titus. Sick in body, and evidently in mind also, Sexby died in the Tower on 13 January 1658 and according to *Mercurius Politicus* was interred in the burial-ground near the Tower chapel two days later. He would appear to have left a wife, of whom nothing is known other than that she visited him during his incarceration.

Alan Marshall

Sources A. S. P. Woodhouse, *Puritanism and liberty: being the army debates (1647–49) from the Clarke manuscripts*, 3rd edn (1986) • W. Allen [E. Sexby], 'Killing noe murder: briefly discourst in three questions (1657)', *Divine right and democracy: an anthology of political writing in Stuart England*, ed. D. Wootton (1988) • C. H. Firth, *The last years of the protectorate, 1656–1658*, 2 vols. (1909) • Thurloe, *State papers* • M. Sindercombe and others, *A true narrative of the late trayterous plot against the person of his Highness the Lord Protector with the votes of Parliament* (1657) • *The whole business of Sindercombe from first to last: it being a perfect narrative of his carriage during the time of his imprisonment in the Tower* (1656–7) • *Diary of Thomas Burton*, ed. J. T. Rutt, 4 vols. (1828) • O. Lutard, *Des révolutions d'Angleterre à la révolution Française, le tyrannicide et 'Killing no murder' (Cromwell, Athalie, Bonaparte)* (1973) • C. H. Firth, 'Killing no murder', *EngHR*, 17 (1902), 308–11 • D. Underdown, *Royalist conspiracy in England, 1649–1660* (1980) • *Mercurius Politicus*, 373 (14–21 Jan 1658) • C. H. Firth, *Cromwell's army*, 3rd edn (1921); repr. (1962) • *DNB* • *CSP dom.*, 1648–50 • S. R. Gardiner, *History of the Commonwealth and protectorate, 1649–1656*, new edn, 4 vols. (1965), iii, iv • C. H. Firth and G. Davies, *The regimental history of Cromwell's army*, 2 vols. (1940) • P. A. Knachel, *England and the Fronde: the impact of the English civil war and revolution on France* (1967) • G. Aylmer, 'Gentleman levellers?', *Past and Present*, 49 (1970), 120–25 • G. Aylmer, ed., *The levellers in the English revolution* (1975) • A. Woolrych, *Soldiers and statesmen* (1987) • J. Morrill and P. Baker, 'The case of the armie truly re-stated', *The Putney debates of 1647*, ed. M. Mendle (2001), 103–24 • *Calendar of the Clarendon state papers preserved in the Bodleian Library*, ed. O. Ogle and others, 5 vols. (1869–1970), vol. 3

Sexton, Sir James (1856–1938), trade unionist, was born on 13 April 1856 in Newcastle upon Tyne, the son of James Sexton. He also had a sister (with whom he shared a house in later life). His Irish parents were itinerant hawkers, but soon settled in St Helens where they ran a market stall. Here Sexton briefly attended Low House elementary school, and took various short-term industrial jobs.

Between 1869 and 1879 Sexton spent several years at sea, worked in the USA, and at a Merseyside chemical factory.

He then obtained employment at the Liverpool docks, following the death of his father. In 1882 he married Christiana, daughter of William Boyle, a painter and decorator; they later separated. A serious industrial injury embittered his feelings towards his employers, and contributed to his becoming a self-employed coal merchant in 1884.

Sexton had passing engagements with trade unionism, but became seriously involved only after the National Union of Dock Labour (NUDL) was established in Liverpool in 1889. He earned prominence in the local unemployed agitation from 1891, and was elected general secretary of the NUDL in 1893, having previously been a branch officer and a trades council delegate. His Irish Catholic background and his former associations with nationalist politics perhaps helped his advancement. In office, however, his competence and probity as an administrator and his management of executive personnel proved his strongest assets. Sexton in addition found time to undertake a fair amount of journalism, writing articles for *The Clarion*, the *Seaman's Gazette*, the *Liverpool Weekly Post*, and the *Workman's Times*. He also wrote stories, and two plays.

Sexton remained at the head of the NUDL until its absorption into the Transport and General Workers' Union (TGWU) in 1922. During this period his organization established itself in many northern and Scottish ports, and briefly in Ireland. Sexton imposed some centralization, and was always keen to secure co-operation with other transport unions. His industrial policies, shaped by the weakness of the NUDL at his accession, were cautious and restrained. He considered the success of combination to depend upon closer mutual understanding with the various employing interests of the industry. The policy matured only after the victorious strikes which dockers, in conjunction with other transport and general workers, conducted in 1911. For Sexton this triumph bore fruit in the agreement signed with the local employers on union recognition and working practices, followed in 1912 by the introduction of the Liverpool 'clearing house' system. This scheme had limited effect in decasualizing dock work, but it confirmed the union's control of access to the waterside.

It was from the solid regional base thus secured that dockers' unionism extended its range and influence during and after the First World War. The official registration of port labour and the development of national trade agreements in 1914–18 led to the establishment of a national minimum wage and the inauguration of a national joint council for port labour in 1920. These achievements were mainly credited to the Transport Workers' Federation, established in 1911. In its formation Sexton played a significant, but not dominant, role, along with J. Havelock Wilson, Ben Tillett, Will Thorne, and Harry Gosling. However, the reforms may also be regarded as the outcome of a strategy with which the union had been particularly identified. Sexton's last significant initiative as secretary was to oversee its merger with the TGWU, in which his later working years were spent as national supervisor of the Dock Labour Group. He was well regarded by the leadership of other unions, holding a seat on the parliamentary committee of the Trades Union Congress almost continuously from 1900 to 1921.

Sexton's politics reflected his trade union experience. He moved from Irish nationalism to socialism in the early 1890s. Although a founding member of the Independent Labour Party, however, and its candidate at Ashton in 1895, he never favoured its tendency to divide the political spokesmen of the working class into the elect and the damned. He found more congenial the broad-churchmanship of the Labour Representation Committee, launched by a resolution in the Trades Union Congress of 1899 which he had seconded. During the war he was a leading representative of Labour's patriotic wing. His short-lived support for a 'trade union' labour party reflected a distaste for anti-war socialists, paralleling his lasting aversion to unofficial militants in his own union. He became MP for St Helens in 1918, holding the seat until 1931.

Entering the Commons at the age of sixty-two Sexton made only a slight contribution to national politics. He did greater service in developing Labour politics as a force in Liverpool. He sat on the council from 1905, and was an alderman from 1930. An important public figure in the city, Sexton was knighted in 1931. He remained attached to his local roots, eventually dying in his niece's home, Wavertree Lodge, Mill Lane, Liverpool, on 27 December 1938. G. A. Phillips

Sources H. A. Clegg, A. Fox, and A. F. Thompson, *A history of British trade unions since 1889*, 3 vols. (1964–94) • K. Coates and T. Topham, *The making of the Transport and General Workers Union: the emergence of the labour movement, 1870–1922*, 1 (1991), pts 1–2 • D. Howell, *British workers and the independent labour party, 1888–1906* (1983) • E. Larkin, *James Larkin: Irish labour leader, 1876–1947* (1965) • G. A. Phillips, 'The National Transport Workers' Federation, 1910–1927', DPhil diss., U. Oxf., 1968 • G. A. Phillips and N. Whiteside, *Casual labour: the unemployment question in the port transport industry, 1880–1970* (1985) • J. Schneer, *Ben Tillett: portrait of a labour leader* (1982) • J. Sexton, *Sir James Sexton, agitator* (1936) • J. Sexton, 'My life story from tramp to MP', *Empire News* (22 Nov 1925–21 Feb 1926) • E. L. Taplin, *The dockers' union: a study of the National Union of Dock Labourers, 1889–1922* (1985) • E. Taplin, 'Sexton, James', *DLB*, vol. 9 • P. J. Waller, *Democracy and sectarianism: a political and social history of Liverpool, 1868–1939* (1981) • *CGPLA Eng. & Wales* (1939)

Archives Labour History Archive and Study Centre, Manchester, papers • Liverpool Reference Library, cuttings, etc. | Liverpool Central Library, corresp. with H. L. J. Jones • U. Warwick Mod. RC, corresp. with Irish Transport Workers' Federation

Likenesses photographs, Liverpool Reference Library

Wealth at death £1819 18*s.* 11*d.*: probate, 15 March 1939, *CGPLA Eng. & Wales*

Sexton, Thomas J. (1848–1932), Irish nationalist, was the eldest son of John Sexton, a constable in the Royal Irish Constabulary. Born at Waterford, he was educated there at the Mount Sion Christian Brothers' School. He worked from the age of twelve to nineteen as a railway clerk, and was active in a local literary and debating society. He contributed articles to *The Nation* newspaper, which subsequently employed him on its editorial staff. A home-ruler and member of the Land League, he was elected MP for Sligo in 1880. Continuously a member of parliament until 1896, he sat successively for Sligo (1880–85), South Sligo

(1885–6), West Belfast (1886–92), and North Kerry (1892–96). He relinquished his parliamentary seat in 1896, frustrated with political dissension. He was a member of the Dublin corporation, high sheriff in 1887, and lord mayor of the city in 1888 and 1889.

Sexton's parliamentary speeches were notable for their effectiveness and substance. He was imprisoned in Kilmainham gaol in 1881 and was one of the signatories to the 'No rent' manifesto. The regard in which he was held by his colleagues was evident from his continuous involvement in the inner circles of the nationalist party, first as one of Parnell's 'lieutenants' and later as a member of the committee of the anti-Parnellite party in the 1890s. He declined the offer of the chairmanship of the anti-Parnellite party in 1896, having already determined to leave parliament.

Sexton's most significant contribution to public life arose from his ability in financial matters, and in this regard he was invaluable to his parliamentary colleagues. As a member of Dublin corporation, and as lord mayor, he transformed the city's financial management, consolidated its debt, and raised its financial credit. This expertise also found expression in his membership of the royal commission on the financial relations between Great Britain and Ireland (1894–6), as chairman of the board of the nationalist newspaper, the *Freeman's Journal*, from 1892 to 1912, and as a member of the viceregal commission on Irish railways between 1906 and 1910. He was chairman of two successful businesses—a bakery and a Roman Catholic insurance society.

After his retirement from parliament, Sexton continued to exercise political influence through his management of the *Freeman's Journal*. He helped to rescue the paper from the crisis caused by its oscillation over Parnell's leadership in 1890–91, but he was also held responsible for its excessively cautious reporting of political activities. The opposition of the newspaper to the Land Act of 1903 is generally attributed to Sexton, who—together with John Dillon and Michael Davitt—considered the legislation too generous to landlords. His skill with figures, joined to his pessimistic temperament, led him into constructing worst-case scenarios for tenant purchasers of their farms, and possibly contributed in some instances to less effective negotiation by them. The campaign against the act, and against the subsequent attempt at conciliation with more moderate landlords, led to the resignation of William O'Brien from his positions in the nationalist movement, and a return to factionalism. Sexton thus played a part in locking the *Freeman's Journal* into a partisan relationship to the party dominated by John Redmond and John Dillon, so linking its fortunes—and ultimately its survival—to that ill-fated enterprise.

Sexton never married, and his latter years were marked by increasing solitude and the eschewing of all connection with politics, although he remained active in the commercial life of Dublin. He died of heart disease at his home, 20 North Frederick Street, Dublin, on 31 October 1932, aged eighty-four, and was buried at St Mary's, Ballygunner, co. Waterford. PHILIP BULL

Sources C. C. O'Brien, *Parnell and his party, 1880–1890* (1957) · F. S. L. Lyons, *The Irish parliamentary party, 1890–1910* (1951) · P. Bew, *Conflict and conciliation in Ireland, 1880–1910* (1987) · P. J. Bull, 'The significance of the nationalist response to the Irish Land Act of 1903', *Irish Historical Studies*, 28 (1992–3), 283–305 · *Irish Independent* (2 Nov 1932) · *Irish Times* (2 Nov 1932) · *The Times* (2 Nov 1932) · *Dod's Parliamentary Companion* (1883–96) · *WWBMP*

Archives TCD, corresp. with John Dillon

Likenesses T. Farrell, bust, exh. Royal Hibernian Academy in or before 1893, City Hall, Dublin · D. O'Brien, portrait, 1910 (after Thaddeus), City Hall, Dublin

Wealth at death £23,371 0s. 11*d.*—in Ireland: probate, 1932, *CGPLA Eng. & Wales*

Seyer, Samuel (1757–1831), antiquary and Church of England clergyman, was born in Bristol, the son of the Revd Samuel Seyer (1719?–1776) and his wife, Ann (*d.* 1809). His father was master of Bristol grammar school and in 1764 became rector of St Michael's, Bristol. Seyer entered Corpus Christi College, Oxford, in 1772, and graduated BA in 1776 and MA in 1780. He was ordained in 1780 and became curate of Westbury-on-Trym in south Gloucestershire. On 18 April 1781 he married Elizabeth Turner (*d.* 1819), of Wraxall, Somerset. He became master of the Royal Fort School in Bristol in 1790, where he acquired a reputation for harsh discipline. From 1790 to 1813 he lived in the gatehouse of the Royal Fort, with his wife and their two daughters, Sybilla and Mary. In 1813 he became perpetual curate of Holy Trinity, Horfield, near Bristol. By this time he had already purchased several small properties in Bristol, among them an inn called the Blue Bell, and had invested in various Bristol companies including Bristol Dock Company, Bristol and Clifton Oil Gas Company, and the New Crown Fire Office. A surviving notebook also contains references to financial dealings in Jamaica. In 1813 he purchased a large house in the recently built Berkeley Square, Clifton, where he lived for the rest of his life. He purchased the advowson of Filton in south Gloucestershire in 1824 and became rector there, resigning the living of Horfield in 1825. His wife, Elizabeth, died in 1819 and was buried at nearby Shirehampton where their unmarried daughter, Mary, lived. The elder daughter, Sybilla, had married the Revd Abel London and lived at Totteridge, Hertfordshire.

Throughout his life Seyer devoted himself to the study of Bristol history, following the example of his friend William Barrett, the Bristol surgeon, whose *History and Antiquities of Bristol* was published in 1789. Seyer's work is distinguished by his detailed study of the available documentary sources. In 1812 he published *Charters and Letters Patent Granted to the Town and City of Bristol*, which provides an English translation of the Latin originals. Bristol city councillors, fearing that the publication of their records would provoke a challenge to some of their privileges and town dues, refused to grant him access to the charters in Bristol and he was obliged to work from transcripts in the Bodleian Library.

In 1821 and 1823 Seyer published the two volumes of his *Memoirs, Historical and Topographical, of Bristol and its Neighbourhood*, with illustrations by Edward Blore. For this work Seyer was allowed unrestricted access to the city records,

Samuel Seyer (1757–1831), by William Walker (after Nathan Cooper Branwhite, 1824)

and throughout the two volumes he based his statements firmly on original sources which he quoted accurately and at length. This was by far the most detailed and reliable history of Bristol which had been published, and it remains a rich source of reliable information. In addition to his historical publications he also published *The Principles of Christianity* (1796), *The Syntax of Latin Verbs* (1798), *Observations on the Causes of Clerical Non-Residence* (1808), *A Treatise on the Modern Use of the Latin Language* (1808), and occasional sermons. Seyer died at his home on 25 August 1831 and was buried beside his wife at Shirehampton.

J. H. Bettey

Sources personal papers and notes relating to Samuel Seyer and the Seyer family, Bristol RO, 12147/26–52 · Samuel Seyer's will, 16 February 1829 and 26 Jan 1830, PRO, PROB 11/1790/544 · Samuel Seyer's notes relating to his parish and property at Horfield, Bristol RO, P/Hor/x/1a–e · details of Seyer's financial and property dealings, Bristol RO, 11178/5c–d; 28777/c/S/2 · Bristol Reference Library, Jefferies Collection, Seyer's notes on Bristol history, 7949 · I. Gray, *Antiquaries of Gloucestershire and Bristol*, Bristol and Gloucestershire Archaeological Society Records Section, 12 (1981) · H. A. Cronne, *Bristol charters, 1378–1499*, Bristol RS, 11 (1945), 3–7 · J. Latimer, *The annals of Bristol in the eighteenth century* (1893), 243, 348, 374, 522, 528 · *GM*, 1st ser., 101/2 (1831), 471–2 · *DNB* · Foster, *Alum. Oxon.*

Archives Bristol Reference Library, topographical MSS · Bristol RO, corresp. and papers relating to his memoirs of Bristol

Likenesses N. Branwhite, portrait, 1824; formerly in possession of his sister-in-law, Anne Turner · W. Pether, portrait · W. Walker, stipple (after N. C. Branwhite, 1824), NPG [*see illus.*] · prints, Bristol City Museum and Art Gallery

Wealth at death house in Berkeley Square; money, stocks, shares; also furniture and personal possessions: will, PRO, PROB 11/1790/544

Seyler, Athene (1889–1990), actress, was born on 31 May 1889 at 18 Goulton Road, Hackney, London, the seventh and youngest child by ten years of Clarence Heinrici Seyler, secretary and financial adviser to a Greek millionaire, and his wife, Clara Thies, a baker's daughter. Both parents were of German extraction. Her father was a Hellenophile; he called all his daughters by Greek names. Athene was educated at Coombe Hill, a progressive co-educational school where the emphasis lay on tutorials not textbooks, and Bedford College, London, where she studied Restoration comedy, of which she was to become a peerless interpreter.

From her first performance as a child, dancing a hornpipe at the Conway Hall and reducing the audience to helpless laughter when her 'draws fell down', Athene Seyler was determined on a stage career. Her father died when Athene was fifteen years old leaving wife and daughter in straightened circumstances, and although both parents had disapproved of her theatrical ambitions, Sir Henry Irving, a one-time neighbour, encouraged the young Athene (she had once fainted while watching his death scene in Tennyson's *Becket*). With his support she applied to the Academy of Dramatic Art, auditioning for Arthur Wing Pinero, Sir Squire Bancroft, and the pioneering female director Lena Ashwell, who took her aside and told her she would never make an actress because of the way she looked. But Athene persevered, recited as Rosalind, and gained a scholarship. She made her début at the academy as Charles the Wrestler in *As You Like It* and graduated as the gold medallist in 1908. It was Ashwell who gave Seyler her first professional role as Pamela Grey in W. T. Coleby's *The Truants* (1909) at the Kingsway Theatre.

Between her début and the end of the First World War, Athene Seyler appeared in almost thirty productions, in London and on tour, but it was not until 1920 at the Lyric, Hammersmith, that she began to attract attention: as Rosalind (her favourite role), and particularly in Sir Nigel Playfair's Restoration revivals, as Melantha in John Dryden's *Marriage à la mode* and Mrs Frail in *Love for Love* by William Congreve. Athene Seyler never stopped working, alternating between the classics and scores of forgotten light comedies, glorying in such wonderfully named characters as Mrs Bucket, Savina Grazia, Mrs Nelly Fell, and Lavinia Mildmay. Classical highlights included three Lady Fidgets in William Wycherley's *The Country Wife* (1924, 1926, and 1934), Titania (1923) and Hermia (1924), another Melantha and Miss Prism back at the Lyric, Hammersmith (1930). She toured Egypt, South Africa, and Australia in the 1930s; played in a season at the St James (1932) as Emilia and Nerissa to Ernest Milton's Othello and Shylock; and in 1933 joined the Old Vic/Sadler's Wells Company as Maria, Mme Ranyevskaya, Lady Bracknell, Mrs Frail, and also as first Weird Sister in *Macbeth*.

In 1937 Athene Seyler shone as Mrs Candour in an all-star (Peggy Ashcroft, John Gielgud, Michael Redgrave, and Alec Guinness) *School for Scandal* by R. B. Sheridan at the Queen's Theatre and in 1941 played another and much admired Ranyevskaya in Chekhov's *The Cherry Orchard*, both directed by Tyrone Guthrie; and was unusually in modern dress for Lillian Hellman's *Watch on the Rhine*

Athene Seyler (1889–1990), by Madame Yevonde

(1942) and as Veta Louise in *Harvey* (1949) by Mary Chase. In the 1950s she played the Nurse at the Old Vic, and Mrs Malaprop. Her final stage appearance was in 1966, with her old friend Dame Sybil Thorndike as the sweetly murderous spinster sisters in *Arsenic and Old Lace* by J. Kesselring.

In a stage career of nearly sixty years Athene Seyler was recognized as one of the great technical experts on the playing of high comedy, relishing with instinctive wit the turn of a phrase or the eloquent manipulation of a fan. In 1943 she co-wrote a book, *The Craft of Comedy*, which took the form of an exchange of letters with the actor Stephen Haggard (1911–1943), who died on active service. They had acted together in the British première of G. B. Shaw's *Candida* (1937) and in Haggard's own play *Weep for the Spring* (1939). The book offered a marvellous series of reflections on the practice of playing comedy. Seyler wrote that 'Comedy is the sparkle on the water, not the depths beneath. But note the waters must run deep', and she developed a system for the getting of laughs: 'Have I been heard? Have I been truthful? Has the feed line been heard?' (Seyler and Haggard, 11).

Athene Seyler made her (silent) film début in 1921 as Rachel Wardle in *The Adventures of Mr Pickwick*, and managed to appear in over sixty films in a career dominated by the stage. She was invariably cast in comic cameos, as eccentric and imperious aunts or dowagers, and unsurprisingly in several more Dickensian adaptations—as Misses La Creevy, Witherfield, and Pross in *Nicholas Nickleby* (1947), in *The Pickwick Papers* (1952), and in *A Tale of Two Cities* (1958). In the 1950s and 1960s she made a few television appearances, in the classics and in *The Avengers*.

On 14 February 1914 Athene Seyler had married James Bury Sterndale-Bennett (1889/90–1941), a journalist, the grandson of Sir William Sterndale-Bennett, composer and entertainer. They had one daughter. In 1922 she met the actor Nicholas 'Beau' Hannen (1881–1972), the son of Sir Nicholas James Hannen and his wife, Jessie Woodhouse, and he was to be the love of her life. She changed her name by deed poll to Hannen in 1928, but they were not to marry until 1960, after the death of his first wife, who had refused a divorce. Although Seyler was appointed CBE in 1959, it was generally assumed that the DBE many thought rightfully hers was withheld on account of her unmarried partnership with Beau.

In 1950 Athene Seyler was elected president of the Royal Academy of Dramatic Art, the first former pupil to hold that post, and in the same year became life president of the Theatrical Ladies Guild. She lived for some fifty years in the Coach House, Chiswick Mall, and would explain to passers-by the finer points of the boat race (and that she was not in fact Margaret Rutherford). She abandoned an autobiography because its leading character bored her but in her hundredth year she was still working, making mischievous appearances on television chat shows and a belated début at the Royal National Theatre on her 101st birthday, vividly recalling G. B. Shaw and Sir Henry Irving, Ellen Terry, and Mrs Patrick Campbell. She died three months later on 12 September 1990 at the Coach House, 26 Upper Mall, Hammersmith, London.

ALEX JENNINGS

Sources I. Herbert, ed., *Who's who in the theatre*, 16th edn (1977) · D. Quinlan, *The illustrated directory of film character actors*, 2nd edn (1989) · A. Seyler and S. Haggard, *The craft of comedy* (1943) · *The Guardian* (31 May 1989) · *The Guardian* (31 May 1990) · *The Guardian* (13–14 Sept 1990) · *The Independent* (13 Sept 1990) · *The Independent* (26–7 Oct 1990) · *The Stage* (24 May 1990) · C. Hassall, *The timeless quest: Stephen Haggard* (1948) · *The Times* (13 Sept 1990) · microfiche of articles on Athene Seyler, BFI · private information (2004) · b. cert. · m. certs. · d. cert.

Archives FILM BFI NFTVA, performance footage | SOUND BL NSA, 'Athene Seyler talks to Bamber Gascoigne', BBC Radio 3, 21 Feb 1968, T125R C1 · BL NSA, documentary recordings · BL NSA, oral history interviews · BL NSA, performance recordings

Likenesses G. Argent, two photographs, 1968, NPG · C. Beaton, photograph, NPG · F. Grey-Edwards, oils, Garr. Club · P. Small, pastel drawing, Royal Academy of Dramatic Art, London · Madame Yevonde, photograph, NPG [*see illus.*]

Seymour, Aaron Crossley Hobart (1789–1870), hymn writer, was born on 19 December 1789 in co. Limerick, the son of John Crossley Seymour, vicar of Caherelly in the diocese of Cashel, and his wife, the eldest daughter of Edward Wight, rector of Meelick, co. Limerick, a member of an old Surrey family. His younger brother was Michael Hobart *Seymour. Aaron received most of his education at home, and was drawn in early life into the religious group formed by Selina Hastings, countess of Huntingdon, whose biography he afterwards wrote (1839). His first work was *Vital Christianity, exhibited in a series of letters on the most important subjects of religion, addressed to young persons* (1810; 2nd edn, 1819). This work, written during an illness, contained most of his hymns; a few of these compositions, including 'Jesus, immortal king, arise', came into general use. In 1816 Seymour published a memoir of Charlotte Brooke, prefixed to an edition of her *Reliques of Ancient Irish Poetry*. He lived in Naples from 1839 until 1847, and subsequently retired to Bristol, where he died at his home, 11 Berkeley Square, on 22 October 1870. He left at least one daughter. Seymour took a deep interest in hymnology, and assisted Joseph Miller in preparing his *Singers and Songs of the Church* (1869).

D. J. O'DONOGHUE, *rev.* LEON LITVACK

Sources J. Julian, ed., *A dictionary of hymnology*, rev. edn (1907); repr. in 2 vols. (1915) • J. Miller, *Singers and songs of the church* (1869) • d. cert. • *CGPLA Eng. & Wales* (1870)

Wealth at death under £1000: probate, 10 Dec 1870, *CGPLA Eng. & Wales*

Seymour, Algernon, seventh duke of Somerset (1684–1750). *See under* Seymour, Charles, sixth duke of Somerset (1662–1748).

Seymour [*married name* Boheme], **Anna Maria** (*c*.1692–1723), actress, is first recorded as playing Clara in Thomas Shadwell's *The Scowrers* on 22 August 1717, at Drury Lane. Most of her later appearances were with the Lincoln's Inn Fields company, which also included Anthony Boheme [*see below*], whom she married on 18 May 1723. According to John Doran, Boheme 'took her off the stage', robbing the company of their 'best actress … to Ryan's great regret as she acted admirably up to him' (Doran, 374). The *British Journal* (13 April 1723), referring to the marriage, described her as 'that celebrated actress'. She played Queen Elizabeth to Lacy Ryan's Richard in *Richard III* and Gertrude to his Hamlet. In fact she appeared as many times, if not more, with James Quin, playing, among other roles, Desdemona to his Othello, Lady Macbeth to his Macbeth, and Mrs Sullen to his Sullen (in George Farquhar's *The Beaux' Stratagem*). In the space of six years between her début at Lincoln's Inn Fields (11 October 1718), as Oriana in James Shirley's *The Traytor*, and her final appearance there, she appeared more than 150 times. By 1720 she was well on the way to becoming an established member of the company. Thomas Davies cites her appearance as Mrs Page in *The Merry Wives of Windsor* as 'the first play at Lincoln's Inn Fields to fix the attention of the public' (Davies, 1.139), and she continued to play this role throughout her career at the theatre. On this first occasion Boheme appeared as Slender; later he took the part of Shallow.

Mrs Seymour played on a number of occasions with her future husband, notably as the eponymous heroine in Elijah Fenton's *Mariamne*, which Doran describes as 'her one great creation' (Doran, 374). Her final appearance at Lincoln's Inn Fields, on 7 June 1723, was in this role. Boheme was Herod to her Mariamne, and an anonymous picture in the Bodleian Library, according to Highfill, shows them together in the play, although, if the date of the painting is 1726, it cannot show Anna Boheme as Mariamne. Other parts she acted with Boheme include Arpasia in Nicholas Rowe's *Tamerlane*, Cordelia, Cressida, Elvira in Joseph Addison's *Cato*, with Boheme this time playing Manuel,

Anna Maria Seymour (*c*.**1692–1723**), by George Vertue, *c*.1723 [as Mariamne with her husband, Anthony Boheme, as Herod in *Mariamne* by Elijah Fenton]

Isabella to his Angelo in *Measure for Measure*, Tamara, Lady Macbeth, Jocasta (a role she also acted in Jane Robe's short-lived *The Fatal Legacy*), and Roxanne in Nathaniel Lee's *The Rival Queens*. However, her appearances were by no means all with Boheme: among other roles were Cynthia in a 'new drest' revival of William Congreve's *The Double Dealer*, Lady Touchwood in the same play, and Laetitia in his *The Old Bachelor*; Lady Brute in Vanbrugh's *The Provok'd Wife*, Imoinda in Thomas Southerne's *Oroonoko*, Lady Macduff, Queen Isabel in *Richard II*, Sylvia in Farquhar's *The Recruiting Officer*, and Aramante in a revival of *The Spanish Curate*, by Beaumont and Fletcher, with Boheme in the part of Bartolus. Like her husband-to-be, she created only a few new roles: Lady Meanwell in a new one-act farce, *The Chimera, or, An Hue or Cry to Change Alley* by Thomas Odell (January 1721); Isabella in *The Fair Captive* by Eliza Heywood (March 1721); and Sabrina in *Hibernia Freed* by William Phillips (February 1722).

Anna Seymour's marriage to Boheme was short-lived, for she died less than two months later in Norwich, perhaps on tour with her husband, on 10 July 1723. A report in the *Daily Journal* of 13 July carried the news of her death:

'that celebrated Actress Mrs Seymour … of a Fever the 10th Instant' (Avery, 2.730). It may be that she was already ill at the time of her marriage, for she was indisposed and unable to play Mrs Page in *The Merry Wives of Windsor* on 21 March 1723, although she had recovered by 25 March and made a number of other appearances at the theatre before her final one (6 June 1723) as Mariamne.

Little is known about the early life of **Anthony Boheme** (*d.* 1732). Highfill suggests that he was probably in his forties by the time his name first occurs in theatrical records. Avery records his first appearance in the capital as 16 October 1718, at Lincoln's Inn Fields, in the role of Decius in *Cato*. According to Doran, he joined the company from Southwark fair, and continued to play there and at Bartholomew fair in the summers of 1720–22. At the fairs he seems to have established a reputation for comedy, although his later reputation was built upon his playing of tragic roles. Performing in the same cast of that début performance at Lincoln's Inn Fields was Anna Seymour, as Lucia, who was later to become his wife. Both of them were to spend virtually all of their London careers at that theatre, although there were rumours of Boheme's imminent departure to Drury Lane at about the time of his marriage.

Boheme turned principally to tragic roles on joining the Lincoln's Inn Fields company. Many of these were Shakespearian, including King Lear, Shylock in *The Jew of Venice* (a version of *The Merchant of Venice*), Ulysses in *Troilus and Cressida*, Cassius in *Julius Caesar*, Brabantio in *Othello*, Titus Andronicus, and Macbeth. Among other major established roles were Oedipus, Alexander in *The Rival Queens*, Theseus in Edmund Smith's *Phaedra and Hippolytus*, Priuli in Thomas Otway's *Venice Preserv'd*, and Tamerlane. However, he seems to have created only a few roles: Lord Gracebank in *The Chimera*, Holly in *The Fair Captive*, Omar in John Sturmy's *Sesostris*, and O'Brien in *Hibernia Freed*.

After the death of Anna Seymour, Boheme married another actress from the company. Even less is known about her than his first wife, and only two appearances are recorded for her. His final performance appears to have been as Alvarez in Vanbrugh's *The Mistake*, on 26 October 1731. Boheme died in early January 1732. The *Daily Journal* of Monday 11 January 1732 reported that he had been interred at Greenwich the previous night: 'The Pall was supported by Mr Quin, Mr [Lacy] Ryan and 4 other Comedians'. ROLAND METCALF

Sources Highfill, Burnim & Langhans, *BDA* • B. R. Schneider, *Index to 'The London stage, 1660–1800'* (1979) • E. L. Avery, ed., *The London stage, 1660–1800*, pt 2: *1700–1729* (1960) • J. Doran and R. W. Lowe, *'Their majesties' servants': annals of the English stage*, rev. edn, 3 vols. (1888) • T. Davies, *Dramatic miscellanies*, 3 vols. (1784) • *IGI*

Likenesses G. Vertue, double portrait, engraving, *c.*1723, Bodl. Oxf. [*see illus.*]

Seymour [*née* Stanhope]**, Anne, duchess of Somerset** (*c.***1510–1587**), noblewoman and literary patron, was the only child of Sir Edward Stanhope (*d.* 1511) of Rampton, Nottinghamshire, by his second wife, Elizabeth (*b.* before 1473, *d.* 1557), daughter of Fulk Bourchier, Lord Fitzwarine, a descendant of Edward III. After her father's death her mother married Sir Richard Page of Beechwood, Hertfordshire. Some time before 9 March 1535 Anne married, as his second wife, Sir Edward *Seymour (*c.*1500–1552) who was ennobled as earl of Hertford in 1537. Henry VIII visited them at Elvetham, Hampshire, in 1535 and at Wolfhall, Wiltshire, in 1539. They were installed at Greenwich Palace in 1536 to chaperone Edward's sister Jane, who succeeded Anne Boleyn as queen.

Anne Seymour gave birth to ten children: Edward (*b.* 1537), who died in infancy; Anne (*b.* 1538); a second Edward (*b.* 1539); Henry (*b.* 1540); Margaret (*b.* 1540); Jane (*b.* 1541); then Mary and Catherine; in 1548 a third Edward, godchild of Edward VI, who died in 1574; and Elizabeth (*b.* 1550). Following royal practice the Seymours offered their three eldest daughters classical instruction. Anne herself participated in Anne of Cleves's reception and served as lady-in-waiting to Katherine Howard and in the privy chamber of Katherine Parr. Validating vague literary tradition, some scholars have identified her with the wolf in Surrey's poem 'Eche beast can chose hys fere according to his minde', which refuses the advances of the lion—that is, a lady who refuses to dance with the poet (Sessions).

After Edward's accession in 1547 and Hertford's elevation as lord protector and duke of Somerset Anne protested against Katherine Parr's marriage to her brother-in-law Thomas, Lord Seymour of Sudeley. John Foxe reported that 'upon what occasion' he knew not 'a displeasure betwixt' the ladies escalated into a conflict between their spouses, and that unconfirmed rumours claimed that Anne had manipulated Somerset into executing Seymour in 1549 (Foxe, 5.283). Embellishing Foxe's comments Nicolas Sander and John Hayward charged Anne, whom they characterized as extremely proud and domineering, with demanding precedence over the queen dowager, a claim lacking contemporary corroboration. It has been argued, moreover, that John Strype misread 'duchess' for 'duke' as the addressee of Sir Thomas Smith's letter of 1547, in which he responded to charges that he lacked religious fervour (Nichols, 380). Modern writers have favoured the Sander–Hayward characterization, perhaps to offset the invention of Somerset as the good duke. Though historians, including M. L. Bush, challenged this invention they mostly validated Strype's judgement of Anne, while omitting references to the extensive evidence of her deep religious faith, such as Foxe's confirmation of John Bale's claim that she gave 10s. to the protestant martyr Anne Askew in 1545.

After Katherine Parr's death in 1548 the duchess briefly sheltered the late queen's infant and assumed her sponsorship of the second volume of the translations of Erasmus's *Paraphrases*, which appeared twice in 1549 with John Olde's dedication to her. In 1549–50, as a patron, she contended with William Paget and Katherine, duchess of Suffolk, for resources for her clients. In 1550, having earlier apologized for his wife's offence, Sir John Cheke thanked Lady Somerset for supporting his court appointment. Between 1548 and 1551 nine additional publications saluted Anne, a larger number than for any other woman in early Tudor England. In her honour Walter Lynne produced three volumes, plus a translation of Bullinger's biblical concordance; Nicholas Lesse two translations (of Francis Lambet and of Augustine); William Samuel his *Abridgement of God's Statutes*; and the family chaplain, Thomas Becon, dedicated to her a work entitled *The Flower of Godly Prayers*, which, reprinted twice, praised her godliness, liberality, 'gentle nature', and patronage of learning. At Martin Bucer's death in 1551 Anne obtained most of his books. Between 1560 and 1570, with their dedications, Becon's *Prayers* was reprinted three times and Lynne's *Concordance* once. In 1570 Edward Crane and in 1585 Ephraim Pagett dedicated translations to her.

When John, duke of Northumberland, imprisoned Somerset for the second time in October 1551 Anne was incarcerated in the Tower, where John Hooper, bishop of Gloucester, visited her. Somerset was executed in 1552 but Anne, though protestant, remained on good terms with Queen Mary, who freed her on 10 August 1553 and granted her Hanworth, Middlesex, in March 1558. Later that year she married her late husband's steward, Francis Newdegate (1519–1582), fifth son of John Newdegate of Harefield, Middlesex, and Anne, daughter of Nicholas Hilton of Cambridge. In 1561, after learning of the secret marriage of Anne's son Edward, then earl of Hertford, and Katherine Grey, a royal claimant, Elizabeth imprisoned them; though Anne denounced their actions she obtained custody of Hertford in 1563–4 and later repeatedly requested his and his wife's freedom. In 1564 the crown questioned Newdegate, a parliamentary member, about his support for Katherine's succession claims. Ultimately both sons of the marriage of Edward and Katherine were placed in Anne's care.

At his death in January 1582 Newdegate bequeathed his entire estate to Anne. In her will, dated 14 July 1586, she left bequests to four of her children: Hertford, whom she favoured as her sole executor; Henry, husband of Joan Percy, daughter of the seventh earl of Northumberland; Mary, wife of Andrew Rogers of Dorset and later of Sir Henry Peyton; and Elizabeth, second wife of Sir Richard Knightly of Northamptonshire. She died at Hanworth Palace, Middlesex, on 16 April 1587 and was buried at Westminster Abbey. RETHA M. WARNICKE

Sources J. Bale, *Select works*, ed. H. Christmas (1849) • *CSP dom.*, *1547–80* • GEC, *Peerage*, new edn, vol. 12/1 • M. L. Bush, *The government policy of Protector Somerset* (1975) • *DNB* • H. Ellis, ed., *Original letters illustrative of English history*, 2nd ser., 2 (1827) • J. Foxe, *The second volume of the ecclesiasticall history, conteyning the acts and monuments of martyrs*, 2nd edn (1570) • P. W. Hasler, *The House of Commons, 1558–1603* (1981) • J. Hayward, *The life and raigne of King Edward the Sixth*, ed. B. L. Beer (1993) • *Report on the Pepys manuscripts*, HMC, 70 (1911) • A. A. Locke, *The Seymour family: history and romance* (1911) • J. G. Nichols, 'Anne duchess of Somerset', *GM*, 2nd ser., 23 (1845), 371–81 [incl. copy of will] • N. Sander, *Rise and growth of the Anglican schism*, ed. D. Lewis (1877) • H. St Maur, *Annals of the Seymours* (1902) • W. A. Sessions, *Henry Howard, the poet earl of Surrey: a life* (1999) • J. Strype, *Annals of the Reformation and establishment of religion … during Queen Elizabeth's happy reign*, new edn, 3/1 (1824) [incl. copy of Newdegate's will] • J. Strype, *Ecclesiastical memorials*, 2/2 (1822) • Magd. Cam., Pepys Library

Archives BL, Lansdowne MSS

Likenesses effigy on a wall monument, 1587, Westminster Abbey • double portrait (with her son, Edward Seymour, first earl of Hertford), priv. coll. • oils, NG Ire.

Seymour, Beatrice May Louisa Kean [*née* Beatrice May Louisa Stapleton] (**1892–1955**), novelist, was born on 23 May 1892 at 100 Fore Street, Devonport, the daughter of Thomas Joseph Stapleton, a journeyman tailor, and his wife, Matilda Louisa, *née* Bone. It is not known whether she had other siblings apart from a sister named Margaret Elizabeth (who did not marry). Her memories were to be of a 'Puritanic upbringing, with its revivalist meetings and distrust of everything which seemed to me to make life worth living' (Seymour, 140). Yet her mother would tell stories as she did the housework and in her turn Beatrice told stories to her classmates. She decided to be a writer early on; after secretarial college she earned her living (Horatio Bottomley was one of her employers), possibly studied English literature at King's College, London, and wrote numerous short stories. Encouraged by one of the teachers at the secretarial college, she had entered and won a short story competition with a story written when she was seventeen. After this she wrote regularly for women's magazines and also had stories accepted by more literary publications such as *Bystander*, *Queen*, and *Magpie*. She could not attempt a full-length book because she 'left the house at nine, and frequently did not return to it until ten' at night (ibid., 139). With her marriage to William Kean Seymour (1887–1975) on 23 August 1915 came the leisure to attempt a novel, since her husband earned a living as a bank clerk (and would later be a bank manager, poet, parodist, and anthologist, and fellow of the Royal Society of Literature). Why she claimed on her marriage certificate that she was twenty-eight (a year older than her husband) instead of twenty-three and why she gave her father's name as David George Stapleton, profession farrier, instead of Thomas Joseph Stapleton (and gave her second name as Mary instead of May) is not known; nor is it known why she continued to pretend to be older than she was until the end of her life, so that when she died she was ostensibly sixty-nine but in fact sixty-three. One has to commend the resourcefulness of Messrs Kunitz and Haycraft who, when compiling their volume *Twentieth-Century Authors* in 1942, commented ruefully that she:

> speaks in one of her novels of 'those beautifully rare people who can be content to know a man or woman's work without wishing to pick over the rags of their private lives'. In her *Who's Who* biography Mrs Seymour [only] records her address, the name of her publishers, the customary list of her books and the name of her husband. (Kunitz and Haycraft, 1265)

After Beatrice Kean Seymour's marriage it took her

> three years to write down, in the intervals of running a small house, cooking the meals, doing odd secretarial jobs, teaching shortand to young women … and … visiting a husband stuck up on a bleak Lincolnshire plain with what was then the Royal Naval Air Force (Seymour, 140)

the novel that was to be *Invisible Tides* (1919). This was in part 'a study of the war years seen by a young woman who hated them and stayed at home' (ibid., 141). Kean Seymour declared her first love to be the short story but wrote novels because she believed only they could be used as a vehicle for social ideas; however, her twenty-seven novels written at the rate of almost one a year over thirty-six years were almost entirely rather aimless upper middle-class family sagas. Alas, it was fairly remarked by her critics that she was unthinkingly verbose; for example Rebecca West called *Intrusion* (1921) 'immensely and incompetently long. Plainly, the idea that art is a selective process as well as a response to life, and demands treatment as well as statement of situations, is not present in Mrs Seymour's mind' (Kunitz and Haycraft, 1265). Nevertheless, her obituarist in *The Times* called her a novelist of 'charm and power' (*The Times*, 2 Nov 1955). *Three Wives* (1927), *Youth Rides Out* (1928), and *False Spring* (1929) were reprinted as early Penguins in 1936, 1937, and 1941. *Daughter to Philip* (1933) is one of her more interesting novels. Like so many other women writers (G. B. Stern, Sheila Kaye-Smith, Margaret Kennedy, and Elizabeth Jenkins, for example) she wrote a study of Jane Austen (in 1937). The Kean Seymours lived in London, spending weekends at Brown's Gate, Bucklebury, Berkshire. Towards the end of Beatrice's life they divorced and William married Rosalind Herschel Wade (1909–1989), also a novelist, who was appointed OBE for her services to literature; they had two sons. Beatrice lived on her own at 49 Elm Park Court, Pinner, Middlesex. She was a great dog lover. Her close friend was Constance Evelyn Redfearn. She died of heart failure on 31 October 1955 at Northwood Cottage Hospital, Ruislip, Middlesex, and was cremated.

NICOLA BEAUMAN

Sources B. K. Seymour, *Beginnings* (1935) • S. J. Kunitz and H. Haycraft, eds., *Twentieth century authors: a biographical dictionary of modern literature* (1942) • b. cert. • m. cert. • d. cert.
Archives BL, corresp. with Society of Authors, Add. MS 63325
Likenesses photograph, repro. in *Good Housekeeping* (Nov 1935), 11 • portrait, repro. in B. Seymour, *False spring*, new edn (1941)
Wealth at death £4132 7*s*. 3*d*.: probate, 1955, *CGPLA Eng. & Wales*

Seymour, Charles, sixth duke of Somerset (1662–1748), politician and courtier, known as the Proud Duke, was born on 13 August 1662 at Preshute, Wiltshire, the sixth and second surviving son of Charles Seymour, second Baron Seymour of Trowbridge (*c*.1621–1665), and his second wife, Elizabeth (*bap*. 1635, *d*. 1691), daughter of William Alington, first Baron Alington of Killard, Ireland. Charles the younger was the only surviving brother and heir of Francis Seymour, fifth duke of Somerset (1658–1678). The fifth duke died, unmarried, on 20 April 1678 after being shot by a Genoese nobleman, Horatio Botti, in revenge for Somerset's allegedly insulting behaviour towards his wife.

Early responsibilities Little is known of the sixth duke's early life. Styled Lord Charles Seymour from 1675 to 1678, he is said to have been educated at Harrow School and Trinity College, Cambridge, but he does not appear in the admissions register of the latter. After a bout of smallpox in spring 1679 he travelled abroad with his tutor, Alexander de Resigade, in October of that year, returning in May 1681. On 30 May 1682 he married the twice-widowed Lady Elizabeth Thynne, *née* Percy (1667–1722) [*see* Seymour, Elizabeth, duchess of Somerset], the greatest heiress in England. From this point, as the possessor of a vast estate (worth perhaps £20,000–£30,000 by the first decade of the eighteenth century) and the second dukedom in the kingdom, he began to receive a steady stream of honours and responsibilities. In November 1682 he became lord lieutenant of the East Riding of Yorkshire, in July 1683 of Somerset. He was nominated knight of the Garter on 10 January 1684 and installed in April. As second duke of the realm he played a prominent part in court ceremonial. At the funeral of Charles II he was second mourner; he would fulfil a similar function at those of William III and Prince George of Denmark as well. In addition he carried the orb at the coronations of Queen Anne, George I, and George II, and was sent to greet the titular king of Spain, Archduke Charles of Austria, in December 1703.

James II named Somerset a gentleman of the bedchamber in May 1685 and colonel of the Queen's regiment of dragoons in August. As lord lieutenant of Somerset he took an active, but not a distinguished, part in the suppression of the duke of Monmouth's rising that year. As commander of the militia of that county he proved a difficult colleague for his fellow lieutenants and other high-ranking military personnel, in part owing to the ridiculous pride of birth which would be his hallmark. However, in summer 1687 he displayed a courage which has been less often noted by historians. When James II requested him, as gentleman of the bedchamber in waiting, to introduce the newly arrived papal nuncio, he refused on the ground that any contact with the Holy See was, in law, treasonous. Upon the sovereign offering him a pardon he refused; when James asked him if he did not know that the king was above the law, Somerset replied that 'whatever the king might be, he himself was not above the law' (*Bishop Burnet's History*, 3.188). This staunch refusal led to the forfeiture of all his posts.

At the revolution of 1688 Somerset abandoned James II and joined the forces of the prince of Orange, but in parliament he voted against the concept that James II, in his flight, had abdicated, for a regency, and against the offer of the crown to William and Mary in January and February 1689. On the other hand, he voted for reversing the judgment in Titus Oates's case. The king stayed with him at Marlborough on his return from Ireland in September 1690 and dined with him at Petworth on his way to Portsmouth in February 1693. Somerset became associated with the opposition when, in 1692, he resisted pressure from the king and queen and accepted Princess Anne's appeal for the loan of Syon House after she and her husband, Prince George, had been expelled from the court. For most of the reign he was classified as a tory and refused to join the Association of 1689. He did join that of 1696, but voted against Sir John Fenwick's attainder and supported the impeachments of the whig ministers. On the other hand he is listed as against the place bill of January 1693. Towards the end of the reign, after Anne had made her own peace with William, he seems to have gravitated towards the court. William III dined with him at

Northumberland House in May 1699 and visited him on his return from Portsmouth in May 1700. He was named a lord justice and a privy councillor on 28 June 1701 and lord president of the council and a lord commissioner of the Board of Trade on 20 January 1702.

Courtier to Queen Anne At the accession of Queen Anne she rewarded Somerset's loyalty in the last reign by making him master of the horse on 20 July 1702; the duchess became a lady of the bedchamber. Somerset was a conscientious and effective master of the horse, which was, during this reign, a cabinet position. He used this place, and his extensive electoral interest, to try to increase his political importance. At the beginning of the reign he was one of the few supporters, in a predominantly tory cabinet, of John Churchill, duke of Marlborough, and a more aggressive land strategy in the War of the Spanish Succession. But Somerset's support was problematic for the ministry because of his reputation for ridiculous pride, prickliness, and indiscretion. Early in the reign he was rumoured to have leaked secrets from cabinet meetings and in 1704 his partisan role as committee chair during the investigation of the 'Scotch plot' led Daniel Finch, earl of Nottingham, secretary of state, to demand his dismissal in April. Instead, Anne purged her cabinet of Nottingham and a number of his fellow tories.

In parliament Somerset was a fairly assiduous attender and, while in office, a frequent appointee to committees and a representative for conferences between the houses. His voting record in Anne's reign was consistently whig, beginning with his votes against the occasional conformity bills of 1703. In 1706 Somerset was a commissioner for the Union and he was sometimes used by the queen to represent her wishes on crucial parliamentary votes, most notably in the case of the abortive attack on Abigail Masham early in 1710. From mid-reign Somerset grew increasingly demanding of Marlborough and Godolphin, presuming on his relationship with the queen and his vast electoral interest to ask numerous favours and especially military posts for his son, Algernon Seymour, styled earl of Hertford [*see below*], and assorted political allies. Some of these individuals were men of real merit, for example James Stanhope, Thomas Meredith, and Hertford himself. However, the duumvirs found the task of placating Somerset increasingly tedious and the Somersets began to use their influence with the queen to make even more demands. In winter 1707–8 Robert Harley, planning to supplant Godolphin as treasurer, attempted to woo Somerset and other great whig court magnates such as John Holles, duke of Newcastle. In the event, Harley failed: at a cabinet meeting on 8 February 1708, which Marlborough and Godolphin boycotted, Harley tried to carry on as principal minister; it was Somerset who stood up, pointed dramatically at the secretary and said that he did not see how business could be conducted without the queen's treasurer and captain-general. This action, supported by the dukes of Devonshire and Newcastle and the earls of Pembroke and Cowper, made clear to Anne that a Harley ministry was premature.

Following this incident the duke and duchess of Somerset, along with a number of other moderate whig peers, began to feel neglected by a ministry increasingly dominated by the junto. As early as December 1708 the duke is reported to have fallen out with the whigs. By the summer of 1709 the Somersets were cultivating Anne behind the Marlboroughs' backs and, possibly, beginning to make common cause with Harley. The first outward sign of a break with the Churchill circle took place over the Sacheverell trial in March 1710: Somerset played an ambiguous part, absenting himself from the vote on the clergyman's guilt, then voting for a light sentence. By June at the latest Somerset was intriguing with Harley and with Charles Talbot, duke of Shrewsbury, to bring down the ministry. Somerset's goal seems to have been to preside himself over a more moderate whig ministry. These intrigues culminated on 8 August with the dismissal of Lord Treasurer Godolphin. By mid-August, as it became clear that the queen would dissolve the predominantly whig parliament and that a tory ministry was in the offing, Somerset began to fall out with Harley. Despite being named keeper of the new park at Hampton Court in October 1710, the duke withdrew from court, became reconciled to the whigs, used his electoral influence for them in the subsequent election, and began sapping operations against the Harley ministry. A brief attempt to resume his seat in the cabinet was scuttled on 12 August 1711 when Henry St John, secretary of state, refused to sit with him. Somerset played an important role in convincing some peers of the queen's support for 'No peace without Spain' in December 1711, and was 'louder than any in the house for the clause against Peace' (J. Swift, *Journal to Stella*, ed. H. Williams, 1948, 433) when, in fact, she supported the treaty. Anne seems to have retained some regard for him until December 1711 when he attempted to deceive her over his opposition vote on the question of whether the duke of Hamilton could take his seat in the House of Lords under his British peerage as duke of Brandon. On 19 January 1712 Somerset was removed as master of the horse. There ensued several days of tense negotiations as the queen and a small circle of court whigs sought to get the duke's permission for the duchess to remain in her post as groom of the stole and thus near the queen. This was eventually granted. Subsequently Somerset was a consistent whig, voting against the French commercial treaty in June 1713 and the Schism Bill in the spring of 1714.

Later career The famous story that on 30 July 1714, during the queen's last illness, Somerset, along with John Campbell, second duke of Argyll, played a crucial role in securing the Hanoverian succession is doubtful. That is, while Somerset and Argyll did rejoin the privy council on that day, they almost certainly did so after the queen had already been persuaded to give the treasurer's staff to the impeccably Hanoverian Shrewsbury. At the accession of George I, Somerset was restored to the mastership of the horse, but he resigned it angrily in October 1715 over the treatment of his son-in-law, Sir William Wyndham, following the Jacobite rising. Somerset had offered to be surety for Wyndham if the latter were allowed to go free, but the cabinet nevertheless voted to place him under arrest. Thenceforward the duke played little active role in public affairs. He is listed as voting for the acquittal of the earl of Oxford (formerly Robert Harley) in 1717 and in 1740–41 as having given his proxy for various motions in support of the removal of Sir Robert Walpole.

In November 1722 the duchess of Somerset died. For a time the duke pursued, with an ardour that belied his years, his late wife's old nemesis, Sarah, duchess of Marlborough. While this resulted in a softening of the duchess of Marlborough's attitude to Somerset—and therefore of his portrayal in her *Conduct of the Dowager Duchess of Marlborough*—it did not result in a marriage. Instead, on 4 February 1726 Somerset married Charlotte, the third daughter of his former antagonist Daniel Finch, second earl of Nottingham and seventh earl of Winchilsea, and Ann, daughter of Christopher, Viscount Hatton of Gretton. She spent much of their marriage nursing him through a variety of ailments. He died on 2 December 1748 at his principal seat, Petworth House, Sussex. He was buried on 26 December at Salisbury Cathedral. The second duchess died on 21 January 1773 and was buried at Chiswick, Middlesex.

Assessment The sixth duke of Somerset was characterized by Macaulay as 'a man in whom the pride of birth and rank amounted almost to a disease' (Macaulay, *History of England*, ed. C. H. Firth, 1914, 2.918), a view borne out by much contemporary testimony. According to Philip Yorke, first earl of Hardwicke, 'This noble lord was so humoursome, proud, and capricious, that he was rather a ministry spoiler than a ministry maker' (*Bishop Burnet's History*, 6.15n.). William Legge, first earl of Dartmouth, wrote: 'He was a man of vast pride, and having had a very low education, shewed it in a very indecent manner' (ibid., 14n.). William, first Earl Cowper, thought him 'a False mean-spirited Knave, at the same time he was a pretender to the greatest Courage and Steddiness' (*The Private Diary of William, First Earl Cowper*, 1833, 50, 16 Dec 1710). There exist numerous anecdotes, most difficult to confirm, of his pride and imperious manner: that he would only communicate with his servants through hand gestures; that he ordered them to clear the roads for his carriage lest he be viewed by the commonalty; that once, when his second wife struck him playfully with her fan, he remarked, coldly, 'Madam, my first wife was a Percy, and she never took such a liberty' (Craik, 4.351). It is said that he always required one of his daughters to stand as a sentry in his presence while taking his afternoon nap; upon awakening one afternoon to find that his daughter, Charlotte, had taken the liberty of sitting, he vowed to reduce her share of his will. He is supposed to have added a codicil reducing her portion by £20,000, although if this is so it had been excised by the time of his death.

On the other hand, Somerset was clearly not without courage, having stood up to both James II and William III, first in opposition to Catholicism, second in defence of Princess Anne. Later he defied Anne's own wishes in his opposition to Harley in 1708, and those of George I in support of his son-in-law in 1715. He was an able master of the horse and managed to be present and play an important role at a number of dramatic moments in British history. Nor was he without taste or an appreciation for scholarship: he was a patron of artists and has been credited with suggesting the Kit-Cat series to Sir Godfrey Kneller and Jacob Tonson, and with beautifying Petworth House. He was chancellor of the University of Cambridge from March 1689 until his death. He was also created DCL at Oxford during the court's progress to Bath in the late summer of 1702. Appropriately, given his position as master of the horse, he was an avid sportsman and his horses won several important cups at Newmarket and elsewhere during the reign of Queen Anne.

Children and grandchildren Somerset and his first duchess had at least four sons and three daughters. Their eldest son, Charles Seymour, known by courtesy as earl of Hertford, was baptized by 22 March 1683 but died and was buried by the following 26 August. Their second but first surviving son, **Algernon Seymour**, seventh duke of Somerset (1684–1750), was born on 11 and baptized on 26 November 1684. For most of his life he was known as the earl of Hertford. Nothing is known of his early education beyond the fact that he undertook the grand tour in 1703 in the company of John Colebatch of Trinity College, Cambridge. Hertford returned in 1706 after narrowly escaping pirates in the channel. He was MP for Marlborough in 1705–8 and for Northumberland in 1708–22 on his father's interest. Frequently absent on campaign until the later years of the War of the Spanish Succession, he voted for 'No peace without Spain' in 1711 and against the expulsion of Richard Steele in 1714. His most significant parliamentary moment came on 24 June 1714 when he proposed a bounty of £100,000 for the apprehension of James Stuart, the Pretender, should he set foot in the British Isles. Hertford was also lord lieutenant of Sussex from 1706 and governor of Tynemouth Castle from 1710 until his death. He was most distinguished as a military man, serving as a volunteer at Oudenarde in 1708, aide de camp to Marlborough at Malplaquet in 1709, and colonel of the fifteenth regiment of foot from 23 October of that year. He saw active service in this capacity during the campaigns of 1710, 1711, and 1712.

Under George I Hertford was gentleman of the bedchamber to the prince of Wales from September 1714 until his resignation in December 1717 and captain of the second troop of Horse Guards from February 1715 to 1740. In parliament he generally supported the ministry: in 1716 he moved for the impeachment of the rebel, William Gordon, sixth Viscount Kenmure, and in 1719 he voted for the Peerage Bill. On his mother's death in 1722 he was summoned to the House of Lords as Baron Percy on the erroneous assumption that the ancient barony of that name had been vested in her. There he supported Walpole. Subsequently he was promoted brigadier-general in 1727; major-general in 1735; lieutenant-general in 1739; and general in 1747. He was governor of Minorca, September 1737–March 1742; governor of Guernsey, March 1742 until his death; and colonel of the Horse Guards regiment from

1740 until his death, with a brief interval in early 1742 when he lost the regiment on the fall of Walpole. Hertford was also president of the Society of Antiquaries from 1724 to 1749. Unlike his father, from whom he was estranged for most of his later life, Hertford seems to have been well regarded by contemporaries, as both a soldier and a patron; Horace Walpole thought him 'as good a man as lives' (Walpole, *Corr.*, 18.522).

Hertford married, soon after 1 March 1715, Frances (1699–1754) [*see* Seymour, Frances, duchess of Somerset], daughter and coheir of Henry Thynne, son of Thomas Thynne, first Viscount Weymouth. Their only son, George Seymour, Viscount Beauchamp, was born on 11 September 1725 and died unmarried in Bologna, Papal States, of smallpox on 11 September 1744. He was buried on 6 July 1745 in Westminster Abbey. On 2–3 October 1749, just over nine months after his father's death, the seventh duke was created Baron Warkworth and earl of Northumberland, and Baron Cockermouth and earl of Egremont, each pair of titles being intended for different branches of his family. He died on 7 February 1750 at Percy Lodge, Iver, Buckinghamshire, and was buried on 24 February in Westminster Abbey. His widow died on 7 July 1754 at Percy Lodge and was buried in Westminster Abbey on 20 July. They were survived by a daughter, Elizabeth (1716–1776) [*see* Percy, Elizabeth], whose husband, Sir Hugh Smithson, fourth baronet (*bap.* 1712, *d.* 1786) [*see* Percy, Hugh], succeeded his father-in-law as earl of Northumberland and Baron Warkworth in 1750 and was created duke of Northumberland in 1766.

The sixth duke and his first duchess had two further sons, Percy, MP for Cockermouth in 1718–21, who died unmarried in 1721; and Charles, who died in 1711. Their three daughters included Elizabeth (*d.* 1734), who married Henry O'Brien, eighth earl of Thomond, and Catherine (*d.* 1731), who married Sir William *Wyndham, baronet. Their son, Sir Charles *Wyndham, succeeded his uncle the seventh duke as earl of Egremont and Baron Cockermouth. Finally, Anne (*d.* 1722), married Peregrine Osborne, third duke of Leeds. Somerset and his second wife had two daughters, Frances (1728–1760), married to John *Manners, marquess of Granby, the military commander and politician, and Charlotte (1730–1805), who married Heneage Finch, Lord Guernsey, who became third earl of Aylesford in 1757. R. O. BUCHOLZ

Sources GEC, *Peerage*, new edn, 12/1.77–81 • G. S. Holmes, *British politics in the age of Anne* (1967), 226–32 • E. Gregg, *Queen Anne* (1980) • R. O. Bucholz, *The Augustan court: Queen Anne and the decline of court culture* (1993) • *The diary of Sir David Hamilton, 1709–1714*, ed. P. Roberts (1975) • *The Marlborough–Godolphin correspondence*, ed. H. L. Snyder, 3 vols. (1975) • G. L. Craik, *Romance of the peerage* (1849), 4.322–51 • *Bishop Burnet's History of his own time*, ed. M. J. Routh, 3, 188–9; 6, 14–15 • N. Luttrell, *A brief historical relation of state affairs from September 1678 to April 1714*, 2–6 (1857) • *CSP dom., 1679–1704* • *The manuscripts of his grace the duke of Portland*, 10 vols., HMC, 29 (1891–1931), vols. 4–5 • E. Cruickshanks, 'Seymour, Algernon', HoP, *Commons, 1715–54* • will, PRO, PROB 11/766, sig. 379

Archives Devon RO, letters • Devon RO, misc. corresp. and letters • W. Sussex RO, papers | Alnwick Castle, misc. corresp. and papers • BL, corresp. with Lord Hardwicke, Add. MSS 35585–35589 • Bodl. Oxf., letters to Sergeant Thomas Pengelly • CKS, letters to Lord Stanhope • CKS, letters to Alexander Stanhope • CUL, corresp. rel. to Cambridge University

Likenesses J. Riley, oils, *c.*1682, Petworth House, West Sussex • J. Riley and J. B. Closterman, oils, after 1684–1688, Petworth House, West Sussex • G. Gibbons, statue, 1691, Trinity Cam. • G. Kneller, oils, *c.*1703 (kit-cat series), NPG • G. Kneller, oils, 1713, Petworth House, West Sussex • J. M. Rysbrack, marble statue, 1756, U. Cam., Senate House

Wealth at death vast: will, PRO, PROB 11/766, sig. 379

Seymour, Edward, duke of Somerset [*known as* Protector Somerset] (*c.***1500–1552**), soldier and royal servant, was the eldest surviving son of Sir John Seymour (1473/4–1536), landowner and courtier, of Wolf Hall, Wiltshire, and his wife, Margery (*d.* 1550), eldest daughter of Sir Henry Wentworth of Nettlestead, Suffolk.

Family and early life Edward Seymour was descended on both sides from ancient families, each having links with the Percys and Cliffords. His father served Henry VII and Henry VIII as a soldier and was sheriff of Wiltshire and of Somerset and Dorset a total of six times between 1498 and 1527. Of his ten children four predeceased him. The others included Thomas *Seymour; *Jane, who became Henry VIII's third wife; Elizabeth, who married successively Sir Anthony Ughtred, Gregory, son of Thomas Cromwell, and William Paulet, first marquess of Winchester; and Dorothy, who married Sir Clement Smith, an important exchequer official. The course of his early life suggests that Edward was born about 1500, probably at Wolf Hall, Wiltshire. He is said to have been educated at both Oxford and Cambridge, although there is little evidence to suggest that he was a learned man.

Edward Seymour married twice. Before 1518 he married Katherine (*d.* in or before 1535?), daughter and coheir of Sir William Fillol, a landowner in Dorset and Essex. They had two sons: John was MP for Wootton Bassett in Wiltshire in 1547 and died on 19 December 1552, being buried at the Savoy Hospital, London. Edward (1529–1593), who was knighted at the battle of Pinkie in September 1547, was restored in blood by act of parliament of 29 March 1554 and settled at Berry Pomeroy, Devon. Reports that Katherine was repudiated by her husband because of misconduct, and that the paternity of her eldest son was suspect, circulated during the seventeenth century.

Seymour married his second wife, Anne (*c.*1510–1587), before 9 March 1535. Anne *Seymour was the daughter of Sir Edward Stanhope of Rampton, Nottinghamshire, and his wife, Elizabeth Bourchier; she was a descendant through her mother of Edward III. Henry Howard, earl of Surrey, addressed to her an ode, 'On a lady who refused to dance with him'. Contemporaries often criticized her arrogance, but she none the less wrote a moving letter in defence of her husband in October 1549 during his fall from power. She later married Francis Newdegate of Hanworth, Middlesex, one of her first husband's stewards, and was buried in Westminster Abbey. Anne and Edward had four sons and six daughters: their eldest surviving son, Edward *Seymour (1539?–1621), became earl of Hertford, while Henry (*b.* 1540) was appointed admiral of the squadron of the narrow seas; he kept close watch on the

Edward Seymour, duke of Somerset (*c*.1500–1552), studio of Nicholas Hilliard, 1560 (after unknown artist)

duke of Parma off the coast of the Netherlands, and played an important part in the battle off Gravelines in 1588. Among their daughters were Anne, Margaret, and Jane. Anne (1538–1587) [*see* Dudley, Anne, *under* Seymour, Lady Jane] was married first to John Dudley, earl of Warwick, eldest son of John Dudley, duke of Northumberland, and second to Sir Edward Unton. Jane *Seymour (1541–1561) was accused of plotting to marry Edward VI, became a maid of honour to Queen Elizabeth, and died unmarried. Lady Margaret *Seymour (*b*. 1540) [*see under* Seymour, Lady Jane], like her siblings, received a humanist education and probably died young.

Early years at court Edward Seymour was introduced to court by his father. In 1514 he was a page of honour to Henry VIII's sister, Mary, when she married Louis XII of France. On 15 July 1517 he was associated with his father in a grant of the constableship of Bristol Castle. He probably attended Charles V when the emperor visited England in 1522, since Eustache Chapuys, the imperial ambassador, later mentioned him as having been in Charles's service. In August 1523 he accompanied the invasion of France led by Charles Brandon, first duke of Suffolk, and was subsequently present at the capture of Bray, Roye, and Montdidier. He was knighted by Suffolk at Roye on 1 November. In the following year he became an esquire of the king's household. On 12 January 1525 he was made a JP for Wiltshire, and in the same year became master of the horse to the duke of Richmond, Henry VIII's illegitimate son. In July 1527 he accompanied Cardinal Thomas Wolsey on his embassy to France, and in 1528 was granted lands of monasteries dissolved for the benefit of Wolsey's colleges. On 5 March 1529 he was made steward of the manors of Henstridge, Somerset, and Charlton, Wiltshire.

On 12 September 1531 Seymour was appointed an esquire of the body to Henry VIII with an annuity of 50 marks. Increasingly in favour with the king, in 1532 Seymour and his father accompanied Henry and Anne Boleyn to Boulogne to meet François I. In the following year he quarrelled with Arthur Plantagenet, Viscount Lisle, and was supported by the latter's stepson, John Dudley, later duke of Northumberland, over lands in Somerset. In October 1535 Henry VIII and Queen Anne visited Seymour at his Hampshire manor of Elvetham, during that year's royal progress. He was made a gentleman of the privy chamber on 3 March 1536, and a few days later, he, his wife, and his sister Jane were installed in the palace at Greenwich in an apartment which the king could reach through a private passage.

Henry VIII married Jane Seymour on 30 May 1536. A week later, on 5 June, her eldest brother Edward—now the king's brother-in-law—was created Viscount Beauchamp of Hache, Somerset. His further advancement at court was a direct consequence of his new position in the royal family. On 7 July he was made governor and captain of Jersey, and in August chancellor of north Wales. He was admitted to the council on 22 May 1537; in the same month he was among the commissioners who tried barons Darcy and Hussey for their role in the Pilgrimage of Grace, having been called upon to provide 200 men to suppress the rebellion in the previous year. On 15 October he carried Princess Elizabeth at Prince Edward's baptism, and three days later was created earl of Hertford. While the death of his sister, Queen Jane, initially diminished his influence at court, and he was subsequently described as 'of small power', albeit 'young and wise' (*LP Henry VIII*, 13/2, no. 732), nevertheless he remained prominent, particularly in military affairs, for the remainder of Henry's reign.

In 1538 Hertford served on commissions for the treason trials of Henry Courtenay, marquess of Exeter, Henry Pole, Baron Montagu, Sir Geoffrey Pole, and others, and in March 1539 he was sent to provide for the defence of Calais and Guînes. In August the king and Thomas Cromwell spent four days with Hertford at Wolf Hall, inherited from his father in 1536. He met Anne of Cleves, Henry's fourth wife, at Calais in December and returned with her to London. Writing to Cromwell he exclaimed that nothing since the birth of Prince Edward had pleased him so much as this marriage.

Hertford not only survived the fall of Cromwell in 1540, but grew steadily more influential during the latter years of Henry VIII. He was elected a knight of the Garter on 9 January 1541, and during the king's progress to the north, between July and November, he managed affairs in London, along with Archbishop Cranmer and Baron Audley. In November he and Cranmer received the charges against Queen Catherine Howard that led to her trial and execution. In September 1542 Hertford was appointed warden of the Scottish marches, but he served there for only a few weeks, resuming attendance on the king in December 1542. Further promotion followed, lord high admiral on 28 December, and lord great chamberlain on 16 February 1543. In April he was closely involved in the prosecution of Henry Howard, earl of Surrey, who was convicted for eating meat during Lent and breaking windows while carousing through the streets of London. During that year the king again visited Hertford at Wolf Hall.

Soldiering in Scotland and France In December 1543 after prolonged indecision the Scottish government broke with England and allied with France. Consequently Hertford was appointed lieutenant-general in the north, embarking from Berwick for Leith in March 1544. Offered the keys to Edinburgh if he would allow all who so desired to leave with their personal property he demanded unconditional surrender on the grounds that the Scots had been faithless to past agreements. When the Scots refused the English soldiers pillaged the city for two days without resistance, and then seized ships at Leith which they loaded with plunder. The operation achieved no lasting result, however, except that it increased Scottish dependence on France and created greater animosity toward England.

Following his Scottish campaign Hertford was appointed lieutenant of the kingdom under Queen Katherine Parr, who was regent while Henry VIII led an army into France. But on 13 August 1544 he joined the king, and was present at the capture of Boulogne on 14 September. Hertford is said to have secured the capture of the town by bribing the French commander. After the war Hertford was active as a diplomat at Calais and Brussels. The negotiations with France and the emperor, Charles V, broke down, however, and fighting resumed. Hertford surveyed the fortifications of Guînes in January 1545 and took command of Boulogne when the French attempted to recapture it. With a force of 4000 foot and 700 horse he took a French army of 14,000 by surprise on 5 February, driving the enemy away in a victory which secured Boulogne for England.

Reversals in Scotland led to the reassignment of Hertford to the north. On 2 May 1545 he was again appointed lieutenant-general, being charged with organizing a new invasion, with the intention of compelling the Scots into union with England through the marriage of the infant Mary, queen of Scots, to Prince Edward. He proposed delaying operations until August because of a lack of soldiers and supplies, and throughout the summer remained near Newcastle to protect the country from an attack from either France or Scotland. He advanced into Scotland on 6 September and proceeded toward Kelso and Jedburgh. Meeting little opposition, in a campaign of systematic devastation later known as the 'rough wooing', the English army burnt castles, monasteries, and villages along its route. He left Scotland in October to attend parliament and apply himself to government business, and remained in and around London until March 1546, when he resumed command of forces defending Boulogne. The next month he began peace negotiations with France which culminated on 7 June in the treaty of Camp, allowing England to occupy Boulogne until 1554 when the French would buy it back. Moving to and fro between London and the continent Hertford was back in England in October where he strengthened his position at court by forging close ties with John Dudley, now Viscount Lisle, who had served with him in Scotland and France, and with Sir William Paget, the king's secretary.

In the last months of Henry VIII's reign the political map was suddenly redrawn by the fall of Thomas Howard, third duke of Norfolk, and his son, the earl of Surrey. Relations between Hertford and Surrey had been strained since at least 1537, when the two men almost came to blows at court. In June 1546 Norfolk sought an alliance with the Seymours by offering to marry his daughter, Mary, duchess of Richmond, to Thomas Seymour, but Surrey was apparently able to persuade his sister to decline, so ensuring that the Seymours and the Howards failed to make a dynastic alliance. Late in 1546 Henry VIII heard reports that Surrey had displayed heraldic decorations that suggested royal ambitions as well as claiming royal blood, and talked of his father's appointment as regent for Prince Edward. These indiscretions provided a pretext for an attack on the powerful Howard family. Hertford and other leading councillors, supported by the king, claimed that the Howards' actions were treasonous, and Surrey, after trial at the Guildhall, was executed, but Norfolk, though attainted by parliament, was saved by Henry VIII's own death.

The fall of the Howards greatly strengthened Hertford's position, though later, as lord protector, he declined to use his authority to order Norfolk's execution, and the aged duke lived on into the reign of Mary. The conflict between Hertford and the Howards involved personal, political, and religious issues. A. F. Pollard and other scholars saw a conflict primarily between the religious conservatism of Norfolk and the reformist programme associated with Hertford, while M. L. Bush argued more persuasively that until the death of Henry VIII Hertford's association with protestants was shadowy and provided no clear evidence of his own beliefs.

Establishing the protectorate The accession of Hertford's nephew, Edward VI, on 28 January 1547 brought his uncle to the pinnacle of his career. Since events at the end of the reign of Henry VIII left Hertford in a position that no other leader could challenge, the controversial events leading to his appointment as lord protector must be seen from the perspective of the recent past. Hertford and Henry's secretary, Sir William Paget, were with the king at his death and agreed to keep the news secret for a short time. They had possession of the king's will (Seymour was given it by Henry), only parts of which were immediately made public, and Seymour hastened to the town of Hertford to escort the new king back to London.

The will of Henry VIII named his son as heir to the throne and appointed a body of sixteen executors who were to govern collectively until the king reached the age of eighteen. The fact that the will was signed with the dry stamp did not affect its legality. Since the king may have regarded his will as provisional it was reasonable for the executors to reject the notion of collective or collegiate government contained in it, and to give the new government what they saw as a more workable form. To this end the executors, with King Edward's assent, on 1 February appointed Hertford to two further offices, those of lord protector of the realm and governor of the king's person. He was also high steward of England for the coronation, lord treasurer, and earl marshal. These positions gave Hertford more power than had been exercised by any subject since the beginning of the Tudor era. In addition he was advanced within the peerage to become duke of Somerset on 17 February, on the grounds that the late king had so wished to strengthen the nobility.

Although Somerset's authority as protector initially required him to govern with the advice and consent of the executors, a patent dated 12 March 1547 empowered him to do anything that a governor of the king's person or protector of the realm ought to do. A second patent of 24 December 1547, though it made Somerset's protectorate dependent on the king's pleasure rather than limiting it as earlier, to Edward's minority, added to his powers in other respects, making it easier for him to bypass the council and govern through a small group of personal advisers, who included Paget, Sir Thomas Smith, William Cecil, and John Hales.

The magnitude of Somerset's power, especially his use of the royal 'we', offended some members of the council, but their opposition was swiftly dealt with through the dismissal of Thomas Wriothesley, first earl of Southampton, as lord chancellor on 6 March 1547. Authoritarian tendencies may likewise be seen in Somerset's use of royal proclamations, on a scale which exceeded that of Henry VIII's reign. Paget became alarmed, and from 1548 sent Somerset a revealing series of letters in which he boldly admonished the protector to alter his policies and reminded him of an earlier promise to follow his advice in all political affairs. But perhaps the greatest challenge to Somerset's position came from his brother Thomas, who had been advanced to the peerage as Baron Seymour of Sudeley.

Thomas Seymour felt that as Edward VI's uncle he should have a larger role in government and demanded promotion as the king's governor. When Somerset refused Thomas began a series of rash initiatives to undermine his brother that ultimately led to his own execution. He courted and married Katherine, the queen dowager, only four months after the death of Henry VIII. Following her death in childbirth he turned his attention to Princess Elizabeth, then fourteen. He also worked to gain personal influence over the king and drew a group of similarly disaffected nobles and gentry to his side. These actions, as well as rumours of a plot to kidnap Edward and Elizabeth, led to Thomas's arrest in January 1549; he was condemned for treason by a parliamentary act of attainder and executed with his brother's reluctant consent on 20 March 1549. Few would deny that Thomas Seymour was an ambitious and irresponsible man, but Somerset's willingness to sanction the execution of his own brother in order to protect his authority irreparably damaged his reputation.

Religious reformation As lord protector Somerset pursued a cautious but consistent programme of religious reform, one that transformed the Henrician church into one that can be described as protestant or evangelical. Archbishop Thomas Cranmer provided the religious leadership, but Somerset and his political allies determined the pace at which the reform programme proceeded. During Somerset's protectorate English became the language of religious services, first in the order of communion (1548) and later in the first Book of Common Prayer (1549). The reformed services not only introduced new liturgies that offended traditionalists but also incorporated a reformed theology that moved the Church of England closer to continental beliefs and practices. In 1547 parliament repealed the conservative Henrician Act of Six Articles, and in January 1549 passed an Act of Uniformity that sought to maintain religious unity through the use of a new English prayer book. Another act of 1549 permitted priests to marry but emphasized unequivocally the superiority of celibacy. Further measures required the complete destruction of religious images, whitewashing of churches, and dissolution of remaining chantries, one of the largest architectural changes of the century. The iconoclasm which resulted in areas where these policies were zealously enforced was greatly resented.

Although the leading evangelicals enthusiastically regarded Somerset as one of their own after 1547, his personal beliefs are not easily defined, and it has been suggested that they were not exactly mirrored in the religious policies of his protectorate. None the less there is evidence that by the late 1540s he favoured reducing the power of bishops while increasing lay participation in religious reform, believed in the superiority of scripture and salvation by faith alone, and regarded images as idolatrous. Such views were fully consistent with an evangelical outlook, as was his close association with three leading protestant reformers, William Turner, Thomas Becon, and John Hooper. Thus Turner, who served Somerset for more than three years as his physician, wrote in opposition to altars, vestments, and organs. Becon, the protector's chaplain, proclaimed the characteristically protestant doctrine that good works were a distinct sign of grace, while Hooper, consecrated as bishop of Gloucester in 1551, was an intimate of Somerset's family who played a major role in the Edwardian reformation, and even challenged the leadership of Archbishop Cranmer, especially over vestments. Somerset also developed a warm relationship with John Calvin, Pietro Martire Vermigli (Peter Martyr), and the Flemish Calvinist Valérand Poullain, who established a community of Flemish weavers on the duke's newly acquired estate in Glastonbury.

Further evidence of Somerset's personal religion may be found in his own devotional writings, which include two translations from Calvin published in 1550, *An Epistle both of Godly Consolacion and also of Advertisement* (a letter sent by the Swiss reformer to Somerset himself following the 1549 risings) and *A Spyrytuall and moost Precyouse Pearle*. His contacts with Geneva suggest that Somerset was moving towards an increasingly radical reformism, just as the prayers he composed in the Tower of London before his death attest to the straightforward religious belief which directed his actions:

Fear of the Lord is the beginning of wisdom.
Put thy trust in the Lord with all thine heart.
Be not wise in thine own conceit, but fear the Lord and flee from evil.
(BL, Stowe MS 1066)

As lord protector Somerset's patronage of protestant writers was recognized by contemporaries like Roger Ascham, who praised him as the supreme patron of letters. Somerset was the successor to Thomas Cromwell in sponsoring Richard Grafton, Edward Whitechurch, William Gray of Reading, and Miles Coverdale, but he 'extended his patronage on a far more sweeping scale' (King, 106). Although no writings were dedicated to him during the reign of Henry VIII, Somerset received twenty-five dedications under Edward VI, and members of his immediate family received twelve more. After his death in 1552 John Foxe, Thomas Becon, and Robert Crowley remembered affectionately his committed support for the protestant cause.

Social and economic policies Somerset's programme of religious reformation was accompanied by bold measures of political, social, and agrarian reform, in areas which included the treason law, inflation of prices, depopulation, social injustice, and university education. Unfortunately the good intentions of commonwealth reformers associated with Somerset often led to bad results. Legislation in 1547 abolished all the treasons and felonies created under Henry VIII and did away with existing legislation against heresy. Two witnesses were required for proof of treason instead of only one. Although the measure received support in, and was in part redrafted by, the House of Commons, its passage contributed to Somerset's reputation for what later historians perceived as his liberalism, even though it brought back treason by words and the offence of concealment of treasons.

Because of the overriding demands of war in Scotland, Somerset's government rejected an early end to the debasement of the coinage as a remedy for price inflation, and turned its attention to illegal enclosure. In a policy intended to reduce depopulation and rural poverty, and at the same time to increase grain production by discouraging sheep grazing, on 1 June 1548 a royal proclamation announced the appointment of commissions to collect evidence and enforce existing legislation restricting enclosures. But the commission achieved little, leading to the issuing of another, on Somerset's authority, on 11 April 1549. It had greater powers than its predecessor, but was likewise ineffective thanks to the widespread opposition of gentry landowners. Other attempts to deal with agrarian problems through parliament faced similarly strong opposition, though the government successfully passed a novel tax on sheep and woollen cloth in 1549. A projected reform of the universities collapsed, however, in the face of opposition and changing political priorities. University visitors appointed by Somerset, who became chancellor of Cambridge in 1547, wished to reform the curriculum in order to place greater emphasis on humanistic studies and to promote the study of civil law in place of that of canon law, abandoned in 1535. Neither end was achieved.

Other measures embodied no worthy motive and did not promote the best interests of the Tudor commonwealth. Thus in 1547 there was harsh legislation against vagabonds, themselves largely a by-product of agrarian poverty and enclosure, which called for branding with hot irons and enslavement; however, the act was never enforced and was repealed in the next session of parliament. The transfer of crown wealth to private hands and the extensive appropriations of episcopal lands which Somerset's government permitted are also difficult to defend. In two years about £20,000 of the crown's annual income was transferred to private hands, about 40 per cent of it in the form of outright gifts. The wealth of the church was also substantially diminished, strikingly so in some cases: the income of the see of Lincoln was reduced by £1300 out of nearly £2000, that of Bath and Wells by £1450 out of £1850. In these two cases the principal beneficiary was Somerset himself, who acquired four large manors and several smaller ones from Lincoln, and seven manors from Bath and Wells, to add to the site (acquired under Henry VIII) of Somerset House in London, which was built on property that had once belonged to the bishops of Worcester and of Coventry and Lichfield.

Relations with Scotland and France An aggressive foreign policy along lines inherited from Henry VIII ran parallel to Somerset's domestic programme. When Henry died the country was preparing for a new attack on Scotland, and Somerset made the defeat of Scotland his highest priority. His ultimate policy was to reassert England's claim of suzerainty and unite the crowns of the two kingdoms by enforcing the marriage of Edward VI to Mary Stewart. His vision of a greater Britain required English domination of the northern kingdom. A gifted soldier, who had learned from his experience of war on the continent, and particularly from recent developments in fortifications, Somerset intended to achieve these objectives by defeating the Scots in the field and then garrisoning the country at strategic points to guarantee compliance. In a break with past military policies Somerset wanted to create an English pale in Scotland, and then to win the loyalty of the Scottish population within the pale and to introduce the reformed religion there. To this end his military campaign was accompanied by an aggressive one of propaganda.

Leading an army of about 19,000 men into Scotland, Somerset won a notable victory over a larger Scottish force at Pinkie, 9 miles east of Edinburgh, on 10 September 1547. But his efforts to garrison the country provoked intervention by France, historically Scotland's ally against England. In June 1548 a French army landed at Leith, attacked English positions, and garrisoned positions sought by the English. At the same time renewed fighting broke out on the continent, where England was committed to the defence of Calais and Boulogne. Although Somerset received praise for defeating the Scots at Pinkie he was also criticized for failing to enforce a naval blockade that would have prevented the French landing, and for inadequate recruitment at home that led to the employment of continental mercenaries instead. Hiring the latter contributed to the most disastrous aspect of Somerset's Scottish policy: its great cost forced his government to supplement insufficient parliamentary appropriations with debasement of the coinage, sale of crown lands, including former chantry and college property, and substantial borrowing. In the end he was forced to withdraw English troops, evacuate many of the garrisons, and consider abandoning his ambitious objectives, leaving nothing except massive debts to show for his great effort.

Although England and France remained formally at peace until August 1549, the French exerted pressure on the English not only in Scotland but also around the recently captured town of Boulogne. By creating a diversion at Boulogne in August 1548 the French made the English position in Scotland more difficult. The construction of a mole extending into the harbour of Boulogne constituted a provocation that caused the French artillery to bombard the town, an action which Somerset countered by threatening to hand Boulogne over to Charles V. But English efforts to secure support from the emperor against France failed when Charles refused to include Boulogne in an alliance that also protected Calais. French attacks on Boulogne continued into spring and summer 1549, leading to the capture of most of the outforts protecting the town, but then strong English resistance forced the French army to settle down 'to the dreary and slow process of siege' (Jordan, *Young King*, 304). Although Somerset was angry about substantial losses and the failure of the commanders, reinforcements were not forthcoming because of the rebellions at home. But it was only in 1550, after his fall from power, that a diplomatic agreement reflecting England's inability to continue the war returned Boulogne to France.

The rebellions of 1549 The greatest test of Somerset's capacity for leadership came from a series of popular rebellions and riots that began in Cornwall in 1548 and spread through more than half the counties of England the next year. Somerset was faced by nothing less than the most extensive English risings of the sixteenth century. The western rising affected Cornwall, Devon, and Somerset, where conservative Henrician clergy with support from the gentry and commons resisted Somerset's religious programme. The new vernacular liturgy contained in the Book of Common Prayer was the most evident grievance of the Cornish rebels, but the other religious changes of recent years and opposition to enclosures were also important. Revolt began in Cornwall in April 1548 when the clergy and commoners resisted the removal of religious images from parish churches and killed a government official, while in Somerset weavers and other commoners pulled down hedges and fences. When the mayor and leaders of Exeter refused to ally with the rebels of Devon in June 1549 that city was besieged. Pacification required a substantial military force, but Somerset responded only after delays that frustrated other councillors, especially John, Baron Russell, who assumed command of the army sent to relieve Exeter in July. But not until the middle of August was the western rising crushed.

Meanwhile in East Anglia agrarian rebels formed camps in July 1549 to protest against landlords who had defied Somerset's efforts to restrict enclosures of common land and misused their control of local government. Robert Kett, a prosperous Wymondham tanner, emerged as the most able rebel leader. The rising in East Anglia reached its high-water mark on 22 July when Kett's men occupied Norwich, England's second largest city, with the support of some of the urban population. Somerset's response to this and the other disturbances can arguably be called populist. In a series of letters he expressed sympathy for the rebels, offered them pardons, and even undertook to recall parliament early so that their grievances could be discussed. He also set up a new enclosure commission (8 July 1549). Such policies infuriated his colleagues, however, and eventually the protector dispatched a small force commanded by William Parr, marquess of Northampton, to Norwich to assert the king's authority, but it failed to pacify the rebels and came to grief in the city streets. Later a larger army commanded by John Dudley, now earl of Warwick, reoccupied Norwich and then crushed Kett's supporters at Dussindale on 27 August, killing at least 2000 rebels.

The outbreak of the rebellions brought Somerset's social programme, especially the enclosures commission, into question. His reluctance to employ force and refusal to assume military leadership merely made matters worse. When peace was restored most of the nobility and gentry had lost confidence in his leadership. Somerset did not at first appreciate this, and in a proclamation issued on 30 September commanded all soldiers to proceed to their appointed commands and to avoid London. On 5 October, however, he issued a letter over the king's signature commanding all subjects to arm themselves and proceed to Hampton Court to defend the king, and followed this up with appeals to Russell and Sir William Herbert for military assistance, and by moving the king from Hampton Court to the fortified castle of Windsor on 6 October. But at the same time his opponents within the council, including Warwick, Southampton, Baron St John (Paulet), Rich, and Northampton, met in London to demand his removal as lord protector, and in this they eventually procured the support of the mayor and aldermen of London. Faced with overwhelming opposition among the ruling élite, and unwilling to endanger king and country in a civil war, Somerset surrendered himself on the 11th, his protectorate was dissolved on the 13th and he was lodged in the Tower of London the next day. Interrogated by his former colleagues he confessed to charges against him contained in twenty-nine articles and threw himself on the mercy of the council. On 14 January 1550 his deposition as lord protector was confirmed by act of parliament, and he was also deprived of all his other positions, of his annuities, and of lands to the value of £2000 a year.

Deposition and rehabilitation The end of Somerset's protectorate was the consequence of the disastrous and costly war with Scotland and France, opposition to his domestic reforms, growing factionalism among nobility and gentry opposed to his authoritarian leadership, and fear that his populist policies would lead to further disorder among the commons. In December 1549 religious conservatives led by Thomas Wriothesley, earl of Southampton, attempted to exploit the charges against Somerset to execute the former protector and discredit Warwick, with the intention of themselves taking control of government. But Warwick faced down the conspiracy and tightened his grip on the council and royal household, and by February felt secure enough to permit Somerset's release from the Tower on the 6th and his pardon on the 8th. For about six weeks the duke and his wife lived under virtual house arrest. Somerset dined with King Edward at Greenwich on 8 April and was readmitted to the council on the 10th. He was restored as a gentleman of the king's chamber on 14 May having resumed attendance at the council on 24 April, when he was given precedence over all other members. Three days later all his property, except those estates which had already been regranted, was restored. There is also evidence of a rapprochement between Somerset and Warwick, for on 3 June the former's eldest daughter, Anne, married John Dudley, Viscount Lisle, Warwick's eldest son, at Sheen in the presence of the king.

A few days later Somerset led a delegation of councillors to attempt to win the conformity of his old adversary, Stephen Gardiner, bishop of Winchester, who was imprisoned in the Tower for opposition to the Edwardian religious reforms. But despite Gardiner's willingness to accept the Book of Common Prayer and articles endorsing the Reformation, the council made further demands that he refused. Later, on 18 October 1550, Somerset suffered a public slight when the council refused to go into mourning on the death of his mother. He was made lord lieutenant of Berkshire and Hampshire on 10 May 1551 and in August took an armed force to Wokingham to pacify commoners who had organized a conspiracy to destroy the local gentry; several offenders were subsequently executed.

Somerset made an exchange of lands with the king in June 1550 whereby he obtained the remaining property of the former abbey of Glastonbury. On this land he helped a group of Flemish protestant refugees establish a community for the manufacture of cloth. Each household was provided with 5 acres of land for the maintenance of two cows along with tools and material for cloth production. Then in 1551 thirty-four more families and ten widows arrived in Glastonbury, together with news that a further ten families were going to join them. Somerset's imprisonment in October 1551 ended involvement in the scheme, but the council accepted responsibility for his commitments to the Glastonbury community.

Early in 1551 rumours began to circulate suggesting that Somerset was becoming restless with his position and wished to regain the power he had lost in 1549. In February 1551 he was said to have quarrelled with Warwick, and about the same time the earl of Shrewsbury was sounded out concerning his feelings about the rival peers. Behind these reports may have lain the activities of lesser men who hoped to profit if Somerset was restored as protector. Thus Richard Whalley, the duke's chamberlain, began to canvas support for his master, while Sir Ralph Vane, another supporter, picked a quarrel with Warwick over pasture rights. There was also talk of Somerset's allying himself with religious conservatives among the peerage in order to advance himself. He may have seen problems ahead in July 1551, when he wrote to Sir John Thynne asking him to bring the necessary books and documents to Syon in Middlesex so that he could prepare his will.

In fact it is likely that Somerset had abandoned serious ambitions of regaining power by summer 1551 because he knew that he lacked a strong political following. Nevertheless Warwick (now duke of Northumberland) regarded him as a threat to effective government and was prepared to believe the allegations of Sir Thomas Palmer that Somerset planned to invite Northumberland and the marquess of Northampton to a banquet where he would cut off their heads, seize the Tower, and raise the people of London. After dining with the king on 16 October, Somerset was arrested on a charge of high treason and sent to the Tower. His wife was arrested two days later.

Trial and execution The trial of Somerset is among the most controversial episodes of his career. His continuing popularity almost certainly explains why the council ordered householders in London to see to their potentially riotous apprentices before the trial began. Tried by his peers on 1 December 1551 with William Paulet, marquess of Winchester presiding as high steward, Somerset pleaded not guilty to all charges against him. He skilfully conducted his own defence and was acquitted of treason but found guilty of felony under the terms of a recent statute (3 & 4 Edward VI c. 5) against bringing together men for a riot. Historians sympathetic to Somerset argue that the indictment was largely fictitious, that the trial was packed with his enemies, and that Northumberland's subtle intrigue was responsible for his conviction. Other historians, however, have noted that Northumberland agreed that the charge of treason should be dropped and that the evidence suggests that Somerset was engaged in a conspiracy against his enemies.

When the trial concluded many Londoners thought Somerset had either been acquitted of all the charges or that his life would be spared despite his conviction for felony. The Christmas holiday celebrations gave him a temporary respite, but the new year ended any hopes that his life would be spared. On 19 January the king and the council decided to proceed with the execution. Somerset prepared himself for death with prayer and Bible reading and on the night before his death wrote a simple but moving prayer on the pocket calendar that he took to the Tower in which he placed his trust in God and repudiated the conceits of the world.

Somerset was brought to Tower Hill at 8 a.m. on 22 January 1552 and beheaded. As the execution risked causing disorder, householders were ordered to remain in their houses until 10, and the king's guard and a thousand men from the city's trained bands attended to guarantee security. Large crowds gathered none the less. On the scaffold Somerset denied that he had ever offended the king in word or deed and proclaimed that he had always been faithful to his country. He admitted, however, that he was condemned to die by the law of the land and exhorted those present to follow the reformed religion that he had promoted. A rumour that he would be pardoned for a moment excited the large crowd assembled for the execution, an incident that provides further evidence of the sympathy Somerset enjoyed among the common people. He was buried in the north aisle of the chapel of St Peter ad Vincula in the Tower, between two queens, Anne Boleyn and Catherine Howard.

Four of Somerset's closest supporters, Sir Thomas Arundell, Sir Miles Partridge, Sir Michael Stanhope, and Sir Ralph Vane, were executed on 26 February. But most of his former associates escaped with their lives, although they suffered financial losses and political disgrace. Sir Thomas Smith had already retired to a quiet life as provost of Eton College, while Sir William Cecil, one of the two principal secretaries, shrewdly looked after his own interests and entered the service of Northumberland. The king's response to the death of his uncle is unclear. In his chronicle Edward VI recorded no emotion or remorse at the death of his closest surviving relative, but according to the early seventeenth-century biography of Edward by Sir John Hayward, the king wept for his uncle and said that his trial had been unfair. The duchess of Somerset, who was sent to the Tower on 18 October 1551 taking with her personal possessions for a long stay, was not released until the accession of Mary in 1553.

Wealth Like other politicians favoured by Henry VIII, Edward Seymour received large grants of land from that king. As protector he was in a position to reward both himself and his friends, and he did so generously. At his father's death he had inherited estates worth about £275 per annum, and also had lands worth some £170 from his first marriage. By the mid-1540s he had increased his estates, mostly through grants and purchases, to about £1700, and enjoyed an income of some £2500 from all sources. Then in the early years of Edward VI's reign he acquired lands worth £3000 more (including those he obtained under Henry VIII's will), and also augmented his income with a further £2000 from his various offices, not including an annuity of 8000 marks to maintain his estate as protector. With a total annual income of around £12,800 Somerset was the crown's wealthiest subject under Edward VI, but, as he was a duke, lord protector, and the king's maternal uncle, his economic status was hardly inconsistent with his position in the political and social hierarchy.

Somerset's acquisitions of lands were largely concentrated in the south of England, and especially in Somerset and Wiltshire. During the reign of Henry VIII he augmented his family estates in those counties with manors formerly belonging to Wolsey in Yorkshire, former monastic property in Hampshire and Somerset, additional manors in Wiltshire and Somerset, the Carthusian priory at Sheen, Surrey, and property belonging to the Howards. After 1547 he acquired episcopal lands formerly held by the bishops of Bath and Wells and of Winchester. He also acquired London property, notably Somerset House in the Strand in 1539/40 which he began building shortly after the death of Henry VIII. The church of St Mary-le-Strand as well as two former episcopal inns were demolished to make room for the new construction. Building materials were obtained by the demolition of the former priory of St John of Jerusalem at Clerkenwell and of part of the cloister on the north side of St Paul's Cathedral and the charnel house there. The burial-ground near the latter was opened and hundreds of human bones were removed and dumped in Finsbury field. Between 1548 and 1551 Somerset spent over £15,000 on Somerset House and Syon House.

Somerset House was the first major Italianate classical building project in early modern England. Its designer is unknown, but Robert Lawes, clerk of works, and Sir John Thynne helped with the initial planning. One of the principal craftsmen was William Cure, who had worked at Nonsuch for Henry VIII. Somerset House was a two-storey building constructed round a quadrangle which was entered from the Strand through a three-storeyed gateway. At either end of the front were bay windows crowned with ornamental attics. This Renaissance palace was completed only after the death of Somerset. He built the hall and provided an ornamental screen, but the arcaded terrace was added under James I. After the duke's death the house passed to Princess Elizabeth, who, following her accession, allowed his son to occupy part of it. Somerset House was demolished in 1776.

Somerset also began to build a majestic country mansion to replace Wolf Hall at the end of 1548. The site chosen was about 3 miles east of Wolf Hall, between Wilton and Great Bedwyn on Bedwyn Brail. Two million bricks and a considerable quantity of Wilton stone were brought to the site, but when his protectorship ended construction stopped. Fine houses and a huge income from landed estates and office-holding permitted Somerset to live in great luxury. At the height of his power he maintained 167 domestic servants, and during three and a half years from 1548 to 1551 he is estimated to have spent a minimum of £14,325 maintaining himself and his household. During that period the expenses of his steward, kitchen, and stable were £1291, £2621, and £427 respectively, while tradesmen's bills amounted to a total of £1445.

By an act of parliament in 1540 Somerset's estates were entailed upon the issue of his second marriage in preference to that of his first. As he was convicted of felony rather than treason his property was not seized until an act of attainder passed on 12 April 1552 declared his dignities forfeited. Edward Seymour, Somerset's eldest surviving son from his second marriage, having been corrupted in blood by his father's attainder, was restored by act of parliament under Mary and was created Baron Beauchamp and earl of Hertford on 13 January 1559 by Elizabeth. Somerset's titles remained in this branch of the family until 1750, when Sir Edward Seymour, bt, a descendant of Somerset and his first wife, succeeded to his ancestor's dukedom.

Conclusion Somerset remains controversial. Zealous contemporary clerical reformers praised him as a champion of protestantism, but Sir William Paget, who knew Somerset well, and Sir John Hayward, the early seventeenth-century biographer of Edward VI, criticized him severely for political failures. From its publication in 1631 until the end of the nineteenth century Hayward's critical biography was the most authoritative work on Somerset and the politics of the reign of Edward VI, and it clearly damaged the duke's reputation. The debate on his character and political career continued into the twentieth century. In 1900 A. F. Pollard portrayed Somerset as a liberal who believed in constitutional freedom, a view he supported by reference to the letters of Paget, even though the latter considered the duke's populism extremely dangerous and a threat to social stability. Pollard's Somerset was a committed protestant and a friend of the poor and oppressed despite his personal acquisitiveness.

Although Pollard was not the last historian to reaffirm the views of Tudor clerical leaders praising Somerset's support of religious reform, in the late twentieth century historians became more critical, emphasizing Somerset's arrogance, his aggressive and costly policy of conquest in Scotland, and his political incompetence as protector. W. K. Jordan (1968–70) recognized the complexity of his character and praised his magnanimity and moderation in religion, as well as drawing attention to his political faults, whereas M. L. Bush (1975), in a largely hostile study, concluded that 'Somerset's political behaviour was directed not by ideals, but by *idées fixes*' (Bush, 5). But more recently still Diarmaid MacCulloch (1999) offered guarded praise for Somerset's concern for the poor who shared his religious enthusiasm.

Somerset, like all leaders of his generation, served his political apprenticeship under Henry VIII, a king who governed with a firm hand. The accession of the nine-year-old Edward VI created challenges for which nobody was prepared. Somerset provided strong leadership that carried England in directions pursued long after his death. Thanks to his religious policies the country developed along protestant lines even though the Church of England was not firmly established until the reign of Elizabeth. His assertive policies toward Scotland—however prejudicial to the northern kingdom—ultimately foreshadowed the Act of Union of 1707. If his rhetorical favour towards the agrarian poor was not matched by his own behaviour, he was hardly the last politician to promise more than he could deliver and open himself to charges of hypocrisy. The absence of royal leadership during the reign of Edward VI forced Somerset to assume responsibilities for which he lacked experience, and might have led to political conflict with disastrous and long-lasting effects. Not the least of his contributions to the structure of authority was his declining to fight for his own place within it in October 1549. It is in deference to such restraint, as well as for the policies he pursued, that it can be concluded that England's surviving the troubled era of Somerset unscathed constitutes one of his enduring achievements.

BARRETT L. BEER

Sources *DNB* • M. L. Bush, *The government policy of Protector Somerset* (1975) • W. K. Jordan, *Edward VI*, 1: *The young king* (1968) • W. Seymour, *Ordeal by ambition: an English family in the shadow of the Tudors* (1972) • W. K. Jordan, *Edward VI*, 2: *The threshold of power* (1970) • B. L. Beer, *Northumberland: the political career of John Dudley, earl of Warwick and duke of Northumberland* (1973) • B. L. Beer, *Rebellion and riot: popular disorder in England during the reign of Edward VI* (1982) • B. L. Beer, ed., 'A critique of the protectorate: an unpublished letter of Sir William Paget to the duke of Somerset', *Huntington Library Quarterly*, 34 (1971), 277–83 • D. Loades, *John Dudley: duke of Northumberland, 1504–1553* (1996) • GEC, *Peerage*, 12/1, 59–65 • J. Hayward, *The life and raigne of King Edward VI*, ed. B. L. Beer (1992) • 'The letters of William Lord Paget of Beaudesert, 1547–1563', ed. B. L. Beer and S. M. Jack, *Camden miscellany, XXV*, CS, 4th ser., 13 (1974) • G. W. Bernard, ed., *The Tudor nobility* (1992) • J. N. King, *English Reformation literature: the Tudor origins of the protestant tradition* (1982) • D. M. Head, *The ebbs and flows of fortune: the life of Thomas Howard third duke of Norfolk* (1995) • P. Williams, *The later Tudors: England, 1547–1603* (1995) • D. E. Hoak, *The king's council in the reign of Edward VI* (1976) • A. F. Pollard, *England under Protector Somerset* (1900) • D. MacCulloch, *Tudor church militant: Edward VI and the protestant Reformation* (1999) • J. Loach, *Edward VI* (1999) • 'Debate' [Protector Somerset and the 1549 rebellions], *EngHR*, 115 (2000), 103–33 • G. R. Elton, *Reform and Reformation* (1977) • L. Stone, *The crisis of the aristocracy, 1558–1641* (1965) • R. B. Wernham, *Before the Armada: the growth of English foreign policy, 1485–1588* (1966) • G. Redworth, *In defence of the church Catholic: the life of Stephen Gardiner* (1990) • *LP Henry VIII* • G. Phillips, *The Anglo-Scots wars, 1513–1550: a military history* (1999) • M. Aston, *The king's bedpost: reformation and iconography in a Tudor group portrait* (1993) • J. Summerson, *Architecture in Britain, 1530–1830* (1991) • R. Strong, *Tudor and Jacobean portraits*, 2 vols. (1969) • BL, Stowe MS 1066 • A. Bryson, '"The speciall men in every shere": the Edwardian regime, 1547–1553', PhD diss., U. St Andr., 2001 • M. Merriman, *The rough wooings: Mary queen of Scots, 1542–1551* (2000) • HoP, *Commons, 1509–58*, 3.292–3

Archives BL, official corresp. and papers, Add. MSS 32648, 32654–32657 • Longleat House, Wiltshire, papers | BL, letters and papers, Cotton MSS • BL, Harley MSS, corresp. with Lord Cobham, and papers • Longleat House, Wiltshire, Thynne MSS • PRO, SP domestic

Likenesses oil on panel, 1535, Sudeley Castle, Gloucestershire • oil on panel, 1537–47 (or later copy), Longleat House, Wiltshire • portrait, 1548, Syon House, Middlesex • portrait, 1548, Claydon House, Buckinghamshire • studio of N. Hilliard, miniature, 1560 (after earlier portrait), Buccleuch estates, Selkirk [*see illus.*] • group portrait, oil on panel, *c*.1570 (*Edward VI and the pope*), NPG

Wealth at death *c*.£12,800 p.a.: Bryson, 'The speciall men in every shere'

Seymour, Edward, first earl of Hertford (1539?–1621), courtier, was the heir of Edward *Seymour, duke of Somerset (*c*.1500–1552), Edward VI's protector, and Anne (*c*.1510–1587), daughter of Sir Edward Stanhope. Somerset had had two sons from an earlier marriage, but his wife, Katherine, was repudiated some time before 1535 and their children disinherited by act of parliament 32 Henry VIII before being restored by 5 and 6 Edward VI. Edward was probably the son born on 22 May 1539 and baptized in the chapel of Beauchamp Place with the dukes of Suffolk and Norfolk as his godfathers. He was educated with

Prince Edward, knighted at his coronation on 20 February 1547, and styled earl of Hertford from 1547 until 1552. On 7 April 1550 he was briefly sent as a hostage to France. In 1551 his father and the marquess of Dorset planned a match between him and Lady Jane Grey.

Somerset's attainder and execution for felony initially did not affect his son's title or estates, but in April 1552 parliament passed a statute declaring forfeit all the Seymour lands and titles. He was made a ward of the crown and granted a few of his father's estates by letters patent of the king, but relied for financial support on his father's former secretary Sir John Thynne. Under Mary his mother was released from the Tower and given custody of her sons. He was a witness to Northumberland's execution, and restored to the blood by an act of parliament. Two months after Elizabeth's accession, on 13 January 1559, she restored to him the lands inherited by his father and created him Baron Beauchamp and earl of Hertford of the second creation.

Marriage to Katherine Grey Some time in November or December 1560 Hertford secretly married Lady Katherine Grey (1540?–1568) [*see* Seymour, Katherine], the queen's cousin, who was heir to the throne according to Henry VIII's will. Soon afterwards, in May 1561, he was sent to France possibly on a minor diplomatic mission and was intended to go from there to Italy as the companion of Thomas Cecil. Although some questions were asked about his suitability to act as a good influence on Cecil, Sir Nicholas Throckmorton (the English ambassador) spoke well of him and it was also said that he had made a good impression on the king of Navarre. On 12 August, however, he was recalled to England because his wife, now heavily pregnant, had confessed their secret marriage to Robert Dudley. On 5 September 1561 Hertford was placed in the Tower, where both he and Katherine were interrogated closely and separately. Later that month a son, Edward [*see below*], was born. Thanks to the leniency of the warder, a second son was conceived and born in the Tower in February 1562. In May an ecclesiastical commission found the marriage invalid and Hertford was fined £15,000 in Star Chamber for deflowering a virgin of the royal blood, breaking his prison, and repeating the fornication. At the same time he was expected to defray Katherine's expenses. Rents from his lands were diverted to the lord treasurer as part of the fine in 1564–5, but not thereafter. In June 1568 Elizabeth agreed to take £200 a year until £10,000 was paid.

On the outbreak of plague in August 1563 Hertford was removed from the Tower and placed in the custody of his mother and stepfather, Francis Newdigate, at Hanworth, Middlesex. On several occasions Anne petitioned William Cecil and Robert Dudley on behalf of her son, but the queen refused to show leniency as she was extremely sensitive about the succession question and possibly suspected a plot against her. Though undoubtedly incorrect about there being political motives behind the marriage, her suspicions seemed confirmed when John Hales wrote a pamphlet defending it and Katherine's right to the succession. As Newdigate was implicated in Hales's activities, Hertford was removed from his care. After a short return to the Tower he was placed in the house of Sir John Mason.

Recovering fortunes After the death of his wife on 27 January 1568 Hertford slowly shook off royal displeasure. He left Mason's custody late in 1568, but was still confined in various country houses until 1571, when he was allowed to attend court. On 2 February 1571 he was admitted to Gray's Inn, and on 30 August 1571 created MA at Cambridge. During 1571 Elizabeth released him from £10,000 of his fine. By October 1572 she had remitted a further £1000 and in December 1577 £1000 more. In 1579 he had only £1813 4*s.* 8½*d.* to pay. He spent much time at court, and was one of the magnates attending the queen during the ceremony of the king's evil in May 1582, hearing the trial of the earl of Essex, and receiving Marshal Biron, the French ambassador, in 1601. Yet, despite his rehabilitation, Hertford secured few rewards or important posts under Elizabeth. In 1578 he appeared on the commission of the peace for Wiltshire and the following year he was joint commissioner of musters. In 1588 he was one of seventeen men ordered to be at court with his personal forces. In 1592 he was appointed a commissioner to take oaths from the JPs of Northumberland, Hampshire, and Wiltshire. At last in 1601 he was appointed lord lieutenant of Wiltshire, Somerset, and Bristol.

While at Elizabeth's court Hertford met Frances Howard, daughter of Lord William Howard of Effingham, sister of the lord admiral, and maid of honour to the queen. By 1575 the two were on intimate terms. John Dee referred to her as the countess of Hertford in 1578, and Hertford's elder son addressed her as mother in 1582. In fact Elizabeth did not consent to their marriage until 1585. The countess died on 14 May 1598 leaving no issue. Three years later Hertford married Frances Prannell [*see* Stuart, Frances (1578–1639)], the widowed daughter of Thomas, Viscount Howard of Bindon. The marriage was performed clandestinely without banns or licence and not in the parish church. They had no children, and she outlived him to die on 8 October 1639 after a third marriage, to Ludovick Stuart, second duke of Lennox and duke of Richmond.

Hertford never fully accepted the verdict of the ecclesiastical court that his first marriage was invalid, and his elder son, Edward, used the courtesy title Lord Beauchamp. Hertford proved an authoritarian father, closely supervising his sons' studies even after they had reached the age of twenty. When he learned in December 1581 that Beauchamp had exchanged vows and a ring with a kinswoman, Honora Rogers (her brother was married to Hertford's sister), he personally intervened to break off the relationship. In August 1585 he even arranged to have his son seized and brought to one of his houses in order to keep him away from Honora. The queen and council, however, took the part of Beauchamp, and Hertford had to accept the marriage as valid.

In 1589 Hertford's second son, Thomas, tried to secure a notarial instrument declaring himself legitimate, and in 1592 he initiated a legal appeal against the sentence that his parents' marriage had been invalid. Details of these proceedings, which were supported by his father, came to light in October 1595 just when the queen and her ministers were growing concerned about the publication of Robert Persons's book dealing with the English succession. The queen therefore acted speedily, and Hertford was sent to the Tower in November 1595, remaining there until 3 January 1596. Thereafter he was careful to avoid any suggestion that he might have an interest in the succession. Thus in 1601, when Arabella Stuart sent a servant to Hertford with a proposition of marriage between herself and his elder grandson, the sixteen-year-old William Seymour, Hertford immediately informed Robert Cecil. On Elizabeth's death Cecil was suspicious that Hertford might promote the candidature of his son, but Hertford immediately declared his recognition of James I.

Under James I James I showed greater favour to Hertford. In June 1603 he was made *custos rotulorum* of Wiltshire. On 19 April 1605 the earl was sent to Brussels as ambassador-extraordinary to ratify the 1604 Anglo-Spanish treaty. In July 1605 and June 1611 he was granted lands. From June 1612 until March 1619 he was high steward of the revenues to Queen Anne. After he began legal proceedings in 1607 to have his elder son declared legitimate, the king agreed in 1608 to give Beauchamp and his heirs the right to inherit the title earl of Hertford on the present earl's death. James, however, would not overturn the bastardy judgment.

The secret marriage of Arabella to Hertford's grandson William in 1611 initially aroused royal suspicions against the earl and he was summoned to court. His willingness, however, to upbraid his grandson soon earned him the council's approval. Despite his anger at the marriage, he allowed William £200 a year, while he remained in Paris. On the occasion of William's second marriage, to the daughter of the earl of Essex in January 1618, Hertford was said to have settled £3000 on his grandson, his heir since Beauchamp's death in 1612.

Both monarchs honoured the earl of Hertford with royal visits. In 1591 Elizabeth stayed with him and Frances at his Hampshire mansion, Elvetham, during which time he put on an elaborate entertainment. Three surviving texts of the Elvetham entertainment have survived, as well as a woodcut illustration. James I visited him at his Wiltshire house, Tottenham Lodge, in 1603 and again in 1617 and 1620. Hertford acted as a patron of the musician John Daniel and possibly the poet Samuel Daniel. In addition, he had a company of players, which toured the provinces between 1582 and 1606 and performed before the queen at court on twelfth night 1592. It is on record that he employed Cornelius Ketel to paint a portrait of the queen in 1579, but no picture by that artist can now be identified. Hertford was also interested in military matters; he wrote a book on his father's victorious expedition to Scotland and was the recipient of a letter detailing a campaign in the Netherlands (1582). His entry-books as lord lieutenant were almost exclusively devoted to military matters. His parliamentary patronage was confined to the seats of Great Bedwyn and Marlborough.

Character Hertford was evidently a quarrelsome man. In addition to his argument with his son, he fell out with his brother Henry on his mother's death in 1587. In 1601 he became involved in a dispute between his sister Mary and her father-in-law, Sir Richard Rogers, about her jointure. He also came into conflict with his half-brother and nephew when a bill settling the Seymour lands came into the Commons first in 1601 and then in April 1604. He was involved in many lawsuits over land, including cases against lords Morley and Wentworth, Henry Knyvett, Henry Middlemore, and the dean and canons of Windsor. He found himself at odds with many gentry families in Somerset and Wiltshire, who tried to obstruct him in his work as lord lieutenant. In May 1606 Sir Henry Poole, the MP for Cricklade, attacked him in the Commons over allowances for the office of muster master, and accused him of favouritism, bullying, and general high-handedness as lord lieutenant. His relationship with his third wife was often strained, and in one letter she implied that he was domineering and obstinate. Sir John Thynne, perhaps his oldest friend, accused him of ingratitude in 1579 for failing to promote a match and grant him some property.

Hertford enjoyed good health. He outlived his sons and grandson Edward, and remained active until his death, despite falling off his horse aged eighty-three. In March 1621 he fell in a palsy, and on 6 April he died at Netley in Hampshire. He was buried in Salisbury Cathedral. His career was not very illustrious for a man of his birth and talents, but his first marriage put paid to his chances of preferment with the queen. Thereafter his political importance lay in the closeness of his sons to the succession and concerns that he would exploit his connections to place one of them on the throne on Elizabeth's death. In this respect, memories of his father's seizure of power in 1547 probably influenced political judgement about him.

Edward Seymour, Viscount Beauchamp (1561–1612), the elder son and heir of Edward Seymour and Katherine Grey, was born in the Tower on 24 September 1561, the date written by his father in a Bible now at Longleat, and baptized two days later. Despite his official illegitimacy he was always given the courtesy title of Lord Beauchamp and owed his importance to inheriting the Suffolk claim to the royal succession.

Beauchamp spent his childhood with his mother and his paternal grandmother, Anne, dowager duchess of Somerset, a formidable woman. He was educated by private tutor at Hanworth, Middlesex. On 22 December 1576 he matriculated from Magdalen College, Oxford, and spent some time studying there, but from correspondence in the Longleat collection it appears he was a poor student and he certainly did not graduate. Some time in 1581 he exchanged vows and a ring with Honora Rogers, the daughter of Sir Richard Rogers of Bryanstone, Dorset, who had been living in his grandmother's household. Cowed by Hertford's fury on learning of the relationship, Beauchamp promised to marry his father's choice and asked Honora to return his tokens and letters. But in September 1582 he admitted that he was legally married to her, and appealed to Walsingham for permission to be with his wife. In March 1584 he was still trying to cohabit with Honora. On his way to London in August 1585 to plead his case before the queen, he was seized at Reading and taken to one of his father's houses. He was in such a distressed state that he threatened to take his own life if he were not set free. Both father and son then petitioned the queen and council, who took the part of Beauchamp. Evidently the family soon became reconciled, as in 1587 Beauchamp and his wife received a legacy from his grandmother, who had earlier been furious at the match. From the marriage three sons were born: Edward (1587–1618), William *Seymour (1587–1660), and Francis *Seymour (1590?–1664).

Beauchamp showed no interest in the succession and consequently did not arouse the suspicions of Elizabeth. No proceedings were taken against him in 1595 when his father appealed against the decision of the invalidity of his first marriage, nor in June 1596 when his brother was implicated in some treasonous activities of Sir John Smith in Essex. James VI, on the other hand, did have anxieties that Beauchamp's following would press his claim to the throne on Elizabeth's death. In 1603, however, only a few insignificant men spoke out for Beauchamp's title while the council ignored it. Various accounts of Elizabeth's death report her rejection of Beauchamp as her successor with the words 'I will have no Rascall to succeed me, as who should succeed me but a King?' (BL, Harley MS 7042, fol. 237r).

Soon after James I's accession a judicial appeal for Beauchamp's legitimacy was considered but apparently rejected. In 1607 Hertford again began legal proceedings to have his son declared legitimate, this time with more success. Although James would not overturn the original decision about his parents' marriage, Beauchamp was granted in 1608 the right to inherit the title earl of Hertford on the present earl's death. In fact, Beauchamp predeceased his father. He died on 13 July 1612 at Wick, Wiltshire, and was buried at Bedwyn Magna; later he was removed to a tomb in Salisbury Cathedral.

SUSAN DORAN

Sources *Calendar of the manuscripts of the marquis of Bath preserved at Longleat, Wiltshire*, 5 vols., HMC, 58 (1904–80), vol. 4 • *Calendar of the manuscripts of the most hon. the marquis of Salisbury*, 1, HMC, 9 (1883); 15 (1930); 17–22 (1938–71) • *CSP dom.*, rev. edn, *1547–53*; *addenda, 1580–1625*; *addenda, 1566–79* • *APC*, *1588*, *1591–2*, *1600–04* • *CPR*, *1558–60*; *1580–82* • *CSP for.*, *1558–63* • *VCH Wiltshire*, vol. 5 • *JHL*, 2 (1578–1614) • *JHC*, 1 (1547–1628) • W. P. D. Murphey, ed., *The earl of Hertford's lieutenancy papers*, Wiltshire RO, Devizes (1969) • *The manuscripts of his grace the duke of Rutland*, 4 vols., HMC, 24 (1888–1905), vol. 1 • *Literary remains of King Edward the Sixth*, ed. J. G. Nichols, 1, Roxburghe Club, 75 (1857) • *The private diary of Dr John Dee*, ed. J. O. Halliwell, CS, 19 (1842) • J. T. Murray, *English dramatic companies, 1558–1642* (1910), vol. 1 • *The letters of Lady Arbella Stuart*, ed. S. J. Steen (1994) • *LP Henry VIII*, vol. 14/1 • C. S. C. Brudenell-Bruce, earl of Cardigan, *The wardens of Savernake forest* (1949) • BL, Harley MS 6286 • Bodl. Oxf., MS Tanner 84, fols. 105–97; MS Tanner 193, fols. 224–9 [letters] • H. Ellis, ed., *Original letters illustrative of English history*, 2nd ser., 2 (1827) • BL, Add. MS 38170, fols. 29, 52, 60, 68 • J. Strype, *Annals of the Reformation and establishment of religion … during Queen Elizabeth's happy reign*, new edn, 3/1 (1824), 507–9, 652–5; 4 (1824), 413–14 • J. Nichols, *The progresses and public processions of Queen Elizabeth*, new edn, 3 (1823) • GEC, *Peerage* • BL, Lansdowne MS 47, no. 33 • *Report on the manuscripts of Lord De L'Isle and Dudley*, 2, HMC, 77 (1933) • PRO, SP 77/7, fols. 97–115, 204v–221 • BL, Cotton MS Vitellius C xvi, art. 22 • BL, Cotton MS Faustus A xi • BL, Add. MS 33749 • BL, Add. MS 63543, fols. 27–82 • opinions from foreign divines about the marriage, CUL, Cambridge MS Ii v 3, fols. 1–96 • J. E. Jackson, 'Wulfhall and the Seymours', *Wiltshire Archaeological and Natural History Magazine*, 15 (1875), 140–207 • J. Strype, *The life and acts of John Whitgift*, new edn, 3 vols. (1822), vol. 2 • BL, Harley MS 7042, fol. 149 • *CSP Scot.*, *1597–1603* • J. B. A. T. Teulet, ed., *Papiers d'état, pièces et documents inédits ou peu connus relatifs à l'histoire de l'Écosse au XVIème siècle*, 3 vols., Bannatyne Club, 107 (Paris, 1852–60), vol. 3 • BL, Cotton MS Caligula C xvi, fol. 412 • BL, Add. MS 38139, fols. 251v, 252 • C. Loomis, 'Elizabeth Southwell's MS account of the death of Queen Elizabeth', *English Literary Review*, 26 (1996), 482–509 [with text]

Archives Alnwick Castle, letter book as Lord Lieutenant of Somerset and Wiltshire • Devon RO, letter book • Longleat, Warminster, MSS

Likenesses portrait, *c.*1565, priv. coll.; repro. in Earl of Cardigan, *Wardens of Savernake Forest* • double portrait (with his mother), priv. coll.; repro. in Earl of Cardigan, *Wardens of Savernake Forest* • tomb effigy, Salisbury Cathedral

Wealth at death land in Hampshire, Wiltshire, and Somerset

Seymour, Edward, Viscount Beauchamp (1561–1612). *See under* Seymour, Edward, first earl of Hertford (1539?–1621).

Seymour, Sir Edward, fourth baronet (1633–1708), speaker of the House of Commons, was the eldest son of Sir Edward Seymour, third baronet (1610–1688), politician, of Berry Pomeroy in Devon, and Anne, daughter of Sir John Portman, first baronet. Seymour's father was the royalist governor of Dartmouth in 1643–5 and a direct descendant of Edward Seymour, Protector Somerset. Little is known of Seymour's early life until he entered parliament in 1661 at a by-election for Hindon, close to the family's Wiltshire estate at Maiden Bradley. However, it may be assumed that the Seymours shared the privations of other sequestered royalists. Resentment at such early experiences, exacerbated by an almost pathological pride in ancestry, may have been responsible for the abrasiveness and arrogance that were features of Seymour's personality. Not even his family were spared. During the negotiations for his first marriage he quarrelled violently with his uncle Henry, causing his father to complain bitterly of Edward's 'pride and undutifulness' (HoP, *Commons, 1660–90*, 3.412). On 7 December 1661 he married Margaret, daughter and coheir of the London merchant Sir William Wale.

Parliamentary apprentice Seymour took to the House of Commons like a duck to water, and was soon speaking regularly in support of the court. Sometimes his bold and aggressive style led him into indiscretion, and on one occasion he 'affronted the Speaker most peremptorily' (HoP, *Commons, 1660–90*, 3.413), but it was useful politically. Although he had served briefly as a gentleman of the privy chamber at the Restoration, his first significant office was as a subcommissioner for prizes in London during the Second Anglo-Dutch War. He also involved himself in various

Sir Edward Seymour, fourth baronet (1633–1708), attrib. Sir Peter Lely, *c.*1679

trading companies, in particular the Royal Fishing Company, and the Royal Adventurers into Africa. His aspirations were far from satisfied, however, and by 1665 he had shifted over to opposition. Two years later he was sufficiently prominent to be selected to open the debate on the earl of Clarendon's impeachment and to carry the impeachment up to the Lords.

By this time Seymour may be identified as a client of George Villiers, second duke of Buckingham, and in this context should be read his arguments in favour of toleration in 1668, and his opposition in the following year to the Conventicles Bill, which he likened to the Spanish Inquisition. The parliamentary diarist John Milward observed cynically that in these speeches Seymour 'drives at an interest more than at religion' (*Diary of John Milward*, 221), and certainly this liberal interlude sits oddly with Seymour's cavalier background and later reputation as a staunch high-churchman. It may also be significant that he was not prepared to suffer long for these beliefs. A punitive dismissal from the commission of the peace served to concentrate his mind and in November 1670, allegedly on the advice of the duchess of York, he turned his coat: in Marvell's words, Seymour and others 'took their leave of their former party and fell to head the King's business' (*Poems and Letters of Andrew Marvell*, ed. H. M. Margoliouth, 2 vols., 1952, 2.305).

Speaker of the house As a ministerial spokesman in the Commons, Seymour proved a great success: busy, ingenious at procedural manipulation, a good manager, and forceful orator. By 1672 he had received a place on the Navy Board, and the following year he was considered as a potential candidate for the speakership. Although he had broken with Buckingham, shades of his former patron's influence may be detected in his vehement enmity towards France, and perhaps in his defence of the declaration of indulgence in parliament in 1673, although this latter intervention also did him no harm at court and may have helped his advance to the chair in February of that year. Seymour was in some respects an unusual choice as speaker, because of his lack of legal training (a deficiency of which he was acutely conscious himself), although on the credit side he had served as chairman of the important committees of supply and ways and means. As far as the court was concerned, he was an ideal choice. Bishop Burnet described him as:

> the most assuming Speaker that ever sat in the chair. He knew the House and every man in it so well that by looking about he could tell the fate of every question. So if anything was put when the court party were not well gathered together, he would have held the House from doing anything by wilful mistaking or mis-stating the question. (*Bishop Burnet's History*, 2.80)

In April 1673 Seymour was sworn a privy councillor, and was then made treasurer of the navy, at a salary of £3800. If rumour is to be believed, the money was badly needed; he is said to have told the king that were it not for the allowance of £1500 per session he would not have been able to take the speakership.

Seymour soon became a *bête noire* of the opposition, and as early as the autumn of 1673 an attempt was made to remove him from the chair because, it was said, his frequent visits to brothels and gaming-houses lowered the reputation of parliament. On one occasion, old friendships were remembered: he was accused of partiality towards Buckingham when his former patron appeared before the Commons in January 1674. Otherwise he proved a strong speaker, unconstrained by constitutional niceties when a firm hand was required. His high-handedness and ignorance of the law exposed him to criticism; on the other hand, members seem to have appreciated that his powerful personality lent authority to the office. During the winter of 1677–8 his arrogance led him into dangerous territory. Four times he adjourned the house by the king's command without putting the question, and in April 1678, to avoid a formal censure, he had to feign a diplomatic illness. When he eventually returned to the chair, however, he showed that he had lost none of his self-confidence, as his interventions strained the speaker's authority to new heights.

By this time Seymour's relations with Lord Treasurer Danby had deteriorated badly. The disclosure of the Popish Plot coincided with the final rupture. Even though in private Seymour did not believe in the veracity of the plot, he none the less acted as though he did, speaking strongly against popery and being the first to recommend limitations on a Catholic monarch. After the election of the first Exclusion Parliament in February 1679, to which he had been returned as knight of the shire for Devon, Seymour was in a difficult position, but his attacks on popery in the preceding session made him popular, despite the enmity which Lord Shaftesbury, his former ally in the Buckingham faction, entertained for him. Thus he was twice elected speaker against a court nominee, only for Charles II to reject him; and it was only in his absence that an alternative candidate was finally accepted by the Commons.

Court and country politics Returned to the ranks of ordinary members, Seymour at first proceeded with caution, taking a moderate line on the plot. His popularity proved short-lived, the more so after he had voted against the first Exclusion Bill. However, this step restored him to favour at court, and especially with the duke of York. For someone as proud as Seymour of the part played by his family in promoting the Reformation in England, and with a long record of opposition to popery, it must have been galling to be accused of sympathy for the Catholic cause. Nevertheless, in November 1680, he made a powerful speech against the second Exclusion Bill, raising the spectre of another civil war which would entail the destruction of English liberties. So effective was his intervention that opposition members manufactured an impeachment against him for alleged malversation of naval funds. Seymour justified himself in a long speech in which he recalled the several occasions on which he had defended the privileges of the house, even resisting royal commands, and had refused a bribe. Such was the level of animosity against him that the motion for impeachment passed, only for the snap dissolution to put a stop to proceedings.

Seymour did not stand for election to the Oxford parliament but attended its meetings as a royal adviser. He was now at the brief zenith of his political power, directing appointments and dismissals (and prompting Dryden to write *Absalom and Achitophel*). His hauteur became unbearable, and when he quarrelled openly with Lord Halifax he finally overstepped the mark. He was removed from office, essentially on personal grounds although some historians have suggested, charitably, that his subsequent withdrawal from public affairs was also prompted by dislike of the shift in royal policy towards France, and a suspicion of Catholic influence at court. Whether or not it was of his own volition, he did not participate in the 'Stuart revenge' of 1681–5, and when he was returned to James II's parliament he denounced royal policy towards the boroughs, warned against the standing army and its Catholic officers, and even referred to the dangers of introducing the 'papist religion and unconstitutional government' (HoP, *Commons, 1660–90*, 3.418). His first wife having died, on 11 August 1685 Seymour married Letitia (*d.* 1729), daughter of Sir Francis Popham of Littlecote, Wiltshire. They had six sons and one daughter.

Williamite tory In 1687 Seymour was dismissed from his local offices, though remaining a privy councillor. He played no part in the opposition to James II in the country, but when the prince of Orange landed he responded quickly, joining William at Exeter, and drafting the local association in support of the Orangist cause and in defence of the protestant religion, the liberty of the subject, and the rule of law. His example was decisive in rallying west-country tories, and the prince made him governor of Exeter. But Seymour could not remain remote from the centre of events and hurried to London. He was especially concerned at the favour being shown to nonconformists, a revealing contrast to his previous public utterances, and further evidence, perhaps, that his political standpoint on religious questions was essentially opportunist. Certainly he was no exemplar of Anglican piety. But he was convinced that churchmen constituted 'the most considerable and most substantial body of the nation', and if the church were not supported 'we should run into a commonwealth and all would be ruined' (*Correspondence of Henry Hyde*, 2.238). Thus reasons of principle, avoiding a recurrence of the upheavals of the 1640s, combined with an awareness of the political advantages to be gained by espousing the interest of the majority of the political nation, determined him to seek his following among tory squires. Moreover, despite the assistance he had given William, he found himself out of favour, possibly because of Danby's influence. Thus he voted in the Convention against the motion that the throne was vacant, and declared his unhappiness at the constitutional implications of the revolution, even if prepared to accept the new regime on pragmatic grounds. Tactlessly, he also gave vent to his natural dislike of the Dutch, in complaints at the behaviour of William's troops in the west country, and complained ceaselessly of mismanagements in the prosecution of the war. This oppositionist stance was continued into the 1690 parliament, in which Seymour appeared as one of the leading 'country tories', pressing inquiries into estimates and expenditure, and missing no opportunity to strike at his personal enemies, Danby and Halifax. With his former colleague from the 'country' opposition in James II's parliament, Sir Christopher Musgrave, he developed a tory critique of the conduct of the war, as benefiting only the Dutch at England's expense, and argued for a greater concentration on naval operations. He also began to make overtures to discontented whigs, like Paul Foley and Robert Harley, in order to develop a combined 'country' opposition.

At this point Seymour found himself badly in need of friends, of any political complexion: his accounts as treasurer of the navy remained unaudited, and he was also vulnerable because of incidental contacts with Jacobite conspirators like Lord Preston. So when he received overtures from a more sympathetic tory minister, Lord Nottingham, he responded positively (whether from fear of exposure or hope of gain), shifting around to a more moderate position. As a result, in the spring of 1692 he was reappointed to the privy council, from which he had been excluded in 1689, and was made a lord of the treasury. He then promptly reversed his former positions on a whole variety of issues—accounts, expenditure, war strategy, naval administration—though remaining consistent on one subject: trade, and in particular his involvement with the affairs of the East India Company. He was a close friend of the interloping merchant Thomas Coulson, whom he brought into parliament for the Devon borough of Totnes.

Seymour's identification with the court did not last long, for the rise to power of the whig junto made it necessary for him to rebuild former friendships and to restore his credit both with high-church back-benchers and 'country' whigs. The crisis came in 1694 when his critical speeches on naval failures provoked the chancellor of the exchequer, Charles Montagu, to a savage response, which for once rendered Seymour speechless. Soon afterwards Seymour was dismissed from the treasury. In opposition once more, he did not find it easy to re-establish his former position. Younger men like Foley and Harley were coming to the fore. Seymour's integrity had been compromised by his several voltes-face, and more harm was to come to his reputation as his misplaced confidence as an oracle of parliamentary procedure drew him into blunders, and investigations into parliamentary corruption over East Indian affairs threatened to implicate him. He even lost his seat at Exeter in 1695 and was obliged to fall back on the less 'popular' constituency of Totnes.

High-church champion Seymour's response to these setbacks was to re-emphasize his own tory credentials, opposing the association of 1696 and the attainder of the Jacobite Sir John Fenwick, and exploiting tory xenophobia by further attacks on the Dutch and on Huguenot refugees. His aversion to government was completed by the foundation of the new East India Company in 1697, which left his own connections out in the cold, and he identified firmly with the old company in its struggle to recover its position. At the same time he was also emphasizing his Devonian roots, showing himself to be a strenuous advocate of local commercial and manufacturing interests. He promoted bills to restrict the export of Irish woollen goods, to benefit the Devon and Somerset cloth industries. His intention was to establish himself as the leader of the high tories in the Commons, with a strong local power base. So while Harley and Foley made the running in the 'new country party' opposition, Seymour settled into a subordinate position at the head of a 'western empire' of tories.

The limits to Seymour's parliamentary influence were clearly seen in 1698, when his vanity persuaded him to stand once again for the speakership, only to be disappointed. He recovered some ground through the virulence of his attacks on the junto ministers, especially over corruption (a charge from which he was himself not entirely safe). But it was Harley rather than Seymour to whom the king turned in the winter of 1700–01 to manage the Commons for the new tory ministry. Although due deference was paid to Seymour he was given no office, and in the 1701 parliament inevitably became restive. Denouncing the old ministry by exposing the secret partition treaty reinforced his position as a tory hero, but embarrassed the king. Indeed, Seymour overplayed his hand to such an extent that, despite his support for the Act of Settlement, and for a generous settlement of the civil list, William not only refused to restore him to office but turned against the tories as a party.

Last campaigns It was only after the accession of Queen Anne that Seymour was restored to power, as comptroller of the household in the Godolphin–Marlborough administration. However, his self-appointed role as leader of the tory interest in the Commons now determined his political stance and he was much less flexible in old age than he had been even in the early 1690s. He never entirely accepted the strategic imperatives imposed by Marlborough, hankering after a 'blue-water' policy of naval rather than land warfare. Worse still, he indulged himself in a display of the full spectrum of tory prejudices, ranting against foreign army officers, union with Scotland, and especially the practice of occasional conformity by which dissenters evaded the requirements of the Test and Corporation Acts. The dismissal of Lord Rochester in 1703, and the consequent reconstruction of the ministry, left Seymour and Nottingham isolated, and when Nottingham departed in 1704 Seymour inevitably followed.

Dismissal from office signalled the end of Seymour's political career. He began to admit the weaknesses of age, and talk of handing the torch to younger men. Reports of decrepitude were briefly disproved at the beginning of the 1705 parliament when he made a number of vigorous speeches, but by late 1706 he had convinced himself, and his physician, that he was dying. Ironically, it was at this point he finally succeeded in clearing his debts as treasurer of the navy. In the event, he survived until 18 February 1708, when he died at Maiden Bradley. He was buried at Maiden Bradley.

Of Seymour's two sons from his first marriage, the elder, Edward, succeeded him in the baronetcy; the younger, William, enjoyed a military career. The eldest son of Seymour's second marriage, Popham Seymour-Conway, succeeded to the considerable estates of his mother's cousin the earl of Conway, in Ireland and England, but was killed in a duel in 1699, so the fortune passed to the next brother, Francis, who assumed the name Conway and was created Baron Conway in 1703. He was the father of the first marquess of Hertford.

D. W. HAYTON

Sources J. P. Ferris, 'Seymour, Edward', HoP, *Commons, 1660–90*, 3.411–23 • M. J. Knights, 'Seymour, Sir Edward', HoP, *Commons, 1690–1715* [draft] • R. W. Clayton, 'The political career of Sir Edward Seymour, bt, 1633–1708', DPhil diss., University of York, 1976 • *The diary of John Milward*, ed. C. Robbins (1938) • A. Grey, ed., *Debates of the House of Commons, from the year 1667 to the year 1694*, 10 vols. (1763) • *The parliamentary diary of Narcissus Luttrell, 1691–1693*, ed. H. Horwitz (1972) • *The parliamentary diary of Sir Richard Cocks, 1698–1702*, ed. D. W. Hayton (1996) • *Bishop Burnet's History* • *Letters illustrative of the reign of William III from 1696 to 1708 addressed to the duke of Shrewsbury by James Vernon*, ed. G. P. R. James, 3 vols. (1841) • *The correspondence of Henry Hyde, earl of Clarendon, and of his brother Laurence Hyde, earl of Rochester*, ed. S. W. Singer, 2 vols. (1828) • *Memoirs of Sir John Reresby*, ed. A. Browning, 2nd edn, ed. M. K. Geiter and W. A. Speck (1991) • *The Marlborough–Godolphin correspondence*, ed. H. L. Snyder, 3 vols. (1975) • D. T. Witcombe, *Charles II and the Cavalier House of Commons, 1663–74* (1966) • P. Seaward, *The Cavalier Parliament and the reconstruction of the old regime, 1661–1667* (1989) • A. Browning, *Thomas Osborne, earl of Danby and duke of Leeds, 1632–1712*, 3 vols. (1944–51) • K. H. D. Haley, *The first earl of Shaftesbury*

(1968) · H. Horwitz, *Parliament, policy and politics in the reign of William III* (1977) · G. S. Holmes, *British politics in the age of Anne* (1967)
Archives Wilts. & Swindon RO, naval, military, and political papers
Likenesses attrib. P. Lely, oils, *c.*1679, NPG [*see illus.*] · J. M. Rysbrack, tomb effigy, 1728, All Saints' Church, Maiden Bradley, Wiltshire · W. Worthington, line engraving, pubd 1821, BM; NPG · J. Lonsdale, oils (after unknown artist), Palace of Westminster, London · Roth, portrait · Worthington, engraving (after Roth)

Seymour, Edward Adolphus, eleventh duke of Somerset (1775–1855), scholar, born on 24 February 1775 at Monkton Farleigh in Wiltshire, was the third, but eldest surviving, son of Webb Seymour, tenth duke (1718–1793), and his wife, Anna Maria (*d.* 1802), daughter and heir of John Bonnell of Stanton Harcourt in Oxfordshire. He was educated at Eton College and matriculated at Christ Church, Oxford, on 31 January 1792. He succeeded to the peerage in 1793, was created MA at Oxford on 2 July 1794, and was made honorary DCL in 1810. From an early age he devoted himself to science and mathematics, displaying genuine aptitude for both studies. He published two mathematical treatises, on the relative properties of circles and ellipses, in 1842 and 1850. He was equally well versed in historical and antiquarian knowledge, and Patrick Fraser Tytler, the historian, valued his judgement in these matters highly. He was elected a fellow of the Royal Society in 1797, of the Society of Antiquaries in 1816, and of the Linnean Society in 1820. He was president of the latter society from 1834 to 1837. He was also a member of the Royal Asiatic Society, was president of the Royal Institution for some years, and from 1801 to 1838 was president of the Royal Literary Fund. On 19 April 1837 he was made a knight of the Garter. He was considered an excellent landlord, and, unlike most large landowners, supported the repeal of the corn laws. In the period of agricultural depression which followed he showed his confidence in the measure by making large purchases of land.

Somerset was twice married: first, on 24 June 1800, to Charlotte (*b.* 6 April 1772), second daughter of Archibald Hamilton, ninth duke of Hamilton; she died on 10 June 1827, leaving three surviving sons (who all succeeded in turn to the title), and four daughters. The eldest son, Edward [*see* St Maur, Edward Adolphus, twelfth duke of Somerset], would become first lord of the Admiralty. Charlotte was noted for the extremes of her economy. The duke married, second, on 28 July 1836, Margaret (*d.* 1880), eldest daughter of Sir Michael Shaw-Stewart of Blackhall, Renfrewshire. Somerset died on 15 August 1855 at his London home, Somerset House, Park Lane, and was buried at Kensal Green cemetery.

E. I. Carlyle, *rev.* K. D. Reynolds

Sources GEC, *Peerage* · *GM*, 2nd ser., 44 (1855), 425 · Foster, *Alum. Oxon.* · G. Ramsden, *Correspondence of two brothers: Edward Adolphus, eleventh duke of Somerset and Lord Webb Seymour* (1906) · *The Times* (16 Aug 1855)
Archives Devon RO, Somerset MSS, 1392M 1392M/L15, 19, 1799Madd2 | BL, correspondence with Charles Babbage, 1823–53, Add. MSS 37183–37201 · BL, correspondence with Greville, 1800–22, Add. MS 58991 · BL OIOC, correspondence with Sir T. S. and Lady Raffles, MSS Eur D 742 · Bucks. RLSS, Ramsden MSS, Acc

Edward Adolphus Seymour, eleventh duke of Somerset (1775–1855), by unknown artist

D/RA · Muncaster Castle, correspondence to and of his wife, NRA 24077
Likenesses J. Stephanoff, drawing, *c.*1821 (*Coronation of George IV*), V&A · G. Hayter, group portrait, oils (*The trial of Queen Caroline, 1820*), NPG · portrait, U. Lond., Senate House [*see illus.*]

Seymour, Edward Adolphus. *See* St Maur, Edward Adolphus, twelfth duke of Somerset (1804–1885).

Seymour, Sir Edward Hobart (1840–1929), naval officer, born at Kinwarton, Warwickshire, on 30 April 1840, was the second son of the Revd Richard Seymour (1806–1880), rector of Kinwarton, and his wife, Frances (*d.* 27 April 1871), third daughter of Charles Smith MP, of Suttons, Essex. He was grandson of Rear-Admiral Sir Michael *Seymour, first baronet (1768–1834), and nephew of Admiral Sir Michael *Seymour (1802–1887). He was educated from 1850 at Radley College (headmaster the Revd W. B. Heathcote), where among his schoolfellows were two other future admirals, Lord Walter Talbot Kerr and Lord Charles Thomas Montagu-Douglas-Scott. Seymour had little difficulty in choosing his profession: 'As soon as I had sense enough to form a real wish, it was to go to sea.' Having been offered a nomination for the Royal Navy, he was sent to Eastman's naval academy at Southsea in the autumn of 1852, and two months later passed the service entrance examination at Portsmouth. A sum in the rule of three and a 'dictation' of twenty lines from *The Spectator* made up the test. The next day he joined the *Encounter*, a screw corvette. He served in her for eight months and was then appointed to the *Terrible*, in the Mediterranean, a paddle-wheel frigate of 21 guns, which was one of the ships of the allied fleet sent to make a demonstration in the Black Sea in January 1854. In the *Terrible*, Seymour sailed for Odessa on the declaration of war with Russia the following April, and thereafter he served in all the operations in the Black Sea until the final evacuation of the Crimea in 1856.

At the end of the Crimean War in 1857, Seymour, still a midshipman, was appointed to the *Calcutta*, flagship of his uncle Sir Michael Seymour, on the China station. He took passage in the sloop *Cruiser*, and his experience in that vessel he afterwards described as 'a first-rate specimen of how youngsters were disregarded and neglected as to their instruction or care of any sort'. He reached China in time to take part in the operations which resulted from the *Arrow* incident. Canton (Guangzhou) was being blockaded and an attack upon a Chinese fleet of about 100 junks was in preparation. Seymour took part in the attack, during which the launch on which he was serving was sunk by a round shot. After the destruction of the fleet of junks the expedition moved up the Canton River to take the city, and Seymour served with the battery of the naval brigade; the other midshipman of the battery was Arthur Knyvet Wilson, afterwards admiral of the fleet. After the capture of Canton (December 1857) the squadron moved to the Gulf of Pecheli (Beizhili) in order to get in touch with the Chinese government at Peking (Beijing). Seymour took part in the severe engagement in which the mouth of the Peiho (Beihe) River, protected by the Taku (Dagu) forts, was forced (May 1858). This was his last service in that war, for shortly afterwards he was invalided home as a result of sunstroke.

On his return to Britain, Seymour passed his examinations and was promoted mate (1859). When he heard that war had again broken out in China, he applied for a ship of that station and sailed for the East in the frigate *Impérieuse*. In Rhio Strait, on the way out, he went overboard to rescue a seaman in waters infested with sharks, for which he received the Royal Humane Society silver medal.

The commander-in-chief on the China station, Sir James Hope, having a blank commission for a lieutenant, gave it to Seymour and took him into his flagship, the *Chesapeake*. In her, Seymour took part in the combined attack by British and French forces on the Taku forts in September 1860. An expedition up the Yang-tse River in a flotilla of light craft and paddle-wheel vessels gave him a new experience; he served first as executive officer, and later was given command of the paddle-steamer *Waterman* on the Canton River. He returned to the flagship in 1861 and took part in the operations against the Taiping rebels (1862), in the capture of Ningpo (Ningbo) and Kahding (Jiading), commanding small-arm parties. In 1863 he returned to Britain. He was twenty-three, and had ten years' continuous active service.

On his return to Britain, Seymour served three years as flag-lieutenant to his uncle Sir Michael Seymour, commander-in-chief at Portsmouth. He then received a 'haul-down' promotion to commander at the age of twenty-six (1866). Posts for commanders were few, and he was on half pay for two years. Anxious to take part in a projected Arctic expedition, he took a cruise in northern waters in a Peterhead whaler, in order to gain experience of the ice. In 1868 he was appointed to the coastguard in Ireland, a position which, although enjoyable, was uncongenial to one whose whole desire was to serve at sea. In June 1869 he obtained his wish as commander of the gunboat *Growler* on the west coast of Africa. In the course of operations on the Congo in 1870 he was shot in the leg. The wound was severe and he was invalided: consequently, when he applied in 1875 for the command of the *Discovery* in the polar expedition under George Nares, he was rejected on medical grounds.

An enforced leisure of eighteen months on half pay was used by Seymour to improve his French by visiting France and Switzerland. In January 1872 he was given command of the paddle-wheel dispatch vessel *Vigilant* for service in the Channel Fleet. In March 1873, at the age of thirty-three, he was promoted post captain. A further period on shore followed, but caused him no deep regret. He spent a year at the Royal Naval College and then travelled in France and Italy. Normally, officers at that time spent at least five years on half pay on promotion, but the Admiralty, taking into consideration Seymour's loss of the command of the *Discovery* in the Arctic expedition, appointed him at his own request to the troopship *Orontes*. Three years' experience, in his own words, 'greatly enlarged my knowledge of that seemingly volatile yet really constant element called "human nature"'. Although he considered that 'trooping was not proper naval work', he saw value in it for the contact which it promoted between the services.

In 1879 Seymour found himself once more on half pay, and used the opportunity to study at the torpedo school and, as before, to travel abroad and refresh his knowledge of French. His service in combined operations with foreign officers in his early days, and later in China as commander-in-chief, impressed him greatly with the need for naval officers to have a knowledge of foreign languages. 'I should make it a rule', he wrote in his memoirs, 'that no boy might become a naval cadet unless he could hold an ordinary conversation in at least one foreign language.' In April 1880 Seymour commissioned the cruiser *Iris* in the Mediterranean, and the following July joined the fleet commanded by Sir Beauchamp Seymour (afterwards Lord Alcester). When the rioting took place at Alexandria in July 1882, Seymour was detached to guard the Suez Canal. Later, he dismantled the forts on the Rosetta mouth of the Nile. In November he succeeded Captain J. A. Fisher in command of the battleship *Inflexible*; he hauled down his pennant in February 1885. Three months later, when war threatened with Russia, he was placed in command of the Cunard liner *Oregon*, commissioned as an auxiliary cruiser—which convinced him that the fighting value of such vessels was very small.

Ten months on half pay followed. From May 1886 to December 1887 Seymour served as flag-captain to Admiral Sir George Willes, commander-in-chief at Portsmouth, and was then made the assistant to the admiral-superintendent of naval reserves; this post he held until his promotion to flag rank at the age of forty-nine (1889). A long period of half pay was then employed in again visiting foreign countries: he travelled in France, Russia, the West Indies, and the United States. In July 1892 he hoisted his flag for the first time on board the *Swiftsure* for the annual manoeuvres, after which he became second-in-command of the channel squadron with his flag on board the *Anson*. It fell to him to take part in the raising of the *Howe* when she grounded at Ferrol, but apart from that particular service the command gave him less work than his energetic mind required. More active work followed when he was appointed, for three years, admiral-superintendent of the reserves.

In December 1897 Seymour was appointed commander-in-chief on the China station. Service there was peaceful until the Boxer uprising in 1900. On 31 May he received news from the British minister, Sir Claude Macdonald, that the situation at Peking was precarious. Having already detached a small force for the defence of the legations, Seymour proceeded at once to the Taku forts. A naval force of ships of several nations shortly assembled, of which, as senior admiral, Seymour assumed command. At a consultation with the foreign commanders it was decided to form a naval brigade under the command of Seymour with his flag-captain John Jellicoe as chief of staff, to march, if necessary, to Peking. Matters moved fast. Immediate help was urgently called for from the legations on 9 June; the next day the brigade—a mixed force of 2000 marines and bluejackets—was landed, and a sharp encounter with the Boxers took place on 11 June at Langfang, about half-way to Peking. Seymour then found himself unable to proceed. He was faced by considerable forces, the railway was cut, and he had no other means of transport. He held on for a week, but was then forced to retire on Tientsin (Tianjin), his short-rationed force harassed by the enemy. At Hsiku (Xigu), an important arsenal, he was attacked by regulars of the Chinese army. He stormed the arsenal and there defended himself against continued assaults until relieved by a body of Russian troops, when he withdrew his brigade and left the operations in the hands of military forces. Seymour's conduct throughout these difficult operations was highly commended, and his command was extended for a further six months. In March 1901 he was promoted to admiral and returned to Britain; he hauled down his flag on 21 August.

In 1902 Seymour accompanied the duke of Connaught on his mission to Madrid for the coronation of Alfonso XIII. In the same year he served on Sir Edward Grey's committee on the staffing of the navy. In 1903 he was appointed to the command at Devonport, which he held until February 1905, when he was made admiral of the fleet. In accordance with custom, he would have then hauled down his flag, but an exception was made on account of his distinguished service, and he kept his flag flying for another month. In 1906 Seymour accompanied Prince Arthur of Connaught on his state visit to Japan, and in 1909 he had the unusual honour of re-hoisting the flag of an admiral of the fleet on board the *Inflexible* when he commanded a squadron sent to Boston, Massachusetts, for the Hudson–Fulton celebration. He retired in 1910 and took no further part in public affairs. He was awarded the Order of Merit (1902), and was made GCB (1901) and GCVO (1906); he was also awarded a Cambridge LLD (1904), and sworn of the privy council (1909).

Seymour was a man of a broad and humane outlook, with a capacity for appreciating others' points of view; this contributed largely to the harmonious relations with foreign officers serving under him. He was widely read and a good linguist. An officer with uncommon intellectual breadth, Seymour was never pushed to his limits, but performed his duties with skill, insight, and dignity. He described his services with modesty in *My Naval Career and Travels* (1911). He was unmarried. He died at his home, Hedsor View, Maidenhead Court, Maidenhead, Berkshire, on 2 March 1929.

H. W. RICHMOND, *rev.* ANDREW LAMBERT

Sources E. H. Seymour, *My naval career and travels* (1911) • R. Bacon, *Life of John Rushworth, Earl Jellicoe* (1936) • W. L. Clowes, *The Royal Navy: a history from the earliest times to the present*, 7 vols. (1897–1903), vol. 7 • P. A. Cohen, *History in three keys: the Boxers as event, experience and myth* (1997) • *WWW* • Burke, *Peerage* (1967) [Culme-Seymour] • *CGPLA Eng. & Wales* (1929)

Archives McGill University, Montreal, McLennan Library, journal and notebook • NL Scot., corresp. and journals • Royal Naval Museum Library, Portsmouth, admiralty library, journal as commander-in-chief of the China squadron | NYPL, report relating to Hudson–Fulton celebration

Likenesses H. G. Herkomer, oils, Admiralty, Devonport • Spy [L. Ward], chromolithograph caricature, NPG; repro. in *VF* (31 Oct 1901)

Wealth at death £54,781 14*s.* 2*d.*: probate, 16 April 1929, *CGPLA Eng. & Wales*

Seymour, Edward James (1796–1866), physician, third son of William Seymour of 65 Margaret Street, Cavendish Square, London, and his wife, Thyphena Letithoea, eldest daughter of Daniel Foulston of London, was born on 30 March 1796, and baptized at the church of St Nicholas, Lower Tooting. His father, a member of a family settled in Lincolnshire in the middle of the seventeenth century, was a solicitor, who lived in Brighton for thirty years and who also practised as a magistrate and deputy lieutenant for Sussex, and chairman of the quarter sessions. Edward Seymour received his education at Richmond School, Surrey, and at Jesus College, Cambridge, where he graduated BA in January 1816, MA in 1819, and MD in 1826. He received a licence *ad practicandum* from his university in 1822. He also studied medicine in London, Edinburgh, and Paris; he was admitted an inceptor candidate of the Royal College of Physicians in 1823, a candidate in 1826, and a fellow in 1827. At the college he subsequently held the posts of Goulstonian lecturer in 1829, censor in 1830, Croonian lecturer in 1831, and *consiliarius* in 1836. On 4 September 1817 Seymour married Maria Searancke of Clapton, London, and they had a family of six sons and four daughters. The eldest son, Lieutenant-Colonel Charles Frederick Seymour CB, of the 84th regiment, was acting adjutant-general at the siege of Lucknow.

The first years of Seymour's career were spent in Italy, mainly at Florence, where he had a large income and made some influential friends who were of use to him on his return to Britain. In 1823 he settled again in England,

and established himself at 23 George Street, Hanover Square, London, soon acquiring a high-class practice. On 28 November 1828 he was elected physician to St George's Hospital; he held the post until 1847, and rose to be senior physician. Seymour had an aptitude for bedside teaching. Shortly after settling in London he became physician to the hospital ship *Dreadnought* at Greenwich, and he subsequently became consulting physician to the Royal Naval Hospital. He was also physician to the duke of Sussex. From 1 September 1831 to 1839 Seymour was a metropolitan commissioner in lunacy; he came to devote much of his attention to cases of insanity, and was one of the first to use opium freely in the treatment of the insane. In 1859 he published a letter, which he addressed to the earl of Shaftesbury, *On the laws which regulate private lunatic asylums, with a comparative view of the process 'de lunatico inquirendo' in England and the law of France*. The letter contains a few observations on the causes of insanity and on the improvement in the treatment of mental diseases during the preceding twenty-five years. On 17 June 1841 Seymour was elected a fellow of the Royal Society; he was also a fellow of the Royal Medical and Chirurgical Society, and a member of the Royal Medical Society and the Wernerian Society of Edinburgh, and of the Imperial and Royal Academy of Science of Siena.

Seymour was an accomplished man outside the range of his professional practice. His main works were *Diseases of the Ovaria* (with a volume of plates, 1830); *Observations on the Medical Treatment of Insanity* (1832); and *Thoughts on the Treatment of Several Severe Diseases of the Human Body* (1847). Seymour suffered from poor health and financial misfortune in his later years and died at his residence, 13 Charles Street, Berkeley Square, London, on 16 April 1866, from organic disease of the stomach and liver. He was survived by his wife. W. W. WEBB, *rev.* MICHAEL BEVAN

Sources *Proceedings of the Medico-Chirurgical Society*, 5 (1867), 251 · Munk, *Roll* · *The Lancet* (28 April 1866) · *Medical Times and Gazette* (28 April 1866), 458 · private information (1897) [Revd E. Seymour, son]

Archives BL, letters to Sir Robert Peel, Add. MSS 40597–40609

Likenesses J. Slater, coloured lithograph, *c.*1830; formerly in possession of the Revd E. Seymour, Bratton Clovelly parsonage, Derbyshire, 1897 · Foley, wax bust; formerly in possession of the Revd E. Seymour, Bratton Clovelly parsonage, Derbyshire, 1897 · E. Morton, lithograph (after J. Slater), Wellcome L.

Wealth at death under £4000: probate, 19 July 1866, *CGPLA Eng. & Wales*

Seymour [*née* Percy], **Elizabeth, duchess of Somerset (1667–1722)**, courtier and politician, was born on 26 January 1667 at Petworth, Sussex, and baptized there on 29 January. She was the only surviving daughter and heir of Joceline Percy, eleventh earl of Northumberland (1644–1670), and Elizabeth (*c.*1646–1690), youngest daughter and coheir of Thomas Wriothesley, fourth earl of Southampton, lord treasurer of England from 1660 to 1667. She was known as Lady Elizabeth Percy from her father's accession to the earldom in 1668 until her marriage in 1679. At her father's death on 21 May 1670, having survived a brother, Henry, who died in 1669, and a sister, Henrietta, who died soon afterwards, she inherited the vast Percy estates and

Elizabeth Seymour, duchess of Somerset (1667–1722), by Michael Dahl

became one of the most sought-after heiresses in England. Upon the marriage of her mother to her second husband, Ralph Montagu (later first duke of Montagu), in 1673 she was placed under the guardianship of her grandmother, Elizabeth, dowager countess of Northumberland (1622/3–1705), at Petworth. In 1679 the dowager countess arranged a marriage for her twelve-year-old granddaughter with the fifteen-year-old Henry Cavendish, styled earl of Ogle (1663–1680), son and heir of Henry, second duke of Newcastle. Ogle, who appears to have been sickly, died on 1 November the following year.

In 1681 the dowager countess arranged a contract of marriage for her granddaughter with Thomas *Thynne (1647/8–1682) of Longleat, Wiltshire, the wealthy and famous 'Tom of Ten Thousand', worth £10,000 per annum. Lady Elizabeth shrank from living with her much older husband, pleading that 'there may be more sin and shame in people's living together than in parting' (*CSP dom.*, *1682*, 49). It is unclear whether she fled or was allowed by Thynne to go abroad to the Netherlands in November 1681. There she was sheltered by Sir William Temple, the English ambassador to The Hague, and sought the assistance of her mother and Ralph Montagu to free her from Thynne. There is evidence of legal proceedings to dissolve the marriage on the grounds of a previous commitment to marry on Thynne's part. The marriage was in fact ended by Thynne's murder on 12 February 1682. While riding in his coach down Pall Mall he was set upon and killed by a group of assailants hired by Charles, Count Königsmark. Königsmark was an adventurer who had become attracted to Lady Elizabeth on a visit to the English court the previous year. While the assailants were soon captured, tried, and executed Königsmark was acquitted and left England. Lady Elizabeth denied any knowledge of the plot but the scandal would forever cast a shadow on her name.

Lady Elizabeth returned to England in March 1682. On 30 May, after an initial refusal, she married Charles *Seymour, sixth duke of Somerset (1662–1748). The original contract stipulated that he was to take the name Percy but she released him from this obligation upon the attainment of her majority. The marriage was well known to be unhappy, largely because of Somerset's imperious temper and overweening pride; according to William Legge, first earl of Dartmouth, Somerset 'treated her with little gratitude or affection, though he owed all he had, except an empty title, to her' (*Bishop Burnet's History*, 6.34n.). Nevertheless, under Queen Anne the Somersets made an effective political team. He was master of the horse and a member of the cabinet; she was named a lady of the bedchamber on 12 May 1702. The duchess seems to have been widely esteemed at court for her gracious disposition and impeccable manners. Dartmouth thought her 'the best bred, as well as the best born lady in England ... She maintained her dignity at court, with great respect to the queen and civility to all others' (ibid.). It is remarkable that this testimony comes from a tory but it is not in fact unique. Towards the end of the queen's reign the tory Anne Wentworth, countess of Strafford, remarked 'If the Duchess must be out, she will leave the Court with a very good grace, for everybody is pleased with her good breeding and civility' (De Fonblanque, 507).

From about mid-reign a genuine friendship developed between the queen and the duchess of Somerset. This was not least because, unlike Sarah Churchill, duchess of Marlborough, and Abigail (later Lady) Masham, the duchess of Somerset 'never press'd the Queen Hard, nothing makes the Queen more Uneasie than that' (*Diary of Sir David Hamilton*, 49). Nevertheless Jonathan Swift thought her 'a most insinuating woman' (Swift, 206). Both the Churchill circle and the tories were convinced that the duchess connived with her husband to bring down the Godolphin ministry in 1710 and to thwart the Harley ministry at every opportunity thereafter. Certainly the Somersets' attendance on the queen stepped up from the summer of 1709. The Churchills suspected that the duchess used this contact to point out the frequent absences from court of the duchess of Marlborough. While the duchess of Somerset was not averse to engaging in political intrigue she tended to do so without the clumsiness of her whig rival, whom she supplanted as groom of the stole on 24 January 1711. Rather her very courtliness could be an effective weapon; thus while attending the queen in the House of Lords during the Sacheverell trial both she and Jane, Lady Hyde, stood with ostentatious correctness while the duchess of Marlborough chose to sit down. At the end of 1711 it was the duchess of Somerset who showed Anne a copy of the *Daily Courant* that contained Johann Kaspar von Bothmer's memorial protesting the preliminary articles of the treaty of Utrecht. As a result Swift thought that the queen's apparent wavering of support for the ministry over 'No Peace without Spain' was 'all your d—d duchess of Somerset's doings' (Swift, 435). And yet in each case the duchess could claim that she was doing nothing that was improper or overtly political.

The Oxford ministry was particularly anxious to neutralize the duchess's influence after this débâcle. In the winter of 1711–12 there was a concerted ministerial campaign to have her removed from her bedchamber post. Swift seconded this with *The Windsor Prophecy*, which referred none too subtly to the duchess's chequered past:

Beware of Carrots from Northumberlond.
Carrots sown Thyn a deep root may get
If so be they are in Sommer set
Their Conyngs mark thou, for I have been told,
They Assassine when young, and Poison when old.

The charge was unfair and it redounded to the author's discredit in the queen's eyes. Nevertheless, when the duke of Somerset was dismissed as master of the horse early in 1712 it looked as if tory hopes might be fulfilled, since he sought to force his wife to resign her court appointments as well. It was only after a concentrated effort by Anne, assisted by William, Lord Cowper, and the queen's physician, Sir David Hamilton, that Somerset was persuaded to allow his wife to remain in office, thus maintaining a whig presence around the queen. In late January, upon the completion of these negotiations, Hamilton wrote 'going into the Queen after the Duchess of Somerset came out from Her, I never saw the Queen Look with a more pleasant and Healthful Countenance, saying that Now, it was done' (*Diary of Sir David Hamilton*, 40). Despite this outcome, and Hamilton's constant urging that the duchess spend less time at Petworth and more time at court, recent historiography finds that the whigs received little tangible advantage from her proximity to the sovereign. This is hardly surprising, given the duchess's characteristic discretion and Anne's growing aversion to being badgered by her bedchamber attendants. Somewhat ironically this failure to press the queen goes far to explain why Somerset was, according to Dartmouth, 'by much the greatest favourite, when the queen died' (*Bishop Burnet's History*, 6.34n.). During the desperate final days of his ministry the earl of Oxford paid tribute to that favour and her reputation for intrigue when he wrote 'Send for the D^chs of Somerset—no body else can save us' (Holmes, 216). In fact there is no evidence that she would—or could—have done so.

In tribute to her birth and rank the duchess of Somerset was chief mourner at the funerals of Mary II in 1695 and Queen Anne in 1714. She died at home at Northumberland House, London, of breast cancer, on 23 November 1722 and was buried on 13 December in Salisbury Cathedral. She gave birth to at least four sons and three daughters. The eldest son, Charles Seymour, styled earl of Hertford, was baptized on 22 March 1683 but died and was buried by the following 26 August. Her second, but first surviving, son was Algernon *Seymour [*see under* Seymour, Charles, sixth duke of Somerset], also styled earl of Hertford in his father's lifetime, Baron Percy from 1722 (the Lords mistakenly assuming that the duchess had held that title), and seventh duke of Somerset from 1748. Her son Percy, MP for Cockermouth from 1718, died in 1721 and her son Charles died in 1711; both had remained unmarried. Her three daughters included Elizabeth (*d.* 1734), who married Henry O'Brien, eighth earl of Thomond (*d.* 1741); Catherine (*d.* 1731), who married Sir William *Wyndham, baronet; and Anne (*d.* 1722), who married Peregrine Osborne, third duke of Leeds. R. O. BUCHOLZ

Sources GEC, *Peerage*, new edn, 12/1.77–9 · E. B. De Fonblanque, *Annals of the house of Percy, from the conquest to the opening of the nineteenth century*, 2 (privately printed, London, 1887), 492–510 · G. L. Craik, *Romance of the peerage* (1849), 4.322–51 · E. Gregg, *Queen Anne* (1980) · R. O. Bucholz, *The Augustan court: Queen Anne and the decline of court culture* (1993) · *The diary of Sir David Hamilton, 1709–1714*, ed. P. Roberts (1975) · G. S. Holmes, *British politics in the age of Anne* (1967) · *The Marlborough–Godolphin correspondence*, ed. H. L. Snyder, 3 vols. (1975) · *Bishop Burnet's History*, 6.34–5 n. · J. Swift, *Journal to Stella*, ed. H. Williams, 2 vols. (1948)

Archives BL, Blenheim MSS, scattered individual letters · Chatsworth House, Derbyshire, Devonshire MSS, scattered individual letters · W. Sussex RO, Petworth House archives, Somerset papers

Likenesses P. Lely, oils, *c.*1669–1670, Syon House, Brentford, Middlesex · studio of P. Lely, oils, 1679–80, Syon House, Brentford, Middlesex · chalk drawing, *c.*1679–1680 (after P. Lely), NPG · J. Riley and J. B. Closterman, double portrait, oils, *c.*1687–1688 (with her son), Petworth House, Sussex · G. Kneller, oils, 1713, Petworth House, Sussex · J. Closterman, oils, Petworth House, Sussex · M. Dahl, oils, Petworth House, Sussex [*see illus.*] · attrib. J. Kerseboom, oils, Petworth House, Sussex · J. vander Vaart, mezzotint (after P. Lely), BM, NPG

Seymour, Lady Elizabeth. *See* Percy, Elizabeth, duchess of Northumberland and *suo jure* Baroness Percy (1716–1776).

Seymour, Frances, countess of Hertford. *See* Stuart, Frances, duchess of Lennox and Richmond (1578–1639).

Seymour [*née* Thynne], **Frances, duchess of Somerset (1699–1754)**, poet and letter writer, was born on 10 May 1699, probably at Longleat House, Wiltshire, the eldest child and coheir of Henry Thynne (1675–1708) and Grace (*c.*1676–1725), daughter and heir of Sir George Strode. Her early upbringing was at Longleat, home of her grandfather Thomas *Thynne, first Viscount Weymouth (*bap.* 1640, *d.* 1714), where she became friendly with Elizabeth Singer, later Rowe (1674–1737). Another early poet friend was her great-aunt Anne Finch, countess of Winchilsea (1661–1720). After her father died in 1708 Frances and her mother moved to Leweston, near Sherborne, home of the Strodes.

On 5 July 1715 Frances, aged sixteen, married the soldier and courtier Algernon *Seymour, earl of Hertford (1684–1750) [*see under* Seymour, Charles, sixth duke of Somerset]. Her husband's parents, the 'proud duke' of Somerset and his duchess, unaccountably hated her. There were two children of the marriage: Elizabeth (1716–1776) [*see* Percy, Elizabeth, duchess of Northumberland] and George, Viscount Beauchamp (1725–1744). An estate at Marlborough, Wiltshire, was settled on Hertford at his marriage; he completed the grand house begun by his father while Lady Hertford improved the landscape. From about 1730 they also had a modest country retreat at St Leonard's Hill, near Windsor; their town house was in Dover Street until 1721, thereafter in Grosvenor Street. In 1723 Lady Hertford was appointed lady of the bedchamber to Caroline, princess of Wales (later Queen Caroline), with a salary of £500 p.a.

Two short poems by Lady Hertford, based on the sentimental story of Inkle and Yarico retold by Steele in *The Spectator*, no. 11, were printed anonymously in *A New Miscellany … Written Chiefly by Persons of Quality* (1725). Isaac Watts published four short poems by her under the pen-name Eusebia ('Piety'), in his *Reliquiae juveniles* (1734); but her unconquerable diffidence ensured that most of her verse remained unpublished in her lifetime. She wrote many lively letters to family members, and to Watts, Elizabeth Rowe, and other friends, including notably Henrietta Knight, Lady Luxborough, and Henrietta Louisa Fermor, countess of Pomfret. Their subjects are, variously, literature, religion, court gossip, family, and the pleasures of a rural life. A few appeared in Rowe's *Miscellaneous Works* (1739) but most remained unpublished in Lady Hertford's lifetime.

Lady Hertford was patron to two generations of poets, including Watts, Rowe, Laurence Eusden (1688–1730), James Thomson (1700–1748), John Dyer (1700–1757), Stephen Duck (1705–1756), her son's tutor John Dalton (1709–1763), William Thompson (1712–1766), and William Shenstone (1714–1763), all of whom complimented her in published verse. Johnson asserted that Thomson, on his first visit to Marlborough, 'took more delight in carousing with lord Hertford and his friends than assisting her ladyship's poetical operations, and therefore never received another summons' (Johnson, 3.287), but the countess did in fact issue further invitations as well as smoothing Thomson's path to royal patronage. Of even more value was her intercession with Queen Caroline in January 1728, which secured a pardon for Thomson's friend Richard Savage (*d.* 1743), poet and convicted murderer.

The queen's death in 1737 ended Lady Hertford's service as lady of the bedchamber, leaving her with a pension of £400 p.a. and time to devote to rural pursuits. The estate at St Leonard's Hill was given up in 1739 when the Seymours acquired nearby Richings, near Colnbrook, Buckinghamshire. They renamed it Percy Lodge and adorned it with a hexagon, a hermitage, and a 'bungola' (bungalow) in the Indian style.

Lady Hertford was a lifelong evangelical Christian. Rowe's posthumous *Devout Exercises of the Heart* (1737), with a preface by Watts, was dedicated to her, and her religious friends and correspondents included, in addition to Rowe and Watts, Selina, countess of Huntington (1707–1791), and Catherine Talbot (1721–1770). Her piety was intensified when her beloved son contracted smallpox on his grand tour and died at Bologna on 11 September 1744, his nineteenth birthday. According to Horace Walpole she then interested herself in spiritualism, influenced by Rowe's famous *Friendship in Death* (Walpole, *Corr.*, 35.179).

On 2 December 1748 Lady Hertford became duchess of Somerset following her father-in-law's death; her husband died on 7 February 1750. She passed her remaining years as dowager duchess of Somerset at Percy Lodge; she died there on 7 July 1754 and was buried on 20 July beside her son and husband in Westminster Abbey.

JAMES SAMBROOK

Sources H. S. Hughes, *The gentle Hertford* (1940) • *Correspondence between Frances, countess of Hartford (afterwards duchess of Somerset) and Henrietta Louisa, countess of Pomfret, between the years 1738 and 1741*, ed. W. Bingley, 3 vols. (1805) • *Select letters between the late duchess of Somerset … and others*, ed. T. Hull, 2 vols. (1778) • *Memoirs of the Rev. Isaac Watts, D.D.*, ed. T. Gibbons (1780), 364–402 • GEC, *Peerage* • S. Johnson, *Lives of the English poets*, ed. G. B. Hill, [new edn], 3 vols. (1905), vol. 2, p. 352; vol. 3, p. 287 • Walpole, *Corr.*, 17.345–6; 18.522; 20.183; 32.283; 35.179 • J. L. Chester, ed., *The marriage, baptismal, and burial registers of the collegiate church or abbey of St Peter, Westminster*, Harleian Society, 10 (1876), 368, 377, 387 • will, PRO, PROB 11/810, fols. 80*r*–82*r*

Archives Alnwick Castle, Northumberland, commonplace books, verses, meditations, and journal, Alnwick MSS 114–117 • U. Birm., letter-book • Yale U., Beinecke L., letters, C 22 | Alnwick Castle, Northumberland, Percy family letters and papers, vols. 21–32 and 77 • BL, letters to Baroness Luxborough, Add. MS 23728 • BL, corresp. with Isaac Watts, Add. MS 33929 • BL, corresp. of the St John family, Add. MS 34196 • Bodl. Oxf., letters to Baroness Luxborough • Wellesley College, Massachusetts, letters to Baroness Luxborough

Likenesses A. Ramsay, oils, repro. in Hughes, *The gentle Hertford*

Wealth at death over £9000; plus landed estate of Percy Lodge; pictures; plate; jewels; furnishings; horses; carriages: will, PRO, PROB 11/810, sig. 211

Seymour, Francis (Ingram). *See* Conway, Francis Ingram-Seymour, second marquess of Hertford (1743–1822).

Seymour, Francis, first Baron Seymour of Trowbridge (1590?–1664), politician, was the third son of Edward *Seymour, Viscount Beauchamp (1561–1612) [*see under* Seymour, Edward (1539?–1621)] and of Honora Rogers. He was a younger brother of William *Seymour, first marquess of Hertford and later duke of Somerset. He was born about 1590 and knighted by James I at Royston on 23 October 1613. About 1620 Seymour married Frances Prynne. They had at least one son, Charles (1621?–1665), but Frances died in childbirth on 6 September 1626. Seymour sat in all the parliaments of the 1620s except that of 1626, representing Wiltshire every time apart from 1624 when he was MP for Marlborough. Throughout this period he was one of Buckingham's most vociferous critics. He was deeply opposed to the Spanish war and thought it parliament's duty to protect the localities from exorbitant financial burdens. His hostility to Buckingham caused him to be pricked as a sheriff in February 1626 in order to exclude him from parliament, and then to be removed from the commission of the peace the following July. Seymour was also passionately committed to defending the rule of law against incursions from the royal prerogative, a stance which led him to refuse the forced loan and to support the petition of right. By contrast, Seymour did not get deeply involved in the protests against Arminianism, and his sympathy for puritan 'godliness' appears to have been limited.

This concern for his locality and attachment to the rule of law continued to motivate Seymour's actions during Charles I's personal rule. In 1634 he led the opposition of Wiltshire justices against a royal commission for reforming the clothing industry, claiming that this was against the dignity of the office of a justice of the peace. He also became a prominent campaigner against ship money and

Francis Seymour, first Baron Seymour of Trowbridge (1590?–1664), attrib. Paul van Somer

in May 1639 was summoned before the privy council. He told the board that:

> he had against his conscience, and upon the importunity of his friends, paid that money twice, but now his conscience would suffer him no more to do a thing (as he thought) so contrary to law and to the liberty of the subject. (Bodl. Oxf., MS Clarendon 16, fols. 125*v*–126*r*)

The same wish to defend legal propriety and the 'liberty of the subject' informed Seymour's speeches in the Short and Long parliaments, and ironically helps to explain his subsequent decision to join the king. On 16 April 1640 he denounced those 'who tell [the king] his prerogative is above all laws', and called the ship-money sheriffs 'as grievous a plague as the task masters of Egypt' (Cope, 142–3). The following November he praised parliament as 'the great physician of the commonwealth' which would remedy the problem of 'ill counsel' (*Journal*, ed. Notestein, 7). As before, Seymour's primary concern was with constitutional and legal propriety; he wished to preserve episcopacy and opposed root-and-branch reform. On 19 February 1641 he was elevated to the Lords as Baron Seymour of

Trowbridge, and in May voted against Strafford's attainder. By the summer of 1641 he had become convinced that the king's leading critics now posed a greater threat to the rule of law and the liberty of the subject than did Charles I. In January 1642 John Coke described him as one of the king's 'chief counsellors' (BL, Add. MS 64922, fol. 88*r*), and the following March, Seymour protested against the militia ordinance. On 18 March he was granted leave to visit his Wiltshire estates and early in April he joined the king at York. He offered to raise twenty horse to support the king's cause, and in August went into Wiltshire to implement the commission of array.

During the first civil war Seymour combined active service in the royalist armies with a strong commitment to peace negotiations. He was appointed chancellor of the duchy of Lancaster in April 1644, and was one of the royalist commissioners at the treaty of Uxbridge. He was at Oxford when it surrendered in June 1646; he begged to compound under the Oxford articles, and his fine was set at £3725. He was one of the peers whom Charles summoned to Hampton Court in October 1647 to advise him, but thereafter he seems to have withdrawn completely from public life. He steered clear of royalist conspiracy and, when Seymour requested exemption from the decimation tax, Cromwell personally intervened to ensure this. Throughout the interregnum Seymour lived in retirement, convinced that the monarchy would eventually be restored, and in a private book of meditations and prayers he hoped that his fellow royalists would rejoice that they were 'counted worthy to suffer in a good cause' (BL, Egerton MS 71, fols. 4*v*–5*r*). At the Restoration, Seymour was sworn a privy councillor and reappointed chancellor of the duchy of Lancaster. He died on 12 July 1664 and was buried in the chancel of Bedwyn Magna church in Wiltshire. Seymour's second wife, Catherine Lee, whom he had married about 1636, lived on until 1701.

DAVID L. SMITH

Sources Longleat House, Wiltshire, Seymour MSS • Devon RO, Seymour of Berry Pomeroy MS 1392/M/L16 • Wilts. & Swindon RO, Ailesbury papers, WRO 1300 • state papers domestic, Charles I, PRO, SP 16 • committee for compounding MSS, PRO, SP 23 • meditations and prayers of Lord Seymour, BL, Egerton MS 71 • *JHL*, 4–10 (1628–48) • E. S. Cope and W. H. Coates, eds., *Proceedings of the Short Parliament of 1640*, CS, 4th ser., 19 (1977) • *The Short Parliament (1640) diary of Sir Thomas Aston*, ed. J. D. Maltby, CS, 4th ser., 35 (1988) • *The journal of Sir Simonds D'Ewes from the beginning of the Long Parliament to the opening of the trial of the earl of Strafford*, ed. W. Notestein (1923) • GEC, *Peerage*, new edn • R. C. Johnson and others, eds., *Proceedings in parliament, 1628*, 6 vols. (1977–83) • D. L. Smith, *Constitutional royalism and the search for settlement, c. 1640–1649* (1994)

Archives Devon RO, MSS • Longleat House, Wiltshire, MSS • St George's Chapel, Windsor, meditations | Wilts. & Swindon RO, Ailesbury MSS

Likenesses attrib. P. van Somer, portrait, Petworth House, Sussex [*see illus.*]

Seymour, Sir Francis, first baronet (1813–1890), army officer, eldest son of Henry Augustus Seymour (1771–1847) of Lisnabrun, co. Down, and his wife, Margaret (*d.* 31 Aug 1867), daughter of the Revd William Williams of Cromlech, Anglesey, was born at Lisnabrun on 2 August 1813, and was commissioned as ensign in the 19th regiment on 2 May 1834. He became lieutenant on 16 June 1837. In 1839, at the request of the king of the Belgians, he accompanied Prince Albert of Saxe-Coburg and Gotha in Italy. In 1840, after Albert's marriage, he was appointed groom-in-waiting to him, and continued in that office until Albert's death.

Seymour was promoted captain on 4 September 1840, and on 21 January 1842 he exchanged into the Scots Fusilier Guards, and obtained his company on 28 June 1850. He went with the 1st battalion to the Crimea in 1854, and was present at Alma, Balaklava, and Inkerman. At the latter he took command of the battalion, and was wounded. He was later wounded again, by a fragment of a shell which struck the back of his head during the siege of Sevastopol, when he was field officer in command in the trenches of the right attack. He was made brevet colonel on 28 November 1854 and CB on 2 January 1857. He received the Légion d'honneur (fourth class) and Mejidiye (fourth class).

Seymour was promoted major in his regiment on 14 June 1858, and lieutenant-colonel on 13 February 1863; he went on half pay on 10 July 1863, and on 25 November 1864 became major-general. He commanded the troops in Malta from 1 January 1872 to 5 April 1874. He was made lieutenant-general on 23 May 1873, colonel of the 11th (North Devon) regiment on 7 February 1874, KCB on 29 May 1875, general on 1 October 1877, and GCB on 24 May 1881. On 1 July 1881 he was retired.

After Prince Albert's death in December 1861, Seymour was appointed groom-in-waiting to the queen. On 7 October 1869 he was made a baronet, and in February 1876 he became master of ceremonies and an extra groom-in-waiting. He was a knight grand cross of the Saxe-Ernestine order.

Seymour married, on 25 August 1869, Agnes Austin, eldest daughter of the Revd H. D. Wickham, rector of Horsington, Somerset, and they had one son and three daughters. He died at Kensington Palace on 10 July 1890.

E. M. LLOYD, *rev.* JAMES FALKNER

Sources *Army List* • *The Times* (12 July 1890) • A. W. Kinglake, *The invasion of the Crimea*, 8 vols. (1863–87) • *Annual Register* (1890) • F. Maurice, *The history of the Scots guards, from the creation of the regiment to the eve of the Great War*, 2 vols. (1934) • Boase, *Mod. Eng. biog.* • Burke, *Peerage*

Archives BL, Add. MS 41167

Likenesses Ape [C. Pellegrini], chromolithograph caricature, NPG; repro. in *VF* (11 Aug 1877) • wood-engraving (in uniform), NPG; repro. in *ILN* (26 July 1890)

Wealth at death £7977 7*s.* 10*d.*: probate, 11 Sept 1890, *CGPLA Eng. & Wales*

Seymour, Frederick Beauchamp Paget, Baron Alcester (1821–1895), naval officer, was born in London on 12 April 1821. He was the son of Colonel Sir Horace Beauchamp Seymour and his first wife, Elizabeth Malet, *née* Palk (*d.* 1827), daughter of Sir Lawrence Palk, bt; his grandfather was Lord Hugh *Seymour, and his uncle Sir George Francis *Seymour. He received his early education at Eton College, and entered the navy in January 1834. He passed his examination in 1840; served as a mate in the *Britannia*, flagship of Sir John Acworth Ommanney, in the Mediterranean, and was promoted lieutenant on 7 March 1842. He was then appointed to the frigate *Thalia* (Captain George Hope) in the Pacific; and from 1844 to 1847 was flag-lieutenant to his uncle, Sir George Seymour, commander-in-chief in the Pacific. On 5 June 1847 he was promoted commander. In 1852 he served as a volunteer on the staff of General Godwin in Burma, and was four times gazetted for distinguished conduct. In May 1853 he commissioned the *Brisk* for the North America and West Indies station, from where he was recalled early in 1854 and sent to the White Sea in the squadron under Commodore Sir Erasmus Ommanney. In May 1855 he was appointed to the floating battery *Meteor*, which he took out to the Crimea, and brought back to Portsmouth in the early summer of 1856. In July 1857 he commissioned the *Pelorus*, which he commanded for nearly six years on the Australian station. Between January and April 1858 the *Pelorus* provided a naval brigade in Burma, playing a vital role in preventing the spread of the mutiny from India. From 1860 to 1861 he commanded the naval brigade in New Zealand during the war there, for which he was made a CB on 16 July 1861.

From 1868 to 1870 Seymour was private secretary to the first lord of the Admiralty, Hugh Childers, and helped to keep the troubled Admiralty board from complete collapse. On 1 April 1870 he was promoted rear-admiral. From December 1870 to May 1872 he commanded the flying squadron, and from 1872 to 1874 was a lord of the Admiralty. From 1874 to 1877 he commanded the Channel Fleet; he was made a vice-admiral on 31 December 1876 and a KCB on 2 June 1877. In 1876 he agreed to a compact with Geoffrey Phipps Hornby and Astley Cooper Key: all three would refuse to accept the post of senior naval lord without securing certain specific reforms of the Admiralty. In 1879 Key took the post, without securing those reforms.

From 1880 to 1883 Seymour was commander-in-chief in the Mediterranean, and so, in 1880, commanded the European squadron sent to the Albanian coast following Turkish refusal to cede Dulcigno to Montenegro. On the dispersal of the fleet after the Porte had yielded, Seymour received the thanks of the government and was made a GCB, on 24 May 1881. In the following year he commanded at the bombardment of the Alexandria fortifications (11 July), and afterwards in the operations on the coast of Egypt. For this he was made Baron Alcester of Alcester in the county of Warwickshire, and received a parliamentary grant of £25,000, the freedom of the City of London, and a sword of honour. From March 1883 to June 1885 he was again a lord of the Admiralty, and on 12 April 1886 was retired.

During the following years Seymour lived principally in London, where his genial nature made him a favourite in society, while his attention to his dress and appearance gained him the name of the 'Ocean Swell'. Latterly his eyesight failed and his health deteriorated. He died at 3 Hanover Terrace, Regent's Park, London, on 30 March 1895, and was buried at Brookwood cemetery, near Woking on 3 April. He was unmarried, and at his death the title became extinct.

After an early career dominated by operations on shore, Seymour matured into an able and active flag officer, both afloat and at the Admiralty. He commanded, at Alexandria, the only battle fleet action between 1855 and 1914. He accepted his peerage, the first conferred for naval service afloat since 1856, on behalf of the service, rather than as a personal reward, and contributed to the efforts made in several quarters to raise the prestige of the service. He was one of the leading flag officers of his generation.

J. K. Laughton, *rev.* Andrew Lambert

Sources J. F. Beeler, *British naval policy in the Gladstone–Disraeli era, 1866–1880* (1997) · N. A. M. Rodger, 'The dark ages of the admiralty, 1869–1885: business methods, 1869–1874', *Mariner's Mirror*, 61 (1975), 331–4 · N. A. M. Rodger, 'The dark ages of the admiralty, 1869–1885: change and decay, 1874–1880', *Mariner's Mirror*, 62 (1976), 33–46 · N. A. M. Rodger, 'The dark ages of the admiralty, 1869–1885: peace, retrenchment and reform, 1880–1885', *Mariner's Mirror*, 62 (1976), 121–8 · P. H. Colomb, *Memoirs of Admiral the Right Honble. Sir Astley Cooper Key* (1898) · C. S. White, 'The bombardment of Alexandria', *Mariner's Mirror*, 66 (1980), 31–52 · J. H. Briggs, *Naval administrations, 1827 to 1892: the experience of 65 years*, ed. Lady Briggs (1898) · Mrs F. Egerton, *Admiral of the fleet: Sir Geoffrey Phipps Hornby, a biography* (1896) · Burke, *Peerage* (1894) · *CGPLA Eng. & Wales* (1895)

Archives NMM | BL, letters to Sir Austen Layard, Add. MSS 38999–39036 · Sheff. Arch., Montagu-Stuart MSS

Likenesses Barraud, photograph, NPG; repro. in *Men and Women of the Day*, 4 (1891) · line engraving (after photograph by J. Maclardy), NPG · photograph, Hult. Arch.

Wealth at death £92,019 15*s*. 4*d*.: probate, 9 May 1895, *CGPLA Eng. & Wales*

Seymour, Sir George Francis (1787–1870), naval officer, the eldest son of Vice-Admiral Lord Hugh *Seymour (1759–1801) and his wife, Anne Horatia (*d*. 1801), the daughter of James Waldegrave, second Earl Waldegrave, was born on 17 September 1787. He entered the navy in October 1797 on board the yacht *Princess Augusta* with Captain Edward Riou, and from March 1798 to September 1801 was with his father in the *Sanspareil* and the *Prince of Wales* in the channel and the West Indies. In 1802–3 he was in the *Endymion*, mostly on the home station, with Captain John Larmour, and afterwards with the Hon. Charles Paget. Towards the end of 1803 he was sent out to the *Victory*, Nelson's flagship in the Mediterranean, and in February 1804 was transferred to the *Madras* as acting lieutenant. A few weeks later he was moved into the *Donegal* with Sir Richard John Strachan, then from early 1805 with Pulteney Malcolm. On 12 October 1804 Seymour was confirmed lieutenant, and, continuing in the *Donegal*, took part in the chase of the allied fleet to the West Indies and back and in the capture of the Spanish ship *El Rayo* immediately after the battle of Trafalgar.

Early in 1806 Seymour joined the *Northumberland*, the flagship of Sir Alexander Forrester Inglis Cochrane, in the West Indies, and on 6 February took part in the battle of Santo Domingo, where he was severely wounded in the jaw by grapeshot. He had already been promoted commander on 22 January 1806, and on 9 February was appointed to the sloop *Kingfisher*, in which, on 14 May, he was in company with Lord Cochrane in the *Pallas*, and was able to rescue him from a dangerous position in the entrance of the Basque Roads. On 29 July 1806 he was posted to command the *Aurora* in the Mediterranean, from which, in February 1808, he was moved to the *Pallas* on the home station. In April 1809 she was attached to the fleet with Lord Gambier off the Basque Roads, and on the 12th Seymour made a gallant effort to support Cochrane in his attempt to destroy the French ships. Afterwards, at the court martial on Lord Gambier, he supported Cochrane's assertion that the whole might have been destroyed.

In September 1809 Seymour was appointed to the frigate *Manilla* (36 guns), which was lost off the Texel in January 1812 during his temporary absence. In February 1811 he married Georgiana Mary (*d.* 1878), the daughter of Admiral Sir George Cranfield Berkeley; they had four daughters and three sons. In June 1812 he was assigned to the *Fortunée*, and from January 1813 to September 1814 he commanded the *Leonidas* in the West Indies. On 4 June 1815 he was nominated a CB, and on 28 May 1816 was awarded a pension of £250 for his wound received in the battle of Santo Domingo. From 1818 to 1841 he was sergeant-at-arms to the House of Lords. In 1827 he commanded the *Briton* for a few months on particular service. He was naval aide-de-camp to William IV from August to November 1830, and from that time until the king's death was master of the robes. In 1831 he was made a KCH and on 9 December 1834 GCH. He was promoted rear-admiral on 23 November 1841.

From September 1841 to May 1844 Seymour was one of the lords of the Admiralty, where he repeatedly quarrelled with the senior naval lord, Sir George Cockburn, on the direction of policy. As a result he was appointed commander-in-chief in the Pacific, where 'the tact, ability, and decision' he showed during the strained relations with France over the 'Pritchard affair' and the negotiations with the United States about the fisheries, were formally recognized by the government. He arrived home in 1848.

On 27 March 1850 Seymour was made vice-admiral and on 7 April 1852 a KCB. From January 1851 to November 1853 he was commander-in-chief on the North America and West Indies station. In late 1853 he was considered for the command of the Baltic fleet, then being prepared, but arrangements to bring him home foundered on the refusal of his nominated successor to take the post. By the time he reached England, in March 1854, the Baltic fleet had been given to Sir Charles Napier, and Seymour served from January 1856 to March 1859 as commander-in-chief at Portsmouth. On 14 May 1857 he was promoted to the rank of admiral. He was nominated a GCB on 18 May 1860, rear-admiral of the United Kingdom in April 1863, vice-admiral in September 1865, and admiral of the fleet on 30 November 1866. He died of bronchitis at his London residence, 115 Eaton Square, on 20 January 1870. Seymour was an intelligent and resourceful officer, successful in all his commands. Although he was a tory, and a personal favourite of William IV, his marriage brought him into contact with the whig naval aristocracy. He impressed Lord Haddington during his time at the Admiralty by his willingness to stand up to the formidable Cockburn.

His eldest son, Francis George Hugh Seymour (1812–1884), in August 1870 succeeded his second cousin as fifth marquess of Hertford. He was appointed groom of the robes in 1833, was lord chamberlain from 1874 to 1879, and died at Ragley on 25 January 1884 from injuries caused by a fall from his horse.

J. K. Laughton, *rev.* Andrew Lambert

Sources B. M. Gough, *The Royal Navy and the north-west coast of North America, 1810–1914* (1971) • H. A. Kay, ed., *HMS Collingwood, 1844–1848, Pacific station* (1986) • J. H. Briggs, *Naval administrations, 1827 to 1892: the experience of 65 years*, ed. Lady Briggs (1897) • K. Bourne, *Britain and the balance of power in North America, 1815–1908* (1967) • A. D. Lambert, *The Crimean War: British grand strategy, 1853–56* (1990) • Cumbria AS, Carlisle, Graham MSS • Burke, *Peerage* (1959)

Archives Warks. CRO | Cumbria AS, Carlisle, Graham MSS

Likenesses F. Holl, stipple, pubd 1852 (after J. Harrison), BM, NPG • H. N. O'Neil, group portrait, oils, 1864 (*The landing of the HRH the Princess Alexandra at Graveshead, 7th March, 1863*), NPG • J. Lucas, oils, Ragley Hall, Warwickshire

Wealth at death under £80,000: probate, 9 Feb 1870, *CGPLA Eng. & Wales*

Seymour, Sir George Hamilton (1797–1880), diplomatist, eldest son of Lord George Seymour (1763–1848) (seventh son of Francis Seymour *Conway, first marquess of Hertford) and Isabella, daughter of the Hon. and Revd George Hamilton (1718–1787), canon of Windsor and third son of the seventh earl of Abercorn, was born at Harrow on 21 September 1797. He was intended at first for the navy but was then sent to Eton College and, in March 1813, appointed gentleman usher in daily waiting on George III. He became a postmaster (award holder) at Merton College, Oxford, and graduated BA in 1818, proceeding MA in 1823. He had already, in March 1817, been appointed an attaché to the British legation at The Hague. From then on his whole career was spent in diplomacy. In December 1819 he became assistant précis writer to the foreign secretary, Lord Castlereagh, précis writer in January 1821, and Castlereagh's private secretary in January 1822. He was with Castlereagh shortly before the latter's suicide in August 1822. In October 1822 he was attached to the duke of Wellington's special mission to Verona. He became secretary of legation at Frankfurt am Main on 18 August 1823 and was transferred on 6 September 1826 to Stuttgart, on 28 December 1827 to Berlin, and on 30 July 1829 to Constantinople.

On 13 November 1830 Seymour was appointed minister-resident at Florence. In 1831 he was sent on an (unsuccessful) special mission to Rome, where Britain had no regular representation at this time, to try to persuade the pope to take a conciliatory line towards the rebels of 1830–31 and guarantee certain civil rights. On 21 July 1831 he married Gertrude Brand (*d.* 1883), third daughter of the twenty-first Lord Dacre; they had four sons and three daughters. On 27 November 1835 he was appointed envoy-extraordinary and minister-plenipotentiary to the Belgian court, where he took part in the negotiations by which the independence of Belgium was finally secured.

On 10 December 1846 he was moved to Lisbon in the same capacity, and he represented the British government through the greater part of the period of insurrection, when the British power supported the Portuguese crown.

In 1850 Seymour gave evidence to the select committee on official salaries and gained some notoriety when he replied to a question, 'Certainly I consider that giving dinners is an essential part of diplomacy … I have no idea of a man being a good diplomat who does not give good dinners' ('Select committee', 15.426). The same year Palmerston wished to send him to Berlin, but Queen Victoria wanted Berlin for Lord Bloomfield and in April 1851 Seymour went to St Petersburg instead. He is best known for the 'Seymour conversations' with the tsar in January–February 1853. The tsar, encouraged by the formation of the Aberdeen coalition in Britain, reopened the question of contingency planning if the Ottoman empire should collapse, which he had discussed with Lord Aberdeen and the then prime minister, Sir Robert Peel, when he visited London in 1844. The conversations were subsequently leaked in the *St Petersburg Gazette* and *The Times* and contributed to the British belief that the tsar was actively plotting the dissolution of the Ottoman empire. Seymour was recalled in February 1854, just before the outbreak of the Crimean War. He was pensioned in October 1854 but was recalled to go as envoy-extraordinary to Vienna in November 1855 to participate in the international discussions which led eventually to the end of the Crimean War and the peace of Paris of 1856. He finally retired in April 1858.

Seymour was made GCH on 16 March 1836 and GCB on 28 January 1847, and was sworn of the privy council on 21 November 1855. He died on 2 February 1880 at his home, 10 Grosvenor Crescent, London, and was buried at Kensal Green cemetery.

C. A. Harris, *rev.* Muriel E. Chamberlain

Sources *FO List* • *The Times* (4 Feb 1880) • Burke, *Peerage* [Hertford] • 'Select committee on official salaries', *Parl. papers* (1850), vol. 15, no. 611 • R. A. Jones, *The British diplomatic service, 1815–1914* (1983) • M. E. Chamberlain, *Lord Aberdeen: a political biography* (1983) • J. Ridley, *Palmerston* (1970) • *Annual Register* (1880) • GEC, *Peerage* • S. T. Bindoff and others, eds., *British diplomatic representatives, 1789–1852*, CS, 3rd ser., 50 (1934) • *DNB*

Archives BL, journals, Add. MSS 60290–60312, 63078 | Balliol Oxf., Morier MSS • BL, Aberdeen MSS • Hants. RO, Harris MSS • Norfolk RO, Bulwer MSS • Notts. Arch., Savile MSS • PRO, FO MSS • PRO, Granville MSS • PRO, Russell MSS • SUL, Palmerston MSS

Likenesses C. Baugniet, lithograph, 1842, BM • H. Watkins, albumen print, 1856–9, NPG • oils (with Bath and Guelphic order), Merton Oxf.

Wealth at death under £400,000: probate, 19 Feb 1880, *CGPLA Eng. & Wales*

Seymour, Henry (*bap.* **1612**, *d.* **1687**), courtier, was baptized on 13 August 1612, the second of the five sons of Sir Edward Seymour, second baronet (*c.*1580–1659), of Berry Pomeroy, Devon, and his wife, Dorothy (*d.* 1643), daughter of Sir Henry Killigrew of Laroch, Cornwall. He was in his youth page of honour to Queen Henrietta Maria, and became a groom of the bedchamber to Prince Charles in May 1638. On the outbreak of the civil war he joined the royalist forces under his kinsman William Seymour, marquess of Hertford, and in September 1642 was the bearer of the challenge from him to the earl of Bedford. He carried the message from Prince Charles to the earl of Warwick in August 1648 summoning him to surrender the parliament's fleet. On 28 January 1649 he delivered the prince's last letter to his father, and received the king's final message to his son and his letter of farewell to Henrietta Maria. In October 1649, as 'a person unbyassed with any faction, and in whose discretion and integrity the king had great confidence' (Carte, 1.337), he was sent by Charles II from Jersey to the marquess of Ormond in Ireland to assess the military situation there. He accompanied Charles to Scotland in 1650, was voted away from the king's person by the Scottish committee, and left for France after the defeat at Dunbar, and the collapse of a plan for a royalist rising by the marquess of Huntly in October. In December 1650 Charles commissioned him to go in search of his brother James, who was then in Brussels, and endeavour to persuade him to return to Paris and follow his mother's advice. In 1651 Seymour was in Paris, and in the following years he undertook several hazardous missions to and from the king and his supporters in England, collecting and distributing money—including the sum of £215 'for redeeming your majesty's seal' (Macray, 2.361)—and transmitting advice and instructions. In October 1652 he had to defend himself before the council of state against the allegation that he was employed by the king. He went back and forth between Paris and the English royalists in 1653 and 1654, and in June 1654 he was arrested and sent to the Tower in the aftermath of the Gerard plot. He was arrested again, 'on suspicion of plotting to stir up forces against Government' (*CSP dom.*, *1655*, 204, 588), in June 1655. Freed from the Tower on bail in April 1656, he was rearrested in October, and having petitioned for release in February 1657 he finally obtained it 'upon hard terms' (Macray, 3.303) at the end of May.

At the general election of 1660 Seymour was elected an MP for East Looe, in Cornwall, which he represented until 1681. In the Convention he was instrumental in securing the exemption of Colonel Matthew Tomlinson from the list of those who were to be denied the benefit of the Act of Indemnity and Oblivion, testifying that in the course of his last interview with Charles I the king had 'signified to him his pleasure, that the colonel should receive favour on account of his civil carriage to him, during his confinement' (*Memoirs of Edmund Ludlow*, 2.286). In the Cavalier Parliament he was generally reckoned to be a supporter, as he was a dependant, of the court. He was not a conspicuously active member, but he seems to have been a mettlesome one. He was narrowly prevented from fighting a duel with Lord St John in 1665; and in 1669 he fought and wounded Roger Vaughan MP. In addition to his post as groom of the bedchamber, which he retained until Charles II's death, he was comptroller of customs in the port of London (1660–69), and clerk of the hanaper (1661–87). He was also granted a number of leases—to the value, it was, most improbably, alleged, of £40,000 (Cobbett, *Parl. hist.*, 4, appx, xxiv)—in the duchy of Cornwall. In 1666 he took up residence at Langley, in Langley Marish, Buckinghamshire, which estate he bought from the trustees of Sir William Parsons in 1669, and where he lived until his death. He married first, about 1661, Elizabeth (*d.* 1671), daughter of Sir Joseph Killigrew, and widow of William Bassett of Claverton, Somerset; she died in 1671. His second marriage, about 1672, was to Ursula, daughter of Sir Robert Austen, first baronet, of Bexley, Kent, and widow of George Stowell, of Cothelstone, Somerset; they had a daughter and a son, Henry, who was created a baronet at seven years of age (4 July 1681) in consideration of his father's services to his sovereign. Seymour died at Langley on 9 March 1687 and was buried there.

W. A. SHAW, *rev.* RONALD CLAYTON

Sources *Calendar of the Clarendon state papers preserved in the Bodleian Library*, 1: *To Jan 1649*, ed. O. Ogle and W. H. Bliss (1872); 2: *1649–1654*, ed. W. D. Macray (1869); 3: *1655–1657*, ed. W. D. Macray (1876) · D. Underdown, *Royalist conspiracy in England, 1649–1660* (1960); repr. (1971) · *CSP dom.*, *1649–60* · M. W. Helms and J. P. Ferris, 'Seymour, Henry I', HoP, *Commons*, *1660–90* · Clarendon, *Hist. rebellion* · *The Nicholas papers*, ed. G. F. Warner, 4 vols., CS, new ser., 40, 50, 57, 3rd ser., 31 (1886–1920) · J. Burke and J. B. Burke, *A genealogical and heraldic history of the extinct and dormant baronetcies of England, Ireland, and Scotland* (1838) · G. Lipscomb, *The history and antiquities of the county of Buckingham*, 4 vols. (1831–47) · W. A. Shaw, ed., *Calendar of treasury books*, 1, PRO (1904); 3 (1908); 7 (1916); 8 (1923) · *A collection of original letters and papers, concerning the affairs of England from the year 1641 to 1660. Found among the duke of Ormonde's papers*, ed. T. Carte, 2 vols. (1739) · C. V. Wedgwood, *The trial of Charles I* (1964) · *VCH Buckinghamshire*, 3.296–7, 300 · *The memoirs of Edmund Ludlow*, ed. C. H. Firth, 2 vols. (1894) · Cobbett, *Parl. hist.*, 4.appx, xxiv

Wealth at death estates in Buckinghamshire, Wiltshire, and Somerset: will, PRO, PROB 11/387, sig. 68, referred to in *VCH Buckinghamshire*, 3.300

Seymour, Henry (1729–1805), politician, was born in London, the son of Francis Seymour (*bap.* 1697, *d.* 1761), MP for Sherborne, and brother of Edward, the eighth duke of Somerset, and Elizabeth Montagu (*d.* 1761), daughter of Alexander Popham of Littlecote, Wiltshire, and widow of Viscount Hinchinbrook. On 24 July 1753 he married Lady Caroline Cowper (*d.* 1773), only daughter of William, the second Earl Cowper. The marriage produced two daughters: Caroline, who married William Danby, the bibliophile and mineralogist, and Georgina, who married Comte Louis de Durfort. Besides his father's estate at Sherborne, Seymour inherited an uncle's property at Knoyle, and also owned Northbrook Lodge, Devon, and Redland Court, near Bristol. He became a groom of the bedchamber to George III, was elected MP for Totnes at a by-election in 1763, and represented Huntingdon (1768–74) and Evesham (1774–80). He spoke on 29 February 1776 in support of Charles James Fox's motion for an inquiry into the miscarriages of the American War of Independence. A widower in June 1773, he married in 1775 Louise Thérèse (*d.* 1821), widow of Comte Guillaume de Panthou; they had one son, Henry (1776–1849), who in 1835 became high sheriff of Dorset.

In 1778 Seymour settled in Paris, obtained letters of domicile to protect his property from forfeiture, and purchased a country house at Prunay, between Versailles and St Germain. He became the neighbour, and may have already been the lover, of Madame Du Barry (*née* Becu) (1743–1793), whose letters he kept, together with a lock of her hair. The letters, about forty in total, are undated, but were probably written in 1780, shortly before a separation from his wife. Seymour also fathered an illegitimate daughter, Henriette Felicité, who was born in France and became the mother of Sir Roger Tichborne, later impersonated by Arthur Orton in the famous Tichborne claimant case. In 1788 Seymour published an anonymous French translation of William Mason's *English Garden*, with views of Prunay. His papers, apparently left behind him on his hasty departure from France in August 1792, were sold in Paris a century later. His heirs later obtained compensation for his losses out of the fund for indemnifying British subjects. Seymour remained in England until his death in 1805.

J. G. ALGER, *rev.* HEATHER SHORE

Sources E. de Goncourt, *Madame Du Barry* (1914) · C. Vatel, *Histoire de Madame Du Barry, d'après ses papiers personnels et les documents des archives publiques*, 3 vols. (1883) · R. B. Douglas, *The life and times of Madame du Barry* (1896) · J. G. Alger, *Englishmen in the French Revolution* (1889) · Burke, *Peerage* (1970) · J. P. Palewski, *Henry Seymour et Madame du Barry* (1938) · GEC, *Peerage* · HoP, *Commons*

Seymour, Lord Henry (1805–1859), patron of the turf, was officially the younger son of Francis Charles Seymour-*Conway, third marquess of Hertford (1777–1842), and his wife, Maria Emily Seymour-*Conway, *née* Fagnani (1770/71–1856) [*see under* Conway, Francis Ingram-Seymour-, second marquess of Hertford], the French adopted daughter of George Augustus Selwyn (1719–1791). It has been suggested that his true father was Count Casimir de Montrond (1768–1843). Lord Henry was born in Paris on 18 January 1805, after the detention of his father, then styled Lord Yarmouth, on landing in France just after the rupture of the treaty of Amiens. Lord Yarmouth was released in 1806 through Fox's intercession with Talleyrand, but his wife remained in France, where Lord Henry lived for the rest of his life.

Lord Henry was a member of the Paris-based English Jockey Club and Pigeon-Shooting Club, founded in 1825 by Thomas Byron. In 1833 the club formed two new but coterminous bodies, the Jockey Club and a society for the encouragement of horse breeding in France. Lord Henry was the first president of the new organizations. He imported British horses, trainers, and jockeys, and won the *prix du Jockey Club* four times, but he quit the turf suddenly in 1842.

A prominent member of the aristocratic society of Paris, Lord Henry was noted for his eccentricities and crude practical jokes, such as giving his friends exploding cigars and powerful purges. In 1856 he inherited his mother's large fortune. He died in Paris, unmarried, on 16 August 1859, and was buried in his mother's vault at the Père Lachaise cemetery in Paris. He bequeathed money for the support of four favourite horses, which were never again to be saddled, and left the residue of his property, about £36,000 a year, to Paris hospitals.

J. G. ALGER, *rev.* WRAY VAMPLEW

Sources R. Longrigg, *The history of horse racing* (1972) • *The Times* (25 Aug 1859) • *GM*, 3rd ser., 7 (1859), 432 • *Annual Register* (1859) • 'Société d'Encouragement pour l'Amélioration des Races de Chevaux en France', *Moniteur Universel* (29 Jan 1834) • Boase, *Mod. Eng. biog.*
Likenesses portrait, repro. in Longrigg, *History of horse racing*

Seymour [*formerly* Seymour Conway], **Lord Hugh** (**1759–1801**), naval officer, was born on 29 April 1759 in London, fifth son of Francis Seymour *Conway, first marquess of Hertford (1718–1794), and his wife, Lady Isabella, *née* Fitzroy (1726–1782), daughter of the duke of Grafton. He used the surname Seymour Conway until his father's death in 1794. He was educated at Bracken's academy, Greenwich, in the late 1760s and appears to have entered the navy as captain's servant in the yacht *William and Mary* on 1 April 1770. He was discharged from her on 31 March 1771, and from 21 April he served for over two years as midshipman in the *Pearl*, commanded by a relation, Captain John Leveson Gower. After spending time on various other ships he joined the *Alarm* on 18 March 1774, and apart from a short spell in the *Trident* served in her until he passed for lieutenant on 11 July 1776; thereupon he was made lieutenant in the same ship, a position he held until 18 June 1778 when he was appointed commander to the xebec *Minorca* in the Mediterranean. He was promoted captain on 8 February 1779 to the *Porcupine*, and then successively to the *Diana*, *Ambuscade*, and *Latona*, mostly in the channel, though the *Latona* was with Richard Howe's fleet at the relief of Gibraltar.

After the peace Seymour Conway with his younger brother George and John Willett Payne took a house in Conduit Street, London where, leading an irregular and convivial life, he became intimate with the prince of Wales. From this fate he was in great measure rescued by his marriage on 3 April 1785 to Lady Anne Horatia Waldegrave (*d.* 1801), daughter of the duchess of Gloucester by her first marriage, to James Waldegrave, second Earl Waldegrave, though he remained on friendly terms with the prince. During the Spanish armament of 1790 he commanded the *Canada*, and while in her received an accidental blow on the head from the lead, as soundings were being taken, so for a time had to live quietly in the country. By February 1793 he was able to resume active service, and was appointed to the *Leviathan*, in which he accompanied Lord Hood to the Mediterranean. After the occupation of Toulon he was sent home with dispatches, but he returned at once and resumed command of the *Leviathan*, which was shortly afterwards sent home to join the fleet under Lord Howe. He had thus a distinguished part in the actions of 28 and 29 May and 1 June 1794.

Early in 1795 Seymour was moved into the *Sanspareil*, and on his promotion to flag rank (1 June 1795) he hoisted his flag on the same ship, in which he took part in the battle off Lorient on 23 June. On 7 March 1795 he was appointed a lord of the Admiralty, and he remained so until 10 September 1798. Although at sea much of the time, there is evidence that he did take some share in the board's work, particularly during the winter. On 14 February 1799 he became a vice-admiral, and he commanded a detached squadron off Brest that summer. He was appointed commander-in-chief at Jamaica on 9 May 1800 and arrived there in August. His command was uneventful, but he was attacked by yellow fever; he went to sea for his health in the *Tisiphone*, but worsened and died at sea off Jamaica on 11 September 1801. His body was sent home in the schooner *Sting*, his wife having died at Clifton, Bristol, shortly before. His loss was much regretted, and he was described even by Lord St Vincent as 'an excellent officer' (*Later Correspondence of George III*, 2453). It is clear that Seymour went to sea from choice and he is said to have been responsible for an improved method of fitting topmasts and for the addition of epaulettes to officers' uniforms (Dillon). He was among the most handsome men of his day, standing over 6 feet tall, had great presence, and was courteous to all. In his will he left most of his money to his wife and then to his children, of whom there were seven: four daughters and three sons; the eldest son, Sir George *Seymour, followed him into the navy. He owned a farm at Hambledon, Hampshire, and an estate at Whittlesey, Cambridgeshire, and his father left him an estate on the island of St John.

A. W. H. Pearsall

Sources W. James, *The naval history of Great Britain, from the declaration of war by France, in February 1793, to the accession of George IV in January 1820*, 5 vols. (1822–4) • *Recollections of James Anthony Gardner*, ed. R. V. Hamilton and J. K. Laughton, Navy RS, 31 (1906) • W. H. Dillon, *A narrative of my professional adventures (1790–1839)*, ed. M. A. Lewis, 2 vols., Navy RS, 93, 97 (1953–6) • *Private papers of George, second Earl Spencer*, ed. J. S. Corbett and H. W. Richmond, 4 vols., Navy RS, 46, 48, 58–9 (1913–24) • *The later correspondence of George III*, ed. A. Aspinall, 5 vols. (1962–70) • *GM*, 1st ser., 71 (1801), 678, 1058 • *Naval Chronicle*, 2 (1799), 357 • *Naval Chronicle*, 6 (1801), 435 • muster books, PRO, ADM 36/7460; 7694; 7751; 7752; 8422 • passing certificate, PRO, ADM 6/87
Archives Warks. CRO, corresp., logs and papers | BL, letters to Lord Bridport, Add. MSS 35195–35201
Likenesses J. Downman, watercolour drawing, 1785, Ragley Hall, Warwickshire • J. Hoppner, oils, 1799, NMM; versions, Althorp, Northamptonshire; Ragley Hall, Warwickshire • J. Hoppner, oils, 1800–25 (after engraving by S. M. Reynolds), Walmer Castle, Kent • Bartolozzi, Landseer, Ryder and Stow, group portrait, line engraving, pubd 1803 (*Commemoration of the victory of June 1st 1794*; after *Naval Victories* by R. Smirke), BM • J. Hoppner, oils, Weston Park, Shropshire

Seymour, James [Jimmy] (**1702?–1752**), painter and draughtsman, was born probably in London, the only son of James Seymour (1658?–1739). The elder Seymour (often styled Colonel, perhaps a militia rank) was described in his obituary in the *Universal Spectator* (27 January 1739) as 'formerly an eminent Banker in Fleet Street, and reckon'd to have understood Diamonds as well as most Men in England'; but the only known evidence of his commercial activities is that he supplied plate for racing trophies, and was involved in organizing race meetings at Guildford. Of greater importance for his son's career was that the elder Seymour was (in the same obituarist's words), 'a compleat Master of the Pen and Pencil' (some heads by him are in the collection of the British Museum and the Huntington Art Gallery, San Marino, California). He collected pictures and 'curiosities', and knew many artists and connoisseurs; he was steward of the Virtuosi of St Luke in 1702, and a subscriber to Kneller's academy in Great Queen Street in 1711.

The younger James Seymour chiefly drew and painted horses, at race meetings and hunts, in stables and riding schools. Few details of his life are recorded, apart from the fact that he attended the academy in St Martin's Lane when it opened in 1720 under the directorship of Louis Chéron and John Vanderbank, paying an extra subscription of 10 guineas in October 1720. His character and career were described by the prudish George Vertue:

> Jimmy Seymor … from his infancy had a genius to drawing of Horses—this he pursued with great Spirit, set out with all sorts & of modish extravagances. the darling of his Father run thro some thousands—livd gay high and loosely—horse raceing gameing women &c. country houses never studied enough to colour or paint well, but his necessityes—obliged him. to work or starve … (Vertue, *Note books*, 3.86)

Vertue's account of Seymour's prodigal career is difficult to reconcile with his prolific output. A large number of finished oils and numerous lively and spontaneous sketches in pen and ink and pencil are known (the latter well represented in the collections of the British Museum, London, and the Yale Center for British Art, New Haven, Connecticut). Seymour's paintings of horses lack that anatomical knowledge which Stubbs was to bring to the art. His originality lay rather in his ability to enliven the conventional horse portrait by conveying, sometimes humorously, some sense of the personality of a horse, and of its accompanying groom or dog. In his most ambitious work, *A Kill at Ashdown Park* (1743; Tate collection), this liveliness animates a scene in which some weaknesses of perspective and composition are obvious. One of Seymour's finest paintings, *Peter Delmé's Hounds on the Hampshire Downs* (1738; Paul Mellon Gift, Virginia Museum of Fine Arts), commissioned by the banker Peter Delmé, gains from greater simplicity, as a small group of riders and hounds set off across the Hampshire downs in a palpably early morning atmosphere. Some of Seymour's finest works were painted for John Jolliffe MP, of Petersfield, Hampshire (priv. coll.).

Seymour's best-known painting, endlessly copied, was *The Chaise Match Run on Newmarket Heath on Wednesday 29th of August 1750*. The event was an improbable wager (the original painting is probably the picture in the Yale Center for British Art, New Haven, Paul Mellon Gift). Seymour's painting was engraved by Charles Grignion, published soon after the event, and often pirated. Numerous engravings after Seymour helped to popularize sporting art; these include Seymour's *Twelve Prints of Hunters and Running Horses, Taken in Various Actions*, mezzotint (*c*.1750), a series of thirty-four racehorse portraits, engraved in mezzotint with rococo borders, published 1741–54, and *Twelve prints, representing managing and training horses, with coursing, shooting, setting, etc.* (n.d.).

Seymour appears to have been a friend and/or associate of John Vanderbank, whose profligacy Vertue similarly deplored; some of their drawings of *haute école* exercises in riding schools may well have been made sitting side by side. Vertue stated that Seymour's extravagances caused his father's bankruptcy, and that the latter part of the artist's life 'was spent in the lowest circumstances & in debt' (Vertue, *Note books*, 3.86). Seymour died, unmarried, on 30 June 1752 at lodgings in Blackman Street, Southwark.

JUDY EGERTON

Sources Vertue, *Note books*, 3.86 • J. Egerton, *The ingenious Mr Seymour* (1978) [exhibition catalogue, William Drummond Gallery, London] • J. Egerton, ed., *British sporting and animal paintings, 1655–1867* (1978), 40–49 • T. Clayton, *The English print, 1688–1802* (1997), 141, 143–4 • E. Waterhouse, *Painting in Britain, 1530–1790* (1953), 206 • I. Bignamini, 'George Vertue, art historian, and art institutions in London, 1689–1768', *Walpole Society*, 54 (1988), 1–148, 92, 94n.27 [Leeds 1991]

Likenesses J. Seymour, pen-and-ink drawing, Yale U. CBA

Seymour, Jane. *See* Jane (1508/9–1537).

Seymour, Lady Jane (1541–1561), writer, was the daughter of Edward *Seymour, duke of Somerset (*c*.1500–1552), lord protector of England in the minority of Edward VI, and thus the niece of Queen Jane Seymour. She was one of the ten children (six daughters, four sons) whom Seymour had with his fiercely protestant second wife, Anne *Seymour (*c*.1510–1587), herself a granddaughter of Thomas of Woodstock, youngest son of Edward III. Together with two of her sisters, **Lady Margaret Seymour** (*b*. 1540) and Anne Seymour [**Anne Dudley**, countess of Warwick (1538–1587)], she received a full humanist education, as did their brother Edward. The education of Jane, Anne, and Margaret seems to be directly connected with their father's political life. He was accused of plotting to marry Jane to her first cousin Edward VI, to which her princess-like education gives some credibility. The sisters were tutored by one John Crane, and then by a French humanist and Pléiade poet in French and Latin, Nicholas Denisot. Their literary ambitions were known outside the family from an early age: Margaret and Jane wrote an undated letter (1548?) to Edward VI, thanking the young king for his 'literary gift', while a letter from Jane to Bucer and Fagius, in Latin, dated 12 June 1549 (when she was eight), thanks them for sending her and her sister books.

The three Seymour sisters seem to have resembled their near-contemporaries, the four daughters of Anthony Cooke, in being conscious of themselves as a group. Their claim to fame is that they collectively composed a collection of 103 Latin distichs for the tomb of Marguerite de Valois, author and queen of Navarre, edited by Denisot and published in Paris in 1550. Margaret, in the judgement of the French humanists, was the most talented. Their work was most respectfully received: the sisters were hailed with a long ode from Ronsard, while a distinguished list of French humanists contributed congratulatory poems to the volume itself. This reception of the sisters' little book is probably to be connected with the high visibility of their father: Ronsard, in another of his odes, celebrates Somerset as the architect of an Anglo-French peace treaty concluded on 24 March 1550, which left the French in possession of Boulogne. The *Hecatodistichon* ran to a second edition, produced in 1551, which shows some interesting differences. Each distich is followed by translations into Greek, Italian, and French, which has the effect of shifting the interest of the collection from the distichs themselves to the translation exercise which they have come to represent. However, the fact that this second edition includes French translations may indicate that the work was attracting genuine interest.

While the sisters were at work on the poem, their father was deposed from the office of lord protector on 14 January 1550. His formal rehabilitation on 10 April of that year was marked by a swiftly arranged marriage between his daughter Anne and John, Lord Lisle, son and heir of his principal enemy, John Dudley, earl of Warwick and duke of Northumberland, on 3 June. The marriage was nearly as brief as the alliance which created it: Lord Lisle was condemned with his father after the fall of Lady Jane Grey, and although Mary spared his life, he died a few days after his release from the Tower in 1554. Meanwhile, Somerset himself had been executed in January 1552. Nothing more is heard of Margaret (who had perhaps died), but Jane became a maid of honour at Mary's court, then at Elizabeth's, and was the prime mover in the disastrous marriage between her brother, Edward Seymour, and Lady Katherine Grey, though she died just before the scandal broke. Jane, in fact, was so entirely responsible for stage-managing the occasion that after her death no single witness to the wedding could be found, and no one knew where to locate the officiating clergyman. This marriage was perceived by Elizabeth as a bid for the succession; it probably was, since the Seymours had Plantagenet blood through their mother, while Lady Katherine was a granddaughter of Mary Tudor, queen of France, and the deeply protestant principles entertained by both sides suggest that the couple had a common interest in reviving the Edwardian religious settlement. Jane died in 1561 and was buried in Westminster Abbey, where a monument was erected to her.

Anne, on the other hand, after only a year of widowhood, married a Berkshire gentleman, Sir Edward Unton, in 1555, rusticated at Faringdon, had seven children in ten years, and in 1566 'fell into lunacy', though according to her son's later testimony, 'she enjoyed lucid intervals'. She seems to have kept the title of countess of Warwick from her brief first marriage, since it is the name used in Chamberlaine's funeral sermon for her. She died in 1587, and was buried at Faringdon. No portrait from life is known, but her second son, Sir Henry *Unton, is remembered by art historians for his memorial portrait (*c*.1596, National Portrait Gallery): a representation of his mother nursing him in infancy is shown on the bottom right.

JANE STEVENSON

Sources B. M. Hosington, 'England's first female-authored encomium: the Seymour sisters' *Hecatodistichon* (1550)', *Studies in Philology*, 93 (1996), 117–63 • C. Jugé, *Nicolas Denisot du Mans (1515–1559): essai sur sa vie et ses œuvres* (Paris, 1907) • B. Chamberlaine, *A sermon preached at Farington in Berkeshire … at the buriall of the … Ladie Anne, countess of Warwick* (1591) • E. Seymour, 'In obitum Dominae Janae Somersetensis', in [W. Camden], *Reges, reginae, nobiles* (1603) • *DNB* • monument, Westminster Abbey

Likenesses portrait, 1596 (Anne Dudley; memorial portrait of Sir Henry Unton), NPG

Seymour [*née* Grey], **Katherine, countess of Hertford** (1540?–1568), noblewoman and royal kinswoman, was the second of three daughters of Henry *Grey, duke of Suffolk (1517–1554), and Frances Brandon (1517–1559). Frances was the second child and elder daughter of Henry VIII's sister *Mary Tudor and Charles *Brandon, duke of Suffolk, and the granddaughter of Henry VII. Katherine's parents inherited the Suffolk title in October 1551. During childhood Lady Katherine lived mainly at Bradgate Hall in Leicestershire, where she was educated by Thomas Aylmer. Unlike Jane Dudley (*née* *Grey), Katherine did not make any impression on Roger Ascham when he visited Bradgate in the summer of 1550, and it is usually assumed from this that she was a far less serious scholar than her elder sister.

The Suffolk family moved to Southwark in late 1550 or 1551. On 21 May 1553, as part of Suffolk's plan to put Lady Jane on the throne, Katherine was either married, or betrothed, to Henry *Herbert (*d.* 1601), the eldest son of William *Herbert, first earl of Pembroke, an ally of the duke of Northumberland. The ceremony took place at the duke's palace, Durham Place, on the same day that Jane married his son. Apparently the marriage was not consummated and Pembroke had it dissolved after Mary I's accession. In 1554, after her father's execution and mother's remarriage, Katherine was placed in the care of Anne, the dowager duchess of Somerset. Despite her father's and sister's treason, Katherine spent time at Mary's court and was treated as a princess of the blood. Although protestant, she outwardly conformed.

Soon after Elizabeth's accession Katherine was appointed maid of honour. On her mother's death in November 1559 she and her younger sister Lady Mary *Keys (1545?–1578) inherited land in Lincolnshire and Warwickshire, but her stepfather, Adrian Stokes, was to enjoy the income from them during his lifetime. She also became heir presumptive according to Henry VIII's will, and consequently attracted the attention of foreign princes and ambitious Englishmen. In August 1559 and March 1560 rumours reached the government that Philip II was planning to persuade her to slip abroad and marry his son. In September 1560 the Scottish council was considering seeking her hand for the earl of Arran. Pembroke, meanwhile, wanted to re-establish her marriage with his son.

Katherine, however, wanted to marry Edward *Seymour, earl of Hertford (1539?–1621), the eldest son of Protector Somerset and his wife, Anne. Katherine's mother had agreed to the match in March 1559 and promised to use her influence with the queen and privy council to obtain their consent. This was crucial because an act of 1536 had made it treason for a person of royal blood to marry without the monarch's approval. Frances, however, died before interceding on the young couple's behalf. Fearful that the queen's permission would not be forthcoming, Katherine and Hertford, abetted by his sister Jane Seymour, decided to risk a clandestine marriage. In November or December 1560 the couple were secretly married at Hertford's house, with only Jane and an unidentified clergyman as witnesses. The marriage was

Katherine Seymour [Grey], **countess of Hertford (1540?–1568),** attrib. Hans Eworth [with her son Edward Seymour, Lord Beauchamp]

immediately consummated in Hertford's bedchamber. In May 1561 Hertford was sent to France to further his education, but by then Katherine was pregnant. Alone and desperate, she confessed her plight in August to Lord Robert Dudley and Elizabeth St Loe, then a gentlewoman of the privy chamber. Dudley immediately informed the queen. Scenting a plot, Elizabeth ordered Katherine to the Tower and summoned Hertford back from Paris. Both were interrogated closely and separately. Although they differed on points of detail, they agreed on the essentials, but the minister could not be found, while Jane Seymour had died the previous March. In the third week of September 1561 Katherine gave birth to a son, Edward *Seymour, Viscount Beauchamp [*see under* Seymour, Edward (1539?–1621)], who was baptized within the Tower. On 31 January 1562 an ecclesiastical high commission headed by Archbishop Parker was appointed to judge the legitimacy of the marriage. With no witnesses or documentary evidence to support its validity, and probably under pressure from the queen, the commission declared on 12 May 1562 that there had been no marriage and that Edward was consequently illegitimate. Meanwhile, Katherine and Hertford were left in the Tower. The lieutenant, Sir Edward Warner, feeling sorry for the couple, disobeyed orders and allowed them secret conjugal visits. As a result, Katherine conceived again and gave birth to a second son, Thomas, in February 1563. For this affront, Hertford was fined £15,000.

For the rest of her life Katherine remained in custody, never to see Hertford again; they could only exchange letters and books. Because of plague in London, she was removed in August 1563 to the house of her uncle, Lord John Grey, at Pyrgo in Essex, where she was kept under strict house arrest. During this time, she and Grey frequently petitioned Dudley and William Cecil to secure her pardon from the queen. Grey described Katherine as 'penitent and soroful', anorexic, and a suicide risk. On his death in November 1564 she was transferred to the custody of Sir William Petre of Ingatestone, Essex. In May 1566 Sir John Wentworth of Horkesley and Gosfield took over her charge until his death. From October 1567 she remained in the custody of Owen Hopton of Cockfield Hall, Yoxford, in Suffolk, who in 1570 became lieutenant of the Tower. Hertford paid for her expenses (66*s*. 8*d*. per week for her diet, 26*s*. 8*d*. for his sons, and 6*s*. 8*d*. for each of her seventeen attendants). Elizabeth assigned to her the rents of the college of Astley in Warwickshire in 1567 to supplement her meagre income.

Katherine was kept in close custody for so long because of the debates on the succession. In early 1563 the MP John Hales wrote a manuscript tract defending her claim to the succession, and also sent Robert Beale abroad to obtain foreign legal opinion that the Hertford marriage was legal. Hales's tract was widely circulated, and news of his activities reached the queen in April 1564. She was incensed, and Hales was sent first to the Fleet and then the Tower. Others came under suspicion, including Lord John Grey, Lord Keeper Bacon, and Hertford's stepfather. Hales's intervention provoked a pamphlet war over the succession issue, which came to a head in the 1566 parliament, where Elizabeth was petitioned unsuccessfully to name her successor. The same year the play *Gorboduc*, written by Thomas Norton and Thomas Sackville, which had originally been performed before the queen on 18 January 1562, was reissued. Some historians believe that it was calling for the parliamentary settlement of the succession on the Suffolk line. Elizabeth, however, was unsympathetic to the claim of Katherine, preferring that of Mary Stewart.

Katherine died on 27 January 1568, perhaps of anorexia, and was buried at Yoxford on 21 February. Her grandson reinterred her remains in the Seymour family tomb at Salisbury Cathedral (the date of death on the monument is incorrect). Her death scene was idealized in a manuscript entitled 'A breefe discowrse of the manner and order of [her] departinge'. In 1572 Thomas Churchyarde wrote a narrative poem based on the discourse, and John Philip also composed a panegyric in verse of her marriage life and death. For years afterwards many argued that her marriage was legal and her sons were consequently heirs to the throne. The union was finally declared legitimate in 1606. SUSAN DORAN

Sources BL, Harleian MS 6286 • BL, Harleian MS 39, art. 45 • proceedings in high commission, 1561, Bodl. Oxf., MS Tanner 84, fols. 105–97 • letters, 1561, Bodl. Oxf., MS Tanner 193, fols. 224–9 • H. Ellis, ed., *Original letters illustrative of English history*, 2nd ser., 2 (1827) • *A collection of state papers … left by William Cecill, Lord Burghley*, ed. S. Haynes, 1 (1740) [material particularly relating to John Hales] • inquisition post mortem, 7 May 1560, on death of Frances, countess of Suffolk, PRO, SP 15/34, fols. 56–57b, 58, 61–4 • livery of Lady Katherine and Lady Mary Grey, 1554, PRO, SP 11/4, fols. 95–6 • miscellaneous letters referring to the marriage and custody of Katherine Grey, PRO, state papers, SP 12, vols. 19, 21, 29, 33, 34, 39, 46 • M. Levine, *The early Elizabethan succession question, 1558–1568* (1966) • R. Davey, *The sisters of Lady Jane Grey and their wicked grandfather* (New York, 1912) • *Calendar of the manuscripts of the most hon. the* *marquis of Salisbury*, 1, HMC, 9 (1883); 13 (1915) • *CSP Spain, 1558–67* • *CSP Venice, 1534–54* • *Calendar of the manuscripts of the marquis of Bath preserved at Longleat, Wiltshire*, 5 vols., HMC, 58 (1904–80) • *The diary of Henry Machyn, citizen and merchant-taylor of London, from AD 1550 to AD 1563*, ed. J. G. Nichols, CS, 42 (1848) • J. A. Giles, *The whole works of Roger Ascham* (1864–5), vol. 1 • *Report on the manuscripts of Lord Middleton*, HMC, 69 (1911) • *CSP for., 1558–62* • J. Phillip, 'The honour of fidelitie', BL, Add. MS 48023, fol. 357 • H. W. Chapman, *Two Tudor portraits: Henry Howard, earl of Surrey and Lady Katherine Grey* (1960) • N. Jones, *The birth of the Elizabethan age: England in the 1560s* (1993) • C. Merton, 'The women who served Queen Mary and Queen Elizabeth: ladies, gentlewomen and maids of the privy chamber, 1553–1603', PhD diss., U. Cam., 1992 • W. M. Schutte, 'Thomas Churchyard's "Doleful discourse" and the death of Lady Katherine Grey', *Sixteenth Century Journal*, 15 (1984), 471–87 • *DNB* • various papers on the marriage, BL, Cotton Vitellius C xvi, art. 22 • tract on the cause of Katherine Grey and Hertford, BL, Cotton Faustus A xi • proceedings of royal commission (eighteenth-century copy), BL, Add. MS 33749 • letters and papers relating to the disputed marriage, BL, Add. MS 63543, fols. 27–82 • opinions from foreign divines about the marriage, CUL, Cambridge MS Ii v 3, fols. 1–96 • *Correspondence of Matthew Parker*, ed. J. Bruce and T. T. Perowne, Parker Society, 42 (1853) • J. E. Jackson, 'Wulfhall and the Seymours', *Wiltshire Archaeological and Natural History Magazine*, 15 (1875), 140–207 • W. L. Rutton, 'Lady Katherine Grey', *N&Q*, 8th ser., 7 (1895), 121–2 • P. Yorke [earl of Hardwicke], ed., *Miscellaneous state papers, 1501–1726*, 2 vols. (1778)

Likenesses attrib. H. Eworth, double portrait, oils (with her son Lord Beauchamp), Petworth House, Sussex [*see illus.*] • H. Holbein, group portrait (with her family) • Hertford monument tomb effigy, Salisbury Cathedral • portrait, priv. coll.; repro. in Chapman, *Two Tudor portraits*

Wealth at death some manors in Warwickshire, Lincolnshire, and Nottinghamshire held jointly with her sister

Seymour, Lady Margaret (*b.* **1540**). *See under* Seymour, Lady Jane (1541–1561).

Seymour, Sir Michael, first baronet (1768–1834), naval officer, second son of the Revd John Seymour (*d.* 1795), one of a younger branch of the family of the dukes of Somerset which settled in Ireland in the time of Elizabeth I, was born at Glebe House, Pallas, co. Limerick, on 8 November 1768. His mother, Griselda, daughter and coheir of William Hobart of High Mount, co. Cork, was related to the family of the earls of Buckinghamshire. Seymour entered the navy in November 1780 on the sloop *Merlin* with Captain James Luttrell, whom he followed in March 1781 to the *Portland*, in April 1782 to the *Mediator*, and in April 1783 to the *Ganges*. When Luttrell retired in September 1783, Seymour was moved into the *Europa*, going to Jamaica with the flag of Vice-Admiral James Gambier. He was transferred to the *Antelope*, and afterwards to the *Janus* (Captain John Pakenham), and in September 1785 he returned to England in the *Ariel*, in bad health. In June 1786 he joined the *Pégase*, guardship at Portsmouth; and in June 1787 the *Magnificent*, with Captain George Cranfield Berkeley, an intimate friend of Luttrell. On Luttrell's death in December 1788, Berkeley brought Seymour's name before the duchess of Gloucester, but it was not until 28 October 1790 that Seymour was promoted lieutenant of the *Magnificent*. In October 1791 the *Magnificent* was paid off, and he spent the next eighteen months with his family in Ireland. In March 1793 he was appointed to the *Marlborough*, then commissioned by Berkeley, and was in her at the battle of 1 June 1794, when he was severely wounded. One of his arms had to be amputated above the elbow, and he was obliged to go on shore to recover. In February 1795 he joined Berkeley in the *Formidable*, moving in June to the *Commerce de Marseilles*, and in August to the *Prince*. On 20 August he was promoted commander. In June 1796 he was appointed to the *Fly*, from which in August he was moved to the sloop *Spitfire*, employed for the next four years in the channel and on the north coast of France. He took many prizes—privateers and armed vessels, as well as small vessels trying to carry on the coasting trade. On 20 January 1789 he married Jane Hawker (*d.* 12 March 1852), daughter of Captain James Hawker; they had a large family, which included Michael *Seymour (1802–1887).

On 11 August 1800 Seymour was promoted captain. During the following years he was appointed to the temporary command of many different ships without being able to get a ship of his own. It was not until June 1806 that he was appointed to the frigate *Amethyst* (36 guns), attached to the Channel Fleet but principally cruising independently off the coast of France, with which, during his long service in the *Spitfire*, he had become well acquainted. On the evening of 10 November 1808, off the Île de Groix, he fell in with the French frigate *Thétis* which had sailed that afternoon from Lorient with a detachment of troops on board for Martinique. Shortly after 9 p.m. he brought her to action, and for three hours there occurred one of the most stubborn and well-contested fights of the war. A few minutes after midnight, being reduced to a wreck and having 236 killed or wounded out of 436 on board, the *Thétis* surrendered. The *Amethyst* lost 70 killed or wounded out of 261; her rigging was cut to pieces, her mizzen-mast fallen, and her mainmast and foremasts were badly damaged. As soon as the two ships were made safe, the *Amethyst* returned to Plymouth, accompanied by her prize in tow of the *Shannon*. Seymour was presented with the gold medal; by the Patriotic Fund with £100 for a sword or a piece of plate; and by the corporations of Limerick and Cork with the freedom of the cities. The first lieutenant of the *Amethyst* and one of the midshipmen nominated by Seymour were promoted, and other officers were appointed to higher rates.

On 8 February 1809 Seymour, still in the *Amethyst*, sailed again, and early on 6 April, off the Île d'Ouessant, fell in with, engaged, and captured the French frigate *Niémen*, which lost 120 men killed and wounded. On his return to England, Seymour was created a baronet on 31 May 1809. During the summer the *Amethyst* was attached to the fleet on the coast of the Netherlands, part of the time with the flag of Sir Richard John Strachan on board; and in October Seymour was appointed to the *Niémen*, the officers and crew of the *Amethyst* being at the same time turned over to her. In her he continued on similar service until May 1812, when he was appointed to the *Hannibal* (74 guns); he commanded her in the channel for the next two years, capturing the French frigate *Sultane* on 26 March 1814.

In September the *Hannibal* was paid off, and Seymour settled down for the next few years near Kingsbridge in Devon. On 3 January 1815 he was nominated a KCB, and in

December of that year the pension for the loss of his arm was increased to £300 a year. In September 1818 he was appointed to the *Northumberland*, guardship at Sheerness; and in August 1819 to the *Prince Regent*, one of the royal yachts, from which, in 1825, he was moved to the *Royal George*, the king's own yacht. During this time he lived principally on shore at Blendworth House, which he had bought, close to Portsmouth. While there he read a great deal and gardened.

In January 1829 Seymour accepted the appointment of commissioner at Portsmouth, a form of semi-active retirement for noted but poor flag officers, which was by custom tenable for life. In 1832 the Admiralty abolished the Navy Board and, with it, the commissionerships at the dockyards. Seymour was offered the choice of holding his office for two more years and then retiring, or of returning to the active list, taking his flag, and going out to South America as commander-in-chief. He chose the latter, his commission as rear-admiral being dated 27 June 1832. With his flag in the *Spartiate* he sailed in February 1833 for Rio de Janiero, where the duties of the station compelled him to remain. In April 1834 he had a severe attack of 'low fever', and on his partial recovery he was landed. On shore, however, he made no satisfactory progress, and he died on 9 July 1834. He was buried in the English cemetery at Rio de Janiero, and a monument to his memory was erected there.

Seymour was a brave and active captain. Although he was not particularly well-connected, especially within the navy, his career brought him to the attention of the prince regent, who supported him after 1815. His relatively slow promotion and inability to find a ship as a captain between 1800 and 1806 were especially revealing. His final command was almost certainly taken to further the career of his son Michael.

J. K. Laughton, *rev.* Andrew Lambert

Sources R. Seymour, *A memoir of Sir M. Seymour* (privately printed, 1878) • *The letters of King George IV, 1812–1830*, ed. A. Aspinall, 3 vols. (1938) • *Letters of … the earl of St Vincent, whilst the first lord of the admiralty, 1801–1804*, ed. D. B. Smith, 2, Navy RS, 61 (1927) • Burke, *Peerage* (1959)

Likenesses H. R. Cook, stipple, pubd 1809 (after J. Northcote), NPG • J. Northcote, portrait; possession of his grandson in 1897 • oils, Rockingham Castle, Northamptonshire

Seymour, Sir Michael (1802–1887), naval officer, third son of Rear-Admiral Sir Michael *Seymour, first baronet (1768–1834), and his wife, Jane Hawker (*d.* 1852), was born on 3 December 1802. He entered the navy in December 1813 on board the *Hannibal*, with his father, but when she was paid off he was sent back to school, and in March 1816 was entered at the Royal Naval College at Portsmouth. On passing out from the college he was appointed in October 1818 to the *Rochefort*, which was going out to the Mediterranean with the flag of Sir Thomas Francis Fremantle. In her, and afterwards in the *Ganymede*, with Captain Robert Cavendish Spencer, he continued until he was promoted lieutenant on 12 September 1822. In July 1823 he joined the *Sybille* (Captain Samuel John Brooke Pechell), and was present at the demonstration against Algiers in 1824. On 6 December 1824 he was promoted commander, and in August 1825 was appointed to the brig *Chameleon* in the channel, and was made captain on 5 August 1826. In January 1827 he was appointed to the *Menai* for the South American station, which then included both the east and west coasts of South America and all the eastern Pacific. In September 1827 he was moved into the *Volage*, in which he returned to England in the spring of 1829. On 22 June 1829 he married his first cousin Dora (or Dorothea; 1807–1875), daughter of Sir William *Knighton. They had a son, Michael Francis Knighton (1841–1909), and three daughters.

In 1832 Seymour's father, who had been appointed to command the South American station, wished to have him as his flag captain. This the Admiralty refused, but in June 1833 he was appointed to the *Challenger*, in which he joined his father at Rio. He was afterwards sent round to the Peruvian coast, but returned to Rio on the news of his father's death. Later, on his way back to the Pacific, the *Challenger*, by an abnormal and previously unknown reversal of the current, was wrecked at Mocquilla Point, near Leubu, on the coast of Chile, on 19 May 1835. The men landed and were rescued after spending seven weeks shipwrecked. Seymour was court-martialled but acquitted of all blame and highly commended for his conduct following the wreck. In 1841 he commanded the *Britannia* as flag captain to Sir John Acworth Ommanney, and then the *Powerful*, which he paid off early in 1842.

From 1845 to 1848 Seymour commanded the *Vindictive* as flag captain to Sir Francis William Austen on the North America and West Indies station. In 1849 he made a prolonged tour in France, visiting the dockyards, arsenals, and engineering works, on which he reported to the Admiralty. In December 1850 he was appointed superintendent of Sheerness Dockyard, from which, in September 1851, he was transferred to Devonport, with the rank of commodore of the first class. In 1854, when war with Russia was imminent, he was appointed captain of the fleet ordered to the Baltic under the command of Sir Charles Napier. In this capacity Seymour had the unenviable responsibility of preparing the equipment and training the ships of the hastily assembled fleet. His reluctance to take the post reflected the obvious difficulties of the task. In addition, Seymour was expected to smooth relations between the irascible Napier, his subordinates, and later his French allies. At the same time he was requested to keep up a correspondence with the first lord, Sir James Graham, and Admiral Sir Maurice Berkeley, the senior naval lord. Promoted rear-admiral on 27 May 1854, Seymour remained in post until the end of the campaign, though he could not prevent a major quarrel developing between Napier and Graham, or the breakdown of relations between the admiral and some of his senior captains. In 1855 Seymour was appointed second in command in the Baltic to Rear-Admiral Sir Richard Dundas, and demonstrated his ability as a combat commander in detached positions. During the campaign he was blinded in one eye when one of the sea mines that had been picked up off Kronstadt exploded while he was examining it.

In the spring of 1856 Seymour went out overland to take command of the China station. Early in October he received news of the seizure of the British coaster *Arrow* by the Chinese authorities at Canton (Guangzhou). The governor of Hong Kong, Sir John Bowring, requested Seymour to bring pressure to bear on the Chinese viceroy. Accordingly Seymour seized the forts that covered the approaches to Canton, and, as the Chinese were obstinate, occupied the Bogue (Humen) forts. Troops were sent out from Britain, and Lord Elgin arrived with full powers to negotiate. However, the troops were ordered instead to India to suppress the mutiny and Lord Elgin followed them to Calcutta. Meantime the Chinese junk fleet was destroyed after a sharp action in the Fatshan (Foshan) Creek on 1 June 1857; on the arrival of other troops and the return of Lord Elgin, as the Chinese viceroy still refused all concessions, Seymour pushed up the river, and, after a clever feint, attacked and captured Canton with very little loss on 28–9 December 1857. The viceroy was captured and sent, a prisoner, to Calcutta. As the Chinese government at Peking (Beijing) refused to negotiate, Lord Elgin considered it necessary to move the scene of action to the north. At the end of April 1858 Seymour, in his flagship, the *Calcutta*, arrived in the Gulf of Pecheli (Beizhili), and, on the request of Elgin, took the forts at the mouth of the Peiho (Beihe) on 20 May, and forced the passage up the river as far as Tientsin (Tianjin), where on 26 June the treaty of Tientsin was signed, in which the Chinese government conceded the demands of the British minister. This campaign reflected the lessons of the Baltic campaigns that, with the proper equipment, coastal forts could be successfully engaged from the sea.

Seymour afterwards escorted Lord Elgin to Japan, returned to Hong Kong, and reached England early in the following summer, at the end of his term of three years. The success of his operations in the Second Opium War was largely due to his foresight and attention to detail, though Lord Elgin publicly accused him of prevarication and delay in moving up to the Peiho and undertaking active operations. The charges were refuted by the Admiralty, and appeared absurd in the light of the failure of Sir James Hope's attack on the same forts in 1859. Seymour was made a GCB on 20 May 1859, and shortly afterwards was presented by the China merchants with a handsome service of plate. On 9 August 1859 he was returned to parliament as Liberal member for Devonport; he resigned his seat in February 1863. In January 1860 the duke of Somerset wanted Seymour to become senior naval lord, but the necessary reshuffling of seats could not be accomplished.

On 1 November 1860 Seymour was promoted vice-admiral, and on 5 March 1864 admiral. From March 1863 to March 1866 he was commander-in-chief at Portsmouth. In 1870 he was put on the retired list, and in 1875 was nominated to the then honorary office of vice-admiral of the United Kingdom. He died at his home, Cadlington House, near Horndean, Hampshire, on 23 February 1887. Seymour was a talented, professional officer who combined nautical accomplishments and diplomatic skill with success in operational command. His early promotion to captain's rank, at a time of very slow movement on the Navy List, was entirely due to the influence of his father.

J. K. LAUGHTON, *rev.* ANDREW LAMBERT

Sources G. S. Graham, *The China station: war and diplomacy, 1830–1860* (1978) • A. D. Lambert, *The Crimean War: British grand strategy, 1853–56* (1990) • D. Bonner-Smith and E. W. R. Lumby, eds., *The Second China War, 1856–1860*, Navy RS, 95 (1954) • BL, Napier MSS • Cumbria AS, Carlisle, Graham MSS • J. W. D. Dundas and C. Napier, *Russian war, 1854, Baltic and Black Sea: official correspondence*, ed. D. Bonner-Smith and A. C. Dewar, Navy RS, 83 (1943) • R. S. Dundas, *Russian war, 1855, Baltic: official correspondence*, ed. D. Bonner-Smith, Navy RS, 84 (1944) • U. Southampton L., Palmerston MSS • personal knowledge (1897) • O'Byrne, *Naval biog. dict.* • W. P. Gossett, *The lost ships of the Royal Navy, 1793–1900* (1986) • Burke, *Peerage* • *CGPLA Eng. & Wales* (1887)

Archives NMM, (LBK) 16 79 | BL, Napier MSS • BL, corresp. with Sir Charles Wood, 1855–8, Add. MS 49558 • Cumbria AS, Carlisle, Graham MSS

Likenesses F. Holl, engraving (after crayon drawing by A. de Salomé) • M. Porter, oils (after A. de Salomé, 1864), admiralty, Portsmouth

Wealth at death £28,637 0s. 6d.: resworn probate, April 1888, *CGPLA Eng. & Wales* (1887)

Seymour, Sir Michael Culme-, third baronet (1836–1920), naval officer, was born on 13 March 1836 at Northchurch, Berkhamsted. He was the son of Sir John Hobart Seymour, second baronet (1800–1880), who took the additional surname Culme after the death of his first wife, Elizabeth, daughter of the Revd Thomas Culme, on 6 March 1841. After attending Harrow School he entered the navy in 1850. He had early experience of active service in the Second Anglo-Burmese War of 1852 and in the Baltic operations of the Russian War in 1854 and then moved to the Black Sea theatre, where he served ashore with the naval brigade at the siege of Sevastopol. He was then appointed to the *Calcutta*, which would carry the flag of his uncle Admiral Sir Michael Seymour, on the China station. Here he benefited from the excellent education provided by the naval instructor John Knox Laughton. He was promoted lieutenant on 25 May 1857, and served as flag-lieutenant during the Second Opium War. He was engaged at the desperate boat action in Fatshan (Foshan) Creek and the capture of Canton (Guangzhou) and the Peiho (Beihe) forts. As flag-lieutenant he was promoted commander on 6 June 1859, when his uncle's command ended. Between June 1861 and July 1864 he commanded the gun-vessel *Wanderer* in the Mediterranean. He was promoted captain on 16 December 1865, and married Mary Georgiana Watson (*d.* 6 March 1912), daughter of Richard Watson MP of Rockingham Castle, Northamptonshire, on 16 October 1866. They had three sons and two daughters.

In 1869 Seymour was appointed naval aide-de-camp to the queen. In 1874–6 he served as private secretary to his near neighbour George Ward-Hunt, the first lord of the Admiralty. In 1876 he commanded the ironclad *Monarch*, and in 1877 moved to the *Temeraire*. She was part of the squadron that Admiral Sir Geoffrey Phipps Hornby led up the Dardanelles in 1878. He served as flag-captain to the commander-in-chief at Portsmouth, Admiral Sir Alfred

Ryder, between 1879 and 1881. He succeeded to the baronetcy on the death of his father in September 1880. Promoted rear-admiral on 6 May 1882, he was appointed to the particular service squadron in 1885 under Hornby, and was then commander-in-chief on the Pacific station from 1885 to 1887. As a vice-admiral (19 June 1888), he was commander-in-chief of the Channel Fleet from 1890 to 1893, and he reached the rank of admiral on 13 May 1893. This would normally have been the end of his sea-going career. However, in July 1893 he was dispatched to command the Mediterranean Fleet by the first lord of the Admiralty, his close friend and relative by marriage Earl Spencer. He replaced Admiral Sir George Tryon, who had been lost with the *Victoria*. The appointment was critical: Britain's international position was intimately identified with the Mediterranean Fleet, and any sign of weakness would encourage the newly formed Franco-Russian alliance to challenge British pre-eminence at sea, upon which rested the whole fabric of the empire.

Seymour remained in the Mediterranean until 1897, restoring the morale and good order of the fleet. He also reversed the radical tactical thinking that Tryon had made a feature of his regime, and it is to his command that Andrew Gordon (in *The Rules of the Game*) attributes a reaffirmation of the signal-driven and over-centralized tactical methods that failed at Jutland. A master of steamship handling and formal evolutions, Seymour selected a staff of future admirals to carry through his counter-reformation, including Francis Bridgeman, John Rushworth Jellicoe, and Hugh Evan-Thomas. Officers who had served in Seymour's fleet held the majority of high commands up to and during the First World War. His impact on the real fighting efficiency of the fleet, particularly gunnery, was less satisfactory. On leaving the Mediterranean he spent the years 1897–1900 as commander-in-chief at Portsmouth, and became principal aide-de-camp to the queen in 1899. He was also awarded the GCB and GCVO during his career, which had benefited from a close family connection with the royal family stretching back to the first baronet. When he retired, on 13 March 1901, he was awarded the honorary rank of vice-admiral of the United Kingdom, which he held until his death. Seymour maintained a lively and well-informed interest in the service for the rest of his life, not only through the career of his eldest son, also called Sir Michael Culme-Seymour (*b.* 29 Aug 1867), but also through his many distinguished subordinates, notably Jellicoe, who always looked back on his period under Seymour's command with particular nostalgia. He died at his home, Wadenhoe House, at Oundle in Northamptonshire, on 11 October 1920. His eldest son, the fourth baronet, held important naval commands before his untimely death on 2 April 1925 as a vice-admiral. Culme-Seymour's association with royalty, and especially with the sailor-prince, later George V, had a curious consequence. There was a fairly persistent rumour, quite unfounded, that George, then Prince George, had in 1890 in Malta married Mary, Culme-Seymour's elder daughter. In February 1911, F. Mylius was prosecuted for perpetrating this libel in a republican squib. Culme-Seymour gave evidence in the king's favour, and Mylius was imprisoned for twelve months. Mary (*d.* 1944), who also gave evidence, as did other members of the family, was in fact legitimately married in 1899 to Vice-Admiral Sir Trevylyan Napier.

A slight, spartan figure with, as an admiral, a white naval beard, Seymour had enormous reserves of physical energy, and continued to win foot races even after his appointment as commander-in-chief of the Mediterranean Fleet. He was also a fearsome martinet with a mania for order. Although his career was made by early promotion, secured by his uncle, his determination and force of character were seen to great advantage in helping the service to recover from the *Victoria* disaster at a time when Britain's international position was threatened.

ANDREW LAMBERT

Sources A. Gordon, *The rules of the game: Jutland and British naval command* (1996) · *WWW* · *Navy List* · A. J. Marder, *The anatomy of British sea power*, American edn (1940) · P. Scott, *Fifty years in the Royal Navy* (1919) · R. Bacon, *Earl Jellicoe* (1936) · W. L. Clowes, *The Royal Navy: a history from the earliest times to the present*, 7 vols. (1897–1903), vol. 7 · B. M. Gough, *The Royal Navy and the north-west coast of North America, 1810–1914* (1971) · K. Rose, *King George V* (1983) · Burke, *Peerage* (1959)

Likenesses photographs, repro. in Gordon, *Rules of the game* · photographs, repro. in Gough, *Royal Navy*

Seymour, Michael Hobart (1800–1874), anti-Catholic polemicist, was born on 29 September 1800 at Limerick, the sixth son of John Crossley Seymour (*d.* 1831), vicar of Caherelly, and Catherine, eldest daughter and coheir of the Revd Edward Wight, rector of Meelick in co. Limerick. He claimed to be the lineal descendant of Sir Henry Seymour, brother of Henry VIII's wife Jane Seymour. Aaron Crossley Hobart *Seymour was his brother. In 1823 he graduated BA from Trinity College, Dublin, and proceeded MA in 1832. He was ordained deacon in 1823 and priest in 1824. He served as a clergyman in Ireland, and also as secretary to the Irish Protestant Association, tirelessly campaigning against the dogmas and practices of the Roman Catholic church. He left Ireland, where he had become unpopular, for England about 1834. In London he was for several years evening lecturer at St George the Martyr, Southwark, and afternoon lecturer at St Ann Blackfriars while also acting as travelling secretary for the Reformation Society. In January 1844 Seymour married, at Walcot church, Bath, Maria, only daughter of General Thomas of the East India Company and widow of Baron Brownmill, physician to Louis XVIII. They had no children. For the next thirty years of his life he made Bath his permanent place of residence and ceased to hold any post in the church.

In September 1844 Seymour and his wife took a long journey to Rome, which he described in his controversial *A Pilgrimage to Rome* (1848) and *Mornings among the Jesuits at Rome: being notes of conversations held with certain Jesuits in that city* (1849). The first book was criticized in *A Brief Review by A. M.* (1849) and the second in *The Rambler* (4, 1849, 144–9). Seymour had a rhetorical way of marshalling his facts, and his deductions could not always be relied upon. He followed up his attack in *Evenings with the Romanists: with an introductory chapter on the moral results of the Romish system* (1854), which was republished in New York and Philadelphia in 1855 and translated into Spanish, finding a large circulation in Mexico. Seymour frequently contributed anti-Catholic pieces to newspapers, and continued to publish pamphlets and lectures against the church of Rome. A lecture on nunneries, published in 1852, involved him in a controversy with Cardinal Nicholas Wiseman, who published a reply. Seymour also brought out a popular new edition of Foxe's *Acts and Monuments of the Church* (that is, the book of martyrs) in 1838, which purported to be 'carefully revised, corrected, and condensed'; this was widely circulated and often reprinted during the Victorian period.

Seymour died at his home, 27 Marlborough Buildings, Bath, on 19 June 1874, and was buried at Locksbrook cemetery, Bath, on 25 June; his wife survived him. He was remembered for his fluency of speech and quick humour as well as for his polemical writings.

W. P. COURTNEY, *rev.* DAVID HUDDLESTON

Sources Allibone, *Dict.* • Burke, *Gen. GB* • *Annual Register* (1874), 156 • *GM*, 2nd ser., 21 (1844), 310 • [J. H. Todd], ed., *A catalogue of graduates who have proceeded to degrees in the University of Dublin, from the earliest recorded commencements to … December 16, 1868* (1869), 510 • Burtchaell & Sadleir, *Alum. Dubl.* • Foster, *Alum. Oxon.* • J. Wolffe, *The protestant crusade in Great Britain, 1829–1860* (1991), 112 • *CGPLA Eng. & Wales* (1874)

Wealth at death under £12,000: resworn probate, Sept 1877, *CGPLA Eng. & Wales* (1874)

Seymour, Robert (1798–1836), illustrator and caricaturist, was born in Somerset, the second son of Henry Seymour and his wife, Elizabeth, *née* Bishop (*d.* 1827). The family moved to London, where Henry Seymour worked as a cabinet-maker for a Mr Seddon. He died during a return visit to Somerset, leaving his wife, two sons, and a daughter in very poor circumstances. Robert was apprenticed in London to a Mr Vaughan as a pattern-drawer in Duke Street, Smithfield, but his ambition was to be a professional painter. He was a frequent visitor to the house of an uncle, Thomas Holmes, in Hoxton, where he met the painter Joseph Severn. In 1822 Seymour's painting depicting a scene taken from Tasso's *Jerusalem Delivered* with over 100 figures was exhibited at the Royal Academy. Another was rejected, and although Seymour continued to paint in oils, he turned to illustration for his livelihood.

In the next five years Seymour produced designs for a wide range of subjects including poetry, melodramas, children's stories, and topographical and scientific works. Among the books which can be identified are William Robinson's *The History of Enfield* (2 vols., 1823); *Public Characters of All Nations* (3 vols., 1823); *Le diable Boiteux* (1824); and Mary Sherwood's *My Uncle Timothy* (1825). A steady supply of work enabled him to live comfortably with sufficient time to enjoy his library, fishing and shooting expeditions, and visits to a gymnasium with Lacey the publisher and George Cruikshank.

In 1827 Seymour's mother died, and he married his cousin Jane Holmes, who later gave birth to a son, Robert, and a daughter, Jane. The same year the publishers Knight and Lacey became bankrupt, owing Seymour a considerable amount of money. Without their regular employment, he now had the opportunity to experiment with the etching process, and was fortunate to have his work accepted by the printseller Thomas McLean. He began producing caricatures in the style of George Cruikshank, signed with the pseudonym Shortshanks, which was quickly discarded when Cruikshank objected to it. Seymour's first etched book illustrations appeared the same year in *Vagaries in Quest of the Wild and Wonderful* by Piers Shafton Grafton (Mr Becke), and Herbert Trevelyan's *Snatches from Oblivion*. These were rather weak efforts, but his abilities developed rapidly, and by the time that works such as *The March of Intellect* (1829) and *The Heiress* (1830) were published, the humorous scenes are well observed and executed with much greater assurance.

Having mastered the art of etching, Seymour turned to lithography, and by 1830 he was using the process for separate prints and book illustrations. In the same year he was invited by Thomas McLean to take over production of the *Looking Glass*, a caricature magazine that had been started in 1830, etched throughout by William Heath. Seymour provided four large lithographed sheets of illustrations every month until his death. Subjects are usually drawn several to a page, reflecting the social behaviour and political events of the time, with some fine full-page designs such as 'W.A.R.: a Masque', similar in style to John Doyle's caricatures. Two sketchbooks containing preparatory drawings for this publication, fine views of Windsor and Eton, figure studies, portraits, and other subjects are now in the Victoria and Albert Museum, London.

Seymour, who by this time was in the first rank of British comic artists, continued to provide drawings for wood-engraved illustrations in books and periodicals, in spite of his misgivings about this medium. In 1831 he began work for a new magazine, *Figaro in London*, producing nearly 300 small drawings to accompany the text of Gilbert À Beckett, often, as was customary at the time, having to work up something humorous from a dull political topic suggested by the editor. The partnership lasted until 1834, when À Beckett suffered a heavy financial loss and refused to pay Seymour money owed to him. Despite Seymour's conciliatory attempt to resolve the matter, À Beckett attacked him publicly in the pages of *Figaro in London*. Seymour resigned, and returned to the paper only after Henry Mayhew had been appointed to replace the former editor.

Independently Seymour launched a new series of lithographs titled *Sketches by Seymour* between 1834 and 1836, devoted largely to the misadventures of cockney sportsmen. Although the designs are poor compared with his other work of this period, the prints were enormously popular, and were reissued several times during the following fifty years. Charles Baudelaire, the French poet, wrote, 'As with the rest of the English, we find in Seymour a violence, a love of the excessive, and a simple, ultra-brutal and direct manner of stating his subject; when it comes to caricature, the English are extremists' (Baudelaire, 188). Seymour is seen at his best in the twenty-four fine but relatively unknown etched plates made in 1835 to illustrate Thomas K. Hervey's *The Book of Christmas* and the twelve plates in *The Squib Annual* for 1836.

Another project was to have been a series of etchings by Seymour depicting the activities of a sporting club. After seeing the first four plates, Edward Chapman, of Chapman and Hall, agreed that the work should be issued in monthly parts with descriptive text, for which he suggested the young Charles Dickens. The first part of the new work, *The Posthumous Papers of the Pickwick Club* appeared, but before the second was completed Dickens had asked Seymour to provide a new plate for 'The Stroller's Tale'. He did so, but was clearly unhappy about the way that his illustrations were now subordinate to the text. Before the second part had been completed, on 20 April 1836, Seymour shot himself with a fowling piece in the summer house to the rear of his home in Liverpool Road, Islington. His obituaries at the time suggest that the feud with À Beckett, the problems with Dickens over 'The Stroller's Tale', overwork, and illness were to blame, but in his last note he wrote, 'Best and dearest of wives—for such you have been to me—blame, I charge you, no one.' Contradictory claims and statements about the origin of *Pickwick Papers* were made long after Seymour's death, but Pickwickian figures can be seen in earlier works such as *The Heiress* and *The Book of Christmas*. In his introduction to Jane Seymour's book on the subject, the Dickens scholar F. G. Kitton states: 'It is probably fair to surmise that had not her husband communicated to Edward Chapman his idea of publishing a series of Cockney Sporting Sketches, *Pickwick* would never have been written' (J. Seymour, introduction). MICHAEL HESELTINE

Sources *DNB* · R. Seymour, *Seymour's humorous sketches* (1866) [with a biographical notice of Robert Seymour by Henry G. Bohn] · R. Seymour, *Seymour's sketches* (1867) [with an account of the artist and his works by John C. Hotten] · Thieme & Becker, *Allgemeines Lexikon* · G. Everitt, *English caricaturists* (1893) · M. Bryant and S. Heneage, eds., *Dictionary of British cartoonists and caricaturists, 1730–1980* (1994) · J. Seymour, *An account of the origin of the 'Pickwick papers'*, ed. F. G. Kitton (1901) · W. Miller and E. H. Strange, *A centenary bibliography of the 'Pickwick papers'* (1936) · M. D. George, *English political caricature: a study of opinion and propaganda*, 2 vols. (1959), vol. 2 · Graves, *RA exhibitors* · C. Baudelaire, 'Some foreign caricaturists', *The painter of modern life and other essays*, ed. J. Mayne (1964)

Likenesses R. Seymour, self-portrait, miniature on ivory, *c*.1827 · R. Seymour, self-portrait, lithograph

Seymour, Thomas, **Baron Seymour of Sudeley** (*b*. in or before **1509**, *d*. **1549**), nobleman, was the fourth of six sons of Sir John Seymour (1473/4–1536), landowner and courtier, of Wolf Hall, Wiltshire, and his wife, Margery (*d*. 1550), daughter of Sir Henry Wentworth of Nettlestead, Suffolk. His elder brothers included Edward *Seymour (*c*.1500–1552), later duke of Somerset and lord protector, and Sir Henry Seymour (*b*. in or before 1503, *d*. 1578) of Marwell in Hampshire, and one of his four sisters was *Jane (1508/9–1537), third wife of *Henry VIII (1491–1547). Sir John Seymour was a minor but reasonably prosperous gentleman with property in Wiltshire and Somerset.

Early career, 1530–1547 By 1530 Thomas Seymour was in service to the leading courtier Sir Francis Bryan (*b*. in or before 1492, *d*. 1550). He rose to prominence on Henry's marriage to Jane on 30 May 1536; he became a gentleman of the privy chamber by 2 October and was named joint master steward of Chirk and Holt in Denbighshire and of other manors and castles in the Welsh marches the following year. On 18 October 1537, six days after Jane gave birth to Edward, prince of Wales (1537–1553), Seymour was knighted. Further reward came with grants of former monastic land in Essex, Hampshire, and Berkshire in March 1538. Thomas Howard, third duke of Norfolk, was keen for an alliance with the Seymour family and on 14 July suggested to the king that his daughter Mary Fitzroy, duchess of Richmond, marry Seymour. Henry approached Seymour, who preferred Sir Thomas Cromwell to have 'the mayning of the matter' (*LP Henry VIII*, 13/1, no. 1375). Seymour was involved in diplomatic missions to François I in 1538 and to Ferdinand in Vienna in summer 1542, witnessing campaigning against the Turks in Hungary. With Dr Nicholas Wotton he was sent as resident ambassador to Mary of Hungary, regent of the Low Countries, on 30 April 1543 with a 'diet' of £1 6*s*. 8*d*. per day. However, he was recalled in mid-July.

Thomas Seymour, Baron Seymour of Sudeley (*b*. in or before 1509, *d*. 1549), by unknown artist

Seymour played a more prominent role in social occasions at court, participating in tournaments at Whitehall Palace on 1, 3, and 5 May 1540. In summer 1543 he was marshal of the English army in the Low Countries, serving under Sir John Wallop. This military experience may explain his appointment as master of the ordnance for life on 18 April 1544, a striking mark of royal favour, and he took part in the capture of Boulogne on 14 September. In

October of that year he was appointed an admiral of the fleet, and he was much involved in naval action in 1545. On 29 November he was rewarded with Hampton Place outside Temple Bar, which he renamed Seymour Place. He was returned as knight of the shire for Wiltshire in 1545, possibly through the influence of Edward Seymour (now earl of Hertford), but his activities in the House of Commons are unrecorded. Various other local offices, rewards, and commissions followed. By the end of Henry's reign Seymour's annual income was an impressive £458 6*s*. 8*d*. In June 1546 Norfolk again asked Henry to arrange marriage between Seymour and his daughter, but Henry Howard, earl of Surrey, was bitterly opposed to the match, saying it was beneath his sister. Seymour himself would have preferred to marry *Katherine (1512–1548), the second child and elder daughter of Sir Thomas Parr of Kendal, Westmorland, and his wife, Maud, and widow of John Neville, third Baron Latimer. He courted Katherine briefly early in 1543 before she caught the king's eye. On 23 January 1547, five days before the king's death, Seymour was sworn of the privy council, possibly despite Henry's objections. Henry named Seymour one of the assistants to the executors of his will and left him £200. According to the principal secretary, Sir William Paget, Henry wished Seymour to be ennobled. He was duly created Baron Seymour of Sudeley on 16 February, with an additional grant of lands valued at £500 per annum, nominated a knight of the Garter the next day, and installed on 23 May.

Lord admiral, privy councillor, and traitor, 1547–1549 At the beginning of Edward VI's reign Hertford seized power and had himself promoted duke of Somerset and installed as lord protector and governor of the king's person. Although he had been ennobled and appointed lord high admiral on 17 February (and relinquished the office of master of the ordnance on 26 March in return), Seymour was dissatisfied with his place in the new regime and embarked on a series of intrigues that ultimately cost him his life. He was incensed that his brother should be both lord protector and governor: those functions should, he claimed, be divided and he should have one. He confessed that he had searched through chronicles for precedents and found them in the minority of Henry VI. So discontent was he that during the Scottish military campaign in autumn 1547, despite his office of lord admiral, he stayed in London while his brother went north to fight. Somerset won a great victory at the battle of Pinkie on 10 September, but then left the borders very hastily without pursuing his military advantage because 'il apprit, par un courier qu'on lui depecha expres, que l'amiral son frere formait a la cour un puissant parti contre lui, et qu'il avait pris des mesures secretes avec le roi meme; pour lui enlever la charge de gouverneur de ce jeune prince' (Abbé de Verdot, 1.129–31). It was probably then that Seymour got the king to write a letter in support of his marriage to Katherine, and possibly prepared a letter to be presented in parliament, which he hoped Edward would sign, stating that Seymour should be governor. Generally Somerset succeeded in keeping his brother away from the king, but Seymour exploited his contacts with John Fowler, one of the grooms of the privy chamber, and the royal tutor Sir John Cheke. On several occasions Seymour gave £5 and £10, and as much as £40, to Fowler and Cheke to give to the king. Seymour had told the king, 'ye are a beggarly king ye have no monie to play or to geve' (Bodl. Oxf., MS Ashmole 1729, fol. 9*r*). He described how Edward moaned, 'my Unkel off Sumerset deylyth very hardly with me and kepyth me so strayt that I cane not have mony at my wylle but my lord Admyral both sendes me mony and gyves me mony' (Hatfield House, Hertfordshire, Cecil MS 150, fol. 112*r*). Seymour was clearly trying to use the king's understandable desire for more spending money to insinuate himself into his favour. If Seymour and Edward had lived longer, such a relationship might have had significant consequences.

Meanwhile Seymour quickly and secretly married Henry's widow, Katherine, probably in May or June. This action openly defied Somerset and the privy council. It was pointed out that had Katherine soon become pregnant, there would have been uncertainty about whether the child was Seymour's or Henry's. The marriage led to friction between the Seymour brothers and their wives, not least over ceremonial precedence, and over Katherine's jewels. Even before Katherine's death on 5 September 1548, shortly after giving birth to Mary Seymour (1548–1550), Seymour had been flirting with Princess Elizabeth, who was resident in their household at Chelsea and Hanworth in Middlesex. Elizabeth's governess and closest servant, Katherine Ashley, testified how:

> He wold com many mornyngs into the said Lady Elizabeths chamber … And if she were up, he wold bid her good Morrow, and ax how she did, and strike hir upon the bak, or on the buttocks familiarly … And if she were in hir bed he wold put open the curteyns, and bid hir good morrow, and make as though he wold come at hir: And she wold go further in the bed, so that he could not com at hir; And one mornyng he strove to have kissed hir in hir Bed. (Hatfield House, Hertfordshire, Cecil MS 150, fol. 85*r*)

'One tyme', according to Ashley, 'the [dowager] Quene, suspecting the often accesse of the Admirall to the Lady Elizabeth's Grace, cam sodenly upon them, wher they were all alone, (he having her in his Armes)' (Hatfield House, Hertfordshire, Cecil MS 150, fol. 80*v*). After Katherine's death Seymour was clearly interested in proposing to Elizabeth; the tone of Ashley's testimony suggests that Elizabeth herself was far from reluctant, though aware of the political sensitivities.

Seymour tried to recruit several noblemen to support his various causes, often speaking with them on their way to or from parliament. Henry Grey, third marquess of Dorset, was won over by Seymour's promise to marry his daughter, Lady Jane Grey, to the king. Thomas Wriothesley, first earl of Southampton, testified how on their way to dinner during parliament, 'after a litle comen talk', Seymour said to him, referring to Southampton's surrender of the office of lord chancellor in early 1547, 'ha my lord of Southampton, you were well handeled touching yor office. Why shuld you not have it again?' (PRO, SP 10/6/15). He also attempted to assemble a group of associates and servants in the Commons. In autumn 1547 he threatened to disrupt the parliament. He was accused of saying, 'I have herd spekyng of a black parlament and they usse me as they doo begyn by goddes preshios soule I wyll make the blakiste parleament that ever was in England' (PRO, SP 10/6/7).

Seymour was very much aware of the need to build local support. To Dorset he said that he should not trust the gentlemen of the county too much 'for they have sumwhat to loose'. Instead:

> I wold rather advise you to make muche of the head yeomen and frankelyns of the cuntreye, specially those that be the ringleaders, for they be the men that be best hable to perswade the multitude and may best bring the number and therefore I wold wishe you to make muche of them, and to goo to their houses, nowe to oon and nowe to an other, caryeng with you a flagon or two of wyne, and a pasty of veneson, and to use a familiaritie with them, for so shall you cause them to love you, and be assured to have them at your commaundemente.

'This maner (I may tel you)', Seymour continued, 'I entende to use miself' (PRO, SP 10/6/7). His 'conception of local power was competitive' (Bernard, 222). He advised Dorset 'to kepe my house in Warwikeshire … because that war a cuntrey full of men, but chiefly to match with my lorde of Warwike [John Dudley, earl of Warwick], so as he should not be hable to matche with me there' (PRO, SP 10/6/7). Sir William Sharington, the under-treasurer of the Bristol mint, testified how Seymour:

> Hathe divers tymes caused me to loke with him uppon a cart of England in the loking wherof he wold many tymes shewe me howe strong he was, what nombres of men he was able to make, how farre his landes and dominions did stretche, And howe his said landes lay betwene his house of Brouham and the Holtehe. (PRO, SP 10/6/13)

Dorset said that Seymour 'used sondry tymes to shewe me as we rodde togithers the cowntrees rounde about sayeng all these which dwell in thes parties be my frendes'. 'And so he did vaunt … that he had as great a nombre of gentlemen that loved hym, as eny noble man in England … And further said that he thought that he had more gentlemen that louved hym than the Lord Protector had and upon that he said he was happye that hath freends in this world what so ever shuld chaunce' (Hatfield House, Hertfordshire, Cecil MS 150, fol. 93*v*). Such evidence was echoed in the charges against him: 'he ment to have matched and sett one Noble man against such an other Noble man, as he thought he cowlde never compasse and wynne to assent to his factyon and false conspiracye' (*Statutes of the Realm*, 11 vols., 1810–28, 3.63).

More significantly still, Seymour was fortifying Holt, at a strategic crossing point on the River Dee that commanded access from north to south Wales. He was also trying to secure more money. He was accused of maintaining pirates and taking a share of their spoil. Seymour asked Sharington, who had been coining testoons for himself and was possibly hoping to be protected from the consequences by high-placed friends, whether he could coin money for him. A later French account hinted that what Seymour planned to do was to kidnap the young king and marry Elizabeth, bringing them to Holt. Significantly, when in custody Seymour denied 'that ever I went about to take the kyng from my lord my brother by force; I never ment it, nor thought it' (Hatfield House, Hertfordshire, Cecil MS 150, fol. 99*v*). Yet Fowler testified how Seymour had once come to St James's Palace at nine o'clock in the morning and voiced his surprise that there were so few people there: 'a man might stele away the king now for there cam more with me than is in all the howse besides' (PRO, SP 10/6/10). If Seymour was indeed plotting to kidnap Edward and Elizabeth, to marry the princess, and to have himself made lord protector in place of his brother, it is not surprising that he was arrested and tried once his plans were discovered.

Fall, 1549 Seymour was arrested on 17 January 1549. Examined on 25 January, he wrote an abject submission to Somerset on 27 January. Many were interrogated. Some members of the privy council were clearly turning this information into articles against Seymour. He was examined on 18 February; the privy council discussed the matter on 22 February; Seymour was examined again on 23 February, but refused to answer unless his accusers stood before him, and would not even subscribe the answers he had earlier begun to make. On 24 February the privy councillors reported to Edward, Somerset 'declaring how sorowfull a case this was unto hym', but regarding his duty to the king greater than that to his brother. They sent once again to Seymour, who would answer no more than three of the articles. On 25 February a bill of attainder was introduced into parliament, unopposed in the House of Lords (Somerset was allowed for natural pity's sake to be absent), but 'very much debated and argued' in the Commons, in which lawyers declared that Seymour's offences 'were in the compasse of High Treason'. On 5 March the bill was passed, the Commons 'being marvailous full almost to the number of iiii[c] persons, not x or xii at the most giving their nays tharunto' (*APC*, 1547–50, 246–7, 256–8, 260). Seymour was beheaded on Tower Hill on 20 March and buried in the Tower, presumably in the chapel of St Peter ad Vincula. It was not any fratricidal bitterness or any factional stirring but quite simply what was found out about his activities and ambitions during the investigations in January and February 1549 that sealed his fate. He had done and said quite enough to have provoked not only his brother but also all his fellow privy councillors. To the end Seymour continued his plotting, for which he was denounced in a sermon by Hugh Latimer. He had allegedly sent papers to Princess Mary and Elizabeth, urging them to conspire against Somerset. These papers had been found in his shoe, sewn between the soles. He had 'made his pen of the aglet of a poynte that he plucked from his hosse'. Latimer declaimed how Seymour 'died very dangerously, irksomely, horribly … He was a man the farthest from the fear of God that I knew or heard of in England' (*Sermons of Hugh Latimer, Sometime Bishop of Worcester, Martyr*, 1555, ed. G. E. Corrie, Parker Society, 22, 1844, 161–5).

Seymour tried to do too much too quickly, and there was as much rhetoric as action. He won insufficient support among his fellow privy councillors: even if Dorset, William Parr, marquess of Northampton, Henry Manners, second earl of Rutland, and Southampton were keener than they allowed themselves to appear in their depositions, Seymour never gained any wholehearted commitment. He hardly had any coherent political programme, even if he agreed with his wife's criticism of the distribution of crown lands, or attacked Somerset's Scottish invasion of 1547 for risking the loss of a great number of men and for costing 'a great summ of Money in vayn', or suggested that Somerset would give up Calais to the French, or declared generally that 'he mislyked the procedinges of the lord Protector and counsayle' and sought 'the alteracion of the state and ordre of the Realme' (Bodl. Oxf., MS Ashmole 1729, fol. 9*r*; Hatfield House, Hertfordshire, Cecil MS 150, fol. 60*v*). Yet, if he had delayed his plots until autumn 1549, he might have gathered more support after the continuing military difficulties and the serious popular rebellions of the summer. Seymour's precipitate approach and consequent failure was as much a matter of temperament. William Wightman, his servant, testified how 'if he had oones conceyved opynion by his owne perswasions, neyther Lawyer nor other could tourne him' (Hatfield House, Hertfordshire, Cecil MS 150, fol. 60*v*). His fiery nature and his soaring ambition told against him, however attractive and charming his personality was. 'This day', said Elizabeth on hearing of his execution, 'died a man with much wit, and very litle judgment' (E. Dent, *Annals of Winchecombe and Sudeley*, 1877, 193).

G. W. BERNARD

Sources Abbé de Verdot, *Ambassades de messieurs de Noailles en Angleterre*, ed. C. Villiart, 5 vols. (Leiden, 1763) • *APC*, 1542–50 • G. W. Bernard, 'The downfall of Sir Thomas Seymour', *The Tudor nobility*, ed. G. W. Bernard (1992), 212–40 • [G. Burnet], *The history of the reformation of the church of England*, ed. J. G. Pocock, 6 vols. (1865) • *CPR*, 1547–51 • GEC, *Peerage* • S. Haynes, ed., *A collection of state papers … left by William Cecill Lord Burghley* (1740) • HoP, *Commons*, 1509–58, 3.290–91, 293–4, 297–301 • W. K. Jordan, *Edward VI*, 1: *The young king* (1968) • G. Leti, *Historia o vero vita di Elisabetta, regina d'Inghilterra*, 2 vols. (Amsterdam, 1693) • *LP Henry VIII*, vols. 5, 11–21 • B. N. de Luna, *The queen declined: an interpretation of Willobie his Avisa with the text of the original addition* (1971) • J. MacLean, *The life of Sir Thomas Seymour* (1869) • J. E. Neale, *Queen Elizabeth* (1960) • *DNB* • state papers, domestic, Edward VI, PRO, SP 10 • L. B. Smith, *Treason in Tudor England: politics and paranoia* (1986) • J. Strype, *Ecclesiastical memorials*, 3 vols. (1822) • Hatfield House, Hertfordshire, Cecil MS 150

Archives Hatfield House, Hertfordshire, Cecil MS 150 • PRO, SP 10 • PRO, SP 46

Likenesses attrib. L. Hornebolt, miniature, *c*.1540–1544, Royal Collection, The Hague • group portrait, oils on panel, *c*.1570 (*Edward VI and the pope*), NPG; identification of Thomas Seymour uncertain • oils (after contemporary portrait), NPG [*see illus.*] • oils, second version (after contemporary portrait), Longleat House, Wiltshire

Seymour, William, first marquess of Hertford and second duke of Somerset (1587–1660), politician and royalist army officer, was born on 1 September 1587, the second but eldest surviving son of Edward *Seymour, Lord Beauchamp (1561–1612) [*see under* Seymour, Edward, first earl of Hertford], and his wife, Honora Rogers. He matriculated at Magdalen College, Oxford, on 16 April 1605 and graduated BA on 9 December 1607. He was later created MA (31 August 1636) and DM (12 August 1645).

Early years: marriages and relations with the court For much of the early Stuart period Seymour's relations with the royal court were somewhat strained. His illicit marriage on 22 June 1610 to James I's cousin Lady Arabella *Stuart (1575–1615) incurred the king's intense displeasure on the grounds that the two parties were cousins, and both had a (remote) claim to the throne. As a result they were imprisoned in the following month, Lady Arabella at Lambeth and Seymour in the Tower. Through the efforts of Lady Arabella's aunt the countess of Shrewsbury they both succeeded in escaping on 3–4 June 1611. However, Lady Arabella was recaptured and confined to the Tower until she died on 27 September 1615, while Seymour, who had managed to flee across the channel, remained in exile until January 1616. His appointment to the Order of the Bath the following November heralded his rehabilitation at court, but the memory of this scandal seemed to dog him, and his offices and honours remained meagre thereafter.

Seymour was elected MP for Marlborough in December 1620, but succeeded his grandfather as second earl of Hertford in the following April. In 1624, although the prince of Wales helped restore him temporarily to favour, Hertford attended the Lords only once, and there is no record that he spoke. He was granted leave of absence from the 1625 parliament, and attended none of its sittings. In 1626, however, he served as chairman of the Lords' committee for privileges which defended the earls of Arundel and Bristol against Charles I's attempts to exclude them. Throughout the 1628 parliament Hertford consistently opposed Buckingham's efforts to introduce a saving clause into the petition of right, and became widely perceived as one of the duke's enemies.

This political alignment may have owed something to Hertford's second marriage, in April 1618, to Lady Frances Devereux (1599–1674), sister of Robert *Devereux, third earl of Essex. Hertford was very friendly with his brother-in-law, another peer marginalized from the court, and in July 1629 wrote warmly to Essex of 'two soe nearly linked in frendship and alliance as wee are' (BL, Add. MS 46188, fol. 114*r*). During the 1630s Essex regularly visited Hertford's Wiltshire houses, supported him in a duel in May 1636, and leased part of Essex House to him for ninety-nine years in return for £1100. Throughout Charles I's personal rule Hertford remained detached from the court: Clarendon later wrote that he:

> had always undergone hard measure from the Court, where he received no countenance, and had no design of making advantage from it. For though he was a man of very good parts, and conversant in books both in Latin and Greek languages, and of a clear courage … he was so wholly given up to a country life, where he lived in splendour, that he had an aversion, even an unaptness, for business. (Clarendon, *Hist. rebellion*, 2.528–9)

Few offices came his way: only belatedly, on 23 March 1639, was he appointed lord lieutenant of Somerset, and then solely because the earl of Pembroke was otherwise engaged in the first of Charles's campaigns against the Scottish covenanters.

The making of a royalist In August 1640 Hertford, like Essex, was among the signatories of the twelve peers' petition urging the king to recall parliament. During the first half of 1641 Charles I sought a rapprochement with several of the twelve peers, and as part of this process Hertford was created a privy councillor (19 February), elevated to the rank of marquess (3 June), and appointed governor to the prince of Wales (10 August). According to Clarendon, from this point onwards Hertford rallied to 'the support and defence of the King's power and dignity, notwithstanding all his allies and those with whom he had the greatest familiarity and friendship were of the opposite party', and he accepted the position of governor to the prince of Wales out of 'pure zeal and affection for the Crown, and the conscience that in this conjuncture his submission might advance the King's service' (Clarendon, *Hist. rebellion*, 1.563–4). Hertford absented himself from the crucial vote on Strafford's attainder on 7 May, and in December he presented a petition from Somerset to the Lords in defence of episcopacy and the prayer book. As civil war approached, his role as governor to the prince of Wales became politically more sensitive, and on 14 January 1642 the two houses of parliament ordered him to ensure that the prince 'bee not carried out of the kingdome' (*JHL*, 4.513). He politely declined to give such an undertaking, and also refused to accept the lord lieutenancy of Somerset under the terms of the militia ordinance. In April he joined the king at York, together with the prince of Wales and the duke of York, and ignored parliamentary orders to return.

Hertford's refusal to be cowed by the houses reflected his growing political stature by the early 1640s, and he remained prominent in royalist counsels throughout the years of civil war. Like a number of other constitutional royalists, including his younger brother Francis *Seymour, his allegiance to the king was not necessarily inconsistent with his earlier history of constitutional 'opposition', notably to the 'saving clause' in the petition of right. The common denominator of both was a consistent commitment to the rule of law and constitutional propriety. Hertford sought to defend these ideals against whoever appeared to pose the greatest threat to them, be it Charles and Buckingham in the later 1620s or the crown's leading parliamentary critics by 1641–2. As the civil war approached, Hertford came to regard the crown as the lesser of two evils, but during the years that followed he pursued a negotiated settlement and avoided the more hardline strand of royalism.

Civil war On 2 August 1642 Hertford was appointed one of the commissioners of array for Somerset, and also lieutenant-general of the south-west and of south Wales. During September, concerted parliamentarian resistance in Somerset obliged him to withdraw his forces into south Wales, where he raised some 2000 men. From there he joined the king at Oxford in January 1643, and then, with Prince Maurice, advanced into Somerset, taking Taunton, Bridgwater, and Dunster Castle. He linked up with Sir Ralph Hopton at Chard on 4 June and they defeated Sir William Waller's forces at Lansdown on 5 July. Hertford then joined up with Prince Rupert to take Bristol on 26 July.

After this successful campaign, growing disputes between Hertford and princes Rupert and Maurice led the king to recall the marquess to Oxford, where he was appointed groom of the stole in January 1644. Hertford occupied rooms in Christ Church, and on 31 October 1643 he was elected chancellor of Oxford University, an office which he held until the visitation of the university by parliamentarian commissioners in the summer of 1647. Throughout the civil wars, Hertford was committed to seeking an accommodation between the king and the houses, and he remained in informal contact with his brother-in-law Essex. For example, during the summer of 1644, shortly before the parliamentarian surrender of Lostwithiel, the king's message to Essex was conveyed by Hertford's son Lord Beauchamp, who was also Essex's nephew. Similarly, Essex's refusal to negotiate without the houses' express permission was related by John Richard, one of Hertford's clients. Hertford was one of the royalist commissioners at the treaty of Uxbridge (January–February 1645), and the following May he was among the commissioners entrusted with the city and university of Oxford during the king's absence on campaign. In December, Hertford, along with the earls of Dorset, Southampton, and Lindsey, again urged Charles to resume negotiations, but the king retorted that he would defend his crown 'with his sword, if those of his friends failed him' (*The Diplomatic Correspondence of Jean de Montereul*, ed. J. G. Fotheringham, 2 vols., Scottish RS, 29–30, 1898–9, 1.70–71). In late April 1646 Hertford and several other royalist peers made a final abortive attempt to reach agreement with the parliamentary army at Woodstock, and on 20 June he was among the signatories of the Oxford articles of surrender.

The following autumn, Hertford begged to compound under the Oxford articles at the rate of one-tenth, or the value of two years' income from his estates. His composition fine was set at £12,603 6*s*. 9*d*. on 21 November 1646, but was subsequently reduced to £8345 in January 1648 because part of his estate was held only for life; there is, however, no firm evidence that the fine was ever paid. In October 1647 Hertford was one of a small circle of royalist peers whom the king summoned to Hampton Court to advise him, and in the autumn of the following year he served as one of the king's commissioners at the treaty of Newport. As late as 12 January 1649 Hertford joined with Richmond, Dorset, 'and divers others of the King's party' in sending 'to the Councell of the Army to engage both their persons and estates that the King shall performe whatsoever he yeilds unto' (Bodl. Oxf., MS Clarendon 34, fol. 74*r*). But this initiative came to nothing, and its failure opened the way to the king's trial, which began on 20 January. Along with Richmond, Southampton, and Lindsey, Hertford remained with Charles during his trial, and on 8 February these four peers acted as pallbearers at the king's funeral at Windsor.

Later years: withdrawal Hertford owned extensive lands, especially in Somerset and Wiltshire, and his importance as a territorial magnate helps to explain why the council of state kept him under close observation during the early years of the interregnum. In July 1650 he was ordered to remain at his seat at Netley, while the following year he was instructed to move to another house in Wiltshire. He was also told to prevent the resort of 'many dangerous and disaffected persons' to his house, and to 'give security for his acting nothing prejudiciall to the Commonwealth' (PRO, SP 25/65, p. 108; SP 25/96, pp. 48–9). Although Hertford himself avoided direct involvement in royalist conspiracy, his eldest son, Lord Beauchamp, took command of the western association, formed in May 1650, and developed an extensive network throughout western England. However, the association was soon infiltrated by government agents, and in April 1651 Beauchamp was imprisoned in the Tower. Hertford, who was the great-grandson of Edward VI's protector Somerset, observed wryly that it seemed the Tower was:

> a place entailed upon our famylie, for wee have now helde it five generations, yeat toe speake the truth I like not the place soe well but that I coulde be very well contented the entayle should be cutt off and settled upon some other familie that better deserves it. (*Rutland MSS*, 2.47)

Beauchamp was released in September 1651, but within two years his health failed, and he died in March 1654 to the great distress not only of his family but also of the exiled royalist court.

Although Hertford had some contact with John Penruddock, he kept his distance from the rising of March 1655, and Major-General Desborough found that the marquess had 'little stomach to meddle' in royalist conspiracy (A. A. Locke, *The Seymour Family*, 1911, 138). Hertford's desire to live quietly and avoid an open confrontation with the regime was further evident in his readiness to pay £515 towards the decimation tax in May 1656; Cromwell reciprocated by granting him a personal exemption. Hertford nevertheless wished to keep the lord protector at arm's length. When Cromwell invited him to dinner, and sought 'his advice what to do', Hertford replied frankly: 'Our young Master, that is abroad, that is, my Master, and the Master of us all, restore him to his crownes, and by doing this, you may have what you please.' Cromwell responded that 'hee had gone so farre, that the young gentleman could not forgive'. Hertford's secretary recorded that they then parted 'and the Marquis had never any prejudice hereby so long as Cromwel lived' (BL, Add. MS 32093, fol. 348*r*–348*v*).

From the mid-1650s onwards Hertford lived more and more quietly. By 1652 his total debts probably stood at about £19,000, and he was twice reported to have gone abroad in 1656–7 in order to escape his creditors. His wife increasingly took over the management of the Seymour estates, taking policy decisions and corresponding with stewards. Hertford was nevertheless an active patron of distressed clergy during the interregnum and a number of ministers received regular payments from the marquess and his wife. He remained deeply reluctant to join in any royalist activism, convinced that a premature insurrection would only jeopardize the Stuart restoration which he always believed would eventually occur.

Hertford's prognosis proved correct, and on 26 May 1660 he was among the peers who welcomed Charles II at Dover. The same day he was restored to his office as chancellor of Oxford University, and the following day he was appointed a knight of the Garter. On 13 September he was restored to the dukedom of Somerset by a private act of parliament (House of Lords RO, 12 Chas. II, Original Act 10). In giving his assent, Charles declared that this was an honour 'of an extraordinary nature … for an extraordinary person, who hath merited as much of the King my father and myself as a subject can do' (*JHL*, 11.173). By this time, however, his health was declining and he died at Essex House on 24 October 1660. He was buried on 1 November at Bedwyn Magna church in Wiltshire. His widow lived on until 24 April 1674 and was buried, also at Bedwyn Magna, on 7 May. DAVID L. SMITH

Sources Clarendon, *Hist. rebellion* • *JHL*, 4–11 (1628–66) • state papers domestic, Charles I, PRO, SP 16 • committee for compounding papers, PRO, SP 23 • GEC, *Peerage*, new edn • Wilts. & Swindon RO, Ailesbury papers, WRO 1300 • HLRO, Main papers collection, HL • *Calendar of the manuscripts of the marquis of Bath preserved at Longleat, Wiltshire*, 5 vols., HMC, 58 (1904–80), vol. 4 • D. L. Smith, *Constitutional royalism and the search for settlement, c.1640–1649* (1994) • Bodl. Oxf., Clarendon MSS • *The Nicholas papers*, ed. G. F. Warner, 4 vols., CS, new ser., 40, 50, 57, 3rd ser., 31 (1886–1920) • *The manuscripts of his grace the duke of Rutland*, 4 vols., HMC, 24 (1888–1905), vol. 2 • BL, Jessop papers, Add. MS 46188 • BL, Malet Collection, Add. MS 32093 • PRO, SP 25/65 • PRO, SP 25/96

Archives priv. coll., papers | Wilts. & Swindon RO, Ailesbury papers, WRO 1300

Likenesses R. Walker, oils, 1656, Syon House, Brentford, Middlesex • Van Dyck, portrait, repro. in M. T. Lewis, *Lives of the friends and contemporaries of Lord Chancellor Clarendon*, 3 (1852); priv. coll. • mezzotint (after A. Van Dyck), NPG • portrait, priv. coll.

Wealth at death £6300 p.a. in Nov 1646: PRO, SP 23/3, 298; SP 23/191, 595, 607–11 • by 1652, heavily in debt, probably by *c.* £19,000

Seymour, William Digby (1822–1895), judge, third son of Charles Seymour, vicar of Kilronan, co. Roscommon, and his wife, Beata, daughter of Fergus Langley of Lich Finn, co. Tipperary, was born in co. Galty, Ireland, on 22 September 1822. He was educated at Edgeworthstown School and at Trinity College, Dublin, where he matriculated on 12 October 1838. He graduated BA in 1844 and LLD in 1872. He entered the Inner Temple on 2 May 1843 but transferred to the Middle Temple on 14 November 1845. He was called to the bar there on 12 June 1846, and practised on the northern circuit. On 1 September 1847 he married Emily, second daughter of Joseph John Wright, solicitor, of Sunderland.

Through the influence of his father-in-law Seymour was returned to parliament as one of the members for Sunderland in 1852, and his support of the Liberal Party was rewarded with the recordership of Newcastle in December 1854. On returning to his constituency for re-election he was defeated. In the meantime he had become connected with various commercial undertakings, notably with the Waller Goldmining Company, of which he was chairman in 1852. These undertakings were unsuccessful and in 1858 he had to make an arrangement with his creditors. In 1859 he was called before the benchers of the Middle Temple to answer charges affecting his character as a barrister in connection with some commercial transactions, and on 23 February was censured by the benchers (*The Times*, 22, 24, 25 Feb 1859 and 4 April 1859). Seymour disputed the fairness of the decision, but he would not publish the evidence, and he was excluded from the bar mess of the northern circuit. None the less, he won nominal damages for libel against the *Law Magazine* for giving a statement of the case with comments.

In May 1859 Seymour was returned for Southampton, securing Conservative support by a pledge not to vote against Derby's government. His failure to observe this promise was commented on by the *Morning Herald*, and Seymour sought to institute a criminal prosecution of that paper, which was refused by Lord Campbell. He claimed to favour an extension of the franchise, provided that this was accompanied by the protection of the ballot, and was opposed to all special religious endowments. Seymour was named a queen's counsel in the county palatine of Lancaster in August 1860, and on 19 February 1861 a queen's counsel for England by Lord Campbell. In the same year he was employed by the government to draw up the Admiralty Reform Act.

Seymour's views grew gradually more Conservative; he unsuccessfully contested Hull in 1857, Southampton in 1865, Nottingham in 1869 and 1870, Stockton in 1880, and South Shields in 1885. Through the influence of his political friends in August 1889 he became judge of the county court circuit no. 1, with his chief court at Newcastle upon Tyne. He held that appointment until his death at Tynemouth, Northumberland, on 16 March 1895.

Seymour published two works on land investment in Ireland as well as texts on shipping law and a translation of the Hebrew psalter.

G. C. BOASE, *rev.* ERIC METCALFE

Sources *WWBMP*, vol. 1 • Boase, *Mod. Eng. biog.* • J. Foster, *Men-at-the-bar: a biographical hand-list of the members of the various inns of court*, 2nd edn (1885) • *The Times* (18 March 1895), 10 • *ILN* (12 Feb 1853), 132 • *ILN* (23 March 1895), 350 • *Pall Mall Budget* (21 March 1895), 4 • *Law Magazine*, new ser., 13 (1862), 158–85, 363–5 • *Law Magazine*, new ser., 14 (1862–3), 181–338

Likenesses C. K. Robinson, portrait, 1894, repro. in *ILN* (23 March 1895), 350 • woodcut (after daguerreotype by Beard), NPG

Wealth at death £7581 4*s*. 10*d*.: probate, 15 Oct 1896, *CGPLA Eng. & Wales*

Shackle, George Lennox Sharman (1903–1992), economist, was born on 14 July 1903 at 1 Mortimer Road, Cambridge, the only child of Robert Walker Shackle (1851–1934), educationist, and his wife, Fanny, *née* Sharman. His father had been a mathematics master at Bradfield College and was a schools examiner who successfully coached John Maynard Keynes for the scholarship examination for Eton. Shackle was educated at the Perse School, Cambridge, from 1910 to 1920. His intellectual Cambridge family could not then afford a university education for him, so he could not accept a place at St Catharine's College. He therefore started his working life as a bank clerk, which after three years and an unhappy year with a tobacco company was followed by ten years as a schoolmaster. During that time he read on his own for a London external BA degree and obtained it in 1931. A Leverhulme research scholarship starting in January 1935 enabled him to read for a PhD at the London School of Economics (LSE), initially under the supervision of Professor F. A. Hayek. However, inspired by Keynes's *General Theory of Employment, Interest, and Money* (1936), he switched with Hayek's generous consent to an interpretation of Keynes's work. He was granted his PhD in 1937, the thesis being published in 1938 as *Expectations, Investment, and Income*. In 1937 Shackle went to New College, Oxford, and while working at the Oxford University Institute of Statistics he also obtained an Oxford DPhil in 1940, for a series of papers.

In March 1939 Shackle was appointed an assistant at St Andrews University, but the Second World War broke out and in September 1939 he was summoned to the Admiralty to join Donald MacDougall and Helen Makower as the first members of Churchill's S-Branch, his personal group of economists, under Professor F. A. Lindemann. At Churchill's resignation after the general election of 1945, S-Branch ceased to exist. Shackle then became a member of the economic section of the Cabinet Office under James Meade.

In April 1950 Shackle was appointed reader in economic theory at the University of Leeds, but in the following year he accepted the Brunner chair of economic science at the University of Liverpool, where he remained until his retirement in 1969. His contributions to economics were wide-ranging but focused on the treatment of time, expectations, and decision-making under conditions of uncertainty, his greatest theoretical innovation being the development of a non-probabilistic theory of decision-making. He was greatly influenced by Keynes and the Swedish school, in particular Gunnar Myrdal, and became widely acknowledged for his interpretation and development of Keynesian economics and Walrasian general equilibrium analysis. It was in 1937 that the notion of 'potential surprise' presented itself to him as a way of emphasizing the role of expectation in the process of choice: his theory of potential surprise proved to be his major analytical contribution, but to his deep disappointment it failed to enter the textbooks of mainstream economics. Four decades later, in April 1977, he finished *Imagination and the Nature of Choice*, and attention was later drawn to his 'important, and virtually novel, emphasis on the role and uses of imagination' (Perlman, 'Fabric of economics', 17). Comparing Shackle's earlier writings with this later work, it emerges that his scheme of thought, though enriched, had not changed in essence. His writings on the implications of uncertainty for economic analysis destroyed any hope of creating universal thought schemes and deterministic models. Instead, in Shackle's writings the focus is on the creative use of *imagination* to build rival scenarios and then consider their plausibility and consequences. Dealing with imagined futures is considered by mainstream economists to be intractable and is therefore ignored, but the relevance of Shackle's ideas for business practice was recognized. He also wrote the dominant historical treatment of the apex of the Cambridge tradition, *The Years of High Theory: Invention and Tradition in Economic Thought, 1926–1939* (1967). This work was proof that he could step back and see certain institutional foundations of his own creativity—particularly unusual since his was nominally not of the Cambridge but of the LSE and perhaps Oxford institutional training.

Shackle was one of the select few who have achieved greatness in economic theory and the history of economic thought in the twentieth century, and increased attention is being paid to his writings, not only by post-Keynesian economists. Yet, despite his outstanding and manifold achievements as a scholar, covering economics, philosophy, and mathematics, and as a writer of considerable distinction, he was a man of genuine humility and extraordinary gentleness. His high scholarship, the striking originality of his thought, and the generosity of his spirit, made him an academic role model for those able and willing to share his analytical insights, especially among the younger generation. His exquisite and effective use of English to convey his thoughts was quite unique.

On 14 March 1939 Shackle married Gertrude Courtney (Susan) Rowe, daughter of Arthur Rowe, civil servant. They had two sons, Robert (*b.* 1941) and Richard (*b.* 1945), and one surviving daughter, Caroline (*b.* 1946). (Frances Harriet (*b.* 1945), the twin of Richard, died aged sixteen months.) The family lived at the Old Vicarage, Easingwold, York, from 1953. They later moved to 15 Devonshire Road, West Kirby, Wirral, Cheshire, and on his early retirement in 1969 to Rudloe, Alde House Drive, Aldeburgh, Suffolk. Following the death of his wife in 1978, which caused him 'heart-breaking grief' (letter, 19 Jan 1979, *Economists in Discussion*), he subsequently found 'a source of serenity and hope' (ibid.) in meeting Catherine Squarey Gibb (*b.* 1909), daughter of Reginald Morgan Weld-Smith of Seend Manor, Wiltshire. She was a former officer in government service and herself a widow, and became his second wife on 30 January 1979. This marriage was a union of exceptional beauty and happiness. Catherine gave him, through her all-embracing presence, intense interest, pertinent comments, and endless care, the strength and energy to renew his writing, disrupted by his first wife's prolonged illness. In his late seventies and early eighties, despite failing eyesight, he produced some of his most brilliant papers (published as a collection in 1988 entitled *Business, Time and Thought*). Among his many honours were visiting professorships at universities in America and Britain, honorary degrees from the universities of Ulster, Birmingham, and Strathclyde, and the fellowship of the British Academy, in 1967.

Already at the time of his retirement in 1969 Shackle had begun to feel rather out of sympathy with recent trends in economics, not least with the tendency to trust in supposedly self-contained mathematical models, the neglect of the history of ideas, and the belief that 'facts' can exist without pre-conceived classifications or concepts. All this seemed to him likely to lead the subject into disrepute. Nevertheless, his interest in the subject remained undiminished. Three months before he died on 3 March 1992 at the Woodhouse Nursing Home, Aldeburgh Road, Aldringham, Suffolk, he wrote: 'I hope to go on working at our subject for some time yet although I am 88 years old. I feel that if I stop working I shall stop living' (letter, 2 Dec 1991, *Economists in Discussion*). He was survived by his second wife, Catherine, and by two sons and one daughter from his first marriage. He was buried on 9 March in the churchyard of the parish church of St Peter and St Paul, Aldeburgh, Suffolk. STEPHEN F. FROWEN

Sources G. L. S. Shackle, 'A student's pilgrimage', *Banca Nazionale del Lavoro Quarterly Review*, 145 (June 1983), 107–16; repr. in *Business, time, and thought: selected papers of G. L. S. Shackle*, ed. S. F. Frowen (1988), 230–39 · G. L. S. Shackle, 'Speech by G. L. S. Shackle at the conference dinner of the George Shackle conference', *Unknowledge and choice in economics: proceedings of a conference in honour of G. L. S. Shackle*, ed. S. F. Frowen (1990), 192–6 · S. F. Frowen and C. Shackle, 'G. L. S. Shackle: bibliography', *Unknowledge and choice in economics: proceedings of a conference in honour of G. L. S. Shackle*, ed. S. F. Frowen (1990), 197–209 · M. Blaug and P. Surges, eds., *Who's who in economics: a biographical dictionary of major economists, 1700–1980* (1983), 348 · P. Arestis and M. Sawyer, eds., *A biographical dictionary of dissenting economists* (1992), 505–10 · C. F. Carter and J. L. Ford, eds., *Uncertainty and expectations in economics: essays in honour of G. L. S. Shackle* (1972) · G. C. Harcourt, 'Introduction: notes on an economic querist', *Unknowledge and choice in economics: proceedings of a conference in honour of G. L. S. Shackle*, ed. S. F. Frowen (1990), xvii–xxvi · M. Perlman, 'Perlman on Shackle', *Contemporary economists in perspective*, ed. H. W. Spiegel and W. J. Samuels (Greenwich, CT, 1984), 579–90 · M. Perlman, 'The fabric of economics and the golden threads of G. L. S. Shackle', *Unknowledge and choice in economics: proceedings of a conference in honour of G. L. S. Shackle*, ed. S. F. Frowen (1990), 9–10 · *Review of Political Economy*, 5/2 (1993) [G. L. S. Shackle memorial issue] · J. L. Ford, *G. L. S. Shackle: the dissenting economist's economist* (1994) · J. L. Ford, 'G. L. S. Shackle (1903–1992): a life with uncertainty', *Economic Journal*, 103 (1993), 583–97 · B. J. Loasby, 'George Lennox Sharman Shackle, 1903–1992', *PBA*, 84 (1994), 505–27 · P. E. Earl and S. F. Frowen, introduction; '1: G. L. S. Shackle, his life and work'; '2: the essence of Shackle's thought'; '3: the chapters in this volume', *Economics as an art of thought: essays in memory of G. L. S. Shackle*, ed. P. E. Earl and S. F. Frowen (2000), xiii–xxvi · K. Cann, 'Catalogue of the Shackle papers [at Cambridge University Library]', *Economics as an art of thought: essays in memory of G. L. S. Shackle*, ed. P. E. Earl and S. F. Frowen (2000), 368–418 · S. C. Littlechild, 'Disreputable adventures: the Shackle papers at Cambridge', *Economics as an art of thought: essays in memory of G. L. S. Shackle*, ed. P. E. Earl and S. F. Frowen (2000), 326–67 · S. F. Frowen, *Economists in discussion: the correspondence between G. L. S. Shackle and S. F. Frowen, 1951–1992* (2003) · private information (2004) · personal knowledge (2004) · b. cert. · m. cert. · d. cert.

Archives CUL, corresp. and papers · U. Lpool L., papers | BLPES, corresp. with editors of *Economic Journal* · CUL, corresp. with S. F. Frowen and H. M. Boettinger · Nuffield Oxf., corresp. with Lord Cherwell

Likenesses Ramsey & Muspratt, photograph, 1949, Cambridge · O. Thomas, drawing, 1983, priv. coll.; repro. in S. F. Frowen, ed., *Business, time, and thought: selected papers of G. L. S. Shackle* · O. Thomas, oils, 1983, priv. coll. · photograph, repro. in *The Independent* · photograph, repro. in *The Times*

Wealth at death £418,628: probate, 23 July 1992, *CGPLA Eng. & Wales*

Shackleton, Abraham (1696–1771), schoolmaster, was born on 27 October 1696 into a family of yeoman farmers, at Shackleton House, Harden, near Bingley, Yorkshire, the youngest of the six children of Richard Shackleton (1643–1705) and his wife, Sarah Brigg (1658–1703) of Keighley. His father, the first of the family to become a Friend, had suffered three years' imprisonment at York Castle for non-attendance at church, and the family home, Shackleton House, became a registered Quaker meeting-house in the year that Abraham was born.

Abraham's parents both died before he was nine, and at the age of twenty he sold his share of the family inheritance to his brother Roger (1691–1766) and took to studying Latin, duly becoming a good prose stylist. He then taught at David Hall's school at Skipton, Yorkshire, and on 7 October 1725 he married Margaret Wilkinson (1688–1768) of Knowlbank, a first cousin of his employer. In 1720 he moved to Ireland and became tutor to the children of two Quaker landowners, John Duckett of Duckett's Grove, co. Carlow, and William Cooper of nearby Cooper's Hill, Queen's county. With their encouragement he established, in 1726, a boarding-school for boys in the tree-lined, Quaker village of Ballitore, co. Kildare. The school was multi-denominational and took both native Irish and Anglo-Irish pupils alike, with a sprinkling from France, Scandinavia, and further afield. He was an extremely diligent and careful teacher, strong on fatherly oversight, and always set a good example of uprightness, temperance, and humility. Because of him Quakerism came to be better understood in Ireland and the Quakers admired. His most famous pupil was the statesman and philosopher Edmund Burke.

Shackleton retired in 1756, having educated over 500 boys in 30 years, and occupied himself with farming and occasional religious journeys, such as travelling around Ireland with Joseph Oxley in 1762 and to the yearly meeting of Friends in London in 1769 (when he also visited Burke at Beaconsfield). He died on 24 June 1771 at Ballitore, where he was interred in the Quaker burial-ground. Burke said of him that 'He was indeed a man of singular piety, rectitude and virtue and he had, along with these qualities, a native elegance of manners which nothing but genuine good nature and unaffected simplicity of heart can give' (Leadbeater, *Memoirs and Letters*, 98). He left one son, Richard [*see below*], and one daughter, Elizabeth Raynor.

Richard Shackleton (1726–1792), schoolmaster and poet, was born at Ballitore on 9 December 1726. He studied Hebrew and the classics, and became one of the leading Quaker scholars of his day. Educated at his father's school and Trinity College, Dublin, he subsequently taught at Ballitore School and was its master from 1756 to 1779. His cheerful, affectionate disposition opened his way with all ranks, and he became a lifelong friend of Edmund Burke, his contemporary at school and university. Sixty-four letters from Burke to him are printed in *The Leadbeater Papers* in a correspondence characterized by wit and by philosophical and moral discussion.

Shackleton greatly relished meeting such men as George Crabbe and Joshua Reynolds in Burke's circle; however, he kept his own worldly ambitions firmly under control. He lived a quiet, virtuous life, became a Quaker elder, and although not a minister he promoted Friends' principles in the school by his example, and through his correspondence greatly encouraged those who were in the ministry. He was a warm, compassionate man who practised daily spiritual retirement, seeking salvation through self-denial and humility. Burke said of him that 'No life was better … [or] more happily spent than his' (Leadbeater, *Papers*, 1.201). He was twice married: his first wife, whom he married on 2 April 1749, was Elizabeth Fuller (1726–1754), with whom he had four children and lived at Fuller's Court in Ballitore. She died on 19 May 1754 and on 17 October in the following year he married Elizabeth Carleton (1726–1804). They first lived at the school, then at Griesebank, and finally at The Retreat, in Ballitore.

In 1767 Shackleton inherited a small estate, with a farm, which was successfully operated by his wife, and a mill, which he rented. In 1779 he was succeeded as master of Ballitore School by his eldest son, Abraham *Shackleton (1752–1818), and thereafter he travelled frequently in Quaker service in Ireland and in England; there he often spent the summer months, attending London yearly meeting and visiting such friends as Burke and the industrialist Abiah Darby, for whom he wrote the poem 'On Travelling to Coalbrook Dale in the Night-Time', in both Latin and English versions, in 1783. With his second wife he had four children, including the writer Mary *Leadbeater (1758–1826), in whose *Poems* (1808) appear seven short compositions by her father. He was a round-faced man, whose portrait, commissioned by Burke, was painted in 1766 by Richard Sisson. He died of a fever, on 28 August 1792, while visiting Mountmellick, Queen's county, and was buried on 30 August in the Quaker burial-ground, Ballitore. PETER LAMB

Sources *DNB* · M. Leadbeater, *The Leadbeater papers*, 2 vols. (1862), esp. vol. 1 · M. Leadbeater, *Memoirs and letters of Richard and Elizabeth Shackleton late of Ballitore, Ireland* (1822) · M. Quane, 'Ballitore School', *Kildare Archaeological Journal*, 14/2 (1966–7), 174–209 · J. Shackleton, *The Shackletons of Ballitore: a genealogy, 1580–1987* (1989) · *A testimony concerning that worthy elder Abraham Shackleton, 26. 2nd mo. 1774*, Carlow monthly meeting (1774) · J. Kendall, ed., *Letters on religious subjects written by divers Friends deceased*, 1 (1802), nos. 22–132; 2 (1805), nos. 53–75 [letters by Richard Shackleton] · *A testimony regarding our dear deceased Friend Richard Shackleton*, Carlow monthly meeting (1793) · M. Leadbeater, *Poems by Mary Leadbeater (late Shackleton)* (1808) · private information (2004) [J. Shackleton] · register of deaths and burials, Carlow monthly meeting, Dublin Friends' Historical Library [Richard Shackleton]

Archives Dublin Friends' Historical Library, letters · Dublin Friends' Historical Library, letters and MS poems [Richard Shackleton] · Hunt. L., corresp. and papers [Richard Shackleton] · NL Ire., MSS [Richard Shackleton] · RS Friends, Lond., letters · RS Friends, Lond., letters and MS poems [Richard Shackleton] · TCD, MSS [Richard Shackleton] · U. Cal., Santa Barbara, MSS [Richard Shackleton] · Yale U., corresp. [Richard Shackleton] · Yale U., Beinecke L., corresp. and papers | NRA, corresp. with his son Richard · Sheff. Arch., corresp. with Edmund Burke [Richard Shackleton]

Likenesses R. Sisson, oils, 1766 (Richard Shackleton), priv. coll. · silhouette, RS Friends, Lond. · silhouette (Richard Shackleton), Religious Society of Friends, Dublin

Wealth at death family property, incl. Ballitore School, farmland, houses, The Retreat, Griesebank, and a mill

Shackleton, Abraham (1752–1818), schoolmaster and theologian, was born on 8 December 1752 at Ballitore, co.

Kildare, the eldest son of the four children of the Quaker Richard *Shackleton (1726–1792) [*see under* Shackleton, Abraham (1696–1771)], master of Ballitore School, and his first wife, Elizabeth Fuller (1726–1754), who died when Abraham was two years old. He was brought up by his stepmother, Elizabeth Carleton (1726–1804) of Dublin, who married his father in 1755; they had four further children, including the writer Mary *Leadbeater (1758–1826), chronicler of Ballitore village.

Shackleton's home, Ballitore (population *c*.400), was a Quaker settlement unique in Europe. Founded in the late seventeenth century and situated in a fertile valley 40 miles south of Dublin, it was a prosperous rural community with its meeting-house (1709), gardens, and orchards. The Shackletons were leading members of the community, being farmers, millers, and owners of the famous school founded in 1726 by Abraham's Yorkshire-born grandfather Abraham *Shackleton (1696–1771), which offered a liberal education to boy boarders from all religious backgrounds; it included among its alumni the statesman Edmund Burke, the United Irishman James Napper Tandy, and in the nineteenth century Cardinal Paul Cullen. Shackleton's father, Richard, a classical scholar, poet, and letter-writer, was a lifelong friend of Burke and an occasional associate of his circle in London; his stepmother, Elizabeth, the school matron, was an adventurous gardener who corresponded with the Quaker plant collector John Fothergill.

Shackleton entered Ballitore School in 1756. He too was a classical scholar and also a keen naturalist and amateur astronomer. He became a teacher and succeeded his father as master in 1779. On 23 February of the same year he married Lydia Mellor (1749–1829), an English schoolmaster's daughter from Edenderry, King's county, with whom he had nine children. He was an outspoken, deeply caring man but also a romantic; he rebuilt the family bolting mill as a castle in 1791 and kept a camel next door in the yard of his home, Griesebank.

Shackleton was a passionate anti-slavery campaigner and pacifist, and he gave up the use of tea, sugar, and all other produce of slave labour in his personal effort to promote the cause of abolition. During the Irish rising of 1798, when Ballitore was occupied by rebel forces, he refused at gunpoint, as a pacifist, to join them, and instead made his house a refuge for the injured of both sides. When the army regained control he negotiated for leniency on behalf of the rebels. His abhorrence of war led him in 1786 to stop teaching certain Latin authors in his school even though this meant a drop in pupil numbers (Latin was then a requirement for university entrance) and eventually the school was forced to close down temporarily in 1801. As his fellow liberal John Hancock wrote, 'to be in extremes was the error of this worthy man' (Hancock, 1). Thereafter he was a successful miller and a farmer given to agricultural improvement.

For many years Shackleton was an esteemed and active Quaker and he was still young when appointed an elder. However, he developed rationalist opinions about the Bible and matters of faith, similar to other Enlightenment thinkers. While admiring the poetical parts of the Old Testament he rejected many of its historical sections, especially that concerning the Canaanite wars. He similarly cherished the sublime morality taught by Christ but rejected the doctrine of the Trinity, expressing his views vigorously both in speech and in writing. He became identified with the New Lights, a group of liberal Quakers in Ulster who were in open rebellion against the Quaker discipline, particularly the marriage regulations. The movement spread, with Shackleton's help, to Leinster, and he was regarded as a particularly dangerous dissident because of his moral and intellectual eminence. His rebellious stand was reinforced by contact with the American Hannah Barnard, a progressive Quaker minister who was in Ireland between 1798 and 1800, and fierce opposition arose against them spearheaded by another visiting American Quaker, the evangelical David Sands, who 'like too many of his countrymen was fond of pushing the exercise of Church power to the uttermost extreme' (*Records and Collections*, 305). Shackleton, the friend of religious and civil liberty, became caught between the opposing forces of Enlightenment on the one hand and of evangelicalism and reaction on the other, and he was disowned by the Carlow monthly meeting in 1801. The wholesale resignations and disownments from the Society of Friends at this time became known as the Irish separation, and the society, considerably weakened by the loss of its spiritual and intellectual élite, fell into a period of stagnation. Shackleton and his fellow liberal John Bewley accompanied Hannah Barnard to England and acted as her counsellors during her dispute with the Quakers in London, but her progress was blocked and she returned to America taking the seeds of discord with her, which in due course led to the Hicksite separation of 1827–8.

Shackleton, who regretted the consequences of the schism, thereafter lived separate from all societies, writing great numbers of essays on philanthropic subjects, which occasionally appeared in periodicals; he also published a volume of poetry, *The Court of Apollo* (1815). Shackleton was intelligent and animated, with a light, well-proportioned physique. He died at home on 2 August 1818 after a short but painful illness, secure in his belief that 'God is Love', and, although a non-member, he was buried two days later in the Quaker burial-ground at Ballitore. He was survived by his wife, who died on 5 February 1829.

PETER LAMB

Sources M. Leadbeater, *The Leadbeater papers*, 2 vols. (1862) • J. Hancock, *A sketch of the character of Abraham Shackleton of Ballitore* (1818) • E. Shackleton, 'Character of her mother and father, Abraham and Lydia Shackleton. Ballitore 6th mo. 1827', MS, Dublin Friends' Historical Library, box B 32 f • W. Rathbone, *Narrative of events among the Quakers in Ireland* (1804) • *The records and recollections of James Jenkins*, ed. J. W. Frost (1984) • R. M. Jones, *The later periods of Quakerism*, 2 vols. (1921) • G. A. J. Hodgett, 'The Shackletons of Ballitore: some aspects of eighteenth-century Irish Quaker life', *Journal of the Friends' Historical Society*, 54 (1976–82), 217–34 • W. Hodgson, *The Society of Friends in the nineteenth century*, 1 (1875), chap. 2 • N. Newhouse, 'The Irish separation of 1800', *Friends Quarterly*, 7 and 10 (1971) • M. Grubb, 'Abraham Shackleton and the Irish separation of 1797–1803', *Journal of the Friends' Historical Society*, 56 (1990–93),

261–71 · M. Quane, 'Ballitore School', *Kildare Archaeological Journal*, 14/2 (1966–7), 174–209 · J. Shackleton, *The Shackletons of Ballitore: a geneology, 1580–1987* (1988) · O. Goodbody, *Guide to Irish Quaker records* (1967) · R. S. Harrison, *A biographical dictionary of Irish Quakers* (1997), 91–2 · Carlow monthly meeting, registry of deaths · Carlow monthly meeting, registry of burials

Archives Hunt. L., letters and MSS · Religious Society of Friends, Dublin, letters and MSS · RS Friends, Lond., letters and MSS · TCD, letters and MSS · U. Cal., Santa Barbara, letters and MSS

Likenesses silhouette (of Shackleton?), RS Friends, Lond.

Wealth at death owned Ballitore School; also mill and mill-house, Griesebank; plus farmland

Shackleton, Sir David James (1863–1938), trade unionist and politician, was born on 21 November 1863 at Cloughfold in north-east Lancashire, the only surviving child of a power-loom weaver, William Shackleton, and his wife, Margaret (*née* Gregory). Educated at a dame-school and then in Wesleyan and Anglican day schools, he began work at the age of nine as a half-timer in a weaving shed, becoming a full-timer at the age of thirteen. In 1883 he married Sarah Broadbent, a fellow mill worker; they had a son and a daughter.

Despite his later attendance at Accrington Mechanics' Institute, Shackleton never improved much on his limited education. Outside family life, in which he was a strong believer, his interests lay predominantly in temperance, trade unionism, and politics. As was the case with many of his contemporaries, his concern with labour questions derived mainly from his own experience. Hard-working, plain-spoken, and pragmatic, he became the best-known of the second generation of cotton union leaders. Fifteen months after joining the Accrington Weavers' Association he became a committee member and then president in 1889. He was briefly the full-time secretary of the Ramsbottom weavers before taking a similar position with the Darwen weavers, a post he held until 1907. In 1904 Shackleton was elected to the council of the TUC and it was a measure of his popularity that, unusually, he was elected president in successive years.

Shackleton had been returned as a Liberal to the Darwen town council in 1894 but contested the parliamentary seat of Clitheroe in 1902 for the new Labour Representation Committee. His return, unopposed by the Liberals, provided a significant boost for the nascent Labour Party, even though his programme was indistinguishable from that of an advanced Liberal. He maintained this stance throughout his short parliamentary career. He served as vice-chairman of his party between 1906 and 1908, but always believed that the trade unions were the most authentic and comprehensive representatives of working-class interests and that they should not be unduly constrained by the Labour Party connection. Coupled with his moderation, this attracted adverse comment from the party's socialists, of whom he was always deeply suspicious. Shackleton was included in a list of those described by Ben Tillett in 1907 as 'softly feline in their purring to Ministers and their patronage … betrayers of the class that willingly supports them' (Elton, 147). Although he was the most obvious successor when

Sir David James Shackleton (1863–1938), by Bassano, 1919

Keir Hardie retired from the chairmanship in 1908 he preferred to stand aside in favour of his closest parliamentary friend, Arthur Henderson.

Although he was never a great orator, Shackleton's stamina, imperturbability, and infectious laugh made him an effective parliamentarian. During discussions of workmen's compensation and factory legislation he acquired a deserved reputation for knowledge and fairness. His major achievement perhaps was to bring before the house the various TUC bills designed to reverse the Taff Vale judgment. When the Liberal government finally introduced appropriate legislation in 1906 his contribution was acknowledged at a Labour Party banquet when Keir Hardie expressed the hope that Shackleton's shadow would never grow less, a sly reference to his imposing physical appearance. Shackleton also spoke regularly against the half-time system then particularly prevalent in the textile industry, and he was instrumental in securing the establishment of a select committee to inquire into the conditions of home workers. Later he was a prime mover behind the introduction of the first Conciliation Bill, designed to further the cause of women's suffrage. As TUC president in 1908 and 1909 he was in constant negotiation with the government about the precise terms under which labour exchanges were set up and he did much to ensure that they did not become blackleg recruitment centres.

After successfully defending his seat in January 1910, Shackleton somewhat surprisingly abandoned both parliament and his trade union work by accepting a post as senior labour adviser at the Home Office. The following year he was made a national health insurance commissioner. In 1916 he was appointed permanent secretary of the newly created Ministry of Labour. This was an unusual but imaginative appointment since the emergency of war required that the new department's chief officer should enjoy the confidence of employers and trade unionists alike. A fellow MP once observed that the unions regarded Shackleton as a great man, and not only in the sense of avoirdupois, but he was never really able to convince them that the ministry's stance was neutral with regard to labour and capital. While his character may have won him the loyalty of his civil servants and ensured harmonious working relationships with ministers from different political traditions, his tenure of office was not entirely successful. He lacked the administrative ability to establish the new ministry on a sound basis and his caution allowed the Treasury to scale down its functions.

Knighted in 1917, Shackleton became chief labour adviser to the reorganized Ministry of Labour from 1920. Even after his official retirement in 1925 his expertise was still called upon and he served as a member of both the Industrial Transference Board and the south Wales miners' arbitration board. Otherwise, retirement to Lytham St Anne's in Lancashire allowed Shackleton to devote more time to his temperance work with the Rechabites, to resume his role as a JP, and to become honorary treasurer of the local branch of the League of Nations Union. He died at 27 Beach Road, Lytham St Anne's, on 1 August 1938 and was buried at Darwen cemetery. He was survived by his wife and a daughter. KENNETH D. BROWN

Sources D. E. Martin, 'Shackleton, Sir David James', *DLB*, 335–9, vol. 2 • R. Lowe, *Adjusting to democracy: the role of the ministry of labour in British politics, 1916–1939* (1986) • R. M. Martin, *TUC: the growth of a pressure group, 1868–1976* (1980) • B. Marsden, 'David James Shackleton, 1863–1938', MA diss., Manchester Polytechnic, 1991 • K. D. Brown, *Labour and unemployment, 1900–1914* (1971) • H. Tracey, ed., *The British labour party: its history, growth, policy, and leaders*, 3 (1948) • Lord Elton [G. Elton], *The life of James Ramsay MacDonald* (1939) • J. Hodge, *Workman's cottage to Windsor Castle* (1931) • M. A. Hamilton, *Arthur Henderson: a biography* (1938) • C. J. Wrigley, *Arthur Henderson* (1990) • d. cert. • *The Times* (2 Aug 1938)

Archives HLRO, papers • Labour History Archive and Study Centre, Manchester, papers

Likenesses W. Stoneman, photographs, 1917–33, NPG • Bassano, photograph, 1919, NPG [*see illus.*] • G. Lord, photograph, NPG

Wealth at death £7288 6*s*. 2*d*.: probate, 8 Nov 1938, *CGPLA Eng. & Wales*

Shackleton, Edward Arthur Alexander, **Baron Shackleton** (**1911–1994**), explorer and politician, was born on 15 July 1911, the younger son and youngest of three children of Sir Ernest Henry *Shackleton (1874–1922), Antarctic explorer, and his wife, Emily Mary (1868–1936), second daughter of Charles Dorman, of Towngate, Wadhurst, Sussex. Although long overshadowed by his famous father, commander of the 1909 national Antarctic expedition, Shackleton hardly knew him. From the age of two until Sir Ernest's death off South Georgia when he was ten, his father was exploring or on naval missions. He was brought up by his mother, Emily, and her Victorian mother, to whom he attributed his self-reliance. Educated at Radley College and then at Magdalen College, Oxford, he arranged the 1932 Oxford expedition to Sarawak, serving as its surveyor. He chose a tropical forest rather than the Antarctic to 'be my own person' and avoid the charge that he was 'playing on my father's reputation' (Parliamentary Profiles files). Having achieved the first known ascent of Borneo's Mount Mulu, he led the 1934–5 Oxford expedition to Ellesmere Island. He recounted these expeditions in *Arctic Journeys* (1937) and *Borneo Jungle* (1938). On 27 April 1938 he married Betty Muriel Marguerite, daughter of Captain Charles Homan, elder brother of Trinity House. (Shackleton himself became an honorary elder brother of Trinity House in 1980.) They had two children, Alexandra (*b*. 1940) and Charles (1942–1979).

After lecturing in Europe and America on his travels, Shackleton joined the BBC as a talks producer in Ulster, whose sectarianism shocked him. He was sacked by the BBC after an abrasive period as a minister of information supervisor of the German service. In 1940 he joined the RAF's Coastal Command as an intelligence officer and anti-U-boat planner. Twice cited in dispatches, he rose to wing commander and, instead of receiving the DFC, was appointed OBE, which he derided as 'Other Buggers' Efforts' and a product of the 'snobbery that operated in high places against Coastal Command' (Parliamentary Profiles files).

Although a former treasurer of the Oxford University Conservative Association, by the late 1930s Shackleton had joined the Labour Party. Beaten by Roy Jenkins as the Labour candidate for winnable Solihull, he did not win much-less-hopeful Epsom and Ewell in June 1945. Despite his slogan of 'With Shackleton to the poll', he also failed against Winston Churchill's favourite, Brendan Bracken, at the November 1945 by-election in hopeless Bournemouth. He finally secured a nomination in Preston to defeat Harmar Nicholls in January 1946. The minister of supply, George Strauss, named him his parliamentary private secretary in 1949, but he was soon 'filched' by Herbert Morrison, leader of the Commons, then foreign secretary and perpetual aspirant to replace Clement Attlee as Labour's leader. When Shackleton's seat was divided, he very narrowly survived in Preston South in 1950 (by 149 votes) and 1951 (by 16). After Labour went into opposition in 1951, Morrison exploited Shackleton's friendship with Richard Crossman, in whose Vincent Square home he had roomed, to try to forge an anti-Attlee link with the left-wing rebels, the 'Bevanites'. Shackleton himself was a non-factional moderate, widely liked and respected, and closest to Roy Jenkins because of their shared pro-Europeanism and liking for proportional representation, which alienated Shackleton from the anti-European Hugh Gaitskell and first-past-the-posters.

Because of the bitter factionalism of the time, Shackleton was not too sorry to lose his seat to Alan Green, subsequently financial secretary to the Treasury, in the 1955 election. He became a director (1955–64 and 1973–82), and deputy chairman (1975–82) of the John Lewis Partnership. He enjoyed himself intellectually, writing the biography of his hero, Fridtjof Nansen (1959), the Norwegian explorer and humanitarian. Still in his forties, Shackleton was a natural choice for Labour's first list of life peers, when created by Harold Macmillan in 1958. He was also a natural choice for the post of minister for the RAF when Labour returned to power in 1964. He was sworn of the privy council in 1966 and became deputy leader of the House of Lords in 1967. Crossman, then leader of the House of Commons, was determined that his friend should nail down the details of the 'Crossman reform', phasing out the voting rights of the mainly Conservative hereditary peers with the collaboration of such reformist tory lords as Jellicoe and Carrington. But foreign secretary George Brown again 'filched' Shackleton for the tricky task of extricating the terrorist-besieged British forces from Aden, despite Crossman's 'We can't spare him' plaint. By his return, the 'Crossman reforms' had aroused the ire of James Callaghan and Iain Macleod, and were talked out in the Commons by Enoch Powell, Michael Foot, and Robert Sheldon.

In 1968 Shackleton became leader of the House of Lords, paymaster-general (taking over security from Lord Wigg), and minister in charge of the civil service. He widened entry to the civil service and improved career prospects for its scientists, implementing many of the recommendations of the Fulton report of 1968. Labour's defeat in 1970 converted him into the leader of the opposition in the Lords until 1974. He parted company with most Labour parliamentarians by joining Roy Jenkins in backing Edward Heath's effort to join the EEC. When Labour unexpectedly returned to power in March 1974, Shackleton made clear that he was not available for full-time politics. He had rejoined the John Lewis board, and had become a director of Rio Tinto Zinc (he was its deputy chairman from 1975 to 1982). In 1973 he told RTZ that the prospects of traffic revenue from a channel tunnel were 'embarrassingly favourable' (Parliamentary Profiles files).

When James Callaghan replaced Harold Wilson as prime minister and leader of the Labour Party in 1976, Shackleton willingly surveyed how to develop the economy of the Falkland Islands by expanding fisheries and by exploiting gas and oil resources. In his report he argued forcibly that, given sufficient investment, the Falkland Islands were economically sustainable. He also emphasized that the majority of the islanders wanted to remain British. He was subsequently a vociferous campaigner for the retention of the ice patrol ship HMS *Endurance* (named after his father's ship) in the south Atlantic. Shackleton's report was updated for Margaret Thatcher six years later, after the Falklands War had underlined his recommendations about the need for an adequate airport and the retention of the *Endurance*, whose withdrawal had precipitated the Argentine invasion. In 1978 Shackleton was called upon to conduct a review of the Prevention of Terrorism Act; he concluded by broadly endorsing its operation. Never a narrow sectarian, he aroused Labour hackles when, with Lord Lever, he endorsed the candidacy of their fellow pro-European Roy Jenkins as the Social Democratic Party candidate for Hillhead, Glasgow, in 1982. He apologized gracefully to Labour peers. For sixteen years he was the chairman of the political honours scrutiny committee. He again achieved public prominence in 1993 by complaining that the Conservative government had handed out titles in return for donations.

Shackleton was remembered as a tall, square-shouldered man, with wavy hair and spectacles, very affable and charming. He under-estimated himself as merely an 'organisational and administrative type, concerned with whether a thing will work or not' (Parliamentary Profiles files). His friend Richard Crossman, never generous with praise, wrote that he was 'as sensible and solid a man as you'll find anywhere' (*Diaries*, 2.704). He was a keen tennis player and swimmer, and swam regularly in the Serpentine on new year's day. In his retirement he windsurfed in Cornwall, hang-glided in Australia, and travelled again to the Arctic to re-acquaint himself with the landscape and its people. He died on 22 September 1994 at Lymington, Hampshire, and was survived by his wife and daughter; his son predeceased him. A memorial service was held in Westminster Abbey on 25 January 1995. ANDREW ROTH

Sources Parliamentary Profiles files · R. H. S. Crossman, *The diaries of a cabinet minister*, 2 (1976) · *The Times* (24 Sept 1994) · *The Independent* (24 Sept 1994) · *The Guardian* (24 Sept 1994) · *WWW*, *1991–5* · Burke, *Peerage* · *CGPLA Eng. & Wales* (1995)

Archives BLPES, interview · HLRO, corresp. and papers; papers · Scott Polar RI, corresp., journal, and papers

Likenesses N. Sinclair, photograph, 1992, NPG · photograph, repro. in *The Times* · photograph, repro. in *The Independent* · photograph, repro. in *The Guardian*

Wealth at death under £125,000: probate, 16 Jan 1995, *CGPLA Eng. & Wales*

Shackleton [*née* Parker], **Elizabeth** (1726–1781), diarist, was the daughter of John Parker (1695–1754), a London-based linen draper, and his wife, Elizabeth Southouse, the daughter of an Essex merchant. She was probably the Elizabeth baptized on 22 December 1726 at St Peter Cornhill, London. In 1728 her father inherited Browsholme Hall in the West Riding of Yorkshire, close to the Lancashire border, and substantial farm lands worth almost £500 in annual rent. After her mother's premature death, some time in the early 1740s, Elizabeth Parker became mistress of this grand house, later described as 'an old magnificent chateau, an extensive and venerable pile' (*GM*, 1st ser., 65/1, 1795, 82). The archive of family letters conjures a much loved only daughter, thought witty, accomplished, clever, and lively, but still dutiful and affectionate. John Parker was considered indulgent of his daughter, and outsiders thought she knew how to manage him. The Parkers and the Southouses had great matrimonial expectations for Elizabeth and shepherded her about the usual stalls in the marriage market—Preston assemblies, the Wakefield races, and the London season—in sumptuous silks.

To the consternation of her kindred, in 1745 Elizabeth revealed her partiality for her second cousin, Robert Parker (1720–1758) of Alkincoats, near Colne in the Lancashire Pennines. As a member of the lesser gentry, Robert was hardly the glittering matrimonial prize that Elizabeth's family had hoped for. Her relatives complained about his small fortune: the Alkincoats estate comprised only 160 acres and yielded a comparatively modest £290 per annum in rent, weaknesses that Robert conceded. However, he was a county office-holder, was reputed to have provided horses to the Jacobites in the rising of 1745, and was a keen sportsman and shot, so he must have cut a dashing figure. More unusually, he had read medicine at Emmanuel College, Cambridge, in the early 1740s, and was famous across the north for his rabies medicine. He showed extraordinary persistence in the face of John Parker's rebuffs and Elizabeth's prevarication, finally wooing her by the old ruse of telling her he was preparing to marry someone else. They were married by special licence on 1 October 1751 and set up home at Alkincoats.

In preparation for Elizabeth's residence Robert Parker initiated rebuilding work in 1751–2 at Alkincoats, intending to make it comfortable but not grand. Judging by friendly reactions, he succeeded in his aim, Elizabeth being teased by her friends that hers would be 'a good, though odd house' (Vickery, *The Gentleman's Daughter*, 20). As her best friend, Jane Scrimshire, remarked, she had elected to 'live in a narrow Compass to pass your days with the man you love' (Lancs. RO, DDB Ac 7886/225). By contrast her brother Edward married the daughter of a baronet in 1754, 'a prudent choice … to keep up the dignity of his family which few in this Giddy Age thinks of' (ibid., DDB/72/77), and thus became related to the nobility of Yorkshire, Westmorland, and Cheshire. Both Edward Parker and his son John were listed on the commission of the peace for the West Riding of Yorkshire, while John Parker became MP for Clitheroe in 1780. Edward Parker's was certainly the milieu of the greater gentry, while his sister's social horizons were, by comparison, decidedly parochial.

However, Elizabeth's happy Lancashire marriage was short-lived. Robert Parker died in 1758, leaving her a widow with three small sons and an estate to manage. Her diaries begin in 1762, and from the early 1770s were divided under three headings: 'Letters to friends and upon business', 'Remarkable occurrences', and 'Ordinary occurrences, memorandums and accounts'. Doubling as household manuals, the thirty-nine volumes reveal her as an indefatigable manager of her children, household, servants, and provisioning, and also catalogue the material culture of the local élite, with its Gillows mahogany, elegant silverware, inherited cabinets, and the newest millinery. She also successfully marketed the anti-rabies medicine inherited from her first husband, which sold across the north of England for a shilling a bottle; the 'Colne medicine' was even celebrated in the *Leeds Mercury*.

In 1765, after seven years of increasingly sociable widowhood, Elizabeth startlingly eloped to Gretna Green with John Shackleton (1744–1788) of nearby Stone Edge, Barrowford. This local woollen merchant was eighteen years her junior and their elopement was a sensation in the area. By her actions Elizabeth forfeited her brother's society for six years and was barred from Browsholme. Why Elizabeth married the young calamanco dealer is not recorded for posterity, but it can only have been her own free choice to do so. The outcome was disastrous.

The Shackletons repented at leisure. Within five years John was deeply discontented, and habitually sought escape from his marriage in hunting, shooting, fishing, and the bottle. Although Elizabeth struggled to maintain her dignity, her husband's drunkenness undermined their social standing, frustrating Elizabeth's management of the household and setting a poor example to her sons and male dependants. She complained bitterly about his drunken roistering with the servants, with tenants, and with workmen in the ale house, in the servant's hall, and even on dreadful occasions in the parlour. He bore little resemblance to the self-controlled gentleman of the conduct books: 'The gentleman came home near 12 at noon & Sans Cermony went snoring to clean bed—where he farted and stunk like a Pole Cat' (Lancs. RO, DDB/81/17, fol. 87). The diaries written between 1772 and 1781 catalogue the steady worsening of relations during the last nine years of marriage. The apparent intensification of strife may be reflected in Elizabeth Shackleton's use of larger diaries in her last years; perhaps she simply had more room to record her husband's misdemeanours, yet the escalation does seem a genuine expression of an ominous shift in the balance of power between the couple. In 1779 things took a further turn for the worse when her son Thomas Parker, who had inherited Alkincoats in 1775, married Elizabeth (Betty) Parker of Newton Hall, Yorkshire, and Elizabeth was forced to move from Alkincoats to John Shackleton's newly built mansion, Pasture House, at Barrowford. 1780 was the Shackletons' worst year together: John was suffering from attacks of gout but his confidence and ill will increased in his own house, while Elizabeth was entering her fatal last illness. Even then Shackleton did not forbear:

> he struck me violently many a time. Took the use out of my Arm, swell'd from my Shoulder to my wrist, the skin knock'd off at my elbow in great Misery and pain he afterwards got up & left my bed, went into a nother room pritty Matrimonial comforts god Bless and help me. (Lancs. RO, DDB/81/39, fol. 204)

Having been dropped by her brother, her most powerful living relative, she was cut off from her most obvious protector, and was probably reluctant to lose face by denouncing as a brute the husband she had eloped with. The private confessional of the diary appears to have been her only outlet. In May 1779 she was already seeking reconciliation with approaching death: 'I left off my old stays & put on my best stays for Good' (ibid., DDB/81/35, fol. 73). Her last entry ends on a characteristic note of mournful dignity: 'A wet close day, my foot most shocking painful. about one Mr. S. & I went off to dine at good old Alkincoats good luck to us' (ibid., DDB/81/39, fol. 231). She died at her home in 1781, probably at the end of August, and was buried on 2 September at Colne parish church.

Elizabeth's diaries demonstrate a strong sense of family continuity (a perennial concern of the lesser gentry), showing her lingering lovingly over her mother's old lace, and passing cherished items on to her sons. These private rituals assured her that some part of her would endure. Her Parker descendants kept her manuscripts for successive generations, eventually depositing them in the Lancashire Record Office; the last love letters were given up by the family in 1995. Although a ravenous reader of novels, pamphlets, and newspapers, and a tireless writer, Elizabeth never sat for her portrait nor left a will, and the only memorials in her time were the bracelet she commissioned in 1776, made from her own hair, and her plaque in Colne church. Her letters and diaries, first systematically exploited by Amanda Vickery in *The Gentleman's Daughter: Women's Lives in Georgian England* (1998), have now revealed her significance as an observer of and participant in the social, cultural, and economic life of women and men in eighteenth-century northern England. Forming a vast archive of immense value to historians, her manuscripts have survived as her lasting monument.

AMANDA VICKERY

Sources Lancs. RO, Parker of Browsholme MSS, DDB • A. Vickery, *The gentleman's daughter: women's lives in Georgian England* (1998) • G. Whittaker and W. M. Spencer, eds., *Parochial chapelry of Colne: register of baptisms and burials, 1774–1789* (1969) [transcribed by G. Whittaker] • *IGI* • A. Vickery, 'Women and the world of goods: a Lancashire consumer and her possessions, 1751–1781', *Consumption and the world of goods*, ed. J. Brewer and R. Porter (1993), 274–304

Archives Lancs. RO, Parker of Browsholme MSS, diaries, DDB/81/1–39

Sir Ernest Henry Shackleton (1874–1922), by Frank Hurley, 1915

Shackleton, Sir Ernest Henry (1874–1922), Antarctic explorer, was born on 15 February 1874 at Kilkea House, co. Kildare, Ireland, the elder son and the second of the ten children of Henry Shackleton (1847–1921), physician, and his wife, Henrietta Letitia Sophia (1845–1926), daughter of Henry John Gavan of Wallstown, Co. Cork. Shackleton's father was Anglo-Irish of Yorkshire descent, while his mother was Irish.

Early life and education Because of the failure of the potato harvest, Henry Shackleton abandoned farming and took his family to Dublin in 1880, returning to Trinity College to read medicine. He qualified in 1884 and settled in England, first briefly in Croydon and then for good in Sydenham, the fashionable London suburb where Ernest Shackleton grew up, not far from the Crystal Palace. Taught at home by a governess until the age of eleven, Ernest's first school was Fir Lodge preparatory school, near his home, Aberdeen House, in West Hill. In 1887 he went to Dulwich College, which was also within walking distance, as a day boy. No conventional scholar (though he came second in English history and literature in his final year), he left school in April 1890 aged sixteen to join the mercantile marine, serving in the White Star Line, the Shire Line, and the Union Castle Line, and making several voyages round the world. He first sailed as boy in the full rigged ship *Hoghton Tower*, 17,000 tons displacement, bound for Valparaiso, and round the Horn. In August 1894 he passed for second mate, soon afterwards transferring to the tramp steamer *Monmouthshire* as third mate. He spent the next five years in voyages to the Far East and America, gaining his master's certificate in April 1898 at the age of twenty-four.

In 1899 Shackleton gained an appointment with the Union Castle Line of mail ships which offered better prospects and a more regular existence than the tramp steamers. Shackleton's first biographer, H. R. Mill, records his arrival on board one of these ships in the East India Dock 'without an overcoat' on a January day, 'carrying one or two books under his arm'. He immediately started to talk of Browning to his fellow officers, giving the impression 'that he was distinctive and a departure from the usual type of young officer'. Later on, Mill's informant continued, 'I found he was several types bound into one volume' (Mill, 51–2). Brought up at home and educated at school to a love of literature, he read widely at sea, enjoying poetry, in particular that of Browning.

During one of Shackleton's spells ashore while employed by the Union Castle Line, he became a fellow of the Royal Geographical Society of London, with which body he had a lifelong association. Meanwhile the outbreak of the Second South African War led to his transfer as third officer in 1899 to the *Tintagel Castle*, 3500 tons register, which was carrying troops from Southampton to the Cape. During two voyages he organized concerts and sports for the men and signalling classes for the officers, plus a spectacular visit from Neptune, on crossing the Line. Together with the surgeon Dr W. McLean, he published a record of the voyage of March 1900, entitled *O.H.M.S.* (on her majesty's service), in the following August. After two more voyages to the Cape as third officer in the *Gaika* and then the *Carisbrooke Castle* of 7600 tons, he was given leave by Union Castle to take up the post of junior officer on board the steam yacht *Discovery*, the newly built wooden barque which carried the members of the national Antarctic expedition of 1901–4 to the Southern Ocean.

The national Antarctic expedition, 1901–1904 Shackleton's chance to achieve distinction came with this appointment. According to H. R. Mill, who met him during the voyage south, the expedition was 'an opportunity and nothing more'—he would have been just as eager to join a treasure-hunting voyage or to search for the island of St Brendan. 'He had no natural affinity for the polar regions, no genius for scientific research', but an 'over-mastering passion' for his future wife gave him the ambition to excel and make himself worthy of her (Mill, 57). The national Antarctic expedition was the brainchild of Sir Clements Markham, elected president of the Royal Geographical Society in 1893. Organized by a joint committee of the Royal Geographical Society and the Royal Society at a time when the interior of the Antarctic continent was unexplored, its aims were both geographical and scientific. The leader was Commander Robert Falcon Scott RN, with Lieutenant A. B. Armitage, Royal Naval Reserve, as second in command. According to H. R. Mill, Shackleton was appointed mainly because of his experience in sail, the *Discovery* being a three-masted barque with an auxiliary engine. Through a chance meeting at sea, he had been recommended by Cedric, son of the expedition's benefactor, Llewellyn Longstaff.

As junior officer, Shackleton was given a commission as sub-lieutenant, Royal Naval Reserve, on 1 July 1901 and the duty of determining the density and salinity of sea-water samples throughout the voyage—a task he found irksome. More congenial was his charge of the stores, after long experience with the Shire Line. He was later given responsibility for the catering on board and, once ashore, put in charge of making up sledging rations and leading one of the very first Antarctic sledge journeys from *Discovery*'s winter quarters at the head of McMurdo Sound. During winter 1902 Shackleton edited and typed the first volume of the *South Polar Times*, which was illustrated largely by his good friend the junior surgeon, Dr Edward Adrian (Billy) Wilson.

Captain Scott chose Shackleton and Wilson to accompany him on the foremost of the summer sledging journeys—towards the south pole, over the 'Great Ice Barrier' (now known as the Ross Ice Shelf) discovered by Captain James Clark Ross. Shackleton was put in charge of the dogs, finding out how to drive them and also practising with ski. Because the dogs died or had to be shot one after another, owing to a diet of Norwegian 'stock-fish' recommended by Dr Fridtjof Nansen, the great Arctic explorer and scientist, their furthest south was a disappointing 82°15′ S opposite a wide valley, which Scott named Shackleton Inlet. Nevertheless, this was the first long-distance sledge journey into the interior of the continent and was less than 500 miles from the south pole. During the return journey all three men showed signs of scurvy and Shackleton coughed blood. He was forbidden to pull the sledge and to do any of the heavy work, but (contrary to Sir Clements Markham's assertion in his posthumously published *Lands of Silence*, 1920), he struggled on and was carried briefly on the sledge only to brake it in a southerly gale.

On the advice of the two surgeons, Shackleton was invalided home in the relief ship *Morning*, his departure being much regretted by his comrades. Scott reported:

> This gentleman has performed his work in a highly satisfactory manner, but unfortunately his constitution has proved unequal to the rigours of a polar climate. It is with great reluctance that I order his return, and trust that it will be made evident that I do so solely on account of his health and that his future prospects may not suffer. (RGS, archives, AA 12/4/1)

On his return to England, Shackleton published an account of his experiences during the national Antarctic expedition (for *Pearson's Magazine*) which praised the devotion and unselfishness of his two companions on the southern journey. He assisted in the fitting-out of the second relief ship, *Terra Nova*, in 1903 and was there to welcome the *Discovery* home to the Thames in September 1904, later receiving the polar medal with most other members of the expedition.

The British Antarctic expedition, 1907–1909 Meanwhile, in January 1904 Shackleton had been appointed secretary of the Royal Scottish Geographical Society in Edinburgh and married Emily Mary Dorman (1868–1936), one of his sisters' friends, in Westminster on 9 April 1904; she was the daughter of Charles Dorman of Wadhurst, Sussex. He fought a bonny but unsuccessful fight in Dundee as Liberal Unionist candidate for parliament at the general election of 1906 and exchanged the secretaryship of the society for one at the Parkhead engineering works at Glasgow, owned by William Beardmore (later Lord Invernairn).

It was Beardmore who first subscribed to Shackleton's British Antarctic expedition of 1907–9 and after three years' hard struggle to raise funds, Shackleton was able to announce the expedition, amid fears of foreign competition, in February 1907. It was a shock to receive a letter from Captain Scott in Gibraltar expressing concern at Shackleton's plans, which conflicted with his own, as yet unannounced. After some tense but restrained correspondence Shackleton agreed not to establish winter quarters in McMurdo Sound or vicinity and to land elsewhere for his attempt on the south pole.

During the months that followed, Shackleton engaged the scientists and shore party, bought an old sealer, *Nimrod* (some 200 tons), and took advice from Nansen and others, making some innovations, including the purchase of Manchurian ponies. Because he could not afford a larger vessel, some of these and other items had to be left behind in New Zealand. The *Nimrod* was towed from Lyttelton by the steamer *Koonya* (Captain F. P. Evans) for 1500 miles through tempestuous seas, as far as the Antarctic circle. Unable to reach King Edward VII Land and unwilling to risk establishing winter quarters on the floating ice shelf (having found that large portions had broken away),

Shackleton very reluctantly made the decision, after much soul-searching, to return west to McMurdo Sound, thus breaking his promise to Scott, the safety of his men being paramount in his mind. Winter quarters were established at Cape Royds on Ross Island, north of the old *Discovery* hut, while *Nimrod* (Captain Rupert England) returned to New Zealand.

The shore party consisted of fifteen men, including Shackleton. Professor T. W. Edgeworth David and Douglas Mawson had embarked at Sydney. Their sledge journey to the south magnetic pole was one of the three foremost achievements of this expedition. The other two achievements were, first, the ascent and survey of Mount Erebus (12,448 feet), the active volcano on Ross Island and, second, the southern sledge journey, which reached within 100 miles of the south pole.

Only four moderately fit ponies had survived, so that Shackleton reduced the pole party to four—J. B. Adams, E. H. Marshall, Frank Wild, and himself. Keeping at a greater distance from the Western Mountains than had Scott, and thus sighting more of the many peaks, Shackleton named an outlying nunatak Mount Hope because it guarded the entrance to the great Beardmore Glacier, the way towards the polar plateau of some 10,000 feet and the south pole. Here they were far beyond Scott, Shackleton, and Wilson's turning point from the *Discovery*. The last pony fell to its death in a crevasse, fortunately not taking Wild too. Suffering sharp pangs of hunger, they struggled on in tattered clothes against bitter winds until on 9 January 1909 Shackleton reluctantly decided at an estimated 88°23′ S that they must go no further. Queen Alexandra's union flag was flown, and in H. R. Mill's words, they 'turned their backs on their unreached goal and started their race of 700 miles, with Death on his pale horse, the blizzard, following close' (Mill, 144–5).

Good fortune enabled them to descend the Beardmore at speed without serious accident and to locate the depots left on the outward journey. The horse flesh gave them dysentery, but they had to march on northwards, fearing that the *Nimrod* (Captain F. P. Evans) would depart for New Zealand before their return. She did in fact wait beyond the appointed date, and after picking up a sledge carrying geological specimens, steamed northwards on 4 March 1909 with all members of the expedition safely on board. Shackleton had made a tremendous advance towards the south and had shown his powers of leadership. He had taken risks, but his decisions turned out to be right. His men called it Shackleton's luck (he called it Providence), and he could claim to have borne out the family motto *Fortitudine vincimus* (By endurance, we conquer).

One of the special features of the expedition was the composition and actual printing in winter quarters of the *Aurora Australis*, copies being bound with boards from the packing cases (reprinted in facsimile, 1986). During his homeward voyage from New Zealand by liner, Shackleton worked with a literary assistant, Edward Saunders, so that his fine two-volume narrative, *The Heart of the Antarctic*, could be published in October 1909. His wife was waiting at Dover, where she had last seen him, and it was to her that he remarked (regarding his decision to turn back when so near the pole), 'better a living donkey than a dead lion' (Mill, 159). Lionized, knighted, and awarded many honours on his return, Shackleton went on to make lecture tours of the British Isles, Canada, and the United States during the latter part of 1909 and 1910. On the continent he met many of the crowned heads of Europe in a world soon to be swept away by war and revolution. Shackleton was fortunate that the expedition's debts of some £20,000 were paid by the government. However, he had no notions of thrift, and gave much of the income from his lectures and book to relatives and charities. One of his imaginative gestures was to have *Nimrod* towed under the Thames bridges to Temple Pier, where the public could go aboard, the proceeds from the venture being given to the London hospitals.

The imperial trans-Antarctic expedition, 1914–1917 Some years passed in the pursuit of business ventures, which failed. During those years Amundsen and Scott had reached the south pole and Peary the north pole. Other Antarctic expeditions had sailed and returned. There was one last great journey—the crossing of the Antarctic continent—that could be made and Shackleton resolved to attempt it. His plan was to secure two ships (in the event, *Endurance* and *Aurora*), in the first of which he would sail to the head of the Weddell Sea. After crossing via the south pole with dog teams, he would be met in McMurdo Sound by the *Aurora*, depots having been laid by the Ross Sea party to be picked up on the second half of the crossing. The announcement of the imperial trans-Antarctic expedition was made in December 1913. After initial difficulties in fund-raising, Sir James Caird of Dundee, the jute manufacturer, gave £24,000, the government £10,000, and the Royal Geographical Society £1000. On the brink of the First World War, *Endurance* was ready to sail. When war broke out Shackleton offered to hand her over with crew and stores to the Admiralty, but the offer was refused. After consulting George V and his benefactor, Sir James Caird, he decided to proceed, *Endurance* setting sail in August, followed in September by Shackleton, who joined her at Buenos Aires in October. Reaching South Georgia in early November, *Endurance* left Grytviken on 5 December, crossing the Antarctic circle on 30 December 1914. Caird Coast was discovered on 11 January 1915.

Thereafter Shackleton's plans went completely awry. No landing on the continent was made from the icebound Weddell Sea. On 18 January 1915 *Endurance* was beset in heavy pack ice and was eventually (27 October 1915) crushed and sunk, leaving expedition members camped on the floes, fortunately drifting northwards. After getting under way from the ice edge on 9 April 1916 they escaped to desolate Elephant Island, which they reached on 15 April in three boats named after his benefactors: the *Stancomb-Wills*, the *Dudley Docker*, and the *James Caird*. Shackleton, Frank Worsley, and four companions left most of the party in Frank Wild's charge, and on 24 April embarked upon the epic voyage of 800 miles in the *Caird*, a 22 foot boat, across the Southern Ocean in some of the stormiest seas in the world, landing at Cape Rosa in South

Georgia on 10 May. To reach the whaling stations on the far side of the island, Shackleton, Worsley, and Crean crossed the unclimbed and unsurveyed Allardyce Range, which is its spine, with a length of rope and a carpenter's adze, arriving at Stromness whaling station on 20 May to the astonishment of the manager and the admiration of the rugged Norwegians. Even before the explorer's reappearance in the war-torn world of 1916, the Admiralty had set about planning a search expedition in the *Discovery*, which her then owners, the Hudson's Bay Company, lent free of charge. However, before she arrived and after three failed attempts, he took off the marooned party from Elephant Island in the Chilean steamer *Yelcho* on 30 August 1916, finding them 'All safe, all well!'

Fêted in South America, Shackleton sailed in a steamer from San Francisco to New Zealand in October 1916 to relieve the stranded Ross Sea party, led by Aeneas Mackintosh, which had been organized by Shackleton to lay deposits for the *Endurance* party once the latter had sledged across the continent from the Weddell Sea. His ship, *Aurora*, had been repaired (after drifting for ten months in the pack ice) with funds provided by the British, Australian, and New Zealand governments, while friends relieved his own financial worries with loans that were repaid when the *Aurora* was eventually sold. Anxious to rescue his men himself, he nevertheless accepted in the end the Australian committee's stipulation that Captain John King Davis should command the relief expedition to the Ross Sea, while Shackleton would be in charge of any land journeys. He signed on as supernumerary officer under Davis in the *Aurora* and the vessel arrived off Cape Royds, his old winter quarters, on 10 January 1917. Soon six men and a dog sledge arrived with a tale to tell of heroism and tragedy.

The depots had indeed been laid as far as the Beardmore Glacier. Travelling for more than 1500 miles in 160 days, the Ross Sea party only narrowly escaped disaster on the return journey. One man died (the Revd Arnold Spencer Smith). Two others (Mackintosh and Victor Hayward) died later when the sea ice, on which they were travelling, broke up. Shackleton later lectured in Australia in aid of Mackintosh's widow. He was also persuaded to dictate the more exciting episodes of the expedition to Edward Saunders, in case he were killed in the war. The book (*South*) was not published until 1919. It was dedicated 'To my comrades who fell in the white warfare of the south and on the red fields of France and Flanders'. In 1974, at a soirée to commemorate Shackleton's birth, Sir Vivian Fuchs, who had made the first crossing of Antarctica in 1957–8, concluded that Shackleton's crossing party might just have made it, given good weather and terrain, experienced drivers, and well-trained dogs (Fuchs, 14–18).

Last years, 1917–1922 Anxious to serve his country and the British empire during the First World War, but—according to H. R. Mill—unable to forgive the Admiralty for not allowing him to enter the navy in 1903 (Mill, 250), Shackleton did not go to sea again, as might have been expected. He carried out a propaganda mission on behalf of the Foreign Office in South America in late 1917 and early 1918. He was then given a commission as major and put in charge of equipment for the winter campaign (1918–19) of the north Russian expeditionary force, based in Murmansk on the staff of Major-General Charles Clarkson Martin Maynard, who found him an easier subordinate than expected. He resigned his commission in February 1919 and returned to business projects.

Shackleton's last voyage was in the little Norwegian sealer which he renamed *Quest*. A proposed expedition to explore the uncharted Beaufort Sea, north of Alaska, fell through, so he turned to the south. 'Programme in a nutshell', he wrote to a friend, 'all the oceanic and sub-Antarctic islands. 2000 miles of Antarctic outline from Enderby Land to Coats Land. Seaplane, kinema, wireless, everything up to date' (Mill, 271). He found a generous backer in his old schoolfriend John Quiller Rowett. The *Quest* was indeed fitted out with numerous aids to exploration and science in St Katharine's Dock, London. George V presented a silk union flag and Queen Alexandra listened to the plans, with all her earlier interest in the Antarctic expeditions. On 18 September 1920 the *Quest* dropped down the Thames, carrying a complement of eighteen, seven of whom had sailed in *Endurance*. Shackleton exchanged 'the hateful ways of business … for the delights of command, where he was supreme alike in his power and in the unquestioning devotion of his crew' (Mill, 273). They reached South Georgia on 4 January 1922 and Shackleton went ashore at Grytviken to visit old friends and to make arrangements for the Antarctic leg of the voyage. While on board the *Quest* at Grytviken he died suddenly of a heart attack at 3.30 a.m. on 5 January 1922, having earlier written his diary, whose last words were, 'In the darkening twilight I saw a lone star hover gem-like above the bay' (diary, Scott Polar RI, quoted in Mill, 277). He was buried on 5 March in the Norwegian cemetery at Grytviken, South Georgia, and a cairn was built at Hope Point in memory of 'the Boss' by his old shipmates on the *Quest*'s return.

Reputation Long eclipsed by Scott, Shackleton's star was in the ascendant during the later years of the twentieth century. The archivist of his old school, organizer of a major Shackleton exhibition there, has well summarized this change:

> Sir Ernest Shackleton is currently something of a cult figure: the mood of our time appears to crave a hero who combines strong leadership with concern for his men, huge powers of physical and moral endurance together with a poetic soul and panache. (J. Piggott, exhibition prospectus, 2000)

Shackleton is even considered a model for businessmen in America (M. Morrell and S. Capparell, *Shackleton's Way: Leadership Lessons from the Great Antarctic Explorer*, 2001), and crowds flocked to the *Endurance* exhibitions there. Like his favourite poet, Browning, he believed (and proved) that great endeavours which fail can be turned into success.

Three biographies of Shackleton have been published. The first (1923) was by H. R. Mill, who knew him well. The second was by James and Margery Fisher (1957), who interviewed and recorded many of his old shipmates, while the third, lengthy and detailed even on the subject of his business ventures and extramarital affairs, was by Roland Huntford (1985). The *James Caird* Society, based at Dulwich College, where the boat is displayed, was founded in 1995 to honour him. A powerful statue by C. S. Jagger stands outside the Royal Geographical Society, South Kensington, while a number of place names in the Antarctic and elsewhere perpetuate his name. It was Apsley Cherry-Garrard who wrote about four of the leaders of the heroic age of Antarctic exploration:

> For a joint scientific and geographical piece of organization, give me Scott; for a Winter Journey, Wilson; for a dash to the Pole and nothing else, Amundsen; and if I am in the devil of a hole and want to get out of it, give me Shackleton every time. (*The Worst Journey in the World*, 1923, p. vi)

Sir Raymond Priestley later paraphrased the latter as, 'get down on your knees and pray for Shackleton' (Priestley, 7). Unlike Scott, Shackleton had little interest in science, but he realized its value when drawing up proposals for an expedition. He chose good scientists in short, unique interviews, so that the scientific results of his expeditions were considerable. On the publication of the Fishers' biography, Dr A. H. Macklin, who had been senior surgeon aboard *Endurance* and was with Shackleton when he died, described him as:

> an outstanding 'personality'—there radiated from him something strong and powerful and purposeful so that even to meet him was an experience ... He was a very exacting person to work for and always expected 'delivery of the goods' no matter how difficult the job. He valued loyalty above everything (and usually got it!) No-one ever questioned his authority. He would listen carefully and weigh advice, but he made up his own mind and his decisions were always his own ... he hated anything in the way of heroics and to label him throughout as the perfect being would of course be ridiculous. (A. H. Macklin, letter to Alfred Lansing, *c*.1957, quoted in Savours, 119–20)

Ann Savours

Sources H. R. Mill, *The life of Sir Ernest Shackleton* (1933) • M. Fisher and J. Fisher, *Shackleton* (1957) • E. H. Shackleton, *The heart of the Antarctic*, 2 vols. (1909) • E. H. Shackleton, *South* (1919); repr. (1920) • R. Huntford, *Shackleton* (1985) • E. H. Shackleton, ed., *South Polar Times*, 1 (1907) [facs.] • E. H. Shackleton, 'Life in the Antarctic', *Pearson's Magazine* (1903), 306–22 • J. Piggott, ed., *Shackleton, the Antarctic and Endurance* (2000) [for an exhibition at Dulwich College, 31 Oct 2000 – 25 Feb 2001] • R. W. Richards, *The Ross Sea shore party, 1914–17* (1962) • V. Fuchs, 'Shackleton', *GJ*, 141 (1975), 14–18 • F. A. Worsley, *Shackleton's boat journey* (1959) • F. A. Worsley, *Endurance*, repr. (1939) • A. Lansing, *Endurance: Shackleton's incredible voyage* (1959) • F. Wild, *Shackleton's last voyage: the story of the Quest* (1923) • R. Priestley, 'Twentieth century man against Antarctica', *Advancement of Science*, 13/50 (1956) [reprint] • A. Savours, 'Some medical aspects of nineteenth and early twentieth century British polar expeditions, seen through the eyes of three surgeons', *Proceedings of the International Symposium on the History of Maritime Medicine, Düsseldorf, 30 Aug 1986*, ed. H. Schadewaldt and K.-H. Leven (1988), 119–20 • private information (2004) [granddaughter] • *CGPLA Eng. & Wales* (1922)

Archives Canterbury Museum, Christchurch, New Zealand, diary • RGS, corresp. and papers • Scott Polar RI, transcripts by M. Fisher and J. Fisher of diaries and letters [originals, priv. coll.] | NMM, letters to Lady Invernairn • RGS, records of the National Antarctic Expedition • Scott Polar RI, HR Mill collections • Scott Polar RI, records of the National Antarctic Expedition • Scott Polar RI, MSS incl. Worsley's *Endurance* journal • Scott Polar RI, letters to Robert Falcon Scott • U. Edin. L., corresp. with Charles Sarolea | FILM BFI NFTVA, 'Bound for the south seas', Gaumont Graphic, 22 Sept 1921 • BFI NFTVA, 'Southward on the *Quest*', 1922 • BFI NFTVA, '*Endurance*: the story of a glorious failure', 1933 • BFI NFTVA, 'South, Sir Ernest Shackleton's glorious epic of the Antarctic', Film Four, 28 July 1999 • BFI NFTVA, 'The *Endurance*: Shackleton's legendary Antarctic expedition', *To the ends of the earth*, Channel 4, 9 Nov 2000 • BFI NFTVA, documentary footage • BFI NFTVA, news footage • BFI NFTVA, *South*, 1914–16 | SOUND NMM, *My south polar expedition*, four-minute wax cylinder record, 1909

Likenesses E. A. Wilson, pencil drawing, 1902, Scott Polar RI • E. A. Wilson, silhouette, 1902, Scott Polar RI • B. Stone, double portrait, photograph, 1904 (with the earl of Balfour), NPG • G. C. Beresford, negative, 1909, NPG • O. Edis, photograph, 1910, NPG • F. Hurley, photograph, 1915, Scott Polar RI [*see illus.*] • R. G. Eves, oils, 1921, NPG • R. G. Eves, oils, 1921, NMM • C. J. Jagger, statue, *c*.1932, RGS • R. G. Eves, charcoal studies and oil studies, Scott Polar RI • Kite, caricature, Hentschel-colourtype, NPG; repro. in *VF* (6 Oct 1909) • B. Kronstrand, oils, priv. coll. • photographs (taken during the expedition), RGS • photographs, Scott Polar RI

Wealth at death £556 2*s*. 7*d*.: probate, 12 May 1922, *CGPLA Eng. & Wales*

Shackleton, John (*d*. 1767), portrait painter, of whose parents nothing is known, is mainly known as principal painter-in-ordinary to George II, a position to which he was appointed on 7 March 1749 as successor to William Kent (1684–1748). He kept the appointment under George III, and continued to be paid for portraits of the king and queen up until 1765–6, although it was Allan Ramsay (1713–1784) who painted the official portraits during this period. Prior to his appointment Shackleton had painted a number of portraits, for example of William Windham (1717–1761) (Felbrigg Hall, Norfolk), and of John Bristowe, steward to the first duke of Newcastle (Reitlinger Museum of Fine Art, Maidenhead). On 25 October 1742 when he was living in the parish of St George's, Hanover Square, London, he married Mary Ann Regnier. In 1755 he was one of the original committee who drew up the first proposal for a royal academy of London, and on 8 March 1758 he was elected a member of the young Society for the Encouragement of Arts, Manufactures, and Commerce. He exhibited at the Free Society of Artists from 1763 to 1766. Shackleton died in London on 14 or 16 March 1767. In his will, dated 8 March 1767, Shackleton left property to his 'dear friend Mrs Sarah Rice', 'two marble heads said to be done by Bernini to my intimate friend Mr Robt [D?]ossie of Wardour Street, Soho', and 'a half-length picture of a Lady by Vandyke and a small landscape by Gaspar Poussin to John Bristow Esqr Keeper of His Majesties Lions in the Tower' (PRO, PROB 11/928, sig. 150). A number of portraits of George II by Shackleton and his studio are in collections in Britain, for example one dated 1755 in the Scottish National Portrait Gallery, Edinburgh; a picture in the Foundling Hospital, London, which was given by the artist in May 1758, upon which he was elected a governor and guardian of the hospital; a painting in the British Museum, London, which was commissioned by the museum in 1759; two examples in the Royal Collection; and others in Fishmongers' Hall, London, and Maidenhead Museum. Engravings after his paintings are in the British Museum.

SARAH HERRING

Sources J. R. Fawcett-Thompson, 'The elusive Mr. Shackleton: light on the principal painter in ordinary to King George II and George III', *The Connoisseur*, 165 (1967), 232–9 • B. Stewart and M. Cutten, *The dictionary of portrait painters in Britain up to 1920* (1997), 417 • Waterhouse, *18c painters*, 341 • J. Kerslake, *National Portrait Gallery: early Georgian portraits*, 1 (1977), 91, 93, 101, 204, 208–9 • O. Millar, *The Tudor, Stuart and early Georgian pictures in the collection of her majesty the queen*, 2 vols. (1963), vol. 1, 26, 150; vol. 2, nos. 567–8 • O. Millar, *The later Georgian pictures in the collection of her majesty the queen*, 1 (1969), xiii n.15, xli • H. Walpole, *Anecdotes of painting in England: with some account of the principal artists*, ed. J. Dallaway, [rev. and enl. edn], 2 (1826), 711 • Redgrave, *Artists* • J. C. Smith, *British mezzotinto portraits*, 1 (1878), 317; 2 (1879), 677–8 • *Engraved Brit. ports.*, 1.245; 2.298, 456; 3.437 • B. Nicholson, *The treasures of the Foundling Hospital, with a catalogue raisonné based on a draft catalogue by John Kerslake* (1972), 32, 34, 50, 78, no. 74 • will, PRO, PROB 11/928, fols. 48*r*–49*r*

Archives PRO, papers

Wealth at death see will, PRO, PROB 11/928, fols. 48*r*–49*r*

Shackleton, Leonard Francis [Len] (**1922–2000**), footballer, was born on 3 May 1922 at 51A Wapping Road, Bradford, Yorkshire, the son of Leonard Price Shackleton, a journeyman house painter, and his wife, Martha Ann Steward. Although his junior school showed little interest in football Shackleton, along with his father, was an avid supporter of the local game. On passing the scholarship exam at the age of eleven he opted to go to Carlton high school, as it had a good reputation for football. Despite being small in stature he made his way into the school team and progressed to play for Bradford schools and, eventually, England schools. While still at school he signed amateur forms for Bradford Park Avenue.

In 1938 Len Shackleton joined the ground staff at Arsenal, London, only to be told at the end of the 1938–1939 season that he was 'not good enough for Arsenal or professional football' (Shackleton, *Clown Prince*, 39). He returned to Bradford and spent the war years both working and playing football. During this period he went back to London for a short spell but was mostly attached to Bradford Park Avenue while working in a factory and, later, as a Bevin boy in the coal mines at Fryston colliery, near Castleford. He married Marjorie Ainley (*b.* 1922/3), a motor engineer's starter winder, at the Methodist church, Crossland Hill, Huddersfield, on 27 May 1944. They had three sons: Graham, Roger, and David.

In 1946, while still at Bradford, Shackleton was chosen to play for England against Scotland in the victory match at Hampden Park, Glasgow. During the same year he was transferred to Newcastle United for a fee of £13,000. In a memorable first game he scored six goals as Newcastle defeated Newport 13–0 in a second-division fixture. He soon came to clash with the authorities over conditions for himself and the other professionals, and after eighteen months he was sold to neighbouring Sunderland in the much heralded 'horse auction' transfer. Sealed bids were taken for his signature, and Sunderland offered £20,050—exactly £50 more than the nearest bid.

Playing as an inside forward, Shackleton spent nine happy years at Sunderland. No trophies were won during this period, yet he endeared himself to the supporters. It was during his stay at Sunderland that he wrote his controversial autobiography, *Clown Prince of Soccer* (1955). An ankle injury, suffered in 1952, proved increasingly irritating and aided his decision to retire from the game after the first match of the 1957–1958 season.

As the 'Clown Prince', Shackleton was one of soccer's greatest characters both on and off the field. He made only five official appearances for England, a fact often credited to his charismatic individuality. His best friend in football, Billy Elliott, admitted that Shackleton was 'not a team player' (*Echo*). On the other hand he was capable of winning games for the team single-handed. He enjoyed the taste of victory and simply 'loved to entertain' (ibid.); legend has it that he would beat a defender and beat him again 'just for the hell of it'. He was 'impish, unpredictable, tantalising' (Harvey), with a perceptible disdain for most forms of authority. He had a wicked sense of humour, characterized by his famous autobiographical blank chapter, headlined 'The average director's knowledge of football'. Even in later life he claimed to have no hard feelings towards Newcastle United—he did not care who defeated them!

While still a professional footballer Shackleton played cricket, appearing for Benwell and Wearmouth in local leagues and making minor county appearances for both Northumberland and co. Durham. He was also keen on classic cars, and in 1990 won a national award for his restoration of a 1939 Jaguar. After leaving football Shackleton remained in the north-east, at one time running his own hairdressing shop. He eventually settled down as a sports journalist for the *Daily Express* and, later, for the *Sunday People*. After retiring he moved from Sunderland to Grange over Sands, in Lancashire, and spent winters at another home, in Tenerife. Towards the end of his life he spent most of his time updating his autobiography, and completed *Return of the Clown Prince* (2000) just before his death. He suffered a heart attack in August 2000 and died at his home in Grange over Sands on 28 November 2000, aged seventy-eight. His wife survived him. A permanent memorial to his life was opened in the museum at Bradford Park Avenue's Horsfall Stadium in April 2001. On the day of his death a poignant minute's silence was observed by 48,000 spectators at Sunderland's Stadium of Light. The team's 3–1 victory over champions Manchester United was recorded in the *Echo* simply by the front-page banner headline 'For Shack'.

KEITH GREGSON

Sources L. Shackleton, *Clown prince of soccer: his autobiography* (1955) • L. Shackleton, *Return of the clown prince* (2000) • C. Harvey, ed., *Encyclopaedia of sport* (1959) • *Evening Chronicle* [Newcastle upon Tyne] (18 Sept 1986) • *Echo* [Sunderland] (29 Nov 2000) • *The Times* (29 Nov 2000) • *Daily Telegraph* (29 Nov 2000) • *The Independent* (29 Nov 2000) • *The Guardian* (29 Nov 2000) • *WWW* • 'All time greats', *Evening Chronicle* [Newcastle upon Tyne] (5 Nov 1990) • E. Andrews and A. Mackay, *Sports report* (1954) • b. cert. • d. cert.

Archives Bradford Park Avenue Museum, Horsfall Stadium | FILM BBC Sports Library, London • Tyne Tees TV Library, Newcastle upon Tyne
Likenesses photograph, repro. in *The Times* • photograph, repro. in *Daily Telegraph* • photograph, repro. in *The Independent* • photograph, repro. in Andrews and Mackay, *Sports report*, 154

Shackleton, Lydia (1828–1914), botanical artist, was born on 22 November 1828 at Grisemount, Ballitore, co. Kildare, Ireland, the third of the thirteen children of George Shackleton (1785–1871), a flour miller, and his wife, Hannah, *née* Fisher (1803–1873). The family were staunch Quakers. Lydia was probably taught at home by a governess, and subsequently studied in the Royal Dublin Society School of Art and Design. In her diary she recalled that 'When at the School of Design I copied a wild violet which was considered by myself and others a chef d'oeuvre. I painted it with excited happy feelings' (Nelson and Sayers). The earliest of her known works date from this period, the late 1840s; two drawings in pencil, of Grisemount and Ballitore, dated 15 November 1848, were reproduced in a privately printed booklet *Lydia Shackleton (1828–1914)* (1947). Being one of the eldest children, Shackleton became responsible for educating her younger brothers and sisters. In the early 1850s she taught her sisters to draw while practising drawing and painting herself. Later, when she lived in Lucan, co. Dublin, she taught her infant nephews and nieces. Shackleton enjoyed teaching, but her preferred occupations were reading, painting, and gardening. She also wrote poetry. In April 1853 Shackleton moved to the family's newly acquired mill at Lyons, co. Kildare, where she was housekeeper for her elder brother Joseph. About 1860, when the Anna Liffey Mills at Lucan, co. Dublin, were purchased by the family, she moved there and lived at 7 The Mall, Lucan, for the rest of her life, except for two lengthy periods (1873–6 and 1888–9) when she was in the United States visiting cousins. While in America she painted; a few naïve sketches and landscapes, and numerous botanical watercolours survive (National Botanic Gardens, Glasnevin, Dublin).

Shackleton's principal work was undertaken for the Royal (now National) Botanic Gardens, Glasnevin, Dublin. She began painting plants growing at Glasnevin about September 1884. Her association continued for twenty-three years, until December 1907, when her deteriorating eyesight forced her to give up painting. In that period she completed about 1500 botanical studies. The majority portray orchids, the particular interest of Frederick Moore (1853–1949), director of the gardens. More than 1000 orchid paintings, each signed L.S., survive in the Glasnevin Gardens, as well as portraits of other miscellaneous garden plants including *Paeonia*, *Sarracenia*, *Helleborus*, and *Lachenalia*. She also painted about one hundred Irish native wild species for the Science and Art Museum, Dublin; these paintings are now in the National Botanic Gardens.

None of Shackleton's paintings was reproduced during her lifetime. However, a plate showing the orchid *Moorea irrorata* (*Neomoorea wallisii*), published under Matilda Smith's name in *Curtis's Botanical Magazine* (1891), and another, published in *The Garden* (16 October 1886), showing two pitcher-plant (*Sarracenia*) hybrids raised at Glasnevin, may have derived from two of her paintings. Shackleton generally used watercolour, and painted on coloured papers which allowed her to employ gouache for white flowers. As a rule she painted a single blossom face on; rarely did she depict whole plants, and very rarely were dissections of the flowers or lateral views included. Thus much of her work cannot be considered truly scientific. Her early botanical portraits are of a consistently high quality but as her eyesight deteriorated in the early 1900s, so too did the precision of her work.

Shackleton is said to have had views, religious and otherwise, ahead of her time which estranged her from her mother who was a 'Quaker of the old school' (Shackleton, [i]). She never married. She died of heart failure at her home, 11 Garville Road, Rathgar, Dublin, on 10 November 1914, and was buried in the Quaker burial-ground, Temple Hill, Blackrock, co. Dublin. E. CHARLES NELSON

Sources E. C. Nelson and E. M. McCracken, *The brightest jewel: a history of the National Botanic Gardens, Glasnevin, Dublin* (1987) • M. J. P. Scannell and H. Lahert, 'Lydia Shackleton, 1828–1914: botanist and artist', *Journal of the County Kildare Archaeological Society*, 16/4 (1983–4), 331–9 • [R. Shackleton], ed., *Lydia Shackleton (1828–1914)* (privately printed, Dundalk, 1947) • E. C. Nelson, 'Lydia Shackleton (1828–1914)', *The Garden*, 107 (1982), 233–5 • E. C. Nelson, 'Orchid paintings at Glasnevin', *Orchid Review*, 89 (1981), 373–7, 384 • B. D. Morley, 'Lydia Shackleton's paintings in the National Botanic Gardens, Glasnevin', *Glasra (Contributions from the National Botanic Gardens, Glasnevin)*, 2 (1978), 25–36 • E. C. Nelson, 'Irish arts and crafts: the cultivation of orchids in the National Botanic Gardens, Glasnevin, Dublin, 1795–1922', *14th World Orchid Conference* [Glasgow 1993], ed. A. Pridgeon (1994), 342–52 • E. C. Nelson, 'A garden of bright images: art treasures at the National Botanic Gardens, Glasnevin', *Irish Arts Review Yearbook*, 14 (1998), 40–51 • E. C. Nelson and B. Sayers, *Orchids of Glasnevin: an illustrated history of orchids at Ireland's National Botanic Gardens* [forthcoming] • d. cert.
Archives priv. coll., diaries
Likenesses photograph, *c*.1885, repro. in Nelson and McCracken, *Brightest jewel*; priv. coll. • photograph, *c*.1900, repro. in Shackleton, ed., *Lydia Shackleton*; priv. coll.
Wealth at death £3163 7*s*. 10*d*.: probate, 14 Jan 1915, *CGPLA Ire.*

Shackleton, Richard (1726–1792). *See under* Shackleton, Abraham (1696–1771).

Shackleton, Robert (1919–1986), university teacher and librarian, was born in Todmorden, Yorkshire, on 25 November 1919, the eldest in the family of two sons and one daughter of (Robert William) Albert Shackleton, shoemaker, and his wife, Emily Sunderland. He attended Broomfield Boys' School and Todmorden secondary school, and subsequently went to Oriel College, Oxford, as a scholar in modern languages, taking a first class in 1940. The next five years were spent in the Royal Corps of Signals, serving in north Africa and Italy. In 1946 he was elected the first modern languages fellow at Brasenose College, Oxford. The college became the physical and affective centre of his life; he resided there, served as senior dean in the difficult post-war years (1954–61), was college librarian (1948–66), and came close to the principalship. An enthusiastic gastronome and a connoisseur of wines, he was a generous host to both young and old.

Born and bred in north country nonconformity, Shackleton was a lifelong Liberal, taking an active part in politics early on and standing for parliament, unsuccessfully, at Blackburn in 1945. A man of unusual elocution—his nasal intonation was a striking characteristic—he was nevertheless a good lecturer. Factually based academic research was, however, one of his real strengths and he soon gained a considerable reputation as both a scholar and an academic administrator. A leading member of his faculty, he was president of the conference of university teachers of French in 1958 and an editor of *French Studies* from 1960, and in 1965 succeeded Enid Starkie as university reader in French literature.

Shackleton's early edition of Bernard de Fontenelle's *Entretiens sur la pluralité des mondes* (1955), linking his childhood love of astronomy with his deep devotion to the European Enlightenment, was followed by his magisterial, if dry, critical biography of Montesquieu (1961), which was translated into French in 1977. Shackleton's identification of Montesquieu's different scribes and the painstaking research behind this volume contributed largely to the resurgence of Montesquieu studies with which his name became synonymous. He took the Oxford degree of DLitt in 1966. A regular traveller abroad and an easy speaker of French and Italian, Shackleton became a major figure in the international learned field, being president of the International Comparative Literature Association (1964–7) and in 1975–9 of the International Society for Eighteenth-Century Studies (where in particular he did much to improve relationships), and chairman of committee of the Voltaire Foundation (from 1983), the transfer of which to Oxford University he did much to assist. From 1972 to 1981 he was a delegate of the Oxford University Press.

An expert committee man, Shackleton was, though often of firm views, notably articulate in their expression and deft at either compromise or the maintenance of an entrenched position. A frequenter of libraries at home and abroad, and from early days a bibliophile and book collector, he became a curator of the Bodleian Library in 1961 and in 1965–6 chaired the special Oxford committee on the university's libraries. Its report, written at the end of the period of post-war expansion, foresaw notable developments in storage, co-operation, and automation, but took funding for granted. The office of Bodley's librarian fell vacant in 1966 and Shackleton was elected to it. Retaining his rooms in Brasenose, he was active in promoting the cause of the Bodleian and that of sharing the labour and cost of cataloguing between major libraries by using automated techniques. He travelled much during these years and lectured throughout the world. Shackleton was an excellent ambassador but less effective as head librarian in the changed financial and academic climate of the 1970s. The desire for a more active participation in the development of the Bodleian by staff, curators, university administrators, and library users did not chime easily with his autocratic management style. Already suffering from a blood complaint, he resigned the librarianship in 1979 in favour of a return to the more strictly academic post of Marshal Foch professor of French literature (1979–86).

This translation required removal from Brasenose to All Souls and, for Shackleton as an unmarried man, to the difficulties of practical domestic life. He had built up a renowned private library, and an informal portrait of him by Margaret Foreman (later placed in the college), standing in his beloved rooms in Brasenose, depicts the man better than his formal portrait by Sir William Coldstream in the Bodleian. His superlative Montesquieu collection, the basis of his 1983–4 Lyell lectures in bibliography, was ultimately bequeathed to the Bodleian while many of his books were sold to the John Rylands University Library of Manchester. He was appointed CBE (1986), was a fellow of the British Academy (1966), of which he was publications secretary (1974–7), and a chevalier of the Légion d'honneur (1982), and he held numerous other awards, including honorary degrees from Bordeaux (1966), Dublin (1967), Manchester (1980), and Leeds (1985).

Shackleton was tall with a domed brow and long arms, which at times made him appear ungainly in his movements. His last professorial years were clouded by illness and he died in Ravello, Italy, on 9 September 1986, a few weeks before he was due to retire. He was buried at the English cemetery in Naples. GILES BARBER, *rev.*

Sources G. Barber and C. P. Courtney, eds., *Enlightenment essays in memory of Robert Shackleton* (1988) [incl. list of pubns] • G. Barber, 'Robert Shackleton, 1919–1986', *PBA*, 73 (1987), 657–84 • *WWW* • *CGPLA Eng. & Wales* (1987) • personal knowledge (2004)

Likenesses W. Coldstream, oils, Bodl. Oxf. • M. Foreman, oils, Brasenose College, Oxford • photograph, repro. in Barber, 'Robert Shackleton'

Wealth at death £168,780: probate, 16 Feb 1987, *CGPLA Eng. & Wales*

Shacklock, Constance Bertha (1913–1999), singer, was born on 16 April 1913 at 79 Port Arthur Road, Nottingham, the daughter of Frederick Randolph Shacklock, farmer, and his wife, Hilda Louise Lucas. At nine she was singing in her local church choir, and a few years later she ran a dramatic group presenting religious drama (she was always a devout Christian), already dreaming of becoming an opera singer. After winning various prizes in the locality, she studied with the baritone Roy Henderson, who also taught Kathleen Ferrier, and joined the semi-professional Nottingham Operatic Society, playing leading roles in the so-called Savoy operas by Gilbert and Sullivan.

In 1939 Shacklock won a scholarship to the Royal Academy of Music in London. She took all the prizes available to a contralto, and in 1944 joined the Council for the Encouragement of Music and Arts, the organization bringing arts to the forces and factories during the war. She also began her concert career and, after appearing with the International Ballet Company as a singer in Milton's *Comus*, was auditioned by Covent Garden in 1946, at the time when the house was forming a resident company from young British singers. She was accepted as leading mezzo-soprano, and there met the musician Eric George Mitchell (1911/1912–1965), son of George Mitchell, a post-office official, whom she married on 23 July 1947. They had one daughter.

Shacklock sang in the very first production by the company, Purcell's *The Fairy Queen*, which it presented jointly with what was then still Sadler's Wells Ballet (later the Royal Ballet). After singing small roles (her début was as Mercédès in *Carmen*, 1947), she soon graduated to major ones, most notably Cherubino in *Le nozze di Figaro*, Magdalene in *Die Meistersinger*, Brangäne in *Tristan und Isolde* (which she sang to Kirsten Flagstad's final Isoldes), and Octavian in *Der Rosenkavalier*, a role for which her rich, vibrant voice and handsome presence were perfectly suited. She was just as well cast as Princess Marina in Peter Brook's controversial staging of *Boris Godunov* and as Herodias in his production of *Salome*, with fantastic designs by Salvador Dali. In Italian repertory she was a noted Azucena (*Il trovatore*) and Amneris (*Aida*), but her interpretation of Carmen was less successful. In 1953 she shared with Joan Cross the role of Queen Elizabeth I in the first performances of Benjamin Britten's coronation opera, *Gloriana*. This was another powerful interpretation, acted with the intelligence and attention to detail that characterized all her work. Her voice of two and a half octaves up to top C enabled her to tackle her wide variety of repertory with ease.

Shacklock also made her mark abroad, at the Berlin State Opera. She had sung under the legendary Erich Kleiber at Covent Garden, and out of the blue he invited her to East Berlin in 1952, the management in London receiving the telegram: 'Please send at once Shacklock to sing Brangäne here. Please wire arrival. Thanks' (*Daily Telegraph*). After many vicissitudes such as were attendant on travelling to Berlin at the time, Shacklock arrived at the state opera and scored a success. She also was a distinguished guest at the Bolshoi in Moscow, where she was the first English singer to appear for thirty years.

After singing for more than 500 performances at Covent Garden, Shacklock left the company in 1956 to work freelance. She soon embarked on a second career in musicals, and had an enormous success in *The Sound of Music*, playing the Mother Abbess from 1960 to 1966 at the Palace Theatre, London, urging audiences to 'climb every mountain, ford every stream'. She later commented that she 'took the veil for six-and-a-half years'. She also became an icon at the last night of the Proms, in which for ten years she led the singing of 'Rule, Britannia' and 'Jerusalem' with a commanding presence and voice to match.

Shacklock was always in demand on the concert platform, most notably as mezzo-soprano in *Messiah* (which she recorded under Hermann Scherchen) and Verdi's Requiem, and as the Angel in *The Dream of Gerontius*, of which a recorded souvenir exists from a performance in Rome under Barbirolli, confirming her emotionally powerful and urgent singing of the part. After retiring, Shacklock turned to teaching. From 1968 she was professor at the Royal Academy of Music, of which she had been elected a fellow in 1953. She was appointed OBE in 1971.

Shacklock was an invaluable stalwart of the resident ensemble at the Royal Opera House following the ravages of war. She attracted an appreciable following for her talented and considered singing. To see and hear her as a concerned Brangäne, a capricious Marina, and, above all, a youthfully ardent Octavian was to appreciate her contribution to the post-war operatic renaissance in Britain, which saw British singers holding their own with their international counterparts. It was an important achievement. She died at her home, East Dorincourt, Kingston Vale, Kingston upon Thames, London, on 29 June 1999.

ALAN BLYTH

Sources *The Times* (1 July 1999) • *Daily Telegraph* (1 July 1999) • *The Guardian* (1 July 1999) • *The Independent* (1 July 1999) • personal knowledge (2004) • private information (2004) • b. cert. • m. cert. • d. cert.

Likenesses C. Ware, photograph, 1949 (with Franz Lechleichner), Hult. Arch. • photograph, 1955, repro. in *Daily Telegraph* • photograph, repro. in *The Times* • photograph, repro. in *The Independent*

Wealth at death £636,582 gross: probate, 14 Jan 2000, *CGPLA Eng. & Wales* • £632,794 net: probate, 14 Jan 2000, *CGPLA Eng. & Wales*

Shacklock, Richard (*d.* before **1588**), religious controversialist, was possibly from the Shacklock family of Mostyn, near Manchester, but exact details of his birth and parentage are unknown. He matriculated as a pensioner at Trinity College, Cambridge, in 1552, took his BA in 1555/6, and was placed eighth in the class list, becoming a fellow of his college in 1555 and proceeding MA in 1559. He soon after abandoned his fellowship, doubtless because he could not swear the oath of supremacy of Queen Elizabeth I. He retired to Louvain in the Spanish Netherlands and took up the study of the civil law at the university there. In the first two decades of Elizabeth's reign a number of Catholic works of controversial theology were published by the 'Louvainists' and then smuggled into England, where they were often rebutted by books written by academics of the established church. Shacklock contributed two such books, in the form of translations from Latin into English of books by continental theologians. The first, published in 1565, was composed by Stanislaus Hosius, bishop of Worms, and was translated as *The Hatchet of Heresies*. The second also appeared in 1565 and was the work of Hieronimus Osorius, a Portuguese bishop, dedicated to Queen Elizabeth I; Shacklock translated it as *A Pearle for a Prynce*. In the original introductory material which he provided to these two books, Shacklock expressed his loyalty to Queen Elizabeth while opposing her religious settlement. In addition, Shacklock wrote a manuscript Latin epitaph on the life of the last Catholic bishop of Chester, Cuthbert Scot, who died in 1564 in Louvain, which was answered by the protestant author Thomas Drant. Shacklock seems to have spent the rest of his life in exile, probably in the Netherlands, and is reported to have died by 1588.

PETER HOLMES

Sources *DNB* • C. Dodd [H. Tootell], *The church history of England, from the year 1500, to the year 1688*, 2 (1739), 131 • S. Hosius, *A most excellent treatise … translated out of Laten and … intituled … 'The hatchet of heresies'*, trans. R. Shacklock (Antwerp, 1565) [Latin orig., *De origine haeresium nostri temporis*] • H. Osorius, *An epistle*, trans. R. Shacklock (Antwerp, 1565); repr. (1977) [running title *A pearle for a prynce*; Latin orig., *Epistola ad serenissimam Elizabetam*] • J. Barker, *A history of the ancient chapel of Blackley* (1854), 179–83 • Cooper, *Ath.*

Cantab., 1.241; 3.114, 156 • J. Strype, *Annals of the Reformation and establishment of religion … during Queen Elizabeth's happy reign*, new edn, 2/2 (1824), 710 • W. Falke, *A defence*, Parker Society (1843), viii • W. Falke, *Answers to Stapleton*, Parker Society (1848), 4 • T. Warton, *The history of English poetry*, new edn, ed. W. C. Hazlitt, 4 vols. (1871), vol. 4, p. 307 • A. C. Southern, *Elizabethan recusant prose, 1559–1582* (1950), 48–9, 112–15, 119–22, 490–92 • W. W. Rouse Ball and J. A. Venn, eds., *Admissions to Trinity College, Cambridge*, 2 (1913), 23 • A. F. Allison and D. M. Rogers, eds., *The contemporary printed literature of the English Counter-Reformation between 1558 and 1640*, 2 (1994), 139 • *Calendar of the manuscripts of the most hon. the marquis of Salisbury*, 13, HMC, 9 (1915), 393–4 • *The pedigree register* (1907–16), 2.249 • *Matricule de l'Université de Louvain*, 4, ed. A. Schillings (1961) • M. Racine, '*A pearle for a prynce*: Jerónimo Osório and early Elizabethan Catholics', *Catholic Historical Review*, 88 (2001), 401–27

Shadrach, Azariah (1774–1844), Independent minister and writer, was born on 24 June 1774 at Garndeifo-fach in the parish of Llanfair Nant-y-gof, near Fishguard, Pembrokeshire, the fifth son of Henry and Ann Shadrach, natives of the neighbouring parish of Nevern. When he was seven, the family moved to Burton, Pembrokeshire, but three years later, Shadrach moved to live with an aunt at Moylgrove. Influenced by the Revd John Phillips, he joined the Independents. He had little formal education but he was later employed as a farm servant by the Revd John Richards, a local Independent minister, and was granted access to his employer's books after his day's work. He decided to enter the Independent ministry and began preaching at his master's church, Rhos-y-Caerau. As a probationary minister, he toured both south and north Wales between 1796 and 1798. While in north Wales, he was persuaded by George Lewis of Llanuwchllyn to undertake the duties of schoolmaster at Hirnant, near Llanfyllin, and then at Pennal and Derwen-las, near Machynlleth. In 1802 he went to Trefriw, near Llanrwst, and by the end of the year had been ordained pastor of the Independent church at Llanrwst, at a salary of £5 a year. Here he was largely instrumental in suppressing the wakes or *mabsantau*, which still flourished in the district. While at Llanrwst, he married Margaret Morris (*c.*1776–1813), on 16 April 1805, with whom he had four children.

In November 1806 Shadrach moved to Cardiganshire, where he had charge of the churches of Tal-y-bont and Llanbadarn Fawr. He began to preach regularly at Aberystwyth in 1816 and, on 30 May 1819, he established an Independent church in the town. Shadrach gave up his ministerial work at Tal-y-bont and Llanbadarn Fawr and concentrated his efforts on the new church at Aberystwyth. He worked tirelessly to collect funds for the erection of Zion Chapel at Penmaes-glas, Aberystwyth in 1821, travelling widely across England and Wales. The chapel remained the meeting-place of the Independents until 1878 when the cause moved to Baker Street.

Shadrach was the author of no fewer than twenty-seven works, all, with one exception, written in Welsh. Some of them ran into several editions, and it is estimated that 60,000 copies of his various books were sold altogether. They were mostly sketches of sermons he had previously delivered. Owing to his liberal use of allegory he was styled, the 'Bunyan of Wales'. Perhaps his best work was *A Looking Glass: neu ddrych y gwrthgiliwr* (1807), which was translated into English by Edward S. Byam, under the title *The backslider's mirror: a popular Welsh treatise, translated from the ancient British language* (1845).

From 1830 Shadrach's son Eliakim was joint pastor with him at Zion, but he left for Dursley, in Gloucestershire in 1834. In August 1835, Shadrach himself resigned his charge, but he continued to preach for some years. He died on 12 January 1844 at Aberystwyth, and was buried there on 18 January in St Michael's churchyard.

D. L. Thomas, *rev.* Mari A. Williams

Sources A. Shadrach, *Cerbyd o goed Libanus* (1840) • J. Jones, *Bywyd a gweithiau Azariah Shadrach* (1863) • E. D. Jones, 'The works of Azariah Shadrach: an attempted bibliography', *Journal of the Welsh Bibliographical Society*, 6 (1943–9), 68–89 • E. D. Jones, 'Azariah Shadrach', *Y Cofiadur* (March 1953) • T. Rees and J. Thomas, *Hanes eglwysi annibynol Cymru*, 4 (1875) • J. T. Jones, *Geiriadur bywgraffyddol o enwogion Cymru*, 2 (1870) • *DWB*
Archives NL Wales | NL Wales, John Williams MSS

Shadwell, Anne (*fl.* 1661–1705). *See under* Shadwell, Thomas (*c.*1640–1692).

Shadwell, Charles (*fl.* 1692–1720). *See under* Shadwell, Thomas (*c.*1640–1692).

Shadwell, Sir Charles Frederick Alexander (1814–1886), naval officer, born on 31 January 1814, was the fourth son of Sir Lancelot *Shadwell (1779–1850) and his wife, Harriet (*d.* 1814), the sister of Sir John Richardson, judge of the court of common pleas. In 1827 he was entered as a scholar at the Royal Naval College, Portsmouth, whence he passed into the navy in 1829. In 1833 he passed his examination, and on 28 June 1838 was made lieutenant. He was then appointed to the frigate *Castor* (36 guns), going out to the Mediterranean, where in 1840 he was present at the operations on the coast of Syria, including the capture of Acre. In December 1841 he was appointed first lieutenant of the *Fly*, and for more than four years was employed in surveying in Torres Strait and on the northern coast of Australia. On the *Fly* being paid out of commission, Shadwell was promoted commander (27 June 1846). He then studied for some time at the Royal Naval College, taking a certificate in 'steam', and devoting himself more especially to nautical astronomy. In February 1850 he was appointed to command the *Sphinx*, which he took out to the East Indies, and in her had an active share in the Second Anglo-Burmese War (1852), for which he twice received the thanks of the governor-general in council; on 7 February 1853 he was advanced to the rank of captain, and on 5 December he was nominated a CB.

In August 1856 Shadwell commissioned the *Highflyer* for the China station, where in 1857 he took part in the operations in the Canton River leading up to the capture of Canton in December, and in the disastrous attack on the Taku (Dagu) forts on 25 June 1859, when, in leading the landing party across the mud flat, he received a severe wound in the ankle, which rendered him permanently lame. In January 1860 he was relieved from the command of the *Highflyer* and returned to England.

From February 1861 to August 1862 Shadwell commanded the *Aboukir* (90 guns) in the Mediterranean and

West Indies, and from October 1862 to June 1864 the *Hastings*, the flagship of Sir Lewis Jones at Queenstown. He was captain-superintendent of the Gosport victualling yard and of Haslar Hospital from June 1864 until his promotion to the rank of rear-admiral on 15 January 1869. From August 1871 to May 1875 he was commander-in-chief in China, and was made KCB on 24 May 1873. He was promoted vice-admiral in 1875 and became an admiral on the retired list in 1879. From 1878 to 1881 he was president of the Royal Naval College at Greenwich, after which he lived in retirement at Meadow Bank, Melksham, in Wiltshire.

Despite his long, and in some instances brilliant, service, Shadwell had rather the temperament of a scholar than of a warrior. He was deeply attached to the study of nautical astronomy, on which he published a number of pamphlets. For many years he was engaged on a work on the subject, which gradually assumed almost encyclopaedic proportions without ever reaching his ideal of completeness, and which remained unfinished at his death. He was elected FRS on 6 June 1861, and was a fellow of the Royal Astronomical and Royal Geographical societies. He died, unmarried, at Meadow Bank, on 1 March 1886.

J. K. LAUGHTON, *rev.* DEREK HOWSE

Sources *Monthly Notices of the Royal Astronomical Society*, 47 (1886–7), 140–41 • *The Times* (4 March 1886), 12 • RAS, fellowship records • election certificate, RS • *BL cat.* • Boase, *Mod. Eng. biog.* • National Portrait Gallery index

Wealth at death £13,186 9*s.* 9*d.*: resworn probate, July 1886, *CGPLA Eng. & Wales*

Shadwell, Charles Lancelot (1840–1919), scholar and college head, was the second son of Lancelot Shadwell (1808–1861), barrister, and his wife, Jane Ellen Nicholl. He was the grandson of Sir Lancelot *Shadwell, the last vice-chancellor of England. Born in London on 16 December 1840, Shadwell was educated at Westminster School and at Christ Church, Oxford, where he became a junior student in 1859 and took a first in classics and a second in law and history in 1863. He was a fellow of Oriel College from 1864 to 1898, and lecturer in jurisprudence there from 1865 to 1875. In 1898 he was elected an honorary fellow.

From 1874 to 1887, as treasurer of the college, Shadwell managed with care and ability the property of the institution, for which he felt an ardent affection that amounted almost to religious fervour. Of its past history, traditions, and muniments he was an indefatigable and competent explorer. The results were shown in the *Registrum Orielense, 1500–1900* (2 vols., 1893, 1902), in a chapter of Andrew Clark's *Colleges of Oxford* (1891), and in privately printed papers. It was characteristic of Shadwell that in the *Colleges of Oxford* he should dwell at length on the remote original foundation, forgotten benefactors, recondite incidents, and obscure earlier developments of the college, but dismiss in two brief sentences the work of Thomas Arnold and John Henry Newman, and ignore all that had happened since the Oxford Movement. Elected provost of Oriel in 1905, he brought to this office (which he held for nine years) the same intense loyalty, with a stately presence which stirred awe rather than invited closer advance. Yet, once captured, he was a firm and hearty friend, never failing to display, for those whom he liked, an appreciation that ignored popular prejudice and palliated individual blemish. He enjoyed dispensing magnificent hospitality, and he was also a generous benefactor of the college. Resigning the provostship in 1914 owing to ill health, he died at his home, 103 Banbury Road, Oxford, on 13 February 1919. He never married.

Shadwell took a large share in the affairs both of the university and of the city of Oxford; a comprehensive grip of minute detail, a fond adherence to immemorial tradition and official form, and a high sense of fit conduct and public duty were inseparable features of his useful service in this connection. He was out of sympathy with many new developments in academic life; the scientist H. T. Tizard recalled his remark, 'Show me a researcher and I'll show you a fool' (Clark, 12). His chief recreation was the study of chess problems and chronograms, to which he joined a literary interest and aptitude that made him pursue assiduously an 'experiment in literal verse translation' of Dante's *Purgatorio* (in a metre favoured by Marvell) which was described by Walter Pater as 'full of the patience of genius'. This bent also gave him the privilege of being, in A. C. Benson's words, the 'closest friend' and 'lifelong companion' of Pater himself. Shadwell had been Pater's pupil and they were both members of the Old Mortality Essay Society at Oxford. Shadwell's handsome appearance as a young man inspired Pater's *Diaphaneitè* (1864), 'an almost classical paean to beautiful youth by an older admirer' (Dowling, 81). They visited Italy together in 1865, and Pater's early studies on the Renaissance were dedicated to Shadwell, who, as his literary executor, fulfilled the duty, Benson says, 'with a rare loyalty and discretion'. In one of the later books issued under his aegis (*Miscellaneous Studies*, 1895), Shadwell's own temperament was finely delineated as that of an 'intellectual guilelessness or integrity that instinctively prefers what is direct and clear' and 'seeks to value everything at its eternal worth' (W. Pater, *Collected Works*, 8, 1910, 251, 248).

L. R. PRICE, *rev.* M. C. CURTHOYS

Sources personal knowledge (1927) • private information (1927) • A. C. Benson, *Walter Pater* (1906) • M. Levey, *The case of Walter Pater* (1978) • J. Foster, *Oxford men and their colleges* (1893) • R. W. Clark, *Tizard* (1965) • L. Dowling, *Hellenism and homosexuality in Victorian Oxford* (1994) • *CGPLA Eng. & Wales* (1919)

Likenesses G. F. Watt, oils, Oriel College, Oxford

Wealth at death £48,391 19*s.* 5*d.*: probate, 29 April 1919, *CGPLA Eng. & Wales*

Shadwell, Sir John (1671–1747), physician, son of Thomas *Shadwell (*c.*1640–1692), poet laureate and playwright, and Anne (*fl.* 1661–1705), actress, daughter of Thomas Gibbs of Norwich, was born in Middlesex, probably at Chelsea. On 15 May 1685 he matriculated from University College, Oxford, later migrating to All Souls College. He graduated BA on 1 June 1689 (3 November 1688, according to the register at All Souls), MA on 26 April 1693, BM on 19 April 1697, and DM on 5 June 1701.

On 30 November 1701 Shadwell was elected a fellow of the Royal Society, and was admitted on 3 December. He read no papers, but one letter he received he set before the society, an 'Account of an extraordinary skeleton' (*PTRS*, 41, 1741, 820). He was appointed physician-extraordinary to Queen Anne on 9 November 1709, and on 9 February 1712 was sworn one of the physicians-in-ordinary, in the place of Martin Lister, being succeeded in his former office by Hans Sloane. He was admitted a fellow of the Royal College of Physicians on 22 December 1712. The accounts of the queen's last illness in December 1713–14 in Abel Boyer's *History of the Reign of Queen Anne* are derived from Shadwell's letters to the duke and duchess of Shrewsbury, sent while Shrewsbury was lord lieutenant of Ireland in 1713. Boyer recorded Shadwell's opinion that the queen died of 'gouty humour translating itself upon the brain' (Boyer, 714). He continued to be physician-in-ordinary to George I and George II, and was knighted on 12 June 1715. For many years he lived in Windmill Street in London, and in 1735 withdrew from practice and retired to France, where he remained until 1740. Following his retirement to the continent, Shadwell was witness to the eruption of Mount Vesuvius in 1737, and supplied an account of this to the Royal Society (*PTRS*, 41, 1739, 252–61).

Shadwell was twice married: with his first wife, who died on 14 April 1722, he had one son and three daughters. He married second Ann Binns, at Somerset House chapel, on 12 March 1725; and on 29 June 1731 he made his will in her favour. Shadwell died at Windmill Street on 4 January 1747. He was buried on 8 January at Bath Abbey, where there is a tomb with an elaborate epitaph to his memory. Lady Shadwell survived until 1777. Shadwell published little other than an edition of his father's works in 1720.

W. W. Webb, *rev.* Patrick Wallis

Sources Foster, *Alum. Oxon.* • Munk, *Roll* • E. Gregg, *Queen Anne* (1980) • 'Extracts of burials from the registers of Bath Abbey', *The Genealogist*, new ser., 6 (1889–90), 92–101, esp. 98 • J. P. Malcolm, *Londinium redivivum, or, An antient history and modern description of London*, 4 vols. (1802–7), vol. 6, p. 295 • A. Boyer, *The history of Queen Anne* (1735) • 'An abstract of a letter from an English gentleman at Naples', *PTRS*, 41 (1739–41), 252–61 • 'Part of a letter to Sir John Shadwell', *PTRS*, 41 (1739–41), 820 • *GM*, 1st ser., 17 (1747), 47 • A. S. Borgman, *Thomas Shadwell: his life and comedies* (1928) • Venn, *Alum. Cant.*

Archives BL, Sloane MSS, corresp. with Sir Hans Sloane

Shadwell, Sir Lancelot (1779–1850), judge, was born on 3 May 1779, the eldest son of Lancelot Shadwell, a barrister and eminent conveyancer, and his wife, Elizabeth Whitmore, third daughter of Charles Whitmore of Southampton. He was educated at Eton College, and then at St John's College, Cambridge, where he matriculated in the Michaelmas term of 1796. In 1800 he became seventh wrangler, obtained the second chancellor's medal, and graduated BA. He was elected a fellow of his college on 23 March 1801, took his MA degree in 1803, and received the honorary degree of LLD in 1842. He was admitted as a member of Lincoln's Inn on 30 June 1797, and was called to the bar on 10 February 1803.

On 8 January 1805 Shadwell married Harriet, daughter of Anthony Richardson, a London merchant; they had six sons including Sir Charles Frederick Alexander *Shadwell (1814–1886), before Harriet's death on 25 May 1814. Shadwell married again on 4 January 1816. His second wife, Frances, was the youngest daughter of Captain Locke, and together they had six sons and five daughters, increasing the Shadwell family to seventeen. Frances survived Shadwell and died on 27 October 1854, aged sixty-six.

After practising for eighteen years, with much success, as a junior in the court of chancery, Shadwell was appointed a king's counsel on 8 December 1821, and took his seat within the bar on the first day of the Hilary term of 1822. As a QC, Shadwell refused to follow the practice of taking briefs in more than one equity court, preferring to give each case his undivided attention. At the general election in June 1826 he obtained a seat in the House of Commons for the borough of Ripon through the influence of Miss Elizabeth Sophia Lawrence, under whose will he subsequently received a handsome bequest. On 14 February 1827 he introduced a bill for the limitation of a writ of right and for the amendment of the law of dower, but it did not get beyond the committee stage. His parliamentary career was short, for on 31 October 1827 he was appointed vice-chancellor of England in the place of Sir Anthony Hart. On 16 November of the same year he was sworn a member of the privy council and knighted.

Shadwell presided in the vice-chancellor's court for nearly twenty-three years. During this period he twice filled the office of a commissioner of the great seal: from 23 April 1835 to 16 January 1836 in conjunction with Sir C. C. Pepys (afterwards Lord Cottenham) and Sir J. B. Bosanquet, and again from 19 June to 15 July 1850 in conjunction with Lord Langdale and Sir R. M. Rolfe (afterwards Lord Cranworth). On 24 June he was seized with a sudden illness, which prevented him from sitting again during the continuance of the second commission. He died at his residence, Barn Elms, Surrey, on 10 August 1850, aged seventy-one, and was buried in Barnes churchyard.

The last person to hold the title of vice-chancellor of England, Shadwell was a learned and able judge, with a reputation for being courteous and polite. He was elected a bencher of Lincoln's Inn on 30 January 1822 and acted as treasurer in 1823. Outside the law, he had many interests. He was president of the Society of Psychrolutes, who bathed out of doors daily from November to March. He was in the habit of bathing every day, whatever the weather, in one of the creeks of the Thames near Barn Elms, and was said while thus engaged once to have granted an injunction. He was a tireless walker when young, and in 1797 he served as a member of the light horse volunteers. Shadwell also enjoyed skating. He was also something of a scholar, having translated both the *Illiad* and the *Gospel According to St Matthew* from Greek into English (1844–7 and 1859 respectively). He was thought of as a witty judge and was regarded as having been the best junior counsel of his time.

The vice-chancellor's eighth son, the second from his second marriage, **Lawrence Shadwell** (1823–1887), army officer, was born in July 1823. He was educated at Eton College and entered the army as ensign in the 98th foot on 26 April 1841. He served in the China expedition of 1842, the Punjab campaign of 1848–9, and in the Crimean War of 1854–6. He held the appointment of assistant quartermaster-general in the Crimea during the greater part of the war. On 2 August 1853 he married Helen Frances, daughter of Edward Coleridge, vicar of Mapledurham. After his return to England he was assistant quartermaster-general to the troops in the northern district from April 1857 to September 1861, in Nova Scotia from January to August 1862, and in the south-western district of England from April 1864 to February 1866. From 1866 to 1871 he was military assistant at the War Office. He was promoted to the rank of major-general on 6 March 1868, and was created a companion of the Bath on 2 June 1869. He was granted a reward for distinguished and meritorious services in January 1874, and was promoted lieutenant-general on 27 April 1879, and general on 1 July 1881. He retired from the army on 25 July 1881, and died at Reading on 16 August 1887; his wife survived him.

G. F. R. Barker, *rev.* Sinéad Agnew

Sources E. Foss, *Biographia juridica: a biographical dictionary of the judges of England … 1066–1870* (1870) • Venn, *Alum. Cant.* • W. P. Baildon, ed., *The records of the Honorable Society of Lincoln's Inn: admissions*, 1 (1896), 470, 560 • *Law Times* (17 Aug 1850), 467 • *Annual Register* (1850), 251–2 • *GM*, 1st ser., 75 (1805), 83 • *GM*, 2nd ser., 15 (1841), 628 • *GM*, 2nd ser., 24 (1845), 423 • *GM*, 2nd ser., 42 (1854), 644 • [Clarke], *The Georgian era: memoirs of the most eminent persons*, 2 (1833), 552 • T. D. Hardy, *Memoirs of … Henry Lord Langdale*, 2 (1852), 258–68 • H. E. C. Stapylton, *The Eton school lists, from 1791 to 1850*, 2nd edn (1864), 14, 21 • S. Maunder, *The biographical treasury*, [14th edn], rev. W. L. R. Cates (1873) • Ward, *Men of the reign*, 803 • Allibone, *Dict.* • *Legal Observer*, 40 (1850), 305 • T. Baker, *History of the college of St John the Evangelist, Cambridge*, ed. J. E. B. Mayor, 1 (1869), 311–12 • *Members of parliament: return to two orders of the honorable the House of Commons*, House of Commons, 2 (1878), 309 • *ILN* (17 Aug 1850) • E. W. Brayley, J. Britton, and E. W. Brayley, jun., *A topographical history of Surrey*, 3 (1844), 437–8 • J. Haydn, *The book of dignities: containing lists of the official personages of the British empire*, ed. H. Ockerby, 3rd edn (1894) • *Army List* • J. B. Moore, *Reports of cases in the common pleas and exchequer chamber* (1824), 4.441 • *LondG* (2 Nov 1827), 2250; (20 Nov 1827), 2385–6 • *Parliamentary debates*, 2nd ser., 16.471–3, 474–5; 17.94, 174 • J. L. Roget, *A history of the 'Old Water-Colour' Society*, 2 (1891), 210–11 • J. Arnould, *Memoir of Thomas, first Lord Denman*, 1 (1873), 17, 25 • *The diary and correspondence of Charles Abbot, Lord Colchester*, ed. Charles, Lord Colchester, 1 (1861), 114 • *CGPLA Eng. & Wales* (1887)

Archives LMA | BL, corresp. Sir Robert Peel, Add. MSS 40398–40568 • Bodl. Oxf., letters to John May

Likenesses T. Phillips, oils, exh. RA 1840, Lincoln's Inn, London • lithograph, BM, NPG

Wealth at death £9991 16*s.* 8*d.*—Lawrence Shadwell: will with two codicils, 3 Sept 1887, *CGPLA Eng & Wales*

Shadwell, Lawrence (1823–1887). *See under* Shadwell, Sir Lancelot (1779–1850).

Shadwell, Thomas (*c.*1640–1692), playwright and poet, was born in Norfolk, either at Santon Hall or Broomhill House, Weeting, the son of John (*d.* 1684) and Sarah Shadwell. His grandfather was George Shadwell, of Linedon (Lyndowne) in Enville, Staffordshire, and theirs was a minor but long-established gentry family from the county. John Shadwell, a lawyer, was of Pembroke College, Cambridge, and the Middle Temple. He inherited a good fortune and substantial property in Thetford, Norfolk, but following his support for the king in the civil war, he was forced to 'sell and spend good part of his Estate' (*Works*, 1.xvii). The family moved to Ireland shortly after the Restoration.

Thomas Shadwell (*c.*1640–1692), by unknown artist, 1690

Early years and education Thomas Shadwell had the 'Birth and Education, without the Fortune of a Gentleman' (*Works*, 3.20). He was one of eleven children, and was described as his father's heir apparent in 1658. He was educated at home where he learnt 'all … gentleman-like exercises' (ibid., 5.292). About 1655 Shadwell attended the grammar school in Bury St Edmunds, which was later the setting for one of his comedies, *Bury Fair*. On 17 December 1656 he matriculated from Gonville and Caius College, Cambridge. In 1687, attacked by Dryden as a weak classical scholar, he was 'provoked' to demonstrate his knowledge by translating the tenth satire of Juvenal, maintaining in the publication's preface that at school and Cambridge he had a reputation as a good Greek and Latin scholar (ibid., 5.292–3). In his will he left his son 'latin and philosophical books', including Hobbes's, but he was no match for Dryden's learning (ibid., 1.ccxxxv–ccxxxvi). He left Cambridge without taking a degree, and entered the Middle Temple on 7 July 1658. He studied there and then travelled, visiting Ireland for four months at the age of twenty-three, probably visiting his family. Some time between 1658 and 1668 he worked as a clerk to the auditor of the exchequer, Sir Robert Long.

Marriage and children Some time between 23 February 1663 and 22 January 1664 Shadwell married Anne Gibbs [**Anne Shadwell** (*fl.* 1661–1705)], daughter of Thomas Gibbs, proctor and public notary at Norwich. She may have been the Anne Gibbs who, aged seventeen, married Thomas Gawdy of Norfolk in 1662. There was a rumour that Shadwell 'hath owned himself … married by a Popish priest' (*Loyal Protestant*, 9 Feb 1681), which he denied, saying only that he had had an active interest in Catholicism for about eight months in 1660–61. Anne acted in several of Shadwell's plays. She performed with the Red Bull Troupe in Oxford in July 1661, and that year was among the eight actresses in Sir William Davenant's Duke's Company in Lincoln's Inn Fields Theatre. She had some musical skill, singing and playing the lute. She may have been still acting as a member of the United Company in 1686–7 and even in 1699, as a member of Christopher Rich's company at Drury Lane. In his will Shadwell called her a 'diligent careful and provident woman and very indulgent to her children' (*Works*, 1.ccxxxvi). She dedicated Shadwell's play *The Volunteers* to the queen in 1693 and was still alive in 1705.

Among the Shadwells' children were George, baptized on 20 January 1674 and buried on 20 February 1678; William, baptized on 21 September 1680 and buried on 27 October 1686; and Anne, who was baptized on the day of William's burial; Shadwell called her 'the greatest comfort to me of all my children' (*Works*, 1.ccxxxvi). Sir John *Shadwell (1671–1747), who matriculated at University College, Oxford, in 1685, and became physician to Queen Anne and George I, was knighted on 12 June 1715, and died on 4 January 1747.

Dramatic work, patronage, and literary controversy, 1668–1680 Shadwell's first play, *The Sullen Lovers*, was premiered on 2 May 1668 by the Duke's Company, for whom Shadwell was to write most of his plays. Anne Shadwell played the 'sullen lover' Emilia. The play, the first of several which Shadwell based on Molière, was acted for twelve days. Its considerable success was due to its 'little witty expressions', royal support, and the fact that 'all the Duke and everybody's talk' was that the self-important know-all Sir Positive At-All was a satire on Dryden's brother-in-law the playwright Sir Robert Howard, whose brother, the playwright Edward Howard, was lampooned as the conceited 'Poet Ninny' (Pepys, 9.185–6, 190–91). Sir Positive represents an attack on the heroic drama of Sir Robert Howard and Dryden. In the preface Shadwell attacks authors who have 'wild Romantick Tales, wherein they strain Love and Honour to that ridiculous Height, that it becomes Burlesque' (*Works*, 1.11).

The following year Edward Howard published a poem, *The British Prince*, and Shadwell wrote one for a series of mock-commendatory poems ridiculing his style. This was the first work produced collaboratively by the circle of court wits led by George Villiers, second duke of Buckingham, in the 1670s. These included the earl of Rochester, Charles Sackville, Lord Buckhurst (later earl of Dorset), John, Lord Vaughan, Sir Charles Sedley, Sir George Etherege, William Wycherley, George Savile, and Fleetwood Sheppard. The group, all whigs, shared Shadwell's literary tastes, and were an important source of patronage. Sedley corrected two of Shadwell's plays and gave him the profits of his own *Bellamira* in 1687, and Shadwell wrote a verse letter to Wycherley 'Inspir'd with high and mighty Ale' (*Works*, 5.227). In 1678 Nell Gwynn said that Dorset 'drinks ale with Shadwell' at the Duke's Theatre 'all day long' (ibid., 5.430). Shadwell's conversational skills and talent for repartee must have been of a high order to allow him intimacy with 'the wittiest men of England' (ibid., 5.291). This group valued impromptu wit in conversation over polished wit in writing. Shadwell behaved as a gentlemanly amateur rather than as the professional writer he really was, a fact ambivalently treated in 'An Allusion to Horace' (1675), where Rochester says 'true Comedy' is only achieved by two 'Moderne Witts', 'hasty Shadwell, and slow Wicherly', but that

> Shadwells unfinisht works doe yet impart,
> Great proofs of force of Nature, none of Art.

After Shadwell's death, Wycherley told Alexander Pope that Shadwell 'knew how to start a fool very well, but that he was never able to run him down': that is, he could not maintain characterization throughout his plays (Spence, 1.205–6).

Shadwell dedicated *The Sullen Lovers* to William Cavendish, duke of Newcastle, who had been Ben Jonson's patron. Shadwell says that Newcastle found him out in his 'obscurity', and helped him several years before he was invited to Welbeck and 'daily admitted into' the duke's 'public and private conversation' (*Works*, 1.19–20). Four more of Shadwell's plays were to have what Dryden called 'northern dedications'. Newcastle employed Shadwell to finish and 'theatricalise' his play *The Triumphant Widow* (acted 1674). In it Shadwell, who wrote more than half of this play, may have satirized Dryden as the hapless, Jonson-hating poet Crambo. Later, Shadwell reused two parts in *Bury Fair*. Shadwell was paid £22 in 1677 for publishing Newcastle's *The Humorous Lovers*, and after the duke's death in 1676 his son Henry, duke of Newcastle, continued the patronage.

Shadwell's play *The Royal Shepherdess* was performed for six days by the Duke's Company in February 1669; Pepys said there was nothing to admire in it but a 'good martial dance of pikemen' (Pepys, 9.459). In 1670 Shadwell's *The Humourists* was severely censored before performance, and 'a numerous party' arrived to damn the play; the actors did not know their words properly and the play was only saved by the kind intervention of a dancer. About this time Shadwell wrote a play, *The Hypocrite*, which is now lost. His adaptation of Molière's *L'Avare*, *The Miser*, was performed in 1672. His next play, his own personal favourite among his works and admired by critics and royalty, was *Epsom-Wells* (1672). It was rumoured to have been written collaboratively with Sedley, who wrote the prologue.

As a child, Shadwell's music master was John Jenkins, musician-in-ordinary to Charles I and Charles II, and Shadwell came to play a significant part in musical culture, working with several professional musicians, including Henry Purcell, and composing the music to at least seven theatre songs. John Dryden refers to a performance Shadwell gave on the Thames to entertain the 'royal barge', by singing and playing on the lute. It was probably Shadwell who revised the adaptation of Shakespeare's *Tempest* by

Dryden and William Davenant into a semi-opera, performed in 1674. With spectacular stage machinery, singing, and splendid dances, *The Tempest, or, The Enchanted Island* was exceptionally popular and profitable. It set a fashion for operatic entertainments, such as Shadwell's own *Psyche* (1675), which had music by Draghi and Matthew Locke. *Psyche* integrated music and dancing into the drama in a way which proved formative for English opera. Shadwell produced for it the first dramatic musical score published in England, its preface proudly claiming he had 'some knowledge' of music, 'having been bred for many Years of [his] Youth to some Performance in it' (*Works*, 2.280).

In 1674 Shadwell joined Dryden and John Crowne in their *Notes and Observations on 'The Empress of Morocco'*, an attack on Elkanah Settle, who had insulted Dryden in the preface to his *Empress of Morocco*. Written in three weeks, Shadwell's Don John play, *The Libertine*, was acted in June 1675. His excellent satire on the Royal Society, *The Virtuoso*, was first performed in May 1676 and remained popular for nearly thirty years. It represented Robert Hooke as Sir Nicholas Gimcrack, who demonstrates phosphorescence by reading a Geneva Bible by the light of a leg of pork, and practises swimming without water, from a book on the subject. In the dedication Dryden is now attacked for 'feminine understanding' displayed by his fondness for repartee ('tattle') and dislike of Jonson. This was the immediate stimulus for Dryden's brilliant satire on Shadwell, *MacFlecknoe*. It was the devastating culmination of a literary disagreement which had begun with Shadwell's 1668 preface to *The Sullen Lovers* and was pursued through the prefaces of Shadwell's plays and the prologues and epilogues of Dryden's, despite their united attack on Settle in 1674. Shadwell favoured the comedy of humours over Dryden's wit-comedies, and thought Dryden's heroic tragedy ridiculous. He considered Jonson faultless, whereas Dryden thought him 'frugal' of wit. Shadwell thought comedy should have an instructive moral purpose, and not show indulgence towards aristocratic vices, whereas Dryden thought it should primarily entertain. Finally, they disagreed over the right of an author to borrow from other authors or the classics: what was imitation to Dryden was plagiarism to Shadwell.

MacFlecknoe has been seen as 'a gauntlet thrown down by the leading professional of one faction', the tory poets led by Mulgrave, 'to the leading professional of another', the whig alliance (Love, *Scribal Publication*, 256). *MacFlecknoe* was written in July–August 1676, and circulated in manuscript (published 1682). It represents the writer Richard Flecknoe as the emperor of Dullness, nominating Shadwell as his successor to the 'realms of nonsense' and the fittest of his sons to wage 'immortal war on wit', thereby lampooning Shadwell's claim to succession to the classical literary heritage and to be the true literary son of Ben Jonson. Shadwell's body—for he resembled Jonson in being enormously fat—'fills the eye', and his coronation rites involve the presentation of a 'mighty mug of potent ale' and a crown of poppies, referring to his heavy drinking and opium addiction. In this mock-laureate, mock-occasional poem, Dryden makes brilliant play with images of laureate activity, attacking Shadwell as a possible rival. His clumsy dunce has come to define Shadwell to posterity.

Shadwell revised Shakespeare's *Timon of Athens* into *The History of Timon of Athens the Man-hater*, adding a love-interest, singing, and a masque of Cupid and Bacchus. First performed in early 1678, it set a fashion for adaptations of Shakespeare's tragedies. Shadwell's *A True Widow*, corrected by Sedley, was performed late in 1678, but was not successful, and he followed it with *The Woman-Captain* in 1679. In September 1680 Shadwell helped John Aubrey to carry the coffin at Samuel Butler's quiet funeral. Butler had had some influence on *The Virtuoso*, and his jocular poem 'To Thomas' is probably addressed to Shadwell. It claims that while he used to be afflicted with 'claps', boozing has now made him so fat that sex is physically impossible.

Political controversies, 1680–1687 Shadwell was a member of the whig propaganda club the Green Ribbon Club, which he probably joined before November 1678. In 1681 Shadwell put on the whig polemic *The Lancashire Witches* whose crude anti-Catholic satire was cut by the censor, though Shadwell later printed the uncut text. It features flying witches and the bigoted, superstitious, and ignorant Irish priest Teague O'Devilly, who proves to be complicit in the Popish Plot. Its consequence was the silencing of Shadwell as a playwright until 1688. In 1682 Shadwell, leading writer of the whigs, and Dryden, leading poet of the tories, clashed yet again, this time over politics, after Dryden published two anti-Shaftesbury poems, *Absalom and Achitophel* (1681) and *The Medal* (1682). In *The Medal of John Bayes* (1682), almost certainly by Shadwell, the author lampoons Dryden as clumsy, 'lumpish', and a 'Hackney-rayler', and the tories as dangerous fools to deny the Popish Plot, while eulogizing Monmouth and Shaftesbury. Among the responses was the second part of *Absalom and Achitophel*, which contained lines by Dryden attacking Shadwell's poetry, his weight, and his habits. He was to be known by Dryden's nickname Og in satires thereafter.

Dramatic work and the laureateship, 1688–1692 In 1688 Shadwell wrote the enormously successful play *The Squire of Alsatia*, which had an unbroken run of thirteen days. Shadwell received the astonishing sum of £130 for the benefit night, from which many had to be turned away. After the revolution of 1688 Dryden was deposed as poet laureate, and Dorset, as lord chamberlain, awarded the post, with that of historiographer royal, to Shadwell, who embarked on a series of tedious laureate poems. His enjoyable comedy *Bury Fair* (1689) was followed by the less successful *Amorous Bigotte* (1690), and *The Scowrers* in late 1690 or early 1691.

For at least four years Shadwell had suffered from gout, the pain of which he relieved with opium; he died from an overdose on 19 or 20 November 1692. He was buried on 24 November at St Luke's Church, Chelsea, and the funeral sermon was preached by Nicholas Brady. In his will, witnessed in 1690 in his Chelsea house, he left mourning rings to his brother, Dorset, Sedley, Edmund Ashton, and William Jephson. His wife, the major beneficiary and executor, inherited leases of two properties in Salisbury Court by the Dorset Garden theatre, rights to the rent for the theatre, and money, some of which was invested in property. She also inherited plate, goods, and chattels. Shadwell's play *The Volunteers* was performed posthumously, and he was succeeded as poet laureate and historiographer royal by Nahum Tate.

Sir John Shadwell published a collected edition of Shadwell's plays in 1720, prefaced with a biographical account of his father as a good patriot and subject, well educated, clever, and a wit. It concluded with Sir John's Latin memorial inscription. This was originally on Shadwell's monument in Poets' Corner, Westminster Abbey, but had to be rewritten after complaints by certain clergymen that it included an 'Encomium' upon plays. Another son, **Charles Shadwell** (*fl.* 1692–1720), was a playwright; his patron was Lady Newtown. He served in the army in Portugal under Major-General Newton, governor of Londonderry, and in 1710 was supervisor of the excise in Kent. His play *The Fair Quaker of Deal* (1710) was successfully performed at the Theatre Royal, Drury Lane, and followed by *The Humours of the Army* (1713). His other plays were acted at the Smock Alley Theatre, Dublin, and printed in 1720: *Irish Hospitality*, *The Plotting Lovers*, *The Hasty Wedding*, *The Sham Prince*, and *Rotherich O'Connor*.

For three centuries Shadwell was seen only as the clumsy dunce hack of Dryden's *MacFlecknoe*, unacceptably 'coarse', and of use only in furnishing details of interest to social historians. From the last years of the twentieth century Shadwell has begun to receive significant attention. New editions have been prepared of his plays, and *The Virtuoso* was revived by the Royal Shakespeare Company in 1991. Scholarship has revealed Shadwell to be a central figure in our understanding of late seventeenth-century theatre, culture, and politics, and he has come into his own as a major Restoration playwright. John Aubrey's comment in 1680 that Shadwell 'is counted the best comedian we have now' (*Brief Lives*, 2.226–7) deserves to be respected.

KATE BENNETT

Sources A. S. Borgman, *Thomas Shadwell* (New York, 1969) • *The works of Thomas Shadwell*, ed. M. Summers, 5 vols. (1927) • J. Ross, 'Addenda to Shadwell's *Complete works*: a checklist', *N&Q*, 220 (1975), 256–9 • P. Beal and others, *Index of English literary manuscripts*, ed. P. J. Croft and others, [4 vols. in 11 pts] (1980–), vol. 2, pt 2 • J. M. Armistead, 'Scholarship on Shadwell since 1980: a survey and annotated chronology', *Restoration*, 20 (1996), 101–18 • Highfill, Burnim & Langhans, *BDA* • B. Corman and T. Gilman, 'The musical life of Thomas Shadwell', *Restoration*, 20 (1996), 149–63 • *The poems of John Dryden*, ed. P. Hammond, 1 (1995) • H. Love, *Scribal publication in seventeenth century England* (1993) • H. Love, 'Shadwell, Rochester, and the crisis of amateurism', *Restoration*, 20 (1996), 119–34 • Pepys, *Diary* • *Brief lives, chiefly of contemporaries, set down by John Aubrey, between the years 1669 and 1696*, ed. A. Clark, 2 vols. (1898) • *The life and times of Anthony Wood*, ed. A. Clark, 1, OHS, 19 (1891) • J. R. Jones, 'The Green Ribbon Club', *Durham University Journal*, 49, new ser., 18 (1956), 20 • J. Spence, *Observations, anecdotes, and characters, of books and men*, ed. J. M. Osborn, new edn, 2 vols. (1966) • parish register, Chelsea, St Luke, 24 Nov 1692 [burial] • parish register, Weeting [birth: sister] • F. Blomefield and C. Parkin, *An essay towards a topographical history of the county of Norfolk*, [2nd edn], 11 vols. (1805–10), vol. 6, p. 197 • parish register, London, St Bride [birth: children]

Archives CKS • Morgan L. • NL Ire. • NRA, literary MSS and papers • PRO | BL, Trumbull MSS • Princeton University Library, New Jersey, general MSS • U. Nott., Portland MSS • Yale U., Osborn collection

Likenesses oils, 1690, NPG [*see illus.*] • F. Bird, marble effigy on monument, 1692, Westminster Abbey • W. Faithorne junior, mezzotint (after J. Kerseboom), NPG • S. Gribelin, engraving (after F. Bird, 1692), repro. in T. Shadwell, *The dramatic works of Thomas Shadwell* (1720)

Shaen, Sir James, first baronet (*d.* **1695**), government official, was the first son of Patrick Shaen. Nothing is known of his youth or education. By 1659 he had married Lady Frances Fitzgerald, daughter of George *Fitzgerald, sixteenth earl of Kildare, and his wife, Joan, daughter of Richard *Boyle, first earl of Cork; they had a son, Arthur.

Shaen served as a cornet of horse in the royalist army in Ulster in the 1640s, though in a petition of 1656 he claimed that he had put his life at risk by declaring for parliament and endeavouring to turn the other soldiers to that interest. His efforts were represented to Lord Deputy Henry Ireton by the Cromwellian commander in Ulster, Colonel Robert Venables. Thereafter Shaen served in Venables's troop of horse, rising to the rank of captain before embarking upon a career in civil government, initially in the Irish land surveys of the early 1650s. While serving as sheriff of Longford and Westmeath in 1655 he was appointed commissioner for allotting lands to Catholics transplanted to Connaught, though he was soon dismissed for taking possession of lands for his own use. In the later 1650s he assisted William Petty in carrying out what was known as the 'own survey'. In the early 1660s Shaen's position improved with the assistance of his wife's uncle, Roger Boyle, earl of Orrery. Appointed for life as principal cessor, collector, and receiver-general for Leinster in October 1660, Shaen was knighted the following December, and in 1661 was elected MP for Clonmel in the Irish parliament. In 1660–61 he served as secretary to the lords justices, and in March 1661 was made principal registrar to the commissioners appointed in accordance with the king's 1660 declaration (which Orrery had been in great part responsible for) for the Irish land settlement. The declaration in turn was to form the basis for the 1662 Act of Settlement, which included a proviso for Shaen as beneficiary of a grant of £8000. Despite the counter-claims of Sir John Perceval to the registrar's office, Shaen also served as chief registrar to the court of claims under the 1662 act.

Although he was suspected of colluding with Orrery in order to deprive James, duke of Ormond, of £10,000, Shaen's career continued to progress during Ormond's viceroyalty in 1662–9. Having journeyed in late 1662 to England to secure a subvention of £60,000 for the government, in 1663 he was created a baronet. In the lead up to the Act of Explanation in 1665, in which he was once again specifically provided for, he was involved in 'a cynical business in Irish land traffic' (Arnold, 72–3), at one point informing two Catholic claimants that his assistance in getting provisos for them in the act would cost £2000. Having long coveted the post of surveyor-general, he was eventually appointed for life in 1668. Although removed in 1689 under the Jacobite regime, he was reappointed in 1690.

In the later 1660s Shaen made several unsuccessful attempts to become involved in the farming of the Irish revenue. However, although not included in the first great farm of 1669–75, the second great farm, of 1675–82, was granted to Shaen and ten partners, on the basis of a £60,000 advance to the crown and a rent of £240,000 a year. Initially Petty had been a partner, but was excluded by the time the final lease was agreed in mid-1676. From the outset the farmers were suspected of corrupt practices. Shaen dominated the farm, although the main security had been provided by William Ryder. An ensuing dispute between Shaen and Ryder was complicated by the interference of the vice-treasurer, Richard Jones, Viscount Ranelagh, a cousin of Shaen's wife, and Ormond after his return as viceroy in 1677, both of whom tried to use the dispute as a way of removing Shaen. However, although the accusations of corruption precipitated a commission of inspection, Shaen retained control because the farm rent continued to be paid. During 1680–82 he was involved in a power struggle with Ranelagh for control of the Irish revenue but, although he was well connected in English political circles, Shaen's honesty had come into doubt with the king. In 1682 the farmers' accounts were called for and the revenue put into the hands of government commissioners. The commissioners commenced proceedings to recover a farm debt of £108,000 in 1683, in which year Shaen was summoned to account before the English Treasury board. At that time Petty wrote of him: 'he never did me good, nor did I ever do him wrong. He is a dangerous friend and a mischievous foe' (Fitzmaurice, 263).

A member of a philosophical society in 1662, Shaen became a fellow of the Royal Society in 1663. While resident in London in the later 1670s he associated with other fellows such as the diarist John Evelyn, Christopher Wren, and Robert Boyle, another uncle of Shaen's wife. Shaen was expelled from the Royal Society in 1685. He sat as MP for Baltinglass, co. Wicklow, in the Irish parliaments of 1692 and 1695. He died on 13 December 1695, and was succeeded by his son, on whose death, on 24 June 1725, the baronetcy became extinct. C. I. McGrath

Sources GEC, *Baronetage*, vol. 3 • J. Lodge, *The peerage of Ireland*, rev. M. Archdall, rev. edn, 1 (1789) • J. Burke and J. B. Burke, *A genealogical and heraldic history of the extinct and dormant baronetcies of England, Ireland and Scotland*, 2nd edn (1841); repr. (1844) • C. W. Fitzgerald, duke of Leinster, *The earls of Kildare and their ancestors, from 1057 to 1773*, 2 vols. (1858) • Evelyn, *Diary*, vol. 4 • S. Egan, 'Finance and the government of Ireland, 1660–85', PhD diss., TCD, 1983 • *CSP Ire., 1647–62; 1666–9* • T. J. Kiernan, *A history of the financial administration of Ireland to 1817* (1930) • K. M. Lynch, *Roger Boyle, first earl of Orrery* (1965) • L. J. Arnold, *The Restoration land settlement in county Dublin, 1660–1688* (1993) • E. Fitzmaurice, *The life of Sir William Petty, 1623–1687* (1895) • R. Dunlop, ed., *Ireland under the Commonwealth*, 2 vols. (1913) • E. Strauss, *Sir William Petty: portrait of a genius* (1954) • *CSP dom., 1675–7* • *Manuscripts of the earl of Egmont: diary of Viscount Percival, afterwards first earl of Egmont*, 3 vols., HMC, 63 (1920–23), vol. 2 • W. A. Shaw, ed., *Calendar of treasury books*, 2, PRO (1905) • R. Lascelles, ed., *Liber munerum publicorum Hiberniae … or, The establishments of Ireland*, later edn, 2 vols. in 7 pts (1852), vol. 1, pt 2 • S. Réamonn, *History of the revenue commissioners* (1981) • *The journals of the House of Commons of the kingdom of Ireland*, 2 (1753) • T. Barnard and J. Fenlon, eds., *The dukes of Ormonde, 1610–1745* (2000)
Archives BL, Carte MSS • NL Ire., Orrery MSS 13177–13225

Shaen, William (1821–1887), radical and lawyer, was born on 31 October 1821 in Hatfield Peverel, Essex, the youngest son of Samuel and Rebecca Shaen, wealthy Unitarians. Samuel Shaen was a lawyer who, following the repeal of the Test and Corporation Acts in 1828, was one of the first of his religious persuasion to be appointed as a country magistrate. William Shaen was educated at the nonconformist Hove House School, Brighton, where he began a lifelong friendship with Peter Taylor (1819–1891), who became a partner in the Courtaulds textile business and an MP. Shaen then attended (1833–6) the recently established University College School in London and read classics at University College, where he graduated in 1840.

Intending to become a barrister, like William Case and James Stansfeld, his friends at University College, Shaen studied law at Edinburgh University and began reading for the bar at the Middle Temple before deciding instead to become a solicitor. He was articled to William Henry Ashurst, then a leading radical solicitor in the City (who acted for many of those refusing to pay church rates, including Samuel Courtauld in the *cause célèbre* Braintree rate case). Shaen was admitted to the profession in 1848.

Through his family, his education, friends, profession, and religion Shaen belonged to a large group of middle-class Unitarians in London working for political and social reform. Shaen admired his principal, Ashurst, and became, with Stansfeld, a close friend of the young Ashursts: William, the only son and his father's partner, and his four sisters, Eliza, Matilda, Caroline (who married Stansfeld), and Emilie. Collectively they, with a few other like-minded friends, were known (from the Ashursts' residence) as the Muswell Hill brigade. Among the causes and people that attracted them, the most influential was the Italian revolutionary Giuseppe Mazzini, and in the early 1840s Shaen helped Mazzini establish a school for Italian children in London.

Shaen was instrumental in founding the Metropolitan and Provincial Law Association in 1848 and was its first secretary. He left Ashurst in order to establish himself in practice in partnership with Richard Roscoe in Bedford Row; they later took into the partnership W. T. Massey and H. A. Henderson. On 2 September 1851 Shaen married Emily Winkworth (1822–1887), daughter of the manufacturer Henry Winkworth, who with her sisters Susanna and Catherine was active in Manchester nonconformist circles. The Winkworth girls, and particularly Emily, were all friends of the novelist Elizabeth Gaskell, and her husband, William, a Unitarian minister in Manchester, conducted the marriage service. They had at least two daughters and a son; in 1860 Emily Shaen became an invalid and remained so until her death in 1887.

Throughout his professional life Shaen combined an

extensive practice with active support for a number of British and international causes and organizations; these included Italian unity and democracy, the abolition of slavery, women's education, female suffrage, and the campaign to secure the repeal of the Contagious Diseases Act. Among the controversial legal cases with which he was concerned were those of Colenso (1863–6), the Jamaica committee in 1866, Voysey in the 1870s, and, in the early 1880s, W. T. Stead, whose articles in the *Pall Mall Gazette* on the sexual exploitation of children led to the Criminal Law Amendment Act of 1885.

Shaen died suddenly on 2 March 1887 at his home, 15 Upper Phillimore Gardens, Kensington, London. He was buried in Kensal Green cemetery. His generosity, enthusiasm, organizing ability, and persistence, combined with intellectual clarity, had won for him the confidence and affection of all who had dealings with him and a considerable reputation as a lawyer and a humanitarian.

JUDY SLINN

Sources *The Inquirer* (12 March 1887) • *Solicitors' Journal*, 31 (1886–7), 320 • E. L. Rasor, 'Shaen, William', *BDMBR*, vol. 2 • J. S. Uglow, *Elizabeth Gaskell: a habit of stories* (1993) • D. C. Coleman, *Courtaulds: an economic and social history*, 3 vols. (1969–80) • *Mazzini's letters to an English family*, ed. E. F. Richards, 3 vols. (1920–22) • D. Mack Smith, *Mazzini* (1994) • M. J. Shaen, *William Shaen: a brief sketch* (1912) • H. Solly, *'These eighty years', or, The story of an unfinished life*, 2 vols. (1893) • J. R. Walkowitz, *Prostitution and Victorian society: women, class and the state* (1980) • m. cert. • d. cert.

Wealth at death £58,909 16*s.* 4*d.*: resworn probate, Dec 1887, *CGPLA Eng. & Wales*

Shaftesbury. For this title name *see* Cooper, Anthony Ashley, first earl of Shaftesbury (1621–1683); Cooper, Anthony Ashley, third earl of Shaftesbury (1671–1713); Cooper, Anthony Ashley-, seventh earl of Shaftesbury (1801–1885).

Shafto, Robert (*c.*1732–1797), landowner and politician, was the eldest of the four children of John Shafto (*d.* 1742) of Whitworth, co. Durham, and his wife, Mary (*d.* 1768), daughter of Thomas Jackson of Nunnington, Yorkshire. The Shafto family estate at Whitworth, co. Durham, was inherited by Shafto's father in 1729 upon the death of his elder brother, Robert. It is not known exactly when or where Shafto was born, but he probably spent most of his childhood at Whitworth, living in the manor house which Robert Surtees described as 'one of the best family mansions in the county' (Surtees, 3.302). The property had been owned by the Shafto family since 1652, when it was bought by Shafto's great-great-grandfather, Mark Shafto, a barrister and, from 1648, recorder of Newcastle upon Tyne.

Shafto was educated at Westminster School, London, from 1740 to 1749, and at Balliol College, Oxford, where he matriculated on 10 November 1749. He succeeded to the family estate on his father's death, 3 April 1742. Shafto's role in public life would follow the examples of the careers of his uncle, Robert (*d.* 1729), and his father, both of whom were MP for the city of Durham, from 1712 to 1713 and 1727 to 1729, and from 1729 to 1742 respectively. Shafto's political career began in 1760, when he defeated the 'regular Whig' (Namier, 'Shafto, Robert', 427) Thomas Clavering to be elected MP for Durham county. He was put up for election by Henry Vane, first earl of Darlington, and his campaign was supported by the bishop of Durham and Thomas Pelham-Holles, duke of Newcastle. Shafto's uncle and father had been tories, and once in the Commons he abandoned his patron Newcastle and, like many other former tories, allied himself with the followers of John Stuart, third earl of Bute. In 1767 he was recorded as a supporter of the Chatham administration. He remained MP for Durham until 1768, when he declined to stand for re-election.

Shafto married Anne Duncombe (*d.* 1783), daughter and heir of Thomas Duncombe of Duncombe Park, Yorkshire, on 18 April 1774 at her uncle's house in Grosvenor Square, London. The ceremony was conducted by Shafto's brother, Thomas Goodfellow Shafto, who was the rector of St Brandon's church, Brancepeth, co. Durham. Shafto and his wife had three children, John (1775–1802), Robert (1776–1848), and Thomas (*b.* 1777).

Shafto was MP for Downton, Wiltshire, from 1780 to 1784, and from 1784 to 1790. His wife, Anne, had inherited property at Downton, and while John Robinson wrote in 1783 that Downton was 'Mr Shafto's borough. He will come in himself. Attention and civility may probably obtain the other seat' (Namier, 'Shafto, Robert', 427), the 1784 election was actually contested by candidates supported by Jacob Pleydell-Bouverie, second earl of Radnor, who was a coheir of the Duncombe property. Shafto was re-elected, but only after the Commons had to decide the merits of rival ballots run by the Shafto and Radnor factions. Namier commented that Shafto 'is not known to have spoken in the House' (ibid.) during his time as MP for Downton; although usually in opposition, he voted with William Pitt the younger during the regency crisis of 1788–9. He did not seek re-election in 1790.

Shafto is remembered as the subject of the popular song 'Bonny Bobby Shafto'. The song was probably written in the eighteenth century, although various additional verses were probably written later. Sir Cuthbert Sharp observed that, as a young man, Robert Shafto was 'popularly called "Bonny Bobby Shaftoe"' (Sharp, 55). Sharp proceeded to state that the song was used for 'electioneering purposes in 1761, when Robert Shafto, of Whitworth, Esq., was the favourite candidate' (ibid.). He particularly refers here to the verse beginning:

> Bobby Shafto's looking out,
> All the ribbons flew about

and says that the first two verses (which begin 'Bobby Shafto's gone to sea' and 'Bobby Shafto bright and fair') 'are the most ancient' (ibid.). The song confusingly, however, tells of a Bobby Shafto who has 'gone to sea', promising to marry the girl he has left behind on his return. Sharp recounts how a 'Miss Bellayse, the heiress of Brancepeth' was believed to have 'died for the love' (ibid.) of Robert Shafto. Bridget Belasyse was the daughter of William Belasyse (*d.* 1769). She lived at Brancepeth Castle, and Shafto's brother Thomas was rector at St Brandon's Church, Brancepeth, so it is very possible that the two knew each other. Bridget died in 1774, two weeks before

Shafto married Anne Duncombe, but the cause of her death has been given as pulmonary tuberculosis rather than a broken heart.

There is no evidence that Shafto 'went to sea', although in 1778 he was appointed to the post of comptroller of fines and forfeitures from the outports. The song alludes to his handsome and fashionable appearance and Shafto is known to have been both of these from the portrait of him by Sir Joshua Reynolds of about 1756. The painting shows an imposing and immaculate figure who is very elegantly dressed: his red suit has gold embroidered buttonholes and lace cuffs, and he wears his wig (or this is possibly his own hair, powdered) tied at the back with black ribbon in the 'solitaire style' (Mannings and Postle, 411). It was suggested by Thomas and George Allan in their *Illustrated Edition of Tyneside Songs and Readings* (1891), acting on the information of W. Brockie, that the song was about Robert Shafto (1760–1781), last of the male line of the branch of the family that lived at Benwell, near Newcastle upon Tyne. All other writers on the subject agree, however, that Robert Shafto of Whitworth is the most likely hero of the song; indeed, some of the later verses of the song are said to have been added in the nineteenth century, when Shafto's grandson, Robert Duncombe Shafto (1806–1889), successfully campaigned to become MP for North Durham in the election of 1861. The song continued to appear in new arrangements, many of which were intended for music teaching purposes, into the beginning of the twenty-first century.

'Bonny Bobby Shafto' is not the only instance of the Shafto name being mentioned in song. Sir Walter Scott included the ballad 'The Raid of Reidswire' in his collection entitled *Minstrelsy of the Scottish Borders* (1833–4). This ballad was written to commemorate a battle between the Scottish and English on 7 June 1575, and is thought to date at least from the early part of the seventeenth century. Stanza xvii begins with:

> Young Henry Schafton, he is hurt;
> A soldier shot him with a bow.

Earlier in the ballad, in stanza x, the battle-cry of the English raiders is 'A Schafton and a Fenwick'.

Shafto's wife, Anne, died on 16 March 1783, and was buried at Downton, Wiltshire. He did not remarry. Shafto died on 24 November 1797, and was buried in the Shafto family crypt beneath Whitworth church. The principal beneficiaries of his will were Susanna Becroft of the Upper Wall, Hammersmith, Susanna Atkinson, late Susanna Becroft, Charlotte Becroft, Dorothy Becroft, and Robert Becroft; they may have been his mistress and a second family born outside wedlock. He was succeeded at Whitworth by his eldest son, John Shafto, who in turn was succeeded by his brother, Robert Eden Duncombe Shafto, MP for the city of Durham from 1804 to 1806. The descendants of Robert Shafto lived at Whitworth until 1981. The house that Shafto knew, however, was destroyed by fire in 1876, only part of the original library and kitchens surviving. The house was rebuilt from a three- to a two-storey building, and became a hotel in 1997. A reproduction of the painting by Reynolds hangs in the entrance lobby, acknowledging the fame of a man of whose private character little is known, but who very probably inspired one of the most popular ballads to come out of north-east England.

JESSICA KILBURN

Sources T. Allan and G. Allan, *Allan's illustrated edition of Tyneside songs and readings* (1891) • R. Surtees, *The history and antiquities of the county palatine of Durham*, 3 vols. (1816–40); facs. edn 4 vols. (1972) • C. Sharp, *The bishoprick garland* (1834); repr., ed. F. Graham (1969) • D. Mannings and M. Postle, *Sir Joshua Reynolds: a complete catalogue of his paintings*, 2 vols. (2000) • *The history of Whitworth* (2001) [leaflet produced by Whitworth Hall Country Park Hotel, co. Durham] • L. B. Namier, 'Shafto, Robert', HoP, *Commons, 1754–90* • W. Scott, *Minstrelsy of the Scottish border*, ed. T. F. Henderson, new edn (1932) • M. Schloesser, *The 'Keel row' and other ballads* (1999) • P. A. White, *Portrait of county Durham* (1967) • *Old Westminsters*, vol. 2 • R. A. Austen-Leigh, ed., *The Eton College register, 1698–1752* (1927) • www.shafto.org [Shafto genealogy], 15 Nov 2001 • H. C. Surtees, *The history of the castle of Brancepeth at Brancepeth, co. Durham* (1920) • L. B. Namier, 'Durham county', HoP, *Commons, 1754–90*, 1.273–4 • J. A. Cannon, 'Downton', HoP, *Commons, 1754–90*, 1.412–13 • Burke, *Gen. GB* (1937) • will, PRO, PROB 11/1301, sig. 62

Likenesses J. Reynolds, oils, *c.*1756, repro. in Mannings and Postle, *Sir Joshua Reynolds*, 20; Sothebys (11 July 1990), lot 49; priv. coll.

Shairp, Sir John, of Houston (*d.* 1607), advocate, was the eldest son of James Shairp, baxter (baker), burgess of Edinburgh, and, probably, his wife, Janet Morys. He matriculated at St Leonard's College at the University of St Andrews in 1553, and graduated MA, probably in the late 1550s. Having accepted protestantism, Shairp was one of those recommended for the ministry to the general assembly of the church in December 1560, but had changed to the law by 8 January 1562, on which date he was admitted to the Faculty of Advocates. His career coincided with a time of increasing numbers and professionalism in those practising at the Scottish bar. He was referred to as dean of the faculty in 1582. Throughout his practice he acted for, and gave legal advice to, the town council of Edinburgh, who on 16 October 1590 made him a burgess and guild-brother free, for his services to the town and in right of his late father.

Shairp had private clients in the professional, mercantile, and landowning community all over Scotland, for whom he not only appeared as an advocate in the courts, but also provided legal advice, drafted legal documents, and initiated legal proceedings. Like many other lawyers, and merchants, he loaned money at interest, taking land in security. About a hundred letters to him from clients and others have survived, forming a unique archive of a sixteenth-century Scottish advocate (NA Scot., Shairp of Houston muniments, GD30). His appearances as advocate in the court of session may be documented in the record of the decisions of that court, over 200 volumes for his working lifetime (NA Scot., registers of acts and decreets, CS7). He became a substantial landowner, purchasing property as far away as the Isle of Whithorn, and in Forfarshire (Angus) where he settled the lands of Ballindoch on a younger son. In 1569 he purchased the estate of Houston in Uphall parish, Linlithgowshire, where, about 1600, he began building a tower house (described as a 'fortalice' in the land transfer to his son).

Shairp was married three times. In his will of 1607 he refers to the children of his first two marriages. He and his first wife, Agnes Moffat (whom he had married by 25 March 1561), had three sons and two daughters, and he and his second wife, Euphemia, daughter of the Edinburgh merchant Alexander Acheson of Gosford, whom he married by a contract dated 14 December 1574, also had three sons and two daughters. In 1591 he married Margaret Collace, the widow of his second wife's cousin Walter Reid, commendator of Kinloss. His eldest son, James, developed a mental illness which prevented his succeeding to the estates, which passed to the second son, John, an advocate. Shairp's favourite son, Alexander, died in France in 1604 while studying at Poitiers. His eldest daughter, Anna, married William Little, 'a man baith honest and civil', but Shairp expressed himself 'somewhat disappointit' in the choice of his second daughter, Agnes. He did, however, accept the love match between his youngest daughter, Isobel, and Robert Dunbar, a relative of her stepmother, 'in respect of the honestie and trewth of the gentilman. I hoip … for ane happie success' (NA Scot., Shairp of Houston muniments, GD30/786). In 1604, while in London as a commissioner for discussions on the abortive parliamentary union between Scotland and England, Shairp was knighted by King James VI and I. He took ill in September 1607 and died at Houston on 10 October. His wife survived him. The burial aisle erected by his family at Uphall church still stands, as does Houston House, converted into a hotel. He left an estate valued at £57,305 Scots. MARGARET H. B. SANDERSON

Sources M. H. B. Sanderson, 'John Shairp, advocate and laird of Houston', *Mary Stewart's people: life in Mary Stewart's Scotland* (1987), 22–33 • NA Scot., Shairp of Houston muniments, GD30 • F. J. Grant, ed., *The Faculty of Advocates in Scotland, 1532–1943*, Scottish RS, 145 (1944), 189 • registers of acts and decreets, NA Scot., CS7 • *John Knox's History of the Reformation in Scotland*, ed. W. C. Dickinson, 2 (1949), 47 • *The works of John Knox*, ed. D. Laing, 6 vols., Bannatyne Club, 112 (1846–64), vol. 4, p. 337, n. 2 • holograph will and settlement, NA Scot., Shairp of Houston muniments, GD 30/787 • protocol book of Alexander Guthrie, 1557–61, NA Scot., B22/1/20, fol. 225

Archives NA Scot., Shairp of Houston muniments

Wealth at death £57,305 3*s*. 4*d*. Scots, *c*. £4775 sterling: will and settlement, NA Scot., Shairp of Houston muniments, GD30/787

Shairp, John Campbell (1819–1885), literary scholar, was born in Houston, in the parish of Uphall, Linlithgowshire, on 30 July 1819, the third son in the family of eleven children of Norman Shairp (1779–1864), a major who had served in the infantry in the army of the Bengal presidency in India from 1799 to 1816, and of Elizabeth Binning Campbell (*d*. 1853), daughter of John Campbell of Kildalloig, Argyllshire.

After preliminary training by a tutor, a Mr Bell from Dumfriesshire, in the family home, Shairp was educated at Edinburgh Academy (1829–32), in George Ferguson's class, where he laid the basis of his scholarship. During 1835 he and his brother attended private classes in Edinburgh, where he was first introduced to the poetry of Wordsworth. From 1836 to 1839 he attended Glasgow University, where he excelled at logic and moral philosophy and was awarded prizes for logic, Greek, ethic (poetical composition), and humanity (translations from the Latin). He was part of a lively social community at Glasgow, centring on the Peel Club, which debated contemporary issues and included members such as Norman Macleod and Henry Douglas (who later became bishop of Bombay, and whose sister Shairp was to marry). In this circle he honed his skills as a public speaker, and developed his passion for literary criticism, especially the criticism of poetry. On leaving Glasgow, he spent a winter in Edinburgh, before moving to Oxford in April 1840, where he won the Snell exhibition to Balliol. Here he attended lectures in logic and moral philosophy, in addition to classics and speculative philosophy. He once more found a lively circle of friends among the brightest undergraduates, which included the poet Arthur Hugh Clough, John Duke Coleridge, and Arthur Stanley (later to be dean of Westminster); much of this period in his life he later chronicled in his poem 'Balliol scholars: a remembrance (1840–43)', published in *Macmillan's Magazine*. During this period at Oxford he became deeply impressed by the leading figures of the Oxford Movement—which was then at its height—especially John Henry Newman and John Keble, although his own religious convictions retained their attachment to the theology of the Church of Scotland. The influence of Matthew Arnold also came to be felt by Shairp during his period at Oxford, and Shairp later admitted that Arnold and Newman were the two biggest influences on his intellectual and religious character. In 1842 he won the Newdigate prize with a poem on Charles XII of Sweden, and it became his first publication. He took his degree in Easter 1844, and unsuccessfully attempted to gain a fellowship at Oriel.

In 1846 Shairp was offered a mastership at Rugby School by A. C. Tait, his former tutor at Balliol, and he remained there until 1857. Although he enjoyed his time at Rugby, with its exceptionally high teaching standards, and where he mixed school lessons with tutoring private pupils, his nationalist feelings were awoken, and he spent several years trying to find a position in his native Scotland. On 23 June 1853 he married Eliza Douglas at Bute House, Petersham, and they had two sons, the first of whom, Norman (*b*. 1855), died in infancy, and the second of whom, John Campbell (*b*. 1858), was to become advocate and sheriff substitute of Argyllshire at Inveraray. In November 1856 Shairp took leave of absence from Rugby to teach Professor Lushington's class at Glasgow University. Soon afterward, however, he secured the position of assistant to the professor of Latin at the United College of St Salvator and St Leonard at St Andrews University. His initial stipend was so low that he was forced to take private pupils, a situation which was resolved in 1861 when he was appointed to the professorship. He made a number of close friendships during this period, particularly with the philosopher John Veitch.

Shairp began to publish regularly from this point on, with articles appearing in *Good Words* and the *North British*

Review. Although he had published his introductory lecture at St Andrews as *The Uses of the Study of Latin Literature* (1858), his first major publication was *Kilmahoe: a Highland Pastoral* which *The Scotsman* viewed favourably, describing it as a 'spring of genuine poetry' (Knight, 234). In 1866 Shairp was unsuccessful in his candidature for the chair of ethics at Glasgow, but continued to publish, with his *John Keble: an Essay* (1866), and his important collection of essays and articles, *Studies in Poetry and Philosophy* (1868). During this latter year he was appointed by the crown to the principalship of the United College at St Andrews, and as a result also took on a large number of administrative duties as a member of the university court. He later became closely involved with the establishment of a college at Dundee (later to become Dundee University).

A steady stream of publications flowed from Shairp's pen during this period: numerous articles in journals such as *Macmillan's Magazine*, and another volume of essays, entitled *Culture and Religion* (1870), which became an instant success, reaching a third edition by 1872, the same year in which his *Studies in Poetry and Philosophy* reached its second. Between 1872 and 1873 Shairp masterminded the publication of *The Life and Letters of J. D. Forbes*, his great friend and fellow academic at St Andrews. The volume was eventually published by Macmillan in 1873, after a prolonged and tortuous editing process. In the following year his edition of Dorothy Wordsworth's *Recollections of a Tour Made in Scotland in AD 1803* further demonstrated his powers as a literary critic, as well as his deep admiration for Wordsworth.

In June 1877 Shairp was elected professor of poetry at Oxford, and awarded the degree of MA. His candidature had been supported by his old mentor, Matthew Arnold. In 1879 his book on Burns, published in the English Men of Letters series, received mixed reviews. His first lectures at Oxford disappointed many, but were published as *Aspects of Poetry* (1881). He held the post jointly with the principalship at St Andrews until his death. The University of Edinburgh honoured him with the degree of doctor of laws in 1884.

Shairp enjoyed walking, especially in the highlands of Scotland, and in the countryside surrounding Yarrow in the borders. It was the Scottish landscape which inspired him to take up poetry. His other passion was for riding, and in particular, hunting. From about 1880, however, his health began to fail, and he eventually died of heart disease at Ormsary House, Ormsary, Argyllshire, on 18 September 1885. He was buried in the ancestral vault at Houston. RICHARD OVENDEN

Sources W. Knight, *Principal Shairp and his friends* (1888) • W. I. Addison, *The Snell exhibitions: from the University of Glasgow to Balliol College, Oxford* (1901) • M. Rodger, *John Campbell Shairp: an address given at the College of San Salvator* (1885) • W. I. Addison, *A roll of graduates of the University of Glasgow from 31st December 1727 to 31st December 1897* (1898) • W. I. Addison, ed., *The matriculation albums of the University of Glasgow from 1728 to 1858* (1913) • [T. Henderson and P. F. Hamilton-Grierson], eds., *The Edinburgh Academy register* (1914) • letters to Messrs Macmillan and Co., 1872–78, BL, Add. MS 55008 • list of prize holders, U. Glas. • *The letters of Matthew Arnold*, ed. C. Y. Lang, 6 vols. (1996–2001), vol. 1 • J. B. H. Simpson, *Rugby since Arnold* (1967) • bap. reg. Scot., 1819 • m. reg. Scot., 1853 • d. cert.

Archives U. St Andr. L., corresp. | BL, corresp. with Macmillans, Add. MS 55008 • Bodl. Oxf., corresp. with A. H. Clough and Mrs Clough • LPL, corresp. with A. C. Tait • Mitchell L., Glas., Glasgow City Archives, letters to Sir William Stirling-Maxwell • NL Scot., letters to J. S. Blackie • NL Scot., letters to Blackwoods • U. Edin. L., letters to David Laing • U. St Andr. L., corresp. with George Forbes

Likenesses R. Herdman, oils, U. St Andr. • mezzotint, NPG

Wealth at death £3125 8*s*. 8*d*.: confirmation, 26 Dec 1885, court books of commissariat of Fife

Shaka (*c*.1783–1828), king of the Zulu, born possibly at Ngunga (near Melmoth), Natal, was the son of Senzangakhona (*c*.1757–1816), chief of the Zulu clan, and Nandi (*c*.1764–1827), daughter of Chief Mbhengi (or possibly of Bhebhe, his father) of the Langa people. Although much has since been written on Shaka, the Zulu were preliterate and there are uncertainties and different versions of key aspects of his life. Shaka was born illegitimate and so not recognized as his father's heir, though his parents may later have married. Nandi was difficult and violent and Senzangakhona exiled her, reportedly for hitting one of his advisers with a knobkerrie. Growing up among his mother's clan, a bullied outsider, Shaka developed a ruthless thirst for power.

As a youth Shaka joined the army of Dingiswayo, chief of the Mthethwa, one of several chiefs then creating expanded paramountcies by employing the traditional circumcision initiation age-mate groupings as military units (*amabutho*). A successful warrior, Shaka won promotion. On Senzangakhona's death Dingiswayo helped Shaka seize the Zulu chiefdom. About 1817 Dingiswayo was killed by his rival Zwide of the Ndwandwe. Shaka expanded his following to counter the Ndwandwe and defeated them about 1818. Some sections of the Ndwandwe then broke away, moving into Mozambique where Soshangane created the Gaza kingdom. Two others, both known as Ngoni, moved on, creating kingdoms in what later became Malawi, Zambia, and Tanzania. The main Ndwandwe body, however, remained a serious threat to Shaka until 1826.

In building his own kingdom Shaka modified the *amabutho* system by keeping the young men on continuous service barracked at a series of royal homesteads until their *butho* was dissolved. This allowed the perfection of tactics of close formation fighting using short stabbing spears wielded from behind a wall of body-length cowhide shields. It also facilitated development of a common loyalty among young men of different home communities. This was reinforced by rituals involving the *inkhata*, a ball of fibres symbolizing their bonding together in the king's service. Each military household tended a section of the royal cattle herds which provided food and hides.

Ambitious, Shaka fought wars of conquest, looting cattle and incorporating conquered peoples into his state. Despotic, ruthless, sadistic, and determined to purge any threat to himself, he ruled partly by terror and ordered repeated executions and massacres. Obsessed by fears of rivals for his kingship, he never officially recognized as his any child: pregnant women of his *isigodlo* (seraglio) aborted, fled into obscurity, or were killed. In August 1824 he was wounded in an assassination attempt but, nursed by the British trader Henry Fynn (whose diary has been published and is an important if controversial source for Shaka's reign), he survived. There has been speculation over his appearance: reportedly he was physically powerful, dark-skinned, and ugly, with buck teeth. Some later writers have alleged he had an aversion to normal sex, was a latent homosexual, or impotent.

The large and efficient army under personally appointed officers (*induna*) strengthened Shaka's kingdom and his personal power. It has been estimated that when he first ruled the Zulu he had no more than 400 warriors, but by 1824 he had increased his army to some 15,000. In expanding his kingdom Shaka's forces drove the Ngwane leader Matiwane onto the eastern Transorangian highveld, adding to the turmoil earlier initiated there by the intrusion of the Hlubi in the era of Dingiswayo and Zwide. They also precipitated the migration of Mzilikazi's Ndebele (Matabele) onto the Transvaal highveld. Shaka's forces were raiding further into Natal by the 1820s, adding to the disruption initiated by other groups which had recently migrated there in the turbulent era of Dingiswayo. In 1824 a party of British traders landed at Port Natal. They bought Zulu ivory, and Shaka allowed them to establish vassal chiefdoms over the local African population. In 1826 they assisted a Zulu army which finally conquered the Ndwandwe.

In August 1827 Nandi died, according to Fynn from dysentery but according to a Zulu tradition, possibly started by his enemies, Shaka himself killed her by spearing her up her anus. After her death he ordered mass killings—possibly to purge opponents—and prolonged mourning, with no sexual intercourse on pain of death. In 1828 he launched a campaign to conquer the Transkei chiefdoms and establish direct contact with Cape Colony. The embassy he had sent in May 1828 to the governor had not returned, however, and fearing British intervention he turned back after receiving the submission of the Npondo. He immediately sent his army to attack Soshangane near Delagoa Bay. While the army was away he rounded up some four or five hundred warriors' wives, accused them of witchcraft, and had them killed. His half-brothers *Dingane and Mhlangana, sensing his growing unpopularity, deserted the military expedition, conspired with his personal attendant, the *induna* Mbopha, and speared Shaka to death on or about 24 September 1828, at his new capital, kwaDukuza, Natal; he was buried there. Dingane, Shaka's successor, moved the capital elsewhere, and later the town of Stanger was built on its site. The exact location of Shaka's grave was no longer known, but in 1932 a memorial was erected nearby to the 'Founder, King and Ruler of the Zulu Nation'.

In his twelve-year reign Shaka created a kingdom knit together by an institutional structure which survived under his successors and generated a sense of common Zulu identity without, however, eliminating earlier lineage chiefdom identifications. The emergence of this kingdom intensified the conflict and migration accompanying the process of change towards the expansion of political scale out of which it had itself been born. His forces contributed directly to causing the major migrations which carried this process to the areas later called Mozambique, Zimbabwe, Malawi, Zambia, and Tanzania. They intensified the dislocation of communities in Natal which had been begun by others. By initiating the Ngwane and Ndebele migrations they also contributed to the widespread dislocations on the South African highveld on the eve of the great Boer trek. JOHN D. OMER-COOPER

Sources C. Hamilton, 'Ideology, oral tradition and the struggle for power in the early Zulu kingdom', MA diss., University of Witwatersrand, 1986 • J. Wright, 'The dynamics of power and conflict in the region in the late 18th and early 19th centuries', PhD diss., University of Witwatersrand, 1990 • C. Hamilton, ed., *The Mfecane aftermath* (1995) • J. Peires, ed., *Before and after Shaka* (1981) • *The James Stuart archive of recorded oral evidence relating to the history of the Zulu and neighbouring peoples*, ed. and trans. C. de B. Webb and J. B. Wright, [5 vols.] (1976–) • *The diary of Henry Francis Fynn*, ed. J. Stuart and M. Malcolm (1950) • J. Laband, *Rope of sand: the rise and fall of the Zulu kingdom in the nineteenth century* (1995) • N. Isaacs, *Travels and adventures in eastern Africa*, ed. L. Herrman, 2 vols. (1936) • A. T. Bryant, *Olden times in Zululand and Natal* (1929) • *DSAB* • D. R. Morris, *The washing of the spears* (1966) • S. Taylor, *Shaka's children: a history of the Zulu people* (1994) • C. M. Thompson, ed., *African societies in southern Africa* (1969) • M. Wilson and L. Thompson, eds., *The Oxford history of South Africa*, 2 vols. (1971), vol. 1 • I. Knight, *Brave men's blood: the epic of the Zulu War, 1879* (1990)

Likenesses J. King, portrait, *c*.1825, repro. in Taylor, *Shaka's children*, facing p. 114

Shakerley, Jeremy [Jeremiah] (1626–1653?), astronomer, was born and baptized at Halifax, Yorkshire, in early November 1626, the son of William Shakerley and his wife, Judith Brig. His parents had married at Halifax on 7 February of that year; as Brig is also written in the registers as Brigge or Briggs, Jeremy could probably claim kinship with the mathematician Henry Briggs of Halifax. He records that he 'was brought up at a Free Schoole, and by the mediation of the Schoolemaster … went into Ireland continuing there until the Rebellion begun there, and then returning to my native place', and that from early 1647 he 'gave my mind to the Mathematicks' (Bodl. Oxf., MS Ashmole 243, fol. 117r). His correspondence with the astrologer William Lilly between January 1648 and March 1650 reveals that he was then living at Carr Hall, near Wheatley Lane, Pendle Forest, Lancashire, the home of the antiquarian Christopher Towneley, 'from whom meat and drinke is all I can expect' (ibid.).

Shakerley thus looked to Lilly to advance his career. He seems genuinely to have shared Lilly's enthusiasm for reforming astrology with the aid of modern astronomy; when another correspondent submitted a problem to his judgement, he declared that without such reform no reliable guidance could be provided. Concerns he mentioned to Lilly included predicting eclipses, translating the third book of Ptolemy, acting as amanuensis to the astrologer John Stephenson, for whom he calculated an ephemeris from Kepler's tables, and conversing with the mathematically minded Nathan Pighells. He composed annual almanacs, one of which was published as *Synopsis compendiariae, or, A Brief Description … MDCLI* (1651).

In February 1649 Shakerley announced that he would 'performe something against Wing' (Bodl. Oxf., MS Ashmole 243, fol. 117r). The result was *The anatomy of Urania practica: … laying open the errors and impertinencies delivered … by Mr Vincent Wing, and Mr William Leybourne, under the title of Urania practica* (1649). In this he argued that papers of the late Jeremy Horrocks (available to him through Towneley) provided a better basis than Wing's for astronomical calculations, especially in lunar theory. Wing replied in *Ens fictum Shakerlaei, or, The Annihilation of Mr Jeremie Shakerley* (1649). The dispute evidently worried Lilly, who had suggested the production of planetary tables in English but now declined to act as their patron. Shakerley records this in a letter of March 1650, and goes on: 'you taxe my tables for being the same with those of Jonas Moore … I make no doubt to cleare my selfe from your suspition of conspiring with Moore against you'; he concluded that 'now you have rid your selfe of mee, you need not long be separated from the friendship of Mr Wing and Mr Leybourne' (ibid., fol. 128r). Here the correspondence ends. Shakerley's tables were published by Robert and William Leybourne as *Tabulae Britannicae: the British Tables* (1653), with a subtitle offering 'logistical arithmetic, the doctrine of the sphere', material on chronology, the calendar, and time, and 'the calculation of the motions of the fixed and wandering stars, and the eclipses of the luminaries. Calculated … from the hypothesis of Bullialdus and the observations of Mr Horrox'. If the volume had any significant influence it was as a source of information about Horrocks's work.

Meanwhile Shakerley had sailed for the Far East, apparently under the auspices of the East India Company. One of his aims was to view a transit of Mercury predicted for 1651; an equivalent observation had been made only once before. A letter of 15 January 1653, addressed to Henry Osborne from Surat, on the north-west coast of India, shows that he successfully observed the transit, made other observations, and planned to collect records of Indian astronomy. He is believed to have died soon afterwards. FRANCES WILLMOTH

Sources Bodl. Oxf., MS Ashmole 242, fols. 94, 95; 243, fols. 111–29 • parish registers, Halifax • *Report on manuscripts in various collections*, 8 vols., HMC, 55 (1901–14), vol. 8, pp. 61–5 • P. Curry, *Prophecy and power: astrology in early modern England* (1989), 32–3 • F. Willmoth, 'Models for the practice of astronomy: Flamsteed, Horrocks and Tycho', *'Flamsteed's stars': new perspectives on the life and work of the first astronomer royal, 1646–1719*, ed. F. Willmoth (1997), 49–75 • V. Wing, *Astronomica Britannica* (1669)

Archives Bodl. Oxf., MSS Ashmole 242–243 • W. Yorks. AS, Leeds, Temple Newsam Estate MSS, TN/Corr.4: 326, 337, 343, 344, 348, 351

Shakespear [*née* Wood], **Dame Ethel Mary Reader** (1871–1946), public servant and geologist, was born on 17 July 1871 at Biddenham, near Bedford, the daughter of the Revd Henry Wood (*c*.1829–1912). After attending Bedford high school, she entered Newnham College, Cambridge, in 1891 and took the natural sciences tripos (second class, part one, 1894; first class, part two, geology, 1895). Among the most prominent and noteworthy of the early Newnham students, she was a tennis champion, an active Liberal member of the Political Club, and a star pianist at college concerts.

Dame Ethel Mary Reader Shakespear (1871–1946), by unknown photographer

In 1896 Wood went to Mason College, Birmingham, as assistant to Charles Lapworth (1842–1920), and shortly thereafter began the collaborative work for which she is best known, the preparation, with her Newnham friend and fellow geologist Gertrude Elles, of the monumental monograph *British Graptolites* (1901–18). Brought out under Lapworth's general editorship, it presented detailed and reliable descriptions of the members of this huge fossil group, critical in zonal demarcation, division, and correlation in Lower Palaeozoic rocks. It was perhaps the single most notable early contribution by women to British stratigraphic geology, and long remained the basis of research in the area. Elles wrote the text and Wood prepared the illustrations, which were particularly outstanding. She published a number of independent papers as well, those on the Lower Palaeozoic rocks of the Welsh borderlands (1900, 1906) being especially notable. A fellow of the Geological Society from 1919, she received the Murchison medal in 1920 for her contributions to the monograph.

Shortly after taking her DSc at Birmingham (1906) Wood married physics lecturer Gilbert Arden Shakespear. Their only child, a daughter, died in infancy. Throughout the

First World War she worked extensively to secure reasonable care and retraining for disabled soldiers, serving on pensions committees and civic associations; for nine years (1917–26) she sat on the special grants committee of the Ministry of Pensions. This public service was recognized with an MBE in 1918 and a DBE in 1920. A justice of the peace for Birmingham from 1922, she was much respected for her work on the bench. Care of children and working-class girls was her major concern. Along with Dame Elizabeth Mary Cadbury, she was closely involved in an early and very successful city of Birmingham plan for the boarding of children with foster parents; she herself was an official family visitor. Over the years she also helped poor women and girls, inviting many into her home for periods of rest. She was president of the Birmingham branch of the National Council of Women (1929–32) and for a time of the Birmingham and midland branch of the Federation of University Women. She died of cancer on 17 January 1946, at her home, Caldwell Hall, Upton Warren, Worcestershire, survived by her husband.

MARY R. S. CREESE

Sources *Newnham College Roll Letter* (1946), 47–9 • *Nature*, 157 (1946), 256–7 • G. L. E., *Quarterly Journal of the Geological Society of London*, 102 (1946), xlvi–xlvii • *The Times* (28 Jan 1946) • [A. B. White and others], eds., *Newnham College register, 1871–1971*, 2nd edn, 1 (1979), 112 • Newnham College, Cambridge, archive • d. cert. • m. cert.

Likenesses two photographs, Newnham College, Cambridge [*see illus.*]

Wealth at death £3501 16*s*. 1*d*.: probate, 23 May 1946, *CGPLA Eng. & Wales*

Shakespear, John (1774–1858), orientalist, born at Lount, near Ashby-de-la-Zouch, Leicestershire, in August 1774, was the son of a small farmer. He was educated at the parish school at Staunton Harold, and afterwards at a school kept by a clergyman, who brought him to the notice of Francis Rawdon Hastings, Lord Rawdon, the lord of the manor. Lord Rawdon, who was contemplating a mission to north Africa, sent Shakespear to learn Arabic in London. In 1793 Lord Rawdon obtained for him a post in the commissariat of a force under his command, which was sent in aid of the royalist insurgents in Brittany but which returned without having achieved anything.

About 1805 Shakespear was appointed to an oriental professorship at the Royal Military College, Marlow. When the East India Company opened its college at Addiscombe in 1809, he was appointed professor of Hindustani. While there he compiled a Hindustani grammar (1813) and dictionary (1817), and various textbooks. Of the first edition of his dictionary he said that it was little more than a revision of one published in Calcutta by William Hunter, but subsequent editions contained the results of his own scholarship. In 1829 he retired from the East India Company's service with a pension. Being frugal he put by a considerable part of his salary and, with the large sums from the sale of his books, he was able on his retirement to buy Langley Priory, near Ashby-de-la-Zouch, thereby fulfilling, it was said, the ambition of his boyhood.

In 1856 Shakespear gave £2500 to the trustees of the fund for preserving William Shakespeare's house at Stratford upon Avon, prompted apparently by the idea that he might have been descended from a branch of the dramatist's family. In his will (which was proved at under £18,000 in 1860) he bequeathed a further sum to the fund but the court of chancery pronounced the bequest invalid. He died at Langley Priory on 10 June 1858, unmarried, the estate passing to his nephew, Charles Bowles, who had followed his uncle and become professor of Hindustani at Addiscombe, and who took the surname of Shakespear.

STEPHEN WHEELER, *rev.* ELIZABETH BAIGENT

Sources H. M. Vibart, *Addiscombe: its heroes and men of note* (1894) • private information (1897) • *CGPLA Eng. & Wales* (1858) • *The Athenaeum* (1858), 85 • advertisement, *The Athenaeum* (21 July 1860), 78 • *GM*, 3rd ser., 5 (1858), 197–8

Likenesses H. P. Briggs, oils, 1835, Langley Priory, near Ashby-de-la-Zouch, Leicestershire • two portraits, Langley Priory, near Ashby-de-la-Zouch, Leicestershire

Wealth at death under £18,000: resworn probate, July 1860, *CGPLA Eng. & Wales* (1858)

Shakespear [*née* Tucker], **Olivia** (1863–1938), novelist, was born on 17 March 1863 at Southlands, Chale, on the Isle of Wight, the second of the three children of Major-General Henry Tod Tucker CB (1808–1896), who served with the British army in Bengal from 1824 until ill health forced his retirement in 1856, and Harriet Maria (1821–1900), second daughter of Sir Henry Allen Johnson (1775–1860). In 1866 the family moved to Framfield in Sussex, and then to Bayswater in London in 1878. Olivia Tucker was privately educated at home; like her cousin Lionel Johnson (1867–1902) she read voraciously from an early age. On 8 December 1885 she married Henry Hope Shakespear (1849–1923), a solicitor from a family with a long history of civil and military service in India. They lived first at 18 Porchester Square, Bayswater, where their only child, Dorothy (1886–1973), was born on 14 September 1886.

The marriage, though outwardly tranquil, was not, from Olivia Shakespear's point of view, a happy one. In April 1894, at the inaugural dinner for the *Yellow Book*, she first encountered William Butler *Yeats (1865–1939); thus began a lifelong relationship which developed, during 1895–6, into a love affair. Olivia Shakespear broke off the affair early in 1897, owing to Yeats's continuing obsession with Maud Gonne (1867–1953), but by 1899 they had resumed contact, and thereafter remained close friends. Olivia Shakespear is a significant presence in Yeats's *The Wind among the Reeds* (1899), and her fourth novel, *Rupert Armstrong* (1898), a *roman-à-clef* about the life of John Millais that attributes his artistic decline to the influence of Effie Ruskin, takes some of its emotional colouring from her affair with Yeats.

Between 1894 and 1909 Olivia Shakespear published six novels, of which the first three, *Love on a Mortal Lease* (1894), *The Journey of High Honour* (1894), and *The False Laurel* (1896), though elegantly written, are conventional 'society' novels. With *Rupert Armstrong* her work becomes more distinctive; *The Devotees* (1904) is a study of a son in thrall to a feckless mother, while *Uncle Hilary* (1909) explores the plight of a young woman who unknowingly marries her stepfather and eventually finds peace in a quasi-Buddhist detachment from the world.

Though not personally ambitious—Yeats remarked that she seemed content 'to have no more of life than leisure, and the talk of her friends' (Yeats, *Memoirs*, 74)—Olivia Shakespear remained actively involved in London literary circles throughout her life. In 1909 she introduced Yeats to Ezra Pound, who married her daughter, Dorothy, in 1914; in 1911 her brother Henry Tudor Tucker (1868–1943) married Edith Ellen Hyde-Lees (1868–1942), whose daughter Bertha George Hyde-Lees (1892–1968) was later to marry Yeats.

After her husband's death in July 1923, Olivia Shakespear moved to 34 Abingdon Court, Kensington. There she died of a heart attack on 3 October 1938. On hearing the news of her death Yeats wrote: 'She was not more lovely than distinguished—no matter what happened she never lost her solitude' (*Letters of W. B. Yeats*, 916).

JOHN HARWOOD

Sources J. Harwood, *Olivia Shakespear and W. B. Yeats* (1989) • W. B. Yeats, *Memoirs*, ed. D. Donoghue (1972) • D. Toomey, 'An afterword on *Rupert Armstrong*', *Yeats Annual*, ed. W. Gould (1986), 99–102 • *The letters of W. B. Yeats*, ed. A. Wade (1954) • b. cert. • m. cert. • d. cert.
Likenesses photograph, *c*.1893, repro. in Harwood, *Olivia Shakespear*, frontispiece • photographs, repro. in Harwood, *Olivia Shakespear*
Wealth at death £23,377: probate, 8 Nov 1938, *CGPLA Eng. & Wales*

Shakespear, Sir Richmond Campbell (1812–1861), army and political officer in India, youngest son of John Talbot Shakespear, of the Bengal civil service, and Emily (eldest daughter of William Makepeace Thackeray of the Bengal civil service and his wife, Amelia Richmond Webb), was born in India on 11 May 1812, and baptized at Krishnagar on 13 April 1813. He came to England with his first cousin, William Makepeace Thackeray, and was with him at a preparatory school—ruled, according to Thackeray, 'by a horrible little tyrant'—and at Charterhouse. After attending Addiscombe College (1827–8) he was commissioned second lieutenant in the Bengal artillery on 12 June 1828. He arrived in India on 10 February 1829 and served at various stations in Bengal until 19 January 1837, when he was appointed assistant in the revenue department and stationed at Gorakhpur.

On 25 September 1838 he joined at Delhi the 6th light field (camel) battery of nine-pounders under Captain Augustus Abbott, and, leaving Delhi on 4 November, marched in the army of the Indus under Major-General Sir Willoughby Cotton and Lieutenant-General Sir John Keane, to Kandahar, arriving in April 1839. He took part in the expedition to Girishk under Sir Robert Sale, returning to Kandahar on 29 May. Like other British officers, he distrusted Shah Shuja.

On 21 June, Shakespear was appointed political assistant in the mission to Herat of Major d'Arcy Todd, the newly appointed envoy to Shah Kamran. Shakespear's special duty was to train the troops at Herat in gunnery and drill. Towards the end of 1839 a Russian expedition under General Perovsky left Orenburg for Khiva; fearing Russian penetration in central Asia, Todd sent Captain James Abbott to persuade the khan of Khiva to release Russian captives sold into slavery, thereby depriving Perovsky of his *casus belli*. Abbott was unsuccessful in his mission but appalling winter weather conditions compelled Perovsky to abandon his march to Khiva.

Sir Richmond Campbell Shakespear (1812–1861), by Charles Grant, 1842

Todd, without news from Abbott, dispatched Shakespear to Khiva on a similar mission. With an escort of eleven picked Heratis he left Herat on 14 May 1840, covering the 433 miles to Khiva by horse and camel by 12 June. He negotiated with the khan of Khiva, and meanwhile proposed to his own superiors a *de facto* British protectorate over Khiva, supporting it by officers and money. Exceeding his instructions and offering the khan a future alliance with Britain, Shakespear persuaded the khan to release the Russian slaves into his care—416 in all, including 18 women and 11 children. With a Khivan escort, Shakespear led them across the desert to Fort Aleksandrovsk on the Caspian and thence to Orenburg on 1 October, where he was received with acclamation. Having delivered his charges he travelled to St Petersburg, arriving on 3 November 1840. He was fêted and was cordially received by the tsar. From St Petersburg, Shakespear carried dispatches to London. On 31 August 1841 he was knighted. He published 'A journey from Herat to Orenburg' in *Blackwood's Edinburgh Magazine* (June 1846).

Shakespear returned to India in 1841. On 3 January 1842

he was appointed military secretary to Major-General George Pollock, commanding the force assembled at Peshawar for the relief of Sir Robert Sale at Jalalabad. He reached Peshawar on 5 February and remained there for two months while the column was organized and reinforcements were brought up. On 31 March he accompanied Pollock to Jamrud, and on 5 April entered the Khyber Pass. He volunteered to accompany Lieutenant-Colonel Taylor as his aide-de-camp in his attack on the heights on the right, and took command of the men who had recently formed the garrison of Ali Masjid, for which he was mentioned in dispatches. He again distinguished himself at Mamu Khel on 24 August, at Jagdalak on 8 September, and at Tezin on 12 and 13 September, and was again mentioned in dispatches. On arrival at Kabul on 15 September he volunteered to accompany 600 Kuzzilbash horsemen to rescue the British captives held by the Afghans at Bamian. The captives, by the exertions of Eldred Pottinger and by liberal bribery, had already effected their own release, but Shakespear, meeting them on 17 September at the foot of the Kalu Pass, escorted them through the disturbed country until, on 20 September, they met Sale's troops. Shakespear arrived at Kabul with the captives on 22 September. In October and November he accompanied Pollock on his return march to India, crossing the Sutlej at Ferozepore on 19 December.

On 28 March 1843 Shakespear was appointed deputy commissioner of Saugor. He was promoted brevet captain on 12 June. In October he was transferred to Gwalior as assistant to Lieutenant-Colonel Sleeman, political agent in Sindhia's dominions, and took part in the war against the Maratha forces, which was considered necessary to establish the government at Gwalior on a firm foundation. He was aide-de-camp to Sir Hugh Gough at the battle of Maharajpur on 29 December 1843. After this he was employed in getting possession of Gwalior Fort and in disbanding the durbar troops. On return to civil duties he remained in political charge of Gwalior until June 1848. During his service at Gwalior, Shakespear married (at Agra), on 5 March 1844, Marion Sophia, third daughter of George Powney Thompson of the Bengal civil service and his wife, Harriet. Lady Shakespear, three sons, and six daughters survived Shakespear, and she died at Bournemouth on 16 December 1899. On 1 May 1846 he was promoted to be regimental captain.

In 1848 sickness compelled Shakespear to go to the hills on leave; but on the outbreak of the Second Anglo-Sikh War he returned to military duty on 20 October. Joining at Ferozepore the army of the Punjab under Sir Hugh Gough, he was present at the action of Ramnagar on 22 November. On 1 December he was promoted to brevet major. On 3 December he was in the action of Sadulapur or passage of the Chenab, and on 13 January 1849 he commanded his battery of six heavy guns at the battle of Chilianwala and was mentioned in dispatches. At the battle of Gujrat on 21 February 1849 Shakespear again commanded his heavy-gun battery. The battle opened with a three hours' bombardment by the British at a range of 1500 yards and at the rate of forty rounds per gun per hour. After this the artillery advanced with exceptional speed, taking up forward positions and steadily driving the enemy back. Shakespear was wounded and was invalided to the hills. He was thanked in dispatches, and on 7 June he was promoted to brevet lieutenant-colonel.

Shakespear returned to civil employment at Gwalior towards the end of 1849. In 1851 he was transferred to the political agency at Jodhpur. He was gazetted to be resident in Nepal in 1853, but did not take this up as the post did not become vacant. He was promoted to brevet colonel in the army on 28 November 1854. In 1857 he was appointed resident at Baroda, and, in February 1858, political commissioner of the district, and received acting command of the northern division of the Bombay army, in addition to his political duties, with the rank of brigadier-general. He was promoted regimental lieutenant-colonel on 27 August 1858.

In July 1859 Shakespear became agent to the governor-general for central India, residing at Indore. He conducted that year negotiations with the begums of Bhopal and installed Sikandar Begam as rani of Bhopal. For his tact in extricating the government from an embarrassing position he was commended by the governor-general in council. He was made CB, civil division, in 1860, and later in the same year (30 December) Lord Canning, in a dispatch to the home government, expressed his high appreciation of Shakespear's conduct of the negotiations with Sindhia. Shakespear had accepted the post of chief commissioner of Mysore and Coorg, and was preparing to take up the appointment when he died of bronchitis on 29 October 1861 at Indore, and was buried at the old cemetery there.

R. H. Vetch, *rev.* James Lunt

Sources Lady Sale, *A journal of the disasters in Affghanistan* (1840) • J. W. Kaye, *History of the war in Afghanistan*, 3rd edn, 3 vols. (1874) • J. W. Kaye, *Lives of Indian officers*, 2 (1867), 253 • J. H. Stocqueler, *Memorials of Afghanistan: being state papers, official documents, dispatches, authentic narratives, etc.* (Calcutta, 1843) • V. Eyre, *Journal of an Afghanistan prisoner* (1843) • G. Pottinger, *The Afghan connection* (1983) • W. M. Thackeray, *Roundabout papers* (1922) • W. Hunter, *Thackerays in India* (1897), 147 • C. R. Low, *The life and correspondence of Field-Marshal Sir George Pollock* (1873) • J. Abbott, *Narrative of a journey from Heraut to Khiva, Moscow, and St Petersburg*, 2 vols. (1843) • U. Low, *Fifty years with John company: from the letters of General Sir John Low, 1822–1858* (1936) • H. C. B. Cook, *The Sikh wars: the British army in the Punjab, 1845–1849* (1975) • *The Times* (6 Dec 1861) • *The Times* (12 Dec 1861) • H. M. Vibart, *Addiscombe: its heroes and men of note* (1894) • M. E. Yapp, *Strategies of British India: Britain, Iran and Afghanistan, 1798–1850* (1980) • V. C. P. Hodson, *List of officers of the Bengal army, 1758–1834*, 4 (1947)
Archives BL OIOC, letters to Lord Elphinstone, MSS Eur. F 87–89
Likenesses C. Grant, engraving, 1842, BL OIOC [*see illus.*] • H. Fanner, crayon; in possession of Lady Shakespear in 1897 • engraving (after drawing by A. Soltykoff), repro. in Low, *Fifty years*

Shakespear, William Henry Irvine (1878–1915), diplomat and explorer, was born at Multan, in what is now Pakistan, on 29 October 1878, the eldest son of William Henry Sullivan Shakespear, of the Indian forestry service, and his wife, Anne Caroline, *née* Davidson. A natural athlete throughout his school career, he was educated at Portsmouth grammar school (1889–1893) and King William's

College in the Isle of Man (1893–1896), and passed out of Sandhurst early in 1898. He never married.

After some six years' service in the Indian army, mostly in Rawlpindi and Bombay, during which he learnt Arabic, Persian, Pushtu, and Urdu, Shakespear transferred to the political department of the government of India. In 1904 he was appointed consul at Bandar-e-ʿAbbas and assistant to the political resident in the Persian Gulf, Sir Percy Cox; at the time of his appointment he was the youngest consul in the Indian administration.

Although Shakespear is best known for his explorations of Arabia, he was also a pioneer motorist. Early in 1907 he bought an 8-horsepower single-cylinder Rover, and left Bushehr in April to drive to England through Persia, Turkey, Greece, Macedonia, Montenegro, and Croatia to Italy. Only one European had made part of this journey by car before, a Romanian driving from Bucharest to Tehran two years earlier. There were no paved roads between Persia and Italy.

In April 1909 Shakespear was appointed political agent in Kuwait, the official position which he held for most of the rest of his life. The years immediately before the First World War were a complex period in the politics of the Arabian peninsula and the gulf. First, Mubarak al-Sabah, amir of Kuwait between 1896 and 1916, who had come to power after assassinating his brother, signed a fairly loose agreement with Britain in 1899 in which he agreed not to grant any part of his territory to a third party without Britain's consent. Second, in January 1902, ʿAbd al-ʿAziz ibn ʿAbd al-Rahman al-Saʿud (Ibn Saʿud), who, together with his family, had long enjoyed the friendship and protection of the amir of Kuwait, recaptured Riyadh from his rivals, the al-Rashid, setting off a chain of events which culminated in the foundation of the modern state of Saudi Arabia some thirty years later. In 1905 the Ottoman state appointed Ibn Saʿud *qa'immaqam* of southern Najd; in 1906 a raiding party under his leadership killed his main rival, the Ottomans' principal ally ʿAbd al-Aziz ibn al-Rashid, and in consequence Turkish forces withdrew from most of northern and north-western Najd.

In 1906 and 1907 Ibn Saʿud made a number of overtures to the government of India through various intermediaries, indicating that he too would value British protection in some form or other. After his appointment to Kuwait in 1909, Shakespear was involved in conveying these wishes to his superiors in India and in the British legation in Constantinople, although both Ibn Saʿud's appeals and Shakespear's tenacious if measured support of them tended to fall on deaf ears.

In February 1910 Shakespear met Ibn Saʿud for the first time, at the palace of Mubarak of Kuwait, and took the first recorded photograph of him. The two men seem to have developed an immediate liking for one another, and the amir invited the political agent to visit him in Riyadh the following year. The meeting took place at Thaj in eastern Arabia, since Ibn Saʿud was on campaign, still intent both on the complete reduction of the al-Rashid, who were still a force to be reckoned with in northern Najd, and on driving the Turks out of Arabia altogether, which had begun to seem more feasible after the Young Turk revolution in 1909. By mid-1913 Ibn Saʿud, in spite of a renewed warning from Shakespear in May that he could expect no support from Britain, dispatched his forces to al-Hasa and ejected the Ottoman garrison. Again Ibn Saʿud asked for British recognition as ruler of the area; again Shakespear was obliged to tell him in December 1913 that this could not be granted. In May 1914 Ibn Saʿud accepted the title of *wali* of Najd (including al-Hasa) from the Ottomans.

In addition to his officially sanctioned political activities Shakespear is known for his meticulously recorded excursions to the interior of Arabia between 1909 and 1914. Each journey was registered with camera and sextant, and with entries in a daily log. His longest journey was undertaken between January and May 1914, from Kuwait to the Suez Canal via Riyadh (where he was the guest of Ibn Saʿud), Burayda, and Jauf, a distance of just over 1800 miles in 111 days, across what was mostly previously uncharted country.

From Egypt, Shakespear went to England in a final attempt to convince his superiors to take Ibn Saʿud more seriously; for a while, it remained an uphill task. However, a few weeks after the outbreak of war it dawned on the India Office that there might, after all, be some value in cultivating an Arabian ruler whose hostility to the Turks was not in doubt. Shakespear was sent back from England to Kuwait to transmit an urgent message to Ibn Saʿud, in effect an offer of the treaty of alliance which he had been seeking for so long. Shakespear left Kuwait on 12 December, and met Ibn Saʿud 200 miles north of Riyadh, where he was campaigning against the Shammar (still firm allies of the Turks) on 31 December. The task of convincing his friend was complicated by the indifference with which the government of India had treated him in the past; nevertheless, Shakespear managed to draft a treaty that Ibn Saʿud agreed to sign, though he could not be sure that it would be acceptable to his own superiors in Simla and London.

On 24 January 1915 Ibn Saʿud's forces fought the Shammar at Jarrab; Shakespear, who refused, as always, to exchange his military uniform for desert dress, was killed by a stray bullet while on a ridge overlooking the battlefield. Ibn Saʿud wrote to Sir Percy Cox:

> our beloved friend Captain Shakespear was hit from a distance by one of the enemy's shots and died. I offer my sincere condolences … We pressed him to leave us before the battle, but he refused to do so and was insistent on being with us. (Winstone, 211)

In December 1915 a treaty between Ibn Saʿud and the government of the United Kingdom was concluded, along the lines of Shakespear's draft (Leatherdale, 372–3). As it turned out, Ibn Saʿud played no great part in the First World War, and the most significant (although perhaps somewhat exaggerated) Arab participation came from the western part of the Arabian peninsula. Subsequently British support was crucial to Ibn Saʿud's survival in the late 1920s (especially to his victory over those of his erstwhile tribal supporters whose growing fanaticism nearly cost him his life) and also to his emergence by the beginning of the 1930s as ruler of the state that bears his family's name.

Much like his contemporary Gerard Leachman, Shakespear was a loner, a poor diplomat and administrator, but a gallant and intrepid soldier and explorer. Although his Arabic was fluent and idiomatic, he remained the quintessential British officer, resisting the temptation (if he ever felt it) to wear Arab dress in the desert. He also lacked the starry-eyed faith of some of his contemporaries in the possible effectiveness of tribal forces in modern warfare. On the other hand, his shrewd assessment of the waning of Ottoman authority in the northern Arabia peninsula, and his understanding of Ibn Saʿud's potential in the politics of the region, cannot be faulted. Had Shakespear lived, and had he in fact succeeded in harnessing Ibn Saʿud's energies more thoroughly to the imperial war effort, a very different post-war Arab world might well have emerged. PETER SLUGLETT

Sources H. V. F. Winstone, *Captain Shakespear: a portrait* (1976) • *GJ*, 45 (1915), 257 • D. Carruthers, 'Captain Shakespear's last journey', *GJ*, 59 (1922), 303–34 • R. H. Kiernan, *The unveiling of Arabia: the story of Arabian travel and discovery* (1937) • G. Troeller, *The birth of Saudi Arabia: Britain and the rise of the House of Sa'ud* (1976) • R. Lacey, *The kingdom* (1981) • C. Leatherdale, *Britain and Saudi Arabia, 1925–1939: the imperial oasis* (1983) • A. Vassiliev, *The history of Saudi Arabia* (2000)

Archives BL OIOC, diary of journey across central Arabia, MS Eur. A 230

Wealth at death £1180 3*s*. 8*d*.: probate, 30 Nov 1915, *CGPLA Eng. & Wales*

Shakespeare, Sir **Geoffrey Hithersay**, **first baronet** **(1893–1980)**, politician, was born at The Wilderness, St Peter Southgate, Norwich, on 23 September 1893, the second son of John Howard *Shakespeare (1857–1928), minister of St Mary's Baptist Church, Norwich, and later secretary of the Baptist Union of Great Britain, and his wife, Amy Gertrude, *née* Goodman. He went to Highgate School and Emmanuel College, Cambridge, where his education was interrupted by the outbreak of war in 1914. He served as a captain with the Norfolk regiment in Gallipoli and Egypt, and returned to Cambridge in 1919, where he was president of the union. He graduated BA and LLB in 1920, and was called to the bar at Middle Temple in 1922.

Shakespeare intended a law career, but in March 1921 he was invited by Lloyd George, a friend of his father, to join his secretariat at 10 Downing Street. He soon entered parliament, winning Wellingborough, Northamptonshire, as a national (that is, Lloyd George) Liberal in the general election of November 1922. He lost the seat in December 1923 before he had even made his maiden speech, and for the next six years pursued a successful career as a political journalist on the *Daily Chronicle* and the *Financial News*. He was briefly famous for predicting the early end of the general strike in 1926. On 16 September 1926 he married Aimée Constance (*d*. 1950), daughter of Walter Loveridge of Codsall, Staffordshire, and widow of Commander Sir Thomas Fisher KBE; they had a son and a daughter.

In the general election of 1929 Shakespeare was returned as a Liberal for Norwich. He made his maiden speech in the debate on the address in July, commenting drily on the Labour government's reliance on Liberal proposals to reduce unemployment:

> I wish the Lord Privy Seal would pin 'We Can Conquer Unemployment' as an appendix to the King's Speech. … I notice that he has already borrowed one or two ideas from it, but he will find out sooner or later that he will take the lot. (*Hansard 5C*, 229, 1929, 126–33)

When the government resigned in August 1931 Shakespeare supported Ramsay MacDonald's National Government, serving from August until October as parliamentary private secretary to (Percy) John Pybus, minister of transport.

Shakespeare now regularly voted independently of the leadership of Lloyd George, and associated instead with the Liberals who coalesced around Sir John Simon. The Simon group was ready to give 'whole-hearted support' to the government's emergency measures, even where these ran contrary to 'cherished formulas', notably free trade (Simon, 171). When in autumn 1931, with a general election impending, the group transformed itself into a party, Shakespeare was in 'the forefront', alongside Leslie Hore-Belisha. As Simon later recalled: 'Few political organisations have ever got into fighting trim so quickly' (ibid., 171). A party headquarters, staff, and campaign fund were swiftly established, and forty-one Liberal National candidates took the field in October, of whom thirty-five were elected. Shakespeare, at Norwich, was among them; he held the seat until 1945.

Shakespeare was made a junior lord of the Treasury in Ramsay MacDonald's National Government in November 1931, and became chief Liberal National whip (the party changed its name to National Liberal in 1948). After the departure from the government in September 1932 of the Liberals led by Sir Herbert Samuel, following the Ottawa trade agreements, Shakespeare supported Simon in trying to preserve the independence of the Liberal Nationals. Though closely allied to the Conservatives, and virtually indistinguishable from them in the eyes of their erstwhile Liberal colleagues, they continued to regard themselves as a wing of Liberalism. They saw themselves as in government to defeat socialism while advancing social reform. Independent Liberals, they reasoned, could do neither.

In the reshuffle following Samuel's departure Shakespeare became parliamentary secretary at the Ministry of Health, where he played a leading part in the national crusade against slums. In July 1936 he moved to the Board of Education, and in May 1937, upon Chamberlain becoming premier, he was appointed parliamentary and financial secretary to the Admiralty. In the next two years he saw first hand Britain's military unpreparedness, which he believed 'underlined the significance of Chamberlain's bid for peace at Munich' (*The Times*, 11 Sept 1980). To the end he loyally supported Chamberlain's foreign policy, writing after the war:

> No nation democratically governed can embark on a war and all it involves unless it has a cast-iron moral case which the nation accepts as conclusive. Chamberlain gave us that moral case by his policy of appeasement and his action at Munich. (Shakespeare, 186)

Although Churchill thought well of Shakespeare's work at the Admiralty, particularly during difficult negotiations with the dockyard workers' unions in March 1940, he approved his transfer to the department of overseas trade in Chamberlain's reshuffle in April 1940. And when Churchill became premier in the following month Shakespeare moved again, becoming parliamentary under-secretary of state for the dominions. He was also chairman of the Children's Overseas Reception Board, in which capacity he made an extended visit to Canada in winter 1941. And in 1944 he visited South Africa as a member of a parliamentary delegation. After losing office in the government reconstruction of March 1942 he sat as a backbencher until his defeat in the 1945 general election; he was created a baronet on 11 July 1942, and sworn of the privy council in June 1945. After the war he remained active in Liberal National affairs, serving as chairman of the party council in 1951.

Outside politics Shakespeare was involved in various commercial activities: he was a director of the Abbey National Building Society (1943–77) and deputy chairman (1965–9); president of the Society of British Gas Industries (1953–4); and chairman of the Industrial Co-partnership Association (1958–68). He also enjoyed country life on his farm in Hertfordshire. After the death of his first wife, Aimée, in 1950, he married on 29 February 1952 Elizabeth, elder daughter of Brigadier-General Robert William Hare; there were no children. Shakespeare died on 8 September 1980 at his home, Great Ash, Lubbock Road, Chislehurst, Kent.

A modest man with an air of quiet detachment, Shakespeare was also resolute and determined. He was often at the edge of great events and recorded his impressions in his memoirs, *Let Candles Be Brought In* (1949). This includes a chapter entitled 'A close-up view of giants—Lloyd George and Winston Churchill compared'. Revealingly, Shakespeare considered Churchill the more loyal to his colleagues, and Shakespeare's own relations with Lloyd George were damaged by his joining the Simon group in 1931. When Shakespeare later agreed to an out-of-court settlement in a legal action that he had brought against Lloyd George, over assistance he had given in the sale of the *Daily Chronicle*, he received only a fraction of what he had expected: it was, recorded Robert Bruce Lockhart, a 'remarkable example of L. G.'s vindictiveness towards any of his henchmen who turned against him' (*Diaries*, 627).

Shakespeare, though, always defended the Liberal National secession, which he believed helped to secure the social reforms of the 1930s. He saw Liberal National support for the Conservatives in much the same light as he saw appeasement, as practical politics. Given this, it was almost inevitable that talks about a Liberal reunion during the war would founder. They broke up over the Liberal National insistence on preserving in peacetime a 'national front' led by Churchill. Violet Bonham Carter, one of the Liberal negotiators, was not surprised at the outcome, and wrote of Shakespeare and his colleagues: 'None of them is the least interested in "politics" or ideas—& they all frankly admit that they lean to the right' (*Champion Redoubtable: the Diaries and Letters of Violet Bonham Carter, 1914–1945*, ed. M. Pottle, 1998–9, 284). In April 1947 the Liberal Nationals formally merged with the Conservative Party, through the Woolton–Teviot agreement, thereafter maintaining only symbols of their former independence. MARK POTTLE

Sources *WWBMP*, vol. 3 • *The Times* (4 July 1946) • *The Times* (18 July 1946) • *The Times* (26 Feb 1951) • *The Times* (11 Sept 1980) • G. H. Shakespeare, *Let candles be brought in* (1949) • *The Churchill war papers*, ed. M. Gilbert, 1: *At the admiralty, September 1939 – May 1940* (1993) • M. Gilbert, *Winston S. Churchill*, 6: *Finest hour, 1939–1941* (1983) • *Hansard 5C* (1923), 161.750, 767, 2102, 163.1614, 166.1195, 1854; (1929), 229.126–33 • *The diaries of Sir Robert Bruce Lockhart*, ed. K. Young, 2 (1980) • *WWW* • [J. Allsebrook, first Viscount Simon], *Retrospect: the memoirs of the Rt. Hon. Viscount Simon* (1952) • *The diaries and letters of Robert Bernays, 1932–1939*, ed. N. Smart (1996) • P. Williamson, *National crisis and national government: British politics, the economy and empire, 1926–1932* (1992) • N. Smart, *The national government, 1931–40* (1999) • D. Dutton, *Simon: a political biography of Sir John Simon* (1992) • *CGPLA Eng. & Wales* (1980) • b. cert. • m. certs. • d. cert.

Archives IWM, papers • NL Wales, papers | BL, letters to Albert Mansbridge, Add. MS 65253 • Bodl. Oxf., corresp. with Lord Simon • CAC Cam., corresp. with Sir E. L. Spears | FILM BFI NFTVA, news footage

Likenesses photograph, repro. in *The Times* (11 Sept 1980)

Wealth at death £61,565: probate, 31 Oct 1980, *CGPLA Eng. & Wales*

Shakespeare, John (*b.* in or before **1530**, *d.* **1601**). *See under* Shakespeare, William (1564–1616).

Shakespeare, John Howard (**1857–1928**), Baptist minister, was born on 16 April 1857 in Malton in the North Riding of Yorkshire, the second of three children of the Revd Benjamin Shakespeare (1817–1887) and his wife, Mary Anne, *née* Hithersay (1825–1886). Both his parents were Baptists. His higher education took place in London between 1878 and 1883: he gained an MA in philosophy at University College and was trained for the Baptist ministry at Regent's Park College. In 1883 he was invited to the pastorate of St Mary's Baptist Church, Norwich, and soon gained a national reputation as a preacher and organizer. On 5 September 1883 he married Amy Gertrude Goodman (1862–1960), the daughter of the Revd William Goodman and his wife, Mary. They had six children, the second of whom was Sir Geoffrey *Shakespeare.

Having been elected to the council of the Baptist Union of Great Britain and Ireland in 1885, Shakespeare made his mark when, in 1892, he delivered a paper appealing for greater co-operative efforts to be made in establishing new churches. In 1898 he was invited to become secretary of the union, taking up residence in Highgate, Middlesex. He immediately began to apply himself to the development of the Baptist Union as a strong, centralized organization directing the affairs of the denomination. His style of leadership was autocratic and the changes he made were rapid and far reaching. He raised a large national fund, primarily for the purpose of building new Baptist churches, and erected a London headquarters for the denomination that was opened in 1903. Previously disparate Baptist activities were increasingly brought under the umbrella of the union. In 1906 Shakespeare's first major work was published by the National Free Church Council, entitled *Baptist and Congregational Pioneers*.

Another major initiative spearheaded by Shakespeare was an attempt to facilitate the movement of Baptist ministers between local churches, and to support those who were in financial need. A significant part of his scheme, as it was eventually implemented in 1916, involved the division of Britain into areas, each overseen by a superintendent minister who was answerable to the union. Some saw this controversial step as the beginnings of episcopacy. Shakespeare was also largely responsible for the formation of the Baptist World Alliance, organizing its inaugural congress in London in 1905 and serving as its European secretary.

Shakespeare was, throughout his ministry, a keen advocate of Free Church unity, and was influenced by earlier leaders of the Free Church Council movement such as the Wesleyan Hugh Price Hughes. He wanted to increase the free churches' effectiveness and to raise their status. At the outbreak of war in 1914, supported by his fellow Baptist David Lloyd George, Shakespeare persuaded the War Office to allow new recruits to register as free churchmen and to commission Free Church chaplains. In December 1914 he created the United Army and Navy Board to nominate chaplains, and served as its chairman and secretary. Throughout the war he remained a loyal supporter and confidant of Lloyd George.

In 1916 Shakespeare was elected president of the National Free Church Council, and proposed the formation of a United Free Church of England. In 1919 the denominations agreed to come together into a federation, and the Federal Council of Evangelical Free Churches was formed, with Shakespeare as its first moderator. His views on church unity were expressed in his second major publication, *The Churches at the Cross Roads* (1918). In it he not only advocated Free Church union, but also made a plea for union with the Church of England. In October 1919 he was honoured for his contribution to the cause of church unity by the archbishop of Canterbury and the prime minister, together with many other church leaders, when a portrait in oils by John Collier and an illuminated address were presented to him. He also received an honorary DD from Glasgow University.

Shakespeare won the respect and co-operation—and often the affection—of those with whom he worked. He was passionate and energetic, frequently working for fifteen hours a day. He often appeared pale and drawn, and suffered from periodic bouts of nervous and physical exhaustion. In 1923 he came to believe his work was over, and retired because of ill health in 1925. He died following a stroke on 12 March 1928 at Fallowhurst, Bow Lane, Finchley, Middlesex, and was buried in the family grave at The Rosary, Norwich. In the tributes that were given at his memorial service in the City Temple in London, he was remembered for his dream of church unity, his statesmanlike leadership of the free churches during the war, his passionate commitment to supporting the Baptist ministry, and his creation of the Baptist Union as an effective national body. PETER SHEPHERD

Sources *Baptist Times* (15 March 1928) • *Baptist Times* (22 March 1928) • G. H. Shakespeare, *Let candles be brought in* (1949) • E. A. Payne, *The Baptist Union: a short history* (1959) • C. M. Townsend, The life and work of J. H. Shakespeare, photocopy of typescript, Angus Library, Regent's Park College, Oxford • Burke, *Peerage* • A. C. Underwood, *A history of the English Baptists* (1947) • R. Hayden, 'Still at the crossroads? Rev. J. H. Shakespeare and ecumenism', *Baptists in the twentieth century*, ed. K. W. Clements (1983) • *CGPLA Eng. & Wales* (1928)

Archives Regent's Park College, Oxford

Likenesses J. Collier, oils, 1919, Baptist Union, Baptist House, Didcot, Oxfordshire

Wealth at death £2130 9s. 0d.: probate, 26 April 1928, *CGPLA Eng. & Wales*

Shakespeare, William (1564–1616), playwright and poet, was baptized, probably by the parish priest, John Bretchgirdle, in Holy Trinity, the parish church of Stratford upon Avon, on 26 April 1564, the third child of John Shakespeare (*d.* 1601) [*see below*] and Mary Arden (*d.* 1608). It seems appropriate that the first of many gaps in the records of his life should be the exact date of Shakespeare's birth, though that is a common problem for the period. He was probably born on 21, 22, or 23 April 1564, given the 1559 prayer book's instructions to parents on the subject of baptisms. But, ever since Joseph Greene, an eighteenth-century Stratford curate, informed the scholar George Steevens that Shakespeare was born on 23 April, with no apparent evidence for his assertion, and Steevens adopted that date in his 1773 edition of Shakespeare, it has been usual to assume that Shakespeare was born on St George's day, so that England's patron saint and the birth of the 'national poet' can be celebrated on the same day. Where he was born is clearer: in 1564 his parents appear to have been living in Henley Street, probably in part of the building now known as Shakespeare's Birthplace but, equally probably, not in that part of the building in which the room traditionally known as the place of Shakespeare's birth is located. The accretion of myth and commerce around Shakespeare's biography and its material legacy produces such paradoxes.

Shakespeare's parents Richard Shakespeare, a husbandman and probably John's father, had settled in Snitterfield near Stratford by 1529 and had died by February 1561, leaving property that he rented from Robert Arden of Wilmcote. Robert Arden was a member of the younger branch of the powerful Arden family; his father, Thomas Arden, lived at Wilmcote and passed lands, probably quite extensive, to his son. Robert married twice: with his first wife, Agnes Hill, *née* Webbe, he had at least eight children, all girls, the youngest of whom was Mary; there appear to have been no children from the second marriage, though there were stepchildren.

The two families, Ardens and Shakespeares, were linked by Richard Shakespeare's tenancy from Robert Arden. But **John Shakespeare** (*b.* in or before 1530, *d.* 1601) did not continue his father's occupation. By the time he married Mary Arden (some time between November 1556 and 1558), he had established himself in Stratford as a glover and whittawer (a dresser of light-coloured leather). He lived in Henley Street, buying a house and garden there in

William Shakespeare (1564–1616), attrib. John Taylor, *c.*1610

1556 and starting to buy further property in town. In this he might well have been helped by his wife's inheritance: in Robert Arden's will of November 1556 she was named one of the two executors and supervised the substantial inventory of his goods and moveables in December 1556 after his death. She also inherited the valuable estate in Wilmcote known as Asbies, land that on her marriage came to her husband.

John and Mary Shakespeare were probably married in Aston Cantlow, the parish church for Wilmcote and the place where Robert Arden wanted to be buried. The exact date of the wedding is unknown but their first child, Joan, was born in September 1558 (and may well have died in infancy); Margaret was baptized in December 1562 and was buried the following April. A year later William was born. He survived the devastating plague that killed one in eight of the town's population later the same year. There were five more children: Gilbert (1566–1612), another Joan (born 1569, indicating that John and Mary's first child must have died by that year; she was the only sibling to outlive William, dying in 1646), Anne (1571–1579), Richard (1574–1613), and Edmund (1580–1607). All but Anne lived to adulthood. William's childhood was thus spent in a steadily increasing family and there were other relatives nearby: his uncle Henry Shakespeare, John's brother, lived in Snitterfield and many of his mother's sisters married local men.

John Shakespeare bought more property in Stratford in 1575, almost certainly including the rest of the 'Birthplace', creating a substantial house which even though it incorporated space for his workshop amounted to a fine home for his expanding family. But this period was also one of ever-increasing civic importance for John Shakespeare. He had risen through the lesser offices of the borough and, by the time of William's birth, was one of the fourteen burgesses of Stratford. In 1565 he became an alderman and in 1568 was elected bailiff for the year, the highest office in the town. In 1571 he became chief alderman and deputy bailiff. At about this time he also seems to have applied for a coat of arms. The family's wealth was also growing and the civic importance and high social standing that John Shakespeare had achieved in a brief period provided the context for William's upbringing.

But in the following years something seems to have gone wrong with John Shakespeare's finances. At the start of the 1570s he was stretching his commercial activities beyond his trade, dealing illegally in wool and also being prosecuted for usury. By the end of the decade he was in debt; in 1578 he mortgaged some of Mary's inheritance and lost it in 1580 when he could not repay the sum, land that would otherwise have been inherited by William in due course. He stopped attending council meetings after 1576 as well, and was replaced as an alderman in 1586. All of this too provided a family context for William's youth; the decline in John Shakespeare's fortunes cannot have been unaccompanied by anxiety.

John Shakespeare and Catholicism In 1592 John was listed by the presenters for the parish of Stratford upon Avon as an obstinate recusant, among nine on the list whose absence was identified by the presenters and by the commissioners to whom they reported as being 'for feare of processe for Debtte' (Schoenbaum, *Documentary Life*, 39). There is no self-evident reason to distrust this statement, though it has been seen as an excuse to cover secret Catholicism. Certainly some Catholics feigned debt as a reason for recusancy but John Shakespeare's debts seem real enough.

In 1790 a bricklayer was reported as having found in 1757 in the roof of the Henley Street house a manuscript now known as John Shakespeare's spiritual testament. Blank copies of this formulaic document, based on one written by Cardinal Borromeo, are claimed to have been circulated in large numbers by Catholic missionaries; this copy was said to have been completed by or on behalf of John Shakespeare. Transcribed by the great Shakespeare scholar Edmond Malone, who later came to doubt its authenticity, it is now lost and its link to John Jordan, a Stratford man well known for inventing materials to satisfy the increasing thirst for Shakespeariana, puts it under suspicion. In the unlikely event that it was genuine it would suggest that John Shakespeare was a Catholic still holding to his original faith and that William was brought up in a household where the double standards of adequate outward observance of protestant orthodoxy and private heterodoxy were largely achieved. There is, of course, no reason to assume that the adult William shared his father's religious views, and the evidence for John's being a Catholic is very far from decisive. It was, after all, during John Shakespeare's time as bailiff in 1568 that the images of the last judgment that decorated the guild chapel in Stratford were whitewashed and defaced as no longer acceptable to state protestantism, though this might simply have been a further example of John's outward conformism.

Players in Stratford In any case, another event during John Shakespeare's tenure as bailiff seems more significant for his son's future career: the visit to Stratford of two theatre companies, the Queen's Players and Worcester's Men, the first time theatre companies are known to have played in Stratford. Since the first performance in any town was usually in front of the town officials, John Shakespeare would have seen the performances and William might well have accompanied him (as other children certainly did in similar circumstances). Further visits followed: Leicester's Men in 1572 and 1576, Warwick's Men in 1574, Worcester's Men in 1574 and 1581, Lord Strange's Men in 1578, Essex's Men in 1578 and 1583, Derby's Men in 1579, Lord Berkeley's Men in 1580 and 1582. Across the period when William was likely to have been continuously resident in Stratford, there were at least thirteen visits by companies of players, bringing a fairly wide repertory of drama, little of which can be confidently identified. None the less, there is a context there for William Shakespeare's early learning about theatre performance and contemporary drama in the work of such professional companies. He might, too, have travelled nearby to see the spectacular entertainments at Kenilworth given by the earl of Leicester for the queen in 1575, or the magnificent cycle drama of mystery plays which was still performed annually at Coventry until 1578, or Coventry's Hocktide play (suppressed in 1568 but performed again at Kenilworth in 1575), or the amateur performances which regularly occurred in Stratford.

Shakespeare's education Shakespeare would also have acted, as part of his education, either in Latin plays or in oratorical declamation, the latter a crucial part of the performative training in classical rhetoric. William's own education was not likely to have been affected by his father's fluctuating fortunes. It was also probably far better than either of his parents had received. There is no evidence that either John or Mary Shakespeare could write: each signed with a kind of mark. But the marks were not the awkward crosses of the totally illiterate: John often drew a fine pair of compasses; Mary's mark in 1579 was a complex design, apparently incorporating her initials and fluently written. Both may well have been able to read: many who could not write could read. Certainly, given John's status in the community, his four sons would have gone to Stratford's grammar school where their education would have been free. Before that William would have attended 'petty school' from about the age of five to about seven, learning to read.

At the King's New School, Stratford's splendid grammar school, William would have learned an immense amount of Latin literature and history, perhaps using the Latin–English dictionary left to the school by John Bretchgirdle who had baptized him. Among the works that Shakespeare later used as sources for his plays are a number that he would have read as part of his grammar-school education: the history of Livy, the speeches of Cicero, the comedies of Plautus and Terence, the tragedies of Seneca, and the poetry of Virgil and, above all, Ovid, who remained his favourite poet. The range of Latin writing that formed the curriculum was, by modern standards, vast. The mode of teaching, by a good teacher assisted by an usher, was one calculated to ensure the arts of memory, facility in composition, and rhetorical skills.

In addition, regular attendance at church, a legal requirement which his father does not appear to have avoided until later, guaranteed prolonged exposure to the Book of Homilies (fairly dull), the Book of Common Prayer (rather more exciting), and, especially, the exhilarating language of the Bible in English, a resource that Shakespeare, like his contemporaries, knew well, used extensively, and embedded deeply into the fabric of his language.

After school, and marriage Leaving school at about fifteen, Shakespeare would have had a series of options open. He might have gone into his father's trade as an apprentice and there is anecdotal evidence to that effect recorded by John Aubrey in the late seventeenth century, also noting that 'when he kill'd a Calfe, he would doe it in a *high style*, & make a Speech' (Schoenbaum, *Documentary Life*, 58), though, since John Shakespeare's trade did not involve slaughtering, this could possibly refer to William's acting in a mumming play or Whitsun 'pastime' of the kind the town council paid for in 1583—pretending to kill a calf was a trick often included in such plays.

John Aubrey's conversation with William Beeston, son of Christopher who had worked with Shakespeare later in the Lord Chamberlain's Men, produced the snippet of information that Shakespeare 'had been in his younger yeares a Schoolmaster in the Countrey' (Schoenbaum, *Documentary Life*, 59). The theory is not impossible and has gained ground in the wake of the re-examination of the evidence surrounding the mention in 1581 of a 'William Shakeshafte' in the will of Alexander de Hoghton of Lea Hall in Lancashire, encouraging Sir Thomas Hesketh to take on Shakeshaft as a servant. Shakeshaft was a common name in Lancashire, not least in the area surrounding the Hoghton family estates, and an extremely uncommon one in Warwickshire; none of the many variant spellings of William Shakespeare's own name even begins to approximate to Shakeshaft.

John Cottom, who was the teacher at Stratford grammar school from 1579 to 1581 and hence during or just after Shakespeare's last year at school, returned to his family in Lancashire; his younger brother was a Catholic priest who was tried with Edmund Campion and executed in 1582. Perhaps, the theory runs, Cottom encouraged Shakespeare, as a member of a recusant Catholic family, to be a schoolteacher in a staunchly Catholic household in the north of England. The evidence is purely circumstantial and the crucial evidence, the mention of William Shakeshaft, is insufficient for proof. In any case, Shakespeare was rather less qualified to be a schoolmaster than any of the Stratford teachers he had studied under.

One advantage of the theory is that it suggests a route for Shakespeare to move to London since there were links between Hesketh and Hoghton and Ferdinando Stanley, Lord Strange (later earl of Derby), whose company of players might well have included Shakespeare but was more certainly the troupe that acted a number of Shakespeare's early plays.

But there is no reason to posit a direct link for Shakespeare between Lancashire and London, if he was ever in Lancashire at all, since by 1582 he was certainly back in Stratford. On 27 November a marriage licence was issued for Shakespeare's marriage to **Anne Hathaway** (1555/6–1623) (though the record in the bishop of Worcester's register mistakenly refers to the bride as Anne Whateley of Temple Grafton) and on the following day a bond was issued binding Fulke Sandells and John Richardson for the sum of £40 as surety for the marriage, a necessary step since William was at eighteen still a minor and needed his father's consent to the match. Sandells and Richardson had both in 1581 been named in the will of Richard Hathaway, Anne's father, a yeoman farmer of Shottery, a village just outside Stratford; the will left Anne 10 marks, to be paid when she married.

Anne (whose name also appears as Agnes) was the eldest of Richard's seven children (three with his first wife and four with his second); William may have been a minor, distinctly young for marriage at this time, but Anne was of a normal marrying age. The Shakespeares and Hathaways knew each other: John Shakespeare had acted as surety for Richard Hathaway and twice paid his debts. Whatever the nature of William's relationship with Anne may have been—and biographers and novelists have frequently speculated about it—by the end of summer 1582 Anne was pregnant and the marriage in November was performed after only a single reading of the banns, rather than the more normal three, presumably in order to speed up the process. The vicar who officiated at Temple Grafton, if that was indeed where they married, was John Frith, known for his ability to cure hawks but also 'Unsound in religion', according to a survey in 1586 of the Warwickshire clergy, again a possible indication of Shakespeare's Catholicism (Schoenbaum, *Documentary Life*, 71).

It is reasonable to give in to temptation and assign Shakespeare's Sonnet 145 to this period, making it Shakespeare's earliest extant work: its final couplet puns on Hathaway ('"I hate" from hate away she threw, / And saved my life, saying "not you."' Sonnet 145, ll. 13–14) and its octosyllabics, unusual in the sonnets, suggest that it may not have been part of the sequence originally. There is no especial reason why a man should write a love poem to a woman only at the beginning of their relationship and the poem need not relate to any actual moment in the history of William and Anne. But, if it were written at the time of the event it appears to describe, then its description of courtship rather than marriage would date it to the early 1580s.

Six months after the marriage, on 26 May 1583, Susanna Shakespeare was baptized, followed on 2 February 1585 by William's and Anne's twins, Hamnet and Judith, probably named after Hamnet and Judith Sadler. Hamnet Sadler, a local baker, was in 1616 one of the witnesses of Shakespeare's will, and his name also appears in local records as Hamlet. With these three children Shakespeare's family seems to have been complete: there are no records of further children. Some have used this as evidence that the marriage was distant or unhappy, though many happily married couples both then and later have had no children at all and it is perhaps relevant that Susanna and Judith had few children (one and three respectively).

The 'lost years' From 1585 to 1592 the records of Shakespeare's life are almost silent. He is briefly referred to in records concerning the attempts of his parents to retrieve property in Wilmcote, part of what had been Mary's inheritance and should have been passed on to William, land that had been mortgaged and was now lost, another indication of John's financial troubles. But the reference does not indicate his presence in Stratford. Biographers have created fanciful narratives for this period; none have any foundation. Perhaps this was when he was 'a Schoolmaster in the Countrey'. The traditional explanation, first set out by Nicholas Rowe in his biographical sketch prefixed to his 1709 edition of Shakespeare's plays, was that William poached deer from Sir Thomas Lucy's estate at Charlecote, was caught and prosecuted, wrote a ballad against Lucy, and was forced to escape to London to avoid further prosecution. Shakespeare's apparent jibe at the Lucy coat of arms in *The Merry Wives of Windsor* (I.i, ll. 13–20) has been explained as belated revenge, though why Shakespeare waited so long and revenged himself so obscurely is not adequately justified.

Shakespeare the player The next print reference to Shakespeare is in *Greenes Groats-Worth of Witte* (1592), a pamphlet ostensibly by Robert Greene (though possibly written by someone else, perhaps Thomas Nashe) and published after Greene's death in September 1592; the pamphlet attacks Shakespeare as:

> an upstart Crow, beautified with our feathers, that with his *Tygers hart wrapt in a Players hyde*, supposes he is as well able to bombast out a blanke verse as the best of you: and beeing an absolute *Iohannes fac totum*, is in his owne conceit the onely Shake-scene in a countrey. (*Greenes Groats-Worth of Witte*, 1592, sig. F1r)

The passage transforms the Duke of York's vicious attack on the even more vicious Queen Margaret in *3 Henry VI*: 'O tiger's heart wrapped in a woman's hide!' (I.iv, l. 138).

Whatever else Shakespeare may have been doing between 1585 and 1592 it is clear that he had been and was still an actor, that he had now become a playwright, and that, whatever other jobs this jack of all trades ('Iohannes fac totum') was doing in the theatre, he had become well enough known to irritate Robert Greene or whoever wrote the pamphlet. The attack was so sharp that Henry Chettle, who had been responsible for its publication, apologized to Shakespeare later that year in his *Kind-Hartes Dreame* for not having 'moderated the heate' in preparing the piece for the press, praising Shakespeare for as 'divers of worship have reported, his uprightnes of dealing, which argues his honesty, and his fa[ce]tious grace in writting, which aprooves his Art' (H. Chettle, *Kind-Hartes Dreame*, 1592, sigs. A3v–4r).

Neither at this period nor later is there any firm evidence of the roles Shakespeare acted or of the quality of his performances. Anecdotes ascribe to him various roles in his own plays, for example Adam in *As You Like It*, a choice which does not suggest any especially great thespian talent. He is named first in the list of 'the Principall Actors in all these Playes' in the collection of his own works in 1623 and appears in the lists of actors in Ben Jonson's *Workes* (1616) for *Every Man in his Humour* ('first Acted, in the yeere 1598') and *Sejanus his Fall* (1603). However much or little he may have acted, it is significant that he was known as a player, for example in the sneer by Ralph Brooke, the York herald, in 1602 at the grant of arms to 'Shakespear the Player' (Schoenbaum, *Documentary Life*, 172).

When Shakespeare became a player is not clear but it is at least possible that he joined the Queen's Men. They played in Stratford in 1587 and their repertory included a play based on Montemayor's *Diana* (the source for Shakespeare's *The Two Gentlemen of Verona*), anonymous plays on the reigns of King John (*The Troublesome Reign*), Richard III (*The True Tragedy*), Henry IV, and Henry V (both covered by *The Famous Victories of Henry V*), all subjects of plays by Shakespeare himself in the 1590s, as well as *King Leir* which, as well as being the major source for Shakespeare's *King Lear*, has possibly left its trace on a number of his earlier works. Though he was influenced by many other plays, not least the work of Christopher Marlowe, in developing his own style in his early works, there is no comparable body of sustained influence. If not actually in the Queen's Men, he certainly seems to have known their work especially well and the plays that belonged to them were crucial to Shakespeare's histories, the works that established the Lord Chamberlain's Men as the pre-eminent company of the age. The Queen's Men's works were virulently anti-Catholic and the company may even have owed its existence to a political aim of touring anti-Catholic propaganda; Shakespeare's plays that owe something of their existence to the Queen's Men's repertory, while hardly being Catholic apologetics, are strikingly less factional in their religion. The idea that Shakespeare joined the company in 1587 after one of their actors, William Knell, died in a fight in Thame, Oxfordshire, is no more improbable than the deer-poaching narrative.

First plays: *Henry VI* Determining what Shakespeare had done to warrant the attack in *Greenes Groats-Worth of Witte* is exceptionally difficult. The dating of Shakespeare's works is often opaque and the early plays pose especial problems. Some scholars argue for the plays to have been written both earlier and in a radically different order from the conventionally accepted sequence. Each reordering produces a new narrative for Shakespeare's contact with other plays and other dramatists, his reading, and his development as a dramatist. While there is uncertainty for the dating of the early plays there is equal uncertainty over authorship. Collaboration was common for playwrights generating drama at high speed to satisfy the appetite of the theatre companies and their customers. The evidence of Philip Henslowe's accounts shows that a minority of plays had a single author, at least for the repertory performed by the companies to which these records relate. If arguments for collaboration in plays in the Shakespeare canon are no longer based solely on a notion of quality (that which is good is by Shakespeare, that which is bad is by a collaborator), the evidence derived from analysis of the plays themselves—their technique, staging, use of rhyme, rare words, common words, feminine endings in blank verse, and other tests—is not susceptible to final verification.

By the time Shakespeare was attacked for his arrogance in being a playwright in 1592, he had certainly written *3 Henry VI*. The other two parts of his exploration of the reign of Henry VI had also been performed. *Part 2*, originally published in 1594 as *The First Part of the Contention betwixt the Two Famous Houses of York and Lancaster*, may have been the first to be performed. It is likely that *Part 3*, published in 1595 as *The True Tragedy of Richard Duke of York*, was next to be written and performed and that *Part 1* was the new play called 'Harey the vj' that Henslowe recorded as performed by Lord Strange's Men at the Rose Theatre on 3 March 1592.

The decision to write plays on English history was a response to the current popularity of such drama. The idea of a two-part play was probably a response to the phenomenal success of Marlowe's *Tamburlaine*, though there were many other two-part plays. There are strong indications, not least in the title by which *2 Henry VI* was first known, that Shakespeare had mapped out the drama as at least a two-part exploration of a catastrophic period of English history. But his decision to create a three-part work was an innovation. Shakespeare's first investigation of English history generated a work on a scale that had no dramatic precedent in the professional theatre. Its nearest analogy was the biblical cycle-drama, the 'mystery' plays which were still being performed in his boyhood. But the move from sacred to secular also produced a form of theatrical analogue to the chronicle histories, the massive prose narratives out of which Shakespeare constructed his plays, particularly Edward Halle's *The Union of the Two Noble and Illustre Families of Lancaster and York* (1548) and Raphael Holinshed's *The Chronicles of England, Scotland, and Ireland* of which Shakespeare used the second edition of 1587. He read other chronicles as well, implying the availability to him of a substantial library, and these plays show the first small traces of his use of works that he would return to for local and general inspiration throughout his career: Apuleius's *The Golden Ass* in Adlington's 1566 translation and Ovid's *Metamorphoses* in Arthur Golding's version completed in 1567.

1 Henry VI in particular was an immediate success. In 1592 Thomas Nashe wondered in *Pierce Penilesse*:

> How would it have joyed brave *Talbot* (the terror of the French) to thinke … hee should triumphe againe on the Stage, and have his bones newe embalmed with the teares of ten thousand spectators at least, (at severall times) who, in the Tragedian that represents his person, imagine they

behold him fresh bleeding. (Schoenbaum, *Documentary Life*, 120)

Nashe's praise might be exaggerated, not least by the likelihood that he co-wrote *Part 1*. It looks as though Shakespeare himself wrote only a comparatively small part of *Part 1* and that Nashe and at least two other dramatists had their hands in it. But the three plays that make up *Henry VI* established Shakespeare as a powerful and popular dramatist.

Early comedies, *Titus Andronicus*, *Richard III*, and 'Sir Thomas More' It is likely that Greene (or whoever wrote the pamphlet) could also have been responding to Shakespeare's first comedies, for *The Two Gentlemen of Verona* and *The Taming of the Shrew* were probably also written at this time. The theatres were closed because of the plague for almost the whole period between June 1592 and June 1594, interrupting Shakespeare's career as a playwright, except for the appearance of *Titus Andronicus*, probably first performed at the Rose Theatre on 24 January 1594. *Titus*, Shakespeare's first tragedy, shows further influences: Ovid's *Metamorphoses* as a profoundly determining source for plots, speeches, language, and emotional power; Seneca's tragedies, filtered now through translations and popular adaptations; and, above all, the need to work through and resolve for himself the challenge presented by the theatrical power achieved by his greatest contemporary, Marlowe. *Titus* also shows Shakespeare working with another collaborator, for George Peele was probably responsible for act I of *Titus*. *Titus Andronicus* was immediately, and remained, popular, also attested by the survival of a drawing by Henry Peacham of a scene derived from the play and by a performance for Sir John Harington at Burley on the Hill in 1596.

The effective closure of the theatres may have also delayed the first performance of *Richard III*. It seems likely that Shakespeare wrote the play not too long after finishing the *Henry VI* trilogy, extending its scope and taking the narrative up to the accession of Henry VII and the inauguration of the Tudor dynasty. But the culminating part is radically different from its predecessors in its exploration of character with its astonishing creation of Richard as comic villain and, in the speech Richard is given on waking after the nightmare appearance of the ghosts of his victims on the night before the battle of Bosworth, with the discovery of a dramatic language never heard before in English drama in its depiction of the inner workings of a disordered mind. It is as if at this moment Shakespeare unlocks the vast potential of dramatic character and of the blank verse form for the first time. Perhaps this may have been a consequence of the delay caused by the plague.

Something of Shakespeare's growing status perhaps at this time is indicated by his participation in the writing of 'Sir Thomas More'. The play, never printed, survives in a manuscript written by a number of hands. It is likely, though not absolutely certain, that Hand D, as it is known, is Shakespeare's and that this is therefore the only piece of his writing other than signatures to survive. The play was first written by Anthony Munday, perhaps with help from Henry Chettle, in 1592 or 1593. At some point thereafter, possibly in 1593 or 1594 (though equally possibly, as some have argued, as late as 1600–04), the play was heavily revised with, among others, Shakespeare (that is, Hand D) being called in to rewrite the scene where More stops the May day riots directed against immigrants in London. Collaborative writing in the period often divided plays up according to different writers' specialisms and Hand D, as a kind of play-doctor, was plainly recognized both as especially proficient in the writing of crowd scenes (as the Jack Cade scenes in *2 Henry VI* had demonstrated) and as someone of proven worth who could effectively resolve the difficulties. Ironically, Sir Edmund Tilney, master of the revels, approved the play provided that the scenes of the 'insurrection' were left out, though this may well refer to the scenes before Shakespeare revised them.

The manuscript itself reveals much about Shakespeare's mode of composition and linguistic preferences with widely varying spellings. Jonson commented (in *Timber*, first printed in 1641), 'the Players have often mentioned it as an honour to *Shakespeare*, that in his writing, (whatsoever he penn'd) hee never blotted out line My answer hath beene, Would he had blotted a thousand' (Vickers, 1.26). But, though the passages by Hand D are far cleaner than many rough drafts, Hand D often changed his mind, blotting and interlineating as he went, often, it would appear, leaving out speech-prefixes of individual members of the crowd (and often marking them simply as 'other' or 'all') as if the dialogue had to be written without the names of speakers really mattering. The sheets in Hand D are as close as we are ever likely to come to Shakespeare in the throes of composition.

About the same date, possibly in 1592 or 1593, Shakespeare contributed a sequence to another play. The main author or authors of *King Edward III* (published in 1596) are unknown but Shakespeare wrote the episode of the king's unsuccessful wooing of the Countess of Salisbury, a witty and moving passage, markedly better than the rest of a mundane play and another indication of Shakespeare's recognition by his fellow dramatists as a writer well worth employing to improve a play.

Narrative poems While the theatre companies toured the provinces and waited for the plague to abate far enough to enable the theatres to be permitted to reopen, Shakespeare turned to another kind of writing, Ovidian narrative poetry. *Venus and Adonis* was published in 1593, printed by Richard Field (*b.* 1561), who had also come to London from Stratford upon Avon and may well have been Shakespeare's friend in childhood. Field had been apprenticed to Thomas Vautrollier, before taking over the business in 1590; Vautrollier had printed in 1579 Sir Thomas North's translation from Plutarch, *The Lives of the Noble Grecians and Romans*, and Field printed a revised edition in 1595, a volume that Shakespeare used extensively in play after play. Perhaps he bought books from Field or, just as likely, borrowed them from his fellow Stratfordian.

The publication of *Venus and Adonis* in 1593, the first

printing of any work by Shakespeare, is perhaps less significant than the poem's dedication, signed by Shakespeare to mark his authorship and offering 'the first heir of my invention' to Henry Wriothesley, third earl of Southampton. A brilliant mixture of comedy and eroticism, *Venus and Adonis* was Shakespeare's most popular work, if the number of reprints is a guide, with at least fifteen editions by 1636. If the tone of this dedication is formal, the language of the dedication to *The Rape of Lucrece*, printed by Field in 1594, speaks of a far closer friendship: 'What I have done is yours; what I have to do is yours, being part in all I have, devoted yours.' In the dedication to *Venus and Adonis*, he vowed to 'take advantage of all idle hours till I have honoured you with some graver labour'; *Lucrece*, with its violently erotic account of rape, passionate description of suicide, and serious portrayal of the overthrow of monarchy, is the powerful outcome of that promise. Both poems were widely alluded to and equally widely praised, apparently the first works by Shakespeare to gain wide approval from young, educated, fashionable male readers; as Gabriel Harvey noted, probably in 1601, 'The younger sort takes much delight in Shakespeares Venus, & Adonis: but his Lucrece, & his tragedie of Hamlet, Prince of Denmarke, have it in them, to please the wiser sort' (Chambers, 2.197).

Shakespeare's toying in *Venus and Adonis* with a desire for the male body that is as much homoerotic as heterosexual might well have endeared the poem to Southampton. Rowe's account in 1709 that Southampton gave Shakespeare the vast sum of £1000 is not credible; however, it might have been exaggerated from a smaller gift. But Rowe describes it as enabling Shakespeare 'to go through with a Purchase which he heard he had a mind to' (*Works*, ed. Rowe, 1.x). There were three possible major pieces of expenditure to which this might relate: the acquisition of a share in the theatre company, the granting of a coat of arms, and the purchase of New Place, all three of which will be considered below. That the poems gained Shakespeare both money and a powerful friend, rather than simply the formal approval of an aristocratic patron, seems likely. A cryptic poem, *Willobie his Avisa* (published in 1594), may, in its comments on H. W. and W. S., allude to a friendship or even a love affair between Southampton and Shakespeare.

The Lord Chamberlain's Men Before the plague most of Shakespeare's plays were probably written for and sold to Lord Strange's Men, later the Earl of Derby's Men, though *2* and *3 Henry VI* and possibly *The Taming of the Shrew* were performed by Pembroke's Men, a company which flourished briefly in London between 1591 and 1593. If one notes the prominence of Lord Stanley, the Earl of Derby, in *Richard III*, then it may be a careful compliment to the current earl of Derby as the players' patron; if one sees the character as a perfect time-server who does his best to stay out of the battle until he can align himself with the winning side, then it may be rather less of a compliment. *Richard III* may be the last play Shakespeare wrote with Strange's Men in mind.

The effect of plague and the difficulty of making a profit by touring affected all the playing companies. The history of the theatre companies in London, their repertory and resources in this period, is as murky as much else to do with Shakespeare's life. *Titus Andronicus*, for instance, was performed by the three different companies named on the title-page of its first printing in 1594: Derby's (that is, Lord Strange's Men), Pembroke's, and Sussex's players; but it could have been either by each successively or by a company containing members of all three. But in May 1594 Henry Carey, Lord Hunsdon, who was lord chamberlain, and his son-in-law Charles, Lord Howard, the lord admiral and previous lord chamberlain, created something approaching a duopoly for their players in London. After the companies had briefly played as a combined company at Newington Butts in June 1594 (including performances of *Titus Andronicus*), the abatement of the plague meant that they could properly return to the city. The Lord Admiral's Men took up residence at the Curtain Theatre. Hunsdon's Men, now known as the Lord Chamberlain's Men, including some of the best actors of Derby's and Pembroke's companies, played at The Theatre to the north-east of the city, beginning their long and unequalled period as the greatest company of actors in the country.

From this point on all Shakespeare's new plays were written for and belonged to the Lord Chamberlain's Men. What is more, payments to the company for their court performances over the Christmas season of 1594 name Shakespeare with William Kemp, the company's clown, and Richard Burbage, their leading actor, as the three payees, indicating their pre-eminent status among the small group of sharers in the company. Though often called actor-sharers, the participants in the Chamberlain's Men were unlikely to have included Shakespeare on the grounds of his acting ability. Uniquely among playwrights of the period, Shakespeare began a long and uninterrupted association with and participation in one particular theatre company, rather than, as it were, accepting freelance work for whoever would pay. Though later dramatists like John Fletcher, Philip Massinger, Richard Brome, and James Shirley had similar links to a particular company—in Brome's case explicitly set out in a contract—none seem to have been sharers. Shakespeare was not only the Chamberlain's Men's house dramatist, producing on average two plays a year for them until his retirement, but also a close participant in their developing business.

Either on the grounds of his reputation as a playwright alone or by virtue of a payment, Shakespeare had acquired a share in the new company and received his share of their fluctuating but sizeable profits over the rest of his life. The share also altered as the number of sharers varied, going from one-tenth in 1599 up to one-eighth when Will Kemp left and down to a twelfth and a fourteenth as further sharers were brought in. If the share was bought it was a shrewd investment, giving Shakespeare a certain amount of security of income, but it also conferred status on him as, in effect, a partner in a profit-sharing collective enterprise.

Plays, 1594–1596 In December 1594 the Chamberlain's Men performed *The Comedy of Errors* at Gray's Inn. The play's design as a classical farce based on Plautus's *Menaechmi*, a play Shakespeare might well have read at school, made it especially suitable for the Christmas revels of the young gentry at one of the inns of court. In the course of the next year or so the company also performed *Love's Labour's Lost*, probably its lost sequel 'Love's Labour's Won', *Richard II*, *Romeo and Juliet*, and *A Midsummer Night's Dream*, an extraordinary output that was perhaps the result of Shakespeare's busy writing activity during the plague time. In the flow of creativity in this period and with the imprecision inevitable in attempting to date the plays' writing and first performances accurately, other work may also belong to this period or even earlier: *King John* was probably written in 1595 or 1596, a history play which, like *Richard II*, was written without being part of a sequence and which, in its extraordinary veering of tone from fully blown tragedy to mocking and satiric comedy, marks Shakespeare's most extreme view of the action of history and the legitimacy of kingship.

Shakespeare's plays were also now beginning to be printed: unauthorized versions of 2 and 3 *Henry VI* appeared in 1594 and 1595 respectively; *Titus Andronicus* was published in 1594. A version of *The Taming of the Shrew*, with different character names and considerable adjustment of the plot, also appeared in 1594 as *The Taming of a Shrew*. Some of this print activity may have been the result of the collapse of the companies which had owned the plays. The publication in 1595 of *Locrine*, 'Newly set foorth, overseene and corrected, By *W.S.*' as the title-page describes it, may, if Shakespeare is the man behind the initials, be evidence of further work, seeing an anonymous play into print.

Shakespeare was now demonstrating his consummate ease in a wide range of genres and theatrical techniques: the frenetic farce within a potentially tragic frame of *The Comedy of Errors*; the learned, witty, verbal games and inconclusive ending of *Love's Labour's Lost*; the lyrical virtuosity and sharply personal politics of *Richard II*; the outrageous sexy comedy, romantic love, and tragic conclusion of *Romeo and Juliet*; and the metrical pyrotechnics and supernatural mechanism of *A Midsummer Night's Dream*. There is in this list a sustained experimentation with form, with theatricality, and with language. There was, as well, a new attitude to the materials out of which his plays were created. For *Romeo and Juliet*, for instance, he went back to a work he had used in part for *The Two Gentlemen of Verona*, Arthur Brooke's *Tragical History of Romeus and Juliet* (1562; reprinted 1587), an immensely long poem in fourteeners, turning Brooke's rather dull epic into an exhilarating and immediate drama while mining the original for details to feed into his drama. But it is striking, too, that neither *Love's Labour's Lost* nor *A Midsummer Night's Dream* has a single narrative source, something that could have offered Shakespeare a clear shape for the plot. Both comedies are also concerned with the nature of theatre itself, embedding into their final sequence a performance (the pageant of the Nine Worthies and the play of Pyramus and Thisbe) that both comments on the drama as a whole and analyses audience response. Shakespeare is clearly reflecting on his own art.

Plays, 1596–1598 Over the next two years, Shakespeare continued to write comedies set in Italy: *The Merchant of Venice* marked the continuing influence of Marlowe, depending on *The Jew of Malta* as *Richard II* had on Marlowe's *Edward II*; *Much Ado about Nothing* turned a traditional trope of mistaken identity into a dark comedy on the social pressures to marry. But he also returned to *Richard II* and began a new cycle of plays, explicitly designed, as the epilogue to *Henry V* would make plain, to connect with his earlier cycle which had dramatized the collapse of rule, empire, and nation after the early death of Henry V. He turned back to the Queen's Men's play *The Famous Victories of Henry V*, with its sharp contrast of the prince's riotous youth and victorious adulthood, as a foundation for a prolonged meditation on the looming threat of succeeding to the crown, on the nature of kingship and the identity of England itself. The two parts of *Henry IV* and *Henry V* created a complete and continuous cycle of eight plays in all, a work of extraordinary ambition and scale, something no English dramatist had attempted before or would attempt again.

But 1 *Henry IV* brought him into conflict with a powerful family. In articulating a tension between the world of politics and an alternative culture in which Prince Henry resists the inevitable future call to the throne, Shakespeare originally named the prince's tavern companion Sir John Oldcastle. Whether deliberately or not, the name was guaranteed to offend the family of William Brooke, Lord Cobham, who had been lord chamberlain from 1596 to his death in 1597, for Oldcastle, the Lollard leader revered as a protestant martyr, was Cobham's ancestor. Under pressure from the family the name was changed to Sir John Falstaff, but only after 1 *Henry IV* had been performed. Other names were changed in the play: Russell became Peto since the family name of the earls of Bedford was Russell, while Harvey became Bardolph since Sir William Harvey was about to marry the countess of Southampton. The politics of naming continued into *The Merry Wives of Windsor* where Master Ford's original name in his disguise, Brook, while allowing watery puns on 'ford', had to be changed to Broom, again after the first performances: Shakespeare may well have first used Brook as a joke at the expense of Lord Cobham's surname.

Rowe reported that Shakespeare wrote *Merry Wives* at Queen Elizabeth's request, the queen being so pleased with the character of Falstaff that she 'commanded him to continue it for one Play more, and to shew him in Love' (*Works*, ed. Rowe, 1.viii–ix). The anecdote is unlikely to be true, but it is far more probable that the play was performed at the celebrations in May 1597 before the installation into the Order of the Garter of Sir George Carey, now Lord Hunsdon, the son of the founder of the Chamberlain's Men and himself now in the same office after Cobham's death. Where there is neither proof nor likelihood that *A Midsummer Night's Dream* was written for and performed at an aristocratic wedding, as is often suggested, *Merry Wives*, while also performed at The Theatre, was adapted to this specific occasion. The company clearly would have wished to praise their patron and mark his high honour and their playwright used his latest play, capitalizing on the exceptional success of Falstaff in the *Henry IV* plays, to provide an appropriate tribute. Plays could earn companies money and goodwill in more ways than through the box office.

Death of Hamnet Shakespeare But the years 1596 and 1597 were also deeply affected by more domestic matters. On 11 August 1596 Hamnet Shakespeare was buried. It is too easy to assume that all expressions of grief in the plays thereafter were a reaction to his son's death, but something of Viola's passionate mourning for the apparent death of her twin brother in *Twelfth Night* could have been generated by the loss of Hamnet, Shakespeare's only male heir. It is not too fanciful to see Shakespeare drawn as a result towards the subject matter of *Hamlet*, where son grieves for father rather than father for son.

The coat of arms and purchase of property in Stratford Two months later John Shakespeare was granted a coat of arms, about twenty-five years after he had first applied for them, but it was probably William who reactivated the application. It was an opportune moment, for the Garter king of arms, Sir William Dethick, was fairly unscrupulous about entitlement and hence was attacked later by the York herald for granting arms not to John Shakespeare but to 'Shakespear the Player'. The draft spoke eloquently but probably fraudulently of the 'valeant service' done by John's 'late grandfather' for which he was 'advanced & rewarded by the most prudent prince King Henry the seventh'. But it more accurately identified John as an erstwhile bailiff in Stratford (albeit getting the date of office wrong). It also noted that John 'hathe Landes & tenementes of good wealth, & substance 500$^{li.}$' (Chambers, 2.19–20). Even allowing for some exaggeration the statement suggests either a remarkable turnaround in John Shakespeare's fortunes or, more probably, an indication of William's rapidly accumulating wealth, enough to make the player and playmaker wish to be able to sign himself as a gentleman. The coat of arms, with gold and silver as its metals, was an expensive option if it was to be reproduced on the bearer's possessions. But the arms are surmounted by an arrogant falcon, punningly displayed shaking its angled spear which, with its silver tip, looks as much like a pen as a weapon. The bird may also be an allusion to the four silver falcons in Southampton's coat of arms. The design and its motto, *Non sancz droict* ('Not without right'), were soon mocked by Jonson whose character Puntarvolo in *Every Man out of his Humour* (Lord Chamberlain's Men, 1599) jeers at Sogliardo, the country clown, by suggesting he should have as his motto 'Not without mustard', an allusion both to Shakespeare's motto and to the yellow colour of his arms.

In 1599 John Shakespeare made an application, probably never approved, to quarter the Arden arms with Shakespeare's and thereby cement the claim to gentility by association with a far more distinguished family. But Dethick's actions were challenged: Brooke, the York herald, identified twenty-three wrongly awarded coats of arms and, though Shakespeare's claim was defended, Shakespeare might never have been confident that the grant of arms had been fair.

Soon afterwards, Shakespeare took another step towards establishing his status and position. While he was in London his wife and children had probably continued to live in Henley Street with his parents; there is no sign that Anne ever moved to London to be with her husband there. In May 1597 Shakespeare bought New Place, reputedly the second largest house in Stratford, with five gables, ten fireplaces, and a frontage of over 60 feet, together with two barns, two gardens, and two orchards. The price is unclear but was probably in excess of £120. There may have been some rebuilding—a load of stone was sold to the town council in 1598 for 10*d*.—and by February 1598 Shakespeare was listed as living in Chapel Street ward, where New Place was situated, when he, together with many of his neighbours, was shown to be hoarding malt. Shakespeare's store (10 quarters or about 80 bushels) was about the average in the ward but, after three bad harvests, such hoarding was a serious action.

Correspondence in 1598 between two Stratford men, Abraham Sturley and Richard Quiney, shows that they thought of Shakespeare both as 'our countriman' and as someone wealthy enough to be worth Quiney's approaching for a loan of £30 to pay his London debts. In London, Quiney wrote a letter to Shakespeare, in which he is addressed as 'Loveinge Contreyman'; though probably never sent, it is the only surviving piece of correspondence with him. Clearly Shakespeare's finances were sufficient to establish him as a highly visible member of the Stratford community and one seeking to rise further as a local worthy, showing him to have been considered a Stratford resident: Sturley's plan to sell Shakespeare 'some od yardeland or other att Shottri or neare about us' was something that 'would advance him in deede' (Chambers, 2.101–2).

Over subsequent years Shakespeare consolidated his position in Stratford and it was there, rather than in London, that he made his major investments, perhaps because property in Stratford was considered, mistakenly, to be less vulnerable to fire than in London. In May 1602 he paid £320, an enormous sum, for 107 acres of land in Old Town in Stratford, bought from John and William Combe, and in September 1602 he acquired a cottage in Chapel Lane, probably to extend his land at New Place. In 1605 he paid £440 for a share in the tithes for Stratford, amounting to approximately one-fifth of the total value and worth £60 a year.

Shakespeare in London, 1598–1601 In the course of less than a decade Shakespeare had earned, borrowed, or been given enough to spend nearly £900 in his home town. By comparison, it is not clear what sort of property Shakespeare lived in while in London at this time. Late in 1596 he was known to have been living in the parish of St Helen's, Bishopsgate, by having failed to pay various levies due at this time. His goods were valued in 1598 at a mere £5, a comparatively small sum. The location was reasonably convenient for walking to The Theatre. He had moved away by 1599 and was now resident in the Clink parish in Surrey, in the Liberty, conveniently close to the site of the new Globe Theatre where the company was resident for the rest of his career. None of this suggests much of a commitment to living in London by comparison with the sustained, substantial, and frequent investment in and around Stratford.

But the move to be near the Globe Theatre marks a new stage in Shakespeare's professional career and it is an apt moment to take stock. He had become a widely known and admired playwright and poet. The *Parnassus* plays, performed by students of St John's College, Cambridge, at the Christmas celebrations between 1598 and 1601, mock Gullio who speaks 'nothinge but pure Shakspeare, and shreds of poetrie that he hath gathered at the theators' and praises 'sweet Mr. Shakspeare!'; Gullio will sleep with 'his Venus, and Adonis under my pillowe' (Chambers, 2.200–01). Poets like Richard Barnfield, John Marston, Robert Tofte, and John Weever referred to Shakespeare's plays and poems in their own poems and epigrams published in 1598 and 1599. In 1598, in *Palladis tamia: Wits Treasury*, Francis Meres praised Shakespeare fulsomely (all Meres's praise is fulsome): 'As *Plautus* and *Seneca* are accounted the best for Comedy and Tragedy among the Latines: so *Shakespeare* among the English is the most excellent in both kinds for the stage', going on to list six comedies and six tragedies (four of which would now be identified as histories) as proof of Shakespeare's status (F. Meres, *Palladis tamia*, fol. 282*r*). In 1600 a collection of quotations, *Belvedere, or, The Garden of the Muses* included over 200 passages from Shakespeare, mostly from *Venus and Adonis*, *Lucrece*, and *Richard II*.

In March 1602 John Manningham, a barrister at the Middle Temple where Shakespeare's *Twelfth Night* had been performed the previous month, noted a bawdy story about Shakespeare and Burbage in his diary; whether true or not, the story (of Shakespeare having sex with a woman who had wanted an assignation with Burbage whom she had fallen for as Richard III) indicates that Shakespeare was a figure to be gossiped about, though Manningham had to remind himself of Shakespeare's first name. Sir George Buc, unsure who had written *George a Greene* (1599), wrote on his copy that Shakespeare had told him it was by 'a minister who ac[ted] the pinner part in it himself' (Honan, 204); Shakespeare's information was probably wrong but Buc saw him as someone worth consulting on such matters. Finally, in this sequence of contacts, Shakespeare's success was sufficient to make one of his colleagues mock him: Jonson's *Every Man out of his Humour* (1599) has a number of satirical allusions to Shakespeare's recent plays as well as to his gentrified status. This amounts to more than a private dig at a friend: Jonson appears to have expected the audience to understand the barbs, yet another sign of Shakespeare's popularity.

Shakespeare's plays were also starting to appear in print both in versions that give unauthorized and often inaccurate versions of the plays and in reasonably carefully prepared versions, the latter often in response to the former: for example the quarto of *Romeo and Juliet* published in 1599, 'Newly corrected, augmented, and amended', in answer to the imperfections of the 1595 quarto. The suspect quartos often bear apparent traces of performance in their more elaborate stage directions. A positive flurry of editions appeared in 1600: *2 Henry IV*, *Henry V*, *The Merchant of Venice*, *A Midsummer Night's Dream*, and *Much Ado about Nothing*, as well as reprints of three other plays and *The Rape of Lucrece*. Some of these published editions of his plays now carried the author's name on their title-pages—for example, *Love's Labour's Lost*, the second quartos of *Richard II* and *Richard III* all published in 1598, or the third quarto of *1 Henry IV* in 1599—another indication of Shakespeare's growing reputation and significance, since playwrights were not usually named on their plays.

In 1605 the placing of Shakespeare's name on the title-page of *The London Prodigal*, a play certainly not by Shakespeare, is a further sign that his name was a good marketing ploy; the same (presumably deliberate) misattribution happened with the publication of Middleton's *A Yorkshire Tragedy* in 1608 (though some have argued that the play is by Shakespeare).

Similarly, in 1599 William Jaggard published the second edition of a collection of poems called *The Passionate Pilgrim* (the date of the first edition is uncertain) which the title-page also attributed to Shakespeare, much to Shakespeare's annoyance that Jaggard, as Thomas Heywood noted, 'altogether unknowne to him … presumed to make so bold with his name' (Schoenbaum, *Documentary Life*, 219). Very little of the collection was by Shakespeare but it included pirated and unattributed printings of three extracts from *Love's Labour's Lost* offered as poems and of two of Shakespeare's sonnets (138 and 144). Meres had noted that 'the sweete wittie soule of *Ovid* lives in mellifluous & hony-tongued *Shakespeare*, witness his *Venus* and *Adonis*, his *Lucrece*, his sugred Sonnets among his private friends, &c.' (F. Meres, *Palladis tamia*, fols. 281*v*–282*r*). Whenever the sonnets were written, these two at least were by 1599 available in versions Jaggard could use.

Plays, 1598–1601 Having completed the second tetralogy in his history cycle, with the epilogue to *Henry V* gesturing to the earlier sequence ('Which oft our stage hath shown'; epilogue, l. 13), Shakespeare might reasonably have thought he had dramatized enough English history and had made enough use of Holinshed's *Chronicles*. He turned to Roman history, a field he had ignored since *Titus Andronicus* but a rich resource for political analysis of contemporary society. *Julius Caesar* was probably the first play the Chamberlain's Men performed at their new theatre where Thomas Platter, a Swiss traveller, saw it on 21 September 1599. Shakespeare's main source was North's Plutarch—perhaps he had now acquired a copy from Richard Field—and Shakespeare kept closer to his source than ever before, dramatizing Plutarch often simply by turning North's prose into verse. Roman historical tragedy may have been successful but *Julius Caesar*, like *Titus*, was not to be the start of a sequence, though *Antony and Cleopatra* would later take up the story.

Women disguising themselves as young men had been a useful plot device in both *The Two Gentlemen of Verona* and *The Merchant of Venice*. Something, perhaps the expertise of a particularly brilliant boy player, made the prospect of making this transformation especially central to a comedy clearly appealing. In *As You Like It* (1599–1600) and *Twelfth Night* (1601), Shakespeare explored the idea to something approaching its limits. For *As You Like It*, his principal source was Thomas Lodge's prose romance *Rosalynde* (1590) but, where Lodge's work is unequivocally placed in the forest of the Ardennes, Shakespeare's play is set ambiguously in France and in the Forest of Arden that had covered the centre of England and from which his mother's family derived its name. In this play Shakespeare also paid a small tribute to Marlowe as Phoebe remembers the words of the 'Dead shepherd': 'Who ever loved that loved not at first sight?' (III.v, ll. 82–3). *Twelfth Night*'s first recorded performance was at the Middle Temple; John Manningham noted its likeness to Plautus's *Menaechmi* and 'most like and neere to that in Italian called *Inganni*' (Chambers, 2.328).

In both plays Shakespeare made use of the talents of the Chamberlain's Men's latest recruit, Robert Armin, who replaced Will Kemp in 1599; Armin's skills as a singer are clear in Touchstone and Feste, the first signs of the line of fools that Shakespeare wrote for him, far more bitter than those for Kemp.

Between the two comedies Shakespeare wrote *Hamlet*, rewriting the 'Hamlet' play that had been playing on the London stage by 1589 and may have been written by Thomas Kyd. Now lost and probably never printed, the earlier play and its own sources can be presumed to have provided a similar narrative but a simpler one. Nothing in them would have been as complex or provocative as Shakespeare's creation of the prince whose thought processes have been so profoundly influential on Western literature. Whatever else made the writing of *Hamlet* happen at this time, the extraordinary talents of Richard Burbage were a major determinant on the creation of the role, his lifelike acting deeply affecting Shakespeare's portrayal of the prince's mind. But, in creating Ophelia, Shakespeare seems also to have remembered a Stratford event, the inquest into the drowning, just outside Stratford in December 1579, of the aptly named Katherine Hamlett.

The Essex uprising *Hamlet* has its topical references to the work of the boys' companies, the popular rivals to the success of the Chamberlain's Men, but Shakespeare's *Henry V* had made a more direct and political reference in its anticipation of the return of Essex, 'the General of our gracious Empress' (v, chorus, l. 30), from subduing the rebellious Irish during the earl of Tyrone's uprising. But when Essex did return, unexpectedly and without permission, the eventual tension placed Shakespeare and the Chamberlain's Men in danger: Essex's ally Sir Gilly Meyrick and others of Essex's faction paid for the company to perform Shakespeare's *Richard II* two days before Essex's attempt at a coup in February 1601, daring to suggest to the audience that Essex would be Elizabeth's Bolingbroke. The actors claimed later, examined in the dangerous days following the failed coup, that they had argued that the play was 'so old and so long out of use' that 'they shold have small or no Company at yt' (Schoenbaum, *Documentary Life*, 160) but were persuaded to perform it for an extra £2. Shakespeare's play was clearly perceived as dangerous and the scene of Richard's deposition was never included in published versions until the fourth quarto (1608). The performance did no lasting damage to Shakespeare or to the theatre company which continued to be summoned to play at court for the Christmas festivities.

Shakespeare in Stratford, 1601–1609 Other events of 1601 link Shakespeare and Stratford upon Avon. In March Thomas Whittington, who had been shepherd to Shakespeare's father-in-law, made his will, bequeathing to the poor the £2 which Anne Shakespeare had and which William therefore owed to his estate. Quite why the money had been loaned or deposited with Anne is unclear but it seems to indicate Shakespeare's absence from her. On 8 September 1601 John Shakespeare was buried in Stratford. No will survives but William, as the eldest son, would have inherited the house in Henley Street, though, with New Place, he had no need of it: his mother and his sister Joan, who had in the 1590s married William Hart, a hatter, together with her family continued to live there.

Unsurprisingly, most of the documents that speak of Shakespeare in connection with Stratford over the next few years concern legal matters: in spring 1604 he sold malt to a neighbour, Philip Rogers, and subsequently lent him 2*s*.; Rogers repaid 6*s*. and Shakespeare sued for the remainder of the debt, 35*s*. 10*d*. There was another suit for a debt owed by John Addenbrooke: Shakespeare pursued him in the courts from August 1608 to June 1609, seeking £6 plus 24*s*. damages. Clearly Shakespeare was not willing to let such matters drop whether the sums were substantial or not, though in 1608 he may have been short of income with the theatres again shut by plague.

Poems and plays, 1601–1603 Shakespeare's densely enigmatic allegorical poem 'The Phoenix and Turtle' was published in 1601, appended to Robert Chester's *Love's Martyr* in a group, *Poeticall Essaies*, including poems by Marston, Chapman, Jonson, and others, offered as a tribute to Sir John Salusbury with whom Shakespeare has no other known connection. In the following year Shakespeare wrote *Troilus and Cressida*, in part a response to George Chapman's translation of Homer's *Iliad*, a section of which had been published in 1598, and in part an engagement with Chaucer's long poem and Henryson's continuation, the first time Shakespeare had made extensive use of Chaucer since *A Midsummer Night's Dream*. Cynical about sexual desire and war, the play's bleakness may have been aimed at a different audience from that of the Globe—if it was performed at all—since, when it was published in 1609, it carried an epistle identifying it as 'a new play, never stal'd with the Stage, never clapper-clawd with the palmes of the vulger' (*Troilus and Cressida*, 1609, sig. ¶2r); the phrase may refer to performance in a space other than the Globe.

The accession of James I brought the Chamberlain's Men an extraordinary honour: soon after arriving in London, James took over the company, now to be known as the King's Men. For the king's entry into London in May 1604, Shakespeare and the other players, like the members of the Queen's Men, Prince Henry's Men, and many other members of the royal household, were each given four and a half yards of red cloth, possibly to march in the procession or line the route. The King's Men frequently performed at the new court: between November 1604 and October 1605 they played eleven different works, seven of which were by Shakespeare, including new plays such as *Measure for Measure* and *Othello* and older ones such as *The Merchant of Venice* (twice) and *The Merry Wives of Windsor*; between the patent of May 1603 and Shakespeare's death they performed at court on at least 107 occasions.

Yet royal patronage could not solve some of the company's problems: performances at the Globe in 1603–4 had been frequently stopped for lengthy periods because of a sequence of plague, Elizabeth's final illness, public mourning, and further outbreaks of plague. The king gave the company £30 to tide them over while they could not perform. Not until April 1604 was public playing allowed again.

Plays, 1603–1606 Shakespeare had hardly been idle during this difficult time for the company: *Measure for Measure*, *Othello*, and *All's Well that Ends Well* belong to 1603–4. They follow the ambiguity of genre that characterizes *Troilus and Cressida* which was variously identified as a comedy in the prefatory epistle, a history on the title-page of the quarto of 1609, and a tragedy in the first folio. They share a world of misplaced sexual desire where one body can be substituted for another either unknowingly as in the bed-tricks of *Measure* and *All's Well* or in fantasy as in Iago's report that Cassio had taken Othello's place in the marriage-bed. While *Othello* is a tragedy using the materials of comic cuckoldry, the other two can be wrenched from potential tragedy towards a comic ending.

In 1605 and 1606 Shakespeare's playwriting energies were spent on unequivocal tragedies: the astonishing sequence of *Timon of Athens*, *King Lear*, *Macbeth*, and *Antony and Cleopatra*. In *Timon*, for the first time since the early stages of his career (depending on exactly when Shakespeare contributed to 'Sir Thomas More'), Shakespeare collaborated with another dramatist, the younger and equally successful Thomas Middleton, the two dividing the play up between them. Middleton was probably also responsible for some of the witches' scenes in *Macbeth* in the only form in which they reached print and he revised *Measure for Measure* in 1621 shortly before it was first printed in the first folio. Shakespeare was not a dramatist who worked in isolation from his fellow playwrights: he was strongly influenced by their plays and by their audiences' responses, just as his work also influenced them. Collaboration became increasingly a part of his playwriting method for the remainder of his career.

Political and other contemporary events affected the plays too. Both *Lear* and *Macbeth* reflect in some ways the accession of King James: James's concern to unite Scotland and England seems to underpin the division of the kingdom in *Lear*, a warning of the consequences of disunity, while his claim of descent from Banquo is explicitly imaged in *Macbeth* where the witches show Macbeth the line of Banquo's descendants stretching towards James himself. *King Lear* also reflects a recent case in 1603 when Brian Annesley's eldest daughter tried to have her father declared insane and was prevented by the loving care of Annesley's youngest daughter, Cordell.

Yet if all these plays cannot be seen as other than tragedies, they are deliberately 'impure'. As Antony Scoloker commented in 1604 in the epistle to his poem *Diaphantus*: a good poem should be 'like *Friendly Shakespeare's Tragedies*, where the *Commedian* rides, when the *Tragedian* stands on Tip-toe: Faith it should please all, like Prince *Hamlet*' (Chambers, 2.214–15). *Lear* and *Macbeth* are both based on events that, for Shakespeare and his audiences, were the stuff of the chronicles: for both the source material lay in Holinshed; both are histories, as the first published edition of *Lear* (1608) is identified on its title-page. Shakespeare continued to rely on sources that had served him well so far: Holinshed and Plutarch above all but also the repertory of the Queen's Men (for the anonymous *King Leir*), Apuleius's *The Golden Ass*, and Ovid.

Friends and lodgings Records of Shakespeare's friends and family provide other suggestions for his life at this time. Augustine Phillips, a fellow sharer in the King's Men, died in 1604, leaving 'my ffellowe william Shakespeare a Thirty shillings peece in gould' (Schoenbaum, *Documentary Life*, 204), as he did to other players but naming Shakespeare first. It is reasonable to assume that his fellows in the theatre company were among his closest friends. William Barksted, a minor playwright, wrote warmly of Shakespeare as 'so deere lov'd a neighbor' (Chambers, 2.216). Perhaps to this period too belong the stories, anecdotal but not contradicted by the evidence of surviving comments, of his close friendship and genial rivalry with Jonson.

As becomes apparent from the records of a case in 1612, Shakespeare was living from 1602 to 1604 as a lodger with Christopher Mountjoy and his family in Silver Street in the respectable neighbourhood of Cripplegate. The case provides rare glimpses of Shakespeare's London life in 1602–4 and in 1612. Mountjoy, a French Huguenot refugee, with his wife and daughter, was a successful tiremaker who made wigs and head-dresses; Shakespeare might have met them through the French wife of the printer Richard Field who lived nearby but theatre companies always needed the services of wigmakers and the Lord Chamberlain's Men may have been the connection. Other dramatists lived near, including Jonson, Dekker, Munday, and Field, while John Heminges and Henry Condell, fellow sharers, were pillars of a local church, St Mary Aldermanbury.

The case of 1612 was brought by Stephen Belott, Mountjoy's former apprentice, who had married Mountjoy's daughter in 1604 and claimed that Mountjoy had failed to pay the dowry promised. Shakespeare was called as a witness and is mentioned by other witnesses. He helped in the marriage negotiations: Mountjoy asked him to encourage Belott to agree to the match and the young couple made their troth-plight in his presence. Six months after the wedding, the Belotts moved out and stayed with George Wilkins, a petty crook who ran a tavern and a brothel. Wilkins was also a writer whose work included a play and a novella, *The Painful Adventures of Pericles Prince of Tyre* (1608), which combines material from Twine's romance *The Pattern of Painful Adventures* (reprinted in 1607) and from Shakespeare's *Pericles*, written in 1607, probably in collaboration with Wilkins who may have contributed the first two acts. Mrs Mountjoy died in October 1608 and the Belotts returned to Silver Street. Arguments continued and Belott sued in 1612 for the unpaid £60 dowry and £200 to be included in Mountjoy's will.

Shakespeare was one of three witnesses examined on 11 May 1612. His deposition brings the closest record of Shakespeare speaking, albeit through the court style of the examiner's clerk. Shakespeare attested that Belott was, in his view, 'A very good and industrious servant' who 'did well and honestly behave himselfe', though he also said that Mountjoy had not 'confesse[d] that he hath gott any great proffitt and comodytye' from Belott's service. He also deposed that the Mountjoys showed Belott 'great good will and affecceon' and that Mrs Mountjoy 'did sollicitt and entreat [him] to move and perswade [Belott] to effect the said marriadge and accordingly [he] did'. On the matter of money Shakespeare could not remember (or chose not to remember) how large the marriage portion was to have been, nor whether there was to have been a sum in Mountjoy's will, nor 'what Implementes and necessaries of houshold stuffe' Mountjoy gave Belott as part of the marriage settlement (Schoenbaum, *Records*, 25). Further witnesses were examined on 19 June but Shakespeare, though named in the margin of the interrogatories, did not depose again.

In the event the matter was referred to the elders of the French church, who ordered Mountjoy to pay Belott 20 nobles; but Mountjoy, who had fathered two bastards and was excommunicated for his dissolute life, never paid. Whatever the neighbourhood may have been, the Mountjoys were hardly the respectable family they might at first have appeared. The case is trivial enough but it shows Shakespeare caught up in the kind of arguments over money and marriage that figured in many plays of the period.

Shakespeare and Stratford, 1606–1608 Events in Shakespeare's family in Stratford in this period balanced good and bad news. In May 1606 his daughter Susanna was listed with other residents of Stratford for refusing to take holy communion at Easter, perhaps a sign that she might be a covert Catholic since such actions were bound to be noticed in the tense aftermath of the Gunpowder Plot. Susanna married in June 1607; her husband, the physician John *Hall (1574/5?–1635), was known to be strongly protestant in his faith. There appears to have been a substantial marriage settlement in which Shakespeare settled on Susanna 105 acres of his land in Old Stratford, probably retaining a life interest in it; it amounts to a very valuable dowry. Shakespeare's younger brother Edmund had become a player, following his eldest brother to London, where both he and his infant son died in 1607; William may well have been the person who paid 20*s.* for his brother's burial in St Saviour's, Southwark, 'with a forenoone knell of the great bell' (Schoenbaum, *Documentary Life*, 26). In February 1608 Shakespeare became a grandfather with the birth of Elizabeth Hall. In September 1608 his mother died.

Plays and publication, 1607–1609 In the meantime, he was developing new forms for his drama. *Pericles* marked a new departure for Shakespeare, a drama whose narrative spreads to and fro across the Mediterranean, with a chorus, the poet John Gower whose poem *Confessio amantis* is one of the play's sources, returned from the grave to tell the tale. From the finality of losing the beloved daughter at the end of *King Lear* to the possibility of a family being reunited at the end of *Pericles* is an enormous distance. *Pericles* was the only play largely written by Shakespeare not to be included in the 1623 first folio but it appeared in a quarto edition in 1608. Its immediate popularity may be indicated by the presence of the French and Venetian ambassadors at a performance in 1608.

If the play marked the start of a new phase in Shakespeare's writing, he made a last exploration of tragedy: *Coriolanus*, once again derived from Plutarch, is his fiercest study of the politics of the state and its citizens, spurred on by the immediate threat of the midlands uprising of 1607–8, a series of outbreaks of popular unrest caused by bad harvests and inflationary food prices. The riots occurred close to Stratford and William Combe, from whom Shakespeare had bought the land in Old Stratford in 1602, warned Lord Salisbury of the risk of sedition.

Shake-Speares Sonnets By 1609 about half of Shakespeare's plays had appeared in print. His long narrative poems continued to be reprinted. In 1609 Thomas Thorpe published *Shake-Speares Sonnets*, printed by George Eld who printed the first quarto of *Troilus and Cressida* in the same year. The foregrounding of Shakespeare's name in the very title of the volume suggests that it may well have been authorized by Shakespeare, who could have sold the sequence to Thorpe for publication; the frequent closures of the theatres yet again because of plague in 1607–9 could have encouraged him to find another source of income. Thomas Heywood indicated in 1612 that Shakespeare's annoyance with the earlier unauthorized publication of some of the sonnets in *The Passionate Pilgrim* had made him take action: 'hee to doe himselfe right, hath since published them in his owne name' (Schoenbaum, *Documentary Life*, 219).

The *Sonnets* were prefaced by an enigmatic dedication (with each word followed by a period) signed with Thorpe's initials, mimicking the form of Ben Jonson's dedication of *Volpone* to the universities (published by Thorpe in 1607): 'To the onlie begetter of these ensuing sonnets Mr W.H. all happinesse and that eternitie promised by our ever-living poet wisheth the well-wishing adventurer in setting forth.' Thorpe included 154 sonnets, following them with the long poem 'A Lover's Complaint'. One of the sonnets may date back to his courtship of Anne Hathaway in 1582; Meres had spoken of his 'sugred Sonnets' circulating in manuscript in 1598; a few had been printed in 1599. But when the bulk of them and 'A Lover's Complaint' were written is a matter for argument. So too are the identities of Mr W. H., who may or may not be the young man to whom most of the sonnets are directed, of the 'dark lady' to whom others are aimed, and of the rival poet who appears in the sequence. Shakespeare, the consummate dramatist, may of course be constructing a drama set out in sonnets without any real figures behind it, but if the poems do tell of events in Shakespeare's life the identities of the participants come to matter greatly.

None of the many attempts at identifying the dark lady or the rival poet are finally convincing. But the case for the young man's being William Herbert, third earl of Pembroke, is more thorough and effective, even if there is a strong counter-claim that 'Mr W. H.' deliberately reverses the initials of Henry Wriothesley, third earl of Southampton, who was Shakespeare's patron in the early 1590s. Shakespeare had little known contact with Herbert, though Herbert and his brother were the dedicatees of the first folio in 1625 and praised there for having 'prosequuted both [Shakespeare's plays], and their Authour living, with so much favour' (sig. $^{\pi}$ A2*r*).

The sonnet sequence begins with a group of seventeen poems, apparently commissioned by the young man's family, that attempt to persuade him to marry and leave versions of himself behind in his children; Herbert had repeatedly refused proposed marriages and it is tempting to date these poems to his seventeenth birthday in 1597, perhaps the ones to which Meres referred. Equally well, if this part of the sequence is earlier than 1597, they could have been written to Southampton. In the absence of any significant external evidence, tests of vocabulary tend to suggest that some of the sonnets belong to the mid-1590s, while other internal indications, including possible allusions to the death of Elizabeth, suggest a date about 1603, when 'A Lover's Complaint' is most likely to have been written as a deliberate coda to the sequence. There is no reason to assume that the sequence was written at one time, nor that its differing segments were originally intended to belong together. Most of the poems, with their account of homoerotic desire between the older poet and a younger and unfaithful man (sonnets 1–126), the counter-attractions of heterosexual desire (127–152), and a continual return to self-humiliation, self-loathing, and sexual disgust, may well have been revised. All one can be sure of is that the poems could not have reached their final form as a sequence, ending with the 'Complaint', until at least 1603 and it is just as likely that they were finally revised shortly before publication. Perhaps the two periods of plague and closure provided Shakespeare with opportunities and reasons to work on his sonnets.

In the whole outpouring of sonnets in England in the period, only Richard Barnfield, in *Cynthia* (1595), wrote poems directed to a man. The *Sonnets* in their repeated punning on Shakespeare's first name make the embedding of the poet himself into the sequence plain. Their explicit homoeroticism suggests that Shakespeare's sexuality was consciously bisexual in its desires, though the modern concept of bisexuality and one appropriate to Shakespeare's lifetime may be significantly different. Whether Shakespeare's homoerotic desires led to or were connected with sexual acts with the young man or indeed any other man is far from clear. Read as biographical, they also make plain that fidelity to Anne was not something Shakespeare was much concerned about, though adulterous sex with the 'dark lady' induced deep shame. Whatever their biographical secrets, the poems have an emotional intensity and poetic complexity that make them among Shakespeare's greatest achievements.

Plays for the Blackfriars In 1608 the King's Men had acquired the lease of the Blackfriars Theatre, an indoor playhouse with a far smaller capacity than the Globe and with far higher admission prices; they acted there from the autumn of 1609. The company played in both venues but Blackfriars was by far the more prestigious. With its greater range of stage machinery, its increased use of music, its habitual division of plays into acts (with music between the acts), and its narrower social range of audience, Blackfriars offered Shakespeare a set of new challenges that he responded to in *The Winter's Tale*, *Cymbeline*, and *The Tempest*, and in his final collaborations with John Fletcher. It appears that Shakespeare was writing plays less frequently than earlier, perhaps now no more than one a year. *The Winter's Tale*, *Cymbeline*, and *The Tempest* belong to the years 1609–11 but the exact order in which they were written is impossible to determine, for all that critics prefer to see a simple sequence according to their own preference for a linear dramaturgical development. Shakespeare turned, as for *Pericles*, to the materials of prose romance narrative, for *The Winter's Tale* using Greene's old tale *Pandosto* (1588). All three play self-conscious games with narrative and its amenability to dramatic form: *The Winter's Tale* is broken-backed, something it shares with *Timon of Athens*, moving from compressed urban tragedy to leisurely pastoral comedy before returning redemptively to the location of its tragic phase; *Cymbeline* ostentatiously foregrounds the long sequence of its own multiple revelations that lead to the drama's resolution, as if teasing the audience to find it merely comic; *The Tempest* uses Prospero's magic to achieve compression into three hours on a metamorphic island. All three are particularly aware of their artifice and of the playwright's own art. If they seem to belong only to the world of romance, they are also full of topicality: *Cymbeline*'s movement to Milford Haven harks back to Richmond's landing to overthrow Richard III, and the play is full of comment on King James's vision of Britain as a newly united nation;

The Tempest plays on the colonizing of America and the encounters with the New World transposed into the Mediterranean. The clashes of worlds, old and new, ancient and modern, near and far, search for new unities.

The style of these plays connects with the drama that Francis Beaumont and John Fletcher were writing at the same time, though the direction of influence is far from clear. Certainly Shakespeare found a new and systematic collaboration with Fletcher desirable and satisfactory, for his next three plays were shared with the younger dramatist who had already written, probably in 1611, a sequel to *The Taming of the Shrew* as *The Woman's Prize, or, The Tamer Tamed*. As with so many contemporary examples of collaboration it is difficult to be sure of the precise shares: each play is perfectly coherent in performance. 'Cardenio', based on an episode in *Don Quixote*, was never printed but a manuscript, now lost, was claimed by Lewis Theobald to be the source for his play *The Double Falsehood* (1728) which shows strong traces of Fletcher in its style. After a prolonged break from the genre, Shakespeare and Fletcher returned to the now unfashionable mode of English history with *Henry VIII*, known to contemporaries as *All is True*. Its worries about competing politics and nostalgia for the optimism at the birth of Elizabeth testify to a cultural nervousness. Finally, if the assumed sequence of the plays is correct, came *The Two Noble Kinsmen*, a return to the chivalric world of Chaucer's 'Knight's tale' but coupled with an unnerving depiction of obsessive desire. Least known of all his work, Shakespeare's final collaborative plays show him continuing to experiment, returning to familiar topics but always in unfamiliar ways.

Lyrics, occasional poems, and revising Following Shakespeare's writings chronologically has obscured two important kinds of work. The first is difficult to determine: a number of lyrics and occasional epigrams have been attributed to Shakespeare but there is little hard evidence for any of them. There are epitaphs on people, with some of whom Shakespeare had a known or possible connection—for example, the verses on John Combe which were claimed to have been on his monument in Holy Trinity Church in Stratford, or the one on Elias James, a brewer who worked close to the Globe Theatre—and with some of whom there is no known link. It is not even certain that Shakespeare wrote the lines that appeared on his own grave, though they were recorded as his by the mid-seventeenth century. It is, though, probable that he wrote some occasional verse, whether songs, epigrams, or epitaphs. In March 1613 he certainly composed the *impresa* (an allegorical insignia with a motto) carried by the earl of Rutland at the king's accession day tilt; he was paid 44*s*., as was Richard Burbage for painting and making it. It is a rare moment linking Shakespeare directly with court events; unlike Ben Jonson, for instance, Shakespeare wrote masques as part of his plays, not for the court, and, though his plays were often performed at court, he was never one of the writers working for court circles.

The second kind of work is Shakespeare's repeated revising and rewriting of his plays. With the plays being part of the stock repertory of the Chamberlain's Men / King's Men, Shakespeare would have had repeated opportunities to reconsider his work. For some plays there is occasional evidence of revision in the stages of the original composition evident in the single text that reached print: a passage repeated with variants in *Love's Labour's Lost*, for instance, seems to show Shakespeare's first and second thoughts for the speech. But for a number of plays that were printed both in quarto and in the first folio, the variants often indicate large- and small-scale revision. Characters' roles are expanded (for example, Emilia in *Othello*); speeches are rethought; lines are added here and there to produce different echoes and connections; lines, speeches, and whole scenes are deleted to alter the dramatic form and the theatrical pacing. In the cases of *King Lear* and *Hamlet* the alterations between the versions are so substantial as to suggest that each survives as two rather significantly different plays, a quarto and a folio text. Texts in the theatre are often unstable entities; actors change lines they dislike and playwrights alter in response to the experience of rehearsal and production. Shakespeare is unlikely to have made the changes only once; rather, many plays, particularly the most popular ones, are likely to have undergone continual alteration over the years, but leaving only two snapshots of the long process, from first composition through years of performances, surviving in the printed texts.

The last years In 1613, at the very end of his playwriting career, Shakespeare made a substantial investment in property in London, buying the gatehouse of the old Dominican priory in Blackfriars, where the Blackfriars Theatre was located, for £140. Burbage had also bought property in the area and Shakespeare's purchase may have been simply an investment, since one John Robinson was a tenant there in 1616. But the gatehouse was large enough for Shakespeare to have let part of it and used the rest himself. Wherever he was living in London after leaving the Mountjoys, he could have been in the Blackfriars gatehouse from 1613. Shakespeare paid £80 of the purchase immediately and mortgaged the remainder. Though he was the purchaser, the property was held by him with three others as trustees: John Heminges of the King's Men, William Johnson, the landlord of the Mermaid Tavern, and John Jackson, possibly the husband of the sister-in-law of Elias James the brewer. The effect may well have been, whether by Shakespeare's design or not, to exclude Anne Shakespeare from having a widow's claim on a third share of the property for her life, her dower right, unless Shakespeare survived the other trustees.

The King's Men remained successful: at the celebrations for the marriage of James I's daughter to the elector palatine in February 1613 they performed fourteen plays, four of which were by Shakespeare (including the not exactly propitious *Othello*). But in June 1613, during a performance of Shakespeare's *Henry VIII*, the Globe Theatre burnt down after some of the stuff shot out of a small cannon, for a sound effect, lodged in the thatch. The sharers decided to rebuild at the cost of over £1400, each sharer contributing between £50 and £60. Shakespeare had certainly sold his share in the company by the time he made his will in 1616; this may have been a good moment to get out.

In 1709 Nicholas Rowe suggested that Shakespeare spent his last years 'in Ease, Retirement, and the Conversation of his Friends ... and is said to have spent some Years before his Death at his native *Stratford*' (*Works*, ed. Rowe, 1.xxxv). But, though the story has taken permanent hold, there is no evidence for Shakespeare's having retired to Stratford. In November 1614 Thomas Greene, Stratford's town clerk from 1603 to 1617, who repeatedly refers to Shakespeare as his cousin, was in London and noted that, Shakespeare 'commyng yesterday to towne I went to see him howe he did' (Schoenbaum, *Documentary Life*, 231). Where Shakespeare came from he does not say—it might well have been Stratford—but Shakespeare still came to London. Greene had been at Middle Temple when *Twelfth Night* was performed there and, with his wife and his children, Anne and William (perhaps the Shakespeares had stood godparents to them), were living in New Place in 1609.

Events in Stratford continued to involve Shakespeare, whether he was there or not. He was one of seventy-one Stratford citizens who subscribed to contribute to the cost of promoting a bill in parliament for the repair of roads, being named first, added in the margin, after the town's officials. A visiting preacher was entertained at New Place in 1614, though it is not clear whether Shakespeare was there at the time. There were family sadnesses too: two of his brothers died, Gilbert in February 1612 and Richard in February 1613, leaving only William and his sister Joan alive in that generation. In July 1613 his daughter Susanna brought a case in the bishop's consistory court that John Lane, a wild young man, had slandered her with an accusation of adultery with Rafe Smith and of having gonorrhoea; she won.

There was a local crisis too that affected Shakespeare. William Combe was the son of the William Combe from whom Shakespeare had bought the land in Old Stratford, and cousin of John Combe who left Shakespeare £5 in his will in 1614. Combe and Arthur Mainwaring, steward to Lord Ellesmere, wanted to enclose land at Welcombe from which Shakespeare and Thomas Greene had tithe income. The Stratford corporation opposed the enclosure. Shakespeare covenanted with Mainwaring's agent to be compensated, along with Greene, 'for all such losse detriment & hinderance' consequent on the enclosure (Schoenbaum, *Documentary Life*, 231). Greene's notes on his conversation with Shakespeare in London in November 1614 showed that Shakespeare knew how much land was intended to be enclosed and that compensation would be fixed the following April. Neither Shakespeare nor his son-in-law, John Hall, believed that the enclosure would go ahead. In December the corporation wrote to Shakespeare and Mainwaring to explain their opposition, not least because a fire in July 1613 had left many residents homeless. Combe's men began enclosing in the same month, but the ditch was filled in by women and children. Combe tried bribing Greene unsuccessfully. The struggle dragged on for years until Combe more or less abandoned his plans. Shakespeare's position in all this seems consistent: he was far more concerned to safeguard his income than to protect the townspeople's rights.

Shakespeare's will In January 1616 Shakespeare summoned his lawyer, Francis Collins, to draft his will. The decision was probably provoked by the impending marriage of his other daughter, Judith, to Thomas Quiney, son of Richard Quiney who had sought a loan from Shakespeare in 1598. Thomas was five years younger than Judith and Shakespeare had good reason to distrust him. The marriage took place in February 1616 in the middle of Lent without a special licence, an ecclesiastical offence for which Quiney was excommunicated. But, far more seriously, in March, Margaret Wheeler died giving birth to Quiney's child. Quiney admitted fornication in the ecclesiastical court and was ordered to do public penance, but paid a fine of 5*s.* instead. The first of the three pages of the will was revised late in March, apparently taking account of his son-in-law's crimes by altering the bequests to Judith.

Perhaps nothing in Shakespeare's plays has provoked quite as much commentary as his will (Chambers, 2.170–74). The three pages with their many corrections and interlineations seem full of afterthoughts and adjustments. Shakespeare's first concern is with Judith who would immediately inherit £100 and a further £50 in return for giving up her rights in a copyhold in Rowington to her sister and a further £150 in three years' time; if she were to die before then and without issue, the money would go to Shakespeare's granddaughter Elizabeth Hall and his sister, Joan Hart. But Judith would only receive the interest on the second tranche if she was married, unless her husband matched the capital sum. Thomas Quiney is never named and the will's phrase about 'such husbond as she shall att thend of the saied three Yeares be marryed unto' at the very least suggests that she might be married to someone other than Quiney by then. Shakespeare moved on to take especial care of his sister. In the event, Joan's husband, William Hart, died in April 1616, a week before Shakespeare; but she was clearly in need of help. She received £20, his clothes, and the house in Henley Street during her lifetime at a peppercorn rent; £5 went to each of Joan's three sons. Shakespeare's plate was to go to his granddaughter Elizabeth except 'my brod silver & gilt bole' which went to Judith. Shakespeare left £10 to the poor of Stratford, not a particularly large sum given his wealth and the fact that his lawyer would receive £13 6*s.* 8*d.*; his sword went to Thomas Combe and there were other bequests to local friends. He had been going to leave a small sum to Richard Tyler but Tyler's name is deleted for some reason. There were extra bequests to buy rings to Hamlet Sadler, his godson William Walker, and others. Of his 'ffellowes' in the King's Men, Shakespeare remembered, belatedly and in an interlineation, only three—Burbage, Heminges, and Condell—who would each receive 26*s.* 8*d.* for rings. Almost everything else went to Susanna, some in reconfirmation of the marriage settlement but the rest carefully tied up for the future for any sons she might have (up to seven) and only then to Elizabeth Hall or thereafter to Judith and her future sons. The generosity to Susanna and therefore to John Hall who were also appointed executors is offset by the tightly limited bequests to Judith. There is no mention of books or papers in the will—hardly a surprise since these would be part of his household goods which the Halls would receive; they did not need special reference.

Interlineated as an afterthought on the third page is the only reference to Anne, like Quiney unnamed: 'Item I gyve unto my wief my second best bed with the furniture'. The second-best bed may well have been the marriage bed with the best bed reserved for guests. But it is not clear whether in Stratford Anne would automatically have received the widow's dower rights of one-third of the estate; there were sharp regional variations in practice. Certainly the will's silence prevents her having control over any part of the estate. Other wills were far more explicit: Burbage's 'wellbeloved' wife was his executor; Henry Condell's 'wellbeloved' wife received all his property (E. A. J. Honigmann and S. Brock, *Playhouse Wills, 1558–1642*, 1993, 113, 157). The lack in Shakespeare's will of even a conventional term of endearment, of specific and substantial bequests to Anne, or even of the right to continue living in New Place amounts to a striking silence.

Death and burial On 23 April 1616 Shakespeare died. John Ward, a clergyman living in Stratford in the 1660s, recorded that 'Shakespear, Drayton, and Ben Jhonson had a merry meeting, and itt seems drank too hard, for Shakespear died of a feavour there contracted' (Chambers, 2.250). The story is not impossible but quite what Shakespeare died from is unknown. He was buried two days later in Holy Trinity, inside the church rather than in the churchyard because his purchase of an interest in the Stratford tithes in 1605 made him a lay rector. The epitaph, possibly written by himself, warning future generations to leave his bones where they lay, was inscribed on the grave, though the grave may not originally have been where the stone is now placed. Anne lived until 1623 (she was buried on 8 August) but her tombstone makes no mention of her husband, and refers to only one daughter; Judith seems to have been ignored.

The Stratford monument, the Droeshout engraving, and other portraits Anne probably lived to see the monument to her husband in Holy Trinity Church (which was certainly in place by 1623) but she could not have seen the publication of *Mr William Shakespeares Comedies, Histories, & Tragedies* (the first folio) in November or December of the same year. The monument and the title-page to the volume are the only two images of Shakespeare to have an especially strong likelihood of accuracy. The former was made by Geerart Janssen, a sculptor of Dutch descent; his father was also a sculptor who had made the tomb for the earl of Southampton, father of Shakespeare's patron. The Janssens had also worked for the earls of Rutland and were commissioned in 1618 to make a tomb for the fifth earl, by the sixth earl for whom Shakespeare and Burbage had made their *impresa* in 1613. Depicted as a writer, his mouth open as he prepares to write on the paper under his left hand (though the earliest reproduction, by Dugdale in 1656, dispensed with pen and paper), the Shakespeare of the monument has seemed too corpulent for some admirers, as if genius should be lean. It is precisely its unremarkable appearance, described by Dover Wilson as that of a 'self-satisfied pork-butcher' (Schoenbaum, *Records*, 161), that has convinced others of its accuracy. Frequently restored and recoloured—it was painted white in 1793 at Edmond Malone's urging but returned to what were assumed to be the original colours in 1861—the monument was used by the Flower brewery in Stratford as the trademark to sell its products and plaster casts derived from it were widely distributed. It is still the representation of Stratford's view of Shakespeare.

London's view may be embodied in the image on the title-page of the collection of his plays. The engraving has usually been ascribed to Martin Droeshout the younger, aged only twenty-one when the portrait was made in 1622, probably initially for separate distribution and not as part of the forthcoming volume, but its old-fashioned style was more likely to be the work of his uncle, Martin Droeshout the elder (*d. c.*1642), a Flemish protestant refugee in England and a leading member of the Painter-Stainers' Company in London at this time. This image of Shakespeare with its massive dome of a forehead 'like another dome of St Paul's' (A. L. Rowse, quoted in Schoenbaum, *Records*, 171), concealing, it seems to imply, a brain of disproportionate size, has become one of the most potent icons of Western culture, the very essence of the originating author making his presence visible in connection with his works. It can now be found on thousands of products, from tea towels to plastic bags to the British Library's computer catalogue (until 1999), but the mere idea of placing an image of an author on the title-page of a collection was unusual. There was no engraving of Ben Jonson on the title-page of Jonson's folio edition of his *Works*, published in 1616. But Jonson's poem on the Shakespeare portrait, placed to face it opposite the title-page, identifies both the image's accuracy and its inadequacy:

> O, could he but have drawne his wit
> As well in brasse, as he hath hit
> His face; the Print would then surpasse
> All that was ever writ in brasse.

The image exists in three distinct states in different copies of the first folio and the deteriorating plate was used for the subsequent folios as well. It was the source for William Marshall's engraving for the pirated 1640 edition of Shakespeare's poems and William Faithorne's for the 1655 edition of *The Rape of Lucrece*. Thereafter it became fair game for anyone seeking to represent their version of Shakespeare.

Droeshout's engraving is also the source of the 'Flower' portrait, now owned by the Royal Shakespeare Company, which was found in 1840 and was then claimed to be Droeshout's source. Its date is unclear and it may even be a nineteenth-century forgery. It reflects the often desperate desire to find authentic images of Shakespeare, like the

Ashbourne portrait (not of Shakespeare at all), first 'identified' in 1847, and the Ely Palace portrait, also a supposed source for Droeshout, discovered in 1845. Others were 'found' earlier, like the Felton or Burdett-Coutts portrait exhibited in 1792 or the Janssen portrait engraved in 1770; still others surfaced much later like the Grafton portrait, unknown before 1907, or the Sanders portrait, publicized in 2001. Sometimes a known image is, for a while, claimed to be of Shakespeare, like the Hilliard miniature which Leslie Hotson identified as Shakespeare in 1977. None of these is likely to be a portrait of Shakespeare independent of the Droeshout engraving or the Stratford bust; many are not even images of Shakespeare at all. Their claims are no more probable than that the plaster cast now in Darmstadt is indeed Shakespeare's death mask.

The only exception to this long succession of dubious manifestations of the bardolatrous desire to have a new image to worship is the Chandos portrait, the most probable of all the claimed portraits. Its provenance secure from 1719 (though earlier owners may have included the actor Thomas Betterton), it eventually came to the Chandos family and was then given by Lord Ellesmere in 1856 as the first picture (still catalogued as 'NPG 1') to enter the infant National Portrait Gallery, an image of the nation's greatest writer with which symbolically to found a collection of British historical portraits. It was copied by Kneller for John Dryden by 1694, Dryden responding with a poem to Kneller praising Shakespeare's 'Majestick Face' (Dryden, 'To Sir Godfrey Kneller', *The Poems and Fables of John Dryden*, ed. James Kinsley, 1962, 497). A version by Michael van der Gucht was part of the frontispiece of Rowe's edition of 1709 and the Tonson family's sequence of Shakespeare editions through the eighteenth century (until 1767) continued the tradition. Indeed, since the Tonsons' address from 1710 was a building they named 'Shakespeare's Head', the Chandos portrait became their commercial trademark. It has been reproduced at least as often as the Droeshout engraving.

Probably painted by John Taylor about 1610 the Chandos image is, if genuine, the only one made before Shakespeare's death. Its swarthiness has created anxieties among some who saw it as too Italian or too Jewish to be Shakespeare's true likeness. Its fashionable gold earring has troubled others at times when male dress was more restrained. It has, more often, been seen as a more acceptably realistic image than either the Droeshout engraving or the Stratford monument.

Elegies and influence on contemporaries Shakespeare's death prompted at least one elegy: William Basse's poem circulated quite widely in manuscript but was not printed until 1633 (as John Donne's). The poem's recommendation that Spenser, Chaucer, and Beaumont should move up in their tombs in Westminster Abbey to leave space for Shakespeare was well enough known for Jonson to allude to it and refute it in his poem 'To the memory of my beloved, the author Mr. William Shakespeare: and what he hath left us' prefixed to the first folio. For Jonson, Shakespeare was:

> a Moniment, without a tombe
> And art alive still, while thy Booke doth live,
> And we have wits to read, and praise to give.
> (W. Shakespeare, *Comedies, Histories, & Tragedies*, 1623, sig. πA4r)

Although Shakespeare's death was not marked by a published collection of verses, an exceptionally rare public effusion for any writer, his work continued to be powerfully influential on contemporary audiences and dramatists alike. Far from his plays and poems coming quickly to be seen as old-fashioned and outdated, references and allusions to his plays and poems in commonplace books, poems, and other writings certainly did not stop with the end of his career. Shakespeare's spectators and readers remained fascinated by his work.

As significantly, just as Shakespeare himself continually reworked scenes, characters, speeches, and thoughts from his own and others' earlier plays into his latest writing, so other playwrights turned to Shakespeare as a major resource for their own development. The late plays and the final collaborations with Fletcher spawned dozens of imitations, as if Shakespeare had defined the age's style. But there were quotations and allusions in numerous plays, ranging from the deliberately resonant to the probably unconscious, as if writing plays now necessitated engagement with his work in a playwriting culture effectively in part defined and even dominated by Shakespeare. When the heroine in Webster's *The Duchess of Malfi* (printed 1623) revives after strangling for a few moments like Desdemona, or when Cornelia in his *The White Devil* (1612) madly distributes herbs like Ophelia, when Middleton's and Rowley's *The Changeling* (performed 1622) has an honest villain like Iago and their Beatrice, like Shakespeare's in *Much Ado*, asks a man to undertake a killing each woman is unable to do for herself, then these great younger contemporaries are, consciously or not, deriving their effects from Shakespeare. But such recycling of Shakespearian materials is not in any way restricted to the work of the best: out of dozens of possible examples, one might note a drama of lovers from rival families in Thomas May's *The Heir* (acted 1620), a murderer who cannot wash the blood from his hands in William Heminges's *The Jews' Tragedy* (*c*.1626), or a play put on for royalty by workers whose leading actor wants to play all the parts in Thomas Rawlins's *The Rebellion* (printed 1640). Shakespeare was not the only dramatist to affect those who came after, nor is it sensible to try to quantify resonances, borrowings, and allusions to determine whether Shakespeare was more or less influential than Jonson. But his plays were already becoming a central store of possibilities which dramatists could raid, largely without acknowledgement.

The first folio Where the raiders could find the work changed substantially with the decision to publish something approximating to a volume of Shakespeare's collected plays. In 1616 the publication of Ben Jonson's *Works* marked the first occasion on which the plays of a vernacular dramatist had been collected. Jonson had spent years on the volume and had included poems and prose works as well. The project to gather Shakespeare's work may have begun with John Heminges and Henry Condell, Shakespeare's fellow actors, though it is tempting to imagine that Shakespeare's bequest of money for rings to them in his will signalled that the plan was Shakespeare's own.

The planning may have been accelerated, and may even have been provoked, by Thomas Pavier's unauthorized publication in 1619 of a group of quartos of plays ostensibly by Shakespeare. Pavier and his printer William Jaggard included two plays certainly not by Shakespeare, *Sir John Oldcastle Part 1* (first printed as Shakespeare's in 1600) and *A Yorkshire Tragedy*, and one other, *Pericles*, that would not be part of the first folio. Some of the title-pages had false dates; all were reprints of previously published plays. Most significantly, the collection of ten plays was sold as a set and the Stationers' Company responded to the lord chamberlain's complaint, presumably instigated by the King's Men as owners of the plays, to prohibit publication of their repertory without their consent.

The publication of a folio of Shakespeare's plays was ambitious and expensive. While Heminges and Condell signed the volume's dedication to the earl of Pembroke, who was lord chamberlain, and his younger brother, and were also the authors of the prefatory letter 'To the great Variety of Readers', they were not necessarily the folio's editors, in the modern sense of the word. The cost of the publishing was, as the volume's colophon indicated, the responsibility of William Jaggard and his son Isaac, Edward Blount, John Smethwick, and William Apsley. The publishers needed to secure the printing rights to a number of plays that had already appeared and Smethwick and Apsley, who owned the rights to four and two plays respectively, may have become involved for that reason.

There were thirty-six plays in the volume: eighteen had never been printed before (including, for instance, *Julius Caesar*, *Twelfth Night*, *Macbeth*, *Antony and Cleopatra*, and *The Tempest*) and sixteen of these were acquired from the King's Men themselves. Isaac Jaggard and Edward Blount entered their rights in sixteen plays in the Stationers' register in November 1623, shortly before the volume appeared, including in their list *Antony and Cleopatra*, which Blount had entered in 1608 but never printed. The publication syndicate had to negotiate with seven other stationers for the rights to other plays. News of the planned folio may have encouraged the reprinting of a number of Shakespeare plays in the early 1620s and the first publication of *Othello* in 1622. Problems over rights may have been the cause of the delay in printing *Troilus and Cressida*, which is not named on the contents page (three copies of the volume without the play survive); though originally intended to follow *Romeo and Juliet*, it was in the end placed ambiguously between the histories and the tragedies, either the last of the former or first of the latter. Of the plays which subsequent bibliographers would assign substantially or significantly to Shakespeare, only collaborative plays (*Pericles*, *The Two Noble Kinsmen*, 'Cardenio', and *Edward III*) were missing.

Printing began early in 1622 and took nearly two years. The compositors' copy came from a variety of sources: for example, scribal copies made by Ralph Crane and others from Shakespeare's manuscripts; quartos annotated by reference to manuscript playbooks used at the theatre; the playbooks themselves; and Shakespeare's 'foul papers'. Having decided not to include Shakespeare's poems (which were not reunited with the plays in any edition until 1790), the editor(s) chose to arrange the volume unconventionally by genre and to allow the genres to be the volume's title: *Mr. William Shakespeare's Comedies, Histories, & Tragedies*. Ben Jonson's naming his volume as his 'works' had attracted some mockery, but the editorial choice of genre as the controlling taxonomy for Shakespeare straitjackets some plays awkwardly. Some had been published with other generic definitions—for example, *Richard II* and *Richard III* had both been published as tragedies, not histories; *King Lear* as history, not tragedy. The folio's organization cast a long shadow over centuries of analysis.

Within the genre of history the plays, which included only English histories (not British or Roman ones), were arranged by chronological order of reign. Comedies and tragedies were fairly randomly sequenced. None of the ordering reflected the chronology of composition or performance, leaving, again, much confusion and sheer hard work to come.

But the choice of format, for all Jonson's precedent, was crucial, giving the volume the instant status of a classic: it is a weighty tome, a book for individuals' libraries, a collection perhaps to be owned rather than read and few surviving copies show traces of early readers. It was also expensive, probably not less than 15*s.* a copy and often costing £1 or more. It remained expensive, with copies in the early twentieth century selling for over $50,000 and one being sold in October 2001 for over $6 million, six times the previous record price for a copy. The first folio's status as a library book probably helped so many copies to survive: over 220 are known, nearly eighty of them in the Folger Shakespeare Library in Washington.

In addition to the plays, preface, portrait, and dedication, the volume included a list of the principal actors in the plays and three prefatory poems, as well as Jonson's two, by Hugh Holland, Leonard Digges, and I. M. (probably James Mabbe). It amounts to a grand but not excessively elaborate quantity of prefatory material.

Without the first folio it is likely that most of the eighteen plays printed there for the first time would never have been printed at all. In effect, half Shakespeare's reputation rests on that publication. No literary volume has generated so much commentary and analysis. Technical study of its printing means that more is known about the processes of its production than for any other early modern book. There have been numerous facsimiles and, of course, innumerable reprintings of its contents.

The volume was first announced in October 1622—prematurely, for copies were not on sale for more than a year. William Jaggard was dead by November 1623 and it is his son's name that appears on the title-page. The first known purchase of a copy, by Sir Edward Dering, was in December 1623. Sales were brisk enough to warrant the printing of a second edition in 1632, with three more prefatory poems, including John Milton's first published poem, and with careful revision of the plays to correct many errors (and introduce some more). The quality of the paper led the scourge of the players, William Prynne, to complain that 'Shackspeers Plaies are printed in the best Crowne paper, far better than most Bibles' (W. Prynne, *Histriomastix*, 1633, sig. **6v). The third folio was published in 1663; a second issue in 1664 added seven more plays, only one of which, *Pericles*, is Shakespeare's while the others (including *The London Prodigal* and *Locrine*) belong to the body of Shakespeare apocrypha, keeping their place in the succession of Shakespeare editions for many years. A fourth folio was printed in 1685 and pages from it were reset to produce a putative 'fifth folio' probably shortly after 1700.

Publication of the poems was markedly less successful. Though *Venus and Adonis* and *The Rape of Lucrece* were frequently published up to the 1630s (at least fifteen and eight times respectively), each was printed only once more before 1700. The *Sonnets* were reprinted by John Benson in 1640 in an unauthorized version which ran a number of sonnets together to form longer works, gave many trivial titles (such as 'Love's relief' or 'The picture of true love'), and altered a few pronouns to reduce the emphasis on homoerotic desire. Benson also included many poems not by Shakespeare at all.

Performances and influences to 1660 The plays continued to be performed through the years before the theatres were closed in 1642. There were performances at the Globe and the Blackfriars but the casts were changing. As actors died or left the King's Men others took over their roles, but some thought it could not be the same: an elegy on the death of Richard Burbage in 1619 mourned:

Kind Leer, the greved Moore, and more beside,
That lived in him, have now for ever dy'de.
(E. K. Chambers, *The Elizabethan Stage*, 1923, 2.309)

There were performances elsewhere: Sir Edward Dering's library contained an adaptation of the two parts of *Henry IV* into a single play, probably for a private performance. Some characters were already dominating their plays: a court performance of *1 Henry IV* on 1 January 1625 was referred to as *Sir John Falstaff*. But a remarkable range of plays which were hardly of the newest fashion were performed at Charles I's court, including *Othello*, *Hamlet*, *Julius Caesar*, *Cymbeline*, and *Richard III*. Charles himself was keen enough on Shakespeare to annotate his copy of the second folio, retitling *Much Ado* as 'Beatrice and Benedict'.

One other admirer at court was Sir William Davenant, whose ode on Shakespeare was published in 1638, the year he became poet laureate. Davenant, whose parents kept an inn in Oxford, variously claimed to be Shakespeare's godson and natural son, the latter especially when drunk.

More ambivalent, inevitably, were the responses of John Milton, who saw his happy man in 'L'Allegro' (*c*.1631), a poem full of Shakespeare echoes, going to the theatre to hear:

sweetest Shakespeare, fancy's child,
Warble his native wood-notes wild
(ll. 133–4)

and whose *Comus* (1634) is pervasively influenced by Shakespeare. But if Shakespeare's work is never far from Milton's mind, especially in *Samson Agonistes* and *Paradise Lost*, his plays also stand, in Milton's prose writing, as tools with which to beat the crown: in *Eikonoklastes* (1649), Charles I is compared with Shakespeare's Richard III.

During the closure of the theatres in the interregnum and probably also in the early years of the Restoration, comic parts of Shakespeare's plays were performed for popular audiences as drolls at fairs, taverns, at the otherwise empty theatres, and elsewhere: versions of the gravedigger scene in *Hamlet* and the Gadshill robbery in *1 Henry IV* were printed in 1662 with a frontispiece showing Falstaff and Mistress Quickly, the first published illustration of Shakespearian characters, while the preface to *The Merry Conceited Humours of Bottom the Weaver* (1661), a very short version of *A Midsummer Night's Dream*, reported performances by apprentices.

Shakespeare adapted When public performances resumed in 1660, Shakespeare was quickly put back into the repertory. The company playing at the Red Bull Theatre in late 1660 performed *Henry IV*, *The Merry Wives of Windsor* (another mark of the especial popularity of Falstaff), and *Othello*, while *Pericles* was at the Cockpit Theatre in Drury Lane. After November 1660 (when the two theatre companies under Thomas Killigrew and Sir William Davenant began competing operations) Killigrew's King's Company, claiming to be the successors to the King's Men, also claimed the rights in their predecessor's repertory, including Shakespeare.

On 11 December 1660 they performed *Othello* with one notable change: a woman played Desdemona. A new prologue 'to introduce the first Woman that came to Act on the Stage' noted the necessity:

For (to speak truth) men act, that are between
Forty and fifty, Wenches of fifteen;
With bone so large, and nerve so incomplyant,
When you call *Desdemona*, enter Giant.
(T. Jordan, *A Royal Arbor of Loyal Poesie*, 1663, 21–2)

The next day, 12 December 1660, Davenant was awarded rights in nine Shakespeare plays (including *King Lear*, *Macbeth*, and *Hamlet*), following his proposition 'of reformeinge some of the most ancient Playes that were playd at Blackfriers and of makeinge them, fitt, for the Company of Actors appointed under his direction and Command' (A. Nicoll, *A History of English Drama, 1660–1900*, 6 vols., 1952, 1.352). It is difficult to know which of the two changes was the more important. The replacement of the boy-actresses with women irrevocably changed the forms of Shakespearian representation. The right to alter plays seen as 'ancient' began the long history of Shakespeare adaptation. Each change had immense impact on Shakespeare in the theatre. A third major change was introduced in June 1661 when Davenant's company moved to the Lincoln's Inn Fields Theatre which was equipped with moveable scenery, the first ever in England. Not everyone was impressed: Richard Flecknoe wrote in 1664 'that which makes our Stage the better, makes our Playes the worse perhaps, they striving now to make them more for sight, then hearing' (R. Flecknoe, *Love's Kingdom*, 1664, sig. G7*v*).

Shakespeare's plays were not especially popular at this time and his name was not one yet able to draw the crowds. Davenant made *Henry VIII* a success in 1663 by spectacular new scenery and costumes and the performance of Thomas Betterton as Henry was exceptional, not least through being part of a tradition: 'he being Instructed in it by Sir *William* [Davenant], who had it from Old Mr. *Lowen*, that had his Instructions from Mr. *Shakespear* himself' (J. Downes, *Roscius Anglicanus*, 1709, 24). Samuel Pepys was regularly impressed by the new scenery and especially by Betterton's acting in Shakespeare, praising his Hamlet as 'beyond imagination' in August 1661 (E. L. Avery and others, *The London Stage, 1660–1700*, 1965, 32). Others were less excited: John Evelyn who saw the production in December 1661 thought that 'now the old playe began to disgust this refined age' (ibid., 43).

Pepys, who often saw Shakespeare plays among his many theatre visits, seeing *Macbeth* and *The Tempest* especially frequently, offers some sense of how a member of the audience estimated Shakespeare's worth. Some plays he admired; others disappointed. *A Midsummer Night's Dream* was 'the most insipid ridiculous play that ever I saw in my life' but relieved by 'some good dancing and some handsome women' (E. L. Avery and others, *The London Stage, 1660–1700*, 1965, 56). Both qualities mattered to Pepys. While he respected *Macbeth* as 'a deep tragedy', he particularly enjoyed the 'variety of dancing and music' (ibid., 100, 107). After his first visit to *The Tempest* he praised a musical echo effect and later noted that the play was 'full of so good variety, that I cannot be more pleased almost in a comedy' (ibid., 123).

In neither case was Pepys seeing Shakespeare's play unaltered. Davenant's *Macbeth* substantially added to the spectacle of the witches' scenes; Downes noted that:

> being drest in all it's Finery, as new Cloath's, new Scenes, Machines, as flyings for the Witches; with all the Singing and Dancing in it … it being all Excellently perform'd, being in the nature of an Opera, it Recompenc'd double the Expence.
> (J. Downes, *Roscius Anglicanus*, 1709, 33)

Less play than opera (for its effects as much as its music), Davenant's version also increased the actresses' roles, emphasized Macbeth's ambition with a dying line 'Farewell vain World, and what's most vain in it, Ambition' ([W. Davenant], *Macbeth*, 1674, 60), and cleaned up the language: Macbeth no longer curses the 'cream-faced loon' asking 'Where gott'st thou that goose look?' (v. iii, ll. 11–12) but politely enquires 'Now Friend, what means thy change of Countenance?' (54). Such linguistic changes were necessary: Shakespeare's vocabulary was difficult, his syntax obscure, and his fascination with metaphor unacceptable since 'the tongue in general is so much refined since Shakespeare's time' as John Dryden noted in 1679 (J. Dryden, *Troilus and Cressida*, 1679, sig. A4*v*).

Davenant's adaptation of *Hamlet* makes similar changes, altering 'To grunt and sweat under a weary life' (III.i, l. 79) into 'To groan and sweat under a weary life', and 'the native hue of resolution' (III.i, l. 86) becomes 'the healthful face of resolution', no longer 'Sicklied o'er with the pale cast of thought' (III.i, l. 87) but now 'Shews sick and pale with thought' ([W. Davenant], *Hamlet*, 1676, 39). Davenant's playing text marked extensive cuts, according to the edition of 1676, in the places 'least prejudicial to the Plot or Sense' because the play was 'too long to be conveniently Acted'. But the edition also includes the full text 'that we may no way wrong the incomparable Author' (sig. [A]2*r*). Clearly, by this date, Shakespeare, simply an old dramatist at the Restoration, was becoming valued.

While Davenant's first Shakespeare adaptation, combining *Measure for Measure* and *Much Ado* into *The Law Against Lovers* (1662), was much more extreme, his version of *The Tempest* as *The Enchanted Island*, a collaboration with Dryden first produced in 1667, was a case of adding to the play's symmetry. Dryden's preface, which saw Fletcher's *The Sea-Voyage* (1622) and Sir John Suckling's *The Goblins* (1638) as earlier responses to the play, praised Davenant for contriving a 'Counterpart to *Shakespear*'s Plot' in balancing Miranda with Hippolito, 'a Man who had never seen a Woman' (Davenant and Dryden, *The Tempest*, 1670, sig. A2*v*). The new action with four lovers is by turns innocent and outrageously sexy. But much more striking is the expansion of the action of rebellion, with more sailors and a broader representation of the chaos of disorder. The adaptation manifests the deep cultural unease of a society only just recovering from civil war, making of Shakespeare's play, as with other early adaptations of pre-Restoration drama and with the new tragi-comedies being written, a fiercely political parable.

Other adaptations sought different solutions to making the plays stage-worthy again: James Howard wrote a happy ending for *Romeo and Juliet* in 1662 with the lovers left alive, the adaptation being played on alternate nights with the tragic original; John Lacy turned Grumio in *Shrew* into a Scot in his farcical adaptation *Sauny the Scot* (1667) in which he starred, with the play now set in London. The Dryden–Davenant *Tempest* was itself adapted by Thomas Shadwell in 1674 into a spectacular version with more machines, stage effects, and much more music, compensated for by cutting the text hard to make room. Howard's play is lost, *Sauny* was popular for a while, but Shadwell's *Tempest*, rescored by Purcell in 1690, lasted over a century. Like Davenant's *Macbeth*, the new version displaced Shakespeare's from the stage. Other plays could be used as, in effect, the raw material for theatrical spectacle, most notably the version of *A Midsummer Night's Dream* as *The Fairy Queen* (1692), again with music by Purcell, whose scenes do not set a single word by Shakespeare. The adaptations also became part of the wars between the theatres: the Duke's Company's success with Shadwell's *The Tempest* provoked the King's Company to put on Thomas Duffett's parody *The Mock-Tempest* (1674), the first in a long line of Shakespeare burlesques. Duffett also mocked the rival company's *Macbeth* in his farce on *The Empress of Morocco* (1674). In both cases it is not Shakespeare that is being mocked; his plays are the convenient vehicle for mocking rivals' theatrical styles.

Praising Shakespeare None of this was incompatible with increasing praise for Shakespeare himself. Dryden, who became as crucial to the next phase of Shakespeare adaptation as Davenant had been at first, defined Shakespeare as the crucial originating natural force which enabled others:

> *Shakespear*, who (taught by none) did first impart
> To *Fletcher* Wit, to labouring *Johnson* Art.
> He Monarch-like gave those his subjects law,
> And is that Nature which they paint and draw.

Dryden here also identifies Shakespeare as the poetic equivalent of divine kingship: '*Shakespear*'s pow'r is sacred as a King's' (Davenant and Dryden, *The Tempest*, 1670, sig. A4*r*). The concepts of Shakespeare as natural genius and as a sacred king were both of immense and potent influence. Throughout his career Dryden sustainedly turns to Shakespeare as a measure of value. It is Shakespeare who is Dryden's example of the supreme dramatist in his *Essay of Dramatic Poesy* (1668), 'the man who of all Modern, and perhaps Ancient Poets, had the largest and most comprehensive soul' (J. Dryden, *Of Dramatick Poesie: an Essay*, 1668, 47). His own *All for Love* (1678) was an attempt 'to intimate the Divine *Shakespeare*' (sig. b4*v*). Even in his preface to his version of *Troilus and Cressida* (1679), a work about which he felt unsure, he identifies Shakespeare as being 'held in the same veneration … by us' as Aeschylus was by the Athenians (sig. A4*v*), while the prologue to the play is spoken by Shakespeare's ghost: 'See, my lov'd *Britons*, see your *Shakespeare* rise' (sig. b4*r*).

But Dryden's degree of praise was still unusual. It was shared by Margaret Cavendish, whose letter on Shakespeare was published in 1664 and ranks as the first lengthy critical assessment of his work. For her, Shakespeare's brilliant characterization would make one 'think he had been Transformed into every one of those Persons he hath Described', an early example of praise of Shakespeare for protean transformation (Thompson and Roberts, 12). Few went as far the other way as the critic Thomas Rymer, who in *A Short View of Tragedy* (1693) damned *Othello* as 'a Bloody Farce' (p. 146), mockingly suggesting that its morals were to advise 'all good Wives that they look well to their Linnen' and 'a lesson to Husbands, that before their Jealousie be Tragical, the proofs may be Mathematical' (p. 89).

Political Shakespeare Nahum Tate was only stating a common view rather than an extreme one when he described *King Lear* as 'a Heap of Jewels, unstrung and unpolisht' (N. Tate, *King Lear*, 1681, sig. A2*v*). His concern to find an 'Expedient to rectifie what was wanting in the Regularity and Probability of the Tale' led to his writing in a love between Edgar and Cordelia and altering the ending to 'conclude in a Success to the innocent distrest Persons' (ibid., sigs. A2*v*–A3*r*). With no Fool to trouble the tragic tone and a new love scene for Edmund and Regan 'amorously Seated' in 'A Grotto' (ibid., 40), Tate's version (1681), the most notorious of the adaptations, may be designed to make the play more manageably moving but it is also a serious attempt to read the play politically, celebrating the king's 'blest Restauration' (ibid., 66). Equally political and topical was his attempt to stage *Richard II* in 1680, first banned outright and then, after two days of performances transposed to Italy as *The Sicilian Usurper*, banned again. Tate was not much luckier with his version of *Coriolanus* as *The Ingratitude of a Commonwealth* (1681), clearly establishment in its politics but not much liked by audiences.

As Tate found, amid the upheavals of the Popish Plot and the exclusion crisis, Shakespeare's plays were means of making dangerous political statements: Ravenscroft's *Titus Andronicus* (1678) was a satire on Titus Oates and the whigs; Otway's *Caius Marius* (1679), from *Romeo and Juliet*, explored the plight of those caught up in political and social struggles. Tate's problems with censorship were not the last: Colley Cibber's *Richard III* (1700), a version long-lived enough to leave traces on Laurence Olivier's film (1955), was first performed without its first act, borrowed from 3 *Henry VI*, since the murder of a king was still unstageable when likely to be seen as a parallel to the death of James II. Cibber carefully distinguished his lines from Shakespeare's in the printed text, again a mark of Shakespeare's growing importance as an originating text.

Adaptations apart, the whole course of drama was being profoundly affected by Shakespeare. Playwrights creating Restoration comedies found their crucial prototypes for the wit-combats of hesitant lovers in Beatrice and Benedick while *Love's Labour's Lost* offered a model for a comedy that did not end with marriage but with future trials, a vital component in the work of Etherege and others. Otway's fascination with Shakespearian tragedy led directly to his brand of pathetic drama: *The History and Fall of Caius Marius* (1680) is the first in a long line of versions of *Romeo and Juliet* to have Juliet (here Lavinia) wake just before Romeo (Otway's Marius Junior) dies, allowing for a last desperate love scene together. It was natural for Nicholas Rowe, writing emotionally affecting tragedies centred on the sufferings of women in Otway's wake, to announce on the title-page that *The Tragedy of Jane Shore* (1714) was 'written in Imitation of Shakespeare's Style', the same phrase that Dryden had used on the title-page of *All for Love*.

Editions by Rowe, Pope, and Theobald Rowe's play was written after his most significant engagement with Shakespeare. In 1709 Jacob Tonson published a six-volume edition of Shakespeare edited by Rowe, the first major attempt to re-edit Shakespeare since the first folio. Tonson had acquired shares in the copyright of many Shakespeare plays in 1707 as part of his self-definition as the pre-eminent publisher of the major works of English literature. The copyright remained with the firm until 1767 and the line of Shakespeare editions it published were reworkings and remarketings of the firm's property. In 1709 Shakespeare was the first in a series of English dramatists—followed by Congreve, Beaumont and Fletcher, Otway, Southerne, and Dryden. Tonson chose Rowe as editor, presumably because an eminent dramatist was the appropriately sympathetic figure to edit the plays.

Rowe modernized Shakespeare's spelling and punctuation, continuing a process begun in the later folios. But he was not a Shakespeare editor in a modern sense: though he knew there were textual problems with lines and scenes absent from the fourth folio (his copy-text) and needing to be supplied, he made such 'corrections' only in a fairly haphazard way, for example by printing the prologue to *Romeo and Juliet*, found in a quarto, at the end of the play. He emended some clear errors introduced by compositors, and one or two that he perceived as Shakespeare's own (in *Troilus*, for example, the anachronistic reference to 'Aristotle' (II.ii, l. 165) was altered to 'graver Sages'). More significantly, Rowe supplied lists of characters and regularized all the plays into five acts, completing a process begun in the first folio and entirely absent from the quartos. For some he also included scene divisions.

Rowe also added a number of scene locators, identifying where the play was set, often at the head of each scene. Many locations he borrowed from contemporary adaptations, so that Shakespeare's plays now appeared as if they were contemporary dramas. Rowe's locations cast a long shadow: Shakespeare's Lear is never out on a heath; Rowe borrowed the placing from Tate's version.

Although less elaborate than other Tonson editions, Rowe's Shakespeare was presented with illustrations, one per play, often derived from contemporary stagings, the first images to appear in print for most of the plays. Rowe also wrote the first substantial Shakespeare biography, 'Some account of the life', prefixed to the first volume, based on a few facts, more legends, and some material that Thomas Betterton had gathered in his 'Veneration for the memory of *Shakespear*' (*Works*, ed. Rowe, 1.xxxiv). Rowe's Shakespeare is a gentleman like Rowe himself, his friends in retirement other 'Gentlemen of the Neighbourhood' (ibid., xxxvi). Rowe's decision to include this short biography was based on his recognition that biographical curiosity is 'very Natural' and 'may sometimes conduce to the better understanding' of an author, even if Shakespeare's works 'may seem to many not to want a Comment' (ibid., ii). The hesitancy over the usefulness of a biography of Shakespeare for understanding the plays would be repeated many times in subsequent centuries.

Tonson retained the extra apocryphal plays added to the third folio but he excluded the poems. They were printed in an extra volume by a rival publisher, Edmund Curll, formatted to match Tonson's plays and edited by Charles Gildon partly from Benson's 1640 text. Gildon also contributed by far the longest critical account of Shakespeare's plays yet to have appeared, carefully evaluating Shakespeare by classical precepts and assuming his pre-eminence among English dramatists.

In the subsequent years the pile of editions and of critical writings on Shakespeare began to grow apace. John Dennis's *Essay upon the Genius and Writings of Shakespeare* (1712), probably the first critical work devoted entirely to Shakespeare, was an extension of his other writing on Shakespeare and his experience as an unsuccessful adapter of *The Merry Wives of Windsor*. Shakespeare was discussed more often than any other literary figure in Steele's periodical *The Tatler*, his finest passages identified and praised, his works harnessed to the defence of English writing against French, his plays alluded to and assumed to be known to Steele's readership.

Rowe revised his edition in 1714 but the whole text was re-edited by Alexander Pope and published in 1725. Pope undertook rather more careful collation of different texts, but his concern was to make contemporary readers appreciate the best passages, marking them with marginal quotation marks and providing a convenient index to them. This fragmenting of the dramas into convenient poetical passages continued in the excerpting of Shakespeare in William Dodd's *The Beauties of Shakespeare* (1752), a lasting anthology that for many, including Goethe, provided an introduction to Shakespeare. Pope also relegated to the foot of the page any passages he decided were weak, especially Shakespeare's increasingly unacceptable puns and conceits. For Pope, Shakespeare was 'the fairest and fullest subject for Criticism, and to afford the most numerous, as well as most conspicuous instances, both of Beauties and Faults of all sorts' (*The Works of Shakespear*, ed. A. Pope, 6 vols., 1725, 1.i). The plays could be regarded as 'an ancient majestick piece of *Gothick* Architecture, compar'd with a neat Modern building' (ibid., xxiii).

While Pope could consult twenty-seven texts for his edition, a sign of the growing libraries of Shakespeare which individuals were beginning to accumulate, Lewis Theobald listed forty-three. Theobald, who had attacked the defects of Pope's edition in *Shakespeare Restored* (1726), published his own in 1733, bringing to Shakespeare the methods of classical and biblical editorial theory and commentary. Careful collation and judicious emendation needed, for Theobald, considerable intellectual skill, though his mockery of Pope's failings only immortalized him as the hero of *The Dunciad* (1728). Theobald also published *The Double Falsehood*, his stage adaptation of what he claimed to be the Shakespeare–Fletcher 'Cardenio'.

Editions and criticism to 1800 More editions followed: Hanmer's opulent one published in Oxford in 1744, Warburton's wilful version for the Tonsons in 1747, Dr Johnson's thoughtful account first outlined in his *Proposals* (1756) and adumbrated throughout his edition (1765) with its preface attempting to defend Shakespeare's generic hybrids against neo-classical orthodoxies. For Johnson, it is Shakespeare's depiction of 'general nature' that overrides local breaches of decorum and Shakespeare, 'the poet of nature', is more vital and more human, showing 'human sentiments in human language' (S. Johnson, *Preface to his Edition of Shakespear's Plays*, 1765, viii, xii). Johnson may blame Shakespeare for his faults, especially his fascination with puns ('the fatal Cleopatra', ibid., xxiii–xxiv), and he may find the tragedies at times laboured, resulting in 'meanness, tediousness and obscurity' (ibid., xxi), but for Johnson Shakespeare is the central figure in British culture and language, as the enormous number of citations in Johnson's *Dictionary* shows.

Other kinds of Shakespeare criticism also started to appear: Charlotte Lennox brought together many of Shakespeare's sources with a commentary in *Shakespeare*

Illustrated (1753–4); Lord Kames made Shakespeare the example of genius as part of his exploration of moral aesthetics in *Elements of Criticism* (1762); Richard Farmer offered careful consideration of Shakespeare's classical learning (1767); Elizabeth Griffith explored *The Morality of Shakespeare's Drama* (1775); Maurice Morgann's *Essay on the Dramatic Character of Sir John Falstaff* (1777) turned from the nature of a single character, widely admired as Shakespeare's crowning achievement, to the nature of Shakespeare's art; Samuel Ayscough's *Index* (1790) was the first reasonably systematic concordance to Shakespeare. Cumulatively it adds up to the development of a critical industry focused on Shakespeare, making his work both a centre of attention and a means of evaluating other concerns, whether moral, aesthetic, or theoretical. But it also defines a literary culture within which the recognition and just evaluation of Shakespeare's worth was increasingly seen as a central emblem of the culture's refinement and taste.

All was, however, still based on the achievements of successive editors. George Steevens reprinted a group of quartos in their original spelling in 1766. Edward Capell was the first to resist the random attempts of his predecessors by an assiduous and accurate collation of early texts, coupled with cautious emendation, resulting in a finely printed text (published in 1768) with brief textual notes. Capell's modesty contrasted with the increasing grandeur of the editions, building on Johnson's, which Steevens published in 1773 and subsequently expanded, with increasingly lengthy introductions, the text vanishing beneath the accumulated notes of editors and the whole a colossal display of the editors' learning.

Edmond Malone's immense achievement was the discovery of numerous records of Shakespeare's life, of the stage conditions of early modern theatres, and of textual materials, the synthesis of this vast archival research into new and remarkable accounts of the chronology of Shakespeare's plays (first published in 1780) and of Shakespeare's biography, and the application in his editing of a scrupulous textual analysis. This was most visible in his ten-volume edition of 1790, the first to include the poems, which was expanded into twenty-one volumes by James Boswell in 1821. Malone's work is the culmination of eighteenth-century editing and the foundation for all subsequent editing to the present, an extraordinary scholarly success. But it is also the sign of the literary icon and library figure that Shakespeare, in this major thread in his afterlife, had become.

By contrast with such scholarship, there was another strand of new editions reflecting performance. Adaptations continued to be written and printed but the theatrical texts, the versions of the plays that were being used with comparatively little adaptation, were also being published. In 1773–4 John Bell printed the first complete works to represent the acting editions 'Regulated from the Prompt Books of each House'. The introductions and commentary by Francis Gentleman identify the theatres' cuts (to deal with the problem of length) and the embarrassing indecencies—aspects of the plays which scholarly editing could play down, but which were glaringly visible in public performance. Later printings by Bell included a number of illustrations, strikingly unlike the fictional scenes in Theobald's or Hanmer's editions, now showing the characters by imaging the actors and actresses who played them.

Garrick The icon that scholarly editors celebrated had himself become increasingly visible elsewhere. In 1735 a bust of Shakespeare was included in the new Temple of British Worthies in Viscount Cobham's garden at Stowe. Money was raised by benefit performances of *Julius Caesar* and *Hamlet* for a more important project: the erection of a statue of Shakespeare in Poets' Corner in Westminster Abbey. Peter Scheemakers's statue, showing Shakespeare leaning on a plinth, was unveiled in 1741. The blank sheet to which Shakespeare was pointing was much mocked and later filled with a misquotation from *The Tempest*. Frequently reproduced, including in the late twentieth century on £20 notes, the statue also appeared on stage in 1741, discovered at the end of *Harlequin Student* at Goodman's Fields Theatre, the untheatrical monument now appropriated for performance. At one performance, the Harlequin in the play was performed by David Garrick.

Nothing that happened in Shakespeare performance in the first half of the eighteenth century quite anticipated the effect of Garrick's arrival. Many Shakespeare plays were established as the backbone of the theatrical repertory: by 1740 nearly a quarter of all London performances were of Shakespeare. There were great actors: for instance, Robert Wilks as Hamlet, Barton Booth as Othello, or James Quin as Falstaff. There was the advocacy of the Shakespeare Ladies' Club which from 1736 successfully pressed for the restoration of more of Shakespeare's plays to the stage. The elevation of Shakespeare to the embodiment of nation meant that adaptation became increasingly seen as unpatriotic: as William Guthrie wondered in 1747, 'Where is the Briton so much a Frenchman to prefer the highest stretch of modern improvement to the meanest spark of Shakespeare's genius?' (W. Guthrie, *An Essay upon English Tragedy*, 1747, 10).

Although many adaptations were still performed, the comedies, in particular, began to be played unadapted and admired: Charles Macklin's Shylock was praised, perhaps by Pope, as 'This is the Jew / That Shakespeare drew' (Bate and Jackson, 66) because, not least, it was Shakespeare's Shylock, not that of Lansdowne's 1701 adaptation, and Macklin played the role from 1740 to 1789.

But Garrick's triumph as Richard III in 1741 changed much. Painted by William Hogarth, one of the growing number of paintings which now sought to represent Shakespeare in performance, Garrick's Richard startled through its power and modernity. Garrick, the most frequently painted figure of the century, was often portrayed in Shakespearian roles in great works by Zoffany and Fuseli, Wilson, and others, adding to the expanding store of visual images of Shakespeare. Throughout his long career, Garrick sought to put more and more of Shakespeare's text back into performance, even while adapting it; his version of *Hamlet* in 1772 was reviled for eliminating almost all of act v but the cuts left space to restore much elsewhere. Shakespeare was, as Garrick wrote, borrowing from *Romeo*, 'the god of my idolatry' (Bate and Jackson, 71), a divinity emphasized by his erection of a temple in the garden of his villa on the Thames with a statue by Roubiliac. On Garrick's death the statue was bequeathed to the British Museum and now stands at the entrance of the British Library. Garrick also left to the museum his large collection of plays, a resource which he freely lent to Capell, Steevens, and other Shakespeare scholars.

Garrick's advocacy of Shakespeare was not always triumphant: his adaptation of *A Midsummer Night's Dream* with George Colman was a failure in 1763 and he was unable to restore the tragic ending of *King Lear*. Other adaptations, especially his *Catherine and Petruchio* (from *Shrew*) and *Florizel and Perdita* (from *The Winter's Tale*), performed as a double bill in 1756, fared better. His Romeo was less passionate than Spranger Barry's, performed at Covent Garden head to head with Garrick's at Drury Lane in 1748, but Garrick's adaptation with its grand funeral scene for Juliet and dying reunion of the lovers was a lasting success. In every role Garrick was minutely examined by the audience; the high points of his performances, especially as Hamlet, Macbeth, and Lear, were seen as overwhelming in the force and range of the emotions he explored. Garrick's dominance was also Shakespeare's and the two were as intertwined in the culture as in the lines on Garrick's Westminster Abbey monument, 'Shakespeare and Garrick like twin stars shall shine', or the comment in a 1752 pamphlet, 'Shakespeare revives! In Garrick breathes again!' (Dobson, 168).

Garrick's most expensive and vulnerable act of homage to Shakespeare was the Stratford jubilee of 1769, his response to Stratford upon Avon's flattery. The event lasted three days, including a masked ball, fireworks, concerts, processions, and a horse race. There was no performance of a Shakespeare play, only of Arne's sacred oratorio *Judith*. The crowning event was Garrick's ode; answering a planted heckling speech complaining that Shakespeare was a provincial nobody, it spoke of Shakespeare's immortality and national significance, his exploration of nature, and his local roots. The success of the ode, which praised Shakespeare as 'The bard of all bards', in combination with Garrick's use in it of the phrase 'The god of our idolatry' from *Romeo*, did much to establish, if not to create, the notion of Shakespeare as a bard to be worshipped by bardolators.

Although rain washed out much of the celebrations, Garrick recouped his losses by staging his brief play *The Jubilee* at Drury Lane the next season, ending with an immense procession of nineteen groups of Shakespeare's characters and a copy of the Shakespeare statue. Garrick's jubilee transformed the social significance of Stratford, putting the quiet town on the national map as Shakespeare's home. Its veneration of Shakespeare emblematized the semi-divine status Shakespeare now occupied. It also helped Garrick's own reputation considerably.

Shakespeare abroad in the eighteenth century While much of the emphasis on Shakespeare's importance was, throughout the eighteenth century, based on his image as virile symbol of the nation, Garrick had tried to persuade French friends to admire the plays. The history of Shakespeare performance outside England starts surprisingly early, with performances of *Hamlet* and *Richard II* in 1607 and 1608 on a ship becalmed off Sierra Leone for an audience of the ship's company and, for *Hamlet*, four African spectators. The performances were permitted, wrote Captain Keeling, 'to keep my people from idleness and unlawful games, or sleep' (I. Kamps and J. G. Singh, *Travel Knowledge*, 2001, 220).

Troupes of English actors touring central Europe (especially Germany and Poland) in the seventeenth century performed short plays, some of which were based on Shakespeare. Initially performing in English, the companies began to include local actors and perform in German. One group performed a *Hamlet* play in Dresden in 1626, though possibly not Shakespeare's. By the later seventeenth century a German company was playing a version of *Hamlet* called *Der bestrafte Brudermord* ('Fratricide punished'), about one-fifth the length of Shakespeare's, with the complexities of action, language, and thought ironed flat into a linear, exciting, and conventionally moral drama. There were versions of *Titus Andronicus* (published in German in 1620), *A Midsummer Night's Dream* (written *c.*1657), *The Merchant of Venice* (perhaps as early as 1611), and others. The English comedians had a profound effect on German theatre, in some respects creating a theatre culture where there had been none, and their repertory influenced the development of a vernacular drama.

In the eighteenth century German translations began to appear. The first, *Julius Caesar* in alexandrines by von Borck in 1741, prompted Lessing's defence of Shakespeare's compatibility with neo-classicism. Lessing's importance led to something approaching a German cult of Shakespeare, aided by Christoph Wieland's prose translations of twenty-two plays (1762–6). Wieland also put on *The Tempest* in Biberach in 1761, the first German production of an 'original' Shakespeare play. Shakespeare rapidly became a rallying cry for avant-garde writers: Herder's praise affected the young Goethe and Schiller, both of whom wrote early plays which were distinctly Shakespearian in ambition. In 1771 Goethe's speech 'On Shakespeare's day', at a domestic version of Garrick's jubilee, eloquently praised Shakespeare.

In Hamburg in 1776, where Lichtenberg's excited descriptions of Garrick's acting in Shakespeare had been published, Friedrich Schröder produced and starred in *Hamlet*, the first of ten Shakespeare plays staged there by 1780, with his *King Lear*, closer to Shakespeare than Tate's, particularly admired. Germany's obsession with *Hamlet* reached one climax in Goethe's *Wilhelm Meister's Apprenticeship* (1795–6), a novel dominated by the play and whose hero performs the role.

In France the process was more complex. Voltaire saw Shakespeare plays performed in England in the late 1720s, translated parts of *Hamlet* (printed 1733), and praised Shakespeare's 'monstrous farces' as signs of his 'genius full of … naturalness, and sublimity, without the least spark of good taste and without the slightest knowledge of the rules' (J. Jusserand, *Shakespeare in France under the Ancien Régime*, 1899, 208). His own plays were based closely on Shakespearian models. But later in life he condemned Shakespeare outright, especially *Hamlet* which was, as Arthur Murphy translated it in 1753 while trying to defend Shakespeare against Voltaire's onslaught, 'a barbarous piece, abounding with such gross absurdities that it would not be tolerated by the vulgar of *France* and Italy' (Vickers, 4.91).

Some scenes from *Hamlet* were published by Pierre-Antoine de la Place in 1746 and a complete translation of the plays by Pierre Le Tourneur appeared in 1776–82. But the plays were slower to reach the stage, though Jean-François Ducis's neo-classical adaptations of *Hamlet* and five others between 1769 and 1792 were all performed at the Comédie-Française.

In Russia there were versions of *Hamlet* (by Sumarokov, 1750), of *Merry Wives* (by Catherine the Great, 1786), and a translation of *Julius Caesar* (by Karamzin, 1787). There was an Italian *Julius Caesar* published in 1756 and a version there of Ducis's *Hamlet* performed in 1774, while a Spanish version was staged in 1772. King Stanislaus of Poland translated *Caesar* into French, while a Czech *Macbeth* was staged in 1786. By the end of the eighteenth century Shakespeare was being translated and performed, praised and attacked across almost the whole of Europe. Whatever ambivalent responses his plays provoked, they could not be ignored.

The Shakspeare Gallery and forgery In England, too, by this point, Shakespeare's plays were part of the common currency of the culture. Alderman Boydell set up his Shakspeare Gallery in 1789 with scenes from Shakespeare painted by Barry, Fuseli, Northcote, Reynolds, Romney, and others. Boydell was concerned both to expand his print business and to establish a new school of English history painting, combining commerce with cultural and national aspirations. Mocked by many, the gallery was auctioned off in 1805. Its most brilliant critic was the caricaturist James Gillray, whose political cartoons frequently use witty and complex allusions to lines from Shakespeare to make his satiric points, another mark of the extent to which Shakespeare's language had penetrated deep into the culture.

Shakespearian documents were also valuable enough in both cultural and financial terms to be worth forging. In 1795–6 William Henry Ireland forged poems and letters, legal deeds and receipts, all supposedly written or signed by Shakespeare. He forged manuscripts for *Hamlet* and *King Lear* and three complete and hitherto unknown plays, *Vortigern* (later staged for one night by Sheridan to howls of derision from the audience), *Henry II*, and *William the Conqueror*. Ireland's father, Samuel, opened his house to display these relics and James Boswell, wholly convinced, knelt before them, giving 'thanks to God that I have lived to see them' (Schoenbaum, *Records*, 129). In 1796 Edmond Malone exposed the forgeries by careful scholarship and William Henry Ireland confessed in print a few years later, though his father died still believing the documents were genuine.

Shakespeare and English Romanticism English Romanticism produced its own particular, immensely powerful and influential versions of Shakespeare. At its greatest, in the criticism of Hazlitt and Coleridge or in the poetry of Keats and Wordsworth, Shelley and Byron, and at its weakest, in their plays, Shakespeare became the touchstone for a new kind of writing, the original genius who embodied the natural rather than the educated, the denier of conventions rather than their slave, the creator of a whole world of characters whose individual consciousnesses explored the full extent of the human mind. As painters found in Shakespeare possibilities of the imagination with little connection to drama or theatre, so poets saw the plays as poems of the mind, spaces of thought and feeling with a kind of power that was unequalled. In 1811 Charles Lamb argued that *King Lear* should not be staged, not only because of the adapters' changes but also because 'while we read it, we see not Lear, but we are Lear,—we are in his mind' (Bate, *Romantics*, 123); for Lamb, reading allowed emotions of delight and terror that staging never could.

Significantly, while continuing the previous generations' praise of *Hamlet*, the poets raised *King Lear* to a new position of accomplishment, Hazlitt, Coleridge, and Shelley explicitly identifying it as Shakespeare's greatest achievement. It was also a play that could be engaged with only in reading, for performances were still of versions derived from Tate. Hazlitt's praise of what he saw as Shakespeare's sympathy with all his characters affected Keats (who heard Hazlitt lecture), who developed his own theory of Shakespeare's 'negative capability'; this was a chameleon quality in which Shakespeare became the ideal of that protean creator with no identity of his own that Keats aspired to be. Coleridge's poetry was the proof of the admiration for Shakespeare he later expressed in his criticism, which survives only in the form of random comments and reports of his lectures. Brilliant in its perception (for instance in his description of one of Iago's soliloquies as 'the motive-hunting of a motiveless malignity'; Bate, *Romantics*, 485) and with a continually startling originality, Coleridge's criticism shows the depth of a great poet's engagement with the complexity of Shakespeare.

All the Romantic poets found themselves, whether they wished or not, deeply influenced by Shakespeare, endlessly alluding to his plays as the ultimate poetic authority for their own writing, defining Shakespeare's genius as their crucial forerunner. If Wordsworth was prepared to criticize Shakespeare, he also embedded him into his attempts at drama like *The Borderers* (1796–7) and in the quotations and references found throughout *The Prelude* and in the rest of his work. It was a conflict of public rejection and poetic acceptance that was also to be pervasively characteristic of Byron who, even as he mockingly rejected Shakespeare as 'the *worst* of models', praised him as 'the most extraordinary of writers' (*Byron's Letters and Journals*, ed. L. Marchand, 12 vols., 1973–82, 8.152). Byron's comedy in *Don Juan*, as much as his tragedy in plays like *Manfred*, is profoundly and openly indebted to Shakespeare, whose work pervades every aspect of Byron's writing.

Kemble, Siddons, and Kean If English Romanticism's responses to Shakespeare were not primarily directed at the stage, they were responsive to it. Late eighteenth-century Shakespeare theatre production was dominated by John Philip Kemble and his sister Sarah Siddons. Her awesome power as Lady Macbeth, especially in the sleep-walking scene, and as Queen Katherine in *Henry VIII* astonished, terrified, and moved audiences. Her preparation for the former, copying a sleepwalker she had seen and trying to find an imaginative sympathy with the character, fed her representation of a dark sublime.

Kemble was most praised for the nobility of his performances, for an aristocratic hauteur that was the essence of a high classical style—hence his success as Shakespeare's Roman heroes. His *Coriolanus*, his own adaptation that used Shakespeare heavily cut for the first three acts and then interwove Shakespeare's play with James Thomson's adaptation (1749), was emphatically in favour of the hero. As a political reading of the play—and Shakespeare was continually being co-opted into contemporary politics as authority and allusion, adaptation and interpretation allowed opposing appropriations of the plays—Kemble's *Coriolanus* disturbed Hazlitt whose liberal politics were at the other pole from this conservative reading. Shakespeare's play, placed in the intersection of theatre, criticism, and contemporary political events, became the site across which politics could be contested.

When Kemble rebuilt Covent Garden Theatre after a fire and raised prices, the resulting riots in 1809 (which lasted sixty-seven nights and which ended only with Kemble's capitulation to the rioters' demands) were a matter of class and power, an argument that Shakespeare belonged to the whole nation, not solely to the aristocratic or the rich. The theatre itself became the place where the tensions of the society could be fully exposed, but Shakespeare as the national bard was the property that was being contested and through him the rights of citizens of that nation. This sense of Shakespeare's presence in the culture is typified, though from a perspective far from that of the rioters, by Henry Crawford's comments in Jane Austen's *Mansfield Park* (1814): 'But Shakespeare one gets acquainted with without knowing how. It is a part of an Englishman's constitution ... one is intimate with him by instinct.'

Against the traditional authority of Kemble were placed the productions of the illegitimate theatres. Their burlesques and travesties, like John Poole's *Hamlet Travestie* (New Theatre, 1811), were a continuation of the eighteenth century's use of Shakespeare as a resource for parody and mockery of contemporary theatre and politics. It was a rich tradition with wonderfully comic work by Charles Selby, Francis Talfourd, William and Robert Brough, and F. C. Burnand, stretching at least as far as W. S. Gilbert's *Rosencrantz and Guildenstern* (staged 1891). But the battle between the patent houses, Kemble's Covent Garden and the rival Drury Lane, was also fought out as a conflict of styles: Kemble's patrician classicism against the new style of Edmund Kean, who from his Drury Lane début in 1814 was the very embodiment of a radical, natural, and emotional force. Kean electrified audiences and destroyed Kemble's authority. Often drunk on stage, full of sexual energy (regularly having sex with a prostitute before and in the intervals of his performances), Kean could be bad as well as brilliant: Coleridge's praise of him as 'like reading Shakspeare [*sic*] by flashes of lightning' is not necessarily a compliment (Bate, *Romantics*, 160). But Kean's was the kind of acting that Romanticism sought.

European Romanticism In the battles of European Romanticism, Shakespeare played a crucial part. August Wilhelm Schlegel's criticism was effective but it was his translation of the plays (1797–1810), later completed by Ludwig Tieck and Tieck's daughter Dorothea, which defined German responses to Shakespeare thereafter. The subtlety of the translations' attempts to capture form as well as meaning, their close links to the style of contemporary German drama, and the ways in which they extended the possibilities of German dramatic verse all made Shakespeare's plays central to German thought and poetry. German Romanticism appropriated Shakespeare and made him its own.

French Romanticism was, by contrast, directly influenced by the cross-channel movement of the theatre company of Charles Kemble, John Philip's brother. In 1823 in *Racine et Shakespeare* Stendhal defined Shakespeare as the vital source for a modern drama. In 1827 Victor Hugo argued in the preface to his play *Cromwell* that 'Shakespeare, c'est le Drame' ('Shakespeare *is* drama' quoted in Bate, *Genius*, 231). Hugo's commitment to Shakespeare underscores his play *Hernani*, whose première in 1830 was the battleground and triumph of French Romantic drama. His son, François-Victor, completed a prose translation of all Shakespeare's works in 1865 and Victor Hugo contributed a long preface, later published separately (in English, French, and German) for the tercentenary of Shakespeare's birth in 1864 and dedicated to England. Hugo's was for long the standard literary translation, though never used in production.

In 1827, the year of Hugo's *Cromwell*, Charles Kemble's company performed *Hamlet* in Paris to an audience which included all the major figures of the French Romantic movement. An extraordinary success, the production overwhelmed Dumas *père* (who wrote later 'I recognised at last that [Shakespeare] was the man who had created most after God'; *Théâtre complet*, 1863–5, 1.15), Eugène Delacroix (who created over the next thirty years a series of powerful lithographs of scenes from the play), and Berlioz (who would later marry Kemble's Ophelia, Harriet Smithson).

Shakespeare and nineteenth-century music and literature Berlioz's greatest music was from then on often explicitly Shakespearian: from the 'Fantasy on *The Tempest*' in *Lélio* (op. 14b, 1830), his overture to *King Lear* (op. 4, 1831), and his dramatic symphony *Roméo et Juliette* (op. 17, 1839) to his quotations from *The Merchant of Venice* for the love scene in *Les Troyens* (1856–8) or the adaptation of *Much Ado about Nothing* as the opera *Béatrice et Bénédict* (1860–62).

If Berlioz is more completely a Shakespearian composer than any other, there was throughout the nineteenth century hardly a major composer who did not at some point write a Shakespeare-influenced piece: Mendelssohn's overture to *A Midsummer Night's Dream* was composed for the concert hall in 1826, with the rest of his incidental music written for the stage in 1843; Schubert wrote songs with Shakespeare texts in 1826; Liszt wrote his *Hamlet* symphonic poem first in 1858 (later revised); Tchaikovsky composed fantasy overtures to *Romeo and Juliet* (1869) and *Hamlet* (1888) and a fantasia on *The Tempest* (1873). Full-scale operas range from Salieri's *Falstaff* (1799) and Rossini's *Otello* (1816, revised 1819 with a happy ending) to Wagner's *Das Liebesverbot* (1836), from *Measure for Measure*, Nicolai's *Die lustigen Weiber von Windsor* (1849), and Ambroise Thomas's *Hamlet* (Paris, 1868). The three greatest nineteenth-century Shakespeare operas are Verdi's *Macbeth* (1847, revised 1865), *Otello* (1887), and *Falstaff* (1893), the last in its exuberance and intelligence fully equal to its source (and for some critics even greater than *Merry Wives*). There are also the fascinating unwritten projects like Mozart's *Tempest* and Verdi's *King Lear*. If initially Shakespeare is no more than a convenient source for a dramatic plot or a romantic mood, he comes to be the literary figure with whom composers must engage: Verdi's *Macbeth* has far less of an imaginative interaction with the full range of Shakespeare's text than his works forty and fifty years later.

Throughout Europe, writers, like composers, worked under the heavy influence, liberating and constricting by turns, of Shakespeare's presence. Shakespeare could enable new national forms of drama: in Russia, for instance, Pushkin's *Boris Godunov* (1825) used Shakespeare's characterization and his approach to historical drama as its model. He could make possible political attack: in Germany Freiligrath used Hamlet's indecision as the stick with which to beat the political pusillanimity of the German intelligentsia in his poem 'Germany is Hamlet' (1844), a reaction to the pro-*Hamlet* attitude after Goethe's celebration of the introspective hero. He could be the source for wholly new styles of writing: Horace Walpole's *The Castle of Otranto* (1765), the instigator of the Gothic novel, was explicit in its Shakespearian method and its mood (derived especially from *Macbeth* and *Hamlet*), as one of its successors, Lewis's *The Monk* (1796) depended on *Measure for Measure*; Sir Walter Scott's effective invention of the historical novel, starting with *Waverley* (1814), depended on a transformation of the range of concerns of Shakespeare's histories into narrative fiction, a metamorphosis sustained by frequent quotation and allusion. Scott could also fictionalize Shakespeare's life: in *Kenilworth* (1821) the chronology is so deliberately confused that in the age of Elizabeth people quote from Shakespeare's last plays, written a decade after the queen's death.

In England in particular, as for Walpole and Scott, the novel was the form in which the nineteenth century's imaginative engagements with Shakespeare were most powerfully present. Charlotte Brontë's *Shirley* (1849) deepens its analysis of industrial relations in the context of the Luddite riots in the Napoleonic era through a web of references to *Coriolanus*. For George Eliot, described as 'the female Shakespeare' (Taylor, 208), Shakespeare's writing was at times unacceptable (the ending of *Two Gentlemen of Verona* was impossible for her) and writing his biography was a task she turned down. But his work was also a means of defining her concerns all the more clearly. In *Daniel Deronda* (1876), for instance, the interplay between Gwendolen Harleth's re-creation of Rosalind in *As You Like It* and Deronda's *Hamlet*-influenced irresolution allows a tension between the plays to reflect the novel's antithesis of realism and Romanticism.

Charles Dickens, who knew Shakespeare as an actor and theatre critic as well as a reader, was unable to write a novel without extensive use of Shakespeare. Benign mockery of provincial Shakespeare production like Crummles's *Romeo and Juliet* in *Nicholas Nickleby* (1839), a novel Dickens dedicated to the great actor–manager Macready, can be more troubling when Mr Wopsle performs *Hamlet* in *Great Expectations* (1861), a novel full of fathers missing, pretending, and returning. Every Dickens novel has a wealth of Shakespeare allusions and quotations, with characters and events demanding to be read against Shakespearian models, amounting in all to many hundreds of references. In some cases, a novel seems especially engaged with a particular play: *Dombey and Son* is permeated by references to *Macbeth*, both as a narrative of children and childlessness and as a drama of melodramatic murder.

Dickens's view of the world was focused through Shakespearian lenses. It is almost as if it is through Shakespeare's characters and action that Dickens saw, thought, and felt. But Shakespeare's presence also pervades much high Victorian poetry and painting, from Tennyson's 'Mariana' and Browning's 'Caliban upon Setebos' to the work of the pre-Raphaelites, Dante Gabriel Rossetti, Holman Hunt, and John Everett Millais.

Lambs' *Tales* and new editions Some attitudes to Shakespeare elsewhere in nineteenth-century society came from quite other needs. Shakespeare's plays needed to be changed to make them accessible to children and acceptable for families. Charles and Mary Lamb produced their *Tales from Shakespeare* in 1807 (mostly written by Mary), turning the plays into placidly and even at times sentimentally moral stories that were also designed to free children's (and especially young girls') imaginations by their encounters with the worlds of the plays. Their versions have never been out of print since and have formed the first encounters with Shakespeare for many generations of children.

But if Shakespeare's plays themselves were to be part of family reading they needed censoring. The Lambs recommended that young boys should read passages from Shakespeare's 'manly book' to their sisters after 'carefully selecting what is proper for a young sister's ear' (Taylor,

207). Henrietta Bowdler's edition of twenty plays in 1807 'endeavoured to remove every thing that could give just offence to the religious and virtuous mind' to produce a text that could be given to boys and girls. *The Family Shakespeare* was completed by her brother, the Revd Thomas Bowdler, in 1818. The cutting and rewritings produced plays that were safe. Both the Lambs' and the Bowdlers' work sold slowly at first but more successfully as the century continued and their values seemed appropriate.

Other kinds of edition were needed as well. The new technologies made cheap Shakespeare possible for nearly all: a complete Shakespeare could be sold for a shilling and other editions were published in penny issues. Shakespeare could become a part of everyone's library alongside the Bible (often the only two books in working-class homes). Other editions were more expensive but were attractive for their extensive illustrations. Charles Knight produced a long series of illustrated texts; his *Pictorial Shakespeare* (1838–41) sold in weekly parts before being available in bound volumes. Staunton's edition was first published at a shilling a play (1856–8) but there were 831 images by Sir John Gilbert. For the wealthy and for scholars, there could now be facsimiles of early texts so that a photographic reproduction of the first folio was published in 1866 and the publication of photolitho quarto facsimiles began in 1858.

Scholars were also helped by the Globe Edition (1863–6), edited by William Clark, William Wright, and John Glover. Their work, the first to be edited by academics, became known as the Cambridge Shakespeare. Its significance lay not only in its careful collations (an extension of Malone's earlier work) and its reprinting of early quartos but also in its inclusion of line numbers, the first version to make referring to a particular line easy and accurate. Abbott's *A Shakespearian Grammar* (1869), Schmidt's *Shakespeare-Lexicon* (1874–5), and Bartlett's accurate complete concordance (1894) provided further important reference works for Shakespeare study. For Shakespeare was now being studied: from 1868 Clark and Wright edited a series of the plays for the Clarendon Press 'to meet the wants of Students in English Literature'; Abbott included questions to test students' understanding of the rules of grammar and prosody. A. W. Verity's Pitt Press Shakespeare (from 1893) and the Warwick Shakespeare served generations of schoolchildren through much of the twentieth century. As English literature emerged as a new and major subject for study at university, and schools also placed literature as a central requirement of children's education, so Shakespeare became the centre of an educational system both in Britain and across the British empire.

Shakespeare societies and the tercentenary, 1864 There were new ways of gathering to talk about Shakespeare, or to listen to lectures, or to preserve the Shakespeare heritage. The Shakespearian Club was founded in Stratford upon Avon in 1824, becoming the Royal Shakespeare Club from 1830 to 1874. Halliwell-Phillipps founded the scholarly Shakespeare Society in 1840 and Furnivall created its successor, the New Shakespeare Society, in 1873. The first major national Shakespeare society was the Deutsche Shakespeare-Gesellschaft, founded in 1864 and a sign of the immense importance of Shakespeare in Germany and of German Shakespeare scholarship to the growth of Shakespeare studies. Its journal *Shakespeare Jahrbuch* began publication in 1865.

The Royal Shakespeare Club had helped the campaign to purchase Shakespeare's birthplace as a national monument in 1847. The Shakespeare Birthplace Trust was formed soon afterwards, acquiring other houses over the years (for example, New Place and Nash's House in 1862, Anne Hathaway's Cottage in 1892)—Stratford had for some time been a place of pilgrimage, with Keats and Scott among the 700 a year visiting the birthplace and/or the grave. The visible material heritage of Shakespeare, redefined as houses associated with his family and his life rather than the theatres he wrote for or indeed the books he wrote, was now preserved for the world's visitors—and their piety superbly mocked by Henry James in his short story 'The Birthplace' (1903).

In 1864 the tercentenary of Shakespeare's birth was celebrated in a typically muddled English way. Perhaps the most public Shakespeare event of the century, it involved competing celebrations in Stratford and London, with two committees, the Stratford one dominated by Edward Fordham Flower whose family became central to Shakespeare in Stratford thereafter. The Stratford events, in spite of the piqued *amour propre* and late withdrawal of the actor Edward Fechter, went well: a banquet for thousands in the specially constructed pavilion, a fancy-dress ball, concerts, two Shakespeare sermons, and even, in contrast to Garrick's 1769 jubilee, performances of and readings from the plays. The National Shakespeare Committee tried chaotically to arrange London's contribution: a tree-planting ceremony on Primrose Hill was mixed up with a demonstration over Garibaldi and came close to a riot; a concert at Crystal Palace was more peaceable. More tangibly, the celebrations led in Stratford ultimately to the opening of the Shakespeare Memorial Theatre in 1879 and the memorial statues by Sir Ronald Gower of Shakespeare, Hamlet, Lady Macbeth, Prince Henry, and Falstaff that were unveiled in 1888.

The connection between the tercentenary tree planting and Garibaldi was not an accident. Instead, it demonstrates the centrality of Shakespeare to nineteenth-century radicalism. From the Chartists onwards, Shakespeare was a crucial part of radicals' literary culture. The few details of his life, with the absence of clear links to the court and his modest background, made him the perfect English exemplum of the ordinary man as poetic genius. His plays were widely used in political oratory, especially when cheap editions of them (like the *Complete Shilling Shakespeare* published by John Thomas Dicks in the 1850s) became available for working-class homes. Reformers read the plays as reformist documents, with his celebration of rural England seen as opposition to enclosures and other forms of dispossession of the rural poor. Shakespeare was identified as a scathing satirist of courts and kings, with plays like *Julius Caesar* co-opted as tracts against tyranny. Chartist newspapers could carefully document precursors to their own political demands throughout Shakespeare's works. Shakespeare became the people's playwright, with radicals fiercely opposing attempts either to appropriate his politics for Conservatism or to claim aristocrats as the true authors of the plays. In 1864 to celebrate Shakespeare and to demonstrate against the government's supposed expulsion of Garibaldi were naturally connected events for radical politics, part of the reclaiming of Shakespeare from the upper classes and their high culture as a different kind of national poet.

The authorship controversy Within the century's enshrining of Shakespeare as the icon of the nation there were also other voices of opposition, especially the growth of the belief that the plays, acknowledged as masterpieces, could not possibly have been the work of the 'man from Stratford', a mere actor and not a poet (there are shades here of the Romantic glorification of the poet removed from the quotidian world). The idea that someone else had written the plays seems first to have been advanced by the Revd James Wilmot in 1785 (his candidate was Francis Bacon) but he destroyed his papers. In 1848 Joseph C. Hart, American consul at Santa Cruz, argued in *The Romance of Yachting* that the plays were written by university graduates and foisted off as Shakespeare's. In 1856 Delia Bacon claimed that Francis Bacon or a committee headed by him had been responsible. Her ascription was repeated, independently, by William Henry Smith the following year. Many editors from Pope onwards had doubted Shakespeare's responsibility for some speeches, scenes, even whole plays—but this was a dislodging of Shakespeare from any authorship of any of his work.

The controversy that followed was energetic. Other candidates emerged, including Edward de Vere, seventeenth earl of Oxford (proposed by J. Thomas Looney in 1920 and supported by Sigmund Freud), the earl of Rutland (the idea of Peter Alvor in Germany in 1906 and popular there for a while), the earl of Derby (first advanced in 1891 but most strongly in France after 1919), Christopher Marlowe (according to William Ziegler in 1895 and advanced even more strenuously by Calvin Hoffman in 1955), and Queen Elizabeth (George Elliott's proposal in 1956). All these claims surmount the contemporary evidence for Shakespeare by arguing for an early modern conspiracy and often a later one among academics and others to suppress the 'truth'. Many resolve the inconveniently early death of their candidate by arguing for posthumous slow release of the plays. Some indulge in cryptograms of mind-boggling complexity to reveal the hidden 'truth' of their assertions. Some, like Delia Bacon, were or became mad in pursuit of their claims. Marlowe apart, whose literary ability is unquestioned, all depend on assumptions that the plays display knowledge available only to an aristocrat, university educated, well travelled, and a habitué of courts. This snobbery is exemplified by the comment of Christmas Humphreys, an Oxfordian and a barrister, in 1955: 'It is offensive to scholarship, to our national dignity, and to our sense of fair play to worship the memory of a petty-minded tradesman' (Bate, *Genius*, 93). All distort evidence for their own ends. None is remotely convincing to scholars, though many others have been and remain steadfastly sure that Shakespeare could not have written Shakespeare.

Shakespeare in America and Russia One of the striking things about the advocates of other authors is that many of the staunchest are Americans. Characterized by a nostalgia for an aristocracy lacking in their democracy and by their proneness to accept conspiracy theories, these anti-Stratfordians are part of the wide range of reactions to Shakespeare generated by Americans in the nineteenth century. By the end of the century there were a hundred Shakespeare societies in America, hardly a surprise in a country with at least four towns called Hamlet, three Othellos, three Romeos, two Violas, two Horatios, and an Iago. The ambivalence of the responses is an eloquent testimony to the interaction of writer and nation. For Emerson, who visited England in 1847, Shakespeare was the perfect poet for his list of *Representative Men* (1850), a genius whose works, half understood in his own time, were fully available only in modern America. Washington Irving's praise of Shakespeare in 1820 was set against his mockery of the Stratford tourist industry where Shakespeare's mulberry tree 'seems to have as extraordinary powers of self-multiplication as the wood of the true cross' (Rawlings, 43).

Some sought to make Shakespeare an honorary American, like Henry Cabot Lodge, who saw his language as close to current American speech in 1895. Others were vehement that there is nothing unique or English about Shakespeare: Melville argued in 1850 that 'Shakespeares are this day being born on the banks of the Ohio' (Rawlings, 165). Still others, in seeking to displace the authority of England, attacked the authority of Shakespeare: Whitman saw the plays as dangerously anti-democratic and demanded that America discard them and 'see that it is, in itself, the final authority and reliance' (ibid., 283). Some writers showed how Shakespeare had penetrated American popular culture, as in Twain's use of *Hamlet* and *Macbeth* in *Huckleberry Finn* (1885), though Twain was never quite sure if Shakespeare was indeed the plays' author.

In many respects this variety of response was intriguingly similar to Russia where, after Mochalov's brilliant performance as Hamlet in 1837, *Hamlet* became as fashionable as throughout much of the rest of Europe, with young men priding themselves on their Hamletism in the wake of the popularity of Goethe's *Wilhelm Meister*. The 'superfluous man', introspective and self-regarding in his Hamlet-like pose, was attacked as useless egotism by Turgenev, especially in his story 'A Hamlet of Shchigrovsky District' (in *Sportsman's Sketches*, 1852) and his lecture on 'Hamlet and Don Quixote' (1860). It was an attack continued in Dostoevsky and in Chekhov but none was attacking Shakespeare; rather, the attack was on Russian intellectuals' misappropriation of Shakespeare. Through Shakespeare—and *Hamlet* in particular—different constructions of social responsibility and political engagement could be fought.

The attack on Shakespeare himself was mounted by Tolstoy in 1906 where the plays, especially *King Lear*, were indicted for poor dramaturgy, ineffective characterization, and, above all, an aristocratic disdain for the common people. Shakespeare is berated, in effect, for failing to be Tolstoy himself. Fanny Burney recorded George III complaining in 1785 'Was there ever ... such stuff as a great part of Shakespeare? Only one must not say so!' (Gross, 113). But Tolstoy dared to say so: his are the most violent of all anti-Shakespearian diatribes, rejecting Shakespeare's drama as universally applicable and infinitely malleable.

Productions in Russia often played Shakespeare to audiences that made immediate political connections, necessitating interventions by censors: Shakespeare was banned in the Ukraine from 1863. Theatres across America, by contrast, often performed Shakespeare with a sense of national pride. The visit of Macready to New York in 1849 resulted in a riot and thirty-one deaths when working-class supporters of Edwin Forrest, the greatest American actor of his time, were encouraged to demonstrate their support for an American actor and against the English visitor and his wealthy American patrons. A number of English stars toured America including George Frederick Cooke and Edmund Kean. American Shakespeare actors toured England, James Hackett making a great success as Falstaff on both sides of the Atlantic for forty years, while the African-American Ira Aldridge starred as Macbeth, Shylock, and Richard III as well as Othello, playing in England and in Russia.

Shakespeare and the nineteenth-century English stage In the interchange, America experienced all the changes in Shakespeare production being explored in England, as England also encountered European performers like Salvini who played Othello in Italian at Drury Lane in 1875 while the rest of the cast spoke English or Ernesto Rossi who played Hamlet, Lear, Macbeth, and Romeo there in 1876, also speaking Italian.

Charles Kemble produced *King John* in 1823 with a designer, James Robinson Planché, commissioned to search for and reproduce historical sources for the play's locations, costumes, and props. It was an extension of the research Charles Macklin undertook for his *Macbeth* in 1773 but it was at the centre of Victorian Shakespeare. The plays, especially the tragedies and histories, became a resource for pictorial splendour with pageantry and stage spectacle, vast sets, and enormous casts of extras, aiming to create on stage the plays as historical narratives. Madame Vestris's ways with the comedies at Covent Garden in the 1840s showed that they too, especially *A Midsummer Night's Dream* (1840), could be spectacles of song and ballet. But elsewhere Shakespeare became the means by which history could be seen. As the centrepiece of English cultural history himself, he had become the sure guide to English and Roman history, now attested by the playbills' references to the British Museum as production resource. Attending a Shakespeare production—and especially looking at a Shakespeare production—was now an education in itself. Authenticity, not to Shakespeare and the conditions of early modern performance but to the historical reality to which it was a kind of window, was the key and the assumption continued through to the BBC television series of the plays (1978–85), where costuming had to be either early modern or of the historical date of the events Shakespeare dramatized.

Macready, concerned with raising the theatre's 'low' image, worked hard to redeem its ways with Shakespeare's texts. Restoring Shakespeare to the stage was one means of improving the theatre's cultural image. But he also prepared his productions more carefully than had been the norm, with frequent rehearsals (and long private work on his own performance) as well as thoughtful staging to manifest the historical accuracy of action and ritual as well as set and costumes. In England and America, which he toured three times, his work was highly praised and much imitated. Much hyped, Macready's restoration of the text was less substantial than his publicity promised: though his production of *King Lear* in 1838 restored Fool, after persuasion, and the tragic ending, never seen since Tate's version was first performed, Macready cut the blinding of Gloucester and his leap at Dover Cliff, the former presumably as too painful, the latter as dangerously close to comic. Macready's *King Lear* was set in an ancient Britain with signs of Stonehenge; his *Coriolanus* was in a modest Rome unlike the splendour of his *Julius Caesar*. But Macready also exploited the stage's technology for grand transformation scenes, for example in the images that backed the Chorus's speeches in his *Henry V*.

Charles Kean, the Eton-educated son of the dissolute Edmund, continued the trend in the 1850s at the Princess's Theatre. The productions became ever more populated, the interpolated scenes (for example Bolingbroke's arrival in London and Richard II's leaving it for prison) ever grander, the historical detail ever more obsessive. Kean was proud of being a fellow of the Society of Antiquaries and his published texts are full of annotation about historical accuracy—the same kind of detail that acted as commentary to Charles Knight's illustrated texts. The Chorus to *Henry V* became Clio, the Muse of History, and the images became *tableaux vivants* displayed behind a gauze, most famously for Henry's return to London. On stage crowds now numbered 200 or more, a visual representation of the nation (be it Rome or England), all exactly costumed, all demonstrating their historicity. The grand processions that had long been part of productions of, for instance, *Coriolanus* or *King Henry VIII* were now inserted wherever space could be made. The effect is, in modern terms, operatic, the text subordinated to the visual. The English style of Shakespeare production influenced and in its turn was influenced by the work of the duke of Saxe-Meiningen's company, with its minutely disciplined crowds, seen in London in 1881.

Samuel Phelps's productions at Sadler's Wells from 1843 to 1862 made Shakespeare his house dramatist, producing thirty-two of the plays. More of Shakespeare's texts were restored but Phelps, while rarely swamping the play, made the diorama his speciality, allowing scenes to metamorphose into others and for characters to be seen journeying between the locations of scenes.

All serious productions were subject to intense scrutiny, not only in the increasingly important work of theatre reviewers who—like Hazlitt earlier, George Lewes in mid-century, and Bernard Shaw, Max Beerbohm, and Henry James at its end—minutely examined a production's adequacy to their individual views of the plays, but also in the mockery of their excesses in the steady stream of travesties.

While Henry Irving and Herbert Beerbohm Tree at the end of the century may have had successes with more plays and while their productions may have been even more spectacular, with Irving employing many fine painters to design his sets, and even more historically accurate, with Tree including the signing of Magna Carta, a scene Shakespeare inconveniently forgot to include in *King John*, there was little that changed the style of work that Macready, Phelps, and Charles Kean had defined. Grandeur dominated in acting as in design, relieved only rarely by the different virtues of domesticity, with extensive musical scores to accompany the action and long gaps while the huge sets were changed by armies of stagehands.

A new style for Shakespeare in the theatre The opposition came first from William Poel, who replaced one form of historical authenticity with another in his search to reproduce early modern theatrical conditions, complete with extras dressed as nobles to sit on stage as if members of the audience. His productions were much affected by the discovery of the De Witt drawing of the Swan Theatre: the first reliable depiction of an Elizabethan theatre interior. Mostly working with amateurs and in short runs in non-commercial spaces, Poel after 1881, when he produced *Hamlet* in first quarto guise, followed his lonely and much-mocked path. More traditionally and less eccentrically, Frank Benson's work, principally at the Shakespeare Memorial Theatre from 1886 to 1919, showed how modest ambition in the service of the text could make Shakespeare both popular and pleasurable.

Edward Gordon Craig, son of Ellen Terry, moved in his theory and practice to a different resistance to the principles of high Victorian spectacular theatre. He explored both abstraction and simplicity, culminating in the use of moveable screens to define space for his *Hamlet*, codirected with Stanislavsky at the Moscow Art Theatre in 1912. Craig's project was explicitly modernist in its assumptions and as startling when underpinning Sally Jacobs's set for Peter Brook's *A Midsummer Night's Dream* (Royal Shakespeare Company, 1970) as when Craig created a church out of light alone for *Much Ado about Nothing* in 1903.

Most influential of all was Harley Granville-Barker, who briefly worked with Poel. His productions of *The Winter's Tale*, *Twelfth Night*, and *A Midsummer Night's Dream* (with a man as Oberon, fairies with gold-leafed faces, and folk tunes as music) at the Savoy (1912–14) revolutionized production technique. But far more influential were his *Prefaces to Shakespeare*, the first of which appeared in 1923. In their mixture of the scholarly and the practical, combining theatrical awareness with close attention to Shakespeare's dramatic technique, they made directors aware of the virtues of the text and students and scholars aware of the plays as dramas. They marked a new meeting of theatre and scholarship in Shakespeare studies.

Shakespeare studies The *Prefaces* were designed for the mythical general reader but Shakespeare studies were increasingly professional and visibly a growth industry. The archival and bibliographical work of Victorian scholars such as James Orchard Halliwell-Phillipps and John Payne Collier, for all the latter's forgeries of documents that might help his arguments (and which continue to confuse scholars), led to further biographical and contextual study. Sidney Lee's work on the many figures surrounding Shakespeare for the *Dictionary of National Biography* helped his much-reprinted and expanded biography (first published in 1898), based on his dictionary entry. The work of Charles William Wallace (1865–1932) and his wife at the Public Record Office added crucial new fragments of knowledge about Shakespeare's life to offset the continuing strain of biographical speculations by, for instance, Oscar Wilde in his fictional *A Portrait of Mr W. H.* (1889) or Frank Harris in his supposedly non-fictional *The Man Shakespeare* (1909).

But there was also a new kind of biographical enquiry, working from the plays to construct a version of Shakespeare's mind. Edward Dowden's *Shakspere: a Critical Study of his Mind and Art* (1875) saw the plays as veiled emotional and intellectual autobiography. Caroline Spurgeon's investigation in *Shakespeare's Imagery and What it Tells Us* (1935) enumerated patterns of images to reveal Shakespeare's own likes and dislikes.

In the first half of the twentieth century the theatrical research of Sir E. K. Chambers and G. E. Bentley and the bibliographical work of Sir W. W. Greg became cornerstones of highly accomplished academic study, often building on the achievements of Germanic classical and Shakespearian scholarship. For Chambers it led towards distinguished work on Shakespeare's biography. The image-centred criticism of Caroline Spurgeon and the historical contextual work of E. M. W. Tillyard, Wilson Knight's thematic criticism and the interest in the history of ideas by Hardin Craig and Theodore Spencer, the growth of the close reading in New Criticism and the work of William Empson, all began major modes of critical interpretative approaches to Shakespeare which profoundly affected the ways the plays were read and taught.

There were new and major series of editions, building on the earlier accomplishments of Malone and hardly changing the premises of such editing: the American-based New Variorum begun by H. H. Furness in 1871 and continued by his son (and still ongoing); the Arden Shakespeare started with *Hamlet*, edited by Edward Dowden, in 1899 and is now in its third complete series; the New Shakespeare, published by Cambridge University Press

(1921–66), was edited by Sir Arthur Quiller-Couch and John Dover Wilson, who was responsible for both its most incisive scholarship and some comically excessive invented stage directions.

Critical interpretations could become best-sellers. In A. C. Bradley's *Shakespearean Tragedy* (1904), for example, though the plays are treated more like novels or biographies of great men, a new orthodoxy of critical reading was defined. Guy Boas argued wittily in 1926:

> I dreamt last night that Shakespeare's ghost
> Sat for a Civil Service post;
> The English paper for the year
> Had several questions on *King Lear*
> Which Shakespeare answered very badly
> Because he hadn't read his Bradley.
> (Gross, 329)

Shakespeare and the British empire Shakespeare, as a cornerstone of Englishness, was part of many kinds of official examination for future administrators of the empire and his work was vigorously championed by, for instance, the British Empire Shakespeare Society, founded in 1901 to encourage reading circles and costume recitals. In 1912 the 'Shakespeare's England' exhibition at Earl's Court in London, complete with the first-ever replica of the Globe Theatre, celebrated Shakespeare as heritage culture in a display of stirring nationalism.

The events in 1916 for the tercentenary of Shakespeare's death, an event marked almost as strongly in Germany as in England, included publication of a major collection of essays on Shakespeare's times, *Shakespeare's England*, as well as a Shakespeare day for schools (complete with a Shakespeare prayer) and, as a sign of Shakespeare's international importance, *A Book of Homage to Shakespeare* edited by Israel Gollancz as secretary of the tercentenary committee, with a poem by Thomas Hardy and with contributions from all corners of the empire carefully placed before those from the rest of the world. Many years later the British Council, as an offshoot of government charged with promoting British culture worldwide, sponsored the Marlowe Society's complete audio recordings of the plays, directed by George Rylands (1958–64), records that functioned as 'official' Shakespeare across the world.

The countries of the empire often developed complexly ambivalent attitudes towards Shakespeare, seeing him both as the embodiment of their colonial masters and as something enticingly able to be appropriated into other forms, ready to be made a part of indigenous dramatic traditions. In India, for instance, Shakespeare was being performed in Calcutta from the 1830s and in Bombay in the 1850s. There were popular adaptations of Shakespeare's plots into Marathi, Gujarati, and Parsi, each culture finding rich resources for its own styles of popular theatre. Aga Hashr Kashmiri, who adapted many Shakespeare plays into Urdu in the late nineteenth and early twentieth centuries, acquired the nickname 'Shakespeare-e-Hind' ('Shakespeare of India'). Indian rulers often commanded private performances of the plays, for example *Cymbeline* performed at the wedding of the maharaja of Baroda in 1879.

English companies toured India (like, later, Geoffrey Kendal's troupe, filmed as *Shakespeare Wallah* in 1965) and the English residents of the raj put on amateur productions. Schools, educating Indian students in the high cultural forms that the proponents of empire thought would raise them to European standards, staged Shakespeare performances as English schools so regularly did. The opposition was replicated throughout the empire: on the one hand, imitations, often amateur or second-rate, of English styles of Shakespeare production; on the other, energized and vital re-imaginations of Shakespeare into other, local, modes of theatre.

Colonial and post-colonial responses to Shakespeare, however, often rewrote Shakespeare as a means of reconsidering the relationship of nation to empire. *The Tempest*, often seen as a narrative of colonialism, became in Octave Mannoni's *Psychology of Colonisation* (1950) the epitome of the process as 'Prospero complex' faced 'Caliban complex'. For many Caribbean writers, like the Barbadian George Lamming in the autobiographical *The Pleasures of Exile* (1960) and the novel *Water with Berries* (1971), Aimé Césaire (from Martinique) in his play *Une tempête* (1968), Edward Brathwaite (from Barbados) in his poem 'Caliban' in *Islands* (1969), and the Cuban Roberto Retamar in 'Caliban' (1974), exploring the play is the way for them, seeing themselves as Calibans, to identify their own political positioning.

Shakespeare worldwide In this these writers were hardly unusual. Across the world in the twentieth century, whether in parts of the (former) British empire or not, writers found in Shakespeare as potent a way of voicing themselves as had earlier generations, and states found Shakespeare co-opted in opposition to their political oppressions. Throughout the Soviet bloc, for instance, Shakespeare was censored as dangerously subversive, controlled into a political acceptability as an example of socialist realism, or banned, as *Hamlet* was under Stalin. Some plays began to be admired because praised by Marx (for example, *Timon of Athens*) or Engels (for example, *The Merry Wives of Windsor*). But writers opposing Sovietism like Blok, Akhmatova, Tsvetaeva, and Pasternak turned to Shakespeare, the last both translating *Hamlet* and *King Lear* (used for Grigori Kozintsev's film versions in 1964 and 1971) and making *Hamlet* the basis of poems in his banned novel *Doctor Zhivago* (1958).

Elsewhere, in less oppressive contexts, Shakespeare was being rethought and remade. In Japan, for instance, *The Merchant of Venice* was played in a Kabuki adaptation in 1885 while the first Japanese translation (*Julius Caesar* by Shoyo Tsubouchi) appeared a few years later. Later translations were crucial in the development of Shingeki, the new theatre that explored modern forms of realism within a Japanese context. Novels and short stories derived from Shakespearian materials were written throughout the century. But perhaps the most visible signs of Japanese Shakespeare have been the films of Akira Kurosawa: *Castle of the Spider's Web* (from *Macbeth*, also known as *Throne of Blood*, 1957), *The Bad Sleep Well* (from *Hamlet*, 1960), and *Ran* (*Chaos*, from *King Lear*, 1985); and the theatre productions of Yukio Ninagawa, especially his *Macbeth* (1980), *The Tempest* (1987), and *A Midsummer Night's Dream* (1994). Where Kurosawa rethought Shakespeare's narratives into Japanese history without using a line of Shakespeare's, Ninagawa used a range of Japanese theatrical styles and cultural concepts to contextualize the plays.

However one looks at it, Shakespeare had become a global phenomenon. There were translations of his plays and poems into a vast array of languages, including Swedish (1813), Greek (1855), Hebrew (1874), Welsh (1874), Dutch (1880), Bulgarian (1881), Yiddish (1886), Arabic (1890s), Korean (1906), Scottish Gaelic (1911), Chinese (1922), and Maori (2000). Academics, teachers, and enthusiasts formed Shakespeare societies to rival the German one in, for example, the USA (1923, refounded 1973), Japan (1962), Korea (1963), France (1977), Australia and New Zealand (1990), the Low Countries (1993), and even Britain (2002). The International Shakespeare Association was created in 1974. A touring exhibition of materials from the Folger Shakespeare Library (1979–81) was justly called 'Shakespeare: the Globe and the World'.

Shakespeare and film Shakespeare's global presence had been altered irrevocably by the development of film. Shakespeare's plays began to be recorded almost as soon as sound recordings began; performances were no longer to be contained within the theatre. Edwin Booth had been recorded in 1890 with a speech from *Othello* and Ellen Terry, Henry Irving, and Beerbohm Tree were also caught on cylinder. *Hamlet* was sold 'complete' on ten 78 r.p.m. discs with John Gielgud, *Macbeth* in Orson Welles's Mercury Theatre production. But the technologies of the LP made full-length recordings more practicable. Great actors—and many not-so-great—could be heard in schools and at home, making the sound of Shakespeare spoken part of the educational and domestic experience of Shakespeare. He entered the home too as part of radio, especially from the BBC which started broadcasting Shakespeare in 1923 and for which Shakespeare has been the backbone of the radio drama repertory ever since. Hundreds of radio productions of the plays have been mounted, often with distinguished casts: Donald Wolfit, John Gielgud, Michael Redgrave, and Alec Guinness have all played Lear on radio. Radio has also generated vast numbers of critical, biographical, and theatrical features on Shakespeare, a significant part of the way that both Shakespeare's life and his work have been thought about.

If Shakespeare on audio disc is necessarily invisible Shakespeare, the first films were necessarily silent Shakespeare. The earliest fragment to survive is the death of King John in Beerbohm Tree's production, filmed in 1899, though how much more was filmed is unclear. The film company, Biograph, was bidding for respectability, and Shakespeare was its route towards it. Sarah Bernhardt was filmed duelling as Hamlet in 1900 and there were further extracts from Georges Méliès in 1907. In the following years there were hundreds of silent Shakespeares, most short, some an hour or more in length—for example, a 1912 American *Richard III* with Frederick Warde and the 1913 *Hamlet* with Sir Johnston Forbes-Robertson.

If initially their style of film acting was overtly theatrical (and in Warde's case could be contrasted with readings and lectures by him 'live' in the gaps between reels at screenings), the film techniques were rapidly becoming sophisticated, encouraging a number of versions of Shakespeare's supernatural plays, *A Midsummer Night's Dream* and *The Tempest*, which could make good use of trick effects. In 1916 Tree was lured to America to film *Macbeth* but was mocked by the British press for succumbing to such commercialism. By the 1920s there were unquestionably major accomplishments in filmed Shakespeare, especially from Germany with Svend Gade's 1920 adaptation of *Hamlet* (with Asta Nielsen as a female prince) and Buchowetski's 1922 *Othello* with Emil Jannings. There were also silent Shakespeare documentaries, fiction films with Shakespeare as a character, and Shakespeare parodies. Most strikingly, silent film was a genuinely international product (and it is significant how many of the films came from Italy and Germany and how few from England), for the intertitles could be easily remade into any language.

There have been fewer Shakespeare sound films in the more than seventy years of the talkies than silent films in the previous thirty. Most of the silents are lost. Many of the sound films are widely available on video and DVD and have become a major element in teaching Shakespeare at school and university. In cinemas and homes, as well as schools, Shakespeare on film is by far the most common experience of Shakespeare in performance. Sound film has formed the modern popular images of performed Shakespeare, a sequence culminating in the success of Shakespeare himself on film in *Shakespeare in Love* (1998), which won seven Oscars with its image of Shakespeare as young romantic genius in search of his muse, the inverse of the Droeshout engraving.

Hollywood quickly recognized the possibilities of Shakespeare for talking pictures. *The Taming of the Shrew* with Mary Pickford and Douglas Fairbanks (1929) was at the bridge between silents and sound, but Warner Brothers' spectacular *A Midsummer Night's Dream* (1935), based on Max Reinhardt's production and with a host of stars, great spectacle, much of Mendelssohn's music, and less than half of Shakespeare's words, showed what could be done. It was not, however, financially successful.

Laurence Olivier, who had played Orlando in a Hollywood *As You Like It* (1936), saw the possibilities for a heroic celebration of England in the middle of the Second World War in making *Henry V* as a form of patriotic epic, starting from a nostalgic vision of the unblitzed London before a performance at the Globe. His broodingly Oedipal *Hamlet* (1948) and comically villainous *Richard III* (1955), another version of Shakespeare as guide to English history, defined English Shakespeare films as safe and traditional. The same was true of the rare American forays (for example, *Julius Caesar* in 1953 and 1970), star-studded epics echoing Hollywood's Roman epics.

Far more brilliantly, Orson Welles, with radical rethinking of the possibilities of cinema and meagre budgets, made incisive and complex versions of *Macbeth* (1948), *Othello* (1952), and the *Henry IV* plays as *Chimes at Midnight* (1966). If the 1960s were dominated by Franco Zeffirelli's popular and lush *The Taming of the Shrew* (1966) and *Romeo and Juliet* (1968), there were powerfully intelligent and superbly cinematic alternatives in Kurosawa's Japanese re-imaginings and Grigori Kozintsev's political readings of *Hamlet* (1964) and *King Lear* (1970), with great performances from Innokenti Smoktunovski as Hamlet and Yuri Yarvets as Lear and the benefits of Shostakovich's fine film-scores.

While there were a number of films that did little more—and often rather less—than record successful stage productions, capturing a shadow of, for example, Olivier's performance as Othello (1965), a new era for popular and commercially successful Shakespeare films began with Kenneth Branagh's *Henry V* (1989). Branagh followed it with *Much Ado about Nothing* (1993) and a full-text, four-hour *Hamlet* (1996). Baz Luhrmann's *William Shakespeare's Romeo + Juliet* (1996) exploited the resources of film as never before, as well as using stars popular with teenage audiences, while Ian McKellen transformed his stage performance of Richard III into a narrative of an alternative twentieth-century history (directed by Richard Loncraine, 1996).

Some of the most thoughtful and experimental work in filming Shakespeare has come from Britain, including Peter Brook's *King Lear* (with Paul Scofield, 1971), Derek Jarman's *The Tempest* (1979), Peter Greenaway's *Prospero's Books* (1991, from *The Tempest*, with John Gielgud playing all the roles), and Christine Edzard's *As You Like It* (1992). But Shakespeare has also been a major source for films that are offshoots, using a Shakespeare play as the underpinning for their own plots, for example *Forbidden Planet* (1956, from *The Tempest*), *Men of Respect* (1990, from *Macbeth*), and *The Lion King* (1994, from *Hamlet*).

Shakespeare and twentieth-century literature Throughout the twentieth century novelists and playwrights continued to work with and from Shakespeare to create their own dramas. The range has been immense and a very few examples in little more than a list must stand for all. *The Tempest* stands behind John Fowles's *The Magus* (1966) and Iris Murdoch's *The Sea, the Sea* (1978) as well as Toni Morrison's *Tar Baby* (1981) and Gloria Naylor's *Mama Day* (1988). Jane Smiley re-imagined *King Lear* in the American midwest in *A Thousand Acres* (1991), while Robert Nye gave an extradramatic life to *Falstaff* (1976) and to *Mrs Shakespeare* (1993). *Hamlet* lies within Virginia Woolf's *Between the Acts* (1941), John Updike's *Gertrude and Claudius* (1999), and many murder mysteries, though the Shakespeare variety reached its apogee in James Thurber's 'The Macbeth murder mystery'. There have also been serious fictional biographies of Shakespeare, for example, Anthony Burgess's *Nothing Like the Sun* (1964), and a superb comic one, Caryl Brahms's and S. J. Simon's *No Bed for Bacon* (1941).

On the stage Shakespeare has become a basis for musicals: for example, *The Boys from Syracuse* (1938, from *The Comedy of Errors*, music by Richard Rodgers), *Kiss Me Kate* (1948, from *The Taming of the Shrew*, music by Cole Porter), and *West Side Story* (1957, from *Romeo and Juliet*, music by Leonard Bernstein). There have been sequels and prequels (for example, Howard Barker's *Seven Lears*, 1990, and Elaine Feinstein's and the Women's Theatre Group's *Lear's Daughters*, 1991), plays developing minor characters (Tom Stoppard's *Rosencrantz and Guildenstern are Dead*, 1966) and rethinking the action (Edward Bond's *Lear*, 1971, Eugène Ionesco's *Macbett*, 1972, Charles Marowitz's collage versions collected as *The Marowitz Shakespeare*, 1978), plays providing cultural relocations (Welcome Msomi's *uMabatha*, 1972) and political reinterpretations (for example, Bertolt Brecht's *Coriolanus*, 1964, or his use of *Richard III* in *The Life of Galileo*, 1943, and *The Resistible Rise of Arturo Ui*, 1957). There have also been major successes in relocating plays to the opera house, especially Benjamin Britten's *A Midsummer Night's Dream* (1960), Samuel Barber's *Antony and Cleopatra* (1966), and Aribert Reimann's *Lear* (1978), and one superb translation to ballet in the successive choreographic interpretations of Prokofiev's *Romeo and Juliet* (1935) by Ashton, Cranko, MacMillan, and others.

Shakespeare on the twentieth-century stage But as well as these adaptations for the stage, the plays themselves have a long and complex history of twentieth-century stage performance. Productions in continental Europe were often thoughtfully political and strikingly modernist in design, for example Leopold Jessner's *Richard III* (1920) and *Othello* (1921), both in Berlin, or the versions of *Julius Caesar* by Leon Schiller (Warsaw, 1928) and Jiří Frejka (Prague, 1936). Such work was echoed by Orson Welles's stage work in America, with his 'voodoo' *Macbeth* and his strongly anti-fascist *Julius Caesar* in 1937.

But little similar was seen in England, with the notable exception of Terence Gray's *Richard III* (Cambridge, 1928) and Theodore Komisarjevsky's productions at Stratford (for example, *King Lear*, 1936). British experiment was more often more restrained: Barry Jackson startled London when his 1925 modern-dress *Hamlet* had Hamlet in plus fours, but there was nothing radical about Jackson's reading of the play. Lilian Baylis's commitment to Shakespeare at the Old Vic Theatre led to all the plays in the first folio being produced there under Robert Atkins, ending in 1923 with *Troilus and Cressida*, a play whose stage history effectively began in the twentieth century. In the aftermath of his triumphant performances as Richard II (1929) and Hamlet (1930), John Gielgud turned to directing: his *Romeo and Juliet* (1935) at the New Theatre, with Laurence Olivier exchanging Mercutio for Romeo during the run, was most remarkable for the sets by the three women designers known as Motley, whose abstracted forms allowed for fluid staging. Their designs transformed Shakespeare productions from Victorian ponderousness to a new light rapidity.

In Stratford the Shakespeare Memorial Theatre reopened in 1932 after a fire in 1926. Its productions, often dull, occasionally brilliant, changed when Peter Brook arrived to direct *Love's Labour's Lost* in 1946 and *Titus Andronicus* in 1955, two previously unfashionable plays whose stageworthiness was newly proven. In 1960 Peter

Hall created the Royal Shakespeare Company (RSC), with a permanent ensemble company and year-round work in Stratford and London. Brook's Beckett-influenced *King Lear* (1962), a production developed from an essay by the Polish Shakespeare critic Jan Kott, and Hall's *The Wars of the Roses* (with John Barton, 1963–4) were early indications that the RSC could create powerful and innovative work to rival the best by European directors as well as their sustained advocacy of plays previously unfashionable, especially *Troilus and Cressida* and *Measure for Measure*. Buzz Goodbody's creation of The Other Place, a small studio-theatre in Stratford, defined radical new ways for the RSC to play Shakespeare in small spaces (for example, her *Hamlet* in 1975 and Trevor Nunn's *Macbeth* in 1976).

In North America the post-war period was most marked by the rapid growth of theatres hosting Shakespeare festivals, like Tyrone Guthrie's at Stratford, Ontario, from 1953 or Joseph Papp's New York Shakespeare Festival in Central Park from 1954 or at Ashland, Oregon. By the end of the century there were seventy Shakespeare festivals across the continent. In western Europe directors, many heavily influenced by Brechtian principles, searched the plays for political meanings, most excitingly in the work of Roger Planchon in France and Giorgio Strehler in Italy (especially *The Tempest* in 1978). In the Soviet bloc after 1968 officially acceptable productions had to compete with productions that used Shakespeare to encode criticism of the state, for example Yuri Lyubimov's *Hamlet* (Moscow, 1971).

In the last quarter of the century English Shakespeare production outside the still-flourishing RSC (under Peter Hall, Trevor Nunn, Terry Hands, and Adrian Noble) and the fine work at the Royal National Theatre varied from the excellent traditional work at the Regent's Park Open Air Theatre in London to the popular and political productions of Michael Bogdanov's and Michael Pennington's English Shakespeare Company (*The Wars of the Roses*, 1987–8) to the defiant northern voices of Barrie Rutter's Northern Broadsides (from 1992). In London a long campaign to build an authentic reconstruction of the Globe, an often uneasy collaboration between Sam Wanamaker's single-minded drive, architects, and scholars, resulted finally in Shakespeare's Globe opening in 1997 and playing thereafter to large and appreciative audiences. If the economics of theatre made Shakespeare's large casts problematic, there were innovative solutions in every corner of the country.

For the first time a significant number of women directed Shakespeare, including Ariane Mnouchkine in France, Karin Beier in Germany, and Deborah Warner and Jude Kelly in England. Productions experimented with cross-cultural influences, especially after the success in the West of Ninagawa's work. Productions could be played with cross-gendered casting, with multilingual casts, with barely a shred of Shakespeare's text, or without a line being cut. Productions could last one hour or six, with casts of fifty or two, with massive sets or none, in daylight or with complex lighting, in theatres large and small or in the street. In Britain, in particular, Shakespeare is also the staple of amateur production with many thousands of performances every year by schoolchildren of all ages, by university societies, and by local groups brand-new and long-established. Shakespeare seems still to be everywhere where theatre is being made: in China in 1986 a Shakespeare festival gathered twenty-eight Chinese productions; in the 1990s there were over forty productions of *Hamlet* in Korea. Always provoking theatre workers and stretching them to their limits, Shakespeare is unquestionably still the major driving force in world theatre.

Shakespeare and education In many of the world's educational systems Shakespeare remains at the core of literary study, compulsory in the English national curriculum at secondary school and all but compulsory in many other countries. At universities his plays are central to the study of literature and drama and, though political battles in the United States to revise the canon of literary study led to Shakespeare no longer being compulsory at many universities, more students than ever take Shakespeare courses there. The editing of Shakespeare has responded to these different needs with innovative editions for schools (for example, Rex Gibson's Cambridge School Shakespeare, from 1991), major student editions of the complete works (for example, edited by Peter Alexander, 1951; the Riverside Shakespeare, 1974, 2nd edn 1997; and the Norton Shakespeare, 1997), and repeated revisions of established series or forms of presentation (for example, the New Cambridge, Oxford, and Arden Third series).

Shakespeare editing has been transformed by new principles of textual bibliography but also by the availability of computers, on-line databases and web-delivered editions. New theories about the early texts, especially that they represent for some plays (for example, *King Lear*) successive stages of Shakespeare's own revision of the plays, have led to the appearance of multiple-text editions, in the wake of the inclusion of both quarto- and folio-derived texts of *Lear* in the Oxford Shakespeare, edited by Stanley Wells and Gary Taylor (1986). Successive movements in scholarship have produced dramatic changes in the understanding of Shakespeare's sources, the printing of the folio, Shakespeare's processes of composition, and the cultural, political, and theatrical contexts within which he wrote.

The development of major resources for scholars has included the Folger Shakespeare Library, opened in 1932 with the collection of Henry Clay Folger and amounting to the world's largest collection of Shakespeare materials, with seventy-nine copies of the first folio; the Shakespeare Centre Library in Stratford upon Avon, which includes the RSC's archives; and the Shakespeare Institute of the University of Birmingham, founded by Allardyce Nicoll in 1951. Shakespeare conferences proliferate, but the annual conference of the Shakespeare Association of America, the biennial International Shakespeare Conference in Stratford upon Avon, and the quinquennial World Shakespeare Congress each gather many hundreds of scholars from all over the world. There are numerous Shakespeare journals, including *Shakespeare Survey* (started by Nicoll in 1948), *Shakespeare Newsletter* (from

1951), two called *Shakespeare Studies* (in Japan from 1961 and the USA since 1965), and, from 1950, the Folger-based *Shakespeare Quarterly*, whose annual listing of publications in its World Shakespeare Bibliography testifies to the colossal output of the academic Shakespeare industry.

There are times when the multiple modes of Shakespeare criticism can seem bewildering—with, in the last quarter of the twentieth century, such dominant strands as new historicism, cultural materialism or feminist studies and gender criticism, queer theory, and cultural studies. Psychoanalytical approaches seem to have little connection with stage- and film-oriented ones. The study of the material culture of early modern England seems to be radically distinct as a mode of academic investigation from the history of Shakespeare translation. The exploration of Renaissance reading habits can seem to sit uncomfortably beside studies in Shakespeare pedagogy.

Not the least important part of this activity has been biographical study. There have been so many biographies of Shakespeare that Samuel Schoenbaum wrote a large as well as entertaining study of the history of Shakespeare biography, *Shakespeare's Lives* (1970). Among the most important biographies of recent years have been Schoenbaum's *William Shakespeare: a Documentary Life* (1975), Park Honan's *Shakespeare: a Life* (1998), and Katherine Duncan-Jones's *Ungentle Shakespeare* (2001)—each contributing significantly to our understanding of the facts and the interpretation of the hypotheses concerning Shakespeare's life.

But the plurality of Shakespeare studies is united by the extraordinary range of meanings provoked by Shakespeare. As much concerned with the history of Shakespeare's afterlife as with close analysis of particular texts, as interested in Shakespeare in twenty-first-century Brazil as in sixteenth-century London, as excited by Shakespeare in nineteenth-century Hebrew as in early modern English, Shakespeare studies engage with every aspect of the culture that produced Shakespeare and the cultures his work has produced.

Shakespeare and popular culture For if Shakespeare has often seemed to some to be the prerogative of English high culture, then throughout the world Shakespeare, his image, and his works have been appropriated for every kind of popular cultural usage, signs both of his cultural authority and of the cultural contestation his works provoke.

In Britain politicians of the left and right rely on Shakespeare as a national and quasi-religious authority for their political creeds. The Labour leader Neil Kinnock, the heir to nineteenth-century political oratory with its predilection for quoting Shakespeare, required his speech-writers to know the Bible and Shakespeare, the twin bedrocks of working-class culture. At the opposite end of the political spectrum, right-wing Conservative politicians like Michael Portillo returned with mechanical frequency to Ulysses's speech on degree in *Troilus and Cressida* as 'proof' that Shakespeare supported the hierarchies and institutions tories were committed to maintain.

Shakespeare's plays are quoted in every kind of popular film and television programme. Episodes in many situation comedies show how contested the place of Shakespeare is in American or British society as children wrestle with Shakespeare homework, parents quote Shakespeare defiantly, or the school Shakespeare production looms. The last of the original *Star Trek* films, *Star Trek VI* (1991), quotes Shakespeare in its subtitle, *The Undiscovered Country*, and jokes about Shakespeare sounding better in the original Klingon, a language invented for the television series whose devotees have indeed 'translated' *Hamlet* into Klingon (2000). There are pornographic films with fragments of Shakespearian plots (both heterosexual and homosexual) and strip clubs that have tried to avoid censorship by having the strippers speak Shakespeare's lines.

In the camp horror film *Theatre of Blood* (1973), a disgruntled Shakespearian actor, played by Vincent Price, murders theatre critics in appropriately Shakespearian ways. The science-fiction film *Forbidden Planet* (1956) spawned a musical stage adaptation, *Return to the Forbidden Planet* (1989), which used classic rock songs and Shakespearian puns ('Beware the Ids that march'). Versions of twelve plays, made as animated 30-minute episodes by S4C, a Welsh television company, in collaboration with Russian animators, were screened in 1992, the texts adapted by Leon Garfield, author of short narrative versions for children, successors to Lambs' *Tales*.

There are strip cartoons which use the entire Shakespeare text in speech bubbles as well as one which shows Shakespeare being given his plots by supernatural beings. A British heavyweight boxer, Frank Bruno, appeared on television in drag in a comedy sketch in which he played Juliet in the balcony scene. Shakespeare's lines appear in rock songs and rap, while a serious popular singer Elvis Costello collaborated with the classical Brodsky Quartet on *The Juliet Letters* (1996), whose lyrics are imaginary letters to Shakespeare's heroine. When listeners to BBC Radio 4's *Today* programme voted Shakespeare the 'Man of the millennium' in 1999, there was hardly any surprise at the choice. Castaways on *Desert Island Discs* on BBC, the world's longest-running radio programme, are always allowed a copy of Shakespeare as well as the Bible for their island.

Shakespeare and his characters have been extensively used for advertising. There are cigars named Hamlet, Romeo y Julieta, Falstaff, and Antonio y Cleopatra. His own image and his characters have been used to sell, for example, Ford cars, Shell petrol, Schweppes soft drinks, and Maxwell House coffee and, since 1986, Coca-Cola, Shreddies breakfast cereal, Typhoo tea, and Carling Black Label lager.

Shakespeare has appeared on English banknotes, as a hologram on British cheque-guarantee cards, and on playing cards. His characters have made up chess sets and cigarette cards. There are statues, streets, squares, piazzas, and avenues named after Shakespeare and after his most famous characters in many cities of the world. There are Shakespeare pubs in many British airports and an American company, Celebriducks, sells plastic Shakespeare ducks for the bath. Souvenirs from Stratford have been available since the eighteenth century and ceramic images of Shakespeare as figurines, on plates, toby jugs, and on the tops of walking-sticks proliferated in the nineteenth.

More seriously, the Shakespeare tourist industry is a vital component of the economic stability of the West Midlands region in England and theatre companies like the Royal Shakespeare Company and Shakespeare's Globe are major employers. There are no figures available for the value of the global Shakespeare economy, but it must run to many billions of pounds per annum. Quite what this extraordinary plethora of Shakespeare material means lies outside the scope of this account. Its mere existence testifies eloquently to the overwhelming presence of Shakespeare, both the man and his works, throughout almost every aspect of the world's culture, in almost every language, in ways often so familiar as hardly to be noticed. His biography, the history of his life and his cultural afterlives, is not only national but triumphantly international. PETER HOLLAND

Sources R. Bearman, *Shakespeare in the Stratford records* (1994) • E. K. Chambers, *William Shakespeare: a study of facts and problems*, 2 vols. (1930) • K. Duncan-Jones, *Ungentle Shakespeare* (2001) • M. Eccles, *Shakespeare in Warwickshire* (1961) • P. Honan, *Shakespeare: a life* (1998) • E. A. J. Honigmann, *Shakespeare: the 'lost' years*, 2nd edn (1998) • S. Schoenbaum, *William Shakespeare: a documentary life* (1975) • S. Schoenbaum, *William Shakespeare: records and images* (1981) • S. Schoenbaum, *William Shakespeare: a compact documentary life*, rev. edn (1987) • P. Thomson, *Shakespeare's professional career* (1992) • S. Wells, *Shakespeare: a dramatic life* (1994) • *William Shakespeare: the complete works*, ed. S. Wells and G. Taylor (1986) • S. Wells and G. Taylor, *William Shakespeare: a textual companion* (1987) • M. Wiggins, *Shakespeare and the drama of his time* (2000) • J. Bate, *Shakespeare and the English Romantic imagination* (1986) • J. Bate, *Shakespearean constitutions* (1989) • J. Bate, *The genius of Shakespeare* (1997) • J. Bate, ed., *The Romantics on Shakespeare* (1992) • J. Bate and R. Jackson, eds., *Shakespeare: an illustrated stage history* (1996) • M. de Grazia and S. Wells, *The Cambridge companion to Shakespeare* (2001) • M. Dobson, *The making of the national poet* (1992) • M. Dobson and S. Wells, *The Oxford companion to Shakespeare* (2001) • J. Gross, *After Shakespeare* (2002) • W. Hortmann, *Shakespeare on the German stage: the twentieth century* (1998) • R. Jackson, ed., *The Cambridge companion to Shakespeare on film* (2000) • D. Scott Kastan, *A companion to Shakespeare* (1999) • D. Kennedy, *Looking at Shakespeare*, 2nd edn (2001) • D. Kennedy, ed., *Foreign Shakespeare* (1993) • D. Lanier, *Shakespeare and modern popular culture* (2002) • A. Loomba and M. Orkin, *Postcolonial Shakespeares* (1998) • P. Rawlings, ed., *Americans on Shakespeare, 1776–1914* (1999) • *The works of William Shakespear*, ed. N. Rowe, 6 vols. (1709) • T. Sasayama and others, eds., *Shakespeare and the Japanese stage* (1998) • G. Taylor, *Reinventing Shakespeare* (1989) • A. Thompson and S. Roberts, eds., *Women reading Shakespeare, 1660–1900* (1997) • B. Vickers, ed., *Shakespeare: the critical heritage, 1623–1801*, 6 vols. (1974–81) • S. Wells and S. Stanton, *The Cambridge companion to Shakespeare on stage* (2002) • S. Williams, *Shakespeare on the German stage, 1586–1914* (1990)

Archives Shakespeare Birthplace Trust RO, Stratford upon Avon, deeds and papers

Likenesses attrib. J. Taylor, oils, *c.*1610 (Chandos portrait), NPG [*see illus.*] • G. Janssen, monument, 1616–23, Holy Trinity Church, Stratford upon Avon • M. Droeshout the elder?, engraving, 1622, repro. in *Mr William Shakespeares comedies, histories, & tragedies* (1623), title-page • W. Marshall, engraving, 1640? (after M. Droeshout), repro. in 1640 edition of Shakespeare's poems • W. Faithorne, engraving, 1655? (after M. Droeshout), repro. in W. Shakespeare, *The rape of Lucrece* (1655) • W. Dugdale, engraving, 1656 (after Janssen), repro. in W. Dugdale, *Antiquities of Warwickshire* (1656) • Kneller, portrait, in or before 1694 (after J. Taylor) • bust, *c.*1735, Stowe • P. Scheemakers, statue, in or after 1741, Westminster Abbey • portrait, engraved 1770 (after Janssen) • portrait, exh. 1792 (Felton or Burdett-Coutts portrait) • R. Gower, statue, *c.*1888, Stratford upon Avon (?) • L. F. Roubiliac, statue, BL • M. Vandergucht, portrait (after J. Taylor), repro. in *The works of William Shakespear*, ed. Rowe (1709), frontispiece • portrait ('Flower' portrait), Royal Shakespeare Company • portrait, Ely Palace

Shakhbut ibn Sultan al-Nahayan, Sheikh (1905–1989), ruler of Abu Dhabi, was born in Abu Dhabi, the son of Sheikh Sultan ibn Zayed (*d.* 1927) and his wife, Sheikha Salamah bint Buti (*c.*1885–1970). Shakhbut's grandfather was Sheikh Zayed ibn Khalifa (*d.* 1909), who had ruled Abu Dhabi since 1855 as leader of the dominant al-Nahayan tribe within the Bani Yas tribal confederation. Life on the eastern edge of the Arabian peninsula had changed little since the Bani Yas first settled there in the eighteenth century: the people lived by fishing, pearling, and simple agriculture. As a boy Shakhbut learned the ways of the desert from Bedouin tribesmen, while a local preacher instructed him in the principles of Sunni Islam. During the 1920s Abu Dhabi's ruling house was racked by murderous rivalries, chiefly centring on money. Shakhbut's father seized control in 1922 by murdering his brother Hamdan, only to be murdered himself in 1927—shot on the stairs as he arrived for dinner—by a third brother, Saqr. Shakhbut fled to neighbouring Sharjah, but his uncle's rule proved brief: he was killed after a year by the slave of a nephew. It was in this context of extreme internal strife that Shakhbut returned to Abu Dhabi in 1928 to become its ruler. Soon afterwards his mother gathered together her sons and made them promise to avoid further bloodshed.

Abu Dhabi's fort served as Shakhbut's residence, which was also the town's only administrative building aside from the custom house. From here he conducted his highly personalized rule, as was traditional. On most days sittings (*majlis*) were held, at which anyone with a problem could present himself to the ruler. His mother's advice guided him during the hard times of the 1930s, when Abu Dhabi's pearling industry was destroyed by the combined effects of world depression and the Japanese invention of the cultured pearl. He took several wives (polygamy being an accepted practice), although one was almost immediately divorced after she quarrelled with his mother. He had several children, the eldest of whom was Said (1930–*c.*1970).

When foreign oil companies began to take an interest in Abu Dhabi in the late 1930s Shakhbut kept a tight rein on developments. His younger brother Zayed (*b.* 1919) acted as guide for the first geological survey team in 1939, but it was not until after the Second World War that oil exploration began in earnest. The immediate result was a flaring up of border disputes: age-old practices of tribal circulation meant that formal lines in the sand had never been drawn. Shakhbut held that the wanderings of the Bani Yas defined the borders of Abu Dhabi, a stance that resulted in a war with neighbouring Dubai between 1945 and 1948. Frustrated by the disruption caused to the oil survey teams, Britain intervened to impose peace, thus beginning a new era of imperialism along the Trucial Coast (so-called because of the truces signed with Arab peoples from the 1830s to halt piracy against East India Company shipping). Britain's previous approach of non-intervention in the internal affairs of the sheikhdoms—while protecting them from outside powers—had effectively fossilized the region along medieval lines. Diplomats posted there in the 1950s would see dismembered hands on display, punishment for theft; there were also no roads and little transport. But now the rulers—and Shakhbut especially—were thrust into the twentieth century because of the demand for oil.

The first oil well was constructed off the coast of Abu Dhabi in 1949. Shakhbut ensured that labour recruitment and conditions of employment were to his liking and in return he provided guards for the oil company. However, he was unable to guarantee security in the hinterland and so in 1951 Britain established the Trucial Oman Levies (renamed the Trucial Oman Scouts in 1956). Its members were drawn mainly from the Abu Dhabi tribes and were led by British officers. A further evolution in Britain's responsibilities took place in 1952 with the creation of the Trucial Council, comprising the British political resident in Bahrain (its senior diplomat along the Trucial Coast) and the local ruling sheikhs. Shakhbut was grateful for the increased presence, especially when Saudi Arabia occupied the Buraimi oasis (100 miles inland from Abu Dhabi town) in August 1952. Anglo-American efforts at a diplomatic solution dragged on until the Eden government gave the go-ahead in October 1955 for Shakhbut to send in the Trucial Levies and force the surrender of the Saudi detachment. During the Suez War of 1956, while the other Arab governments were in uproar, the ruler of Abu Dhabi presented a gold sword to a British official in demonstration of his loyalty.

Shakhbut nevertheless remained wary of Britain's redefined policy of promoting modern government in the sheikhdoms. A visit to Britain in 1953 failed to impress on him the need to build schools and hospitals. In anticipation of commercial offshore oil production in 1958, Britain's diplomatic representative in Abu Dhabi was upgraded from political officer to political agent in 1957. The pressure on Shakhbut increased still further with the start of onshore production in 1962, and faced with the prospect of profound changes to Abu Dhabi he became yet more intransigent. To the north, Kuwait's newly acquired wealth was a cautionary tale. When the British suggested he renegotiate the oil agreements to secure greater revenues, he replied: 'What I've got, I keep. And if it says "one shilling a barrel", I want one shilling a barrel. I refuse to change it' (Middleton).

Oil revenues were retained under Shakhbut's close supervision and, to the mounting frustration of his family, he refused to delegate any authority over financial matters. In the mid-sixties stories appeared in the Western press depicting him sleeping on wads of banknotes whose corners had been nibbled away by mice. In truth the money was kept in the local Ottoman bank, but this did not stop him from regularly visiting the premises to count it (and even check the serial numbers on individual notes). His deeply conservative attitude was unwavering: 'I am a Bedou and all my people are Bedou. We are accustomed to living with a camel or a goat in the desert. If we spend the money, it will ruin us' (Pipes). His younger brother Sheikh Zayed disagreed, however, and advocated expenditure on grandiose modernization projects.

In 1966 British officials, working with Shakhbut's mother, engineered a peaceful coup whereby Zayed succeeded Shakhbut. All were anxious to avoid repeating the bloodshed of the 1920s. The chain of events began with Zayed visiting London and presenting a letter to a Foreign Office official during a garden party at Buckingham Palace. The letter confirmed the ruling family's desire to have Shakhbut ousted. On 6 August Shakhbut's absence on a sailing trip triggered the take-over. His family held a meeting that day and formally replaced him.

After four years of exile in Bahrain Shakhbut was allowed to return to Abu Dhabi and he lived in a palace in al-ʿAin, a town in the Buraimi area. He was given a generous allowance by Zayed, who went on to form and preside over the United Arab Emirates following Britain's withdrawal from the Persian Gulf in December 1971. Shakhbut cut a forlorn figure in his last years, and was rumoured to have become a manic depressive. In the mid-seventies he received treatment at Wellington Hospital in London—suggesting that he bore no grudge against the British. He died in al-ʿAin on 11 February 1989. By the end of the century Abu Dhabi—with Zayed still president of a federation of eastern sheikhdoms—had become the richest state on earth per capita. Shakhbut was one of a kind: an oil-rich ruler who refused to spend the money. Like Abu Dhabi's traditional ways of life, he was cursed by wealth.

MICHAEL T. THORNHILL

Sources H. Boustead, *The wind of the morning* (1975) · P. Lienhardt, *Shaikhdoms of eastern Arabia*, ed. A. al Shahi (2001) · F. Heard-Bey, *From Trucial states to UAE* (1982) · L. Blandford, *Oil sheiks* (1976) · C. Morris, *The desert falcon: the story of H. H. Sheikh Zayed bin Sultan al Nahiyan* (1974) · G. Balfour-Paul, *The end of the empire in the Middle East* (1991) · G. Butt, *The lion in the sand: the British in the Middle East* (1995) · B. Burrows, *Footnotes in the sand* (1990) · H. Ladjevardi, interview with Sir George Middleton, 14 Oct 1985, Harvard U., Iranian oral history project, Center for Middle Eastern Studies · D. Pipes, 'The curse of oil wealth', *The Atlantic* (July 1982) · private information (2004)

Archives U. Durham, William Luce MSS

Likenesses photographs, repro. in Lienhardt, *Shaikhdoms of eastern Arabia* · photographs, repro. in Balfour-Paul, *The end of the empire*

Wealth at death very wealthy: Blandford, *Oil sheiks*

Shalders, George (*c.*1825–1873), watercolour painter, was born in Portsmouth and began to exhibit in London at the Royal Academy and the Society of British Artists in Suffolk Street in 1848. He showed fifteen paintings at the Royal Academy, the last in 1864. In 1863 he became an associate of the New Society of Painters in Water Colours, and a member in 1864, and subsequently he exhibited only there. He painted landscapes, usually views in Hampshire, Surrey, Yorkshire, Wales, and Ireland, often containing cattle or sheep. Reviewing the 1865 exhibition at the New Watercolour Society, in which his *Fresh Pasture* was exhibited, the critic writing for the *Art Journal* commented that 'Sheep are folded and driven to field by Mr Shalders with a truth and beauty which finds no rivals' (*Art Journal*, 27, 1 June 1865, 176). His *Cows in a Landscape* is in the Victoria and Albert Museum, London. Shalders died a widower on 27 January 1873 at his home, 10 Berkeley Gardens, Campden Hill, London, leaving three young daughters. His early death was said to have been caused by overwork, following the death of his wife two years earlier.

F. M. O'DONOGHUE, *rev.* ANNE PIMLOTT BAKER

Sources *Art Journal*, 35 (1873), 80–127 • S. Wilcox and C. Newall, *Victorian landscape watercolors* (1992), 126 [exhibition catalogue, New Haven, CT, Cleveland, OH, and Birmingham, 9 Sept 1992 – 12 April 1993] • Boase, *Mod. Eng. biog.* • Mallalieu, *Watercolour artists*, vols. 1–2 • Wood, *Vic. painters*, 3rd edn • Graves, *RA exhibitors* • L. Lambourne and J. Hamilton, eds., *British watercolours in the Victoria and Albert Museum* (1980) • J. Johnson, ed., *Works exhibited at the Royal Society of British Artists, 1824–1893, and the New English Art Club, 1888–1917*, 2 vols. (1975) • *CGPLA Eng. & Wales* (1873)

Wealth at death under £450: administration, 4 Aug 1873, *CGPLA Eng. & Wales*

Shanawdithit [*called* Nancy] (*c.*1801–1829), the last of the Beothuk, was the daughter of Doodebewshet and granddaughter of Moo-meshduck. Her people, the Beothuk, were a small population of Algonquian hunter-gatherers who were the aboriginal occupants of the island of Newfoundland.

When Europeans arrived in Newfoundland, the Beothuk were dependent in due season on the seals, fish, and seabirds of the coast and the caribou of the interior. During the sixteenth century, when Newfoundland was the locus of a migratory European fishery, the Beothuk largely avoided European contact, choosing instead to scavenge metal objects from seasonally abandoned fishing premises. With the beginning of permanent European settlement in the early seventeenth century, they retreated from the areas of the coast occupied by Europeans. By the beginning of the nineteenth century the much-diminished Beothuk population had fallen back to the Red Indian Lake–Exploits River system. Denied regular access to the resources of the coast, they were forced to depend on the sometimes unreliable interior caribou herds.

Shanawdithit was born into this world, where her people faced starvation as well as harassment from an expanding English population whose fur trappers and salmon fishers were in competition with her people. Because of the long-standing pattern of avoiding European contact, no links existed between the two peoples, despite the efforts of a number of British governors to establish peaceful relations. One such effort, apparently witnessed by Shanawdithit, had occurred in 1811, when Lieutenant David Buchan and a small detachment encountered a Beothuk camp on Red Indian Lake. Despite a promising beginning, the Beothuk misunderstood Buchan's intentions and killed two of his marines. Shanawdithit was also present in March 1819 when Demasduit (Mary March) was captured by a group of English settlers led by John Peyton jun., a local entrepreneur whose salmon fishing operations had been disrupted by the Beothuk. After Demasduit's death from illness, Buchan brought her remains back to Red Indian Lake, an event which Shanawdithit later recorded in a drawing.

By March 1823 the Beothuk population had shrunk to a remnant of fifteen individuals. Weak and starving, Shanawdithit, her mother, Doodebewshet, and her elder sister made their way to the coast, where they gave themselves up to a white settler. They were taken to Peyton's premises on Exploits Island, and then to the capital, St John's, where an observer noted of Shanawdithit that 'her complexion was swarthy, … her features were handsome; she was a tall fine figure … In her manners she was bland, affable, and affectionate' (Wilson, 313). After a short stay in St John's, Shanawdithit and the other two women were sent back to their people in Exploits Bay, but, unable to find them, the three women returned to the Peyton household, where Shanawdithit's sister and mother died.

Shanawdithit remained with Peyton until September 1828 when several members of the newly formed Beothuk Institution brought her to St John's. There she provided the founder of the institution, William Cormack, with invaluable information, partly in the form of drawings, about her people. Shanawdithit died of pulmonary tuberculosis in St John's on 6 June 1829, the last known member of the Beothuk people. She was buried in the naval and military cemetery in St John's. Her tragic life has been described in many, mostly inaccurate, popular accounts.

RALPH T. PASTORE

Sources J. P. Howley, *The Beothucks or Red Indians: the aboriginal inhabitants of Newfoundland* (1915) • R. T. Pastore, 'Fishermen, furriers and Beothuks: the economy of extinction', *Man in the Northeast*, 33 (1987), 47–62 • William Carson to Christopher Ayre, 17 Nov 1830, Provincial Archives of Newfoundland and Labrador, St John's, GN 2/2, 325–8 • W. Wilson, *Newfoundland and its missionaries* (1866) • *Public Ledger* [St John's, Nfld] (12 June 1829) • *Newfoundlander* [St John's, Nfld] (11 June 1829) • I. Marshall, *A history and ethnography of the Beothuk* (1996) • J. Hewson, *Beothuk vocabularies* (1978) • I. Marshall, 'Newfoundland Beothuk illustrated', *Man in the Northeast*, 35 (1988), 47–70 • G. C. Pulling, 'A few facts by G. C. Pulling respecting the native Indians of the Isle of Newfoundland, Anno Domini 1792', BL, Add. MS 38352, fols. 18–47 • R. T. Pastore, 'The collapse of the Beothuk world', *Acadiensis*, 19 (1989), 52–71 • L. F. S. Upton, 'The extermination of the Beothuks of Newfoundland', *Canadian Historical Review*, 58 (1977), 133–53

Archives Newfoundland Museum, St John's, Newfoundland

Shand, Alexander Allan (1844–1930), banker, was born on 11 February 1844 at Turriff, Aberdeenshire, son of James Shand, surgeon, and his wife, Margaret Allan. According to his *Times* obituary he was trained in a Scottish bank before he joined the Chartered Mercantile Bank of India, London, and China in the early 1860s in Hong Kong. By 1864, at the age of twenty, he had arrived in Yokohama, Japan, as acting manager of the bank's sub-branch. Takayoshi Kido (1833–1877), one of the most influential and gifted of the newly empowered Japanese oligarchs, anxious to set the new Japan on a sound financial basis, made friends with Shand and, impressed by his clear discussion of banking problems, recommended him to the Japanese ministry of finance.

Tempted by the extraordinarily high salary of 450 yen a month (a Japanese cabinet minister earned 500 yen a month), Shand started work for the ministry by writing, in English, a book on bank accountancy. *The Detailed Account of Bank Bookkeeping* was published, in Japanese, by the ministry in December 1873.

In November 1874 Shand, who had earlier been on home leave in Britain, organized lecture courses on economics and public finance in the ministry. More than 300 aspiring young Japanese bankers attended. Joseph Heco (Hikozo Hamada; 1837–1897) was Shand's chief interpreter and translator. Early in 1875 he undertook the first Western-style bank inspections, following the collapse of a long-standing finance house, Ono. Shand advised the Japanese to establish a central bank, but this was a concept the Japanese were then unable to accept. (The Bank of Japan was established in 1882 by Masayoshi Matsukata.) Shand recommended that Japanese bankers follow English and Scottish banking rules. Before leaving Japanese service Shand himself produced another two books, *On Banking* (1877) and the *Manual of National Banking* (1877–8). He left Japan in March 1877; his sponsor, Takayoshi Kido, died, aged forty-three, in May 1877.

During his stay in Japan, Shand married Emmeline Christmas (1848–1913). They had eight children, including Montague, who died as a child of dysentery in Japan. The other children were Margaret, Helen, Ida, Winifred, Norman, Evan, and Hubert.

Back in London by 1878 Shand entered the service of the Alliance Bank in London. On the amalgamation of the bank with Parr's Bank in 1892 he assumed the managership of the Lombard Street branch. From 1896 Shand was head office manager of Parr's Bank at Bartholomew Lane. In the early years of the twentieth century, especially during the Russo-Japanese War of 1904–5, Shand was a crucial figure in forming syndicates to launch successful Japanese loans on the London money market. His Japanese partner in this endeavour was Korekiyo Takahashi (1854–1936), then deputy governor of the Bank of Japan and later finance and prime minister, who had in the 1860s been messenger boy for Shand in Yokohama. For these services, over several years, particularly during the Russo-Japanese War, the emperor Meiji conferred on him the fourth order of the Rising Sun in 1902, the third order of the Sacred Treasure in 1904, the third order of the Rising Sun in 1906, and the second order of the Sacred Treasure in 1908. Parr's Bank also expressed its thanks to Shand by awarding him several substantial gifts of money. In 1908 Shand was elected to the board of directors; he finally retired from Parr's Bank in 1918, when it merged with the Westminster Bank.

Shand retired to Ardmore, Ardmore Road, Parkstone, Dorset, with his daughters Ida and Winifred. His wife, Emmeline, had died in 1913 in Upper Norwood. On 12 April 1930 he died at his Dorset home from influenza; he was cremated on 16 April at Brookwood, Surrey. Shand's estate (his will was probated at £7582) was not great, probably the result of losses he sustained following the great earthquake in Yokohama and Tokyo in September 1923.

NORIO TAMAKI

Sources *The diary of Kido Takayoshi*, ed. S. D. Brown and A. Hirota, 3 vols. (1983) • O. Checkland, *Britain's encounter with Meiji Japan, 1868–1912* (1989) • T. E. Gregory and A. Henderson, *The Westminster Bank through a century*, 2 vols. (privately printed, London, 1936) • K. Nishikawa, *Nihon bokishidan* (1971) ['Studies on the history of accountancy in Japan'] • N. Tamaki, *Japanese banking* (1995) • *The Times* (16 April 1930) • T. Tsuchiya, 'Alexander Allan Shand no jireki to ningenzo nitsuite', *Proceedings of Japan Academy* (1976) ['Character and career of A. A. Shand'] • N. Umetani, *The role of foreign employees in the Meiji era in Japan* (1971) • General RO of Scotland, batch C112476/0715

Wealth at death £7582 1s. 9d.: probate, 19 June 1930, *CGPLA Eng. & Wales*

Shand, Alexander Burns, Baron Shand (1828–1904), judge, was born at Aberdeen on 13 December 1828, the son of Alexander Shand, merchant in Aberdeen, and his wife, Louisa Whyte, of Banff. Shand was in early boyhood when his father died, and his mother married William Burns, a solicitor in Glasgow. Shand worked in his stepfather's office while attending law classes at the University of Glasgow (1842–8); later at the University of Edinburgh (1848–52) and also spent a short time at the University of Heidelberg in 1852.

Shand was admitted as an advocate at the Scottish bar in 1853 and his practice then seemed to develop rapidly. While at the bar he joined the reserves, being for a time a member of the Advocates' company of the City of Edinburgh volunteer rifles. He was also an active whig, though his membership of the political club coincided with its social rather than political period. Shand married Emily Merelina Meymott in 1857. She died in 1911. They had no family.

In 1860 Shand was appointed advocate-depute. In 1862 he became sheriff of Kincardine and in 1869 he was made sheriff of Haddington and Berwick. He was raised to the bench in 1872 at the early age of forty-four. He served with distinction, especially in matters of commercial law, and his services were most valued in relation to the great volume of litigation that arose out of the liquidation of the City of Glasgow Bank. In 1888 Shand had a long and serious illness and he returned to the bench for only two years before retiring. Being afraid of the severity of the Edinburgh winter, he moved to London.

In 1890 Shand was sworn of the privy council and as a privy councillor who had held a high judicial position he took his seat at the board of the judicial committee. In 1892 he entered the House of Lords as Baron Shand of Woodhouse, in Dumfriesshire, and thereafter for twelve years he sat in the House of Lords as a judicial peer: he was under no obligation to attend and he did so without remuneration or reward of any kind.

Lord Shand was an unusually small man. He was a strong and independent judge. He was much involved in public matters in Scotland and he sat on several commissions of inquiry. He wrote letters to *The Times* on law reform, and he often delivered lectures to public bodies involved in that subject. He identified strongly with the whigs and later the Liberal Party, and he was a friend of Adam Black, a prominent Edinburgh reformer, and Sir Henry Campbell-Bannerman. He received several honorary degrees.

Lord Shand died at his home, 32 Bryanston Square, Marylebone, London, on 6 March 1904. An important appeal against the judgment of the Court of Session in the famous 'Free Church' case judgment was reserved. Shand was believed to have upheld the Court of Session's decision which had rejected the claim of the minority of the Free Church of Scotland to the whole property of the Free Church on its union with the United Presbyterians. In consequence of his death the case was reheard and the Court of Session's judgment was reversed, with much public speculation as to how the matter would have been decided had Lord Shand been able to give his speech. The case was of intense interest in Scotland.

ROBERT SHIELS

Sources *DNB* • *Scots Law Times* (12 March 1904) • NL Scot., MSS 12343, fol. 89; 12266, fol. 57; 12349, fol. 235; 9657, fol. 193; 1845, fol. 190 • *Index of manuscripts in the British library*, 9 (1985) • *Summary catalogue of the Advocates' manuscripts*, National Library of Scotland (1970) • W. I. Addison, *A roll of graduates of the University of Glasgow from 31st December 1727 to 31st December 1897* (1898) • W. I. Addison, ed., *The matriculation albums of the University of Glasgow from 1728 to 1858* (1913) • Irving, *Scots.* • G. W. T. Omond, *The lord advocates of Scotland, second series, 1834–1880* (1914) • *Book of the Old Edinburgh Club*, 3 (1910) • D. M. Walker, *The Oxford companion to law* (1980) • d. cert. • *CGPLA Eng. & Wales* (1904)

Archives BL, Campbell-Bannerman MSS • NL Scot., Minto MSS • NL Scot., Advocates MSS

Likenesses photograph, 1904, repro. in *Scots Law Times* • G. Reid, oils, 1912, Gray's Inn, London • Spy [L. Ward], caricature, NPG; repro. in *VF* (23 July 1903)

Wealth at death £3569 15*s.*: probate, 23 March 1904, *CGPLA Eng. & Wales*

Shand, Alexander Innes (1832–1907), journalist and author, born at Fettercairn, Kincardineshire, on 2 July 1832, was the only child of William Shand of Arnhalt, Fettercairn, and his second wife, Christina (*d.* 1855), daughter of Alexander Innes of Pitmedden, Aberdeenshire. His father possessed a considerable estate in Demerara, but his income was greatly reduced on the abolition of slavery in the 1830s. The family moved to Aberdeen where Alexander, after being educated at Blair Lodge School, entered the university, graduating MA in 1852. Declining an offer of a commission in the 12th Bengal cavalry, owing to his widowed mother's objection to his going abroad, Shand turned to the law. But in 1855, on his mother's death, he began a series of long and systematic European tours. When at home he frequented the estate of Major John Ramsay, a cousin, at Straloch in Aberdeenshire.

In 1865 Shand was admitted to the Scottish bar. He married, on 25 July 1865, Elizabeth Blanche, daughter of William Champion Streatfield, of Chart's Edge, Westerham, Kent; she was an invalid and died childless on 6 June 1882. They settled in Edinburgh but because of his wife's health the Shands moved to Sydenham, and there he discovered his true vocation. After contributing papers on Turkey, America, and other subjects during 1867 to the *Imperial Review*, a short-lived Conservative paper edited by Henry Cecil Raikes, Shand began writing for *The Times* and for *Blackwood's Edinburgh Magazine*, and also joined the staff of John Douglas Cook, editor of the *Saturday Review*. To each of these he contributed for the rest of his life. Shand wrote too rapidly and fluently to be concise or always accurate, but his habit of constant travel, wide reading, good memory, and powers of observation made him in other respects a good journalist. To *The Times* he contributed biographies of, among others, Tennyson, Lord Beaconsfield, and Napoleon III (A. I. Shand, 'Memories of The Times', *Cornhill Magazine*, April 1904), as well as descriptive articles from abroad, and from the west of Ireland and the highlands of Scotland, several series of which were collected for separate issue. He was also an occasional correspondent for the newspaper during the Franco-Russian War (1870), republishing his articles as *On the Trail of the War* (1870).

Shand wrote moderately successful novels, such as *Against Time* (1870), *Shooting the Rapids* (1872), *Fortune's Wheel* (1886), *Kilcurra* (1891), and *The Lady Grange* (1897), but he was more effective as a biographer, as in *Wellington's Lieutenants* (1902), the lives of Sir Edward Hamley (1895) and of John Jacob (1900), and a memoir attached to the 1890 edition of A. W. Kinglake's *Eothen*. *Old World Travel* (1903), and *Days of the Past* (1905), consisting mainly of later sketches in the *Saturday Review*, give an attractive picture of Shand's character, of his capacity for making friends with 'poachers, gamekeepers, railway guards, coach drivers, railway porters, and Swiss guides', and of his experience of London clubs, where he was at home in all circles. He united strongly tory personal convictions with large-hearted tolerance. Among his friends were George Meredith, Laurence Oliphant, and George Smith the publisher. He was devoted to children and all animals, especially dogs, was a fine rider, good shot, and expert angler. He published *Mountain, Stream and Covert* (1897), *The Gun Room* (1903), and *Dogs* (1903). He knew how to cook the game he killed, and wrote well on culinary matters, contributing on cookery to eight volumes of the *Fur, Fin, and Feather* series (1898–1905).

In 1893 he was British commissioner, with Sir Philip Cunliffe Owen, at the Paris Exhibition. He was busily engaged in writing until his death, which took place on 20 September 1907 at his house, Oakdale, Edenbridge, Kent; he was buried in the churchyard of Crookham Hill. Two of his books were posthumously published: *Soldiers of Fortune* (1907), and *Memories of Gardens* (with a memoir by Rowland Blennerhassett) (1908).

W. B. DUFFIELD, *rev.* H. C. G. MATTHEW

Sources R. Blennerhassett, 'Memoir', in A. I. Shand, *Memories of gardens* (1908) • *The Times* (23 Sept 1907)

Archives NL Scot., correspondence with Blackwoods

Wealth at death £3219 2*s.* 6*d.*: probate, 3 Dec 1907, *CGPLA Eng. & Wales*

Shand, Sir James [Jimmy] (1908–2000), accordionist and dance band leader, was born on 28 January 1908 in the village of East Wemyss, Fife, the sixth of the nine children of Erskine Shand (*d.* 1933), pithead contractor, and his wife,

Mary (*d.* 1929). After attending the local school, at the age of fourteen he began work at the local colliery and continued there until the general strike of 1926, after which he took employment where and when it could be found, including a period making concrete blocks. His father was a keen musician with a particular love of brass bands and young Jimmy, after a brief apprenticeship on the mouth-organ, soon graduated to playing the family's melodeon. His obvious expertise in handling a button-key accordion that he tested in a Dundee music shop led to a job offer from the proprietor Charlie Forbes, as a salesman and demonstrator; it was Forbes too who provided the financial backing for Shand to make his first recording in 1933. In the following year Shand made his first radio broadcast. His virtuosity on the accordion was widely acknowledged, but his talent was accompanied by a sound knowledge of the instrument's construction, and he worked with the German manufacturers Hohner to produce an improved accordion that was known as the Shand Morino. On 24 January 1936 he married Anne G. Anderson, with whom he had two sons.

Shand played at dances during the war as often as his work as a fireman allowed. With the return of peace he formed his famous band, which quickly became established on the Scottish music scene, featuring regularly on the radio and touring widely, though he was prepared to return home from some improbably distant venues for the sake of sleeping in his own bed. Demand from the Scottish diaspora resulted in tours to North America, Australia, and New Zealand. Shand's performing style was so economical that he scarcely appeared to be playing his instrument at all and the band's adherence to strict tempo was ideally suited both to dancing and to live radio broadcasts. In 1955 he enjoyed chart-topping success with his *Bluebell Polka* and he attracted the kind of crowds and enthusiasm that soon became more associated with rock and roll. He became still better known through television and his association with, first, *The Kilt is my Delight* and later *The White Heather Club*, a programme of Scottish music and dancing compered by Andy Stewart. The animated presenter contrasted with the reserved and apparently unsmiling Shand; though he was a consummate professional, Shand was, by his own admission, never comfortable in the role of a public performer and the demands of his calling took their toll on his health. He was dogged by various ailments, including a perforated ulcer that forced him to take a break from performing. In 1957 Shand moved with his family from their modest semi-detached home in Dundee to a more spacious house in Auchtermuchty, in his native Fife. Thereafter he returned to touring with a reconstituted band. His eventual retirement in 1972 did not preclude charity work and his appearance for a concert and a country dance in Letham village hall in 1990 with his son Jimmy Shand junior introduced him to another medium, the music video. The resulting product, entitled *Dancing with the Shands*, eventually appeared in 1994 and made it into the music video chart top ten.

Honours bestowed on Shand began with his appointment as MBE in 1962, though in collecting it he was only renewing acquaintanceship with a royal family with whom he was already a great favourite. Possibly he was just as pleased to be awarded the freedom of the burgh of Auchtermuchty in 1974. Such recognition culminated in the award of a knighthood in 1999. Formal honours counted for little compared to the affection in which he was held; every Scot felt that they knew Jimmy Shand. If at one point his image was perhaps associated with an exaggerated Scottishness that bordered on self-caricature, the passage of time has seen the rediscovery and re-evaluation of his work. Charlie Watts, the Rolling Stones drummer, unexpectedly revealed himself as a fan, and the folk-rock singer–songwriter Richard Thompson celebrated him in his song 'Don't sit on my Jimmy Shands', which concluded that 'no shindig is half complete/without that famous polka beat'.

Shand remained unaffected by his celebrity: he retained his plain tastes, gentlemanly demeanour, and broad Fife tones. Despite his demanding schedule, he had unlimited time for his fans and an ability to be on the spot when friends or family fell ill. Outside music his passion was for speed, largely expressed through his ownership of a succession of motor cycles. In 1995 Shand's portrait by George Bruce was unveiled at the Scottish National Portrait Gallery in Edinburgh. Appropriately it was hung next to that of Niel Gow, the eighteenth-century fiddler, to whom Shand has often been compared in terms of their pre-eminent influence on the music of their respective eras. Jimmy Shand died in Perth Royal Infirmary on 23 December 2000. His funeral took place at Auchtermuchty parish church on 29 December.

LIONEL ALEXANDER RITCHIE

Sources I. Cameron, *The Jimmy Shand story* (1998) • D. Phillips, *Jimmy Shand* (1974) • *The Scotsman* (26 Dec 2000) • *The Times* (26 Dec 2000) • *The Guardian* (27 Dec 2000) • *The Independent* (26 Dec 2000) • *Daily Telegraph* (26 Dec 2000) • *The Stage* (4 Jan 2001) • *WW* (2001) • 'In memory of Sir Jimmy Shand', www.accordions.com/memorials, 29 Oct 2001
Archives SOUND BL NSA
Likenesses G. Bruce, oils, Scot. NPG
Wealth at death £180,591.23: confirmation, 17 April 2001, *CCI*

Shandon. For this title name *see* O'Brien, Ignatius John, Baron Shandon (1857–1930).

Shank, John (*d.* 1636), actor, is of unknown origins. Fortunately his personal and professional life are better documented, thanks largely to testimony he gave to the lord chamberlain in 1635 and to the will he signed on 31 December in the same year. He had a long career as a professional actor, in 1635 describing himself as 'an old man in this quality' ('Dramatic records', 367). His will records him as 'one of his Maiesties servants the players and Citizen and Weauer of london' (Honigmann and Brock, 186). He almost certainly lived in London all his life. Shank married Winifred Porter on 12 February 1610 in the parish of St Dunstan-in-the-West. They seem to have spent their married life in the parish of St Giles Cripplegate, where they may have run a boarding house. Of their several children only Elizabeth (*bap.* 1612), John (possibly baptized on 16 March 1616), and James (*bap.* 1619) seem to have survived into adult life. Elizabeth married someone called Bowen and had a daughter, another Winifred. John Shank's elder son was, possibly, a player at the Red Bull and the Fortune, a circumstance that has led to a certain amount of confusion between him and his father, although the younger man survived him by twenty years or so.

The older Shank began his acting career with Pembroke's Men some time after 1592. Later he joined the Queen Elizabeth's Men. By 1610 he was a member of the company whose patron was Prince Henry. He is named as a groom of Prince Henry's chamber on a livery list of 8 November 1612 and his name appears on a patent of 11 January 1613. This was issued when the company came under the patronage of the elector palatine or Palsgrave, a move necessitated by the death of Prince Henry in November 1612. Perhaps Shank supplied the company with the wherewithal for costumes, since on 24 December 1614 a John Shank of St Giles was involved with receiving goods stolen from a linen draper. By the end of 1618 he had left Palatine's Men and had joined the company with which he was to be associated for the rest of his life, the King's Men. Between March 1619 and May 1629 his name appears on six of their patents and livery lists. In 1624, when the King's Men got into trouble for playing *The Spanish Viceroy* without permission, he was a signatory on their letter of apology to Sir Henry Herbert, the master of the revels. He appeared in several plays known to have been in the repertoire of the King's Men. He is included on the list of principal actors in the great 1623 folio of Shakespeare's plays. No specific Shakespearian roles have been assigned to him. He seems to have specialized in comic roles and he was probably extremely thin. In Philip Massinger's *The Picture* (licensed on 8 June 1629), for example, he played the clown Hilario, one of a number of parts that may have capitalized on his physical characteristics. He appeared as Hodge A Countrey Fellowe in John Clavell's *The Soddered Citizen* (*c*.1630), a play in which one of his apprentices also took part. In or about 1632 the King's Men revived *The Wild Goose Chase*, in which he was cast as an impudent but unnamed servant. Diagoras in *The Maid's Tragedy* (revived *c*.1630) is another servant role he may have played. There are several early allusions to Shank which associate him with other comic performers, pointing out how he used to sing his own rhymes, and commenting on his dancing. He also wrote and performed jigs. His own entertainment, 'Shank's Ordinarie', no longer extant, was licensed for the King's Men on 16 March 1624.

As well as acting, writing, and providing costumes Shank performed other services for the King's Men. He was on occasions their financial agent and he also 'supplyed the company … with boyes' ('Dramatic records', 369). These included Thomas Pollard, John Thompson, John Honeyman, Thomas Holcome, and Nicholas Burt. Some were his apprentices; it was customary for senior members of the company to teach the boy players their art. He may also have run some kind of training and/or boarding establishment for boys.

Shank invested in the King's Men, holding shares that had originally belonged to John Heminges. On his death in 1630 the heir, Heminges's son William sold them to Shank. It was these shares and those of the surviving members of the Burbage family that were the subject of the dispute recorded in the Sharers' Papers of 1635. Robert Benfield, Eyllaerdt Swanston, and Thomas Pollard, fellow King's Men, petitioned the lord chamberlain to allow them to purchase shares in the Blackfriars and the Globe theatres. Richard Burbage's widow, Winifred, by then remarried, and her brother-in-law Cuthbert objected, as did John Shank. An order was made to allow the petitioners to buy some of Shank's shares, but no agreement was reached about the price. So on 1 August 1635 the case was passed to Sir Henry Herbert for arbitration. The matter had still not been finally resolved by Shank's death in January 1636. He was buried at St Giles Cripplegate on the 27th of that month. Winifred Shank remarried some time before 26 August 1639, when she was a legatee in the will of Richard Benfield, a kinsman of the King's player.

M. E. WILLIAMS

Sources parish register, London, St Giles Cripplegate, GL, MS 6419/3 [burial] • parish register, London, St Dunstan-in-the-West, GL, MS 10343 [marriage] • E. A. J. Honigmann and S. Brock, eds., *Playhouse wills, 1558–1642: an edition of wills by Shakespeare and his contemporaries in the London theatre* (1993) • 'Dramatic records: the lord chamberlain's office', *Malone Society Collections*, 2 (1913–31), 321–416, esp. 362–73 • M. Eccles, 'Elizabethan actors, IV: S to end', *N&Q*, 238 (1993), 165–76 • G. E. Bentley, *The Jacobean and Caroline stage*, 7 vols. (1941–68) • E. Nungezer, *A dictionary of actors* (1929) • A. Gurr, *The Shakespearian playing companies* (1996) • *The control and censorship of Caroline drama: the records of Sir Henry Herbert, master of the revels, 1623–73*, ed. N. W. Bawcutt (1996) • G. E. Bentley, *The profession of player in Shakespeare's time, 1590–1642* (1984) • T. J. King, *Casting Shakespeare's plays: London actors and their roles, 1590–1642* (1992) • D. George, 'Pre-1642 cast lists and a new one for "The Maid's Tragedy"', *Theatre Notebook*, 31 (1977), 22–7 • B. Maxwell, *Studies in Beaumont, Fletcher and Massinger* (1939) • *DNB*

Wealth at death no value given: will, PRO, PROB 10/545; Honigmann and Brock, *Playhouse wills*, 186–90

Shankly, William [Bill] **(1913–1981)**, football manager, was born on 2 September 1913 at Manse Place, Glenbuck, Ayrshire, the last of five sons and penultimate of ten children of John Shankly, then a postman and later tailor, and his wife, Barbara Gray, *née* Blyth. Glenbuck was a pit village of about 800 people and, after elementary schooling, Shankly worked as a loader above and below ground. Glenbuck's principal male recreation was football. Over time it produced some fifty league professionals, including six Scottish internationals. Though their inter-war pay was generally inferior to that of stars of the entertainment world and their average length of career was seven years (Fishwick, 80), football appealed over most ordinary working-class occupations. At Glenbuck, where mines were failing, other options were few; and all five Shankly boys became footballers, as had their two maternal uncles: Robert Blyth who played for Glasgow Rangers, then Portsmouth, of which he became chairman, and William, who played for Preston North End, then Carlisle United, of which he became director.

This Uncle Billy, who was also a publican in Carlisle, gave Shankly his opening as a professional, when Shankly signed for the club in July 1932. He was paid £4 10s. a week

William [Bill] **Shankly** (**1913–1981**), by unknown photographer, *c.*1970

when he made his first-team début against Rochdale on 31 December. After another fifteen appearances in the third division north he was sold for £500 to second-division Preston and received £50, a signing-on fee of £10, and weekly wages of £5. Shankly remained on Preston's books for the rest of his playing career—though he turned out for other teams during the war—and accumulated 297 league appearances, mostly at right-half, the first of them against Hull City on 9 December 1933, the last against Sunderland on 19 March 1949. His weekly pay was raised to £8 (£6 in summer) after his first season, when Preston were promoted to the first division; after 1946, it became £10.

Shankly was above all an energetic player, a tough tackler, fair reader of the game, and keen motivator. He scored rarely, altogether only thirteen times in the league for Preston, including eight penalties, and his first goal did not come until 2 February 1938, ironically in view of his eventual reputation, against Liverpool. He was a losing FA cup finalist in 1937 and a winner in 1938, the year he was first capped for Scotland. He played five internationals before the war, and seven during, when, as an airman who never flew, he was assigned routine jobs at various bases. At Glasgow he met a slater's clerk enlisted with the WRAF, Agnes Wren Stewart (Nessie) Fisher, daughter of James Fisher, a motor mechanic-cum-garage proprietor. They married according to Church of Scotland rites on 29 June 1944, when she was twenty-three and Shankly thirty. Two daughters, Barbara (*b.* 1945) and Jeanette (*b.* 1951), resulted. Nessie, a strong character, provided Shankly with a lifelong shield. He paid his own handsome tribute: 'I'd break my wife's legs if I played against her' (Kelly, 299).

Shankly's tenacity, uncompromising style, and experience as player marked him out for management, though it was personal connection that provided the initial invitation to take charge of Carlisle in March 1949. He moved to Grimsby in July 1951, then to Workington in January 1954; all three clubs were in the third division north and remained there under Shankly's management. Nor did he achieve promotion from the second division with Huddersfield Town, which he joined in December 1955. This undistinguished record is in part explained by scarce resources; investment in players and facilities was either unavailable or withheld, though no amount of attention could turn a dead-end club such as Workington into world champions. Shankly's forcefulness and ambition were otherwise recognized, and in December 1959 he was appointed manager of Liverpool—a post he had failed to get in 1951—at £2500 per annum. Here was a big club, then underachieving in the second division, where the team was placed below Huddersfield. Promotion was gained in 1962 and by 1974, when Shankly retired, Liverpool had won the league championship three times (1964, 1966, 1973) and were twice runners-up; the FA cup was also won twice (1965 and 1974), and Liverpool were beaten finalists in 1971. In Europe, Liverpool carried off the UEFA cup in 1973, having reached the finals of the European cup-winners' cup in 1966, and the semi-finals of the European cup in 1965 and of the UEFA cup in 1971.

Shankly's outlook was shaped by his origins in a particular place and family. Teamwork, necessary as much as natural in a mining community, became the cornerstone of his philosophy as football manager. Labour's political processes held no attraction. All politicians, even Labour's, were 'two-faced, even three-faced' (Kelly, 290). Shankly's socialism derived from Robbie Burns, not Karl Marx. It was with a life of the poet that he chose to console himself on *Desert Island Discs* in 1965; more important, in the category of luxury item—which must, according to the rules of the programme, have no practical use—he wanted to take with him the impractical football. As Shanks himself became a folk hero, he was courted by politicians who itched for his popularity to rub off on them. The OBE was conferred in 1974 and, at his death, delegates at the Labour Party conference in Brighton stood in silent respect. He always voted Labour but, at Glenbuck, he had seen trade-union officials manipulate the lives of miners just as company bosses did, and he cared for neither. The wider world, with its larger organizations and varied cultures, remained strange to Shankly, who regarded it with suspicion, even hostility. When Liverpool Football Club first entered European competitions, he blamed foreign skulduggery, corrupt officialdom, and bad luck for their defeat. This xenophobia was not reserved for foreign nationals. Abroad included everyone outside the club. His highest praise for any non-Liverpool player was 'fair … nae bad'. More commonly, they were 'rubbish … not fit to tie your bootlaces', as Ray Wilson, a member of England's world cup-winning side of 1966, discovered because, though he played for Shankly at Huddersfield, he had meanwhile joined Everton.

Shankly recognized that there were two teams in Liverpool, but Everton was not one of them: they were Liverpool and Liverpool reserves. He never tired of lauding his own players. Don Revie, manager of some outstanding Leeds teams, received regular Sunday morning telephone calls from Shankly following a Liverpool win, when every Liverpool player would be hailed as the world's best in his position. Absolute to the point of absurdity—'Some people think football is a matter of life and death. I can assure them it's much more serious than that' (*Sunday Times*, 4 Oct 1981)—Shankly exuded will-power, and his charismatic conviction animated players and supporters alike. With the Kop end at Liverpool's Anfield Stadium, where 24,000 of the most fervent fans stood, swayed, and sang, Shankly had a special affinity. He saluted them, with raised arms and hypnotic intensity of eyes, just as they saluted him. 'The Kop', he always said, 'was worth a goal start' (Kelly, 286). Characteristically, when required to register in hotels, he gave Anfield as his home address. It became a football fortress or, as some would have it, a shrine at which Shankly's Red Devils were worshipped. This nickname referred to the all-red strip which his team first adopted for a European cup match against Belgian champions Anderlecht in 1965. Liverpool had played in red shirt with white shorts and socks since 1896: it was Shankly, together with his centre-forward Ian St John, who conceived of their transformation, as a warning that Liverpool intended to become the dominant European side as Real Madrid had been in their all-white strip. That achievement eluded Shankly's teams, and he betrayed jealousy when the teams managed by his successor, Bob Paisley, did so, while Paisley, the ever unassuming former assistant, acknowledged Shankly's inspirational force as the foundation.

Deification by Liverpool fans, who kissed his feet at Wembley following the cup final victory in 1974, increasingly weighed on Shankly. Expected to heal the sick during hospital visits, he needed to explain: 'I'm no God. People seem to think I'm a miracle-maker' (Kelly, 290). The fortunes of his team—and of Everton, who won the FA cup and were twice league champions during the Shankly era—mattered the more in a city in catastrophic economic decline; yet Liverpool in the 1960s and 1970s was also a popular cultural capital, and the cult of Shankly's personality echoed the theatre of hysteria surrounding the Beatles and other pop musicians, and allied artists, poets, and comedians. Shankly's standing cannot be measured without reckoning the structure of Liverpool Football Club, however. The Littlewoods magnate John Moores was a crucial figure. This was less visible than at Everton, where he became chairman and virtual dictator in 1960; but Moores was also a principal shareholder at Liverpool and he installed Eric Sawyer—the first non-family director of Littlewoods (Clegg, 166)—as his nominee on the board. This released money and, while Shankly never enjoyed unlimited powers to buy or sell, Sawyer's backing secured the pivotal players of the Shankly era, St John as leader of the forward line and Ron Yeats as defensive colossus. The support of the directors, chaired by first Tom Williams—another friend of Moores—and then by John Smith, and of the club secretary Peter Robinson, was therefore vital, though Shankly was never comfortable in their presence, conscious of his class origins and want of education. Posh homes and cars, and the country-club circuit of golf and bridge, were alien to Shankly, whose family resided in an unpretentious three-bedroomed semi, and whose off-duty recreations were limited to weeding (unselectively: flowers were at risk) in the garden and scouring clean the cooker. He was no great reader, still less a penman; but as a wordsmith, spitting phrases out in machine-gun style, raw, abrasive, and aphoristic, he excelled. The model here was James Cagney in his cocky, tough-talking screen roles; gangster and cowboy films were Shankly's favourites and, on television, *The Untouchables* series about Eliot Ness. Boxing thrilled him too; otherwise he was a football totalitarian: he talked about it tirelessly to journalists and anyone, and was always ready for a game, with his players on the training ground or with scratch boys and dads on car-park asphalt and urban wastes. Moreover, the match must continue until Shankly's side won.

Leadership at football came naturally to Shankly. The objects were clear-cut, to score goals and not to concede them. These were secured by collective and individual effort and skill. Their right combination involved complex, even mysterious, chemistry but Shankly believed it could be manufactured from quite simple ingredients and processes. A prerequisite was physicality. Most manual labourers were muscular but suffered wear and tear, from occupational hazards and ageing and also from self-inflicted or socially acquired disabilities, such as excessive alcohol and tobacco consumption or unsuitable diet. Shankly never drank, gave up cigarettes early, and always kept in condition. Like his father, a competitive runner, he would be one of the fittest men to die. In his own playing career he was rarely unavailable through injury and, as manager, he was unsympathetic to those that were. After discovering that the champion boxer Joe Louis had been sustained by steak, Shankly insisted on this (with chips and salad) for his Liverpool teams. Their training emphasized stamina; he was proud that they pressurized opponents to the final whistle. Tom Finney, whom Shankly had known at Preston, he revered as supreme, but it was his fitness as much as ball-dribbling that impressed: 'He was grizzly strong; he could run for a week. I'd have played him in his overcoat' (Kelly, 53, 213). Shankly thought the less of America, which he visited in 1964, for never having heard of Finney.

All this indicates that Shankly's greatest gift was as a motivator rather than tactician. In that sphere the fabled Anfield 'bootroom'—the support staff of mostly former players, such as Reuben Bennett, Joe Fagan, Ronnie Moran, and, above all, Bob Paisley—was influential: scouting, coaching, scheming. Shankly tried to guard against his own impulsiveness and, in his early days at Liverpool, would consult his friend Matt Busby, shrewd manager of the great rivals Manchester United. Yet Shankly had his methodical strengths, and the institution of five-a-side games, training players in quick control, simple passing, and intelligent use of space, was central to his system. He understood too the need to conduct change within a stable framework. Like most managers at the start of his regime, he showed some ruthlessness in clearing out players whom he had inherited, where he assessed them as wanting; but the trickiest decision, having constructed a winning team, is thereafter to preserve continuity while simultaneously rebuilding. Shankly, for all his aggressive image, was sometimes thought too soft and slow about dropping star players who were past their peak; but he valued loyalty both as an ethic and as a device, and his sustained success at Liverpool entitles him to be ranked with the best managers of his generation, next to Jock Stein (of Glasgow Celtic) and Matt Busby, fellow Scots from similar backgrounds.

Retirement for Shankly was painful. He soon regretted his decision to resign, tried to retract it, and felt hurt about being sidelined by the club he had so well served, though this was essential for Paisley to establish his own authority. On 26 September 1981 Shankly was admitted to Broadgreen Hospital, Liverpool, following a heart attack; he died there on 29 September, with his wife at his bedside. He was cremated at Priory Road crematorium, Liverpool, on 2 October. In life stocky, Shankly's stature was enhanced after death when in 1997 Tom Murphy's 7 feet 6 inch bronze figure of him, weighing three-quarters of a ton, was planted near the entrance to the Anfield Kop. It captured the famous attitude: club scarf about the neck, arms aloft, intense, pugnacious, victorious.

PHILIP WALLER

Sources S. F. Kelly, *Bill Shankly: it's much more important than that: a biography* (1996) · D. Bowler, *Shanks: the authorised biography of Bill Shankly* (1996) · *Liverpool Daily Post* (29 Sept 1981) · *Liverpool Daily Post* (30 Sept 1981) · *Daily Telegraph* (5 Dec 1997) · N. Fishwick, *English football and society, 1910–1950* (1989) · www.shankly.com · B. Clegg, *The man who made Littlewoods: the story of John Moores* (1993) · b. cert. · m. cert. · d. cert.

Archives FILM BFI NFTVA, *Arena*, BBC 2, 28 March 1997 · BFI NFTVA, documentary footage

Likenesses photograph, *c*.1970, Hult. Arch. [*see illus.*] · S. Hale, photograph, 1975, Anfield stadium, Liverpool · T. Murphy, bronze statue, 1997, Anfield stadium, Liverpool

Wealth at death £99,867: probate, 21 Oct 1981, *CGPLA Eng. & Wales*

Shanks, Alexander (1801–1845), engineer and lawnmower manufacturer, was born at Milnetown of Bridgetown, Forfarshire, on 3 September 1801, the son of Alexander Shanks, a wright, and his wife, Elizabeth Ferguson. Very little is known about his early life, with the exception that he had extensive family connections in the flax industry. In 1825 he established his own spinning and machine making firm in Ogilvy Place, Arbroath. His interest at this time was primarily in the mechanization of the labour-intensive process of converting raw flax into linen. In 1834 his efforts were rewarded when he successfully patented a process 'for preparing and dressing hemp and other fibrous substances'. On 23 March 1829 he married Ann Braid, of the parish of St Vigeans in Forfarshire; her brothers Alexander and William subsequently assisted Shanks in the development of his company. Their son James [*see below*], was born at West Kaptie Street, Arbroath.

In 1840 Shanks founded the firm of Alexander Shanks & Son, with its works in Dens Road, Arbroath, where iron castings, steam engines, and excavating machinery were produced. In 1842 he took out his first patent for a lawnmower which could both cut and roll the grass in a single operation. The successful trial of the machine in July 1842 was drawn to the attention of the *Mechanical Magazine*, which published a glowing review. The anonymous author of the account acclaimed Shanks's machine as superior to its competitors, thereby permitting the Arbroath firm to describe itself as 'manufacturers of the first effective lawnmower'. Shanks's lawnmower was horse-drawn, the driver walking behind, guiding the machine and controlling the horse's reins. The mower's promotion was assisted by William Fullerton, and by Lindsay Carnegie of Boysack, who placed an order for a pony-drawn mower, 27 inches wide, for use on his 2.5 acre lawn at Kinblethmont.

On 16 July 1845 Alexander Shanks died of consumption at the premature age of forty-four; he was buried at Arbroath churchyard. His son **James Shanks** (1829–1909), who was trained in business and law, then forsook his job in the town clerk's office to run the business, and the firm's subsequent rapid expansion owed a great deal to the energetic and committed way in which he marketed the lawnmower. The Great Exhibition held at the Crystal Palace in 1851 provided him with the opportunity to display his 42 inch machine, aptly nicknamed 'Shanks's five-drummer'. On 25 May 1855 a patent was awarded for improvements. Four years later James Shanks took an improved version to the Paris Exhibition of Industry. This was purchased by Emperor Napoleon III for the Imperial Gardens at St Cloud. In order to promote the lawnmower further, James Shanks acquired a London showroom and office at 27 Leadenhall Street about 1860.

Under James Shanks's control the firm expanded rapidly; it abandoned the earlier diverse manufactures to concentrate on the production of agricultural and horticultural implements, and of marine and land engines, in addition to lawnmowers. It was due to his inventive disposition, energy, and research that the firm was able to acquire its national and international reputation.

Shanks was succeeded by his four sons, Alexander, James, Frederick, and David, who took control of the activities of this traditional family business. In 1894 the business became a limited liability company. James Shanks died in 1909 at 8 Alexandra Place, Arbroath, and was buried at the western cemetery. In spite of mixed fortunes in the twentieth century the firm survived until it was taken over in the 1960s.

Alexander Shanks has been widely regarded as the originator of the first successful lawnmower. He is also widely acknowledged for the role he played in establishing Alexander Shanks & Son. His claim to fame merits some revision. Firstly, there is controversy about who actually invented the first lawnmower, though he undoubtedly designed the first efficient machine. Secondly, the role played by his son James in the subsequent technical development and popularization of the lawnmower should be recognized. The nineteenth-century convention of retaining the father's Christian name as part of the company name sustained Alexander's reputation long after his untimely death, when his son James was developing the business.

In spite of the fact that the original lawnmower was horse-drawn, the Shanks family was not associated with the well-known nineteenth-century expression, 'Shanks's pony', the origin of which rather surprisingly predates both Alexander Shanks and his son. JOHN MARTIN

Sources *Arbroath Herald* (5 June 1909) • *Arbroath Guide* (19 March 1955) • 'The great lawnmower debate', *Arbroath Herald Christmas Annual* (1983) • Catalogues and trade brochures of Alexander Shanks and Son, Dens Iron Work, Arbroath, Arbroath Museum, Arbroath • Mr Rae, 'Alexander Shanks and Son', Arbroath Museum, Arbroath [unpublished article] • Kinnettles parish register, Kinnettles, Forfarshire, 3 Sept 1801 [birth] • Arbroath parish register, Arbroath churchyard, Arbroath, Forfarshire, 16 July 1845 [death] • A. Hall, 'The history of the lawn mower, part I: 1800–1900', *Farm and horticultural equipment collector*, 18 (JanxFeb 1995), 6–8 • A. Hall, 'The history of the lawn mower, part II: 1830–1900', *Farm and horticultural equipment collector*, 19 (MarchxApril 1995), 12–13

Archives Arbroath Museum, Arbroath

Shanks, James (1800–1867), chemical engineer, was born on 24 April 1800 in Lochwinnoch, near Johnstone, Renfrewshire, the eldest of at least nine children of William Shanks, millwright and engineer. His mother was Isabel Anderson. In 1821, after assisting in his father's engineering works for several years, he went to Glasgow University, where he studied chemistry, under Andrew Ure, and medicine to qualify as a doctor. He returned to Johnstone and practised medicine for three years, during which time he also gave scientific lectures at Johnstone's Mechanics' Institute. He then abandoned medicine in favour of the chemical industry. He started a small chemical works in Paisley, manufacturing alum and potassium chromate. This did not prove a success and he subsequently accepted positions in Worcester, and later in Newcastle upon Tyne.

In 1836 William Gossage appointed him, together with George Elliott, to assist in the erection and development of Gossage's absorption towers (patented in 1836) at the British Alkali works in Stoke Prior, Worcestershire. In 1841 he moved to St Helens and erected Gossage towers for Gamble and Crosfields. When the Gamble and Crosfields partnership was dissolved in 1845, Shanks became a partner in the new firm, Crosfield Bros. & Co., a position he held for the rest of his life. The firm became Crosfield and Shanks.

Shanks took out the first of several patents for alkali manufacture in the spring of 1841, for improvements in the manufacture of carbonate of soda. In September 1858 he patented a process for preparing chlorine using calcium chromate, for which he was awarded a medal at the 1862 international exhibition. His final patent, taken out in 1863, for improvements in the manufacture of caustic soda and caustic potash, seems never to have gone beyond the experimental stage.

Shanks's name is permanently associated with the system of vats, known as 'Shanks's vats', introduced in 1861 for the extraction of the soda from black ash in the Leblanc method for the production of alkali, but these were never the subject of a patent. Although there is a claim that these vats were introduced by Charles Tennant Dunlop and Heinrich Buff of Giessen, it is generally accepted that Shanks was responsible for their development.

Shanks was president of the Mechanics' Institute of St Helens. He also assisted the St Helens Permanent Building Society. An upright and honest man, he was a Baptist and regularly attended the Myrtle Street Chapel in Liverpool, where the Revd Hugh Stowell Brown was minister. He also worked hard to promote the formation of a Baptist church in St Helens.

Shanks was married twice but had no children. The maiden name of one of his wives (probably the second) was Watt. He died on 13 August 1867 in St Helens. His estate, valued at under £16,000, was distributed between his numerous nephews and nieces.

ANN K. NEWMARK, *rev.*

Sources J. Fenwick Allen, *Some founders of the chemical industry: men to be remembered* (1906) • D. W. F. Hardie, *A history of the chemical industry in Widnes* (1950) • J. F. Iselin and P. Le Neve Foster, eds., *Reports by the juries on the…[International] Exhibition* (1863), 221

Wealth at death under £16,000: probate, 26 Sept 1867, *CGPLA Eng. & Wales*

Shanks, James (1829–1909). *See under* Shanks, Alexander (1801–1845).

Shanks, John. *See* Shank, John (*d.* 1636).

Shanks, Michael James (1927–1984), journalist and economist, was born on 12 April 1927 in London, the only son and the eldest of three children of (Alan) James Shanks of Mill Hill, managing director in the firm of Moussec drinks, and his wife, Margaret Lee. He was educated at Blundell's School, Tiverton, and at Balliol College, Oxford, which initially he attended in Trinity term 1945. He then joined the Royal Artillery and was demobilized as a lieutenant in 1947. He was at Balliol again from 1948 to 1950 and obtained a second-class degree in the short course for philosophy, politics, and economics (1950).

In 1950–51 Shanks lectured in economics at Williams College, Massachusetts, USA. He then started on his first career as an economic observer and commentator. During the ten years from 1954 he served successively as leader and feature writer, labour correspondent, and industrial editor on the *Financial Times*. During this period he travelled extensively in western and eastern Europe as well as in North America. Other part-time assignments included consultancy jobs with Granada Television and Penguin Books Ltd. In addition he became one of the best-known commentators on current affairs and made frequent appearances on both radio and television. In 1964–5 he was economic correspondent for the *Sunday Times*.

At the beginning of 1965 Shanks started his second career, as a public servant. When the Labour government set up the Department of Economic Affairs he joined it and became its industrial policy co-ordinator with co-responsibility for industrial policy, thus leading its team of industrial advisers. Having left the department in 1967 he started the connections with industry and business that became so prominent later in his life. He was appointed economic adviser to Leyland Motors and helped to create the British Leyland Motor Corporation, for which he worked as director of marketing services and planning from 1968 to 1971. During this time he was also special writer on economic and management topics for the business section of *The Times*. In 1971 he moved to British Oxygen, where he was chief executive (finance and planning) and subsequently, from January 1973, director of group strategy.

Shanks was always an internationalist; he knew that the world was too small a place for lessons learned in one country to go unheeded in his own. So it was no surprise that when the United Kingdom joined the European Economic Community he chose to return to public service. He was appointed in June 1973 as one of the four British directors-general, in charge of employment policy and social affairs. During his period at the commission he inaugurated and implemented the community's first ever social action programme. French was his working language during this period; he was also able to work in German.

In January 1976 Shanks resigned from his post at the commission in order to return to business interests in Britain. He was a leading consultant at this time and he became a director of a number of companies, including BOC International Ltd in 1976 and P-E Consultants Ltd in 1977. From 1976 he was a director of Barmel Associates Ltd and, from 1977, of the Henley Centre for Forecasting and Environmental Resources Ltd. At the time of his death he was also a director of Rouger SA, and chairman of Barratt & Co. Ltd. From 1977 to 1982 he was chairman of Datastream plc, and he was appointed chairman of George Bassett (Holdings) in 1982, having been a director since 1977.

At the same time Shanks continued to devote a considerable portion of his time to public service. He succeeded Michael Young as chairman of the National Consumer Council in 1977. Founded in 1975 the council was still young and uncertain of its direction. Shanks consolidated its position and led its attempt to map out a specifically consumer view of the economic world in two major pieces of economic analysis—*Real Money, Real Choice* (1978) and *The Consumer and the State* (1978). He was reappointed twice as chairman, and under his leadership the council achieved a reputation for clear thinking and positive action on behalf of consumers.

In 1953 Shanks married Elizabeth Juliet, daughter of Geoffrey Bower Richardson, general practitioner in Penzance and surgeon at the West Cornwall Hospital; they had three sons and one daughter. Elizabeth died in 1972, and in 1973 Shanks married a widow, Patricia Jaffe, who had six children. She was the daughter of Thomas Aspin, schoolmaster. There were no children from this second marriage. Shanks was a prolific author; he wrote a number of books and contributed to many journals, pamphlets, and symposia. Perhaps the most influential of his books was *The Stagnant Society* (1961), which diagnosed Britain's economic ills.

Shanks had a wide circle of friends among his colleagues in the many different worlds he inhabited. All remember his friendliness, quickness, and wit; his friends and colleagues valued also his deep concern with the fundamental obligations of decency in society—a concern which surfaced clearly in his last book, *What's wrong with the modern world* (1978). He could never have held together his different careers—economic commentator, public servant, businessman, and industrialist—without enormous energy. Shanks died in hospital in Sheffield on 13 January 1984. M. J. MONTAGUE, *rev.*

Sources *The Times* (14 Jan 1984) · D. Kynaston, *The Financial Times: a centenary history* (1988) · *WWW* · D. Griffiths, ed., *The encyclopedia of the British press, 1422–1992* (1992) · *CGPLA Eng. & Wales* (1984)
Archives SOUND BL NSA, current affairs recording · BL NSA, oral history interview
Wealth at death £307,894: probate, 15 June 1984, *CGPLA Eng. & Wales*

Shannon. For this title name *see* Boyle, Henry, first earl of Shannon (1681x7–1764).

Shannon, Charles Haslewood (1863–1937), lithographer and painter, was born on 26 April 1863 at Quarrington rectory, Lincolnshire, the second son of Frederick William Shannon (*c.*1821–1909?), rector of Quarrington with Old Sleaford, and his first wife, Catherine Emma (*b. c.*1835), the daughter of Dr Daniel Manthorp, of Thorpe Abbey, Thorpe-le-Soken, Essex. Shannon's father remarried after 1881. Shannon had four sisters, three brothers, and one half-brother. He attended St John's School, Leatherhead, from 1873 to 1881, and then studied at the City and Guilds Technical Art School, an extension of the Lambeth Art School, from 1881 to 1885. He worked under Charles Roberts, a reproductive wood-engraver, and was joined in 1882 by Charles de Sousy *Ricketts (1866–1931), who was three years younger than him. It was the start of a lifelong friendship, which was strengthened by their uncommon artistic idealism and their interests in literature, the Pre-Raphaelites, and French symbolism. Their training proved useless as a means of employment, since the photographic process had generally replaced engraving; so, as both young artists were gifted draughtsmen, they exhibited and sent illustrations to periodicals, while Shannon also taught part-time at Croydon School of Art. However, by 1888 they had devised a strategy for their joint career by which Ricketts was to provide their income while Shannon perfected his abilities as a painter without exhibiting; this policy was vindicated in 1897, when Shannon finally sent two paintings and some lithographs to Munich,

Charles Haslewood Shannon (1863–1937), self-portrait, 1897

where he was awarded a gold medal. Shannon's admirable self-portrait, *The Man in a Black Shirt* (National Portrait Gallery, London) was completed that year.

Ricketts was the dominant figure in the artistic and literary circle which formed around them in Chelsea (1888–98) and then more privately at Richmond (1898–1902). William Rothenstein remembered that the artists' partnership in the nineties 'seemed perfect; each set off the other in looks as in mind', Shannon being as 'quiet and inarticulate as Ricketts was restless and eloquent'. They were believed by some to have been lovers, but there is no conclusive evidence about this. Joint activities included their magazine *The Dial* (1889–97), design and illustration for Oscar Wilde's books, and wood-engravings for editions of *Daphnis and Chloe* (1893) and *Hero and Leander* (1894). Then a bequest from Ricketts's grandfather enabled him, partnered by a wealthy lawyer, William Llewellyn Hacon, to set up in 1896 an imprint of their own, the Vale Press (1896–1904), which they complemented with a shop where work by Shannon and their friends could be bought.

Shannon's artistic career was now on course, mainly as a portraitist, but also as a painter of idylls and other figure subjects. The two facets of his art had already been evident in his lithographs, which many colleagues in the nineties felt were his outstanding achievement. Shannon had his own lithographic press, which enabled him to experiment, for example, with a method of scraping away the chalk on a lithographic stone—as in *A Lithograph in White Line* (1891)—achieving delicate and silvery tone in prints such as *Summer* (1892) or *The Shepherd in a Mist* (1892), and producing felicitous portraits of friends, such as *Lucien Pissarro* (1895), *Alphonse Legros* (1896), or *Thomas Sturge Moore in a Cloak* (1896). Shannon returned to lithography in 1904, but his aesthetic aims were by then more emphatic, his line stronger, and his figure subjects less idealized. Nevertheless, his *œuvre* as a lithographer, containing more than a hundred works, is a major British contribution to print-making.

Shannon's standing as a painter may be gauged from work in both British and foreign collections. His traditional technique, deriving from the Venetians and the English eighteenth century, his thoughtful compositions, and his restrained palette were the bases of his contemplative art. An early success was *The Lady with a Cyclamen*, formerly in the collection of the Hon. Mrs Chaloner Dowdall (1899, Walker Art Gallery, Liverpool); a favourite sitter, Kathleen Bruce, is seen as *The Sculptress* (1904, Musée d'Orsay, Paris) and in *The Winged Hat* (Johannesburg Art Gallery). Among the works in the Tate collection are *The Bath of Venus* (1898–1904) and one of several portraits of Mrs Patrick Campbell (1908); a portrait of Princess Patricia of Connaught (1918–19) is at the National Gallery of Canada in Ottawa.

From 1902 Ricketts and Shannon returned to London to live in a flat in a block in Lansdowne Road, Holland Park, built by their friend and patron Sir Edmund Davis. It was here and at Chilham, the Davises' Kent residence (the artists had the Norman keep), that they worked and entertained. Their resources, however, were stretched by travel and a passion for collecting in a variety of fields, whether old masters (especially drawings), Egyptian and classical antiquities, or Japanese prints. Their fine collection largely remains at the British Museum and the Fitzwilliam Museum, Cambridge, a testimony to their knowledge and judgement.

Shannon was a tall man, fair haired in youth and calm in manner. He became an active exhibitor, for example, at the New English Art Club and the International Society, and was elected ARA in 1911 and RA in 1920. He never married; Kathleen Bruce, to his dismay, married the Antarctic explorer Captain Robert Falconer Scott; several affairs with women imperilled his life with Ricketts, but none lasted. In January 1929 he suffered a fall while hanging a picture on the stairs of Townshend House, Regent's Park, where they had moved in 1923. He suffered brain damage, and never recovered. Ricketts sold some works from the collection to pay nursing expenses, and more went after Ricketts's death in 1931. Shannon died at 21 Kew Gardens Road, Richmond, on 18 March 1937, and his ashes were buried at Quarrington, Lincolnshire.

JOSEPH DARRACOTT

Sources *DNB* • J. G. P. Delaney, *Charles Ricketts: a biography* (1990) • J. G. P. Delaney, *The lithographs of Charles Shannon, 1863–1937* (1978) • J. Darracott, ed., *All for art: the Ricketts and Shannon collection* (1979) [exhibition catalogue, Fitzwilliam Museum, Cambridge, 9 Oct – 3 Dec 1979] • J. Darracott, *The world of Charles Ricketts* (1980) • Shannon file, Usher Gallery, Lincoln • *CGPLA Eng. & Wales* (1937) • b. cert.

Archives BL, corresp., papers, and travel journals, Add. MSS 58085–58097, 58110–58118, 61713–61724 | Boston PL, letters to Harry Quilter • FM Cam., letters to Sir William Rothenstein • Harvard U., Houghton L., letters to Sir William Rothenstein • Hunt. L., letters, mainly to Harold Dowdall • NYPL, letters to John Quinn

Likenesses A. Legros, drawings, 1896–7, FM Cam. • W. Rothenstein, lithograph, 1897 (with Charles Ricketts), NPG • C. Shannon, self-portrait, oils, 1897, NPG [*see illus.*] • W. Rothenstein, pastel drawing, 1903, BM • photographs, 1903–7, NPG • J. E. Blanche, oils,

1904 (with Charles Ricketts), Tate collection • F. Dodd, chalk drawing, 1905, FM Cam. • M. Beerbohm, watercolour and pen caricature, 1907 (with Charles Ricketts), FM Cam. • M. Beerbohm, caricature, 1911 (with Charles Ricketts; after painting by Rossetti), Johannesburg Art Gallery, South Africa • E. Dulac, watercolour and pen caricature, 1914? (with Charles Ricketts), FM Cam. • C. Shannon, self-portrait, oils, 1917, FM Cam. • C. Shannon, self-portrait, lithograph, 1918, BM, NPG • K. Kennet, bronze statuette, Leeds City Art Gallery • C. Shannon, self-portrait, lithograph, Carlisle City Art Gallery • R. F. Wells, bronze sculpture, FM Cam.

Wealth at death £41,385 19*s*. 3*d*.: probate, 26 May 1937, *CGPLA Eng. & Wales*

Shannon, Sir James Jebusa (1862–1923), portrait painter, was born on 3 February 1862 at Auburn, New York, USA, one of seven children of Patrick Shannon (*d*. *c*.1896) and his wife, Mary, *née* Nicholson, both of whom were Irish. Patrick Shannon's profession as a contractor and railway builder required frequent relocation. After some interim moves the family settled in St Catherines, Ontario, Canada, about 1875, and it was there that Shannon reportedly received his first art instruction from one Wright (probably William E. Wright, (*fl*. 1865–1882)). In 1878 he enrolled at the National Art Training School, South Kensington, London (now the Royal College of Art), where he studied for three years under the guidance of Edward John Poynter. His training culminated in 1880, when he was awarded the gold medal in the school's annual competition and received a commission from Queen Victoria to paint a portrait of the Hon. Horatia Stopford, who had been appointed woman of the bedchamber in 1877 (Royal Collection). The painting was displayed, on the queen's command, at the Royal Academy's summer exhibition in 1881. Shannon exhibited at the academy every year thereafter (excepting 1885 and 1890) until his death. Canvases from this early phase of his professional activity display tightly handled brushwork and a tentative, academic approach to his sitters. Soon, however, his portraits compared favourably with contemporary portrait productions by Sir John Everett Millais and James Sant (for example, *Madame Patey*, 1884; Tate collection).

By 1885 Shannon was occupying rooms at the Merton Villas Studios in Manresa Road, Chelsea, where his circle of friends included Henry Herbert La Thangue. Under the influence of La Thangue and other French-trained artist friends he occasionally adopted the square-brush facture inspired by the art of Jules Bastien-Lepage. He established a pattern of submitting his more conservative paintings to the Royal Academy and showing his aesthetically progressive works at, for example, the New English Art Club (of which he was a founding member), the Grosvenor Gallery, the Society of British Artists, the New Gallery, and the Institute of Painters in Oil Colours. His *Henry Vigne, Master of the Epping Forest Harriers* gained wide critical notice when it was shown at the Grosvenor Gallery in 1888 and at the Paris Universal Exhibition in 1889, where it won a gold medal. At this juncture Shannon's art captured the attention of Violet Manners, marchioness of Granby (later duchess of Rutland), who became his most consistent patron. His dramatic rise as a favoured painter of the upper classes was witnessed in 1892 by his acquisition of a large studio-cum-residence on the prestigious Holland Park Road. His garden often provided the setting for the romanticizing, neo-Georgian-type portraits for which he was popular (for example, *Lady Dickson-Poynder and her Daughter Joan* (exh. RA, 1905; priv. coll.).

In 1886 Shannon married Florence Mary Cartwright (*d*. 1948), a former student at the South Kensington School of Needlework; their only child, Katherine Marjorie (Kitty), was born on 3 February 1887. Both Florence and Kitty Shannon sat regularly for what were referred to as Shannon's 'subject pictures' (for example, *Jungle Tales*, 1895; Metropolitan Museum of Art, New York), an aspect of his art that was featured in a one-man exhibition at the Fine Art Society, London, in 1896. Shannon's stylistic eclecticism is best revealed in these uncommissioned works, whose techniques range from a colourful, modified impressionist mode—acquired during his sojourns at the artists' colony of Egmond ann Zee, in the Netherlands, with the American painters George Hitchcock and Gari Melchers, and exemplified by *The Purple Stocking* (*c*.1894; South African National Gallery, Cape Town)—to the sombre realism that defines the 1902 portrait of his friend the illustrator Phil May (Tate collection).

Shannon spent three consecutive winter seasons, beginning in 1904–5, painting in the United States; over that period he secured more than thirty commissions from notable American families and enjoyed three small, one-man exhibitions at M. Knoedler & Co., New York. For the most part, however, he maintained a thoroughly English identity, exhibiting in the British sections of international exhibitions. He was elected associate of the Royal Academy in 1897 and Royal Academician in 1909 (his diploma work, *Black and Silver*, is a portrait of his daughter). In addition to being a founder of the Society of Portrait Painters (which under the term of his presidency, from 1910 to 1923, attained royal patronage) and a founder of the Chelsea Arts Club he was a member of the Belgian Royal Academy of Sciences, Letters, and Arts; the Royal Hibernian Academy; and the Royal British Colonial Society of America. He was knighted in 1922.

Shannon died at 198 Cromwell Road, Kensington, a London nursing home, on 6 March 1923, of complications from a steadily advancing paralysis that began after a riding accident about 1911. Memorial exhibitions were mounted at several venues in the United States, at the Leicester Galleries, London, and at the winter exhibition at the Royal Academy in 1928. Shannon's output was decidedly uneven in quality and his reputation has been understandably overshadowed by that of his more brilliant contemporary John Singer Sargent. However, his finest works attest to his deserving a place among the upper ranks of portrait specialists of his time.

BARBARA DAYER GALLATI

Sources B. Gallati, 'Portraits of artistry and artifice: the career of Sir James Jebusa Shannon, 1862–1923', PhD diss., City University of New York, 1992 • K. Shannon, *For my children* (1933) • J. Creelman, 'An American painter of the English court', *Munsey's Magazine*, 14 (Nov 1895), 128–37 • A. L. Baldry, 'J. J. Shannon, painter', *The Magazine of Art* (20 Nov 1896), 1–5 • M. Roberts, 'A colony of artists', *Scottish Art Review*, 2 (Aug 1889), 72–7 • L. Hind, 'The work of J. J.

Shannon', *The Studio*, 8 (July 1896), 66–75 • F. Rinder, 'J. J. Shannon, A. R. A.', *Art Journal*, 53 (1901), 41–5 • C. Brinton, 'Shannon and pictorial portraiture', *Harper's Monthly Magazine*, 111 (1905), 204–13 • C. Brinton, 'A painter of fair women', *Munsey's Magazine*, 35 (May 1906), 132–43 • C. Dakers, *The Holland Park circle* (1999) • G. P. Jacomb-Hood, *With brush and pencil* (1925) • K. Anderson, 'Anderson's impressions', *The Bellman*, 8 (March 1910), 292–4 • *CGPLA Eng. & Wales* (1923) • private information (2004) [descendants] • *The Times* (7 March 1923)

Likenesses J. J. Shannon, self-portrait, oils, 1884, priv. coll.; repro. in B. Gallati, 'James Jebusa Shannon', *The Magazine Antiques*, 134 (Nov 1988), 1132–41 • photograph, *c*.1896, repro. in Hind, 'The work of J. J. Shannon', 67, • J. J. Shannon, group portrait, self-portrait, *c*.1901 (*My family*), priv. coll.; repro. in Rinder, 'J. J. Shannon, A. R. A.', 41 • O. Rouland, oils, *c*.1910, National Museum of American Art, Washington, DC • J. J. Shannon, self-portrait, oils, *c*.1919, NPG

Wealth at death £21,162 4*s*. 11*d*.: probate, 27 April 1923, *CGPLA Eng. & Wales*

Shapley [*married names* Salt, Gorton], **Olive Mary** (1910–1999), broadcaster, was born on 10 April 1910 at 10 Tresco Road, Peckham, London, the only daughter and youngest of the three children of William Gilbert Shapley (1870/71–1939), local government officer, and his wife, Kate Sophie, *née* Reimann (1871/2–1958), who had worked as a servant before her marriage. Her father was a sanitary inspector for London county council and, later, chief inspector of the public health department. Her oldest brother, Frank, eleven years her senior, was killed in the battle of Jutland in 1916. Bill, who was five years older than her, became a journalist. Both parents were Unitarians and, although Olive later declared herself agnostic, she returned to Unitarianism towards the end of her life. At the age of ten she started at the Mary Datchelor Girls' School, Camberwell Green, where she remained until she was nineteen. In 1929 she won a place at St Hugh's College, Oxford, to study history. There she established a lifelong friendship with Barbara Betts (later Barbara Castle) and discovered the mysteries of sex and communism with which she, like so many of her generation, flirted while an undergraduate. She graduated in 1932 with a third-class degree and stayed on at Oxford to take a postgraduate certificate in education. After a spell as a Workers' Education Association lecturer in Surrey and training as a nursery school teacher she applied, in late 1934, for a post at the BBC, in Manchester, to organize *Children's Hour*. To her surprise she was offered the job and so began a lifetime's involvement with the BBC.

The BBC's regional programme had started in 1930 and Manchester was the production centre for the whole of the north region, from the Scottish borders to the Peak District. For a brief period before the war it was the most exciting place to work in the BBC. Shapley's activities soon went well beyond *Children's Hour*. She produced a memorable radio drama, *Plague at Eyam*, about the coming of the black death to a Derbyshire village. But her enduring contribution to broadcasting was with her recorded 'actuality' programmes about the lives and experiences of working-class men and women in the north of England at that time. She produced remarkable programmes, using the BBC's one and only 7-ton recording van, about shopping, the homeless, barge people, an all-night transport cafe, miners' wives, and the BBC itself. Her two most ambitious productions, of which recordings still exist, were *They Speak for themselves*, about Mass-Observation (1 June 1939), and *The Classic Soil* (6 July 1939), written by Joan Littlewood, which compared the living conditions of the working class in Manchester with those described by Frederick Engels 100 years earlier.

On 14 July 1939 Shapley married John Scarlett Alexander Salt (1905–1947) (great-grandson of Sir Titus Salt of Saltaire), then director of programmes in Manchester. Much to her indignation, she had to resign from the BBC to conform with its policy on staff inter-marriage. Her freelance services, however, were in immediate demand when war was declared, and her sympathetic skills as a documentary maker were now applied to the impact of evacuation and the blitz on people's lives. Late in 1941 Salt was posted to the BBC's North America office in New York. From there Olive produced a regular *Letter from America* (the title was subsequently taken over by Alistair Cooke, in whose apartment the Salts lived for some months) for transmission on *Children's Hour* in London. She suffered a severe nervous breakdown in 1942, from which psychoanalysis helped her to recover. Her first son, Daniel Alexander, was born in New York on 15 August 1943. Back in Manchester she gave birth to her second child, Nicholas John, on 7 December 1945, and to a daughter, Christina Mary, on 11 May 1947. Within months her husband was stricken with inoperable stomach cancer, and died in the same year on the morning of Boxing day.

With three small children to support, Shapley returned to full-time work. In 1949 she moved to London to become the presenter of *Woman's Hour*, with which she was associated for the next twenty years. Unobtrusively she introduced talk about a whole range of matters of concern to women that had hitherto been unmentionable: not only medical and sexual topics, but also psychology and human relationships. Listeners were advised that they might wish to turn down their radios, especially if there were young children about. Throughout the 1950s Shapley was busy, writing a regular features column for *Modern Woman*, taking in lodgers, and working on early BBC television, for which she presented a series of interviews with prominent women called *Women Today* and, for children, *Olive Shapley Tells a Story*.

On 31 October 1952 Shapley married Christopher Bellhouse Gorton (1894–1959), fifteen years her senior, who worked for the Manchester textile firm Tootals. The following year they moved back to Manchester and bought a large Victorian villa in Didsbury, called Rose Hill, where Shapley lived very happily for nearly thirty years. She continued to work as a presenter for television in London, but in 1959 switched to production. Her most successful programme, in her own judgement, was *Something to Read*, for which she recruited Brian Redhead, then a young journalist with the *Manchester Guardian*, as presenter. In the same year, and again with devastating suddenness, her second husband died of a heart attack on 2 November, leaving her once more alone with three children.

The immediate impact of Christopher's death was the

gradual return of depression and a breakdown. With the help of friends and BBC colleagues Shapley recovered and continued to support and care for her family and to work in radio and television. In her later professional years she presented the Manchester edition of *Woman's Hour*, three series of *The Shapley File* on social issues, as well as many individual contributions to radio magazine and feature programmes. She finally retired from broadcasting in 1973. After her children had left home she established the Rose Hill Trust and for fourteen years ran it as a refuge for unsupported mothers and babies. In 1979 she took in some of the Vietnamese 'boat people'. In 1982 she sold Rose Hill and moved into a small terraced house in Didsbury, and in 1992 moved to Llanidloes, in Radnorshire, to be near her son Nicholas. Meanwhile she had taken to travelling and became a regular visitor to India and the Himalayas in her sixties. In her seventies she campaigned vigorously, but without success, to establish a community for older single people like herself. On this topic she wrote to Katherine Whitehorn:

> I am 72 years old, but *will* not be tidied away neatly and there are many like me. I have just come back from a rough tour in India where I travelled with my 9 year old grandson and it was grand to feel part of the human race again. But living alone in a small neat house is simply not on as far as I am concerned. (Shapley files, BBC WAC 341/48/1, 1 July 1982)

In 1996 Shapley's autobiography, *Broadcasting a Life*, was published with the help of her daughter Christina. She wrote the story of her life in part so that her three children should know something of their father, whose untimely death was most movingly described in her book. It was also the record of a life in broadcasting, by one who was committed to letting people speak for themselves on radio and television. Much of what appeared in the book was first broadcast by Shapley herself over a thirty-year period. Her life story, with its difficulties and triumphs, exemplifies what it was to be a professional working woman, wife, and often single mother in the twentieth century. Shortly after the book was published Shapley suffered a stroke and lost much of her speech. She died in a home for the elderly, Crosfield House, Dark Lane, Rhayader, Radnorshire, on 13 March 1999, and was survived by her three children. She was buried at Thorpe Arch church, Boston Spa, next to her first husband, John Salt, on 3 July 1999. PADDY SCANNELL

Sources O. Shapley, *Broadcasting a life* (1996) • BBC WAC • P. Scannell and D. Cardiff, *A social history of British broadcasting*, [1] (1991) • *The Guardian* (15 March 1999) • *The Independent* (20 March 1999) • *The Times* (13 April 1999) • private information (2004) [Nicholas Salt] • m. cert. • d. cert.

Archives BBC WAC, personal papers and recordings and scripts • priv. coll. | BBC WAC | SOUND BBC sound archives

Likenesses photograph, 1939, repro. in *The Independent* • photograph, repro. in *The Guardian* • photograph, repro. in *The Times*

Wealth at death £25,000—net: probate, 17 June 1999, *CGPLA Eng. & Wales*

Shardlow [Shardelowe], **Sir John** (*d.* **1344**), justice, was probably born at Thompson, Norfolk, though the name of the family may have been derived from the village of Shardlow in Derbyshire. He became a serjeant-at-law in 1318, and in August 1319 received the first of more than 130 commissions of oyer and terminer recorded to him in the chancery rolls. During the London eyre of 1321 he acted as pleader in twenty-nine cases, and received a fee of 40*s*. for his services on behalf of the city of London after the conclusion of the eyre. In July 1326 he is mentioned as chief justice of the common bench in Ireland but seems never to have taken up his duties there. During Michaelmas term 1329 he acted temporarily as justice of the king's bench; a permanent appointment to the common pleas followed in January 1332. In this year he also became a knight of the Bath. Shardlow appears in year-book reports from Michaelmas 1320 onwards, though his contributions cannot always be clearly identified, because the abbreviated form of his surname may sometimes refer to his colleagues William Shareshull (*d.* 1370) or Robert Scarborough. Apart from his work in the common pleas he also frequently acted as justice of assize on the eastern circuit and as justice of gaol delivery, as well as on special commissions; in October 1337 for instance he was appointed to deal with deserters from the royal army in the north of England.

After Edward III's unexpected return to London on 30 November 1340 Shardlow's career seemed to have come to an end when, despite a commission to act as justice of oyer and terminer addressed to him on 8 January 1341, he was among those royal officials who by 13 January had been arrested and subjected to the scrutiny of a judicial commission. In the following month he was among the thirteen justices against whom accusations and complaints were invited. His disgrace lasted for more than a year until on 16 May 1342 he was again appointed justice of the common pleas. In the second phase of his career he received several commissions to investigate smuggling, the import of counterfeit money, and other economic offences. This was part of a concerted campaign in several counties; Shardlow concentrated mainly on East Anglia. Summoned to parliament in July 1332 he also heard petitions from Scotland, Wales, Ireland, Gascony, and other areas during the Easter parliament of 1343.

The income from Shardlow's legal practice enabled him to lend substantial sums of money (£20, £40) to neighbouring landholders in 1324/5, and after 1332 he purchased several estates in Cambridgeshire and Suffolk. At the time of his death, on 5 March 1344, he held parts of the two manors of Fulbourn (near Cambridge) and Leverington (near Wisbech), three shops in Wisbech, and lands and rents to the value of £1 6*s*. 8*d*. in six places in Suffolk, as well as estates in Norfolk. In 1349 his sons John and Thomas founded a chantry for him and his wife, Agnes, in the church of Thompson, Norfolk.

JENS RÖHRKASTEN

Sources G. O. Sayles, ed., *Select cases in the court of king's bench*, 7 vols., SeldS, 55, 57–8, 74, 76, 82, 88 (1936–71), vol. 4 • N. M. Fryde, 'Edward III's removal of his ministers and judges, 1340–1', *BIHR*, 48 (1975), 149–61 • H. M. Cam, ed., *The eyre of London, 14 Edward II, AD 1321*, 2 vols., SeldS, 85–6 (1968–9) • A. J. Horwood and L. O. Pike, eds. and trans., *Year books of the reign of King Edward the Third*, 15 vols., Rolls Series, 31b (1883–1911), vols, 1, 2 • *Chancery records* • *CIPM*, 8, 365 • F. Blomefield and C. Parkin, *An essay towards a topographical* *history of the county of Norfolk*, [2nd edn], 11 vols. (1805–10), vol. 2, p. 367

Wealth at death see *CIPM*, vol. 8, p. 365

Shareshill [Sareshel], **Alfred of** [*called* Alfred the Englishman] (*fl. c.*1197–*c.*1222), scientist and translator of Aristotelian works, came from Shareshill, which is probably the village of that name 10 miles west of Lichfield, and so is likely to be the 'Magister Alueredus de Sarutehill canonicus Lich.' who appears in a charter of Ralph Neville, dean of Lichfield from 1214 to 1222 (BL, Harley MS 4799, fol. 62*va*). Other than this, very little is known of the details of his life. He was associated (as witnessed by the dedications of his works) with a group of English scholars that included Roger of Hereford and Alexander Neckham, and must therefore have flourished in the last years of the twelfth century and the first years of the thirteenth.

Two more facts are significant. Alfred of Shareshill continued the programme of translating the corpus of texts on Aristotelian natural science set out in order in al-Farabi's *On the Classification of the Sciences*, from the point where Gerardo da Cremona (*d.* 1187), the Toledan-based translator of texts from Arabic into Latin, left off. Whereas Gerardo had translated Aristotle's *Physics*, *On Generation and Corruption*, *On the Heavens*, and completed the *Meteorology*, Alfred took the texts next in order: *On Minerals* and *On Plants* (the series was to be completed by another Briton working in Toledo, Michael Scot, who translated Aristotle's books on animals). This strongly suggests that Alfred himself spent some time in Toledo, a hypothesis strengthened by the fact that several Spanish vernacular words are included in his translations. It was probably here that he studied with a Master Salomon Avenraza, 'Israelita celeberrimus et modernorum philosophorum precipuus' ('the most famous Jew and leader of modern philosophers'; Alfred of Sareshel, *Commentary on the 'Metheora'*, 51). Furthermore, Alfred wrote commentaries on many of these texts on natural science. His commentaries were quoted with respect by Oxford masters lecturing on Aristotle's natural science in the mid-thirteenth century, such as Adam of Bockenfield and 'R. de Stanington'. It is possible, therefore, that Alfred was himself a master at the university in its early days.

The works on plants and mineralogy that Alfred of Shareshill translated as part of an Aristotelian corpus were the *De plantis* of Nicholas of Damascus (dedicated by Alfred to Roger of Hereford), and two chapters, on stones and on metals, from Avicenna's *Shifa*ʾ, becoming three chapters in Latin. He wrote commentaries on these works and on the *Meteorology*, and refers to his own commentary on *On Generation and Corruption*. According to a medieval catalogue of the manuscripts of Beauvais Cathedral, he also wrote commentaries on Aristotle's *On the Soul*, *On Sleep*, *On Death and Life*, and *On the Heavens*.

Alfred of Shareshill's independent treatise—*On the Movement of the Heart* (*De motu cordis*)—was dedicated to *magister magnus* Alexander Neckham, probably before *c.*1197 when Alexander left Oxford to become a canon of Cirencester. It is concerned with the conditions necessary for life and ensoulment (a topic also covered in his commentary on *On Plants*), and adopts a strictly Aristotelian view in making the heart rather than the brain the seat of the soul. This work is remarkable for the large number of scientific texts it cites, which include, in addition to the above-mentioned works, Aristotle's *Physics*, *On Respiration*, *Metaphysics* ('*in Postphisicis*'), and *Ethics*, Qusta b. Luqa's *On the Difference between the Spirit and the Soul*, Alexander of Aphrodisias's commentary on the *Meteorology*, and texts by Arabic authors. Alfred undoubtedly played an important role in that critical period during which Aristotle was being established as the key authority in natural science, but that role is obscured by the lack of surviving works, and by the fact that his commentaries are buried in the masses of glosses that accompany the university copies of Aristotle's texts. CHARLES BURNETT

Sources D. A. Callus, 'Introduction of Aristotelian learning to Oxford', *PBA*, 29 (1943), 229–81 • Alfred of Sareshel, *Commentary on the 'Metheora' of Aristotle*, ed. J. K. Otte (1988), 3–15 • R. W. Southern, *Robert Grosseteste: the growth of an English mind in medieval Europe*, 2nd edn (1992), 90–92 • N. Damascenus, *De plantis*, ed. H. J. Drossaart Lulofs and E. L. Poortman (1989), 465–73 • R. J. Long, 'Alfred of Sareshel's commentary on the pseudo-Aristotelian *De plantis*: a critical edition', *Mediaeval Studies*, 47 (1985), 125–67 • *Des Alfred von Sareshel (Alfredus Anglicus) Schrift 'De motu cordis'*, ed. C. Baeumker, Beiträge zur Geschichte der Philosophie des Mittelalters, 23 (1923), 1–2

Shareshull, Sir William (1289/90–1370), justice, was born in Staffordshire, at Shareshull or possibly Walsall, into a family which may have ranked among the lesser gentry; perhaps he was a younger son of Adam Shareshull and Katherine. His highly successful career brought him estates in Oxfordshire (especially Barton Odonis), Staffordshire, Worcestershire, and Shropshire. He married twice, soon after 1316 and again in the summer of 1357, each time to a woman named Dionisia. His first marriage probably linked him to the Purcells, a family of slightly higher status than his own. His second marriage, to the daughter and heir of William Bottiler, greatly extended his landholding. His only son, William, predeceased him. His three daughters, Katherine, Elizabeth, and Agnes, made what were considered good marriages, reflecting their father's social rise; Agnes, for example, married Sir Richard *Abberbury (*c.*1330–1399) [*see under* Abberbury family].

Shareshull first appears in the legal records, which document so much of his life, in the 1310s, both as a litigant and a juror in his home county. His first appearance in the common pleas came in 1316; he first acted as an attorney, for the man who probably was (or would soon become) his father-in-law, in 1319. Having served a period as an apprentice-at-law, his career reached a new stage by 1324 when he was promoted to serjeant-at-law. Appointments to a variety of judicial commissions began in the same year and continued for four decades; moreover, from this time the yearbooks begin to mention him frequently as a pleader. His first assize commission came in March 1329. The regard of men important in the king's government, and in the law courts, no doubt lay behind Shareshull's appointment as king's serjeant at the end of

1330. In Easter term 1333 he became a justice of the common bench, receiving the status of knight-banneret with his appointment. For two terms in 1334 he moved to the king's bench, replacing Geoffrey Scrope, but then returned to his former post until Edward III removed him (along with other officials) in the crisis of 1340–41.

Shareshull was temporarily disgraced and confined in Caerphilly Castle, but was never formally charged and was soon back in favour and at work as a justice; he returned to the common bench in 1342 and was again a frequent holder of judicial commissions. On 3 July 1344 he became chief baron of the exchequer, leaving this post in Hilary term 1346 to become second justice of the common bench. From Easter 1350 to Easter 1361 he sat as chief justice of the king's bench. His biographer, Bertha Putnam, argued that he was highly influential in the legislation regulating labour after the plague of 1348–9, and in the statutory definition of treason, that he was a determined upholder of law and order, and a tireless collector of sizeable amounts of revenue through judicial fines.

For thirty years Shareshull served Edward, the Black Prince, as well as his father; he came to be retained as a 'bachelor' of the prince, conducted judicial inquests in his lands, and sat frequently on his council. He was likewise considered a close adviser in matters of law by such lords as the abbots of Glastonbury and Ramsey. Such service must have been well rewarded despite the oath, required by the ordinance of 1346, that justices give no counsel to litigants in matters concerning the king and take no fees, robes, or gifts.

Shareshull was not universally popular; in the Middle English poem 'Wynnere and Wastoure', for example, he is denounced by name. Moreover, he personally encountered the violence that troubled his era. He was attacked and abducted in June 1329, possibly as an attempt to keep him out of court; two prominent knights attacked his household in York in 1333; armed force was threatened against his sessions in Wiltshire in 1336, and may have hastened his departure into a neighbouring county; two of his houses were attacked in 1337, and other break-ins came in 1355 and 1358; his judicial sessions at Tredington were broken up by force in 1347; a clerk and others, probably labourers, were brought to court in 1358, charged with having announced that they would gladly strike Shareshull, given the chance. The most interesting incident occurred in 1344 at Ipswich, following oyer and terminer sessions that had yielded particularly heavy fines. A man who had 'busied himself about the king's business there before William de Shareshull and his fellows' had been killed, and as soon as the justices left, the townspeople, rich and poor, feasted the killers with delicacies and honoured them with gifts, 'as if God had come down from Heaven'. Then from the very steps of the hall of pleas they 'caused proclamation to be made that William of Shareshull was to appear before them under penalty of a hundred pounds … in mockery of the king's justices and ministers in his service' (Sayles, 6.37). Ipswich soon had its liberties taken into the king's hands.

Shareshull's religion may have been of a conventional sort. If he sounded a secular note in his judicial opinions, he could speak in tones of standard piety in a letter to his friend John Monington, abbot of Glastonbury. His bequests were likewise typical of his age and status. His piety was certainly not lacking in that degree of independence so often seen among the privileged ranks of the laity. In the dispute between Thomas Lisle, bishop of Ely (*d.* 1361), and Blanche, Lady Wake, who was the king's cousin, Shareshull and other royal justices and officials were cited in 1357 to appear in the papal court at Avignon; they disregarded this citation and fell under papal excommunication. The excommunication was lifted some time later, but Shareshull had earned the king's gratitude for his stand. His vigour lasted nearly to the end of his life. Even after his retirement from the king's bench, Shareshull continued to serve on a variety of judicial commissions. Early in 1369, however, he entered the Franciscan convent in Oxford as a novice and died, and was buried there early in the following year. RICHARD W. KAEUPER

Sources B. H. Putnam, *The place in legal history of Sir William Shareshull, chief justice of the king's bench, 1350–1361* (1950) · J. R. Maddicott, 'Law and lordship: royal justices as retainers in thirteenth- and fourteenth-century England', *Past and Present*, suppl. 4 (1978) · D. W. Sutherland, ed., *The eyre of Northamptonshire: 3–4 Edward III, AD 1329–1330*, 2 vols., SeldS, 97–8 (1983) · G. O. Sayles, ed., *Select cases in the court of king's bench*, 7 vols., SeldS, 55, 57–8, 74, 76, 82, 88 (1936–71), vols. 3–4, 5–6 · *Chancery records* · M. C. B. Dawes, ed., *Register of Edward, the Black Prince*, 4 vols., PRO (1930–33) · G. Wrottesley, ed., 'Extracts from the plea rolls, 1 to 15 Edward III', *Collections for a history of Staffordshire*, William Salt Archaeological Society, 11 (1890) · M. S. Arnold, ed., *Select cases of trespass from the king's courts, 1307–1399*, 1 (1985) · Baker, *Serjeants*

Sharington, Sir William (*c.*1495–1553), administrator and embezzler, was the first son of Thomas Sharington (*d.* 1527?) of Norfolk and his wife, Katherine, daughter and heir of William Pyrton of Little Bentley, Essex. Despite the obscurity of his early years, it seems clear that two men were instrumental in his rise to importance: Sir Francis Bryan, diplomat and soldier, of whose affinity he was by 1538; and (also in Bryan's service) Sir Thomas Seymour, the younger brother of Protector Somerset. To the former Sharington was related by marriage by virtue of his taking as his first wife Ursula, the illegitimate daughter of John Bourchier, second Lord Berners, who was Bryan's brother-in-law; to the latter he became 'my friend' (PRO, SP 10/1, no. 43). By 1539 Sharington was page of the king's robes and in 1540 was appointed groom. In the following year he became page of the privy chamber and then, in 1542, when he also became joint steward and constable of Castle Rising, Norfolk, groom. As such, he had close personal access to Henry VIII and was ideally placed to gain further preferment. In 1546 he was made under-treasurer, or head, of the newly established mint in Bristol; in 1547 he was appointed to commissions to investigate the mints and the admiralty; and in the following year he became a chantry commissioner for Gloucester, Gloucestershire, and Bristol. The king is said to have trusted him, and so too must Queen Katherine Parr, who had welcomed him into

Sir William Sharington (*c*.1495–1553), by Hans Holbein the younger

her household by 1544. Sadly, as the investigations into the treasonous activities of Thomas Seymour subsequently revealed, this trust was entirely misplaced.

According to the act of attainder of 1549 by which Sir William Sharington (he had been knighted at the coronation of Edward VI in 1547) was condemned, he had been guilty of four offences: coining £2000 in testoons, or shilling pieces, without warrant; coining a further £10,000 in testoons, also without warrant; gaining over £4000 profit by making his coins too light; and covering his tracks by compiling false records and burning the originals. Each was a serious charge but what gave them especial significance was that in rushing to Seymour, obviously with the intention of obtaining his protective support should his misdeeds be discovered, Sharington had succumbed to Seymour's plots. On being asked whether he could make £10,000, sufficient to keep 10,000 men in the field for a month, Sharington had agreed that he could, provided bullion were available, and, moreover, he had said that so long as there was a mint in Bristol, Seymour 'should lack no money' (PRO, SP 10/6, no. 13). What had started out as simple fraud—the result, according to his own confession, of his fear that his minting activities would leave him significantly out of pocket, but possibly also of his overspending on building activities at his principal seat of Lacock Abbey, Wiltshire, which he had purchased in 1540 for £783—had ended in disaster. Lacock and other properties, mostly in Wiltshire, which he had purchased for £3800 were confiscated, as were 1937 ounces of plate and other goods including £1000 in ingots and old gold, and gold and silver which it was estimated would have made up to £14,000 in coin. However, having interceded for help with the earls of Shrewsbury and Southampton and with Somerset directly for mercy, his life was spared; the simple reason being that once Seymour had been executed Sir William was no political threat at all. On 5 November 1549 he was pardoned and subsequently restored to his estates on payment of £12,867. In a sermon by Hugh Latimer preached before Edward VI in Lent 1549—a sermon in which Seymour was castigated and through which it was said Latimer earned the 'great hatred of many' (BL, Add. MS 48023, fol. 351)—Sharington was depicted as 'an honest gentleman, and one that God loveth … a chosen man of God, and one of his elected' (Latimer, 227).

Restored to lands and favour, Sharington was appointed in April 1550 with Sir Maurice Dennis, treasurer of Calais, to take receipt in France of 200,000 crowns, the first payment for the sale of Boulogne back to the French. He continued on the commission of the peace for Wiltshire, to which he had been appointed in 1547; in 1553 he became one of the commissioners in Wiltshire for the confiscation of church goods; and, on the ennoblement of Sir William Herbert in October 1551, he was returned at a by-election as an MP for Wiltshire, a position to which he had been elected in 1547 but from which he had been ejected upon his disgrace in 1549. Earlier on he had served as MP for Heytesbury (1545) and Bramber (1547). His appointment as sheriff of Wiltshire in 1552 effectively stymied his possible candidature for the parliament of 1553.

Over and above the rents that came from his lands and his salary of £133 6*s*. 8*d*. at the mint, Sharington enjoyed an income from moneylending, which he appears to have practised on some scale, dealing with, among others, Sir William Herbert, Sir Miles Partridge, and Protector Somerset. Then there were his trading activities. In 1542, on Henry VIII's recommendation, he was made an honorary freeman of London and it was from there through his factor that he traded with Antwerp, importing in 1549, for example, 'Tapistry, Tiks and Lynnen Clothe for my Lorde Admirall [Thomas Seymour] hymself, and sum other of his Frends' (Haynes, 64), worth over £2000. He also traded extensively in lead and English wool, owned ships, and ventured capital with Bristol merchants, on one occasion 'Southward', on another to 'Thisles of Portingale for Frute' (ibid., 65).

A man of culture, as evidenced by the Renaissance-style features of his building works at Lacock, Sharington survives through a drawing of him by Holbein, now at Windsor Castle. He married as his second wife Eleanor, daughter of William Walsingham, and in 1542, as his third wife, Grace, *née* Farrington, widow of Robert Paget, alderman of London, but left no children, and when he died, before 22 November 1553, he was succeeded by his brother Henry.

C. E. Challis

Sources *CSP dom.*, 1547–53 • *Calendar of the manuscripts of the most hon. the marquis of Salisbury*, 24 vols., HMC, 9 (1883–1976), vols. 1, 13 • S. Haynes, ed., *A collection of state papers* (1740) [part-printing of HMC, London, *Salisbury MSS*; microfilm, BL, M485] • A. Luders and others, eds., *Statutes of the realm*, 11 vols. in 12, RC (1810–28), vol. 4, pt 1, pp. 60–61, 112–13 • BL, Add. MSS 5751B, fol. 36, 48023, fol. 351 • *APC*, 1547–50; 1552–4 • *DNB* • HoP, *Commons*, 1509–58, 3.302–4 • *The ledger of John Smythe, 1538–1550*, ed. J. Vanes, Bristol RS, 28 (1974) • C. E. Challis, 'Mint officials and moneyers of the Tudor period', *British Numismatic Journal*, 45 (1975), 51–76, esp. 68 • C. E. Challis, *The Tudor coinage* (1978) • H. Latimer, *Sermons* (1906) • PRO, state papers domestic, Edward VI, SP 10/1, no. 43; SP 10/6, no. 13

Archives BL, Salisbury MSS, M483 • PRO, state papers, SP 10

Likenesses H. Holbein the younger, chalk drawing, Royal Collection [*see illus.*]

Sharman, Isabel (1865–1917), nursery nurse teacher and administrator, was born on 27 August 1865 at Oxford Street, Wellingborough, one of eleven children of Matthew Reid Sharman, solicitor, and his wife, Mary Elizabeth, formerly Dulley. She moved to London in 1883 to undertake her training as a teacher. She completed her training at the recently opened Norland Place School under the eagle eye of Miss Emily Lord, its founder. On qualification she worked for a while as kindergarten mistress at Shrewsbury high school, and then returned to London, at the request of Lord, to help inaugurate the Norland Institute in the suite of rooms at the Norland Place School that Lord had vacated upon her marriage to Walter Ward in the previous year (1891). Together with Mrs Ward she sought support from the opinion leaders of the time for an institute dedicated to the training of gentlewomen as children's nurses. Sadly the two women achieved very little encouragement from their friends and peers. However, their perseverance, foresight, and planning led to the opening of the Norland Institute in September 1892. Indeed, Sharman was principal of the institute from its foundation until her death in 1917, and she was its longest-serving incumbent in the twentieth century.

In 1904 Sharman introduced the maiden scheme to the institute, by which women of slender means would be able to train at Norland. In return for one year's service of light housework, the annual Norland training fees were reduced from £80 to £12. Sharman did not wish to create a separate class of student and, in order to disguise their identity during this period of domestic service, maidens would forfeit their first names and answer to the name of Honour, Verity, Prudence, and Mercy.

Sharman's great talent lay in her cogent organizing ability: it enabled her to sift Mrs Ward's vigorous, determined innovation and inspiration, which she controlled and organized, then brought to fruition. She was utterly dependable, calm, and practical, and possessed a quiet strength and cool simplicity. She was known as Shar to her colleagues on the institute staff and as Bella to her friend and mentor. In the early days of the institute she undertook much of the work herself. This involved instruction on the washing of flannels and the care of hairbrushes, in addition to the teaching of theories of education and all the secretarial work. Indeed, in these early days of the institute she was 'the Staff'. She would always visit the nurseries at bath time and she enjoyed every aspect of life at the institute. She was a true teacher, and always felt praise went much further than blame. She was thus an inspiration to many a young trainee struggling with aspects of the course. Although Miss Sharman preferred the nurses to continue to wear uniform when in employment, she agreed to the award of a badge, which had been requested by those who did not wear uniform. It was her wish that the badge or medal should not be given on attainment of a position of private nurse but as a mark of fresh honour. The badge was regarded as an outward sign of integrity, of loyalty, and of faithful service to the employer, the institute, and the children entrusted to the nurse's care. It was awarded after five years' faithful service, three of which were with one employer. In June 1902 the first badges were donated by the countess of Dudley and awarded to fifty nurses who fulfilled the necessary criteria. At the same time a gold badge was given to Miss Sharman by Mrs Ward, together with a gold chain presented to her by the badge nurses in recognition of her ten years' work as principal. She was a devout Christian and worshipped regularly at the Allen Street Chapel in Kensington.

Isabel never enjoyed robust health and in 1916 it was necessary for her (temporarily, it was hoped) to lay down her responsibilities at the Norland Institute, but having spent the summer at her old family home, Ivy Lodge, Wellingborough, she died there, from cancer, on 11 January of the following year. She was buried at Wellingborough cemetery on 13 January.

Perhaps the most fitting epitaph for Isabel Sharman is the words of Emily Ward, writing in the *Norland Quarterly* after the death of her friend: 'the keynote of her life was her extraordinary simplicity and integrity and her abhorrence of all extravagance'; the fund that bears her name and was set up on her death is also a fitting memorial. It is dedicated to providing help to Norland students who encounter financial difficulties during their training. In 1992 Isabel Sharman's name was lent to the modern equivalent of the maiden scheme: Sharman students are able to fund up to half of their training fees by undertaking a year's domestic work in college prior to commencing their studies.

LOUISE E. DAVIS

Sources Norland College Archives, Denford Park, Hungerford, Isabel Sharman MSS • *Norland Quarterly* (1892–1917) • P. Stokes, *Norland, 1892–1992: the story of the first one hundred years* (1992) • b. cert. • d. cert.

Wealth at death £3168 12*s*. 10*d*.: probate, 21 Feb 1917, *CGPLA Eng. & Wales*

PICTURE CREDITS

Sassoon family (*per.* c.1830–1961)—© reserved
Sassoon, Siegfried Loraine (1886–1967)—© Cecil Beaton Archive, Sotheby's; collection National Portrait Gallery, London
Saumarez, James, first Baron de Saumarez (1757–1836)—private collection. Photograph: Photographic Survey, Courtauld Institute of Art, London
Saunders, Edith Rebecca (1865–1945)—by permission of the Linnean Society of London
Saunders, Thomas William (1814–1890)—© National Portrait Gallery, London
Saunders, William Wilson (1809–1879)—© National Portrait Gallery, London
Saunderson, Edward James (1837–1906)—© National Portrait Gallery, London
Saunderson, Nicholas (*bap.* 1683, *d.* 1739)—© Fitzwilliam Museum, University of Cambridge
Saussure, César-François de (1705–1783)—Musée Historique de Lausanne
Savile, George, first marquess of Halifax (1633–1695)—© National Portrait Gallery, London
Savile, Sir George, eighth baronet (1726–1784)—photograph by courtesy Sotheby's Picture Library, London
Savile, Sir Henry (1549–1622)—© Bodleian Library, University of Oxford
Saville, Victor Myer (1897–1979)—© reserved; British Film Institute
Savory, Sir William Scovell, first baronet (1826–1895)—St Bartholomew's Hospital Archives and Museum. Photograph: Photographic Survey, Courtauld Institute of Art, London
Savundra, Emil (1923–1976)—© News International Newspapers Ltd
Saxby, Jessie Margaret Edmondston (1842–1940)—Scottish National Portrait Gallery
Sayers, Dorothy Leigh (1893–1957)—© National Portrait Gallery, London
Sayers, Tom (1826–1865)—V&A Images, The Victoria and Albert Museum
Scambler, Edmund (c.1520–1594)—© National Portrait Gallery, London
Scarburgh, Sir Charles (1615–1694)—by permission of the Royal College of Physicians, London
Scarlett, Sir James Yorke (1799–1871)—Towneley Hall Art Gallery & Museum, Burnley / Bridgeman Art Library
Schafer, Sir Edward Albert Sharpey-(1850–1935)—© National Portrait Gallery, London
Schapiro, Leonard Bertram (1908–1983)—© reserved; Royal Academy of Arts, London
Scharf, Sir George (1820–1895)—© National Portrait Gallery, London
Scharf, George Johann (1788–1860)—© National Portrait Gallery, London
Scharlieb, Dame Mary Ann Dacomb (1845–1930)—© reserved; collection Royal Free Hospital, London; photograph National Portrait Gallery, London
Schechter, Solomon (1847x50–1915)—Library of the Jewish Theological Seminary of America, New York; photograph National Portrait Gallery, London
Scheemakers, Peter Gaspar (*bap.* 1691, *d.* 1781)—© National Portrait Gallery, London
Schimmelpenninck, Mary Anne (1778–1856)—© National Portrait Gallery, London
Schlich, Sir William Philipp Daniel (1840–1925)—© National Portrait Gallery, London
Schmitz, Leonhard (1807–1890)—© National Portrait Gallery, London
Schnadhorst, Francis (1840–1900)—© National Portrait Gallery, London
Scholes, Percy Alfred (1877–1958)—© National Portrait Gallery, London
Schomberg, Sir Alexander (1720–1804)—© National Maritime Museum, London
Schomberg, Frederick Herman de, first duke of Schomberg (1615–1690)—© National Portrait Gallery, London
Schomberg, Isaac (1714–1780)—The Huntington Library, Art Collections and Botanical Gardens, San Marino, CA, USA
Schomburgk, Sir Robert Hermann (1804–1865)—© National Portrait Gallery, London
Schorlemmer, Carl (1834–1892)—© National Portrait Gallery, London
Schreiber [Guest], Lady Charlotte Elizabeth (1812–1895)—Glamorgan Record Office
Schreiner, William Philip (1857–1919)—© National Portrait Gallery, London
Schröder, (Rudolph) Bruno, Baron Schröder in the Prussian nobility (1867–1940)—The de László Foundation; Witt Library, Courtauld Institute of Art, London
Schumacher, Ernst Friedrich [Fritz] (1911–1977)—© Sophie Baker
Schuster, Sir Arthur (1851–1934)—© The Royal Society
Schuster, Sir Felix Otto, first baronet (1854–1936)—© National Portrait Gallery, London
Schwabe, Randolph (1885–1948)—© Estate of Francis Dodd; collection National Portrait Gallery, London
Scoresby, William, junior (1789–1857)—Scottish National Portrait Gallery
Scott, Alexander John (1768–1840)—© National Maritime Museum, London
Scott, Anna, duchess of Monmouth and *suo jure* duchess of Buccleuch (1651–1732)—in the collection of the Duke of Buccleuch and Queensberry KT
Scott, Charles Prestwich (1846–1932)—© Estate of Francis Dodd; collection National Portrait Gallery, London
Scott, Charlotte Angas (1858–1931)—The Mistress and Fellows, Girton College, Cambridge
Scott, Clement William (1841–1904)—© National Portrait Gallery, London
Scott, David (1806–1849)—Scottish National Portrait Gallery
Scott, Edward Taylor (1883–1932)—© The Guardian
Scott, Sir George Gilbert (1811–1878)—RIBA Library Photographs Collection
Scott, Sir Giles Gilbert (1880–1960)—© National Portrait Gallery, London
Scott, Sir Harold Richard (1887–1969)—© National Portrait Gallery, London
Scott, Henry, third duke of Buccleuch and fifth duke of Queensberry (1746–1812)—in the collection of the Duke of Buccleuch and Queensberry KT; photograph courtesy the Scottish National Portrait Gallery
Scott, Henry Young Darracott (1822–1883)—© National Portrait Gallery, London
Scott [Crofts], James, duke of Monmouth and first duke of Buccleuch (1649–1685)—private collection; photograph National Galleries of Scotland
Scott, John, first earl of Clonmell (1739–1798)—unknown collection; photograph Sotheby's Picture Library, London / National Portrait Gallery, London
Scott, John, first earl of Eldon (1751–1838)—printed by kind permission of the Trustees of the Cowdray Settled Estate. Photograph: Photographic Survey, Courtauld Institute of Art, London
Scott, John (1794–1871)—© National Portrait Gallery, London
Scott, (Edith Agnes) Kathleen, Lady Scott (1878–1947)—© Photo RMN - Jean Schormans
Scott, Mackay Hugh Baillie (1865–1945)—RIBA Library Photographs Collection
Scott, Lady Margaret Rachel (1874–1938)—© National Portrait Gallery, London
Scott, Michael (1789–1835)—© Scottish National Portrait Gallery
Scott, Paul Mark (1920–1978)—© Mark Gerson; collection National Portrait Gallery, London
Scott, Sir Percy Moreton, first baronet (1853–1924)—© National Portrait Gallery, London
Scott, Sir Peter Markham (1909–1989)—© National Portrait Gallery, London
Scott, Robert (1811–1887)—© National Portrait Gallery, London
Scott, Robert Falcon (1868–1912)—© Popperfoto; collection National Portrait Gallery, London
Scott, Ronald [Ronnie] (1927–1996)—© Philip Sayer; collection National Portrait Gallery, London
Scott, Sir Terence Charles Stuart Morrison- (1908–1991)—© National Portrait Gallery, London
Scott, Thomas (*d.* 1626)—© National Portrait Gallery, London
Scott, Thomas (1747–1821)—© National Portrait Gallery, London
Scott, Thomas (1808–1878)—© National Portrait Gallery, London
Scott, Sir Walter (1771–1832)—in the collection of the Duke of Buccleuch and Queensberry KT
Scott, Walter Francis Montagu-Douglas-, fifth duke of Buccleuch and seventh duke of Queensberry (1806–1884)—The Lord Montagu of Beaulieu. Photograph: Photographic Survey, Courtauld Institute of Art, London
Scott, William, Baron Stowell (1745–1836)—reproduced by permission of the Masters of the Bench of the Honourable Society of the Middle Temple
Scott, William Bell (1811–1890)—© National Portrait Gallery, London
Scovell, Sir George (1774–1861)—© National Portrait Gallery, London
Scroggs, Sir William (c.1623–1683)—© National Portrait Gallery, London
Scrope, Adrian (1601–1660)—© National Portrait Gallery, London
Scrope, George Poulett (1797–1876)—Ashmolean Museum, Oxford
Scrope, Richard (c.1350–1405)—reproduced by kind permission of the Dean and Chapter of York
Scudamore, Frank Ives (1823–1884)—© National Portrait Gallery, London
Seacole, Mary Jane (1805–1881)—Institute of Jamaica; photograph National Portrait Gallery, London
Searle, Humphrey (1915–1982)—© Estate of Michael Ayrton; collection National Portrait Gallery, London
Sebright, Sir John Saunders, seventh baronet (1767–1846)—© National Portrait Gallery, London
Secker, Thomas (1693–1768)—reproduced by kind permission of His Grace the Archbishop of Canterbury and the Church Commissioners. Photograph: Photographic Survey, Courtauld Institute of Art, London
Sedding, John Dando (1838–1891)—RIBA Library Photographs Collection
Seddon, Richard John (1845–1906)—Alexander Turnbull Library, National Library of New Zealand, Te Puna Matauranga o Aotearoa / Seddon Family Collection (F-47794-1/2)
Sedgwick, Adam (1785–1873)—Sedgwick Museum of Geology
Sedley, Catharine, *suo jure* countess of Dorchester, and countess of Portmore (1657–1717)—© National Portrait Gallery, London
Sedley, Sir Charles, fifth baronet (*bap.* 1639, *d.* 1701)—private collection.

Photograph: Photographic Survey, Courtauld Institute of Art, London

Seebohm, Frederic (1833–1912)—private collection

Seeley, Harry Govier (1839–1909)—by permission of the Geological Society of London

Seeley, Sir John Robert (1834–1895)—© National Portrait Gallery, London

Seely, John Edward Bernard, first Baron Mottistone (1868–1947)—© National Portrait Gallery, London

Seemann, Berthold Carl (1825–1871)—© National Portrait Gallery, London

Segar, Sir William (*b.* in or before 1564, *d.* 1633)—© National Portrait Gallery, London

Seilern und Aspang, Count Antoine Edward (1901–1978)—The Courtauld Institute Gallery, Somerset House, London

Selden, John (1584–1654)—Yale Law School

Selfridge, Harry Gordon (1858–1947)—Estate of William Orpen / Witt Library, Courtauld Institute of Art, London

Seligman, Charles Gabriel (1873–1940)—© Estate of Sir William Rothenstein / National Portrait Gallery, London

Selincourt, Ernest De (1870–1943)—© National Portrait Gallery, London

Sellers, Peter (1925–1980)—© National Portrait Gallery, London

Selous, Frederick Courteney (1851–1917)—© National Portrait Gallery, London

Selwyn, George Augustus (1719–1791)—private collection

Selwyn, George Augustus (1809–1878)—© National Portrait Gallery, London

Semon, Sir Felix (1849–1921)—by kind permission of the Royal Society of Medicine, London

Semprini, (Fernando Riccardo) Alberto (1908–1990)—Camera Press

Sen, Keshub Chunder (1838–1884)—© National Portrait Gallery, London

Senanayake, Don Stephen (1884–1952)—© National Portrait Gallery, London

Senior, Nassau William (1790–1864)—© National Portrait Gallery, London

Sennett, (Alice) Maud Mary Arncliffe (1862–1936)—Mary Evans / The Women's Library

Seppings, Sir Robert (1767–1840)—© National Maritime Museum, London

Septimius Severus, Lucius (145/6–211)—© Copyright The British Museum

Séquard, Charles Édouard Brown- (1817–1894)—© National Portrait Gallery, London

Serbati, Antonio Rosmini- (1797–1855)—© National Portrait Gallery, London

Series, George William (1920–1995)—private collection

Serres, Dominic (1722–1793)—© National Portrait Gallery, London

Serres, Olivia (1772–1835)—© reserved; private collection

Service, James (1823–1899)—© National Portrait Gallery, London

Service, Robert William (1874–1958)—© reserved; photograph National Portrait Gallery, London

Seton, Alexander, first earl of Dunfermline (1556–1622)—Scottish National Portrait Gallery

Seton, George, fifth Lord Seton (*c.*1530–1586)—National Gallery of Scotland, on loan to the Scottish National Portrait Gallery

Severn, Joseph (1793–1879)—© National Portrait Gallery, London

Sewall, Samuel (1652–1730)—Copyright 2004 Museum of Fine Arts, Boston; bequest of William L. Barnard (by exchange), and Emily L. Ainsley Fund

Seward, Sir Albert Charles (1863–1941)—reproduced by permission of Curtis Brown Group Ltd, on behalf of the Estate of Harold Knight. © Harold Knight; collection Department of Plant Sciences in the University of Cambridge

Seward, Anna (1742–1809)—© National Portrait Gallery, London

Sewel, Willem (1653–1720)—Rijksprentenkabinet, Rijksmuseum, Amsterdam

Sewell, Anna (1820–1878)—© National Portrait Gallery, London

Seyer, Samuel (1757–1831)—© National Portrait Gallery, London

Seyler, Athene (1889–1990)—© Yevonde Portrait Archive; collection National Portrait Gallery, London

Seymour, Anna Maria (*c.*1692–1723)—© Bodleian Library, University of Oxford

Seymour, Edward, duke of Somerset (*c.*1500–1552)—in the collection of the Duke of Buccleuch and Queensberry KT

Seymour, Sir Edward, fourth baronet (1633–1708)—© National Portrait Gallery, London

Seymour, Edward Adolphus, eleventh duke of Somerset (1775–1855)—Witt Library, Courtauld Institute of Art, London

Seymour, Elizabeth, duchess of Somerset (1667–1722)—The Lord Egremont. Photograph: Photographic Survey, Courtauld Institute of Art, London

Seymour, Francis, first Baron Seymour of Trowbridge (1590?–1664)—National Trust Photographic Library / John Hammond

Seymour [Grey], Katherine, countess of Hertford (1540?–1568)—The Lord Egremont. Photograph: Photographic Survey, Courtauld Institute of Art, London

Seymour, Thomas, Baron Seymour of Sudeley (*b.* in or before 1509, *d.* 1549)—© National Portrait Gallery, London

Shackleton, Sir David James (1863–1938)—© National Portrait Gallery, London

Shackleton, Sir Ernest Henry (1874–1922)—reproduced by permission of the Scott Polar Research Institute

Shadwell, Thomas (*c.*1640–1692)—© National Portrait Gallery, London

Shakespear, Dame Ethel Mary Reader (1871–1946)—The Principal and Fellows, Newnham College, Cambridge

Shakespear, Sir Richmond Campbell (1812–1861)—The British Library

Shakespeare, William (1564–1616)—© National Portrait Gallery, London

Shankly, William [Bill] (1913–1981)—Getty Images - Hulton Archive

Shannon, Charles Haslewood (1863–1937)—© National Portrait Gallery, London

Sharington, Sir William (*c.*1495–1553)—The Royal Collection © 2004 HM Queen Elizabeth II